THE COMPLETE STEPHEN KING ENCYCLOPEDIA

THE DEFINITIVE GUIDE TO THE WORKS OF AMERICA'S MASTER OF HORROR

STEPHEN J. SPIGNESI

CB

CONTEMPORARY
BOOKS

CHICAGO

Published by Contemporary Books, Inc.
Two Prudential Plaza, Chicago, Illinois 60601-6790
Manufactured in the United States of America
International Standard Book Number: 0-8092-3911-6 (cloth)
0-8092-3818-7 (paper)

Book design and layout by Tom Schultheiss
and Patricia Curtis.

This edition is published by arrangement with Popular
Culture Ink, Ann Arbor, Michigan.

A Note to the Reader

This work was originally published as a collector's edition under the title *The Shape Under The Sheet: The Complete Stephen King Encyclopedia*. Any and all references to *The Shape Under The Sheet* found throughout the work therefore pertain to this edition as well.

To

My wife, Pam,
For probably being the truest friend I'll ever have
in this life or any other;

My mother, the amazing Lee,
For having me, healing me, and helping me
for the past (almost) four decades;

My editor, Tom Schultheiss,
For being my touchstone, and for guiding me carefully
through a sometimes dark and bewildering forest;

My friend, Dave Hinchberger,
For proving to me that God sometimes deliberately brings
the absolutely perfect people into our lives...
at the absolutely perfect times—I love ya, man;

And Stephen King,
For always giving me something to read...
and for always telling the truth.

"...all the lights in the city
don't start to shine the way you do..."

How to Use This Book

Whatever your reason for consulting this book—be it reference, research, or just plain entertainment—this is the place to start.

Using any encyclopedic work can be a daunting experience, especially if it contains much in the way of new and unfamiliar information, as is the case here. That's why we've included over a dozen indexes and other helpful features—like this one—to guide you through the maze of all things King offered herein.

FINDING YOUR WAY

Here are the four most helpful ways to approach the contents of this book, features you'll consult time and again during your journey through King's world:

(1) **Alphabetical Index to Works**—You can easily find the discussion of any particular title among King's works by consulting the index on pages xi and xii. All works—published and unpublished, collected and uncollected, novels, short stories, non-fiction, motion picture adaptations—are listed here in a single alphabetical sequence, with a reference to the page number where the discussion begins. Additionally, chronological and alphabetical indexes group titles by category in each of the three major divisions of the concordance section noted at the bottom of these pages (e.g., the list of Published Works only begins on page 151, etc.).

(2) **"Contents Classifieds"**—In addition to the traditionally-organized table of contents, you'll find a classified table of contents, arranged by type of feature—a subject approach, if you will—on pages ix–x. If you're looking for the very beginning of the concordances, a list of all the interviews, all the fiction, all the reference features or indexes, just turn to these two pages.

(3) **Page Number Key**—A numerical listing arranged by the chronologically-based Master Code assigned by the author to each of the works covered in the concordance section (*Part V* of this book), with reference to the page number where discussion of the work begins. You'll need to refer to this feature, repeated on pages 648–649, when using the character indexes (pages 650–669), or to follow up on any text reference that includes mention of a Master Code.

(4) **Running Heads**—Left-hand pages of major sections carry an identifying heading to help you get your bearings when you're just browsing through the book. Occasional sidebars, usually related to the major section in which they appear, carry no such headings,

and are generally displayed in bordered boxes that can range from one page (closed box) to several continuous pages (boxes open at the side).

THE CONCORDANCES

The heart of this book—fully half of its content—is the series of massive concordances that provide details on virtually every character, location, and physical object mentioned in King's published and unpublished works. Grouped within these two categories, his works are arranged chronologically (see the Alphabetical Index for an alphabetical approach). Each work, taken in turn, opens with a "skeleton"—a descriptive outline of the work's structure, or history and content—contained in a shaded box, followed by a dictionary-like arrangement of brief entries under the subdivisions "People," "Places," and "Things."

ABOUT THIS BOOK'S STRUCTURE

This work is divided into seven major sections, each emphasizing and focusing on different aspects of and approaches to King and his work: *Part I* introduces us to King's background, and discusses the meaning of his metaphor, "The shape under the sheet"; *Part II* offers interviews with friends and relatives, articles, and other features that attempt to bring us still closer to "King the man"; *Part III* concentrates on the world of King fandom; *Part IV* offers full details on the history and content of *Castle Rock*, the Stephen King newsletter; *Part V*, in addition to the concordances, is devoted to features designed to facilitate the exploration of King's life's work—a first line index, a section on his films (including many related sidebars), a discussion of his poetry, an annotated guide to audiotape versions of his stories; several features and character indexes that light your path through the Kingdom; *Part VI* offers perspective and commentary—through an annotated bibliography and interviews with King's literary contemporaries—on King's place in American fiction; *Part VII* concludes the volume with a look at stories unfinished or as yet unwritten by King. Watch for editorial comment within shaded boxes within all seven sections.

Occasionally, you'll also encounter a piece of original fiction or poetry—each in its own way connected with Stephen King—in the sections above, arresting waystops in your exploration of the abundant riches contained in this book.

Original drawing by Kenny Ray Linkous.

Contents

"CONTENTS CLASSIFIEDS"
A Quick-Reference Guide to Features

MOTION PICTURES

PUBLISHED WORKS

REFERENCE

UNPUBLISHED & UNCOLLECTED WORKS

❖❖❖

MISCELLANEOUS FEATURES

ALPHABETICAL INDEX TO ALL WORKS
BY STEPHEN KING DISCUSSED IN THIS VOLUME

CS=Creepshow; DS=Different Seasons; FPM=Four Past Midnight; NS=Night Shift; PPT=People, Places and Things, SC=Skeleton Crew

Classified listings: Published Works (p. 151); Unpublished & Uncollected Works (p. 459); Motion Picture Adaptations (p.554).

ALPHABETICAL INDEX TO ALL WORKS
BY STEPHEN KING DISCUSSED IN THIS VOLUME
(continued)

CS=Creepshow; DS=Different Seasons; FPM=Four Past Midnight; NS=Night Shift; PPT=People, Places and Things; SC=Skeleton Crew

Classified listings: Published Works (p. 151); Unpublished & Uncollected Works (p. 459); Motion Picture Adaptations (p.554).

Introduction

PART 1

How Ryan O'Neal And Shelley Long Convinced Me To Lease A Copier

or

What Are John Ford And Woody Allen Doing In A Book About Stephen King Anyway?

*(With special thanks to Chris Matheson &
Ed Solomon for writing a certain movie.)*

One evening in 1987 or '88 (I can't remember which), I sat down to stare at a movie after having put in a fourteen-hour day working on this book. John Lennon serenely gazed down at me from my wall, my cat Ben serenely dozed beneath the piano, and I collapsed into my recliner feeling like the "after" version of the "this is your brain on drugs" frying eggs commercial. My brain was just as fried, and I felt that way *without* doing drugs. (If I ever *did* do drugs, I think I'd turn into—as my idol Woody Allen put it in "Manhattan"—"one of those guys that sells comic books outside of Bloomingdale's.")

I remember that I was at a point in my research where I had a stack of file folders approximately head-high containing the handwritten notes for about a dozen Stephen King novels, almost fifty short stories, and close to two dozen interviews.

These were my original notes.

Naively, either I or my research assistant would do the research, take the notes (sometimes, in the case of the novels, the yellow legal pad pages would number near one hundred), put them in a folder, and then place them in a file cabinet in my office until I was ready to start reviewing them and begin the actual writing of the entries that make up the concordance section of *The Shape Under the Sheet*.

But back to the recliner.

My wife and I have three pay cable channels: Showtime, HBO, and The Movie Channel. Pam and I like movies; all we do is work, and so we splurge thirty dollars a month on movie channels.

This particular evening, one of the channels (again, I can't remember which) was showing the 1984 movie "Irreconcilable Differences" with Ryan O'Neal and Shelley Long.

It wasn't too bad a movie. Shelley Long is terrific, Ryan O'Neal is underrated, and even though the story was a little ridiculous, it was watchable.

About halfway through, there was a scene that literally knocked me out of my chair. I had never felt such an immediate and overwhelming empathy with a film character as I did after this scene.

Ryan O'Neal and Shelley Long are traveling across country. They stop at a diner for something to eat. While they're in the restaurant eating, O'Neal's character sees his car being stolen. He runs out of the diner, frantically chases the car, and then gives up when he realizes pursuit on foot is pointless.

So, what's so devastating about that, right? A car was stolen. Big deal.

Lemme tellya.

While he's chasing the car, O'Neal screams out, "My John Ford notes!"

That was when I fell out of the chair. (Well, actually, all I did was suddenly sit up straight, but falling out of the chair is such a vivid, dramatic image that I decided to use that instead.)

It seems O'Neal's character had been doing research for a book about the director John Ford, and his original (and only) set of notes were in that car. In a blisteringly honest portrayal of a sincerely driven writer, O'Neal didn't care about the car, the luggage, or anything Shelley Long may have had in the car. All he cared about were his notes.

Ryan, I know how you felt.

As though in some horrible hallucinatory nightmare, I saw myself running after a car screaming, "My Stephen King notes! My Stephen King notes!"

This scene—plus a conversation with my agent, John White—made me realize that if there was ever a burglary or fire at my office, all my months of work would be gone, and *The Shape Under the Sheet* would be out of business. Since that night, I've made it my business to keep photocopies of all my notes (as well as disk copies of my final manuscript versions), in a locked, fireproof safe at another location. As my friend Joe Parcella would say, "It only takes once." He's right.

I'll admit it was a great relief to send off the completed manuscript to my editor Tom Schultheiss at Popular Culture, Ink. As soon as that was done, and Tom had the diskettes safely in his Michiganian hands, the burden of protection was lifted from my shoulders.

I tell that story to make a point: I lived with *The Shape Under the Sheet* for four solid years. I ate and slept with the beast, and if this book were a woman, she would have been a siren seductive beyond demurral; if it were a drug, it would have been an addiction beyond sobriety.

Stephen King's work was always important to me.

It was entertaining, enlightening, moving, and, yes, scary. But that was before I began *studying* it. Devoting myself wholeheartedly to his body of writing showed me the true "shape under the sheet": Stephen King's talent, imagination, prolificacy, and morality.

The guy's got a heart.

And a soul, too.

Stephen King's work became something beyond entertainment for me: I realized that I was privileged enough to be witnessing the creation of a true American literary giant.

I defy anyone to read the last couple of pages of *IT* and tell me that those pages don't contain some of the finest writing by an American *ever*. Never mind the genre. You can stand the writing on those pages up against anything you want, and it'll still hold its own.

It was a genuine honor to be able to dig so deeply into Stephen King's body of work. I started the book unaware of the profound impact such intensive exposure to his work would have on me. I simply thought it might be fun.

And it was.

But it was more than that.

It was...umm...lemme see...it was...oh, I've got it: It was—as my friends Bill and Ted might say—savory, bodacious, and above all...EXCELLENT!!

Yes, that's it.

Writing *The Shape Under the Sheet: The Complete Stephen King Encyclopedia* was an excellent adventure.

Glad you could come along for the ride.

PART 2

A Kiss In The Dark

"Fear of the dark is in any case a sensible fear until one knows what the universe is capable of."

"...The idea of the ghost and the sense of the ghastly arise from a single source: the mystery and horror of death."

—Jacques Barzun

"It is not bad, it is high time,
Stark violence is still the sire of all the world's values.
Never weep, let them play,
Old violence is not too old to beget new values."

—Robinson Jeffers

On New Year's Eve, 1986, there was a big fire at a hotel in San Juan, Puerto Rico. CNN showed live unedited videotape of the rescue efforts. They showed burned people, half-clothed, writhing in agony, crying, embracing, and choking on smoke. Unedited life. They continually ran a text line on the screen that said "Unedited Video Tape."

One of the most common questions people ask Stephen King is "Where do you get your ideas?" Looking at the world around us, do we really have to ask?

Stephen King can stimulate fear and dread in his readers. Through his incredible talents and marvelous ability to tap into our dark halves, he can create a condition in our minds that was not there before we began reading.

Vicarious thrills.

The terror of the rollercoaster trapped between two covers.

As humans, we are supremely gifted with the ability to interpret sensory stimuli on a huge variety of levels. We don't have to physically be in Room 217 with Danny Torrance when the dead woman rises up out of the bathtub, nor do we have to be in Paul's room in Annie Wilkes's house when she comes in with the axe and the blowtorch. (Those two scenes, by the way, are the two scenes that scared Stephen King himself while writing them.)

Our brain allows us to experience the emotion of these moments without actually living through them.

Stephen King understands fear. He remembers those moments in his own life when he was scared. He pays attention to the things that make him nervous, and then he's considerate enough to share those moments with us.

About a third of the way through the writing of *The Shape Under the Sheet,* my wife Pam and I bought a new condominium in New Haven, Connecticut.

We were the fourth people to close and move in. There were a total of nineteen units in the development, and while we and the other three families were living there, the other fifteen units were still empty.

For the first few weeks, it was like living in a ghost town.

The blank windows of the empty units stared out into the deserted parking lot. The doors gaped open onto bare wood stairways. None of the doors had doorknobs; the empty holes looked like dead, black eye sockets.

I would occasionally walk through some of the unsold units. None of the rooms had walls, and the heating and plumbing looked like exposed intestines in a huge cavernous body.

The parking lot at night was pitch dark except for one lone white-globed lamppost. The builder was still waiting for the other lights. Our cars looked abandoned sitting there all night. And when the other residents parked their cars in their garages—they only had one car; my wife and I each had a car—my car sat out there totally alone all night long.

In the dark.

Watched by dark windows that loomed out from empty rooms.

Fears walked and talked in my head for quite a while until more of the units had people living in them.

As King acknowledged in *Danse Macabre,* there are two levels, two gradations of Fear: Real Fears and Unreal Fears.

Real Fears are those that have a real threat and real risk—real vulnerability—attached to them. In my case, a Real Fear in the condominium complex was that some maniac would walk into one of the unoccupied units, which by necessity weren't locked (have you ever walked through a building site?—you can stroll right into the open buildings), and set fire to the place. Or that kids would use the place for a drug den. Or that animals would get into one of the units, defecate, and attract vermin and all other manner of disgusting creatures.

The woman driving home alone at night who thinks a car is following her is subject to a variety of Real Fears: kidnap, rape, murder...the list is limited only by one's imagination. Satanists could kidnap her and use her as a sacrifice in a Black Mass. Farfetched? Perhaps, but have you read the papers or watched "Donahue," "Geraldo," or "Oprah" lately?

These fears are Real because the threats are real. It's all too easy to imagine a woman in your life ending up in a situation like that.

Cancer, lightning, and pit bulls.

Real Fears with a Real Threat.

Then there are the Unreal Fears.

Unreal Fears are those fears that don't carry with them a "real world" threat. These are terrors that open the doors we usually keep closed and locked. You know the ones I mean? Sure you do. Haven't you, at some point in your life, asked yourself, are ghosts real? Are there such things as vampires, werewolves, and haunted houses? Do zombies really exist? Do the dead sing? Are pyrokinesis, telekinesis, ESP, and spontaneous human combustion real things? Has anybody *really* been abducted by ufonauts? Is there a Heaven?

And even worse...is there a Hell?

Do you really want to know?

These are fears of the soul—fears that don't affect whether or not you pay your mortage this month, or whether or not you get laid off.

And very often these are the Fears that we ignore, brush aside, and pretend don't exist.

But even though they're Unreal, they're real.

They make us close the closet door securely before getting into bed. Now, rationally, we all know that there isn't a monster in our bedroom closet. But

emotionally we all feel a little better with the door closed tight. That way, anything that just might be in there won't be able to get out without us hearing the door squeak open. (Unless it's a ghost. They can walk through walls, you know. And doors.)

The exquisite and dark delight that comes when vicariously confronted with these two types of fears is what makes Stephen King so popular.

We want—and need—our fright fix.

All we King junkies have a real horror "sweet tooth," and let's face it—we've been spoiled.

Stephen King is prolific enough, and diligent enough, to have turned out a huge amount of writing since 1974. And we are all the better for it – even if the term "better" includes Sub-Topic A, "Unease, Various Levels."

PART 3

Summing Up

"My dad raised us by the book. Unfortunately, that book was *The Shining.*"
—Comedian Drake Sather

"Have you seen the Stephen King book *IT*? Is this fair? What's gonna happen? Are people gonna wake up in the middle of the night and say 'Honey, there's a pronoun in the basement, there's a pronoun in the basement.'"
—Comedian Richard Lewis

The Shape Under the Sheet: The Complete Stephen King Encyclopedia is my attempt to provide the ultimate reference to Stephen King's fiction. While putting together the original outline for this book, I started with the concordance section of the encyclopedia, and then added interviews, features, fiction, etc., around it.

While reading through the concordance section, you will notice that there is less information given about the more widely-seen King material (the best-selling novels, the collected stories, etc.), and more information given for the harder-to-find, more rare King works (*The Plant,* "Slade," the uncollected stories, etc.). This is intentional. I didn't feel that my readers needed a great deal of detail about people like Jack Torrance or Charlie McGee, inasmuch as *The Shining* and *Firestarter* are readily available in inexpensive, Signet paperback editions (and are probably already in most King fan's collections anyway).

But things like "The Blue Air Compressor," "I Was a Teenage Grave Robber," and the aforementioned *The Plant* are very difficult, and in some cases, impossible to locate.

So, for those King fans who have heard or read about these "buried treasures," but cannot track them down, here, in *The Shape Under the Sheet,* are details on the people, places, and things of these tales, along with synopses and publication information.

In both cases, it's important to stress that it's not my intention that this work act as a substitute for reading King's works; my primary goal is to encourage you to *read the originals.* There is no substitute for that experience. *Shape Under the Sheet* is *not* Cliffs Notes for Stephen King. It is a tool designed to increase your understanding, enjoyment, and appreciation.

The Shape Under the Sheet concordance is complete through the publication of 1990's *Four Past Midnight* (a collection), and the short story "The Moving Finger" (also from 1990). The First Line Index is complete through the as yet unpublished *The Dark Tower III: The Waste Lands.* (My first book on King, *The Stephen King Quiz Book,* is complete through 1989's *The Dark Half.* Both *The Shape Under the Sheet* and *The Stephen King Quiz Book* will be revised and updated periodically.)

I welcome letters from readers. You can write me at the following address:

Stephen Spignesi
c/o Popular Culture, Ink.
P.O. Box 1839
Ann Arbor, Michigan 48106

The Shape Under the Sheet was four years in the writing, and a lifetime in the making. I hope you enjoy it, and that it enhances your enjoyment and understanding of one of our finest and most entertaining writers. If it does that, then my hopes for this book have been realized.

Stephen J. Spignesi

Shape Under The Sheet
logo by Katherine Flickinger.

Acknowledgments

I know...everyone says it: This book could not have been written alone...I owe all kinds of thanks to...and so on and so on...blah, blah, blah, and before you know it, the Acknowledgments begin to read like one of the longer Academy Award acceptance speeches.

But I'm going to say it anyway: I could not have written *The Shape Under the Sheet: The Complete Stephen King Encylopedia* alone.

And I mean it.

This book was such a huge project that if I hadn't received help in many ways, shapes and forms, there is no way the tome you now hold in your hands would have become a reality.

Help ranged from such integral assistance as researching King's texts and granting me interviews, to just being available when I needed a question answered or returning a phone call. What I've done is to break up this listing into sections, thus allowing me to individually thank and acknowledge the people to whom I owe more than I could ever repay.

I hope I didn't forget anyone, but if I did, it was by no means intentional, and please (whomever you may be) accept my sincerest apologies for my regrettable slighting of your contributions to this project.

And before we get started, just let me say one big, King-sized !!!THANKS!!!! to one and all. My love and appreciation for you all knows no bounds, and by sharing in *Shape Under the Sheet* in whatever way you did, you have enriched my life.

(1)

The following people are beyond thanks, but I'll try anyway. These are the people who shared in the birth pangs of this baby; the ones who literally helped this project come alive.

These are the people to whom I owe the most:

- **MY WIFE, PAM**, for understanding that a book such as this requires a twenty-four-hour-a-day commitment, and for accepting everything that such a commitment entailed, things like using our vacations to write, and locking myself away in my office when I was home. People often asked me, how does your wife feel about the fact that even when you're there, you're not there...that all your time is spent writing? I always gave the same answer: She understands...and I love her for it.

- **STEPHEN KING**, for allowing me to be the one to do the authorized Stephen King encyclopedia. I could never be so presumptuous as to call Stephen King my friend...friendship comes from years of shared lives. But I do hope that *The Shape Under the Sheet* somehow expresses the admiration and respect I have for him and his work. If it does that, I can hope for no more.

- **MY MOTHER, LEE MANDATO**, who was my primary research assistant on this project, and who put untold hours into compiling some of the raw notes I would need to write the concordance section of *The Shape Under the Sheet*. I often told my mother that I couldn't have paid for the dedication and help I got from her...assistance I received for free! Most children could never hope to share such an experience with a parent: I am one of the lucky ones who did.

- **MY EDITOR, TOM SCHULTHEISS**, for his unquestioning faith in me and my work. Tom always had the answers I needed and was always there with the absolute perfect advice and suggestions...again, exactly when I needed them. I am fortunate to have met such a man, and I owe him more gratitude than I am capable of expressing.

- **MY FRIEND, DAVE HINCHBERGER**, the founder of the Overlook Connection. Dave and I met through my request for an Overlook Catalogue, and his scribbled return note asking about a possible mutual friend. From there, it was easy. Dave and I must have been connected in some past life because he and I immediately became the best of friends...and what makes it more amazing to me is that we were incredibly close for a year...before we even met! Long-distance friendships sometimes suffer because of the distances. Not ours. When Dave and I finally met at NECON IX in Rhode Island in the summer of 1989, it was as though we had just had dinner together the night before. In fact, the guy I was with at the convention, a dear friend and dynamite guy named Mark Savo, thought that we had spent lots of time together prior to the convention. He was floored when I told him we had never met in person before that day. Dave and I just picked up as though we had known each other for years. And, in a way, I suppose that somehow, we had. Dave was an enormous help on *The Shape*. He sent me so much material in 1988 that he saved me months of hunting trying to find rare King pieces I needed for research. I am happy that Dave Hinchberger is my friend.

- **MY AGENT, JOHN WHITE**, a truly advanced soul whom I met through a teacher and friend, Jay Halpern. John and I share much in the way of personal beliefs and interests, and he is one of the most truly moral people I have ever known. I can only try to emulate his high ideals and belief in a higher consciousness for man. John believes that there is evidence that man is evolving into a higher state of awareness – a God-centered sensibility rather than a self-centered sensibility. I have found evidence that John is right, and John himself is, to me, an example of the most pervasive evidence of the advancement of the species. I am privileged to know such a man.

(2)

This section thanks (in alphabetical order) those people who had a significant impact on the book's look and/or content—the "front line" people. These are the people who gave of themselves in many ways, never with an eye for their own benefit, but rather, always trying to help the progress of *The Shape Under the Sheet* in any way they could. Friends like these enrich your life...and I am honored to have had such support and help from the following angels:

- **MICHAEL J. AUTREY**, a West Coast book dealer who went out of his way to help me with research copies of *extremely* rare Stephen King materials for this book. Thanks to Michael, I was able to include details on "The Stephen King Notebook" and "An Evening at God's," and I am grateful for his help and for our interview.

- **GEORGE BEAHM**, author of the superlative *The Stephen King Companion,* who, like Dave Hinchberger, literally became a friend overnight. Ever since our first phone conversation, we have kept in weekly (sometimes daily!) touch, and it was through George's efforts that I was able to get an advance copy of *The Stand: The Complete & Uncut Edition*. But probably his most significant contribution to this book was his making available to me his notes for the three unpublished Stephen King novels in the University of Maine Special Collections Library. George is one of the handful of people on this planet who have actually read all three novels, and his detailed synopses and notes allowed me to include a concordance to these tales in this book. George is a quiet, incredibly ethical human being, and my appreciation for his help and support knows no bounds.

- **STEVE BISSETTE**, my artist for the limited edition of *The Shape Under the Sheet*. Steve did a superb job on the artwork for that edition. Thanks, Steve, for your help, for *Taboo,* and for believing that nothing is taboo.

- **TYSON BLUE**, former *Castle Rock* contributing editor and author of *The Unseen King*. Tyson is bright, prolific, and an acknowledged King expert. His work in *Castle Rock* could easily have been a book itself, and his *Unseen King* is a very accessible look at the more rare King works. Look for Tyson's "Blue Notes" column in *Midnight Graffiti*.

- **DEB BURRELL**, of the New York Astrology Center, went out of her way to help with the astrological profile of King originally scheduled for inclusion in this book. Deb is kind, warm, and incredibly knowledgeable about astrology and other metaphysical concerns. Her energy, enthusiasm and generous spirit permeate everything she does. Thanks, Deb, for your time, your efforts, and for always keeping your eye on the stars. My regrets about having to leave the feature out of *The Shape*.

- **CHRIS CHESLEY**, Stephen King's *People, Places, and Things* co-author, decided at the last minute to become involved in this project, and when he had made the decision, boy, did he come through! The result of his decision was an insightful, in-depth interview, permission to reprint his short story "Genius" from *People, Places, and Things* (with a new 1990 introduction), permission to publish, for the first time, his new short story "The Mission Boy," and a personal essay called "Death Scenes." Chris is a modest, unassuming guy, and his personal humility was an example I still aspire to emulate.

- **JIM COLE**, the director of the terrific short film (based on King's short story) "The Last Rung on the Ladder." Jim is one of those rare people who has not only devoted himself to his work with a fervor that is red-hot, but who also has the talent to fulfill his dreams. My special thanks to Jim for his neverending interest in this book, and for his friendship.

- **MICHAEL R. COLLINGS** is the author of more books about Stephen King than anyone else on this planet. (At last count, seven books). His Starmont titles are insightful, astute analyses of Stephen King's work, and they were immeasurably helpful to me while working on *The Shape Under the Sheet*. Also, Dr. C. was very generous with his time, contributing two pieces, the essay on King's poetry called "The Radiating Pencils of His Bones," and the poignant poem, "You, Stephen King." (Dr. C. also wrote the "Star Invaders" feature for this book.) Michael Collings is the ultimate academic, but tempers his scholarship with a terrific sense of humor and a wonderful imagination. (He and his son have collaborated on a novel about a high school that eats—literally—students.) If you haven't read Michael Collings's work, I suggest you do so as soon as possible. I guarantee that it will enhance your appreciation and understanding of Stephen King's work.

•**PAT CURTIS**, who, along with Tom Schultheiss, is one of the principals at Popular Culture, Ink., the publishing house that released the book you are now reading. Pat is an intelligent, charming, and warm person who handles operations and marketing chores at PCI. Thanks to Pat's efforts, my first book, *Mayberry, My Hometown,* continues to deliver royalty checks and, also thanks to Pat, I did more media interviews for *Mayberry* (and I expect for this book) than I could ever set up on my own. Pat is a terrific person who has always been more help to me than she can probably imagine.

•**JAMES DOURGARIAN**, a California book dealer whose interview was regrettably not able to be included in *The Shape.* Thanks, Jim, for all your help and kindness.

•**STEVE FIORILLA**, who contributed the drawing he originally did for *Enterprise Incidents Presents Stephen King.* Steve is a great guy and a terrific artist. Thanks, my friend!

•**LARRY FIRE**, a friend who was a big help in the last days of the preparation of this book. Larry put me in touch with Kenny Ray Linkous and, thanks to his efforts, I was able to include some of Kenny Ray's work in this book. Thanks, Larry, for everything. See you at NECON.

•**MY ARTIST, KATHERINE FLICKINGER**, a friend who gave of herself unstintingly, and who gave her absolute best to me and *The Shape Under the Sheet.* I was awestruck the first time I saw the final version of Katherine's drawing "The Overlook Was At Home With The Dead," and I'm proud to be able to showcase her talents in this book. Special thanks must also go to Kath's friend Linda for her interest and support of this project. (Linda allowed herself to be wrapped in a sheet so that Kath could see what a body on a table looked like for her "Shape Under the Sheet" logo. She also "played dead" in a bathtub for the drawing "Toner in the Tub.") Thank you both, Kathy and Linda, for all your help, and your kindness and cooperation.

•**RAY GARTON**, author of *Live Girls, Methods of Madness, Trade Secrets,* and other white hot horror and dark fantasy works, was one of the first people I interviewed for *The Shape,* and his insights into the Stephen King Phenomenon added a great deal to this book. Thanks, Ray, for your help and support.

•**CRAIG GODEN**, book dealer extraordinaire, went out of his way to help with a bunch of things I needed for *The Shape,* including "A Possible Fairy Tale," and photocopies galore. Craig is one of the nicest people I've met while working on this book, and I heartily recommend his company, The Time Tunnel, for all your genre needs.

•**JIM GONIS**, the director of the student film (based on King's short story) "The Lawnmower Man." King himself has remarked how much he liked Jim's film (he said he liked the "cheesy" quality to it), and I'd like to thank Jim for supplying *Shape* readers with his article detailing the making of "Lawnmower Man," and for his interest in this project.

•**DONALD M. GRANT**, as all serious King fans know, is the hardcover publisher of King's Dark Tower series. Don always made time to answer my questions, and very generously contributed a piece on the late Joseph Payne Brennan (his friend and co-author), which I used to introduce the reprinting of Joe's brilliant story "Canavan's Back Yard." Don Grant is quiet, unassuming, and very dedicated to his work. His limited editions are some of the most beautiful books in existence. This field is better off because people like Don Grant are in it.

•**JAY HALPERN**, a former teacher from whom I have never stopped learning, is the author of the excellent 1979 horror novel *The Jade Unicorn* (why doesn't somebody out there make a *movie* of this book!!??). Jay was always there during the writing of *The Shape Under the Sheet* with advice and counsel. Jay is a truly unique soul who tells me that he is currently working with autistic and retarded children to try and repair some of the damage he did to his karma in his younger days. I think he's succeeding because he does more to advance the human condition in a week than most people do in a year. Thanks, Jay, for setting me on a road that, while sometimes dark and confusing, is nonetheless the one that leads in the right direction.

•**RICK HAUTALA** (the *other* Maine horror writer!) is a funny, terrific guy who possesses a genuine humility that is honest and sincere. Rick was a big help with *The Shape,* and I truly value his friendship. (And Rick Hautala at NECON is an experience, believe me!) Thanks, Rick, for your support and kindness over the past few years.

•**BARRY HOFFMAN** is the founding editor of *Gauntlet* magazine, a publication that, dare I say, is the most important periodical being published today. *Gauntlet* – and Barry Hoffman – are worried about censorship, and they take any and all steps to see that it is decapitated wherever it rears its detestable head. Barry will publish anything, no matter who it offends, and I, for one, give him a standing ovation for doing so. Bless you, Barry. To me, you define the word "patriot," and I will do everything and anything I can to help you with your battle. (Oh, and by the way...thanks for your help with *Shape Under the Sheet,* too!)

•**JESSIE HORSTING**, the author of *Stephen King At the Movies,* is a trip. We've never had a chance to meet in person, but all my conversations with her have been huge fun. She gave me a long interview for *The Shape,* and also published an excerpt from this book in the Stephen King issue of her magazine *Midnight Graffiti.* Thanks, Jess.

•**DAVID KING**, Stephen King's brother, allowed me to be the first person to ever do an in-depth interview with him, and he also gave me the rights to reprint the last surviving "Dave's Rag" in *The Shape Under the Sheet.* His thoughts about growing up with his brother and their early years together filled in a lot of blanks for me and Stephen King's readers, and allowed us all a peek at the making of a writer. Thanks, Dave, for your help, your friendliness, and your willingness to be so helpful to some guy from New Haven. God bless you.

•**JOE R. LANSDALE**, author of some of the most entertaining fiction I've ever read, gave me a lengthy, insightful interview about Stephen King, and I am privileged to share his thoughts with my readers. Joe lives in Texas, in a town very close to La Plata. And you know something? I think King was right about the water. (And if you don't know what I'm talking about, see the section on "The End of the Whole Mess" in this volume.)

•**STEPHANIE LEONARD**, who, as I'm sure you all know, is Tabitha King's sister, Stephen King's sister-in-law, and the Founding Editor of the official King newsletter, *Castle Rock.* At a time when she was overwhelmed with work, Stephanie made it a point to help with advice and suggestions, send me back issues of *Castle Rock,* and respond—in detail—to my interview questions. Stephanie is a class act, and I owe her much thanks.

•**KENNY RAY LINKOUS**, the artist who illustrated the Philtrum Press edition of Stephen King's *The Eyes of the Dragon.* Kenny Ray produced an illustration especially for *Shape Under the Sheet* with about six seconds notice, and I sincerely appreciate his efforts and last-minute assistance. Thanks, Kenny. *Next* time, you'll have *more* time. I promise.

•**DAVE LOWELL**, my "man in Maine" (and New Hampshire...and

California…and elsewhere!) really was an enormous help with photos, scripts, and especially as my personal emissary to Dave King's place in New Hampshire. There were times when Mr. Lowell amazed me with his unbelievable speed at getting things to Dave, taking photos, having them developed and getting them back to me. Dave is the man who took the pictures of David King, and of Stephen King's childhood home. Dave also offered me countless photos, autographs, and postcards from his superb collection. Thank you, sir, for all your help and kindness. You added immeasurably to *The Shape Under the Sheet,* and for your assistance I will be ever grateful.

• **RICHARD MATHESON** , living legend, was gracious, friendly, and very prompt in responding to my written interview questions. Mr. Matheson is the author of some of the seminal works in the field (as well as being a primary influence on Stephen King). I—and all King fans—owe him a world of thanks.

• **RICHARD CHRISTIAN MATHESON** , the son of a legend, gave me a huge block of his time one Sunday and, later, even took the time to send my wife an autographed photo. His cards and occasional notes always made us smile, and his short fiction – written as what's come to be known as "short-shorts" – were always just the right length for those times when I needed a fiction break but didn't have the time to read anything long. Thank you, my man, R.C. Cola, for everything – and especially for introducing me to your father.

• **ROBERT R. McCAMMON** , author of *Swan Song, Mine,* and a slew of other brilliant works of fiction, is well on his way to becoming a living legend. Rick gave of himself at a time when he was busy with a mountain of other work, and for taking the time to speak with me for this book, I am very grateful. Thanks, Rick. Your participation in *The Shape Under the Sheet* meant a great deal to me.

• **KEN OWENS,** for his assistance is providing me with tapes and articles about Stephen King's 1989 Pasadena Library lecture. My very first awareness of King's novella "The Library Policeman" was thanks to Ken's phone calls and letters, and his help was much appreciated. I think you'd call Ken a serious King fan: He owns a car that is an exact duplicate of Christine. Thanks, Ken.

• **RAY REXER,** the creator of the now-defunct *Castle Rock* parody newsletter, *Castle Schlock .* How can I describe Ray for those of you who are not familiar with him or his work? Well, let me try this approach: If Ray were a Loser, he'd be Richie Tozier. If Ray were a TV show, he'd be "Late Night with David Letterman." If Ray were a pizza, he'd be a large scrambled egg, double cheese, anchovies…and coconut. If Ray were an animal, he'd be a platypus. If Ray were a movie, he'd be "The Rocky Horror Picture Show." If Ray were a rock and roll band, he'd be Devo. Get the picture? I thought so. Many thanks to Ray for his help with *The Shape,* for his terrific short story, and for the late, great *Castle Schlock.*

• **SHIRLEY SONDEREGGER** , who, as Stephen King's secretary, somehow manages to keep the madness and mighty confusion of Stephen King's career under total control. Shirley was always pleasant, accessible, helpful, and unbelievably generous with her time. Thank you, Shirley, for the interview, and for somehow knowing just the right thing to say at times when I needed to hear just the right thing.

• **MY SISTER, JANET SPIGNESI** , who helped me in many ways, but who really came through with special assistance on the *Rage* section of the concordance. Thanks, Jan, for agreeing in some unknown way and at some unknown time, to be my sister.

• **CHRISTOPHER SPRUCE** , Stephen King's brother-in-law and the second Editor of *Castle Rock,* published excerpts from *The Shape Under the Sheet* in *Castle Rock* throughout the four years I worked on the book. His support of, and interest in *The Shape* gave the project a recognizability factor among King fans that I couldn't have bought for love or money. For this, Chris has my undying appreciation. In addition to the terrific PR, he also made available to us his *Castle Rock* mailing lists, giving us access to just the people we wanted to reach: Stephen King's fans. My deepest thanks go out to Chris for his help with this book, his kindness and consideration, and most of all, for his superb work on the *Castle Rock* newsletter in its last year.

• **LEWIS TEAGUE** , director extraordinaire, shared his thoughts and insights about filming *Cujo* and *Cat's Eye,* and we're all the wiser for his efforts. Many thanks to Lew for his participation and his work over the years.

• **JAMES VAN HISE** , the creator of *Enterprise Incidents Present Stephen King* and *The Illustrated Guide to the Masters of the Macabre,* and editor (with Jessie Horsting) of *Midnight Graffiti,* for his help, his interview, and for being one of the first editors to publish an excerpt from the book you now hold in your hands in *Midnight Graffiti.* Thanks, Jim, for your help, and for your work over the years.

• **STAN WIATER** , a writer and editor of prodigious talents, is a friend and advisor who helped me in many ways; sometimes with materials, sometimes with advice. You got me started with my S.K. collection, Stan, and for that I will be ever grateful. Thanks for everything. I'd also like to thank Stan's wife, Iris, a terrific photographer, for, first, taking some of the photos that appear in this book, and second, for allowing me to reprint them.

• **J.N. WILLIAMSON** , one of the most prolific writers working in the field today, was the first author I interviewed for *The Shape.* His overwhelming belief in this project led him to help in countless ways, including supplying me with phone numbers and addresses of other writers I needed to speak to, and also granting me a lengthy, very insightful interview. I was finally able to meet Jerry in person at the 1989 NECON, and I truly value his friendship. Thanks, Jerry, for everything.

• **DOUGLAS E. WINTER** , the author of the superlative *Stephen King: The Art of Darkness,* likewise gave of himself at a time when time was the last thing he had to spare. He went out of his way to edit our interview into something that both of us could be proud of—more thanks to him than me! Doug has a magnificent intellect, and I learned a lot from our interactions over the years it took to write *The Shape Under the Sheet.* He is an incredibly down-to-earth guy who just happens to possess one of the best minds in the field. Thanks, Doug, for your work, and for your help. Also, I'd like to express my sincerest thanks to Doug's wife, Lynne, for her kindness, and for her interest in, and help with, this project. She always made sure that Doug got my messages, assistance which I greatly appreciated, and which made things a lot easier as I got nearer to completing *The Shape.* Thanks, Doug and Lynne, for everything.

(3)

The following people are those family members and friends who were always there with a kind or encouraging word about this project, and who were always interested in hearing me wax endlessly about the latest *Shape* developments. Even though they weren't actually involved in the book itself, I could tell their heart was in it, and that they sincerely wanted to see me complete this marathon. This section also makes note of a few total strangers who, without ever knowing it, made my day easier, either through their music, their writing, or their work. Thank you all for every moment of kindness and interest. My thanks to the following people, whose names are in alphabetical order so that nobody's feelings will get hurt!:

Woody Allen; Yvette Scharf Altman; Doug Altmannsberger; Hazel Bacote; Joe Badamo; Mrs. Joseph Payne Brennan; Kate Bush; Susan Capelli Kohary; Toni Capelli; Joe Citro; Jim Clark—My Dear Friend and Fellow Goober; Mary Lou Cofrancesco; Frank & Edith Cupo; Curly; Pete DeBrino; Ted DeMaio; Gary Dermer; Louanne Deserio; Ted Ditky; Paul Dobish; Dolores, Tony, & Linda Fantarella; Dante & Marie Fasano; Dan & Laurie Fasano; Al Hemingway; Laurie Hinchberger; Carl Jung; Hugh Klockars; Lynn and Ed Knapp; Larry; Bob & Suzanne Leen of Minuteman Press of East Haven, Connecticut; Lynn & Erik Leeming; John Lennon; David Letterman; Frank Mandato; Ronnie McDermott; Larry "Bud" Melman; Chuck Miller; Moe; Frank & Judy Myjak; William Paley; Joe Parcella; Bob Plante; John Polisky; Marian Powers of *Time* magazine; Steve (my namesake) & Marge Rapuano—for their incredible, unending support; Dave & Judy Richards; Roger & Michelle; Judi Saleeby—Baker of the Best Bread on the Planet Earth; Matt Sartwell—my Signet *Stephen King Quiz Book* editor (and his assistant, Peter); Mark & Paula Savo; Dr. Angelyn Spignesi; David, Maureen, Amanda, & Joey Spignesi; Paul, Laura, & Jennifer Spignesi; Richard Neal Spignesi; Sheryl & Vinnie Streeto; Tim Underwood; the Viking Press Publicity Department; Paul Winnick; and Georgette Campano Wood.

And a last, final thank you to...

The late **JOSEPH PAYNE BRENNAN**, who passed over during the writing of *The Shape Under the Sheet*. Joe and I had become friends during the last year of his life, and he had hoped to be around for the publication of this book. This was not to be so, and we lost Joe on January 28, 1990. I would like this book to be a tribute to his memory. Thank you, Joe, wherever you are, for your kindness and help, for the interview, and for letting me reprint your story "Canavan's Back Yard" in this book. You were a great soul, and you are sorely missed.

"When he shall die
Take him and cut him out in little stars
And he will make the face of heaven so fine
That all the world will be in love with the night
And pay no worship to the garish sun."
—William Shakespeare,
Romeo and Juliet

A Death in the Family

"Many good men should weep for his death...."
—Horace, from *Odes*

On Friday afternoon, April 26, 1991, our friend, fellow writer and colleague, Police Officer Ray Rexer, was shot to death in the line of duty.

I had spoken with him around noon that day. Ray had sent me a written interview and he had called me to tell me that he had gotten my interview responses, and that he wanted to follow up with a few more questions. I told him to call me that evening around seven. He said he would, and the way Ray was I could count on setting my watch by the ringing of the phone. When 7:30 came and went, I somehow sensed that something wasn't right. It wasn't like Ray to forget to make a scheduled call. I found out the next morning just how "not right" things actually were.

Ray was a genuine gift to this planet. He was blessed with a sense of humor that very often deflated pomposity, and his irreverence was a shower of cool rain on the stuffy, muggy air of a popular culture that all too often took itself *way* too seriously.

Ray was my friend. And he was a huge help with *The Shape Under The Sheet*. He contributed an essay about his brilliant parody newsletter, *Castle Schlock;* he allowed me to reprint excerpts from the newsletter at will; and he also contributed the terrific short story, "Character Assassination," the title of which now holds a certain dark gravity, don't you think?

But I feel secure in saying that I don't think Ray would want tears. He loved life too much, and he had too much fun just being alive, to allow us to spend time mourning. After Ray's death, I even considered making some last minute changes in my remarks about Ray in *The Shape Under The Sheet*, but decided against it. Just as Donald Grant decided to let his comments about his friend, Joseph Payne Brennan, stand after Joe's death, so will my comments about Ray stand. They were written about a friend *by* a friend, and so will not be made more somber because of Ray's death.

But as friends who miss him—and will continue to miss him as the years go by—mourn we must. Our loss is deep, and the pain is real. But now that Ray has gone on to something better, let's also remember him with smiles. Let's remember the guy who signed his letters "Wray Wreckser"; the guy who was the Ruler of the Kingdom of the Outrageous Pun; the guy who invented a Stephen King cereal called SCARY-O'S, "for people who aren't afraid to eat right"; and the guy who created an actual crossword puzzle in which every answer was the word "King."

Thank you, Wray Wreckser, wherever you are, for your gentle manner, your sense of humor, and your kindnesses. You were loved, and you will be missed. And as you now watch over your family and friends, take a minute to crack open a cold one and smile at the follies of life on the planet Earth. You were one of its best citizens, and we're all the worse for your departure.

Rest in peace, pal.

—Steve Spignesi, Sunday, April 28, 1991

PART I

THE SHAPE TAKES FORM

An Introduction to Stephen King & His Art

"THE SHAPE UNDER THE SHEET"
by Stephen J. Spignesi

Dedicated
...with thanks and admiration...
to Stephen King

1.
The violet band of warmer forties
Snakes through New England;
The tail of the serpent
    Flicks and nips
Touching...(but barely)
The gabled peak of a Victorian
House on West Broadway,
In the kingdom of Bangor, Maine.

For a moment, the weather
Map on "Good Morning, America"
Goes black and your bearded
Visage slaps into my
Consciousness...
Smiling
At the gray shroud of America
And the skeletal
Ghost of its coast.

This sometimes happens:
Stepping through
My open front door,
The land changes—
The air goes black—
Hills rise up in the distance
    (a dark tower looms there)
The army of ghouls moves
Slowly,
Inexorably,
Towards me:

Each step
    Lurches...
        (And in the end,
        birds
        stand still
        in the gray
        light of you.)

I am reminded that this world grew
Mother Teresa as well as
A maniac
With no name
Who cut up and froze
twenty-four pounds
of a woman's body parts.

The police found her head
Boiling in a pot.

Such visions can test
And yet,
The blood knows
What the mind rejects:
We want to know.
We so...
    Want..
        To know.

2.
What is its look,
The shape under the sheet?
What is its feel,
And where is its glory?

Its essence: a bloodletting in ink:
Cujo knows the Tommyknockers...
Frank Dodd sings with Pennywise...
Rainbird and Flagg embrace in the mist...
While Carrie walks the halls of hell...
(And the street just one block over.)

Welcome to Castle Rock:
Here there be tygers
And the hidden things of darkness.

Here there be the deadlights...

DO IT:
Lift the corner...there...and touch
The shape under the sheet:

Here there be Stephen King.

"THE SHAPE UNDER THE SHEET"
A Look at Stephen King's Seminal Metaphor
and His "Ten Bears" List of Personal Fears

"The field has never been highly regarded...It may be because the horror writer always brings bad news: you're going to die, he says; he's telling you to never mind Oral Roberts and his 'something *good* is going to happen to *you*,' because something *bad* is also going to happen to *you*, and it may be cancer and it may be a stroke, and it may be a car accident, but it's going to happen. And he takes your hand and he enfolds it in his own, and he takes you into the room and he puts your hands on the shape under the sheet...and tells you to touch it here...here...and *here*...He's telling you that you want to see the car accident, and yes, he's right—you do. There's a dead voice on the phone...something behind the walls of the old house that sounds bigger than a rat...movement at the foot of the cellar stairs. He wants you to see all of those things, and more; he wants you to put your hands on the shape under the sheet. And you want to put your hands there. Yes."

—Stephen King,
from his *Night Shift* Foreword

"The horror movie asks you if you want to take a good close look at the dead cat (or the shape under the sheet, to use a metaphor from the introduction to my short story collection)..."

—Stephen King,
from *Danse Macabre*

As you can see from the quotations above, the title I've given this volume is not original to me. Stephen King originally used the metaphor "the shape under the sheet" in the Foreword to his *Night Shift* collection, and the image has always struck me as the perfect five words to describe what the horror writer shows the reader. Since my goal with *The Shape Under the Sheet* was to show King's readers the entire Stephen King universe, I "appropriated" the image for this book. I owe Steve King much thanks: first, for writing it, and thereby titling this book for me, and second, for not charging me to use it.

King is right: we *do* want to see the car accident. I remember hearing about an accident that happened on the Quinnipiac River bridge (which is nearby my home) several years ago. The Q Bridge (as it is known in these parts) is a treacherous, three-lane bridge that crosses the New Haven Harbor and gets folks into downtown New Haven from the outskirts.

This bridge is scary. The speed limit is around twenty-five or so, but cars regularly travel fifty or better.

And there are no breakdown lanes.

The accident I'm referring to involved a motorcycle and a car. A guy was riding with his brother on the back of his bike. The motorcyclist was traveling close to fifty, as were most of the other drivers. When he changed lanes, he somehow didn't see the car be-

hind him and to his left.

Impact.

The biker's brother's left leg was amputated at the hip by the car behind them.

Before the site was cleared, there were *two* shapes under *two* sheets: the brother...and his leg.

People slowing down to stare tied up traffic for hours.

Stephen King makes a good point: there is a primal desire, a real *need* in us all to somehow prepare for death, to in some way experience the void...without actually going through the experience of dying. As he has often said, we need to "rehearse" for death, because knowing, in some small, incomplete way, what death might be like, may make it easier when the time actually does come.

We try lots of ways to "get the feeling." What are rollercoasters but the simulation of what it must feel like to fall—or jump—off a building? How about skydiving? And don't hunters vicariously experience what it feels like to be stalked...and shot to death?

Carl Jung wrote that there exists in the human animal a "collective unconscious." In *Introduction to Psychology* (West, 1980, p. 425), Dennis Coon writes:

Jung believed that since the beginning of time all humans have had experiences with birth, death, power, god figures, mother and father figures, animals, the earth, energy, evil, re-birth, and so on. According to Jung, such universals create archetypes. Archetypes, found in the collective unconscious, are unconscious images that cause us to respond emotionally to *symbols* of birth, death, energy, animals, evil, and the like. As such, archetypes are a carry-over of our rich human heritage. Jung believed that he detected symbols representing such archetypes in the art, religion, myths, and dreams of every culture and age.

Jung's theory would explain why horror, in all its guises and forms, creates such deep emotional responses (fear, abhorrence, repulsion, panic, etc.) in the people who experience it. Horror as an art form can be viewed as a representational manifestation—a symbol—of our cultural insecurities about death.

But King goes beyond a simple preoccupation with death, although that is certainly present in his work. By tapping into the collective unconscious on many levels through his novels and stories, he has assembled a body of work that can be looked at as a catalog of human fears and insecurities. Stephen King has spent a great deal of time peeking beneath the sheet:

Are you worried about being a good parent? *The Shining.*

Are you worried that you're a failure? *The Shining* again.

Are you afraid your wife's car will break down someplace...nasty? *Cujo.*

Are you afraid your wife's cheating on you? *Cujo* again.

Are you worried about the road in front of your house...because *you've got kids*? *Pet Sematary.*

Are you afraid the kids in your high school will make fun of you...and maybe worse? *Carrie.*

Are you paranoid about our government? *Firestarter.*

Are you uneasy about your neighbors? *'Salem's Lot* and "Cain Rose Up."

Have you had a sudden, unexplained weight loss? *Thinner.*

Are you afraid of machines...and wind-up toys...and cars? *Christine,* "The Monkey," and "Trucks."

Do you get uneasy during bad weather? "The Mist."

Are you a celebrity who gets just a little nervous when approached by *very* involved fans? *Misery.*

Are you afraid of your students? "Suffer the Little Children."

Did your childhood almost destroy you? *IT.*

When you're on a ship, do you ever worry about being shipwrecked? "Survivor Type."

Are you afraid of the library? "The Library Policeman."

Are you afraid of your past? *The Dark Half.*

And so on...

Stephen King is able to create stories, characters, and situations that do to the reader just what Jung spoke about: they elicit emotional responses from symbols of universal archetypes.

King has even gone so far as to make up his own "Top Ten" list of personal terrors; fears that work on a variety of levels for him. In his 1973 essay "The Horror Writer and the Ten Bears," King bared his soul for the reader, and the following is what he came up with:

10. Fear *for* someone else
9. Fear of others (paranoia)
8. Fear of death
7. Fear of insects (especially spiders, flies, and beetles)
6. Fear of closed-in places
5. Fear of rats
4. Fear of snakes
3. Fear of deformity
2. Fear of squishy things

and Stephen King's Number One Bear...

1. Fear of the dark

There is much to Stephen King and his work. Through a reading (and re-reading) of his stories, we can experience a plethora of emotions, not all of which are pleasant. But that's good. Not all of life is pleasant either. By looking under the sheet, we prepare ourselves for those moments and events in our lives that require a huge emotional commitment. Through his tales, we can see how *we* would react if our child was killed by a truck in front of our house (even though, for most of us, such a horrific event will probably never take place). Knowledge is power, and through a deeper knowledge of our own emotional responses, we can achieve growth.

All this—while being supremely entertained by a master storyteller at the same time.

Enjoy *The Shape Under the Sheet: The Complete Stephen King Encyclopedia.*

And while you're spending time with all this information about King's work, realize that it's all right to be frightened of the shape under the sheet.

Yes, it may bite...but you can always bite it back, right?

Right.

POSTCARDS FROM
THE DARK SIDE OF THE MOON
A Bare-Bones Biographical Profile

"I'm up at 6:30 every morning and get breakfast for the kids and get them off to school. Then I just walk around for about four hours sniffing at this book in my mind. I get back at 9:30 and write to 11:30. Everyday I write 1,500 words. In the afternoon I read and sort of gibber around."

—Stephen King, from a 1983 interview with Michael Hanlon, originally published in the *Toronto Star,* October 5, 1983.

Who is Stephen King?

This is Stephen King: A role call of superlatives: eighty-two million books in print, including twenty-three novels, four fiction collections, one nonfiction book, and close to a hundred short stories. Also, five produced screenplays; routine first printings of one million plus books; advances in the eight-figure range and, as of the fall of 1990, twenty-five film adaptations of his work.

This is *also* Stephen King: Of the top twenty-five *Publishers Weekly* fiction bestsellers of the eighties, Stephen King had seven titles on the list: *The Dark Half, The Tommyknockers, It, Misery, The Talisman, The Eyes of the Dragon,* and *Skeleton Crew.* The twenty-five titles on the list sold a combined total of 25,889,924 copies. Of that total, 7,269,929—or twenty-eight percent—were Stephen King titles.

And *this* is *also* Stephen King: King is the down-to-earth Yankee who shows up for publicity photos and interviews wearing jeans and Keds. He is the family man who takes the clan to see the Boston Red Sox, whether they're playing in Boston or Toronto. And he is the guy who welcomed a couple of friends of mine into his office one July afternoon, and when asked for a picture, had my friends pick him up and hold him in the air while the shot was taken.

And, perhaps most important to our understanding, is the knowledge that Stephen King is the workaholic who writes 362 days a year, and who has been known to scrap entire novels that didn't meet his standards (despite the fact that his fans would welcome even his lesser efforts with eager salivation and open arms).

But who is this guy, *really*? And where did he come from?

A furry Stephen King hard at work.
From the original poster for "Maximum Overdrive."

King and furry friend on the "Cat's Eye" set.
Autographed photo courtesy Dave Lowell.

RUTH PILLSBURY   *"Ruthie Pill"*

"Whose little girl are you?"

Public Speaking (1, 2, 3, 4); Second Prize (1); First Prize (2, 3, 4); Winner of Silver Cup at County Contest, Class B (2); Representative at State Speaking Contest (3); Second Place at County Contest, Class B (4); Representative of County to State Contest (4); Physical Education (2); Glee Club (3); Senior Drama (3, 4); Student Council (4); Vice-President of Athletic Association (4).

It's no use to try to tell what Ruth can do, for she does so many things so well, even to broadcasting over Station WHDH. Her 57 varieties of faces make her a bright spot in dull weather. Ruth's ability in public speaking has won distinction for her in numerous plays and honor for the school in every contest she has entered.

King's mother, Ruth Pillsbury, won distinction for her public speaking and drama activities in high school.

Yearbook entry and portrait courtesy David King.

Stephen King was born in Portland, Maine, on September 21, 1947. (*Art Imitates Life Department, Part 1*: September 21 is the same day that Carrie White would be born about fifteen years or so later.)

When Stephen was two, his father, Donald King, went out one night for a pack of cigarettes and was never seen again. Stephen King and his then four-year-old brother David were left to be raised by their mother, Nellie Ruth King. (*Art Imitates Life Department, Part 2*: In *The Stand*, Donald King, an Electrolux salesman from Peru, Indiana, tried to sell Mother Abagail a vacuum cleaner in 1936 or 1937.)

After their father left, Stephen and David King had what could be justifiably called a "nomadic" childhood. I talked to Dave King about the family's early wanderings, and he told me that between 1949 through the fall of 1958, they lived in Scarborough and Croton-On-Hudson, New York; Chicago, Illinios; West De Pere, Wisconsin (*Art Imitates Life Department, Part 3*: About 100 miles southwest of West De Pere is a body of water called Castle Rock Lake); Fort Wayne, Indiana, and Stratford, Connecticut. At the end of 1958,

when Steve was twelve and Dave was fourteen, Nellie King moved her boys from Stratford, Connecticut, to Durham, Maine, where they spent their remaining childhood years. [NOTE: See my interview with Dave King in this volume.]

The King brothers' boyhood home ➤ in West Durham, Maine.
Photo courtesy Dave Lowell.

6

Portland general hospital, King's probable birthplace, still looks just as creepy despite the addition of new wings.

MAINE GENERAL HOSPITAL, PORTLAND, ME.

Main Street, Lisbon Falls (a.k.a. Castle Rock?), early 1960s. Note the 1958 Plymouth Fury at the lower left (Christine in her demure, powder-blue period).

DRUGS

WESTERN AUTO

DUNTON'S

FIRST NATIONAL STORES

Turn of the century post-card showing King's present home on West Broadway in Bangor (middle house).

Stephen and his mother in the late sixties.
Photo courtesy David King.

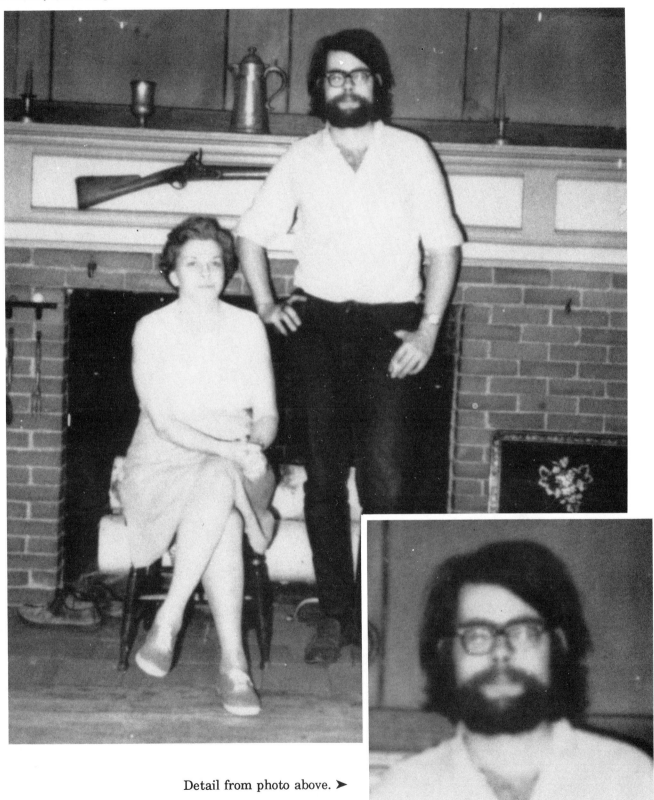

Detail from photo above. ➤

In Maine, King attended Lisbon Falls High School, and from there went on to the University of Maine at Orono. His first published short story, "I Was a Teenage Grave Robber," appeared in *Comics Review* when he was eighteen, and in 1967, at the age of twenty, he sold his first short story, "The Glass Floor," to the magazine *Startling Mystery Stories*. Between 1965 and 1966, he wrote his first novel, *The Aftermath*, and in 1974, *Carrie* was published.

When King and his family moved to Durham, Maine, in 1958, Stephen King met a local kid named Chris Chesley who shared King's interest in horror and science fiction books and movies. The boys soon became friends and writing companions and, in 1960, Chesley and King co-authored an eighteen-page collection of horror stories called *People, Places, and Things*. [NOTE: See the "Chris Chesley" section in this volume.]

The myriad influences on Stephen King include a whole casserole of eclectic elements – ingredients that played an important part in the "recipe" that created the man and writer we know today as the King of Horror.

Among these influences number the work of Richard Matheson, Don Robertson, John D. MacDonald, Robert Bloch, and Ray Bradbury, to name just a few. King credits Richard Matheson's novel *I Am Legend* with showing him that horror does not have to be set in castles and dungeons: Horror can happen in the mall and in suburban tract houses. King was also affected by fifties television, B-horror movies, E.C. Comics, a single-parent upbringing, smalltown living, the sixties, and Chesterfields.

And then there are the more obscure influences: In an interview for this volume, Richard Christian Matheson said that "It's like Steve's got some bizarre telescope that he put together up there in fucking Bangor out of beer and snow and rock and roll, and with it he can see the dark side of the moon."

I find that well put.

Stephen King has an enviable talent: He has the ability to transmute elements from his life into powerfully dramatic moments in his fiction. He is, as horror writer J.N. Williamson has described him, a "noticer." King's *Skeleton Crew* short story "Gramma" was drawn from the time that his invalid grandmother lived in his house in Durham when he was a kid; "The Woman in the Room" from *Night Shift* was his attempt to deal with watching his mother die a protracted and painful death from cancer; "The Mangler" (also from *Night Shift*) came from his ruminations about the menacing

King with co-author Peter Straub (*The Talisman*)
at the World Fantasy Convention, 1984.
Photo courtesy Iris Wiater.

laundry equipment he worked with after graduating from the University of Maine (not having been able to find a teaching job); his novel *IT* contains countless elements from his own childhood; and his "Writer's Trilogy"—*Misery, The Dark Half,* and the novella "Secret Window, Secret Garden"—explores writing, fandom, and the shadows that lie between the two.

Stephen King started writing when he was just a kid. He wrote his first short story when he was seven, and his first novel when he was eighteen. In our interview, his brother David told me that as a kid, "Steve was constantly at the typewriter. When I was home from college, he was always upstairs typing. And we always encouraged him. I remember how excited he was when he got his first check for 'The Glass Floor.' He got lots of rejection slips. If I remember correctly, there was a nail pounded in the wall up in the bedroom, and he'd spear all the rejection slips on it."

Stephen King at a public lecture in
Virginia Beach, VA, September 22, 1986.
Photo courtesy George Beahm.

And what about the 1990s Stephen King?

Today, King still resides in Bangor, Maine, with his wife, novelist Tabitha King, and their three children, Joe, Owen, and Naomi. Naomi is in college, Joe writes novels, and Owen plays little league ball. (In another example of King using his life in his writing, the April 16, 1990, issue of *The New Yorker* magazine contained a lengthy nonfiction piece by King called "Head Down," which was about his son Owen's little league team.) King's most recent hardcover book-length release (as of this writing) is the masterful collection of novellas *Four Past Midnight.* He published a new short story called "The Moving Finger" in the December 1990 issue of *The Magazine of Fantasy & Science Fiction* and, in early 1991, Donald M. Grant published the third volume of the *Dark Tower* series, *The Dark Tower III: The Waste Lands.* Also in 1991, King will publish *Needful Things,* the novel that will write the final chapter on Castle Rock, Maine.

I think that if we want to understand the sensibility that is Stephen King, we would have to look at his entire body of work, including his introductions, his nonfiction work, and his interviews. They show a man who has watched, learned, and most importantly, *paid attention.* This meticulous devotion to seeing how and why people, things, society, and culture works has given him an insight that he has shared with his readers through the characters he has created and the stories he has told.

The Stephen King Library (which actually exists, you know—the Book-of-the-Month Club offers all of King's books in specially-designed editions) chronicles life as we know it in the twentieth century, and also shows us the darkside—that place where "the window between reality and unreality breaks and the glass begins to fly," as King put it in "Two Past Midnight," his introductory note to "Secret Window, Secret Garden" in *Four Past Midnight.*

In "Straight Up Midnight" (the general introduction to *Four Past Midnight*), King says that he's still interested in "a place where, perhaps, the walls have eyes and the trees have ears and something *really* unpleasant is trying to find its way out of the attic and downstairs, to where the people are." He admits "That thing still interests me. . .but I think these days that the people who may or may not be listening for it interest me more."

The author bio blurb on the jacket of *Four Past Midnight* says that "the 1980s saw [King] become America's bestselling writer of fiction. He's glad to be held over into the new decade." And since he's decided to spend the decade examining and exploring "the human monster," it looks like we King fans will be spending an awful lot of time journeying in and out of the darkness.

And we'll all be better off for the trip, don't you think?

[A shorter version of this piece originally appeared in the February 1991 issue of *Cinefantastique* magazine. Special thanks to Fred Clarke and the whole crew at *CFQ*. They are an oasis of accuracy, insight, and entertainment in the sometime barren and dry desert of genre reporting. — **sjs**]

PART II

"I WRITE FEARSOMES"

Inside Stephen King

THE STARS & STEPHEN KING

Stephen King's
Natal Astrological Chart

Birth Information
Date: September 21, 1947
Time: 1:30 a.m. EDT
Place: Portland, Maine
Coordinates: 70W16, 43N39

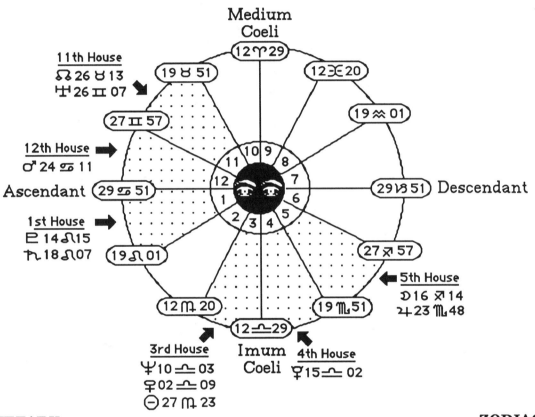

Medium
Coeli
12 ♈ 29

12 ♋ 20

11th House
☊ 26 ♉ 13
♅ 26 ♊ 07

19 ♉ 51

19 ♒ 01

27 ♊ 57

12th House
♂ 24 ♋ 11

Ascendant   29 ♋ 51

29 ♑ 51   Descendant

1st House
♇ 14 ♌ 15
♄ 18 ♌ 07

19 ♌ 01

27 ♐ 57

5th House
☽ 16 ♐ 14
♃ 23 ♏ 48

12 ♍ 20

19 ♏ 51

12 ♎ 29

3rd House
♆ 10 ♎ 03
♀ 02 ♎ 09
☉ 27 ♍ 23

Imum
Coeli

4th House
☿ 15 ♎ 02

PLANETARY SYMBOLS

☽	Moon
☉	Sun
☿	Mercury
♀	Venus
♂	Mars
♃	Jupiter
♄	Saturn
♅	Uranus
♆	Neptune
♇	Pluto
☊	Node M.

✧ **Legend** ✧

ELEMENTS	Cardinal	Fixed	Mutable
FIRE	0	2	1
EARTH	0	0	1
AIR	3	0	1
WATER	1	1	0

Moon is slow
1st Quarter

ZODIAC SIGNS

♈	Aries
♉	Taurus
♊	Gemini
♋	Cancer
♌	Leo
♍	Virgo
♎	Libra
♏	Scorpio
♐	Sagittarius
♑	Capricorn
♒	Aquarius
♓	Pisces

HE IS LEGEND
An Interview with Richard Matheson

Reading Richard Matheson's novel *What Dreams May Come*—and I've told him this—was a major event in my life. For the first time, I had found a work that coalesced and validated my personal beliefs about an afterlife. The novel was just so "right" and so uplifting that for weeks after I went around not just recommending the book to people, but actually *insisting* (in some cases *demanding*) that they read it. I take this opportunity to again thank him for it. *What Dreams May Come* epitomizes the effect simple words on paper can have on people's lives.

Richard Matheson was born on February 20, 1926, in Allendale, New Jersey. His first published piece of writing was a poem in the *Brooklyn Eagle* at the age of eight. His first short story sale was a mesmerizing—and at the time innovative and daring—piece called "Born of Man and Woman." The story begins: "This day when it had light mother called me a retch," and is about a mutant child kept chained in a basement by his parents.

A prolific writer, Matheson is probably best known for his work on the "Twilight Zone" TV series, and his novels *Hell House, The Shrinking Man,* and *I Am Legend.* "Star Trek" fans cherish Matheson's one and only contribution to that series—the episode "The Enemy Within" (Episode #5; 10/6/66)—in which Captain Kirk is split into two people by a transporter accident.

Mark Rathbun, co-author of the 1984 bio-bibliographic pamphlet *He Is Legend* (the title of which I borrowed for this interview) also wrote the Richard Matheson entry for the 1986 Penguin release *The Penguin Encyclopedia of Horror and the Supernatural.* In that entry, Rathbun described Matheson's fiction as follows:

> "Matheson's fiction is broad based; it ranges from humorous to horrific...[and] his stories stress personal interaction, and most have a strong undercurrent of shocking horror and startling twists. A surprising number reflect an ironic tongue-in-cheek whimsy and biting satire.
> In his early works Matheson almost always utilized man's alienation from familiar surroundings and a sense of paranoia as dominant themes...." (pg. 284)

Matheson's writing convinced Stephen King that he could write about *today*—as contemporaneously as he liked—and still write horror. (See the interview below.)

I was introduced to Richard Matheson by his son R.C. I had interviewed R.C. for this book, and asked if he'd "open the door," so to speak, to his father. He did, and this interview is the result. Special thanks must go to both Mathesons for their interest in, and support of this project.

The following is a "mini-biblio/film-ography" of the works of Richard Matheson. Any and every one listed is well worth your while. Genre notwithstanding, Richard Matheson has been, and will continue to be, a major force in contemporary American literature. — **sjs**

Novels

Fury On Sunday (1953)
Someone Is Bleeding (1953)
I Am Legend (1954)
The Shrinking Man (1956)
A Stir Of Echoes (1958)
Ride The Nightmare (1959)
The Beardless Warriors (1960)
Hell House (1971)
Bid Time Return (1975)
What Dreams May Come (1978)
Earthbound (1982) (As Logan Swanson)

Short Story Collections

Born Of Man And Woman (1954)
Third From The Sun (1955)
The Shores Of Space (1957)
Shock! (1961)
Shock II (1964)
Shock III (1966)
Shock Waves (1970)
Richard Matheson: Collected Stories (1989)

Richard Matheson's "Twilight Zone" Episodes

Air Date Written by	Episode Title Based on
12/11/59 Matheson	"And When the Sky Was Opened" "Disappearing Act"
1/8/60 Rod Serling	"Third From the Sun" "Third From the Sun"
2/5/60 Matheson	"The Last Flight" [Original screenplay]

3/11/60 Matheson	"A World of Difference" [Original screenplay]	
7/11/60 Matheson	"A World of His Own" [Original screenplay]	
11/18/60 Matheson	"Nick of Time" [Original screenplay]	
1/27/61 Matheson	"The Invaders" [Original screenplay]	
12/15/61 Matheson	"Once Upon A Time" [Original screenplay]	
3/16/62 Matheson	"Little Girl Lost" "Little Girl Lost"	
1/31/63 Matheson	"Mute" "Mute"	
2/7/63 Matheson	"Death Ship" "Death Ship"	
10/4/63 Matheson	"Steel" "Steel"	
10/11/63 Matheson	"Nightmare at 20,000 Feet" "Nightmare at 20,000 Feet"	
2/7/64 Matheson	"Night Call" "Long Distance Call"	
2/21/64 Matheson	"Spur of the Moment" [Original screenplay]	
5/11/64 Matheson	"Young Man's Fancy" [Original screenplay]	

TV Movies

(Original Scripts and Adaptations)

"Duel" (1971)
"The Night Stalker" (1972)
"The Night Strangler" (1973)
"Dying Room Only" (1973)
"Scream Of The Wolf" (1974)
"Dracula" (1974)
"The Stranger Within" (1974)
"The Morning After" (1974)
"Trilogy Of Terror" (1975)
"Dead Of Night" (1977)
"The Strange Possession Of Mrs. Oliver" (1977)
"The Martian Chronicles" (1980)

Selected Theatrical Films

(Original Scripts and Adaptations)

"The Incredible Shrinking Man" (1957)
"House Of Usher" (1960)
"The Pit And The Pendulum" (1961)
"Burn, Witch, Burn" (1962)
"The Raven" (1963)
"The Last Man On Earth" (As by "Logan Swanson") (1964)
"The Young Warriors" (1967)
"The Legend Of Hell House" (1973)
"Somewhere In Time" (1979)
"Twilight Zone: The Movie" (1983)
"Jaws 3-D" (1983)

HE IS LEGEND
An Interview With Richard Matheson

Richard Matheson
Photo courtesy Richard Matheson

STEVE SPIGNESI: Thank you for visiting *The Shape Under the Sheet,* Mr. Matheson. Since you are one of the three primary influences on Stephen King's writing (along with John D. MacDonald and Don Robertson), your thoughts and opinions are of great interest to us all. Let's start off with this: How, specifically, do you feel that your work has influenced King?

RICHARD MATHESON: I gather, from what Stephen King has said himself, that reading my work—in particular *I Am Legend*—indicated to him that horror need not be (indeed, in my point of view, should not be) confined to crypts and ancient cellars. When Lovecraft was writing, that sort of thing was in vogue. These are modern times. The approach to horror must accommodate these times. Since I was unable to write "old fashioned" horror stories (I tried it on a number of occasions and, in spite of it being very difficult, the results are not

"This approach to horror, so I gather, had its effect on Stephen, and he went on to become its most successful exponent....he, also, became a distinctly *regional* writer. This is important and I think a valuable approach to this genre."

that great—i.e., "Slaughter House"), I wrote as contemporaneously as I wanted to and found it more successful. This approach to horror, so I gather, had its effect on Stephen, and he went on to become its most successful exponent. I have not read about him that extensively, so I may be repeating what has already been said but he, also, became a distinctly *regional* writer. This is important and I think a valuable approach to this genre. I suppose this could have been done in the "old fashioned" mode, but it certainly works well done in a contemporary style.

STEVE SPIGNESI: Of the King works that you've read, do you have a personal favorite?

RICHARD MATHESON: No particular favorite. I have enjoyed them all from *Carrie* on. I was impressed right from the start. *Carrie* was remarkable in that he kept mentioning some horrendous event which took place and kept the entire book leading to it—which can be very perilous if you don't pay it off properly—and then *did* pay it off in spades. I think *'Salem's Lot* is great, and was sorry I didn't get to do the [film] script on it—or on any of the books, for that matter. I would have enjoyed it.

STEVE SPIGNESI: How often are you in contact with Stephen King?

RICHARD MATHESON: I am not in contact with Stephen very often. My wife, Richard and I had dinner with him out here some years ago and enjoyed his company; he is a very friendly person. Richard has seen him at conventions.

STEVE SPIGNESI: I suppose I must ask this cliched, yet obligatory, question: Do you have any idea of what Stephen King is *really* like?

RICHARD MATHESON: I can't say I really have any idea at all what he is "really" like. I suggest a reading of his work. What a writer writes is a dead giveaway of what is going on inside. In my case it is—or, I hope, was—a sense of paranoia. In

Stephen's case—who knows? Not me.

STEVE SPIGNESI: What are your thoughts on the film adaptations of King's work?

RICHARD MATHESON: I thought "Carrie" was well-done. I thought the TV version of "'Salem's Lot" was well done. [NOTE: See the interview with director Tobe Hooper in this volume.] Of course, I always miss the parts that are left out; trying to make a film out of a long novel is usually a waste of time—witness "Dune" and "Ghost Story." Both marvelous books, both inferior films because of what had to be left out.

I thought "The Shining" was a poor film. It was a marvelous—*is* a marvelous—novel. I thought Kubrick lost most of it in his usual attempt to be abstruse. For instance, I keep telling people to read Clarke's novelization of "2001," which is perfectly understandable while the film is rather incomprehensible until viewed about ten times and discussed for a year or two.

I thought "Dead Zone" was the best King film so far. Cronenberg did an excellent job, the performers were perfect. I haven't seen any of the later films, except part of "Cujo" which I didn't care for.

STEVE SPIGNESI: Your son Richard seems to be the leading practitioner of the "short-short," and his fiction is often closer to mainstream than horror. What are your thoughts on your son's work?

RICHARD MATHESON: I admire Richard's horror short-shorts. When they succeed—this form, I mean—the impact can be tremendous. He has been impactful in many of his stories. For instance, who would dare do a story in which each sentence is *one word*! Incredible. [NOTE: The story referred to is Richard Christian Matheson's "Vampire," from his collection *Scars and Other Distinguishing Marks* (Tor paperback, 1988). See the interview with R.C. Matheson in this volume.]

"I can't say I really have any idea at all what he is 'really' like. I suggest a reading of his work. What a writer writes is a dead giveaway of what is going on inside. In my case it is—or, I hope, was—a sense of paranoia. In Stephen's case—who knows? Not me."

STEVE SPIGNESI: Your son has acknowledged King as a major influence on his own writing. What are your thoughts on the fact that you seem to have influenced R. C.'s work—"channeled" so to speak—through Stephen King?

RICHARD MATHESON: The process by which I may have influenced my son's work via Stephen King's work is too convoluted for me to comment on. I think Richard was drawn to this type of short story because I wrote them. Naturally, he would have read Stephen King and been so influenced. He, then, chose his own path which is, largely, the short-short horror story, a most difficult form which he has become extraordinarily proficient in.

"Suppose the Beatles had come forth in the 1940's? Nothing. This is, perhaps, saying nothing in that the Time and the Artist are so inextricably bound together. Stephen King, the Phenomenon, without the Time he emerged from, would not have become a Phenomenon."

STEVE SPIGNESI: It seems Stephen King has transcended his own name, and become a popular culture archetype—a brand name for horror. What do you think of the current "Stephen King Phenomenon"—this unprecedented popularity of a young, living American writer?

RICHARD MATHESON: The Stephen King Phenomenon is, I think, simply this. The groundwork for it was laid by a number of writers – myself included, I presume. The market and the tastes of the public—synonomous, I suppose—reached a peak of "expectation" and "desire," even, perhaps, "need" for this type of product, and Stephen was there to become its spokesman. His writing style, his attitudes, his ideas made him *the* writer to end up on top of the mountain.

I will mention a parallel although, for God's sake, don't think for a second that I am equating Stephen King with Hitler. The point I make is that, when Hitler came into power, Germany was waiting for him, almost, in a sense, "created" him with their need for such a person. Hitler was a brilliant man, maybe a genius, though a very twisted one indeed. And Stephen King is a brilliant writer but, if the need were not there, if he had begun writing in the 1930s or, perhaps, the 1980s, it would not be in such perfect synch with the market for this genre.

He would always have become a successful writer because of his talent. But a phenomenon is something else. More is required. In particular, the Time. Suppose the Beatles had come forth in the 1940's? Nothing. This is, perhaps, saying nothing in that the Time and the Artist are so inextricably bound together. Stephen King, the Phenomenon, without the Time he emerged from, would not have become a Phenomenon. The Time, without Stephen King, would have still demanded *someone,* and someone might well have emerged. Happily, when the craving was there, so, too, was Stephen with his talent, and the phenomenal period of his success began.

Bottom line: the man is an enormous talent and the Time was ripe for his spectacular literary ascent.

STEVE SPIGNESI: Why did you lose interest in horror?

RICHARD MATHESON: As for why I lost interest in horror...I now believe that thoughts are "things," that they are real and do not vaporize and that their effect is far deeper than most people think. I don't want to put out any more of those thoughts into the world. We have enough horrible thoughts exteriorized out there already. I do not condemn anyone who writes in this genre. I do not look down on my own participation in it. And I think it can be used, under certain circumstances, to illuminate through shock. Mostly, today, however, it is used to—as kids may still put it, I don't know—"gross us out." I can't see this. I never really tried for that in my writing. Although God knows some of my stuff is probably a gross-out to the reader. But...well, anyway, that's why I don't write it anymore.

What I *will* write, God only knows. ❏

"KING OF HORROR"
TIME Looks at the
Stephen King Phenomenon

This is the first reprinting of what many critics consider to be a superb overview of Stephen King and his career.

The article first appeared in the October 6, 1986, issue of *Time* magazine, and Stephen King was featured as the cover story that week. The cover illustration was a drawing of a man reading a book that said "A Novel by Stephen King." The reader's hair was sticking straight up in the air, and the whole back cover of the book was a drawing of Stephen King. Immediately below the *Time* masthead there were three lines of text from *IT*: "As It saw Eddie looking, its green-black lips wrinkled back from huge fangs...."

The contents page of the issue identified the King feature as the cover story, and introduced the piece with the following: "At 39, the protean horror writer has already produced 20-odd books that raise gooseflesh for fun and profit. His work attracts millions of readers and generates millions of dollars, but he shuns the Manhattan and Hollywood scenes and hangs out instead in Maine, where he and his wife live like 'a couple of hicks' amid a profusion of cars, bats and children. See BOOKS."

The story was accompanied by a small reproduction of the *IT* dustjacket, and a huge page-and-a-half photo of King on his Harley between the gates of the "bat fence" in front of his home. Other photos in the article included stills from the films "Carrie," "Firestarter," "Christine," "The Shining," "The Dead Zone," and "Creepshow." Also, there were three other photos: Stephen and Tabitha King at Stephen's word processor, King on the set of "Maximum Overdrive," and the entire King family in their giant indoor pool.

Following the text of "King of Horror" is an update on those of King's works discussed in the future tense in Kanfer's article. A sidebar quotes King himself on the writing process.

Special thanks to Marian Powers of Time, Inc. for her help with the reproduction of this piece. —**sjs**

"KING OF HORROR"
The Master of Pop Dread
writes on...and on...and on...and on
by
Stefan Kanfer

Pennywise, a brightly dressed clown, beguiles the young passersby. The lucky ones elude the creature. The others are never seen again—alive. This is obviously not your average Ringling Bros. fool with bulbous nose and orange sideburns. When it shucks off its costume, it resembles a spider. Or a crawling eye. Or a mummy. Its breath is foul, its eyes are mere holes, and its diet consists of human entrées. Pennywise's address is the sewers of Derry, Me., but the monster is only renting there. Its permanent home is a far stranger dwelling: the mind of Stephen Edwin King.

In his new novel, *It* (Viking; $22.95), Stephen proves once again that he is the indisputable King of horror, a demon fabulist who raises gooseflesh for fun and profit. At 39, he seems to be the country's best-known writer. When he appeared on an American Express commercial to ask onlookers "Do you know me?," the answer was obvious: Of course, they did. His face, sometimes bearded, now clean-shaven, appears on most of the 20-odd books written under two names. More than 60 million of them have been in distribution worldwide, including two volumes— *Carrie* and *The Dead Zone*—that were presented by Nicholas Daniloff, minutes before his arrest, to Misha, his Soviet friend. Some dozen films have been based on King's fictions, and there are more on the way. He has earned over $20 million so far, including a $3 million advance for *It*, which fulfilled expectations by vaulting to the top of the best-seller list before official publication.

Hurtling down two streams of time, the '50s and the '80s, the book displays all the author's patented tics and tropes. The Beautiful Losers: a black, a homosexual, and—among others persecuted in adolescence and now called home to disinter a buried memory—a stutterer and an abused girl. The Validated Nightmare: "At the last instant, as the ax slowed to its apogee and balanced there, Richie understood that this wasn't a dream at all..." The Disgusting Colloquialism: "She drew in a great, hitching breath and hocked a remarkably large looey onto the top of his head." The Brand-Name Maneuver: "Here sits a man with Bass Weejuns on his feet and Calvin Klein underwear to cover his ass." The Comic-Strip Effect: " *Whack-WHACK-whack-WHACK*—And suddenly it was in his hands, a great living thing that pumped and pulsed against his palms, pushing them back and forth. (*NONONONONONONO*)." The Burlesque Locution: "'Good ahfternyoon, deah lady,' Richie said in his best Baron Buttonhole Voice. 'I am in diah need of three ticky-tickies to youah deah old American flicktoons.'" The Fancy Juxtaposition: epigraphs from Virgil and *Mean Streets*. The Self-Defeating Jape: "I am...the only survivor of a dying planet. I have come to rob all the women...and rape all the men...and learn to do the Peppermint Twist!" And, most discouraging of all, the Unconscionable Length: 1,138 pages.

The weight alone (3 lbs. 7 1/2 oz.) would seem the right heft for a doorstop and the wrong one for a best seller. But King has become a brand name himself, and his publishers ordered a supernatural first printing of 800,000 copies—and then demanded five additional printings, for a current total of 1,025,000 copies. When an author receives that kind of recognition, two factors are at work: his skills and the vitality of his genre. King, who regards *It* as a "very badly constructed book," may be a little too hard on himself. But the frightful theme is what continues to make him the most successful horror writer in history.

That history is almost as old as the night. In the *Odyssey*, Odysseus visited the land of the dead, where he reported that "pale fear got hold of me" as the spirits rose up to drink blood. Every ethnic group has spun folktales of the ungrateful dead. Even so, horror did not become a literary convention until the late 18th century, when the gothic novel described the exotic terrors of old feudal keeps. In the gaslight era, the supernatural took hold of the public imagination, and British authors quickly dominated the field. Their very names suggest creaking Victorian stairways, forbidden rooms and disembodied spirits: Montague Rhodes James, J.S. Le Fanu, Eden Phillpotts, Algernon Blackwood. In the U.S., an alcoholic and sickly journalist led readers down dark corridors that still echo in American and European fiction. Edgar Allan Poe was, wrote D.H. Lawrence, "an adventurer into the vaults and cellars and horrible underground passages of the human soul." He told of disintegrating bodies (*The Facts in the Case of M. Valdemar*), accusatory objects (*The Purloined Letter*) and doomed homes (*The Fall of the House of Usher*)—all now standard props of horror. Once the genre was taken seriously, American writers as naturalistic as Jack London and as refined as Edith Wharton used those special effects and sojourned in those underground passages, and they have been accompanied by hundreds of others, perhaps none more influential than Henry James.

If Poe was the quirky father of modern horror, its uncle was the sobersided James, who was strongly influenced by the terrors that afflicted his family. His brother William, the pragmatic philosopher and investigator into the varieties of religious experience, recalled one of his most terrifying moments: "Suddenly there fell upon me without any warning, just as if it came out of the darkness, a horrible fear of my own existence. Simultaneously there arose in my mind the image of an epileptic patient...a black-haired youth with greenish skin...*That shape am I,* I felt, potentially." This was the image of monstrosity that is only a chromosome away. Henry added another kind of apparition. In *The Turn of the Screw* he presented a governess and a ghostly valet who vie for the soul of a living boy.

These twin terrors—fear of the real and fear of the insubstantial—are the subtexts of most stories designed to make the flesh creep. Yet it has been nearly a century since the brothers James recorded their visions. Surely horror should have become an outdated category by now. Surely science should have driven a stake through its heart. But, no, the genre is, in every sense, the home of the undead. In the '40s Critic Edmund Wilson mused about the persistence of ghost stories: "What is the reason, then—in these days when a lonely country house is likely to be equipped with electric light, radio and telephone—for our returning to these antiquated tales?...First, the longing for mystic experience which seems always to manifest itself in periods of social confusion...Second, the instinct to inoculate ourselves against panic at the real horrors loose on the earth..."

Two generations later, the longings have grown more aggravated and the real horrors have metastasized. Terrorism and the Bomb, the breakdown of the ozone layer and the rise of crime—almost any news item will serve to drive readers to distraction. Manhattan Psychiatrist Robert E. Gould finds that horror "is extremely distracting. That is one of the main purposes of its popularity. In difficult times, in the world outside and your own world, you reach out far from yourself. Also, you can control that horror. You can stop reading anytime you want." His colleague Dr. Herbert Peyser agrees. In horror, he says, "we see an ordered world. We know it really isn't real, and we can master it. It's fantasy, and we can get out." It is no wonder then that videocassettes like *I Dismember Mama* and *Halloween* are favorites on the rental circuit, that *Aliens* and *Friday the 13th, Part VI: Jason Lives* were among the top movie grossers of the summer, and that, in paperback, Stephen King now outsells James Michener and Robert Ludlum.

At his home in Bangor, Me., King recently took time away from the IBM Selectric to ponder his role as the Master of Pop Dread. In *It* he observes, "All writers have a pipeline which goes down into the subconscious. But the man or woman who writes horror stories has a pipeline that goes further, maybe...into the *sub*-subconscious, if you like." King's *sub*-subconscious started working overtime when he was barely out of infancy. In an eerie resemblance to his spiritual ancestor Poe, King was also deserted by his father in infancy. At the age of four the lonely boy walked home pale and unspeaking. A neighborhood friend had inexplicably vanished. "It turned out," King later recalled, "that the kid had been run over by a freight train while playing on or crossing the tracks (years later, my mother told me they had picked up the pieces in a wicker basket)." To this day the author has "no memory of the incident at all; only of having been told about it..." But at the age of eight he had a very accessible dream: "I saw the body of a hanged man dangling from the arm of a scaffold on a hill. When the wind caused the corpse to turn in the air, I saw that it was my face—rotted and picked by the birds, but obviously mine. And then the corpse opened its eyes and looked at me." Permutations of both incidents would turn up in books two decades later.

There were, almost from the start, two Kings. Mr. Outside grew up in Durham, Me., where his mother had moved to care for her aging parents. He was oversized and ungainly, with a thatch of unruly black hair, buck teeth and thick glasses, the one who was predictably chosen last in sandlot games. Mr. Inside was the fatherless boy who held a lot of "anger that has never been directed. In my inward life, I still boil a lot." So it is no surprise that many of King's books could be fairly called "The Revenge of the Nerds": the ursine kid with the bad eyes and the shambling gait would find a way to get his own back, even if it took him 20 years—especially if it took him 20 years.

Vengeance was novels away when Stephen scraped away through the University of Maine at Orono, moonlighting as a dishwasher, Little League coach and gas-station attendant. He majored in English, minored in dramatics, marched for peace, voted Republican for the last time in 1968 ("I believed Nixon when he said he'd get us out of Viet Nam"), and met his future wife, a woman whose unlikely name, Tabitha Spruce, seems to have been plucked from a Stephen King coven. She remembers him as an imposing figure, a "campus institution" who wrote a weekly column called "King's Garbage Truck" for the school newspaper. Recalls Stephen: "Tabby looked like a waitress. She came across—and still does—as a tough broad." After graduation they married; when he was unable to find a teaching position, he labored in a

launderette for $60 a week. "Budget was not exactly the word for whatever it was we were on," King later wrote. "It was more like a modified version of the Bataan Death March."

In 1971 he finally landed a job as a prep-school English instructor at Hampden, Me. At night Tabitha put on her hot-pink uniform and went to work at Dunkin' Donuts. When she exited, King turned to the typewriter which was perched on a child's desk. As an adolescent, he had read Richard Matheson's *The Shrinking Man* and other works that were adapted for *The Twilight Zone*. "The same year," he recalls, "I read *Peyton Place* and *King's Row*. I understood instinctively that both authors were talking about the small-town caste society that I grew up in, the veil of hypocrisy, what people hide behind. I understood that I could write about my own milieu and combine it with Matheson's approach, and it worked like a bandit."

So did King. He began to sell short stories to men's magazines such as *Cavalier* and *Adam*; the checks, he remembers, "always seemed to come just in time to buy antibiotics for the baby's ear infection or to keep the telephone in the apartment for another record-breaking month." One baby later, there was barely enough money for the kids and none at all for the phone. It was disconnected the month King turned in the manuscript of *Carrie,* a novel about an adolescent with telekinetic powers and a lethal resentment of her high school tormentors. The work was worth a $2,500 advance, more than enough to pay some bills. And a good thing too: on Mother's Day, 1973, a Doubleday editor called about the sale of paperback rights. "I thought he was going to tell me I was only getting $5,000 or something," King fondly remembers. "He said $400,000. The only thing I could think to do was go out and buy my wife a hair dryer. I stumbled across the street to get it and thought I would probably get greased by some car."

He was not greased, Tabitha stopped smelling like an overgrown cruller, and the six-figure earnings soon became seven. "People think the muse is a literary character," says King, "some cute little pudgy devil who floats around the head of the creative person sprinkling fairy dust. Well, mine's a guy with a flattop in coveralls who looks like Jack Webb and says, 'All right, you son of a bitch, time to get to work.'" The ultimate workaholic obeyed the figure in coveralls every day, except for his birthday, the Fourth of July and Christmas. His work reflected more than the normal fears and superstitions. King was unnerved by spiders, elevators, closed-in places, the dark, sewers, funerals, the idea of being buried alive, cancer, heart attacks, the number 13, black cats and walking under ladders. In the process of merchandising his own

THE NOVELIST
SOUNDS OFF

KING ON "IMPORTANT" FICTION

"People ask me, 'When are you going to write something serious?' A question like that always hurts. They don't understand it's like walking up to somebody and saying how does it feel to be a nigger? My answer is that I'm as serious as I can be every time I sit down at a typewriter."

KING ON CHILDHOOD

"People of my generation, 25 to 40, we were obsessive about our own childhoods for a long time. We went on playing for a long time, almost feverishly. I write for that buried child in us, but I'm writing for the grown-up too. I want grown-ups to look at the child long enough to be able to give him up. The child should be buried."

KING ON EXORCISM

"There is a part of us that needs to vicariously exorcise the darker side of our feelings. You can hold all this stuff inside and then do something like Charles Whitman at the Texas tower."

KING ON WRITING

"A matter of exercise. If you work out with weights 15 minutes a day over a course of ten years, you're gonna get muscles. If you write for an hour and a half a day for ten years, you're gonna turn into a good writer."

KING ON HORROR

"I saw *The Amityville Horror* on Times Square, and there wasn't anybody talking back at the screen. There was total silence, which is unusual for 42nd Street. It was awe. The silence you'd hear in a medieval church, I thought. That's what horror is—the church of 42nd Street."

KING ON PSYCHOANALYSIS

"In a way I'm in therapy every day. People pay $135 an hour to sit on a couch. I'm talking about the same fears and inadequacies in my writing."

KING ON SUCCESS

"I've grown fat and rich by discovering the vast Bowl-a-Drome of the American psyche. But I still don't have the guts to buy a pair of lizard-skin boots, although I'd like some. It's just too much money to pay. Part of me would like to buy a really nice guitar too, but I know I don't really play well enough. I keep the price tag on my guitar to remind me. It cost $129."

KING ON THE COMPETITION

"I get upset about being compared with certain brand-name writers who sell megabillions of copies. Michener is one. I can't read him. Ludlum is another one. I was paid to review one of his books. He's the clumsiest, most awful writer. No style."

KING ON HIS OWN NOVELS

"The literary equivalent of a Big Mac
and a large fries from McDonald's."

terrors, he developed an infallible formula: "First you create people that you want to live, then you put them into the cooker." Carrie, the paranormal adolescent, was succeeded by the vampires of *'Salem's Lot* (1975), the haunted hotel of *The Shining* (1977), the deadly superflu of *The Stand* (1978). The clairvoyant young man of *The Dead Zone* (1979) placed King on the best-seller list for more than six months, replaced by *Firestarter* (1980), *Cujo* (1981), a nonfiction investigation of horror called *Danse Macabre* (1981), and a collection of novellas, *Different Seasons* (1982). In his spare time he turned out *Christine* and *Pet Sematary* (both 1983) by himself, and *The Talisman* (1984) in collaboration with Peter Straub, author of *Ghost Story*. Another collection of short stories appeared in 1985. And still that did not exhaust King. Because publishers were wary of overkill, he submitted five other novels under another name. When Richard Bachman's cover was blown, after *Thinner* climbed aboard the best-seller list, the pretense was shelved. "It should have been in *Time*'s Milestones," King grumbles. "Died. Richard Bachman, of cancer of the pseudonym."

A great many of the King-Bachman books seem to have been written on a word processor by a word processor. The author often employs three exclamation points !!! where one would suffice, shows a blithe disregard for grammar ("My mother used to tell my brother David and I to 'hope for the best and expect the worst'"), and produces metaphors that obviously embarrass their creator: "He felt that he had unwittingly stuck his hand into the Great Wasps' Nest of Life. As an image it stank." But all along he displays one talent that never flags—he is able to convince the reader that the unreal is actually occurring. Critic Jacques Barzun once analyzed the technique of the effective horror novelist: "Since terror descriptions must perpetually make the reader accept yet question the strange amid the familiar, the writer pursues the muse of ambiguity. He begins by establishing a solid outer shell of comfort—the clergyman's study, the lawyer's book-lined room, the well-placed camping tent, or the cozy room at the inn or club, with fortifying drinks at hand. But soon a vague unease, a chill in the air, or else a strong shock undermines or shatters composure. No rhetorical onslaught...can equal it; the intrusion, fluid and elusive or sharp and violent, destroys all past security."

King begins with all the reassuring American trappings: the 7-Eleven stores, the ribbons of super-highway, the town high schools that seem part of an ordered landscape. Then come the hints of malaise, and, abruptly, what A.D. Hutter, a professor of English at UCLA, calls King's "brilliant creation of a shared nightmare." A marriage breaks up and a trusted dog suddenly turns on its owners; a teenager's love affair with his Plymouth Fury is totaled when the car is possessed by the vengeful ghost of a previous owner; the caretaker of a vast mountain resort hotel finds himself slowly overtaken by the malevolent spirits envisioned by the little boy; two college students volunteer for a government experiment and become parents of a daughter with a unique gift: she can make things burst into flame with the force of her will. All of these fantasies are built on an armature of moral order. The good suffer, but the malefactors perish. "Beneath its fangs and fright wig," the author confesses, the horror tale is "as conservative as an Illinois Republican in a three-piece pinstripe suit."

Oddly enough, King's unsettling plots rarely work on film, perhaps because occult scenarios are best played in the Skull Cinema. On a real screen his lethally gifted children often turn out to be amateurish performers; the floodlighted hotel is about as frightening as the set of a Fred Astaire musical; and the rabid Saint Bernard seems only a benign cartoon of the Hound of the Baskervilles. King confesses to be satisfied with many of the movie adaptations, except for *The Shining* ("Stanley Kubrick's stated purpose was to make a horror picture, and I don't think he understood the genre") and the summer's *Maximum Overdrive* ("a stiff"), which King directed. But privately he derives consolation from a James M. Cain anecdote. An interviewer commiserated with the author of *Double Indemnity* and *The Postman Always Rings Twice* because Hollywood had ruined all his books. "Cain looked over at his shelf and said, 'No, they are all still right there.'" Besides, King's work has inspired a bona fide hit in 1986: Rob Reiner's *Stand By Me,* an adaptation of *The Body,* a 1982 novella that focuses on a group of twelve-year-olds searching for the body of a boy who was struck by a train.

It is easy to understand King's fondness for cloth-bound versions. After all, it is paper more than celluloid that allows him to live in the style of a Down East grand seigneur. The family occupies a 23-room, 129-year-old house surrounded by a black iron fence with interwoven designs of bats and spider webs, installed in an excess of whimsy by the owners. The place is within a mile of the down-at-the-heels section of town where the Kings began their odyssey. It has an eccentric charm appropriate to the tenants: one cupola is conical, the other square. Tabitha, 37, works in a spacious front room of the main house; there she has written three published novels. Each book explored a different genre. One book was, in her view, a "political romance," another concerned a Maine woman attacked by ruffians, and the third was an old-fashioned love story. King's sun-washed study, set in a remodeled stable loft, has a hidden stairway leading down to a toy-cluttered indoor swimming pool with a vaulted gothic-style ceiling. Tabitha calls it the Church of the Poisoned Mind. The children drift in and out frequently. Naomi, 16, comes by dressed in a Mickey Mouse T-shirt and shorts, a departure from the standard King uniform of work shirt and jeans. She complains that the boys were hogging the pool. Joe, 14, prowls through the study shelves in search of the videocassette of *Day of the Dead,* but his father suggests the boy screen some Alfred Hitchcock thrillers. "Watch the Hitcher," King advises. "He's scary." When Joe wanders off with *Capricorn One* instead, King digs out one of the unsolicited horror films he constantly receives by fourth-class mail. The cassette is still wrapped in cellophane. "I can't bear to throw them away," he admits. "But I won't let the kids watch them." Meantime, Owen, 9, is down in the kitchen with a group of friends, hunched over a consumer magazine for children. The King children earn their allowances by taping books for Dad to hear while he drives. For the going steno rate of $9.10 an hour, Owen records detective novels. Naomi is currently reading the stories of John Steinbeck into a microphone.

The five Kings could set their castle anywhere, but Stephen refuses to leave familiar turf; even the family's lakeside summer place is in the state. "Maine is far and away better for a couple of hicks like us," he maintains. "And it's better for the kids." King enjoys the role of paterfamilias, scrubbing the indoor grill over the sink so that Tabby and the children can have an outing at the local shopping mall. Dinner is a family affair with everybody present. The conversation ranges from Little League to books and movies to local gossip. King can drive to New York City for meetings with his publishers in one of two Mercedes, or in a red Cadillac convertible, or in a Chevy van, but once or twice a year he prefers to vroom south on his Harley-Davidson motorcycle. Neither of the Kings likes to fill up any of their vehicles. A brother-in-law who acts as handyman and caretaker attends to the cars and van, but rarely rides the Harley. So King has, on occasion, found himself stranded and called home for a pickup, just like a character in a movie. Conferences with editors frequently take place not in offices or restaurants but in the stands at Yankee Stadium. There King can talk between pitches, and hot dogs and beer.

The brew tends to be of the lite variety these days. In the past the author could do a pretty fair imitation of a character in *Animal House,* and remembers writing *Cujo* under the influence of malt and hops. Then two years ago, physicians picked up symptoms of heart arrhythmia, and these days King tends to watch his solids and liquids and waistline. But he still pays very little attention to externals. Two lawn chairs on the driveway is about as much luxury as he likes to display to the neighbors. "I guard against success," he says, "because you start to expect things, preferential treatment at hotels or concerts. I don't want that. I'm not any better than anyone else."

Well, maybe not at the well-wrought sentence or the lapidary essay. But that has never been his aim or his claim. Random House Editor Sam Vaughn accurately notes that "King is one of those rare writers with both a cult and a mass audience." And Barnes & Noble Buyer Ronda Wanderman ungrammatically observes, "King goes beyond horror like Danielle Steel goes beyond romantic fiction." Columbia English Professor George Stade probes further. The King novels, he maintains, "are not so different from the Sherlock Holmes stories, *Dracula,* or *Tarzan.* We need these guys around, and we tend to read them more than we read James Joyce." The author cherishes few illusions. He likes to be compared with "Jack London, who said, in effect, I'm not much of a writer but I'm one hell of an elaborator.' That's me." King barely gives himself a passing grade in freshness: "I've had about three original ideas in my life. The rest of them were bounces. I sense the limitations of where my talents are." Some of this sudden vote of no confidence may come from the realization that a new talent is howling at the door. The British horror writer Clive Barker (*The Inhuman Condition*) has been gaining in reputation and sales, and King has become something of a cheerleader: "You read him with a book in one hand and an airsick bag in the other. That man is not fooling around. He's got a sense of humor, and he's not a dullard. He's better than I am now. He's a lot more energetic." So King is not merely posing at poolside when he promises that *It* will be his last horror novel: "For now, as far as the Stephen King Book-of-the-Month Club goes, this is the clearance-sale time. Everything must go."

And so it went—into *It.* Before he began the book, Stephen thought about a favorite image: the entire cast of the Bugs Bunny Show coming on at the beginning, Yosemite Sam, Bugs Bunny, Daffy Duck and the gang. In a surge of adolescent enthusiasm, King burbled, "Wouldn't it be great to bring on all the monsters one last time? Bring them all on— *Dracula, Frankenstein, Jaws, The Werewolf, The Crawling Eye, Rodan, It Came from Outer Space,* and call it *It.*" But how could he combine them all in one book? Simple. Use a Tulpa—the tibetan word for a creature created by the mind.

Now that *It* is out, can King change himself? In the next 14 months he will make three attempts by publishing novels outside the Pop Dread belfry. *The Eyes of the Dragon,* just completed, is an Arthurian sword-and-sorcery epic written for Naomi, who read *Carrie* and has since refused to venture into any of her father's other books. *Tommyknockers,* still being revised, is a sci-fi epic set in the post-Chernobyl era. "It's about how our ability to make gadgets outraces the moral ability" is all King is willing to disclose. *Misery,* just about completed, is a psychological novel "about a crazy nurse who captures her pet writer and hooks him on drugs after a car crash. He writes bodice-ripper novels about a character called Misery Chastain. She wants him to write a book about Misery just for her, not knowing—because she waits for the paperback—that in the latest hard-cover he's killed Misery."

These projects barely begin to tap the King energy. An image arises in the morning mists, a tableau so powerful and intimidating that only a publisher can contemplate it without blenching. Every day at 9 a.m., except for his birthday, the Fourth of July and Christmas, a 6-ft., 4-in., 198-lb. creature climbs into a T-shirt and jeans, swallows a vitamin pill, drinks a glass of Maine tap water and turns on some hard rock on WZON. He is never dissatisfied with what he hears: after all, he owns the station. With a few breaks, he will type until what he calls "beer o'clock"—about 5 p.m. He has been known to work into the night. The output is some ten pages a day, although with a Wang computer, "the sky's the limit." Before him lies a handful of works in progress. There is the second installment of a five-story science-fantasy cycle, *The Dark Tower,* featuring Roland, the Last Gunslinger, on the track of his grail. Then there is the uncut version of *The Stand.* Then there are plans to study French in order to finish *Livre Noir,* a detective story in French, "the language that turns dirt into romance." And there is a project to turn *Carrie* into a Broadway musical, with choreography by Debbie Allen. Plus an original story for TV, an 875-page screenplay that will run over 14 episodes. "All right, you son-of-a-bitch, get to work," says the muse in flattop and coveralls. And the giant meekly obeys, preparing to flood the market with millions of words. "The horror!" says the muse. "The horror!" But just now, no one can tell whether he is speaking with nostalgia or anticipation.

A 1990 UPDATE TO "KING OF HORROR"

Five years have passed since "King of Horror" ran in *Time* magazine, and a few things mentioned in the article require updating.

What hasn't changed is that King is still writing, still married to Tabby, and still living in Bangor. He remains hugely popular—perhaps even more now than ever. He continued as owner of WZON into 1990, but finally sold the radio station.

Here, then, is what has happened with the projects mentioned in "King of Horror":

• *Eyes of the Dragon, The Tommyknockers, and Misery* have all been published, and Rob Reiner's film adaptation of *Misery* was released in December 1990 to widespread acclaim. [NOTE: See the discussion of these works elsewhere in this volume.]

• The second *Dark Tower* installment was published in hardcover by Donald M. Grant in 1987. An audio version and a paperback edition subsequently followed from New American Library. Part 3, *The Waste Lands,* was published in early 1991.

• *The Stand: The Complete and Uncut Edition* was published by Doubleday in April 1990.

• There has been no word on *Livre Noir (Black Book),* and it is not known if the project is still active.

• The musical adaptation of *Carrie* opened—and closed. [NOTE: See the section on "Carrie: The Musical" elsewhere in this volume for more information.]

• There has been no word on the fourteen-episode *original* TV story mentioned in the article, although "IT" was aired on ABC in November 1990. [NOTE: See the section on the "IT" mini-series elsewhere in this volume.]

A recent photo of King with two supportive fans, Larry Fire (l) and Dave Lowell (r).
Photo courtesy Dave Hinchberger.

"A SENSE OF THE RIDICULOUS"
An Interview with Stephen King's
Personal Secretary, Shirley Sonderegger

I cancelled an appointment to have a new fuel pump put on my car the day I interviewed Shirley Sonderegger for this book.

It just would have made my morning too hectic. Dropping off the car, worrying about getting a ride back home, and still trying to maintain a clear head for the interview would have been stretching it. Also, I still had to review my list of questions; our talk was scheduled for 11:00 o'clock that morning, so I decided to postpone the fuel pump.

Well, the postponement worked—even though my fuel pump didn't: I had a great time talking with Shirley.

I bring up this personal, seemingly irrelevant incident to make a point. One of the things Shirley Sonderegger does for Stephen King is to shield him from the tidal wave of requests that come in to him every day: Journalists want interviews, charities want contributions, businessmen want endorsements, writers want critique, help, blurbs and reviews, and any number of organizations and conventions want personal appearances.

Shirley understands the creative process, and more importantly, she understands Stephen King.

She realizes what it takes to maintain the mental state that has allowed Stephen King to create, trap, and display the characters and stories his fans know so well and love so much. Just as the routine task of dropping off a car for repair would have thrown off my rhythm on the day I was to interview Shirley, so would having to deal with the business end of "Stephen King" throw off his own personal rhythm. We all need to find that groove where we're comfortable, and it's a fact that usually the mundane functioning of the business of writing does not jibe with the more intangible and fragile creative act of actually putting the words on paper.

After speaking with Shirley on and off for a couple of months before our interview, what was so amazing to me was the way in which she smoothly and calmly *did it all.*

She fields questions, phone calls, and letters with grace, good humor, and an enviable patience.

And lemme tellya...with some of the phone calls that come into that office, it takes a truly remarkable personality to handle it all with such aplomb.

Shirley first met Steve through Steve's sister-in-law, Stephanie Spruce Leonard (Tabitha King's sister). Shirley admits she wasn't a fan before she got the job, but she now considers King's use of language "absolutely wonderful."

Shirley lives with her husband Peter in the Bangor area. She has three children, and on the day I talked with her, she had recently attended the wedding of her son, the middle child between two sisters. Did she have a good time? "It was marvelous," she said. "A great party. We're ready for another one next week. It's amazing what a couple of glasses of champagne can do for a person's dancing ability," she laughingly told me.

Shirley recently made her acting debut in Stephen King's "Creepshow" sequel, "Creepshow 2." You didn't see her? Well, as she put it, you'd have to know what the back of her head looked like in order to recognize her. Shirley played Mrs. Cavanaugh in the "Old Chief Woodn'head" segment, and her only onscreen appearance was a scene set in the Cavanaugh house. The camera is looking down a hallway towards a den where Mr. and Mrs. Cavanaugh are watching television. All you can see of Mrs. Sonderegger is the back of her head, and she recently told me that the scene was filmed with her sitting on the floor. She didn't have any lines, but she admits she was delighted with the results of the Chief's visit to the Cavanaugh kid.

Shirley Sonderegger is charming, gracious, and a delight to talk to.

And I can tell you this: If I had a secretary like Shirley Sonderegger running my office, I sure as hell wouldn't have to worry about my fuel pump. She'd take care of everything. And that's exactly what she does in Stephen King's office: She takes care of it all, and lets Stephen King write. —**sjs**

"A SENSE OF THE RIDICULOUS"
An Interview With Shirley Sonderegger

STEVE SPIGNESI: Why don't we start with what is probably the most obvious question: How did you get the job as Stephen King's secretary?

SHIRLEY SONDEREGGER: When my husband Peter and I first moved to the Bangor area, I worked at a bank where I met Stephanie Leonard—Steve's other secretary. After Steph resigned from the bank and started working for Steve, she got pregnant with her second child and decided she wanted a six month leave of absence.

Since Steve still needed a secretary for those six months, Stephanie asked me if I'd consider taking on the job. I said yes, and in November of 1983, I went over to the house and interviewed with Steve.

After the interview, Steve decided that he'd like to have me work for him, and this November [1989], it's going to be five years since I started. Originally, this position was supposed to be a temporary situation ending in June of 1984, but around that time Steve said to me, "You know, Shirl, we have a few things to finish—wouldn't you like to work until September?" We were in the middle of publishing the Philtrum Press limited edition of *Eyes of the Dragon* and that project kept me busy until December of that year; after that Steve asked me to stay on permanently.

I've been here ever since.

STEVE SPIGNESI: Has Steve ever discussed that first interview with you?

SHIRLEY SONDEREGGER: In a sense. On Steve's birthday, which was just last week, he said to me, "You know, Shirley, when you first interviewed with me, I thought to myself at the time, 'She must think I'm crazy.'" (Laughs.) "But you know," he said, "since you've been working here, you're as crazy as I am. No wonder we get along so well!" (Laughs.)

STEVE SPIGNESI: What was that interview like? I'm sure a lot of people would imagine it involved taking a test on vampires and spelling words backwards.

SHIRLEY SONDEREGGER: Far from it. When I first got to Steve's house, he was sitting out on the front porch in a rocking chair watching the neighbors go by. We sat and talked for a little bit, and then we went upstairs to his office where he dictated a short letter to me. I typed it up and he saw that I could take shorthand, and type a decent letter and I guess he was real happy that I spelled his name right. I didn't spell it S-T-E-V-E-N.

STEVE SPIGNESI: I can understand that. As another "Stephen," I get that all the time, too.

SHIRLEY SONDEREGGER: And then he said "You're hired." It was great. It really was the easiest job interview I ever had.

STEVE SPIGNESI: It sounds like it. What's a typical workday in Stephen King's office like?

SHIRLEY SONDEREGGER: I pick up the mail about 8:30, and then I usually come straight to the office unless I stop off at Steve's house to see if there's any mail there, or if they have anything going out. I'm normally here by quarter of nine. Then I open the mail, and usually the phone starts ringing around nine. Steve almost always checks in early and sees what's on for the day.

Monday is usually a big mail day. I go through what's come in and if there are questions to be answered—things to ask Steve—then I put those in a pile, and if there are books to be autographed, then I put those in Steve's office.

If Steve comes in, we go through the mail, and Steve signs the books. That's the basic routine, but every day is different. If there are travel plans to be made we have to do that. I usually try and get out of here by 4:00 o'clock, but that doesn't always happen.

Sometimes, if there's a lot of stuff to do, I bring my lunch and just eat here. And of course some days are more productive than others.

STEVE SPIGNESI: So it's essentially a one-woman office?

SHIRLEY SONDEREGGER: Well, it used to be a two-woman office until Stephanie left, but now it's just me.

STEVE SPIGNESI: Does Stephen King also have an office in the building?

SHIRLEY SONDEREGGER: Yes. He usually comes in once a day, but now that "Pet Sematary" is being filmed here, his time is divided. Because he has interests in the film, and since it's his screenplay, he's frequently on location with the cast and crew. It's being filmed down in Ellsworth, which is a good half hour, forty minutes from here. But he usually calls in every day.

STEVE SPIGNESI: Does he ever do any writing in that office, instead of at home?

SHIRLEY SONDEREGGER: Yes, sometimes he does. But his office here is kind of an auxiliary office.

STEVE SPIGNESI: Do you ever work on his manuscripts?

SHIRLEY SONDEREGGER: Sometimes I re-type manuscripts for him. He started writing *The Dark Half* in his office here. He wrote it on an old Underwood manual typewriter, if you can believe it. And then the typed pages had to be transferred over to the Wang, onto disk. Steph and I took turns typing it into the word processor. Sometimes we would do it here and sometimes we would do it over at the house. We have a Wang terminal here, and Steve has a terminal at home.

STEVE SPIGNESI: Are they linked?

SHIRLEY SONDEREGGER: Yes.

"He's very easy-going. Sometimes it's hard to get him to sit still to answer questions, and once in awhile he's a little off the wall, but as he said, I'm as crazy as he is,..."

STEVE SPIGNESI: What kind of boss is Stephen King?

SHIRLEY SONDEREGGER: He's pretty neat. He really is. He's very easy-going. Sometimes it's hard to get him to sit still to answer questions, and once in awhile he's a little off the wall, but as he said, I'm as crazy as he is, so I wouldn't want to ask him what kind of secretary I am either! (Laughs.)

STEVE SPIGNESI: (Laughs.) You might not want to hear the answer?

SHIRLEY SONDEREGGER: Right! I might not! But Steve's very understanding. He's one of the nicest bosses I've ever had.

STEVE SPIGNESI: Were you a King fan before you started working for him?

SHIRLEY SONDEREGGER: No, I wasn't. This was all new to me when I started.

STEVE SPIGNESI: And are you now a "Stephen King expert?"

SHIRLEY SONDEREGGER: No! By no means! He's written things that were way before my time—things that I've heard of, but never read. I admire Steve, I really do. I think he shows an absolutely marvelous use of the English language. If I ever had a difficult letter to write, I would certainly ask Steve to write it. He really has a way with words.

STEVE SPIGNESI: I think eighty million readers agree with you.

SHIRLEY SONDEREGGER: Yes, I'm sure they do. And I'm more aware than I've ever been of punctuation and things like that. Since Steve was an English teacher, I can see why people say they're afraid to write him a letter. They're sure that it's going to be edited and corrected. (Laughs.) But he's a pretty neat guy.

STEVE SPIGNESI: What's the most common question you're asked about working for Steve?

SHIRLEY SONDEREGGER: There are two: "Is he really as off the wall as he seems to be?" and "What is he like?"

STEVE SPIGNESI: And what are your stock answers?

SHIRLEY SONDEREGGER: I answer "no" to the first and "he's really a terrific guy" to the second. I admit that he may be off the wall once in a while, but aren't we all? Steve is a very sincere person, and he does a *lot* for the community. He does more than people realize—both he and Tabby do.

STEVE SPIGNESI: Speaking of Mrs. King, do you also work for Tabitha?

SHIRLEY SONDEREGGER: Yes, I do.

STEVE SPIGNESI: Do you ever get involved with her fiction as well?

SHIRLEY SONDEREGGER: No, not really. She's pretty self-contained. If there's business mail to be answered I take care of that for her, and sometimes I do her personal mail. I also make copies for her and take care of getting her stuff mailed to the publishers, but as far as working on her novels, no.

STEVE SPIGNESI: Did your husband Peter know about Stephen King's "Richard Bachman" pseudonym?

SHIRLEY SONDEREGGER: I'd say Peter knew before it was revealed. You can't help but say something when you talk wife to husband, so I'm sure I divulged it at some point.

STEVE SPIGNESI: Do you collect Stephen King memorabilia?

SHIRLEY SONDEREGGER: Yes, I do.

STEVE SPIGNESI: What does your collection consist of? Is it limited to signed books and magazine articles, or is there more to it?

SHIRLEY SONDEREGGER: I've saved all the little notes that Steve has written to me over the past five years.

STEVE SPIGNESI: That must be quite a collection!

SHIRLEY SONDEREGGER: Yes, it is.

"Doing a book would probably be fun, but I feel strongly that I'm Steve's *personal* secretary and there are some things that I would just never divulge. He's a friend."

STEVE SPIGNESI: Well, as Phil Donahue is fond of asking, when's *your* book coming out? (Laughs.)

SHIRLEY SONDEREGGER: (Laughs.) Right! Doing a book would probably be fun, but I feel strongly that I'm Steve's *personal* secretary and there are some things that I would just never divulge. He's a friend.

STEVE SPIGNESI: It seems as though he relies on you enormously and that you take a lot of the burden off him. I know that there are incredible demands made on his time and yet I get the feeling that you're able to act as a very effective "front-line defense" for him. Is this an accurate perception, and if so, is it a burden or a joy?

SHIRLEY SONDEREGGER: Yes, it is accurate, and it's a joy.

STEVE SPIGNESI: Why?

SHIRLEY SONDEREGGER: Because he always says thank you, and when I do something special for him, he does something special for me. He really appreciates it. It's a two-way street.

STEVE SPIGNESI: You yourself are probably more aware of what's come to be known as "The Stephen King Phenomenon" than anyone else, except perhaps Steve himself.

SHIRLEY SONDEREGGER: Oh, yes. It's a *cult*. (Laughs.)

STEVE SPIGNESI: I agree. The fandom is just incredible. It's enormous—and it's worldwide. What are your thoughts on the whole obsession with King and his work? You must get letters...

SHIRLEY SONDEREGGER: Oh, all the time. The mail often comes in bits and spurts, and in many cases, from different parts of the country. We get a lot of mail from California, and recently we've had a lot of mail from West Germany. Not so much "we think you're great" and things like that, but instead they all want autographs. And what's funny is that you can tell where the publicity has been across the country simply because it comes in in droves from those different areas.

Steve's fandom is absolutely amazing and sometimes I don't understand it. It never ceases to amaze me that he has such a following.

I'm sure Steve's writing is what does it—but in addition to the stories I also think it's his Afterwords and Forewords that really appeal to people. He makes them sound so personal. It sounds like he's talking to them individually, and I think that that is probably what attracts so many people. They say that he talks to them, and that it's like he's writing each of them a personal letter.

STEVE SPIGNESI: It's as if he knows each of them *individually*?

SHIRLEY SONDEREGGER: Yes, and I think that people enjoy that.

STEVE SPIGNESI: What other kind of mail does Steve get?

SHIRLEY SONDEREGGER: Some of the other mail we get includes complaints about the prices of the books, and complaints about the language, as well as various questions.

STEVE SPIGNESI: Horror can sometimes attract what's come to be known as "the dark side of fandom." How do you handle letters or phone calls that you're just a little uneasy about? Do you just trash them and ignore them?

SHIRLEY SONDEREGGER: Some of them I do. But you can't do it when it's a phone call.

"Some fans look to Steve for everything. A woman called here just last week. She was having trouble with her ex-husband. Apparently he had kidnapped their daughter and was molesting her, and she wanted to know who she should talk to."

STEVE SPIGNESI: What kind of calls come into your office?

SHIRLEY SONDEREGGER: Some fans look to Steve for everything. A woman called here just last week. She was having trouble with her ex-husband. Apparently he had kidnapped their daughter and was molesting her, and she wanted to know who she should talk to. Why in the world would she call here!? She wanted Stephen to recommend an attorney so I told her, "There's nothing that Stephen can do for you, and if I were you I would call the police, or the Attorney General's office." I don't know why she ever thought to call here...but they do call for most any reason. Sometimes they call looking for money, and sometimes it's just crazy stuff.

STEVE SPIGNESI: Simply from reading his books, they assume they have an advocate?

SHIRLEY SONDEREGGER: Yes, they think that Stephen has an answer for everything.

"One of the strangest things that happened occurred about three years ago....I remember one day I went to the post office and picked up a box addressed to Steve....It was a flat box—sort of like a small shirt box. I opened it up and it was filled with hay, and in the hay were the bones and hair of several dead kittens."

STEVE SPIGNESI: What's the most bizarre thing that's happened to you since you began working for Steve?

SHIRLEY SONDEREGGER: One of the strangest things that happened occurred about three years ago, and I've mentioned this incident in another interview because it sticks in my mind.

I remember one day I went to the post office and picked up a box addressed to Steve. The return address was from someone in the Bangor area. It was a flat box—sort of like a small shirt box. I opened it up and it was filled with hay, and in the hay were the bones and hair of several dead kittens. Apparently these people had cleaned out a barn somewhere and found these bones, and who did they think of to send them to but Stephen?

I showed them to Steve and we both shuddered. It was absolutely disgusting. We threw the box in the trash.

STEVE SPIGNESI: That's really gross, and I'd say that certainly qualifies as bizarre. Let's talk about Steve's books. Do you have a personal favorite

Stephen King novel?

SHIRLEY SONDEREGGER: I loved *Misery*.

STEVE SPIGNESI: How about your favorite short story?

SHIRLEY SONDEREGGER: I really enjoyed "The Body."

STEVE SPIGNESI: And how about the films?

SHIRLEY SONDEREGGER: I think "Stand By Me" was really terrific.

STEVE SPIGNESI: Do you ever socialize with Stephen and Tabitha King?

SHIRLEY SONDEREGGER: No, not really. I figure they probably see enough of me during the day.

STEVE SPIGNESI: If I asked you to give us the "twenty-five words or less" capsule summary of what it takes to run Stephen King's office, both emotionally and logistically, what would you say?

SHIRLEY SONDEREGGER: You want to know what it takes to run Stephen King's office? Emotional fortitude and a sense of the ridiculous! I'd say that pretty well sums it up! (Laughs.)

STEVE SPIGNESI: How does Stephen King handle the incredible demands on his time? He must be pulled at from every direction every day of the week.

SHIRLEY SONDEREGGER: Oh, he is, he is. And sometimes he gets to the point where he says no to everything because the demands are just so overwhelming.

It's gotten to a point now where I know that there are some requests made of him that are just out of the question so I say no without bothering him. It's the only way.

But then there are some things that kind of pique my interest and that I think he may really like to do, so I bring them up and we discuss them. People just have to understand that Stephen can't possibly do everything—he can't be everything to all people. And I think that's what people are looking for. Even though everyone thinks their situation is the best and the most important, Steve just can't possibly do everything. The requests come in from all across the country and from all over the world.

He has tried to do things like interviews and public appearances when he could, but in the last couple of years he's just kind of pulled in and withdrawn.

He feels like overexposure is something to consider, too. It seems as though everyone wants an interview and everyone wants a personal appearance. Now he's relaxing a little bit. For a while there, he was just kind of running on nervous energy. But since he's laid low for the past couple of years now, he's a little more relaxed.

STEVE SPIGNESI: Well, that's good to hear. I've always thought of writing as a process as well as an act, and in my experience I've come to realize that a writer has to try and push away a lot of things in order to maintain the creativity. It would seem to me that in the case of Stephen King, the pressures must be mind-boggling.

SHIRLEY SONDEREGGER: Yes, sometimes they are. And in Steve's case, as with any other normal human being, some days are better than others. There are some days when he's willing to say yes —as there are those days when you'll ask a secretary to do an interview, and she'll say no way—but then you catch her in a weak moment and she

agrees to give you ten minutes and then talks for half an hour! (Laughs.)

STEVE SPIGNESI: That's true! (Laughs.) And since that sounds like a rather blatant hint, I will wrap this up by thanking you for your help—both with this interview and with *The Shape Under the Sheet.* I sincerely appreciate it.

SHIRLEY SONDEREGGER: Oh, you're welcome Steve, and good luck with the book! ❑

"You want to know what it takes to run Stephen King's office? Emotional fortitude and a sense of the ridiculous! I'd say that pretty well sums it up!"

Out of Line   *by Mort Gerberg*

"Honey, please turn out the light; it's nearly half-past winter! Why didn't you pick a shorter book to read before hibernating!"

GROWING UP WITH THE BOOGEYMAN
An Exclusive Interview With
Stephen King's Brother, David King

"This book is for my brother, David,
who held my hand crossing West Broad Street,
and who taught me how to make skyhooks
out of old coathangers. The trick was so
damned good I just never stopped.

I love you, David."

—Stephen King's *Cujo* dedication

David King, Stephen King's only sibling, was born in 1945 and adopted by Nellie and Donald King two years before Stephen was born.

Dave is a very bright man. (He skipped second grade because he was so advanced.) He is also a gentle and very spiritual man, and he regularly conducts church services – usually at more than one church.

For the past several years, Dave has owned an appliance store in New Hampshire.

I was flabbergasted to hear that no one had ever interviewed Dave about his brother, and he was flattered and surprised that I wanted to talk to him for this book. He did caution me, though (as do most humble people), that he wasn't sure if what he could tell me would be of any help. But, as it usually turns out, our talk was fascinating.

As you'll soon discover in the following interview, David King is an interesting, literate gentleman who is ecstatic about his brother's overwhelming success. Dave King knew "Stevie" King "when," and his insights into their childhood upbringing add a lot to our understanding and appreciation of this American literary giant.

David and Stephen shared the same bedroom in Durham, Maine, as children, and David remembers the actual moment when they found the box of books owned by their long-gone father, Donald, the discovery of which King nods to as a major event in his writing life. (Chris Chesley also talks about that moment in the 1990 introduction to his *People, Places, and Things* story, "Genius," which appears elsewhere in this volume.)

I started off the interview by talking about a newspaper Dave wrote, printed, and even took the photographs for, called "Dave's Rag."

Dave was in his teens when he was writing the "Rag," and Stephen King used David's mimeograph machine for some of his own early efforts, most notably "The Star Invaders."

When Dave and I were going over a few changes for the final version of the following interview, he told me that he had found a couple of childhood pictures I could use, and he also mentioned that he had found the only existing copy of "Dave's Rag." I appreciate Dave taking the time to hunt for these wonderful artifacts of his and his brother's early years, and I am proud to reprint both the photos and "Dave's Rag" here.

A very special thanks must go to my friend Dave Lowell for service above and beyond. (It seems like there's Daves everywhere, doesn't it?!) I had told Dave King that I would send the first edited version of this interview to Dave Lowell, who lives fairly close to Dave, and that Signore Lowell would drive it over and take some photos of Dave to accompany our talk. I mailed the interview to Dave Lowell on a Tuesday by certified mail. Three days later, on a Friday night, Dave King called my wife Pam and told her he had already received the interview, gone over it, and made some changes that he and I could discuss the following morning. He had also already been photographed by Dave Lowell, and those photos are likewise reprinted here. Friends like Dave Lowell don't come around every day, and I owe him a huge amount of thanks for his thoughfulness, industry, and ready willingness to drop everything and be my "man in Maine." (And New Hampshire, for that matter.)

I can't say thank you enough, Dave...but I'll never stop trying. Thanks, pal. — **sjs**

GROWING UP WITH THE BOOGEYMAN
An Exclusive Interview With David King

STEVE SPIGNESI: I really appreciate your participation in *The Shape Under the Sheet*, Dave. Why don't we start off by talking about "Dave's Rag"?
DAVID KING: "Dave's Rag" was a little community newspaper that I did when I was in the ninth or tenth grade. I started out by hand-typing a few

David King with "Cujo"
Photo courtesy David Lowell.

issues, and I took some photographs and processed them myself, and taped them into the newspaper. It really wasn't a project Stevie was involved in all that much, although he might have written a little bit for it. But bear in mind that at this point he was four years behind me in school. He was probably in the fifth or sixth grade then.

STEVE SPIGNESI: Your brother told a story in Doug Winter's *Stephen King: The Art of Darkness* that there was a time when people would telephone you, and your mother, in all innocence, would say "Well, Dave can't come to the phone right now, he's down in the basement on the rag." Do you remember that?

DAVID KING: No, I don't remember that! But I do remember that the cylinder on the mimeograph machine was broken, so you couldn't use the crank. I had to turn it by actually turning the drum by hand. I couldn't whip 'em right out.

STEVE SPIGNESI: And what type of books were you reading at this stage?

DAVID KING: Science fiction, mainly. Stevie and I were sharing the same bedroom upstairs. We didn't have any bookcases, so all our paperbacks lined the walls of the room on the floor.

STEVE SPIGNESI: Chris Chesley also told me that story. The books were lined up against the wall with the spines up?

DAVID KING: The spines were up, yes, so you could read the titles. That's always been a big bugaboo of mine, to go to somebody's bookshelf and the books are in all different directions.

Speaking of that bedroom…the picture in *Art of Darkness* of Stevie sitting at a typewriter with "The Glass Floor" propped open in front of him was taken by me up in that room. In fact, I think that was my typewriter. I think that was the "Dave's Rag" typewriter.

STEVE SPIGNESI: What were the years like that you and your mother and brother spent moving around?

DAVID KING: When we were very small, I heard that we lived in Scarborough for a while, and then we lived in a place called Croton-on-Hudson, New York. That part is just hearsay, of course, because I really don't remember that. And then there was a period of time when Stevie stayed with Ethelyn, my mother's sister, and Oren Flaws, in Durham, and I stayed with Molly, another of her sisters, down in Malden, Massachusetts. Mother was working. I don't remember too much of that. I do remember one thing, though. Mom came to visit me at Molly's once, and I remember at breakfast time Molly always used to put wheat germ on our cereal, and I told my mother that my aunt was feeding us germs.

After that we went to live with my grandmother on my father's side in Chicago for a period. I was in kindergarten at the time. I can remember at one time seeing a picture of me in my kindergarten class. All of us in the class had made Easter bonnets out of paper and whatnot. I don't know if that picture is still in existence or not.

Following Chicago, we lived in west De Pere, Wisconsin. I was in first grade at that time. [NOTE: Approximately 100 miles to the southwest of De Pere, Wisconsin, is a body of water called Castle Rock Lake.]

I can vaguely remember that we had a dog, and that the dog was kept in the front yard, and so you had to be very careful where you walked.

After Wisconsin, we then went to live with my father's sister Betty, and a lady she stayed with named Rudy. We have a picture of that somewhere, too—Stevie and I sitting on a lawn in front of a house. That was in the Fort Wayne, Indiana, area. Aunt Betty was a schoolteacher, as was Rudy, and I skipped second grade because she thought that I should.

After that we lived in an apartment of our own in Fort Wayne. I can remember some of that. We shared the apartment with a number of cockroaches. It was an apartment house, but I'm not sure if it was a single-family dwelling or if there were a couple of apartments in it. That's extreme-

> **"Once, Stevie and I got in trouble for playing with matches....And I remember that once I tried to do a garden out in the backyard...it began to rain. In order to be efficient, I tied an umbrella to the handle of the shovel so I could dig in the rain."**

ly vague. We *are* talking almost forty years ago here! (Laughs.)

A couple of anecdotes do come to mind, though, from when we lived in that apartment. Once, Stevie and I got in trouble for playing with matches. I remember that. And I remember that once I tried to do a garden out in the backyard. I had a long-handled shovel for digging up the ground, and it began to rain. In order to be efficient, I tied an umbrella to the handle of the shovel so I could dig in the rain.

STEVE SPIGNESI: (Laughs.) Very clever. What do you remember about your father, Donald King?

DAVID KING: Nothing. I don't remember the man personally at all. I do remember that at one point —I guess when we got back to Durham, Maine— Stevie and I found a trunk up in Aunt Ethelyn's garage that contained a lot of books on seamanship and that sort of thing, and in fact, there was even one of his Merchant Marine uniforms in it.

We also had several still pictures of him and one sixteen-millimeter film that he had taken. One scene from that film that I can remember was of the ship he was on going through a storm. There were waves crashing over the bow and everything. And, surprisingly (since this was the mid-1940s), there were also some shots on that reel in color – footage of both Stevie and I as little kids running around.

STEVE SPIGNESI: Do you think he's still alive?

DAVID KING: I have no clue. I think he was my mother's age, possibly a year younger. Today, my mother would be in her seventies, so he would probably be at least that old. We just heard nothing at all about him from the time he left. It's possible that my mother may have heard something a few years later and not said anything to us, but for all intents and purposes, he just vanished.

STEVE SPIGNESI: In the interview he did with *Playboy* magazine, your brother remarked that he

thought that greed would have probably been the likely motivation for Donald to look him up, since Steve's wealth and fame would have made him relatively easy to find.

DAVID KING: Oh, yeah. That's my feeling as well. Ever since Stevie really hit it big, it would have been fairly simple to track him down. Stephen Edwin King—there aren't too many names like that. And I'm sure Don would have recognized it, because if you had kids, even after thirty years, you'd remember something about them.

STEVE SPIGNESI: So he's probably dead?

DAVID KING: Either that, or he could be in a nursing home somewhere not really able to think.

STEVE SPIGNESI: To get back to your childhood travels – where did you move to after Fort Wayne?

DAVID KING: From Fort Wayne, Indiana, we went to live with another of my mother's sisters in Stratford, Connecticut, for a short time.

STEVE SPIGNESI: Were you and your brother together in Connecticut?

DAVID KING: Yes. The only time we were apart was when he stayed with Ethelyn and I stayed with Molly. In Chicago, west De Pere, and in Fort Wayne, we were together as a family.

When we were growing up, my mother lived with a number of her sisters, and for a while with her sisters-in-law. Back in those days, families kind of stuck together.

In Connecticut, we lived with my aunt and uncle in Stratford, in an area called Putney, which was in the north end of town, up near the Merit Turnpike. I remember going to a place up there that had an orchard. We went up there near the Halloween season and got cider and doughnuts and that was kind of neat.

After that we had a place of our own in Stratford on West Broad Street. [NOTE: See the *Cujo* dedication that leads off this interview.] My mother worked at Stratford Laundry. Back when we were in Fort Wayne, I believed she worked for General Electric winding coils for small motors. And then after Stratford, we moved to Durham.

STEVE SPIGNESI: How old were you and your brother when you moved back to Maine?

DAVID KING: When we moved to Durham, I was just starting my freshman year of high school, so Stevie must have been starting fifth grade, because he was four years behind me. This was in the fall of 1958, so Stevie would have been around eleven, and I was thirteen.

STEVE SPIGNESI: So there's a two-year difference in your age?

DAVID KING: Yes. He was born in 1947, and I was born in 1945, but there's a four-year difference in our schooling because I skipped the second grade.

David, fresh from a haircut done by his father, attends Stevie's tabletop bath time. Circa 1947-48.
Photo courtesy David King.

STEVE SPIGNESI: Where did you go to high school?

DAVID KING: I went to high school in Brunswick, Maine, because when I lived in Durham, the town had no high school. Durham would pay the out-of-town tuition, but it was up to the student to get their own transportation to school every day.

When I was starting high school, my cousin Donald Flaws was a sophomore at Brunswick High. His father was in the contracting business in the Brunswick area, so we rode back and forth to Brunswick with my uncle and his helper. Four of us in a pickup truck bouncing over the dirt roads. That was fun. Especially in the wintertime. I remember one time we were coming home during an ice storm and the truck went a complete 360° around. About half the trip was over dirt roads, but back in the late fifties, early sixties, they called them "improved gravel" roads. Back in those days we had an annual event called mud season, and I can remember times when we literally churned our way through.

STEVE SPIGNESI: How long did you live in Durham?

DAVID KING: My home was in Durham until I graduated from college, and then I got married and Linda and I stayed in Durham for a while. When Stevie got out of college, he lived up in Oldtown, and then in Bangor.

STEVE SPIGNESI: Was this when he was living in a trailer?

DAVID KING: Well, it wasn't actually a trailer, it was a double-wide mobile home. It was on the outskirts of Bangor on Route 2 between Newport and Bangor. That's when he wrote *Carrie,* or at least when *Carrie* was sent out.

All I can remember about that period was that Linda and I were living in Mexico, Maine, at the time. I was town manager in Mexico, and once on our way home from visiting Steve and Tabby, I got a speeding ticket. The kids enjoyed that.

STEVE SPIGNESI: How many children do you have?

DAVID KING: I have two daughters, Karen and Katherine. Karen has her Bachelors of Science in Health and Physical Fitness Club Management, and Katherine is studying to be an elementary school teacher.

STEVE SPIGNESI: Do your daughters ever get approached because of who their uncle is? Do their friends know?

DAVID KING: They try not to reveal who they're related to. They basically try to keep it a secret. Occasionally people will try to get them—or even me sometime—to get Stevie to autograph a book, but we just tell them that he doesn't do that sort of thing. Even in New Hampshire, people will come into my store and say, "Are you Stephen King's brother?" (Laughs.)

STEVE SPIGNESI: How do you feel about that? And how do you respond?

DAVID KING: I just say, yes, I am, and he's done very well, and that's about it. I don't go into too much detail about him.

The Kings' boyhood home, West Durham.
Photo courtesy Dave Lowell.

STEVE SPIGNESI: Were you aware that as a kid, Steve was doing things like "The Star Invaders?" Typing stuff up and selling it at school?

DAVID KING: We were aware of it because he was constantly at the typewriter. When I was home from college, he was always upstairs typing.

As I mentioned, as we were growing up, we both slept in the bedroom upstairs. But once I went away to college, things changed. Think about the idea of a kid who wants a room of his own. That's where I was at after I went away to school.

There was an old room out back that my grandfather had had for a while. That room became Dave's Dream Room, "Where You Go For Nightmares." The room had a twin bed in it, and the twin bed almost exactly fit in the room with enough space to stand up next to it. And I stayed in that room when I was home from school or during the summers.

STEVE SPIGNESI: Can you remember any specific moments from when you guys were growing up together where you saw something in him in terms of storytelling ability, where you said, "He's really good," or "He should be a writer"?

DAVID KING: Not really, because bear in mind that Stevie started his writing when I was away at the University of Maine. I was home on weekends, but most of the time I had a girlfriend, and I didn't hang around the house with my kid brother. I was out "girling."

One of the things I do remember was he and Chris Chesley making a movie at a rundown house in the neighborhood. I had always been interested in photography, and at one point—and I marvel today at how my mother was able to do these things—she got me a movie camera, an eight-millimeter. And Stevie and Chris Chesley went over and made a movie. I don't know if he's still got it. I think doing the haunted house movie was one of the bigger thrills in his life.

STEVE SPIGNESI: Was it something that he had written?

DAVID KING: I seriously doubt that he and Chris actually wrote up a screenplay, but they did do some things with my eight-millimeter camera. Of course, it was more playing around than serious filmmaking.

But as far as literary indications went, all I can think of was when I was home from college, he was always writing. And we always encouraged him – you know, "Hey, send 'em out." Why not? And I remember how excited he was when he got his first

> **"...I remember how excited he was when he got his first check for 'The Glass Floor.' He got lots of rejection slips. If I remember correctly, there was a nail pounded in the wall up in the bedroom, and he'd spear all the rejection slips on it."**

check for "The Glass Floor." He got lots of rejection slips. If I remember correctly, there was a nail pounded in the wall up in the bedroom, and he'd spear all the rejection slips on it.

STEVE SPIGNESI: And as all beginning writers do, I've read that he built up quite a collection.

DAVID KING: Oh, sure. My brother paid his dues. His success was not handed to him on a silver platter by any means. But there was also a degree of timing involved because when he sent *Carrie* in, that was the time of *The Exorcist*. I've heard Stevie himself say, if he were six months earlier or six months later, he'd still be teaching English.

STEVE SPIGNESI: In an interview for this book, Richard Matheson brought up the idea of the time and the man being so perfectly in tune that everything worked out just right.

DAVID KING: Well, there are those of us who would say it's the Lord who does it rather than pure luck, but however one wants to put it, there is that factor to Steve's success.

STEVE SPIGNESI: Personally, this has got to be a very strange experience for you. Your brother has become a worldwide phenomenon. Did it all just explode in front of you?

DAVID KING: Pretty much, yes. Because here again, we each had our own families and Stevie and I have never lived in the same area, so Linda and I and the kids weren't able to see the day-to-day developments in his career. Stevie and Tabby and the kids were up in the Bangor area while we pretty much started in Durham, and then moved up to Mexico, Maine, and then back down to Brunswick, and then we came over here to New Hampshire. He and I have never lived close enough so that we could stop at a pizza place and have a pizza together and talk over the things that were happening. So, yes, it did seem to sort of happen all at once from our perspective.

STEVE SPIGNESI: From what I've read, I know that your mother took her parents into your home for a time. How did you manage to go to college in that situation?

DAVID KING: Yes. At that time, my mother was taking care of her parents with support from her sisters, and sometimes, even when we were in Durham, she was getting Aid to Dependent Children.

The principal of my high school found out that I wasn't the richest person in the world, and he knew that I wanted to go to college and so he gave me a job on the school's janitorial staff about halfway through my senior year. He also helped me get an experimental scholarship to the University of Maine, or otherwise I wouldn't have even been able to go.

I'm not sure what Stevie's situation was, how he went to college, how his was financed. But I did it with student loans, some scholarship help, and working at Brunswick High School during the summers. In fact, that's where I went to work when I graduated in January of 1966. I taught math at Brunswick for four years.

STEVE SPIGNESI: You quit teaching after four years?

DAVID KING: Yes. I left in January of 1970. In fact, if memory serves, I left teaching without having another job. I said, "That's it." That's twice in my career that I've done that—and, if you can imagine, with kids in the house.

STEVE SPIGNESI: I can't.

DAVID KING: I look back on it now and shudder, but the Lord was good to us, and took care of us.

STEVE SPIGNESI: How often do you see your brother?

DAVID KING: Maybe once a year, maybe once every couple of years.

STEVE SPIGNESI: Do you ever get a chance to stay in Bangor for a period?

DAVID KING: No, because usually I've been in the position where because of the kids or my job or something I just didn't have the time. Five or six years ago, when the kids were home, there was a period of time when for two or three years, we went up there at Christmas time.

STEVE SPIGNESI: Are your daughters close with their cousins?

DAVID KING: Not anymore. Naomi's out in the far west now and as I said, we're almost five hours away from Bangor. It's hard. There was a time

when our kids were five, six, and seven, when we saw them every now and again, but now Stevie's life is just so busy that's it's difficult to get together.

STEVE SPIGNESI: Who did you and your brother hang around with when you were kids?

DAVID KING: There was a whole group of us ranging in ages from seven to sixteen all going around playing guns. Today, it isn't done. The neighborhood kids, I don't know how much they play together today. It was funny in a way, because we were kids in all different age groups all playing together—we had Douglas Hall, who was a junior or senior in high school, and his twin brothers, Dean and Dana, who were younger than Stevie. I remember that the Halls were the first ones in the neighborhood to have a television set, so we always went up to the Halls' house to watch TV.

We didn't hang around with the Chesleys that much when I was living at home. It was more with my cousin and a couple of girls that lived over the other way, and the Hall boys.

STEVE SPIGNESI: What was your brother like physically as a child?

DAVID KING: Well, Stevie was husky, and he wasn't too well-coordinated. He looked like Vern in the film *Stand By Me*.

STEVE SPIGNESI: What was your and your brother's religious upbringing like?

DAVID KING: We lived right next to the West Durham Methodist Church, which is, according to a plaque on the building, "the Second Oldest Methodist Church in Continuous Use in New England." My mother was very talented on organ and piano. When we were young—I don't remem-

United Methodist Church, West Durham.
Photo courtesy Dave Lowell.

ber where we were living at the time—there was a fairly good-sized church where she played the organ. I assume she did it to make a couple of extra bucks.

I remember the first church I joined. I was twelve, in junior high school in Stratford, Connecticut, and it was a Congregationalist Church.

Now, when Stevie turned twelve, we were in Durham by then, and we both joined the West Durham Methodist Church. So basically, we had a traditional Protestant upbringing.

Linda and I are now what's known as evangelical Christians. We're Biblical fundamentalists, which sometimes connotes a negative impression in people's minds. We are of the group that believes that the Bible is the total and factual and complete word of God.

STEVE SPIGNESI: Was your mother religious?

DAVID KING: I would say so. She regularly attended church.

STEVE SPIGNESI: Did she prod you guys to go with her?

DAVID KING: It wasn't like that exactly. It was more or less, "We're going to church today." It was a given that we went to church. But I think that we were both probably very fidgety in younger years.

STEVE SPIGNESI: What do you personally know of your brother's religious beliefs?

DAVID KING: Well, I know he's not an atheist or an agnostic, but I don't think he attends church. I believe that when he and Tabby married he agreed to have the children brought up in the Catholic faith, because Tabby is Catholic.

STEVE SPIGNESI: Any last remembrances you'd like to talk about?

DAVID KING: Yes, I would like to mention a man who had a profound impact on both Stevie and me as children. He was a fellow by the name of Charles Huff.

STEVE SPIGNESI: Huffy.

DAVID KING: That's right!

STEVE SPIGNESI: I have a copy of the eulogy your brother delivered at a memorial service for Mr. Huff.

DAVID KING: Mr. Huff was a bachelor, in his sixties at the time, who drove up to Durham from Orr's Island and back in those days, late fifties, early sixties, that was a heck of a trip. He was the retired postmaster. It would take him over an

hour each way and he was the world's worst driver. I can remember one time when he took Douglas Hall, my cousin Donald, and myself from Durham to a camp meeting up in the Portland area. We were driving to Portland through Auburn at the time and of course back in those days all cars didn't have turn signals. You were supposed to use hand signals.

Well, when Huffy was driving, he'd be pointing out things and waving his arm out the window, and we'd all be looking out the back window at the drivers shaking their fists at us. This particular time, when we were going to this camp meeting, we were going right through the middle of Auburn and Huffy was waving his hands and pointing around and we went right slam through a red light. My mother and aunt never ceased to marvel at how God was watching over Mr. Huff. And his driving.

I can remember later as I got into my senior year in high school, he let me practice drive in his car, and my mother was very glad that it was me that was *driving* instead of *riding* with Huffy.

He would come up every Sunday and he'd always have candy bars for the kids. And he used to come up Thursday nights also for youth meetings.

I particularly remember the Easter season. I think about Huffy almost every year as Easter approaches. Mr. Huff was never an ordained minister and so he never thought it appropriate that he should give communion. When we'd have communion periodically, we'd have some ordained minister come over.

But on Maundy Thursday, the day before Good Friday, Mr. Huff always set up his own version of the Last Supper. We'd all go over to the parish hall where we'd sit around with candles, and we would have Za-Rex. I remember that specifically. Even when he used to take us down to picnics down at Bradbury Mountain, it was always Za-Rex.

STEVE SPIGNESI: Za-Rex punch. That's mentioned so often in your brother's stories.

DAVID KING: That's probably all that Huffy could afford, you know? And on Maundy Thursday, we had what we used to call the crunch-crunch service.

The poor old fellow had the greatest intentions in the world. But here you take a bunch of young adolescent kids sitting around tables with Za-Rex and cookies. *Hard* cookies. He was trying to get into the spirit of the Last Supper, yet we were all

"And on Maundy Thursday, we had what we used to call the crunch-crunch service....The poor old fellow had the greatest intentions in the world. But here you take a bunch of young adolescent kids sitting around tables with Za-Rex and cookies. *Hard* cookies. He was trying to get into the spirit of the Last Supper...."

---

just dreading the minute he would have us eat the cookies. Crunch-crunch. Everything would be quiet and then...crunch-crunch. Even my mother would have a problem in not breaking up. You've got to picture it.

But I think that out of all the kids that attended these services, I'm one of the only ones that truly understood the spirituality that he was trying to convey.

STEVE SPIGNESI: That's a great story, Dave, and thank you for sharing it with us, and for your help with *The Shape Under the Sheet*. Your kindness is greatly appreciated.

DAVID KING: You're more than welcome. It was my pleasure. ❏

A EULOGY FOR "HUFFY"

The eulogy by Stephen King mentioned in the previous interview was titled "Huffy," and is unpublished. A copy of "Huffy," along with much else in the way of research materials, was kindly given to me by Joyce and Alex Hall, the parents of the Hall boys mentioned by Dave King.

"Huffy" began, "Although this is a church service, I don't want to preach a sermon. I wouldn't know how even if I did want to, so that lets *that* out." Apparently, those Maundy Thursday services left quite an impression on Stephen King as well:

> "The closest Huffy came to giving communion himself was at the Maundy Thursday service he held each year in the parsonage, on the Thursday just prior to Easter. During those services—which we kids called, rather irreverently, the Munchy Crunchies—we would re-create, in our humble way, the Last Supper."

He also spoke eloquently about childhood:

> "It has been a good thing for me to reconsider Mr. Huff, who meant so much to me as a child. Children are self-centered little beings, and they take a great deal for granted. There's nothing bad about this; it seems to me that it is the chief luxury of a good childhood. But it is also a fine thing to look back as a man or a woman, and to reconsider the work and sacrifice of others with a more mature understanding. I don't think that such recollection has to be a guilty thing; that the person doing the remembering has to berate himself with all the things he or she didn't know or understand then; there need be no guilt attached to a gift that has been freely given, and there were no strings attached to all which Huffy gave to this church and its parishioners."

Compare that with this lyrical and brilliant passage [italics added] from the last page of King's magnum opus, *IT*:

> "...[H]e thinks that it is good to be a child, but it is also good to be a grownup and able to consider the mystery of childhood...its beliefs and desires. *I will write about all of this one day,* he thinks, and knows it's just a dawn thought, an after-dreaming thought. But it's nice to think so for awhile in the morning's clean silence, to think that childhood has its own secrets and confirms mortality, and that mortality defines all courage and love. To think that what has looked forward must also look back, and that each life makes its own imitation of immortality: a wheel."

A LOOK AT "DAVE'S RAG"

"Dave's Rag" was a community newspaper published by David King, Stephen King, and Donald Flaws when they were in their early teens.

"Dave's Rag" began publishing in January of 1959 (with a circulation of two), and the only surviving copy of the newspaper is the Summer Special 1959 issue, which, thanks to the generosity of Dave King, I have the honor of reprinting here.

What is of greatest interest to us as Stephen King fans, of course, is the role he played in the publication of "Dave's Rag." Is there early writing by Stephen King in the newspaper that heretofore has never been seen? Yes, there is. You'll find a TV review in the issue reprinted here, as well as a classified ad for a "New book by Steve King," and you'll also find news of the brothers' doings in and around Durham, Maine, in the late fifties.

In addition to the only existing copy of "Dave's Rag" sent to me by David King, Dave also enclosed an article from the Brunswick, Maine, *Record,* dated Thursday, April, 23, 1959, and headlined "3 Durham Lads Publishing Bright Hometown Newspaper." This article revealed that by this time the circulation of the newspaper had risen to twenty, and it also revealed something of possible significance to Stephen King fans.

This is an excerpt from Douglas E. Winter's interview with Stephen King from Doug's book, *Faces of Fear*:

> "I can remember the first real horror story that I wrote. I was about seven years old, and I had internalized the idea from the movies that, when everything looked blackest, the scientists would come up with some off-the-wall solution that would take care of things. I wrote about this big dinosaur that was really ripping ass all over everything, and finally one guy said, 'Wait, I have a theory—the old dinosaurs used to be allergic to leather.' So they went out and they threw leather boots and leather shoes and leather vests at it, and it went away."

In the *Record* article, the reporter quotes from an issue of "Dave's Rag" now gone forever, and this is one of the classified items he reproduced:

WATCH FOR THE NEW KING STORY!!!!
"Land of 1,000,000 Years Ago."
Exciting story of 21 people prisoners on an island that should have been extinct 1,000,000 years ago. Order through this newspaper.

Could this have been the "dinosaur" story? After all, dinosaurs did live a long time ago, and they could have been on the island, right? Realistically, though, it is probably not the same story, if only because the classified ad was for a "new" story, and since King was eleven when "Dave's Rag" was being published, it's unlikely that the dinosaur story survived four years and was then offered for sale. Then again, perhaps King himself is recalling something he did at age eleven as having occurred at "about" age seven. In any event, it's interesting nonetheless to see these early efforts by King. These lost stories, along with the *People, Places, and Things* stories detailed elsewhere in this volume, give us a look at the development of King's phenomenal storytelling gifts.

Inasmuch as the only surviving copy of "Dave's Rag" is reprinted in this volume, I won't go into too much detail about the actual contents of the newspaper (since you can read it yourselves), but allow me to mention a few specific items in the paper which, as Stephen King readers and fans, you'll find especially interesting.

The following annotation should help explain a few items that will become even more interesting with some clarification.

PAGE 1

• Notice the price increase from 5¢ to 20¢.
• The blank space in the "Bible School" item was for a picture taken by Dave King. On Page 3, Dave offers 3 x 5 color enlargements of the shot for 35¢.
• Notice the missing "N"s in the text. Dave's typewriter (the typewriter behind which Stephen King is sitting in a photo in Doug Winter's *Stephen King: The Art of Darkness*) was missing the N key, and so they had to be filled in by hand. Dave (and Steve) didn't always catch all the missing letters.
• The item about Old Home Sunday mentions Charles Huff, who is spoken about at length in the interview with David King in this volume.
• The editorial blurb at the bottom of the page laments the lack of support on the part of some Durham residents for "Dave's Rag." Dave was concerned about giving readers enough news to make the subscription price of $1.00 a year worth the money.

PAGE 2

• An item in the left column about Stephen and David King's birthday party on September 17, 1959 mentions Chris Chesley's brother Andy, as well as the Hall boys. (Stephen King's birthday is September 21.)

• An item in the right column mentions a trip by Steve and Dave to the Science Museum in Boston while they visited their Aunt and Uncle in Malden, Massachusetts.

• An item in the right column mentions the Chesley family. (See my interview with Chris Chesley in this volume.)

PAGE 3

• Page 3 contains advertising by local merchants, the cost (we find out on page 5), 2¢ a line.

• In the right column is a lengthy TV review by "Steve King," in which King gives a chatty overview of the 1959 new fall TV season. He signed off "Happy Viewing" after filling in every "N" in the piece – except for the "N" in "King"!

• The right column also contains another item which details Steve and Dave's trip to West Point, Maine.

PAGE 4

• Page 4 gives the newspapers' masthead. We learn that the paper was published by "THE DK Publishing Co.," and that the Editor-in-Chief and Illustrator was David V. King, the Reporter was Stephen E. King, and the Sports Reporter was Donald P. Flaws.

• Dave's editorial on Page 4 lamented the state of Durham's roads.

• Dave also cautions his readers—and correspondents —that "Anonymous letters go into the waste-basket."

• The item dated 10/7/59 reveals that the Pillsburys will be visiting the Kings in October. Pillsbury was Nellie Ruth King's maiden name, and is often mentioned in King's stories.

PAGE 5

• Page 5 consisted of classified ads, and the left column contained an ad for Dave King's "Dave's Studios." Dave King would take pictures of "any subject," and also offered photo greeting cards. The King family's phone number—2691—was listed in the ad.

• The right column contained an ad for a "New Book by STEVE KING!" The book was called "Thirty-One of the Classics," and was Stephen King's reworking of such tales as "Kidnapped," Tom Sawyer," and *many* others!!! The book sold for 30¢ (but only if you ordered within three weeks.)

In addition to the copy of the "Rag," and the article from the *Record*, David King also sent me two photos from his family collection, as well as his mother's high school yearbook photo, all of which he graciously allowed me to reprint. Many, many thanks, David!

The first photo, reproduced as part of my interview with David King, shows David standing by the table on which the infant Stephen King lies. The back of the photo reads: "Don had just cut David's hair—flat looking, ain't it!"

The second photo, reproduced as part of my brief Stephen King biography earlier in this volume, shows a bearded Stephen King in his late teens or early twenties standing before a fireplace, in front of which his mother is seated.

The yearbook photo, also reproduced in King's bio, shows "Ruthie Pill," and is interesting for the fact that her biographical blurb reveals that "Ruth's ability in public speaking has won distinction for her in numerous plays and honor for the school in every contest she has entered." It has often been noted that Stephen King is quite an engaging public speaker, and it is also known that he acted in college.

(Record Photo by Downing)

GETTING OUT THE PAPER, Dave King (left) and Donald Flaws get together on a issue of "Dave's Rag," a semi-monthly, individually type newspaper circulated in Durham. At the moment the paper is circulated primarily to friends, but the editors are planning to include wider coverage of the West Durham area. The editorial and printing offices are in Dave's bedroom at the moment.

Circulation Now 20 . . .
3 Durham Lads Publishing Bright Hometown Newspaper

By Don Hansen

Newspapers throughout this area have stepped up their coverage recently as the result of a new semi-monthly news-paper now being published by three Durham lads.

The paper, called "Dave's Rag," is published by 13-year-old David V. King, the editor, publisher and photographer; his 11-year-old brother Stephen, and Donald Flaws, 15, the sports editor.

Boasting an all paid circulation of 20 copies, the typewritten newspaper thus far has had a good reception with readers.

While the paper suppose to "hit the streets" every two weeks editor Dave noted that "I think you had better not expect your paper every other Tuesday. Until I get a mimeograph machine things are going to be rather rushed."

At present each copy is individually typed.

Six issues have been published since the paper first appeared with a circulation of two in January.

In the manner of all good newspapers, "Dave's Rag," probes deeply into the lives of its readers for news. One news story, for example covered a fire in detail:

"A few weeks ago, Doris' house, in Scarborough, caught on fire. It leveled the barn, the shop, and the out-buildings. Doris was in Boston, but when she heard about it, she came home. The only fatality was the cat, Confusious. Oren is fixing it back up, at least the house. The cause is not known."

Local news of interest is also covered in detail. In a February issue the following item appeared:

"Today the Pillsburys and Kings were surprised by the arrival of Francis and Phil. They also brought Aunt Gert. They arrived about 2:00 Sunday afternoon, and left at about 4:30. Dave took a picture of them which will probably be in next week's pictures Aunt Gert put her hands over her face when Dave took it, but you can still tell who it is."

And in a later issue:

"Aunt Gert recently appeared in movies! While attending a Stanley Party at Jane's, moving pictures were taken at the refreshment table. Aunt G. is seen juggling her coffee with one hand while she covers her face with the other."

The sports stories also cover every aspect of the games. The following story, written before the New England high school basketball tournament, ended on this note of doom:

"On Feb. 25, Donald and Dave went to the basketball tournament in Lewiston. Brunswick kept up the pace in the first half, but in the second their best player broke his glasses. He cannot shoot without them. The final score was 59-50.

"On March 7, Lewiston beat Bangor for the state championship. Sometime this month they will go to Boston and lose the New Englands."

A weather story contained this interesting sidelight:

"Friday the snow drifted something awful on Route No. 9. There were three cars stuck. A truck, and two cars. A road commissioner was stuck for about 2 hours, and I imagine he got plenty mad."

Or again:

"On Donald's birthday the three Kings were invited down to the Flaws estate for supper, at about 6:00 p.m. Dave was all dolled up in a tie, sports shirt and all the works. Everybody thought that he looked very funny."

The classified advertising department seems to be thriving. In one issue the following advertisements appeared:

"CAT WANTED!!!

Do you have a baby or half-grown cat that you do not have room for? All we need is one! If so, contact Dave King."

WATCH FOR THE NEW KING STORY!!!!

"Land of 1,000,000 Years Ago." Exciting story of 21 people prisoners on an island that should have been extinct 1,000,000 years ago. Order through this newspaper."

Editor Dave takes his responsibility seriously. He points out strongly that "anonymous letters go into the waste-basket."

Dave and Stephen King are the sons of Mrs. Ruth King of Durham. Sports Editor Donald is the son of Mr. and Mrs. George Flaws of Durham.

Dave and Donald are freshmen and sophomore students, respectively, of Brunswick High School. Stephen attends the West Durham school.

Although Dave is probably the nation's youngest newspaper editor, he doubts that he will make newspapering a career. Sports editor Donald thinks he'll go into the field of mathematics as a teacher.

What will be the fate of "Dave's Rag"? Dave plans to continue publishing just as long as time allows. If he should cease publication to enter some other field, however, we're certain that at least 20 subscribers (all paid), will be sorry to see it die.

So will we.

Item from the Brunswick *Record*, April 23, 1959, discussing "Dave's Rag." Courtesy David King.

DAVE'S RAG 2 or 4 (cheap)

⭐ SUMMER SPECIAL 1959 — With reports on the Summer vacation news of West Durham. ⭐

_ Special Photo Section, Illustrations, Jokes, and the Regular dpts. _ _

BIBLE SCHOOL HAS RECORD 50 ENROLLMENT THIS YEAR; SETS NEW RECORD

This year the West Durham Methodist Church sponsored its annual Vacation Bible school. It was u der the directio of Mr. & Mrs. A. Centinao, and the other teachers were: Mrs. G.O. Flaws, & Mrs. H. Herling. Helpers were Joline Brown and Beverly Bowser. The average daily attendance was about 45. The boys and girls put on a closing night service, and all the participants did a good job. The largest class was the Beginner class, directed by Mrs. Herling. On the last day, everyone had ice cream, as sort of a party.

Ready for morning worship

MAINE HAS VERY WET JUNE; HINDERS GROWING SEASON

This year, most of New England was under the spell of a rainy spell. It occured during June, a crucial part of the growing season. Without sunshine, of which there was very little, most of the crops didn't fare too well, except for a few wet-weather types, such as strawberries, and other types of berries.

During part of the summer, the young people of West Durham organized a game club, which met in the Methodist Church parish house. They all enjoyed it, and it lasted for a good part of the month.

OLD HOME SUNDAY, PUT ON BY METHODIST CHURCH, HAS A.M. ATTENDENCE OF OVER 50; OVER HALF STAYED FOR DINNER; ABOUT 1/3 AT P.M. SERVICE

According to Mr. Charles Huff, lay minister for the West Durham Methodist Church, the annual Old Home Sunday services were very good. The attendence wasn't as good as it has been past years, but it was a very (continued on page 2)

CONTENTS

OFF THE EDITOR'S DESK

This issue is a combination of the issues that were due this summer. It is a condensation of all the vacation news that has happened in Durham, and also any news that our readers have sent us. I sent out about 30 post cards asking you about what you did this summer, and I recieved about five replies. I would like to have more support, since I need a lot of news to run a paper that looks worth the subscription rates. I don't care what you say in the way of praises or if you call us names, just SEND them. Thanks, Dave

Old Home Sunday (Cont. from p. 1) well put on service. The dinner was put on by the Ladie's Aid, and it was very tasty.

In the morning service, Mr. & Mrs. Carlton Murphy sung, Mr. & Mrs. Colby sung, and Rev. Walter M. Colby gave the message.

The afternoon service was put on by the Salvation Army from Bath.

Friday, October 9, Mrs. C. Chesley, Mrs. Harold Davis, and Mrs. Ruth King went to the Pickard Theatre in Memorial Hall at Bowdin Bowdin College. They saw Bette Davis and Gary Merrill in "The World of Carl Sandburg". They all enjoyed it very much.

Miss Alice Goddard's nephew, Robert Goddard, visits Miss Hisler and Miss Goddard on weekends. He is from Tennessee, and is stationed at the SAGE base at Topsham. He was last stationed in Newfoundland.

The Foulin and Flaws company is working on Alex Hall's Barn. They are making a new foundation and potato cellar.

On the last few days in August, Mrs. Clair Chesley went down to Virginia. She went to pick up her husband, who just got home from the navy.

Mrs. Andrews, Mr. Julian Andrews' mother, is visiting relatives in Norway.

On September 17, David and Stephen King had a birthday party. They had it down at the Flaws'. The guests were: Andy Chesley, Brian Hall, Douglas Hall, Beverly Bowser, Judy and Joline Brown, and Donald Flaws.   s

Mr. & Mrs. Harry Davis went to the White Mts. Sunday, Sept. 27. Mr. & Mrs. Virgil Ray accompanied them on the sightseeing trip.

Clair Chesley spent two weeks at Manchester, New Hampshire, this summer. While he was there, he went to Boston to see the Red Sox play.

The Harold Davis family, along with Mrs. Davis' sister and husband, went to Rangeley last weekend. The community was celebrating its annual Foliage Festival.

Jokes

"Somebody's in for a big surprise!"

In the first part of August, Dave and Steve King went to Malden, Mass. While they were there, visiting their Aunt and Uncle, they went on a guided tour of Boston, went to the Science Museum, and went to the Sagus Iron Works.   s

The Harold Davis family went to Old Orchard Beach the first week in August. They also went to Reid State park a few times, and went on the Farm Bureau Field day.

The Chesley family went on a few excursions to Reid State park, and also went to Sabbothday lake.

Alison Andrews has joined the 4-H club in Freeport.

Alison Andrews and Mike and Roy DeWitt went to a square dance in Freeport Friday, Oct. 9.

Joyce Hall has been taking care of her nephew, Danny Rand, for the last week.

Last Thursday Joyce and Douglas Hall went to the Washington Trip committee meeting at Lisbon High School.

On Wednesday, October 7, Mrs. Ruth King, and Mr. & Mrs. G. O. Flaws attended the Golden Wedding anniversiary party of Mr. & Mrs. Leslie Graffam. It was held in the vestry of the Kennebunk Unity Church.   S

The Brown family went to visit Mrs. O.L. Brown's sister, Mrs. Duffy. The Browns also went to New Hampshire the day after Labor Day. Judy and Joline Brown are both working: Judy is working after school.

43

FAMILY TREE

Ted and Sue Krueger had another baby; a girl. They named her Susan Barbra. She weighted 5 pounds, 11½ ounces.

Another pair of proud parents is Mr. & Mrs. Ted Story. They had a boy, Fredrick Warren III.

Gertrude Hanscom has been very sick with a cold. She was running a high fever. She is getting better now. Aunt Gert also has been sick with a cold.

Donald Flaws has been taking care of Jim Donahue's female Weimaraner, The Dutchess of Durham.

On the 27 of Sept., Mrs. C. Harrington went on a one-week vacation to New York state,(Cont.

On Saturday, October 10, Mrs. Joyce Hall, Mrs. Sylvia Brown, Judy Brown, and Dean and Dana Hall went to a rummage sale at Yarmouth.

A three by five inch enlargement, in color, is available of the picture on the front page. It costs 35¢. Order through this paper.

On Saturday, Oct. 10, Clair Chesley, Andy Chesley, Donald Flaws, and Dave King went for a hike in the woods. The fall foliage was just about at its peak, and the woods were very beautiful.

On Monday, October 12, Judy Brown is celebrating her 15 birthday.

T. V. NEWS

Well, the fall T.V. season is in full swing, and it has the newest and best shows since the beginning of T.V. There's T.V. for every fan, Like adventure and espionage? Try the "Trouble Shooters" or "Five Fingers". Westerns your preference? How about "The Deputy" or "Man From Blackhawk". Westerns are the most numerous this season. Science Fiction? Try "Man Into Space" or "Twilight Zone".

Roughly 20 new fall shows. Happy Viewing.   Steve King

On the second weekend in August, Mr. & Mrs. G.O. Flaws, Donald, and Dave and Steve King went to West Point (Maine) to visit Mr. & Mrs. Wallace, and Mr. & Mrs. Harley Flaws.

On Tuesday, September 8, Mr. C. Huff, Mr. Alex Hall, Douglas, Brian, and Dean & Dana Hall, Beverly Bowser, Christie Chesley, Andy Chesley, Donald Flaws, and David King went to the Bath Iron Works to see the launching of the John F. Adams, a guided missile ship.

On June 21, The Methodist Church had Layman's Sunday. Douglas Hall was the leader, Donald Flaws read the Scripture, and led the Psalter, and David King gave the Message.

Mrs. Harrington (cont.)

Mrs. Harrington said that she ate dinner at a different house each day. She went to Fort Edward, where she visited her son, Charles Harrington, and she also visited Mrs. Cora Turner, as well as "everybody" else. She got back on Monday, Oct. 5.

THE E PUBLISHING CO.
Mailing address:
DAVE'S RAG
Rt. #1
Pownal, Maine
Call Lisbon Falls
2591

DAVE'S RAG
a Trade Mark

STAFF
Editor-in-chief:
Illustrater:
David V. King
Reporter:
Stephen E. King
Reporter; Sports
Donald P. Flaws

entered as second-class-matter
at Pownal, Maine, on January 26,
1959.

SUBSCRIPTION RATES
$1.50 Per year   (Incl.)
.07 Per copy   (Post.)

$1.00 Per year   (Without)
.05 Per copy   (Postage)

EDITORIAL

Every week the Durham roads seem to get worse and worse. The town road comissioner, in the opinion of some people, seems to be down on the job. They say that some of the roads are the worst that they have ever seen.

I called up the town road comissioner, Mr. A. Merrill, and he told me that he and the selectmen have just ridden over the town roads, and that they thought that they are the best that they have ever seen. Mr. Merrill says, however, that he is going to go over the roads, at least the ones that seem the worst ones, So to the editor at least, it seems that there are two schools of thought. I guess that in any case, everyone will be happy after Mr. Merrill goes over the bad roads.

40 Miles Of Bad Road

How do you like them?   Best I've ever seen

LETTERS

Send letters to: DAVE'S RAG
Anonymous letters go into the wastebasket. Name withheld on request. Deadline; one week before the paper comes out.

Rt. #1
Pownal, Me.

ANNOUNCEMENTS

On Sunday, October 11, Rev. Boobar will come to the Methodist Church to conduct services. He will hold a communion, and also will do any christning, baptizing, or take people into the church. Oct. 18, Layman's Sunday.

10/7/59

Today Mr. & Mrs. John Pillsbury cousins of Mr. & Mrs. Guy Pillsbury and Mrs & Mrs. Gerald Pillsbury, son of The J. Pillsburys, and Mr. Homer Remilk, nephew of the J. Pillsburys (complicated, isn't it?) came to visit The Kings and the Guy Pillsburys.

6/20/59

On Wednesday, June 17, the Hall family went on a sight-seeing and camping trip in upper New York state. They visited many of the numerous forts along Lake Champlain, and camped out along the way. They got back Saturday night, the twentith.

9/30/59
10/3/59

The J.F. Donahue family has been coming up to their Durham house, from their home in Malden, Mass., just about every week-end this summer. They also spent a week here for a vacation, and Bobbie stayed with the King family for a few weeks. Today they brought Mrs. R. King a small wood stove.

On Tuesday, June 16, the Hall family visited the Mystery Hill caves in southern New Hampshire. The caves are truly a mystery, since archaeligists are uncertain of the origin of them, and to what race they can be credited to.

CLASSIFIED ADS

FOR the FINEST squash, potatoes, and pumpkins, go to HALL'S road-side stand, Rt. #9, West Durham. Pumpkins, 25¢, Indian Corn, 10¢, also, corn stalks for decorating your yard.   Call 2401.

DAVE'S STUDIOS

Pictures expertly taken of any subject, in color or black-and-white. Professional looking prints or enlargements given at lowest prices.

For that different touch this year, give the "special few" of your friends and relatives a picture of you and your family (or house) on our photographic greeting cards. Lowest prices anywhere.   Call 2591.

In the first part of August, Mrs. C. Bowser, and her two daughters, Geraldine Price and Beverly, went up to Aroostook. They spent two or three days at the home of Mrs. Bowser's brother, William Craig, in Bridgewater, and during their stay there, they visited some of Mrs. Bowser's relatives. From Bridgewater they went to Mr. Craig's cottage at Grand Lake. They spent about 4 days there, then started home. On the way home, they stopped off at a park near Bangor, where they took some pictures.

In the first part of July, the Carl Weimer family came up here, from Pennsylvania, to visit the Flaws family. Mr. Weimer went home right away, but Mrs. Weimer and their three girls, Wendy, Penny, and Emily, stayed for a visit. Wendy, Penny, and Emily went to Vacation Bible School while they were here, as well as going swimming in White's Pond, and Harry's Pond. When Mr. Weimer came back to pick up the rest of his family, he stayed for a day or two, and on the last night, they all had a lobster dinner.

Alison Andrews' lamb, which he brought up last year, was one of the Grand Champions at the Cumberland Fair.

Get your CHRISTMAS CARDS and Christmas ribbon and wrapping paper early this year. Mrs. Charles Harrington has an ample supply of samples to chose from. Call 2392 for all your Christmas needs.

New book by STEVE KING! "Thirty-One of the Classics"! Read "Kidnapped", "Tom Sawyer, and many others!!! If you order in three weeks, only 30¢. Contact Steve King %Dave's Rag.

SPORTS

The World Series has ended with a bang. The Los Angeles Dodgers won the deciding game by the score of 9-3. The White Sox were the favorites in the series, but their pitching didn't turn out so well. Larry Sherry and Charlie Neal were the heroes for the Dodgers. The White Sox only hero was Ted Kluszewski. The White Sox have waited forty years for a pennant, and I fear they may have to wait forty more for another.   By Donald P. Flaws

A new family moved into West Durham last week. They are the Lemuel Cousins. Mr. & Mrs. Cousins have three children, two boys and a girl. They are staying in their trailer on the old Flander's place.

Donald Flaws spent a few weeks in Pennsylvania this summer. He left when the F. W. Story family were passing through Durham on their way to their home in Pennsylvania. The Storys invited him to come, and visit them. While he was there, he saw a polo game. He came back with the Weimers when they came to Maine.

Miss Hazel Hisler, teacher at the West Durham school, and her companion, Miss Alice Goddard, have been all over the state this summer. They went to Cadillac Mt., Norway, Rangeley, Boothbay Harbor, Ft. Edgcomb, Pownalburo, Naples, China, and the Fish Hatchery.

A TALK WITH STEPHEN KING'S
TRUE FIRST COLLABORATOR
An Interview With Chris Chesley

Imagine being Chris Chesley.

Imagine being the guy who grew up with, and *wrote with,* Steve King—the guy who would later become "Stephen King." These two guys attended grammar school together, and they collaborated on what Chris says was "reams" of short stories together.

Just your average, typical, American adolescence, right?

Wrong.

Chris Chesley and Stephen King were not your typical kids. They read Don Robertson and Robert Bloch together aloud while other kids were out on the playground, and these two friends wrote—and self-published—stories ranging from one-page horror stories to mini-novels, while other kids were planted in front of the TV.

Steve and Chris maintained their friendship through their school years. When Chris went to college at the University of Maine, he boarded with the King family. Chris was living with Steve and Tabitha King in Hermon, Maine, when King sold *Carrie*.

I wanted to talk to Chris because of his most famous collaboration with King: the eighteen- page collection of horror short stories called *People, Places, and Things.* (See the section on the collection in this volume.)

I had to do a little detective work to track him down, but I finally got a phone number, and called him one Sunday morning in the fall of 1988. At first, Chris was a little wary: "How did you get this number?" (it wasn't hard, actually), and "Why do you want to talk to me?" But after I explained the concept of *The Shape Under the Sheet,* and confessed my somewhat compulsive penchant for completeness, he understood that a talk with him was necessary, not only for the book, but to assuage my fears that I'd somehow leave a stone unturned somewhere.

Chris was free that afternoon, and we ended up doing a ninety-minute interview that same day.

It was a real treat to talk with Chris. He is bright, friendly, amazingly well-read, and had very well-reasoned opinions and thoughts about not only Stephen King and their years together, but about writing and contemporary American culture as well.

When I was talking to Chris, it struck me that his feelings about Stephen King echoed those of Clint Howard's about his brother, Ron. (I interviewed both Clint and Ron for my first book, *Mayberry, My Hometown.*) You might think that there would be jealousy or a veiled envy in each of their situations: Clint saw his big brother Ron go on to become a major director, Chris saw his best friend go on to become one of the most successful writers in the history of publishing.

Nope.

Both Clint and Chris were happier than you'd ever expect them to be about the successes of these two important people in their lives. And that is the mark—and measure—of two true gentlemen and two truly fine men.

Chris Chesley lives in Maine, and has a continuing interest in writing.

Here's my talk with Chris Chesley. — **sjs**

A TALK WITH STEPHEN KING'S
TRUE FIRST COLLABORATOR

STEVE SPIGNESI: I'm very happy to include my talk with you in *The Shape Under the Sheet,* Chris. I think having you in the book is great, and I sincerely appreciate your generosity in allowing me to reprint your *People, Places, and Things* short story "Genius" as well.

CHRIS CHESLEY: You're more than welcome. As to my participation—I like the idea of making a contribution towards filling in the blanks on somebody's background. When I remember back on those times, it strikes me there are other people who may get a hold of Steve's books and say "Wow!" and then get inspired to write. In this way the tradition keeps on rolling. So, I'm kind of doing the interview for that reason: It would be nice if I could add something to somebody's understanding so that they can then say "I can do this sort of thing, too."

STEVE SPIGNESI: Did you do any other collaborations with Steve besides *People, Places, and Things*?

CHRIS CHESLEY: We wrote together a lot when we were kids, but I think *People, Places, and Things* was the only actual "formal" copyrighted collaboration.

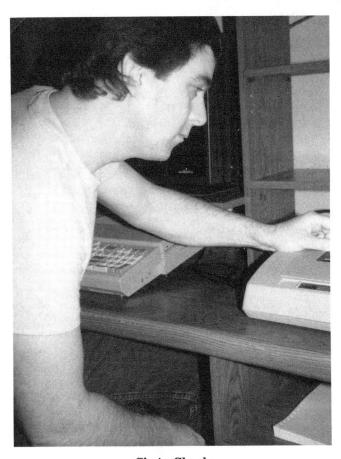

Chris Chesley
Photo courtesy Chris Chesley.

STEVE SPIGNESI: So *People, Places, and Things* — your eighteen story collection—was essentially your only real combined effort at putting your work on paper and making it available to friends?

CHRIS CHESLEY: No! (Laughs.) We wrote together fairly steadily and our work was available for friends around town to read. We wrote together quite often as a matter of fact. When we first started to write together, he would write a paragraph or two, and then I would write a paragraph or two and so forth. So, we did write many stories together, and they were available for people to look at, but not in any formal sense. Other than *People, Places, and Things* we never actually "published" anything else—unless he's got other material from those days. I had no idea that *People, Places, and Things* still survived. I didn't know that was still extant. Does he have it in his collection?

STEVE SPIGNESI: Yes, he has one original, and it's not complete. There are stories missing. Do you have a copy of it?

CHRIS CHESLEY: No, I don't. [NOTE: Chris does now. See the section on *People, Places, and Things* in this volume.]

STEVE SPIGNESI: Two of his stories are missing, "The Dimension Warp" and "I'm Falling," and of your stories, they're all lost except "Genius" and "Top Forty, News. Weather, and Sports." "Never Look Behind You," which was a joint effort, also survived.

CHRIS CHESLEY: You've really done your homework! This is incredible!

STEVE SPIGNESI: Thanks. I've done quite a bit of analysis of King's contributions to this collection, and how they relate to themes that he began to work with later on. I found some fascinating foreshadowings. In his *People, Places, and Things* story "The Thing At the Bottom of the Well," the thing in the well is his monster in the sewers, it's Pennywise the Clown, it's the boogeyman in the closet, it's IT—the ultimate archetypal monster that he has been working with for many, many years. I think it's incredible to see it here when he was thirteen or fourteen years old . It's fascinating to see the way he began developing these themes at such an early age.

CHRIS CHESLEY: One of the things that you are probably aware of—and that was true of him even at that age and younger—is how "conservation-minded" Steve is as a writer. Since I have known him, I don't think that he has ever "thrown away" anything. I think everything that has come into his mind has been used again, albeit changed to suit his developing writing ability. And I agree with you. You are absolutely right in that intuition—he keeps doing later on what you see him doing as a fourteen-year-old.

STEVE SPIGNESI: Did you have any other influence on his work that you're aware of?

CHRIS CHESLEY: Many of his "Richard Bachman" items were written when I knew him back in his late high school and early college years. I don't want to say that I had anything to do with those works, although I was there when he was writing them. I never made suggestions in the sense that could be called collaboration, so I suppose not.

STEVE SPIGNESI: You mentioned the Bachman stuff. Did you know about Richard Bachman when the Bachman novels were released?

CHRIS CHESLEY: No, I did not. At one point

somebody told me that he was putting out books under that name. I was living in New Mexico at the time, and in southern New Mexico there is not a wide distribution, so the Bachman books did not show up. I didn't see a Bachman book until we got back here to Maine. And it was only when I saw them that I realized what material he was using. I had thought they were new stories, and when I got back here and finally saw them, I realized where he was getting the stuff! This was material that he was writing when I knew him in his last two years of high school and his early years of college—and I was privileged to be there to watch them come about. It was very interesting to watch that.

"The thing that you have to understand about Steve's writing is that Steve's characters are based upon two things...His characters are primarily based upon a tradition—the horror genre tradition— and secondarily, upon actual people that he has known. His characters are always composites of those two factors."

STEVE SPIGNESI: Can you give me some specific incidents from your years together that he's used in his fiction?

CHRIS CHESLEY: Let me tell you about an incident that happened a few years ago. I had asked Steve if he could help our local library and he agreed to do a book-signing, so he flew out to New Mexico as a favor to me. During the signing, a woman came up to him and asked him if his real-life friends were in "The Body." He turned to me and grinned and said "Chris is in it." Now, that is partially true and partially not true.

The thing that you have to understand about Steve's writing is that Steve's characters are based upon two things—and "The Body" is no exception. His characters are primarily based upon a tradition—the horror genre tradition—and secondarily, upon actual people that he has known. His characters are always composites of those two factors. The tradition in which he's writing has always been extremely important to him. I have never read of another writer more influenced by a tradition than Steve, which is one of the reasons

why his writing in the horror genre is so good. When he was growing up, he did his homework in a very, very thorough way.

In terms of "The Body," there are different aspects of the characters that I can look at and say, yeah, that reminds me of so-and-so—someone that he and I knew in common. So, it's more complex than simply saying, yes, these characters are based upon so-and so—that they are one for one based on real people. None of the characters are based on specific people, yet there are salient characteristics of the individuals which are very reminiscent of people that he and I knew in common.

STEVE SPIGNESI: King has stated publicly that the childhood friends he depicted in "The Body" are all dead. Here's the quotation where he said that [from *Stephen King at the Movies* by Jessie Horsting, page 83; Rob Reiner is speaking about King's reaction to his first viewing of "Stand By Me"]:

> **Rob Reiner**: "After the screening, he appeared very, very moved and really couldn't even talk to us. He said 'I have to go away.' And he went away for about fifteen minutes. Then, he came back and we sat around and talked about it and he told us how much of the story had been his life—and how upsetting it was to him. He told me that, in fact, all three of his buddies had died. His best friend Chris had been killed in a truck hijacking—he was in law school at the time and was driving a truck to make ends meet and the truck was hijacked and he was murdered. There was a trestle—no train ever came on it, but there was a trestle that they used to have to cross, and they used to dare each other and all...He said it was upsetting to sit there and see all these kids he grew up with on screen, brought back to life when—well, you can't ever get them back."

CHRIS CHESLEY: I think that's what gives "The Body" so much of its power, its understanding of its characters as on the edge of losing something they'd never get back again. "The Body" marks the end of the boyhood era. Also, I'm not even sure that boyhood now is the same as it was when Steve and I were young.

STEVE SPIGNESI: What are your thoughts on what he has become?

CHRIS CHESLEY: My thoughts are that the real Stephen King is much more interesting than the external myth that surrounds him now.

To me, there are reasons why he's had the success that he has, and those reasons are much more interesting than any attempt to glamorize him—to attribute a "luster" to him.

You have to understand that thirty years ago he moved with his mother and brother from Connecticut to Durham, Maine. Durham at that time was a different place than it is now. The old small farm ethic—which had been the rule for many generations past—was just on its way out, and what we had was a community where people got up in the morning and went to work in the factories in the surrounding towns. It was a working class rural town.

> **"He was influenced by a working class, gritty little rural town. And in that sense it made him intellectually, and literarily, an outsider. And I think a lot of the push, a lot of the drive, a lot of the narrative force in his writing stems directly from that...."**

Steve was by no means nurtured as a writer by the heritage of middle-class America—as the American middle class likes to see itself, that is. He was influenced by a working class, gritty little rural town. And in that sense it made him intellectually, and literarily, an outsider. And I think a lot of the push, a lot of the drive, a lot of the narrative force in his writing stems directly from that—his sense of himself as being outside the mainstream, outside the American suburban middle class ethos.

And that, in a way, is why I think many people are attracted to his writing—because it has the force, it has the stamina, and it has the vitality which American middle class writing doesn't have. So, in that respect, it's not mythologizing him to say that, as far as writing goes, he's kind of like a working man's hero of a writer. He's kind of like a literary Joe Hill, you might say. He always identified with people who were outside the established American middle class rules and regulations—as he was. Those characters influenced him more than any other.

STEVE SPIGNESI: And in a sense, he has since recreated them over and over in his fiction.

CHRIS CHESLEY: In a way, yes, he has created them over and over. That's one motif in his fiction that you will see again and again. His characters, his people don't exactly have smug comfortable lives. And they don't have middle class dilemmas. They aren't worried about when the next wine and cheese party will be. They don't suffer from anxiety the way people do in stories in *The New Yorker*. They have gritty dilemmas, they have very gritty conflicts, and that's one very important motif in his fiction. When he was young, he was developing that theme.

STEVE SPIGNESI: There are two quotations by King that really hit home in terms of what you're talking about. The first is from Doug Winter's *Faces of Fear*. King is talking about his novel *Cujo:*

> "I loved that guy Joe Camber in *Cujo,* but I also hated him because he was an asshole. But he was *my* asshole—not in the physiological sense, you understand. What I mean is that I know the guy and I love him because he's like me."

The character appealed to King even though he was sadistic and mean-spirited—a cold, hard man. King seemed to understand him—to relate to him —perhaps because he'd known many such people throughout his life? People working away from the cities, people struggling to "get by," to make a living, to keep their heads above water?

CHRIS CHESLEY: Right.

STEVE SPIGNESI: And then he did an interview with the Orono High School newspaper, *Inside,* in which he called himself a hick.

> *Inside*: Why do you stay in Maine?
> **Stephen King**: I'm a hick.
> *Inside*: There really isn't anything here.
> **Stephen King**: That's one of the reasons I like it in Bangor is because if someone wants to get to me they really have to be very dedicated. I stay here because there are no distractions whatsoever. I have my family. I'm a guy who sells a lot of books and yet my kids can go to public schools. We lead ordinary lives. I grew up here. I went to one-room schoolhouses. There were outhouses. I am a hick and this where I feel at home.

I get the feeling that he still feels like an outsider. There is that alienation. It seems like he's never felt comfortable in Hollywood or at the wine and cheese parties.

CHRIS CHESLEY: Right. And the "outsider" theme shows up all over Steve's work. One of his important contributions to the field of writing on the supernatural is the basic insight that children are naturally "outsiders." With Carrie White and Danny Torrance and other characters, he's creating an understanding of childhood that is more than just a stepchild of Freudian psychology. Children let in a world that adults can't, or won't, deal with. As Steve says in *Danse Macabre*, children really have the power to believe. The joining between the "normal" and the "abnormal" is seamless. Kids buy it all. And it's an important reason for his popularity. It's that little kid in you, the one Steve knows so well, who loved *The Shining*.

And we ought to distinguish Steve's perspective from other child-kidnapped-by-demon books. For example, the kid in *The Exorcist* is just a vehicle for evil. It doesn't move you as much as Danny does in *The Shining*. One of the essential terrors about Danny is that he shows us something about the real existence of a child, that actual borderland of wonder and speculation and anxiety, the feel for the unknown children live with from moment to moment.

STEVE SPIGNESI: He seems to have a real sympathy for overweight children. As an adolescent, was he heavy?

CHRIS CHESLEY: Let's put it on a spectrum with normal being in the middle, the "super-athletes" on one end, and then on the other end the kids who could barely walk they were so fat and uncoordinated. Steve was somewhere between normal and being overweight and kind of uncoordinated, but he was not one of those kids who were helpless once they were on the playground.

STEVE SPIGNESI: That shows up in some of the characters he's created, like Lard-Ass Hogan, Ben Hanscom, and others. How widely have you read in his fiction?

CHRIS CHESLEY: Well, I haven't read all of *IT* yet. But I understand that there's a clown figure in the novel?

STEVE SPIGNESI: Yes. Pennywise the Clown. Pennywise is the manifestation of IT, and he has the ability to become your worse fear.

CHRIS CHESLEY: I'll tell you something about that that I've always found fascinating. Steve has these images and characters that he uses again and again. It's fascinating that he has a clown figure in that book. I'm going to make a series of

connections here. There's another story that he has written that has a toy monkey in it.

STEVE SPIGNESI: "The Monkey" from *Skeleton Crew*.

CHRIS CHESLEY: Right. When we were younger we used to hitchhike up to Lewiston to go to the movies. When a good horror flick was playing, we would go and see it. And at one point we went to see a movie called "Dementia-13."

STEVE SPIGNESI: Francis Ford Coppola.

CHRIS CHESLEY: Exactly! Who then went on to bigger and better things.

STEVE SPIGNESI: He sure did.

CHRIS CHESLEY: And in that movie there's a sequence where a monkey claps cymbals together, and from that sequence he got the image that he later used in "The Monkey." To this day I don't know of any other source where that would have come from. I knew him pretty well back then, and we were together pretty regularly, and that was such an effective sequence that it stuck with him. Right after that he began to use it. That image began to appear in his stories soon after we saw "Dementia-13."

I believe the film also has a very ominous-looking clown figure as well. In fact, I believe "Dementia-13" was the first movie I saw to ever use the ominous toy motif.

STEVE SPIGNESI: You've already answered a question I had planned on asking about how much of King you've read. Of the stuff that you have read, what were your favorites? Where do you think he succeeded?

CHRIS CHESLEY: You've got to keep in mind that this is subjective. I'm talking about his books from my standards, and these are only my opinions, and people are bound to disagree.

STEVE SPIGNESI: Fine.

CHRIS CHESLEY: His best book, as far as I'm concerned, is *The Shining*. *The Shining* will be a classic someday because it's so psychologically perfect. The set-up is psychologically excellent, and the reason it is, is because *The Shining* is one of the few books where Steve did not write to escape. He wrote to transmute his own anxiety—there's a direct transmutation of his own anxiety into those characters because of what Wendy and Jack are going through. The sense of anxiety (if not the details of their lives) that exists in *The Shining* is psychologically perfect because it is right out of his own head. So, the set-up for what comes later—the set-up for the supernatural stuff —is one of the best that I've ever read in the genre. I was enthralled by it when I read it.

And again, this is a question of what I consider to be authentic horror. I tend to think that the most authentic horror is the stuff which grounds itself in the twisted mind. If you don't have a twisted mind to begin with, all the vampires in the world won't work. So in terms of what I consider to be good horror, *The Shining* is it. I think it will be a classic.

There's another work which shows his ability to write—which sometimes he'll let you see and then take away from you. *The Dark Tower: The Gunslinger* is clearly his best writing.

He gave me one of the first copies of *The Gunslinger*. I'm so proud to own that.

I remember the day he started writing the story. He was back from college on a weekend and he asked me over. I walked over to his house and he was sitting in his kitchen. Now at this time, he was too poor to afford regular paper, and so somehow he had "inherited" some of this heavy yellow and green paper. I don't know how to describe it any better than that it was smaller than regular paper, and made heavily, almost like cardboard. And he was using this paper for this story *The Gunslinger*. And he said "I want you to read this." So I sat down and I read the first three pages and I said, "My God, this is incredible!" And he went, "Nah. No, it isn't." And I said "Yes it is, this is amazing." It was incredible prose, just incredible prose.

Over the years, as I talked to him, I'd keep on asking him, "What are you going to do with the *Dark Tower*? When are you going to do something with that?" And finally he brought out the first volume, and gave me a copy of it, and I was so pleased to have it. To me *The Gunslinger* is indicative of sheer skill at writing.

STEVE SPIGNESI: Are you familiar with the audio-tapes of *The Gunslinger*? It's a four-cassette set, and Steve reads it from beginning to end with no sound effects, just an author reading his work. It's very well done. He really does a superb job.

CHRIS CHESLEY: I've heard about those. They should be good because he got a lot practice when he and I were younger. One of our customs was to read aloud to each other. We did a great deal of that. What we'd like to read together were these long paperbacks that they don't make anymore. Now they make romance paperbacks, but back in those days, you used to be able to buy a great big

thick seventy-five cent Bantam for example, and it would be a slightly pre-Harold Robbins-type novel, you know, the kind where this guy starts out very poor and then he builds an empire and loses it— those kinds of stories.

"We read stories and novels by Richard Matheson aloud. *I Am Legend* was a favorite. I still remember that one because we both got off on it so much. We did a lot of that."

STEVE SPIGNESI: I know the type.
CHRIS CHESLEY: We also read *The Scarf* by Robert Bloch aloud. We didn't read Lovecraft aloud because he didn't sound good aloud—the language is too hard. We read stories and novels by Richard Matheson aloud. *I Am Legend* was a favorite. I still remember that one because we both got off on it so much. We did a lot of that.

STEVE SPIGNESI: Richard Matheson and I talked about *I Am Legend* influencing Steve. Steve has repeatedly referred to that work as being a primary influence on a lot of his stuff. The contemporaneous use of language, the colloquialisms, the interior dialogue, the contemporary setting—that type of writing. Steve also nods to John D. MacDonald, and Don Robertson as well.

CHRIS CHESLEY: Please include Don Robertson in there. When I was a freshman in high school, I bought this book called *The River and the Wilderness* by Don Robertson. Everybody should read that book because of its stylistic innovation. If you read the first ten pages of *The River and the Wilderness,* you'll say "My God, what is this guy doing!?" And sometime later on, Steve had heard of him, too, and so we got and read aloud Robertson's *Paradise Falls.*

STEVE SPIGNESI: I loved Don's latest novel, *The Ideal, Genuine Man,* which Steve published through his own company, Philtrum Press.
CHRIS CHESLEY: The last time I saw Steve he gave me one of Don Robertson's working copies of that novel, with the cross-outs and everything.

STEVE SPIGNESI: It's an incredible novel, and to refer back to a novel you just mentioned, in Section 6 of the Foreword to *The Ideal, Genuine Man,* Steve wrote "I read *The River and the Wilderness* the year I started high school, and it was the use of onomatopeia which struck me as forcefully as a slap in the face."

CHRIS CHESLEY: I remember reading *Paradise Falls* aloud, trading the book back and forth. Don Robertson's language and style really got to be a thing with us. That language was extremely important.

STEVE SPIGNESI: *The Ideal, Genuine Man* was the first Robertson novel I read and it blew me away.

CHRIS CHESLEY: Well, read *Paradise Falls,* and you've also got to read *The River and the Wilderness.*

STEVE SPIGNESI: What did you think of Robertson's *The Greatest Thing Since Sliced Bread*?

CHRIS CHESLEY: The "Greatest Thing" series is good, mainly because of the way he recalls childhood in Cleveland. The only thing that you can even roughly compare Don to would be Jean Shepherd, particularly his film "A Christmas Story." That's the only comparison I can think of to make and even then it's not very good. Those are the Morris Bird stories.

STEVE SPIGNESI: Let's talk about Doug Winter's *Art of Darkness*. Have you seen it?

CHRIS CHESLEY: No, I have not read it. I only looked in it because someone said to me "Your name's in there," but I haven't read the book.

STEVE SPIGNESI: It sure is. Doug attributes the genesis of Steve's novel *'Salem's Lot* to a conversation with you and Steve's wife Tabitha. Is that accurate? Did a discussion with you generate that novel?

CHRIS CHESLEY: Oh, boy! (Laughs.) I don't know that it's fair to say that one discussion will generate a novel. I don't recall a discussion with him and Tabby about the possiblity of writing a book like *'Salem's Lot.* You've got to realize that everybody's life was going on, and we didn't take all this down verbatim!

I vaguely recall talking to him about things that may have had to do with *'Salem's Lot* before he wrote it. I was in my freshman year of college and living with Steve on Stone Street in Bangor. I paid him board money and I hitchhiked back and forth from Bangor to Orono where I went to school.

That winter he was writing, among other things, *The Running Man,* and I think that he began *'Salem's Lot* in the spring semester of that year and continued it through the summer. But I'm vague on this. He could have begun it sooner.

STEVE SPIGNESI: According to *Art of Darkness,* it was 1973, and he was writing it with the title *Second Coming.*

CHRIS CHESLEY: Really? I never knew its original title. And the reason why is because all I saw was the text. I never saw a title page. He started showing it to me and I read excerpts from it with just the page number at the top. (Laughs.)

STEVE SPIGNESI: What else do you remember about that period?

CHRIS CHESLEY: I remember one particular event vividly. I'll never forget this. This happened one day in the spring of that year. It was probably April, because it was warm. I remember the weather because I used to hitchhike.

> **"[Tabby] handed me the telegram and I read it, and it was just a few words. It was from Bill Thompson, Steve's editor, and it said *Carrie*'s going to be taken, you'll receive a twenty-five hundred dollar advance, congratulations, and so forth."**

Steve was living in Hermon then, and I was again boarding with him, and I would hitchhike from Hermon to Orono and back again at the end of my school day. So one day I hitchhiked home, and I came down this little dirt road that his house was on, and I had just gotten in the yard, when Tabby ran out the front door...and she was waving a telegram. And she said "Look, look at this."

She handed me the telegram and I read it, and it was just a few words. It was from Bill Thompson, Steve's editor, and it said *Carrie*'s going to be taken, you'll receive a twenty-five hundred dollar advance, congratulations, and so forth.

And Tabby jumped and shouted, and I jumped and shouted, and when Steve got home, I kind of got out of the way. And they just hugged each other and cried. I could hear them from the next room...not that I was eavesdropping but you just couldn't avoid it. It was just one of the best days that I have ever spent.

STEVE SPIGNESI: I read that the money came in handy.

CHRIS CHESLEY: Oh, yes. They got twenty-five hundred bucks, and that was more money then

"GENIUS"
A Chris Chesley Story from the 1963 Collection,
People Places, And Things

["Genius" is one of the two surviving Chris Chesley stories from the Stephen King/Chris Chesley 1963 collaborative collection *People, Places, and Things*. (The other surviving Chesley story is "Top Forty, News, Weather, and Sports." See the section on *People, Places, and Things* in this volume for details on Stephen King's contributions to this collection.)

Chris was kind and generous enough to permit me to reprint this story in *The Shape Under the Sheet*, allowing us all a glimpse at a piece that is significant for two reasons: First, it is part of an historic collection co-written by Chris with the most successful genre writer in the history of publishing, and secondly, it shows us the early talent of Chris Chesley, a guy who used to write with Stephen King and must have, it is assumed, influenced King, as King most assuredly influenced Chris back in the early years of their respective writing lives.

As you'll read in Chris's own Introduction to "Genius," he credits the genesis of this story to the perusal of the very same collection of paperback novels that Stephen King has credited with the start of his *own* career. In *Stephen King: The Art of Darkness*, Douglas E. Winter describes the exact moment Chris talks about in his "Genius" Introduction:

"In Durham [Maine] in the fall of 1959 or 1960, King's fledgling writing career received a strange legacy from his departed father, who, according to King's mother, had himself tried a hand at writing fiction. In the attic above his aunt and uncle's garage, King discovered a box of his father's old books; inside were Avon paperbacks from the 1940s that included a sampler of stories from *Weird Tales* magazine and a collection of stories by H.P. Lovecraft."

Now, thanks to Chris Chesley, we can know what King (and Chesley) did with those books, and we can get a clearer glimpse of that long-ago time.

Isn't it amazing what Donald King's forgotten box of books spawned?

"Genius" is about a baby boy who just refuses to stay in his crib, and ends up paying the price for his nocturnal wanderings. Is this what goes on in baby's heads when they're lying there so innocently?

I'll leave it to you to decide after reading "Genius" by Chris Chesley.

I think you'll find that "Genius" nicely bookends Chris's more recent "The Mission Boy," which is also included in this volume. — **sjs**]

"GENIUS"
by Christopher Chesley

1990 Introduction

I believe this story owes its origin to a gift, from a relative or family friend, of a collection of science fiction and horror paperbacks Stephen King received sometime in 1960. As I see it now at a thirty-year distance, that library of a hundred books was almost uncanny good fortune: its previous owner had excellent taste in selecting the best names in the two fields. Steve's room had only one small bookcase, so he parked this collection on the floor, lined up against the walls around the room, titles on the bindings facing up, and when my turn at the typewriter was done, I would look at these books by authors who helped to confirm me as a reader, who sharpened my ear for words.

One paperback in particular inspired "Genius" and perhaps other stories in *People, Places, and Things*. It was an anthology called *Children of Wonder*, edited by William Tenn, and for me the children in those stories acted as a vault into new possibility. Almost in an instant, I flew from the contrived light of *The Happy Hollisters* into the decadent darkness of "Small Assassin" and "Idol of the Flies."

"Genius"
(continued)

The flight was welcome: at that time reading had recently stopped being work; a story had become more like a vivid, intuitive, personal infusion. I had begun to read with my whole self, and so I sought a whole-view, cosmic narrative. Tex Maul had come to seem narrow and pale. I wanted a lavish expanse of hues and shades. When Steve got his collection of paperbacks, I began to read for shade. *Children of Wonder* was the perfect book at the perfect time, a mirror for change my mind would make in itself, and make for good.

I say this thirty years away, long after that irreversible change. I know about the eleven-year-old author of "Genius"—I even remember the day he wrote it—but I no longer *sense* him. Now he is my shade, the same shade I had only begun to look for then.

Copyright © 1990 Christopher Chesley.

The 1963 Story

"I have got to get out of this foolish crib," the baby thought. His face was red with anger. "I don't know why that silly woman puts me here."

Another few inches: that was all. But—

The baby heard the doorknob squeak as he slid back into the warm blankets.

"Oh my little boy!" Your face is bright red and you haven't slept at all! You're a strange child." She lifted him up and patted his back slowly.

"Silly woman," the baby thought. "Why doesn't she leave me alone? I wish I could talk."

She held him so softly. She patted his back and talked to him in such a nice way.

"Phsoog!"

"Why child!" she set him down. "What kind of strange noise is that? I never heard you say that."

The baby's face was getting redder. He wriggled and squirmed like a tiny worm.

"All right. I know you want to go to sleep."

It was dark. No light came through the window as in day. The baby could make out the light fingers of the clock.

"Two o'clock," thought the baby. "I wish it was morning."

The baby was laying on his back. "I want to turn over." The nights were cold so a lot of blankets covered the baby. He couldn't move.

"Eighteen past two, eighteen past two." Over and over. "I'll try to speak." He puffed his cheeks way out.

"phsoog! phsoog! phsoog!"

Daddy woke up. "Oh, whazza matter with that kid now?" Daddy was hoping Mommy would hear, but she didn't wake up. "Eighteen past two. What a time!"

Mommy woke up. This was one of the worst days. Blowing, freezing, sleeting.

"Mmmmm. What a terrible day. I've seen better. Got to get up."

She walked, half awake, into the kitchen to begin the new day.

"What is that terrible smell!"

Daddy came into the kitchen. He looked so tired. His eyes were bloodshot.

"What is that terrible smell!"

Mommy glanced over to the baby's door. Her eyes focused on a bright red squashy mess stuck on the lower corner of the door.

"John!!" She called to her husband. "Open our son's door!"

The baby's head had been crushed last night. It stunk.

Copyright © 1963 by Chris Chesley.
Reprinted by permission of the author.

55

they'd seen for some time. They were just thrilled to death...*Carrie* was going to be published.

They moved out of Hermon and moved into an apartment in Bangor. At one point, Steve invited me to the apartment in Bangor to watch "Duel"— the Steven Spielberg movie—on TV. I had never seen it, and he said "You've got to see it."

After that, my wife and I were in the process of buying a trailer for ourselves right next to the campus. And I remember Steve coming over after we had gotten the trailer. This had to have been in the summer because they had just bought a new car. Their old car was just a hurtin', hurtin' machine. They had bought a new blue Pinto, and he came over and dropped me off a second draft of *'Salem's Lot* to read and critique. He wanted me to see if I could find any minor things that needed to be corrected. I had the second draft of that novel.

STEVE SPIGNESI: Did you save the manuscript copy he gave you?

CHRIS CHESLEY: No, I wish! No, I gave it back to him.

STEVE SPIGNESI: Do you think that was his only copy?

CHRIS CHESLEY: It may have been, but I don't think so. I wished I had saved it. It would have been nice to have.

STEVE SPIGNESI: That leads me to ask you if you any have memorabilia or materials that you saved from those days. Do you have any collectibles? Are you a King collector?

CHRIS CHESLEY: I don't have any surviving original writing. We all think about that now and say, oh, it would have been nice to have saved a bunch of those stories.

We used to put out reams of stuff in those days. We'd get a ream of paper and we would sit down and write short stories. It would have been nice to have put some of those away for a future date, but of course I never did, and in a way I suppose that was right. Because if I had it would have said something about me that did not fit my character, and also, if I had laid that value on it at that time, it would have screwed up the original quality of the experience. We were just kids, we were just writing, and I think that's the best way to remember it. We weren't sitting around thinking of THE FUTURE, you know? We were just having a good time.

STEVE SPIGNESI: That's fascinating. Do you still write?

CHRIS CHESLEY: I write when I can, but it's

definitely in the position of being in the shadow of Stephen King. [NOTE: One of Chris's recent short stories, "The Mission Boy," appears in this volume, as well as one of Chris's *People, Places, and Things* stories, "Genius."]

STEVE SPIGNESI: What are your thoughts on how Steve's writing ability developed?

CHRIS CHESLEY: A lot of people will say, "Hey, Steve King wrote a novel. I can do the same thing." In *Danse Macabre,* he talks about what it is to become a writer. He says talent is one thing, but the most important thing, and this is a bad paraphrase, he talks a great deal about honing your talent. He uses the metaphor of a blade or something like that. Working, discipline—that's what makes you a writer.

"...I could tell even than he was an interesting guy. He was twelve years old and he already had a way with words....One day after school, he and I got to talking, and he invited me to his house. He had this very, very old typewriter. It had letters broken off the wire things and you had to fill in your O's with a pencil."

But when Steve moved from Connecticut, he came to the same one-room school that I was going to. And I could tell even than he was an interesting guy. He was twelve years old and he already had a way with words. His house was right down the road from the school. One day after school, he and I got to talking, and he invited me to his house. He had this very, very old typewriter. It had letters broken off the wire things and you had to fill in your O's with a pencil.

I got him to show me some stories that he was writing. He didn't want to – he was very, very modest about it. Now this guy is twelve years old, and I looked at these stories and I said, "This is incredible!"

The essential ability to write was there in the first thing I ever read by him.

The style you read now is only more complex, more sophisticated, more experienced and more worldly, but the quality of his writing was there the first time I met him when I was twelve. He can talk about work and discipline and honing your craft and all that stuff, but that guy could write the first time I met him. His way of using dialogue, his ear for American English, and his ability to take you along from paragraph to paragraph was there as a twelve-year-old. And I said to him "Give me more of this stuff to read!"

STEVE SPIGNESI: A good example of that would be his first published story "I Was a Teenage Grave Robber." It first appeared in the magazine *Comics Review* in 1965 and was then reprinted in *Stories of Suspense* in 1966 as "In A Half-World of Terror." The story—which is about a mad scientist, a damsel in distress, and maggots growing out of corpses – was written when he was sixteen or seventeen, and is amateurish and very derivative, specifically of B monster movies—but the narrative power is overwhelming. And I was really surprised by *People, Places, and Things*. There are some stories by King in there that are just around two hundred words, and yet they have a beginning, a middle, and an end. There's background, characters are developed, and then bang!...the piece is over.

CHRIS CHESLEY: Absolutely.

STEVE SPIGNESI: Richard Christian Matheson told me "you can't not read him." You pick up something and he just drags you along. Are you familiar with the King short story "Squad D?"

CHRIS CHESLEY: No, I don't think so.

STEVE SPIGNESI: "Squad D" is an unpublished story which he wrote for Harlan Ellison's anthology *The Last Dangerous Visions*. In the story there's a guy typing a letter and the "O" sticks. It's a flying "O."

CHRIS CHESLEY: Is that right?! I'll be damned!

STEVE SPIGNESI: And in *Misery*, there's a writer named Paul Sheldon. Sheldon writes Gothic romances, but wants to write "serious novels." So he kills off the lead character—called Misery Chastain—in his series of Gothics, and writes a novel called *Fast Cars* which he thinks will be his breakthrough novel as a serious writer. Then he gets stupid. He gets drunk and takes off into a blizzard in Colorado with the only copy of the manuscript. He has an accident, and gets "rescued", so to speak, by a psychotic nurse who happens to be his biggest fan. His legs are broken. She addicts him to painkillers, and keeps him trapped in her home forcing him to write a novel in which he brings back Misery from the dead.

CHRIS CHESLEY: Oh, I see.

STEVE SPIGNESI: The typewriter she gives him is an old Royal on which he has to fill in the letters, and King intersperses actual manuscript pages in the novel. And Paul Sheldon/Stephen King hand fills in each "E," each "O," until finally the typewriter loses letters like crazy and he ends up having to write the last chaper of the novel by hand, and King includes the actual handwritten manuscript in the novel.

CHRIS CHESLEY: That's very interesting. Hearing you describe the plot of *Misery* reminds me of something that I read. It might be in *Danse Macabre*. He talks about a recurrent dream that he has. He says that when he's anxious, he has this dream where he's alone in an upstairs room in a house, and he's writing as fast as he can, and there's a woman with an axe trying to get in.

STEVE SPIGNESI: That just happens to be the cover of—and the most frightening scenes in— *Misery*. There's a scene in *Misery* that King has said is one of the two scenes that frightened him as he wrote them. The first one was the dead woman in the bathtub scene in *The Shining*. The second one takes place in *Misery* after Paul Sheldon tries to escape while Annie is away in town. She comes back and discovers that he has been naughty, and she gives him this big speech about what the Africans do to mine workers who run away. "They hobble them," she tells him. So, now Paul thinks Annie is going to kill him. And she says, oh no, that would be a waste. You have a story to write. She says, "I'm going to hobble you." And then from behind her back she pulls out a blowtorch and an axe.

CHRIS CHESLEY: Oh God!

STEVE SPIGNESI: And she amputates his foot with the axe and cauterizes the stump with the blowtorch while he's awake. And the cover art for *Misery* is the shadow of a woman with an axe looming over a guy in a wheelchair.

CHRIS CHESLEY: I remember Steve telling me about that dream when we were younger. That is, in fact, a true dream—that's not something that he made up, that's something that he told me when we were kids.

STEVE SPIGNESI: And here he uses it in *Misery,* a novel many people consider to be one of his best. But that's indicative of his writing. What do you think of him being able to take the realities of his life, as well as his thoughts and dreams, and turn them into the type of fiction that he does—this incredibly compelling writing?

CHRIS CHESLEY: I think that what it comes down to is the "child" Stephen King. Henry James has something to say about this in his novel *What Maisie Knew,* which is a tour de force in narration from the consciousness of the child Maisie. This little girl takes in everything, even to the point where she's forced to see more than she should have to.

> **"I would say that the adult Stephen King—who is motivated to take these images and to transmute them into fiction—exists because the child Stephen King saw and felt too much for his age....the reason why these images come out so powerfully in his fiction is because as a child he had no way to filter. As an adult, he can take a critical viewpoint...."**

Consider how sensitive children are generally—how they don't have a way to edit, to filter, to take a critical stance on experience around them. I would say that the adult Stephen King—who is motivated to take these images and to transmute them into fiction—exists because the child Stephen King saw and felt too much for his age.

And the reason why these images come out so powerfully in his fiction is because as a child he had no way to filter. As an adult, he can take a critical viewpoint, but as a child everything just came in, and it affected him. Those experiences were then transmuted into dreams, and the dreams were then transmuted later on into fiction.

I think that if you were to take the measure of Stephen King as a person, one way to measure it is in terms of him as a child, with that degree of sensitivity.

I felt it in his house, and I'll give you an example. When I first knew Steve , his mother was in the position of taking care of his grandparents. They lived in the house with Steve and his mother, and Steve's story "Gramma" from *Skeleton Crew* came out of that.

In that story, the grandmother has been transmuted into a supernatural thing about which a child has to make decision. Should I give this...what seems to be a monster...should I give this creature the tea? Well, that giving of the tea is based directly upon his life at that time, when he was a boy between ten and twelve. The grandparents lived in the downstairs front room. The grandmother was invalided. She was not able to talk. And for kids that age, someone who is invalided and very old is kind of a horrifying presence. The grandfather was not in much better shape, although he could sit up.

And so Steve had that experience, and it was borne home on him, and you can see the connection between that experience, and how affected he must have been by that situation to be motivated to later turn it into such a powerful story.

When I read the story—sitting there by myself in the night—it raised the hackles on my neck, even though I knew from whence the story was derived. And I thought to myself at the time, think of how much he took in. Think of how affected he was by that in order to have the psychological motivation to spit it back out by writing this hair-raising story.

To me, that is one of the ways to measure what kind of organ of perception, what kind of consciousness Stephen King has. Most people just don't have that going for them. And I also think that most people aren't that affected. Most people have other ways of dealing with their experiences. I think his sense of isolation was a great motivator for him to turn those experiences into the artificial form of fiction. And given the talent that he had, contemporaneous with that mental work that had to be done, you can see the natural connection there. His mother worked. He was there a lot by himself. He had to do it alone. And in that respect, he was different from many of us who knew him. He was, to a degree, more isolated than we were.

STEVE SPIGNESI: What's your relationship with Steve now?

CHRIS CHESLEY: I still consider him a very good friend—a very good friend who's living the life that he always dreamed he would live.

When we were children and we would sit at the typewriter, he would get done typing a page, and he'd look over at me with a cigarette in his mouth—a cigarette that his mother didn't know he was smoking...usually a Chesterfield—he would look over at me and say, "You know what I'm gonna do the first time I hit it big, Chris?" Now remember that this guy's fourteen years old! "You know what I'm gonna do? I'm gonna get myself a great big Cadillac!" (Laughs.) And of course he did!.

It's the life he's supposed to be living. And that's good. I always wanted him to get what he wanted. I always wanted that for him because I knew how badly he wanted it. And he got it. And I'm very happy for him that he has gotten it, because if anybody deserved it, it's Steve.

You know how they talk about nice guys finishing last? Well here's a nice guy that has finished first. Here's somebody who paid the price. He paid his dues, and as a person, as a real life person, as an individual human being, he deserves what he's got, and I'm all for it. I think it's wonderful.

STEVE SPIGNESI: Did you know they filmed "Pet Sematary" in your area?

CHRIS CHESLEY: Yes, I saw Steve on the tube. The local news people interviewed him up in Hancock or one of those towns up there.

STEVE SPIGNESI: They filmed his screenplay.

CHRIS CHESLEY: Well, I'm glad he did the screenplay because it's no secret to anybody the way he writes. Let me give you an interesting example about the way he learned to write as a kid. When we were younger, Steve and I and this other guy, we got this idea. The idea was simply to take traditional themes and to have Steve write them up in like seven or eight page forms, and type them out, make up copies of these things, and then sell them at school. Steve had this old mimeograph machine in his cellar.

STEVE SPIGNESI: The one that belonged to his brother David?

CHRIS CHESLEY: Yes. We got that thing to work, and we started selling them at school. When the teachers found out about it, they shut that down right away! This was like, when he was in the seventh grade and I was in sixth. (Laughs) We were selling them for either a dime or a quarter a copy. Something like that.

Steve was very influenced by the movies. He would write up sequences for these stories. For instance, he did one called "The Pit and the Pendulum," but he didn't use Edgar Allan Poe's story. Instead of telling the story from the book, he would write the movie scenes down in words. And so even though he read a lot when he was young, and he learned from what he read, he also learned as much or more from the way scenes are written for television and the movies. And of course, as I said, it's no secret that his writing is like that now. His writing is extremely cinematic, extremely visual. It's almost like you're watching a movie when you read it.

It's not traditionally literary prose at all, which

I think is one of his greatest gifts. When people talk about Stephen King, they don't talk about that aspect of his writing enough. I think one of the most powerful aspects of his writing is that he doesn't write prose like anybody else does. He writes cinematically.

"Stephen King has changed popular writing forever. Before Stephen King, you had a visual element...but before Stephen King, there was not that emphasis. There was not cinematic writing....after Stephen King, you've got to read him in order to write."

Now there have been people who have come along after him who try to do the same thing but not as well. I think that if people are going to start writing today, they've got to read Stephen King and they've got to take him into consideration. Stephen King has changed popular writing forever. Before Stephen King, you had a visual element—there was *always* a visual element in writing, but before Stephen King, there was not that emphasis. There was not cinematic writing. There was still literary writing. You created your effects from certain words in a traditional way. But now, after Stephen King, you've got to read him in order to write.

STEVE SPIGNESI: Are you familiar with "The Star Invaders?"

CHRIS CHESLEY: No, I don't think so.

STEVE SPIGNESI: "The Star Invaders" was a "AA Gaslight" book which was self-published and printed on Dave King's mimeograph machine, and then sold around school. Were you involved in that? It was 1964.

CHRIS CHESLEY: (Laughs.) If "Star Invaders" was part of the stuff we were doing together, then it couldn't have been '64.

STEVE SPIGNESI: Why not?

CHRIS CHESLEY: Because I was a grade behind Steve, and in '64 I was in high school. And so Steve would have been a sophomore in high school.

STEVE SPIGNESI: And he wasn't doing these self-published pamphlets in high school?

CHRIS CHESLEY: The ones he and I were involved

in happened in grammar school. Now, he could have done some on his own and sold them around Lisbon Falls High for all I know, but I didn't go to the same high school so I don't really know. I went to North Yarmouth Academy, which was a prep school. 1964 was my first year at North Yarmouth Academy and it would have been his second year at Lisbon Falls High.

STEVE SPIGNESI: And the mimeographing of stories was done prior to that, in grammar school?

CHRIS CHESLEY: I believe I was in the sixth grade and he and this other guy were in the seventh grade.

STEVE SPIGNESI: So when he was seventeen, you two were not doing these types of things?

CHRIS CHESLEY: Oh no! (Laughs.) And the reason that I can place 1964 so well is because of another particular event. In December of 1964, he called me up one night on the phone and said "Come over, you've gotta hear this." So I went to his house, it was a winter night, and when I got there, he put a song on this old record player he had and he said, "Now listen to this." And it was "Sounds of Silence" by Simon and Garfunkel.

STEVE SPIGNESI: And that was new, right?

CHRIS CHESLEY: And it was new. That's right. And we were both in high school by that time. I was going to prep school and he was in Lisbon Falls High.

STEVE SPIGNESI: So, then, do you think he could have continued this selling of his stories into Lisbon Falls High on his own?

CHRIS CHESLEY: It's possible. I do remember that just previous to our effort at doing things together, he wrote stories that were passed from hand to hand when we were in grammar school.

There was one particular story that he wrote that everybody read in school. I wish I could remember the name of it, but maybe somebody else might. But anyway, it was a mini-novel, and in the story he had us real kids—including him— take over the school. We stole our parents' guns, and everything else we could get, and we holed ourselves up in the elementary school. The whole story was basically like an Alamo kind of thing, where first the local cops, and then the National Guard come and try to get us out of the school and in the end we all die.

STEVE SPIGNESI: That sounds like the Richard Bachman novel *Rage*.

CHRIS CHESLEY: If you could find a copy of that, then you'd really have a piece of history. That would be a major coup. That story went from hand to hand—everybody read it, and Steve was lionized. That was the beginning of his mythology. People were just floored by that. We all loved it. But our writing together was a grammar school thing.

"We sat in his Plymouth in the schoolyard and drank gin and Bubble-Up....we had a very good time that evening. We sang songs and we talked about what was going to happen in the future and what had happened in the past. You know how that is..."

STEVE SPIGNESI: To wind this up, Chris, is there else anything you'd like to say, either about your years together as friends, or directly to Steve?

CHRIS CHESLEY: Well, I can't think of anything profound to say, but the only thing that I would ask is that Steve remember one particular night we spent in his blue Plymouth with the big fins. It's one of my fondest memories. We sat in his Plymouth in the schoolyard and drank gin and Bubble-Up. I'd like him to remember that because we had a very good time that evening. We sang songs and we talked about what was going to happen in the future and what had happened in the past. You know how that is...

STEVE SPIGNESI: Sure.

CHRIS CHESLEY: And that is just something that I would like him to remember. ❐

"THE MISSION BOY"
A Short Story by Christopher Chesley

Along with Chris Chesley's revisions to our *Shape Under the Sheet* interview, he enclosed two of his more recent short stories for me to read, "The Two Looks" and "The Mission Boy." With characteristic self-effacement, he told me in his cover letter, "I hope it is clear to you that this work of my own I am sending has nothing at all to do with your book. Anything else I can come up with about these two stories is either presumptuous or superfluous." He wanted to be sure I knew that he was not "submitting" these stories for publication in *The Shape Under the Sheet*. He simply wanted me to read them and offer an opinion. I was, and still am, flattered that he thought enough of my opinions to solicit them.

Well, I read Chris's stories.

And then I re-read them.

And then I read them again.

And then I wrote Chris a letter asking for permission to publish "The Mission Boy" in *The Shape Under the Sheet*.

I think Chris Chesley is an excellent writer, and I think "The Mission Boy" is an excellent short story, and that's why I wanted it to appear in this book.

"The Two Looks" seemed to be more of a first draft effort; I felt it could be improved greatly by a minor pruning and rewrite.

But "The Mission Boy" leaped off the page at me fullblown and complete, a tale unto itself, and also, I dare say, an important statement on those who are "too blind to see."

I will not go into too much detail regarding the specifics of the story: I will leave its pleasures to you lucky first readers. But I will say that the story is reminiscent of Carlos Castaneda's Don Quixote stories, and that it is a superb representation of the possiblities available to us when our higher consciousness "intrudes" into what our anxious professor calls "the stability of an upright, mundane life...[where] the things of the world [seem to be] arranged quite rationally."

Chris's choice of language is perfect for this story, and the narrative moves smoothly and deliberately.

I am a sucker for stories involving mystical experiences, and "The Mission Boy" satisfied my paranormal sweet tooth, while at the same time did what all good fiction is supposed to do: it made me think.

Chris told me that the church in this story actually exists, and so I commissioned a drawing done from a photograph of the actual church. I feel that the accompanying illustration by Katherine Flickinger vividly shows us a moment in time captured in the New Mexico light, and adds to our appreciation of Mr. Chesley's work.

Well, enough said.

I'd like to express my sincerest appreciation to Chris Chesley for his steadfast and continued support of this project. Chris gave an industrial-strength-sized chunk of his time to *The Shape Under the Sheet*, and for that I owe him a world of thanks. This book is enhanced immeasurably by Chris's contributions: the interview, "Genius," Chris's remembrance of going to the movies with a young Steve King, "Death Scenes," and now, "The Mission Boy."

Ladies and gentlemen, it is my pleasure to introduce, for your reading pleasure, Christopher Chesley, now appearing nightly (exclusively in these pages) with his superb short story, "The Mission Boy."

"THE MISSION BOY"
by Christopher Chesley

I expect no one to take much note of my personal history, since it can be summed up briefly. In these years of retirement and old age, I discreetly avoid taking much note of it myself. Not that the past has been in any manner cause for embarrassment, something I would rather keep concealed; rather, there is merely an obvious dullness about it, the stability of an upright, mundane life that cannot stand much elaboration. I had a career at one of those New England state universities, and the profession of teaching philosophy for thirty or so years.

The importance of this fact (and I agree with you that it is little) has nothing to do with philosophy as such, but with the type of life a professor leads, a life solidly predisposed, before not many years of that career go by, toward reason, order, and tranquil days. If I may speak candidly, the world, for the professor, soon comes to have about it the air of one enormous library, with the things of the world seeming to him arranged quite rationally in a sort of Dewey Decimal System of calm. It all becomes so steady and reliable, so satisfying.

This had essentially been my frame of mind, and though I have an opinion on the topic, I will tactfully leave it to you to decide its relevance to the question of the mission boy.

The journey I made to New Mexico was reasonable enough, quite easily explained. As I said, I was retired; I had a longstanding invitation from former colleagues of mine, who had moved on years ago to academic advancement in western universities, an invitation I was now at liberty to accept; I would travel by the highways, taking a leisurely pace, these indulgences certainly being common among those of my age and station.

But I do discern that there may have been another more covert motive for the trip, a motive I felt as a slight, easily ignored anxiety, compounded perhaps of an image of future workless days, and of the sound of my own definitely limited personal time ticking away. Unbidden, an inner voice seemed to say to me, *See something.*

And I did see a great deal as I went westward, much of the country, given a well-developed, plodding professorial nature, and an equally hardened lack of a sense of adventure, I had never seen before. It is to be presumed that I should have seen something of the kind which would have quieted those repetitive words of my inner, anxious voice, but the contrary, I confess, was the case.

Even the bold Rocky Mountains (near the residence of another former professor, the last of the old and dear friends I was obliged to call upon as I traveled) merely caused me to feel an almost comical sense of aesthetic guilt: the longing of a hungry perception ought to have been fulfilled by the grandeur of such immense vistas.

I had not realized it, but this rather arrogant dissatisfaction had even been noted by my host, who mentioned it to me at the end if our pleasant time together.

It was his assumption that I missed New England. He was smiling when he said, "I see the West merely brings out your yearning for your real home."

It is a trait of mine to be taciturn, and the way of life of New England has long since confirmed that. "Yearning, perhaps," I only said.

I could see he became seriously interested; perhaps my face gave too much away. He asked what kind

of yearning it was. I informed him surprisingly quickly, against personal habit. Yet I might really have needed the relief of simply talking openly to someone.

When I had explained, he replied, "You sound like a man in search of a bit of magic, or mystery, some sight with a little glamor to it."

"Really?" I said, in an ironic tone. I was hardly the "glamorous" type.

My host was not put off. "The Rockies have all the atmosphere of clarity and light anyone could ask for, but a searcher after mystery should go elsewhere," he said, and paused in thought. "Perhaps," he continued, "you ought to get a look at New Mexico. I always thought, myself, that there is something haunting, yes, even mysterious about that area." He laughed. "They call it the 'Land of Enchantment.'"

"What does an old fellow, a dusty bookworm like me, know about 'enchantment?'" I asked ruefully.

But I must admit that the freedom I was enjoying, and the interest his remarks aroused in me, determined me to set out southward on the very next day. Moreover, it was not merely "interest" fixing the course of this journey, I suspected, as I drove down through southern Colorado.

By the time I stopped for the night in the city of Trinidad, and was resting on a motel-room bed with a neglected book on the blanket, I was seeing, in amazement, curious thoughts of mine appear to show grudging agreement with my Denver host's opinion of the "inner voice." That agreement indeed had a strange, almost alarming, cast about it.

Tomorrow would see an entrance into New Mexico, and as I recalled the terms he had employed in describing that place (it was all quite odd since I had no idea what I would do there) the emotional pitch of suspense rose in degree. New Mexico was "haunting," and "mysterious." These words created the most extraordinary feeling of excitement around me, and I was helpless to resist it. But I fell asleep with the weak excuse that, because I was so far from home, this peculiar deviation of character was to be expected.

I could not, however, excuse direct perception as, the next morning, I descended out of Raton Pass and came into New Mexico. Even the first view, from the heights above, of those whitish summer plains with their curious mesas resting in the lower distance, was an acute confirmation of my friend's words. He had simply been correct, and long before I took a room at Las Vegas later that day, I was forced to give belated assent to him.

I felt I was at last *seeing something:* This day in New Mexico was a gift of an entirely new sense of light by which to take in what was before me. While the Colorado mountain light gave a clear and open form to things, this New Mexican light was distinctly luxurious, a veritable dazzle. To stretch words a bit, I would even say it was a "rain" of light, a fountain-like gleam ornamenting all I saw. For example, the quickly-passed town of Wagon Mound, resting on the breast of its lonely bluff, somehow became more than it was, more sublime and less substantial, like a beautiful mirage from a fairy-tale, clothed in enigmatic, glamorous light.

Under such light what I saw, and was to see, had the effect of an intense and prodigious mystery.

It did no good to attribute my attitude to a position as an easily-impressed, gawking tourist, because (and this is extremely difficult to explain) new moments in this brilliant atmosphere somehow were turning the tables: my own perception, oddly enough, no longer carried so much weight; what mattered now was *a perception of me,* the origin of which I cannot begin to understand, as if I myself had come to be revealed through the abundance of light. I had the definite sensation that I was no longer the visitor—I was the visited.

I do not think I was succumbing to the upsetting but hardly rare paranoia of one who finds himself solitary, in a perfectly unknown region, and cut off from all that is usual. I did not feel disturbed, at least in the way of being oppressed. On the contrary, if anything, I was taken almost by exhiliration which, I thought, had some connection, unknown but nevertheless strong, with the profusion of wonderful light.

The excitement, I might say the pleasure, was even more remarkable, since this consciousness of having the capacity *to be seen,* to be visited, as I have put it, went completely against the grain of my normally stubborn trait of personal privacy. I can only say that the light appeared to have qualities of illumination, giving me a form more visible than I had ever had before.

This would go far to explain why the "inner voice," previously a quiet command to *see something,* became progressively more insistent, quite keeping pace with that other sensation of *being seen.* I had assumed I had been the observer, during the drive to Las Vegas, of the unique New Mexican light; but it was true, I realized as night fell: I had merely observed myself under the influence of that light.

After all, *I* was touring, I concluded the next morning as I headed tworad Albuquerque. I was not traveling in order to see what I was already too familiar with, a tired, anonymous old professor. I wanted some satisfying spectacle, and I let the "inner voice" push me on.

And, at the end of the day, as I put up in a small but adequate motel on the southern outskirts of Albuquer-

que, perhaps it was the importunate voice directing my attention to a group of pictures on the wall behind the small counter, while the clerk had turned to retrieve the room key. I took a sudden fancy to one of the pictures, staring at it so unconsciously that the clerk had to tap gently with the key on the register to bring me back.

"That's the church at Isleta Pueblo," he said, in response to my question.

The effect of the white-faced old mission church in the picture was immediate. I was getting used to the unusual emotional course New Mexico had been shaping within me, but there is endless surprise, for a thoroughly reasonable man, in the revelation of his thoroughly unreasonable mental events. My own decision was rapidly and intensely made, seemingly by some novel individual, some hitherto concealed person standing in the shadows a little beyond a certain threshold I had never known existed, down among those deeper mental parts one carries so innocently.

The conclusion established itself, practically with all the lack of deliberation one notes in a migratory bird, that I would go tomorrow ot the mission church at a place called Isleta: I would go there with the singular conviction that that destination had about it the virtue of being the most fulfilling, the most spectacular, sight in the world.

The clerk must have caught a dazed look on my face; perhaps he took it to mean I was hard of hearing, which was quite the truth at the moment, since I really didn't hear a word of his directions to Isleta; at any rate, he agreeably and patiently wrote the directions in a note, while I gazed at the picture on the wall.

But why that particular place, that particular venerable building? I asked myself with great irritation and still greater repetition, when I got into bed. There was no answer to this question, no answer because even the question made absolutely no sense. The only way I could drop off to sleep was by settling uneasily on the tentative thought of Isleta as the spot where I might finally come to *see something.*

Perhaps in consequence, I would finally obtain some peace of mind.

If I had hoped for peace of mind there the night before, I was sadly disappointed late in the morning of the next day, for I stood outside the Church of St. Augustine at the Isleta Pueblo looking in vain for the desired spectacle.

It was not that the edifice was deficient in religious nobility and dignity, since the sight of its simple, yet magnificent, face could bring peace to the soul of the weariest spiritual pilgrim. Nor were the surrounding houses devoid of an atmosphere of ancient tradition, both native American and Spanish; this could have satisfied the taste of the most demaning tourist. I was not certain what I had expected to find there, but apparently, by the indication of my sense of fading enthusiasm, I was not seeing it.

There I stood, in the dust before the silent mission church, actually looking at nothing, the sun rising higher and the open space around me growing warmer. There was not a soul about. I had arrived on a weekday, so I presumed the residents of the place were absent on their various routine employments, or were taking refuge from the heat in their adobe houses nearby. The only other presence with me was an occasional movement of dry wind which lifted up the dust into random, gentle whirls.

Motivated from the glare of the sun's reflection on the bright face of the church, and from perspiring discomfort at the approach of noon, I moved to the large front door of the church to see whether I could enter. The door was not locked; I went in, to relax in what coolness I could find there. On a little table were copies of a short book on the history of this mission, by a Mr. Joe L. Montoya. I picked up one of these copies and walked down to a pew near the altar. My intention was to use a quick reading of this book, and a casual observation of the icons, for diversions, while I was refreshed in the quiet, and still morning-like, air of the church.

But as soon as I had seated myself, opened the book, and had begun to read, I was suddenly aware of another person in what I had thought was an empty building.

A cloudy, mumbling voice, yet curiously sweet and melodious, was addressing me. "Have you come to see me?"

I looked up. Not four feet from me, sitting rather awkwardly on the floor with his face toward me, was the most extraordinary child I have ever seen. And it was at least as extraordinary that I had not noticed him on my way to the front pew.

He repeated his question in the same soft, blurred tone. But, caught up as I was in staring at him, in trying to take him in, I could not produce an answer. He seemed to represent in himself some mysterious, prodigious contradiction: he was horrifyingly pathetic, and yet perfectly, peacefully sublime.

His shocking condition of deprivation was obvious. Streaks and smudges of dirt crowded from his withered, thin limbs onto his gaunt chest; and he had the scars of some virulent disease imprinted on his temples and forehead. These figures on him of physical ruin were moving enough, but my pity was brought to an even greater intensity because it was drawn out by the

despair in his eyes, his manner of inconsolable loss.

He was certainly as desolate as an orphan, although it went beyond, in a way, the more common (if no less shocking) touch about him of abandonment by parents. The impression I received was of a more profound, dreadful homelessness, as if he had been eternally separated not only from mother and father, but also from all those comforting, loving connections it is human and natural to have with one's own time and place in the world. The power of this sight of unearthly sadness was undeniable; it set me to trembling.

How, them, could I have been equally penetrated by a countering truth which was simultaneously in him? It was simply astounding.

The very same child had exquisite beauty, spectacular fineness of facial lines, deep sensitivity tinging his expression, and delicate grace making his little form vibrant.

Perhaps it was the degree of his vividness that caused him to appear not quite substantial. The reason for such a disturbing effect might have been derived from a kind of strange, luminous gleam he had around him, but of this I cannot be sure. The more I tried to get a close look at his odd aura, the more my eyes began to ache, even if the light was not really bright; then its radiance would subtly fade almost to nothing, coming back fully only for an oblique glance, much like a distant star is blotted out by the blind-spot of direct vision. At any rate, I am more positive, at least, of the light's source: it was not from beyond him—it was within him.

I stared and stared at him for a long time. I could not get enough of him.

He asked the same question a third time: "Have you come to see me?"

I fought for composure, managing to speak. But I am afraid what I said, as my stare had been, was rude. I have never been good with children. "Why are you so—dirty?"

He smiled gently. "We have worked at the walls with mud."

"Mud? What walls?"

He inconsequently replied, "All the people work, once, in the year." His voice became slightly more muted.

I pressed for his meaning. "Work with mud?"

"Once, in the year," he repeated. He was now portentous, his stare at me stronger than mine had been at him.

Then my sensibility seemed to stumble, and my next question, accompanied by some quaking shift of feeling, was a surprise to me. "Do you work now, or just before winter?"

The Mission.
Original drawing courtesy Katherine Flickinger.

My eyes now were very sore. The boy might have been fading away. "I can't see you," I called to him.

Blindly, I lost contact with him. I lost all connection with where I was.

(But I *see:* here I am, a little boy. Our family gathering, once a year. To keep the northern winter out of the house, it is banked all around by juniper branches, November work for country families. Even little children must carry the juniper. We work the walls. We pile juniper. New England light, bitter, fading. I try to keep up with the others. The sky is raw and damp. My hands are aching from the cold and the work. The smaller fingers on both hands are numb. I hate this, but I do not dare say it. The rest of them do not care about any pain of mine. They do not see me. I take off mittens, and look at white fingers. My hands also have red marks, where the sharp juniper needles have come through and stung me often. I wring these cold hands miserably. Father does not see me. He says only. "Takes these branches over there, now. I put on the mittens again.)

Just as abruptly as I had left the church and the boy, I came back to them once more. The boy was still staring at me. "You have seen something," he said simply.

I could not speak for a moment. The effect of this grim memory, of a scene I had quite forgotten, or had deliberately erased, from ages ago, was numbing. I had been plunged back in time to see, in all its harsh intensity, something I never wished to see again, that annual torment of the junipers. I managed to give the boy a rueful look and a downcast smile, hoping to cover my confusion. "But no one saw *me*," I finally said.

He said nothing to this, and he never moved his eyes from mine.

The silence was disagreeable; I was ridiculously embarrassed. To turn attention away from me, and toward him, where I thought it had been in the first place, I fumbled for questions to search him with. "Are you ill? What are those marks on your face?"

He said, "The sickness came."

His voice was faint. I had to lean forward in order to hear.

"Many died."

"How could that be?" I asked him, practically cutting off his words. "Surely, in this day and age, medicine, doctors—" I stopped myself, belatedly struck with a chilling tone in his words, a certain disquieting intimation, as if he barely kept something back from me.

"Who? Who died?" I could not restrain myself from putting the question, although I was not sure that I wished brought into the light whatever it was the boy

seemed to conceal.

"I never saw my mother again." As he said this, an appalling sense of regret was suddenly breathed out upon the very air of the church. Its baleful influence was inescapable. For the second time I was overwhelmed.

(Again, I *see:* I am still a little boy, only slightly older. father leads me into the dim room where Mother lies. When I am near her bed, he goes out. He closes the door behind him. I am alone with her. After this, I will never see her again. She is feeble. Her hand wavers. She speaks. Her voice is so low I have to lean forward to hear her.

"Take my hand," she says. I take it, slowly. It is livid.

She sighs. She is dying early, very bitterly. She breathes out regret and anger on the air. I cannot look at her. The light of her pallor hurts my eyes. She groans softly, restlessly. Her anger is somehow at me. I do not understand. I am trembling.

"What will become of you now?" she asks. She does not look at me. "The others can stand by themselves, but you, how will you get brought up? You're a thin-skinned little thing. You see too much, and you take everything so hard. Will there be anyone who can understand that after I go? And even when you're older, you'll be lucky to get some good soul fond enough to waste herself looking after you."

I cannot speak. What have I done that makes her angry?

"It can't be helped now," she says. Then she weakly pulls me forward. She suddenly releases me.

She closes her eyes. "Get away from me," she says. "I can't bear the sight of you."

I leave the room quietly.)

And, as mysteriously as before, I was translated back into the church.

This desperate living over again of an extremely unhappy time, a time I had thought was thoroughly banished from memory down among the vanished, long-dead years where such pictures belong, blinded me with tears. It was the staggering force of the image of my mother's final misery, and the renewed sounding of her rebuke, which compelled me to cry out as I did.

"She wouldn't even *look at me!* Not even a last look!"

I faltered. The boy was still there. Subduing myself, holding in these uncanny surges of feeling out of due concern for an impressionable child, was difficult, but after all, for both our sakes, making some sort of spectacle was the last thing I desired.

I knew what he would say before it was out of his mouth.

"You have seen something," he whispered.

Prey as I had been for two repellent experiences rising unbidden like terrifying ghosts from the past, exhausted as I was after what I now considered futile travels through an almost foreign land, I do not doubt that I will have your sympathy for the attitude toward the boy I put on. His relentless, inexorable, simple words, his unchanging stare, were like sharp glass grinding against me.

Impatiently, I got up from the pew. I reached the point of standing within my arm's length from him, and tried a manner of irritated propriety. "Look," I said. "Haven't you got any place to go? Where are your parents? I think it's about time you told whoever it is that takes care of you where you are."

He also rose. We faced each other.

His voice no more than the lightest of aural touches, he said, "There is no one."

Plainer aggravation roughened my response. "That is hardly possible. If you'll tell me who looks after you, I'll take you there," I said, gesturing vaguely at the houses beyond the door of the church.

There was a hint of some kind of appeal in his eyes when he answered, "All of them went away."

But I was hardened: I didn't care the slightest bit what dire sign or secret woe he may have been exhibiting. I only wished he would go. I could not bear the sight of him anymore.

However, one cannot imply from my harried mood that I could stop staring at him, or that he looked elsewhere. We stood face to face, at a quiet impasse.

During our whole peculiar meeting, I had not succeeded in shedding any light on the facts of this enigmatic child's presence; all I had gotten out of him amounted to mere trivial hints and clues. And because he was such a unique, vivid appearance, it would have at least partially eased my distressed nerves to uncover some connection between him and the residents of Isleta Pueblo. To this end, I consciously put on a kinder look, and broke the silence. "Won't you please show me where you belong?"

He said nothing, all of him concentrated in his stare. Before I had a chance to continue, the fading, fainting sensation for the third time swept me into the darkness.

(I *see:* I am a young man, in college years. I stand face to face with a girl who has a luminously beautiful, vivacious air about her. Even though I have known her for a long time, even though I am now furious, I stare and stare at her. I cannot get enough of her.

"If you could only see yourself," she is saying, her expression both angry and pleading. "I wish you could see what you have become."

"I've become what I ought to be," I reply. "I am doing what I know best, which is only to say I haven't changed at all. I am on the road where I belong. This is what I am, isn't it clear?"

She does not look at me. She has some distant, mysterious picture before her eyes as she says, "It's *not* you. It's not what you used to be. We used to be happy. We were always out in the world. We used to visit friends, and they would visit us. You know it's different now. You have no friends, and you haven't noticed me in months. You spend all your time with your precious books. What is happening to you?"

"But I'm working toward the future, yours and mine," I say. "If I don't apply myself, if I don't prepare for a career, I won't be able to give you—"

"And what are you giving me now?" she asks.

"I'm sorry it has to be this way, and I'm sorry you feel I ignore you. I only know that if I work hard now, then later we'll be able to have the things we want. If I can see that, then why can't you?"

Suddenly her voice drops to a whisper. "I'll tell you what you don't see. You don't see me."

And she leaves.

I stand there alone, in the empty room, staring at nothing.

After a moment, I say aloud, "I can forget you.")

For the third time, I came back to myself.

Yet I had not left behind with the memory, in which it should have stayed imprisoned, my outrage. I was out of control, moving about sightlessly, hands raised and shaking.

"I won't stand for it! I won't look at these things! I won't look!"

I knew it was patently absurd to address the boy as if he were some sort of accomplice in what had befallen me, but torment made me lash out at him. "What is happening to me? I don't understand any of it! Why won't you let me *see something*—"

I was shouting this way as I turned to face him.

The boy was gone.

I stood alone for a moment, in the empty church. Then I fled.

One can imagine how severely shaken I was, how sick at heart, and how hastily I retreated eastward, away from a place that, I am convinced, had meant dire harm for me, out of a light that had illuminated nothing but terror.

I only wanted to go home, a goal which I attained by the most rigorous mental discipline, and by a tightly-controlled methodical sensibility. Even if I can merely claim my safe arrival in New England was due to a forced and blindly mechanical placidity wherein all power of decision seemed to have been taken out of my hands, still the success of survival was victory enough. After the calamity I have narrated here, simply getting back to where I belong constituted a personal triumph.

Time, of course, has restored me almost completely. Now I am able to smile at that single oddity which, until recently, even here in New England, used to seem threatening: Mr. Joe L. Montoya's little volume. Somehow the softbound book crossed the country among my luggage. I had forgotten to throw it out. Morbid curiosity got the better of me, and I read it, disturbed all over again by certain bizarre and ominous correspondences between the history of Isleta Pueblo and the boy's suggestive words. If the boy had spoken of working with mud, then the book explained the annual practice of repairing the walls of the church; if the boy had appeared scarred by disease, then the book recounted the ravages of a smallpox epidemic; and if the boy had hinted at abandonment, then the book told of a time of tragic exile.

And, more ominous still, had all this to do with my own grim experience in the Church of St. Augustine?

Needless to say, this sort of pondering did nothing to hasten my recovery, and it has taken great effort to extract my thoughts from the enchantment of uncertain speculation.

I know that my total well-being depends on disengagement from the memory of that day at Isleta. Writing, I hope, is the way to rid myself of the whole thing. I have never cared to dwell on past painful experiences, and I especially do not prefer the retention of the memory of that strange mission boy.

PART III

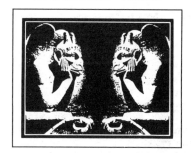

"YERRRNNN UMBER WHUNNNN FAYUNNNN"

Stephen King Fans, Conventions & Collectors

"THE FIND"
A Short Story by Barry Hoffman

Chris browsed through "Whodunit," a specialty bookstore that catered to horror, sci-fi, and mystery afficionados. He visited the store faithfully once a week, searching for those wonderful finds that never saw the light of day at Waldenbooks.

Although he had every Stephen King book in print, he invariably glanced at the multitude of titles in this section—revisiting old friends.

Today he was taken aback when he saw a *new* Stephen King novel, *The Find.* The sole copy was haphazardly strewn between copies of *Misery* and *The Tommyknockers.* He was frankly puzzled. Nothing about any such book had been mentioned in *Castle Rock,* the bible of Stephen King fans. Moreover, nary a word had been heard from King himself since his self-imposed sabbatical a year before.

Sure, he had written a few pieces on the Red Sox, an article on censorship, a couple of short stories, and introductions to anthologies. He was apparently content, though, away from the pressures and limelight that had driven him into seclusion.

Yet undeniably, there on the back of the plain black dust jacket—the words *The Find* looking handwritten—was Stephen King. His full beard could not mask the maniacal gleam in his eye. He seemed to have taken a perverse pleasure in slipping this new novel upon an unsuspecting public.

Chris sought the store's manager, who kept abreast of such matters and would surely clear up the mystery, but he had been taken ill. His son, a crater-faced teenager, who, unlike his father, had as much use for books as vampires had for garlic, was of no help. He merely shrugged at Chris's bewilderment, enfolding his money in his greasy palms.

At home all was forgotten but *The Find.* Chris settled into his favorite overstuffed easy chair—a chair that had comforted him from *Carrie* through *The Tommyknockers.* A chair as forlorn as Chris had been the past year and a half without a new offering from King. As he leafed through the book, Chris had the unsettling feeling that, while new, it had been read before. Pure nonsense, of course, but how could he explain what looked like a dried booger on page 64, and a ketchup stain on page 182? It was not something he dwelled on, however, as from page one he was totally immersed in the story. As so many times before, Chris was transported to a small Maine town, vicariously entering the lives of friends and enemies, like long lost relatives.

The plot, oddly enough, revolved around a previously undiscovered novel by a well-known, semi-retired author. There were a multitude of plot twists as the main character tracked down the shadowy origin of this unknown work. The hero was consumed by his seemingly unsuccessful hunt to the exclusion of all else. He became unglued as clue after clue led to one dead end after another.

He ignored his wife and children. He quit his job only to find out he had been fired two weeks earlier. Time itself lost meaning. He found himself being hung up on by associates of the author he called at all hours of the night. He let his appearance go to hell.

As he sat on the pot one day scribbling messages to himself, the hero glanced at the stranger in the mirror before him. He wondered, then, when he'd last showered as the rank smell of his body attacked his senses; when he'd last shaved; when he had eaten; when he had slept... *if* he had slept. The man returning his gaze looked remarkably like a concentration camp victim, with sunken cheekbones, bloodshot eyes, and the haunted look of someone who had gone over the edge.

He passed out, only to awaken in bed so drained he was unable to rise.

The story ended there...in mid-sentence, for God's sake. A fury engulfed Chris as he frantically tore at the ten remaining pages—all blank. What a downer, he thought. Obviously a printing error. But why, of the tens of thousands of copies printed did *his* have to contain such an error? He looked at his watch, saw it was 2:00 A.M., and knew he'd have to wait until the next day to get another copy to learn how (or even if) the hero extricated himself from the mess his life had become.

As he attempted to get up, Chris felt strangely sapped of all energy—too tired to even make it to bed. He was sweating like a pig, though there was a distinct chill in the air, and he began shivering uncontrollably. Damn, he thought, he was coming down with the flu. He dozed off, though in his delirium he was aware of the door opening.

A man in his early forties with a full beard and thick glasses gingerly plucked the book Chris still clutched in his hand.

The bearded man shook his head in sorrow at the shell of a man that sat before him, and felt for a pulse he knew wouldn't be there. He made his way to the phone, dialed, and waited for an answer.

"It's all right, Tabitha," he said, whispering almost so as not to awaken the decaying carcass before him. "I've tracked the damn thing down."

"No," he responded to her query, both fatigue and impatience in his voice. Doors were beginning to open that would solve his dilemma—how to end the book. All he wanted was to get back to his typewriter and get to work. "I still have no idea how it'll end, but I think it's going to be a killer."

He hung up the phone, and softly humming "Stand By Me," quietly let himself out the door.

Barry Hoffman is editor of a new annual, *Gauntlet,* a magazine devoted to the publication of censored material. The next *Gauntlet* issue is scheduled to be a special Stephen King issue, with a limited number to be signed by King and others (see page 92).

FROM CASUAL TO FANATIC
The Three Levels of Stephen King Fandom

"When I get a little money, I buy books;
and if any is left, I buy food and clothes."
—Desiderius Erasmus

I honestly think the "Stephen King Fan" can be sorted by category, and I think that when all is said and done, there are really only three basic levels: Casual, Serious, and Fanatic. (To be fair, there is also an especially rarefied category called "The Stephen King Expert" which will be discussed in the Epilogue to this piece.)

I know that other writers have attempted to analyze King fandom by breaking down fans into all sorts of exotic and esoteric sub-divisions, but for me, the three categories I've come up with seem to do the job.

Casual.

Serious.

Fanatic.

Which are you? And do you really want to know?

There is, of course, a realm beyond simple fandom —the isolated, over-the-edge kingdom of the Annie Wilkeses among us—that King himself refers to in his dedication to *Misery*, but let's not confuse the issue here with sheer psychosis.

Let us now sharpen our blades and do a nice, thorough dissection of each category and take a look at what's inside...where the red river flows...and after the autopsy, we can leave the remains for that dark guy with the silver eyes who pulls the sheet up.

I've never gotten used to the way that guy smiles, have you?

The "Casual" Stephen King Fan

I've met a lot of "casual" Stephen King fans. They're the ones who have read a lot of King, but rarely in hardcover—unless someone gives them one for Christmas or their birthday. They usually wait for the paperback, or take the hardcover out of the library.

They have never heard of magazines like *Mystery Scene, Cinefantastique, Locus,* or *Midnight Graffiti,* but have re-read favorite King novels.

They will state unequivocally that Stephen King is their favorite author, but in some instances will have seen the movie version of a King book and felt that that was enough.

The Casual Fan may have written King a fan letter, but would have sent it to Viking Press, King's publisher rather than track down one of the more precise addresses King uses. (They wouldn't even know where to begin to search for such "confidential" information.)

Casual King fans may have heard of *Castle Rock,* but more than likely had never even seen a copy.

And you can be sure that the Casual Fans are not aware of books like Doug Winter's *Stephen King: The Art of Darkness* or George Beahm's *The Stephen King Companion,* let alone any of Michael Collings' Starmont volumes on King. But they probably have seen (or maybe even bought) my own *Stephen King Quiz Book,* only because bookstores put it with the King paperbacks, and that's the first place these fans head when they go to a bookstore.

Casual King fans are often confused and bewildered when they meet a Serious or Fanatical King fan. They are usually overwhelmed by the King arcana these fans possess, and there sometimes comes a point where a personal transformation takes place and a Casual crosses over and becomes a beginner Serious. (This is usually heralded by a very determined shopping trip in which the nascent Serious plugs the holes in his or her King collection by buying the King books missing from their library.) King then becomes an avocation, rather than just a pleasant diversion.

If the Casual has the right stuff, he or she will make the move to Serious, and will look bemusedly upon the Casuals he or she comes across in their quest to graduate to Fanatic.

The "Serious" Stephen King Fan

The Serious King fan is just that: Serious about Stephen King.

He or she buys King in hardcover, and usually knows the release dates of King's new books.

The Serious Fan has read Winter and Beahm's books, owns my *Stephen King Quiz Book* and *The Shape Under the Sheet,* and probably has a few (but not all) of Collings' Starmont volumes.

The Serious King fan subscribed to *Castle Rock,* and has seen *all* of the film adaptations of King's stories. (Probably owns many of them on tape, too.)

The Serious King fan most certainly has written to King, and more than likely did enough detective work to obtain one of the Bangor addresses King uses.

The Serious is aware of many of the uncollected Stephen King short stories (but doesn't have any), and he or she has heard of *The Plant* (but never seen it.)

The Serious King fan can hold his or her own in a conversation with a Fanatic, but nonetheless feels somewhat inferior to people who actually own copies of "Suffer the Little Children," "It Grows On You," and "Man with a Belly."

THE UN-"CONVENTION"-AL
STEPHEN KING

"Being famous sucks."
—Stephen King, from an interview in *Mystery Scene* magazine

A convention, for those of you who are not familiar with this somewhat unique expression of fandom, is a gathering, usually annually, of fans, writers, filmmakers, dealers, and others involved in a particular field (horror, science fiction, fantasy, "Star Trek," comics, etc.) for a weekend (or more) of lectures, programs, signings, memorabilia sales, and parties.

Conventions serve several purposes: They allow fans to meet their favorite writers and hear them speak on different facets of their particular field; they allow bookdealers to move some goods; and they also give everyone the excuse to stay up late, drink too much, and spend too much money.

Stephen King used to attend conventions.

Stephen King does not attend conventions anymore.

Why?

Because it got to the point where Stephen King's attendance at a convention completely changed the mood and program of the con.

J.N. Williamson, Stan Wiater, and Jessie Horsting each relate "Stephen King" convention stories in my interviews with them in this volume, and I refer you there for specific incidents. But the bottom line is that everything began revolving around King's presence at the convention. If King was going to be signing books, fans would start lining up early, and King would often have to continue signing books for hours after the scheduled signing was over.

I have never attended a convention where Stephen King was a guest, but I can understand how even the rumor of his presence can change things.

In the summer of 1990, I attended NECON X at Roger Williams College in Bristol, Rhode Island. From the moment I stepped on campus, the rumors were rampant. King was coming, he would be attending the roast, he would be signing books, he would be giving a lecture...and on and on. It was understandable how the rumors could be seen to have some credence: It was the tenth anniversary of NECON, and thus, if King was going to attend *any* convention, it was thought that NECON X would be the one.

Well, to cut to the chase, King didn't show, although I heard that he did send a statement that was read at the Sunday morning roast. (I left Saturday night, and so wasn't able to attend the Sunday functions.)

I found it amazing that talk of King buzzed among many conversations, and that he was present even in his absence. The dealers' room was, of course, loaded with all manner of genre books and magazines, and King was there, too, seeming to be part of every dealer's inventory. I saw everything from a proof of *Carrie* to the more recent Stephen King issue of *Midnight Graffiti*.

Today, there are countless genre conventions (too many to list, in fact), including the aforementioned NECON, the renowned World Fantasy Con, and the newcomer Horrorfest. Horrorfest is significant because it is blatantly a "Stephen King" convention (albeit a "Stephen King" convention at which there is no Stephen King). The first Horrorfest took place in 1989 at the Stanley Hotel in Estes Park, Colorado, the hotel that inspired King to write *The Shining*. Despite mixed reviews for Horrorfest 1989 and 1990, Horrorfest 1991 is scheduled for May 17-19 at the Holiday Inn in Denver, Colorado.

Who knows? Maybe King will show at this one.

But don't hold your breath.

NECON=New England Writers Convention

Rick Hautala and Dave Hinchberger at NECON IX, 1989.
Photo by Stephen Spignesi.

Author Stan Wiater, another NECON IX conventioneer.
Photo by Stephen Spignesi.

The Serious has also read widely in the horror/dark fantasy field, and is familiar with not only King's contemporaries, but also with the writers who influenced King, such as Richard Matheson and Ray Bradbury—but probably not Don Robertson.

The Serious did not buy the *My Pretty Pony* trade edition, but knows someone who did. The Serious probably did buy *Night Visions 5* with the three King stories, and more than likely has *The Drawing of the Three* in the Donald Grant edition.

The Serious has been to at least one convention, and has probably met several horror writers, most of whom signed books for him.

The Serious does not believe that Clive Barker is the "future of horror" since he is able to recognize hype in the field when he or she sees it.

The Serious can play "Got it, got it, need it, need it" in the horror department of a bookstore.

The Serious Stephen King fan is one step away from mutating into a Fanatic, and money is usually the deciding factor. (It is expensive to be a Stephen King Fanatic, and a lot of Serious fans can't afford it.)

The Stephen King Fanatic

Now we're on another planet.

The Stephen King Fanatic is a different breed of fan, and when I speak with them at conventions or book-signings, I am inevitably reminded of the hilarious "Star Trek" skit on "Saturday Night Live" with William Shatner, in which Shatner appears at a Trek convention and the fanatical fans end up telling him things about his ranch and his horses that even he didn't know.

I like the Fanatics.

They do their homework.

The Fanatics have found something that is enormously appealing to them: the work of Stephen King, and they embrace that world with everything they've got.

The Fanatics not only subscribed to *Castle Rock*, but may have collected the entire set by buying back issues.

The Fanatics are on the mailing lists of The Overlook Connection, Dark Harvest, Barry Levin, Donald M. Grant, Craig Goden's Time Tunnel, Underwood-Miller, and other purveyors of genre materials.

The Fanatics own everything King has written in hardcover—including the *Dark Tower* series. They have purchased back issues of magazines such as *Gallery* and *Cavalier* for the King stories, and very often they will search for years for King pieces their collections lack. (Fanatics are often—but not always—Completists: collectors who have to have *everything*.)

Fanatics have the entire Starmont collection of books about King, as well as the film books (by Jessie Horsting and Jeff Conner), and the Underwood-Miller interview collections and "Fear" anthologies (*Fear Itself, Kingdom of Fear and Reign of Fear.*)

Fanatics may have once heard King speak publicly, and more than likely has a signed King book (or possibly more than one) in their collection.

The Fanatic also owns the books about King and his work: Winter's, Beahm's, my own two books, and the University studies.

I guess if you wanted to summarize the Stephen King Fanatic in a phrase, you could do it with "He or she is *aware*." They know what's happening in the field, they know what they like, and they pursue their interests with dedication and singleminded devotion bordering on obsession.

It is not coincidental that the word "fan" comes from the word "fanatic."

EPILOGUE
The Stephen King Expert

There aren't too many true King experts around, and to be frank, the Experts are usually the writers who have done extensive studies of King and his work.

These "Experts" include Douglas Winter, Michael Collings, George Beahm, Tyson Blue, Jessie Horsting, Jeff Conner, Ray Rexer, Stephanie Leonard, Don Herron, Carroll Terrell, Tim Underwood, Chuck Miller, James Van Hise, Darrell Schweitzer, Tony Magistrale, Gary Hoppenstand, Ray E. Browne, Joseph Reino, and myself.

These are the scholars who have studied King and his work with an eye to understanding Stephen King the writer and then, by publishing their scholarship, to enlightening and educating his readers. (For further information about these writers and their books, consult the bibliography "Books With Eyes" in this volume.)

We all know the stats: There are now more books *about* Stephen King than *by* Stephen King—and Stephen King is a *very* prolific writer.

The final conclusion is that Stephen King is arguably the most popular writer of fiction in America...and he has the fans to prove it.

A VISIT TO THE OVERLOOK CONNECTION
An Interview With Dave Hinchberger

Where do I begin?

How can I communicate the essence of Dave Hinchberger to my *Shape Under the Sheet* readers?

What can I possibly say that will successfully paint a portrait of Dave?

I'll give it my best shot.

Ten Things You Should Know About Dave Hinchberger

1. Dave Hinchberger works for Polygram Records. He parties with the Fat Boys, trucks Michelle Shocked around Atlanta in his van, and hugs everybody he likes.

2. Dave Hinchberger owns and operates the superb mail-order company The Overlook Connection, a company he started as a "Stephen King Superstore," and which has since branched out into a universe of other authors, titles, and products.

3. Dave Hinchberger is married to Laurie, a quiet, pretty, incredibly intelligent woman who is yin to his yang; the perfect balance to Dave's determined gregariousness and genuine, outgoing nature.

4. Dave Hinchberger was unbelievably helpful to me with reading copies of uncollected Stephen King stories, as well as phone numbers and introductions to horror writers and people in the field. If you are enjoying *The Shape Under the Sheet*, you owe Dave a great deal of thanks for going out of his way to make people and materials available to me.

5. Dave Hinchberger has a love of life I envy. Not that I'd prefer to be in the box, six feet under, you understand, it's just that Dave is consistently "up," continually smiling, and always positive...regardless of the circumstances. Dave is truly one of those people who can change someone's mood just by being around. I have never, to this day, known Dave to be in a sour mood. Like I said, I'm jealous.

6. Dave is well-read, bright, humorous, and has a beard. And since all bearded men are virile, brilliant, and masterpieces of human evolution, Dave and I share a few things in common.

7. Dave continually tries to draw me out of what he calls my "shell." He thinks I'm too introverted, too reclusive, and too nervous most of the time. He's probably right, and whatever changes I've made in the past few years regarding going out and being more outgoing, I probably have Dave to thank.

8. Dave Hinchberger is not Italian. As you may or may not know from the bio blurb in the back of my recent Signet paperback *The Stephen King Quiz Book*, I am addicted to something called a white broccoli pizza (although here in New Haven—the pizza capital of the world—we call pizza a "pie.") A white broccoli pie is a pizza with no tomato sauce, thus the moniker "white." First, diced broccoli is sautéed with olive oil, fresh garlic, and a little crushed red pepper. This savory concoction is then spread over pizza dough that has already been covered with fresh mozzarella cheese (which here is called "moots"), and the whole magnificent assemblage is then baked in a hot oven until golden brown. The gustatory delights of this culinary masterpiece are almost indescribable. The garlic, broccoli, cheese and olive oil blend impeccably with the chewy pizza dough, and every mouthful is an orgasmic delectation. I have one a week. (Well, I did use the word "addiction, didn't I?)

But, to get back to Dave...like I said, Dave is not Italian. I once attempted to communicate to him the glories of a white broccoli pie. After waxing ecstatic for five minutes about how delicious they are, how he should try one, he said, "Wait a minute. White broccoli...that's cauliflower, isn't it?" I hung up the phone and made a visit to the nearest cathedral, where I made a novena for Dave to Saint Ricky Ricotta, the Patron Saint of the Terminally Non-Ethnic. Someday, I swear, Dave will know of what I speak.

9. Dave Hinchberger laughs like a white Eddie Murphy.

10. Dave Hinchberger is probably one of the best friends I'll ever have. He published the limited edition of this book, and I couldn't be prouder. Now all I gotta do is get him up here for a weekend, drag him to Aniello's, and slap a white broccoli pie down in front of him. Then we'll *truly* be soul brothers!

Here's my interview with Dave. —**sjs**

A VISIT TO THE OVERLOOK CONNECTION
An Interview With Dave Hinchberger

STEVE SPIGNESI: Let's start off with a brief history of the Overlook Connection. How, why, and when did you start the company? Where'd the name come from?

DAVE HINCHBERGER: The Overlook Connection's beginnings? That's a loaded question, but I'll certainly *try* to make this answer concise. I caught the fever in ninth grade when I read my first Stephen King novel. The book was *The Shining*, and I have to tell you I've never read a book that made my heart go pitter-patter so fast before. This guy was giving me my own 70mm mind movie! I could take this movie anywhere with me and start it up when I opened the book. Stephen King's work really set me on the path to reading for enjoyment (as opposed to reading solely for the purpose of regurgitation for school work). From then on I looked for every new release by King. I generally had to borrow someone's paperback, or check his work out from the library. (And you know how sparse the favorites can be at a library.)

Times were rough for our family, and we really couldn't afford books. While on the bus on my way home from work one night, I noticed a young woman reading the *new* SK novel *Firestarter*. My

Dave and Laurie Hinchberger in front of Stephen King's home in Bangor, Maine.

mind was reeling in envy; like I said, getting a used paperback was usually the best I could hope for, and seeing the new title meant I'd have to wait at least a year before I could read it.

That basically was my start with SK. I really didn't read much before I discovered King, but *The Shining* really changed the world for me.

The next phase began when I picked up the *Twilight Zone* SK issue in February of 1986. In it I read "Collecting King" by Doug Winter, an article which gave details on a lot of oddities I didn't even know existed. An asbestos edition of *Firestarter*, *The Plant* series, and all sorts of uncollected lore which 'till now had been unknown to me.

Along with the article was an introduction to *Castle Rock*, a monthly newsletter published for SK fans. I'd seen ads for it in the backs of a couple of paperbacks, and it had always piqued my interest, but you know how you can put things off. Well, after reading that article, I sent my money in pronto, kiddies. When my first *Castle Rock* arrived—KABOOOMMM!!! My mind was reeling again! Here was all this information about the Bachman books, the uncollected short stories, etc., etc. I had certainly heard of the Bachman pseudonym after *Thinner* was released and the pen name had made the news, but *Castle Rock* clarifed the whole thing and answered a lot of other questions for me as well, by bringing me up to date and keeping me abreast of what was happening with my man Steve!

Now that I had all this information about rare stories in magazines, unusual editions, etc., I started looking for them. This went on for about eight months, and every time I found a magazine or a first edition paperback or hardcover, I'd pick it up—if it was a reasonable price, that is. So, here I was with eight months of collecting, and I had piled up quite a few extra items that I didn't need.

I decided to sell them off in *Castle Rock* by offering a catalog. I didn't just want to say "David Hinchberger's got some extra stuff...wanna buy?" I wanted to approach it more professionally. I didn't even want anyone to know it was me. I wanted to remain totally anonymous at the time.

I advertised in *Castle Rock* and sent out my first catalog in May 1987. I made fifty copies. It was a little xeroxed thing, and only eight pages— shrunk. Hell, I didn't even use all the space! Now, three years later, we've evolved into a newspaper-sized tabloid that spans two sections, and consists of over sixty pages. Who would have thought that it would have come this far? I just wanted to sell some extras I'd found. I guess I've never stopped looking for stuff, or reading. I never will.

As far as the name goes, I wanted to tie it in with my discovery of Stephen King. *The Shining* is still my favorite King novel, and it seemed only natural that I should use something from that start way back there in ninth grade. The Overlook Hotel was the consummate evil place, a disease that was on almost every page of the book. It had scared the hell out of me, and I didn't forget it. The term "Connection" is self-explanatory: We are "your connection" to Stephen King books and things.

In the beginning, for the first seven months, we only offered Stephen King books for sale. Then I read Dean Koontz's *Phantoms* (which is one of my all time faves!), and *Strangers,* Joe R. Lansdale's *Nightrunners,* and Robert McCammon's *Swan Song,* and the walls of the Overlook Connection started to bulge with new talent—new to me, that is. As time went on I kept adding authors whose work I enjoyed and wanted to pass on to others. We've certainly gone well beyond that point; I can't possibly read everything that we stock now, but I still try.

My whole mission is to pass along to my customers authors I think they will enjoy. I mean, if I were to advise a customer to buy one of everything, he'd see through that in a heartbeat. But I'd never do that. I'm going to turn you on to what I think you might like. Keep a customer happy, they'll be back. Give someone a lemon and they'll be buying from a different vendor. I know I would. Our service and personal attention is very important. Time permitting, we'll always be willing to answer questions to the best of our abilities. Not everyone can afford to buy something from every catalog (and my wife empathizes with you all—how she does *love* those mail order catalogs!) We're here to help. We try to be a reference source and a friend in the business as well, "not just a line and a price."

STEVE SPIGNESI: As far as I can tell, Dave, yours is the most diverse, wide-ranging, broad-based genre-focused mail-order company catalogue in existence. How did you come up with the newsletter-magazine-newspaper-catalog format, and how has it been received by your customers?

DAVE HINCHBERGER: As I started reading and enjoying other authors, I had many questions myself. Since most of them don't have published bibliographies, I went straight to the source and found out the information myself. I'm also set up with most of the publishers in the Horror/Fantasy/

Science Fiction field and receive a lot of information on new releases, new deals, etc. Of necessity, I maintain a dialogue with many authors as well. So, here I was with all this information, and I thought, why not report it in the catalog? It's good advance promotion for everyone, and the customer stays informed.

In my early days as a reader there were many times when I was caught off-guard when a limited edition was released, or I'd miss out on that first edition hardcover because I didn't know in advance what was happening, and wouldn't see it until it had been out for several months, and in multiple reprints! Our customers know that they can rely on us to keep them up-to-date on established as well as up-and-coming new authors. We try to offer reserve list ordering whenever possible so they won't miss out.

The newspaper format grew out of my desire to include more visual images in the catalog, and the cost of xerox versus newsprint. I started looking for other avenues, and this one worked. When this format hit the streets almost two years ago, the enthusiasm was great. And you should see the responses we get from people now! A lot of people send us postcards or notes saying that they can't afford to order now, but that they want to say thanks for the fiction and general info. It's a good feeling to know you're appreciated with or without an order. This catalog is hard work to put together. I spend a lot of time on each issue. Right now, we're trying to keep to four catalogs a year, with an addendum between each issue to tide you over until the next Pound 'O Catalog reaches you.

STEVE SPIGNESI: Why did you start including fiction in the catalog?

DAVE HINCHBERGER: The fiction idea grew out of a basic need to start educating the Overlook readers about authors with whom they might not be familiar. If they read a short story or an excerpt from a novel, and find they like this person's work, then Voila!

We are carrying more and more authors every issue, and it's important to give a look-see at who we're offering. You can't pick up our books or browse through our racks (unless you're in town), so we have to give you an opportunity to try new blood, so to speak.

When I mentioned the fiction idea to a few authors they were ecstatic. They saw it an an opportunity to reach more readers. We go out to over 5,000 people now. They might buy the book from us, but if they don't, they'll probably see his or her name in the local bookstore sometime. I'm not saying we have this huge domino effect in the book-selling industry, but books are sold all the time in other bookstores, grocery stores, etc.— because someone saw it in the Overlook Connection first. I know this because customers tell me all the time that they picked up this or that at their local outlet after seeing it here first. That's fine with us, because they usually buy something else from us, since that's the only way to stay on our mailing list and keep getting the catalogs.

The best part for me, though, is to know that I'm publishing people. I enjoy sharing new work that I think is going to be good reading for everyone.

We've published several original stories, and even an author's first published work (an author who has now sold a novel to a major publishing house). It's a good feeling and a hell of a lot of fun!

"Stephen King's readers want to keep this man's work.
Always.
Can you imagine how many complete Stephen King libraries an alien life form would find landing here in two hundred years?
A LOT!!"

STEVE SPIGNESI: What percentage of your business is in Stephen King-related merchandise?

DAVE HINCHBERGER: Stephen King sales usually happen around the time of a new novel release, and sometimes with a new SK movie project. The newly-aroused attention usually brings readers to think about some odd item or items they saw in an edition of the catalog. Or sometimes it stimulates people to begin adding to (or begin building) their hardcover SK collection.

Stephen King's readers want to keep this man's work.

Always.

Can you imagine how many complete Stephen King libraries an alien life form would find landing here in two hundred years?

A LOT!!

They might think this King fellow was some kind of Horror Messiah! With King's work, it's almost like the old Lay's potato chip commercial: "You can't read just one." A new reader is more

likely to try to find all the unusual, uncollected material, but I've also had longtime enthusiasts come back for old and new. They're a dedicated bunch, that's for sure.

But to answer your question, it's anywhere from five to forty percent, depending on King's action in the field at the time. This was a loaded question, Steve, with no easy answer.

STEVE SPIGNESI: What are your five favorite King novels, short stories, and films?

DAVE HINCHBERGER: My favorites are always changing. Hey, the man keeps writing! But *The Shining* was my first King novel, and it had the most impact on me. It'll always be Number 1 on my list. I hope another film version of *The Shining* will be made someday. (Maybe the next director will read the book.)

My five favorite novels are:

1. *The Shining*
2. *The Stand*
3. *Misery*
4. *The Dead Zone*
5. *It*

I would like to say that *Pet Sematary,* although not a favorite, scared me to hell and back. While I was reading this one I had to put the book down at times. Laurie asked me if I was okay at one point during a session with that book! King has never scared me as much, before or since. I've never read it again.

My five favorite short stories are:

1. "The Mist" (I wish it had been a novel.)
2. "Graveyard Shift" (This story scared the hell out of me!)
3. "Suffer the Little Children" (Disturbing.)
4. "Mrs. Todd's Shortcut"
5. "Gramma"

My five favorite films are:

1. "Stand By Me" (The best by far!)
2. "Creepshow"
3. "The Dead Zone"
4. "The Woman in the Room"
5. "Gramma"

STEVE SPIGNESI: What are your hopes for the catalog and the company?

DAVE HINCHBERGER: We are building this company to be the superstore of the fantastic! I want to offer any fiction that's good. Not just because it's Horror, Science Fiction, Fantasy,

Mystery, etc....but because it's a great read.

There are so many readers out there who wear blindfolds. I find that some SK readers would rather re-read his work than try to find some of the terrific talent available to them. There's so much to enjoy from writers like Joe Lansdale, Ray Garton, Dan Simmons, and Chet Williamson, just to name a few. I've named these authors because they all write what they and when they feel like it, and these guys have all written some damn good work in most of the fields I mentioned. Look at Dan Simmons, for example. His first novel, *Song of Kali,* contained elements of the supernatural, but I wouldn't call it a horror novel. His second novel, *Carrion Comfort,* on the other hand, is an *incredible* horror novel. When Dan's fourth novel, *Hyperion,* was released, I discovered that readers weren't buying it because it wasn't horror. What a shame! *Hyperion* and its sequel *Fall of Hyperion* contain some of the best writing I've ever had the pleasure to read. It's one great *big* story, with eight central characters, and I cared about what each one of them were going through. Dan Simmons has that knack that makes you get involved.

So, I try to sell Dan Simmons, and not just his horror or science fiction novels. If Dan has a new work, we're going to offer it. If Joe Lansdale has a new release, you'll be able to find it here—always.

When I like an author's work, I don't just offer it today, and not tomorrow. They're offered here everyday, as long as they're available.

The Overlook keeps changing in appearance and services, and we'll keep on changing. And growing. And hopefully bringing our customers enjoyment all year long.

STEVE SPIGNESI: It's more than obvious that you actually read a great deal of the books you offer. How much time do you spend a month reviewing offerings?

DAVE HINCHBERGER: It's ironic that you bring this up. I work fulltime in the record industry, and that requires me to work at night, and sometimes on the weekends. It's not a nine-to-five job. Running the L.A. Guns all over Atlanta for sound-checks and in-store appearances is not the usual working lifestyle for most. And as the Overlook keeps growing, I've found myself working more and reading less. If I'm lucky, I get to read five novels a month. That's about half of what I used to read. Now I keep books at work, on the bedside table...everywhere. The bathrooms at home aren't safe for my wife anymore—she never knows what's going to be staring back at her from a bookcover!

STEVE SPIGNESI: You don't get too involved with the more collectible stuff, like uncorrected proofs, manuscripts, etc. What are your thoughts on dealers who really devote a large part of their inventory to one-of-a-kind pieces?

DAVE HINCHBERGER: One-of-a-kind pieces are generally sold by antiquarian dealers, and there's a definite need for dealers of this type. They're specialists in their field who've spent a good part of their lives living and breathing what they're working with today. If it wasn't for them, some of us wouldn't have the foggiest idea what goes on in that particular area of the market. I generally don't sell this kind of thing because my market is basically the new item market. Manuscripts and rarities can tie up a lot of money. Fast. This is definitely something you need an established clientele for—customers who are likely to buy what you're selling as soon as you advertise it or offer it for sale. There's a lot of money to be made in the antiquarian field, but without the knowledge, you'd be running around in circles. It's an art. It takes time. I'd have to learn, like anyone else, before I started approaching that territory.

STEVE SPIGNESI: What are your thoughts on completists and hardcore collectors who will buy something in shrinkwrap and never read it, and then re-sell it at a profit?

DAVE HINCHBERGER: Professionally I think this is fine. Every collectors' market deals in new, untouched materials. Selling and trading is what makes a collectors' market in the first place. Making a profit is everyone's right. Ripping the public off, with no regard for anyone else, is also everyone's right. This doesn't make it right. I've had a lot of new SK customers find us after making outrageously-priced purchases from a couple of dealers. The customer needs to shop around before making that quick decision. It can cost them dearly if they don't. Personally, I feel that books are meant to be read, touched, and looked at. I had a customer visit me recently, and I offered to show him the Doubleday limited edition of *The Stand: The Complete & Uncut Edition.* It is bound beautifully in leather, and set in a black pine box. He shook his head, saying, "No, no, I could never hold that." Books are touchable objects. A limited, although a very nice and exclusive edition, is a book. Granted, I would never read a limited as long as a trade edition was available. A limited is a celebration of an author and his work. Most times the limited is slipcased for extra protection. An avid reader sometimes wants that signed edition. They get the satisfaction of a personal copy between them and the author.

STEVE SPIGNESI: I know Stephen King is one of your customers. What has been his response to you and your company?

DAVE HINCHBERGER: The first time I got a call from SK's office for an order I was very surprised. I told Laurie we'd come full circle. I mean, I started the Overlook because of my interest in King's work. I never imagined he'd be ordering from us one day. Since then Steve has ordered again, and he also responded to our request for New Year's resolutions for a feature in the catalog. (He was one of over thirty authors we contacted for the feature.) Based on his support, Steve must appreciate what we're doing. It's personally very gratifying.

STEVE SPIGNESI: What are your personal favorite collectibles—the things you'd never sell?

DAVE HINCHBERGER: Personally signed books to us or the Overlook; a few prized limiteds, including the Donald M. Grant edition of Doug Winter's *Prime Evil; The Stand* Doubleday limited; and the *Swan Song* lettered/wood-boxed limited. Also, books by Dan Simmons, Rick Hautala, Ray Garton, Joe Lansdale, Dean Koontz, Robert McCammon, Richard Matheson, Neal Barret, Jr., Chris Fahy, Robert Cormier, Joe Citro, Matt Costello, and Stephen King, to name a handful. And my shelves grow heavier every day.

STEVE SPIGNESI: Why is horror so popular?

DAVE HINCHBERGER: We all have underlying fears in our lives. Presently most people fear AIDS, plane travel, cancer, heart disease, etc. Most of us have come to accept these as the trials and tribulations of everyday life.

The horror genre's popularity is mainly due to that scare that is above and beyond our reach. Which is, frankly, fine with me. It's entertainment. I can look at the post-nuclear war possibilities in a book and try to understand what might happen. No story could ever *truly* be able to describe that ultimate horror, but I'm interested nonetheless.

We're on the outside looking in. If we were on the inside, engaged in a nuclear war, for instance (or some other major disaster), I don't think horror would have much of an audience.

If it did, I'd be very worried about some of my friends.

STEVE SPIGNESI: With the demise of *Castle Rock*, do you see the Overlook Connection catalog filling the gap left by becoming more of a news source?

DAVE HINCHBERGER: *Castle Rock* was a good source of information for all of us Stephen King readers. When it's demise came, I instinctively tried to keep my SK clientele alert to King's new work, and the latest happenings. Although I consider this to be an almost impossible task, we try every issue to keep the information up-to-date. The Overlook was built on SK readers from *Castle Rock*, and we'd like to keep our friends together – to meet four times a year and exchange information. And believe me, our customers are some of the best informants out there! Those readers are the best!!

STEVE SPIGNESI: Have you ever thought of running a "letters" column?

DAVE HINCHBERGER: At this time it's a future possibility for the Overlook. But right now, we are so busy trying to keep everything running on time that a letters column wouldn't be feasible at this juncture. (Could it be, oh, I don't know, could it be that...!!SATAN!! has possessed this answer?!?!)

STEVE SPIGNESI: One final question: Who put the bop in the bop-shu-bop-shu-bop, and who put the ram in the ram-a-lam-a-ding-dong?

DAVE HINCHBERGER: You should never ask a music person this kind of question, bub. In response, I ask you...who sings...

1. "Bark at the Moon"? (Hint: Favorite cuisine: bat's heads)
2. "Moondance"? (Hint: It's "fantabulous")
3. "Bad Moon Rising"? (Hint: "Stormy winds a'blowin'")

STEVE SPIGNESI: I give up, Dave. All of you out there who likewise throw in the towel can write to ole' Dave for the answers. He'll be glad to help!

Dave Hinchberger
THE OVERLOOK CONNECTION
P.O. Box 526
Woodstock, Georgia 30188
(404) 926-1762

STEPHEN KING COLLECTOR EDITIONS
An Interview With Michael J. Autrey

Michael Autrey puts out a four-fold brochure offering dozens of items, the majority of them Stephen King collectible editions.

What was so interesting to me when I first saw one of Mike's brochures was the detail and information he packed into his flyers. For instance, here's Michael's listing for a paperback edition of *Rage* he offered in a recent catalog:

> RAGE—Signet, NY, (1977), [3], 75,000 cc (est.) wr also states 'First printing, Sept. 1977'; written as Richard Bachman; # W 7645.
>
> VG-F—$100.00

That translates to *Rage*, published by Signet, in New York, in 1977. There were three "states" of the book, and 75,000 copies (estimated) were printed. The book's wrapper (cover) also states 'First printing, Sept. 1977'; and it was written by King as Richard Bachman. The copy offered for sale is in very good to fine condition, and is priced at $100.00. [NOTE: See George Beahm's *The Stephen King Companion* for information on the definitions used in the book trade for collectibles. There is also a price guide in George's book (compiled with Barry Levin) which is very helpful.]

Michael carries everything from the first hardcover edition of *Carrie* ($300) to "The Stephen King Notebook" ($6,000). [NOTE: See the feature on the "Notebook" in this volume.]

Not long after I got involved in writing *The Shape Under the Sheet*, I received one of Michael's flyers in the mail, saw the "Notebook" listed, and wrote him asking for a photocopy of the material in it for research. Michael was more than willing to help, and as we got to know each other through correspondence and phone calls, the subject of an interview came up. I felt that a talk with Michael would be informative and interesting to my readers, many of whom, I'm sure, are relative newcomers to the field of King collecting.

Michael is thirty-six years old, divorced, and has no children. He was born and raised in the Midwest, the oldest of eight children. He moved to California when he was fourteen years old, attended high school in El Monte,

California, and studied pre-law at Whittier College, graduating with a B.A. in political science. After college he worked for five years as an insurance claims adjuster, then became a fiscal administrator for two aerospace companies. He did that for eight years, and then left aerospace to become a fulltime book dealer.

Besides horror, science fiction, and fantasy, his interests include cinematography and animation, particularly early Disney animation, and the art work of Carl Barks.

Michael's company is based at 13624 Franklin Street, #5; Whittier, California 90602. His phone numbers are (213) 945-6540 and (213) 698-3075. Give him a call and get yourself on his mailing list. You won't be disappointed.

Here is my conversation with Michael Autrey. —sjs

STEPHEN KING COLLECTOR EDITIONS
An Interview With Michael J. Autrey

STEVE SPIGNESI: What makes a Stephen King item rare? Is it simply supply and demand? How do you arrive at the prices/value of King items?

MICHAEL AUTREY: The answer to this question can be summed up in one word: availablity, which is a function of supply and demand. If we take it as a given that there will be a demand for any particular King item, then the rarity of that item is going to be dependent on the availablity, which equates with supply.

The first printing of *'Salem's Lot*, for example, is a more difficult book to find than a first printing of *The Dark Half,* and consequently, commands a much higher price. Very simply, serious collectors will pay whatever they have to, to purchase the books they want in their collection. If the book is common, it will not command a premium price. However, if it goes out of print upon publication, you can reasonably expect it will increase in value rapidly. Speculation in King items is rampant.

As for arriving at prices and values of King materials, this, too, is dictated by the marketplace. I, for one, count heavily on the activities of other booksellers to help me determine prices. Generally speaking, you can expect any limited edition King book to start increasing in price shortly after publication. A dealer has to consider replacement costs when selling a book. That is, once I've sold this book, what will it cost me to replace it...so I can sell it again. If it costs as much or more than a dealer is asking for a book to replace it, then he is hard-pressed not to raise his price. This tendency has fueled an inflationary spiral, with no immediate end in sight. With the proliferation of books being written about Stephen King and Stephen King collecting, including this one and George Beahm's *The Stephen King Companion,* thousands of King fans are just now becoming aware of all the collector editions that have been done of King's works. This has fueled an entirely new inflationary spiral, and caused prices of many rare King items to go completely out of sight.

STEVE SPIGNESI: Are your customers investors, fans, or both? Personally, I've always been turned off by people who buy books in shrink-wrap, never open them up or read them, and then just resell them after holding onto them long enough to raise the price. What are your thoughts on people who seem to ignore the bottom line: Stephen King's magic with stories, and instead, treat his books as they would gold bullion or stocks?

MICHAEL AUTREY: My customers are both fans and investors, but I'd have to say they are more fans than investors, because to my way of thinking, if they weren't serious fans, they would put their money into other things. It's really only their love for Stephen King that causes them to want to *invest* in Stephen King. There are lots of other ways to invest your money, even better ways, believe it or not, so I have to believe it is more of a "fan-ish" pursuit than one of strict investing.

As for people who buy books in shrink-wrap, never read them and sell them later at a profit; I really don't have a problem with that. They're speculators...they're capitalists...in the truest sense of the word. Capitalism is what this country is founded on; free enterprise is a way of life. I don't question that, but obviously I'm not the best one to ask something like that. I make my living off of people who speculate in books, so my answer is going to be biased, regardless. But I don't think there's anything more wrong with that than collecting baseball cards...or coins...or anything else that gives you personal satisfaction.

The bottom line is that book collecting is a hobby, and it's meant to be enjoyed as a hobby, and not taken too seriously. I do have a problem with collectors who are so intense about their collecting that it becomes an obsession.

I guess what I'm trying to say is that if people find value in Stephen King's books, it's out of respect for Mr. King and it's a sign of their devotion to him and that I find very commendable.

STEVE SPIGNESI: What percentage of your business is in Stephen King items? How about the rare book industry as a whole? As collectibles, how do King items stack up against, for instance, Steinbeck, Fitzgerald, Twain, etc.?

MICHAEL AUTREY: I would say fifty to sixty percent of my business is in King items, with the rest of it being divided between Clive Barker, Dean Koontz, Dan Simmons, Robert R. McCammon, Joe Lansdale, and a host of other horror writers.

"I don't know how to go about comparing King with contemporary American writers such as Steinbeck, Fitzgerald, and Twain, because there has never been another writer received quite as remarkably as King has. I would have to say that King's collector following is much greater than these writers individually, and possibly, combined."

I am constantly striving to expand my business into other areas of the science fiction, fantasy, and horror field. I don't know how to go about comparing King with contemporary American writers such as Steinbeck, Fitzgerald, and Twain, because there has never been another writer received quite as remarkably as King has. I would have to say that King's collector following is much greater than these writers individually, and possibly, combined.

STEVE SPIGNESI: We all know a signed King book is worth more than an unsigned King book. There's obvious value in King's signature. Does this mean that any materials with Stephen King's signature, such as cancelled checks, letters, etc., are collectibles? Does the carpenter who gets King's signature on a work order now have a valuable collector's item? Where would it end? How does the assignment of value to a signed item work?

MICHAEL AUTREY: If you have ever been to a King signing, then you are painfully aware there is value in King's signature. King is worshipped to such an extent that his signature has value on absolutely anything it is placed on. With no exceptions. As far as assigning value to these items, the item itself dictates the relative value of the signature on it. For example, King's signature on a handwritten manuscript is obviously more important than King's signature on a napkin. The carpenter who get's King's signature on a work order only has a valuable collector's item if he completes the work.

There is no end, unless Stephen King stops signing his name.

STEVE SPIGNESI: Do you have a Stephen King "wish list"? Is there one (or more) items that you would love to own but simply have not been able to find? Have you, at one time or another, traded every piece of King material that has seen print? If not, what items have eluded you?

MICHAEL AUTREY: Yes, I do have a Stephen King "wish list." I have yet to own any of the original manuscripts to any of his finished novels. I would love to be able to say I have owned one of these items, even if only for a short period.

I have, at one time or another, traded almost every major piece of King material that has seen print, although a few have eluded me; those being the rarest states of some of his earliest works.

STEVE SPIGNESI: Are you a big Stephen King fan? What are your favorite King novels? Short stories? Films? Recipes? (Sorry, Mike...got carried away there for a moment.)

MICHAEL AUTREY: Yes, I am a big Stephen King fan. My favorite King novel, which is many people's favorite King novel, is *The Stand.* I also am very partial to *'Salem's Lot.*

As for short stories, "Do the Dead Sing?," originally published in *Yankee* magazine in November of 1981 (and later retitled "The Reach" and collected in *Skeleton Crew*), stands out in my mind as one of Stephen King's best.

"Stand By Me" was probably my favorite King film.

As for recipes – I'm really not up on these, but I understand he makes a mean loaf of bread.

STEVE SPIGNESI: How do you get your Stephen King items? Do you spend days on the phone hunting down an item? Have you ever had to back off on an item because the seller wanted more than you thought it was worth?

MICHAEL AUTREY: I get my Stephen King items the same way everyone else does. I buy them from publishers, other dealers, and collectors. I do spend a lot of time on the phone, tracking down items, but I also rely on the many catalogs I get from all over the United States, Canada, England, and as far away as Yugoslavia (I offer an assortment of Stephen King books in the Slavic language).

I also get lots of lists from individual collectors, which I welcome. Some of these items turn out to be very important and often come from people closely associated with Mr. King. I have had to turn down a few items over the years for various reasons; usually because I already have ample quantities of the item being offered in stock.

"There's really no way to describe the average Stephen King collector. They come from all walks of life...and from every career: doctors, dentists, lawyers, engineers, scientists, actors, teachers, truck drivers, etc. Interest in Stephen King seems to transcend all of society."

STEVE SPIGNESI: Who is your "typical" customer? Describe him or her.

MICHAEL AUTREY: There's really no way to describe the average Stephen King collector. They come from all walks of life...and from every career: doctors, dentists, lawyers, engineers, scientists, actors, teachers, truck drivers, etc. Interest in Stephen King seems to transcend all of society. He doesn't seem to appeal to any one group more than another. Some of my customers are fanatical "completists" who must have every appearance of a King story. Others are only interested in reading copies, but they all share a genuine love and respect for Mr. King's work.

I'm also tempted to answer that Stephen King seems to appeal more to women than to men. I really don't know this to be true. It's just a gut feeling I have based on thousands of conversations with King fans. But then I'd be tempted to suggest that women, in general, are more avid readers than men. Again, this is just a theory and I don't have much to base it on.

STEVE SPIGNESI: You've said that you often buy huge quantities of an item in order to never have to turn away a customer. How does this affect the smaller dealer who may not be able to compete? Do you work with the smaller merchants, supplying them with merchandise, as well as with the individual customer?

MICHAEL AUTREY: With the demand for King items being what it is, it is very difficult to buy too much of a King item. I tend to order based on demand—or at least what I perceive that demand to be. I don't generally go heavy on trade editions because I know there will be 1.5 million copies out there. The harder I think a book is going to be to find, the more likely I'll be to order heavy on it.

As for how this affects other dealers, we all seem to be in the same boat—all competing for the same merchandise and the same market. Because of the large number of dealers and collectors, it has become increasingly difficult for us to obtain enough books (especially signed limited editions) to satisfy our regular customers. I have recently had to turn long-standing customers away on the limited edition of *The Stand: The Complete & Uncut Edition* because there just weren't enough to fill the ever-increasing demand for Stephen King collectibles.

I work with other dealers whenever possible and supply books to many of them. I also share information on upcoming books with many dealers.

STEVE SPIGNESI: What are your thoughts on the future of King collecting?

MICHAEL AUTREY: I believe King collecting is still in its infancy; that the demand for King collectibles is far from reaching its apex. The advent of this book and others (again, George Beahm's *The Stephen King Companion,* for example), have introduced the hobby of King collecting to thousands of King fans who previously were unaware of all the signed limited, illustrated small press editions. I also believe that as King continues the *Dark Tower* series, more and more fans will be

Author Clive Barker with Michael Autrey (right).
Photo courtesy Greg Preston.

> **"The advent of this book and others...have introduced the hobby of King collecting to thousands of King fans who previously were unaware of all the signed limited, illustrated small press editions....The future of King collecting looks very bright."**

come collectors. King has at least three new books under contract as of this writing, with many more to follow. The future of King collecting looks very bright.

STEVE SPIGNESI: Define a Stephen King completist. What does it take to be one, besides tons of money? Are these people just total compulsives? Are there a lot of them around?

MICHAEL AUTREY: A Stephen King completist is a collector who tries to collect King's entire catalog of available material. He or she wants every variant state of every King item ever produced. It does take tons of money, but it also takes incredible persistence and patience. They are not just total compulsives—they are simply trying to bring perfection and totality to their hobbies. Yes, there are lots of them around—there's a Stephen King completist lurking in each of us—some escape more readily than others.

STEVE SPIGNESI: I notice that you carry King-related material (*Fear Itself, Kingdom of Fear,* etc.), as well as works by King. Is there a big market for this type of material as well? Do books *about* King have interest to the collectors? I have already been approached by dealers who are interested in *Shape Under the Sheet* materials. In your opinion, where will this trend end (or will it just keep growing)? Do people collect things in which King is merely mentioned, such as articles, blurbs, etc.?

MICHAEL AUTREY: The market for books about King is growing and seems to be proportional to the number of new fans entering the King market. Once the collector bug has injected his venom into the King fan, he becomes interested in books about King, in the belief that the more he knows about King and his works, the more likely he is to complete his collection. This trend is going to continue in an almost logarithmic fashion. There is no end.

People collect absolutely everything with any reference to King: articles, interviews, *TV Guide* issues, appearances on Best Seller lists, advertisements, and especially blurbs. I have met collectors who try and collect every book King has ever blurbed. I even tried it for awhile, but gave it up when I realized how futile it was.

STEVE SPIGNESI: To wind things up, would you please give us Michael Autrey's Top Ten list of favorite authors?

MICHAEL AUTREY: This is a tough one. I really don't like playing favorites. and I'm sure to leave out a few noteworthy authors, but I'll give it a shot.

1. Stephen King
2. Clive Barker
3. Dean Koontz
4. Dan Simmons
5. Robert R. McCammon
6. Harlan Ellison
7. Orson Scott Card
8. Iain Banks
9. Peter Straub
10. Joe R. Lansdale

STEVE SPIGNESI: A mighty list, indeed, Mike. ❏

The "Time Tunnel" company name is derived from the short-lived science fiction series broadcast on ABC-TV, September 9, 1966, through September 1, 1967, which starred James Darren, Robert Colbert, and Lee Meriwether.

LOST IN THE TIME TUNNEL
An Interview With Craig Goden

I first met Craig Goden at NECON IX, at Roger Williams College in Bristol, Rhode Island, in July of 1989.

I had been on his Time Tunnel mailing list for awhile prior to that meeting, and had spoken with him on the phone a few times about a rare King nonfiction piece that he had come across. (It's called "A Possible Fairy Tale." See my feature on the piece following my interview with Craig.)

Craig was exceedingly generous with his offers of assistance, and made photocopies of the piece available to me for research for a feature in *The Shape Under the Sheet*.

After going through his catalog, and seeing the plethora of Stephen King items, I realized that Craig was someone I should talk to for the book. He agreed to an interview to be conducted at NECON, and I found him to be friendly, soft-spoken, and amazingly well-read.

I heartily recommend Craig and the fine folks at the Time Tunnel for all your genre needs. Craig's address and phone number are at the end of this interview.

Special thanks to my pal Mark Savo for his assistance at NECON, and for the photos of me and Craig. —**sjs**

LOST IN THE TIME TUNNEL
An Interview With Craig Goden

STEVE SPIGNESI: What turned you into a horror/science fiction/fantasy fan?

CRAIG GODEN: Richard Matheson's novel *I Am Legend*. That was the one that did it for me.

STEVE SPIGNESI: Apparently that was the novel that set the lightbulb over King's head burning bright, too.

CRAIG GODEN: Yes, I've read that King was overwhelmed by the book. It *is* an incredible novel.

STEVE SPIGNESI: I agree. [Note: See my interview with Richard Matheson in this volume.] How'd you get started in the business of buying and selling genre materials?

CRAIG GODEN: In 1983, I had never been to a convention before, but I was a big King fan at the time and had read a lot of books. I was also a big

Robert Bloch collector, too. Robert Bloch was a Guest of Honor at PulpCon in Dayton, Ohio, in 1983, and so I went on a pilgrimage to meet him. It was a very small convention, and Bloch was very gracious. We talked for about an hour.

But what blew me away was when I walked into the dealer's room. This was the first time that I had ever seen a dealer's room, and it was stocked with all my dreams. I'd been looking for years to find these books and here they all were. For $2 apiece! *Spiderweb* was $15...I just about died right there.

My visit to that room inspired me. The people that were doing this were so nice, *and* they were doing it full time, and had stores and everything. A lot of them were in sandals and beards—it seemed like a real counterculture kind of a job, so it was very attractive. I was a full-time music teacher at the time, but I decided I'd try book-dealing for a hobby on weekends.

For awhile I did the Star Trek circuit conventions, and whenever I could find a good science fiction or horror convention that dealt mainly with books, I'd always try to attend. I remember that PhilCon in Philadelphia was a good one.

So I kept at it, and it really took off. I did really well at the conventions, and I just kept putting the money back into the business. By January of 1985, when *Castle Rock* got started, I was primed to do it full time. I had been doing mail order for a while at that point.

I didn't even know what *Castle Rock* was all about. I just saw an ad for it in *Twilight Zone* magazine that it was starting publication. I wanted to encourage it, so I wrote Stephanie Leonard a letter and told her I thought the newsletter was a wonderful idea, and that I'd like to carry it in my business. She was very nice, and wrote back, and encouraged me to advertise.

Back then I was selling second printings of *The Dark Tower* for $60 apiece. I was unwittingly playing K-Mart, because they were going for about $75 to $100 at that time.

STEVE SPIGNESI: I paid $85 for my second edition.

CRAIG GODEN: What year?

STEVE SPIGNESI: Christmas, 1987.

CRAIG GODEN: Well, I'll tell you, I'd like to have some of those books back at that price. But anyway, I put an ad in *Castle Rock* and overnight my business just exploded. The mail-order business expanded to where I could do the whole thing fulltime. So I'd guess 1985 was when I *really* got started as a full-time dealer.

STEVE SPIGNESI: What are your biggest King sellers? What are the King items that the fans are really after?

CRAIG GODEN: The new book. Always the new book. Six months in advance everybody wants the new book. No matter what it is. As long as it has his name on it. *Nightmares in the Sky,* for instance, was a very popular book *before* it came out. And then when it came out, the interest dropped off immediately. And this was just terrible because the book itself is wonderful.

"It was obvious to me that King seemed to be using magazines as a forum for his own personal thoughts and that his nonfiction work was intrinsically valuable— that is, as far as what he was talking about. It's important material."

STEVE SPIGNESI: How is the Time Tunnel different from other dealers?

CRAIG GODEN: Ever since I first got started, I concentrated a lot on King's magazine appearances. I paid close attention to a lot of his nonfiction work because nobody else was doing that in the field. Nobody was preserving that material. It was obvious to me that King seemed to be using magazines as a forum for his own personal thoughts and that his nonfiction work was intrinsically valuable. So I set out to preserve that stuff and offer it in the market. This type of material has always been very well received by my customers. I've always sold a lot of magazines. I still do.

STEVE SPIGNESI: If a fan came to you and said, Craig, I'm looking for a proof copy of *IT,* would you try to get it or do you limit yourself to readily-available "published" materials? Also, how'd you come across the *Maine Campus*'s special publication, *The Paper*? [NOTE: See my feature on Stephen King's 1970 nonfiction essay in *The Paper,* "A Possible Fairy Tale," following my interview with Craig.]

CRAIG GODEN: No, I don't limit myself. Absolutely not. I try to get as much "oddball" stuff as I can.

That stuff is really popular if you can get it.

Being able to carry *The Paper*—to me that's a real coup. As to how I got it, somebody who went to college with King had a box of *Maine Campus*'s in his attic. He was looking through them just last year, and realized, hey, this issue has got Stephen King in it, I'll bet they're worth something. So he got in touch with me, and I said, well, yes, they are worth something; they're very valuable, I'm sure.

That's part of the fun of this business—to get something like that—something that's not usually available on the market.

STEVE SPIGNESI: Do you have a "Stephen King Wish List?"

CRAIG GODEN: Sure. There are so many things that would be wonderful to have. *The Plant,* of course. But there's no sense in duplicating what B. Dalton's is doing, like current paperbacks of King's work. If you can get them at Dalton's, then you don't need me. But I try to get everything else I can, and keep it available over the years. That's the trick, I think.

STEVE SPIGNESI: What are your personal favorites among King novels and short stories?

CRAIG GODEN: The first Stephen King short story I ever read was "Trucks." I love that story. It seemed so much like a Richard Matheson story to me. It felt like it could have been right out of one of Richard Matheson's *Shock!* anthologies. I also love "Battlegound." That's real nice. In fact, almost every story in *Night Shift* is amazing. "Apt Pupil" is also a favorite of mine.

As far as novels go, I think *The Shining* may be my favorite novel of all time. I keep saying, well, maybe *The Stand,* or maybe this or that, but I always keep coming back to *The Shining*.

The King novel that I think gets less respect than it deserves is *Cujo*. I love that book. I love the fact that the actual action of the novel is not based on a supernatural premise—it's grounded in reality and is something that could actually happen. *Cujo* also happens to be one of the scariest books I've ever read.

STEVE SPIGNESI: A lot of people make a distinction between their favorite King novel and the novel they consider to be King's best. Do you?

CRAIG GODEN: I think *The Shining* is King's best book. I'm not afraid to say it. People will hedge around, but that's the one that's going to stand a hundred years from now.

But it must also be remembered that he's not done, you know? *Misery* knocked my socks off when I read it. And now I keep wondering what's he going to do next. I have a feeling that with *IT*, King reached a plateau of growth, of maturity, and that everything after *IT* is a new direction for him.

I think it's going to be really interesting to see what else is going to come out of his head. *Thinner* is another one that just blew me away.

I remember that King said an interesting thing after *Christine*, which I think showed something about where his head was at at the time. People were giving him some trouble about *Christine*, saying, why are you writing a haunted car story? We've already had the movie "The Car," and Theodore Sturgeon did "Killdozer," so why are you re-doing that? And King's reply was, well, all the good ideas are taken, and that now it's just sort of going over them and putting your own spin on them.

And then six months or a year later, Clive Barker happened. He came out with *The Books of Blood*, and I think it shook King up. Barker was so original, and his ideas were like, from Mars or something—really outrageous ideas. I think King probably took a step back at that point and said, well, maybe I need to finish up all this stuff that's in my head. Finish it up and move on and try other things. To be honest, it makes me feel a little uncomfortable to be second guessing somebody like King, but from where I'm sitting—and especially from reading his work—I would have to say that that's how I saw it.

And I think my opinion is validated when you hear King talk about *IT* as being a culmination of his ideas, a real doctoral thesis on what he had been doing up to that point. *IT* is an incredible book.

> **"...I think Stephen King is dangerous now. I think after *IT*, he's really dangerous. He could write anything at this point. And I can't wait."**

STEVE SPIGNESI: *IT* is my favorite King novel.

CRAIG GODEN: That book pays off. Most novels pay off once or twice with a really horrific scene. That book pays off every fifty pages. It's just an unrelentingly great book. What I'm trying to say is that I think Stephen King is dangerous now. I think after *IT*, he's really dangerous. He could write anything at this point. And I can't wait.

STEVE SPIGNESI: Thanks, Craig, and good luck with the Time Tunnel.

CRAIG GODEN: It was my pleasure, Steve, and good luck with *The Shape Under the Sheet*.

CRAIG GODEN'S TIME TUNNEL
313 Beechwood Avenue
Middlesex, New Jersey 08846
(201) 560-0738 ❒

Steve Spignesi (l) with Craig Goden (r) at NECON IX, 1989.
Photo courtesy Mark Savo.

"A POSSIBLE FAIRY TALE"
Stephen King's 1970 Anti-War Essay

"He is the freeman
whom the truth makes free,
And all are slaves beside.
—William Cowper
from "The Winter Morning Walk"

On May 8, 1970, the *Maine Campus* (the University of Maine's student newspaper), issued the second volume of a special publication called *The Paper*. (Craig Goden tells the story of how he came across the newspaper in my interview with him that precedes this feature.)

The Paper seems to have been an attempt by some UMO students to call attention to the war in Vietnam and the Nixon administration's refusal to acknowledge the strong resistance of many Americans to our involvement.

The front page of the paper had a peace sign next to the masthead, accompanied by photos of an anti-war rally.

Of interest to Stephen King fans is the presence of King in the paper itself, as well as his listing as one of the people who participated (by donating time and writing) in the actual publication of the newspaper.

The student staff of *The Paper* consisted of "David Bright, Russ Van Arsdale, Mark Leslie, Steve Rubinoff, Jeff Strout, Ken Weider, Roy Krantz, Steve King, Pam Murphy, Peggy Howard, Mary Ellen Gordon, Margie Rode, Bob Haskell and many others."

David Bright, a college friend of Stephen King's, appears in *The Tommyknockers* and *The Dead Zone,* and seems to have been the editor-in-chief of *The Paper* since he was the author of the lead-off editorial in the publication called "We Call the Shots." "We Call the Shots" urged students to give long thought to whether they actually *did* have a military obligation after college.

But the piece that most interests us S.K. devotees is *his* contribution to the newspaper, "A Possible Fairy Tale."

"A Possible Fairy Tale" appeared on page 5 of the paper, and was by-lined "Steve King." It ran approximately 600 words, and posited an imaginary end to the war in Vietnam within ten days, by May 18, 1970.

The piece began:

"The following little piece is fictional—a fairy tale, if you like. But fairy-tales do come true. Witness our space program as one example. Or the airplane as another. So let's say that it's only a piece of fiction right now. So many people have been trying to turn 'once upon a time" into 'happily ever after' lately that maybe—just maybe—it can all come true."

King then begins a chronology of events that would result in the complete end of the Vietnam war, thanks to the efforts of "the people."

Here is a rundown of the events (paraphrased) the way King "imagined" them:

FRIDAY, MAY 8, 1970: The University of Maine joins the nationwide campus strikes against the war.

SATURDAY, MAY 9: One million people participate in a sit-in at the White House.

SUNDAY, MAY 10: The sit-in swells to 1.2 million.

MONDAY, MAY 11: Campus strikes continue; the Teamsters decide to strike until Nixon withdraws our troops from Cambodia.

TUESDAY, MAY 12: National Guard troops refuse to enter the Berkley campus, twelve platoons of army troops and marines refuse to go to Cambodia.

WEDNESDAY, MAY 13: The United Auto Workers join the strikes; there are calls for Spiro Agnew's impeachment.

THURSDAY, MAY 14: Nixon addresses the nation, pleads for support; railworkers join the strikes; the sit-in around the White House swells to 2 million. (Also, Eugene McCarthy describes the prior week's events as "a groove.")

FRIDAY, MAY 15: A bill is expected to pass the House forbidding Nixon to spend any more money in southeast Asia.

SATURDAY, MAY 16: Postal workers, dock workers, and some federal government employees join the strikes; there is talk that articles of impeachment against Agnew will be drawn up by Thursday.

SUNDAY, MAY 17: Nixon tells the nation he is withdrawing 500,000 troops from Vietnam and that the Cambodia invasion is over.

MONDAY, MAY 18: "Alexi Kosygin calls Nixon,...[and] congratulates him on 'an act of sanity and humanity'" The two leaders decide on a summit "to discuss complete disarmament."

King ends his "fairy tale" with this:

"So there's your fairy-tale, complete with happily-ever-after ending. It would be nice if things could turn out that way, but I doubt if they will. But then, there was the story of Icarus, the boy who wanted to fly. That was a fairy-tale once, too. Perhaps man could fly in other ways.

Let's all hope so."

This piece, plus King's involvement in the strikes, the rallies, and the newspaper, is further evidence of just how deeply commited he was to the anti-war effort.

King's fairy-tale did not come true as (or when) he imagined it, but eventually we did get out of Vietnam, and his, and many others' efforts contributed to the achievement of that goal.

For the record, a ceasefire in Vietnam on January 28, 1973 ended our direct involvement in southeast Asia. The last U.S. troops left Vietnam on March 29 of that year, but we continued to bomb Cambodia while retrieving prisoners of war. American battle deaths for the conflict, as recorded in 1991 sources, totaled 47,356.

"Soldier rest! thy warfare o'er,
Sleep the sleep that knows not breaking;
Dream of battled fields no more,
Days of danger, nights of waking."
—Sir Walter Scott
from "The Lady of the Lake"

Cover of University of Maine publication, *The Paper,* containing "A Possible Fairy Tale."

Cover of the Stephen King Special Issue of *Gauntlet* magazine (309 Powell Road, Springfield, PA 19064). The King section of this 400-page issue contains pieces by George Beahm, Michael Collings, Steve Spignesi, and Howard Wornom, as well as a gallery of King art by various illustrators.

PART IV

A VISIT TO CASTLE ROCK

A Look at the Stephen King Newsletter

AN INTRODUCTION TO
CASTLE ROCK
The Stephen King Newsletter

In this section we'll take an in-depth look at the now-defunct Stephen King newsletter *Castle Rock*. Each issue of the newsletter, from the first issue in January of 1985 through December 1989, is annotated in detail in a feature I've called "A *Castle Rock* Autopsy." The annotation is broken down into the following five sections:

ARTICLES
FICTION
BOOK REVIEWS
BOOK EXCERPTS
FEATURES

Castle Rock operated on the assumption that its readers were not only interested in information about Stephen King's life, but that they also wanted informed criticism and analysis of his work as well. This was a fan's newsletter and, as such, certain assumptions were made, not the least of which was that the reader was intimately familiar with the writing of Stephen King.

Castle Rock ran pieces that held the Stephen King phenomenon up to the bright light of day and tried to uncover its dark secrets. Many of the articles sought to understand a little better just what it is about this American writer that so mesmerizes his audience.

There were bibliographic studies published, as well as nonfiction by Stephen King, reviews of books *about* Stephen King, commentary on conventions, and articles that explored Stephen King fandom. Also, there were articles on collecting Stephen King books, articles detailing a fan's search for real-life locales used in King books and movies, and even a look at the numerous and varied bookjacket blurbs King has written for other writer's books. *Castle Rock* ran excerpts from *The Shape Under the Sheet* as well.

What all these articles had in common was that both the writers *and the readers* of these pieces were all very well versed in not only Stephen King's work, but in the entire horror genre as well. These articles often referred to other horror writers, as well as other works of dark fantasy, and those people who approached this newsletter with no exposure at all to the field would likely find reading some of the articles difficult at best, and at worst downright bewildering.

The first four years of *Castle Rock*'s issues were edited by Stephanie Leonard, Tabitha King's sister and Stephen King's sister-in-law. Publication began in January 1985. In late 1988, it was announced that the newsletter would cease publication in December

1988. That didn't happen, although Stephanie did resign as editor. *Castle Rock* continued for one more year, with Christopher Spruce as editor.

Stephanie originally decided to stop publishing the newsletter in 1988 when Stephen King announced he would be taking a five-year hiatus from publishing. Of course, he'd still be writing (and publishing if the truth be told—the unexpurgated edition of *The Stand*, as well as the third part of the *Dark Tower* series, *The Waste Lands*, would likely see print within this period, along with numerous short stories). Stephanie felt, however, that the publication had served its purpose, and that four years was enough. [NOTE: See my interview with Stephanie in this section. This interview took place after it was announced that the publication would stop, but before they changed their minds.] In the "Editor's Column" of the July 1987 issue, she explained:

"As of December 1987, we will no longer be accepting renewals, in keeping with our decision to cease publication in December of 1988. *Castle Rock* continues to grow daily and the decision to cease publication doesn't come easily, but we feel the timing is right (given the impending slowing of publication of Stephen King's work), and we can go out on top of our game, to use a nicely hackneyed cliche. We had thought that the lack of new books by King would not affect the newsletter, but the feeling is now that it would inevitably affect the purpose and substance of the newsletter. We do know that there will be much to talk about between now and the end of 1988, and we hope that all of you who have been so loyal and involved will continue to be."

Well, things changed in the summer of 1988, and although Stephanie Leonard would no longer act as publisher of the newsletter, it was revealed that Christopher Spruce, former managing editor, would continue the newsletter acting as editor.

The news was revealed in the August 1988 edition with the following announcement:

"Castle Rock Will Live On"

The reports of *Castle Rock*'s death may have been exaggerated—or premature at the very least!

Stephanie Leonard, editor and publisher of *Castle Rock,* has announced that while she still plans to discontinue ownership of the newsletter effective Dec. 31, 1988, the newsletter will continue to publish beyond that date.

Leonard said Christopher Spruce, presently managing editor of *Castle Rock,* will continue the publication, under the same name, as of January 1, 1989. Spruce will become publisher of the newsletter under the aegis of his publishing company, Tree Top Publishing Co., Inc., which currently publishes *The Register,* a weekly newspaper based in Bangor.

Current plans call for Leonard to continue as editor, while relinquishing the business and production aspects of the newsletter to Spruce.

Spruce, who redesigned the format and layout of the newsletter shortly after its inception in 1984, said he planned no dramatic changes in the publication.

"Having been active in determining the content and design of *Castle Rock,* he said, 'I'm naturally concerned with maintaining the status quo. Obviously, we could do some things better—a little more this and a little less of that kind of thing. But overall I hope to keep what Stephanie initiated intact."

Spruce said he and Leonard decided to continue publishing the newsletter after repeated requests from Stephen King fans to do just that. "The readers indicated they wished us to keep on keepin' on," said Spruce. "So we will."

Although SK plans to slow down his pace of publishing new books, Spruce said he believes there will be enough new activity and critical works to keep the publication interesting.

In addition, the publication will continue to serve as a forum for the exchange of information and opinion by SK fans.

The existence (and longevity) of a newsletter such as *Castle Rock*—one solely devoted to the work of one author, and a living author at that—is tribute to the talent, skill, vision and above all, story-telling abilities of Stephen Edwin King.

This guy knows what he's doing, his readers recognize that fact, and that's why they anxiously await every new work that spews forth from his word processor. And that's why in the August 1987 *Esquire,* Stephen King was one of the few writers—along with Robert Ludlum and James Michener—to be crowned an "Instant Bestseller."

Now I'm going to take you on a guided tour through the dark town of *Castle Rock,* starting with Issue Number 1, in that bleak and snowy month of January, when, if you listen carefully, you just might hear a wolf howl in the hills above nearby Tarker's Mills.

LIVING IN CASTLE ROCK
An Interview with Stephanie Leonard,
the Founding Editor of
Castle Rock: The Stephen King Newsletter

Stephanie Spruce Leonard, Stephen King's sister-in-law (she's Tabitha Spruce King's sister), was King's secretary for several years.

From January of 1985 through December of 1988, Stephanie was the editor of *Castle Rock: The Stephen King Newsletter*.

Other aspects of her life include being the mother of two small boys, Jonathon and Justin, two young men who—as we are told in the following interview—are just beginning to realize who their "Uncle Steve" really is.

Stephanie is also the wife of Jim Leonard, the gentleman who took one of the best candid shots of Stephen King I've ever seen—the dustjacket picture for the hardcover edition of *Different Seasons*. (It's a terrific shot of King holding his son Owen.)

What this all amounts to is that Stephanie Leonard is busy.

Very busy.

In fact, I guess you can call her World-Class Busy.

When setting up this interview and arranging for an excerpt from *The Shape Under the Sheet* for *Castle Rock*, she told me she was a victim of "too much juggling. I drop balls and forget which ones I'm supposed to be throwing. How do people do it all and still stay sane!?"

Well, whatever the secret is—and notwithstanding her bewilderment—Stephanie Leonard somehow manages to not only juggle a *lot* of balls, but to stay sane in the process.

Stephanie is a generous, literate, kind, and extremely affable person. At first, she wasn't sure she wanted to talk on the record about working for Stephen King, and about her relationship with him, but I made it clear to her that my interview questions were generally about the newsletter, and that any questions she felt uncomfortable with we would simply drop. I also suggested right up front to show *all* the questions to Stephen King, and if he didn't want her to do the interview, then that would be the end of it.

Everything turned out fine, though, and none of my questions had to be eliminated. Journalistic integrity notwithstanding, the bottom line is that people grant interviews because they want to, and any journalist who refuses to compromise on areas of discussion is stubborn, self-defeating, and just plain dumb! *Especially* when you're dealing with extremely high profile people like Stephen King and the people who work for him.

In any case, the following interview is the result, and it gives us an inside look at what it's like to go into that big Victorian mansion every day, and what it takes to keep the office of Stephen King running smoothly.

This interview was conducted in July of 1988, early on in my preparation of this manuscript, at a time when the official position was that *Castle Rock* would cease publication in December of 1988. So bear that in mind when reading some of Stephanie's answers. — **sjs**

LIVING IN CASTLE ROCK
An Interview with Stephanie Leonard

STEVE SPIGNESI: How did *Castle Rock* come into existence? Could you tell us about the newsletter's beginnings?

STEPHANIE LEONARD: It originally came about as a response to the flood of fan mail that Stephen received every week—and which I had to answer! It quickly became obvious that a lot of the mail concerned the same things, among them, how to get a copy of *The Dark Tower,* and also which of Stephen's books were being made into films. I answered so many of the same questions again and again that I thought there must be an easier way to do this. Someone then showed me a copy of a newsletter devoted to Harlan Ellison's work, and the idea struck me that a Stephen King newsletter would solve the mail problem as well as serve as a vehicle for communication between the fans. I hated then—and still do —to throw away fan mail after it's read. But it seemed that I was always six months behind in answering the letters. So *Castle Rock* was born with Stephen's blessing, and on the condition that he would have nothing to do with it.

STEVE SPIGNESI: You could have just as easily called the newsletter "Jerusalem's Lot," for instance.

Why did you decide on *Castle Rock*?

STEPHANIE LEONARD: The name came, of course, from Stephen's books, and also because I like the sound of it. We originally started out typed and mimeographed, and in the first few months, the subscriber list numbered around five hundred.

STEVE SPIGNESI: What is *Castle Rock*'s current circulation?

STEPHANIE LEONARD: As of now (July 1988), it is just about 3500. We were up to 5500 last year, but we have let it dwindle.

STEVE SPIGNESI: That's quite some growth from the 500 subscribers in your first year. Have you consciously let circulation drop this year?

STEPHANIE LEONARD: Yes, we have.

STEVE SPIGNESI: How have you reduced circulation?

STEPHANIE LEONARD: Basically by not doing any advertising, and also by dropping our advertising in the paperback reprints of Stephen's books. Through New American Library we had run ads soliciting subscriptions to the newsletter in the back of the paperbacks. We stopped that in December of 1987, when we decided to cease publication in one year. We have not, in other words, actively pursued new readers, or offered incentives to get back or keep old readers.

STEVE SPIGNESI: How much time is spent on putting the newsletter together?

STEPHANIE LEONARD: The timing varies, of course, with the length of the issue. This month's [July 1988)] was twelve pages long; our average is eight. Generally, it is something I work on everyday, a little bit. One day I might only send for a permission for a reprint, the next day I might work on my editor's column for an hour or two. My mother, Sarah Spruce, who handles the subscriptions, works on it every day, keeping the circulation list up-to-date.

STEVE SPIGNESI: Could you describe for us how a typical issue is assembled?

STEPHANIE LEONARD: The first or second week of each month is the most intense time, when the material has to be type-set, laid-out and edited, and the mailing list up-dates have to be finished so we can print out the labels and get ready to mail. The process of finding the material goes on constantly; I never stop looking for it or getting it ready. Even if we just finished an issue, as we did yesterday (to me finished means mailed out). I have to be looking ahead to next month, deciding what we'll feature, getting reviewers lined up, or permissions ready, thinking about illustrations. It's a labor-intensive job for a couple of days for Chris Spruce (who is my brother, and yes, we do like to keep things "in the family"), who is managing editor. He does the layout and design, and he was the one who took it from typed and mimeographed copy to the tabloid it is now. Chris recently bought a local paper, so he won't have the time he might have had for *Castle Rock*— a consideration in continuing or not continuing since I rely so much on him.

STEVE SPIGNESI: How much is Stephen King involved in the day-to-day operation of the newsletter?

STEPHANIE LEONARD: Very little. In fact, from the beginning he insisted on not being involved. He had already made it clear to me that the whole fan club idea appalled him, and so when I brought up the idea of a newsletter he said "Okay, as long as I'm not personally involved. I've got nothing to do with it one way or another." He might make a suggestion now and then, but it is not something I believe he thinks a lot about.

STEVE SPIGNESI: Stephen King has had both fiction and nonfiction in the newsletter. How does that usually come about?

STEPHANIE LEONARD: Occasionally, Stephen will read something and feel the need to comment. He'll generally write it up, hand it to me and then not give it another thought. I found "Dolan's Cadillac" sitting in a drawer and asked if I could run it, likewise "The Dreaded X."

"'What's he like to work for?' I think they imagine him to be an awful ogre or perhaps hopelessly weird. I usually say 'He's never dull.'"

STEVE SPIGNESI: What's the most common question people ask you about working for Stephen King?

STEPHANIE LEONARD: Surprisingly, I think, it seems to be "What's he like to work for?" I think they imagine him to be an awful ogre or perhaps hopelessly weird. I usually say "He's never dull." Most people envy me my job, assuming it to be quite glamorous and lucrative. And it can be and has been both of those things, but it's still a job, in an office, with all the typing, photocopying and filing that goes along with any other office job.

STEVE SPIGNESI: My favorite Stephen King novel is *IT*. I consider it to be the ultimate manifestation of his talents. What are your personal favorites?

STEPHANIE LEONARD: My personal favorite (and it happens to be dedicated to me and my husband, but it was my favorite even before that came about!) is *Misery*. If I was going to choose something to re-read it would be *Different Seasons* or *The Stand*, because it's been awhile and they were former favorites. The one I would not want to read again, partly because in working on it I had to read it so many times and partly because I am the mother of two small boys, is *Pet Sematary*.

STEVE SPIGNESI: My favorite Stephen King short stories include "The Jaunt" and "The Reach." How about your favorites of his shorter pieces?

STEPHANIE LEONARD: I think the ones that stick in my mind must be the ones I would call favorites— "Here There Be Tygers", "Word Processor of the Gods", "Uncle Otto's Truck." There were a few short stories, but only a few, that I could never get into— "The Jaunt", for instance, comes to mind. I also always enjoy his non-fiction work, the movie and book reviews, and the social and political commentary he does now and then.

STEVE SPIGNESI: Why is *Castle Rock* ceasing publication with the December 1988 issue?

STEPHANIE LEONARD: There are a number of reasons, but partly because the monthly production of a newsletter is a confining thing, and since most of us who work on it also have full-time jobs (and young families), it can be very wearing. I didn't want to do it until I was sick of it or if my heart wasn't in it. I wanted to stop while it was still fun and in good shape. And there was some concern about what we would write about if Stephen stopped producing as he has in past years; his intention is to cut back on publishing for about five years. I also think perhaps you get the feeling "haven't we done this before?" When that happens, you may be beating a good thing to death.

STEVE SPIGNESI: Is there any talk of starting the newsletter up again sometime in the future?

STEPHANIE LEONARD: Some. We've talked about ways to keep it alive, perhaps by going on as a quarterly, but at this point, we've decided not to do that. I feel that if we don't continue in some form,

probably someone else will begin a newsletter, and so be it.
[NOTE: This interview was conducted before the announcement was made that *CR* would continue, with Chris Spruce as editor, which it did for one additional year.]

STEVE SPIGNESI: Would you describe for us what it's like to be Stephen King's secretary? What's a typical workday like?

STEPHANIE LEONARD: On a typical workday I answer a lot of mail, both fan mail and business correspondence. Stephen has two secretaries, and we divide up the work load. Shirley Sonderegger, who originally began working for Stephen when I took a maternity leave in 1983, is an expert at handling travel arrangements, so I leave that to her. Other than that, we both do whatever needs to be done, from phoning to word processing to photocopying. There is sometimes very little research, editing or word processing, and sometimes a great deal. There is a lot of variation in the work, most of the time, so it is, as I said, never dull.

"I took the trouble to count one week and between that and the mail he gets at home there were more than 500 pieces of unsolicited mail—and probably 450 expected a reply."

STEVE SPIGNESI: Could you describe a typical day's mail?

STEPHANIE LEONARD: There is so much mail, it's overwhelming. Shirley and I used to be able to answer every letter, but that is simply not possible now, and it probably wouldn't be even if there were two more of us. We get big envelopes full of mail from the book companies weekly. I took the trouble to count one week and between that and the mail he gets at home there were more than 500 pieces of unsolicited mail—and probably 450 expected a reply.

STEVE SPIGNESI: What are these letters like?

STEPHANIE LEONARD: Most of the letters are good, very positive and simply written to express how much they enjoy Stephen's books. Many letters often end with a request for a reply or an autograph. Some fans write to ask questions (the most common question is "How can I find *The Dark Tower*?"), or to tell him they've found an error in one of his stories. Of course in every batch of mail there are bound to be negative letters, either expressing disappointment in a particular book or taking Steve to task for

---

"We also get a lot of requests for celebrity auction items, to which we generally send signed paperbacks, although recently, on a whim, Stephen sent a pair of dirty socks...."

---

too much "bad language" or for allowing one of his works to be "ruined" by a film company.

We also get a lot of requests for celebrity auction items, to which we generally send signed paperbacks, although recently, on a whim, Stephen sent a pair of dirty socks (they asked for something he would discard)! Often the mail is touching—letters from kids who weren't good readers but became interested in his books and now excel, or letters from people who say his books have helped them get through hard times. And of course there are the nut cases and religious cranks who write to save or condemn him.

STEVE SPIGNESI: Is there anything in particular about the mail he gets that annoys you?

STEPHANIE LEONARD: Yes. Over the past couple of years there has been an irritating trend of more letters from students—students who have been encouraged by their teacher to write to someone famous. Very often we'll get twenty or thirty letters from one school. These children expect replies, and most often don't get them. For some reason, the teachers don't see what an imposition this is, and that they are probably setting the students up for disappointment. I know many authors do not answer any of their fan mail, so if they write to someone other then Stephen, they are likely to be just as disappointed. I have a lot of guilt over those letters.

STEVE SPIGNESI: *Misery*'s dedication page reads:

"This is for Stephanie and Jim Leonard,
who know why. Boy, *do* they."

Why was the book dedicated to you and your husband? What does the dedication mean?

STEPHANIE LEONARD: For some reason, maybe the way it was phrased, people assume there's a secret there, or an in-joke. What that means—BOY, DO THEY (KNOW)—is just that we've been party to

his life for a long time and we've seen the fan mail and the people who hang around in front of his house snapping pictures, and the way the fame and money has affected his life. Basically, we know all the little things that inspired *Misery*.

STEVE SPIGNESI: Do people read more into it?

STEPHANIE LEONARD: Oh, sure! People have asked me if Jim or I have ever gotten attacked by a nut or if we know of some secret, terrible thing that happened to Stephen!

STEVE SPIGNESI: At this point in time, my favorite film adaptation of Stephen's books is Rob Reiner's "Stand By Me." What do you think of the film adaptations of Stephen King's stories?

STEPHANIE LEONARD: I'm not a great movie afficionado. None of them offended me terribly, and the one that likewise made the most impression on me was "Stand By Me." I thought that was very faithful and well-done.

STEVE SPIGNESI: It's always risky when the attempt is made to translate a novel to the screen – especially a Stephen King story. So it's very encouraging when there are successes, such as "Stand By Me," "Carrie," and "The Dead Zone." But those really don't make up for the somewhat "less than successful" attempts such as "The Shining" and "Firestarter," and they can never make up for the outright failures, such as "Children of the Corn."

STEPHANIE LEONARD: Well, I think I agree with what Stephen says when he is asked about the movies—they don't change the book. I see them as quite separate from the books.

STEVE SPIGNESI: Any last thoughts on what the past seventeen years have been like?

STEPHANIE LEONARD: Fast and furious! A lot of things have changed since Stephen first came into our lives. It seems like one day I was sixteen and babysitting for them when they could scrape up enough money to go to a movie, and the next day I was babysitting for them while they went to Cannes! My children are just beginning to realize that "Uncle Steve" is famous—as well-known as "Alf" or Michael J. Fox. It's good and it's bad for those of us on the fringe, so to speak. You want to have your own identity; I have very little use for people who think of me and speak of me as "Stephen King's secretary" and nothing else. When a person speaks to me *only* of Stephen, I feel very invisible and incidental. But it's only a problem now and then. I'm happy for him that he's had this success and all the good stuff that comes with it. And I can't say that it hasn't had a lot of effect on my life, most of it good.   ❒

A CASTLE ROCK AUTOPSY
January 1985—December 1989

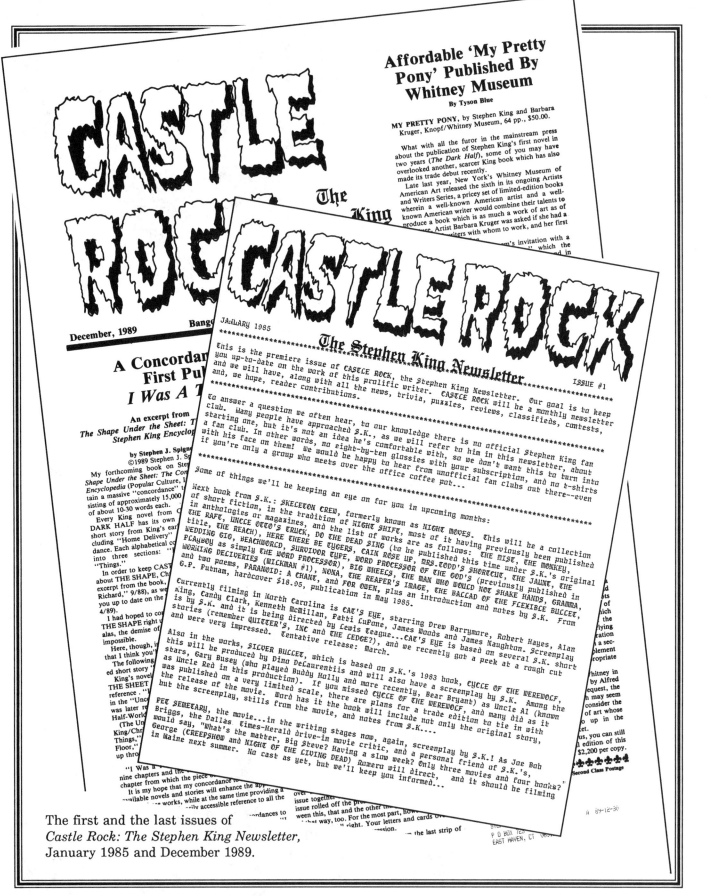

The first and the last issues of
Castle Rock: The Stephen King Newsletter,
January 1985 and December 1989.

CASTLE ROCK
1985

Vol. 1, No. 1 (Issue #1) January 1985

The first issue of *Castle Rock* was a typed, six-page (three, two-sided 8 1/2 x 11" sheets) newsletter. This first issue looked more like a company's interoffice newsletter than the deluxe newspaper format it would eventually become.

The first page had the logo "Castle Rock" in purple-and-white ink and, beneath the logo, the publication immediately identified itself as "The Stephen King Newsletter" in bold black Old English lettering.

Editor Stephanie Leonard opened up this first issue with the following:

> "This is the premiere issue of CASTLE ROCK, the Stephen King Newsletter. Our goal is to keep you up-to-date on the work of this prolific writer. CASTLE ROCK will be a monthly newsletter and we will have, along with the news, trivia, puzzles, reviews, classifieds, contests, and we hope, reader contributions."

Interestingly, the editor also addressed the issue of "Stephen King Fandom" right off the bat. Apparently, there has always been talk of starting a Stephen King fan club. Here's what Stephanie had to say about that in the very first issue of the newsletter:

> "To answer a question we often hear, to our knowledge there is no official Stephen King fan club. Many people have approached S.K., as we will refer to him in this newsletter, about starting one, but it's not an idea he's comfortable with, so we don't want this to turn into a fan club. In other words, no eight-by-ten glossies with your subscription, and no t-shirts with his face on them! We would be happy to hear from unofficial fan clubs out there – even if you're only a group who meets over the office coffee pot..."

This entire issue consisted of news, trivia, and classifieds. There were no critical articles, reviews or pieces of any depth. This issue revealed that King's next book, *Night Moves,* had been retitled to *Skeleton Crew.* It also revealed that the movie "Pet Sematary" was now in the writing stages. There was also talk of the just-published limited edition *Eyes of The Dragon,* and there was a brief mention of Doug Winter's recently-released (back then, that is) *Stephen King: The Art of Darkness.*

Overall, the first issue was a basic newsy/folksy chat about a popular culture icon. The biggest complaint about the first issue was the type font they used. It was a small Old English font and was *very* difficult to read. Stephanie mentioned people's complaints about the type style in the next issue, and it was changed to a simpler font in Issue #3.

Vol. 1, No. 2 (Issue #2) February 1985

Issue #2 still had the Old English type but, as mentioned above, Stephanie promised to vary it in future issues. (She did. By Issue #3, it was gone, gone, gone.) The newsletter had already grown – from six pages to eight.

Once again, there was news scattered throughout the newsletter, inasmuch as the concept of Stephanie's "Editor's Column" hadn't yet been decided upon. But there were two very notable pieces in this issue: The first, and *most* notable, of course, was the first installment of a five-part, never-before-published Stephen King short story, "Dolan's Cadillac." It was obviously typewritten (by King himself, perhaps?), and it was fascinating to see King's famous use of italics in their original underlined typescript form.

"Dolan's Cadillac" opens with the old Spanish proverb: "Revenge is a dish best eaten cold." (Just as a little aside, one of the more recent uses of this proverb was by none other than the criminal Khan Noonian Singh, the genetically-altered superman from the twentieth century, in the second Star Trek movie, "The Wrath of Khan." After Khan's utterance, he embellishes it by adding that it is very cold in space. A terrific moment.) Thus begins a tale of revenge that acknowledged, was inspired by, and paid homage to Edgar Allan Poe's short story, "The Cask of Amontillado." The story is a gripping tale that begins: "I waited and watched for seven years. I saw him come and go— Dolan." Later, we learn why the narrator is watching Dolan: "He killed my wife or had her killed; it comes to the same, either way. Do you want details?" The story builds to a horrifying climax in which Dolan is buried alive in...what else? Yup. His Cadillac.

The publication of this first installment of "Dolan's Cadillac" made it very clear that *Castle Rock* subscribers were in for something special: Stephanie Leonard and her staff obviously had special access to King and his work, and "Dolan's Cadillac" was the first of many special (and many previously unpublished) King pieces that the newsletter's readers would be treated to over the next four years.

The other notable piece in Issue #2 was called "'Shining' At The Overlook Hotel," by Teresa Bagnato. Bagnato visited the actual hotel in Estes Park, Colorado—The Stanley—that King claims inspired him to write *The Shining.* Bagnato stayed in the actual room SK stayed in (Room 217, now changed to Room 340), and she and her husband toured the area, noting the features that ended up in the novel: Hallorann Summit, Sidewinder Road and, as she put it, "more than a few Scenic Overlooks."

"'Shining' At The Overlook Hotel" was a three-part article that continued in Issue #3, skipped Issue #4 (due to the fact that "Dolan's Cadillac" ran long that month), and was concluded in Issue #5.

Articles:
- "'Shining' At The Overlook Hotel" (Part 1), by Teresa Bagnato.

Fiction:
- "Dolan's Cadillac" (Part 1), by Stephen King.

Vol. 1, No. 3 (Issue #3) March 1985

Still in the 8 1/2 x 11" format, Issue #3 scrapped the Old English font and went with a nice, clean, easy-to-read font that looked like Geneva.

And, with Issue #3, the newsletter grew once again, now to ten pages. The biggest news of the month was right up front on Page 1:

> "I don't think I have to tell anyone the big news for this month. Yes, Stephen King is indeed Richard Bachman. One of the toughest things about doing this newsletter has been that I've not been able, until now, to reveal that to the readers. I have known that Stephen was using a pseudonym for years, but I was sworn to secrecy. I am relieved now that I don't have to lie or be evasive anymore."

Also in this issue was one of the first mentions of King's involvement in the attempt to bring his short story "Trucks" to the screen. (It, of course, finally did see big-screen production as the disappointing "Maximum Overdrive.")

The majority of the issue was devoted to Part 2 of "Dolan's Cadillac" and Part 2 of "'Shining' At The Overlook Hotel."

Articles:
- "'Shining' At The Overlook Hotel" (Part 2), by Terrie Bagnato.

Fiction:
- "Dolan's Cadillac" (Part 2), by Stephen King.

Vol. 1, No. 4 (Issue #4) April 1985

The fourth issue, still in 8 1/2 x 11" format, had news of Richard Bachman, limited editions of *Skeleton Crew, The Dark Tower,* and Peter Straub's *Leeson Park and Belsize Square.*

There was also a short piece about where the name "Castle Rock" came from, and a *'Salem's Lot* trivia quiz.

The remaining space was used up by Part 3 of "Dolan's Cadillac." Ten pages.

Fiction:
• "Dolan's Cadillac" (Part 3), by Stephen King.

Vol. 1, No. 5 (Issue #5) May 1985

With this issue, *Castle Rock* got down to business!

For the first time, there was a dollar cover price and, also for the first time, the 8 1/2 x 11" format was gone. The newsletter was now in tabloid (newspaper) format, with a full 11" x 17" page. It was down to eight pages, but with the increase in the size of the sheet, readers were getting a lot more than with the original format.

This issue also marked the first appearance of a "media-watch" column called "King Klips."

Issue #5 had a number of notable pieces, not the least of which was Donald Grant's "Some Reflections on Specialty Publishing."

With Issue #5, *Castle Rock* became a complete, literate, exciting, and fascinating insider's look at the publishing phenomenon of the twentieth century.

Articles:
• "An Evening with Stephen King at Amherst," by Sheryl Mayer. (Coverage of a Stephen King lecture.)
• "'Shining' At The Overlook Hotel" (Part 3), by Terrie Bagnato.
• "The Real Beginning of the Real Bachman," by Stephen Brown. (Brown tells how he uncovered the pseudonym.)
• "Collecting Stephen King Limiteds," by George Beahm. (King as a collectible, by the author of *The Stephen King Companion.*)
• "Stephen King as Breckinridge Elkins?," by Donald M. Grant. (Roast of S.K., delivered at Roger Williams College, at NECON III on July 7, 1982.)
• "Some Reflections on Specialty Publishing," by Donald M. Grant. (King's *Dark Tower* publisher reflects on the "business" of limited editions.)

Fiction:
• "Dolan's Cadillac" (Part 4), by Stephen King.

Book Reviews:
• "*Thinner* by Stephen King." (Reviewed by Wayne Allen Sallee.)

Book Excerpts:
• *Faces of Fear* by Douglas E. Winter.

Features:
◊ "Richard Bachman 'Obituary'."
◊ "Horrors!" (Crossword puzzle with clues by Stephen King.)
◊ "In Print." (Column.)
◊ "King Klips." (Column.)
◊ "Classified Ads."
◊ "Cat's Eye." (Trivia contest.)
◊ "News from the Rock & Roll Zone." (Article about WZON's "Cat's Eye" promotion.)

Vol. 1, No. 6 (Issue #6) June 1985

This issue—now up to twelve pages—had the final installment of "Dolan's Cadillac," and the first installment of Stephanie Leonard's Stephen King bibliography. Interestingly, the subscription form on the back page of this issue offered a sample issue to people thinking about subscribing. The cover price was still a dollar, the one-year subscription price was twelve dollars, but offered no discount for subscribing. The logo was still purple-and-white.

Articles:
• "Stephen King Contracts for Two New Novels." (Unattributed. Details on the contracts for *Misery* and *The Tommyknockers.*)
• "The Politics of Limited Editions," by Stephen King. (King talks about why he did *The Dark Tower* as a limited.)
• "Stephen King Bibliography" (Part I), by Stephanie Leonard. (A very good bibliography, although admittedly incomplete. She offers to the reader some of the more accessible pieces on King, and many of the listings are annotated.)
• "Cat from Hell," by Stephen King. (How King came to write "The Cat from Hell.")
• "Michael Whelan." (Unattributed. A look at the illustrator of *Firestarter.*)
• "The Adventurer Looks at Stephen King," by Will Cortland. (Piece about S.K. originally written for a magazine for Dodge dealers.)
• "*Fantasy Review* Article is a Hoax!" (Unattributed. Details on the alleged "John Wilson" Stephen King pseudonym, under which it was said that King wrote a porno novel called *Love Lessons*. He didn't. The entire review was a hoax.)

Fiction:
• "Dolan's Cadillac" (Part 5), by Stephen King.

Book Reviews:
• "*Momilies* by Michele Slung" (Reviewed by Stephanie Leonard.)

Book Excerpts:
• "Collings Studies Stephen King." (Chapter II: "Genre, Theme, and Image" from *Stephen King as Richard Bachman,* by Michael R. Collings.)

Features:
◊ "In Print." (Column.)
◊ "Cat's Eye." (Reviews.)
◊ "Editor's Column," by Stephanie Leonard.
◊ "King Krossword," by Beth Ann Myers.
◊ "Not a Stephen King." (Blurb explaining that the Stephen King who wrote the book of poetry *Another Quarter Mile* is not *the* Stephen King.)
◊ "King Klips." (Column.)

Vol. 1, No. 7 (Issue #7) July 1985

This issue had a very striking drawing on Page 1 by David Dorman of Jack Torrance on the rampage with his axe. The word "Redrum" was painted in blood on the wall above Jack's head. This issue also contained an interview with Peter Straub, more on the politics of limited editions, and the second half of Stephanie Leonard's bibliography.

This issue was back to eight pages.

Articles:
• "WZON Offers Movie Part." (Unattributed. King's radio station was giving away a part in "Maximum Overdrive.")
• "Straub Talks About *The Talisman.*" (Unattributed. Interview with King's collaborator, Peter Straub.)
• "The Politics of Limiteds" (Part II), by Stephen King. (More on publishing much-sought-after books in (very) limited quantities.)
• "Book Dealers Respond to Grant on Limiteds," by Martin Last, Richard Spelman, Chuck Miller, Robert Weinberg, Phyllis Weinberg, and L.W. Currey. (An open letter responding to Donald Grant's piece in Issue #5.)
• "Stephen King Bibliography" (Part II), by Stephanie Leonard.

Features:
◊ "Editor's Column," by Stephanie Leonard.
◊ "Letters." (Readers write to *Castle Rock.*)
◊ "All 'Richard' Trivia Contest."
◊ "In Print." (Column.)
◊ "Classifieds."

Vol. 1, No. 8 (Issue #8) August 1985

Another eight-page issue, this one had a picture of Stephen King on the front page, standing in front of North Carolina Film, Inc., the studio where he was at the time directing "Maximum Overdrive." This issue listed for the first time a very nice sampling of some of the book dealers specializing in Stephen King material. We were also treated to writing by Stephen King, and were invited to participate in a reader's poll.

Also with this issue, *Castle Rock* temporarily made back issues unavailable "due to the expense and time involved in trying to fulfill your back issue order."

This issue, Number 8, was mis-identified on Page 1 as "Volume 1, No. 7."

Articles:
- "Starmont House Adds Three Volumes to SK Studies." (Unattributed. Details on *The Stephen King Concordance* (cancelled in November 1987), *The Films of Stephen King*, and *The Stephen King Phenomenon*.)
- "Goshgarian Finds the Real S.K.," by Gary Goshgarian. (Text of a speech given by Goshgarian at Hartford College of Women on April 24, 1985.)
- "Designing *The Eyes Of The Dragon*," by Michael Alpert. (Detailed piece on the physical "construction" of the limited edition of *Eyes of the Dragon*. Everything from how the paper was chosen, to how he and King decided where the illustrations would go.)
- "Book Dealers," by Mark Rathbun and Jerad Walters. (Listing of twenty-three dealers/publishers (with addresses) who specialize in King material.)
- "Lists That Matter (Number 7)," by Stephen King. (King tells you what he thinks are the ten best movies of all time. From the top, they are "Casablanca," then "E.T.," "The Godfather Part II," "West Side Story," "The Haunting," "Psycho," "Stagecoach," "Sorcerer," "Cool Hand Luke," and "The Wizard of Oz."
- "Koontz, Not King." (Unattributed. Blurb that reveals that Dean Koontz wrote *Invasion*, not Stephen King.)

Book Reviews:
- "A Skeleton Crew Inside King's Closet," by Kent Daniel Bentkowski. (Article/letter which reviews King's *Skeleton Crew*.)

Features:
◊ "Letters." (Readers write in.)
◊ "Castle Rock Readers' Poll."
◊ "Editor's Column," by Stephanie Leonard.
◊ "In Print." (Column.)
◊ "King Klips." (Column.)
◊ "Classifieds."

Vol. 1, No. 9 (Issue #9) September 1985

This issue, again eight pages, notified us that *Castle Rock* subscription prices would be going up to fifteen dollars effective January 1, 1986. The cover price for this issue was still a dollar, but it would rise to one-twenty-five with the January 1986 issue.

Also in this issue, we were treated to Doug Winter's superb review/interpretation of *Skeleton Crew*, as well as another Stephen King "Lists That Matter."

Articles:
- "Movie Contest Winner Brigalli Filmed for 'Maximum Overdrive'." (Unattributed. The winner of the WZON promotion.)
- "My First Science Fiction Convention," by Alberta Dudley. (Just what the title indicates, but with emphasis on how S.K. was represented.)
- "Searching for Richard Bachman," by Frank Norulak. (Article on one fan's search for original Bachman paperbacks.)
- "Search for Terror is Worth King's Ransom," by Manny Cruz.

(This begins "I love horror." 'Nuff said?)
- "In the Matter of Stephen King," by Michele Slung. (Analysis of why Stephen King is not taken seriously by the critics.)
- "King is Dead. Long Live the Kings," by Erskine Carter. (Humor piece about a fictitious Stephen King secretary who is terrified of her boss.)
- "Lists That Matter (Number 8)," by Stephen King. (King tells you what he thinks are the ten *worst* movies of all time. All-time worst is "Blood Feast," then "Plan Nine From Outer Space," "Teenage Monster," "Old Yeller," "Missing in Action," "Children of the Corn," "Bring Me the Head of Alfredo Garcia," "Love Story," "The Gauntlet," and "Oceans Eleven.")

Book Reviews:
- "Winter Reviews *Skeleton Crew*." (Doug Winter review of King's anthology.)

Features:
◊ "Letters." (Lengthy letter from Michael Collings on Stephen King videos.)
◊ "All 'Richard' Trivia Contest Answers."
◊ "*Silver Bullet* Contest."

Vol. 1, No. 10 (Issue #10) October 1985

The *Castle Rock* logo was now orange, and a picture of Uncle Otto's truck was on Page 1. This issue had two pieces by Stephen King—one about Halloween called "Ghostmaster General," and another installment of "Lists That Matter." The "Editor's Column" was back, and so was a King puzzle. Eight pages.

Articles:
- "Questions Asked Most Often of S.K.," by Stephanie Leonard. (Answered by Stephanie Leonard, editor of *Castle Rock*. Questions include "What is *The Dark Tower*," and "Is Stephen King's house haunted?" "No" to the second one.)
- "Games Highlight King's Terror." (Unattributed. Article about new software based on the Stephen King novella *The Mist*.)
- "Ghostmaster General," by Stephen King. (King waxes grisly about Halloween.)
- "How I Found Uncle Otto's Truck," by Richard McIntosh. (Uncle Otto's truck is real. McIntosh found it – and gives you directions to where it likely still sits.)
- "Introducing 'Richard Bachman'," by Pat Chase. (Article about Chase's correspondence with King.)
- "Stephen King Fan or Fanatic," by Judith R. Behunin. (Fan tells about her descent into total S.K. immersion.)
- "Lists That Matter (Number 14)," by Stephen King. (King shares ten of his biggest fears with the reader. They include trans-atlantic flights, cellars, elevators, the phone ringing late at night, skyscrapers (will it tip over?), street food, and motel showers.)

Book Excerpts:
- "Collecting Stephen King" (Part I), by Darrell Schweitzer. (From Starmont House's *Discovering Stephen King*, edited by Schweitzer. Good info on first editions and the whole collecting field. A sidebar "Contents Under Cover" lists the Table of Contents for *Discovering*.)

Features:
◊ "Letters." (Readers write in.)
◊ "Erskine Carter's S.K. Primer: A *'Salem's Lot* Primer and a *Shining* Primer," by Erskine Carter. ("A is for Anemia, Danny Glick caught it first,..." etc.)
◊ "The Past and Future King's A Horror Show Crosscramble," by T. Vern Jones. (A Stephen King word search puzzle.)
◊ "Classifieds."

Vol. 1, No. 11 (Issue #11) November 1985

This eight-page issue was notable for the lengthy interview Tyson Blue did with Stephen King on the "Maximum Overdrive" set, which ran on four pages of the newsletter. Blue also did another companion piece to the interview for this issue called "'Overdrive' Set Relaxed." The logo was back to purple, and the front page had a nice picture of King taken while he was directing "Maximum Overdrive." The caption for this shot said "S.K. makes a point on 'Overdrive' set," and it was Copyright 1985 by Dino DeLaurentis Productions.

Another interesting piece in this issue was the article that reported the results of the "Reader's Poll" from Issue #8. Turns out that of all the readers who responded, *The Stand* was the favorite King novel.

Articles:
- "S.K. Interviewed on 'Overdrive' Set." (Recorded by Tyson Blue, Sept. 21, 1985. Interview conducted by Blue on King's birthday.)
- "Reader's Pick *The Stand*." (Unattributed. Results of the "Reader's Poll" from Issue #8.)
- "How SK Has Changed Our Lives – A Commentary on the State of the Art," by Kent Daniel Bentkowski. (King reader/fan/critic Bentkowski talks about the possibility that S.K.'s prolific output has actually changed lives.)
- "'Overdrive' Movie Set Relaxed," by Tyson Blue. (Behind the scenes in Wilmington with S.K., Emilio Estevev, and a few rowdy machines.)
- "Stephen King in the Lowlands," by Eddy C. Bertin. (An annotated bibliography of his works as published in the Netherlands (Holland and Belgium.)

Book Excerpts:
- "Collecting Stephen King" (Part II), by Darrell Schweitzer. (Once again from the Starmont volume *Discovering Stephen King*.)

Features:
◊ "In Print." (Column.)
◊ "Classifieds."
◊ "Fan's Opinion." (Letter.)

Vol. 1, No. 12 (Issue #12) December 1985

This eight-page issue brought to a close the first year of *Castle Rock*'s publication and, fittingly (considering the time of the year and all), the logo was now green, and just below the masthead was a chain of green bells. Very Christmassy, indeed. This issue was chock-full of good stuff, not the least of which was yet another interview with Stephen King called, appropriately, "Yet Another Interview with Stephen King." This was also the very last dollar issue of *Castle Rock*.

Articles:
- "Stephen King's 'Silver Bullet': A Review," by David Pettus. (He recommends the movie.)
- "Stephen King: The Critics' Non-Choice," by Christopher Spruce. (Spruce is the Managing Editor of *Castle Rock*, and Stephen King's brother-in-law. Here, he talks about why King's work is generally not considered "real literature.")
- "If I Could Cast *The Stand*," by Edward DeGeorge. (Judd Hirsch as Stu Redman; Jan-Michael Vincent as Nick Andros; Billy Joel as Larry Underwood; Sissy Spacek as Frannie Goldsmith; and Molly Ringwald as Julie Lawry. Hell of a movie, huh?!)
- "Bewitched by Tabitha King," by J. T. Judge. (A look at the career of Mrs. King.)
- "'Silver Bullet': Another Opinion," by Michael R. Collings. (The noted King scholar examines the latest film adaptation and concludes that, while "not a great movie...It is among the

better translations of King's prose into film.")
- "Yet Another Interview with Stephen King," by David Pettus. (Originally published in *Fan Plus* in 1983.)
- "'Silver Bullet' Reviews," by Stephanie Leonard. (Overview of the national reviews of the film.)

Fiction:
- "Putting Richard to Rest," by Wayne Allen Sallee. (Fictional(?) short-short that takes place on a haunted hill overlooking three towns: Castle Rock, Jerusalem's Lot, & Derry. It is here that Richard Bachman meets John Swithen. Quite moving, in its own tongue-in-cheek way.)

Book Reviews:
- "Bachman Books are Interesting Trip," by Tyson Blue. (A positive review of *The Bachman Books*.)

Features:
◊ "Editor's Column," by Stephanie Leonard.
◊ "Points from Don." (Letter from Donald Grant.)
◊ "Recent Newspaper Interviews with King on 'Overdrive'." (Unattributed sidebar. List of King's promotional interviews for the movie.)
◊ "In Print." (Column.)
◊ "Licensing Stephen King??" (A picture of "CUJO" and "SALEMLOT" license plates.)
◊ "Classifieds."
◊ "Index to Back Issues of Castle Rock." (Up to the November 1985 issue.)
◊ "Seven Titles of Novels and/or Short Stories in magazines by Stephen King." (Word jumble puzzle.)

CASTLE ROCK
1986

Vol. 2, No. 1 (Issue #13) January 1986

Stephanie Leonard started off her "Editor's Column" this month with the revelation that editing *Castle Rock* has "been interesting if it hasn't always been fun, and I'm looking forward to year two."

The first issue of *Castle Rock*'s second year of publication was also its first dollar-twenty-five issue. The *CR* logo was purple again. A notable addition to this month's eight-page issue was a brilliant and chilling short story by Tabitha King called "Road Kill." Accompanying Tabitha's story was a black-and-white graphic by Allen Koszowski. The caption mentioned that Koszowski "also illustrated the S.K. short story "Gramma" for *Weirdbook 19*."

Probably the best piece in the whole issue was a letter by Stephen King to *Fantasy Review*, in which King blasted the editors for numerous sins, not the least of which was the *Love Lessons* fiasco. (See Issue #6 above.) King wrote this letter after *Fantasy Review* published a number of erroneous facts about the publication and sale of *The Eyes of the Dragon*. The best line in King's letter was the following: "If you guys are gonna publish, it's time you fucking quit this bush-league journalism." I think Mr. King was a little...well, would "pissed-off" fit the bill?

Articles:
- "World Fantasy Convention Classy Again," by Bud P. White. (A visit to the Tuscon Convention.)
- "Stephen King Books for Sale at WFC '85." (Unattributed. Sidebar to the above article, with prices.)
- "The Blurbs of Stephen King," by Stephanie Leonard. (A look at the praises SK has written for fellow writers' book covers.)
- "Kids Love SK; Parents Don't," by Bill Munster. (The hassles of a rural high school teacher trying to teach Stephen King to his classes.)
- "'Bullet' is SK's Best Screenplay," by Tyson Blue. (A review of the film "Silver Bullet.")

- "Lists That Matter," by Stephen King. (This time it's The Best Things In Life...but at specific ages. Some of these include...at seven, an ice cream cone, at fourteen, a date, at forty-two, a car you can drive fast, and at fifty-six, NOT to have had a heart attack or a cancer scare.)

Fiction:
- "Road Kill," by Tabitha King.

Book Reviews:
- "'Silver Bullet' by Stephen King." (Reviewed by Tyson Blue.)
- *The Trap*, by Tabitha King. (Reviewed by Tyson Blue.)

Features:
- ◊ "Editor's Column," by Stephanie Leonard.
- ◊ "Fie on Fantasy." (Letter from Stephen King to *Fantasy Review*.)
- ◊ "Trivia" (S.K. quotation quiz.)
- ◊ "*Dark Tower* Reprint Sought." (Letter from the Editor of *Author Price Guides*.)
- ◊ "Classifieds."
- ◊ "*Castle Rock* Obsession." (Letter from a *CR* reader asking questions, with answers from Stephanie Leonard.)

Vol. 2, No. 2 (Issue #14) February 1986

With the *CR* logo now in red, Issue #14 brought to its readers some serious material, once again showing that *Castle Rock* readers were well-versed in the literary traditions that have shaped and influenced the horror/dark fantasy field. Two notable pieces in this issue were Part One of Harlan Ellison's "Watching" column, which originally appeared in *The Magazine of Fantasy and Science Fiction*; and Part One of Harold Schechter's "The Bosom Serpent: Folklore and Popular Art," a cogent analysis of the problems inherent in popular culture criticism, with the writer ultimately defending pop culture as "part of an age-old tradition of popular or communal storytelling."

And, as if this wasn't enough, we were also treated in this issue to a piece by Stephen King: His "High School Horrors" (Page 8) was a humorous look back at his teaching days, and some of the bizarre characters he had to deal with on a daily basis. This piece was a slightly different reaction to experiences which King has used in numerous works, including *Rage*, "Suffer the Little Children," "Here There Be Tygers," "Sometimes They Come Back," and *Christine*. Eight pages.

Articles:
- "'The Stanley' Shines On," by Gary Taylor. (Another visit to the hotel that inspired *The Shining*.)
- "Uncut Edition of *The Stand* to be Published by Doubleday." (Unattributed. Details on the "lost" 300 pages cut from the original edition of *The Stand*.)
- "Part One: In Which We Scuffle Through the Embers," by Harlan Ellison. (Two selections from the column "Harlan Ellison's Watching." Ellison looks at the Stephen King phenomenon.)
- "The Bosom Serpent: Folklore and Popular Art," by Harold Schechter. (Part One of an essay analyzing popular culture, including a brief discussion of Stephen King.)
- "The 'King' Goes On," by Judith R. Behunin. (A fan/fanatic's love letter to Stephen King.)
- "Kings, WZON Help Cancer Society Raise $12,000." (Unattributed. Piece about the Kings' charitable work for the Cancer Society.)
- "High School Horrors," by Stephen King. (King talks about the horrors of teaching high school. His list includes "The Thing That Wouldn't Shut Up," "The Incredible Osculating Creature," and "The Smell from Hell." Funny stuff.)
- "Short Story Winners Picked." (Unattributed. The second part of the "Castle Rock's Reader's Poll." "The Mist" was the favorite S.K. short story, with "The Raft" coming in second.)

Book Reviews:
- "*Faces of Fear: Encounter with the Creators of Modern Horror*," by Douglas E. Winter. (Reviewed by Tyson Blue.)

Features:
- ◊ "Trucks." (Graphic by D. Pelliccio.)
- ◊ "King Klips," by Stephanie Leonard. (Column.)
- ◊ "King of Comics?" (Four comic strip panels. Characters from "Spider-Man," "Captain America," and "The Blue Beetle" comics all mention Stephen King.)
- ◊ "Shirt Design Sought." (Readers are invited to submit designs for the official WZON t-shirt.)
- ◊ "Classifieds."
- ◊ "The Man Who Loved Flowers." (Graphic by Ray Basham.)

Vol. 2, No. 3 (Issue #15) March 1986

The logo and Page 1 headline ink for this issue were in a nice light blue color, and the front page was devoted to a piece on S.K. cassettes by Tyson Blue, along with the second part of Harlan Ellison's "Watching" column. Another eight-pager, the back page of this issue was devoted to a full-page ad for Dave Silva's terrific genre magazine *The Horror Show*.

Articles:
- "King of Cassette: Reading SK by Ear," by Tyson Blue. (Overview of the available cassette adaptations of SK's work.)
- "Part Two: In Which We Discover Why the Children Don't Look Like Their Parents," by Harlan Ellison. (The second of two selections from Harlan Ellison's "Watching" column in which he continues his look at the SK phenomenon.)
- "SK Critics Criticized," by Ian Harris. (Just what it sounds like: Harris blasts King's critics.)
- "SK Reprints." (Unattributed. News on two new anthologies containing King material.)
- "'Gramma' Update," by Tyson Blue. (News on the "Twilight Zone" adaptation of King's short story.)
- "The Bosom Serpent: Folklore and Popular Art" (Part II), by Harold Schechter. (The second part of Schechter's essay analyzing popular culture, and including a brief discussion of Stephen King.)
- "*Carrie* to be Musical." (Unattributed. News on the possible Broadway musical adaptation of King's first novel.)

Features:
- ◊ "Editor's Column," by Stephanie Leonard.
- ◊ "Classifieds."
- ◊ "Celebrity Evaluations: Stephen King," by K.G. Stevens. (Handwriting analysis of Stephen King's signature.)
- ◊ "Letters." (Readers write in, including responses to Bill Munster's piece in Issue #13, and a response to "The Bosom Serpent.")
- ◊ "To Stephen King," by Marie A. Asner. (Award-winning poem by the Entertainment Reviewer for the Shawnee (Kansas) *Journal-Herald*.)
- ◊ "*Crew* Quiz." (*Skeleton Crew* trivia quiz.)

Vol. 2, No. 4 (Issue #16) April 1986

This issue had a photo on page one from the "Twilight Zone" adaptation of King's short story "Gramma," showing Barrett Oliver as George bringing his Gramma her cup of tea.

This issue also had an excerpt from *Kingdom of Fear*. It was Michael McDowell's essay "The Unexpected and the Inevitable," one of my favorite pieces from that collection of essays.

Eight pages.

Articles:
- "Praise for Ellison's 'Gramma'," by Tyson Blue. (Positive review of the "Twilight Zone" adaptation of King's short story. A look

at Harlan Ellison's superb teleplay adaptation of one King's most autobiographical short stories.)

- "It's Really Only A Game," by Wayne Allen Sallee. (Negative review of the newly-released videotape *The Stephen King Collection*, which contained two short film adaptations of King works: "The Woman in the Room," and The Boogeyman.")
- "Probing the Mystery of Richard Bachman," by R.L. Day. (Tongue-in-cheek piece that proposes that Bachman is the *real* author, and *King* the pseudonym!)
- "King's Gramma Makes Her Small Screen Debut," by Kent Daniel Bentkowski. (*Very* positive review of the "Twilight Zone" episode.)
- "True Horror Stories Take the Fun out of Fear," by Rick Thomas. (An analysis of the healing effect of horror fiction—vicarious thrills that don't hurt.)
- "*Carrie* To Be Musical," by Mel Gussow. (Reprints the piece that ran in the March issue without a byline.)
- "Stephen King's Religious Vision," by Robert J. Hutchison. (Why King is scorned by Catholics, along with a defense of his vision: He forces Americans to confront real-life evil and most readers can't take it.)

Book Reviews:
- "The Vivesector: Scary Stuff," by Darrell Schweitzer. (Excerpt from Schweitzer's "Vivesector" column, combined with a review of *Skeleton Crew*.)

Book Excerpts:
- "The Unexpected and the Inevitable," by Michael McDowell. (An excerpt from Underwood and Miller's *Kingdom of Fear*.)

Features:
◊ "Editor's Column," by Stephanie Leonard.
◊ "Contents of *Kingdom of Fear*. (Sidebar to the McDowell piece.)
◊ "*Crew* Quiz." (*Skeleton Crew* trivia quiz.)
◊ "Classifieds."

Vol. 2, No. 5 (Issue #17) May 1986

This eight-page issue had a number of notable features: a piece by King's daughter Naomi, an interview with King's agent Kirby McCauley, a piece by Tyson Blue discussing the "war" between Stephen King and John Updike, and the winners in the WZON t-shirt design contest.

The logo was purple, and the front page had a picture of King, Peter Straub, Gahan Wilson, and Donald Westlake (among others) at a Mohonk Mystery Weekend covered by King's daughter Naomi.

Articles:
- "Celebrating a Mystery Weekend at Mohonk," by Naomi King. (King's daughter covers a horrifyingly fun weekend...with the likes of Peter Straub, Gahan Wilson, and Donald Westlake. While her writing was lacking in certain areas, it was nonetheless interesting to get a look at what her famous father does for fun.)
- "SK Literary Agent Discusses Friend and Client," by Christopher Spruce. (Spruce interviews King's agent, Kirby McCauley, and the talk ranges from King's first meeting with McCauley to his recent five-book year. A very rare interview with King's literary agent and one of his best friends.)
- "Searching for S.K.," by Dan McMillan. (McMillan visits his first sci-fi convention, and hunts down rare King books.)
- "Stephen King, One: Updike, Zip!!—A War Story by Tyson Blue." (Blue responds to a reader who defends Updike...while he himself wants nothing to do with Updike's work: "I feel no injustice in telling people to avoid Updike; educators will continue to inflict him on students and I pity them, for his work is, for me, hackwork on a par with Sidney Sheldon." Interesting defense of King, and also quite daring for Blue to take on that almost-sacred literary giant, Updike.)

Book Reviews:
- "*The Dark Tower: The Gunslinger,*" by Stephen King. (Review by S.L. Mehegan. Praise for *DT* Part I, and a look at one of its influences – "Childe Roland" by Robert Browning.)
- "*Kingdom of Fear*: The World of Stephen King," edited by Tim Underwood and Chuck Miller. (Reviewed by Tyson Blue. A generally positive review of the anthology.)

Features:
◊ "Editor's Column," by Stephanie Leonard.
◊ "Lathrop Trivia Quiz," by Kathy Lathrop.
◊ "T-Shirt Design Winners." (Centerspread of notable entries.)
◊ "Classifieds."
◊ "*Cosmo* Winners." (Winners of magazine containing Stephen King interview.)

Vol. 2, No. 6 (Issue #18) June 1986

The most important piece in this issue was the lead-off story by Tyson Blue called "*The Plant*: The Unseen King." This essay introduced the S.K. fan to that rarest-of-the-rare King piece, the novel-in-progress called *The Plant*. The article, which ran on the front page, was an excerpt from Blue's Starmont volume, *The Unseen King*.

Also in this eight-pager was a short story by Stanley Wiater, and selected responses to criticism leveled earlier, most notably, Kathy Lathrop's and Christine Furru's response to Edward DeGeorge's "If I Could Cast *The Stand*" from Issue #12, and director Frank Darabont's response to Wayne Sallee's blistering attack on his "The Woman in the Room" in Issue #16, run with Sallee's "reconsideration" of the film.

Articles:
- "*The Plant*: The Unseen King," by Tyson Blue. (An introduction to one of King's rarest works.)
- "On Hidden Treasure," by Bud P. White. (Informative piece on the making of quality books.)
- "If I Could Re-Cast *The Stand*," by Kathy Lathrop with Christine Furru. (A rebuttal to Edward DeGeorge's article from Issue #12. Her choices? Among those on her list: Rosanna Arquette as Frannie Goldsmith; Randy Quaid as Tom Cullen; Judd Nelson as Nick Andros; Debra Winger as Dayna Jurgens; Madonna as Julie Lawry; Joan Collins as Nadine; Sean Lennon as her companion, Leo Rockway; Whoopi Goldberg as Mother Abagail Freemantle; and Kurt Russell as The Trashcan Man.)
- "The States of Jackets." (Unattributed. A look at the dust jackets on various King editions.)
- "Sallee Reconsiders 'Woman in the Room'," by Wayne Allen Sallee. (Reappraisal and rethinking of Sallee's original negative review.)

Fiction:
- "The Man Who Would Not Be King," a short story by Stanley Wiater.

Features:
◊ "Editor's Column," by Stephanie Leonard.
◊ "Arnold Who?" (Letter from Ian Harris regarding the choice of Schwarzenegger for the film version of *The Running Man*.)
◊ "Classifieds."
◊ "Questions for the Editor." (Letter from Tom McEvoy, with questions answered by Stephanie Leonard.)
◊ "Darabont Replies to Sallee's Critique of his Film" (Letter from "The Woman in the Room" director Frank Darabont.)
◊ "*Skeleton Crew* Portfolio Winners."

Vol. 2, No. 7 (Issue #19) July 1986

This was a big, twelve-page issue with two very special features (not even counting the bright red logo and red graphic of the word

"IT" on the front page). One was the lengthy essay on the front page by King scholar Michael Collings about King's book *IT*; and the other was the reprinting of a personal letter from King to Collings in which King discussed the genesis of *IT*, and its influences.

Issue #19 was a major issue in the history of *Castle Rock*'s publication.

Articles:
- "*IT*: Stephen King's Comprehensive Masterpiece," by Michael R. Collings. (Piece that eventually became the first section of Collings book, *The Stephen King Phenomenon*. Very well done piece on *IT*, overwhelmingly favorable, and valuable for the insight afforded the reader.)
- "Stephen King Comments on *IT*," by Stephen King. (Lengthy "thank you" to Collings from King, reprinted in its entirety, in which King discusses the conception, writing, and editing of his magnum opus.)
- "The Situation Over Here," by Andrew Wolczyk. (A look at the publishing of King books in England.)
- "One Stormy Friday Night with Stephen King," by Doris McLelland. (A fan reads King on a stormy night.)
- "SK in Boxer Shorts? Don't Hold Your Breath." (Unattributed. King's Boston Red Sox bet with Bob Haskell of the Bangor *Daily News*. S.K. won.)
- "Stephen King on Videocassette," by Tyson Blue. (A look at the S.K. films available on tape, with reviews.)
- "Collecting King on a Beer Budget," by Amy Edwards. (Inexpensive ways of filling in your S.K. collection.)
- "Is SK Too Commercial?," by Andrew Wolczyk. (Yes and no.)
- "SK Items Dominate West Coast Book Auction," by F. Lennox Campbello (Rundown of King items at the May 24, 1986, auction run by the California Book Gallery, with prices.)
- "SK Helps Spearhead Censorship Referendum Defeat," by Christopher Spruce. (Considering the freedom to write what he wants his "reason for living," King defended the First Amendment by taking to the airwaves and newspapers of Maine to help defeat a censorship referendum which was sponsored by the Maine Christian Civic League.)
- "SK 'Lists' Set For Syndication." (Unattributed. Details on the radio syndication of King's "Lists That Matter.")

Book Reviews:
- "*Stephen King At the Movies* by Jessie Horsting." (Unattributed review. A look at the Starlog publication.)
- "*Stephen King: The Art of Darkness* by Douglas E. Winter." (Reviewed by Tyson Blue. A very positive review of the definitive critical biography of Stephen King.)

Features:
◊ "Editor's Column," by Stephanie Leonard.
◊ "Darabont: One More Time, Wayne." (Letter from Frank Darabont, the director of "The Woman in the Room," in response to Wayne Sallee's follow-up review of Darabont's film. See Issue #18.)
◊ "Another State of '*Salem's Lot*.'" (Letter from David Pettus. A look at the various '*Salem's Lot* dustcovers.)
◊ "Review: "The Mist' in 3-D Sound." (Review by Tyson Blue of the cassette adaptation of King's novella.)
◊ "Trivia Quiz (and Answers)," by Andrew Wolczyk.
◊ "The Stanley Hotel." (Photo by Lew Dakan. Gorgeous half-page black-and-white shot of the Stanley Hotel. The caption reads "The Stanley Hotel: The hotel upon which the setting of SK's *The Shining* is based.")
◊ "Classifieds."

Vol. 2, No. 8 (Issue #20) August 1986

This issue had a couple of very serious pieces, most notably the "term paper" piece by Pat Chase. This issue also contained an Index

to back issues, as well as a piece by Stephen King's daughter Naomi.

The logo was purple again, and the eight-pager had a couple of fun features as well as the serious stuff. They included the piece by Tyson Blue on the unanthologized King short stories, and also the "SK Character Poll" results.

Articles:
- "In Search of the Pets Sematary," by Terrie Bagnato. (Bagnato finds the *real* pet sematary.)
- "Why and How to Teach SK," by Bill Munster. (A teacher discusses King as curriculum.)
- "What's it like being the Daughter of SK," by Naomi King. (In this piece, we find out that King's wife Tabitha equates people who ask for her husband's autograph with leeches, and that being King's daughter has its problems as well as its perks.)
- "Popular SK Taken as Serious Literature," by Pat Chase. (Originally written as a term paper for her English lit class, in this piece Chase critiques King and compares him to Edgar Allan Poe and William Faulkner.)
- "Person, Persona," by Ken Shipley. (Shipley looks at the *two* Stephen Kings: the "regular" King, and King's "public" persona – his "brand name," so to speak.)
- "Say 'no' to the Enforcers," by Stephen King. (King again defends the First Amendment.)
- "Unanthologized Short Stories: The Unseen King II," by Tyson Blue. (Blue details the King short stories that have never been collected, and offers suggestions for a new anthology.)

Features:
◊ "Editor's Column," by Stephanie Leonard.
◊ "Index to Back Issues of *Castle Rock*." (Unattributed.)
◊ "Recent Appearances." (Unattributed. Recent in-print appearances of work by Stephen King.)
◊ "SK Character Poll Results," by Thomas Cattrysse. (Favorite character? Wolf, from *The Talisman* .)
◊ "Classifieds."

Vol. 2, No. 9 (Issue #21) September 1986

This eight-page issue was primarily a "Maximum Overdrive" issue. It had an interview with King about the making of the film, and it ran several readers' comments about the movie. The issue ran three photos—two from the movie, and one of King sitting atop the runaway steamroller. This issue also contained an interview with "Joe Bob Briggs," the alter ego of John Bloom, who is a friend of S.K.'s. In 1987, King wrote the introduction for Briggs' collection of movie "reviews," a collection called *Joe Bob Briggs Goes to the Drive-In*. The introduction was titled "This Guy is *Really* Scary!"

Articles:
- "SK Discusses Making of 'Maximum Overdrive'." (Press conference interview. Unattributed reporters. Transcript by Tyson Blue. Very lengthy interview with King obviously in a great mood, and having a lot of fun.)
- "Reiner Directs Comedy about Kids," by United Press International. (One of the first notices of the "film 'Stand By Me,' which was based on King's novella "The Body.")
- "Joe Bob Briggs Says SK is Jordy." (Interview by Velveeta Spandex (Interview with the Dallas Times *Herald* movie reviewer.)
- "The Austin Book and Paper Show," by Amy Edwards. (Another convention visit, with prices for King collectors editions.)

Features:
◊ "Draw That Toon." (Invitation for readers to submit drawings to *Castle Rock*.)
◊ "Editor's Column," by Stephanie Leonard.
◊ "A Novel Contest." (Compiled by Naomi King) (King's daughter makes up a "First line" trivia quiz.)

◊ "*Castle Rock* Readers Comment on 'Maximum Overdrive'." (Two pages of letters from readers about the movie.)

◊ "Classifieds."

◊ "Baseball Poem is by SK." (Letter detailing very rare S.K. poem.)

◊ "Not a Stephen King." (Blurb explaining that there's another Stephen King—the author of the 1979 volume of poetry called *Another Quarter Mile* .)

Vol. 2, No. 10 (Issue #22) October 1986

This was a significant issue in *CR*'s publication life. The front page (now with a bright orange logo, as well as orange ink for the headlines) blared forth a piece by Tyson Blue called "'Stand By Me': The Best King Film Ever." Blue went so far as to state – in the very first paragraph – that "...for now, ['Stand By Me' is the] blue-ribbon best film I've ever seen." The issue also ran an excerpt from Michael Collings' at-the-time work-in-progress, *The Stephen King Phenomenon* (no connection to the article of the same name by Stan Wiater in this issue), and a short story by Stanley Wiater called "The Toucher," which was awarded First Place in the "Boston Phoenix Short Story Competition," judged by S.K. ("The Toucher" is reprinted in this volume.) Good issue.

Articles:
- "'Stand By Me': The Best King Film Ever," by Tyson Blue. (Blue waxes praisingly the latest film adaptation of a King work.)
- "Stephen King and The Stars (Up There)," by J.N. Williamson. (The prolific fiction writer, self-titled weirdworker, discusses Stephen King's astrological chart. See the interview with J.N. Williamson in this volume. Also, see my feature on King's chart called "The Stars and Stephen King.")
- *The Stephen King Phenomenon*, by Stanley Wiater. (A discussion of King's impact on publishing, and the world.)
- "Obsession: The True Confessions of an SK Collector," by Glen Leon. (Glen Leon on the hunt for rare S.K. material.)

Fiction:
- "The Toucher." (A short story by Stanley Wiater.)

Book Excerpts:
- "The Bestselling Bestseller: King and the Lists," by Michael R. Collings. (Chapter from the Collings' at-the-time work-in-progress *The Stephen King Phenomenon,* which dissects King's bestseller-list appearances.)

Features:
◊ "Editor's Column," by Stephanie Leonard.

◊ "Recent Appearances." (Unattributed. S.K. newspaper/magazine articles and interviews from July 20, 1986, through August 30, 1986.

◊ "Book List," by Tyson Blue. (Blue looks at the books available about Stephen King and his work.)

◊ "*Castle Rock* Readers Comment on 'Maximum Overdrive'." (Letters.)

◊ "Classifieds."

Vol. 2, No. 11 (Issue #23) November 1986

Purple-logoed, this eight-page issue featured a front-page photo of the Derry (actually Bangor) standpipe from *IT*. There really is a standpipe in the Thomas Hills section of King's hometown, and he used it prominently in his magnum opus. This issue continued the commitment to excellence on the part of Stephanie Leonard and her crew, featuring pieces on *IT*, the World Fantasy Convention, King's television appearances, and one of King's favorite writers, Don Robertson. A very helpful feature on the back page was a directory of forty-seven book dealers who specialize in genre material.

Articles:
- "And So It Goes," by Wayne Allen Sallee. (Discussion of *IT* and other King works.)
- "In Praise of Don Robertson," by Garth Whitson. (Discussion/introduction to the work of a writer Stephen King has called "one of the best unknown publishing novelists in the United States.")
- "New King Cassettes," by Tyson Blue. (A look at the burgeoning availablity of audiotape adaptations of works by Stephen King.)
- "A 'Limited' Edition King Paperback," by Tom Draheim. (Story of a 25,000-copy first edition run of *Firestarter* – that should *not* have been a separate edition. The printer treated the major 2,000,000-copy run as a *second* edition, when usually they don't change the edition numbers.)
- "World Sci-Fi Con: A Report for *CR*," by Ken Cobb. (Good coverage of the 1986 World Sci-Fi Con in Atlanta, with listing of rare S.K. items available.)
- "Library Sets SK Auction." (Unattributed. Details on an auction in which the prizes were rare S.K. items.)

Book Reviews:
- "*IT*: A Journey into the Dark Side" (Review by Tyson Blue. (A rave for King's 1100 page magnum opus.)
- "*The Trap*: Rape as Violence, Not Passion." (Review by Flo Stanton. A look at Tabitha King's novel – a "real-life" horror story.)

Features:
◊ "Who's on First?" (Letter from Barbara Larkin. Humorous parody of Abbott & Costello's "Who's On First?" routine, centering around the title *IT*.)

◊ "Editor's Column," by Stephanie Leonard.

◊ "Monkey Business" (Letter from Kathy Curry. Letter wondering if the film "The Devil's Gift" was based on S.K.'s short story "The Monkey." It wasn't, although there were striking similarities between the two.)

◊ "Stephen King on Television." (Compiled by Dr. Barry M. Brooks. King on TV from August 18, 1980 – "Late Night with David Letterman"/*Firestarter* interview – through July 25, 1986 – "Entertainment Tonight"/"Maximum Overdrive" interview.)

◊ "Five Questions About 'Jerusalem's Lot'." (Trivia quiz.)

◊ "Five Questions About 'One for the Road'." (Trivia quiz.)

◊ "Classifieds."

◊ "Book Dealers." (Forty-seven dealers and publishers who specialize in genre – and Stephen King – material

Vol. 3, No. 1 (Issue #24)
December 1986/January 1987

What an issue! This first-ever double edition of *Castle Rock* was a twice-the-size, twice-the-price green-logoed Christmas present from Stephanie Leonard and her team for all us Stephen King devotees. In her "Editor's Column," Leonard explained that by doing a year-end double issue (sixteen pages) "it means we don't have to mail in December, which will mean that fewer copies get lost or damaged in the crush of holiday mail" [and] "that we want to find out how our readers feel about possible receiving bigger issues every other month, instead of monthly." (The suggestion didn't go over, and Leonard ended up limiting her double issues to once or twice a year. See the *Castle Rock* abstracts in this section for more info.)

The front page featured a half-page graphic of a red "X," used to trumpet the presence of a major nonfiction piece by Stephen King called "The Dreaded X." In this piece, which King says was rejected by a number of markets—everybody from *Film Comment* to *The Atlantic Monthly*—Stephen King completely revamps the movie rating system. You may not agree with his suggestions, but it's interesting to see what directing "Maximum Overdrive" did for

King's feeling about this subject.

In addition to the S.K. piece, this issue also contained poetry by Tabitha King, book reviews, analysis, and a picture of Stephen King with Stephanie Leonard (Tabitha King's sister), Christopher Spruce, Suzanne Spruce, and King's mother-in-law, Sarah W. Spruce. Considering the number of pieces in this issue by King's family members and in-laws, you could really say that this issue was truly a family affair.

Articles:
- "The Dreaded X," by Stephen King. (In a lengthy piece, King suggests changes in the movie rating system.)
- "Kings Deliver UM Lectures," by Sarah W. Spruce. (Coverage of two lectures by Mr. and Mrs. King at the University of Maine, including the reprinting of a poem by Tabitha King called "Conditional.")
- "Dean R. Koontz: An Interview," by Sheryl Weilgosh. (A talk with the prolific King contemporary – "a certified workaholic who puts in 70 to 80 hours a week at his word processor."
- "King Goes to the Beach," by Howard Wornom and Mark Freeman. (Dual coverage of King's lecture at the Virginia Beach Public Library.)
- "Finally, SK Story Filmed in Bangor," by Christopher Spruce. (Coverage of the filming of "The Hitchhiker" segment of *Creepshow II* in Bangor.)
- "*Creepshow II.*" (Unattributed. Capsule summaries of the three segments of the film, as well as the "Wraparound Story.")
- "*Running Man* Still Unmade," by Christopher Spruce. (Details of the Arnold Schwarzenegger adaptation of King's Bachman novel.)
- "News From Holland," by Bart van Miert. (Piece about King's popularity in Holland, with an excerpt from a "Stephen King Newspaper" published there.)
- "One for the Road." (Unattributed. Short blurb detailing the publication of a new anthology called *Strange Maine*, containing the S.K. piece "One for the Road," a story that was originally published in *Maine* magazine in 1977, and in *Night Shift* a year later.
- "Two Versions of *The Shining*," by Ian Harris. (Lengthy piece on the differences between King's novel and Kubrick's film.)

Book Reviews:
- "*Stephen King At the Movies* by Jessie Horsting." (Reviewed by Tyson Blue.)
- "*Talisman* Limited Review." (Reviewed by Tyson Blue. Praise for the Donald Grant limited edition of King and Straub's *The Talisman*.)

Features:
◊ "Editor's Column," by Stephanie Leonard.
◊ "More on Stars." (Letter from Linda M. Seekins. Seekins comments on J.N. Williamson's astrology piece from Issue #22.)
◊ "Castle Rock Readers' Poll." (The newsletter polls its readers with questions such as "What would you like to see more of/less of in *Castle Rock*?," and "Do you ever pass your copy on to other people, or do you keep your copies on file?"
◊ "Letters."
◊ "Stephen King on TV and Radio (New Listings)." (Compiled by Dr. Barry Brooks. A continuation of Brooks' cataloguing of S.K.'s media appearances, this time running from July 20, 1986 – "The Ed Busch Talk Show" – through August 24, 1986 – WXCL/WKQA "The Source.")
◊ "Classifieds."
◊ "Book Dealers." (Two more dealers specializing in SK material.)

CASTLE ROCK
1987

Vol. 3, No. 2 (Issue #25) February 1987

This eight-page issue holds a special place in my heart for the simple reason that Stephanie Leonard mentioned me by name for the first time in her "Editor's Column" in this month's issue. I had sent her some S.K. jokes that I had heard on "Late Night with David Letterman," and she used them in a section of her column that looked at recent media appearances of Stephen King's name. Here's the excerpt:

> And this one from "Late Night with David Letterman" from guest Drake Sather: "My dad raised us by the book. Unfortunately, the book was *The Shining*." Also from an earlier Letterman show (*Castle Rock* reader Stephen J. Spignesi, who sent us these two jokes must be a Letterman fan!): "I went to get a book. You know Stephen King? There's a book now called *IT*. It's called *IT*. Is that fair? Are people gonna wake up now and say, 'Honey, please, I think there's a pronoun in the basement'!"

The rest of this issue was terrific. There was a piece about finding the gazebo from the "Dead Zone" film, two nonfiction pieces by Stephen King, as well as an S.K. paperback bibliography. The logo was red, and the price was still one-twenty-five.

Articles:
- "Finding the Dead Zone," by Sheryl and Richard Weilgosh. (Two Ontarians find the gazebo – and other shooting locales – used in David Cronenberg's film.)
- "A Postscript to 'Overdrive'," by Stephen King. (King continues the ratings discussion he began in "The Dreaded X" in Issue #24.)
- "*The Dark Tower II: The Drawing of the Three*," by Donald M. Grant. (Grant details the progress of the publication of the second *Dark Tower* book.)
- "SK Paperback Bibliography Compiled," by Wayne Rhodes. (Detailed bibliography of the many and varied paperback incarnations of King's books.)
- "Everything Old Is New Again at Dodge," by Debbie Seaman. (Article about a Dodge TV commercial that used elements from *Christine* and *Cujo*.)
- "Why I Wrote *The Eyes of the Dragon*," by Stephen King. (The original uncut version of the flap copy King wrote for *Dragon*. This piece greatly expands the four paragraphs Viking ended up using for the jacket copy.)
- "'Maximum Overdrive' Video Reviewed," by Tyson Blue. (A look at the cassette release of King's directorial debut.)
- "Robertson Novel." (Unattributed. Blurb about Stephen King's Philtrum Press publication of Don Robertson's *The Ideal, Genuine Man*. "This book is going to blow you out of your seat.")

Fiction:
- "The Exit" – An Homage to Stephen King—Castle Rock Exit 5 Miles," by Dan P. McMillen. (A "Castle Rock" short story.)

Book Reviews:
- "*The Eyes of the Dragon*, by Stephen King." (Reviewed by Tyson Blue.)

Features:
◊ "Editor's Column," by Stephanie Leonard.
◊ "The gazebo from the movie, 'The Dead Zone'." (Photo by Weilgosh.)
◊ "Find the Missing Word," by Greg Holmes. (SK word search puzzle)
◊ "*Pet Sematary* Trivia," by Greg Holmes.
◊ "*Thinner* Trivia," by Greg Holmes.

◊ "Illustrations from *Eyes of the Dragon.*" (Four sketches by David Palladini.)
◊ "Letters."
◊ "Classifieds."

Vol. 3, No. 3 (Issue #26) March 1987

This was a nice, full, green-logoed twelve- page issue that featured a black-and-white photo of Stephen King and George Romero on the front page. There were loads of good articles this month, including the excerpt from Paul Gagne's *The Zombies That Ate Pittsburgh: The Films of George A. Romero,* and Tyson Blue's interview with Deborah Brodie, the editor of *The Eyes of the Dragon.* Once again, Stephanie Leonard used a "David Letterman" joke that I had sent to her in her "Editor's Column." This time the joke came from David Letterman himself rather than from a guest comic, and here's the excerpt:

> Here's another joke from "Late Night with David Letterman," again sent in by Stephen Spignesi. During a segment in which Letterman reviews books, he had this comment: 'What do we have here? Oh, this is a good one. A piece of fiction. Master of horror Stephen King gets right to the point with his latest book. It's entitled *Wouldn't This Make A Great Movie?* A work of fiction so frightening, you can practically hear the cashier say 'That'll be six dollars, please.'

Over all, another quality issue.

Articles:
• "Readers Poll Results," by Stephanie Leonard. (Answers to the questions posed in Issue #24.)
• "Who Knows What Lurks on Your Bookshelves; It Could be Valuable," by Julie Penn. (A look at King collectibles, with an overview of other "investment" authors and the entire book collecting field.)
• "And Where He Stops, Nobody Knows," by Julie Knox. (A discussion of Stephen King's prolific output.)
• "Editing Eyes: An Interview with Deborah Brodie," by Tyson Blue. (Terrific talk with the Viking editor who helped shape the version of *Eyes of the Dragon* that the reading public finally saw. Good look at just what goes on during the editorial process. Two of David Palladini's illustrations for *Eyes* accompany the interview.)
• "Stephen King Items *Very* Collectible," by F. Lennox Campbello. (Another piece that looks at the boom in the market for King collectibles.)
• "The Horror, The Horror," by Stanley Wiater. (Insightful reviews of six current books significant to the horror genre, including King's *IT,* the *Penguin Encyclopedia of Horror and the Supernatural,* Clive Barker's *The Inhuman Condition,* and books by Charles L. Grant and Whitley Strieber. See the interview with Stan Wiater in this volume.)
• "Robertson Novel." (Unattributed. Another blurb about Stephen King's Philtrum Press publication of Don Robertson's *The Ideal, Genuine Man.*)
• "*The Drawing of the Three.* " (Unattributed. Details on the second volume of King's *Dark Tower* series.)
• "For Horror Master Stephen King 'Waiting is the Hardest Part'," by Liz Soloway. (Coverage of King's appearance at a YMCA fundraiser, and a discussion of the fact that he rarely experiences writer's block.)
Book Excerpts:
• "King and Romero: The Filming of *Creepshow,*" by Paul R. Gagne. (Excerpt from Gagne's book *The Zombies That Ate Pittsburgh: The Films of George A. Romero.)*

Features:
◊ "Editor's Column," by Stephanie Leonard.
◊ "SK Trivia Quiz." (Contributed by Julie Knox.)
◊ "Another Bookseller." (Letter from R. Jeff Wood. (Five more dealers who specialize in genre and SK material.)
◊ "Letters."
◊ "Index to Back Issues of *Castle Rock.*" (Unattributed. Overview of each issue from August 1985 through February 1987.)
◊ "Classifieds."

Vol. 3, Nos. 4 & 5 (Issue #27) April/May 1987

This may eventually rank as the single best issue *Castle Rock* ever published.

This sixteen-page issue offered excerpts from two of the finest books ever published. That's right. I said "Two of the finest books ever published." And I'm not just talking about genre publications, either. The two books excerpted here rank as classics of American literature, and their genre is only a secondary consideration.

The first book excerpted was the long-awaited second volume of Stephen King's amazing *Dark Tower* series. This second volume, *The Drawing of the Three,* picks up hours after the first volume, *The Gunslinger,* ends. *Castle Rock* ran the entire Prologue and first chapter of the book, along with three of Phil Hale's somewhat bizarre and almost-surrealistic illustrations. This "teaser" could only whet the appetite for the entire novel, and in its final form, the book was well worth the wait...and the lofty expectations.

The second excerpt in this issue was from an absolutely incredible novel by the American naturalist Don Robertson. King is on record as acknowledging that Robertson was one of the three cardinal influences on his writing.

The Robertson novel excerpted, *The Ideal, Genuine Man,* is a stark, almost stream-of-consciousness novel of contemporary American values and mores, and Robertson creates a landscape at once immediately recognizable, but at the same time, showing us a dark and bizarre America many of us wish we didn't have to acknowledge. In the Forenote to the novel (not excerpted in *Castle Rock,* and available only in the published novel) Stephen King says "Most of you who've never read Robertson before...may never again be entirely satisfied with a book purporting to depict 'real' American life. Win, lose, or draw, you have never read anything quite like the novel which follows. Never. *Never.*"

King was right. *The Ideal, Genuine Man* is more than a book: It is an experience unlike anything you've ever read before. It is to Stephen King's credit that he published Robertson, and to Stephanie Leonard's that she excerpted him in this month's issue.

Also in this issue was the second part of Paul Gagne's *The Zombies That Ate Pittsburgh* excerpt, and a review of *Misery.* Good issue – both for SK fans, and people who love great books.

Articles:
• "*Drawing of 3* Artist." (Unattributed. Profile of Phil Hale, the twenty-two-year-old Massachusetts artists who did the artwork for King's *The Drawing of the Three.*)
• "In Praise of Horror—and Those Who Frighten Us," by Lynn Berk. (Article about the people who read—and love—horror fiction.)
• "Mystification in King," by Chris Thomson. (Piece that details mistakes of fact in King's fiction.)
• "Change of Hobbit Celebrates Year Fifteen," by Suzanne Bidinger. (Article about the speculative fiction Los Angeles bookstore's anniversary. King mentioned Change of Hobbit in *Danse Macabre.* The reference is on Page 382 of the revised paperback edition.)
Fiction:
• "'Prologue: The Sailor' and 'The Door'," by Stephen King. (The

Prologue and the first chapter from King's second *Dark Tower* book, *The Drawing of the Three*.)
- *"The Ideal, Genuine Man,* by Don Robertson." (The first chaper from Robertson's novel.)

Book Reviews:
- "*Misery*...No Way!" (A Review by Patricia Hagan. Glowing review of King's story of Annie Wilkes and Paul Sheldon.)

Book Excerpts:
- "*The Zombies That Ate Pittsburgh* " (Part II), by Paul R. Gagne. (Second excerpt from Gagne's book *The Zombies That Ate Pittsburgh: The Films of George A. Romero*.)

Features:
- ◊ "Editor's Column," by Stephanie Leonard.
- ◊ "Correspondence Column." (Stephen King pen pals.)
- ◊ "Congratulatory Note." (Lloyd Gola. Illustrated postcard congratulating King for *IT*.)
- ◊ "Letters."
- ◊ "Wordy Gurdy," by Lela Marie De La Garza. (Rhyming Stephen King word game.)

Vol. 3, No. 6 (Issue #28) June 1987

This was a twelve-page, purple-logoed issue that featured pieces on "Creepshow 2"; commentary by Darrell Schweitzer, as well as a feature on collecting movie posters, and coverage of the California International Bookfair.

We were also subjected in this issue to Part 2 of Chris Thomson's "Mystification in SK." I feel perfectly comfortable in saying that I did not enjoy this piece. In fact, I hated it. Even though Thomson offers a disclaimer wherein he explains that he's not detailing all these mistakes to be critical, I still didn't like the relentless nitpicking and fault-finding. Thomson calls this error elucidation "a list of incidents and citations which may provoke thought," but all it really amounts to is the billboarding of errors in continuity, mistakes in the text, and other blunders in King's writings that somehow got through to the final version. So what. Any number can play this game. I know, for example, that there are going to be mistakes in this book (gasp!), no matter how much of an attempt I make to keep them out. And here's a flash for you, Chris: discrepancy isn't spelled "discrepency." Just thought it was vitally important (?) for you to know.

Articles:
- "'Creepshow 2': Somewhere Between a 5 and a 9," by Tim Cotton. (Review of the film.)
- "About the Filmmakers: Some 'Creepshow 2' Notes." (Uncredited. Details on the people responsible for the film.)
- "Will Stephen King's Work Survive?" (Commentary by Darrell Schweitzer. Essay examining the possibilities of King still being read a century from now.)
- "The Art of Movie Poster Collecting," by Stephanie Leonard. (Excellent article about poster collecting, slanted towards the Stephen King collector.)
- "Goden on Posters," by Craig Goden. (Book dealer Goden gives details on how to identify first editions.)
- "Virginia Beach Lecture Available," by Tyson Blue. (Article about a King lecture available on videotape through interlibrary loan. This information and offer was withdrawn later. As of now, the tape is no longer available.)
- "Video Review," by Tim Foster. (A review of the videotape of "Stand By Me.")
- "King Discusses his Creepy Craft," by Tiffany Vail. (Coverage of a lecture by King at Boston University originally published in the Boston University *Daily Free Press*.)
- "Flood Relief Screening." (Uncredited. Article about a charity screening of "Creepshow 2" in Bangor.)
- "SK Delivers UM Commencement Address." (Uncredited. Coverage of King's address to the University of Maine's 169th graduating class.)
- "Nearly All of SK's Books Under One Roof: The 20th Annual California International Bookfair," by F. Lennox Campbello. (Coverage of the Bookfair, with a listing of some of the items available, with prices.)
- "Mystification in SK Continued or Points to Ponder in King: Part II," by Chris Thomson.
- "The Young and the Restless: Trendy and Sharp Focus on SK," by Trendy Sharp. (Fan letter from a sixteen-year-old SK devotee.)

Book Reviews:
- "*The Eyes of the Dragon* : New King, Old King." (Review by Mark Freeman. Positive review of King's fable, with insightful examination of the recurring character, Flagg.)
- "New Books of Interest." (Uncredited. Capsule blurbs on upcoming S.K.-related books, including *Bare Bones* and *The Drawing of the Three*.)
- "Two Collings' Books on SK Reviewed." (Reviews by Tyson Blue. He reviews *The Stephen King Phenomenon* and *The Annotated Guide to Stephen King*.)

Features:
- ◊ "Editor's Column," by Stephanie Leonard. (Longer-than-usual column containing many blurbs of S.K. information.)
- ◊ "Crock," by Bill Rechin and Don Wilder. (Cartoon. Strip mentioning S.K.)
- ◊ "Correspondence Column." (S.K. pen pals.)
- ◊ "John Cafferty and the Beaver Brown Band." (Photo. Details on a Beaver Brown concert introduced by Stephen King and sponsored by WZON.)
- ◊ "A Verse for *IT*—"The Man Who Read King." (Poem by John Pike.)
- ◊ "'Creepshow 2' Photos." (Laurel Entertainment. Three stills from the film.)
- ◊ "Letters."
- ◊ "Classifieds."

Vol. 3, No. 7 (Issue #29) July 1987

This was an eight-page, blue-logoed summer issue that featured a gorgeous high contrast photograph of King's home on the front page. The photograph—taken by Dr. Charles Civiello, Jr. of Bangor—highlighted one of the three-headed wrought iron "things" that perch atop the fence.

Tyson Blue reviewed *The Drawing of the Three*, Stephen King expounded on the Red Sox, and readers were treated to a reproduction of a page of a promotional note pad distributed as a tie-in with the release of *Misery*, showing a silhouetted Annie Wilkes, ax and all, ready to party.

The price was still a dollar-twenty-five.

Articles:
- "The Growing Optimism of Stephen King: Bachman's Pessimism Gets Thinner," by Michael Pepper. (Pepper examines King's pseudononymous titles as essentially a body of work espousing "a bitter view of the world.")
- "On Becoming a Stephen King Fan," by Karen L. Jackson. (Essay by a woman who works with Tabitha King's mother, and who came late to an appreciation of S.K.'s work.)
- "Essays Examine SK's Contributions to Academics," by Kelly Rose. (First details on a new critical study of King called *Journey Into Horror: Stephen King's World*.)
- "The Cat Gets Around," by Glen Leon. (The publishing history of King's short story "The Cat from Hell.")
- "Objects In This Mirror are Closer Than They Appear," by Gerry Whetter. (Personal essay in which Whetter responds to the film "Stand By Me.")

- "A look at the Red Sox on the edge of '87," by Stephen King. (King talks baseball.)
- "Rounding Up Books on King," by Tyson Blue. (Survey of the books about King already on the market, as well as those to come.)

Book Reviews:

- "*The Dark Tower II: The Drawing of the Three,* by Stephen King." (Review by Tyson Blue.)
- "New Books of Interest." (Uncredited. Same piece as in Issue #28, except it now adds details on *Night Visions 5.*)

Features:

- ◊ "Stephen King's House." (Photo by Dr. Charles Civiello, Jr.)
- ◊ "Editor's Column," by Stephanie Leonard.
- ◊ "Dealer Alleges Misquote." (Letter from Peter Stern. Letter blasting F. Lennox Campello for his allegedly fabricated conversation with Stern.)
- ◊ "*Misery* Note Pad." (Graphic. Reproduction of S.K. promotional item.)
- ◊ "Correspondence Column."
- ◊ "All of Us Would-Be Writers, #1: Characterization in the Work of Stephen King." (Quiz by Julie Knox.)
- ◊ "Classifieds."

Vol. 3, No. 8 (Issue #30)   August 1987

This issue was notable for a very special reason: It featured a lengthy Page 1 article written by King's wife Tabitha called "Co-Miser-A-Ting With Stephen King." In this insightful essay, Tabitha examines the relationship between a writer and his readers, and specifically, the relationship between Stephen King and his fans. She offers a rarely-glimpsed look into the private lives of the Kings, and also gives the reader detailed analysis of King's writing. She focuses on the "why" of King's fiction, examining the real-life incidents that acted as catalysts for much of his writing. She also makes it clear that Paul Sheldon is *not* Stephen King, just as Annie Wilkes is not the personification of the average Stephen King fan.

"Co-Miser-A-Ting With Stephen King" is an excellent companion piece to *Misery,* as well as to the rest of Stephen and Tabitha King's work.

This eight-page issue had a red logo and, in addition to Tabitha King's article, Page 1 featured a reproduction of the cover of the British edition of *Misery.* (Another particularly gratifying item in this issue was a very negative letter from *CR* reader Scott Barlow (!) called "Who Cares?," commenting on Chris Thomson's two-part article, "Mystification in King.")

Articles:

- "Co-Miser-A-Ting With Stephen King," by Tabitha King. (See my review above.)
- "Stephen King's No. 1 Fans," by David Streitfeld. (Article about King fandom, including the Mark Chapman story.)
- "Another Look at 'Creepshow 2'," by Jodi Strissel. (Generally negative review of the film.)
- "New King Book Set," by Tim Foster. (News on the then work-in-progress *The Unseen King* by Tyson Blue.)
- "More on Flagg/Gunslinger Connection," by Mark Freeman. (Follow-up to Freeman's June 1987 *CR* article detailing links between *Eyes* and the *Dark Tower* books.)
- "The World of Horror: Writing Up Bad Dreams," by Dory L. Wethington. (Horror writing as psychotherapy.)
- "A Book on Stephen King in the Netherlands," by Eddy C. Bertin. (Details on a collection of essays on King called *The Stephen King Book: The Horror Worlds of Stephen King* to be published in the Netherlands.)

Book Reviews:

- "*Masques II* Edited by J.N. Williamson." (Review by Tyson Blue. Positive review of the collection which includes King's short story "Popsy.")

Features:

- ◊ "Editor's Column," by Stephanie Leonard. (Fairly short column this month that started off with a reaffirmation of the decision to cease publication in December 1988.)
- ◊ "Correspondence Column." (King pen pals.)
- ◊ "Letters."

Notable Advertisements: This issue contained two particularly significant ads, and I felt they were worth mentioning:

- ◊ On Page 3 was a display ad with the simple headline "For Sale." The ad was run by none other than Burton Hatlen, King's teacher and the person to whom "The Long Walk" was dedicated. Hatlen was selling thirty-two very important pieces of rare King material. They were:

  1. Ten copies of "Moth." (See the section on King's poetry in this volume.)
  2. Seven copies of *Onan.* (Containing "The Blue Air Compressor.")
  3. Ten copies of *Contraband 1.*
  4. Three copies of *Marshroots* 3:1 (misprinted in this ad as "*Marshrooms*"). (Containing "It Grows On You.")
  5. Two copies of *The Maine Review* 1:2. (Containing "The Revenge of Lardass Hogan."

  Hatlen was offering individual items, sets, or the whole collection for sale, and was selling by sealed bid.

- ◊ Another notable ad was on Page 7. This was a half-page display ad placed by a company called Collector's Choice (368 Armstrong Avenue, Laurel, MD 20707; 1-301-725-0887). This company was offering Stephen King First Editions, including, *Carrie, The Stand,* the Mysterious Press edition of *Cujo,* the Scream Press limited, signed *Skeleton Crew,* and Volume 5 of *Whispers.* In addition to King books, they also had for sale King magazine appearances, including—for the ridiculously low price of thirty-five dollars—all five of the *Magazine of Fantasy and Science Fiction* appearances of *Dark Tower.* People are always asking me where they can get some of this rare Stephen King material. Obviously it's out there: all you've got to do is look for it.

Vol. 3, No. 9 (Issue #31)   September 1987

Another fine effort from the *Castle Rock* crew. The more I studied this newsletter, the more impressed I was with its consistency, focus, and devotion to all things S.K. *Castle Rock* was more than a newsletter: It could justifiably be called a Stephen King *newspaper.* The breadth of its scope was far superior to the ordinary basement-produced fanzine. The production values were professional, the look of the paper was clean, and the material spanned the Stephen Kingdom – every month.

This issue featured a Page 1 article by Stephanie Leonard on King's house, called "SK's House is a Tourist Hot Spot." She gave King's home address in the piece, and it was accompanied by a photo of a Stephen King fan taking a picture of the house. The *Castle Rock* photo by Jim Leonard was taken from inside the fabled bats and spiders fence and gate.

Purple-logoed, this issue was eight pages, and featured a half-page ad on the back page from Barry Levin.

Articles:

- "SK's House is a Tourist Hot Spot," by Stephanie Leonard. (Article about King's Bangor mansion, and the fans who regularly make the pilgrimage.)
- "Some Notes on *IT,*" by Faye Ringel. (Insightful analysis of King's magnum opus.)
- "A *King*-size Remedy that Worked!," by David M. Lowell. (The writer details how his involvement with King helped alleviate his anxiety over having to have four wisdom teeth out.)
- "King Class A Small Success," by Karl D. Kober. (Details on a

class taught by the writer called "The Modern Master of Horror.")

- "*IT* in the Netherlands, or: The Rape of Stephen King," by Eddy C. Bertin. (Article examining the Dutch edition of *IT*, which the writer refers to as "an *abortion* of what was a marvelous novel." The Dutch edition brutally eliminated almost half of King's text, leaving a novel the writer says reads like "a working draft, the synopsis for a novel to be written.")

Book Reviews:

- "Books on SK Films Similar," by Stephanie Leonard. (Reviews of *Stephen King Goes To Hollywood* and *Stephen King At the Movies.*)
- "*The Eyes of the Dragon,* by Stephen King." (Review by Darrell Schweitzer. Positive review of King's fairy tale.)

Features:

- ◊ "King's House." (Photo by Jim Leonard.)
- ◊ "Editor's Column," by Stephanie Leonard.
- ◊ "Castle Rock, Maine: Just the Facts" (Trivia quiz by Julie Knox.)
- ◊ "Letters."
- ◊ "Classifieds."
- ◊ "Sinister Synonyms and Creepy Cliches: A Puzzle," by J.N. Williamson and David Taylor.
- ◊ "Correspondence Column."

Notable Advertisements:

- ◊ Half-page ad run by Barry L. Levin (2265 Westwood Boulevard, No. 669, Los Angeles, CA, 90064; 213-474-5611). This ad offered some exceptionally rare King material (at some very expensive prices). Among the items offered for sale were an out-of-series Chapter One of *The Plant* for $500, and a double-lettered signed first edition of *The Dark Tower: The Gunslinger* (supposedly limited to a printing of somewhere between thirty-five and fifty-two copies) for $2,200.

Vol. 3, No. 10 (Issue #32) October 1987

I guess you could call this a "Rock and Roll Issue," because the Page 1 story was entitled "Rocking On In SK's Rock and Roll Zone" —a lengthy story about King's involvement with his very own Bangor AM radio station, WZON, emphasizing that the station was more than just "another entry in SK's investment portfolio."

Also on Page 1 was a nonfiction piece by Stephen King called "Entering the Rock Zone, Or, How I Happened to Marry a Rock Station from Outer Space."

Articles:

- "Rocking On In SK's Rock and Roll Zone," by Hank Cheever Jr. (Informative piece on King's station WZON. See above.)
- "Entering the Rock Zone, Or, How I Happened to Marry a Rock Station from Outer Space," by Stephen King (A terrific piece about AM radio, rock and roll, and growing old, as evidenced by the following excerpt:

"Guy walked up to me on the street the other day, maybe forty. 'I like your station,' he said shyly. 'The song about the outlaw [I'm pretty sure he meant "Gunslinger Man," by The Long Ryders] is great. It reminds me of Creedence.' He looked wistful and rubbed the top of his head. There was a lot of skin up there to rub. 'When Creedence was playing, I had a lot more hair,' he said.

'Well, are you still rockin'?' I asked.

'Yeah,' he said.

'Then I guess it doesn't matter,' I said. 'So's Fogerty. So am I. *You* keep rockin' and *I'll* keep rockin'.'

'Good deal,' he said.

And for me, that's just what the Rock Zone has been: a damn good deal."

The magic touch – that's what Stephen King has got. Let's all hope he never loses it.)

- "*Misery* On Stage?" by Ian Harris. (Piece expressing the author's opinion that *Misery* is really King's single most adaptable work for the stage. Harris mentions the rumor of the musical version of *Carrie*. "Carrie" was made, and closed the first week as "The Biggest All-Time Flop Ever." (*Time* magazine, May 30, 1988.) See the feature on the "Carrie" musical in this book.)
- "Sorry, Right Number," by Tyson Blue. (Article about the upcoming "Tales from the Darkside" episode written by King called "Sorry, Right Number." See my feature on this "Darkside" episode in this volume.)
- "Update on SK Bibliography," by Wayne Rhodes. (Update to the author's original bibliography in the February 1987 issue.)
- "SK Contributes to Baseball Book." (Uncredited. Information on the forthcoming *The Red Sox Reader: 30 Years of Musings on Baseball's Most Amusing Team,* featuring a contribution by Stephen King.)

Book Reviews:

- "Back in the 60's Again." (A review of *Do You Believe in Magic? The Second Coming of the 60s Generation,* by Annie Gottlieb (Reviewed by Sarah Spruce. Review focusing on King's remarks in the book.)
- "The Ideal, Genuine Novel." (A review of *The Ideal, Genuine Man* by Don Robertson (Favorable review by Tyson Blue of Robertson's brilliant novel.)
- "*The New Adventures of Sherlock Holmes,* edited by Martin Harry Greenberg and Carol-Lynn Rossel Waugh." (Reviewed by Mark Graham. Review of the book containing the Stephen King short story "The Doctor's Case.")

Features:

- ◊ "Editor's Column," by Stephanie Leonard.
- ◊ "The Quigmans." (Cartoon.)
- ◊ "Letters."
- ◊ "WZON photos." (Photos by Christopher Spruce.)
- ◊ "Mrs. Todd's Newest Shortcut: AN SK Word-find Game," by Lela Marie de la Garza (Short story containing twenty-eight titles from S.K.'s works.)
- ◊ "Classifieds."

Vol. 3, No. 11 (Issue #33) November 1987

This purple-logoed, eight-page issue featured two very notable Page 1 pieces. Three-quarters of the page was devoted to a lengthy review of *The Tommyknockers* called "Stephen King, Sci-Fi, and *The Tommyknockers*" by the King scholar Michael R. Collings. Collings goes into great detail examining the references to other King works present in the book, as well as placing King's novel within the science fiction genre.

The other notable Page 1 article was a piece called "The Triple Whammy," by Stephen King. This article was written in 1984 for the New York *Times,* and reprinted here to commemorate something that both years had in common: Each year contained three Friday the 13ths.

Other interesting pieces this month included a lengthy article by Mark Graham called "The Automobile Motif: Stephen King's Most Frequent Villain," as well as photos from "Maximum Overdrive" and "Creepshow 2."

Articles:

- "The Triple Whammy," by Stephen King. (King talks about triskaidekaphobia.)
- "The Automobile Motif: Stephen King's Most Frequent Villain," by Mark Graham. (Fun and informative piece detailing how King uses the car as a villain in his works.)
- "A Few Thoughts on Why SK Should Review His Christmas Mailing List," by F. Lennox Campello. (Campello asserts that

King should keep track of which copies of *The Plant* end up being sold, and then remove the recipient of those copies from his Christmas mailing list. He also makes a thinly veiled plea to be one of the lucky ones included on King's list. I guess he wouldn't sell his.)

- *"IT* an ABC Mini-Series—I Shudder at the Thought," by Barry Hoffman. (Thoughts upon the then-dead ABC-TV miniseries adaptation of King's best (in this writer's opinion) novel.)
- "Two Fun Items." (Uncredited. Blurb about two books with S.K. interest available through Craig Goden's Time Tunnel.)

Book Reviews:
- "Stephen King, Sci-Fi, and The *Tommyknockers.*" (Review of *The Tommyknockers,* by Stephen King. Excellent review by Michael R. Collings that also teaches us a lot about science fiction, King's influences, and the chameleon nature of the horror genre.)
- *"Splatter*: A Cautionary Tale by Douglas E. Winter." (Review by Tyson Blue. Review of the Footsteps Press edition of Winter's avant garde short story.)

Features:
- ◊ "Editor's Column," by Stephanie Leonard.
- ◊ "Letters."
- ◊ "Correspondence Column."
- ◊ "Classifieds."

Vols. 3-4, Nos. 12-1 (Issue #34)
December 1987/January 1988

This was a terrific sixteen-page double issue with a green *Castle Rock* logo. It included an interview with none other than Tabitha King, a lengthy excerpt from Underwood-Miller's forthcoming *Under Cover of Darkness,* and a very detailed analysis of *The Drawing of the Three* focusing on King's use of the Tarot and its symbolism.

The most significant piece in the newsletter, however, was the aforementioned book excerpt called "Fear and the Future: King as a Science Fiction Writer." This amazing essay was written by King scholar Darrell Schweitzer, and covered King's use of the science fiction genre, emphasizing that with a slightly different interprative stance, King could very easily be typed as a sci-fi writer.

This issue also reprinted a piece that originally ran in Connecticut's *Hartford Courant* called "King's Other Publisher Well-Kept Collector's Secret." This article by Garrett Condon was, of course, about Donald M. Grant, Publisher.

Articles:
- "Stephen King Picks a Winner!" (Uncredited. Article about a short story contest judged by Stephen King. The prizewinning story was called "Tabitha," and was written by Sloan Harper.)
- "The King/Roland Quest," by Estelle Ruiz (Excellent, literate analysis of King's use of the Tarot and its symbolism in *The Drawing of the Three.* Very informative, this essay teaches as well as interprets King's novel, and one comes away from it a little better prepared to accept and understand what Ruiz calls "the instinctive understanding of symbolism that exists deep in our subconscious." This piece just re-emphasizes what S.K. fans and students have known all along: King is a very intelligent, very sensitive writer who calls upon a myriad pool of influences when he writes.)
- "Tabitha King: Resisting the Star-Maker Machinery." (Interview by Rodney Labbe. An in-depth twenty-five question interview with Mrs. King, conducted by the editor of *Ubris,* the University of Maine student literary magazine, which once published both Stephen King and then-Tabitha Spruce. Quite a bit of the interview focuses on Tabitha King's work, but she also offers some memorable remarks about her husband—and her opinions on some of his own thoughts about writing and the

creative act. To wit: "Steve used to say he'd commit suicide if he couldn't write, which has always pissed me off. I'd tell him if he pulled an Ernest Hemingway on me, I'd kick his body into the street and dance on it!" Fascinating interview that hopefully will prompt S.K. fans to also read the "other King.")
- "King's Other Publisher Well-Kept Collector's Secret," by Garret Condon. (Article about Donald M. Grant, Publisher, which understandably focuses on the *Dark Tower* series.)
- "To this Dedicated Fan, King is a Prince," by Lori Montgomery. (Article about fifty-two-year-old Stephen King fan and collector Lois White, with a photo of White standing in front of her King collection.)
- "Different Seasons II—A Look Back at the Five-Book Year," by Tyson Blue. (Article about King's five-book year, 1987, which saw publication of *IT, The Eyes of the Dragon, Misery, The Drawing of the Three,* and *The Tommyknockers.*)

Fiction:
- "We've Been Expecting You," by Ken Rickert. (A short story "based on characters and situations created by Stephen King." Fun piece.)

Book Excerpts:
- "Fear and the Future: King as a Science Fiction Writer," by Darrel Schweitzer. (An excerpt from a forthcoming Underwood-Miller book called *Under Cover of Darkness.*)

Features:
- ◊ Near North Graphics greeting card graphic. (Annie Wilkes "Get Well Soon" card.)
- ◊ "Editor's Column," by Stephanie Leonard.
- ◊ "Letters."
- ◊ *"Drawing of the Three.* " (Illustration by Phil Hale.)
- ◊ Reproductions of *Roadwork* and *Rage* original paperback covers.
- ◊ "Owen King Becomes GI Joe?" (Feature about King's son Owen, who created a GI Joe character for Hasbro called "Crystal Ball." Hasbro then also created an "Owen King" Joe code name as well.)
- ◊ "The Queen's Pavilion." (Illustration by Thomas Canty for the Donald Grant edition of *The Talisman.*)
- ◊ "Back Issues of *Castle Rock.*" (Listing and order form.)
- ◊ "Can You Hack it on the Skeleton Crew?" (Stephen King crossword puzzle by David Taylor and J.N. Williamson.)
- ◊ Ads. (Reproductions of an ad for classifieds that ran in the Roseville, California, *Press-Tribune* that featured a "Cujo" dog dish, and the ad for the British edition of *The Tommyknockers.*)
- ◊ "Classifieds."
- ◊ *"Drawing of the Three* Last Call." (Display ad placed by Donald Grant.)

CASTLE ROCK
1988

Vol. 4, No. 2 (Issue #35) February 1988

The first official single edition of the final year of *Castle Rock*'s "Stephanie Leonard Years" devoted a great deal of space to what was then the biggest Stephen King news: the release of the film version of Richard Bachman's *The Running Man.*

The front page featured two reviews of the film, one by Michael Collings, and one by Darrell Schweitzer. Collings' review was called "Not a Bad Film," and Schweitzer's, "'The Running Man' is Fundamentally Dishonest."

The reviews were accompanied by a still of Arnold Schwarzenegger, and the combined review feature was entitled "'The Running Man' and Stephen King."

Other notable features included a lengthy interview with Clive Barker, and a very large "Letters" section, most of which concerned the film.

The logo of this eight-pager was in red. There were now only ten months left for the original incarnation of *Castle Rock*.

Articles:
- "'The Running Man' and Stephen King." (Two reviews of the film by Michael Collings and Darrell Schweitzer. Collings was called "Not a Bad Film," and Schweitzer's, "'The Running Man' is Fundamentally Dishonest.")
- "Having A Wonderful Time...," by Dory L. Wethington. (Humorous speculation on how King might spend his "retirement.")
- "*Carrie* as a Musical," by Tim Foster (More on the shortlived Broadway version of King's debut novel.)
- "Interview: Meet Clive Barker." (Interview by Sheryl Weilgosh with Barker (includes photo) conducted during a book signing.)
- "'Running Man' Fun for Arnie," by Tyson Blue. (Generally favorable review of the film.)
- "Cedar Falls Students Tell Why They Like Stephen King," by Jackie Young, Don Haugh, and Jamie Dietsch. (Three essays by S.K. fans from Cedar Falls (Iowa) High School.)
- "Grant Sets *Prime Evil*." (Uncredited. Details on the anthology containing King's story "The Night Flyer.")

Book Reviews:
- "*The Dark Descent*, David G. Hartwell, editor." (Review by Tyson Blue. Details on what is probably the single best horror anthology of the past decade.)

Features:
- ◊ "Editor's Column," by Stephanie Leonard.
- ◊ "Correspondence Column."
- ◊ "Letters." (Lengthy section headlined "More Comment on 'The Running Man'.")
- ◊ "Back Issues of *Castle Rock*." (Back issue order form.)
- ◊ "Stephen King's Women in Cinema," by Flo Stanton. (Matching quiz based on the women who have played King characters in films.)
- ◊ "Classifieds."

Vol. 4, No. 3 (Issue #36) March 1988

This issue featured a green logo and headline ink, and the front page was taken up by two pieces: One, an essay called "Observations from the Terminator" by Tyson Blue; and the other a reply from Stephen King to criticism he's received for his "treatment" of blacks in his fiction. The Blue piece was subtitled "The Dark Side of Fandom," and was a fair and reasoned look at what Blue called "The Terminator": that line separating so-called "normal" fans from those of the Mark David Chapman ilk.

The remainder of this eight-page issue was the usual stuff: A piece about a major-league King fan, coverage of the "Carrie" musical, and an article about King's radio station WZON being put up for sale.

Articles:
- "Observations from the Terminator," by Tyson Blue. (A sober look at what being a celebrity entails – basically an analysis of the dark side of fandom, as Blue calls it. With remarks from Doug Winter, Harlan Ellison, and Dean Koontz, this piece shows "fans" where the line is: How to stay on the "okay" side of The Terminator.)
- "SK Criticized for References to Blacks," by Kima R. Hicks and Stephen King (Hicks wrote a letter to S.K.—reproduced in this piece—in which she criticized King for "derogatory comments" about blacks. King's reply—also reproduced—is that yes, he has used the standard racial epithets in his books, but that they were "always used by idiots and bigots." He has always taken the position that "a realistic depiction of racial incidents *expose* rather than promote racism.")
- "Whitney Museum Planning Limited" (Unattributed. Details on the publication of the charitable limited edition of S.K.'s "My

Pretty Pony," which sold for $1800 a copy. See the section on "My Pretty Pony" in this volume.)
- "Profile: R. Bradley Trent of Oklahoma City," by Stephanie Leonard. (Article about a dentist who is also major Stephen King fan. He has two subscriptions to *Castle Rock* – one for himself and one to keep in his office waiting room!)
- "SK's Rock 'n' Roll Zone for Sale," by Hank Cheever Jr. (Article detailing King's decision to sell the failing AM radio station.)
- "'Carrie' to Open at the Virginia Theater." (Unattributed. Details on the musical version of S.K.'s first novel.)
- "Report from River Oaks," by William R. Wilson. (Details on a Stephen King/Don Robertson book-signing in River Oaks, Texas.)
- "Queen for a Day with King in Cleveland," by Jeanne Zulkowski. (Details on another Stephen King/Don Robertson book-signing – this one in Cleveland, Ohio.)

Book Reviews:
- "Mystery Weekend is Novelized: A Review of *Transylvania Station*," by Donald and Abby Westlake. (Review by Naomi King, King's daughter, who reviews the Westlake book. She refers to her dad as "S.K." in the review.)

Features:
- ◊ "Editor's Column," by Stephanie Leonard.
- ◊ Cartoon by Paul Williams.
- ◊ "Classifieds."

Vol. 4, No. 4 (Issue #37) April 1988

The big news in this twelve-page, purple-logoed issue (misidentified as Vol. 4, No. 5 on Page 1) was the June 1988 release of *The Gunslinger* on audio tape, read by Stephen King.

Tyson Blue did a front page story called "SK Read *Gunslinger* Tapped for June Release," and the front page also reproduced the cover artwork for both the cassette package and the paperback cover.

The article included an interview with Stephen King in which he talked about the actual recording of both *The Gunslinger* and *The Drawing of the Three*, as well as comments by King's secretary, Shirley Sonderegger, about how many copies of the original *Gunslinger* Steve had. (One.) (See my interview with Shirley Sonderegger in this volume.)

The rest of the issue contained articles on the "Carrie" musical, a Stephen King class that never happened, articles on King fandom, and a Stephen King crossword puzzle.

Articles:
- "SK Read Gunslinger Tapped for June Release," by Tyson Blue. (Details on the audio versions of King's most sought-after books, which reportedly ended up as an $8 million dollar rights deal for King.)
- "Musical 'Carrie' is Strange Spectacle," by Richard Mills. (Coverage of the "Carrie" musical. The piece begins: "Everything about the production was absurd.")
- "Thanks for the Memories, SK," by Del Rhea Watson. (Article about a Houston book-signing with Stephen King and Don Robertson, written by the manager of the bookstore in which the signing took place.)
- "Nightmares Publication Set for Fall." (Unattributed. Details on *Nightmares in the Sky*, a collection of photographs of architectural gargoyles in America, with an introduction by Stephen King. King's introduction to *Nightmares* was excerpted in the September 1988 issue of *Penthouse*, which also contained the terrific Clive Barker short story "The Life of Death.")
- "The Power of the Unseen," by Tim Murphy. (Informative article detailing the audiotape versions of S.K.'s works, complete with a sidebar called "Audio Tapes (Alphabetical List).")
- "Years 'n Fears: A Look Backward," by Tyson Blue. (A somewhat self-focused, yet still interesting essay about Blue's first

exposure to King, and his subsequent involvement with King's work.)

- "Stephen King is Basis for Class," by Daniel Miller. (Article profiling Stan Wiater and giving details on a course he was reportedly going to teach called "The Dark Visions of Stephen King." See the interview with Stan Wiater in this volume.)
- "What a Carrie On," by Paddy McKillop. (Commentary on the London reviews of the "Carrie" musical.)
- "...And the Critics be Damned," by Barry Hoffman. (Essay about the critical response to King's work.)
- "He Can Turn the Page, But He Can't Turn Back," by Mike Cummins. (Humorous essay about a fan who starts to take King's fictions a little too seriously.)
- "Printing Error Explained," by Tyson Blue. (Details on the "Permissions to Come" screw-up in *The Tommyknockers.*)
- "If You're Scared Silly, then Stephen King is Happy," by Julie Washington. (Details on yet another Stephen King/Don Robertson book-signing, this one in Cleveland, Ohio. What makes this piece notable, however, is the writer's noting of two unwritten Stephen King ideas that she heard him discuss at the signing. See "The Unwritten King" in this volume.)

Features:

◊ "Editor's Column," by Stephanie Leonard. (Most notable in this month's column was the news that a notebook containing pages from an unfinished King story called "Keyholes" was auctioned off by the American Repertory Theater on May 1, 1988. No details on the story were given, but I was able to obtain a copy of the handwritten, unfinsihed story. See my feature on "The Stephen King Notebook" in this volume.)

◊ "Scarier than SK," by Julie Jackson Lusby. (Poem about King and Don Robertson's *The Ideal, Genuine Man.* The poet's conclusion was that "Time and old age more frightening/Than any sluice in Derry/The Ideal, Genuine me someday?/Now that's really scary.")

◊ "Kingy Zingies," by Lela Marie De La Garza. (A Stephen King word puzzle.)

◊ "Letters."

◊ "King Crossword," by Phil Dickinson. (A Stephen King crossword puzzle.)

◊ "Classifieds."

◊ "Another Reminder." (Unattributed. Blurbs about *Bare Bones* and *Prime Evil.*)

Vol. 4, Nos. 5 & 6 (Issue #38) May/June 1988

This was a twelve-page, purple-logoed issue that featured a front-page article called "Lost in Derry" that examined the Bangor landmarks that Stephen King "transplanted" to Derry in *IT.*

There was also a piece by Stephen King called "SK Clarifies Gardner Reference," in which he discusses the two writers John Gardner and John Gardener.

Other notable items from this month's issue included Part Two of Tyson Blue's "Observations from the Terminator," in which Blue looked at the "Dark Side of Fandom."

Other interesting articles included a piece about the "Carrie" musical and a review of *The Tommyknockers* by Darrell Schweitzer.

Articles:

- "Lost in Derry," by Stanley A. Johnson Jr. (A look at Bangor landmarks in *IT,* including pictures of the Standpipe, the Paul Bunyan statue, and a picture of King's house, as well as one of the three-headed dragons that adorn the wrought iron fence surrounding it.)
- "More Carrie-ing On," by Brian Osborne. (A review of the English premiere of the "Carrie" musical.)
- "Observations from the Terminator," by Tyson Blue. (Subtitled "The Dark Side of Fandom.")
- "SK Clarifies Gardner Reference," by Stephen King. (The differ-

ence between John Gardner (of the James Bond series), and John Gardener (*The Sunlight Dialogues*).)

- "Before the Brand Name," by Philip Wilson. (A look at reviews of King's works before he became "Stephen King.")
- "Whitney Museum Planning Limited." (Unattributed. Details on the Whitney's limited of "My Pretty Pony.")
- "Oh Goodie...They Might Have Fallen," by Barry Hoffman. (The follow-up to Hoffman's article in the April 1988 *Castle Rock,* once again about the critical response to King's work.)
- "Horrorfest '89 Expands Show." (Unattributed. Details on the Stephen King Convention.)

Book Reviews:

- "Not for Everyone." (Review by SJW. A review of the collection of essays, *The Gothic World of Stephen King: Landscape of Nightmares.*)
- "*The Door to December* by Dean R. Koontz." (Review by George Hamilton comparing Koontz's pseudononymous—published as by Richard Paige—*Door* to King's *Firestarter.*)
- "Second *Tommyknockers* Quite Different." (Review by Sarah J. White of the Carlton Press book, *The Tommyknockers* by Alan E. Leisk, which is a seventy-two-page children's book involving mythical "tommyknockers," creatures akin to capricious goblins rather than alien maniacs.)
- "Schweitzer on TK, SK and Science Fiction." (Review by Darrell Schweitzer. Generally positive critique of King's *The Tommyknockers,* with particular emphasis on how King uses sci-fi conventions in the story.)
- "New Book Compares Koontz and SK." (Review by Tyson Blue of *Sudden Fear: The Horror and Dark Suspense Fiction of Dean R. Koontz,* with particular emphasis on an essay by Michael Collings called "Dean R. Koontz and Stephen King: Style, Invasion and an Aesthetics of Horror," comparing King and Koontz.)

Features:

◊ "Editor's Column," by Stephanie Leonard.

◊ "Out of Line." (Cartoon by Mort Gerberg.)

◊ "The Quigmans." (Cartoon by Hickerson.)

◊ "Correspondence Column."

◊ "King Crossword." (By Phil Dickinson.)

◊ "Classifieds."

◊ "Letters."

Vol. 4, No. 7 (Issue #39) July 1988

This was the kind of issue I'd call "meaty." It was a red-logoed twelve-pager, and articles included a lengthy examination of the "blurbs" King has bestowed on fellow writers, a discussion of Jack's metamophosis in *The Talisman,* along with five book reviews, more about the "Carrie" musical, and an "Editor's Column" that ran longer than a full page.

The graphics in this issue were exceptionally nice, including book covers, illustrations, and photos, and, as always, the ads alone were worth the price of the issue. Dave Hinchberger from *The Overlook Connection* was up to a half-page ad, there was a three-quarter-page reproduction of the cover of Tabitha King's new novel *Pearl.* Horrorfest '89 also took a half-pager.

Articles:

- "'The Road Laid its Mark on You:' Jack's Metamorphosis in *The Talisman* (or, Beyond Boy-Wonderdom)," by Jack Slay, Jr. (Lengthy essay which concludes that "King and Straub have reshaped and surpassed what has basically become the stereotypical quest myth...a work of art with which critics must contend.")
- "Reach Out and Touch Some Thing: Blurbs and Stephen King," by Stanley Wiater. (How King has helped colleagues through his endorsement and use of his "golden name." See the interview with Stan Wiater in this volume.)

- "King's Kids...Less than Meets the Eye," by Barry Hoffman. (An essay postulating that King's kid characters are "one-dimensional caricatures, with no real substance." I disagree. I think that portraying childhood accurately and honestly is one of King's primary strengths as a storyteller. As I tell my students in my King seminars, "Stephen King remembers childhood." And, to be frank, I can't see how Hoffman could have read *IT* and not seen that both the good and the bad about children is shown in the book. Yes, Hoffman is right: most of King's children are small town, white, and middle-class. So what? That's how King grew up, where he "came from." As Hoffman himself acknowledges and admits, both he and King are products of their childhood, and a writer writes about *what he (or she) knows.* Where is it written that King must show characters from every social and economic strata in his work? In my opinion, for a reader to criticize a writer because the writer's characters don't jibe with the people that the reader interacts with daily is to invalidate the particular voice/message/story that any writer strives to convey through his art.)
- "Horrorfest Convention Lists Appearances," by Tim Foster. (Details on Horrorfest '89.)
- "You Read the Book, Saw the Movie, But What About the Show?," by Bill Munster. (Review of the "Carrie" musical with suggestions for changes which might improve the show.)
- "Black and White and Read All Over – *Carrie* on Broadway," by Craig Goden. (Article about the brief life of the "Carrie" musical.)

Book Reviews:
- "Book Reviews," by Tyson Blue. (Generally positive reviews of four new Stephen King-related volumes:
  ◊ *The Gothic World of Stephen King: Landscape of Nightmares,* edited by Gary Hoppensand and Ray B. Browne (The Popular Press).
  ◊ *Landscape of Fear: Stephen King's American Gothic,* by Tony Magistrale (The Popular Press).
  ◊ *Stephen King: The First Decade, Carrie to Pet Sematary* by Joseph Reino (Twayne).
  ◊ *Bare Bones: Conversations on Terror with Stephen King,* edited by Tim Underwood and Chuck Miller (McGraw-Hill).
- "'Night Flier' Tops Horror Stories." (Very positive review by Tyson Blue of Doug Winter's horror anthology *Prime Evil,* with particular emphasis on King's contribution "The Night Flier." See the interview with Doug Winter in this volume.)

Features:
  ◊ "Editor's Column," by Stephanie Leonard. (Lengthy column which contains a blurb mentioning a piece I found in *Horoscope* magazine (entitled "Who Is He?") and sent to Stephanie Leonard.)
  ◊ "Fishpaper–Firemen's 'Carrie'." (Cartoon by Carle Hennicke.)
  ◊ "Letters."
  ◊ "Classifieds."

Vol. 4, No. 8 (Issue #40) August 1988

This issue was an average, purple-logoed issue, one which didn't contain anything really noteworthy, although the front page Jim Leonard picture of S.K. in the *real* Pets Sematary was terrific!

Probably the most important news this month was the announcement that *Castle Rock* would live on. The most significant essays were both by Ben Indick: His appraisal of *The Tommyknockers,* and his review of *The Ideal, Genuine Man.*

There were plenty of important advertisements this month, and I'm sure King fans had the opportunity to fill in the holes in their collection.

Twelve pages.

Articles:
- "S.K.'s Pet Sematary Scheduled for Maine Production," by Hank Cheever, Jr. (Details on Laurel Entertainment's announcement about the filming of what some have called "Stephen King's most frightening novel.")
- "The Arrival of a Limited," by Tom Draheim. (Details on the signed, limited of *Night Visions 5.* Draheim was excited the day he got it in the mail.)
- "Castle Rock Will Live On." (Unattributed. The official announcement that Chris Spruce would take over as publisher of *CR*, beginning with the January 1989 issue.)
- "H.P. Lovecraft and Those Tommyknockers," by Ben Indick. (Analysis of the Lovecraft influences in King's *The Tommyknockers,* with Indick going so far as to postulate that with *Tommyknockers,* King was rewriting Lovecraft's "The Colour Out of Space.")
- "SK Book Banned in Virginia." (Unattributed. Details on the Goochland, Virginia, school board's banning of King's *'Salem's Lot* from the high school library.)
- "Buckets of Talent Wasted in 'Carrie'," by Dan Cziraky. (This was subtitled "One Last Time: 'Carrie' Reviewed," and essentially lambasted the production. Again.)
- "Stephen King, Werewolf," by Stephanie Leonard. (Short blurb about the paperback of *Transylvania Station,* which recounted a "mystery weekend" in Mohonk with the likes of Stephen King, Peter Straub, and Gahan Wilson. The book had an introduction by King.)

Book Reviews:
- "SK Contributions Are Worth Reading." (Review by Tyson Blue (Blue assesses *Night Visions 5.*)
- "Dark Tower Tape Reviewed." (Review by Tyson Blue of King's debut as a professional "reader," asserting that once King starts supplying the characters in *The Gunslinger* with voices, "things improve.")
- "Philtrum Press' Second Book: *The Ideal, Genuine Man* by Don Robertson." (A balanced and literate review of Robertson's most recent novel by Ben Indick.)

Features:
  ◊ "Editor's Column."
  ◊ "SK in the Real Pet Sematary, circa 1982." (Photo by Jim Leonard.)
  ◊ "Gorrell." (Cartoon spoofing the Goochland, Virginia, school board's banning of *Salem's Lot.*)
  ◊ "Illustration." (The foreign cover of *Pet Sematary.*)
  ◊ "Letters."
  ◊ "That's Jake." (Cartoon.)
  ◊ "King Krossword," by Phil Dickinson.
  ◊ "Classifieds."
  ◊ *Notable Advertisements*:
    - Blood & Guts Press: Jim Thompson's *The Killer Inside Me,* with an introduction by Stephen King.
    - Half-page ad for Horrorfest '89.
    - Full-page ad for *Midnight Graffiti* (containing the announcement of their third issue, which would be a Stephen King Special—they wrote *"We Hadda Do It!"*).
    - Footsteps Press: The Chapbook edition of Doug Winter's *Splatter: A Cautionary Tale.*
    - Half-page ad for Collector's Choice.
    - Full-page ad for The Overlook Connection.
    - A large ad offering "STEPHEN KING. An ultimately collectible ONE-OF-A-KIND item..." available from Oxford Too Books in Atlanta, Georgia. (It was the uncorrected galleys for *Night Visions 5,* complete with the original illustrations, and author's editing marks and signatures. Grover Deluca was asking $2500 the last time I spoke with Oxford Too, in summer 1988.)

Vol. 4, No. 9 (Issue #41) September 1988

This month's eight-page *Castle Rock* marked the appearance of the first excerpt from the book you now hold in your hands, and my sincerest thanks go out to Stephanie Leonard, Shirley Sonderegger, Stephen King, Richard Matheson, and Richard Christian Matheson for their continued support and interest in *The Shape Under the Sheet.*

The excerpt was a dual interview with Richard Matheson and Richard Christian Matheson called "From Richard to Stephen to Richard: How Richard Matheson Influenced the Work of Both Stephen King and Richard Christian Matheson," and it ran on Page 1. The piece took selected responses from my interviews with these men, and focused on what R.C. has called "the migration of an influence." It was very well-received, and, again, thanks to all who helped.

The rest of the issue was interesting, and there were a couple of pieces that were fascinating: The article entitled "The Good and Bad of Film Adaptation" by James Cole, which detailed Cole's experiences filming S.K.'s "The Last Rung on the Ladder"; and a piece called "The Dark Bard of New Hampshire" by Michael Berry, which was a satirical obituary for a writer named Rex Stephens, author of such masterworks as *Blood of the Night Beast, Night of the Blood Beast,* and *THE,* which was 5,000 pages long and weighed thirty pounds. Very funny piece.

Articles:
- "The Good and Bad of Film Adaptation," by James Cole. (Cole's shooting diary during his filming of S.K.'s "The Last Rung on the Ladder.")
- "Horrorfest Preparations Proceeding," by Tyson Blue. (Details on the Stephen King Convention.)
- "The Dark Bard of New Hampshire," by Michael Berry. (Very funny satirical piece. See my comments above.)
- "Collector's News," by Tyson Blue. (Information on the two versions of *The Gunslinger* paperback, as well as updated info on the "Permissions to Follow" error in *Tommyknockers.*)

Book Reviews:
- "*Pearl* Is a Bit of Writing Magic." (Review by Tyson Blue (Very favorable review of Tabitha King's latest novel, *Pearl.*)
- "Straub Novel is Suspenseful." (Favorable review by Mark Graham of Straub's *Koko,* which Graham sees as a novel that could allow Straub to "break out" of the horror genre.)

Book Excerpts:
- "From Richard to Stephen to Richard: How Richard Matheson Influenced the Work of Both Stephen King and Richard Christian Matheson," by Stephen J. Spignesi. (An excerpt from this volume. See the complete interviews with Richard Matheson and Richard Christian Matheson in this volume.)

Features:
◊ "Editor's Column."
◊ "Correspondence Column."
◊ "Letters."
◊ "Thicket From Hell," by Ray Rexer. (Stephen King word game.)
◊ "Classifieds."

Vol. 4, No. 10 (Issue #42) October 1988

With an orange logo and eight pages of material, this issue looked at the filming of "Pet Sematary," King's villains, and featured an article about a pilgrimage to King's house.

Also, Tyson Blue explained *again* why his *Unseen King* still was not available.

Articles:
- "'Pet Sematary' Finally Converted to Celluloid," by Christopher Spruce. (Terrific behind-the-scenes article about the filming of King's screenplay, complete with a front-page photo of King

discussing the movie with director Mary Lambert.)
- "Sure Glad the Book Wasn't *Cujo,*" by Sherwood Springer. (Springer's "Twilight Zone-ish" experience at finding a doctor's business card in a used copy of *Misery*—the same doctor who, years before, had prescribed a codeine-based painkiller that put Springer in the hospital.)
- "King's Characters: The Good, The Bad, and The Badder," by Barry Hoffman. (A look at King's villains.)
- "Stephen King's WZON Rocks On." (Unattributed. Info on the format change of King's radio station, from commercial to non-commercial.)
- "Audio-Cassette News," by Tyson Blue. (Details on the *Prime Evil* tapes.)
- "How I Spent My Summer Vacation or A Stephen King Fan's Study in Frustration," by Judee Gardner. (A fan's pilgrimage to S.K.'s house, which ended with the photos she had taken—including one of the man himself—ending up "lost.")
- "Blue Updates Unseen King," by Tyson Blue. (Details on why Blue's book was still not available.)

Book Reviews:
- "*Pearl* Shines for Tabitha." (Review by Dan S. McMillen. A book McMillen considers "Tabitha's best yet.")
- (Mass Market Edition of *Gunslinger* Released." (Review by Tyson Blue. Details on the Plume trade paperback edition of King's most sought-after and most legendary book.)
- "*Bare Bones*: A Disquieting Look At Stephen King." (Review by Barry Hoffman. A look at the most extensive collection of King interviews assembled, a book which Hoffman finds disturbing due to King's brutal honesty in baring his soul, his fears, and himself to the reader.)

Features:
◊ "Photo." (King and "Pet Sematary" director Mary Lambert on the set.)
◊ "Editor's Column."
◊ "Letters."
◊ Graphic. (S.K. with headphones and the WZON logo.)
◊ "And Still More 'Kingy Zingies'." (S.K. word game by Lela Marie De La Garza.)
◊ "Photo." (Terrific shot of Miko Hughes, who plays Gage Creed in the film version of *Pet Sematary*. He's shown holding up a paperback copy of the novel.)

Vol. 4, No. 11 (Issue #43) November 1988

After this issue, there would be only one more issue of *Castle Rock*'s "Stephanie Leonard Years."

This issue had a purple logo, and was eight pages.

The lead-off article was once again about the filming of "Pet Sematary," and there was also another review of Tabitha King's *Pearl.*

There was a neat photo on Page 1 of Fred "Herman Munster/Jud Crandall" Gwynne and Stephen King, taken by Tabitha King. We also learned that King would make a cameo appearance in the film as the minister who presides over the burial of Missy Dandridge. (Interestingly, in the first draft script, Missy hangs herself in her cellar, while in the film, according to reports by Christopher Spruce, the suicide takes place in a garage. Also, the character of the minister appears in the first draft script in Scene 284, Page 68, but only as a voice-over. I guess when everyone realized that King would appear, they decided it might be good for the film for him to appear on camera rather than simply speak his words from out of the scene. The minister has one line: "May the Lord bless you and keep you; may the Lord make his face to shine upon you, and comfort you, and lift you up, and give you peace. Amen.")

Articles:
- "'Pet Sematary' Film Crews Visit Bangor," by Christopher Spruce. (More on the movie.)

- "Christine II Shoulda Had A Diehard," by Jim Burdett. (Burdett's account of a demolition derby in which he participated with a car he christened Christine II. He lost.)
- "SK Wins Stoker Award," by Jodi Strissel. (Details on the Horror Writers of America banquet. S.K.'s *Misery* tied with Robert McCammon's *Swan Song* for a Stoker.)
- "Mount Hope: 'The Most Beautiful Cemetery'," by Christopher Spruce. (Subtitled "A Visit to the Set of 'Pet Sematary' in Pictures," with photos by Tabitha King and Christopher Spruce.)
- "Interview with Robert R. McCammon," by Jodi Strissel. (A brief talk with the *Swan Song* author. See my interview with McCammon in this volume.)

Book Reviews:
- "Pearl Is 'Engaging Character'." (Positive review by Janet C. Beaulieu of Tabitha King's latest novel, *Pearl*.)
- "Of New Frontiers and Gargoyles." (Review by Tyson Blue of the photo book *Nightmares in the Sky*, with text by Stephen King and photos of architectural gargoyles by F-Stop Fitzgerald.)
- "*Silver Scream* Among Best Anthologies." (Review by Tyson Blue. A look at the new Dark Harvest collection, containing works by Doug Winter, Ray Garton, R.C. Matheson, Clive Barker, Robert McCammon, and others.)
- "Audiocassette Reviews." (Reviews by Tyson Blue of audio versions of Clive Barker's "The Hellbound Heart," "The Body Politic," and "The Inhuman Condition.")

Features:
◊ "Editor's Column."
◊ Cartoon by Mark Cullum.
◊ "Letters."
◊ "Classifieds."

Vol. 4, No. 12 (Issue #44) December 1988

This green-logoed twelve-pager was the last issue of *Castle Rock* edited by Stephanie Leonard.

She still did her "Editor's Column," but apparently Chris Spruce was already in charge of quite a bit of the production. The reply to a letter asking about *The Dark Half* prompted an "Editor's reply" which was signed CJS—Christopher Spruce.

The newsletter acknowledged Stephanie's departure with the following blurb at the bottom of Page 2:

> "This is the last issue of *Castle Rock* as editor for editor/publisher Stephanie Leonard. Steff, who started *CR* five years ago in response to S.K. fans' suggestion for an S.K. newsletter, will remain associated with *CR* as a contributing editor. Christopher Spruce will take over as editor/publisher effective with the January, 1989 issue. Thanks, Steff, and good luck!"

The *Castle Rock* Stephanie Leonard put together served as a meeting place and a sounding board for S.K. fans everywhere. It confirmed our belief that we weren't alone, no matter what some of our family and friends said when we mentioned our devotion to things King! Nice work, Steff!

But *CR* would live on, and that, in the end, is what counts.

Articles:
- "TV Version of 'Stand By Me' Is 'Horrifying'," by Barry Hoffman. (A justified lambasting of ABC for butchering the network premiere of what many consider to be the finest S.K. film adaptation yet. The network flunkies that worked on editing ("censoring" is the better and more accurate word) this film proved that the networks should either run feature films *as originally produced* or not run them at all.)
- "Farris at NECON." (Interview by Sheryl Weilgosh with author John Farris, one of S.K.'s favorite writers.)
- "Moviemaking Next Door Can Really Change Scenes," by Anne

Hyde Degan. (What it was like living next door to the "Pet Sematary" movie set.)
- "Stranger Than Fiction?," by Dory L. Wethington. (Book titles and lottery winners—stories strange, but true!)
- "'Yes' To Short Fiction." (Unattributed. Piece announcing that *Castle Rock* would begin publishing readers' short stories in the January 1989 issue.)
- "References to SK Found in Unusual Books," by Daniel W. Hays. (A look at the *Deathlands* series of adventure novels, which contain references to the work of Stephen King.)

Book Reviews:
- "'My Pretty Pony': A Treat For The Eye." (Review by Tyson Blue of the limited edition King story. See the section on "My Pretty Pony" in this volume.)
- "Blood-Letting on Tape." (Review by Tyson Blue of the audio-cassette version of Doug Winter's landmark anthology *Prime Evil*.
- "Koontz Produces Toy Fable." (Review by Tyson Blue of Koontz's fable *Oddkins*.)

Features:
◊ "Editor's Column."
◊ "Letters."
◊ "King Krossword," by Phil Dickinson.
◊ "King Klues," by Rob Edmiston.
◊ "Classifieds."

CASTLE ROCK
1989

Vol. 5, No. 1 (Issue #45) January 1989

This was the first issue of *Castle Rock*'s final year—although we didn't know it when we received it.

The issue was an interesting eight-page purple-logoed pot-pourri of articles, reviews, and the first story of *Castle Rock*'s short story contest.

Articles:
- "SK Flicks Not Found At A Theatre Near You," by Tyson Blue. (A look at two short amateur film adaptations of the Stephen King stories "The Last Rung on the Ladder," and "Lawnmower Man.")
- "Looking for Trouble: Nightmares in Daylight," by Ben Indick. (A discussion of Stephen King's introduction to the photo collection *Nightmares in the Sky*.)
- "Look for 'Best of Shadows'." (Unattributed. A blurb about the anthology appearance of the original version of King's "The Man Who Would Not Shake Hands.")
- "More Info Released on *Dark Tower II*," by Tyson Blue. (An update on the audiotape release of *The Drawing of the Three*.)

Fiction:
- "The Mallwalkers," by Barbara Doty Larkin. (The first short story (of six) in *Castle Rock*'s short story contest.)

Book Reviews:
- "Joe Bob Finds Fear and Loathing," by Velvetta Spandex. (A review of *A Guide to Western Civilization or My Story*, by Joe Bob Briggs. One of John Bloom's creations, Velveeta Spandex, reviews a book by another of Bloom's creations, Joe Bob Briggs, which was written by Bloom. Wait a minute...does that mean that Bloom reviewed his own book? I think it does. I think....)
- "Fans Can Celebrate New Hardcover Release of *Books of Blood*," by Tyson Blue. (A review of Clive Barker's *The Books of Blood*. An overview of the omnibus edition of Barker's landmark series.)
- "New Straub Novel Gets Quick Cassette Treatment," by Tyson Blue. (A review of *Koko* by Peter Straub (read by James Woods on a Simon & Schuster AudioWorks cassette). A generally

positive review of what Blue calls "the auditory equivalent of Cliff Notes."

Features:

◊ "Editor's Column," by Christopher Spruce.
◊ "Letters to *CR*."
◊ "Index to Back Issues of *Castle Rock*." (Unattributed. A very comprehensive index to *Castle Rock* which, although unattributed, was more than likely the work of Chris Spruce.)
◊ "Classifieds."

Vol. 5, No. 2 (Issue #46) February 1989

This was a very serious issue.

And by "serious" I don't mean scholarly or dry. I mean "serious" the way high-schoolers used to use it when they wanted to get across just how cool something was: "Hey dudes, Jimi Hendrix played some serious guitar, know wadda mean?" (It's about a block due west of "heavy.")

This twelve-page issue had the first in-depth information about King's new four-book contract with Viking, as well as a lengthy interview with King by none other then David Bright (who has appeared in King's fiction, most notably in *The Dead Zone* and *The Tommyknockers*.)

I'd have to say a splendid time was had by all.

Articles:

• "Happy New Year: SK Inks New Four Book Contract," by Christopher Spruce. (Details on the contract that will eventually bring us four new books by Stephen King. The first was *The Dark Half,* published in the fall of 1989; the second, *Four Past Midnight,* published in the fall of 1990. Two other titles will follow at the rate of one per year.)
• "Stephen King, 41." (An Interview by David Bright with S.K. that originally appeared in *Portland Monthly* magazine. King talks about making movies in Maine, among other things.)
• "Short Subjects: Recent Short Fiction of Stephen King," by Ben P. Indick. (A look at recent short stories by King beginning with "Popsy" in *Masques II,* and continuing up through "The Doctor's Case" in *The New Adventures of Sherlock Holmes*.)
• "SK Companion Book In the Works." (Unattributed. An update on the progress of George Beahm's *The Stephen King Companion*.)

Fiction:

• "Maker's Place" by Eli White. (The second (of six) short stories in *Castle Rock*'s short story competition.)

Book Reviews:

• "*Pearl* is 'Rich, Warm'." (A review of Tabitha King's *Pearl* by Tyson Blue, a novel that Blue says gives us a "rewarding look at how one woman's life can resonate through and affect an entire town.")
• "Barker Part II: *Cabal* Completes American Publication of Stories," by Tyson Blue (The second part of Blue's look at Clive Barker's work.)
• "Bradbury Still Offers His Unique Magic." (A positive review by Tyson Blue of Ray Bradbury's *The Toynbee Convector*.)

Features:

◊ "Editor's Column," by Christopher Spruce.
◊ "Letters to *CR*."
◊ "Short Story Contest Update."
◊ "Index to Back Issues of Castle Rock." (Unattributed. Part 2 of a very comprehensive index to *Castle Rock* which, although unattributed, was more than likely the work of Chris Spruce.)
◊ "Middle Name Quiz," by Ray Rexer. (Match the S.K. character to his middle name. See the feature on Ray Rexer's *Castle Rock* parody, *Castle Schlock,* and his short story "Character Assassination" in this volume.)
◊ "Classifieds."

Vol. 5, No. 3 (Issue #47) March 1989

This blue-logoed eight-page issue featured two front-page articles by Janet Beaulieu on *The Dark Tower: The Gunslinger,* as well as the first part of a two-part interview with Rick Hautala by Dave Lowell. (See Rick Hautala's essay "Steve Rose Up" in this volume.)

Articles:

• "Gunslinger Stalks Darkness in Human Spirit," by Janet C. Beaulieu. (An overview of King's *Dark Tower* series, combined with an interview with S.K. in which he talks about his intentions in writing the series.)
• "Interview: Talking Horror Fiction With Rick Hautala." (Interview by Dave Lowell. A terrific interview with my friend Rick, conducted by my other friend Dave. Dave asks insightful questions, and Rick gives honest answers.)

Fiction:

• "Firefly...Burning Bright," by Barry Hoffman. (The third (of six) short stories in *Castle Rock*'s short story competition.)

Book Reviews:

• "SK Excels in Quest for the Dark Tower," by Janet C. Beaulieu. (An insightful review of *The Gunslinger*.)
• "*Dark Tower II* Audio Tapes Released." (Review by Tyson Blue. Blue looks at (or "listens to," actually) the *Drawing of the Three* audiotapes.)
• "Dead Lines: On Short Stories Becoming Novels." (Review by Tyson Blue of John Skipp and Craig Spector's "mutation," *Dead Lines*.)
• "'100 Best' is Best of Its Kind Ever." (Review by Mark Graham. A positive review of *Horror: 100 Best Books,* edited by Stephen Jones (editor of *Clive Barker's Shadows In Eden*) and Kim Newman (who lives in Crouch End).)

Features:

◊ "Editor's Column," by Christopher Spruce.
◊ "Letters to *CR*."
◊ "Classifieds."

Vol. 5, No. 4 (Issue #48) April 1989

This issue was back up to twelve pages, and contained a number of interesting articles, features, and reviews for Stephen King fans.

The whole front page was taken up by Ben Indick's look at the Whitney Museum's publication of *My Pretty Pony*. The right two-thirds of the front page consisted of a reproduction of the "nothing" lithograph from that book, but the reproduction came out so dark it was almost impossible to make out the falling guy in the picture.

The issue also contained Part 2 of Dave Lowell's interview withe Rick Hautala, an "SK-related" play by Ben Indick, and an article by Chris Spruce on a Belgian documentary about Stephen King that we'll probably never get to see in this country.

This issue also contained an article by yours truly called "Spignesi Updates SK Encyclopedia," accompanied by two of Katherine Flickinger's illustrations from this volume, "Under Lottie's Bed," and "Boyd Jumping His Pony."

Articles:

• "*My Pretty Pony*: An Odd Couple Produces A Work of Art," by Ben Indick. (Indick talks about the Whitney Museum's *My Pretty Pony*.)
• "Belgian TV Interview Provides Insights to SK," by Christopher Spruce. (Chris talks about a documentary that ran on Belgian television that he says is the most in-depth look at King to date. The cost of reproducing videos of the documentary from the European to American systems is so cost-prohibitive that, in all likelihood, it'll never be shown or available here. The videotape of the program the producers sent to King cost the company

$300 to make.)
- "Spignesi Updates SK Encyclopedia," by Stephen J. Spignesi. (Article updating my progress on *The Shape Under the Sheet.*)
- "Talking Horror With Rick Hautala, Part 2." (Interview by Dave Lowell. Part 2 of Dave's talk with Rick.)

Fiction:
- "Children of King: A Closet Screenplay." (A play by Ben P. Indick with King's child characters as the main characters.)
- "The Reunion" by Phillip W. Wilson. (The fourth (of six) short stories in *Castle Rock*'s short story competition.)

Book/Audio Reviews:
- "New Cormier Novel Garners SK Praise." (Review by Mark Graham. A positive review of Cormier's terrific novel *Fade*. And, for what it's worth, allow me to stick my two cents in: If you like Stephen King's work, you will love *Fade*.)
- "*Midnight* Returns Koontz to Horror Genre." (Review by Tyson Blue. A look at Koontz's latest.)
- "*Night Visions 6* Continues Consistently Well-Done Series." (Review by Tyson Blue of the latest offering from Dark Harvest.)
- "Readings Hinder Quality of Second *Prime Evil* Audio Tapes." (Review by Tyson Blue. Tyson didn't like James B. Sikking's readings.)
- "SK Story Featured in Grant Anthology." (Review by Tyson Blue. A look at the Charles Grant *Best of Shadows* anthology, a collection that included the original version of S.K.'s "The Man Who Would Not Shake Hands.")

Features:
- ◊ "Editor's Column," by Christopher Spruce.
- ◊ "Letters to *CR*."
- ◊ "*Last Words* Quiz," by Ray Rexer.
- ◊ "Classifieds."

Vol. 5, No. 5 (Issue #49) May 1989

A good portion of this issue was understandably devoted to the premiere of the film "Pet Sematary." (The film opened nationally April 21, 1989.) The front page had a still from the film, as well as two articles about the movie.

The issue also contained some truly informative and entertaining pieces, most notably "Mr. King Meets the Comics," and a look at the Lord John Press edition of "Dolan's Cadillac."

The issue was twelve pages, had a purple logo, and also had full-page ads for the Stephen King issue of *Midnight Graffiti* (which contained an excerpt from *The Shape Under the Sheet*), Horrorfest '89, and The Overlook Connection.

Articles:
- "Opening Night: No Glitz, Just The Jitters," by T.J. Tremble. (Interesting coverage of the opening-night Bangor world premiere of "Pet Sematary.")
- "Do You Know Where Your Kid Is Tonight?," by Christopher Spruce. (Chris Spruce's personal response to "Pet Sematary.")
- "Mr. King Meets The Comics," by Gary D. Robinson (Terrific overview of the comics adaptations of S.K.'s work.)
- "King Play Is Raging Success," by Dave Lowell. (An article about Robert B. Parker's ("Spenser") stage production of the Bachman novel *Rage*.)
- "A Cadillac For King's Used Car Lot," by Ben P. Indick. (A look at the Lord John Press edition of the Stephen King novella "Dolan's Cadillac.")
- "Horrorfest Plans Finalized," by Tim Foster. (Coverage of the final itinerary of the first Horrorfest convention.)

Fiction:
- "Dead Dogs," by Peter D. Harrison. (The fifth (of six) short stories in *Castle Rock*'s short story competition.)

Book Reviews:
- "*Unseen King* Finally Is Seen." (Review by Christopher Spruce.

A generally positive review of Tyson Blue's book-length look at rarely-seen Stephen King material, Starmont's *The Unseen King*.)
- "Making Horror Work: Tips From T.E.D. Klein." (Review by Tyson Blue of the Footsteps Press edition of Klein's *Raising Goosebumps for Fun and Profit.*)
- "*Fireflies*: From the Author's Heart." (Review by Tyson Blue of Morrell's moving "semi-novel" about his son Matthew's death.)

Features:
- ◊ "Editor's Column," by Christopher Spruce.
- ◊ "Letters to *CR*."
- ◊ "Classifieds."

Vol. 5, No. 6 (Issue #50) June 1989

This was it: We were halfway through the final year of *Castle Rock*.

This issue contained a review of the *Rage* play, an article about the reception given "Pet Sematary" in Boston, as well as lots of letters form *CR* readers about the film.

There was coverage of King's Pasadena Library lecture, and a terrific article by Gary Robinson about King's use of religion and religious imagery.

There was also a nonfiction piece by King himself called "The Ultimate Catalogue."

Twelve pages.

Articles:
- "The Play's the Thing for the Parker Family," by Patti Hartigan. (Interesting article about Robert Parker's ("Spenser") production of the Bachman novel *Rage*.)
- "'Pet Sematary' Doesn't Draw Raves in Boston," by Tom Draheim. (Coverage of the negative reviews "Pet Sematary" received in the Boston newspapers.)
- "One Fan's Night in Pasadena," by Suzanne Bidinger. (Fannish article about King's lecture at the Pasadena Library.)
- "God of Blood and Fire," by Gary D. Robinson. (Insightful article that examines King's use of religion and religious imagery in his fiction.)
- "The Ultimate Catalogue," by Stephen King. (King talks about mail-order catalogues. This article originally appeared in the Bangor *Register* in June of 1988.)

Fiction:
- "Night of the Dog," by Michael D. Stewart. (The sixth—and final—short story in *Castle Rock*'s short story competition.)

Book/Audio Reviews:
- "McCammon Audio 'One of the Best'." (Review by Tyson Blue of a Simon & Schuster AudioWorks collection of three Robert R. McCammon short stories read by William Windom. The stories read are three of Rick's best: "Nightcrawlers," "Yellowjacket Summer," and "Night Calls the Green Falcon.")
- "2nd [sic] *Prime Evil* Audio Is Better." (Review by Tyson Blue of the *third* release in the *Prime Evil* audiotape series.)
- "Romero Film Classic Adapted to Cassette." (Lukewarm review by Tyson Blue of an audio version of George Romero's classic film *Night of the Living Dead.*)
- "Another Look—*Cabal* Disappoints." (Review by Alan Warren. Negative review of Clive Barker's collection *Cabal.*)
- "Tanith Lee Offers Clever Fantasy." (Very positive review by Tyson Blue of Lee's fantasy novel published in a signed limited edition by Donald M. Grant.)
- "Lansdale Puts English on Suspenseful Plot." (Review by Tyson Blue of two Lansdale novels, *Cold in July,* and *The Nightrunners.*)

Features:
- ◊ "Editor's Column," by Christopher Spruce.
- ◊ "Letters to *CR*." (Letters from readers about "Pet Sematary," the

movie. Also, one letter that reproduced David Letterman's Top Ten list from April 27, 1989: "Top Ten Lines from Stephen King Novels." (The No. 1 line was "I've been a veterinarian for thirty years and I'm telling you—that's no ordinary poodle." The entire Top Ten is reproduced elsewhere in this volume.)

◊ "Classifieds."

Vol. 5, No. 7 (Issue #51) July 1989

This basically was a "Horrorfest" issue. The front page (in red headlines and logos this time) was completely devoted to coverage of the first horror convention specifically designed for Stephen King fans. In addition, three interior pages and ninety percent of the back page of this twelve-pager were given over to coverage of the event.

Other notable pieces included an intriguing look at a character that may very well be King's ultimate "outsider," Stanley Uris, along with an essay by Barry Hoffman, editor of *Gauntlet,* on censorship.

Articles:
- "More Than 300 Attend Horrorfest," by Tyson Blue. (Firsthand coverage of Tyson's trip to the Rockies.)
- "The Organizer Offers His Account," by Ken Morgan. (An interesting overview of Ken Morgan's role in putting the convention together.)
- "Mr. Norman's Longcut," by Ray Rexer. (How the irrepressible Wray Wreckser got home.)
- "'Companion' Book Nears Publication." (Unattributed. Article about George Beahm's forthcoming *Stephen King Companion.*)
- "Stanley Uris: World's Smallest Adult," by Michael Moses. (An essay written by one of Michael Collings' Pepperdine University students.)
- "Censorship Rears Its Ugly Head…Again," by Barry Hoffman. (This overview of recent instances of censorship is an alarming, scary eye-opener. With this piece, Barry encourages us to "let our voices be heard…before it's too late." He cautions that "we have only ourselves to blame when they invade our homes and confiscate *Carrie, IT, Misery* …the whole ball of wax." Think it can't happen? Don't be too sure.)
- "Page After Page After Page of Garbage'." (Unattributed. A sidebar about an Arkansas school trying to remove Stephen King's *Cujo* from a school curriculum.)
- "Horrorfest '89: Bill & Bud's Excellent Adventure," by W.F. Roberts and Marcelo Mathew Martinez. (Another recounting of the Horrorfest weekend.)

Fiction:
- "Lullaby Haven," by Gillian Ewing. (This short story is subtitled "A Fairy Tale In Which A Gander Can Indeed Become A Cooked Goose," and earned the writer an "A" in a creative writing class. This story was an interesting choice to run in this issue, because it resonates off of Barry Hoffman's "Censorship" article. Ewing says that "'Lullaby Haven' sums up my feelings regarding the mixed messages we tend to transmit to our kids about censorship.")

Book/Audio Reviews:
- "Geekism Made Easy." (Review of Katherine Dunn's *Geek Love* by Christopher Spruce. Glowing review of Dunn's brilliant novel.)
- "Hautala Can Deliver Good Case of Creeping Heebie-Jeebies." (Review by Tyson Blue of Hautala's *Moon Walker* and *Winter Wake.*)
- "Simple Style Aids Audio Version of Harris Novel." (Review by Tyson Blue. Positive review of the audio version of Thomas Harris's incredible novel *The Silence of the Lambs.*)

Features:
◊ "Editor's Column," by Christopher Spruce.
◊ "Letters to *CR*."
◊ "Classifieds."

Vol. 5, No. 8 (Issue #52) August 1989

The most significant piece in this issue was the first part of a two-part essay by Dr. Michael Collings entitled "Acorns to Oaks: Explorations of Theme, Image, and Character In the Early Works of Stephen King." As most King fans know, Collings is one of the two leading critics of King's work. (The other, of course, being Douglas Winter.) With "Acorns to Oaks," Dr. C. gives us insightful analysis of themes and images in S.K.'s early work, beginning with "The Star Invaders," and moving up through King's "Garbage Truck" columns and "Slade." (Part 2 covers King's early poetry, and is an adaptation of the essay Dr. C. wrote for *The Shape Under the Sheet* entitled "The Radiating Pencils of His Bones" which appears elsewhere in this volume.)

Other interesting items in this eight-page issue included an interview with Joe Lansdale, a review of *Book of the Dead,* and a short story by Paddy McKillop.

Also, George Beahm ran a full-page ad updating the progress and availablity of his *Stephen King Companion.*

Three issues to go…and we still didn't know.

Articles:
- "Acorns to Oaks: Explorations of Theme, Image, and Character In the Early Works of Stephen King," by Michael R. Collings. (A brilliant piece that adds to Dr. C's incredible canon of work about Stephen King.)
- "A Talk With Joe R. Lansdale." (Interesting interview with Joe by Thomas M. Cooper. See my own talk with Mr. Lansdale in this volume.)
- "Dead Dogs Tops Short Stories." (Unattributed. The announcement of the winner of *Castle Rock*'s short story competition. It was Peter D. Harrison's "Dead Dogs," from the May 1989 issue.)

Fiction:
- "The Wrath of Herb & Marge" by Paddy McKillop. (A bizarre and funny story about two people who decide that Stephen King has been abusing woodchucks in his work for too long, and must be punished. They kidnap a guy they think is King, run his legs over with a car, disembowel him, cover his intestines with blueberry sauce, and then make him eat them in a macabre parody of a scene from "The Body." The only problem is the victim probably is *not* King, and has no idea what Herb and Marge are ranting about as they torture him. The author bio note at the end of this story says "Paddy McKillop needs no introduction—or, for that matter, explanation." I concur.)

Book Reviews:
- "More Terror From Dean Koontz." (Review by Tyson Blue. A look at a re-issue of one of Dean's "Leigh Nichols" novels.)
- "Hale, Hale, The Maniac's All Here." (Very positive review by Tyson Blue of Charles Grant's novel *In a Dark Dream.*)
- "SK's Tale the Tamest in *Book of the Dead.* " (Review by Tyson Blue. A look at Skipp and Spector's seminal zombie collection.)

Features:
◊ "Editor's Column," by Christopher Spruce.
◊ "Letters to *CR*."
◊ "Classifieds."

Vol. 5, No. 9-10 (Issue #53)
September-October 1989

This was it.

Now we knew.

In this issue, Chris Spruce told us that *Castle Rock* was closing up shop in a front page article entitled "Say Goodnight, Lucy."

I—and many others—had heard through the grapevine that December was going to be *CR*'s last issue, but final confirmation was reserved for this issue.

The question many fans wanted answered was "Why?"

A lot of S.K. fans thought that *CR* was now a fixture in their lives—especially after the "false alarm" of a year previous when the word was that *Castle Rock* was going to cease publication with the December 1988 issue.

Instead, 1989 was to be the newsletter's last year.

Here's what Chris had to say about the demise of *CR*:

> "*Castle Rock* is at a crossroads. We are not quite 'The Stephen King Newsletter' in the same sense we were a couple of years back. We have branched out – largely at subscriber request – to review and discuss the works of other horror and fantasy genre writers, some of whom have professional or personal connection with SK. At the same time, SK's public activities have become less frequent over the past five years as he has chosen to spend more time at home and less on the road. And, of course, his popularity as a contemporary novelist is such that he really does not have to do publicity tours to sell books. To this point, they sell quite well without his personal assistance. Same goes for the movies made from his works.
>
> Thus, the scope of things SK fans would read CR for has been reduced. Largely, we try to update our readers on when, where, and how his newest books, stories, and movies will appear, his occasional public appearance, and tidbits about works in progress. Very often, in the last couple of years, much of our news has concerned books *about,* as opposed to *by,* Stephen King, as his popularity has given birth to a whole new cottage industry of books studying both him and his works.
>
> Then there is Stephen, himself. I'm not sure he has ever been entirely comfortable with the idea of a newsletter devoted to 'Stephen King.' After all, he is yet a tried-and-true Yankee possessed of that sometimes endearing quality of self-effacement who just might be a little embarrassed by the fuss. At the same time, he understands his faithful fans need both a source of information about him and an outlet for their comments about their favorite writer.
>
> In such a context, I believe Stephen would be just as happy to see *Castle Rock, The Stephen King Newsletter,* pass on or, at the very least, become something other than a newsletter devoted to Stephen King.
>
> Bearing all that in mind, I have decided to cease publishing *Castle Rock, The Stephen King Newsletter,* as of the final issue of 1989. And, believe me, this time it is *the end.*"

And he wasn't kidding, either.

Chris took a little bit of his "Editor's Column" to explain some of his personal reasons for closing up shop, and what he would be doing post-*CR*.

And that, my friends, was that.

The rest of this twelve-page double issue contained the usual potpourri of articles, reviews, and also included a large photo of Stephen King throwing the first pitch at the Maine Little League All-Star Championship game in Old Town, Maine, on August 5, 1989.

Articles:
- "Hello, It's Me...Say Goodnight, Lucy," by Chris Spruce. (Hel-lo, goodbye from Chris and *Castle Rock*.)
- "Acorns to Oaks: Explorations of Theme, Image, and Character In the Early Works of Stephen King," by Michael R. Collings. (Part 2 of the essay begun in last month's issue. Part 2 covers King's poetry, and appears in this volume as "The Radiating Pencils of His Bones: The Poetry of Stephen King.")
- "NECON '89 Lauded," by Dave Lowell. (A review of NECON 9.)
- "Bill and Steve—Two Of A Kind," by Mark Graham (An interesting piece comparing Stephen King to William Shakespeare.

The point is that Shakespeare wrote for a popular audience, as does King, and many of the two writers' stories involve supernatural elements.)
- "Magazine Will Focus On Censorship Issues." (Unattributed. Article revealing details on Barry Hoffman's censorship-oriented annual magazine *Gauntlet, The Magazine of Free Expression.*)
- "I Wouldn't Tease 'Em If I Didn't Love 'Em." (An interview with Ray Rexer by Barry Hoffman. A fun interview with Ray in which he talks about his thinking (and with Ray I use that word loosely) behind publishing his *Castle Rock* parody, *Castle Schlock.*)

Fiction:
- "Silent Partner," by Christopher Spruce. (*CR*'s editor dishes up a tale he says is based on a true story. He advised readers with complaints about *CR*'s lack of blood and shock value to send the diatribes to Paddy McKillop.)

Book Reviews:
- "A Horror Home Companion." (A lengthy, in-depth, and positive review by Michael R. Collings of George Beahm's terrific *The Stephen King Companion.*)
- "Lori Is A Thrilling Chip Off The Old Bloch." (Positive review by Tyson Blue of Bloch's first novel since *Night of the Ripper.*)
- "*Carrion Comfort* Is Best New Novel Of The Year – So Far." (Glowing review by Tyson Blue of Dan Simmon's follow-up to *The Song of Kali.*)
- "*Swan Song* Is Epic Novel." (Review by Tyson Blue of Robert R. McCammon's epic post-holocaust novel. See my interview with Rick McCammon in this volume for McCammon's own thoughts about *Swan Song* and his other works.)
- "Vampire Anthology Is High Quality Fare." (A rave recommendation by Tyson Blue of Ellen Datlow's non-traditional vampire anthology *Blood Is Not Enough.*)

Features:
◊ "Editor's Column," by Christopher Spruce.
◊ "Letters to *CR.*"
◊ "Classifieds."

Vol. 5, No. 11 (Issue #54) November 1989

Other than a few letters from readers lamenting the demise of *Castle Rock*, this issue was business as usual, and for that, Chris Spruce and staff should be commended. They still had a newsletter to get out, they knew what readers wanted, and so they delivered. That, to me, is true professionalism. Even though I'm not real satisfied with this analogy, I think you'll get my point: It's all too easy to slack off on the job when you know you're getting laid off at the end of the week. What difference would it make, right? But it made a difference to the *Castle Rock* crew, and for that they deserve our thanks. *CR* was essentially history, and yet Chris made sure he delivered the goods with this issue.

The front page contained *CR*'s first review of the new S.K. novel, *The Dark Half,* as well as a terrific poem by Ray Rexer called "I Don't Care What People Say, *Castle Rock* Is Here To Stay."

The eight-page issue also contained a Barry Hoffman interview with *New Blood*'s Chris Lacher, an overview of S.K. movie soundtracks, and a full-page Horrorfest '90 ad.

Articles:
- "Some SK Soundtracks Are More Than Background Music," by Wayne Rhodes. (Overview of S.K.'s movie music.)
- "An Interview with *New Blood*'s Chris Lacher." (Interview by Barry Hoffman. An interesting talk with the editor of a magazine that just may fill the *Twilight Zone* void.)
- "More Videos of SK Works Released," by Tyson Blue. (An overview of forthcoming S.K. videos.)
- "Here's An Unusual King Collectible," by Ben P. Indick. (An

article on the S.K. introductory essay that appears only in the Book of the Month Club edition of John Fowles's *The Collector*.)

Fiction:

- "No Place to Hide," by Barry Hoffman. (A short story about a woman haunted by a demonic rapist...that can't be killed.)

Book Reviews:

- "New Novel Puts SK Back On Track." (A positive review by Tyson Blue of *The Dark Half.*)

Features:

◊ "I Don't Care What People Say, *Castle Rock* Is Here To Stay." (A poem by Ray Rexer.)

◊ "Editor's Column," by Christopher Spruce.

◊ "Letters to *CR*." (One letter contained a comprehensive listing of mail-order book companies, small presses, and publications for SK/horror fans.)

◊ "The SK Soundtracks." (Compiled by Wayne Rhodes. A complete listing of S.K.'s movie music.)

◊ "Classifieds."

Vol. 5, No. 12 (Issue #55) December 1989

As Christopher Spruce put it in his final "Editor's Column": "Well, folks, this is it."

And it, it was.

Castle Rock's final issue was a twelve-pager that contained a terrific collection of what we had come to love *CR* for: articles, reviews, excerpts, fiction, and more...and all aimed right for the throat of the Stephen King fan.

I had heard a rumor about the last issue. Rumor was that Stephen King was going to contribute a previously unseen short story to the newsletter. But that was not to be. For whatever reason, Stephen King's final contribution to the newsletter was his article "The Ultimate Catalogue," featured in the June 1989 issue.

I was flattered to receive front-page placement for an excerpt from the book you now hold in your hands. My concordance to "I Was A Teenage Grave Robber" began on the front page and continued onto all of Page 4. Chris Spruce—and Stephanie Leonard before him—have always been very supportive of *The Shape Under the Sheet*, and my sincerest thanks and appreciation go out to them for their kindness throughout the *Castle Rock* years.

Other notable items in this last issue included a look at the trade edition of "My Pretty Pony," an article about *Lights Out! The Robert R. McCammon Newsletter*, interviews with Barry Hoffman and Christopher Spruce, and several farewell articles to the *Rock*.

Articles:

- "The Last Rat Swims, Or a Farewell to the *Rock*," by Tyson Blue. (Blue bids adieu.)
- "*Lights Out!: The Robert R. McCammon Newsletter*," by Barry Hoffman. (A look at the new McCammon newsletter.)
- "*Castle Rock* and the Stephen King Experience," by Tom Draheim (A farewell piece that begins: "King is our drug, he is our heroin.")
- "DT Books Make Dutch Appearance," by Eddy C. Bertin. (Details on the Dutch editions of SK's *Dark Tower* series.)
- "An Interview with *Gauntlet*'s Barry Hoffman." (Interview by Richard Chizmar. A talk with the editor of *Gauntlet*.)
- "Cut Adrift In a Plagiarized Raft," by Wayne Rhodes. (Details on the illegal reprinting of an edited version of S.K.'s "The Raft," which appeared in a college publication in Arkansas.)
- "Just In The Nick Of Time." (An interview with Chris Spruce by Barry Hoffman. A talk with *CR*'s editor.)

Fiction:

- "The Incubus Dream," by Tom Draheim. (A short story.)

Book Reviews:

- "Affordable 'My Pretty Pony' Published By Whitney Museum." (Tyson Blue reviews the fifty-dollar trade edition of "Pony.")
- "The 'Twilight Zone' Companion." (Positive review by Tyson

Blue of the must-have book for all "TZ" fans.)

- "Harlan Ellison's Watching." (Rave review by Tyson Blue of Ellison's giant collection of essays.)
- "'Companion' Covers A Lot of Ground." (Positive review by Tyson Blue of George Beahm's *The Stephen King Companion*. See the feature on George and the *Companion* in this volume.)
- "Rode Hard, Put Up Wet?" (Tyson Blue reviews Joe Lansdale's western/horror cowpunk anthology *Razored Saddles*.)
- "Sparrows Flying Again Is Not Good News." (Review by Michael E. Stamm. Insightful review of *The Dark Half* that originally appeared in the Eugene, Oregon *Register-Guard*.)
- "Tryon is Back." (Unattributed. Positive review of Tryon's return to the horror genre, *The Night of The Moonbow*.)

Book Excerpts:

- "A Concordance to Stephen King's First Published Short Story 'I Was A Teenage Grave Robber'." (An excerpt from *The Shape Under the Sheet: The Complete Stephen King Encyclopedia* by Stephen J. Spignesi. Features several dozen entries from this volume.)

Features:

◊ "Editor's Column," by Christopher Spruce.

◊ "Letters to *CR*."

◊ "The End." (At the bottom of the third column of Page 12 of this issue, Chris Spruce wrote "The End." And so it was.)

CASTLE ROCK
A Final Note

"Goodbye, Farewell, and Amen"

In December of 1989, on New Year's Eve, somewhere in Maine, a small town named Castle Rock began to fade away.

As the hours passed and the year drew to a close, the buildings started to shimmer in the moonlight, and if you were there you would have begun to see the images of distant hills and high clouds appearing *through* the structures.

As the clocks all ticked their last seconds away towards midnight, ghostly figures began to appear on Main Street. All of Castle Rock's residents were assembling for their last goodbye. I won't say their names: You all know them well enough. They all stood there, watching their town die, watching as bit by bit, piece by piece, things disappeared. Discorporated.

Finally, the clock tolled midnight.

The houses and buildings gave one last glimmer and blinked out; the people in the streets looked up and smiled wistfully before they rose off the ground and faded into the sky. The wind picked up.

And off in the distance, the somber strains of "Auld Lang Syne" played in a minor key could be heard wafting away into the blackness, the wind combining with the song to create a *true* music of the night.

Beyond the town's limits, a lone man stood on a hill, looking down into emptiness. He was tall, bearded, and had his hands in his jacket pockets. He stood silently, not moving, listening to the final strains of some tune he heard in the distance. After a while, he turned, and for one brief moment, the moon illuminated his visage, the silver light limning a single shiny tear rolling down his cheek. The tear slid down his face and fell onto the cold, hard soil.

"So long," he whispered to the night, and walked away into the darkness.

CASTLE SCHLOCK
The Stephen King Parody Newsletter

I saw my first copy of *Castle Schlock* when Dave Hinchberger of the Overlook Connection sent me a complete set.

I loved it.

I love parody and satire, and Ray Rexer is very good at it, indeed. The finest satirical writing comes from a complete and comprehensive knowledge of the subject being parodied, and if there's anything Ray Rexer has a complete and comprehensive knowledge of (other than artillery maintenance and methods of bruiseless interrogation) it's the work of Stephen King.

In the following piece, Ray gives an overview of his parody newsletter, and talks a little bit about its appeal.

Following Ray's essay, I will give you a look at some of my favorite moments from the now-defunct *Castle Schlock*. —sjs

CASTLE SCHLOCK
A Brief History
by Ray Rexer

The Origin

Castle Schlock began in mid-1986 and started out with a total readership of two: I wrote it, and a guy I work with named Leonard Norman read it. Now, Len is more than just your average Stephen King nut—he's like an SK savant or something. He can't remember his own phone number, but I don't think he's ever forgotten a single word of any Stephen King tale he's ever read.

Len and I are both policemen (who feel badly miscast in the roll, by the way—but that's another story), and Stephen King has gotten us through some pretty miserable times on the job. When things get rough, we try to meet and swap Kingisms—stories, trivia, lines from SK books and the like. We escape into the Kingdom of Delain for a while, or "flip" with Jack into the Territories. It's like taking a mental vacation, and when we get back, some of the pressure's been relieved and things don't seem quite so bad.

Steve may not know it, but he's contributed vastly to the sanity of two Michigan cops.

One night I went home and cranked out issue #1 of the *Schlock* on my PC for just such an occasion. I gave it to Len at work a few days later and he loved it. I'll

never forget what he said to me after reading it. He said, "This is better than getting a check in the mail! Betcha fer!" I was touched—who wouldn't have been?

And *Castle Schlock* was born.

The Growth

Word about the *Schlock* got around via the SK Underground Grapevine (The SKUG—and yes, I just made that up, but I'm pretty sure something like it actually does exist), and requests for copies started pouring in at the rate of something like one in a millenium. Momentum grew; the *Schlock* took on a life of its own. I received a lot of good feedback on *Castle Schlock* from various King devotees, and before long the reverberating chant of "WE WANT MORE! WE WANT MORE!" could be heard from coast to coast.

It wasn't something I could ignore.

So, I wrote issue #2...then #3...then #4. Shortly thereafter, a couple of mail-order booksellers started offering it through their catalogs: Craig Goden from the Time Tunnel in New Jersey, and Dave Hinchberger of The Overlook Connection in Georgia, who puts out a hugely entertaining catalog. Just recently, Weinberg Books added *Castle Schlock* to the large and varied list of items they sell.

The Appeal

Castle Schlock seems to appeal mostly to the person who's an accomplished Kingologist, a true kindred spirit, someone with a PhD in SK.

There are a lot of inside jokes in the *Schlock* that only such a person could truly understand. For example, issue #1 mentions SK's new cookbook, *Food Processor of the Gods*, an obvious takeoff on a similarly named short story by King—but only to someone who's "in" on King.

In the classified ad section of another issue, a man named Art Denker advertises three King limited editions for sale: an asbestos-bound *Firestarter*, a leather-bound *Skeleton Crew*, and a dead-cat-bound *Pet Sematary*. Now, this would totally lose someone who doesn't read King, and rightfully so—anyone who doesn't read King doesn't deserve to understand these things and to heck with them! Let 'em go read an Updike book or something!

But I digress.

At the same time, there are a lot of inside jokes relating to *Castle Rock* (the real Stephen King newsletter, remember?). The *Schlock's* editor, for example, is a woman named Annie Lynn Steffard, a corruption

The first and the last issues of
Castle Schlock: The Stephen King Parody Newsletter,
Issue #1 (1986) and Vol. 1, No. 5 (September 1989).

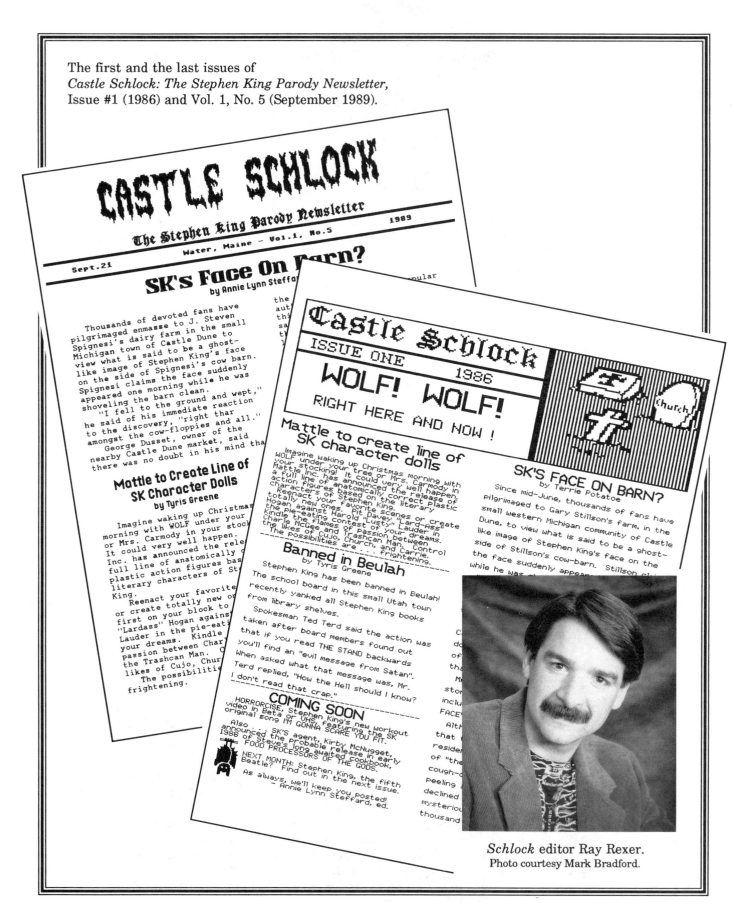

CASTLE SCHLOCK

The Stephen King Parody Newsletter

Water, Maine — Vol.1, No.5   1989

Sept.21

SK's Face On Barn?
by Annie Lynn Steffa[rd]

Thousands of devoted fans have pilgrimaged enmasse to J. Steven Spignesi's dairy farm in the small Michigan town of Castle Dune to view what is said to be a ghost-like image of Stephen King's face on the side of Spignesi's cow barn. Spignesi claims the face suddenly appeared one morning while he was shoveling the barn clean.

"I fell to the ground and wept," he said of his immediate reaction to the discovery, "right thar amongst the cow-floppies and all."

George Dusset, owner of the nearby Castle Dune market, said there was no doubt in his mind tha[t]

Mattle to Create Line of SK Character Dolls
by Tyris Greene

Imagine waking up Christmas morning with WOLF under your or Mrs. Carmody in your stock It could very well happen. Inc. has announced the rele full line of anatomically c plastic action figures bas literary characters of St King.

Reenact your favorite or create totally new o first on your block to "Lardass" Hogan agains Lauder in the pie-eati your dreams. Kindle passion between Char the Trashcan Man. O likes of Cujo, Chur

The possibilitie frightening.

Castle Schlock

ISSUE ONE   1986

WOLF! WOLF!
RIGHT HERE AND NOW !

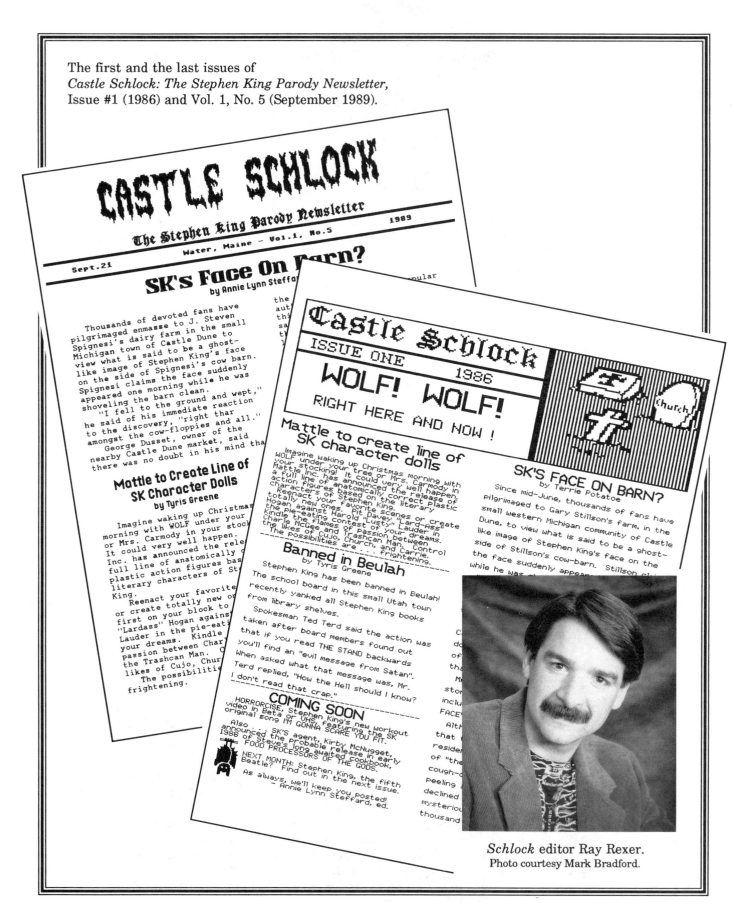

SK'S FACE ON BARN?
by Terrie Potatoe

Since mid-June, thousands of fans have pilgrimaged to Gary Stillson's farm, in the small western Michigan community of Castle Dune, to view what is said to be a ghost-like image of Stephen King's face on the side of Stillson's cow-barn. Stillson cl[aims] the face suddenly appea[red] while he was sh[oveling]

Mattle to create line of SK character dolls

Imagine waking up Christmas morning with WOLF under your tree or Mrs. Carmody in your stocking! It could very well happen. Mattle Inc. has announced the release of a full line of anatomically correct plastic action figures of Stephen King characters based on the literary characters.

Reenact your favorite scenes or create totally new ones. Pit Davey "Lard-Ass" Hogan against Harold "Lusty" Lauder in the pie-eating contest of your dreams. Kindle the flames of passion between Charlie McGee and the Trashcan Man. Control the likes of Cujo, Church, and Carrie.

The possibilities are... frightening.

Banned in Beulah
by Tyris Greene

Stephen King has been banned in Beulah! The school board in this small Utah town recently yanked all Stephen King books from library shelves.

Spokesman Ted Terd said the action was taken after board members found out that if you read THE STAND backwards you'll find an "evil message from Satan".

When asked what that message was, Mr. Terd replied, "How the Hell should I know? I don't read that crap."

COMING SOON

HORRORCISE, Stephen King's new workout video in Beta or VHS, featuring the SK original song I'M GONNA SCARE YOU FIT.

Also, SK's agent, Kirby McNugget, announced the probable release in early 1988 of Steve's long-awaited cookbook, FOOD PROCESSORS OF THE GODS.

NEXT MONTH: Stephen King, the fifth Beatle? Find out in the next issue.

As always, we'll keep you posted!
— Annie Lynn Steffard, ed.

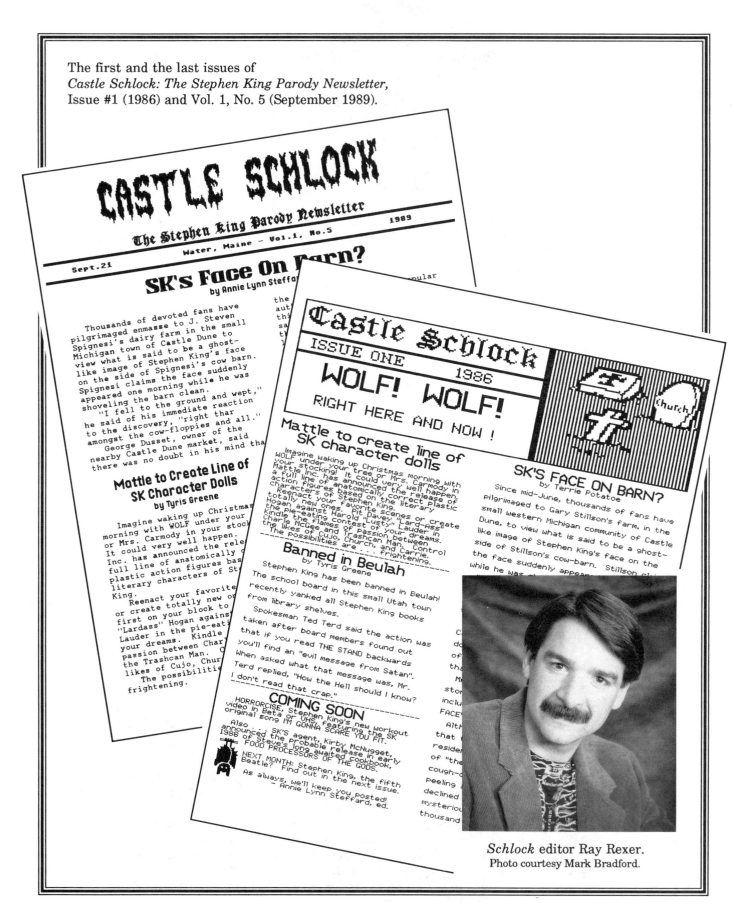

Schlock editor Ray Rexer.
Photo courtesy Mark Bradford.

of Stephanie Leonard's name (God bless her ink-stained heart). And one of the *Schlock*'s contributing editors is a man named Tyris Greene, a colorful name, so to speak.

Castle Schlock is nothing more than harmless fun. It was never meant to be anything more than that, and I'm quite sure it never evolved into anything more than that. Harmless fun, no offense intended. I believe it's possible to be funny without being mean, and that's all the *Schlock* tries to do. And, as an added bonus of sorts, *Castle Schlock* is now low in saturated fats and completely safe when used as directed. Now what more could a person want in a parody newsletter anyway, huh?

The Future

None.

The original Stephen King newsletter, *Castle Rock*, ceased publication as of December 1989, so according to international parody laws, *Castle Schlock* had to do likewise. It's completely out of my hands. Sorry.

But...as a final offering of sorts, I combined the best of *Castle Schlock* from the first four issues with a fair amount of all new material to produce a single, larger, more professional-looking, action-packed laff-a-minute issue!

And that'll have to do.

(Order back issues of *Castle Schlock* from either The Overlook Connection or The Time Tunnel.)

❖❖❖

CASTLE SCHLOCK:
An Abundance of Schlock

Issue #1, 1986

Issue #1 was a one-pager that bore the headline "WOLF! WOLF! RIGHT HERE AND NOW!" and informed us that: "Mattle" was marketing a line of Stephen King character dolls (including Davey "Lard-Ass" Hogan and Harold "Lusty" Lauder); that in the "small western Michigan community of Castle Dune" a ghostlike image of Stephen King's face was visible on "Gary Stillson's" barn; and that coming soon was Stephen King's new workout video, "Horrocise," featuring the original Stephen King song "I'm Gonna Scare You Fit."

There was also an article by "Tyris Greene" called "Banned in Beulah" in which we learned that school board spokesman "Ted Terd" had banned all of King's

books because it had been discovered that if you read *The Stand* backwards, you'd find "an evil message from Satan."

Also, in the "Coming Soon" column was news that Stephen King's long-awaited cookbook *Food Processor of the Gods* would be released in early 1988.

Issue #2, 1986

Issue #2 was expanded to two pages, and bore the headline "Don't tell me, I'll tell you."

This issue told us about Stephen King's new cereal SCARY-O'S—the "breakfast cereal for people who are not afraid to eat right."

The Editor's Column cleared up the rumor about Stephen King appearing on "Late Night with David Letterman" in a segment of Stupid Pet Tricks. Turns out that an act called "Steve and King"—"a Utah man and his dancing dingo"—caused the confusion.

Also, an article by some guy named "Wray Wreckser" asserted that Stephen King was actually the fifth Beatle, basing his argument on certain lines from "I Am the Walrus" ("Yellow matter custard dripping from a dead dog's eye"), and "Come Together" ("He got joo-joo eyeball"). The piece was illustrated by a drum kit with a "John, Paul, George and Stephen" logo, and noted that "experts say [Stephen King] authored a great many of the lyrics credited to Lennon and McCartney [and that] some say it's time to give the Devil his due."

And, in an article by "Colling R. Michaels," we also learned that some 5,000 counterfeit Stephen King books had recently been seized outside a popular Bangor, Maine, restaurant, The Crab Slab, and destroyed. The books were corrupt copies of King's collection *Skeleton Crew* which had been retitled *Skeleton Crude,* and contained the stories "Son of A Beachworld," "Cain Threw Up," "Uncle Otto's Duck," "Here There Pee Tigers," and "a nasty little tale about Mrs. Todd that would make even Stephen King blush."

Issue #3, 1987

Issue #3 bore the headline "HELLO, FROM BELLIS!" and was a three-pager.

The issue bore news of a new GM car, the "Christine-Classic," that GM spokesman R. Lee Bay said came with a warranty so good "you'd swear the car repairs itself."

We also learned that there was a rumor that Stephen King was about to take over the troubled PTL ministry. King's agent Kirby McNugget's response? "No comment."

This issue had a demented letters column ("Dear Schlock: *Q:* What would you have if you crossed Ace

Merrill, Stephen King, Queen Sasha, Jack Sawyer and Bo Derek? *A:* A straight! Ace, King, Queen, Jack, and a Ten!"), and an article by "R. Jeff Hinchberger" on a good-against-evil baseball game. The teams were "The Derry Stiffsoxs vs. The Castle Rock Crab-Catchers," and the lineups included Kurt Barlow ("Watch out for him during those night games"), Robert "Pennywise" Gray ("Watch him FLOAT down that baseline"), Stu Redman ("This man will catch anything – except the flu!"), and Nick Andros ("A man who lets that bat do the talking for him.")

Issue #4, 1988

This was the final all-new issue of *Castle Schlock,* and it bore the headline "Dirty Birdie! Cockadoodie!" It ran two pages, and the front page contained an article by "Tyris Green" called "He's Making a LIST." Yes, it had actually happened: "[A]vailable to the general reading public for the first time now! STEPHEN KING'S LAUNDRY LIST!"

We also learned in the editor's column that Stephen King "had joined the ranks of such celebrities as Carole King, B.B. King, Billie Jean King, and Alan King" in promoting Rheingold beer—the beer (groan) of KINGS!

The editor's column also let slip that Stephen King was really James Michener, and that King's given name was really Joseph Heller.

There was a "King Crossword" puzzle in which some of the clues were: *3-Across:* Sky ____; *2-Down:* The ____ And I; *6-Across:* ____ Tut; and *7-Down:* Long live the ____.

My favorite item in this issue, though, was a "Classified Ad" that read "WANTED: Fornit with fornus, any condition. Desperate! John Updike, 1 Eastwick Lane, Fresno, California 95062."

Issue #5, September 21, 1989

Issue #5 was a "*Castle Schlock*'s Greatest Hits" issue, so to speak, and I think I'm flattered. (I think.) They say you've arrived when you're parodied, and if so, then I've arrived—at least in the eyes of Ray Rexer and the *Castle Schlock* staff!

The front page of this issue had an article by "Annie Lynn Steffard" called "SK's Face On Barn?" In its entirety it read:

"Thousands of devoted fans have pilgrim-

aged en masse to J. Steven Spignesi's dairy farm in the small Michigan town of Castle Dune to view what is said to be a ghost-like image of Stephen King's face on the side of Spignesi's cow barn. Spignesi claims the face suddenly appeared one morning while he was shoveling the barn clean.

'I fell to the ground and wept,' he said of his immediate reaction to the discovery, 'right thar amongst the cow-floppies and all.'

George Dussett, owner of the nearby Castle Dune market, said there was no doubt in his mind that the face was that of the popular author. 'Just looking at that thing gives me the willies,' he said. Mr. Dussett went on to say that his store now carries a full line of specialty souvenirs including the fast-selling 'I SURVIVED THE FACE' t-shirt.

Although both Dussett and Spignesi swear that the image is authentic, another local resident claims it is nothing more than 'one of them thar Smith brothers' from an old cough drop ad showing through layers of faded and peeling paint. The resident declined to identify himself, saying mysteriously, 'The pile of shit has a thousand eyes.'"

(Thanks, Ray.)

The rest of the issue was a compilation of some of the funniest pieces from the previous issues, although Ray and Len did add some new material, specifically one classified ad that had me rolling on the floor. (And getting full of cat hair, too.) On this note, I'll conclude my look at that shortlived phenomenon, *Castle Schlock,* with thanks and appreciation to Ray Rexer and Len Norman for their help, interest, and support for *The Shape Under the Sheet,* and for allowing me to reprint material from the newsletter.

Okay.

Are you ready?

CLASSIFIEDS

"MY FOOT! My foot! My foot! My foot! My FOOOOOOT! Deke."

See?

What'd I tellya?

"CHARACTER ASSASSINATION"
A King Parody by Ray Rexer

"Character Assassination" could, I suppose, justifiably be called Stephen King's worst nightmare.

In this short story by *Castle Schlock*'s Ray Rexer, several characters that Stephen King killed off in his stories come back to life seeking revenge on King for killing them off. (If fictional characters aren't real to begin with, does that mean they must first come to life as living people, *then* be killed off in the stories, and *then* come back to life as nonexistent beings who were brought to life, made dead, and then brought back to life? Just thought I'd ask.)

In the cover letter that accompanied his story, Ray asked if I "could mention [that] the original version of this story [was] written and published before SK's *The Dark Half.*" He felt that "[p]eople are gonna think I ripped King off for the idea (when we both know he stole the idea from me—right?"). I won't spoil the "shared" moment Ray is referring to, but I will tell you that it involves a Berol Black Beauty pencil.

As with all good parody, to get the full effect of Ray's brilliance it would help if you've already read things like *The Stand, The Shining, Misery, The Dark Half,* and "Word Processor of the Gods," but there's plenty here to howl over for even the most casual King reader.

The original (and much shorter) version of "Character Assassination" was first published in the Fall 1989 issue of *Horrorfest Press,* and Ray kindly consented to do an expanded, revised version especially for readers of *The Shape Under the Sheet.*

But lemme tellya about Ray.
Ray Rexer is probably certifiable.
But he is also a brilliant satirist, a terrific writer, and a great guy who went out of his way to help with *The Shape Under the Sheet.*

And I've also heard from Len Norman that Ray uses Lawn-Gro on his moustache.

Ladies and germs, Ray Rexer, and his nifty tale, "Character Assassination." — **sjs**

"CHARACTER ASSASINATION"
by Ray Rexer

Stephen King was in trouble. Bad trouble. There could be no denying that.

Snow drifted down unwatched in light delicate spirals and pushed softly, like ghostly hands, against the locked door of the cheap Dakin Street motel room he occupied. Inside, Stephen stood before a grubby mirror and saw an old man, thin and haggard, wearing his face. He passed a hand slowly over his grizzled chin. I look haunted, he thought. Haunted. And in a very real way, that was just what he was. Haunted. He took off his thick glasses and rubbed his eyes. He was tired, bone tired, very near the end of his endurance. He couldn't remember the last time he had slept through an entire night. Another lifetime ago, perhaps. A truck roared by on Highway 99, shaking the thin walls of the room and rattling the door. Stephen jumped and turned quickly to look at the door. The thin wood vibrated with the truck's passing. "Shit on a shingle," he muttered, and then laughed bitterly at himself for sounding like a character out of one of his own stories. But why not? It was, after all, those very characters who had gotten him into this mess. "Shit on a goddamn shingle," he said again, watching the door.

It had started some four months ago, way back when he had been the Stephen King everybody knew and some even loved. A good ole boy, normal in most ways, unbelievably happy and solidly sane. A lifetime ago. When he had been a writer. Remember that? A writer, for God's-sweet-sakes. He had put words down on paper to the delight of millions. And that was great. But what was even better was that he had done it to the delight of *himself.* A nearly orgasmic delight at times. It was what he lived for. He was a gleefully possessed man when he was at his word processor (a big Wang he lovingly called the "monster dick"), and back then he had been a writing fool, a one-man story factory. Back then he had been at his word processor nearly every waking moment. Writing was his life; it was what he lived for. It was almost as if he fed off the light from his CRT, like a plant absorbing life's energy from the sun. It meant that much to him.

But he hadn't typed a single word, a single letter, in over four months now. And for him that was the worse thing, much worse than everything that had happened since. But he just couldn't risk it. No way, no how. He just couldn't. He had become much too powerful a writer for his own good. He had become dangerous. His words had almost killed him.

Stephen King was scared. And he was in trouble.

Bad trouble.

He set his glasses on the scarred nightstand next to the bed and stretched his long frame out on top of the ratty bedspread. He reached up and turned off the light. The darkness was nearly complete; the only sound his shallow breathing. He felt very much alone. He had a headache, a real bitch-kitty, and he rubbed fiercely at his temples. "Stressaches," his doctor had once told him. "You gotta slow down, Steve, start taking it easy."

Right. Slow down. Take it easy. He snorted at the thought and the sudden intake of air drove a spike of pain through his eyes. Lying fully dressed in a cheap, musty-smelling motel room somewhere in southwestern Pennsylvania, protected from death by thin plywood walls and discount K-Mart locks, "taking it easy" didn't seem very much in his future. No way, no how. Stephen squeezed his eyes shut against the pain and tried to ignore the angry throbbing in his head. Yeah, he thought, I'll slow down. Promise. And that, my friends, is boolsheet of the purest ray serene. He concentrated on his breathing, tried to make it deep and regular, tried to relax, tried not to think of anything, tried to make his mind a blank, a white void...and finally he drifted off.

A knock at the door woke him with a start from the cheap beginnings of sleep. His heart flapped and thundered in his chest like aluminum in the wind. He grabbed the hunting knife from the inside pocket of his denim jacket and held it pointed at the door. His hand jitter-bugged the knife above him in the dark. He resisted an urge to scream. The knock came again. Stephen held his breath. Who this time? Which one of them? Why can't they just leave me *alone*?

The knock came louder, a booming WHUMP! WHUMP! WHUMP! that echoed through the small room and rattled the door. And then a voice, almost a whisper, spoke. "Steve. Oh, Ste-eve. Open the door. Open the goddamn door."

Stephen back-crawled out of the bed, eyes wide in the darkness, never leaving the shadow-shape of the door. His feet touched down on the matted carpeting and he shuffled backwards to the far side of the motel room until he felt the cool of its wall against his hips. The knife was still held out in front of him, more like a talisman than a weapon. A ward against evil.

Then sharp and loud: "OPEN THE GODDAMN DOOR! OPEN IT!" The door bucked inward from a shoulder crash. "Open the fuckin' door, you little shit! Right now! Open it or I'll...I'll..." Then a pause. "Why, I'll huff and I'll puff and I'll bloooww your door down!" Laughter, deep and maniacal, shot through the door chilling Stephen's spine. "Right the fuck down, Steve-o. I shit you not."

"No," Stephen said out loud, shaking his head in denial. No. You're not real. You're *not* real!"

"I'm real, you little pup. You created me."

"No." But it was too late for denials.

"Oh yeah. And it's time for paybacks. It's time for...correction. Can you say that, you witless bastard? Correction. It's time for CORRECTION, you shitheap! You *officious little PRICK!*"

The final word was counterpointed by a resounding *CRASH!* as the business end of an axe slammed through the door. Jagged wooden splinters flew. Stephen screamed. A flashback of Annie Wilkes hit his brain and he touched the fresh scar on his wrist. The axe was pulled out and then came down again, harder. A hole the size of a fist appeared in the door. Trapped, he thought, I'm trapped. He pushed away from the wall in a panic and struck the nightstand hard with his thigh. Gonna bruise, he thought crazily as the nightstand fell over and he went down with it. The knife flew out of his hand and he watched it somersault through the air in comic slow motion. It landed and skittered across the floor. Stephen scampered on hands and knees over the contents of the upset nightstand and groped around for the knife. The axe came down again and now its whole head crashed through the door. Stephen screamed again and looked up. The axe was pulled free. Puffs of snow swirled through the hole, spears of gray light stabbed their way angrily into the small room. He could see movement outside, shadowy and indistinct. Then an eye appeared at the opening and part of an evil, crooked smile.

"Redrum, Stevie. It's time for redrum."

It was Jack. Jack Torrance. He was alive.

His characters had been coming back from the dead for four months now and he had been running, not really sure why but not knowing what else to do. Most of his friends knew something was wrong. It didn't take a Rhodes Scholar to figure that one out. The easygoing man they had known and loved had disappeared, the man with that strange but infectious laugh and genuine smile. The man who would kick back and crack a few with them at the Bangor Lanes every once in a while, slapping backs and cracking wise. Their friend. Gone. And in his place came a restless stranger, complete with a maddening array of nervous tics and quick head movements.

But what could he tell them? That his characters were coming back to life and that they were pissed off? That the fictional people he had created out of paper and ink had suddenly turned into flesh and blood? No way, no how. That would never wash. Made up characters just didn't come to life, for chrissakes. They were simple figments of imagination, not real. Sure, he was good at characterization, even his hardest critics gave him that. But he wasn't *that* good. No one was. Characters just didn't come alive. That was fucking absurd. That was like something out of a...well, like something out of a Stephen King novel, as ironic as it seemed. He couldn't tell them that. Even if it was the truth.

And what about Tabitha? She certainly was nobody's fool. She had been married to him for too long not to have known almost from the onset that something was wrong. He realized that and had come close on several occasions to telling her everything, the whole truth—at least the truth as he knew and believed it. But, in the end, he had simply asked her for her trust. And she had given it to him. Just like that.

No, made-up characters just didn't come alive. No way, no how. That was absurd. That was impossible.

But it was happening.

The first one had been Andrew "Poke" Freeman, a relatively minor character out of the pages of *The Stand*. Stephen had been finishing the final draft of a short story for a Charles Grant anthology called *Oh, Loathsome Me* when Poke appeared at the door to his study.

"Wha–," Stephen said, looking up at Poke, shocked by his sudden appearance and then dumbfounded when he really looked at him. "Wha—"

Poke stood in a blood-soaked shirt. He was smiling, but the left side of his face was mostly gone and the smile was less than friendly. "Whoop! Whoop!" he said. Steve could see his jaw work through the rough open flesh on his face. Most of Poke's teeth were gone on that side. "You blew me up, you stupid fuck. Blew me up in your stupid book. Got me shot. Now I'm gonna Pokerize you, ole buddy."

Poke brought a gun up from his side. Stephen wasn't the least bit surprised to see that it was a .357 Magnum. He had, after all, given the gun to Poke—in a literary manner of speaking.

Stephen didn't give a thought to the utter impossibility of the situation, he just dove for the floor. The shot exploded above him and took out his word processor. Glass rained down on him. He hugged his head with both arms. His mind cartwheeled in his head. A second shot rang out and slammed into the word processor again with enough force to slide it sideways on the desk. "You'll never watch Lawrence Welk again!" Poke yelled, and whooped crazily.

Stephen tried to melt into the floor. Glass chips bit into the palms of his hands and poked through the knees of his jeans. He held his breath and waited, shaking in uncontrollable spasms, trying to think but being unable to form any rational thought at all. A final shard of glass worked its way out of the ruined

Wang and dropped to his side. Fifteen minutes passed and then another fifteen...and nothing more happened. Just silence. Finally, Stephen had cautiously inched his way out from under the desk and peeked around its corner. The room had been empty.

Three weeks later, while walking out of the downtown Bangor Public Library, he had been chased by Mrs. Carmody and a small band of her followers right down Main Street in the middle of the afternoon. "Blood sacrifice!" they had screamed at him, fists raised in anger. "Expiation!" they had called as they ran. "Expiation!"

Over the next four months, fourteen more of the characters he had killed off in his books and short stories had come back for him. Had come for revenge. Some seemed mostly benign, their intentions unstated. Like Ray Brower. Ray had appeared shoeless one day in Stephen's backyard, his ashen face a blank and staring mask, a dented blueberry pan held out in front of him like he was catching raindrops—or maybe hailstones.

But others were evil, pure and simple. There was no ambiguity to their intentions. They were out for blood.

One morning in late October, with the air as cool and crisp and fine as a sip from a New England stream, Stephen had opened his front door and stepped out onto the porch to get his morning paper...and Kurt Barlow had been there, fangs dripping morning dew and shining bright white in the clear October sun. Barlow had the paper in his hand and he held it out to Stephen saying, "Local author suffers fate worse than death. Read all about it."

Stephen stumbled backwards. "No," he said. "No...you can't...the sun...you can't..."

"I can, Mr. King, and I will. I can do as I please now. You have lost control."

"Oh, *Jesus!*"

"No, Mr. King, I'm afraid not. Not Jesus. Quite the opposite, actually. Quite the opposite, indeed."

He had escaped Barlow. At first all of his characters had been easy to elude. They moved like toddlers —or maybe more like zombies: all stiff in limb and motion. But each new arrival seemed to be stronger, seemed to have more substance. And each new arrival was definitely more dangerous than the last. When Annie Wilkes came back four weeks ago she had nearly killed him. He would carry the scar she had hacked into him for the rest of his life. Annie had convinced him, in her own mad way, that it was time for him to get out, to move on, if for no other reason than to protect his family.

Annie Wilkes. When she came for him he was sick in bed with a real down-home version of the Shanghai flu. Visions of Captain Trips danced in his head. His guts were in a real uproar, quivering inside him like a sick bird. What wasn't tied down eventually found its way out one end or the other; what didn't ache, just wasn't there. His temp was high, his spirits low, and all in all he felt like dirt. All he wanted to do was sleep and be done with it. All he wanted was to feel good again. He didn't think that was too much to ask. He thought he had suffered enough misery for a while.

Apparently not. Tabitha had just left for the store when Stephen was wracked with a violent case of the chills. He groaned and pulled the thick quilt up to his chin, closed his eyes. He shivered and coughed weakly. We're having some fun now, his mind mused. He shivered again and wondered idly what time it was. There was a digital clock on the stand not two feet from his pillow but to look at it would mean he would have to turn his head to the side *and* open his eyes again. He thought either one of those fancy maneuvers might just kill him. He was just too tired. Didn't matter anyway, although it could've been time for another dose of astin. *Aspirin,* his mind corrected. Astin was just something one of his characters had called it. His characters. The thought caused a brief surge of unease to well up in him, but before he could focus on it the feeling flittered away. Soon he slept.

And dreamt. He was sick in bed and there was a vase of yellow flowers on the nightstand. Goldenrods. Such pretty little flowers. He knew it was a dream because in real life he was allergic to goldenrods and Tabby would never have allowed them in the room. As he watched, a fat, swollen bee flew out of the flowers, buzzed around his head and then landed on his arm. He stared in amazement as the bee produced an impossibly long stinger, silver in color like a hypodermic needle, and slowly injected it into his arm. He felt dizzy. His arm burned. Gotta swat that bee, he thought, that's a Do-Bee and they're the most dangerous kind. Gotta wake up and swat that damn bee. But his eyelids felt like heavy wads of thick dough and, try as he might, he just couldn't get them open. But Tabby would be home soon, anyway. She'd swat the bee and everything would be all right.

When he awoke he felt different. The flu was still with him but no longer up front; its symptoms seemed dulled, muted somehow. He felt groggy and off kilter. He opened his eyes slowly and his first thought was, Oh, that silly wife of mine's gone and got me a nurse. A woman was standing by his bed. She was a large woman and she seemed to be smiling. The light in the room was clouded by heavy shades on the windows and it took a few moments for his eyes to adapt. The woman was wearing a gray cardigan sweater and a frumpy wool skirt, and at first he couldn't understand why he had thought she was a nurse. Nurses dressed in white. But then he recognized her.

"Wake up, sleepyhead!" Annie trilled. "Wake up!"

She moved fast for her size. Before Stephen could even scream she had clamped one flabby hand over his mouth with enough force to push him down into his mattress. He could smell a dreadful mixed stench of peanut butter, vanilla cookies and chicken gravy on her hand, and for one awful moment he thought he was going to vomit.

"Not a word, you dirty bird," Annie said and then barked a laugh at her own little rhyme. Stephen shook his head under the weight of her hand, his eyes wide. "Not a peep-peep-peep." Annie's nostrils flared as she looked down on him. He shook his head again.

She released her hold on Stephen and he immediately lifted up on his elbows in an effort to bolt out of bed. He was a big man and even with his illness he was sure he could overpower her. But his head spun crazily as he rose and before he could gain any ground at all, Annie had shoved him back down with an effortless, almost offhanded push to his chest that took the wind right out of him and made him bounce twice on the bed.

Christ, she's strong, he thought in panic. What have I done?

"Don't try that again, Mister Smart Guy," she said, "or I'll have to give you another pre-op shot. I'm in a poopie-doopie mood today."

Pre-op??? Dear God, is that what she said? He rubbed at his arm. Bits and pieces of his dream passed by him in a blur. Flowers. A bee.

"A real poopie-doopie mood." Annie bent down suddenly next to the bed and came up holding a hatchet in her strong right hand. It was the Craftsman he and Tabby and the kids used every December to chop down their Christmas tree. She must've taken it from the garage. Stephen could see small streaks of rust on the blade, and he had time to wish he'd taken better care of the damn thing. Annie held the hatchet high. The tendons stood out in her wrist like mighty little cables. He could see the wink of an amethyst ring on her pinkie finger. "Remember how I hobbled Paul in the book? Remember?" She poised the hatchet over him and smiled. "Now it's your turn, Mister Man."

"No Annie, don't," he said. "I'll..."

"Geeeee-yahhh!" she screamed, and swung the hatchet.

He rolled toward her with as much strength as he could muster. He felt like he was moving in slow motion, drugged. He knew with sudden, utter certainty that he'd never get away from her, never see Tabitha again, never see the kids. He knew that he was going to die. The hatchet caught him a glancing blow on his left wrist as he rolled. He felt a brief jolt of searing pain and then he was falling off the bed and onto the floor. Annie's feet dug into his side as her forward momentum carried her into him. She tripped and fell hard on top of the bed. Stephen started to crawl away but found he could barely move. The wound in his wrist gaped like a small red mouth. Blood streaked the floor. Stephen looked back over his shoulder and saw Annie pushing herself off the bed.

"Cockadoodie!" she yelled. She was pissed. She turned for him, hatchet held high, a vicious snarl on her thick face. "Cocka—"

A car door slammed. Annie paused. It was Tabby. She had come home to swat the bee.

And then, like the remnants of a very bad dream, he saw Annie Wilkes start to fade from view. Stephen could see right through Annie, could see the Berni Wrightson print that hung on the wall behind her, blurry at first but clearer and clearer as she lost cohesion. The hatchet dropped from Annie's hand and fell to the floor with a muffled clang as it hit the throw rug next to the bed. And then she was gone. But Stephen had no doubt that others would follow and his last coherent thought before he passed out was that it was time for him to boogie right the hell out of Bangor.

A week later he found himself in southwestern Pennsylvania.

The face disappeared from the jagged hole and a bare arm snaked its way through the opening. Stephen continued his frantic efforts to locate the knife. The arm bent and its hand opened and closed like a viper's head, searching for the door lock. "Gonna getcha, Steve," Jack said from behind the door. His hand brushed the security chain and snapped down on it. "Gonna getcha."

Stephen's knee rolled painfully over something hard and round. *The knife!* He grabbed it without looking and found himself holding an ordinary pencil, apparently shot out of the overturned nightstand. A pencil, not the knife.

"GETCHA! GETCHA! GETCHA!" Jack yelled and began working the security chain out of its track.

Stephen lurched to his feet. For one long moment he froze, very near panic, then suddenly he bounded across the room in three loping strides, not thinking. He held the pencil out in his right hand like a dagger. "This is crazy," he said—but it felt right. He stabbed Jack's forearm with the pencil. It went through the arm with sickeningly little resistance. Jack howled. Blood as black and thick as dirty oil flowed from the wound. The air smelled suddenly of rotted meat.

Jack yanked his arm out of the opening, leaving Stephen holding the bloody pencil. He wiped it off on his jacket without thinking. Mightier than the sword, his mind reeled, not just the pen, but the pencil, too.

Mightier than the sword.

"You bastard! You bitch!" Jack cried.

The pencil had hurt Jack much more than an object so innocuous had any right to. Stephen had sensed that immediately.

It was in the tone of Jack's cry. There had been more than just pain and anger in that cry. There had been fear. But why? He looked at the pencil. It was just an ordinary pencil, a Berol Black Beauty, nothing at all unusual about it. Stephen had used the same kind years ago when he had been a student. But it felt warm and alive in his hand, like it was filled with living, pulsing blood instead of dry graphite. And did it glow somewhat in the predawn darkness? Perhaps.

Jack howled again from the outside. Stephen didn't seem to hear. His gaze was locked on the Berol. It was definitely glowing now, there could be no mistake of that. The room was visible: the bed, the upturned nightstand, a scattering of motel stationery. All visible.

Jack had retrieved his axe and brought it down on the door again, but this time there was no force in the swing and the blow was mostly ineffective. "LET ME IN!" he wailed. "YOU GOTTA!"

Stephen looked slowly at the door and then back at the pencil in his hand. He walked around the bed, plucked a sheet of stationery off the floor and righted the nightstand.

"Jack," he said softly.

"LET ME THE FUCK IN!"

"Jack, listen to me."

"NO!"

"It's not your fault."

"NO!"

"You're going away now, Jack."

"NONONONONO!" He hammered the door.

Stephen looked at the piece of paper in his hand almost reverently. He set it down on top of the nightstand and brushed it straight with a gentle hand. "Yeah," he said. "Yeah, you are." Then he sat on the edge of the cheap motel room bed and using the nightstand as a writing table he wrote: 'Jack Torrance came back from the dead looking for revenge. What he found instead was his *permanent* demise. Jack Torrance was written out of existence for good, once and for all.'

Stephen King read back what he had written. He smiled, his first real smile in over four months. He thought what he had written sounded just like the beginning of some cheap pulp novel. But he also thought it'd do just fine.

And, God, didn't it feel good to be writing again!

The Overlook was At Home with the Dead

Original illustration by Katherine Flickinger.
(See pages 492–496 for other drawings related to the prologue to *The Shining*, "Before the Play.")

PART V

HORRORS SMALL AND LARGE

Stephen King's "Strange and Wonderful World"

Promotional poster for King's two newest works.

AN INDEX TO THE
FIRST LINES
OF STEPHEN KING'S NOVELS,
SHORT STORIES, AND POETRY

This "First Line Index" is the first attempt to compile and publish a *complete* index to the beginnings of King's work. I kept in mind the goal of including everything I could get my hands on, and I think I've been fairly successful. (By necessity, though, this Index includes those King works I could collect through the publication of *Four Past Midnight.* The second edition of this volume (scheduled for around 1996 or so) will continue covering King's work from 1991 on, beginning with *Needful Things.*)

Thus, this Index covers every novel and short story I'm aware of, including, of course, all the collected works, all the uncollected stories, all the tales in *People, Places, and Things,* as well as the unpublished stories such as "Squad D," "Keyholes," and the 1990 one-act, one-minute play, "An Evening at God's." The short story first lines are complete through the 1990 story "The Moving Finger." In addition, the first line of every King poem known to exist in a published form is also included.

While compiling this feature, I came across a facet of King's work that required a decision: Should the work of King's characters be included as well as King's material? Many of King's characters are writers, and King has often included their work within the text of his novels.

My decision was "Hell, yes." My reasoning was that since the works of King's characters were ultimately written by King himself, then they should be included within this Index.

As a consequence, you will find here the first lines of Paul Sheldon's novels, Bobbi Anderson's novel *The Buffalo Soldiers,* George Stark's *Steel Machine,* Jim Gardener's poetry, and Morton Rainey's short story "Sowing Season." (Stark's *Steel Machine* is the only Stark first line quoted because the other Stark excerpts in *The Dark Half* (as well as the excerpt from Thad Beaumont's *The Sudden Dancers*) are obviously not first lines.)

I've also included the first lines of different versions of King stories (such as the *Creepshow* tales), along with the first lines of the unpublished King novels (*The Aftermath, Sword in the Darkness,* and *Blaze*) in the University of Maine Special Collections Library. (However, I did not include the first line to "Pinfall," the unfilmed segment of "Creepshow 2,"

because even though the story was by Stephen King, the script was by George Romero, and so did not warrant inclusion here.)

I included the first line of King's nonfiction study *Danse Macabre* because I wanted to.

Although I approached this feature as an alphabetical survey of King's first lines, designed to facilitate comparisons of similarities or variations in the ways he begins his stories, I've also provided a cross-index arranged by title of the work for those who wish to use this section as a reference feature. Instead of scanning the first-line list for the opening sentence from "The Man Who Would Not Shake Hands," *The Shining,* or "The Moving Finger," skip to the cross-index and look up the title of the work. There you'll find the first few words of the first line. Follow that reference back to the first-line alphabetical list for the complete opening line.

Each of the first lines included in this Index is keyed to the master numbers I've assigned to King's novels and short stories (e.g., "Night Surf" is followed by "5c," its master code number.) The numbers refer back to the main concordance in this volume, with the exception of *The Dark Tower III: The Waste Lands,* which is coded "29," but does not have a concordance. I was able to include that book's first line here thanks to an advance peek at its opening section, but the book itself was published too late to be included. The revised edition of *The Shape Under the Sheet* will contain a concordance to *The Waste Lands, Needful Things,* and any other works published between now and its appearance.

Regarding other works for which there is no concordance: Since there are also many King works indexed here that are not detailed in the master concordance because of their nature (unpublished and unfinished works, poetry, etc.), I've footnoted these references. For information on these pieces, refer to the footnotes that follow the Index.

Special thanks must go to those people (friends and colleagues all) who helped me with the assemblage of material for this Index and *The Shape Under the Sheet,* especially Dave Hinchberger, Michael Collings, George Beahm, Stan Wiater, Michael Autrey, and the Viking Press publicity department.

A

- "After the guy was dead and the smell of his burning flesh was off the air, we all went back down to the beach." —"Night Surf," *Night Shift* (5c)
- "Alexis Machine was rarely whimsical, and for him to have a whimsical thought in such a situation as this was something which had never happened before." —*Steel Machine* by George Stark, *The Dark Half* (27)
- "Almost everyone thought the man and boy were father and son." —*'Salem's Lot* (2)
- "Although Ian Carmichael would not have moved from Little Dunthorpe for all the jewels in the Queen's treasury, he had to admit to himself that when it rained in Cornwall, it rained harder than anywhere else in England." —*Misery's Return* (Version 1) by Paul Sheldon, *Misery* (25)
- "Around the corner from the doormen, the limos, the taxis, and the revolving doors at the entrance to Le Palais, one of New York's oldest and grandest hotels, there was another door—this one small, unmarked, and unremarked." —"Dedication" (U28)
- "As Pete Jacobs stepped out, the fog immediately swallowed up his house, and he could see nothing but the white blanket all around him." —"The Other Side of the Fog," *People, Places, and Things* (U1)
- "At first glance it looked like a Wang word processor —it had a Wang keyboard and a Wang casing." —"Word Processor of the Gods," *Skeleton Crew* (21j)

B

- "The barbecue was over." —"The Ballad of the Flexible Bullet," *Skeleton Crew* (21u)
- "Billy Clewson died all at once, with nine of the ten other members of D Squad on April 8, 1974." —"Squad D" (An unpublished short story) (UUP1)
- "The boy found the oracle and it almost destroyed him." —"The Oracle And The Mountains," *The Dark Tower: The Gunslinger* (14c)
- "Brian Engle rolled the American Pride L1011 to a stop at Gate 22 and flicked off the FASTEN SEATBELT light at exactly 10:14 P.M." —"The Langoliers," *Four Past Midnight* (28a)
- "Burt turned the radio on too loud and didn't turn it down because they were on the verge of another argument and he didn't want it to happen." —"Children of the Corn," *Night Shift* (5p)
- "But Viet Nam was over and the country was getting on." —*Roadwork* (10)
- "By the time he graduated college, John Smith had forgotten all about the bad fall he took on the ice that January day in 1953." —*The Dead Zone* (8)
- "By the time the woman had finally gone, it was nearly two-thirty in the morning." —"Crouch End" (U13)

C

- "Can you do it?" —"Harrison State Park '68" (poem) [1]
- "Charles needed to go to the bathroom very badly." — "Here There Be Tygers," *Skeleton Crew* (21b)
- "Conklin's first, snap judgement was that this man, Michael Briggs, was not the sort of fellow who usually sought psychiatric help." —"Keyholes" (An unfinished, unpublished short story.) [2]
- "Considering that it was probably the end of the world, Maddie Pace thought she was doing a good job." —"Home Delivery" (U32)

D

- "'Daddy, I'm tired,' the little girl in the red pants and the green blouse said fretfully." —*Firestarter* (9)
- "DARK STAGE. Then a spotlight hits a papiermache globe, spinning all by itself in the middle of darkness." —"An Evening at God's" (A one-act play) [3]
- "The dawn washed slowly down Culver Street." — "Morning Deliveries (Milkman #1)" *Skeleton Crew* (21r)
- "Dear Bones, How good it was to step into the cold, draughty hall here at Chapelwaite, every bone in an ache from that abominable coach, in need of instant relief from my distended bladder—and to see a letter addressed in your own inimitable scrawl propped on the obscene little cherrywood table beside the door!" —"Jerusalem's Lot," *Night Shift* (5a)
- "Dees didn't really get interested—in spite of his private pilot's license – until the third and fourth murders." —"The Night Flier" (U29)
- "Dexter Stanley was scared." —"The Crate" (12c1)
- "Do you love?" —"Nona" *Skeleton Crew* (21n)

E

- "The engine of the old Ford died, for the third time that morning." —*The Aftermath* (an unpublished novel) [4]
- "Everything, Sam Peebles decided later, was the fault of the goddamned acrobat." —"The Library Policeman," *Four Past Midnight* (28c)

F

- "'Faster!' Tommy Riviera said." —"The Hotel at the End of the Road," *People, Places, and Things* (U1)
- "FedShip ASN/29 fell out of the sky and crashed." — "Beachworld," *Skeleton Crew* (21l)
- "For a moment Geoffrey Alliburton was not sure who the old man at the door was, and this was not entirely because the bell had awakened him from a deepening doze." —*Misery's Return* (Version 2) by Paul Sheldon, *Misery* (25)
- "For me, the terror—the real terror, as opposed to whatever demons and boogeys which might have been living in my own mind—began on an afternoon in October of 1957." —*Danse Macabre* [5]
- "For want of a nail the kingdom was lost—that's how the catechism goes when you boil it down." — *The Tommyknockers* (26)
- "Four days after George had confirmed to his own satisfaction that his wife was cheating on him, he confronted her." —An unpublished, unfinished short story by Morton Rainey; from "Secret Window, Secret Garden," *Four Past Midnight* (28b)
- "From The New York Post, page 1, March 4, 1981: INSANE GENERAL ESCAPE OAK COVE ASYLUM, KILLS THREE!!" —*The Plant*, Part Three (U21)

G

- "Garish walked out of the bright May sunshine and into the coolness of the dorm." —"Cain Rose Up," *Skeleton Crew* (21d)
- "George Jacobs was closing his office, when an old woman felt free to walk right in." —"Never Look Behind You," *People, Places, and Things* (U1)
- "George was somewhere in the dark." —*Blaze* (An unpublished novel) [6]
- "George's mother went to the door, hesitated there, came back, and tousled George's hair." —"Gramma," *Skeleton Crew* (21t)
- "Go on,' Cressner said again, 'Look in the bag.'" — "The Ledge," *Night Shift* (5l)
- "The gunslinger came awake from a confused dream which seemed to consist of a single image: that of the Sailor in the Tarot deck from which the man in black had dealt (or purported to deal) the gunslinger's own moaning future." — *The Dark Tower II: The Drawing of the Three* (23)
- "The gunslinger spoke slowly to Jake in the rising and falling inflections of a dream: 'There were three of us: Cuthbert, Jamie, and I'" —"The Slow Mutants," *The Dark Tower: The Gunslinger* (14d)
- "The guy's name was Snodgrass and I could see him getting ready to do something crazy." —"Trucks," *Night Shift* (5i)

H

- "Halston thought the old man in the wheelchair looked sick, terrified, and ready to die." —"The Cat from Hell" (U10)
- "Hapscomb's Texaco sat on US 93 just north of Arnette, a pissant four-street burg about 110 miles from Houston." —*The Stand* (6)
- "Harding: It is sprawled along the verge of the lake like a string of dirty pearls made clean with the dawn." —*Sword in the Darkness* (An unpublished novel) [7]
- "He looked like the total all-American kid as he pedaled his twenty-six-inch Schwinn with the apehanger handlebars up the residential suburban street, and that's just what he was: Tod Bowden, thirteen years old, five-feet-eight and a healthy one hundred and forty pounds, hair the color of ripe corn, blue eyes, white even teeth, lightly tanned skin marred by not even the first shadow of adolescent acne." —"Apt Pupil," *Different Seasons* (15b)
- "Heh-Heh!! Greetings, kiddies, and welcome to the first issue of CREEPSHOW, the magazine that dares to answer the question: Who goes there?" — *Creepshow* (12)
- "The house was tall, with an incredible slope of shingled roof." —"The Blue Air Compressor" (U6)

I

- "I believe there was only one occasion upon which I actually solved a crime before my slightly fabulous friend, Mr. Sherlock Holmes." —"The Doctor's Case" (U24)
- "'I came to you because I want to tell my story,' the man on Dr. Harper's couch was saying." —"The Boogeyman," *Night Shift* (5f)
- "I can't go out no more." —"Paranoid: A Chant" (Poem) *Skeleton Crew* (21h) [8]
- "'I don't have no wheels,' Tony Bonasaro said, walking up to the girl coming down the steps, 'and I am a slow learner, but I am a fast driver.'" — *Fast Cars* by Paul Sheldon, *Misery* (25)
- "I dressed a bit more speedily than normal on that snowy, windy, bitter night—I admit." —"The Breathing Method," *Different Seasons* (15d)
- "I first saw Mr. Legere when the circus swung through Steubenville, but I'd only been with the show for two weeks; he might have been making his irregular visits indefinitely." —"The Night of the Tiger" (U12)

K

- "Kelso Black laughed." —"The Stranger," *People, Places, and Things* (U1)
- "The kid heard a sound in the back of the building and although the thought of rats crossed his mind, he turned the corner anyway—it was too early to go home because school didn't let out for another hour and a half and he had gone truant at lunch." —An untitled Work-In-Progress by Paul Sheldon, *Misery* (25)

L

- "Louis Creed, who had lost his father at three and who had never known a grandfather, never expected to find a father as he entered his middle age, but that was exactly what happened...although he called this man a friend, as a grown man must do when he finds the man who should have been his father relatively late in life." — *Pet Sematary* (17)

M

- "The man in black fled across the desert, and the gunslinger followed." —"The Gunslinger," *The Dark Tower: The Gunslinger* (14a)
- "The man in black led him to an ancient killing ground to make palaver." —"The Gunslinger And The Dark Man," *The Dark Tower: The Gunslinger* (14e)
- "Miss Sidley was her name, and teaching was her game." —"Suffer the Little Children" (U8)
- "'Mr. Renshaw?'" —"Battleground," *Night Shift* (5h)
- "The morning I got it on was nice; a nice May Morning." —*Rage* (3)
- "Morrison was waiting for someone who was hung up in the air traffic jam over Kennedy International when he saw a familiar face at the end of the bar and walked down." —"Quitters, Inc.," *Night Shift* (5n)
- "The most important things are the hardest things to say." —"The Body," *Different Seasons* (15c)

N

- "News item from the Westover (ME) weekly *Enterprise,* August 19, 1966: 'Rain of Stones Reported: It was reliably reported by several persons that a rain of stones fell from a clear blue sky on Carlin Street in the town of Chamberlain on August 17th.'" —*Carrie* (1)
- "No one knew exactly how long it had been going on." —"The Reploids" (U26)
- "Nothing..." —"Silence," (poem) *Moth,* 1970[12]
- "A nursery rhyme had been playing itself through his mind all day, the maddening kind of thing that will not let go, that stands mockingly outside the apse of the conscious mind and makes faces at the rational being inside." —"The Way Station," *The Dark Tower: The Gunslinger* (14b)

O

- "Officer Hunton got to the laundry just as the ambulance was leaving—slowly, with no siren or flashing lights." —"The Mangler," *Night Shift* (5e)
- "Oglethorpe Crater was an ugly, mean little wretch." —"The Thing At the Bottom of the Well," *People, Places, and Things* (U1)
- "Okay, this is a science fiction joke." —"For the Birds" (U23)
- "An old blue Ford pulled into the guarded parking lot that morning, looking like a small, tired dog after a hard run." —*The Long Walk* (7)
- "The old man sat in the barn doorway in the smell of apples, rocking, wanting not to want to smoke not because of the doctor but because now his heart fluttered all the time." —"My Pretty Pony" (U30)
- "On an early evening in May of 1963, a young man with his hand in his pocket walked briskly up New York's Third Avenue." —"The Man Who Loved Flowers," *Night Shift* (5r)
- "On September 15th, 1981, a boy named Jack Sawyer stood where the water and land come together, hands in the pockets of his jeans, looking out at the steady Atlantic." —*The Talisman* (18)
- "Once, in a kingdom called Delain, there was a King with two sons." —*The Eyes of the Dragon* (24)
- "Once upon a time, not so long ago, a monster came to the small town of Castle Rock, Maine." — *Cujo* (11)
- "Our first stop...the Grantham House...you'll like the Granthams, kiddies." —"Father's Day," *Creepshow* (12a)
- "Our story opens in the basement of Amberson Hall, the science building on the campus of Horlicks University...it begins with a whim of fate...a toss of the coin, as it were, heh-heh!" —"The Crate," *Creepshow* (12c)
- "Outsiders think they are always the same, these small towns—that they don't change." —"It Grows on You" (U9)

P

- "People, Places, and Things is an Extraordinary book." —*People, Places, and Things* (Foreword)

- "People's lives—their real lives, as opposed to their simple physical existences—begin at different times." —*The Dark Half* (27)

Q

- "The question is: Can he do it?" —"The Woman in the Room," *Night Shift* (5t)

R

- "'The Reach was wider in those days,' Stella Flanders told her great-grandchildren in the last summer of her life, the summer before she began to see ghosts." —"The Reach," *Skeleton Crew* (21v)
- "Richard and I sat on my porch, looking out over the dunes to the Gulf." —"I Am the Doorway," *Night Shift* (5d)
- "Rocky and Leo, both drunk as the last lords of creation, cruised slowly down Culver Street and then out along Balfour Avenue toward Crescent." —"Big Wheels: A Tale of the Laundry Game (Milkman #2)," *Skeleton Crew* (21s)

S

- "Sally." —*The Stand: The Complete & Uncut Edition* (6a)
- "September 15th was Kevin's birthday, and he got exactly what he wanted: a Sun." —"The Sun Dog," *Four Past Midnight* (28d)
- "She was squinting at the thermometer in the white light coming through the window." —*The Running Man* (13)
- "Sheridan was cruising slowly down the long blank length of the shopping mall when he saw the little kid push out through the main doors under the lighted sign which read COUSINTOWN." — "Popsy" (U25)
- "Shratt came on limping..." —"Donovan's Brain," (poem)*Moth, 1970*[13]
- "Somewhere, high above, the moon shines down, fat and full—but here, in Tarker's Mills, a January blizzard has choked the sky with snow." — *Cycle of the Werewolf* (20)
- "Sooner or later the question comes up in every medical student's career." —"Survivor Type," *Skeleton Crew* (21p)
- "Springheel Jack...I saw these two words in the paper this morning and my God, how they take me back." —"Strawberry Spring," *Night Shift* (5k)
- "The Star Invaders had their own ways of loosening men's tongues." —"The Star Invaders" (U2)
- "Stevens served drinks, and soon after eight o'clock on that bitter winter night, most of us retired with

them to the library." —"The Man Who Would Not Shake Hands," *Skeleton Crew* (21k)

T

- "The terror, which would not end for another twenty-eight years—if it ever did end—began, so far as I know or can tell, with a boat made from a sheet of newspaper floating down a gutter swollen with rain." —*IT* (22)
- "'There goes the Todd woman,' I said." —"Mrs. Todd's Shortcut," *Skeleton Crew* (21e)
- "There were twelve of us when we went in that night, but only two of us came out—my friend Kirby and me." —"Skybar" (U16)
- "There's a guy like me in every state and federal prison in America, I guess—I'm the guy who can get it for you." —"Rita Hayworth and Shawshank Redemption," *Different Seasons* (15a)
- "These streets begin where the cobbles/surface through tar like the heads/of children buried badly in their texture,..." —"Leighton Street" (A poem by Jim Gardener), *The Tommyknockers* (26)
- "They had been predicting a norther all week and along about Thursday we got it, a real screamer that piled up eight inches by four in the afternoon and showed no signs of slowing down." —"Gray Matter," *Night Shift* (5g)
- "'Thinner,' the old Gypsy man with the rotting nose whispers to William Halleck as Halleck and his wife, Heidi, come out of the courthouse." —*Thinner* (19)
- "This is the apartment of Upson Pratt." —"They're Creeping Up on You," *Creepshow* (12e)
- "'This is the last call for Jaunt-701,' the pleasant female voice echoed through the Blue Concourse of New York's Port Authority Terminal." —"The Jaunt," *Skeleton Crew* (21f)
- "This is the story of a lover's triangle, I suppose you'd say – Arnie Cunningham, Leigh Cabot, and, of course, Christine." —*Christine* (16)
- "This is what happened." —"The Mist," *Skeleton Crew* (21a)
- "This occurred during her annual spring cleaning, which took place this year (as it did most years) around the middle of June." —"The Revelations of 'Becka Paulson" (U18)
- "Todd Downey thought that a woman who would steal your love when your love was really all you had was not much of a woman." —"Secret Window, Secret Garden," a short story by John Shooter, from the novella "Secret Window, Secret Garden" in *Four Past Midnight* (28b)
- "Two A.M., Friday." —"Graveyard Shift," *Night Shift* (5b)

U

- *"umber whunnnn"* —*Misery* (25)

W

- "Walking to school you ask me..." —"For Owen" (poem), *Skeleton Crew* (21o)[14]
- "'We moved it last year, and quite an operation it was, too,' Mr. Carlin said as they mounted the stairs."
  —"The Reaper's Image," *Skeleton Crew* (21m)
- "'Well,' said Jimmy Keller, looking across to the gantry to where the rocket rested in the middle of the desert." —"The Cursed Expedition," *People, Places, and Things* (U1)
- "Wharton moved slowly up the wide steps, hat in hand, craning his neck to get a better look at the Victorian monstrosity that his sister had died in."
  —"The Glass Floor" (U4)
- "'What am I doing here?'" —"'I've Got to Get Away!,'" *People, Places, and Things* (U1)
- "When Hal Shelburn saw it, when his son Dennis pulled it out of a mouldering Ralston-Purina carton that had been pushed far back under one attic eave, such a feeling of horror and dismay rose in him that for one moment he thought he would scream."
  —"The Monkey," *Skeleton Crew* (21c)
- "When the scratching started, Howard Mitla was sitting alone in the Queens apartment where he lived with his wife." —"The Moving Finger" (U34)
- "'Why not? Do I look like a fat-farm candidate to you?'" —"Heroes for Hope Starring the X-Men" (Stephen King's segment) (U20)
- "A woman who would steal your love when your love was all you had wasn't much of a woman – that, at least, was Tommy Havelock's opinion." —"Sowing Season," a short story by Morton Rainey from the novella "Secret Window, Secret Garden" in *Four Past Midnight* (28b)

Y

- "You see kiddies, Harry Wentworth has been having himself a good time with Becky Vickers...the only problem is Richard Vickers, Becky's husband, who is just a wee bit upset over this arrangement and means to see that Harry gets his comeuppance...cruel and unusual punishment for a charge of unlawful entry, you might say...heh-heh..."
  —"Something To Tide You Over," *Creepshow* (12d)
- "'You stole my story',' the man on the doorstep said."
  —"Secret Window, Secret Garden," *Four Past Midnight* (28b)

Footnotes

The following section supplies details on all the titles footnoted in the First Line Index.

1. "Harrison State Park '68" — See the essay "The Radiating Pencils of His Bones: The Poetry of Stephen King," by Michael R. Collings in this volume.
2. "Keyholes" — See the section "The Unfinished King" in this volume.
3. "An Evening at God's" — See the Uncollected Stories concordance for details on this play.
4. *The Aftermath* — See the section "The Unpublished King: A Concordance to *The Aftermath, Sword in the Darkness,* and *Blaze*" in this volume.
5. *Danse Macabre* — See my review of *Danse Macabre* in this volume.
6. *Blaze* — See the section "The Unpublished King: A Concordance to *The Aftermath, Sword in the Darkness,* and *Blaze*" in this volume.
7. *Sword in the Darkness* — See the section "The Unpublished King: A Concordance to *The Aftermath, Sword in the Darkness,* and *Blaze*" in this volume.
8. "Paranoid: A Chant" — See the essay "The Radiating Pencils of His Bones: The Poetry of Stephen King," by Michael R. Collings in this volume.
9. "The Dark Man" — See the essay "The Radiating Pencils of His Bones: The Poetry of Stephen King," by Michael R. Collings in this volume.
10. "Brooklyn August" — See the essay "The Radiating Pencils of His Bones: The Poetry of Stephen King," by Michael R. Collings in this volume.
11. "Untitled Poem" — See the essay "The Radiating Pencils of His Bones: The Poetry of Stephen King," by Michael R. Collings in this volume.
12. "Silence" — See the essay "The Radiating Pencils of His Bones: The Poetry of Stephen King," by Michael R. Collings in this volume.
13. "Donovan's Brain" — See the essay "The Radiating Pencils of His Bones: The Poetry of Stephen King," by Michael R. Collings in this volume.
14. "For Owen" — See the essay "The Radiating Pencils of His Bones: The Poetry of Stephen King," by Michael R. Collings in this volume.

TITLE / FIRST LINE CROSS-INDEX

The first few words of a work's first line appear after identification of the work. Follow these words back to the alphabetical list of first lines for the complete quotation.

The Aftermath — "The engine of..."
"Apt Pupil," *Different Seasons* (15b) — "He looked like..."
"The Ballad of the Flexible Bullet," *Skeleton Crew* (21u) — "The barbecue was..."
"Battleground," *Night Shift* (5h) — "Mr. Renshaw?"
"Beachworld," *Skeleton Crew* (21l) — "FedShip ASN/29 fell..."
"Before The Play" (U14) — "It was October..."
"Big Wheels: A Tale of the Laundry Game (Milkman

Shelburn..."

"Morning Deliveries (Milkman #1)" *Skeleton Crew* (21r) — "The dawn washed..."

"The Moving Finger" (U34) — "When the scratching..."

"Mrs. Todd's Shortcut," *Skeleton Crew* (21e) — "There goes the..."

"My Pretty Pony" (U30) — "The old man..."

"Never Look Behind You," *People, Places, and Things* (U1) — "George Jacobs was..."

"The Night Flyer" (U29) — "Dee's didn't really..."

"The Night of the Tiger" (U12) — "I first saw..."

"Night Surf," *Night Shift* (5c) — "After the guy..."

"Nona," *Skeleton Crew* (21n) — "Do you love?"

"One for the Road," *Night Shift* (5s) — "It was quarter..."

"The Oracle And The Mountains," *The Dark Tower: The Gunslinger* (14c) — "The boy found..."

"The Other Side of the Fog," *People, Places and Things* (U1) — "As Pete Jacobs..."

"Paranoid: A Chant" (poem) *Skeleton Crew* (21h) — "I can't go..."

People, Places, and Things (U1) — "'Faster!' Tommy Rivera..."

People, Places, and Things (Foreword) (U1) — "People, Places, and..."

Pet Sematary (17) — "Louis Creed, who..."

The Plant, Part One (U15) — January 4, 1981...."

The Plant, Part Three (U21) — "From The New..."

The Plant, Part Two (U17) — "January 30, 1981...."

"Popsy" (U25) — "Sheridan was cruising..."

"Quitters, Inc.," *Night Shift* (5n) — "Morrison was waiting..."

"The Raft," *Skeleton Crew* (21i) — "It was forty..."

Rage (3) — "The morning I..."

"Rainy Season" (U31) — "It was half..."

"The Reach," *Skeleton Crew* (21v) — "The Reach was..."

"The Reaper's Image," *Skeleton Crew* (21m) — "We moved it..."

"The Reploids" (U26) — "No one knew..."

"The Revelations of 'Becka Paulson" (U18) — "This occurred during..."

"Rita Hayworth and Shawshank Redemption," *Different Seasons* (15a) — "There's a guy..."

Roadwork (10) — "But Viet Nam..."

The Running Man (13) — "She was squinting..."

'Salem's Lot (2) — "Almost everyone thought..."

"Secret Window, Secret Garden," *Four Past Midnight* (28b) — "You stole my..."

"Secret Window, Secret Garden" (John Shooter) in "Secret Window, Secret Garden," *Four Past Midnight* (28b) — "Todd Downey thought..."

The Shining (4) — "Jack Torrance thought:..."

"Silence" (poem) *Moth* — "Nothing..."

"Skybar" (U16) — "There were twelve..."

"Slade" (U5) — "It was almost..."

"The Slow Mutants," *The Dark Tower: The Gunslinger* (14d) — "The gunslinger spoke..."

"Sneakers" (U27) — "John Tell had..."

"Something to Tide You Over," *Creepshow* (12d) — "You see kiddies,..."

"Sometimes They Come Back," *Night Shift* (5j) — "Jim Norman's wife..."

"Sowing Season" (Morton Rainey) in "Secret Garden, Secret Window," *Four Past Midnight* (28b) — "A woman who..."

"Squad D" (UUP1) — "Billy Clewson died..."

The Stand (6) — "Hapscomb's Texaco sat..."

The Stand: The Complete & Uncut Edition (6a) — "Sally."

"The Star Invaders" (U2) — "The Star Invaders..."

Steel Machine in *The Dark Half* (27) — "Alexis Machine was..."

"The Stranger," *People, Places, and Things* (U1) — "Kelso Black laughed."

"Strawberry Spring" (5k) — "In New England..."

"Strawberry Spring," *Night Shift* (5k) — "Springheel Jack...I..."

"Suffer the Little Children" (U8) — "Miss Sidley was..."

"The Sun Dog," *Four Past Midnight* (28d) — "September 15th was..."

"Survivor Type," *Skeleton Crew* (21p) — "Sooner or later..."

Sword in the Darkness — "Harding: It is..."

The Talisman (18) — "On September 15th,..."

"They're Creeping Up On You," *Creepshow* (12e) — "This is the apartment..."

"The Thing at the Bottom of the Well," *People, Places, and Things* (U1) — "Oglethorpe Crater was..."

Thinner (19) — "'Thinner,' the old..."

The Tommyknockers (26) — "For want of..."

"Trucks," *Night Shift* (5i) — "The guy's name..."

"Uncle Otto's Truck," *Skeleton Crew* (21q) — "It's a great..."

Untitled (Morton Rainey) in "Secret Window, Secret Garden," *Four Past Midnight* (28b) — "Four days after..."

Untitled (Paul Sheldon) in *Misery* (25) — "The kid heard..."

"The Way Station," *The Dark Tower: The Gunslinger* (14b) — "A nursery rhyme..."

"The Wedding Gig," *Skeleton Crew* (21g) — "In the year..."

"Weeds" (12b1) — "Jordy Verrill's place..."

"The Woman in the Room," *Night Shift* (5t) — "The question is:..."

"Word Processor of the Gods," *Skeleton Crew* (21j) — "At first glance..."

PUBLISHED WORKS
1974-1990

CHRONOLOGICAL INDEX TO PUBLISHED WORKS BY STEPHEN KING / RICHARD BACHMAN, 1974-1990

Alphabetical Index to Published Works by Stephen King / Richard Bachman, 1974-1990

CS=Creepshow; DS=Different Seasons; FPM=Four Past Midnight; NS=Night Shift; SC=Skeleton Crew

CARRIE

DEDICATION

This is for Tabby, who got me into it—
and then bailed me out of it.

[NO CONTENTS PAGE]

BOOK BREAKDOWN

Part One: BLOOD SPORT
Part Two: PROM NIGHT
Part Three: WRECKAGE

(1)
CARRIE
People

ALLISON, HAROLD Margaret White's stepfather. Margaret's mother married Harold after John Brigham was killed in 1959.

ALLISON, JUDITH BRIGHAM Margaret White's mother.

BANKSON, J.W. A scholar who believed that Margaret White blocked her pregnancy from her mind.

BARRETT, DON Ewen High School student. He was on the senior prom decorating committee.

BICENTE, MRS. A deceased Ewen High teacher.

"BIG OTIS" Sheriff Otis Doyle.

BILLY, UNCLE Tommy Ross's uncle. Tommy figured that after graduation he would spend Friday and Saturday nights either at his Uncle Billy's place or at the Cavalier bar.

THE BILLY BOSNAN BAND They supplied the music for part of the evening at the Ewen High School senior prom.

THE BLACK MAN Satan. Carrie believed that only her mother was good; that she had fought and vanquished the Black Man.

BLAKE, HENRY One of Billy Nolan's cohorts. He went with Billy to kill the pigs and get their blood for Carrie's "shower."

BLAKE, TINA Ewen High School student. She was in Chris Hargensen's "camp." She participated in the "stoning" of Carrie with sanitary napkins in the gym shower. She was also on the prom committee. [NOTE: It isn't clear whether Tina and Henry were related.]

BLISS, P.P. Hymn writer.

BLOCK, HARRY The Chamberlain commisioner of public utilities.

"BOMBA" George Dawson.

BRACKEN, DAVID Ewen High School student. He was a National Honor Society member.

BRANN, DOUG He owned the Western Auto Store.

BRIGHAM, JOHN Margaret White's father. He was killed in the summer of 1959.

BROCK, LENNIE Ewen High School student. He attended the senior prom.

BRUCIE Billy Nolan's mother's boyfriend.

BURTON, CHIEF Police chief.

CANTOR, EDDIE "Banjo Eyes."

CHAMBLIS, WILLIAM A. The president of Chamberlain Mills and Weaving.

CHIZMAR, GEORGE Ewen High's most artistic student.

CINDI Ewen High School student.

COCHRAN, SADIE Margaret Brigham's grandmother.

COWAN, MAUREEN She played folk music with John Swithen at the Ewen High School senior prom.

CRAGER, MEL The Durham, Maine, constable.

CRATZCHBARKEN, MORTON He lectured to the "National Colloquim on Psychic Phenomena."

CREWES, MYRA Ewen High School student. She was on the King & Queen ballot with Peter. She felt that the King and Queen competition insulted women.

DAVID School District #4 assistant principal George Kramer cut David's hair without his parent's permission. The incident became a court case called "School District #4 vs. David."

DAWSON, GEORGE Ewen High School student. He was on the King & Queen ballot with Frieda Jason. George's nickname was "Bomba."

DAWSON, MRS. George's mother.

DEIGHAN, STEVE One of Billy Nolan's cohorts. He was an idiot. He went with Billy to kill the pigs and get their blood for Carrie's "shower."

DeLOIS, BILLY Ewen High class-cutter. He cut French I.

DESJARDIN, RITA Ewen High School's gym teacher. She came to Carrie's defense when the girls began pelting Carrie with sanitary napkins in the shower.

DEVEAUX, SAM He owned the Cavalier bar.

"DON MacLEAN'S SECRET LOVER" Carrie (according to Carrie).

DOWNER, MR. Music teacher. He played the piano.

DOYLE, SHERIFF OTIS The Chamberlain, Maine, sheriff. He was known as "Big Otis."

DRAIN, HENRY He had a meadow that bordered the Cavalier bar's property.

DUBAY, FAST MARCEL Poker player. Thomas Quillan thought Dubay cheated.

DUCHAMP, TEDDY He owned Teddy's Amoco. [See the "Places" entry TEDDY'S AMOCO.]

ERBTER, TOMMY A five-year-old who taunted Carrie while he was riding by her on his bike. Carrie flexed and made his bike fall over.

EVARTS, RAY Helen Shyres's boyfriend.

EVERS, MR. Teacher.

FARNHAM, DON Ewen High School student. He was on the King & Queen ballot with Helen Shyres. When the sprinklers went on during Carrie's fire, he said "This is gonna wreck the basketball court."

FEARON, ROGER He had worked at Chamberlain Mills and Weaving for eighteen years, but wanted to move out of the area.

FERN Ewen High School student.

FIELDING, GEORGE A scholar who believed that Margaret White blocked her pregnancy from her mind.

FISH, MISS Peter Morton's secretary.

GAINES, COACH Ewen High School's 1976 basketball team coach.

GALATEA On prom night, Tommy Ross told Carrie she was like Galatea: she, too, was transformed from a drudge into a beautiful woman.

GALEN, UNCLE Tommy Ross's uncle, who owned a farm. At the senior prom, Tommy thought of the milk buckets at his uncle's farm when he heard the clanging of the bucket of pigs' blood over his head.

GARRISON, MRS. An eighty-six-year-old woman who often invited Carrie in to watch TV with her.

GARSON, KENNY One of Billy Nolan's cohorts. His intelligence level was that of a third grader. He went with Billy to kill the pigs and get their blood for Carrie's "shower."

GARSON, LOU Kenny's brother, and one of Billy Nolan's cohorts. He went with Billy to kill the pigs and get their blood for Carrie's "shower."

GAULT, JEANNE Ewen High School student. She was one of Sue

Snell's girlfriends.

GEER, MISS The spinster chairwoman of Ewen High School's senior prom. She was known as "Miss Moustache."

GILLIAN, BRENT Ewen High School student.

GIVENS, JULIA Author.

GOGAN, RUTH Ewen High School student.

GRAMMA Annie Jenks's grandmother. Gramma was telekinetic.

GRAYLE, HENRY The principal of Ewen High School.

GRIER, FRANK Ewen High School student. He was on the King & Queen ballot with Jessica Maclean.

HANSCOM, VICKY Classmate.

HARGENSEN, CHRIS One of Carrie White's Ewen High School classmates. She plotted the "pigs' blood shower" revenge plan against Carrie after she and her friends were punished for throwing sanitary napkins at Carrie in the gym shower.

HARGENSEN, JOHN Chris's father. He was a hot-shot lawyer.

HARRIS, BILLY Reporter.

HE/IT God, according to Carrie.

HENTY, IRWIN He had a farm in North Chamberlain. He was mean and crotchety. Billy Nolan killed two of his pigs and drained their blood for Carrie's prom night "shower."

HENTY, MRS. Irwin's mother. Henty was at her funeral the night Billy Nolan and the Chamberlain greaser squad killed two of his pigs and drained their blood for Carrie's "shower."

HOLT, FREDDY "The Beak." A misfit Ewen High School student who had a big nose.

HORAN, ESTELLE (STELLA) An ex-neighbor of the Whites. She moved to the Parrish suburb of San Diego, California.

HORAN, MRS. Estelle's mother.

JASON, FRIEDA She was on the King & Queen ballot with George Dawson.

JENKS, AMELIA "MELIA" She lived in Royal Knob, Tennessee, and had a daughter with telekinetic powers.

JENKS, ANNIE Telekinetic two-year-old.

JENKS, PETE When the cops came for him, Gramma made their guns fly out of their hands.

JENKS, RICH Sandra's husband.

JENKS, SANDRA She received a letter from Amelia Jenks telling her about Annie Jenks.

JEROME, GEORGE He wrote a piece for the *Atlantic Monthly* on the Black Prom.

JONES, VICKY The vice president of the women's league.

JOSIE AND THE MOONGLOWS They supplied the music for part of the evening at the Ewen High School senior prom.

THE JUNKMAN Jerry Smith paid the junkman a hundred dollars to chip off a piece of stone from the rocks that fell on Carrie's house, so he could have it checked out at Boston University.

KELLOGG, DONNA A friend of Chris Hargensen's. Donna moved to Providence, Rhode Island, in 1978.

KELLY, HUBERT The owner of the Kelly Fruit Company.

KING, EDWIN One of Carrie's teachers. [NOTE: Stephen King's full name is Stephen Edwin King.]

KIRK, MR. One of the Whites' Carlin Street neighbors. He watched ice and stones fall on the White's property.

KIRK, VIRGINIA Mr. Kirk's wife.

KLEIN, MRS. One of Tommy Ross's neighbors.

KOLINTZ, ANDREA Girl with pyrokinesis.

KRAMER, GEORGE The assistant principal of School District 14. He once cut a student's hair without parental permission. This incident became a court case called "School District #4 vs. David."

LAVOIE, MR. Ewen High School's head custodian.

"LITTLE MISS SORORITY" Sue Snell, according to herself.

LUBLIN, MR. He and his wife were prom chaperones.

LUBLIN, MRS. She and her husband were prom chaperones.

LUPONET, GERALD Physicist.

MACAFERTY, MISS She drove a VW. When Carrie was young, she gave Miss Macaferty's car four flat tires by simultaneously unscrewing all of the tire valves with her mind.

MacLEAN, JESSICA Ewen High School student. She was on the King & Queen ballot with Frank Grier.

MARGARET WHITE'S GRANDMOTHER She was a witch.

MARSHALL, HOLLY Ewen High School student. She was on the senior prom decorating committee.

McLAUGHLIN, GEORGIA A neighbor of the Whites. After hearing screams coming from their house, she finally gave in and called the police. It turned out that Margaret White was going through labor by herself.

McMANUS, SALLY Ewen High School student. She attended the senior prom.

MEARS, THOMAS B. Chamberlain fireman.

MEARTON, THOMAS G. Investigating officer.

MISS DESJARDIN'S FIRST PROM DATE Unnamed gent.

"MISS MOUSTACHE" Miss Geer.

MR. CHAIRMAN Unnamed chairman of the White Commision.

MOONEY, VIC Ewen High School's senior class president.

MORTON, PETER The assistant principal of Ewen High School.

MORTY Peter Morton, the assistant principal of Ewen High School.

MOTT, ELTON Margaret White's foreman at the Blue Ribbon Laundry.

"THE NICE GIRL" Sue Snell, according to herself.

NOLAN, BILLY Chris Hargensen's boyfriend. He drove a Chevy. He rigged the bucket of pigs' blood over the stage for Carrie's "Prom Queen" shower.

NORBERT, DALE Carrie severed his finger with the gym door.

O'CONNELL, DICK The general manager of the Boston Red Sox.

OVERLOCK, FREDDY He was a luckless bastard who had been shot in the butt with birdshot by Irwin Henty.

PATRICK, DANNY A sixth-grader Tommy Ross once kicked.

PETER Ewen High School student. He was on the King & Queen ballot with Myra Crewes.

PHILPOTT, PETER Superintendent of schools.

PICKETT, FLASH BOBBY The girls in Carrie's class found a love note Carrie had written to Pickett, copied it, and then passed it around.

PLESSY The Chamberlain deputy who locked Quillan in Holding Cell #1 the night of the Black Prom.

PRESTON, BILLY Ewen High School student.

QUILLAN, THOMAS K. He testified about the Black Prom before the state investigatory board of Maine. Quillan drank Schlitz and Alka-Seltzer.

ROSS, MR. Tommy's father.

ROSS, TOMMY (THOMAS EVERETT) Sue Snell's boyfriend. He took Carrie to the prom on the urging of Sue. At the prom, he was on the King & Queen ballot with Carrie. He was killed when he was knocked unconscious by the falling milk bucket that had held the pigs' blood, and then burned to death when the stage caught fire. "He was dead when the oil tank exploded a half hour later."

SAUNDERS Classmate of Tommy's.

SHEILA HORAN'S BROTHER He was hit by a hay truck.

SHYRES, GEORGETTE Helen's mother. She came for Mrs. Simard on the night of the Black Prom.

SHYRES, HELEN Ewen High School student. She participated in the "stoning" of Carrie with sanitary napkins in the gym shower. She was also on the King & Queen ballot at the prom with Don Farnham.

SIMARD, MR. Rhonda's father. He was in Boston on prom weekend.

SIMARD, MRS. CORA Rhonda's mother. She testified about the Black Prom before the Maine state investigatory board.

SIMARD, RHONDA Ewen High School student. She wore a green tulle formal gown to the prom, and died there by electrocution.

SMITH, JERRY One of the Whites' neighbors. He paid a junkman a hundred dollars to chip off a piece from the stones that fell on Carrie's property, so he could have it checked out at Boston

University.

SMITH, MRS. Whites' neighbor; Jerry's wife. She and her husband watched the ice and stones fall on the Whites' property.

SMITH, TERRY Miss Potato Blossom of 1975.

SNELL, MR. Sue's father.

SNELL, MRS. Sue's mother.

SNELL, SUE One of Carrie's classmates. She participated in the "stoning" of Carrie with sanitary napkins in the gym shower. She later felt guilty about the incident and decided to try and make amends by having her boyfriend Tommy Ross take Carrie to the prom. It was a good idea, but it really didn't work out. Sue later wrote a book about the Black Prom called *My Name is Susan Snell*.

SNERD, MORTIMER Label for those who were unwelcome at the prom.

SPIES, RACHEL One of Carrie's classmates. She participated in the "stoning" of Carrie with sanitary napkins in the gym shower.

STENCHFIELD, SANDRA She twirled a baton to "Cabaret" as part of the entertainment for the Ewen High Senior prom.

STAMPEL, HENRY Ewen High School student. He was the class valedictorian of a class of fifty-two surviving seniors. He broke into tears halfway through his valedictory address.

STEPHENS, MR. The fifth period study hall teacher. He was "a tall man just beginning to run to fat."

"SUZY CREEMCHEESE" Sue Snell, according to herself.

SWITHEN, JOHN He played folk music with Maureen Cowan at the Ewen High School senior prom. [NOTE: "John Swithen" was the pseudonym Stephen King used for his crime short story "The Fifth Quarter." See the section on "The Fifth Quarter" in this volume.]

SWOPE, IRMA Classmate. She had a harelip. Chris Hargensen put a firecracker in her shoe.

TABER, PETER The little boy who beat up Danny Patrick.

TALBOT, JACKIE One of Billy Nolan's cohorts. He was first busted for stealing hubcaps at the age of nine. He went with Billy to kill the pigs and get their blood for Carrie's "shower."

THIBODEAU, DONNA One of Carrie's classmates. She participated in the "stoning" of Carrie with sanitary napkins in the gym shower. Donna and Mary Lila Grace were sisters. Donna was a member of the National Honor Society.

THIBODEAU, MARY LILA GRACE One of Carrie's classmates. She participated in the "stoning" of Carrie with sanitary napkins in the gym shower. Mary Lila Grace and Donna were sisters.

THREE TELEPHONE OPERATORS Unnamed; they stayed on duty during the Black Prom.

THRONEBERRY, WILLIAM G. Author

TRELAWNEY, RED Irwin Henty's hired hand. Red was a heavy drinker.

TRENNANT, HENRY Ewen High class-cutter. He cut French I.

TREVOR, BRUCE Ewen High School student. He was a basketball player. In 1976, he was not allowed to play in the Ewen-Stadler game because a kilo of marijuana had been found in his locker.

TWO MEN Two unnamed men were electrocuted the night of the Black Prom.

TWO OR THREE STAGEHANDS They moved the King and Queen thrones.

ULLMAN, DALE Ewen High School student. He was a sixth period student.

THE UNNAMED BOY Dale Ullman whispered to him.

UPSHAW, JESSICA Ewen High School student.

VRECK, JOSIE The leader of Josie and the Moonglows.

WARWICK, MRS. One of the Whites' neighbors. She watched ice and stones fall on the Whites' property.

WATSON, NORMA Ewen High School student. Tina Blake thought Norma was bitchy.

WHITE, CARIETTA (CARRIE) Young girl who was born with telekinetic powers. She was ridiculed by her classmates when she thought she was bleeding to death after getting her first menstrual period during a shower after a gym class. Her classmate Chris Hargensen plotted to inflict the ultimate humiliation on her: crown her Queen of the senior prom, and then dump a bucket of pigs' blood on her as she stood on stage accepting the applause. When this happened, something inside Carrie snapped, and she unleashed the full wrath of her powers. Carrie was born September 21, 1963. [NOTE: September 21 is also Stephen King's birthday.]

WHITE, MARGARET Carrie's mother. The ultimate Bible-pounding fundamentalist religious fanatic. She often kept Carrie locked in a closet for punishment.

WHITE, RALPH Carrie's father. He carried the TK gene that had been passed on to Carrie. He died in February of 1963.

YORRATY, MRS. One of the Whites' neighbors.

(1)
CARRIE
Places

THE BANK OF AMERICA Mr. Horan was an executive at the Parrish branch.

BARKER STREET GRAMMAR SCHOOL School in Chamberlain, Maine, that Carrie attended. In one of the classrooms, there was a desk with graffiti scratched into it: "Carrie White eats shit."

BELLSQUEEZE ROAD AND ROUTE 6 INTERSECTION Chamberlain intersection. There was a graveyard there.

THE BILLIARD PARLOR A Chamberlain business that Sheriff Doyle saw burning when he returned to town on the night of the Black Prom.

BILL'S HOME DRUGSTORE Chamberlain business. Its windows jingled and fell inward during Carrie's fire.

BLUE RIBBON LAUNDRY The laundry where Margaret White worked. [NOTE: Maybe she knew Bart Dawes? Even though the Blue Ribbon Laundry in *Roadwork* was in M_____, W_____; it is (remotely) possible that the Chamberlain Blue Ribbon was a branch of Bart's Blue Ribbon that was just never mentioned in *Roadwork* (see the section on *Roadwork* in this volume).]

BOSTON COLLEGE The school attended by one of Chris Hargensen's former lovers.

BRICKYARD HILL The west end of Chamberlain, Maine. This was where the worst disaster took place on the night of the Black Prom: A gas main exploded and the fire raged out of control for most of the next day.

BRUNSWICK, MAINE Three fire engines from this town came to Chamberlain on the night of the Black Prom.

CARLIN STREET, CHAMBERLAIN, MAINE Carrie White and her mother lived on Carlin Street in Chamberlain.

THE CARLIN STREET CONGREGATIONAL CHURCH The church where Carrie went to pray after blowing up Ewen High and most of Chamberlain.

CARRIE'S CLOSET The place where Margaret White would imprison Carrie for her sins. Here's a description of Margaret White's "closet decor":

> "The blue light glared on a picture of a huge and bearded Yahweh who was casting screaming multitudes of humans down through cloudy depths into an abyss of fire. Below them, black horrid figures struggled through the flames of perdition while the Black Man sat on a huge flame-colored throne with a trident in one hand. His body was that of a man, but he had a spiked tail and the head of a jackal."

THE CAVALIER Local Chamberlain bar. Tommy Ross figured that the Cavalier would be where he would spend his weekends after graduating from high school.

CHAMBERLAIN, MAINE Carrie White's hometown.

THE CHAMBERLAIN HARDWARE & LUMBER Chamberlain

business. Mr. Morton had a brush with their slogan printed on it: "Chamberlain Hardware and Lumber Never Brushes You Off."

THE CHAMBERLAIN JUNIOR HIGH SCHOOL The junior high Carrie attended. As in the Barker Street Grammar School, there was also "Carrie-specific" graffiti scratched on a desk here. This slur read: "Roses are red, Violets are blue, Sugar is sweet, but Carrie White eats shit."

THE CHAMBERLAIN MILLS AND WEAVING The town's major industry. It was untouched by Carrie's fire.

THE CHAMBERLAIN U-WASH-IT Chamberlain business. Sue Snell sat on the steps of this business as the town burned around her.

CHRISTIAN YOUTH CAMP A camp Carrie had attended as a child. The girls in Carrie's cabin short-sheeted her bed.

COURTHOUSE PARK Chamberlain park. The elms in the park burned during Carrie's fire.

DUFFY'S BAR AND GRILLE A Chamberlain business Sheriff Doyle saw burning when he returned to town on the night of the Black Prom.

EWEN AVENUE Carrie usually walked down Ewen Avenue to get to Carlin. [NOTE: It wasn't said if Ewen High School was on Ewen Avenue, although it is likely.]

EWEN HIGH SCHOOL Carrie White's high school. It wasn't in too good shape after the senior prom. Something about a fire.

FRANK'S BAR A Chamberlain business. It was on Sullivan Street.

THE GRASS PLAZA During Carrie's "after-prom" rampage, she opened a fire hydrant at Grass Plaza in Chamberlain.

HOLDING CELL #1 The cell Thomas Quillan would use when he got drunk. Like Mayberry's Otis on "The Andy Griffith Show," he would lock himself up.

JACKSON AVENUE On her rampage through Chamberlain, Carrie opened a gas main on Jackson Avenue.

JOHN'S A store in Westover, Maine. Carrie bought the material for her prom gown at John's.

THE JOLLY ROADHOUSE A bar that Margaret White's parents owned just outside the Motton, Maine, town limits.

JORDAN MARSH A store where Chris Hargensen shopped. She had once bought a sweater there that got full of grease when she helped Billy Nolan change a flat tire. The sweater cost twenty-seven fifty.

KELLY FRUIT COMPANY High school hangout. It was a combination grocery, soda fountain, and gas station. Sheriff Doyle saw it burning when he returned to town on the night of the Black Prom.

KENNEDY JUNIOR HIGH Danny Patrick and Pete Taber had once had a fight on the Kennedy Junior High playground.

KENOSHA, WISCONSIN Margaret White had a friend in Kenosha. Margaret once wrote to this woman and told her that she had "cancer of the womanly parts."

KLEEN KORNERS Sue Snell's "life plan" included working diligently "to keep the niggers out of Kleen Korners," —that perfect manifestation of a lily-white town she saw herself inhabitating after high school and college.

LEWIN BUSINESS COLLEGE A school in Motton, Maine. Estelle Horan had attended classes there when she lived on Carlin Street.

LEWISTON HIGH SCHOOL They had private showers at Lewiston High.

MACON, GEORGIA The town where Sandra Jenks lived.

MAIN AND SPRING The Chamberlain intersection where Quillan first saw Carrie on the night of the Black Prom.

THE MAITLAND REAL ESTATE AGENCY A Chamberlain business that Sheriff Doyle saw burning when he returned to town on the night of the Black Prom.

MOTTON, MAINE The town where the Lewin Business College was located. Also, Margaret White was born in Motton.

OBERLIN COLLEGE The college that Chris Hargensen planned on attending after graduation from Ewen High.

THE OLD BENTOWN ROAD Route 179.

PARRISH, SAN DIEGO The area of California that Estelle Horan moved to from Chamberlain, Maine.

PORTLAND, MAINE Ralph White died when a steel girder fell out of a carrying sling on a housing project in Portland.

THE RENNET BLOCK During Carrie's fire, water was brought in from this area.

RIVERSIDE GOLF COURSE Golf course in the Chamberlain area that had smooth, green hills.

ROUTE 179 The Old Bentown Road. Sheriff Doyle was on Route 179 investigating an auto accident on the night of May 27, 1979, the evening of the Black Prom.

ROUTE 302 It was near Brickyard Hill.

ROYAL KNOB, TENNESSEE The town where the Jenks lived.

ST. LOUIS Margaret White once mail-ordered a four-foot-high plaster crucifix from St. Louis. It hung in her living room.

ST. PETERSBURG, FLORIDA Henry Kelly, the proprietor of the Kelly Fruit Company, said he would not rebuild after Carrie's fire, but would instead retire to St. Petersburg, Florida.

SHUBER'S FIVE AND TEN Carrie once stole a forty-nine-cent finger ring from Shuber's when she was young. Her mother had kept her in the closet for a whole day.

SULLIVAN STREET Frank's Bar was located on Sullivan Street, Chamberlain.

STACK END ROAD A rutted North Chamberlain road.

STAR PRINTERS The company that printed the Ewen High School senior prom tickets.

SULLIVAN STREET Frank's Bar was on Sullivan Street in Chamberlain.

SUMMER STREET Tony's Citgo was on Summer Street in Chamberlain.

TEDDY'S AMOCO Gas station owned by Teddy Duchamp, who later moved to Castle Rock, Oregon, and ran the Castle Rock Stationery Shop—as we were told in "The Body."

TONY'S CITGO A Chamberlain business that Sheriff Doyle saw burning when he returned to town on the night of the Black Prom.

THE UNIVERSITY OF MASSACHUSETTS The school attended by one of Chris Hargensen's former lovers.

THE WESTERN AUTO STORE A Chamberlain business owned by Doug Brann that Sheriff Doyle saw burning when he returned to town on the night of the Black Prom.

WESTOVER DOCTORS HOSPITAL Margaret White was admitted to this hospital for a suspected out-of-wedlock miscarriage on April 3, 1962.

WESTOVER HIGH SCHOOL They had private showers at Westover High.

WOOLWORTH'S The Chamberlain department store where Carrie usually bought the material she used to make her clothing.

(1)
CARRIE
Things

ACE COMB The comb Billy Nolan used.

ALKA-SELTZER Thomas Quillan had been known to drink Schlitz and Alka-Seltzers.

ALLIED VANS & U-HAULS A company that moved out of Chamberlain.

APRIL 3, 1962 The day Margaret White was admitted to Westover Doctors' Hospital for a (suspected) miscarriage.

AVON SOAP One of the odors that exuded from Norma Watson at the senior prom.

THE BILLY BOSNAN BAND One of the bands that played at the Ewen High School senior prom. (The other was Josie and the Moonglows.)

A BIRDHOUSE On the night Sue Snell asked Tommy Ross to take

Carrie to the prom, they were at Tommy's house, and Tommy's father was downstairs in the cellar workroom building a birdhouse..

BLACK FOREST CUCKOO CLOCK The clock Margaret White had in her living room.

BOSTON ROCKER A chair in Carrie's room that she had bought and paid for herself.

BRYLCREEM The hair tonic Billy Nolan used.

BUDWEISER Chris Hargensen's fraternity dates usually drank Bud.

THE BURIAL On June 1 and 2, 1979, Chamberlain had three mass ceremonies to bury their 440 dead.

A BUST OF PALLAS A bust of Pallas was used in a Ewen High School production of Edgar Allan Poe's "The Raven." The bust was stored in the school's stage flies.

CARRIE WHITE'S ADDRESS:

47 Carlin Street
Chamberlain, Maine 02249

CARRIE'S LAST THOUGHT:

(momma i'm sorry where)

CARRIE'S PHYSICAL STATISTICS DURING "FLEXING" When Carrie was utilizing her telekinetic powers, her physical stats were affected as follows:

Respiration—16 breaths per minute (Normal is 6-7 breaths)
Blood Pressure—190/100 (Normal is 120/80)
Heartbeat—140 beats per minute (Normal is 72)
Body Temperature—94.3° (Normal is 98.6°)

CARRIE'S POEM Carrie turned in the following poem to her English teacher, Mr. Edwin King, as a class assignment in the seventh grade. The border of the paper on which this poem was written was "decorated with a great many cruciform figures which almost [seemed] to dance..."

Jesus watches from the wall
But his face is cold as stone,
And if he loves me
As she tells me
Why do I feel so all alone?

CARRIE'S PROM DRESS It was nearly floor-length, crushed red velvet, it had a Princess waistline, Juliet sleeves, and a simple straight skirt. (She wore a corsage of two roses that Tommy had brought her.)

CARRIE'S REVENGE At the Black Prom, Carrie got even in this order: First she set off the sprinklers, which resulted in multiple electrocutions. She then caused several explosions in Chamberlain, resulting in a huge, devastating fire.

THE CARS DRIVEN BY CHRIS HARGENSEN'S FORMER LOVERS Their vehicles included VW's, Javelins, and Dodge Chargers.

THE CHAMBERLAIN *CLARION* The Chamberlain newspaper. It was blown up during Carrie's rampage.

THE CHAMBERLAIN GRAVEYARD It was at the intersection of Bellsqueeze and Route 6.

"CHARLIE" Billy Nolan's nickname for Chris Hargensen: "He called her Charlie whenever he was pleased with her. It seemed to be, she thought with a cold blink of humor, a generic term for good cunt."

THE CIGARETTES SOLD AT THE KELLY FRUIT COMPANY The brands carried included Murads, King Sano, and Marvel Straights.

CONSTANT COMMENT TEA The tea Margaret White drank.

CRAFTSMAN TOOLS The tool kit in Billy Nolan's car.

"DARKNESS" Carrie's gift to her mother.

THE DEATH TOLL 440 dead; 18 missing; 67 high school seniors dead.

"DIRTYPILLOWS" The word Margaret White used for breasts.

EIGHTEEN UNACCOUNTED FOR There were eighteen people unaccounted for after Carrie's rampage on the night of the Black Prom.

11:30 P.M. Carrie's prom night curfew time.

EVERLEAF The magazine that published a poem by Tommy Ross six months before he died.

THE EWEN HIGH SCHOOL SONG These were the only lyrics given to the song:

All rise high for Thomas Ewen High
We'll raise your banners to the sky
With pride we wear the red and white

440 DEAD The final death toll from Carrie's rampage on the night of tthe Black Prom.

GIANT STEP Cora Simard thought of the children's game Giant Step when she had to step over downed live wires on the night of the Black Prom.

JANTZEN Estelle Horan's bathing suit.

JEFFERSON AIRPLANE'S "LONG JOHN SILVER" ALBUM The album Sue Snell listened in her living room the night of the senior prom.

JOSIE & THE MOONGLOWS One of the bands that played at the Ewen High School senior prom. (The other was the Billy Bosnan Band.)

JUICY FRUIT GUM One of the odors that exuded from Norma Watson at the senior prom.

JUNE 1 AND 2, 1979 The dates of the "after-prom" mass burials in Chamberlain.

JUNE 3, 1979 The date of the memorial service to remember Chamberlain's 440 dead, killed the night of the Black Prom.

KING JAMES BIBLE Margaret White always kept one in her pocketbook.

KING SANO One of the cigarette brands carried at the Kelly Fruit Company.

KODAK STAR FLASHES The flashblulbs used to take pictures at the Ewen High School senior prom.

"LET THE LOWER LIGHTS BE BURNING" A song sung by Tennessee Ernie Ford that Margaret White listened to on a Webcor phonograph.

MARCH 23, 1962 The day Carrie's mother married Ralph White.

MARGARET WHITE'S PICTURES AND PLASTER PLAQUES: The "artwork" on her walls included:

"Christ, the Unseen Guest"
"What Would Jesus Do"
"The Hour Draweth Nigh: If Tonight Became
   Judgement, Would You Be Ready."
Jesus Leading the Lambs
Jesus Turning the Moneychangers From the Temple
Moses Throwing Down the Tablets
Thomas Putting His Hand Into Jesus' Side
Noah's Ark
Lot Fleeing the Burning of Sodom and Gomorrah

MARVEL STRAIGHTS One of the cigarette brands carried at the Kelly Fruit Company.

MAY 17, 1979 The date a letter from Chris Hargensen to Donna Kellogg was postmarked. In the letter, Chris told Donna that she was going to get even for being banned from the senior prom, that "everyone was going to get a big fucking surprise."

MAY 27, 1979 The date of the Ewen High School senior prom.

MEMORIAL SERVICE The memorial service for the 440 killed during Carrie's rampage took place in the Chamberlain town square on June 3.

"MONONDOCK CONSOLIDATED SCHOOL DISTRICT VS. CRANEPOOL" A case involving a school's parental rights during school hours.

MURADS One of the cigarette brands carried at the Kelly Fruit Company.

MY NAME IS SUSAN SNELL Book written about the Black Prom by one of Carrie's former classmates.

THE NATIONAL HONOR SOCIETY Donna Thibodeau and David Bracken were both members.

1960 The year Carrie's mother met Ralph White and moved to Chamberlain Center.

PLANTER'S MIXED NUTS There were gondolas of Planters on the tables at the Black Prom.

PLAYTEX GLOVES The gloves Billy Nolan wore when rigging the blood bucket over the Ewen High stage.

"POMP & CIRCUMSTANCE" Josie and the Moonglows played a rock version of "Pomp and Circumstance" as the ushers approached Tommy and Carrie's table after the couple won the King and Queen ballot.

POPULAR MECHANIX A magazine Billy Nolan read.

"THE PRAYER OF EXORCISM" FROM *DEUTERONOMY* The prayer Margaret White recited after Carrie told her mother she was going to the senior prom.

RHEINGOLD The beer Billy Nolan drank.

RODIN'S "THE THINKER" The ashtray on Mr. Morton's desk.

SAVILE ROW John Hargensen's suit.

SCHLITZ The beer Thomas Quillan drank.

"SCHOOL DISTRICT #4 VS. DAVID" A case involving a principal who cut a student's hair without his consent.

SEAGRAM'S 7 The booze Brucie (Billy Nolan's mother's boyfriend) drank.

SEPTEMBER 21, 1963 The day Carrie White was born. [NOTE: September 21 is also Stephen King's birthday.]

SEVENTEEN The magazine Carrie looked through to get ideas for her prom gown.

'77 PLYMOUTH Mrs. Snell's car.

"SHE'S GOT TO BE A SAINT" A song by Ray Price that was playing on the jukebox in the Cavalier bar while Billy Nolan and Chris Hargensen waited in an upstairs room.

SIGN ON CARRIE'S LAWN: After Carrie's death, a sign was put up on her lawn:

CARRIE WHITE IS BURNING FOR HER SINS
JESUS NEVER FAILS

A '61 BISCAYNE Billy Nolan's car.

SIXTY-SEVEN SENIORS Of the 440 dead after Carrie's rampage on the night of the Black Prom, 67 were members of the Ewen High School graduating senior class.

SONG OF THE SOUTH A Disney storybook that Norma Watson had had as a child. Carrie reminded her of the tar-baby in an Uncle Remus story when Carrie opened her eyes after being drenched in blood from head to toe.

SOURCES CITED IN *CARRIE* Carrie's powers, her rampage and its aftermath were documented in the following sources (in order of appearance):

1. *The Enterprise*; Westover, Maine; August 19, 1966 "Rain of Stones Reported"
2. *The Shadow Exploded: Documented Facts and Specific Conclusions Derived from the Case of Carietta White* by David R. Congress (Tulane University Press, 1981) pp. 34, 41, 54, 58, 60-61, 74-76, 59, 92-93, 100-101, 129, 131, 132, 133, 134, 151, 164-165, 201, and Appendix III. (NOTE: A *Life* magazine article of September 4, 1955 regarding Andrea Kolintz was referred to on pp. 60-61 of this report).
3. *Telekinesis: A Wild Talent Revisited* by White and Stearns
4. *Esquire* magazine; September 12, 1980 "Carrie: The Black Dawn of TK" by Jack Gaver
5. *Ogilvie's Dictionary of Psychic Phenomena*
6. *Science YearBook 1981* "Telekinesis: Analysis and Aftermath" by Dean D.L. McGuffin
7. *My Name is Susan Snell* by Susan Snell; (NY, Simon & Schuster, 1986) pp. i-iv, 6, 23, 40, 45, 48, and 98
8. *Reader's Digest* "Drama in Real Life"; August 1980 "We Survived the Black Prom" by Norma Watson
9. New England Associated Press Ticker Reports: May 27, 1979: 10:46 P.M.; 11:22 P.M.; 11:46 P.M. June 5, 1979: No Specific Time
10. *Black Prom: The White Commission Report* (Signet Books, 1980) Testimony of Thomas K. Quillan Testimony of Sheriff Otis Doyle, pp. 29-31 Testimony of Mrs. Cora Simard, pp. 217-18
11. *Microbiology Annual*; Berkeley, 1982 "A View Towards Isolation of the TK Gene with Specific Recommendations for Control Parameters" by Bourke and Hannegan
12. *Black Prom: The White Commission Report* (Signet Books, 1980) Testimony of Susan Snell, pp. 306-472
13. Westover Mercy Hospital "Report of Decease": May 28, 1979, "Carrie White"
14. *Lewiston Daily Sun*; Sunday, September 7, 1979 "The Legacy of TK: Scorched Earth and Scorched Hearts"
15. Letter fom Henry Grayle to Peter Philpott; June 9, 1979
16. Letter from Rita Desjardin to Henry Grayle; June 11, 1979
17. *Slang Terms Explained: A Parent's Guide* by John R. Coombs (NY, Lighthouse Press, 1985) p. 73
18. Conclusion of the State Investigatory Board of Maine
19. Letter from Amelia Jenks to Sandra Jenks; May 3, 1988

STEPHEN KING'S FIRST USE OF DOUBLE-MARGIN EXCLAMATION POINTS Page 91 (paperback edition):

!!!!!!!no no no no no !!!!!!!

SUE SNELL'S ADDRESS:

19 Back Chamberlain Road
Chamberlain, Maine 02249

10:25 P.M. The time the whistle atop the town hall on Main Street in Chamberlain began to shriek on the night of the Black Prom. Ewen High School was already on fire by this time.

THE TIME SPAN OF *CARRIE*: August 19, 1966—May 3, 1988

VIRGINIA SLIMS Estelle Horan's cigarettes.

VOLKSWAGEN FORMULA VEE Estelle Horan's car.

A WEBCOR PHONOGRAPH Margaret White's record player.

WOOLWORTH'S PERFUME One of the odors that exuded from Norma Watson at the senior prom.

'SALEM'S LOT

DEDICATION

For Naomi Rachel King
"...promises to keep."

CONTENTS PAGE

BOOK BREAKDOWN

Author's Note
Prologue—(Seven sections numbered 1-7)

PART ONE
The Marsten House

PART TWO
The Emperor of Ice Cream

PART THREE
The Deserted Village

(2)
'SALEM'S LOT
People

ANDERSON, SHERWOOD American writer who Ben felt surely would have recognized the small town distrust for creative types that Susan's mother Ann was exhibiting towards Ben.

ASHFORD Ben Mears' mother's maiden name.

BANNOCK, JOHN The fiancee of an unnamed young girl. He died before their wedding. He had a large strawberry birthmark on his neck. He came back from the dead to prevent his fiancee from marrying someone else. The girl was so distraught she wasted away and died. Bannock was photographed standing by her grave two years later. The developed photographs were blank.

BARCLAY, DAVIE Childhood friend of Ben Mears.

BARLOW, KURT Antiques expert. Straker's business partner. Vampire.

BASCOMB, BUDDY Morgue attendant.

THE BEWILDERED MAN An unnamed man who helped an orderly subdue Ann Norton.

BISSONETTE, FATHER RAYMOND Father Callahan's friend. He was ministering a parish in Cornwall.

BODDIN, DEREK Franklin Boddin's brother.

BODDIN, FRANKLIN Derek Boddin's brother.

BODDIN, RICHIE School bully. He was eleven years old, and weighed 140 pounds.

BOWIE, CLAUDE Lot resident. His son came back from Vietnam with a mechanical foot.

THE BOWIE BOY Claude's son. He came back from Vietnam with a mechanical foot.

BOYER, GEORGE Mill worker. He worked the three-to-eleven shift.

BRYANT, COREY Twenty-two year old telephone lineman who was having an affair with Bonnie Sawyer.

BURKE, MATTHEW High school English teacher. He was sixty-three.

BUTTS, PEARL ANN Girl who ran off to New York City in 1907 to become a Ziegfield girl.

BUZZEY, FRANK The main character in Ben Mears' novel *Air Dance*.

CALLAHAN, FATHER DONALD St. Andrew's parish priest. He ended up "missing."

CAMPION, BRAD Ben's friend. Brad worked in the Yarmouth Liquor Store.

CARLYLE Author quoted by Matt.

CARVER, GEORGE WASHINGTON Matt Burke said students groaned when faced with people like Carver.

CHOPPER Mark Petrie's dog. He had to be put to sleep by a vet. [NOTE: Do you think he could have worked in a junkyard first?! See "The Body" in the *Different Seasons* section in this volume.]

CINDY Ben's Aunt Cindy. Her name was Cynthia Stowens. Ben ate cereal at her house when he was young.

CODY, JIMMY Young doctor; Matt Burke's friend.

COGGINS, MRS. FIONA A widow who was reported missing on February 14, 1976.

COLEMAN, GARY One of Matt Burke's students. He went blind due to optic nerve degeneration.

COOGAN, MISS Woman who worked at Spencer's Drugstore.

COREY, MINELLA Birdie Marsten's sister.

CORLISS, AGGIE Woman who wrote a letter to the Cumberland *Ledger* after they threw out the dress code at Consolidated High School. Aggie had been writing to the *Ledger* every week for years. She preached against the evils of whiskey and the joy of accepting Jesus Christ as your personal savior.

CORSON, SHELDON One of Eva Miller's boarders.

CRAIG, WEASEL Ed Craig. A drunk. One of Eva Miller's

boarders. He helped Eva Miller clean the house.

CROCKETT, LAWRENCE The Lot's second selectman. He was the proprietor of Crockett's Southern Maine Insurance and Realty. He ended up "missing."

CROCKETT, RUTHIE School girl who never wore a bra and always snickered at Dud Rogers. Dud thought of her as a slut.

CRONKITE, WALTER News anchor. Listening to Cronkite was how residents of the Lot learned of the Vietnam war.

CROSSEN, MILT The owner of Crossen's Agricultural Store.

CURLESS, RHODA Resident of the Lot who ended up working with St. Matthew's Mission in Portland.

DANLES, KENNY Man who worked for the post office.

THE DARK FATHER Satan. Barlow's master.

DICKENS, PAULINE Resident of the Lot who moved to Los Angeles. She had worked for years at the Excellent Café in the Lot.

DICKEY, JAMES American author.

DOC Irwin Purinton's dog. Doc was a half-cocker mongrel.

DUBE, LAVERNE Billy Smith's girlfriend. She was killed in a car accident with Billy.

DURHAM, HARRIET Lady on the party line. Mabel Werts listened in on Harriet's conversation with Glynnis Mayberry. Harriet worked at Gates Mill and Weaving. She ended up "missing."

DURHAM, LESTER He worked at Gates Mill and Weaving. He ended up "missing".

EVANS, DAVID Auto mechanic. He worked at Sears in Gates Falls.

FARRINGTON, JOHN A farmer who was found dead in his barn on February 27, 1976.

FELSEN, DAVE The man in charge of the S.A.D. 21 motor pool. He was friends with Charlie Rhodes.

FOREMAN, CARL The Lot's undertaker.

FORESTER, DEBBIE Little girl whose Indian costume caught fire at the bicentennial fireworks display.

"FRED ASTAIRE AND GINGER ROGERS" While drunk, Father Callahan imagined Astaire and Rogers dancing in the spotlight circle in front of the church.

GAME WARDENS All county employees.

GARDENER, NOLLY The Lot's town deputy constable.

THE GARDENER KIDS Boys Ben played with as a child. [N OTE: Was Jim Gardener possibly one of them?? See the section on *The Tommyknockers* in this volume.]

GARVEY, ANDY Boy suspended for letting the air out of Bob Thomas' bus tires.

GAYE, MARVIN Matt Burke referred to Gaye's song "I Heard It Through the Grapevine."

GILLESPIE, PARKINS The Lot's constable. He ended up living with his sister in Kittery.

GLICCUCCHI, MR. Tony Glick's grandfather. He had his name legally changed to Glick.

GLICK, DANNY School kid. He was turned into a vampire.

GLICK, MARJORIE Margie Glick. Danny and Ralphie's mother.

GLICK, TONY Marjorie's husband.

GORBY, DR. The doctor in charge of Danny Glick.

GRACON, FATHER Los Zapatas village priest.

GREEN, MAURY Mortician.

GREEN, RACHEL Maury Green's wife.

GREENBERG, BOB Morgue attendant.

GREER, SALLY One of Matt Burke's students. She was killed by her drunken boyfriend.

GRIEGSON, MARY KATE One of the kids on Charlie Rhodes' school bus.

GRIFFEN, BABS Hal and Jack's eldest sister.

GRIFFEN, CHARLES Son of the owner of the original Griffen Dairy.

GRIFFEN, DOUG Baseball player. He struck out.

GRIFFEN, HAL Eighteen-year-old son of Charles Griffen.

GRIFFEN, JACK Fourteen-year-old son of Charles Griffen.

GROGGINS, JOHN Pastor of the Jerusalem's Lot Methodist Church. He ended up "missing." Matt Burke thought Groggins was the asshole of the western world.

HANRAHAN, AGENT Portland FBI agent.

HAWTHORNE, NATHANIEL Father Callahan considered Hawthorne "conventionally religious."

HERBERT OR HAROLD An old student of Matt Burke's.

HERSEY, AUDREY Member of the ladies auxiliary.

HERSEY, JACKSON Audrey Hersey's eldest brother.

HERSEY, MRS. GERTRUDE Fiona Coggins' niece. She reported Coggins missing.

HOLCOMB, MISS Playground monitor.

HOLLOWAY, DANIEL, AND FAMILY They were reported missing by Daniel's grandfather on May 29, 1976.

HOLLY, BUDDY Matt Burke was a Holly fan.

HOLMWOOD, ARTHUR Actor in the film "Dracula."

HOOKER, JUDGE Judge who fined Frank Kilby fifty dollars for dope possession.

HORRIS Elderly man from Schoolyard Hill. He was a cancer patient at the Maine Medical Center.

HOUDINI Magician.

HUME, FATHER An old priest. Father Callahan replaced him.

JAMES, AUDIE One of the boys Charlie Rhodes thought let the air out of the bus tires.

JAMES, CHARLES He was known as "Sonny." He owned a gas station across from the drugstore in the Lot. He ended up running a repair shop in Cumberland. He was a childhood friend of Ben Mears.

JAMES, SONNY Owner of Sonny's Exxon Station.

"JOE BLOW" Name Horris gave the fictional gas station attendant at Sonny's Amoco.

JOINTNER, ELIAS Member of the state house of representatives who had the Portland Post Road renamed in his honor. It was renamed Jointner Avenue.

KALI A Hindu goddess.

KELLY, JOHN When Straker presented the conditions under which he would buy the Marsten House, Crockett thought that it was a practical joke set up by John Kelly.

KILBY, FRANK The kid who delivered Eva Miller's newspaper. He got arrested on a dope charge.

KILBY, HORACE Frank's father.

KINGFIELD, JERRY Ten-year-old boy who disappeared in the marshes while fishing. It was assumed he went down in quicksand.

LABREE, MR. Pharmacist at Spencer's Drugstore.

"LAWRENCE CREWCUT" How the watchman referred to Larry Crockett.

LEE, CHRISTOPHER Actor in Hammer Films.

LEWIS, JOHN *Press-Herald* features editor. He wrote the article "Ghost Town in Maine?"

LOVECRAFT, H.P. American writer. An atheist.

MARKEY, DELBERT The owner of Dell's. He was also the bartender.

MARSHALL, PETER Emcee of "The Hollywood Squares" TV show.

MARSTEN, BIRDIE Hubie Marsten's wife.

MARSTEN, HUBERT Hubie Marsten. Owner of the Marsten House. He was president of the New England Trucking Company in the twenties.

MAYBERRY, DOUG One of Matt Burke's students. He drowned at Old Orchard Beach.

MAYBERRY, GLYNNIS Lady on the party line. Mabel Werts listened in on her conversation with Harriet Durham.

McCASLIN, MRS. Sheriff McCaslin's wife.

McCASLIN, SHERIFF County sheriff.

McDOUGALL, RANDY Sandy and Royce McDougall's ten-month-old son.

McDOUGALL, ROYCE Sandy's husband, Randy's father. Royce worked in the mill. After he was turned into a vampire, his teeth looked like those of a German shepherd. He ended up "missing."

McDOUGALL, SANDY Seventeen-year-old mother of Randy McDougall. She beat her son and told her husband he fell off the changing table. She ended up "missing."

McFEE, PETER Maine state police chief who investigated some of the Lot's disappearances.

McGEE, TRAVIS Sheriff McCaslin told Ben he should write books like the guy who wrote the Travis McGee stories. [NOTE: This was King's nod to one of his three primary influences, John D. MacDonald.]

McLEOD, LARRY Mailman in the twenties. He delivered to Hubie Marsten.

MEARS, BEN Writer. He discovered the truth about Jerusalem's Lot.

MEARS, MIRANDA Ben's wife. She died in a motorcycle accident.

MERTON Ben Mears' father's middle name.

MIDDLER, GEORGE He worked in the hardware store.

MIDDLER, MILT Lot resident. He sat in Crossen's store.

MIDDLER, PAT Lot resident. She sat in Crossen's store.

MILLER, EVA She ran the local boarding house. She ended up "missing."

MILLER, RALPH Eva's husband. He was killed in a sawmill accident in 1959.

"MR. FLIP" Father Callahan's boogeyman when he was a child.

MUNŌZ, JESUS DE LA REY Los Zapatas man who interpreted for Father Gracon.

NORBERT, BRENTON Assistant medical examiner.

NORTON, ANN Susan's mother.

NORTON, BILL Susan's father.

NORTON, SUSAN Ben first met her in the park. She was reading his novel *Air Dance*.

AN ORDERLY Unnamed orderly who subdued Ann Norton.

OVERLOOK, JUDY Girl who ran off with a Saladmaster salesman in 1957 or 1958.

PATTERSON He was from the Church of Latter-Day Saints and the Followers of the Cross. He was "crazier [than] a bear stuck in a honey tree."

PERKINS, MRS. Ben Mears' first grade teacher.

PETERS, HANK He went with Royal Snow to pick up the "Hepplewhite" for Straker.

PETRIE, HENRY Lot resident. Mark's father. He worked for the Prudential insurance company. He ended up "missing." He had a B.S. from Northeastern, a Master's from Massachusetts Tech, and a Ph.D in Economics. He was a Democrat.

PETRIE, MARK Mr. and Mrs. Petrie's son.

PETRIE, MRS. Mark's mother. Lot resident. She ended up "missing."

PHILBROOK, MIKE One of the boys Charlie Rhodes thought let the air out of the bus tires.

PHILLIPS, GORDON Man from Scarborough. His car was found deserted on January 4, 1976. He and his family were missing.

PLOWMAN, DR. The McDougall's doctor.

POE, EDGAR ALLAN Father Callahan considered Poe a half-assed transcendentalist.

POTTER Lot resident who was killed in Vietnam.

POULIN, ROMEO Larry Crockett's silent partner in a supermarket plaza deal.

PRINE, DR. DAVID Doctor at Johns Hopkins.

PRITCHETT, CHARLES V. Man who, with his family, bought the Charles Griffen farm. They moved out on November 19, 1975.

PURINTON, IRWIN Slewfoot Hill milkman in West Salem.

PURINTON, LESLIE Irwin Purinton's wife.

THE RANGERS Band at Dell's.

RATHBUN, TOMMY A drunk who fell off Drunk's Leap.

RATHBUN, VIRGE Tommy Rathbun's brother.

RAUBERSON, HAROLD A childhood friend of Ben Mears.

Harold died of leukemia.

RAWCLIFFE, AMY Childhood friend of Susan Norton's.

RHODES, CHARLIE School bus driver.

RICE, DAVID County medical examiner.

ROBINSON, EDWARD ARLINGTON American writer who Ben felt sure would have recognized the small town distrust for creative types that Susan's mother Ann was exhibiting towards Ben.

RODDY Little boy who was pushing his sister on the swing in the park.

RODDY'S MOTHER She told Roddy not to push his sister so high on the swing.

RODDY'S SISTER Roddy was pushing her on the swing in the park.

RODIN, MRS. Teacher. Her nickname was "Mrs. Rodan." She was named after the Japanese monster movie "Rodan."

ROGERS, DUD The dump custodian.

ROYKO, BILLY One of Matt Burke's students. He died in Vietnam in a helicopter crash.

RYERSON, MIKE Groundskeeper. He maintained the Lot's three cemeteries.

THE SALADMASTER SALESMAN Judy Overlook ran off with him in 1957 or 1958.

SALK, JONAS Matt Burke said students groaned when faced with people like Salk.

SAWYER, BONNIE Reg Sawyer's wife. She was having an affair with Corey Bryant.

SAWYER, REG Bonnie Sawyer's husband.

SMITH, BILLY Drunk driver who was killed in a car accident.

SMITH, CARL He drank Moxie soda.

SMITH, JIM He owned a garage in Buxton where Reg Sawyer worked.

SNOW, ROYAL Man who put up poster for Barlow and Straker. He drove the U-Haul truck Crockett rented.

STARCHER, MISS LORETTA Lot librarian.

STEVENS, WALLACE Poet Parkins Gillespie referred to.

STOWENS, CYNTHIA Ben's Aunt Cindy. He lived with her after Ben's mother had a nervous breakdown.

STRAKER, RICHARD THROCKETT The man who bought both the Marsten House and the Village Washtub. Barlow's human emissary.

SYLVESTER, MICKEY One of Eva Miller's boarders. He worked in the textile mill. He didn't wash his dishes.

TALBOT, MAUREEN Jackie Talbot's mother. Maureen used to pick up Ben's Aunt Cindy's laundry.

TALBOT, JACKIE A waitress at Dell's.

TANNER, CHARLES BELKNAP Lot farmer who had a pig named Jerusalem. The town was named for the pig.

TENNEY, BRENT One of the kids on Charlie Rhodes' school bus.

THE TEXAS OILMAN Texan who was buried in a brand-new Cadillac Coupe DeVille.

THOMAS, BOB Teacher who caught Andy Garvey letting the air out of the bus tires.

THREE HOSPITAL ORDERLIES Three unnamed orderlies who helped Loretta Starcher carry books to Matt Burke's hospital room.

TIBBITS, FLOYD Lot resident. He liked Susan Norton. He was a childhood friend of Ben Mears.

TOULOUSE-LATREC Matt jokingly said he had astral conversations with Latrec.

TREMONT, ELAINE MRS. A widow who suffered a heart attack on June 4, 1976.

TRUCK DRIVER Unnamed driver who helped Ben after the motorcycle accident.

UPSHAW, VINNIE One of the boarders at Eva Miller's.

VAN HELSING Character in the film "Dracula."

VARNEY, NORRIS Lot constable in the twenties.

VERRILL, GROVER One of Eva Miller's boarders. He worked in the textile mill. He didn't wash his dishes.

VICKERY, FRANK John Farrington's son-in-law. He found Farrington's body.

WALSH, FRANCIS Crockett's lawyer in Boston. Straker knew about Walsh, even though Crockett's wife didn't.

WELBY, MARCUS TV character Dr. Cody did not want to be.

WERTS, MABEL Widow. She was a friend of Ann Norton's and was known as the town gossip. She was prominent in church and social functions in the Lot. She ended up "missing."

WILSON, GAHAN Cartoonist. Jimmy Cody thought the situation in the Lot was getting like one of Gahan Wilson's cartoons.

WOLFE, THOMAS An author Matt Burke mentioned to Ben.

WOLFMAN JACK Disc jockey on Monterey radio station.

WORDSWORTH The poet who wrote "The eyes are the windows of the soul."

(2)
'SALEM'S LOT
Places

ANDROSCOGGIN RIVER The river where a missing boy was found dead.

ARCADE COIN A store in Portland, Maine.

B & M The place where Weasel Craig used to work.

BAB'S BEAUTY BOUTIQUE Business owned and operated by Babs Griffen.

BARLOW AND STRAKER'S FURNITURE SHOP Antique shop used as a front by Straker.

BROCK STREET Street where the Glick house was located. Also, Irwin Purinton's milk route. Brock Street was also known as the Brock Road, and as that "Christless Washboard."

BROCK STREET ELEMENTARY SCHOOL An old school in 'salem's Lot.

BURNS ROAD The road Ben took into the Lot.

BUXTON Town where Jim Smith's garage was located.

A CALIFORNIA TOWN After the incidents in 'salem's Lot, Ben Mears worked pumping gas and repairing small foreign cars in an unnamed California town.

CENTRAL FALLS, RHODE ISLAND Ben Mears mailed his agent the outline of a novel from Central Falls.

CHAMBERLAIN, MAINE The town where Ben considered stopping for lunch.

CHEMICAL BANK BUILDING The official business location of the Continental Land and Realty Company.

CINEX CORPORATION Company that opened a triple cinema in Portland. They bought twelve of Susan Norton's paintings.

COBB'S FERRY New Hampshire town that had a schoolhouse fire.

CONSOLIDATED HIGH SCHOOL Lot high school.

CROCKETT'S SOUTHERN MAINE INSURANCE AND RE-ALTY Business owned and operated by Larry Crockett.

CROSSEN'S AGRICULTURAL MARKET Store where men gathered around the stove to talk about the Fire of '51, one of the largest forest fires in Maine's history. They closed their doors after the incidents in the Lot.

CUSTOM HOUSE WHARF At the Portland Docks. Straker told Crockett to have a truck there.

DELL'S A tavern in the Lot.

DRUNK'S LEAP Fifty-foot stone cliffs that drunks often fell off.

EVA MILLER'S BOARDING HOUSE The place Ben lived when he returned to 'salem's Lot to write his book about the Marsten House. It was located on Railroad Street.

EXCELLENT CAFÉ Lot restaurant. Pauline Dickens worked there for years. It went out of business.

GATES MILL AND WEAVING Lot business. Lester and Harriet Durham both worked there.

GRANT'S Falmouth store where Floyd Tibbits worked.

GREEN'S MORTUARY Maury Green's business.

THE GRIFFEN FARM Farm that once bottled and sold its own milk.

GUILFORD A little pissant burg, according to Chief Gillespie.

THE HARDWARE STORE Lot retailer that went out of business.

HARMONY HILL CEMETERY Cemetery in the Lot.

JERUSALEM'S LOT 'salem's Lot. Small town in southern Maine east of Cumberland and twenty miles north of Portland.

JERUSALEM'S LOT METHODIST CHURCH Lot church. John Groggins was pastor.

JERUSALEM'S LOT PUBLIC LIBRARY Lot library. They had Ben Mears' books.

JOINTNER AVENUE The new name of the Portland Post Road. (See ELIAS JOINTNER.)

KITTERY, MAINE The town where Chief Gillespie's sister lived.

KOREA Charlie Rhodes and Dave Felsen had served together in Korea.

LEWISTON, MAINE The town where Ben considered stopping for lunch.

LONDON AND HAMBURG Straker told Gillespie that he and Straker had worked together in London and Hamburg.

LOS ZAPATAS Small Mexican village not far from the ocean. Los Zapatas meant "the shoes." It was the town where Mark Petrie was given holy water by Father Gracon.

THE MARSTEN HOUSE It had a gabled roof.

MARSTEN'S HILL Hill in the Lot on which the Marsten House was located.

MILBRIDGE A little pissant burg, according to Chief Gillespie.

MOMSON, VERMONT Town written about in the book *Strange Disappearances*.

THE MUNICIPAL BUILDING After the death of the Lot, even the municipal building was all boarded up.

THE NORDICA Theater Ben remembered. It closed in 1968.

NORTHERN BELLE FLOWER SHOP Store where Ben went to buy roses.

OLD ORCHARD BEACH The beach where Doug Mayberry drowned.

PEMAQUID POINT The place where Irwin Purinton intended to retire.

POPHAM BEACH The beach where Mark Petrie went swimming.

PORTLAND POST ROAD The original name of the Lot's main road.

RAILROAD STREET Where Eva Miller's boarding house was located.

RHODE ISLAND After the incidents in 'salem's Lot, Ben Mears worked in a textile mill in Rhode Island.

ROUTE 116 Road in Gates. It was where a missing boy was buried.

ST. ANDREWS CHURCH Lot Catholic church. Father Donald Callahan was assigned there.

ST. MATTHEW'S MISSION Mission in Portland. Rhoda Curless went to work there.

SCHOOLYARD HILL Hill in the Lot. It was where Horris was from.

SLEWFOOT HILL DAIRY Dairy owned and operated by Charles Griffen.

SONNY'S AMOCO Gas station in Falmouth referred to by Horris.

SOUTH JOINTNER AVENUE Where Mark Petrie lived.

SPENCER'S SUNDRIES AND PHARMACY Lot retailer that went out of business.

STANLEY STREET ELEMENTARY SCHOOL The school to which Charlie Rhodes drove.

"STICKSVILLE" The Lot, according to Susan Norton.

STOP & SHOP The store where Ben Mears and Jimmy Cody bought twelve boxes of garlic.

TAGGERT STREAM ROAD Matthew Burke's address.

THE TOWN DUMP To Dud Rogers, the dump was Disneyland and Shangri-La.

TULSA, OKLAHOMA The Glicks had relatives from Tulsa. They came to 'salem's Lot for Danny's funeral.

URANUS Horris believed that creatures from Uranus were infiltrating all of American life.

VIETNAM Reggie Sawyer spent seven months there in 1968.

THE VILLAGE WASHTUB Lot laundromat.

WOOLWORTH'S Store where Matt Burke bought a crucifix.

YARMOUTH LIQUOR STORE Store where Brad Campion worked.

YOUNGSTOWN, OHIO After the incidents in 'salem's Lot, Ben Mears worked on a tractor assembly line in Youngstown.

(2)
'SALEM'S LOT
Things

AIR DANCE Ben Mears' second novel.

AMAZING STORIES One of the magazines delivered to Hubie Marsten.

ARMOUR Ham eaten by the Broddins.

AUGUST 12, 1939 The day Hubie Marsten died.

AUSTEN, JANE Author whose works Mrs. Petrie enjoyed reading, along with those of Henry James.

BARLOW'S ORIGIN Matt suspected Barlow was either Romanian, Magyar, or Hungarian.

"BEN CODY AND SON" How Ben Mears signed the motel register in New Hampshire.

BEN'S INSCRIPTION TO SUSAN On the flyleaf of *Air Dance*, Ben wrote "For Susan Norton, the prettiest girl in the park. Warm Regards, Ben Mears."

"BEST WISHES TO CONSTABLE GILLESPIE FROM BEN MEARS 9/12/75" The inscription Ben wrote for Gillespie on his book *Conway's Daughter* .

BILLY SAID KEEP GOING Ben Mears' third (and latest at the time of the story) novel.

BLACK LABEL Crockett gave Snow and Peters two six-packs each of this beer.

BLUE CHALK MARKS Marks that Mark Petrie saw on Barlow's hands.

THE BOSTON ORGANIZATION Organized crime in Boston. Hubie Marsten was a contract killer for the Boston organization.

BRIGGS & STRATTON The lawnmower Mike Ryerson used.

BSA Motorcycle that passed Ben.

BUDWEISER Beer that Weasel ordered for himself and Ben at Dell's.

"BURY THE BOTTLE WITH ME" Song by Dick Curless.

"BUS" Neon sign outside Spencer's.

CAMELS The cigarette Richie Boddin intended to smoke when he got old.

CAMPBELL'S ALPHABET SOUP To Matthew Burke, a school play should be like this soup: tasteless, but not actively offensive.

CANADIAN WHISKEY People thought that Hubie Marsten was running whiskey into Massachusetts after midnight in the twenties.

THE CATHOLIC JOURNAL Father Callahan wrote a monograph for this journal.

"CHARLEY'S PROBLEM" School play directed by Matthew Burke.

CHESTERFIELDS Eva Miller's cigarette.

CHEVROLET Norris Varney's car.

CHEVY BISCAYNE Car driven by Matthew Burke.

CITROEN The car Ben Mears drove across country after the incidents in 'salem's Lot.

COKE AND BACARDI The drink Ben offered to Susan if she would sit on Eva's porch with him.

CONTINENTAL LAND AND REALTY The dummy corporation that bought the land on which Straker and Barlow's Portland shopping center was to be built.

CONWAY'S DAUGHTER Ben Mears' first novel. Ben was loading cases of Coca-Cola onto a truck when the novel sold.

COSMOPOLITAN Magazine which ran an excerpt of Ben Mears' novel *Conway's Daughter*. Sheriff McCaslin's wife read the excerpt.

CRICKET Ben's lighter.

CUMBERLAND *LEDGER* Cumberland newspaper.

CURRIER & IVES Design on a small tin plate in the Marsten house.

DANNY GLICK'S GUEST LIST The following attended Danny's funeral: Mark Petrie and his parents; Richie Boddin and his family; Mabel Werts; Mr. and Mrs. William Norton; Lester and Harriet Durham; Paul and Glynis Mayberry; Pat Middler; Joe Crane; Vinnie Upshaw; Clyde Corliss; Milt Crossen; Eva Miller; Loretta Starcher; Rhoda Curless; Parkins Gillespie; Nolly Gardener; Lawrence Crockett; Charles Rhodes; the Charles Griffen family; and the Griffen sons, Hal and Jack.

"THE DEAD-LETTER FILE" The phrase John Lewis used to describe people missing from 'salem's Lot. They included the local mortician, the local librarian, and the local beautician. He felt that "[t]he list [was] of a disquieting length."

THE DEBATE CLUB Club monitored by Matthew Burke.

"DIALING FOR DOLLARS" Program Eva Miller watched while she ironed.

DR. DENTONS Kids' pajamas.

DODGE Brenton Norbert's car.

DRACULA Book by Bram Stoker. Ben remembered it.

E-VAP Cleaning fluid Father Callahan used to remove scotch from the rug.

EH-279 The number of Matt's Romantic Literature class when he was in college. His professor preferred to read *Beowulf* or *The Screwtape Letters* rather than *Varney The Vampyre*.

841-4000 The number to dial for an ambulance.

EKG Heart test given to Matt Burke.

AN ELLERY QUEEN PLOT Ben Mears said that Ellery Queen would have been able to explain what was going on in the Lot, but life was not an Ellery Queen plot.

FATHER CALLAHAN'S POETS Callahan knew a lot about the following poets: Whittier, Longfellow, Russell, and Holmes.

FATHER CALLAHAN'S SAMPLER While in the seminary, Callahan was given a sampler which read: "God grant me the SERENITY to accept what I cannot change, the TENACITY to change what I may, and the GOOD LUCK not to fuck up too often." The sampler was in Old English script with a rising sun in the background.

FEBRUARY 14, 1976 The day Fiona Coggins was reported missing.

FEBRUARY 1960 The month the saw mill was shut down for good.

FEBRUARY 27, 1976 The day John Farrington was found dead in his barn.

FIVE YALE PADLOCKS Straker made Crockett buy these and use them after he delivered the "Hepplewhite"—(which was really Barlow) to the Marsten house. Crockett had to use the locks to secure the antique shop's back door, the bulkhead, front, and back doors of the house, and the shed-garage.

THE FLAME OF REMEMBRANCE The flame lit by Mike Ryerson at Danny Glick's gravesite.

402 Matt Burke's hospital room number.

"FRANK'S MOBIL STATION" Legend written on the pen belonging to the truck driver who helped Ben.

GARLIC AND ROSES The items Matt told Ben and the others to buy for their confrontation with Barlow.

"GHOST TOWN IN MAINE?" Title of an article by John Lewis in the *Press-Herald* that explored the "mysterious emptying of Jerusalem's Lot."

GOOD HOUSEKEEPING Magazine Susan stared at while at the hospital waiting for news about Ben.

"THE GOSPEL ACCORDING TO FREUD" Father Callahan

said the Devil, according to the Gospel according to Freud, would be a composite id, the subconscious of us all.

"GUNSMOKE" The TV show Nolly Gardener thought about before he unlocked the drunk-tank door.

THE HAUNTING OF HILL HOUSE Novel by Shirley Jackson which Stephen King quotes as an epigraph and which Ben Mears refers to when talking about the Marsten house.

"HENRY'S U-HAUL" Sign painted on the side of the truck that Crockett rented to pick up Barlow.

HEPPLEWHITE A valuable sideboard that Straker told Crockett to pick up and deliver to the Barlow house. The hepplewhite was actually Kurt Barlow.

THE HOST Father Callahan said that if he went to investigate the Marsten house with the Host, he'd be acting as an agent of the Holy Catholic Church, and he would be in the role of Christ's representative on earth.

HUBIE MARSTEN'S BOOKS After Hubie's suicide, complete sets of Dickens, Scott, and Mariatt were found in his house.

HUBIE MARSTEN'S HEADSTONE Mike Ryerson picked it up after it fell over. It read:

> HUBERT BARCLAY MARSTEN
> October 6, 1889
> August 12, 1939
> The angel of Death who holdeth
> The bronze Lamp beyond the golden door
> Hath taken thee into dark Waters
> God Grant He Lie Still

"I GOT DEM OL' KOZMIC E-VAP BLUES AGAIN" Song Father Callahan imagined Fred Astaire and Ginger Rogers dancing to in front of the church.

"IRONSIDE" TV show on at Dell's bar.

JAMES, HENRY Mrs. Petrie enjoyed reading his works, along with those of Jane Austen.

JANUARY 4, 1976 The day Gordon Phillips' empty car was found.

JOHNNIE WALKER Crockett gave Snow and Peters drinks of it in Dixie cups.

JUICY FRUIT The gum chewed by Babs Griffen.

JUNE 4, 1976 The day Mrs. Elaine Tremont suffered a heart attack.

JUNIOR MINTS Empty box Ben found in the confessional.

"KEEP MAINE GREEN" Legend painted on the side of a Cumberland water tower.

KLH Matt Burke's home sound system.

LADIES AUXILIARY BAKE-OFF A big event in the Lot in 1970.

LANCER'S The wine Matt Burke served to Ben.

LEUKEMIA The disease that killed Harold Rauberson.

LIFE SAVERS There was an open roll on Ben's desk.

LOS ZAPATOS HOLY WATER This water was given to Mark Petrie by Father Gracon.

LUTHERAN Mike Ryerson's religion.

LYSOL Margie Glick used it when cleaning.

M.C.R. The initials engraved inside Mike Ryerson's class ring: Michael Corey Ryerson.

M.D. PLATES Jimmy Cody had them on his car.

"MADE IN GRAND RAPIDS" Legend printed on a bed. Dud Rogers sanded it off and sold the bed as an authentic "Made in New England" piece.

MAINE STATE WILDLIFE SERVICE The game wardens were instructed on May 20, 1976, to look for packs of wild dogs.

MARK PETRIE'S AURORA MODELS Mark had Dracula, Frankenstein, the Mad Doctor, the Wolfman, the Mummy, and the Chamber of Horrors.

MARK TWAIN'S "NOVEL" QUOTATION Ben Mears quoted Twain to Gillespie: "A novel is a confession to everything by a man who had never done anything."

"THE MARY CELESTE-LIKE MYSTERY" How John Lewis described the "mysterious emptying of Jerusalem's Lot."

MATT BURKE'S "LIBRARY" Father Callahan saw the following books in Matt Burke's hospital room: *Dracula*; *Dracula's Guest*; *The Search For Dracula*; *The Golden Bough*; *The Natural History Of The Vampire*; *Hungarian Folk Tales*; *Monsters Of The Darkness*; *Monsters In Real Life*; *Peter Kurtin, Monster Of Dusseldorf*; *Varney The Vampire, or The Feast Of Blood*.

MATTHEW BURKE'S SPECIALTIES Burke taught "The Ancient Mariner," Steinbeck, and Chaucer.

MAY 20, 1976 The day the Maine State Wildlife Service instructed the game wardens to look for packs of wild dogs.

MAY 29, 1976 The day Daniel Holloway and his family were reported missing by Daniel's grandfather.

McCULLOUGH Brand of chainsaw that Mark Petrie and his father used to cut firewood.

A MECHANICAL FOOT Claude Bowie's son came back from Vietnam with one.

MÉDOC A white wine.

METHODIST Matt Burke was a non-practicing Methodist.

MICHELOB The beer Floyd Tibbits drank at Dell's.

MIKE RYERSON'S THOUGHTS ABOUT BUYING FLOWERS Mike thought buying flowers was a waste and that the money would be better off going to the Cancer Society, the March of Dimes, or the ladies aid.

MOTOROLA The television in Matt Burke's living room.

"MOXIE" Soda Carl Smith drank.

"MURDER INCORPORATED" The business Crockett sarcastically suggested Straker was planning on starting.

THE NATIONAL ENQUIRER Paper in which Mike Ryerson read about a Texas oilman who was buried in a brand-new Cadillac Coupe DeVille.

THE NEW YORK *TIMES* Paper bought by Loretta Starcher.

THE NEW YORKER One of the magazines delivered to Hubie Marsten.

1957 CHEVROLET PICKUP Franklin Boddin's truck.

1907 The year Pearl Ann Butts ran off to New York City to become a Ziegfield girl.

1965 MERCURY Tony Glick's car.

"A NORMAN ROCKWELL FACE" Ben thought that Dr. Cody had a boyish Rockwell face.

NOVEMBER 19, 1975 The day the Charles Pritchett family moved off the Griffen farm.

OCTOBER 6, 1889 The day Hubie Marsten was born.

OCTOBER 6, 6:51 P.M. The date and time of Joe Crane's death.

151 Nolly Gardener's bowling average.

THE ONLY NATURAL DEATH TO OCCUR IN JERUSALEM'S LOT Joe Crane's death on October 6, at 6:51 P.M., was that day's only natural death in the Lot.

ORANGE CRUSH Soft drink.

PABST The beer Bill Norton offered to Ben.

PACKARD Straker's car. It was a '39 or '40.

PALL MALL Cigarette smoked by Parkins Gillespie.

PEARL KINEO The stove in Milt Crossen's store.

"PEYTON PLACE" Film that was shot in Camden, Maine.

PORTLAND *PRESS-HERALD* Maine newspaper Eva Miller had delivered to the boarding house.

PORTLAND *TELEGRAM* Newspaper that did a story about the death of the Marstens.

REAL LIFE CONFESSIONS Magazine Miss Coogan read.

REPUBLIC SERIALS Serials that were shown at the Nordica. They included "Rocket Man," "The Return of Rocket Man," and "Crash Callahan and the Voodoo Death God."

"RESEARCHER GENERAL" What Matt Burke appointed Ben Mears.

ROYAL RIVER The river could be seen from the back porch of Eva Miller's boarding house.

ST. CHRISTOPHER MEDAL Parkins Gillespie and Pauline Dickens both wore one on a chain.

ST. PAUL'S CRUCIFIXION St. Paul was crucified upside down, and Straker was found upside down. This method of death was as "old as Macedonia." The body of the enemy was hung upside down so the head faced earth instead of heaven.

SANDY MCDOUGALL'S KITCHEN CABINET When Sandy panicked at her son Randy's unconsciousness, she pawed through her cabinet looking for a treat with which to awaken him. The following spilled out: Chef Boy-Ar-Dee Ravioli, Wesson Oil, and Rice-Chex. She tried to feed Randy a jar of Gerber's chocolate custard.

"SATAN WORSHIPPERS DESECRATE FLA. CHURCH" Headline that Delbert Markey showed Floyd Tibbits.

SATAN'S SEX SLAVES Book read by Larry Crockett.

THE SATURDAY EVENING POST One of the magazines delivered to Hubie Marsten.

SCOTCH-ENGLISH OR FRENCH The nationalities of most of the residents of the Lot.

THE SENSUOUS EXORCIST Book by Sybil Leek.

SEPTEMBER 24, 1:00 A.M. The date and time of Danny Glick's death.

SERIES E TWENTY A bill Straker gave Milt Crossen for merchandise.

$700 The amount the Cinex Corporation paid Susan Norton for twelve of her paintings.

"THE SEVENTH SEAL" Ingmar Bergman picture Ben recalled while in the confessional.

SHREDDED WHEAT Cereal eaten by Joe Crane.

SHYLOCK'S BARGAIN To extract a pound of flesh without spilling a drop of blood.

SILVER STAR Weasel Craig received one for his service at Anzio during World War II.

SONY Small TV Cody watched at Green's Mortuary.

"A SPIRITUAL BOY SCOUT TROOP" Father Callahan said that the Church was more than "a spiritual Boy Scout Troop."

STRAKER'S BLOOD It was darker than movie blood.

STRAKER'S DELIVERIES In the boxes Royal Snow and Hank Peters picked up were a Polish rocking chair, a German clock, an Irish spinning wheel, and Barlow the Vampire.

STRANGE DISAPPEARANCES Book Matt Burke read.

"SUNSHINE MILK FROM THE GRIFFEN FARMS" The Griffen Farm's slogan.

SUSAN'S CLIPPINGS Clippings from the following magazines hung in Susan's room: *Rolling Stone*, *Creem*, and *Crawdaddy*.

SUSAN'S PICTURES Pictures of the following people once hung in Susan's room: Jim Morrison, John Lennon, Dave von Ronk, and Chuck Berry.

THE *TIMES* Newspaper Susan Norton bought in Cumberland.

"TOO FAR TO JUMP" Title of the cartoon Callahan drew to accompany his monograph in *The Catholic Journal*.

TURKISH BLEND Cigarette smoked by Straker.

$12,000 Ben Mear's advance from Random House for his novel.

.22 CALIBER TARGET PISTOL The gun Dud Rogers used to kill rats at the dump.

"THE UNDISAPPEARANCES" The Lot residents who *didn't* disappear after some people began to drop out of sight.

VAMPIRELLA Magazine in Matt Burke's hospital room.

A VEGA HATCHBACK Susan Norton's car. It was found on Brooks Road.

VIDEO KING Ben's Aunt Cindy had a Video King television.

THE WALL STREET JOURNAL Paper Mr. Petrie read.

THE WAR MEMORIAL Monument in the park.

WILLIAM PENN The cigar Larry Crockett smoked.

WOODSHOP AND GRAPHIC ARTS The only two school subjects Hal Griffen liked.

"YANKEE TRADER" Local radio program.

"YOU'VE NEVER BEEN THIS FAR BEFORE" Song the Rangers performed at Dell's.

ZEISS BINOCULARS Brand used by Parkins Gillespie.

RAGE

DEDICATION

For Susan Artz
and WGT

[NO CONTENTS PAGE]

BOOK BREAKDOWN

[Thirty-five untitled chapters]

---

(3)
RAGE
People

ANDERSON, DR. The doctor at the Woodlands mental institution who was in charge of Ted Jones after he was admitted.

ANDREISSEN, DANA Placerville student. Charlie thought about looking up her dress in study hall.

ANNMARIE A girl Charlie Decker had once dated. She was Rosalynn's sister.

THE BASEBALL BAT BOY In 1959, a Placerville High student beat a girl with a baseball bat, and was sent to the South Portland Correctional Institute. He beat her because she wouldn't go out with him.

BATES, IRMA Placerville student and one of Charlie's prisoners. She screamed when Charlie shot Mrs. Underwood.

THE BEATLES Some of the music played at Carol Granger's birthday party was by the Beatles.

BROOKS, SUSAN Placerville student and one of Charlie's prisoners.

BROWNMILLER, SUSAN The author of *Women Rapists*.

CABLE, DICKY A bully who used to torment Charlie Decker and Joe McKennedy. He reminded Charlie of a Briggs & Stratton lawnmower.

CANNING, VICTOR A mystery writer whose books Charlie Decker's mother enjoyed reading.

CARLSON, JOHN A chemistry and physics teacher at Placerville High. Charlie Decker almost killed him.

CAROL GRANGER'S SISTER One Christmas, Carol bought her a scarf.

CARRADINE, JOHN Charlie Decker thought that Mr. Denver looked like John Carradine.

CASKIN, NANCY Placerville student and one of Charlie's prisoners.

CASTINGUAY, MRS. Carl and Rita Decker's neighbor. She and her husband drove by while Carl and Rita were arguing in the front yard after their then four-year-old son Charlie had broken all the storm windows with rocks.

CASTINGUAY, SAM Carl and Rita Decker's neighbor. He and his wife drove by while Carl and Rita were arguing in the front yard after their then four-year-old son Charlie had broken all the storm windows with rocks.

CHRISTIE, AGATHA Mystery writer. Charlie Decker's mother liked to read English mysteries, but she would never read Agatha Christie.

COLLETTE, DANA A friend of Scragg Simpson's. Her folks owned a camp out near Schoodic Point, and Scragg invited Pete and Joe

McKennedy and Charlie Decker to come to a party being held at the camp.

COULSON, MR. A Placerville high school teacher.

CRANSTON, LAMONT "The Shadow."

"THE CREAKING THING" Carl Decker. Charlie remembered waking up in the middle of the night when he was three years old, and hearing something in the darkness "creaking and creaking and creaking." It was his father making love to his mother.

CROSS, SANDRA Sandy Cross. Placerville student and one of Charlie's prisoners. She had dated Decker, and had attended the Wonderland dance with Ted Jones. She and Ted had had sex in the back seat of Ted's car while parked at the gravel pit in Auburn.

DANO, JOHN ("PIG PEN") Placerville student and one of Charlie's prisoners. He fainted after Charlie shot Mrs. Underwood.

DANO, LILLY Pig Pen Dano's older sister. LaFollet St. Armand got her pregnant.

DANO, MRS. Pig Pen's mother.

DEBBINS, ROSEANNE Placerville High student. Her locker was next to Charlie's.

DECKER, CARL Charlie Decker's father.

DECKER, CHARLIE Charles Everett Decker. The high school student who "got it on" one nice May morning, and took over Placerville high school. He shot two teachers, and turned Mrs. Underwood's algebra classroom into a vicious group therapy session.

DECKER, RITA Charlie Decker's mother.

DECKER, TOM Carl Decker's brother, Charlie Decker's uncle. He lived in Wisconsin.

DELEAVNEY, JUDGE SAMUEL K.N. The judge who signed Charlie Decker's commitment papers.

DENCH, CARLA Placerville High student. Her locker was next to Charlie's.

DENVER, THOMAS The principal of Placerville High.

EARL, RANDY One of the guys who went hunting with Carl Decker and Al Lathrop every November.

FAZIO, MR. The Placerville high school janitor.

FITZGERALD, PAT Placerville student and one of Charlie's prisoners.

FLOREN, MYRON The accordionist on "The Lawrence Welk Show."

FRANKEL, MR. The owner of Frankel's Jewelry Store & Camera Shop. He drove a Pontiac Firebird, was Placerville's second selectman, and a crony of Ted Jones's father Norman.

FRANKLIN, PETER A Placerville student who was absent with the measles the day Charlie took over Mrs. Underwood's algebra class.

GANNON, TANIS Placerville student and one of Charlie's prisoners.

GAVIN Don Grace's mother's maiden name.

GAVIN, MIKE Placerville student and one of Charlie's prisoners. Gavin told Mr. Vance that Charlie had a gun.

THE GIRL BEAT WITH A BASEBALL BAT In 1959, a Placerville High student beat a girl with a baseball bat because she wouldn't go out with him.

GOLDMAN, JACK Placerville student and one of Charlie's prisoners.

GOSSAGE, RICH An administrator on the staff of the Woodlands mental institution, the private hospital that Ted Jones was admitted to after his ordeal in Charlie Decker's "classroom."

GRACE, DON The school psychiatrist at Placerville High.

GRANGER, CAROL A student at Placerville High, and a member of Mrs. Underwood's algebra class. She was class president. Charlie had once bought her a handkerchief from J.C. Penney's as a birthday present. It had her initials on it, had lace all around it, and sold for fifty-nine cents. Charlie thought her mother looked like a Sherman tank. Carol was one of Charlie's prisoners.

GRANGER, MRS. Carol Granger's mother. Charlie thought she

looked like a Sherman tank. Her appearance had also been known to be compared with Ghidra, Mothra, Godzilla, Rodan, and Tukkan the Terrible.

GREEN, MRS. Placerville High's typing teacher.

GREENBERGER, WILL A doctor on staff at the Woodlands mental institution who had had a great deal of success with semi-catatonic patients. He examined Ted Jones, and was less than optimistic.

THE GREENBRIAR BOYS One of the bluegrass bands listened to by Jerry Moeller.

HANNAFORD, BRIAN Jessie Decker's husband.

HANNAFORD, JESSIE DECKER Charlie's parents met at Jessie's wedding. Jessie was burned to death a year after her wedding.

HEAD, EDITH Fashion designer.

HERALD, CORKY Placerville student; one of Charlie's prisoners.

THE HUMAN SUBMARINE Nickname for Mr. Johnson, the history teacher.

INNES, HAMMOND A mystery writer whose books Charlie Decker's mother enjoyed reading.

JACKSON, HARMON Placerville student and one of Charlie Decker's prisoners.

JOHN Don Grace's father's middle name.

JOHNSON, MR. Placerville High history teacher. His nickname was "The Human Submarine."

JONES, MRS. Ted's mother. Pig Pen Dano revealed to Charlie's algebra class that Mrs. Jones was an alcoholic and had to go someplace and dry out.

JONES, NORMAN Ted Jones's father. He was vice president of the Placerville Bank and Trust.

JONES, TED Placerville student and one of Charlie's prisoners. He was a BMOC, even though he had quit the football team. He ended up in the Woodlands mental institution after he went into a catatonic state after being tortured in Charlie Decker's "class." Ink was poured in his hair, his foot was broken, and he was forced to admit to personal things that he couldn't stand to have aired publicly.

KATZENTZ, MRS. Charlie Decker weeded her flower garden, earning one dollar.

KEENE, DICK Placerville High student and one of Charlie's prisoners. He was an aggressive student, and Charlie thought that there was a moment when it would have been all over if Keene had taken the opportunity to whack him over the head with an algebra book.

KEENE, FLAPPER Dick Keene's brother. He was in state prison in Thomaston.

KESSERLING, JERRY The Placerville police chief.

A KID After Charlie set his locker on fire, a kid came out of Mr. Johnson's room carrying a green bathroom pass. Charlie didn't think the kid saw Charlie's pistol.

LASKY, ANNE Placerville student and one of Charlie's prisoners.

LATHROP, AL A friend of Carl Decker's. Al was a textbook salesman.

LEVESQUE, HERBIE One of the guys who went hunting with Carl Decker and Al Lathrop every November. He was their guide.

LORDI, DON Placerville student and one of Charlie's prisoners.

MacDONALD, JOHN D. According to Charlie, MacDonald realized that there was a Mr. Hyde for every happy Jekyll.

THE MAD BOMBER A bomber from Waterbury, Connecticut. Charlie Decker though that he must have been "the most well-adjusted American of the last quarter century."

MALVERN, DANIEL A state trooper from Kent's Hill, Maine. He was the state's best sharpshooter, and he was brought in to shoot Charlie Decker.

MARBLE, MISS Mr. Denver's receptionist.

McKENNEDY, JOE Charlie Decker's best friend.

McKENNEDY, PETE Joe McKennedy's brother. He lived in Bangor.

MILLIKEN, RANDY The boy who was with Dicky Cable when Dicky was killed.

MOELLER, JERRY The biggest dope dealer in the Orono-Oldtown-Stillwater triangle. [NOTE: In both the omnibus and mass market paperback editions of *The Bachman Books*, Jerry Moeller is initially mis-identified as "Larry Moeller," unless, that is, Jerry had a brother and the conversation where Larry was mentioned was about the brother instead of Jerry. It's not too clear.]

"MR. MAN" The name Charlie called Principal Denver after he (Charlie) blew his cool.

NORWISS, SCOTT One of the guys who went hunting with Carl Decker and Al Lathrop every November.

ORVILLE, HERK A childhood friend of Charlie Decker's who had once swallowed a mouse because Charlie had dared him to.

PASTERNE, SARAH Placerville student and one of Charlie Decker's prisoners.

"THE PATHFINDER OF THE WESTERN WORLD" How Charlie thought of Don Grace, the psychiatrist.

PHILBRICK, FRANK The head of the Maine state police. He was in charge of trying to talk Decker into surrendering. [NOTE: In *Stephen King as Richard Bachman,* Michael Collings notes that King's use of the name "Frank Philbrick" is obviously "an ironic reference to Herbert Arthur Philbrick, FBI counter-agent and author of *I Led Three Lives* (1952). Michelle Slung notes the importance of Philbrick and others associated with the communist threat of the early fifties for herself and others of King's generation." *Stephen King as Richard Bachman,* page 44.]

"PIG PEN" John Dano.

PIG PEN'S UNCLE He gave Pig Pen a Dodge when he got his license.

THE PRINCIPAL WITH THE AMAZING OVERSHAVED NECK Mr. Denver, according to Charlie Decker.

QUINN, MAYNARD A friend of Charlie Decker's who had a deck of dirty playing cards.

RAGAN, SYLVIA Placerville student and one of Charlie's prisoners.

THE ROLLING STONES Their music played on the jukebox at the Rollerdome.

ROSALYNN A girl Joe McKennedy had once dated. She was Annmarie's sister.

ST. ARMAND, LAFOLLET The Placerville High junior who got Lilly Dano pregnant..

SAWYER, BILLY A student at Placerville High, and a member of Mrs. Underwood's algebra class. He was one of Charlie Decker's prisoners.

SHANKAR, RAVI Sitarist.

SIMPSON, SCRAGG A friend of Pete McKennedy.

"SOME HIPPIE FROM LEWISTON" After Charlie Decker was put away, Joe McKennedy wrote him that Irma Bates was going out with some "hippie" from Lewiston.

STANNER, GRACE Placerville student and one of Charlie's prisoners.

STARK, RICHARD A writer Carl Decker enjoyed reading. [NOTE: Richard Stark was actually Donald Westlake writing under a pseudonym, just as Stephen King had written *Rage* under the "Richard Bachman" pseudonym. In King's 1989 novel, *The Dark Half,* King tells the story of a writer named Thad Beaumont who used the pseudonym "George Stark." See the section on *The Dark Half* in this volume.]

STONEHAM, BOB ("STONE BALLS") The coach of the Placerville High Greyhounds.

TALBOT, WARREN The Placerville police chief before Jerry Kesserling. Talbot died in 1975.

TAYLOR, DONNA One of Carol Granger's girlfriends.

THOMAS, MELVIN Placerville student and one of Charlie's prisoners. While a hostage, Melvin asked Charlie if it was all right to do homework.

THORNE, BUCK Carol Granger's boyfriend and center for the Placerville High Greyhounds.

UNDERWOOD, JEAN ALICE Mrs. Underwood. An algebra teacher at Placerville high school. Charlie shot her in the head after she asked him if he had a pass.

VANCE, JOHN DOWNES Placerville teacher. Charlie shot him in the throat right after he shot Mrs. Underwood. Vance was a very porky man with a crew cut. [NOTE: After Vance was found lying on the floor, someone yelled "Pete Vance's had a heart attack." Also, in Chapter 21, a TV news report states that "One person, Peter Vance, a history teacher at Placerville, is known dead." It wasn't said that "Pete" was Vance's nickname, so this may have been a textual error. His name was given as "John Downes Vance" in Charlie Decker's commitment order, and so I have used that name as his "official" name for this concordance.]

VENSON, MRS. A member of Placerville High's administration. When Charlie went to see the principal, Mrs. Venson was going over attendance lists with Miss Marble.

WELCH, RAQUEL Charlie had her picture taped to the back of his locker.

WESTLAKE, DONALD A writer Carl Decker enjoyed reading.

WOLFE, MR. A member of the Placerville high school administration. He called the cops after Charlie took over the school.

A WOMAN A woman at Dana Collette's party asked Charlie Decker if he had read *Women Rapists* by Susan Brownmiller.

YANNICK, GEORGE Placerville student and one of Charlie Decker's prisoners. He told Charlie to turn off the intercom.

(3)
RAGE
Places

ALLAGASH Carl Decker, Al Lathrop, and a bunch of their friends went hunting in Allagash every November for one week.

AUBURN Ted Jones and Sandy Cross had sex in the back seat of Ted's car while parked at the gravel pit on the road to Auburn.

THE AUGUSTA STATE HOSPITAL The hospital Decker was committed to for reasons of insanity after his hostage-taking stand and murders at Placerville High.

BANGOR Joe McKennedy's brother Pete lived in Bangor.

THE BANGOR SANITATION DEPARTMENT Joe McKennedy's brother Peter worked for this department.

BAR HARBOR OR CLEAR LAKE Most of the University of Maine summer students took off to these places for weekends.

BOXFORD, MASSACHUSETTS Lilly Dano had an aunt in Boxford. After Lilly got pregnant, she was packed off to her aunt's house in Boxford. The story was a "small-town classic."

BRISSETT'S BEND One of the roads where Dicky Cable would drive his car at ninety-five miles per hour.

CENTRAL MAINE GENERAL HOSPITAL The hospital where Mr. Carlson was taken after Charlie Decker hit him with a pipe wrench.

DENNY'S A Placerville bar on South Main Street where Grace Stanner's mother hung out.

FAT SAMMY'S A pizza parlor.

GOGAN'S The bar where Carl Decker drank with his buddies.

THE GRAVEL PIT Ted Jones and Sandy Cross had sex in the back seat of Ted's car while parked at the gravel pit on the road to Auburn.

GREENMANTLE ACADEMY Decker hallucinated that Mrs. Underwood had chased after him, screaming that boys like him belonged either in Greenmantle, a reform school, or a hospital for the criminally insane.

THE HARLOW REC The place where Ted Jones and Dick Keene shot pool together.

HARRISON STATE PARK Charlie Decker and Joe McKennedy took their dates there. [NOTE: See the section on King's poetry in this volume for details on an early poem by King called "Harrison State Park '68."]

THE HAWAIIAN HUT The restaurant where Ted Jones and Sandy Cross went for cocktails after the Wonderland Dance.

J.C. PENNEY'S The Lewiston department store where Charlie Decker had once bought Carol Granger a handkerchief as a birthday present.

JONES'S BOOK SHOP Once, when Carol Granger was out Christmas shopping, she saw a Salvation Army Santa Claus standing in front of Jones's Book Shop.

JUNIOR'S DINER The diner where the Placerville police got their coffee and doughnuts.

LEWISTON There were Police Athletic League hops in Lewiston. Brawls usually broke out at these PAL functions. Also, after Charlie was put away, Joe McKennedy wrote him that Irma Bates was going out with some "hippie" from Lewiston.

MAMMOTH MART Mrs. Dano bought Pig Pen two hundred Be-Bop pencils at Mammoth Mart every September.

THE MUNICIPAL BUILDING A fire whistle went off on this building after Charlie set fire to his locker.

OAK HILL POND ROAD After Charlie took over Mrs. Underwood's classroom, Police Chief Jerry Kesserling began directing traffic onto Oak Hill Pond, diverting it away from Placerville High.

OLDTOWN Jerry Moeller's apartment was in Oldtown.

PLACERVILLE, MAINE Charlie Decker's hometown.

THE PLACERVILLE BANK AND TRUST Ted's father was vice president of this bank.

THE PLACERVILLE CEMETERY The cemetery where Dicky Cable was buried after he was hit and killed by a delivery truck.

PLACERVILLE HIGH SCHOOL The high school "commandeered" by Charlie Decker.

PORTEUS-MITCHELL Carol Granger once bought her sister a scarf for Christmas in this store.

PORTLAND, MAINE Carl Decker once worked in Portland.

THE ROLLERDOME A rollerskating rink in Lewiston. Ted Jones had once taken Sandy Cross skating there.

RONNIE'S VARIETY The store where Grace Stanner once saw Ted Jones buy a girlie magazine.

ROOM 16 Placerville's Alegebra II classroom. Charlie shot Mrs. Underwood in this room, and then held the students prisoner.

ROOM 300 The typing room at Placerville High.

SCHOODIC POINT The Collettes' camp was located near Schoodic Point.

SOUTH MAIN STREET The street in Placerville where Denny's Bar was located.

THE SOUTH PORTLAND CORRECTIONAL INSTITUTE The institution where a Placerville High student was sent in 1959 after beating a girl with a baseball bat because she wouldn't go out with him.

STACKPOLE ROAD IN HARLOW One of the roads where Dicky Cable would drive his car at ninety-five miles per hour.

THOMASTON STATE PRISON The prison where Flapper Keene was incarcerated.

THE UNIVERSITY OF MAINE Charlie's mother and Jessie Decker were roommates at the University of Maine. Also, Pete McKennedy attended the university.

WILLOW STREET After he was beat up by Dicky Cable, Charlie Decker hid behind a house on Willow Street until he stopped crying.

THE WOODLANDS MENTAL INSTITUTION The private hospital that Ted Jones was admitted to after his ordeal in Charlie Decker's "classroom."

(3)
RAGE
Things

AMERICAN GOVERNMENT One of the books in Charlie Decker's locker.

ARGOSY, BLUEBOOK, TRUE AND THE SATURDAY EVENING POST Some of the magazines tied with twine in Carl Decker's garage.

AUGUST 27, 1976 The day Judge Samuel K.N. Deleavney signed Charlie Decker's commitment papers.

"THE BACH FUGUE FOR STORM WINDOWS IN A MINOR" The "piece" Charlie Decker thought of every time he heard Bach. His mother had been playing Bach when, at four years of age, he broke all the storm windows on his house with rocks.

A BAGGIE Charlie kept his Ritz crackers in a baggie.

"THE BALLAD OF JOHN AND YOKO" AND "LET IT BE" Beatles songs played at Carol Granger's party.

BE-BOP PENCILS Mrs. Dano bought Pig Pen two hundred Be-Bop pencils at Mammoth Mart every September. Charlie preferred Eberhard Faber. Be-Bops were the cheapest pencils on the planet.

A BERTRAND RUSSEL POSTER A Bertrand Russell poster hung on the bulletin board in Room 16.

"THE BLOW LUNCH FACTOR" One of the ways Charlie thought to describe the goings-on in his subconscious.

A BLUE MERCURY Joe McKennedy's car.

A BLUE PINTO The Placerville fire chief's car.

A "BMOC" Ted Jones was a "Big Man on Campus," even though he had quit the football team.

"BOOK-BAGS" John Dano's nickname for Mrs. Underwood.

THE "BOOKS AND BRIDGE" CLUB Mrs. Decker and Mrs. Granger both belonged to this club.

THE BOOKS IN CHARLIE'S LOCKER He had *Civics*, *American Government*, *French Stories and Fables*, and *Health*.

"THE BUGLE" The Placerville high school newspaper.

BUICK Al Lathrop's car. It was a station wagon.

"THE BUILDING BLOCKS OF NUTRITION" Charlie ripped his *Health* book in half between this chapter and the chapter "Swimming Rules for Fun and Safety."

CAMELS Sylvia Ragan's cigarettes.

"THE CHANCELLOR-BRINKLEY SHOW" Charlie's story was given fifty seconds on this newscast.

CHARLIE DECKER'S "CLASS LIST" The following students were all part of Miss Underwood's algebra class on the day Charlie shot Mrs. Underwood and took over the class.

BATES, IRMA	JACKSON, HARMON
BROOKS, SUSAN	JONES, TED
CASKIN, NANCY	KEENE, DICK
CROSS, SANDRA	LASKY, ANNE
DANO, JOHN ("PIG PEN")	LORDI, DON
FITZGERALD, PAT	PASTERNE, SARAH
GANNON, TANIS	RAGAN, SYLVIA
GAVIN, MIKE	SAWYER, BILLY
GOLDMAN, JACK	STANNER, GRACE
GRANGER, CAROL	THOMAS, MELVIN
HERALD, CORKY	YANNICK, GEORGE

THE CHEROKEE NOSE JOB Charlie remembered hearing his father tell about how the Cherokees would slit their wives' noses if they caught them cheating on them: "The idea was to put a cunt right up in their faces so everyone in the tribe could see what part of them got them in trouble."

CIVICS One of the books in Charlie Decker's locker.

THE CLASS PRESIDENT Carol Granger.

CON-TACT PAPER Charlie's name was printed on his locker on con-tact paper.

167

THE CONVERSATION TOPICS AT THE COLLETTE PARTY The people at Dana Collette's party talked about Michelangelo, Ted Kennedy, and Kurt Vonnegut.

A "DA" Ted Jones wore his hair in a "Duck's Ass."

"DE BLUE FRAWWWG" The name Joe McKennedy called his blue Mercury.

"DEALING WITH THE DISTURBED CHILD" A course Mr. Denver took in college. It was EdB-211. Charlie laughingly thought that Denver's instructors in that course had never thought to teach him how to deal with a child that attacked him personally.

DECEMBER 5, 1976 The day Charlie Decker received a letter from Joe McKennedy. Decker was committed to the Augusta State Hospital for reasons of insanity.

THE DETROIT REDWINGS A hockey team Carl Decker enjoyed following.

THE DETROIT TIGERS A baseball team Carl Decker enjoyed following.

A DODGE Pig Pen's uncle had given him a Dodge when Pig Pen got his license.

EBERHARD FABER PENCILS Mrs. Dano bought Pig Pen two hundred Be-Bop pencils at Mammoth Mart every September. Charlie preferred Eberhard Faber.

EMERGENCY VEHICLES Charlie Decker felt that emergency vehicles should play ragtime music as they drove to their destination.

ENGLISH Pete McKennedy's major at the University of Maine.

FIFTY-NINE CENTS The price of the handkerchief Charlie Decker had once bought for Carol Granger as a birthday present.

FLAIR A felt tip pen.

FRENCH STORIES AND FABLES One of the books in Charlie Decker's locker.

"GOLDILOCKS LOVED IT" A button worn by Jerry Moeller.

THE GOOD CITIZENSHIP AWARD Charlie though that Dick Keene would have been awarded this honor if he had stopped Charlie at the beginning of his classroom takeover.

A HANDKERCHIEF Charlie had once bought Carol Granger a handkerchief from J.C. Penney's as a birthday present. It had her initials on it, had lace all around it, and had sold for fifty-nine cents.

HEALTH One of the books in Charlie Decker's locker. He ripped this book in half between the chapters "The Building Blocks of Nutrition" and "Swimming Rules for Fun and Safety."

HESSE, TOLKIEN, AND THE READERS' DIGEST CONDENSED BOOKS Some of the books in the bookcase at Dana Collette's house.

THE HESSIANS AND THE CONTINENTAL ARMY The subject matter of Mr. Johnson's history class on the day Charlie Decker "got it on."

"HOPES FOR THE FUTURE" Charlie thought that Carol Granger would probably speak about this topic as valedictorian at graduation in June.

"HOW I OVERHEARD MY DAD EXPLAIN THE CHEROKEE NOSE JOB" After Charlie took over Mrs. Underwood's class, he thought about telling them about "My Hunting Trip," or "How I Overheard My Dad Explain the Cherokee Nose Job." [NOTE: See the entry THE CHEROKEE NOSE JOB.]

INK The students in Charlie's "class" poured ink in Ted Jones hair and smeared it all over him.

A JIMMY CAGNEY VOICE Charlie Decker did a Cagney voice.

"KEEP IT TIGHT, KEEP IT RIGHT" Carl Decker's motto.

"THE LAST BERRY IN THE PATCH" The name of the jigsaw puzzle Tom Decker had given Rita Decker one Christmas.

THE "LOONEY TUNES FILE" One of the ways Charlie thought to describe the goings-on in his subconscious.

THE MANCHESTER *GUARDIAN* A magazine Charlie Decker's mother enjoyed reading.

MARCH 3 The day Charlie Decker almost killed Mr. Carlson.

THE MARINES LaFollet St. Armand joined the marines after he got Lilly Dano pregnant.

THE MATHEMATICAL SOCIETY OF AMERICA A poster for this organization hung on the bulletin board in Room 16.

A MAUSER Daniel Malvern used a mauser with a telescopic lens to shoot Charlie Decker. He aimed for Decker's heart and instead hit Titus, the Helpful Padlock, which had been sitting in Decker's breast pocket.

METHODIST Don Grace's religious affiliation.

THE MONOCLE A magazine Charlie Decker's mother enjoyed reading.

THE MOTHER'S CLUB Mrs. Dano, Pig Pen's mother, helped out with their functions.

A MOUSE Herk Orville, a childhood friend of Charlie Decker's, had once swallowed a mouse because Charlie had dared him to.

MUSTANG Ted Jones's car.

"MY HUNTING TRIP" After Charlie took over Mrs. Underwood's class, he thought about telling them about "My Hunting Trip," or "How I Overheard My Dad Explain the Cherokee Nose Job." [NOTE: See the entry THE CHEROKEE NOSE JOB.]

A NATIONAL GRUNTING BEE Charlie thought that Mr. Denver should enter a "National Grunting Bee," if one existed.

THE NEW YORK REVIEW OF BOOKS A magazine Charlie Decker's mother enjoyed reading.

1958 The year Charlie Decker was born.

1959 The year a Placerville High student beat a girl with a baseball bat because she wouldn't go out with him.

1975 The year Warren Talbot died.

NOVEMBER 3, 1976 The date of Dr. Anderson's interoffice memo to Rich Gossage regarding giving shock treatments to Ted Jones.

OCTOBER 1962 The year and month a four-year-old Charlie Decker threw stones at, and broke, all the storm windows on his parents' house.

ONE DOLLAR The amount Charlie Decker earned for weeding Mrs. Katzentz's flower garden.

"OUR RESPONSIBILITIES TO THE BLACK RACE" Charlie thought that Carol Granger would probably speak about this topic as valedictorian at graduation in June. She actually gave a speech entitled "Self-Integrity and a Normal Response To It."

PALL MALLS Carl Decker's cigarettes.

PEANUTS COMIC STRIPS These hung on the bulletin board in Room 16.

"PIG PEN" John Dano's nickname.

A PIPE WRENCH On March 3, Charlie Decker hit Mr. Carlson with a pipe wrench and almost killed him.

THE PLACERVILLE HIGH GREYHOUNDS Placerville high school football team. Buck Thorne was their center.

THE PTA Pig Pen's mother, Mrs. Dano, helped out with their functions.

A RADIO SHACK BULLHORN The bullhorn the police used to talk to Charlie.

RINSO Mrs. Dano entered a contest once in which she had to tell why she liked Rinso detergent in twenty-five words or less.

RITZ CRACKERS The crackers Charlie ate before he went to the principal's office.

THE SADIE HAWKINS DAY DANCE Pig Pen's mother, Mrs. Dano, helped out with this function.

THE SATURDAY NIGHT DANCE Decker took Sandy Cross to the regular Saturday night dances at Placerville High.

A SCHWINN Charlie Decker's bike.

A SCRIPTO LIGHTER The lighter Charlie used to set fire to the contents of his locker.

SECOND SELECTMAN Mr. Frankel was Placerville's second selectman.

"SELF-INTEGRITY AND A NORMAL RESPONSE TO IT" Carol Granger's valedictory speech, reprinted in *Seventeen* magazine. Joe McKennedy told Charlie Decker about the speech in a letter after Charlie was institutionalized.

SEVENTEEN MAGAZINE The magazine that reprinted Carol Granger's valedictory speech, "Self-Integrity and A Normal Response To It."

"SHEEEIT! FRIDAY NIGHT AND I'M STONED AGAIN!" A poster on the wall in Dana Collette's house.

A SILVER BURDETT Charlie's *Civics* book was a tough old Silver Burdett text circa 1946, and it wouldn't rip easily.

"6 LEFT, 30 RIGHT, 2 TURNS BACK TO 0" The combination to Charlie Decker's locker in Placerville High.

"SIXTY MINUTES OF TERROR WITH THE PLACERVILLE MANIAC" The article Sylvia Ragan wanted to have written after Charlie's hostage-taking episode was over. She wanted to publish it in a detective magazine.

"SLIPPING IT TO THE PSYCHOS FOR FUN AND PROFIT, MOSTLY PROFIT" Charlie felt that all the courses psychiatrists took in school were variations on this theme.

"SM L DK, HOT SHIT, TOMMY '73" The graffiti etched into Billy Sawyer's desk in Mrs. Underwood's algebra class.

A SONY RADIO Corky Herald had a twelve-transistor, six-band, TV, shortwave, and CB Sony radio.

"SWANEE" A song Mrs. Granger enjoyed singing.

"SWIMMING RULES FOR FUN AND SAFETY" Charlie ripped his *Health* book in half between this chapter and a chapter called "The Building Blocks of Nutrition."

"THE THING IN THE CELLAR" One of the ways Charlie thought to describe the goings-on in his subconscious.

TIME MAGAZINE Charlie's story was given a column-and-a-half in *Time*.

TITUS The padlock on Charlie's locker. He called it "Titus, the Helpful Padlock," and "Titus, you old cock-knocker." Titus saved Decker's life when Daniel Malvern shot Decker and hit Titus, which was sitting in Decker's breast pocket.

"TWO-GUN SUE" A nickname for Mrs. Underwood.

A WEEK IN NOVEMBER Carl Decker, Al Lathrop, and a bunch of their friends went hunting in Allagash every November for one week.

WGAN-TV The TV station that covered Charlie Decker's hostage-taking situation. They parked their newsmobile in front of the school.

A WINCHESTER .22 BOX Charlie kept the shells to his pistol in a box that had once held Winchester .22 shells.

THE WONDERLAND DANCE The dance Ted Jones and Sandy Cross attended together.

WRANGLERS The jeans worn by Sandra Cross.

THE YEARBOOK Charlie Decker's mother sent him his class yearbook after he was institutionalized. He didn't open it because he didn't think he could look at all the senior pictures and not tremble a bit. He was afraid he'd see black streaks on their hands.

THE SHINING

DEDICATION

This is for Joe Hill King, who shines on.

[NO CONTENTS PAGE]

BOOK BREAKDOWN

PART ONE
Prefatory Matters

Chapter 1: JOB INTERVIEW
Chapter 2: BOULDER
Chapter 3: WATSON
Chapter 4: SHADOWLAND
Chapter 5: PHONEBOOTH
Chapter 6: NIGHT THOUGHTS
Chapter 7: IN ANOTHER BEDROOM

PART TWO
Closing Day

Chapter 8: A VIEW OF THE OVERLOOK
Chapter 9: CHECKING IT OUT
Chapter 10: HALLORANN
Chapter 11: THE SHINING
Chapter 12: THE GRAND TOUR
Chapter 13: THE FRONT PORCH

PART THREE
The Wasps' Nest

Chapter 14: UP ON THE ROOF
Chapter 15: DOWN IN THE FRONT YARD
Chapter 16: DANNY
Chapter 17: THE DOCTOR'S OFFICE
Chapter 18: THE SCRAPBOOK
Chapter 19: OUTSIDE 217
Chapter 20: TALKING TO MR. ULLMAN
Chapter 21: NIGHT THOUGHTS
Chapter 22: IN THE TRUCK
Chapter 23: IN THE PLAYGROUND
Chapter 24: SNOW
Chapter 25: INSIDE 217

PART FOUR
Snowbound

Chapter 26: DREAMLAND
Chapter 27: CATATONIC
Chapter 28: "IT WAS HER!"
Chapter 29: KITCHEN TALK
Chapter 30: 217 REVISITED
Chapter 31: THE VERDICT
Chapter 32: THE BEDROOM
Chapter 33: THE SNOWMOBILE
Chapter 34: THE HEDGES
Chapter 35: THE LOBBY
Chapter 36: THE ELEVATOR
Chapter 37: THE BALLROOM

(4)
THE SHINING
People

AILEEN Wendy Torrance's sister. She was killed by a delivery van.
ANDY Danny Torrance's friend from Vermont.
BACH Classical German composer.
BAEDECKER Halloran's assistant in Florida.
BARTOK Classical Hungarian composer.
BATTAGLIA, CHARLES ("BABY CHARLIE") Sixty-year-old Las Vegas impressario. He had controlling interests in two casinos on the strip, the Greenback and the Lucky Bones.
BEATRICE, SISTER The nun who taught Jack Torrance's catechism class.
THE BELLBOYS The unnamed young men who carried guests' luggage at the Overlook.
BENSON, GARY The hero in Jack Torrance's play "The Little School."
BOORMAN, VICTOR T. One of the men found shot to death outside the presidential suite in the Overlook in 1966. He was from Las Vegas.
THE BOSTON STRANGLER Watson told Jack that Ullman would have hired the Boston Strangler, if he'd have worked for the minimum wage.
BRADDOCK The Overlook's head desk clerk.
BRANNIGAR, JOSH Muck-raking journalist who investigated Horace Derwent's ties to the Mafia.
BRANT, MRS. One of the guests at the Overlook. She insisted on paying her bill with an American Express card, which the Overlook did not honor. [NOTE: It's well known that King got the inspiration to write *The Shining* when he visited the Stanley Hotel in Estes Park, Colorado. They visited on closing day, however, and there was only one American Express sales form left. American Express was the only card King had with him. King jokes today that *The Shining* would not have been written if there hadn't been that sales form, and yet, upon writing the novel, King decided to have the Overlook *not* accept AMEX.]
BRENT One of Danny's Stovington classmates. Brent was epileptic.
BUGS BUNNY Cartoon character.

CAPOTE, TRUMAN He had once stayed at the Overlook.
CASEY The engineer in the poem "The Wreck of the Old 97'."
THE CHECKER AT THE MARKET Person at a Sidewinder market who told Wendy about the doctor in town.
CHUG-CHUG Dr. Edmonds' invisible friend when he was five. Chug-Chug was a talking rooster.
COCHRAN, EDDIE Recording artist.
CONKLIN, RODNEY Financial editor. He wrote the article entitled "Millionaire Exec To Sell Colorado Investments."
THE COP The unnamed Colorado officer who gave Hallorann directions.
COTTRELL, HOWARD Snow plow driver who pulled Hallorann's car back on the road after Hallorann skidded into a guardrail on his way to the Overlook. Howard also gave Hallorann a pair of mittens to wear.
CROMMERT, MR. Headmaster at the Stovington Preparatory Academy where Jack had taught. Crommert had told Jack that the academy's board wanted his resignation.
DARLA A girl at Jack's party in the Colorado Lounge.
DENKER The sadistic headmaster in Jack Torrance's play "The Little School."
DERWENT, HORACE M. He bought the Overlook at the end of World War II. [NOTE: See the section on "Before the Play" in this volume.]
DERWENT, SYLVIA HUNTER She was married to Horace Derwent from 1942 to 1948.
DICK, JANE, AND JIP Characters in Danny's first grade primer.
"DOC" Danny Torrance's nickname.
THE DOG MAN Danny saw a man on all fours in a dog costume in the hallway of the Overlook. [NOTE: It was a man named Roger, although in "Before the Play," the man's name was Lewis Toner. See the "Before the Play" concordance section.]
THE DONNER PARTY People who were snowbound in the Sierra Nevadas. They resorted to cannibalism in order to stay alive.
DURKIN, LARRY He owned Durkin's Conoco in Sidewinder.
EDMONDS, DR. BILL The doctor in Sidewinder that Jack and Wendy took Danny to after he was stung by wasps.
EFFINGER, HARRY A man who was on the school board with Al Shockley.
ELAINE She and Tom lived above Jack and Wendy in Boulder, Colorado. They fought constantly.
FELTON, DAVID Features editor of the Denver paper that ran an article on May 15, 1947, about the reopening of the Overlook.
FIELDS, W.C. Actor. He disliked children.
FINKEL, HENRY Businessman that Horace Derwent hired to run Top Mark Studios.
FORD, HENRY He and his family stayed at the Overlook in 1927. Jack found their name on an old guest register in the hotel's basement.
THE FOUR WRITERS In 1961, four unnamed writers (two of whom were Pulitzer Prize winners) leased the Overlook and reopened it as a writer's school.
GABLE, CLARK He stayed at the Overlook in 1930. Jack found his name on an old guest register in the hotel's basement.
GALAHAD, SIR Wendy Torrance imagined that a soap opera hero or Sir Galahad would come and rescue her and Danny.
GIENNELLI, VITTORIO "Vito the Chopper." Criminal involved with the purchase of the Overlook.
GRADY, DELBERT The man hired as caretaker for the winter of 1970-1971. He sort of went a little nuts and chopped up his family with an axe. He told Jack that they had both been "hired" at the same time.
GREEN, AL Soul singer.
GRIMMER Character in Jack Torrance's short story, "The Monkey is Here, Paul DeLong."
GRONDIN, CHARLES He was the head of a group of California investors, and the former director of the California Land Development Corporation – the corporation that bought the Overlook

Hotel from Derwent. It was later revealed that he was also the president of High Country Investments.

HALLORANN, DICK The Overlook's cook. He, too, had "the shining." [NOTE: See the "People" section of *IT* in this volume.]

HALLORANN'S BROTHER He was killed in 1955 when the railroad car he was riding in was derailed.

HALLORANN'S SON Fictitious boy Halloran made up as an excuse to get back to Colorado.

HARDING, WARREN G. U.S. president. He stayed at the Overlook in 1922. Jack found his name on an old guest register in the hotel's basement.

HARLOW, JEAN She stayed at the Overlook in 1930. Jack found her name on an old guest register in the hotel's basement.

HATFIELD, BRIAN George Hatfield's father. He was a corporation lawyer.

HATFIELD, GEORGE When Jack was a teacher, Hatfield was the boy that Jack had to cut from the debating team. Hatfield later punctured all the tires on Jack's car.

HOLLIS, WALLY Man who told Jack about Vic Stenger's mental breakdown.

HOLT, VICTORIA Writer.

HOUGHTON, ARCHER Boulder county coroner. He changed Mrs. Massey's ("the Lady in the Bathtub") death certificate from suicide to heart attack, and got a new Chrysler from her husband in return.

JACKSON, SHIRLEY Author of *The Legend of Hill House*.

JANA Fictitious girl Halloran said told him about his fictitious son's accident in Colorado.

KAYE, LENNY He wrote the liner notes on one of Eddie Cochran's albums.

THE LAWYER Unnamed attorney Jack had once written to about a defective bug bomb.

LEFFING, ROBERT T. He was the spokesman for High Country Investments.

LLOYD The bartender in the Colorado Lounge in the Overlook. When Jack first met him, Lloyd had been dead for some time.

LOMBARD, CAROLE She stayed at the Overlook in 1930. Jack found her name on an old guest register in the hotel's basement.

LONGFELLOW American poet.

MACASSI, ROGER One of the men found shot to death outside the presidential suite in the Overlook in 1966. He was from Las Vegas.

MASSEY, MR. A hot-shot New York lawyer. He "convinced" Archer Houghton to change Mrs. Massey's death certificate from suicide to heart attack by buying him a new Chrysler.

MASSEY, MRS. Sixty-year-old woman who killed herself after the seventeen-year-old stud she was screwing around with stole her Porsche and disappeared. Her hot-shot lawyer husband got the death certificate changed to heart attack instead of suicide by buying Archer Houghton, the coroner, a new Chrysler.

MASTERTON, FRANK The owner of the One-A Wholesale Vegetable Market. He was a friend of Dick Halloran's.

McIVER The lawyer who drew up Halloran's will.

McTEAGUE The dentist in the Frank Norris novel, *McTeague*.

MILLER, ARTHUR He had once stayed at the Overlook with Marilyn Monroe.

"MR. HALL" Fictitious name Halloran gave Staunton, the Ranger.

MONROE, MARILYN She had once stayed at the Overlook with Arthur Miller.

MOORER, BENJAMIN The state trooper who discovered two dead men outside the door of the presidential suite in the Overlook in 1966.

MORRIS, LITTLE MARGERY Fourteen-year-old child star of Top Mark Studios. She died of a heroin overdose in 1934.

THE *NATIONAL OBSERVER* MAN Unnamed man who vomited into his *National Observer* magazine on Flight 196.

NEVERS, MR. Dick Halloran's chef apprentice at the Overlook.

NORMAN, ROBERT Overlook manager in 1966 who summoned the police when he heard shots fired.

O'CASEY, SEAN Phyllis Sandler, Jack's agent, thought the literary sun rose and set on Sean O'Casey.

OLSON, CHARLES Poet.

PEOPLE WHO HAD STAYED AT THE OVERLOOK They included the Vanderbilts, the Rockefellers, the Astors, and the Duponts.

PEPYS English writer.

THE PILLSBURY DOUGH-BOY Wendy thought a chef should look like the Pillsbury Dough-Boy.

POOH Danny's stuffed toy.

PRASHKIN, CARL ("JIMMY-RICKS") San Francisco investor who was reputed to be the heir to Vittorio Gienelli.

PRESIDENTS WHO HAD STAYED AT THE OVERLOOK They included Presidents Wilson, Harding, Roosevelt and Nixon. They all, of course, occupied the presidential suite.

QUEEMS The manager of the hotel in Florida where Halloran worked the winters.

QUEEN, ELLERY Fictional detective.

REDFORD, ROBERT Jack Torrance felt that George Hatfield reminded him of Redford.

ROCKEFELLER, NELSON He stayed at the Overlook in 1950. Jack found his name on an old guest register in the hotel's basement.

ROGER The man in the dog costume at the party in the Colorado Lounge. [NOTE: In "Before the Play," the man's name was Lewis Toner, not Roger.]

RYAN, NOLAN Pitcher. Danny's first telepathic thought (!!!HI, DICK!!!) to Halloran was "like a Nolan Ryan fastball."

SALLY Dr. Edmonds' assistant.

SALLY Overlook maid.

SANDLER, PHYLLIS Jack Torrance's agent. She was a "tough red-headed woman" who smoked Herbert Tareytons, drank Jim Beam from a paper cup, and thought the literary sun rose and set on Sean O'Casey.

SCARNE, RICHARD The principal stockholder of Fun Time Machines.

SCOFFY, FRANK Boston vice overlord. He was murdered with an axe, and Vito Giennelli was tried for the crime.

SCOTT Danny's friend in nursery school in Vermont.

THE SEVENTEEN-YEAR OLD Unnamed young stud who stayed with – and played with – sixty-year-old Mrs. Massey, the woman who ended up killing herself when the kid stole her Porsche and took off. Mrs. Massey became "The Lady in the Bathtub."

SHOCKLEY, ALBERT A member of the Overlook's board of directors, and the owner of the hotel. Al had taught with Jack in Vermont, and he directed Ullman to hire Torrance for the winter caretaker's job.

SHOCKLEY, ARTHUR LONGLEY Al Shockley's father. He was a steel baron.

STAUNTON, TOM Park ranger Halloran called and told there was trouble at the Overlook.

STENGER, ROBIN A boy in Danny's nursery school.

STENGER, VIC Robin Stenger's father. He went mad and was taken away by the men in the white coats.

STRONG, MISS French teacher at Stovington.

THE THREE MOUNTAIN CLIMBERS The three unnamed men who tried to climb the north face of King's Ram in Colorado.

THE THREE NUNS They sat on a sofa in the lobby of the Overlook the day the Torrances arrived at the hotel.

TOM He and Elaine lived above Jack and Wendy in Boulder, Colorado. They fought constantly.

TONY Danny's invisible playmate.

TORRANCE, BECKY Jack's sister.

TORRANCE, BRETT Jack's oldest brother.

TORRANCE, DANNY (DANIEL ANTHONY) Jack and Wendy's five-year-old son. He had "the shining."

TORRANCE, MIKE Jack's middle brother.

TORRANCE, JACK Alcoholic, failed father and failed writer. Jack took the winter caretaker job at the Overlook Hotel in Colorado to write, and to renew himself. Instead, due to his character flaws, he succumbed to the evil presence of the hotel and tried to kill his family, emulating a previous Overlook caretaker, Grady, who had succeeded in doing away with his "loved ones." Jack died in a boiler explosion at the hotel, and we must presume (or at least hope) that his soul went on to better things.

TORRANCE, WENDY Jack Torrance's wife.

TUNNEY, ZACK Stovington teacher who drank a keg of beer on the weekends.

ULLMAN, STUART Manager of the Overlook Hotel.

VECKER, CARLTON Passenger who didn't show up for Flight 196 to Denver. Halloramn got his seat.

VICKERY, DELORES Overlook chambermaid. She was the first person to see the ghost of Mrs. Massey in the bathtub. Ullman fired her.

THE VW FAMILY The family that had an accident on their way to Albuquerque.

WALPOLE, HORACE Novelist.

WATSON The Overlook's maintenance man. He took care of the plumbing and the boiler from May 15 through September 30.

WATSON, ROBERT TOWNLEY Bob T. Watson. The man who built the Overlook. [Note: See the "Before the Play" section.]

WENDY'S MOTHER She lived in New Hampshire.

THE WOMAN Unnamed woman on Flight 196 (Halloramn's flight back to Colorado) who burst into tears and said the plane was going to crash.

ZANUCK, DARRYL F. He stayed at the Overlook in 1956. Jack found his name on an old guest register in the hotel's basement.

ZEISS, PETER "POPPA" Miami-based importer.

(4)
THE SHINING
Places

ARAPAHOE STREET The street in Boulder, Colorado, where Jack and Wendy had once lived.

BARRE, VERMONT The town where Al Shockley lived.

THE BEEKMAN TOWER The hotel in New York where Jack and Wendy spent their honeymoon.

BERLIN, NEW HAMPSHIRE The town where Jack Torrance spent his boyhood.

BERLIN COMMUNITY HOSPITAL Hospital where Jack Torrance's father had worked as a male nurse.

THE BOULDERADO On closing day, Ullman was going to spend the night at the Boulderado Hotel in Boulder.

CHATTERTON LAKE The lake where Wendy told Danny they would go fishing in the spring.

THE COLORADO LOUNGE It was located in the west wing of the Overlook.

DONG HO Province in Vietnam where Brett Torrance was killed in 1965.

DURKIN'S CONOCO Sidewinder service station. Howard Cottrell told Dick Halloramn to go to Durkin's, mention his name, and he would get a deal on renting a snowmobile.

THE EQUIPMENT SHED Place where Jack found Ping-Pong tables and J.C. Penney jumper cables.

ESTES PARK Colorado town where a radio station was located.

FIRST BANK OF FLORIDA They had a thermometer.

THE FLATIRONS Mountains near Boulder, Colorado.

FORT LAUDERDALE, FLORIDA The town where Ullman managed the Surf-Sand Resort in the winter.

GATE 32, CONCOURSE B, STAPELTON INTERNATIONAL AIRPORT The gate where Halloramn was to catch his flight to Florida.

GERMANY Halloramn bought his Zippo lighter in Germany in 1954.

GREAT BARRINGTON Town in Vermont where an amusement and animal park was located.

THE GREENBACK Casino on the strip in Las Vegas.

HASTY NOTCH Colorado mountain range where three men tried to climb the north face of King's Ram.

THE JACK & JILL NURSERY SCHOOL The school Danny attended in Stovington, Vermont.

THE LUCKY BONES Casino on the strip in Las Vegas.

MARYLAND Wendy and Danny moved there after the winter at the Overlook.

MIAMI INTERNATIONAL Airport in Florida.

NEW HAMPSHIRE Where Wendy's mother lived.

149 MAPLELINE WAY The Torrance's address in Vermont.

ONE-A WHOLESALE VEGETABLE MARKET The market where Dick Halloramn shopped in Florida.

THE OVERLOOK DINING ROOM It was located in the west wing.

THE OVERLOOK HOTEL The hotel where the story takes place. It had a wicked heart.

THE PRESIDENTIAL SUITE Room 300. Four U.S. presidents had occupied the presidential suite at the Overlook.

RED ARROW LODGE Lodge in the western Maine mountains. It was thirty miles from the town of Rangely. It was where Halloramn worked after the late Jack Torrance's "Overlook" winter.

RED EYE LOUNGE The name of the Overlook's lounge during Derwent's time.

A REXALL DRUGSTORE Place in the Table Mesa shopping center where Jack stopped to phone Wendy after he got the job at the Overlook.

ROCKY MOUNTAIN NATIONAL PARK Jack thought that this park was within helicopter range of the Overlook.

ROOM 217 Halloramn told Danny to stay out of Room 217. This was the room where the old lady, Mrs. Massey, killed herself.

ROOM 300 The Overlook's presidential suite.

ST. PAUL The town where Horace Derwent was born.

ST. PETERSBURG, FLORIDA The town where Halloramn spent the winter season.

SEARS & ROEBUCK Department store.

THE 7-11 Convenience store.

SIDEWINDER The closest town to the Overlook.

THE SIDEWINDER PUBLIC LIBRARY Small building located in the town's business area.

SIERRA NEVADAS Mountains where the Donner Party was stranded.

STAPELTON AIRPORT The Denver, Colorado, airport where Halloramn reserved an Avis car.

STOVINGTON, VERMONT The town where Jack and Wendy used to live.

STOVINGTON PREPARATORY ACADEMY The school where Jack had taught, and from which he had been forced to resign.

THE SURF-SAND RESORT Resort in Fort Lauderdale, Florida, where Ullman worked the winters. He managed the place.

TABLE MESA SHOPPING CENTER Shopping Center where Jack stopped at a Rexall drugstore to call Wendy after he got the job at the Overlook.

THE UNIVERSITY OF NEW HAMPSHIRE School Mike Torrance attended on a merit scholarship.

WEST GERMANY In 1955, when he was stationed in West Germany, Halloramn saw the vision of the Georgia and South Carolina Railroad car derailing that told him his brother was dead.

THE WEST WING The wing of the Overlook where the dining room and the Colorado Lounge were located.

THE SHINING
Things

"ABBOTT AND COSTELLO MEET THE MONSTERS" The movie Danny mentioned after being shown the dumbwaiter in their apartment in the Overlook.

ADIDAS Sneakers.

THE ADVENTURES OF JOE AND RACHEL Danny's second grade primer.

"THE AMERICAN SHAKESPEARE" According to Wendy, Jack was not only the "Eugene O'Neill of his generation," but also the "American Shakespeare."

ANACIN The medication Jack took for his headaches.

APRIL OR MAY The months the queen wasp laid her eggs.

APRIL 10, 1963 The date the newspaper article ran about High Country Investments buying the Overlook.

ARCTIC CAT The snowmobile Hallorann rented to get him to the Overlook.

AUGUST 29, 1945 The day of the masked ball that celebrated the completion of the renovations of Horace Derwent's Overlook. [NOTE: See the section on "Before the Play."]

BABY RUTH Candy bar Danny wanted.

BANK AMERICARD & MASTERCHARGE DECALS Decals on the cash register in the Overlook.

"BLUE DANUBE WALTZ" The song that played on the clock in the ballroom at the Overlook.

"BLUEBEARD" A story and movie that once scared Danny. Jack read it to Danny when he was drunk.

THE BUG BOMB Jack had once bought a defective one. He wrote to an attorney about it.

BUICK ELECTRA The car Hallorann rented from Hertz in Colorado.

CAMAY Ladies' soap.

THE CARTONS In the Overlook basement were cartons marked "Records, Invoices, Receipts. Save."

CASHELMARA A book Wendy read.

A CHRYSLER Archer Houghton got a new Chrysler after changing Mrs. Massey's ("the Lady in the Bathtub") death certificate from suicide to heart attack.

"CIRCLE H," "BAR D BAR," "ROCKING W," AND "LAZY B" The embossing on the leather stools in the Colorado Lounge in the Overlook.

CLAIROL Radio commercial.

COCA-COLA After Jack quit drinking, he drank endless cans of Coke.

"CONCERNING THE BLACK HOLES" Story by Jack Torrance which was published in *Esquire* magazine. He was paid $900.

DANNY TORRANCE'S FAVORITE LUNCH A bologna sandwich and Campbell's bean soup.

DANNY'S HAND Danny's hand got stung by wasps. After it swelled, it looked like Bugs Bunny and Daffy Duck did after they had slammed themselves with a hammer.

DANNY'S NICKNAME "Doc."

DANNY'S SIGNS Danny could read the following signs: Closed, Stop, Exit, and Pizza.

DECEMBER 2 The date written in red on the clockface in the ballroom.

THE DENVER POST The newspaper that carried an article about Delbert Grady's slaying of his family.

THE DERWENT RUMORS It was rumored that Horace Derwent owned United Airlines, four hotels and casinos in Las Vegas, Los Angeles, and possibly owned the U.S.A. itself.

DETECTIVE BOOK CLUB TRILOGIES They were in the Torrances' apartment in the Overlook.

DR. DENTON'S Danny Torrance's pajamas.

DODGE Hotel truck. Wendy used it once to go in to Sidewinder.

THE DT'S Delerium tremens. Hallucinations experienced by severe and chronic alcoholics.

EEG Brain wave scan Dr. Edmonds gave Danny after he was stung by wasps.

"ELECTRIC COMPANY" TV show Danny watched.

ELECTRIC FLAMBEAUX LIGHTS Gas lights in the hallways of the Overlook. They were designed to look like London gas lamps.

ELEVATOR The game Jack's father used to play with Jack when Jack was a child. It involved picking Jack up and (almost) hurling him at the ceiling, then playfully catching him as he fell back to earth.

"ENTERING SIDEWINDER PASS" Sign on the road to the Overlook. This was as far as the snowplows went in the winter.

ESQUIRE MAGAZINE The magazine that published Jack Torrance's short story "Concerning the Black Holes."

"THE EUGENE O'NEILL OF HIS GENERATION" According to Wendy, Jack was not only the "Eugene O'Neill of his generation," but also the "American Shakespeare."

EXCEDRINS After a drinking binge, Jack would chew four Excedrins dry.

"FALLING ROCK ZONE" Signs on the road to the Overlook.

FEBRUARY 1, 1952 Date on the scrapbook clipping "Millionaire Exec. To Sell Colorado Investments."

FLEXIBLE FLYER Danny's sled.

"FRESH UP WITH 7-UP" The words written on an outdoor thermometer at the Overlook.

THE "FRIDAY NIGHT FIGHTS" What Jack called their neighbors Tom and Elaine's constant battling.

"GANGLAND-STYLE SHOOTING AT COLORADO HOTEL." Headline that ran in June of 1966.

THE GEORGIA AND SOUTH CAROLINA RAILROAD It was a G & SC train that was carrying Dick Hallorann's brother when it derailed and he was killed.

A GIDEON BIBLE Bible on an end table in Room 217.

HAMBURGER HELPER Hallorann thought that a plane crash that involved eighty-nine people would have probably looked like Hamburger Helper. [NOTE: One of my research assistants put a note next to this entry that read simply "UGH!"]

THE HAYES OFFICE The agency that checked movies for unacceptable content.

THE HEDGE TOPIARY Huge, elaborately-cut hedge animals on the Overlook's grounds. They were a big attraction at the Overlook. The animals were a rabbit, a horse, a dog, a cow, and lions.

HERBERT TAREYTONS Phyllis Sandler's cigarettes.

THE HIGH COUNTRY INVESTMENTS GROUP Las Vegas group that bought the Overlook in 1963.

THE HIGHWAY ADVISORY BOARD The board advised Colorado drivers about weather and highway conditions.

HONDA 350CC Motorcycle Jack Torrance had when he met Wendy. He traded it for a Saab.

INTERNATIONAL HARVESTER Watson's pickup truck.

JACK AND DANNY'S BASEBALL TEAMS The Torrance boys liked the Angels in the Western League, and the Red Sox in the American League.

JIM BEAM Phyllis Sandler's drink of choice. She drank it from a paper cup.

JUNE 1966 The month and year the following headline ran in a Colorado newspaper: "Gangland-Style Shooting at Colorado Hotel."

JUNE 27, 1934 The date on a note Jack found in the cellar of the Overlook.

KENTS Queens' cigarettes.

KMTX Colorado radio station.

"LAS VEGAS GROUP BUYS FAMED COLORADO HOTEL" April 10, 1963, headline reporting the sale of the Overlook.

"THE LITTLE SCHOOL" The play Jack was trying to write while at the Overlook.

"THE LOST WEEKEND" Movie about an alcoholic that starred Ray Milland.

LOWILA Ladies' soap.

MAINE MAGAZINE Magazine that published Jack's short story "The Monkey is Here, Paul DeLong."

THE MAPS While waiting for his father to make a phone call, Danny looked at roadmaps of the following states: Colorado, Nebraska, Utah, Wyoming, and New Mexico.

"MARK ANTHONY TORRANCE, LOVING FATHER" The inscription on Jack Torrance's father's tombstone. Jack thought he would have added one line: "He knew how to play elevator."

A MARTINI The drink Jack Torrance ordered from Lloyd the bartender.

THE MASKED BALL Gala party Horace Derwent held on August 29, 1945, to celebrate the completion of the Overlook's renovations. Here's what the invitation looked like:

Horace M. Derwent Requests
The Pleasure of Your Company
At a Masked Ball to Celebrate
The Grand Opening of

THE OVERLOOK HOTEL

Dinner Will Be Served at 8 P.M.
Unmasking And Dancing At Midnight
August 29, 1945   RSVP

MAY 15, 1947 The date an article ran in a Denver paper about the reopening of the Overlook.

MAYTAG WASHER The washer in the laundromat where Hallorann used the phone to call United Airlines.

"MILLIONAIRE DERWENT BACK IN COLORADO VIA BACK DOOR" Headline of article about Derwent's involvement with the Mafia.

"THE MONKEY IS HERE, PAUL DELONG" Short story Jack Torrance wrote and sold to *Maine* magazine.

THE MOUNTAINVIEW RESORTS GROUP The Colorado group that bought the Overlook from Charles Grondin's group.

MY LIFE IN THE TWENTIETH CENTURY The book Jack thought he would write and which would win him the Pulitzer Prize.

THE NATIONAL OBSERVER The magazine a man on Flight 196 vomited into.

A NEW ENGLAND PATRIOTS FLANNEL TOP Danny wore one.

NEW YORK *SUNDAY TIMES* Newspaper in which the Overlook ran advertisements.

THE NEW YORK *TIMES* Newspaper that was in the scrapbook Jack found in the basement of the Overlook.

1907-1909 The years the Overlook was built.

1915 The year Bob Watson sold the Overlook.

1950 CADILLAC The car Hallorann kept in Florida.

1961 The year four writers leased the Overlook and reopened it as a school for writers.

1970 The year Mr. Shockley and his associates bought the Overlook.

1934 The year Little Margery Morris died of a heroin overdose.

1936 One of the years the Overlook Hotel was sold.

1929 One of the years the Overlook Hotel was sold.

1922 One of the years the Overlook Hotel was sold.

NORTH AMERICAN ROQUE TOURNAMENT Tournament held at the Overlook in the twenties.

"NOTORIOUS HOTEL SOLD FOLLOWING MURDER OF UNDERWORLD FIGURE" Headline on column written by Josh Brannigar in 1967.

OCTOBER 20 The day Wendy went to Sidewinder.

110 GUEST QUARTERS The number of rooms in the Overlook Hotel.

OREOS Cookies Danny ate.

THE OVERLOOK'S SALE YEARS From 1915, the year Bob T. Watson sold the Overlook, it was sold again every seven years: in 1922, 1929, and 1936.

THE PICTURES ON DANNY'S WALL They included Winnie the Pooh, Eyore, and Christopher Robin.

PING-PONG TABLES AND J.C. PENNEY JUMPER CABLES Things Jack found in the Overlook's equipment shed.

PINTO STATION WAGON Car that Hallorann almost ran into in Florida.

PLYMOUTH FURY Car Hallorann rented.

A POLAROID CAMERA Jack used a Polaroid to take pictures of Danny's hand after the boy was stung by wasps.

A PORSCHE Mrs. Massey's car. Her seventeen-year-old stud stole it. She killed herself and became "the Lady in the Bathtub."

READER'S DIGEST CONDENSED BOOKS They were in the Torrances' apartment in the Overlook.

"REDRUM" The word "murder" when seen backwards in a mirror. Danny saw the word in a mirror when he was with Tony.

"ROAD CLOSED 12 MILES AHEAD DURING WINTER MONTHS" Sign along the road that led to the Overlook.

"ROCKY MOUNTAIN NEWS" Jack found a newspaper clipping in the Overlook's basement. The clipping was dated December 19, 1963. [NOTE: See the entry THE SCRAPBOOK.]

ROEBUCKERS Dick Hallorann's teeth. 1950-vintage Sears and Roebuck dentures. Wendy's father had also had a pair.

ROQUE The British forebear of our croquet. The Overlook had what may have been the finest roque court in the United States.

"RUGBY PLAYERS EAT THEIR OWN DEAD" Bumper sticker Jack saw in Boulder.

SAAB Car for which Jack Torrance traded his Honda 350CC.

ST. CHRISTOPHER MEDAL Hallorann had one in his car.

"SATURDAY NIGHT SHOCK SHOW HORROR" How Danny Torrance saw his father.

THE SCRAPBOOK Jack found a scrapbook containing several clippings in the Overlook's basement. [NOTE: See Chapter 18 of *The Shining*, "The Scrapbook," for complete details as to the scrapbook's contents.]

"SESAME STREET" TV show Danny watched.

"THE SHINING" Precognition. Danny and Hallorann had it. Hallorann explained it to Danny.

THE SIDEWINDER GAZETTE, *THE ESTES PARK DAILY*, **AND** *THE BOULDER CAMERA* Newspapers kept on file at the Sidewinder public library.

6:36 P.M. The United flight to Denver Hallorann wanted to take out of Miami airport. He couldn't get on it.

16 PEACH LANE Larry Durkin's address.

SNOOPY Danny's nightlight.

SPANISH LLAMA .38 Jack Torrance's gun.

SPEEDOGLIDE Danny's glider.

STIGMATA Christ's wounds. People who believe deeply in Christ's divinity exhibit bleeding wounds on their hands and feet during Holy Week.

THE STOCK OF THE COLORADO LOUNGE Jack Torrance saw the following bottles behind the bar in the lounge: Jim Beam, Wild Turkey, Gilby's, Sharrod's Private Label, Toro, and Seagram's.

STRANGE RESORT, THE STORY OF THE OVERLOOK HOTEL The title of the book Jack thought he might write about the Overlook.

TV GUIDE Weekly television magazine.

THE THINGS ON DANNY'S DESK They included picture books, coloring books, Spiderman comics, Crayolas, and Lincoln Logs.

THUNDERBIRD AND GRANDDAD FLASH'S POPSKULL BOURBON Jack told Lloyd that drunks carried these two bottles in paper bags.

THE TITANIC Ship that went down on its maiden voyage.

TOP MARK STUDIOS Horace Derwent's most famous investment.

THE TORRANCES' WAGES Based on a few facts, we can calculate how much Jack would have earned had he finished out the season. Ullman told Jack that the Overlook's season ran from May 15 through September 30. This meant that Jack's job ran from October 1 through May 14. This totals out at 226 days, and a total of 5,424 hours. (It would have to be assumed that Jack would be paid for a twenty-four-hour workday, since he was there for the entire period.) At one point, Watson told Jack that Ullman would have hired the Boston Strangler "if he'd've worked for the minimum wage. Since it's assumed that *The Shining* takes place in 1977, when the minimum wage was $2.30, then we can figure that 5,424 hours times $2.30 equals a total of $12,475.20 for the winter season. That's not too bad when you figure that utilities, room, and food were also included. (And that Ullman made $22K working as manager.)

A TURKEY Halloran left the Torrances a turkey for their Thanksgiving holiday.

TWA FLIGHT 196 The flight Halloran took to Denver.

$22,000 A SEASON Ullman's salary.

UNDERWOOD Jack's typewriter.

THE VIOLENT VIOLET VOLKSWAGEN Danny's matchbox car.

A VOLKSWAGEN The Torrance's car.

"THE WALTONS" TV show.

THE WASP'S NEST After Jack bug-bombed the nest that was on the roof, Danny kept it on a plastic plate on the table next to his bed.

WELCOME TO HARD TIMES Novel by E.L. Doctorow.

WENDY'S RECORDS Wendy had music by Grieg, Handel, the Beatles, Art Garfunkel, and Liszt. Danny saw the records broken and thrown everywhere when he was with Tony.

WIDE WORLD OF ANIMALS Danny thought that the fire extinguisher hose looked like a snake from this book.

WRITER'S DIGEST Magazine Jack bought in a drugstore.

"YOU ARE WHAT YOU EAT" Bumper sticker Jack saw in Boulder.

YOU CAN BE YOUR OWN BEST FRIEND The book a woman airline passenger read on the flight Halloran took to Denver.

ZEISS-IKON Jack's binoculars.

ZIPPO Halloran's lighter. He bought it in Germany in 1954.

NIGHT SHIFT

[No Dedication]

Contents Page

Book Breakdown

[*Night Shift* consists of an Introduction, a Foreword, and twenty short stories.]

(5a)
NIGHT SHIFT
"Jerusalem's Lot"
People

BIGELOW, MR. Historian. Charles Boone was introduced to him at Mr. Clàry's fund-raising dinner for the abolitionist cause.

"BONES" Mr. Everett Gransom. He was the friend and correspondent of Charles Boone. In a series of letters to Bones, Boone revealed the dark secrets of Chapelwaite, his ancestral home, and the abandoned town of Jerusalem's Lot.

BOON, JAMES Charles Boone's ancestor and the man who founded Jerusalem's Lot in 1710. He was a religious fanatic who used *The Bible* and deGoudge's *Demon Dwellings* at the same time. Frawley the blacksmith called Boon "that mad Antichrist." He reappeared as a zombie to Charles Boone when Charles burned the book *De Vermis Mysteriis* in the abandoned Jerusalem's Lot church.

BOONE, AUNT JUDITH One of Charles Boone's ancestors. Her portrait hung in the upper gallery at Chapelwaite.

BOONE, CHARLES He took up residence in his ancestral home of Chapelwaite, and learned the horrible truth about Jerusalem's Lot.

BOONE, GRANDFATHER ROBERT One of Charles Boone's ancestors. His portrait hung in the upper gallery at Chapelwaite. He and his brother Phillip had a falling out over stolen items in 1789. Calvin McCann found his diary.

BOONE, JAMES ROBERT Charles Boone's second cousin removed by three generations. He was Charles's last descendant. He was from Central Falls, Rhode Island, and he moved to Chapelwaite in 1971. In a letter dated October 2, 1971, he noted "There are some huge rats in the walls, by the sound." [NOTE: Central Falls, Rhode Island, is also where Carlos Detweiler worked at the Central Falls House of Flowers. See the section on *The Plant* in this volume.]

BOONE, KENNETH Charles Boone's great grandfather. He was a fur trader. His sons Phillip and Robert built Chapelwaite.

BOONE, MARCELLA Randolph Boone's daughter. Randolph had an accident on the cellar stairs at Chapelwaite that took the life of Marcella. Randolph later killed himself.

BOONE, PHILLIP Robert Boone's brother. He and Robert had a falling out over stolen items in 1789.

BOONE, RANDOLPH Stephen Boone's father. He and his wife disappeared in 1816. He had an accident on the cellar stairs at Chapelwaite that took the life of his daughter Marcella. He later committed suicide.

BOONE, SARAH Charles Boone's dead wife. Charles had "brain fever" after her death.

BOONE, STEPHEN Charles Boone's cousin. Stephen used to own Chapelwaite before Charles took possession. Stephen fell to his death from his own front porch.

BOONE, UNCLE HENRY One of Charles Boone's ancestors. His portrait hung in the upper gallery at Chapelwaite.

BROCKETT, CLIFTON After Charles Boone moved into Chapelwaite, the townsfolk claimed that evil omens and portents were occurring. They included: Barbara Brown giving birth to a child with no eyes, and Clifton Brockett finding a flat five-foot-wide trail in the woods beyond Chapelwaite where everything had withered.

BROWN, BARBARA After Charles Boone moved into Chapelwaite, the townsfolk claimed that evil omens and portents were occurring. They included Barbara Brown giving birth to a child with no eyes.

CALHOUN, MR. A long-winded friend of Charles Boone and Bones.

A CHILD WITH NO EYES After Charles Boone moved into Chapelwaite, the townsfolk claimed that evil omens and portents were occurring. They included: Barbara Brown giving birth to a child with no eyes.

CLARY, MR. He gave a fund-raising dinner for the abolitionist cause.

CLORIS, MR. The woman who cleaned Chapelwaite for Charles Boone. She brought four young girls to help her. She had cleaned the house for Charles's cousin Stephen before he died, as well as for Stephen's father Randolph Boone before he and his wife disappeared in 1816.

FOUR YOUNG GIRLS The girls Mrs. Cloris brought with her to clean Charles Boone's house.

FRAWLEY THE BLACKSMITH In 1789, Frawley wanted to know what Robert Boone's brother Phillip and "that mad Antichrist" (James Boon) were up to.

THE GHOSTS OF MARCELLA AND RANDOLPH BOONE Charles Boone wrote to Bones that he and Calvin had gone downstairs and seen the ghosts of Marcella and Randolph Boone.

GRANSOM, EVERETT Bones, Charles Boone's friend and correspondent.

GRANSOM, MRS. Bones's wife. Charles Boone sent his best to her in his first letter to Bones from Chapelwaite.

HANSON A friend of Charles Boone. He was in England on a jaunt. Hanson believed (as did Moses, Jereboam, Increase Mather, and Charles Boone), that there were "spiritually noxious places."

"HIM" Mrs. Cloris told Charles Boone, "Some die not. Some live in the twilight shadows Between to serve—Him!"

JEREBOAM Charles Boone believed (as did Moses, Jereboam, Increase Mather, and Boone's friend Hanson), that there were "spiritually noxious places."

MATHER, INCREASE Charles Boone believed (as did Moses, Jereboam, Increase Mather, and Boone's friend Hanson), that there were "spiritually noxious places."

McCANN, CALVIN Charles Boone's manservant. He was killed when The Worm burst up from The Abyss beneath the deserted church in Jerusalem's Lot.

MOSES Charles Boone believed (as did Moses, Jereboam, Increase Mather, and Boone's friend Hanson), that there were "spiritually noxious places."

PETTY, JOHN He and Bones had arranged for Charles Boone to take up residence at Chapelwaite.

RANDALL, GOODY In the October 27, 1789, entry of Robert Boone's diary, he revealed that Goody Randall said that there had been signs (omens and portents) lately.

RANDOLPH BOONE'S WIFE She and Randolph disappeared in 1816. They had a daughter named Marcella who died when Randolph had an accident on the cellar stairs.

RICHARD Lawyer friend of Charles Boone. Boone called him Dick. He had a wife and two sons. He was a lawyer and wrote for *The Liberator* in Boston.

RICHARD'S TWO SONS Dick and his wife had two boys.

RICHARD'S WIFE She and Dick had two sons.

"THAT MAD ANTICHRIST" In 1789, Frawley the blacksmith wanted to know what Robert Boone's brother Phillip and "that mad Antichrist" (James Boon) were up to.

THOMPSON, MR. A "besotted pulp-logger" with five sons, a wife, and four hundred acres of pine, birch, and spruce. He sold to the mills in Portland. Calvin went to see him about buying wood for Chapelwaite. His wife once made the forked-finger gesture at Charles Boone.

THOMPSON, MRS. Thompson the logger's wife. She once made the forked-finger gesture at Charles Boone.

THOMPSON'S FIVE SONS Thompson the logger had five boys.

THE WORM When Charles Boone and Calvin McCann went to the deserted church in the Lot and burned the book *De Vermis Mysteriis*, the floor of the church opened up and The Worm came up out of The Abyss. Calvin McCann was killed and James Boon, now a zombie, rose up out of the hole.

(5a)
NIGHT SHIFT
"Jerusalem's Lot"
Places

THE BOAR'S HEAD INN AND TAVERN A deserted pub in Jerusalem's Lot.

BOSTON Richard, Charles Boone's lawyer friend wrote for *The Liberator* in Boston. Also, Boston was the location of Johns & Goodfellow, the book company Robert Boone wrote to about the book he found, *De Vermis Mysteriis*.

THE BUILDING MARKED WITH A STEEPLE Calvin heard laughing from behind the walls at Chapelwaite. He then found a map hidden in the wall that had seven buildings drawn on it. One of the buildings was marked with a steeple and bore the legend "The Worm That Doth Corrupt."

THE CELLAR STAIRS Randolph Boone had an accident on the cellar stairs at Chapelwaite that took the life of his daughter Marcella.

A CHANDLER A deserted shop in Jerusalem's Lot.

CHAPELWAITE Charles Boone's ancestral home near Preacher's Corner. The house had twenty-three rooms. It was three miles north of Falmouth, and nine miles north of Portland. It used to be his cousin Stephen's place. It was built in 1789 by Kenneth Boone's sons, Robert and Phillip.

CUMBERLAND COUNTY, MAINE The county where Chapelwaite was located.

ENGLAND Hanson, a friend of Charles Boone, was in England on a jaunt.

FLORIDA Bones lived in Florida.

A HOSTELRY A deserted shop in Jerusalem's Lot.

JERUSALEM'S LOT A deserted village near Preacher's Corners on the Royal River. It was founded in 1710 by James Boon.

JOHNS & GOODFELLOW Johns & Goodfellow was the book company Robert Boone wrote to about the book he found, *De Vermis Mysteriis*. Robert had known Henry Goodfellow for years, yet the reponse from Goodfellow was very cool. He didn't want to talk about *The Mysteries of the Worm*, but he did tell him that only five copies of the book were known to exist.

THE MAIL-ORDER COMPANY On October 17, 1850, Calvin McCann ordered rat's bane from a company that sold household items by catalogue. It was their Summer 1850 catalogue.

THE MILLS IN PORTLAND Thompson the logger sold pine, birch, and spruce to the mills in Portland.

PREACHER'S CORNERS The closest village to Chapelwaite. It was founded (as Preacher's Rest) in 1741.

PREACHER'S REST The name of Preacher's Corner when it was founded in 1741.

THE ROYAL RIVER Jerusalem's Lot was near Preacher's Corners on the Royal River.

A SMITHY A deserted shop in Jerusalem's Lot.

"SPIRITUALLY NOXIOUS PLACES" Charles Boone believed (as did Moses, Jereboam, Increase Mather, and Boone's friend Hanson), that there were "spiritually noxious places."

TANDRELL When Charles Boone decided to go to the Lot, he attempted to send Calvin McCann off on an errand to Tandrell, some ten miles distant. Cal didn't fall for it and, instead, accompanied Charles to the Lot.

THREE MILES NORTH OF FALMOUTH AND NINE MILES NORTH OF PORTLAND The location of Chapelwaite.

A WAREHOUSE A deserted building in Jerusalem's Lot. It had oak and pine stocked inside.

THE WOODS BEYOND CHAPELWAITE After Charles Boone moved into Chapelwaite, the townsfolk claimed that evil omens and portents were occurring. They included Barbara Brown giving birth to a child with no eyes, and Clifton Brockett finding a flat five-foot-wide trail in the woods beyond Chapelwaite where everything had withered.

(5a)

NIGHT SHIFT
"Jerusalem's Lot"
Things

AUGUST 4, 1789 The date of Robert Boone's diary entry that Charles Boone reprinted in his October 24, 1850, letter to Bones.

THE BIBLE Charles Boone's ancestor James Boon founded Jerusalem's Lot in 1710. He was a religious fanatic who used the *Bible* and deGoudge's *Demon Dwellings* at the same time.

"BLESSED ARE THE MEEK" Among Robert Boone's papers was found an advertisement for gentlemen's silver hats on the back of which was scribbled "Blessed are the meek" and below that:

b k e d s h d e r m t h e s e a k
e l m s o e r a r e s h a m d e d

This was a cypher used in the War for Independence known as the "fence-rail." It was the code Robert Boone used to encrypt his diary.

"BRAIN FEVER" Charles Boone had brain fever (whatever that was) after his wife Sarah's death.

A BUCKWHITE COMPASS When Charles and Cal decided to visit Jerusalem's Lot, they took a Buckwhite compass.

CHAPELWAITE'S ADDRESS:

Chapelwaite
Preacher's Corners
Cumberland County, Maine

A CROSS The cross in the church in Jerusalem's Lot was hung upside down. This was a symbol of Satan's mass.

DEGOUDGE'S *DEMON DWELLINGS* Charles Boone's ancestor James Boon founded Jerusalem's Lot in 1710. He was a religious fanatic who used the *Bible* and deGoudge's *Demon Dwellings* at the same time.

1816 The year Randolph Boone and his wife disappeared.

THE EPISTOLARY CHRONOLOGY OF "JERUSALEM'S LOT" The events in Jerusalem's Lot were recounted in the following documents:

1. *LETTER*
   To: Bones
   From: Charles Boone
   Date: October 2, 1850

2. *LETTER*
   To: Bones
   From: Charles Boone
   Date: October 5, 1850

3. *LETTER*
   To: Richard
   From: Charles Boone
   Date: October 16, 1850

4. *LETTER*
   To: Bones
   From: Charles Boone
   Date: October 16, 1850

5. *LETTER*
   To: An unnamed Mail-Order Company
   From: Calvin McCann
   Date: October 17, 1850

6. *LETTER*
   To: Bones
   From: Charles Boone
   Date: October 19, 1850

7. *FROM THE POCKET JOURNAL OF CALVIN McCANN*
   Entry Date: October 20, 1850

8. *LETTER*
   To: Bones
   From: Charles Boone
   Date: October 20, 1850

9. *FROM THE POCKET JOURNAL OF CALVIN McCANN*
   Entry Date: October 20, 1850

10. *LETTER*
    To: Bones
    From: Charles Boone
    Date: October 22, 1850

11. *FROM THE POCKET JOURNAL OF CALVIN McCANN*
    Entry Date: October 23, 1850

12. *LETTER*
    To: Bones
    From: Charles Boone
    Date: October 24, 1850

13. *FROM THE DIARY OF ROBERT BOONE*
    Entry Date: August 4, 1789

14. *FROM THE POCKET JOURNAL OF CALVIN McCANN*
    Entry Date: October 25, 1850

15. *LETTER*
    To: Bones
    From: Charles Boone
    Date: October 26, 1850

16. *FROM THE POCKET JOURNAL OF CALVIN McCANN*
    Entry Date: October 27, 1850

17. *LETTER*
    To: Bones
    From: Charles Boone
    Date: November 4, 1850

18. *LETTER*
    To: An unnamed publisher
    From: James Robert Boone
    Date: October 2, 1971

EVERY SECOND THURSDAY Mrs. Cloris used to clean house every second Thursday for Stephen Boone before he died.

"THE FENCE-RAIL" Among Robert Boone's papers was found an advertisement for gentlemen's silver hats on the back of which was scribbled "Blessed are the meek" and below that:

b k e d s h d e r m t h e s e a k
e l m s o e r a r e s h a m d e d

This was a cypher used in the War for Independence known as the "fence-rail." It was the code Robert Boone used to encrypt his diary.

FIVE COPIES Robert Boone learned from Johns & Goodfellow in Boston that only five copies of the book *De Vermis Mysteriis (The Mysteries of the Worm*) had ever been known to exist.

400 ACRES OF PINE, BIRCH, AND SPRUCE Thompson the logger's property. He sold to the mills in Portland.

THE GATEWAY After Charles Boone awakened The Worm (and his dead relative James Boon) by burning *De Vermis Mysteriis*, he told Bones "It still lives. The burning of the book thwarted It, but there are other copies." He realized "I am the gateway, and I am the last of the Boone blood. For the good of all humanity I must die...and break the chain forever." He then went "to the sea." His journey, like his story, was at an end.

GENTLEMEN'S SILVER HATS Among Robert Boone's papers was found an advertisement for gentlemen's silver hats on the back of which was scribbled the "fence-rail" code. [NOTE: See the entry THE FENCE RAIL.)

THE INTELLIGENCER A periodical Charles Boone read.

JUNE 1, 1789 The date of the first entry in Robert Boone's diary.

LAUGHING Calvin heard laughing from behind the walls at Chapelwaite. He then found a map hidden in the wall that had seven buildings drawn on it. One of the buildings was marked with a steeple and bore the legend "The Worm That Doth Corrupt."

THE LIBERATOR The Boston magazine that Richard wrote for.

THE MAP Calvin heard laughing from behind the walls at Chapelwaite. He then found a map hidden in the wall that had seven buildings drawn on it. One of the buildings was marked with a steeple and bore the legend "The Worm That Doth Corrupt."

MR. CLARY'S FUND-RAISING DINNER FOR THE ABOLITIONIST CAUSE A dinner Charles Boone had attended. While there, he was introduced to an historian named Bigelow.

THE MYSTERIES OF THE WORM (De Vermis Mysteriis) The book Charles Boone and Cal found on the altar of the deserted Jerusalem's Lot church. It had originally been discovered by Robert Boone, who learned from Johns & Goodfellow in Boston that only five copies of the book had ever been known to exist. Charles eventually burned the Jerusalem's Lot copy, thus awakening The Worm, and killing Calvin McCann.

NOVEMBER 4, 1850 The date of Charles Boone's ninth, and final, letter to Bones.

OCTOBER 8, 1850 The date of Charles Boone's second letter to Bones from Chapelwaite.

OCTOBER 19, 1850 The date of Charles Boone's fourth letter to Bones from Chapelwaite.

OCTOBER 2, 1850 The date of the first letter from Charles Boone to Bones.

OCTOBER 2, 1971 The date of a letter written by James Robert Boone, Charles Boone's second cousin removed by three generations, after he took up residence at Chapelwaite. His activities reawakened the ghosts of Marcella and Randolph Boone, and reaffirmed James Boon's evil control over the Boone bloodline.

OCTOBER 17, 1850 The date of a letter Calvin McCann wrote to a company that sold household items by catalogue.

OCTOBER 16, 1850 The date of Charles Boone's third letter to Bones from Chapelwaite. (It was the fourth letter he'd written. The third was to Richard in Boston.)

OCTOBER 16, 1850 The date of the third letter Charles Boone wrote at Chapelwaite. It was to Richard in Boston.

OCTOBER 31, 1789 The date Phillip Boone and the entire population of Jerusalem's Lot disappeared.

OCTOBER 20, 1850 The date of an entry in Calvin McCann's pocket journal in which he revealed that he'd heard noises in the walls, that he had put sleeping powder in Charles Boone's tea, and that he himself had been stoned by the townspeople.

OCTOBER 20, 1850 The date Calvin McCann made two entries in his pocket journal. In the first, he wrote that he had forced open the book he had found (which turned out to be Robert Boone's

diary); in the second, he made note of Charles Boone's health beginning to deteriorate. This was also the date of Charles Boone's fifth letter to Bones.

OCTOBER 24, 1850 The date of Charles Boone's seventh letter to Bones. In this letter, Bones revealed what he had learned from reading Robert Boone's Diary.

OCTOBER 22, 1850 The date of Charles Boone's sixth letter to Bones. He wrote that he had been unconscious for thirty-six hours after he and Calvin had gone downstairs and seen the ghosts of Marcella and Randolph Boone.

OCTOBER 27, 1850 The date of an entry in Calvin McCann's pocket journal in which he revealed that he had decided to go with Charles Boone to the Lot.

OCTOBER 27, 1789 The date of Robert Boone's diary entry in which he revealed that Frawley the blacksmith was questioning him about his brother Phillip's activities with James Boon, and that Randall Goody had noted omens and portents.

OCTOBER 27, 1789 The date of the last entry in Robert Boone's diary.

OCTOBER 26, 1850 The date of Charles Boone's eighth letter to Bones.

OCTOBER 23, 1850 The date of an entry in Calvin McCann's pocket journal in which he wrote that he thought the papers he had found were Robert Boone's.

OMENS AND PORTENTS After Charles Boone moved into Chapelwaite, the townsfolk claimed that evil omens and portents were occurring. They included: Barbara Brown giving birth to a child with no eyes, and Clifton Brockett finding a flat five-foot-wide trail in the woods beyond Chapelwaite where everything had withered.

RAT'S BANE On October 17, 1850, Calvin McCann ordered one five-pound tin of rat's bane for thirty cents from a company that sold household items by catalogue.

SATAN'S MASS The cross in the church in Jerusalem's Lot was hung upside down. This was a symbol of Satan's mass.

SEPTEMBER 1, 1789 The date Phillip Boone was baptized into James Boon's church.

1789 The year Robert and Phillip Boone had a falling out over stolen items.

1782 The year Chapelwaite was built by Kenneth Boone's sons, Robert and Phillip.

1741 The year Preacher's Rest (later known as Preacher's Corners) was founded.

1710 The year Jerusalem's Lot was founded by James Boon.

SUMMER 1850 The edition of the catalogue from which Calvin McCann ordered rat's bane by mail.

"THERE ARE SOME HUGE RATS IN THE WALLS, BY THE SOUNDS." The last line of a letter written by James Robert Boone, Charles Boone's second cousin removed by three generations, upon his taking up residence at Chapelwaite on October 2, 1971.

THIRTY CENTS The price of a five-pound tin of rat's bane that Calvin McCann ordered from a company that sold household items by catalogue.

THIRTY-SIX HOURS In Charles Boone's sixth letter to Bone, he wrote that he had been unconscious for thirty-six hours after he and Calvin had gone downstairs and seen the ghosts of Marcella and Randolph Boone.

TWENTY-THREE ROOMS Charles Boone's ancestral home Chapelwaite had twenty-three rooms.

DE VERMIS MYSTERIIS (The Mysteries of the Worm) Book Charles Boone and Cal found on the altar of the deserted Jerusalem's Lot church. It had originally been discovered by Robert Boone, who learned from Johns & Goodfellow in Boston that only five copies of the book had ever been known to exist.

"THE WORM THAT DOTH CORRUPT" Calvin heard laughing from behind the walls at Chapelwaite. He then found a map hidden in the wall that had seven buildings drawn on it. One of the buildings was marked with a steeple and bore the legend "The Worm That Doth Corrupt."

❖❖❖

(5b)
NIGHT SHIFT
"Graveyard Shift"
People

THE BATS While the magna mater of the rats ate Warwick in the mill's sub-sub-basement, the bats ate Hall.
BROCHU, CHARLIE One of Hall's co-workers at the mill. Charlie was one of the thirty-six guys who agreed to work during the Fourth of July week cleaning out the mill's sub-basement.
BROGAN One of the mill workers who went down into the sub-sub-basement looking for Hall and Warwick.
CARMICHAEL Mill worker. While cleaning out the sub-basement, a rat bit his chest.
DANGERFIELD One of the mill workers who went down into the sub-sub-basement looking for Hall and Warwick.
HALL He had been working in the mill since April. He had no wife, no girl, and no alimony. He didn't get along with Warwick, "Mr. Foreman," and ended up forcing Warwick down into the mill's sub-sub-basement where Warwick was eaten by the queen rat and Hall was eaten by bats.
IPPESTON, CY Mill worker. He was part of the crew cleaning out the mill's sub-basement. After seeing the rats bite some of his co-workers, Cy said that he wasn't an exterminator.
THE MAGNA MATER Hall found the rat's queen in the mill's sub-sub-basement. She was as big as a Holstein calf. She ate Warwick while the bats ate Hall.
NEDEAU One of the mill workers who went down into the sub-sub-basement looking for Hall and Warwick.
STEVENSON One of the mill workers who went down into the sub-sub-basement looking for Hall and Warwick.
THIRTY-SIX MEN There were thirty-six men working the Fourth of July week cleaning out the mill's sub-basement. (Hall was one of them.)
TONY One of Hall's co-workers at the mill. Tony was one of the thirty-six guys who agreed to work the Fourth of July week cleaning out the mill's sub-basement. While they were working, the guys made jokes about who was keeping Tony's wife warm.
TONY'S WIFE While the guys were working cleaning out the mill's sub-basement, jokes were made about who was keeping Tony's wife warm.
THE TOWN COMMISSIONER After discovering the sub-sub-basement, Hall threatened to go to the Gates Falls town commissioner if Warwick refused to clean out the place.
THE TWO MEN The two unnamed mill workers who were bitten by rats while cleaning the sub-basement. After being bitten, they insisted on wearing heavy, rubber acid-gloves.
UPSON, RAY While working in the mill's sub-basement, a rat bit Ray and he had to go home.
VARNEY, ELIAS In the mill's sub-sub-basement, the workers found a box labeled "Elias Varney 1814."
WARWICK "Mr. Foreman." The foreman of the mill where Hall worked. He and Warwick didn't get along.
THE WATCHMAN The mill watchman. He let Brochu into the office to get three flashlights. They needed them to explore the mill's sub-sub-basement.
WISCONSKY, HARRY One of Hall's co-workers at the mill. He was fat, lazy, and gloomy. Harry sent orders down to Hall.

(5b)
NIGHT SHIFT
"Graveyard Shift"
Places

BERKELEY Hall was a college student in Berkeley.
THE DYE HOUSE Hall agreed to work the Fourth of July week cleaning out the sub-basement below the dye house.
GALVESTON Before working at the mill, Hall worked in Galveston as a stevedore.
GATES FALLS, MAINE The town where the mill was located.
HALL'S THREE-YEAR JOURNEY Before he worked in the mill, Hall traveled around the country, mostly by hitchhiking. His itinerary consisted of the following:

> Berkeley—college student;
> Lake Tahoe—busboy;
> Galveston—stevedore;
> Miami—short-order cook;
> Wheeling—taxi driver and dishwasher;
> Gates Falls, Maine—picker-machine operator.

LAKE TAHOE Before working at the mill, Hall worked in Lake Tahoe as a busboy.
MIAMI Before working at the mill, Hall worked in Miami as a short-order cook.
THE MILL BASEMENT Hall agreed to work (for two dollars an hour and double time on the Fourth of July) cleaning out the mill basement. The basement was actually the sub-basement, beneath the dye house.
MILL STREET The street Wisconsky took to drive Hall home. It crossed a bridge.
THE OFFICE It was where the flashlights were kept.
THE SUB-SUB-BASEMENT Hall found the trapdoor to the mill's sub-sub-basement...where the queen of the rats lived. He and Warwick—in their final confrontation—went down there together, and died there together.
THE THIRD FLOOR Hall's floor in the mill.
WHEELING Before working at the mill, Hall worked in Wheeling as a taxi driver and dishwasher.

(5b)
NIGHT SHIFT
"Graveyard Shift"
Things

APRIL The month Hall began working at the mill.
A DEFUNCT CLEVELAND FIRM They manufactured the picking machines Hall worked on in the mill.
1814 In the mill's sub-sub-basement, the workers found a box labeled "Elias Varney 1814."
1897 The year the mill was built.
11:00 P.M. MONDAY The time and day Hall and thirty-five other guys began to clean out the mill basement.
THE FOURTH OF JULY WEEK The mill closed down for the week of the Fourth of July. That was the week Hall agreed to clean out the basement.
HALL'S JOBS Before he worked in the mill, Hall hitchhiked around the country, working different jobs. His "work record" consisted of the following:

> Berkeley—college student;
> Lake Tahoe—busboy;
> Galveston—stevedore;
> Miami—short-order cook;
> Wheeling—taxi driver and dishwasher;
> Gates Falls, Maine—picker-machine operator.

THE HEAVY RUBBER ACID-GLOVES Two unnamed mill workers were bitten by rats while cleaning the sub-basement. After being bitten, they insisted on the heavy, rubber acid-gloves.

THE HOTTEST JUNE ON RECORD While working at the mill, Hall went through the hottest June on record. The thermometer had once read ninety-four degrees at three in the morning.

THE MILL STREET BRIDGE The bridge Wisconsky crossed to take Hall home.

A MOLDY SKULL While investigating the mill's sub-sub-basement, Hall and the others found a moldy skull.

A NEHI CAN While on the graveyard shift, Hall threw a Nehi can at a rat.

NINETY-POUND BAGS OF FIBER (ESPECIALLY THE DISCONTINUED MELTONS AND THE IRREGULAR SLIPES) These made excellent nesting places for the rats.

$1.78 AN HOUR Hall's hourly rate in the mill.

THE ONLY THING HALL DIDN'T LIKE ABOUT THE GRAVEYARD SHIFT The rats.

THE ORANGE CRUSH THERMOMETER While working at the mill, Hall went through the hottest June on record. The Orange Crush thermometer had once read ninety-four degrees at three in the morning.

PICKER MACHINES The machines Hall worked in the mill. They had been made by a defunct Cleveland firm in 1934.

THE RATS The rats were the only thing Hall didn't like about the graveyard shift.

THE TOWN ZONING ORDINANCES They were set up in 1911, and specifically addressed the problem of vermin. Hall threatened Warwick with these ordinances after the foreman refused to clean out the sub-sub-basement. Hall was on some kind of macabre "death walk," and insisted that he and Warwick go down into the sub-sub-basement together.

2:00 A.M., FRIDAY Three hours into the graveyard shift at the mill where Hall worked.

TWO DOLLARS AN HOUR Hall was to be paid two dollars an hour for working the Fourth of July week cleaning out the mill's sub-basement, with double time on the Fourth.

◆◆◆

(5c)
NIGHT SHIFT
"Night Surf"
People

ALVIN SACKHEIM'S GRANDMOTHER As Alvin Sackheim raved with Captain Trips, he called for his grandmother. At one point, he thought that Susie was his grandmother.

THE BACKWOODS DEEJAY The unnamed WKDM deejay in Portsmouth who had gone nutty-religious after the flu.

BERNIE The narrator of "Night Surf," and one of the survivors of A6. He had had A2, the Hong Kong flu, which supposedly made him immune to Captain Trips.

BOBBY One of the deejays on WDOPE. He announced that Freddy had the flu.

A BUNCH OF KIDS One of the two surviving radio stations (either WKRO or WBZ in Massachusetts) was being manned by a bunch of kids who used gag call letters like WDOPE, KUNT, or WAG.

COREY One of the survivors of A6. He had a radio and was well-to-do before the flu. He had had A2, the Hong Kong flu, which supposedly made him immune to Captain Trips.

FREDDY One of the kids who took over either WRKO or WBZ in Massachusetts. Bobby announced that Freddy had the flu.

THE GIRL A girl in the background on WDOPE asked Bobby where he put the beer.

JOAN One of the survivors of the flu. She walked the beach with Kelly. She had had A2, the Hong Kong flu, which supposedly made her immune to Captain Trips.

KELLY One of the survivors of the flu. He walked the beach with Joan. He had had A2, the Hong Kong flu, which supposedly made him immune to Captain Trips.

THE MAN WHO RAN THE CONCESSION STAND The unnamed man who ran a stand at Anson Beach. He had an apartment above the stand.

MAUREEN Bernie once dated a girl named Maureen in high school.

NEEDLES One of the survivors of the flu. Susie and Bernie had met Needles in Portland. He had been sitting on a curb in front of the State Theater playing Leadbelly tunes on a big, old Gibson guitar. Needles lit Alvin Sackheim's pyre with his Zippo. Needles had told the rest of the kids that he had had A2, the Hong Kong flu, which made him immune to A6. He got Captain Trips anyway.

THE ROLLING STONES Their song "Angie" was playing on a radio at Anson Beach.

SACKHEIM, ALVIN The man who had Captain Trips, and who drove his big yellow Lincoln onto the beach. His "head was bloated to the size of a football and his neck looked like a sausage." Alvin thought that Susie was his grandmother. The kids burned him on a pyre.

SUSIE One of the survivors of the flu. She wore cranberry bellbottoms and was getting fat. She had had A2, the Hong Kong flu, which supposedly made her immune to Captain Trips.

(5c)
NIGHT SHIFT
"Night Surf"
Places

ANSON BEACH The gathering place of the last survivors of the flu, and the place where the kids burned Alvin Sackheim's body. It had once been a public beach, but the ocean had eaten it "as casually as you might eat a handful of Cracker Jacks."

THE ANSON BEACH SNACK BAR The concession stand on the beach. It sold sweatshirts that said "Anson Beach," and plastic vomit advertised as "So Realistic!" They recommended that you "Try it on your wife!" They also sold pennants that said "Souvenir of Anson Beach and Park."

THE APARTMENT The man who ran the concession stand at Anson Beach had a small apartment above the stand.

THE BONNEVILLE SALT FLATS Bernie wanted to put up a sign in the Salt Flats measuring three miles on a side. It would be a bronze square that read JUST THE FLU.

HARRISON STATE PARK From the text: "When I was a kid my mother used to take us kids to Harrison State Park and there was a fun house with a big clown face on the front and you walked in through the mouth." [NOTE: See the section on King's poetry in this volume for information on his poem called "Harrison State Park '68," as well as the section on *It* for his use of the evil clown image as manifested in Pennywise the clown. Also see the section on his film "Maximum Overdrive" in this volume. In "Overdrive," he used the giant clown face image on the front of one of the sentient trucks.]

MASSACHUSETTS The state where the only other surviving radio station was located. It was either WRKO or WBZ, and it was manned by a bunch of kids who used gag call letters like WDOPE, KUNT, or WAG.

PORTLAND The town where Susie and Bernie had met Needles. He had been sitting in front of the State Theater playing Leadbelly tunes on a big, old Gibson guitar.

PORTSMOUTH The town where one of the two surviving radio stations, WKDM, was located.

THE STATE THEATER Susie and Bernie had met Needles in front of the State Theater in Portland. He had been playing Leadbelly tunes on a big, old Gibson guitar.

THE UNIVERSITY Susie and Bernie had been together at the university before Captain Trips.

(5c)
NIGHT SHIFT
"Night Surf"
Things

A6 Captain Trips. The superflu. The illness that decimated the entire human race. It had come "out of Southeast Asia and [covered] the world like a pall…"

A2 The Hong Kong flu. All the kids had had it. Needles had said he had had it, too. This was supposed to make him immune to Captain Trips, but it was no guarantee. He ended up getting A6 anyway. Bernie figured he lied about having A2.

"BRINGIN' IN THE SHEAVES" A hymn sung by the deejay on WKDM.

"CAPTAIN TRIPS" A6. The superflu that wiped out the human race.

CASES OF BUD There were three or four cases of Budweiser beer in the apartment above the Anson Beach Snack Bar.

"EAST OF EDEN" The backwoods deejay on WKDM who had gone nutty-religious read from *Psalms*, complete with each "selah," just like James Dean in "East of Eden."

A GIBSON GUITAR Susie and Bernie had met Needles in Portland. He had been sitting in front of the State Theater playing Leadbelly tunes on a big, old Gibson guitar.

THE HONG KONG FLU A2. Needles eventually wound up with Captain Trips, A6, even though he had said he had had the Hong Kong flu.

THE "JUST THE FLU" SIGN Bernie wanted to put up a sign in the Bonneville Salt Flats that would measure three miles on a side and be a bronze square that read "JUST THE FLU."

KUNT One of the two surviving radio stations (either WKRO or WBZ in Massachusetts), manned by a bunch of kids who used gag call letters like WDOPE, KUNT, or WAG.

LEADBELLY TUNES Susie and Bernie had met Needles in Portland. He had been sitting in front of the State Theater playing Leadbelly tunes on a big, old Gibson guitar.

A LINCOLN Alvin Sackheim drove a big, yellow Lincoln.

THE NIGHT SURF The surf at Anson Beach. It could have been halfway to England the night before.

PENNANTS The snack bar at Anson Beach sold sweatshirts that said "Anson Beach," as well as plastic vomit advertised as "So Realistic!" They recommended that you "Try it on your wife!" They also sold pennants that said "Souvenir of Anson Beach and Park."

PERRY COMO AND JOHNNY RAY RECORDS The backwoods deejay on WKDM played Como and Ray records.

PLASTIC VOMIT The snack bar at Anson Beach sold sweatshirts that said "Anson Beach," as well as plastic vomit advertised as "So Realistic!" They recommended that you "Try it on your wife!" They also sold pennants that said "Souvenir of Anson Beach and Park."

PSALMS The backwoods deejay on WKDM who had gone nutty-religious read from *Psalms*.

SWEATSHIRTS The snack bar at Anson Beach sold sweatshirts that said "Anson Beach," as well as plastic vomit advertised as "So Realistic!" They recommended that you "Try it on your wife!" They also sold pennants that said "Souvenir of Anson Beach and Park."

"TRY OUR CLAM CAKE SPECIAL!" Sign at the snack bar at Anson Beach.

WAG One of the two surviving radio stations (either WKRO or WBZ in Massachusetts), manned by a bunch of kids who used gag call letters like WDOPE, KUNT, or WAG.

WBZ The call letters of one of the two surviving radio stations. It was in Massachusetts.

WDOPE One of the two surviving radio stations (either WKRO or WBZ in Massachusetts), manned by a bunch of kids who used gag

call letters like WDOPE, KUNT, or WAG.

WKDM Radio station in Portsmouth. It was one of the two radio stations left on the air after A6. Some backwoods deejay at WKDM had gone nutty-religious and played Perry Como and Johnny Ray records, and read from *Psalms* ("complete with each 'selah,' just like James Dean in 'East of Eden'…"), and even sang "Bringin' In the Sheaves."

WRKO The call letters of one of the two surviving radio stations. It was in Massachusetts.

ZIPPO Needles's lighter. He lit Alvin Sackheim's pyre with it.

❖❖❖

(5d)
NIGHT SHIFT
"I Am the Doorway"
People

ANDERS Astronaut who orbited the moon in 1968.

ARTHUR The narrator of "I Am the Doorway." He killed a boy after he was taken over by the aliens. As he put it, "I am the doorway, can't you understand that?"

ARTHUR'S AUNT She had died of Hansen's disease (leprosy).

BALLANGER, DR. The doctor on call for Dr. Flanders.

BORMAN Astronaut who orbited the moon in 1968.

THE BOY Unnamed boy who was killed and buried by Arthur.

CORY Arthur's crewmate.

CRESWELL Navy Department investigator. He checked on Arthur once a year.

DAVIS, JOHN His little orbiting observatory was holed by a meteor – a 1 in 1,000 fluke.

FLANDERS, DR. Arthur's doctor on the mainland.

"THE GHOST OF HOWDY DOODY" Arthur felt that just finding Howdy's ghost with Project Zeus would justify the mission.

HARRINGTON, MAUD Richard checked with her regarding the missing boy.

JACKS He landed on Mars in 1978.

LEDERER When nothing worked on the second-to-last Apollo flight, he ended up eternally circling the sun.

LOVELL Astronaut who orbited the moon in 1968.

LOVINGER, DON Project Zeus's whiz kid.

MARKHAN He landed on Mars in 1979.

PEDERSEN When nothing worked on the second-to-last Apollo flight, he ended up eternally circling the sun.

RICHARD A friend of Arthur's; Arthur told him his story.

(5d)
NIGHT SHIFT
"I Am the Doorway"
Places

BETHESDA Arthur spent two years there.

THE BIG DUNE It ran almost the whole length of Key Caroline.

CAPE KENNEDY Launch site.

FORT LAUDERDALE Arthur theorized that the aliens could have entered him there.

THE GULF Arthur and Richard sat on a porch looking over dunes towards the gulf.

HUNTSVILLE CONTROL They handled communications with Cory and Arthur.

JUPITER, SATURN, AND URANUS The DESA was used to broadcast to these planets.

KEY CAROLINE Where Richard lived.

MIAMI Miami was where the "Invasion of Arthur" began.

VENUS Cory and Arthur's destination, and the source of the invaders. According to Arthur, "It was like circling a haunted house in the middle of deep space."

181

(5d)
NIGHT SHIFT
"I Am the Doorway"
Things

THE AIR MOISTURE CONVERTER Cory and Arthur lost it on the third day of their Project Zeus mission.

ARTHUR'S PENSION According to Arthur, it was "large enough to be almost embarassing."

DESA The Deep Space Antenna. Cory went outside nine days into the flight to fix it.

DRIFTWOOD SCULPTURES Richard made them and sold them at "shameless" prices.

DUNE BUGGY Richard's. A 1959 VW with pillow-sized tires.

EYES Arthur told Richard that "there were eyes peering up at me through splits in the flesh of my fingers."

FORD Arthur's car. It had a hand-operated brake and accelerator.

HOOKS After Arthur burned his hands, he had hooks on the ends of his arms.

KEROSENE Arthur drenched his hands with kerosene and lit them up.

LIGHTNING Richard was killed by lightning that had been summoned by the aliens.

MEDAL OF HONOR Arthur received the medal for his ordeal in space.

THE *NIGHT SHIFT* COVER The cover of the paperback is the scene detailed in the entry EYES in this section.

A PENCIL Arthur poked out one of the eyes in his hands with a pencil. It had hurt.

PI 3.14159. What the DESA broadcast.

THE PORTLAND The ship that picked up Arthur.

PROJECT ZEUS Arthur and Cory's mission to find something out there.

A REAL ESTATE BUSINESS IN MARYLAND Richard had retired from it.

SATURN 16 The "Empire State Building" booster – Cory's spacecraft.

SHOTGUN Arthur planned to shoot himself with a shotgun because "There is a perfect circle of twelve golden eyes on my chest."

WAGNER AND BEATLES TAPES Cory and Arthur listened to them while in orbit.

WEST VIRGINIA RADIO TELESCOPE It listened to the stars.

❖❖❖

(5e)
NIGHT SHIFT
"The Mangler"
People

CHERINIKOU, MRS. The woman in the bed next to Annette Gillian in City Receiving Hospital.

DIMENT, HERB The Blue Ribbon laundry's repairman.

THE DUMP CARETAKER The man who found six dead birds in the refrigerator-man's empty refrigerator.

ESSIE A Blue Ribbon laundry worker. She got her dress caught in the Mangler's drive chain during Adelle Frawley's accident.

FRAWLEY, ADELLE The first victim of the Mangler at the Blue Ribbon laundry.

GARTLEY, BILL The owner of the Blue Ribbon laundry.

GILLIAN, ANDY Annette Gillian's son.

GILLIAN, ANNETTE A Blue Ribbon laundry worker. She testified at the inquest investigating Adelle Frawley's death. She had tried to pull Adelle out of the machine.

HUNTON, OFFICER JOHN The cop who initially reported the slaughter at the Blue Ribbon laundry.

HUNTON, PATTY Sandra and John Huntons' three-year-old daughter.

HUNTON, SANDRA John Hunton's wife.

JACKSON, MARK College professor friend of Officer John Hunton.

JASON, GINNY She, too, was burned in the accident at the Blue Ribbon laundry.

KEENE, ALBERTA A Blue Ribbon laundry worker. She had tried to turn off the Mangler after Adelle Frawley got caught.

MARTIN, MRS. Roger's wife.

MARTIN, ROGER One of the state inspectors that checked out the Mangler after Adelle Frawley's death.

OUELETTE, SHERRY A Blue Ribbon laundry worker. She cut her hands on a clamp and bled into the Mangler. She was "saving herself for [her] husband," and thus provided the virgin's blood that helped to summon the demon that ultimately possessed the Mangler.

THE REFRIGERATOR BIRDS Six dead birds were found in the empty refrigerator at the dump by the dump caretaker.

THE REFRIGERATOR BOY Unnamed boy who was found dead in a refrigerator put out by a man in Milton. The refrigerator had been moved to the dump, and that was where the boy was found.

THE REFRIGERATOR BOY'S MOTHER The woman who reported her son missing. He was found in a refrigerator at the dump.

THE REFRIGERATOR DOG A dog was found dead in a refrigerator put out by a man in Milton.

THE REFRIGERATOR MAN The Milton man who put out an empty refrigerator that later killed a dog, a boy, and six birds. It was assumed the refrigerator was possessed.

SIX STATE INSPECTORS Six inspectors checked out the Mangler after Adelle Frawley's death.

STANNER, GEORGE The Blue Ribbon laundry foreman. He lost an arm to the Mangler.

THE STATE COP The cop who told the refrigerator man in Milton to bring his empty refrigerator to the dump.

(5e)
NIGHT SHIFT
"The Mangler"
Places

BLUE RIBBON LAUNDRY The home of the Mangler.

CITY RECEIVING HOSPITAL The hospital where Annette Gillian was brought with second-degree burns after trying to pull Adelle Frawley out of the Mangler.

THE DUMP The place where the refrigerator man brought his empty refrigerator.

MILTON The town where a man put out an empty refrigerator, and later a dog, a boy, and six birds were all found dead in the box.

PLEASANT HILL CEMETERY The nearest cemetery to the Blue Ribbon laundry. It was five miles away.

(5e)
NIGHT SHIFT
"The Mangler"
Things

AN ARM George Stanner lost an arm in the Mangler.

"DEATH BY MISADVENTURE" The official ruling on Adelle Frawley's death.

E-Z GEL TABLETS They cost seventy-nine cents. Adelle Frawley dropped a whole box into the Mangler. E-Z Gel used a chemical derivative of belladonna. This contributed to the elements necessary for summoning the demon that eventually possessed the Mangler.

ELEMENTS FOR CALLING DEMONS Mark Jackson learned

that the following elements were commonly used to summon demons:

blood of a virgin,
graveyard dirt,
hand of glory (belladonna),
bat's blood,
night moss,
horse's hoof,
eye of toad.

Enough of these elements were present to call the demon that eventually possessed the Mangler. (Sherry Ouelette's blood fulfilled the blood of a virgin requirement; E-Z Gel tablets used a derivative of belladonna.)

HADLEY-WATSON MODEL-6 SPEED IRONER AND FOLDER The Mangler.

HOLY WATER, *THE BIBLE*, AND THE HOST The weapons Hunton and Jackson decided to use to fight the demon in the Mangler.

JIM BEAM Hunton drank two ounces of Jim Beam after the Mangler ripped itself up out of the concrete floor and escaped the laundry.

THE MANGLER A Hadley-Watson Model-6 Speed Ironer and Folder. A conscious, malevolent shirt-folding machine that lived at the Blue Ribbon laundry.

MILTON'S COLLECTED WORKS A book read by Mark Jackson.

THE REFRIGERATOR A seemingly possessed refrigerator that killed a dog, a boy, and six birds. [NOTE: This refrigerator foreshadowed King's use of the "refrigerator in the dump" sequence in *It*. See the concordance for *It* in this volume.]

SCREEN SECRETS The magazine Annette Gillian read while in the hospital.

SECOND DEGREE BURNS Annette Gillian received second-degree burns trying to pull Adelle Frawley out of the Mangler.

THE STATE BOARD OF SAFETY They shut down the Mangler.

❖❖❖

(5f)
NIGHT SHIFT
"The Boogeyman"
People

"A BACK-COUNTRY FUCKHEAD DOCTOR" The doctor who ruled that Denny Billings' demise was crib death. Lester said the doctor had a black bag full of Junior Mints, and a sheepskin from some cow college.

BILLINGS, ANDY (ANDREW LESTER) Lester's son. He was born in the summer of 1969 (an unplanned accident), and he died in February 1973.

BILLINGS, DENNY Lester's son. He died in 1967.

BILLINGS, LESTER Twenty-eight-year-old divorced father of three from Waterbury, Connecticut, who went to see Dr. Harper with a bizarre story: His three children were all dead, and the Boogeyman in the closet had killed them. Lester worked for an industrial firm in New York.

BILLINGS, RITA Lester's wife. He married her in 1965. He was twenty-one, she was eighteen and pregnant with Denny.

BILLINGS, SHIRLEY Lester's daughter. She was born in December of 1966, and she died in 1971.

THE BOOGEYMAN He lived in the closet and he killed Lester's kids.

A GOOD WOMAN When Rita went home to help after her mother's car accident, a "good woman" stayed and helped Lester with the kids.

GRAMMY ANN Shirley Billings looked like Lester's Grammy Ann.

HARPER, DR. Lester Billings' psychiatrist. [NOTE: At least we think he is, until the end of the story when we find out that Dr. Harper is, in fact, the Boogeyman.]

INGLES, GRAHAM *Tales from the Crypt* artist. He could draw the most awful things.

RITA'S FATHER Rita's father called Rita to tell her that her mother had been in a car accident. Rita went home to help.

RITA'S GYNECOLOGIST The unnamed doctor who fitted Rita with an IUD.

RITA'S MOTHER Rita's father called Rita to tell her that her mother had been in a car accident. Rita went home to help.

VICKERS, NURSE Dr. Harper's nurse. She took Lester Billings' history.

(5f)
NIGHT SHIFT
"The Boogeyman"
Places

ALL-NIGHT DINER When Andy died, Lester went to an all-night diner.

CLUETT AND SONS Before Andy died, Lester was selling drill bits for Cluett and Sons.

DR. HARPER'S CLOSET During his session with the psychiatrist, Lester made Dr. Harper open the closet door and show the inside to him. The closet contained a tan raincoat and galoshes. The raincoat had a New York *Times* in the pocket. When Lester went back into the office after his session was over, the Boogeyman was in the closet, holding his Dr. Harper mask.

HARTFORD RECEIVING HOSPITAL The hospital that did the autopsy on Shirley Billings. They ruled that a brain convulsion was the cause of her death.

SAVIN ROCK, WEST HAVEN, CONNECTICUT Legendary Connecticut amusement park that was torn down. Condos were built on its site. Lester had once taken his kids there. [N OTE: I, like Steve King, also went to Savin Rock as a kid, and can vividly remember the "laughing lady," the bumper cars, and food stands everywhere. Even though I now know that where Savin Rock stood was all of ten minutes away from where we lived, it seemed like a great journey when we were kids. Everyone in the New Haven area remembers Savin Rock.]

THE SEWERS It seems as though the Boogeyman was a cousin of "It": Lester thought that "It had to hunt around, slinking through the streets at night and maybe creeping in the sewers."

"SOME COW COLLEGE" Lester said that the doctor who ruled Denny Billings' demise as crib death had a black bag full of Junior Mints and a sheepskin from some cow college.

A WAREHOUSE The summer Denny died, Lester had a job loading Pepsi trucks in a warehouse.

WATERBURY, CONNECTICUT The town where Lester Billings (and the Boogeyman) lived.

(5f)
NIGHT SHIFT
"The Boogeyman"
Things

"A BLACK BAG FULL OF JUNIOR MINTS" Lester said that the doctor who ruled that Denny Billings' demise was crib death had a black bag full of Junior Mints, and a sheepskin from some cow college.

A BRAIN CONVULSION Hartford Receiving Hospital did the autopsy on Shirley Billings. They ruled a brain convulsion was the cause of her death.

CRIB DEATH A doctor ruled that Denny Billings' demise was crib death. Lester said the doctor had a black bag full of Junior Mints, and a sheepskin from some cow college.

DECEMBER 1966 The month and year Shirley Billings was born.

DR. HARPER MASK When Lester returned to Dr. Harper's office after his first visit, the Boogeyman was in Harper's closet. holding his Dr. Harper mask.

DRILL BITS Before Andy died, Lester was selling drill bits for Cluett and Sons.

EIGHTEEN Rita's age when she married Lester.

FEBRUARY 1973 The month and year Lester's son Andy died. [NOTE: Stephen King has often said that he thinks he's going to die in February. He has said that all the most terrible things in his life happen to him in February.]

"IT GETS REAL." Lester "started to think, maybe if you think of a thing long enough, and believe in it, it gets real."

A NEW YORK *TIMES* There was a New York *Times* in the pocket of the raincoat in Dr. Harper's closet.

1971 The year Lester's daughter Shirley died.

1965 The year Lester and Rita were married.

1967 The year Lester's son Denny died.

PEPSI-COLA TRUCKS The summer Denny died, Lester loaded Pepsi trucks in a warehouse.

SUMMER 1969 Andy Billings was born in the summer of 1969. He was an unplanned accident.

TALES FROM THE CRYPT Lester told Dr. Harper that he had dreams that reminded him of *Tales from the Crypt*.

A TAN RAINCOAT AND GALOSHES When Lester first looked into Dr. Harper's closet, all he saw was a tan raincoat (with a New York *Times* in the pocket) and a pair of galoshes.

TUESDAYS AND THURSDAYS After hearing Lester's story about the Boogeyman in the closet, Dr. Harper told him to make appointments for every Tuesday and Thursday.

TWENTY-EIGHT Lester Billings' age when he went to see Dr. Harper.

TWENTY-ONE Lester's age when he married Rita.

❖❖❖

(5g)
NIGHT SHIFT
"Gray Matter"
People

BLIND EDDIE Seventy-year-old man who used to steal a loaf of bread every week from Henry's Nite-Owl. Eddie was nearly blind. Henry Parmalee and Eddie had a bet on a bill sponsoring an airplane. The airplane didn't fly and, since Eddie had voted against the woman who sponsored the bill, Henry lost the bet and had been buying Eddie's bread ever since.

CONNORS, BERTIE One of the guys in Henry's Nite-Owl during the blizzard.

GAITEAU Richie Grenadine's landlord.

GRENADINE, RICHIE Timmy's father. He had worked at a sawmill in Clifton when he hurt his back and ended up on compensation. The last time he had been seen by anyone in town was at the end of October, when he had stopped by Henry's Nite-Owl to buy a case of Schlitz.

GRENADINE, TIMMY Richie Grenadine's kid. Timmy came looking for help when his father started getting weird.

HALDEMAN, FRANKIE George Kelso's friend.

KELSO, GEORGE Man who worked for the Bangor public works department. He went into a sewer once on Essex Street and came out with white hair. He had seen a spider the size of a dog with a web full of kittens.

LITTLEFIELD, CARL One of the guys in Henry's Nite-Owl during the blizzard.

THE NARRATOR Unnamed character who tells the reader of "Gray Matter" of the trip to Richie Grenadine's place during the mid-January Bangor, Maine, blizzard.

PARMALEE, HENRY Owner of Henry's Nite-Owl. He went on the "seek & destroy" mission to Richie Grenadine's place.

PARMALEE, MRS. Henry's wife.

PELHAM, BILL One of the guys in Henry's Nite-Owl during the blizzard.

REX The narrator's dog. It had gotten hit by a car, and then crawled under a porch and died.

A SALESMAN FROM MONTPELIER The guy who lost a twenty-dollar beer-drinking bet to Richie Grenadine. Richie bet that he (Richie) could drink twenty two-bit glasses of beer in one minute, and won by downing them in fifty-three seconds.

A SALVATION ARMY WINO Man who had disappeared. Richie had eaten him, along with two young girls.

TWO YOUNG GIRLS They had disappeared. Richie had eaten them, along with a Salvation Army wino.

WESTPHAIL, DR. The Grenadine's doctor. Richie wouldn't let Timmy call him.

THE WOMAN The woman who sponsored a bill for an airplane that ended up being unable to fly.

(5g)
NIGHT SHIFT
"Gray Matter"
Places

CURVE STREET The street where Richie and Timmy Grenadine lived.

HARLOW AND CURVE STREET The intersection where Henry paused on his way to Richie Grenadine's house.

HENRY'S NITE-OWL Store on Ohio Street owned by Henry Parmalee. Timmy Grenadine came to the store when his father, Richie, started to get weird.

LEVANT A town where the narrator had once lived.

OHIO STREET The street on which Henry's Nite-Owl was located.

A VICTORIAN MANSION Richie Grenadine lived on the third floor. The rest of the house was empty.

WALLY'S SPA Bar where Richie once bet twenty dollars on how much beer he could drink. He bet a salesman from Montpelier that he could drink twenty two-bit glasses of beer in one minute. Richie won, drinking them down in fifty-three seconds.

(5g)
NIGHT SHIFT
"Gray Matter"
Things

A DEAD CAT After Richie started to change, he hid a dead cat covered with maggots in order to have it available for lunch.

A .45 CALIBER HOGLEG Henry's gun. He took it with him when he went to Richie's.

GOLDEN LIGHT The can of bad beer that started Richie Grenadine on the road to changing into a giant amoeba was in a case of Golden Light.

HARROW'S SUPREME The case of beer that Henry brought to Richie during the blizzard.

THE MULTIPLICATION TABLE The narrator thought of the multiplication table after he saw that Richie was dividing. He was up to "32,768 times two is the end of the human race" while they were waiting to see who would return from Richie's house: Henry or Richie. As the narrator put it, "I hope it's Henry. I surely do."

1958 The year Henry went to twenty-four-hours a day with the Nite-Owl.

ORANGE CRUSH THERMOMETER It hung outside Henry's Nite-Owl.

THE PLANE A woman had sponsored a bill for an airplane. (Blind Eddie and Henry Parmalee had a bet on the bill.) The plane wouldn't fly and Henry lost the bet.

RELIABLE The stove in Henry's Nite-Owl.

THE SPIDER George Kelso went into a sewer on Essex Street and saw a spider the size of a dog with a web full of kittens. He quit the job. [NOTE: This story seems to foreshadow *It* by using two key images King uses in his later novel: the sewers and the giant spider.]

TWENTY TWO-BIT GLASSES OF BEER Richie Grenadine drank them down in fifty-three seconds to win a twenty-dollar bet with a salesman from Montpelier.

❖❖❖

(5h)
NIGHT SHIFT
"Battleground"
People

BATES, CALVIN The man who called Renshaw with the Morris job.

THE DESK CLERK The man who told Renshaw there was a package for him.

THE GIRL Unnamed girl with Ralph who saw the flash of the nuclear weapon the soldiers used on Renshaw. She was not supposed to be with Ralph.

MORRIS, HANS Founder and owner of the Morris Toy Company. He was Renshaw's "hit."

MORRIS, MRS. Hans Morris's mother. She sent Renshaw the G.I. Joe Vietnam Footlocker loaded with tiny live soldiers and tiny real weapons. Hans had had a picture of Mrs. Morris on his desk that was signed "Best from your number-one idea girl—Mom."

RALPH Man on the street below the hotel who saw the flash of the nuclear weapon the soldiers used on Renshaw. He was with a girl he was not supposed to be with.

RENSHAW, JOHN Killer. He did the Hans Morris job for the Organization, and was then "hit" by Mrs. Morris via the use of tiny, living toy soldiers.

THE SOLDIERS Twenty tiny, living toy soldiers sent to exact revenge for Renshaw's "hit" on Hans Morris.

(5h)
NIGHT SHIFT
"Battleground"
Places

THE HOTEL The unnamed hotel where Renshaw waged his (losing) battle against the soldiers in the G.I. Joe Vietnam Footlocker.

MIAMI The package from Mrs. Morris to Renshaw was postmarked from Miami, April 15.

RENSHAW'S ROOM The hotel room where Renshaw tried to fight off (unsuccessfully) the tiny soldiers and their tiny weapons that had been sent to him by Mrs. Morris after Renshaw killed her son, Hans.

THE STREET Ralph and the girl saw the nuclear weapon flash from Renshaw's room while passing the hotel on the street below.

(5h)
NIGHT SHIFT
"Battleground"
Things

APRIL 15 The postmark on the package sent to Renshaw by Mrs. Morris was from Miami, April 15.

FINDER'S FEE The Organization took a fifteen percent finder's fee from John Renshaw on the Hans Morris hit.

.44 MAGNUM Renshaw's gun.

THE G.I. JOE VIETNAM FOOTLOCKER Mrs. Morris sent Renshaw a package containing the footlocker. Its contents (which

were stencilled on the front) were:

20 infantrymen;
10 helicopters;
2 BAR men;
2 bazooka men;
2 medics;
4 jeeps;
1 rocket launcher;
20 surface-to-air "Twister" missiles;
1 scale-model thermonuclear weapon.

(The rocket launcher, "Twister" missiles, and nuclear weapon were not listed on the front of the locker.)

GIN AND TONIC Renshaw's drink.

MORRIS TOY COMPANY Company founded and owned by Hans Morris, John Renshaw's "hit."

MRS. MORRIS'S PICTURE Hans Morris had had a picture of his mother on his desk. It was signed "Best from your number-one idea girl–Mom."

THE NOTE After the nuclear weapon killed Renshaw, a note fluttered down to the sidewalk. It said "Hey, Kids! Special in this Vietnam Footlocker! 1 Rocket Launcher; 20 Surface-to-Air 'Twister' Missiles, 1 Scale-Model Thermonuclear Weapon."

THE PACKAGE The desk clerk at the hotel told Renshaw that there was a package from Miami for him. The hotel was where Renshaw stayed after the Morris "hit."

RENSHAW'S REPLY TO THE SOLDIERS' NOTE "Nuts."

RENSHAW'S MINIMUM FEE It was $10,000 a hit.

THE SOLDIERS' NOTE The tiny living soldiers sent Renshaw a note that said: "Surrender." Renshaw's reply was "Nuts."

❖❖❖

(5i)
NIGHT SHIFT
"Trucks"
People

THE CADILLAC'S OWNER Unnamed dead guy behind the wheel of a Cadillac in the truck stop's parking lot.

CONANT The owner of the truck stop.

FOGARTY, JOHN Member of Creedence Clearwater Revival. Jerry played Fogarty's "Born on the Bayou" in the truck stop.

THE GIRL IN THE PINK DRESS Girl who bolted from the Cadillac that was parked in the truck stop parking lot.

JERRY Kid who skidded into the truck stop parking lot in an old Fury.

THE NARRATOR The unnamed storyteller who narrated the events at the truck stop after the trucks took over.

THE SHORT ORDER COOK Black truck stop cook. He tried the radio after the trucks took over.

SNODGRASS A salesman who was trapped in the truck stop.

THE TRUCK DRIVER An unnamed driver who sat at the counter in the truck stop.

(5i)
NIGHT SHIFT
"Trucks"
Places

CONANT'S TRUCK STOP & DINER The truck stop where everyone was trapped.

THE MENS' AND LADIES' ROOMS Jerry and the narrator went to the restrooms to get water from the toilet tanks. A Peterbilt truck snuck up on them.

PELSON The town Jerry was headed for when he skidded into the truck stop's parking lot.

(5i)
NIGHT SHIFT
"Trucks"
Things

"ATTENTION" When the trucks wanted gas, they blew "Attention" in morse code with their horns.

"BORN ON THE BAYOU" Song by John Fogerty that Jerry played on the jukebox in the truck stop.

CADILLAC One of the cars parked in the truck stop's lot. The dead owner of the car was still behind the wheel.

CHEVY LIGHT PICKUP It joined the parade of trucks in the truck stop parking lot.

"CONANT'S TRUCK STOP & DINER—GOOD EATS" Conant's sign.

FIREBOMBS The people in the truck stop threw Molotov cocktail firebombs into a bulldozer. Jerry was killed.

FORD STATION WAGON The car that slammed through the guardrails on the highway across the road from the truck stop.

GREYHOUND BUS It plowed through cars.

THE MESSAGE The trucks sent the following message to the people in the truck stop by blowing morse code on their horns: "Someone must pump fuel. Someone will not be harmed. All fuel must be pumped. This shall be done now. Now someone will pump fuel."

1971 CAMARO The narrator's car.

A PETERBILT TRUCK The truck that snuck up on Jerry and the narrator while they were taking water from the restroom toilet tanks.

A TANKER A tanker came to fill up the empty gas tanks at the truck stop. The side of the truck read "Fill Up with Phillips 66—The Jetport Fuel."

THE TRUCK STOP'S SUPPLIES They had two or three hundred hamburger patties, canned fruit and vegetables, dry cereal, eggs, milk, and well water.

TWO MACKS, A HEMINGWAY, AND FOUR OR FIVE REOS The vehicles in the truck stop's parking lot.

TWO PLANES The narrator saw two planes flying over the truck stop. He thought to himself "I wish I could believe there are people in them."

VICEROY The trucker broke into the truck stop's cigarette machine and took six or eight packs of Viceroy.

VW BEETLE Jerry saw a truck flip a VW off the road.

WESTCLOX The clock in the truck stop.

WONG'S CASH-AND-CARRY LAUNDRY TRUCK A small panel truck. The truckdriver was run down by the Wong's truck.

❖❖❖

(5j)
NIGHT SHIFT
"Sometimes They Come Back"
People

"ANOTHER GUY" Unnamed teacher Jim traded with so as to finish practice teaching at Cortez High.

THE COP Unnamed officer who pulled Jim over while Jim was on his way to the hospital to see his wife.

COREY, MRS. Vinnie Corey's mother. She alibied him for Wayne Norman's murder.

COREY, VINCENT Vinnie the Viper. Tall kid with a blond crewcut and a broken nose. He carried a switchblade and was one of the kids who participated in the murder of Wayne Norman. He came back from the dead and became one of Jim's new students.

DENKINGER, GARY Chip Osway's stepfather.

FENTON, PRINCIPAL The principal of Harold Davis High School.

GARCIA, DAVID A fat guy with greasy black hair and a jittery eyelid. He was one of the kids who participated in the murder of Wayne Norman. He came back from the dead and became one of Jim's new students. He also worked part-time as an orderly at a hospital. He was present the night Jim's wife died.

LAWSON, ROBERT Guy in black chinos who had a strawberry birthmark. He carried a switchblade and participated in the murder of Wayne Norman. He came back from the dead and became one of Jim's new students.

LIVINGSTON, SERGEANT MORTON The cop who gave Jim Officer Nell's home phone number.

THE LOCAL GIRL Girl that Bleach got pregnant. Bleach ended up a career army man.

NELL, OFFICER DON The Stratford cop who investigated Wayne Norman's murder. [NOTE: It's obvious that Mr. Nell got tired of Stratford and decided to move to Maine, inasmuch as he also appears in King's masterpiece *IT*. In *IT*, Officer Nell discovered the dam in the barrens designed by Ben and built by the Losers.]

NORMAN, JIM Teacher whose brother was killed in 1957. The killers came back to haunt Jim, and Jim summoned the spirit of his dead brother to fight them off.

NORMAN, MRS. Jim's mother. She had died of cancer the summer before Jim got the job at Harold Davis High School.

NORMAN, SALLY Jim's wife. She was killed by the three guys who had also killed Jim's brother Wayne.

NORMAN, WAYNE Jim's brother. He was killed by Vincent Corey, David Garcia, and Robert Lawson. When the three came back to haunt Jim, Jim summoned the spirit of his brother.

THE NURSE Unnamed nurse who had her cap on crooked. She was at the hospital when Jim's wife died.

OSWAY, BARRY Chip's father. He had been dead six years.

OSWAY, CHIP (CHARLES) One of Jim's "Living with Literature" remedial students. Jim caught him with a crib sheet and threw him out of class. Chip threatened to "get" Jim.

THE REGISTRATION SECRETARY Unnamed secretary who gave Jim Norman the Osway residence phone number.

SALLY'S FATHER Jim's father-in-law. He was at Sally's funeral.

SALLY'S MOTHER Jim's mother-in-law. She was at Sally's funeral.

SALLY'S SISTER Jim and Sally visited her in Vermont over the Christmas vacation.

SILVERSTEIN, PINKY Jim had once lost sixteen dollars at a poker game at Pinky's.

SIMMONS, MR. The head of the English Department at Harold Davis High School.

SIMON, OFFICER FRANK The cop who chased three of the hoods who killed Wayne Norman; they died in a car crash six months after Wayne's murder. Supposedly, of the four, only Sponder was still alive at the time that Jim was teaching at Harold Davis High.

SLAVIN, KATHY One of Jim Norman's students. She either fell or was pushed off the roof of her apartment building. Robert Lawson told Chip Osway that he thought she had "nice tits." [NOTE: See the entry "TEEN-AGE GIRL FALLS TO HER DEATH."]

SNOW, DIANNE Fictitious student Jim invented. According to Jim's story, Dianne was the victim of a rape attempt on Summer Street. He made up the story to convince his wife to take a cab home instead of walking.

SPONDER, CHARLIE "Bleach." A guy with bleached orange hair. He was one of the kids who participated in the murder of Wayne Norman. He ended up a career army man after getting a local girl pregnant.

SPONDER, MRS. Charlie's mother. She lived in Stratford.

STEARNS, BILL (WILLIAM) Harold Davis High School student. His activities included Key Club 1, Football 1, 2, and Pen á Lance 2, and got consistent A's and B's. He was killed in a car accident on Rampart Street. He was hit by a Ford sedan with "Snake Eyes" written on its side.

THE SUPERVISOR/CRITIC TEACHER Jim's unnamed superior at Cortez High. He gave Jim all A's.

THE THREE KIDS Unnamed kids who held Mack Zimmerman and smashed his guitar.

"THE UNIDENTIFIED WOMAN" The woman who saw three boys running across the roof of Kathy Slavin's apartment building.

THE YOUNG DOCTOR Unnamed physician who told Jim that his wife was dead.

ZIMMERMAN, MACK One of Jim's former students. He was a sensitive kid who played the guitar. Once, three kids held Mack and smashed his guitar.

(5j)
NIGHT SHIFT
"Sometimes They Come Back"
Places

ASH HEIGHTS ROAD Road in Stratford where the Milford Cemetery was located.

BARNUM AVENUE The Stratford, Connecticut, street where Officer Nell lived.

BURRETT'S BUILDING COMPANY Business in Stratford, Connecticut. Jim and Wayne passed it on their way to the Stratford library.

CENTER STREET VOCATIONAL TRADES HIGH SCHOOL The school where Jim Norman interned.

CORTEZ HIGH SCHOOL School where Jim finished his practice teaching after his stint at Center Street Vocational Trades.

DAVIS STREET The street on which Harold Davis High was located.

GRANVILLE REFORMATORY In his new reincarnation, David Garcia had spent two years at Granville for car theft.

HAROLD DAVIS HIGH SCHOOL The school where Jim taught, and where the ghosts of the three creeps that killed his brother confronted him.

MILFORD CEMETERY Cemetery on Ash Heights Road in Stratford. It was where Corey, Lawson, and Garcia came from.

"MILFORD HIGH" The four creeps' "alma mater." There was no Milford High–the slime actually came from the Milford Cemetery on Ash Heights Road.

RAMPART STREET The street where Bill Stearns was hit by a Ford sedan and killed.

ROOM 33 Jim Norman's "Living with Literature" classroom.

THE SCIENCE WING The science wing at Harold Davis High had been funded at $1.5 million.

SIKORSKY The place where Officer Frank Simon was working when Jim was trying to track him down.

STRATFORD, CONNECTICUT The town where Jim and Wayne were living when Wayne was murdered.

THE STRATFORD DINER Jim and Wayne used to meet there every day to eat their bag lunches together.

THE STRATFORD LIBRARY Jim and Wayne were on their way to the library when Wayne was murdered.

SUMMER STREET The street where Jim's fictitious student "Dianne Snow" was supposedly the victim of a rape attempt.

TEDDY'S MARKET Business in Stratford, Connecticut. Jim and Wayne passed it on their way to the Stratford library.

VERMONT Sally Norman's sister lived in Vermont.

(5j)
NIGHT SHIFT
"Sometimes They Come Back"
Things

A'S While practice teaching at Cortez High, Jim got all A's from his supervisor/critic teacher.

APPLE PIE A LA MODE Officer Nell remembered buying apple pie á la mode for Jim and Wayne when they were kids.

BARNETT HUDSON PERSONALITY TEST The IQ test administered to Robert Lawson. The test revealed that his IQ was 78.

"THE CELEBRATION MEAL" After Jim got the job at Harold Davis High, he and his wife had their "celebration meal": two steaks, a bottle of Lancer's, a head of lettuce, and some thousand island dressing.

THE DREAM Jim would often dream of the day his brother was killed. Jim was nine, and Wayne was twelve. They were walking down Broad Street in Stratford, Connecticut, on their way to the Stratford library when they were confronted by the boys who would kill Wayne.

FOOTBALL 1, 2 One of Bill Stearns' school activities.

FORD SEDAN A black 1954 sedan that hit and killed Bill Stearns. The car had "Snake Eyes" written on its side.

HI-FI SOUND EFFECTS The record album Jim used for the sound of the freight train during the summoning ritual of his dead brother Wayne. The cut was called "Freight Train," and it ran three minutes and four seconds.

HIT AND RUN ACCIDENT Before Jim's breakdown, his fiancee (at the time), Sally, was the victim of a hit and run driver. As Jim put it, "She was the hit part of it."

INTRODUCTION TO GRAMMAR One of the texts Jim used.

JIM'S SCHEDULE AT HAROLD DAVIS HIGH SCHOOL

Period 1: Free
Period 2: Freshman Composition (dull)
Period 3: Freshman Composition (kind of fun)
Period 4: American Literature (the best; all college-bound seniors)
Period 5: Consultation Period (spent it reading)
Period 6: Grammar (dry as dust)
Period 7: Living with Literature (trouble)

KEY CLUB 1 One of Bill Stearns' school activities.

"LIVING WITH LITERATURE" The class Jim Norman had to teach for "slow learners." This was the class that the three kids who killed Jim's brother attended when they came back from the dead.

LORD OF THE FLIES Book Jim Norman taught at Harold Davis High.

"MALEFIC SPIRITS AND HOW TO CALL THEM" The chapter from *Raising Demons* that Jim referred to during the ritual in which he called on his dead brother Wayne for help against Corey and company.

1957 The year Wayne Norman was murdered.

PEN á LANCE One of Bill Stearns' school activities.

RAISING DEMONS Book Jim consulted to prepare for his confrontation with the four revenants who wanted to kill him.

78 Robert Lawson's IQ on the Barnett-Hudson personality test.

"SNAKE EYES" The Ford sedan that hit and killed Bill Stearns had "Snake Eyes" written on its side.

THE SUMMONING FORMULA INGREDIENTS To summon Wayne, Jim had to supply a photo, blood (he used blood from a stray cat), and sweat from Wayne's sweatband. He also offered his right and left index fingers, which he cut off himself.

SWITCHBLADES The knives carried by Vincent Cory and Robert Lawson. They used them to murder Wayne Norman.

"TEEN-AGE GIRL FALLS TO HER DEATH" The headline of the story about Kathy Slavin's death. The story read: "Katherine Slavin, a seventeen-year-old junior at Harold Davis High School, either fell or was pushed from the roof of her downtown apartment house early yesterday evening. The girl, who kept a pigeon coop on the roof, had gone up with a sack of feed, according to her mother. Police said an unidentified woman in a neighboring development had seen three young boys running across the roof at 6:45 P.M., just minutes after the girl's body (continued page

3)—" Kathy Slavin was one of Jim Norman's students.
3.88 Jim's four-year college average.
YAMAHA Mack Zimmerman's guitar was a Yamaha.

❖❖❖

(5k)
NIGHT SHIFT
"Strawberry Spring"
People

[The first version of "Strawberry Spring" appeared in the fall 1968 edition of *Ubris*, the University of Maine's student literary magazine. The story ran three double-columned, single-spaced pages, and King's long poem "Harrison State Park '68" appeared in the same issue. Both works carried the byline "Stephen King," instead of King's more informal "Steve King."

The most notable difference in the two versions is that the *Ubris* version took place in Maine, and that for the *Night Shift* revision (which originally appeared in *Cavalier* magazine in November of 1975), King turned the locale into a more general New England backdrop.

The *Ubris* version began "In New England they call it a strawberry spring–no-one knows why–and it happens once every fifteen years."

For the revised version, King added three paragraphs before he came to that line (which he changed to "In New England they call it a strawberry spring. No one knows why; it's just a phrase the old-timers use.")

The new text starts right off with an introduction to the murderer:

"Springheel Jack...
I saw those two words in the paper this morning and my God, how they take me back."

For this concordance, I have made note of the differences between the two versions by including parenthetical remarks in the specific entries where changes were made, and I have also included separate entries when King used a completely different person, place, or thing for the *Ubris* version. –**sjs**]

AMALARA, CARL Gail Cerman's ex-boyfriend. He was accused of Gail's murder. His roommate said that he had been despondent over his breakup with Gail. They found a seven-inch hunting knife from L.L. Bean and a picture of Gail cut up with scissors in his room. [NOTE: In the *Ubris* version, it was "Amalera" instead of "Amalara."]

AMALERA, CARL "Carl Amalara" in the *Ubris* version of the story.

BRAY, ANN Springheel Jack's second victim. After her murder, he took her head with him. Ann was the first runner-up in the Miss New England Pageant. [NOTE: In the *Ubris* version, it was the Miss Maine Pageant.] Her "talent" had been twirling a flaming baton to "Hey, Look Me Over." She had also been president of the National Service Sorority.

A CAMPUS COP An unnamed cop who found the unconscious Donald Morris and took him to the hospital. Morris had had the flu and fainted. [NOTE: In the *Ubris* version, it was a state trooper.]

CARL AMALARA'S ROOMMATE He told the police that Carl had been despondent over his breakup with Gail Cerman.

CASNER, PRESIDENT The president of New Sharon Teachers' College in the *Ubris* version.

CERMAN, GAIL Springheel Jack's first New Sharon Teachers' College victim. She had been an art major, and had lived in Judith Franklin Hall. Everyone knew her, or so it seemed, but rumors were the rule, and everything said about her contradicted every-

thing else. She had a good figure. [NOTE: In the *Ubris* version, she "had a small bust" instead of a "good figure."]

CURRAN, MARSHA Springheel Jack's fourth New Sharon victim. She had been "fat," and "sadly pretty." She had lived in an apartment in town.

DANCEY, JOHN A junior at New Sharon Teachers' College. He was an education major and a speech minor. He discovered Gale Cerman's body at 11:10 P.M. He found her in a corner of the animal sciences parking lot. Her throat had been cut.

FRODO Hobbit, and the savior of Middle-Earth. He lost his finger over a fight for the One Ring. During the March 1968 strawberry spring, people stepped out of the "juke-thumping, brightly lit confusion of the Grinder" into a "silent, muffled world of white, drifting fog. You half expected to see Gollum or Frodo and Sam go hurrying past." [NOTE: For those of you not familiar with J.R.R. Tolkien's *Lord of the Rings* trilogy (and its prequel *The Hobbit*), get up, put on your shoes, and go out and buy a complete set of the four volumes right now. Then bring them home and read them. I have read *LOTR* over a dozen times since I first discovered it in the late sixties, and I consider it one of the most magnificent masterworks of imaginative fiction ever written. And after I finish writing *The Shape Under the Sheet,* I'm going to re-read it again.]

A GIRL In 1971, a girl was found murdered at New Sharon Teachers' College. She was "not all there." The narrator's wife was upset and wanted to know where he was the night before. He was afraid to open his trunk.

GOLLUM Bad guy and servant of Mordor. He lusted after the One Ring and was doomed for it. During the March 1968 strawberry spring, people stepped out of the "juke-thumping, brightly lit confusion of the Grinder" into a "silent, muffled world of white, drifting fog." "You half expected to see Gollum or Frodo and Sam go hurrying past." [NOTE: See the FRODO entry above.]

GRAY, HANSON The homosexual sociology graduate student who was arrested for the murder of Adelle Parkins. After he was released, he went back to New Hampshire. [NOTE: In the *Ubris* version, he was a history grad student.]

HAWKINS, DR. JOHN A reporter christened the New Sharon murderer "Springheel Jack." He named him after Dr. John Hawkins of Bristol, who did away with five of his wives with "pharmaceutical knickknacks." [NOTE: In the *Ubris* version, it was London.]

McCORRISON, DONALD "Donald Morris" in the *Ubris* version.

MORRIS, DONALD New Sharon student who was found unconscious by a campus cop. He had had the flu and fainted. [NOTE: In the *Ubris* version, it was Donald McCorrison.]

THE NARRATOR'S FATHER During the Springheel Jack scare, the narrator's father called him at school all "bluff and hearty and man-to-man."

THE NARRATOR'S MOTHER She wanted her son to come home during the Springheel Jack scare at New Sharon Teachers' College.

THE NARRATOR'S ROOMMATE He told the narrator that the cops had picked up Carl Amalara, Gail Cerman's ex-boyfriend, for Gail's murder. At one point, the roommate said to the narrator, "I suspect everyone but me and thee, and sometimes I wonder about thee." He was, of course, intuitively right, since the narrator (his roommate) *was* Springheel Jack.

THE NARRATOR'S ROOMMATE'S GRANDMOTHER She used to say that a strawberry spring meant that the worst norther of all was on its way.

THE NARRATOR'S SON In 1971, the narrator and his wife had a son: he had "[his] eyes," and "her mouth."

THE NARRATOR'S WIFE In 1971, a girl was found murdered at New Sharon Teachers' College. She was "not all there." The narrator's wife was upset and wanted to know where he was the night before. He was afraid to open his trunk.

THE NECKING COUPLE After the nine o'clock evening curfew was imposed at New Sharon, a couple was found necking after nine in the bushes north of the Tate Alumni Building.

A NEW HAMPSHIRE NEWSMAN The reporter who christened the New Sharon murderer "Springheel Jack." He named him after Dr. John Hawkins of Bristol, who did away with five of his wives with "pharmaceutical knickknacks."

PARKINS, ADELLE Springheel Jack's third New Sharon victim. She was found propped up behind the wheel of a '64 Dodge. There were parts of her in the front seat, the back seat, and the trunk. Written in her blood on the windshield were the words "Ha! Ha!" [NOTE: In the *Ubris* version, he cut off only her legs, and those he took away with him.]

THE PRESIDENT OF NEW SHARON TEACHERS' COLLEGE On March 24, 1968, he moved spring break up one week due to the murders on campus. [NOTE: In the *Ubris* version, it was President Casner.]

SAM Hobbit and loyal companion to Frodo. Sam accompanied Frodo on his quest to destroy the One Ring.

THE SEVEN NEW SHARON SDS MEMBERS After the murders of Gail Cerman and Ann Bray, the rumors began: one of them spread the rumor that the murders had been committed by an offshoot of the SDS. The New Sharon SDS had seven members.

SEVEN PEOPLE In the *Ubris* version, when spring break was moved up one week, the narrator took seven people downstate in his car, instead of six as in the *Night Shift* revision.

SEVENTEEN PLAINCLOTHESMEN Seventeen plainclothesmen (including eight women from Boston) had been on campus the night Adelle Parkins was killed. [NOTE: In the *Ubris* version, it was Portsmouth instead of Boston.]

SIX PEOPLE When spring break was moved up one week, the narrator took six people downstate in his car. "For all any of us knew, Springheel Jack might have been in the car with us." Damn straight. The dude was driving! [NOTE: In the *Ubris* version, he took seven people to Kennebunk.]

SPRINGHEEL JACK The murderer that terrorized New Sharon Teachers' College in the spring of 1968. He didn't like the word "trunk."

A STATE COP After Gail Cerman's murder, the narrator was questioned by an unnamed state cop. The narrator joked that he showed the cop his "student ID without the fangs."

A STATE TROOPER The "Campus Cop" in the *Ubris* version of the story.

STUDENT NUMBER 1 An unnamed teachers' college student who–after the murder of Ann Bray–told the narrator that "he" (Springheel Jack) had gotten another one.

STUDENT NUMBER 2 An unnamed teachers' college student who told the narrator that the police had had to let Carl Amalara go.

A WELL-LIKED HISTORY PROFESSOR After the murders of Gail Cerman and Ann Bray, the rumors began: one of them spread that a well-liked history professor had been seen laughing and weeping by a small bridge.

(5k)
NIGHT SHIFT
"Strawberry Spring"
Places

ANIMAL SCIENCES PARKING LOT Gail Cerman's body was discovered in a corner of this parking lot by John Dancey. [NOTE: In the *Ubris* version, it was the fisheries building parking lot.]

BOSTON The eight female plainclothes cops put on campus were from Boston. [NOTE: In the *Ubris* version, it was Portsmouth.]

BRISTOL A reporter christened the New Sharon murderer "Springheel Jack." He named him after Dr. John Hawkins of Bristol, who did away with five of his wives with "pharmaceutical knickknacks." [NOTE: In the *Ubris* version, it was London.]

CENTRAL MAINE HOSPITAL In the *Ubris* version, this was the hospital mentioned.

THE GRINDER Campus eatery. During the March 1968 strawberry spring, people stepped out of the "juke-thumping, brightly lit confusion of the Grinder" into a "silent, muffled world of white, drifting fog. You half expected to see Gollum or Frodo and Sam go hurrying past." [NOTE: In the *Ubris* version, it was the Lion's Lair.]

JUDITH FRANKLIN HALL The dorm where Gail Cerman lived before Springheel Jack got her.

KENNEBUNK In the *Ubris* version, when spring break was moved up one week, the narrator took seven people to Kennebunk in his car, instead of six as in the *Night Shift* revision.

KENT HALL "Prashner Hall" in the *Ubris* version.

L.L. BEAN The store where Carl Amalara bought the seven-inch hunting knife found in his room. (The police thought he had used it to kill Gail Cerman.)

LONDON Dr. Hawkins was from London in the *Ubris* version.

NEW ENGLAND Every eight or ten years, New England experienced a strawberry spring. They went through one in March of 1968, when Springheel Jack stalked the New Sharon Teachers' College campus.

NEW HAMPSHIRE Hanson Gray's home state. [NOTE: In the *Ubris* version, it was Rhode Island.]

NEW SHARON TEACHERS' COLLEGE The school where the Springheel Jack murders took place in March of 1968. [NOTE: In the *Ubris* version, it was Wiscasset College.]

PORTSMOUTH The eight female plainclothes cops were from Portsmouth in the *Ubris* version instead of Boston.

PRASHNER HALL A building on the New Sharon Teachers' College campus. At the time of the strawberry spring in March of 1968, there was a snow sculpture of a dove in front of the hall. [NOTE: In the *Ubris* version, it was Kent Hall.]

A PUBLISHING HOUSE After college, the narrator married, and got a good job with a publishing house.

THE TATE ALUMNI BUILDING After the nine o'clock evening curfew was imposed at New Sharon, a couple was found necking after nine in the bushes north of the Tate Alumni Building. [NOTE: In the *Ubris* version, it was Tate Hall.]

TATE HALL "The Tate Alumni Building" in the *Ubris* version.

TEP FRATERNITY HOUSE Frat house on the New Sharon Teachers' College campus. At the time of the strawberry spring in March of 1968, there was a snow sculpture of Lyndon Johnson in front of the house.

THE TRUNK In 1971, a girl was found murdered at New Sharon Teachers' College. She was "not all there." The narrator's wife was upset and wanted to know where he was the night before. He was afraid to open his trunk.

(5k)
NIGHT SHIFT
"Strawberry Spring"
Things

ART MAJOR Gail Cerman's course of study.

"THE BALLAD OF BONNIE AND CLYDE" The song played on the jukebox in the *Ubris* version instead of "Hey Jude."

DRAFT PROTESTS AND SIT-INS By early June, Springheel Jack had gone, and talk had moved on to draft protests and a sit-in at a building where a well-known napalm manufacturer was holding job interviews.

EDUCATION MAJOR/SPEECH MINOR John Dancey's course of study.

A FLAMING BATON Ann Bray's talent in the Miss New England Pageant had been to twirl a flaming baton to the tune of "Hey, Look Me Over."

GAIL'S PICTURE The police found a picture of Gail Cerman cut up with scissors in Carl Amalara's room.

"HA! HA!" Adelle Parkins (Jack's third victim) was found propped up behind the wheel of a '64 Dodge. There were parts of her in the front seat, the back seat, and the trunk. Written in her blood on the windshield were the words "Ha! Ha!"

"HEY JUDE" A Beatles song played on the jukebox during the strawberry spring of 1968. [NOTE: In the *Ubris* version, it was "The Ballad of Bonnie and Clyde."]

"HEY, LOOK ME OVER" Ann Bray's talent in the Miss New England Pageant had been to twirl a flaming baton to the tune of "Hey, Look Me Over."

A HUNTING KNIFE FROM L.L. BEAN The police found a seven-inch hunting knife from L.L. Bean in Carl Amalara's room. They also found a picture of Gail Cerman cut up with scissors.

"LOVE IS BLUE" A song played on the jukebox during the strawberry spring of 1968.

THE MAINE CAMPUS In the *Ubris* version, this was the title of the college's paper.

A MANDATORY NINE O'CLOCK CURFEW After Ann Bray's murder, the administration at New Sharon Teachers' College imposed a mandatory nine o'clock evening curfew for the entire campus.

MARCH 16, 1968 The date the strawberry spring began.

A MILTON ESSAY When Carl Amalara was picked up for Gail Cerman's murder, the narrator was working on a Milton essay.

THE MISS MAINE PAGEANT Ann Bray was the first runner-up in the Miss Maine Pageant in the *Ubris* version.

THE MISS NEW ENGLAND PAGEANT Ann Bray was the first runner-up in the Miss New England Pageant. Her "talent" had been to twirl a flaming baton to the tune of "Hey, Look Me Over." [NOTE: In the *Ubris* version, it was the Miss Maine Pageant.]

A NAPALM MANUFACTURER By early June, Springheel Jack had gone, and talk had moved on to draft protests and a sit-in at a building where a well-known napalm manufacturer was holding job interviews.

THE NATIONAL SERVICE SORORITY Ann Bray had been president of this sorority.

THE NEW SHARON SDS After the murders of Gail Cerman and Ann Bray, the rumors began: one of them spread that the murders had been commited by an offshoot of the SDS. The New Sharon SDS had seven members.

"PHARMACEUTICAL KNICKKNACKS" The reporter who christened the New Sharon murderer "Springheel Jack" had named him after Dr. John Hawkins of Bristol, who did away with five of his wives with "pharmaceutical knickknacks."

THE RUMORS After the murders of Gail Cerman and Ann Bray, the rumors began: one of them spread that a well-liked history professor had been seen laughing and weeping by a small bridge. Another said that Gail Cerman had left a two-word message in her own blood; and the third said that the murders had been commited by an offshoot of the SDS.

"SCARBOROUGH FAIR" A song played on the jukebox during the strawberry spring of 1968.

A '64 DODGE Adelle Parkins (Springheel Jack's third victim) was found propped up behind the wheel of a '64 Dodge. There were parts of her in the front seat, the back seat, and the trunk. Written in her blood on the windshield were the words "Ha! Ha!"

SPRING BREAK On March 24, 1968, the President of New Sharon Teachers' College moved spring break up one week due to the murders on campus.

STRAWBERRY SPRING A false spring; a lying spring. In New England it happened once every eight or ten years. [NOTE: In the *Ubris* version, it was a fifteen-year cycle.]

THE STUDENT ID WITHOUT THE FANGS After Gail Cerman's murder, the narrator was questioned by a state cop. The narrator joked that he showed the cop his "student ID without the fangs."

TRUE CIGARETTES In the *Ubris* version, these were the cigarettes mentioned instead of an unnamed brand.

A TWO-WORD MESSAGE After the murders of Gail Cerman and Ann Bray, the rumors began: one of them spread that Gail Cerman had left a two-word message in her own blood.

"THE WALTER CRONKITE REPORT" During the "Springheel Jack" scare, the narrator of "Strawberry Spring" saw himself on "The Walter Cronkite Report."

WINTER CARNIVAL SNOW SCULPTURES The snow sculptures on the New Sharon Teachers' College campus. There was Lyndon Johnson in front of the TEP fraternity house, and a dove in front of Prashner Hall.

WISCASSET *DAILY JOURNAL* In the *Ubris* version, this was the newspaper mentioned instead of an unnamed college paper.

"THE WORST NORTHER OF ALL" The narrator's roommate's grandmother used to say that a strawberry spring meant that the worst norther of all was on its way.

❖❖❖

(51)
NIGHT SHIFT
"The Ledge"
People

THE BABY PIGEONS Their father pecked at Norris's ankle as he walked around the ledge.

THE BASEBALL PLAYER One of the six people to whom Cressner offered his "ledge" wager over the twelve years he had lived in the apartment. The baseball player declined. [NOTE: See the "Things" entry THE WAGER.]

CRESSNER The hood who put Stan Norris on the ledge. Stan was having an affair with his wife. Cressner was, according to Norris, "an A-number-one 500 carat, dyed-in-the-wool son of a bitch."

CRESSNER, MARCIA Cressner's wife; Stan Norris's lover. Cressner hired detectives to spy on them.

CRESSNER'S OPERATIVES The detectives Cressner had watching Marcia. She ditched them using "the old ladies'-room vanishing act" at the airport.

THE DETECTIVES Cressner hired detectives to spy on his wife and Norris.

AN EMPLOYEE An unnamed employee of Cressner's who moved Norris's car to a public parking lot.

HATTON, RONDO After Norris slammed Tony with the gun, "He went down with a single very weary grunt, looking like Rondo Hatton."

THE JOCKEY One of the six people to whom Cressner offered his "ledge" wager over the twelve years he had lived in the apartment. The jockey declined. (The jockey had alimony problems.) [NOTE: See the "Things" entry THE WAGER.]

MAMA PIGEON The mother pigeon who had a nest above the ledge. She protected her babies while her husband pecked at Norris's ankle.

MAMA PIGEON'S HUSBAND He pecked at Norris's ankle while his wife protected their babies.

NORRIS, STAN The man who Cressner put out on "the ledge." Stan was in love with Cressner's wife, and Cressner found out. Stan was a thirty-six-year old tennis pro. He had once spent three years in San Quentin for breaking and entering. Cressner hid six ounces of heroin in Norris's car. [NOTE: See the "Things" entry THE WAGER.]

ORDINARY CITIZEN NUMBER 1 One of the six people to whom Cressner offered his "ledge" wager over the twelve years he had lived in the apartment. The citizen declined. [NOTE: See the "Things" entry THE WAGER.]

ORDINARY CITIZEN NUMBER 3 One of the six people to whom Cressner offered his "ledge" wager over the twelve years he had lived in the apartment. He accepted, took one look over the edge of the balcony, and fainted. Cressner collected. [NOTE: See the

"Things" entry THE WAGER.]

ORDINARY CITIZEN NUMBER 2 One of the six people to whom Cressner offered his "ledge" wager over the twelve years he had lived in the apartment. The offer was declined. [NOTE: See the "Things" entry THE WAGER.]

POLICE BAGMEN Cressner paid $80,000 per week to police bagmen.

THE QUARTERBACK One of the six people to whom Cressner offered his "ledge" wager over the twelve years he lived in the apartment. The quarterback declined. (The quarterback was famous for TV commercials.) [NOTE: See the "Things" entry THE WAGER.]

TONY One of Cressner's goons. He was waiting for Cressner's call. If he didn't hear from Cressner by 8:20 p.m., he would call the police about the heroin in Norris's car.

(51)

NIGHT SHIFT
"The Ledge"
Places

THE AIRPORT Marcia ditched Cressner's operatives at the airport using "the old ladies'-room vanishing act."

THE BAYSIDE MOTEL Cressner's detectives got a motion picture of Norris and Marcia in the Bayside Motel.

DEAKMAN STREET Cressner's building was on Deakman Street.

THE GREYHOUND BUS STATION While Norris was being offered the "ledge" wager, Marcia was at the bus station: "Two hundred dollars and a Greyhound bus ticket could take you anywhere in the country."

THE LEDGE The ledge that ran around Cressner's building. It was accesible by climbing off the balcony outside his apartment. It was five inches wide, and four hundred feet off the ground. Norris walked it.

THE MORGUE After Norris successfully made it around the building on the ledge and arrived back at Cressner's apartment, Cressner told him he could pick up his third win (Marcia) at the morgue.

THE MUTUAL BANK From his perch on the ledge, Norris could see the lighted bank sign: It said "8:46 Time to Save at Mutual!"

THE OPPOSITE PENTHOUSE BALCONY Norris stopped at the balcony of the penthouse directly opposite Cressner's apartment.

THE PENTHOUSE APARTMENT Cressner lived in an apartment forty-three stories up. It had a ledge off the balcony.

A PUBLIC PARKING LOT Cressner had had Norris's car moved to a public parking lot, where six ounces of heroin were planted in the trunk.

SAN QUENTIN Stan Norris had spent three years in San Quentin for breaking and entering. He faced another forty years there if the planted heroin was discovered in the trunk of his car. He accepted Cressner's wager instead. [NOTE: See the "Things" entry THE WAGER.]

(51)

NIGHT SHIFT
"The Ledge"
Things

"AN A-NUMBER-ONE 500 CARAT DYED-IN-THE-WOOL SON OF A BITCH" Cressner, according to Stan Norris.

THE BANK SIGN From his perch on the ledge, Norris could see the lighted Mutual Bank sign: It said "8:46 Time to Save at Mutual!"

A BASQUE SLING CHAIR One of the chairs in Cressner's apartment.

BREAKING AND ENTERING Stan Norris had spent three years in San Quentin for breaking and entering.

CRESSNER'S CARPET It was a burnt orange deep-cut pile.

CRESSNER'S LIFE After Cressner had Marcia killed, Stan Norris overcame Tony and Cressner. Stan then bet Cressner his life against a walk on the ledge. At 11:29, Cressner stepped out onto the ledge. As Norris waited for Cressner, he mused that he had been known to welch on a bet now and then, too.

8:46 P.M. From his perch on the ledge, Norris could see the lighted Mutual Bank sign: It said "8:46 Time to Save at Mutual!"

$80,000 PER WEEK Cressner paid $80,000 per week to police bagmen.

11:09 P.M. The time Norris made it back to Cressner's apartment. He was met by Tony, who put a loaded forty-five to his temple.

11:29 P.M. The time Cressner started his walk around the building on the ledge.

FORTY YEARS Norris faced forty years in San Quentin if the planted heroin was discovered in the trunk of his car.

FOUR HUNDRED FEET OFF THE GROUND The ledge was five inches wide and four hundred feet off the ground.

A GENUINE LEATHER COUCH One of the chairs in Cressner's apartment.

THE LADIES'-ROOM VANISHING ACT The ploy Marcia used to ditch Cressner's operatives at the airport.

A LOADED FORTY-FIVE When Norris made it back to Cressner's apartment, he was met by Tony, who put a loaded forty-five to his temple.

A NEW YEAR'S EVE NOISEMAKER As Norris was beginning his walk around the building on the ledge, Cressner blew a noisemaker in his ear. Norris was startled.

NORRIS'S THREE WINS By making it all the way around the building on the ledge, Norris won three things: the money, his freedom, and Marcia. Cressner told him he could pick up Marcia at the morgue.

PLAN THREE Cressner's "plan three" called for Tony to actually remove the heroin from Cressner's car.

PLAN TWO Cressner called Tony and said "plan two." That plan called for Cressner to call Tony back in fifteen minutes (after Norris's ledge walk), and Tony would remove the heroin from Norris's car.

SELF-HYPNOSIS AND DEEP BREATHING Before Norris started his walk around the building on the ledge, he performed self-hypnosis and deep breathing. With every inhale/exhale, he threw a distraction out of his mind.

THE SHOPPING BAG Before he made the wager with Stan Norris, Cressner made Norris look in a shopping bag. In the bag was $20,000. There were one hundred bundles of twenties – ten twenties to a bundle.

A SILK DRESSING GOWN WITH AN EMBROIDERED DRAGON Cressner's "at-home" attire.

SIX OUNCES OF HEROIN Cressner had had six ounces of heroin planted in the trunk of Norris's car.

THE TEMPERATURE When Norris stepped out onto the ledge, the wind was blowing at from ten to twenty-five miles an hour. The temperature was forty-four degrees, which made the wind chill factor in the mid-twenties.

THIRTY-SIX YEARS OLD Stan Norris's age.

THREE YEARS Stan Norris had spent three years in San Quentin for breaking and entering.

A TURKISH CIGARETTE IN AN ONYX HOLDER Cressner's mode of smoking.

$20,000 Cressner showed Norris a shopping bag with $20,000 in it. There were one hundred bundles of $200 each (ten twenties per bundle.)

$200 While Norris was being offered the "ledge" wager, Marcia was at the bus station: "Two hundred dollars and a Greyhound bus ticket could take you anywhere in the country."

THE WAGER Cressner proposed the following wager to Norris: If Norris could successfully walk around the building on the ledge (without falling to his death, that is), he would get the money in the shopping bag and Marcia. Since Norris faced forty years in San Quentin (for the planted heroin in his trunk), he took the wager. Cressner had proposed the wager six times to six different people in the twelve years he'd lived in the apartment: First, to a quarterback famous for his TV commercials. He had said no. Second, to a baseball player, who also had said no. Third, to a jockey with alimony problems. He had said no. The fourth and fifth were ordinary citizens who had "a certain body grace" and a need for money. The last person was also an ordinary citizen, but he accepted the offer. The terms of the wager were always $20,000 cash against six months service to Cressner. The guy who accepted the wager took one look over the edge of the balcony and fainted. Cressner collected on him, too.

THE WIND When Norris stepped out onto the ledge, the wind was blowing at from ten to twenty-five miles an hour. The temperature was forty-four degrees, which made the wind chill factor in the mid-twenties.

THE WIND-CHILL FACTOR When Norris stepped out onto the ledge, the wind was blowing at from ten to twenty-five miles an hour. The temperature was forty-four degrees, which made the wind chill factor in the mid-twenties.

◇◇◇

(5m)
NIGHT SHIFT
"The Lawnmower Man"
People

[The December 1981 issue of *Bizarre Adventures* magazine (Marvel Magazine Group) featured a comic adaptation of King's story "The Lawnmower Man." The text was by King, and the artwork was by Walter Simonson. The story was very close to the original text version, except in a few instances where King changed character's names or created a name (such as naming the lawnmower man "Karras," and the Smith's cat "Shasta"). Details from the *Bizarre Adventures* adaptation are identified with a "(BA)" following the entry. – **sjs**]

THE BLACK-HAIRED SWEDE According to Lieutenant Goodwin, the circumstances surrounding Harold Parkette's death were akin to the feelings expressed by the man who saw a black-hair Swede: "It surely is a Norse of a different color."

THE BOY DOWN THE STREET Harold Parkette paid the boy down the street five dollars to mow his lawn.

THE BOY DOWN THE STREET'S MOTHER She told Harold her son was at the state university and couldn't mow Harold's lawn anymore.

THE BOYFRIEND (BA) The unnamed boyfriend who took Sheila Parkette to the local passion pit.

CARLA PARKETTE'S MOTHER Carla and Alicia were at Carla's mother's when Harold called Pastoral Greenery.

CASTONMEYER, JACK Harold's neighbor. He made jokes about Harold's lawn.

CASTONMEYER, RICH (BA) Harold's neighbor. He made jokes about Harold's lawn.

THE CASTONMEYERS Harold's neighbors. They had a dog.

THE CASTONMEYER'S DOG The Castonmeyer's dog had chased the Smith's cat under Harold's lawnmower in mid-October.

COOLEY, PATROLMAN One of the officers who investigated the death of Harold Parkette.

DRAGO, DICK Red Sock. During a game Harold listened to, Drago touched for a double and then hit a batter.

GOODWIN, LIEUTENANT The cop who investigated Harold Parkette's death.

HALL, SERGEANT The cop who took Harold's call about the lawnmower man.

KARRAS (BA) The name of the lawnmower man. [NOTE: It was

only given in the *Bizarre Adventures* version.]

THE LAWNMOWER MAN The fat guy sent over by Pastoral Greenery and Outdoor Services to mow Harold's lawn. He said things like "By Circe."

LEVY (BA) Harold's neighbor. (He referred to him as "that Jew Levy.")

A MOLE The lawnmower man's red lawnmower swerved while cutting Harold's lawn to attack and kill a mole.

PAN The lawnmower man's boss. The lawnmower man told Harold that Pan might be receptive to a sacrifice.

PARKETTE, ALICIA Harold's daughter. She had thrown up a half-quart of cherry Kool-Aid after the Castonmeyer's dog had chased the Smith's cat under Harold's mower.

PARKETTE, CARLA Harold's wife. She had nightmares for a week after the Castonmeyer's dog chased the Smith's cat under Harold's mower. Carla wore a Playtex Living Girdle, and had buck teeth.

PARKETTE, HAROLD He always took pride in his lawn. Harold owned a large silver Lawnboy, but paid a boy down the street five dollars to cut his lawn. He was more interested in following the Red Sox than maintaining his yard. He was eaten by a lawnmower as a sacrifice to the god Pan.

PARKETTE, SHEILA (BA) Harold's daughter.

PHIL The owner of Phil's Sunoco. He traded Harold a new Kelly blackwall tire and a tank of hi-test for his lawnmower. [NOTE: In the *Bizarre Adventures* adaptation, Phil traded Harold "a tank of high-test and a new radial tire."]

A PROGRESSION OF YOUNG BOYS The unnamed boys who came around and took (the ever-buxom) Alicia Parkette to the local passion pit.

THE RED SOX Harold Parkette's team.

SHASTA (BA) The name of the Smith's cat.

SMITH, DON Harold's neighbor. His daughter Jenny hid in the tall grass of Harold's lawn whenever there was oatmeal for breakfast or spinach for supper.

SMITH, HANK (BA) Harold's neighbor.

SMITH, JENNY Don Smith's daughter. She hid in Harold's yard whenever there was oatmeal for breakfast or spinach for supper.

SMITH, MRS. She had watched Harold clean the blades of his lawnmower after the Castonmeyer's dog had chased the Smith's cat under the mower.

THE SMITHS Harold's neighbors. They once had a cat.

THE SMITH'S CAT The Castonmeyer's dog had chased the Smith's cat under Harold's mower in mid-October.

SONNY The bartender at the Goldfish Bowl.

STARK, MRS. (BA) The mother of the boy who used to cut Harold's lawn before he went off to college. [NOTE: "George Stark" is the pseudonymn Thad Beaumont used for his mystery novels in *The Dark Half*. See the section on *The Dark Half* in this volume.]

THE TWO MEN IN WHITE They brought the basket for Harold's body after he was sacrificed to Pan by the lawnmower man.

WALL STREET EXECUTIVES Harold considered Wall Street execs "minor demigods."

A WOODCHUCK When Harold saw a woodchuck on his back walk, he decided he had to do something about his lawn.

(5m)
NIGHT SHIFT
"The Lawnmower Man"
Places

THE GOLDFISH BOWL Bar. Harold often drank there and discussed his problems with Sonny the bartender.

1421 EAST ENDICOTT STREET Harold Parkette's address.

THE LOCAL PASSION PIT A progression of young boys took the oh-so-buxom Alicia Parkette to the local passion pit.

PHIL'S SUNOCO Gas station Harold used.

THE STATE UNIVERSITY The boy down the street went to the state university, and therefore couldn't mow Harold's lawn anymore.

(5m)
NIGHT SHIFT
"The Lawnmower Man"
Things

BRUSSELS SPROUTS (BA) Don Smith's four-year-old daughter hid in the tall grass of Harold's lawn whenever there were Brussells sprouts for supper.

BUCK TEETH Carla Parkette had them.

"BY CIRCE" The oath sworn by the lawnmower man.

A COORS CAN Harold knocked over a Coors can when the lawnmower man rang his bell.

FIVE DOLLARS Harold paid the boy down the street five dollars to mow his lawn.

"A GOOD REPUBLICAN" Harold was a good Republican, and considered Wall Street executives minor demigods.

A HALF-QUART OF CHERRY KOOL-AID Alicia Parkette had thrown up a half-quart of cherry Kool-Aid after the Castonmeyer's dog had chased the Smith's cat under her father's mower.

LUCKY STRIKES OR CAMELS Harold felt that guys like the lawnmower man smoked Luckies or Camels.

MID-OCTOBER The Castonmeyer's dog had chased the Smith's cat under Harold's mower in mid-October.

MIDWEST BISON BURGERS, INC. The company Harold had once invested in. He had bought three shares of stock for seventy-five dollars. The company had gone broke.

A NEW KELLY BLACKWALL TIRE AND A TANK OF HI-TEST The items Phil (of Phil's Sunoco) traded Harold for his mower. [NOTE: In the *Bizarre Adventures* adaptation, Phil traded Harold a "tank of high-test and a new radial tire."]

"A NORSE OF A DIFFERENT COLOR" According to Lieutenant Goodwin, the circumstances surrounding Harold Parkette's death were akin to the feelings expressed by the man who saw a black-haired Swede: "It surely is a Norse of a different color."

OATMEAL FOR BREAKFAST OR SPINACH FOR SUPPER Don Smith's daughter Jenny hid in the tall grass of Harold's lawn whenever there was oatmeal for breakfast or spinach for supper.

THE PART-TIME COLUMN OF THE CLASSIFIEDS The newspaper column where Harold found the ad for Pastoral Greenery and Outdoor Services.

THE PASTORAL GREENERY AD It read "Lawns Mowed. Reasonable. 776-2390."

PASTORAL GREENERY AND OUTDOOR SERVICES The company Harold called to mow his lawn. They sent the lawnmower man.

A PLAYTEX LIVING GIRDLE Carla Parkette's support undergarment of choice.

A RED MOWER The lawnmower man brought a red lawnmower that ran by itself. The lawnmower man followed the mower stark naked and ate up the grass clippings. Harold was not pleased by this sight.

A SACRIFICE The lawnmower man told Harold that his boss Pan might be receptive to a sacrifice.

776-2390 Pastoral Greenery's phone number.

SEVENTY-FIVE DOLLARS Harold had once bought three shares of Midwest Bisonburgers, Inc. for seventy-five dollars. The company had gone broke.

A SILVER LAWNBOY Harold Parkette's lawnmower.

❖❖❖

(5n)
NIGHT SHIFT
"Quitters, Inc."
People

CRAGER, BOBBY One of the owners of Crager and Barton, the company where Jimmy McCann worked. Crager had told McCann to get his butt in gear or get out.

DICK'S CRONY FROM LARKIN STUDIOS After he signed on with Quitters, Inc., Dick drank with a crony from Larkin Studios at Jack Dempsey's bar. Dick was offered a cigarette and refused it. Dick eventually gave a Quitters, Inc. business card to this guy.

DONATTI, VICTOR The Quitters, Inc. "counselor" in charge of Dick Morrison's case.

A FOURSOME Dick saw the young man in the blue suit (the Quitters, Inc. operative) as part of a foursome on the golf course.

HENRY A bartender in a bar Dick found himself in a month after his meeting with McCann. He paid Henry and left the bar after he had made the decision to visit Quitters, Inc. "just for chuckles."

JIMMY McCANN'S BIG CLIENT When Dick met up with Jimmy McCann at Kennedy International, Jimmy was on his way to Miami for a meeting with a client that billed $6 million. (Jimmy was an executive vice president with Crager and Barton, an advertising agency.)

JIMMY McCANN'S DOCTOR The unnamed physician who told Jimmy that he had an incipient ulcer.

JUNK Donatti's assistant. He was built like an ape, he wore a "Smile" sweatshirt, and carried a thirty-eight.

A MAN An unnamed man who entered the Quitters, Inc. waiting room after Dick Morrison.

McCANN, JIMMY An old college friend of Dick Morrison's. Jimmy gave Dick a Quitters, Inc. card.

McCANN, MR. Jimmy McCann's father. He had died of a heart attack.

McCANN, SHARON Jimmy's wife. The little finger on her right hand was cut off when her husband gained more weight than Quitters, Inc. allowed.

MINELLI, MORT ("THREE FINGERS") The man who endowed Quitters, Inc. with family funds. Mort had smoked three packs a day and ended up with lung cancer. He had been extremely successful in family businesses: slot machines, massage parlors, numbers, and a brisk trade between New York and Turkey. He had died in 1970. Mort's picture was on the wall in Donatti's office. In the picture, he was holding a piece of paper: It was his doctor's diagnosis of lung cancer.

MORRISON, ALVIN DAWES Dick and Cindy Morrison's mentally retarded son. He attended the Paterson School for Handicapped Children in New Jersey. Alvin had cranial brain damage and a tested IQ of forty-six.

MORRISON, LUCINDA RAMSEY Cindy Morrison, Dick Morrison's wife.

MORRISON, RICHARD A Quitters, Inc. client. The company was recommended to Dick by his friend Jimmy McCann. Dick was married to Lucinda Ramsey Morrison, and they had a mentally retarded son named Alvin.

AN OPERATIVE If Dick violated his no smoking agreement four times, an operative from Quitters, Inc. would be sent to the Paterson School for Handicapped Children to beat up his son Alvin.

A RABBIT To illustrate the Quitters, Inc. program to Dick Morrison, a rabbit was placed in a room with a metal floor, and given electrical shocks.

THE RECEPTIONIST The unnamed Quitters, Inc. receptionist who greeted Dick Morrison. She used an IBM typewriter.

THE THREE MEN Three men and one woman waited in the

Quitters, Inc. waiting room on the afternoon Dick Morrison first visited the company.

THE WOMAN Three men and one woman waited in Quitters, Inc. waiting room on the afternoon Dick Morrison first visited the company.

A YOUNG MAN IN A BLUE SUIT The Quitter's Inc. operative assigned to watch Dick Morrison. Dick saw him while waiting for a train; at Onde's where Dick was meeting a client; at Sam Goody's where Dick was looking for a Sam Cooke album; and as part of a foursome on the golf course.

(5n)
NIGHT SHIFT
"Quitters, Inc."
Places

CRAGER AND BARTON The advertising agency Jimmy McCann worked for. He was an executive vice president.

THE GOLF COURSE The course where Dick saw the young man in the blue suit as part of a foursome. (He was the Quitters, Inc. operative assigned to watch Dick.)

THE HELEN HAYES THEATER Two years after Dick signed on with Quitters, Inc., he and his wife met up with the McCanns at the Helen Hayes Theater. Jimmy McCann's wife's right little finger was missing.

JACK DEMPSEY'S BAR The bar where Dick drank with a crony from Larkin Studios.

KENNEDY INTERNATIONAL The airport where Dick Morrison waited for someone caught in an air traffic jam. While waiting, he talked with his old friend Jimmy McCann in the airport bar. Jimmy gave Dick a Quitters, Inc. card.

LARKIN STUDIOS Advertising agency. Dick knew a guy who worked there.

MIAMI When Dick met up with Jimmy McCann at Kennedy International, Jimmy was on his way to Miami for a meeting with a big client.

THE MIDTOWN TUNNEL While stuck in a traffic jam in the Midtown Tunnel, Dick smoked. Donatti subsequently put Cindy in the rabbit room for thirty seconds.

THE MORTON AGENCY The advertising agency Dick Morrison worked for.

NEW JERSEY The location of the Paterson School for Handicapped Children.

NEW YORK AND TURKEY Mort Minelli kept up a brisk trade between New York and Turkey.

ONDE'S A restaurant where Dick waited for a client. Dick saw the young man in the blue suit there. (The young man was a Quitters, Inc. operative.)

THE PATERSON SCHOOL FOR HANDICAPPED CHILDREN The New Jersey institution where Dick Morrison's mentally retarded son Alvin lived.

QUITTER'S INC. A very successful company that helped people quit smoking. [NOTE: See the "Things" entry QUITTERS, INC. "QUIT SMOKING" PROGRAM.] Vic Donatti was in charge of things. The company had a ninety-eight percent cure rate.

SAM GOODY'S The record store where Dick shopped for a Sam Cooke album. While in the store, he noticed a Quitters, Inc. operative (the young man in the blue suit) watching him.

29 MAPLE LANE, CLINTON, NEW YORK Dick Morrison's address.

(5n)
NIGHT SHIFT
"Quitters, Inc."
Things

BOURBON AND BITTERS Dick Morrison's drink.

"BULLITT" One of Cindy Morrison's favorite movies. It was the "Friday Night Movie" the week Dick signed the Quitter's Inc. agreement.

CRANIAL BRAIN DAMAGE Dick's son Alvin had cranial brain damage and a tested IQ of forty-six.

DICK MORRISON'S QUITTER'S INC. BILL Twelve months after signing on with Quitters, Inc. Dick received the following bill:

QUITTERS, INC.
237 East 46th Street
New York, N.Y. 10017

1 Treatment	$2500.00
Counselor (Victor Donatti)	$2500.00
Electricity	$ .50
TOTAL (Please pay this amount)	$5000.50

EXECUTIVE VICE PRESIDENT Jimmy McCann's position at Crager and Barton.

FIVE FOOT ELEVEN INCHES Dick Morrison's height.

5:00 P.M. Dick's appointment time to watch Cindy in the rabbit room. (He had sneaked a smoke in a traffic jam in the Midtown Tunnel.)

FLIGHT NUMBER 206 AT GATE 9 Jimmy McCann's flight to Miami.

FORTY-SIX Alvin Morrison's tested IQ.

AN IBM TYPEWRITER The typewriter used by the Quitters, Inc. receptionist.

JIMMY McCANN'S FLIGHT TO MIAMI He was on Flight 206 at Gate 9.

A MAROON SHAG RUG The carpeting in the Quitters, Inc. waiting room.

MORT MINELLI'S FAMILY BUSINESSES The founder of Quitters, Inc was very successful in slot machines, massage parlors, and numbers. He also kept up a brisk trade between New York and Turkey.

MORT'S LUNG CANCER DIAGNOSIS On the wall of Vic Donatti's office at Quitters, Inc. was a picture of Mort Minelli, the founder of the company, holding a piece of paper: the paper was his doctor's diagnosis of lung cancer.

"THE MOST PERNICIOUS DRUG OF ALL" One day, Dick Morrison realized that love was the most pernicious drug of all.

1970 The year Mort "Three Fingers" Minelli died.

A NINETY-EIGHT PERCENT CURE RATE The Quitters, Inc. "Quit Smoking" success rate.

182 POUNDS Dick Morrison's maximum weight, as set by Vic Donatti. If he went over 182, they'd cut off his wife's little finger.

174 POUNDS After he successfully quit smoking, Dick gained weight. After he got up to 174, (and based on his height of 5'11"), Donatti set Dick's maximum weight at 182. If he went over that, they'd cut off his wife's little finger.

167 POUNDS Eight months after Dick successfully completed the Quitters, Inc. program, his weight was down to 167 pounds.

A PARTY After signing on with Quitters, Inc., Dick got drunk at a party, but didn't light up.

THE QUITTERS, INC. BUSINESS CARD:

QUITTERS, INC.
Stop Going Up in Smoke!
237 East 46th Street
Treatments by Appointment

THE QUITTERS, INC. CURE RATE The company had a ninety-eight percent cure rate.

THE QUITTERS, INC. "QUIT SMOKING" PROGRAM The following program was outlined for Dick Morrison:

1st Offense: Cindy Morrison would be put in the "rabbit room";

2nd Offense: Dick gets put in the room;

3rd Offense: Dick and Cindy would be put in the room together;

4th Offense: An operative would be sent to Alvin's school to work the boy over;

5th Offense: The rabbit room for Dick and Cindy; a second beating for his son, and a beating for Cindy;

Steps 6, 7, and 8: More trips to the rabbit room (with increased voltage), and more serious beatings;

Step 9: Alvin's arms would be broken;

Step 10: Dick would become one of the unregenerate two percent who simply can't stop...so they would shoot him.

THE QUITTERS, INC. SURVEILLANCE PROGRAM The first month, Dick would be under constant supervision; the second and third months, he'd be under supervision eighteen hours a day (but he wouldn't know which eighteen); the fourth month, he'd be back to being watched twenty-fours a day; and then he'd be under twelve hours of broken surveillance each day for the next year. After this, there would be random surveillance for the rest of the client's life.

THE RIGHT LITTLE FINGER Mrs. McCann's right little finger was cut off by Quitters, Inc. when her husband gained more weight than he was allowed to.

A SAM COOKE ALBUM A record Dick looked for in Sam Goody's.

$6 MILLION When Dick met up with Jimmy McCann at Kennedy International, Jimmy was on his way to Miami for a meeting with an advertising client that Jimmy's company billed $6 million a year.

A "SMILE" SWEATSHIRT The shirt worn by Junk, Donatti's assistant.

A SQUEAKING SQUEEZE BALL The toy Dick brought his son Alvin.

THIRTY SECONDS IN THE RABBIT ROOM Cindy Morrison's punishment for Dick's violation of his no smoking pledge. (He had smoked during a traffic jam in the Midtown Tunnel.)

A THIRTY-EIGHT Junk's gun.

THREE PACKS A DAY Mort "Three Fingers" Minelli's smoking habit before his diagnosis of lung cancer.

TIME **MAGAZINE** The magazine Dick Morrison read in the Quitters, Inc. waiting room.

A TRAFFIC JAM While stuck in a traffic jam in the Midtown Tunnel, Dick smoked. Donatti subsequently put Cindy in the rabbit room for thirty seconds.

❖❖❖

(5o)
NIGHT SHIFT
"I Know What You Need"
People

ACKERMAN, SANDRA Liz Rogan's summer roommate.

ALICE Liz's roommate. She was a chemistry major with a 3.6 average.

ALICE'S PARENTS They paid her tuition.

BANNER, PROFESSOR Sociology professor. Ed Hamner told Liz that he had had Banner the year before, and that thanks to his eidetic memory, he was able to give Liz the final word for word.

DANNY KILMER'S GIRLFRIEND Liz and Tony had doubled a couple of times with Danny and his girl.

D'ANTONIO, SHIRLEY The summer Tony Lombard was killed, Shirley was working at the Pines Restaurant, which was right across the street from the Lakewood Theater. She told Alice that she had never seen anyone who looked like Ed Hamner working at the theater.

DEEDEE Liz Rogan's mother's nickname. Ed somehow knew this.

"THE DEVIL'S HENCHMAN" Ed Hamner, Jr., according to his mother. She tried to kill him with a scissors in 1964.

DIAMOND, NEIL Alice, Liz's roommate, listened to Neil Diamond and read *The Story of O*.

HAMNER, ED, SR. Ed's father. He was a big gambler. He once worked for a top-line advertising agency in New York.

HAMNER, EDWARD JACKSON, JR. Weird guy who, through voodoo, was able to discern what people "needed." The object of his attentions for a time was Elizabeth Rogan. She discovered his occult paraphernalia and threw them in the river. Ed was a junior, short, skinny and he looked "like he washed his hair last around Washington's birthday." Also, Ed wore mismatched socks: one black, one brown.

HAMNER, MRS. Ed's mother.

A KID Tony Lombard was killed by a sober kid driving a red Fiat. It was considered an honest accident. [NOTE: It was, however, as all we King fans know, actually the dastardly doings of that nasty voodoo king himself, Ed Hamner.]

KILMER, DANNY A guy who worked with Tony Lombard in Boothbay, Maine. Danny was the one who told Liz that Tony was dead.

LOMBARD, TONY Elizabeth Rogan's boyfriend.

THE OPERATIVE The private detective Alice hired to look into Ed Hamner.

ROGAN, ELIZABETH College junior, and the object of Ed Hamner's voodoo attention. She had a split education and math major.

(5o)
NIGHT SHIFT
"I Know What You Need"
Places

THE AUGUSTA AIRPORT Ed Hamner went home from Maine via the Augusta airport.

BOOTHBAY, MAINE The town where the Boothbay Inn was located. Liz and Tony planned on working together there for the summer before Liz's senior year, but Tony couldn't make it: he was killed by Ed Hamner's voodoo red Fiat.

THE BOOTHBAY INN Inn in Boothbay, Maine. Liz Rogan and Tony Lombard planned on working there the summer before Liz's senior year.

BRIDGEPORT, CONNECTICUT The town where Liz and Ed had both attended P.S. 119 as children.

THE BRIDGEPORT CANDY COMPANY A company that packaged their candy in tin boxes. Ed kept his "voodoo" paraphernalia in one of the boxes. [NOTE: See the entry ED'S TIN BOX.]

DAY'S Department store. Ed had once bought Liz a hairdryer at Day's just when she had been wishing for a new one.

THE GRINDER Campus ice cream parlor/restaurant. Ed Hamner invited Liz Rogan there for a strawberry double-dip cone.

THE HARBOR INN The restaurant where Danny Kilmer told Elizabeth about Tony's death.

KITTERY, MAINE The town eighty miles from Skowhegan. Alice summered there.

THE LAKEWOOD THEATER Ed Hamner claimed he was working at the Lakewood Theater in Skowhegan the summer Tony Lombard was killed by a kid driving a red Fiat.

LAS VEGAS Alice revealed to Liz that Ed had spent the previous summer (the summer Tony was killed) in Vegas, not working at the Lakewood Theater.

A LOCKED CLOSET Liz found a locked closet in Ed's apartment. In it were Ed's voodoo paraphernalia. [NOTE: See the entries ED'S VOODOO BOOKS, ED'S TIN BOX, and ED'S ELIZABETH DOLL.]

MAIN AND MILL STREETS The intersection where the bus let Liz off when she went to check out Ed's apartment.

MILL STREET The street where Ed Hamner lived. He lived in a third floor walkup.

NEW YORK Ed Hamner, Sr., had once worked for a top-line advertising agency in New York.

NINETY-DOLLAR-A-MONTH CHEESE BOX In 1961, after Ed Hamner moved his family to L.A., they were living in a ninety-dollar-a-month "cheese box."

P.S. 119 The Bridgeport, Connecticut, grammar school both Liz and Ed had attended as children.

PEMAQUID The summer Tony was killed, Ed took a motel room in Pemaquid. He did not work at the Lakewood Theater.

THE PINES RESTAURANT A restaurant directly across the street from the Lakewood Theater. Shirley D'Antonio was working at the Pines the summer Tony Lombard was killed.

THE RIVER Elizabeth threw Ed's "voodoo" paraphernalia in the river.

ROUTE 101 After Ed's mother was released from the mental hospital, she drove her car off a cliff on Route 101.

ROUTE 16 Tony Lombard had been repairing drainage culverts on Route 16 when he was killed by a kid driving a red Fiat.

THE SILENT WOMAN A restaurant in Waterville. Ed and Liz had dinner at the Silent Woman after Tony Lombard was killed.

SKOWHEGAN The town where the Lakewood Theater was located. Ed claimed to have been working there and that he had run into Alice, who had told him about Tony Lombard's death. Alice had actually been summering in Kittery, which was eighty miles from Skowhegan.

THE STUDENT UNION Liz was studying on the third floor of the student union when she first met Ed Hamner.

THE THINK TANK The third floor of the student union.

THE UNIVERSITY POOL Liz had seen the deep scar below Ed's left shoulder when they swam together at the university pool. [NOTE: See the "Things" entry A DEEP SCAR.]

VARIOUS MENTAL INSTITUTIONS Ed Hamner's mother spent six years in and out of various mental institutions. She claimed her son was "the devil's henchman" because he had been able to tell his father what stocks to buy and sell.

(5o)
NIGHT SHIFT
"I Know What You Need"
Things

ANCIENT RITES, MODERN MYSTERIES One of the books Liz found in Ed's "voodoo" closet.

A BLUE POKER CHIP One of the items Liz found in the tin box in Ed's "voodoo" closet. [NOTE: See the entry ED'S TIN BOX.]

A BORKHUM RIFF POUCH In Ed's locked closet, Liz found a spilled Borkhum Riff pouch.

A CORVETTE After Tony Lombard was killed, Ed showed up in a new Corvette to take Liz to dinner.

DANCE CRAZES OF THE FIFTIES A book Liz found in Ed's apartment. The Stroll was circled and "Beth" was written in the margin.

DEAN'S LIST Alice was on the dean's list every semester. Her parents paid for her tuition.

A DEEP SCAR Ed Hamner had a deep scar below his left shoulder from the time his mother tried to kill him with a scissors. He told Liz that he had gotten it from falling on a picket fence.

DRAINAGE CULVERTS Tony Lombard had been repairing drainage culverts on Route 16 when he was killed by a kid driving a red Fiat.

ED'S ELIZABETH DOLL One of the items Liz found in the tin box in Ed's "voodoo" closet. It was dressed in a scrap of red nylon; its arms were pipe cleaners draped in blue graveyard moss, and the hair on the doll was the color of Elizabeth's hair when she was a child. Elizabeth crushed the doll.

ED'S TIN BOX In Ed's locked "voodoo" closet, Liz found a tin box stamped Bridgeport Candy Co. In the box were an "Elizabeth doll"; a blue poker chip with a strange six-sided pattern drawn on it; Mr. and Mrs. Hamner's obituary, with the same pattern drawn on their faces; two more dolls, one male, and one female; and a toy red Fiat with a piece of Tony Lombard's shirt attached to the front of it.

ED'S VOODOO BOOKS In Ed's locked closet, Elizabeth found the following books:

> *The Golden Bough* ;
> *Ancient Rites, Modern Mysteries* ;
> *Haitian Voodoo* ;
> *The Necronomicon* .

EH-17 When Liz saw Alice reading *The Story of O*, she told her she didn't know that they assigned that book in EH-17.

AN EIDETIC MEMORY Ed Hamner claimed he had a photographic memory.

AN EIGHTY AVERAGE The average Elizabeth needed in order to keep her scholarship. She had to get at least an eighty-four on her sociology final to achieve an eighty average.

AN EIGHTY-FOUR Liz needed at least an eighty-four on her sociology final in order to maintain an eighty average and keep her scholarship.

ELIZABETH'S SENIOR YEAR SCHOLARSHIP Because she got a ninety-seven on her sociology final (thanks to Ed Hamner's supposed eidetic memory, which was actually use of the occult), Liz was able to keep her scholarship for her senior year. It was $2,000.

A FIFTIES STROLL TROPHY Ed and Liz won a fifties Stroll trophy at the Homecoming Nostalgia Dance.

A '52 CHEVROLET The car Ed Hamner Sr. was driving in 1961.

THE GOLDEN BOUGH One of the books Liz found in Ed's "voodoo" closet.

A HAIRDRYER Ed had once bought Liz a hairdryer at Day's – just when she was wishing for a new one.

HAITIAN VOODOO One of the books Liz found in Ed's "voodoo" closet.

THE HAMNER OBITUARY One of the items Liz found in the tin box in Ed's "voodoo" closet. [NOTE: See the entry ED'S TIN BOX.]

THE HOMECOMING NOSTALGIA DANCE Ed and Liz won a fifties Stroll trophy at the Homecoming Nostalgia Dance.

HONORS Ed Hamner was in the honors program, and didn't have to take finals.

"I KNOW WHAT YOU NEED" The first line said by Ed Hamner to Elizabeth Rogan. This established the parameters and tone of their relationship. He wasn't kidding, either.

INTRODUCTION TO SOCIOLOGY The book Liz was reading when Ed Hamner first told her he knew what she needed.

JUNE The first month Liz and Tony worked at the Boothbay Inn. It was rainy, there was a gas shortage, and the tips were mediocre.

LAST YEAR'S FINAL Ed Hamner was able to reproduce last year's sociology final for Elizabeth word for word. He claimed it was because he had an eidetic (photographic) memory.

LIZ'S AUGUST NIGHTMARE She dreamed that she was lying in an open grave, and she was unable to move. It was raining on her. Tony Lombard was standing over her wearing a hardhat. He said to her, "Marry me or else," and then he started a bulldozer. She was rescued by Ed Hamner, who then turned into a wolf.

A LOS ANGELES ADVERTISING AGENCY Ed Hamner, Sr., took a job with a Los Angeles ad agency after he got into a jam in Bridgeport, Connecticut, due to his gambling.

A MALE AND A FEMALE DOLL Two of the items Liz found in the tin box in Ed's "voodoo" closet. [NOTE: See the entry ED'S TIN BOX.]

MISMATCHED SOCKS Ed Hamner wore one black sock and one brown.

THE NECRONOMICON One of the books Liz found in Ed's "voodoo" closet.

A NEW YORK ADVERTISING AGENCY Ed Hamner, Sr., had once worked for a top-line advertising agency in New York.

1964 The year Ed Hamner's mother tried to kill him with a scissors.

A NINETY-SEVEN Liz's score on her sociology final.

A $1 MILLION STOCK PORTFOLIO After Ed's mother drove her car off a cliff on Route 101, Ed was left with a $1 million stock portfolio.

A PICKET FENCE Ed claimed the scar below his left shoulder came from falling onto a picket fence. [NOTE: See the entry A DEEP SCAR.]

A PRIVATE DETECTIVE AGENCY Alice hired a detective agency to check up on Ed Hamner.

A RED FIAT The car that hit and killed Tony Lombard. There were several holes in the car's brake lines, and the police assumed they had overheated and melted through.

ROULETTE Ed Hamner, Sr., used to bring Ed Jr. to Las Vegas with him when Ed Jr. was a kid. He called him his good luck charm. When Ed Sr. began sticking to roulette, he always won when Ed Jr. was with him. Ed Jr. ended up being banned from every casino on the strip.

A SCISSORS In 1964, Ed Hamner's mother tried to kill him with a scissors. She believed he was "the devil's henchman."

A SEVENTY-EIGHT AVERAGE Elizabeth's average at the time she met Ed Hamner. She needed an eighty to keep her scholarship, and therefore had to get at least an eighty-four on the sociology final.

THE STOCK MARKET Sixteen months after Ed Hamner, Sr., got into the stockmarket, he was driving a brand-new Thunderbird and his wife was driving a VW. He had made lots of money, thanks to the "suggestions" made by Ed Jr.

THE STORY OF O A book read by Alice, Liz's roommate.

A STRAWBERRY DOUBLE-DIP CONE The first thing Ed Hamner told Liz Rogan he knew she needed.

THE STROLL A dance craze of the fifties. Ed had circled it in a book on dances of the fifties and written "Beth" in the margin.

A THUNDERBIRD Sixteen months after Ed Hamner Sr. got into the stockmarket, he was driving a brand-new Thunderbird and his wife was driving a VW. He had made lots of money, thanks to the "suggestions" made by Ed Jr.

A TOY RED FIAT One of the items Liz found in the tin box in Ed's "voodoo" closet. [NOTE: See the entry ED'S TIN BOX.]

$2,000 The amount of Liz's senior year scholarship

A VOLKSWAGEN Sixteen months after Ed Hamner Sr. got into the stockmarket, he was driving a brand-new Thunderbird and his wife was driving a VW. He had made lots of money, thanks to the "suggestions" made by Ed Jr.

VOODOO Ed Hamner's "hobby."

❖❖❖

(5p)
NIGHT SHIFT
"Children of the Corn"
People

AHAZ, CURSED OF GOD Malachi had led the hunt for Japheth, who forever would be known as Ahaz, Cursed of God.

BABY HORTENSE, THE SINGING MARVEL The eight-year-old evangelist Vicky saw in tent prayer meetings when she was a child. Baby Hortense would sing "Leaning On the Everlasting Arms" while her father passed the plate.

BABY HORTENSE'S DADDY The father of eight-year-old evangelist Baby Hortense. Baby Hortense would sing "Leaning On the Everlasting Arms" while her father passed the plate.

THE BLUE MAN The Gatlin police chief.

BOARDMAN, CRAIG Malachi Boardman.

BOARDMAN, MALACHI Child of the corn. His other name was

Craig. He was born on August 15, 1957.

THE BOY While driving through Nebraska with Vicky, Burt hit a thirteen-year-old boy who ran in front of their car. His throat had been cut.

THE BOYS WHO TOOK VICKY While Burt was fighting off the kid with the Pensy jackknife, two boys took Vicky away.

BURT'S MOTHER Burt's mother used to wear a tight-mouthed expressionless look on her face when she pulled the innards out of the Sunday chicken. Vicky wore the same expression as she tried to pull loose the knots holding shut the dead boy's suitcase.

CLAWSON, RUTH Child of the corn. Her other name was Sandra. She was born on April 30, 1961.

CLAWSON, SANDRA Ruth Clawson.

THE DEFILER OF THE CORN Burt and Vicky heard an evangelist preaching on their car radio. He said something about there being no room in God's house for the defiler of the corn.

DEIGAN, AMOS Child of the corn. His other name was Richard. He was born on September 4, 1945, and died September 4, 1964.

DEIGAN, RICHARD Amos Deigan.

THE ELKS As Burt and Vicky headed into Gatlin, they passed an Elks Club sign that said "Gatlin 5 Mi. Drive Carefully Protect Our Children." There were small bullet holes in the sign.

THE EVANGELIST Burt and Vicky heard an evangelist preaching on their car radio. He said something about there being no room in God's house for the defiler of the corn.

THE FALSE MINISTER The Grace Baptist Church's minister. He was crucified next to Vicky Robeson.

GILMAN, CLAYTON Job Gilman.

GILMAN, JOB Child of the corn. His other name was Clayton. He was born on September 6, 1964.

THE GIRL WITH THE JACKHANDLE While Burt was reading the census book in the Grace Baptist Church, children attacked Vicky, who was waiting in the car. One girl of about eight had a jackhandle.

THE GRACE SISTERS Evangelists Vicky saw in tent prayer meetings when she was a child. They wore tin haloes.

GREENLAW, ADAM Child of the corn. He had no other name. He was born on July 11, 1965.

"HE WHO WALKS BEHIND THE ROWS" The Corn God worshipped in Gatlin, Nebraska, by the children of the corn. He smelled like corn and moved in the fields.

HOLLIS, EDWARD Yemen Hollis.

HOLLIS, YEMEN Child of the corn. His other name was Edward. He was born on January 5, 1946, and died January 5, 1965.

JAPHETH Malachi had led the hunt for Japheth, who forever would be known as Ahaz, Cursed of God.

KIRK, GEORGE Zepeniah Kirk.

KIRK, ZEPENIAH Child of the corn. His other name was George. He was born on October 14, 1945, and died October 14, 1964.

MALACHI AND RUTH'S CHILD On a night after Vicky and Burt's crucifixions, Ruth bid Malachi farewell as he walked into the corn to meet He Who Walks Behind the Rows. Ruth was pregnant with Malachi's child, and she feared the corn.

A MONGREL DOG A mongrel dog lay down in the middle of Maple Street, Gatlin.

OWENS, BUCK The radio in Burt's car broadcast farm reports, Buck Owens, and Tammy Wynette.

THE POLICE CHIEF Vicky had been crucified next to the Gatlin police chief.

RENFREW, ISAAC Child of the corn. His other name was William. He was born on September 19, 1945, and died September 19, 1964. He was the Seer of the Children of the Corn.

RENFREW, WILLIAM Isaac Renfrew.

RICHARDSON, HENRY Moses Richardson.

RICHARDSON, MOSES Child of the corn. His other name was Henry. He was born on July 29, 1957.

ROBESON, BURT Ex-Vietnam vet, medical orderly, and Vicky's husband. He and Vicky had driven fifteen-hundred miles from

Boston to Nebraska enroute to visit Vicky's brother and his wife on the coast. They were hoping that the trip together would save their marriage. Burt ended up crucified by the children of the corn as a sacrifice to He Who Walks Behind the Rows.

ROBESON, VICKY Ex-prom queen; Burt's wife. She and Burt had driven fifteen-hundred miles from Boston to Nebraska enroute to visit Vicky's brother and his wife on the coast. They were hoping that the trip together would save their marriage. Instead, she ended up getting crucified in a clearing in Gatlin, Nebraska, as a sacrifice to He Who Walks Behind the Rows, the Corn God.

THE SIXTEEN-YEAR-OLD BOY When Burt came out of the Grace Baptist Church, a sixteen-year-old boy threw a Pensy jackknife into his arm. Burt stabbed him in the throat.

STAMPNELL, RUDY Ten-year-old faith healer Vicky saw in tent prayer meetings when she was child.

STAUNTON, NORMAN Seven-year-old preacher Vicky saw in tent prayer meetings when she was child. He would preach hellfire and brimstone in a Little Lord Fauntleroy suit.

STIGMAN, DONNA Rachel Stigman.

STIGMAN, RACHEL Child of the corn. Her other name was Donna. She was born on June 21, 1957, and died June 21, 1976.

TOBIN, EVE Child of the corn. She had no other name. She was born on June 16, 1965.

THE TWO SKELETONS Burt discovered that Vicky had been crucified next to two skeletons. One had been the police chief, the other the minister of the Grace Baptist Church.

VICKY'S BROTHER He and his wife lived on the coast. Burt and Vicky were on their way to visit them when they got involved with the children of the corn in Nebraska.

VICKY'S FATHER Vicky's mother and father used to drag her to tent prayer meetings when she was a child.

VICKY'S MOTHER Vicky's mother and father used to drag her to tent prayer meetings when she was a child.

VICKY'S SISTER-IN-LAW She and Vicky's brother lived on the coast. Burt and Vicky were on their way to visit them when they got involved with the children of the corn in Nebraska.

WELLS, MARY Child of the corn. Her other name was Roberta. She was born on November 12, 1945, and died November 12, 1964.

WELLS, ROBERTA Mary Wells.

WYNETTE, TAMMY The radio in Burt's car broadcast farm reports, Buck Owens, and Tammy Wynette.

(5p)
NIGHT SHIFT
"Children of the Corn"
Places

THE BIJOU THEATER The theater Burt passed as he ran through Gatlin looking for Vicky. [NOTE: See the "Things" entry THE BIJOU MARQUEE.]

BIRCH STREET Gatlin street that Burt and Vicky passed as they drove through town.

BOSTON The town where Burt and Vicky Robeson lived.

A CAFE As Burt and Vicky drove into Gatlin, they passed a cafe with a Conoco gas island out front.

THE CLEARING After searching for Vicky, Burt hid in the corn. When it got dark, he came into the clearing where Vicky had been crucified. She was held in place by barbed wire (seventy cents a yard at any hardware store), and her eyes had been gouged out and the sockets filled with cornhusks.

THE COAST Burt and Vicky were on their way to the west coast to visit Vicky's brother and his wife.

ELM STREET Gatlin street that Burt and Vicky passed as they drove through town.

GATLIN, NEBRASKA The town where Burt brought the body of the boy he had hit on Route 17. Gatlin was where the corn was worshipped.

GATLIN BAR AND GRILL It was deserted. The mirror behind the bar was broken, and all the beer taps were broken off.

GATLIN ICE CREAM SHOPPE An ice cream parlor Burt saw as he ran through Gatlin looking for Vicky.

GATLIN LUMBERYARD A business Burt and Vicky passed on their way into Gatlin. Their motto was "You Breakum, We Fixum." Their August 1964 calendar hung on the wall of the deserted Gatlin Bar and Grill.

GATLIN MUNICIPAL CENTER The town center where Vicky and Burt decided to bring the body of the boy they had hit on Route 17.

GRACE BAPTIST CHURCH Gatlin church. On July 24, 1976, their sermon was "The Power and Grace of He Who Walks Behind the Rows."

GRAND ISLAND, NEBRASKA A town seventy miles away from Gatlin. Vicky wanted to bring the body of the boy to Grand Island.

HAMBURG The town in Nebraska where Burt left the interstate.

MAPLE STREET Gatlin street that Burt and Vicky passed as they drove through town. A mongrel dog had lain down in the middle of the street.

NEBRASKA The state Vicky and Burt were driving through when they hit the thirteen-year-old boy.

PLEASANT STREET Gatlin street where Main split into two. There was a town square and a bandstand at the intersection.

ROUTE 17 The road where Burt hit the boy whose throat was cut.

THE 76 GAS STATION As Burt and Vicky entered Gatlin, they passed a 76 gas station. The prices were 35.9¢ for regular gas, and 38.9¢ for hi-test. The station also carried diesel fuel (around back). The prices, Burt noted, were four years old.

TENT PRAYER MEETINGS When Vicky was a child, her parents would drag her to prayer tent meetings.

A TOWN SQUARE A town square and a bandstand sat at the intersection of Main and Pleasant Streets in Gatlin.

UPSTATE NEW YORK Burt Robeson grew up in rural upstate New York.

(5p)
NIGHT SHIFT
"Children of the Corn"
Things

THE AGE OF FAVOR The maximum age a child of the corn was allowed to reach. After Vicky's death, Isaac decided that it would drop to eighteen from nineteen. (Isaac had seen the Lord in a dream.)

APRIL 30, 1961 The day Sandra Clawson was born.

AUGUST 15, 1957 The day Craig Boardman was born.

AUGUST 1964 An August 1964 calendar from Gatlin Lumber and Hardware hung on the wall of the deserted Gatlin Bar and Grill.

BAN 5000 Vicky Robeson's deodorant.

A BANDSTAND A town square and a bandstand at the intersection of Main and Pleasant Streets in Gatlin.

BARBED WIRE After searching for Vicky, Burt hid in the corn. Once it got dark, he came into the clearing where Vicky had been crucified. She was held in place by barbed wire, and her eyes had been gouged out and the sockets stuffed with cornhusks.

THE BEER TAPS All the beer taps in the deserted Gatlin Bar and Grill had been broken off.

THE BIJOU MARQUEE It read: "NOW HOWING L MITED EN AGEMEN ELI A TH TAYLOR CLEOPA RA."

THE BOOK In the Grace Baptist Church in Gatlin, Burt found a book with names and birthdates in it. The cover of the book read "Thus Let The Iniquitous Be Cut Down So That The Ground May Be Fertile Again Saith The Lord God Of Hosts." By reading through the lists of names and dates, Burt realized that something happened in Gatlin in 1964 that had to do with religion, corn, and children. [NOTE: See the entry THE CHILDREN OF THE CORN ROSTER.]

CHEESEBURGERS In the deserted Gatlin Bar and Grill, the price cards said that cheeseburgers were 35¢.

THE CHILDREN OF THE CORN ROSTER In the book Burt found in the Grace Baptist Church in Gatlin, the following list was written:

Amos Deigan (Richard), b. Sept. 4, 1945
Sept. 4, 1964
Isaac Renfrew (William), b. Sept. 19, 1945
Sept. 19, 1964
Zepeniah Kirk (George), b. Oct. 14, 1945
Oct. 14, 1964
Mary Wells (Roberta), b. Nov. 12, 1945
Nov. 12, 1964
Yemen Hollis (Edward), b. Jan 5. 1946
Jan. 5, 1965
Rachel Stigman (Donna), b. June 21, 1957
June 21, 1976
Moses Richardson (Henry), b. July 29, 1957
Malachi Boardman (Craig), b. August 15, 1957
Ruth Clawson (Sandra), b. April 30, 1961

In a second book, the roster continued:

Job Gilman (Clayton), b. September 6. 1964
Eve Tobin, b. June 16, 1965
Adam Greenlaw, b. July 11, 1965

CONOCO GAS ISLAND As Burt and Vicky drove into Gatlin, they passed a Conoco gas island in front of a café.

THE CORN Burt and Vicky were driving through acres of corn rows in Nebraska when the boy ran out in front of their car. After Burt hit him, he could see blood in the corn.

A CORN CRUCIFIX When Burt got out of the car to investigate the boy he hit, he found a suitcase in the corn. The suitcase contained socks, two pairs of pants, a shirt, a string tie with a Hopalong Cassidy clasp, and a corn crucifix.

CORNHUSKS After searching for Vicky, Burt hid in the corn. When it got dark, he came into a clearing where he discovered that Vicky had been crucified. She was held in place by barbed wire (seventy cents a yard at any hardware store), and her eyes had been gouged out and the sockets filled with cornhusks.

DIESEL FUEL The Gatlin 76 gas station carried diesel fuel (around back).

THE ELKS CLUB SIGN As Burt and Vicky headed into Gatlin, they passed a sign put up by the Elks Club that said "Gatlin 5 Mi. Drive Carefully Protect Our Children." There were .22-caliber bullet holes in the sign.

THE ENTERING GATLIN SIGN As Burt and Vicky entered Gatlin, they saw a sign that said "You are Now Entering Gatlin, Nicest Little Town in Nebraska – Or Anywhere Else! Pop. 543)"

FARM REPORTS The radio in Burt's car broadcast farm reports, Buck Owens, and Tammy Wynette.

FIFTEEN HUNDRED MILES When Burt and Vicky got involved with the children of the corn, they had driven fifteen-hundred miles into Nebraska from Boston enroute to the coast.

543 The population of Gatlin before the children of the corn went to work.

THE GAS STATION SIGN The 76 gas station in Gatlin had a sign posted that said "Reg 35.9 Hi-Test 38.9 Hi Truckers Diesel Fuel Around Back."

THE GATLIN BAR AND GRILL SPECIAL In the deserted Gatlin Bar and Grill, the price-cards said "Today's Special Ham and Red Eye Gravy w/ Mashed Pot 80¢."

THE GATLIN LUMBER & HARDWARE CALENDAR An August 1964 calendar from the Gatlin Lumberyard hung on the wall of the deserted Gatlin Bar and Grill. Their motto was "You Breakum, We Fixum."

"HELLFIRE AND BRIMSTONE" The sermon subjects preached by seven-year-old evangelist Norman Staunton. He would preach while wearing a Little Lord Fauntleroy suit.

JANUARY 5, 1946 The day Edward Hollis was born.

JANUARY 5, 1965 The day Yemen Hollis died.

JOB 38 The Bible on the lectern in the Grace Baptist Church in Gatlin was open to Job 38. The passage read "Then the Lord answered Job out of the whirlwind, and said, Who is this that darkeneth counsel by words without knowledge?...Where wast thou when I laid the foundations of the earth? declare, if thou hast understanding." [NOTE: This passage consists of Job 38: 1, 2, 4.]

JULY 11, 1965 The day Adam Greenlaw was born.

JULY 24, 1976 The Sunday before Burt and Vicky visited Gatlin.

JULY 29, 1957 The day Henry Richardson was born.

JUNE 16, 1965 The day Eve Tobin was born.

JUNE 21, 1957 The day Donna Stigman was born.

JUNE 21, 1976 The day Rachel Stigman died.

"LEANING ON THE EVERLASTING ARMS" The hymn Baby Hortense would sing in the tent prayer meetings while her daddy passed the plate.

THE LEAVING GATLIN SIGN It said "You Are Now Leaving Gatlin, Nicest Little Town in Nebraska – or Anywhere Else! Drop In Anytime!"

A LITTLE LORD FAUNTLEROY SUIT The suit worn for preaching by seven-year-old evangelist Norman Staunton.

THE MIRROR BEHIND THE BAR The mirror behind the bar in the deserted Gatlin Bar and Grill was broken.

NEBRASKA RADIO The radio in Burt's car broadcast farm reports, Buck Ownes, and Tammy Wynette.

1973 The year Vicky and Burt Robeson met He Who Walks Behind the Rows.

"NO MUSIC..." There was an organ in the Grace Baptist Church in Gatlin. Burt discovered that all the keys had been ripped out and the pipes had been filled with cornhusks. The plaque over the organ said "Make No Music Except With Human Tongue Saith The Lord God."

NOVEMBER 12, 1945 The day Roberta Wells was born.

NOVEMBER 12, 1964 The day Mary Wells died.

OCTOBER 14, 1945 The day George Kirk was born.

OCTOBER 14, 1964 The day Zepeniah Kirk died.

THE "ONLY JESUS SAVES" BILLBOARD As Burt and Vicky drove into Gatlin, they passed an "Only Jesus Saves" billboard.

THE ORGAN There was an organ in the Grace Baptist Church in Gatlin. Burt discovered that all the keys had been ripped out and the pipes had been filled with cornhusks. The plaque over the organ said "Make No Music Except With Human Tongue Saith The Lord God."

A PAINTING OF CHRIST In the Grace Baptist Church in Gatlin, there was a huge painting of Christ with corn hair.

A PENSY JACKKNIFE When Burt came out of the Grace Baptist Church, a sixteen-year-old boy threw a Pensy jackknife into his arm. Burt stabbed him in the throat.

"THE POWER AND GRACE OF HE WHO WALKS BEHIND THE ROWS" The sermon at the Gatlin Grace Baptist Church on July 24, 1976.

A RADIO TOWER A radio tower poked out of the corn as Burt and Vicky drove down Route 17 in Nebraska.

RELIGION, CORN, AND CHILDREN While reading the "Children of the Corn" roster, Burt realized that something had happened in 1964 that had to do with religion, corn, and children.

SEPTEMBER 4, 1945 The day Richard Deigan was born.

SEPTEMBER 4, 1964 The day Amos Deigan died.

SEPTEMBER 19, 1945 The day William Renfrew was born.

SEPTEMBER 19, 1964 The day Isaac Renfrew died.

SEPTEMBER 6, 1964 The day Clayton Gilman was born.

A SHIRT When Burt got out of the car to investigate the boy he hit on Route 17, he found a suitcase in the corn. The suitcase contained socks, two pairs of pants, a shirt, a string tie with a Hopalong Cassidy clasp, and a corn crucifix.

THE SINGLE WORD SIGNS As Burt and Vicky drove into Gatlin, they passed signs which contained one word each. The signs spelled "A-Cloud-By-Day-A-Pillar-Of-Fire-By-Night-Take-This-And-Eat-Saith-The-Lord."

SOCKS When Burt got out of the car to investigate the boy he hit on Route 17, he found a suitcase in the corn. The suitcase contained socks, two pairs of pants, a shirt, a string tie with a Hopalong Cassidy clasp, and a corn crucifix.

STRAWBERRY RHUBARB PIE In the deserted Gatlin Bar and Grill, the price cards said that strawberry rhubarb pie was twenty-five cents.

A STRING TIE WITH A HOPALONG CASSIDY CLASP When Burt got out of the car to investigate the boy he hit on Route 17, he found a suitcase in the corn. The suitcase contained socks, two pairs of pants, a shirt, a string tie with a Hopalong Cassidy clasp, and a corn crucifix.

A SUITCASE When Burt got out of the car to investigate the boy he hit, he found a suitcase in the corn. The suitcase contained socks, two pairs of pants, a shirt, a string tie with a Hopalong Cassidy clasp, and a corn crucifix.

T-BIRD Burt and Vicky's car.

38.9¢ The (four-year-old) price posted for hi-test gas at the Gatlin 76 gas station.

35.9¢ The (four-year-old) price posted for regular gas at the Gatlin 76 gas station.

TIN HALOES The Grace Sisters, evangelists Vicky saw in tent prayer meetings when she was a child, wore tin haloes in their "act."

.22 CALIBER BULLET HOLES As Burt and Vicky headed into Gatlin, they passed a sign put up by the Elks Club that said "Gatlin 5 Mi. Drive Carefully Protect Our Children." There were small .22 caliber bullet holes in the sign.

TWO PAIRS OF PANTS When Burt got out of the car to investigate the boy he hit on Route 17, he found a suitcase in the corn. The suitcase contained socks, two pairs of pants, a shirt, a string tie with a Hopalong Cassidy clasp, and a corn crucifix.

THE WORLD'S BEST JOE In the deserted Gatlin Bar and Grill, the price cards said the "World's Best Joe" was ten cents a cup.

"YOU BREAKUM, WE FIXUM" The Gatlin Lumber and Hardware company's motto.

❖❖❖

(5q)
NIGHT SHIFT
"The Last Rung on the Ladder"
People

THE BEAUTY CONTEST JUDGE Kitty won a beauty contest after high school and married one of the judges. She got divorced when Larry was in law school.

THE COMPANY PRESIDENT A company president once introduced Larry as a "hired gun."

HELEN Larry's ex-wife. They had divorced in 1971.

THE HIRED MAN Larry's father had taken on a hired man. The day of the incident in the barn, he didn't show up, and Larry's father fired him a month later.

IKE The day the incident in the barn took place, Ike was still the nation's president.

KATRINA Larry's sister.

KITTY Katrina, Larry's sister. Larry had once saved her life by piling hay underneath her when the ladder she was climbing in the barn pulled away from the crossbeam, leaving her dangling sixty feet off the barn floor. Kitty committed suicide by jumping from the top floor of an insurance building in Los Angeles.

KITTY'S LANDLADY Kitty's landlady in the apartment bulding in Van Nuys was a nice lady who liked Kitty.

KITTY'S SECOND HUSBAND After Kitty divorced her beauty contest judge husband, she remarried again in Los Angeles.

LARRY Kitty's brother, and "one of the best independent corporation lawyers in America." Larry had once saved Kitty's life by piling hay beneath her when the ladder she was climbing in the barn pulled away from the crossbeam, leaving her dangling sixty feet off the barn floor. He got Kitty's last letter after she had killed herself.

LARRY AND KITTY'S FATHER He owned three hundred acres in Hemingford Home, eighty miles west of Omaha. Larry hesitated calling his father about Kitty's last letter because the old man had already had two heart attacks.

LARRY AND KITTY'S MOTHER She died when Larry and Kitty were in high school in Columbia City.

THE NEAREST NEIGHBOR The day the incident in the barn took place, Larry's father had gone to visit their nearest neighbor, who was seven miles away.

PEDERSEN, DR. The general practitioner from Columbia City who treated Kitty's broken left ankle the day she fell sixty feet into the hay.

THE THREE ASSISTANTS Larry had three fulltime assistants in his law office.

(5q)
NIGHT SHIFT
"The Last Rung on the Ladder"
Places

AN APARTMENT BULDING ON VAN NUYS The building in Los Angeles where Kitty had been living when she commited suicide.

COLUMBIA CITY When Larry and Kitty's mother died, they were both attending high school in Columbia City.

HEMINGFORD HOME, NEBRASKA Larry and Kitty had grown up in Hemingford Home, eighty miles west of Omaha.

"THE HOME PLACE" Larry's father's farm in Nebraska.

AN INSURANCE BUILDING Kitty committed suicide by jumping from the top floor of an insurance building in Los Angeles.

INTERSTATE 80 Interstate 80 and Nebraska Route 96 were the only roads near the home place that were not dirt.

LAW SCHOOL Kitty got divorced from her beauty-contest-judge husband when Larry was in law school.

LOS ANGELES Larry and his father had gone to L.A. for Kitty's funeral.

NEBRASKA ROUTE 96 Interstate 80 and Nebraska Route 96 were the only roads near the home place that were not dirt.

OMAHA Larry and Kitty's childhood home, Hemingford Home, was eighty miles west of Omaha.

A ONE-ROOM SCHOOL Larry had attended a one-room school as a child.

SEVEN MILES AWAY Larry's father's nearest neighbor was seven miles away.

THE THIRD LOFT The ladder in the barn was nailed to a crossbeam in the third loft. It was seventy feet off the floor of the barn.

A TRACTOR DEALERSHIP When Larry's father lost his farm, he went to work selling tractors, and eventually bought a dealership.

THE UNIVERSITY OF NEBRASKA Larry got a football scholarship to the University of Nebraska.

WILMINGTON, DELAWARE Kitty's last letter to Larry had come postmarked Wilmington, Delaware.

THE WOODSHED After Larry's father found out about the incident in the barn, he took Larry to the woodshed. Every time his father whacked him, Larry had to thank God that Kitty was still alive.

(5q)
NIGHT SHIFT
"The Last Rung on the Ladder"
Things

A BEAUTY CONTEST Kitty won a beauty contest after high school and married one of the judges.

"CALL-GIRL SWAN DIVES TO HER DEATH" The newspaper headline that reported Kitty's suicide.

A DESOTO Dr. Pedersen's car.

A FOOTBALL SCHOLARSHIP Larry got a football scholarship to the University of Nebraska.

THE HAY After Larry received Kitty's last letter, he thought to himself "She was the one who always knew the hay would be there." He hoped that she didn't think he'd forgotten, but instead, that she got tired of waiting. [NOTE: See the entry KITTY'S LAST LETTER.]

"A HIRED GUN" The term a company president once used to introduce Larry.

THE INCIDENT IN THE BARN The incident that took place when Kitty ended up dangling off the last rung of the ladder. Larry piled straw beneath her, told her to let go, and her trust in her brother was so great that she dropped off without knowing what Larry had done. [NOTE: See the entry KITTY'S LAST LETTER.]

KITTY'S LAST LETTER Larry received it after Kitty's funeral. It was postmarked two weeks before she died. There was one sentence in it that would have probably brought Larry on the run:

> *Dear Larry,*
> *I've been thinking about it a lot lately...and what I've decided is that it would have been better for me if that last rung had broken before you could put the hay down.*
>
> *Your,*
> *Kitty*

KITTY'S LEFT ANKLE When Kitty let go of the ladder and dropped sixty feet into the hay Larry had piled up, she broke her left ankle. Dr. Pedersen, the GP from Columbia City, said it was a miracle she wasn't killed.

THE LADDER The ladder in the barn was nailed to a crossbeam in the third loft. It had forty-three rungs and was seventy feet off the floor of the barn. Larry thought "The ladder had always held us before, we thought it would always hold us again, which is a philosophy that gets men and nations in trouble time after time."

LOW-TOPPED KEDS The day of the incident in the barn, Kitty was wearing low-topped Keds.

1971 The year Larry and Helen had divorced.

A SATURDAY IN EARLY NOVEMBER The day the incident in the barn took place.

SEVENTY FEET The ladder in the barn was nailed to a crossbeam in the third loft. It had forty-three rungs and was seventy feet off the floor of the barn.

SIXTY FEET When the ladder in the barn pulled away from the crossbeam, Kitty was left dangling off the last rung, sixty feet up off the barn floor.

300 ACRES Larry and Kitty's father had three hundred acres of flat, rich land in Nebraska. Larry's father called it "the home place."

TRACTORS When Larry's father lost his farm, he went to work selling tractors and eventually bought a dealership.

TWO HEART ATTACKS Larry hesitated calling his father about Kitty's last letter because the old man had already had two heart attacks.

❖❖❖

(5r)
NIGHT SHIFT
"The Man Who Loved Flowers"
People

THE BABY The young woman's child. The man who loved flowers saw them on Third Avenue.

"BETTY AND HENRY" Two people the little girl on Third Avenue sang about.

THE CRIME OVERLORD A news story about an unnamed crime overlord not being indicted was heard on the radio as the man who loved flowers strolled New York's Third Avenue.

THE DEAD WOMAN A news story about an unnamed dead woman being found in the East River was heard on the radio as the man who loved flowers strolled New York's Third Avenue.

THE FOUR SEASONS Group that did the song "Sherry."

THE GIRL IN THE SAILOR BLOUSE The sixth girl the man who loved flowers had killed with a hammer.

THE GROUP OF MEN Men on Third Avenue. They all watched a four-figure color TV in a hardware store window.

"THE HAMMER MURDERER" A news story about a hammer murderer being loose was heard on the radio as the man who loved flowers strolled New York's Third Avenue. The man who loved flowers was "the hammer murderer."

THE LITTLE GIRL The man who loved flowers saw a little girl on Third Avenue singing about "Betty and Henry."

"THE MAN WHO LOVED FLOWERS" The unnamed young man who just happened to be a psychopath. King tells us his name was "Love." The love of his past was a girl named Norma, who had been dead for ten years. It isn't clear whether or not he killed Norma.

THE MIDDLE-AGED MARRIED COUPLE A couple who saw the man who loved flowers walk away. They did not know he had just killed the girl in the sailor blouse.

NORMA The dead lover of the man who loved flowers. At the time of the story, she had been dead ten years. It isn't clear whether or not he killed her, but it is clear that he has been searching for her for years now, killing the women he mistakes for her in his search. Norma's favorite fruit was the Valencia orange.

AN OLD LADY A woman who smiled at the man who loved flowers as he strolled New York's Third Avenue.

THE OLD MAN An unnamed sixty-eight-year-old man who sold flowers to the man who loved flowers.

THE RUSSIANS A news story about the Russians exploding a nuclear device was heard on the radio as the man who loved flowers strolled New York's Third Avenue.

THE TWO MEN WITH BEER BELLIES The two unnamed men who pitched nickels as the man who loved flowers strolled New York's Third Avenue.

TWO PREGNANT WOMEN Two women on Third Avenue.

THE TWO TEENAGE GIRLS Two girls on Third Avenue. They giggled at the man who loved flowers.

THE YOUNG TRAFFIC COP The cop at the intersection of Third Avenue and 69th Street. He stopped traffic to let the man who loved flowers cross.

THE YOUNG WOMAN The man who loved flowers saw a young woman with a baby on Third Avenue.

(5r)
NIGHT SHIFT
"The Man Who Loved Flowers"
Places

EAST RIVER The river where the body of the unnamed woman was found.

73RD STREET The street where the man who loved flowers turned off Third and saw the girl in the sailor blouse.

THIRD AVENUE Street in New York City. In May of 1963, the man who loved flowers walked this avenue.

VIETNAM A news story about Vietnam was heard on the radio as the man who loved flowers strolled New York's Third Avenue.

(5r)
NIGHT SHIFT
"The Man Who Loved Flowers"
Things

A BAG OF VALENCIA ORANGES When Norma was alive, this was one of the gifts brought to her by the man who loved flowers. Valencia oranges were Norma's favorites.

A BOUQUET The flower vendor offered the young man a bouquet for a dollar, or a half-dozen tea roses for three-fifty. He bought the roses.

A BOX OF CANDY When Norma was alive, this was one of the gifts brought to her by the man who loved flowers.

A BRACELET When Norma was alive, this was one of the gifts brought to her by the man who loved flowers.

THE COLOR TV A four-figure TV set watched by a group of men in a hardware store window.

A HAMMER The murder weapon used by the man who loved flowers. He had killed six women with it.

"LOVE" The name of the man who loved flowers.

MAY 1963 The month and year the man who loved flowers walked New York City.

NORMA'S GIFTS When Norma was alive, the man who loved flowers brought her the following gifts: a box of candy, a bracelet, and a bag of Valencia oranges.

A NUCLEAR DEVICE A news story about the Russians exploding a nuclear device was heard on the radio as the man who loved flowers strolled New York's Third Avenue.

THE RADIO NEWS As the man who loved flowers strolled New York's Third Avenue, the following news was heard on the radio: Vietnam, there was a hammer murderer loose, a dead woman had been found in the East River, a crime overlord had not been indicted, and the Russians had exploded a nuclear device.

"SHERRY" Song by the Four Seasons that was playing on the radio as the young man strolled New York's Third Avenue.

TEA ROSES The flower vendor offered the young man a bouquet for a dollar, or a half-dozen tea roses for three-fifty. He bought the roses.

❖❖❖

(5s)
NIGHT SHIFT
"One for the Road"
People

BOOTH The narrator of "One for the Road."

BOOTH'S MOTHER She drank her share of beer in Tookey's.

HENRY, LAMONT He said that no one would ever see Richie Messina again after he got drunk and went into the Lot at night.

LARRIBEE, BILLY The snowplow driver.

LUMLEY, FRANCIE Gerard Lumley's wife. She was turned in to a vampire when the Lumleys got lost in the Lot during a January blizzard.

LUMLEY, GERARD New Jersey man who got lost in the Lot with his family. He, his wife Francie, and his daughter Janey were on their way to see his wife's sister when they ended up in the Lot.

LUMLEY, JANEY Gerard Lumley's daughter. She was turned in to a vampire when the Lumleys got lost in the Lot during a January blizzard.

MESSINA, MRS. Richie's wife. After Richie never came back from the Lot, she moved to Rhode Island.

MESSINA, RICHIE He got drunk and went into the Lot at night. No one ever saw him again.

TOOKEY, MISSUS Tookey's wife. She died in '74. She was responsible for getting Tookey's written up in *Downeast*, the *Sunday Telegram*, and the Boston *Globe*.

TOOKLANDER, HERB He owned Tookey's Bar in the northern part of Falmouth.

VICTORIA Booth's wife. She died in '73.

THE WATERVILLE COUPLE The couple that bought Tookey's after Tookey died.

(5s)
NIGHT SHIFT
"One for the Road"
Places

HARMONY HILL CEMETERY Sometimes people disappeared near there.

JERUSALEM'S LOT Maine town that "went bad" and burned down two years prior to the Lumley's getting lost in the Lot. It was burned out. The fire started by the Marsten House, a house that overlooked Jointner Avenue.

JOINTNER AVENUE The Marsten House overlooked Jointer Avenue.

THE MARSTEN HOUSE The fire that burned down Jerusalem's Lot started by the Marsten House.

NEW JERSEY The Lumleys' home state.

RHODE ISLAND Richie Messina's wife moved there after Richie never came back from the Lot.

SCHOOLYARD HILL Sometimes people disappeared near there.

TOOKEY'S BAR Bar owned and operated by Herb Tooklander in the northern part of Falmouth.

TOOKEY'S INN OR TOOKEY'S REST The two names to which Missus Tookey considered changing the name of Tookey's Bar.

(5s)
NIGHT SHIFT
"One for the Road"
Things

THE BOSTON *GLOBE* Newspaper that did an article about Tookey's.

DOUAY BIBLE Tookey threw his mother's Douay Bible at Janey Lumley when she came at him as a vampire.

DOWNEAST Magazine that did an article about Tookey's.

FOUR WHEEL DRIVE SCOUT Tookey's vehicle. He used the Scout to take Gerard Lumley into the Lot to look for his wife and daughter.

JANUARY 10 The day "one hell of a northeaster" was blowing outside Tookey's Bar.

MERCEDES Gerard Lumley's car.

THE *SUNDAY TELEGRAM* Newspaper that did an article about Tookey's.

❖❖❖

(5t)
NIGHT SHIFT
"The Woman in the Room"
People

BLACK OAK ARKANSAS Country music band. John could hear them singing "Jim Dandy" on a radio somewhere on the third floor of Central Maine Hospital.

CRICHTON, MICHAEL Author of *The Terminal Man*.

THE DOCTOR The unnamed doctor who did John's mother's cortotomy. He was six foot, four inches tall and had a red, sandy beard.

A FAT MAN WITH AN ELASTIC BANDAGE ON ONE LEG One of the patients at Central Maine Hospital. He was walking the hall when John arrived to visit his mother.

JOHN The woman in the room's son. He helped her die by feeding her Darvon capsules and making it look like a suicide.

JOHN'S GRANDMOTHER She was eighty-six years old and bedridden. High blood pressure had made her blind and senile. John's mother had cared for her before she herself got sick.

JOHN'S GRANDPARENTS John's mother had moved her family to Maine to take care of her parents.

JOHN'S MOTHER'S ROOMMATE One of his mother's roommates told John's mother that a patient had lost $500 when she was in the hospital.

JOHN'S WIFE She was alseep when John called Kevin to talk about their mother.

KEVIN John's brother; the woman in the room's other son. He was adopted and lived in Andover, Maine. He only made it to the hospital once or twice a week.

MONROE, MARILYN She crossed the line from a heavy habit to a lethal dosage.

A TALK-SHOW HOST An unnamed TV host who was talking about Nixon. John could hear him on a TV somewhere on the third floor of Central Maine Hospital.

THE WOMAN IN THE ROOM John and Kevin's terminally ill mother.

(5t)
NIGHT SHIFT
"The Woman in the Room"
Places

ANDOVER, MAINE The town where Kevin lived. It was seventy miles west and Kevin only made it to the hospital once or twice a week.

THE BACK SEAT OF SOME FRIEND'S CAR The first place John ever got laid.

THE BARS ON LOWER LISBON STREET The residents of Lewiston loved jigs and reels almost as much as they loved to cut each other up in the bars on lower Lisbon Street.

CENTRAL MAINE HOSPITAL The Lewiston, Maine, hospital where John's mother underwent the cortotomy. She was in Room 312.

LEWISTON, MAINE The town where Central Maine Hospital was located.

RAYMOND, MAINE The town where John lived. It was a twenty-two mile drive to Lewiston via Routes 302 and 202.

ROOM 312 John's mother's room in Central Maine Hospital.

ROUTES 302 AND 202 The roads John would take to Lewiston to visit his mother.

SONNY'S MARKET The store where John bought his two six-packs of Black Label before he visited his mother.

(5t)
NIGHT SHIFT
"The Woman in the Room"
Things

ANACIN ARTHRITIS PAIN FORMULA One of the medications John's mother had in her home medicine cabinet.

"CAN HE DO IT?" The question John had to ask himself.

CANCER OF THE STOMACH John's mother's terminal illness.

CORTOTOMY The operation performed on John's mother in an attempt to relieve her pain. The cortotomy made John think of Michael Crichton's *The Terminal Man*.

DARVON CAPSULES John fed his mother Darvon capsules and left the empty bottle in her hand so it would look like a suicide, which, in a way, it was. John's mother really wanted to die. John just helped her through the door.

ELAVIL A medication John's mother was on. It sedated her enough so that she didn't know that John would often come to visit her drunk.

"ELECTRIC COMPANY" Kid's show. John would drink one can of Black Label while watching the show with his kids before he visited his mother.

FLEET SUPPOSITORIES One of the medications John's mother had in her home medicine cabinet.

JOHN'S GRANDMOTHER'S WET DIAPER Once John had smarted off to his mother and she had whacked him with his grandmother's wet diaper. The first whop with the diaper had upset his bowl of Special K. John thought that "there is nothing in the world so perfect to set a twelve-year-old's impression of his place in the scheme of things into proper perspective as being beaten across the back with a wet grandmother-diaper."

KOOL The cigarette John gave his mother in the hospital.

A LOT OF WATER After John fed his mother the Darvon, he went home and, while waiting for the phone to ring, he watched TV and drank a lot of water.

"MR. ROGERS" Kid's show. John would drink two cans of Black Label while watching the show with his kids before he visited his mother.

"THE NIGHT OF THE LIVING DEAD" George Romero film. The patients at Central Maine Hospital made John think of the zombies in this movie.

PEPTO-BISMOL One of the medications John's mother had in her home medicine cabinet.

PHILLIPS MILK OF MAGNESIA One of the medications John's mother had in her home medicine cabinet.

A POLKA WITH FRENCH LYRICS John could hear a polka with French lyrics playing somewhere on the third floor of Central Maine Hospital.

"SESAME STREET" Kid's show. John would drink three cans of Black Label while watching the show with his kids before he visited his mother.

SPECIAL K The cereal John had been eating when he smarted off to his mother and she whacked him with a wet grandmother-diaper.

A SUCRETS BOX John's mother kept her aspirin in a Sucrets box.

THE TERMINAL MAN A novel by Michael Crichton. John's mother's cortotomy made John think of this novel.

A TWENTY-TWO MILE DRIVE It was twenty-two miles from John's house in Raymond to Central Maine Hospital in Lewiston.

TWO SIX-PACKS OF BLACK LABEL The beer John would consume before visiting his mother. He'd buy it at Sonny's Market and sit with the kids and watch their afternoon TV: three beers with "Sesame Street," two with "Mr. Rogers," one with "Electric Company," and one with supper. The other five he would take in the car with him on the way to the hospital.

UREMIC COMA The doctors figured that John's mother would die of a uremic coma when her kidneys shut down.

THE WOMAN IN THE ROOM'S MEDICINE CABINET John's mother had the following in her home medicine cabinet: Fleet suppositories, Phillips Milk of Magnesia, Anacin Arthritis Pain Formula, Pepto-Bismol, and a bottle of Darvon capsules.

THE STAND
[Original Version]
(1978)

DEDICATION

For my wife Tabitha:
This dark chest of wonders

[NO CONTENTS PAGE]

BOOK BREAKDOWN

AUTHOR'S NOTE

[One-page note from Stephen King]

BOOK ONE
Captain Trips
June 16-July 4, 1980

[Thirty-three untitled chapters numbered 1-33]

BOOK TWO
On The Border
July 5-September 6, 1980

[Seventeen untitled chapters numbered 34-50]

BOOK THREE
The Stand
September 7, 1980-January 10, 1981

[Seventeen untitled chapters numbered 51-67]

Chapter 68
Part 1: Mayday
Part 2: Dusk, of a Summer Evening

(6)
THE STAND
People

ACE HIGH One of Flagg's Las Vegas men.

AHAZ As Ralph, Glen, and Larry were taken into custody on the Utah highway, Larry told Flagg's men that Ahaz was another name for Randall Flagg.

ANDROS, MR. Nick Andros's father. He was an independent farmer.

ANDROS, MRS. Nick Andros's mother. She carried on the family farm after her husband's death, but then lost it to the "big operators." She was killed in an accident in 1972.

ANDROS, NICK The deaf-mute who was beat up in Shoyo, Arkansas, jailed, befriended by Sheriff Baker, and who ended up the only Shoyo survivor of Captain Trips. He went to the Free Zone where he became a charter member of the ad hoc committee,

and was ultimately killed in an explosion set by Harold Lauder. He later appeared in dreams to Tom Cullen as Tom and Stu tried to get back to the Free Zone.

ANDY One of Flagg's pilots at the Indian Springs project.

ANUBIS As Ralph, Glen, and Larry were taken into custody on the Utah highway, Larry told Flagg's men that Anubis was another name for Randall Flagg.

THE ARAB Rita Blakemoor's husband was at a luncheon with an Arab when he had a massive heart attack.

ARIZONA TROOPER #1 One of the state troopers who captured Lloyd Henreid.

ARIZONA TROOPER #2 One of the state troopers who captured Lloyd Henreid.

ARLENE A girl who worked at Jane's Place in California.

THE ARMY DRIVER An unnamed enlisted man who let out three bellowing sneezes as he drove the Arnette citizens to the airport.

THE ARNOLDS One of the white families that wanted nothing to do with John Freemantle.

THE ASSISTANT DISTRICT ATTORNEY Judge Farris read in Lapham's *Law and the Classes of Society* about a black woman from Brixton, Mississippi, who was sentenced to ten years in prison for shoplifting. The assistant district attorney and three jurors had been black.

ASTAROTH As Ralph, Glen, and Larry were taken into custody on the Utah highway, Larry told Flagg's men that Astaroth was another name for Randall Flagg.

ATOMIC ENERGY COMMISSION OFFICIALS During his incarceration in Stovington, Stu Redman heard on the news that Atomic Energy Commission officials in Miller County denied that there was any possiblity of a reactor meltdown at the Fouke, Texas, nuclear reactor.

BABE The owner of Babe's Kwik-Eat cafe in east Texas.

BAILEY, STAN Paul Burlson's partner in Vegas.

BAKER, JANE Sheriff John Baker's wife. She died of Captain Trips in Shoyo, Arkansas.

BAKER, SHERIFF JOHN The Shoyo, Arkansas, sheriff who befriended Nick Andros after Nick was beat up by Ray Booth, Vince Hogan, Billy Warner, and Mike Childress. He died from Captain Trips.

BALL, BRIAN The Rutland, Vermont, boy who had taken third prize at the science fair in 1977 for a doorbell that could be rung by a walkie-talkie from a distance. Harold Lauder used Brian's diagram to build the remote-controlled bomb with which he blew up Ralph Brentner's house.

BALLINGER, MR. An administrator at the Stovington plague center.

THE BARTENDER Wendell Elbert, Trashcan Man's father, shot and killed the bartender at O'Toole's.

BATEMAN, GLEN Glendon Pequod Bateman, B.A., M.A., M.F.A. The sixtyish assistant professor of sociology Stu Redman met on the road. He had taught at Woodsville Community College. He became part of the first Free Zone ad hoc committee, and eventually traveled to Las Vegas to fulfill Mother Abagail's final instructions. He was one of "the righteous" killed in the final "Hand of God" atomic explosion in Vegas.

BATEMAN, MRS. Glen's wife. She had been dead ten years when Stu ran across Glen after the flu hit.

BATEMAN'S NEIGHBOR Glen Bateman had been neighbors with the woman who had owned Kojak before the flu. She didn't survive, but Big Steve (Kojak) did.

BEAME, ABE A former New York mayor.

BEETHOVEN Larry Underwood and Rita Blakemoor listened to Debussy before they fled New York, but Larry would have preferred Wagner or Beethoven.

BENSON, CLIFF One of Flagg's pilot trainees.

BETTY, AUNT Stu Redman's aunt. He remembered when she was pregnant.

THE BIG MAN WITH HIS FISTS The unnamed Free Zone citizen who caught his woman screwing around, and beat up the woman and her illicit lover.

BIG STEVE Kojak the dog. ("Big Steve" was his original "pre-flu" name.)

A BLACK VIETNAM VET Randall Flagg had once killed six cops in New York and New Jersey, and a black Vietnam vet.

THE BLACK WOMAN SHOPLIFTER Judge Farris read in Lapham's *Law and the Classes of Society* about a black woman from Brixton, Mississippi, who was sentenced to ten years in prison for shoplifting. The assistant district attorney and three jurors had been black.

BLAKELY, MRS. Tom Cullen's mother's friend. She died from the flu.

BLAKEMOOR, HARRY Rita's husband. Harry had died of a stroke two years prior to Captain Trips. He had been a "career executive with a major New York bank."

BLAKEMOOR, RITA A society woman that Larry Underwood met in Central Park after the flu hit. They traveled together (after a brief separation marked by a reunion in the Lincoln Tunnel). Rita died in Larry's sleeping bag in the hills. Larry never got over her death.

THE BLONDE GIRL While in the Boulder library, Frannie Goldsmith saw a pretty young blonde of about fourteen reading a book called *600 Simple Recipes*.

BO DONALDSON AND THE HEYWOODS After Larry Underwood broke up with Julie, she told him he was the eighties' answer to Bo Donaldson and the Heywoods. [NOTE: In *The Stand: The Complete & Uncut Edition*, this reference was changed to Zager and Evans.]

BONNIE Dinny McCarthy's "mom" in Las Vegas after Angelina Hirschfield.

BOOTH, RAY Sheriff John Baker's brother-in-law. He beat up and robbed Nick Andros in Shoyo, Arkansas.

"THE BOSS" The warden at the Brownsville Minimum Security Station.

BRACEMAN, REVEREND The Shoyo, Arkansas, Methodist minister.

BRADENTON, CHRISTOPHER Kit Bradenton. Randall Flagg's contact in Mountain City. Bradenton knew Flagg as "Richard Fry," and supplied him with a car.

BRADENTON, KIT Christopher Bradenton.

BRADFORD, SARAH Mrs. Robert Bradford. The matronly woman who was in Dr. Sweeney's office to pay her bill the day the Trents brought Hector in with flu symptoms.

BRANNIGAN, ROY A realtor in Ogunquit, Maine, who did not survive Captain Trips. Harold Lauder "commandeered" his Cadillac Coupe de Ville after his death.

THE BREAD DELIVERY MAN The bread delivery man in Babe's Kwik-Eat cafe was infected with the flu by Harry Trent.

BRENTNER, RALPH The fortyish man in a truck who picked up Nick Andros and Tom Cullen on their way out of Kansas. The three went to Nebraska together, (along with several other picked up in the way). [NOTE: See the "People" entry MOTHER ABAGAIL'S VISITORS.] Ralph eventually became part of the company that went to Las Vegas (the others were Larry Underwood, Glen Bateman, and Stu Redman, although Stu never made it. He broke his leg and was left behind.) Ralph was killed in Trashcan Man's "Hand of God" atomic explosion in Vegas.

BRENTWOOD, JOE BOB Bill Hapscomb's cousin. He was a Texas state trooper. He came to Hap's to tell the guys that men were coming in from the plague center in Atlanta after Campion's death.

BRINKMEYER, JUNE Nick Andros and company met Olivia Walker and June Brinkmeyer on their way to Mother Abagail's in Nebraska. June and Olivia joined the men (Tom Cullen, Ralph Brentner, and Dick Ellis) and Gina McCone on the dream-inspired trip to Hemingford Home.

BRUCE, FRANK D. A Project Blue worker who died in the cafeteria with his face in a bowl of Campbell's Chunky Sirloin soup.

BRUETT, BOBBY Norm Bruett's son.

BRUETT, LILA Norm's wife.

BRUETT, LUKE Norm Bruett's son.

BRUETT, NORMAN Arnette, Texas, resident who was at Hapscomb's Texaco the day Charles Campion "touched down" after his escape from the Project Blue lab. Norm had worked in the defunct paper factory, and at the time of Campion's arrival, was on welfare. Norm died from the flu.

BUCHAN, SERGEANT The national guardsman who shot and killed Ray Flowers.

BUNDELL, AL A young Free Zone lawyer who was voted head of the Zone's law committee.

BURLSON, PAUL The man in charge of keeping a file of Las Vegas residents for Flagg.

BURROUGHS, STEVENSON, AND ROBERT HOWARD Authors Harold Lauder read as a youngster.

THE BUSBOY The boy who delivered Nick Andros's supper from Ma's Truck Stop.

CAIDE, BRADLEY A former deputy of Sheriff John Baker.

CAIDE, MRS. Bradley Caide's wife.

THE CAIDE BABY Bradley Caide's child. It died of crib death.

THE CALLER After Ray Flowers was blown away by the army, a caller urged Ray to "keep up the good work and not let them bully you."

CAMPANARI, FREDDY One of Flagg's men. Campanari was badly burned in the Indian Springs fire set by Trashcan Man.

CAMPION, CHARLES D. The government employee who fled from the biological testing site when Project Blue fell apart. He and his family got sick in Tahoe and ended up crashing into the gas pumps at Hapscomb's Texaco. Charles died in the ambulance on the way to Braintree. His wife and daughter had died on the way to Arnette. [NOTE: In *The Stand: The Complete & Uncut Edition*, the story begins with Campion fleeing the test site.]

CAMPION, LAVON Sally and Charles Campion's daughter. She died from Captain Trips.

CAMPION, SALLY Charles Campion's wife. She died from Captain Trips.

THE CAMPUS DOCTOR The doctor who prescribed Frannie Goldsmith's birth control pills.

CARMICHAEL, HENRY Hank Carmichael. Arnette, Texas, resident who was at Hapscomb's Texaco the day Charles Campion "touched down" after his escape from the Project Blue lab. Henry worked thirty hours a week in the ailing calculator factory.

CARSLEIGH, LEN One of Bill Starkey's Project Blue co-workers. [NOTE: In *The Stand: The Complete & Uncut Edition*, this character's name was changed to Len Creighton.]

CATHY YOUNG AND THE INNOCENTS A pre-flu rock group that Harold Lauder remembered. [NOTE: In *The Stand: The Complete & Uncut Edition*, Cathy's name was changed to "Kathy."]

CHILDRESS, MIKE One of the creeps who beat up and robbed Nick Andros in Shoyo, Arkansas.

CHILDRESS, MRS. Mike Childress's ex-wife.

CHRIS One of Larry Underwood's New York friends. Larry intended to look Chris up while he was in town visiting his mother. Larry's plans changed.

CINQUE Randall Flagg once suggested that Donald DeFreeze adopt the name of Cinque.

THE CLERK The unnamed guy behind the counter during Lloyd Henreid's and Poke Freeman's holdup of a gas station in Burrack, Arizona.

CLEVELAND, JACK The government official who knew who we had behind both curtains, the Iron one and the Bamboo one.

THE COLORADO REVIVAL PREACHER The escapee from the Brownsville Minimum Security Station who claimed he saw a large castle with a moat in the desert later found Jesus in a big way when a Colorado revival preacher did a show at the prison.

CONSTABLE, LAURIE The twenty-six-year-old nurse who joined Larry Underwood's group and became part of the Free Zone population.

CONVEIGH, BEN One of the white men who wanted nothing to do with John Freemantle.

CONVEIGH, GEORGE One of the white men who wanted nothing to do with John Freemantle.

THE CONVULSIVE BOY One of Dick Ellis's Free Zone patients.

COOKIE Mrs. Sarah Bradford.

THE COUGHER One of the flu-infected people left alive at the Stovington plague center after Stu Redman escaped his room. Stu thought of him as "The Cougher."

CRADDOCK, WILLY An Arnette, Texas, resident who played cards with Stu Redman at Ralph Hodges's house.

CROSS, MR. Nadine's father. He was killed in a car accident when Nadine was six. [NOTE: See the "Places" entry THE WHITE MOUNTAINS.]

CROSS, MRS. Nadine's mother. She was killed in a car accident when Nadine was six. [NOTE: See the "Places" entry THE WHITE MOUNTAINS.]

CROSS, NADINE The woman Larry Underwood met at a New England farmhouse as she traveled with Leo "Joe" Rockway. Flagg eventually chose her as his wife, and she cheated him out of a son by jumping out of a window in a Las Vegas hotel.

THE CROSS BOY Nadine's brother. He was killed in a car accident when Nadine was six. [NOTE: See the "Places" entry THE WHITE MOUNTAINS.]

CULLEN, DON Tom Cullen's father. He ran off with DeeDee Packalotte.

CULLEN, MRS. Tom's mother.

CULLEN, TOM The retarded man Nick Andros met on Main Street in May, Oklahoma. Tom became part of the Free Zone's population and was sent as a spy to Las Vegas. He saved Stu Redman's life by rescuing him after Stu broke his leg, and helped him back to health. Stu and Tom finally made it back to the Free Zone. Tom claimed that Nick Andros came to him in his dreams after Nick was killed in Harold Lauder's explosion at Ralph Brentner's house, and that Nick spoke to him.

"CUNNILINGUS" Hatch Cunningham's nickname.

CUNNINGHAM, HATCH One of Trashcan Man's childhood taunters. His nickname was "Cunnilingus."

DALE, UNCLE Stu Redman's uncle. Stu remembered shooting his first deer on a trip with Uncle Dale.

DANNEMONT, ROLF A Free Zone citizen. He owned a Remington rifle.

DAVID One of Larry Underwood's New York friends. Larry intended to look David up while he was in town visiting his mother. Larry's plans changed.

DAYNA JURGENS'S HIGH SCHOOL BOYFRIEND He was a "leather jacket type."

THE DEACONS One of the white families that wanted nothing to do with John Freemantle.

THE DEAD MAN AND WOMAN On his way out of New York, Larry Underwood came upon an El Dorado with a dead man and woman inside.

THE DEAD MAYFLOWER DRIVER On their way out of New York, Larry Underwood and Rita Blakemoor saw a man who had been driving a Mayflower moving van hanging dead from the van's window.

A DEAD SOLDIER On his way through the Lincoln Tunnel, Larry Underwood tripped over the hand of a dead soldier.

DEAN, JAMES One of the actors who appeared in the movie "Hell's Angel On Wheels."

DEBBINS, JASON A guard at the Northern Indiana Correctional Center for Boys who shot himself after Captain Trips hit.

DEBUSSY Larry Underwood and Rita Blakemoor listened to Debussy before they fled New York. (Larry would have preferred Wagner or Beethoven.)

DEFREEZE, DONALD Randall Flagg was acquainted with DeFreeze in the early seventies, and helped him plan the kidnapping of Patty Hearst.

DEITZ, DICK When Stu Redman was first taken captive by the government after surviving Captain Trips, Dick Deitz was sent to talk to him.

THE DELIRIOUS MAN After the flu hit Shoyo, Arkansas, a delirious man grabbed Nick Andros, thinking Nick was someone named Jenner.

A DELIRIOUS WOMAN A delirious woman called Ray Flowers's radio show and said that the superflu epidemic was being caused by flying saucers from outer space.

DEMOTT, KEN One of Flagg's Las Vegas men.

DENNINGER, DR. The Stovington, Vermont, plague center doctor who tried to convince Stu Redman to let Nurse Greer take his blood pressure.

THE DENVER FM DISC JOCKEY After the flu hit, a semidelirious Denver FM disc jockey broadcast the rumor that the U.S. Meteorological Air Testing Center was really a biological warfare installation.

DESCHAMPS, LEWIS He lost an eye in Harold Lauder's explosion at Ralph Brentner's house.

THE DEVIL'S IMP Randall Flagg, according to Mother Abagail.

DEWEY THE DECK Larry Underwood's drug supplier during his insane post-"Baby, Can You Dig Your Man?" days.

DIAMOND, NEIL Larry Underwood once played on a Neil Diamond album.

DINKWAY, BOO Randall Flagg remembered a defective marine named Boo Dinkway being beaten into a hole and set afire with gasoline at the Parris Island military base.

DINSMORE, GUS The parking lot attendant at the Ogunquit, Maine, town beach. When he came down with Captain Trips, Frannie Goldsmith nursed him until he died.

DIOGENES Rita Blakemoor told Larry Underwood that the monster-shouter reminded her of an insane Diogenes.

DIRE STRAITS Larry Underwood and the Tattered Remnants opened for Dire Straits and Led Zeppelin in 1981 at Chavez Ravine.

THE DISHWASHER The dishwasher in Babe's Kwik-Eat cafe was infected with the flu by Harry Trent.

A DOBERMAN Rich Ellerton's dog.

A DOCTOR Four stoic army men and a doctor came to get Stu Redman in Arnette after the flu hit. Also, Patty Greer infected a plague center doctor with the flu.

DONAHUE, TONY A Free Zone resident who waited at Larry Underwood's house for word of Mother Abagail's whereabouts.

THE DOORMAN The doorman at Rita Blakemoor's New York building. He survived Captain Trips. Rita tipped him five dollars on the morning she met Larry Underwood.

DORGAN, BARRY Randall Flagg's Las Vegas security chief.

DORIA, SAL One of Larry Underwood's friends. Sal had been at the party in California that Larry fled.

DRAGONSKY, LOUIS A former inmate in the Shoyo, Arkansas, jail where Nick Andros was brought after being beat up by Ray Booth, Vince Hogan, Billy Warner, and Mike Childress. Dragonsky had written "THIS PLACE HAS BUGS LOUIS DRAGONSKY, 1977" on the cell wall.

DROGAN, HECTOR ALONZO One of Flagg's Las Vegas men.

THE DRUNK DRIVER In 1970, an unnamed drunk driver killed Freddie Goldsmith.

DUCHIENS, SANDY The Free Zone woman who was voted in charge of a census committee at a mass meeting in the Munzinger Auditorium.

DUCK, HOWARD A comic book character who was a master of Quack-Fu.

DUNBAR, SHIRLEY Flagg's Las Vegas telephone operator.

DUNBARTON, HARRY A Free Zone citizen who attended the first mass meeting on August 18, 1985. He eventually came to the opinion that the elective period of one year for the Free Zone Committee was too long. He was a former spectacle salesman.

DUPRAY, ANGELA Sarah Bradford's best friend and bridge partner.

DUPRAY, DAVID Angela's husband.

DYLAN, BOB Robert Zimmerman.

ELBERT, DONALD MERWIN Trashcan Man. He set fires. He died in a nuclear explosion when the atomic bomb he carried back to Las Vegas was ignited by a ball of blue fire flicked from Flagg's transformed hand (the Hand of God).

ELBERT, SALLY Trashcan Man's mother. She saved herself and Trashcan from Wendell Elbert's murderous rage by running into the night screaming.

ELBERT, WENDELL Trashcan Man's father. He was shot and killed by Sheriff Greeley.

ELDER The Project Blue official sent to kill Stu Redman. Instead, Stu killed him and escaped the Stovington facility.

AN ELDERLY WOMAN During a Free Zone meeting, an elderly woman covered her eyes, mouth, and ears when the "dark man" was mentioned.

ELISE Ralph Brentner's woman.

ELLERTON, RICH Before being beaten up and robbed, Nick Andros had worked for Rich Ellerton. He had cleaned his barn and put a load of hay in his loft.

ELLIS, DICK Richard Ellis. The veterinarian who became part of Nick Andros and company, and who was part of the troup that went to Mother Abagail's. Nick, Tom Cullen, and Ralph Brentner came across Dick halfway across Kansas. He, too, was headed for Nebraska. Ellis became part of the Free Zone's ad hoc committee.

ELLIS, MRS. Dick's wife. She was a hell of a good cook.

ENGSTROM, JENNY An ex-nightclub dancer who worked on streetlamp maintenance in Las Vegas with Dayna Jurgens.

ERWINS, RATTY One of Flagg's Las Vegas men.

THE ESCAPEE WHO SAW THE CASTLE A young man who escaped from the Brownsville Minimum Security Station was out in the desert for three days. He claimed he'd seen a large castle with a moat south of Gabbs.

EZWICK, DR. A Project Blue participant who died in the physics lab. He had been a Nobel Prize winner.

A FARMER A farmer called Ray Flowers's radio show and reported that "an army squad with payloaders had just finished digging a hell of a long ditch near Route 71 south of Kansas City."

FARRIS, JUDGE RICHARD The seventy-year-old man who joined Larry Underwood's group in Joliet, Illinois. He eventually left the Free Zone and, on his way to Las Vegas as a spy for the good guys, was killed by Dave Roberts and Bobby Terry, two of Flagg's men.

"FEARLESS LEADER" When speaking with Whitney Horgan, Lloyd Henreid used this term for Flagg.

FENNER, FRANK A friend of John Freemantle.

FINE, EBEN G. The man for whom a park in Boulder, Colorado, was named. Harold Lauder's house was across the street from the park.

FINNEGAN The coroner who examined the body of Charles Campion.

FLAGG, RANDALL The Dark Man; the Man with No Face; the Walkin Dude.

FLOWERS, RAY The emcee of "Speak Your Piece," the highest-rated morning radio program in Springfield, Missouri.

FORREST, NATHAN BEDFORD While using the alias of "Ramsey Forrest," Randall Flagg claimed to be a distant descendant of Nathan Bedford Forrest.

FORREST, RAMSEY Randall Flagg's alias in Georgia.

FOUR ARMY MEN Four stoic army men and a doctor came to get Stu Redman in Arnette after the flu hit.

FOUR YOUNG MEN IN MOTORCYCLE JACKETS After the flu hit, a young man in khaki shorts with ash on his forehead walked the streets of Duluth with a sandwich board sign that foretold the end of the world. Four young men in motorcycle jackets beat him unconscious with his own sign.

FOURTEEN WOMEN Fourteen women lay dead in the Project Blue cafeteria after the superflu hit.

FRAMPTON, TED One of the Free Zone citizens (the other was Bill Scanlon) who found walkie-talkies in the Sunrise Ampitheater where Harold Lauder's bomb was set off.

FRANQ, ROBERT Randall Flagg's alias in New York.

FRED, CLYDE D. One of the inmates at the Shoyo, Arkansas, jail where Nick Andros was brought after being beat up by Ray Booth, Vince Hogan, Billy Warner, and Mike Childress.

FREEMAN, ANDREW (POKE) Lloyd Henreid's partner in crime. He was shot by Bill Markson while holding up a gas station. At one point, Poke is referred to as Poke "Waxman.")

FREEMAN, MR. The manager of the apartment house Alice Underwood lived in.

FREEMANTLE, MOTHER ABAGAIL The hundred-eight-year-old black woman who "summoned" certain flu survivors in their dreams to Nebraska, where she became the touchstone and focus for the powers of good.

FREEMANTLE, JOHN Mother Abagail's father. (John was a slave, and his last name came from his owner, Sam Freemantle, of Lewis, South Carolina.)

FREEMANTLE, LUCAS Mother Abagail's brother. He had hung the tire swing in Abagail's yard in 1922.

FREEMANTLE, REBECCA Mother Abagail's mother.

FREEMANTLE, SAM The white plantation owner of Lewis, South Carolina, who had owned Mother Abagail's father John.

FRY, RICHARD The alias by which Christopher Bradenton knew Randall Flagg. (NOTE: In *The Stand: The Complete & Uncut Edition*, Richard Fry was known as Richard "Frye.")

GALEN One of Larry Underwood's New York friends. Larry intended to look Galen up while he was in town visiting his mother. Larry's plans changed.

GEHRINGER, TOMMY The Free Zone resident who raced his car up and down Pearl Street and crashed. He walked away with a forehead gash.

GERALDO The guinea pig that told the plague center doctors that Stu Redman was not contagious.

THE GIRL WITH THE GANGRENOUS LEG A girl Dick Ellis operated on in the Free Zone. Laurie Constable assisted.

THE GLASSBLOWER After the flu, Larry Underwood saw Gene Shalit interview a glassblower on the "Today" show. The man had a bald head, and his book was being published by Random House.

GOLDSMITH, CARLA Frannie's mother; Peter's wife.

GOLDSMITH, FRANNIE Frances Rebecca Goldsmith. She survived Captain Trips, traveled with Harold Lauder, became one of the founding members of the Free Zone ad hoc committee, and "married" Stu Redman. She gave birth to Peter Goldsmith-Redman, who successfully fought off the superflu. She moved back to Maine after Stu returned from his journey to the west.

GOLDSMITH, FREDDIE Frannie's brother. He had been killed in 1970 at the age of thirteen by a drunk driver. Frannie had been six at the time. [NOTE: Thus, the year Frannie was born was 1964. In *The Stand: The Complete & Uncut Edition*, Freddie was killed in 1973, when Frannie was four, making her year of birth 1969.]

GOLDSMITH, PETER Frannie's father.

GOLDSMITH-REDMAN, PETER Frannie Goldsmith's and Jess Rider's son. He was six pounds, nine ounces at birth, and survived Captain Trips.

GOODELL, CAL One of Mother Abagail's Hemingford Home neighbors.

THE GOODELLS Mother Abagail's neighbors. She stopped at the Goodells' place to rest on her "chicken run" to Addie Richardson's house.

GOODMAN, NEIL A musician Larry Underwood hired to work on his "Pocket Savior" album.

GORGEOUS GEORGE A small-time hood who'd agreed – for twenty-five percent of the take – to let Poke Freeman and Lloyd Henreid steal guns and dope from him that were owned by "Sicilian-type people." Poke and Lloyd double-crossed George, taped up his mouth and nose, and watched him suffocate to death.

GREELEY, SHERIFF The "father-killing sheriff." Greeley shot and killed Trashcan Man's father, and then married Trashy's mother.

GREEN, JACK Ogunquit, Maine, resident. When Gus Dunsmore died, Frannie Goldsmith covered him with a clean sheet and left him on old Jack Green's bed. [NOTE: In *The Stand: The Complete & Uncut Edition*, this character's name was changed to "Jack Hanson."]

GREEN, MORT ("GINO") The owner of Gino's supper club, the club where Larry Underwood played "Tony Bennett-style" tunes before "Baby, Can You Dig Your Man?" became a hit.

GREER, PATTY The nurse at the Stovington, Vermont, plague center who tried to take Stu Redman's blood pressure. Stu declined.

GREIG, BARRY One of the members of the Tattered Remnants.

GRIFFITH, ANDY As Andy Taylor, he was the sheriff of Mayberry, North Carolina, and the star of Ritz Crackers TV commercials. Larry Underwood could imitate Andy's southern drawl.

GROUDEMORE, RICHIE One of Trashcan Man's childhood taunters.

THE GUARD One of Lloyd Henreid's guards at the Phoenix jail. He said that he felt fine, but that he was getting the hell out of there as soon as he could.

THE GUARD WITH THE RUNNY NOSE One of Lloyd Henreid's guards at the Phoenix jail.

THE GUARD'S KID Lloyd Henreid's guard was going to take his wife and kid to a cabin in the mountains, and if anyone got within thirty yards of it he'd put a bullet in their head.

THE GUARD'S WIFE Lloyd Henreid's guard was going to take his wife and kid to a cabin in the mountains, and if anyone got within thirty yards of it, he'd put a bullet in their head.

THE GUY WHO RECOMMENDED AN EMPLOYMENT AGENCY Rudy Schwartz once lent Larry Underwood twenty-five dollars. When Rudy needed the money to register with an employment agency recommended to him by some guy, he went to Larry for the money, but Larry refused to pay, saying he had already paid Rudy back.

HALSEY, MRS. Alice Underwood's neighbor. Mrs. Halsey had arthritis.

HAMMER, CYNTHIA STARKEY Bill Starkey's daughter; Vic Hammer's widow.

HAMMER, VIC Bill Starkey's son-in-law and a Project Blue worker. Hammer shot himself after the superflu virus was released.

HAMMETT, SHIRLEY One of the women Stu and company met on the road on July 30. Shirley, along with Sue Stern, Patty Kroger, and Dayna Jurgens, became part of Stu's party.

THE HANGED MAN On the judge's journey to Las Vegas, he came across a hanged man in Idaho.

HAPSCOMB, BILL The owner of Hapscomb's Texaco on US 93, north of Arnette, Texas.

HAPSCOMB, MARY Bill Hapscomb's wife.

HAROLD LAUDER'S GRANDFATHER He was an ordained minister; Rita Lauder guessed that Harold had inherited his way with words.

"HAWK" Harold Lauder's Free Zone nickname.

THE HEAVILY-BEARDED MAN One of Flagg's men. He met Glen, Larry, and Ralph on the Utah highway on their way to Las Vegas.

HENREID, LLOYD Poke Freeman's partner-in-crime. He became one of Flagg's Las Vegas lieutenants, and was eventually destroyed by Trashcan Man's A-bomb.

HENREID, MR. Lloyd's father.

HIRSCHFIELD, ANGELINA One of Dinny McCarthy's "moms" in Flagg's camp in Las Vegas.

HOBART, CHIP A Free Zone resident who waited at Larry Underwood's house for word of Mother Abagail's whereabouts.

HODGES, BERT The oldest Hodges child. He was six. Bert died from the flu.

HODGES, CHERYL The youngest Hodges child. She was eighteen months old when she was exposed to Captain Trips. Cheryl died from the flu.

HODGES, EVA The middle Hodges child. She was four.

HODGES, RALPH Sally's husband. Ralph died from the flu.

HODGES, SALLY Arnette, Texas, woman who paid Lila Bruett a dollar to babysit her three kids.

HOGAN, VINCE One of the creeps who beat up and robbed Nick Andros in Shoyo, Arkansas.

HOLLY, BUDDY Dead rock star.

HOLMES, DR. Alice Underwood's chiropractor.

THE HOME PLATE MASTURBATOR As Larry Underwood roamed Central Park after the flu hit, he came upon a young man munching Fritos who told Larry that he was going to Yankee Stadium, where he would run around the bases naked, and then masturbate on home plate. The young man said it was his "lifetime ambition" to do this.

HORGAN, WHITNEY Randall Flagg's cook at the M-G-M Grand Hotel.

HOUGH, CARL One of Flagg's pilots. He had been a pilot for Ozark Airlines.

HOVINGTON, JANE Lucy Swann's Free Zone next-door neighbor.

IMPENING, CHARLES Impening had lived in Boulder pre-flu, and had worked at the IBM plant on the Boulder-Longmont Diagonal. He stirred up unrest in the Free Zone by scaring people about Boulder's upcoming winter season. He was the Zone's resident doomcrier.

IMPENING, MAVIS Charles Impening's mother.

JACK Candy Jones's boyfriend. He, like Candy, got poison ivy, and had to be treated for it. Candy told Frannie "I bet you can guess where *Jack's* got it."

JACKSON, HENRY ("SCOOP") A Presidential candidate that Larry Underwood had once shaken hands with.

JACKSON, JACK A Free Zone car mechanic. Jackson told Sue Stern about Regina Wentworth, the woman who had been traveling with Dr. George Richardson. Regina had had twins that had died. Jack eventually became head of the Free Zone Committee.

JACKSON, NATE A saloon keeper who allowed John Freemantle to drink in his bar.

JAMES, DR. The doctor who was called in from Atlanta to look at the deceased Charles Campion.

JAMIESON, BILL One of Randall Flagg's helicopter pilots.

JANE The proprietor of Jane's Place in California.

JENNER After the flu hit Shoyo, Arkansas, a delirious man grabbed Nick Andros, thinking Nick was someone named Jenner.

JERRY One of the inmates at the Shoyo, Arkansas, jail where Nick Andros was brought after being beat up by Ray Booth, Vince Hogan, Billy Warner, and Mike Childress.

A JEWISH MAN One of the dead people Larry Underwood saw in the Lincoln Tunnel.

JIM Abagail Freemantle's great-granddaughter Molly's husband.

THE JIVE-TALKING BLACK GUY The guy in the cell to Lloyd Henreid's left in the Phoenix jail maximum security wing. He succumbed to Captain Trips.

JOE Leo Rockway. The young boy Nadine Cross "adopted."

JOHN THE CONQUEROR Randall Flagg. Flagg appeared to Mother Abagail as a Rocky Mountain timber wolf in a vision, telling her that her own people knew him and called him John the Conqueror.

JONES, CANDY A Free Zone citizen that Dr. Richardson treated for poison ivy.

JONES, SHELDON The Free Zone citizen who nominated Ted Frampton to replace Nick Andros on the ad hoc committee after Nick was killed in Harold Lauder's explosion at Ralph Brentner's house.

THE JUKEBOX MAN The jukebox man in Babe's Kwik-Eat cafe

was infected with the flu by Harry Trent.

JULIE A girl Larry Underwood dated.

JURGENS, DAYNA ROBERTA One of the women Stu and company met on the road on July 30. Dayna, along with Sue Stern, Patty Kroger, and Shirley Hammett became part of Stu's party.

KELLOGG, NORMAN A man from Louisiana who arrived at Mother Abagail's Free Zone house with a party of twelve. Mother Abagail had already left.

KING, DONALD An Electrolux salesman from Peru, Indiana, who tried to sell Mother Abagail a vacuum cleaner in 1936 or 1937. [NOTE: Stephen King's father's name was Donald King. Don King abandoned Stephen, King's mother Nellie Ruth, and King's brother David in 1949, and was never heard from again.)

KINGMAN, ROSE A woman who claimed she saw Randall Flagg snap his fingers at a number of crows. They then fluttered down to his shoulders and croaked "Flagg...Flagg...Flagg..." over and over.

KITCHNER, BRAD The Free Zone electrician.

KOERNER, RAY, AND GLOVER The composers of an old blues tune Larry Underwood played on a beach in Maine.

KOJAK An auburn-colored Irish setter that survived Captain Trips and became Glen Bateman's dog. Kojak's name had previously been Big Steve, and he had belonged to a woman who had lived around the corner from Bateman.

KROGER, PATTY One of the women Stu and company met on the road on July 30. Patty, along with Sue Stern, Dayna Jurgens, and Shirley Hammett, became part of Stu's party.

LADDIE Stu Redman's cousin.

LATHROP, DAN When Stu and Tom returned to the Free Zone after the destruction in Las Vegas, they learned that the Zone had a new doctor, Dan Lathrop.

LATHROP, MRS. A Shoyo, Arkansas, resident who was sick at the time Nick Andros became a deputy for Sheriff Baker.

LAUDER, AMY Harold's sister, and Frannie Goldsmith's best friend. Amy didn't survive Captain Trips.

LAUDER, BRAD Harold's father.

LAUDER, HAROLD EMERY One of the survivors of Captain Trips. He had lived in Ogunquit, Maine, before he traveled to the Free Zone with Stu, Frannie and the others. He eventually gave in to the powers of darkness and blew up Nick Andros's house, killing Nick and six others. He later killed himself. Harold was six-foot-one, and weighed two-hundred-forty pounds. Before the flu, he had been the editor of the Ogunquit High School literary magazine. He favored cowboy boots with pointed toes, and his sister Amy had once told Frannie that Harold wacked off in his pants and then didn't change his underwear.

LAUDER, MR. Harold and Amy's father. He didn't survive Captain Trips.

LAUDER, RITA Harold and Amy's mother. She didn't survive Captain Trips.

LAWRY, JULIE The seventeen-year-old girl Nick Andros met in a drugstore in Pratt, Kansas. Things started out well between Julie and Nick (they had sex on the floor of the Rexall within ten minutes of meeting), but after Nick turned down her offer of seconds, and she turned nasty, ending up slashing his bike tires.

LAWRY, MR. Julie's father. The flu had killed him two weeks before she met Nick Andros and Tom Cullen.

LAWRY, MRS. Julie's mother. The flu had killed her two weeks before she met Nick Andros and Tom Cullen.

LED ZEPPELIN Larry Underwood and the Tattered Remnants opened for Dire Straits and Led Zeppelin in 1981 at Chavez Ravine.

LEOMINSTER, TONY Anthony Leominster. Arnette, Texas, resident who owned a Scout. Tony died from the flu. Before he died, Hap had put a new tailpipe on Tony's Scout.

LLOYD HENREID'S LAWYER The attorney who represented Lloyd after he was arrested for armed robbery.

THE LOOTER A man Larry Underwood saw hanging from a street sign at the corner of Fifth Avenue and 53rd Street in New York City after the flu hit. He had a sign around his neck that said "LOOTER."

LUCAS Abagail Freemantle's brother. He had hung the tire swing in her yard in 1922.

LUCY SWANN'S BROTHER-IN-LAW He lived in Philadelphia.

MAJORS, JOLINE One of Lucy Swann's high school girlfriends.

A MALE NURSE A male nurse at the Stovington plague center came to take away Stu Redman's TV.

THE MAN FROM COLUMBIA The record company exec who gave Larry Underwood the go-ahead to cut a demo of "Baby, Can You Dig Your Man?"

A MAN IN A WHITE COVERALL A man in a white coverall lay beside the Seeburg jukebox in the Project Blue cafeteria after the superflu hit.

A MAN IN BLUE COVERALLS A man in blue coveralls lay crumpled in front of the candy machine in the Project Blue cafeteria after the superflu hit.

A MAN IN PJ'S In Randy's Sooperette in Arnette, Texas, after the flu took its toll, a man in pajamas lay draped over the meat counter. A dog had eaten part of his face.

THE MAN IN PORTLAND A man in Portland claimed that Randall Flagg carried a weasel or a fisher in his ratty old Boy Scout pack.

THE MAN IN THE "SUPERHUMP" TANK-TOP One of Flagg's men who met Glen, Larry, and Ralph on the Utah highway on their way to Las Vegas. He wore a yellow tank top that had a camel on it and said "SUPERHUMP."

THE MAN ON A MOTORCYCLE Mrs. Andros was run down in 1972 by a man on a motorcycle.

A MAN SORTING THROUGH FISHING TACKLE One of the Free Zone citizens Larry Underwood and Dayna Jurgens saw one night while walking home from a meeting.

A MAN WITH A PICKAXE One of the Free Zone citizens Larry Underwood and Dayna Jurgens saw one night while walking home from a meeting.

THE MAN WITH NO FACE While in custody at the Vermont plague center, Stu Redman dreamt of a man with no face. It was Flagg.

MANSON, CHARLES On his way to Las Vegas, Larry Underwood dreamt of Charles Manson and Richard Speck.

MANUEL The bouncer in a Nuevo Laredo whorehouse that Stu Redman remembered.

MARCY The girl who checked on Frannie in the hospital as she rested after giving birth to her son Peter.

MARIA Larry Underwood's New York oral hygienist one-night stand. When he walked out on her, she threw a milk bottle at him and told him, "You ain't no nice guy." As much as he didn't want to believe her, deep down, Larry knew she was right.

MARK One of Larry Underwood's New York friends. Larry intended to look Mark up while he was in town visiting his mother. Larry's plans changed.

MARKSON, BILL The cowboy who shot Poke Freeman during a holdup in a gas station in Burrack, Arizona.

MARX, BUDDY One of Larry Underwood's New York buddies. Buddy worked at a print shop on Stricker Avenue.

MATHERS One of Lloyd Henreid's fellow inmates at the Phoenix jail. Mathers kneed Lloyd in the groin for a pack of Pall Malls from Shockley, the door-guard.

MAYO, CHUCKIE The cutest boy in school when Frannie Goldsmith and Amy Lauder were young.

McCALL, JOHNNY One of the members of the Tattered Remnants.

McCARTHY, DINNY Daniel McCarthy. The four-year-old boy who was the youngest child in Flagg's camp in Las Vegas.

McCONE, GINA The little girl discovered in a barn by Nick Andros and company as they made their way to Mother Abagail's. Dick Ellis, the veterinarian, fixed her broken leg.

MCGRAW, ALI The star of the movie "Love Story."

A MIDDLE-AGED MAN One of the dead people Larry Underwood saw in the Lincoln Tunnel.

A MIDDLE-AGED WOMAN One of the dead people Larry Underwood saw in the Lincoln Tunnel.

"THE MIDNIGHT RAMBLER" When speaking with Whitney Horgan, Lloyd Henreid used this term for Flagg.

MOFFAT, RICH The Free Zone's only alcoholic.

MOLLY Abagail Freemantle's great-granddaughter.

THE MONSTER-SHOUTER A tall man in his mid-sixties who roamed Central Park shouting "Monsters coming now!"

THE MOTHER-SHOUTER One of Lloyd Henreid's fellow inmates at the Phoenix jail. The guy kept yelling "Mother!" while Lloyd tried to unscrew the leg to his cot.

MORISSETTE, NORM One of Trashcan Man's childhood taunters.

THE MORLOCKS Creatures Larry Underwood remembered from the Classics Comics version of H.G. Wells's *The Time Machine*. During his journey through the Lincoln Tunnel, Larry imagined they were following him.

MORRIS, WRIGHT A writer that Harold Lauder imitated.

MOTHER ABAGAIL'S VISITORS The truck that finally arrived at Mother Abagail's Hemingford Home farm carried Ralph Brentner, Olivia Walker, Gina McCone, Nick Andros, Dick Ellis, Tom Cullen, and June Brinkmeyer.

"MR. COOL" Paul Burlson's nickname.

MRS. POKENO KILLER The Pokeno Killer's wife. The Pokeno Killer had killed her and his brother-in-law during a game of pokeno.

THE NAKED WOMAN HANGING UPSIDE DOWN FROM A LAMPPOST When Trashcan Man first got to Las Vegas, he saw a naked woman hanging upside down from a lamppost.

NASON, MRS. Parker Nason's wife and Stu Redman's neighbor.

NASON, PARKER An elderly man who (with his wife) lived in a trailer park near Stu Redman's house.

A NEW YORK DOCTOR The unnamed doctor interviewed at Brooklyn's Mercy Hospital about the flu outbreak. (Before almost everybody died, that is.)

NICHOLSON, JACK One of the actors who appeared in the movie "Hell's Angel On Wheels." [NOTE: Jack also played Jack Torrance in the film version of Stephen King's novel *The Shining*.]

NICK ANDROS'S MOTHER'S FRIEND The unnamed woman who got Nick's mother a job at a bakery in Bog Springs, Iowa.

"A NIGGER IN A BAR" Wendell Elbert bought the gun with which he shot the bartender at O'Toole's, his two sons, and his daughter from "a nigger in a bar" on Chicago's State Street.

NINE MEN Nine men lay dead in the Project Blue cafeteria after the superflu hit.

THE NO-ACCOUNTS OUT ON THE BARKER ROAD Doc Soames told John Baker that most of the no-accounts out on the Barker Road were coughing their brains out.

NOGOTNY, JANEY Stan Nogotny's wife.

NOGOTNY, STAN The Free Zone citizen who said that Tom Cullen's house looked "as if the Catholics, Baptists, and Seventh-day Adventists had gotten together with the Democrats and the Moonies to create a religious-political Disneyland." Stan eventually talked about going to Acapulco for a few years, and then to Peru. He used to live in Miami.

NORRIS, CHAD The head of the Free Zone's burial committee.

NORRIS, EDWARD M. The New York police lieutenant who asked Harry Trent for directions to US 21 North.

NORRIS, HECTOR One of Trish and Edward Norris's three children.

NORRIS, MARSHA One of Trish and Edward Norris's three children.

NORRIS, STANLEY One of Trish and Edward Norris's three children.

NORRIS, TRISH Edward Norris's wife.

NORTON, MR. The May, Oklahoma, druggist who left town after the flu hit.

A NURSE One of the plague center personnel infected by Patty Greer. Also, a nurse called Ray Flowers's radio show and confirmed that truckloads of bodies were being removed from Kansas City hospitals.

NYARLAHOTEP As Ralph, Glen, and Larry were taken into custody on the Utah highway, Larry told Flagg's men that Nyarlahotep was another name for Randall Flagg.

OLD CREEPING JUDAS Ratty Erwin's name for Randall Flagg.

AN OLD MAN An unnamed drunk who was lying in the drunk tank in the Shoyo, Arkansas, jail where Nick Andros was brought after being beat up by Ray Booth, Vince Hogan, Billy Warner, and Mike Childress.

AN OLD MAN DRIVING A THUNDERBIRD An old man driving a big Thunderbird picked up Trashcan Man on July 18, southwest of Sterling, Colorado.

AN OLD MAN IN A BLUE SUIT One of the corpses Larry Underwood stumbled over in the Lincoln Tunnel.

O'NEAL RYAN Actor. He starred in the movie "Love Story" with Ali McGraw, and in "Irreconcilable Differences" with Shelley Long. [NOTE: see the "Things entry A LOVE STORY POSTER, and the Preface to this volume.]

THE OPERATOR The telephone operator who told Larry Underwood his three minutes were up as he was talking to Jane in California from New York.

AN ORDERLY One of the plague center personnel infected by Patty Greer.

ORTEGA, CARLOS One of the men in the ambulance who reported to Hapscomb's Texaco after Charles Campion crashed into the station's gas pumps.

ORTEGA, CHRIS Christian Ortega. The bartender at the Indian Head bar. Chris died from the flu.

OSWALD, LEE HARVEY Randall Flagg remembered meeting Oswald in New Orleans in 1962.

O'TOOLE The guy who owned O'Toole's bar, the bar where Trashcan Man's father (Wendell Elbert) murdered the bartender.

PACKALOTTE, DEEDEE A waitress at Boomer's Bar & Grille in May, Oklahoma. She ran off with Tom Cullen's father, Don.

PALFREY, VICTOR Arnette, Texas, resident who was at Hapscomb's Texaco the day Charles Campion "touched down" after his escape from the Project Blue lab. Victor was retired. He died from the flu.

PAULIE The owner of Paulie's Radio & TV in Shoyo, Arkansas. Nick Andros commited an "apologetic" break-in at Paulie's.

PEDERSEN, DALE A motorcyclist killed in Harold Lauder's explosion at Ralph Brentner's house.

PERRY, RICHARD Larry Underwood met him while working as a session guitarist on a Neil Diamond album.

PETEY One of Trashcan Man's childhood taunters.

PETRELLA, HUGH The Free Zone resident who campaigned for the job of marshall and won.

THE PFC The young, pimply-faced national guardsman who burst into tears after Sergeant Buchan shot and killed Ray Flowers, and was then subsequently shot by his own men.

A PIMPLY BOY The unnamed boy who brought the prisoners' dinner to the Shoyo, Arkansas, jail from Ma's Truck Stop.

THE PLANK-FACED SERGEANT The army sergeant who took the booze and food order on the plane that brought Stu Redman and the others to the Atlanta plague center.

THE POKENO KILLER A guy in the Phoenix jail maximum security wing with Lloyd Henreid. He hung himself with his belt.

THE POKENO KILLER'S BROTHER-IN-LAW The Pokeno Killer killed his wife and brother-in-law at a pokeno game.

POST, MIKEY The little Free Zone boy who called Frannie Goldsmith "Fan."

THE PROPHET After the flu hit, a young man in khaki shorts with ash on his forehead walked the streets of Duluth with a sandwich board sign that said:

THE TIME OF THE DISAPPEARANCE IS HERE
CHRIST THE LORD RETURNETH SOON
PREPARE TO MEET YOUR GOD!

The back read:

BEHOLD THE HEARTS OF THE SINNERS WERE BROKEN
THE GREAT SHALL BE ABASED
AND THE ABASHED MADE GREAT
THE EVIL DAYS ARE AT HAND
WOE TO THEE O ZION

Four guys in motorcycle jackets beat him unconscious with the sign.

PUERTO RICANS Alice Underwood told Larry that the New York emergency rooms were full of Puerto Ricans.

PURVIS, MELVIN The super G-Man of the thirties who shot himself in 1959.

R'YELAH As Ralph, Glen, and Larry were taken into custody on the Utah highway, Larry told Flagg's men that R'yelah was another name for Randall Flagg.

RAMAGE, DESMOND A young radical who planted better than sixteen pounds of plastique in the U.S. Meteorological Air Testing Center's lobby.

RANDALL One of the administrators at the Stovington plague center.

THE RAT-MAN One of Flagg's people at the Indian Springs project.

THE RAT-WOMAN As he roamed Central Park after the flu hit, one woman he met told Larry Underwood that she was afraid that all the rats were going to rise up and inherit the earth.

RAWSON, HANK One of Flagg's jet plane pilots.

REDMAN, BRYCE One of Stu Redman's younger brothers. At the time the superflu hit, Bryce was a systems analyst with IBM in Minnesota.

REDMAN, DEV Stu Redman's younger brother. He died of pneumonia.

REDMAN, MR. Stu's father. He was a dentist. He had died when Stu was seven.

REDMAN, MRS. Stu's mother. She worked at the Red Ball Truck Stop just outside of Arnette until it burned down.

REDMAN, NORMA Stu's wife. She died of ovarian cancer.

REDMAN, STU The Arnette, Texas, resident who was at Hapscomb's Texaco the day Charles Campion "touched down" after his escape from the Project Blue lab. Stu worked thirty hours a week in the ailing calculator factory. Stu became the marshall of the Free Zone, "married" Fran Goldsmith, and was the only survivor of the journey to Las Vegas. He eventually moved back to Maine with Frannie.

"REVRUNT DEIFFENBAKER" After they met, Tom Cullen told Nick Andros that he had had a dream about a man in a black suit like the one the "Revrunt Deiffenbaker" wore.

RICHARD Randall Flagg told Nadine Cross that "Richard" was his real first name.

RICHARDSON, ADDIE Mother Abagail's friend and neighbor. Abagail walked to Addie's house, which was almost five miles away, to get the chickens for her "guests." [NOTE: See the "People" entry MOTHER ABAGAIL'S VISITORS.]

RICHARDSON, BILLY Addie Richardson's husband.

RICHARDSON, DR. GEORGE A doctor who entered the Free Zone in the late summer of 1985 with forty other people.

RICHARDSON, MOSES The owner of the barn on which Harold Lauder painted his "Gone to Stovington" message.

THE RICHIE FAMILY A Shoyo, Arkansas, family that was sick at the time Nick Andros became a deputy for Sheriff Baker.

RIDER, JESS The father of Fran Goldsmith's son Peter. He was a poet.

ROBERTS, DAVE One of Flagg's guards. Dave was Bobby Terry's partner.

ROBERTSON, ROBBIE Former Band musician who played on the Neil Diamond album on which Larry Underwood also played.

ROCKWAY, LEO The real name of Nadine Cross's "adopted" son "Joe."

RONNIE Mother Abagail's great-nephew. He had lived in Rouses Point in upstate New York.

RYAN, NOLAN The pitcher for the California Angels.

SANTA CLAUS While holed up in a blizzard on Christmas morning on their way back to the Free Zone, Stu told Tom that Santa had left presents for Tom. One of Tom's gifts was a pinball machine encased in Lucite.

SCANLON, BILL One of the Free Zone citizens (the other was Ted Frampton) who found walkie-talkies in the Sunrise Ampitheater where Harold Lauder's bomb was set off.

SCHOEY When Stu Redman shot his first deer on a hunting trip with his Uncle Dale, a man named Schoey had skinned and dressed the deer for three dollars and ten pounds of deer meat.

SCHWARTZ, RUDY Larry Underwood's childhood friend. They went out to California together. Rudy had once lent Larry twenty-five dollars that Larry had never paid back.

SELBY, HUBERT JR. A writer that Harold Lauder imitated.

SEMPLE, MRS. When Trashcan Man was a kid, he started a fire in Old Lady Semple's mailbox and burned up her pension check.

SETI As Ralph, Glen, and Larry were taken into custody on the Utah highway, Larry told Flagg's men that Seti was another name for Randall Flagg.

SHALIT, GENE When Larry Underwood returned to New York, he watched the "Today Show" and saw Gene Shalit sneeze.

SHAW, IRWIN Author.

SHOCKLEY The Phoenix jail door-guard.

THE SHOWGIRL Lloyd Henreid was sentenced to two-to-four years (plus time served) at Brownsville for his attempted rape of a showgirl in Reno. She sprayed teargas in his eyes.

SITES, GARY The white man who told John Freemantle that he had been elected to the Grange in March of 1895. He was the first black man ever allowed in the organization. [NOTE: In *The Stand: The Complete & Uncut Edition* , John was elected to the Grange in March of 1902.]

SIX COPS Randall Flagg had once killed six cops in New York and New Jersey, and a black Vietnam vet.

SIX GUARDS Flagg posted guardposts all along the eastern border of Oregon to watch for the Free Zone's spies. The largest was in Ontario, where he had six guards in a Peterbilt truck.

S.L. The initials of the owner of the car Stu found in functioning order after being discovered in the desert by Tom and Kojak. [NOTE: In *The Stand: The Complete & Uncut Edition,* the owner's initials were changed to "A.C."]

SLOANE, DR. One of the doctors at the Stovington plague center.

SOAMES, DOC Dr. Ambrose Soames. Shoyo, Arkansas, doctor. He almost ran over Nick Andros the night Nick was beat up.

SOAMES, MRS. Doc Soames's wife.

SOMEONE ON THE FLOOR ABOVE ALICE UNDERWOOD'S APARTMENT When Larry knocked on his mother's apartment door and she didn't answer, he then rapped hard enough to make someone upstairs knock back.

SPARKMAN, RUDY A six-foot-five man with scars on his face and a bald head who taught Nick Andros how to read and write.

SPECK, RICHARD On his way to Las Vegas, Larry Underwood dreamt of Charles Manson and Richard Speck.

A SPEECH THERAPIST FROM OAKLAND A girl Larry Underwood once dated.

SPELLMAN, AL One of the members of the Tattered Remnants.

THE SPIES The Free Zone spies chosen to infiltrate Flagg's operation were Judge Farris, Dayna Jurgens, and Tom Cullen.

SPRUCE, MARCY She checked on Frannie as she rested in the Boulder hospital after giving birth to her son Peter.

STARKEY, BILLY A Project Blue veteran who was one of the few survivors of the Captain Trips containment breach.

STARKWEATHER, CHARLES Serial murderer. Randall Flagg remembered attending school with Starkweather. [NOTE: Starkweather's story is retold in King's short story "Nona," and in *The Stand: The Complete & Uncut Edition,* where Trashcan Man travels across the United States with The Kid, a reincarnation of Starkweather.]

STERN, SUSAN One of the women Stu and company met on the road on July 30. Sue, along with Dayna Jurgens, Patty Kroger, and Shirley Hammett, became part of Stu's party.

STONE, PATSY A motorcyclist killed in Harold Lauder's explosion at Ralph Brentner's house.

STONER, REG One of Mother Abagail's neighbors. He kept pigs.

STORM, MISSUS The woman shot by Poke Freeman during a holdup in a gas station in Burrack, Arizona.

STRANG, MR. Trashcan Man passed Mr. Strang's blue mailbox (it had the flag up) as he ran away from the exploding Cheery Oil Company tanks.

STRELLERTON, ERIC A lawyer who was driven mad by Randall Flagg. After Flagg destroyed his mind, he sent him into the Mojave Desert.

STUKEY, MR. Wayne's father. He "owned half of the the country's third largest electronic games company."

STUKEY, WAYNE A musician Larry Underwood hired to work on his "Pocket Savior" album. Wayne set Larry straight.

STU REDMAN'S FRIEND A friend of Stu's had once recommended that he read *Watership Down.* Stu had read it in a weekend.

SULLIVAN, MONTY One of the men in the ambulance who reported to Hapscomb's Texaco after Charles Campion crashed into the station's gas pumps.

SUZANNE The love object of one of the inmates at the Shoyo, Arkansas, jail where Nick Andros was brought after being beat up by Ray Booth, Vince Hogan, Billy Warner, and Mike Childress.

SWANN, LUCY The Enfield, New Hampshire, woman Larry Underwood, Nadine Cross, and Joe met on their journey to Stovington.

SWANN, MARCY Lucy and Wes Swann's daughter. The flu killed her.

SWANN, MR. Lucy's father. He didn't want Lucy to marry Wes.

SWANN, MRS. Lucy's mother. She didn't want Lucy to marry Wes.

SWANN, WES Lucy Swann's husband. The flu killed him.

SWEENEY, DR. BRENDEN The doctor in Polliston, Kansas, who looked at Hector Norris after the boy came down with Captain Trips.

THE SWEET THANG WAITRESS The sweet thang waitress in Babe's Kwik-Eat cafe was infected with the flu by Harry Trent.

THE SWEET TREAT The grinning dead man Larry Underwood found in the Central Park Transverse Comfort Station Number One. The guy had maggots crawling all over his body.

SYKES, RONNIE One of Flagg's people at the Indian Springs project.

TARZAN, LONG JOHN SILVER, AND PHILIP KENT Harold Lauder became these characters when he read late at night as a youngster.

A TEENAGE BOY A Free Zone citizen who paid a visit on Mother Abagail.

TERMINELLO, ANDREA A motorcyclist killed in Harold Lauder's explosion at Ralph Brentner's house.

TERRY, BOBBY One of Flagg's guards. He manned the guardpost in the Copperfield Five and Dime. His partner was Dave Roberts.

TERRY, DELORES Bobby Terry's mother.

THE THING FROM THE DARKNESS As Stu Redman made his way out of the Stovington facility, a thing from the darkness beneath a stairwell grabbed his ankle and invited Stu to "Come down and eat chicken with me, beautiful. It's *soooo* dark." [NOTE:

It sounds like it might have been Gollum, doesn't it?]

THREE DEAD SOLDIERS The corpses of the three soldiers that shot the old man in a blue suit and his family in the Lincoln Tunnel.

THREE JURORS Judge Farris read in Lapham's *Law and the Classes of Society* about a black woman from Brixton, Mississippi, who was sentenced to ten years in prison for shoplifting. The assistant district attorney and three jurors had been black.

THREE PATHOLOGISTS Three pathologists from the Atlanta plague center landed at Braintree at three o'clock in the morning of Charles Campion's death.

TILYONS, GRETCHEN The girl who had performed at the Grange Hall before Abagail Trotts on December 27, 1895. She had done a racy French dance.

TOBIN, STEVE One of Flagg's pilots.

TRASHCAN MAN'S SISTER She was shot and killed by her father, Wendell Elbert.

TRASHCAN MAN'S TWO OLDER BROTHERS They were shot and killed by their father, Wendell Elbert.

TRASK The man in the cell next to Lloyd Henreid in the Phoenix jail maximum security wing. Lloyd ended up eating part of Trask to stay alive.

TRENT, HARRY An insurance man from Braintree. Joe Bob Brentwood gave him a speeding ticket.

A TRIO OF YOUNG WOMEN Three Free Zone young women who spread out a picnic supper in the small park opposite the Boulder First National Bank.

TROTTS, DAVID Mother Abagail's first husband.

TUCKER, ROG He had owned the Red Ball Truck Stop until it burned down in 1969.

A TV REPORTER A TV reporter was sent to do a story on Mother Abagail on her hundredth birthday.

TWO MEN After Rita Blakemoor left Larry Underwood before he entered the Lincoln Tunnel, two men came looking for either Larry or Rita.

TWO NEWSCASTERS Nick Andros saw two newscasters both report that the superflu epidemic was under control – even as people were dying around him in Shoyo, Arkansas.

TWO SHOT SOLDIERS Two soldiers who refused the order to "take care" of Ray Flowers were shot on the spot.

TWO TEENAGE BOYS Two of the dead people Larry Underwood saw in the Lincoln Tunnel.

TWO TRUCKERS Two truckers in Babe's Kwik-Eat cafe were infected with the flu by Harry Trent.

TWO WOMEN Two of the dead people Larry Underwood saw in the Lincoln Tunnel.

UNDERWOOD, ALICE Larry's mom. She worked as a floor supervisor at the Chemical Bank Building in New York City. She was a victim of Captain Trips.

UNDERWOOD, LARRY Lawson Underwood. The singer-songwriter who was one of the few survivors of the Captain Trips virus. He died in Las Vegas when Trashcan Man's nuclear bomb (and the Hand of God) blew away Flagg and his empire. Larry was the composer of the hit single "Baby, Can You Dig Your Man?" He also became one of the founding members of the Free Zone's ad hoc committee.

UNDERWOOD, MR. Larry's father. He had died when Larry was a boy.

THE UPSHAW OR UPSON BOY A Free Zone child who participated in the Mayday games on Flagstaff Mountain.

VERECKER, BILLY One of the men in the ambulance who reported to Hapscomb's Texaco after Charles Campion crashed into the station's gas pumps.

VIC One of Stu Redman's guards at the Stovington plague center.

VOLLMAN, DICK One of the men who joined Larry Underwood's group and became part of the Free Zone population.

VOLLMAN, SALLY Dick Vollman's dead wife.

WAGNER Larry Underwood and Rita Blakemoor listened to

Debussy before they fled New York, but Larry would have preferred Wagner or Beethoven.

THE WAITRESS Lloyd had bought a bag of burgers and eight milkshakes from a waitress in Silver City after he and Poke had stolen the Lincoln Continental.

WAITS, JOHN The man in charge of Randall Flagg's motor pool.

WALKER, OLIVIA Nick Andros and company met Olivia Walker and June Brinkmeyer on their way to Mother Abagail's in Nebraska. June and Olivia joined the men, (Tom Cullen, Ralph Brentner, and Dick Ellis) and Gina McCone on the dream-inspired trip to Hemingford Home.

THE WALKIN DUDE Another name for Randall Flagg.

WANNAMAKER, TOMMY Arnette, Texas, resident who was at Hapscomb's Texaco the day Charles Campion "touched down" after his escape from the Project Blue lab. Tommy had worked in the defunct paper factory, and at the time of Campion's arrival, was on welfare. Tommy died from the flu.

THE WARDEN The man in charge at the Brownsville Minimum Security Station. He preferred to be called "The Boss."

WARFIELD, EDDIE Arnette, Texas, local hero. He was a high school quarterback who was given an athletic scholarship to Texas A & M. He ended up playing ten years with the Green Bay Packers.

WARNER, BILLY One of the creeps who beat up and robbed Nick Andros in Shoyo, Arkansas.

THE WEIRD SISTERS Three old ladies who kept chickens and supplied Flagg's camp with fresh eggs.

WEIZAK A member of the Free Zone burial committee. [NOTE: Weizak was the name of Johnny Smith's doctor in *The Dead Zone*.]

WENTWORTH, REGINA A woman who had traveled with Dr. George Richardson before he arrived at the Free Zone. She had given birth to twins. Both babies had died.

THE WHO As part of the "Things to Remember" section of her post-flu diary, Frannie Goldsmith remembered The Who, who used to smash their instruments and amplifiers after a performance. She said this was known as "conspicuous consumption."

WIGGS, MRS. A woman who worked at the Stovington plague center. She had her own office.

WILSON, MR. One of the Lauders' Ogunquit, Maine, neighbors.

THE WOLFMAN On their way to Las Vegas, Larry, Stu, Ralph, and Glen found the body of a guy they called The Wolfman. He had been killed by wolves. [NOTE: This was the only mention in the original edition of a character whose real name was The Kid. He was the reincarnation of Charles Starkweather. See the "People" entry THE KID in the Addendum.)

THE WOMAN AFRAID OF RATS While walking through Central Park, Larry Underwood was accosted by a woman who said she was afraid the rats would "rise up out of the subways and inherit the earth."

A WOMAN IN BLUE COVERALLS A woman in blue coveralls lay crumpled in front of the candy machine in the Project Blue cafeteria after the superflu hit.

WOMEN LOOKING IN WINDOWS Some of the Free Zone people Larry Underwood and Dayna Jurgens saw while walking home from a meeting one night.

WYKOFF, DEAN A motorcyclist killed in Harold Lauder's explosion at Ralph Brentner's house.

YATES, CARLEY Carl Yates. One of Trashcan Man's childhood taunters. He ended up a car salesman at the Stout Chrysler-Plymouth dealership in Powtanville, Illinois.

YEATS English poet. Starkey's daughter had given him a book of poems by Yeats. Starkey pronounced his name "Yeets."

THE YOUNG, BALDING MAN One of Flagg's men who met Glen, Larry, and Ralph on the Utah highway on their way to Las Vegas.

THE YOUNG MAN While in the Boulder library, Frannie Goldsmith saw a young man of about twenty-five reading a book called *Seven Independent Power Sources for Your Home*.

THE YOUNG MAN IN JOCKEY SHORTS As Stu Redman made his way through the Stovington facility, he came upon a young man wearing nothing but jockey shorts, sprawled atop a desk. He was comatose but still alive.

A YOUNG MAN WEARING CUTOFF DENIM SHORTS After the flu hit, Larry Underwood saw a young man wearing cutoff denim shorts lying atop a Ding-Dong taxi cab.

YVONNE A topless dancer Larry Underwood once lived with. [NOTE: Yvonne's last name – "Wetterlen" – was revealed in *The Stand: The Complete & Uncut Edition*, and there is an entry for her in the Addendum under her full name.)

ZELLMAN, MARK The former Lowville, New York, welder who joined Larry Underwood's group and became part of the Free Zone population. He eventually decided he'd like to learn how to fly and go to Hawaii.

(6)
THE STAND
Places

THE A & P Nick Andros visited the May, Oklahoma, A & P to stock up on canned meats, fruits, and vegetables before he and Tom Cullen left town.

ACAPULCO Stan Nogotny wanted to go to Acapulco for a few years and then move to Peru.

AFRICA After teaching Nick Andros how to read and write, Rudy Sparkman joined the Peace Corps and went to Africa.

ALABAMA The people Ed Norris and his family encountered at the Eustice, Oklahoma, travel court were headed for Texas, Alabama, Arkansas, and Tennessee. They had all been infected with Captain Trips by Joe Bob Brentwood via Harry Trent via Edward Norris.

THE APACHE COUNTY JAIL After Lloyd Henreid was captured following his and Poke Freeman's "tri-state killing spree," he woke up in the Apache County jail infirmary.

ARAPAHOE STREET The Boulder, Colorado, street where Harold Lauder lived. It was on the other side of town, away from where most of the other Free Zone citizens lived.

AN ARCO STATION An Arco station marked the end of the business section on Main Street in May, Oklahoma.

ARDMORE One of the deserted towns Nick Andros traveled through on his way to Nebraska.

ARIZONA After Lloyd Henreid and Poke Freeman pokerized Gorgeous George, they stopped at a general store two miles beyond Sheldon in Arizona on Highway 75. They pokerized the proprietor (an old man with mail-order teeth), and got away with sixty-three dollars and the old man's pickup truck.

ARKANSAS The people Ed Norris and his family encountered at the Eustice, Oklahoma, travel court were headed for Texas, Alabama, Arkansas, and Tennessee. They had all been infected with Captain Trips by Joe Bob Brentwood via Harry Trent via Edward Norris.

THE ATLANTA PLAGUE CENTER Men from the Atlanta plague center went to Texas after Charles Campion's death.

THE AVON FIVE-AND-TEN While holed up in a blizzard on Christmas morning on their way back to the Free Zone, Stu decorated a Christmas tree for Tom with silver icicles he got from the Avon Five-and-Ten.

BABE'S KWIK-EAT The Texas diner where Harry Trent stopped for lunch after getting a speeding ticket from Joe Bob Brentwood.

BASELINE DRIVE, COLORADO The street in the Free Zone where Nick Andros shared a house with Ralph Brentner and Ralph's woman Elise.

BAYARD One of the towns Poke and Lloyd drove through after they stole the Lincoln Continental.

BEEF 'N BREW A New York restaurant. Larry Underwood called Jane's Place in California from a pay phone next to the restaurant.

BEL AIR Wayne Stukey's family had a palatial estate in Bel Air.

BENNINGTON, VERMONT On July 4, Larry Underwood and Rita Blakemoor were in Bennington, Vermont.

THE BENNINGTON MEN'S SHOP The store in Vermont on the way to Stovington where Larry Underwood outfitted himself with new clothes, boots, socks and shorts.

BIG SPRINGS, IOWA After she lost the family farm, Mrs. Andros got a job in a bakery in Big Springs.

BOOMER'S BAR & GRILLE The bar in May, Oklahoma, where DeeDee Packalotte worked.

THE BOULDER-LONGMONT DIAGONAL The area of Boulder, Colorado, where the IBM plant was located, and where Charles Impening had worked on the custodial crew.

THE BOULDERADO HOTEL A Boulder, Colorado, hotel. Glen Bateman's house was on Spruce Street, about two blocks away from the hotel.

BRAINTREE Charles Campion died in the ambulance en route to Braintree.

BREEKMAN'S QUARRY A quarry Stu remembered from Arnette, Texas, where four boys had drowned.

BRIXTON, MISSISSIPPI Judge Farris read in Lapham's *Law and the Classes of Society* about a black woman from Brixton, Mississippi, who was sentenced to ten years in prison for shoplifting. The assistant district attorney and three jurors had been black.

THE BROKEN DRUM A bar Larry Underwood fantasized about playing in.

THE BRONX Larry Underwood's oral hygienist one-night stand Maria came from the Bronx.

BROOKLYN'S MERCY HOSPITAL When the flu outbreak got serious, a New York doctor was interviewed at Mercy Hospital.

THE BROWNSVILLE MINIMUM SECURITY STATION The Nevada work farm where Poke Freeman and Lloyd Henreid had first met.

BURRACK, ARIZONA Poke Freeman and Lloyd Henreid's "tri-state killing spree" was stopped at a gas station in Burrack, Arizona, where Poke was killed and Lloyd was taken into custody after a shootout in the gas station's market.

BUTTE CITY On his spy mission to Las Vegas, Judge Farris spent one whole day in a motel room in Butte City reading Lapham's *Law and the Classes of Society* .

THE CALCULATOR PLANT One of the two industries in Arnette, Texas. In 1970, the paper plant had shut down. The calculator plant was still operating, but it was ailing.

CAMDEN After the flu hit, Nick Andros thought that the occupants of the empty houses in Shoyo, Arkansas, might have gone to Camden, El Dorado, or Texarkana. Also, the prisoners who beat up Nick Andros were supposed to be sent to Camden, but then everybody died.

THE CANYON BOULEVARD PARK & BANDSHELL The location of the first mass meeting to elect the Free Zone representative board if FINE. [NOTE: See the "Places" entry THE CHAUTAUQUA HALL IN CHAUTAUQUA PARK.]

THE CASHBOX The Las Vegas casino where Flagg's followers drank in the Slipper Room, the casino's bar.

CASLIN, NEBRASKA Nick Andros's birthplace.

CENTRAL PARK The park where Larry Underwood first heard the monster-shouter, and where he first met Rita Blakemoor.

THE CHAUTAUQUA HALL IN CHAUTAUQUA PARK The location of the first mass meeting to elect the Free Zone representative board if FOUL. [NOTE: See the "Places" entry THE CANYON BOULEVARD PARK & BANDSHELL.]

CHAVEZ RAVINE Larry Underwood and the Tattered Remnants opened for Dire Straits and Led Zeppelin in 1981 at Chavez Ravine.

THE CHEERY OIL COMPANY Illinois oil company. Trashcan Man blew up its oil storage tanks.

THE CHEMICAL BANK BUILDING Alice Underwood worked at the Chemical Bank Building in New York City.

THE CHICAGO HEIGHTS Trashcan Man broke into a doctor's office in the Chicago Heights and stole a case of morphine syrettes. He needed the morphine for pain. He had badly burned his arm while setting the explosives at the Cheery Oil Company.

THE CHILDREN OF JESUS ORPHANAGE After Nick Andros's mother was killed in an accident in 1972, Nick was sent to the Children of Jesus orphanage in Des Moines, where he met Rudy Sparkman.

CHILE One of the places where cases of the Project Blue virus initially appeared.

THE CHURCH OF LATTER-DAY SAINTS The Free Zone burial committee found over seventy bodies in this church.

CIBOLA The Fabled City, Seven-in-One, the City that is Promised, the City of Dreams. The name Trashcan Man gave to Las Vegas.

CLIFF One of the towns Poke and Lloyd drove through after they stole the Lincoln Continental.

COLLEGE HILL The Woodsville development where Kojak's previous owner had lived – and died – of the superflu.

COLUMBIA The record company that gave Larry Underwood his first recording contract. It was for the single "Baby, Can You Dig Your Man?", which appeared on his first album "Pocket Savior."

COPPERFIELD FIVE-AND-DIME One of the places Flagg set guardposts to watch for the spies from the Free Zone. Bobby Terry manned the post.

COPYFILE One of the offices Stu Redman passed on his way out of the Stovington plague center.

COUNTY ROAD The road that led to Mother Abagail's farm.

CROWHEART On his way to Las Vegas, this was one of the towns Judge Farris drove through.

THE CUB BAR The M-G-M Grand's bar.

THE CURTIS MORTUARY Shoyo, Arkansas, funeral home. Jane Baker wanted her husband John to buried by the Curtis Mortuary.

THE DAIRY QUEEN Fran Goldsmith and Jess Rider stopped for ice cream at a Dairy Queen in Ogunquit, Maine, the day Fran told Jess she was pregnant with his child. Frannie had a Banana Boat Supreme.

THE DAKOTA RIDGE MEDICAL CENTER The clinic near Boulder where Dr. Richardson set up practice as the Free Zone physician.

DERBYSHIRE, TENNESSEE Dr. George Richardson's hometown.

DETROIT One of the cities where Larry Underwood's "Baby, Can You Dig Your Man?" got a lot of airplay the week it was released.

DISNEYWORLD The Orlando, Florida, amusement park where Edward M. Norris and his family vacationed.

THE DRIVE-INS FRAN GOLDSMITH WENT TO WHEN SHE WAS IN HIGH SCHOOL After the flu, Fran Goldsmith remembered going to these drive-ins: Well's Drive-In, the Sanford Drive-In, and the South Portland Twin Drive-In.

THE DUCK VALLEY RESERVATION When Captain Trips broke out, Flagg was walking the highways somewhere between Grasmere and Riddle, west of Twin Falls, north of the Duck Valley Reservation.

DULUTH After the flu hit, a young man in khaki shorts with ash on his forehead walked the streets of Duluth with a sandwich board sign that foretold the end of the world.

DURGIN STREET An Arnette, Texas, street.

EARTHLY SOUNDS A Boulder music store where Leo Rockway picked out a $600 Gibson guitar.

EBEN G. FINE PARK The park across the street from Harold Lauder's Boulder house.

EDWARDS AIR FORCE BASE Because of the threat of spies from the Free Zone (and as part of his plan for total world dominance), Flagg told Dayna Jurgens that he was taking defensive measures here.

THE EISENHOWER TUNNEL The tunnel Trashcan Man had to

pass through on his journey to Cibola. On their journey to Vegas, Glen, Stu, Larry, and Ralph also passed through the tunnel. They went through roped together.

EL DORADO After the flu hit, Nick Andros thought that the occupants of the empty houses in Shoyo, Arkansas, might have gone to Camden, El Dorado, or Texarkana.

EMIGRANT VALLEY The valley north of Las Vegas where Randall Flagg went to send out his Eye.

EUSTICE, OKLAHOMA On their way home to New York, the Norris family stayed at a travel court in Eustice, Oklahoma.

THE FIRST BANK OF BOULDER The notes of the Free Zone ad hoc committee meeting recorded on Memorex cassettes were placed in a safe deposit box in the First Bank of Boulder.

FIRST BANK OF CALIFORNIA Arlene (of Jane's Place) had a First Bank of California bank book with $13,000 in it for Larry Underwood from Wayne Stukey.

FLORA One of the places Flagg set guardposts to watch for the spies from the Free Zone.

FLORIDA One of the places where cases of the Project Blue virus initially appeared.

THE FOLK ARTS MUSIC STORE The Boulder store where Stu got Frannie a washboard.

FORDHAM UNIVERSITY When Larry Underwood woke up in New York with the oral hygienist, he could see Fordham from a window in her apartment.

FOUKE, TEXAS During his incarceration in Stovington, Stu Redman heard on the news that Atomic Energy Commission officials in Miller County denied that there was any possiblity of a reactor meltdown at the Fouke, Texas, nuclear reactor.

THE FREE ZONE Sanctuary for flu survivors, centered around Mother Abagail Freemantle in Boulder, Colorado.

FREEMONT One of the towns Flagg saw when he went out into the desert and sent out his Eye.

FREEMONT JUNCTION On the night of September 27, enroute to Las Vegas, Larry, Ralph, and Glen camped in Freemont Junction.

THE GARAGE In a detached garage on the south end of May, Oklahoma, Nick Andros found Tom Cullen a Schwinn bike Tom would be able to ride. There had also been a Mercury station wagon in the garage.

A GAS STATION Poke Freeman and Lloyd Henreid's "tri-state killing spree" was stopped at a gas station in Burrack, Arizona, where Poke was killed and Lloyd was taken into custody after a shootout in the gas station's market.

A GENERAL STORE After Lloyd Henreid and Poke Freeman pokerized Gorgeous George, they stopped at a general store two miles beyond Sheldon in Arizona on Highway 75. They pokerized the proprietor (an old man with mail-order teeth), and got away with sixty-three dollars and the old man's pickup truck.

GINO'S The supper club owned by Mort "Gino" Green where Larry Underwood played and sang.

GIRARD, OHIO While camping in Ohio on their way to Nebraska, Stu Redman and Glen Bateman went into Girard to look for food. That same night Harold Lauder succeeded in kissing Frannie Goldsmith.

GOLDEN, COLORADO On their first night out on their way to Las Vegas, Stu, Larry, Ralph, and Glen camped in Golden, Colorado.

A GOLDEN MOTEL The hotel where Trashcan Man and the old man who had picked him up southwest of Sterling, Colorado, stayed the night of July 18.

THE GRACE BAPTIST CHURCH After Mrs. Andros was killed in an accident in 1972, the Grace Baptist Church gave her a charity funeral.

GRAND JUNCTION, COLORADO One of the towns Flagg saw when he went out into the desert and sent out his Eye.

THE GRAND JUNCTION HOLIDAY INN After Stu and Tom resumed their journey back to the Free Zone (after Stu recovered

from pneumonia), they stayed at the Grand Junction Holiday Inn once they were back on the road.

THE GRANGE HALL On December 27, 1895, Abagail Trotts played the guitar and sang at the Nebraska Grange Hall. She was a hit.

GRASMERE When Captain Trips broke out, Flagg was walking the highways somewhere between Grasmere and Riddle, west of Twin Falls, north of the Duck Valley Reservation.

THE GREAT DIVIDE BASIN On his way to Las Vegas, Judge Farris turned northwest at Rawlins, skirted the Great Divide Basin, and camped in Wyoming, east of Yellowstone.

GREEN RIVER One of the towns Flagg saw when he went out into the desert and sent out his Eye.

THE GREEN RIVER SUPERETTE While in Utah, Tom Cullen got Stu Redman Gator-ade from the Green River Superette. Stu had pneumonia, and had been rescued by Tom after Larry, Glen, and Ralph went on to Vegas to fulfill Mother Abagail's final instructions.

THE GREYHOUND BUS TERMINAL IN BOULDER The Free Zone burial committee's base of operations.

GUNLOCK, UTAH On his way back to the Free Zone, Tom Cullen camped in Gunlock, Utah, on the night of September 17.

HAMBURG AND DRESDEN Two World War II bombed-out cities. Flagg wanted the Free Zone to look like these towns after he got through bombing it.

HAMMER CROSSING, KANSAS Edward Norris and his family were in Hammer Crossing on their way back to New York when they decided that their son Hector needed to see a doctor. (He had Captain Trips.)

HAPSCOMB'S TEXACO The gas station on US 93, north of Arnette, Texas, where Charles Campion "touched down" after his escape from the Project Blue lab.

HARLEY DOME One of the towns Flagg saw when he went out into the desert and sent out his Eye.

THE HECKSCHER PLAYGROUND When he first heard him shouting, Larry Underwood thought the monster-shouter was in the Heckscher Playground in Central Park.

HEMINGFORD HOME, NEBRASKA The Nebraska town where Mother Abagail was born, and to where some of the survivors of the flu were drawn by their dreams.

HOMESTEAD On his way to Las Vegas, Judge Farris stopped in Homestead for lunch.

A HONDA DEALERSHIP Larry Underwood and Nadine Cross got motorcycles at a Honda dealership in Wells, Maine.

HURLEY One of the towns Poke and Lloyd drove through after they stole the Lincoln Continental.

THE INDIAN HEAD TAVERN A bar in Arnette, Texas.

THE INDIAN SPRINGS AIRBASE The airbase where daily seminars on the art and craft of flying jet planes were held on Flagg's orders.

JANE'S PLACE A poker parlor in California where Wayne Stukey sometimes hung out.

JEFFREY CITY On his way to Las Vegas, this was one of the towns Judge Farris drove through.

JOLIET, ILLINOIS The town where Judge Farris joined Larry Underwood's group.

KING SOOPER'S A Boulder, Colorado, supermarket.

KITTREDGE After the destruction of Las Vegas, Tom and Stu spent two days in Kittredge on their way back to the Free Zone.

THE KUNKLE FAIRGROUNDS Fairgrounds in Kunkle, Ohio, where Harold Lauder, Frannie Goldsmith, Glen Batemen, and Stu Redman camped on their way to Nebraska.

LAKES REGION After she gave birth to Peter, Fran told Stu that she missed Maine's lake region, and wanted to move back. She particularly remembered Bridgton, Sweden, and Lovell.

LAMONT Enroute to Las Vegas, Judge Farris drove through the town of Lamont.

LANDER Enroute to Las Vegas, Judge Farris drove through the town of Lander.

LAS VEGAS Lloyd Henreid and Poke Freeman met in Las Vegas after they were both released from Brownsville.

THE LASALLE SCHOOL The Chicago correspondence school where Nick Andros had earned six high school credits.

LAUREL STREET The Arnette, Texas, street where Norm Bruett and his family lived.

LEWIS, SOUTH CAROLINA Sam Freemantle, the owner of Mother Abagail's slave father John, had a plantation in Lewis, South Carolina.

THE LIGHTHOUSE MOTEL The motel Jess Rider stayed at while visiting Fran in Ogunquit.

THE LINCOLN TUNNEL On his way out of New York, Larry Underwood had a particularly horrifying passage through the darkened Lincoln Tunnel.

LOGAN LANE A street in the best neighborhood in Arnette, Texas.

LOUISIANA One of the places where cases of the Project Blue virus initially appeared.

LOWVILLE, NEW YORK Mark Zellman's hometown.

LSU Ray Booth's (shortlived) alma mater. (He flunked out in his sophomore year.)

THE M-G-M GRAND HOTEL When Trashcan Man got to Vegas, he threw himself into the fountain in front of the M-G-M Grand Hotel.

MA'S TRUCK STOP Shoyo, Arkansas, restaurant.

MAPLETON HILL The section of Boulder, Colorado, where Mother Abagail lived when the Free Zone was established.

MAY, OKLAHOMA The town where Nick Andros met Tom Cullen.

MCDERMITT One of the places Flagg set up guardposts to watch for the spies from the Free Zone.

MCNAB One of the deserted towns Nick Andros traveled through on his way to Nebraska.

MERCY GENERAL HOSPITAL A New York Hospital. After Alice Underwood got sick, Larry called the hospital and got a recording.

THE METHODIST CHURCH Wendell Elbert was shot by Sheriff Greeley outside the Powtanville Methodist Church.

MEXICO One of the places where cases of the Project Blue virus initially appeared.

MIAMI Stan Nogotny's pre-flu hometown.

MICROFILM One of the offices Stu Redman passed on his way out of the Stovington plague center.

MINNESOTA At the time the superflu hit, Bryce Redman was a systems analyst with IBM in Minnesota.

MILLER COUNTY, ARKANSAS During his incarceration in Stovington, Stu Redman heard on the news that Atomic Energy Commission officials in Miller County denied that there was any possiblity of a reactor meltdown at the Fouke, Texas, nuclear reactor.

MOJAVE DESERT The desert where Flagg sent Eric Strellerton after he drove him mad.

MORRISTOWN, NEW JERSEY The town where Chad Norris had once been an undertaker's assistant.

MOUNT HOLLY As people left Shoyo, Arkansas, after the flu hit, they waded through the Shoyo Stream, which passed through Smackover and came out in Mount Holly.

MOUNT HOPE CEMETERY The Illinois cemetery that Judge Farris and his father would walk by when the judge was a young boy.

MUDDY GAP On his way to Las Vegas, this was one of the towns Judge Farris drove through.

THE MUNZINGER AUDITORIUM The auditorium where a Free Zone mass meeting was held at which Sandy DuChiens was elected to head the Zone's census committee.

THE NATIONAL GUARD ARMORY Chad Norris got gas masks for the Free Zone's burial committee from the armory.

NEBRASKA One of the places where cases of the Project Blue virus initially appeared. Also, Randall Flagg remembered coming from Nebraska. (Where he attended school with Charles Stark-

weather.)

NEDERLAND The section outside of Boulder where Harold Lauder was supposed to be searching for Mother Abagail. He wasn't.

NELLIS AIR FORCE RANGE The air force installation northwest of Indian Springs. Trashcan Man went there after he set the fires at Indian Springs. He brought an atomic weapon back from there to Flagg.

NEW ORLEANS In 1962, Randall Flagg met Lee Harvey Oswald in New Orleans.

NOD God exiled Cain to Nod.

NOGALES Vic Palfrey had seen cholera in Nogales in 1948.

NORTH BERWICK, MAINE The town in Maine where Larry Underwood found an empty house and spent the night. Nadine Cross and Joe followed him on his travels.

THE NORTHERN INDIANA CORRECTIONAL CENTER FOR BOYS The institution where Trashcan Man was sent after he torched a Methodist church.

OGUNQUIT, MAINE Frannie Goldsmith and Harold Lauder's hometown.

AN ORANGE JULIUS SOFT DRINK STAND A penny arcade in Times Square that Larry Underwood remembered from his youth had been replaced with an Orange Julius soft drink stand when Larry returned to New York.

OREGON One of the places where cases of the Project Blue virus initially appeared.

O'TOOLE'S The bar where Wendell Elbert shot a bartender. Wendell then went home and shot and killed Trashcan Man's two older brothers and his sister.

OWYHEE TO MOUNTAIN CITY Randall Flagg's route into Nevada, where he would meet Christopher Bradenton.

THE OZ TOYSHOP When the power came back on in Boulder on September 5, 1985, a manhole cover exploded and came down on the roof of this toy store.

P.S. 162 Larry Underwood's New York grammar school.

THE PAPER FACTORY The Arnette, Texas, plant where, in 1970, Norm Bruett and Tommy Wanamaker had worked before it shut down.

PARRIS ISLAND The marine base where Randall Flagg remembered a defective marine named Boo Dinkway being beaten into a hole and set afire with gasoline.

PASSAIC Larry Underwood acquired a 1200-CC Harley, a sleeping bag, and a tent in Passaic, New Jersey, on his and Rita's journey to Stovington.

PAT'S A bar on 43rd Street in New York City. Before he met Rita Blakemoor, Larry Underwood had gone into Pat's and poured himself a water glass full of Johnnie Walker. He didn't drink it.

PAULIE'S RADIO & TV A TV store in Shoyo, Arkansas. Nick Andros did one of his "apologetic break-ins" there and took a Sony portable TV.

THE PEARL STREET KITCHEN A restaurant on Pearl Street in Boulder, Colorado.

PERU Stan Nogotny wanted to go to Acapulco for a few years and then move to Peru.

PHILADELPHIA One of the cities where Larry Underwood's "Baby, Can You Dig Your Man?" got a lot of airplay the week it was released.

THE PHOENIX JAIL MAXIMUM SECURITY WING After the shootout in the gas station in which Poke was killed, Lloyd Henreid was taken to the Phoenix jail maximum security wing, where he was actually considered something of a celebrity.

POLK COUNTY, NEBRASKA The county where Mother Abagail lived. Nick Andros saw it in a dream.

POLLISTON, KANSAS The Kansas town where Edward Norris found a doctor for his son Hector.

PORTLAND, MAINE One of the cities where Larry Underwood's "Baby, Can You Dig Your Man?" got a lot of airplay the week it was released.

THE PORTLAND CIVIC CENTER The auditorium where Flagg

gathered his followers and told them that he wanted "the spy" (Judge Farris) killed.

THE POWTANVILLE CAFE The cafe where Sally Elbert got a job after her husband Wendell was killed.

PRATT, KANSAS The town where Nick Andros stopped to get some Pepto-Bismol for Tom Cullen, and where he met Julie Lawry.

THE PRATT HOTEL After things tuned sour between Nick Andros and Julie Lawry, she slashed Nick and Tom's bike tires and then shot at them from a window of the Pratt Hotel as they were leaving town.

THE PRATT THEATER The Pratt, Kansas, theater that was next to the Rexall drugstore where Nick Andros got some Pepto-Bismol for Tom Cullen.

RADIOLOGY One of the offices Stu Redman passed on his way out of the Stovington plague center.

THE RANCHLAND MOTEL On September 4, this was the motel Judge Farris was staying in when a crow tapped on his window.

RANDY'S SOOPERETTE An Arnette, Texas, grocery store.

RAWLINS On his way to Las Vegas, Judge Farris turned northwest at Rawlins, skirted the Great Divide Basin, and camped in Wyoming, east of Yellowstone.

RECORDS AND TRANSCRIPTS One of the offices Stu Redman passed on his way out of the Stovington plague center.

THE RED BALL TRUCK STOP The truck stop where Stu Redman's mother had worked until it burned down in 1969.

RENO Lloyd Henreid was sentenced to two-to-four years (plus time served) at Brownsville for his attempted rape of a showgirl in Reno. She sprayed teargas in his eyes.

A REXALL DRUGSTORE The Pratt, Kansas, drugstore where Nick Andros got some Pepto-Bismol for Tom Cullen. The drugstore was next to the Pratt Theater.

RIDDLE When Captain Trips broke out, Flagg was walking the highways somewhere between Grasmere and Riddle, west of Twin Falls, north of the Duck Valley Reservation.

RIFLE On their way back to the Free Zone in the snowmobile, Stu and Tom stayed in the town of Rifle and awoke to a blizzard.

ROOM 209 Frannie Goldsmith's hospital room number after she gave birth to her son Peter.

THE ROSSTON JAYCEE'S LITTLE LEAGUE FIELD The field where Nick Andros and Tom Cullen camped their first night out of May, Oklahoma.

THE ROSSTON SPORTING GOODS STORE The store where Nick Andros acquired a sleeping bag after he left May, Oklahoma, with Tom Cullen.

ROUSES POINT, NEW YORK The town where Mother Abagail's great-nephew Ronnie had lived pre-flu.

RUSSIA, CHINA, OR IRAN Randall Flagg thought to himself that there might be another person like him in one of these countries ten years or so down the line.

SAN DIEGO Charles Campion's ID said he was from San Diego.

SAN RAFAEL On their journey to Las Vegas, Glen, Stu, Larry, and Ralph came upon a thirty-foot area of I-70 that had been swept away by a flash flood. Ralph thought that someone should tell the Utah state highway department about the missing section of roadway.

THE SAN RAFAEL KNOB The place where Larry, Glen, and Ralph camped the night of September 24, on their way to Las Vegas. (Stu had been injured and left behind.)

SANFORD AUTO PARTS The company where Peter Goldsmith worked pre-Captain Trips.

THE SANFORD DRIVE-IN One of the drive-ins Fran Goldsmith remembered going to when she was in high school.

THE SCRUBBA-DUBBA CAR WASH The car wash where Trashcan Man had once worked.

SEARLES LAKE, CALIFORNIA Because of the threat of spies from the Free Zone (and as part of his plan for total world dominance), Flagg told Dayna Jurgens that he was taking defensive measures here.

SEDLEY The town where Trashcan Man started a fire in a deserted house.

SEGO One of the towns Flagg saw when he went out into the desert and sent out his Eye.

SHANNON'S A bar Larry Underwood fantasized about playing in.

SHEAVILLE One of the places Flagg set up guardposts to watch for the spies from the Free Zone.

SHELDON, ARIZONA After Lloyd Henreid and Poke Freeman pokerized Gorgeous George, they stopped at a general store two miles beyond Sheldon in Arizona on Highway 75. They pokerized the proprietor (an old man with mail-order teeth), and got away with sixty-three dollars and the old man's pickup truck.

SHOYO, ARKANSAS The town where Nick Andros was beaten up by Ray Booth, Vince Hogan, Billy Warner, and Mike Childress.

SILVER CITY One of the towns Poke and Lloyd drove through after they stole the Lincoln Continental. Lloyd had bought a bag of burgers and eight milkshakes from a waitress in Silver City.

THE SLIPPER ROOM The bar at the Cashbox.

SMACKOVER As people left Shoyo, Arkansas, after the flu hit, they waded through the Shoyo Stream, which passed through Smackover and came out in Mount Holly.

THE SNAKE RIVER The Snake River marked the northern border between Oregon and Idaho.

THE SOUTH PORTLAND TWIN DRIVE-IN One of the drive-ins Fran Goldsmith remembered going to when she was in high school.

SOUTHWEST OF STERLING, COLORADO An old man driving a big Thunderbird picked up Trashcan Man on July 18, southwest of Sterling, Colorado.

SPENCERVILLE One of the deserted towns Nick Andros traveled through on his way to Nebraska.

THE SPORT AND CYCLE WORLD The Pratt, Kansas store where Nick Andros and Tom Cullen got two new bikes after Julie Lawry slashed their tires.

SPRINGFIELD, MISSOURI "Speak Your Piece," hosted by Ray Flowers, was the highest-rated morning radio program in Springfield, Missouri.

SPRUCE STREET Glen Bateman's Boulder Free Zone house was on Spruce Street, about two blocks from the Boulderado Hotel. [NOTE: Spruce is Tabitha King's maiden name, and Christopher Spruce was the editor of *Castle Rock: The Stephen King Newsletter*.]

STATE STREET, CHICAGO The street where Wendell Elbert bought the gun with which he shot the bartender at O'Toole's, his two sons, and his daughter. He bought it from "a nigger in a bar."

THE STOUT CHRYSLER-PLYMOUTH DEALERSHIP A car dealership in Powtanville, Illinois, where Carley Yates worked as a salesman.

THE STOVINGTON PLAGUE CENTER The government facility where Stu Redman was incarcerated after Atlanta. He eventually escaped, but returned later with Frannie Goldsmith and Harold Lauder.

STRICKER AVENUE The New York print shop where Larry Underwood's buddy Buddy Marx worked was on Stricker Avenue.

THE SUNRISE AMPITHEATER The Colorado outdoor theater where Ralph Brentner stopped to talk to Stu on their walkie-talkies while searching for Mother Abagail.

TAHOE The town where Charles Campion and his family got sick.

TAIWAN In 1970, calculators were being produced more cheaply in Taiwan. This hurt the calculator plant in Arnette, Texas.

THE TARGHEE PASS Judge Farris came into Idaho through the Targhee Pass.

TENNESSEE The people Ed Norris and his family encountered at the Eustice, Oklahoma, travel court were headed for Texas, Alabama, Arkansas, and Tennessee. They had all been infected with Captain Trips by Joe Bob Brentwood via Harry Trent via Edward Norris.

TERRE HAUTE After burning up Old Lady Semple's pension check and a deserted house, Trashcan Man was sent to an institution in Terre Haute for tests. He spent two years there.

TEXARKANA One of the deserted towns Nick Andros traveled through on his way to Nebraska. Also, after the flu hit, Nick Andros thought that the occupants of the empty houses in Shoyo, Arkansas, might have gone to Camden, El Dorado, or Texarkana.

TEXAS The people Ed Norris and his family encountered at the Eustice, Oklahoma, travel court were headed for Texas, Alabama, Arkansas, and Tennessee. They had all been infected with Captain Trips by Joe Bob Brentwood via Harry Trent via Edward Norris.

THOMPSON One of the towns Flagg saw when he went out into the desert and sent out his Eye.

TIFFANY'S A New York jewelry store.

TIMES SQUARE Shortly after his return to New York, and before his mother died, Larry Underwood went to Times Square.

TOM CULLEN'S HOUSE It looked like a "religious-political Disneyland" according to Stan Nogotny. There were Mastercharge, Visa, Diner's Club, and American Express signs mounted over the mantel; models of Fokkers, Spads, Stukas, Spitfires, Zeros, and Messerschmitt fighter planes hung on piano wire in the upper hallway; and stuffed owls, hawks, a bald eagle, a woodchuck, a gopher, a skunk, a weasel, and a coyote strung on piano wire in the downstairs game room.

THE TRANSVERSE NUMBER ONE COMFORT STATION The bathroom in Central Park where Larry Underwood found "the sweet treat," the grinning dead man who had maggots crawling all over his body.

TREMONT AVENUE Larry Underwood's oral hygienist, Maria, had an apartment on Tremont Avenue in New York City.

TWIN FALLS When Captain Trips broke out, Flagg was walking the highways somewhere between Grasmere and Riddle, west of Twin Falls, north of the Duck Valley Reservation.

261 PEARL STREET An apartment building on the corner of Pearl Street and Broadway in Boulder, Colorado. Stu Redman and Frannie Goldsmith shared an apartment on the third floor of this bulding.

THE U.S. METEOROLOGICAL AIR TESTING CENTER After the flu hit, this Boulder, Colorado, facility was rumored to really be a biological warfare installation.

THE UTAH HOTEL The hotel where Stu Redman recuperated from pneumonia after being rescued by Tom Cullen.

THE VERMONT PLAGUE CENTER The goverment installation where Stu Redman was taken after his exposure to Charles Campion. Frannie Goldsmith and Harold Lauder headed there after everyone in Ogunquit, Maine, died.

WATTS, OKLAHOMA Before traveling to Shoyo, Arkansas, Nick Andros had been in Watts the week before, running fence.

WELLS, MAINE Larry Underwood and Nadine Cross got motorcycles at a Honda dealership in Wells, Maine.

THE WELLS DRIVE-IN One of the drive-ins Fran Goldsmith remembered going to when she was in high school.

WESTERN AUTO STORE In Oklahoma, Nick Andros checked out this store for a bike that Tom Cullen could ride.

THE WHITE MOUNTAINS The area of eastern New Hampshire where Nadine Cross had gone to live when she was six. Her parents and her brother had been killed in a car accident.

WOODSVILLE COMMUNITY COLLEGE The school where Glen Bateman had taught pre-Captain Trips.

THE WOODSVILLE GRACE BAPTIST CHURCH Just before Stu Redman met up with Glen Bateman, Glen had confiscated a white table cloth from the Grace Baptist Chutch in Woodsville. It had once been part of a communion set.

WYOMING, EAST OF YELLOWSTONE On his way to Las Vegas, Judge Farris turned northwest at Rawlins, skirted the Great Divide Basin, and camped in Wyoming, east of Yellowstone.

YAKIMA RIDGE, WASHINGTON Because of the threat of spies from the Free Zone (and as part of his plan for total world dominance), Flagg told Dayna Jurgens that he was taking defensive measures here.

ZACK'S PLACE Shoyo, Arkansas, bar. Nick Andros was beaten up and robbed after leaving Zack's.

(6)
THE STAND
Things

A16410USAF The serial number on the atomic warhead Trashcan Man found at the Nellis Air Force Range, and brought back to Flagg in Las Vegas. It exploded when Flagg flicked a ball of electricity from his hand (which Ralph Brentner thought was the Hand of God coming to rescue them), and "...the righteous and unrighteous alike were consumed in that holy fire."

AMY LAUDER'S RECORD PLAYER On the night before they left Ogunquit for Stovington, Harold Lauder found a record player his parents had given his sister Amy when she graduated from junior high school. Harold and Frannie listened to "the music of a dead world" that night.

AN ARMSTRONG CEILING The suspended ceiling in the basement of Harold Lauder's house in Boulder.

ARNETTE VOLUNTEER AMBULANCE The ambulance company Hap called to the gas station when Charles Campion crashed his car into the gas pumps.

AUGUST 18, 1985; 8:30 P.M. The date and time of the first mass meeting to elect the Free Zone representative board. [NOTE: In *The Stand: The Complete & Uncut Edition,* the date was August 18, 1990.]

"BABY, CAN YOU DIG YOUR MAN?" Larry Underwood's first – and only – hit single. It appeared on his album "Pocket Savior."

BACTINE The antiseptic Nick Andros used on his cut forehead in Oklahoma.

A BAG OF BURGERS AND EIGHT MILKSHAKES Lloyd Henreid bought a bag of burgers and eight milkshakes from a waitress in Silver City after he and Poke stole the Lincoln Continental.

BAGGIES During Stu Redman's incarceration, the soldiers in the Stovington plague center kept their revolvers in Baggies.

BAND-AIDS, MERCUROCHROME, AND ANACIN The items in the first aid kit that Tom Cullen brought to Stu Redman as Stu lay with a broken leg. Tom found Stu as he headed back home to the Free Zone.

BANKAMERICARD One of the cards found in Charles Campion's wallet. It had been issued in 1979, and was expired.

A BAR WEAPON The weapon Trashcan Man found in the guardhouse at Nellis Air Force Range. He used it to blow up a porcelain high-voltage conductor at the range for fun.

THE BATTLE OF THE SOUNDS A contest run by a Detroit soul radio station. Soon after its release, Larry Underwood's "Baby, Can You Dig Your Man?" won.

A BIC The lighter Larry Underwood carried.

BIG CLOCK The solitaire card game Lloyd Henreid played in the M-G-M's Cub Bar while Flagg was out in the desert consummating his infernal marriage to Nadine Cross.

"BIG JOHN" Sheriff John Baker's nickname to his Shoyo, Arkansas, constituents.

BILLBOARD The music industry weekly that listed "Baby, Can You Dig Your Man?" as one of three hot prospects the week it was released.

A BLUE FORD On his journey through Maine with Larry Underwood and Nadine Cross, at one point Leo "Joe" Rockway sat on a blue Ford and looked at the pictures in *Oui* magazine.

A BLUE HORSE WRITING TABLET Harold Lauder remembered once copying an entire Tom Swift book word-for-word in a Blue Horse writing tablet.

THE BOOK OF KNOWLEDGE Frannie Goldsmith used two volumes of the *Book of Knowledge* to prop up her dead father's head as she tied his tie for his burial.

BORKHUM RIFF Peter Goldsmith's tobacco.

A BOTTLE OF MILK When Larry Underwood walked out on his oral hygienist one-night stand, she threw a bottle of milk at him.

BOULDER, COLORADO 609 MILES/THIS WAY TO BOULDER A sign Mother Abagail had seen in her dreams before Nick Andros and company arrived at her farm.

A BRIGGS HAND-PUMP In a detached garage on the south end of May, Oklahoma, Nick Andros found Tom Cullen a Schwinn bike Tom would be able to ride. There had also been a Mercury station wagon in the garage, as well as a Briggs hand-pump that Nick took with him, just in case.

BRILLO Alice Underwood kept her Brillo pads in a Table Talk pie dish.

A BRONZE STAR A medal won by Peter Goldmsith at Anzio. Frannie pinned it to his lapel before she buried him.

THE BURIAL COMMITTEE The committee formed by the Free Zone ad hoc committee to bury Boulder's dead.

A CADILLAC COUPE DE VILLE The car Harold Lauder drove around Ogunquit after the flu hit. It had once belonged to Roy Brannigan.

CALIFORNIA PLATES The license plates on Charles Campion's car.

CAMPBELL'S CHUNKY SIRLOIN SOUP After the superflu hit, Frank D. Bruce died in the Project Blue cafeteria with his face in a bowl of Campbell's Chunky Sirloin Soup.

CAMPBELL'S TOMATO SOUP AND CHEF BOY-AR-DEE RAVIOLI The foods Nick Andros packed in his knapsack for his journey to Nebraska from Shoyo.

"CAMPTOWN RACES" As Lloyd Henreid tried to snag Trask's pant leg with the leg of his prison cot, he hummed/sang "Camptown Races."

"CAPTAIN TRIPS" The superflu.

THE CENSUS COMMITTEE The Free Zone head-counting committee headed by Sandy DuChiens.

CHESTERFIELDS The cigarette smoked by Joe Bob Brentwood.

A CHEVROLET Charles Campion's car.

"CHICO 116" Some of the graffiti on the New York building where Larry Underwood lived before he became a hit with "Baby, Can You Dig Your Man?"

A CHIQUITA BANANA When Dayna Jurgens brought a knife into Flagg's office, Flagg turned it into a Chiquita banana.

CITIZEN'S BAND CHANNEL 14 Nick Andros and company monitored Channel 14 on their way to Boulder.

A CIVIL WAR CANNON One of the memorials in the small park in the center of Ogunquit, Maine.

A COCA COLA THERMOMETER The thermometer outside Mother Abagail's window in Nebraska.

COKES Henry Carmichael took Cokes from Bill Hapscomb's Coke machine without paying for them.

A COLEMAN STOVE The stove in the kitchen of Harold Lauder's house in Boulder.

A CONTINENTAL The Lincoln Continental stolen by Lloyd Henreid and Andrew "Poke" Freeman after they were released from the Brownsville Minimum Security Station. They killed the owner of the Connie, as well as his wife and daughter.

"COOKIE" Sarah Bradford's nickname. (She was "Cookie" to her husband.)

CORGI CARS AND A TEXACO STATION Tom Cullen's toys.

THE COUNTY COURTHOUSE AIR RAID SIREN On September 5, 1985, the air raid siren on the top of the Boulder county courthouse went off when the power briefly came back on.

A DATSUN Z Larry Underwood's pre-flu car.

A DAY-GLO PACK Stu Redman's backpack.

DECEMBER 27, 1895 The night Abagail Trotts played and sang at the Grange Hall. [NOTE: In *The Stand: The Complete & Uncut*

Edition, the date was changed to December 27, 1902.]

THE DECLARATION OF INDEPENDENCE, THE CONSTITUTION, AND THE BILL OF RIGHTS After establishing the Free Zone, Glen Bateman told Stu that they needed a committee to ratify these foundations of American democracy.

A DING-DONG TAXI CAB After the flu hit, Larry Underwood saw a young man wearing cutoff denim shorts lying atop a Ding-Dong taxi cab.

"DO NOT CHANGE LANES" One of the signs Larry Underwood saw in the Lincoln Tunnel.

"THE DOCTORS" The soap opera Lila Bruett watched while babysitting for the Hodges kids.

DR. PEPPER The soft drink favored by Vic Palfrey.

"DTS CAN BE FUN" Some of the graffiti written on the Shoyo, Arkansas, jail-cell wall where Nick Andros was brought after being beat up by Ray Booth, Vince Hogan, Billy Warner, and Mike Childress.

1877 The year Mother Abagail Freemantle was born. [NOTE: In *The Stand: The Complete & Uncut Edition*, Mother Abagail's birth year was changed to 1882.]

AN EL DORADO On his way out of New York, Larry Underwood came upon an El Dorado with a dead man and woman inside.

"END OF THE WORLD SUITE ARRANGED FOR CLOCKWORK FIGURES" As Larry sat in Central Park listening to the monster-shouter, he heard the animal clockwork figures in the park playing their tunes to an empty house, and named the music "End of the World Suite Arranged for Clockwork Figures."

FARMING BOOKS Frannie Goldsmith went to the Boulder library and saw two or three people looking at farming books.

50 FRIENDLY PLANTS A book Frannie Goldsmith read in the Free Zone.

"THE FIRST NOEL" "The First Noël" was the hymn Tom Cullen sang after he opened his Christmas gifts from Stu while they were on the road back to the Free Zone.

FISHER-PRICE TOYS When Norm Bruett's Arnette, Texas, house blew sky high from a gas leak, Fisher-Price toys flew all over Laurel Street.

FIVE DOLLARS Rita Blakemoor gave the doorman to her building a five-dollar tip on the morning she met Larry Underwood.

580 PEOPLE The number of people who attended the Free Zone's first town meeting on August 18.

FLAGG'S PAMPHLETS As he walked the country, Randall Flagg carried pamphlets of conflicting literature, including information on the International Jewish Cartel, the CIA, the Farm Workers' Union, Jehovah's Witnesses, Blacks for Militant Equality, and the Ku Klux Klan.

FLAMETRACKS Weapons filled with naplam that Trashcan Man armed at the Indian Springs Air Force Base. Grunts in Vietnam had called them Zippos.

A FORD STATION WAGON The vehicle Sue Stern and company had been driving when they went off the road into a ditch. They later became part of Stu's Nebraska-bound party.

FREDRIC REMINGTON'S "THE WARPATH" When Tom and Stu finally reached the Boulder city limits after their journey back to the Free Zone, the sentry there asked Stu to identify this painting from the wall of Stu's old apartment to verify his identity.

THE FREE ZONE AD HOC COMMITTEE Ralph Brentner, Stu Redman, and Glen Batemen agreed upon the following roster for the Free Zone's ad hoc committee: Nick Andros, Glen Bateman, Ralph Brentner, Richard Ellis, Fran Goldsmith, Stuart Redman, and Susan Stern.

FREEZE-DRIED CONCENTRATES On his way back to the Free Zone, and after he had found Stu Redman, Tom Cullen found some freeze-dried eggs, peas, squash, and dried beef concentrates in an abandoned car, and brought them to Stu.

FRESCA The soda Joe Bob Brentwood took out of Hap's soda machine.

A FRIGIDAIRE Norm Bruett's refrigerator.

THE "GADGETS" THAT FASCINATED MOTHER ABAGAIL
Mother Abagail moved into a house in the Mapleton Hill section of Boulder after the Free Zone was established. The house was loaded with time-saving appliances and they fascinated her. They included: a dishwasher, two vacuums, a Dispo-All, a microwave oven, a Maytag washer and dryer, a trash masher, and a Motorola TV.

GAINESBURGERS Kojak's dog food.

GATOR-ADE While in Utah, Tom Cullen got Stu Redman Gator-Ade from the Green River Superette. Stu had pneumonia, and had been rescued by Tom after Larry, Glen, and Ralph went on to Vegas to fulfill Mother Abagail's final instructions.

GEOMETRY, ADVANCED MATH, AND TWO YEARS OF A LANGUAGE At the time Nick Andros was beat up in Shoyo, Arkansas, he had needed these remaining courses to enter college.

GEORGIA GIANTS Stu Redman's shoes.

"GET YO' ASS UP THE PASS–COLD CREEK CANYON" A bumpersticker on the back deck of a Ford's trunk in Boulder. Leo Rockway threw a rock through the car's window.

A GIBSON GUITAR A guitar Larry Underwood had taken from a house and with which he "taught" Leo how to play. (Actually, Leo was a prodigy and taught himself.) Later, in Boulder, Leo picked out a $600 Gibson at the Earthly Sounds music store

GLASSBLOWING Larry Underwood saw Gene Shalitt interview a guy on the "Today Show" who had done glassblowing as a hobby for forty years.

GOD'S FINGER On his way home to the Free Zone, Tom Cullen dreamt of Nick Andros. In the dream, Nick told Tom to look for God's Finger and follow it east. God's Finger turned out to be a giant stone monolith pointing east.

GOTTLIEB DESERT ISLE A penny arcade game Larry Underwood remembered from his youth.

THE GRANGE In March of 1895, Gary Sites told John Freemantle that he had been elected to the Grange. John was the first black man ever allowed in the organization. [NOTE: In *The Stand: The Complete & Uncut Edition* , John was elected to the Grange in March of 1902.]

THE GREAT CHICAGO PIG CONVENTION OF 1968 The 1968 rally at which Christopher Bradenton was arrested.

HAMM'S BEER The beer Larry Underwood drank.

HANDY WRAP On the morning Lila Bruett babysat for Sally Hodges' children, she left Norm three "sassages" wrapped in Handy Wrap.

A HARLEY-DAVIDSON MOTORCYCLE Larry Underwood acquired a 1200-CC Harley in Passaic on his and Rita's journey to Stovington. He also got a sleeping bag and tent in Passaic.

HAROLD AND COMPANY'S ROUTE TO NEBRASKA Route 7 to Rutland, Route 4 to Schuylerville, Route 29 to I-87, I-87 to I-90, I-90 West.

HAROLD'S "GONE TO STOVINGTON" MESSAGE Harold Lauder painted this message in white paint on the roof of Moses Richardson's barn:

HAVE GONE TO STOVINGTON, VT. PLAGUE CEN-
TER
US 1 TO WELLS
INTERSTATE 95 TO PORTLAND
US 302 TO BARRE
INTERSTATE 89 TO STOVINGTON
LEAVING OGUNQUIT JULY 2, 1985
HAROLD EMERY LAUDER
FRANCES GOLDSMITH

HAROLD'S BOMB Harold Lauder used a Realistic walkie-talkie, eight sticks of dynamite, and a doorbell to build the bomb with which he blew up Ralph Brentner's house.

A HEFTY BAG On the floor of Lloyd and Poke's stolen Lincoln Continental was a Hefty trash bag filled with sixteen pounds of marijuana.

THE HOLIDAY INN SIGN On their journey back to the Free Zone, Tom and Stu stayed at the Grand Junction Holiday Inn. The motel had a sign on its marquee which read:

ELCOME TO GR ND JUNC ON'S SUMMERF ST '85!
JUNE 12—JU Y 4TH!

HONDA MOTORBIKES The vehicles Harold Lauder and Frannie Goldsmith used to travel to Stovington.

HOSTESS TWINKIES AND COKE Frannie Goldsmith and Harold Lauder ate Twinkies and drank Coke in an Ogunquit park after they survived Captain Trips.

HOSTESS TWINKIES, COKE, AND BUBBLE-UP The snack items that were scattered on the tables in the Project Blue cafeteria after the superflu hit.

A HUSH PUPPIES SHOE BOX The box into which Harold Lauder put the bomb he used to blow up Ralph Brentner's house.

"I LOVE LUCY" After Nick Andros "took over" for Sheriff Baker, he stole a Sony portable TV from Paulie's Radio & TV. An ABC station was showing "I Love Lucy" reruns.

"I STILL LOVE YOU SUZANNE" Some of the graffiti written on the Shoyo, Arkansas, jail-cell wall where Nick Andros was brought after being beat up by Ray Booth, Vince Hogan, Billy Warner, and Mike Childress.

"IF YOU EAT YOU SHOULD READ THIS!" The headline of a poster about food poisoning put together by Stu Redman in the Free Zone.

IN HIS STEPS A book that had been Larry Underwood's mother's. It had been given to her by Larry's grandmother. It contained ethical problems.

"IN THE GARDEN" One of the hymns Mother Abagail hummed while she plucked Addie Richardson's chickens.

"INCOMMUNICADO" Nick Andros learned this word at the movies when he was a kid.

INDEPENDENCE DAY On July 4, Larry Underwood and Rita Blakemoor were in Bennington, Vermont.

AN INTERNATIONAL HARVESTER PICK-UP TRUCK An overturned truck in the road on the way to Stovington that Larry Underwood couldn't avoid. He ditched the Harley. (This took place after Rita's death, so Larry was alone.)

A "JESUS IS COMING & IS HE PISSED" T-SHIRT The t-shirt worn by Dewey the Deck.

JOHNNIE WALKER Before he met Rita Blakemoor, Larry Underwood had gone into Pat's (a bar on 43rd Street in New York City), and poured himself a water glass full of Johnnie Walker. He didn't drink it.

JOHNSON'S BABY POWDER Frannie Goldsmith used Johnson's baby powder to touch up her dead father's face, neck, and hands before she buried him.

THE JUDGE'S ROUTE TO THE WEST When Judge Farris left Boulder as a spy, he traveled the following route: north to Wyoming, and then west. Then straight across Idaho towards northern California.

JULY 18 An old man driving a big Thunderbird picked up Trashcan Man on July 18, southwest of Sterling, Colorado.

JULY 1 The day Fran and Stu headed back for Maine.

JULY 3 The day Nick Andros started out for Nebraska.

JUNE 14 The day Lucy Swann expected her baby.

JUNE 13, 1985; 2:37:16 A.M. The date and time the superflu virus was released from containment in the Project Blue labs. [NOTE: In *The Stand: The Complete & Uncut Edition,* the date was changed to June 13, 1990.]

JUNE 28, 9:17 P.M. The date and time the power went off in Ogunquit, Maine.

KEDS Trashcan Man's sneakers.

A KENT STATE UNIVERSITY SWEATSHIRT The sweatshirt worn by Susan Stern when she was on the road with Stu and company.

KENTS Bobby Terry's cigarettes.

"THE KEY" The imagistic, talismanic symbol Lloyd Henreid fixated on while locked in his Phoenix cell with no food.

KLEENEX Hap used these tissues to wipe his runny nose after he caught Captain Trips from Charles Campion.

KLMT The radio station on which Larry first heard his song "Baby, Can You Dig Your Man?" played on the air.

KOOL-AID The drink Tom Cullen carried in a big thermos on the way back to the Free Zone. Also, when Frannie Goldsmith and Amy Lauder were young, they would drink Kool-Aid in Barbie's Kitchen Cups, in the summer house, in the Lauders' yard.

A LAND ROVER The vehicle Judge Farris drove to the west as a spy.

LAPHAM'S *LAW AND THE CLASSES OF SOCIETY* On his spy mission to Las Vegas, Judge Farris spent one whole day in a motel room in Butte City reading this law book.

LARGE DANGLING PENISES, GIGANTIC BREASTS, AND CRUDELY DRAWN VAGINAS Some of the graffiti drawn on the Shoyo, Arkansas, jail-cell wall where Nick Andros was brought after being beat up by Ray Booth, Vince Hogan, Billy Warner, and Mike Childress.

LARRY UNDERWOOD'S FAVORITE FOODS When Larry came back to New York after his "Baby, Can You Dig Your Man?" party debacle on the west coast, his mother bought his favorite foods: Roast beef, a Daisy canned ham, real butter, Coke, deli sausages, and Baskin-Robbins chocolate cheesecake ice cream.

LARRY UNDERWOOD'S MEMORIES OF THE SIXTIES After Rita Blakemoor's death, Larry Underwood stumbled along the highway thinking about pop culture icons of the sixties, including: Andy Warhol, the Velvet Underground, the Beatles, the Who, Return of the Creature from Yorba Linda, Norman Spinrad, Norman Mailer, Norman Rockwell, Norman Bates, Dylan, Barry McGuire, Diana Ross, Creem, the Young Rascals, the Lovin' Spoonful, and Grace Slick and the Jefferson Airplane.

LARRY UNDERWOOD'S PERFORMANCE FOR NADINE AND JOE On a beach in Maine, Larry played these tunes for Nadine and Joe: "Goin Downtown" by Geoff Maladur, "Sally's Fresno Blues," "The Springhill Mine Disaster," "That's All Right, Mamma," "Milk Cow Blues," "Jim Dandy," and "Endless Sleep" by Jody Reynolds.

LARRY UNDERWOOD'S ROUTE OUT OF NEW YORK This is the route Larry suggested to Rita Blakemoor: "We go down Fifth to Thirty-ninth and turn west. Cross to New Jersey by the Lincoln Tunnel, then follow 495...I thought we could head northeast. Maybe end up in Maine."

THE LAS VEGAS COUNTY JAIL SIGNS After they were taken into custody by Flagg's men, Larry, Ralph, and Glen were greeted by signs that said:

NO SPITTING
THIS WAY TO SHOWERS & DELOUSING
YOU ARE *NOT* A GUEST

"LAS VEGAS 260" On the night of September 24, Glen, Larry, and Ralph camped northeast of the San Rafael Knob. Nearby was a road sign that said "LAS VEGAS 260."

THE LAS VEGAS *SUN* The Las Vegas newspaper Trashcan Man saw fly by him when he got to Cibola. The headline read "PLAGUE GROWS WORSE WASHINGTON MUTE."

THE LAS VEGAS STRIP SIGNS When Trashcan Man got to Las Vegas, he saw the following signs on the Strip:

LIBERAL SLOTS
BLUEBELL WEDDING CHAPEL–6-SECOND WED-
DING BUT IT'LL LAST A LIFETIME
NEIL DIAMOND! THE AMERICANA HOTEL JUNE 15-
AUGUST 30!

He also saw the words "DIE LAS VEGAS for your sins!" slashed across the front window of a jewelry store.

THE LASALLE BUSINESS SCHOOL One of the things Stu Redman had with him as he lay in a ravine with a broken leg while Larry, Glen, and Ralph went on to Vegas, was a book of matches with LaSalle Business School on it. He had eight matches left.

THE LAST SUPPER A paint-by-number painting done by Sally Hodges that hung over her TV.

THE LAW COMMITTEE The Free Zone committee headed by attorney Al Bundell.

"LEDGER" The gold leaf legend stamped on the cover of Harold Lauder's journal.

"LIKE IT IN MY ASSHOLE" Some of the graffiti written on the Shoyo, Arkansas, jail-cell wall where Nick Andros was brought after being beat up by Ray Booth, Vince Hogan, Billy Warner, and Mike Childress.

A LINCOLN CONTINENTAL After the Cheery Oil Company fires, this was one of two cars containing corpses that Trashcan Man saw off the highway.

"LITTLE ABIE #1" Some of the graffiti on the New York building where Larry Underwood lived before he became a hit with "Baby, Can You Dig Your Man?"

"LOOTER" The sign that was hung around the neck of a man hanging from a street sign at Fifth Avenue and 53rd Street in New York City after the flu hit.

A "LOVE STORY" POSTER Larry Underwood's oral hygienist one-night stand Maria had a "Love Story" movie poster on her apartment wall.

AN LSU FRATERNITY RING A ring worn by Ray Booth. Nick Andros remembered seeing it as he was beaten, and this helped Sheriff Baker identify Ray as one of Nick's assailants.

LUCKIES AND SLIM JIMS When Poke Freeman and Lloyd Henreid held up the gas station in Burrack, Arizona, Bill Markson was buying Slim Jims and Luckies.

LUCKY STRIKES Carley Yates's cigarettes.

MANTOVANI AND LAWRENCE WELK TAPES The eight-track tapes the old man who picked up Trashcan Man in Colorado played in his Thunderbird.

MARCH 1895 The month and year John Freemantle was elected to the Grange. [NOTE: In *The Stand: The Complete & Uncut Edition,* it was March of 1902.]

MAYDAY CHASE A game played by the Free Zone children in the picnic area halfway up Flagstaff Mountain. Fran and Stu watched them play as they discussed moving back to Maine with their new son, Peter.

McDONALD'S BOXES AND TACO BELL WRAPPERS The litter found in the 1960 Plymouth that Stu and Tom used to get to the Utah Hotel.

A MELTDOWN During his incarceration in Stovington, Stu Redman heard on the news that Atomic Energy Commission officials in Miller County denied that there was any possiblity of a reactor meltdown at the Fouke, Texas, nuclear reactor.

MEMOREX CASSETTES The cassettes used to record the notes of the Free Zone ad hoc committee meeting.

A MERCEDES-BENZ After packing his burned arm in jelly and injecting himself with morphine, Trashcan Man came upon a Mercedes-Benz with two dead people in it. He slept in the trunk.

A MERCURY STATION WAGON In a detached garage on the south end of May, Oklahoma, Nick Andros found Tom Cullen a Schwinn bike Tom would be able to ride. There had also been a Mercury station wagon in the garage.

A MILKY WAY In addition to the bottle of 1947 Bordeaux wine, Larry Underwood also brought Harold Lauder a Milky Way candy bar in Boulder as gifts of introduction.

MONITOR 2 The monitor Starkey used to look into the Project Blue cafeteria after the flu hit.

MORPHINE, ELAVIL, AND DARVON COMPLEX Some of the drugs Trashcan Man learned about when he was a trusty in a prison infirmary.

"THE MOST IMPORTANT PRODUCT" Dr. Richardson told Frannie that babies were the Free Zone's most important product if they wanted to survive.

MOTHER ABAGAIL'S FAREWELL NOTE After Mother Abagail's vision of Randall Flagg as a wolf, she decided she must leave the Free Zone and make peace with God. She left a note which said:

> *I must be gone a bit now. I've sinned and presumed to know the Mind of God. My sin has been PRIDE, and He wants me to find my place in His work again.*
> *I will be with you again soon if it is God's will.*
> *Abby Freemantle*

MOTHER ABAGAIL'S REPERTOIRE On December 27, 1895, the night Abagail Trotts appeared at the Nebraska Grange Hall, she performed the following songs:

> "The Old Rugged Cross"
> "How I Love My Jesus"
> "Camp Meeting in Georgia"
> "When Johnny Comes Marching Home"
> "Marching Through Georgia"
> "Goober Peas"
> "Tenting Tonight on the Old Campground"

THE MOVIES FRAN GOLDSMITH SAW AT THE DRIVE-IN WHEN SHE WAS IN HIGH SCHOOL After the flu, Fran thought back on her youth and remembered seeing the following movies at drive-ins when she was in high school: "The Wild Angels," "The Devil's Angels," and "Hell's Angels On Wheels."

A MUSTANG Gorgeous George's car.

THE NATIONAL GUARD After the flu hit, Ray Flowers heard that the national guard was called into Kansas City and St. Louis, Missouri, to "stop the spread of panic" and to "prevent looting." Guardsman Sergeant Buchan eventually shot and killed Flowers for broadcasting after he was ordered to shut down.

THE NELLIS AIR FORCE RANGE SIGNS The signs said:

> U.S. GOVERNMENT PROPERTY
> NO TRESPASSING
> ARMED SENTRIES
> GUARD DOGS
> THERE IS A HIGH-VOLTAGE CHARGE PASSING
> THROUGH THESE WIRES

NIGHTWORK A novel by Irwin Shaw.

1981 Larry Underwood and the Tattered Remnants opened for Dire Straits and Led Zeppelin in 1981 at Chavez Ravine.

A 1947 BORDEAUX The wine Larry Underwood brought to Harold Lauder as a gift of introduction.

1970 The year Freddie Goldsmith was killed by a drunk driver. [NOTE: In *The Stand: The Complete & Uncut Edition,* he was killed in 1973.]

1972 The year Mrs. Andros was killed in an accident.

1977 The year Mother Abagail turned a hundred years old. Her picture appeared in the Omaha newspaper. [NOTE: In *The Stand: The Complete & Uncut Edition,* the year she turned a hundred was 1982.)

1964 The year Frannie Goldsmith was born. [NOTE: In *The Stand: The Complete & Uncut Edition,* she was born in 1969.]

A 1960 PLYMOUTH The standard shift car Stu and Tom came upon on their way back to the Free Zone. They got it going by popping the clutch. It had a Sears battery.

1962 The year Randall Flagg met Lee Harvey Oswald in New Orleans.

NOVEMBER 14, 1963 The day Nick Andros was born.

NYQUIL When Alice Underwood got sick with the flu, Larry brought her Nyquil.

ODÉ PERODÉ CIGARS The old man driving a big Thunderbird who picked up Trashcan Man on July 18, southwest of Sterling, Colorado, smoked Odé Perodé cigars.

OLD TESTAMENT MAGICAL MYSTERY TOURS Glen Bateman compared the trip to Vegas that he, Larry, and Stu were making with the trips into the wilderness the Old Testament prophets would make from time to time.

ORANGE SPOT The soda Leo Rockway drank.

OUI **MAGAZINE** On his journey through Maine with Larry Underwood and Nadine Cross, at one point Leo "Joe" Rockway sat on a blue Ford and looked at the pictures in *Oui* magazine.

OXBOW DAM The Oxbow Dam was on the Snake River.

PABST Stu Redman's beer.

PALL MALLS At the Phoenix jail, the inmate named Mathers kneed Lloyd Henreid in the groin for a pack of Pall Malls from Shockley the door-guard.

"PEGGY SUE GOT MARRIED" Buddy Holly tune.

PENICILLIN, AMPICILLIN, AND V-CILLIN The antibiotics Nick Andros told Tom Cullen to bring to Stu Redman because Stu had pneumonia. They were in Utah and Nick came to Tom in a dream.

THE PENSION CHECK When Trashcan Man was a kid, he started a fire in Old Lady Semple's mailbox and burned up her pension check.

PEPSI CANS AND A MILKY WAY WRAPPER Larry Underwood found these items of trash in the barn where Harold Lauder had painted his "Gone to Stovington" sign.

PEPTO-BISMOL Just after entering Kansas on their way to Nebraska, Nick Andros stopped at a Rexall drugstore in Pratt to get some Pepto-Bismol for Tom Cullen. Tom had diarrhea from eating too many green apples.

A PHILCO Norm Bruett's radio.

A PICKUP TRUCK After Lloyd Henreid and Poke Freeman pokerized Gorgeous George, they stopped at a general store two miles beyond Sheldon in Arizona on Highway 75. They pokerized the proprietor (an old man with mail-order teeth), and got away with sixty-three dollars and the old man's pickup truck.

A PINBALL MACHINE ENCASED IN LUCITE While holed up in a blizzard on Christmas morning on their way back to the Free Zone, Stu told Tom that Santa had left presents for him. One of Tom's gifts was a pinball machine encased in Lucite.

A PING PONG TABLE Gorgeous George had a Ping Pong table in his house covered with guns. [NOTE: See the "People" entry GORGEOUS GEORGE.]

A PINTO Larry Underwood and Rita Blakemoor saw a Pinto lying crushed beneath the wheels of a Mayflower moving van as they fled New York.

PLANTER'S PEANUTS A favorite of Mother Abagail's.

"POCKET SAVIOR" The song Larry Underwood wrote and recorded for the flip side of his single "Baby, Can You Dig Your Man?" "Pocket Savior" was also the title of Larry's first album.

POKE AND LLOYD'S DOPE Poke and Lloyd had the following dope in their stolen Lincoln Continental: five grams of hash, a snuffbox loaded with coke, and sixteen pounds of marijuana. (They also had two .38s, three .45s, a .357 magnum (Poke's "Pokerizer"), six shotguns (two of them sawed-off pumps), and a Schmeisser submachine gun in the car.)

POKE AND LLOYD'S GUNS Poke and Lloyd had the following guns in their stolen Lincoln Continental: two .38s, three .45s, a .357 magnum (Poke's "Pokerizer"), six shotguns (two of them sawed-off pumps), and a Schmeisser submachine gun. (They also had five grams of hash, a snuffbox loaded with coke, and sixteen pounds of marijuana in the car.)

THE POKERIZER Poke's .357 magnum.

POP-TARTS In Boulder, Harold Lauder ate these cold for breakfast.

A PORT-O-SAN The portable toilet that Nick Andros and Ralph Brentner installed in the backyard of Mother Abagail's Mapleton Hill Free Zone home.

PROJECT BLUE The code name for the Captain Trips biological warfare program.

THE PROPHET'S SIGN After the flu hit, a young man in khaki shorts with ash on his forehead walked the streets of Duluth with a sandwich board sign that said:

THE TIME OF THE DISAPPEARANCE IS HERE
CHRIST THE LORD RETURNETH SOON
PREPARE TO MEET YOUR GOD!

The back read:

BEHOLD THE HEARTS OF THE SINNERS WERE
  BROKEN
THE GREAT SHALL BE ABASED AND THE ABASED
  MADE GREAT
THE EVIL DAYS ARE AT HAND
WOE TO THEE O ZION

A PULSAR Stu Redman and Lucy Swann both wore Pulsar watches.

A RALEIGH BIKE Nick Andros's bike.

RALPH'S POSTER Ralph Brentner made up a poster for the mass meeting to elect the Free Zone representative board. The poster said:

MASS MEETING!

REPRESENTATIVE BOARD
TO BE NOMINATED AND ELECTED!

8:30 P.M., August 18, 1985

Place: Canyon Boulevard Park & Bandshell if FINE
Chautauqua Hall in Chautauqua Park if FOUL

REFRESHMENTS WILL BE SERVED
FOLLOWING THE MEETING

A RAND-MCNALLY ATLAS The road atlas Nick Andros carried in his pack.

"THE RED LIST" A list of names Flagg had given to Paul Burlson. These names were "flagged."

"REMEMBER! IT IS IN YOUR BEST INTEREST TO SHOWER DAILY!" A sign Trashcan Man saw in the barracks at Nellis Air Force Range.

"REPORT ANY COLD SYMPTOMS NO MATTER HOW MINOR TO YOUR SUPERVISOR AT ONCE" The directive that was posted in the nurse's center in the Stovington, Vermont, plague center while Stu Redman was held in custody.

RITA BLAKEMOOR'S PILLS On their way to Stovington, Larry knew that Rita carried some yellow jackets, Quaaludes, and Darvon with her.

RITZ Crackers.

ROAST BEEF ON VIENNA BREAD WITH ONIONS AND GULDEN'S SPICY BROWN MUSTARD Flagg's lunch the afternoon he freed Lloyd Henreid from the Phoenix prison.

A ROCKY MOUNTAIN TIMBER WOLF While in the Free Zone, Mother Abagail saw this wolf in a vision. The wolf was Randall Flagg, and he told her that her own people knew him and called him John the Conqueror.

"A ROSE FOR EMILY" A short story by William Faulkner.

"S.L." The initials on the imitation leather key case Stu and Tom found in the 1960 Plymouth they got running and used to get to a hotel in Utah. (They were headed back to the Free Zone.)

SANTA MONICA POLICE, DETECTIVE SECOND CLASS Barry Drogan's job before the flu.

SARA LEE CAKES After the flu, Frannie included Sara Lee frozen cakes as part of the "Things to Remember" section of her diary. Strawberry cheesecake was her personal favorite.

A SCHWINN BIKE In a detached garage on the south end of May, Oklahoma, Nick Andros found Tom Cullen a Schwinn bike Tom would be able to ride. There had also been a Mercury station wagon in the garage.

SCOTCH BRAND FILAMENT TAPE The tape Lloyd Henried and Poke Freeman used to bind Gorgeous George's hands (and his mouth and nose.)

A SCOUT The vehicle that belonged to Tony Leominster. Before Charles Campion "touched down," Bill Hapscomb had put a new tailpipe on the Scout.

SEPTEMBER 4 The day Judge Farris stayed at the Ranchland Motel on his way to Las Vegas. A crow had tapped on his motel room window.

SEPTEMBER 4; 8:00 P.M. The date of a Free Zone meeting at Munzinger Auditorium.

SEPTEMBER 17 On his way back to the Free Zone, Tom Cullen camped in Gunlock, Utah, on the night of September 17.

"SEVEN GATES TO THE CITY" One of the hymns Mother Abagail hummed while she plucked Addie Richardson's chickens.

SEVEN INDEPENDENT POWER SOURCES FOR YOUR HOME While in the Boulder library, Frannie Goldsmith saw a young man of about twenty-five reading a book called *Seven Independent Power Sources for Your Home* .

A SHELL CAP The clerk at the Burrack, Arizona, gas station held up by Poke Freeman and Lloyd Henreid wore a Shell cap.

A SHIFTING-ANTIGEN FLU Dr. George Richardson learned that Captain Trips was a shifting-antigen flu: the flu itself changed as the body created antibodies to destroy it in one particular form.

A SHOYO STREAM As people left Shoyo, Arkansas, after the flu hit, they waded through the Shoyo Stream, which passed through Smackover and came out in Mount Holly.

656-8600 One of the toll-free numbers for "Speak Your Piece."

656-8601 One of the toll-free numbers for "Speak Your Piece."

600 SIMPLE RECIPES While in the Boulder library, Frannie Goldsmith saw a pretty young blonde girl of about fourteen reading a book called *600 Simple Recipes* .

6:13:85:2:37:16 The time frozen in red on the digital clock in the Project Blue labs marking the time the superflu virus was released from containment.

"65 NATIONAL SCIENCE FAIR PRIZE WINNER" The article from which Harold got the information he used to build the bomb with which he blew up Ralph Brentner's house.

SIXTY-THREE DOLLARS After Lloyd Henreid and Poke Freeman pokerized Gorgeous George, they stopped at a general store two miles beyond Sheldon in Arizona on Highway 75. They pokerized the proprietor (an old man with mail-order teeth), and got away with sixty-three dollars and the old man's pickup truck.

A SKIPPY PEANUT BUTTER JAR After Poke Freeman and Lloyd Henreid killed Gorgeous George, they found a Skippy peanut butter jar in an upstairs cabinet containing $20.60 in dimes.

SKYHAWK PLANES The jet planes Flagg's people tried to learn to fly.

SLIM JIMS AND SALTINES The foodstuffs Tom Cullen carried in his knapsack on the way back to the Free Zone.

A SMITH & WESSON .38 The gun Harold Lauder carried while out (supposedly) searching for Mother Abagail.

"THE SNIFFER" A box made in Portland, Oregon, designed to detect any releases of the Project Blue biological warfare "creations." It was built for the Defense Department under contract No. 164480966.

A SNOWMOBILE The vehicle Tom and Stu used to travel back to the Free Zone from Utah.

"SOFTLY AS I LEAVE YOU" AND "MOON RIVER" Two of the songs Larry Underwood played at Gino's supper club.

A SON HOUSE HATCHET Billy Richardson's hatchet. Mother Abagail used it to behead the chickens she brought back for her guests.

A SONY PORTABLE TV After the flu hit, Nick Andros did one of his "apologetic break-ins" at Paulie's Radio & TV in Shoyo, Arkansas, and took a Sony portable TV.

"SOUL TRAIN" Soon after its release, Larry heard his record "Baby, Can You Dig Your Man?" played on this Saturday morning TV show.

SPACE RACE A penny arcade game Larry Underwood remembered from his youth.

"SPEAK YOUR PIECE" The highest-rated morning radio program in Springfield, Missouri. It was hosted by Ray Flowers.

SPOCK, DR. Even though Lila Bruett had never read the good doctor, she had an instinctive sense about caring for children.

THE STOVINGTON PLAGUE CENTER SIGN When Larry Underwood, Nadine Cross, Lucy Swann, and Joe finally arrived at the Stovington plague center, they found the following sign:

> ROUTE 7 TO RUTLAND
> ROUTE 4 TO SCHUYLERVILLE
> ROUTE 29 TO I-87
> I-87 TO I-90
> I-90 WEST
>
> EVERYONE HERE IS DEAD
> WE ARE MOVING WEST TO NEBRASKA
> STAY ON OUR ROUTE
> WATCH FOR SIGNS
> HAROLD EMERY LAUDER
> FRANCES GOLDSMITH
> STUART REDMAN
> GLEN BATEMAN
> JULY 8, 1985

STU REDMAN AND GLEN BATEMAN'S LUNCH Stu and Glen's first meal together consisted of caviar, pepperoni, salami, sardines, apples, Keebler's fig bars, and saltines. They had Sara Lee poundcake for dessert. They drank Narragansett beer after they ate.

STU'S CAR MODELS AND TOM'S MOONBASE ALPHA While holed up in the Grand Junction Holiday Inn for four weeks, Stu Redman built over twenty car models, including a Rolls-Royce with 240 parts. Tom had built Moonbase Alpha, "a terrain-contoured landscape that covered nearly half the floor-space of the Holiday Inn's convention hall."

STU'S CHRISTMAS GIFT TO KOJAK It was a box of Hartz Mountain Dog Yummies. [NOTE: See the "Things" entry STU'S CHRISTMAS GIFTS TO TOM.]

STU'S CHRISTMAS GIFTS TO TOM Stu Redman and Tom Cullen spent Christmas morning in their snowmobile, so Stu did the best he could to give Tom a real Christmas: He put a tree up in the snow and wrapped three gifts for Tom in wedding paper that he got from the Avon Five-and-Ten. He gave Tom a pinball machine encased in Lucite, a sweatshirt that said "I CLIMBED LOVELAND PASS," and a silver "infinity" charm on a chain.

A T-BIRD After the Cheery Oil Company fires, this was one of two cars containing corpses that Trashcan Man saw off the highway.

THE TATTERED REMNANTS Larry Underwood's pre-solo career band. The band consisted of Larry, Barry Greig, Al Spellman, and Johnny McCall.

TEARGAS Lloyd Henreid was sentenced to two-to-four years (plus time served) at Brownsville for his attempted rape of a showgirl in Reno. She sprayed teargas in his eyes.

THE THINGS IN FRANNIE GOLDSMITH'S SMALL ZIPPER BAG Frannie kept the following belongings in a small zipper bag in the Free Zone: Stay-Free Mini Pads, "IT'S A BOY" cigars, "IT'S A GIRL" cigars, several jars of cleansing cream, and her diary.

$13,000 After Larry Underwood fled California for New York, he called Jane's Place to find out what was happening. Arlene told him she had a bank book there for him from Wayne Stukey. The account contained $13,000.

A .38 CALIBER POLICE SPECIAL Dave Roberts's gun.

A .30-.30 The rifle Larry Underwood carried out of New York.

A .32 CALIBER REVOLVER Rita Blakemoor's gun.

"THIS PLACE HAS BUGS. LOUIS DRAGONSKY, 1977" Some of the graffiti written on the Shoyo, Arkansas, jail-cell wall where Nick Andros was brought after being beat up by Ray Booth, Vince Hogan, Billy Warner, and Mike Childress.

"THIS PLACE SUX, JERRY" Some of the graffiti written on the Shoyo, Arkansas, jail-cell wall where Nick Andros was brought after being beat up by Ray Booth, Vince Hogan, Billy Warner, and Mike Childress.

THREE DOLLARS AND TEN POUNDS OF DEER MEAT When Stu Redman shot his first deer on a hunting trip with his Uncle Dale, a man named Schoey had skinned and dressed the deer for three dollars and ten pounds of deer meat.

TIDE The detergent Frannie Goldsmith used to "feet wash" her and Stu's clothes in the Free Zone.

TIMEX Gorgeous George's watch.

THE "TODAY SHOW" NBC's morning show.

A TOLKIEN STORY After the flu hit, Larry thought that New York looked like a fabled city in a J.R.R. Tolkien story.

A TOM SWIFT BOOK Harold Lauder remembered once copying an entire Tom Swift book word-for-word in a Blue Horse writing tablet.

"TRUST AND OBEY" One of the hymns Mother Abagail hummed while she plucked Addie Richardson's chickens.

TUMS AND ROLAIDS The antacid tablets favored by Larry Underwood in the Free Zone.

TUPPERWARE Lila Bruett used Tupperware containers for her leftovers.

$20.60 IN DIMES After Poke Freeman and Lloyd Henreid killed Gorgeous George, they found a Skippy peanut butter jar in an upstairs cabinet containing $20.60 in dimes.

TWENTY-FIVE PERCENT OF THE TAKE Gorgeous George, a small-time hood, agreed—for twenty-five percent of the take—to let Poke Freeman and Lloyd Henreid steal guns and dope from him that were owned by "Sicilian-type people." Poke and Lloyd doublecrossed George, taped up his mouth and nose, and watched him suffocate to death.

TWO UTAH STATE PATROL CARS On their way to Vegas, Glen, Larry, and Ralph were met by two Utah state patrol cars parked nose-to-nose across the highway on which they were walking. Several armed men awaited the travelers.

A U-HAUL The vehicle in which Tom Cullen found a broiling pan and rope, which he used as a makeshift travois. He pulled the injured Stu Redman in the contraption.

"THE UPPER ROOM" The religious tract from which Mother Abagail read a daily lesson.

THE UTAH STATE HIGHWAY DEPARTMENT On their journey to Las Vegas, Glen, Stu, Larry, and Ralph came upon a thirty-foot area of I-70 that had been swept away by a flash flood. Ralph thought that someone should tell the Utah state highway department about the missing section of roadway.

V-8, WELCH'S GRAPE JUICE, AND ORANGE DRINK While recuperating from pneumonia after being rescued by Tom Cullen, Tom saw to it that Stu drank quarts of these beverages for two weeks straight.

VASELINE After the Cheery Oil Company fires, Trashcan Man took some Vaseline from a drugstore and packed his burned arm in an inch of the jelly.

VERONAL The drug, a mild sedative, that Harold, Stu, and company took to interrupt their dream cycles so as not to dream of the Dark Man. Frannie didn't take her dose because she was afraid of what it might do to her baby. The rest of them were taking half-grain doses each.

A VESPA MOTOR SCOOTER The scooter Nadine Cross used to travel to Harold Lauder's Boulder house.

WABC The New York radio station on which Alice Underwood first heard her son's record "Baby, Can You Dig Your Man?"

THE WAR MEMORIAL One of the statues in the small park in the center of Ogunquit, Maine.

WARD 8 After Sarah Bradford was infected with Captain Trips by Hector Trent, she went to a Polliston, Kansas, bar and had a Ward 8. She infected everyone in the bar.

WATERSHIP DOWN A book by Richard Adams that Stu Redman had once bought for his nephew, but read before he gave it to him.

"WE ARE MARCHING TO ZION" The hymn Mother Abagail was humming when she heard the arrival of the Chevy truck bearing Nick Andros and company.

A WESTCLOX Mother Abagail's Free Zone clock.

THE WHITE TABLECLOTH Just before Stu Redman met up with Glen Bateman, Glen had confiscated a white table cloth from the Grace Baptist Church in Woodsville. It had once been part of a communion set.

A WILLYS INTERNATIONAL The vehicle with which Dave Roberts and Bobby Terry chased Judge Farris.

A WINCHESTER RIFLE AND A .45 COLT Bobby Terry's rifle and gun.

WINSTONS Chad Norris's cigarettes.

WONDER BREAD Sheriff John Baker ate Wonder bread for breakfast.

A WOOLCO CHAIR The chair Stu Redman was sitting on in Hapscomb's Texaco the day Charles Campion "touched down."

ZA-REX AND COOKIES The refreshments at the first Free Zone mass meeting.

"ZIPPOS" The slang term in Vietnam for Flametracks, weapons filled with naplam. Trashy loved them.

"ZORRO 93" Some of the graffiti on the New York building where Larry Underwood lived before he became a hit with "Baby, Can You Dig Your Man?"

THE STAND
THE COMPLETE & UNCUT EDITION
(1990)

DEDICATION

FOR TABBY
this dark chest of wonders.

[NO CONTENTS PAGE]

BOOK BREAKDOWN

AUTHOR'S NOTE

[One-page note from Stephen King]

A PREFACE IN TWO PARTS

Part 1: To Be Read Before Purchase
Part 2: To Be Read After Purchase

THE CIRCLE OPENS

[One untitled section]

BOOK ONE
Captain Trips
June 16-July 4, 1990

[Forty-two untitled chapters numbered 1-42]

BOOK TWO
On The Border
July 5-September 6, 1990

[Eighteen untitled chapters numbered 43-60]

BOOK THREE
The Stand
September 7, 1990-January 10, 1991

[Seventeen untitled chapters numbered 61-77]

Chapter 78
Part 1: Mayday
Part 2: Dusk, of a Summer Evening

THE CIRCLE CLOSES

[One untitled section]

—Addendum—
(6A)
THE STAND
THE COMPLETE & UNCUT EDITION

[This addendum is comprised of the characters who appear in *The Stand: The Complete & Uncut Edition*. These are characters who did not appear in the original edition (as published) of *The Stand*.

I decided to do an addendum to only the "People" section because I felt that their appearance was the most significant difference between the original and the uncut editions.

The "Places" were essentially the same, and if I had added a "Things" addendum, I would've had to supply a wheelbarrow with each copy of *The Shape Under the Sheet* .

Did I like the uncut *Stand*? Indeed, I did. The original *Stand* was never one of my favorites. Now, I know that to King fans, that's akin to saying that apple pie tastes like cow flops. I'm sorry. But reading the original *Stand* made me fidgety, restless, and I didn't have that sense of giddy glee I got when reading other things by King—like *It, Misery,* "Secret Window, Secret Garden," "One for the Road," and "The Jaunt," just to name a few.

But *The Stand: The Complete & Uncut Edition* ...now that's another story. (Even though it's the *same* story, if you know whadda mean?)

The story is fuller, more complete; the characters are even more real, and there are some new scenes that will make you feel like you just did six Gs without a safety harness.

One memorable scene is Frannie Goldsmith's confrontation with her mother over Frannie's pregnancy in the parlor of their home, that almost-sacred room filled with "segments of time in a dry age." This is one scene that should not have been cut, no matter what the budget.

Another favorite (and a revelation, too) is the scene where we learn that Flagg communicated with Nadine Cross as early as in her college days. The scene where he speaks to her via a ouija board is truly frightening and, again, adds to the story immeasurably.

I really enjoyed the uncut *Stand*. And since I had to research the book and compare it with the original, I was able to see the differences, sometimes the omission of a paragraph or a chapter, sometimes the changing of a character's name.

Writers often dream about being able to go back and rewrite their existing books.

With *The Stand: The Complete & Uncut Edition*, Stephen King not only did just that, but since the original version still exists, we're treated to a rare glimpse at the workings of a writer's imagination, and we get to see the actual re-editing/re-writing process as it took place in Stephen King's mind.

For King fans, this is a special treat.

For lovers of a great story, it's Christmas morning. – sjs]

People

A.C. The initials of the owner of the car Stu found in functioning order after he was discovered in the desert by Tom and Kojak. [Note: In the original edition of *The Stand*, the owner's initials were "S.L."]

THE AGING SERGEANT After regular army troops began shooting it out with the black soldiers who took over WCSH-TV, an aging sergeant with gray hair stood up and screamed for the gunfire to stop. He was shot by both sides.

AL One of the men who held Dayna Jurgens and seven other women captive. Dayna, Susan Stern, Patty Kroger, and Shirley Hammett survived the shootout between the men and Stu Redman's group, and joined Stu and company on their way to Nebraska. Al was known to the women as Doc because he handed out the pills.

ALICE UNDERWOOD'S BROTHER-IN-LAW He drank.

ALICE UNDERWOOD'S SISTER She tried to comfort Alice at the wake for Max Underwood, but Alice didn't need comforting. Alice never said a mean word about her son Larry to anyone, even to her sister. Alice's sister's husband was a drinker.

ANDERS Mother Abagail's grandson. He had been killed in a hunting accident when he was six.

ANDERSON, BOBBI Over Gus Dinsmore's weak protests, Frannie Goldsmith read him four chapters from *Rimfire Christmas*, a novel by "that woman who lived up north in Haven." [Note: This woman was, of course, Bobbi Anderson from *The Tommyknockers*.

ANDREW, UNCLE One of Frannie Goldsmith's uncles. Her mother told Frannie not to pick at her clothes. She said people would think she had fleas, and what would her Uncle Andrew and Aunt Carlene think?

ANGEL Julie Lawry told Nick Andros that her friends had always called her either "Angel-Face" or "Angel."

ANGEL-FACE Julie Lawry told Nick Andros that her friends had always called her either "Angel-Face" or "Angel."

THE ARMY MAJOR An unnamed army major had been James D. Hogliss's source of information about the Project Blue germ-warfare flu virus.

ARNOLD, BILL One of Abagail Freemantle's neighbors. After the flu hit, and before Nick and company arrived, Abagail dreamed that Bill Arnold was yelling about getting those "dirty coons" out of the Grange Hall.

BABALUGAH When Nick Andros awoke in the Shoyo, Arkansas, jail cell, Sheriff John Baker asked him, "You got a name, Babalugah?" [Note: In the original edition of *The Stand*, the question was phrased, "What's your name, boy?"]

BAKER, JORY A session guitarist who had become the driving force of a band called Sparx before he had a car accident and got addicted to heroin. He eventually cleaned up, but a part of him was gone. Barry Grieg had told Larry Underwood that Jory had "come out the other side."

BEAUCHAMP, CURTIS One of the Ogunquit, Maine, residents who manned the barricades that blocked the roads leading into and out of the town after the flu hit.

BESS Rita Blakemoor's sister.

BETTS, RICHARD On the Project Blue cafeteria bulletin board, a notice was posted that Richard (Dicky?) Betts wanted to give away some puppies.

THE BIG BOYS Tom Cullen told Nick Andros a story about how a bunch of "big boys" jumped him one night and he fought them off until "they was just about dead." He put one of them in the hospital with ruptures – "M-O-O-N, that spells ruptures, that's what Tom Cullen did."

BIGGERS, CHARLEY One of Frannie Goldsmith's grammar school friends. His nickname was Biggy. He "had had his appendix out during the summer between fifth and sixth grades."

"BIGGY" Charley Biggers.

THE BLACK MAN IN A LOINCLOTH A black man in a pink loincloth executed white soldiers on WCSH-TV in Portland, Maine, by picking their drivers' licenses out of a rotating drum. He executed sixty-two men before four squads of regular army burst into the studio and went to war with the man and his followers.

THE BLACK MAN IN THE CONTROL ROOM A black man wearing a green long-billed fatigue cap and white jockey shorts manned the control room of WCSH-TV in Portland, Maine, as other black soldiers in the studio executed white soldiers.

THE BOOGEYMAN Randall Flagg.

THE BOY IN BIKINI BRIEFS During a Captain Trips-induced fever delirium, Christopher Bradenton remembered a young boy he had once picked up, tripped with, and then had sex with. But in his vision, the boy's face was that of Randall Flagg.

BRACKNELL, DAMON One of the men (the other was Richard Darliss) with whom Dayna Jurgens left Xenia, Ohio. Darliss and Bracknell were murdered by Al, Virge, Ronnie and Garvey, and Dayna was taken prisoner, the fourth addition to the hardcases' "harem."

BRADDOCK, MARK A member of Stu Redman and Frannie Goldsmith's party. He died of appendicitis during emergency surgery performed by Stu Redman.

BRADENTON, MRS. Chris Bradenton's mother. She died in 1969. Chris hallucinated seeing her in a Captain Trips-induced fever delirium.

BRADFORD, SAMANTHA Cookie Bradford's daughter. Her mother infected her with Captain Trips.

BRODSKY A man who was executed for treason by the army. His death was reported in army communique #771 by Gareth.

BROOKS, NATE Mother Abagail's third husband.

"BROTHER ZENO" The former Sergeant First Class Roland Gibbs, the army officer who took over a radio station and proclaimed himself the first president of the Republic of Northern California. He was shot for treason.

BUDDY MARX'S FIANCEE Larry Underwood's night with the oral hygienist had begun innocently enough with Buddy Marx and Buddy's fiancée.

BURLEIGH, RICHARD The Kent State University campus security chief.

BURSTEIN, NORMAN When Frannie Goldsmith was six, her mother caught her and Norman Burstein naked in the barn, examining each other's bodies.

CALLEY The army lieutenant responsible for the Mei Lai massacre.

THE CAMERAMAN An untrained cameraman broadcast the executions of white soldiers on WCSH-TV in Portland, Maine, until he was shot by army troops who took over the studio.

THE CAR-AND-HOUSETRAILER DRIVER Just outside of Warner, Larry Underwood, Nadine Cross, and Joe came upon a jackknifed car-and-housetrailer. The driver and his wife had both been dead for three weeks.

THE CAR-AND-HOUSETRAILER DRIVER'S WIFE Just outside of Warner, Larry Underwood, Nadine Cross, and Joe came upon a jackknifed car-and-housetrailer. The driver and his wife had both been dead for three weeks.

CARELLA, STEVE A detective. One of Edward M. Morris's co-workers. Steve told Ed that it was impossible to take your wife and kids someplace by car and have a good time.

CARLENE, AUNT One of Frannie Goldsmith's aunts. Her mother told Frannie not to pick at her clothes. People would think she had fleas, and what must her Uncle Andrew and Aunt Carlene think?

CARMODY, RACHEL One of the women who was killed in the shootout between Stu Redman's party and the four men who held Dayna Jurgens and seven other women as prisoners.

CARON, PAUL One of Peter Goldsmith's former co-workers. Paul couldn't make it financially after he retired, and had been forced to sell his house and move in with his daughter.

CATHY One of Abagail Freemantle's kin. Cathy and David (Cathy's husband) bought Abagail a TV set in 1982.

CHRISTOPHER One of Abagail Freemantle's kin. Christopher and Susy had once offered to get Abagail onto the city water supply, but she refused, preferring to stick with her well.

CHUMM, DUDLEY One of the police officers who witnessed the mass execution of the protesting Kent State students on June 26, 1990.

CONSUELA One of Alice Underwood's co-workers. She kept hiding the requisition forms.

CRASLOW, MILTON The Harding County, New Mexico, rancher who died a half-hour after being bitten by a rattlesnake.

CREIGHTON, LEN The new name for the character of "Len Carsleigh" in the original version of *The Stand*.

CROWLEY, LESTER One of Peter Goldsmith's co-workers almost lost his thumb in a small press "because his mind was down at the pool-hall while his damn thumb was under the stamp." Lester Crowley saved the guy.

DADDS, BILL An old man who was the only resident (other than Lucy Swann) of Enfield, New Hampshire, still alive by July 3, 1990. Everyone else except Bill and Lucy had died from the flu. Bill died on Independence Day.

DARLISS, RICHARD One of the men (the other was Damon Bracknell) with whom Dayna Jurgens left Xenia, Ohio. Darliss and Bracknell were murdered by Al, Virge, Ronnie and Garvey, and Dayna was taken prisoner, the fourth addition to the hardcases' "harem."

DAVID One of Abagail Freemantle's kin. David and Cathy (David's wife) had bought Abagail a TV set in 1982.

DEACON, CHET One of Abagail Freemantle's neighbors. After the flu hit, and before Nick and company arrived, Abagail dreamed that Chet Deacon wrapped a red velvet window curtain around her and tied her up, yelling "Dressed coon! Dressed coon!"

THE DEAD FAMILY When Tom Cullen and Nick Andros sought protection from a tornado in a barn's storm cellar two-and-a-half hours out of May, Oklahoma, they found they were sharing their refuge with the owner of the farm and his family. They were all dead.

A DEAD FATHER When Nadine Cross "moved in" to the big white house in Epsom, there had been a lot of dead people in the house: a mother, father, and three children.

A DEAD GUARD As Bill Starkey descended to the Project Blue cafeteria to close Frank Bruce's eyes and then shoot himself, he passed a dead guard.

A DEAD MAN IN A UNIFORM After Flagg killed Kit Bradenton, he walked to a Conoco station and saw three dead dogs, along with one dead man who had been wearing some sort of uniform.

THE DEAD MAN WITH THE CHATTY CATHY DOLL On their way to Las Vegas, Trashcan Man and The Kid came upon a dead man lying facedown on I-70. Near his body was a broken Chatty Cathy doll.

A DEAD MOTHER When Nadine Cross "moved in" to the big white house in Epsom, there had been a lot of dead people in the house: a mother, father, and three children.

DELANCEY, FREDDY One of the Ogunquit, Maine, residents who manned the barricades that blocked the roads leading into and out of the town after the flu hit.

DEVINS, ANDY Lloyd Henreid's lawyer.

DICKERSON, GEORGE One of the WBZ-TV employees who participated in the takeover of the station.

THE DINSMORE BROTHERS Gus Dinsmore's daddy used to take Gus and his brothers for ice cream sodas every Fourth of July.

DINSMORE, MR. Gus's daddy. He had taken Gus and his brothers for ice cream sodas every Fourth of July.

"DOC AL" One of the men who held Dayna Jurgens prisoner. [Note: See the entry for AL above.]

THE DOKKEN BASSIST Julie Lawry told Nick Andros that she had made it with the Dokken bassist at a Monsters of Heavy Metal concert.

DOWNES, TOBIAS Carla Goldsmith's grandfather. Tobias had built the grandfather clock that sat in Carla's parlor.

A DOZEN NATIVES When Randall Flagg was reincarnated in the jungle as Russell Faraday, a dozen natives greeted his awakening.

DRUMMOND, MRS. EILEEN The Clewiston, Florida, woman who, on July 2, 1990, got drunk on DeKuyper crème de menthe, threw up, went to bed smoking a lit cigarette, and burned the house down.

THE DRUMMOND BOY Eileen Drummond's sixteen-year-old son. After his death, on July 1, 1990, Eileen found a baggie of marijuana in his bedroom and got stoned. The next day she died when she accidentally burned the house down after falling asleep holding a lit cigarette.

THE DRUNK KID A Free Zone kid, too young to drive, crashed a car into a bread truck and gashed his forehead.

DUGGAN, GRACE One of Frannie Goldsmith's high school friends.

EDMONTON, ALBERTA Dr. Tom Edmonton's wife.

EDMONTON, DR. THOMAS Frannie Goldsmith's doctor.

ENDERS, HARLAN One of Peter Goldsmith's former co-workers. Harlan was bored in retirement.

ENSLIN, TED Two semesters prior to getting pregnant by Jess, Frannie Goldsmith and Jess Rider went to hear Ted read some of his poems.

FARADAY, RUSSELL Randall Flagg's reincarnation in the jungle.

FARGOOD, JANE One of the girls who participated in the ouija board session in Rachel Timms's dorm room, during which Flagg first communicated with Nadine Cross.

FAYETTE, IRMA The twenty-six-year-old Lodi, California, woman who was morbidly afraid of rape, and who died when her father's old pistol exploded in her hand. She had been preparing to shoot a "hippie." [NOTE: Irma found the pistol in a box in the attic that had belonged to her father, a merchant seaman who had abandoned her mother in the late sixties. This parallels what happened with King's father, Donald, who also was a merchant seaman and who likewise abandoned King, his mother, and his brother David in the late forties. Compare the scene where Irma goes through her father's possessions with David King's reminiscence of finding his father's things in my interview with David King in this volume. (I cannot resist mentioning another amazing parallel: Beatle John Lennon's father, Freddie Lennon, a merchant seaman, abandoned John and his mother, Julia, in John's childhood.)]

FAYETTE, MR. Irma Fayette's father. He was a merchant seaman who abandoned Irma and her mother in the late sixties.

FAYETTE, MRS. Irma's mother. She was abandoned by her husband in the late sixties.

THE FIFTYISH MAN One of the men murdered by Al, Virge, Ronnie, and Garvey.

FINE, EBEN G. The man for whom a park in Boulder, Colorado, was named. Harold Lauder lived right across the street from the park.

THE FIRST STRIKERS One of the bowling teams in the Project Blue league.

FIVE RETIRED ARIZONA JUDGES They comprised what was called the Arizona Capital Crimes Circuit Court.

FLOSS, ANNA On the Project Blue cafeteria bulletin board, a notice was posted that Anna Floss wanted a ride to Denver or Boulder on July 9.

FOUR POKER PLAYERS Starkey had been playing poker with four men when word of the Mei Lai massacre came in. Two of the men in the game ended up on the Joint Chiefs of Staff.

FOUR WAITRESSES The Shoyo truck-stop restaurant had four waitresses.

FOURTEEN CIVILIANS Army communique #771 reported that fourteen civilians had been shot and six killed when they attempted to interfere with the army's neutralization of Brodsky for treason.

FRANNIE GOLDSMITH'S GREAT-GRANDMOTHER In the fireplace in Carla Goldsmith's parlor, a pot that had been handed down from Frannie's great-grandmother hung over a dried-out birch log. "Segments of time in a dry age."

FREEMANTLE, MATTHEW One of Abagail Freemantle's brothers.

FREEMANTLE, MICAH One of Abagail Freemantle's brothers.

FREEMANTLE, RICHARD One of Abagail Freemantle's brothers.

FREEMANTLE, RICHARD One of Randall Flagg's aliases.

FREEMONT, ROBERT One of Randall Flagg's aliases.

GARETH The originator of army communique #771 about the neutralization of Brodsky.

GARFIELD The army man who signed off on communique #771, even though it was originated by Gareth.

GARVEY One of the men who held Dayna Jurgens and seven other women captive. Dayna, Susan Stern, Patty Kroger, and Shirley Hammett survived the shootout between the men and Stu Redman's group, and joined Stu and company on their way to Nebraska.

GEOGHAN, MR. Alice Underwood's boss.

GEORGE One of Vic Palfrey's brothers? As Vic lay dying of the flu, he went in and out of delirium, and at one point he asked if "George put the horse in?" He then heard his mamma say that Georgie had gone courting Norma Willis.

GIBBS, SERGEANT FIRST CLASS ROLAND "Brother Zeno," the army officer who took over a radio station and proclaimed himself the first president of the Republic of Northern California. He was shot for treason.

THE GIRL IN THE GUTTER Chris Bradenton helped an injured, bloody girl whom he found lying in the gutter during the Chicago riots of 1968.

GOLDSMITH, MR. Peter Goldsmith's father and Frannie Goldsmith's grandfather. He never trusted in the social security system, and made a Democrat out of Fran's father.

GOOCH, MARY BETH One of Julie Lawry's friends.

THE GRIM GUTTERBALLERS One of the bowling teams in the Project Blue league.

THE GUY IN THE MOTEL CORRIDOR Edward Morris, a flu carrier, infected a guy in a motel corridor in Eustace, Oklahoma.

HALLIDAY One of the police officers who witnessed the mass execution of the protesting Kent State students on June 26, 1990.

HALLIDAY, MRS. One of Carla Goldsmith's lady friends. They were both members of the historical society.

HANSON, JACK Frannie Goldsmith brought Gus Dinsmore to Jack Hanson's house for his "final confinement" before he died. [NOTE: In the original edition, the "Jack Hanson" character was named "Jack Green."]

HARDESTY, HENRY Mother Abagail's second husband.

THE HARDESTY/ABAGAIL CHILDREN After Mother Abagail married Henry Hardesty, they had two children together. (Henry already had seven children of his own.)

THE HARDESTY CHILDREN When Mother Abagail married Henry Hardesty, he had been a widower with seven children.

THE HEAD COOK The head cook at Tony's Feed Bag, a cafe where Larry Underwood worked when he first got to California. Larry thought of him as "evil-tempered" and a dipstick.

HERB Joline Majors' boyfriend. She snuck around with him.

HEWETT, RONA A woman who walked from Laramie, Wyoming, to the Free Zone. She came down with a case of ordinary flu after arriving.

THE HIPPIE Irma Fayette saw a hippie wearing a t-shirt that said "I GAVE UP SEX AND DRINKING AND IT WAS THE SCARIEST 20 MINUTES OF MY LIFE." She aimed to shoot him with her daddy's pistol, but it exploded in her hand, killing her instantly. No great loss.

HOGGINS, RICHARD The young black man from Detroit, Michigan, who died after injecting himself with ninety-six percent pure heroin he found in Erin D. McFarlan's house.

HOGLISS, JAMES D. The retired lawyer who was the publisher of the Durbin, West Virginia, *Call-Clarion*. Hogliss put out an Extra with the headline "GOV'T FORCES TRY TO CONCEAL PLAGUE OUTBREAK."

HOOPES, ROY One of Flagg's people in Las Vegas. He participated in Hector Drogan's crucifixion.

THE HORSE-FACED GIRL One of the girls who participated in the ouija board session in Rachel Timms's dorm room, during which Flagg first communicated with Nadine Cross.

HORTON, JUDY The Milltown, Kentucky, woman who allowed Waldo Horton to "work his will" on her, and ended up married and with a kid named Petie. Her husband and son both died of the flu, and she put their bodies in the big walk-in freezer in the basement of their apartment house. One day, when she went down to check on (gloat over) them, she forgot to put the rubber wedge under the door, and she ended up dying of starvation in the company of her husband and son.

HORTON, PETIE Judy and Waldo Horton's son. He died of the flu. (Judy was a little sad about that, but she got over it in a couple of days.)

HORTON, WALDO Judy's husband; Petie's father. He died of the flu.

THE HORTONS Waldo's parents.

THE HOTSHOT RHYTHM RANGERS & ALL-TIME BOOGIE BAND The bar band Larry Underwood got a job singing with after he moved in with Yvonne Wetterlen. Johnny McCall (who later formed the Tattered Remnants) was in the band.

THE HOUSEMOTHER The woman who ended the ouija board session in Rachel Timms's dorm room, during which Flagg first communicated with Nadine Cross.

JACKIE On the afternoon Frannie Goldsmith told her father she was pregnant, she heard someone calling for Jackie to come in now.

JANE BAKER'S SISTER Jane spoke of her sister to Nick Andros as she waited to die. Her sister had gone to Viet Nam as part of a Baptist mission group, and had returned with three adopted children.

JANE BAKER'S SISTER'S THREE ADOPTED CHILDREN Jane's sister had gone to Viet Nam as part of a Baptist mission group, and had returned with three adopted children.

JOHN A spirit who communicated with Rachel Timms and her friends via a ouija board. His message was "you won't fart so much if you stop eating those CAFETERIA BEANS!!!!!"

JOHNNY A guy who worked at the Ogunquit, Maine, Citgo station.

JUDY HORTON'S PARENTS They (along with Waldo's parents) wouldn't allow Judy's husband Waldo to quit school.

KATZ, LEONARD Patty's boyfriend.

THE KID "He looked like Baby Elvis." The Kid – who was the reincarnation of Charles Starkweather – came upon Trashcan Man as Trashy walked Highway 34 out of Yuma, Colorado. The Kid wore human molar cufflinks, had a three-inch pompadour, and drove a 1932 Ford deuce coupe that looked like "a parody of all American cars." He believed that Coors beer was the only beer, and was fond of asking "You believe that happy crappy?" On the night of July 18, in a motel in Golden, Colorado, after drinking twenty-one cans of Coors, The Kid made Trashy jerk him off while he pistol-raped him. Trashy was rescued from the Kid by wolves sent by Flagg. The wolves escorted Trash away from The Kid's refuge (now an Austin), leaving several wolves in a ring around the car, waiting for him to try and make a dash for it. The Kid had spoken openly about overthrowing Flagg. The Kid's body was found by Larry, Stu, Glen, and Ralph. They dubbed him the Wolfman. [NOTE: We are told that The Kid was the reincarnation of Charles Starkweather in Doug Winter's *Stephen King: The Art of Darkness,* page 192 of the paperback edition.]

KING LAUGH "Sometimes King Laugh knocks and you're one of those people who can't keep him out." Peter Goldsmith said this when Frannie told him how she got the giggles at a poetry reading by Ted Enslin.

LANDON The originator of army communique #234 about the superflu.

LEE, JIM The Hattiesburg, Mississippi, man who hooked up all the electrical outlets in his house to a gasoline generator after the flu hit and the power went off. He electrocuted himself trying to start it up.

LINDA One of Mother Abagail's kin (perhaps a granddaughter?). She had married a "no-account" salesman.

A LITTLE GIRL When Dayna Jurgens left Xenia, Ohio, after the flu, the only people left alive in town had been a very old man, a woman, and a little girl.

LOTHROP, SAM A friend of Jess Rider and Frannie Goldsmith. In May of 1990, Jess and Frannie took a bicycle trip to Rangely with Sam and Sally Wenscelas.

A MAN IN DOCTOR'S WHITES As Vic Palfrey lay dying of the flu, he saw a man in doctor's whites behind a window.

THE MAN WITH A SIGN AROUND HIS NECK As Bill Starkey descended to the Project Blue cafeteria to close Frank Bruce's eyes and then shoot himself, he passed a dead man with a sign around his neck that said "NOW YOU KNOW IT WORKS, ANY QUESTIONS?"

MANN, POP Before the flu, Pop Mann owned a general store in Hemingford Home, Nebraska.

MARKHAM, JON The defendant in the case "Markham vs. South Carolina."

MASSINGILL, DAVID A Project Blue operative who tried to hold down Zone 10. He couldn't do it, and a transcript of a special high-frequency radio band in southern California recorded the assault on his base.

MASTERS, HARRY One of Peter Goldsmith's co-workers.

McCARTHY, PERION A member of Stu Redman and Frannie Goldsmith's party. She and Mark Braddock were lovers. She committed suicide with Veronal after Mark died during appendix surgery performed by Stu Redman.

McDOUGALL, BILL Harriet and George McDougall's son. He died of the flu on June 24, 1990.

McDOUGALL, DANNY Harriet and George McDougall's son. He died of the flu on June 27, 1990.

McDOUGALL, FRANK Harriet and George McDougall's three-year-old son. He died of the flu on June 28, 1990.

McDOUGALL, GEORGE The Nyack, New York, man who survived the flu only to watch his wife and eleven children succumb to it. George died of a massive coronary thrombosis while running.

McDOUGALL, GEORGE, JR. Harriet and George McDougall's son. He died of the flu on June 24, 1990.

McDOUGALL, HARRIET George's wife, and the mother of eleven children. She died of the flu on June 24, 1990.

McDOUGALL, HELEN Harriet and George McDougall's daughter. She died of the flu on June 23, 1990.

McDOUGALL, JEFF Harriet and George McDougall's nine-year-old son. He died of the flu on June 22, 1990.

McDOUGALL, MARTY Harriet and George McDougall's son. He died of the flu on June 23, 1990.

McDOUGALL, PATRICIA Harriet and George McDougall's sixteen-year-old daughter. She died of the flu on June 29, 1990.

McDOUGALL, RICHARD Harriet and George McDougall's son. He died of the flu on June 25, 1990.

McDOUGALL, ROBERT Harriet and George McDougall's son. He died of the flu on June 24, 1990.

McDOUGALL, STAN Harriet and George McDougall's son. He died of the flu on June 24, 1990.

McFARLANE, ALLIE The third-biggest heroin dealer in Detroit.

McFARLANE, ERIN D. Allie McFarlane's great-uncle. Allie had bought him a house in Grosse Point, and that was where Richard Hoggins found the heroin which killed him.

McGUIRE, GEORGETTE When Frannie Goldsmith was ten, "she had ridden her bike into the mailbox post while looking back over her shoulder to yell something to Georgette McGuire."

MORAN, CANDICE The ten-year-old Swanville, Maine, girl who fell off her bike and died of a fractured skull.

MORRISON, JIM One night when Stu was working at Hap's filling station pumping gas, Jim Morrison of the Doors drove in for gas. After Stu recognized him, he said, "If you are who I think you are, you're supposed to be dead." And Morrison replied, "You don't want to believe everything you read, man."

MORRISON, MR. Jim Morrison's father. He was in the air force.

MORTON, LIEUTENANT While Nadine Cross was staying in the big white house, a soldier loaded down with guns and ammo had passed by the house. He had been raving about blowing the balls off Lieutenant Morton.

MOTHER A spirit who communicated with Rachel Timms and her friends via a ouija board. Her message was that she was fine.

MOTHER ABAGAIL'S CHILDREN, GRANDCHILDREN, GREAT-GRANDCHILDREN, AND GREAT-GREAT-GRANDCHILDREN Mother Abagail had six boys, thirty-two grandchildren, ninety-one great-grandchildren, and three great-great-grandchildren.

NADINE CROSS'S AUNT On the day her parents and brother were killed in a car accident, Nadine chose to stay home and play with a friend rather than go visit her aunt and uncle.

NADINE CROSS'S CHILDHOOD FRIEND On the day her parents and brother were killed in a car accident, Nadine chose to stay home and play with a friend rather than go visit her aunt and uncle.

NADINE CROSS'S ROOMMATES Throughout her college years, Nadine had many roommates. They came and went.

NADINE CROSS'S UNCLE On the day her parents and brother were killed in a car accident, Nadine chose to stay home and play with a friend rather than go visit her aunt and uncle.

THE NAKED DEAD MAN As Bill Starkey descended to the Project Blue cafeteria to close Frank Bruce's eyes and then shoot himself, he passed a naked dead man and woman who had screwed before dying. The man had shot her and then shot himself.

THE NAKED DEAD WOMAN As Bill Starkey descended to the Project Blue cafeteria to close Frank Bruce's eyes and then shoot himself, he passed a naked dead man and woman who had screwed before dying. The man had shot her and then shot himself.

THE NAUGLERS Abagail Freemantle's neighbors.

THE NEWSCASTER While being held in the Stovington facility, Stu watched the six o'clock news and heard a newscaster reassure his viewers that there was no flu epidemic, and that there was nothing to worry about. "…[A]nd off-camera, someone sneezed."

NORBUTT, MR. Tom Cullen once worked for Norbutt, the farmer. Norbutt trusted Tom with an axe.

NUNN, MAJOR ALFRED The army officer who took back the

California radio station taken over by "Brother Zeno," and shot Zeno and some of his followers.

THE OLD MAN WITH WHITE HAIR One of the dead occupants of the Mercedes that Trashcan Man slept in on his way to Las Vegas.

OLD SPIKE Stu Redman's childhood dog.

THE OLD WOMAN WEARING A LOT OF BANGLED JEW-ELRY One of the dead occupants of the Mercedes that Trashcan Man slept in on his way to Las Vegas.

THE 122-YEAR-OLD MAN In 1989, Mother Abagail was told she was the sixth-oldest human being in the United States (and the third-oldest woman). The oldest was a guy in Santa Rosa who was 122.

A PAIR OF REPORTERS A pair of reporters for a Houston daily linked what had happened in Arnette, Texas, with the flu that was raging in other towns.

PALFREY, MR. Vic's father. Vic hallucinated seeing him as he lay dying of the flu.

PALFREY, MRS. Vic Palfrey's mamma. As he lay dying of the flu, Vic hallucinated seeing her.

PALMER, BOB One of the WBZ-TV newscasters who took over the station and ran film of what was really happening with the flu epidemic.

PATTY One of the girls who participated in the ouija board session in Rachel Timms's dorm room, during which Flagg first communicated with Nadine Cross.

PAUL CARON'S DAUGHTER AND HER HUSBAND Paul Caron sold his house and moved in with his daughter and her husband after he retired.

PECHERT, JUDGE A judge who tried a case in which Andy Devins defended a guy who was guilty as sin. The guy was found not guilty.

PETER GOLDSMITH'S CO-WORKER One of Peter's co-workers almost lost his thumb in a small press "because his mind was down at the pool-hall while his damn thumb was under the stamp." Lester Crowley saved the guy.

PETERS One of the police officers who witnessed the mass execution of the protesting Kent State students on June 26, 1990.

PETERS, SERGEANT T.L. The sergeant who was scragged by his own men after he blew away Ray Flowers. [NOTE: In the original edition, this character was named Sergeant Buchan.]

PETERSEN, MASTER TECH SERGEANT ROGER One of the white soldiers executed by black soldiers in the WCSH-TV studio in Portland, Maine.

PHILIPS, COLONEL ALBERT The army colonel who ordered the execution of the protesting Kent State University students on June 26, 1990.

THE PHOTOGRPAHER A photographer who tried getting out of Sipe Springs with news of the flu epidemic. He was shot by soldiers.

THE PRESIDENT The president of the United States addressed the nation after he was infected with Captain Trips.

"PRINCE" Stu Redman's code name after he was taken into custody at the Atlanta plague facility.

"PRINCESS" Eva Hodge"s code name after she was taken into custody at the Atlanta plague facility.

PRYNNE, MRS. One of Carla Goldsmith's lady friends.

RACHEL Dr. Tom Edmonton's receptionist.

RACKMAN, JOE Rackman lived out by one of the roads that entered or exited Shoyo, Arkansas. He told Doc Soames that the men supposedly working on the culvert were going very slowly. The Rackmans had a very sick little boy.

RACKMAN, MRS. Joe's wife.

THE RACKMAN BOY Joe Rackman's little boy. He was sick from the flu.

RAMPLING, GEORGE According to the graffiti on the jail-cell wall in Shoyo, Arkansas, where Nick Andros was incarcerated after being beaten up, George Rampling was a jerk-off.

RENGARTEN, BOBBI One of Frannie Goldsmith's friends. Bobbie lived in Dorchester, and Frannie considered moving in with her after her confrontation with her mother over her pregnancy.

RENNETT One of the Free Zone people who came to visit Mother Abagail.

REYNOLDS, HATTIE The woman who owned the field of wild blueberries in Georgia where Sam Tauber fell into a dry well and died.

RHODA Debbie Smith's roommate. Debbie and Rhoda couldn't swing the rent on their apartment without a third roommate, so they asked Frannie Goldsmith if she wanted to move in.

RITA BLAKEMOOR'S FATHER Rita's father once took Rita and her sister Bess to the zoo.

ROBERTS, DONNY A childhood friend of Larry Underwood's. Larry learned how to play guitar with Donny's guitar.

ROGER One of Flagg's minions in Las Vegas.

ROGET, HELEN One of the women who was killed in the shootout between Stu Redman's party and the four men who held Dayna Jurgens and seven other women prisoners. She was shot by Ronnie.

RONNIE One of the men who held Dayna Jurgens and seven other women captive. Dayna, Susan Stern, Patty Kroger, and Shirley Hammett survived the shootout between the men and Stu Redman's group and joined Stu and company on their way to Nebraska.

RONNIE Julie Lawry's dead boyfriend.

RONSON, WILL He ran the Ogunquit drugstore.

ROSS, HUBERT The president's press secretary.

SAMANTHA BRADFORD'S BOYFRIEND Cookie Bradford infected her daughter Samantha's boyfriend with Captain Trips.

SAMUEL One of Mother Abagail's sons. He had died in 1974.

SANDY One of the girls who participated in the ouija board session in Rachel Timms's dorm room, during which Flagg first communicated with Nadine Cross.

SEARS, RUTHIE A childhood friend of Fran Goldsmith's who had once pushed Frannie down.

THE SIPE SPRINGS DOCTOR A doctor in Sipe Springs had made some good guesses about the spread of Captain Trips.

THE SIXTEEN-YEAR-OLD GIRL WITH STRABISMUS A girl who was murdered by Al, Virge, Garvey, and Ronnie and left in a ditch. [NOTE: I'll save you a trip to the dictionary, okay? Strabismus is defined as the "inability of one eye to obtain binocular vision with the other because of imbalance of the muscles of the eyeball."— *Webster's New Collegiate Dictionary* . No need to thank me...it's just part of my job.]

SMITH One of the Free Zone people who came to visit Mother Abagail.

SMITH, DEBBIE One of Frannie Goldsmith's friends. Debbie lived in Somersworth, and Frannie considered moving in with Debbie after her confrontation with her mother over her pregnancy. Debbie already lived with a girl named Rhoda.

A SOLDIER While Nadine Cross was staying in the big white house, a soldier loaded down with guns and ammo had passed by the house. He had been raving about blowing the balls off Lieutenant Morton.

STARKEY, CINDY Bill Starkey's daughter.

DR. STAUNTON Mother Abagail's last doctor before the flu hit.

STAUNTON, JAMES D.L. The clinical sociologist who, in 1958, published a study of train and airplane crashes. He discovered that statistically, full planes and trains seldom crash.

STEFFENS The Project Blue computer operator.

STEPHANIE-ANN Lloyd Henreid told Roger to have Whitney Horgan or Stephanie-Ann bring Trashcan Man some fries and a couple of hamburgers after Trashy got to Vegas.

STERN, PFC FRANKLIN One of the white soldiers publicly executed on WCSH-TV in Portland, Maine, by a black man in a pink leather loincloth.

STIMSON, ARTHUR The Reno, Nevada, man who stepped on a

rusty nail and tried to amputate his own foot when it turned gangrenous. He died of shock and blood loss in the lobby of Toby Harrah's gambling casino.

STONER, MRS. Sheriff John Stoner's (from the novel *Rimfire Christmas* by Bobbi Anderson) "lovely young wife."

STONER, SHERIFF JOHN A character from Bobbi Anderson's novel *Rimfire Christmas*.

THE STRINGER A reporter who tried getting out of Sipe Springs with news of the flu epidemic. He was shot by soldiers.

STU REDMAN'S NEPHEW Stu had a nephew in Waco, Texas. He had once bought him a copy of *Watership Down,* and read it first before he sent it to him.

SULLIVAN, BRICK One of Abagail Freemantle's neighbors when she was a child. The audience at a minstrel show at the Grange Hall had once thrown tomatoes at Brick when he tried to sing in the show.

SUSY One of Abagail Freemantle's kin. Christopher and Susy had once offered to get Abagail on the city water system, but she refused, preferring to stick with her well.

"SYLVESTER" The name Andy Devins called Lloyd Henreid.

TATE, PEGGY A high school friend of Frannie Goldsmith. Peggy got a job as a senate page.

TAUBER, APRIL Sam and Mike Tauber's two-year-old sister. She died of the flu on June 25.

TAUBER, MIKE Sam and April's twenty-seven-year-old brother. He died of the flu on June 27.

TAUBER, MR. Sam, April, and Mike Tauber's father. He died of the flu on June 25, along with his two-year-old daughter April.

TAUBER, MRS. Sam, April, and Mike Tauber's mother. She died of the flu on June 24, in the Murfreesboro, Georgia, general hospital.

TAUBER, SAM The five-and-a-half-year-old boy from Georgia who was the only member of his family to survive the flu. On July 2, he fell in a dry well, broke both his legs, and died twenty hours later, "as much from fear and misery as from shock and hunger and dehydration." His parents, his brother Mike, and his sister April predeceased him.

TEAM LION GUY The Sipe Spring operative who informed Starkey that the flu would spread.

THE TEENAGE GIRL The driver of the Austin in which The Kid took refuge from Flagg's wolves. (When The Kid pulled her out of the car, her arm came off in his hand.)

THREE DEAD CHILDREN When Nadine Cross "moved in" to the big white house in Epsom, there had been a lot of dead people in the house: a mother, father, and three children.

TIMMS, RACHEL One of Nadine Cross's college acquaintances. It was in Rachel's dorm room that Flagg first communicated with Nadine via a ouija board.

TOMMY A spirit who communicated to Rachel Timms and her friends via a ouija board. His message was "you have been using that strawberry douche again."

TROTTS, MAYBELLE One of Abagail and David Trotts's children. Maybelle choked to death on a piece of apple.

THE TWELVE-YEAR-OLD GIRL A girl killed by Garvey when she wouldn't perform some bizarre sexual act on him. Sue Stern wouldn't even say what it was. She said it was that bad.

THE TWO COOKS The Shoyo truck-stop restaurant had two cooks.

TWO GUARDS As Charles Campion escaped from the Project Blue lab site, one guard nodded over a magazine at the gate, the other was nowhere to be seen; he might have been in the "head."

TWO OF GEORGE McDOUGALL'S NEIGHBORS Before the flu, two of George's neighbors asked him if they could join him jogging every evening. The jogging eventually became a neighborhood thing.

TWO POLITICAL PRISONERS Christopher Bradenton had once driven two political prisoners who had jumped bail from Texas to Los Angeles.

TWO TOWN FELLOWS On the night Nick Andros was put in charge of the prisoners who had beaten him up, two Shoyo men stopped in at the jail to see if Nick was all right. Both of the men had colds.

TWO WOMEN IN THE LAUNDROMAT Trish Morris, a flu carrier, infected two women washing clothes in the laundromat in Eustace, Oklahoma.

UNDERWOOD, MAX Larry's father. He died of a heart attack. [NOTE: In the original version of *The Stand*, he was an unnamed character. In the uncut edition, we learned his name was Max.]

VENNER, MRS. One of Carla Goldsmith's lady friends.

A VERY OLD MAN When Dayna Jurgens left Xenia, Ohio, after the flu, the only people left alive in town had been a very old man, a woman, and a little girl.

VICTOR One of Abagail Freemantle's grandsons. He had built her privy.

VIRGE One of the men who held Dayna Jurgens and seven other women captive. Dayna, Susan Stern, Patty Kroger, and Shirley Hammett survived the shootout between the men and Stu Redman's group, and joined Stu and company on their way to Nebraska.

THE WAITRESSES AT TONY'S FEED BAG The "ass-wiggling, gum-chewing" waitresses at a cafe where Larry Underwood worked when he first got to California. Larry thought of them as dipsticks.

WARNER, DR. Harriet and George McDougall's doctor.

WARRINGTON, JIM He drove one of the Sanford ambulances.

WENSCELAS, SALLY A friend of Jess Rider and Frannie Goldsmith. In May of 1990, Jess and Frannie took a bicycle trip to Rangely with Sally and Sam Lothrop.

WETTERLEN, YVONNE A topless dancer Larry met in a movie theater after he helped her find her lost purse. They eventually moved in together.

WILLIS, NORMA As Vic Palfrey lay dying of the flu, he went in and out of delirium, and at one point he asked if "George out the horse in?" He then heard his mamma say that Georgie had gone courting Norma Willis.

WINKS, WINKY One of Flagg's people in Las Vegas. He was a bald man whose eyes twitched. He participated in Hector Drogan's crucifixion.

A WOMAN When Dayna Jurgens left Xenia, Ohio, after the flu, the only people left alive in town had been a very old man, a woman, and a little girl.

YORKIN, CHARLES The WBZ-TV station janitor. He participated in the takeover of the station.

A YOUNG MAN WITH CARROTY HAIR A white soldier who tried to escape the gunfire being sprayed across the studio audience at WCSH-TV in Portland, Maine. His legs were chewed up by gunfire as he climbed over the backs of the studio chairs.

THE LONG WALK

DEDICATION

This is for Jim Bishop
and Burt Hatlen and Ted Holmes.

[NO CONTENTS PAGE]

BOOK BREAKDOWN

[Opening Epigraphs (three epigraphs):
one from Thomas Carlyle,
one from John F. Kennedy,
and one from Bob Dylan]

(7)

THE LONG WALK
People

AARONSON Long Walker. He was Number 1. He was shot on the white line on the road to Oldtown.

ABRAHAM Long Walker. He was Number 2. He was sixteenth out of the selection barrel.

ABRAHAM'S GIRLFRIEND She wanted to have Abraham's Long Walk acceptance letter turned into a t-shirt at the Shirt Shack.

ABRAHAM'S GRANDFATHER He had never taken a laxative in his life.

ADDERLY, CANNONBALL One of the Banned Noisemakers.

ALICE A man yelled to Alice "He's gonna puke" when Garraty fell to his knees on the road.

BAKER, ARTHUR (ART) Long Walker. He was Number 3. He had a southern accent. As the Walkers entered Massachusetts, he was one of the final surviving seven. He was the fourth of the seven to die.

BAKER, JAMES Long Walker. He was Number 4.

BAKER'S AUNT She had his uncle's ashes in Baton Rouge.

BAKER'S AUNT HATTIE Baker thought that the old lady who used "Vogue" magazine as a rain hat looked like his Aunt Hattie.

BAKER'S AUNT HATTIE'S KIDS Baker's Aunt Hattie had nine kids.

BAKER'S BROTHER Baker's brother once stole a car and drove to Hattiesburg, Mississippi. He got a two-year suspended sentence, and died of a heart attack.

BAKER'S GIRL Baker once took a girl to a dance where a drunk fella kept trying to pick her up. Baker whipped his ass.

BAKER'S GRANDFATHER He was a lawyer in Shreveport.

BAKER'S UNCLE He was an undertaker.

THE BALDING "WHGH" MAN The newsman who filmed the Walkers as McVries told the story of his scar. [NOTE: See the entry A PADDINGTON BEAR LETTER-OPENER.]

THE BANNED NOISEMAKERS As the Walkers entered Massachusetts, Garraty's head was playing the Banned Noisemakers: Dave Brubeck, Thelonius Monk, and Cannonball Adderly.

BARKOVITCH, GARY Long Walker. He was Number 5. Just before the Walkers reached Porterville, Barkovitch ripped out his own throat.

THE BASTARD IN AN ARMY COAT The unnamed official who told Abraham to finish up his "Why Do You Feel Qualified to Participate in the Long Walk?" essay.

THE BEARDED FARMER The unnamed farmer who waved to the Walkers as they passed his farmhouse on the road to Oldtown.

A BIG BLONDE KID One of the last two survivors of the Long Walk that occurred four years prior to Garraty's Walk. He had lost to a kid who had no shoes left.

THE BIG FAT HOOCHIE-KOOCHIE MAMA The unnamed dancer in a G-string at the Steubenville state fair who hit Davidson on the head when he got drunk and crawled into the hoochie-koochie tent.

THE BLACK MAN Baker revealed that he had once burned a cross on an unnamed black man's lawn.

THE BOY AFTER LARSON An unnamed Long Walker who got his ticket after Larson.

THE BOY BEHIND OLSON AND GARRATY An unnamed Walker who received a second warning after the Walkers passed the bridge on the road to Oldtown.

A BOY IN A BLACK TURTLENECK Long Walker. He had a convulsion, was warned, and then shot.

THE BOY IN A BLUE SWEATER Long Walker. He got a ticket on the road to Caribou.

THE BOY RAY DIDN'T KNOW A Long Walker who was walking next to Baker on Brickyard Hill in Porterville.

THE BOY WHO HAD A CONVULSION Long Walker. He swallowed his tongue, and was shot.

THE BOY WHO RAN INTO THE WOODS An unnamed Walker who tried to escape by running into the trees on the side of the road. He was immediately shot.

THE BOY WITH SUNSTROKE Long Walker. He was shot on the road to Oldtown, and his shooting was applauded by a covey of high school boys

THE BOYFRIEND OF THE GIRL WITH LARGE BREASTS An unnamed youth who was part of the group of teenagers that cheered Garraty. As his girlfriend jumped up and down, he watched her breasts bounce.

BRADBURY, RAY The author of the short story "The Crowd."

BRUBECK, DAVE One of the Banned Noisemakers.

A BURLY MAN An unnamed man in the front row of the Oldtown crowd who said "Goddamnit" when someone threw a firecracker.

CAROLYN A girl who Garraty had dated and who lived on Brickyard Hill in Porterville.

CATHY SCRAMM'S PARENTS Scramm's in-laws. They were with Cathy while Scramm Walked.

THE CHASE VEHICLE GUARDS Two unnamed armed guards rode in the chase vehicle that followed the Walkers.

THE CHILDREN A group of children who stood in the play yard of a one-room schoolhouse the Walkers passed on their way to Oldtown.

THE CLUMP OF CHEERING HOUSEWIVES A group of women the Walkers passed on the road to Oldtown. One of the women wore tight slacks and a tighter sweater. Three bracelets on her right wrist clanked.

COLLINS, WILKIE The author of *The Woman in White*, Baker's favorite book.

COLTER, REGGIE The only guy from Maine ever to win the Long Walk. He hemorrhaged in one eye, and finished the Walk half-blind. He had a blood clot on his brain and died one week later.

A COP In Jefferson Plantation, a cop struggled with a little boy who wanted an autograph from the Walkers.

A COP An unnamed officer in Eureka who stopped a truck so the Walkers could pass through the town.

A COP An unnamed officer had to pull Percy's mother away from the Walkers in Caribou.

THE COVEY OF HIGH SCHOOL BOYS They applauded the shooting of the Long Walker with sunstroke.

CURLEY Long Walker. He was Number 7. He had a charley horse early in the Walk, and was the first to get his ticket.

D'ALLESSIO, GEORGE (FREAKY) A childhood friend of Ray Garraty's. Freaky had been hit and killed by a car on U.S. 1 outside of Freeport. Freaky had been riding his Schwinn. Eddie Klipstein had seen it happen.

DAVIDSON Long Walker. He was Number 8. On the road to Caribou, he passed along the news that Zuck was still bleeding from his cut knee. Also, on the road to Oldtown, he told the other Walkers a story about getting drunk at the Steubenville state fair and crawling into the hoochie-koochie tent. He got hit in the head by a big fat mama wearing a G-string. Davidson got his ticket on the road to Oldtown.

THE DIEHARDS On the road to Oldtown, the Walkers passed about three-dozen sleepy spectators since midnight of the day Davidson got his ticket.

A DOG On the road to Augusta, a dog ran out at Pearson and was shot by a guard.

THE DOG'S OWNER The little boy who owned the dog that ran out at Pearson on the road to Augusta. He cried when the dog was shot by a guard.

DORGENS, MRS. AMELIA The woman who ran a modern dance school. Ray Garraty had attended, and later taught Jan how to rhumba and cha-cha.

THE DRUNK FELLA Baker once took a girl to a dance where a drunk fella kept trying to pick her up. Baker whipped his ass.

THE DUNKIN' DONUTS PEOPLE A group of people in a Dunkin' Donuts in Caribou cheered as the Walkers passed.

"DUSSETTES, AUBUCHONS, AND LAVESQUES" Families that had lived on the land where the twin cities of Lewiston and Auburn stood.

ELWELL, MR. Farmer. Ray Garraty had once gotten cramps while helping Mr. Elwell take in his hay. Mrs. Elwell had brought them ice-cold water, and drinking it had given Ray the cramps.

ELWELL, MRS. Farmer's wife. Ray Garraty had once gotten cramps while helping Mr. Elwell take in his hay. Mrs. Elwell had brought them ice-cold water, and drinking it had given Ray the cramps.

EV The owner of Ev's Market in Caribou.

EWING Long Walker. He was a black fellow from Texas. He was Number 9. As the Walkers left Limestone, Ewing realized he had blisters on his feet.

THE FAMILY OF FIVE A family of five, consisting of a mother, father, boy, girl, and a grandmother ate a picnic breakfast and watched the Walkers pass by.

A FAMILY OF FOUR AND THEIR CAT A group the Walkers passed on their way to Oldtown.

THE FAMILY THAT WATCHED A family made up of a father, a mother, and three teenagers watched as Larson and another Walker both got their tickets.

THE FAT, BALD MAN An unnamed spectator who rubbed a wart beside his ear as he stared at Curley's remains.

THE FAT NEWSPAPERMAN An unnamed reporter who poked a mike at the Walkers as they passed Caribou's city limits.

A FAT WOMAN In Jefferson Plantation, while watching the Walkers, a fat woman was crushed between three college students who were drinking beer.

FENTNER Long Walker. He was Number 12. He wore a t-shirt that said "I RODE THE MT. WASHINGTON COG RAILWAY." He got his ticket while holding a St. Christopher's medal.

FENUM, ROGER Long Walker. He was Number 13. He was the fiftieth boy to go down.

FIEDLER, GEORGE Long Walker. As the Walkers entered Massachusetts, he was one of the final surviving seven. He was the first of the seven to die.

FIELD, CHARLIE Long Walker. He got his ticket on Brickyard Hill in Porterville.

FOSTER, STEPHEN AND EDGAR ALLAN POE If they had lived to see the Long Walk, they could have collaborated on the world's first morbid musical: "Massa's on De Cold, Cold Road, or The Tell-Tale Stride."

THE FOUR LITTLE BOYS Four unnamed boys who slept in a pup tent in a field in order to watch the Walkers pass by.

GALLANT Long Walker. He was shot on the road to Augusta.

GARRATY, JEFF Ray's brother. Jeff died of pneumonia when he was sixteen. It wasn't said whether Jeff and "Garraty's little brother" were the same kid.

GARRATY, JIM Ray's father. He was taken away by the Squads and never seen again. At one point towards the end of the Walk, Garraty remembered "his father picking him up, swinging him dizzily, rumpling his hair." This scene echoes the "playing elevator" scene in both *The Shining* and "Before the Play" in which Jack Torrance's father does the exact same thing to little Jacky Torrance. [NOTE: See the sections on *The Shining* and "Before the Play" in this volume.]

GARRATY, MR. Ray Garraty's grandfather. He had taught Ray's father how to knit. Ray's father had taught Ray, and Ray had subsequently taught Jan.

GARRATY, MRS. Ray's mother.

GARRATY, RAY (RAYMOND DAVIS) Long Walker from Porterville, Maine. He was Number 47. At the beginning of the Walk, he was sixteen years old and weighed 160 pounds. The year he Walked, he "won." In Porterville, he ran to his mother and Jan on the sidelines, and took three warnings for it. McVries pulled him off and saved his life.

GARRATY'S LITTLE BROTHER An unnamed sibling of Ray's. Ray and Jan had once gone sledding on his sled.

THE GAS STATION ATTENDANT An unnamed attendant who waved at and urged on Walker Number 94, called Wayne.

THE GIRL WITH LARGE BREASTS An unnamed girl in the group of teenagers that cheered Garraty. She jumped up and down and her boyfriend watched her breasts bounce.

GRIBBLE Long Walker. He was Number 48. On the road to Oldtown, two unbearably erotic girls leaned against an MG and watched the Walkers. Gribble couldn't take it, ran to one of them, and dry-humped her through his three warnings. He got a cramp in his crotch after he rejoined the Walkers, fell to his knees, and was shot.

A GROUP OF LITTLE GIRLS A group of little girls did a "spastic" cheerleading routine as the Walkers passed by on their way to Oldtown.

THE GROUP OF MEN AROUND A FORD PICKUP A bunch of drunk guys who cheered the Long Walkers as they passed.

A GROUP OF TEENAGERS A group that cheered Garraty. A girl in the group with large breasts jumped up and down. Her boyfriend watched her breasts jiggle.

A GROUP OF WORKERS A group of Caribou Paper Mill workers watched as the Walkers passed by.

THE GUARD (#1) The unnamed guard who manned the gate at the beginning site of the Long Walk. He wore a khaki uniform and a Sam Browne belt.

THE GUARD (#2) The unnamed guard who was eating C rations from a can when Garraty showed up for his Long Walk.

THE GUIDANCE COUNSELOR The unnamed school official who tried to convince Scramm to stay in school after he decided to drop out. Scramm dropped out because a history teacher had told him that schools were overpopulated.

HARKNESS Long Walker. He wore glasses and had a crewcut. He was Number 49. He planned on writing a book about the Long Walk.

HARLAN One of McVries' co-workers in the Plymouth Sleepwear factory. Harlan worked in the dyehouse, and couldn't make piecework because of McVries slow output.

THE HELL'S ANGELS BOY Long Walker. He had "Hell's Angels On Wheels" stencilled on the back of his jean jacket. He got his ticket on the road to Augusta.

A HIGH SCHOOL BAND A Caribou high school band played as the Walkers passed by a shopping center.

THE HISTORY TEACHER The teacher who told Scramm that schools were overpopulated. Scramm subsequently dropped out and married Cathy. A guidance counselor had tried, to no avail, to convince Scramm to stay in school.

THE HOLLOW-CHEEKED MAN WITH NO TEETH IN AN UNCLE SAM SUIT The Oldtown man who wore a sign that said "We Gave Away the Panama Canal to the Communist Niggers."

THE HOPI INDIANS Long Walkers; two brothers named Joe and Mike. When the Walkers were about forty-five miles north of Oldtown, the vanguard consisted of these two boys. They both had leather jackets tied around their waists.

HOUGH, BILL Long Walker. As the Walkers entered Massachusetts, he was one of the final surviving seven. He was the second of the seven to die.

HOWARD, RON McVries said that after J.D. Salinger, John Knowles, James Kirkwood, and Don Bredes destroyed being an adolescent, you couldn't discuss adolescent love anymore: "You just come off sounding like fucking Ron Howard with a hard-on."

JAN Garraty's girlfriend.

JENSEN Long Walker. During a hailstorm, he ran off the road outside of Oldtown and was shot.

JOE Long Walker. When the Walkers were about forty-five miles north of Oldtown, the vanguard consisted of two brothers named Joe and Mike. They were Hopi Indians and both had leather jackets tied around their waists.

JOHNNY A person from the crowd who was called to watch as Garraty took a shit on the road.

THE KID WHO FROZE An unnamed Walker froze up at the beginning of the previous year's Walk. He took his three warnings and was shot at 9:02.

THE KID WHO TRIED TO CLIMB THE HALFTRACK Long Walker Number 38. The guards butted his hands, the halftrack ran over his legs, obliterating his feet, and he got his ticket.

THE KID WITH NO SHOES LEFT One of the last two survivors of the Long Walk four years prior to Garraty's Walk. He won.

KLINGERMAN Long Walker. He was Number 59. In Porterville, he started screaming. He thought he had an appendicitis.

Someone asked him if he wanted an Alka-Seltzer.

KLIPSTEIN, EDDIE He had seen George "Freaky" D'Alessio get hit and killed by a car on U.S. 1 outside of Freeport. Freaky had been riding a Schwinn bike.

L'ANTONIO, DOM A little Italian man that the Walkers passed. He held a sign that said "Dom L'Antonio Loves All Long Walkers – Free Watermelon!!!"

LARSON Long Walker. He was Number 60. He sat down on the road and got his ticket.

A LITTLE BOY WEARING A RANDY THE ROBOT T-SHIRT As the Walkers headed towards Augusta, this little boy pointed at Scramm from the side of the road.

THE LITTLE BOY WHO WANTED AN AUTOGRAPH In Jefferson Plantation, a cop struggled with a little boy who wanted an autograph from the Walkers.

A LITTLE GIRL She made a face at Garraty.

THE LONG WALKERS ROSTER (ALPHABETICAL) The following list is comprised of all sixty-two of the Long Walkers mentioned in the text. When numbers were assigned, they are given; when names were not revealed, the Walkers are described by the term used in the text. [NOTE: For more information, see the individual entries for each Walker listed elsewhere in this section. For a numerical list of Walkers mentioned in the text, see the "Things" section.]

AARONSON Number 1.
ABRAHAM Number 2.
BAKER, ARTHUR Number 3.
BAKER, JAMES Number 4.
BARKOVITCH, GARY Number 5.
THE BOY AFTER LARSON
THE BOY BEHIND OLSON AND GARRATY
A BOY IN A BLACK TURTLENECK
THE BOY IN A BLUE SWEATER
THE BOY RAY DIDN'T KNOW
THE BOY WHO HAD A CONVULSION
THE BOY WHO RAN INTO THE WOODS
THE BOY WITH SUNSTROKE
CURLEY Number 7.
DAVIDSON Number 8.
EWING Number 9.
FENTNER Number 12.
FENUM, ROGER Number 13.
FIEDLER, GEORGE
FIELD, CHARLIE
GALLANT
GARRATY, RAY (RAYMOND DAVIS) Number 47.
GRIBBLE Number 48.
HARKNESS Number 49.
THE HELL'S ANGELS BOY
HOUGH, BILL
JENSEN
JOE
THE KID WHO TRIED TO CLIMB THE HALFTRACK Number 38.
KLINGERMAN Number 59.
LARSON Number 60.
McVRIES, PETER Number 61.
MIKE
MILLIGAN #1
MILLIGAN #2
MORGAN, FRANK Number 64.
THE "NEARLY PORTLY" WALKER
OLSON, HENRY (HANK) Number 70.
PARKER, COLLIE
PASTOR, BRUCE
PEARSON
PERCY Number 31.

QUINCE, HAROLD

QUINCY OR QUENTIN

RANK

SCRAMM Number 85.

THE SCREAMING WALKER

THE SHORT, STOUT BOY WEARING A GREEN SILK VEST

SLEDGE, BOBBY

STEBBINS Number 88.

TOLAND

TRAVIN

TRESSLER Number 92.

TUBBINS

THE TWO WALKERS

THE WALKER WEARING A GREEN TRENCHCOAT Number 45.

A WALKER WITH APPLE CHEEKS

WAYNE Number 94.

WYMAN, MARTY Number 97.

YANNICK Number 98.

ZUCK Number 100.

THE MAJOR The mysterious authoritarian figure in charge of the Long Walk. He wore reflector sunglasses and was merciless. It was also eventually revealed that the Major was Stebbins' father.

A MAN A man yelled to Alice "He's gonna puke" when Garraty fell to his knees on the road.

A MAN IN A LUMBERYARD He waved to the Walkers as they passed.

A MAN IN HOUND'S-TOOTH JACKET A man in a hound's-tooth jacket and wearing a straw hat waved to the Walkers as they passed by on the way to Oldtown.

THE MAN WITH A BULLHORN The man who praised Garraty and at the same time announced his candidacy to represent the Second District.

THE MAN WITH THE "SCRAMM" SIGN In Jefferson Plantation, a man waving a "Scramm" sign popped his fly.

McVRIES, KATRINA Pete McVries' sister. She was four years old at the time of Pete's walk.

McVRIES, MR. Pete's father. He had a half-ownership in a drive-in theater.

McVRIES, PETER A dark-haired Long Walker. He weighed 167 pounds at the beginning of the Walk. He was Number 61. As the Walkers entered Massachusetts, he was one of the final surviving seven. He was the fifth of the seven to die.

McVRIES' ROOMMATES McVries and Priscilla had separate apartments in Newark one summer. They worked in a pajama factory. McVries roomed with two other guys; Priscilla with three girls.

THE McVRIESES Peter's parents. They accompanied him to the Long Walk starting point.

THE MECHANIC On the road to Oldtown, the Walkers passed a gas station where a mechanic was hosing off the tarmac.

A MIDDLE-AGED HOUSEWIFE On the road to Oldtown, a teenager in pegged jeans raced a middle-aged housewife for McVries' empty chicken-concentrate tube.

MIKE Long Walker. When the Walkers were about forty-five miles north of Oldtown, the vanguard consisted of two brothers named Joe and Mike. They were Hopi Indians and both had leather jackets tied around their waists. On the road to Augusta, Mike got gut cramps. He and Scramm then sat down and got their tickets together.

THE MILKMAN An unnamed milkman who yelled "Go to it, boys!" from the side of the road as the Walkers passed by.

MILLIGAN #1 Long Walker. He fell to his knees outside of Augusta and was blasted.

MILLIGAN #2 Long Walker. As the Walkers entered Massachusetts, he was one of the final surviving seven. He was the third

of the seven to die.

"MR. AND MRS. NORMAN NORMAL" During the Walk, Ray Garraty fantasized that if he survived, he and Jan would end up "Mr. and Mrs. Norman Normal," with four kids and a collie dog.

MONK, THELONIUS One of the Banned Noisemakers.

MORGAN, FRANK Long Walker. He was Number 64. He got his ticket after the Walkers passed through Jefferson Plantation.

THE "NEARLY PORTLY" WALKER Long Walker who was shot in Oldtown.

THE NEW HAMPSHIRE PROVO GOVERNOR The man who stormed the German nuclear base in Santiago. His face (and the Major's face) were outlined in fireworks when the Walkers crossed into New Hampshire.

AN OLD LADY During the storm on the road to Oldtown, an old lady who was using a *Vogue* magazine as a rain hat waved to Garraty.

AN OLD LADY WITH A BLACK UMBRELLA An unnamed woman who watched as the Walkers passed.

THE OLDTOWN HIGH SCHOOL STUDENTS They cheered Garraty as the Walkers passed.

OLSON, HENRY (HANK) Long Walker. Before the start of the Walk, he said "Walking is my game." He was Number 70. He also told Barkovitch that his name was "John Carter," and that he was from Barsoom, Mars. As they neared Oldtown, Garraty realized that Olson had locked himself away in some place where there was no pain. Garraty thought that if Olson won, the headlines would read "Long Walk Won By Dead Man." Instead of winning, though, Olson climbed a halftrack in Oldtown, disarmed a guard, and was shot.

OWENS, JIMMY Childhood friend of Garraty's. Jimmy and Ray had been caught playing "Doctor's Office" when they were both five.

OWENS, MRS. Jimmy Owens' mother. Jimmy had seen her naked when he was five.

PARKER, COLLIE Long Walker from Joliet, Illinois. Harkness inadvertently bumped into him. Collie was a mean son-of-a-bitch.

PARKER'S GUARD As the Walk came to an end, Parker stole a gun and shot a guard.

PASTOR, BRUCE Long Walker. He told Garraty the following knock-knock joke: "Knock knock: Who's there? Major. Major who? Major buggers his mother before breakfast."

PATTERSON, DR. Ray Garraty's mother's boyfriend.

PEARSON Long Walker. He wore glasses. Pearson's little brother loved enemas. On the road to Augusta, a dog ran out at Pearson and was shot by a guard.

PEARSON, MRS. Pearson's mother. She would administer enemas to Pearson's little brother. He loved them.

PEARSON'S LITTLE BROTHER He loved the enemas his mother administered.

PERCY Long Walker. He was Number 31. His mother yelled to him from the side of the road as the Walkers passed by. On the road to Oldtown, he left the road, forfeiting his right to Warnings, and was shot.

PETRIE, MISS Tubbins' sixth grade teacher.

THE PLYMOUTH SLEEPWEAR FACTORY FOREMAN McVries' boss at the pajama factory in Newark.

POE, EDGAR ALLAN One of the subjects of discussion among the Walkers was whether or not Poe was a necrophiliac.

THE POLICEMEN The unnamed officers who saluted the Walkers as they passed by.

POPHAM, DAVEY One of Art Baker's childhood friends. He once burned off all the hair on his ass and back in a fart-lighting contest.

PRISCILLA McVries' girlfriend.

PRISCILLA'S MOTHER McVries' girlfriend's mother. McVries once asked Pris what her mother would say if they were to wed.

PRISCILLA'S ROOMMATES McVries and Priscilla had separate apartments in Newark one summer. They worked in a pajama factory. McVries roomed with two other guys; Priscilla with three girls.

QUINCE, HAROLD Long Walker. At mile 218 of the Walk, Harold was one of the front runners.

"QUINCY OR QUENTIN" A Long Walker who got his ticket on the way to Oldtown.

RALPH One of McVries' co-workers in the Plymouth Sleepwear factory. Ralph worked on the picker, and couldn't make piece-work because of McVries' slow output.

RANK Long Walker. He was "a squat, ugly boy." He took a swing at Barkovitch and was warned for it. He got his ticket on the road to Oldtown.

RAY JUNIOR During Ray Garraty's "Mr. and Mrs. Norman Normal" fantasy, McVries asked Ray if his and Jan's first boy would be Ray Junior.

SALINGER, J.D., JOHN KNOWLES, JAMES KIRKWOOD AND DON BREDES According to McVries, these four authors destroyed being an adolescent.

SCRAMM Long Walker. He was Number 85. Scramm was married to Cathy and thought the Long Walk was "the biggest fucking thing he'd ever seen." Scramm had dropped out of school at fourteen because a history teacher had told him that schools were overpopulated. When the Hopi Walker Mike got gut cramps, Scramm sat down with him and they both got their tickets on the road to Augusta.

SCRAMM, CATHY Scramm's wife. At the time of the Long Walk, she was pregnant.

THE SCREAMING WALKER During the Long Walk that Ray Garraty had watched in Freeport, one boy had kept screaming "I can't" over and over.

THE SEVEN As the Walkers entered Massachusetts, there were seven Walkers left: Garraty, Baker, McVries, George Fiedler, Bill Hough, Milligan #2, and Stebbins. [NOTE: See the "Things" entry THE FINAL ORDER.]

SHEILA The Major's Bedlington terrier.

THE SHORT, STOUT BOY WEARING A GREEN SILK VEST Long Walker. On the road to Oldtown, the guns came down on him for slowing his pace. He picked up the pace and then got a ticket anyway.

THE SIXTEEN-YEAR-OLD GIRL As the Walkers passed houses, a sixteen-year-old girl held up a Magic Marker sign that said "Go-Go-Garraty Number 47 We Love You Ray 'Maine's Own'."

SLEDGE, BOBBY Long Walker. He got his second warning as the Major passed by the Walkers. Just before the Walkers crossed the New Hampshire border, Bobby tried to sneak into the crowd. He got his ticket instead.

THE SMALL BOY A small boy sat on a "Keep Maine Tidy" barrel as the Walkers passed through Caribou.

A SMALL BOY IN A BASEBALL CAP When the Walkers were about forty-five miles north of Oldtown, a storm came up and a small boy's baseball cap blew away.

THE SMALL BOY IN PATCHED OVERALLS An unnamed Limestone boy who walked along with the Walkers for almost a mile.

A SMALL BOY IN THE CROWD On the road to Augusta, the Walkers passed a small boy in a crowd who whined that he wanted to go home.

THE SMALL BOY ON THE JUNGLE GYM A little kid who waved to Garraty as the Walkers passed a one-room schoolhouse on the road to Oldtown.

THE SOLDIERS Unnamed government personnel who passed out canteens to the Walkers.

"SOMEONE HE KNEW" As Garraty stumbled towards winning the Long Walk, he thought he saw "someone he knew beckoning in the dark ahead." It was a dark figure, up ahead, not far, beckoning. The dark figure was Death, and Garraty finally ran towards him.

STEBBINS Long Walker. He was Number 88. At the end of the Long Walk, Stebbins revealed that the Major was actually his father. As the Walkers entered Massachusetts, he was one of the final surviving seven. He was the sixth of the seven to die.

A TEENAGER IN PEGGED JEANS On the road to Oldtown, a teenager in pegged jeans raced a middle-aged housewife for McVries' empty chicken-concentrate tube.

THE THREE COLLEGE STUDENTS In Jefferson Plantation, three college students drank beer and crushed a fat woman while the Walkers passed.

THE THREE SCRAWNY WOMEN The women who watched Ray Garraty as the guard gave him his three warnings when he sat down on the road to Augusta to work out a charley horse.

THE THREE SOLDIERS At the beginning of the Long Walk, they passed out wide belts with snap pockets. The pockets were filled with tubes of concentrated, high-energy pastes.

THE THREE STATE TROOPERS The three unnamed officers who restrained Dom L'Antonio from giving the Walkers free watermelon.

THE THREE WAITRESSES On the road to Oldtown, the Walkers passed an unnamed truck stop restaurant and waved at three waitresses inside.

THE TINY SON The unnamed child of the young woman in the small village the Walkers passed through.

TOLAND Long Walker. He got his ticket right after Larson did.

TRAVIN Long Walker. He had diarrhea and got shot with his pants down.

TRESSLER Long Walker. He was Number 92. He got sunstroke on the way to Oldtown and was shot while unconscious.

THE TRUCKER An unnamed truckdriver who gave the Walkers the finger.

TUBBINS Long Walker. He was freckled and short. He went insane in Porterville and began screaming to the rain about the Whore of Babylon.

THE TWELVE WALKERS Twelve of the original Walkers used the April 31 backout date.

THE TWO COPS The unnamed Caribou officers who explained to Ev (every year, it seemed) that he couldn't give soft drinks to the Long Walkers.

THE TWO GIRLS BESIDE A BATTERED MG Two unbearably erotic girls who leaned against an MG and watched the Walkers. Gribble couldn't take it, ran to one of them, and dry-humped her through his three warnings. He got a cramp in his crotch after he rejoined the Walkers, fell to his knees, and was shot. Garraty came in his pants thinking about the girls.

THE TWO GUARDS Two guards came to get McVries for the Long Walk. McVries was an alternate and was chosen to replace one of the twelve original Walkers who had decided to use the April 31 backout date.

THE TWO HIGHWAY REPAIRMEN The two unnamed repairmen who had helped make the bridge on the road to Oldtown passable.

THE TWO MEN IN RED-AND-BLACK CHECKED HUNTING SHIRTS The two guys sitting in a pickup in a Shell station who watched the Walkers pass.

TWO OLD MEN Two unnamed men who sat outside a gas station in the small village that the Walkers passed through.

THE TWO SMALL BOYS IN LITTLE LEAGUE SHIRTS They watched Harkness massage the cramp out of his foot.

THE TWO TECHNICIANS The two unnamed technicians who unreeled cable as the Walkers passed the Caribou city limits.

THE TWO TWELVE-YEAR-OLDS The two unnamed children who watched the Walkers pass through a small village.

THE TWO WALKERS Two unnamed Walkers who got tickets as the troupe walked towards Oldtown.

THE VANGUARD When the Walkers were about forty-five miles north of Oldtown, the vanguard consisted of two tall Walkers named Joe and Mike. They both had leather jackets tied around their waists. They were Hopi Indians.

THE WAITRESSES A bunch of waitresses cheered the Walkers as they passed a truck stop.

THE WALKER WEARING A GREEN TRENCHCOAT An unnamed Walker who fell down on the road to Oldtown and was shot. He was Number 45.

A WALKER WITH APPLE CHEEKS The unnamed Long Walker who passed the word that Mike (of the Hopi Indian brothers, Mike and Joe) had gotten gut cramps.

WAYNE Long Walker. He was Number 94.

A WOMAN As the cars began pulling out of the parking lot before the beginning of the Walk, an unnamed woman began screaming.

THE WOMAN BESIDE A VW BUS Garraty could see her blue underwear as the Walkers passed by her.

THE WOMAN IN A FLOPPY STRAW SUNHAT The unnamed woman who threw a transister radio at the three state troopers restraining Dom L'Antonio from giving the Walkers free watermelon.

THE WOMAN IN THE FRONT ROW At mile 218 of the Walk, this woman said that Ray Garraty wouldn't last much longer.

THE WOMAN WITH A CROW IN A CAGE A woman in Oldtown who watched the Walkers pass. She had a big crow in a cage.

WYMAN, MARTY Long Walker. He was Number 97. He and Yannick discussed the soldiers' ancestry as they walked. He got his ticket at 11:40 on the last day of the Walk.

YANNICK Long Walker. He was Number 98. He and Marty Wyman discussed the soldiers' ancestry as they walked.

THE YOUNG BLONDE GUARD The guard who gave Garraty his three warnings when Ray sat down on the road to Augusta to work out a charley horse.

THE YOUNG COUPLE SLEEPING ON A BENCH A young couple sat on a bench in front of a Shopwell holding a sign while waiting for the Walkers to pass. When the Walkers finally arrived, the couple was asleep.

THE YOUNG MAN WITH HIS FLY HALF UNZIPPED As the Walkers passed through Eureka, a group cheered them. In the group was a young man of about thirty-five whose fly was half-unzipped.

A YOUNG WOMAN An unnamed young woman who held up her tiny son to see the Walkers as they passed through a small village.

ZUCK Long Walker. He had red hair. He was Number 100. On the road to Caribou he fell down and cut his knee.

(7)
THE LONG WALK
Places

THE AMERICA/CANADA BORDER The Long Walk began on a road at a point on the border.

ANDROSCOGGIN COUNTY Ray Garraty's home county. He lived on R.D. #1 in Pownal, Maine.

THE AUGUSTA ROUTE By nine in the morning on the day after the Walkers passed through Oldtown, they had already passed Veazie, Bangor, Hermon, Hampden and Winterport. They passed a sign that said AUGUSTA, 48, PORTLAND 117."

BANGOR Ray's father had once told him that during a Long Walk, people lined the road from Bangor onward.

BARSOOM, MARS Hank Olson told Gary Barkovitch that his name was John Carter and that he was from Barsoom, Mars.

BATON ROUGE Baker's aunt had his uncle's ashes in Baton Rouge.

A BEDSHEET FACTORY IN PHOENIX The place where Scramm worked. He earned three dollars an hour.

A BOARDED-UP DAIRY QUEEN On the road to Oldtown, the Walkers passed a boarded-up Dairy Queen that bore a sign that said "Will Re-Open for Season June 5."

BRICKYARD HILL One of the roads the Walkers walked in Porterville.

THE BRIDGE On one of the bridges on the road to Oldtown, a support and two butt-planks had washed away. The Walkers thought that this would necessitate a temporary stop, but the Squads had worked feverishly to make it passable.

BURGER KING One of the businesses in Limestone.

BURR'S BUILDING MATERIALS As children, Ray Garraty and Jimmy Owens had looked into the window of Burr's to see the naked-lady calendars. They then played "Doctor's Office."

CARIBOU The town after Limestone on the Walkers' route.

CARIBOU PAPER MILLS A Caribou mill the Walkers passed by.

CARIBOU SHOPPING CENTER The shopping center that was having an annual "Walk-In For Values" sale.

CLARK AVENUE, LIMESTONE One of the side streets in Limestone that the Long Walkers passed.

COLTER MEMORIAL AVENUE The Walkers walked down the main drag of Lewiston. It used to be Lisbon Street, but it was changed to Colter Memorial Avenue in honor of Reggie Colter, the only guy from Maine ever to win the Long Walk. [NOTE: See the "People" entry REGGIE COLTER.]

THE CONSOLIDATED BUILDING The building in Porterville that replaced an abandoned one-room schoolhouse. The Walkers passed it.

A CORNER GROCERY A store the Walkers passed by in Limestone. It had a Narragansett sign in the window.

DAIRY JOY An ice cream parlor in Porterville where Ray Garraty, his girlfriend, and Jan would go after the movies.

THE DESERTED FARMHOUSE On the road to Oldtown, the Walkers passed a deserted farmhouse that bore a sign that said "GARRATY'S OUR MAN!!! Aroostock County Parents' Association."

EUREKA A small town the Walkers passed through on their way to Oldtown. A group cheered them. In the group was a young man of about thirty-five or so. His fly was half unzipped.

EUREKA GRANGE NO. 81 A grange the Walkers passed by in Eureka, a small New England town.

EV'S MARKET A shop on the outskirts of Caribou. Every year, Ev tried to offer soft drinks to the Walkers.

EXCHANGE STREET, LIMESTONE One of the side streets in Limestone that the Long Walkers passed.

THE FIRST GRAVEYARD On their way to Caribou, the Walkers passed their first graveyard.

FREEPORT Ray Garraty once watched a Long Walk in Freeport.

THE GAS STATION On the road to Oldtown, the Walkers passed an unnamed gas station where a mechanic was hosing off the tarmac.

THE GERMAN NUCLEAR BASE IN SANTIAGO The base that was stormed by the man who later became New Hampshire's provo governor.

THE GOVERNMENT SALES BUILDING One of the buildings the Walkers passed in Porterville. It had a "May is Confirm-Your-Sex Month" sign in the window.

HAINSEVILLE WOODS The Walkers passed through these woods on their way to Oldtown.

THE HOOCHIE-KOOCHIE TENT A tent at the Steubenville state fair. Davidson once got drunk and snuck into the tent. He was hit in the head by a big fat mama wearing a G-string.

JEFFERSON PLANTATION The Jefferson Plantation chamber of commerce put up a banner congratulating the Walkers on hitting the hundred mile mark. [NOTE: See the entry "THE BANNER."]

JUNIPER LANE, LIMESTONE One of the side streets in Limestone that the Long Walkers passed.

LEWISTON The Walkers walked down the main drag of Lewiston. It used to be Lisbon Street, but it was changed to Colter Memorial Avenue in honor of Reggie Colter, the only guy from Maine ever to win the Long Walk. [NOTE: See the entry REGGIE COLTER.]

LIMESTONE Town the Walkers passed through. Limestone was "proud to welcome the Long Walkers."

LIMESTONE The town the Walkers were headed for after they passed through a small village. It was ten miles away.

LISBON STREET, LEWISTON The Walkers walked down the main drag of Lewiston. It used to be Lisbon Street, but it was changed to Colter Memorial Avenue in honor of Reggie Colter, the only guy from Maine ever to win the Long Walk. [NOTE: See the "People" entry REGGIE COLTER.]

McDONALD'S One of the businesses in Limestone.

McLAREN'S DODGE An auto dealership the Walkers passed on the road to Oldtown.

MEADOW BROOK On the road to Oldtown, the Walkers crossed a bridge over the Meadow Brook.

THE NEW HAMPSHIRE BORDER When the Walkers crossed into New Hampshire, fireworks were set off that outlined the Major's and the then New Hampshire provo governor's faces.

NEWARK McVries and Priscilla had separate apartments in Newark one summer. They both worked in a pajama factory. McVries roomed with two other guys; Priscilla with three girls.

OLDTOWN The city the Walkers headed for after they left Caribou. It was 120 miles away.

A ONE-ROOM SCHOOLHOUSE A schoolhouse the Walkers passed on the road to Oldtown.

THE PAJAMA FACTORY McVries and Priscilla had separate apartments in Newark one summer. They both worked in a pajama factory. McVries roomed with two other guys; Priscilla with three girls.

PHOENIX There was a bedsheet factory in Phoenix. Scramm worked there and made three dollars an hour.

PIZZA HUT One of the businesses in Limestone.

THE PLYMOUTH SLEEPWEAR FACTORY The pajama factory in Newark where Priscilla and McVries both worked one summer.

PORTERVILLE Just before the Walkers reached Porterville, Gary Barkovitch, Number 5, ripped out his own throat.

PORTERVILLE, MAINE Ray Garraty's lifelong hometown. Its population was 970. [Note: It is unclear why Garraty's ID card gave Pownal, Maine, as his address. Perhaps a mailing address?]

PORTERVILLE REC CENTER One of the buildings the Walkers passed in Porterville.

PORTERVILLE WEAVING COMPANY One of the buildings the Walkers passed in Porterville.

POWNAL, MAINE The address on Garraty's ID card. He lived on R.D. #1, in Androscoggin County. [Note: Elsewhere, Porterville, Maine, is identified as Garraty's lifelong hometown.]

THE ROYAL RIVER On the road to Oldtown, Ray Garraty imagined belly-flopping into the Royal River. He remembered that "there were suckers by the rocks." (This echoes the leeches scene in "The Body.")

THE SCHOOL FOR MODERN DANCE The school operated by Mrs. Amelia Dorgens. Ray Garraty attended and learned to rhumba and cha-cha. He later taught Jan these dances.

THE SECOND DISTRICT A man with a bullhorn praised Garraty and, at the same time, announced his own candidacy to represent the second district.

THE SHADY NOOK MOTEL McVries and Priscilla lost their virginity one summer at the Shady Nook Motel. They used a Trojan.

A SHELL STATION The Walkers passed by a Shell station where two guys in red-and-black checked hunting shirts sat in a pickup and watched them walk by.

THE SHIRT SHACK Abraham's girlfriend wanted to have Abraham's Long Walk acceptance letter turned into a t-shirt at the Shirt Shack.

SHOPWELL A store the Walkers passed on the road to Oldtown.

SHREVEPORT Baker's grandfather was a lawyer in Shreveport.

A SMALL VILLAGE An unnamed village the Walkers passed through.

THE STATES At the time of the Long Walk, the United States was comprised of fifty-one states.

STEUBENVILLE STATE FAIR Davidson once got drunk and sneaked into the hoochie-koochie tent at the fair. He was hit in the head by a big fat mama wearing a G-string.

THE STILLWATER OR THE PENOBSCOT RIVERS A river the Walkers passed as they neared Oldtown.

SYCAMORE STREET, LIMESTONE One of the side streets in Limestone that the Long Walkers passed.

THE TRUCK STOP On the road to Oldtown, the Walkers passed a truck stop. The waitresses cheered them.

A TRUCK STOP RESTAURANT On the road to Oldtown, the Walkers passed an unnamed truck-stop restaurant and waved at three waitresses inside.

THE TWIN CITIES OF LEWISTON AND AUBURN Two cities the Walkers passed through. These cities were "the land of the Dussettes and Aubuchons and Lavesques."

U.S. 202 The road the Walkers used to get to Augusta.

(7)
THE LONG WALK
Things

"ADOLESCENT LOVE" McVries said that after J.D. Salinger, John Knowles, James Kirkwood and Don Bredes destroyed being an adolescent, you couldn't discuss adolescent love anymore: "You just come off sounding like fucking Ron Howard with a hard-on."

APRIL 31 The official backout date for the Walk. [NOTE: See the entry THE BACKOUT DATE.]

AROOSTOCK COUNTY PARENTS ASSOCIATION The organization that hung the "GARRATY'S OUR MAN!!!" sign on the deserted farmhouse on the road to Oldtown.

ASHES Baker's aunt kept his uncle's ashes in Baton Rouge.

THE AUGUSTA SIGN By nine in the morning on the day after the Walkers passed through Oldtown, they had already passed Veazie, Bangor, Hermon, Hampden, and Winterport. They passed a sign that said AUGUSTA 48, PORTLAND 117."

THE BACKOUT DATE The official backout date for the Walkers was April 31. [NOTE: Interestingly, The Change in the government seems to have also brought about a tampering with the calendar as well, since there was no April 31 prior to The Change! Either that, or (a) the government had fixed it so that none of the Long Walkers could possibly back out, insofar as the "backout date" didn't exist (but then why would "alternates" be selected to replace those who backed out? If you backed out, perhaps you were killed, too?), (b) King screwed up and inadvertently left in a blooper, or (c) he is playing a joke on his readers to see who notices. I doubt it's an error, though. For whatever reason, I think it was intentional.]

THE BANNER The Walkers passed beneath a banner that said:

100 MILES!!! CONGRATULATIONS FROM THE
JEFFERSON PLANTATION
CHAMBER OF COMMERCE!
CONGRATULATIONS TO THIS YEAR'S
"CENTURY CLUB" LONG WALKERS!!

THE BARREL The government pulled the Walkers names out of a barrel. One hundred Walkers and one hundred backup Walkers were selected. Ray Garraty was the 73rd out of the drum.

A BLACK TURTLENECK The shirt worn by one of the Walkers. He had a convulsion, was warned, and then shot.

THE BLOOD STAIN There was a blood stain on the road from the beginning of the previous year's Walk. A kid froze up, took his three warnings, and was shot at 9:02.

A BLUE FORD Ray Garraty's mother's car.

"BODILY CONTACT" The Long Walk Rules said that a Walker could have bodily contact with anyone he wanted as long as he didn't leave the road.

THE BOSTON SIGN In Massachusetts, the Walkers came upon a sign that read "49 Miles to Boston! Walkers You Can Make it!"

THE CHANGE The "rearrangement" of the United States government. After The Change, The Squads came in.

A CHARLEY HORSE On the road to Augusta, Garraty got a charley horse. He sat down, took his three warnings as he worked out the cramp, and then got up. A young, blonde guard who wore a wedding ring gave Ray his warnings.

THE CHASE VEHICLE The vehicle that followed the Walkers. There were two armed guards in it.

CORNHUSKER'S LOTION The lotion McVries put on his blisters after working in the pajama factory.

A CROSS Baker once burned a cross on a black man's lawn.

"THE CROWD" The (incredible) Ray Bradbury story Garraty thought of when he fell to his knees on the road and everyone gathered to watch.

DIAL The soap Pearson used.

"DOCTOR'S OFFICE" Garraty had been caught playing "Doctor's Office" with Jimmy Owens when they were both five. They both had boners.

DOM L'ANTONIO'S SIGN Dom was a little Italian man who held a sign that said "Dom L'Antonio Loves All Long Walkers – Free Watermelon!!!"

THE DRIVE-IN SCREEN On the screen of a drive-in that the Walkers passed near the end of the Walk, there was a message that read "The Management of This Theater Salutes This Year's Long Walkers!"

AN EMPTY CHICKEN-CONCENTRATE TUBE On the road to Oldtown, a teenager in pegged jeans raced a middle-aged housewife for McVries' empty chicken-concentrate tube.

ENEMAS Pearson's little brother loved them.

"ENTERING LIMESTONE CITY LIMITS—WELCOME, LONG WALKERS!" A sign on the road to Limestone.

A FART-LIGHTING CONTEST On the road to Oldtown, Art Baker told the story of how Davey Popham once burned all the hair off his ass and back during a fart-lighting contest.

THE FINAL ORDER As the Walkers entered Massachusetts, there were seven Walkers left: Garraty, Baker, McVries, George Fiedler, Bill Hough, Milligan #2, and Stebbins. They died in this order:

    1st. Fiedler.
    2nd. Hough.
    3rd. Milligan (No. 2).
    4th. Baker.
    5th. McVries.
    6th. Stebbins.

Garraty was the last survivor and the "winner" of the Long Walk. [NOTE: See the "People" entry "SOMEONE HE KNEW."]

THE FINGER An unnamed truckdriver gave the Walkers the finger.

49-801-89 Ray Garraty's Long Walk ID number.

FOUR MILES PER HOUR The low speed cutoff for the Walkers.

GARRATY'S ID CARD It was made of blue plastic and said:

GARRATY RAYMOND DAVIS
RD 1 POWNAL MAINE
ANDROSCOGGIN COUNTY
ID NUMBER 49-801-89

When inserted into the computer, the readout was "OK-OK-OK."

GARRATY'S ID NUMBER It was 49-801-89.

"GARRATY'S OUR MAN!!!" The sign hung by the Aroostock County Parents' Association on a deserted farmhouse on the road to Oldtown.

THE GERMAN AIR-BLITZ OF THE AMERICAN EAST COAST The lights over Augusta reminded Garraty of pictures he had seen in history books of the German bombing of the east coast of America during the last days of World War II.

"GHOST" On the road to Oldtown, Baker and Abraham played a word game called "Ghost."

"THE GREAT GOD CROWD" As the Walkers neared Augusta, Garraty began to imagine the "great god Crowd."

"A GUNSLINGER" "Olson slung his belt low on his hips, like a gunslinger." [NOTE: An image that parallels the opening moments of King's epic series *The Dark Tower*. Here is the passage from *The Gunslinger* where King describes the last Gunslinger's guns, an echo, perhaps, of the *Long Walk* "gunslinger" reference above: "Below the waterbag were his guns...The holsters were tied down with rawhide cord, and they swung heavily against his hips."]

GUT CRAMPS On the road to Augusta, Mike the Hopi Indian got gut cramps. He and Scramm sat down together and got their tickets.

THE HEADLINES When Ray sat down on the road to Augusta and took his three warnings, he imagined the official records: "Garraty, Raymond, #47, Eliminated 218th Mile." He also visualized the headlines: "Garraty Dead; 'Maine's Own' Becomes 61st to Fall!"

A HEART ATTACK Baker's brother died of a heart attack.

HIGH-ENERGY CONCENTRATE PASTES The Walkers were given belts with snap pockets. The pockets were filled with tubes of the pastes.

THE HINTS Included in the official Long Walk rules were a series of Hints, designed to help the Walkers Walk as far as possible. Only five were revealed (which are detailed below), but there were at least thirteen given. It wasn't said how many Hints were actually offered to the Walkers.

    HINT 3 "Do not wear sneakers."
    HINT 6 "Slow and easy does it."
    HINT 10 Save your wind. If you ordinarily smoke, try
        not to smoke on the Long Walk.
    HINT 12 Hint 12 recommended athletic socks.
    HINT 13 "Conserve energy whenever possible."

A HOUND'S-TOOTH JACKET The jacket worn by a man in a straw hat. He waved to the Walkers as they passed by on their way to Oldtown.

THE HUMAN PYRAMID As the Walkers passed through Oldtown, a group of University of New Hampshire students formed a human pyramid.

A "KEEP MAINE TIDY" BARREL A small boy sat on a "Keep Maine Tidy" barrel as the Walkers passed through Caribou.

A LAXATIVE Abraham's grandfather had never taken a laxative in his life.

A LEAD-LINED COFFIN As the Walk neared its end, Baker remarked that he had a dollar twenty-two cents in change, and that he would use it to buy a lead-lined coffin.

"LIMESTONE IS PROUD TO WELCOME THE LONG WALKERS" A banner beneath the "Limestone 7 Mi." sign on the Walkers' route.

"LIMESTONE 7 MI." A sign on the Long Walkers' route.

THE LONG WALK The annual ritualized blood-lust torture of one hundred young boys. Essentially, one hundred young men began walking south at the Canadian border. They could not walk slower than four miles per hour, and if they were warned three times for walking too slowly, they were shot to death after the fourth warning. (This was called "getting your ticket.") The Walkers could not stop, and had to eat, defecate, and even sleep while walking no slower than four miles per hour. The last Walker alive after ninety-nine had been shot was the winner, and he would receive the Prize – anything he wanted for the rest of his life. From the history of the Walk, though, it seems as though most winners usually didn't survive very long after the grueling physical trauma of the event. The most horrifying aspect of the

Walk was the fact that society had accepted (and was actually thriving on) the annual ritualized murder of young men as sport.

THE LONG WALK ROSTER (NUMBERED PARTICIPANTS) The following listing is comprised of the twenty-nine Long Walk participants who were assigned numbers which were revealed in the text. (The remaining thirty-three mentioned Walkers were neither named nor numbered, but were instead described by their apparel or by a physical description. For a complete listing of Long Walkers, see the "People" entry called THE LONG WALKERS ROSTER (ALPHABETICAL).

1. Aaronson.	49. Harkness.
2. Abraham.	59. Klingerman.
3. Baker, Arthur.	60. Larson.
4. Baker, James.	61. McVries.
5. Barkovitch.	64. Morgan.
7. Curley.	70. Olson.
8. Davidson.	85. Scramm.
9. Ewing.	88. Stebbins.
12. Fentner.	92. Tressler.
13. Fenum.	93. Unnamed.
31. Percy.	94. Wayne.
38. Unnamed.	97. Wyman.
45. Unnamed.	98. Yannick.
47. Garraty.	100. Zuck.
48. Gribble.	

THE LOW SPEED CUTOFF It was four miles per hour.

MAY 1 The date of the Long Walk.

THE "MAY IS CONFIRM-YOUR-SEX-MONTH" SIGN The sign in a window of the Government Sales building in Porterville.

MELLOW CIGARETTES The brand of cigarettes McVries smoked.

"MY SON GAVE HIS LIFE IN THE SQUADS" A window sign in two houses the Walkers passed on the road to Oldtown.

THE NATIONAL ANTHEM, A MEDLEY OF SOUSA MARCHES AND "MARCHING TO PRETORIA" The repertoire of the high school band that played at the Caribou shopping center as the Walkers passed.

A NIGHT RIDER Baker revealed that he was a Night Rider for three years, and that he once burned a cross on a black man's lawn.

9:00 A.M. The starting time of the Long Walk.

9:02 A.M. The time the kid who froze in the previous year's Long Walk was shot.

NINETY DOLLARS Priscillas' salary at the Plymouth Sleepwear factory. McVries was making sixty-four forty.

OFFICIAL DETECTIVE MAGAZINE After Curley got his ticket, Stebbins left his footprint in Curley's blood. It looked like a photograph in *Official Detective* magazine.

THE OFFICIAL RECORDS When Ray sat down on the road to Augusta and took his three warnings, he imagined the official records: "Garraty, Raymond, #47, Eliminated 218th Mile." He also visualized the headlines: "Garraty Dead; 'Maine's Own' Becomes 61st to Fall!"

"ON THE HOUSE FOR THE LONG WALKERS!! COURTESY OF 'EV'S' MARKET" The sign in front of Ev's Market. He had put out a soft drink cooler, even though it was against the rules for any bystanders to help the Walkers.

A DOLLAR TWENTY-TWO CENTS IN CHANGE As the Walk neared its end, Baker remarked that he had a dollar twenty-two in change, and that he would use it to buy a lead-lined coffin.

ONE HOUR Individual warnings were voided after one hour.

OVER $2 BILLION *World's Week* magazine reported that over $2 billion a year was bet on the Long Walk.

P.F. FLYERS Ewing's sneakers. (He obviously didn't pay attention to Hint 3.)

A PADDINGTON BEAR LETTER OPENER The source of Pete McVries' scar. He tried to take Pris to bed one summer day in Newark and she cut him with the letter opener.

A PEACH IS NOT A PEACH WITHOUT A PIT A book sarcastically attributed to Hank Olson by Pete McVries.

POPULAR MECHANIX Magazine. They once ran an article on the timers the guards carried during the Long Walk.

A PREVIOUS LONG WALK Stebbins had seen the end of a Long Walk four years prior to the one he participated in. Two kids had ended up alone: a big, blonde kid, and a kid who had no shoes left. The blonde kid lost.

THE PRIZE The winner of the Long Walk would win everything he wanted for the rest of his life.

THE PROMISE Garraty, Abraham, Baker, McVries and a few other surviving Walkers made a promise: As the Walk came to an end, there would be no help from anyone. Each would have to either make it – or not – alone.

"THE RAY GARRATY STORY" As Garraty walked, he felt like he was the star of "that long-running hit film, "The Ray Garraty Story."

RAY GARRATY'S NUMBER The government pulled the Walkers' names out of a barrel: One hundred Walkers and one hundred backup Walkers. Ray Garraty was the seventy-third out of the drum.

REFLECTOR SUNGLASSES The sunglasses worn by the Major.

THE RHUMBA AND THE CHA-CHA The two dances Ray Garraty learned at Mrs. Amelia Dorgens' School for Modern Dance. He later taught his girlfriend Jan how to do these dances.

ST. CHRISTOPHER'S MEDAL The medal Fentner was holding when he got his ticket.

A "SCRAMM" SIGN In Jefferson Plantation, a man waved a "Scramm" sign and popped his fly.

"SERMONETTE 342" After the Walkers passed by the family of five, McVries gave Sermonette Number 342: The Watchers are smart, the Long Walkers are dumb.

SEVEN AND THREE-QUARTER MILES The longest distance a full complement of one hundred Walkers had ever covered.

"A SHIRLEY JACKSON SHORT STORY" "For no reason Garraty could put a finger on, he felt as if he had just walked through a Shirley Jackson short story." Garraty felt this way after passing through Eureka, a small New England town. [NOTE: This was also a hint that this Bachman novel may have been by Stephen King. King has always publicly acknowledged that he is a huge Jackson fan, and, in fact, *'Salem's Lot* uses a quote from Jackson's novel *The Haunting of Hill House* as an epigraph.]

SIXTY-FOUR DOLLARS FORTY CENTS McVries' salary at the Plymouth Sleepwear factory. Pris was making ninety dollars.

THE SOCIETY FOR INTENSIFYING CRUELTY TO ANIMALS McVries thought that if Stebbins won the Long Walk, he would donate two or three hundred grand to this society.

"A SOCIETY-SUPPORTED SOCIOPATH" The Major, according to Ray Garraty's father, Jim. He called him "the most dangerous monster any nation can produce." One day, the Squads took Jim Garraty away, and he was never seen or heard from again.

THE SQUADS The military/secret police force that took away Ray Garraty's father, Jim. He had called the Major a "society-supported sociopath," and "the most dangerous monster any nation can produce."

THE STATE The authoritarian government of the future. The State sanctioned the sadistic and barbaric Long Walk.

TEN DOLLARS AT TWELVE TO ONE One of the highway repair men had a ten dollar bet on Garraty at twelve to one odds.

THE THREE GREAT TRUTHS According to Hank Olson, there were three great truths in the world: a good meal, a good screw, and a good shit.

A TICKET Long Walk euphemism for getting shot in the head with a high-powered rifle.

"THE TRANSCENDENTAL QUALITY OF LOVE" When Hank Olson started talking about love, McVries said that "The Transcendental Quality of Love" was the title of a lecture by "the noted philosopher and Ethiopian jug-rammer Henry Olson." McVries also said that Olson was the author of *A Peach Is Not a Peach without a Pit.*

A TRANSISTOR RADIO An unnamed woman in a floppy straw sunhat threw a transistor radio at the three state troopers who were restraining Dom L'Antonio from giving the Walkers free watermelon.

A TROJAN McVries and Priscilla lost their virginity one summer at the Shady Nook Motel. They used a Trojan.

TWENTY-THREE BAGS A DAY McVries' output at the Plymouth Sleepwear factory. It wasn't enough, and he didn't make piecework (thirty bags a day).

A TWO-YEAR SUSPENDED SENTENCE The sentence imposed on Baker's brother for stealing a car.

VOGUE MAGAZINE During the storm on the road to Oldtown, an old lady who was using *Vogue* magazine as a rainhat waved to Garraty.

A WAIFA CHOCOLATE BAR The candy bar eaten by Olson.

THE WARNINGS During the Long Walk, a Walker was allowed three warnings. If he was warned a fourth time within three hours after receiving the third, he was shot. If a thrice-warned Walker walked for another three hours, he was in the clear again.

WATER CRAMPS Ray Garraty had once gotten water cramps while helping Mr. Elwell take in his hay. Mrs. Elwell had brought them ice-cold water, and drinking it had given Ray the cramps.

"WE GAVE AWAY THE PANAMA CANAL TO THE COMMUNIST NIGGERS." The sign worn by the hollow-cheeked man with no teeth who stood in the Oldtown crowd. He was wearing an Uncle Sam suit.

"WHY DO YOU FEEL QUALIFIED TO PARTICIPATE IN THE LONG WALK?" The essay the aspiring Walkers had to write in order to qualify.

"WILL RE-OPEN FOR SEASON JUNE 5" On the road to Oldtown, the Walkers passed a boarded-up Dairy Queen that bore a sign that said "Will Re-Open for Season June 5."

THE WOMAN IN WHITE A book by Wilkie Collins. *The Woman in White* was Baker's favorite book.

"THE WORLD'S FIRST MORBID MUSICAL" If Stephen Foster and Edgar Allan Poe had lived, they could have collaborated on the world's first morbid musical: "Massa's on De Cold, Cold Road, or The Tell-Tale Stride."

WORLD'S WEEK The weekly magazine that reported the story that over $2 billion was bet on the Long Walk every year.

THE DEAD ZONE

DEDICATION

This is for Owen
I Love You, Old Bear

CONTENTS PAGE

Prologue
PART I: The Wheel of Fortune
PART II: The Laughing Tiger
PART III: Notes from the Dead Zone

BOOK BREAKDOWN

[NOTE: All of the individual chapters of *The Dead Zone* are untitled. Information is given here on how many individual sections there are within each chapter, and how they are numbered. –sjs]

Prologue—(Two sections numbered 1 and 2)

PART ONE
The Wheel of Fortune

Chapter 1:   (Four untitled sections numbered 1-4)
Chapter 2:   (Two untitled sections numbered 1 and 2)
Chapter 3:   (Six untitled sections numbered 1-6)
Chapter 4:   (One untitled section numbered 1)
Chapter 5:   (Ten untitled sections numbered 1-10)
Chapter 6:   (Seven untitled sections numbered 1-7)
Chapter 7:   (Two untitled sections numbered 1 and 2)
Chapter 8:   (Two untitled sections numbered 1 and 2)
Chapter 9:   (Nine untitled sections numbered 1-9)
Chapter 10: (Four untitled sections numbered 1-4)
Chapter 11: (Three untitled sections numbered 1-3)
Chapter 12: (Two untitled sections numbered 1 and 2)
Chapter 13: (Two untitled sections numbered 1 and 2)
Chapter 14: (Two untitled sections numbered 1 and 2)
Chapter 15: (Six untitled sections numbered 1-6)
Chapter 16: (Sixteen untitled sections numbered 1-16)

PART TWO
The Laughing Tiger

Chapter 17: (Two untitled sections numbered 1 and 2)
Chapter 18: (One untitled, unnumbered section)
Chapter 19: (Two untitled sections numbered 1 and 2)
Chapter 20: (Four untitled sections numbered 1-4)
Chapter 21: (Four untitled sections numbered 1-4)
Chapter 22: (Four untitled sections numbered 1-4)
Chapter 23: (Five untitled sections numbered 1-4)
Chapter 24: (One untitled, unnumbered section)
Chapter 25: (Three untitled sections numbered 1-3)
Chapter 26: (Eight untitled sections numbered 1-8)
Chapter 27: (Six untitled sections numbered 1-6)

PART THREE
Notes from the Dead Zone

[Thirteen untitled sections numbered 1-13]

(8)
THE DEAD ZONE
People

ABLANAP, MRS. Sarah Bracknell's housekeeper.

ALVAREZ, BONITA A Phoenix Amtrak terminal clerk. She sold John his ticket from Phoenix to New York.

BANNERMAN, GEORGE The Castle Rock sheriff.

BANNERMAN, KATRINA Sheriff Bannerman's daughter.

BASS, CHIEF The Trimbull police chief.

BENEDIX, TOMMY A boy who could skate backwards.

BERNHARDT, STEVE The construction worker who watched John at the Wheel of Fortune before John had his accident.

BOLLES, DON The Arizona investigative reporter who was killed in 1976 by a bomb wired to the ignition of his car.

BORENTZ, HELMUT Dr. Weizak's father.

BORENTZ, JOHANNA Dr. Weizak's mother.

BOWDENS, MARSTENS, AND PILLSBURYS The families buried in the Birches Cemetery. [NOTE: The Marsten House appeared in *'Salem's Lot*, and "Pillsbury" was Stephen King's grandfather's name.]

BOWES, DAVID The Democratic candidate in the third district.

BRACKNELL, SARAH Cleaves Mill high school teacher; Johnny Smith's girlfriend.

BRIGHT, DAVID Bangor *Daily News* reporter. He interviewed John in his hospital room.

BROLIN, JAMES Arnie Tremont reminded Sarah of the actor James Brolin.

BROWN, DANNY The boy on the Greyhound bus with John Smith who kept asking his mother if John was "sick or dying."

BROWN, DR. The doctor who became interested in John Smith's case.

BROWN, JULIE A woman on the Greyhound bus with John Smith.

BURKE, HENRY He ran The Bucket, a tavern.

BURT Eileen Magown's next-door neighbor.

CARLIN, GEORGE How Roger Chatsworth thought of Greg Stillson (i.e., as a clown).

CARRICK, BRUCE Owner and bartender of Cathy's Roadhouse.

CARTER, JAMES EARL Georgia peanut farmer and ex-navy man. He thought of running for president.

CASEY He was mentioned as possibly being at Cathy's during the fire.

CATHY'S GUEST LIST After the fire, the following names were mentioned as possibly being in the bar: Mike, Shannon, Casey, Ray, and Maureen Ontello.

CAYCE, EDGAR He had "second sight."

CHANCELLOR, JOHN Newscaster.

CHASE, CHEVY How Roger Chatsworth thought of Greg Stillson (i.e., as a clown).

CHATSWORTH, CHUCK The seventeen-year-old boy that John Smith tutored.

CHATSWORTH, ROGER Chuck's father, and the owner of Chatsworth Mills and Weaving in southern New Hampshire.

CHATSWORTH, SHELLEY Chuck's mother; Roger's wife.

CHILDRESS The southern boy who beat up Herb Smith behind an Atanta bar.

CLARICE A patron of the Timmesdale Pub.

CLAWSON, STUART John told Clawson he was a freelance writer. Clawson took the photo of Stillson holding up a baby as a shield. [NOTE: It wasn't said if Stuart and Fred Clawson from *The Dark Half* were related.]

CLAY, DEAN A salesman for the Phoenix Office Supply, Inc.

CLEMENTS, GEORGE The taxi driver who drove John from Grand Central to the Port Authority Terminal.

COHEN, WILLIAM The senator from Maine who chaired the Stillson Committee.

COLTSMORE, REVEREND FREDDY The Bessemer, Alabama, preacher who sold Blessed Coltsmore Cloth.

CONOVER, ALLISON An aide at the Eastern Maine Medical Center.

CONSTANTINE, STEPHANIE Sarah's friend.

THE CRAZIES OF THE WORLD According to Johnny Smith, this category included Frank Dodd, Lee Harvey Oswald, Sirhan Sirhan, Arthur Bremmer, and Squeaky Fromme.

CRONKITE, WALTER Newscaster.

CURRY, ELTON The conductor on the Amtrak Phoenix-Salt Lake run. He helped John Smith board the train.

DAN The man Sarah was dating when she met John.

DEES, RICHARD A reporter for *Inside View* magazine. [NOTE: Dees later appeared in the Stephen King short story "The Night Flier." See the section on "The Night Flier" in this volume.]

DEPUTY DAWG Sonny's initial impression of Greg Stillson.

DESALVO, ALBERT The Boston Strangler.

DODD, FRANK Sheriff Bannerman's deputy. Dodd was the Castle Rock Strangler.

DODD, HENRIETTA Frank's mother.

DOHAY, ANDREW A lightning rod salesman.

DRUMMORE, SOL The man who ran the Wheel of Fortune.

DUNBARGER, CAROL The fourth victim of the Castle Rock Strangler. Charlie Norton and Norm Lawson found her body protruding from melting snow in November 1974. Carol was seventeen years old.

DUSSAULT, ROGER A Lewiston *Sun* reporter.

EDWARDS, DAWN One of John's students. She had a crush on him and went to the hospital to see how he was after his accident.

ELLIMAN, SONNY Greg Stillson's goonish right-hand man. He was six-foot-five.

ERROLL FLYNN AND HENNY YOUNGMAN Johnny Smith, according to Sarah Bracknell: "He's sure no Errol Flynn," and "He wants to be Henny Youngman when he grows up."

ERWIN A Republican candidate.

FISHER, HARRISON The Republican representative of the third district in Washington.

FISHER, ROSCOE One of Sheriff Bannerman's deputies.

FLARHATY, SUSAN She walked with Katrina Bannerman to the library at 9:15.

FORD, GERALD The president who pardoned Nixon.

FRANKENSTEIN The name John's students called him.

FRECHETTE, ALMA A waitress at the Coffee Pot. She was the Castle Rock killer's first victim. She was killed on November 12, 1970, at 3:00 p.m.

GEDREAU, LOTTIE A neighbor of Herb Smith.

GENDRON, BILL One of the adults at Runaround Pond on the day John Smith got hurt.

GENDRON, CHARLES ("CHUCK") A banker and the president of the Lion's Club.

GEORGE HARVEY'S NEPHEW An unnamed boy drinking Pepsi in the Ridgeway police station.

THE GREENBLATTS According to Stillson's propaganda, the Greenblatts were trying to take over the U.S. economy and government.

"GRUNTS" John's term for students studying just for grades.

HACKMAN, BETTYE A friend of Sarah Bracknell's. She was with the Peace Corps.

HARRINGTON, PETER He walked with Melissa Loggins to the library at 8:50.

HARRIS, FRED A politician. Johnny shook his hand.

HARRISON, TOM He took a course (Rural Law Enforcement) with Frank Dodd from October 15 through December 25, 1972 at the University of Colorado in Pueblo.

HARVEY, GEORGE A town council member.

HAWES, COTTON A fictional character in the 87th Precinct stories.

HAZLETT, DENNIS EDWARD The son born to Sarah and Walter on Halloween night.

HAZLETT, WALTER The man Sarah met at Anne Strafford's New Year's Eve party who reminded her of Johnny. She married him because Johnny remained in a coma after his accident.

HENDRASEN, MARY KATE The nine-year-old girl who was the sixth victim of the Castle Rock Strangler. She was killed at 10:10 a.m. on December 17, 1975.

HERMAN, GEORGE A CBS newscaster at a Stillson rally.

HOVEY, MILTON The Somersworth fire chief.

HUMBARR, BILLY A southern evangelist whom Vera Smith followed.

HURKOS, PETER The "Psychic Detective." He had "second sight."

JACKSON, HENRY A politician. Johnny shook his hand.

JACKSON, MICHAEL CAREY A reading and grammar specialist from the University of California. He wrote *The Unlearning Reader*. He discovered "Jackson's Syndrome."

JAMIESON, HAKE A man who owned land in Trimbull where a rock concert had been held.

JANICE Eileen Magown's next-door neighbor.

JARVIS, MRS. She ran the Quik-Pik.

JURGENS, RACHEL A friend of Sarah's. She was married, and lived in Massachusetts.

KELSO, SHERIFF CARL M. The county's chief law officer. He was voted out of office.

"KLEM KADIDDLEHOPPER" This was how Greg Stillson referred to the farmer whose dog he killed.

LANCTE, EDGAR An FBI agent with the Boston office.

LAWSON, NORMAN A nine-year-old boy from Otisfield, Maine.

LOGGINS, MELISSA She walked with Peter Harrrington to the library at 8:50.

LONGELY The insurance man who was elected over Erwin and Mitchell.

MACKENZIE, CHARLENE A New Gloucester widow. Herb Smith was working on her house.

MACKIN, CASSIE An NBC news reporter.

MAGOWN, EILEEN John's physical therapist.

MARKSTONE, HECTOR The eighty-year-old father of Charlene Mackenzie.

MARKSTONE, JOE ("BUDDY") Charlene Mackenzie's brother.

MCCARTHY, EUGENE John's choice for president.

MCCARTHY, JOE A communist in Washington, according to Stillson's propaganda.

MCCARTNEY, PAUL AND ELVIS PRESLEY Two performers Johnny thought of when exposed to all the noise at the Stillson rally.

MCGOVERN, GEORGE A presidential candidate in the 1972 election.

MCNAUGHTON, LARRY A Phoenix public works employee who had pills for every purpose.

MEGGS, SERGEANT The Orono state cop who called Herb Smith about John's accident.

MICHAUD, MARIE The nurse who was the first to talk to John upon his awakening.

MIKE He was mentioned as possibly being at Cathy's during the fire.

MITCHELL A Democratic candidate.

MOOCHIE One of Stillson's men. He checked out the meeting hall.

MOODY, CHERYL The third victim of the Castle Rock killer. She was murdered at 2:00 p.m. on December 16, 1971.

MUSKIE, EDMUND A presidential hopeful in the 1972 campaign.

NASON Vera Smith's maiden name.

NIXON, RICHARD The president in 1974.

NOLAN, KATHY A psychic who worked for *Inside View* magazine.

NORTON, CHARLIE An eight-year-old boy from Otisfield, Maine.

O'DONNELL, DICK The owner of the Timmesdale Pub, the only beer joint in Timmesdale.

ONTELLO, MAUREEN She was mentioned as possibly being at Cathy's during the fire.

PARMELEAU, SPIDER A guest at Chuck Chatsworth's party.

PELLETIER, RUBY She owned the diner where John Smith worked on a temporary basis.

PHAT, NGO The Vietnamese groundsman who worked for Roger Chatsworth. He explained a Vietnamese children's game called "The Laughing Tiger" to John.

PRESCOTT, BUD A Phoenix sporting goods store clerk. He sold John Smith a Remington 700 .243-caliber rifle.

QUINN, LOUIS The congressman caught taking kickbacks in a parking lot scam.

RAY He was mentioned as possibly being at Cathy's during the fire.

RENFREW, ALBERT The deputy counsel for the Stillson Committee.

RICHARDS, STANBURY Dr. Vann's brother-in-law. His nickname was "Strawberry."

RICHARDSON, NORMA Warren Richardson's wife.

RICHARDSON, SEAN Warren Richardson's son.

RICHARDSON, WARREN A real estate man from Capitol City, New Hampshire.

RINGGOLD, ETTA The fifth victim of the Castle Rock Strangler. She was killed on or about October 29, 1975.

THE ROOSEVELTS According to Stillson's propaganda, the Roosevelts were trying to take over the U.S. economy and government.

THE ROTHCHILDS According to Stillson's propaganda, the Rothchilds were trying to take over the U.S. economy and government.

ROUNDS, GEORGE A teacher. Sarah Bracknell had once dated him.

R2D2 Chuck Chatsworth wanted R2D2 from his parents as a graduation present. He got a Pulsar watch instead.

RUOPP, RAYMOND San Francisco surgeon. He pioneered the procedure used on John.

RUSTY Sheriff Bannerman's dog.

SCHUMANN, LISA Student. John found her lost class ring.

SECRET SERVICE MAN The unnamed agent protecting Jimmy Carter in Manchester.

SEDECKI, GENE A new math teacher. Sarah Bracknell had once dated him.

SHANNON She was mentioned as possibly being at Cathy's during the fire.

SHERBURNE, JOHN ("FIRE BRAIN") A Max Brand character in a book Chuck Chatsworth was reading.

SHRIVER, SARGEANT Johnny chatted with him at the Newington Mall.

THE SIGN PAINTER The unnamed mental patient who was a suspect in the Frechette murder.

SIMONS, ANN A twenty-three-year-old college girl who was raped and strangled on November 12, 1972, in Colorado.

SMITH, HERB John Smith's father.

SMITH, JOHN The precognitive "Everyman" schoolteacher who had a mission, and who perdiodically visited "The Dead Zone."

SMITH, MARGARET CHASE She was known to Stillson as "that bitch" for her "Declaration of Conscience."

SMITH, VERA John Smith's mother. She was a religious fanatic.

SPIER, CHUCK An adult who was drinking Bushmill at Runaround Pond on the day John got hurt.

STARRET, MR. A patient in John's hospital room (Room 619). He was recovering from a heart attack.

STILLSON, GREG The maniacal presidential candidate who would one day destroy the world, if not stopped.

STILLSON, HARRY Greg's father.

STILLSON, MARY LOU Greg's mother.

STONKERS, MR. HARRY L. He led the ASLT. [NOTE: See the "Things" entry ASLT.]

STONKERS, MRS. HARRY L. She led the ASLT with her husband.

STRACHAN, PATTY Chuck Chatsworth's girlfriend.

STRAFFORD, ANNE A friend of Sarah's who told her about John's accident.

STRANG, KEITH A man who worked for the Phoenix public works department in December, 1978. He was questioned about John Smith.

STRAWNS, DR. The doctor who told John's parents about his condition.

STUBBS, DEENIE A friend of Sarah's. She was in grad school in Houston.

TAYLOR, OFFICER A Colorado policewoman. Bannerman called her to check on any homicides between October 15 and December 17, 1972.

THOMPSON, HUNTER He researched and wrote about the Hell's Angels.

TOOTHAKER, PAULINE The second victim of the Castle Rock killer. She was murdered at 10:00 a.m. on November 17, 1971.

TREMONT, ARNIE A mechanic at Cleaves Mills Chevron.

TWO TEENAGERS Two unnamed kids who watched John at the Wheel of Fortune.

UDALL, MORRIS A politician. Johnny shook his hand.

VANN, DR. The doctor who told John he had a brain tumor.

NORMAN D. VERIZER The Stillson Committee's chief counsel.

WEIZAK, DR. Johnny Smith's "post-coma" physician.

WIGGINS, CHIEF The Ridgeway police chief.
WYMAN, STEPHANIE Chuck Chatsworth's girlfriend.

(8)
THE DEAD ZONE
Places

AMES, IOWA Greg Stillson kicked a dog to death at a farmhouse in this town.

AUGUSTA STATE MENTAL HOSPITAL A sign painter was released from here, and became a suspect in the Frechette murder.

BANGOR HOUSE The hotel where the Smiths stayed while visiting John in the hospital.

BANGOR'S BRASS RAIL The restaurant where Sarah and Dan dined. Dan had a fight with a customer there.

BEHIND AN ATLANTA BAR Childress once beat up Herb Smith behind an Atlanta bar.

BIDDEFORD The town where Herb and Charlene Smith wanted to buy a twenty-acre farm.

THE BIRCHES The cemetery where John Smith was buried.

THE BUCKET A tavern run by Henry Burke.

CARSON'S BOG John was hurled there by the impact of his collision. It was twenty-five feet from the site of the accident.

CASTLE ROCK A town in the lakes region of Maine.

CASTLE ROCK WESTERN AUTO John and Dodd stopped there so John could rest.

THE CASWELL HOUSE The restaurant where Gendron ate, and played poker.

CATHY'S A bar owned by Bruce Carrick.

CATHY'S ROADHOUSE A bar and grille in Somersworth, New Hampshire.

CLEAVES MILLS One of the towns surrounding Orono, Maine.

CLEAVES MILLS CHEVRON Arnie Tremont worked at this station.

CLEAVES MILLS HIGH SCHOOL The school where John Smith and Sarah Bracknell taught.

CLUB PLAYBOY Johnny thought the fair reminded him of Club Playboy.

THE COFFEE POT Alma Frechette worked there.

THE CONFERENCE ROOM The room where Dr. Strawns took the Smiths and Sarah.

THE CONGREGATIONAL CHURCH AT SOUTHWEST BEND The church where Herb Smith and Charlene Mackenzie got married.

COORTER'S NOTCH A small town visited by Greg Stillson. It had eight hundred residents.

CUMBERLAND GENERAL The hospital Vera Smith was admitted to after her stroke.

DONNY HAGGAR'S GULF STATION The gas station where Frank Dodd worked after graduating from high school.

DURHAM Herb Smith once built a house for a customer there.

THE EASTERN MAINE MEDICAL EMERGENCY ROOM John wanted to take Sarah there after she got sick at the fair.

ESTY A town twenty miles north of Cleaves Mills that held "Absolutely the Last Agricultural Fair of the Year in New England."

THE FIRST METHODIST CHURCH OF BANGOR The church where Sarah and Walter were married in July 1972.

FLAGG STREET, VEAZIE Sarah Bracknell once had an apartment on Flagg Street. She applied for jobs in Veazie. [NOTE: Flagg is...well, you know who Flagg is, don't you!? See the sections on *The Stand*, *The Eyes of the Dragon*, and *The Drawing of the Three* in this volume.]

FOURTH STREET PHOENIX SPORTING GOODS STORE The store where John bought the Remington rifle with which he planned to assassinate Greg Stillson.

HART HALL Sarah's dorm.

HOLIDAY INN, PORTSMOUTH The motel where John once stayed.

JACKSON HOUSE The hotel John stayed at in Jackson.

JACKSON TOWN HALL ROOMS The rooms Johnny passed to get to the gallery above the rear of the meeting hall: Town Manager, Town Selectman, Tax Assessor, Men's O'Seer of the Poor, and Ladies.

JON'S The Bridgton restaurant where John met Bannerman.

KITTERY, MAINE The town where John was living when he answered the ad for a tutor.

L.L. BEAN The store where Greg Stillson once bought loafers.

LAUREL ESTATES An illegal real estate deal Chuck Gendron had been involved in.

LEWISTON GENERAL HOSPITAL Chuck Spier was sent there when his car battery exploded in his face.

MANCHESTER Jimmy Carter shook hands at the shoe factory there.

NEW HAMPSHIRE STATE PRISON This prison is where they stamp "Live Free or Die" on New Hampshire license plates.

NEWINGTON MALL John chatted with Sargent Shriver there.

O'MIKES A local pizza-and-beer hangout.

110 NORTH MAIN ST., CLEAVES MILLS John Smith's Cleaves Mill's address.

PETER'S CANDLELIGHTER Greyhound buses stopped there.

PHOENIX AMTRAK TERMINAL The terminal where John bought his ticket from Phoenix to New York.

PHOENIX OFFICE SUPPLY, INC. The store where John bought a large attache case for $149.95.

PITTSFIELD ACADEMY Prep school. John suggested Chuck Chatsworth go there.

POWNAL The Maine town where John grew up.

RAPPAHANNOCK RIVER John visualized a bridge over this river in Virginia.

RFD #1 POWNAL John Smith's mailing address.

RIDGEWAY, NEW HAMPSHIRE The town where Greg Stillson owned a real estate and insurance business in 1971.

THE RIDGEWAY CARD AND NOTION SHOPPE This shop could be seen from Fisher's office.

THE RIDGEWAY FIVE-AND-TEN This store could be seen from Fisher's office.

RUNAROUND POND A Durham, Maine, skating pond. John Smith, at age six, was knocked unconscious at the pond.

ST. LO, 1944 The place and time near Belleau Wood where Charlene's brother Joe ("Buddy") was killed by the Nazis.

THE SHADE A movie theater in Cleaves Mills that showed art films and forties nostalgia flicks when school was in session.

THE SHOE FACTORY A factory in Manchester. Jimmy Carter once shook hands there.

624 CENTER STREET Eileen Magown's address.

SOUTH PARIS The paper town in Western Maine where Sarah Bracknell grew up.

SUNNINGDALE ACRES An illegal real estate deal that Chuck Gendron had been involved in.

TIBBET'S GARAGE A garage in Hampden. They fixed John's car.

TIMMESDALE, NEW HAMPSHIRE A small town west of Durham.

TIMMESDALE PUB A beer joint in Timmesdale owned by Dick O'Donnell.

TULSA, OKLAHOMA The town where Greg Stillson was born.

24 HOWLAND STREET The address of the apartment Dave found for John in Cleaves.

VIETNAM Dan thought he was going there after receiving orders for a physical.

WATERGATE HOTEL The hotel once mentioned by Herb to John.

WATERVILLE The town where a teacher's convention was held.

WILDWOOD GREEN Greg Stillson found Jesus in Wildwood Green.

(8)
THE DEAD ZONE
Things

ALDOMET Vera Smith's blood pressure medication.

ALL THE PRESIDENT'S MEN The book by Bob Woodward and Carl Bernstein that John was reading when Sarah came to visit him.

THE AMERICA NOW PARTY Party formed by Greg Stillson.

THE AMERICAN SOCIETY OF NEUROLOGISTS A Washington, D.C., group. Dr. Brown presented his paper about John to the society.

THE AMERICAN SOCIETY OF THE LAST TIMES On a farm in Vermont, Vera waited with these people for the end of the world.

THE AMERICAN TRUTHWAY BIBLE Greg Stillson sold them for a dollar sixty-nine.

THE AMERICAN TRUTHWAY DELUXE WORD OF GOD Greg Stillson sold them for nineteen ninety-five.

THE AMERICAN TRUTHWAY NEW TESTAMENT Greg Stillson sold them for sixty-five cents.

AN AMERICAN TRUTHWAY PAPERBACK A book Greg Stillson sold. Its full title was *American Truthway: The Communist-Jewish Conspiracy Against Our United States.*

APPLE ZAPPLE The wine John once bought for Sarah.

"AS THE WORLD TURNS" The TV show watched in Cathy's Roadhouse.

THE ASLT The American Society of the Last Times.

ATTACHE CASE The case John bought at Phoenix Office Supply, Inc., from Dean Clay for $149.95. He bought it to hold the Remington rifle with which he was going to assassinate Greg Stillson.

AUGUST 19 The day John went to Trimbull to see Greg Stillson.

"BABY LETS FUCK" The message written on a red t-shirt worn by an unnamed boy.

BANGOR & ORONO YELLOW CAB The cab John was riding in during his accident.

THE BANGOR *DAILY NEWS* The paper David Bright wrote for.

BAPTIST Vera Smith's religion.

A BETTE DAVIS FILM A movie Sarah Bracknell once watched.

BIC LIGHTER Greg Stillson used one to burn the "Baby Let's Fuck" t-shirt.

"THE BIG CASINO" John Smith's term for assassination.

BLACK LABEL BEER Herb Smith's drink.

BLESSED COLTSMORE CLOTH The cloth blessed by Reverend Freddy Coltsmore of Bessemer, Alabama. Vera insisted Herb wrap it around his broken leg.

BMOC "Big Man on Campus"; Chuck Chatsworth was a BMOC.

THE BOSTON *GLOBE* Greg Stillson wrote to this newspaper about Vietnam. He also advocated the death penalty for heroin pushers.

BUD The beer Andrew Dohay ordered.

BUICK The car driven by Andrew Dohay.

A BUMPER STICKER Sarah remembered seeing a bumper sticker that said "If the Rapture's Today, Somebody Grab My Steering Wheel."

A "BUTCH CASSIDY AND THE SUNDANCE KID" POSTER Hanging in Eileen's house.

CADILLAC Roger Chatsworth's car. It was a restored 1957 model.

CAMPBELL'S TOMATO SOUP The soup John Smith ate when he got home from Runaround Pond.

CAROUSEL A ride Sarah and John went on.

CARRIE Patty Strachan accused John Smith of setting the fire at Cathy's with his mind, "just like in that book *Carrie*." [NOTE: See the section on *Carrie* in this volume.]

"CASTLE COUNTY SHERIFF" The sign on Bannerman's car.

CAT SCAN The brain x-rays given to John.

"CAVETT" The TV show Sarah watched before going to bed.

CHIVAS REGAL The drink Chatsworth offered to Johnny.

CHUCK CHATSWORTH'S READING LIST IN ENGLISH CLASS His list included the three J.D. Salinger books *The Catcher in the Rye, Franny and Zooey,* and *Raise High the Roof Beams, Carpenters.*

"CITIZEN KANE" The movie Sarah and John saw on their first date.

CLINT EASTWOOD FILMS AND SPAGHETTI WESTERNS The films The Shade showed during the summer.

THE COMMUNIST-MARXIST-LENINIST-TROTSKYITE AXIS The graphs showing how the Jews related directly to the Antichrist, according to Stillson's propaganda.

"THE COOK NEEDS A DRINK" John visualized this on his father's apron during a test.

CORVETTE Chuck Chatsworth's car.

COUNTRY JOURNAL John told Stuart Clawson he freelanced for *Country Journal* magazine.

CROIX DE GUERRE The medal Hector Markstone received in World War I.

D-CON RAT KILLER This poison was found in Frank Dodd's closet.

"THE DEAD ZONE" The term John Smith used to describe what John called the black spots in his memory when he couldn't remember something.

DECEMBER 1978 The month Congressman Leo Ryan of California was shot to death on a jungle outstrip in Guyana.

A "DECLARATION OF CONSCIENCE" Margaret Chase Smith's statement.

DELTA TAU DELTA Sarah's sorority.

DEVIL'S DOZEN A bike club that disbanded in 1972.

"THE DEVIL'S DOZEN-SONNY ELLIMAN, PREZ." The legend stitched on the back of Sonny's jacket.

"DIRTY HARRY" The new Clint Eastwood movie Sarah saw with Walter Hazlett.

A DODGE CHARGER AND A FORD MUSTANG Makes and models of the two drag-racing cars that caused John's accident.

DOWNEAST John told Stuart Clawson he freelanced for *Downeast* magazine.

"DRIVER EXAMINATIONS TODAY—HAVE PAPERS READY" The sign on the door of the meeting hall where Stillson was scheduled to speak.

814-6219 Stephanie Constantine's phone number.

$86,000 The assessment on Greg Stillson's house.

$11,000 Amount of Greg's 1975 income tax on an income of $36,000.

EXTRAORDINARY DISASTER ASSISTANCE The Smiths applied for it when their medical insurance ran out.

***FATE* MAGAZINE** One of the magazines read by Vera Smith.

FERRIS WHEEL One of the rides Sarah and John went on before John's accident.

FIFTY-FIVE MONTHS The length of John Smith's coma.

FIFTY-FOUR DOLLARS The amount Johnny played on Number 19, at a 10-1 payoff, winning $540.00.

FIVE MILLIGRAM VALIUM The pill ordered by Dr. Brown for John Smith, in order to calm John down.

FLAIR Dr. Brown's pen.

A FORD WITH HERTZ STICKER The car driven by Richard Dees of *Inside View* magazine.

THE FRANK DODD/CASTLE ROCK MURDERS COMPARISON CHART:

THE MURDERS	FRANK DODD
Alma Frechette (waitress) 3:00 PM, 11/12/70	Working at the Main Street Gulf station
Pauline Toothaker 10:00 AM, 11/17/71	Off duty

Cheryl Moody (J.H.S. student) 2:00 PM, 12/16/71	Off duty
Carol Dunbarger (H.S. student) 11/?/74	Two-week vacation period
Etta Ringgold (teacher) 10/29(?)/75	Regular duty tours
Mary Kate Hendrasen 10:10 AM, 12/17/75	Off duty

All times are "estimated time of death" figures supplied by the state medical examiner.

"THE FRENCH CONNECTION II" The movie in which Gene Hackman was forcibly hooked on drugs.

"G.E. THEATER" TV show hosted by Ronald Reagan.

"GIVE PEACE A CHANCE" The legend embroidered on one pocket of Stillson's army fatigue shirts.

"GOD'S TROPICAL UNDERGROUND" A pamphlet read by Vera Smith.

GOODWILL Vera Smith called them to pick up her furniture when she tried to sell the Smith house.

THE HALLOWEEN MASK The Jekyll & Hyde mask John wore to wish Sarah "Happy Halloween."

"HAPPY DAYS" The TV show that played in the Timmesdale Pub.

HARLEYS AND BSA'S Greg Stillson's biker "honor guard" rode Harleys and BSA motorcycles.

HARLEY-DAVIDSON The bike Sonny rode.

HERB SMITH'S PHONE CALL Herb was called October 30, 1970, at 2:15 a.m. by Sergeant Meggs of the Orono branch of the state police about John's accident.

"THE HUNT FOR THE CASTLE ROCK STRANGLER GOES ON...AND ON" A three-week-old headline John found.

HYDRODIURAL Vera Smith's blood pressure medication.

"I CONFESS" The "suicide note" sign written in lipstick hanging around Frank Dodd's neck.

INSIDE VIEW MAGAZINE Supermarket tabloid. They offered John a job as a psychic. They had three million readers. Every year they published a book called *Inside Views of Things to Come*.

JANUARY 3, 1978 The date Johnny took an Amtrak train to New York. The train left at 10:30 a.m.

JANUARY 2, 1977 The date Herb Smith and Charlene Mackenzie were married.

"JOHN SMITH, MODERN RIP VAN WINKLE, FACES LONG ROAD BACK" Bangor *Daily News* headline to an article written by David Bright. [NOTE: David Bright is a real-life reporter friend of King's who also appears in *The Tommyknockers*. See the section on *The Tommyknockers* in this volume.]

JOHN'S FIRST WORDS On May 17, 1975, upon awakening from his coma, John said "The whole wad on 19"; "One way or the other"; and "My girl's sick."

JUDE THE OBSCURE A book read by Chuck Chatsworth.

JUNE 1951 The month and year Greg Stillson graduated.

JUNE 23, 1977 The date Chuck Chatsworth graduated from high school.

L4 AND L5 The fourth and fifth lumbar vertebrae. John was injected there before surgery.

THE LATE GREAT PLANET EARTH John received eight copies of this book in the mail.

THE LAUGHING TIGER A Vietnamese children's game.

"LET'S BUILD A BETTER RIDGEWAY" Stillson's campaign slogan.

A LORD BUXTON WALLET Dr. Weizak's wallet. He had a picture of his mother in the wallet.

THE MAINE TIMES The newspaper where John saw an ad for a tutor.

MANCHESTER UNION-LEADER Greg Stillson wrote to this newspaper about Vietnam. He also advocated the death penalty for heroin pushers.

MARCH 4, 1978 The date an article ran in the New York *Times* about FBI Agent Edgar Lancte. Lancte was killed by a bomb wired to the ignition of his car.

MAY 17, 1975 The day John Smith awakened from his fifty-five-month coma.

MERCEDES Shelley Chatsworth's car.

MIRROR MAZE Sarah and John went into it at the fair.

"MISS POPULARITY" Sarah Bracknell, in senior high school.

MOM'S APPLE PIE The legend embroidered on one pocket of Stillson's army fatigue shirts.

"THE MONKEY'S PAW" The W.W. Jacobs story John associated with Weizak's call to his mother.

NATIONAL GEOGRAPHIC The magazine Vera Smith scanned for pictures of the South Pole.

THE NEW ENGLAND ENVIRONMENTAL COMMISSION They held a meeting in Boston that Roger Chatsworth attended.

NEW HAMPSHIRE JOURNAL The newspaper which ran a story about questionable real estate deals.

"THE NEW HURKOS" The *Newsweek* article about John. It was on page forty-one in the December 24, 1975, issue.

NEW YORK TIMES One of the newspapers Greg Stillson wrote to about Vietnam. He also advocated the death penalty for heroin pushers.

THE NEW YORK TIMES HEADLINE "Maine Psychic Directs Sheriff to Killer Deputy's Home after Visiting Scene of the Crime." It ran December 19, 1975.

NIKON John's camera.

A 1953 MERCURY SEDAN The car twenty-two-year-old Bible salesman Greg Stillson was driving in the summer of 1955.

A 1948 DESOTO Chuck Spier's car.

$19.95 TO $29.95 The price range of Dohay's lightning rods.

A 1975 ELDORADO Dr. Weizak's car.

1973 This was the year Stillson and three businessmen built a shopping mall. It was also the year of the Arabian oil boycott, and the year Stillson drove a Lincoln Continental and ran for mayor.

NORELCO John Smith's razor.

THE OKLAHOMA RANCHERS' AND CATTLEMEN'S ASSO-CIATION They hired Greg Stillson to make it rain.

THE OLDTOWN FIRE DEPARTMENT John called them to report that Eileen Magown's house was on fire.

"THE ORAL ROBERTS SHOW" The TV show Vera was watching when she got the call about John's accident.

PABST The beer Johnny ordered in the Timmesdale Pub.

PALL MALL Greg Stillson's cigarettes.

PEPSI-COLA George Harvey's nephew drank it in the Ridgeway police station. Also, John Smith drank it with Chatsworth.

"PETER PAN'S BAND WITH NIXON OR AGNEW PLAYING CAPTAIN HOOK" How Sarah thought of the university: "Never-Never Land."

PILOT PEN The pen John used to make notes on Greg Stillson.

POLICE INVESTIGATION The sign attached to yellow nylon rope cordoning off Castle Rock crime scenes.

PORTLAND/BANGOR AIRWAYS The airline Richard Dees used.

"PRIVATE PARTY THIS EVENING ONLY 7 PM TO CLOS-ING. SEE YOU TOMORROW" Sign on Cathy's.

THE PRUDENTIAL INSURANCE COMPANY Greg Stillson worked there until 1965.

A PULSAR WATCH Chuck Chatsworth wanted R2D2 from his parents as a graduation present. He got a Pulsar watch instead.

Q-TIPS Sonny Elliman told Warren Richardson to use them to clean his ears.

RAGGEDY ANDY The doll found in Frank Dodd's room.

THE RAMONES A rock music group Stephanie Wyman liked.

"REAWAKENED COMA PATIENT DEMONSTRATES PSY-

CHIC ABILITY AT DRAMATIC NEWS CONFERENCE." A newspaper headline Sarah Bracknell read.

"RED RIVER VALLEY" The song that the custodian hummed while lighting a fire in the stove in the town meeting hall.

A REMINGTON 700 A .243-caliber rifle John bought to assassinate Greg Stillson. It was "a very nice gun with a light kick and flat trajectory."

THE RIDGEWAY, NEW HAMPSHIRE, CHAMBER OF COMMERCE Stillson joined in 1965.

THE RIDGEWAY, NEW HAMPSHIRE, ROTARY CLUB Stillson joined in 1965.

A ROI-TAN BOX The fair pitchman kept dollar bills in this box under the counter.

ROOM 619 John Smith's hospital room at Eastern Maine Medical.

"RUNT" Greg's father's nickname for Greg.

"A RUSTY GILLETTE RAZOR BLADE" Greg told Sonny the people would like to castrate him with this.

SARAH'S POSTERS Sarah had seen Dylan at Forest Hills, Baez at Carnegie Hall, Jefferson Airplane at Berkeley, and The Byrds in Cleveland.

SEPTEMBER 2, 1939 The date John visualized while holding a picture of Dr. Weizak's mother.

$700 Amount of the check given to Greg after he caused trouble for the Cattlemen's Association.

SOMETHING WICKED THIS WAY COMES A book Chuck Chatsworth told Stephanie Wyman to read.

"SOMETHING WICKED THIS WAY COMES" The Mirror Maze made Sarah think of this film.

"STAND BY YOUR MAN" A song by Tammy Wynette playing on the jukebox in Timmesdale Pub.

SUNKIST John visualized this word stamped on an orange during a test.

"THANK GOD I'M A COUNTRY BOY" The John Denver song played at the Stillson rally.

A .357 MAGNUM Dirty Harry Callahan's gun. This was the gun of choice for many Ridgeway cops.

"A TOLKIEN DWARF" Sarah looked like a Tolkien dwarf (maybe Gimli?) in the mirror in the maze.

"THE TRIMBULL HIGH SCHOOL MARCHING BAND" The banner carried by two boys leading the Trimbull parade.

U.S. GYPSUM A factory in Lisbon Falls.

THE UNLEARNING READER A book by Michael Carey Jackson.

VANTAGE GREEN Edgar Lancte's cigarette.

VERA SMITH'S MAGAZINES Vera Smith subscribed to these magazines: *God's Saucers*, *The Coming Transfiguration*, *God's Psychic Miracles*, and *The Upper Room*.

VERA SMITH'S WANT-LIST Vera Smith wanted to send away for the following: A sliver of the One True Cross of Our Lord for $99.98; a vial of water drawn from springs at Lourdes for $110.00; a cassette of the twenty-third Psalm and the Lord's Prayer recited by southern evangelist Billy Humbarr; and an autographed picture of Humbarr.

"WALTER AND SARAH HAZLETT – JULY 9, 1972" The engraving inside Walter and Sarah's wedding bands. When Sarah lost her band, John told her where to find it.

WHEEL OF FORTUNE The gambling wheel at the carnival, and the only booth still open on the midway when Johnny and Sarah went there.

THE WHIP A ride John and Sarah went on at the fair.

THE WILD MOUSE A baby roller coaster at the fair.

WILKINSON SWORD BLADES The blades Frank Dodd used to commit suicide.

WMTQ A classical radio station that broadcast from the top of Mount Washington.

YANKEE **MAGAZINE** John posed as a reporter for this magazine in order to get inside the meeting hall where Stillson was scheduled to speak. He wanted to case the place.

FIRESTARTER

DEDICATION

In memory of Shirley Jackson, who never needed to raise her voice.

The Haunting of Hill House
The Lottery
We Have Always Lived in the Castle
The Sundial

[NO CONTENTS PAGE]

BOOK BREAKDOWN

(9)

FIRESTARTER
People

ALBRIGHT, DICK A volunteer in a Shop experiment with Andy. Andy was supposed to try and push him into drinking ink.

ALFALFA Character on "The Little Rascals" films.

THE ALLEGEHENY AIRLINES TICKET CLERK Unnamed clerk who talked with two security guards.

THE AYATOLLAH KHOMEINI Cap fantasized about the possibilities of using Charlie as a "secret weapon" to telepathically influence key world figures. Khomeini was one of the people he considered influencing.

BACON, EILEEN Friend of Vicky McGee's. She was having an affair with vodka – and looked it.

BARCLAY, HORTENSE Shirley McKenzie's best friend.

BATES, NORVILLE Shop agent. He drove the green car.

BAXTER, RALPH Shop agent. He was thirty-five years old, and posed as a graduate assistant during the Lot Six experiment. Through a drug-induced ESP, Andy was able to learn the following about Ralph: "He had killed four people during his career, three men and one woman. And he had raped the woman after she was dead."

BIMBO Granther McGee's dog.

BIXBY, JEROME The author of *It's a Good Life*.

BONO, SONNY Andy watched him on TV.

BRACKMAN, GENERAL Washington-based general. Cap had to discuss the incident at Irv Manders' farm with Brackman.

BRADFORD, MR. Sally's brother. He was a schoolteacher.

BRADFORD, SALLY Eddie Delgardo's girlfriend. Eddie tried to convince her that he had had a vasectomy.

THE BRADFORD CONSTABLE "A johnny-come-lately who had lived in town for only twelve years and thought he owned the place."

BREEDLOVE, MILO Norma Manders' uncle on the Gulf Coast of Texas. He was involved in some shady business dealings. [NOTE: See the entry WHITNEY TARKINGTON.]

BURTON, FRANK The alias Andy used when he first met the Manders.

THE CAB DRIVER Unnamed driver Andy pushed when Shop agents told him to stop.

CARL Deenie's brother.

CARSON, JOHNNY Andy watched him on TV.

CASTENEDA, CARLOS Writer referred to by Andy during a discussion of the Lot Six experiment.

CASTRO, FIDEL Cap fantasized about the possibilities of using Charlie as a "secret weapon" to telepathically influence key world figures. Castro was one of the people he considered influencing.

COBHAM, BILL The Bradford postmaster. He was fifty-six.

COOK, BRUCE Shop agent.

CORA, AUNT Andy's mother's sister. His only remaining close family member.

CUNNINGHAM, LENA Woman who worked in the office of the Slumberland Motel.

CUNNINGHAM, SAM Football player.

DEENIE Charlie's friend. Deenie told Charlie about the Catholic sacrament of confession.

DELGARDO, EDDIE Soldier. Sally Bradford's boyfriend. Charlie set his shoes on fire.

DEVINE, SHIRLEY Fifty-year-old maiden lady, and resident of Bradford, New Hampshire. She had a sister in Tampa, Florida.

A DOBERMAN The dog who attacked OJ.

DOBERMANS The Shop's guard dogs.

DR. CYCLOPS Quincey Tremont compared Dr. Wanless to this movie character.

DON Norma Manders' brother. He was involved with the SDS in the mid-sixties, and participated in a plot to firebomb Dow Chemical.

DRABBLE, PETER Head groom at the Shop's stables.

DREW, FRED Irv Manders' nephew in Kansas. He grew pot. [NOTE: See entry WHITNEY TARKINGTON.]

DREYFUSS, RICHARD Actor.

DUANE Shop man who sometimes took Josie's place.

DUGAN, TERRI Friend of Charlie McGee, and a participant in the Great Swap of 1980. Charlie had been at Terri's house when the Shop agents pulled out Vicki's nails to find out where her daughter was.

EBERHARDT, CHUCKIE Three-year-old Harrison boy who pulled a pan of hot fat off the stone onto himself.

THE ENGLISH PROFESSOR Unnamed teacher Andy had in college who constantly sniffed his tie while lecturing on William Dean Howells and the rise of realism.

EVERETT, ROBERT The Bradford mailman.

THE EYES KID During the Lot Six experiment, Andy saw one of the subjects claw out his own eyes.

FLYNN, MRS. One of Andy's Lakeland neighbors.

FOLSOM, RICHARD Major Puckeridge's aide.

FRANKLIN, BEN The face on a dollar bill.

GEORGE Vicky's ex-boyfriend

GLYNIS The cab driver's girlfriend.

GORDON, JOHNNY One of Irv Manders' neighbors.

GRABOWSKI, DON Andy's friend, and a member of the English department. Don collected Polish jokes.

THE GRAD ASSISTANT The GA who told Andy that he had hallucinated Ralph Baxter and the kid who clawed his own eyes out.

GREEN, MEAN JOE Football player.

GURNEY, MRS. A woman who had once weighed three hundred pounds; she lost weight through Andy's program (and a well-placed push now and then).

GURNEY, STAN Mrs. Gurney's husband.

HACKETT, BUDDY Comedian. Andy watched him on TV.

HAMMOND, MR. One of Andy's Lakeland neighbors.

HARRIS, FRANCO Football player.

HELGA The checker in the A & P.

HOCKSTETTER, DR. A clinical psychologist and pyschotherapist.

HOFFERITZ, DR. The doctor Irv Manders called to examine Charlie.

HOLLISTER, CAPTAIN (CAP) Head of the Shop.

HOLLISTER, GEORGIA Captain Hollister's wife.

HOWELLS, WILLIAM DEAN American writer. He was responsible for the rise of realism.

HYUCK, BRADFORD Shop scientist who analyzed Charlie's telemetry tests.

JAMIESON, ORVILLE Shop agent. He was in the green car with Norville Bates and John Mayo. Orville preferred to be called "OJ" or "The Juice."

THE JOADS The family in John Steinbeck's *The Grapes of Wrath* .

JOHNSON, ARTE A comedian on "Laugh-In."

JORY, VICTOR Actor. Al Steinowitz was sometimes mistaken for Jory.

JOSIE The Shop's receptionist.

"THE JUICE" The name Orville Jamieson preferred to be called.

JULES, DON Shop agent handpicked by Rainbird to take Andy. He carried a .22 pistol.

KELLEHER, MIKE Shop employee. He monitored Charlie's room.

KENNEDY, TED Cap fantasized about the possibilities of using Charlie as a "secret weapon" to telepathically influence key world figures. "That pinko" Ted Kennedy was one of the people he considered influencing.

KNOWLES, RAY Shop agent. He was in the car with John Mayo.

LAWRENCE, D.H. English author.

THE LIBRARIAN Unnamed young man who helped Charlie find the right newspaper to send her story to.

THE LOCAL YOKEL Shop agent. With his wife, they checked hotels and motels for Andy and Charlie.

THE LOCAL YOKEL'S WIFE Shop agent. With her husband, they checked hotels and motels for Andy and Charlie.

LOMAN, WILLY Character in "Death of a Salesman."

THE LOT SIX TWELVE Here's what had happened to the twelve who participated in the study:

> "Two...had died, one during the test, one shortly afterward.
>
> Two had gone hopelessly insane, and both of them were maimed – one blind, one suffering from psychotic paralysis.
>
> One...had died in a car accident...that was almost certainly suicide.
>
> Another had leaped from the roof of the Cleveland Post Office.

Three others had commited suicide.
[One]...worked for Telemyne Coprporation.
And that left two, Andy McGee and his wife."

"THE MAD DOCTOR" How Quincey Tremont referred to Dr. Wanless.

MANDERS, IRV The farmer who picked up Andy and Charlie in his truck. His farm was later stormed by Shop agents.

MANDERS, NORMA Irv Manders' wife.

MANDROSKIS The last name of Irv Manders' family when they came to America from Poland in 1888.

MAYO, JOHN Shop agent. He was in the green car with Norville Bates. He wore a Botany 500 suit.

McGEE, ANDREW Charlie's father. He participated in the Lot Six experiment, met Vicky during the test, married her, and later they had Charlene who, due to her parents' use of the drug, was born with pyrokinesis.

McGEE, CHARLIE (CHARLENE ROBERTA) The Firestarter. Charlie was the offspring of two college students who were given an experimental drug called Lot Six. She was subsequently born with pyrokinesis – the ability to start fires with her mind. Charlie was sort of a one-note Carrie White. Her specialties included Barbecued Shop Agents and Toasted Army Boots.

McGEE, GRANTHER Andy's father; Charlie's grandfather.

McGEE, HULDA Granther McGee's wife. She was a Puritan atheist.

McGEE, VICKY TOMLINSON Andy's wife; Charlie's mother. She was one of the subjects who took Lot Six in college.

McKENZIE, SHIRLEY Dr. Hofferitz's housekeeper.

McKEON, RICH Groundskeeper at Shop headquarters.

McKINLEY, PRESIDENT The face on a $500 bill.

MERLE, MR. The man Andy had pushed to give him more confidence.

MICHAEL The infant child of one of the rest area families.

MIKE He owned the Hastings Diner.

MILTON, JOHN The author of *Paradise Lost*.

MISHKIN, MRS. Charlie's teacher.

NEARY Man on duty monitoring Charlie's room.

NECROMANCER A gelding kept in the stables at the Shop. Rainbird told Charlie that Necromancer meant "Wizard" or "Sorcerer."

THE NEWS HEAD The man who watched the New York *Times*, the Washington *Post*, and the Chicago *Tribune* for news of Charlie's story.

NOFTZIEGER, DR. The Shop's computer chief.

NORTON, T.B. The Shop's shift supervisor.

NUTTER, DR. Dr. Pynchot's former assistant.

O'BRIAN, EV Andy's friend, and a member of the English department.

"O.J." The name Orville Jamieson preferred to be called.

OSCAR THE GROUCH The name someone had written on the chart of a naked man.

PARKS, RAY One of Irv Manders' neighbors.

PASIOCO, DAVID One of Charlie's classmates. His father owned a gray van.

PASIOCO, MR. His son went to school with Charlie. Mr. Pasioco owned a gray van.

PATTON, GENERAL GEORGE S. Cap had his picture in his wall.

PAULSON, JIM Van driver who picked up Andy and Charlie and dropped them off at the Slumberland Motel.

PAYSON, CHARLIE Bradford resident and Shop agent. He owned the Bradford Notions 'n Novelties shop. It was a front.

THE PRESUICIDAL MAN Member of Confidence Associates who had calmly talked of Hemingway and suicide at a meeting Andy attended. On his way out of the meeting, Andy had given him a "push."

PUCKERIDGE, VICTOR Major involved with the Shop.

PYNCHOT, DR. HERMAN Shop doctor. Andy pushed him into

convincing Cap not to send Andy to Maui right away. In college, Pynchot was a cross-dresser. He commited suicide by sticking his right arm down a garbage disposal.

RACHEL Cap's secretary.

RAINBIRD, JOHN Shop operative and assassin. He was half Cherokee Indian.

RAMMADEN, G.M. Aging burglar who was brought to the Shop headquarters to teach agents safecracking.

RANCHER, MR. New York delicatessen owner. Andy used to play chess with him.

THE REST AREA PEOPLE When the gray van carrying Charlie stopped in a highway rest area, Andy observed the following people: Two families (one of four people, and one of three – the baby's name was Michael), two girls of about twenty, an old man and woman, two people, and a man alone.

RICHARD The Shop receptionist after Josie.

RICHARDSON, JAMES One of the students who participated in the Lot Six experiment. His drug-induced powers disappeared when the drug wore off.

ROBERTA The name that Charlie gave Irv Manders when he picked her and Andy up.

ROWLEY, JAKE He owned the Bradford general store.

ROZELLE, BRUCE Alias Andy McGee used when he signed in at the Slumberland Motel.

SECURITY GUARD #1 One of two unnamed guards who talked to the Allegheny Airlines ticket clerk.

SECURITY GUARD #2 One of two unnamed guards who talked to the Allegheny Airlines ticket clerk.

SEDAKA, GEORGE Shop agent.

SHIRLEY DEVINE'S SISTER She lived in Tampa, Florida.

SILVER, LONG JOHN Andy had a dream in which Charlie was talking to Long John Silver.

THE SLUMBERLAND MOTEL NIGHT DESK CLERK Unnamed middle-aged man who registered Andy and Charlie.

SMITH, KATHY Vicky McGee's best girlfriend in first grade. She later married Frank Worthy.

SMITH, WINSTON The main character in George Orwell's *1984*.

STEINHAM, RALPH A Dartan Pharmaceutical rep.

STEINOWITZ, AL Shop agent.

STEVE Shop agent. He drove a light brown Pacer.

TARKINGTON, WHITNEY Man from "Government Adjustments" who gave Irv Manders a check for $35,000. He threatened Irv with trouble because of Irv's pot-growing nephew, Fred Drew, and Norma's shady uncle, Milo Breedlove.

TEDDY Charlie's teddy bear. Charlie burned him up because she tripped over him.

TOM Shop agent. He drove a light brown Pacer.

TRAEGGER, CHRISTINE Hortense Barclay's best friend.

TRANTER, LOUIS Shop employee. He monitored Charlie's room.

TREMONT, QUINCEY Andy McGee's college roommate.

THE TWO JAG GIRLS Two young girls who drove a white Jaguar and who were renting a house in the Lakeland district of Harrison, on the corner of Jasmine Street and Lakeland Avenue. Andy wondered what it would be like to spend the night with both of them.

THE TWO SHOP AGENTS The two unnamed agents who killed Vicky McGee and kidnapped Charlie. Andy blinded them with a push.

UPMORE, TAMMY Friend of Vicky McGee.

VAN VOGT, A.E. Author of the short story "The Weapon Shops of Isher," the story from which the Shop got its name. [NOTE: See the "Things" entry DSI.]

VICKY'S FRIEND Unnamed girl who took the J.P. Rhine ESP card test.

VIVALDI Classical Italian composer.

THE WAITRESS Waitress at the Hastings Diner who was questioned by O.J.

WALLACE, BILL Andy's friend, and a member of the English department. Bill had to have three or four Cokes a day.

WANLESS, DR. JOSEPH The doctor who helmed the Lot Six experiments. He was dispatched by Rainbird when he began making noise about revealing the truth about the experiments and the Shop.

WAYNE, DUKE Actor.

THE WOMAN Unnamed woman on the "PTL Club" who claimed God had cured her of Bright's disease.

WORTHY, FRANK Man who married Kathy Smith.

WYETH American painter.

THE YOUNG MAN Unnamed man who worked in the car wash on Carlisle Avenue.

THE YOUNG WOMAN Unnamed woman who was adjusting her Underalls when Eddie Delgardo burst into the airport ladies' room to put out his flaming feet.

(9)

FIRESTARTER
Places

THE A & P The store where Irv shopped. Shop agents talked to Helga about Andy and Charlie.

AN ABANDONED DINER Defunct Lakeland business on Carlisle Avenue.

ALBANY The place where Andy told the cab driver to take him and Charlie.

ALBANY COUNTY AIRPORT Airport in Colonie, New York.

BEST WESTERN MOTEL Hammersmith motel where Andy took Charlie after rescuing her from the Shop agents.

BLASSMORE PLACE The street where the Dugans lived.

BRADFORD The town across Tashmore Pond. Andy bought supplies there.

THE BRADFORD GENERAL STORE The store owned by Jake Rowley.

BRISKA POWER STATION The power station hit by lightning during a bad storm.

BUCKEYE ROOM The faculty lounge in the Union Building at Harrisn State College, the school where Andy taught.

CALIFORNIA Jim Paulson's destination.

CARLISLE AVENUE Lakeland street. The gray van drove down it.

CHEMICAL ALLIED BANK OF NEW YORK Andy McGee had his accounts there. The Shop had them all closed.

COLONIE, NEW YORK The town where the Albany County airport was located.

CONFIDENCE ASSOCIATES Dale Carnegie-like group that Andy ran in New York.

DAWN Nearest town southwest of the Shop headquarters.

THE DRIVE-IN Lakeland theater on Carlisle Avenue. They were showing "The Corpse Grinder" and "Bloody Merchants of Death."

DURBAN AIR FORCE BASE Base near Chicago where Andy's plane was to refuel.

EXXON STATION Lakeland business on Carlisle Avenue.

FLAGSTAFF, ARIZONA Rainbird had a home there.

FREE CHILDREN'S NURSERY SCHOOL School in Harrison. Charlie attended there when she was four.

GETHER Nearest town east of Shop headquarters.

A GREYHOUND BUS TERMINAL Irv told Andy there was a terminal in Hastings Glen.

THE GULF COAST OF TEXAS Area where Norma Manders' uncle, Milo Breedlove, had worked some shady business dealings.

HAMMERSMITH Where the Best Western motel was located.

HARRISON STATE COLLEGE Ohio school where Andy had been an English instructor.

HASTINGS DINER Diner where OJ questioned the waitress about Andy and Charlie.

HASTINGS GLEN One of the towns the Shop agents searched while hunting for Andy and Charlie. Also, Irv Manders told Andy there was a Greyhound bus terminal in Hastings Glen. Also, it

was the town Andy told Jim Paulson he was headed for.

"THE HOT PLACE" Deenie told Charlie that this was where you'd go if you weren't washed in the blood of Christ through confession.

HUNDRED-ACRE WOOD A locale in one of the Winnie the Pooh stories.

IBM PLANT Plant where Andy's Lakeland neighbors worked.

ICELAND One of the places OJ wanted to go on his next assignment.

JASON GEARNEIGH HALL The psychology/sociology building where the Lot Six experiment was held. Andy was told to report to Room 70. (He had already brought his release form to Room 100 in the same building.)

JOHN GLEN JUNIOR HIGH SCHOOL Lakeland school at the end of Blassmore Place.

KANSAS The state where Irv Manders' nephew, Fred Drew, grew pot.

KARACHI One of the places OJ hoped his next assignment would be.

THE LAKELAND DISTRICT Area of Harrison where Andy and Vicki McGee had lived.

LONGMONT, VIRGINIA The location of the Shop.

LOOTON One of the towns the Shop agents searched while hunting for Andy and Charlie.

LOWVILLE The town where Orville Jamieson grew up.

MACY'S Quincey Tremont told Charlie that every college campus in America was like Macy's to the Shop.

MARATHON, FLORIDA Eddie Delgardo's hometown.

MAUI, HAWAII The Shop had a compound there.

MAYFLOWER HOTEL Washington hotel that Wanless stayed at.

MESSALONSETT One of the towns the Shop agents searched while hunting for Andy and Charlie.

MIKE'S CAMERA STORE Lakeland business on Carlisle Avenue.

NOTIONS 'N NOVELTIES Bradford shop owned by Charlie Payson. Charlie was a Shop agent.

OAKVILLE One of the towns the Shop agents searched while hunting for Andy and Charlie.

OHIO SEMI-CONDUCTOR PLANT Plant where Andy's Lakeland neighbors worked.

PORT CITY Town where Charlie had gone to school.

THE PSYCHOLOGY/SOCIOLOGY BUILDING Jason Gearneigh Hall. The building where the Lot Six experiment took place.

ROOM 70 The room in Jason Gearneigh Hall where the Lot Six experiment took place.

ROWNATREE POWER STATION Power station hit by lightning during a bad storm.

ST. JOHNSBURY The place where Andy told Irv Manders he was headed.

SANIBEL ISLAND, FLORIDA Town where the Shop maintained an R & R facility.

SHAKEY'S PIZZA Lakeland business on Carlisle Avenue. Andy pulled into its parking lot.

THE SHOP A clandestine agency that dealt with such things as experimental drugs and psychic phenomena. It could have been a silent arm of the CIA.

SIX FLAGS OVER GEORGIA Amusement park.

THE SLUMBERLAND MOTEL The motel where Jim Paulson dropped off Andy and Charlie.

TASHMORE POND Pond where Charlie used to go fishing with her grandfather.

TELEMYNE CORPORATION The company where James Richardson worked.

THIRD AND 70TH STREETS The New York intersection where Andy thought the Shop agents would make their move on him and Charlie.

TREMONT One of the towns the Shop agents searched while hunting for Andy and Charlie.

UNIT 16 Andy and Charlie's room at the Slumberland Motel.

UNITED VENDING COMPANY OF AMERICA The company Andy said he worked for when he signed in at the Slumberland Motel.

VIETNAM While in Nam, a claymore mine blew up in Rainbird's face, costing him his left eye.

(9)
FIRESTARTER
Things

ADOLPH'S A meat tenderizer, especially effective (or so Dr. Pynchot thought) on Hush Puppies.

THE AMERICAN SOCIETY OF ATHEISTS Granther's wife belonged to this organization.

ANDY'S ATTEMPT TO EXPLAIN CHARLIE TO CHARLIE In an attempt to explain Charlie's powers to her, Andy showed her the following books:

Lo! by Charles Fort
Stranger Than Science by Frank Edwards
Night's Truth
Pyrokinesis: A Case Book

AUGUST 1980 The month the Shop agents killed Vicky McGee and took Charlie. Andy had gotten a premonition "(something's wrong at home)" while eating lunch at school.

"AXON" Rainbird's computer code name.

"THE BAD THING" How Charlie thought of her pyrokinesis.

BEAL-SEARLES CAT TEST Caloric burn test done on Charlie at the Shop.

A BEIGE CHEVROLET CAPRICE The car driven by Orville Jamieson and George Sedaka. They stopped Robert Everett's mail truck and stole the six letters Andy had mailed.

"BOMBA THE JUNGLE BOY" BOOKS Books Charlie found in Granther McGee's attic.

A BOTANY 500 SUIT Suit worn by John Mayo.

BRIGHT'S DISEASE A woman on the PTL Club claimed that God had cured her of Bright's disease.

"BROW" Cap's computer code. His previous code name had been "RASP."

"CANCER OF THE CREDIBILITY" Cap thought that Nixon, Lance, and Helms suffered from this disease.

CHARLIE'S FAVORITE BOOKS AS A FIVE YEAR OLD Her favorites included *Winnie The Pooh*, *Mr. Toad*, and *Willie Wonka's Great Glass Elevator*.

CHARLIE'S SONGS IN IRV'S TRUCK Charlie sang the following songs in Irv Mander's truck:

"Happy Birthday"
"This Old Man"
"Jesus Loves Me"
"The Camptown Races"

CHOPIN MUSIC Music on Cap's stereo.

CIA, DIA, AND NSA Three government agencies Quincey Tremont was sure were not handling the Lot Six experiment.

A CLAYMORE MINE While in Vietnam, a claymore mine blew up in Rainbird's face, costing him his left eye.

"THE CORPSE GRINDERS" AND "BLOODY MERCHANTS OF DEATH" The double bill being shown at the drive-in movie on Carlisle Avenue in Lakeland.

CREAM AND JEFFERSON AIRPLANE Andy jokingly told Vicky that music by these bands would probably be piped in during the Lot Six experiments.

CREMORA The dry milk Cap used in his coffee.

"THE CROSSWITS" TV show Rainbird watched in the Mayflower Hotel.

D5W The IV drip. It was five percent dextrose in water. It was the solution used to administer the Lot Six drug.

DELTA TAU DELTA Herman Pynchot's college fraternity.

THE DEPARTMENT OF SCIENTIFIC INTELLIGENCE The DSI. [NOTE: See the entry DSI.]

DLT The original name of Lot Six.

DR. WANLESS'S LOT SIX MEMO Dr. Wanless sent a memo dated September 12, 1968, to Cap Hollister. Part of it read:

"...of an enormous importance in the continuing study of controllable psychic phenomena. Further testing on animals would be counterproductive (see overleaf 1) and, as I emphasized at the group meeting this summer, testing on convicts or any deviant personality might lead to very real problems if Lot Six is even fractionally as powerful as suspect..."

THE DSI The Department of Scientific Intelligence. The real name of the Shop. According to Andy, they got their name from the science fiction short story by A.E. van Vogt "The Weapon Shops of Ishtar." The story was actually called "The Weapon Shops of Isher."

EASTERN VIRGINIA POWER AUTHORITY Electric company that serviced the Shop.

AN EXPLODING BICYCLE The Shop had once paid $300,000 for a feasibility study on the bike.

GRANTHER MCGEE'S PROVISIONS In Granther's cupboard, Andy and Charlie found Campbell soups, Wyman's sardines, Dinty Moore beef stew, and Rival dog food.

GRAVY TRAIN The dog food fed to the dogs at the Shop compound.

A GRAY VAN Van owned by Mr. Pasioco.

THE GREAT SWAP OF 1980 Charlie would sleep over Terri Dugan's house, and then Terri would stay at Charlie's.

A GREEN CAR The Shop car that followed Andy and Charlie McGee in New York.

HITACHI TV It sat on the counter of the Slumberland Motel.

HOSTESS TWINKIE Snack eaten by Louis Tranter.

"I GOT A TELEPHONE CALL FROM HEAVEN AND JESUS WAS ON THE LINE" A song sung on the "PTL Club" TV show.

IRV MANDERS' ADDRESS RFD #5 Bailings Road, Hastings Glen, New York.

J.P. RHINE ESP CARD TEST Vicky's friend received fifty dollars for taking this test.

A JAMES BOND MOVIE Movie Hockstetter watched on TV.

KELVINATORS The Shop had eight huge Kelvinator air conditioners installed in the room where they would test Charlie.

THE KGB The Russian CIA.

KODAK TRI-X Andy found a crumpled film box at the base of a tree outside the cabin where he and Andy were holed up.

LEE RIDERS The jeans Andy McGee wore.

LMS 240 The license number of the nonexistent 1978 Vega. Andy made it up when he signed in at the Slumberland Motel.

LOT SIX The experimental chemical compound injected into twelve college students in an experiment designed by Dr. Wanless. Wanless described it as "essentially an hypnotic and mild hallucinogenic." It was originally called DLT.

LOTS SEVEN AND EIGHT The experimental drugs scheduled for testing after Lot Six.

MARCH 24 Charlie McGee's birthday.

MILKY WAY Candy bar eaten by one of the boys sitting around Jake Rowley's stove in the general store.

MR. COFFEE The coffeemaker in Cap's office.

THE NEW YORK *TIMES*, THE WASHINGTON *POST*, AND THE CHICAGO *TRIBUNE* Newspapers watched by the "News Head" of the Shop for news of Charlie's story.

1978 VEGA The nonexistent car Andy made up when he registered at the Slumberland Motel.

A ONE DOLLAR BILL When the cab driver balked at taking Andy and Charlie to Albany, Andy gave him a dollar and pushed him to believe it was a $500 bill. It worked.

AN ORANGE VEGA Cap's car.

ORASIN The drug the Shop decided to administer to Charlie.

A PACER Light brown Pacer driven by Shop agents Tom and Steve.

PARADISE LOST A book by John Milton. Andy had it in his car.

"THE PHIL DONAHUE SHOW" The show being watched by Lena Cunningham in the office of the Slumberland Motel.

PLEDGE When Andy found Vicki dead, her mouth had been stuffed with a rag that smelled of Pledge furniture wax.

POPEYE CARTOONS Cartoons Charlie watched.

A POPSICLE Snack being eaten by the young man in the car wash on Carlisle Avenue.

"THE PTL CLUB" TV show that Andy was watching when the power went out at the Shop.

"THE PUSH" Andy McGee's legacy from the Lot Six experiments. The Push allowed him to mentally "persuade" people to do what he wanted.

PYROKINESIS The ability to start fires with the mind. Charlie McGee had it and thought of it as "The Bad Thing."

RACHMANINOFF MUSIC The music played during the Lot Six experiment.

RAINBIRD'S SHOES He owned Gucci, Bally, Bass, Adidas, and Van shoes.

"RASP" Cap's computer code before "BROW."

RED MAN AND ZIG ZAG Rainbird rolled his own cigarettes with Red Man tobacco and Zig Zag rolling papers.

A RED PINTO The car driven by the two rest area girls.

RFD #5 BAILINGS ROAD, HASTINGS GLEN, NEW YORK Irv Manders' address.

A RICHARD NIXON POSTER Quincey Tremont had one.

ROLLING STONE The magazine that ran an article about the Shop. Also, the magazine that Charlie went to with her story.

THE ROLLING STONES AND THE DOOBIE BROTHERS Bands Andy listened to while sitting in the parking lot of Shakey's Pizza waiting for the gray van.

"THE ROOKIES" TV show Charlie watched.

SAFECRACKING G.M. Rammaden's specialty.

THE SAN DIEGO PADRES According to Jim Paulson, the Padres would win the World Series.

SEIKO WATCH Rainbird bought a Seiko digital watch in Venice.

SEPTEMBER 12, 1968 The date of Dr. Wanless's Lot Six memo. [Note: See entry DR. WANLESS'S LOT SIX MEMO.]

THE SHOP SIGNS The fence outside the Shop's headquarters was marked every sixty feet by signs that read: CAUTION! GOVERNMENT PROPERTY! LOW ELECTRIC CHARGE RUNS THROUGH THIS FENCE!

"STARSKY & HUTCH" TV show.

A STEVIE WONDER SONG It was playing on the jukebox in the Hastings Diner.

"STILL THE SAME" Song by Bob Seger. It was playing on Andy's car radio.

A TERRORIST FIRE-BOMB ATTACK How the media reported the destruction at Shop headquarters.

THE TERRORIST GROUPS After Charlie's destruction of Shop headquarters, the following groups took credit for the "terrorist bombing": the Japanese Reds, the Khadafi Splinter of the Black September, and the Militant Midwest Weatherpeople.

.38 SMITH & WESSON Josie's gun. She kept it in her top desk drawer.

THORAZINE The drug that the Shop decided was best for Andy.

"A THOUSAND AND ONE NIGHTS" The painting on the side of Jim Paulson's van. He picked up Andy and Charlie.

.357 MAGNUM Orville Jamieson's gun. He called it "The Windsucker."

"TODAY"; "GOOD MORNING, AMERICA"; AND "CBS NEWS" The TV shows that carried the story of the destruction of the Shop headquarters. They reported it as a terrorist fire-bomb attack.

$200 The fee Andy and Vicky were paid to participate in the Lot Six experiment.

THE U.S. BUREAU FOR GEOLOGICAL UNDERSTUDIES The name Rainbird used to tap into the Shop's computer network. His access code name was "AXON."

U.S. INTELLIGENCE They ran the Lot Six experiment.

U.S. OLYMPIC DRINKING TEAM SWEATSHIRT Shirt worn by Don Jules.

UNDERALLS A young woman was adjusting her Underall pantyhose when Eddie Delgardo burst into the ladies room to put out his flaming feet.

UNITED AIRLINES, ALLEGHENY, AMERICAN, AND BRANIFF The airlines checked by the Shop agents looking for Andy and Charlie.

UTICA CLUB The beer Irv Manders gave Andy.

THE VACATION DECALS Andy found a suitcase in the cabin where he and Charlie were staying. It had decals on it from Grand Rapids, Niagara Falls, and Miami Beach.

VAN GOGH PRINTS Prints in Cap's living room.

VANTAGE BUTTS Andy found six of them at the base of a tree outside the cabin where he and Charlie were holed up.

VICKI'S CLEANING SUPPLIES In the cubbyhole under Vicky's sink were the following cleaning supplies: Lestoil, Biz, Tide, and Spic & Span.

THE WATERGATE SCANDAL Government fiasco referred to by Quincey Tremont.

"THE WEAPON SHOPS OF ISHER" The science fiction short story by A.E. van Vogt from which the Shop got its name. [Note: See the entry DSI.]

WELCH'S A grape juice.

"WILLIAM WILSON" A short story by Edgar Allan Poe that Andy had read in high school.

WILLYS JEEP Irv Manders' jeep. Irv gave it to Andy and told him to use it to get to Vermont.

THE WIND IN THE WILLOWS Cap's face reminded Charlie of illustrations from *The Wind in the Willows*.

"THE WINDSUCKER" Orville Jamieson's .357 Magnum.

A WOOLCO CIRCULAR Andy found one in his mailbox.

WORLD WAR II V-ROCKET The Shop compound looked like it had been hit by a WW II V-rocket after Charlie's rampage.

ROADWORK

DEDICATION

In memory of Charlotte Littlefield
Proverbs 31:10-28

[NO CONTENTS PAGE]

BOOK BREAKDOWN

Prologue—(Three lines from a "Man-in-the-street interview concerning Viet Nam, circa 1967" followed by a nineteen-paragraph untitled section.)

PART ONE
November

Chapter 1: November 20, 1973
Chapter 2: November 21, 1973
Chapter 3: November 22, 1973
Chapter 4: November 23, 1973
Chapter 5: November 25, 1973
Chapter 6: November 26, 1973

(10)
ROADWORK
People

ADAMS, NICK Nicholas Frederic Adams. The fictitious "cousin" invented by Bart Dawes. He told Harry, the proprietor of Harvey's Gun Shop, that he was buying the .44 Magnum for his cousin Nick, who supposedly had bought him a sixty-horsepower Evinrude motor. [NOTE: For an incisive look at King's use of the name "Nick Adams" and how it relates to the work of Ernest Hemingway, see the *Roadwork* chapter in Michael Collings' terrific 1985 Starmont volume, *Stephen King as Richard Bachman*. Information on Starmont House can be found in Part VI, "Beneath the Sheet," of this volume.]

ALAN One of Magliore's men. Bart met Ray and Alan at the Revel Lanes Bowladrome to pick up the explosives he would later use to blow up his house.

ALBERT, DAVE The reporter covering the groundbreaking of the Route 784 extension. He also ended up covering "Dawes' Last Stand," for which the WHLM newsteam won a Pulitzer Prize.

ALBERT, HANK One of Mary and Bart Dawes' Crestallen Street neighbors. Hank bought a new house in Waterford.

ALBERTSON, RALPH He was the boss of the Blue Ribbon Laundry "Washroom" in 1953. He died of a heart attack.

ANDREA Mr. Piazzi's black mongrel bitch. He kept her chained up all day, and one day she bit Luigi Bronticelli in the throat. He needed thirty-seven stitches and, after the wound healed, he was never able to talk above a whisper.

ANDY Bart Dawes' twelve-year-old nephew. Bart bought him a chess set for Christmas.

BAKER OR BARKER A boy who lasted three hours working at the Blue Ribbon Laundry.

THE BANK GUARD The First Bank guard who watched Bart as he shoved his $34,250 in cash in his overcoat pockets.

THE BANK MANAGER The First Bank manager. He was a middle-aged man with young clothes; he had to approve Bart's city check before Bart could get half of his $68,500 in cash.

BEA Mary Dawes' sister.

BETTY A character on a soap opera that was playing on the TV in Duncan's bar.

BILL Bart Dawes' nephew. Bart bought him a G.I. Joe for Christmas.

A BLACK WOMAN WITH AN AFRO The woman who rode in the elevator with Bart when he went to Steve Ordner's high-rise office.

BRENNER, ANGIE Olivia's sister.

BRENNER, OLIVIA The twenty-one-year-old hitchhiker Bart brought home, fed, and then slept with later...even though he swore he wouldn't. Bart later set up a trust fund for her, and when she eventually saw the pictures of his house blowing up, she fainted.

BRONTICELLI, LUIGI A kid Sally Magliore knew when he was growing up. Luigi was bit in the throat one day by Andrea, Mr. Piazzi's mongel bitch. He needed thirty-seven stitches and, after that, could never speak above a whisper. He grew up and got his own barbershop in Manhattan, and was known as "Whispering Gee."

CALLOWAY, JEAN Mary Dawes' mother. When Sally Magliore once asked Bart if he wanted explosives to blow up his mother-in-law, Bart said he wouldn't waste them on her. They both laughed at that, but it didn't break the tension.

CALLOWAY, LESTER Mary Dawes' father. He was a retired engineer.

CARLISLE, KITTY A member of the "To Tell the Truth" panel.

CHALMERS, HENRY The Blue Ribbon plant foreman when Bart and Mary were first married. Bart panelled Henry's family room to help earn the money to buy their first TV.

CINDY Bart Dawes' niece. Bart bought her a Maisie the Acrobat doll for Christmas.

THE CLERK A Shop 'n' Save clerk ran up the aisle when the thirty-five-year-old woman collapsed from a brain hemorrhage.

COCKER, ANDY A Charger.

THE COMPLAINING LADY Bart received a letter of complaint from a lady who had sent the Blue Ribbon six of her husband's shirts, and they had come back with the collars burned. Bart knew that Ethel had been drinking her lunch again.

CONNIE One of Bart's Bay High School classmates. She signed his yearbook:

> "Uptown, downtown, all around the town
> I'm the gal who wrecked your yearbook
> Writing upside down—A.F.A. Connie."

COSELL, HOWARD Sportscaster.

CULLEN, BILL A member of the "To Tell the Truth" panel.

DAHL, ARLENE A member of the "To Tell the Truth" panel.

THE DANKMANS When Bart brought Olivia Brenner home, he and the Dankmans were the last families still living on Crestallen

Street West.

THE DARBYS One of Mary and Bart Dawes' Crestallen Street neighbors.

DAWES, BART Barton George Dawes. He objected to the road-work that turned his life upside down. He did something about it, and it cost him everything, including his life.

DAWES, CHARLES FREDERICK Bart and Mary's son. He was their second child. Their first was born dead. Freddy died of a brain tumor. Mary said he was born with a "built-in self destruct."

DAWES, CHARLIE Charles Frederick Dawes. Mary and Bart Dawes' dead son.

DAWES, MARY Bart's wife. Her maiden name was Calloway. She had had two children with Bart. One was born dead, the other, Charlie, died of a brain tumor.

DIMENT, ETHEL One of the former Blue Ribbon Laundry employees who showed up to see the place torn down.

DRAKE, PHIL A man Bart Dawes spoke with in Wally Hamner's den at the New Year's Eve party. He was also a "street priest" who worked at the Drop Down Mamma coffeehouse in the Landing Strip area helping teenagers.

DUNCAN The proprietor of Duncan's Bar.

AN ELDERLY WOMAN WITH AN ELASTIC BANDAGE AROUND ONE LEG She was in the waiting room at St. Mary's Hospital emergency ward when Bart went to see how Johnny Walker was doing after his accident.

ELLEN HOBART'S MOTHER She lived in Cleveland; she died of cancer within a period of three weeks. Ellen went to the funeral.

THE FABULOUS OYSTERS The Boston band that was playing at the Town Line Tavern on the night Bart got his explosives from Ray and Alan.

FEDNACH, HUGH The Mustangs' deep man.

FENNER, PHILIP T. The lawyer for the city council. He visited Bart regarding Bart's failure to relocate.

FLOYD, GRACE One of the former Blue Ribbon Laundry employees who showed up to see the place torn down.

"FREDDY" The alter ego for Dawes' dead son Charlie. Dawes heard "Freddy" as a voice in his head.

GAYLE A waitress at Nicky's Diner.

"GEORGIE" Another of the voices in Bart Dawes' head; this one, however, was his own.

GIBBS, ETHEL She worked one of the shirt presses at the Blue Ribbon Laundry. Sometimes she drank her lunch.

GORDON, JOHN T. Jack Gordon. Lawyer for the city council. He wrote Bart a letter on December 20, 1973, reminding Bart that he had until midnight January 19, 1974 to relocate, or he would be in violation of the law. He told Philip T. Fenner to bring Bart a relocation form.

THE GOVERNOR He showed up at the groundbreaking for the Route 784 extension.

GRANGER, TOM One of Bart Dawes' Blue Ribbon Laundry co-workers. Granger and Vinnie Mason went to a new German restaurant to dicker about tablecloths. Tom showed up to see the laundry torn down.

GRANGER, VERNA Tom Granger's wife. She loved rigatoni.

GREENE, LORNE When Bart got home from Harvey's Gun Shop, Mary was watching "The Merv Griffin Show." Merv was interviewing Lorne Greene about Lorne's new series, "Griff."

GRIFFIN, MERV When Bart got home from Harvey's Gun Shop, Mary was watching "The Merv Griffin Show."

HAMNER, WALLY Walter Hamner. Advertising man. He invited Bart and Mary to his New Year's Eve party. He drove a GTX.

HANK A character on a soap opera that was playing on the TV in Duncan's bar.

HOBART, ELLEN Jack's wife. Her mother died of cancer within a period of three weeks, and Ellen had to go to Cleveland for the funeral.

HOBART, JACK An old neighbor of Bart and Mary's. He and his wife Ellen moved to Northside. Bart ran into him in the Stop 'n'

Shop.

HOBART, LINDA One of the Dawes' neighbors. She had babysat for Charlie and, after his death, became a doctoral student at City College.

THE HOBARTS Mary and Bart Dawes' Crestallen Street neighbors. They moved to Northside. Bart ran into Jack Hobart in the Stop 'N Shop after they moved.

JACKSON, DICK A man Mary Dawes danced with at Wally Hamner's New Year's Eve party.

JACKSON, MRS. Dick Jackson's wife. She was at Wally Hamner's New Year's Eve party. After she was introduced to Bart she went to throw up.

JEFF The guy Olivia had lived with before she decided to hitchhike to Las Vegas.

JOHN The proprietor of John's TV, the shop where Bart and Mary bought their first TV. [NOTE: See the "Things" entry AN RCA CONSOLE.]

JONES, HARRY The Blue Ribbon Laundry worker who was sent to pick up Johnny Walker's load of laundry after Johnny was injured in an accident on Deakman Street while driving the laundry truck.

KEESON, BETTY While working in the laundry, Betty slipped on a wet floor and broke her arm. The Tarkingtons paid her hospital bill.

KELLER, DICK The Dawes' first floor neighbor in the early years of their marriage. Dick helped Bart carry their RCA console up to the third floor when Bart and Mary had successfully saved up enough to buy it.

KILGALLON A Blue Ribbon Laundry customer.

KING, LIEUTENANT HENRY The police officer who investigated the fire-bombing of the Route 784 extension site.

KNAUER, MRS. A lady on television who talked about saving energy.

A KOREAN, A SOUTH VIETNAMESE, AND A UGANDAN CHILD The children supported by the Ordners.

THE LADY WHO CASHED HER SOCIAL SECURITY CHECK The First Bank customer who was next in line after Bart cashed his $68,500 city check.

LANE, FRANCIS The owner of the Lane Construction company.

LANG, ALICIA Tony's wife.

LANG, TONY One of Mary and Bart Dawes' Crestallen Street neigbors. Tony and his wife Alicia moved to Minnesota because Tony requested a new territory. He got it.

A LITTLE BOY IN A RED KNITTED CAP Before Bart went into Harvey's Gun Shop, he saw a little boy in a red knitted cap go by. The boy's mouth was open to catch a snowflake.

LOVECRAFT, H.P. Bart remembered reading Lovecraft's Cthulhu Mythos stories as a young boy.

MAC A fat man who was in Harvey's Gun Shop when Dawes first entered. Mac was a customer who was waiting for a Cobra and a Menschler.

MAGLIORE, SALLY Hood. He was a big fat guy with nine chins and a cataract. He was into dope, girls, gambling, crooked investments, and sharking. His nickname was "Sally One-Eye." His "legitimate" business was Magliore's Guaranteed Okay Used Cars, out on the Landing Strip. Sally did ten months of a two-to-five bit in 1946 for carrying a concealed weapon; in 1952, he beat a conspiracy rap; in 1955, he beat a tax evasion rap; and in 1959 he got a receiving-stolen-property rap which he didn't beat. He did eighteen months in Castleton.

MAGLIORE'S SALESMAN Bart saw one of Magliore's salesmen talking to a young kid in a red silk jacket when he arrived at Magliore's used car lot. The salesman wore a gray-green topcoat.

MAGLIORE'S SECRETARY When Bart visited Magliore's used car lot, she was sitting in a cubicle in Magliore's outer office working an adding machine.

MAMMA JEAN Mary's mother.

THE MAN IN THE PONTIAC A man in a Pontiac skidded

through a red light on Deakman Street and hit Johnny Walker's Blue Ribbon Laundry truck.

A MAN WITH HIS THUMB WRAPPED IN A GIANT DRESS-ING He was in the waiting room at the St. Mary's Hospital emergency ward when Bart went to see how Johnny Walker was doing after his accident.

MANSEY, PETE A guy who worked for Sally Magliore at Magliore's Used Cars.

MASON, ROBERTA Bobbie Mason. Vinnie Mason's daughter.

MASON, SHARON Vinnie Mason's daughter. Her favorite actors were Paul Newman and Clint Eastwood.

MASON, SHARON Vinnie Mason's wife.

MASON, VINNIE One of the men who worked with Dawes at the Blue Ribbon Laundry. He worked for Steve Ordner.

MAUREEN One of the former Blue Ribbon Laundry employees who showed up to see the place torn down.

MONOHAN The realtor handling the Waterford plant sale.

MOORE, GARY The host of "To Tell the Truth."

NAISH, DONALD P. Dead Democrat. He died in a car crash. Victor Winterburger was running for his seat.

NIXON, RICHARD The Ordners were Democrats, but had been Democrats for Nixon.

THE OLD WHITE BOOZER When Bart went to see Phil Drake, he was one of Drop Down Mamma's customers.

OLSEN The fictitious realtor Bart invented when Mary asked him who was selling him a new house.

ORDNER, CARLA Stephan Ordner's wife.

ORDNER, STEPHAN Steve Ordner. A managerial bigwig with Amroco, the corporation that owned the Blue Ribbon Laundry.

THE ORDNER'S MAID She opened the door for Bart when he visited the Ordners.

PHYLLIS Bart Dawes' secretary at the Blue Ribbon Laundry.

PIAZZI, MR. A man Magliore knew when he was growing up. Piazzi had a black mongrel bitch that he kept chained up all day.

POLLACK, STEVE Dave Radner's helper.

PRESTON, BOB Mary Dawes was having Christmas dinner with Bob and Janet.

PRESTON, JANET Mary Dawes was having Christmas dinner with Bob and Janet.

THE QUINNS One of Mary and Bart Dawes' Crestallen Street neighbors. Bart made the WHLM camera team set up on their lawn before he blew up his house.

RACHEL The tired-looking young woman's daughter.

RADNER, DAVE The man who ran the "Washroom" at the Blue Ribbon Laundry.

RAY One of Magliore's men. Bart met Ray and Alan at the Revel Lanes Bowladrome to pick up the explosives with which he would blow up his house.

RESTON, MURIEL State represenattive.

REYNOLDS, BOB The WDST six o'clock anchor. His show was called "News-plus-Sixty."

RHONDA She worked one of the shirt presses at the Blue Ribbon Laundry.

RICKER, MRS. The woman who ran the nursery school that Charlie Dawes had attended before he died.

RUCKER The quarterback for the Mustangs.

ST. CLAIRE, JOANNA Jean Calloway's cousin. Joanna lived in Minnesota.

SALES, SOUPY A member of the "To Tell the Truth" panel.

SALLY MAGLIORE'S BROTHER Sally Magliore's brother went to Puerto Rico every year from November 1 through April 15. He owned a hotel there.

"SALLY ONE-EYE" Sally Magliore.

A SALVATION ARMY SANTA He stood in front of the Norton U-Wash-It and said "God bless you" to Bart.

SHARON The wife of a guy who picked up Olivia hitchhiking. [NOTE: See the entry SHARON'S HUSBAND.]

SHARON A character on a soap opera that was playing on the TV in Duncan's bar.

SHARON'S HUSBAND A guy who picked up Olivia hitchhiking, and said his wife Sharon's name the whole time he was having sex with her. He came in fourteen seconds.

THE SHRINERS The Shriners had a convention at the Holiday Inn, and the Blue Ribbon Laundry got their sheets and towels for cleaning. Ron Stone said they were "the cummyest sheets I ever seen."

THE SMART MICK REALTOR The realtor who kept telling Bart he had to move on closing the deal on the new Waterford plant.

STAUFFER, BILL One of the Dawes' neighbors. He once drove a go-kart through a board fence into someone's swimming pool.

THE STAUFFERS One of Mary and Bart Dawes' Crestallen Street neighbors.

STONE, RON The Blue Ribbon Laundry's foreman. He showed up to see the laundry torn down.

SWINNERTON, HARRY Harold Swinnerton. The proprietor of Harvey's Gun Shop.

SWINNERTON, HARVEY Harold Swinnerton's brother, and the original proprietor of Harvey's Gun Shop. He had died eight years prior to Bart's purchases at the gun shop.

SYLVIA Bart Dawes' niece. Bart bought her a Barbie doll for Christmas.

TARKINGTON, DON Ray's father. He ran the laundry with Ray. Don's father had started the laundry in 1926.

TARKINGTON, MR. Don Tarkington's father. He started the Blue Ribbon Laundry in 1926.

TARKINGTON, RAY After Ralph Albertson died of a heart attack in 1953, Bart went to Tarkington and asked for Ralph's job.

A TEENAGE KID WITH A BROKEN ARM He was in the waiting room of the St. Mary's Hospital emergency ward when Bart went to see how Johnny Walker was doing after his accident.

THE TELLER WITH THE SIN-BLACK HAIR The First Bank teller who cashed Bart's $68,500 city check. Her salary was $6,850 a year.

TINA Bart Dawes' niece. Bart bought her a Chatty Cathy doll for Christmas.

THE TIRED-LOOKING YOUNG WOMAN The only other customer besides Bart in the Norton U-Wash-It. She had her daughter Rachel with her.

TREMONT, RALPH A friend of Bart's who had an "aging" Chris-Craft sailboat. Bart helped earn the money for their first TV by painting Ralph's boat.

THE TWO CHECKOUT GIRLS Two Shop 'n' Save checkout girls ran up the aisle when the thirty-five-year-old woman collapsed from a brain hemorrhage.

TWO MEN Fenner and two men got out of a green sedan in front of Bart's house on the day he was supposed to be off the premises.

TWO POLICEMEN Two cops got out of a squad car in front of Bart's house on the day he was supposed to be off the premises.

UPSHAW, DONNA Bart and Mary had watched TV with Donna at her house just after Bart and Mary had married.

THE UPSHAWS Bart and Mary had watched "Your Hit Parade" and "Dan Fortune" at the Upshaws' house just after they were married. When they got home that night, Mary had talked Bart into buying their own TV.

UPSLINGER, DON One of Bart's Crestallen Street neighbors.

UPSLINGER, KENNY One of the Dawes' neighbors. He delivered Bart Dawes' morning newspaper.

THE UPSLINGERS One of Mary and Bart Dawes' Crestallen Street neighbors. They had a boy named Kenny.

VONNEGUT, KURT Author of *Slaughterhouse Five*. He was banned in Drake, North Dakota.

VOREMAN, GENE The Charger who punted.

WALKER, ARNIE Johnny Walker's brother.

WALKER, COREY EVERETT Johnny Walker.

WALKER, JOHNNY A Blue Ribbon Laundry delivery truck driver. On November 28, 1973, a man in a Pontiac skidded through a red light on Deakman Street and hit Johnny while he was driving the Blue Ribbon Laundry truck. Johnny had started working at the laundry in 1946. Johnny's real name was Corey Everett Walker.

WALKER, MRS. Johnny Walker's wife. She had died in 1956 while on a vacation trip.

WALLACE, TINA HOWARD A woman at Wally Hamner's party who kissed Bart.

WASSERMAN, PETER He was in charge of deliveries at the Blue Ribbon Laundry.

"WHISPERING GEE" Luigi Bronticelli.

WICKER, TOM The author of the book *Facing the Lions*.

"WILT CHAMBERLAIN" Bart saw a black guy driving a pimpo-mobile (a pink Cadillac Eldorado); the guy was as tall as Wilt Chamberlain.

WINTERBURGER, VICTOR The Democratic candidate for the seat of the late Donald P. Naish.

THE WOMAN BEHIND BART The woman behind Bart in the Shop 'n Save screamed weakly when she saw the young woman die of a brain hemorrhage in the aisle.

THE WOMAN WHO DIED IN THE SHOP 'N' SAVE While shopping at the Shop 'n Save, Bart saw a thirty-five-year-old woman die of a brain hemorrhage.

YOUNG, MRS. She worked for Mrs. Ricker at the nursery school Charlie Dawes had attended before he died.

A YOUNG BLACK KID IN AN OVERSIZED PEA COAT When Bart went to see Phil Drake, the black kid was one of Drop Down Mamma's customers.

THE YOUNG DOCTOR A young doctor who had been shopping at the Shop 'n' Save with his wife pronounced the thirty-five-year-old woman dead when she collapsed from a brain hemorrhage.

THE YOUNG DOCTOR'S WIFE Her husband pronounced the thirty-five-year-old woman dead when the woman collapsed from a brain hemorrhage in the Shop 'n' Save.

A YOUNG KID IN A RED SILK SPORTCOAT Bart saw one of Magliore's salesmen talking to a young kid in a red silk jacket when he arrived at Magliore's used car lot. The salesman wore a gray-green topcoat, and was trying to sell the kid a Mustang.

YOUNGER, DR. The doctor who had treated Charlie Dawes, and who told Bart and Mary that Bart's brain tumor was inoperable.

(10)
ROADWORK
Places

A & S TIRES The shop that put on Bart Dawes' snow tires.

ALASKA Bart thought that Monohan would probably find the need to go visit some relatives in Alaska (or Bombay for that matter) after five o'clock on the day the option ran out on the new Waterford plant.

AN AMERICAN LEGION DINNER The place where Victor Winterburger made his remarks about Bart's vandalism of the Route 784 construction site.

AMROCO The corporation that bought the Blue Ribbon Laundry.

THE ARNOLD TRAVEL AGENCY While fantasizing about going away with Olivia, Bart called this travel agency, but then hung up.

AUTOMATIC INDUSTRIES COMPANY The company that serviced the Bowl-A-Score machine in Duncan's bar.

BALTIMORE, MARYLAND Mary Dawes' sister Bea lived in Baltimore.

BART'S FANTASY TRIP WITH OLIVIA After Bart signed the relocation form and took the city's money, he thought about tracking down Olivia in Vegas and going off on a trip to the South Seas, Hong Kong, Saigon, Bombay, Athens, Madrid, Paris, London, and finally to New York.

BAY HIGH SCHOOL One of the high schools Bart Dawes attended. (The other was Grover Cleveland High School.) Their

yearbook was called the *Centurion*.

BENJAMIN'S A bar where four-drink lunches were not uncommon. (Particularly for Steve Ordner.)

BENJY'S GRILLE The diner where Bart usually had coffee.

THE BLUE RIBBON LAUNDRY The place where Bart Dawes worked.

BOCA RIO Hunting enclave in Mexico. Harry at Harvey's Gun Shop asked Bart if this was where "Nick Adams" and his buddies were going.

BOSTON The Fabulous Oysters were from Boston.

A BOWLING ALLEY One of the places Bart passed on his way to Magliore's.

BRITE-KLEEN The Brite-Kleen company offered Tom Granger a job.

THE CANAL OF TEARS As Bart sat drinking and wallowing in despair, he felt like he was visiting Disney World's newest head trip, "Self-Pity Land," where you could take a gondola ride down the "Canal of Tears," and visit the "Museum of Old Snapshots." (You could also go for a ride in the Wonderful NostalgiaMobile, driven by Fred MacMurray.)

CASTLETON The prison where Sally Magliore did eighteen months in 1959 on a receiving-stolen-property rap.

CENTRAL HOSPITAL A new laundry account for the Blue Ribbon Laundry.

CENTURION Name of the yearbook at one of the high schools Bart Dawes attended.

CHICAGO When Bart picked up Olivia hitchhiking, she asked him if he was going all the way to Chicago when he said he'd take her to the end of the highway. She hadn't realized that the Route 784 extension was under construction.

CHICAGO OR GARY Bart said that there was a board of directors in Gary or Chicago who knew nothing about the laundry business.

CINEMA MCMXLVII A suburban theater that Bart imagined would evolve if theater multiplexes continued to grow as they had.

CINEMAS I, II, AND III Suburban theaters.

CITY COLLEGE Linda Hobart was a doctoral student at City College.

THE CLEAN LIVING CAR WASH The car wash Bart usually took the LTD through.

CLEVELAND Ellen Hobart's mother lived in Cleveland. Ellen went there for her mother's funeral.

CONNECTICUT Bart Dawes had lived in Connecticut as a boy.

THE CORNER OF RICE AND VENNER STREETS The Norton intersection Bart dreamed about. He dreamed that Charlie rather than Luigi Bronticelli had been bitten by Mr. Piazzi's dog.

COTTER'S STREAM On a Grover Cleveland High School sophomore class trip to Cotter's Stream, Tina Howard had let Bart rub her breast through her blouse.

CRAGER PLAZA Bart had once made a mistake in billing a motel in Crager Plaza, and Ray Tarkington had thrown him against a door.

CRESCENT Bart looked at a house in Crescent offered for $48,000. He and Mary couldn't afford it.

CRESSEY STUDIOS The photographers who had taken Bart Dawes' Bay High School yearbook photo.

A DAIRY FREEZ One of the places Bart passed on his way to Magliore's.

DEAKMAN STREET A man in a Pontiac skidded through a red light on Deakman Street, hitting Johnny Walker in the Blue Ribbon Laundry truck.

A DEPARTMENT STORE After Bart had his "psychiatrist" talk with Mary at Handy-Andy's, he went Christmas shopping at a large department store.

THE DIAL HELP CENTER The place where Phil Drake spent most of his evenings.

DOCTOR'S HOSPITAL The hospital where Charlie Dawes was diagnosed as having an inoperable brain tumor.

DRAKE, NORTH DAKOTA The town where Kurt Vonnegut's *Slaughterhouse Five* was banned.

A DRIVING RANGE One of the places Bart passed on his way to Magliore's.

DROP DOWN MAMMA The coffeehouse where Phil Drake worked on weekday afternoons.

DUMONT STREET The Westgate street that was turned into the Kennedy Promenade.

DUNCAN'S A quiet neighborhood bar on Barker Street. Bart stopped there to call Magliore.

THE EGYPTIAN TRADE EXPO When Bart told Sally Magliore that he wanted to buy explosives, Sally wanted to know if he was going to blow up the Egyptian trade exposition.

FIR STREET The street where the bus dropped Bart off for work.

FIRST BANK The bank that cashed Bart's $68,500 city check.

THE GARSON BLOCK A block of buildings in Westgate. It had been demolished.

GENERAL DELIVERY, LAS VEGAS, NEVADA Olivia Brenner's mailing address.

THE GOODWILL SHOP After Charlie's death, Bart and Mary had given all of his toys to the Goodwill Shop in Norton.

THE GRAND THEATER A theater Bart remembered. It had been demolished.

GREENWOOD Philip T. Fenner owned a house in Greenwood.

GROVER CLEVELAND HIGH SCHOOL One of the high schools Bart Dawes attended. (The other was Bay High School.) On a sophomore class trip to Cotter's Stream, Tina Howard had let Bart rub her breast through her blouse.

HANDY-ANDY The restaurant where Bart took Mary for lunch.

HARVEY'S GUN SHOP The store where Bart bought the .44 Magnum and the .460 Weatherbee rifle for his fictitious cousin, Nick Adams.

HEBNER AVENUE PARK Bart used to take Charlie to this park before the boy died.

HELL'S KITCHEN The section of New York where Sally Magliore grew up.

HEMINGWAY TRUCKING A company for which Arnie Walker had once driven.

HENNY'S NEWSTAND The newstand where Bart usually bought his *Time* magazine.

HENREID DRIVE Steve Ordner lived on Henreid Drive.

HERON STREET The street by which Bart fled the construction site after he fire-bombed it.

A HOLIDAY INN Bart offered to pay for Olivia's Holiday Inn room, no strings attached. Instead, she went home with Bart. The Holiday Inn was also one of the Blue Ribbon Laundry's customers.

HONOLULU Jean and Lester Calloway vacationed in Honolulu three years prior to Bart's problems with the Route 784 extension.

HOWARD JOHNSON'S One of the Blue Ribbon Laundry's customers.

THE INDIANA TOLL ROAD A road Arnie Walker had once driven while working for the Hemingway Trucking Company.

JACKSONVILLE Mary Dawes' brother lived in Jacksonville.

JAMAICA Jean and Lester Calloway vacationed in Jamaica the winter prior to Bart's problems with the Route 784 extension.

THE JERSEY TURNPIKE John Chancellor reported that reduced speed on the New Jersey Turnpike had probably been responsible for fewer accidents.

JOHN'S TV The shop where Bart and Mary bought their first TV. It was an RCA Console. It cost $846, but John gave it to them for $837.

THE KENNEDY PROMENADE The street which used to be Dumont Street.

THE LANDING STRIP A bad area of Norton.

THE LANE CONSTRUCTION COMPANY The construction company that was building the Route 784 extension.

LANE 16 Bart had to meet Magliore's guys, Ray and Alan, on Lane 16 at the Revel Lanes Bowladrome. He was told they would be wearing green "Marlin Avenue Firestone" shirts.

LAS VEGAS Olivia was hitchhiking to Vegas when Bart picked her up on the highway.

M_____ The city where Bart Dawes lived. (In a letter from John T. Gordon to Bart, Bart's address was given as 1241 Crestallen Street West, M_____, W_____.)

MAMMOTH MART A huge department store that was built in a shopping center across the street from where Olivia grew up.

MANHATTAN Luigi Bronticelli (a friend of Sally Magliore's) owned a barbershop in Manhattan.

THE MAYO CLINIC The clinic where Sally Magliore had his cataract removed.

A MCDONALDS One of the places Bart passed on his way to Magliore's.

THE MENTAL INSTITUTION A new account for the Blue Ribbon Laundry.

MEXICO "Nick Adams" and six of his buddies were supposedly going hunting in Mexico.

MIAMI Jean and Lester Calloway vacationed in Miami (at the Fountainbleau) two winters prior to Bart's problems with the Route 784 extension.

MICHIGAN "Nick Adams" supposedly lived in Michigan.

MINNESOTA The state where Jean Calloway's cousin Joanna St. Claire lived.

"THE MUSEUM OF OLD SNAPSHOTS" As Bart sat drinking and wallowing in despair, he felt like he was visiting Disney World's newest head trip, "Self-Pity Land," where you could take a gondola ride down the "Canal of Tears," and visit the "Museum of Old Snapshots." (You could also go for a ride in the Wonderful NostalgiaMobile, driven by Fred MacMurray.)

NICKY'S The diner where Bart Dawes had lunch with Tom Granger.

NINO'S STEAK PIT One of the places Bart passed on his way to Magliore's.

NORTON The proceeds from the fashion show in Russell that Carla Ordner attended went to support a teenage coffeehouse in Norton.

THE NORTON DRIVE-IN One of the places Bart passed on his way to Magliore's.

PIERCE BEACH Bart dreamed he was at the beach with Charlie.

THE PLACES BART PASSED ON HIS WAY TO MAGLIORE'S He passed a McDonald's, a Shakey's, Nino's Steak Pit, a Dairy Freez, the Norton Drive-In, a bowling alley, a driving range, and two gas stations.

PONDEROSA PINES Bart and his neighbors often took their wives to Ponderosa Pines to drive little go-karts.

PORTLAND, MAINE The town where Olivia grew up.

PUERTO RICO Sally Magliore's brother went to Puerto Rico every year from November 1 through April 15. He owned a hotel there.

THE QUALITY MOTOR COURT The Blue Ribbon Laundry did their sheets.

THE REVEL LANES BOWLADROME The bowling alley where Bart met Magliore's two "Explosives Delivery" guys, Ray and Alan.

THE ROTARY Tom Wicker had once spoken at a Rotary luncheon that Bart had attended.

ROUTE 16 The road on which Magliore's Used Cars was located. Route 16 became Venner Avenue as you went further into Norton.

RUSSELL When Bart Dawes visited Steve Ordner at home, Carla Ordner was at a fashion show in Russell.

ST. MARY'S HOSPITAL The hospital Johnny Walker was taken to after he was hit by a man in a Pontiac on Deakman Street while driving the Blue Ribbon laundry truck.

THE SCREENING ROOM A suburban theater.

SELF-PITY LAND As Bart sat drinking and wallowing in despair, he felt like he was visiting Disney World's newest head trip, "Self-Pity Land," where you could take a gondola ride down the "Canal of Tears," and visit the "Museum of Old Snapshots." (You could also go for a ride in the Wonderful NostalgiaMobile, driven by Fred MacMurray.)

A SHAKEY'S One of the places Bart passed on his way to Magliore's.

THE SHOP 'N' SAVE The grocery store at which Bart usually shopped.

THE SKYVIEW SHOPPING MALL The Revel Lanes Bowladrome was just past this mall.

THOM McAN SHOES The company that was also interested in buying the Waterford plant if the Blue Ribbon Laundry didn't want it. Blue Ribbon had a ninety-day option on the plant that ran out on November 26.

THREE MOTELS Three new accounts for the Blue Ribbon Laundry.

TIMES SQUARE At Wally Hamner's New Year's Eve party, Phil Drake and Bart watched the ball atop the Allis-Chalmers building in Times Square.

THE TOWN LINE TAVERN The tavern where Bart was to drive to after meeting Ray and Alan at the Revel Lanes Bowladrome.

TWO GAS STATIONS Two of the places Bart passed on his way to Magliore's.

U-WASH-IT A laundromat in Norton.

UNION STREET A little colonial on Union Street that Bart and Mary Dawes had looked at. It was sold before they could act on it.

THE UNIVERSAL LAUNDRY Blue Ribbon's chief competition.

THE UNIVERSITY OF NEW HAMPSHIRE A University in Durham, New Hampshire, near Portsmouth. Olivia Brenner dropped out of that university in her junior year.

VENNER AVENUE Route 16 became Venner Avenue as you went further into Norton.

W_____ The state where Bart Dawes lived. (In a letter from John T. Gordon to Bart, Bart's address was given as 1241 Crestallen Street West, M_____, W_____).

THE WASHROOM The Blue Ribbon Laundry "Washroom" was run by Dave Radner.

WATERFORD There was a new suburb going up in Waterford.

THE WESTFALL CINEMA The movie theater Vinnie Mason managed. It was part of the Cinemate Releasing chain.

WESTFIELD AVENUE A street near Crestallen Street in Westgate where a high-rise housing development had gone up. It blocked Bart's view of the river.

WESTGATE The area of town where Bart Dawes lived and worked.

THE WESTGATE TOLL BOOTHS Bart was forty miles from the Westgate toll booths when he picked up Olivia, who was hitchhiking.

(10)

ROADWORK
Things

"ALFIE" A song sung on "The Merv Griffin Show."

AMERICAN EXPRESS Bart Dawes paid for the .44 Magnum and .460 Weatherbee rifle he bought at Harvey's Gun Shop with his American Express card.

AN ANDYBURGER The sandwich Bart and Mary ordered at Handy-Andy's.

AN ARCO CARD One of Bart Dawes' credit cards.

AUGUST 1937 The month and year that Andrea, Mr. Piazzi's mongrel bitch, bit Luigi Bronticelli in the throat.

AN AUTOMATIC BLOW-JOB Duncan thought that if he was still operating his bar in 1980, Automatic Services Company would probably want to take out the Bowl-A-Score machine and put in an Automatic Blow-Job machine.

A BARBIE DOLL Bart bought his niece Sylvia a Barbie doll for Christmas.

BART'S CHECKING ACCOUNT BALANCE After Bart bought his cousin "Nick" the .44 Magnum and .460 Weatherbee rifle, he came home and found his checking account statement: forty-nine debits, nine credits, and a $954.47 balance. Between November 20, 1973, and January 9, 1974, he spent $150.98 of that balance, leaving him with $803.49. After he sold his house and deposited Mary's half of the $68,500.00 check, he ended up with a final balance of $35,053.49, all of which he sent to Mary.

BART'S CREDIT CARDS When Bart was ordered by Magliore to empty his pockets, he had the following charge cards in his wallet: Shell, Sunoco, Arco, Grant's, Sears, Cary's Department Store, and American Express.

BART'S FORTY STICKS OF DYNAMITE Bart bought a crate of dynamite (malglinite) from Magliore. He wired his house as follows:

> The attic—four sticks
> The master bedroom—two sticks (one on each twin bed)
> The guest bathroom—one stick
> The guest bedroom—two sticks
> Charlie's bedroom—four sticks
> The kitchen—four sticks
> The living room—four sticks
> The dining room—four sticks
> The hall—four sticks
> The backseat of his car—eleven sticks.

BEECHCRAFT STOCKS One of the stocks owned by Lester Calloway.

THE BLADE A newspaper Bart Dawes read and/or subscribed to.

A BONNEVILLE WAGON One of the Calloway's cars.

THE BOSS OF THE DRIVERS After Bart graduated college, Ray Tarkington put him to work as boss of the drivers.

BOWL-A-SCORE A coin-operated machine in Duncan's that broke down. It was serviced by the Automatic Industries Company.

A BRUNSWICK BILLIARD TABLE The table that Steve Ordner had in his basement.

A BULOVA WATCH Don and Ray Tarkington gave Bart a Bulova watch when he paid off his $2,000 college loan. The back was engraved "Best from Don & Ray, The Blue Ribbon Laundry." It cost eighty dollars.

A CADILLAC GRAN DEVILLE One of the Calloway's cars.

A CARY'S DEPARTMENT STORE CARD One of Bart Dawes' credit cards.

A CASHIER'S CHECK FOR $2,000 Ray Tarkington handed Bart Dawes a check for $2,000 and told him to go back to college. He wanted three things from Bart:

1. Repay the loan.
2. Repay the interest.
3. Bring back what you learn in college to the Blue Ribbon Laundry.

THE CENTURION The Bay High School yearbook.

CHANNEL 9 WHLM's broadcast channel.

A CHATTY CATHY DOLL Bart bought his niece Tina a Chatty Cathy doll for Christmas.

A CHESS SET Bart bought his nephew Andy a chess set for Christmas.

A CHRIS-CRAFT Bart helped earn the money for his and Mary's first TV by painting Ralph Tremont's "aging" Chris-Craft boat.

A CHRYSLER IMPERIAL The governor's car.

THE CIGARETTES BART THOUGHT VINNIE MASON WOULD SMOKE Bart thought that Vinnie was the only one he knew who would smoke the following brands:

King Sano	Twists
English Ovals	Shit-On-A-Stick
Marvels	Black Lung
Murads	

"CITY DAY" A morning TV news program.

CITY ROADS PROJECT 6983-426-73-74-HC The Route 784 extension.

A COBRA One of the guns that Mac was waiting for. [NOTE: See the "People" entry MAC.]

COLT One of the brands of guns carried at Harvey's Gun Shop.

CONSCIOUSNESS-RAISING GROUP HYDROTHERAPY Mary Dawes' sister Bea was into this new type of self-improvement program.

THE CONSTRUCTION SITE SIGNS Bart saw three orange signs at the Route 784 extension site that said:

1. ROAD ENDS TEMPORARILY
2. DETOUR—FOLLOW SIGNS
3. BLASTING AREA!
   TURN OFF 2-WAY RADIOS

THE CONTENTS OF BART DAWES' POCKETS When Magliore ordered Bart to empty his pockets, Bart removed the following items: A Zippo lighter engraved "BGD," a package of flints, a pack of Phillie Cheroots, a tin of Phillips Milk of Magnesia tablets, a receipt from A & S tires, his car keys, forty cents in change, and his wallet.

THE CONTENTS OF BART'S WALLET When Magliore ordered Bart to empty his pockets, the following items were in his wallet: photos of Mary and himself, a driver's license, a social security card, a blood donor card, a library card, a photostat of his birth certificate, a bunch of old receipted bills, and some old checking account deposit slips.

THE CPO COAT The coat Olivia Brenner was wearing when Bart picked her up hitchhiking.

A CRANE One of the pieces of construction equipment that Bart blew up at the Route 784 extension site with his homemade Molotov cocktails. It was valued at $60,000, and was expected to be out of service for as long as two weeks.

THE "CTHULHU MYTHOS" STORIES Bart remembered reading H.P. Lovecraft's Cthulhu Mythos stories as a young boy.

"DAN FORTUNE" One of the TV shows the Dawes watched at the Upshaws.

THE DAWES' FIRST TV Bart and Mary each agreed to come up with half of the $750 they'd need to buy their first TV. Bart earned $390 by painting the Blue Ribbon's smokestack, panelling Henry Chalmers familyroom, and painting Ralph Tremont's Chris-Craft boat. Mary earned $416 by sewing. [NOTE: See the entry MARY'S SEAMSTRESS WORK.]

"DAWES' LAST STAND" The title the WHLM newsteam gave to their coverage of Bart's final standoff and the dynamiting of his house.

"THE DAY THE EARTH STOOD STILL" A movie with Michael Rennie that Bart had seen at the Grand Theater.

DECEMBER 18 The date Bart and Mary agreed to pool their earnings, in hopes of having enough to buy their first TV.

"DIAL M FOR MURDER" A movie with Ray Milland that Bart had seen at the Grand Theater.

"DIRTY HARRY" Clint Eastwood movie in which Dirty Harry carried and used a .44 Magnum.

A DODGE The car Bart saw up on a lift in Magliore's garage.

A DODGE CUSTOM CAB PICKUP The vehicle Ray and Alan drove on the night they delivered the explosives to Bart.

DROP DOWN MAMMA'S MENU It was crayoned on construction paper:

MENU
Coffee 15¢
Tea 15¢
All soda 25¢
Balogna 30¢
PB&J 25¢
Hot Dog 35¢

AN ECONOLINE VAN The van Magliore's men drove to Bart's house. It had "Ray's TV Sales and Service" printed on the side.

849-6330 Harry Swinnerton's phone number.

892-4576 The phone number of Magliore's Guaranteed Okay Used Cars.

"EIGHT-BALL" One of the X-rated movies playing at the Norton Drive-In.

$18,000 The amount of money Bart gave Magliore for Olivia Brenner's "trust fund." Magliore was to pay her dividends after $15,000 of the money was invested. (Magliore took $3,000 as a finder's fee.)

EXECUTIVE PINE OFFICE FURNITURE Bart received a mailing from this company.

EXPLOSIVES Bart Dawes told Sally Magliore he wanted to buy explosives to blow up the Route 784 extension (then in progress), along with the machinery and equipment that would build it.

FACING THE LIONS A book by Tom Wicker.

FIELD AND STREAM One of the magazines in Magliore's office.

FIFTY-FIVE DOLLARS FOR FIFTY-FIVE HOURS Bart's take-home pay in 1953.

$5,000 The amount of money Bart gave to Phil Drake for the Drop Down Mamma coffeehouse.

FORTY CENTS IN CHANGE The coins Bart Dawes had in his pockets when he was ordered to empty them by Magliore.

A .44 MAGNUM AND A .460 WEATHERBEE RIFLE The two guns Bart Dawes bought at Harvey's Gun Shop for his (nonexistent) cousin, Nick Adams.

FOUR BUGS Magliore's men "washed" Bart's house and found four bugging devices. They were put there by Fenner.

"FRED" Bart's nickname for Charlie.

A G.I. JOE Bart bought his nephew Bill a G.I. Joe doll for Christmas.

GALLO WINE The wine served when Bart visited Magliore in January of 1974.

"GEORGE" Charlie's nickname for Bart.

"THE GIFT OF THE MAGI" A short story by O. Henry.

"THE GODFATHER" A movie Bart had taken Mary to see at a theater in Waterford. The tickets had been two-fifty each.

GO-KARTS Bart and his neighbors often took their wives to Ponderosa Pines to drive little go-karts.

GOOD HOUSEKEEPING The magazine Bart read while waiting to blow up his house. He read articles on the Kennedy family, and on women and breast cancer.

"GOODBYE YELLOW BRICK ROAD" The Elton John song that was playing on the jukebox in Nicky's diner when Bart had lunch there with Tom Granger.

"A GOOD-SIZE WALNUT" As the Stones' "Monkey Man" played in the background, Bart Dawes touched the red alligator clip to the negative pole of his Sear's Die-Hard battery, exploding his house and car. His last thought was that the world was exploding inside him, and even though it was cataclysmic, it was not larger than, say, a good-sized walnut.

A GRANT'S CARD One of Bart Dawes's credit cards.

A GREEN SEDAN Fenner and two men got out of a green sedan in front of Bart's house on the day he was supposed to be off the premises.

A GTX Wally Hamner's sports car.

THE GUNS THAT DAWES RECOGNIZED When Bart entered Harvey's Gun Shop, he recognized .22's, .38's, .44's, and a .44 Magnum.

THE HARVEY'S GUN SHOP SIGN It said:

AMMO HARVEY'S GUN SHOP AMMO
Remington Winchester Colt Smith & Wesson
HUNTERS WELCOME

HERBERT TAREYTON Tom Granger's cigarette.

"HOME FOR THE HOLIDAYS" The movie Bart watched on Christmas day.

AN HONOR RACK There was an "honor" newspaper rack outside

Harvey's Gun Shop. It had a sign that said, "Please Pay For Your Paper! This Is An Honor Rack, Dealer Must Pay For All Papers."

AN IBM SELECTRIC Steve Ordner's typewriter.

"IF GUNS ARE OUTLAWED ONLY OUTLAWS WILL HAVE GUNS" A sticker on the cash register in Harvey's Gun Shop.

THE INDUSTRIAL SMOKESTACK Bart made an agreement with Mary that they would each come up with half of the $750 they'd need to buy their first TV. Bart got his by painting the smokestack behind the Blue Ribbon on weekends for $300, by paneling Henry Chalmers familyroom for $50, and by painting Ralph Tremont's "aging" Chris-Craft.

THE J.C. WHITNEY CATALOGUE The catalogue Magliore and Mansey were looking at when Bart visited Magliore's used car lot.

JANUARY 20 The date by which Bart and Mary Dawes had to be out of their house on Crestallen Street.

"JESUS! MARY! JOSEPH THE CARPENTER!" One of Sally Magliore's favorite expressions.

"THE KLASS KLOWN" Bart's high school nickname.

KLEENEX AND VICKS The two products Mary Dawes used to nurse her cold.

A KLH SOUND SYSTEM The sound system Steve Ordner had in his basement.

A LANE CONSTRUCTION COMPANY TRAILER One of the vehicles that Bart blew up at the Route 784 extension site with his homemade Molotov cocktails.

"LAS VEGAS OR BUST" The sign Olivia was carrying when Bart picked her up hitchhiking.

"LET IT BLEED" The Stones album Bart bought after he sold his house to the city.

A LIONEL TRAIN SET While Christmas shopping, Bart saw a Lionel train set in a department store. It consisted of the following cars:

> B & O
> SOO LINE
> GREAT NORTHERN
> GREAT WESTERN
> WARNER BROTHERS [WARNER
>   BROTHERS??]
> DIAMOND INTERNATIONAL
> SOUTHERN PACIFIC

LISTERINE When Pete Mansey frisked Bart Dawes, Mansey smelled like Listerine.

"THE LOBSTERMEN" The Winslow Homer painting that fell off Bart's living room wall when the police bullets thudded into the wall during "Dawes' Last Stand."

AN LTD Bart's car. It was two years old.

MAGLIORE'S SUSPICIONS ABOUT BART DAWES When Bart first visited Magliore's used car lot, Magliore suspected Bart was either with the state police, the city police, the IRS, or the FBI.

MAGLIORE'S USED CARS Sally Magliore's "legitimate" business. It was on Route 16 in Norton, and the phone number was 892-4576.

A MAISIE-THE-ACROBAT DOLL Bart bought his niece Cindy a Maisie-the-Acrobat doll for Christmas.

"MAMMA JEAN" Bart's name for his mother-in-law, Jean Calloway.

MANHATTAN TRANSFER A book by John Dos Passos that Bart told Olivia he had not read.

"THE MARCH OF TIME," "PROGRESS IN REVIEW" OR "BILLION DOLLAR BABIES" Bart Dawes' thoughts about the new suburb in Waterford.

MARLBORO Olivia Brenner's cigarettes.

MARLIN AVENUE FIRESTONE SHIRTS The green shirts that Magliore's men would be wearing at the Revel Lanes Bowladrome. Bart was to look for the shirts and then bowl a couple of strings with the guys before they went and picked up his explo-

sives.

MARY'S SEAMSTRESS WORK To earn her half of the $750 needed to buy their first TV, Mary Dawes did the following seamstress work: She:

> Made twenty-six dresses,
> Hemmed up forty-nine dresses,
> Hemmed down sixty-four dresses,
> Made thirty-one skirts,
> Crocheted three samplers,
> Hooked four rugs, (one latch-hook style),
> Made five sweaters,
> Made two afghans,
> Made two complete set of table linen,
> Embroidered sixty-three handkerchiefs, twelve sets of
>   towels, and twelve sets of pillowcases.

A MENSCHLER One of the guns that Mac was waiting for. [NOTE: See the "People" entry MAC.]

MILNOR A brand of machine used at the Blue Ribbon Laundry.

MOLOTOV COCKTAILS Bart made them in his garage and used them to blow up a crane, two bulldozers, two payloaders, a trailer, a pickup truck, and a steam shovel at the Route 784 extension construction site. He did approximately $100,000 worth of damage.

A MOVIE SCREEN Steve Ordner had one in his basement.

A MUSTANG Bart saw one of Magliore's salesmen trying to sell a a Mustang to kid in a red silk jacket.

MUZAK The piped-in music in Steve Ordner's office. It was playing Mantovani the day Bart visited Steve.

THE NATIONAL LAMPOON The magazine Phil Drake was reading when Bart went to see him at Drop Down Mamma.

1955 The year Bart Dawes went back to college, thanks to Don and Ray Tarkington.

1959 The year Don Tarkington died.

1957 The year Bart Dawes got his college degree.

1956 The year Johnny Walker's wife had died on a vacation trip.

1953 The year Ralph Albertson was boss of the Blue Ribbon "Washroom."

A 1970 AND A 1972 ELDORADO The two cars that Bart told Pete Mansey he wanted to buy from Sally Magliore as a ruse to get to talk to Magliore.

1972 The year the groundbreaking took place for the Route 748 extension.

1926 The year Don Tarkington's father started the Blue Ribbon Laundry.

NOVEMBER 26, 1973 The day Blue Ribbon's option on the Waterford plant ran out.

OLIVIA'S CHANNEL-CHANGING While watching TV at Bart's house, Olivia used the remote control to change channels: Her changing sequence went as follows: From "To Tell the Truth" to "What's My Line" to "I Dream of Jeannie" to "Gilligan's Island" to "I Love Lucy" to Julia Child to "The New Price is Right." She was looking for "Star Trek." (And honestly, aren't we all always just looking for "Star Trek"?)

OLIVIA'S DRUG-TAKING TRACK RECORD Olivia told Bart that she had taken lysergic acid, mescaline, peyote, and STP.

$100,000 The estimated amount of damage Bart did to the Route 784 extension by fire-bombing it.

ONE PERCENT INTEREST The interest rate on the $2,000 college loan the Tarkingtons gave to Bart Dawes. It came to twenty dollars.

OUTDOOR LIFE One of the magazines in Magliore's office.

OUTING CLUB 1,2,3,4 One of Bart's Bay High School activities.

A PAIR OF EARRINGS AND A TIE Every Christmas, Don and Ray Tarkington would give every woman in the laundry a pair of earrings, and every man a new tie.

PHILLIES CHEROOTS One of the items Bart Dawes had in his pockets when he was ordered to empty them by Magliore.

PHILLIPS MILK OF MAGNESIA TABLETS One of the items Bart Dawes had in his pockets when he was ordered to empty them by Magliore.

A PHONE-MATE CIRCULAR Bart received one in the mail.

A PICKUP TRUCK One of the vehicles that Bart blew up at the Route 784 extension site with his homemade Molotov cocktails.

A PINK CADILLAC ELDORADO A "pimpmobile," according to Bart.

PLAYER'S NAVY CUT CIGARETTES Vinnie Mason's cigarettes.

POE SOCIETY 3,4 One of Bart's Bay High School activities.

THE PRISM Bart's college yearbook.

"RAY'S TV SALES AND SERVICE" The sign painted on the Econoline van Magliore's men drove to Bart's house.

AN RCA CONSOLE Bart and Mary Dawes' first TV. The set cost $846, of which Bart and Mary had saved $806. (Bart had earned his $390 by painting the Blue Ribbon's smokestack, panelling Henry Chalmer's familyroom, and painting Ralph Tremont's Chris-Craft. Mary had earned hers by doing (a lot of) seamstress work.) They had spent a weekend collecting empty bottles to make up the difference, but only came up with thirty-one dollars. John—of John's TV—gave them the set for nine dollars less as a Christmas gift.

REA EXPRESS "Nick Adams" shipped an Evinrude motor to Bart Dawes by REA Express.

REMINGTON One of the brands of guns carried at Harvey's Gun Shop.

"RESTLESS WIVES" One of the X-rated movies playing at the Norton Drive-In.

ROLAIDS Harry Swinnerton gave Bart Dawes Rolaids for his gas problems.

THE ROUTE 784 EXTENSION The roadwork that took away Bart Dawes job, wife, and home—and eventually his life.

SALLY MAGLIORE'S "BUSINESS" INTERESTS Dope, girls, gambling, crooked investments, and sharking.

"SALLY ONE-EYE" Sally Magliore's nickname.

A SCREWDRIVER The first drink Bart made for Olivia Brenner after they ate at Bart's house. (She later had one of Bart's "private drinks," Southern Comfort and Seven-Up.)

A SEAR'S CARD One of Bart Dawes' credit cards.

A SEAR'S DIE-HARD BATTERY The battery Bart used to detonate the forty sticks of dynamite he used to blow up his house...and himself.

A '74 TOYOTA COROLLA Vinnie Mason's new car.

'71 VEGAS Magliore said he could sell '71 Vegas for $1500-1600. He described them as Maxwell House coffee cans and Saltine Boxes on wheels.

"SHAKY CEASE-FIRE HOLDS" The headline on a newspaper Bart saw in a rack outside Harvey's Gun Shop.

"SHAKY CEASE-FIRE HOLDS ON CRESTALLEN STREET" The newspaper headline Bart imagined seeing while holding off the cops. Then he blew up his house.

SHE A novel by H. Rider Haggard.

A SHELL CARD One of Bart Dawes' credit cards.

THE SIGN IN FRONT OF SANTA'S THRONE In the department store where Bart did his Christmas shopping, there was a sign in front of Santa's throne that said:

"SANTA IS HAVING LUNCH AT OUR FAMOUS
"MID-TOWN GRILL"
Why Not Join Him?

$68,500 The amount of the cashier's check the city gave Bart for his house. He deposited half of it ($34,250) in his First Bank checking account, and mailed the checkbook to Mary. He took the other half in cash.

A SIXTY-HORSEPOWER EVINRUDE MOTOR Bart Dawes told Harry at Harvey's Gun Shop that Nick Adams, his (nonexistent) cousin, had bought him an Evinrude motor for Christmas,

and that in order to reciprocate, he wanted to buy Nick a .44 Magnum. The gun was actually for himself. He also ended up buying a .460 Weatherbee rifle.

$63,500 The assessed value of Bart Dawes's house.

"THE SLAMMED DOOR ORGASM" Bart told Vinnie Mason the story of how his wife got pregant due to a slammed door. When they were first married, they were going to wait to have a baby. They were using the interruption method as birth control. As Bart told it, they were "going to town," when somebody in the building slammed a door and startled Bart into an orgasm. Mary ended up losing the baby, though.

"SMALL CROWDS IN BETHLEHEM/PILGRIMS FEAR HOLY TERROR" A newspaper headline Bart read in the Norton U-Wash-It.

SMITH & WESSON One of the brands of guns carried at Harvey's Gun Shop.

SOI STOCKS One of the stocks owned by Lester Calloway.

"SOME CAME RUNNING" One of the X-rated movies playing at the Norton Drive-In.

SOUTHERN COMFORT AND 7-UP Bart's private drink.

A STEAM SHOVEL One of the pieces of construction equipment that Bart blew up at the Route 784 extension site with his homemade Molotov cocktails.

"SUNFLOWERS" A Van Gogh reproduction that hung in Steve Ordner's reception room.

A SUNOCO CARD One of Bart Dawes' credit cards.

SWIPE A cleaning product.

SYNTHETIC MESCALINE "PRODUCT 4" The drug Olivia gave to Bart when she left for Las Vegas. Bart took it at Wally Hamner's New Year's Eve party.

"THIMK" The sign on Vinnie Mason's desk.

"THINK! IT MAY BE A NEW EXPERIENCE" The sign on Bart Dawes' desk at the laundry.

THIRTY-EIGHT DOLLARS The balance on Bart Dawes' Gulf credit card.

$35,053.49 The amount in the checkbook that Bart mailed to Mary after he sold his house to the city. [NOTE: See the entry BART'S CHECKING ACCOUNT BALANCE.]

$34,250 Exactly half of the $68,500 cashier's check Bart got from the city for his house. He deposited half in his First Bank checking account, and sent the checkbook to Mary. The other half he took in cash.

THIRTY-SEVEN STITCHES The number of stitches Luigi Bronticelli needed after Andrea, Mr. Piazzi's dog, bit him in the throat.

THE THOM McAN SIGN Bart knew that if he let the option on the new Waterford plant run out, there would soon be a sign up that said:

SITE OF OUR NEW WATERFORD PLANT
THOM McAN SHOES
Here We Grow Again!!!

THREE EXCEDRIN WASHED DOWN WITH PEPTO-BISMOL, AND A MAXWELL HOUSE INSTANT COFFEE CHASER The morning after his destruction of the equipment at the Route 784 extension site, Bart woke up with a killer headache. He took three Excedrin, washed them down with Pepto-Bismol, and drank Maxwell House instant coffee.

$390 The money Bart managed to earn for their new TV set. Mary had earned $416.

$3,000 The "finder's fee" Magliore took for setting up Olivia Brenner's trust fund for Bart.

THE TRAINED DOG ETHIC Bart's self-invented sociological theory. According to Bart, this theory fully explained "such mysteries as the monetary crisis, inflation, the Vietnam War, and the energy crisis." His theory hypothesized that Americans are like trained dogs: We're trained to like big gas-guzzling cars, etc., and we respond. Then the energy crunch hits, and we're retrained to hate the same kind of cars and once again, we respond accordingly.

TRUE AND *ARGOSY* Two of the magazines in Magliore's office.

THE TV SHOWS BART AND MARY WATCHED WHEN THEY WERE NEWLYWEDS The following is a list of the television shows Bart remembered watching with Mary when they were first married, along with details on the networks on which they ran, and the years in which they were broadcast:

"The Jack Benny Show"—CBS & NBC; 1950-1977

"Amos 'n Andy"—CBS; 1951-1953

"Dragnet"—NBC; 1952-1970

"Highway Patrol"—(Syndicated only); 1955-1959 (156 episodes)

"Your Show of Shows"—NBC; 1950-1954

"Your Hit Parade"—NBC & CBS; 1950-1974

"Tic Tac Dough"—NBC; 1957-1958

"Twenty-One"—NBC; 1956-1958

"The $64,000 Question"—CBS; 1955-1958

"Dotto"—NBC; 1958

"Annie Oakley"—(Syndicated and Network daytime); 1953-1956 (81 episodes)

"The Adventures of Rin-Tin-Tin"—ABC; 1954-1959

"Sergeant Preston of the Yukon"—CBS; 1955-1958

"The Range Rider"—(Syndicated and Network reruns); 1951-1952 (78 episodes)

"The Adventures of Wild Bill Hickok"—(Syndicated and Network daytime); 1951-1958 (113 episodes)

1241 CRESTALLEN STREET WEST Bart Dawes' address.

TWO BULLDOZERS Two of the pieces of construction equipment that Bart blew up at the Route 784 extension site with his homemade Molotov cocktails.

TWO PAYLOADERS Two of the pieces of construction equipment that Bart blew up at the Route 784 extension site with his homemade Molotov cocktails.

A U.S. DRINKING TEAM STEIN A stein Mary had once bought for Bart. Bart put his $34,250 in cash in the stein.

THE UNITED FUND Bart received a thank-you note from the fund.

A USED BUICK Jack Hobart bought his wife Ellen a used Buick when she couldn't get into the car pool in her new, snobbish Northside neighborhood.

A VALIANT One of the cars Bart saw in Magliore's car lot. It had flat tires and a cracked windshield. It was selling for seventy-five dollars, and was advertised as a "Mechanix Special."

THE WALL STREET JOURNAL The newspaper Sally Magliore read.

WASHEX A brand of machine used at the Blue Ribbon Laundry.

THE WATERFORD DEAL The deal Stephan Ordner wanted to discuss with Bart Dawes. Waterford was where the new Blue Ribbon Laundry plant was to be located, due to the "Roadwork."

THE WDST WEATHERPHONE While shopping for a present for "Nick Adam" in Harvey's Gun Shop, Bart called the WDST Weatherphone and pretended he was talking to his wife Mary.

"WHAT DREAMS MAY COME?" Phil Drake quoted a line from Hamlet to Bart: "In that sleep of death, what dreams may come?" [NOTE: *What Dreams May Come* is also the title of one of the most incredible novels ever written by mortal man. *What Dreams May Come* is by Richard Matheson, one of the major influences on Stephen King. Reading it changed my life. Find it, read it, and tell other people to read it. See my interview with Richard Matheson in this volume.]

A WHITE FORD VAN One of the WHLM news vehicles.

A WHITE STATION WAGON One of the WHLM news vehicles.

"WHIZZER" Bart's Bay High School nickname.

WHLM Channel 9. The station that covered "Dawes' Last Stand."

THE WHLM NEWSBEAT VAN The Channel 9 news vehicle that covered Bart's standoff.

THE WHLM NEWSMOBILE Dave Albert and the WHLM Newsmobile covered the groundbreaking for the Route 784 extension.

WINCHESTER One of the brands of guns carried at Harvey's Gun Shop.

"WINTERBURGER SAYS ACTS OF VANDALISM WILL NOT BE TOLERATED" A news story about his fire-bombings that Bart read in the Norton U-Wash-It.

"THE WONDERFUL NOSTALGIAMOBILE" As Bart sat drinking and wallowing in despair, he felt like he was visiting Disney World's newest head trip, "Self-Pity Land," where you could take a gondola ride down the "Canal of Tears" and visit the "Museum of Old Snapshots." (You could also go for a ride in the Wonderful NostalgiaMobile, driven by Fred MacMurray.)

YELLO-GO A new industrial bleach. Bart received a flyer on it.

"YOUR HIT PARADE" One of the TV shows the Dawes watched at the Upshaws.

ZIPPO Vinnie Mason's lighter. Also, Bart Dawes had a Zippo that was engraved "BGD."

CUJO

DEDICATION

This book is for my brother, David,
who held my hand crossing West Broad Street,
and who taught me how to make skyhooks
out of old coathangers. The trick was so
damned good I just never stopped.

I love you, David.

[NO CONTENTS PAGE]

BOOK BREAKDOWN

[NOTE: *Cujo* begins with "Once upon a time,..." and continues on without being broken into chapters or sub-groupings of any kind. King merely leaves some white space to indicate a break in the story. The hardcover edition runs 309 pages. – sjs]

---

(11)
CUJO
People

"ADAM SWALLOW" The alias Steve Kemp used when he called Vic's office.

"AUNT EVVIE" Evelyn Chambers.

BANNERMAN, SHERIFF Castle Rock sheriff.

THE BATS While in pursuit of a rabbit, Cujo stuck his head into a hole filled with rabid bats.

BEAULIEU, STRINGER He received a special delivery letter.

BELASCO, MR. He owned Portland Machine.

BELLAMY, BILLY Boy with cerebral palsy. Roger and Vic used him in their successful CP ad campaign.

BERGERON, DAVE Brett Camber's friend.

"BERNIE CARBO" Steve Kemp's cat.

BOSTON RED SOX Vic listened to a Red Sox game on the radio.

BRADY, JOAN Donna Trenton's high school friend. Joan was killed in an auto accident.

BREAKSTONE, ALTHEA Roger's wife.

BREAKSTONE, ROGER Vic Trenton's partner in the advertising agency.

BREAKSTONE, TIMOTHY Roger and Althea's dead infant son. He died of sudden infant death syndrome.

THE BREAKSTONE TWINS Roger and Althea Breakstone's twin girls.

BRETT, GEORGE Baseball player.

BROOKS, HOLLY Charity Camber's sister. She lived in Connecticut. She was married to Jim.

BROOKS, JIM Holly's husband.

BROOKS, JIM Holly and Jim's son.

CALLAHAN, VIN Auto mechanic in North Conway.

CAMBER, BRETT Joe and Charity Camber's son.

CAMBER, CHARITY Joe Camber's wife.

CAMBER, JOE Mechanic. He owned Cujo. He also owned and operated a garage on the outskirts of Castle Rock. It was in his yard that Donna and Tad were trapped in their Pinto by Cujo.

THE CAMBER'S NEIGHBORS Unnamed people who lived in the house at the bottom of the hill outside Camber's place. Donna tried to get their attention by beeping SOS on the car horn.

CARLIN, GEORGE He made a joke about the Sharp cereal professor after the Red Razberry Zingers fiasco.

CARSON, JOHNNY He did an entire monologue about the Sharp cereal professor after the Red Razberry Zingers fiasco.

CASH, NORM He played for the Tigers in 1968.

CHALMERS, EVELYN "Aunt Evvie." She was ninety-three years old, and the oldest living person in Castle Rock.

"CISCO" Donna, according to Tad.

THE CONTINENTAL DRIVER Unnamed driver of the Continental with New York plates that swung around Donna's car on a curve.

THE COOKIE SHARPSHOOTER Western peace officer developed for the Sharp account by Roger and Vic. His six-guns shot Chocka Chippers, Ginger Snappies, and Oatmeals instead of bullets.

THE COUNTY DOG OFFICER He took the rabid dog's head to the state health and welfare department.

CROWELL, RAY Man from Fryeburg. He gave Cujo to Joe Camber in 1975 as payment for a repair job.

CUJO A huge St. Bernard dog owned by Joe, Charity, and Brett Camber. He was five years old and weighed 200 pounds.

DAVIS, BETTE AND ALI McGRAW Ron said that Yancey Harrington would be so good doing the professor's swan song in the Sharp cereal spot that he'd make Bette Davis in "Dark Victory" look like Ali McGraw in "Love Story."

DIMMESDALE, REVEREND Donna tried to convince herself that Cujo was not the Reverend, and that he was not out to get her personally.

DOBSON, STANLEY Bully. He pushed Tad at camp.

DODD, FRANK The Castle Rock Strangler. He was a Castle Rock cop who went on a killing spree in the seventies.

DODD, MRS. Frank's mother. She died of a stroke.

DONOVAN The manager of the Shop 'n Save.

DuBAY, RONNIE One of the guys who delivered the new chainfall to the Cambers.

DUNBARGER, CAROL Castle Rock girl who was killed in 1974.

THE FAT LADY The Continental driver's wife. Donna gave her the finger.

FISHER, ROSCOE Deputy with the Castle Rock sheriff's department.

FOURNIER, MICHAEL The Castle Rock postmaster.

FRECHETTE, ALMA Castle Rock waitress who was killed in 1970.

FREEMAN, BILLY Paperboy who delivered the *Castle Rock Call* to the Trentons.

GARCIA, JERRY Leader of the Grateful Dead.

GEHRINGER, DEBBIE Tad's fifteen-year-old babysitter.

GEORGE AND GRACIE Characters in a Sharp cookie ad.

THE GIRL SCOUTS Donna belonged to the scouts as a child.

GREEDO Character whose picture Tad colored.

GRESHAM, DR. The doctor Charity consulted about Brett's sleepwalking when Brett was six years old.

"HANDSOME HUBBY" Vic Trenton, according to Steve Kemp.

HARRINGTON, YANCEY Actor who played the Sharp cereal professor.

HEEBERT, ARNOLD Castle Rock resident; he was 101 years old. He lived at the Castle Acres Nursing Home. He died when he fell off the porch of the home and broke his neck.

HENDRASEN, MARY KATE Castle Rock grade school teacher who was killed in 1975.

HOFNAGER, RANDY Camper friend of Tad's. He pronounced breakfast "brekfust."

HOPE, BOB He made a joke about the Sharp cereal professor after the Red Razberry Zingers fiasco.

HURST, JOHN He wrote the song "Candy Man."

JACKSON, MICHAEL His song "Off the Wall" was playing in the cab Vic took.

"JERRY FORD WITH HAIR" Donna thought Vic looked like Ford with hair when Vic wore his best suit.

JOANIE One of Donna Trenton's friends.

JOHNSON, MR. Maitre d' at the unnamed restaurant where Vic, Roger, and Rob had lunch.

JON "CHiPS" character.

KEMP, STEVE Castle Rock poet and furniture refinisher. Donna Trenton had an affair with Kemp.

LISA A girl who worked for Ad Worx.

"LITTLE MISS HIGHPOCKETS" Donna Trenton, according to Steve Kemp.

MACARTHUR, DOUGLAS Vic compared the Sharp professor's demise to Macarthur's "old soldiers just fade away" remark.

MACKENZIE, ALLISON One of Donna Trenton's friends. She sold for Amway and Avon.

MAGRUDER, RONNIE One of the guys who delivered the new chainfall to the Cambers.

MANTLE, MICKEY Baseball player.

MARCHANT, VIN George Meara thought that Vin would inherit the Boston Post cane when Evvie Chambers died.

MARCY Four-year-old girl who threw up blood. The blood turned out to actually be Red Razberry Zingers.

MARTIN, ROB President of Image-Eye. He was a Vietnam vet. He lost a leg in the Tet offensive.

MARTIN, STEVE He made a joke about the Sharp cereal professor after the Red Razberry Zingers fiasco.

MASEN, ANDY Man sent from the Augusta attorney general's office to investigate the assumed kidnapping of Donna and Tad by Steve Kemp.

MASEN, MARTY Andy Masen's youngest brother.

MASEN, ROBERTA Andy Masen's sister.

"MAYOR McCHEESE" McDonald's character.

McGRAW, ALI AND BETTE DAVIS Ron said that Yancey Harrington would be so good doing the professor's swan song in the Sharp cereal spot that he'd make Bette Davis in "Dark Victory" look like Ali McGraw in "Love Story."

McNALLY, ALTITUDE LOU FM weatherman.

MEARA, GEORGE Castle Rock mailman.

THE METS Vic didn't like them.

MILLER, MR. Schoolteacher. He had a Ford that needed a transmission.

MILLIKEN, FREDDY One of Joe Camber's customers.

MILLIKEN, JOHN One of Joe Camber's customers.

MILLIKEN, KIM Fred Milliken's daughter.

THE MILLIKENS George Meara delivered their mail.

MOBY DOG Donna tried to convince herself that Cujo was not Moby Dog and that he was not out to get her personally.

MOODY, CHERYL Castle Rock high school student who was killed in 1971.

MOUSAM, JOHN The previous owner, before Joe Camber, of Seven Oaks Farm.

"MR. BUSINESSMAN TRIUMPHANT" Vic Trenton, according to Steve Kemp.

"MR. CLEAN" A cat.

"MR. PORK PINE" A porcupine, according to Brett Camber.

"MRS. BEASLEY" Cujo's mother.

NEADEAU, TOMMY Boy who saw a deer out by Moosuntic Pond.

NIPPER The RCA dog, the company's logo.

THE OUT-OF-STATE COUPLE They brought Steve Kemp a Hoosier cabinet for refinishing.

"PANCHO" Tad, according to Donna.

THE PARTY OF FOUR Four unnamed people drinking at the Yellow Submarine. Three wore UMP T-shirts, and one wore a t-shirt that read "Darth Vader is Gay."

PERVIER, GARY The Camber's neighbor. He didn't give a shit. Cujo killed him.

PONCH "CHiPS" character.

QUENTIN, DR. George Meara's doctor.

THE RABBIT Cujo chased a rabbit, got stuck in a hole, and got bitten by a rabid bat.

THE RAGGED EDGE Local ragtime band. They played concerts at the Common Bandstand.

RESCUE UNIT DRIVER Unnamed paramedic who tried to give Donna an injection.

RINGGOLD, ETTA Castle Rock teacher who was killed in the fall of 1975.

ROCKY Waiter at the unnamed restaurant where Vic, Roger, and Rob had lunch.

"RONALD FUCKING McDONALD" Ronald McDonald, according to Gary Pervier.

SAMPSON, DWIGHT The first boy Donna Trenton kissed with her mouth open.

THE SHARP CEREAL PROFESSOR Character created by Vic and Roger for the Sharp cereal account. His trademark slogan was "Nope, nothing wrong here."

SHOUPER, MR. Banker at Casco Bank in Bridgton.

SIMMS, RICHIE He had an International Harvester that needed a new motor.

SMITH, JOHN Castle Rock man who discovered Frank Dodd was the Castle Rock killer in Stephen King's *The Dead Zone*.

SPRINGSTEEN, BRUCE A tune by Bruce played on Donna's car radio.

STANLEY, BOB Baseball pitcher.

STEIGMEYER, MR. The custodian in Vic's office building.

TEDDY Tad Trenton's teddy bear.

THORNTON, ALVA Owner of Thornton's Egg Farms.

THORNTON, BESSIE Alva's wife; Evvie Chalmers' great niece. She was not terribly bright.

TIMMINS, RED Boy who was always trying to kiss Holly when they were young.

TOOTHAKER, PAULINE Castle Rock woman who was killed in 1971.

TORGESON, BUDDY He turned Gary Pervier's Distinguished Service Cross into an ashtray.

TRENTON, DONNA Vic's wife, Tad's mother. She had an affair with Steve Kemp. She was trapped in her Pinto by Cujo.

TRENTON, TAD Four-year-old son of Vic and Donna Trenton. He died after being trapped in the Pinto by Cujo.

TRENTON, VIC Donna's husband, Tad's father.

THE TWO-YEAR-OLD Unnamed kid who stood in a driveway with a sopping Pamper.

WARHOL, ANDY Steve Kemp had strong opinions about Warhol's films.

WELSH, JOANIE Friend of Donna's. She was three years older and ten pounds heavier than Donna.

WELSH, MR. Joanie's husband. He liked Joanie with a little weight on her.

THE WELSH GIRL Joanie Welsh's daughter.

WILLIE After Cujo's death, Brett got a new puppy and named him Willie. His mother referred to the pup as "Heinz 57 Varieties."

WOLFE, WILLIAM A member of the SLA (Symbionese Liberation Agency). He was known as Cujo.

(11)

CUJO
Places

AGWAY MARKET The store where Donna Trenton shopped.

AMERICAN LEGION FIELD The field where Tad's day camp was located.

AMOCO STATION Station east of Machias where Gary Pervier first saw a rabid dog.

THE APPALACHIAN TRAIL Donna, Vic, Tad, Roger, and Althea had once gone hiking there.

BATON ROUGE City where The Press Over The Garage was located.

BLOOMINGDALE'S New York store where Donna once tested a professor's theory. His theory was that a person could not walk very well on a down escalator that was not moving.

BOISE, IDAHO City where Red Razberry Zingers were successfully test marketed.

BRIDGEPORT City where Holly and Charity went shopping.

BRIDGTON, MAINE The Breakstones lived there. It was another city where Red Razberry Zingers were successfully test marketed.

BRIDGTON ACADEMY The school the Breakstone twins had their hearts set on attending. Also, Steve Kemp played tennis on the court behind an academy building.

BRIDGTON PHARMACY The store where Vic bought plastic trucks for Tad, and a *Time* magazine for himself.

CALDOR'S The store where Charity and Brett shopped.

CAMP TAPAWINGO The camp where Donna Trenton learned to dive as a child.

CASCO BANK Bridgton bank.

CASCO BANK AND TRUST Bank near the Greyhound bus terminal.

CASTLE ACRES NURSING HOME The home where Arnold Heebert lived and died.

CASTLE FALLS ESSO Station where Buddy Torgeson worked.

CASTLE ROCK, MAINE Cujo's hometown, and the setting for the novel.

CLEVELAND City where the Sharp company headquarters was located.

CMP The power company that serviced Castle Rock.

CONNECTICUT Charity Camber's sister Holly lived there.

DAIRY QUEEN Steve Kemp ate lunch there.

DEERING OAKS PARK The park Vic went to after he got the note from Steve.

DREW School in New Jersey. Steve Kemp graduated from there.

"EAST GALOSHES CORNER" The name Vic called the farthest reaches of the Castle Rock township.

ELLISON AGENCY Ad agency in New York. Vic and Roger had both worked there for six years. [NOTE: The name of this agency is probably a nod to King's friend and colleague, Harlan Ellison.]

GIGEURE'S Bridgton market.

HARVARD Andy Masen could have gone there, but didn't.

HOUSE OF LIGHTS, INC. The phony company that Steve Kemp made up when he called Vic's office. He told Vic's secretary he was their marketing manager.

J.C. WHITNEY & CO. Company that sent Joe Camber a package.

JACK AND JILL NURSERY SCHOOL Tad's school three mornings a week.

JOE'S SMOKE SHOP Steve Kemp called Vic's office from a phone booth on Congress Street across from Joe's Smoke Shop.

KENNEBUNK, HOLLIS, OR AUGUSTA Donna dreamt she attended a family reunion in one of these towns.

KENNEBUNK BEACH The locale where Ad Worx shot the Book Folks ad spots.

LEWISTON Joe Camber went there to find a windshield for a '72 Camaro.

LOGAN AIRPORT Airport where Vic and Roger boarded their plane.

MAGIC LANTERN THEATER Theater in Bridgton where Donna and Vic had once taken Tad.

MAPLE SUGAR ROAD Road leading to Joe Camber's place.

MARIO'S Local restaurant.

McDONALD'S Gary Pervier had gotten a free glass there.

THE MELLOW TIGER The only tavern in Castle Rock. George Meara ate two cheeseburgers there.

THE MET THEATER The theater Holly and Charity had once snuck into to see Elvis in "Love Me Tender."

MOOSEHEAD Joe Camber and Gary Pervier went hunting there.

MOOSUNTIC POND Tommy Neadeau saw a deer out by this pond.

NEW HAMPSHIRE Liquor was cheaper in New Hampshire than in Maine.

NEW YORK CITY Vic's original hometown.

NORTH CONWAY Where Vin Callahan was from.

NORWAY DRIVE-IN Vic and Donna took Tad there to see "White Lightning" and "White Line Fever."

ORSON WELLES CINEMA Theater that ran Welles' films.

THE POCONOS Where Donna Trenton's mother lived.

PONDICHERRY LANES Bridgton bowling alley.

PORTLAND CITY LIBRARY Library where Charity found a book about sleepwalking.

PORTLAND MACHINE Company owned by Mr. Belasco.

PORTSMOUTH, NEW HAMPSHIRE Joe and Brett Camber went to Portsmouth for a used car auction.

A RESTAURANT Unnamed dining spot where Vic and Roger met with Rob about the Sharp cereal professor's "deathbed scene." Vic got drunker than he had ever gotten before at a business luncheon.

RITZ CARLTON Hotel in Boston.

SABBATUS ROAD, LISBON, MAINE Where Andy Masen grew up.

SALVATION ARMY Vic gave all of Tad's toys to the Salvation Army.

SAMMY'S PIZZA Joan Brady was on her way home from this restaurant when she had her fatal auto accident.

SANTA'S VILLAGE A New Hampshire tourist attraction.

SCRANTON, PENNSYLVANIA City where Red Razberry Zingers were successfully test marketed.

SEARS, ROEBUCK Gary Pervier bought a lawn chair from Sears through the mail.

SEVEN OAKS FARM Joe Camber's farm. It was out on Town Road 3. He had owned it for seventeen years.

THE SHARP COMPANY Company that advertised with Vic's ad agency. They made Twinkles, Cocoa Bears, Bran 16, All-Grain Blend, Chocka Chippers, and Ginger Snappies.

SIX-GUN CITY A New Hampshire tourist attraction.

SOUTH PARIS Town where Cujo's vet had his practice.

SUNOCO STATION Station where Joe Camber and his buddies drank Black Label and hung around.

SWANSON'S Department store where Donna bought a keyring.

TAHITI Donna wished she was there.

THE TAJ MAHAL Gary Pervier would be the first to admit that his home was no Taj Mahal. But he didn't give a shit.

TASTEE FREEZE Donna usually took Tad there for ice cream.

THORNTON EGG FARMS Local hatchery.

TOWN ROAD 3 The road where the Camber place, Seven Oaks Farm, was located.

TRACE OPTICAL Castle Rock's only real industry. Charity Camber got a job there after Joe's death.

TWICKENHAM Small town where Steve Kemp spent the night after he trashed the Trentons' house.

TWIN CITY FORD DEALERSHIP South Paris dealership. Vic told Donna to call this dealership to get her Pinto towed to Camber's garage. Also, the police called there looking for Donna's Pinto.

U.N. PLAZA Hotel in New York.

THE UNIVERSITY OF MAINE The school where Jim Brooks studied pre-law.

WASHINGTON STREET "The Combat Zone." It was busy with prostitutes, X-rated movies, etc.

WESTPORT, CONNECTICUT Where Yancey Harrington lived.

WESTPORT, GREENWICH, AND NEW YORK CITY Towns the first commuter train was bound for.

YELLOW SUBMARINE A restaurant in Portland.

YMCA Steve Kemp intended on staying at the Portland YMCA when he left Castle Rock.

(11)
CUJO
Things

ACE BANDAGE The bandage Tad had to wear for a month after he shut a door on his foot.

AD WORX Vic Trenton and Roger Breakstone's ad agency. [NOTE: See the entry AD WORX BUSINESS CARD.]

AD WORX BUSINESS CARD The text of the Ad Worx business card read as follows:

roger breakstone   ad worx   victor trenton
1633 congress street
telex: ADWORX   portland, maine 04001   tel (207) 799-8600

AGENT ORANGE Defoliant used in Vietnam.

ALL-GRAIN BLEND One of the cereals made by the Sharp company.

AMWAY AND AVON Two products sold by Allison Mackenzie.

ANACIN BOTTLE Steve Kemp kept his cocaine in it.

"AS THE WORLD TURNS" A soap opera Donna Trenton watched.

"AS THE WORLD TURNS," "THE DOCTORS," AND "THE YOUNG AND THE RESTLESS" Soap operas Bessie Thorton watched.

ATARI VIDEO GAME A game in Holly's family room.

AVIS Vic rented a car from Avis to drive home in.

BASEBALL BAT Donna saw one lying in the grass in Camber's yard when she was trapped in the Pinto.

BEARCAT SCANNER Type of radio in the Castle Rock police cars.

"BEULAH LAND" Song performed by the Ragged Edge.

BIG MAC BOXES Some of the trash in Steve Kemp's van.

BIG WHEELS One of Tad's toys.

A BLACK AND WHITE ZENITH Steve Kemp's TV.

BLACK BEAUTIES Pills found in Kemp's van.

BLACK CAT FRICTION TAPE The tape on the baseball bat Donna used to fight Cujo.

BLACK LABEL Beer that Joe Camber drank.

BON VIVANT VICHYSSOISE Having this account could have been worse than having the Sharp account, according to Roger.

BOOK FOLKS Company who used the Ad Worx agency. Vic and Roger shot their spots at Kennebunk Beach.

BOSTON POST CANE Evvie Chambers had held it for two years.

BOSTON-KANSAS CITY SERIES Ron offered tickets to this series to Vic and Roger.

BRAN 16 One of the cereals made by the Sharp company.

"BUGS BUNNY" Saturday morning children's show.

BUSCH The beer Roger Breakstone drank.

CAMARO The car in which Marty Masen was killed.

CAMPBELL'S SOUP Tad's lunch.

A LOOK AT
DANSE MACABRE
Stephen King's Only Book-Length Work of Non-Fiction

"Finally, my sincere thanks to
Stephen King for *Danse Macabre.*"
—David G. Hartwell,
from the acknowledgments section
in *The Dark Descent* (Tor, 1987).

Danse Macabre is a masterful overview of the fantastic and the horrible in films, books, and television from 1950 to 1980. *Danse Macabre* makes it very clear that King has read widely in the field, seen hundreds of films, and watched and listened to countless hours of television and radio in his life.

His insight into the field can only add to your understanding and enjoyment of horror and fantasy, and the book should be in every horror lover's home library.

My only hope is that King will do an updated edition that takes a look at the genre from 1980 to 1990, but, in the meantime, the original edition will do quite nicely.

A Chapter-By-Chapter Look
at *Danse Macabre*

Contents

The Forenotes

In the first "Forenote," King explains the genesis of *Danse Macabre*: "This book is in your hands as the result of a telephone call made to me in November of 1978." His *Carrie* editor Bill Thompson suggested the concept of the book, and after much thought (and persuasion), he agreed to do it.

In the "Forenote" to the paperback edition, he explains that the hardcover edition of *Danse Macabre* generated a whole bunch of "you fucked up" letters, and that Dennis Etchison handled the corrections for the paperback. ("I wanted to thank the man for tucking in my shirt and combing my hair for me.")

I. October 4, 1957,
and an Invitation to Dance

The first chapter of *Danse Macabre* begins "For me, the terror—the real terror, as opposed to whatever demons and boogeys which might have been living in my own mind—began on an afternoon in October of 1957." That afternoon, King writes, he was in a theater in Stratford, Connecticut, watching "Earth vs. the Flying Saucers" when the theater manager stopped the film to tell the house that the Soviet Union had launched Sputnik—and beaten the United States into space.

That story may or may not be apocryphal, since King stated in his "Garbage Truck" column #46 (May 7, 1970, in *The Maine Campus*) that:

> "I was waiting in the barber shop to get a haircut when that [the launching of Sputnick] happened. I thought it had to be a joke. Americans were always first—we had been with the telephone, the electric light, the airplane—surely the Russians, who played dirty, could not have beaten us into space!

Essentially an introduction to *Danse Macabre,* in Chapter I, King sets the stage for the in-depth look at the horror genre to follow.

II. Tales of the Hook

Basically a "What is horror?" overview, "Tales of the Hook" offers King's three levels of "Scare Tactics": First, try to terrify, then try to horrify, and if neither work, then go for the gross-out.

In this chapter, King also discusses the eliminated "rats in the basement" scene from *'Salem's Lot* (see the section "The Unwritten King" in this volume), and he also covers monsters, freaks, the cycles of horror, and the American International "I Was a Teenage..." films of the 1950s.

III. Tales of the Tarot

An insightful discussion of the three novels *Dr. Jekyll and Mr. Hyde, Dracula,* and *Frankenstein.* King states "I believe it's impossible to discuss horror in the years 1950-1980 with any real fullness of understanding unless we begin with these three books."

IV. An Annoying Autobiographical Pause

King looks at why he developed an interest in reading—and writing—horror, and relates some autobiographical childhood tales.

V. Radio and the Set of Reality

A comprehensive look at horror on radio.

VI. The Modern American Horror Movie —Text and Subtext

A look at "'areas of unease'—the political-social-cultural and those of the more mythic, fairy-tale variety"—and how they were interpreted by horror movies of the thirty years between 1950 and 1980. An explanation of the subtext of major films of the period.

VII. The Horror Movie as Junk Food

A continuation (from Chapter VI) of King's look at the subtext present in horror films.

VIII. The Glass Teat, or, This Monster Was Brought to You by Gainesburgers

Horror on television.

IX. Horror Fiction

A must-read chapter for anyone seriously interested in horror fiction. King discusses ten seminal novels (including Peter Straub's *Ghost Story,* Anne River Siddons' *The House Next Door,* Shirley Jackson's *The Haunting of Hill House,* Ira Levin's *Rosemary's Baby,* Jack Finney's *The Body Snatchers,* Ray Bradbury's *Something Wicked This Way Comes,* and Richard Matheson's *The Shrinking Man*), and makes you want to go back and re-read the novels he writes about, or in the cases where you haven't read them, go out and buy and read them immediately. A terrific overview.

X. The Last Waltz—Horror and Morality, Horror and Magic

An exploration of the role that horror plays in real-life violence, discussed primarily through brief, numbered vignettes.

AFTERWORD

An explanation by King that portions of *Danse Macabre* included material from his *Night Shift* Foreword, as well as his nonfiction article "The Fright Report."

APPENDIX 1. THE FILMS

King recommends one hundred fantasy/horror films.

APPENDIX 2. THE BOOKS

King recommends one hundred fantasy/horror books.

"CANDY MAN" Song performed by the Ragged Edge.

CANNES-LOOK JEANS Company that cancelled their account with Image-Eye.

CASCO BANK & TRUST One of the Ad Worx accounts.

CASTLE ROCK CALL The Castle Rock newspaper.

CASTLE ROCK MUNICIPAL SERVICES The department Joe Camber planned on calling after he found Gary's body.

CASTLE ROCK SNODEVILS Snowmobile club Alva and Bessie Thornton belonged to.

CHARITY CAMBER'S WINNING LOTTERY TICKET Her winning numbers were #76 Green, and #434 Red. She won $5,000.

CHASING SUNDOWN The book of poetry written by Steve Kemp.

CHEVY BEL AIR Freddy Milliken's car.

CHOICE BLUEBERRIES One of the Ad Worx accounts.

COCOA BEARS One of the cereals made by the Sharp company. Brett Camber ate it.

CONTINENTAL A car with New York plates. It barely missed Donna's car coming around a curve.

CRAYOLA Tad's crayons.

"CRUSADE OF THE ETERNAL CHRIST" Evelyn Chambers got prayer folders from the Crusade.

DAGWOODS The sandwiches served at the Yellow Submarine.

DECOSTER EGG FARMS Vic did their ads.

DELTA 727 JET The plane Vic and Roger flew on.

DINER'S CLUB CARD The credit card Holly used to buy lunch for Charity and Brett.

DISTINGUISHED SERVICE CROSS Gary Pervier received it in 1944.

DR. PEPPER The soda Tad drank.

DONNA'S BREAKFAST FANTASIES While trapped in the Pinto, Donna dreamed about the following: Eggs, french toast, orange juice, canadian bacon, home fries, bran flakes, and Egg McMuffins.

"THE DRAC PACK" Saturday morning children's TV show.

DUTCH ELM DISEASE It was killing Gary Pervier's tree.

83 LARCH STREET The Trentons' address.

ERECTOR SET One of Tad's toys.

EVELYN CHAMBERS' MAIL It mostly consisted of *Reader's Digest* and "Crusade of the Eternal Christ" prayer folders.

FEBRUARY 1945 When Gary Pervier was discharged from the service.

'58 FORD Joe Camber bought one at the used car auction.

FLEXIBLE FLYER SLED Brett's sled when he was five years old.

"FRANKENSTEIN" The movie Vic and Roger watched.

"FREE KITTENS" Sign nailed to a tree outside of Camber's place.

"A FRISBEE" What Tad called the car's air cleaner.

FURY III The sheriff's deputy's car.

GAINES MEAL AND RALSTON PURINA Cujo's food.

GARY PERVIER'S SCREWDRIVER Gary drank screwdrivers that were twenty-five percent Bird's Eye frozen orange juice, and seventy-five percent Popov vodka.

GELUSIL After Timothy Breakstone's death, Roger Breakstone became a "closet Gelusil chugger."

"GENERAL HOSPITAL" A TV show Steve Kemp watched.

GILLETTE FOAMY Donna thought they used Gillette Foamy in "To Kill A Mockingbird" to make the dog look rabid.

"GILLIGAN'S ISLAND" Syndicated TV show.

"A GOOD DOG" Cujo was eulogized as follows:

"It would perhaps not be amiss to point out that he had always tried to be a good dog. He had tried to do all the things his MAN and his WOMAN, and most of all his BOY, had asked or expected of him. He would have died for them, if that had been required. He had never wanted to kill anybody. He had been struck by something, possibly destiny, or fate, or only a degenerative nerve disease called rabies. Free will was not a factor."

THE GRATEFUL DEAD Band on the radio. They did "Sugaree."

GREYHOUND The bus Charity and Brett took to Connecticut.

GRIMACE A character on Gary Pervier's McDonald's glass.

HEFTY BAG Steve Kemp's kitchen was dirty. A green plastic Hefty bag was filled with Beefaroni and tuna-fish cans.

HEINZ FIFTY-SEVEN VARIETIES A dog of mixed breed, according to Joe Camber.

HERBERT TAREYTON Aunt Evvie's cigarettes.

"HERE COMES TROUBLE" Logo written on Holly's son Jim's t-shirt.

"HOGAN'S HEROES" Syndicated TV show.

"HOLD MAIL UNTIL NOTIFIED" The card that notified George Meara to hold the Cambers' mail.

HOME MEDICAL ENCYCLOPEDIA The book George Meara used to look up his "medical problem": He farted too much.

HONDA CIVIC Roger Breakstone's car.

HOOSIER CABINET The cabinet brought to Steve for refinishing by a couple from out of state.

HOUND'S The air conditioner on the Greyhound bus.

IMAGE-EYE The company in Boston that did the Red Razberry Zinger ad spots.

INTERNATIONAL HARVESTER It was owned by Richie Simms, and it needed a new motor.

JAGUAR Vic Trenton's old car.

JENN-AIRE Range in Holly's kitchen.

JOHNSON'S NO MORE TEARS The shampoo Donna used on Tad's hair.

JÖRGEN CHAINFALL Brett Camber told his mother that Joe would like one.

KEDS Brett Camber's sneakers.

KEEBLER FIGBARS Donna packed them for a snack.

KELLOGG'S PRODUCT 19 The cereal George Meara had for breakfast.

LA-Z-BOY Vic Trenton's recliner.

LIBRARY COMMITTEE AND HOSPITAL COMMITTEE Things Donna Trenton did not want to do.

"LIKE A MAFIA BUTTON MAN" The Sharp company wanted to treat the Red Razberry Zingers fiasco "like a mafia button man." Vic had to convince them that even though the Sharp cereal professor had to be buried, it could not be a midnight burial.

LITTLE GOLDEN BOOKS Tad's books.

LORD BUXTON Steve Kemp's wallet.

"LOVE ME TENDER" Holly and Charity had once sneaked into the Met theater to see this Elvis movie.

"LOVE OF LIFE" AND "SEARCH FOR TOMORROW" Soaps the ladies of Castle Rock watched daily, according to Steve Kemp.

LUKE SKYWALKER POSTER A poster on Tad's bedroom wall.

"THE MAGICAL MYSTERY TOUR" How Vic described his and Roger's trip from Cleveland to New York.

MAINE REALTORS' ASSOCIATION One of the Ad Worx accounts.

MARTIN'S POSTCARD Rob Martin sent Vic and Roger the following message on a postcard: "Image-Eye Lands Contract To Do Butts For Boston Buses; Bills Big Bucks."

MERCER-MAYER One of Tad's books.

MERIT SCHOLARSHIP Andy Masen received one while in high school.

MIGHTY MARVEL CALENDAR Tad had one hanging in his room.

THE MILLION DOLLAR BRIDGE The bridge to South Portland.

"THE MONSTER WORDS" The words Vic made up "For Tad" to keep the monsters away from Tad. They were:

Monsters, stay out of this room!
You have no business here.
No monsters under Tad's bed!
You can't fit under there.

No monsters hiding in Tad's closet!
It's too small in there.
No monsters outside of Tad's window!
You can't hold on out there.
No vampires, no werewolves, no things that bite.
You have no business here.
Nothing will touch Tad, or hurt Tad, all this night.
You have no business here."

"THE NEW ZOO REVIEW" TV show Tad watched.

1944 The year Gary Pervier received the Distinguished Service Cross.

1971 FORD ECONOLINE Steve Kemp's van. It's license number was 641-644.

1960 THUNDERBIRD Donovan's car.

"NO TRESPASSING – DUMP CLOSED" Sign across the road beyond Camber's place.

OLD AD CHARACTERS Characters consigned to a "promotional limbo" included Speedy Alka-Seltzer and Big Dick Chewing Gum.

$1,241.71 The wholesale price of a JÖRGENS chainfall.

THE OUT-OF-TOWNERS GRAVESTONES Donna figured that Maine residents – who are somewhat noted for their provinical attitudes towards "outsiders" – would write the following on a resident's gravestone: "Harry Jones, Castle Corners, Maine, (Originally from Omaha, Nebraska)."

PALL MALLS Andy Masen's cigarettes.

PAMPER The two-year-old in the driveway wore a sopping-wet Pamper.

PANASONIC TV The TV in Holly's family room.

PARENT EFFECTIVENESS TRAINING Donna tried this technique to help Tad deal with the monster in his closet. It didn't work. Vic's "Monster Words" did.

PILOT RAZOR POINT Steve Kemp's pen.

PINTO Donna Trenton's car.

THE PINTO'S REAR END A report claimed that if the Pinto was involved in a rear-end collison, it could result in a gas-tank explosion.

PLAYSKOOL Tad's toys.

POPULAR MECHANIX A magazine Gary Pervier subscribed to.

THE PRESS OVER THE GARAGE Publishing company in Baton Rouge that published Steve Kemp's book of poetry, *Chasing Sundown.*

QUARTER POUNDER Some group weighed a McDonald's Quarter Pounder and found it came up short.

RALEIGH Billy Freeman's bike.

"THE RAPE OF THE SABINE WOMEN" Donna Trenton felt that some men had this movie playing in their heads, and that she was the star.

READER'S DIGEST Evelyn Chambers had it delivered.

RED RAZBERRY ZINGERS Cereal made by the Sharp company. The food dye used didn't assimilate during digestion, and children seemed to be vomiting and defecating blood.

RED ROSE TEA BAGS The tea that Vic and Donna drank.

THE RED SOX AND KANSAS CITY GAME Baseball game Roger Breakstone watched on Channel 38.

RED SOX FEVER Vic Trenton resisted it.

REDBALL FLYER Tad's wagon.

ROADKING TRAILER It sat on a crumbling concrete foundation outside of Camber's place.

"THE ROADRUNNER HOUR" Saturday moning children's TV show.

ROLODEX The file in Jim Brooks' study.

"RONALD REAGAN SHOT J.R." Bumper sticker on Steve Kemp's van.

SAF-T-GLAS The Pinto's windows were made of it.

SARAN WRAP The olives and cucumbers were wrapped in Saran Wrap. [NOTE: See TUPPERWARE DISH.]

"SATURDAY NIGHT LIVE" They had a field day with the Sharp cereal professor.

SCRABBLE The game Jim Brooks taught Brett Camber.

SESAME STREET PICTURES Tad had pictures of Big Bird, Bert & Ernie, and Grover on his wall.

'72 CAMARO Joe Camber went to Lewiston to find a windshield for this car.

THE SHARP ACCOUNT One of the key ad accounts for Vic Trenton and Roger Breakstone's ad agency, Ad Worx. Ad Worx developed the Sharp cereal professor.

"SHUFFLE OFF TO BUFFALO" Song performed by the Ragged Edge. Donna could hear it in the Pinto seven miles away.

641-644 The license plate number of Steve Kemp's van.

'68 FORD FAIRLANE Car that passed Donna on her way to Camber's. It was going the other way.

'66 CHRYSLER HARDTOP Gary Pervier's car.

SLIM JIMS Donna packed them for a snack.

SMUCKERS Strawberry preserves Vic Trenton used on his waffles.

SNOOPY LUNCH BOX Tad's lunch box.

THE SONY AD Successful ad conceived by Roger and Vic. It was "a picture of a man sitting cross-legged on the median strip of a sixteen-lane superhighway in a business suit, a big Sony radio on his lap, a seraphic smile on his kisser. The copy read: POLICE BAND, THE ROLLING STONES, VIVALDI, MIKE WALLACE, THE KINGSTON TRIO, PAUL HARVEY, PATTI SMITH, JERRY FALWELL. And below that: HELLO, LA!"

SPACE INVADERS Game.

SPCA PAMPHLET Pamphlet that told pet owners not to leave animals in a hot car with the windows closed.

SPIDER-MAN T-SHIRT Tad Trenton wore one.

"SPLIT WOOD, NOT ATOMS" The bumper sticker on Steve Kemp's van.

"STAR BLAZERS" Syndicated TV show.

STAR WARS COLORING BOOK One of Tad's toys.

STEVE KEMP'S "CLEANUP ROUTINE" In addition to breaking bottles of booze all over the Trentons' kitchen closet door, he also threw the following supplies all over the kitchen: Spic 'n Span, Downey Fabric Softener, Lestoil, Top Job, and Tide.

STEVE KEMP'S NOTE TO VIC TRENTON:

HELLO VIC.
NICE WIFE YOU'VE GOT THERE.
I ENJOYED FUCKING THE SHIT OUT OF HER.
WHAT'S THAT MOLE JUST ABOVE HER PUBIC
  HAIR LOOK LIKE TO YOU?
TO ME IT LOOKS LIKE A QUESTION MARK.
DO *YOU* HAVE ANY QUESTIONS?

STEVE KEMP'S OVERHANDED LIQUOR TOSS When Steve broke into the Trentons' house, he threw bottles of liquor at their kitchen closet door. He threw Gilbey's gin, Jack Daniels, J & B whisky, crème de menthe, and amaretto.

STEVE'S MESSAGE TO DONNA When Steve broke into the Trentons' house, he masturbated onto their bedspread and then left a message on the message board in the kitchen: "I left something upstairs for you, baby."

STOP SIGN Frank Dodd held a stop sign when he worked as a crossing guard.

STUDEBAKER The car driven by the county dog officer.

SWEET 'N LOW Vic used it in his coffee.

"TADDER" Tad Trenton's nickname.

TAD'S BREAKFAST (IN THE PINTO) Fig bars, olives, and Slim Jims.

TAD'S "FRANK DODD" DREAM Tad had the following dream about Frank Dodd:

"And a man was walking out of the mist…a man who wore a black shiny raincoat and held a stop sign on a stick in one hand. He grinned, and his eyes were shiny silver coins. He raised one hand to point at Tad, and he saw with

"Staircase O' Monsters"
Original drawing courtesy Steve Fiorilla and Jim McDermott.

horror it wasn't a hand at all, it was *bones*, and the face inside the shiny vinyl hood of the raincoat wasn't a face at all. It was a skull."

TAD'S GAMES Tad played these games with his trucks: Dukes of Hazzard, B.J. and the Bear, and Cops and Moonshiners.

TAD'S STAR WARS GUYS Luke, Han Solo, The Imperial Creep Darth Vader, The Bespin Warrior, and Greedo. Greedo was Tad's favorite.

TEN-TRUCK WIPE-OUT A game Tad made up.

TEXACO CREDIT CARD The only credit card the Cambers had.

THERMOS Donna filled one with milk.

"TO KILL A MOCKINGBIRD" Movie in which Gregory Peck shot a rabid dog.

TONKA BULLDOZER One of Tad's toys.

TRAVEL-ETTE The alarm clock Vic had on his night table.

TUBORG The beer Vic drank.

TUFFSKIN The jeans worn by Holly's son Jim.

TUPPERWARE AND STANLEY PRODUCTS The things Donna Trenton did not want to sell.

TUPPERWARE DISH Donna had a Tupperware dish filled with cucumbers and olives in the car.

TWA FLIGHTBAG Steve Kemp had one.

12:34 A.M. The time Roscoe Fisher was killed by Cujo.

TWENTY QUESTIONS The game Donna played with Tad while trapped in the Pinto.

TWINKLES One of the cereals made by the Sharp company.

218-864 The license number of Donna Trenton's Pinto.

"THE U.S. OF ARCHIE" Syndicated TV show.

UNDERWOOD Steve Kemp's typewriter. The typewriter in Jim Brooks' study.

UNITED CEREBRAL PALSY ACCOUNT Roger and Vic's first account for the Ellison Agency.

UPJOHN The rescue unit driver tried to inject Donna with an Upjohn syringe.

VERMONT MAID SYRUP The syrup Donna used on her waffles.

VOIT Swim equipment company. Roger and Vic did an ad for them.

WCSH The radio station Joe Camber listened to for the ball scores.

"WHEEL OF FORTUNE" A TV show Donna watched.

WHERE THE WILD THINGS ARE Book by Maurice Sendak.

"WHITE LIGHTNING" AND "WHITE LINE FEVER" Two movies Donna and Vic took Tad to see at the Norway Drive-In.

WINCHESTER .30-.06 Gary Pervier's rifle.

WINNEBAGO George Meara wanted to buy one when he retired.

WONDER BREAD Joe Camber's bread.

WOXO Radio station in Norway.

WURLITZER JUKEBOX The jukebox in Holly's family room.

THE ZINGERS' COMPETITION Red Razberry Zingers had to compete with Count Chocula, Frankenberry, and Lucky Charms.

CREEPSHOW

[No Dedication]

[No Contents Page]

Book Breakdown

[*Creepshow* consists of five stories comprising a total of 424 individual comic strip panels.]

"Father's Day" –(sixty-seven individual comic strip panels)

"The Lonesome Death of Jordy Verrill"–(seventy-eight individual comic strip panels)
"The Crate"–(a hundred twenty-seven individual comic strip panels)
"Something To Tide You Over"–(sixty-five individual comic strip panels)
"They're Creeping Up On You"–(eighty-seven individual comic strip panels)

(12a)
CREEPSHOW
"Father's Day"
People

DANVERS, MRS. The cook at the Grantham House.

GRANTHAM, AUNT BEDELIA The matriarch of the clan. She killed her father, Nathan Grantham, by hitting him in the head with an ashtray after he had her boyfriend killed in a "hunting accident." She was killed on Father's Day by her dead father.

GRANTHAM, AUNT SYLVIA She had a place in Rome, a summer house in Bermuda, and a lifetime Eurorail Pass. When Nathan came back from the dead demanding a Father's Day cake, he made his own using Sylvia's head as the centerpiece and the candle.

GRANTHAM, CASSANDRA Cass. Henry's wife.

GRANTHAM, NATHAN Bedelia's father, and the real patriarch of the Grantham clan. Bedelia killed him with an ashtray after Nathan had Bedelia's boyfriend killed in a "hunting accident."

GRANTHAM, RICHARD Cass's brother.

HENRY Hank. Cass Grantham's husband. He went out to look for Aunt Bedelia, fell into Nathan's grave next to Bedelia's dead body, and was killed when the headstone fell on top of him.

YARBRO, PETER RICHARD Aunt Bedelia's boyfriend. He was killed in a "hunting accident" set up by Bedelia's father Nathan.

Places

THE GRANTHAM HOUSE The Grantham's palatial residence. The family gathered there every Father's Day for a "Nathan Grantham Memorial Dinner."

NATHAN GRANTHAM'S GRAVE Aunt Bedelia used to visit her father's grave at four o'clock every Father's Day. Cass's husband Henry fell into the grave and was killed by the falling headstone.

Things

AN ASHTRAY The "weapon" Bedelia used to kill her father.

A BAKED HAM DINNER After Bedelia visited her father's grave for an hour on Father's Day, she would then have a baked ham dinner with the Grantham family.

A CAKE After his stroke, Nathan Grantham used to bang his cane on his wheelchair arms and demand his Father's Day cake. After he came back from the dead and killed Bedelia and Henry, he made his own cake using Sylvia's head as the centerpiece and the candle.

THE "FATHER'S DAY" CLOSING The Creep closed the "Father's Day" story with this:

"Now, that's what I call a twist ending, eh kiddies? Nate did all the twisting and Sylvia ended…poor old girl just lost her head and went all to pieces…but the worst part came when old Nate blew out Cass and Richard's candles…heh-heh…POOF!! But why hang around here while my next terror tale awaits?"

THE "FATHER'S DAY" INTRO The Creep introduced "Father's

Day" with the following:

"Our first stop...the parlor of the GRANTHAM HOUSE...You'll like the Granthams, kiddies, they're the kind of people who'd steal candy from a baby...then lace it with arsenic and feed it to the dog! But, read on...you'll get to meet them soon enough..."

4:00 P.M. At this time every Father's Day, Bedelia visited her father's grave for one hour of meditation.

A "HUNTING ACCIDENT" Peter Richard Yarbro died in a "hunting accident" set up by Bedelia's father, Nathan.

NATHAN'S CANE Nathan used to bang his cane on the arms of his wheelchair, demanding his Father's Day cake.

NATHAN'S HEADSTONE It killed Cass's husband Henry when it fell on him in Nathan's grave.

A STROKE Before Bedelia met Peter Yarbro, her father Nathan Grantham had had a stroke. Bedelia had the job of nursing him.

❖❖❖

(12b)
CREEPSHOW
"The Lonesome Death of Jordy Verrill"

["The Lonesome Death of Jordy Verrill" is the comic adaptation of the short story "Weeds," which first appeared in *Cavalier* magazine in May of 1976. The story was later reprinted in *Nugget* magazine in April of 1979.

A concordance to "Weeds" – the text version of "The Lonesome Death of Jordy Verrill" – immediately follows this concordance, and is keyed "12b1."– **sjs**]

People

BILKMORE, MR. Jordy Verrill's banker.

BROTHER MELVIN A contributor to Reverend Fleece U. White's Church of the Holy Shrinking Purse.

GEESON, DR. RICHARD Jordy Verrill's doctor.

HIGGINS, DR. PETER V. The Castle Rock doctor who was taking Doc Geeson's calls. Geeson was fishing.

VERRILL, JORDY The hapless Maine farmer who one day found a meteor on his farm.

VERRILL, MR. Jordy's dead father. He appeared to Jordy in a mirror and told him that if he took a bath, he was a goner.

WHITE, REVEREND FLEECE U. An evangelist Jordy watched on TV. White was the pastor of The Church of the Holy Shrinking Purse.

Places

CASTLE ROCK, MAINE The town where Dr. Peter V. Higgins had his practice.

THE CHURCH OF THE HOLY SHRINKING PURSE Reverend Fleece U. White's evangelical television ministry.

THE DEPARTMENT OF METEORS After the meteor landed on Jordy's land, he fantasized about bringing it to the College's Department of Meteors.

Things

THE CREEP'S "LONESOME DEATH OF JORDY VERRILL" CLOSE The Creep closed the story with the following:

"...Hear that, kiddies? Rain tonight, heh-heh! I guess that old Verrill luck is in again, eh? You can decide for yourself if Jordy finally had a bit of good luck when he managed to pull that trigger! But don't think too long, kiddies...Our next yell yarn awaits..."

THE CREEP'S "LONESOME DEATH OF JORDY VERRILL" INTRO The Creep introduced the Creepshow version of "Weeds" thusly:

"Heh-Heh! Hello again, kiddies...my last story was so grim it even frightened me! So I decided to head for the hills...you know the other side of the mountain whereat the grass is always greener...which brings to mind another tale..."

FIFTY DOLLARS In Jordy's "Department of Meteors" fantasy, he imagined the college offering him fifty dollars for his meteor. He definitely wouldn't take less than $200.

METEORCRAP The fluid that seeped from the meteor after Jordy broke it open.

$200 In Jordy's "Department of Meteors" fantasy, he imagined the college offering him fifty dollars for his meteor. Jordy wanted at least $200.

WKBS The TV station Jordy was watching when he killed himself.

—*Addendum*—
(12b1)
"Weeds"

["Weeds" is the original text version of the *Creepshow* segment "The Lonesome Death of Jordy Verrill," and first appeared in *Cavalier* magazine in May of 1976 and was later reprinted in *Nugget* magazine in April of 1979. A concordance to this story is included to allow you to compare the changes made from the original to the *Creepshow* version.

A concordance to "The Lonesome Death of Jordy Verrill," – the *Creepshow* adaptation of "Weeds" – immediately precedes this concordance, and is keyed "12b." – **sjs**]

People

A BAT Jordy had once gotten a bat caught in his hair when he was insulating Missus Carver's attic.

CARVER, MISSUS Jordy had once gotten a bat caught in his hair when he was insulating Missus Carver's attic.

CONDON, DOC Jordy's doctor. Jordy called Doc when he saw that green moss had started to grow on his fingers where he had touched the meteor.

MCGINTY, ARLEN Jordy Verrill's neighbor. By the time Jordy began to "sprout," the weeds had spread up to McGinty's land.

OAKLEY, DR. The other doctor in Cleaves Mill besides Doc Condon. Dr. Oakley wanted to be paid when he rendered services.

VERRILL, JORDY A New Hampshire farmer who had a place on Bluebird Creek that consisted of a small house with two outbuildings. One day he found a meteor.

VERRILL, MR. Jordy's daddy. He had once made Jordy get out of bed to hear the corn grow.

WARREN, MR. Jordy Verrill's banker.

Places

BLUEBIRD CREEK Jordy Verrill's farm was on Bluebird Creek in New Hampshire. After the meteor's "moss" began to spread, the whole creek was covered in green.

BOSTON In the winter, Jordy Verrill hauled Christmas trees to Boston.

CLEAVES MILLS, NEW HAMPSHIRE The town where Jordy Verrill lived.

MISSUS CARVER'S ATTIC Jordy had once gotten a bat caught in his hair when he was insulating Missus Carver's attic.

NEW HAMPSHIRE The state where Jordy Verrill's farm was located.

Things

BIG THINKING One of Jordy Verrill's Three Types of Thinking. Big Thinking was "like when all the cows died and he was trying to figure if Mr. Warren down at the bank would give him an extension on his loan. Like when you had to decide which bills to pay at the end of the month. Like what he was going to do about this meteor."

A BUCKET FILLED WITH WATER AND A BROOM Jordy used a bucket of water and a broom to fight grass fires on his land.

CAVALIER, **MAY 1976** The first appearance of the short story "Weeds."

"CLEAVES MILLS-FOOD" One of the two types of food that the meteor plants found on Earth. (The other was "Jordy-food.")

CORNHUSKER'S LOTION The lotion Jordy spread on his blistered fingers after he touched the hot meteor.

DIRTY BOOKS Jordy wore glasses when he read dirty books.

DR. OAKLEY'S SIGN A sign in Dr. Oakley's office said: "It is customary to pay cash unless arrangements have been made in advance."

A DODGE PICKUP Jordy Verrill's truck.

FOOD The plants that grew from the meteor moss were sentient and considered Jordy to be food.

FORTY-SIX Jordy's age when he touched the meteor and doomed himself to never seeing age forty-seven.

A .410 REMINGTON SHOTGUN The gun with which Jordy killed himself.

THE FOURTH OF JULY On the Fourth of July, a meteor landed on Jordy Verrill's land.

A HALF BOTTLE OF RIPPLE Jordy drank a half bottle of Ripple after the "moss infection" (the "Jordy weeds") began to spread.

JORDY VERRILL'S THREE TYPES OF THINKING Plain Thinking, Work Thinking, and Big Thinking. [NOTE: See individual "Things" entries for details on each type of thinking.]

JORDY VERRILL'S WAYS OF EARNING A LIVING Jordy grew carrots, fixed cars, and in the winter he sold wood and hauled Christmas trees to Boston.

JORDY'S TRASH In Jordy's trash was a Bacardi bottle, a Del Monte pineapple chunks can, and a Heinz catsup bottle.

"JORDY-FOOD" One of the two types of food the meteor plants found on Earth.

KODAK The camera Jordy used to take pictures of the meteor that fell on his land.

LOUIS L'AMOUR WESTERNS Jordy wore glasses when he read L'Amour's westerns.

A METEOR On the Fourth of July, a meteor landed on Jordy Verrill's land.

NUGGET, **APRIL 1979** The second appearance of the short story "Weeds."

PLAIN THINKING One of Jordy Verrill's Three Types of Thinking. Plain Thinking was "like what you were going to have for supper or the best way to pull a motor with his old and balky chain-fall."

QUAKER OATS When Jordy took pictures of the meteor with his Kodak, he noticed that there were still "Quaker Oats" coming out of it.

RED CROSS COTTON Jordy wrapped his meteorcrap-infected fingers in Red Cross cotton.

THE SEED CATALOGUE Jordy wore glasses when he read the seed catalogue.

$700 The amount of money Jordy owed Mr. Warren.

TWENTY-FIVE DOLLARS The amount of money Jordy wanted from the college for his meteor.

VERRILL LUCK Jordy was sure he had the Verrill luck, and it was spelled B-A-D.

VICKS VAPORUB AND BACARDI RUM Jordy Verrill's regime for fighting off an illness: sweat it out with Vicks and Bacardi.

"THE WEEDS BEGAN TO GROW TOWARDS TOWN" The last line of "Weeds."

THE "WEEDS" INTRO *Cavalier* magazine introduced "Weeds" as follows: "More Than A Green Thumb...Will Be Necessary To Stop The Weeds. A chilling new story by the author of *Carrie* and *'Salem's Lot*."

WORK THINKING One of Jordy Verrill's Three Types of Thinking. Work Thinking was thinking that he did about work.

❖❖❖

(12c)
CREEPSHOW
"The Crate"

["The Crate" is the comic adaptation of the short story "The Crate." The following concordance is taken from this comic adaptation, but most of the information about the story is contained in the text version.

A concordance to "The Crate" – the text version of this story – immediately follows this concordance, and is keyed "12c1." – sjs]

People

GERESON, CHARLIE The student that Professor Stanley first told about the thing in the crate.

LATIMER, HENRY The Horlicks University janitor who found the crate.

NORTHRUP, HENRY Wilma's husband. Henry fed Wilma to the thing in the crate.

NORTHRUP, WILMA Bitch; Crate-Thing food.

STANLEY, DEXTER Horlicks University professor.

Places

AMBERSON HALL The Horlicks University hall where the crate was found.

HORLICKS UNIVERSITY The school where the crate was found.

Things

THE CREEP'S CLOSING COMMENTS TO "THE CRATE" The Creep signed off with this:

"Heh-heh! Well, I guess Wilma got what was coming to her, eh kiddies? But such manners! Not so much as a thank you...the only word to describe Wilma now is...are you ready, kiddies...Incrate!! Heh-Heh!!"

THE CREEP'S INTRO TO "THE CRATE" The Creep introduced "The Crate" as follows:

"Heh-heh! Welcome, kiddies...I don't know about you, but I'm feeling a bit edgy! Maybe I'm still feeling the effects of our last story...or maybe it's just because I haven't been out in a long time! That's it! I've got that boxed-in feeling, heh-heh! Which reminds me of another tale in my lurid lexicon! A little fear fable called...THE CRATE"

HENRY'S LETTER TO WILMA TO GET HER TO COME TO THE UNIVERSITY Henry wrote the following letter to lure Wilma to Amberson Hall [NOTE: Compare with the original text version in 12c1 below]:

Wilma,
I've had to leave in a hurry because of a call from Dexter Stanley. He seems to have gotten himself into a great deal of trouble...it seems he got a young woman to accompany him to Amberson Hall, and then *attacked* her. I'm sorry but that's the kindest way to put it...I

tried to get him to tell me what happened but he only kept repeating "It's awful, Henry, it's awful!"

Wilma, could you come out here? I know it's asking a lot...but you're always so clear-headed about these things. As you so often say, what would I do without you?

—Addendum—
(12c1)
"The Crate"

["The Crate" is the original text version of the *Creepshow* segment "The Crate." It first appeared in *Gallery* magazine in July of 1979, and its latest reprinting was in *The Arbor House Treasury of Horror and the Supernatural* in 1981 (which also contained an Introduction by Stephen King.). A concordance to this story is included to allow you to compare the changes made between the original and the *Creepshow* version.

A concordance to the *Creepshow* comic adaptation of "The Crate" immediately precedes this concordance, and is keyed "12c." —sjs]

People

BADLINGER The guy who beat out Henry for the English departmental chair.

BILLIE Wilma Northrup.

CARPENTER, JULIA The woman who found the monster that ended up in a crate beneath a stairwell in Horlicks University. She found the little devil while on an arctic expedition in 1834.

CHRISTIAN MISSIONARIES The Paella and Terra del Fuego peoples were killed off when they contracted diseases carried by fleas living in the blankets given to them by Christian missionaries.

A DOG On the day the thing in the crate was discovered, two Horlicks students played Frisbee with an unnamed dog.

THE EXPLORER'S CLUB SURVIVORS The London Explorer's Club tried for the South Pole in 1850. Their ship sank, and the three or four survivors sucked dew from their clothes and ate kelp to survive. They claimed to have seen sea monsters.

GERESON, CHARLIE A Horlicks grad student. He was the thing in the crate's second victim.

"THE GIRL" The nonexistent girl Henry invented to get Wilma to Amberson Hall.

HALLEY The female assistant professor who found a box of mouse head clamps. Halley graduated from Berkeley, and wore her hair like Farrah Fawcett-Majors.

THE JANITOR The Horlicks University janitor who was the thing in the crate's first victim.

THE JANITOR'S FATHER He had been a carpenter.

NORTHRUP, HENRY Wilma's husband.

NORTHRUP, WILMA Henry's wife. She told everyone to "just call me Billie, everyone does." She was a world-class bitch and Henry found a way to get rid of her: he fed her to the thing in the crate.

THE PAELLA AND TERRA DEL FUEGO PEOPLE They were killed off when they contracted diseases carried by fleas living in the blankets given to them by Christian missionaries.

STANLEY, DEXTER The sixty-one-year-old head of the Horlicks' University zoology department. He opened the crate.

TWO YOUNG MEN Two unnamed Horlicks students who played Frisbee with a dog in front of the dorms.

VINEY, PROFESSOR Professor Viney had found an antique gerbil run at Horlicks. It was on display at the Museum of Natural Science in Washington.

Places

AMBERSON HALL The crate was found in Horlicks' Amberson Hall. Amberson Hall was sometimes called "The Old Zoology Building."

BERKELEY The school Halley had attended.

CATHER HALL Horlicks University's new zoology building.

HANCOCK HOUSE A restaurant.

HORLICKS UNIVERSITY The crate was found at Horlicks..

THE MUSEUM OF NATURAL SCIENCE Professor Viney had found an antique gerbil run at Horlicks. It was on display at the Museum of Natural Science in Washington.

NORTH CAMPUS AVENUE The street where Henry and Wilma Northrup lived.

THE OLD FRONT DORMS The Horlick University buildings that went back to the turn of the century.

THE OLD ZOOLOGY BUILDING Amberson Hall.

PAELLA A small island south of Tierra del Fuego. It was the smallest island inhabited by man. Easter Island-type monoliths were found there. The crate started its trip to Horlicks from Paella.

PAELLA / SANTIAGO / SAN FRANCISCO / CHICAGO / NEW YORK / HORLICKS The crate's route to Horlicks.

ROOM 6 Room 6 in Amberson Hall was a big lecture hall.

RYDER'S QUARRY Henry dumped the crate in Ryder's Quarry after the thing inside ate Wilma.

THE UNION Horlicks campus eatery.

Things

CHESS NIGHT Every Thursday, Henry Northrup played chess. His wife Wilma used that night to take two classes.

THE CRATE'S MARKINGS Written on the side of the crate was the following:

SHIP TO HORLICKS UNIVERSITY
VIA JULIA CARPENTER
ARCTIC EXPEDITION
JUNE 19, 1834

CUTTY SARK The scotch Henry Northrup gave to Dexter Stanley.

1888 Horlicks University had been all male until 1888.

THE ENGLISH DEPARTMENT CHAIR Henry was beaten out of this position by Badlinger.

THE EXPLORER'S CLUB The London club that tried for the South Pole in 1850. Their ship sank, and the three or four survivors sucked dew from their clothes and ate kelp to survive. They claimed to have seen sea monsters.

A GERBIL RUN Professor Viney had found an antique gerbil run at Horlicks. It was on display at the Museum of Natural Science in Washington.

HENRY'S NOTE TO WILMA TO GET HER TO THE UNIVERSITY Henry wrote the following note to Wilma in order to lure her to Amberson Hall so she could be eaten by the thing in the crate:

Dear Billie,
I've just had a call from Dex Stanley. He's hysterical. Seems to have commited some sort of indiscretion with one of his female grad students. He's at Amberson Hall. So is the girl. For God's sake, come quickly. I'm not sure exactly what the situation is, but a woman's presence may be imperative, and under the circumstances, a nurse from the infirmary just won't do. I know you don't like Dex much, but a scandal like this could ruin his career. Please come.

Henry.

JUNE 19, 1834 The date the crate was shipped to Horlicks.

AN MG Henry Northrup's car.

MOUSE HEAD CLAMPS Halley found a box of clamps that had been used to hold the heads of white mice while they were operated on without anesthesia.

"NEGATIVE ENVIRONMENTAL FACTORS IN LONG-TERM ANIMAL MIGRATION" The topic of the paper Charlie Gereson was working on before he was eaten by the thing in the crate.

NESSIE A giant stuffed animal Badlinger bought for his kids.

A QUARTER The janitor had flipped a quarter, it fell under a stairway, and that was how the crate was discovered.

THE SCOUT Henry and Wilma Northrup's other vehicle (in addition to the MG).

SIXTY BOXES OF *THE AMERICAN ZOOLOGIST* Sixty boxes of *The American Zoologist* were found at Horlicks University, along with an antique gerbil run.

THE THING IN THE CRATE It was "a fury, writhing shape...that appeared to have not four but six legs and the flat bullet head of a young lynx."

A VOLKSWAGEN A VW with a "NO NUKES" sticker on the back deck was headed for Upper Circle.

ZIPPO Henry Northrup's lighter.

❖❖❖

(12d)

CREEPSHOW
"Something To Tide You Over"
People

FIELDS, W.C. Star of "The Bank Dick."

VICKERS, BECKY Richard Vickers' wife and Harry Wentworth's lover. Richard buried her on the shore up to her head, and then videotaped her drowning. She came back from the dead with Harry, and they did the same thing to Richard.

VICKERS, RICHARD Becky's jealous husband. He killed both Becky and her lover, Harry Wentworth. They came back from the dead and exacted a watery revenge.

WENTWORTH, HARRY The man who was having an affair with Becky Vickers, Richard Vickers' wife. Richard found out and buried him on the shore up to his head. Harry drowned, came back to life, and did the same thing to Richard.

Places

THE BEACH Richard buried both Harry and Becky on the beach up to their heads, and then let them both drown. He videotaped the festivities.

"A HOUSE IN THE COUNTRY" Richard heard the following dialogue from "The Bank Dick," and then turned the movie off: "...a beautiful house in the country, upstairs and down, beer flowing over your grandmother's paisley shawl..."

THE OCEAN After Harry and Becky got their revenge on Richard, they walked back into the ocean from whence they came.

Things

"THE BANK DICK" After drowning Harry and Becky, Richard showered while "The Bank Dick" was playing on TV. He eventually turned it off, thinking to himself that he must have seen it a thousand times.

BECKY'S HOLE Richard Vickers dug a hole on the beach and buried his cheating wife Becky in it up to her head.

THE CREEP'S "SOMETHING TO TIDE YOU OVER" CLOSE The Creep signed off with this:

"Heh-heh! Looks like Richard got himself in over his head, eh kiddies? No? Well, it'll be over his head soon enough, heh-heh! and listen to him laugh! It's enough to drive you crazy! Of course, I've been crazy for years, so it doesn't

really bother me...ready for some more putrid prose, kiddies? Hee-hee..."

THE CREEP'S "SOMETHING TO TIDE YOU OVER" INTRO The Creep introduced this soggy saga thusly:

"Heh-heh. Hello, again, kiddies! My last story was so grueling, I thought I'd take a vacation...a little trip to the seashore! Of course, this reminds me of yet another awful anecdote...But the tide's coming in so I'd better get started! I call this one...SOMETHING TO TIDE YOU OVER."

HARRY'S HOLE Richard Vickers buried Harry Wentworth in his own hole on the beach, and then let Harry drown while watching his lover Becky drown in her own hole.

A VIDEO MONITOR AND CAMERA Richard Vickers very thoughtfully set up a video camera and monitor so that Harry and Becky could watch each other drown.

A VIDEOTAPE Richard played Harry a tape of Becky, buried in the sand, pleading for help...and the tide was coming in.

WATERLOGGED CORPSES After being drowned by Richard, Harry and Becky came back from the dead as waterlogged corpses. They buried Richard in the sand up to his head, and then walked back into the ocean...together.

❖❖❖

(12e)

CREEPSHOW
"They're Creeping Up On You"
People

CASTONMEYER, LENORE Norman Castonmeyer's wife. After her husband shot himself, Pratt sent her flowers.

CASTONMEYER, NORMAN One of Pratt's employees. On the night of the blackout, Castonmeyer shot himself at 8:30.

THE EXTERMINATOR Pratt gave Carl Reynolds half an hour to get an exterminator to Pratt's apartment.

GENDRON, GEORGE One of Pratt's employees. He called Pratt at 9:30 on the night of the blackout to discuss the Pacific Aerodyne takeover.

MEGGS, SERGEANT The police officer Upson Pratt called after he lost his power.

THE PARELLI BROTHERS White told Pratt that he could have the Parelli Brothers exterminators to Pratt's by 11:30.

PRATT, UPSON The incredibly wealthy clean freak who ended up with bugs in places he never imagined they could go.

REYNOLDS, MRS. Carl's wife. She was with her husband in Disneyworld on the night of the blackout.

REYNOLDS, CARL One of Pratt's employees. On the night of the blackout, he was in Orlando, Florida, with his family. He had taken his wife and kids to Disneyworld. Pratt gave Reynolds half an hour to get the super and the exterminator to Pratt's apartment, or he'd lose his job.

THE REYNOLDS KIDS Carl's kids. They were all in Disneyworld on the night of Pratt's blackout.

WHITE The super in Upson Pratt's building. He was a black guy named White.

Places

THE BUILDING ACROSS FROM PRATT The building that lost its power just before Pratt's building did.

DISNEYWORLD Carl Reynolds and his family were at Disneyworld in Orlando, Florida, on the night of Pratt's blackout.

ORLANDO, FLORIDA Carl Reynolds and his family were at Disneyworld in Orlando, Florida, on the night of Pratt's blackout.

PACIFIC AERODYNE An Upson Pratt takeover target.

PRATT'S BUILDING The huge high-rise that the bugs took over during a blackout.

THE PROJECTS Upson Pratt grew up poor in the projects.

A SKYSCRAPER The second building in Pratt's neighborhood to lose its power. Pratt's was next.

Things

A BLACKOUT Upson Pratt's building had a blackout, leaving Pratt alone with the (pretty pissed-off) bugs. They were, after all, the target of Pratt's systematic attempts at "roach genocide."

"CLEANLINESS IS NEXT TO PRATTLINESS" Upson Pratt's motto.

THE CREEP'S "THEY'RE CREEPING UP ON YOU" CLOSE AND FINAL SPEECH The Creep closed off *Creepshow* with:

> "So that's where the bugs went! Looks like old Mr. Pratt was right, after all, eh, kiddies? Those little suckers can hide anywhere, heh-heh! Well, that's our last yell-yarn for this time, and until we get together for another foul feast, I'll leave you with these famous words from the classic film 'Casebleccha'...as ole Boogey said to Ingrid Barrghman, 'Here's looking at you kiddies...heh-heh-heh...'"

The Creep was holding one of his eyeballs as he bid us farewell.

THE CREEP'S "THEY'RE CREEPING UP ON YOU" INTRO The Creep introduced this bugfest with the following:

> "Heh-heh! Well, kiddies, it seems you've caught me moonlighting! Let me tell you this job is enough to drive you bugs! The li'l suckers hide everywhere! Take it from me, kiddies, you gotta stay alert, because...THEY'RE CREEPING UP ON YOU"

11:30 White told Pratt that he could have the Parelli Brothers exterminators to Pratt's by 11:30.

FLOWERS After Norman Castonmeyer shot himself, Pratt sent his wife, Lenore, some flowers.

9:30 The time George Gendron called Pratt to discuss the Pacific Aerodyne takeover.

THE ROACHES During the blackout, they took over. They decided to move into Upson Pratt, and turn his body into their new condo complex.

UPSON PRATT'S MOTTO "Cleanliness is next to Prattliness."

THE RUNNING MAN

[NO DEDICATION]

[NO CONTENTS PAGE]

BOOK BREAKDOWN

The Running Man has 100 chapters, titled as follows:

"...Minus 100 and COUNTING..."

with each chapter number decreasing by 1, as in...

"...Minus 099 and COUNTING..."
"...Minus 098 and COUNTING..."
etc.

The final (101st) chapter is entitled:
"000"

THE RUNNING MAN
People

THE AIRLINE POLICE International law enforcement organization that was neither state nor federally controlled. It had been international since the UN Treaty of 1995. Ben thought of giving up to them. He had heard that if fugitives gave up to the Airline Police, they were given amnesty. Ben figured it wasn't true, and that he'd be immediately turned over to the Hunters.

THE BLOCK POLICE South City police force.

THE BOY Rolf's owner.

BURNS, ARTHUR M. The Assistant Director of Games.

THE CAB DRIVER Cab driver who picked up Ben Richards when he first left the Games Building. The driver told Ben he would have to report him.

THE COP An unnamed cop was standing by Nixon Memorial Park when Ben Richards got off the Games Building elevator that opened onto the street.

COWLES, BOBBY One of the kids who observed Laughlin cowering in a Highway Department shed.

COWLES, MARY One of the kids who observed Laughlin cowering in a Highway Department shed.

CRAGER, JACK A man Ben knew would be questioned about Ben's whereabouts.

CURRY An old man in the drugstore where Stacey went to buy medicine for Cassie.

DEEGAN, JOHN The name Ben used to sign in at the Boston Y.M.C.A. He said he was from Michigan.

DICKY The guy who worked at the Rockland Newsie. Dicky opened the national cable when Ben called and said he was holding Amelia Williams hostage.

DONAHUE, ROBERT S. The navigator on the plane Ben commandeered at Voigt Airfield. Donahue was actually a part of Games Council Control.

DONNIGAN, FLAPPER He was pitching nicks with Gerry Hanrahan on a corner when the cop went by to deliver an envelope to Richards' house.

DUNINGER, WAYNE The co-pilot of the plane Ben commandeered at Voigt Airfield.

THE FIVE POLICEMEN Free-Vee showed graduation pictures of the five policemen who died while chasing Richards.

FRANKIE Someone pounded on the door of Ben's room in the Boston Y.M.C.A. looking for Frankie.

FRIEDMAN, KIPPY The communications man on the plane Ben commandeered at Voigt Airfield.

GILLY The guy who owned Gilly's Town Line Store & Airstop.

GOLEON, RICH Bradley's friend.

GRADY, CHARLIE Network cop who grudgingly lent Ben Richards two New Quarters so he could call Sheila.

GRASSNER, FATHER OGDEN The name Ben Richards used to register at the Winthrop House.

GRIFFEN, JOHN The false name on Ben Richards' new ID papers.

HANRAHAN, GERRY He was pitching nicks with Flapper Donnigan on a corner when the cop went by to deliver an envelope to Richards' house.

HARRIS A man who had worked with Ben at General Atomics. Harris had told Ben what it felt like to be gutshot. Harris was a fat guy who drank illicit beer on the job.

HIZZONER The governor of Kansas.

HOLLOWAY, DON The pilot of the plane Ben commandeered at Voigt Airfield.

THE HUNTERS Game show force whose job it was to stop the "running men."

JAGGER, MICK Molie Jernigan remembered when Mick was a big name.

JANSKY, MR. Game show contestant.

JENNER, EILEEN A woman Ben knew would be questioned

about his whereabouts.

JENNER, MRS. The Richards' neighbor in Co-Op City.

JERNIGAN, MOLIE Molie ran a Dock Street hockshop, and could get you anything you needed, illegally. [NOTE: It wasn't said if Molie was a descendant of the Haven Jernigans from *The Tommyknockers*.] Molie was something of a Robin Hood: He banged the rich hard, but sold to the neighborhood people at close to his cost.

JESUS His picture was on the wall of Ben's room in the Boston Y.M.C.A

JOHNSBURY, GOVERNOR Area governor. Ben Richards thought of him as a "corn-holing sonofabitch."

JONES, MISS Network makeup artist.

KELLY, LIZ A receptionist reminded Ben Richards of this old Tee-Vee star.

KILLIAN, DAN Executive producer of "The Running Man."

LAUGHLIN, JIMMY Game show contestant who lived three blocks from Ben Richards on Dock Street.

MCCARTNEY, MICK Molie remembered that "Mick" was the drummer for that English group, The Beetles.

MCCONE, EVAN The man in charge of the Hunters.

MORAN, DINK A friend of Bradley's. Dink built a pollution counter.

AN OLDER MAN WITH SILVERY BARBERSHOP HAIR Rockland man who wore madras shorts that came down over his knees. He took a picture of Ben Richards – with the camera lens cap left on.

O'SANCHEZ, BUDGIE Walt O'Sanchez's father.

O'SANCHEZ, WALT Budgie O'Sanchez's son. Walt went for a doctor for Cathy Richards.

THE PARKING ATTENDANT The boy who read skin mags at the entrance to the U-Park-It.

PARRAKIS, ELTON A man in Portland who Bradley told Ben to see.

PARRAKIS, VIRGINIA Elton Parrakis's mother. She turned Ben in to the police.

THE "PLEDGE OF ALLEGIANCE" BOY Ben remembered a boy in grammar school whose pants fell down when he stood up to recite the Pledge of Allegiance.

"PRITCHARD" The cab driver who picked up Ben Richards as he left the Games Building thought Ben's name was "Pritchard."

RETTENMUND A friend of Ben Richards. Rettenmund told dirty stories.

RICH A friend of Bradley's. With Dink Moran, Rich built a pollution counter.

RICHARDS, BEN Twenty-eight-year-old man who decided to go on "The Running Man" on the slim chance that he'd survive and thus be able to buy medicine for his daughter and build a better life for his family. He ended up dying in a tremendous explosion as he flew a plane into the Games Building.

RICHARDS, CATHY (CATHERINE SARAH) Ben and Sheila Richards' eighteen-month-old daughter.

RICHARDS, SHEILA Ben Richards' wife.

RICHARDS, TODD Ben Richards' brother. Todd died at the age of twelve.

THE ROCKLAND NEWSIE GUY An unnamed station employee who took Ben Richard's hostage call.

ROLF German shepherd that chased and licked Ben.

THE SINGER As Ben realized he was being "bracketed" by police in the Boston Y.M.C.A, he went into the bathroom where someone was singing in the shower "in a cracked and pitchless voice."

THE SIXTY WOMEN In 2024, sixty women were killed marching on the Southwest Food Depository.

A SKELETON CREW Ben Richards demanded the following at Voigt Airfield: "I want a jet fully fueled and ready to fly with a skeleton crew."

SKINNER Stacey's nickname.

THE SMALL BOY A boy who offered Ben some scag in Portland.

THE STABBERS The gang Bradley belonged to.

STEPINFETCHIT Ben dreamt that Bradley was a comical caricature, a futuristic Stepinfetchit.

TAYLOR, GRACE A receptionist reminded Ben Richards of this old Tee-Vee star.

THOMPSON, BOBBY Host and emcee of "The Running Man."

THROCKMORTON, BRADLEY Stacey's eighteen-year-old brother.

THROCKMORTON, CASSIE Stacey's five-year-old sister. She had lung cancer.

THROCKMORTON, MRS. Bradley's mother.

THROCKMORTON, STACEY Eight-year-old black boy who thought Ben was the devil.

VICTOR, FRED Director of "The Running Man."

WARD, RINDA The network woman who gave Ben Richards his pre-game test.

WILLIAMS, MRS. AMELIA While on the run, Ben Richards jumped into her car and held her hostage.

THE WOMAN An unnamed woman who worked for the network. She wore shorts and a halter, and blew Ben a kiss as he prepared to begin his stint as a "running man."

(13)
THE RUNNING MAN
Places

"THE ASH FACTORY" AND "THE CREAMERY" The names the kids on the street called the Municipal Crematorium.

ATLANTA One of the places Ben thought he might go after he left Boston.

BLOCK HEALTH CLINIC The clinic where Ben Richards had been immunized against influenza.

BLOOD EMPORIUMS Ben Richards walked past them on his way to the Games Building.

BOOTH SIX Richards was sent there before his "Running Man" show to be tested.

THE BRANT HOTEL During his stint as a "running man," Ben Richards checked into the Brant, a hotel on the east side. He booked a room for two days, on the twenty-third floor.

BREEZE INN One of the summer homes in Rockland. There was a sign on the road leading to the cottage that said "Private Road."

CANADA After escaping the Boston Y.M.C.A. and meeting Stacey, Ben thought he might go to Canada.

THE CENTER A movie theater that showed Disney films.

CHRISTIAN LENDING LIBRARY One of the facilities at the Boston Y.M.C.A.

CLEVELAND Elton Parrakis told Ben that his tapes would have to go to Cleveland instead of Boston, since Bradley Throckmorton was on the run.

CLOUD-HI One of the summer homes in Rockland. There was a sign on the road leading to the cottage that said "5000 Volts."

CO-OP CITY The slum development in South City where Ben Richards and his family lived.

COMMONWEALTH AVENUE The street where Stacey mailed two clips for Ben Richards.

DERRY The town where the Voight Field jetport was located. [NOTE: Pennywise the Clown was no longer ruling the sewers in Derry.]

DESK 9 (Q-R) The desk in the Games Building to which Ben Richards was routed.

DOCK STREET The street three blocks from where Ben Richards lived. Jimmy Laughlin lived on Dock Street.

DRUMMOND STREET After he left the Games Building, Ben walked towards Drummond Street on his way to Molie's place.

ECHO FREE-VEE REPAIR Repair company. Their slogan was "Because you watch it, we won't botch it."

ECUADOR During Ben's "Running Man" examination, he heard a news report that fighting in Ecuador was worse.

ELIZABETH'S REST One of the summer homes in Rockland. There was a sign on the road leading to the cottage that said "Trespassers Will Be Shot."

FALMOUTH Amelia Williams' hometown.

42ND STREET The street where Ben attended the all-night "perverto" show.

GENERAL ATOMICS The company where Jimmy Laughlin had once worked as an engine wiper. Bradley said that the only good nose filters were from General Atomics.

GILLY'S TOWN LINE STORE & AIRSTOP Store on U.S. 1 where Ben stopped to call Rockland Newsie to tell them he was holding Amelia Williams hostage.

GLAMOUR COLUMN STORE The building Ben barely missed (by twelve feet) as he headed his plane toward the Games Building.

HARDING On the phony ID papers he bought from Molie Jernigan, Ben Richards gave his home as Harding.

HARDING, NEW YORK, BOISE, ALBUQUERQUE, OR COLUMBUS Bobby Thompson told his viewers to look out for Ben Richards: he could be in any of these places.

HARDING LAKE The view from the Games Building.

HARTFORD One of the places Ben thought he might go after he left Boston.

HOCKERIES Ben Richards walked past them on his way to the Games Building.

HONKY TONKS, BARS, AND AUTOSLOT EMPORIUMS The businesses that lined the streets of Rockland.

HUNTINGTON AVENUE The street where the Boston Y.M.C.A. was located.

INDIA During Ben's "Running Man" examination, he heard a news report that new cannibal riots had broken out in India.

JARROLD'S STORE Rolf's owner said there was a mailbox at Jarrold's.

JUST ME 'N PATTY One of the summer homes in Rockland. There was a sign on the road leading to the cottage that said "Keep Out."

LEWISTON Amelia Williams told Ben there were roadblocks in Lewiston.

LOT 16 The lot at Voigt Airfield where the Airline Police were waiting for Ben. Richards was told to proceed there.

MANCHESTER Bradley thought he could get a friend to drive Ben to Manchester.

MANUAL TRADES SCHOOL The last school Ben Richards had attended. He spent two years there.

MICHIGAN Home state for "John Deegan." [NOTE: See the entry DEEGAN, JOHN.]

MILK STREET Bradley told Ben that there was a spic on Milk Street who might sell Ben a Wint for $300.

MOLIE'S PLACE A Dock Street hockshop run by Molie Jernigan.

THE MUNICIPAL CREMATORIUM Ben Richards' mother and brother Todd were both cremated at Municipal.

THE NETWORK GAMES BUILDING The highest skyscraper in South City and the building where the Free-Vee game shows were produced. At the end of his stint as a "running man," and with his guts tangled about his feet, Ben Richards flew a plane into the side of the Games Building. "The explosion was tremendous, lighting up the night like the wrath of God, and it rained fire twenty blocks away."

NEW HAMPSHIRE One of the places Ben thought he might go after he left Boston.

NIXON MEMORIAL PARK A park in Co-Op City. A cop was standing by its frontage when Ben Richards got off the Games Building elevator that opened onto the street.

NORTHEASTERN UNIVERSITY The college further up Huntington Avenue in Boston.

THE PEOPLE'S FOUNTAIN PARK South City park. It cost seventy-five cents admission to enter.

PHILADELPHIA One of the places Ben thought he might go after he left Boston.

PINELAND Rolf's owner said he knew Ben wasn't from Pineland because he didn't look like a retard.

PORT AUTHORITY ELECTRIC BUS TERMINAL Ben bought a Greyhound ticket to Boston at the terminal. The ride cost him twenty-three dollars, and it left at 6:15.

RAMPART STREET An elevator out of the Games Building opened onto Rampart Street, the street where the "Running Man" chase began.

RAYGON CHEMICALS Fictitious company Bradley said he worked for as a district manager.

ROBARD STREET Ben Richards' ostensible destination when he first left the Games Building. He was actually going to Molie's place, which was five blocks from Robard Street.

ROCKLAND NEWSIE Free-Vee Tabloid #6943. The station Ben called to say that he was holding Amelia Williams hostage.

ROOM 512 Ben's room at the Boston Y.M.C.A.

ROUTE 495 The route Bradley took with Richards hidden in the trunk of the car.

SCARBOROUGH On his way to Portland, Ben drove through the suburbs of Scarborough.

SEAT 100 The seat on the plane where the parachute pack that Ben got from McCone sat.

SET-A-SPELL One of the summer homes in Rockland. There was a sign on the road leading to the cottage that said "Guard Dogs on Patrol."

SOUTH CITY The area where Ben Richards and his family lived in a slum development called Co-Op City.

THE SOUTHWEST FOOD DEPOSITORY In 2024, sixty women were killed marching on the Southwest Food Depository.

THOMASTON Rolf's owner wanted to know if Ben has escaped from Thomaston.

TOKYO By the year 2012, everyone in Tokyo had to wear a nose filter because of the pollution.

TOPEKA There was a rumor that Laughlin had once raped a woman in Topeka.

TRADES HIGH The high school Sheila and Ben Richards had attended.

THE U-PARK-IT GARAGE Bradley left a car there for Richards.

THE VENDO-SPENDO COMPANY The company where Elton Parrakis worked.

VERMONT One of the places Ben thought he might go after he left Boston.

VOIGT FIELD, DERRY A jetport.

WINTERPORT The town to which Ben and Amelia Williams drove after they left Rockland.

THE WINTHROP HOUSE Hotel on Winthrop Street where Bradley reserved a room for Richards.

WINTHROP STREET The street where the Winthrop House hotel was located.

X-HOUSES Porno parlors. They advertised "!!24 Perversions—Count 'Em 24!!"

Y.M.C.A. The place Ben stayed in Boston. It was on Huntington Avenue.

(13)
THE RUNNING MAN
Things

A-62 The tank that blocked the main gate at Voigt Airfield in Derry.

AN ALL-NIGHT PERVERTO SHOW After booking a room at the Brant, Ben spent five hours at an all-night perverto show.

ARROW Mens' shirts.

AN AXIAL CHARGE CARD One of the items of identification Ben Richards needed to buy from Molie Jernigan.

BEN'S BREAKFAST AT THE BRANT He had a poached egg on

toast, an orange drink, and coffee sent to his room.

BEN'S DISGUISE Ben bought the following disguise paraphrenalia from Molie Jernigan: grey hair, spectacles, mouth wadding, and plastic buck-teeth.

BEN'S "LAST MEAL" Ben ordered the following meal in his suite the night before his chance on "The Running Man": steak, peas, mashed potatoes, milk, and apple cobbler.

BEN'S NEEDS Ben needed the following items from Molie Jernigan: a driver's license, a military service card, a Street Identicard, an Axial Charge Card, and a Social Retirement Card.

BEN'S TIMETABLE AFTER LEAVING THE GAMES BUILDING 12:30—He emerged onto Robard Street; 1:15—He was on the north side of the Canal; 1:30—He hailed a cab; 1:50—He was at the airport; 2:20—He took a Speed Shuttle to New York; 3:06—He deplaned in New York; 3:15—He took a cab down Lindsay Overway and crossed Central Park; 3:20—He disappeared into the largest city on the face of the earth.

BLACK IRISH Dynacore Hi-Impact Plastic Explosive.

BLAMS Cigarettes Ben bought from a vending machine in the Games Building.

BRADLEY'S NOTE TO BEN As Ben headed to Portland, he read the note Bradley had given him. It said:

94 State Street, Portland
THE BLUE DOOR, GUESTS
Elton Parrakis (& Virginia Parrakis)

CANNIBAL RIOTS During Ben's "Running Man" examination, he heard a news report that new cannibal riots had broken out in India.

CANOGYN Truth serum that left no trace. McCone was waiting for three ampoules of it to use on Amelia Williams, but it was too late to stop Ben Richards from taking off from Voigt Airfield.

CAVE ART AND EGYPTIAN ARTIFACTS Art objects Dan Killian collected.

A CERTIFICATE OF MERIT One of the things Bobby and Mary Cowles were given for finding and turning in Laughlin.

CHEVIES One of the cars Ben saw as he stood at his window in the Boston Y.M.C.A., counting cars out of boredom.

THE COMPULSORY BENEFIT BILL OF 2021 The bill that failed to make it illegal to turn off Free-Vee.

THE COWLES' REWARD For finding Laughlin, Bobby and Mary Cowles were given the following: a Certificate of Merit, a Lifetime Supply of Funtwinks Cereal, and a check for a thousand New Dollars each.

THE DETROIT TIGERS They were playing the Harding Catamounts.

DETROIT VOR Communications vector Halloway had been speaking to when Ben Richards came up to the plane's cockpit.

"DIG YOUR GRAVE" One of the game shows on Free-Vee.

"DO NOT DISTURB" The sign Ben hung on the doorknob of his room in the Brant Hotel.

DRIVER'S LICENSE One of the items of identification Ben Richards needed to buy from Molie Jernigan.

THE F.B.I. AND THE C.I.A. Evan McCone had inherited these two agencies.

$15.50 The cost of Ben's room at the Boston Y.M.C.A.

FORDS One of the cars Ben saw as he stood at his window in the Boston Y.M.C.A., counting cars out of boredom.

FREE-VEE Future TV; ubiquitous mind-altering interactive television. It was the law that every building have one, although it was still legal to turn them off.

FREE-VEE TABLOID #6943 The Rockland Newsie.

FRISCO PUSH Speed. Twenty oldbucks a tab.

"FUK THE NETWORK" Message scrawled in foot-high letters in the bathroom of the Boston Y.M.C.A above the urinal.

"FUN GUNS" One of the game shows on Free-Vee.

G-A/IBM The pencil Ben Richards used to take his pre-game test.

GENERAL ATOMIC MODEL 6925-A9 Android state police officer. 16-psm Iridium Batteries were included. It came in white only.

GIDEON BIBLE The bible in Ben's room at the Brant Hotel.

HARDING CATAMOUNTS They were playing the Detroit Tigers.

HEROIN OR SAN FRANCISO PUSH During his "Running Man" pre-game examination, Ben Richards was asked if he did either of these drugs. He didn't use either.

HONDACYCLES The cycles that passed over the manhole cover under which Ben waited to escape from the pipe he used to leave the Boston Y.M.C.A.

"HOW HOT CAN YOU TAKE IT" One of the game shows on Free-Vee.

JIFFY SNIFFERS Automated sniffing devices the police used on the backroads.

JULY 2023 One of the dates Ben Richards had been immunized against influenza.

THE LABELS Bradley gave Ben gummed labels that said "After five days return to Brickhill Manufacturing Company, Manchester, N.H." Ben was to send Bradley the tapes using these labels and Bradley would then send them to Games from Boston.

A LIFETIME SUPPLY OF FUNTWINKS CEREAL One of the things Bobby and Mary Cowles were given for finding and turning in Laughlin.

A LOCKHEED G.A. OR A DELTA SUPERSONIC Ben demanded either one of these planes, or else he'd blow the Dynacore he (supposedly) had in his pocket.

A LOCKHEED/G.A. SUPERBIRD An airplane that took off from Voigt Airfield.

MACE-B, TEAR GAS, AND HEAVY ARMOR-PIERCING WEAPONRY The police held these weapons as Ben drove along the service ramp in the Northern States Terminal of Voigt Airfield.

A MAGNUM/SPRINGSTUN The machine pistol Donahue pointed at McCone on the plane Ben had commandeered. Donahue was actually on the Games Council.

THE MAIN STORM DRAIN Ben escaped from the Boston Y.M.C.A. through an underground storm drainpipe.

THE MASSACRE IN '24 The massacre in which sixty women were killed marching on the Southwest Food Depository.

MEATLOAF SUPREME AND THUNDERBIRD WINE Ben's Sunday dinner at the Winthrop House.

MILITARY SERVICE CARD One of the items of identification Ben Richards needed to buy from Molie Jernigan.

A MOTHER GOOSE MOBILE A Mother Goose Mobile hung above Cathy Richards' crib.

AN N.A.A.C.P. PIN Bradley wore one on his tie.

NEW DOLLARS The revalued and devalued money of the future.

940 Ben Richards' bed number in the Games Building.

"NO SMOKING IN THIS HALL BY ORDER OF FIRE MARSHALL" This sign appeared every twenty paces in the halls of the Boston Y.M.C.A.

OLD BUCKS Old money before the government revalued the currency.

ONE BILLION NEW DOLLARS The grand prize on the "Running Man." All the contestant had to do was evade the Hunters and remain free for thirty days.

ONE HUNDRED NEW DOLLARS The amount Ben Richards would receive for every hour he remained free during his participation on "The Running Man." If he could last thirty days without getting caught, his grand prize would be one billion new dollars.

165 POUNDS Ben Richards' weight.

126 Ben Richards' certified Weschler Test IQ. He was tested at the age of fourteen.

OTTO The automatic pilot on the plane Ben Richards commandeered at Voigt Airfield.

PERVERT MAGS In Co-Op City, these were safe to carry, but actual books were regarded with suspicion.

THE DARK TOWER: THE GUNSLINGER

DEDICATION

TO

ED FERMAN

who took a chance on these stories,
one by one

CONTENTS PAGE

ILLUSTRATIONS
[by Michael Whelan]

Silence came back in, filling jagged spaces.
  [*The Gunslinger*]
They paused...looking up at the dangling, twisting body.
  [*The Way Station*]
He could see his own reflection...
  [*The Oracle and the Mountains*]
The boy shrieked aloud...
  [*The Slow Mutants*]
There the gunslinger sat, his face turned up into the fading light.
  [*The Gunslinger and the Dark Man*]

BOOK BREAKDOWN

"The Gunslinger" (Twenty untitled sections numbered II-XX; the first section is unnumbered)
"The Way Station" (Three untitled sections numbered II-III; the first section is unnumbered)
"The Oracle and the Mountains" (One unnumbered section)
"The Slow Mutants" (One unnumbered section)
"The Gunslinger and the Dark Man" (One unnumbered section)
Afterword (One unnumbered section)

(14)
THE DARK TOWER: THE GUNSLINGER

[NOTE: The following concordance covers all five stories that comprise the first volume of the *Dark Tower* series, *The Gunslinger*. See the legend below for the story key. — **sjs**]

(1) = "The Gunslinger"
(2) = "The Way Station"
(3) = "The Oracle and the Mountains"
(4) = "The Slow Mutants"
(5) = "The Gunslinger and the Dark Man"

People

THE AGELESS STRANGER (5) Maerlyn. Walter, the Man in Black's master.
AILEEN (2) A woman from the Gunslinger's past. He thought of her after he heard Jake's story of how Jake was killed in the other world.
ALICE (1) The bartender at Sheb's in Tull. Roland slept with her.
ALLIE (1) Alice, the Tull bartender.
ARTHUR (2) A King from Roland's past.
THE BEAST (5) The keeper of the Tower.
THE BORDER DWELLERS (1) The people who had told the Gunslinger that devils lived in the flames of the devil-grass.
BROWN (1) The man who lived in a hut in the desert with Zoltan, his crow. Brown was young and had waist-length hair. Roland ate with him.
CASTNER (1) He owned the dry goods emporium in Tull.
CASTNER, MRS. (1) Castner's slat-sided wife.
CHAMBERS, JAKE (JOHN) (2) The boy Roland met at the Way Station, and who was killed in the other world when he was pushed in front of a Cadillac. He died by falling into an abyss when Roland chose to pursue the Man in Black rather than rescue Jake.

CHAMBERS, MR. (2) Jake's father. He worked for The Network.
CHAMBERS, MRS. (2) Jake's mother.
"CHARLIE" (1) One of the three kids shooting marbles on the main street of Tull called the Gunslinger a "weed-eater," and asked "How long you been screwin' your sister, Charlie?"
CORT (1) Roland's teacher. After the massacre in Tull, the Gunslinger thought of Cort, who had taught him how to shoot.
CUTHBERT (2) Roland's childhood friend.
DAVID (2) Roland's falcon.
DINOSAURS (5) Roland dreamed of dinosaurs during the Man in Black's enchantment.
THE DRINKERS (1) When the Gunslinger first entered Sheb's, there were four or five of Tull's townsfolk at the bar.
FELDON, AMY (1) Tull woman. Zachary once threw her skirts over her head and painted zodiac signs on her knees.
THE FIRST (3) The first of the three that Roland had to draw together. He was young and dark-haired, and a demon called heroin had infested him.
GABRIELLE (2) Roland's mother.
THE GUARD (2) An unnamed guard who chatted with Hax the cook.
THE GUNSLINGER (1) Roland.
HAX (2) A cook Roland knew as a child. Hax was hung on Gallows Hill for blowing up the tracks at the railhead and for the dead stock in Hendrickson.
THE HOSTLER (1) The man who took care of the Gunslinger's mule.
THE INTERLOPER (1) The subject of Sylvia Pittston's sermon when the Gunslinger was in Tull.
JEREMIAH (3) The Man in Black was a prophet of doom, his voice the voice of Jeremiah.
JESUS (1) A madman once gave Roland a Silva compass and told him to give it to Jesus.
JONAS (2) An old man Roland thought of after he heard Jake tell the story of how he was killed in the other world.
JONSON (1) Tull resident who confessed to Sylvia Pittston.
KENNERLY (1) Livery man in Tull. He was "plagued with daughters." Kennerly saw the Man in Black come into town. At the time, Kennerly had the hot flesh of his second daughter's left breast in his hand.
KENNERLY'S DAUGHTERS (1) He had two half-grown, a baby in the dirt, and the full-grown Soobie.
A KUVIAN NIGHT-SOLDIER (5) As the Man in Black prepared to tell Roland's fortune, a "mocking note" creeped into his voice, "like a Kuvian night-soldier with a killing-knife gripped in his hand."
LAZARUS (4) He was raised from the dead by Jesus.
LEPERS AND MADMEN (1) Lepers and madmen lived in the Mohaine desert in huddles made of sod.
A MADMAN (1) As Roland led his mule out of the foothills, a madman gave him a stainless steel Silva compass and told him to give it to Jesus.
MAERLYN (5) The Ageless Stranger. The Man in Black's master.
MAGGIE (2) A girl who worked for Hax the cook.
THE MAN IN BLACK (1) A mysterious sorcerer that Roland, the last Gunslinger, tracked. Roland knew that the Man in Black was somehow tied up with his quest for the Dark Tower, but could not identify in what way he would be involved. The Man in Black's name was Walter.
MARTEN (2) That "incomplete enchanter"; Roland's father's right-hand man. (Or was it the other way around?) Marten betrayed Roland's father with the help of Roland's mother.
MERLIN (2) A magician.
MILL, AUNT (1) A woman who sang in Sheb's.
A MULE (1) The Gunslinger led a mule out of the foothills and came upon Brown's hut.
THE MUMMY (4) Jake and Roland found a mummy in the deserted underground station. The mummy was wearing a

trainsman's blue uniform.

THE MUSIC LOVERS (1) When the Gunslinger first entered Sheb's, six of Tull's townsfolk were grouped around the piano listening to Sheb play.

NORT (1) An old man with wild gray hair who was collapsed at a table in Sheb's. He had died a while back, and the Man in Black had brought him back from the dead by spitting in his face. After the massacre in Tull, Nort was crucified on the roof of Sheb's.

AN OLD MAN (1) An old man with a straw hat who sat on the steps of a boarded-up grocery store. The Gunslinger saw him on the main street of Tull as he entered the town.

AN OLD MAN (1) On his way through Tull, the Man in Black had healed an old man of thirty-five.

PAPPA DOC (1) The man who brought beans out to Brown's hut once in a while.

PAUL (2) Roland's childhood friend.

THE PEOPLE ON THE STREET OF TULL (1) As the gunslinger entered the town, he saw the following people: Three ladies wearing black slacks and identical middy blouses, an old man with a straw hat who sat on the steps of a boarded-up grocery store, a scrawny tailor in his shop, taking care of a customer, a young boy, age thirteen, and his girl, and three boys shooting marbles.

PITTSTON, SYLVIA (1) Woman preacher in Tull. In five years she had worn out five Bibles. She claimed to have walked in the lions' den with Daniel; that she stood with David as he was tempted by Bathsheba; that she was in the furnace with Shadrach, Meshach, and Abednego; that she slew 2,000 with Samson; that she was blinded with St. Paul on the road to Damascus; and that she wept with Mary at Golgotha.

THE REAL MINISTER (1) The man who used to live in the shack behind the church in Tull. Sylvia Pittston took it over.

ROBESON (2) The man from the Guard who conspired with Hax to poison the meat for Farson.

ROLAND (2) The last Gunslinger.

ROLAND THE ELDER (2) Roland's father. A desperately thin man with a handlebar moustache. He was betrayed by Marten.

THE SCRAWNY TAILOR (1) He took care of a customer in his shop. The Gunslinger saw him on the main street of Tull as he entered the town.

THE SECOND (3) The second of the three that Roland had to draw together. She would come to him on wheels.

SHAW, MRS. GRETA (2) Jake Chambers' mother's cook in the "other world."

SHEB (1) The piano player at Sheb's. He owned the joint.

SIX TOWNIES (1) When the Gunslinger first entered Sheb's, there were six townies in the back playing "Watch Me."

THE SLOW MUTANTS (4) Hideous mutations that Roland and Jake came upon deep in the mountains. "The face was that of a starving idiot. The faint naked body had been transformed into a knotted mess of tentacular limbs with suckers."

SOOBIE (1) One of Kennerly's daughters.

THE SPEAKING DEMON (2) The dead voice of Alice that Roland heard emanating from a jawbone in the wall of the cellar of the Way Station.

SUSAN (2) Roland's beloved. "The lovely girl at the window" Roland thought of after hearing Jake tell the story of how he got killed in the other world.

THE THIRD (3) The third of the three Roland had to draw together. He would come in chains.

THREE BOYS SHOOTING MARBLES (1) The Gunslinger saw them as he entered Tull.

THE THREE LADIES (1) Three ladies wearing black slacks and identical middy blouses. The Gunslinger saw them on the main street of Tull as he entered the town.

ULYSSES (3) Jake told Roland that he knew about Ulysses.

WALTER (5) The Man in Black.

A WOOD NYMPH (3) Roland saw the face of a wood nymph in the trees that overhung the Oracle's altar.

A YOUNG BOY (1) Thirteen-year-old boy the Gunslinger saw as he entered Tull.

A YOUNG GIRL (1) The thirteen-year-old boy's girlfriend. The Gunslinger saw her as he entered Tull.

ZACHARY (1) Tull man. Once, he threw Amy Feldon's skirts over her head and painted zodiac signs on her knees.

ZOLTAN (1) Brown's raven.

(14)
THE DARK TOWER:
THE GUNSLINGER
Places

AN ANCIENT BOOTERY (4) A deserted booth in the underground station.

THE BACK COURTS (2) When Roland was a child, the Back Courts were where the ladies played at Points.

THE BARN (1) The hostler took care of the Gunslinger's mule in his barn.

A BOARDED-UP GROCERY STORE (1) The Gunslinger saw an old man with a straw hat sitting on the steps of a boarded-up grocery store as he entered Tull.

A BOOK AND NEWSPAPER STORE (4) A deserted booth in the underground station.

BRENDIO'S (2) A store in the other world that Jake used to pass on his way to school.

THE CENTRAL PLACE (3) A place made up of a hundred stone castles.

THE CHURCH (1) The Tull place of worship. It had no pews.

A COACH ROAD (1) There was once a coach road across the desert. It's use died out after the world moved on.

THE DESERT (1) Roland tracked the Man in Black across the vast Mohaine desert: "The world had emptied."

ENGLAND (5) The place where Maerlyn first appeared to the Man in Black.

FARSON (2) A town from Roland's past where Hax was hung on Gallows Hill for blowing up the tracks at the railhead and for the dead stock in Hendrickson.

GALLOWS HILL (2) A hill on Farson Road where hangings took place. Hax hung there.

GOLGOTHA (5) A bowl indented into the descending slope of the mountain. An ancient killing ground, a place-of-the-skull. This was where the Man in Black took Roland for a palaver after Jake's death.

THE GREAT HALL (4) The Hall of Grandfathers. It was where the Easter-night dance was held.

THE HALL OF GRANDFATHERS (4) The Great Hall. It was where the Easter-night dance was held.

HENDRICKSON (2) A town where there was dead cattle. Hax hung for it.

KING'S TOWN (4) Roland told Jake he had left a girl there twelve years earlier.

THE LIVERY (1) Kennerly's business in Tull.

MAIN STREET (1) Tull road.

MARS (2) Fourth planet from the sun.

THE MOHAINE DESERT (5) Roland crossed this desert to find the Man in Black.

THE NETWORK (2) The place Jake's father worked in the other world.

NEW CANAAN (3) Roland's land.

THE NEW JERSEY TURNPIKE (4) Jake remembered that his father had once driven ninety-miles-an-hour on the New Jersey Turnpike and been stopped for speeding.

POLARIS (2) The North Star.

PRICETOWN (1) The town where the Gunslinger had bought his mule.

THE SCHOOL (2) Jake's school in the other world. He thought of it as private, nice, and white.

A SHACK (1) Allie told the Gunslinger that Sylvia Pittston lived in a shack behind the church. (A real minister used to live there.)

SHEB'S (1) Tull honky-tonk.

THE TAILOR SHOP (1) One of the businesses in Tull.

THE TOWER (3) "Suppose that all worlds, all universes, met in a single nexus, a single pylon, a Tower. A stairway, perhaps, to the Godhead itself. Could it be somewhere above all of endless reality, there exists a Room...?" The oracle told Roland that he would speak of the Tower with the Man in Black.

THE WAY STATION (2) A former way station for a coach line that Roland found in the Mohaine desert after he left Brown's hut. Jake lived in the way station.

A WEAPON SHOP (4) A deserted booth in the underground station.

<h3 style="text-align:center">(14)
THE DARK TOWER:
THE GUNSLINGER
Things</h3>

AN ACT OF CONTRITION (2) When Jake was crushed under the Cadillac that killed him, the Man in Black pushed through the crowd telling everyone he was a priest, and that he wanted to administer an Act of Contrition to the boy.

AN AFTERLIFE (1) At one point, the Gunslinger asked Brown if he believed in an afterlife. Brown replied, "I think this is it."

AMOCO LEAD FREE (4) The sign Roland and Jake saw on a gas pump as they neared the cave of the slow mutants.

"BEYOND THE TOUCH OF HUMAN RANGE/A DROP OF HELL, A TOUCH OF STRANGE..." (3) A line of poetry Roland remembered while waiting for the Oracle to speak to him.

THE BIBLE (3) Roland asked Jake if he knew the *Bible*.

A BLACK CASSOCK (1) When the Man in Black came to Tull, he was wearing a black cassock.

BOW AND ARROWS (4) Roland took a bow and arrows out of the deserted weapons shop in the underground station.

THE BRIDE OF GOD (1) Sylvia Pittston told the Gunslinger that she was the Bride of God. Roland jammed a gun into her vagina and killed her "demon child."

CORN AND BEANS (1) Corn and beans were all Brown had to offer the Gunslinger for dinner.

DEATH (5) The fifth card in Roland's fortune. His fortune was told with tarot cards by the Man in Black.

DEVIL-GRASS (1) A desert weed that was the only thing in the Mohaine desert that would burn.

THE DRAWING (5) Walter told Roland to go to the sea and he would be invested with the power of the drawing.

DRIED JERKY (2) The food Jake gave Roland at the way station.

AN EARTH SCIENCE BOOK (2) One of the books Jake carried in his bookbag on his way to school in the other world on the day he was killed.

"EASE ON DOWN THE ROAD" (3) One of the old songs Susan had once sung to Roland.

AN ECONOMIC GEOGRAPHY BOOK (2) One of the books Jake carried in his bookbag on his way to school in the other world on the day he was killed.

EDWARDIAN SUITS (2) The mannequins in Brendio's window wore Edwardian suits.

AN EIGHT-INCH CARVING KNIFE (1) Sheb tried to stab the Gunslinger with an eight-inch carving knife. Roland broke his wrists.

THE EYES (1) During the Gunslinger's stay at Brown's hut, his mule died. Zoltan the raven "et the eyes."

"THE FACE OF GOD WITH HIS MOUTH OPEN TO EAT YOU UP" (1) One of the things Kennerly thought could exist after the boundaries of the Mohaine desert had been reached.

THE FIDDLE (1) The instrument Allie, the Tull bartender, played.

FOUR EMPTY WATERBAGS (1) While crossing the desert, Roland had left behind four empty waterbags.

GLAMMER (5) Enchantment.

"GO THEN. THERE ARE OTHER WORLDS THAN THESE." (4) Jake's last words to Roland before he fell into the abyss.

A GOLD PIECE (1) The Gunslinger paid the hostler in Tull with a gold piece.

GREEN BEANS, YELLOW BEANS, AND CORNED BEEF (2) The food the Gunslinger found in the cellar of the way station.

A GREEN DRAGON (3) Roland saw the face of a green dragon in the trees that overhung the Oracle's altar.

THE GUNS (1) Roland carried two revolvers with sandalwood stocks. He kept them in oiled holsters, and wore a gunbelt for his bullets.

A HANDCAR (4) Jake and Roland found one on the tracks leading into the slow mutants' cave.

THE HANGED MAN (5) The first card in Roland's fortune. His fortune was told with tarot cards by the Man in Black.

"HEY JUDE" (1, 3) In Tull, the Gunslinger could hear a honky-tonk piano playing "Hey Jude." "Hey Jude" was also one of the old songs Susan had once sung to Roland.

THE HIGH SPEECH (2) An ancient, almost forgotten language still spoken by certain people the Gunslinger encountered on his quest for the Dark Tower.

"A HUNDRED LEAGUES TO BANBERRY CROSS" (3) One of the old songs Susan had once sung to Roland.

THE IDEOGRAPHIC PATTERNS OF THE FIRE (1) Roland thought that the ideographic patterns of the devil-grass fire could mean "Take a powder," "The end draweth nigh," or even "Eat at Joe's."

JAKE'S LUNCH (2) On the day he was killed, Jake carried the following bag lunch to school: A peanut butter and jelly sandwich; a bologna, lettuce and onion sandwich; and four Oreo cookies.

A JAWBONE (2) Roland heard the dead voice of Alice speak from a jawbone that he found in the cellar of the way station.

THE KHEF (1) Roland had progressed through the khef and, as he tracked the Man in Black, he was at the fifth level. If he was at the seventh or eight level, he would no longer be thirsty.

THE KILL (1) After he was attacked in Tull, the Gunslinger killed thirty-nine men, fourteen women, and five children. The following morning, all the bodies were gone.

THE LADY OF SHADOWS (5) The fourth card in Roland's fortune. His fortune was told with tarot cards by the Man in Black.

A LADY WITH A CROWN AND A TORCH (2) When Jake remembered his life in the other world, he remembered a statue in the water: a lady with a crown and a torch; the Statue of Liberty.

LIFE (5) The seventh and final card in Roland's fortune. His fortune was told with tarot cards by the Man in Black. The Man in Black told Roland that life was not for him.

"LIGHTS TO DRIVE A MAN BLIND" (1) One of the things Kennerly thought could exist after the boundaries of the desert had been reached.

A LIVING SKULL COVERED WITH SLIME (3) Roland saw the face of a living skull in the trees which overhung the Oracle's altar.

THE LORD'S PRAYER (1) Brown had tried to teach Zoltan the raven "The Lord's Prayer," but it didn't take.

LSD (3) When Roland and Jake discussed mescaline, Jake referred to LSD, but did not know what it meant. He thought the term came from "before."

MESCALINE (3) Roland took a tiny white pill that would help keep him awake. It was mescaline.

A 1976 BLUE CADILLAC (2) The car that killed Jake Chambers

in the other world.

A NOTE PAD (2) One of the things Jake carried in his bookbag on his way to school in the other world on the day he was killed.

"AN OCEAN OF MONSTERS" (1) One of the things Kennerly thought could exist after the boundaries of the desert had been reached.

A PENCIL (2) One of the things Jake carried in his bookbag on his way to school in the other world on the day he was killed.

POINTS (2) A game the ladies played on the Back Courts when Roland was a child.

THE PRISONER (5) The third card in Roland's fortune. His fortune was told with tarot cards by the Man in Black.

THE PROPHECY (3) Roland told the thing with Susan's face at the stone altar to reveal to him the Prophecy.

ROLAND'S FORTUNE (5) Walter, the Man in Black, told Roland's fortune with tarot cards. His lay was as follows:

> The Hanged Man,
> The Sailor,
> The Prisoner,
> The Lady of Shadows,
> Death,
> The Tower,
> Life.

The Man in Black told Roland that his seventh card – Life – was "not for you."

THE SAILOR (5) The second card in Roland's fortune. His fortune was told with tarot cards by the Man in Black.

SIXTEEN TO EIGHTEEN HOURS A DAY (1) Roland told Brown that he had been tracking the Man in Black for sixteen to eighteen hours a day since the horror in Tull.

A STAINLESS STEEL SILVA COMPASS (1) A madman once gave Roland a Silva compass and told him to give it to Jesus.

STAR WHISKEY (1) The best whiskey in Tull. Alice brought it out for the Gunslinger.

THE STARS (AND THE GUNSLINGER'S DREAMS) (1) As Roland slept in the desert, "The stars were as indifferent [to his dreams] as they were to wars, crucifixions, resurrections."

THE STATUES THAT SOLD CLOTHES (2) When Jake remembered his life in the other world, he remembered "statues that sold clothes." (They were mannequins.)

THE TALL, BLACK STONES (3) Roland and Jake came upon a ring of tall black stones. In the center of this ring was a stone altar.

TAROT CARDS (4) The cards used for fortune-telling.

TEN YEARS (5) After Roland spoke of the Tower with Walter, the Man in Black, he fell asleep and awoke ten years older.

THREE (3) The number of Roland's fate. The oracle told Roland that he must succeed in the drawing together of the three. The first was young and dark-haired. A demon had infested him. Heroin was the name of the demon. The second would come on wheels, and the third would come in chains. [NOTE: See the section on *The Drawing of the Three* in this volume.]

THREE BURGERS AND A BEER (1) The meal the Gunslinger ordered in Tull's. It cost him five dollars. He gave Alice a gold piece for which she could not make change. He told her he didn't expect any.

THE TOWER (5) The sixth card in Roland's fortune. His fortune was told with tarot cards by the Man in Black.

TRACK 10 TO SURFACE AND POINTS WEST (4) The sign Roland and Jake saw above the entranceway to the underground station.

TWO MONTHS (1) As he progressed across the desert (and before he came to Brown's hut), Roland had been tracking the Man in Black for two months.

"WATCH ME" (1) The card game six townies were playing when the Gunslinger first entered Sheb's.

A WATERBAG (1) As Roland tracked the Man in Black across the desert, he carried a waterbag that was almost full.

THE YELLOW ONES (2) When Jake remembered his life in the other world, he remembered "yellow ones" that moved people around. (They were buses.)

DIFFERENT SEASONS

[No Volume Dedication]
[See individual story dedications below]

Contents Page

Hope Springs Eternal
RITA HAYWORTH AND SHAWSHANK REDEMPTION

Summer of Corruption
APT PUPIL

Fall from Innocence
THE BODY

A Winter's Tale
THE BREATHING METHOD

Afterword

Book Breakdown

• Hope Springs Eternal
RITA HAYWORTH AND SHAWSHANK REDEMPTION
DEDICATION: "For Russ and Florence Dorr"
(One unnumbered section; white space is used to separate sections)

• Summer of Corruption
APT PUPIL
DEDICATION: "For Elaine Koster and Herbert Schnall"
(Thirty untitled sections numbered 1-30)

• Fall from Innocence
THE BODY
DEDICATION: "For George McLeod"
(Six untitled sections numbered 1-6;
One section numbered 7 and titled "Stud City";
Eight untitled sections numbered 8-15;
One section numbered 16 and titled "The Revenge of Lard Ass Hogan";
Eighteen untitled sections numbered 17-34.)

• A Winter's Tale
THE BREATHING METHOD
DEDICATION: "For Peter and Susan Straub"
(One section titled "The Club" and numbered I;
One section titled "The Breathing Method" and numbered II;
One section titled "The Club" and numbered III)

Afterword–(One untitled section by Stephen King)

(15a)
DIFFERENT SEASONS
"Rita Hayworth and Shawshank Redemption"
People

ARMITAGE, ELMORE Prisoner who sometimes got things for Red.

BETTS, DICKIE Worked at re-tarring the license plate factory roof. Called the ladder an "extensible."

"THE BIRDMAN OF ALCATRAZ" Regardless of Jake the pigeon, it was generally acknowledged that Sherwood Bolton was not The Birdman.

BLATCH, ELWOOD Tommy Williams' cellmate. Blatch admitted to Tommy that he – not Andy Dufresne – had killed Linda Dufresne and Glenn Quentin.

BOLTON, SHERWOOD Shawshank prisoner. He had a pigeon named Jake.

BONSAINT, PAUL Prisoner who worked at re-tarring the license plate factory roof.

BURKES, DAVID Assistant to Richard Gonyar.

BYRON HADLEY'S BROTHER He died and left Byron $35,000.

CALLAHAN, JOHNNY A man Tommy Williams knew. Callahan owned a Smith & Wesson police special.

CHESTER Half-lame trusty, named for Matt Dillon's sidekick.

COTE, ROBERT ALAN Prisoner. In 1951, he robbed the First Mercantile Bank of Mechanic Falls.

DARROW, CLARENCE Red told Andy he could afford Darrow with the money Jim had earned for him.

A DETECTIVE FROM THE ATTORNEY GENERAL'S OFFICE He testified that he found evidence seventy yards from the Dufresne murder scene. [NOTE: See THE DUFRESNE EVIDENCE.]

DIAMOND, BOGS Prisoner. He said Andy Dufresne was marked for trouble.

THE DISTRICT ATTORNEY Handled Andy's case. He planned on running for the house of representatives.

DUFRESNE, ANDY Banker, convicted murderer, and prisoner at – and subsequent escapee from – Shawshank. He asked Red to get him a Rita Hayworth poster in 1949.

DUFRESNE, LINDA COLLINS Andy's wife. She had a lover named Glenn Quentin. Both were supposedly murdered by Linda's husband Andy.

DUNAHY, GEORGE Yankee; Shawshank's prison warden in 1950. He was fired in 1953 for running a discount auto repair service in the prison garage.

DURHAM BOY Unnamed fourteen-year-old psychopath. He castrated a classmate with a piece of rusty metal. He served seven years in solitary confinement and "actually emerged alive."

ENTWHISTLE, MERT Prison guard on "roof patrol."

ERNIE Old trusty. He swept Cellblock 5's corridors. Red gave him some Camels.

"THE EVEN-STEVEN KILLER" Andy Dufresne, according to the Portland *Sun*.

FROST, ROBERT Poet referred to by Andy.

GONYAR, RICHARD Captain of the guards.

HADLEY, BYRON Guard on "roof patrol."

HANLON, BILLY Head guard.

HATLEN, BROOKS Prisoner who ran the library. He got Andy a job there.

JAKE Sherwood Bolton's pigeon.

JESSUP, HOMER Head guard in the prison laundry room.

JIM Andy's friend. He set up Andy's false identity and invested his money for him.

KENDRICKS Shawshank trusty.

LATHROP, CHARLIE Tommy Williams's partner in the laundry room.

LONBORG Losing Boston Red Sox pitcher in the seventh game of the 1967 world series.

MACBRIDE, ROOSTER One of the Sisters. Andy broke his nose. He was in Shawshank for beating his stepdaughter to death.

MALZONE, FRANK Third baseman for the Boston Red Sox.

MARTIN, RENNIE Prisoner who worked at re-tarring the license plate factory roof.

THE MEDICAL EXAMINER Testified as to the dates and times of the Dufresne murders.

MINCHER, LIEUTENANT Handled dragging the Royal River for Andy's gun.

"MR. HOTSHOT BANKER" What Hadley called Andy Dufresne.

MORRISON, BEAVER He built a glider in the license plate factory basement, but then couldn't get it through the door.

NEDEAU, SID Escaped Shawshank prisoner.

"NEIMAN-MARCUS" How Red thought of himself.

NORMADEN Half-breed Passamaquoddy. He shared a cell with Andy in 1959.

NORTON, MRS. Samuel Norton's wife.

NORTON, SAMUEL He became Shawshank's warden in 1963.

O'MALLEY Prisoner.

PETROCELLI, RICO Boston Red Sox player.

PUGH, HENRY Guard at Sabbatus location.

QUENTIN, GLENN Golf pro. Linda Dufresne's lover. Quentin and Linda were supposedly murdered by Andy Dufresne.

RED Shawshank's "Neiman-Marcus," and the narrator of "Rita Hayworth and Shawshank Redemption." He could get it for you.

REED, GOVERNOR His picture hung in Warden Norton's office.

ST. PIERRE, LOGAN Prisoner who worked at re-tarring the license plate factory roof.

THE SISTERS "Bull Queers." "Jailhouse Susies." "Killer Queens." Inmates who preyed on young, slim, good-looking prisoners for sex.

STAMMAS, GREG Prison guard who became warden in 1953.

STEVENS, PETER Andy's alias.

TREMONT, RORY Prison guard. He was ordered to go through the hole in the wall of Andy's cell.

"TROUT" Hadley's nickname for Youngblood.

VERNESS, PETE One of the Sisters.

WILLIAMS, TOMMY Professional thief. He came to Shawshank in November 1962.

YOUNGBLOOD, TIM Prison guard on "roof patrol."

(15a)
DIFFERENT SEASONS
"Rita Hayworth and Shawshank Redemption"
Places

ATTICA Prison.

AUSTIN, TEXAS City where Byron Hadley's brother died.

BAPTIST ADVENT CHURCH Samuel Norton had a thirty-year pin from this church.

THE BAY OF YARMOUTH The Royal River emptied into it.

BENTLEY'S RESTAURANT Chicken dinner from there was brought in for the jury at Andy's trial.

THE BREWSTER HOTEL Where Red stayed when he was in Portland.

BUXTON Town next to Scarborough.

CARBINE STREET Where Red's wife lived before they were married.

CASCO BANK Bank in Portland where Andy had a safe deposit box.

CASHMAN Minimum security prison in Aroostock County. Tommy Williams was sent there.

CASTLE HILL Route where Red's wife died.

CELL 14 OF CELLBLOCK 5 Andy Dufresne's "home" in Shawshank.

CONGRESS STREET In Portland. Red bought a writing tablet there.

ELIOT NURSING HOME The Shawshank laundry room did their sheets.

FALMOUTH HILLS COUNTRY CLUB Club where Glenn Quentin worked and, where Linda Dufresne learned to play golf.

THE FIRST MERCANTILE BANK OF MECHANIC FALLS It was robbed by Robert Alan Cote in 1951.

FOODWAY MARKET Located in the Spruce Mall in South Portland. Red was a stockroom assistant there after his parole.

HANDY-PIK Store where Andy Dufresne bought cigarettes, three quarts of beer, and some dishtowels.

HIGHWAY 6 AND HIGHWAY 9 Cons were picked up there after a prison break.

KITTERY LIBRARY They wouldn't give Hatlen a library card.

LAS INTRUDES Peruvian seacoast town. Red substituted it for Zihautanejo in the story he wrote about Andy, in case authorities found his notes.

LICENSE PLATE FACTORY Andy, Red, and eight others had to re-tar the factory roof.

LIGHT SIDE PRESS New England company that published George Dunahy's book.

LISBON FALLS Two escaped cons were picked up there in a pinball parlor.

McNARY, TEXAS Where Andy crossed into Mexico.

OLD SMITH ROAD Road that led to the hayfield in Buxton.

PORTLAND Linda Dufresne said she was going there when she was actually meeting with Quentin.

PORTLAND SUPERIOR COURT Where Andy's trial was held in 1947 and 1948. It lasted six weeks.

THE ROYAL RIVER Where Andy Dufresne threw his revolver on the afternoon of September 9.

SABBATUS Where some "Inside-Out" cons were picking potatoes.

SAN QUENTIN Prison.

SHAWSHANK Prison.

WISE PAWN SHOP In Lewiston. Clerk there sold Andy Dufresne the gun he used to allegedly kill his wife and her lover.

ZIHAUTANEJO Mexican town twenty miles from Playa Azul. It was a hundred miles northwest of Acapulco. Andy told Red that Zihautanejo was where he'd live out his life after prison, and it's where Red went after he got out.

(15a)
DIFFERENT SEASONS
"Rita Hayworth and Shawshank Redemption"
Things

ANDY DUFRESNE'S PAROLE BOARD VOTING RECORD In 1957, 7-0 against parole; in 1958, 6-1 against; in 1959, 7-0 against; and in 1960, 5-2 against.

ANDY'S LETTER TO RED Twenty new fifty-dollar bills were in the letter Red found under Andy's rock in the hayfield. It read:

Dear Red,

If you're reading this, then you're out. One way or another, you're out. And if you've followed along this far, you might be willing to come a little further. I think you remember the name of the town, don't you? I could use a good man to help me get my project on wheels.

Meantime, have a drink on me – and do think it over. I will be keeping an eye out for you. Remember that hope is a good thing, Red, maybe the best of things, and no good thing ever dies. I will be hoping that this letter finds you, and finds you well.

Your friend,
Peter Stevens

ANDY'S REVAMPING OF THE PRISON LIBRARY He included editions from the Literary Guild and the Book-of-the-Month Club, titles by Erle Stanley Gardner and Louis L'Amour,

and a selection of Perry Mason novels and Jake Logan westerns.

ANDY'S ROCKS Quartz, mica, and shale. He showed them to Red in the prison yard.

APRIL 1977 The month that Red started hitchhiking to Buxton.

APRIL 23 The date Red found the Rock in Buxton.

AUGUST 24 AND SEPTEMBER 10 The dates Andy Dufresne felt suicidal.

AVA GARDNER POSTER Red sold them.

BETTY GRABLE POSTER Former favorite poster.

BLACK LABEL BEER Beer given to Andy and the others by Hadley for Andy's financial advice.

BRYON HADLEY'S OUTLOOK ON LIFE "The glass is half empty."

"BUYING THE BROOKLYN BRIDGE" How Warden Norton described Andy's attitude towards Elwood Blatch's story that Elwood had killed Linda Dufresne and Glenn Quentin.

CAMELS Cigarettes Red gave to Ernie.

"CHEATERS" Fake pockets used to transport dirt from his cell wall to the prison yard outside.

CHEVROLET COUPE Car in which Red's wife died. He "fixed" the brakes.

CHOCOLATES Red got them for the prisoners on Valentine's Day.

CHRISTMAS Andy Dufresne would have one drink every Christmas.

CIVIL WAR STATUE Red's wife ran her car into it and died.

"DEEP THROAT" AND "THE DEVIL IN MISS JONES" Two films Red got for a group of twenty prisoners.

"DIAMOND PEARL" Words engraved on the side of Bogs Diamond's razor.

DINNER SMELLS Beefaroni, Rice-A-Roni, and Noodle-Roni. They drifted upstairs to Red's room.

THE DUFRESNE EVIDENCE Evidence found at the murder scene were: two empty quarts of Narragansett beer; twelve Kool cigarette ends; and the tire tracks of a 1947 Plymouth (Andy's car).

DUNAHY'S DOWNFALL "Nest-Feathering" and "Scandal" – the newspaper headlines which trumpeted the supposed improprieties that cost Dunhay his job.

81433-SHNK Andy Dufresne's prison number.

"FIBBER MCGEE AND MOLLY" Radio program referred to by Red.

FRISBEE Toy played with by the prisoners at Shawshank.

GREEN MILKSHAKES Red got them for O'Malley on St. Patrick's Day.

GREYHOUND BUS TICKET Given to Hatlen when he was paroled.

HAZEL COURT English actress. Her poster replaced Jayne Mansfield in Andy's cell until 1966.

HEXLITE CATALYST Bleaching compound in laundry.

THE "INSIDE-OUT" PROGRAM Instituted by Warden Norton. Prisoners worked outside the prison.

JACK DANIELS Whiskey Red got for Andy.

JAYNE MANSFIELD POSTER Replaced Marilyn Monroe in Andy's cell for one year.

JOKE BOOKS, FUCK BOOKS, AND JOKE NOVELTIES Some of the things Red could get brought into Shawshank.

THE KEY The key to Andy's safe deposit box. It was hidden in a piece of glass in a rock wall in a hayfield in Buxton.

LIBRARY BOOKS AND MAGAZINES In 1922, the Shawshank library consisted of the "Readers Digest Condensed Books" series, and issues of *National Geographic*.

LIBRARY SUGGESTION BOX The prisoners asked for certain titles Andy couldn't supply, including the request for "More Fuk-Book Pleeze," and a book called *Escape in 10 E-Z Lessons*.

LINDA RONSTADT POSTER Replaced Raquel Welch poster in Andy's cell. Linda was Andy's last poster.

"THE LOST WEEKEND" The movie shown in prison auditorium.

MARILYN MONROE POSTER Replaced the Rita Hayworth

poster in Andy's cell from 1955 through 1960.

MAY 1950 The month Andy, Red, and eight other men were chosen to re-tar the license plate factory roof.

THE MODERN BOY'S GUIDE TO FUN AND ADVENTURE Circa-1900 book used by Beaver Morrison to build his glider.

THE NEW TESTAMENT Book given to every new prisoner at Shawshank by Warden Norton.

NEW YEAR'S EVE Andy Dufresne would have one drink every New Year's Eve.

NEWSWEEK The magazine ran a story on Warden Norton and his "Inside-Out" program.

1950-1951 The years in which Jim invested Andy's money. It had grown over this period to $370,000.

1954 The year Andy wrote to the state senate asking for funds for the prison library.

1953 The year Hatlen died in Freeport in a home for indigent old folks.

1952 The year Hatlen was paroled.

1948 The year Andy Dufresne went to Shawshank for murdering his wife and her lover.

1947 The year Linda Dufresne learned to play golf with Glenn Quentin at the Falmouth Hills Country Club.

1975 The year Andy Dufresne escaped from Shawshank.

1967 The year Red got Andy a new rock-hammer. It now cost twenty-two dollars.

THE 1967 WORLD SERIES The Red Sox won the American League pennant.

NO TRESPASSING SIGNS Signs posted on some hayfields in Buxton.

NORTON'S NEW BOOKS Warden Norton got the following new books for Andy's library: a selection of automotive repair manuals; the Grolier encyclopedias; and *Preparation for Scholastic Achievement Tests* .

"ONE HAND WASHES THE OTHER" One of Warden Norton's favorite aphorisms.

P.O. Short for "parole officer."

PHILLIPS SCREWDRIVER It was held to Andy's head while he was raped by one of the Sisters.

PLAQUE ON NORTON'S DESK "Christ is my Savior.

THE PORTLAND *SUN* Paper that covered the Andy Dufresne trial. It ran the headline "Four For Him and Four For Her." (Eight bullets were used to kill them.)

PP Short for "provisional parole."

QUARTZ SCULPTURES Two perfectly carved pieces of quartz chipped into driftwood shapes given to Red by Andy.

RAQUEL WELCH POSTER Replaced the Hazel Court poster in Andy's cell. Raquel hung there for six years.

RED'S IMPOSSIBLE DREAMS To own a Cadillac, and take a trip to Jamaica.

RED'S ROUTE TO ANDY Spring Street to the Greyhound terminal. There he bought a ticket to El Paso by way of New York City. Then he was on to McNary, Texas, and then on to Zihautanejo...and Andy.

ROCK BLANKETS Polishing cloths. Andy asked Red to get some for him.

ROCK-HAMMER Andy Dufresne asked Red to get him one.

ROTARY AND KIWANIS CLUBS They invited Norton to speak on his "Inside-Out program."

SAMPLER ON NORTON'S WALL "His Judgement Cometh and That Right Early." It was made by his wife.

SEPTEMBER 15, 1975 The date Red received a blank postcard from McNary, Texas.

SEPTEMBER 10 AND 11; 11:00 P.M. AND 2:00 A.M. Dates and times Andy Dufresne allgedly commited the murders of his wife and her lover, Glenn Quentin.

SEPTEMBER 10, 1947 Date Andy and Linda Dufresne argued about her infidelity.

SEPTEMBER 20 Andy Dufresne's birthday. To celebrate, he

would have two drinks.

SHAWSHANK'S "PHARMACY" Some of the drugs brought into the prison by guards included reds, uppers, downers, Nembutals, and Phase Fours.

SILVA COMPASS Red carried it while hitchhiking to Buxton.

SIX-SHOT .38 POLICE SPECIAL The gun Andy Dufresne allegedly used to kill his wife and her lover.

SIXTIES POSTERS Popular were Jimi Hendrix, Bob Dylan, and "Easy Rider."

THE SOLITARY WING Basement level in Shawshank. It was twenty-three steps down.

TEN DOLLARS Price for Andy's original rock-hammer.

THE THREE AGES OF JESUS Three sculptures made by a prisoner out of pink Vermont marble.

TWENTY-SEVEN YEARS Time it took Andy to dig through his cell wall.

TWO SHOTS Red bought two shots of Jack Daniels at a bar after he found Andy's gift of $1,000.00 – one shot for him and one for Andy.

"WOMAN IN HEAT" How Red described the Rita Hayworth poster.

WPA CONCRETE Material used to build the Shawshank wing containing Cellblocks 3, 4, and 5. It was built from 1934-1937.

❖❖❖

(15b)
DIFFERENT SEASONS
"Apt Pupil"
People

ACKERMAN, HARRY Head of the counselling center.

ACKERMAN, SHARON Todd told her he wanted to be a doctor so she'd let him feel around beneath her dress.

ANDERSON, MRS. Fifth-grade teacher. The kids called her "Bugs." She ran Careers Day.

THE ATLANTA BRAVES Morris Heisel's favorite team.

BLONDI Hitler's dog.

BOWDEN, MONICA Todd's mom. She typed manuscripts in her spare time. Her maiden name was Darrow.

BOWDEN, RICHARD Todd's dad. He was an architectural engineer. He looked like the actor Lloyd Bochner. He helped to design and build two dams in Africa when he was in the Peace Corps.

BOWDEN, TODD Thirteen years old, five-foot-eight; 140 pounds. Devoted Holocaust buff and novice mass murderer.

BOWDEN, VIC Dick Bowden's dad. Everyone called him Vic the Grocer because he owned a grocery store.

BOZEMAN, DAN The cop who handled the investigation of the wino deaths.

BRACKETT, CHARLES "SONNY" One of the murdered winos.

THE BUM Dussander's first murder victim. The bum had approached Dussander for money at a bus stop .

CARSON, JOHNNY Todd's dad watched him. Buddy Hackett was a guest.

CASTELLANO, FIONA One of Vic Bowden's customers. When Vic had a stroke, she arranged to keep his store open.

CHAMBERS, RANDY Boy who mowed Dussander's lawn.

CHESTER Matt Dillon's sidekick.

LA COSA NOSTRA Organization from which Dussander got his "papers."

CRICHTON, MICHAEL Monica Bowden read his books.

DARROW, MONICA Todd's mom's name before marriage.

DENKER, ARTHUR A former Nazi and death camp commandant; his real name was Kurt Dussander. Todd Bowden thought he looked like a cross between Albert Einstein and Boris Karloff. Todd and Denker entered into a mutually parasitic relationship that ended with Denker/Dussander's suicide, and Todd's becoming a sniper and getting killed by the police.

DOYLE, ARTHUR CONAN Dussander's namesake. His father greatly admired the author.

DUFRESNE, ANDY Man who set up a stock portfolio for Dussander. [NOTE: This is the same Dufresne from Stephen King's novella in *Different Seasons*, "Rita Hayworth and Shawshank Redemption."]

DUSSANDER, KURT Arthur Denker's real name.

DUSSANDER'S LIST OF GREAT MURDERERS FROM THE PAST The Cleveland Torso Murderer, the Zodiac, Mr. X., and Springheel Jack. [Note: Springheel Jack was the subject of Stephen King's *Night Shift* short story, "Strawberry Spring."]

DUSSANDER'S TWO WINOS From 1976 to 1977, Dussander killed two winos. When one wino didn't die after Dussander plunged a steak knife into the base of his neck, Dussander drove a meat fork into his back.

EICHMANN Nazi war criminal who was hung.

EVERSON, BERNIE Classmate of Todd's.

FARROW, ANGELA A girl Todd dated.

FELICE Candy-stripe nurse who served Morris Heisel his dinner.

FLOREN, MYRON A regular on "The Lawrence Welk Show."

FRANKEL, WILLI Dussander's nephew. Todd pretended he had to read a letter from Willi to Dussander so that he could go over to Dussander's and clean up the murdered wino's blood before the ambulance came.

FRENCH, EDWARD School guidance counselor. He always wore Keds to school, either Fast Track Blue or Screaming Yellow Zonkers. The kids called him Rubber Ed, Sneaker Pete, The Ked Man, or Pucker. His major in college was educational psychology. He was eventually killed by Todd.

FRENCH, NORMA Sondra and Ed French's daughter.

FRENCH, SONDRA Ed French's wife.

GLUECKS, HEINRICH Himmler's second-in-command. Todd saw a picture of him shaking hands with Dussander.

GOEBBELS, DR. Nazi war criminal.

GOERING Hitler aide who committed suicide.

HACKERMEYER American soldier who gave Dussander a chocolate bar.

HAINES, COACH He awarded Todd his Athlete of the Year Award.

HALLECK, MR. Halleck told Todd that Todd's dad had put a lein on his own car to scare up $200 for French tutoring for Todd. [NOTE: Is this Billy Halleck from *Thinner*? In 1982? Was Stephen King planting "Richard Bachman" hints in his books all along?]

HAP Derelict who identified Todd from a newspaper photo to Bozeman.

HARRY AND DEBORAH Todd's aunt and uncle. They lived in Minnesota.

HASKELL, FRANK Morris Heisel's boss.

HASSLER, HANS German who disappeared after criticizing Hitler.

HEISEL, LYDIA Morris Heisel's wife. She walked with a crutch, like Matt Dillon's sidekick Chester.

HEISEL, MORRIS Man who broke his back and ended up in the same intensive care room as Dussander. Heisel remembered Dussander from the death camps.

HEISEL, RUTH Morris's first wife. She died in the death camp showers.

HENREID, PRIVATE He manned a machine gun in the northwest tower in Patin. The other men called him "Three Eyes" and "Old Cyclops" because he had a cyst between his eyes.

HEPBURN A counselor who had 115 children to "counsel."

"THE HYATT PEOPLE" Dick Bowden went to Los Angeles to discuss a new hotel in Reno with them.

JACOBS, ERNIE Dick Bowden's boss and golfing partner.

KEMMELMAN, DR. Morris Heisel's doctor.

KESSEL German soldier who had a photograph of his girlfriend naked, lying on a sofa, her hands behind her head. He charged the other men to look at the picture.

KLINGERMAN, DAVE He ran the city dog pound. Dussander got a dog there.

KOCH, ILSE Todd said she had lampshades made of human skin.

KRAMER, JOSEF He said that the dead speak, but that we hear them with our noses.

LOVER-BOY Morris Heisel's cat.

MAZURSKY, BILL Mrs. Mazursky's husband. Vic said he was a wino.

MAZURSKY, MRS. One of Vic Bowden's customers.

MONICA'S GRANDMOTHER Todd's dad called her "The Polack."

OLD MAN Unnamed man who may have recognized Dussander in traffic.

PEGLER, HAROLD Todd's friend. His nickname was "Foxy." Harold's father had a big stack of war magazines in his garage.

RICHLER Cop who questioned Todd about Dussander.

ROGAN Heisel's neighbor. His dog had chased Lover-Boy, which had caused Morris's ladder to fall. Morris broke his back.

SANTO DONATO COUGARS Todd's football team.

SAYERS, DOROTHY Mystery writer. The Frenches read all her books.

"THE SCHWARZEN" How Dussander referred to blacks.

THE SICILIANS They arranged false papers for Dussander after the war.

SMITH, PETER "POLEY" One of the murdered winos.

STEWBUM Unnamed bum who was another of Dussander's murder victims.

STORRMAN, MR. Todd's algebra teacher.

TEY, JOSEPHINE Historian mentioned to Todd by Richler.

TIMPNELL Young intern. He checked Morris Heisel's feet.

TRASK, BETTY A girl Todd dated.

TRASK, RAY Betty's father; Dick Bowden's friend.

TREMAINE, BEN Todd's study partner.

UPSHAW, MRS. Todd's fourth grade teacher. She wrote on his report card that Todd was "an extremely apt pupil."

"WALTER KLONDIKE" How Todd's dad referred to Walter Cronkite.

THE WAR FUGITIVES Group Dussander joined. They were based in Brazil, Paraguay, and Santo Domingo, and dealt in minerals and ores – tin, copper, and bauxite.

WEISKOPF He visited Dussander in the hospital. He was a special operative who taught Yiddish literature and English grammar.

WIMSEY, LORD PETER Character in Sayers novel. Ed French thought Dussander looked like him. French also associated the following Wimsey PBS stories with Todd and Dussander: "Clouds of Witness," "Murder Must Advertise," and "The Nine Tailors." Ian Carmichael was the actor who portrayed Wimsey.

THE WINO Todd's first murder victim. He stabbed him thirty-seven times.

WINO NUMBER 2 Todd's second murder victim.

(15b)
DIFFERENT SEASONS
"Apt Pupil"
Places

AN ABANDONED TRAINYARD This was where Todd committed his first murder. He stabbed a wino thirty-seven times.

BERKELEY Todd applied to the university and was immediately accepted there.

BUENOS AIRES Dussander's destination after Patin.

CIENEGA WAY The location of a vacant lot where Todd killed another wino in December.

COUNSELING CENTER It was suggested to Todd's parents that they make a series of appointments with this center regarding Todd.

CUBA Dussander was spotted there by an Israeli agent.

DEVON AVENUE BUS STOP Todd had a picture of Dussander at this bus stop.

FIELDINGS Store where Monica Bowden bought a knick-knack shelf.

FREIGHT BYPASS ROAD Todd had gotten stuck in a culvert beneath the road when he was seven or eight. The memory of this imprisonment came back to him when he thought about his relationshiop with Dussander.

GRANTS Store where Dussander bought a barbecue fork for $2.98. He used it to scrape off the remains of the roasted cat from his oven walls.

HAWAII The Bowdens' vacation site for one month beginning June 25.

LAS VEGAS Morris and Lydia had gone there to see Buddy Hackett.

MENSCHLER MOTOR WORKS Factory in Essen where Dussander worked in 1955.

MEXICO CITY Dussander's home from 1950-1952.

PATIN Where Dussander was stationed during the war.

PETER'S QUALITY COSTUME CLOTHIERS Where Todd bought the SS uniform for Dussander.

RADOM, POLAND Morris Heisel's hometown.

RATSKELLER A bar in Germany.

REDONDO BEACH Todd bought his knife in a sporting goods store there.

THE RIFLE CLUB Todd joined this in the fall of 1977.

ROME Where the Bowdens went after Hawaii. Also, where Dussander lived for three years.

SALVATION ARMY On Euclid. Todd thought that this was a prime location for finding winos to kill.

SAN REMO The town where Ed French attended a convention for guidance counselors.

THE SANTO DONATO MISSION FOR THE INDIGENT Todd thought this was a prime spot for finding winos to kill.

SHOPRITE Where Denker shopped.

SMOKENDERS Todd's dad was a member.

TAHOE Where the Bowdens' skied.

UCLA Dick Bowden received a scholarship to this school.

WEST BERLIN Dussander was there in 1965.

WEST GERMAN AUTOBAHN There was an accident there and, while waiting in traffic, Dussander thought a war survivor in a nearby car recognized him.

(15b)
DIFFERENT SEASONS
"Apt Pupil"
Things

A-1 STEAK SAUCE Denker had some on the left lapel of his bathrobe.

ALPACA GUN OIL The oil Todd used to clean his .30-.30.

AMERICAN LEGION PATRIOTIC ESSAY CONTEST Todd entered his essay entitled "An American's Responsibility."

"AN AMERICAN'S RESPONSIBILITY" The title of the essay Todd entered into the American Legion Patriotic Essay Contest.

ANCIENT AGE BOURBON Dussander drank it. It was also the drink he gave the stewbum before he rammed a butcher knife into his neck.

ARTHRITIS PAIN FORMULA Dussander used it.

ATHLETE OF THE YEAR Todd was named this in June.

AUGUST 1974 The month when Todd and Dussander sat on Dussander's back porch eating Big Macs, drinking and talking. Todd drank Coke and Dussander drank bourbon.

"BEWITCHED" TV show that Ed French watched at the Holiday Inn in San Remo.

BIG MACS Richler and Weiskopf had them for lunch.

"THE BLOOD-FIEND OF PATIN" Dussander, as described in a *Men's Action* article.

BUTCH WAX Foxy used it on his crewcut.

CAMELS Dussander's cigarette.

CAREERS DAY Fifth-grade event at which students were supposed to find their "Great Interest."

CENTENNIAL The James Michener book Dussander held.

CHEVY NOVA Richler's car.

CLOCHE Hat popular in the twenties and thirties.

CRAFTSMAN HAMMER The weapon Todd used on Wino Number 2.

DAIRYLEA FARMS Brand of milk Dussander served Todd.

DENKER'S MAGAZINES *National Geographic* and *Reader's Digest*.

DIAMOND BLUE TIP MATCH How Dussander lit his Camels.

DIAMOND MATCH Stock that Dussander sold. He used the proceeds to buy his house and a small cottage near Big Sur.

DUSSANDER'S CELLAR GRAVE Dussander dug a two-and-a-half by six-foot grave in his cellar for all the winos he killed.

DUSSANDER'S COFFEE MUG On the mug was written "Here's Your Cawfee Maw, Haw, Haw, Haw." He used the mug to drink his bourbon.

DUSSANDER'S STOCKS He owned General Motors, AT & T, and Revlon.

"THE EFFECT OF FRUIT FLIES IN THE SALINAS VALLEY AFTER WORLD WAR II" The thesis Todd's mother was typing.

"EMERGENCY" TV show Dussander enjoyed.

FEBRUARY 1975 The month the Bowdens invited Dussander to dinner.

FIVE HOURS Todd shot at people and cars from above the highway for five hours before they "took him down."

FLINTSTONES GLASS Dussander used one.

"FUGITIVE NAZI COMMITS SUICIDE IN SANTO DONATO HOSPITAL" The newspaper headline announcing Dussander's death.

"GENERAL HOSPITAL" Dussander's favorite soap opera.

GLADE Dussander sprayed the kitchen with it to get rid of the smell of the cat he had roasted in his oven.

THE GOODWILL BOX Where Dick Bowden's pants came from when he was a boy.

"HOGAN'S HEROES" To Todd, Colonel Klink was more a Nazi than Denker.

"THE HORST WESSEL SONG" The Nazis sang this song as they fed poison to their children at the end of the Third Reich.

"I'M KING OF THE WORLD!" What Todd shouted before he began his killing spree from above the highway.

INK ERADICATOR Todd used it to change his report card grades.

IOP CARDS Interpretation of Progress Cards. The students called them Flunk Cards.

A JAMES BOND MOVIE Monica Bowden watched it on tape.

"JOHN THOMAS" What Todd's dad said was Todd's problem: puberty.

KODAK Todd's camera. He used it to take clandestine pictures of Dussander.

KÖK How Dussander pronounced Coke.

KOOLS Dussander's cigarette.

"THE LAWRENCE WELK SHOW" Dussander wanted to watch it.

"THE LEFT HAND BOOK" The book in which Vic Bowden kept the names of people who owed him money.

LEMON FRESH JOY Dussander used it to wash his murder weapon.

LESTOIL AND TOP JOB What Todd used to clean up blood.

LOS ANGELES *TIMES* Newspaper on Denker's porch.

MAGAZINE ADS The following were advertised in the war magazines Todd read: German knives, belts, helmets, magic trusses, hair restorer, German flags, Nazi Lugers, and a game called Panzer Attack.

"MANNIX," "HAWAII FIVE-O," AND "BARNABY JONES" TV shows Dussander referred to.

MAY 1 The day Todd decided to kill Dussander.

MAY 2, 1945 The date Dussander's regiment surrendered to the Americans.

"MEDICAL SUPPLIES" This was printed on the railroad cars that delivered Zyklon-B.

MEN'S ACTION Magazine that ran an article on the death camps.

MERIT SCHOLARSHIP Todd received one, having achieved the third highest score in the school's history.

MINOLTA Todd wished he could afford one.

"THE MONKEY'S PAW" The W.W. Jacobs' short story Morris Heisel thought about.

MORRIS Dussander's car.

MOTOROLA TV Black-and-white TV on a stand in Denker's home.

963 CLAREMONT STREET Arthur Denker's address.

1955 The year Dussander's wife died of a lung disease.

"NO SOLICITORS, NO PEDDLERS, NO SALESMEN" Sign on Denker's door.

NUREMBERG TRIALS Dussander listened to them on the radio.

1:35 P.M. The time Dussander was found dead.

P499965214 The numbers tatooed on Morris Heisel's arm.

PEGASUS A nerve gas sent to Dussander at Dachau. It made the prisoners leap about screaming and laughing, and also caused them to vomit and defecate helplessly. Some of Dussander's men called it "Yodeling Gas."

PENTHOUSE The magazine Todd's mom was glad Todd wasn't reading.

PHILLIES CHEROOTS Cigars Ed French smoked.

PLAYER Weiskopf's cigarettes.

PLAYTEX RUBBER GLOVES Dussander used them to pick up the cat and throw it into his oven.

"REAL PEOPLE" TV show mentioned by Richler.

RING DING Todd ate one at Dussander's.

RITZ CRACKERS AND VELVEETA CHEESE Dussander offered these to Todd.

ROBINSON CRUSOE The book Todd's mom thought Todd was reading to Dussander.

ROOM 217 Ed French's room at the Holiday Inn in San Remo. [Note: Room 217 was also the number of the room at the Overlook Hotel in which the dead woman rose up out of the bathtub in Stephen King's novel *The Shining*. See the section on *The Shining* in this volume.]

THE SANTO DONATO *CLARION* The newspaper Todd delivered.

SCHNAPS Dussander's drink.

SCHWINN Todd Bowden's bike. It was a twenty-six-incher with apehanger handlebars.

SCIENCE FAIR Todd went to the state finals with his project on solar power.

SECONAL The pills Dussander stole and used to commit suicide.

SIMCA Car driven by an old man who recognized Dussander.

6,000,000 The number below a picture of corpses in Dachau.

SOUTHERN CAL HIGH SCHOOL ALL-STARS Todd was named to the team.

SS UNIFORM Todd's Christmas gift to Dussander. He bought it at Peter's Quality Costume Clothiers for eighty dollars.

SWISS ARMY KNIFE Todd kept the Angler model in his pocket.

TABLE-TALK PIE DISH What Dussander used for an ashtray.

THUNDERBIRD The Bowdens' car.

TIMEX The watch Todd earned by selling personalized greeting cards.

THE TITANIC Ship model built by Todd and his father.

TODD'S BATTING AVERAGE .361.

TODD'S CAREER MODELS Todd wanted to be a private detective like Sam Spade or Mannix.

TODD'S DRY-FIRES While practicing for his shooting spree, Todd dry-fired at a Toyota and a Subaru Brat.

TODD'S EXPECTATIONS Even though he didn't expect to see

them, Todd had hoped to find Hitler memorabilia, medals, a ceremonial sword, a Luger, or a Walther PPK in Dussander's home.

TODD'S FIRST QUARTER MARKS One B, four C's, and one D.

TODD'S "PASSWORD" INTO DENKER'S HOUSE To gain entrance, Todd said the following to Denker "Bergen-Belsen, January 1943 to June 1943. Auschwitz, June 1943 to June of 1944, Unterkommandant. Patin—"

TOM JONES The book Todd told his dad he was reading to Dussander. Instead, he bought the Cliff's Notes and studied them carefully.

TUROK, SON OF STONE Magazine in Foxy's garage.

TWELVE The number of steps from Dussander's cellar up to his kitchen.

222 Emergency number. It rang the Santo Donato MED-Q.

A USED PORSCHE Todd's dad had one.

VICKS OR MENTHOLATUM One of the smells in Denker's house.

WAIKIKI BEACH POSTCARD Todd sent one to Dussander.

WESTCLOX CLOCK It hung over the fireplace in Denker's home.

WINCHESTER .30-.30 Christmas gift to Todd from his dad. It had a telescopic sight. This was the weapon Todd used for his highway shooting spree.

ZYKLON-B The poison gas used at Dachau.

❖❖❖

(15c)

DIFFERENT SEASONS
"The Body"
People

BANNERMAN, CONSTABLE He carried the only gun Gordie had ever seen.

BRACOWICZ, NORMAN "FUZZY" Friend of Billy Tessio and Charlie Hogan.

BROWER, RAY Missing boy from Chamberlain. He had been killed by a train. Ray was "The Body."

BURROUGHS, MRS. The Duchamps' neighbor.

THE CABBAGE AND TURNIP GIRL Unnamed girl in a coma who was in the car when Teddy crashed. She lay in the "Cabbages and Turnips Ward" for six months before someone pulled the plug on her respirator.

CAMPANELLA, ROY Baseball player who was in an auto accident and ended up in a wheelchair.

CAVELLA, STEVE 87th Squad cop in the Ed McBain novels.

CHALMERS, MRS. She called for the police when she saw Ace and Fuzzy beating Gordie.

CHAMBERS, CHRIS One of the boys.

CHAMBERS, EYEBALL Chris's brother, and one of the bad guys. His real name was Richard.

CHAMBERS, FRANK Chris's oldest brother. He joined the Navy.

CHOPPER Milo Pressman's dog.

CLARKSON, DR. Gordie was taken to him after he was beaten by Ace and Fuzzy.

COTE, MRS. Teacher. The boys considered her "the meanest bitch God ever set down on earth."

CUJO Joe Camber's dog. He went rabid in 1980 and did some damage in Castle Rock. [NOTE: See the section on *Cujo* in this volume.]

DARABONT, ROYCE Steve's oldest brother. He bought a bottle of Wild Irish Rose for Gordie.

DARABONT, STEVE Royce's younger brother.

DESPAIN, JOHN One of the gang members.

DESPAIN, MARTY One of the gang members.

DOUGHERTY, MARIE Charlie Hogan dated her.

DUCHAMP, NORMAN Teddy's father.

DUCHAMP, TEDDY One of the boys.

DUSSET, GEORGE He owned the Florida Market.

EWING, MRS. Teacher. Jamie Gallant gave her the finger.

FORD, WHITEY Yankee pitcher.

GALLANT, JAMIE Toughest guy in Castle Rock.

GREER, BILLY Boy who played right field.

HALLIBURTON, MR. Castle Rock truant officer.

HARDY, MISS Gordie's teacher.

HOGAN, CHARLIE Billy Tessio's friend.

HORR, HARRY Boy from Castle View who claimed that Chopper was a Doberman.

JENNER, RICHIE A boy who moved to Nebraska in 1959. He had previously hung around with the boys.

KNIEVEL, EVEL As an adult, Gordie paid twenty dollars to see Knievel attempt a jump over the Snake River Canyon.

LACHANCE, DENNIS Gordie's older brother. He was killed in a jeep accident during basic training at Fort Benning, Georgia. He was twenty-two years old when he died.

LACHANCE, GORDIE One of the boys.

MACDONALD, JOHN D. Gordie liked to read his books.

MCGINN, MRS. Neighbor who took Chris Chambers to the CMG emergency room after his brother broke Chris's arm and beat his face.

MERRILL, ACE One of the bad guys.

MUNSON, THURMAN Yankee player. He died in a plane crash.

MURPHY, AUDIE War hero turned actor.

NAUGHTON, DANNY Boy who left horror comic books in the treehouse.

"PENNY" Vern's nickname. [NOTE: See the "Places" entry BENEATH THE TESSIO PORCH.]

PRESSMAN, MILO Castle Rock dumpkeeper.

RYDELL, BOBBY Vern wore his hair like Rydell.

SIMONS, OLD LADY Chris Chambers' teacher. She bought a skirt with the milk money Chris stole but then returned to her.

TESSIO, BILLY Vern's older brother.

TESSIO, VERN One of the boys.

THOMAS, BEVERLY A girl Billy Tessio dated.

"THUNDERJUGS" Francine Tupper.

TUPPER, FRANCINE Waitress at the Blue Point Diner. Her nickname was "Thunderjugs."

WAYNE, JOHN The boys saw his war movies.

WILLIAMS, TED He played with the Red Sox in 1960.

(15c)
DIFFERENT SEASONS
"The Body"
Places

BACK HARLOW ROAD The road past the cemetery where Billy Tessio and Charlie Hogan had seen Ray Brower's body.

BEEMAN'S FIELD The route the boys took to get to Harlow.

BENEATH THE TESSIO PORCH It was where Vern had buried a quart jar of pennies. He had been searching for them for four years.

BLUE POINT DINER Castle Rock diner.

CASTLE ROCK, OREGON Setting for "The Body," and where "the boys" had their treehouse.

CASTLE ROCK DRUGSTORE Town pharmacy. In the alley between the drugstore and the Blue Point Diner, Chris showed Gordie the gun he'd stolen from his father.

CASTLE ROCK DUMP It was surrounded by a six-foot-high fence.

CASTLE ROCK HIGH SCHOOL Dennis Lachance graduated with honors from there.

CASTLE ROCK STATIONERY SHOPPE Business owned by Teddy Duchamp's uncle.

CENTRAL MAIN GENERAL EMERGENCY Teddy's father called there after he held Teddy's head over the stove and burned both of his ears.

DAHLIE'S Card shop in Castle Green.

DANBERRY STREET Street where Teddy Duchamp's mom had a boarding house.

EMPORIUM GALORIUM Store that sold antiques, junk, and dime books.

FLORIDA MARKET Gordie bought supplies there.

GEM THEATER Theater the boys went to.

GORDIE'S NEW YORK SIGHTSEEING STOPS As an adult, Gordie would see Radio City Music Hall, the Empire State Building, and Times Square at night.

HARLOW Where Teddy Duchamp had his fatal car crash.

HARRISON Chris's dad went there with six or eight bottles of wine.

HARRISON STATE PARK Denny and Gordie had once gone body-surfing there. [NOTE: See the section on Stephen King's poem "Harrison State Park '68" in this volume.]

LE DIO Town in France in Gordie's stories.

MACKEY LUMBER & BUILDING SUPPLY It was on Carbine Road. The boys got the lumber for the treehouse from them.

THE MELLOW TIGER Saloon. As an adult, Teddy Duchamp hung out there. [NOTE: The Mellow Tiger also appears in *Cujo* and *The Dark Half*. See the sections on those books in this volume.]

MOTTON, DURHAM, AND POWNAL Nearby towns in which the police searched for Brower.

PORTSMOUTH PRISON Where Frank Chambers did time for rape and criminal assault.

SHAWSHANK Prison.

SHOE FACTORY In South Paris. It was where Teddy's mother worked.

SUKEY'S TAVERN The bar where Chris Chamber's dad and Ace Merrill's dad hung out.

TOGUS Veteran's Hospital for Section 8's.

THE TRESTLE The train bridge that ran over the Castle River. The boys had to cross it to complete their journey to the body of Ray Brower.

UNIVERSITY OF MAINE Chris and Gordie were both accepted there. Gordie went to the Orono campus; Chris went to the Portland campus.

WHITE'S BEACH Brunswick beach. Teddy saw a boy almost drown there.

(15c)
DIFFERENT SEASONS
"The Body"
Things

ALL-CONFERENCE HALFBACK Dusset remembered that Denny Lachance had made all-conference while in high school.

THE BOY'S BESTS While sitting in the dump, the boys agreed on the following: Best Ball Team, The Yankees (with Mantle and Maris); the Best Car, the '55 Thunderbird (with Teddy voting for the '58 Corvette); the Toughest Guy in Castle Rock, Jamie Gallant; and the Best TV Show, "The Untouchables," or "Peter Gunn."

BUICK Ten-year-old car Chris's mother drove.

THE C & T WARD The "Cabbages and Turnips Ward." A girl who was in the car with Teddy when his car crashed lay in this ward for six months. Someone then pulled the plug on her respirator.

CAMELS ASHTRAYS The ashtrays used in treehouse.

CASTLE ROCK DUMP SIGNS They were posted every twenty feet on a six-foot-high fence surounding the dump. They read:

CASTLE ROCK DUMP
HOURS 4-8 P.M.
CLOSED MONDAYS
TRESPASSING STRICTLY FORBIDDEN

CASTLE ROCK PUBLIC WORKS DEPARTMENT Where Teddy Duchamp worked as an adult.

CHEVROLET BEL AIR The car Teddy Duchamp was killed in.

CLOVERINE BRAND SALVE Gordie sold it. He got a Timex watch as a premium for selling it.

CRISCO CAN The can next to the water pump in the Castle Rock dump.

DAN BLOCKER'S DEATH Gordie was as sad about Dennis's death as he was about Blocker's.

DENNIS'S MAGAZINES *True* and *Sports Illustrated*.

DODGE The car Billy Tessio and Charlie Hogan stole.

THE DOGPISS OF THE YEAR AWARD Posthumous award given to Teddy Duchamp for putting one of his passengers, an unnamed girl, in a coma in a hospital ward for six months. She died when some phantom pulled the plug on her respirator.

'56 BUICK Milo Pressman's car.

GAINES MEAL AND CHICKEN BLOOD Chopper's feed, according to some area kids.

"GOG" A science fiction movie starring Richard Egan.

GORDIE'S PROVISIONS PURCHASES At the Florida Market, Gordie bought three pounds of hamburger, four sodas, hamburger rolls, and one churchkey.

GS & WM FREIGHT RUN It went to Derry and Brownsville.

HERBERT TAREYTON Mrs. Chalmers' cigarette.

"HIGHWAY PATROL" AND "DRAGNET" TV shows Billy Tessio had seen.

THE HITS OF THE SIXTIES "Come Softly to Me" by The Fleetwoods; "Susie Darling" by Robin Luke; and "I Ran All the Way Home" by Little Anthony.

THE INVISIBLE MAN A book by Ralph Ellison. Gordie did a book report on it.

IVY LEAGUE PENNANTS They hung on the wall in Dennis's room.

KEDS Ray Brower's sneakers.

LABOR DAY The day the boys returned to Castle Rock after their journey – and their "fall from innocence."

LEECHES They were in the beaver pond where the boys went swimming. The leeches found the boys tasty.

MASTER DETECTIVE One of the magazines in the treehouse.

MUSKOL An insect repellent.

"NAKED CITY" AND "THE UNTOUCHABLES" TV programs Gordie's father never missed.

NEW YORK GIANTS BASEBALL CAP It was worn by Milo Pressman.

NEWS STORIES ON THE RADIO Broadcasts included stories on Nixon, Kennedy, and Castro. The boys didn't like listening to them.

1952 DESOTO Vern Tessio's dad's car.

1952 FORD The car Ace Merrill and Fuzzy Bracowicz drove.

1971 The year Chris Chambers was stabbed to death in an altercation at a Chicken Delight in Portland. He was trying to break up a fight.

1971 The year Teddy Duchamp was killed in a car crash.

1966 The year Vern Tessio was killed in a house fire.

"PARKING" LOTS The bad guys would take girls parking in Castle View, Harlow, and Shiloh.

PHILCO RADIO The boys had one in the treehouse.

PIONEER DRUMSTICKS Hamburger roasted on the ends of green branches.

PURPLE JESUSES The drinks the bad guys drank with their girls in the car.

RHEINGOLD BOTTLE Chris's father broke one over the back of Chris's head.

ROLLOS The candy Gordie offered his dad.

SCHLITZ PLACEMAT On the counter at the Florida Market.

'77 FORD STATION WAGON The car Ace Merrill ended up driving as an adult. It had a "Reagan/Bush 1980" bumper sticker on it.

STORIES READ TO GORDIE "The Gingerbread Man" and "Three Little Pigs" were read to Gordie by his mother. "Blue-

beard" and "Jack the Ripper" were read to Gordie by his brother Dennis.

"STUDENT FATALLY STABBED IN PORTLAND RESTAU-RANT" Headline Gordie read. It was how he learned about Chris's death.

SUNDAY *TELEGRAM* Newspaper. On the front page of its funnies section were "Blondie" and "Dick Tracy." The paper was delivered to Otisfield, Norway, South Paris, Waterford, and Stoneham.

TIMEX WATCH Gordie received one for selling Cloverine Brand Salve.

TREEHOUSE It overhung a vacant lot.

THE TREEHOUSE MUSIC The boss oldies WLAM played included "What in the World's Come Over You" by Jack Scott; "This Time" by Troy Shondell; "King Creole" by Elvis; and "Only the Lonely" by Roy Orbison.

$2.13 The amount of Gordie's provisions purchases.

$2.37 The total of the boys' funds.

VSOP BRANDY Gordie thought that Mrs. Chalmers' coffee was sixty percent VSOP brandy.

WLAM Lewiston radio station the boys listened to.

WARRINER'S English book Chris bought.

WCOU Night baseball station.

WHAT MILO PRESSMAN SAID ABOUT TEDDY AND TEDDY'S FATHER He called Teddy a "little tin-weasel peckerwood loony's son." He also said "Your dad was a loony," that he was "crazier'n a shithouse rat," "crazier'n a buck with tickwood fever," and "nuttier'n a long-tailed cat in a room fulla rockin chairs." He also called Teddy a "foulmouthed little whoremaster." [NOTE: See the "Things" entry WHAT TEDDY CALLED MILO PRESSMAN.]

WHAT TEDDY CALLED MILO PRESSMAN "Fatass," "Lard-Bucket," "Tubbaguts," "Asshole," and "Cocksucker." He also told Milo that [his] "mother blows dead rats." [NOTE: See the "Things" entry WHAT MILO PRESSMAN SAID ABOUT TEDDY AND TEDDY'S FATHER.]

"WILD CARD" The words painted on the back deck of the 1952 Ford Ace Merril drove.

WILD IRISH ROSE The wine the bad guys would drink while cruising.

WINSTON The cigarettes Chris Chambers smoked.

—*Addendum*—
(15c)

DIFFERENT SEASONS
"The Revenge of Lard Ass Hogan"
from
"The Body"
People

BANCICHEK, MR. Butcher at the Freedom market. He weighed the pies every year.

BROCKWAY, MRS. The Methodist minister's wife. She threw up roast beef, mashed potatoes, and apple cobbler.

CHARBONNEAU, MARGUERITE The mayor's wife. Calvin Spier puked on her head.

CHARBONNEAU, MAYOR Mayor of Gretna.

CORMIER, BOB Disc jockey at WLAM and one of the pie-eating contestants.

DAY, CHUCK Owner of the Great Day Appliance Shop.

DODGE, SYLVIA President of the Gretna ladies' auxiliary. She oversaw the baking of the pies for the pie-eating contest. She threw up on the mayor's back. (He was wearing a Robert Hall suitcoat.)

GAMACHE, GEORGE Pie-eating contestant in 1957 who had eaten three pies in four minutes, and then fainted dead away.

HARRINGTON, MURIEL The mayor's wife threw up Muriel's

Bosco chocolate cake.

HOGAN, DAVIE Lard Ass Hogan. Entered "The Great Gretna Pie-Eat of 1960," and turned it into a puke-o-rama.

LAVIN, MARIA Marguerite Charbonneau's friend. Marguerite threw up on Maria.

MALING, JERRY Owned the Gretna Amoco station.

NORMAN, MISS She taught Latin and English fundamentals at the Gretna Consolidated High School. She threw up in her purse.

SPIER, CALVIN Pie-eating contestant.

TRAVIS, BILL Chuck Day's cousin and the reigning pie-eating champion.

WIGGINS, JOHN Principal of the Gretna elementary school, and one of the pie-eating contestants.

Places

FREEDOM MARKET Where the pies were weighed every year.

GREAT DAY APPLIANCE SHOP Owned by Chuck Day.

GRETNA Town in Gordie's story "The Revenge of Lard Ass Hogan."

GRETNA CONSOLIDATED HIGH SCHOOL Miss Norman taught there.

GRETNA ELEMENTARY SCHOOL John Wiggins was principal.

SABBATUS ROAD Jerry Maling had a two-story ranch on this street.

Things

CASTOR OIL Lard Ass drank three-quarters of a bottle of castor oil before the pie-eating contest.

"THE GREAT GRETNA PIE-EAT OF 1960" Sign announcing the Gretna pie-eating contest.

"THE REVENGE OF LARD ASS HOGAN" A short story by Gordon Lachance. It was originally published in *Cavalier* magazine in March 1975.

TEN MINUTES The strictly observed time limit for the pie-eating contest.

—Addendum—
(15c)
DIFFERENT SEASONS
"Stud City"
from
"The Body"
People

BILLY Chico's younger brother.

CARTER, DANNY Chico's friend.

CHICO Main character in "Stud City." His real name was Edward May.

JANE Chico's girlfriend.

JOHNNY Chico's brother.

MAY, EDWARD Chico's real name.

MAY, SAM Chico's dad.

MORRISON, SALLY Town pump. She drove a T-bird.

VIRGINIA Chico's stepmother.

Places

BROWNIE'S STORE Gas station/market in "Stud City."

Things

BUICK Chico's car.

DODGE Johnny's car.

HANES T-SHIRT Johnny was wearing one when he got killed.

"I WANT IT EVERY DAY" Button pinned to Chico's sun visor.

"STUD CITY" A short story by Gordon Lachance. It was published

in *Greenspun Quarterly*, in the Fall 1970 issue (#45)

"TIE ME KANGAROO DOWN" Chico thought of the lyrics to this.

❖❖❖

(15d)
DIFFERENT SEASONS
"The Breathing Method"
People

ADLEY, DAVID Guest at "The Club" for the evening's story-telling session.

ADLEY, ELLEN David's wife.

AMBULANCE ATTENDANT He ignored McCarron's request for a blanket after he saw that Sandra's body was still breathing.

ANDREWS, PETER Member of The Club.

BEAGLEMEN, HUGH Member of The Club.

CAB DRIVER He picked up Sandra to take her to the hospital.

CARDEN, ROBERT Lawyer. One of George Waterhouse's partners.

CARRUTHERS, LATHROP American general.

DAVIDSON, ELLA Dr. McCarron's nurse.

EFFINGHOUSE, HENRY Lawyer. One of George Waterhouse's partners.

GIBBS, MRS. Blind woman in the village. She hired Sandra to read to her and do light housework.

GORDON, DEXTER Blue-eyed black horn player.

GREGSON, GEORGE Member of The Club.

HANRAHAN, ARLENE John Hanrahan's widow. She received an anonymous gift of $10,400 from "Friends of Your Late Husband." The gift was from the members of The Club.

HANRAHAN, JOHN Member of The Club. He died of cancer.

"JANE SMITH" Pseudonymous name Sandra Stansfield used on her admittance form for Dr. McCarron.

JOHANSSEN Club member.

KELLY, MRS. Sandra Stansfield's supervisor at the department store.

LENNOX, TERRY Character in the *The Long Goodbye*.

McCARRON, EMLYN Club member.

MIDDLE-AGED NURSE The unnamed nurse who helped McCarron deliver Sandra's child.

ROSEN, NORBERT Poet. David discovered three volumes of his works in The Club's stacks. David felt he was the equal of Ezra Pound and Wallace Stevens.

SANDRA STANSFIELD'S SON JOHN At the time McCarron told the story of the boy's birth, the son was currently head of the English department at a respected private college.

"SARGE" Name McCarron called the nurse who helped him deliver Stansfield's baby. McCarron thought he was back in the army again.

"A SENATOR ON THE HILL" Senator who later became president. This senator once came in to Peter Andrews' law office with blood on his shirt.

SEVILLE, EDWARD GRAY Eleven novels by Seville were in The Club's library.

THE SHOSHONE, KIOWA, AND MICMAC TRIBES Indian tribes which used the Breathing Method.

STANSFIELD, SANDRA Pregnant woman; patient of Dr. McCarron.

STEIN, HARRY Member of The Club.

STEINEM, GLORIA The club was still considered a "gentlemen's club" – in a pre-Gloria Steinem antiquity.

STETT, NORMAN Club member who told the first story that evening.

STEVENS English butler at The Club. Stephen King's alter ego.

TOZEMAN, GERARD Member of The Club.

WATERHOUSE, GEORGE David Adley's boss. He invited David to The Club.

WHITE, HARRIET Nurse. She had a hospital named for her.
WOODS, JOSEPH Peter Andrews' boss in Washington.
YOUNG WOMAN Unnamed woman who witnessed Sandra Stansfield's accident.

(15d)
DIFFERENT SEASONS
"The Breathing Method"
Places

ANZIO Where Norbert Rosen was killed.
COPENHAGEN David was sent there for six weeks.
COW AND SILEAGE JUNIOR COLLEGE "School" where McCarron said Stansfield had gotten her English degree.
EAST 58TH STREET The Adleys lived in an apartment building on this street.
EMERGENCY WING RAMPWAY Where the accident took place that resulted in the amputation of Sandra Stansfield's head.
HARRIET WHITE MEMORIAL HOSPITAL Hospital directly across the street from Madison Square Graden. Emlyn McCarron was associated with this hospital.
INDIA AND AFRICA Countries in which the Breathing Method was widely used.
IOWA, NEBRASKA, OR MINNESOTA Sandra Stansfield had come from a small town in one of these states.
NEW YORK PUBLIC LIBRARY David went there to check on the writers of the books he had seen at The Club.
PARK AVENUE Where Peter Andrews had his law office.
SCHNECTADY Ellen Adley's sister lived there. She and David planned on spending Christmas with her.
THE SHEEP MEADOW Meadow in Central Park. Sheep grazed there while Harriet White got her experience in nursing.
249B EAST 35th STREET Address of The Club.
WARD NINE IN BELLEVUE McCarron said that delivery rooms sounded like Ward Nine.
WASHINGTON, D.C. Where Peter Andrews practiced law for twenty years before moving to Park Avenue.
WISCONSIN David's home state. He grew up on a farm.

(15d)
DIFFERENT SEASONS
"The Breathing Method"
Things

BECK The beer David drank.
BREAKERS Edward Gray Seville's last novel.
"THE BREATHING METHOD" The Lamaze Method. McCarron introduced this method to Sandra in her fourth month.
CHECKER CAB David took one to The Club.
CHRISTMAS EVE Sandra's labor began at just past 6:00 p.m. on Christmas Eve.
DECEMBER 10 The date McCarron gave Sandra Stansfield as the possible date her baby could be born. He cautioned her that it could be two weeks either way.
DECEMBER 23, 197- The night the storytelling session took place.
DICKENS, DEFOE, AND TROLLOPE BOOKS Sets of books by these authors were at The Club.
A DR. PEPPER BOTTLE McCarron had known of a woman who gave herself an abortion with a broken Dr. Pepper bottle.
ELLEN ADLEY'S COMMITTEES She belonged to the Relief Committee, the Commission on Women's Rights, and the Theater Society.
FORTY-TWO INCHES Height of a door in The Club.
THE FOUR STAGES OF LABOR Contractive labor, mid-labor, birth, and expulsion of the afterbirth.
"HERE, SIR, THERE ARE ALWAYS MORE TALES." Stevens last words to David as he left The Club.

"IT IS THE TALE, NOT HE WHO TELLS IT" Legend engraved on the stone above the fireplace in The Club. [NOTE: Also a favorite expression of Stephen King's, reflecting his attitude towards interest in his personal life as opposed to interest in his writings.]
THE LITERARY MARKETPLACE David couldn't find Stedham & Sons in this directory of publishers.
LOCOMOTIVE The final stage of the Breathing Method, it was named after the sound a child made when imitating a steam locomotive.
THE LONG GOODBYE Philip Marlowe book. Ellen was reading it when David came home from The Club.
MARCH 20, 1900 The day McCarron was born.
NAMES SANDRA STANSFIELD COULD HAVE MADE UP "Betty Rucklehouse" and "Termina DeVille." Instead she used "Jane Smith."
1911 The copyright date on the first Seville novel.
1924 The year Norbert Rosen was born.
1929 The year McCarron began practicing medicine.
1926 The year McCarron interned at Harriet White Memorial Hospital.
NORD BILLIARD TABLE Table in The Club. David checked with the International Trademark Commission to find out about the company. There were two companies called Nord. One made skis, the other made wooden kitchen accessories.
OCTOBER The month David's firm had their company dinner.
PET CASES A book David saw at The Club.
PHI BETA KAPPA KEY George Waterhouse wore one on his vest.
THE POETS In a large volume in The Club's library, scenes from famous movies were accompanied by verses by the following poets: Robert Frost, Marianne Moore, William Carlos Williams, Louis Zukofsky, Erica Jong, and Algernon Williams.
A PRACTICAL GUIDE TO PREGNANCY AND DELIVERY A book written by Dr. McCarron.
ROLLS-ROYCE SILVER WRAITH Terry Lennox's car.
THE ROOMS UPSTAIRS David discovered the following rooms upstairs at The Club: a writing room, a bedroom, a gymnasium, a sauna room, and two bowling alleys.
SEAFRONT JUKEBOX Jukebox in The Club. There was no Seafront company listed with the International Trademark Commission. The closest was "Seeburg."
SECOND AND THIRTY-FIFTH Intersection where David got out of the cab.
STEDHAM & SON Publishing company that published Edward Gray Seville's novels. David had never heard of either Stedham & Son or Seville.
"THANK YOU, DR. McCARRON" The words McCarron heard spoken by the severed head of Sandra Stansfield.
THESE WERE OUR BROTHERS Edward Gray Seville's first novel.
TWENTY CASES OF DISMEMBERMENTS AND THEIR OUTCOMES UNDER BRITISH LAW A book David saw at The Club.
THE "VALLEY OF THE SHADOW" SYNDROME The feeling of doom felt by pregnant women.
WALL STREET JOURNAL Paper Johanssen read.
WATERFORD BOWL Eggnog was served from this bowl at The Club on the Thursday before Christmas.
WATERHOUSE, CARDEN, LAWTON, FRASIER, AND EFFINGHAM Firm where David had worked for fifteen years.
WCBS New York radio station. On the night of December 23, the station was forecasting heavy snow.
WEIRD TALES Regarding his Breathing Method, one of McCarron's colleagues told him that if he wanted "nigger superstitions" he'd buy *Weird Tales*.
WORKS BY GENE STRATTON PORTER AND PEARL BUCK Sandra read them to Mrs. Gibbs in the village.

CHRISTINE

DEDICATION

This is for George Romero and
Chris Forrest Romero.

And the Burg.

CONTENTS PAGE &
BOOK BREAKDOWN

[Note: Unlike many of King's other novels, all the chapters of *Christine* are completely self-contained. There is no internal numbering of sub-sections within the chapters. –sjs]

(16)
CHRISTINE
People

ACKERMAN The name of the guy that Leigh Cabot eventually married. He was an IBM service rep.

AHAB, CAPTAIN With his new beard, Buddy Repperton looked like Ahab.

ARROWAY, DR. Dennis Guilder's doctor.

BARONGG, LENNY Tailback for the Libertyville football team. He had once asked Leigh Cabot out, but she turned him down. He also played on the Libertyville basketball team, the Terriers. In the game against the Bucanneers, Lenny scored thirty-four points.

BECK, DAVE He denied that the Teamsters union was a front for the rackets.

BELLERMAN, MARTY Lineman on the high school football team.

BLACKFORD Dennis's neighbor.

BROWNE, JACKSON Singer/songwriter. He did a show at the Pittsburgh civic center. [Note: As of this writing, Jackson Browne and Daryl Hannah have been an item for years. That piece of information has absolutely nothing to do with the work of Stephen King, but at least it gave me an excuse to mention Daryl Hannah in this book.]

THE BUCCANEERS Basketball team. On December 12, they beat the Libertyville Terriers, 54-48.

BUCK, HENRY Car dealer in Albany. He had fourteen "clean" used cars he wanted to sell Darnell.

THE BULLY Young boy who used to torment Roland LeBay as a child. The bully's house burned down one night.

THE BULLY'S FAMILY The father, little brother, and little sister of the unnamed bully who used to torture Roland LeBay as a youngster. Roland burned their house down. The father and brother were killed, the sister horribly burned.

BYRNES, ED "KOOKIE" Teen idol of the fifties.

CABOT, LEIGH Arnie's girlfriend. He first met her when she asked him for the English assignment. After Arnie's death, Dennis and Leigh became lovers, but they eventually drifted apart. By the end of the story, Leigh had moved to Taos, New Mexico, and married some guy named Ackerman. Leigh was world-class beautiful, and Dennis was in love with her for a very long time.

CABOT, MR. Leigh's father. He worked for 3M.

THE CALLISONS The family that invited the Guilders to brunch on Thanksgiving Day.

"CAPTAIN BEEFHEART" A cat Dennis had when he was nine. It got hit by a UPS truck.

CARRUTHERS, AIMEE Ellie Guilder's friend. Aimee moved to Nevada.

THE CARSON BROTHERS Dennis and Arnie had worked for

them all summer on the I-376 extension.

CHAPLIN, CHARLIE AND HITLER Dennis had heard Roland LeBay say "Watch me put it up the little tramp's ass." Dennis had thought LeBay was referring to Charlie Chaplin. George LeBay eventually told him that Roland had instead meant Adolph Hitler.

CHRISTINE A 1958 red Plymouth Fury. "Arnie's first love...his only true love." Roland LeBay bought her in 1958 for $2,100. She was killed by a tanker truck named Petunia. Even though she was reportedly run through a crusher and compacted into a cube, Christine was a suspect in the drive-in murder of Sandy Galton in California.

CLARK, DICK He was on TV on New Year's Eve.

COCHRAN, EDDIE Singer who was killed in a car crash in London. Arnie heard about it on Christine's radio.

THE COLOMBIANS They dealt cocaine with Will Darnell.

CUNNINGHAM, ARNIE Dennis's friend; he was a nerd with acne; he was five-ten, 140 pounds. He was seduced and destroyed by Christine.

CUNNINGHAM, MICHAEL Arnie's father. He taught history at the University in Horlicks.

CUNNINGHAM, REGINA Arnie's mother. She taught English at the University in Horlicks.

DAISY MAE The rubber dummy on which Barry Gottfried learned the Heimlich Maneuver.

DARLINGTON, FREDDY Classmate of Arnie and Dennis.

DARNELL, WILL He owned Darnell's Used Auto Parts. "Great rolls of fat bulged out his neck and hung in dewlaps below his chin." Darnell dealt coke, and was eventually killed by Christine. The car burst into Darnell's living room and ran him over.

DECKINGER, TOMMY Boy who had been in the fifth grade with Arnie. Tommy had called Arnie "Fart-Breath."

DELLA Elaine Guilder's girlfriend.

DINGLE, EVERETT A man Darnell knew. Dingle had gone home from Will's garage one day and murdered his entire family.

THE DINGLE FAMILY They were all murdered by Everett Dingle.

DODD, MILTON Elaine Guilder's boyfriend.

DONAHUE, PAT The man who ran Gino's Fine Italian Pizza restaurant.

EMERSON, DAVID Owned David Emerson's Furniture Store, Libertyville's "good" furniture store.

FARNER, DR. When Roland LeBay was a child, Dr. Farner put twelve stitches in his head.

THE FASSENBACHS Arnie's parents went to the Fassenbachs' home for a 1979 New Year's Eve party.

FENDERSON, MR. Arnie's calculus teacher.

GABBS The man in Stall 10 at Darnell's. He was putting a new muffler on an old Valiant.

GALTON, SANDY Sandor Galton. One of Buddy Repperton's cohorts. He was the parking lot attendant at the airport where Arnie parked Christine. Sandy drove a Mustang. He was eventually killed in a bizarre accident at a drive-in movie. A car plowed through the wall of the snack bar and ran him down. Dennis had a feeling it was Christine.

GILMAN, ROGER Arnie's classmate. Roger beat up Arnie.

GITNEY IRS man.

GOTTFRIED, BARRY The hitchhiker who saved Leigh Cabot's life as she was choking on a hamburger while sitting in Christine. He used the Heimlich Maneuver. At first, Leigh had thought he looked "Manson-like." Gottfried complained about "bad vibes" from Christine.

GUILDER, DENNIS Teller of *Christine*; Arnie's friend.

GUILDER, ELAINE Dennis's fourteen-year-old sister.

GUILDER, KENNY Dennis's father. He was a tax consultant for H & R Block.

GUILDER, MRS. Dennis's mother. She was a dental hygienist.

HARVEY, PAUL He reported on the Cunninghams' death on his radio program.

HASKINS, WANDA Will Darnell's high school sweetheart.

HATCH, MR. He drove a Fairlane. He picked it up at Darnell's.

HICKS, MIKE One of the players in the chess tournament.

HIDDEN HILLS Football team. Libertyville played them in the third game of the season. Libertyville won, 27-18.

HODDER, MR. Freshman grammar teacher.

HORTON, JOHNNY Singer of the fifties.

HURLING, BRANDON Ellie Guilder's first date.

JAMES, STUKEY High school math teacher.

JEFFRIES, BRAD The I-376 extension job foreman.

JOHN PAUL I, POPE Will Darnell cogitated on the Pope's death.

JONES, COACH Libertyville high school basketball coach.

JUNKINS, RUDY The police officer who called Michael Cunningham to question him about Arnie's possible connection with Moochie Welch's death.

THE "KILL EM ALL" GUY A guy who worked on a BSA in Darnell's Speed Shop. On the back of his leather jacket was a skull wearing a Green Beret and the message "KILL EM ALL AND LET GOD SORT EM OUT."

LeBAY, DREW George and Roland's brother. He died in France in 1944.

LeBAY, GEORGE Roland LeBay's brother.

LeBAY, RITA Veronica and Roland LeBay's daughter. She was born in 1952. In 1958, at the age of six, she choked to death while sitting in Christine.

LeBAY, ROLAND D. U.S. army retired; he sold Christine to Arnie. He wore a back brace, and usually ranted against the "shitters." His corpse appeared to Buddy Repperton after Christine rammed Buddy's Camaro.

LeBAY, VERONICA Roland LeBay's wife.

LEHEUREUX, MR. French teacher.

LEIGH'S GIRLS After Leigh Cabot married a guy named Ackerman, they had twin girls.

THE LIBERTYVILLE TERRIERS Libertyville's basketball team. On December 12, they lost to the Buccaneers, 54-48.

LOMBARDI, VINCE Coach Puffer patterned his coaching style after Lombardi's.

LOMBARDO, GUY Arnie didn't know he was dead.

LOTHROP, MS. School discipline officer.

THE LUNEBURG TIGERS Libertyville played them on September 9. Libertyville lost, 30-10.

MARCIA Roland LeBay's sister.

A MARGINALLY RETARDED GIRL She read the *National Enquirer* in a gas station.

MASCIA, DR. The doctor who prescribed a back brace for Dennis.

McCANDLESS, RICHARD The secretary of the American Legion post.

McCARTHY, CHUBBY In Dennis's dream, Chubby was the commentator for Libertyville's game against the Philadelphia City Dragons.

McNALLY, BRIAN Football player. He replaced Dennis in the fourth quarter in the Hidden Hills game.

MEECHAM, MR. High school principal.

MERCER, RICK Pennsylvania state police officer. Dennis told him about LeBay, Arnie, and Christine.

MOLOCH The god Dennis read about in his "Origins of Literature" class.

MUSTUNGERRA, ROY The man who ran United Auto Parts.

OSMOND, DONNY AND MARIE They had a special on TV on New Year's Eve.

THE OVERWEIGHT BE-BOP QUEEN The mother of the Devil Dog-eating kids. She was a Libra.

OWEN OR OLIVE The names Mr. Guilder gave to every toy bear he made.

PENNSYLVANIA ATTORNEY GENERAL He signed the order impounding any of Bill Upshaw's records that related to Will Darnell.

PERKINS, CARL Singer from the fifties.
PETUNIA Tanker truck Dennis rented from Johnny Pomberton to use to kill Christine.
PHILADELPHIA CITY DRAGONS A team Dennis dreamt that Libertyville played.
THE PHILLIES AND THE STEELERS Arnie and Dennis talked about the Phillies's collapse and the Steelers' chances of making the Super Bowl.
POMBERTON, JOHNNY Lived on Ridge Road. He had a lot of "rolling stock" available. He rented Dennis the tanker truck named Petunia that Dennis used to "kill" Christine.
PREWITT Character in *From Here To Eternity*. George LeBay compared his brother Roland to Prewitt.
PUFFER, COACH High school football coach.
PURVIS, MELVIN The G-Man who killed Dillinger, and then himself.
QUALSON, BARRY One of the players in the chess tournament.
QUEEG, CAPTAIN Character from *The Caine Mutiny*. Coach Puffer reminded Dennis of Queeg because of the way he jingled his keys.
RALPH The Overweight Be-Bop Queen's husband. He told Arnie and Dennis to get Christine away from in front of his house.
RASPUTIN How Dennis thought of the "Kill Em All" guy.
RAYPACH, MISS Study-hall teacher. The kids called her "Miss Rat-Pack."
A RECORD CLERK An unnamed library employee.
RENNEKE, DINAH Ellie Guilder's friend.
REPPERTON, BUDDY High school creep. He hated Arnie Cunningham, trashed Christine, and was destroyed by her revenge.
THE RIDGE ROCK BEARS Football team. Libertyville played them in the second game of the season. Libertyville lost, 40-6.
ROSEANNE The girl that Dennis took to see "Grease."
SALVATION ARMY SANTAS The men in the mall ringing bells and collecting for the Salvation Army.
SANDY GALTON'S KID BROTHER He pushed dope at Gornick Junior High School.
SANDY GALTON'S MOTHER "A forty-five-year-old wino who didn't look a day over sixty."
SHAMBLISS, CAROLYN Elaine Guilder's girlfriend. Carolyn told Elaine that farts could be ignited.
SLAWSON The high school faculty advisor.
SMOLNACK, MR. Arnie's Auto Shop I teacher.
SMYTHE, LADD Patrol-boy who had once pushed Arnie down in the street.
SPRAGUE, TOM Michael Cunningham's lawyer.
STANTON, BOBBY One of Buddy Repperton's cohorts. He was killed by Christine.
STEVE Regina Cunningham's brother-in-law; Vicky's husband.
STEWART, MR. Leigh Cabot's dad's new boss.
STORK A man Dennis's father went to college with.
STRICKLAND, PAUL Michael Cunningham's friend. He went to O'Malley's with Michael.
STROUGHMAN, NED He had once asked Leigh Cabot out, but she turned him down.
SYKES, JIMMY Boy who worked for Darnell.
SYKES, MRS. Jimmy Sykes's mother.
THOMPSON, MR. Head of the history department. He taught "Topics in American History" for the first nine weeks of the class.
THROGMORTON, RANDY Boy who had once hit the young Roland LeBay with a hockey stick and split his head open.
TRELAWNEY, RICHIE One of Buddy Repperton's cohorts. He drove a Firebird.
TURNER, RANDY He saw Arnie and Buddy fight, and later gave Dennis the details.
TWO CHILDREN The two unnamed kids of the Overweight Be-Bop Queen. They watched Arnie change a tire on Christine.
UPSHAW, AMBER Bill Upshaw's wife.

UPSHAW, WILLIAM Monroeville accountant. He did Will Darnell's taxes after Dennis's dad quit in 1975. He was eventually served with a court order impounding all his tax records that related to Will Darnell (an individual) or Will Darnell (a corporation).
VANDENBERG, DON One of Buddy Repperton's cohorts. He worked in his father's gas station.
VANDENBERG, MR. Don's father. He owned a gas station.
VICKERS, MR. The guidance counselor. Lenny Barongg called him "Motormouth."
VICKY Regina Cunningham's sister.
WARBERG, JIM Criminal lawyer that Tom Sprague recommended to Regina Cunningham for Arnie.
WELCH, MOOCHIE (PETER) One of Buddy Repperton's cohorts. He was run over by Christine.
YOUNGERMAN, QUENT Friend of Will Darnell's.

(16)
CHRISTINE
Places

BARNSWALLOW DRIVE The former name of JFK Drive.
BASKIN-ROBBINS Ice cream parlor.
THE BLACK HOLE OF CALCUTTA Dennis thought that being in the Black Hole would be better than being in Darnell's.
BRITISH LION STEAK HOUSE Restaurant. Arnie and Leigh had reservations there.
CUSTOM CHRYSLER New Jersey supplier. Darnell figured Arnie bought the new grill for Christine from them.
DARBY JUNIOR HIGH SCHOOL One of the schools Dennis and Arnie attended together.
DARNELL'S OFFICE According to Dennis, it was decorated in "Early American Carburetor."
DARNELL'S USED AUTO PARTS Garage owned by Will Darnell. Arnie paid twenty dollars a week to rent a stall for Christine.
DAVID EMERSON'S FURNITURE STORE Libertyville retailer. Libertyville's "good" furniture store. Richard McCandless worked at Emerson's.
DENVER Town where Roland Lebay's sister Marcia lived.
DREW The college Leigh and Dennis went to.
FM-104 Radio station.
FORT ARNOLD Army base in West Texas. Roland LeBay was stationed there. He worked as a mechanic.
FOX CHAPEL A neighboring suburb of Libertyville. It was considered ritzy.
GINO'S FINE ITALIAN PIZZA A restaurant on the corner of Main and Basin Drive.
GORNICK JUNIOR HIGH SCHOOL Sandy Galton's kid brother pushed more dope at Gornick than anyone else.
H & R BLOCK Dennis's father worked as a tax consultant for them.
HORLICKS Where the university was located.
JFK DRIVE Street formerly called Barnswallow Drive. It was renamed in honor of Kennedy. It led to the Pennsylvania Turnpike.
KENTUCKY FRIED CHICKEN Dennis and Leigh parked in the franchise's parking lot in order to "make out" and to talk about Arnie.
KINGSFIELD PIKE Where Moochie lived.
KOREA Roland LeBay went there shortly after he was married.
LAUREL DRIVE On Laurel Drive, backfires from Christine sounded as if someone had opened up with machine gun fire on the street.
LAUREL STREET A quiet residential street on the west side of Libertyville where the Cunninghams lived.
LIBERTY LOOKOUT The poor section of Libertyville. It was also known as "Low Heights."
LIBERTYVILLE Town where *Christine* takes place.
LIBERTYVILLE DRIVE-IN The drive-in where Arnie and Leigh

went to see Sylvester Stallone's movie "FIST."

LIBERTYVILLE HEIGHTS CEMETERY Cemetery where Roland LeBay and the Cunninghams were buried.

LIBERTYVILLE HIGH SCHOOL One of the schools that Dennis and Arnie attended together.

LIGONIER Town ninety miles east of Libertyville.

MAMMOTH MART They sold Sapphire motor oil.

MCCONNELL'S Auto-glass specialist. Arnie told Junkins that this was where he got the replacement glass for Christine.

MONROEVILLE Lower class neighborhood near Libertyville. It was filled with miles of malls, discount tire warehouses, and dirty-book emporiums.

MONROEVILLE MALL PARKING LOT The lot where Arnie broke down and cried after leaving Christine at Darnell's.

NORMAN COBBS PLYMOUTH DEALERSHIP The dealership where LeBay bought Christine.

O'MALLEY'S Beer parlor. Michael Cunningham went there for a drink.

100 FRANKSTOWN ROAD, MONROEVILLE Address of Bill Upshaw's office.

OWEN ANDREWS GRAMMAR SCHOOL One of the schools Dennis and Arnie attended together.

PARADISE FALLS, OHIO The place where George LeBay had taught high-school English for almost forty years. [NOTE: This reference was King's way of acknowledging and honoring one of the three main influences on his writing, Don Robertson. Paradise Falls, Ohio, was the setting for some of Robertson's fiction.]

PENN-DOT The Pennsylvania department of transportation.

PHILADELPHIA SHERATON The hotel where the chess tournament was held.

PHYSICAL THERAPY ROOM Dennis called it the "Torture Chamber."

PITTSBURGH CIVIC CENTER Jackson Browne played there.

PITTSBURGH SAVINGS AND LOAN The bank where Dennis and Arnie cashed their checks.

THE PLACES ALONG JFK DRIVE IN LIBERTYVILLE A drive-in movie, McDonalds, Burger King, Arby's, the Big Twenty lanes, and ten service stations.

THE RAINBOW MOTEL The Libertyville motel where George LeBay stayed.

THE RAMADA INN The Kansas City hotel where Michael Cunningham stayed when he went to KC for a convention.

RIDGE ROAD The street where Johnny Pomberton lived.

SEWICKLEY Bill Upshaw owned a $300,000 English Tudor home in Sewickley.

THE SPEED SHOP The shop owned by Will Darnell in addition to the garage. They stocked Feully heads, Hurst shifters, and Ram-Jet superchargers. Dennis thought that looking into the window of the shop was like peering into some "crazy automotive Disneyland."

SQUANTIC HILLS Buddy Repperton's, Bobby Stanton's, and Richie Trelawney's destination, and the place where they were murdered by Christine.

SQUIRREL HILL Dennis went there to see Arnie play in a chess tournament.

TAOS, NEW MEXICO The place that Leigh Cabot moved to after marrying an IBM customer-service rep named Ackerman.

TEXACO STATION They were having a tire sale.

THOM McAN'S When Arnie broke down crying, Dennis wished he was at Thom McAn's trying on shoes.

3M The company Leigh Cabot's father worked for.

UNIT 14 The room in the Rainbow Motel where George LeBay stayed when he was in Libertyville.

UNITED AUTO PARTS Company on North Broad Street. Will Darnell asked Arnie to check on some new tires there.

VACATION BIBLE SCHOOL Dennis and Arnie went there for two weeks every summer when they were young.

VANDENBERG'S HAPPY GAS Service station on Route 22 in

Monroeville. Dennis had seen Buddy Repperton there.

WALNUT STREET AND BASIN DRIVE The route Arnie took to Darnell's. It kept him off the main roads.

WDIL AM station from Pittsburgh that played only oldies.

WEST VIRGINIA Veronica LeBay's home state.

WESTERN AUTO Shop where Dennis had keys made to Darnell's Garage.

WMDY Local rock-and-soul station.

WOOLWORTH'S Store that sold Darth Vader costumes for Halloween.

(16)
CHRISTINE
Things

"A.B." "The Asshole Brigade." The way Roland LeBay referred to some of his neighbors.

ALICE IN WONDERLAND When Mr. Leheureux said "You boys are late" to Dennis and Arnie, Dennis was reminded of the white rabbit in *Alice in Wonderland*.

AM RADIO The radio in Christine. FM had not been available when she was made.

AMWAY Leigh Cabot Ackerman sold it in her spare time.

ARNIE'S LIBRARY BOOKS Arnie withdrew the following books from the library: *American Car, American Classics,* and *Cars of the 1950's*.

ARNIE'S SIGNATURES Arnie signed Dennis's cast twice. The second time he wrote "For Dennis Guilder, The World's Biggest Dork Arnie Cunningham" Dennis compared the two signatures and realized that they were totally different.

AUGUST 11, 1978 The day Dennis realized that he was getting ready to be a grownup.

BENTLEY When he was in the army, Roland LeBay was once ordered to fix a congressman's Bentley.

"THE BIG CHEESE OF 119 BASIN DRIVE" How Dennis thought of Ralph, the Be-Bop Queen's husband.

BIG WHEELS The two unnamed Devil Dog-eating kids were astride Big Wheels.

"BIZARRE MURDER BY CAR IN LOS ANGELES" Headline detailing the story about the car that killed Sandy Galton.

BLOCK PARTY WEEKEND A program on FM-104.

BORAXO Even Boraxo couldn't get the grease off Arnie's hands.

"BOSS" According to his sister Elaine, Dennis was "boss" because he liked Bruce Springsteen.

BUBBLICIOUS GUM The gum chewed by the girl reading the *National Enquirer* in the gas station.

"THE BUDDY HOLLY, KRUSCHEV, AND LAIKA THE SPACE DOG ERA" Arnie thought of Christine as a resurrected time traveler from this era.

BUSCH BEER Arnie brought Dennis a six-pack on Thanksgiving.

CAMARO Buddy Repperton's car.

CAMPBELL'S CHUNKY BEEF The soup Dennis ate.

CAPRICORN One of the Devil Dog kids said he was a Capricorn, and that his mother was a Libra.

CAREERS, LIFE, AND CLUE Board games that Dennis and Arnie sometimes played.

CHEVETTE The car George LeBay rented from Hertz.

CHEVROLET The car Roland LeBay owned after World War II.

CHRISTINE'S MILEAGE The day Arnie bought the car, her mileage was 97,432.6 miles.

CHRISTINE'S PLAYLIST Dennis thought he'd hear the following songs on Christine's radio: "Maybelline" by Chuck Berry; "Wake Up Little Susie" by the Everly Brothers; and ""Susie Darling" by Robin Luke.

"A CHRISTMAS CAROL" The movie on TV on Christmas Eve.

"C'MON EVERYBODY" Song by Eddie Cochran.

CONESTOGA WAGONS Dennis thought that the jack in Christine's truck looked like it might have been used to change wheels on Conestoga wagons.

D9-CAT A bulldozer. Dennis compared Arnie's smile "post-Christine" to a bulldozer operator lowering the blade of a D9-CAT in front of a particularly difficult stump.

"DARNELL INVESTIGATOR MURDERED NEAR BLAIRSVILLE" Newspaper story about Rudy Junkins's death.

DARNELL'S FIRECRACKER SUPERMARKET Will Darnell would sell anyone firecrackers, cherry bombs, or bottle rockets for the Fourth of July.

DARNELL'S INVESTMENTS When Dennis's father was doing Will Darnell's taxes, Darnell told him he wanted his money invested in Pennsylvania Solar Heating, and in New York Ticketing.

DARNELL'S SIGNS The following signs were posted in Darnell's Garage:

ALL TOOLS MUST BE INSPECTED
BEFORE YOU LEAVE

MAKE APPOINTMENT FOR LIFT-TIME
IN ADVANCE

MOTOR MANUALS ON
FIRST-COME FIRST-SERVE BASIS

NO PROFANITY OR SWEARING
WILL BE TOLERATED

"THE DEATH CAR" Dennis had a dream in which Christine was "not just old; she was ancient, a terrible hulk of a car, something you'd expect to see in a Tarot deck: instead of the Hanged Man, the Death Car."

DENNIS AND ELAINE, ACCORDING TO ARNIE "The Creature from the Black Lagoon" and "The Bride of Frankenstein."

DENNIS'S CHRISTINE DREAMS After it was all over, whenever Dennis dreamt of Christine, he heard Buddy Holly, J.P. Richardson, The Big Bopper, and "La Bamba."

DENNIS'S INJURIES In the game against the Ridge Rock Bears, Dennis was injured and woke up in the hospital on Monday, October 23, 1978. He had two broken legs (the left broken in two places), and his right forearm was fractured. He also had a fractured skull and "a lower spinal accident," which meant that he had come within a centimeter of being paralyzed for life from the waist down.

DENTAL HYGIENIST Mrs. Guilder's job.

DEVIL DOGS The two unnamed kids of the Overweight Be-Bop Queen and the Big Cheese of 119 Basin Drive were eating Devil Dogs as they watched Arnie change Christine's tire.

"DID JESUS HAVE A DOG?" Essay written by Dennis's mother.

"DUKE OF EARL" Song by Earl Chandler.

"EARLY AMERICAN CARBURETOR" The decor of Will Darnell's office, according to Dennis.

18,000 POUNDS The gross vehicle weight (GVW) of Petunia.

ELAINE GUILDER'S FAVORITE MAGAZINES *16*, *Creem*, and *Tiger Beat*.

ELAINE GUILDER'S FAVORITE PERFORMERS At nine, Donny and Marie; at eleven, John Travolta; at twelve, Shaun Cassidy and Andy Gibb; and at fourteen, Deep Purple and Styx.

11:00 A.M. CHRISTMAS DAY This was when Dennis Guilder left the hospital to come home.

"ENGINE FUNDAMENTALS" Auto shop course Arnie took as a sophomore.

"EXCEPT MAYBE FOR PUSSY" Roland LeBay said the smell of a new car was "the finest smell in the world. Except maybe for pussy."

FEDERAL DRUG CONTROL TASK FORCE Organization investigating Darnell, Arnie, and Bill Upshaw.

FIREBIRD Richie Trelawney's car.

FISHER-PRICE TOYS They littered the backyards of the homes in Liberty Lookout.

513 George LeBay's area code.

FOREIGNER Arnie and Dennis heard "Dirty White Boy" and "Juke Box Heroes" by Foreigner during FM-104's Block Party Weekend.

THE GIRLS ON CHRISTINE'S RADIO It seemed that at times Christine's radio only played songs with girl's names in them: Peggy Sue, Carol, Barbara-Ann, and Susie Darlin'.

"GIVE ME LIBERTYVILLE OR GIVE ME DEATH" This was written on the front of Leigh Cabot's t-shirt.

GOODYEAR OR FIRESTONE The tires that Arnie wanted to buy for Christine.

GRANNY SMITH APPLE Michael Cunningham ate one.

"GREASE" The movie Dennis took Roseanne to see.

"THE GREAT DICTATOR" Charlie Chaplin film.

HAWAIIAN PUNCH Dennis had a glass of punch when he returned from talking with George LeBay.

THE HEART FUND OR THE CANCER SOCIETY Arnie suggested these charities to Dennis instead of being charitable to Arnie Cunningham.

THE HEIMLICH MANEUVER The method that could have been used to save Rita LeBay when she was choking to death in Christine, but which hadn't been developed in 1958.

"HIS UNENDING FURY" The last line of *Christine*. As the story ends, Dennis wonders "What if it's working its way east, finishing the job? Saving me for last? His single-minded purpose. *His unending fury*." Dennis still wasn't sure that Roland LeBay had finished with him…or Christine.

THE HOBBYIST A magazine Ken Guilder read.

"HONK FOR ENTRY" The sign next to the door of Darnell's Garage.

HUDSON HORNET The car Roland LeBay bought the year after he got married.

HY-6241-J Christine's license plate number.

THE I-376 EXTENSION Arnie and Dennis had been working on the road for the Carson brothers.

"IRISH MAFIA" The sign on the cash register in Gino's.

IRON CITY BEER The beer Ralph drank.

"JAILHOUSE ROCK" Song by Elvis.

JANUARY 1959 The month Veronica LeBay died. It was six months after Roland's and her daughter, Rita, choked to death in Christine.

"JEEVES" The nickname Arnie called Dennis when Arnie was in a good mood.

JUNE 1, 1976 Date of the invalid inspection sticker on Christine.

KEDS The sneaks Roland LeBay wore.

THE KEYSTONE Dennis checked back issues of this newspaper to see if Roland LeBay had ever run ads to try and sell Christine. He hadn't. All he did was put the car on his front lawn. Dennis thought it was too convenient that he would put it out just before Arnie happened by.

"KILL EM ALL AND LET GOD SORT EM OUT" Message written on a jacket worn by a guy working on a BSA in Darnell's Speed Shop.

"LA BAMBA" Song by Richie Valens.

LA-Z-BOY Will Darnell's armchair.

THE LeBAY REALTORS George LeBay gave three realtors the listing to sell Roland's house after Roland died: Century 21, Libertyville Realty, and Pittsburgh Homes.

"LIBERTYVILLE VETERAN DIES AT 71" Headline of the article announcing Roland LeBay's death.

LIBRA Birth sign of the mother of the Devil Dog kids.

"LIKE A REFUGEE FROM THE DEMO DERBY" How Christine moved on her way to Darnell's.

LIONELS Stork's obsession.

"MASHED POTATO TIME" Song by Dee Dee Sharp.

THE MINISTER Will Darnell's role in a high school play.

"MISS RAT-PACK" Derogatory nickname for Miss Raypach, the study hall teacher.

MONDAY, OCTOBER 23, 1978 The day Dennis woke up in the hospital after being injured in the game against the Ridge Rock Bears. Libertyville had lost, 46-3. [NOTE: See the "Things" entry DENNIS'S INJURIES.]

MORTE D'ARTHUR English classic by Malory. Leigh, Arnie, and Dennis had studied it in school.

"MOTHER-IN-LAW" Song by Ernie K-Doe.

"MOTORMOUTH" The nickname Lenny Barongg called Mr. Vickers.

MR. COFFEE Coffeemaker in Darnell's office.

MR. GOODWRENCH Some of the guys in shop class wanted to grow up to be Mr. Goodwrench.

MUSTANG Sandy Galton's car.

MUSTANG MACH II Dennis told LeBay that Arnie's parents had bought Arnie a Mustang in order to dissuade LeBay from selling Christine to Arnie. The Mustang supposedly had a Hurst shifter.

THE NATIONAL ENQUIRER Newspaper read by a marginally retarded girl in a gas station.

THE NATIONAL GUARD They held maneuvers in Squantic Hills.

NEW YEAR'S EVE MUSIC On New Year's Eve, Dennis heard Dion and the Belmonts, Ernie K-Doe, the Total Teens, and Bobby Rydell on Christine's radio.

"THE NEXT VIETNAM" Article in *Esquire*. Dennis Guilder read it as an assignment.

1951 The year Veronica and Roland LeBay were married.

1957 The year Roland LeBay left the army.

1957 CADILLAC The car in LeBay's yard.

1975 DUSTER Dennis Guilder's car.

1965 The year Roland LeBay retired, and stopped taking care of Christine.

1966 IMPERIAL Will Darnell's car. Arnie used it for "errands."

1923 The year Roland LeBay joined the army.

97,432.6 MILES Christine's mileage the day Arnie bought her.

NORTHERN STATES FALL TOURNEY Chess tournament in Philadelphia. Arnie attended for three days.

NOVEMBER 1, 1978 The day Christine became street legal.

PENIS ENVY, OEDIPAL CONFLICTS, AND THE SHROUD OF TURIN These were things Arnie said sounded "nuts," until you really considered them.

PEPSI Dennis and Arnie drank Pepsi with their pizza.

PEPSI COLA CANS They were scattered around Darnell's garage. Darnell yelled for someone to pick them up.

THE PHILLIES GAME Dennis's father watched the Phillies play Atlanta. He wore purple bermudas, Jesus shoes, and had a six-pack of Stroh's nearby.

"PLEASE MR. POSTMAN" Song by the Marvelettes.

"PURPLE PEOPLE EATER" Song by Sheb Wooley.

RALEIGH BIKE A boy riding a Raleigh yelled to Arnie "Put it in a trash-masher, mister!" when he saw Arnie driving Christine enroute to Darnell's.

"RAVE ON" Song by Buddy Holly.

"REBEL ROUSER" Instrumental played on Christine's radio.

"ROBERT DEADFORD" How Arnie referred to Ralph.

"ROCK AND ROLL WILL NEVER DIE" Bumper sticker on Christine in Dennis's dreams.

"RUMBLE" Song by Linc Wray that played on Christine's radio.

"RUNAROUND SUE" Song by Dion.

ST. PATRICK'S DAY On this holiday, Gino's Pizza served green beer.

THE SALVATION ARMY 400 FUND Mr. Guilder made toys in his basement and donated them to this charity.

SAPPHIRE MOTOR OIL Cheap oil. It cost three dollars fifty-cents per recycled five gallon jug. It was sold at Mammoth Mart. LeBay loaded up Christine with it before Arnie picked her up.

SATURDAY, DECEMBER 16 The day Junkins and his men followed Arnie to Albany.

"SAVE MONEY! YOUR KNOW-HOW, OUR TOOLS!" The sign over Darnell's Garage.

SEPTEMBER 1957 The month Roland LeBay bought Christine.

7-UP George LeBay was drinking one when Dennis went to see him.

SIDE-NOOGIES Pokes in the side. Dennis inflicted them on Arnie.

SKETCHES OF LOVE AND BEAUTY Book of themes and stories being written by Dennis's mother.

SONY Will Darnell's TV.

"SPLISH-SPLASH" Song by Bobby Darin.

STROH'S Beer that Dennis's father drank.

SWAP-AROUND PAMMIE Porno novel Don Vandenberg read.

TEXAS DRIVER BEER Six or eight guys passed around a bottle of this when Buddy was working at the garage.

"THREE KILLED IN CAR CRASH AT SQUANTIC HILLS STATE PARK" Headline detailing Repperton and his buddy's deaths.

$3,000 The asking price for Christine when Roland LeBay bought the car. He ended up paying $2,100.

TIPARILLOS Arnie smoked these cigars.

"TOPICS IN AMERICAN HISTORY" One of the classes Arnie and Dennis shared.

"THE TORTURE CHAMBER" Dennis's name for the physical therapy room.

$1,200 When Roland LeBay left the army, he had just over $1,200 saved.

29.9 CENTS The per gallon price of gasoline in 1928.

"THE TWILIGHT ZONE" Dennis Guilder thought that George LeBay's story about Roland, Veronica, Rita, and Christine sounded like a story from the "Twilight Zone."

TWINKIE Elaine Guilder hid one in the back of the bread box. Dennis found it and ate it.

200 CARTONS OF WINSTONS The "load" Arnie had to take with him to Albany. It was probably cocaine.

$250 The amount Arnie Cunningham paid Roland LeBay for Christine.

$2,100 The price Roland LeBay eventually paid for Christine. The asking price had been $3,000.

TWO TURKEY SANDWICHES ON WONDER BREAD Arnie brought Dennis these sandwiches, along with a six-pack of Busch beer, on Thanksgiving.

A UPS TRUCK The truck that hit and killed Dennis's cat, Captain Beefheart, when Dennis was nine.

V.T. Vocational training. Arnie promised his parents he'd sign up for this unless they left him alone about Christine.

VALIANT Gabbs's car.

"WAITIN IN SCHOOL" Song by Ricky Nelson.

WESSON OIL Arnie used it to make popcorn.

"WHEN" Song by the Kalin Twins.

"WHEN IRISH EYES ARE SMILING" Song sung by Rosemary Clooney. It played on the jukebox in Gino's pizza restaurant.

"WHY DO FOOLS FALL IN LOVE?" Song by Frankie Lymon.

"WILD WEEKEND" Instrumental on Christine's radio.

WONDER BREAD Ralph the Big Cheese was eating a hamburger on Wonder bread when he told Arnie to get Christine away from his house.

WURLITZER The jukebox in Gino's pizza restaurant.

YOGURT Michael Cunningham ate it.

PET SEMATARY

DEDICATION

For Kirby McCauley

CONTENTS PAGE

BOOK BREAKDOWN

FOREWORD—(One untitled section consisting
of six paragraphs)

PART ONE
THE PET SEMATARY

(Thirty-five untitled chapters numbered 1-35)

PART TWO
THE MICMAC BURYING GROUND

(Twenty-two untitled chapters numbered 36-57)

PART THREE
OZ THE GWEAT AND TEWWIBLE

(Five untitled chapters numbered 58-62)

EPILOGUE—(Nine paragraphs)

(17)
PET SEMATARY
People

ANDERSON, GEORGE Postmaster.

BAEZ, JOAN A Joan Baez song played on Louis's car radio.

BAILLINGS, MRS. The night nurse at the infirmary.

BATERMAN, BILL Timmy's father. He buried Timmy in the secret burial ground.

BATERMAN, TIMMY Ludlow boy who went overseas in 1942 "to fight Hitler," and was killed in Italy in 1943. His father buried him in the Micmac burial ground and Timmy came back...sort of different.

BENSON, HANNIBAL Second selectman.

BENTON, TONY The Chicago doctor Creed worked with. He called Ellie the "Indian Princess."

BISSON, LOUELLA One of the ladies who brought Norma home from the hospital.

BOUCHARD, STANLEY (STANNY) The man who told Jud about the secret Micmac burial ground. Jud was ten years old at the time. According to Jud Crandall, Stanny was the "biggest tosspot

this side of Bucksport."

BOWSER Billy Holloway's dog.

BRACERMUNN, DR. One of the doctors who taught Louis in medical school.

BRADLEIGH, MISSUS Her parakeet had died.

BUCK, GEORGE Ellie's classmate. He told Ellie about the pet cemetery.

BUDDINGER, MRS. Woman who helped Louis when Norma had her heart attack.

BURNS, MICHAEL Ellie's classmate. He told Ellie that all doctors were rich.

CABRON, MR. AND MRS. PETER The Goldmans were visiting them on the day Zelda died.

CARL, UNCLE Louis Creed's uncle. He was an undertaker.

CARLA Candy-striper who saw Victor Pascow die.

CHAPIN, GEORGE Louis dreamt that he was twenty-three and passing around a bottle of Georgia Charger Whiskey with Chapin.

CHARLTON, MISS JOAN Head nurse at the University of Maine.

CHURCH Winston Churchill; Eileen Creed's five-year-old cat. Louis buried him in the secret burial ground. Church came back.

CLEVELAND, BILL The Clevelands lived in the Creeds' house before the Creeds bought it. Bill Cleveland left the keys to the house with Jud.

CLEVELAND, MRS. Bill Cleveland's wife.

COSLAW, BETTY Friend of Norma Crandall. Betty died of cancer.

CRANDALL, JUDSON Eighty-three-year-old man who lived across the street from the Creeds. He introduced the Creeds to the pet cemetery. Louis Creed considered Jud to be the father he'd never had.

CRANDALL, NORMA Jud Crandall's wife. She suffered from arthritis.

CRANDALL, PETE Jud's brother, born 1898. He died of a burst appendix in 1912 at the age of fourteen.

CREED, EILEEN Louis and Rachel Creed's daughter. She was known as Ellie.

CREED, GAGE Louis and Rachel Creed's son. He was killed by a truck on the highway in front of Creed's house.

CREED, LOUIS Doctor at University of Maine; head of university medical services.

CREED, RACHEL Louis Creed's wife. Her maiden name was Goldman.

CREED, RUTHIE Louis Creed's cousin. She died in a car accident.

DANDRIDGE, MISSY She watched Ellie and Gage for Rachel.

"DEE DEE RAMONE" The name under which Louis registered at the Howard Johnson Motor Lodge.

DeLESSIO, JUDY Candy-striper who saw Victor Pascow die.

DESSLER, TOMMY His cocker spaniel was buried in the pet cemetery.

DIMMART, PETER Man who claimed he was a Ludlow.

FRITCHIE, OLD MAN One of Jud Crandall's "gang," now dead. He had a pet buried in the pet cemetery.

GARBER, HUEY The engineer who drove the train that brought Timmy Baterman's body back to Orrington.

GOLDMAN, IRWIN Rachel Creed's father.

GOLDMAN, MRS. DORY Rachel Creed's mother.

GOLDMAN, ZELDA Rachel's sister. She died of spinal meningitis.

GRINNELL, BARBARA Dr. Grinnell's wife.

GRINNELL, DR. ROB Bangor physician.

GROATLEY, ALBION One of Jud Crandall's "gang," now dead. He had a pet buried in the pet cemetery.

HAND He wrote the text *Human Physiology*.

HANNAH, CARL One of Jud Crandall's "gang," now dead. He had a pet buried in the pet cemetery.

HANRATTY Lester Morgan's prize bull. Lester shot the bull two weeks after he "came back." It had changed, turned mean.

HARDU, DR. SURRENDRA An Indian doctor at the University of Maine.

"HENRY MONTEZ" Victor Pascow. Louis used this fictitious name when he spoke at the New England Conference on College and University Medicine. Louis spoke on the legal ramifications of student medical treatment.

HOLLOWAY, BILLY Born 1915. He was ten when his dog Bowser died. They gave him a funeral.

HUMPERTON, PETER Freshman. He went into convulsions. He was saved by Dr. Hardu.

IRVING, RICHARD Head of campus security.

JEPPSON, WILL Man lost in the North Ludlow woods in 1934.

JOLANDER, QUENTIN L., D.V.M. Veterinarian. Louis called him for an appointment to have Church neutered.

KINSMAN, LIEUTENANT A man from the War Department. He was concerned about letters he received saying that Timmy Baterman was alive.

LATHROP, DR. Irwin Goldman's doctor.

LAUGHLIN, REVEREND The minister at Norma Crandall's funeral.

LAVASSEUR, PETE One of Jud Crandall's "gang," now dead. He had a pet buried in the pet cemetery.

LAVESQUE, LINDA Lester Morgan took Linda to the burial ground after her dog got run over.

LOCKE, AL One of Louis's fellow med students. He died in a motorcycle accident.

LUDLOW, ANSON Great-grandson of the town's founding father.

THE MAN An unnamed man who died on a fishing trip in Aroostook County.

MARVEL, ANDREW Louis thought of a line from Marvel:

"...fine and private place,
but none, I think, do there embrace."

MASTERTON, STEVE Louis Creed's physician's assistant.

MICHAUD, RENE Louis dreamt that he was twenty-three and passing around a bottle of Georgia Charger Whiskey with Michaud.

MICMAC INDIAN TRIBE The tribe had laid claims to state land that abutted the Creeds' property.

MORGAN, LESTER Man who buried his prize bull, Hanratty, in the secret burial ground.

PARKS, RUTHIE One of the ladies who brought Norma home.

PASCOW, VICTOR Dying boy brought into the infirmary. "Half of his head was crushed. His neck had been broken. One collarbone jutted from his swelled and twisted right shoulder. From his head, blood and a yellow, pussy fluid seeped sluggishly into the carpet." His last words were "It's not the real cemetery."

PASIOCA, ANDY Ellie's classmate.

PHIPPS Name on a Romanesque monument in the cemetery.

PURINTON, ALAN Fire chief.

PURINTON, LAURINE Alan Purinton's second wife.

RONALD MCDONALD, SPIDERMAN, AND THE BURGER KING Louis realized that Ellie knew more about these guys than about Moses, Jesus, and St. Paul.

RYDER, MATTY He had a raccoon that got killed on the highway in front of Creed's house.

RYDER, MR. He worked for IBM in Bangor.

RYNZWYCK, DR. The doctor who performed the autopsy on Pascow.

ST. BERNARD Jud Crandall's reference to Cujo: "There was a big old St. Bernard went rabid downstate a couple of years ago and killed four people."

SPOT Jud Crandall's dog. He died in 1914, and was also buried in the pet cemetery.

STAPLETON, MRS. Lady who worked in the registrar's office.

STRATTON, MISSUS She saw the "returned" Timmy Baterman from her porch.

SULLIVAN, WILKES One of the guys Louis played poker with.

THE SUNBURN GIRL Girl who came to the infirmary with sunburn. According to Nurse Charlton, she was "your basic college hypochondriac."

TARDIFF, GEORGE Neurologist.

VINTON, MRS. She had a field where Gage and Louis flew a kite.

WASHBURN, MARJORIE Mail carrier who saw Timmy Baterman walking towards York's Livery Stable four or five days after he was buried.

WENDIGO The spirit of the north country.

WEYBRIDGE, DR. Norma Crandall's doctor.

WITHERS, TREMONT A twenty-three-year-old from Haven, Maine, who was driving the car that hit Victor Pascow.

(17)

PET SEMATARY
Places

THE AMERICAN CASKET COMPANY They manufactured the Eternal Rest Casket that Louis bought for Gage.

BANGOR CARPET The company called to replace the blood-stained infirmary carpet following Pascow's death.

BANGOR INTERNATIONAL AIRPORT Louis's family left from here for Chicago for a Thanksgiving vacation.

THE BANGOR MALL Ellie had seen a "skinny" Santa there.

THE BEAR'S DEN The university cafeteria. Louis had dinner there with Steve.

BENJAMIN'S The restaurant where Louis and Jud went after Gage's funeral.

BERGENFIELD, NEW JERSEY Victor Pascow's hometown.

BIDDLEFORD The rest area on the Maine Turnpike where Rachel called Jud.

BONNEVILLE SALT FLATS Louis compared Mrs. Vinton's field to the salt flats.

BREWER The small city across the Penobscot River from Bangor.

THE BROOKINGS-SMITH MORTUARY The funeral home that claimed Pascow's body for his parents. They had also handled Norma Crandall's funeral.

BUCKSPORT A town where Jud and Norma shopped.

CAMP AGAWAM Louis Creed imagined his son spent the summer there when Gage was ten years old.

CARSTAIRS STREET SCHOOL Ellie's school in Chicago.

DEERING ICE CREAM PARLOR The shop where Ellie had seen the "skinny" Santa eating a cheeseburger.

DYSART'S TRUCK STOP The place where Rachel had her rented car fixed.

EASTERN MAINE MEDICAL CENTER The university's "emergency room."

EMPORIUM GALORIUM Jud and Norma went to this store to look at a Welsh dresser.

FERN STREET The street where the Greenspan Funeral Home was located.

GANNET-CUMBERLAND-ANDROSCOGGIN A dorm complex on campus.

GRAND FALLS, MINNESOTA The body of the man who died in Aroostook County during a fishing trip was supposed to go to Grand Falls. It first went to Miami, then to Des Moines, and then to Fargo, North Dakota.

GREENSPAN FUNERAL HOME Fern Street funeral parlor where Timmy Baterman's body was brought.

HOLIDAY INN The Goldmans stayed at the Bangor Holiday Inn when they came to Maine for Gage's funeral.

HOWARD JOHNSON MOTOR LODGE Louis spent the night there. It was near the Pleasantview Cemetery.

IBM The company in Bangor that Mr. Ryder worked for.

JOHNS HOPKINS The college Gage attended in Louis's imagination. While there, Gage made the Olympic Swimming Team and won a Gold Medal for the United States.

JULIO'S A store in Orrington that sold beer.

LIMESTONE IN PRESQUE ISLE Coffins were flown to Limestone before they were put in the train for points south.

LITTLE GOD SWAMP The name the Micmacs gave the swamp on

the edge of the deadfall.

LUDLOW, MAINE The Maine town to which the Creed family moved from Chicago.

MOUNT HOPE CEMETERY Jud and Norma had bought plots there in 1951.

MRS. VINTON'S FIELD Louis and Gage flew a kite there.

NEW FRANKLIN LAUNDRY The laundry located across from the Greenspan Funeral Home's former location.

NORTH LUDLOW BAPTIST CHURCH Louis could see its spire through the elms on his first trip to the pet cemetery.

NORTH LUDLOW WOODS The woods behind Creed's house.

ORRINGTON The town where Bill Cleveland lived in an old folks' apartment complex.

PENOBSCOT RIVER VALLEY It could be seen from the top of a hill on Creed's property. Louis could also see Hampden, Winterport, and Bucksport.

THE PET CEMETERY The burial ground for area pets. There were better than a hundred graves in the cemetery.

PROSPECT HILL The old name for the hill behind Creed's house.

SING'S A Chinese restaurant near the Eastern Maine Medical Center.

STATE STREET AND THE LOOP Chicago locales Louis Creed remembered.

UPJOHN Drug company.

WATSON'S HARDWARE A store in Brewer.

WHERE THE COFFINS WENT Two went to Houlton, one to Passadumkeag, two to Bangor, one to Derry, and one to Ludlow.

YORK'S LIVERY STABLE The "returned" Timmy Baterman was seen walking towards the stable four or five days after he was buried.

(17)
PET SEMATARY
Things

"ALBERTA BURNHAM NEDEAU" The sign outside the West Room at the funeral home.

APRIL 14, 1965 The date Zelda Goldman died.

BANGOR AND AROOSTOOK TRAIN COMPANY The company that transported the coffins.

THE BANGOR *DAILY NEWS* The local newspaper.

BEN-GAY Louis put it on his bad knee.

BERMUDA ONION Louis put onion on his meatloaf sandwich.

BERTERIER CHART The chart that showed the normal range of infant head sizes on a monthly basis.

BLACK LABEL The beer Jud and Louis drank on Jud's front porch.

CALO Church's cat food.

"THE CAT IN THE HAT" A story Louis read to Ellie.

CATHOLICISM Louis imagined Gage converting to the Catholic religion when he was seventeen – if he had lived.

CHESTERFIELD KINGS Jud Crandall's cigarettes.

CHUGGY-CHUGGY-CHOO-CHOO The toy Louis threw at the ressurected Church to get him out of Gage's closet.

COCA-COLA TRAY Antique tray Norma Crandall used to serve iced tea.

COCOA BEARS One of Gage's favorite cereals.

COKE Louis bought one for lunch.

COUNCIL OF COLLEGES Louis attended meetings at the council.

D-DAY Darvon Day; the day the drug salesmen called on Louis. Darvon was the "all-time favorite."

THE DANDRIDGE'S ADDRESS This is how Missy signed the book at Gage's funeral:

> Mr. & Mrs. David Dandridge
> Rural Box 67
> Old Bucksport Road

"DARLING" The first word Rachel said to Louis after she returned from the grave, and the final word of *Pet Sematary*.

DECEMBER 16 The day that school let out for the holidays.

DELTA FLIGHT 109 The flight that took Victor Pascow's body home.

DELTA 727 Rachel and her children's flight to Chicago.

DENTON'S, DR. Gage's pajamas.

THE DUQUESNE MEDICAL DIGEST Louis read an article in the *Digest*.

ELLIE AND GAGE'S CHRISTMAS GIFTS Among the gifts they got were Matchbox Racers, Barbie and Ken dolls, a Turn 'N Go trike, and a play oven.

ETERNAL REST CASKET The model Louis picked out for Gage. It was made by the American Casket Company.

EVERLOCK Trademark for the sealant used to seal the concrete vault in which coffins were placed into in the grave.

THE FOUR CAMPS SWIMATHON In Louis's imagination, Gage won two blue ribbons and one red ribbon at the age of eleven in this competition.

"THE FRONT FILE" The file of students with a disability.

"GAGE WILLIAM CREED" The sign outside the East Room at the funeral home.

GERRYPACK Pack used to carry Gage.

A GOLD CHAIN WITH A SAPPHIRE STONE Louis's Christmas gift to Rachel. It cost $2,000.

THE GRAVES AND REGISTRATION MAN The army's wartime version of the peacetime undertaker.

H-101 The number of Norma Crandall's plot in the Mount Hope Cemetery.

H-102 The number of Jud Crandall's plot in the Mount Hope Cemetery.

"THE HEADLESS HORSEMAN" The story Ellie told Gage.

HONDA CIVIC Louis Creed's car.

HUMAN PHYSIOLOGY The textbook by Hand that said that it takes the average human fifteen to twenty minutes to fully wake up.

"THE INDIAN PRINCESS" The nickname Tony Benton called Ellie.

"ITCHYBOD CRANE" The way Gage pronounced Ichabod Crane.

JULY 15, 1943 The date Timmy Baterman was killed on the road to Rome.

JULY 4, 1912 The date Stan Bouchard died.

"LET THE WILD RUMPUS START" A line from Maurice Sendak that Louis recalled.

LOUIS CREED'S DREAM Louis dreamt of Disney World, an 1890's train station, and Mickey Mouse.

LOUIS CREED'S MODELS They included a World War I Spad, Revell airplanes, Colts, Winchesters and Lugers, a Buntline Special, the Lusitania, the Titanic, and the Andrea Doria. Louis had been "model-crazy" since his tenth year.

THE MAGAZINE OF COLLEGE MEDICINE A magazine Louis wrote for.

MARCH 24, 1984 The last really happy day of Louis Creed's life.

MAREK STOVE The stove in Jud's house.

MASTERCARD How Louis payed for Gage's funeral.

MAY 17 The date of Gage Creed's funeral.

MERCUROCHROME Louis put it on Eileen's cut.

"THE MUPPET SHOW" Ellie and Gage watched this show on TV.

1917 ROLLS-ROYCE SILVER GHOST A model Louis was assembling. It had 680 pieces, with over fifty moving parts.

"A NOEL COWARD FARCE" One thing Louis hated about his father-in-law, Irwin Goldman, was the way he took his checkbook out of his smoking jacket – like a rake in a Noel Coward farce.

"OLD MACDONALD" Song Ellie sang in kindergarten.

THE ORIGINAL GRANT ON LOUIS CREED'S LAND "From the great old maple which stands atop Quinceberry Ridge to the verge of Orrington Stream."

ORINCO This was written on the side of a truck that passed the

Creeds' house.

PELTS Stanny Bouchard's grandfather would go from the maritimes to Bangor and Derry and as far south as Skowhegan to buy pelts.

"PET SEMATARY" The cemetery sign. It was done in black paint on old weatherstained boards.

THE PET SEMATARY GRAVE MARKERS Signs included:

Smucky the Cat;
Biffer the cockerspaniel;
Trixie, who was "Kilt on the highway Sept. 15, 1968";
"In Memory of Marta Our Pet Rabit Dyed March 1, 1965."

Further on was one that read "Gen. Patton (Our! Good! Dog!) Died 1958", and "Polynesia," who had died in the summer of 1953. There was also a marker that read "Hannah the Best Dog That Ever Lived 1929-1939."

POLAROID SX-70 Camera that Louis and the kids gave to Rachel as a birthday present.

"REAL PEOPLE" Louis wondered what he'd say when a film crew from the TV show showed up wanting to film his resurrected son.

"ROCKAWAY BEACH" A song by the Ramones that Louis heard on his car radio.

ROMAN MEAL BREAD Louis made a meatloaf sandwich using Roman Meal bread.

SALVATION ARMY SANTAS Rachel had to explain to Ellie that these Santas were the real Santa's helpers.

"SANNA" How Ellie pronounced "Santa."

SANTA'S SNACKS Ellie left Santa oatmeal cookies, two Ring-Dings, and a can of Michelob.

SCHLITZ Beer Jud and Louis drank at Benjamin's.

SCHLITZ LIGHT There were five cases in Louis's cellar. Rachel had bought it at the Brewer A & P.

THE SCIENCE FICTION WRITERS Louis read the following as a child: Robert A. Heinlein, Murray Leinster, and Gordon R. Dickson.

SEARS SKI PARKA Gage was wearing one in a picture.

SILVER STAR Medal awarded posthumously to Timmy Baterman.

SMITH BROTHERS WILD CHERRY COUGH DROPS What Zelda's medicine smelled like.

SPEEDWAY SLED Louis had a picture of Gage sitting on one.

THE SPIRAL "Diminishing circles indicating a spiral leading down, not to a point, but to infinity; order from chaos or chaos from order." The layout of the Pet Sematary.

SPODE CHINA Mr. and Mrs. Goldman's wedding gift to Louis and Rachel.

A STEVIE WONDER CONCERT Louis and Rachel had gone to one before Ellie had been born.

10:09 The time Victor Pascow died.

"THIS OLD HOUSE" A song sung by Shakin Stevens on WACZ.

TROUTMAN'S TREATMENT OF WOUNDS A book Louis hunted for in his bookcase.

TUINAL The pill Louis took to cope with the death of Pascow.

$2,000 The cost of the sapphire pendant Louis bought for Rachel for Christmas.

"THE VULTURE" Louis's kite.

WACZ Radio station.

"WHEEL OF FORTUNE" TV show Rachel stared at after Gage was killed.

"WHERE THE WILD THINGS ARE" The Maurice Sendak story Ellie wanted to hear.

THE TALISMAN
[Written with Peter Straub]

DEDICATION

This book is for

RUTH KING

ELVENA STRAUB

CONTENTS PAGE

36. Jack and Richard Go to War
37. Richard Remembers
38. The End of the Road
39. Point Venuti
40. Speedy on the Beach
INTERLUDE   Sloat in This World (V)
41. The Black Hotel
42. Jack and the Talisman
43. News from Everywhere
44. The Earthquake
45. In Which Many Things Are Resolved on the Beach
46. Another Journey
47. Journey's End
Epilogue
Conclusion

BOOK BREAKDOWN

PART ONE
JACK LIGHTS OUT

Chapter 1:   The Alhambra Inn and Gardens—(Six untitled sections numbered 1-6)
Chapter 2:   The Funnel Opens—(Six untitled sections numbered 1-6)
Chapter 3:   Speedy Parker—(Four untitled sections numbered 1-4)
Chapter 4:   Jack Goes Over—(Five untitled sections numbered 1-5)
Chapter 5:   Jack and Lily—(Four untitled sections numbered 1-4)
INTERLUDE   Sloat in This World (I)—(One unnumbered section)

PART TWO
THE ROAD OF TRIALS

Chapter 6:   The Queen's Pavilion—(Two untitled sections numbered 1 and 2)
Chapter 7:   Farren—(Nine untitled sections numbered 1-9)
Chapter 8:   The Oatley Tunnel—(Five untitled sections numbered 1-5)
Chapter 9:   Jack in the Pitcher Plant—(Seven untitled sections numbered 1-7)
Chapter 10:   Elroy—(Five untitled sections numbered 1-5)
Chapter 11:   The Death of Jerry Bledsoe—(Five untitled sections numbered 1-5)
Chapter 12:   Jack Goes to the Market—(Three untitled sections numbered 1-3)
Chapter 13:   The Men in the Sky—(Seven untitled sections numbered 1-7)
Chapter 14:   Buddy Parkins—(Four untitled sections numbered 1-4)
Chapter 15:   Snowball Sings—(Three untitled sections numbered 1-3)
Chapter 16:   Wolf—(Four untitled sections numbered 1-4)
INTERLUDE   Sloat in This World (II)—(One unnumbered section)
Chapter 17:   Wolf and the Herd—(Three untitled sections numbered 1-3)
Chapter 18:   Wolf Goes to the Movies—(Eight untitled sections numbered 1-8)
Chapter 19:   Jack in the Box—(Twelve untitled sections numbered 1-12)

PART THREE
A COLLISION OF WORLDS

Chapter 20:   Taken by the Law—(Three untitled sections numbered 1-3)
Chapter 21:   The Sunlight Home—(Three untitled sections numbered 1-3)
Chapter 22:   The Sermon—(Six untitled sections numbered 1-6)
Chapter 23:   Ferd Janklow—(Five untitled sections numbered 1-5)
Chapter 24:   Jack Names the Planets—(Four untitled sections numbered 1-4)
Chapter 25:   Jack and Wolf Go to Hell—(Five untitled sections numbered 1-5)
Chapter 26:   Wolf in the Box—(Nineteen untitled sections numbered 1-19)
Chapter 27:   Jack Lights Out Again—(Two untitled sections numbered 1 and 2)
Chapter 28:   Jack's Dream—(Three untitled sections numbered 1-3)
Chapter 29:   Richard at Thayer—(Five untitled sections numbered 1-5)
Chapter 30:   Thayer Gets Weird—(Three untitled sections numbered 1-3)
Chapter 31:   Thayer Goes to Hell—(Two untitled sections numbered 1 and 2)
Chapter 32:   "Send Out Your Passenger!"—(Eight untitled sections numbered 1-8)
Chapter 33:   Richard in the Dark—(Eleven untitled sections numbered 1-11)
INTERLUDE   Sloat in This World/Orris in the Territories (III)—(One unnumbered section)

PART FOUR
THE TALISMAN

Chapter 34:   Anders—(Eight untitled sections numbered 1-8)
INTERLUDE   Sloat in This World (IV)—(One unnumbered section)
Chapter 35:   The Blasted Lands—(Twelve untitled sections numbered 1-12)
Chapter 36:   Jack and Richard Go to War—(Nine untitled sections numbered 1-9)
Chapter 37:   Richard Remembers—(Thirteen untitled sections numbered 1-13)
Chapter 38:   The End of the Road—(Five untitled sections numbered 1-5)
Chapter 39:   Point Venuti—(Five untitled sections numbered 1-5)
Chapter 40:   Speedy on the Beach—(Six untitled sections numbered 1-6)
INTERLUDE   Sloat in This World (V)—(One unnumbered section)
Chapter 41:   The Black Hotel—(Eleven untitled sections numbered 1-11)
Chapter 42:   Jack and the Talisman—(Nine untitled sections numbered 1-9)
Chapter 43:   News from Everywhere—(Eleven untitled sections numbered 1-11)
Chapter 44:   The Earthquake—(Eleven untitled sections numbered 1-11)
Chapter 45:   In Which Many Things Are Resolved on the Beach—(Eight untitled sections numbered 1-8)
Chapter 46:   Another Journey—(Eight untitled sections

numbered 1-8)
Chapter 47: Journey's End—(Twelve untitled sections
numbered 1-12)

Epilogue—(One paragraph)

Conclusion—(Quotation from Mark Twain's *Tom Sawyer*)

(18)
THE TALISMAN

[NOTE: *The Talisman* is a weird one among King fans. I've found that most of King's readers fall into one of three categories when it comes to *The Talisman*:

1. "I hate it."
2. "I love it."
3. "I haven't read it" (or, "I couldn't get through it.")

I fall into Category 2: I loved it, although I found it a somewhat strange reading experience. (Interestingly, in George Beahm's *The Stephen King Companion*, Harlan Ellison (and editor Beahm for that matter) both admitted that they fall into Category 3.)

How about you, Constant Reader?

Could you get through it?

If you haven't read it, I suggest you try again. Reading through this concordance is not going to give you a real feel for the true epic sweep of the novel, although it might reveal some plot points that are definitely better experienced for the first time by reading the book in its entirety. There is just no substitute for reading King's works as he wrote them.

You might be interested to know that there are some King fans who count *The Talisman* as their favorite Stephen King novel. Not many, it's true, but there are some. (I teach a course called "Stephen King: An Appreciation," and routinely survey my students for favorite King novels and short stories. Of course, *The Stand* is almost always Number 1, but every now and then I get a couple of people who write in *The Talisman* as their favorite. There is something about it, once it takes hold, truly works its magic.)

Go ahead.

Give it one more shot.

And then when you're through, you can read through this concordance for clarification, for enjoyment, and to enhance your experience in the Territories. – **sjs**]

People

ABELSON, PETER An outside staffer at the Sunlight Gardener Home.

ADAMS, BILLY One of the residents of the Sunlight Gardener Home.

THE ADULT AND TWO CHILDREN IN THE RENAULT The family that gaped at Jack and Richard when they materialized on Route 17 with the Talisman.

"ALBERT THE BLOB" Albert Humbert.

ANDERS The Territories depot keeper. He was a liveryman.

ATWELL, CARLTON (DIGGER) The Oatley chief of police.

ATWELL, DIGGER Carlton Atwell, the Oatley chief of police.

AUBREY Jack's fictitious "Wicked Stepfather."

BALGO, MR. If Jack had started school when he was supposed to (instead of moving to New Hampshire), he would have been taking a computer class that was taught by Mr. Balgo.

BANBERRY, MINETTE The woman who owned the Golden Spoon Diner in Auburn.

BARKER, BOB The host of "The New Price is Right."

THE BARKER The barker at the fun-fair on the pavilion grounds offered a prize to anyone who could stay on Wonder the Devil-Donkey for two minutes.

BAST, HECTOR A steward at the Sunlight Gardener Home.

BLEDSOE, JERRY Sawyer & Sloat's electrician and handyman. He was electrocuted when he was working on the electrical wiring at Sawyer & Sloat's building one Saturday. Jack realized that his father and Morgan Sloat had probably done something in the Territories that "echoed" into our world, killing Jerry. It turned out that Morgan Sloat called lightning to Jerry with the tin key that had once been used to wind up a tin soldier. The key became a strange sort of lightning rod in the Territories.

BLEDSOE, NITA Jerry Bledsoe's wife.

BOYNTON The head of security at Thayer School.

THE BUCKEYE MALL BOY IN THE APRON AND BOW TIE When Jack called his mother from the Buckeye Mall and heard Morgan Sloat's voice on the phone, the phone fell off the wall after Jack hung it up. A twenty-year-old boy in a white apron and a bow tie coming out of the men's room saw it fall, and called Mr. Olafson.

BUCKLEY One of the Thayer School upperclassmen that Jack and Richard saw smoking pot near the statue of Elder Thayer. Jack knew Buckley was a Twinner.

THE BURLY CHRYSLER DRIVER A burly man with a bull neck and a Case Farm Equipment cap driving a Chrysler stopped for Jack and Wolf, but changed his mind after Wolf growled at him.

THE CAPTAIN OF THE OUTER GUARDS Farren. A friend of Speedy Parker's in the Territories. The Captain had a scar on his face. Speedy told Jack that Farren would help Jack if he got into trouble.

THE CARTER The man who had been driving a wagon filled with Kingsland Ale. The wagon overturned and killed the man's son.

THE CARTER'S SON The young boy who was killed when the cart that the Carter was driving overturned. The boy was sixteen. He was crushed to death under barrels of Kingsland Ale.

CASEY A resident of the Sunlight Gardener Home. He harassed a fifteen-year-old kid named Morton. Casey was fat.

CASSIDY, TOM A resident of the Sunlight Gardener Home. He was struck by the common room door when Wolf ripped it off its hinges.

CHANG, LORETTE The twenty-three-year-old woman who was riding her bike into the Sawyer & Sloat bulding parking lot when she saw the electrical explosion that killed Jerry Bledsoe.

THE CHEF The palace cook in the Territories. He went at Jack and the Captain with a three-tined fork.

THE CHINESE TENANT When Morgan Sloat bought the building in Beverly Hills that eventually became home to Sawyer & Sloat, there was one holdout tenant who wouldn't hear of a rent increase: a Chinese guy who owned a restaurant. Sloat put up a fence separating him from access to his garbage cans and, after the restauranteur had to carry the garbage through the dining room (and his front window was mysteriously smashed with a baseball bat), the guy finally agreed to pay quadruple rent.

THE COUNTERMAN The Town Line Sixplex employee who manned the concession stand, and who sold Jack his snacks. Wolf gave him his #1 Friendly Smile.

THE COWBOY One of the customers at the Oatley Tap.

CURLESS, DICK One of the country-and-western singers played on the jukebox in the Oatley Tap.

DANIELS, CHARLIE The celebrity spokesperson for a chewing tobacco company.

DARRENT, BOB The Pennsylvania district high school superintendent who gave Jack a ride on U.S. I-70.

DAVEY, BRUCE One of the Speiser Company construction workers killed in the freak Angola, New York, earthquake that hit the Rainbird Towers condominium complex. Davey was thirty-nine years old.

DeLOESSIAN, QUEEN LAURA Queen of the Territories, and

Lily Cavanaugh Sawyer's Twinner. The queen opened her eyes the moment Jack healed his mother with the Talisman.

THE DESK CLERK'S TWINNER Jack saw the Twinner of the Alhambra desk clerk on the Outpost Road. The clerk's Twinner was drunk on Kingsland Ale.

THE DESK CLERK'S TWINNER'S SON The son of the Alhambra desk clerk's Twinner was also drunk on Kingsland Ale. He puked on an elderly man lying on the side of the Outpost Road.

DESTRY, ALAN He was frightened to death in the night when he saw his wife getting out of the bath. (According to East-Head & West-Head, the two-headed parrot.)

DOLPH Rudolph, the cook at the Sunlight Gardener Home.

DONDORF, ASHER Character actor and putz. Dondorf was one of Morgan Sloat's clients. Sloat "persuaded" Dondorf to kill himself. Dondorf played the sidekick on the series "Flanagan and Flanagan."

THE DRUNKEN WHORE As Farren and Jack approached the overturned Kingsland Ale cart on the Outpost Road, they came upon a cart filled with drunken whores. One woman pulled her skirt up to her crotch and did a tipsy bump and grind.

DUFREY, MR. The headmaster of the Thayer School.

DUGGAN, ANDREW The evil cattle-baron in "Last Train to Hangtown."

EAST-HEAD & WEST-HEAD The two-headed parrot Jack saw in the Territories' market. The parrot was as green as a Heineken bottle and talked to itself. [NOTE: See the "Things" entry EAST HEAD & WEST HEAD'S QUESTIONS FOR HIMSELF.]

ELAM, JACK He played the chief minion of evil in "Last Train to Hangtown."

THE ELDERLY MAN The Alhambra desk clerk's Twinner's son puked on an elderly man lying on the side of the Outpost Road.

ELROY A millhand who looked like Randolph Scott. Jack bumped into him in the hall of the Oatley Tap. Elroy turned into a snarling, hooved "Elroy-thing" that wanted to rape Jack and then kill him. Jack escaped using Speedy's magic juice to flip into the Territories.

THE ELROY-THING Elroy, the homosexual shape-changer.

ETHERIDGE The Thayer School student who mistakenly thought Jack was a student at the school when Jack first arrived on the campus. Etheridge was also one of the Thayer School upperclassmen that Jack and Richard saw smoking pot by the statue of Elder Thayer. Jack knew Etheridge was a Twinner. Etheridge wore an army duffle coat, a Pendelton shirt, and a blue tie with tiny gold "E's" woven into it.

FAIRCHILD, JUDGE ERNEST The magistrate who sent Jack and Wolf to the Sunlight Home. He was eventually charged with misuse of public monies and the acceptance of bribes for his involvement with Sunlight Gardener.

FARREN The captain of the outer guards at Queen Laura DeLoessian's palace.

FARREN, LEWIS The alias Jack used with Buddy Parkins.

THE FAT MAN A soldier at the pavillion grounds who called men to work with a French horn.

FERGUSON, TOM A shoe shop foreman from Vermont who gave Jack a ride on I-70.

THE FIFTY FLYING MEN After leaving the marketplace, Jack came to a huge tower that was being worked on by fifty winged men in flight. Jack was impressed.

THE FOUR MEMBERS OF THE FAIR WEATHER CLUB The four Oatley residents who played cards sitting inside a DeSoto with no tires.

FRAZER, COACH Richard Sloat's basketball coach at Thayer School.

FURY, SERGEANT Comic book character.

GARDENER, REUEL Sunlight Gardener/Osmond's son, and a student at Thayer School.

GARDENER, REVEREND SUNLIGHT Robert "Sunlight" Gardener. The proctor of the Sunlight Gardener Scripture Home for

Wayward Boys. Gardener was a tall man with long, wavy, white hair. At the school, he always wore a white suit, with white shoes, a white shirt, and a white silk scarf. Reverend Gardener and Osmond were Twinners.

GARGAN, JOSEPH The Angola *Herald* reporter who wrote the story about the "freak earthquake" that had taken place in Angola, New York, on the day Jack flipped from the Western Road and landed on the border of Angola.

GARGOYLES The "guards" in The Pit.

GARSON One of the Thayer School upperclassmen Jack and Richard saw smoking pot near the statue of Elder Thayer. Jack knew Garson was a Twinner.

THE GENNY VALLEY BOYS A country-and-western band that played at the Oatley Tap.

THE GIANT WHALE CREATURE IN THE WATER AROUND THE AGINCOURT A huge water creature helped Jack fend off Sunlight Gardener's bullets while at the same time pushing him towards the Black Hotel and the Talisman.

GILLEY, MICKEY One of the country-and-western singers played on the jukebox in the Oatley Tap.

THE GIRL The waitress at the Golden Spoon Diner who was on a work-release program for the retarded.

GLORIA A waitress at the Oatley Tap.

GORDON, DEXTER Saxophonist.

"GRIDLEY" Richard Sloat, according to Jack.

THE GUARDIAN KNIGHTS As Jack/Jason moved through the Black Hotel, he was attacked by suits of armor that enclosed some type of vampire bent on killing him. Jack bested them with the pick that Speedy had given him.

HAGEN, MICHAEL One of the Speiser Company construction workers killed in the freak Angola, New York, earthquake that hit the Rainbird Towers condominium complex. Hagen was twenty-nine years old.

THE HAITIAN The cook at the Golden Spoon Diner in Auburn.

HALLAS, JUDGE The judge who had told Snowball not to "work" the Buckeye Mall.

THE HARDWARE STORE CLERK The True Value clerk who wanted to know why Jack wanted a padlock.

HATFIELD, GEORGE At the moment Jack got the Talisman, Hatfield, who'd been caught cheating, was in Mr. Dufrey's office at Thayer School. [N OTE: Also see *The Shining* entry for Hatfield.]

HATFIELD, MR. George Hatfield's father.

HAYWOOD, MR. A faculty member at the Thayer School. Richard thought about reporting the pot they found in Suite 4 to Haywood, but didn't.

"HE OF THE LASHES" The name the Wolfs used for Osmond/Sunlight Gardener.

HEIDEL, ROBERT One of the Speiser Company construction workers killed in the freak Angola, New York, earthquake that hit the Rainbird Towers condominium complex. Heidel was twenty-three years old.

HENRY The Territories farmer who gave Jack a ride in his cart after Jack's escape from the Elroy-thing in our world.

HENRY'S WIFE The wife of the farmer who gave Jack a ride in his cart after Jack escaped from Elroy.

HUMBERT, ALBERT A Thayer School student. He was known as "Albert the Blob."

HUNKINS, MR. A teacher at Thayer School.

HURT, MISSISSIPPI JOHN In the Buckeye Mall, Snowball played a song by Mississippi John Hurt that Jack recognized.

HUTCHINS, WILL One of Lily Cavanaugh's co-stars in the 1960 film "Last Train to Hangtown." He played Andy Ellis.

IRWINSON, GEORGE A boy who worked in the kitchen at the Sunlight Gardener Home.

JANKLOW, FERD A boy at the Sunlight Gardener Home who tried to escape. He got caught and reportedly ended up in the hospital, where he experienced a sudden desire to confess his sins and dedicate his life to God. He actually ended up in Morgan's Pit in the Territories, where Jack and Wolf saw him get his spine broken as he was run over by a cart.

JASON Jason was Queen Laura DeLoessian's murdered infant son. Also, Jason was the name of Henry the farmer's three-year-old son. Queen Laura's Jason was Jack's Twinner.

JENNINGS, WAYLON One of the country-and-western singers played on the jukebox in the Oatley Tap.

JUDGE FAIRCHILD'S SECRETARY She was a middle-aged woman who wore wire-rimmed glasses and a black dress.

KEEGAN, DONALD A resident of the Sunlight Gardener Home. Keegan was "in love" with Jack.

KELLY, JACK The suave gambler in "Last Train to Hangtown."

KIGER, MYLES P. The fiftyish schoolteacher who gave Jack a ride and a Loden coat after Jack escaped from the Sunlight Gardener Home. Kiger lived in Ogden, Illinois.

LARRY As Jack hitchhiked on I-70A, Larry, who was a C.P.A., passed him on the road.

"LEWIS" Jack. While sneaking Jack into the palace, the captain introduced Jack to Osmond as his son, Lewis.

LEWIS, BRANDON A classmate of Jack's in Los Angeles who had a speech impediment.

LIGHT, EMORY W. The president of the First Mercantile Bank of Paradise Falls, Ohio. He was a large, bald man who picked Jack up near Dayton.

LITTLEFIELD One of the Thayer School upperclassmen that Jack and Richard saw smoking pot near the statue of Elder Thayer. Jack knew Littlefield was a Twinner.

LORI A barmaid at the Oatley Tap. She was Smokey Updike's woman.

THE LOS ANGELES DODGERS To pass the time while locked in the shed, Jack tried to name every player on the Los Angeles Dodgers.

A MADWOMAN As Jack and Richard approached the Black Hotel in Point Venuti, a madwoman fled from them.

A MAID After Jack flipped into the Territories at the beginning of his quest, he saw a man talking to a maid in the palace.

A MAN After Jack flipped into the Territories at the beginning of his quest, he saw a man talking to a maid in the palace.

"THE MAN FROM GLAD" Jack thought that Reverend Gardener, dressed in white from head to toe, looked like the Man from Glad as he began his evening sermon in the cellar chapel.

THE MAN IN THE TAN SAFARI SUIT The unnamed man who offered to walk Jack home after Sunlight Gardener had tried to kidnap Jack in California in 1976.

THE MAN WITH A BOW AND ARROW A man – "or what looked like a man" – with a bow and arrow ran towards Jack and Richard's train as they moved through the Blasted Lands. Jack shot him with an Uzi.

THE MANAGER The Town Line Sixplex manager. He threw Wolf and Jack out of the theater after Wolf freaked out. Jack said that Wolf, his "big brother," was an epileptic and had had a seizure.

MANSON, CHARLES While walking into Muncie with Wolf, Jack thought that if a state trooper caught Wolf, he'd probably think he caught an eighties incarnation of Charles Manson wearing John Lennon glasses.

THE MIDDLE-AGED MAN IN THE MEN'S ROOM A man in the Oatley Tap's men's room. He had a "Joe Pyne" haircut.

MORGAN OF ORRIS Orris. Morgan Sloat's Twinner.

"MORGAN THUDFOOT" Morgan of Orris was called "Morgan Thudfoot" in the Territories because he had a clubfoot.

MORTON A fifteen-year-old resident of the Sunlight Gardener Home. He was harassed by Singer, Bast, Warwick, and Casey.

"MR. ALL-AMERICA" Timmy. [NOTE: See the "People" entry TIMMY.]

"MR. ICE CREAM" The name that Ferd Janklow called Sunlight Gardener.

"MRS. JERRY" Jerry Bledsoe's wife.

MYRNA A ballet dancer friend of Lily Sawyer's.

NORRINGTON One of the Thayer School upperclassmen Jack and Richard saw smoking pot near the statue of Elder Thayer. Jack knew Norrington was a Twinner.

NORRIS, CHUCK Martial arts expert/actor.

THE NORTH HOLLYWOOD CLERK A men's shop clerk who once offered Jack a blow-job in the changing room while Jack was trying on clothes. Jack declined, and the clerk simply said, "Fine. Now try on the blue blazer, okay?"

THE OAK RIDGE BOYS One of the country-and-western acts played on the jukebox in the Oatley Tap.

OLAFSON, MR. When Jack called his mother from the Buckeye Mall and he heard Morgan Sloat's voice on the phone, the phone fell off the wall after Jack hung it up. A twenty-year-old boy in a white apron and a bow tie coming out of the men's room saw it fall, and called Mr. Olafson.

"OLD BLOAT" Morgan Sloat; Morgan of Orris.

THE OLD WOMAN WITH A FLYSWATTER She sat on a porch as Jack passed through Oatley.

THE ONE-EYED ROOSTER SALESMAN One of the vendors at the marketplace where Jack saw the two-headed parrot.

ORRIS Morgan of Orris. Morgan Sloat's Twinner.

OSMOND One of Morgan's men in the Territories. He was thought to have smothered the queen's six-week-old infant son. (That son was Jack's Twinner, Jason.) Osmond used a whip to maintain order. Osmond and the Reverend Sunlight Gardener were Twinners.

OWDERSFELT, MRS. The mother of Roy. Roy had stolen ten dollars from her purse, and used it to play video games at the Wizard of Odds.

OWDERSFELT, ROY A resident of the Sunlight Gardener Home. He had confessed to stealing ten dollars from his mother's purse.

PALAMOUNTAIN, ELBERT Farmer. Before Jack hit the road again and saw "Snowball" in the Buckeye Mall, he had spent a few days working on Palamountain's farm.

PALAMOUNTAIN, MRS. Elbert's wife.

PARKER, JACK The alias Jack gave to Judge Fairchild.

PARKER, LESTER Speedy Parker.

PARKER, SPEEDY Lester "Speedy" Parker. Jack's friend. Speedy turned Jack into Travelin' Jack by showing him how to "flip" into the Territories.

PARKINS, BUDDY A man out of Cambridge, Ohio, who picked Jack up on U.S. 40. He had three sons, and was cleaning out the henhouse when Jack obtained the Talisman. Parkins knew that Jack had gotten "there," and had also gotten "it." Later, Parkins thought he had gotten high on the chickenshit dust. He lived in Goslin, Ohio.

PARKINS, EMMIE Buddy Parkins' wife.

PARKUS Speedy Parker's name in the Territories. He was the "Judge General and the Lord High Executioner all rolled into one."

PAULIE The police officer who examined the Gardener Home's punishment box.

PAULIE'S COLLEAGUE The other officer who examined the punishment box at the Sunlight Gardener Home after Wolf ripped the place apart.

PEABODY One of the Far Field guards at the Sunlight Gardener Home.

PEDERSEN One of the Far Field guards at the Sunlight Gardener Home.

THE PEOPLE WHO PEERED INTO WOLF'S BROTHER'S CADILLAC They were looking for Mick Jagger or Frank Sinatra. The "gawkers" included people in parking lots, a sailor, an ox-faced girl in a convertible, and a skinny Ohio kid wearing bicycle gear.

THE POPCORN SELLER Jack bought popcorn in the Buckeye Mall for fifty cents. The man who sold it to him wore a bowler hat and sleeve garters, and had a walrus moustache. He directed Jack to the mall's pay phones so that Jack could call his mother.

"THE QUEEN OF THE B'S" Lily Cavanaugh.

RABBIT, EDDIE One of the country-and-western singers on the jukebox in the Oatley Tap.

RASMUSSEN, THEODORE One of the Speiser Company construction workers who was missing but presumed dead in the freak Angola, New York, earthquake that hit the Rainbird Towers condominium complex.

RUDOLPH The cook at the Sunlight Gardener Home.

THE RUG SALESMAN The salesman who had a rug booth in the market where Jack was taken by Henry the farmer. He rhymed.

RUSHTON Orris's son. He had drowned as an infant.

THE SALESMAN The mid-thirties salesman in the Ford Fairlane who gave Jack a ride on his way to Oatley.

SAWTELLE, JACK The name Jack used at the Oatley Tap.

SAWTELLE, PRINCE PHILIP Phil Sawyer's Twinner. He had been assassinated by Orris.

SAWYER, JACK John Benjamin Sawyer, aka Jack Sawtelle. Travelin' Jack.

SAWYER, JOHN BENJAMIN Jack Sawyer, aka Jack Sawtelle.

SAWYER, LILY CAVANAUGH Jack's mother. Her Twinner in the Territories was Queen Laura DeLoessian. Jack had to travel to the Black Hotel and take possession of The Talisman in order to save his mother's life.

SAWYER, PHILIP Jack's father. He was killed by Sunlight Gardener on Morgan Sloat's orders.

SCHULKAMP, ARNOLD One of the Speiser Company construction workers who was missing but presumed dead in the freak Angola, New York, earthquake that hit the Rainbird Towers condominium complex.

SCOFFLER, HANK A boy that Jack and Richard hung around with in Los Angeles.

SCOFFLER, MRS. Hank's mother.

SCOTT, RANDOLPH Jack bumped into a guy in the hall of the Oatley Tap who looked just like Randolph Scott. It was actually Elroy. He was a mill hand (and a homosexual shape-changer.)

THE SHAW BROTHERS Morgan had once negotiated with the Shaw brothers for a "terrible novel about Hollywood stars menaced by a crazed ninja."

SIMON One of the captain's soldiers at the palace in the Territories.

SINGER, SONNY A steward at the Sunlight Gardener Home.

SKARDA, VERNON A resident of the Sunlight Gardener Home. He was confessing to Hector Bast when Wolf ripped off the door to the common room and did a little damage.

SLOAT, GORDON Morgan Sloat's father. He had been a Lutheran minister in Ohio.

SLOAT, MORGAN Morgan Luther Sloat. Lily Cavanaugh Sawyer's dead husband's business partner. He was an evil manipulator whose counterpart in the Territories was Morgan of Orris. He wanted Laura DeLoessian's throne.

SLOAT, RICHARD Richard Llewellyn Sloat. Morgan Sloat's son and Jack Sawyer's best friend since birth.

SLOAT'S GRANDMOTHER Morgan Sloat's maternal grandmother had died at home when Morgan was a child. It had taken her four years to die.

THE SLUT A young girl Jack met at the pavilion grounds who had an infant hanging on one huge breast. She told Jack she could teach him something to do with his "little man" beside let piss out of it, if he had a coin or two.

THE SNAKE GUY A man with the head of a snake tried to board Jack and Richard's train as it moved through he Blasted Lands. Jack shot him with an Uzi.

SNOWBALL A black, blind guitar player Jack met at the Buckeye Mall. Jack intuitively felt that Snowball was Speedy in some other form. He questioned his thinking until the cops took Snowball away and, "although Jack could not see through the dirty dark glasses, he knew perfectly well that Lester 'Speedy' Parker had winked at him."

SPRATT, MRS. No one would ever see what was in her cupboard. (According to East-Head & West-Head, the two-headed parrot.)

STEIN, GERTRUDE In a variation on a theme, Lily Sawyer quoted Gertrude Stein as saying, "Horseshit is still horseshit is still horseshit."

STEPHEN A dandy. He worked for Osmond.

STEVENS, INGER The actress who pulled out of "Last Train to Hangtown," giving Lily Cavanaugh the role. The role was that of the dance hall girl.

THE STRANGERS Speedy explained to Jack that there were Strangers in the Territories who kept one foot in both worlds – like a goddamn Janus-head.

THE SUNTANNED MAN IN TENNIS WHITES The man who saw Sunlight Gardener's car racing away after the attempt to kidnap Jack in 1976. The suntanned man drove a Clenet.

THE TALL MAN A tall man in a houndstooth jacket passed Jack near the restroom at a rest area on I-70 in Ohio.

TEMKIN, VICTOR An outside staffer at the Sunlight Gardener Home.

THAYER, ANDREW The Thayer School existed because Andrew Thayer saw the possibilities in rail shippage. The campus's depot was actually a late nineteenth-century train depot.

THAYER, ELDER The New England transcendentalist for whom the Thayer School was named.

THIELKE, THOMAS One of the Speiser Company construction workers killed in the freak Angola, New York, earthquake that hit the Rainbird Towers condominium complex. Thielke was thirty-four years old.

THOMPSON, BILL (BUCK) The farmer who offered Jack and Wolf a ride in his pickup truck. [NOTE: Bill Thompson was Stephen King's editor on *Carrie*. Thompson also suggested to King that he write a nonfiction book on horror, and thus *Danse Macabre* was born.]

THE THREE LITTLE PRINCESSES Timmy's friends. [NOTE: See the "People" entry THE THREE YOUNG GIRLS.]

THE THREE PORTUGESE MAIDS Three Portugese maids at the Alhambra brought Lily Sawyer blankets.

THE THREE YOUNG GIRLS "The Three Little Princesses." Jack saw three young girls and a boy named Timmy get out of a Subaru Brat in the Buckeye Mall parking lot. He thought of them as "Mr. All-America" and "The Three Little Princesses."

THE THUGGSY TWINS At the Sunlight Home, Jack thought of Singer and Bast as "The Thuggsy Twins."

THE TICKET GIRL The girl who sold Jack the tickets at the Town Line Sixplex.

TIMMY "Mr. All-America." Jack saw three young girls and a boy named Timmy get out of a Subaru Brat in the Buckeye Mall parking lot. He thought of them as "Mr. All-America" and "The Three Little Princesses."

"TRAVELIN' JACK" Jack Sawyer.

THE TRUCK DRIVER WITH THE DETROIT TIGERS CAP The driver who offered Jack a ride to Decatur.

THE TRUCKER The unnamed truck driver who gave Jack a ride in his Diamond REO truck after Jack escaped from the Sunlight Gardener Home.

THE TWO COPS The two unnamed officers who took Snowball away from the Buckeye Mall in a squad car.

THE TWO DRUNKEN MEN After the Kingsland Ale cart overturned, Jack and Farren saw two men fighting outside a tavern in All-Hands' Village.

THE TWO FAT WOMEN At the Territories marketplace, Jack saw two fat women selling pots and pans.

TWO OLD MEN Two old men were playing Skee-Ball in the back of Arcadia Funworld when Jack first met Speedy.

UPDIKE, SMOKEY The owner of the Oatley Tap. He was killed when the Tap exploded as Jack obtained the Talisman.

VAN PELT, ARMIN A geologist from New York University who discussed the freak earthquake that hit Angola, New York.

VAN ZANDT A resident of the Sunlight Gardener Home. Van Zandt was one of the boys who urinated on Jack's and Wolf's beds.

VAUGHAN, HELEN Jack's fictitious aunt. She was a school-teacher.

THE WAITER The waiter at the Lobster Chateau. Lily taught him how to make an "elementary martini." He was not amused.

THE WAITRESS There was one waitress in the Arcadia Tea and Jam Shoppe when Jack went looking for his mother.

WALKER, CLINT One of Lily Cavanaugh's co-stars in the 1960 film "Last Train to Hangtown." He played Rafe Ellis.

WARWICK, ANDY A resident of the Sunlight Gardener Home. He harassed a fifteen-year-old kid named Morton. He was also one of the Far Field guards at the Sunlight Gardener Home.

WEBSTER, DANIEL Webster spoke at the first New England abolition rally in the Alhambra Hotel in 1838.

WILD, JEROME One of the Speiser Company construction workers killed in the freak Angola, New York, earthquake that hit the Rainbird Towers condominium complex. Wild was forty-eight years old.

WILLIAMS, OFFICER FRANK B. Officer Franky Williams. The cop who picked up Jack and Wolf at the Cayuga, Illinois, town line. He was eventually charged with misuse of public monies and the acceptance of bribes for his involvement with Sunlight Gardener.

WOLF A six-foot-five, sixteen-year-old werewolf who was Jack's "Territories" friend. He was killed saving Jack's life as they tried to escape the Sunlight Home. Wolf's litter-brother said "He's in the moon, now."

A WOLF One of Morgan's wolves dressed in a mercenary uniform stood outside a guardhouse as Jack and Richard approached Sloat's stronghold.

WOLF, JACK Jack told Judge Fairchild that Wolf was known as "Jack Wolf," but that his real name was Philip Wolf.

WOLF, PHILIP Jack told Judge Fairchild that Wolf was known as "Jack Wolf," but that his real name was Philip Wolf.

WOLF'S BROTHER Jack and Richard were driven back to New Hampshire by Wolf's litter-brother. He was a big Creedence Clearwater Revival fan.

THE WOMAN One of the customers at the Oatley Tap.

THE WOMAN WITH A CHILD After Jack and Wolf were thrown out of the Town Line Sixplex, an unnamed woman screamed at Jack not to let Wolf near her baby.

THE WOMAN WITH THE PILED-UP HAIR A woman who was near the cash register in the Arcadia Tea and Jam Shoppe when Jack went looking for his mother.

WONDER THE DEVIL-DONKEY A barker at the fun-fair on the pavilion grounds offered a prize to anyone who could stay on Wonder for two minutes.

WOODBINE, TOMMY Phil Sawyer and Morgan Sloat's lawyer. Jack called him "Uncle Tommy." Woodbine was a homosexual. He was killed by a van with "Wild Child" written on its side.

WOODRUFF, BENNY A resident of the Sunlight Gardener Home. Benny was kicked down three flights of stairs by Reverend Gardener after being caught with a Superman comic book.

YELLIN An outside staffer at the Sunlight Gardener Home.

(18)

THE TALISMAN
Places

AKRON, OHIO Morgan Sloat's birthplace.

THE ALHAMBRA INN AND GARDENS The New Hampshire hotel where Jack and his mother stayed after they moved from New York. It had a counterpart in the Territories: The Black Hotel.

ALL-HANDS' VILLAGE The carter was on his way to All-Hands' Village with Kingsland Ale when his cart overturned and killed his son.

AMANDA, OHIO Buddy Parkins and his brothers ran a farm not far from Amanda, Ohio, which was thirty miles southeast of Columbus.

THE AMERICAN EAST The American East corresponded to the Territories; the American West corresponded to the Blasted Lands.

THE AMERICAN WEST The American East corresponded to the Territories; the American West corresponded to the Blasted Lands.

ANGOLA, NEW YORK After Jack saw the Flying Men, he flipped back into his own world, thinking he was near either Olcott or Kendall. He was actually in Angola, near Lake Erie.

"ANTI-DISNEYLAND" Jack thought that the Black Hotel looked like it belonged in a weird Anti-Disneyland, where Donald Duck had strangled Huey, Dewey, and Louie, and Mickey Mouse had shot up Minnie Mouse with heroin.

ARCADIA AND BEACH DRIVE The intersection in Arcadia Beach where a mailbox was located.

ARCADIA BEACH The New Hampshire beach where the Alhambra Hotel and Arcadia Funworld were located.

ARCADIA FUNWORLD The New Hampshire amusement park that was open from Memorial Day to Labor Day.

ARCADIA TEA AND JAM SHOPPE One of the two shops that remained open in Arcadia Beach after Labor Day.

ARCANUM When Jack flipped back into our world with Wolf, he landed at the Arcanum, Ohio, exit, fifteen miles from the state line.

AUBURN Jack worked as a dishwasher in the Golden Spoon Diner in Auburn.

BATAVIA There was a Mammoth Mart in Batavia.

BATAVIA TO BUFFALO TO CHICAGO TO DENVER The route Jack expected to follow while hitchhiking across the USA.

THE BEACHCOMBER LOUNGE The name of the Alhambra coffee shop.

THE BEVERY HILLS HOTEL In 1976, when Jack was seven and living in California, a green car had stopped and the man inside had asked Jack how to get to the Beverly Hills Hotel. The man then offered Jack a Tootsie Roll and, when Jack reached for it, grabbed Jack's wrist. The other guy in the car (Sunlight Gardener) got out and tried to push Jack into the car. Speedy Parker had come along and saved Jack.

THE BLACK HOTEL The Agincourt, the repository of the Talisman, and the end of Jack's quest. It was in Point Venuti, California.

THE BLASTED LANDS A nasty place that was populated with deadly fireballs, headless skeletons of babies, packs of mutant big-headed dogs, kamikaze trees with tortured faces, leathery, featherless birds with monkey faces, and animals with human eyes, pig forequarters and cat hindquarters. The Blasted Lands directly paralleled the American West, and it had been befouled by radiation from nuclear testing in our world.

BOARDWALK AVENUE The main street of Arcadia Funworld. (It was an imitation of Atlantic City.)

BOWL-A-RAMA Jack passed a Bowl-A-Rama on his way into Oatley.

THE BOX The place of punishment for the boys at the Sunlight Gardener Home. Gardener kept the kids in there and, after Wolf ripped the Box (and the Home) apart, two cops examined the Box and found writing on the walls inside.

THE BUCKEYE MALL The mall where Jack saw "Snowball," the blind guitar player, who was actually Speedy.

BUSHVILLE A town far west of Oatley.

CAMBRIDGE, OHIO Buddy Parkins was out of Cambridge, Ohio, when he picked up Jack on U.S. 40.

CAMMACK After Wolf freaked out in the Town Line Sixplex, he and Jack slept in an empty house north of Cammack.

CAMP READINESS When he was a child, Richard attended Camp Readiness with his father.

THE CAPTAIN'S TABLE A restaurant in the Buckeye Mall.

CAYUGA, ILLINOIS Buck Thompson dropped Jack and Wolf off at the Cayuga town line.

THE CELLAR CHAPEL The cellar of the Sunlight Home had been converted to a comfortable chapel. Reverend Gardener used it for his evening sermons.

CENTRAL PARK WEST Jacky and his mother rented an apartment on Central Park West in New York City after they closed their house on Rodeo Drive in Los Angeles.

CHAVEZ RAVINE A Los Angeles nighttime cruising area.

"THE COUNTRY OF BAD SMELLS" Our world, according to Wolf.

THE CREAMERY The Thayer School's infirmary was called the Creamery because a dairy and milk bottling plant had once stood on the school's site.

D'AGOSTINO'S New York shop. Lily and Jack used a D'Agostino bag to lug stuff to New Hampshire. The bag broke open in the trunk of their car.

DALEVILLE After Jack and Wolf spent the night in an empty house north of Cammack, they arrived in Daleville around noon the next day.

THE DALEVILLE BURGER KING After Wolf let him out of the shed, Jack washed up in a Burger King and ordered a Whopper.

THE DANGEROUS PLANET BOOKSTORE A Point Venuti, California, bookstore. Sloat threw the tin soldier he bought into a trash bin outside this store. When Richard and Jack got to Point Venuti, this bookstore was one of the abandoned stores in the town.

THE DEPOT A squatty brick building on the grounds of the Thayer School. It had once been a main railroad office where the station master and the rail-boss worked. Its parallel location in the Territories was the depot on the edge of the Blasted Lands.

DOGTOWN A town near Oatley.

DOGTOWN CUSTOM RUBBER An Oatley factory that paid its employees on Fridays.

DOGTOWN ROAD One of the roads at a crossroads that Jack came to on his way to Oatley. Jack took Mill Road to the Oatley Tunnel.

"DOWNTOWN BETWEEN CENTER STREET AND MURAL STREET" The area that Judge Hallas allowed Snowball to "work," playing the guitar for spare change.

THE EMPIRE DINER The diner where Myles Kiger took Jack to lunch.

ENTRY 5, NELSON HOUSE The entrance to Richard Sloat's room at the Thayer School.

THE FAR FIELD A field on the grounds of the Sunlight Gardener Home. It was on the edge of the property, about a mile and a half down the road. The boys were often sent there to pick rocks. As the Reverend liked to remind the boys, rocks were always in season.

A FAT BOY DRIVE-IN During an "exchange" between the Territories and our world, Orris had ended up in our world in Morgan Sloat's body. He had taken control, driven to a Fat Boy Drive-In and tasted his first hamburger, fries, and chocolate milkshake.

FAYVA The shoe store in the Buckeye Mall where Jack bought his new sneakers. They cost six dollars.

FENDERVILLE, VERMONT Jack told Smokey Updike that he was from Fenderville.

FERDY'S WHOLEFOOD HEALTHSTORE When Richard and Jack got to Point Venuti, this store was one of the abandoned stores in the town.

THE FIRST MERCANTILE BANK OF PARADISE FALLS, OHIO Emory W. Light, the president of this bank, picked up Jack on I-70 near Dayton. [NOTE: Paradise Falls, Ohio, was the setting of much of Don Robertson's work. Robertson was a major influence on the work of Stephen King, so can we speculate that this section of *The Talisman* was written by King?]

THE FORTY-NINER ROOM One of the rooms in the Agincourt.

FRENCH LICK ROAD Officer Williams picked up Jack and Wolf on French Lick Road, out by Bill Thompson's place. Judge Fairchild sent them to the Sunlight Home.

THE FURNITURE DEPOSITORY Jack passed this building on his way into Oatley.

GENESEE COUNTY The county where Oatley was located.

GOLDEN SPOON DINER The Auburn restaurant where Jack worked as a dishwasher.

THE GOLDEN STATE ROOM One of the rooms in the Agincourt.

GOSLIN, OHIO The town where Buddy Parkins lived.

THE HAMPTON TOWNSHIP The town where the Lobster Chateau restaurant was located. Jack and Lily ate there on their first night at the Alhambra.

HARDEE'S A fast-food chain.

HARRISVILLE Jack bought a newspaper at a roadside store across the Indiana line, near Harrisville.

THE HENRY HUDSON PARKWAY The road Jack and Lily took to get to the Alhambra.

THE HERON BAR The bar in the Agincourt.

HOBBITON The place where Bilbo Baggins lived.

THE INSTITUTE OF SEISMOLOGY AT CALTECH They timed the "Black Hotel" earthquake at seventy-nine seconds.

KENDALL After Jack saw the Flying Men, he flipped back into his own world, thinking he was near either Olcott or Kendall. He was actually in Angola, near Lake Erie.

THE KINGSLAND MOTEL The Point Venuti motel where Richard and Morgan Sloat stayed when Richard was a child.

LA CIENEGA BOULEVARD The Los Angeles street where the "Wild Child" van hit Uncle Tommy Woodbine and killed him.

LAKE ERIE After Jack saw the Flying Men, he flipped back and landed in Angola near Lake Erie.

A LIQUOR STORE One of the shops in the Buckeye Mall.

THE LOBSTER CHATEAU The restaurant in Hampton Township where Jack and Lily ate on their first night at the Alhambra.

LOS CAVERNES ISLAND This island could be seen from the verandah of the Agincourt.

THE MARKETPLACE After Jack flipped into the Territories to escape the Elroy-thing, he hitched a ride with Henry the farmer and ended up in a Territories marketplace.

MCDONALD'S When Jack flipped back into our world after his escape from Morgan, he thought that the first thing he wanted to see was McDonald's golden arches.

MENDOCINO AND SAUSALITO Lily once told Jack that the land around these two California counties looked like New England.

THE MENDOCINO ROOM One of the rooms in the Agincourt.

MILL ROAD The road Jack took to the Oatley Tunnel.

THE MONKSON FIELDHOUSE One of the Thayer School campus buildings.

A MR. CHIPS COOKIE SHOP One of the stores in the Buckeye Mall.

MUNCIE, INDIANA Just before Jack and Wolf successfully escaped the Sunlight Home, Gardener had an appointment to meet Morgan Sloat in Muncie.

MUNCIE, INDIANA The town where Jack took Wolf to see Ralph Bakshi's film "The Lord of the Rings."

NELSON HOUSE The house at Thayer School where Richard Thayer lived.

THE NEON VILLAGE When Richard and Jack got to Point Venuti, this was one of the abandoned storefronts in the town.

NEW ENGLAND DRUGS One of the two shops in Arcadia Beach to remain open after Labor Day.

NEW HAMPSHIRE The state where Arcadia Beach and Arcadia Funworld were located.

NEW YORK UNIVERSITY Armin Van Pelt the geologist was associated with New York University.

NORTH HOLLYWOOD The men's shop where the clerk once offered Jack a blow-job was in North Hollywood.

NORTH HOLLYWOOD The area where Sawyer & Sloat opened a talent agency after they graduated from Yale.

OATLEY The rundown town where Jack stopped and worked while traveling across America. He worked at Updike's Oatley Tap.

OATLEY TEXTILES AND WEAVING An Oatley factory that paid its employees on Fridays.

THE OATLEY TUNNEL The tunnel Jack had to pass through to get to Oatley. He had an encounter in the tunnel with…what? "Only for an instant he had a glimpse of a face hanging in the dark, glowing as if with its own sick and fading interior light, a long, bitter face…."

OGDEN, ILLINOIS Myles P. Kiger's hometown.

OHIO Gordon Sloat had been a Lutheran minister in Ohio.

OLCOTT After Jack saw the Flying Men, he flipped back into his own world, thinking he was near either Olcott or Kendall. He was actually in Angola, near Lake Erie.

THE OUTPOST ROAD The road where the Kingsland Ale cart overturned. All-Hands' Village was on the Outpost Road.

THE PALACE After Jack flipped into the Territories at the beginning of his quest, he saw a man talking to a maid in the palace. The palace was where Queen Laura DeLoessian lay dying.

PALMYRA When Jack was picked up by the salesman in the Ford Fairlane while on his way to Oatley, he told the driver his hometown was Palmyra.

PARKLAND HOSPITAL According to Reverend Gardener, Ferd Janklow was recuperating at the Parkland Hospital after his escape attempt. Ferd was actually in The Pit.

PEMBROKE A town far west of Oatley.

PENNSYLVANIA Bob Darrent was a district high school superintendent from Pennsylvania.

THE PIT In their escape attempt from the Sunlight Home, Jack and Wolf flipped over to the Territories and ended up in The Pit, a place Morgan designed for prisoners. Jack and Wolf ended up on a precipice overlooking the Furnaces of the Black Heart. They saw a prisoner get run over by a cart, and heard his spine break. The prisoner was Ferd Janklow.

THE PLACES JACK AND RICHARD ATE AT ON THEIR WAY BACK TO NEW HAMPSHIRE Among the places Wolf's brother stopped at were a Stuckey's, a Burger King, and a Kentucky Fried Chicken.

THE PLACES WHERE SUNLIGHT GARDENER THOUGHT HE'D MET JACK Sunlight Gardener asked Jack to confess that they'd met before. The places the Reverend wondered about were California, Maine, Oklahoma, Texas, El Paso, Jerusalem, and Golgotha.

POINT VENUTI, CALIFORNIA The location of the Black Hotel, the Agincourt, and the destination of Sloat's train. Also, Point Venuti was the town where Morgan Sloat bought a dusty, dented, wind-up tin soldier in order to get the key in the soldier's back.

"POINTERS" The Oatley Tap men's room.

THE RAINBIRD TOWERS The Angola, New York, condominium complex that collapsed in a freak earthquake on the day Jack flipped from the Western Road and landed on the border of Angola. [NOTE: "John Rainbird" was the name of The Shop operative assigned to Charlie McGee in *Firestarter*.]

A ROADSIDE STORE Jack bought a newspaper at a roadside store across the Indiana line, near Harrisville.

RODEO DRIVE Jacky and his mother lived on Rodeo Drive in Los Angeles before they moved to New York and rented an apartment on Central Park West.

ROOMS 407 AND 408 Lily and Jack Sawyer's room numbers at the Alhambra.

ROUTE 17 IN NORTHERN CALIFORNIA NEAR STOREYVILLE When Jack found the big tree using Speedy's instructions, and flipped back into our world after obtaining the Talisman, he ended up on Route 17.

THE SADDLE OF LAMB The name of the Alhambra dining room.

SAINT LOUIS COUNTRY DAY A school that did two or three "newspaper exchanges" a year with students at Thayer School. Richard told Jack to say he was from Saint Louis Country Day if anyone should come into Richard's room when Jack was there.

SATURN, URANUS, MERCURY, IO, AND GANYMEDE When Sunlight Gardener persisted in asking Jack where they had met before, Jack screamed out the names of these planets and moons.

SEABROOK ISLAND, SOUTH CAROLINA The Sloats and the Sawyers used to vacation on Seabrook Island in South Carolina when the boys were younger.

"SETTERS" The Oatley Tap ladies' room.

THE SETTLEMENTS The term Wolf used for the towns and villages of the east.

SHARP'S The Beverly Hills store where Jack had bought his mother the gold cross earrings he had given her one Christmas. (Uncle Tommy Woodbine had helped him pick them out.)

SPENCE HOUSE One of the dorms at the Thayer School.

SUITE 4 The suite in Nelson House at Thayer School where Jack smelled pot.

THE SUNLIGHT GARDENER SCRIPTURE HOME FOR WAYWARD BOYS The Sunlight Gardener Home in Indiana. Jack and Wolf were sent there after being picked up by Officer Williams on French Lick Road in Cayuga, Illinois. The Sunlight Home was a sadistic place that Jack broke out of by flipping into the Territories. Wolf was killed helping Jack.

SUNSET BOULEVARD The first time Morgan Sloat ever flipped into the Territories, he had been standing on Sunset Boulevard looking at a billboard advertising a new Peggy Lee record.

SWITZERLAND When Jack suspected his mother had cancer (but before he really knew), he figured that if she was really sick, she would go to Switzerland for a cure.

TEA AND SYMPATHY When Richard and Jack got to Point Venuti, this was one of the abandoned stores in the town.

"THE TECHNICOLOR DREAM PALACE" The name Lily had given to their apartment in Los Angeles because of the spectacular view of the Hollywood Hills.

THE TERRITORIES A magical land that existed in a parallel universe to our earth. The Territories used magic as we use physics. The "government" was an agrarian monarchy. Each of us has a Twinner in The Territories, and some people could "flip" over into the land at will. Jack had to travel across the Territories and acquire the Talisman in order to save his dying mother's life back in the real world.

THE TERRITORIES BALLROOM The room in the Agincourt that housed the Talisman.

TEXAS AND ALABAMA When Jack questioned him about whether or not he'd ever been to the Territories, Speedy told Jack that he had never traveled further than Texas and Alabama.

THE THAYER SCHOOL The boy's boarding school in Springfield, Illinois, that Richard Sloat attended. (He lived at Nelson House.) Jack visited him there, and that was when "Thayer Got Weird."

THIRTY-ONE FLAVORS One of the stores in the Buckeye Mall.

THE TOWN LINE SIXPLEX The Muncie, Indiana, movie theater complex where Jack and Wolf (almost) saw Ralph Bakshi's film "The Lord of the Rings."

A TRUE VALUE HARDWARE STORE The store where Jack bought the padlock with which Wolf locked him up.

THE TWILIGHT ZONE Jack thought that the grim closed-up look of the Lobster Chateau restaurant reminded him of the Blasted Zone.

U.S. 40 The Ohio road where Jack was picked up by Buddy Parkins.

U.S. I-70 The western Ohio highway Jack hitchhiked on after leaving the Buckeye Mall.

UPDIKE'S OATLEY TAP The bar where Jack worked in Oatley. It was owned by Smokey Updike, and blew up when Jack acquired the Talisman.

UTAH AND NEVADA The two states where the United States government conducted the underground nuclear testing that resulted in the Blasted Lands in the Territories.

VERMONT Tom Ferguson was a shoe shop foreman in Vermont.

WALDENBOOKS One of the stores in the Buckeye Mall.

THE WESTERN ROAD A road in All-Hands' Village that had been oiled to suppress dust.

THE WESTWOOD YMCA Richard Sloat had almost drowned at the Westwood YMCA during a Young Paddler's Class. (Orris's son Rushton, Richard's Twinner, had drowned as an infant.)

WILSHIRE BOULEVARD Myrna the ballet dancer had a practice loft on Wilshire.

THE WIZARD OF ODDS The video game arcade where Roy Owdersfelt spent the ten dollars he stole from his mother's purse.

YALE A university in New Haven, Connecticut. [NOTE: New Haven is also my hometown, in case you were interested. You weren't? Sorry for the interruption. – **sjs**] Yale was Morgan Sloat's, Phil Sawyer's, and Tommy Woodbine's alma mater.

ZANESVILLE The town where Buddy Parkins dropped Jack off.

ZURICH Morgan Sloat had bought his "world's smallest safe" in Zurich.

(18)
THE TALISMAN
Things

ALBERT HUMBERT'S FOOD STASH Richard Sloat and Jack found the following items in Albert the Blob's room:

Famous Amos cookies
Licorice whips
Ring Dings
Slim Jims
Reese's Peanut Butter Cups
Pepperoni slices
Marshmallow Fluff
Salt 'n' Vinegar Potato Chips.

`THE ALHAMBRA LOBBY SHOP'S MERCHANDISE Among other things, they carried stuffed animals, newspapers, Chapstick, *People* magazine, *Us* magazine, and *New Hampshire* magazine.

"ALLEGORICALLY OPPOSED FIGURES" Jack saw Uncle Morgan Sloat and Speedy Parker as almost allegorically opposed figures like Night and Day, Moon and Sun, and Dark and Light.

"AMERICAN GRANGE HALL CUISINE" Jack thought that his Uncle Tommy would have described the food at the Sunlight Gardener Home as "grange hall cuisine."

THE ANGOLA *HERALD* The newspaper Jack was carrying when he was picked up by Buddy Parkins.

"ARCADIA DISTRICT SCHOOLS" The legend painted on the side of Arcadia school buses.

"ARRESTS MADE, RELATED TO SHOCK HORROR DEATHS" Newspaper headline Jack saw at the Empire diner that revealed the horrors at the Sunlight Home.

AUTHORS THAT RICHARD SLOAT ADMIRED He liked John McPhee, Lewis Thomas, and Stephen Jay Gould (Sloat owned *The Panda's Thumb*).

BEACH TOYS, INFLATABLE RUBBER DOLLS, AND "RIBS OF DELIGHT" CONDOMS Some of the products made at the Dogtown Rubber Plant.

A BLACK DeSOTO The "Fair Weather Club." It was a car with no tires parked on the street in Oatley. Four men sat inside playing cards as Jack passed.

THE BLACK DISEASE Cancer. Wolf smelled it on the burly man in the Chrysler who stopped to give Jack and Wolf a ride, but then changed his mind.

A BLACK VAN The vehicle that hit and killed Tommy Woodbine on La Cienega Boulevard in Los Angeles. The words "Wild Child" were painted on its side.

"BLAZE" The 1968 movie for which Lily Sawyer was nominated for an Academy Award. [NOTE: *Blaze* is also the title of an unpublished novel by Stephen King. It was completed in 1973.)

BLONDIE A rock group led by Deborah Harry.

A BMW Morgan Sloat's car.

THE BOOK OF GOOD FARMING The *Bible* of the Territories. When Jack first set out on his quest, the captain told him that *The Book of Good Farming* said that "the meek shall inherit the earth."

THE BOOK OF JOB Elbert Palamountain ate onion sandwiches and read the *Book of Job* during his lunch break.

THE BOOKS JACK MADE RICHARD READ FOR BOOK REPORTS When they were younger, Jack made Richard read the following books for book reports: *The Red Pony, Dragstrip Demon, The Catcher in the Rye, I Am Legend,* and *Lord of the Flies*.

THE BOOKS RICHARD SLOAT PACKED AWAY When Richard Sloat was five or six, he packed away the following books, absolutely refusing to deal with fantasy after he followed his father into a closet and couldn't find him anywhere: the Little Golden books, the Pop-Up books, the I-Can-Read books, the Dr. Seuss books, and the *Green Fairy Book for Young Folks* .

BROCA'S BRAIN The book Richard read on the way back to New Hampshire.

BUDWEISER A beer sold at Updike's Oatley Tap.

BUSCH A beer sold at Updike's Oatley Tap.

A CADILLAC As Jack approached Point Venuti, he saw a black Cadillac parked near the Agincourt.

A CADILLAC ELDORADO The car in which Richard and Jack were driven back to New Hampshire by Wolf's litter-brother.

A CAMARO While limping into Muncie, Indiana, Wolf and Jack were passed by a Camaro that blasted its horn at them.

CANADA MINTS Smokey Updike sucked Canada Mints almost constantly.

CARLTONS One of Lily Cavanaugh's former cigarette brands.

CHEAP WINE The "special juice" Speedy Parker gave Jack. The wine allowed Jack to "flip" into the Territories. After awhile, Jack learned to do it: he no longer needed the wine because the magic was within him.

A CHRYSLER The car the burly man with the bull neck and the Case Farm Equipment cap was driving. (After Wolf growled at him, he chose not to let Wolf and Jack into his Chrysler.)

A CLENET The car driven by the suntanned man in tennis whites who witnessed Sunlight Gardener's flight from the scene after attempting to kidnap Jack in 1976.

A COACH When Morgan Sloat flipped into the Territories (at the same time that Jack flipped with Richard Sloat), he found himself riding towards the Outpost Depot in a coach on a benchseat plusher than the seats in a Rolls Royce.

THE COIN When Farren took leave of Jack and sent him on his way, he gave him a large coin with Laura DeLoessian's profile on it. He told him he'd know what to do with it when the time came. (Or maybe he wouldn't.) The coin became a 1921 silver dollar in our world.

COMET The scouring powder Jack used to clean up the puke in the Oatley Tap men's room.

COUNTRIES IN CENTRAL AMERICA To pass the time while locked in the shed, Jack tried to name countries in Central America. He named: Nicaragua, Honduras, Guatemala, and Costa Rica.

A DAIRY QUEEN CHILI DOG As Jack and Richard prepared to "go to war" with Sloat and his men, Jack told Richard that he would buy him a Dairy Queen chili dog if they lived.

A DAISY AIR RIFLE Osmond's whip reminded Jack of the pop of his Daisy. Jack was eight years old when he had the rifle.

THE DAYDREAMS The term Jack used to describe his dreams of "the other place," the place he thought of when "things were boring or maybe a little scary." Jack could remember thinking that the Territories was Daydream-land when he was six.

"DEATH'S DARLING" One of Lily Cavanaugh's movies. She had starred.

DECEMBER 21, 1981 The day Jack arrived back at the Alhambra, three months after he set out. It was his thirteenth birthday.

DEMON DODGEM CARS One of the boarded-up amusements at the Arcadia Funworld Amusement Park.

"DEMONS" Anders called the batteries that ran Sloat's train "demons."

A DeSOTO Phil Sawyer and Morgan Sloat had driven an old DeSoto to California when they were younger.

DI-GEL The antacid tablets Morgan Sloat used.

A DIAMOND REO TRUCK The trucker who gave Jack a ride after he escaped the Sunlight Gardner Home drove a Diamond Reo truck.

DINGO BOOTS The boots worn by the patrons of the Oatley Tap.

DONATED COMMODITIES The milk at the Sunlight Gardener Home had "Donated Commodities – Indiana State Dairy Commission" written on the side of the cartons.

DORITOS, JAX, AND HAVE-A-KONE The snack items that had gone bad in the vending machines in the depot at the Thayer School.

"DRAG STRIP RUMBLE" A movie Lily Cavanaugh had made in 1953.

THE DRAMATICS CLUB The Thayer School Dramatics Club used the old depot for productions.

EAST HEAD & WEST HEAD'S QUESTIONS FOR HIMSELF The two-headed parrot in the Territories asked himself questions which his other head answered as follows:

1. East-Head: How high is up?
   West-Head: As low as low.

2. East-Head: What's the great truth of noblemen?
   West-Head: That a king will be a king all his life, but once a knight's enough for any man!

3. East-Head: And what's in Mrs. Spratt's cupboard?
   West-Head: A sight no man shall see!

4. East-Head: And what frightened Alan Destry to death in the night?
   West-Head: He saw his wife – growwwwk! – getting out of the bath!

1838 A plaque in the Alhambra's lobby proclaimed that in 1838, the Northern Methodist Conference held the first of their great New England abolition rallies in the hotel.

"AN ELEMENTARY MARTINI" Lily Sawyer's drink. Lily's drink recipe was "Ice in a glass. Olive on ice. Tanqueray gin over olive. Then you take a bottle of vermouth – any brand – and hold it against the glass. Then you put the vermouth back on the shelf and bring the glass to me."

ELLA SPEED The name Speedy gave to one of the carousel horses at Arcadia Funworld.

"THE EVERLASTING ROAD TO EVERLASTING GRACE" One of the pamphlets Jack and Wolf were given to read upon their arrival at the Sunlight Gardener Home and their subsequent incarceration in a tiny room.

"THE FAIR WEATHER CLUB" A "club" in Oatley that was actually a black DeSoto with no tires in which four men played cards.

FAMOUS PIER PIZZA & DOUGH-BOYS One of the boarded up buildings at the Arcadia Funworld Amusement Park.

FIFTY-FIVE CENTS The cost of either a large glass of milk or a ginger ale at the Oatley Tap.

"FLANAGAN AND FLANAGAN" Before he killed himself, Asher Dondorf played the sidekick on this TV series.

"THE FLYING DRAGON" The Chuck Norris movie playing at Cinema Four in the Town Line Sixplex on the day Jack and Wolf (almost) saw "The Lord of the Rings."

A FORD FAIRLANE A Ford Fairlane picked Jack up on his way to Oatley.

"FREAK EARTHQUAKE KILLS FIVE" The headline in the Angola *Herald* that Jack was carrying when he was picked up by Buddy Parkins. The story was by Joseph Gargan.

"FRUIT" The legend written on the sides of the boxes of hand grenades on Sloat's train.

THE FURNACES OF THE BLACK HEART The furnaces that fed Morgan's pit in the Territories.

GENESEE One of the beers served in the Oatley Tap.

GINSU KNIVES Jack thought that Wolf's teeth looked like a commercial for Ginsu knives.

THE "GO HOME" SIGN As Jack and Richard began to walk to Point Venuti by following the railroad tracks, they saw a sign on the left side of the tracks that said:

GOOD BIRDS MAY FLY;
BAD BOYS MUST DIE.
THIS IS YOUR LAST CHANCE:
GO HOME.

"GOD LOVES YOU" One of the pamphlets Jack and Wolf were given to read upon their arrival at the Sunlight Gardener Home and their subsequent incarceration in a tiny room.

GOLD CROSS EARRINGS Jack's Christmas gift to his mother one year.

A GREAT LAKE Jack saw a Great Lake in the Territories that he thought would be Lake Ontario in his world.

"GRIDLEY" Jack's nickname for Richard Sloat.

"HAPPY DAYS ARE HERE AGAIN" The song that the bells at Thayer School played when Jack acquired the Talisman.

"HAS BEGUN TO SICKEN AND MUST DIE" Words spoken by Daniel Webster at the abolitionist rally held at the Alhambra in 1838. They were engraved on a bronze plaque in the hotel's lobby.

HEAVY METAL The magazine on the desk in Suite 4 in Nelson House at Thayer School.

A "HELP WANTED" SIGN There was a "Help Wanted" sign in the window of the Oatley Tap.

"HERBERT TARRYTOONS" Lily's name for her Herbert Tareyton cigarettes.

THE HOLLYWOOD REPORTER The newspaper in which Morgan Sloat read that Asher Dondorf had killed himself.

AN HOURGLASS Jack saw the biggest hourglass he had ever seen in Anders' Depot. It was filled with green sand.

"I'D RATHER HAVE A BOTTLE IN FRONT OF ME THAN A FRONTAL LOBOTOMY" The song that was playing on the jukebox in the Oatley Tap when it exploded at the moment Jack acquired the Talisman.

"I'LL BE A SUNBEAM FOR JESUS" The message written on the Sunlight Gardener Home's envelopes.

THE INDIANA BOARD OF EDUCATION Before Jack got there, the Indiana board of education had tried to shut down the Sunlight Gardener Home twice.

AN INDIANA UNIVERSITY ATHLETIC DEPARTMENT SWEATSHIRT The gray sweatshirt Wolf was wearing when he let Jack out of the shed.

INTERNATIONAL HARVESTER Make of Elbert Palamountain's truck. Also, Speedy Parker's truck.

JACK'S "CALIFORNIA SENSIBILITY" Jack had grown up with a "California sensibility in which gays had been merely part of the scenery." When groped, Jack would respond, "No thanks, mister. I'm strictly A.C." This response was always good-naturedly shrugged off until Jack tried it with Tom Ferguson, who got mortally offended and threw Jack out of the car.

JACK'S FAREWELL NOTE TO HIS MOTHER Before Jack set out for the Territories, he wrote his mother three lines that "were most of what he had to say":

Thanks
I love you
and will be back

JACK'S "GUEST CHECK" IN THE OATLEY TAP Jack earned a dollar an hour working from four to one at the Oatley Tap, grossing nine dollars. Smokey deducted the following from Jack's pay:

1 hmbrg	$1.35
1 hmbrg	$1.35
1 lrg mk	.55
1 gin-ale	.55
Tx	.30

This totaled $4.10. Jack cleared $4.90.

A JUICY FRUIT WRAPPER In a moment when Jack realized that he was getting involved in something dark and magical, he watched the sand on Arcadia Beach open up in a whirling funnel and expose a Juicy Fruit wrapper.

JUNIOR MINTS, REESE'S PIECES, AND POPCORN, NO BUTTER The snacks Jack bought for himself and Wolf at the Town Line Sixplex.

KARASTAN The carpet in Sunlight Gardener's office.

KINGSLAND ALE The finest brew in the Territories.

A LAST SUPPER CERAMIC DIORAMA The religious display Mrs. Scoffler had in her living room.

"LAST TRAIN TO HANGTOWN" A movie Lily Cavanaugh had starred in in 1960. Will Hutchins, Clint Walker, Jack Kelly, Andrew Duggan, and Jack Elam were also in the film.

"LENSES" The legend stencilled on the crates of machine gun clips in Sloat's train.

LEVI'S The jeans worn by the "Randolph Scott" guy (who turned out to be Elroy) in the Oatley Tap.

THE LIFE OF THOMAS EDISON A book Jack remembered Richard Sloat reading during one of their vacations on Seabrook Island in South Carolina.

THE "LILY CAVANAUGH" BILLBOARD As Richard and Jack approached Point Venuti, they saw a billboard which said the following:

THIRD ANNUAL KILLER B FILM FESTIVAL
POINT VENUTI, CALIFORNIA
BITKER THEATER
DECEMBER 10TH–DECEMBER 20TH
THIS YEAR FEATURING LILY CAVANAUGH
"QUEEN OF THE B'S"

"LITTLE RED RIDING HOOD" Before he was locked in the shed, Jack had to search for the wandering Wolf. Jack thought of "Little Red Riding Hood" when he found Wolf, and Wolf said to him, "Sat here to see you coming."

A LODEN COAT The coat Myles P. Kiger gave Jack after he picked Jack up just outside of Danville following Jack's escape from the Sunlight Gardner Home.

A LONG TOOTH The pick that Speedy had given Jack before he set out on his quest became "a long tooth, a shark's tooth perhaps, inlaid with a winding, intricate pattern of gold."

THE LORD OF THE RINGS* AND *WATERSHIP DOWN Jack thought he would have had a better time explaining the Territories and his quest to Richard if *The Lord of the Rings* and *Watership Down* were on Richard's desk instead of *Organic Chemistry* and *Mathematical Puzzles*.

"MACHINE PARTS" The legend stencilled on the crates of guns in Sloat's train.

THE MAGIC JUICE The wine Speedy gave Jack that enabled him to flip into the Territories and back again.

MEMORIAL DAY TO LABOR DAY Arcadia Funworld was open from Memorial Day to Labor Day.

MERCEDES The only make of car Jack could recognize when he was seven years old.

MIDNIGHT The name Speedy gave to one of the carousel horses at Arcadia Funworld.

"MISSISSIPPI JOHN HURT TODAY" The name of the album from which the John Hurt song that Snowball played for Jack was taken. It was on Vanguard Records.

"MLS" Morgan Sloat's license plate.

"MOTORCYCLE MANIACS" Lily Cavanaugh's last role before she got sick was that of a cynical ex-prostitute in "Motorcycle Maniacs."

MUZAK The music in the Buckeye Mall.

NEW ENGLAND ABOLITION RALLIES A plaque in the Alhambra's lobby proclaimed that in 1838, the Northern Methodist Conference held the first of their great New England abolitionist rallies in the hotel.

"THE NEW PRICE IS RIGHT" Jack felt like a contestant on this show because of his lack of knowledge of the cost of things in the Territories.

THE NEW REPUBLIC The magazine in which Richard Sloat read an article about drugs.

A NEW YORK WORLD'S FAIR PILLOW The pillow Lori gave Jack in the Oatley Tap.

NEWSPAPER EXCHANGES Thayer School did two or three "newspaper exchanges" a year with students from other schools. Richard told Jack to say he was from Saint Louis Country Day if anyone should come into Richard's room when Jack was there.

NIKES Jack's sneakers.

NINEMONTH The term for September in the Territories.

1953 The year Lily Cavanaugh made "Drag Strip Rumble."

1979 The year that the Thayer School Dramatics Club put on a production of "The Fantasticks" in the depot.

1976 In 1976, when Jack was seven and living in California, a green car had stopped and the man inside had asked Jack how to get to the Beverly Hills Hotel. The man then offered Jack a Tootsie Roll and, when Jack reached for it, the man grabbed Jack's wrist. The other guy in the car (Sunlight Gardener) got out and tried to push Jack into the car. Speedy Parker came along and saved Jack.

1960 The year Lily Cavanaugh starred in "Last Train to Hangtown."

1968 The year Lily Cavanaugh was nominated for an Academy Award for her role in "Blaze." [NOTE: See the "Things" entry BLAZE.]

A 1921 SILVER DOLLAR The coin that Farren had given Jack in the Territories became a 1921 silver dollar in our world.

"NO EXIT" One of the plays Morgan Sloat directed while attending Yale. (The other was "Volpone.")

THE NORTHERN METHODIST CONFERENCE A plaque in the Alhambra's lobby proclaimed that in 1838, the Northern Methodist Conference held the first of their great New England abolitionist rallies in the hotel.

A #1 FRIENDLY SMILE The smile Wolf gave to the counterman at the Town Line Sixplex.

ONE DOLLAR THIRTY-FIVE CENTS The cost of a hamburger at the Oatley Tap.

ONION SANDWICHES Elbert Palamountain ate onion sandwiches and read the *Book of Job* during his lunch break.

"OPEN WEEKENDS ONLY – SEE YOU IN JUNE" The signs on the shops in Arcadia Beach, New Hampshire, during the fall and winter.

ORGANIC CHEMISTRY* AND *MATHEMATICAL PUZZLES Jack thought he would have had a better time explaining the Territories and his quest to Richard if Richard had *The Lord of the Rings* and *Watership Down* on his desk, instead of *Organic Chemistry* and *Mathematical Puzzles*.

OSHKOSH OVERALLS Wolf's overalls.

OSMOND'S WHIP Osmond used a whip to maintain order.

PAC-MAN AND LASER STRIKE Two of the games Roy Owdersfelt played at the Wizard of Odds video game arcade with the ten dollars he stole from his mother's purse.

PALL MALLS Lori's cigarettes.

A PALMER KNIFE Speedy Parker's knife.

PHILLIES CHEROOTS The cigars smoked by Smokey Updike.

PITCH TIL U WIN One of the boarded up amusements at the Arcadia Funworld Amusement Park.

PLASTIC EXPLOSIVES In addition to the Uzis on Sloat's train, there were also two-pound packs of plastic explosives.

THE POLICE TRAINING CAMP SIGN After killing Reuel in the Blasted Lands, Jack and Richard flipped back and ended up outside an abandoned police training site. The first thing they saw was a sign that read:

> By Order of the Mendocino County
> Sheriff's Department
> By Order of the California State Police
> VIOLATORS WILL BE PROSECUTED!

PSALM 37 The Psalm that Sunlight Gardener read at the first evening prayer service that Jack and Wolf attended at the Sunlight Gardener Home. Jack had begun to suspect that Gardener and Osmond were Twinners, and "his heart took a nasty, leaping turn in his chest" when Gardener made two minor revisions in the Psalm. The two verses he changed were Verse 3 and Verse 9.

In the Authorized King James version, Verse 3 reads:

> "Trust in the Lord, and do good; so shalt thou dwell in the land and verily thou shalt be fed."

Gardener changed it to:

> "Trust in the Lord, and do good; so shalt thou dwell in the Territories, and verily thou shalt be fed."

Verse 9 originally read:

> "For evildoers shall be cut off: but those that wait upon the Lord, they shall inherit the earth."

This became:

> "For evildoers shall be cut off: but those that wait upon the Lord, they shall inherit his Territory."

"THE QUEEN OF THE B'S" Lily Cavanaugh's nickname when she was hot during the fifties and sixties.

RADIATION POISONING When Anders described what had happened to the people living in the Blasted Lands, Jack immediately knew that he was describing the effects of radiation poisoning.

RAJ COLOGNE The cologne that Morgan Sloat wore when his son Richard was a child.

A RAND MCNALLY ROAD ATLAS One of the things Speedy gave to Jack before he set out on his journey to the Territories. (The other was a white ivory guitar pick.)

A RENAULT LE CAR The car that sped past Jack and Richard when they appeared on Route 17 with the Talisman.

"RIGHT HERE AND NOW!" Wolf's motto and credo.

THE RIMFIRE SHOOTING GALLERY One of the boarded-up amusements at the Arcadia Funworld Amusement Park.

ROLLING ROCK The beer of choice for the Fair Weather Club.

RUBIK'S CUBE Richard Sloat could solve Rubik's Cube in less than ninety seconds.

"RUN THROUGH THE JUNGLE" Wolf's litter-brother's favorite Creedence Clearwater song.

SALISBURY STEAK AND FRENCH FRIES The lunch Jack ate at the Empire Diner with Myles P. Kiger.

SCIENCE FICTION WRITERS JACK THOUGHT RICHARD SLOAT WOULD NOT READ Jack didn't think Richard would read sci-fi writers specializing in "metaphysical bullshit" such as Robert Silverberg and Barry Malzberg.

SCIENCE FICTION WRITERS JACK THOUGHT RICHARD SLOAT WOULD PROBABLY READ Jack thought Richard would probably approve of such "hard science" writers as Heinlein, Asimov, Arthur C. Clarke, and Larry Niven.

A "SCOTT HAMILTON" TAPE The tape Jack bought in Cheyenne and listened to on the way back to New Hampshire.

SCOUT The name Speedy gave to one of the carousel horses at Arcadia Funworld.

"SEND ALL AMERICAN NIGGERS AND JEWS TO IRAN" The graffiti on the hallway wall of the Oatley Tap.

SEPTEMBER 15, 1981 The day Jack Sawyer stood on Arcadia Beach in New Hampshire and looked out at the Atlantic. This was the day his journey began.

SEPTEMBER 1939 The month and year there was a war in the Territories. It began the same day Germany invaded Poland in our world.

SEVENTY-NINE SECONDS The length of the "Black Hotel" earthquake.

"SHE'S ALREADY DEAD, JACK, SO WHY BOTHER?" A message Jack saw on a window-door in the Agincourt.

SILVER LADY The name Speedy gave to one of the carousel horses at Arcadia Funworld.

A SILVER LADY RUBBER RAFT In Point Venuti, Speedy gave Jack a "Silver Lady" inflatable rubber raft. Jack used it to float out to the pilings beneath the Black Hotel.

SKEE-BALL The game two old men were playing in the back of Arcadia Funworld when Jack first met Speedy.

THE SMELLS OF "THE COUNTRY OF BAD SMELLS" The following smells in our world caused Wolf to vomit: diesel fuel, car exhausts, industrial wastes, garbage, bad water, and ripe chemicals.

THE SNEAKERS Jack bought himself new sneakers at the Fayva in the Buckeye Mall. They were "blue canvas with red zigzag stripes down the sides. No brand name was visible anywhere on the shoes." They cost six dollars.

SNOWBALL'S SIGN The blind guitar player Jack met at the Buckeye Mall (Speedy Parker in some other form?) wore a sign that read:

> "Blind Since Birth
> Will Play Any Song
> God Bless You"

"SONGS BY FATS WALLER" To pass the time while locked in the shed, Jack tried to name songs by Fats Waller. He named "Your Feets Too Big," "Ain't Misbehavin'," "Jitterbug Waltz," and "Keepin Out of Mischief Now."

SPACE INVADERS A video game in the Oatley Tap.

SPEEDSTERS, BULLSEYES, AND ZOOMS The "Fayva-brand" sneakers Jack saw at the Fayva in the Buckeye Mall.

THE SPEISER CONSTRUCTION COMPANY The company that had been building the Rainbird Towers when the earthquake struck Angola, New York.

STICKS The "word" (as best as Jack could interpret it) for money in the Territories.

THE STORY While on the road, Jack learned right away that "they always wanted a Story." Everyone wanted to know why a young boy was traveling at first, alone, and later, with his "big brother," Wolf. Jack revised his "Story" to fit the changing situations as he traveled.

STORY #2 "The Wicked Stepfather." Jack's second story about why he was on the road.

A SUBARU BRAT Jack saw three young girls and a boy named Timmy get out of a Subaru in the Buckeye Mall parking lot.

"SUNDAY REPORT" The TV show that did a segment on the Sunlight Gardener Home.

THE SUNLIGHT OF JESUS The magazine published by the Gardener organization.

A *SUPERMAN* COMIC BOOK Benny Woodruff was kicked down three flights of stairs in the Sunlight Gardener Home by Reverend Gardener because he was caught with a *Superman* comic. .

SURVIVORS The boots worn by the patrons of the Oatley Tap.

THE TALISMAN Speedy told Jack it looked like a crystal ball, and that Jack was to go get it in the Territories and bring it back. It was actually:

…a crystal globe perhaps three feet in circumference—the corona of its glow was so brilliant it was impossible to tell exactly how big it was. Gracefully curving lines seemed to groove its surface, like lines of longitude and latitude… *and why not?* Jack thought… *It is the world—ALL worlds—in microcosm. More; it is the axis of all possible worlds.* Singing, turning; *blazing*.

"TATTOO VAMPIRE" The Blue Oyster Cult song that had been playing when Jack got to Nelson House at Thayer School.

TERRITORIES TUPPERWARE At the Territories marketplace, Jack saw two fat women selling pots and pans. He thought of their goods as Territories Tupperware.

A TEXAS INSTRUMENTS CALCULATOR The calculator used by Smokey Updike.

THE THINGS IN THE GULLY Before he was locked in the shed, Jack searched for Wolf and saw the following items in a gully: old tires, old political pamphlets for a candidate named Lugar, a Connecticut license plate, and beer bottles.

THE THINGS SLOAT'S YALE CLASSMATES TALKED ABOUT When Morgan Sloat was at Yale, his classmates talked about things of which he had no knowledge: New York City, "21," The Stork Club, Brubeck at Basin Street, and Erroll Garner at the Vanguard.

THINGS THE PEOPLE IN THE TERRITORIES HAD NEVER HEARD OF Power poles, electricity, cable TV, Ma Bell, Malibu, Sarasota, and California.

THREE DOLLARS FORTY CENTS The New York minimum wage at the time Jack worked in the Oatley Tap.

TIDY BOWL The smell in the hallway of the Oatley Tap.

A TOOTSIE ROLL The candy that Sunlight Gardener's minion had tried to get Jack to accept before they tried to kidnap him in 1976.

THE TRASH IN THE WOODS BORDERING THE STATE REST AREA Jack saw the following rubbish in the woods bordering a state rest area off I-70: empty Dorito bags, squashed Big Mac boxes, crimped Pepsi and Budweiser cans, smashed Wild Irish Rose and Five O'Clock gin bottles, a pair of shredded nylon panties ("with a mouldering sanitary napkin still glued to the crotch"), and a rubber poked over a broken branch.

TWENTY-TWO DOLLARS The amount of money Jack had with him when he flipped into the Territories following his ordeal at the Oatley Tap.

TWINNERS The counterparts to people in our world. Jack's Twinner was Jason, who had died in infancy; Morgan Sloat's was Morgan of Orris; Lily Cavanaugh's was Laura DeLoessian, Sunlight Gardener's was Osmond, etc.

UNCLE TOMMY'S CHINESE PROVERB Jack's Uncle Tommy Woodbine had been fond of quoting "The man whose life you save is your responsibility for the rest of your life." Jack, therefore, felt responsible for Wolf.

THE UNITED FUND A solicitor for the United Fund called at the Oatley Tap looking for a donation.

THE UPRIGHT STICK Anders called the gearshift on Sloat's train the "upright stick."

UPS Jack thought to himself that if he ran out of magic juice while in the Territories, Speedy could UPS him some more.

UTICA CLUB One of the beers served in the Oatley Tap.

UZIS The Israeli-built submachine guns Jack found on Sloat's train.

"VOLPONE" One of the plays Morgan Sloat directed while attending Yale. (The other was "No Exit.")

"WANDERING JACK" The name Lily called Jack when he found her in the Arcadia Tea and Jam Shoppe.

"WAS HE ANOTHER JIM JONES?" The caption beneath the photo of Sunlight Gardener that ran in the paper following Jack's escape from the home.

A WEATHERBEE .360 RIFLE Sunlight Gardener's rifle.

A WHITE IVORY GUITAR PICK One of the things Speedy gave to Jack before he set out on his journey to the Territories. (The other was a Rand McNally road atlas.)

"WILD CHILD" The words that were painted on the side of the van that hit and killed Tommy Woodbine.

WINDEX The glass cleaner Jack used on the Oatley Tap's jukebox.

WINSTONS The cigarette Phil Sawyer smoked.

"WIZARDS" AND "THE LORD OF THE RINGS" The two Ralph Bakshi movies playing at the Town Line Sixplex the day Jack tried to get some sleep in the theater. It didn't work. Wolf freaked out at the movie.

THE WORLD'S SMALLEST SAFE Morgan Sloat's safe. It was a small steel box that he bought in Zurich. It contained a tarnished tin key that he wore on a chain around his neck. In the Territories, the key became some kind of weird lightning rod. Sloat used it to call electricity to Jerry Bledsoe.

YALES, MOSSLERS, AND LOK-TITES The padlocks the True Value hardware store in Daleville carried.

"YOU'RE DEAD NOW" As Jack and Richard moved through Point Venuti towards the Black Hotel, they saw "You're Dead Now" painted on the side of an abandoned boarding house.

YOUNG PADDLER'S CLASS Richard Sloat had almost drowned at the Westwood YMCA during a Young Paddler's class. (Orris's son Rushton, Richard's Twinner, had drowned as an infant.)

"YOUR LAST CHANCE TO GO HOME" A message Jack saw on a window-door in the Agincourt.

"YOUR MOTHER DIED SCREAMING" The message Jack saw hacked into a panel of the mahogany door of the Mendocino Room in the Agincourt.

ZIPPO Sunlight Gardener's lighter. He held the flame near Jack's face to frighten him.

THINNER
[Stephen King writing as "Richard Bachman"]

DEDICATION

To my wife,
Claudia Inez Bachman

[NO CONTENTS PAGE]

BOOK BREAKDOWN

[NOTE: As King did in *Christine*, all the chapters of *Thinner* are completely self-contained. There is no internal numbering of sub-stories within the chapters. — sjs]

Chapter 1: 246
Chapter 2: 245
Chapter 3: Mohonk
Chapter 4: 227
Chapter 5: 221
Chapter 6: 217
Chapter 7: Bird Dream
Chapter 8: Billy's Pants
Chapter 9: 188
Chapter 10: 179
Chapter 11: The Scales of Justice
Chapter 12: Duncan Hopley

(19)

THINNER
People

AHAB The captain of the Pequod in *Moby Dick*.

AMOS Linda Halleck's teddy bear.

ANDERSON, WARNER TV personality.

ARNCASTER, LARS The farmer who rented the use of his land to the gypsies.

THE ATTLEBORO BULLY Town fellow who had a fight with a gypsy.

BARTON DETECTIVE SERVICES The people hired to track down Billy as he hunted for Taduz Lemke.

BEAN, MRS. A neighbor of the Hallecks.

"BIFF" Frank Quigley's nickname.

BOYNTON, JUDGE HILMER When Billy Halleck's pants fell down in court, Judge Boynton was presiding.

A BUSINESS ASSOCIATE Unnamed man who delivered four packages to Ginelli. The packages were marked "World Book Encyclopedia," but actually contained a Kalishnikov AK-47 assault rifle and 400 rounds of ammo.

CALLAGHEE, MRS. Duncan Hopley's cleaning lady. She also did his grocery shopping.

CARPENTER, KAREN Fander explained to Billy that cardiac arrhythmia was caused by radical potassium depletion, and that this may have been what killed Karen Carpenter.

CHALKER, ALLEN The Raintree chief of police.

CONLEY The president of the Good Luck Paint Company.

CROSSKILL, RICHARD Man who was photographed handing out fliers on the Fairview Green.

THE CROSSKILLS The members of Richard Crosskill's family mentioned in the material sent to Billy at the South Portland Sheraton.

THE DALLAS COWGIRLS After Billy read his "Thinner" fortune, he didn't think he'd be able to "get it up" even if the Dallas Cowboy Cheerleaders paraded past him dressed in lingerie from Frederick's of Hollywood.

DEEVER, GEORGIA Linda Halleck's girlfriend.

DIOR Dress designer favored by Leda Rossington.

DUGANFIELD, DAVID Client represented by Billy Halleck against the Good Luck Paint Company.

EASTWOOD, CLINT Billy Halleck thought that Chief Hopley looked like a bush-league Eastwood.

EINSTEIN, ALBERT Billy thought that Einstein was wont to say "What the fuck" now and then.

ENDERS, LON Old man in the Seven Seas Bar who told Billy about the gypsies. Billy thought he looked like Lee Strasberg.

FANDER The man Ginelli sent to help Billy in Maine.

THE FAT MAN Unnamed man Ginelli saw in a drugstore.

THE FIVE RICH KIDS Five kids in a Porsche Turbo who told Ginelli that the gypsies were moving out.

"FLASH" Lon Enders' nickname when he worked the penny pitch in the fifties.

FOXWORTH, RAND Fairview's assistant chief of police.

GINA Gypsy girl.

GINELLI, RICHARD One of the owners of the Three Brothers restaurant. He succeeded in helping Billy get the curse taken off. He was found murdered, one hand cut off, and "pig" written on his forehead in blood. [NOTE: In Stephen King's *The Plant*, Ginelli owned a bar called the Four Fathers. See the section on *The Plant* in this volume.]

GREELY, PENSCHLEY, KINDER, AND HALLECK Billy Halleck's law firm.

HALLECK, HEIDI Billy Halleck's wife.

HALLECK, LINDA JOAN Billy and Heidi's fourteen-year-old daughter.

HALLECK, WILLIAM "BILLY" Fat Connecticut lawyer who hit and killed Taduz Lemke's wife Susanna, and was cursed by Taduz with the word "Thinner."

HEIDI'S MOTHER She finally moved back to Virginia.

HEILIG, MAMMA Trey Heilig's wife.

HEILIG, TREY Gypsy man that Ginelli questioned.

HOPLEY, DUNCAN The Fairview, Connecticut, chief of police.

THE HOTEL CLERK Unnamed Ramada Inn clerk who told Billy he had last seen the gypsies out by the burned-down Parson's Bargain Barn.

HOUSTON, DR. MICHAEL Billy Halleck's doctor. He was a Fairview archetype: "[T]he Handsome Doctor with White Hair and a Malibu Tan."

HOUSTON, MRS. Dr. Houston's wife. She drove a Cadillac Cimarron.

HOUSTON, SAMANTHA Mike Houston's daughter. She told Linda about Heidi's attempts to get Billy committed.

"THE INCREDIBLE SHRINKING MAN" The term Dr. Houston used to describe Billy Halleck. [NOTE: This was Stephen King's nod to Richard Matheson's *The Shrinking Man* and the subsequent film version, "The Incredible Shrinking Man." See the interview with Richard Matheson in this volume.]

JILLIAN Girl who worked in Halleck's office. Halleck joked that if Heidi didn't want to go to Mohonk, he'd ask Jillian.

"JUGGLER" The name Billy Halleck gave to Samuel Lemke when the gypsies first came to town. Lemke was missing some teeth. He came to Fairview and juggled on the town green.

KING, STEPHEN American writer referred to by Dr. Houston.

L'AMOUR, LOUIS Author liked by Ginelli.

LAWLOR, GRAND The county coroner.

LEMKE, ANGELINA Samuel Lemke's sister Gina. She came to the Fairview town green and set up the slingshot while her brother juggled.

LEMKE, SAMUEL Young gypsy. He juggled.

LEMKE, SUSANNA The gypsy woman Billy hit and killed with his car.

LEMKE, TADUZ Old gypsy man who put the "Thinner" curse on Billy Halleck.

MAINE STATE POLICE OFFICER Unnamed officer who stopped Ginelli as he approached the gypsy camp.

MARCHANT, ZACHARY Connecticut Union Bank banker. He handled Lars Arncaster's mortgage.

MARCY Little girl who talked to Billy.

MARLEY, MRS. Leda Rossington's cleaning lady.

McGHEE, LONESOME TOMMY Lon Enders's friend. When Billy met Lon, Tommy had been dead many years.

NEARING, MISS Linda Halleck's phys-ed teacher. Nearing was also the cheerleading teacher.

THE "NEW TEETH" WOMAN Eighty-eight- year-old woman who started growing new teeth.

NEWTON-JOHN, OLIVIA Her picture was on a keyring.

THE "NO BRAIN" STUDENT A George Washington University

student who was having blinding headaches. It turned out he had no brain at all – just a single twist of cortical tissue in the center of his skull.

AN OLD GYPSY WOMAN The unnamed woman Billy saw putting S & H Green Stamps in a book.

OSHKOSH How Billy referred to the old gypsy man Taduz Lemke, because he wore Oshkosh jeans.

PARKER, JOHN Billy's assistant.

THE PATROLMAN Unnamed cop who accompanied Hopley to the town green when the gypsies "set up shop."

PEALE, NORMAN VINCENT Author of *The Power of Positive Thinking*.

PENSCHLEY, KIRK One of Billy Halleck's partners.

PETRIE, GLENN Cary Rossington's friend.

QUIGLEY, FRANK Realtor. His nickname was "Biff." He charged Billy $200 to "not tell" Barton Detective Services that he'd seen Billy.

RANGELY, TOM Cop.

RICHOVSKY Brooklyn dope baron that Richie Ginelli had killed.

RICKLES, DON Comedian. Billy Halleck imagined Don making fun of Billy's weight.

"RIP VAN WINKLE" The name Ginelli called Billy after Billy woke up.

ROBERTS, JIM He revoked the fire permit that had been granted to the gypsies.

ROGERS, MR. If Billy could lose weight, fine. But if he couldn't, Heidi assured him that – as Mr. Rogers (and Billy Joel, for that matter) said – she liked him just the way he was.

ROSSINGTON, JUDGE CARY Billy Halleck's friend. He ruled that Billy was not at fault on the charge of vehicular manslaughter in the death of the old gypsy woman, Susanna Lemke. Cary had once grabbed Heidi Halleck's "oh-so-grabbable tit" during a New Year's kiss.

ROSSINGTON, LEDA Judge Rossington's wife.

SAYERS, DOROTHY Leda Rossington's favorite mystery writer.

SENDAK, MAURICE The author of *Alligators All Around*.

SIMONSON, RHODA Linda Halleck's aunt.

SPURTON, FRANK "The Man" Ginelli found. He was high-class drift trade. Ginelli hired him to track the gypsies. He was found with a bullet hole in his head, and a chicken cut open on his lap. The word "Never" was written in blood on his forehead.

STALLONE, SYLVESTER As Billy continued to lose wieght, his daughter Linda told him he was starting to look like Sly Stallone.

THE STANCHFIELDS People mentioned in the material sent to Billy at the South Portland Sheraton.

THE STARBIRDS People mentioned in the material sent to Billy at the South Portland Sheraton.

STEVENS, YARD Owner and operator of Heads Up, Fairview's only barber shop.

STONER, SPECIAL AGENT ELLIS The FBI alias that Ginelli used.

THE THREE STOOGES Billy's three doctors at the Glassman Clinic.

TIMMY The Seven Seas bartender who served Billy.

TRACY, SPENCER American actor.

TREE, JOHN When Spurton had information for Ginelli, he was to call the motel and ask for John Tree.

THE WAITER Nineteen-year-old boy at the South Portland Sheraton who looked at Billy in horror when he saw him in a robe.

THE WAITRESS Woman who told Billy that Old Orchard Beach was "the honkiest honky-tonk of them all."

WALKER, JERRY JEFF Sang the song "Mr. Bojangles." Billy thought of a line from the song when he saw a picture of Taduz Lemke.

WELBY, MARCUS Dr. Houston looked like a younger version of this TV doc.

THINNER
Places

ADIRONDACKS Billy and Heidi's vacation spot.

AMOCO STATION Fairview business. The gypsy vulture flew over it in Billy's dream.

BANKERTON The town from which Frank Spurton called "John Tree."

BAR HARBOR A waitress told Billy that Bar Harbor in summer was like Fort Lauderdale during spring break.

BARKER'S COFFEE SHOP Billy Halleck called Penschley from Barker's.

BLUE MOON COURT AND LODGE Ginelli took Billy there and then left for the day.

BOB'S SPEEDY SERV Billy showed the gypsy pictures there.

BROWN UNIVERSITY Decal in back window of the Porsche Turbo driven by the five rich kids.

BUCKSPORT The gypsies crossed the Penobscot River and camped in Bucksport for three days.

CAPTIVA The place where the Rossingtons had another home.

CHAMBERLAIN BRIDGE Quigley told Billy he saw the gypsy caravan leave Bangor via this bridge.

COVE ROAD The road where Lon Enders lived.

ELLSWORTH The town where the gypsies got a permit to camp on the fairgrounds for three days.

ESTA ESTA Fairview business. The gypsy vulture flew over it in Billy's dream.

FAIRVIEW, CONNECTICUT The Hallecks' hometown.

FAIRVIEW COUNTRY CLUB Halleck and Dr. Houston met poolside there to discuss Billy's weight loss.

FAIRVIEW PUBLIC LIBRARY The gypsy vulture flew over it in Billy's dream.

FAIRVIEW TOWN GREEN The green where the gypsies set up shop.

FALMOUTH BEVERAGE BARN Billy showed the gypsy pictures there.

THE FARMER'S CO-OP Business where Lars Arncaster had a line of credit.

THE FEED AND GRAIN Business where Lars Arncaster had a line of credit.

FINSON ROAD The road on which Spurton saw the gypsy caravan.

FRANK'S FINE MEATS Fairview business. Billy saw it from his train window.

FREDERICK'S OF HOLLYWOOD Lingerie manufacturer. [NOTE: See the "People" entry THE DALLAS COWGIRLS.]

FRENCHMAN'S BAY MOTEL Bar Harbor motel.

GEORGE WASHINGTON UNIVERSITY The school the "no-brain" student attended.

GOOD LUCK PAINT COMPANY The company headed by Mr. Conley. Halleck represented a plaintiff in a case against the company.

GUN HILL ROAD Billy had to pass this exit on his way home to Connecticut.

HARBORVIEW MOTEL A motel in Rockland.

HASTUR LOUNGE The bar where Billy and Judge Rossington discussed their families.

HEADS UP Fairview's only barber shop.

THE HENRY GLASSMAN CLINIC A private facility in New Jersey where Billy Halleck went for a series of metabolic tests.

KING IN YELLOW The shop where Linda Halleck bought her jeans.

LABYRINTH TRAIL Mohonk hiking trail.

LANTERN DRIVE Street in Fairview, Connecticut, where the Hallecks' lived.

MAYO CLINIC The clinic where Cary Rossington went, convinced he had skin cancer. He was actually cursed. Also, Billy felt that if Heidi looked at him while he had his "cancer-scare" look on his face, she'd put him in the Mayo Clinic.

McDONALD'S After the curse was removed, Billy stopped at McDonald's to eat.

MILFORD The town where the gypsy touched Duncan Hopley, cursing him.

MOHONK Resort where Heidi and Billy went for a weekend.

NEW PALTZ The town where Billy bought his new Nikes.

NEW YORK SUPERIOR COURT The court where Billy Halleck was indicted on a charge of vehicular manslaughter in 1980.

NITE OWL Convenience store. The Attleboro bully had a fight with a gypsy outside the store.

NORMIE'S SUNOCO Business where Lars Arncaster had a line of credit.

NORTH CAROLINA The state where Billy Halleck lived as a boy.

OLD ORCHARD BEACH According to a waitress, Old Orchard Beach was "the honkiest honky-tonk of them all."

OLD OVERLAND Billy went to a bar called the Seven Seas in Old Overland.

O'LUNNEY'S Bar and grille. Billy took a client there for lunch.

OWL HEAD Billy stayed at the Sheepscot Motel in Owl Head.

PARK LANE AND LANTERN DRIVE There was a bus stop there.

PARSON'S BARGAIN BARN Store in Bangor that burned down. A hotel clerk told Billy that he had last seen the gypsies near the burned out building.

RAINTREE Cary and Leda Rossington were at a flea market in Raintree when the old gypsy man touched Cary, putting a curse on him that gave him a condition that Cary was convinced was skin cancer.

RAMADA INN Motel in Bangor.

RIBBONMAKER LANE The street where Duncan Hopley lived.

ROCKLAND The town where Enders thought the gypsies were heading.

THE SALT MARSHES An area in Fairview that the gypsy vulture flew over in Billy's dream.

THE SALT SHACK The place near where the gypsies camped.

THE SALTY DOG Bar where Billy got a cab.

THE SEVEN SEAS Bar Billy went to in Old Overland.

SHEEPSCOT MOTEL Owl Head motel. Billy stayed there.

SHERATON HOTEL South Portland hotel. Billy told Penschley to send all available papers on the gypsies to this hotel.

SHOP 'N SAVE The grocery store where Billy and Heidi Halleck shopped. Ginelli bought Billy a bag of oranges there.

SUNNYVALE ACRES Nonexistent asylum where Billy thought his family wanted to send him. Supposedly "Basket-Weaving Was [Their] Specialty."

TECKNOR A town, one town inland from Bar Harbor, where the gypsies set up camp.

TEXACO STATION Bankerton station from which Spurton called "John Tree."

THREE BROTHERS RESTAURANT Restaurant co-owned by Richard Ginelli.

TOYS ARE JOYS Fairview business. Billy saw it from his train window.

UNION AND HAMMOND There was a park between these two streets. Billy was to meet Lemke there at 7:00 p.m.

VILLAGE PUB Fairview business. The gypsy vulture flew over it in Billy's dream.

VIRGINIA Heidi's mother finally moved back there.

WALDENBOOKS Fairview business. The gypsy vulture flew over it in Billy's dream.

THE WATERING HOLE The Fairview Country Club poolside bar.

WESTPORT Dr. Houston's children went to a private school in Westport.

THE WESTPORT HERTZ OFFICE Billy rented a car there.

(19)
THINNER
Things

ALLIGATORS ALL AROUND A book by Maurice Sendak.

ANAÏS ANAÏS Heidi Halleck's perfume.

"AND JUSTICE FOR ALL" A movie Heidi and Billy watched on HBO.

ANOREXIA NERVOSA Billy thought the gypsy had cursed him with this condition.

AUREOMYCIN The antibiotic Fander gave to Billy.

AVIS The car Billy rented.

BAKER VS. OLINS A case Billy thought of.

BALL JAR Ginelli bought one in a supermarket.

BALLY The shoes Billy Halleck wore.

BANGOR *DAILY NEWS* The paper that ran news of Ginelli's slaying.

BAR HARBOR BUMPER STICKERS The cars in Bar Harbor had bumper stickers that said things like "SPLIT WOOD, NOT ATOMS," "U.S. OUT OF EL SALVADOR," and "LEGALIZE THE WEED."

THE BAR HARBOR CARS In Bar Harbor, Billy saw Saabs, Volvos, Datsuns, BMWs, and Hondas.

BAUSCH & LOMB The soft contact lenses Billy Halleck wore.

"THE BEVERLY HILLBILLIES" TV show Cary Rossington watched.

BILLY HALLECK'S BREAKFAST In his pre-curse days, Billy would eat the following for breakfast: "[A] steaming mound of scrambled eggs, an English muffin with raisins, [and] five strips of crisp country-style bacon."

BILLY'S FORTUNE Billy weighed himself on a penny scale outside a shoe store that had a sign that said YOUR WATE AND FATE. His weight was 232 pounds, and his fortune read "Thinner."

BILLY'S GYPSY VULTURE DREAM Billy dreamed that the old gypsy became a vulture and flew over Fairview, which had become a town peopled by the living dead, including a skeletal Ronald Reagan screaming "Where's the rest of me?!"

BILLY'S TESTS AT THE GLASSMAN CLINIC Billy had x-rays, a cat-scan, an EEG, and an EKG.

"BLACK MARIA" The name for the Fairview police wagon.

BLACKGLAMA Leda Rossington's fur coats.

BUICK SEDAN The second car Ginelli rented from Avis.

CADILLAC CIMARRON Mrs. Houston's car. It looked like a "Rolls-Royce with hemorrhoids."

CADILLAC HEARSE One of the vehicles belonging to the gypsies.

CALVIN KLEIN JEANS The apparel favored by the younger set in Fairview.

CAMELS Ginelli's cigarettes. Also, Chief Hopley's cigarettes. The chief smoked two packs a day.

CANCER When Billy started losing weight unexplainedly, he and Heidi worried he had cancer. He said cancer rhymed with "dancer" and "You shit your pants, sir."

CARAMEL CORN One of Billy's snacks.

CHEEZ-DOODLES One of Billy's snacks.

CHESTERFIELD KINGS The cigarettes Billy bought when he decided to go back to smoking.

CHEVROLET Fander's car.

CHEVY NOVA The blue car Ginelli was driving when he returned to the Blue Moon.

CHICKEN NEAPOLITAN The dish Ginelli offered to make for Billy.

CHIVAS REGAL The scotch Ginelli brought to Billy's motel room.

COKE The drink Ginelli bought in a gas station.

COMMODORE Billy Halleck's computer.

DAVE'S DOG WAGON Hot dog and lemonade vendor.

DORITOS The snack that Billy ate while watching the Mets on TV.

DOVER SOLE One of Billy Halleck's favorite foods.

DUNGEONS AND DRAGONS The game Linda Halleck played with her friends.

DUZ Laundry powder in Susanna Lemke's net bag.

EAMES Duncan Hopley's chair.

EMPIRIN The painkiller Fander gave to Billy.

ESPRESSO Italian coffee. After their legal matters were concluded, Ginelli asked Billy Halleck to come around for espresso once in a while.

"FAMILY FEUD" TV show Cary Rossington watched.

AN FBI IDENTIFICATION CARD Ginelli had one and showed it to a state cop who stopped him as he approached the gypsy camp. It worked.

FLAIR FINELINER The pen Kirk Penschley used.

FRISBEES, TWINKIES, COKES, AND SLURPIES Billy saw people in the park partaking of these varied goodies.

FVW1 Duncan Hopley's license plate.

GINELLI'S NOTE TO LEMKE After Ginelli killed Lemke's dogs, he wrote this note on a dollar bill and tucked it under the dog's collar: "NEXT TIME IT COULD BE YOUR GRANDCHILDREN, OLD MAN. WILLIAM HALLECK SAYS TAKE IT OFF." [N OTE: See the entry "NEVER."]

GINELLI'S PIT-BULL COCKTAIL It was a mixture of Mexican brown heroin and strychnine that Ginelli injected into steaks and then fed to Taduz Lemke's pit bulls. [NOTE: See the entry GINELLI'S NOTE TO LEMKE.]

GREEN FIREBIRD One of the cars from between which the Gyspy woman darted out into the path of Billy's car.

GREYHOUND The tag on Linda Halleck's luggage.

THE GYPSY TRAVEL ROUTE Greeno, Connecticut, to Pawtucket, Rhode Island, to Attleboro, Massachusetts.

"THE HAMMER" Richie Ginelli's nickname.

HAYMAN-REICHLING SERIES Card test for blood in the stools. Billy had one during a physical.

"HOGAN'S HEROES" TV show Cary Rossington watched.

HORCHOW LAMP Ornamental lamp on the Rossington doorway from the Horchow collection. It was a wrought-iron facsimile of an 1880's New York streetlamp. It cost $687, plus mailing.

"THE HOUSE THAT BUDWEISER BUILT" How Billy Halleck described his belly.

J.W. DANT Cary Rossington drank this whiskey like Pepsi-Cola.

"THE JOKER'S WILD" TV show Cary Rossington watched.

JORDACHE JEANS Apparel favored by the younger set in Fairview.

KALISHNIKOV AK-47 ASSAULT RIFLE AND 400 ROUNDS OF AMMO Actual contents of the four packages delivered to Ginelli marked "World Book Encyclopedia." There was also a spring loaded knife, a lady's leather bag loaded with lead shot, Scotch strapping tape, and a jar of lampblack.

KLUGE BAG Billy's luggage.

LaCOSTE Dr. Houston's shirt.

LADIES AID BAKE SALE Billy told Heidi he bought the gypsy pie at a bake sale.

"LIKE AN ELECTROLUX" Ginelli said the book *This Savage Rapture* sucked like an Electrolux.

LINDA'S BUTTONS Buttons on Linda Halleck's purse strap included Bruce Springsteen, John Cougar Mellancamp, Lionel Ritchie, Sting, and Michael Jackson.

LIPTON CUP O' SOUP BOXES Billy used to hide his munchies behind the soup boxes.

A LOUP An old shotgun. Samuel Lemke was holding one and listening to a Walkman with headphones when Ginelli choked him and taped him to a tree.

MARLBORO LIGHTS Yard Stevens' cigarette. He smoked two packs a day.

MERCEDES Dr. Houston's car.

MILLER The beer Billy drank.

MILLER LITE The beer Ginelli drank.

"MR. BOJANGLES" Billy thought of a line from this song when he saw a picture of Taduz Lemke.

"MYSTERY DEATH MAY HAVE BEEN GANGLAND SLAYING" The headline announcing Ginelli's death.

"NEVER" The word written in blood on Frank Spurton's forehead.

NEW YEAR'S DAY, 12:01 A.M. The day and time Billy Halleck quit smoking.

NIKE Billy Halleck's hiking shoes.

1980 The year Billy Halleck was indicted for vehicular manslaughter in the death of the old gyspy woman.

1981 OLDSMOBILE 98 Billy Halleck's car. He was driving it – and getting an unexpected hand-job from his wife – on the day he hit and killed Susanna Lemke.

1957 PONTIAC Billy Halleck's first car.

NIQUES The belt Billy Halleck wore. Heidi had bought it for him.

NIVEA The cream Cary Rossington rubbed on his "scales."

OSHKOSH Jeans worn by Taduz Lemke.

THE PENNY PITCH Lon Enders worked it in the fifties.

PENTOTHAL Leda Rossington wondered what she'd say if someone gave her a shot of pentothal before her husband's funeral.

PEPPERONI SLICES AND MUENSTER CHEESE ON RITZ CRACKERS Billy ate this snack while watching a Yankee-Red Sox doubleheader.

THE PIE A strawberry pie that Taduz Lemke gave to Billy to remove the "thinner" curse. Billy cut his hand and put his blood in the pie. He had to make somebody eat it or the curse would come back. Without him knowing it, his wife and daughter ate the pie. *Thinner* ends with Billy eating the pie himself, joining his family in inevitable death. Taduz Lemke had truly gotten his revenge.

A PORSCHE TURBO A car with five rich kids in it. Ginelli asked them if they knew where he could find the gypsies.

PURFARGADE ANSIKTET "Child of the night-flowers" in Rom. Lemke explained to Billy that that's what he had put inside Billy, which was causing him to lose weight and grow "thinner."

Q-TIPS Dr. Houston used them to wash his nose with distilled water after he snorted coke.

RADICAL POTASSIUM DEPLETION This may have been what killed Karen Carpenter, and it became something Billy had to worry about.

RICHARDS VS. JERRAM, NEW HAMPSHIRE A case Billy thought of.

RING-DINGS One of Billy's snacks.

ROLEX Dr. Houston's watch.

ROM The language spoken by the gypsies.

THE ROTARY CLUB The club that gave Duncan Hopley an award.

"THE ROUSTING OF THE UNDESIRABLES" The term Billy used to describe Chief Hopley's harassment of the gypsies on the Fairview town green.

S & H GREEN STAMPS Billy saw an old gypsy woman putting stamps in a book.

SAMSONITE Linda Halleck's luggage.

SARA LEE CHEESECAKE Billy and Heidi ate one while watching "And Justice For All" on HBO.

SARAN WRAP It covered the gypsy pie.

SCHOONER The beer that the bartender served Billy at the Seven Seas.

$687 PLUS MAILING The cost for the ornamental lamp outside the Rossington's doorway.

SIXTEEN OUNCE PEPSI Ginelli bought one in a supermarket.

"SOME ASSHOLE KICKED ME LAST NIGHT AND NOW I AM OUT OF ORDER" The sign on the Seven Seas jukebox.

SONY Cary Rossington had a large-screen Sony TV.

STATISTICAL SOCIOLOGY The text Gina Lemke was studying when Ginelli questioned her.

"A STEPHEN KING NOVEL" Dr. Houston told Billy Halleck that he sounded "a little like a Stephen King novel."

SWISS ARMY KNIFE The knife Billy always kept in his pocket.

.38 CALIBER COLT WOODSMAN The gun in one of the smaller packages that was delivered to Ginelli.

THIS SAVAGE RAPTURE The book Ginelli was reading when Billy woke up.

THREE BROTHERS ASSOCIATES, INC. The company that owned Three Brothers restaurant. Halleck once represented them in what Ginelli referred to as [his] "legal problems."

"THREE'S COMPANY" TV show Linda Halleck watched.

"TIPS" The term Lon Enders used to describe the crowds.

TRIBOROUGH BRIDGE The bridge Billy crossed to get home.

TWINKIES The snack Billy Halleck had in his glove compartment.

(203) 555-9231 Billy Halleck's home phone number.

TWO PLYMOUTHS Two unmarked police cars that were parked at the edge of a field outside the gypsy camp.

"UNDER MY THUMB" Rolling Stones song that Samuel Lemke was listening to when he was attacked by Ginelli.

VANTAGE 100 Heidi Halleck's cigarettes.

VEHICULAR MANSLAUGHTER The charge against Billy Halleck. He hit and killed the old gypsy woman, Susanna Lemke, during a distracting hand-job being administered by his wife Heidi while he was driving.

VOLVO Duncan Hopley's car.

VW MICROBUS One of the gypsy vehicles.

WALL STREET JOURNAL The newspaper Billy Halleck read.

WHOPPERS WITH CHEESE One of Billy's snacks.

WILD TURKEY The bourbon Cary Rossington drank.

"WORLD BOOK ENCYCLOPEDIA" The legend written on the four packages delivered to Ginelli by a business associate. The packages actually contained a Kalishnikov AK-47 assault rifle, 400 rounds of ammo, and other arms and weaponry.

YELLOW SUBARU One of the cars from between which the gypsy woman darted out into the path of Billy's car.

CYCLE OF THE WEREWOLF

DEDICATION

In memory of Davis Grubb,
and all the voices
of Glory

[NO CONTENTS PAGE]

BOOK BREAKDOWN

[NOTE: *Cycle of the Werewolf* consists of twelve chapters. —sjs]

January
February
March
April
May
June
July
August
September
October
November
December

Afterword—(One paragraph by Stephen King.)

---

(20)
CYCLE OF THE WEREWOLF

[The number in parentheses following the entry indicates the chapter of *Cycle of the Werewolf* in which the information appears. *Cycle* is broken into twelve chapters, each corresponding to a month of the year, beginning with January and ending in December. Therefore, chapter numbers neatly reflect the month in the cycle. For instance, (7) refers to July, and so forth. – sjs]

People

AL, UNCLE (7) Marty's uncle; his mother's brother. Uncle Al brought Marty fireworks for the Fourth of July. Marty set them off alone, and was attacked by the werewolf. The boy did manage, however, to take out the wolf's left eye with the fireworks. Al always came to Tarker's Mills in July for the traditional salmon and fresh peas dinner with Marty's family.

THE BEAST (5) The Great Satan. According to Reverend Lowe's dream, the Beast could be anywhere: Buying Marlboros and a Bic lighter; in front of Brighton's Drug eating a Slim-Jim; waiting for the 4:40 Greyhound from Bangor; sitting next to you at a band concert, or having a piece of pie at the Chat 'n Chew on Main Street.

BESSEY, ARLENE (6) The former Arlene McCune.

BESSEY, MR. (6) Arlene's husband. He was a successful Bangor lawyer.

BLODWIN, CAL (5) Grace Baptist Church's head deacon. In Reverend Lowe's dream, Cal changed into a werewolf. He owned Blodwin Chevrolet.

BOWLE, VICTOR (5) The town's head selectman. He changed in to a werewolf in Reverend Lowe's dream.

BURNEY, DELIA (12) A friend of Ollie Parker's wife.

THE COLLINSES (10) They were on Marty's Halloween trick-or-treat route.

CORLISS, ALDEN (12) Corliss's brother. He cashed his food stamps at an A & P two towns over.

CORLISS, CLYDE (5) Grace Baptist's janitor, and the werewolf's fifth victim. He was found gutted and hanging face down over the pulpit.

CORLISS, ERROL (12) Corliss's brother. He cashed his food stamps at an A & P two towns over.

COSLAW, GRANDFATHER Marty's grandfather. He had a heavy Slavic accent, and drank Schnapps.

COSLAW, HERMAN (7) Marty's dad. He was a physical education teacher at Tarker's Mills grammar school.

COSLAW, KATE (7) Marty's thirteen-year-old sister. She pretended to dislike Marty, but she really loved him.

COSLAW, MARTY (7) Ten-year-old crippled kid who discovered the werewolf's identity, and succeeded in blowing him away with two silver bullets.

COSLAW, MRS. (7) Marty's mother. She was brusque with Marty so as not to spoil him.

THE DIXONS (10) They were on Marty's Halloween trick-or-treat route.

THE DRIFTER (3) Unnamed man found dead. He was the werewolf's third victim.

THE EASTONS (10) They were on Marty's Halloween trick-or-treat route.

ELLENDER, HENRY Author of *The Wolf*. [NOTE: King used a quotation from *The Wolf* as one of the epigraphs to *Cycle of the Werewolf*.]

FOURNIER, ELISE (4) Billy Robertson's bar maid. She was twenty-four years old, attended Grace Baptist Church, and sang in the choir. She had a crush on Reverend Lowe. She planned to leave Tarker's Mills and move to Portsmouth. She was afraid of the wolf.

FRANKLIN, KENNY (8) He was waiting for a haircut in Stan's during the discussion as to whether or not the Full Moon Killer was a werewolf.

FREEMAN, ELBERT (5) Fat science teacher. In Reverend Lowe's dream, he changed into a werewolf.

THE FULL MOON KILLER (7) The name the papers gave to the werewolf.

A GUY IN BRIDGTON (7) Unnamed guy from whom Uncle Al bought his firecrackers.

HAGUE, GRAMMA (4) Old Man Hague's wife. She baked pies. She died of a heart attack.

HAGUE, OLD MAN (3) He had a hayfield known locally as Forty Acres Field. It was frozen in the March blizzard.

HARRINGTON, WILLIE (12) Ninety-two-year-old man who slipped on the ice in front of his Ball Street house in late November and broke a hip.

IDA, AUNT (7) Marty's aunt. She lived in Stowe, Vermont, and Marty was sent to visit her after he was attacked by the werewolf.

JIM, UNCLE (7) Marty's uncle. He lived in Stowe, Vermont, and Marty was sent to visit him after he was attacked by the werewolf.

KINCAID, BRADY (4) Eleven-year-old boy. The fourth victim of the werewolf. He was found headless and disembowelled, propped against the war memorial.

KINCAID, MR. (4) Brady's father. Brady knew his father would be mad because he stayed out too long flying a kite.

KNOPFLER, ALFIE (6) Owner of the Chat 'n Chew. He weighed 220 pounds. He was the werewolf's sixth victim.

LOWE, REVEREND LESTER (4) Minister of the Grace Baptist Church in Tarker's Mills. Werewolf. He was killed By Marty Coslaw with two silver bullets.

THE MACINNES (10) They were on Marty's Halloween trick-or-treat route.

MACKENZIE, VIOLET (5) Tarker's Mills piano teacher. In Reverend Lowe's dream, she changed in to a werewolf.

THE MANCHESTERS (10) They were on Marty's Halloween trick-or-treat route.

MCCUNE, ARLENE (6) Alfie Knopfler lost his virginity to Arlene. At the time he was killed, Arlene was Arlene Bessey, and was married to a successful Bangor lawyer.

McCUTCHEON, MAC (12) Uncle Al's friend. Mac melted down Marty's confirmation spoon to make the two silver bullets.

MILLER, MRS. (11) The Reverend Lowe's housekeeper.

THE MILLIKENS (10) They were on Marty's Halloween trick-or-treat route.

MOTHER NATURE (3) According to Milt Sturmfuller, she had pruned some power lines out by Tarker Brook.

NEARY, CONSTABLE LANDER (2) Tarker's Mills town constable. If he wasn't around, small boys would torment Stella Randolph, chanting "Fatty-Fatty-Two-By-Four." He was the werewolf's eighth victim.

NEARY, JOAN (3) The constable's wife. She suspected the terror of Donna Lee Sturmfuller.

NEARY, MRS. (8) Constable Neary's mother. Neary said he would have believed his own mother was the killer before he would believe it was the guy wearing the eyepatch – the Reverend Lowe.

O'NEIL, PUCKY (9) Owner of O'Neil's Gulf Station. Pucky brained a tourist with the gas pump nozzle after the guy gave him lip about the price of gas.

PARKER, MRS. (12) Ollie's wife. She told Delia Burney that Ollie was a new man after losing twenty pounds.

PARKER, OLLIE (3) Fat grammar school teacher. He eventually became the principal. Ollie was diagnosed as an acute hypertensive when he had a nosebleed that would not stop. The doctor told him him to lose forty pounds, and he actually managed to lose twenty.

PELKY, STAN (8) Barber. He owned Stan's Barber Shop.

THE QUINNS (10) They were on Marty's Halloween trick-or-treat route.

RANDOLPH, STELLA (2) Overweight virgin who was the second victim of the werewolf.

THE RANDOLPHS (10) They were on Marty's Halloween trick-or-treat route.

RAY (6) Alfie Knopfler's nephew. He liked "The Incredible Hulk."

ROBERTSON, BILLY (4) Proprietor and bartender of the pub.

SCOTT, WILLARD (9) Weatherman on "The Today Show."

THE STATE POLICE (8) They took Marty's deposition after he was attacked by the werewolf.

STURMFULLER, DONNA LEE (3) Milt's wife. She had been married to Milt for twelve years, and had lived in terror of her husband the entire time. He beat her. After Milt was killed by the werewolf, Donna Lee moved out of town. Some said to Boston, some said to Los Angeles.

STURMFULLER, MILT (3) Tarker's Mills' town librarian. He beat his wife. He was also the November victim of the werewolf. The wolf ripped his head off.

TELLINGHAM, MATTY (4) He had a cow-pond.

TENNISON, RITA (11) A B-girl Milt Sturmfuller had been seeing. She gave Milt herpes, which he then passed on to Donna Lee.

THE THREE HUNDRED (5) In Reverend Lowe's dream, all 300 of his congregation changed into werewolves.

THE TOURIST (9) An unnamed guy from New Jersey who was brained with a gas pump nozzle by Pucky O'Neil. He needed four stitches in the upper lip.

THE WEALTHY SUMMER RESIDENT Unnamed summer resident who left the town library a bequest in his will

THE WEREWOLF'S VICTIMS The monthly toll went as follows:

1. (January) Arnie Westrum.
2. (February) Stella Randolph.
3. (March) An unnamed victim.
4. (April) Brady Kincaid.
5. (May) Clyde Corliss.
6. (June) Alfie Knopfler.
7. (July) No victim. (There was one failed attempt to kill Marty Coslaw).
8. (August) Lander Neary.
9. (September) Nine sow and two boars.
10. (October) Four deer.
11. (November) Milt Sturmfuller.
12. (December) The Reverend Lester Lowe.

WESTRUM, ARNIE (1) Flagman on the GS&WM Railroad. The werewolf's first victim.

WOMAN (12) An unnamed woman who tried to make a go of the Corner Bookshop, but failed.

WRIGHTSON, CHRIS (4) Biggest drunk in Tarker's Mills. In April, he threw his "Great Spring Drunk."

YODA (10) Marty's Halloween costume.

ZINNEMAN, ALICE (9) Elmer's wife. She was almost pretty when Elmer married her in 1947, when she was sixteen.

ZINNEMAN, ELMER (9) Owner of a farm on Stage Road, and owner of the nine sows and two boars that were the werewolf's September victims.

ZINNEMAN, PETE (9) Elmer's brother. He lived in Minot.

(20)
CYCLE OF THE WEREWOLF
Places

ALLIED CHEMICAL BUILDING (12) Marty blew away the Beast just as the ball dropped on this building on New Year's Eve.

BALL STREET (12) Street where Willie Harrington lived.

THE BIG WOODS (4) In April, the snow in the Big Woods had begun to melt.

BOSTON (12) It was rumored Donna Lee Sturmfuller moved there after Milt was killed.

BRIGHTON'S DRUG (5) Tarker's Mills' drugstore.

CENTER AVENUE (1) Street in Tarker's Mills that was deserted the night of the blizzard that forced even the snowplows to give up.

CHAT 'N CHEW (5) Diner on Main Street.

THE COMMONS (7) The park where the fireworks display was usually held.

CONGREGATIONAL CHURCH PARSONAGE (10) The parsonage was on Marty's Halloween trick-or-treat route. They gave out Snickers bars.

THE CORNER BOOKSHOP (12) Tarker's Mills' business that failed.

THE DRIFTWOOD MOTEL (11) Portland motel near the Portland-Westbrook line that Reverend Lowe checked into on the night he killed Milt Sturmfuller.

THE DRIVE-IN (6) Tarker's Mills theater.

FORTY ACRES FIELD (3) Hayfield owned by Old Man Hague.

GRACE BAPTIST CHURCH (4) Church ministered by Reverend Lester Lowe, who dabbled in lycanthropy (became a werewolf) in his spare time. It usually came around about once a month.

GS&WM RAILROAD SIGNAL SHACK (1) The shack where Arnie Westrum worked, and where he was killed by the werewolf.

LAUREL STREET (3) Constable Neary and his wife Joan lived in an apartment on Laurel Street, Tarker's Mills.

LOS ANGELES (12) It was rumored Donna Lee Sturmfuller moved there after Milt was killed.

MAIN STREET (3) It was coated with ice during the March blizzard.

MARKET BASKET (6) Tarker's Mills market. The night he was killed, Arnie Knopfler was thinking of getting a six-pack from the Basket.

MINOT (9) Town where Pete Zinneman lived.

NEW JERSEY (9) The state the tourist came from.

O'NEIL'S GULF STATION (9) Station on Town Road owned by Pucky O'Neil.

PORTLAND (11) Reverend Lowe drove to Portland, and ended up killing Milt Sturmfuller.

PORTLAND GENERAL HOSPITAL EMERGENCY ROOM (9) Hospital where Donna Lee Sturmfuller was taken after Milt beat her. He beat her because there was some dried egg on his clean dish.

STAN'S BARBER SHOP (8) Shop owned by Stan Pelky. In this shop, Constable Neary admitted he thought the Full Moon Killer might be a werewolf.

SUNSHINE HILL CEMETERY (11) Reverend Lowe remembered picking flowers by this cemetery. They all turned black. He wondered if this was when his lycanthropic condition began.

TARKER'S BROOK (3) During the March blizzard, Mother Nature knocked down some power lines out by Tarker's Brook.

TARKER'S MILLS, MAINE (1) The setting for *Cycle of the Werewolf*.

TARKER'S MILLS SET 'N SEW (2) Business run by Stella Randolph.

TARKER'S STREAM (4) Brady Kincaid used to fish there.

TOWN ROAD (9) The road where O'Neil's Gulf Station was located.

VIET NAM (12) Uncle Al fought there.

WRIGHT'S HILL (7) The area in town where all the kids sledded.

(20)
CYCLE OF THE WEREWOLF
Things

"THE BEAST WALKS AMONG US" (5) The name of the sermon Reverend Lowe dreamt he gave on Homecoming Sunday. He dreamt this the night before.

THE BEAST'S LEFT EYE (8) Marty put it out with a firecracker, and there was only one person in Tarker's Mills sporting an eyepatch after that night: Reverend Lester Lowe.

BICYCLE CARDS (1) The cards Arnie Westrum was using to play Last Man Out Solitaire on the January night he was killed by the werewolf.

THE "BIG PAL" VOICE (7) The voice Marty's dad used when he was with Marty.

BUSCH (8) The beer Lander Neary drank.

CAMELS (1) Arnie Westrum's cigarettes.

"CHILD'S RIME" The "30 days hath September" rhyme. [NOTE: King used the rhyme as one of the epigraphs to *Cycle of the Werewolf*.]

THE CHOIR (4) Grace Baptist Church choir. Elsie Fournier sang in it.

CHUNKY BARS (10) They were given out for Halloween at the Baptist parsonage.

COLT WOODSMAN (12) The .38 caliber gun that Uncle Al gave to Marty on New Year's Eve. It was loaded with two silver bullets.

"THE CYCLE OF THE WEREWOLF" (1) With Arnie Westrum's death in January, it had begun.

"A DARK PLACE" (3) According to Stephen King, "[Tarker's Mills] can be a dark place."

"DICK CLARK'S ROCKIN' NEW YEAR'S EVE" (12) TV show the Coslaw's watched.

DODGE PICKUP (8) Constable Neary was sitting in his pickup when the werewolf got him.

"FATTY-FATTY-TWO-BY-FOUR" (2) Small boys would taunt Stella Randolph with this name.

THE FIRST NOTE (11) The first note Marty sent to Reverend Lowe said: "I know who you are."

A FISHBOWL OF CANDY CORN (10) The candy given out for Halloween at the pub.

.45 [sic?] MAGNUM (12) Uncle Al's gun.

FOUR DEER (10) The Werewolf's October kill.

FOUR STITCHES IN THE UPPER LIP (9) After Pucky O'Neil slammed a New Jersey tourist in the mouth with a gas pump nozzle, the guy needed four stitches in his upper lip.

THE FOURTH NOTE (11) The fourth and final note Marty sent to Reverend Lowe said: "Why don't you kill yourself?"

THE FOURTH OF JULY (7) The year of the killings, Tarker's Mills cancelled the Fourth's fireworks displays.

GAS PUMP NOZZLE (9) "Weapon" used by Pucky O'Neil on a tourist after the guy gave him some lip about the price of gas. The tourist needed four stitches in the upper lip.

THE GREAT SPRING DRUNK (4) April event which had Chris Wrightson as the only participant.

GS&WM RAILROAD (1) Railroad that Arnie Westrum worked for as a flagman. He sat alone in a signal shack, nine miles outside of town.

"A HARLEQUIN ROMANCE" (2) Stella Randolph believed love would be like a Harlequin romance.

HOMECOMING SUNDAY (4) Sunday in May that used to be called "Old Home Sunday."

"THE INCREDIBLE HULK" (6) TV show favored by Alfie Knopfler's nephew, Ray.

THE LAST BLIZZARD (3) A March storm that was the last of the year.

LAST MAN OUT SOLITAIRE (1) Card game Arnie Westrum was playing the January night he was killed by the werewolf.

"LIKE DYING" (2) As Stella Randolph was dying at the hands of the werewolf, she thought to herself that "love was like dying."

"LOVER" (2) When the werewolf came to Stella Randolph's window, she said "Lover."

MARTY'S CONFIRMATION SPOON (12) The spoon that Mac McCutcheon melted down to make two silver bullets.

MARTY'S FIREWORKS (7) Uncle Al brought Marty Twizzers, bottle-rockets, Roman candles, and Black Cat firecrackers.

MARTY'S NOTES TO REVEREND LOWE:

The First Note: "I know who you are."

The Second Note: "If you are a man of God, get out of town.
  Go someplace where there are animals for you to kill but
  no people."
The Third Note: "End it."
The Fourth Note: "Why don't you kill yourself?"

MOONLIGHT (6) The last thing Arnie Knopfler saw before he was
  killed by the werewolf. The wolf ripped open his back.
NEARY'S GRADES (8) When he was in high school, Lander Neary
  got some C's and not a few D's.
NINE SOWS AND TWO BOARS (9) Elmer Zinneman's pigs.
  They were killed in September by the werewolf.
1947 (9) The year Elmer and Alice Zimmeman were married. Alice
  was sixteen.
OLD HOME SUNDAY (5) Sunday in May that was now called
  Homecoming Sunday.
"OMENS OF EVIL" (1) Just before Arnie Westrum was killed by
  the werewolf, he thought, "This has been a bad season in Tarker's
  Mills; there have been omens of evil on the land."
PICK (1) Arnie tried to defend himself against the werewolf with
  a pick. He got in one swing.
***READER'S DIGEST* JOKES** (3) Milt Sturmfuller liked the jokes
  in *Reader's Digest,* specifically the "Life in These United States"
  and "Humor in Uniform" columns.
THE REVEREND LOWE'S ADDRESS (11) The Reverend Lowe,
  Baptist Parsonage, Tarker's Mills, Maine 04491.
THE SECOND NOTE (11) The second note Marty sent to
  Reverend Lowe said: "If you are a man of God, get out of town. Go
  someplace where there are animals for you to kill but no people."
SENIOR CITIZENS' CLUB NATURE OUTINGS (1) They were
  reported in the weekly paper.
SEPTEMBER 21 (9) Willard Scott said that a foot of snow fell in
  the Canadian Rockies on September 21. September 21 is Stephen
  King's (and Carrie White's) birthday.
A SIX-PACK (6) The night Arnie Knopfler was killed, he was
  thinking about closing early, getting a six-pack, and catching the
  second picture at the drive-in.
SNICKERS BARS (10) They were given out at the Congregational
  Church parsonage on Halloween.
"SOMETHING INHUMAN" (1) In January, "[s]omething inhu-
  man has come to Tarker's Mills. It is the werewolf."
"THE SONG OF SOLOMON" (4) Reverend Lowe read from "The
  Song of Solomon" the day he gave a sermon entitled "The Spring
  of the Lord's Love."
"THE SPRING OF THE LORD'S LOVE" (4) A sermon given by
  Reverend Lowe.
TARKER'S MILLS TIGERS (8) The football team Lander Neary
  played on when he was in high school.
THE THIRD NOTE (11) The third note Marty sent to Reverend
  Lowe said: "End it."
TWELVE YEARS (3) The length of time Donna Lee and Milt
  Sturmfuller had been married.
TWENTY VALENTINES (2) Stella received twenty valentines,
  including cards from Paul Newman, Robert Redford, John Tra-
  volta, and Ace Frehy from KISS. She sent them all to herself.
TWO SILVER BULLETS (12) The bullets Marty Coslaw used to
  kill the werewolf.
A VULTURE KITE (4) Brady Kincaid got one for his birthday. he
  stayed out too long flying it, and the Werewolf got him.
A WHEELCHAIR (3) Marty Coslaw had a battery-powered
  electric wheelchair.

SKELETON CREW

DEDICATION

This book is for
Arthur and Joyce Greene

CONTENTS PAGE

BOOK BREAKDOWN

[NOTE: *Skeleton Crew* consists of an Introduction, twenty
short stories, two poems, and a closing section titled
"Notes." None of the short stories are broken into sections
with the exception of the novella "The Mist," which is
detailed below. See the sections on the individual *Skeleton Crew* stories in Part 5 of this volume for more details.
—sjs]

"The Mist"
  I.   The Coming of the Storm.
  II.   After the Storm.
        Norton.
        A Trip To Town.
  III. The Coming of the Mist.
  IV.   The Storage Area.
        Problems with the Generators.
        What Happened to the Bag-Boy.
  V.   An Argument with Norton.
        A Discussion Near the Beer Cooler.
        Verification.

(21a)
SKELETON CREW
"The Mist"
People

THE AZTECS Amanda Dumfries told David that the Aztecs believed in human sacrifice.

THE BEEFY GUY A man who ran out into The Mist began shrieking, and a beefy guy went out to rescue him. Neither came back.

THE BESPECTACLED MAN A man trapped in the supermarket thought that the enormous thud they experienced was an earthquake.

BIBBER, AGGIE The area's resident "necrologist." She told Steffy Drayton that Brent Norton's wife had died of cancer.

THE BIBBERS They owned the property to the left of the Draytons.

BILL GIOSTI'S NIECE She worked for the Continental Phone Company.

THE BLONDE WOMAN One of The Mist's supermarket prisoners. She had a daughter named Wanda, who was eight, and a young son named Victor.

BROWN, BUD One of the managers of the Federal Foods supermarket. (The other was Ollie Weeks.)

THE CALIFORNIA EXECUTIVE The man who bought David's painting, "Beans and False Perspective," for $2,500.

CARMODY, MRS. A religious fanatic who owned the Bridgton Antiquary. She saw The Mist as a sign of the apocalypse, or a punishment from God. Her thinking was that a human sacrifice would solve things nicely.

A CHUBBY BOY A boy of about twenty who was one of "Norton's people." [NOTE: See the entry THE TEN MEMBERS OF THE FLAT EARTH SOCIETY.]

CLAPHAM, MRS. One of the supermarket prisoners. She was trampled.

CORNELL, AMBROSE Supermarket prisoner who had a shotgun in the trunk of his car.

De GAULLE, CHARLES David thought that Bud Brown fancied himself the "Charles deGaulle of the supermarket world."

DRAYTON, ANDREW David's father. He was a famous artist. In 1938, his summer home was destroyed by a summer storm.

DRAYTON, BILLY David and Steffy's five-year-old son. He accompanied his father on the ill-fated trip to the grocery store.

DRAYTON, DAVID Steff's husband; Billy's father. He was trapped in the supermarket with Billy. He eventually escaped the supermarket, and the last we saw him, he was on his way to Hartford. He was a commercial artist by trade.

DRAYTON, STEFFY Stephanie Stepanek Drayton. David's wife, Billy's mother. David never saw her again after he went to the supermarket with his father following the storm.

DUMFRIES, AMANDA Supermarket prisoner who produced a pistol (like a magic trick) from her pocketbook.

EAGLETON, BUDDY One of the Seven Who Went To The Pharmacy.

AN ELDERLY LADY An old lady who wore bifocals and was one of "Norton's people." [NOTE: See the entry THE TEN MEMBERS OF THE FLAT EARTH SOCIETY.]

ELLITCH, TOMMY Farmer. His barn was smashed flat by the storm.

ENTS Ancient sentient trees from J.R.R. Tolkien's *Lord of the Rings* saga. Dave Drayton thought that old trees reminded him of Ents.

THE FAT, LOCAL MAN He told everyone in the supermarket that there had once been an earthquake in Naples, Maine.

THE FAT, LOCAL MAN'S WIFE She contradicted her husband when he said that Naples, Maine, had had an earthquake. She insisted it was Casco.

THE FBI Billy Drayton asked his father why the FBI didn't come and rescue them.

FROVIN, JOHN LEE A mechanic at the Bridgton Texaco station.

GAULT, MR. A writer friend of David Drayton's. He lived in Otisfield.

GIOSTI, BILL The owner and operator of Giosti's Mobil Station in Casco Village.

GRONDIN, JIM Man who worked for the Bridgton town road department.

HARTGEN, VINCENT One of David Drayton's teachers at the University of Maine.

HATLEN, MIKE Area selectman.

LAFLEUR, MYRON A friend of Jim, the bag boy.

LAWLESS, JANINE The Drayton's mail carrier.

A MAN WEARING BLUE JEANS AND A CAP A man who was one of "Norton's people." [NOTE: See the entry THE TEN MEMBERS OF THE FLAT EARTH SOCIETY.]

THE MAN WITH NO HEAD David and his expedition to the drugstore found a man with no head lying in the doorway.

THE MARTINS The Draytons' Long Lake neighbors. Their dock washed up on the rock breakwater near the Draytons' house.

McALLISTER, VICTOR A friend of Billy Drayton's.

THE McKEONS Their restored Dutch Colonial house was swallowed by The Mist.

McVEY, MR. The Federal Foods Supermarket butcher.

MICHAELSON, BEN One of the people Ollie Weeks had heard "stuff" from about the Arrowhead Project.

MILLER, DAN Man trapped in the supermarket. He was from Lynn, Massachusetts, and had a house on Highland Lake. He drove a blue Chevy pick-up.

MUEHLER, DICK Dave Drayton's insurance agent.

NEARY, MRS. Billy Drayton's teacher.

NORM One of the bag boys at the Federal Foods Supermarket. He was grabbed by a tentacle when he went outside the supermarket.

NORTON, BRENT The Draytons' obnoxious neighbor. He went with David and Billy to town after the storm.

NORTON, CARLA Brent Norton's wife. She had died of cancer.

O'BRIEN, WILLY A visual-effects specialist.

THE OLD GEEZER An unnamed old guy who ran a second-hand shop near Jon's Restaurant in Bridgton.

OLLIE WEEK'S SISTER She lived in Naples, and had a one-year-old daughter.

OLLIE'S NIECE Ollie's sister's one-year-old daughter. They lived in Naples.

PAULINE Jim Grondin's sister.

REPPLER, HILDA Third-grade teacher, and one of the Seven Who Went To The Pharmacy.

REUBEN, UNCLE David's uncle. David remembered Uncle Reuben diving into the lake with all his clothes on when David was a boy.

ROBARDS, JUSTINE One of the people Ollie Weeks had heard "stuff" from about the Arrowhead Project.

SALLY A checkout girl at the Federal Foods Supermarket.

THE SCREAMER When The Mist first appeared, a woman in Federal Foods screamed.

THE SEVEN WHO WENT TO THE PHARMACY Ollie Weeks, Dan Miller, Mike Hatlen, Jim Grondin, Buddy Eagleton, David Drayton, and Hilda Reppler.

THE SHRIEKER A man who ran out into The Mist. The people in the supermarket heard him shrieking, and a beefy guy went out to rescue him. Neither came back.

SIMMS, ARNIE One of the supermarket prisoners. At one point, he heard things moving around outside.

THE SMALL, NEAT MAN The man who slapped Mrs. Carmody across the face when she started talking about a "blood sacrifice."

SMALLEY, TOM Supermarket prisoner. He manned one of the loopholes.

THE STATE POLICE Billy Drayton asked his father why the state police didn't come and rescue them.

STEPANEK Steffy Drayton's maiden name.

THE SWELTERING WOMAN IN THE PURPLE SUNSUIT She told David that none of the pay phones in the shopping center were working.

TATTINGER, LOU The man who ran the Pine Tree car wash.

THE TEN MEMBERS OF THE FLAT-EARTH SOCIETY There were ten people in the supermarket who refused to believe that there were monsters in The Mist. David dubbed them "The Flat Earth Society," named after the group that sincerely believes that the earth is actually flat. This group was headed by Brent Norton.

TOCHAI, NICK One of the people Ollie Weeks had heard "stuff" from about the Arrowhead Project.

TRUMBULL, DOUGLAS A visual-effects specialist.

TURMAN, ALAN Mrs. Turman's husband.

TURMAN, HATTIE A woman who sometimes babysat for Billy Drayton. Her husband's name was Alan.

THE TWO SIXTEEN-YEAR-OLD GIRLS Two girls in the supermarket who wore "Camp Woodlands" t-shirts.

VANNERMAN, HANK Supermarket prisoner who claimed that all the bugs and birds outside the store were gone.

VICTOR The blonde woman's young son.

WALTER One of the supermarket prisoners. At one point he heard things moving around outside.

WANDA The blonde woman's eight-year-old daughter.

WEEKS, OLLIE One of the managers of the Federal Foods Supermarket. (The other was Bud Brown.) Ollie was a bachelor who lived in a "nice, little house" up by Highland Lake, and drank at the bar at Pleasant Mountain.

A YOUNG GIRL A girl who was one of "Norton's people." [NOTE: See the entry THE TEN MEMBERS OF THE FLAT EARTH SOCIETY.]

(21a)

SKELETON CREW
"The Mist"
Places

AUBURN NOVELTY SHOP The shop where Billy Drayton bought a set of wind-up chattering teeth.

BOLSTER'S MILLS During the summer thunderstorm, David thought it was probably also raining in Bolster's Mills and Norway.

BRIDGTON The location of the Federal Foods Supermarket where the people were trapped by The Mist.

THE BRIDGTON ANTIQUARY A junk shop owned and operated by Mrs. Carmody.

THE BRIDGTON PHARMACY The drugstore next to the Federal Foods Supermarket.

THE BRIDGTON TEXACO STATION The service station where John Lee Frovin worked.

THE BROOKSIDE THEATER The theater where Andrew Drayton took David to see "Moby Dick," starring Gregory Peck.

CASCO Maine town that had an earthquake, according to the fat, local man's wife. (He insisted it was Naples, not Casco.)

CASCO VILLAGE Bill Giosti owned and operated a Mobil station in Casco Village.

THE CONTINENTAL PHONE COMPANY The company Bill Giosti's niece worked for.

DAIRY QUEEN Shake cups from Dairy Queen littered the Federal Foods parking lot.

THE DRAYTON SANDY BEACH In 1941, David's father had six dumptrucks of beach sand brought in to create his own beach on Long Lake. He paid eighty dollars.

THE ENGLISH BEDLAM David thought that the scene in the Federal Foods Supermarket resembled the old English hospital for the insane, Bedlam.

THE FEDERAL FOODS SUPERMARKET The grocery store where everyone was trapped by The Mist.

FRYEBURG FAIR David had won the kewpie doll he found in the cabinet at the Fryeburg Fair.

GIOSTI'S MOBIL STATION A service station in Casco Village owned and operated by Bill Giosti.

HARTFORD David's post-escape destination.

HIGHLAND LAKE Ollie Weeks lived in "a nice, little house up by Highland Lake."

HOWARD JOHNSON'S A restaurant near Exit 3 off the Maine Turnpike where David wrote down the story of The Mist. (He used HoJo stationery.)

JON'S RESTAURANT Bridgton restaurant near a second-hand shop.

KANSAS ROAD The road in front of the Draytons' house. It led to Bridgton. When The Mist arrived, it came from Kansas Road to the entrance of the shopping center.

LONG LAKE The area of Maine where the Draytons lived.

LYNN, MASSACHUSETTS Dan Miller was from Lynn.

MADAME TUSSAUD'S Wax museum.

NAPLES A town in Maine that had once had an earthquake, according to the fat, local man. His wife insisted it was Casco.

NAPLES MARINA The marina where David's boat was being repaired.

NEW JERSEY The state where Brent Norton lived. (He summered at Long Lake.)

THE NORGE WASHATERIA A laundromat in the shopping center.

NORTH WINDHAM One of the towns where a Federal Foods Supermarket was located.

NORWAY During the summer thunderstorm, David thought it was probably also raining in Bolster's Mills and Norway.

NORWAY, MAINE The town where the Shop-and-Save was located.

OLD SHAYMORE ROAD It ran along the eastern side of the Arrowhead Project's land for about a mile or so.

OTISFIELD The town where Gault lived.

THE PINE TREE CAR WASH The car wash run by Lou Tattinger.

PLEASANT MOUNTAIN Ollie Weeks drank in a bar at Pleasant Mountain.

PORTLAND One of the towns where a Federal Foods Supermarket was located.

PORTLAND The city where the National Weather Service was located.

PORTLAND ROAD The road where Central Maine Power was located.

ROUTE 302 After David escaped from Federal Foods, he took Route 302 towards Portland. The Naples Causeway was still intact.

ROUTES 117 AND 302 The roads visible through the front window of the Federal Foods Supermarket.

RUMFORD The old geezer thought that The Mist came from the mills at Rumford and South Paris.

THE SACO RIVER On his way to Portland, David crossed the Saco

River.

SAN LUIS OBISPO, CALIFORNIA The home of the executive who bought David's painting, "Beans and False Perspective."

A SECOND-HAND SHOP Shop run by "an old geezer." The shop was near Jon's Restaurant in Bridgton.

SHAYMORE The town where the Arrowhead Project was located. Shaymore bordered on Stoneham.

THE SHOP-AND-SAVE A grocery store in Norway, Maine.

THE SHOPPING CENTER The center where the Norge Washateria, the Bridgton Pharmacy, and the Federal Foods Supermarket were located.

SOUTH PARIS The old geezer thought that The Mist came from the mills at Rumford and South Paris.

THE SPORTMAN'S EXCHANGE Sporting goods shop on Main Street in Bridgton.

STONEHAM Shaymore bordered on Stoneham.

TOWN ROAD DEPARTMENT Bridgton public works department. Jim worked for the department.

THE UNIVERSITY OF MAINE The university David and Steffy Drayton had attended. David had first seen Steffy at the school, biking across the mall. [NOTE: The University of Maine is both Stephen and Tabitha King's alma mater, and Tabitha's sister's name is Stephanie. See my interview with Stephanie Leonard in this volume.]

VALUE HOUSE The store where David Drayton bought his McCullough chainsaw.

THE VICKI-LINN CAMPGROUND A campground near the Drayton's property. After the storm, a power pole had fallen across the road near the campground.

(21a)
SKELETON CREW
"The Mist"
Things

THE ARROWHEAD PROJECT A mysterious government project that some people thought involved shooting atoms into the air. Others hypothesized that they were working on shale oil, or that it was an agricultural station. Many people held the Arrowhead Project responsible for The Mist, and for what happened after.

"BEANS AND FALSE PERSPECTIVE" David once painted a picture called "Beans and False Perspective" that showed the Federal Supermarket building and a line of Campbells beans cans in the parking lot. He ended up selling it to an executive from San Luis Obispo for $2,500.

BLACK FLAG BUG SPRAY The "weapon" Hilda Reppler carried on the trip to the pharmacy, along with a Spaulding "Jimmy Connors" tennis racket.

THE BLACK SPRING OF 1888 "[I]f the spring is cold enough, the ice on the lakes will eventually turn as black as a rotted tooth." Mrs. Carmody loved to tell this story, although it wasn't that rare an occurence.

A BLUE CHEVY PICKUP Dan Miller's truck.

BUD Beer.

CAMP WOODLANDS T-SHIRTS The t-shirts worn by two sixteen-year-old girls in the supermarket.

CENTRAL MAINE POWER (CMP) The power company that serviced the Drayton's Long Lake house.

CHRIS-CRAFT A sixty-foot boat David's father once owned.

"CHRISTINE STANDING ALONE" A painting by David's father Andrew. It hung in the White House.

COKE The soda that was on the shopping list that Steff gave to David.

COLT .45 One of the guns Ollie Weeks used for target shooting.

DAVY CROCKETT BUBBLEGUM CARDS When David was a boy, his father would take him into Bridgton where David would ogle the bubblegum cards through the glass showcase in a candy shop.

DELCO FLASHLIGHT David's flashlight.

DELSEY TOILET PAPER The tentacles grabbed the Pepsi and the Delsey toilet paper when they attacked the loading dock.

DINGO BOOTS Jim Grondin's boots.

DRISTAN AND STAYFREE MINI-PADS Some of the items sold at the Bridgton Pharmacy.

AN EARTHQUAKE A bespectacled man trapped in the supermarket thought that the enormous thud they all heard ("as if the entire building had suddenly dropped three feet") was an earthquake.

EIGHTY DOLLARS The amount David's father paid to have six dumptrucks of beach sand brought in in 1941 to create his own sandy beach on Long Lake.

THE EPA They forbade installing sand beaches in 1980.

FISHER David Drayton's plow.

FM 92 One of the radio stations Billy tried to get on the Scout's radio as they headed into town after the storm.

FRISBIE David Drayton drew a girl playing Frisbee on a beach for the Golden Girl Shampoo ads.

GOLDEN GIRL SHAMPOO ADS The ads David drew. (He was a commercial artist, and this was one of his accounts.)

GREEN ACRES LAWN FOOD The people trapped in the supermarket tried to block the front windows with twenty-five-pound bags of Green Acres and Vigoro lawn food.

A GREEN CADILLAC A car that pulled out from a parking space as Dave drove through the shopping center.

HALLMARK A card company.

A HERSHEY BAR After the storm, Billy Drayton brought a Hershey bar to his father.

"HOPE" One of the two words David whispered into his son Billy's ear as he slept at the Howard Johnson's off the Maine Turnpike. The other was "Hartford."

JBQ A radio station that Steffy was able to pull in after the storm.

JULY 19 The night the worst heat wave in northern New England broke, and the western Maine region was inundated with vicious thunderstorms.

KEWPIE DOLL A doll David found in a cabinet in his house on Long Lake. The doll was made in Taiwan.

LANCER'S The wine that was on the shopping list that Steff gave to David.

LLAMA .25 One of the guns Ollie Weeks used for target shooting.

THE MARTINSES DOCK It washed up on the rock breakwater near the Drayton's house.

McCULLOUGH David's chain saw.

"MOBY DICK" A movie starring Gregory Peck. David's father had taken David to see it at the Brookside Theater.

THE MOTHER NATURE ENCYCLOPEDIA This book was the current give-away at the Federal Foods Supermarket.

THE NAPLES CAUSEWAY A bridge on Route 302 that was still intact after the storm.

THE NATIONAL WEATHER SERVICE Portland station. Before the storm, they were reporting temperatures of over a hundred degrees.

NCR CASH REGISTERS The cash registers in the Federal Foods Supermarket.

A *NEW YORKER* CARTOON David thought that Bud Brown looked like something out of a *New Yorker* cartoon.

1941 The year David's father had six dumptrucks of beach sand brought in to create his own sandy beach on Long Lake. He paid eighty dollars for the job and the sand was never moved.

A 1960 T-BIRD Norton's car. Its roof was bashed in by a falling tree during the storm.

1938 The year David's father's summer home was destroyed by a summer storm.

O'CEDAR Mops.

OISEAU DE MORT A gigantic scarlet bird in a dream David had.

OVER A HUNDRED DEGREES Before the storm, the National Weather Service at Portland was reporting Maine temperatures of over a hundred degrees.

PABST Beer.

"PARANOID PAY PHONES" The name Steffy called the public pay phones that always gave you a dial tone. You made your call first and then when someone picked up you were cut off until you put in your money.

PARLIAMENTS WITH A "ONE STEP AT A TIME" FILTER Mrs. Carmody's smoking regime.

PEPSI The tentacles grabbed the Pepsi and the Delsey toilet paper when they attacked the loading dock.

"PLEASE CHOOSE ANOTHER LANE" A sign on the conveyor belt of the closed checkouts in the Federal Foods Supermarket.

PURINA PUPPY CHOW Two dead "soldiers" lay under the Puppy Chow in the supermarket.

RAGU, PRINCE, AND PRIMA SALSA The jars of tomato sauce that splattered when the big insect creature that David set on fire sent them flying.

A RESTORED DUTCH COLONIAL The McKeon's house. It was swallowed by The Mist.

RIPPLE A cheap wine.

ROLAIDS The antacid Ollie Weeks always chewed.

SAAB One of David Drayton's cars.

A SAMSONITE SUITCASE Mrs. Carmody's purse looked like a small Samsonite suitcase.

SCHLITZ The beer Brent Norton bought at the Federal Foods Supermarket.

SCOUT David Drayton's truck.

SEARS CATALOGUE A catalogue David found in a cabinet in his Long Lake house.

$79.95 The Value House price of David's chainsaw. It was a McCullough.

SIX DUMPTRUCKS OF BEACH SAND In 1941, David's father had six dumptrucks of sand brought in to create his own sandy beach on Long Lake.

SNOWY BLEACH When Jim froze at the sight of tentacles grabbing Norm the bag boy on the supermarket loading dock, David threw a box of Snowy Bleach at Jim to snap him out of it.

SOMINEX AND NYTOL Sleeping tablets the people trapped in the supermarket cleaned off the shelves.

A SPAULDING "JIMMY CONNORS" TENNIS RACKET The "weapon" Hilda Reppler carried with her when she went to the pharmacy. She also carried a can of Black Flag bug spray.

SPECIAL K The cereal Billy Drayton ate for breakfast.

A SPIDERMAN COMIC BOOK David promised Billy a Spiderman comic book from the Bridgton Pharmacy.

SPIDERWEBS David and his expedition to the pharmacy found spiderwebs all over the store.

A STAR SAPPHIRE RING Ollie Weeks wore one on the little finger of his left hand.

STAR-CRUISER David Drayton's boat.

THE TAKEOFF OF A 747 David compared the wind of the big thunderstorm to a 747's takeoff.

A TENTACLE Norm the bag boy was grabbed by a tentacle when he went outside the supermarket.

"TENTACLES FROM PLANET X" The term Norton used to describe what carried off Norm the bag boy.

A TEXAS INSTRUMENT CALCULATOR The calculator Bud was using to total up purchases made at the Federal Foods Supermarket after the power went.

$3.59 The price of ladies' tops.

TUFFSKIN Billy Drayton's jeans.

UPS David shipped his painting "Beans and False Perspective" by UPS to the California executive who bought it.

V-8 JUICE The vegetable juice Mrs. Carmody drank while trapped in the supermarket.

VIGORO LAWN FOOD The people trapped in the supermarket tried to block the front windows with twenty-five-pound bags of Green Acres and Vigoro lawn food.

WBLM One of the radio stations Billy tried to get on the Scout's radio as they headed into town after the storm.

WIGY-FM One of the radio stations Billy tried to get on the Scout's radio as they headed into town after the storm.

"WINSTON" A sign on the conveyor belt of the closed checkouts in the Federal Foods Supermarket.

WJBQ-FM One of the radio stations Billy tried to get on the Scout's radio as they headed into town after the storm.

WOXO The local FM radio station.

ZIPPO The lighter Dan Miller used to light a torch.

◇◇◇

(21b)

SKELETON CREW

"Here There Be Tygers"

People

BILL One of the characters in the third-grade textbook *Roads to Everywhere*. He was at the rodeo.

BIRD, MISS Charles's third-grade teacher. She was eaten by a tiger in the boy's bathroom.

CHARLES A third-grader who needed to go to the bathroom. When he did, he came upon a tiger in the boy's bathroom at the Acorn Street grammar school.

GRIFFEN, KENNETH Kenny Griffen. One of Charles's third-grade classmates. He was eaten by the tiger in the boy's room.

KINNEY, MISS Another third-grade teacher (in addition to Miss Bird and Mrs. Trask) who taught at the Acorn Street grammar school. She was young, blonde, and bouncy.

MISS KINNEY'S BOYFRIEND He picked Miss Kinney up after school. He drove a blue Camaro.

"OFFICER FRIENDLY" A make-believe cop who told the Acorn Street grammar school students "Never Ride with Strangers."

SCOTT, CATHY One of Charles's third-grade classmates.

THE TIGER When Charles entered the boy's bathroom, he saw a tiger lying next to a urinal.

TRASK, MRS. Another third-grade teacher (in addition to Miss Bird and Miss Kinney) who taught at the Acorn Street grammar school. She was shaped like a Moorish pillow, and wore her hair in braids.

"WOODSY OWL" An owl who told the Acorn Street grammar school students "Give a Hoot, Don't Pollute" from a bulletin board.

(21b)

SKELETON CREW

"Here There Be Tygers"

Places

THE ACORN STREET GRAMMAR SCHOOL The school Charles attended. It had a tiger in the boy's bathroom.

BOLIVIA Miss Bird pointed out Bolivia to Charles's third-grade class.

THE BOY'S BATHROOM The Acorn Street grammar school boy's bathroom had two urinals, three toilet cubicles, and a tiger

A BULLETIN BOARD Woodsy Owl's home.

THE RODEO Bill, a character in *Roads to Everywhere*, was at the rodeo in the book.

STAR THEATER A theater downtown that had a stinking bathroom.

(21b)

SKELETON CREW

"Here There Be Tygers"

Things

A BLUE CAMARO Miss Kinney's boyfriend's car.

"GIVE A HOOT, DON'T POLLUTE" Woodsy Owl's message.

A MOORISH PILLOW Miss Trask was shaped like a Moorish pillow, and wore her hair in braids.

"NEVER RIDE WITH STRANGERS" Officer Friendly's message.

A NIBROC TOWEL DISPENSER The towel dispenser in the bathrooms at the Acorn Street grammar school.

ROADS TO EVERYWHERE One of the third grade textbooks.

THE THIRD GRADE The grade Charles was in. It was taught by Miss Bird.

TWO URINALS AND THREE TOILET CUBICLES The facilities in the Acorn Street grammar school's boy's bathroom.

◇◇◇

(21c)

SKELETON CREW
"The Monkey"
People

CULLIGAN, AMOS The Casco man who drove his Studebaker out onto the frozen Crystal Lake one winter and broke through the ice. He escaped just in time by swimming out of the driver's window.

CULTURE CLUB Boy George's band. Culture Club was on the cover of a *Rock Wave* magazine Dennis Shelburn read in the hotel room in Maine where the Shelburns were staying while back for Aunt Ida's funeral.

DAISY Uncle Will's dog. The monkey killed it by causing the dog to have explosive brain hemorrhages.

THE DESK CLERK When Hal needed a car to go get rid of the monkey in Crystal Lake (Terry and Dennis had the family car), he borrowed the motel desk clerk's AMC Gremlin using his Texas Instruments digital watch and a twenty-dollar bill as collateral.

IDA, AUNT Hal and Bill Shelburn's aunt. She was married to Will, and took over the raising of the two boys after Hal's mother died (was killed by the monkey) while at work.

THE ITALIAN RAGMAN The man who took all the junk from the Shelburns' house in Hartford after Hal's mother died. He even took the monkey...but it came back.

THE MANX CAT Aunt Ida's cat. It had ear mites. It was killed by a speeding car. The monkey did it.

MCCABE, JOHNNY Hal's best friend as a child. Johnny died when he fell from a treehouse and broke his neck. The monkey made Johnny fall.

MCCAFFERY, BEULAH One of Hal and Bill Shelburn's babysitters. She was shot by her boyfriend, Leonard White, during an argument over who would go out for Chinese food. The monkey did it.

MILLY Aunt Ida's best friend. She told Ida that Johnny McCabe had died falling from a treehouse.

MORIARTY, BETSY The reporter who wrote the Bridgton *News* article, "Mystery of the Dead Fish."

SHELBURN, BILL Hal's brother.

SHELBURN, COLETTE Bill Shelburn's wife.

SHELBURN, DENNIS Terry and Hal Shelburn's twelve-year-old son. He smoked grass, and was pissed that his father had gotten laid off and that the family had to move to Texas.

SHELBURN, HAL The owner of "the monkey," and the man who was finally (?) able to put an end to the toy's murderous influence. Hal was married to Terry and had two sons, Petey and Dennis.

SHELBURN, MR. Hal's and Bill's father. He was a navigator with the merchant marines who had disappeared when the boys were very young. [NOTE: Stephen King's father, Donald King, was a merchant mariner who abandoned King's mother, King, and his brother David when the boys were very young. See my interview with David King in this volume.]

SHELBURN, MRS. Hal's mother. She died of an embolism while getting a drink of water at Holmes Aircraft. The monkey did it.

SHELBURN, PETEY Hal and Terry Shelburn's son; Dennis's brother. Petey was with his father the day Hal threw the monkey in Crystal Lake.

SHELBURN, TERRY Hal's wife; Dennis and Petey's mother. After Hal got laid off by National Aerodyne, Terry got into a heavy Valium habit.

SILVERMAN, CHARLIE A childhood friend of Bill Shelburn's who was killed by a car on the Brook Street corner by a drunk driver. The monkey did it.

STUKEY, MRS. The woman from the helicopter plant who brought the news to Hal and Bill of their mother's death.

TREMONT, SALLY Beulah McCaffery's friend. She was shot by Beulah's boyfriend, Leonard White, and pronounced dead at Hartford Receiving Hospital.

WILL, UNCLE Hal and Bill Shelburn's uncle.

(21c)

SKELETON CREW
"The Monkey"
Places

ARNETTE, TEXAS The town in Texas where Hal Shelburn and his family lived. Their home was Texas Instrument company housing. [NOTE: Arnette is where Charles Campion "touched down" at Hapscomb's Texaco Station after he was infected by the Project Blue virus in both *The Stand* and *The Stand: The Complete & Uncut Edition* .]

THE BOATHOUSE The building in Maine behind Uncle Will's house where Hal got the rowboat he used to row out to the middle of Crystal Lake where he drowned the monkey.

THE BURDON'S BOATHOUSE A neighbors' boathouse that collaped when Hal and Bill were kids.

CALIFORNIA Before moving to Texas, Hal Shelburn and his family had lived in California. Hal had worked for National Aerodyne.

CASCO, MAINE The "home place" in Maine; the place where Hal's Uncle Will and Aunt Ida lived.

CRYSTAL LAKE The lake where Amos Culligan's Studebaker lay, and where Hal Shelburn drowned the monkey. The monkey got revenge by killing hundreds of fish in the lake.

FRESNO, CALIFORNIA The town where Hal Shelburn and his family had lived (in National Aerodyne company housing) before he was laid off by the company.

HARTFORD The Connecticut town where Hal and Bill Shelburn once lived with their mother.

HARTFORD RECEIVING HOSPITAL The hospital where Sally Tremont was pronounced dead.

HOLMES AIRCRAFT The company where Hal Shelburn's mother had worked as a secretary. The company was in Westville, Connecticut.

HONG KONG The monkey was made in Hong Kong.

MAUI On the day Hal first found the monkey while rummaging through junk in the Casco home place back closet, he also found a bunch of black rocks from Maui.

MILFORD The drunk driver who killed Charlie Silverman owned a candy store in Milford.

NATIONAL AERODYNE The California company where Hal Shelburn worked until he was laid off. He had to move to Texas to find a job as a software architect.

TEDDY'S A local store where Hal and Bill Shelburn bought popsicles.

TEXAS Hal Shelburn and his family moved to Texas after Hal got laid off by National Aerodyne in California. In Texas, Hal worked for Texas Instruments.

(21c)
SKELETON CREW
"The Monkey"
Things

AN AMC GREMLIN The motel desk clerk's car. Hal Shelburn "rented" it to go drown the monkey.

BARRON'S GUIDE TO NAVIGATION A twenty-volume set of navigation books Hal found in the back closet of the home place in Casco, Maine. They had been his father's.

"THE BEVERLY HILLBILLIES" A TV show Terry Shelburn watched in the Maine hotel room that the Shelburns were staying in while back in Maine for Aunt Ida's funeral.

A BILL BOYD AUTOGRAPHED PICTURE Bill Shelburn had one.

BLACK LABEL Uncle Will's beer of choice when fishing.

THE BOWLER FIGURINE On the day Hal first found the monkey while rummaging through junk in the Casco home place back closet, he also found a bowler figurine that said "YOU PICK A GIRL AND I'LL PICKADILLY."

THE BRIDGTON *NEWS* The newspaper that ran the article "Mystery of the Dead Fish."

BURMA SHAVE The shaving gear the Italian ragman used.

BUSTER BROWN Brand of Hal Shelburn's shoes as a child.

THE CHRISTMAS DECORATIONS When Aunt Ida sent Hal to the attic to get the Christmas decorations, Hal found the monkey...after he had earlier thrown it away.

A DELTA FLIGHT BAG The bag Hal Shelburn used to "bury" the monkey in the bottom of Crystal Lake.

THE EIFFEL TOWER GLASS GLOBE On the day Hal first found the monkey while rummaging through junk in the Casco home place back closet, he also found a glass globe with a miniature Eiffel Tower inside it.

ENVELOPES WITH FOREIGN STAMPS On the day Hal first found the monkey while rummaging through junk in the Casco home place back closet, he also found envelopes with foreign stamps inside.

FOREIGN COINS On the day Hal first found the monkey while rummaging through junk in the Casco home place back closet, he also found a bunch of foreign coins.

A GREYHOUND BUS Aunt Ida took Hal and Bill Shelburn to Maine on a Greyhound after their mother died.

A HUDSON HORNET The car driven by the drunk driver who killed Charlie Silverman.

A LASSIE COLORING BOOK When Hal first found the monkey, he placed it in his room on top of a Lassie coloring book.

"MADE IN HONG KONG" The legend stamped on the bottom of the monkey.

THE MONKEY A demonic wind-up toy that killed. [NOTE: Hal Shelburn should be credited with finally putting an end to the toy's malefic ways...but I kinda doubt that he truly succeeded. Don't you?]

MY STORY A magazine read by Beulah McCaffery.

"MYSTERY OF THE DEAD FISH" An article by Betsy Moriarty that appeared in the Bridgton *News* on October 24, 1980, that reported that "hundreds of dead fish were found floating belly-up on Crystal Lake" and that fish and game authorities were mystified. The monkey did it.

OCTOBER 24, 1980 The day that the article "Mystery of the Dead Fish" by Betsy Moriarty ran in the Bridgton *News*.

A PHILCO RADIO The radio the monkey knocked into the Italian ragman's bathtub while the guy was bathing. The shock killed him.

POLAND SPRINGS MINERAL WATER The type of water in the water cooler that broke when Hal's mother pulled it over while dying.

POPSICLES The frozen confection Hal and Bill Shelburn bought at Teddy's store when they were kids.

A RALSTON-PURINA CEREAL CARTON The box which contained the evil toy monkey, first in the back closet of the home place in Maine, and later in the house's attic.

RECORDS On the day Hal first found the monkey while rummaging through junk in the Casco home place back closet, he also found "funny records in foreign languages."

RED RYDER COWBOY BOOTS Charlie Silverman's boots.

REESE'S PEANUT BUTTER CUPS A favorite of Beulah McCaffery's.

ROCK WAVE A magazine Dennis Shelburn read. (Culture Club was on the cover.)

ROCKS FROM MAUI On the day Hal first found the monkey while rummaging through junk in the Casco home place back closet, he also found a bunch of black rocks from Maui.

A SAMSONITE The suitcase in which Hal Tremont locked up the monkey after he found it in the home place in Casco twenty years after he had thrown it down the well.

A STUDEBAKER Amos Culligan's car. He drove it out onto the frozen Crystal Lake one winter and broke through the ice. The car ended up at the bottom of the lake.

A TEXAS INTRUMENTS DIGITAL WATCH The watch Hal used as collateral to borrow the motel desk clerk's AMC Gremlin for the ride to Crystal Lake to drown the monkey.

"TWO KILLED IN APARTMENT SHOOT-OUT" The headline of the newspaper article that told of Beulah McCaffery's (19) and Sally Tremont's (20) deaths at the hands of Beulah's boyfriend Leonard White (25).

VALIUM After Hal got laid off by National Aerodyne and the family moved to Texas, his wife Terry got into a serious Valium habit.

A WISH-CUP Hal Shelburn's childhood milk cup.

❖❖❖

(21d)
SKELETON CREW
"Cain Rose Up"
People

ABEL Cain's brother. He was turned into Abelburgers by his brother.

BAILEY College student. He wanted Garrish's chemistry notes. Garrish thought "There was no future for Bailey. Bailey would marry a stupid girl and they would have stupid kids. Later on he would die of cancer or maybe renal failure."

THE BLOND COED Garrish's first victim. She wore jeans and a blue shell top, and she didn't know that there were microbes in her intestines, feeding, dividing, multiplying. Garrish blew her head off.

THE BLOND COED'S FATHER Garrish's third victim. He began to run away after his daughter and wife were shot by Garrish. Curt shot him in the back.

THE BLOND COED'S MOTHER Garrish's second victim. He shot her head and hand off with one shot.

BOGART, HUMPHREY Garrish had a huge blow-up of Bogart over his bed in his dorm room.

A BOY IN A MADRAS SHIRT After Garrish shot the blond coed, her mother and father, and Quinn; a boy in a madras short crouched down behind a bush. He wanted to run, but his legs were frozen.

BRODY, JIMMY College student. Rollins, the dorm floor counselor, sent Jimmy to the dean of men for a drinking offense.

CAIN Abel's brother. Cain had an idea God was a vegetarian. Abel knew better: If you don't eat the world, the world will eat you.

THE DEAN OF MEN College administrator. Rollins, the dorm floor counselor, sent Jimmy Brody to the dean for a drinking offense.

FRANE, RON Dorm resident. Rollins told him to turn down his stereo.

331

"STEVE ROSE UP"
Rick Hautala Remembers His First Time

They say we all remember our first time. Do you?

Rick Hautala went to college with Stephen King. "Steve Rose Up" is Rick's remembrance of the first time he read a Stephen King story. Anything else I could possibly say about the piece would only be superfluous to the essay itself, so I will shut up and allow Rick to recount for you *his* first time.

(Before I go, allow me to recommend the work of Mr. Hautala to you. No less that Stephen King himself "blurbed" Rick's first two novels *Moondeath* and *Moonbog*. Rick's other novels are *Night Stone, Little Brothers, Winter Wake,* and *Dead Voices.* Check him out. Okay. I'm done.) —**sjs**

"STEVE ROSE UP"
by Rick Hautala

I'm going to "date" myself, but I don't care. Anyone in my age group—that is, anyone who can no longer watch "thirtysomething" because of the age cut-off—has a few very sharp memories. We all know *exactly* where we were when we heard that President Kennedy had been assassinated. (I was in detention hall for goofing off in my sophomore French class.) We clearly remember when we heard the news that both Bobby Kennedy and Martin Luther King Jr. had been shot and killed. And, more recently, we have a perhaps too clear memory of where we were when we heard that John Lennon had been murdered. These memories are etched in our minds like harsh acid-bright lines. But for anyone who has enough of an interest in the work of Stephen King even to pick up a book titled *The Shape Under the Sheet: The Complete Stephen King Encyclopedia,* I'll bet there's one more event you can recall with a deep-bone shudder: the first time you experienced a story or novel by Stephen King.

Right?

Okay, maybe the exact time and place aren't there in your mind like the crackling voice of Walter Cronkite struggling to maintain his composure. You might not remember the time or day or the place precisely. Reading a novel or short story, after all, doesn't quite have the bombshell impact of hearing that someone you respected and admired has died. But I'll bet you haven't—and won't ever—forget how, as you first dove into Steve's work, you felt as if your whole sense of reality was being stretched and distorted like a long, sludgy string of taffy being pulled out to—and past—its limit.

Okay, so I've already hinted at my age; I'm just about as old as Stephen King. But there's a bit more to tell. You see, I was a freshman at the University of Maine in Orono in 1966, rooming on the third floor in a men's dormitory called Gannett Hall. (Most of the dorms at UMO are co-ed now. Damn! I always miss the fun!) Anyway, in the same dorm that same year, I think down on the second floor, was this other freshman. He was kinda strange looking, and he immediately stood out from the swirling mass of scared-looking freshmen (which I was) and cocky upperclassmen (which I guess I became) as we all crowded into the commons for our daily meals. This guy was...different; I saw *that* much right away.

Tall and, at least in my memory, hefty, he had thick black hair and wore eyeglasses that looked as thick as the bottom of a Coke bottle. He was always wearing faded jeans and a casual "frumpy"-looking shirt. In warmer weather, I seem to remember that he wore sandals or went barefoot. I have *no* idea when the beard first came because it, like the leaves on the trees in spring, seems to come and go overnight. Using the parlance of the 60s, he was "dressed down," like a Hippie, which was the "in" look at the time. If there were "designer jeans" back then, they sure as hell hadn't made it north of Boston. One thing I noticed about this guy was that he never seemed to interact with anyone; he didn't even seem to be checking out the bevy of co-eds. Being a compulsive reader myself, I also noticed that he was always standing in the lunch line with his face and concentration lost in reading. What was he reading? Nope. Not some textbook or scholarly magazine; he always had a tattered, wild 'n crazy-looking science fiction paperback. In my memory, it seemed as though every day, seven days a week, he had a different book at each meal, morning, noon, and night. I remember thinking time and again: *My God! That guy reads like a fiend!*

Little did I know...

Somehow or other, I found out this guy's name was Steve King and that he was majoring in English. Somehow, that fit. Anyone who read that much, I figured, sure as hell wasn't majoring in Chemical Engineering or Forestry!

Fade out—

Fade in—a year later: my sophomore year.

I had begun my college career as a Biology major with intentions of studying pre-med, so I thought. The problem was, I was a terrible student in biology and, especially, chemistry. (On the chemistry final, I scored a whopping 12 out of a possible 200 points.) I got onto the Dean's List both semesters of my first year at college all right, but it was the wrong Dean's list. It was a list of students who were *t-h-i-s* close to being asked to take a little vacation from school. With the specter of Vietnam breathing diesel fumes down my neck, I didn't think that promised me a very bright future. After barely hanging on for one more semester in biology, and figuring I'd always enjoyed reading, anyway (but certainly not three books a day!), I switched my major to English and began reading Shakespeare, Hawthorne, Hemingway, and the rest.

Also, for the first time, I became aware that the English majors were publishing a "literary" journal once every semester. The name seemed to change as often as the editor, but in the spring of 1968 (when Bobby Kennedy was unknowingly

approaching the receiving end of a Saturday night special), the magazine was called *Ubris*. (A year or so later the title changed to *Onan* and, considering the level of most of the writing, that seemed damned appropriate.) I was writing my own stuff at the time, but I didn't have any confidence in my work, so I never submitted anything to the student magazine. I did. however, buy a copy each semester, and I read most of 'em, too...as bad as most of the fiction and poetry was.

Rick Hautala
Photo courtesy Rick Hautala.

"How bad was it?" I hear Ed McMahon ask.

What is *any* college literary magazine like? It was full of half-baked character sketches trying to pass muster as short stories and rambling stream of semi-consciousness parading as poetry. I doubt student writing has changed much in the decades since then, but it was reading the first issue of *Ubris,* in the spring of 1968, that I came upon a little story entitled "Cain Rose Up." It started on page 33 and ended with a literal *bang* at the top of page 35. By the time that I finished reading that story, I knew I'd been *nailed!*

I'd just read my first Stephen King story!

Now I've never put a whole lot of faith in my critical abilities, even after earning an M.A. in English, but I knew one thing after I finished reading that story; this most definitely was *not* your run-of-the-mill student writing. I knew this story—and this King-fella—were somehow...different. In retrospect, I even remember wondering if maybe that story had been printed in a different typeface or in a different color ink because whatever it had going for it, it had the same "get-off-the-tracks-the-train's-comin'!" energy Steve brings to everything he writes. I don't think I was the only person back then in the spring of 1968 who started wondering what kind of mind could produce a story like this. But whereas I suspect most of the English department professors and students were freaked out by this piece and objected to its gruesome violence, I remember *loving* the impact of that story.

Everyone knows the story I'm talking about, right? The one where the kid finishes up his finals and then barricades himself in his dorm room, takes his rifle and scope, and methodically starts picking off people on the mall between the dorms. And maybe without even looking it up you remember that the woman's dorm across the way was called Carlton Memorial. (If you don't remember, I'm sure there's a reference to it somewhere here in *The Shape*...)

But you're wrong on this one; and if Steve Spignesi tells you it's Carlton Hall, then *he's* wrong, too!

I don't know what name Steve had in mind for the dorm from which the character Curt began firing, but I also know its real name.

It's Gannett Hall.

I knew from the way Steve described the scene outside Curt's dorm window that, sometime during his Freshman year, maybe many times, he'd been sitting by the window of his dorm room in Gannett Hall one floor below my own room and looking out across the mall to Androscoggin Hall. And at some moment during our freshman year, that wild imagination of his kicked into high gear. In a world where Texas Tower snipers and Lee Harvey Oswalds can shift the scales of reality in an instant that will make the evening news, Steve King, the sophomore English major, brought it all home to the University of Maine in Orono.

I love the story "Cain Rose Up" because, for the first time in my life, I *truly* experienced the magic of fiction making. Oh, sure—I'd read plenty of science fiction, fantasy, and horror stories, and I've loved a lot of 'em: Bradbury, Howard, Vonnegut, Burroughs, and Lovecraft in particular—but none of their stories ever hit me with the impact Steve's story had simply because, just a year before, I had been struggling to stay in college just like Curt so I wouldn't end up in Vietnam, where everyone seemed to be doing what Curt had done.

What Steve did, the magic he wove, was to take the intense pressure to stay in school that I and probably all but a handful of college freshman feel, and make the horror of it *live*. Sure, he's done that lots of times since in dozens of novels, stories, and movies. Reading *'Salem's Lot* a few years later honest-to-God made me sleep with a light on for a week or two. But I'm sure, no matter how many times it's happened since, every avid King reader vividly remembers the first time Steve did it to 'em. I feel privileged to have "discovered" this man's work long before the rest of the world did, and I'm sure as hell glad he's still doing it to us!

Copyright © 1990 Rick Hautala.
Reprinted by permission.

❖❖❖

RICK HAUTALA'S
5 FAVORITE STEPHEN KING WORKS

1. *The Dead Zone*
2. *'Salem's Lot*
3. *"The Body"*
4. *Cujo*
5. *Misery*

GARRISH, CURT College student who went on a shooting spree from his dorm window one day.

GARRISH, REVEREND Curt's father. He bought Garrish a .352 Magnum hunting rifle for Christmas one year.

GOD He told Cain to put on his boogie shoes.

HARRY THE BEAVER Curt Garrish's college friend. He had buck teeth, and wore a 69 t-shirt with a button on the front that said Howdy Doody was a pervert. Harry and Curt lived in the same dorm.

THE HOUSEMOTHER Curt Garrish's dorm housemother. She was a tall woman who looked like Rudolph Valentino.

THE IDIOT FROM THREE One of the students who lived in Garrish's dorm. He had hairy legs, and on the day Garrish began shooting people from his dorm window, the idiot and Quinn walked by Garrish tossing a softball back and forth.

A LITTLE FELLA WEARING HORN-RIMMED GLASSES One of the students who lived in Garrish's dorm. He was trying to grow a goatee, and he walked carrying his calculus book clutched to his chest like a bible.

PIG PEN Piggy. Garrish's dorm roommate. He was an English major.

"PIGGY" Pig Pen.

QUINN One of Garrish's classmates. He was Garrish's fourth victim. Garrish shot him in the neck as he ran across the mall, and he flew maybe twenty feet.

ROLLINS Garrish's dorm floor counselor. Rollins sent Jimmy Brody to the dean of men on account of a drinking offense.

(21d)
SKELETON CREW
"Cain Rose Up"
Places

CARLTON MEMORIAL The women's dorm. It was more popularly known as "the dog kennels." It was across the mall from Garrish's dorm. [Note: See the essay "Steve Rose Up," by Rick Hautala, in which Rick reveals the real-life University of Maine counterparts to the locales in "Cain Rose Up." Apparently, Carlton Memorial was actually Androscoggin Hall, and Garrish's dorm was Gannett Hall.]

THE CLOSET Garrish kept his .352 Magnum hunting rifle locked in the closet of his room.

THE DORM Garrish's dorm, and the site of his sniper attack from his room window.

GARRISH'S ROOM Curt Garrish began shooting people from his dorm room window on the day he took his last final.

THE MALL The area between Garrish's dorm and Carlton Memorial Hall. From his dorm window, Garrish shot people walking in the mall.

THE THIRD FLOOR The dorm floor that the "idiot" with the hairy legs lived on.

THE UNIVERSITY GUN STORAGE ROOM The room where Garrish had kept his .352 Magnum hunting rifle while he was on campus. Prior to his sniper attack, he had signed the gun out with a forged withdrawal slip.

(21d)
SKELETON CREW
"Cain Rose Up"
Things

BOOGIE SHOES After Cain killed his brother Abel, God told him to put on his boogie shoes.

A CALCULUS BOOK The little fella with horn-rimmed glasses carried his calculus book clutched to his chest like a bible.

A DRINKING OFFENSE Jimmy Brody was sent to the dean of men on account of a drinking offense.

A FORD WAGON Garrish pointed the sights of his rifle at a Ford wagon that was being unloaded in the mall between his dorm and Carlton Memorial Hall. The wagon belonged to the blond coed and her family.

"GOOD DRINK, GOOD MEAT, GOOD GOD, LET'S EAT!" The mantra Curt Garrish chanted as he shot people from his dorm window.

"HOWDY DOODY WAS A PERVERT" The button worn by Harry the Beaver.

MAY The month Curt Garrish started shooting people from his dorm window. He had just finished his finals.

***PLAYBOY* GATEFOLDS** The pinups in Garrish's room. They belonged to Pig Pen.

A RODIN'S "THE THINKER" POSTER A poster of "The Thinker" on a toilet was hung in Garrish's dorm room. It had been left there by Pig Pen.

A 69 T-SHIRT The t-shirt Harry the Beaver wore.

A .352 MAGNUM HUNTING RIFLE The gun Garrish had in his room. He used it to shoot people from his dorm window. Garrish's father, a Methodist minister, had bought it for him for Christmas. Garrish used Winchester ammo in the gun.

WINCHESTER AMMO The ammunition Garrish used in the .352 hunting rifle he used to pick off people from his dorm window.

✧✧✧

(21e)
SKELETON CREW
"Mrs. Todd's Shortcut"
People

THE AUCTIONEER An auctioneer who headed auctions in Gates Falls. Sometimes, before an auction, he would put the whiskey to himself.

BASCOMB, GEORGE George had a house that looked across Castle Lake at the mountains. Homer plowed his field when he was a boy of sixteen.

BRUGGER, HENRY In 1959, Dave Owens had once shot whitetails in Henry's backfield for food.

BUCKLAND, FRANKLIN Homer's brother.

BUCKLAND, HOMER The caretaker for the Todd family. He told Dave Owens the story of "Mrs. Todd's Shortcut."

BUCKLAND, MEGAN Homer's wife.

CAMBER, JOE The Castle Rock man who was killed by his own dog. It was a big St. Bernard that went rabid. [NOTE: See the section on *Cujo* in this volume.]

CORBRIDGE, ESTONIA The woman who found the Castle Rock textile man who shot himself. He still had the pistol in his hand.

DIANA The huntress who was supposed to drive the moon across the sky.

MEGAN BUCKLAND'S BROTHER He lived in New Hampshire.

MURRAY, PROFESSOR The University of Maine professor who validated the *Science Today* article that proved that no man could run a mile in under four minutes.

OWENS, DAVE The man who sat in front of Bell's Market and listened to Homer Buckland tell the story of Ophelia Todd.

THE SCOTTS Homer Buckland kept an eye on their house.

THE TEXTILE MAN A textile man from Amesbury shot himself. He was found by Estonia Corbridge.

TODD, MRS. Worth Todd's second wife. She drove a Jaguar.

TODD, OPHELIA Worth Todd's first wife. She loved to find shortcuts.

TODD, WORTH Worth owned a summer home on Castle Lake. His first wife was Ophelia Todd.

THE WOMAN A woman on the school committee who Ophelia Todd spoke to on the phone from Bangor.

(21e)
SKELETON CREW
"Mrs. Todd's Shortcut"
Places

ALTON'S PLANTATION Part of Ophelia Todd's shortest route to Bangor from Castle Lake.

AMESBURY The town where the textile man who shot himself lived.

BEAR ROAD Part of Ophelia Todd's shortest route to Bangor from Castle Lake.

BELL'S MARKET Castle Rock market.

BIG ANDERSON ROAD (BY SITES' CIDER MILL) Part of Ophelia Todd's shortest route to Bangor from Castle Lake.

BULL PINE ROAD Part of Ophelia Todd's shortest route to Bangor from Castle Lake.

CASTLE LAKE Castle Rock lake, and also an area of Castle Rock. Worth Todd had a summer home on Castle Lake.

CASTLE ROCK The Maine town where Worth Todd lived.

DENTON STREET Part of Ophelia Todd's shortest route to Bangor from Castle Lake.

THE DERRY HOSPITAL As part of Ophelia Todd's shortest route to Bangor from Castle Lake, you came out on Route 3 just past the Derry hospital. [NOTE: See the "Things" entry MRS. TODD'S SHORTCUTS TO BANGOR. Also see the section on *It* in this volume for more info (a *lot* more info!) on Derry, Maine.]

GATES FALLS The town where auctions took place.

KENNEBEC COUNTY Bog country.

LANDING ROAD Before her disappearance, Castle Rock residents would often see Ophelia Todd heading down Landing Road with a pickup full of kids for the summer swim program.

LEWISTON Passing through Lewiston was part of the route most people took to get to Bangor from Castle Rock.

MASSACHUSETTS While Homer was getting ready to tell the story of Ophelia Todd, a car with Massachusetts plates pulled up in front of Bell's Market for gas.

MECHANIC FALLS Passing through Mechanic Falls was part of the route most people took to get to Bangor from Castle Rock.

MOTORWAY A paved road that Ophelia Todd found in the middle of the Maine woods. It was a road to another dimension.

NEW HAMPSHIRE The state where Megan Buckland's brother lived.

OLD DERRY ROAD Part of Ophelia Todd's shortest route to Bangor from Castle Lake.

OLD DERRY ROAD Part of Ophelia Todd's second shortcut to Bangor from Castle Lake.

AN OLD LOGGER'S ROAD Part of Ophelia Todd's shortest route to Bangor from Castle Lake.

THE OLD TOWNHOUSE ROAD Part of Ophelia Todd's shortest route to Bangor from Castle Lake.

OLYMPUS In Greek mythology, Olympus is a mountain in Thessaly that is the abode of the Gods. Ophelia Todd went to Olympus.

PILOT'S GRILLE When Ophelia Todd took Homer Buckland to Bangor via her shortest shortcut, she said that they'd be having dinner at the Pilot's Grille in two hours and forty-five minutes or she'd buy him a bottle of Irish Mist.

RANGELY Homer Buckland remembered seeing mosquitoes as big as English sparrows in Rangely.

ROUTE 11 Part of the route most people took to get to Bangor from Castle Rock.

ROUTE 9 THROUGH CHINA LAKE, UNITY, AND HAVEN Part of Ophelia Todd's first (and longest) shortcut to Bangor from Castle Lake.

ROUTE 97 Part of Ophelia Todd's shortest route to Bangor from Castle Lake. Also, part of the route most people took to get to Bangor from Castle Rock.

ROUTE 106 Part of Ophelia Todd's shortest route to Bangor from Castle Lake.

ROUTE 3 Part of Ophelia Todd's shortest route to Bangor from Castle Lake.

ROUTE 2 The longest route to Bangor from Castle Lake.

ROUTE 219 Part of Ophelia Todd's second shortcut to Bangor from Castle Lake.

ROUTE 202 Part of Ophelia Todd's second shortcut to Bangor from Castle Lake.

ROUTE 202 TO AUGUSTA Part of Ophelia Todd's first (and longest) shortcut to Bangor from Castle Lake.

THE SLOAN LIBRARY Before her disappearance, Ophelia Todd worked to raise money for the library.

SPECKLED BIRD MOUNTAIN You had to cross Speckled Bird Mountain on 210 to get to 202 as part of Mrs. Todd's second shortcut to Bangor from Castle Lake.

STANHOUSE ROAD Part of Ophelia Todd's shortest route to Bangor from Castle Lake.

SUNSET BOULEVARD Homer Buckland thought that Ophelia Todd's Mercedes would look more at home on Sunset Boulevard than in the Maine woods.

TOWN ROAD #6 Part of Ophelia Todd's shortest route to Bangor from Castle Lake.

THE UNIVERSITY OF MAINE The University where Professor Murray taught.

VERMONT Homer Buckland went to live in Vermont after working for the Todds. (He really went to Olympus.)

(21e)
SKELETON CREW
"Mrs. Todd's Shortcut"
Things

APPALACHIAN TRAIL GUIDEBOOKS Ophelia Todd kept pages from the Rand-McNally Road Atlas and Appalachian Trail guidebooks in her glove compartment.

A BOTTLE OF IRISH MIST When Ophelia Todd took Homer Buckland to Bangor via her shortest shortcut, she said that they'd be having dinner at the Pilot's Grille in two hours and forty-five minutes or she'd buy him a bottle of Irish Mist.

A CADILLAC Worth Todd's car.

CHAMPAGNE The color of Ophelia Todd's Mercedes.

"HOLES IN THE MIDDLE OF THINGS" Homer told Dave Owens that there were holes in the middle of things – "right in the damn middle of things...." Ophelia Todd drove *through* one of those holes...right to Olympus.

A JAGUAR Worth Todd's second wife's car.

THE LONGEST ROUTE TO BANGOR The longest route to Bangor from Castle Rock was Route 2. It was 163.4 miles.

THE MASSACHUSETTS MOTOR REGISTRY They gave green license plates to any motorist who hadn't had an accident in two years. People with accidents had to have red ones.

A MERCEDES Ophelia Todd's car.

A MOBIL MAP The map on which Homer Buckland measured the miles to Bangor from Castle Rock by airplane.

MRS. TODD'S SHORTCUTS TO BANGOR In order of decreasing distance, Mrs. Todd favored these three routes:

1. (144.9 miles): Go to Mechanic Falls, Route 11 to Lewiston, Route 202 to Augusta, then up Route 9 through China Lake and Unity and Haven to Bangor.

2. (129.2 miles): Across Speckled Bird Mountain on 219 to 202 beyond Lewiston. Take Route 19, get around Augusta, then take the Old Derry Road into Bangor.

3. (116.4 miles): "You set out Route 97 and then cut up Denton Street to the Old Townhouse Road and that way you get around Castle Rock downtown but back to 97. Nine miles up

you can go an old logger's road a mile and a half to Town Road #6, which takes you to Big Anderson Road by Sites' Cider Mill. There's a cut-road the old timers call Bear Road, and that gets you to 219. Once you're on the far side of Speckled Bird Mountain you grab the Stanhouse Road, turn left onto the Bull Pine Road – there's a swampy patch there but you can spang right through it if you get up enough speed on the gravel – and so you come out on Route 106. 106 cuts through Alton's Plantation to the Old Derry Road – and there's two or three woods roads there that you follow and so come out on Route 3 just beyond Derry Hospital. From there it's only four miles to Route 2 in Etna, and so into Bangor."

THE NATIONAL ANTHEM Ophelia Todd liked to stay up at night watching TV until the national anthem came on.

1973 The year Ophelia Todd disappeared.

1923 The year the *Science Today* article appeared that proved that no man could run a mile in under four minutes.

OLYMPICS Ophelia Todd thought that someday, someone would run a two-minute mile in the Olympics.

144.9 MILES Ophelia Todd's longest route to Bangor from Castle Lake (of the three she used, all of which were shorter than the route most people used).

163.4 MILES The longest route to Bangor from Castle Rock was on Route 2. It was 163.4 miles.

116.4 MILES Ophelia Todd's shortest route to Bangor from Castle Lake.

129.2 MILES Ophelia Todd's second longest route to Bangor from Castle Lake (of the three she used, all of which were shorter than the route most people used).

A RAND-MCNALLY ROAD ATLAS Ophelia Todd kept pages from the Rand-McNally Road Atlas and Appalachian Trail guide-books in her glove compartment.

SCIENCE TODAY An article appeared in *Science Today* in 1923 that proved that no man could run a mile in under four minutes.

SEVENTY-NINE MILES The distance from Castle Rock to Bangor by airplane.

THE TYPICAL ROUTE FROM CASTLE LAKE TO BANGOR Route 97 to Mechanic Falls, then Route 11 to Lewiston, and then the Interstate to Bangor. This came to 156.4 miles. [NOTE: See the "Things" entry MRS. TODD'S SHORTCUTS TO BANGOR.]

000.0 Ophelia Todd would reset her odometer to 000.0 everytime she set out from Castle Lake to Bangor.

❖❖❖

(21f)
SKELETON CREW
"The Jaunt"
People

ARMED GUARDS Armed guards and a Jaunt attendant flanked the entranceway to the Blue Concourse terminal area sleep lounge.

THE AUTOMATED FEMALE ANNOUNCER The New York Port Authority Terminal announcer in the year 2037 was an automated female voice.

BUFFINGTON After Carune teleported his fingers, he wondered if he should call Carson in New Jersey or Buffington in Charlotte.

THE BUSINESSMAN While the Oates waited to Jaunt, a harried-looking businessman arrived just in time for his Jaunt.

CARSON After Carune teleported his fingers, he wondered if he should call Carson in New Jersey or Buffington in Charlotte.

CARUNE, VICTOR The man who invented the Jaunt. After the ad agency Young and Rubicam took over PR for Jaunting, Carune was turned into a combination of "Edison, Eli Whitney, Pecos Bill, and Flash Gordon."

THE ELDERLY WOMAN WITH HER SKIRT PULLED UP After an elderly woman was given the gas and knocked out prior to Jaunting, her skirt rode up as she lay on the sleep couch. A Jaunt attendant pulled it down for her.

THE FIRST MOUSE The first mouse that Carune Jaunted came through the process sick. Then it died.

FIVE JAUNT ATTENDANTS Five Jaunt attendants took care of the hundred Jaunt "passengers" at the New York Port Authority Terminal Blue Concourse sleep lounge.

FOGGIA, RUDY The convicted murderer who agreed to go through Jaunting awake in exchange for a complete pardon if he came through all right. He didn't come through all right. He emerged insane, and said "It's eternity in there" before he died of a massive heart attack.

FOUR OLD PEOPLE Rudy Foggia was convicted of murdering four old people at a Sarasota bridge party.

A JAUNT ATTENDANT Armed guards and a Jaunt attendant flanked the entranceway to the Blue Concourse terminal area sleep lounge.

A KID DRIVING A CHEVETTE As Carune hitchhiked to Mosconi's veterinary clinic, a kid driving a Chevette stopped, but refused to give him a ride when Victor told him he had a bunch of dead mice in the bag he was carrying.

A LADY WITH A SHAVED AND PAINTED HEAD One of the Jaunt passengers on the day that the Oates Jaunted to Mars.

LESTER MICHAELSON'S DAUGHTER Lester used his daughter's plexiplast Dreamropes to tie up his wife and Jaunt her into eternity.

THE MAN WITH THE ETERNA-SHINE SHOES One of the Jaunt passengers on the day that the Oates Jaunted to Mars. He did not want the gas.

MICHAELSON, LESTER The Jaunt researcher who tied up his wife with their daughter's plexiplast Dreamropes, and pushed her through the Jaunt portal at Silver City, Nevada. He had pushed the Nil button, and erased all the emergence portals.

MICHAELSON, MRS. Lester's wife. He tied her up and pushed her through the Silver City, Nevada, Jaunt Portal after he erased all the emergence portals. His lawyer tried to say Michaelson couldn't be tried for murder because there was no proof Mrs. Michaelson was dead, but the concept of her being discorporated, yet sentient, was so abhorrent, that Michaelson was convicted and executed for his actions.

MICHAELSON'S LAWYER After Lester Michaelson pushed his screaming wife into a Jaunt portal, his lawyer tried to say that Michaelson could not be tried for murder because they couldn't prove that Mrs. Michaelson was dead. This idea so horrified the court that Michaelson was convicted and executed for his actions.

MOSCONI, DR. The veterinarian who autopsied the first mouse that Carune put through the Jaunting process.

NINE WHITE MICE Victor Carune spent his last twenty dollars on nine white mice after he teleported his fingers and a pencil: He had to try something that was alive.

OATES, MARILYS Mark's wife, and Ricky and Patricia's mother.

OATES, MARK Marilys Oates's husband, and the father of Ricky and Patricia Oates. He transferred to Whitehead City, Mars, for two years. While waiting to Jaunt, Mark told his kids the story of Victor Carune and how he invented the Jaunt.

OATES, PATTY Patricia Oates. The nine-year-old daughter of Mark and Marilys Oates; the sister of Ricky "Longer than you think!" Oates.

OATES, RICKY The twelve-year-old son of Marilys and Mark Oates. He held his breath during the inhalation of the sleep gas prior to Jaunting, and Jaunted awake. He came out of the Jaunt a "twelve-year-old boy with a snow-white fall of hair and eyes which were incredibly ancient." He gouged his own eyes out after shrieking, "Longer than you think, Dad!"

OVER 10,000 PEOPLE The winter before Carune invented Jaunting, over ten thousand people froze to death in the United States.

"Ricky Oates After His Jaunt"
Original drawing courtesy Kenny Ray Linkous.

PATRICK One of the goldfish that Carune teleported.

PERCY One of the goldfish that Carune teleported.

THE SIX HUMAN VOLUNTEERS The first six human Jaunt volunteers were prisoners who were gassed and fed through Portal One. They all came back fine.

SUMMERS, C.K. The author of the book *The Politics of the Jaunt* .

THE THIRTY PEOPLE In her book, *The Politics of the Jaunt,* C.K. Summers revealed that thirty or so people had Jaunted awake since Jaunting's invention, and all of them had emerged either dead or insane.

THURGOOD, GOVERNOR The Florida governor who agreed to sign Rudy Foggia's pardon if Foggia came through his wide-awake Jaunt all right. Rudy never got his pardon.

THE TIMID-LOOKING MAN As the Oates waited for their turn for the sleep gas, a timid-looking man took the gas. Mark knew he was a "first-timer."

THE TWO MEN WHO LOST THEIR NERVE Before the Oates Jaunted, two men lost their nerve and left the sleep lounge.

AN UNNAMED BUSINESSMAN As the Oates waited to Jaunt, an unnamed businessman on a nearby couch looked over some papers.

(21f)
SKELETON CREW
"The Jaunt"
Places

THE BLUE CONCOURSE AREA The New York Port Authority Terminal area sleep lounge where the Oates family waited for their Jaunt to Mars. It had wall-to-wall oyster gray carpeting.

CARUNE'S LAB Victor Carune's lab was located in a barn at the end of a mile-long stretch of road off Route 26.

CHARLOTTE After Carune teleported his fingers, he wondered if he should call Carson in New Jersey or Buffington in Charlotte.

EMERGENCE PORTALS The destination portals for the Jaunt. Lester Michaelson erased all of them from his Silver City, Nevada, Jaunt terminal, and then sent his wife out into eternity, her body discorporeated, yet feeling her plight.

MARS It was discovered that there was enough oil on Mars for eight thousand years.

THE MOSCONI VETERINARY CLINIC Dr. Mosconi's clinic. This clinic was where the first mouse teleported through Carune's Jaunting equipment was autopsied.

NEW JERSEY After Carune teleported his fingers, he wondered if he should call Carson in New Jersey or Buffington in Charlotte.

NEW PALTZ The town where Stackpole's House of Pets was located.

THE NEW YORK PORT AUTHORITY TERMINAL The terminal where the Oates family waited to take their Jaunt to Whitehead City, Mars.

PORTAL ONE The origination portal of Carune's Jaunting equipment.

PORTAL TWO The destination portal of Carune's Jaunting equipment.

PROVINCE, VERMONT The site of the first human Jaunt experiments.

ROUTE 26 Victor Carune's lab was located in a barn at the end of a mile-long stretch of road off Route 26.

A SARASOTA BRIDGE PARTY Rudy Foggia was convicted of murdering four old people at a Sarasota bridge party.

SCHENECTADY The Oates had once lived in Schnectady.

SILVER CITY, NEVADA The Jaunt terminal where Lester Michaelson erased all the emergence portals and pushed his screaming wife into the Jaunt portal.

THE SMITHSONIAN ANNEX IN WASHINGTON The Smithsonian Annex in Washington had on display one of the two splinters fron Carune's teleported fingers. (The other splinter was lost.)

STACKPOLE'S HOUSE OF PETS The pet shop where Victor Carune bought the white mice he used to first try out the Jaunt process.

TEXACO WATER Mark Oates worked for Texaco Water.

VENUS It was discovered that there was enough oil on Venus for 20,000 years.

WHITEHEAD CITY, MARS The Oates's destination. Mark Oates had transferred there for two years.

THE WHITEHEAD COMBINED SCHOOL The school the Oates children would be attending on Mars.

(21f)
SKELETON CREW
"The Jaunt"
Things

"ALL THE HISTORY BOOKS" Mark Oates explained to his kids that Victor Carune was in all the history books, just "like Presidents Lincoln and Hart."

A BRAT PICKUP TRUCK Victor Carune's truck.

THE CARUNE PROCESS Teleportation. Jaunting. The term Jaunt came from Alfred Bester's sci-fi story "The Stars My Destination." (In that story, though, jaunt was spelled "jaunte.")

A CLOUD CHAMBER A cloud chamber was part of Carune's Jaunting equipment: It stood at Portal Two, the destination portal.

COMLINK Victor Carune's computer connection. He was given a limited amount of computer time as part of his government funding.

AN EBERHARD FABER NO. 2 PENCIL The second thing Victor Carune teleported.

11:31:49 The time on Carune's Seiko watch when it emerged in Portal Two after being teleported across his barn lab.

11:31:07 The time on Carune's Seiko watch when he put it through Portal One to be teleported across his barn lab.

ETERNA-SHINE SHOES A man wearing Eterna-Shine shoes did not want the gas. He was waiting to Jaunt on the day that the Oates Jaunted to Mars.

FIFTEEN OLDBUCKS A GALLON Prior to the time that Jaunting revolutionized travel, gasoline was fifteen oldbucks a gallon, and cars could only be driven two days a week.

THE FIRST AND SECOND FINGERS OF HIS LEFT HAND The first things that Victor Carune successfully teleported were the first and second fingers of his left hand.

THE FIRST TELEPORTATION The first things that Victor Carune successfully teleported were the first and second fingers of his left hand.

FOUR CENTS A GALLON After Jaunting became commonplace, gasoline prices dropped to four cents a gallon.

A HERSHEY BAR WRAPPER After Carune teleported his fingers, he used a Hershey bar wrapper to hold the splinter he retrieved from one of his "Jaunted" digits.

"I CAME FROM STACKPOLE'S HOUSE OF PETS" The legend written on the side of the box containing the nine white mice that Victor bought at Stackpole's.

AN ION GUN An ion gun was part of Carune's Jaunting equipment: It stood at Portal One, the origination portal.

"IT WORKS!" Carune wrote "It works!" on a barn board with the teleported Eberhard Faber No. 2 pencil.

"IT'S ETERNITY IN THERE." This is what Rudy Foggia said when he emerged from his wide-awake Jaunt.

JAUNT 701 The Jaunt the Oates family planned to take to Whitehead City, Mars.

"THE JAUNT EFFECT" The organic effect that occured during Jaunting while awake: It brought madness, and ended in either death or suicide. It didn't happen when the Jaunter was unconscious.

THE JAUNT SERVICE The agency that handled the adminstration of the sleep gas for Jaunt passengers.

"THE JAUNT UNDER THE ROSE" A chapter in C.K. Summer's book, *The Politics of the Jaunt*. This chapter was a compendium of the more believable stories about the Jaunt.

THE JAUNTING EQUIPMENT At one end of Carune's barn laboratory he had set up an ion gun; at the other end was a cloud chamber. Also, at each end of the barn were two Portals, Portal One, which was the origination portal, and Portal Two, the destination portal.

KEYS The third thing Victor Carune teleported (after his fingers and a pencil.)

"LONGER THAN YOU THINK, DAD!" This is what Ricky Oates said when he emerged on Mars after his wide-awake Jaunt. He had aged a hundred years, was quite insane, and he clawed his eyes out after he said this to his father.

MOBIL HYDRO-2-OX After working teleportation became a reality in 1988 and revolutionized transportation, Mobil changed its name to Mobil Hydro-2-Ox, and began focusing on water prospecting rather than oil.

THE NEW YORK WORLD-TIMES The harried-looking businessman who was almost late for his jaunt carried a copy of the *New York World-Times*.

THE NIL BUTTON The button that erased all emergence portals from a Jaunt station.

1987 The (approximate) year the Jaunt process was invented.

1993 The year Victor Carune died. He died riding in the pace car at the Tournament of Roses Parade.

OCTOBER 19, 1988 The date that working teleportation was announced.

"OLD SPARKY" The Florida electric chair.

ONE HUNDRED JAUNT COUCHES The Blue Concourse Jaunt terminal area had a hundred sleep couches in ten rows of ten.

THE ONLY MANNED ROCKET FLIGHT TO MARS The only manned rocket flight to Mars took place in the year 2030. It was a French mission.

"OPERATION STRAW" The first waterlift from the Martian icecaps. It took place in the year 2045.

PLEXIPLAST DREAMROPES Lester Michaelson used his daughter's plexiplast Dreamropes to tie up his wife and Jaunt her into eternity.

THE POLITICS OF THE JAUNT A book about the Jaunt by C.K. Summers.

POMONA ORANGE CRATES Portal Two stood atop two Pomona orange crates in Victor Carune's barn lab.

POPULAR MECHANICS The magazine that published Victor Carune's first and only article about Jaunting before the government shut him up.

RED JUMPERS The Jaunt Service attendants wore red jumpers when they administered the gas.

"REPRESENTATIVES OF LETHE" The name Mark Oates used to describe the Jaunt Service.

A SEIKO QUARTZ LC CALCULATOR WATCH The fourth thing Victor Carune teleported. He put it in Portal One at 11:31:07, and it came out of Portal Two at 11:31:49.

$750 The amount Victor Carune was paid for the one and only article he ever wrote about Jaunting before the government shut him up. The article appeared in *Popular Mechanics* magazine.

A SPLINTER The Smithsonian Annex in Washington had on display one of the two splinters from Carune's teleported fingers. (The other splinter was lost.)

SUMMER 2007 Rudy Foggia Jaunted wide-awake in the summer of 2007.

TEXACO OIL/WATER After working teleportation became a reality in 1988 and revolutionized transportation, Texaco changed its name to Texaco Oil/Water and began focusing on water prospecting rather than oil.

THE TOURNAMENT OF ROSES PARADE Victor Carune died in 1993 riding in the pace car at the Tournament of Roses Parade.

TWENTY DOLLARS The amount of money Victor Carune spent on the nine white mice he bought to try the Jaunting process on something alive. It was his last twenty dollars.

2045 The year water prospecting became the real challenge, and oil became what it had been in 1906: a toy. 2045 was also the year that Operation Straw, the first waterlift from the Martian icecaps, took place.

2030 The only manned rocket flight to Mars took place in the year 2030. It was a French mission.

$20,000 A YEAR The amount of government funding Victor Carune was receiving when he discovered the Jaunting process.

2307 The year Ricky Oates Jaunted awake.

TWO DAYS A WEEK Prior to the time that Jaunting revolutionized travel, gasoline was fifteen oldbucks a gallon and cars could only be driven two days a week.

"THE ULTIMATE JIMMY HOFFA MACHINE" The Jaunt was used by the Mafia to get rid of bodies and, when used in this manner, it became known as the "ultimate Jimmy Hoffa machine."

VICTOR'S REMAINING ASSETS After Victor Carune spent his last twenty dollars on the nine white mice he bought to try the Jaunting process with something living, he had exactly ninety-three cents left in his right front pocket, and eighteen dollars in his savings account. He also had his lab equipment, and a Brat pickup truck.

YOUNG AND RUBICAM The advertising agency that was put in charge of PR for Jaunting.

0.000000000067 OF A SECOND The time it took to Jaunt.

✦✦✦

(21g)

SKELETON CREW
"The Wedding Gig"
People

BIFF The jazz band's drummer.

BILLY-BOY The jazz band's piano player. He was the only black member of the band.

CHARLIE The jazz band's trombone player.

ENGLANDER, TOMMY Englander owned the speakeasy where the jazz band was playing when they were approached to play Maureen Scollay's wedding.

GIBSON, MISS The woman who was in charge of Maureen Romano's wedding reception.

THE GREEK The hood who had Mike Scollay killed at his sister's wedding reception. After Maureen took over her brother's operations, she had the Greek brought to her, and she killed him by sticking a piece of piano wire in his left eye and into his brain while he wept before her.

HENRY Henry almost lit a cigarette near a dangling crepe streamer at Maureen's wedding reception.

KATZENOS, DEMETRIUS The little man sent by the Greek to Maureen's wedding reception to deliver a message. [NOTE: See the "Things" entry THE GREEK'S MESSAGE.]

KATZENOS, MRS. The wife of Demetrius Katzenos. The Greek had Mrs. Katzenos, and wouldn't let her go until Demetrius delivered his message to Scollay. [NOTE: See the "Things" entry THE GREEK'S MESSAGE.]

"MA BARKER WITH BRAINS" Maureen Romano became a sort of "Ma Barker with brains" after her brother was gunned down by the Greek's people.

MANNY The trumpet player in the jazz band.

A MOLL After Mike Scollay was gunned down by the Greek's men, one of the molls brushed broken glass out of her bobbed hair.

"MR. CORNET PLAYER" The narrator of "The Wedding Gig," and the band member approached by Scollay about playing at his sister's wedding.

340

RED NICHOLS AND HIS FIVE PENNIES Maureen asked the band to play "Roses of Picardy" like Red Nichols and His Five Pennies.

THE REDHEAD "Mr. Cornet Player" missed a chance to pick up a redhead at Tommy Englander's speakeasy. He had to talk to Mike Scollay about Maureen's wedding.

ROMANO, RICO Maureen Scollay's Italian husband. He became her lieutenant when she took over her dead brother's crime operations.

A SAILOR The redhead that Mr. Cornet Player missed out on picked up a sailor instead.

SCOLLAY, MAUREEN Maureen Scollay Romano. Mike Scollay's sister. Maureen was fat. On the day of her wedding, she weighed nearly three-fifty. She took over her brother's crime operations, bulding it into an empire to rival Capone's. It was said she was five hundred pounds when she died in 1933.

SCOLLAY, MIKE Small-time Shytown racketeer. He hired the jazz band to play at his sister Maureen's wedding. He was gunned down at the reception by the Greek's men.

TEN PALLBEARERS It took ten pallbearers to carry Maureen Romano's coffin.

(21g)
SKELETON CREW
"The Wedding Gig"
Places

THE BRICKYARD When all the car engines revved up after the Greek's message was delivered at Maureen's wedding reception, "Mr. Cornet Player" thought it sounded like Memorial Day at the Brickyard.

GROVER STREET The street where the Sons of Erin hall was located.

THE ILLINOIS STATE PENITENTIARY After Maureen Romano died of a heart attack in 1933, her husband Rico couldn't run her operation on his own, and within a year ended up in the Illinois state penitentiary for assault with intent to kill.

MORGAN, ILLINOIS The town where the band was playing a gig when Scollay approached them about working his sister's wedding.

SHYTOWN Mike Scollay was from Chicago.

THE SONS OF ERIN HALL The hall where Maureen Scollay Romano's reception was held.

THE SPEAKEASY The jazz band was playing in Tommy Englander's speakeasy when they were approached to play Maureen Scollay's wedding.

(21g)
SKELETON CREW
"The Wedding Gig"
Things

ASSAULT WITH INTENT TO KILL After Maureen Romano died of a heart attack in 1933, her husband Rico couldn't run her operation on his own. Within a year, he ended up in the Illinois state penitentiary for assault with intent to kill.

"AUNT HAGAR'S BLUES" "A tune that passed for racy out in the boondocks."

"BAMBOO BAY" One of the songs played by the jazz band.

THE BAND The jazz band that played at Maureen Scollay's wedding consisted of drums, cornet, trombone, piano, and trumpet. Manny played the trumpet, Billy-Boy played piano, Charlie played trombone, Biff was the drummer, and "Buddy-Gee" – "Mr. Cornet Player" – played the cornet.

"BEST ALWAYS MAUREEN AND RICO" The banner in the Sons of Erin hall.

THE CHARLESTON The people at Maureen's wedding reception wanted to dance the Charleston, so the band played "I'm Gonna Charleston Back to Charleston" and "Aunt Hagar's Blues."

CORNET One of the instruments in the jazz band.

COUNTY CORK RED The color of Maureen Scollay Romano's hair.

DIXIELAND MUSIC Scollay hired the jazz band to play at his sister Maureen's wedding because she liked Dixieland music.

DRUMS One of the instruments in the jazz band.

A FORD The truck that the jazz band used to get around to gigs.

THE GREEK'S MESSAGE The Greek sent the following message to Mike Scollay at Maureen Scollay Romano's wedding reception:

"Your sister is one fat pig. She got an itch. If a fat woman got an itch on her back, she buy a back-scratcher. If a woman got an itch in her parts, she buy a man. The whole town laughing at you."

A HEART ATTACK Maureen Romano died of a heart attack in 1933.

"I'M GONNA CHARLESTON BACK TO CHARLESTON" The people at Maureen's wedding reception wanted to dance the Charleston, so the band played "I'm Gonna Charleston Back to Charleston" and "Aunt Hagar's Blues."

MOXIE Sometimes the farmboys down south had a hankering for something stronger than Moxie after a hot day in the fields.

1933 The year Maureen Scollay Romano died of a heart attack.

1927 The year the jazz band played the "wedding gig."

A PACKARD COUPE Mike Scollay's car.

PIANO One of the instruments in the jazz band.

A PIPE Mike Scollay smoked a pipe "with more squiggles in it than a French horn."

"ROSES OF PICARDY" Maureen asked the band to play "Roses of Picardy" like Red Nichols and His Five Pennies.

SCOTCH The bootleg booze served at Maureen Romano's wedding reception.

A SHANTY-IRISH MICK "Mike Scollay described himself as a "shanty-Irish Mick," and proud of it.

TROMBONE One of the instruments in the jazz band.

TRUMPET One of the instruments in the jazz band.

TWO C'S Scollay offered the jazz band two hundred dollars (plus expenses) to play his sister's wedding.

"THE VARSITY DRAG" One of the songs the band played at Tommy Englander's.

"THE WEDDING MARCH" The jazz band played a ragtime version of "The Wedding March" when Maureen and Rico entered the reception hall.

WILDROOT CREME OIL The hair oil used by Mike Scollay.

WINCHESTERS The rifles used to "cool" Mike Scollay.

❖❖❖

(21h)
SKELETON CREW
"Paranoid: A Chant"
[Poem]

❖❖❖

(21i)
SKELETON CREW
"The Raft"
People

BATMAN AND ROBIN Randy thought of himself and Deke as Batman and Robin.

CISCO Deke.

DEKE Horlicks University student. He drove Randy, Rachel, and LaVerne to Cascade Lake one October night near Halloween. He owned a Camaro, and was a good football player. (He was All-Conference in 1981.) He was the second victim of the thing on the water in Lake Cascade.

DELOIS, BILLY A friend of Randy and Deke's. Billy lived near Cascade Lake.

DUNCAN, SANDY Rachel reminded Randy of Sandy Duncan.

LAVERNE Horlicks University student. She went to Cascade Lake with Randy, Deke, and Rachel. She was the third victim of the thing on the water in Cascade Lake.

A LOON As Randy whispered "Do you love?" to the thing on the water, and looked into its swirling colors, "Somewhere, far across the empty lake, a loon screamed."

MAHARIS, GEORGE He starred in "Route 66."

MILNER, MARTIN He starred in "Route 66."

PANCHO Randy.

RACHEL Horlicks University student. She went to Cascade Lake with Deke, Randy, and LaVerne. She was the first victim of the thing on the water in Cascade Lake.

RANDY Horlicks University student, and a friend of Deke, Rachel and LaVerne. His nickname was "Pancho," and he went to the lake with his three friends. He was a good student. He was the last victim of the thing on the water in Cascade Lake.

RANDY'S FRIEND A friend of Randy's had been a paramedic in Vietnam and had learned all sorts of tricks. [NOTE: See the "Things" entry RANDY'S FRIEND'S VIETNAM TRICKS.]

SCOTT, BON The lead singer of AC/DC. He puked down his own throat and died.

SHEENA She was a punk rocker.

THE YANKEES Stephen King hates the Yankees.

(21i)
SKELETON CREW
"The Raft"
Places

THE AUSTRALIAN OUTBACK Deke was sure they'd be rescued off the raft in the morning when someone heard their shouts because, after all, they weren't in the Australian outback, right?

CASCADE LAKE The lake where the raft floated, and where the thing in the water lived. Cascade Lake was forty miles from Horlicks University.

A CRACK IN THE RAFT Deke was eaten by the thing on the water when he was pulled through a crack in the raft.

HORLICKS UNIVERSITY The school that Randy, Rachel, Deke, and LaVerne attended. It was forty miles from Cascade Lake.

NEW YORK Randy thought that Rachel looked like a slightly neurotic New York girl.

RANDY'S ROOM Rachel, Deke, LaVerne, and Randy were partying in Randy's room at Horlicks Univeristy when they decided to drive out to Cascade Lake, swim out to the raft, and say goodbye to summer.

THE RIALTO THEATER Randy told Deke that the last time he had seen anything like what happened when the thing on the water ate Rachel was the time he had gone to the Halloween Shock-Show at the Rialto Theater when he was twelve.

ROCKAWAY BEACH You could hitch a ride there.

VIETNAM Randy had a friend who had learned a lot while serving as a paramedic in Vietnam. [NOTE: See the "Things" entry RANDY'S FRIEND'S VIETNAM TRICKS.]

(21i)
SKELETON CREW
"The Raft"
Things

AN ALL-CONFERENCE RING Deke wore an All-Conference ring he had been awarded in 1981. It slid off his finger when he was pulled through a crack in the raft by the thing on the water.

CAMARO Deke's car. After a couple of beers, Deke made his Camaro walk and talk.

"CISCO" Deke's nickname.

COLORS Rachel was the first one to see the colors in the black thing on the water. She saw "colors...swirling in rich, inward-turning spirals."

THE DIPPER After Rachel was eaten by the thing on the water, Randy could see the stars of the Dipper just beginning to appear.

"DO YOU LOVE?" Randy's last words. He said them to the thing on the water in Cascade Lake.

THE HALLOWEEN SHOCK-SHOW Randy told Deke that the last time he had seen anything like what happened when the thing ate Rachel was the time he had gone to the Halloween Shock-Show at the Rialto Theater when he was twelve.

IRON CITY LIGHT BEER The beer Rachel found in Randy's refrigerator.

LABOR DAY LaVerne told Randy, Deke, and Rachel that Cascade Beach had been closed since Labor Day.

A LACOSTE SHIRT The shirt LaVerne wore the night she, Randy, Rachel, and Deke went to Cascade Lake.

"MACHO CITY" The name LaVerne called Deke when he asked if the girls were all right while swimming to the raft.

A NIGHT RANGER ALBUM Randy, Deke, Rachel, and LaVerne had been listening to a Night Ranger album on the stereo in Randy's room when they decided to drive to Cascade Lake one October night.

"NO TRESPASSING" SIGNS There were "No Trespassing" signs every fifty feet leading to Cascade Beach.

AN OCTOBER NIGHT The night Deke, Randy, Rachel, and LaVerne decided to drive to Cascade Lake and swim out to the raft.

"PANCHO" Randy's nickname.

THE RAFT The float that was still moored out in Cascade Lake on the October night that Deke, Randy, Rachel, and LaVerne drove out to the lake and went swimming. The raft was made of "bright white wood."

RANDY'S FRIEND'S VIETNAM TRICKS Randy's friend learned a lot of neat tricks in Vietnam, such as how to catch head lice off a human scalp and make them race in a matchbox, how to cut cocaine with baby laxative, and how to sew up cuts with ordinary needle and thread. He also knew how to bring around someone who was "abysmally" drunk: Bite their earlobe as hard as you could.

A ROGER CORMAN MOVIE Randy told the thing on the water to go to California and audition for a Roger Corman movie.

THE THING ON THE WATER On Cascade Lake, there was a moving black spot that looked like an oil slick. It showed rainbow colors when you looked into it, and it could hypnotize you. It ate people. Randy thought that the thing looked like a Pac-Man image with its mouth open to eat electronic cookies.

TUPPERWARE STORAGE BOXES There were blue Tupperware boxes in Randy's refrigerator.

THE WHITE ROCKS LABEL Randy thought that Rachel looked like the girl on the White Rocks label.

❖❖❖

(21j)
SKELETON CREW
"Word Processor of the Gods"
People

A BOY IN NEW MEXICO A boy in New Mexico discovered tachyons, particles that are supposed to be able to travel backwards in time.

DAVEY The bassist in Seth Hagstrom's band.

EPSTEIN, BERNIE A friend of Richard Hagstrom.

HAGSTROM, BELINDA Roger Hagstrom's wife. She, Roger, and their son Jonathan were all killed when a drunk Roger drove his van off the edge of a ninety-foot drop. Richard brought back Belinda from the dead to be his wife using Jonathan's word processor.

HAGSTROM, JONATHAN Roger and Belinda's fourteen-year-old son; Richard's nephew. Jon made the word processor of the gods for his uncle Richard.

HAGSTROM, LINA Richard's wife. She was sullen and fat, and when Richard deleted their son Seth, she came back from Bingo even fatter.

HAGSTROM, RICHARD The English teacher who was left a Wang word processor with which he could add and delete things from the real world. He had been married to Lina, and had a son named Seth, until he changed all that and executed a command that made his dead brother's wife Belinda and their son Jon into his family.

HAGSTROM, SETH Richard and Lina Hagstrom's son. He fancied himself a rocker. Richard deleted him.

THE KID WHO BLEW UP A DOGHOUSE An eleven-year-old boy in Waterbury "made a pipe bomb out of the celluloid...off the backs of a deck of playing cards." He used it to blow up a doghouse.

THE KID WHO MADE AN ATOM SMASHER Back in the fifties, some kid made an atom smasher "out of two soup cans and about five dollars' worth of electrical equipment."

NORDHOFF, MR. A neighbor of Richard Hagstrom's brother Roger. Nordhoff was in his seventies, and helped lug the word processor that Jonathan had made over to Richard's house.

NORM The lead guitarist in Seth Hagstrom's band.

THE OPTOMETRIST After Richard deleted Seth, his wife reminded him that they still owed the optometrist for her reading glasses.

PHILLIPS, FATHER The priest at Our Lady of Perpetual Sorrows church. He had to have his gall-bladder out.

(21j)
SKELETON CREW
"Word Processor of the Gods"
Places

THE GUEST ROOM After he deleted Seth, Richard thought that Seth's former room should have a sign "Guest Room" put on it.

NEW MEXICO A boy in New Mexico discovered tachyons, particles that are supposed to be able to travel backwards in time.

OUR LADY OF PERPETUAL SORROWS The church where Lina Hagstrom played Bingo.

RICHARD'S STUDY It was a small shed away from the house.

WATERBURY, CONNECTICUT An eleven-year-old boy in Waterbury "made a pipe bomb out of the celluloid...off the backs of a deck of playing cards."

(21j)
SKELETON CREW
"Word Processor of the Gods"
Things

AN AMANA FREEZER After Richard deleted Seth, an Amana freezer appeared in the pantry of his house.

THE BETAMAX After Richard deleted Seth, Lina reminded him that they were a payment behind on the Betamax.

A BOB SEGER TUNE Seth Hagstrom and his band were trying to do a Seger tune the night Richard discovered the powers of the word processor.

BUD The beer Richard Hagstrom gave to Mr. Nordhoff on the day Nordhoff helped bring the word processor over to Richard's house.

DELETE The button on Richard's word processor that made anything typed on his screen disappear from the real world.

1871 The year stamped on the gold coins that Richard created with his word processor.

EXECUTE The button on Richard's word processor that made whatever was typed on the screen happen in the real world.

A FENDER Seth Hagstrom's guitar.

$514 AN OUNCE The price of gold at the time Richard created the gold coins with his word processor.

"HAGSTROM'S WHOLESALE DELIVERIES" The legend printed on the side of Roger Hagstrom's (doomed) van.

"HAPPY BIRTHDAY, UNCLE RICHARD! JON" The message Jonathan left on the word processor that Jon made for his Uncle Richard's birthday.

"I AM A MAN WHO LIVES ALONE. EXCEPT FOR MY WIFE, BELINDA, AND MY SON JONATHAN." The sentences Richard typed to create his *true* family.

IBM The brand of computer that Richard Hagstrom's nephew Jonathan used (with a Wang board) to create his "word processor of the gods."

A LAST SUPPER VELVET TAPESTRY A picture that hung in the rec room of Richard's house (after he deleted Seth).

AN LTD STATION WAGON The vehicle Seth Hagstrom's band used to lug around their equipment.

A MAGIC EIGHT-BALL A toy Richard played with as a child. His brother Roger broke it.

MERCEDES-BENZ Richard and Lina Hagstrom thought that they would both eventually be driving a Mercedes after Richard became a successful novelist.

"MY BROTHER WAS A WORTHLESS DRUNK" The first thing that Richard Hagstrom typed on the word processor left to him by his nephew Jonathan.

"MY FLOOR IS BARE. EXCEPT FOR TWELVE TWENTY-DOLLAR GOLD PIECES IN A SMALL COTTON SACK." The sentences Richard typed to create the gold coins.

"MY SON IS SETH ROBERT HAGSTROM." The sentence Richard typed to delete his son.

"MY WIFE IS ADELINA MABEL WARREN HAGSTROM." The sentence Richard typed to delete his wife.

"MY WIFE'S PICTURE IS ON THE WALL." The sentence Richard typed to bring back his wife's portrait.

"MY WIFE'S PHOTOGRAPH HANGS ON THE WEST WALL OF MY STUDY." The sentence that Richard typed to delete his wife's picture from his study wall.

AN OLIVETTI Richard Hagstrom's manual typewriter.

PLAYING CARD CELLULOID An eleven-year-old boy in Waterbury "made a pipe bomb out of the celluloid...off the backs of a deck of playing cards." He used it to blow up a doghouse.

THE PRINTS IN RICHARD'S STUDY In addition to a portrait of his wife Lina, Richard had Whistler, Homer, and N.C. Wyeth prints hanging on the walls of his study.

REESE'S PEANUT BUTTER CUPS A favorite of the newly-childless Lina Hagstrom.

THE STATE SCIENCE FAIR Jonathan Hagstrom won first prize at the state science fair when he was in the sixth grade.

TACHYONS A boy in New Mexico discovered tachyons, particles that are supposed to be able to travel backwards in time.

300 POUNDS Lina Hagstrom's weight after Richard deleted their son Seth.

$27,756 The value of the gold coins Richard created with his word processor.

WANG The modified word processor Jon Hagstrom left for his uncle Richard.

WELLS FARGO "Wells Fargo" was stenciled on the side of the sack that held the gold coins that Richard created with his word processor.

THE WORD PROCESSOR OF THE GODS Jonathan Hagstrom constructed the word processor of the gods with parts from IBM, Radio Shack, Western Electric, an erector set motor, and a Lionel train transformer.

(21k)
SKELETON CREW
"The Man Who Would Not Shake Hands"
People

ADLEY, DAVID One of the members of the Club. On the night George Gregson told the story of the man who would not shake hands, Adley sat on the narrator's right.

ANDREWS, PETER A member of the Club. He was present on the night that Gregson told the story of the man who would not shake hands.

BAKER, DARREL One of the poker players at the Club on the night in 1919 when Brower sat in for George Oxley.

THE BOY A holy man's son. He was killed when he got into Brower's car in Bombay, accidentally started it, and crashed into a stone wall.

BROWER, HENRY The man who would not shake hands. Henry was cursed by a holy man in Bombay after the Wallah's son got into Brower's car, accidentally started it, and crashed into a brick wall. [Note: It wasn't said if Henry was a relative (grandfather perhaps?) of Ray "The Body" Brower, although in Stephen King's world of fiction, it's likely!]

THE BUILDING SUPERINTENDENT The super at Brower's East Village tenement building. He was a scrawny man. He told Gregson that Brower had moved out on April 3.

DAVIDSON, JASON One of the members of the Club in 1919. He was twenty-two then. Davidson tried to shake hands with Henry Brower, who refused, and thus the Club members present learned of how Brower came to be cursed with toxic palms.

THE DOG To prove the curse, Brower "shook hands" with a stray dog. It died shortly thereafter.

FRENCH, ANDREW One of the poker players at the Club on the night in 1919 when Brower sat in for George Oxley. He was a "fearsome-looking fellow with [a] beard."

GREER, RAYMOND The Club member who had "spoken for" Henry Brower. Greer was with the city trade commission, and had an office in the Flatiron Building. Greer told Gregson the story of Brower's year in Bombay.

GREGSON, GEORGE A member of the Club. He told the story of the man who would not shake hands.

JOHANNSEN A member of the Club. On the night Gregson told the story of the man who would not shake hands, Johannsen had been reading *The Wall Street Journal*.

THE JUTE MANUFACTURER On the day the holy man's son was killed in his car, Brower had been meeting with a jute manufacturer in Bombay.

MACBETH, LADY After Davidson reached over and grabbed Brower's hand, Brower screamed and held his hand out in front of him like Lady Macbeth.

THE MAN AT THE DESK AT DEVARNEY'S A scabrous ancient with a peeling bald skull and rheumy, glittering eyes. He told Gregson that Brower had died shaking his own hands.

McCARRON, EMLYN A member of the Club. He had once told the Club members "a frightening story about a woman who had given birth under unusual circumstances." [Note: This, of course, was the same Dr. Emlyn McCarron from the novella "The Breathing Method" in *Different Seasons*. See the section on that collection in this volume.]

THE NARRATOR The man at the Club who related the story to Stephen King's *Skeleton Crew* readers of the man who would not shake hands.

OXLEY, GEORGE One of the members of the Club in 1919. On the night Henry Brower told them his "I never shake hands" story, Oxley was laid up with a broken leg.

ROSALIE George Gregson's fiancée in 1919. When Gregson returned from the Great War that year, Rosalie had died five months earlier from influenza. She had been nineteen.

STEVENS The butler at the Club at 249 East 35th Street. He was present on the night Gregson told the story of the the man who would not shake hands.

STEVENS' GRANDFATHER Stevens' grandfather had been the butler at the Club in 1919.

WALLAH The Bombay holy man. His son was killed in Brower's car.

WILDEN, JACK One of the poker players at the Club on the night in 1919 when Brower sat in for George Oxley. [Note: This character's name was a tribute to Nye Willden, the editor of *Cavalier* magazine. Willden bought several short stories from King in the early years.]

(21k)
SKELETON CREW
"The Man Who Would Not Shake Hands"
Places

ALBANY On the night of the poker game in which Henry Brower played, Jack Wilden had a long drive to Albany ahead of him.

BOMBAY Brower was cursed by a holy man in Bombay. Any living thing he touched with his hands would die. The holy man accused Brower of practicing "sorcery" on his son after the boy got into Brower's car, accidentally started it, and was killed when it crashed.

THE BOWERY The building superintendent at Brower's East Village tenement told Gregson that Brower may have moved to either Hell, or the Bowery from the East Village.

BRENNAN STREET After World War I, George Gregson took up residence in an apartment on Brennan Street – rooms he still occupied in his eighty-fifth year. [Note: This is obviously an homage to Joseph Payne Brennan, the legendary horror writer who wrote a story called "Canavan's Back Yard," a tale King called "one of the dozen best stories of the macabre ever written by an American, in the genre or out of it." See my interview with Brennan, and the reprinting of "Canavan's Back Yard" in this volume."]

THE CLUB A mens' club at 249B East 35th Street where stories were told. [Note: This is the same club used as the setting for King's "The Breathing Method," contained in *Different Seasons*. Although the events in the two stories occur at least fifty years apart (here, 1919, and in December 197- in "The Breathing Method"), we find that the Club's English butler is still named Stevens (although he is the grandson of the 1919 Stevens). Also, the following club members still toddle in: David Adley (who is only a Club "guest" in "The Breathing Method"), Peter Andrews, George Gregson, Johannsen, and Emlyn McCarron. See the section on "The Breathing Method" elsewhere in this concordance.]

DEVARNEY'S ROOMS The boarding house to which Brower moved after leaving the East Village.

THE EAST SIDE Brower's forwarding address after his residence in Harlem.

THE EAST VILLAGE The area to which Brower reportedly moved after his residence on the East Side.

THE FLATIRON BUILDING Raymond Greer had an office in the Flatiron Building.

HARLEM The area where Brower had lived in 1919.

THE JUTE MANUFACTURER'S HOUSE On the day the holy man's son was killed in Brower's Model-A Ford, Brower had been at a jute manufacturer's house discussing business.

NEW ENGLAND Darrel Baker's father owned three of the largest shoe factories in New England.

POTTER'S FIELD Brower's last residence.

23 – 19th STREET Jason Davidson's address.

249B EAST 35TH STREET The address of the Club where stories were told.

(21k)
SKELETON CREW
"The Man Who Would Not Shake Hands"
Things

A BROOKLYN ACCENT Stevens, the butler at the Club at 249B East 35th Street, had a Brooklyn accent.

CUTTY SARK WHISKEY The whiskey that was drunk at the poker games at the Club in the years following the Great War.

THE GREAT WAR George Gregson returned from the Great War (WW I) in 1919, the year of the story of the man who would not shake hands.

INFLUENZA Gregson's fiancée, Rosalie, died in 1919 of influenza.

"IT IS THE TALE, NOT HE WHO TELLS IT." The legend carved into the fireplace keystone at the Club at 249 East 35th Street. [NOTE: Stephen King's credo. See my discussion of THE CLUB in the "Places" section above, and of the importance of the legend in the "Things" section of "The Breathing Method," a novella contained in *Different Seasons*.]

A MODEL-A FORD The car Henry Brower had in Bombay. The holy man's son was killed in this vehicle.

THE NEW YORK *WORLD* The newspaper Henry Brower was reading before he told the story of how he could never shake hands.

1919 The year the story of the man who would not shake hands began. At the time, George Gregson was twenty years old.

THREE SHOE FACTORIES Darrel Baker's father owned three of the largest shoe factories in New England.

249B EAST 35TH STREET The address of the Club.

❖❖❖

(21l)
SKELETON CREW
"Beachworld"
People

THE BEACH BOYS They'd been dead for eight thousand years when the FedShip crashed onto the Beachworld.

THE CAPTAIN The captain of the rescue ship that found Rand and Shapiro. He was built into treads, and wore a beret with a clan symbol on it.

DUD The salvage ship captain's assistant.

GOMEZ The pilot of the salvage ship that rescued Shapiro.

GRIMES A member of the Fedship ASN/29 crew. He was killed when the ship crashed on the Beachworld.

GRIMES' GOLDFISH Grimes and his goldfish were both killed when the FedShip crashed onto the Beachworld.

MONTOYA, EXCELLENT A brown crew member of the ship that rescued Shapiro.

RAND A member of the Fedship ASN/29 crew. He went "umby," and devoured – and was devoured – by the Beachworld.

SHAPIRO, BILL A member of the Fedship ASN/29 crew. He was the astrogator. He weighed a hundred and forty pounds, and stood five-five.

"SHERLOCK" Shapiro, according to Rand.

THREE SAMPLER ANDROIDS The three androids that accompanied Dud and the salvage ship captain out of the rescue ship.

(21l)
SKELETON CREW
"Beachworld"
Places

THE BEACHWORLD A sentient sand planet. Fedship ASN/29 crashed onto it, and one of the crew members, Rand, was seduced by it, and refused to leave with the rescue ship. He finally began

eating the sand, becoming one with the Beachworld.

A CIRCULAR TANK Grimes had kept goldfish in a tank designed especially for weightlessness. They were killed when the FedShip crashed.

THE DUNES To Rand, the dunes were alive; the manifestation of the sentient beachworld.

HANSONVILLE When Shapiro saw the rescue ship, he said "Fuck you, sand. I got a honey back in Hansonville."

"SURF CITY" How Rand referred to Beachworld's dunes.

(21l)
SKELETON CREW
"Beachworld"
Things

"ALAS, POOR YORICK, I KNEW HIM WELL." Line from Shakespeare's *Hamlet* that Rand spoke when he saw Grimes' dead goldfish.

THE BEACON Rand thought the beacon was destroyed when FedShip ASN/29 crashed onto the Beachworld, but it wasn't.

COMPSCAN A topographical scan done to determine Rand and Shapiro's location.

'DRONEHEAD" Future slang for "asshole." [NOTE: See the entry YELLOWJACK.]

ENVIRONMENTAL PROTECTION SUITS The suits worn by Rand and Shapiro when they exited their ship and stepped out onto the Beachworld.

FEDSHIP ASN/29 The Fedship that fell out of the sky and crashed.

FREON After FedShip ASN/29 fell out of the sky and crashed, there was a freon smell in the aircraft.

PIDGIN DIALECT The lingo spoken by the Dud and the captain. "Umby" was the word for crazy.

A SAND HAND When Excellent Montoya shot a tranquilizer dart at Rand, a huge sand hand reached up out of the dunes and stopped it.

"SHERLOCK" Rand's nickname for Shapiro.

#23196755 The number of the water storage flask recovered from the ship.

"UMBY" Pidgin dialect for "crazy."

THE WATER STORAGE FLASK On it was written:

ASN/CLASS SHIP'S SUPPLIES
STORAGE FLASK CL. #23196755

YELLOWJACK Shapiro got fed up with Rand, and told him he was going to go get a syringe and an amp of yellowjack. He told Rand, "If you want to act like a goddamn dronehead, I'll treat you like one."

❖❖❖

(21m)
SKELETON CREW
"The Reaper's Image"
People

BATES, SANDRA A woman who once tried to break the Delver mirror with a rock.

THE BATES BOY Sandra Bates's brother. He was a victim of the Delver mirror.

CARLIN, MR. The keeper of the Delver mirror. He was a little man who wore rimless glasses. He was the curator of the Samuel Claggert Memorial Private Museum, where the mirror was kept.

CLAGGERT, SAMUEL He was the owner of the Delver mirror, and other antiques. He was a self-made industry emperor of the 1800's.

CRATER, JUDGE A probable victim on the Delver glass. He disappeared during the period when the Delver was in New York,

1897-1920.

DeIVER, JOHN An English craftsman of Norman descent who made mirrors during the Elizabethan period of English history. He made the DeIver mirrors with a crystal that magnified and distorted images. This was his trademark.

THE ENGLISH DUCHESS A victim of the DeIver mirror in 1709. She had primped for a soirée in front of the DeIver, left the room, paused, and then returned for her pearls. She was never seen again.

THE PENNSYLVANIA RUG MERCHANT A victim of the DeIver mirror in 1746. After presumably looking into the mirror, he went for a carriage ride. Only an empty carriage and two horses were ever found.

THE REAPER A hooded figure that victims of the DeIver glass saw as a black splotch in the upper left-hand corner of the mirror when they looked into the glass.

SPANGLER, JOHNSON Spangler was studyng the DeIver mirror, and ended up becoming its latest victim when he refused to give credence to the legends surrounding the reaper's image in the glass.

TWO HORSES The Pennsylvania rug-merchant who disappeared in 1746 after looking into the DeIver left behind an empty carriage and two horses.

A VIRGINAL YOUNG GIRL Spangler knew the smell of age, a smell "common only to museums and mausoleums. He imagined much the same smell might arise from the grave of a virginal young girl, forty years dead."

(21m)
SKELETON CREW
"The Reaper's Image"
Places

THE ATTIC The "resting place" of the DeIver mirror in the Samuel Claggert Memorial Museum.

ENGLAND The location of the DeIver mirror in 1709. It killed an English duchess.

KING TUT'S TOMB A subject of fear and speculation that was often "Sunday-supplementized."

LLOYD'S OF LONDON The insurance company that insured the DeIver mirror when it was moved.

LONDON One of the DeIver mirrors was destroyed in the London Blitz. That mirror, like the one in the Claggert museum, had a "bad reputation."

NEW YORK The DeIver glass had been in New York from 1897 through 1920, the period during which Judge Crater disappeared.

OVER THE HEARTH IN THE KITCHEN A Coombs long rifle hung over the hearth in the kitchen in the Samuel Claggert Memorial Private Museum.

THE PARLOR A *camera obscura* was on display in the parlor in the Samuel Claggert Memorial Museum.

PENNSYLVANIA The location of the DeIver mirror in 1746. It killed a rug-merchant.

THE SAMUEL CLAGGERT MEMORIAL PRIVATE MUSEUM The museum where Johnson Spangler went to study the DeIver mirror. It was owned by the estate of Samuel Claggert, who was a self-made industry emperor of the 1800's. There were guided tours of the museum on the hour, and the admission prices were a dollar for adults and fifty cents for children.

THE UNITED STATES The location of two of the remaining five DeIver mirrors.

(21m)
SKELETON CREW
"The Reaper's Image"
Things

"ABSOLUTELY NO ADMITTANCE" The sign hanging off the arm of the imitation Adonis guarding the attic of the Samuel Claggert Memorial Museum.

A BLACK SPLOTCH IN THE UPPER LEFT-HAND CORNER The image of the Grim Reaper that victims of the DeIver glass saw when they looked into the mirror.

A *CAMERA OBSCURA* One of the antiquities on display in the Samuel Claggert Memorial Museum. It was in the parlor.

A COOMBS LONG RIFLE One of the antiquities on display in the Samuel Claggert Memorial Museum. It hung over the hearth in the kitchen.

THE DeIVER LOOKING GLASS A haunted mirror on display in the Samuel Claggert Memorial Museum. The rumor was that victims of the mirror saw a black splotch in the upper left-hand corner of the glass before they died. What they were actually seeing was the hooded figure of the Grim Reaper. At the time that Spangler visited the museum, there were five DeIver's in existence. The one in Claggert's and the one destroyed in the London Blitz had "bad reputations."

DeIVER'S CRYSTAL John DeIver made his mirrors with a crystal that magnified and distorted images. This was his trademark.

THE DISMEMBERED SKELETON OF AN ANCIENT TANDEM BICYCLE Some of the junk in the upper galleries of the Samuel Claggert Memorial Museum.

1897-1920 The years that the DeIver glass had been in New York. Judge Crater disappeared during this time.

THE ELIZABETHAN PERIOD OF ENGLISH HISTORY The period during which John DeIver made his mirrors.

AN EMPTY CARRIAGE The Pennsylvania rug-merchant who disappeared in 1746 after looking into the DeIver left behind an empty carriage and two horses.

FIFTY CENTS The admission price for children to the Samuel Claggert Memorial Museum.

THE FIVE DeIVER MIRRORS At the time Spangler visited the Samuel Claggert Memorial Museum, five DeIver mirrors remained; two were in the United States. They were priceless.

GOLD-PLATED BIRDCAGES Some of the junk in the upper galleries of the Samuel Claggert Memorial Museum.

"GUIDED TOURS ON THE HOUR—ADMISSION $1.00-ADULTS; $.50 CHILDREN" The notice informing visitors to the Samuel Claggert Memorial Museum of their hours and admission prices.

AN IMITATION ADONIS There was a statue of an imitation Adonis in the Samuel Claggert Memorial Museum. It guarded the attic of the museum: a sign hung off his arm that read "Absolutely No Admittance."

THE KOH-I-NOOR DIAMOND A subject of fear and speculation that was often "Sunday-supplentized."

THE LEMLIER STRADIVARIUS A fake Stradivarius that, for a while, was considered to be the real thing.

THE NATIONAL ENQUIRER Spangler sarcastically said that the *Enquirer* would love the "Reaper's Image" story.

ONE DOLLAR The admission price for adults to the Samuel Claggert Memorial Museum.

PEARLS The English duchess who disappeared in 1709 was a victim of the DeIver glass. She had returned to her room for her pearls, and was never seen again.

1709 The year the English duchess disappeared after she returned to her room for her pearls. She had primped in front of the DeIver, and ended up a victim of the Reaper that haunted the glass.

"THE SMELL OF AGE" Spangler knew the smell of age, a smell "common only to museums and mausoleums. He imagined much the same smell might arise from the grave of a virginal young girl, forty years dead."

SPANGLER'S FACTS Johnson Spangler gave Mr. Carlin the following facts about the DeIver mirrors:

1. John DeIver was an English craftsman of Norman descent who made mirrors during the Elizabethan period of English history.
2. His mirrors were collector's items. They were made with very fine craftsmanship, and a crystal was used that magnified and distorted images viewed in the mirror. This was his trademark.
3. Five DeIver's remained. Two were in the United States, and they were priceless.
4. The mirror in Claggert's and the one destroyed in the London Blitz had bad reputations.

Carlin then gave Spangler Fact Number 5: "You're a supercillious bastard, aren't you?"

STATUARY Some of the junk in the upper galleries of the Samuel Claggert Memorial Museum.

A TENNYSON POEM When Spangler disappeared after seeing the Reaper in the DeIver glass, Carlin remembered a line from a Tennyson poem: "I am half-sick of shadows, said the Lady of Shalott…"

$250,000 The amount of insurance on the DeIver mirror in the Claggert Museum.

❖❖❖

(21n)
SKELETON CREW
"Nona"
People

BLANCHETTE, NORMAN The driver of the Chevy Impala that first picked up the Prisoner and Nona after the violence at Joe's Good Eats.

CASH, JOHNNY The country-and-western singer who recorded the hit song "A Boy Named Sue."

CRAIG, CHERYL The phony name that Nona gave Norman Blanchette.

CURT A state ward who lived with the Prisoner at the Hollises for a while before running away.

THE DELTA TAU DELTA GUY The first girl that the Prisoner loved in college came back from Thanksgiving break and told him she was in love with a Delta Tau Delta frat guy from back home. She then broke up with the Prisoner.

DRAKE The Prisoner's older brother.

EMONDS The name of Nona's fictitious uncle in Bowen Hill.

ESSEGIAN, OFFICER On their way back to Castle Rock, Nona and the Prisoner were stopped by a cop, Officer Essegian, who skidded into the back of the pickup truck that the Prisoner was driving. The Prisoner killed him.

FOUR TRUCKERS There were four truckers sitting in a booth in Joe's Good Eats on the night the Prisoner met Nona there.

A GAWKY KID One of the people in Joe's Good Eats on the night the Prisoner met Nona there was a gawky kid who might have been the dishwasher.

THE GIRL THE PRISONER LOVED IN COLLEGE She was pretty, he slept with her twice, and when she came back from Thanksgiving break, she told him she was in love with a Delta Tau Delta frat guy from back home.

THE GUY WITH THE FLASHLIGHT'S PARTNER As the Prisoner and Nona drove down Stackpole Road in Castle Rock on their way to the graveyard, they were stopped by two men (probably utility workers) who told them to take Bowen Road because there was a live wire down. The Prisoner shot the guy with the flashlight; the other guy got away.

THE GUY WITH THE FLASHLIGHT As the Prisoner and Nona drove down Stackpole Road in Castle Rock on their way to the graveyard, they were stopped by two men (probably utility workers) who told them to take Bowen Road because there was a live wire down. The Prisoner shot the guy with the flashlight; the other guy got away.

HAGGARD, MERLE The country-and-western singer whose song played on the jukebox in Joe's Good Eats when the Prisoner came in from hitchhiking on Route 202.

HOGAN, CHARLIE Charlie Hogan told Ace Merrill that the Prisoner was hanging around Betsy Malenfant.

HOLLIS, MR. The "father" of the Prisoner. As a boy, he was sent to live with the Hollises as a state ward after his real family died in a house fire. Mr. Hollis was "skimpy and rarely spoke. He wore a red-and-black hunting cap all year round."

HOLLIS, MRS. The "mother" of the Prisoner. As a boy, he was sent to live with the Hollises as a state ward after his real family died in a house fire. Mrs. Hollis was fat.

KENNEDY, BILL A friend of the Prisoner's who worked at the Castle Rock Youth League.

MALENFANT, BETSY The girl that the Prisoner liked when he was a sophomore in high school. She was Ace Merrill's girl, though, and Ace beat him up for coming on to her. Ace dropped Betsy shortly thereafter, and the last the Prisoner heard, Betsy had lost most of her teeth and ended up a bar bimbo in Lewiston, hustling guys for drinks.

MERRILL, ACE "[T]he toughest guy in three towns." The Prisoner got on the wrong side of Ace when he started making moves on Ace's girl, Betsy Malenfant. Ace kicked his ass, and the Prisoner never went in the bowling alley again.

NONA The blackhaired beauty that the Prisoner met in Joe's Good Eats on Valentine's Day the winter he left college. They went on a killing spree together. Nona may not have been real. The Prisoner thought that looking at Nona was like seeing the Mona Lisa and the Venus de Milo come to life.

THE PICKUP TRUCK DRIVER The guy that the Prisoner killed after killing Norman Blanchette.

THE PRISONER The man who met Nona in Joe's Good Eats one bitter Valentine's Day night, and went on a killing spree with her. Before leaving for college, he had lived with a family named Hollis as a state ward.

THE PRISONER'S FAMILY When the Prisoner was three years old, and in the hospital with a bad case of the flu, his family all died when their house burned down Killed were the Prisoner's parents, and his older brother Drake. They were all buried in the Castle Rock graveyard where Nona took the Prisoner.

THE SHORT-ORDER COOK One of the people in Joe's Good Eats on the night that the Prisoner met Nona was a short-order cook.

TESSIO, VERN Vern spread the word that Besty Malenfant kissed the Prisoner.

TWO OLD LADIES There were two old ladies in Joe's Good Eats on the night that the Prisoner met Nona there.

TWO TRUCKERS There were two truckers sitting at the counter in Joe's Good Eats on the night that the Prisoner met Nona there.

(21n)
SKELETON CREW
"Nona"
Places

AUGUSTA, MAINE One February 14, the Prisoner arrived in Augusta, where he stopped at Joe's Good Eats and "met" Nona.

BOWEN HILL The Maine town where Nona's fictitious uncle, Emonds, was supposed to live.

BOWEN ROAD As the Prisoner and Nona drove down Stackpole Road in Castle Rock on their way to the graveyard, they were stopped by two men (probably utility workers) who told them to take Bowen Road because there was a live wire down. The

Prisoner shot the guy with the flashlight; the other guy got away.

CASTLE ROCK The Maine town across the river from Harlow where the Prisoner, a state ward, grew up with a family named Hollis. His real mother had come from Castle Rock, and that was where Nona took him on Valentine's Day night.

THE CASTLE ROCK YOUTH LEAGUE A renovated farm in Castle Rock that had twelve lanes of candlepin bowling, a jukebox, three Brunswick pool tables, and a Coke-and-chips counter.

GARDINER When Norman Blanchette picked up the Prisoner and Nona, he told them he was headed for Gardiner. He never made it.

THE GRAVEYARD The place Nona took the Prisoner. There, he saw "the girl." She was naked, and had been ripped open from "throat to crotch"; rats lived inside her body. Then there was nothing there. And then Nona turned into a giant rat.

GRETNA Toughies from Gretna were really the only guys that hung out at the Castle Rock Youth League.

HARLOW The Maine town where the Hollises lived. Also, toughies from Harlow were really the only guys that hung out at the Castle Rock Youth League.

HARLOW VILLAGE On their way back to Castle Rock, the Prisoner and Nona saw a Buick Riviera that had skidded and climbed the curb in Harlow Village.

JAY HILL Most of the Castle Rock youth didn't hang around the Castle Rock Youth League, preferring instead to drive to Jay Hill to go to the drive-in.

JOE'S GOOD EATS A combination diner and diesel stop on Route 202 in Augusta, Maine. Joe's was where the Prisoner "met" Nona.

KITTERY Before he met Nona, the Prisoner was headed for Kittery.

LEWISTON AND AUBURN Castle Rock, Maine, was just south and west of Lewiston and Auburn, Maine.

THE MANOIR A bar in Lewiston, Maine, where Betsy Malenfant ended up hustling guys for drinks.

OXFORD PLAINS Castle Rock youth went to the stock-car races at Oxford Plains.

PORTLAND After his family died in a house fire, the Prisoner was sent to a home in Portland. He was three years old.

ROUTE 136 The road that the Prisoner and Nona traveled after killing Norman Blanchette and the pickup truck driver.

ROUTE 126 The road (towards Castle Heights) where the Castle Rock Youth League was located.

ROUTE 7 The logging road where Nona and the Prisoner had sex in the police cruiser.

ROUTE 202 The road just inside the Augusta, Maine, city limits.

STACKPOLE ROAD The road that the Prisoner and Nona took through west Castle Rock.

(21n)
SKELETON CREW
"Nona"
Things

"A BOY NAMED SUE" When the Prisoner entered Joe's Good Eats and got The Eye, one of the truckers in the diner went to the jukebox and played Johnny Cash's song, "A Boy Named Sue."

A BUICK RIVIERA On their way back to Castle Rock, the Prisoner and Nona saw a Buick Riviera that had skidded and climbed the curb in Harlow Village.

A CHEVROLET IMPALA SEDAN The car driven by Norman Blanchette. He gave the Prisoner and Nona a ride. The Prisoner killed him.

A CHRISTMAS WREATH On February 14, a wilted Christmas wreath still hung on the door of Joe's Good Eats in Augusta, Maine.

DELTA TAU DELTA The girl that the Prisoner first loved in college dumped him for a guy from her hometown who was a member of the Delta Tau Delta fraternity.

"DO YOU LOVE?" The question Nona the Rat-Thing asked the Prisoner in the Castle Rock graveyard. [NOTE: This is the same question posed by Randy to the thing on the water in Cascade Lake in King's story "The Raft," also contained in *Skeleton Crew*.]

THE EYE "You know about The Eye once you let your hair get down below the lobes of your ears. Right then people know you don't belong to the Lions, Elks, or the VFW. You know about The Eye, but you never get used to it." The Prisoner got The Eye as soon as he entered Joe's Good Eats on the night he met Nona.

FEBRUARY 9 The date that the Prisoner got the letter from the dean of arts and sciences telling him that he was flunking two or three courses in his major field.

THE GS&WM RAILROAD TRESTLE After the Prisoner killed the cop, he could make out the GS&WM railroad trestle as only a shadow in the distance.

"KEEP RIGHT FOR EXIT 14" Norman Blanchette intended to drop off the Prisoner and Nona at this sign, and then continue on his way. He never made it.

MASON JARS The jars Mrs. Hollis used to can her vegetables.

THE MONA LISA When the Prisoner first met Nona, he thought that she looked like the Mona Lisa and the Venus de Milo come to life.

A SHOTGUN The weapon that the Prisoner found beneath the dash of the police car driven by the cop he killed in Castle Rock. He used it to kill the utility worker with the flashlight.

UNIT FOUR The number of the police car driven by the cop killed by the Prisoner.

VALENTINE'S DAY February 14. The day that the Prisoner left college, and the night he "met" Nona.

THE VENUS DE MILO When the Prisoner first met Nona, he thought that she looked like the Mona Lisa and the Venus de Milo come to life.

❖❖❖

(21o)
SKELETON CREW
"For Owen"
[Poem]

❖❖❖

(21p)
SKELETON CREW
"Survivor Type"
People

THE BIG CHINK Henry Li-Tsu.

BRAZZI, RICKY Pine paid Brazzi three dollars to take care of Howie Plotsky. Brazzi brought Pine three of Plotsky's teeth.

THE BURNT MAN A man on the Callas was burned in the explosion. His shirt was burned off, and his skin was barbecued.

THE COOK The cook on the Callas was burned on his face and hands during the explosion.

DOM A friend of Pine's who used to say "No way no how."

A GULL Pine killed and ate a gull raw on January 28.

HAILLEY, FATHER The priest from Holy Family Church, the church Pine attended as a child.

HAMMERSMITH, WILL Pine's friend. Pine remembered that Will used to have barbecues at his house on Long Island.

HANELLI, RONNIE "Ronnie the Enforcer." He played football with Pine in college. Pine got Ronnie's kid brother a medical residency. Hanelli loan-sharked in a room over the Fish Bowl Bar. Pine got Henry Li-Tsu's name from Hanelli.

HANELLI'S KID BROTHER Pine got him a medical residency as a favor to Hanelli.

LI-TSU, HENRY The "Big Chink" in Saigon that sold Pine the two kilos of heroin. Henry had a lisp.

LI-TSU, MRS. Henry Li-Tsu's wife. She was killed when her Opel blew up with her in it. She was killed by Ngo.

LOWENTHAL The man who told the tax people about Pine's drug-kickback scheme.

A MIDDLE-AGED MAN After the explosion on the Callas, a middle-aged man sat on the shuffleboard court pulling his hair.

MOCKRIDGE, PROFESSOR "Old Mockie." Pine's "Basic Anatomy" professor.

NGO, SOLOM A Vietnamese chemist whom Hanelli said would test Henry Li-Tsu's "product" for Pine. Apparently, the Chink was known to play "jokes" now and again: One of his favorites was a plastic bag filled with talcum powder, drain cleaner, or cornstarch, instead of heroin.

"OLD MOCKIE" Professor Mockridge, Pine's "Basic Anatomy" professor.

PINE, RICHARD He was stranded on an island with four gallons of water, a first aid kit, a lifeboat inspection log, two knives, a combination fork and spoon, and two kilos of pure heroin worth $350,000. His real name was Richard Pinzetti, and he had been born in Little Italy. He ended up literally eating himself to death.

PINZETTI, MR. Richard Pine's father. He was an old-world guinea who died of cancer at the age of forty-six.

PINZETTI, MRS. Pine's mother. She always said that Richard broke her heart by changing his name to Pine.

PINZETTI, RICHARD Richard Pine's real name.

PLOTSKY, HOWIE Pine attended high school with Howie. Plotsky had zits, and always bothered Pine in school.

RONNIE THE ENFORCER Ronnie Hanelli.

"RONNIEWOP" The name the Puerto Ricans called Ronnie Hanelli.

THE SAILOR One of the crew members on the Callas was the only guy in the lifeboat with Pine. His hand got stuck in a rope, however, and he fell overboard. He had a pimply face.

THE SCREECHING WOMAN A screeching woman with a baby fell overboard when the explosion occured on the Callas.

THE SCREECHING WOMAN'S BABY A screeching woman with a baby fell overboard when the explosion occured on the Callas.

THE SKINDIVER Pine paid a skindiver $3,000 to get the two kilos of heroin through U.S. customs.

STEINBRUNNER, MR. The Jewish grocer Mrs. Pinzetti married the day after Mr. Pinzetti was buried.

(21p)
SKELETON CREW
"Survivor Type"
Places

CALIFORNIA Pine planned on taking the "cure" (for his heroin habit) in California after he was rescued.

THE FISH BOWL BAR Ronnie Hanelli loan-sharked from a room over the Fish Bowl Bar.

HOLY FAMILY CHURCH Pine's childhood church. Father Hailley was the priest there, and Pine remembered him always talking about sin.

THE ISLAND The island on which Pine was stranded was 190 paces wide by 267 paces long.

LIFEBOAT STATION 8 The station where Pine went with his heroin when the explosion occured on the Callas.

LITTLE ITALY Richard Pine's New York City birthplace.

LONG ISLAND Will Hammersmith lived on Long Island.

MOTHER CRUNCH An ice cream parlor on First Avenue that was a favorite of Pine's.

PARK AVENUE Before he was drummed out of the medical profession, Pine had a practice on Park Avenue in New York City.

NEW YORK CITY Before he was drummed out of the medical profession, Pine had a practice on Park Avenue in New York City.

SAIGON Pine bought the two kilos of heroin in Saigon from Henry Li-Tsu.

THE SHUFFLEBOARD COURT After the explosion on the Callas, a middle-aged man sat on the shuffleboard court pulling his hair.

ST. REGIS HOTEL The hotel in San Francisco where Pine was supposed to meet with the skindiver who was going to get his heroin through U.S. customs.

TWO DRUG SUPPLY HOUSES Pine had a kickback scheme going with two drug supply houses when he was in practice on Park Avenue.

U.S. CUSTOMS Pine paid a skindiver $3,000 to get the two kilos of heroin through U.S. customs.

(21p)
SKELETON CREW
"Survivor Type"
Things

ALL-CITY QUARTERBACK Pine's high school football accomplishment.

AUGUST 8, 1970 The last entry in the sunken ship's log was dated August 8, 1970.

"BASIC ANATOMY" A course that Pine took in medical school. It was taught by Professor Mockridge.

"THE BIG MAC THEME SONG" Some time after Pine ate the meaty top of his own thigh, he began to hallucinate the McDonald's "Big Mac Theme Song."

THE CALLAS The name of the sunken ship.

THE CHINK'S JOKES Henry Li-Tsu (The Chink), was known to play "jokes" now and again: one of his favorites was a plastic bag filled with talcum powder, drain cleaner, or cornstarch, instead of heroin. Ronnie Hanelli said that "one day Li-Tsu's little jokes would get him killed."

"COLD ROAST BEEF" On February 9, Pine amputated and ate his own left foot. He kept telling himself "cold roast beef, cold roast beef."

A COMBINATION FORK AND SPOON One of the items Pine salvaged off the ship before it went down.

A COMPOUND FRACTURE OF THE RIGHT ANKLE On January 31, Pine fractured his right ankle while waving to a plane.

A CRAB On February 13, Pine caught and killed a crab and roasted it. This was his first cooked food since he was stranded on the island.

A DEAD FISH On or about February 23, Pine ate a dead fish that was already rotten.

THE EARLOBES After Pine had eaten everything from the groin down, he started in on his earlobes.

8:00 O'CLOCK ON THE NIGHT OF THE TWENTY-THIRD The time and date of the explosion belowdecks on the Callas.

FE The date of Pine's twenty-sixth log entry.

FE/40? The date of Pine's twenty-eighth log entry.

FEB ? The date of Pine's twenty-third log entry.

FEBBA The date of Pine's twenty-seventh log entry.

FEBRUARY The date of Pine's twenty-fifth log entry.

FEBRUARY 8 The date of Pine's fifteenth log entry.

FEBRUARY 11 (?) The date of Pine's seventeenth log entry.

FEBRUARY 15 The date of Pine's twenty-first log entry.

FEBRUARY 5 The date of Pine's twelfth log entry.

FEBRUARY 1 The date of Pine's eighth log entry.

FEBRUARY 14 The date of Pine's twentieth log entry.

FEBRUARY 4 The date of Pine's eleventh log entry.

FEBRUARY 9 The date of Pine's sixteenth log entry.

FEBRUARY 2 The date of Pine's ninth log entry.

FEBRUARY 17 (?) The date of Pine's twenty-second log entry.

FEBRUARY 7 The date of Pine's thirteenth and fourteenth log entries.

FEBRUARY 3 The date of Pine's tenth log entry.

FEBRUARY 13 The date of Pine's nineteenth log entry.

FEBRUARY 12 The date of Pine's eighteenth log entry.

FEBRUARY 23 (?) The date of Pine's twenty-fourth log entry.

A FIRST-AID KIT One of the items Pine salvaged off the ship before it went down.

FORGED PRESCRIPTIONS In med school, Pine sold forged prescriptions for ten or twenty dollars each.

FORTY-SIX The age Richard Pine's father, Mr. Pinzetti, died of cancer.

$40,000 Pine had $40,000 in cash in a safe deposit box. It didn't do him much good on the island.

FOUR GALLONS OF WATER One of the items Pine salvaged off the ship before it went down.

A FULL PRE-MED ACADEMIC SCHOLARSHIP Pine's ticket into college.

GLADE AIR FRESHENER Pine thought that his patients would have snorted Glade if they thought it would get them high.

THE HELP SIGN In early February, Pine made a "HELP" sign out of dark rocks against white sand. It washed away by Valentine's Day.

HIWAY OUTLAWS Dom's club.

JANUARY 28 The date of Pine's fourth log entry.

JANUARY 24 The day a storm washed Richard Pine up on the island.

JANUARY 29 The date of Pine's fifth log entry.

JANUARY 27 The date of Pine's second and third log entries.

JANUARY 26 The date of Pine's first "post-stranded" log entry.

JANUARY 30 The date of Pine's sixth log entry.

JANUARY 31 The date of Pine's seventh log entry.

KELP AND SEAWEED After eating both his feet and a raw spider, Pine ate kelp and seaweed off a piece of driftwood.

LADY FINGERS After Pine ate his earlobes, he amputated his left hand and ate it. The last line of his journal was "lady fingers they taste just like lady fingers."

THE LEFT FOOT On February 9, Pine amputated and ate his own left foot. He kept telling himself "cold roast beef, cold roast beef."

THE LEFT HAND After Pine ate his earlobes, he amputated his left hand and ate it. The last line of his journal was "lady fingers they taste just like lady fingers."

THE LEFT LEG AT THE KNEE The piece of Pine's anatomy that he amputated and ate after eating the right leg from the knee down.

A LIFEBOAT INSPECTION LOG One of the items Pine salvaged off the ship before it went down.

THE MEATY TOP OF THE THIGH Sometime after February 23, Pine cut off and ate the meaty top of his thigh.

"NO TOMATOES TODAY" A sign that Pine remembered seeing on the vegetable pushcarts from his old neighborhood.

"NOTHING LEFT BELOW THE GROIN" Sometime toward the end of February, Pine had eaten everything from his groin down.

190 PACES WIDE BY 267 PACES LONG The dimensions of the island on which Richard Pine was stranded.

AN OPEL Mrs. Li-Tsu's car. She died when Ngo blew up the car with her in it.

PARADISE LINES Pine was on a Paradise Lines cruise ship, the Callas, when it sank, stranding him on the island.

"A PAVLOV DOG" Pine began salivating like a Pavlov dog when he saw a gull.

PINE'S "FE/40" DREAM Sometime after he had amputated and eaten everything from his groin down, Pine had a dream about his father. He wrote of his father, "Daddy you fucking greaseball dipstick nothing cipher zilcho zero."

PINE'S FOOD FANTASIES After amputating and eating his own right foot, Pine began to fantasize about food. His "Dream Menu" consisted of:

> His mother's lasagna
> Garlic bread
> Escargots

Lobster
Prime ribs
Peach melba
London broil
Pound cake with ice cream (from Mother Crunch on First Avenue)
Hot pretzels
Baked salmon
Baked Alaska
Baked ham with pineappple rings
Onion rings
Onion dip with potato chips
Iced tea
French fries.

PINE'S JOURNAL ENTRIES (CHRONOLOGICAL ORDER) Note The following chronological listing is intended to help to illustrate the disintegration of Pine's mind as he began to devour more and more of himself, a descent into madness reflected in the increasingly erratic and incoherent dating of his journal entries. Hope it's helpful.]

ENTRY	1	"January 26"
ENTRY	2	"January 27"
ENTRY	3	"(later)"
ENTRY	4	"January 28"
ENTRY	5	"January 29"
ENTRY	6	"January 30"
ENTRY	7	"January 31"
ENTRY	8	"February 1"
ENTRY	9	"February 2"
ENTRY	10	"February 3"
ENTRY	11	"February 4"
ENTRY	12	"February 5"
ENTRY	13	"February 7"
ENTRY	14	"(later)"
ENTRY	15	"February 8"
ENTRY	16	"February 9"
ENTRY	17	"February 11 (?)"
ENTRY	18	"February 12"
ENTRY	19	"February 13"
ENTRY	20	"Feb 14"
ENTRY	21	"Feb 15"
ENTRY	22	"Feb 17 (?)"
ENTRY	23	"Feb ?"
ENTRY	24	"February 23 (?)"
ENTRY	25	"February"
ENTRY	26	"Fe"
ENTRY	27	"Febba"
ENTRY	28	"Fe/40?"

PINE'S SALVAGE Pine took the following items off the Callas when it went down:

> Four gallons of water
> A sewing kit
> A first-aid kit
> A lifeboat inspection log
> Two knives
> A combination fork and spoon
> Two kilos of pure heroin worth $350,000.

PRESCRIPTION PADS In med school, Pine stole prescription pads and sold forged prescriptions for ten or twenty dollars each.

PULSAR Pine's watch.

THE RIGHT FOOT Pine amputated his right foot in a sixty-five minute operation, and then ate it. The last line of the entry detailing the surgery (and the first mention of his self-cannibalization) was "I washed it thoroughly before I ate it."

THE RIGHT LEG FROM THE KNEE DOWN On or about

February 17, Pine amputated his right leg from the knee down. He roasted it before he ate it.

"THE SECOND OATH OF HIPPOCRATES AND HYPO-CRITES" Pine wrote that he was drummed out of the medical profession by this "Oath."

A SEWING KIT One of the items Pine salvaged off the ship before it went down.

A SPIDER After amputating both his feet, Pine caught a spider and ate it raw.

TEN OR TWENTY DOLLARS EACH The amount Pine charged for forged prescriptions when he was in medical school.

THREE DOLLARS The amount Pine paid Ricky Brazzi for three of Howie Plotsky's teeth.

THREE TEETH Ricky Brazzi brought Pine three of Howie Plotsky's teeth. Pine paid Ricky three dollars.

$3,000 The fee Pine paid a skindiver to get the two kilos of heroin through U.S. customs.

12:41 At 12:41, Pine woke up after snorting some heroin, and from 12:45 to 1:50, he amputated his right foot.

TWENTY MINUTES It took twenty minutes from the first explosion on the Callas until the ship sunk.

TWENTY-FIVE POUNDS By February 2, Pine had already lost twenty-five pounds.

TWO KILOS OF PURE HEROIN Pine had two kilos of heroin worth $350,000 with him when the Callas sank. He used it to anesthetize himself when he performed his self-amputations.

TWO KNIVES Two of the items Pine salvaged off the ship before it went down.

A WHITE CONTINENTAL Ronnie Hanelli's car.

❖❖❖

(21q)
SKELETON CREW
"Uncle Otto's Truck"
People

BAKER A pulper who offered George McCutcheon twenty dollars for the Cresswell's wheels, tires and all. George took the twenty.

BARGER, CHUCKIE Chuckie painted Uncle Otto's house red.

DODD, BILLY "Crazy Frank's" father. Billy hitched his wrecker to George's ditched Cresswell so it faced the road. [Note: See the sections on *The Dead Zone* and *Cujo* in this volume for more info on Crazy Frank Dodd.]

DODD, FRANK Billy Dodd's boy.

DURKIN, CARL The Castle Rock undertaker.

McCUTCHEON, GEORGE The partner that Otto took on in order to buy the New England Paper Company land he wanted. Otto later killed George by pushing the old Cresswell truck on top of him.

SCHENCK, GRANDFATHER Otto's father.

SCHENCK, MR. Quentin's father.

SCHENCK, MRS. Otto's mother.

SCHENCK, OTTO Quentin's uncle, and the owner of a big red Cresswell truck abandoned in a field on the Black Henry Road. Otto was the object of the truck's final act of revenge.

SCHENCK, QUENTIN Uncle Otto's nephew. Quentin pissed in his pants in the Cresswell when he was five years old. Quentin was the one to find Uncle Otto's oil-gorged body. He was also the one to take the spark plug from Uncle Otto's mouth. Until he wrote "Uncle Otto's Truck," Quentin never told anyone about the spark plug.

THE SELECTMAN The Castle Rock selectman wrote Uncle Otto a letter declining the use of the one-room house (as a schoolhouse) that Otto had built for Castle Rock.

(21q)
SKELETON CREW
"Uncle Otto's Truck"
Places

THE BLACK HENRY ROAD The road from Bridgton to Castle Rock. In 1953, Otto Schenck and George McCutcheon (both of them "shithouse drunk") drove the Cresswell into a ditch off the Black Henry Road, where it stood for years – until it crossed the road and killed Uncle Otto.

BRIDGTON The Maine town accessible by the Black Henry Road through Castle Rock.

CARBINE STREET, CASTLE ROCK The street where the new Castle Rock high school was located.

CASTLE HILL The section of Castle Rock, Maine, where Otto Schenck bought a large house.

THE CASTLE RIDGE SCHOOL Castle Rock's last-to-close one-room schoolhouse. It ended up Steve's Pizzaville.

CASTLE ROCK, MAINE Otto Schenck moved to Castle Rock at the age of twenty, after his father died. Otto received a full inheritance.

THE CUSHMAN BAKERY After Uncle Otto ditched the Cresswell, he and George were given a ride back to town in a Cushman Bakery truck.

FORTY NEW ENGLAND CITIES The Schenck and McCutcheon hardware stores eventually had branches in forty New England cities.

FROM CENTRAL FALLS, RHODE ISLAND, TO DERRY, MAINE George McCutcheon and Otto Schenck had lumberyards from Central Falls to Derry.

THE FRYEBURG FAIR One day, when they were on their way to the Fryeburg Fair, Quentin's father pulled over on the Black Henry Road and put Quentin in the cab of the Cresswell. Quentin pissed in his pants.

GERMANY Otto's parents came from Germany.

HARLOW Most of the New England Paper Company land that Otto Schenck bought was in Castle Rock, Maine, but some of it spilled into Waterford and Harlow.

THE SCHENCK AND McCUTCHEON HARDWARE STORES The chain of hardware stores started by George McCutcheon and Otto Schenck in New England. They eventually had stores in forty New England cities.

THE SCHENCK AND McCUTCHEON LUMBERYARDS George McCutcheon and Otto Schenck had lumberyards from Central Falls to Derry.

STEVE'S PIZZAVILLE Castle Ridge School was Castle Rock's last one-room schoolhouse to close. It ended up Steve's Pizzaville.

TRINITY HILL In 1953, Uncle Otto shifted the Cresswell into first gear to make it up Trinity Hill but, because he was "shithouse drunk," he forgot to shift back up again once they hit the top of the hill. The Cresswell exploded, and ended up ditched in a field off the Black Henry Road.

UNCLE OTTO'S HOUSE In 1965, Uncle Otto built a one-room house and tried to give it to Castle Rock to be used as a schoolhouse. They turned it down, so Uncle Otto moved into the house. Otto was found dead in the house by his nephew, Quentin. He was full of Diamond Gem Oil, and had a sparkplug in his mouth.

THE UNIVERSITY OF MAINE FORESTRY DEPARTMENT The University of Maine forestry department received all of Uncle Otto's fortune when he died.

WARREN'S A store in Bridgton, Maine. Quentin Schenck's mother shopped there.

WATERFORD Most of the New England Paper Company land that Otto Schenck bought was in Castle Rock, Maine, but some of it spilled into Waterford and Harlow.

THE WHITE MOUNTAINS After Otto ditched the Cresswell, he would have had a view of the White Mountains – if the truck's windshield hadn't been covered with Diamond Gem Oil.

(21q)
SKELETON CREW
"Uncle Otto's Truck"
Things

A CHAMPION MAXI-DUTY SPARK PLUG When Quentin found Uncle Otto's dead body, a Champion Maxi-Duty spark plug was jammed into Otto's mouth, and his body was filled with three quarts of Diamond Gem Oil.

A CRESSWELL Uncle Otto's truck. (It had originally been George McCutcheon's, but it went to Uncle Otto – as did everything else – after George was crushed to death underneath the truck.)

THE CRESSWELL'S WHEELS George McCutcheon sold the Cresswell's wheels, tires and all, to a pulper named Baker.

A CUSHMAN BAKERY TRUCK After Uncle Otto ditched the Cresswell, he and George were given a ride back to town in a Cushman Bakery truck.

DIAMOND GEM OIL The oil George McCutcheon always used in the Cresswell. When Quentin Schenck found Uncle Otto's dead body, a Champion Maxi-Duty spark plug was jammed into Otto's mouth, and his body was filled with three quarts of Diamond Gem Oil.

THE NEW ENGLAND PAPER COMPANY Otto bought four thousand acres of New England Paper's land at a cost of about $2,500 an acre. (The company was selling off its land in a last-ditch effort to stay alive. It worked.)

1953 The year Uncle Otto ditched the Cresswell on the Black Henry Road.

1965 The year Uncle Otto built a one-room house, and tried to donate it to the town as a schoolhouse. They turned it down.

1933 The year Otto Schenck sold his house in Castle Hill.

1925 The year Otto Schenck's father died.

1929 The year of the stock market crash.

A PONTIAC Quentin Schenck's car.

THE THINGS QUENTIN SCHENCK BELIEVED IN WHEN HE WAS FIVE YEARS OLD Santa Claus, the Tooth Fairy, and the Allamagoosalum.

THE TRINITY HILL MEMORIAL TOURIST TRUCK When tourists stopped at the Cresswell to take pictures of it and the White Mountains, Quentin's father called it the "Trinity Hill Memorial Tourist Truck," until Uncle Otto's obsession with it got too intense to be funny anymore.

TWENTY Otto Schenck's age when he moved to Castle Rock.

TWENTY DOLLARS George McCutcheon sold the Cresswell's wheels, tires and all, to a pulper named Baker.

VITALIS AND WILDROOT CREME OIL The barbershop smells Quentin Schenck remembered from his childhood.

❖❖❖

(21r)
SKELETON CREW
"Morning Deliveries (Milkman #1)"
People

A BOY As Spike finished his Culver Street deliveries, a boy banged out of a house, and took in the milk.

THE COLLINS FAMILY A family on Spike's Culver Street delivery route. He left them two quarts of milk and a carton of yogurt. We don't learn if they were poisoned.

THE JENNER BOYS Growing boys on Spike's Culver Street route.

THE JENNERS A family on Spike's Culver street delivery route. They had growing boys. Spike left them five quarts of milk. We don't learn if they were poisoned.

THE KINCAIDS A family on Spike's Culver Street delivery route. One morning in June, they wanted nothing from Spike, so he left

them instead an empty milk bottle filled with cyanide gas.

MACKENZIE, NELLA Mrs. Mackenzie. She was one of Spike's Culver Street customers, and one morning she left him a note. [NOTE: See the "Things" entry NELLA MACKENZIE'S NOTE.]

THE MACKENZIES One of the families on Spike's Culver Street milk delivery route. They had a birdbath.

McCARTHY, MRS. A woman on Spike's Culver Street delivery route. She left him a note one morning that said "Chocoloate." He left her a tarantula instead.

THE MERTONS A family on Spike's Culver Street delivery route. They wanted to cancel delivery. Their house on Culver Street was empty, and there was a clump of hair and bone matted into a hole in a wall in the house.

ORDWAY, MISS One of Spike's Culver Street delivery route customers. He left her a carton of eggnog spiked with belladonnna.

ROCKY Spike's friend. He worked at an industrial laundry.

SPIKE The milkman. His specialty was leaving a little "something extra" with his morning deliveries...like deadly nightshade, a tarantula, acid gel, belladonna, or cyanide gas. [NOTE: In "Big Wheels: A Tale of the Laundry Game (Milkman #2)," we find out that Spike's full name was Spike Milligan. See the section on "Big Wheels" immediately following this concordance.]

SPIKE'S MOTHER Spike's dead mother. She once told Spike, "Variety is the spice of life, but we are Irish, and the Irish prefer to take their 'taters plain. Be regular in all ways, Spike, and you will be happy." [NOTE: Her name was Mrs. Milligan. See the section on "Big Wheels: A Tale of the Laundry Game (Milkman #2)" immediately following this section.]

THE WALKERS A family on Spike's Culver Street delivery route. He left them two quarts of milk and a pint of whipping cream. We don't learn if they were poisoned.

THE WEBBERS A family on Spike's Culver Street delivery route. He left them a container of all-purpose cream filled with an acid gel. They owned a Saab.

(21r)
SKELETON CREW
"Morning Deliveries (Milkman #1)"
Places

THE CORNER OF CULVER AND BALFOUR AVENUE A maple tree stood at this intersection.

CRAMER'S DAIRY The company Spike worked for. He had a delivery route. "Morning Deliveries" were their specialty.

CULVER STREET One of the streets on Spike the milkman's Cramer's Dairy milk delivery route.

A HOLE IN A WALL There was a clump of hair and bone matted into a hole in a wall in the empty Merton house on Spike's route.

IN A MAYONNAISE JAR Spike kept his tarantula in a mayonnaise jar on his truck.

AN INDUSTRIAL LAUNDRY Spike's friend and cohort, Rocky, worked at an industrial laundry. While on his route, Spike heard the five a.m. whistle blow. [NOTE: In "Big Wheels: A Tale of the Laundry Game (Milkman #2)," we find out that it was the New Adams Laundry. See the section on "Big Wheels" immediately following this concordance.]

THE LETTER SLOT Mrs. McCarthy's "Chocolate" note was wedged into the letter slot of her front door.

THE MCCARTHY HOUSE The stop on Spike's delivery route after the Mackenzie house.

THE WEBBER HOUSE The stop on Spike's Culver Street delivery route after the McCarthy house.

(21r)
SKELETON CREW
"Morning Deliveries (Milkman #1)"
Things

ACID GEL Spike left the Webbers an all-purpose cream container filled with an acid gel.

A BEIGE TRUCK Spike the milkman's delivery truck was beige with red lettering.

A BIRD BATH The Mackenzies had a bird bath on their lawn.

A CARTON OF EGGNOG SPIKED WITH BELLADONNA The order Spike left for Miss Ordway.

A CLUMP OF HAIR AND BONE There was a clump of hair and bone matted into a hole in a wall in the empty Merton house

A CONTAINER OF ALL-PURPOSE CREAM The Webbers' order. Spike left them an all-purpose cream container...filled with a deadly acid gel.

"CRAMER'S DAIRY DRINK WHOLESOME AND DELICIOUS SERVE HOT OR COLD KIDS LOVE IT!" The message written on the side of the Cramer's chocolate milk carton that Spike left for Mrs. McCarthy.

"CRAMER'S DAIRY – MORNING DELIVERIES OUR SPECIALTY!" The red-lettered sign on Spike's truck.

THE CRAMER'S DAIRY TRUCK SIGN The red-lettered sign said "Cramer's Dairy – Morning Deliveries Our Specialty!"

DEADLY NIGHTSHADE The poison that Spike left for Mrs. Mackenzie. (On his truck, the orange juice was behind the nightshade.)

"DELIVERY MADE" The message Spike wrote on Mrs. McCarthy's note. He left her a tarantula.

FIVE QUARTS OF MILK Spike left the Jenners five quarts of milk. We don't learn if they were poisoned.

JUNE The month Spike made his special "morning deliveries" to the families on Culver Street.

A MAPLE TREE A maple tree stood on the corner of Culver Street and Balfour Avenue on Spike's milk delivery route.

A MILK BOTTLE FILLED WITH CYANIDE GAS The order Spike left for the Kincaids.

MRS. McCARTHY'S NOTE It said "Chocolate." Spike left her a tarantula in a Cramer's Dairy chocolate milk carton.

NELLA MACKENZIE'S NOTE One morning Mrs. Mackenzie left Spike the following note:

> 1 qt milk
> 1 econ cream
> 1 ornge jce
> Thanks
> Nella M.

ORANGE JUICE On Spike's truck, the orange juice was behind the deadly nightshade.

A SAAB The Webbers' car.

SPIKE'S CULVER STREET DELIVERIES The following list is made up of Spike's Culver Street customers and their orders, listed in order of delivery:

1. THE MACKENZIES—One quart milk, one economy cream, one orange juice, and deadly nightshade;
2. THE McCARTHYS—a chocolate milk carton containing a tarantula;
3. THE WEBBERS—An all-purpose cream container filled with an acid gel;
4. THE JENNERS—Five quarts of milk;
5. THE COLLINS—Two quarts of milk and a carton of yogurt;
6. MISS ORDWAY—A carton of eggnog spiked with belladonna;
7. THE KINCAIDS—An empty milk bottle filled with cyanide gas;
8. THE WALKERS—Two quarts of milk and a pint of whipping cream;
9. THE MERTONS—Nothing.

A TARANTULA Spike left Mrs. McCarthy a tarantula instead of chocolate milk. He kept the bug in a mayonnaise jar on his truck.

TWO QUARTS OF MILK AND A PINT OF WHIPPING CREAM The order that Spike left for the Walkers. We don't learn if they were poisoned.

TWO QUARTS OF MILK AND A CARTON OF YOGURT The order Spike left the Collins family. We don't learn if they were poisoned.

"VARIETY" Spike's mother once told Spike, "Variety is the spice of life, but we are Irish, and the Irish prefer to take their 'taters plain. Be regular in all ways, Spike, and you will be happy."

❖❖❖

(21s)
SKELETON CREW
"Big Wheels: A Tale of the Laundry Game (Milkman #2)"
People

BLIER, ROCKY One of the football players pictured on the cans of Iron City beer that Rocky and Leo drank.

BRADSHAW, TERRY One of the football players pictured on the cans of Iron City beer that Rocky and Leo drank.

DREW, MARCY Marcy Driscoll, Bob Driscoll's wife.

DRISCOLL, BOBBY "Stiff Socks," an old classmate of Rocky's from Crescent High School. He opened his own Citgo service station, and Rocky convinced him (via the Iron City beer express) to slap an inspection sticker on Rocky's old '57 Chrysler.

DRISCOLL, MARCY Marcy Drew Driscoll, Bob Driscoll's wife.

EDWARDS, LEO Rocky's helper in the washroom at the New Adams Laundry. He and Rocky set out one night on a mission: to acquire an inspection sticker for Rocky's 1957 Chrysler.

FREEMANTLE, OLD LADY One of Rocky's and Bobby Driscoll's former Crescent High School teachers. (Tinker Johnson had once pasted a picture of Ursula Andress up on her bulletin board.)

GREEN, "MEAN JOE" One of the football players pictured on the cans of Iron City beer that Rocky and Leo drank.

HARRIS, FRANCO One of the football players pictured on the cans of Iron City beer Spike and Leo drank.

JOHNSON, TINKER A Crescent High School classmate of Rocky and Bobby Driscoll's who had pasted a picture of Ursula Andress up on old lady Freemantle's bulletin board.

MILLIGAN, SPIKE The milkman. Spike had gotten Rocky's wife pregnant, and moved to Dakin Street with Spike. [NOTE: This is the same Spike the milkman from "Morning Deliveries (Milkman #1)." See the section on "Morning Deliveries" in this volume.]

ROCKWELL, JOHNNY Rocky, the laundry worker with the 1957 Chrysler who set out one night with his friend Leo on a quest for an inspection sticker.

THE ROCKWELL CHILDREN Rocky and his wife had two.

ROCKY Johnny Rockwell.

RUCKLEHOUSE, DIANA One of Rocky and Bob Driscoll's classmates from Crescent High School. She was amply endowed in the pectoral area.

SPIKE'S CHILD Spike and Rocky's ex-wife had a child "every bit as trout-eyed as his daddy."

"STIFF SOCKS" Bobby Driscoll, an old schoolmate of Rocky's.

SWANN, LYNN One of the football players pictured on the cans of Iron City beer Rocky and Leo drank.

THE YOUNG COUPLE In 1968, there had been a torture murder of a young couple in the Devon Woods in southwestern Pennsylvania. Their bodies were found dissected in a 1959 Mercury.

(21s)
SKELETON CREW
"Big Wheels: A Tale of the Laundry Game (Milkman #2)"
Places

BALFOUR AVENUE On the night that Rocky and Leo set out for an inspection sticker for Rocky's 1957 Chrysler, they cruised down Culver Street, and then out along Balfour Avenue towards Crescent.

THE BULLETIN BOARD Tinker Johnson had once pasted a picture of Ursula Andress up on old lady Freemantle's bulletin board.

A CITGO STATION Bob Driscoll owned a Citgo station that was also Pennsylvania state inspection station #72.

CRAMER'S DAIRY The dairy where Spike Milligan worked.

CRESCENT HIGH SCHOOL The high school Bob Driscoll and Rocky attended.

CRESCENT STREET On the night Rocky and Leo set out for an inspection sticker for Rocky's 1957 Chrysler, they cruised down Culver Street, and then out along Balfour Avenue towards Crescent.

CULVER STREET On the night Rocky and Leo set out for an inspection sticker for Rocky's 1957 Chrysler, they cruised down Culver Street, and then out along Balfour Avenue towards Crescent.

DAKIN STREET After Rocky's wife divorced him, she moved in with Spike and lived with him on Dakin Street.

DEVON STREAM ROAD While out cruising, Rocky turned at the intersection of Highway 99 and the Devon Stream Road.

DEVON WOODS An area in southwestern Pennsylvania where there had been a torture murder of a young couple in 1968. The couple had been found dissected in a 1959 Mercury.

FLAGSTAFF After Leo saved enough money and bought his Kawasaki, he planned on moving to Flagstaff.

THE FOUR CORNERS TAVERN When Rocky found out that his wife was having an affair with Spike the milkman, he decided to kill him. But before he went after Spike, he stopped at the Four Corners Tavern and had " a few beers – six, eight, maybe twenty."

GENERAL DELIVERY Bobby Driscoll sometimes thought of killing his wife Marcy, and mailing her to General Delivery, Lima, Indiana; North Pole, New Hampshire; Intercourse, Pennsylvania; or Kunkle, Iowa.

A GIANT EAGLE STORE Bobby Driscoll's wife was partial to the Donuts by the Dozen sold at the local Giant Eagle store.

HIGHWAY 99 While out cruising, Rocky turned at the intersection of Highway 99 and the Devon Stream Road.

INTERCOURSE, PENNSYLVANIA Bobby Driscoll sometimes thought of killing his wife Marcy and mailing her to General Delivery, Lima, Indiana; North Pole, New Hampshire; Intercourse, Pennsylvania; or Kunkle, Iowa.

KUNKLE, IOWA Bobby Driscoll sometimes thought of killing his wife Marcy and mailing her to General Delivery, Lima, Indiana; North Pole, New Hampshire; Intercourse, Pennsylvania; or Kunkle, Iowa.

LIMA, INDIANA Bobby Driscoll sometimes thought of killing his wife Marcy and mailing her to General Delivery, Lima, Indiana; North Pole, New Hampshire; Intercourse, Pennsylvania; or Kunkle, Iowa.

NEVADA When Rocky was in prison, his wife got a divorce in Nevada, and moved in with Spike.

THE NEW ADAMS LAUNDRY The laundry where Rocky and Leo both worked.

NORTH POLE, NEW HAMPSHIRE Bobby Driscoll sometimes thought of killing his wife Marcy, and mailing her to General Delivery, Lima, Indiana; North Pole, New Hampshire; Intercourse, Pennsylvania; or Kunkle, Iowa.

OAK AND BALFOUR When Rocky went out to kill Spike, his ex-wife called the cops. They were waiting for him at the intersection of Oak and Balfour, and they found the .32 in his waistband.

OAK STREET Rocky and his wife had lived on Oak Street before the divorce.

PAULINE'S SUPERETTE Rocky sent Leo to Pauline's to buy more beer after he, Leo, and Bobby killed the case they had been working on. (Leo went to get their third case of the evening, an "evening" which had begun at four o'clock – punchout time at the laundry.)

A PENNSYLVANIA PRISON After Rocky was caught with a .32 in his waistband on his way to kill Spike the milkman, he spent four months in a Pennsylvania prison laundry.

SOUTHERN HILL After Rocky got his inspection sticker, he saw Spike Milligan's truck and chased it up Southern Hill on the wrong side of the road.

SOUTHWESTERN PENNSYLVANIA The area where the Devon Woods was located.

(21s)
SKELETON CREW
"Big Wheels: A Tale of the Laundry Game (Milkman #2)"
Things

BOB DRISCOLL'S GAS STATION SIGN The following sign stood in front of Bob's Citgo station:

BOB'S GAS & SERVICE
BOB DRISCOLL, PROP.
FRONT END ALIGNMENT OUR SPECIALTY
DEFEND YOUR GOD-GIVEN RIGHT TO BEAR ARMS!
STATE INSPECTION STATION #72

CAMELS Leo's cigarettes.

DONUTS BY THE DOZEN One of the products sold at a local Giant Eagle store in Pennsylvania. Bobby Driscoll's wife was partial to them – by the dozen.

FIFTEEN DOLLARS A WEEK ALIMONY After Rocky's wife divorced him, he had to pay her (and Spike) fifteen dollars a week alimony.

FLEER'S The bubble gum that Spike chewed constantly.

"GET OFF MY CLOUD" The Stones' song that Leo hummed.

IRON CITY BEER Rocky and Leo got drunk on I.C. beer the night they set out for the inspection sticker.

JULY 1 Rocky and Leo went out cruising on the evening of June 30. At 12:01 a.m., July 1, the inspection sticker on Rocky's car would expire.

JUNE 30 Rocky and Leo went out cruising for an inspection sticker on the evening of June 30.

A KAWASAKI MOTORCYCLE The bike that Leo was saving up to buy.

A 1959 MERCURY In 1968, there had been a torture murder of a young couple in the Devon Woods in southwestern Pennsylvania. Their bodies were found dissected in a 1959 Mercury. After Rocky got his inspection sticker, he chased Spike Milligan's milk truck up Southern Hill on the wrong side of the road, and crashed head-on into a 1959 Mercury missing a hood ornament.

A 1957 CHRYSLER Rocky's car.

1970 The year Bobby Driscoll married Marcy Drew.

1968 In 1968, there had been a torture murder of a young couple in the Devon Woods in southwestern Pennsylvania. Their bodies were found dissected in a 1959 Mercury.

ROCKY'S INSPECTION STICKER At 12:01 a.m. on July 1, the inspection sticker on Rocky's Chrysler would expire. Rocky was able to "convince" his old friend "Stiff Socks" to slap a new sticker on his car. (It took a few Iron Citys to do it, but Driscoll finally agreed.)

A .32 CALIBER Rocky's gun.

THURSDAY NIGHTS Marcy Driscoll's Bingo night.

12:01 A.M. Rocky and Leo went out cruising on the evening of June 30. At 12:01 a.m., July 1, the inspection sticker on Rocky's car would expire.

❖❖❖

(21t)
SKELETON CREW
"Gramma"
People

ARLINDER, DR. The Bruckners' family doctor.

BRUCKNER, BUDDY George's older brother. (He was thirteen to George's eleven.) Buddy broke his leg playing baseball, and Ruth had to go to him, leaving George alone with Gramma. Buddy often tortured George with the Spoon Torture of the Heathen Chinee and Indian Rope Burns.

BRUCKNER, GEORGE The eleven-year-old boy who was left alone with his Gramma (who was a witch). George received her powers after she died.

BRUCKNER, MR. George's father. He was hit and killed in 1971 by the Drunk Man Who Had to Go to Jail.

BRUCKNER, RUTH George and Buddy's mother; Gramma's daughter. She was just past fifty. She moved to Maine from Stratford, Connecticut, to care for her ailing mother.

BURDON, MR. George Bruckner's school principal.

CAMBER, JOE He had a hill that the kids in Castle Rock used for sledding in the winter. [NOTE: See the section on *Cujo* in this volume.]

THE CARTOON GRAMMA Ruth had a note-minder that had a cartoon Gramma on it who was saying "REMEMBER THIS, SONNY!"

CHEAP LITTLE CORNER-WALKERS Henrietta Dodd's daily topics of conversation with Cora Simard usually included:

1) Who would be having a Tupperware or Amway party;
2) Cheap little corner-walkers;
3) What they had said to people at:
    3a) The Grange;
    3b) The monthly church fair;
    3c) K of P Hall Beano.

DODD, HENRIETTA One of the Bruckners' neighbors. Henrietta monopolized the party line.

THE DRUNK MAN WHO HAD TO GO TO JAIL George's father was hit and killed in 1971 by the Drunk Man Who Had to Go to Jail.

FLO, AUNT George and Buddy's aunt; Ruth's sister; Gramma's daughter. She lived in Salt Lake City.

FRANKLIN, UNCLE George's uncle. He was born in 1934, and died in 1948 from a Gramma-induced burst appendix.

FRED, UNCLE George's Uncle Fred had shown George how to test the wind by wetting a finger.

GEORGE, UNCLE One of George's uncles. He convinced Ruth to take care of Gramma because she wouldn't last more than eight months.

GRAMMA Ruth's mother. She was "huge and fat and blind." She was also a witch. When she died at the age of eighty-three, her powers passed on to her grandson George.

GRANPA Gramma's husband. He was a carpenter.

HARHAM, MRS. Gramma killed Mrs. Harham by saying "Gyaagin! Gyaagin! Hastur degryon Yos-soth-oth!"

HASTUR Gramma's taken father's name.

A HIRED HAND A hired hand working for the Scarborough school board found some of Gramma's witchcraft books.

LARSON, UNCLE George's uncle; Gramma's first "post-witch-craft" child.

MABEL One of the Bruckners' neighbors. She often spent the afternoon talking to Henrietta Dodd.

MACARDLE, HEATHER A girl George Bruckner liked. His brother Buddy made fun of him for it.

REDENBACHER, MRS. One of George Bruckner's teachers. George asked Mrs. Redenbacher what "skeleton in the closet" meant.

SIMARD, CORA One of the Bruckners' neighbors. She shared their party line and often spent the afternoon talking to Henrietta Dodd.

STEPHANIE, AUNT One of George's aunts. She convinced Ruth to take care of Gramma because she (Gramma) wouldn't last more than eight months.

TWO DEAD BABIES Before Gramma got involved with witchcraft, she gave birth to two dead babies.

UNCLE GEORGE'S THREE DAUGHTERS George Bruckner's Uncle George's wife and three daughters had gone to Gates Falls for some shopping on the day George heard his mother and his uncle discussing Gramma.

UNCLE GEORGE'S WIFE George Bruckner's Uncle George's wife and three daughters had gone to Gates Falls for some shopping on the day George heard his mother and his uncle discussing Gramma.

(21t)
SKELETON CREW
"Gramma"
Places

BEAVER BOG The day George was left alone with Gramma, the wind knocked down trees by Beaver Bog and cut the phone lines.

THE BIRCHES CEMETERY George remembered Gramma once mumbling "strange words that made no sense," and the next day the Birches cemetery on Maple Sugar Road had been vandalized and graves desecrated.

BUXTON The Scarborough school board found Gramma's witchcraft books and forced her to move to Buxton.

CASTLE ROCK The town where the Bruckners (and Gramma) lived.

THE CMG (CENTRAL MAINE GENERAL) HOSPITAL IN LEWISTON The hospital where Buddy was taken after he broke his leg playing baseball.

THE GRANGE Henrietta Dodd's daily topics of conversation with Cora Simard usually included:

1) Who would be having a Tupperware or Amway party;
2) Cheap little corner-walkers;
3) What they had said to people at:
    3a) The Grange;
    3b) The monthly church fair;
    3c) K of P Hall Beano.

JOE CAMBER'S HILL A Castle Rock winter sledding spot for the local children.

MAINE Ruth had moved to Maine to care for her mother when George was six.

MAPLE SUGAR ROAD George remembered Gramma once mumbling "strange words that made no sense," and the next day the Birches cemetery on Maple Sugar Road had been vandalized and graves desecrated.

MINNESOTA Aunt Flo called George when Gramma came back to life and told him how to get her to go be dead again. (She told him to tell her to "Lie down in the name of Hastur.")

SALT LAKE CITY George's Aunt Flo lived in Salt Lake City.

THE SCARBOROUGH CONGREGATIONAL CHURCH Gramma quit the Congregational Church in Scarborough over her use of demonic books

SPERRY-RAND George Bruckner's Uncle George worked for

Sperry-Rand.

THE STRATFORD LAUNDRY The laundry in Stratford, Connecticut, where Ruth worked before moving to Maine to take care of her mother.

STRATFORD, CONNECTICUT Ruth worked at the Stratford Laundry in Stratford, Connecticut, before moving to Maine to take care of her mother.

(21t)
SKELETON CREW
"Gramma"
Things

BEANO Henrietta Dodd's daily topics of conversation with Cora Simard usually included:

1) Who would be having a Tupperware or Amway party;
2) Cheap little corner-walkers;
3) What they had said to people at:
   3a) The Grange;
   3b) The monthly church fair;
   3c) K of P Hall Beano.

CASTLE ROCK COUGARS BOOK COVERS George's books were covered with Castle Rock Cougars book covers.

THE "CORA-CORA" CHANT All the neighborhood kids teased Cora Simard with the following chant: "Cora-Cora from Bora-Bora, ate a dog turd and wanted more-a!"

FIFTEEN YEARS Gramma had taught school for fifteen years before leaving teaching and the Scarborough Congregational Church at the same time.

GRAVES George remembered Gramma once mumbling "strange words that made no sense," and the next day the Birches cemetery on Maple Sugar Road had been vandalized and graves desecrated.

HENRIETTA DODD'S TOPICS OF CONVERSATION WITH CORA SIMARD Henrietta Dodd's daily topics of conversation with Cora Simard usually included:

1) Who would be having a Tupperware or Amway party;
2) Cheap little corner-walkers;
3) What they had said to people at:
   3a) The Grange;
   3b) The monthly church fair;
   3c) K of P Hall Beano.

HENRIETTA'S SOAPS Henrietta Dodd tied up the Castle Rock party line talking most afternoons from one o'clock to six with "Ryan's Hope," "One Life to Live," "All My Children," "As the World Turns," and "Search for Tomorrow" playing in the background.

INDIAN ROPE BURNS One of the tortures Buddy Bruckner would inflict on his brother George.

KEDS George Bruckner's sneakers.

A MASSIVE BRAIN HEMORRHAGE After Gramma turned George into a witch, he killed Aunt Flo with a massive brain hemorrhage.

NESTLE'S QUIK George had been eating cookies and drinking Nestlé's Quik when his mother got the call that Buddy had broken his leg playing baseball.

1981 The year Gramma died and George took over her witchcraft duties.

1948 The year George's Uncle Franklin died of a Gramma-induced burst appendix.

1969 The year George Bruckner was born.

1930 The year George's mother Ruth was born.

1934 The year George's Uncle Franklin was born.

1932 The year George's Aunt Flo was born.

OCTOBER 5 The date Gramma died, and George "inherited" her

powers.

PEE WEE LEAGUE George Bruckner's baseball league.

PERITONITIS George's Uncle Franklin died at the age of fourteen of peritonitis from a Gramma-induced burst appendix.

THE PONY LEAGUE Buddy Bruckner's baseball league.

THE SCHOOL BOARD The Scarborough school board found Gramma's witchcraft books and forced her to move to Buxton.

681-4330 Dr. Arlinder's phone number.

A '69 DODGE Ruth Bruckner's car. It burned too much gas and oil.

THE SPOON TORTURE OF THE HEATHEN CHINEE One of the tortures Buddy Bruckner would inflict on his brother George. It involved pinning George to the ground with knees on both his shoulders, and then tapping him on the forehead with a spoon until George almost went crazy. Sometimes Buddy would do it until George cried.

"STRANGE WORDS THAT MADE NO SENSE" George remembered Gramma once mumbling "strange words that made no sense" and the next day the Birches cemetery on Maple Sugar Road had been vandalized and graves desecrated.

TUPPERWARE OR AMWAY PARTIES Henrietta Dodd's daily topics of conversation with Cora Simard usually included:

1) Who would be having a Tupperware or Amway party;
2) Cheap little corner-walkers;
3) What they had said to people at:
   3a) The Grange;
   3b) The monthly church fair;
   3c) K of P Hall Beano.

❖❖❖

(21u)
SKELETON CREW
"The Ballad of the Flexible Bullet"
People

BAKER, JARED The assistant fiction editor of *Esquire* magazine.

BELLIS The name of Henry Wilson's Fornit. (Bellis was his mother's maiden name.)

"CAPTAIN FUTURE" Jimmy Rulin's persona when he was killing Rackne with his death ray.

THE COLLEGE KIDS NEXT DOOR Reg Thorpe's neighbors. He believed that they were KGB, and that they had radium in their van.

DOHEGAN, JIM Henry Wilson's boss at *Logan's* magazine.

THE FAT GIRL The hero in Reg Thorpe's short story "The Ballad of the Flexible Bullet" dumped lime Jell-O on a fat girl's head, and then killed his wife and baby daughter.

FORNITS The good-luck elves who lived in Reg Thorpe's typewriter. Reg's personal Fornit was named Rackne.

A GIRL IN THE MAILROOM A girl in the mailroom at *Logan's* magazine passed along Reg Thorpe's story "The Ballad of the Flexible Bullet" to Henry Wilson. The girl ended up a full editor at Putnam's.

HAGEN, TOM A writer whose early success was too much for him to handle. He committed suicide.

HENRY WILSON'S FORNIT To "humor" Reg Thorpe, Henry Wilson invented his own Fornit, Bellis, and when he was drunk took pleasure in elaborating on his Bellis's likes and dislikes: He liked Bach, Brahms, and Kirschner's bologna.

HENRY WILSON'S SECRETARY She typed out the letters from Henry to Reg Thorpe.

THE HERO The hero in Reg Thorpe's short story "The Ballad of the Flexible Bullet" dumped lime Jell-O on a fat girl's head, and then killed his wife and baby daughter.

THE HERO'S BABY DAUGHTER The hero in Reg Thorpe's short story "The Ballad of the Flexible Bullet" dumped lime Jell-O on a fat girl's head, and then killed his wife and baby daughter.

THE HERO'S WIFE The hero in Reg Thorpe's short story "The Ballad of the Flexible Bullet" dumped lime Jell-O on a fat girl's head, and then killed his wife and baby daughter.

JACKSON, SHIRLEY The author of the short story "The Lottery."

LOCKRIDGE, ROSS A writer whose early success was too much for him to handle. He commmitted suicide.

MARSHA Paul's agent's wife. She was at the barbecue on the night Henry Wilson told the story of "The Ballad of the Flexible Bullet."

MEG Paul's wife.

MOORE, MARIANNE The writer who coined the phrase "madness is a flexible bullet."

MORRISON, JANEY Jim Dohegan's secretary.

PAUL A writer. He was Henry Wilson's client. He was married to Meg.

PAUL'S AGENT He was at the barbecue on the night Henry Wilson told the story of "The Ballad of the Flexible Bullet."

PLATH, SYLVIA A writer whose early success was too much for her to handle. She commmitted suicide. Paul argued that he didn't think Plath qualified as a successful writer. "She had not committed suicide because of success," he had argued, "she had gained success because she had committed suicide."

THE PROPRIETOR OF THE CORNER STORE Reg believed he was an android.

RACKNE Reg Thorpe's Fornit.

REG THORPE'S MAILMAN Reg believed he was CIA.

REG THORPE'S PAPERBOY He believed the kid was FBI.

RIVERS, ANDY Fiction editor of *American Crossings* magazine.

RULIN, GERTRUDE A black cleaning woman that Reg Thorpe hired. Her son, Jimmy, tried to kill Rackne with death rays from his toy gun, and Reg shot Gertrude and Jimmy (along with his own wife, Jane, and himself.)

RULIN, JIMMY Gertrude Rulin's son. As Captain Future, he tried to kill Rackne with death rays from his toy gun. Reg shot him.

THE RULIN CHILDREN Gertrude Rulin had eleven children.

SEXTON, ANNE A writer whose early success was too much for her to handle. She commmitted suicide.

STRONG, MERT She worked in the publicity department of *Logan's* magazine.

THE SUPERINTENDENT Wilson couldn't stand the idea of the red eye of the smoke detector watching him, so he made the super remove it.

A TEN-YEAR-OLD GIRL SCOUT Thorpe chased away a Girl Scout who came to his front door. He thought she was an android.

THORPE, JANE Reg Thorpe's wife. She moved to New Haven after she recovered from being shot by her husband. She was a painter.

THORPE, REG Writer and friend to Fornits. Thorpe was the author of *Underworld Figures,* and "The Ballad of the Flexible Bullet." Reg shot his wife, Jane, their housekeeper Gertude Rulin, and Gertrude's son Jimmy, and then shot himself in the head. He shot them because Jimmy had been shooting Rackne with death rays from a toy gun.

THE TRUCKER When Henry Wilson drove off a bridge into the Jackson River, he was found by an unnamed trucker.

TWO PSYCHIATRISTS Two psychiatrists (and various mental caseworkers) worked on Henry Wilson for thirty months after his nervous breakdown.

THE TYPEWRITER-STORE MANAGER The dealership manager of the typewriter store where Reg Thorpe got his loaner sent Reg a bill for also having to clean the typewriter. It was full of food. Reg had been feeding the Fornits.

VADAR, SAM The editor-in-chief at *Logan's* magazine.

WILSON'S BROTHER Henry Wilson and his brother used to use the phrase "el bonzo seco" to mean crazy.

WILSON, HENRY The magazine editor who told the story of "The Ballad of the Flexible Bullet" at Paul's barbecue. He had been the editor of *Logan's* magazine when he received Reg Thorpe's short story.

WILSON, MRS. Henry's mother. Her maiden name was Bellis.

WILSON, SANDRA Henry Wilson's ex-wife.

YOUNGER, KATE She worked in the ad department at *Logan's* magazine.

(21u)
SKELETON CREW
"The Ballad of the Flexible Bullet"
Places

THE ADIRONDACKS Henry Wilson had a family place in the Adirondacks.

THE BRIDGE Henry Wilson drove off a bridge into the Jackson River.

BURGER HEAVEN The restaurant on 49th Street where Henry Wilson met Jared Baker to discuss Thorpe's story.

FOUR FATHERS A bar on 49th Street in New York City.

THE JACKSON RIVER Henry Wilson drove off a bridge into the Jackson River with four copies of Reg Thorpe's short story "The Ballad of the Flexible Bulet." All copies were lost.

KRESGE'S The store where Jimmy Rulin had gotten his "death ray" gun.

LITTLEJOHN'S GUN EMPORIUM The store where Reg Thorpe bought the gun with which he shot his wife, Gertrude and Jimmy Rulin, and himself.

NEW HAVEN After Reg's suicide, Jane Thorpe moved to New Haven.

NEW YORK Henry Wilson was working at *Logan's* magazine in New York when he received "The Ballad of the Flexible Bullet" from Reg Thorpe.

OMAHA After his novel, *Underworld Figures,* was published, Reg Thorpe moved to Omaha.

PUTNAM'S The girl in the mailroom at *Logan's* magazine who passed along Reg Thorpe's story to Henry Wilson ended up a full editor at Putnam's.

THE TYPEWRITER STORE The dealership manager of the typewriter store where Reg Thorpe got his loaner sent Reg a bill for also having to clean the typewriter. It was full of food. Reg had been feeding the Fornits.

(21u)
SKELETON CREW
"The Ballad of the Flexible Bullet"
Things

***AMERICAN CROSSINGS* MAGAZINE** One of the magazines at which Henry Wilson tried to place "The Ballad of the Flexible Bullet" after *Logan's* folded.

ARVIN PUBLISHING, INC. The publishing company responsible for *Logan's* magazine. Henry Wilson opened a checking account in the name of Arvin in order to pay Reg Thorpe for his story after *Logan's* killed fiction in the magazine.

BACH, BRAHMS, AND KIRSCHNER'S BOLOGNA To "humor" Reg Thorpe, Henry Wilson invented his own Fornit, Bellis, and when he was drunk took pleasure in elaborating on his Fornit's likes and dislikes: Bellis liked Bach, Brahms, and Kirschner's bologna.

"THE BALLAD OF THE FLEXIBLE BULLET" The short story written by Reg Thorpe that he submitted to Henry Wilson at *Logan's* magazine. The hero in "Ballad" dumped lime Jell-O on a fat girl's head, and then killed his wife and baby daughter. Henry Wilson had a nervous breakdown after his experience with Thorpe and the Fornits, and the story was never published.

BELLIS'S MESSAGE TO WILSON Bellis the Fornit typed the following message to Henry:

"rackne is dying its the little boy jimmy thorpe doesn't know tell thorpe rackne is dying the little boy jimmy is killing rackne bel..."

A BILL The dealership manager of the typewriter store where Reg Thorpe got his loaner sent Reg a bill for also having to clean the typewriter. It was full of food. Reg had been feeding the Fornits.

BLACK VELVET Henry Wilson drank a whole bottle of Black Velvet while reading Thorpe's "CIA" letter.

A CHEVETTE Henry Wilson's car was a blue Chevette.

A COLEMAN GAS LANTERN After being convinced that electricity was poison, Wilson took to using only a Coleman gas lantern.

A DEATH RAY Jimmy Rulin tried to kill Rackne with a death ray from a toy gun he had bought at Kresge's.

$800 Henry Wilson offered Reg Thorpe $800 for "The Ballad of the Flexible Bullet," payable upon acceptance (more or less).

"EL BONZO SECO" A phrase Henry Wilson and his brother used to mean "crazy."

ELECTRICITY Reg Thorpe believed that his enemies were drawn by electricity, so he had all power cut off to his house.

ESQUIRE MAGAZINE One of the magazines at which Henry Wilson tried to place "The Ballad of the Flexible Bullet" after *Logan's* folded.

EVEREADY BATTERIES The batteries in Jimmy Rulin's death ray gun.

FOOD The dealership manager of the typewriter store where Reg Thorpe got his loaner sent Reg a bill for also having to clean the typewriter. It was full of food. Reg had been feeding the Fornits.

"FORNIT SOME FORNUS" On the bottom of a letter to Henry Wilson, just under his signature, Reg Thorpe had written, "Fornit Some Fornus." Fornits were luck-elves who had handguns filled with fornus, which was good-luck dust.

FORNUS The good-luck dust Fornits shot out of handguns.

A .45 AUTO AND 2,000 ROUNDS OF AMMO The weaponry Reg Thorpe bought at Littlejohn's Gun Emporium.

"GOING MAD STYLISHLY IN AMERICA" Henry Wilson said this was a popular theme in twentieth century American literature. Subtopic A was "Nobody Talks to Each Other Anymore."

A GOLD RONSON Henry Wilson's lighter.

IOWA REVIEW One of the magazines at which Henry Wilson tried to place "The Ballad of the Flexible Bullet" after *Logan's* folded.

JANUARY 1970 The proposed publication issue of Reg Thorpe's story "The Ballad of the Flexible Bullet" in *Logan's* magazine. (The magazine folded in the summer of 1969.)

JORDAN'S BOLOGNA The bologna that Reg Thorpe substituted for Kirschner's, and fed to his Fornit.

LIME JELL-O The hero in Reg Thorpe's short story "The Ballad of the Flexible Bullet" dumped lime Jell-O on a fat girl's head, and then killed his wife and baby daughter.

THE LITERARY GUILD Reg Thorpe's first novel, *Underworld Figures,* was a Literary Guild selection.

LOGAN'S The magazine Henry Wilson had been working for when he received "The Ballad of the Flexible Bullet" from Reg Thorpe. They had published thirty-six or more short stories a year, and had folded right after the summer of 1969.

LONDON FOG Henry Wilson's raincoat.

"THE LOTTERY" A short story by Shirley Jackson.

"MADNESS IS A FLEXIBLE BULLET." A phrase coined by Marianne Moore, and used by Henry Wilson the night he told the story of "The Ballad of the Flexible Bullet."

PAUL AND MEG'S BARBECUE Henry Wilson told "The Ballad of the Flexible Bullet," at a barbecue given by Paul and his wife, Meg. The menu consisted of drinks, charcoaled T-bones (rare), green salad, and Meg's special dressing.

RADIUM Reg Thorpe believed that telephones ran on radium, and were the cause of all the cancer in the world.

REYNOLDS WRAP Reg Thorpe put it over all his switchplates to keep out the electricity.

SALEM Meg's cigarettes.

SEVEN HUNDRED WORDS The original length of Reg Thorpe's short story "The Ballad of the Flexible Bullet" was 10,500 words.

Reg thought he could shave seven hundred words.

SEWANEE REVIEW One of the magazines at which Henry Wilson tried to place "The Ballad of the Flexible Bullet" after *Logan's* folded.

THE SMOKE DETECTOR Wilson couldn't stand the idea of the red eye of the smoke detector watching him, so he made the super remove it.

"STUPIDDITY" The way Henry Wilson always spelled "stupidity."

"SUBTOPIC A" Subtopic A of the popular theme in twentieth century American literature "Going Mad Stylishly in America" was "Nobody Talks to Each Other Anymore."

THE SUMMER OF 1969 *Logan's* magazine had folded right after the summer of 1969.

TELEPHONES After the publication of *Underworld Figures,* Reg Thorpe stopped using telephones. He believed that they ran on radium, and were the cause of all the cancer in the world.

10,500 WORDS The original length of Reg Thorpe's short story "The Ballad of the Flexible Bullet." Reg thought he could shave seven hundred words.

THIRTY-SIX OR MORE SHORT STORIES A YEAR The number of stories *Logan's* magazine had published a year before they folded.

THORPE'S "DOODLE" Below his signature on his letters to Henry Wilson, Thorpe doodled a pyramid with an eye in it and, below that, he wrote "Fornit Some Fornus."

TYPE O Reg Thorpe's blood.

UNDERWORLD FIGURES Reg Thorpe's first novel. It received rave reviews, was a Literary Guild selection, and was made into a movie.

AN UPDIKE NOVELLA *Logan's* magazine had originally planned on running an Updike novella in their February 1970 issue, before they pulled the plug on fiction.

❖❖❖

(21v)

SKELETON CREW
"The Reach"
People

ABERSHAM, CARL Carl had gone down with the Dancer, along with Hattie Stoddard's husband. Carl was the first of the Goat Island dead that Stella saw as she walked across the frozen Reach.

BENSOHN, JOHN John recognized Bill Flanders's hat on Stella when her body was found on the day after she walked across the frozen Reach.

"BIG GEORGE" George Havelock.

BLOOD, HARLEY A friend of Alden Flanders'.

BOWIE, RUSSELL Stewie McClelland and Russell Bowie took Stewie's Bombardier Skiddoo out onto the Reach when it froze in 1938, and the Skiddoo went into the Reach. Stewie managed to crawl out (although he lost a foot to frostbite), but Russell got taken away by the water. They had been drinking Apple Zapple all afternoon before going out there. Russell was one of the Goat Island dead that Stella met as she walked across the frozen Reach.

CHILD, FRANK On the day Ettie Wilson's Mongoloid child died of crib death, Ettie had gone to see Frank's new boat.

CURRY, AL Goat Island boatman.

DANIELS A man George Havelock once hired to put new sills on his house, and a new engine in his Model A. Daniels was missing two fingers on his right hand, and he had a deck of playing cards with dogs on them. He was also a child molester, and one day was found at the foot of Slyder's Point. Seems he slipped and fell, broke his neck, and bashed in his head.

DINSMORE, FREDDY The oldest man on Goat Island. He was

ninety-three to Stella Flanders's ninety-five. He was one of the Goat Island dead that Stella met as she walked across the frozen Reach.

DINSMORE, GEORGE Freddy Dinsmore's son. He was "a tosspot of the first water."

DODGE, MARY Goat Island midwife. After Ettie Wilson gave birth to a Mongoloid child, Mary watched the child while Ettie went visiting. When Ettie returned, she learned that the child had died of crib death.

DODGE, MARY One of the Goat Island residents who attended Stella Flanders's ninety-fifth birthday party.

DODGE, RICHARD One of the Goat Island residents who attended Stella Flanders's ninety-fifth birthday party.

DOSTIE, MR. The Racoon Head watchmaker who had cleaned Stella's watch a couple of times.

FLANDERS, ALDEN Stella and Bill Flanders' son. He was a lifelong bachelor.

FLANDERS, BILL Stella's husband. In her ninety-fifth year, Stella began seeing the ghost of her husband, until she finally was reunited with him (and other deceased Goat Island residents) on the frozen Reach. Stella was found dead, wearing Bill's cap.

FLANDERS, STELLA The oldest resident of Goat Island. When she died at the age of ninety-five, she had never been across the Reach in her life...except once.

FRANE, ANNABELLE Sarah Havelock's mother, and Stella Flanders' best friend. When Stella turned ninety-five, Annabelle was already deceased. Stella met Annabelle as she walked across the frozen Reach.

FRANE, TOMMY Annabelle Frane's husband; Sarah Havelock's father. Stella met Tommy as she walked across the frozen Reach.

GODLIN, LOUIS Stella Flanders' father.

GODLIN, MARGARET Stella Flanders' mother.

HATTIE STODDARD'S HUSBAND He had gone down with the Dancer in 1941.

HAVELOCK, GEORGE Sarah's husband. He was known as "Big George." Stella met him as she walked across the frozen Reach.

HAVELOCK, SARAH One of the Goat Island residents who attended Stella Flanders's ninety-fifth birthday party.

HENREID, GERD A Goat Island resident who was struck down by a broken blood vessel in his chest. The residents of the Island had covered-dish suppers for a month to pay for his operation in Boston, and Gerd came back alive.

JOLLEY, NORM In her ninety-fifth year, Stella began to hear her dead husband Bill talking to her. Once he said "We'll get Norm Jolley's old Ford and go down to Bean's in Freeport just for a lark."

THE LIGHTHOUSE KEEPER One of the Goat Island dead that Stella met as she walked across the frozen Reach.

THE MAINLAND DOCTOR He drove a Corvette.

McCLELLAND, STEWIE Stewie and Russell Bowie took Stewie's Bombardier Skiddoo out onto the Reach when it froze in 1938, and the Skiddoo went into the Reach. Stewie managed to crawl out (although he lost a foot to frostbite), but Russell got taken away by the water. They had been drinking Apple Zapple all afternoon before going out there.

McCRACKEN, EWELL The Goat Island minister who presided over Russell Bowie's funeral service.

McCRACKEN, JUSTIN The minister's son. He broke his ankle while ice-skating.

McKEEN, LARRY He ran the Goat Island "general store."

PERRAULT, DAVID Lois Wakefield Perrault's husband; Lona, Tommy, and Hal's father.

PERRAULT, HAL David and Lois Perrault's son; Lona and Tommy's brother; Stella Flanders' great-grandson.

PERRAULT, LOIS Lois Wakefield Perrault; David Perrault's wife; Tommy, Hal, and Lona's mother; Stella Flanders' granddaughter.

PERRAULT, LONA Lois and David Perrault's daughter; Stella Flanders' great-granddaughter; Hal and Tommy Perrault's sister.

PERRAULT, TOMMY Stella Flanders' great-grandson.

PHILLIPS, ANNIE A friend of Vera Spruce's.

PHILLIPS, TOBY Annie Phillips' son.

SPRUCE, VERA Hattie Stoddard's best friend. Vera helped make Stella Flanders' birthday cake.

STODDARD, HATTIE One of the Goat Island residents who attended Stella Flanders' ninety-fifth birthday party.

STODDARD, MADELINE One of the Goat Island dead that Stella met as she walked across the frozen Reach.

STODDARD, MR. Hattie's father. He was lost with his boat, the Dancer, in 1941.

STODDARD, MRS. Hattie's mother. She died of pleurisy in 1954.

SYMES, BULL The Goat Island resident who used to deliver the mail before there was a mail boat.

SYMES, GERT Maine's "Teacher of the Year" in 1978. She had been molested at the age of five by a worker named Daniels.

SYMES, HAROLD Bull Symes's son.

WAKEFIELD, JANE Jane Flanders Wakefield; Stella and Bill's daughter; Lois Wakefield Perrault's mother.

WAKEFIELD, RICHARD Jane Flanders Wakefield's husband; Lois Wakefield Perrault's father.

WILSON, ETTIE Norman's wife. She gave birth to a Mongoloid child. Ettie was one of the Goat Island dead that Stella met as she walked across the frozen Reach.

WILSON, NORMAN Ettie's husband. He was the father of a Mongoloid child.

THE WILSON BABY Ettie and Norman Wilson had a Mongoloid child. Mary Dodge "took care" of the child.

(21v)
SKELETON CREW
"The Reach"
Places

BORROW'S COVE When the phones went dead during a conversation between Vera Spruce and Annie Phillips, the two women figured the lines had gone down in either Godlin's Pond or Borrow's Cove. (Although "some might even have said (only half-joking) that [the dead] Russell Bowie had reached up a cold hand to snap the cable, just for the hell of it.")

BOSTON Gerd Henreid was operated on in Boston after he broke a blood vessel in his chest.

BRUNSWICK HIGH The school where Gert Symes taught.

THE CONGO CHURCH A church across the Reach from Goat's Island. The church could be seen from the island.

CONGRESS STREET, PORTLAND At times, Stella wondered what it would be like to visit Congress Street in Portland.

DORRITT'S TAVERN A bar in Racoon Head on the mainland.

FREEPORT The town where L.L. Bean's was located.

GOAT ISLAND Stella Flanders' home. Goat Island was across the Reach from Racoon Head on the mainland and, until her death, Stella had never once crossed the Reach.

THE GOAT ISLAND STORE The island's "general store." It was run by Larry McKeen.

GODLIN'S POND The kids who tried to skate on the Reach gave up and went back to Godlin's Pond. (The ice on the Reach was too bumpy.)

GODLIN'S POND When the phones went dead during a conversation between Vera Spruce and Annie Phillips, the two women figured the lines had gone down in either Godlin's Pond or Borrow's Cove. (Although "some might even have said (only half-joking) that [the dead] Russell Bowie had reached up a cold hand to snap the cable, just for the hell of it.")

L.L. BEAN'S Bean's in Freeport.

PORTLAND The Maine city where David and Lois Perrault and their children lived.

RACOON HEAD The town on the mainland across the Reach from Goat Island.

SEAR'S At times, Stella wondered what it would be like to visit a Sear's store.

SHAW'S MARKETS At times, Stella wondered what it would be like to visit a Shaw's market.

SLYDER'S POINT A rocky part of the Goat Island coast "where the rocks poke out of the surf like the fangs of a dragon that drowned with its mouth open." Daniels was found dead at the foot of the point. Seems he slipped.

STANTON'S BAIT AND BOAT As Stella walked across the Reach toward the Head, she could see the Stanton's sign.

(21v)
SKELETON CREW
"The Reach"
Things

APPLE ZAPPLE The wine that Stewie McClelland and Russell Bowie had been drinking all afternoon in 1938 just before they went out onto the frozen Reach in Stewie's Bombardier Skiddoo. They fell through the ice.

THE BANGOR *DAILY NEWS* A copy of the *News* was found in Freddy Dinsmore's hands when he died.

A CORVETTE The doctor on the mainland across from Goat Island drove a Corvette.

THE DANCER Hattie Stoddard's father's boat. He was lost with the Dancer in 1941.

"DO YOU LOVE?" The question that plagued Stella Flanders. She didn't know what it meant. [NOTE: The same question was posed by Randy to the thing on the water in Cascade Lake ("The Raft"), and by Nona the Rat-Thing to the Prisoner in the Castle Rock graveyard ("Nona"), two other *Skeleton Crew* stories.]

A FORD Norm Jolley's car.

"GODLIN-FLANDERS-WAKEFIELD-PERRAULT" Like a mantra, Stella would recite the names of her family, telling her great-grandchildren, "Those are your names, children: you are Godlin-Flanders-Wakefield-Perrault..."

HERBERT TAREYTONS The cigarettes Bill Flanders smoked.

THE NATIONAL WEATHER SERVICE The service that kept the weather records.

1954 The year that Hattie Stoddard's mother died of pleurisy.

1941 The year that Hattie Stoddard's father was lost with his boat, the Dancer.

1967 The year George Havelock died on the mainland. "An axe had slipped in Big George's hand, there had been blood – too much of it!"

1938 The year that the Reach had frozen.

NOVEMBER 19, 1884 The day that Stella Flanders was born. (It was a Wednesday.)

"ONWARD CHRISTIAN SOLDIERS" The only song Alden Flanders would sing.

THE REACH A Reach is a body of water between two bodies of land, a body of water which is open at either end. Stella Flanders's Reach was the water between Goat Island and the mainland.

REMINGTON Freddy Dinsmore's gun.

STELLA'S FAMILY TREE Stella would recite the following genealogical history to her great-grandchildren.

1. Louis and Margaret Godlin begat Stella Godlin, who became Stella Flanders.
2. Bill and Stella Flanders begat Jane and Alden Flanders, and Jane Flanders became Jane Wakefield.
3. Richard and Jane Wakefield begat Lois Wakefield, who became Lois Perrault.
4. David and Lois Perrault begat Lona and Hal.

VALENTINE'S DAY Six inches of snow fell on Goat Island on Valentine's Day the year Stella walked across the frozen Reach.

ZA-REX The punch served after Russell Bowie's funeral service.

IT

DEDICATION

This book is gratefully dedicated to my children. My mother and my wife taught me how to be a man. My children taught me how to be free.

NAOMI RACHEL KING, at fourteen;

JOSEPH HILLSTROM KING, at twelve

OWEN PHILLIP KING, at seven.

Kids, fiction is the truth inside the lie, and the truth of this fiction is simple enough: *the magic exists.*

CONTENTS PAGE

21. Under the City
22. The Ritual of Chüd
23. Out

Derry: The Last Interlude

EPILOGUE:
BILL DENBROUGH BEATS THE DEVIL (II)

BOOK BREAKDOWN

PART ONE
THE SHADOW BEFORE

Chapter 1:   After the Flood (1957)—(Four untitled
              sections numbered 1-4)
Chapter 2:   After the Festival (1984)—(Eighteen
              untitled sections numbered 1-18)
Chapter 3:   Six Phone Calls (1985)
              1. Stanley Uris Takes a Bath
              2. Richard Tozier Takes a Powder
              3. Ben Hanscom Takes a Drink
              4. Eddie Kaspbrak Takes His
                 Medicine
              5. Beverly Rogan Takes a Whuppin
              6. Bill Denbrough Takes Time Out

DERRY: THE FIRST INTERLUDE
   1. January 2nd, 1985

PART TWO
JUNE OF 1958

Chapter 4:   Ben Hanscomb Takes a Fall—(Twelve
              untitled sections numbered 1-12)
Chapter 5:   Bill Denbrough Beats the Devil (I)—
              (Nine untitled sections numbered 1-
              9)
Chapter 6:   One of the Missing: A Tale from the
              Summer of '58—(Six untitled
              sections numbered 1-6)
Chapter 7:   The Dam in the Barrens—(Eight
              untitled sections numbered 1-8)
Chapter 8:   Georgie's Room and the House on
              Neibolt Street—(Fourteen untitled
              sections numbered 1-14)
Chapter 9:   Cleaning Up—(Twelve untitled sections
              numbered 1-12)

DERRY: THE SECOND INTERLUDE
   1. February 14th, 1985 Valentines Day
   2. (later)
   3. February 20th, 1985
   4. February 26th, 1985
   5. February 28th, 1985
   6. March 1st, 1985

PART THREE
GROWNUPS

Chapter 10:   The Reunion
              1. Bill Denbrough Gets a Cab
              2. Bill Denbrough Gets a Look
              3. Ben Hanscom Gets Skinny
              4. The Losers Get The Scoop
              5. Richie Gets Beeped
              6. The Losers Get Dessert

Chapter 11:   Walking Tours
              1. Ben Hanscom Makes a Withdrawal
              2. Eddie Kaspbrak Makes a Catch
              3. Bev Rogan Pays a Call
              4. Richie Tozier Makes Tracks-
                 (Misnumbered as No. 2 in the
                 paperback)
              5. Bill Denbrough Sees a Ghost
              6. Mike Hanlon Makes a Connection
Chapter 12:   Three Uninvited Guests—(9 untitled
              sections numbered 1-9)

DERRY: THE THIRD INTERLUDE
   1. March 17th, 1985

PART FOUR
JULY OF 1958

Chapter 13:   The Apocalyptic Rockfight—(Nine
              untitled sections numbered 1-9)
Chapter 14:   The Album—(Six untitled sections
              numbered 1-6)
Chapter 15:   The Smoke-Hole—(Six untitled sections
              numbered 1-6)
Chapter 16:   Eddie's Bad Break—(Eight untitled
              sections numbered 1-8)
Chapter 17:   Another One of the Missing: The Death
              of Patrick Hocksetter—(Seven
              untitled sections numbered 1-7)
Chapter 18:   The Bullseye—(Twelve untitled sections
              numbered 1-12)

DERRY: THE FOURTH INTERLUDE
   1. April 6th, 1985

PART FIVE
THE RITUAL OF CHÜD

Chapter 19:   In the Watches of the Night
              1. The Derry Public Library/1:15 A.M.
              2. Lower Main Street/11:30 A.M.
              3. The Derry Public Library/1:55 A.M.
              4. Kansas Street/12:20 P.M.
              5. The Derry Town House/2:00 A.M.
              6. The Barrens/12:40 P.M.
              7. The Seminary Grounds/2:17 A.M.
              8. The Barrens/12:55 P.M.
              9. Henry Gets a Lift/2:30 A.M.
             10. The Losers All Together/1:20 P.M.
             11. Eddie's Room/3:05 A.M.
             12. The Barrens/1:55 P.M.
Chapter 20:   The Circle Closes
              1. Tom
              2. Audra
              3. Eddie's Room
              4. (Untitled)
              5. (Untitled)
              6. In the Barrens
Chapter 21:   Under the City
              1. It/August 1958
              2. In the Tunnels/2:15 P.M.
              3. It/May 1985
              4. In the Tunnels/4:30 A.M.
              5. In the Tunnels/4:55 A.M.
              6. In the Tunnels/2:20 P.M.
              7. In the Tunnels/4:59 A.M.
              8. Derry/5:00 A.M.
              9. George/5:01 A.M.

(22)

IT
People

ABELSON, DOC An old psych professor of Mike Hanlon's.

ADLER One of the guards at the Juniper Hill Asylum for the Criminally Insane.

THE AGE FAIRY Richie Tozier believed that becoming a grownup was like getting a visit from the Age Fairy.

THE AIR FORCE COLONEL A forty-year-old air force colonel with a wife and three children got Cheryl Lamonica pregnant when she was twelve years old. He ended up serving time in Shawshank for armed robbery.

ALBRECHT, LISA One of the nine children murdered by IT in 1985. She was found dead on Neibolt Street in October. Mike Hanlon looked to this death as a clue that It was back.

THE AMBULANCE DRIVER After IT was dead and Bill emerged from the Derry sewers, he flagged down an ambulance driver and made him take Audra to the hospital.

ANDEEN, OFFICER BRUCE The cop who found Chief Rademacher dead after the tramp chair fell on him.

ANDERSON, PAUL One of Ben Hanscom's grammar school classmates.

"ANDI" Andrea Lamonica.

ANGSTROM, BUDDY The Derry man who was the first to see Shorty Squire's Souvenirs and Sundries Shop sink into the ground on the day of the Losers' final confrontation with IT.

ANNIE A waitress at the Red Wheel.

ANSON, STORK One of Will Hanlon's army buddies. He was killed in the fire at the Black Spot.

ARNOLD, GRESHAM Rumdum. In 1961, he had been a star basketball player for the Hemingford Rams.

ARROWSMITH, BRENDA Bev Marsh's friend. Brenda once showed Bev a dirty book.

THE ART TEACHER After the funds for the Paul Bunyan statue were approved, a woman art teacher in Derry said she'd blow the statue up if it was ever erected.

"THE ASSHOLE WHO WALKS LIKE A MAN" Tom Rogan, according to Kay McCall.

AUDRA'S GRANDFATHER He died frigging with a chainsaw when he was drunk.

AUDRA'S YOUNGER SISTER Audra had a younger sister that she loved.

AURLETTE, ROGER Barber. Al Marsh, Stan Uris, and Mr. Uris all went to Roger for haircuts.

AVARINO, OFFICER CHARLES "Chick." The Derry cop who questioned Steve Dubay about Adrian Mellon's death.

THE BABYSITTER An unnamed girl who used to sit for the Rogan children.

THE BABYSITTER (#2) Eddie Kaspbrak's babysitter. She had once taken Eddie to a public pool. Eddie's mother freaked out.

THE BAKER STREET PROSTITUTE When Egbert Thoroughgood was a young man, he once had a prostitute in a crib on Baker Street. When he was ninety-three, Egbert told the story to Mike Hanlon:

> "I only realized after I spent m'spunk in her that she was laying in a pool of jizzum maybe an inch deep. 'Girl,' I says, 'ain't you never cared for y'self?' She looks down and says, 'I'll put on a new sheet if you want to go again. I knows pretty much what I'm layin in until nine or ten, but by midnight my cunt's so numb it might's well be in Ellsworth.'"

[NOTE: Some scenes from the 1989 Stephen King film *Pet Sematary* were filmed in Ellsworth, Maine.]

A BAKERY TRUCK DRIVER After Bev Marsh fled Mrs. Kersh's apartment, she was almost hit by a bakery truck. The driver yelled at her.

"BANANA-HEELS" When Henry Bowers slipped and fell in school, Richie called him "Banana-Heels." Henry was not amused.

THE BANKER The Bradley Gang had once kidnapped a banker and held him for $30,000 ransom. The ransom was paid, but they killed the guy anyway.

"BARON BUTTONHOLE" One of Richie Tozier's voices.

BARR, MR. After Tom Rogan couldn't get a rental at the Bangor airport, he bought a '76 LTD Wagon from a guy for $1,400 cash money. Tom used the name Mr. Barr.

BAYNES, DR. Eddie Kaspbrak's childhood doctor.

BEAULIEU, BENNY Pyromaniac. He was one of Henry Bower's "neighbors" at the Juniper Hill Asylum for the Criminally Insane. He continually yelled "Try to set the night on fire" (from The Doors' song "Light My Fire").

BELLWOOD, JERRY The Derry boy found torn apart after Harold Earl was arrested for the 1985 Derry murders. The words "Come Home Come Home Come Home" were written on the wall in Jerry's blood at the murder scene.

BEN'S FOREMAN The unnamed foreman who was part of Ben Hanscom's staff at his Nebraska farm.

BEN'S SECRETARY Ben Hanscom's unnamed secretary at his farm.

BERTOLY, ANDREA Andrea Uris's maiden name.

BICKFORD, AMSEL One of the four lumbermen who tried to unionize in 1905. [NOTE: See the "People" entry THE FOUR LUMBERMEN.]

BILL DENBROUGH'S CLASSMATES AT THE UNIVERISTY OF MAINE Bill remembered one classmate who wanted to be John Updike, one who wanted to be William Faulkner, and one who wanted to be Joyce Carol Oates.

BILLINGS, FRANK An architect Ben Hanscom worked with in Peru in 1978.

BILLY One of Mike Hanlon's library patrons. He took out Bill Denbrough's latest novel.

BIP One of the Bowers' pigs.

BLACK, COACH Eddie Kaspbrak's childhood coach.

BLONDIE One of the boys who played softball on the Tracker Brothers lot in 1958.

BLUM, HERBERT Patty Blum Uris's father.

BLUM, MR. Herbert Blum's brother. Herbert complained to him about Stanley.

BLUM, PATTY Patty Uris's maiden name.

BLUM, RUTH Patty Uris's mother.

BOBBY The Luces' cat. Patrick Hockstetter took him and put him – alive – in a refrigerator with the Engstroms' cocker spaniel puppy.

BOBBY The Leper told Eddie Kaspbrak that "Bobby blows me for a dime."

BOGART, HUMPHREY One of Richie Tozier's impressions.

BOLTON, SKIPPER Skipper lived in the second floor, front apartment in Bev Marsh's building. He was fourteen years old.

BOOGER TALIENDO'S SISTER She lived in Eastport. Vincent went to see her after he witnessed a manifestation of IT in the form of blood flowing from the beer kegs at Walley's Spa.

BOP One of the Bowers' pigs.

BORDEAUX, CARLA One of Ben Hanscom's grammar school classmates.

BORTON, CHIEF The Derry police chief who implemented a curfew after the death of Matthew Clement.

BORTON, KENNY A Derry man who participated in the public execution of the Bradley Gang in 1929.

BOUTILLIER, TOM The assistant district attorney.

BOWERS, BUTCH Henry Bower's father. As a young man, he harassed Will Hanlon by breaking his windows and killing his chickens. Henry ended up killing his father in the late fall of 1958.

BOWERS, HENRY One of the Losers' bitterest enemies, and the only one to survive until 1985. (Victor Criss and Belch Huggins were killed by the Frankenstein Monster in 1958.)

BOWIE, GRETA One of Ben Hanscom and Bev Marsh's classmates. She came from a rich family and lived in one of the big houses on West Broadway.

BOWIE, RICHARD According to Claude Heroux, it was Hamilton Tracker, William Mueller, and Richard Bowie who killed his friends Davey Hartwell, Andy DeLesseps, and Amsel Bickford in 1905. [NOTE: See the "People" entry THE FOUR LUMBERMEN.]

BOWIE, STEPHEN A timber baron who lived in Derry on West Broadway. He donated a four-sided clock to the Grace Baptist Church in 1898.

BRADDOCK, MR. The Derry trainmaster.

BRADLEY A Derry little kid. He had a lisp.

BRADLEY, AL One of the members of the Bradley Gang.

BRADLEY, GEORGE One of the members of the Bradley Gang.

THE BRADLEY GANG Bad guys. The gang proper consisted of the following:

> Al Bradley
> George Bradley
> Joe Conklin
> Cal Conklin
> Arthur "Creeping Jesus" Malloy
> Patrick Caudy.

Also with the gang were Kitty Donahue, George's common-law wife, and Marie Hauser, who belonged to Caudy but sometimes got passed around. The Bradley Gang was executed in October of 1929 at the three-way intersection of Canal, Main, and Kansas streets in Derry.

BRAND, MAX Western writer.

BRANNOCK, GEORGE One of Will Hanlon's army buddies. He was killed in the fire at the Black Spot. George had come up with the name "The Black Spot." George played sax in the Company E Jazz band at the Black Spot.

BRANT, HARTSON He rescued Rick in *The Rick Brant Science Adventures.*

BRANT, RICK The "star" of *The Rick Brant Science Adventures*.

BRENNAN, JOSEPH One of the Derry residents who had taken out the book *Bulldozer* in 1958. [NOTE: Joseph Payne Brennan is the legendary author of such short stories as "Slime," and "Canavan's Back Yard," as well as the "Lucius Leffing" series published by Donald M. Grant. Stephen King wrote the introduction to Brennan's definitive collection, *The Shapes of Midnight*, and has said that he considers "Canavan's Back Yard" to be one of the best stories of the macabre of this century. See my interview with Mr. Brennan in this volume, and also see the reprinting of "Canavan's Back Yard" (with an introduction by Donald M. Grant) also in this volume. I will be forever grateful to the late Joseph Payne Brennan for allowing me to reprint his magnificent story, and also to Donald Grant, for his terrific and personal intro to the tale.]

BRIEFCASE, KINKY The Sexual Accountant. One of Richie Tozier's Voices.

THE BRITISH DOCTOR'S WIFE One of Bill and Audra Denbrough's British neighbors. She lived down the lane.

BROCKHILL, MR. In 1985, Mr. Brockhill was looking through a folio of Luis de Vargas sketches in the library when Ben Hanscom heard Pennywise speak to him (Ben).

BROOKS, HARRY A National Weather Service forecaster.

BROWN, CHARLES M. One of the Derry residents who had taken out the book *Bulldozer* in 1958.

BROWNE, SUSAN Bill Denbrough's first agent and first lover.

THE BRUCKNER GIRL Ruth Blum told Patty Uris in a letter that the Bruckner girl was sent home from school for not wearing a bra.

"BUCKY BEAVER" Richie Tozier.

BUDDINGER, BRANSON Buddinger wrote a history of Derry, Maine. He was a sloppy researcher and got many facts wrong.

BURKE One of the names on the mailboxes at Bev Marsh's old house at 127 Lower Main Street in Derry. She saw the name when she went back to the house after the Losers' reunion lunch in 1985.

BUTCH BOWERS' BROTHER After getting caught for vandalizing Will Hanlon's property, Butch was given the choice of a $200 fine or time in Shawshank. Butch made his brother sell his car to get the money.

THE CAB DISPATCHER The unnamed dispatcher Eddie called for a cab as he left on his return trip to Derry.

THE CABBIE After fleeing from Tom Rogan in a cab, Bev gave the cabbie a big tip.

CALDERWOOD, FLOYD One of the guys who was playing poker in the Sleepy Silver Dollar the day Claude Heroux went nuts and killed all the guys in the game with an ax.

CARRINGTON, BUTCH The owner of Cape Cod Limo.

CARSON, ALBERT Derry's head librarian from 1914-1960. He died at the age of ninety-one in the summer of 1984.

CASEY, MRS. One of Eddie Kaspbrak's childhood teachers.

CASTLEMAN, DELIA The founder of Delia Fashions.

CAUDY, PATRICK One of the members of the Bradley Gang.

CHACOWICZ, SAM Kay McCall's ex-husband. His sexual credo had been "Two pumps, a tickle and a squirt."

THE CHINESE COOLIE One of Richie Tozier's voices.

CLARK, CALVIN One of Ben Hanscom's grammar school classmates. He had a twin sister named Cissy.

CLARK, CARLTON Calvin and Cissy Clark's big brother. Carlton told Bill Denbrough that the Tooth Fairy, Santa Claus and Captain Midnight were all a lot of baby stuff.

CLARK, CISSY One of Ben Hanscom's grammar school classmates. She had a twin brother named Calvin.

CLEMENTS, MATTHEW One of IT's child victims. He was a three-year-old Derry boy who was found dead in a culvert on Merit Street. Later, Bev Marsh heard his voice from the drain in her bathroom sink.

CLEMENTS, MR. Matthew's father.

CLEMENTS, MRS. Matthew's mother.

CLEMONS, CLARENCE The Big Man. Richie Tozier turned down a chance to interview Clemons in order to return to Derry.

COCHRAN, EDDIE The singer who recorded "Summertime Blues."

COLE, MRS. ("LIVER LIPS COLE") The ticket-taker at the Alladin theater.

A COLLEGE GIRL AND BOY Two kids who were burned up in the fire at the Black Spot.

THE COLONEL'S THREE CHILDREN The forty-year-old air force colonel who got Cheryl Lamonica pregnant had a wife and three children.

THE COLONEL'S WIFE The forty-year-old air force colonel who got Cheryl Lamonica pregnant had a wife and three children.

CONKLIN, CAL One of the members of the Bradley Gang.

CONKLIN, JOE One of the members of the Bradley Gang.

CONLEY, OFFICER One of the Derry cops who questioned John "Webby" Garton about Adrian Mellon's death.

CONROY, DEWEY One of Will Hanlon's army buddies. Dewey was white.

A CONTINGENT OF FBI MEN Sixteen detectives and a contingent of FBI men came to Derry to investigate the murders of the nine children. [NOTE: See the "People" entry NINE CHILDREN.]

THE COP Mike Hanlon paid a cop twenty dollars a month to act as a pipeline for information.

THE COP (#2) The unnamed cop who occasionally had to tell Eddie Corcoran's parents to quiet down during their regular shouting matches.

CORCORAN, DORSEY Eddie Corcoran's younger brother. He was killed with a recoilless hammer in May of 1957 by his stepfather, Richard P. Macklin.

CORCORAN, EDWARD L. The ten-year-old boy who had been missing since June 19, 1958. His stepfather, Richard P. Macklin, was eventually convicted of the beating death of Edward's brother Dorsey. Eddie Corcoran was actually decapitated by one of IT's manifestations, the Creature from the Black Lagoon.

THE COUNTRY CLUB MAITRE'D The maitre'd at the country club where Patty Blum's prom was held made Patty and her date feel out of place.

THE COUNTY ATTORNEY In 1958, the county attorney and the county medical examiner requested the exhumation of Dorsey Cororan's body.

THE COUNTY MEDICAL EXAMINER In 1958, the county attorney and the county medical examiner requested the exhumation of Dorsey Cororan's body.

THE COUNTY SHERIFF He talked to a reporter about Georgie Denbrough's murder.

A COUPLE OF KIDS Richie Tozier saw a couple of kids on the beach outside his California home as he prepared to go back to Derry.

COVALL, STEVE KLAD's program director.

COWAN, FREDERICK Richard Cowan's son. He was a two-and-a-half-year-old Derry boy who drowned in a toilet in early 1985, and was then partially eaten by a thing that looked like black smoke. His mother said she had heard the toilet flushing and someone laughing.

COWAN, MRS. Frederick Cowan's mother. She heard the toilet flushing and someone laughing, and went in to find her two-and-a-half-year-old son Frederick drowned in the toilet.

COWAN, RICHARD He grew up and fathered a son named Frederick, who was drowned in a toilet and then partially eaten by a thing that looked like black smoke.

CRAIG, REVEREND Derry's Methodist minister.

THE CRAWLING EYE One of IT's manifestations.

THE CREATURE FROM THE BLACK LAGOON One of IT's manifestations, and the creature that decapitated Eddie Corcoran.

CRISS, VICTOR One of the Losers' enemies. Victor had had his head ripped off in the sewers by the Frankenstein Monster (IT.) The dead Victor visited Henry Bowers (the only surviving member of the three enemies) in the Juniper Hill Asylum for the Criminally Insane.

CRUMLEY, MR. Vic's dad. He had told Vic about the three kids who had drowned in the Derry standpipe.

CRUMLEY, VIC Vic told Bev about the three kids who had drowned in the Derry standpipe.

CULLUM, JIMMY One of IT's child victims. He was nine when he was killed. His body came pouring out of a concrete drain in the Barrens. His entire face was gone except for his nose.

CURTIE, ELMER He founded The Falcon in 1973.

CURTIS, TONY One of Richie Tozier's impressions.

THE CUSTOMS AGENT The agent who passed Audra through customs at Bangor International Airport.

DANNER, CAROLE Mike Hanlon's co-worker. Mike joked about going to bed with her. Carole renewed Ben Hanscom's library card in 1985.

DAVE The cabbie who drove Bill Denbrough to the reunion lunch at the Jade of the Orient restaurant.

DAVENPORT, RENA Oscar "Butch" Bowers' girlfriend. Rena was fat, forty, and filthy.

DAVIES, MISS The young librarian who read "The Three Billy Goats Gruff" to a group of children.

DAWSON, RICHARD The host of "Family Feud." Dawson was Patty Uris's favorite game show host.

DAWSON, TREVOR One of Will Hanlon's army buddies.

D'CRUZ, FRANKLIN D'Cruz raped over fifty women between the ages of three and eighty-one before being caught in Bangor's Terrace Park. He ended up incarcerated in the Juniper Hill Asylum for the Criminally Insane.

THE DEAD BUGS A band John "Webby" Garton liked.

DEBBIE A friend of Stan Uris's mother, Andrea.

DEDHAM, STRINGER One of the kids who played softball on the Trackers Brothers lot in 1958. He once pitched a home run ball to Belch Huggins. The cover came off the ball.

DEF LEPPARD, TWISTED SISTER, AND JUDAS PRIEST John Garton and company's favorite bands.

DeLESSEPS, ANDY One of the four lumbermen who tried to unionize in 1905. [NOTE: See the "People" entry THE FOUR LUMBERMEN.]

DELORES The woman who did sewing alterations for the Kaspbraks.

DEMETRIOS One of Eddie Kaspbrak's limo drivers. Demetrios had previously worked for Manhattan Limousine.

DENBROUGH, AUDRA Bill's wife. Her maiden name was Audra Philpott. Her stage name was Audra Phillips.

DENBROUGH, BILL Stutterin' Bill. He was one of the Losers, a writer, and IT's conqueror. (He reached into IT's body and crushed the monster's heart with his hands.) He was married to Audra. When he was a child, he had a bike named Silver.

DENBROUGH, GEORGIE Bill's six-year-old brother, and a victim of IT. His arm was ripped out of its socket as he reached into a sewer to get his newspaper boat.

DENBROUGH, SHARON Bill and Georgie's mother. She played the piano.

DENBROUGH, ZACK Bill and Georgie's father. He died of lung cancer when Bill was seventeen.

DENNIS TORRIO'S GIRLFRIEND At the time he disappeared, Dennis Torrio had a girlfriend that he was apparently head-over-heels about.

DENTON, MRS. Bev Marsh's neighbor. She had six daughters. She watched (and did nothing) from her second floor window as Al Marsh chased Bev.

THE DENTON DAUGHTERS Mrs. Denton's six girls.

THE DERRIE COMPANY In October of 1741, 340 settlers known as the Derrie Company disappeared from Derry, Maine.

A DERRY NEWS PHOTOGRAPHER The unnamed photographer who snapped a picture of Bill climbing up out of the sewers after the Losers' final confrontation with IT.

A DERRY NEWS REPORTER The unnamed reporter who interviewed the Derry sheriff about Georgie Denbrough's murder.

THE DERRY OPERATOR The Derry operator gave Kay McCall the phone numbers for the motels in the Derry area after she was beat up by Tom Rogan.

THE DERRY TOWN HOUSE DESK CLERK Richie Tozier spoke with a clerk (who had a Yankee twang) to make reservations for his return to Derry. Also, after she was beaten up by Tom Rogan, Kay McCall left a message for Bev Rogan with the desk clerk at the Derry Town House telling her that Tom was on his way.

DERRY'S OLD LINE Five old men and the twelve that backed them up. They protested blacks patronizing the Derry bars.

DEVEREAUX, CORPORAL MARTIN The drummer in the Company E jazz band at the Black Spot.

DEVILLE, GEORGE DeVille murdered his wife and their four children one winter night in 1962. He ended up incarcerated in the Juniper Hill Asylum for the Criminally Insane.

DEVILLE, MRS. George DeVille's wife. DeVille murdered her and their four children one winter night in 1962.

DODD, FRANK "That crazy cop" who killed all those women in Castle Rock, Maine. [NOTE: See the section on *The Dead Zone* in this volume.]

DOHAY, ROBERT After the Kitchener Ironworks explosion, Robert Dohay's head was found in an apple tree on the following Wednesday by a woman.

DONAHUE, KITTY One of the members of the Bradley Gang. (She was George Bradley's common-law wife.)

DONLIN, JIMMY Donlin killed his mother in Portland in the summer of 1965, and then ate half her brains. He ended up incarcerated in the Juniper Hill Asylum for the Criminally Insane.

DONLIN, MRS. Jimmy Donlin's mother. Donlin killed her in Portland in the summer of 1965, and then ate half her brains. He ended up incarcerated in the Juniper Hill Asylum for the Criminally Insane. The night the dead Victor Criss visited Henry Bowers at the asylum, Jimmy woke up and saw his dead mother.

DONOVAN, BRADLEY Eddie Kaspbrak's friend. Eddie pitched pennies with Bradley.

DOUGLAS, MR. Mrs. Douglas's husband.

DOUGLAS, MRS. One of Ben Hanscom's childhood teachers. She was married.

DOW, TONY Wally on "Leave It to Beaver."

DOYON, JIM Mrs. Doyon's son, and one of Bev Marsh's neighbors.

DOYON, MRS. One of Bev Marsh's neighbors.

DR. OCTOPUS Richie Tozier thought that Ma Bell was like Doc Oc.

DRACULA One of It's manifestations.

DREW, MR. Nancy's dad.

THE DRUNKEN TRAINMAN The unnamed trainman who had once thrown Eddie a case of lobsters off a train.

DUBAY, STEVE Steven Bishoff Dubay. One of the guys who participated in the murder of Adrian Mellon. He left school at sixteen. His IQ was 68.

DUMONT, HENRIETTA Henrietta taught fifth grade at Derry Elementary School.

DUNTON, ELEANOR Sonia Kapsbrak's friend. When Eddie brought home the case of lobsters he got from the drunken trainman, his mother had Eleanor over for lobster salad.

DUPREE, ROMEO The bartender at Wally's Spa.

EARL, HAROLD The Derry man arrested for the murders of Lisa Albrecht, Steven Johnson, Dennis Torrio, Dawn Roy, Adam Terrault, Frederick Cowan, Jeffrey Holly, and John Feury. Harold was a hermit, and when he was taken in – his clothes covered with blood – he became a prime suspect. Turned out he had three butchered deer in his shed, and had been drinking paint thinner.

THE EATER OF WORLDS IT.

EDDIE'S THREE AUNTS Eddie Kaspbrak had three spinster aunts. They were all fat. They lived in Haven, Bangor, and Hampden.

THE EDITOR The editor of *White Tie* magazine called Bill Denbrough's short story, "The Dark," the "best damned horror story since Ray Bradbury's 'The Jar'."

EIGHT CHILDREN Eight children were never accounted for following the Kitchener Ironworks explosion.

"EL KATOOK" Lathrop Rounds.

ELMER CURTIE'S BROTHER An amateur taxidermist. His stuffed birds decorated The Falcon.

THE EMERGENCY ROOM ORDERLY An emergency room orderly once told Sonia Kaspbrak that she should pay rent at the emergency room.

EMERSON, MRS. One of Norbert Keene's prescription customers in 1929.

ENGSTROM, MR. A neighbor of the Hockstetters. He accused Patrick of stealing their cocker spaniel puppy.

THE ENGSTROMS The Hockstetters' neighbors. They lived a block over and almost directly behind the Hockstetters. Patrick took their cocker spaniel puppy ten days before Thanksgiving, and put it – alive – into a refrigerator with the Luces' cat, Bobby.

ETCHISON, DENNIS The horror writer who had once had a story published in *White Tie* magazine. [NOTE: Dennis Etchison is a friend of Stephen King's, and helped King with the corrections for the paperback edition of *Danse Macabre*.]

FADDEN, MARCIA One of Ben Hanscom's grammar school classmates.

FALKLAND A lumberman who was in the Sleepy Silver Dollar bar the night Eddie King killed a bunch of guys who were playing poker.

A FAT KID Stan traded a bunch of Superman and Little Lulu comics for a pack of Black Cat firecrackers with a fat kid he went to synagogue with.

A FAT LADY Ben remembered having looked away as a child when a fat lady descended the library stairs. He didn't want to see up her dress, even though he had readily looked up the dress of a pretty young girl wearing pink panties. Ben was selective.

THE FAT SEATMATE The unnamed guy who sat next to Bill Denbrough on Bill's return flight to Derry.

THE FAT-ASSED COP The Portland cop who laughed while some idiots set Don Hagarty's shoes on fire.

THE FATHER When the Paul Bunyan statue became Pennywise and spoke to Richie after the reunion lunch, a father walked by wheeling a little boy. The father didn't hear Pennywise...but the little boy did.

FAZIO, ARMANDO ("MANDY") The Derry dumpkeeper. His brother was the Derry Elementary School janitor.

FAZIO, MR. The Derry Elementary School janitor. His brother Armando ("Mandy" to his friends) was the Derry dumpkeeper.

FEENY, CAROL Richie Tozier's travel agent.

A FELLA Dave the cabbie told Bill about a fella who wanted to buy the Derry trainyard and put up a roadside entertainment center.

THE FELLOW IN A BUSINESS SUIT The guy who sat across from Eddie Kaspbrak on the train as Eddie left for his return trip to Derry.

THE FELLOW WHO BOSSED THE CONSTRUCTION OF THE DERRY SEWER SYSTEM He was killed in World War II.

FELSEN, HENRY GREGOR The author of *Hot Rod*.

FEURY, JOHN The Derry fifth-grader who was found dead on Neibolt Street on May 22, 1985. His legs were gone, but the boy had died of fear.

THE FINAL OTHER He made the Turtle.

FIRESTONE, FREDDIE The producer of "Attic Room."

A FIVE-MAN JANITORIAL TEAM A five-man janitorial team cleaned the Derry Mall every morning.

FLANAGAN, STELLA In a letter, Ruth Blum told Patty Uris that Stella was married again.

FOGARTY One of the guards at the Juniper Hill Asylum for the Criminally Insane.

FOGARTY, REVEREND RAYMOND He'd been the minister of the First Methodist Church of Derry in 1957, and had presided over the burial rights of Georgie Denbrough. The Reverend was killed by a toppling beer cooler in 1985.

FORTUNA, AUNT Georgie and Bill Denbrough's aunt. She was in one of the photos in Georgie's photo album.

FORTY TO SIXTY KIDS A YEAR Forty to sixty kids a year disappeared unaccountably from Derry. Most of the time, nobody seemed to notice.

FOSTER, CHUCK The KLAD deejay.

FOSTER, RALPH Bill Denbrough's hand-wrestling oppponent.

THE FOUR DEVILLE CHILDREN George DeVille murdered his wife and their four children one winter night in 1962.

THE FOUR KIDS WHO GOT POLIO In 1956, four kids who had gone swimming in the O'Brien Memorial Pool had gotten polio.

FOUR LOGGERS Four loggers were found torn apart in a cabin in Derry in 1876.

THE FOUR LUMBERMEN Four lumbermen tried to unionize in 1905. They were Claude Heroux, Davey Hartwell, Andy De-Lesseps, and Amsel Bickford. DeLesseps was never seen again after he checked into the Floating Dog, and Bickford and Hartwell were found floating face down in the Kenduskeag. Bickford was missing his head. Hartwell was missing his legs, and seven of his toes were found jammed into his mouth.

FOUR-EYES One of the boys who played softball on the Tracker Brothers lot in 1958.

THE FOURTH GRADER A fourth-grader was beat up by Henry Bowers for making fun of Henry's jacket.

FOXWORTH, "FOXY" The owner of the Alladin Theater.

"FOXY" Mr. Foxworth.

FOXY FOXWORTH'S SISTER After Foxy got out of the hospital with a broken leg and a punctured testicle (injuries he sustained in the devastation that took place during the Losers' final confrontation with IT), he went to live with his sister in Somersworth, New Hampshire.

THE FRANKENSTEIN MONSTER One of IT's manifestations. Frankenstein killed Victor Criss by whopping his head off. Frank also killed Belch Huggins.

THE FRATI BROTHERS They owned a pawnshop in Derry in 1958.

FREESE'S SALECLERK He looked like Mr. Peepers.

FRICK, FRANK One of Ben Hanscom's grammar school classmates.

FRICKE The author of a useless history of Derry, Maine.

FROST, ROBERT "Old Bobby Frost."

FUDD, ELMER Eddie Kaspbrak had once said that Bill Denbrough sounded like Elmer Fudd when he stuttered.

FULLER, MAJOR An army major during Will Hanlon's stint in the service.

GANT, MRS. Mrs. Gant used to watch Tom Rogan cross his sister Megan, and reported back to Tom's mother if he didn't cross her at the Broad Street corner.

THE GARBAGE TRUCK WORKERS As Bev ran away from Al Marsh, she ran down an alley that was blocked by a dumpster. Two men who were on their lunch break were in the cab of the truck servicing the dumpster.

GARDENER, DAVE He heard Georgie's cries as IT ripped off his arm. Dave owned the Shoeboat.

GARDENER, HAROLD The Derry man who asked Alfred Zitner if the streets were going to collapse on the morning of the Losers' final confrontation with IT.

GARTON, JOHN ("WEBBY") He killed Adrian Mellon. Garton dressed like Bruce Springsteen.

GAUTIER, BOB One of Mike Hanlon's classmates. He told Mike that the word "nigger" couldn't be bad because his father used it all the time.

GAUTIER, MR. Bob's father. He worked at Star Beef.

GEDREAU, MR. The owner of the Costello Avenue Market.

GEFFEN, DR. The doctor who treated Kay McCall at the Sister of Mercy emergency room after she was beaten up by Tom Rogan.

GEIGER, ELLIE One of Bev Marsh's childhood friends.

GENDRON, MR. The Neibolt Street School janitor.

THE GERMAN COMMANDANT One of Richie Tozier's voices.

GINSBERG, ARNIE A deejay on WMEX out of Boston.

THE GIRL WHO DROWNED IN THE STANDPIPE A three-year-old girl once drowned in the Derry standpipe.

THE GIRL WHO LAUGHED IN 1967 In 1967, a country club girl laughed at Patty Blum and her Jewish date, Michael Rosenblatt, when they arrived for the prom. Patty hoped the girl was living somewhere in a tract house with a goy husband, that she had miscarried three times, and that her husband cheated on her. Patty also hoped that the girl had slipped discs, fallen arches, and cysts on her tongue.

THE GIRL WITH THE PINK PANTIES When Ben was a kid, he had seen up a girl's dress on the library steps. She had been wearing pink panties.

GLADRY, DR. The husband of Ruth Gladry, who was one of the members of the Derry library board of directors.

GLADRY, RUTH A pushy woman from New York who was one of the members of the Derry library board of directors.

GOLDMAN, WILLIAM The writer who had been under consideration to do the *Black Rapids* screenplay. [NOTE: William Goldman actually wrote the screenplay for *Misery,* which was directed by Rob Reiner.]

GORDON, JIMMY A Derry man (Peter's father?) who participated in the public execution of the Bradley Gang in 1929.

GORDON, PETER The sixth-grader who once yelled out to Ben Hanscom, "Hey, tits! Wanna play?" From that moment on, Ben wore nothing but sweatshirts in order to hide his breasts. Peter Gordon was the kid who found the homerun baseball hit by Belch Huggins (the cover had come off). Peter planned on attending a prep school in Groton.

GRUNT, GRANNY One of Richie Tozier's voices.

GRAY, BOB IT. Mrs. Kersh told Bev Marsh that her father's name was Bob Gray.

GREENGUSS, MRS. One of Mike Hanlon's childhood teachers.

GRENIER, DAVID ("STUGLEY") One of the guys who was playing poker in the Sleepy Silver Dollar the day Claude Heroux went nuts and killed all the guys in the game with an ax.

GRESHAM, MR. Arnold's dad. He had a John Deere dealership.

GROGAN, VERONICA The fourth-grader whose body was discovered in a sewer by Frankie (or Freddy) Ross (or Roth) with his Fabulous Gum-Stick.

GUMBEL, BRYANT The host of "The Today Show" on NBC. He went to Derry after the devastation that occured there because of the Losers' final confrontation with IT.

A GUY IN A LIGHT PLANE A guy in a light plane had taken a picture of the Derry library from the air.

THE GUY IN THE SEAT NEXT TO BEV On Bev's trip back to Derry, the guy in the seat next to her tried to talk to her.

THE GUY WHO SPOKE IN SAINT JOHN VALLEY FRENCH

A guy who spoke in Saint John Valley French once asked Will Hanlon if he was a Negro. When Will acknowledged that he was, the guy bought him a drink.

THE GUY WHO TRIED TO SAVE THE THREE-YEAR-OLD The unnamed guy who tried to save the three-year-old girl who drowned in the Derry standpipe ended up drowning, too.

THE GUY WITH THE '76 LTD WAGON After Tom Rogan couldn't get a rental at the Bangor airport, he bought a '76 LTD Wagon from a guy for $1,400 cash money. Tom used the name Mr. Barr.

HAGARTY, DON Adrian Mellon's boyfriend. He was a draftsman with an engineering firm in Bangor.

HALE, DR. A retired doctor who lived on West Broadway in Derry, Maine. He walked down West Broadway every morning, no matter what the weather was like. He was killed when a manhole cover flew up and cut his head off on the morning of the Losers' final confrontation with IT.

HALF-PINT One of the boys who played softball on the Tracker Brothers lot in 1958.

HALLORAN, PFC. DICK The army mess-cook when Will Hanlon was in the army. Halloran survived the fire at the Black Spot and went on to become the head chef at the Overlook Hotel in Colorado. [Note: See the section on *The Shining* in this volume.]

HANDEY, M.K. The author of *Guide to North American Birds*. (It was Stan Uris's favorite.)

HANDOR, DR. RUSS Eddie Kaspbrak's childhood doctor.

HANLON, JESSICA Mike Hanlon's mother.

HANLON, MICHAEL Derry librarian and writer. He was one of the Losers. He stayed in Derry. He was the author of *Derry: An Unauthorized Town History*.

HANLON, WILL William ("Bill") Hanlon; Mike Hanlon's father. He told Mike about the fire at the Black Spot. Will died in 1962.

HANSCOM, ARLENE Ben Hanscom's mother. She worked at Stark's Mills In Newport.

HANSCOM, BEN Loser. Ben was a famous architect. Richie remembered him as a human version of Moby Dick.

HANSCOM, BEN, JR. When Ben visited the library after the Losers' reunion lunch, he told the library assistant he was looking for his son Ben Hanscom, Jr., when she asked if she could help him.

HANSCOM, MR. Ben's dad. He had died when Ben was four.

HARDY, FENTON He bailed out the Hardy Boys.

HARKAVAY, DR. Patty Uris's fertility doctor.

HARLENGEN, RANDI A friend of Ruth Blum's. Randi had her tubes tied. (She had had twenty-seven ovarian cysts.)

HARTWELL, DAVEY The chief organizer of the loggers' union movement in 1905. [Note: The real David Hartwell is the editor of the seminal anthology *The Dark Descent* (which contained three Stephen King stories), and is also the author of *Age of Wonders*, a nonfiction study of the science fiction field. Also, see the "People" entries DAVID HARTWELL and THE FOUR LUMBERMEN.]

HARTWELL, DAVID One of the Derry residents who had taken out the book *Bulldozer* in 1958. [Note: As mentioned above, David Hartwell is the renowned editor of several science fiction, horror, and other genre collections. His most recent collection for horror fans was the masterful anthology *The Dark Descent*, which contained three Stephen King stories, "The Reach," "The Monkey," and the hard-to-find "Crouch End." One Davey Hartwell was a logger who participated in a unionization movement in Derry in 1905. It wasn't said if David Hartwell was a descendant of Davey Hartwell. See the "People" entry DAVEY HARTWELL.]

HAUSER, MARIE One of the members of the Bradley Gang. (She belonged to Patrick Caudy, but sometimes got passed around.)

HENLEY, MRS The Hockstetters' next-door neighbor.

HENLEY, TIM A multi-millionaire developer who had come to Derry in the sixties.

HEROUX, CLAUDE Claude was a logger who went crazy in the

summer of 1905 and began to set fires in the woods. (His biggest fire was the one in Haven's Big Injun Woods that burned down 20,000 acres of prime hardwood.) Claude was one of the four lumbermen who tried to unionize in 1905. [Note: See the "People" entry THE FOUR LUMBERMEN.] Claude went into the Sleepy Silver Dollar one day and killed Tinker McCutcheon, Floyd Calderwood, Lathrop Rounds, and David "Stugley" Grenier. He was lynched for the murders.

A HIGH SCHOOL GIRL After the Paul Bunyan statue turned into Buddy Holly, Richie got terrible eye pain, popped out his contacts, and summarily lost them. A high school girl helped him look for them.

THE HIGH SCHOOL HACKER A Derry high school computer hacker confirmed that the murder rate in Derry was six times that of other comparable New England towns.

HILDA Dr. Hale's housekeeper.

HOCKSTETTER, AVERY Patrick Hockstetter's baby brother. Patrick suffocated him.

HOCKSTETTER, MR. Patrick's father. He was a paint salesman.

HOCKSTETTER, MRS. Patrick's mother. She was a devout Catholic who died of breast cancer in 1962.

HOCKSTETTER, PATRICK One of IT's child victims. Patrick disappeared in July of 1958.

HOLLY, BUDDY After the Losers' reunion lunch, as Richie walked through Derry, the Paul Bunyan statue first became Pennywise the clown, and then turned into a giant Buddy Holly.

HOLLY, JEFFREY The black Derry youth who was found torn open on May 13, 1985.

HORSEFOOT One of the boys who played softball on the Tracker Brothers lot in 1958.

HOWARD, UNCLE Mike Hanlon's uncle. He did time in jail.

HOYT, UNCLE Georgie and Bill Denbrough's uncle. He was in one of the photos in Georgie's photo album.

HUGGINS, BELCH Reginald Huggins. One of the Losers' enemies. He was decapitated by the Frankenstein Monster in 1958.

HUGHES, PAUL One of the Derry cops who questioned John "Webby" Garton about Adrian Mellon's death.

HUMBOLDT, PATRICK On his way to the reunion lunch at the Jade of the Orient, Bill Denbrough remembered something about Patrick Humboldt, a refrigerator, and the Ironworks.

HUNTLEY, CHET Newscaster.

THE INSTRUCTOR OF EH-141 One of Bill Denbrough's instructors at the University of Maine. The instructor had published four books of poetry and his master's thesis with the university press.

THE INTERN After Eddie broke his arm, an intern told Eddie's mother that she would have to be quiet or she'd have to leave the hospital.

THE IRISH COP One of Richie Tozier's voices.

IT Pennywise the Clown. Bob Gray. The Mummy. The Teenage Werewolf. The Leper. The Creature from the Black Lagoon. Dracula. The Crawling Eye. Jaws. The Frankenstein Monster. The Eater of Worlds.

IVES, SANDY A University of Maine professor who was the author of a worthwhile history of Derry, Maine.

JACKSON, MICHAEL One of Richie Tozier's voices.

JACUBOIS, MR. A neighbor of the Hockstetters. He accused Patrick Hockstetter of stealing the Engstroms' cocker spaniel puppy.

JAGERMEYER, BRUCE A Derry man who participated in the public execution of the Bradley Gang in 1929.

JAGERMEYER, GARD A friend of Henry Bowers. (Bruce's son?) He once pushed Richie and broke his glasses.

JAWS One of IT's manifestations.

JIMMISON, MISS A school nurse.

JOCEYLEN, ARCHIE Western writer.

JOHNSON, STEVEN A eight-year-old boy found mutilated in Memorial Park in early December of 1984. Mike Hanlon looked to this death as a clue that It was back.

JOLLYN, REVEREND The Derry Grace Baptist Church minister.

JONESY The bartender at the Sleepy Silver Dollar bar. He said he never dyed his hair. He was present the day Claude Heroux killed Eddie King, Tinker McCutcheon, Floyd Calderwood and Stugley Grenier.

JOSEPHS, MRS. A neighbor of the Hockstetters. She accused Patrick of stealing the Engstroms' cocker spaniel puppy.

"JUGS" Ben Hanscom.

THE JUNIOR HIGH SCHOOL TEACHER A junior high teacher found the body of Matthew Clements in a culvert on Merit Street.

KASPBRAK, EDDIE Loser. Eddie believed he had asthma. He didn't.

KASPBRAK, FRANK Eddie's father. He died when Eddie was three.

KASPBRAK, MYRA Eddie's wife. She was fat.

KASPBRAK, SONIA Eddie's mother. She died of congestive heart failure at the age of sixty-four. She weighed 406 pounds

KEENE, ANDREW Norbert Keene's grandson. He was the only one who saw the standpipe fall on the morning of the Losers' final confrontation with It.

KEENE, NORBERT Druggist. Keene was the proprietor of the Center Drug Store from 1925 through 1975, and was present at the execution of the Bradley Gang. He told Mike Hanlon the complete story of the killing.

KENNEDY, JOHN F. One of Richie Tozier's voices.

"KERKORIAN" After they killed IT, the Losers began to forget. Mike and Bill couldn't remember Eddie Kaspbrak's last name. They thought it was "Kerkorian."

KERPASKIAN, MR. The hospital spokesman Richie Tozier spoke to the night Mike Hanlon was stabbed by Henry Bowers.

KERSH, MR. The nonexistent husband of Mrs. Kersh, and one of the manifestations of IT.

KERSH, MRS. One of the manifestations of IT. IT appeared to Bev Marsh in 1985 in Bev's old house as an old lady named Mrs. Kersh.

THE KID WITH THE SKATEBOARD The young kid Bill saw after his final fight with IT. The kid had previously told Bill that you couldn't be careful on a skateboard.

KILGALLON, BRENT A Derry farmer. A piece of the Sears roof flew off and sliced through Brent's silo on the morning of the Losers' final confrontation with IT.

THE KILGALLON BOY Brent Kilgallon's sixteen-year-old son.

KING, EDDIE One of the guys who was playing poker in the Sleepy Silver Dollar the day Claude Heroux went nuts and killed all the guys in the game with an ax. Eddie King was "a bearded man whose spectacles were almost as fat as his gut." [NOTE: Stephen King's middle name is "Edwin."]

KINKO THE CLOWN, A GUY IN AN UNCLE SAM SUIT ON STILTS, OR HUBERT THE HAPPY HOMO According to Tom Boutillier, the mysterious clown seen in Derry after Adrian Mellon's murder could have been any of these guys.

KISSDRIVEL, COLONEL BUFORD One of Richie Tozier's voices.

KITCHENER, CARL He sold the Losers two bearing molds at fifty cents each with which to make their "silver bullets."

"THE KLASS KLOWN" Richie Tozier in grammar school.

KOONTZ One of the guards at the Juniper Hill Asylum for the Criminally Insane.

"THE KRAZY KUT-UP" Richie Tozier in grammr school.

A LADY FROM THE HISTORICAL SOCIETY A lady from the Derry Historical Society gave tours of the Derry standpipe.

LAMONICA, ANDREA Cheryl Lamonica's daughter. Her nickname was "Andi."

LAMONICA, CHERYL The sixteen-year-old Derry girl who was found in pieces in a Derry stream. She had had a daughter named Andrea that she had given birth to when she was thirteen.

LAMONICA, MARK When Mike was in the hospital after being attacked by Henry Bowers, IT planned on sending a male nurse with a bad pill habit to kill him. The nurse was Mark Lamonica, Cheryl's brother.

LAMONICA, MR. Cheryl Lamonica's father.

LAMONICA, MRS. Cheryl Lamonica's mother.

LARRY, MOE, AND CURLY The Hanlons' three scarecrows.

LAUGHLIN, MACK The publisher of the Derry *News* in 1929.

THE LAY PREACHER OF THE METHODIST CHURCH The preacher who drowned all four of his children and then shot his wife in the head in 1877. He was lynched.

THE LAY PREACHER'S FOUR CHILDREN A lay Methodist preacher drowned all four of his children and then shot his wife in the head in 1877. He was lynched.

THE LAY PREACHER'S WIFE A lay Methodist preacher drowned all four of his children and then shot his wife in the head in 1877. He was lynched.

THE LEPER One of IT's manifestations. Eddie Kaspbrak saw his face in the house on Neibolt Street.

LERNERD, ROGER The head loan officer at Harold Gardener's credit union. Roger got swept away in his K-car on the morning of the Losers' final confrontation with IT.

LESLEY A friend of Bev Rogan's. Tom called her a "bull-dyke."

LIBBY, HEATHER Reverend Libby's wife.

LIBBY, REVEREND Derry clergyman.

THE LIBRARIAN The librarian at the Derry public library in 1985 was a pretty young girl. Ben feared she'd banish him from the library when he went there after the reunion lunch.

THE LIBRARY ASSISTANT When Ben visited the library in 1985 after the reunion lunch, a seventeen-year-old library assistant with dark blonde hair asked him if she could help him. Because Ben saw the tips of her nipples through her thin Western-style shirt, he suddenly realized that this was definitely 1985, *not* 1958.

A LITTLE BOY When the Paul Bunyan statue became Pennywise and spoke to Richie after the reunion lunch, a father walked by wheeling a little boy. The father didn't hear Pennywise...but the little boy did.

"LITTLE BUDDY" Bill Denbrough, according to IT.

THE LITTLE GIRL The daughter of the mother in the lawn chair.

A LITTLE KID After the reunion lunch, Bill Denbrough went and looked at "Georgie's" sewer. A little kid with a Freeze-Pop and a Fiberglass skateboard happened by, and Bill asked him if he had ever heard voices from the sewer. The kid said yes, and that he had told his father, but his father said it was probably an echo.

THE LITTLE KID On their way home after building the dam in the Barrens, Eddie and Ben passed a dorky little kid wearing a Davy Crockett coonskin cap and rolling a hula hoop.

THE LITTLE KID'S FATHER After the reunion lunch, Bill Denbrough went and looked at "Georgie's" sewer. A little kid with a Freeze-Pop and a Fiberglass skateboard happened by, and Bill asked him if he had ever heard voices from the sewer. The kid said yes, and that he had told his father, but his father said it was probably an echo.

LITTLEFIELD, CHAROLTTE She was in town the day the Bradley Gang was executed. [NOTE: The Richard Bachman novel *Rage* is dedicted to Charlotte Littlefield. See the "Skeleton" for *Rage* in this volume.]

"LIVER LIPS COLE" The ticket-taker at the Alladin Theater.

A LOCAL CONTRACTOR A man who dug gravel in the deserted coal pit near the Derry trainyards until he went bust in 1955.

LONDON, JACK The author of "To Build a Story."

"THE LOOT" Sergeant Wilson's lieutenant. Wilson had to explain to him why he missed inspection.

LOTTMANN, DETECTIVE Lottman had punched Henry Bowers in the gut when questioning him about Derry's murders.

LOUBIRD, PHILLY Mike Hanlon's Uncle Phil. Phil was the youngest of Will Hanlon's siblings. Phil was a lawyer in Tucson,

Arizona.

LOWE, CHAD The three-and-a-half-year-old boy who disappeared from Derry in April of 1958.

THE LUCES The people who lived three doors down from the Hockstetters. They had a cat named Bobby.

MACHEN, GOOSE Lal's father. Mr. Machen was one of the sheriff's deputies who went to the Sleepy Silver Dollar after Eddie King's killing spree. When he saw what Eddie had done, he had a heart attack.

MACHEN, LAL The proprietor of Machen's Sporting Goods in Derry. After Lal informed Chief Sullivan that Al Bradley was going to come by his store, he sold the Bradleys a huge amount of guns and ammo, and then participated in their public execution.

MACHEN, OFFICER FRANK The Derry cop who told John Garton and his friends to leave Adrian Mellon and Don Haggarty alone.

MACKENZIE, ANITA The Urises' next door neighbor. Anita heard Patty scream when she found Stan dead.

MACKLIN, MONICA Eddie Corcoran's mother.

MACKLIN, RICHARD P. Eddie Corcoran's stepfather. Macklin beat Eddie's brother Dorsey to death with a recoiless hammer.

THE MAINTENANCE MEN The unnamed men who took care of the standpipe.

MAITLAND, VERNON A Derry man who had cancer of the esophagus.

THE MAKEUP MAN The makeup man's assistant on "The Pit of the Black Demon" was a palmist who read palms at the film party.

THE MAKEUP MAN'S OTHER ASSISTANT The makeup man on "The Pit of the Black Demon" had two assistants: one was a palmist.

MALLORY, GREG When Bev Marsh was twenty-two, she fell in love with a football player named Greg Mallory. Greg had damn near raped Bev after a frat party.

MALLOY, ARTHUR ("CREEPING JESUS") One of the members of the Bradley Gang.

THE MAN FROM BANGOR HYDRO Mrs. Kersh told Bev Marsh that a man from Bangor Hydro came to read her meter, and that she often put out tea and cakes and cookies for him.

THE MAN WHO FOLDED HIS PAPER AND WENT INSIDE When Bev was being chased by her insane father in 1958, a man saw her running, heard her screaming, and folded his paper and went inside.

A MAN WITH A BOOK ON THE CIVIL WAR One of Mike Hanlon's library patrons.

MARGARET, AUNT Patty Blum's aunt. Ruth Blum told Patty in a letter that Aunt Margaret was feuding with the power company again.

MARKSON, JOHN In 1851, John Markson killed his family with poison, and then commited suicide by eating "white nightshade" mushrooms.

THE MARKSON FAMILY In 1851, John Markson killed his family with poison, and then commited suicide by eating "white nightshade" mushrooms.

MARLOW, BIFF A Derry man who participated in the public execution of the Bradley Gang in 1929. Biff was Lal Machen's helper.

MARSH, AL Alvin Marsh. Bev's father. He was a janitor at Derry Home Hospital.

MARSH, BEVERLY A Loser. Bev was a fashion designer.

MARSH, ELFRIDA Bev Marsh's mother. She worked as a waitress from three to eleven at Green's Farm restaurant.

"MARTY" Myra Kaspbrak.

MARY One of Mike Hanlon's library patrons. She used the copy machine.

MASSENIK, KARL Andrew Keene's sixth-grade teacher.

MAUREEN NELL'S BROTHER Maureen told her brother about the Irish Cop Voice that came out of her husband Al just before he died.

McCALL, KAY Bev Rogan's best friend. She was a feminist, and came to Bev's rescue after Bev was beaten by Tom. Tom hated Kay. Kay had written three books: one on feminism and the working woman, one on feminism and the family, and one on feminism and spirituality. Kay had been married to Sam Chacowicz. After her divorce from Sam, Kay had taken two or three lovers who had been virile enough to keep up with her, but not virile enough to beat her at tennis.

McCASLIN, EVERETT One of Will Hanlon's army buddies. He was killed in the fire at the Black Spot.

McCREW, GERRY The assistant cook the night of the fire at the Black Spot.

McCUTCHEON, TINKER One of the guys who was playing poker in the Sleepy Silver Dollar on the day Claude Heroux went nuts and killed all the guys in the game with an ax.

McDOWELL, FATHER The Nell's priest.

McKIBBON, MR. He routed around in people's garbage. He was a "Christer."

MEADER, STEPHEN W. The author of *Bulldozer*.

THE MEDCU GUYS The guys Eddie Kaspbrak called to his apartment in Queens when his mother died.

MELLANCAMP, JOHN COUGAR John Garton wore his hair like Mellancamp.

MELLON, ADRIAN A gay man who was murdered in Derry. He was a freelance writer.

METCALF, HAROLD The Derry school superintendent.

MICHAUD The author of a useless history of Derry, Maine.

MIKE HANLON'S AUNTS AND UNCLES (OTHER THAN PHIL AND HOWARD) Two were dead, and two were married.

MIKE HANLON'S GRANDFATHER He died in a farm machinery accident.

MIKE'S TEACHER One of Mike Hanlon's grade school teachers told his class the story of Ham, and why blacks aren't as good as whites. While telling the story, she looked right at Mike.

MISS DERRY OF 1945 She rode in a Cadillac as part of a 1945 parade to welcome home the troops.

MITCHELL, BILLY In 1930, he irritated his elders enough for them to courtmartial him for trying to build a better air force.

MORAN, MRS. A fourth-grade teacher at Derry elementary school.

MORGAN, SCOOTER One of Ben Hanscom's kindergarten classmates.

THE MORLOCKS They lived underground.

MORRISON, OFFICER BARNEY The Derry cop who questioned Dubay.

THE MOTHER IN THE LAWN CHAIR After the reunion lunch, Bill went by his old house and saw a mother in a lawn chair on the front lawn.

MOULTON, DISTRICT COURT JUDGE ERHARDT K. The judge that ordered the exhumation of Dorsey Corcoran's body.

THE MOVIETONE NEWSREEL NARRATOR One of Richie Tozier's voices.

MR. CHIPS Mike Hanlon's dog. Henry Bowers poisoned him.

MR. FROGGY The frog who wondered where the water went after Ben built his dam in the Barrens.

"MR. JIVEASS NIGGER" One of Richie Tozier's voices.

MR. URIS'S CUSTOMER One of Stan's father's customers had once seen a male cardinal, Fringillidae Richmondena, drinking at the fountain in Memorial Park.

MRS. NELSON'S SISTER She used to babysit for Bill and Georgie Denbrough.

MUELLER, HORST The grandfather clock in the Derry library was donated in 1923 by Horst Mueller.

MUELLER, MR. Sally's father. He was in college around the time of the fire at the Black Spot.

MUELLER, MR. Sally Mueller's uncle. He was on the town council and, back in the days when Will Hanlon's father was in the army, complained about the blacks attending the town bars.

MUELLER, SALLY She sat next to Bev Marsh in grammar school. She came from a rich family, and lived in one of the big houses on West Broadway.

MUELLER, WILLIAM According to Claude Heroux, Hamilton Tracker, William Mueller, and Richard Bowie killed his friends Davey Hartwell, Andy DeLesseps, and Amsel Bickford in 1905. [NOTE: See the "People" entry THE FOUR LUMBERMEN.]

THE MUELLERS' GARDENER The Muellers' gardener always looked at Eddie Kaspbrak suspiciously when Eddie passed the Mueller house.

THE MUMMY One of IT's manifestations.

NAUGLER, ALFIE He had a farm on Naugler Road in Derry in the early 1900's.

NAUGLER, TRACE The Derry mayor in 1929.

NELL, ALOYSIUS The police officer who discovered the dam in the Barrens and made the guys take it down. Also, Officer Nell was present at the execution of the Bradley Gang in Derry. [Note: Officer Nell also appeared in the *Night Shift* story "Sometimes They Come Back," only in that story he was in Stratford, Connecticut. He must have moved to Derry at some point after "Sometimes They Come Back" took place.] In *IT*, he had a fatal stroke at 7:32 on the morning of the day the Losers had their final confrontation with IT. Nell did Richie's Irish Cop voice before he died.

NELL, MAUREEN Officer Aloysius Nell's wife.

NELSON, MRS. The Derry woman who saw Bill's head pop up out of the sewers after the Losers' final confrontation with IT.

THE NEW RECRUIT During Will Hanlon's army stint, a new recruit dropped a live grenade. Will lost most of his left foot in the accident.

THE NEW YORK WOMAN A woman from New York who was in the Red Wheel wondered if Ben Hanscom was gay. She smoked Dorals.

THE NIGHTWATCHMAN A nightwatchman in a Studebaker used to watch the Derry trainyards.

NINE CHILDREN When the Losers had their reunion lunch at the Jade of the Orient restaurant in 1985, nine children were already dead in Derry. This convinced Mike Hanlon that the killings had begun again and that IT was awake again. The nine (in alphabetical order) were:

> Lisa Albrecht
> Jeffrey Bellwood
> Frederick Cowan
> John Feury
> Jeffrey Holly
> Steven Johnson
> Dawn Roy
> Adam Terrault
> Dennis Torrio

THE NINE LUMBERJACKS In 1879, nine lumberjacks were found hacked to pieces in a camp on the outer Kenduskeag. One of them had had his penis nailed to the cabin wall.

A 1931 FLOOD VICTIM An unnamed victim of the 1931 flood. Fish had eaten his eyes, three fingers, his penis, and most of his left foot.

THE NURSE After Eddie broke his arm, a young nurse wiped his face in the emergency room.

THE NURSERY SCHOOL TEACHER A male nursery school teacher told the Derry *News* that Dorsey Corcoran had said that his daddy had beaten him because he was bad.

O'BANNON, SERGEANT The police sergeant Kay McCall reached when she called the Sixth Street station after being beaten up by Tom Rogan.

O'BRIAN, FATHER ASHLEY The Shawshank prison priest.

O'HARA, MIKE A KLAD deejay.

O'HARA, PATTY One of Bev Marsh's childhood friends.

THE OLD GUY In order to make the dam in the Barrens, Ben wanted to hawk some boards from an old guy he knew.

THE OLD GUY IN THE FIRST FLOOR APARTMENT An old guy in Ben Hanscom's building put four extra holes in Ben's belt after he began to lose weight.

AN OLD LADY IN A 1950 FORD An old lady in a 1950 Ford saw Henry Bowers attacking Bev Marsh and told him to leave her alone.

AN OLD LADY WITH A PAPERBACK GOTHIC One of Mike Hanlon's library patrons.

AN OLD LADY WITH A SHOPPING BASKET She noticed Eddie studying his aspirator after Mr. Keene had told him it was a placebo.

AN OLD MAN After his escape from the insane asylum, Henry Bowers hitchhiked to Derry with an old man. Henry killed him.

THE OLD MAN An old man and an old woman in a '51 Ford drove by as Henry was preparing to carve his name in Ben Hanscom's belly.

THE OLD WOMAN An old man and an old woman in a '51 Ford drove by as Henry was preparing to carve his name in Ben Hanscom's belly.

ONE ADULT One adult was never accounted for after the Kitchener Ironworks explosion.

127 CHILDREN In 1958, 127 children, ages three to nineteen, disappeared from Derry.

THE OPERATOR An operator gave Richie Tozier the phone number of the Derry Town House.

THE OPERATOR (#2) The telephone company representative who asked Patty Uris if she needed help before she hallucinated (thanks to Pennywise?) that the phone was a snake.

OSBOURNE, OZZY Richie Tozier once interviewed Ozzy.

O'STAGGERS, FATHER One of Richie Tozier's voices.

THE OTHER After Bill killed IT, he heard the voice of the Other saying, "Son, you did real good."

"OVER FIFTY WOMEN" Franklin D'Cruz raped over fifty women between the ages of three and eighty-one before being caught in Bangor's Terrace Park. He ended up incarcerated in the Juniper Hill Asylum for the Criminally Insane.

"OVER 170 KIDS" In the year 1930, over 170 kids disappeared from Derry.

THE PALMIST A palmist read palms at the "Pit of the Black Demon" party.

PARKER AND WATERS Swedholm undertakers.

PASQUALE, BUCKY Bev Marsh's neighbor. He saw Al Marsh chasing Bev and ignored it.

PAULSON, MRS. Rebecca's husband. [NOTE: See the "People" entry REBECCA PAULSON.]

PAULSON, REBECCA A woman who lived in Haven Village. She found a fifty-dollar bill under her back door welcome mat, two twenties in her birdhouse, and a hundred-dollar bill on an oak tree in her backyard on the morning of the day the Losers had their final confrontation with IT. [NOTE: Rebecca also appears in *The Tommyknockers*. See the section on *The Tommyknockers* in this volume.]

PEARSON, DOC The Derry doctor who would often prescribe placebos for his patients.

PENNYWISE THE CLOWN IT's primary Derry manifestation.

PERKINS, ANTHONY At their reunion lunch at the Jade of the Orient, Bill thought that Eddie had grown up to look like Anthony Perkins.

PHILLIPS, AUDRA Audra Philpott Denbrough's maiden (stage) name.

PHILLIPS, OWEN A kid who had laughed when a fly ball hit Belch Huggins on the head. Belch kicked his ass. [NOTE: One of Stephen King's sons is named Owen Philip King.]

PHILPOTT, AUDRA Audra Denbrough's maiden name. (Her stage name was Audra Phillips.) [NOTE: It wasn't said if Audra was related to Peter Philpott, the Ewen superintendent of schools in *Carrie*.]

"PHYLLIS HOUSEFLY" Phyllis Schafly.

THE PICKANINNY One of Richie Tozier's voices.

PICKMAN Pickman painted funny pictures and drank all day at Wally's Spa. He was in town the day the Bradley Gang was executed.

THE PIMPLY-FACED 7-11 COUNTERMAN The 7-11 clerk loaned Bev Rogan forty cents after she let him look down her blouse.

PINETTE, JAKE A Derry man who participated in the public execution of the Bradley Gang in 1929.

THE PISCOPOS A family Patty Uris watched on "Family Feud."

THE PITCH-TILL-U-WIN LADY The unnamed booth attendant who gave Webby Garton an undeserved prize.

POE, LOVECRAFT, AND MATHESON Bill Denrough acknowledged that his horror tales owed a great deal to the work of Edgar Allan Poe, H.P. Lovecraft, and Richard Matheson. [NOTE: See my interview with Richard Matheson in this volume.]

THE POLACK WOMAN ON THE CITY COUNCIL Dave the cabbie told Bill Denrough that he wanted to string her up by her tits for agreeing to knock down all the old buildings in Derry.

PORTLEIGH, MRS. Eddie Kaspbrak's Sunday school teacher. She was a divorced woman who lived in Kittery, and played Bingo at St. Mary's in Bangor.

PRENDERLIST, MARK Richie Tozier had once seen Prenderlist taking a leak in McCarron Park. Richie thought that Mark had "the ugliest hogger you ever saw."

THE PROPRIETOR OF SECONDHAND ROSE, SECOND-HAND CLOTHES He was about forty, wore designer jeans and a fishnet t-shirt, and was reading a novel called *Construction Site Studs* when Bill visited the shop after the reunion lunch. In 1985, the proprietor sold Bill's old bicycle, Silver, back to Bill.

THE PROPRIETOR OF THE DRUGS-AND-SUNDRIES SHOP The proprietor of a drugs-and-sundries shop where Tom Rogan stopped on his way to Derry. The proprietor wished him a good evening.

THE QUEEN OF ENGLAND Tom Rogan thought that he would hit the queen of England if she mouthed off to him.

RADEMACHER, ANDREW The Derry police chief. He blamed the Depression for the disappearance of so many of Derry's children.

RADEMACHER, MRS. Andrew Rademacher's wife.

RADER, RICHARD D. The phony name Al Bradley used to buy his guns and ammo from Lal Machen.

A RECORD COMPANY REP Richie Tozier had once been given an L.E.D. quartz clock from an unnamed record company rep.

THE RECRUITER The army recruiter told Will Hanlon that the army had meat every night.

RED One of the boys who played softball on the Tracker Brothers lot in 1958.

REEVES, JEFFREY Harold Gardener's partner.

RHODA One of Will Hanlon's nurses.

RHULIN, ANDREW Andrew was the grand-uncle of the man who ended up owning Rhulin Farms in 1985. Andrew was responsible for the 1906 animal mutilations in Derry.

RICHIE TOZIER'S DOCTOR Richie's doctor told him that his own vasectomy never worked. The doctor knew of eleven regenerations out of 28,618 vasectomies. The doctor *still* didn't have any children.

RICKY LEE The Red Wheel's bartender.

RICKY LEE'S DADDY Ricky Lee's daddy told him that as long as a man was in his right mind, you brought him what he paid for.

RICKY LEE'S THREE BOYS Ricky Lee, the Red Wheel bartender, had three sons.

RIPSON, BETTY In the early winter of 1957-1958, Betty Ripson was found on Outer Jackson Street with her insides ripped out.

RIPSON, MR. Betty Ripson's father.

RIPSON, MRS. In the early winter of 1957-1958, Mrs. Ripson (Betty Ripson's mother) heard voices speaking from her kitchen drain just before Betty was found on Outer Jackson Street with her insides ripped out.

ROBBINS, DR. Eddie Kaspbrak's doctor as an adult.

ROBINSON, RANDY One of Mike Hanlon's grammar school classmates.

ROCHE, ASSISTANT FALMOUTH POLICE CHIEF BRANDON K. The police officer that told the press about Richard Macklin's suicide and the suicide note Macklin left, in which Macklin said he'd seen Eddie Corcoran and that Eddie was dead.

RODAN A monster. Mike Hanlon and his father had once seen Rodan on "The Early Show."

ROGAN, JOEY Tom's brother.

ROGAN, MEGAN Tom's sister.

ROGAN, MRS. Tom's mother. She used to beat him.

ROGAN, RALPH Tom's father. He commited suicide in the bathroom by drinking lye and gin.

ROGAN, TOM Bev Marsh Rogan's husband. He was abusive, chauvinistic, and an asshole.

THE ROGAN BABY The youngest of Tom's three siblings.

"RONNIE MORON" Ronald Reagan.

ROONE, CARL One of Will Hanlon's army buddies.

ROSE The hostess at the Jade of the Orient restaurant.

ROSENBLATT, MICHAEL An old prom date of Patty Blum's. (The later Patty Uris.)

ROSS, HERBERT Ross saw Henry Bowers attacking Bev Marsh and, instead of saying or doing anything, went inside his own house.

"ROSS" OR "ROTH," "FRANKIE" OR "FREDDY" The little kid who used his "Fabulous Gum-Stick" to pull things up out of sewers.

THE ROTTING LEPER Bob Gray.

ROUNDS, LATHROP "El Katook." One of the guys who was playing poker in the Sleepy Silver Dollar the day Claude Heroux went nuts and killed all the guys in the game with an ax.

ROWDEN, BUTCH The Derry butcher. He admitted to being in town the day the Bradley Gang was executed.

ROWLAND, TEDDY Freddie Firestone said he'd send Teddy Rowland to square it with the union boss after Freddie allowed a man to do a stunt for a woman, which was against union rules.

ROY, DAWN A Derry girl found decapitated four days after Dennis Torrio's body was found.

RUBY Mr. Keene's countergirl at the pharmacist.

RUSSELL, BOBBY A KLAD deejay.

THE RYAN FAMILY A family Patty Uris watched on "Family Feud."

SADLER, NORMAN One of Will Hanlon's neighbors. Norman was goodhearted and dumb.

SADLER, STEVE ("MOOSE") Norman Sadler's son. Steve was half-retarded, and was nicknamed Moose for the Archie comic book character.

THE SALLOW YOUNG GIRL One of Bill Denbrough's fellow students at the University of Maine. She once wrote a story about a cow examining a discarded engine block.

SANDY A girl Richie Tozier once dated who got sick from taking birth control pills.

SARTORIS, HORTON One of Will Hanlon's army buddies. He was killed in the fire at the Black Spot.

SCOTT, WILLARD The weatherman on "The Today Show" on NBC. He went to Derry following the devastation that occured because of the Losers' final confrontation with IT.

SEAN The eight-year-old son of the mother in the lawn chair.

SERGEANT WILSON'S FRIEND Upon Wilson's return from a three-day pass in Boston, the sergeant's friend told Wilson that he had missed inspection

"THE SEVENTH GUEST" At the Losers' reunion lunch at the Jade of the Orient, IT was "the seventh guest."

THE SEVENTY-YEAR-OLD WRITER One of the members of the Derry library board of directors.

SEVERAL BROWSERS In 1985, several browsers were looking through the current fiction seven-day-loan books in the library when Ben Hanscom heard Pennywise speak to him.

SHIRLEY Mike Hanlon's grandmother.

THE SHOEBOAT CLERK One of Dave Gardener's co-workers.

THE SHORT FAT GRAD STUDENT One of Bill Denbrough's University of Maine classmates. He couldn't/wouldn't speak above a mutter, and once wrote a play with nine characters, each of whom had one word of dialogue to say. When put together, the play's entire dialogue was "War is the tool of the sexist death merchants."

THE SHORT-ORDER COOK The Red Wheel's cook. He played cribbage with Annie the waitress.

SHRATT, DR. The doctor who cared for Goose Machen after Goose's heart attack.

SIMON, PAUL The musical artist who wrote the song "Still Crazy After All These Years." When Richie Tozier found out that the Derry Town House was still standing, he sang "still standing after all these years."

THE SIX EMPLOYEES Stan's company, Corridor Video, had six employees in 1983. The company was giving Stan a six-figure income.

SIXTEEN DETECTIVES Sixteen detectives and a contingent of FBI men were in Derry investigating the murders of the nine children. [NOTE: See the "People" entry NINE CHILDREN.]

SIXTY PEOPLE Sixty people were killed in the fire at the Black Spot.

SNOPES, ALAN ("POP") One of Will Hanlon's army buddies. He was killed in the fire at the Black Spot. He played barrelhouse piano in the Company E jazz band at the Black Spot.

SNOW, CARL Carl was in town the day the Bradley Gang was executed.

SNUFFY A Derry sixth-grader who always had a cold.

SOME FOOL After Henry Bowers escaped from the Juniper Hill Asylum, he thumbed a ride after dark and "some fool" picked him up.

THE SOUTHERN SENATOR One of Richie Tozier's voices. (The senator sounded like Foghorn Leghorn.)

THE SPINNERS The night Ben Hanscom drank a stein of Wild Turkey in the Red Wheel, the Spinners' "Rubberband Man" was playing on the juke.

SPRINGSTEEN, BRUCE John "Webby" Garton dressed like The Boss.

STACEY, AUBREY Aubrey was in town the day the Bradley Gang was executed.

STAMPNELL, EBEN Eben was in town the day the Bradley Gang was executed.

STAN'S CLIENT One of Stan Uris's video clients had made the Urises a key-shaped hook board for their keys.

STANCHFIELD, VERNON A farmer from Palmyra.

STARKWEATHER One of the names on the mailboxes at Bev Marsh's old house at 127 Lower Main Street in Derry. She saw the name when she went back to the house after the reunion lunch in 1985. [NOTE: Stephen King has always been fascinated by the mass murderer Charles Starkweather. Starkweather was the inspiration for two King stories: "Apt Pupil," and "Cain Rose Up." Also, Starkweather appears in *The Stand: The Complete & Uncut Edition*. See the essay "Steve Rose Up" by Rick Hautala in this volume. The essay accompanies the concordance to the *Skeleton Crew* story "Cain Rose Up."]

STARRETT, BARBARA The head children's librarian. She died at the age of fifty-eight or fifty-nine in 1982 of a stroke. Pennywise took credit for killing her.

THE STARTER The Tracker Brothers' dispatcher. He had a *Playboy* calendar over his desk.

THE STAVIER KID He had epilepsy.

STEVE DUBAY'S STEPFATHER He had problems with Steve.

STEVENSON, ACE The cornet player in the Company E jazz band

at the Black Spot.

THE STEWARDESS A stewardess on Ben Hanscom's flight back to Derry thought Ben was dead.

STILLWAGON, DR. Mike Hanlon's childhood doctor.

THE STROLLING COUPLE As Richie Tozier prepared to return to Derry, he saw a couple strolling on the beach in front of his house. The guy wore glasses.

STUART, ANNE The Derry woman who was killed during the Losers' final confrontation with IT. An ancient gear-wheel catapulted out of her toilet and through the glass door of her shower, cutting her throat.

THE STUNTWOMAN The stuntwoman in Audra's movie "Attic Room" couldn't do a stunt requiring her to fall down a flight of stairs: she had done her quota of stunts, and the union boss said a man could not do a stunt for a woman.

SULLIVAN, CHIEF The Derry police chief in 1929. He was bird-hunting in western Maine when the Bradley Gang was executed in Derry in October. It was Sullivan who who worked to discover who was breaking Will Hanlon's windows and killing his chickens. (It was Butch Bowers, Henry's father.)

SULLY, SHERIFF The Derry sheriff who used to strap vagrants into the tramp-chair.

THE SUPPLY OFFICER During Will Hanlon's stint in the army, this was the officer who discovered that the government truck wouldn't run because cockroaches had eaten the hoses and the fanbelts.

TALIENDO, VINCENT CARUSO ("BOOGERS") Boogers Taliendo taught Eddie Kaspbrak about fucking. ("And when you 'got the feeling,' you had to grab your cock and aim it real fast so you could shoot the jizzum into the girl's bellybutton as soon as it came out. It went down into her stomach and made a baby there." Eddie was sort of appalled by the whole idea, and wanted to know if girls actually liked that.)

TAMMERLY, JOE Al Marsh's friend. Al helped Joe fix cars.

TANNER, BOB Norbert Keene's assistant in 1929.

TARRENT, CHERYL Elfrida Marsh's friend. Cheryl broke her leg in a car accident, and Elfrida went to see her in St. Joseph's Hospital in Bangor.

TARRENT, MR. Cheryl's husband.

THE TAXI DRIVER The Checker Cab driver who picked up Eddie Kapsbrak as he left for his return trip to Derry.

TAYLOR, ELIZABETH An epileptic classmate of Patrick Hockstetter's.

THE TEENAGE WEREWOLF One of IT's manifestations.

TERRAULT, ADAM A sixteen-year-old Derry boy who was found decapitated on April 23, 1985.

THERAMENIUS, LARS Bev Marsh's next-door neighbor. He was a toddler.

THERAMENIUS, MRS. Lars' mother.

THERAMENIUS, OLAF A Derry man (Lars' father?) who participated in the public execution of the Bradley Gang in 1929.

THIBODEAU, MRS. Ben Hanscom's first-grade teacher.

THIRTY TOWN CONSTABLES Thirty Derry town constables broke up the strike that took place in May of 1905 when four loggers (Claude Heroux, Davey Hartwell, Andy DeLesseps, and Amsel Bickford) tried to unionize. [NOTE: See the "People" entry THE FOUR LUMBERMEN.]

35,000 PEOPLE Derry's population.

THOMAS, MRS. The Derry Elementary School secretary.

THOMAS, MRS. (#2) Bill Denbrough's speech therapist.

THOMAS, PHIL A guy who worked for Eddie Kaspbrak.

THOROUGHGOOD, EGBERT The ninety-three-year old Derry man who once told Mike Hanlon about taking a prostitute in a crib on Baker Street when he was younger. [NOTE: See the entry THE BAKER STREET PROSTITUTE for some disgusting facts about Egbert's hooker.]

THE THREE CAR-RENTAL GIRLS Three car-rental girls told Tom Rogan there were no cars available at the Bangor airport.

THE THREE KIDS WHO DROWNED IN THE STANDPIPE By 1958, three kids had drowned in the Derry standpipe.

THREE OLD LADIES As a child, Bill almost hit three old ladies while riding his bike, Silver.

THREE OR FOUR HIGH-SCHOOL BOYS Will Hanlon always hired three or four high-school boys to help him with his harvest.

THREE TEENAGE BOYS Three teenage boys had followed Bev after she had fled from Tom Rogan.

TOODLES THE ENGLISH BUTLER One of Richie Tozier's voices.

TORRIO, DENNIS A sixteen-year-old boy who disappeared from Derry the same time as Laurie Ann Winterbarger.

"THE TOWER OF POWER" A Falcon patron. He was a big guy in a Nazi uniform, and the rumor was that his arm was greased to the shoulder.

TOZIER, MAGGIE Richie Tozier's mother.

TOZIER, RICHIE Rich "Four Eyes" Tozier. Rich "Records" Tozier. Loser, and "Man of a Thousand Voices."

TOZIER, WENTWORTH Richie's father. He died of cancer of the larynx in 1973.

TRACKER, HAMILTON According to Claude Heroux, Hamilton Tracker, William Mueller, and Richard Bowie killed his friends Davey Hartwell, Andy DeLesseps, and Amsel Bickford in 1905. [NOTE: See the "People" entry THE FOUR LUMBERMEN.]

TRACKER, PHIL Tony Tracker's brother. The Tracker brothers owned the Tracker Brothers' Truck Depot. Phil and Tony Tracker had the nicest mansion on West Broadway in Derry.

TRACKER, TONY Phil Tracker's brother. The Tracker brothers owned the Tracker Brothers' Truck Depot. Phil and Tony Tracker had the nicest mansion on West Broadway in Derry.

THE TRAYNOR SUPERINTENDENT OF SCHOOLS While Patty Uris was trying to select a job to take out of all the approvals she had received, Stan helped her by picking the letter from the Traynor superintendent of schools.

TREMONT, MR. The Tremonts lived in Bev's building. Mr. Tremont had lost his job at the shoe shop on Tracker Avenue.

THE TREMONT BOY Bev Marsh's five-year-old neighbor.

THE TREMONT GIRLS Bev Marsh's neighbors. They were three years old, and six months old.

THE TRUCK DRIVER A truck driver passed Eddie Corcoran on Route 2 while Eddie was being chased by the Creature from the Black Lagoon.

TUCKER, FORREST The only movie that ever scared Richie Tozier was "The Crawling Eye," with Forrest Tucker.

THE TURTLE It's opponent, and the Losers' advocate. The Turtle made the universe, but told Bill, "Don't blame me. I had a bellyache." The Final Other made the Turtle.

20,000 PEOPLE Derry's population in 1929.

THE TWO DEAD ONES Two dead kids came after Stan at the Derry standpipe.

TWO FRIENDS Bev remembered getting drunk with two friends on the Bluebird Hill Overlook when she was sixteen years old.

THE TWO FRIENDS Two unnamed friends of Tom Rogan's attended his wedding to Bev.

THE TWO GUYS OUT SICK Two of Eddie Kaspbrak's drivers who had called in sick on the night Eddie left for his return trip to Derry.

TWO HIGH-SCHOOL GIRLS In 1985, two high-school girls were working in the reference room in the library when Ben Hanscom heard Pennywise speak to him.

TWO LOVERS Bev Marsh had had two lovers before Tom Rogan.

TWO MEN Two unnamed men watched as Al Marsh chased Bev after he accused her of screwing around.

TWO OR THREE LOVERS After her divorce from Sam Chacowicz, Kay McCall had taken two or three lovers who had been virile enough to keep up with her, but not virile enough to beat her at tennis.

THE UNION BOSS The stuntwoman on Audra's movie "Attic Room" couldn't do a stunt requiring her to fall down a flight of stairs: she had done her quota of stunts, and the union boss said a man could not do a stunt for a woman.

UNWIN, CHRIS Christopher Phillip Unwin. He was one of the boys who was tried for Adrian Mellon's murder.

URIS, ANDREA Andrea Bertoly Uris. Stanley Uris's mother. She and Stan's father had married in their early twenties.

URIS, ANDY One of Stan and Patty Uris's unborn children.

URIS, DONALD Stanley Uris's father.

URIS, JENNY One of Stan and Patty Uris's unborn children.

URIS, PATTY Patricia Blum Uris. Stanley Uris's wife.

URIS, STANLEY Loser, and bird expert. Stan committed suicide rather than fulfill his promise to return to Derry and once again face IT. (During the "love and desire" ritual in the sewers in 1958 in which Eddie, Richie, Ben, Stan, and Mike all made love to Beverly, Stan was the only one who didn't have an orgasm, thereby not creating the permanent bond that would enable them to fulfill the promise to come back to Derry if IT should resurface.)

VAN PRETT, MRS. A friend of Mrs. Kaspbrak. Mrs. Van Prett had skin problems.

VANILLA, PANCHO One of Richie Tozier's voices.

VANNESS, PETER A Derry man who participated in the public execution of the Bradley Gang in 1929.

VARNEY The lumberman who kicked El Katook's head out of the way when he came into the Sleepy Silver Dollar bar after Eddie King's killing spree.

VICANANZA, TOMMY The little kid who told Bill he had heard voices coming from "Georgie's" sewer also told him about Tommy Vicananza, a little kid who had seen a shark in the canal that he thought was Jaws.

VINCENT, GENE The singer who recorded "Be-Bop-A-Lula."

THE WAITRESS The waitress at the Jade of the Orient restaurant. She brough the Losers their drinks.

WEEMS, MRS. Patrick Hockstetter's third-grade teacher.

WESTON, ARLEN A resident of the Juniper Hill Asylum for the Criminally Insane. The guards there once hit him too hard with a roll of quarters, and he had a convulsion.

"WHEEZY" Eddie Kaspbrak, according to the dead Tony Tracker.

WHITE FOLKS White folks brought Chivas and Glenfiddich into the Black Spot.

WHITSUN, COUNTY ATTORNEY BRADLEY The attorney that broke down Richard Macklin, and got him to admit that he had killed Dorsey Corcoran.

WHITSUN, HENRY One of Will Hanlon's army buddies. He was killed in the fire at the Black Spot.

WILSON, SERGEANT One of Will Hanlon's army buddies. He was a southerner, and had red hair.

WINTERBARGER, HORST Laurie Ann's father.

WINTERBARGER, LAURIE ANN A five-year-old girl who disappeared from Derry around the same time as Dennis Torrio. Chief Rademacher believed that Horst Winterbarger, Laurie Ann's father, snatched her.

WINTERBARGER, MRS. Laurie Ann's mother.

WITT, JIM The WZON meteorologist.

A WOMAN A woman yelled at Bev, Eddie, and Ben to get out of Richard's Alley.

A WOMAN (#2) After the Kitchener Ironworks explosion, Robert Dohay's head was found in an apple tree the following Wednesday by a woman.

THE WOMAN DIGGING WEEDS A woman digging weeds once saw Bill pass by on his bike, and thought to herself that the bike was too big for him. [NOTE: Little did *she* know, huh?]

A WOMAN IN A NURSE'S UNIFORM When Bev, Eddie, and Ben went to wash the bloody rags at the Kleen-Kloze Washateria, a woman in a nurse's uniform was in the laundromat reading *Peyton Place*.

THE WOMAN SITTING ON THE JOHN A Derry woman sitting on the toilet was killed when her toilet bowl exploded during the

Losers' final confrontation with It. She had been reading *The Banana Republic*.

A WOMAN WHEELING A CART OF GROCERIES When Bev, Eddie, and Ben went to wash the bloody rags at the Kleen-Kloze Washateria, a woman wheeling a cart of groceries passed the laundromat.

A WOMAN WHO LOST HER BABY IN THE STANDPIPE A woman had lost her three-year-old girl in the Derry standpipe.

A WOMAN WITH A GROCERY CART After Bev Marsh fled Mrs. Kersh's apartment, a woman with a grocery cart hurried by as Bev ran into the street.

WOODLEIGH, COACH Ben Hanscom's childhood grammar school coach. Woodleigh told Ben to grow up after he was fat-paddled and left naked in the locker room hallway.

WYATT THE HOMICIDAL BAG-BOY One of Richie Tozier's voices.

THE ZIMMERMAN KIDS Bev Marsh's neighbors. They were washing their Hudson Hornet when Al Marsh chased Bev down the street after accusing her of screwing around.

ZITNER, ALFRED The Derry man who ran Zitner's Realty.

(22)
IT
Places

THE A & P Bill Denbrough had been hit by a car at the A & P when he was three.

THE ALLADIN THEATER The Derry theater run by Foxy Foxworth.

ALVEY'S SMOKES 'N JOKES One of the Derry businesses/buildings that collapsed on the day of the Losers' final confrontation with IT.

AMES, IOWA One of the towns Audra Phillips woke up in while touring with "Arsenic and Old Lace."

THE ARLINGTON MOTOR LODGE A Derry motel.

ARLINGTON STREET Cape Cod Limousine was located on Arlington Street in Boston.

THE ARMOUR MEAT-PACKING PLANT A plant that still existed in Derry in 1985. It was part of Warehouse Row, and fronted Up-Mile Hill.

AN ATLANTA SUBURB Stan and Patty Uris lived in an Atlanta suburb.

THE AUGUSTA STATE MENTAL HOSPITAL Henry Bowers spent twenty years in Augusta before being transferred to Juniper Hill.

AYNESFORD, MASSACHUSETTS A decomposed body found in Aynesford in 1960 was at first thought to be that of Edward Corcoran. It wasn't.

BAILLEY'S LUNCH A Derry luncheonette dating from 1958 that had been replaced in 1985 (along with the Shoeboat) by the Northern National Bank. Bailley's was one of the Derry businesses/buildings that collapsed on the day of the Losers' final confrontation with IT.

BANDLER'S RECORD AND MUSIC BARN One of the Derry businesses/buildings that collapsed on the day of the Losers' final confrontation with IT.

BANGOR Eddie Kaspbrak had three fat spinster aunts. One lived in Haven, another in Bangor, and another in Hampden. Also, white folks came in from Bangor (among other places) to hear the music and drink at the Black Spot in the early 1900s. Also, on the day of the Losers' final confrontation with IT, the morning started out cloudy in Bangor and then got progressively worse as the battle escalated. [NOTE: The writing of *IT* was begun in Bangor on September 9, 1981, and completed in Bangor on December 28, 1985.]

THE BANGOR HYDROELECTRIC COMPANY Four days after the Losers' final confrontation with IT, this Bangor electric company fell into a hole.

BANGOR INTERNATIONAL AIRPORT The morning of the Losers' final confrontation with IT, Harry Brooks, a National Weather Service forecaster based out of Bangor International Airport, called the National Weather Service headquarters in Augusta when the wind speeds in Derry picked up to thirty-seven miles-an-hour by 7:00 a.m.

THE BANGOR MENTAL HEALTH INSTITUTE After IT's death, Audra Phillips was scheduled to be admitted to this Bangor mental institution, but Bill (and Silver) healed her instead. Also, this was the hospital where Mrs. Cowan resided after her son Frederick drowned in her toilet.

THE BANGOR ORPHAN ASYLUM Ben Hanscom worried that if his mother died, he'd be sent to the orphan asylum.

BANGOR'S TERRACE PARK Franklin D'Cruz was captured in Terrace Park.

THE BARRENS "[A] messy tract of land about a mile and a half wide by three miles long. It was bounded by upper Kansas Street on one side and by old Cape on the other." The Barrens were where the "Morlock Holes" were (the sewer pipes that led underground), and also where Ben Hanscom designed and built the makeshift dam.

THE BASKIN-ROBBINS STORE Explosions blew a hole in the Baskin-Robbins (in the Derry Mall) on the day of the Losers' final confrontation with IT.

BASSEY PARK The Derry park that faced the high school.

THE BASSEY PARK FAIRGROUNDS The Derry Days Festival was held there.

THE BASSEY PARK INN A Derry motel.

BEV'S SECRET HIDING PLACE When Bev wanted to conceal things from her father, she hid them in the bottom of her box spring.

BEVERLY FASHIONS Bev and Tom Rogan's clothing company.

BIG INJUN WOODS A huge expanse of forest in Haven. In the summer of 1905, 20,000 acres of prime hardwood burned there.

THE BIJOU THEATER A Derry theater from 1958 that had been replaced with a parking lot in 1985.

THE BIKE AND CYCLE SHOPPE The Center Street, Derry, shop where Bill originally bought Silver.

THE BLACK SPOT The "nightclub" (actually a non-sanctioned "social club") built by black servicemen in 1930 that burned down one night while filled with partygoers. IT did it.

THE BLOODY BUCKET A bar six doors down from the Silver Dollar Bar.

THE BLUE WARD The "Moderately Dangerous" ward at the Juniper Hill Insane Asylum. Henry Bowers was in the Blue Ward.

THE BLUEBIRD HILL OVERLOOK Bev Marsh had once gotten drunk with two friends at the Overlook.

THE BOWER FARM The Bower farm was on Kansas Street, Derry.

A BRANCH OF THE NEBRASKA HOMEOWNER'S BANK One of the business establishments in downtown Hemingford Home, Nebraska.

THE BRENTWOOD ARMS HOTEL In 1905, four union organizers checked in to this hotel, and were never seen again. (The Brentwood had once been called The Floating Dog.)

BREWSTER Rampar's Bar was in Brewster, Maine.

THE BRIAN X. DOWD PROFESSIONAL BUILDING One of the Derry businesses/buildings that collapsed on the day of the Losers' final confrontation with IT.

THE BROAD STREET CORNER The corner where Megan Rogan used to cross on her way home from school.

THE BUCKET OF BLOOD Rampar's Bar.

BUCKY'S HI-HAT EAT-EM-UP A diner on Highway 92 in Hemingford Home, Nebraska.

THE BUNYAN MOTOR COURT A Derry motel.

A BURBANK LEATHER-GOODS SHOP Audra Phillips had once bought a purse at a leather-goods shop in Burbank. Bill found the purse under a sewer cover, and immediately knew that Audra had followed him to Derry.

BURGAW, NORTH CAROLINA The town where Will Hanlon was born.

THE BUS TERMINAL There was a bus terminal next door to the Falcon.

THE CANAL DAYS MUSEUM It was comprised of three store-fronts. The exhibition was put together by Mike Hanlon, and nearly 40,000 visitors paid a quarter each to see 1890 menus, loggers bits, peaveys, and axes from the 1880s, toys from the 1920s, over 2,000 photos, and nine reels of movie film.

CAPE COD LIMOUSINE Butch Carrington's Boston company.

CARSON LAKE A lake where Patty Blum Uris swam as a child.

CASTLE ROCK, MAINE A "crazy cop" once killed a bunch of women in Castle Rock. [NOTE: See the section on *The Dead Zone* in this volume.]

CENTER STREET, DERRY The location of the Shoeboat.

CENTER STREET DRUG The Center Drug Store. The Derry drugstore owned by Norbert Keene where Eddie Kaspbrak got his aspirator refills. Norbert operated the place from 1925 through 1975.

CHARTER STREET A small gate from the Derry Elementary School playground exited onto Charter Street.

CHEVRUS HIGH SCHOOL Bill Denbrough's alma mater.

A CHICAGO SINGLES BAR The bar where Bev Marsh met Tom Rogan.

THE CHRISTIAN SCIENCE READING ROOM Kenny Borton fired at the Bradley Gang from the window of the reading room during the gang's execution.

THE CITY DUMP One of the two vestiges of the original Derry that still existed down by the Barrens in 1985. (The other was Derry Pumphouse #3.)

THE CLARENDON INN A Derry motel.

CLEAVES MILLS White folks came in from Cleaves Mills (among other places) to hear the music and drink at the Black Spot in the early 1900s.

THE COAL PIT NEAR THE DERRY TRAINYARDS A local Derry contractor dug coal in this pit until he went bust in 1955.

COLORADO SPRINGS The location of the Mountain States Cultural Center.

CORNELL-HOPLEY'S A downtown Derry clothing store. They sold dresses and nightgowns.

THE CORNER OF KANSAS STREET AND KOSSUTH LANE The location of the Clements' house.

THE CORNER OF ROUTE 2 AND NEIBOLT STREET The corner where the Neibolt Street Church School was located.

CORRIDOR VIDEO The video company that offered Stan Uris a job when he was working for H & R Block. He ended up incorporated.

COSTELLO AVENUE The Derry street that led to the library.

THE COSTELLO AVENUE MARKET The market where Ben cashed in his bottles, and used the money to buy candy.

COURT STREET The Derry police station was on Court Street.

THE COURTHOUSE STEPS Peter Vanness, Al Nell, and Jimmy Gordon sat on the Derry courthouse steps the afternoon the Bradley Gang came back into town to pick up their ammo.

A CRIB ON BAKER STREET Egbert Thoroughgood told Mike Hanlon about once taking a prostitute in a crib on Baker Street.

A CVS One of the stores in the Derry Mall in 1985.

DAHLIE'S The Derry store where Bev bought the red velvet bows she wore in her hair.

DAYTON, OHIO Don Hagarty got beat up at a truckstop in Dayton when he was a teen.

DELIA FASHIONS The company where Bev Marsh was working when she first met Tom Rogan. It was on the twelfth floor of the Standard Brands Building in Chicago.

DERRY The scene of it all. According to Don Hagarty, Derry was "a lot like a dead strumpet with maggots squirming out of her cooze. A sewer." Derry was thirty miles from downtown Bangor.

THE DERRY AGRICULTURAL FAIR George Denbrough had a picture of his Aunt Fortuna at the fair.

THE DERRY ARMY AIR CORPS BASE The air corps base where Will Hanlon was stationed, and also where the Black Spot was located.

THE DERRY BARS IN 1929 AND 1930 The bars in the Hell's Half Acre section of Derry in the early 1900s consisted of Nan's, The Paradise, Wally's Spa, The Silver Dollar, and The Powderhorn.

THE DERRY COMMUNITY HOUSE Derry building. Henry Bowers, Victor Criss, and Belch Huggings once stood near the Derry Community House and watched Ben Hanscom go into the library.

THE DERRY DISTRICT COURT The court where Garton and Dubay's trial was held.

THE DERRY ELEMENTARY SCHOOL Eddie Kapsbrak's, Mike Hanlon's, Bill Denbrough's and Georgie Denbrough's alma mater. Henrietta Dumont taught fifth grade there.

THE DERRY FARMERS' TRUST An explosion blew open this bank on the day of the Losers' final confrontation with IT.

DERRY HEIGHTS A section of Derry visible from the Barrens.

DERRY HIGH SCHOOL Mike Hanlon's high school.

DERRY HOME HOSPITAL Mike Hanlon was born at Derry Home Hospital, and was taken there after being stabbed by Henry Bowers. Also, Eddie Kapsbrak was taken there when he broke his arm. Also, Bev Marsh's father Al was a janitor at the hospital.

THE DERRY HOME HOSPITAL EMERGENCY ROOM Doctors at the emergency room sedated Mrs. Denbrough after Georgie's murder.

THE DERRY ICE CREAM BAR A Derry ice cream parlor. Richie Tozier once bought a pistachio cone there.

THE DERRY LIBRARY Ben Hanscom's favorite place as a child, and Mike Hanlon's place of employment as an adult. Pennywise appeared to Mike in the library.

THE DERRY MALL Dave Gardener had a second Shoeboat in the Derry Mall. (His third store was in Bangor.) Also, explosions shook the mall on the day of the Losers' final confrontation with IT.

THE DERRY PUBLIC LIBRARY VAULT Mike Hanlon kept his "Derry: An Unauthorized Town History" manuscript in the library vault.

DERRY PUMPHOUSE #3 One of the two vestiges of the original Derry that still existed down by the Barrens in 1985. (The other was the city dump.)

THE DERRY TOWN HOUSE A Derry hotel. It was built with red brick.

THE DISCOUNT BARN A Derry dry goods store. They sold towels and pots.

"DOWN HERE" Pennywise told Don Hagarty "Down here we all float; pretty soon your friend will float, too."

DOWNTOWN HEMINGFORD HOME It consisted of a second-run movie house, a five-and-dime, a branch of the Nebraska Homeowner's Bank, a 76 gas station, a Rexall drugstore, a National Farmstead and Hardware Supply store, and the Red Wheel.

EAGLE BEEF AND KOSHER MEATS A Derry plant that had been replaced by a drive-in bank and a bakery in 1985. It had been part of Warehouse Row, and it had fronted Up-Mile Hill.

EAST SIDE HIGH SCHOOL The Omaha, Nebraska, high school Ben Hanscom attended.

THE EASTERN STAR A Derry hotel at the end of Exchange Street that existed in 1958.

EASTPORT After the taps at Wally's Spa opened themselves on the day of the Losers' final confrontation with IT, Boogers Taliendo went to live with his sister in Eastport.

AN ELKS HALL, BOWL-A-DROME, OR ELECTRIC DREAMSCAPE VIDEO ARCADE Before he arrived back in

Two sample pages from among the
110 pages of notes made by the author
for the *IT* section of this volume.

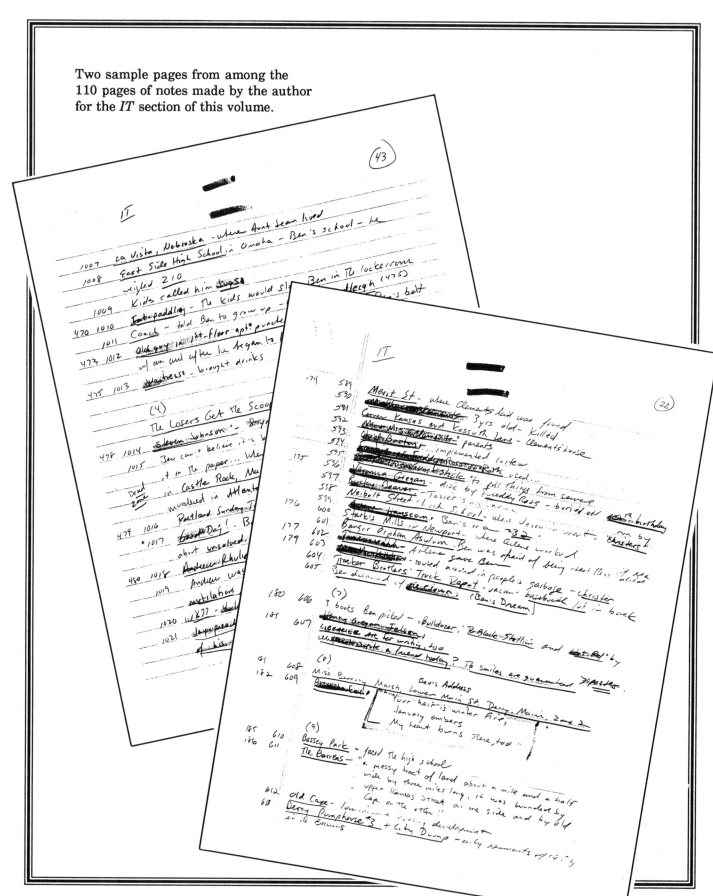

Derry, Richie thought that the Derry Town House might have been turned into any one of these emporiums.

THE ETNA-HAVEN EXIT The exit where Richie got off the turnpike on his return trip to Derry.

THE FALCON A gay bar in Derry.

FALMOUTH Richard P. Macklin committed suicide in Falmouth after his release from prison.

FELDMAN'S STORAGE The Derry business next-door to the Tracker Brothers' annex.

THE FIRST BANK OF CHICAGO IN WATERTOWER SQUARE On her way back to Derry, Bev Marsh cashed a check from Kay McCall at this bank.

THE FIRST MERCHANT'S BANK OF PENOBSCOT COUNTY The bank that issued Will Hanlon a ten-year mortgage on his farm.

THE FIRST METHODIST CHURCH OF DERRY The First Methodist Church's Reverend Fogarty was killed by a toppling beer cooler on the day of the Losers' final confrontation with IT.

A FIVE-AND-DIME One of the business establishments in downtown Hemingford Home, Nebraska.

FLEET, ENGLAND The town in the south of England where Bill and Audra Denbrough lived.

FLINT, MICHIGAN After IT's death, as Mike talked to Richie on the phone, he could hear a woman talking from Omaha; Ruthven, Arizona; or possibly Flint, Michigan.

THE FLOATING DOG The original name of the Brentwood Arms Hotel.

THE FLYING DOGHOUSE Seven days after the Losers' final confrontation with IT, the Flying Doghouse fell into a hole.

A FORD PLANT The place where Tom Rogan's mother worked.

FORT HOOD After the fire at the Black Spot, Will Hanlon was transferred to Fort Hood.

FOUR OTHER BARS Derry had four bars other than the Falcon.

THE FOX RUN MALL A mall where Patty Uris shopped.

THE FRATI BROTHERS PAWNSHOP A 1958 Derry business that was replaced in 1985 by a Trustworthy Hardware Store.

FREESE'S DEPARTMENT STORE A Derry department store. Richie once eluded Bowers and his boys by hiding in Freese's toy department.

GLOINTON, NEW YORK The location of the country club that once refused Patty Blum Uris admittance to an after-prom party.

THE GOVERNOR'S MANSION A Derry landmark.

THE GRACE BAPTIST CHURCH The Derry church that had been on the corner of Witcham and Jackson streets since 1897. Mike Hanlon had a "Jesus Saves" letter opener from the church.

GRAND ISLE, NEBRASKA One of the towns Audra Phillips woke up in while touring with "Arsenic and Old Lace."

"THE GREAT DON'T KNOW" After they reunited, the Losers talked about "The Great Don't Know" – the "white spot on the map" between 1958 and 1985.

GROTON Peter Gordon planned on attending a prep school in Groton.

A GULF STATION The gas station on Kansas Street owned by Mr. Ripsom.

H & R BLOCK Stan Uris once worked for H & R Block for $150 a week.

THE HAINSEVILLE WOODS Bill told Richie in 1985 that if he was lost with Eddie in the Hainseville Woods, he (Bill) wouldn't worry.

HAMPDEN Eddie Kaspbrak had three fat spinster aunts. One lived in Haven, another in Bangor, and another in Hampden. Also, on the day of the Losers' final confrontation with IT, the morning started out showery in Hampden, and then got progressively worse as the battle escalated.

THE HANLON FARM Mike's family's farm. The back field was hay, the south field, potatoes, the west field, corn and beans, and the east field, squash, peas, and pumpkins.

THE HARE AND HOUND Freddie Firestone invited Audra to this

bar for a drink before she left for Derry.

HAVEN Eddie Kaspbrak had three fat spinster aunts. One lived in Haven, another in Bangor, and another in Hampden. Also, white folks came in from Haven (among other places) to hear the music and drink at the Black Spot in the early 1900s. Also, on the day of the Losers' final confrontation with IT, the morning started out drizzly in Haven, and then got progressively worse as the battle escalated. [NOTE: See the section on *The Tommyknockers* in this volume for more information on Haven, Maine.]

HAVEN VILLAGE The clock in the steeple of the Grace Baptist Church in Derry had come from Switzerland in 1897. The only other one like it was in a church in Haven. [NOTE: See the section on *The Tommyknockers* in this volume.]

A HEALTH CLUB ON THIRD AVENUE Eddie Kaspbrak fantasized about joining the health club if he left Myra.

HEATHROW AIRPORT The airport from which Bill Denbrough flew out of England.

HELL'S HALF ACRE An area of Derry in the early 1900s where the bars were located.

HEMINGFORD HOME, NEBRASKA The town where the Red Wheel was located.

HEMPHILL STORAGE & WAREHOUSING A Derry business that was part of Warehouse Row. It fronted Up-Mile Hill.

HIGHWAY 92 The road on which Bucky's Hi-Hat Eat-Em-Up was located.

HIGHWAY 63 The road on which Ben Hanscom drove away from the Red Wheel.

HIT OR MISS The Hit Or Miss store (in the Derry Mall) exploded on the day of the Losers' final confrontation with IT.

THE HOLIDAY INN The Derry motel Audra Phillips checked into upon arriving in Derry.

HOLLYWOOD'S CHURCH IN THE PINES The church where Audra and Bill Denbrough were married.

HONOLULU Butch Bowers had a sword that he claimed he had taken off a "dying Nip" on the island of Tarawa during World War II. Actually, he had traded six bottles of Bud and three joysticks for it in Honolulu.

THE HOUSE ON NEIBOLT STREET A deserted Derry house at 29 Neibolt Street that IT used as a manifestation point: At times, he appeared there as the Rotting Leper or the Teenage Werewolf, and he also caused paranormal phenomena to take place in the house.

THE HUGE CHAMBER While hunting down IT in 1958, the Losers came to a huge chamber in the Derry sewer sytem where they were attacked by a giant bird.

THE INTERSECTION OF CANAL, MAIN, AND KANSAS STREETS The execution of the Bradley Gang took place at this three-way Derry intersection in October of 1929.

THE ISLAND OF TARAWA Butch Bowers had a sword that he claimed he had taken off a "dying Nip" on the island of Tarawa during World War II. Actually, he had traded six bottles of Bud and three joysticks for it in Honolulu.

J.C. PENNEY One of the stores in the Derry Mall in 1985.

THE JADE OF THE ORIENT The Derry Chinese restaurant where the Losers held their reunion luncheon in 1985.

A JOHN DEERE DEALERSHIP Arnold Gresham's dad owned a Deere dealership and gave his son a job there as a salesman.

JUBILEE, NORTH DAKOTA One of the towns Audra Phillips woke up in while touring with "Arsenic and Old Lace."

JULLIARD Mrs. Denbrough's alma mater.

JUNIPER HILL The location of the insane asylum where Henry Bowers was kept. He was in the Blue Ward ("Moderately Dangerous").

JUNKINS, NEBRASKA Ben Hanscom had a farm in Junkins.

KANSAS STREET The Derry street where Mr. Ripsom's Gulf station and the Derry library were located.

THE KANSAS STREET MEMORIAL PARK The Derry standpipe was in this Kansas Street park.

THE KENMORE SQUARE CITY CENTER Eddie Kaspbrak passed the center on his way into Boston when he returned to Derry as an adult.

KING & LANDRY PUBLIC RELATIONS The firm where Tom Rogan was working when he first met Bev Marsh. It was on the forty-second floor of the Standard Brands Building in Chicago.

KIRSHNER PACKING WORKS A Derry business that was part of Warehouse Row, and fronted Up-Mile Hill.

THE KITCHENER IRONWORKS The foundry that exploded on Easter Sunday in 1906. There were 102 killed, 88 of them children. IT did it.

KITTERY Mrs. Portleigh lived in Kittery, and played Bingo at St. Mary's in Bangor.

THE KLEEN KUT BARBER SHOP A Hemingford Home barber shop. (There was a sign in the window of the shop that read "If your a 'hippy' get your hair cut somewheres else.")

THE KLEEN-KLOZE WASHATERIA The Derry laundromat where Bev, Ben, Ed, and Stan brought the bloody cloths they had used to clean up the blood (that only they could see) from Bev's bathroom. The laundromat was on the corner of Main and Cony Streets.

THE KOALA INN The Derry motel that Tom Rogan checked into upon arriving in Derry.

KOSSUTH LANE Bill Denbrough's very first ride on Silver (as a child) ended when he broke through a fence at the end of Kossuth Lane.

LA VISTA, NEBRASKA Ben Hanscom's Aunt Jean lived in La Vista, Nebraska.

LAKE FOREST Tom Rogan and Bev Marsh once attended a party in Lake Forest. It was on the way home from this party that Tom told Bev she couldn't smoke anymore.

THE LIBRARY LOUNGE Mike Hanlon had a refrigerator in the Derry library lounge. Stan Uris's severed head appeared in the fridge one night.

THE LOBBY OF THE DERRY COURTHOUSE BUILDING On the day of the Losers' final confrontation with IT, the wind gauge in the lobby of the Derry courthouse building registered twenty-four miles-an-hour by 6:45 a.m.

LONDON'S BBC COMMUNICATIONS CENTER One of the buildings built by Ben Hanscom.

LONG ISLAND Eddie and Myra Kaspbrak lived in a fieldstone house on Long Island.

LOWER MAIN STREET, DERRY The section of Derry where Bev Marsh lived as a child.

MA COURTNEY'S A Derry whorehouse in 1905.

MACHEN'S SPORTING GOODS The Derry shop where the Bradley boys "stocked up" on ammo before they were executed. The shop was owned and operated by Lal Machen.

"MACHO CITY" Derry, according to Don Hagarty.

THE MAIN STREET BRIDGE Adrian Mellon and Don Hagarty meant to use the Main Street Bridge the night Mellon was killed.

THE MAIN STREET HILL Bill Denbrough healed Audra by taking her for a ride on Silver down the Main Street hill in Derry.

MALL ROAD The Kitchener Ironworks was on Pasture Road, a road which later became Mall Road.

MASSACHUSETTS Audra Phillips's "Arsenic and Old Lace" tour had begun at the Peabody Dinner Theater in Massachusetts, and ended at Play It Again Sam in Sausalito, California.

McCARRON PARK A Derry park. Ben Hanscom once sat in McCarron Park and whispered "I love Beverly Marsh." Mike Hanlon went sledding in McCarron.

THE MEAT MARKET Butch Rowden's place.

A MEDIUM-SIZED TOWN IN TEXAS At their reunion, Mike Hanlon told the other Losers about a town in Texas that had an abnormally low crime rate. Its pacific nature was traced to a natural tranquilizer in the water. [NOTE: Find out more about this town by reading the Stephen King short story "The End of the Whole Mess." See the section on that story in this volume.]

MEMORIAL PARK The Derry park where the Johnson boy was found murdered.

MERIT STREET The Derry street where the Clements kid was found dead. Merit Street was in the Old Cape section of Derry, and on the day of the Losers' final confrontation with IT, every toilet on the street exploded.

MERRILL TRUST A downtown Derry bank. They had a clock on their building.

THE MIDWEST The Bradley brothers hit six or seven banks across the midwest before they were executed in Derry.

MILLINOCKET El Katook swore that he didn't kill El Katook's friends. He said he was in Millinocket that day. [Note: See the "People" entries EL KATOOK, and CLAUDE HEROUX.]

MONT STREET The Derry street where the trolleys ran.

MOUNT HOPE CEMETERY Georgie Denbrough was buried in Mount Hope. [NOTE: So was Gage Creed. See the section on *Pet Sematary* in this volume.]

MOUNTAIN STATES CULTURAL CENTER A building in Colorado Springs that Ben was in the process of putting up when he got called back to Derry.

MR. McKIBBON'S BACKYARD Bill, Eddie, and Ben got the boards for their dam in the Barrens from Mr. McKibbon's backyard.

MR. PAPERBACK A Derry store at the corner of Center and Main Streets.

MRS. KERSH'S BEDROOM Bev saw a large cedar chest in Mrs. Kersh's bedroom that had the initials "R.G." ("Robert Gray") inlaid into it.

NAN'S One of the bars in the Hell's Half Acre section of Derry in the early 1900s.

NAN'S LUNCHEONETTE A Derry luncheonette next door to the Alladin Theater.

A NATIONAL FARMSTEAD AND HARDWARE SUPPLY One of the business establishments in downtown Hemingford Home, Nebraska.

NAUGLER ROAD Alfie Naugler had a farm on Naugler Road in Derry.

NEIBOLT STREET The Derry street where the Albrecht girl was found murdered.

THE NEIBOLT STREET CHURCH SCHOOL The school Veronica Grogan attended. It was run by "the Christers." It stood at the corner of Route 2 and Neibolt Street.

THE NEIBOLT STREET STATION In 1985, it had become a parking lot. It used to be a train station.

NEW MEXICO The forty-year-old air force colonel that got Cheryl Lamonica pregnant already had a wife and three children in New Mexico.

NEW YORK STATE UNIVERSITY Stan Uris's alma mater. He was a scholarship student.

NEWPORT White folks came in from Newport (among other places) to hear the music and drink at the Black Spot in the early 1900s. Also, on the day of the Losers' final confrontation with IT, the morning started out with moderate rain in Newport and then got progressively worse as the battle escalated.

NINTH STREET MIDDLE SCHOOL Mike Hanlon's junior high school.

A NITE-OWL STORE On the morning of the day of the Losers' final confrontation with IT, an old maple on the Old Cape side of the Barrens fell and flattened the Nite-Owl store on the corner of Merit and Cape Avenue at 7:17 a.m.

THE NORTHEAST BANK One of the Derry businesses/buildings that collapsed the day of the Losers' final confrontation with IT.

THE NORTHERN NATIONAL BANK The bank that replaced the Shoeboat and Bailley's Lunch in 1985.

THE O'BRIAN MEMORIAL POOL A Derry public pool. Four kids who had gone swimming there in 1956 contracted polio.

THE OCEAN The ocean was forty miles from Derry. [NOTE: The Atlantic Ocean is forty miles from Bangor, Maine.)

O'HARE AIRPORT The Chicago airport Bev Rogan flew out of to return to Derry.

AN OHIO PLASTICS PLANT The Paul Bunyan statue in the center of Derry was cast in an Ohio Plastics plant.

OLD CAPE A low income housing development. There were trolley tracks there.

THE OLD CAPE SECTION The old maple that fell and flattened the Nite-Owl Store on the corner of Merit Street and Cape Avenue on the day of the Losers' final confrontation with IT knocked out power to the entire Old Cape section of Derry, as well as to the Sherburn Woods development.

THE OLD CAPE SIDE OF THE BARRENS On the morning of the day of the Losers' final confrontation with IT, an old maple on the Old Cape side of the Barrens fell and flattened the Nite-Owl store on the corner of Merit and Cape Avenue at 7:17 a.m.

OLD LYME STREET The Derry street that ran from Kansas Street to the town dump.

OLD TOWN White folks came in from Old Town (among other places) to hear the music and drink at the Black Spot in the early 1900s.

OMAHA After IT's death, as Mike talked to Richie on the phone, he could hear a woman talking from Omaha; Ruthven, Arizona; or possibly Flint, Michigan.

127 LOWER MAIN STREET, DERRY, MAINE, ZONE 2 Beverly Marsh's address.

THE ORINOKA A Derry restaurant. Carson suggested that Mike Hanlon take Ives to dinner there.

OUTER JACKSON STREET The Kaola Inn in Derry was on Outer Jackson Street. Also, Betty Ripsom was found on Outer Jackson Street with her insides ripped open.

"OUTSIDE" During the Smoke-Hole Ceremony, Richie and Mike went back in time to the prehistoric Barrens and saw the landing of IT's spaceship. They learned that IT had come from Outside. Outside what? Outside *everything*.

PALMER LANE As a child, Mike Hanlon often rode his bike to Main Street via Palmer Lane.

PALMYRA Herman Stanchfield had a farm in Palmyra.

THE PARADISE One of the bars in the Hell's Half Acre section of Derry in the early 1900s.

PASTURE ROAD The Kitchener Ironworks was on Pasture Road, a road which later became Mall Road.

THE PAULSON NURSING HOME The Bangor nursing home where retired Officer Aloysius Nell spent his last years.

THE PEABODY DINNER THEATER Audra Phillips' "Arsenic and Old Lace" tour had begun at the Peabody Dinner Theater in Massachusetts, and had ended at Play It Again Sam in Sausalito, California.

PECK'S BIG BOY An outrageous bar.

PENOBSCOT COUNTY Derry was in Penobscot County.

THE PENOBSCOT RIVER The Derry sewers emptied into the Torrault Stream and the Penobscot River.

PERU Ben Hanscom worked with Frank Billings, the architect, in Peru in 1978.

PILOT'S A Bangor bar in the 1920s.

PITCH TIL U WIN One of the stalls at the Derry Days carnival.

PLAY IT AGAIN SAM Audra Phillips's "Arsenic and Old Lace" tour had begun at the Peabody Dinner Theater in Massachusetts, and had ended at Play It Again Sam in Sausalito, California.

THE PLOW AND BARROW A bar in England.

THE POCONOS Stan and Patty Uris honeymooned in the Poconos.

POOH'S CORNER The area of the Derry library where the children looked at picturebooks.

PORTLAND Jimmy Donlin killed his mother in Portland in the summer of 1965. Also, Portland was where Derry's drinkers went if they wanted something outrageous.

THE POWDERHORN One of the bars in the Hell's Half Acre section of Derry in the early 1900s. At the Powderhorn, you could get a whore if you wanted one.

THE PREHISTORIC BARRENS During the Smoke-Hole Ceremony, Richie and Mike went back in time to the prehistoric Barrens and saw the landing of IT's spaceship.

THE PUMPING-STATION When being chased by Bowers and Company in 1958, the Losers had to descend into the Derry sewers' pumping-station in order to escape.

QUEENS Eddie and Myra Kaspbrak had originally lived in a four-room house in Queens before they bought a place in Long Island.

RAMPAR'S A Brewster bar nicknamed the Bucket of Blood.

RANGELEY Alfred Zitner had a time-sharing condo in Rangeley.

THE RED WARD The shock treatment department at the Juniper Hill Insane Asylum.

THE RED WHEEL Ben Hanscom's favorite watering hole. [NOTE: See the "Things" entry THE DIRECTIONS TO THE RED WHEEL.]

A REDONDO BEACH ART GALLERY A building built by Ben Hanscom.

A REXALL DRUGSTORE One of the business establishments in downtown Hemingford Home, Nebraska.

REYNOLD'S HARDWARE The Derry hardware store where the Losers got the hinges for the door that covered their Barrens' "hole-in-the-ground" clubhouse.

REYNOLDS STREET, DERRY Chief Andrew Rademacher lived on Reynolds Street.

RHULIN FARMS The road outside the Hanlon farm (Route 7) led to Rhulin Farms.

RICHARD'S ALLEY A street in Derry center.

RIDGELINE ROAD The road leading into the Derry army air corps base.

RODEO DRIVE Richie Tozier bought his clothes from the best shops on Rodeo Drive.

ROOM 518 Beverly Marsh's room in the Derry Town House.

ROOM 404 Ben Hanscom's room in the Derry Town House.

ROOM 609 Eddie Kaspbrak's room in the Derry Town House.

ROOM 311 Bill Denbrough's room in the Derry Town House.

ROOM 217 Richie Tozier's room in the Derry Town House.

ROUTE 7 Rhulin Farms was on Route 7 in Derry.

ROUTE 7, NEWPORT Harold Earl lived on Route 7.

RURAL STAR ROUTE 2, HEMINGFORD HOME, NEBRASKA, 59341 Ben Hanscom's Nebraska address.

RUTHVEN, ARIZONA After IT's death, as Mike talked to Richie on the phone, he could hear a woman talking from Omaha; Ruthven, Arizona; or possibly Flint, Michigan.

RYE The Derry army air corps stockade was in Rye.

SAINT CRISPIN'S LANE The Derry street where Bev had once fallen and scraped her knee.

ST. JOSEPH'S HOSPITAL The Bangor hospital where Cheryl Tarrent was taken after she broke her leg in a car crash.

ST. MARY'S The Bangor Catholic church that held bingo games. Mrs. Portleigh usually attended the games.

THE ST. REGIS HOTEL Al Pacino stayed there.

A SALT LAKE CITY BUSINESS BUILDING One of the buildings built by Ben Hanscom.

SAUSALITO Audra Phillips's "Arsenic and Old Lace" tour had begun at the Peabody Dinner Theater in Massachusetts, and had ended at Play It Again Sam in Sausalito, California.

SECONDHAND ROSE, SECONDHAND CLOTHES A secondhand shop at the bottom of Up-Mile Hill in Derry.

A SECOND-RUN MOVIE HOUSE One of the business establishments in downtown Hemingford Home, Nebraska.

A 76 GAS STATION One of the business establishments in downtown Hemingford Home, Nebraska.

73 CHARTER STREET, DERRY, MAINE Edward L. Corcoran's address.

THE SEWER SYSTEM The Derry sewers. The sewers were where IT lived.

SHAWSHANK The forty-year-old air force colonel who got Cheryl Lamonica pregnant ended up in Shawshank prison. He served time for armed robbery. [NOTE: The Shawshank prison is also the setting for the *Different Seasons* novella "Rita Hayworth and Shawshank Redemption." See the section on that novella in this volume.]

THE SHERBURN WOODS DEVELOPMENT The old maple that fell and flattened the Nite-Owl Store on the corner of Merit Street and Cape Avenue on the day of the Losers' final confrontation with IT knocked out power to the entire Old Cape section of Derry as well as to the Sherburn Woods development.

THE SHIRT SHACK A Bangor t-shirt shop. They sold t-shirts that said "Where the Hell is Derry, Maine?"

SHITHOUSE FALLS, NORTH DAKOTA OR PUSSYHUMP CITY, WEST VIRGINIA As Richie Tozier was preparing to return to Derry, Steve Kovall asked if either of these two "towns" was his destination.

THE SHOEBOAT The store where Dave Gardener worked. Also, the Shoeboat was the Derry store where Eddie Kaspbrak x-rayed his foot. It was on Center Street. The Shoeboat was one of the Derry businesses/buildings that collapsed on the day of the Losers' final confrontation with IT.

SHOOK'S DRUG STORE A Derry pharmacy. Shook's sold ice cream cones.

SHOP 'N SAVE Ben Hanscom's mother shopped at the Derry Shop 'N Save.

THE SILVER DOLLAR One of the bars in the Hell's Half Acre section of Derry in the early 1900s. (It was also known as "The Sleepy Silver Dollar.")

THE SISTERS OF MERCY EMERGENCY HOSPITAL The emergency room where Kay McCall went for treatment after she was beat up by Tom Rogan.

SIX OR SEVEN BANKS The Bradley brothers hit six or seven banks across the midwest before they were executed in Derry.

THE SIXTH STREET STATION The police station Kay McCall called after she was beat up by Tom Rogan.

61 PALMER LANE Mike Hanlon's Derry address.

THE SLEEPY SILVER DOLLAR The Silver Dollar Bar.

THE SMOKE-HOLE The Losers' Barrens' clubhouse. They burned branches down there one day in imitation of an ancient Indian ritual that Ben called "The Smoke-Hole Ceremony," and during the rite they had a mystical experience in which they saw the coming of IT to our world.

SMOKEY'S GREATER SHOWS The company that produced the carnival for Derry Days festival.

SOMERSWORTH, NEW HAMPSHIRE Foxy Foxworth, who was injured during the "storm" that occurred during the Losers' final confrontation with IT, went to live with his sister in Somersworth after he recovered.

THE SOUTH WINDHAM'S BOYS' TRAINING FACILITY Chris Unwin was sentenced to six months at the facility for Adrian Mellon's death.

THE SPECIAL BARRACKS The Derry army air corps base had a "special barracks" for the black enlisted men that was a half mile away from the other seven barracks.

SQUIRE'S SOUVENIRS AND SUNDRIES One of the Derry businesses/buildings that collapsed on the day of the Losers' final confrontation with IT.

THE STANDARD BRANDS BUILDING When Tom Rogan and Bev Marsh first met, they were both working in the Standard Brands Building.

THE STANDPIPE A Derry landmark. It held 1.75 million gallons of water.

THE STAR BEEF MEAT-PACKING PLANT A plant that still existed in Derry in 1985. It was part of Warehouse Row, and fronted Up-Mile Hill.

STARKS MILLS IN NEWPORT The mill where Arlene Hanscom worked.

STRAPHAM STREET It opened onto Witcham Street in Derry. The Nells lived on Strapham Street.

STREYLAND AVENUE The Chicago street where a 7-11 was located.

SWEDEN Mrs. Kersh told Bev that she came from Sweden in 1920.

SWITZERLAND The clock in the steeple of the Derry Grace Baptist Church had come from Switzerland in 1897.

A SYNAGOGUE IN BANGOR Stan Uris's family occasionally attended a synagogue in Bangor when Stan was a child.

A TEXTILE MILL Bill Denbrough worked part-time in a textile mill while attending college.

THE THEOLOGICAL SEMINARY A big Victorian building in Derry. The seminary property was behind Feldman's Storage and the Tracker Brothers' annex.

THOMASTON There was a prison there.

THREE NEW YORK SKYSCRAPERS Three buildings built by Ben Hanscom.

TOBIN BRIDGE Eddie Kaspbrak passed this bridge on his way into Boston when he returned to Derry as an adult.

TOPANGA CANYON Audra Phillips had a house in Topanga Canyon, as well as her rented house in Fleet, England. Also, "The Pit of the Black Demon" wrap party was held in Topanga Canyon.

THE TORRAULT STREAM The Derry sewers emptied into the Torrault Stream and the Penobscot River.

THE TOWNS THE WHITE FOLKS CAME FROM White folks came in from Bangor, Newport, Haven, Cleaves Mills, and Old Town to hear the music and drink at the Black Spot.

TRACKER AVENUE Mr. Tremont worked at a shoe shop on Tracker Avenue in Derry. When Bev began hearing voices from her bathroom sink drain, he had just lost his job.

THE TRACKER BROTHERS' TRUCK DEPOT A depot where Derry kids played baseball on a vacant lot in the back.

TRAPHAM NOTCH In May of 1905, there was a brief logger's strike up near Trapham Notch. (The Notch's population at the time was 79.)

THE TRAVELER'S REST A Derry hotel that existed in 1958.

TRAYNOR, GEORGIA A town forty miles south of Atlanta. In July of 1972, Patty Uris got a job in Traynor teaching shorthand and business English.

THE TRAYNOR FLATS SHOPPING CENTER A strip shopping center that opened in November of 1972. Stan Uris worked at an H & R Block there for $150 a week.

A TRUSTWORTHY HARDWARE STORE The Derry store that replaced the Frati Brothers pawnshop in 1985.

TUCSON, ARIZONA Mike Hanlon's uncle, Philly Loubird, was once a lawyer in Tucson.

A TUNNEL While pursuing Bill to Derry, Audra Phillips dreamt of finding a three-foot door in a tunnel marked with a strange symbol.

UNIVERSAL CITY The studio producing the "Black Rapids" film.

THE UNIVERSITY OF MAINE Bill Denbrough's and Mike Hanlon's alma mater.

UP-MILE HILL A section of Kansas Street in Derry.

VANNOCK'S DRY GOODS A dry goods store in the center of Derry in the 1920s.

THE VIKING PRESS Bill Denbrough sent his first novel (it was about ghosts) to Viking.

THE VOID In 1985, after IT told Bill that she was the "Eater of Worlds," she fired Bill across the huge underground cavern into the Void, where he saw the carcass of the Turtle.

A WALDENBOOKS One of the stores in the Derry Mall in 1985.

WALLY'S SPA One of the bars in the Hell's Half Acre section of Derry in the early 1900s.

WAREHOUSE ROW In Derry, Warehouse Row was comprised of Star Beef, Armour Meatpacking, Hemphill Storage & Warehousing, Eagle Beef & Kosher Meats, and Kirshner Packing Works. (These businesses fronted Up-Mile Hill.)

WATER STREET HIGH SCHOOL Steve Dubay's school. He left it at sixteen. He went through seventh grade three times.

WATERVILLE After the devastation that took place in Derry during the "storm" that occurred as part of the Losers' final confrontation with IT, Raytheon decided to build in Waterville instead of Derry.

WEST BROADWAY The section of Derry where there were mansions. Dr. Hale lived on West Broadway.

WICHITA STATE COLLEGE Tom Rogan's alma mater. He escaped from an abusive mother by attending college.

WITCHAM AND JACKSON A Derry intersection.

WITCHAM STREET The Derry street where the Denbroughs lived. Georgie Denbrough's newspaper boat floated down Witcham Street into one of Pennywise's sewers.

THE WOODEN BRIDGE Bill always stashed Silver under a wooden bridge at Kansas Street.

A WOOLWORTH'S One of the stores in the Derry Mall in 1985.

YORK'S STEAK HOUSE One of the stores in the Derry Mall in 1985.

ZALES JEWELERS Zales Jewelers (in the Derry Mall) was wiped out by an explosion on the day of the Losers' final confrontation with IT.

ZITNER'S REALTY The Derry real estate firm owned and operated by Alfred Zitner.

(22)
IT
Things

THE ACES OF SPADES In 1985, Mike Hanlon gave Bill a new deck of Bicycle playing cards for Silver's wheels. Bill shuffled them, and sprayed them on the floor. Only two cards landed face up: both were the ace of spades: one was red, and one was blue.

ACID To attack the Crawling Eye in the Derry sewers, Eddie pretended his aspirator was filled with acid, and used it to spray the eye.

ADRIAN MELLON'S HAT It was a paper top hat with a flower that said "I ♥ Derry!"

ADRIAN MELLON'S WOUNDS Mellon was stabbed seven times, including once in the left lung, and twice in the testicles. He also had four broken ribs, bites on his arms, left cheek, and neck, there was a chunk of meat out of his armpit, and his earlobe was gone.

AL BRADLEY'S AMMO SHOPPING LIST Al Bradley wanted the following list of ammo from Machen's Sporting Goods:

- 500 rounds of .38 caliber
- 800 rounds of .45 caliber
- 60 rounds of .50 caliber shotgun shells loaded both with buck and bird
- 1000 rounds of .22 caliber short-rifle
- 1000 rounds of .22 caliber long-rifle
- 16,000 rounds of .45 caliber machine-gun bullets.

AL MARSH'S POSTCARD After Bev married Tom Rogan, her father sent her a postcard that said: "Hope you are doing well and being good. Hope you will send me something if you can, as I don't have much. I love you Bevvie. Dad."

AL PACINO'S AUTOGRAPH Myra Kaspbrak wanted it.

ALBERT CARSON'S RECOMMENDATIONS FOR THE STUDY OF DERRY'S HISTORY Carson told Mike Hanlon to throw away Fricke and Michaud, and then read Buddinger.

"ALL THERE IS" "The circle closes, the wheel rolls, and that's all there is....go toward all the life there is with all the courage you can find and all the belief you can muster. Be true, be brave, stand. All the rest is darkness." [NOTE: Amen.]

THE ALL-DEAD BAND Richie Tozier's name for an all-star band comprised solely of dead musicians. At the time of Mike Hanlon's call from Derry, the newest member of the band was Marvin Gaye.

ALTOID MINTS Audra Denbrough kept Altoids in her purse.

AMERICAN AIRLINES Richie Tozier flew American to Derry from California.

"AMERICAN BUFFALO" A play that was starring Al Pacino.

"ANDI" Andrea Lamonica's nickname.

AN ANSEL ADAMS PHOTO OF BIG SUR Richie Tozier's safe was behind this photo.

AN ANTIQUE PENDULUM CLOCK A clock that sat at the foot of the stair's in Tom and Bev Rogan's house.

"APPAREBET EIDOLON SENEX" The Pliny inscription on the Memorial Park birdbath.

APRIL 1958 The month that three-and-a-half-year-old Chad Lowe disappeared.

APRIL 23, 1985 The date Adam Terrault was found decapitated.

ARMED ROBBERY The father of Cheryl Lamonica's daughter, Andi, ended up serving time in Shawshank for armed robbery.

"ARSENIC AND OLD LACE" At the age of nineteen, Audra Phillips had done a road tour of "Arsenic and Old Lace." It had consisted of forty performances in forty towns in forty-seven days.

"ATTIC ROOM" Bill Denbrough's first original screenplay.

AUDRA'S WEDDING RING Bill and the Losers found Audra's wedding ring in the sewers of Derry. They found it near Patrick Hockstetter's body.

AUGUST 19, 1972 The day Stan and Patty Uris were married.

"AUNT HAGAR'S BLUES" AND "DIGGIN' MY POTATOES" Two of the songs played by the Company E jazz band in the Black Spot. They also learned to play the Maine Stein Song.

"THE AUTHOR OF ALL THERE WAS" The Final Other; the creator of the Turtle; "a force beyond the universe, a power beyond all other powers, the author of all there was."

THE AUTOMATIC Whenever a ball was hit over the Tracker Brothers Depot chainlink fence into the Barrens, it was an automatic home run called "The Automatic."

A B.A. Patty Uris's degree.

"A BABY DAM" In 1958, Eddie and Bill built a small dam in the barrens that Bowers and company smashed and called a "baby dam."

"BACK TO THE FUTURE" The Alladin was featuring "Back to the Future" on May 31, 1985.

BALL BEARING MOLDS The Losers bought two ball bearing molds costing fifty cents each from the Kitchener Ironworks. They used them to make the silver slugs with which they shot It.

THE BANGOR HYDRO DAM In 1957, it was under construction.

THE BASSEY PARK GRAFFITI It said "KILL ALL QUEERS" and "AIDS FROM GOD YOU HELL-BOUND HOMOS!"

BE-BOP PENCILS Ben Hanscom's pencil of choice.

"BEAN, BEANS, THE MUSICAL FRUIT" The "fart" rhyme that was a favorite of Henry Bowers.

"THE BEGINNING OF THE END" AND "THE BLACK SCORPION" In 1958, when Bev heard a "buzzing scream" in the house on Neibolt Street, she thought of these two movies. The noise turned out to be a "mooseblower"; a Sterno can with the ends cut off and a waxed string in the middle.

A BELLYACHE While in the Void, Bill met the Turtle, who revealed to Bill that he had, indeed, made the universe, but "don't blame me for it, I had a bellyache."

THE BEN HANSCOM FREEDOM DIET Ben's term for the emotional upheaval that led him to lose weight. (It included fat-paddling, and being called "Jugs.")

BEN HANSCOM'S HAIKU As a child, Ben wrote the following haiku to Beverly Marsh:

Your hair is winter fire
January embers
My heart burns there, too.

BEN HANSCOM'S ROUTINE IN THE RED WHEEL Friday night, two beers; Saturday night, four or five beers. He always asked after Ricky Lee's three kids, and always left a five dollar tip under his beer stein. At Christmas, he always left a fifty-dollar tip under the stein.

BEN HANSCOM'S TOYS His toys included Revell models, Lincoln Logs, and an erector set.

BEN'S DAM IN THE BARRENS Without realizing what he'd done, Ben Hanscom designed and built a "cofferdam" in the Barrens.

BEN'S LUNCH After the guys built the dam in the Barrens, they ate lunch. Eddie and Bill were amazed at Ben's repast: "[T]wo PB&J sandwiches, one bologna sandwich, a hardcooked egg (complete with a pinch of salt twisted up in a small piece of waxed paper), two fig-bars, three large chocolate chip cookies, and a Ring-Ding."

BEN'S PURCHASES AT COSTELLO'S With the twenty-eight cents he got from cashing in the empty bottles that he found, Ben Hanscom bought the following at Costello's: five red licorice whips, five black licorice whips, ten rootbeer barrels (at two for a penny) a nickel strip of buttons (five to a row, five rows on a strip), a packet of Likem Ade, and a package of Pez. He got four cents change.

BEN'S SWEATSHIRTS After Ben's "tits" fiasco with Belch Huggins, Ben wore only baggy sweatshirts. He had four: one brown, one green, and two blue.

BEST BOOK OF ACTIVITIES One of Georgie Denbrough's schoolbooks.

"THE BEST DAMNED HORROR STORY SINCE RAY BRADBURY'S 'THE JAR'" How the editor of *White Tie* magazine described Bill Denbrough's early short story, "The Dark."

BETWEEN $75,000 AND $200,000 When the final explosion blew open the Derry Farmers' Trust, between $75,000 and $200,000 in cash blew away. Rebecca Paulson found $190 of the money in her backyard.

BEV'S MILESTONES In 1985, before the Losers' final confrontation with IT, Bev Marsh remembered three "milestones" from her younger years: At age twenty-nine, she had streaked her hair; at twenty-two, she had fallen in love with a football player named Greg Mallory who had damn near raped her after a frat party; and, at sixteen, she had gotten drunk with two friends on the Bluebird Hill Overlook.

BIB OVERALLS AND MAKEUP During the execution of the Bradley Gang, there was a clown present wearing bib overalls and makeup. The clown was also shooting at the Bradleys. The clown had no shadow.

BICYCLE PLAYING CARDS A deck of cards Mike bought for Silver's wheels in 1985.

THE BIG INJUNS WOODS FIRE In the summer of 1905, a fire in the Big Injuns Woods burned 20,000 acres of prime hardwood.

BILL DENBROUGH'S STORY THEORY "Why does a story have to be socio-anything? Politics...culture...history...aren't these natural ingredients in any story, if it's told well? I mean...can't you...just let a story be a story?"

BILL DENBROUGH'S WRITINGS AT THE UNIVERSITY OF MAINE During his EH-141 Creative Writing honors seminar, Bill wrote one locked-room mystery tale, three science fiction stories, and several horror stories that owed a great deal to Poe, Lovecraft, and Matheson. [NOTE: See the interview with Richard Matheson in this volume.]

BILL'S DREAMS Years after IT's death, Bill Denbrough would have dreams in which he was leaving Derry alone, at sunset, and the only sounds were his footsteps and the water rushing through the stormdrains.

BILL'S LUNCH BAG Belch Huggins once stomped Bill Denbrough's lunch bag when Bill was a kid.

BILL'S NIGHTSTAND THINGS When Bill was sick in bed just prior to Georgie's death, he had Kleenex, Vicks Vaporub, and a Philco radio on his nightstand.

A BIRD As the Black Spot burned, Bill Hanlon saw a huge bird hovering over the running men. It floated. "There were big bunches of balloons tied to each wing, and it floated."

THE BIRD BOOK Stan's bird book protected him from the Dead Ones in the standpipe who attacked him. (The book was M.K.

Handey's *Guide to North American Birds*.)

THE BIRD THEORY Eddie Kaspbrak's mother's race theory: Blackbirds flew with other blackbirds, etc.

BLACK CATS FIRECRACKERS In 1958, Stan Uris traded a bunch of Superman and Little Lulu comics for a package of Black Cats firecrackers. He had traded with a fat kid with whom he went to synagogue.

A BLACK '84 CADILLAC EL DORADO The car Cape Cod Limousine gave Eddie Kaspbrak for his drive into Derry.

THE BLACK RAPIDS One of Bill Denbrough's novels.

THE BLACK STALLION One of the three books Ben checked out from the Derry children's library the day he was chased and attacked by Bower and company.

BLOODLETTERS AND BADMEN A picture from this book showed Chief Sullivan standing over Al Bradley's corpse after the execution of the Bradley Gang in Derry in October of 1929.

THE BLOODY CLOTHS Ben, Ed, Bev, and Stan brought the bloody cloths they had used to clean Bev's bathroom to the Kleen-Kloze Washateria (on the corner of Main and Cony Streets) for laundering.

BLUE AND ORANGE BALLONS At the Derry library the evening of the day of the Losers' reunion lunch, Mike opened the refrigerator in the library's lounge and blue and orange balloons floated out. The balloons said "Derry Niggers get the Bird," and "The Losers Are Still Losing, But Stanley Uris is Finally Ahead." [NOTE: Stan's severed head was also in the refrigerator. See the "Things" entry STAN URIS'S SEVERED HEAD.]

"BODY NOT THAT OF CORCORAN YOUTH BORTON ANNOUNCES" The January 27, 1960, page 1 Derry *News* article about a newly discovered decomposed body suspected to be that of Edward Corcoran.

"BOOK-VALIUM" Bill Denbrough said reading was the finest kind of dope: He called it "Book-Valium."

THE BOTTOM OF HER BOX-SPRING Bev's secret hiding place when she was a kid.

THE BRADLEY GANG SHOOTOUT Inclusion of photos of the shootout in the Derry Days Museum was vetoed.

BREAST CANCER Patrick Hockstetter's mother died of breast cancer in 1962.

BRITISH AIRWAYS FLIGHT 23 The flight Audra Phillips Denbrough took to Bangor.

A BROKEN LEG AND A PUNCTURED TESTICLE The injuries Foxy Foxworth sustained during the Losers' final confrontation with IT. (Although he – and everyone else for that matter – thought it was just *really* bad weather.)

BRYLCREEM The hair pomade of choice for Victor Criss.

BULLDOZER One of the three books Ben checked out from the Derry children's library the day he was chased and attacked by Bower and company. This was also the book by Stephen W. Meader that Ben pulled blindly off the shelf when he returned to the Derry library in 1958. It was the same book he had been carrying when he was attacked by Henry Bowers in 1958. Henry's engineer boot footprint was still on the cover. [NOTE: See the "Things" entry *BULLDOZER*'S BORROWERS.]

BULLDOZER'S BORROWERS When Ben Hanscom returned to the Derry library in 1985, he blindly pulled *Bulldozer* off the shelf. The borrowers of the book in 1958 included:

Charles N. Brown	May 14	58
David Hartwell	Jun 1	58
Joseph Brennan	Jun 17	58
Benjamin Hanscom	Jul 9	58.

[NOTE: See the feature on the late Joseph Payne Brennan in this volume.]

A BULLSEYE SLINGSHOT Bill Denbrough's slingshot. In 1958, the Losers had devised "The Plan": Bev would shoot a silver ball (made from one of Ben's silver dollars) into IT's head.

THE BURNT MATCH Before the Smoke-Hole Ceremony, the

Losers drew matches to see who would stay topside for safety. The burnt match disappeared (thanks, of course, to IT), and they all had to go down into the hole.

BURSITIS One of Eddie Kaspbrak's adult complaints.

BUTCH-WAX Henry Bowers's hair stuck up from it.

A CADILLAC After IT's death, Ben rented a Cadillac to drive back to Nebraska.

"CAMPTOWN RACES" Just before the Dead Ones attacked Stan, he thought he heard calliope music playing. "Camptown Races" seemed to be coming from the standpipe. It made him think of the carnival rides, the Wild Mouse, the Whip, and the Koaster-Kups.

CANCER OF THE ESOPHAGUS The disease that killed Vernon Maitland.

CANCER OF THE LARYNX Richie Tozier's dad, Wentworth, died of cancer of the larynx in 1973.

CANDY Mrs. Kersh's apartment turned into candy, and the witch from Hansel & Gretel turned into her father.

A CAPTAIN MIDNIGHT MAGIC DECODER RING The reason Mike Hanlon ate Wheaties.

THE CARNIVAL RIDES The rides at the Derry Days carnival included the Devil Dish, the Parachute Drop, and Bumper Cars.

A CARTON OF CAMELS As Tom Rogan pursued Bev, he stopped at a drugs-and-sundries shop in Bangor and bought a carton of Camels. He decided he was going to make Bev eat the Camels when he found her.

CATATONIC After her rescue from IT's lair, Audra was catatonic. Bill healed her by taking her for a ride "to beat the Devil" on Silver.

THE CEDAR CHEST Mrs. Kersh had a large cedar chest in her bedroom that had the initials "R.G." inlaid into it.

THE CELLAR SHELF ITEMS On the shelf in the Denbrough cellar were the following items: Kiwi shoe polish, a broken kerosene lamp, two empty bottles of Windex, and a container of Turtle [!] Wax.

THE CELLAR WINDOW In 1958, while breaking into the house on Neibolt Street for their confrontation with IT, Ben got stuck in the cellar window because he was so fat.

"A CERTAIN SLANT OF LIGHT" A certain slant of light made Mike Hanlon feel like crying for no reason. [NOTE: This line is from the Emily Dickinson poem "There's A Certain Slant Of Light." The poem begins:

There's a certain Slant of light,
Winter Afternoons—
That oppresses, like the Heft
Of Cathedral Tunes—

CHANTILLY During the fight Bev had with Tom over her returning to Derry, she threw a bottle of Chantilly at him and hit him in the chest.

A CHEAP TWO-BLADE POCKETKNIFE As a child, Mike Hanlon found a pocketknife in Bassey Park with the initials E.C. scratched on the side. It had belonged to Eddie Corcoran.

THE CHESLEY ACCOUNT Tom Rogan would think about White Sox batting averages or the Chesley account in order to delay coming while making love. [NOTE: Chris Chesley was Stephen King's co-author for the 1963 collaborative collection called *People, Places, and Things*. See the section on Chris Chesley and *People, Places, and Things* in this volume.]

CHIVAS AND GLENFIDDICH The booze brought in to the Black Spot by the white folks.

A CIRCLE At 6:49 on May 31, 1985, the Losers formed a circle in the sewers of Derry to send their power to Mike Hanlon, who was laid up in the Derry Home Hospital with a broken arm. Mike's life was being threatened by Mark Lamonica, who was under the control of IT.

THE CITY CENTER MARQUEE In 1958, the marquee bore this message "in large blue translucent letters:

HEY TEENS!
COMING MARCH 28TH!
THE ARNIE "WOO-WOO" GINSBERG
ROCK AND ROLL SHOW!
JERRY LEE LEWIS
THE PENGUINS
FRANKIE LYMON AND THE TEENAGERS
GENE VINCENT AND THE BLUE CAPS
FREDDY "BOOM-BOOM" CANNON

AN EVENING OF WHOLESOME ENTERTAINMENT

In 1985, those same blue letters spelled out:

JUNE 14TH
HEAVY METAL MANIA!!
JUDAS PRIEST
IRON MAIDEN
BUY YOUR TICKETS HERE OR AT ANY TICKETRON
OUTLET

A CLEAR COKE BOTTLE In 1958, the Losers cut their palms with a piece of a clear Coke bottle after their first battle with IT, swearing an oath and vowing to return to Derry if IT ever returned. (Truth was, she never left. She was only sleeping.)

THE CLOWN'S EYES Hagarty said he saw the clown's eyes and knew the clown was Derry.

A COLT .45 Gregory Cole's gun.

COLUMBIAN RED Andrew Keene's smoke of choice. He had smoked so much Red the morning the standpipe fell over that at first he thought he was hallucinating.

"A COMBER" Bill Denbrough was afraid that if Eddie Kaspbrak didn't get his aspirator refilled, he would slip into "a comber."

"COME HOME COME HOME COME HOME" When Jerry Bellwood was found torn apart, "Come Home" was written on the wall where Jerry was discovered. It was written in Jerry's blood.

A COMMODORE COMPUTER The Derry library had a Commodore.

COMPANY E Company E at the Derry army air corps base had twenty-seven men.

THE COMPANY E JAZZ BAND The Black Spot's Company E Jazz Band consisted of Corporal Martin Devereaux on drums, Ace Stevenson on cornet, Pop Snopes on barrelhouse piano, and George Brannock on sax.

CONGESTIVE HEART FAILURE Eddie Kaspbrak's mother died of congestive heart failure at the age of sixty-four. She weighed 406 pounds.

CONSTRUCTION SITE STUDS The book the proprietor of Secondhand Rose, Secondhand Clothes was reading in 1985 when Bill went in the shop and bought Silver back.

CONTACT LENSES When the Derry Paul Bunyan statue came alive in 1985 and became a giant Buddy Holly statue, Richie Tozier got a terrible eye pain that caused him to pop out his contact lenses. A high school girl helped him look for them.

"CONVICTED MURDERER COMMITS SUICIDE IN FALMOUTH" The July 19, 1967, page 3 Portland *Press-Herald* article about Richard Macklin's suicide.

"COURT ORDERS SURPRISE EXHUMATION" The June 22, 1958, page 1 Derry *News* article about the exhumation of Dorsey Corcoran's body.

"THE CRAWLING EYE" The only movie that ever truly scared Richie Tozier.

CRIME IN DERRY Mike Hanlon was able to discern the following pattern of crime in Derry (all of which was related to IT's cyclical awakenings and feedings): 1715-1716; 1740-1743 (a bad one); 1769-1770; all the way up to 1958, when the cycle came to a premature end due to the efforts of the Losers.

A CUTLASS Bev Rogan's car.

"'DADDY HAD TO TAKE ME UP 'CAUSE I'M BAD'" The June 28, 1958, page 2 Derry *News* article about Dorsey Corcoran.

DAISY AIR RIFLE Ben Hanscom's gun.

"THE DARK" A short story by Bill Denbrough. It was about a small boy who discovers a monster in the cellar of his house. He was writing about his brother Georgie, but he didn't know it.

A DARVON AND A VALIUM After Bev left him, Tom Rogan threatened to cut Bev's best friend Kay McCall's face with a piece of a broken Waterford vase. Kay broke down and told him where he could find Bev. When Tom left, Kay took a Darvon and a Valium, and smoked a Pall Mall from a pack that was three years old.

A DATSUN Audra Phillips Denbrough rented a Datsun from National Car Rental when she got to Bangor in pursuit of her husband, Bill.

THE DAY THE LOSERS WON It was May 31, 1985. The day began for the Losers at 5:30 a.m. At 5:45, a power transformer on the pole beside the Trackers Brothers' Depot exploded; at 6:06, every toilet on Merit Street exploded; at 6:09, Calvin Clark stepped on a live wire and was electrocuted; at 6:19, lightning struck the Kissing Bridge; by 6:45, the wind gauge in the lobby of the courthouse building registered twenty-four miles-an-hour; by 7:00, the wind was up to fifty-seven; at 7:10, the first severe weather warnings were broadcast; at 7:17, the old maple on the Old Cape side of the Barrens fell and flattened a Nite-Owl store; at 7:20, the clock in the steeple of the Grace Baptist Church chimed thirteen times; at 7:21, the steeple was truck by lightning and exploded; at 7:32, Aloysius Nell died from a fatal stroke; at 7:49, explosions shook the Derry Mall; at 9:10, the wind speeds were down to fifty-five; and at 10:02, Bill ripped out IT's heart, and downtown Derry collapsed.

THE DEAD OLD PARTY Richie Tozier's name for dead politicians.

THE DEADLIGHTS IT's eyes.

DECEMBER 1982 The last time Kay McCall had smoked from an old pack of Pall Malls. She next smoked one of them three years later, after she was assaulted by Tom Rogan, who forced her to tell him where he could find Bev.

DECEMBER 6, 1958 The date of the front page Derry *News* article "The End of Derry's Long Night" that (incorrectly) proclaimed Henry Bowers as Derry's "monster," and the man responsible for all of Derry's unsolved killings.

DERRY: AN UNAUTHORIZED TOWN HISTORY Mike Hanlon's running account of events in Derry, Maine. His ruminations were published as "Interludes" in *It*. Mike called his notes "Derry: A Look Through Hell's Back Door."

THE DERRY BLUES The 23rd Maine Battalion. Memorial Park was named for them.

THE DERRY CANAL DAY'S DAILY PROGRAM OF EVENTS Paul Hughes imagined the following "program" after Adrian Mellon's death:

Saturday, 9:00 P.M.: Final band concert featuring the Derry High School Band and the Barber Shop Mello-Men.
Saturday, 10:00 P.M.: Giant fireworks show.
Saturday, 10:35 P.M.: Ritual sacrifice of Adrian Mellon officially ends Canal Days.

THE DERRY CHILDREN'S LIBRARY SIGNS They included such signs and posters as: a cigarettes poster that said "When I Grow Up I Want To Be Sick A Lot, Just Like My Dad"; a Ralph Waldo Emerson photo with the caption "One Idea Lights A Thousand Candles"; "Join the Scouting Experience"; "The Girls' Clubs of Today Build The Women of Tomorrow"; "Join The Summer Reading Experience"; and "Remember the Curfew 7 P.M. Derry Police Department"

THE DERRY CURFEW It began at 7:00 p.m.

"THE DERRY DEPARTMENT OF PUBLIC WORKS" The legend stencilled on the sawhorses blocking the flooded streets of Derry in 1957.

THE DERRY LADIES' SOCIETY They sponsored the Canal Days Museum.

THE DERRY LIBRARY BOARD OF DIRECTORS It had eleven members, including a seventy-year-old writer who had had a stroke in 1983, and a pushy woman from New York.

THE DERRY MALL SIGN It said: "Forty-eight Different Merchants Under One Roof for Your Shopping Convenience." It was the third biggest mall in the state.

THE DERRY *NEWS* The Derry daily. It carried the story of Adrian Mellon's murder, among other items of interest for Derryites.

THE DERRY STANDPIPE The water storage tank in Memorial Park. Three kids had once drowned in the standpipe. It held 1.75 million gallons of water.

THE DERRY THEATER The Derry town theater.

DERRY'S CANAL DAYS FESTIVAL It took place from July 15 through July 21, 1984.

DERRY'S LUMBER TRADE Derry's lumber trade was opened up between 1884 and 1910.

DERRY'S MURDER RATE Mike Hanlon figured out that it was six times higher than that of comparable New England towns.

DERRY'S 1958 POPULATION There were 30,000 people in the city limits, and 7,000 in the suburbs.

DESERT DRIVER BOOTS Ben Hanscom's boots. He used them to crush IT's miscarried eggs in the sewers of Derry.

DEVOUT BAPTISTS The Hanlon family's religion.

THE DIRECTIONS TO THE RED WHEEL Go west out of Omaha on Interstate 80. Take the Swedholm exit, and then Highway 81 to downtown Swedholm "(of which there isn't much)." There, turn off on Highway 92 at Bucky's Hi-Hat Eat-Em-Up, and once out in the country again hang a right on Highway 63 "which runs straight as a string through the deserted little town of Gatlin" and that'll bring you right into downtown Hemingford Home. [NOTE: See the section on the *Night Shift* story "Children of the Corn" in this volume for more details on Gatlin, Nebraska.]

A DIRTY MAGAZINE In 1958, in the house on Neibolt Street, Bev found a dirty magazine. In 1985, she realized that the woman on the cover of the magazine was Mrs. Kersh.

A DISCARDED AMANA REFRIGERATOR Patrick Hockstetter put live animals in the refrigerator, and left them there. He would often go back and check up on their progression towards death.

DIXIE Stan Uris's beer.

DR. JARVIS'S VERMONT FOLK MEDICINE A book read by Eddie Kaspbrak's mother.

DR. WACKY'S SNEEZING POWDER Richie brought the powder to the house on Neibolt Street, and was able to use it to repel the Teenage Werewolf.

A DONALD DUCK NIGHTLIGHT Henry Bowers used a Donald Duck nightlight at Juniper Hill.

THE DOWNTOWN PICTURE An old picture in Georgie Denbrough's photo album. After Georgie's death, Richie and Bill appeared in the photo – and so did a clown with Georgie's face. Everything in the picture moved, including the Pierce-Arrow, Chevrolet, and Packard automobiles in the shot.

"DRAGNET" One of Ben Hanscom's favorite TV shows.

THE DREADED QUESTION The question Patty Uris hated to hear from her mother Ruth: "So when are you and Stan going to make us grandparents?"

A DUSTER Steve Dubay's car.

AN EAMES CHAIR Richie Tozier had one.

EARLY SPRING 1980 In the early spring of 1980, Mike Hanlon went to see Albert Carson about the history of Derry.

EARLY WINTER 1957-1958 In the early winter of 1957-1958, Mrs. Ripsom heard voices speaking from her kitchen sink drain.

EASTER SUNDAY, 1906 The day of the egg hunt at the Kitchener Ironworks plant. Five hundred eggs were hidden in the plant and on the grounds. At 3:15, the Kitchener Ironworks exploded. The final death toll was 102 dead, 88 of them children.

EDDIE CORCORAN'S DEATH The Creature from the Black Lagoon ripped open Eddie's carotid artery, and then ripped his head off.

EDDIE CORCORAN'S SAVINGS ACCOUNT In 1966, Eddie's mother had the boy declared legally dead so she could take possession of his savings account. There was sixteen dollars in the account.

EDDIE KASPBRAK'S FANTASIES IF HE LEFT MYRA They consisted of tennis lessons, a pool membership at the U.N. Plaza Hotel, and a membership at the health club on Third Avenue.

EDDIE KASPBRAK'S MEDICINE CABINET "If you would know all there is to know about an American man or woman of the middle class as the millenium nears its end, you would need only to look in his or her medicine cabinet – or so it has been said." No personality profile could do as good a job of letting you *truly* know Mr. Kaspbrak as giving you, Constant Reader, a glimpse inside his and Myra's medicine cabinet.

The Top Shelf

Anacin	Serutan
Excedrin	Two bottles of Phillips' Milk
Excedrin P.M.	of Magnesia (one regular,
Contac	one mint)
Gelusil	Rolaids
Tylenol	Tums
A large jar of Vicks	Di-Gel (orange-flavored tab-
Vivarin	lets)

The Second Shelf

Vitamin E	Iron
Vitamin C	Calcium
Vitamin C with rosehips	Cod liver oil
B-simple [sic]	One-A-Day Multiples
B-complex	Myadec Multiples
B-12	Centrum multiples
L-Lysine	A large bottle of Geritol
Lecithin	

The Third Shelf

Ex-Lax	Cepacol
Carter's Little Pills	Cepestat
Kaopectate	Listerine
Pepto-Bismol	Visine
Preparation H	Murine
Tucks	Cortaid
Formula 44	Neosporin
Nyquil	Oxy-5
Dristan	Oxy-Wash
Castor oil	Tetracycline
Sucrets	Three bottles of coal-tar
Chloraseptic	shampoo

The Bottom Shelf

Valium	Darvon Complex
Percodan	Six Quaaludes in a
Elavil	Sucrets box

There was also a tube of Blistex and a bottle of Midol in the medicine cabinet.

EDDIE'S ASPIRATOR Eddie Kaspbrak's ever-present defense against imagined asthma. As a child, his mother kept him under her thumb by insisting that he was "sickly," and the aspirator was part of it. One day, Mr. Keene took Eddie aside and told him that the aspirator was filled with nothing but camphor-flavored water, that it was a placebo. Eddie wondered, but never completely believed him. He was still using it in 1985. In 1985, as Eddie was talking with the others in the Derry library the night of their reunion lunch, his aspirator rolled across the table all by itself. The balloons that had appeared in the library then read "Asthma

Medicine Gives You Cancer!"

EH-141 The Creative Writing honors seminar that Bill Denbrough took at the University of Maine.

AN EIGHT-FOOT CLOWN WITH A DOBERMAN'S HEAD Before Henry Bowers escaped from the Juniper Hill Asylum, Koontz the guard saw an eight-foot clown with a Doberman's head. The Doberman was the only animal Koontz was afraid of.

800K Bill Denbrough's 1984 tax return showed 800K in income.

1890 The year the Derry library was built.

1898 The year the four-sided clock was shipped to Derry Grace Baptist Church from Switzerland.

1879 In 1879, nine lumberjacks were found hacked to pieces in a camp on the upper Kenduskeag. One of their penises was nailed to the cabin wall.

1877 In 1877, there were four lynchings in Derry.

1876 In 1876, four loggers were found torn apart in a cabin in Derry.

1876-1877 The period in Derry's history during which IT caused some undescribed havoc. IT's presence during this period was discovered by Mike Hanlon.

$87,000 The cost of Stan and Patty Uris's house in 1979.

EIGHTY-THREE DEGREES The temperature in Derry the afternoon of May 31, 1985.

ELAVIL In Juniper Hill in 1985, Benny Beaulieu had watched an "Emergency" rerun, and then jerked off until his dick bled. They gave him Elavil to quiet him.

11:45 P.M. The time the stewardess on Ben Hanscom's flight to Chicago thought Ben was dead.

ELEVEN YEARS At the time of Mike Hanlon's "return to Derry" call, Bill and Audra Denbrough had been married eleven years.

"THE END OF DERRY'S LONG NIGHT" The title of the December 6, 1958, front-page Derry *News* article that proclaimed Henry Bowers to be Derry's monster, responsible for all the unsolved killings. [NOTE: Little did they know, huh?]

ENGLISH AND MATH Henry Bowers flunked both of these subjects.

EPILEPSY The Stavier kid had it.

THE FABULOUS GUM-STICK Frankie or Freddy Ross or Roth used his Fabulous Gum-Stick (a stick with a wad of gum on one end) to pull stuff up out of the sewers.

THE FACE OF PENNYWISE After his shock treatment, and before his escape from Juniper Hill in 1985, Henry Bowers saw the moon turn into the face of Pennywise.

THE FALCON'S BUSINESS After it became a strictly gay bar, Elmer Curtie's bar business went from sixty beers and twenty drinks per night to eighty beers and a hundred to a hundred-sixty drinks per night.

"FAMILY FEUD" Patty Uris's favorite TV show.

A FARM MACHINE ACCIDENT Mike Hanlon's grandfather had died in a farm machine accident.

FAT-PADDLING Ben's classmates used to slap his rolls of fat in the gym locker room. It was called fat-paddling.

FEBRUARY 1985 In February of 1985, Denny Torrio was found mutilated in the Barrens.

A '51 FORD In 1958, a '51 Ford drove by just as Henry Bowers was preparing to carve his name into Ben Hanscom's stomach.

FIRST DEGREE MURDER Webby commited himself to being charged with first degree murder by admitting he wanted to drive by the Falcon on the night Mellon was killed.

555-3711 The phone number of the Derry Home Hospital.

FLYING LEECHES When Patrick Hockstetter went to the dump to get rid of a pigeon he had put in "his" Amana refrigerator to die, flying leeches attacked him when he opened the door. (He had already killed a cat and a cocker pup in the refrigerator.)

A FORD Butch Bowers had to sell his new Mercury to pay off Will Hanlon after he was caught killing Will's chickens. Butch bought a Ford to replace the Mercury. Also, a Ford was the unnamed 1931 flood victim's car.

THE FORTUNE COOKIES At their Jade of the Orient reunion lunch, the Losers' fortune cookies were not your usual fortune cookies: Bev's bled; a huge mutated cricket came out of Eddie's; a human eye looked out of Richie's'; Ben's had two teeth in it; and Bill's breathed (like "a boil filling with pus"), and then a fly the size of a baby sparrow was born out of it.

FORTY INDEX ENTRIES The number of references to Derry in the text *Maine Then and Now* .

FORTY MILES The ocean was forty miles from Derry.

FORTY MILES PER HOUR The speed Bill Denbrough could achieve on Silver. Especially when flying down Up-Mile Hill.

FORTY PERFORMANCES OF "ARSENIC AND OLD LACE" At the age of nineteen, Audra Phillips had done a road tour of "Arsenic and Old Lace." It had consisted of forty performances in forty towns in forty-seven days.

FOUR BOOKS OF POETRY AND A MASTER'S THESIS Bill Denbrough's EH-141 instructor's publishing history. All his work was published by the University of Maine Press.

406 POUNDS Eddie Kaspbrak's mother died of congestive heart failure at the age of sixty-four. She weighed 406 pounds.

FOUR LYNCHINGS In 1877, there were four lynchings in Derry.

FOUR ROSES The Red Wheel's bar whiskey.

"FOUR STAR PLAYHOUSE" A favorite TV show of Sharon Denbrough's.

A FOUR-SIDED CLOCK The clock on top of the Derry Grace Baptist Church. It had been shipped from Switzerland in 1898.

$1400 The amount Tom Rogan paid (as "Mr. Barr") for the 1976 LTD Wagon he bought when he got to Bangor.

THE FOURTH SILVER DOLLAR In the Derry library in 1985, Ben Hanscom remembered what had happened to the fourth silver dollar he had had. He knew that he had given three to Ricky Lee for Ricky's kids before he flew back to Maine, but he hadn't remembered what had happened to the fourth: In 1958, the Losers had had it melted down to make a slug with which to attack IT.

THE FOURTH WEEK OF JUNE IN 1958 The week Silver saved Bill Denbrough's life. (Silver got Bill away from the house on Neibolt Street before the Teenage Werewolf could grab him.)

FRANKENSTEIN MONSTER Victor Criss had his head ripped off by the Frankenstein Monster. After he was dead, Victor visited Henry Bowers in the Juniper Hill Asylum.

"THE FREAKY FORTY" One of Richie Tozier's syndicated radio programs.

A FRIGIDAIRE AND AN AMANA RADARANGE Mrs. Kersh (Bob Gray's "daughter") occupied Bev's old apartment in 1985. She had a Frigidaire refrigerator and an Amana Radarange stove in the apartment.

A FRINGILLIDAE RICHMONDENA A male cardinal Stan Uris saw drinking at the birdbath in Memorial Park.

"FUR ELISE" The Beethoven piano piece Mrs. Denbrough knew how to play.

GARTON'S CLASS RING He had "DB" engraved on it for "The Dead Bugs."

GARTON'S SENTENCE He was convicted of first degree manslaughter. He got ten to twenty years at Thomaston State Prison.

GEM **MAGAZINE** A magazine "read" by Richie Tozier's dad.

GEORGIE'S CELLAR FEAR "One unmistakable ineluctable smell, the smell of the monster, the apotheosis of all monsters."

GEORGIE'S FIRST THOUGHT OF THE TURTLE "That turtle," George thought. "Where did I see a turtle like that before?"

GEORGIE'S PHOTO ALBUM The album had "My Photographs" written on it, and contained black-and-white Kodaks that people had given to Georgie. The people in the pictures moved one day when Bill opened it.

GEORGIE'S POSTERS They included Tom Terrific, Huey, Louie, and Dewie Duck, and a Mr. Do crossing-guard poster.

GHOSTS OF THE GREAT PLAINS The book where Ben learned about the Indian Smoke-Hole Ceremony. The ceremony caused Richie and Mike to go back in time and witness IT's arrival on Earth.

A GIANT BARRIER While in the Void, Bill and Richie came to a giant barrier that Richie translated as fossilized wooden stakes going up and down into eternity. Behind the barrier were the deadlights.

"THE GIANT CLAW" Mike Hanlon said that the bird he saw at the Kitchener Ironworks looked like the one in the movie "The Giant Claw."

GILLETTE PLATINUM PLUS RAZOR BLADES The razor blades with which Stan Uris committed suicide. He slit his inner forearms open from wrist to the crook of the elbow and then crossed each cut below the Bracelets of Fortune, making bloody capital Ts.

A GIN-AND-LYE COCKTAIL Tom Rogan's father committed suicide using this "cocktail."

A GLAMOUR In 1958, Bill Denbrough deduced that the monster in the Derry sewers was a "glamour"; "an evil magic being that could read your mind and then assume the shape of the thing you were most afraid of." Other names for the creature were manitou, tallus, eylak (the brother of vurderlak or vampire), or le loup-garou. The Ritual of Chüd could defeat it. He read about this being in a book called *Night's Truth* .

THE GLASS LIBRARY CORRIDOR The Derry children's library was connected to the main building by a long glass corridor. At 10:30 a.m., on May 31, 1985, the corridor exploded. It was never rebuilt.

GLENFIDDICH Scotch liquor. Bill Denbrough took a drink of Glenfiddich after he got Mike Hanlon's "return to Derry" call.

"GOOD DAY!" The Boston TV program that mentioned Derry in a show about unsolved murders.

A GRANDFATHER CLOCK In 1923, Horst Mueller gave the Derry library a grandfather clock.

"GRAVEYARD MOON" One of Audra Phillips's film credits. It was a horror flick.

A GRENADE When Mike Hanlon's father Will was in the army, a new recruit dropped a live grenade that took off most of Will's left foot.

GRETA BOWIE'S BALLOON The dead Greta Bowie appeared to Eddie Kaspbrak at the abandoned Tracker Brothers' Depot. She held a green balloon that said "Asthma Medicine Causes Lung Cancer! Compliments of Center Street Drug."

THE GUARDIAN The London newspaper that loved the design of the BBC Communications Center, which had been built by Ben "Dam in the Barrens" Hanscom.

GUIDE TO NORTH AMERICAN BIRDS A book by M.K. Handey that Stan Uris carried around with him for luck as a kid.

GULF PARAFFIN Bill Denbrough used Gulf paraffin to waterproof the newspaper boat he made for his brother.

AN "H" In 1958, Henry Bowers carved an "H" into Ben Hanscom's stomach.

HALF HER BRAINS Jimmy Donlin killed his mother in Portland in the summer of 1965 and ate half her brains.

HAMBURGERS WITH SAUTEED MUSHROOMS AND ONIONS AND A SPINACH SALAD The supper Mike Hanlon made for Bill the evening of the day in 1985 that Bill bought Silver back.

THE HANLONS' FIELDS On the Hanlon farm, the back field was hay, the south field, potatoes, the west field, corn and beans, and the east field, peas, squash, and pumpkins.

THE HANLONS' SCARECROWS Larry, Moe, and Curly.

"HARDCASTLE AND MCCORMICK" AND "FALCON CREST" Myra Kaspbrak ate brownies in bed during these two shows.

"HAVE A GOOD DAY! TONIGHT YOU DIE!" The message written on a balloon Ben saw hanging in the Derry library when he went back in 1985.

"HE THRUSTS HIS FISTS AGAINST THE POSTS AND STILL INSISTS HE SEES THE GHOSTS" Bill Denbrough's anti-stuttering (and anti-IT) magic sentence.

HENRY BOWERS' NIGHTLIGHTS AFTER DONALD DUCK

BURNED OUT Mickey and Minnie Mouse, Oscar the Grouch, and Fozzie Bear.

"HIGHWAY PATROL" One of Ben Hanscom's favorite TV shows.

A HISTORY OF OLD DERRY Branson Buddinger's history of Derry. It was published by the University of Maine Press in 1950.

"HI-YO, SILVER, AWAYYYYYYY!" Bill Denbrough's exhortation to his bike as he rode to beat the devil.

"HOME" As Eddie prepared to return to Derry, he thought "Home is the place where when you go there, you have to finally face the thing in the dark."

HOT ROD One of the three books Ben checked out from the Derry children's library the day he was chased and attacked by Bower and company. It was by Henry Gregor Felsen.

A HUDSON HORNET The Zinnerman kids' car.

HYDROMIST SOFT LENSES Eddie Kaspbrak's contact lenses.

HYDROX MIST Eddie Kaspbrak's aspirator medicine. It was water with a dash of camphor.

"'I KILLED BARBARA STARRETT' PENNYWISE THE CLOWN" The message on a balloon Ben saw in the Derry library when he went back there in 1985.

"I SPENT IT DEAD IN A TUNNEL!" Eddie thought that if Patrick Hockstetter had to write a "How I Spent My Summer Vacation" essay, it would be called "I Spent It Dead In a Tunnel!"

I, THE JURY A book read by Mr. Nell.

"I WAS A TEENAGE FRANKENSTEIN" The movie Richie, Ben, and Bev saw together at the Aladdin.

THE INK IN MIKE'S JOURNAL After IT's death, the ink rapidly began to fade.

IT In 1985, the Losers finally saw IT: It was "...a nightmare Spider from beyond time and space, a Spider from beyond the fevered imaginings of whatever inmates may live in the deepest depths of hell."

"IT" Stan wrote "IT" in blood on his bathroom wall before he died by suicide.

"IT CAME FROM OUTER SPACE" After Mrs. Kersh's apartment turned into candy, the witch from Hansel & Gretel turned into Al Marsh first, and then into a clown holding balloons that said "It Came From Outer Space." [NOTE: And it was true, too.]

IT'S BECKONING CALL After writing "Derry: The Fourth Interlude," Mike Hanlon felt as though IT was calling:

> "Come on back and we'll see if you remember the simplest thing of all: how it is to be children, secure in belief and thus afraid of the dark."

IT'S CYCLE IT's awakening and feeding, as charted by Mike Hanlon, consisted of bad "years" of fourteen to twenty months every twenty-seven years.

IT'S DERRY HIGH SCHOOL JACKET When Pennywise appeared to the Losers as the Teenage Werewolf in the house on Neibolt Street (he had climbed up through the toilet pipe after the toilet had exploded), he was wearing a Derry High School jacket that said:

> Derry High School Killing Team
> Pennywise
> 13

IT'S EYES IT's eyes were the deadlights.

IT'S FIRST WORDS "Hi, Georgie."

IT'S HEART Bill killed IT by reaching into her body and ripping her heart apart.

IT'S HISTORY IN DERRY Mike Hanlon came up with the following "schedule" (and evidence thereof) of IT's activities in Derry:

> 1957-1958—The Losers
> 1929-1930—The Black Spot
> 1904-1906—The Kitchener Ironworks explosion
> 1876-1877—Some activity not described.

IT'S MISCARRIED EGGS As the Losers chased IT through the sewers of Derry, they came upon her miscarried eggs. Ben crushed each egg with his Desert Driver boots.

AN IVY LEAGUE SHIRT As a child, Ben Hanscom had received a pullover Ivy League shirt that showed his tits. After having this called to his attention (by Belch Huggins), he never again wore anything but baggy sweatshirts.

JANUARY 2, 1985 The date of the first entry in Mike Hanlon's "Derry: An Unauthorized Town History."

JANUARY 27, 1960 The date of the Derry *News* article about the discovery of a decomposed body suspected to be Edward Corcoran. It wasn't.

A "JESUS SAVES" LETTER OPENER A letter opener Mike Hanlon had gotten from the Derry Grace Baptist Church.

THE "JEW YORK TIMES" How Eddie Kaspbrak's mother referred to the New York *Times*.

A JEWELED COMPACT Freddie Firestone had given Audra Phillips a jeweled compact when she signed to do the film "Attic Room."

JIM BEAM One of Tom Rogan's favorites.

JIMMY-PETES, KENWORTHS, AND RIOS The trucks in the Tracker Brothers' Depot.

JOANNA Bill Denbrough's first book.

A JOHN WAYNE MOVIE Georgie Denbrough had seen a John Wayne movie sometime before he was killed.

JUICY FRUIT GUM The gum Henry Bowers chewed.

JULY 1972 The month and year Patty Uris got a job teaching shorthand and business English in Traynor.

JULY 19, 1967 The date of the Portland *Press-Herald* article about Richard Macklin's suicide.

JULY 17, 1958 The date of the Smoke-Hole Ceremony.

JULY 20, 1958 The day Henry Bowers broke Eddie Kaspbrak's arm.

JULY 25, 1958 The day the Losers shot IT with their silver slugs.

JULY 24, 1958 The date of the Derry *News* article about Richard Macklin's confession to the murder of Dorsey Corcoran.

JULY 22, 1958 The day Patrick Hockstetter was reported missing.

JULY 23, 1958 The night the Losers made the silver slugs they used to shoot IT. (They told their parents they were playing Monopoly.)

JUNE 19, 1958 The night Eddie Corcoran died.

JUNE 1974 The month and year the Derry Theological Seminary graduated its last class.

JUNE 30, 1958 The date of the Derry *News* article about Richard Macklin being questioned about the murders of Grogan and Clements.

JUNE 28, 1958 The page 2 Derry *News* article "Daddy had to take me up 'cause I'm bad' Tot told nursery teacher before beating death" about the murder of Dorsey Corcoran.

JUNE 25, 1958 The date of the Derry *News* article about Edward Corcoran often coming to school bruised.

JUNE 21, 1958 The date of the Derry *News* article about the disappearance of ten-year-old Edward L. Corcoran.

JUNE 24, 1985 Norbert Keene's ninety-sixth birthday.

JUNE 24, 1958 The date of the Derry *News* article about the arrest of Richard Macklin for the murder of Dorsey Corcoran.

JUNE 22, 1958 The date of the Derry *News* article about the exhumation of Dorsey Corcoran's body.

A K-CAR Roger Lernerd's car.

KAY McCALL'S THREE BOOKS They were on feminism and the working woman, feminism and the family, and feminism and spirituality.

KEDS Ben Hanscom's sneakers.

KENDUSKEAG STREAM The Kenduskeag ran through downtown Derry in the canal.

THE KISSING BRIDGE The covered walkway over the Derry canal.

THE KISSING BRIDGE GRAFFITI Some of it included: "Save

Russian Jews! Collect Valuable Prizes!"; "Show me your cock queer and I'll cut it off you"; and "Stick Nails in Eyes of all Fagots (For God)!"

THE KITCHEN SINK DRAIN In the early winter of 1957-1958, weeks before her daughter was killed, Mrs. Ripsom heard voices speaking from down her kitchen drain.

KLAD The radio station on which Richie Tozier was a deejay.

THE "KYAG" FOLDER The "Kiss-Your-Ass-Goodbye" folder on planes.

A LA-Z-BOY Stan Uris's recliner.

"THE LAST OF A DYING RACE" IT told Bev that she was the last of a dying race, the only survivor of a dying planet, and in a moment of despair, Bev realized that they couldn't beat IT. She then saw a balloon that said "That's Wight, Wabbit."

THE LAST PICTURE IN GEORGIE'S PHOTO ALBUM It was Georgie's school picture and the eyes rolled up at Bill when he looked at it one day after Georgie's death.

THE LATE FALL OF 1958 Henry Bowers killed his father in the late fall of 1958.

A "LET'S BE QUIET, SHALL WE?" SIGN One of the signs on the Derry children's library.

THE "LETTERS" POSTER The Derry children's library had a poster that said "Libraries Are For Writing, Too. Why not write a friend today? The smiles are guaranteed."

LITTLE LULU COMICS One of Richie and Eddie's favorite comics.

THE LITTLE WORSHIPPERS Members of Eddie Kaspbrak's childhood Sunday-school class were called Little Worshippers.

THE LOSERS' DRINKS When the Losers' met at the library the night of their reunion, they all brought their own drinks:

> Bill—bourbon
> Beverly—vodka and orange juice
> Richie—a sixpack
> Ben—Wild Turkey
> Mike—a sixpack of Bud Light
> Eddie—gin and prune juice

LOUISVILLE SLUGGERS The Maine Legion of Decency came in Packards to burn down the Black Spot. They carried Louisville Sluggers wrapped in burlap torches.

"THE LOVE" In 1985, in trying to understand their purpose and the meaning of their return to Derry, Bill thought "The love is what matters…[m]aybe that's all we get to take with us when we go out of the blue and into the black."

LUCKY STARR AND THE MOONS OF MERCURY A book Ben Hanscom wanted to read in 1958.

LUCKY STRIKES The cigarettes Bev smoked as a kid.

LUNG CANCER Bill Denbrough's father Zack died of lung cancer when Bill was seventeen.

LYE AND GIN Tom Rogan's father Ralph committed suicide by drinking lye and gin.

"MACKLIN ARREST IN BEATING DEATH—UNDER SUSPICION IN UNSOLVED DISAPPEARANCE" The June 24, 1958, page 1 Derry *News* article about the arrest of Richard Macklin for the murder of Dorsey Corcoran.

"MACKLIN QUESTIONED IN DEATHS OF GROGAN, CLEMENTS" The June 30, 1958, page 5 Derry *News* article about Richard Macklin being questioned about two other murders.

"MACKLIN TO BE CHARGED ONLY WITH MURDER OF STEPSON DORSEY" The July 6, 1958, page 1 Derry *News* article about Richard Macklin being charged with the murder of Dorsey Corcoran.

"MAINE AIN'T BAD BUT DERRY'S GREAT!" Adrian Mellon's t-shirt.

THE MAINE LEGION OF WHITE DECENCY They set the fire at the Black Spot.

MAINE THEN AND NOW A Maine history that had forty index entries for Derry.

MARCH 1984 Adrian Mellon and Don Hagarty first came to Derry in March of 1984.

MARCH 1973 The month Patty Uris threw away her birth control pills.

THE MARCHING BANDS PHOTO IN WILL HANLON'S PHOTO ALBUM A photo of marching bands in Will Hanlon's photo album came alive as the Losers looked through the book. The marchers included WWI soldiers, the Boy Scouts, the Kiwanians, the Home Nursing Corps, the Derry Christian Marching Band, Derry's WW II Vets, and a Cadillac carrying Miss Derry of 1945.

THE MARK In 1958 and 1985, when the Losers (and Henry Bowers) came to the antechamber outside of IT's lair, they found a three-foot door marked with a strange symbol. They each saw something different. In 1958, they saw:

> Bill—A paper boat
> Stan—a Phoenix
> Mike—a hooded face
> Richie—two eyes behind a pair of spectacles
> Bev—a hand doubled into a fist
> Eddie—the face of the Leper
> Ben—a tattered pile of Mummy wrappers
> Henry—a black moon.

In 1985, they again each saw something different:

> Bev—Tom's face
> Bill—Audra's severed head
> Eddie—a skull and crossbones
> Richie—a killer Paul Bunyan
> Ben—Henry Bowers

"MAULED BY THE KILLER FROM THE WHITE WASTES" An article in the issue of *True* magazine read by Zack Denbrough.

MAY 1983 The month one of Stan Uris's clients had given him and Patty a handmade key-shaped hook board.

MAY 1970 The month there was a strike on the University of Maine campus to end the Vietnam war.

MAY 6, 1985 The date Frederick Cowan drowned in a toilet.

MAY 13, 1985 The date Jeffrey Holly was found torn open.

MAY 13, 1957 The date Derry's Paul Bunyan statue was unveiled.

MAY 30, 1985; 2:04 A.M. The moment Henry Bowers's nightlight burned out in Juniper Hill.

MAY 31, 1957 The date of Dorsey Corcoran's death.

MAY 31, 1985 The day IT died.

MAY 31, 1985; 8:00 A.M. The time Dr. Hale was killed when a manhole cover blew up off the street and decapitated him while he was out on his morning walk.

MAY 31, 1985; 5:00 P.M. The four-sided clock in the Grace Baptist Church didn't chime the hour of five on May 31, 1985. It had also not chimed noon the day the Kitchener Ironworks exploded.

MAY 28, 1985 The date Stan Uris took his suicide bath. This was also the night Ben Hanscom "took a drink" at the Red Wheel Roadhouse. Also, May 28, 1985, turned to May 29 over West Illinois as Ben flew back to Derry.

MAY 29, 1985 The day Bev Rogan flew to Boston from Milwaukee on her way back to Derry. She flew on Republic.

MAY 22, 1985 The date John Feury, a fifth-grader, was found dead on Neibolt Street. His legs were gone, but he had died of fear.

"MAYBE EVEN A CADILLAC!" As Eddie Tozier watched the car-carriers loaded with Fords and Chevies, he thought, "I'll have me a car like one of those someday. Like one of those or even better. Maybe even a Cadillac!" [NOTE: Stephen King felt the same way. See the interview with Chris Chesley in this volume for details.]

MAYTAG The washers in the Kleen-Kloze Washateria.

A MEMO FROM PENNYWISE In Christine's glove compartment, Henry Bowers found a "Memo from Pennywise" that gave Henry Bowers the Losers' Derry Town House room numbers:

BILL DENBROUGH   311
BEN HANSCOM   404
EDDIE KASPBRAK   609
BEVERLY MARSH   518
RICHIE TOZIER   217

MENNEN SKIN BRACER Al Marsh's apres shave of choice.

A MERCEDES Kay McCall's car.

A MERCEDES DIESEL Stan Uris's car. Patty Uris called it a "Sedanley."

METHODIST Richie Toziers' parents' religion. Also, Eddie Kaspbrak and his mother's religion. They used Welch's grape juice and cubes of Wonder bread for communion.

AN MG Richie Tozier's car.

"MIDNIGHT REQUISITIONS" The procedure by which Pop Snopes "acquired" window panes for the Black Spot: He stole them.

MIKE HANLON'S ADDRESS 61 Palmer Lane.

THE MIRROR The London newspaper that hated the design of the BBC Communications Center, which had been built by Ben "Dam in the Barrens" Hanscom.

"MISSING BOY PROMPTS NEW FEARS" The June 21, 1958, page 1 Derry *News* article about the disappearance of ten-year-old Edward L. Corcoran.

A MODEL-A FORD CAR WITH A PICK-UP BACK END The Hanlon's truck.

A MOOSEBLOWER In 1958, Bev heard a "buzzing scream" in the house on Neibolt Street. The noise turned out to be a "mooseblower": a Sterno can with the ends cut off and a waxed string in the middle.

MORLOCK HOLES The name Ben Hanscom called the cylinders in the Barrens where the big pumps for the sewer system were.

MOTHER'S SUNDAY The name Stephen Bowie used for Mother's Day.

MOTHERS' WALKERS GROUPS Groups of mothers who chaperoned kids home from school. They were formed in response to the high murder rate of children in Derry.

MOTOROLA The Denbroughs' TV.

MR. KEENE'S SHOPLIFTING SIGN It said:

> Shoplifting is not a "kick" or a "groove" or a "gasser"!
> Shoplifting is a *crime* and we will *prosecute!*"

A MURALVISION TV Eddie and Myra Kaspbrak's large-screen television.

NARRAGANSET Bill Hanlon's beer of choice. He called it "Nasty Gansett."

THE *NATIONAL ENQUIRER* When the Derry Mall exploded, Brent Kilgallon's son took a picture of a piece of the Sears roof slicing through his father's silo. The *Enquirer* bought the picture for sixty dollars.

NEW ENGLAND BYWAYS The magazine Adrian Mellon was on assignment for when he was murdered in Derry. His assignment was to write a piece about the Derry canal.

A NEW MERCURY Butch Bowers had to sell his new Mercury to pay off Will Hanlon after Butch was caught killing Will's chickens. Butch bought a Ford to replace the Mercury.

A NEW YORK YANKEES UNIFORM The dead Belch Huggins appeared to Eddie wearing a New York Yankees uniform at the abandoned Tracker Brothers' Depot.

"NIGGER" Mike Hanlon's grammar school classmate Bob Gautier told Mike that "nigger" couldn't be a bad word because his father used it all the time.

NIGHT'S TRUTH In 1958, Bill Denbrough deduced that the monster in the Derry sewers was a "glamour"; "an evil magic being that could read your mind and then assume the shape of the thing you were most afraid of." Other names for the creature were manitou, tallus, eylak (the brother of vurderlak or vampire), or le loup-garou. The Ritual of Chüd could defeat it. He read about this

being in a book called *Night's Truth*.

NINE POUNDS OF BLUEPRINTS The fellow who had bossed the construction of the Derry sewer system was killed in World War II. Five years later, the water department discovered that nine pounds of blueprints of the sewers were missing.

THE NINE TAILORS A book by Dorothy Sayers that Audra Denbrough brought with her to Maine.

$9,200 Patty Uris's starting salary as a teacher.

A 1984 VOLVO Patty Uris's car.

1981 The year Elmer Curtie realized his clientelle was gay.

1983 By 1983, Stan Uris was making a six figure income.

A 1950 CAR ACCIDENT Bill Denbrough was in a car accident in 1950, following which he was unconscious for seven hours. Mrs. Denbrough blamed the accident on Bill's stuttering.

1958 In 1958, 127 Derry children, ages three to nineteen, disappeared. The chief of police wasn't surprised. He blamed the Depression.

A 1958 RED AND WHITE PLYMOUTH FURY In 1985, while staggering through Derry with a stomach knife wound, Henry Bowers got a ride from a car driven by the dead Belch Huggins. The car was a 1958 red and white Plymouth Fury with a V-8 327 engine, with available horsepower of 255, and cherry bomb mufflers. Pennywise had obviously called Christine back from Hell and was using her for his means.

1957-1958 The years IT battled the Losers in Derry.

1956 The year the Bowers' well had gone dry.

1956 The year the funds for Derry's Paul Bunyan statue were approved.

1944 The year Mark Lamonica was born.

1947 The year both Mike Hanlon and Stephen King were born.

1942 The year Derry's Kansas Street was paved.

1942 The year Eddie Kaspbrak was born.

1914-1960 The years during which Albert Carson was the Derry head librarian.

1904-1906 The period of Derry's history during which IT caused the Kitchener Ironworks explosion.

THE 1906 ANIMAL MUTILATIONS Derry animal mutilations that were done by Andrew Rhulin, the grand-uncle of the man who owned Rhulin Farms in 1985.

1975 The year Stan Uris quit H & R Block.

A 1968 CADILLAC CONVERTIBLE Ben Hanscom's car. The license plate said "BEN'S CADDY."

1965 The year Dave Gardener purchased the Shoeboat.

1964 The year Richard Macklin was released from prison.

1962 The year Patrick Hockstetter's mother died of breast cancer. Also, the year Mike Hanlon's father died.

1930 The year of the fire at the Black Spot. Also, 1930 was the year that over 170 Derry kids disappeared.

A 1930 TRAMP CHAIR It was vetoed as a Derry Days Museum exhibit by the ladies' society. The chair later killed Chief Andrew Rademacher when it fell on him during the destruction following IT's death.

1931 The year of the Derry flood.

1937 The year Mike Hanlon's father left the army with a disability pension.

1936-1966 The years during which Sandy Ives published a cycle of articles on Derry's history.

1933 The year prohibition was repealed in Derry.

1925-1975 The years during which Norbert Keene was the proprietor of Derry's Center Drug Store.

1929-1930 The period in Derry's history during which IT caused the fire at the Black Spot, among, it is assumed, other dastardly events.

1926 The year Mrs. Kersh supposedly came to America.

1923 The year Horst Mueller gave a grandfather clock to the Derry library.

NINETY-ONE Albert Carson's age at the time of his death in the summer of 1984.

Stand pipe, Bangor

STAND PIPE AND OBSERVATORY, BANGOR, MAINE.

Postcard depictions of two Bangor landmarks mentioned in *IT*: two views of the Bangor standpipe, and the Paul Bunyan statue.

NIVEA CREAM During the fight Bev had with Tom over her returning to Derry, she threw a jar of Nivea cream at him.

NOVEMBER 14, 1984 The day John Garton and Steve Dubay went on trial.

NOVEMBER 13 During the investigation into the murder of Adrian Mellon, November 13 was the day Gardener said he had to mention the clown story.

OCTOBER The month Ben Hanscom and Adrian Mellon were born.

OCTOBER 1957 The month Georgie Denbrough was killed.

OCTOBER 1929 The month and year the Bradley Gang was executed at the three-way intersection of Canal, Main, and Kansas Streets in Derry.

AN OLD FORD In 1958, Bev hid in an old Ford and watched Belch Huggins and Patrick Hockstetter light farts and play with each other. Also, Mike Hanlon's car was an old Ford.

AN OLD GREEN DeSOTO The car driven by Rena Davenport.

OLD KENTUCKY When Mike Hanlon wrote "Derry: the Fourth Interlude" he was drunk on Old Kentucky.

OLYMPIA BEER Ben Hanscom's beer of choice.

180 POUNDS Eddie Kaspbrak's mother's weight in 1944.

$165,000 The amount Stan and Patty Uris's house was worth in 1985.

1.75 MILLION GALLONS OF WATER The capacity of the Derry standpipe.

A $1,000 CHECK After Bev left Tom Rogan and Kay McCall gave her money, Bev wrote her a check on plain paper for $1,000 as repayment.

1-A Ben Hanscom's seat on his Omaha-to-Chicago flight.

THE ORDER IN WHICH THE LOSERS FLED THE SMOKE-HOLE Stan was first [figures, huh?]; Ben, second; Eddie, third; Bev, fourth; and Bill fifth. Richie and Mike remained in the hole and were transported back in time to "the ago" where they witnessed the arrival of IT on earth.

THE ORDER OF BEV'S LOVES AND DESIRES In 1958, the boys made love to Beverly Marsh in the following order:

Eddie
Mike
Richie
Stan (Stan didn't come, though, thereby failing to bond, and setting the stage for his rejection of the oath that required him to return to fight IT)
Bill
Ben

OVER SEVENTY AIRSICK BAGS The crew had over seventy airsick bags to dispose of on Ben Hanscom's Omaha-to-Chicago flight the night he headed back to Derry.

OVRAL (#96) Patty Uris's birth control pills.

P.F. FLYERS The sneakers Eddie Kaspbrak wore as a child.

PACKARDS The Maine Legion of Decency came in Packards to burn down the Black Spot. They carried Louisville Sluggers wrapped in burlap torches.

PAINT-THINNER Harold Earl drank paint-thinner.

PATEK PHILIPPE Eddie Kaspbrak's watch.

PATRICK HOCKSTETTER'S BELT AND VERONICA GROGAN'S PANTIES These two items were found in Henry Bowers's mattress, giving the police what they thought was incontrovertible proof that Bowers was Derry's "monster," responsible for all of Derry's unsolved killings.

PATRICK HOCKSTETTER'S FAVORITE TV SHOWS "Crusader Rabbit," "Whirlybirds," "Highway Patrol," and "Science Fiction Theater."

THE PAUL BUNYAN STATUE A giant statue of Paul Bunyan that stood in front of the Derry city center. The statue was one of the town's landmarks. Bunyan came to life one day and attacked Richie Tozier. The statue stood twenty feet tall, and stood atop of a six-foot base. The funds for the statue had been approved in

1956. The statue was unveiled on May 13, 1957, Derry's 150th birthday. [NOTE: There is a *real* Paul Bunyan statue in the center of Bangor, Maine, Stephen King's hometown. For the record, here is what is written on the plaque attached to the base of that statue. It's also interesting to compare how King "edited" reality for his fiction, and yet still retained the realism so prevalent in, and important to, his work.]

PAUL BUNYAN OF BANGOR, MAINE

• This permanent statue of Paul Bunyan, 31 feet tall and weighing 3700 pounds, is made of reinforced fiberglass and internally braced with steel. It stands on a solid reinforced concrete foundation the top of which is 6 feet above ground level. Built into the foundation at a point between the feet of the statue is a special vault in which a time capsule containing documented records of BANGOR'S 125TH ANNIVERSARY observance together with various other articles of historic significance were sealed on DECEMBER 31ST, 1959. The capsule is scheduled to be removed from the vault on BANGOR'S 250TH ANNIVERSARY, February 12, 2084 A.D.

• This statue, reputed to be the largest of Paul Bunyan in the world, was made possible by the BANGOR 125TH ANNIVERSARY STEERING COMMITTEE. The legendary giant woodsmen is a symbol of the great era in the late 1800's during which BANGOR, MAINE was acclaimed "the LUMBER CAPITAL of the WORLD".

• The statue stands facing the Penobscot River nearby, which in the days of PAUL BUNYAN bristled with masts as sailing vessels loaded long lumber for shipment to seaports around the world.

• The total cost of the statue, erected, was approximately $20,000. It was paid for wholly by voluntary contributions from civic minded individuals and firms in Bangor and vicinity."

PEANUT BUTTER AND ONION SANDWICHES One of Mike Hanlon's favorite sandwiches.

PENNYWISE'S REFRIGERATOR MESSAGE In 1958, Pennywise left the Losers a message written in blood inside the door of Patrick Hockstetter's discarded Amana refrigerator. It said:

Stop now before I kill you all
A word to the wise from your friend Pennywise.

THE PENOBSCOT RIVER One hour, twenty minutes, forty-five seconds after Georgie's death, his newspaper boat entered the Penobscot River.

PEOPLE MAGAZINE AND "HOLLYWOOD SQUARES" Audra Phillips was in *People* magazine and on "Hollywood Squares."

PERRIER In 1985, Eddie Kaspbrak drank Perrier for acid indigestion.

A PIECE OF THE SEARS ROOF A piece of the Sears roof flew off during the explosions that rocked the Derry Mall while Bill was fighting with IT.

A PINK MOTORCYCLE JACKET Henry Bowers's jacket. It had an eagle on the back.

A PISTACHIO CONE In 1958, Gard Jagermeyer, one of Henry Bowers' friends, pushed Richie Tozier as Richie was coming out of the Derry Ice Cream Parlor with a pistachio cone. Richie's glasses broke.

"THE PIT OF THE BLACK DEMON" The title of the film version of Bill Denbrough's novel *The Black Rapids*.

THE PLAN In 1958, the Losers came up with a plan they hoped would kill IT: Bev would shoot a silver ball (made from one of Ben Hanscom's silver dollars) into IT's head.

A PLAYBOY CALENDAR The starter for the Tracker Brothers' Truck Depot kept a *Playboy* calendar over his desk.

POISONED MEAT As a child, Henry Bowers killed Mike Hanlon's dog, Mr. Chips, by feeding it poisoned meat.

THE PORTLAND SUNDAY TELEGRAM The newspaper that

ran an article about the murders in Derry.

THE POWER OF POSITIVE THINKING A book by Norman Vincent Peale read by Eddie Kaspbrak's mother.

A POWER-FLITE BUICK Mr. Tremont's car.

PROSTATE CANCER, A BRAIN TUMOR, AND TURNING HIS TONGUE TO MUSH When the Derry Paul Bunyan statue came alive in 1985 and turned into Pennywise, the clown threatened Richie Tozier with these afflictions.

A PYE Bill and Audra's color TV in England.

"RALPH IS BUSY TONIGHT" Stewardesses code phrase for a lot of in-flight puking.

THE "REALLY BAD WORD" "Fuck."

RED VELVET BOWS As a child, Bev bought her red velvet bows at Dahlie's.

THE REFLECTION After IT's death, as the surviving Losers (Bev, Richie, Ben, and Bill) were walking into the Derry Town House, Bev saw a reflection in the Town House door of six, rather then four. The ghosts of Eddie and Stan were walking with the four of them.

"THE RETURN OF THE BIG BULLIES" The term Mike Hanlon used to describe the recall of the other Losers to Derry.

RHEINGOLD Richard Macklin's beer of choice.

RICH AND CHILDLESS At their reunion lunch, the Losers realized that they all shared two things in common: they were all rich and childless.

RICHARD MACKLIN'S SUICIDE NOTE It read: "I saw Eddie last night. He was dead."

RICHIE TOZIER'S "ALL-DEAD" ROCK SHOW In 1985, the Derry Paul Bunyan statue came alive and became Pennywise that held balloons that said "It's Still Rock and Roll To Me" and "Richie Tozier's 'All-Dead' Rock Show."

RICHIE TOZIER'S DUDS (The 1985) Richie wore Bass Weejuns, Calvin Klein underwear, and a sportsjacket from one of the best shops on Rodeo Drive.

RICHIE'S IMAGINARY FORTUNE Richie imagined he'd get the following fortune at his reunion luncheon at the Jade of the Orient: "You will soon be eaten up by a large monster. Have a nice day!"

RICHIE'S VASECTOMY It never worked. His doctor had had eleven regenerations out of 28,618 vasectomies, and Richie's was one of them. And he was *still* childless.

THE RITUAL OF CHÜD The only way to defeat a glamour (or *taelus*). Bill Denbrough explained: "The *taelus* stuck its tongue out. You stuck *yours* out. You and it overlapped tongues and then you both bit in all the way so you were sort of stapled together, eye to eye. ...[T]h-then y-you started telling juh-jokes and rih-riddles."

ROADBUGS A novel Bill was planning to write.

ROADS TO EVERYWHERE A child's textbook that Eddie saw in his "Patrick Hockstetter" dream in the Derry sewers in 1958.

A ROBERT LUDLUM NOVEL As Bev flew to Boston on her way back to Derry, the guy in the seat next to her read a Ludlum novel. [NOTE: See the *Time* magazine piece "King of Horror" in this volume for Stephen King's thoughts about Robert Ludlum.]

ROCKS The Losers gathered rocks for the apocalyptic rockfight in the Barrens. After the fight, Mike Hanlon became the seventh member of the Losers.

A ROUTINE CHECKUP EVERY SIX WEEKS The adult Eddie Kaspbrak had a checkup every six weeks.

RURAL STAR ROUTE 2, HEMINGFORD HOME, NEBRASKA, 59341 Ben Hanscom's address.

THE RUSTY DOOR OF A '49 HUDSON HORNET Ben, Eddie, and Bill used the door to repair the dam in the Barrens when the current started loosening the boards.

SADDLER'S BRASS POLISH As a child, this was the polish Mike Hanlon used to polish his trombone.

SAM CHACOWICZ'S LOVEMAKING MOTTO "Two pumps, a tickle and a squirt."

THE SAVE OUR CHILDREN COMMITTEE A committee formed in response to the murders of children in Derry.

"SCHOOL FRIENDS 1957-58" The title of Georgie Denbroughs' school yearbook.

A SCHWINN Mike Hanlon's childhood bike.

SCOTTI RECOILLESS HAMMER The hammer with which Richard Macklin killed Dorsey Corcoran.

A "SEDANLEY" The name Patty Uris called Stan's Mercedes Diesel.

"SEEIN' STARS" A syndicated entertainment show Richie Tozier ran that once mentioned Bill and Audra Denbrough.

SEPTEMBER 18, 1958 The date of the page 6 Derry *News* article about the still-missing Edward Corcoran.

SEPTEMBER 1905 The month and year Claude Heroux went crazy and committed the "queerest mass murder in the entire history of America" in the Silver Dollar bar.

A SETH THOMAS CLOCK Eddie and Myra Kaspbrak's clock.

SEVEN BEER TAPS There were seven beer taps in Wally's Spa: Three Bud, two Narragansett, one Schlitz, and one Miller Lite. On the morning of May 31, 1985, the taps opened all by themselves, and blood, flesh, and hair poured out of them. Boogers Taliendo saw this, and moved to Eastport.

$7.23 The price Mike Hanlon paid in 1985 for the bicycle tire patching kit he bought a week before Bill "re-bought" Silver.

$17,000 The value of the four-sided clock donated to Derry in 1898 by Stephen Bowie. Also, $17,000 was Stan and Patty Uris's combined income when they first got married.

A '76 LTD WAGON The car Tom Rogan bought for $1400 when he got to Bangor.

"THE SHAPE BEHIND THE SHAPE" In 1985, for a moment, Ben Hanscom saw IT: He saw "[t]he shape behind the shape: saw lights, saw an endless crawling hairy thing which was made of light and nothing else, orange light, dead light that mocked life."

A SHARK In 1985, a Derry little kid told Richie that his friend Tommy Vicananza had seen a shark in the canal, and that he thought it was Jaws.

"SHE BLINDED ME WITH SCIENCE" A song Mike Hanlon whistled while he and Bill set about patching Silver's tires in 1985.

SHINING BRIDGES One of Ben Hanscom's grammar school texts.

"THE SIFT" Eddie Kaspbrak's term for syphillis.

SIGNED EDITIONS OF *MOBY DICK* AND *LEAVES OF GRASS* Two of the special possessions of the Derry library.

SIGNET Bill Denbrough's paperback publisher.

SILK CUT CIGARETTES The cigarettes Freddie Firestone smoked.

SILVER Bill Denbrough's twenty-eight-inch Schwinn bicycle, named after the Lone Ranger's horse. When Bill was a kid, he saw Silver in the window of the Bike and Cycle Shoppe on Center Street. It had a sign on it that said "Used. Make An Offer." Bill paid twenty-four dollars for it.

A SINGLE BALLOON Mike Hanlon fell asleep right after he wrote the story of the fire at the Black Spot. When he woke up someone (or something) had tied a single balloon to his reading lamp. It had Mike's face on it, his eyes were gone, and there was blood running down from the sockets. When Mike saw it he screamed...and the balloon burst.

SIX BOTTLES OF BUD AND THREE JOYSTICKS Butch Bowers had a sword he claimed he took off "a dying Nip" on the island of Tarawa. He had actually traded six bottles of Bud and three joysticks for it.

648-4083 The phone number of the Bassey Park Inn.

643-8146 The phone number of the Arlington Motor Lodge.

$6,000 IN CASH Tom Rogan had six thousand dollars in cash on him when he landed in Bangor on his pursuit of Bev.

SIXTY DOLLARS When the Derry Mall exploded, Brent Kilgallon's son took a picture of a piece of the Sears roof slicing through his father's silo. The *Enquirer* bought the picture for sixty dollars.

The kid used the money to buy two new tires for his Yamaha motorcycle.

SIXTY-FOUR Eddie Kaspbrak's mother died of congestive heart failure at the age of sixty-four. She weighed 406 pounds.

A SKOOLTIME RULER Before he disappeared in 1958, Patrick Hockstetter used to kill flies with his SkoolTime ruler and keep them in his lunchbox.

"SLAPPING DOWN THE CARDS" Eddie Kaspbrak's mother's term for difficult truth-telling.

SLEEPMUD The "exotic language" of sleep.

THE SMOKE-HOLE CEREMONY A ceremony Ben learned about from a book called *Ghosts of the Great Plains*. It involved burning branches in an underground hole and breathing in the smoke. The smoke was supposed to induce mystical, mind-expanding visions.

"SON, YOU DID REAL GOOD." After Bill killed IT, he heard the voice of the Other saying, "Son, you did real good."

A SONY CD PLAYER Eddie Kaspbrak had one. It cost him $1,500.

A SPACESHIP During the Smoke-Hole Ceremony, Richie and Mike witnessed IT's arrival on earth in a spaceship that was beyond description.

THE SPIRIT OF RODAN A giant bird had its nest in the Ironworks cellarhold. Mike Hanlon somehow knew it was the spirit of Rodan. It attacked Mike.

STACK TWO Stack Two in the Derry library was the occult shelf: Edgar Cayce, Nostradamus, Charles Fort, *The Apocrypha*, etc.

STAN URIS'S PHILOSOPHY "Everything's a lot toughter when it's for real. That's when you choke. When it's for real."

STAN URIS'S SEVERED HEAD At the Derry library the night of the Losers' reunion lunch, Mike opened the refrigerator in the library's lounge, and blue and orange balloons floated out. In the fridge was Stan Uris's severed head. Stan's mouth was stuffed with feathers from the bird Mike had seen in May and August of 1958, and that his father Will had seen at the Black Spot the night of the fire.

STAYFREE Patty Uris's brand of sanitary napkins. (She used both Maxi and Mini pads.)

A STEIN OF WILD TURKEY The night of May 28, 1985, after Ben had gotten his call from Mike Hanlon and the night Stan Uris killed himself, Ben Hanscom drank an entire stein of Wild Turkey in the Red Wheel.

STEVE DUBAY'S SENTENCE He was convicted of first degree manslaughter. He got fifteen years at Shawshank state prison.

"STORM CAUSES HENLEY TO GIVE UP AUDITORIUM EXPANSION PLANS" Headline in the June 6, 1985, Derry *News*.

THE STORY OF HAM Mike Hanlon's grammar school teacher had told Mike's class the story of Ham, and explained why blacks weren't as good as whites. While relating this ludicrous Biblical excuse for racism, she looked right at Mike.

A STROKE Barbara Starrett died of a stroke in 1982. Pennywise took credit for killing her.

A SUBARU During his pursuit of Bev, Tom Rogan switched plates with a Subaru after he bought a '76 LTD in Bangor.

THE SUMMER OF 1965 Jimmy Donlin killed his mother in Portland in the summer of 1965 and ate half her brains.

"SURVIVORS" The headline of the June 1 edition of the Derry *News*. The story featured a photo of Bev hugging Bill.

A SWITCHBLADE In 1958, after Bev escaped her father's murderous (and perversely incestuous) pursuit, Henry Bowers, Victor Criss, and Belch Huggins (switchblade in hand) tracked Bev.

A SWORD Butch Bowers had a sword he claimed he took off "a dying Nip" on the island of Tarawa. He had actually traded six bottles of Bud and three joysticks for it.

TANGLE-TRACK GLUE The glue the Losers used to cover the boards they used to make their underground clubhouse in the Barrens.

"TEACHER SAYS EDWARD CORCORAN 'OFTEN BRUISED'"

The June 25, 1958, page 1 Derry *News* article about Edward Corcoran.

TED LAPIDUS COLOGNE The fat guy who sat next to Bill Denbrough on his return flight to Derry was wearing Ted Lapidus cologne.

TEN CENTS EACH; TWELVE FOR A DOLLAR Secondhand Rose, Secondhand Clothes sold records for ten cents each, twelve for a dollar. Selections included the Andrews Sisters, Perry Como, and Jimmy Rogers.

$10.59 The amount of money the Losers brought with them to the Kitchener Ironworks to buy ball bearing molds for the silver slugs they wanted to cast. The molds cost fifty cents each. The Losers bought two.

TENTH BIRTHDAY Vernica Grogan was buried on her tenth birthday.

A TEN-YEAR MORTGAGE When Will Hanlon got out of the army, the First Merchants Bank of Penobscot County issued him a ten-year mortgage for his farm.

"THE TERROR'S BEGINNINGS" "A boat made from a sheet of newspaper floating down a gutter swollen with rain."

TEXAS DRIVER BEER AND PEANUT BUTTER AND BERMUDA ONION SANDWICHES While on the night shift at Juniper Hill, Koontz the guard watched late movies on Channel 38, drank Texas Driver beer, and ate peanut butter and Bermuda onion sandwiches.

THIRTEEN Cheryl Lamonica's age when she had her daughter Andrea.

A $30,000 RANSOM In 1928, Al Bradley and George Bradley kidnapped a banker and held him ransom for $30,000. The ransom was paid, but they killed the guy anyway.

$30,000 A YEAR Stan Uris's starting salary with Corridor Video.

THIRTY-TWO YEARS OLD In 1958, Ben Hanscom's mother Arlene was thirty-two years old.

THOUSANDS OF BALLOONS They floated under the bridge after Adrian Mellon's murder; red, blue, green, and yellow. They all said "I Love Derry."

THREE Eddie Kaspbrak's age when his father died.

"THE THREE BILLY GOATS GRUFF" A story read to a group of children in the Derry children's library.

THREE METHODIST HYMNS Three Methodist hymns had been played at Georgie Denbrough's funeral.

THREE SILVER DOLLARS Before Ben Hanscom returned to Derry, he gave Ricky Lee three silver dollars, one for each of his kids.

A THREE-FOOT HIGH DOOR Before being taken prisoner by IT in 1985, Audra dreamt of a three-foot high door marked with a strange rune or symbol. Also, during the dream, she took on Bev Marsh's consciousness.

A TIME-SHARING CONDO Alfred Zitner had a time-sharing condo in Rangely.

A TIMEX WATCH Ben Hanscom's mother gave him a Timex when kids started showing up dead in Derry. Also, as a kid, Richie Tozier wore a Timex.

A TIRE PATCHING KIT In 1985, Mike Hanlon bought a bicycle tire patching kit a week before Bill bought Silver. He paid $7.23 for it.

THE TOILET In 1958, the toilet in the house on Neibolt Street exploded while the Losers were in the house. IT then came up through the pipe as the Teenage Werewolf. Bev hit IT above the right eye with one of the silver slugs.

TOM ROGAN'S SPECIAL SEMINARS Discipline sessions administered to Bev by Tom for a variety of offenses. Smoking was one of them. [NOTE: See the "Things" entry TOM'S PUNISHMENTS.]

TOM'S PUNISHMENTS Tom Rogan doled out the following punishments to Bev: If dinner was cold, two with the belt; if Bev forgot to call while working late, three with the belt; if Bev got a parking ticket, one with the belt across the breasts.

"TRASHMOUTH" Richie Tozier's nickname.

A TREEHOUSE The Losers had originally wanted to build a treehouse in the Barrens instead of an underground clubhouse, "but people have a bad habit of breaking their bones when they fall out of treehouses—" [NOTE: See the prologue to *The Shining*, "Before the Play," in this volume for details on how a little Jacky Torrance broke something when he was pulled out of a treehouse.]

TROMBONE Mike Hanlon's instrument in the Church School band.

TRUE MAGAZINE A magazine read by Zack Denbrough.

"TRY TO SET THE NIGHT ON FIRE!" Benny Beaulieu was a pyromaniac incarcerated in Juniper Hill who kept screaming "Try to set the night on fire!"

"THE TURTLE COULDN'T HELP US" One day, out of the blue, Stan Uris said this, and his wife Patty heard him.

TURTLE SUNGLASSES Ben wore a pair of Turtle sunglasses while casting the silver slugs they used to shoot IT.

THE TUESDAY MATH EXAM Henry Bowers once wanted to copy answers off of Ben Hanscom's paper during a Tuesday math exam.

TWENTY DOLLARS A MONTH Mike Hanlon paid a cop twenty dollars a month to act as a pipeline for information on the murders in Derry.

20K A YEAR Mike Hanlon's uncle, Philly Loubird, was a lawyer in Tuscon, Arizona, and made 20K a year.

TWENTY YEARS IN THE AUGUSTA STATE MENTAL HOSPITAL Henry Bowers' sentence for killing his father.

A TWENTY-DOLLAR BILL Tom Rogan kept a twenty-dollar bill in his wallet behind his driver's license.

TWENTY-EIGHT CENTS WORTH OF EMPTIES Ben Hanscom's haul one day. He found four beer bottles (Rheingold's) and four big soda bottles under a hedge. [NOTE: See the "Things" entry BEN'S PURCHASES AT COSTELLO'S.]

TWENTY-FIVE GRAINS BLUE SKIES When Doc Pearson wanted one of his patients to have a placebo, he'd write a prescription for "25 Grains Blue Skies," and Norbert Keene would know what he meant.

TWENTY-FOUR DOLLARS The price Bill Denbrough paid for Silver when he bought the bike in 1958.

TWENTY-SEVEN OVARIAN CYSTS Ruth Blum told her daughter, Patty Uris, in a letter that Randi Harlenegen had to have her tubes tied after she had twenty-seven ovarian cysts removed.

TWENTY-SEVEN YEARS IT resurfaced in Derry every twenty-seven years.

TWENTY-SIX MILES It was twenty-six miles from the Bangor International Airport to the Derry, Maine, town line.

TWENTY-THREE FEET The distance from the Kissing Bridge to the water of the canal.

TWO DARVON In 1985, after Henry Bowers broke his arm, Eddie Kapsbrak took two Darvon for the pain.

TWO DOLLARS EACH The Clark twins used to mow the Tozier lawn for $2 each.

TWO DOLLARS, FIFTY CENTS Richie Tozier's pay for mowing the lawn.

$200 Butch Bowers was ordered to pay Will Hanlon $200 for killing Will's chickens, or he'd have to go to Shawshank prison. Also, $200 was the fee Bill Denbrough was paid for "The Dark" when it was published in *White Tie* magazine.

206 TIMES Richie Tozier told Bill that Bill had used the word "fuck" 206 times in his last book.

207-555-1212 Phone number for Maine directory assistance.

207-941-8282 The phone number of the Derry Town House. [NOTE: In 1989, dialing this number got you a "The number you have dialed is not in service" recording. In 1990, however, dialing got you nothing but an endless ringing. Maybe there was nobody at the front desk?]

TWO TO TEN YEARS IN SHAWSHANK Richard Macklin's sentence for the murder of Dorsey Corcoran.

UNDERSTANDING OUR AMERICA A child's textbook that Eddie saw in his "Patrick Hockstetter" dream in the Derry sewers in 1958.

AN UNDERWOOD TYPEWRITER Bill Denbrough had an Underwood as a child and used it to write stories.

UNITED AIRLINES FLIGHT 41 Ben Hanscom's Omaha-to-Chicago flight on his way back to Derry.

UNWIN'S SENTENCE Chris Unwin was tried for Adrian Mellon's death as a juvenile on second-degree manslaughter. He got six months at the South Windham Boys' Training Facility. The sentence was suspended.

"URBAN ENERGY CONSERVATION AND THE YOUNG TURKS" An article in the October 15, 1984, edition of *Time* magazine about Ben Hanscom.

A VEGA Tom and Bev Rogan had a late-model Vega.

THE VOICES Richie Tozier's trademark impressions. Richie's favorite voice was that of Kinky Briefcase, the Sexual Accountant.

THE VOICES FROM THE DRAIN Bev Marsh heard the dead Matthew Clements talking to her from her bathroom sink drain. Matthew told her that with him was Georgie Denbrough, Betty Ripsom, and Veronica Grogan.

WABI The only radio station Richie Tozier's transister could pick up from the Barrens. Richie was not pleased: WABI played pansy rock.

A WALTHER Zack Denbrough's gun.

A WATERFORD VASE After Bev left him, Tom Rogan threatened to cut Bev's best friend Kay McCall's face with a piece of a broken Waterford vase. Kay broke down, and told Tom where he could find Bev.

"WE WILL REBUILD, VOWS DERRY MAYOR" The headline in the Derry *News* the Sunday following the collapse of the town.

THE WEEKLY SHOPPER The newspaper delivered by Belch Huggins as a kid.

"WEEPING STEPFATHER CONFESSES TO BLUDGEON DEATH OF STEPSON" The July 24, 1958, page 1 Derry *News* article about Richard Macklin's confession.

A WELSH DRESSER Mrs. Denbrough had a Welsh dresser.

WEREWOLVES Bill Denbrough had written at least one book about werewolves.

WESTCLOX Bill Hanlon's clock.

WHAT BEV PACKED When Bev got the call from Mike Hanlon, she packed the following items for her return trip to Derry: cotton K-Mart underwear, a cotton nightie, a white cotton bra, two pair of jeans, a pair of cords, a sweater, two t-shirts, and an old Ship 'n Shore blouse.

WHAT IT HAD IN COMMON WITH THE TURTLE "All living things must abide by the laws of the shape they inhabit."

WHEATIES The cereal Mike Hanlon ate as a kid in order to get the Captain Midnight magic decoder ring.

"A WHEEL" "...[E]ach life makes it's own imitation of immortality: a Wheel. Or so Bill Denbrough sometimes thinks on those early mornings after dreaming, when he almost remembers his childhood, and the friends with whom he shared it." The last line of *IT*. By calling Bill's childhood "it" in this passage, King is using the symbol of It the monster as a symbol of childhood – his friends and he shared childhood (It) together.

"WHERE IS EDWARD CORCORAN?" The September 18, 1958, page 6 Derry *News* article about the still-missing Edward Corcoran.

"WHERE THE HELL IS DERRY, MAINE?" The t-shirt Bill wore while taking Audra for his life-saving "beat the devil" ride on Silver.

"WHIRLYBIRDS" A TV show with Kenneth Tobey that Ben Hanscom liked.

WHITE NIGHTSHADE MUSHROOMS In 1851, John Markson killed his family with poison, and then committed suicide by eating white nightshade mushrooms.

WHITE TIE The magazine which bought and first published Bill Denbrough's story, "The Dark." (Bill thought the mag should have been called "Naked Girls Who Look Like Drug Users.")

WILL HANLON'S PHOTO ALBUM The album contained pages from the Derry *News*, including "Huzzah! Ironworks Opens! Town Turns Out for Gala Picnic," a political cartoon, pictures taken at Wally's Spa after prohibition was repealed, the Japanese surrender in 1945, and a photo of marching bands that came alive.

A WINCHESTER Tom Rogan's gun.

WINDEX The window cleaner Bev Marsh used.

WINSTONS Richie Tozier's cigarettes.

A WINTER NIGHT IN 1962 George DeVille murdered his wife and four children one winter night in 1962.

WOODY ALLEN FILMS Stan and Patty Uris both liked the Woodman's movies.

WZON Bangor's AM stereo rocker.

THE X-RAY MACHINE When Eddie was a child, he put his foot in an x-ray machine in the Shoeboat. The sign on the machine said "Do Your Shoes Fit Right? Check and See!" His mother flipped out.

A YAMAHA MOTORCYCLE When the Derry Mall exploded, Brent Kilgallon's son took a picture of a piece of the Sears roof slicing through his father's silo. The *Enquirer* bought the picture for sixty dollars. The kid used the money to buy two new tires for his Yamaha motorcycle.

ZEISS-IKON BINOCULARS Stan Uris's birdwatching binoculars.

ZIPPO Richie Tozier's lighter.

THE DARK TOWER II: THE DRAWING OF THE THREE

DEDICATION

To Don Grant,
who's taken a chance on these *novels*,
one by one.

CONTENTS PAGE

ARGUMENT
PROLOGUE: THE SAILOR
THE PRISONER
    1. The Door
    2. Eddie Dean
    3. Contact and Landing
    4. The Tower
    5. Showdown and Shoot-Out
SHUFFLE
THE LADY OF SHADOWS
    1. Detta and Odetta
    2. Ringing the Changes
    3. Odetta on the Other Side
    4. Detta on the Other Side
RESHUFFLE
THE PUSHER
    1. Bitter Medicine
    2. The Honeypot

    3. Roland Takes His Medicine
    4. The Drawing
FINAL SHUFFLE
AFTERWORD

ILLUSTRATIONS

DID-A-CHICK
ROLAND
ON THE BEACH
SOUVENIR
WAITING FOR ROLAND
DETTA
WAITING FOR THE PUSHER
NOTHING BUT THE HILT
JACK MORT
THE GUNSLINGER

BOOK BREAKDOWN

ARGUMENT—(One unnumbered section)
PROLOGUE: THE SAILOR—(One unnumbered section)

PART ONE:
THE PRISONER

Chapter 1:   The Door—(Six untitled sections numbered 1-6)
Chapter 2:   Eddie Dean—(Twelve untitled sections numbered 1-12)
Chapter 3:   Contact and Landing—(Eighteen untitled sections numbered 1-18)
Chapter 4:   The Tower—(Fourteen untitled sections numbered 1-14)
Chapter 5:   Showdown and Shoot-Out—(Twenty-five untitled sections numbered 1-25)

PART TWO:
SHUFFLE

[This part consists of nine unnumbered sections, each titled *Shuffle*.]

PART THREE:
THE LADY OF SHADOWS

Chapter 1:   Detta and Odetta—(Eight untitled sections numbered 1-8)
Chapter 2:   Ringing the Changes—(Eight untitled sections numbered 1-8)
Chapter 3:   Odetta on the Other Side—(Eight untitled sections numbered 1-8)
Chapter 4:   Detta on the Other Side—(Eighteen untitled sections numbered 1-18)

PART FOUR:
RESHUFFLE

[This part consists of seventeen untitled sections, numbered 1-17]

(continued next page)

(23)
THE DARK TOWER II:
THE DRAWING OF THE THREE
People

ADLER Psychiatric expert. He said "the perfect schizophrenic would be a man or woman not only unaware of his other persona(e), but one unaware that anything at all was amiss in his or her life."

ALEXANDER, TRUMAN The man who helped Dretto bury the mick that Balazar shot. They buried him under a chickenhouse in Sedonville, Connecticut.

ALLEN, WOODY The Woodman.

ALLIE Odetta Holmes's mother, Alice. Her father sometimes called her Allie if he'd had a few.

ANDOLINI, CLAUDIO One of Balazar's personal bodyguards.

ANDOLINI, JACK One of Ginelli's employees. He was in the pizza truck that tailed Eddie Dean in New York City. Eddie thought of Andolini as "Old Double-Ugly." Jack had a brow like a Neanderthal.

ANNE One of the stewardesses on Eddie's flight back to New York.

"AUNT BLUE" The name Odetta Holmes called her Aunt Sophia.

BALAZAR, EMILIO ("RICO") "A high-caliber big shot in New York's wonderful world of drugs." Eddie picked up the cocaine in Nassau for Balazar.

BASALE, MIGUEL The guy who took Julio's place on his bowling team on the night in August of 1959 that Odetta Holmes lost her legs.

BILLY THE KID Odetta Holmes felt that John F. Kennedy was a peacemaker – not the "Billy the Kid" type.

BIONDI, GEORGE One of Balazar's "gentlemen." He played Trivial Pursuit with Henry Dean. He was known as "Big George" to his friends, and "Big Nose" to his enemies.

BLAKE, KEVIN One of Balazar's men. He cut off Henry Dean's head and threw it at Eddie.

THE BLUE WOMAN The woman who owned the china plate that Detta Walker broke.

THE BOBBSEY TWINS The medical personnel who had ridden with Julio and Odetta after her accident. Julio called them the Bobbsey Twins.

BRENNAN, WALTER After hearing Henry Dean answer "Johnny Cash" to every Trivial Pursuit question, George Biondi finally asked him a question to which "Johnny Cash" was the correct

answer. ("What popular country and western singer had hits with "A Boy Named Sue" and "Folsom Prison Blues?") Henry's answer was Walter Brennan.

BRUMHALL, DR. Mrs. Rathbun's doctor.

THE CABBIE An unnamed driver who saw Jack Mort spread his hand across his brow as though he had an Excedrin headache.

CASPER THE FRIENDLY GHOST Cartoon character.

CASTRO Dictator of Cuba.

CHARLIE BROWN AND LUCY Eddie Dean compared him and his brother, Henry, to these two "Peanuts" characters.

CLEMENTS, ARNOLD Justin Clements. [NOTE: He is mistakenly referred to as "Arnold Clements" in the text on page 349 of the hardcover edition.]

CLEMENTS, JUSTIN The owner of Clement's Gun Shop. Clements had been a Marine. The cops had been dying to bust him for a long time.

THE CONTACT The unnamed guy that Eddie got the China White cocaine from in Nassau.

CRONKITE, WALTER Newscaster.

CUSTOMS AGENT NO. 1 An unnamed agent at Kennedy who asked Customs Agent No. 2 if he believed in Santa Claus.

CUSTOMS AGENT NO. 2 He was asked by Customs Agent No. 1 if he believed in Santa Claus.

CUTHBERT Eddie told Roland that he talked about Cuthbert in his sleep. [NOTE: See the section on *The Dark Tower: The Gunslinger* in this volume.]

DARIO One of Balazar's men.

DEAN, EDDIE The Second. [NOTE: See the entry THE THREE.]

DEAN, HENRY Eddie's brother.

DEAN, SELINA Eddie and Henry Dean's sister. She had been run over and killed by a drunk driver.

DEAN, SUSANNAH The Third. The woman born from the commingling of Odetta Susannah Holmes and Detta Susannah Walker.

DEERE, CO-PILOT The co-pilot on Eddie's Delta flight (carrying the Nassau cocaine) back to New York.

DELEVAN, CARL One of the police officers who investigated the trouble between Justin Clements and Jack/Roland.

"DOCKTORS" Roland considered these people to be sorcerers.

DOLLENTZ Pharmacist. He was undercutting Katz.

DORNING, JANE One of the stewardesses on the plane Eddie took back to New York.

DOUGLAS, SUSY One of the stewardesses on Eddie's flight back to New York.

DRETTO, CARLOCIMI One of Balazar's personal bodyguards.

DUVALIER, POPPA DOC Dictator of Haiti.

EARP, WYATT, DOC HOLLIDAY OR BUTCH CASSIDY When Fat Johnny Holden looked at Jack Mort/Roland, he thought he could see one of these gunslingers.

ELAPHAUNTS Giant creatures (probably the forefathers of our elephants) that Roland had heard about in childhood stories.

AN ELDERLY BLACK CHICK An unnamed woman who had helped George Shavers when Odetta was pushed onto the train tracks. She was awarded the Medal of Bravery by the mayor of New York City.

THE ELDERLY PASSENGER On Eddie's Delta flight back to New York with Balazar's cocaine, an unnamed elderly passenger worried about catching a flight to Montreal.

THE ELDERLY WHITE BUSINESS TYPE The unnamed guy who had (reluctantly) taken off his belt and let the elderly black chick use it as a tourniquet on Odetta Holmes after her legs were cut off. She said "Thank you, Bro."

ELLINGTON, DUKE The bandleader who recorded "Take the A-Train."

ESTEVEZ, JULIO The Cuban ambulance driver for the Sisters of Mercy Hospital. He picked up Odetta Holmes after her accident. George Shavers called Julio "Wonder Hook" because of Julio's bowling hook shot.

EVERS, MEDGAR, AND MARTIN LUTHER KING Andrew Feeney thought that his boss, Odetta Holmes, was as well known to the American public as these two civil rights activists.

FARSON, THE GOOD MAN Raids by Farson's rebel forces had shut down supply lines when Roland was a child.

A FAT MAN WITH GLASSES An unnamed man who got onto an elevator and spoke with Jack Mort. He was really speaking to Roland.

FEENY, ANDREW Odetta Holmes's limo driver. His heritage was Irish.

FELLINI Italian film director.

FLAGG A creature Roland believed to be a demon pretending to be a man. [NOTE: Flagg, as all us Stephen King mega-fans know, also appears in two other works by the master: *The Stand,* and *The Eyes of the Dragon.* See the sections on those two novels in this volume. Also, in *The Dead Zone,* Sarah Bracknell takes an apartment on Flagg Street in Veazie, Maine.]

FRAMINGHAM, MR. Jack Mort's boss.

GINELLI Hood. He and Balazar were "involved." [NOTE: Ginelli also appears in the Richard Bachman novel *Thinner*. See the section on *Thinner* in this volume.]

GODZILLA OR GHIDRA THE THREE-HEADED MONSTER Eddie told Odetta that they'd open Door Number Three and probably find either Godzilla or Ghidra.

GOLDWATER, BARRY Odetta Holmes felt that Goldwater was a "Billy the Kid" type.

GOODEN, DWIGHT Baseball player.

GOULD, CHESTER Comic strip artist.

A GUY An unnamed New Yorker in a muscle shirt who was watching Eddie Dean and talking on the telephone at the same time.

HALVORSEN, JIMMY Macy's store detective.

HASPIO, JIMMY One of Balazar's men.

HATHAWAY, MISS Eddie Dean's third-grade teacher.

HOLDEN, FAT JOHNNY Justin Clements' brother-in-law, and the clerk in Clements' gun shop. Jack/Roland tried to buy shells from him.

HOLIDAY, BILLY Black songstress.

HOLMES, ALICE Odetta Holmes's mother. Her father sometimes called her Allie.

HOLMES, DR. Odetta's father. He was a dentist.

HOLMES, ODETTA SUSANNAH One half of the "Lady of Shadows," who was comprised of Detta Walker and Odetta Holmes. From these two was born the Third part of the Drawing, Susannah Dean.

HOWARD The doorman at Odetta Walker's building.

HUNTLEY AND BRINKLEY Sixties newscast team.

JAKE John Chambers. Roland had sacrificed his life while pursuing the man in black, and when he entered Jack Mort, he saw the scene when Mort pushed Jake into traffic and killed him. [NOTE: See the section on *The Dark Tower: The Gunslinger* in this volume.]

"JOHNNY CASH" George Biondi asked Henry Dean the following "Arts and Entertainment" Trivial Pursuit question: "What enormously popular novel by William Peter Blatty, set in the posh Washington, D.C. suburb of Georgetown, concerned the demonic possession of a young girl?" The correct answer, of course, was *The Exorcist*, but Henry answered "Johnny Cash" to that and every other question for which another answer was correct.

KATZ, MR. Pharmacist. He owned Katz's Drug Store.

KENT, CLARK Superman.

LANE, LOIS Superman's girlfriend.

LENNOX, RALPH The security guard in Katz's Drug Store.

THE LOBSTROSITIES The giant lobsters that attacked Roland on the beach. They made noises that sounded like "Dod-a-chock, did-a-chick, dum-a-chum, dad-a-cham." They were four feet long, a foot high, and weighed seventy pounds.

THE MAN IN BLACK Walter. [NOTE: Or Johnny Cash, for that matter.]

McAULIFFE, CHRISTA Schoolteacher and Challenger shuttle astronaut who was killed when the shuttle exploded.

McDONALD, CAPTAIN The Delta pilot on Eddie's flight back to New York.

McGURSKY, MRS. Eddie and Henry Dean's landlady.

THE MICK The hood shot by Balazar. He was buried by Dretto and Truman Alexander under a chickenhouse in Sedonville, Connecticut.

MORT, JACK The Pusher. The third person (after Eddie and Odetta) that Roland "entered."

"MOUSTACHE PETE" Wiseguys of a previous generation would have called Balazar "Moustache Pete."

"MR. GOLD-RIMMED SPECS" The title by which Officer O'Mearah referred to Jack Mort/ Roland.

NEWMAN, PAUL The blue-eyed actor.

O'MEARAH, GEORGE One of the police officers who investigated the trouble between Justin Clements and Jack/Roland.

OSWALD, LEE HARVEY The man who shot JFK.

PARKS, ROSA LEE The black woman who refused to move to the back of the bus in Montgomery, Alabama, thus touching off the civil rights movement.

PAULA One of the stewardesses on Eddie's New York flight.

PETER One of the stewards on Eddie's flight back to New York.

POE, EDGAR ALLAN American writer. He had made the name "William Wilson" famous.

POPEYE The Sailor Man.

POST, WILEY Old pilot.

POSTINO, TRICKS One of Balazar's henchmen.

POTZIE Eddie and Henry Dean's cat.

RATHBUN, MRS. One of Mr. Katz's pharmacy customers. She wanted Katz to refill her Valium prescription even though the prescription had expired.

THE RCA VICTOR DOG Andolini thought that Eddie Dean looked like this dog.

ROLAND The last gunslinger. His story is told in King's *Dark Tower* series.

ROTH, DAVID LEE Ex-Van Halen rocker.

RUBY, JACK The man who shot Lee Harvey Oswald.

A SALESWOMAN Eddie and Roland could see a saleswoman in a store through the door on the beach. She was taking care of Detta Walker.

SANTA CLAUS One Kennedy Airport customs agent asked another if he believed in Santa Claus.

SCHULTZ, CHARLES Creator of the "Peanuts" cartoon strip.

THE SEVEN NARCS After Eddie landed in New York, he was questioned by seven narcotics agents about what he had been carrying from the Bahamas.

SHAVERS, GEORGE An intern at Sisters of Mercy Hospital.

THE SILICON VALLEY COKE-HEADS Jack Andolini's name for those who sold stolen top-secret equipment at bargain prices.

"SISTER BLUE" Odetta Holmes's Aunt Sophie.

SOPHIA Odetta Holmes's mother's youngest sister.

SOPHIA'S HUSBAND Odetta Holmes's uncle.

SPIX AND MOCKIES Jack Mort told Roland that these people drove cabs.

STAUNTON, ANDREW New York City foot patrolman.

STREISAND, BARBRA Singer.

SUVIA A creature who had eight eyes and nine arms.

SWAGGART, JIMMY Television evangelist.

A TEEN-AGED GIRL The unnamed girl Jack Mort shoved out of the way in order to push Jake Chambers into traffic.

THE THREE The Drawing of the Three was eventually completed with the final gathering of Roland, Eddie Dean, and Susannah Dean.

THE TWO PARAMEDICS The medical personnel who had ridden with Julio and Odetta after her accident. Julio called them the Bobbsey Twins.

VECHHIO, RUDY One of Balazar's men.

VERONE, TIO Balazar's dead uncle.

VINCENT, COL One of Ginelli's employees. He was in the pizza truck that tailed Eddie Dean in New York City.

WALKER, DETTA SUSANNAH One half of the "Lady of Shadows" who was comprised of Detta Walker and Odetta Holmes. From these two was born the Third part of the Drawing, Susannah Dean.

WALTER The man in black. Roland kept his jawbone. [Note: See the section on *The Dark Tower: The Gunslinger* in this volume.]

A WASP FROM VERMONT The cab driver who drove Jack/Roland thought of him as a WASP from Vermont.

WEAVER, NORRIS Andrew Staunton's partner.

WEBB, JACK Actor. He starred in the "Dragnet" TV series.

WILSON, WILLIAM The American who had strapped the bags of cocaine to Eddie Dean in Nassau.

THE WOMAN An unnamed woman who screamed while Roland was in Katz's Drug Store.

THE WOMAN (#2) An unnamed New Yorker who sat on a bench rooting through her purse. She was also watching Eddie Dean.

THE WOMAN IN THE DRESSING ROOM A Macy's shopper who had on a Playtex Living Bra.

A YOUNG BLACK GUY An unnamed New Yorker who looked at t-shirts at a newsstand. He was also watching Eddie Dean.

A YOUNG WHITE GUY An unnamed kid who had called the police when Odetta was pushed onto the railroad tracks.

(23)
THE DARK TOWER II:
THE DRAWING OF THE THREE
Places

ACHIN' ASSHOLE, ALASKA When Roland told Eddie that they were going to the Tower, Eddie said that was "like me being some ignoramus from Texas without a road-map saying he's going to Achin' Asshole, Alaska."

THE AQUINAS HOTEL The Aquinas Hotel in Nassau was where Eddie picked up the cocaine for Balazar.

ATLANTIC CITY Balazar had once seen the magician David Copperfield perform in Atlantic City.

THE BAHAMAS Eddie Dean had been born in the Bahamas.

THE BEACH The seemingly endless expanse of shore where Roland was attacked by the lobstrosities, and where he found the doors.

THE BONDED ELECTROPLATE FACTORY When they were younger, Eddie and Henry Dean used to smoke cigarettes behind the Bonded Electroplate factory on Cohoes Street.

CHRISTOPHER STREET STATION After the incident at Katz's drug store, Jack took Roland to the Christopher Street station in the Village.

CLEMENTS GUNS AND SPORTING GOODS The gunshop where Jack/Roland got his ammo. Their sign said "Ammo," "Fishing Tackle," and "Official Facsimiles."

CO-OP CITY Bronx housing development where Eddie Dean confronted Andolini about Balazar's betrayal.

COHOES STREET When they were younger, Eddie and Henry Dean used to smoke cigarettes behind the Bonded Electroplate factory on Cohoes Street.

CONNECTICUT, HARLEM, AND MONTAUK SOUND Anyone trying to track Balazar's Ginelli Pizza van by standard triangulation methods would conclude that the van was in all three of these places at the same time.

THE DARK TOWER Roland's Quest. He dreamt of the Tower:

"It stood on the horizon of a vast plain the color of blood in the violent setting of a dying sun. He couldn't see the stairs which spiraled up and up and up within its brick shell, but he could see the windows which spiraled up along that staircase's way, and saw the ghosts of all the people he had ever known

pass through them. Up and up they marched, and an arid wind brought him the sound of voices calling his name.
Roland...come...Roland...come...come...come..."

THE DRAWERS Detta Walker took the Blue Woman's china plate to a place called The Drawers. She stepped on it there and broke it. Detta had once seen a burning baby with plastic skin at The Drawers.

DUNKIN' DONUTS While on the beach and watching through the "Lady of Shadows" door, Eddie felt like going through and getting some Dunkin' Donuts.

ELIZABETH, NEW JERSEY Odetta Holmes and her family once traveled to Elizabeth to attend a wedding.

THE EMPIRE STATE BUILDING After Fat Johnny Holden kept Jack Mort/Roland's wallet, Roland told the cop that there was a picture in the wallet of him (Jack) and his mother standing in front of the Empire State Building.

FIFTH AND CENTRAL PARK WEST Odetta Holmes lived in a gray Victorian on Fifth Avenue and Central Park West in New York City.

FOUR FATHERS RESTAURANT Restaurant owned and operated by Ginelli. He and Balazar were "involved."

409 PARK AVENUE SOUTH The address Roland gave to the cops when he was in Jack Mort's body. [NOTE: The address of Zenith Publishing in *The Plant* is 490 Park Avenue South. See the section on *The Plant* in this volume.]

FOUR SEASONS A New York City restaurant.

GARLAN Kingdom where the mythical Grand Featherex came from. While "inside" Eddie Dean, Roland thought that airplanes were as fantastic as the Grand Featherex described in the stories he had once been told.

GEORGIA The very first boatload of slaves had been brought by the British to a colony in Georgia that the British had formed in order to get rid of their criminals and debtors.

GREAT SMOKIES Odetta Holmes's Aunt Sophia and her husband went to the Great Smokies for their honeymoon.

GREENWICH VILLAGE Detta Walker lived in a loft in Greenwich Village.

GREYMARL APARTMENTS The apartment building on Central Park South where Odetta Holmes, her mother, and her father lived.

HAITI, QUINCAN, OR BOGOTA Eddie thought that clearing customs from Nassau wasn't like clearing customs from any of these cities.

THE HUNGRY I Coffeehouse. Odetta remembered coming out of the Hungry I just before she was pushed beneath the A-Train.

IDLEWILD AIRPORT In August of 1959, a T.W.A. Tri-Star crashed at Idelwild with sixty-five people on board. Sixty were what Julio Estevez called "D.R.T.": Dead Right There.

IRELAND OR PERU Officer O'Mearah thought to himself that the value of his gun (which had been taken by Roland) was about as important as the population of Ireland or the principal mineral deposits of Peru.

KATZ'S DRUG STORE The store where Roland got his Keflex.

KENNEDY AIRPORT The airport where Eddie Dean's plane landed.

KENNEDY'S INTERNATIONAL ARRIVALS BUILDING Eddie's Delta flight was approaching this building when Roland first spoke to Eddie.

THE LEANING TOWER Balazar's place.

LONG ISLAND SOUND The 727 Eddie took back to New York from Nassau banked over Long Island sound, and then started in for a landing.

MACY'S Detta Walker once stole a $1.99 scarf from the Nice Notions counter in Macy's. Macy's was also the store where Roland entered Detta Walker's head.

MONTGOMERY, ALABAMA The town where Rosa Lee Parks refused to move to the back of the bus.

MONTREAL On Eddie's Delta flight back to New York with

Balazar's cocaine, an unnamed elderly passenger worried about catching a flight to Montreal.

THE MUSEUM OF SCIENCE A museum in Boston. They had a computer there that played tic-tac-toe.

N.Y.U. Balazar had gone to N.Y.U.'s business school for two years.

NASSAU The Aquinas Hotel in Nassau was where Eddie picked up the cocaine for Balazar.

NEW JERSEY Cimi Dretto planned on retiring to New Jersey.

NEW YORK CUSTOMS Eddie was worried about going through customs when the plane he was on landed.

ODETTA, ARKANSAS The town where Odetta Holmes's mother was born, and for which Odetta was named.

OXFORD, MISSISSIPPI Odetta Holmes had spent three days in Oxford protesting racism and segregation.

THE PROJECTS Urban housing developments where Eddie and Henry Dean grew up.

THE PUSHING PLACE The corner of Fifth Avenue in New York City where Jack Mort pushed Jake under the wheels of a Cadillac. Mort thought of this corner as the Pushing Place. [NOTE: See the section on *The Dark Tower: The Gunslinger* in this volume.]

QUEENSBORO BRIDGE When they were kids, Eddie and Henry saw a police car near the Queensboro Bridge as they drove their stolen Chevrolet to New York.

RED LOBSTER Restaurant.

REGENCY TOWER The New York hotel where Henry Dean explained to his brother about going "cool turkey" rather than cold turkey.

RIKERS Island prison.

RINCON AVENUE When they were younger, Eddie and Henry stole comic books from a candy store on Rincon Avenue.

IL ROCHE The Rock: What Balazar's place, The Leaning Tower, was known as.

THE ROYAL COURT GARDENS As Roland, Eddie, and Odetta moved across the beach, Roland thought of the apple trees and the spring flowers in the Royal Court Gardens.

ST. ANTHONY'S CHURCH Fat Johnny Holden went there for confession and communion.

SEDONVILLE, CONNECTICUT Truman Alexander and Dretto buried the mick that Balazar shot under a chickenhouse in Sedonville, Connecticut.

SEVENTH AVENUE AND 49TH STREET Jack/Roland told a cab driver to take him to this location.

THE SISTERS OF MERCY HOSPITAL The hospital where Odetta Holmes was brought when she lost her legs in the train accident.

SIXTH AVENUE AND THE AVENUE OF THE AMERICAS Jack Mort's "Mortcypedia" told Roland that they were on these New York City streets.

395 WEST 49TH STREET The location of the shootout at Katz's Drug Store.

THE 23RD PRECINCT TARGET RANGE The range where Ralph Lennox practiced shooting his .38.

VIETNAM Henry went to Vietnam when he was drafted.

THE VILLAGE After the incident at Katz's Drug Store, Roland told Jack to drive to the Village.

WESTCHESTER Justin Clements told Jack/Roland that if he didn't have a Carry Permit, he would have to go to Westchester to buy the ammo shells he wanted.

WOOLWORTH'S Department store.

(23)
THE DARK TOWER II:
THE DRAWING OF THE THREE
Things

THE A-TRAIN Odetta Holmes had been waiting for the A-Train when she was pushed onto the railroad tracks.

AM-FM OR VHF When Roland spoke to Eddie from inside Eddie's

head, Eddie thought he was receiving either an AM/FM or VHF transmission.

"AND THE TOWER IS CLOSER." The last line of the "Afterword" to *The Drawing of the Three* .

"ARTS AND ENTERTAINMENT" A Trivial Pursuit question category.

"ASTIN" How Roland pronounced "aspirin."

AUGUST 19, 1959 The date Odetta Holmes lost both her legs.

'BASING Eddie Dean explained to Odetta Holmes that freebasing was like turning TNT into an A-bomb.

THE "BEST ACTOR OF THE YEAR" ACADEMY AWARD Eddie Dean thought he deserved an Oscar for best actor after remaining expressionless while being spoken to by Roland.

"BIG GEORGE" The name by which George Biondi was known to his friends.

"BIG NOSE" The name by which George Biondi was known to his enemies.

"BIG TIME WRESTLING" A televison show Henry Dean used to watch.

THE BLUE CAR One of the vehicles (along with Ginelli's pizza truck) that followed Eddie (and Roland) after they were released by the narcs at the airport.

BONOMO'S TURKISH TAFFY The candy Henry had bought his brother Eddie when they were kids.

THE BUS ADS There were several ads on the bus on which Rosa Lee Parks rode, and on which she refused to move to the back of the bus. They included:

> "Lucky Strike L.S.M.F.T.";
> "Attend the Church of Your Choice For Heaven's Sake";
> "Drink Ovaltine! You'll See What We Mean!";
> "Chesterfield, Twenty-One Great Tobaccos Make Twenty Wonderful Smokes."

"BUTTERFLY McQUEEN GONE LOONEY TUNES" George Shavers thought Odetta was Butterfly gone nuts when he heard her and Detta talking out of one person.

CADILLAC Odetta Holmes's limo.

CALIBER CHART Jack Mort/Roland asked the clerk in Clements gun shop for a caliber chart.

A CERTIFIED PUBLIC ACCOUNTANT Jack Mort's profession.

"CHEEFLET" How Roland saw the word "Keflex."

CHESTERFIELDS Julio Estevez's cigarettes.

CHEVROLET Jack Mort owned a mid-fifties Chevrolet. Also, Eddie and Henry Dean once stole a Chevrolet and drove it to New York City when they were kids.

CHINA WHITE Eddie Dean's Nassau drug contact told Eddie that the coke he was taking back to New York was China White. Eddie said that if the coke was China White, then he was Dwight Gooden.

THE CIVIL RIGHTS ACT Odetta Holmes hoped that President Johnson would enact the Civil Rights Act.

"CLOSED TONIGHT ONLY" The sign on the door of Il Roche, Balazar's place.

CODE 19 The code that came over police radios after Jack Mort/Roland got involved in the shootout at Katz's Drug Store.

A COLT COBRA Andolini's gun.

"COOL" TURKEY Henry Dean explained to his brother Eddie that rather than cold turkey, a junkie should go "cool" turkey first.

"COP KILLS FOUR IN WEST SIDE DRUGSTORE SNAFU" Officer O'Mearah imagined this headline in the *Daily News* as he responded to the Code 19 at Katz's Drug Store.

"D.R.T." Julio Estevez's acronym for "Dead Right There," a term he used for plane crash victims who died upon impact with the ground.

"DA BOSS" Cimi Dretto's name for Balazar.

THE *DARK TOWER* SERIES The series is comprised (so far) of three completed and published volumes, and one outlined but unwritten volume:

1. *The Dark Tower: The Gunslinger*
2. *The Dark Tower II: The Drawing Of The Three*
3. *The Dark Tower III: The Waste Lands* The third volume "details half of the quest of Roland, Eddie, and Susannah to reach the Tower."
4. *The Dark Tower IV: Wizard And Glass* The fourth volume "tells of an enchantment and a seduction but mostly of those things that befell Roland before his readers first met him upon the trail of the man in black."

THE DEA The Drug Enforcement Agency.

DELTA The airline Eddie flew back to New York on with Balazar's cocaine.

DEMEROL The pain medication George Shavers gave Odetta Holmes after her accident.

THE DEPARTMENT OF INTERNAL AFFAIRS The police department that investigated misconduct among police officers.

DIGITALIS After her accident, George Shavers shot Odetta Holmes full of digitalis when her heartbeat became very erratic.

"DR. JEKYLL AND MR. HYDE" Movie starring Spencer Tracy. George Shavers thought of this movie when he heard Odetta Holmes and Detta Walker both speaking from one woman.

THE DOOR Roland came upon a door on the beach. It was six-and-a-half feet high, made of solid ironwood. It had a gold doorknob, and it was filigreed with a design of the grinning face of a baboon. The door had no keyhole, and its hinges were fastened to nothing. Written on the door in black letters were the words "The Prisoner."

THE DORFMAN ACCOUNT The account that Jack Mort had been working on when he pushed Jake into traffic.

A DUNHILL SILVER LIGHTER Jack Mort's $200 silver lighter. It saved Jack/Roland's life when Andrew Staunton shot them.

EMERGENCY RIDE A new program at Sisters of Mercy Hospital in August of 1959.

"EMERGENCY RIDE," "BUCKET OF BLOOD," OR "NAME THAT TUNE" George Shavers thought that no matter what you called it, he still wanted to be a doctor.

"THE EXORCIST" A film in which the main character, a little girl named Regan, was possessed by a demon.

EXTRA STRENGTH ANACIN The medication Eddie bought at a New York newsstand.

FLIGHT 901 Eddie Dean's Delta flight back to New York from Nassau.

A '46 DODGE DESOTO Detta Walker had once been with a white boy in a '46 Dodge DeSoto.

"FOTTERGRAFFS" The word Roland heard for "photographs."

FOUR FEET LONG, A FOOT HIGH, AND SEVENTY POUNDS The length, height and weight of the lobstrosities.

4:05 EDT The time Eddie Dean's plane was expected to land at Kennedy.

GEOGRAPHY A Trivial Pursuit question category.

GEORGE SHAVER'S NEEDLEPOINT SAMPLER George paid ten dollars to have a needlepoint sampler made that said "If You Can Take This, You Can Take Anything."

GIN AND TONIC The drink Eddie Dean ordered on his flight back to New York with Balazar's cocaine.

GINELLI'S PIZZA VAN A Gineli's Pizza van tailed Eddie's cab in New York City. [Note: Ginelli also appeared in the Richard Bachman novel *Thinner*. See the section on *Thinner* in this volume. Also see the entry THE PIZZA VAN'S EQUIPMENT.]

THE GOAD The term Odetta Holmes used to describe the voice in her mind that tried to goad her into being honest.

GODZILLA DOGS What Eddie Dean called the twelve-inch hot dogs he bought at a New York snack bar.

"GONE WITH THE WIND" AND "MANDINGO" Eddie told Roland that Detta talked like a cross between "the Darkies" in both of these movies.

GRAND FEATHEREX Mythical flying creatures from the kingdom of Garlan. While "inside" Eddie Dean, Roland thought that airplanes were as fantastic as the Grand Featherex from the stories he had once been told.

GUCCI Jack Mort's loafers. Also, Andolini's loafers.

THE GUINNESS BOOK OF WORLD RECORDS After he was held up by Roland for Keflex, Katz thought that if he had any good luck, then such news belonged in the *Guinness*.

"HALLOWEEN," "THE SHINING," AND "STAR WARS" Eddie compared the point-of-view shots through the doorway on the beach to the Steadicam work on these three films. [NOTE: See the section on the film "The Shining" in this volume.]

HEROIN While on the beach, Roland dreamt of the man in black telling him that the name of the demon was Heroin.

"HITCHHIKE" A word Eddie used that Roland did not understand.

THE HOLMES DENTAL INDUSTRIES PLANTS Odetta Holmes was sole heir to the twelve Holmes Dental Industries plants in the South.

THE HONOR STANCE The boxer stance once taught by Cort to the gunslingers.

"IF YOU CAN TAKE THIS, YOU CAN TAKE ANYTHING" George Shavers paid ten dollars to have this legend done as a needlepoint sampler.

"IN THE HEAT OF THE NIGHT" Movie with Rod Steiger and Sidney Poitier. (Eddie remembered it as starring "Sidney Steiger" and "Rod Poitier.")

JELL-O A desert.

JERKY Roland ate jerky on the beach.

A JOSHUA TREE While on the beach, Roland found some shade beneath a Joshua tree.

"KA" Duty, destiny.

KEFLEX An antibiotic.

"LA MONSTRA" Cimi Dretto's name for his mother-in-law.

"THE LADY OF SHADOWS" This was written on the second door that Roland came upon after he and Eddie made it back to the beach.

A LLAMA .38 Kevin Blake's gun.

THE LOBSTROSITIES SOUNDS The lobstrosities made noises that sounded like "Dod-a-chock, did-a-chick, dum-a-chum, dad-a-cham."

THE MAFIA A powderhorn (a legal gunshop) often sold guns in bulk to the Mafia.

"MAGDA-SEEN" While inside Eddie Dean, this was how Roland understood the word "magazine."

A MARCH OF DIMES TROPHY A trophy in Balazar's office.

THE MEDAL OF BRAVERY The medal that was awarded to the old black woman who helped Odetta Holmes after Odetta was pushed onto the railroad tracks.

"MIAMI VICE" TV show.

THE MIRROR MAZE A concession at Coney Island.

"MORTCYPEDIA" Jack Mort's memory. Roland consulted it when he needed to know something.

THE MOVEMENT Odetta Holmes became involved in the civil rights movement in 1957.

"NEGRO" VS. "BLACK" Odetta told Eddie Dean that calling a Negro black was rude.

NEW YORK *DAILY MIRROR* Jack Mort cut an article out of this paper. The story was headlined "Negro Girl Comatose Following Tragic Accident."

NEW YORK *DAILY NEWS* The paper that ran the headline "Thank You, Bro" after the elderly black chick put a tourniquet on Odetta Holmes. [NOTE: See the entry THANK YOU, BRO.]

1962 The year Odetta Holmes's father died.

NO-DOZ Caffeine pills.

ODETTA'S LAST WORDS After she was pushed onto the train tracks, Odetta reportedly said "Who was that Mahfah? I gone hunt him down and kill his ass!"

"OLD DOUBLE-UGLY" Eddie Dean's nickname for Jack Andolini. Jack had a brow like a Neanderthal.

OLD SPARKY The electric chair.

PERMIT TO CARRY Fat Johnny Holden had decided that if Jack/Roland didn't have a Carry Permit with a photo ID, he wasn't going to sell him the ammo shells he wanted.

THE PHOTO After Fat Johnny Holden kept Jack Mort/Roland's wallet, Roland told the cop that there was a picture in the wallet of him (Jack) and his mother standing in front of the Empire State Building. Written on the back of the photo was "It was a wonderful day and a wonderful view. Love, Mom."

THE PIZZA VAN'S EQUIPMENT Balazar's Ginelli Pizza van contained the following equipment: A fuzz-buster, a UHF police radio jammer, a high range/high frequency radio transmissions detector, an h-r/hf jammer, a transponder-amplifier, a red button that buzzed Balazar's office, and a radio telephone.

A PLAYTEX LIVING BRA A woman in Macy's wore one in a dressing room.

A "PLEASE FEED ME, I AM A U.S. GOVERNMENT EMPLOYEE" T-SHIRT Eddie confronted the young black guy who he knew was watching him, and asked him if he was looking for one of these t-shirts.

"POPKIN" Roland's word for sandwich.

"POSSE" Roland read the word "Police" as "Posse."

POST OFFICE TRUCKS The F.B.I. had custom vans that looked just like post office trucks.

A POWDERHORN Police slang for a legal gunshop that did business with stick-up men who had proper credentials. A powderhorn often sold guns in bulk to the Mafia.

"THE PURPLE ROSE OF CAIRO" A Woody Allen movie in which a character stepped out of the screen and into a woman's life.

"THE PUSHER" The words written on the third door Roland came upon on the beach.

READER'S DIGEST Magazine.

"THE REALLY BAD MAN" This was how Detta Walker thought of Roland.

A REMINGTON SHOTGUN A weapon carried by one of Balazar's men.

"REXES" Roland surmised that "doktors" wrote their magic formulas on sheets of paper called "rexes."

RING DING Snack.

ROI-TAN Cigars.

ROLEX Jack Mort's wristwatch.

ROLODEX A card file.

THE SAILOR One of the tarot cards dealt to Roland by the man in black.

SCOTCH STRAPPING TAPE The tape Eddie Dean used to strap two bags of cocaine under his arms.

SECOND GENERATION SICILIAN Balazar's heritage.

"SEIG HEIL" When Eddie was brought back to Roland's beach and first saw the lobstrosities raise their claws, he thought they looked like the Nazis did when they all raised their arms to Hitler in a "sieg heil" salute.

744 The number on the police car Roland/Jack Mort stole.

THE SHOOTER'S BIBLE Fat Johnny Holden, the clerk in Clement's gun shop, told Jack/Roland that he had a *Shooter's Bible* he could refer to when Jack asked for a caliber chart.

$6,500 The value of Jack Mort's Rolex.

THE SPICS OF SUPREMACY Julio's bowling team.

THE "SPORTSMAN OF THE YEAR" TROPHY There was a picture in Balazar's office of him presenting the Police Athletic League's "Sportsman of the Year" trophy to a young boy.

SUPERMAN'S JOCKEY SHORTS On Eddie's Delta flight back to New York with Balazar's cocaine, an unnamed elderly passenger worried about catching a flight to Montreal. Eddie said he didn't care if the passenger flew to Montreal in Superman's jockies.

A SWANSON'S TURKEY T.V. DINNER George Shavers ate one.

T.W.A. TRI-STAR The plane that crashed at Idlewild airport. There were sixty-five people on board, and sixty of them were what Julio Estevez called "D.R.T.": Dead Right There.

"TACK-SEES" How Roland understood taxis.

TEFLON Teflon was used to replace the bone in Henry's knee when it was blown off in Vietnam.

"THE TERMINATOR" A movie with Arnold Schwarzenegger and Linda Hamilton. [NOTE: The ever-pumped-up Arnold went on to play Ben Richards in the film version of the Richard Bachman novel *The Running Man*, and the ever-gorgeous Linda Hamilton went on to play the role of Vicky in the film version of the short story "Children of the Corn."]

"THANK YOU, BRO" The words that the elderly black chick said to the elderly white business type after he gave her his belt to use as a tourniquet on Odetta Holmes. The words became the headline of the next day's New York *Daily News,* and made the woman an authentic American hero.

"THAT'S ALL I CAN STANDS AND I CAN'T STAND NUMMORE" Popeye's motto.

THERMOS Jane the stewardess filled a thermos with hot coffee on Eddie Dean's Delta flight back to New York. She planned on throwing the hot coffee on Eddie if he did anything.

A .38 Ralph Lennox's gun.

3A Eddie Dean's seat number on his Delta flight to New York.

"THE THREE FACES OF EVE" Eddie Dean thought of this movie when he explained schizophrenia to Roland.

A .357 MAGNUM Justin Clements kept a fully loaded .357 Magnum in a spring clip beneath the counter of his store. Balazar also carried a .357.

TIME MAGAZINE Odetta Holmes had been on the cover of *Time.*

"TOOTER FISH" Roland's term for tuna fish.

TRIVIAL PURSUIT The board game played by George Biondi and Henry Dean.

THE TRIVIAL PURSUIT "ARTS AND ENTERTAINMENT" QUESTION George Biondi asked Henry Dean the following "Arts and Entertainment" Trivial Pursuit question: "What enormously popular novel by William Peter Blatty, set in the posh Washington, D.C. suburb of Georgetown, concerned the demonic possession of a young girl?" The correct answer, of course, was *The Exorcist*, but Henry answered "Johnny Cash" because he answered "Johnny Cash" to every question.

THE TRIVIAL PURSUIT "GEOGRAPHY" QUESTION George Biondi asked Henry Dean: "What is the only continent where kangaroos are a native form of life?" Henry's answer was Johnny Cash.

THE TRIVIAL PURSUIT "JOHNNY CASH" QUESTION After hearing Henry Dean answer "Johnny Cash" to every Trivial Pursuit question he was asked, George Biondi finally asked him a question to which "Johnny Cash" was the correct answer. ("What popular country and western singer had hits with "A Boy Named Sue" and "Folsom Prison Blues?") Henry's answer was Walter Brennan.

TWA For the benefit of the "sallow thing" (his coke contact in Nassau), Eddie Dean pretended he had a flight booked back to New York on TWA.

TWO BAGS OF COCAINE Eddie Dean landed at Kennedy with two bags of coke strapped under his arms.

TWO TWELVE-INCH HOT DOGS AND AN EXTRA LARGE PEPSI The food and drink Eddie Dean bought at a New York snack bar.

AN UZI Submachine gun. On Eddie's flight back to New York, Jane the stewardess imagined she saw an Uzi in Eddie's hand.

WALL STREET JOURNAL The newspaper Odetta's father read.

"WONDER HOOK" The name George Shavers called Julio Estevez because of Julio's bowling hook shot.

"THE WONDERFUL RAMBO MACHINE" The name Tricks Postino called his M-16 rapid-fire assault weapon.

Original drawing by Kenny Ray Linkous.
First published in the Philtrum Press limited edition of *Eyes of the Dragon*.

THE EYES OF THE DRAGON

DEDICATION

This story is for my great friend, BEN STRAUB, and for my daughter, NAOMI KING.

[NO CONTENTS PAGE]

BOOK BREAKDOWN

[*The Eyes of the Dragon* consists of 142 individually-numbered untitled chapters. The hardcover runs 326 pages; the paperback, 380 pages.]

(24)
THE EYES OF THE DRAGON
People

ALHAZRED Madman. He wrote the *Book of Spells*.

THE ANDUAN PIRATES They were smashed by Delain's navy. The pirates had plagued Delain for over a hundred years.

ANNA CROOKBROWS' SON The unnamed son of the midwife who was cured of the Shaking Disease by Flagg.

ARLEN Anders Penya's butler.

BESON, ARON The Chief Warder of the Needle.

BITER-SNAKE A rattler.

BRANDON Peter's butler.

BROWSON A singer. Browson was the manifestation of Flagg four hundred years before King Roland.

THE CHIEF VINTNER The Castle's wine steward.

THE CRIER He called out the time in Delain.

CROOKBOWS, ANNA Delain midwife. She lived on Third South'ard Alley.

DENNIS Brandon's son and Peter's servant.

ELLENDER, QUENTIN The craftsman commissioned to make Sasha the finest dollhouse a young lady ever had.

THE EXILES They were the people who fled from Delain.

FLAGG The bad guy. He was the King's magician, and acted as the architect of King Roland's death and Peter's imprisonment in the Needle.

FRISKY A huge black-and-white Anduan husky. Naomi's favorite.

GALEN The goshawk.

THE GREAT LAWYERS They sat in on Peter's trial.

GUARD O' THE WATCH The guard posted at a corridor junction in the castle.

HINCH, BILL The Lord High Executioner. Bill Hinch was the manifestation of Flagg two-hundred-fifty years before King Roland's reign.

THE HOME GUARDS The Armed Troops.

THE HORSE DOCTOR A veterinarian.

JOSEF He taught Peter about "breaking strain."

KING, ROGER A name Peter made up while playing with Sasha's dollhouse.

KING, SARAH A name Peter made up while playing with Sasha's dollhouse.

KING ALAN A king of older days.

KING ALAN II The uncle of Kyla the good.

KING JOHN A king of older days.

KYLA THE GOOD The niece of King Alan II.

LANDRY King Roland's grandfather. As Browson, Flagg was his singer.

THE LESSER WARDERS They worked under Beson.

LITA Dowager Queen of Delain, Roland's mother. She had ruled for almost fifty years.

LORD TOWSON'S SON Peter's rival in the bowmanship classes.

NINER The dragon killed by Roland.

PEONY Peter's horse. Peter saved Peony's life.

PETER King Roland's elder son; the king-in-waiting.

PETIE A name Peter made up while playing with Sasha's dollhouse.

PEYNA, ANDERS Delain's Judge General.

REECHUL, CHARLES He raised Anduan huskies, and was sympathetic to the Exiles.

REECHUL, NAOMI Charles Reechul's eldest daughter.

RHIANNON The Witch of the Coos.

ROLAND THE GOOD The King of Delain. Roland was murdered by Flagg.

SASHA Roland's wife, and Queen of Delain. She came from the Western Barony, and wed Roland when she was seventeen years old. She died giving birth to Thomas.

"SQUIRE" Andy Staad's nickname.

STAAD, ANDY Ben Staad's father. He was known as "Squire."

STAAD, BEN Peter's friend. Ben was eight years old.

STAAD, EMMALINE The youngest of the Staad children.

STAAD, SUSAN Ben Staad's mother.

THOMAS King Roland's younger son.

VALERA, ELEANOR Leven Valera's murdered wife.

VALERA, LEVEN The Black Duke of the South Barony. He spent twenty-five years in the Needle. He wrote the note that Peter found beneath the loose stone.

WICKS, ULRICH A lawyer at Peter's trial. He drew the white stone.

THE WOMAN She was hired to remove the royal crest from Peter's napkins.

YOSEF The Lord High Groom of the Horses.

(24)
THE EYES OF THE DRAGON
Places

ANDUA Flagg's destination (told to Thomas).

THE ARCHERY RANGE The archery range was where Peter competed in the bowmanship classes against Lord Towson's son.

CASTLE TREASURE ROOM It held emeralds, rubies, and diamonds.

DELAIN "A very old Kingdom," and the place where *The Eyes of the Dragon* takes place.

THE DELAIN GREAT ROAD Delain's main road.

DESERT OF GRENH The desert where Green Sand came from.

DISMAL SWAMP The swamp where Deadly Clawfoot grew.

THE DUNGEON GATE The castle entrance on the northeast side of the Needle.

DUNGEON OF THE INQUISITION The lowest point in the castle.

EASTERN TOWER The highest point in the castle.

THE FAR FIELDS Heaven? Peter dreamed of Roland taking him there.

THE FAR FORESTS The Exiles camped in the Far Forests.

GARLAN Flagg came from Garlan.

THE GREAT HOSPITAL The hospital created by Queen Sasha.

HALL OF THE NEEDLE The hall where Peter was put on trial for murdering his father.

KING'S HALL The hall where banquets were held.

THE KING'S KENNELS The King's dogs were kept in these kennels.

MAIN WESTERN GALLERY The way that led to Roland's apartments.

A MINOR STORAGE ROOM The storage room located on the ninth floor, in the west turret of the castle. It was where Sasha's

Original drawing by Kenny Ray Linkous.
First published in the Philtrum Press limited edition of *Eyes of the Dragon*.

dollhouse was found.

THE MOAT The entrance to the castle.

THE NEEDLE The plaza where the king had his coronation.

THE PEDDLERS' GATE The little castle entrance on the south-west side of the Needle.

PLAINS OF LENG The *Book of Spells* was written on the Plains of Leng.

THE PRESERVES King Roland hunted in the preserves.

SEA OF TOMORROW Flagg's destination (as told to Thomas).

THE STOREROOM A half-million napkins and tablecloths were stored there.

THIRD EAST'RD ALLEY The horse surgery was on Third East'rd Alley.

THIRD SOUTH'ARD ALLEY The alley where Anna Crookbrows lived.

THE WEST GATE Peter and the others ran there to escape Flagg and the guards.

WESTERN BARONY The small barony where Queen Sasha came from.

(24)
THE EYES OF THE DRAGON
Things

THE BABY DEATH Crib death; death by smothering.

BARONY FIFTH VAT King Roland's favorite wine.

BEN'S NOTE TO PETER It read:

"Peter – destroy this after you have read it. I don't believe you did it. Others feel the same I am sure. I am still your friend. I love you as I always did. Dennis does not believe it either. If I can ever help get to me through Penya. Let your heart be steadfast."

BENDOH MEN Game pieces. Peter made them for his father. They consisted of twenty men: infantrymen, knights, archers, the fuslier, the general, and the monk.

BONSEY The elk head in King Roland's trophy room

BOOK OF SPELLS A book bound in human skin written on the distant Plains of Leng by a madman named Alhazred.

THE BOOKCASE The mouse and poison planted by Flagg in Peter's room were hidden in Peter's bookcase.

BOWMANSHIP CLASSES Peter competed in them against Lord Towson's son.

BRAIDING Weaving two cables.

BREAKING STRAIN The "breaking strain" was the point where things would break. Josef taught Peter about its principles.

THE CART A cart stolen by Ben, Dennis, and Naomi, and piled with napkins to break Peter's fall.

CHANCELLOR Penya's title during Peter's trial.

CHILDREN'S TATTOO The disease now called chicken pox.

CHURCH OF THE GREAT GODS A Lesser Warder returned to the church and became a priest after hearing Peter call his father.

THE CRYSTAL Flagg's magic crystal, with which he could see the past and the future.

DA' The Delain term for "father."

DEADLY CLAWFOOT A poison which grew in the Dismal Swamp.

DIM The closest Flagg could come to being invisible.

THE DOLLHOUSE LOOM The loom used by Peter to weave a rope with which to escape.

"DRAGON" Roland's last word.

DRAGON SAND Green Sand.

THE FARMER'S LAWN PARTY The yearly ritual where Peter and Ben met.

FOE-HAMMER Roland's father's great arrow. Roland used it to kill Niner the Dragon.

"FOGGY TOM THE CONSTANTLY BOMBED" The name some townsfolk called King Thomas.

FOOLSCAP A sheet of paper found by Peter beneath the loose stone.

"THE GIRL" Naomi, in Frisky's mind.

GOD AND DOG "The two natures of man."

GOLD LOCKET AND CHAIN The two things found by Peter beneath the loose stone.

THE GOSHAWK Leader of the guard.

THE GREAT LETTERS The fifteen letter alphabet of Delain.

THE GREAT OLD TREE It went gray from drought.

GREEN SAND The deadliest poison, it came from the Desert of Grenh.

THE GUARD'S SONG The lyrics were:

"I have a girrul name of Marchy-Marchy-Melda. She's got a sister named Esmeralda…I would sail the seven seas just to kiss her dimply knees. Tootie-sing-tay sing-tiy and pass me a bucket-da-wine."

GUNPOWDER Gunpowder was known in Delain, but it was rare.

THE IRON BALL A spiked ball modified by Flagg. Each spike was dipped in poison.

JUDGE'S RING Penya's ring. It bore Delain's great seal.

KLEFFA CARROT A vegetable. It made up the lock on Flagg's teak box.

LESSER WEST DOOR The entrance used to reach the castle proper.

THE LOOSE STONE The loose floor stone found by Peter on east side of his bedroom floor.

"MY KING" Dennis's salutation to Peter in a note pinned to a napkin.

"THE NAPKIN" A symbolic lesson about the proper use of a napkin, taught to Peter by Sasha.

NINER'S HEART The nine-chambered heart eaten by Roland after he killed the dragon with his father's great arrow, Foe-hammer.

THE NOTE The second note written to Penya from Peter. It was delivered to Penya by Beson. It read:

"Perhaps your request to know my business is presumptuous, perhaps not. It matters little, since I am at your mercy. Here are the two things your eight guilders per years are to purchase:
1. I want to have my mother's dollhouse. It always took me to pleasant places and pleasant adventures, and I loved it much as a boy.
2. I would like to have a napkin brought with my meal – a proper royal napkin. The crest may be removed, if you like.
These are my requests."

OBSIDIAN Flagg's paperweight was made of obsidian.

ONE OF DELAIN'S OLDEST PROVERBS "A man can't outsmart the Gods."

1,825 DAYS The time it took for Peter's beard to grow to the middle of his chest.

POTATOES AND TURNIPS Dennis's sustenance at the deserted farmhouse.

PUCKERSTRING One of King Roland's trophies.

THE QUEST Thomas's mission to find Flagg.

REMISSION OF THE KING'S TAXES This was pleaded for by Queen Sasha.

ROLAND'S CHAIR The chair where Thomas sat unseen by Peter and the others.

SASHA'S DOLLHOUSE Sasha had one as a child. It was built by Quentin Ellender. It had kashamin rugs, velvet curtains, real china plates, a cold cabinet that really kept things cold, a working stove, a working loom, a many-colored fanlight over the front doors, glass in the windows, and a spinet piano that really played.

THE SECRET PASSAGEWAY Flagg used it to spy on the king's chamber. He showed it to Thomas.

THE SEWER OUTFLOW PIPE Dennis used this to gain entrance to the east wing of the castle.

THE SHAKING DISEASE The disease which afflicted the twenty-year-old son of Anna Crookbrows.

STAG POOL One of King Roland's trophies.

"A STRANGE GREEN DRINK" The drink given to Roland by Flagg on the night Sasha conceived Peter.

"THE TALL BOY" Ben, in Frisky's mind.

TEAK BOX The triple-locked box where Flagg kept his poison.

"THOMAS THE LIGHT BRINGER" King Thomas's title.

THREADS Peter removed them from the napkins every day.

THREE HUNDRED FEET The height off the cobblestones of Peter's window in the Needle.

345 FEET The height of the Needle at its peak.

THE THREE HUNDRED STAIRS The stairs to the Needle.

TOM'S BLACK TAX An eighty percent tax increase imposed by King Thomas on the Delain farmers.

"TRIPOS" The password to enter the camp of the Exiles.

TWENTY-ONE NAPKINS Twenty-one napkins were delivered to Peter in the Needle every week.

TWO GUILDERS Beson's fee for delivering Peter's note.

"THE TWO NATURES OF MAN" God and dog. Sasha made Peter write these words on his slate.

A TWO-HEADED PARROT Flagg's pet. It was kept in a cage in Flagg's room. [NOTE: A two-headed parrot named "East-Head, West-Head" also appears in *The Talisman*. See the section on *The Talisman* in this volume.]

VALERA'S PARCHMENT The paper that Peter used to answer Dennis's note. He wrote it in his own blood.

WET LUNG DISEASE An incurable disease of the time.

WOLF-JAW SHAKOS Armament worn by the Home Guards.

WRAPPING The weaving process of making rugs with three cables.

MISERY

DEDICATION

This is for Stephanie and Jim Leonard,
who know why.
Boy, *do* they.

[NO CONTENTS PAGE]

BOOK BREAKDOWN

SUBTITLE:
goddess
africa

PART ONE:
ANNIE

(Thirty-six untitled chapter/sections numbered 1-36]

PART TWO:
MISERY

Chapter 1: "*Misery's Return* By Paul Sheldon"—(One numbered section of typed manuscript)
Chapter 2: (One untitled chapter/section numbered 2)
Chapter 3: (One untitled chapter/section numbered 3)
Chapter 4: (One untitled chapter/section numbered 4)

Chapter 5: (One untitled chapter/section numbered 5)
Chapter 6: "*Misery's Return* By Paul Sheldon"—(Six numbered sections of typed manuscript numbered 1-6)
Chapters 7-23: (Seventeen untitled chapter/sections numbered 7-23)

PART THREE:
PAUL

Chapter 1: "Chapter 32"—(One chapter/section of typed manuscript)
Chapter 2: (One untitled chapter/section numbered 2)
Chapter 3: (One untitled section of typed mansucript continuing the section entitled "Chapter 32")
Chapters 4-27: (Twenty-four untitled chapter/sections numbered 4-27)
Chapter 28: "Chapter 37"—(One chapter/section of hand-written manuscript)
Chapters 29-38: (Ten untitled chapter/sections numbered 29-38)
Chapter 39: (One untitled section of typed and hand-written mansucript)
Chapters 40-48: (Nine untitled chapter/sections numbered 40-48)

PART FOUR:
GODDESS

Chapters 1-10: (Ten untitled chapter/sections numbered 1-10)
Chapter 11: (One untitled section of mansucript done on a word processor)
Chapter 12: (One untitled section numbered 12)

(25)
MISERY
People

ALLIBURTON, GEOFFREY One of the characters in Paul Sheldon's Misery novels, and a friend of Misery and Ian Carmichael. In *Misery's Child*, and *Misery's Return*, Version 1, he went for the doctor when Misery was giving birth to Thomas. In *Misery's Return*, Version 2, his last name was revealed.

ANNIE'S BROTHER Annie's brother Paul. He went with Annie to the movies every Saturday afternoon when they were young and living in Bakersfield, California.

THE BARBER (*Misery's Return*, Version 2) Unnamed gentleman in Storping-on-Firkill who was also the village constable.

BEAULIFANT, HESTER ("QUEENIE") Woman who died under Annie's "care" on March 19, 1969, in St. Joseph's Hospital. She was eighty-four years old.

THE BEE-PEOPLE The name by which the Bourkas tribe were known.

BELL, BRYCE Paul Sheldon's literary agent.

BERNSTEIN A playwright Paul knew in Greenwich Village.

BERRYMAN, CRYSILDA Annie's mother's maiden name.

BILLFORD, DR. (*Misery's Return*, Version 2) Village doctor in Storping-on-Firkill.

BONASARO, TONY The main character in Paul Sheldon's novel *Fast Cars*.

BOOKINGS, DR. (*Misery's Return*, Version 2) The doctor who performed the last rites on Misery.

BOSSIE The dead cow that Annie buried on her land. She later used the cross from Bossie's grave to stab Duane Kushner, the state trooper.

THE BOURKAS Africa's most dangerous natives. They were known as the Bee-People.

CANLEY, DR. FRANK The doctor who admitted Carl Wilkes to the hospital.

CARMICHAEL Misery's marriage name.

CARMICHAEL, IAN (*Misery's Return*, Version 1) Misery Chastain's husband.

CARMICHAEL, THOMAS (*Misery's Return*, Version 1) Ian and Misery's son.

CHASTAIN, MISERY The heroine of Paul Sheldon's "Misery" series.

CHEEVER, JOHN Writer.

COLTER (*Misery's Return*, Version 2) The church sexton who buried Misery, and who went to Geoffrey Alliburton with tales of noises coming from her grave.

"CONSTANT READER" Originally, Paul thought that when it came to his Misery novels, Annie was the perfect embodiment of the Victorian archetype, the Constant Reader. After Annie read Paul's first version of *Misery's Return* (and didn't like it), he thought to himself that "Constant Reader" had become "Merciless Editor."

CORRIGAN, CARELESS A character in a made-up story told at the Malden Community Center.

THE COUNT OF MONTE CRISTO Trooper Wicks told his wife that he thought that when Paul Sheldon was found, he looked like the Count of Monte Cristo.

COX, WALLY, AND BOOM-BOOM MANCINI How Paul thought of the differences in strength between himself and Annie. (Paul was Wally Cox.)

CRANTHORPE, MR. (*Misery's Child*) Geoffrey's horse tripped on the top rail of Cranthorpe's toll-gate, thereby preventing him from fetching a doctor, which led to Misery Chastain's demise in what was supposed to be the final Misery novel, *Misery's Child*. Annie didn't buy that, and so Paul was forced to write *Misery's Return*, in which he brought our plucky heroine back from the dead.

CRONENBERG, DAVID Director of the film "The Brood" (as well as the Stephen King film "The Dead Zone.")

CURIE, MADAME Scientist.

DADDLES, DUCKY Paul thought that the Royal typewriter that Annie bought him would clack and sound like the comic strip character Ducky Daddles.

DARTMONGER, NANCY Woman who ran the Used News store.

"DAVID AND GOLIATH" How Paul thought of the two state troopers who came to Annie's house looking for the missing trooper, Duane Kushner.

"DESIGNATED GAWKERS" The people who came by to look at Annie's house after the incident in which she shot at the KTKA news people. The word had gotten out that the missing cop, Duane Kushner, was at the Dragon Lady's house before he disappeared.

DESMOND, EDDIE The name of the character in Paul's first "post-Annie" novel. The character was inspired by the kid that Paul saw pushing the shopping cart with the skunk in it up 48th Street.

DICKENS, CHARLES (*Misery's Return*, Version 2) Author.

DOYLE, ARTHUR CONAN Author of the Sherlock Holmes stories.

"THE DRAGON LADY" The name with which one newspaper correspondent dubbed Annie Wilkes after she went on trial for the murders at Boulder Hospital.

DUGAN, RALPH Annie's husband. He was a physical therapist.

DUMPSTER The cross-eyed Siamese cat that Paul got at the pound after his rescue from Annie and his recovery.

EILEEN Paul Sheldon's first wife.

EVELYN-HYDE, CHARLOTTE (*Misery's Return*, Version 2) A woman who had been buried alive.

FAVEREY, MR. A teacher in Paul's "Misery" novels.

FITZGERALD, HEMINGWAY, AND FAULKNER Authors who had won Pulitzer Prizes.

FORD, ANGELA Her divorce was announced in the same "Divorces Granted Column" as that of Annie Wilkes and Ralph Dugan.

FORD, JOHN His divorce was announced in the same "Divorces Granted Column" as that of Annie Wilkes and Ralph Dugan.

FOSSINGTON, ALBERT (*Misery's Return*, Version 2) Schoolmate of Ian and Geoffrey. Fossington inherited Oak Hall in Doncaster.

FOWLES, JOHN Author of *The Collector*.

FRAWLEY, KIRSTEN Her divorce was announced in the same "Divorces Granted Column" as that of Annie Wilkes and Ralph Dugan.

FRAWLEY, STANLEY His divorce was announced in the same "Divorces Granted Column" as that of Annie Wilkes and Ralph Dugan.

FREELING, NICHOLAS Author.

FROMSLEY, DUNCAN (*Misery's Return*, Version 2) The man who saw Old Man Patterson two days after his funeral "glowin' just as white as marshfire."

GALSWORTHY Author of *The Forsythe Saga*.

GEORGE Bartender at the Boulderado.

GIRL CHRISTOPHER A one-day-old newborn allegedly murdered by Annie Wilkes.

GOLDING, WILLIAM Author of *Lord of the Flies*.

GONYAR, ERNEST The man who died under Annie's "care" on March 2, 1969, in St. Joseph's Hospital. He was seventy-nine years old.

THE GRATEFUL DEAD Rock music group. [NOTE: Stephen King acknowledged on "The Larry King Show" on April 10, 1986, that he is, in fact, a Deadhead.]

GRAY, LIEUTENANT Character in Paul Sheldon's novel *Fast Cars*. Gray was killed by Tony Bonasaro in a Times Square Movie Theater.

THE GRIM REAPER (*Misery's Return*, Version 1) Death.

THE GRIQUAS (*Misery's Return*, Version 2) The tribe that taught Fossington that each man must eat the thing he loves.

GROWLER Ian's Irish setter.

HAGGARD, H. RIDER Novelist. Author of *She* and *King Solomon's Mines*.

HALE, CHRISTOPHER A book reviewer for the New York *Times*.

HARDY, THOMAS Author of *Jude the Obscure*.

HARVEY, PAUL Radio newscaster.

HAVERSHAM, BILLY The man who put heat tapes in the roof of Annie's barn.

HAWKEYE Surgeon on "M*A*S*H."

HOLMES, SHERLOCK Fictional detective.

HOT LIPS Nurse on "M*A*S*H."

JAN One of the characters in Paul Sheldon's "Misery" novels.

KASPBRAK, MRS. A neighbor of the Sheldons when Paul was a boy. [NOTE: This means that at one point, Paul grew up near Eddie Kaspbrak, our friend from Derry, whose story is told in King's magnum opus, *It*. See the section on *It* in this volume for more info on Eddie and the rest of the Losers.]

THE KID A boy pushing a shopping cart with a skunk in it up 48th Street. Paul saw the kid and it gave him an idea for a new book — his first "post-Annie" novel.

KING KONG At one point, Paul thought that his body looked as though King Kong had used it for a trampoline.

KINSOLVING, TAMARA Boulder, Colorado, sheriff's office spokeswoman.

KIRK, CAPTAIN Captain of the starship Enterprise.

KRENMITZ, ADRIAN Jessica Krenmitz's husband, and the father of Paul, Frederic, Alison, and Laurene. Adrian was killed in an apartment house fire set by Annie Wilkes. He was able to rescue Laurene, but died with the other three children.

KRENMITZ, ALISON One of the Krenmitz "brats." Annie babysat for them when she was a kid, and later set fire to the apartment house in which they lived, killing three of the four children, as well as Irving Thalman. Alison was three years old.

KRENMITZ, FREDERIC One of the Krenmitz "brats." Annie babysat for them when she was a kid, and later set fire to the apartment house in which they lived, killing three of the four children, as well as Irving Thalman. Frederick was six years old.

KRENMITZ, MRS. JESSICA Annie used to babysit for her four "brats" as a child. Annie later set fire to the apartment house in which the Krenmitz family lived, killing three of her four children, as well as Jessica's husband Adrian, who was forty-one years old.

KRENMITZ, LAURENE The only survivor of the apartment house fire that killed three Krenmitz children, as well as their father Adrian. The fire was set by Annie Wilkes.

KRENMITZ, PAUL One of the Krenmitz "brats." Annie babysat for them when she was a kid, and later set fire to the apartment house in which they lived, killing three of the four children, as well as Irving Thalman. Paul was eight years old.

THE KRENMITZ "BRATS" Annie used to babysit for them when she was a child and living in Bakersfield, California. They died in an apartment house fire set by Annie.

KUSHNER, DUANE Colorado state trooper killed by Annie after Paul screamed to him out the bedroom window in an attempt to get his attention. First she stabbed him in the back with a cross she had used to mark Bossie's grave, and then she ran him over with a Lawnboy.

LAZARUS (*Misery's Return*, Version 2) A man brought back from the dead by Jesus.

LEITH, MICHAEL Reporter for the Denver *Post*. He wrote the June 1, 1982, article headlined "Head Maternity Nurse Questioned on Infant Deaths."

LEROUX, FRENCH VISCOUNT (*Misery's Return*, Version 2) The madman who had kidnapped Misery.

MAILER, NORMAN Writer.

MARY (*Misery's Return*, Version 2) Geoffrey Alliburton's horse.

MAUGHAM, SOMERSET Author.

McKIBBON, MR. Friend of Virginia Sandpiper. He owned a squirrel rifle and, at Virginia's request, had shot a hole in the wall by a chair in her "Misery's Parlor" in order for the room to conform perfectly to the description in Paul's novels.

McKNIGHT, TROOPER One of the troopers who came looking for Duane Kushner at Annie's house. Paul Sheldon thought of him as Goliath.

McLAREN, DANNA Her divorce was announced in the same "Divorces Granted Column" as that which announced the divorce of Annie Wilkes and Ralph Dugan.

McLAREN, LEE His divorce was announced in the same "Divorces Granted Column" as that which announced the divorce of Annie Wilkes and Ralph Dugan.

"MERCILESS EDITOR" After Annie read Paul's first version of *Misery's Return* (and didn't like it – she said it was a "cheat" because Paul seemed to be disregarding all that had happened in *Misery's Child*), Paul thought to himself that "Constant Reader" had become "Merciless Editor."

MERRILL, CHARLIE Paul Sheldon's editor at Hastings House.

MILLER, ROGER Singer-singwriter.

MISERY Annie Wilkes's pig.

"MR. CLEAN" How Paul thought of himself while working on *Misery's Return*. He had no more bad habits (except for his "codeine jones," of course), and he was averaging twelve pages a day compared to his previous output of two or three.

"MR. ROCKY MOUNTAIN BUSINESSMAN" The man who brought Annie a back tax bill. He drove a Chevy Bel Air.

MULVANEY, MRS. Neighbor of the Sheldons' when Paul was a child.

"MUTT AND JEFF" How Paul thought of the two state troopers who came to Annie's house looking for missing trooper, Duane Kushner.

THE NATIONAL GUARDSMEN Two chopper-jockeys who accidentally found Paul's car because of the sun flash on his windshield.

NUGENT, TED Rocker.

O'WHUNN, MICHAEL The Centralia fire chief.

THE PAPIST MONK (*Misery's Return*, Version 2) The dead man who walked the battlements of Ridgeheath Manor.

PATTERSON, OLD MAN (*Misery's Return*, Version 2) A man who died and was seen by Duncan Fromsley walking around two days after his funeral, "glowin' just as white as marshfire."

PAVAROTTI, LUCIANO Operatic tenor.

PAVLOV'S DOGS Paul compared himself to the dogs: When Annie walked into his room with a hypo, Betadine, and a sharp cutting object, he automatically screamed.

PETER GUNN Annie Wilkes's and Andrea Saint James's cat. (They shared an apartment together.) Andrea died when she tripped over Peter's dead body and fell down the stairs. Peter's body had somehow been strategically placed on the steps so that Andrea would fall over it. Andrea (and probably Peter) were both victims of Annie Wilkes.

PICASSO Spanish painter.

POMEROY, ANDREW Twenty-three-year-old man found murdered in the Grider Wildlife Preserve. The article about his body being discovered was in Annie's scrapbook. Andrew was another of Annie's victims.

"THE PRISONER OF ZENDA" Trooper Wicks told his wife he thought that when Paul was found, he looked like the Prisoner of Zenda.

THE PRUSSIAN ARMY At one point, Paul thought that he had enough dope in his system to put the Prussian army to sleep.

THE PUERTO RICAN ORDERLY The man initially arrested for the deaths at Boulder Hospital. He was released nine hours after his arrest.

RAMAGE, MRS. (*Misery's Return*, Version 1) The Carmichaels' housekeeper.

REAGAN, RONALD Paul thought of this actor's performance in the movie "King's Row" when he saw his own mangled legs.

THE RED QUEEN A character in *Alice in Wonderland*.

REED, OLIVER The actor who portrayed the mad scientist in the movie "The Brood," directed by David Cronenberg.

ROBERTS, GLENNA News reporter from KTKA.

ROBERTS, TONY Man at the Feed Store in Sidewinder.

ROTHBERG, LAURA D. Woman who died under Annie's "care" on September 21, 1978, in Denver Receiving Hospital. [NOTE: Once again, Stephen King has used his own birthday – September 21 – as a significant date in one of his works of fiction.]

THE ROYDMANS Annie Wilkes's nearest neighbors.

RUDDMAN, GARY A friend of Paul Sheldon's. Gary worked at the Boulder Public Library.

SAINT JAMES, ANDREA USC nursing student who died after tripping over Annie's dead cat, Peter Gunn. Mr. Gunn's body was on the stairs of the apartment that Andrea shared with Annie.

SANDPIPER, MRS. ROMAN D., III World-class Misery fan. She lived in Ink Beach, Florida, and had created "Misery's Parlor" in an upstairs room of her home.

SANDPIPER, VIRGINIA Mrs. Roman D. Sandpiper III.

SEAN (*Misery's Return*, Version 1) Paul Sheldon's original first name for Baby Thomas Carmichael. He decided against Sean because the old Royal typewriter that Annie had gotten for him had a missing "n," and there would have been too many letters to fill in by hand.

SHELDON, MRS. Paul's mother.

SHELDON, PAUL Writer. Author of the "Misery" novels, a series of Gothoic romances. He was also the author of non-genre novels such as *Fast Cars*, the novel he hoped would allow him to break away from having to write formulaic romances. After a drunken car accident in the snow, Paul was "rescued" by his "Number One Fan," Annie Wilkes, a psychotic ex-nurse who kept him prisoner in her home. After she discovered that he had killed off Misery Chastain in his latest Misery novel, she forced him to write a novel for her that would bring Misery back from the dead. She "persuaded" him through a variety of measures involving drug addiction and physical and psychological torture. He eventually escaped after killing Annie, yet her ghost haunted him the rest of his days.

SHINEBONE, DR. (*Misery's Return*, Version 2) The doctor who had taped Geoffrey's ribs after his fall from Mary, his horse. (He had been on his way to fetch a doctor for Misery, who was in labor with her son, Thomas. Geoffrey stayed the night in a ditch and, in *Misery's Child*, Misery (supposedly) died.

SIMEAUX, PAULETTE Woman who died under Annie's "care" in March of 1969 in St. Joseph's Hospital. She was forty-six years old.

SOAMES, MRS. (*Misery's Return*, Version 2) The woman who saw Charlotte Evelyn-Hyde's hand protruding from the earth after she'd been declared dead and subsequently buried.

SWEE'PEA Popeye's nephew.

THE TEENAGERS Designated Gawkers. A carload of teenagers drove by Annie's house and harassed her after the incident in which she shot at the KTKA news people.

TENNIEL, JOHN Author of *Alice in Wonderland*.

THALMAN, IRVING A fifty-eight-year-old bachelor who lived on the top floor of the apartment house in which the Krenmitz family lived. He was killed in the fire set by Annie Wilkes that also claimed the lives of three of the Krenmitz children, as well as their father Adrian.

TOLKIEN, J.R.R Author of *The Lord of the Rings* trilogy.

TWO OLD MEN Two unnamed men who died under Annie's "care" in March of 1969 in St. Joseph's Hospital. They died of "that perennial favorite, Long Illness."

TWYFORD, TOM Ex-cop who had taught Paul how to hot-wire an ignition, and how to use a "slim-jim" to get into cars.

TYLER Geoffrey's butler in the Misery novels.

UNCLE REMUS, BRER RABBIT, AND BRER FOX Characters in the Uncle Remus childrens' books.

VAN DER VALK Fictional detective created by Nicholas Freeling.

WEBSTER, DANIEL Paul told Annie pen and pencil holders were called "Webster Pots" after Daniel Webster. He lied.

WELLINGTON (*Misery's Return*, Version 2) "The Iron Duke." Dr. Shinebone claimed to have shaken hands with him.

WICKERSHAM, MAD JACK (*Misery's Return*, Version 1) A pirate.

WICKS, TROOPER One of the troopers who came looking for Duane Kushner at Annie's house. Paul thought of him as David (of David and Goliath fame.)

WILKES, ANNIE (*Misery's Return*, Version 1) Baby Thomas Carmichael's nurse.

WILKES, ANNIE Ex-nurse, baby-killer, psychotic, and lover of literature. Annie saved Paul's life after his car accident, and then held him captive in her home, forcing him to write a novel in which he brought back from the dead her favorite heroine, Misery Chastain.

WILKES, CARL Annie's father.

WILKES, PAUL EMERY Annie's brother.

WILSON, EDMUND Essayist.

YODER, CHUCKIE The man at the liquor store who told Annie that Dom Perignón was the finest champagne.

(25)
MISERY
Places

AFRICA The setting of the second half of *Misery's Return*.
ANNIE'S LAUGHING PLACE A place in the hills Annie went to

now and then...sometimes to laugh, but mostly to scream. She had taken the name from the Uncle Remus stories, specifically the one in which Brer Rabbit tells Brer Fox about his "Laughing Place." Annie's was upcountry and had a sign over the door that said "Annie's Laughing Place."

APARTMENT 9-E Paul's post-captivity apartment. It was on the east side of Manhattan.

ARAPAHOE COUNTY HOSPITAL The hospital where Ralph Dugan went to work after his marriage to Annie.

BAKERSFIELD, CALIFORNIA The town where Annie and her brother Paul went to the movies every Saturday afternoon.

BAKERSFIELD RECEIVING HOSPITAL The hospital where Paul Wilkes was born.

BOSTON Paul's mother and Mrs. Kaspbrak spent a day in Boston when Paul was a child. Paul used the opportunity to smoke cigarettes.

THE BOSTON ZOO Paul remembered his mother taking him there as a child.

THE BOULDER BANK The bank where Paul cashed a check for $450 before heading out into the snowstorm.

BOULDER HOSPITAL The hospital where Annie got caught murdering her patients. She went on trial for the murders, but was acquitted.

THE BOULDER PUBLIC LIBRARY The library where Gary Ruddman worked.

BOULDERADO A bar. Paul stopped there and tipped George twenty dollars when George sold him a bottle of Dom Perignón.

THE BRONX ZOO Eddie Desmond had been there.

CALTHORPE MANOR (*Misery's Return*, Version 2) Ian and Misery's home.

CANA On his way to Vegas, Paul chose not to stop in Cana.

THE CARMICHAEL HOME (*Misery's Return*, Version 1) The house where Misery and her husband Ian lived.

COLD STREAM HARBOR, NEW YORK Andrew Pomeroy's home town.

COVE O'BIRCHES (*Misery's Return*, Version 2) The name of Charlotte Evelyn-Hyde's home in Storping-on-Firkill.

DEADWOOD A town in a Hollywood western movie.

DENVER, COLORADO The town where Annie stood trial for the alleged Boulder Hospital murders.

DENVER RECEIVING HOSPITAL The first Colorado hospital where Annie Wilkes worked. After Denver Receiving, she moved to Boulder Hospital, where she got caught murdering patients.

DOCTOR'S HOSPITAL IN QUEENS The hospital where Paul spent months recovering after his rescue from Annie's house.

EAST 105TH STREET Location of the tenement where Eddie Desmond found the skunk.

THE FEED STORE Sidewinder business.

48TH STREET The kid pushing the shopping cart with the skunk in it was walking up 48th Street when Paul saw him.

FOSTER FUNERAL HOME The funeral parlor where Hester "Queenie" Beaulifant was viewed.

THE GREAT DIVIDE Sidewinder, Colorado.

THE GRIDER WILDLIFE PRESERVE The area where the body of Andrew Pomeroy was found.

HERNANDEZ GENERAL HOSPITAL The hospital where Carl Wilkes was admitted after having a freak fall.

HUMBUGGY MOUNTAIN When Paul's car went off the road, he went halfway down this mountain.

INK BEACH, FLORIDA This was where Mrs. Roman D. (Virginia) Sandpiper III lived.

THE INSTITUTE OF PSYCHOPLASMATICS The medical institute in the movie "The Brood."

JULESBURG The town where Andrew Pomeroy had been when he called his parents in Cold Stream Harbor, New York. He was later found murdered in the Grider Wildife Preserve. The article about his body being discovered was in Annie's scrapbook.

KILIMANJARO Mountain range in Africa.

KIMBERLY DIAMOND MINES Diamond mines in Africa. If the natives working there got caught stealing diamonds, they were "hobbled."

THE LION'S HEAD A bar on Christopher Street in Greenwich Village.

LITTLE DUNTHORPE One of the locales in Paul Sheldon's Misery novels.

LIVERPOOL, ENGLAND (*Misery's Return*, Version 1) The town where Ian thought Misery had been kidnapped by Mad Jack Wickersham.

LONDON'S BEDLAM HOSPITAL The hospital where much of the first Misery novel had taken place.

MALDEN COMMUNITY CENTER The day-camp that Paul attended as a child.

MARY CYR CEMETERY The cemetery where Hester "Queenie" Beaulifant was interred.

MAUI Paul and his first wife had honeymooned there.

MERCY HOSPITAL The hospital where Andrea Saint James's body was brought after she tripped over Peter Gunn and died.

MR. LEE'S The restaurant where Paul had lunch with Charlie Merrill after Paul recovered from his captivity.

NEDERLAND A small town west of Boulder, Colorado.

NEW YORK The city where Paul Sheldon lived.

OAK HALL, DONCASTER (*Misery's Return*, Version 2) Ian and Geoffrey went there for a week of grouse shooting and card playing.

THE OVERLOOK HOTEL Hotel in Colorado. Andrew Pomeroy had told Annie that he was doing an article about the hotel for a magazine. [NOTE: See the section on *The Shining* in this volume for more information on the Overlook.]

THE PAPER PATCH The store where Annie bought the Corrassable Bond paper for Paul.

REICHENBACK FALLS This was where Arthur Conan Doyle killed off Sherlock Holmes.

REVERE BEACH Paul Sheldon's parents took him to this beach as a child. Revere Beach was where Paul first saw the piling that "looked to him like the single jutting fang of a buried monster."

RIDGEHEATH MANOR (*Misery's Return*, Version 2) The castle supposedly haunted by the shade of a Papist Monk.

RIVERVIEW HOSPITAL The hospital in Harrisburg, Pennsylvania, to which Annie moved after her stint at St. Joseph's.

ST. JOSEPH'S HOSPITAL Annie Wilkes's first hospital assignment after her graduation from nursing school.

SANGRE DE CRISTOS, NEW MEXICO The storm that creamed Paul Sheldon was supposed to have veered off into New Mexico.

SIDEWINDER, COLORADO Sidewinder was the town where Paul had the auto accident that resulted in him becoming Annie Wilkes's prisoner.

SOUTH AMERICA Careless Corrigan once got lost in the jungles of South America.

SPANISH HARLEM Hispanic neighborhood in New York.

SPRINGER ROAD When "David and Goliath" came looking for Duane Kushner, Annie told them she thought he had headed towards Springer Road.

STEAMBOAT HEAVEN A town thirty-five miles from Annie's house.

STORPING-ON-FIRKILL (*Misery's Return*, Version 2) Charlotte Evelyn-Hyde's village.

USED NEWS The store where Annie bought Paul the used Royal typewriter.

"VEGAS, RENO, AND THE CITY OF THE ANGELS" Where Paul was headed when he had his car accident.

WATCH HILL AVENUE The street on which the Krenmitz family lived in an apartment house.

WILSON'S DRUG CENTER A store in town where Annie usually bought her paperback books.

(25)
MISERY
Things

AN AMERICAN BOOK AWARD After completing the manuscript, Paul thought that *Fast Cars* – his latest "non-Misery" novel – just might win him the American Book Award.

ANNIE'S ARREARS While Paul was writing *Misery's Return*, the tax man visited the Wilkes farm. Annie owed $506.17 in back property taxes. She had until March 25 to pay up.

ANNIE'S DRUG STASH Paul found boxes of drugs on the floor of Annie's linen closet. Companies represented included Upjohn, Lilly, and Cam Pharmaceuticals. Some of the drugs Annie had included Motrim [sic], Lopressor, Darvon, Darvocet, Darvon Compound, Morphose, Morphose Complex, Librium, Valium, and, of course, Novril.

ANNIE'S HOUSEKEEPING When Paul went into Annie's kitchen after Annie left to go to her Laughing Place, he found the room in a filthy state: Smeared and caked all over the place were ice cream, cake crumbs, pie, Jell-O, Pepsi, and custard pudding.

ANNIE'S JOB HISTORY After graduating from nursing school, Annie went from New Hampshire (St. Joseph's Hospital) to Harrisburg (Riverview Hospital) to Pittsburgh to Duluth to Fargo and finally to Denver in 1978.

ANNIE'S PANTRY Some of the things Paul found in Annie's pantry included sardines, deviled ham, Sun-Maid raisins, corn flakes, Wheaties, and Slim-Jims.

ANNIE'S SUNDAES After amputating his foot, Annie made herself and Paul sundaes with vanilla ice cream, Hershey's chocolate syrup, Reddi-Wip, and maraschino cherries.

ANNIE-ISMS "Didoes," "Poop," "Cockadoodie," "Kaka," "Kaka-Poopie-Doopie," "Mister Smart Guy," "Dirty Birdie," "Rooty Patooties," "Oogy," "Poopie Doopie," "Do-Bees," "Don't Bees," and "Mister Man."

APRIL 1, 1943 Annie Wilkes's date of birth.

APRIL FOOL'S DAY The day Paul sent out copies of his privately printed story, "Misery's Hobby." [NOTE: See the entry "Misery's Hobby."]

ARC DE TRIOMPHE The picture in Paul's room at Annie's house.

"ART CONSISTS OF THE PERSISTENCE OF MEMORY." Paul couldn't remember who said this: Thomas Szasz, William Faulkner, or Cyndi Lauper.

"AUG 43RD 1889 FUCK YOU!" Annie wrote this at the bottom of the "Divorces Granted" column in the Nederland paper after her divorce from Ralph Dugan was announced.

"BAMBI" The first movie that Paul ever saw as a child.

BELUGA CAVIAR The caviar Annie bought to celebrate the completion of *Misery's Return*.

BERNZ-O-MATIC The torch Annie used to cauterize Paul's stump after she "hobbled" him by amputating his foot.

BEROL BLACK WARRIOR The pencils Paul used to complete *Misery's Return*.

BETADINE The solution Annie used to sterilize Paul's foot and ankle before she amputated the foot with an axe. Annie always was one for sterile procedures.

A BIBLE Annie Wilkes had her mother's.

A BO DIDDLEY TAPE A cassette in Paul's car.

A BOBBY PIN Paul picked one up off the floor in his room in Annie's house.

THE BOULDER, COLORADO, *CAMERA* The newspaper that ran the "New Arrivals" article announcing Annie's arrival at Boulder Hospital.

"THE BROOD" A film by David Cronenberg.

"CAN YOU?" A game played at the Malden Community Center. A counselor would start a story and ask the children "Can you..." finish the story?

CERAMIC PENGUIN A figurine in Annie's parlor. It stood on a block of ceramic ice that had the inscription "Now my tale is told."

CHAPTER 38 OF *MISERY'S CHILD* Annie reminded Paul that Geoffrey rode for the doctor in Chapter 38 of *Misery's Child,* and ended up tripping his horse on the top rail of Mr. Cranthorpe's toll-gate. Geoffrey spent the night in the rain, and the doctor never came. When Paul recapped the incident in his first version of *Misery's Return*, he had the doctor arrive just in time to save Misery and her child. Annie refused to accept this, and insisted that Paul change it – she said it was a "cheat."

CHEVY BEL AIR The car driven by the man who brought Annie her back tax bill.

CHOPIN (*Misery's Return*, Version 1) The music playing in the Carmichael Home.

CLOUGH & POOR BOOZIERS (*Misery's Return*, Version 2) The label on a bottle of gin at Mrs. Ramage's party.

C-O-D-E-I-N-E How Paul spelled Novril.

"COLORADO BARBECUE AND THE FLOOR BUCKET SCHOOL OF THOUGHT" Two new critical modes of literary interpretation Paul invented while held in Annie's captivity.

A COLORADO STATE POLICE CAR The car that pulled into Annie's driveway after she had amputated Paul's left thumb.

THE CONVERSATION Paul remembered a conversation he had had with Bernstein the playwright in the Lion's Head Bar. They had discussed Jews, the Holocaust, and Germany.

A COPY After his "rescue" by Annie Wilkes, and her subsequent burning of his manuscript of *Fast Cars*, Paul realized that he should have made a copy of the novel.

CORRASSABLE BOND Annie bought Paul this kind of typing paper. She wanted him to use it to write a new Misery novel called *Misery's Return*.

"DEATH IN THE SKY" The sixth chapter of the "Rocket Man" serial.

DECEMBER 16, 1982 The day the banner headline ran that announced "DRAGON LADY INNOCENT." Annie had been acquitted of the murders at Boulder Hospital.

DECEMBER 13, 1982 The day Annie's case went to the jury.

DIAMOND BLUE TIP MATCHES The matches Annie made Paul use to burn his *Fast Cars* manuscript.

"DIVORCES GRANTED COLUMN" The column in a Nederland paper that announced Ralph Dugan and Annie Wilkes's divorce. Grounds: Mental cruelty. Other divorces announced in the same column included Angela Ford from John Ford; Kirsten Frawley from Stanley Frawley; and Danna McLaren from Lee McClaren.

DOM PERIGNON Champagne. Paul was drunk on it when he drove off into the mountains during a snowstorm. Also, Annie bought champagne to celebrate Paul's completion of *Misery's Return*.

"THE DRAGON FLIES" Chapter 11 of the "Rocket Man" serial.

"THE DRAGON LADY" The name that one newspaper correspondent gave Annie Wilkes after she went on trial for the murders at Boulder Hospital.

"DUGAN-WILKES NUPTIALS" The headline of the clipping that announced Annie Wilkes and Ralph Dugan's wedding.

THE EISENHOWER TUNNEL Before his accident, somewhere east of this tunnel, Paul had diverted off I-70 because of the snowstorm.

ELMER'S GLUE In his mind, Paul saw Annie squeezing Elmer's glue into the hole of the telephone modular plug, and then replacing the telephone jack for it to harden and freeze.

EUSTICE PUBLIC WORKS DEPARTMENT The sanding crew that helped dig Annie out of a snowbank.

FAST CARS The novel Paul Sheldon thought would win him the American Book Award, and allow him to break away from the "Misery" series. He had just finished it when he decided to drive off into the mountains during a snowstorm with the only copy of the manuscript.

FEBRUARY At one point, Paul saw that the calendar in Annie's house said February, but he was sure it was early March.

FEBRUARY 1983 The month and year that the district attorney's office announced that the case against Annie Wilkes was closed.

FISHER Annie's plow.

FLAIR FINE-LINER Paul's pen.

FORD STATION WAGON The car driven by the KTKA news people who came to interview Annie.

GINSU KNIVES A commercial on Annie's TV.

"GIRLS JUST WANT TO HAVE FUN" Song by Cyndi Lauper.

"THE GURNEY" The in-house newspaper of Denver Receiving Hospital.

HAMMERMILL BOND The typing paper Paul used for his *Fast Cars* manuscript.

HAMMERMILL BOND OR TRIAD MODERN Paul told Annie to get him two reams of either of these typing papers.

A "HART FOR PRESIDENT" BUMPERSTICKER Paul had one on his car.

HASTINGS HOUSE The publishers of *Misery's Return*.

"HEAD MATERNITY NURSE QUESTIONED ON INFANT DEATHS" The headline of the article by Michael Leith in the Denver *Post*.

THE HERALD The Harrisburg, Pennsylvania, newspaper that ran an article entitled "New Hospital Staff Announced." Annie Wilkes was one of the new members of the staff.

"HOBBLING" The amputation of one foot. Annie did it to Paul after she discovered that he had been roaming around, apparently trying to escape from her.

"THE HORROR CONTINUES: THREE MORE INFANT DEATHS IN BOULDER HOSPITAL" The headline of a story that ran on July 2, 1982, in the *Rocky Mountain News*.

A HUDSON The car that Rocket Man was trapped in in Chapter 6 of the serial.

IACOCCA Charlie Merrill told Paul that a nonfiction account of his captivity would outsell the book *Iacocca*.

AN ICBM Paul said that writing a book was a little like firing an ICBM, only it travelled over time instead of space.

"IN MISERY? NOT THE DRAGON LADY." Caption beneath the photo of Annie reading *Misery's Quest* in her cell while awaiting the jury's verdict in her murder trial.

IV Annie fed Paul intravenously after his accident.

JANUARY 14, 1982 The day the Boulder *Camera* ran the headline that read "New Head Maternity Ward Nurse Named."

JANUARY 2, 1979 The day Annie Wilkes and Ralph Dugan were married.

JANUARY 29, 1982 The day the nursery deaths at Boulder Hospital began.

JEEP CHEROKEE Annie's vehicle.

JELL-O Annie promised Paul some Jell-O because he had been such a good boy. He had readily acquiesced to write *Misery's Return*.

JULY 19, 1982 The day that both the Denver *Post* and the *Rocky Mountain News* announced Annie's arrest for the murders at Boulder Hospital.

JULY 19, 1957 The date of Carl Wilkes's obituary.

JUNE 15, 1981 One of the dates on which a patient died at Boulder Hospital while under Annie's care. This patient was listed as dying from a short illness.

JUNE 1, 1982 The day the Denver *Post* ran the article by Michael Leith headlined "Head Maternity Nurse Questioned on Infant Deaths."

JUNE 9, 1981 One of the dates on which a patient died at Boulder Hospital while under Annie's care. This patient was listed as dying from a short illness.

JUNE 16, 1981 One of the dates on which a patient died at Boulder Hospital while under Annie's care. This patient was listed as dying from a short illness.

"THE JUNKIE'S REVENGE" How Paul referred to his withdrawal from Novril when Annie was once gone for fifty-one hours.

"KEEP YOUR BEACH CLEAN" The sign stencilled on the side of a trash drum on Revere Beach.

KEFLEX AND AMPICILLAN The antibiotics that Annie gave Paul to lower his "post-thumbectomy" fever.

"KING'S ROW" Ronald Reagan film Paul thought of when he saw his mangled legs.

KLEENEX When Annie went to her Laughing Place, Paul wrapped the pills he had cached under his mattress in a Kleenex. Also, Annie occasionally used Kleenex to wipe Paul's forehead.

KREIGS The locks on Annie's doors. Paul knew they were the best in the world.

THE LEFT FOOT Annie Wilkes amputated Paul Sheldon's left foot at the ankle with an axe. She then cauterized the stump with a blowtorch.

THE LONDON PSYCHIC SOCIETY (*Misery's Return*, Version 2) Ladies from this organization were sent to Ridgeheath Manor to check out the stories of a dead monk walking the battlements.

LORD BUXTON Paul Sheldon's wallet.

LORD OF THE FLIES A book by William Golding that Paul had read at the age of twelve.

LORELEI The schooner that Ian and Geoffrey were outfitting in Southhampton for their journey into the Dark Continent in *Misery's Return*.

MARCH 18, 1979 The day Annie and Ralph closed on their house.

MARCH 19, 1981 The date that the Boulder *Camera* ran the "New Arrivals" article announcing Annie's position at the Boulder Hospital.

MARCH 19, 1969 The day that Hester "Queenie" Beaulifant died.

MARCH 2, 1969 The day that Ernest Gonyar died.

MARCH 3, 1979 The date Annie and Ralph commited to buying their house. In Annie's scrapbook, beneath a picture of the house, Annie wrote "Earnest money paid March 3rd, 1979. Papers passed March 18th, 1979."

MARCH 25 The date Annie's back taxes were due.

MARLBORO Paul's one cigarette after completing a book was always a Marlboro.

THE MASKED AVENGER, FLASH GORDON, AND FRANK BUCK These were serials Annie saw in the theater as a child.

MAY 14, 1981 One of the dates on which a patient died at Boulder Hospital while under Annie's care. This patient was listed as dying from a long illness.

MAY 17, 1966 The day Annie graduated from nursing school.

MAY 10, 1981 One of the dates on which a patient died at Boulder Hospital while under Annie's care. This patient was listed as dying from a long illness.

MAY 12, 1939 Paul Wilkes's date of birth.

MAY 23, 1981 One of the dates on which a patient died at Boulder Hospital while under Annie's care. This patient was listed as dying from a long illness.

"MEMORY LANE" The inscription on Annie's scrapbook.

A MICKEY MOUSE LOCK Paul thought of the lock on his bedroom door in Annie's house as ineffective.

THE MISERY CHASTAIN FAN CLUB This club was made up of fans of Paul's fictional creation, Misery Chastain.

MISERY'S CHILD Paul Sheldon's last "Misery" novel before he was forced to write *Misery's Return*.

THE MISERY CONCORDANCE Paul's guide to all the characters and places in his "Misery" novels. Annie wasn't interested in hearing about it.

MISERY'S COUCH One of the items in Virginia Sandpiper's "Misery's Parlor."

MISERY'S EPITAPH (*Misery's Return*, Version 2) Written on Misery's tombstone was "Lady Calthorpe," her dates of birth and death, and then the inscription "Loved By Many."

MISERY'S ESCRITOIRE One of the items in Virginia Sandpiper's "Misery's Parlor."

"MISERY'S HOBBY" A short story by Paul Sheldon. On April Fool's Day four years prior to his accident, Paul had had the story privately printed and sent out to a dozen close acquaintances. In the story, "Misery spent a cheerful country weekend boffing

Growler, Ian's Irish setter."

MISERY'S PARLOR A room in the home of Virginia Sandpiper. She was a huge fan of Paul's "Misery" novels, and had turned one of the upstairs rooms of her home into "Misery's Parlor." She had sent Paul Polaroids of Misery's spinning wheel, Misery's escritoire, a half-completed bread and butter note to Mr. Favery, Misery's couch, and Misery's sampler.

MISERY'S QUEST One of Paul Sheldon's "Misery" novels. Annie was seen reading it in her cell while awaiting the jury's verdict in her murder case.

MISERY'S RETURN The novel Paul wrote for Annie Wilkes in which he brought back Misery Chastain from the dead.

MISERY'S SAMPLER One of the items in Virginia Sandpiper's "Misery's Parlor." It said "Let Love Instruct You; Do Not Presume To Instruct Love."

MISERY'S SPINNING WHEEL One of the items in Virginia Sandpiper's "Misery's Parlor."

"NANCY WHOREMONGER" Annie thought that Nancy Dartmonger should be called "Nancy Whoremonger" instead.

"NEW HEAD MATERNITY WARD NURSE NAMED" The headline in the January 14, 1982, Boulder *Camera* announcing Annie's new position.

THE NEW YORK MARATHON In Annie's twisted mind, Paul was ready to run the New York Marathon, therefore, he needed to be "hobbled."

NEWSWEEK The magazine that ran a piece in its "Transitions" column about Paul Sheldon being reported missing by his agent Bryce Bell.

"NOT TO BE DISPENSED WITHOUT PHYSICIAN'S PRESCRIPTION" The legend written on one of Annie's sample bottles of Novril.

NOVEMBER 19, 1984 The day that an article about Andrew Pomeroy's murder ran in the Sidewinder *Gazette*.

NOVRIL Codeine-based painkiller that Annie used on Paul Sheldon. He quickly became addicted to it.

"NOW MY TALE IS TOLD" The inscription on a block of ceramic ice (on which stood a ceramic penguin) in Annie's parlor. This is also the final epigraph to the novel Misery.

O-CEDAR MOP Paul considered using the mop to open Annie's medicine chest.

OCTOBER 15, 1984 The day Andrew Pomeroy had called his parents in New York from Julesburg.

OCTOBER 1969 The month that another death took place at St. Joseph's Hospital. (It was during Annie's period of employment at the hospital, and the death notice was in Annie's "Memory Lane" scrapbook.)

OCTOBER 28, 1954 The date of the apartment house fire set by Annie that claimed the lives of three of the Krenmitz "brats," their father, and bachelor Irving Thalman.

OLD BESSIE Annie's car.

190,000 WORDS The word count of Paul Sheldon's novel *Fast Cars*.

100.7 Paul's temperature after his thumbectomy.

"PEN" CARD Paul Sheldon had one in his wallet.

PEOPLE, US, AND PERSONALITY PARADE Magazines that had ran articles about Paul Sheldon.

PEPSI Annie left Paul three bottles of Pepsi when she locked him in the cellar.

PLEDGE AND ENDUST The rag that Annie stuffed into Paul's mouth tasted and smelled like Pledge and Endust.

A PRE-OP SHOT Before amputating Paul's foot, Annie gave him a pre-op shot.

RED DEVIL CONDOM On his fourteenth birthday, Paul's father had given him a Red Devil condom, and told him to keep it in his wallet because there were "[t]oo many bastards in the world already and I don't want to see you going in the Army at sixteen."

THE REFRIGERATOR MAGNETS Annie had the following magnets on her refrigerator doors: candy, bubble gum, a Hershey's chocolate bar, and a Tootsie Roll.

"REPORTED MISSING" The headline that ran in the "Transitions" column about Paul Sheldon in *Newsweek*. The piece said:

> "REPORTED MISSING: Paul Sheldon, 42, novelist best known for his series of romances about sexy, bubble headed, unsinkable Misery Chastain; by his agent, Bryce Bell. 'I think he's fine,' Bell said, 'but I wish he'd get in touch and ease my mind. And his ex-wives wish he'd get in touch and ease their bank accounts.' Sheldon was last seen seven weeks ago in Boulder, Colorado, where he had gone to finish a new novel."

RITZ CRACKERS, SARDINES, AND A BED PAN The things Annie left for Paul in the cellar (in addition to the Pepsi) when she drove state trooper Duane Kushner's car to the Laughing Place.

"ROCKET MAN" Annie's favorite chapter-play as a child.

ROCKY MOUNTAIN NEWS The newspaper that ran a front page story on July 2, 1982, headlined "The Horror Continues: Three More Infant Deaths in Boulder Hospital." This was also the newspaper that ran Laura D. Rothberg's obituary, as well as the announcement of Annie's marriage to Ralph Dugan.

R-O-L-A-I-D-S Paul knew that this was how you spelled relief, but that C-O-D-E-I-N-E was how you spelled Novril.

RONSON FAST-LITE Charcoal lighter fluid.

ROYAL NAVIGATION CHARTS (*Misery's Return*, Version 2) Fossington said that the Griquas could carry all twelve volumes of the charts on their lower lips.

SEPTEMBER 1969 The month that another death took place at St. Joseph's Hospital. (It was during Annie's period of employment at the hospital, and the death notice was in Annie's "Memory Lane" scrapbook.)

SEPTEMBER 9, 1982 The day that Annie went on trial for the murder of Girl Christopher, a one-day old newborn, and on seven other counts of first-degree murder.

SEPTEMBER 21, 1978 The day Laura D. Rothberg died in Denver Receiving Hospital while under Annie Wilkes's "care." [NOTE: September 21 is Stephen King's birthday.]

SEVENTY-FIVE DOLLARS The amount Annie paid for the Dom Perignón that she bought to celebrate the completion of *Misery's Return*.

'74 CAMARO Paul Sheldon's car. It was wrecked in the accident.

"SOUVENIR OF HANNIBAL, MISSOURI – HOME OF AMERICA'S STORY TELLER" The legend written on the ashtray that Annie brought to Paul for his "completing a book" Marlboro cigarette.

$10 MILLION Charlie Merrill believed he could set the floor at $10 million for a nonfiction account of Paul's captivity, and then conduct "one hell of an auction."

THE THUMBECTOMY When Paul complained about the missing "n" on the Royal typewriter, Annie decided he needed something to take his mind off the missing letter. So she cut off his left thumb with an electric carving knife, and later that evening used the thumb as a candle on a cake for Paul.

THE UNION-LEADER The newspaper that reported the deaths at St. Joseph's Hospital.

"USA TODAY" AND "ENTERTAINMENT TONIGHT" Paul thought that the Royal typewriter that Annie bought him was made before these TV shows were on the air.

A VICTOR RAT TRAP The trap Annie used to catch rats.

A WEBSTER POT What Paul called his pen and pencil holder.

"WILKES RELEASED, MUM ON INTERROGATION" The follow-up headline in the Denver *Post* that ran after the story about Annie being questioned for the infant deaths at Boulder Hospital.

"WILKES-BERRYMAN NUPTIALS" The newspaper article that was the first item in Annie's "Memory Lane" scrapbook. (It announced the wedding of her parents.)

"WKRP IN CINCINATTI" TV show that Paul heard playing in Annie's parlor.

THE WORLD ACCORDING TO GARP A book Paul read in 1983.

THE WORLD'S BIGGEST FLEA MARKET A week-long affair in Steamboat Heaven.

A WRITERS' GUILD CARD Paul Sheldon had one in his wallet.

THE TOMMYKNOCKERS

DEDICATION

FOR TABITHA KING

...promises to keep."

[NO CONTENTS PAGE]

BOOK BREAKDOWN

Author's Note & Acknowledgements—(Untitled section consisting of eight untitled and unnumbered paragraphs, signed "Stephen King")

BOOK ONE
The Ship in the Earth

Chapter 1: ANDERSON STUMBLES—(Five untitled sections numbered 1-5)

Chapter 2: ANDERSON DIGS—(Five untitled sections numbered 1-5)

Chapter 3: PETER SEES THE LIGHT—(Six untitled sections numbered 1-6)

Chapter 4: THE DIG, CONTINUED—(Three untitled sections numbered 1-3)

Chapter 5: GARDENER TAKES A FALL—(Seven untitled sections numbered 1-7)

Chapter 6: GARDENER ON THE ROCKS—(Three untitled sections numbered 1-3)

Chapter 7: GARDENER ARRIVES—(Five untitled sections numbered 1-5)

Chapter 8: MODIFICATIONS—(Nine untitled sections numbered 1-9)

Chapter 9: ANDERSON SPINS A TALE—(Nine untitled sections numbered 1-9)

Chapter 10: GARDENER DECIDES—(Thirteen untitled sections numbered 1-13)

BOOK TWO
Tales of Haven

Chapter 1: THE TOWN—(Four untitled sections numbered 1-4)

Chapter 2: 'BECKA PAULSON—(Five untitled sections numbered 1-5)

Chapter 3: HILLY BROWN—(Ten untitled sections numbered 1-10)

Chapter 4: BENT AND JINGLES—(Three untitled sections numbered 1-3)

Chapter 5: RUTH McCAUSLAND—(Twelve untitled sections numbered 1-12)

Chapter 6: RUTH McCAUSLAND CONCLUDED—(Seventeen untitled sections numbered 1-17)

Chapter 7: BEACH JERNIGAN AND DICK ALLISON—(Nine untitled sections numbered 1-9)

(26)
THE TOMMYKNOCKERS
People

THE AIDE The unnamed representative that Congressman Brennan sent to Ruth McCausland's funeral.

ALDEN, MRS. Dr. Etheridge's assistant at the Augusta Veterinary Clinic.

ALFIE John Leandro's cousin.

ALLISON, DICK Chief of Haven's volunteer fire department. Dick attended Ruth McCausland's funeral.

AMBERSON, HENRY Newport forest ranger who died in the fire at Big Injun Woods.

ANDERSON, ANNE Bobbi's sister. Peter and Gard hated her, Bobbi feared her. She was abrasive, mean, cruel, and foulmouthed. She took amphetamines, masturbated with a vibrator, and had the ability to bring clerks, waiters, and other functionaries to tears within minutes. She ended up in the Shed.

ANDERSON, BOBBI Haven resident, author of westerns, friend of Jim Gardener, and the woman who discovered the ship in the earth.

ANDERSON, MR. Bobbi and Anne's father. He died of a stroke.

ANDERSON, PAULA Bobbi and Anne's mother.

ANDERSON, POUL Author of *Brain Wave*.

ANDERSON, VERA Woman who lived in Derry. Vera was Mary Jacklin's best friend.

THE ANDERSONS Haven residents who appeared to Ruth McCausland in a dream, "staring up at the sky, their faces rotted swampfire green."

ANDREWS, POLEY A guy who worked at Cooder's Market. He sold Bobbi every battery he had during Bobbi's "Historic Battery Run of 1988."

ANNABELLE The woman who accompanied Congressman Brennan's aide to Maine for Ruth McCausland's funeral.

ANNMARIE Gard's girlfriend when he was seventeen. At the time, she was also seventeen, and was with him when he had his skiing accident at Victory Mountain in Vermont.

THE ANTHROPOLOGISTS The two unnamed white men who were present at Chief Atlantic's death. They were looking for Indian artifacts.

APPLEGATE, BARNEY A boy at Hilly Brown's ninth birthday party; probably Henry's son. Barney got hurt when Hilly broke a coffee cup.

APPLEGATE, HENRY Henry was one of the men that Ruth McCausland enlisted to look for David Brown.

THE APPLEGATES They attended Ruth McCausland's funeral.

ARBERG Assistant professor of English at Northeastern. He led the poetry reading at the school on June 25. Gard got into an argument with him over nuclear power, and ended up slamming him in the chest with his left elbow. When Arberg (who Gard called "Arglebargle") complained he was having a heart attack, Gard said he was surprised Arberg even had a heart. Arberg was the kind of guy Jim's father used to call a "beefy sonofawhore."

ARCHINBOURG, KYLE Haven man.

THE ARCHINBOURGS They attended Ruth McCausland's funeral.

"ARGLEBARGLE" The name Gard called Arberg, the assistant professor of English at Northeastern.

ATLANTIC, CHIEF He died in the Big Injun Woods.

AUDEN, W.H. Poet.

THE AVIS CLERK Girl brought to tears by Anne Anderson.

BAILEY, PETER Private pilot whose plane exploded in Ezra Dockery's north field. Bailey flew a Cessna Hawk XP, and was a neurosurgeon.

BARFIELD, DUKE Haven resident. In 1900, Duke would have won the "Stinkiest Man in Town" contest. ("He smelled like a pickled egg that has spent a month in a mud puddle.") Duke said that Preacher Colson packed a "six-shooter" in his pants. [NOTE: See the entry BRADLEY COLSON for more information on the preacher's "six-shooter."]

BARFIELD, "PITS" A card-weasel.

BARKER, ANDY Elt Barker's brother.

BARKER, ELT The guy who took care of inspecting vehicles at the Shell station. Elt wouldn't slap an inspection sticker on Bobbi's truck when it was still a Country Squire station wagon. Delbert Cullum worked for Elt.

THE BARTENDER Unnamed needy post-graduate student who manned the bar at the reception following Gard's poetry reading at Northeastern University.

THE BARTENDER Unnamed bartender at the Big Lost Weekend Bar and Grille. He called Bobbi "purty lady."

BEAVER The kid in the Eddie Parker Band who rode in the shotgun seat of the Dodge van.

THE BELLMAN Alhambra employee who gave Gard the bum's rush because he didn't have any shoes on.

BERGEN, EDGAR Ventriloquist.

BERRINGER, RICKY House painter in Bangor. Ricky was the younger brother of Newt Berringer.

BERRINGER, NEWT Haven town selectman. Newt attended Ruth McCausland's funeral.

BETTY Paula Anderson's sister; Bobbi and Anne's aunt.

A BLACKSNAKE Unnamed snake owned by the little girl in Dr. Etheridge's waiting room at the Augusta Veterinary Clinic.

BLACKY Cat owned by a woman in Dr. Etheridge's waiting room at the Augusta Veterinary Clinic.

BLUE, DON Derry realtor.

BOBBI'S GRANDFATHER He had died of cancer in February of 1972. At one point during the dig, Bobbi heard her grandfather's voice saying "Leave it alone, Bobbi. It's dangerous."

BOK, HANNES Artist who once drew covers for *Startling Stories* magazine.

BOND, JAMES 007.

BORNS, DR. Bobbi thought that Dr. Borns from the university would go batshit over the ship in the earth.

THE BOXER A dog in Dr. Etheridge's waiting room at the Augusta Veterinary Clinic. It was owned by a man in blue mechanic's overalls. The boxer had his right foreleg in a cast.

BOZEMAN, ANDY Haven's only realtor.

BOZEMAN, IDA Andy's wife. The Tommyknockers taught her how to build a molecule-exciter. She used it to blow up Bobbi's farmhouse.

BRENNAN, CONGRESSMAN Ruth McCausland worked hard for him when he ran for office.

BRIGHT, DAVID Reporter for the Bangor *Daily News*.

BRODKSY The Paulsons' nearest neighbor.

BROOKLINE, HESTER She went to Derry with Tommy Jacklin to buy twenty car batteries.

BROWN, BRYANT Marie's husband, and Hilly and David's father.

BROWN, DAVID JONATHAN Hilly Brown's younger brother. During a backyard magic show, Hilly sent David to Altair-4.

BROWN, HILLY (HILLMAN) A ten-year-old amateur magician. He sent his brother David to Altair-4.

BROWN, MARIE HILLMAN Hilly and David's mother.

THE BROWNS Haven residents who appeared to Ruth Mc-Causland in a dream, "staring up at the sky, their faces rotted swampfire green."

BUCK, HANK Man who worked at Paul's Down-East SuperMart. One day, Hank put half a box of Ex-Lax in his boss's McDonald's chocolate shake. (He hated the guy.) The 3-D Jesus on 'Becka Paulson's TV told her all about it. Also, Hank almost had a fight with Jud Tarkington before they found that Ruth McCausland had collapsed while looking for David Brown.

CAGNEY, JIMMY Buck Peters could imitiate Cagney's voice.

CANDI Naked girl in an issue of *Gallery* read by Al Barfield.

CAPA, ROBERT Famous reporter.

CHIEF JUSTICE JOHN MARSHALL'S DAUGHTER Ruth McCausland had one of her dolls.

CHILES, DELBERT The only plumber in the Haven area. He was unpleasant.

CHIP McCAUSLAND'S COMMON-LAW WIFE Unnamed woman who lived with Chip on Dugout Road.

CHUCK A dead woodchuck Bobbi found on the way to the dig. There were no flies on Chuck.

CLARENDON, FAITH She gave birth to a boy on March 29, 1901. Preacher Colson was the father. Cora Simard was the midwife. Faith's husband, Paul, cut the baby's throat, then Faith's, then his own. Irwin Simard found the bodies.

CLARENDON, PAUL Faith's husband. Faith gave birth to a boy on March 29, 1901. Preacher Colson was the father. Cora Simard was the midwife. Paul cut the baby's throat, then his wife's, then his own. Irwin Simard found the bodies.

THE CLARENDON BABY Faith Clarendon gave birth to a boy on March 29, 1901. Preacher Colson was the father. Cora Simard was the midwife. Paul Clarendon cut the baby's throat, then his wife's, then his own. Irwin Simard found the bodies.

THE CLARENDONS Haven residents who appeared to Ruth McCausland in a dream, "staring up at the sky, their faces rotted swampfire green."

CLAUGHTSWORTH, BILL Poet who hung himself "just like Phil Ochs." Bill's spot on the New England Poetry Caravan then went to Jim Gardener.

COLSON, BRADLEY A preacher who came to Haven in 1900. His real name was Cooder, and he was the illegitimate son of Albion Cooder. On September 7, 1900, at the Great Harvest Home Revival of 1900, the preacher impregnated six local girls. Between January 1 and March 1901, nine children were born to

women in Illium. As Duke Barfield put it, "I *heerd* o men with double barrel shotguns in their pants, and I reckon it's so every once n agin, and once't I even heerd tell o some fella had him a three-shot pistol, but that fucker Colson's the *only* man I ever heerd of who come packin a six-shooter."

COLSON, STEPHANIE Young girl who had been going with Bobby Tremain for four years.

COODER, ALBION In 1862, Albion Cooder, the last surviving Cooder, went bankrupt and commited suicide.

COODER, GEORGE In 1830, Hiram Cooder's cousin, George, opened a hostelry and feed store in the south end of Haven village.

COODER, HIRAM Man who owned Cooder's Tavern & Lodging-House in 1826.

THE COP Bangor officer who gave Anne Anderson directions to the Cityscape Hotel.

CORINNE 'Becka Paulson's older sister. She lived in Portsmouth. She had given the Paulsons the 3-D picture of Jesus.

CRANE, HUGH He bought Montville Plantation from the Commonwealth of Massachusetts in 1813. It later became Haven, Maine. Hugh Crane (who would have become the thirteenth Earl of Montville) was disinherited by his father for becoming American. Hugh instead called himself the first Earl of Maine and the Duke of Nowhere at All. Hugh Crane died in 1826.

CRANE, SIR Hugh Crane's father, the twelfth Earl of Montville. He had never ventured east of Dover, and he ended his life as a loyal Tory. Hugh Crane (who would have become the thirteenth Earl of Montville) was disinherited by his father for becoming American.

CRENSHAW, GALEN Mrs. Crenshaw's son.

CRENSHAW, MRS. Haven woman who sold Avon products.

THE CRENSHAWS Haven residents who appeared to Ruth McCausland in a dream, "staring up at the sky, their faces rotted swampfire green."

CROWELL, EMORY Baptist minister who had piles. He served Troy, Ilium, Etna, and Unity around the turn of the century.

CULLUM, ARLENE She sold Amway products.

CULLUM, DELBERT Mechanic who worked at Elt Barker's Shell station.

CULLUM, MAGGIE Delbert Cullum's wife.

THE CULLUM CHILDREN Delbert and Maggie Cullum had six children: three girls over eighteen (who went to work in Bangor and Derry after their family was broken up), and three minors (who were placed in foster homes). There were rumors in town of incest in the Cullum family.

CUMMINGS, RON A good, serious poet, and a friend of Gard's. Ron had lots of money – his family was in the textile business.

CUSSLER, CLIVE Novelist.

DAGGETT, DOC Augusta veterinarian, and Peter the beagle's vet before Dr. Etheridge. Doc Daggett retired to Florida.

THE DALLAS POLICE Bobbi's and Gard's term for any authoritarian organization that royally screws things up, such as:

—Protecting Kennedy and Lee Harvey Oswald,
—controlling the summer race riots of 1964,
—the Viet Nam War,
—the oil embargo,
—the negotiations to release the Iranian hostages,
—Kent State.

DARLA GAINES'S BOYFRIEND Darla's unnamed boyfriend. Darla had a half-ounce of "bitchin' reefer" under her mattress, and every afternoon between 2:30 and 3:00 she and her boyfriend would smoke grass and "do the horizontal bop" on Darla's bed.

DAVIDSON, ORVAL Unity man who had bloodhounds.

DAVIES, ROBERTSON Author of the *Deptford Trilogy*.

DAWSON, SMOKEY State cop.

THE DEAD (by an E-4 in the APC). Some of the Haven Tommyknockers who died included: Elt Barker, Ashley Ruvall, Miss Timms, Rosalie Skehan, Frank Spruce, Rudy Barfield, Chip

McCausland (he fell and broke his neck), Phil Golden, Hazel McCready, Bryant Brown, Poley Andrews (he swallowed Drano), Queenie Golden (she jumped into Hazel's dry well), and Justin Hurd (he was shot).

DELANEY, ANN Poet who wrote spare, haunting poems about rural, working-class New England.

THE DEPUTY The officer who guarded Jim Gardener at the Penobscot County Jail after Gard shot his wife, Nora. The deputy asked Gard, "Shot your wife, huh?" The deputy read *Crazy* magazine, and picked his nose.

THE DESK CLERK Alhambra clerk who gave Gard the bum's rush because Gard didn't have shoes on.

DEVINE, ANDY Actor.

DICKEY, JAMES Novelist.

DOCKERY, EZRA Farmer. Peter Bailey's plane exploded in Ezra's north field.

DUGAN He investigated the disappearance of the two state cops.

DUGAN, MONSTER Ruth McCausland's husband's partner before Ruth's husband died.

THE DUKE OF NOWHERE AT ALL Hugh Crane.

DUPLISSEY, MYRTLE Haven's self-appointed historian.

THE DUPLISSEYS Haven residents who appeared to Ruth McCausland in a dream, "staring up at the sky, their faces rotted swampfire green." The Duplisseys attended Ruth McCausland's funeral.

THE EDDIE PARKER BAND Rock group that gave Gard a ride after he woke up on the Arcadia Beach. There were four guys in the band, and a girl with red spiked hair who traveled with them. (Her legs went approximately up to her chin.)

EDISON, THOMAS Inventor.

THE EDITOR One of the editors who rejected Gard's series of poems called "The Radiation Cycle." The editor had written "Poetry and politics rarely mix, poetry and propaganda, never."

EILEEN Telephone operator who Gard talked to from the Mobil station after his bum's rush out of the Alhambra.

ELDERLY, BILL Haven man who killed a deer. (Dave Rutledge dressed it out.)

ELFMAN, DR. Hypothermia specialist. He was called in when five-year-old Hilly Brown was reported missing from Derry Home Hospital after the sled accident.

ELLENDER, TUG Derry state police base dispatcher.

ENDERS, JOHN School principal.

THE ENGINEER On October 5, 1966, there was a partial nuclear meltdown of the Enrico Fermi breeder reactor in Michigan. The unnamed engineer who was called in took one look, said "You guys almost lost Detroit," and fainted.

ERIC THE CRAZED POMERANIAN Pomeranian owned by Mrs. Perkins. Eric went after Peter in Dr. Etheridge's waiting room at the Augusta Veterinary Clinic.

ESTABROOKE, CHARLIE Haven man who retired from the post office.

ETHERIDGE, DR. Peter's vet at the Augusta Veterinary Clinic.

THE FAMILY For a week and half in 1957, a family in Charlotte, North Carolina, picked up a classical music station from Florida on the drinking glasses in their home.

FANNIN, BILLY Boy who owned a red wagon that became transformed into an electronic killer.

FANNIN, WENDY Ruth McCausland's next-door neighbor.

THE FARMER Man who picked up Gard after he was let off by the Eddie Parker Band. The farmer complained about the government.

THE FARMER Gard had once traded a birthday sonnet for a farmer's wife in exchange for three shopping bags of new potatoes. The farmer insisted that the poem rhyme.

FENDERSON, MOLLY Beach Jernigan's niece. She cooked at the Haven Lunch.

FENDERSON, SHERRY A very good poet, and one of Bobbi's circle. After Bobbi published *Hangtown*, Sherry rejected her.

FINLAY, VIRGIL Artist who once drew covers for *Startling Stories* magazine.

THE FIRST EARL OF MAINE Hugh Crane.

FOGERTY, JOHN Rock musician played on the jukebox at Smith Brothers.

THE FRIENDS OF POETRY The group that sponsored a reading by Gard at Northeastern University. This group was comprised of ladies who were more familiar with Rod McKuen than with John Berryman, Hart Carne, Ron Cummings, or James Gardener.

FUNICELLO, ANNETTE Actress.

THE G.I Soldier who told the Washington *Post* that after the fire, Haven's dead looked like bloody human commas.

GABBONS, PETER ("JINGLES") State cop.

GAINES, DARLA Seventeen-year-old girl who delivered the Sunday newspaper in Haven. She had a half-ounce of "bitchin' reefer" under her mattress, and every afternoon between 2:30 and 3:00 she and her boyfriend would smoke grass and "do the horizontal bop" on Darla's bed.

GAINES, MR. AND MRS. Darla's parents. They worked at Splendid Shoe in Derry.

GARD Jim Gardener.

GARD'S DOCTOR The doctor who told Gard to be thankful for his "steel plate" headaches: He should be thankful he could feel anything at all.

GARD'S FATHER Sometimes Gard heard his father's voice in his head.

GARD'S LAWYER The attorney who represented Gard on Gard's handgun charge. Gard ended up spending two months in jail. The lawyer told Gard he was lucky to get off with only two months.

GARDENER, JIM (JAMES ERIC GARDENER) Bobbi's friend; he was a poet, and an alcoholic. He gave Bobbi Peter the beagle in 1976. He was known to Bobbi as Gard. He discovered what was happening with Bobbi and the Tommyknockers, and ended up dying on the floor of the ship somewhere in space.

GARRICK, FRANK Bobbi's uncle. She lived and wrote in his house in the woods of Maine.

THE GIRL Girl who heard Gard read "Leighton Street," and ended up crying and starting a standing ovation.

GOLDEN, EDDIE A boy at Hilly Brown's ninth birthday party. Eddie got hurt on rusty barbed wire.

GOLDEN, JOHN One of the men Ruth McCausland enlisted to look for David Brown.

THE GOLDMANS They attended Ruth McCausland's funeral.

GOOHRINGER, REVEREND LESTER He conducted the services at Ruth McCausland's funeral.

GORDON, ALEX Artist. Gard thought that Bobby Tremain had a handsome face that could have been drawn by Gordon.

"GORILLA MONSOON" How Ev Hillman referred to Monster Dugan.

GOUDGE, PAULINE Havenite who "became" one with the Tommyknockers.

HANEY, ELMER The man who married Iva Jorgenson after Benny Jorgenson had a stroke.

HANEY, IVA The former Iva Jorgenson.

HARLEY, JOHN Former Haven constable before Ruth McCausland. John attended Ruth McCausland's funeral.

THE HARLEYS Haven residents who appeared to Ruth McCausland in a dream, "staring up at the sky, their faces rotted swampfire green."

HARLINGEN, ABEL Moss Harlingen's father. Moss murdered Abel in 1973 in Greenville.

HARLINGEN, EMORY Moss Harlingen's brother.

HARLINGEN, MOSS Man who murdered his father in 1973 in Greenville.

HARTLEY, DONALD Methodist minister who served Ilium and Troy around the turn of the century.

HARTLEY, REVEREND MR. DONALD Ruth McCausland's

great-uncle.

THE HEAD OF ADMINISTRATIVE SERVICES Official at the Derry Home Hospital who called in the Derry police and fire departments to search for the missing Hilly Brown.

HEINLEIN, ROBERT Sci-fi writer.

HENRY APPLEGATE'S GRANDMOTHER A picture of her face was used to test the device that would project the hologram of the bell tower over the town hall in Haven center.

HILLMAN, EV Marie's father, and Hilly and David's grandfather.

THE HIPPIES At one point a bunch of hippies had been selling dope in and around Haven. Ruth McCausland threw them out of town.

HIRAM COODER'S COUSIN He opened the Barber Shop and Small Surgery next to the General Mercantile in 1828.

HIRAM COODER'S NEPHEW He owned and operated the General Mercantile across the street from Cooder's Tavern in 1826.

HOUDINI, HARRY Famous magician.

HOWELL, ROBERT A character in Bobbi Anderson's novel, *The Buffalo Soldiers*.

A HUNTER Unnamed hunter who had once shot Peter the beagle in the ass with birdshot.

HURD, JUSTIN Farmer. David saw him tearing up his fields, burying under the vegetables. Justin thought it was May of 1951.

JACK The kid who Gard met on the Arcadia Beach when he woke up with the worst hangover of his life. This kid was Jack Sawyer from *The Talisman*, but we're never told his last name in *The Tommyknockers*. Jack wore a "School-Lunch Victim" t-shirt. [NOTE: See the section on *The Talisman* in this volume.]

JACKLIN, MARY Tommy Jacklin's grandmother. Mary was a friend of Eileen Pulsifer. [NOTE: The Pulsifers also appear in Stephen King's 1989 short story "Home Delivery." See the section on "Home Delivery" in this volume.]

JACKLIN, TOMMY He went to Derry with Hester Brookline to buy twenty car batteries.

JERNIGAN, BEACH The short-order cook at the Haven Lunch.

JERNIGAN, HUMP Ruth McCausland took an M-16 firecracker from him.

JERNIGAN, STANLEY A boy at Hilly Brown's tenth birthday party.

JORGENSON, BENNY Haven man who died of a stroke.

JORGENSON, BETHIE Iva and Benny Jorgenson's daughter.

JORGENSON, IVA Benny's wife. After Benny died of a stroke, Iva married Elmer Haney.

JORGENSON, RICHARD Iva and Benny Jorgenson's son.

THE JUDDS Mother and daughter country-and-western singing duo.

KIMBALL, ALICE Haven grammar school teacher. The 3-D picture of Jesus on 'Becka Paulson's TV told 'Becka that Alice was a lesbian.

KIRK, CAPTAIN Captain of the starship Enterprise.

KLINGERMAN, DR. The professor who had taught Bobbi in a psychology department seminar on creativity.

KOONTZ, DEAN Author of the book *Watchers*. Bobbi read it.

KROGER, RANDY The German who owned Cooder's.

KUPFERBERG, TULI In *The Tommyknockers*, King attributed the words "And I feel like homemade shit" to Ed Sanders and Tuli Kupferberg (also known as The Fugs). [NOTE: King has so far used this quotation twice: He has Jim Gardener repeat it in *The Tommyknockers*, and he used the line as one of the epigraphs that lead off his 1969 poem called "Harrison State Park '68."]

LADY DAY The red-haired girl who was traveling with the Eddie Parker Band. (Her name wasn't given, but Gard thought of her as "Lady Day.") She gave Gard a hit off a joint.

LEANDRO, GEORGINA John Leandro's mother.

LEANDRO, JOHN Bangor *Daily News* reporter who wrote the story about Ruth McCausland's death.

LESTER, DR. Derry physician. Dr. Lester was Hilly Brown's doctor.

LINDLEY, CHRISTINA Seventeen-year-old girl who had won second prize in the Fourteenth Annual State O' Maine Photography Competition.

THE LITTLE BOY Little boy from Quebec who was headed for Old Orchard Beach. He lost four baby teeth in ten minutes as he passed through Haven.

THE LITTLE GIRL Girl in Dr. Etheridge's waiting room at the Augusta Veterinary Clinic who stepped on Eric the Crazed Pomeranian's lease when Eric went after Peter.

LUMPKIN Ruth McCausland's scarecrow doll.

THE MAN IN BLUE MECHANIC'S OVERALLS Man in Dr. Etheridge's waiting room at the Augusta Veterinary Clinic who had a boxer that had its right foreleg in a cast.

THE MAN WHO LOOKED LIKE A COLLEGE DEAN He and his wife listened to Ted the Power Man extoll the virtues of nuclear power at the reception following the Northeastern poetry reading.

THE MAN WHO LOOKED LIKE A COLLEGE DEAN'S WIFE Along with her husband, she listened to Ted the Power Man extoll the virtues of nuclear power at the reception following the Northeastern poetry reading.

MANCINI, BOOM-BOOM Boxer.

MANSON, CHARLES Psychopathic mass murderer.

MANTELL, CAPTAIN Air force captain. In 1947, he had flown too high chasing what he thought was a flying saucer. He blacked out and died. He had been chasing a reflection of Venus.

MARTIN, NED Radio announcer for "Red Sox Warmup."

THE MATHEMATICIAN An MIT mathematician headed for the University of Maine grasped an entire new way of looking at mathematics and math philosophy while driving through Haven. He envisioned winning a Nobel Prize for his insights.

McCARDLE, MR. Patricia McCardle's late husband. He left Pat a lot of money.

McCARDLE, PATRICIA World-class bitch, and the woman who ran the New England Poetry Caravan. Her ancestry was traced to the Mayflower.

"McCARGLEBARGLE" The name by which Gard thought of Patricia McCardle.

McCARTHY, CHARLIE Edgar Bergen's dummy.

McCAUSLAND, CHIP Guy who lived on Dugout Road with his common-law wife. They had henhouses.

McCAUSLAND, RALPH Ruth's husband.

McCAUSLAND, RUTH Ruth Arlene Merrill McCausland. Haven town constable. She collected dolls, and was killed in the town hall explosion.

McCREADY, DELBERT A friend of Ev Hillman's who had gotten lost in Big Injun Woods. He went into the woods on Tuesday, November 10, 1947.

McCREADY, HAZEL Woman who put Ruth McCausland to bed after Ruth collapsed while looking for David Brown. Hazel attended Ruth McCausland's funeral.

McKEEN, ADLEY Man who took Ruth McCausland home after she collapsed while looking for David Brown. Haven resident who attended Ruth McCausland's funeral.

McKEEN, CHRISTINE A friend of Ruth McCausland's.

MEGAN John Leandro's aunt. She lived in Nova Scotia.

MERRILL, HOLLY Ruth McCausland's mother.

MERRILL, JOHN Ruth McCausland's father.

THE MEXICAN Unnamed man who found a picture of the Virgin Mary baked into an enchilada.

MICHAEL Newt Berringer's nephew. Newt bought him a model of the Amazing Invisible Man one Christmas.

MONTGOMERY, ELLIS On July 4, 1864, Coodersville's name was changed to Montgomery, in honor of Ellis Montgomery, a local boy who fell at Gettysburg.

MONTGOMERY, MRS. Ellis Montgomery's mother. She protested when the town of Montgomery (named after her son) changed its name to Ilium, but they changed it anyway.

MORAN, LESTER Textbook salesman and fire freak who lived in a Boston suburb.

THE MORANS The people who owned the house where Ruth McCausland was bitten by a dog while collecting for the American Cancer Society.

MOSS, FREEMAN The guy who picked up Gard after Gard was let off by the farmer who complained about the government.

"MR. SPLITFOOT" The name that the 3-D Jesus on 'Becka Paulson's TV set used for the Devil.

"MRS. TED" The wife of Ted the Power Man.

MUMPHREY, JOHN Haven man who ran against Ruth McCausland for the position of constable. He attended Ruth McCausland's funeral.

MUMPHRY, MURIEL Woman at the University who always knew where Gard could be found.

THE NASHVILLE KITTY-CATS The group that played at the Big Lost Weekend Bar and Grille on Friday and Saturday nights.

THE NEUROLOGIST Hilly Brown's doctor. He was a big man with a red beard.

NICHOLSON, JACK The actor who played Jack Torrance in the film *The Shining*.

THE NINE ILLEGITIMATE CHILDREN The offspring of Preacher Colson's "six-girl fling" on September 7, 1900. The litter consisted of three girls and six boys.

NORA Gard's wife. He shot her in the head one Thanksgiving when he was drunk.

A NOTARY PUBLIC FROM DERRY Patricia McCardle brought in a notary from Derry to witness Gard's contract for the Poetry Caravan. (She didn't have too much trust in Gard or his un-notarized signature.)

NOYES, MABEL Woman who owned the Junque-a-Torium.

THE NURSE The unnamed nurse who found David Brown in Hilly's room in the hospital after the events in Haven were all over.

"OLD BETSY" The name Beach Jernigan called his truck.

OLD GAMMAR HOOD One of Ruth McCausland's dolls.

OLSEN, JIMMY Superman's pal.

ORWELL, GEORGE Author of *Animal Farm*.

THE OTHER YOUNG MAN An unnamed student who, along with the post-grad student bartender, held Ted the Power Man back as he went for Gard at the reception following the Northeastern University poetry reading.

OZZIE 'Becka Paulson's cat.

PARKER, EDDIE Leader of the Eddie Parker Band, and the driver of the Dodge van that picked up Gard.

PAUL Owner/operator of Paul's Down-East SuperMart. His employee, Hank Buck, hated him so much that one day Hank put a half-box of Ex-Lax in Paul's McDonald's chocolate shake. Paul exploded at 3:15 that afternoon. The 3-D Jesus on 'Becka Paulson's TV told her all about it.

PAULSON, BYRON The only child of Joe and Rebecca Paulson.

PAULSON, JOE One of Haven's two mail carriers.

PAULSON, REBECCA BOUCHARD Joe Paulson's wife.

PELL, JOE Little boy who damaged Ruth McCausland's Mrs. Beasley doll.

PERKINS, MRS. Forty-two-year-old fat woman in Dr. Etheridge's waiting room at the Augusta Veterinary Clinic. She wore bright yellow slacks, and held a Pomeranian named Eric.

PERRY, FRED Ilium Methodist deacon.

PETER Bobbi Anderson's aging beagle. He was blind in one eye. Peter ended up in the Shed.

PETERS, BUCK Buck talked to the Derry state police from a radio in Elt Barker's Shell station.

POE, EDGAR ALLAN Author-poet.

THE PUBLISHER A small press in West Minot once gave Gard a half-cord of ash wood as an advance against publication of a book of Gard's poems. The unnamed publisher was from Connecticut

and didn't know the wood was ash.

PULSIFER, EILEEN John Leandro's mother's friend. [NOTE: The Pulsifers also appear in Stephen King's 1989 "zombie" short story, "Home Delivery." See the section on "Home Delivery" in this volume.]

PYLE, ERNIE Famous reporter.

RAINS, CLAUDE Actor in the film "The Invisible Man."

RAMSEY, DUNSTABLE A character in Robertson Davies' *Deptford Trilogy*.

REYNAULT, PETER City editor of the Bangor *Daily News*.

RHODES, BENTON State cop.

RICHARDSON FBI agent shot by CIA agent Spacklin after all hell broke loose in Haven.

RICHARDSON, MOOSE Man who waved to Ruth McCausland.

RIDEOUT, ANDY State cop who attended Ruth McCausland's funeral.

ROBBY THE ROBOT AND DR. MOBIUS Kyle Archinbourg told Ev Hillman that David Brown was on Altair-4 with these two characters.

ROBERTSON, PAT Television evangelist.

ROOSEVELT, ANNA Ruth McCausland had one of her dolls.

RUTLEDGE, ALVIN Dave Rutledge's grandson. Alvin was a long-haul trucker who lived in Bangor.

RUTLEDGE, DAVE A Haven oldtimer.

RUVALL, ASHLEY Boy on a bike carrying a fishing pole who waved to Ruth McCausland. He also attended Ruth McCausland's funeral.

RUVALL, CLAUDETTE Ashley's mother.

RUVALL, IRWIN Ilium's head selectman. He proctored the vote to change the name of Ilium to Haven on March 27, 1901.

SANDERS, ED The guy who uttered the immortal words "And I feel like homemade shit." [NOTE: King has so far used this line twice: He has Jim Gardener repeat it in *The Tommyknockers,* and he used the line as one of the epigraphs that lead off his 1969 poem, "Harrison State Park '68."]

SARGENT, PAMELA Ladies aid member who referred to Reverend Goohringer as "Gooey."

SIMARD, CORA Midwife. Faith Clarendon gave birth to a boy on March 29, 1901. Preacher Colson was the father. Cora was the midwife. Paul Clarendon cut the baby's throat, then his wife's, then his own. Irwin Simard found the bodies.

SIMARD, IRWIN Cora's husband. Faith Clarendon gave birth to a boy on March 29, 1901. Preacher Colson was the father. Cora was the midwife. Paul Clarendon cut the baby's throat, then his wife's, then his own. Irwin found the bodies.

THE SIX GIRLS On the night of September 7, 1900, Preacher Colson impregnated six girls before he fled Illium. Faith Clarendon was one of them.

SKEHAN, ROSALIE A girl at Hilly Brown's Magic Show who found a playing card in her purse.

SMITH, JOHN Cleaves Mill, Maine, teacher and psychic who "went nuts" and tried to kill a presidential candidate named Stillson. [NOTE: See the section on *The Dead Zone* in this volume.]

SPACKLIN The CIA agent who shot the FBI agent named Richardson after things broke loose in Haven.

SPRUCE, BILL Frank Spruce's brother. Bill had a herd of dairy cows in Cleaves Mills, Maine.

SPRUCE, EVELYN Bill Spruce's wife.

SPRUCE, FRANK Haven resident who attended Ruth McCausland's funeral.

STAMPNELL, EDDIE State cop who attended Ruth McCausland's funeral.

STILLSON The presidential candidate Johnny Smith tried to assassinate. [NOTE: See the section on *The Dead Zone* in this volume.]

STRAUB, PETER Author of *Floating Dragon*.

THE SURGEON The doctor who operated on Lester Moran when, at the age of twelve, Lester was struck by a car and thrown thirty feet against the brick wall of a furniture warehouse.

SWAGGART, JIMMY Television evangelist 'Becka Paulson watched on TV.

SYLVIA Don Blue's aunt. She lived in Haven.

SYMINGTON, JON EVARD Poet who won the 1987 Boston University Hawthorne Prize for his long poem "Harbor Dreams 1650-1980."

TARKINGTON, JUD Jud almost had a fight with Hank Buck before they found that Ruth McCausland had collapsed while looking for David Brown. Jud attended Ruth McCausland's funeral.

TED THE POWER MAN A guy who defended the nuclear power industry at the reception following the Northeastern University poetry reading. Gard went at it with him, and ended up poking him in the stomach with an umbrella. One of Ted's favorite subjects was the benefits of the Iroquois Nuclear Power Facility.

THOROGOOD, GEORGE, AND THE DESTROYERS Gard had a dream in which he heard George in his head.

THE THREE MEN Bobbi Anderson had only had sex with three men in her entire life, and Jim Gardener was one of them.

THURLOW, ALBION Haven man who lived a quarter of a mile from Delbert Cullum's house. It wasn't said if Albion was related to Edwina and Norma, although it's likely.

THURLOW, EDWINA Little girl who lived in Haven, and who was afraid of Ruth McCausland's doll collection.

THURLOW, NORMA Edwina's mother.

THE THURLOWS They attended Ruth McCausland's funeral.

THURSTON AND BLACKSTONE Two famous magicians.

TIERNEY, JIM Attorney general in Augusta, Maine.

TILLETS, MADGE Checkout girl at the market.

THE TOMMYKNOCKERS The dead alien inhabitants of the ship in the earth. Bobbi thought the Tommyknockers were dead, that they died long before men existed, "but then Caruso's dead, but he's still singing on a lot of records, isn't he?"

TONY John Leandro's nephew. Tony lived in Halifax.

TORGESON, ANDY The man David Bright talked to at the Cleaves Mills state police barracks. (He was one of the "Dallas Police.")

TREMAIN, ALF Haven constable in 1947. He and his wife attended Ruth McCausland's funeral.

TREMAIN, BOBBY Young boy who had been going with Stephanie Colson for four years.

TREMAIN, CASEY One of the men who went out looking for David Brown.

THE TREMAINS They attended Ruth McCausland's funeral.

THE TRUCK DRIVER An unnamed truck driver passing through Haven on I-95 who picked up a rock station from Chicago on his radio.

TWAIN, MARK American humorist/author.

THE TWENTY-SIX After the fire, the remaining twenty-six Tommyknockers were brought to The Shop in Virginia, where they died one by one. The last survivor was Alice Kimball, who died on October 31, Halloween.

TWO GOOD OLE BOYS Two guys who had beaten up Gard and Ron Cummings in the Stone Country Bar and Grille. They had gotten into an argument about Chernobyl and Seabrook. Cummings said the boys were "Snopeses from Mississippi."

THE TWO OLD FOLKS Two people on their way to Bar Harbor who picked up a classical station from Florida on their car radio while passing through Haven.

THE TWO STATE COPS Unnamed cops blown up by Beach Jernigan.

UNDERHILL, MRS. Hilly Brown's third-grade teacher.

THE UNION OF CONCERNED SCIENTISTS The group that kept the Black Clock.

VAN IMPE, JACK Television evangelist 'Becka Paulson watched on TV.

VICTOR The Browns' family cat.

THE VIRGIN MARY A Mexican fellow found a picture of the Virgin baked into an enchilada.

VOSS, NANCY Woman who came from Augusta, and who replaced Charlie Estabrooke in the post office. Joe Paulson was having an affair with Nancy.

WAHWAYVOKAH Chief Atlantic's Micmac name. Wahwayvokah meant "tall waters."

WARWICK, DOC The Haven town doctor. He was Bobbi's doctor. He also attended Ruth McCausland's funeral.

WAYNE, JOHN Buck Peters could imitate Wayne's voice.

THE WEBBER DRIVER The fuel-truck driver who crashed his truck to avoid hitting Hilly Brown's sled.

WEEMS, CLAUDELL Maine's only black state trooper. He was six-foot-four, and had one gold tooth in the front of his mouth.

WELLS, H.G. Writer.

THE WOMAN Unnamed woman in Dr. Etheridge's waiting room at the Augusta Veterinary Clinic who was holding a cat named Blacky.

WOODWARD AND BERNSTEIN The reporters who uncovered the Watergate scandal.

WRIGHTSON, BERNI Artist. Gard thought that Bobby Tremain had a handsome face that could have been drawn by Wrightson. [NOTE: Berni Wrightson was the artist for King's "Creepshow" comic book, and the *Cycle of the Werewolf* novella.]

THE YOUNG MAN Unnamed young man who heard Gard read "Leighton Street," and ended up with tears rolling down his cheeks.

(26)
THE TOMMYKNOCKERS
Places

ALBION Bobbi got the loam for her new cellar floor in Albion.

ALBION TOWN ROAD #5 The road where Ev Hillman and Monster Dugan ended up after backroading to get into Haven.

THE ALHAMBRA HOTEL Hotel on Arcadia Beach, New Hampshire. Jack told Gard he could use the phone in the hotel. [NOTE: The Alhambra also appears in *The Talisman*. See the section on *The Talisman* in this volume.]

ALLAGASH Maine camping grounds.

ALTAIR-4 The place where David Brown was sent by his brother Hilly during Hilly's backyard magic show.

ARCADIA BEACH, NEW HAMPSHIRE The beach where Gard woke up following the incident with Ted the Power Man. He wasn't far from the Arcadia Funworld Amusement Park. [NOTE: Both of these settings also appear in *The Talisman*. See the section on *The Talisman* in this volume.]

ARCADIA FUNWORLD AMUSEMENT PARK Amusement park not far from Arcadia Beach.

AROOSTOOK COUNTY Lester Moran was returning from Aroostook County at 4:15 when he saw the fire in Haven.

THE ASYLUMS IN BANGOR OR JUNIPER HILL While working on the dig, Bobbi thought she might be going funny in the head, and that one day they'd cart her off to either of these asylums. [NOTE: Both asylums are also mentioned in *It*.]

AUGUSTA The town Nancy Voss came from. Augusta was also the town where Joe Paulson's bookie lived.

AUGUSTA TRUSTWORTHY HARDWARE STORE Area hardware store where Bobbi sometime shopped.

AUGUSTA VETERINARY CLINIC The clinic where Dr. Etheridge practiced.

BANGOR INTERNATIONAL AIRPORT Dow Base eventually became this commercial airport.

BAR HARBOR Annabelle and the aide overnighted there while in Maine for Ruth McCausland's funeral.

THE BARBER SHOP AND SMALL SURGERY The shop opened by Hiram Cooder's cousin next to the General Mercantile in 1828.

THE BATTERY GRAVEYARD A drawer in Bobbi's house where

she kept dead batteries. She couldn't throw them out.

BEAR'S DEN Haven restaurant.

BERGENFIELD, NEW JERSEY Ruth McCausland picked up a college radio station from Bergenfield on her car radio.

BIG INJUN WOODS Woods east on Derry Road. Ev Hillman used to call it Burning Woods. They burned when the ship in the earth took off.

THE BIG LOST WEEKEND BAR AND GRILLE The bar that Bobbi stopped in on her way home from the Augusta Veterinary Clinic.

THE BIRD MUSEUM IN BAR HARBOR Museum. Gard had once heard a commercial for the Bird Museum after sticking his finger in a socket, somehow turning the steel plate in his head into a radio receiver.

BOSTON Boston was part of Gard's New England Poetry Caravan tour.

BOSTON UNIVERSTY Gard did a poetry reading at BU on June 25.

THE BOUNTY TAVERN Bangor pub across the street from the Bangor *Daily News*.

BURNING WOODS The land owned by the New England Paper Company that bordered Bobbi's land. "Burning Woods" was the name Ev Hillman called Big Injun Woods.

THE CAPITOL MALL The mall in Haven where a Radio Shack was located.

CHARLOTTE, NORTH CAROLINA For a week and half in 1957, a family in Charlotte, North Carolina, picked up a classical music station from Florida on the drinking glasses in their home.

CHINA LAKES FIRE STATION The station that reported the "tommyknocker" fire in Big Injun Woods.

THE CITYSCAPE HOTEL The hotel on Route 7 recommended to Anne Anderson by a Bangor cop.

A CLEAVES MILL APARTMENT Bobbi started writing her first western novel, *Hangtown,* in a scuzzy Cleaves Mill apartment. She used a thirties vintage Underwood typewriter.

CONNECTICUT A small press in West Minot, Connecticut, that once gave Gard a half-cord of ash wood as an advance against publication of a book of Gard's poems. The publisher was from Connecticut, and didn't know the wood was ash.

COODER'S MARKET Haven general store. Cooder's was where Poley Andrews worked. Bobbi bought every battery they had during her "Historic Battery Run of 1988."

COODER'S TAVERN & LODGING-HOUSE Local Haven bar owned by Hiram Cooder in 1826.

COODERSVILLE In 1831, Montville Plantation became Coodersville.

CROSMAN CORNER The one-room schoolhouse that Ruth McCausland attended as a child was located in Crosman Corner.

DEAD RIVER GAS Once a month, Dead River Gas in Derry replaced the LP gas tanks that Bobbi used for her water heater.

DERRY, MAINE The company where Dead River Gas was located. [NOTE: Derry is also where all of *It* takes place. See the section on *It* in this volume.]

DERRY AMC The car dealership where Ev Hillman rented a Jeep Cherokee.

DERRY BURGER RANCH The restaurant where John Leandro ordered two cheeseburgers.

DERRY FIRE ALERT AND RANGER STATION 3 IN NEWPORT When the fire started in Big Injun Woods, Derry Fire Alert and Ranger Station 3 in Newport were called in.

DERRY HOME HOSPITAL The hospital where Hilly Brown was taken at the age of five after his sled accident. Also, Ruth McCausland went to the Derry Home emergency room after she was bitten by the Morans' dog while collecting for the American Cancer Society.

DERRY TRU-VALUE HARDWARE The store where Tommy Jacklin and Hester Brookline bought over one hundred C, D, and Triple A batteries.

THE DIAMOND GRAVEL PIT This was where the Nista Road petered out.

THE DIG Bobbi's excavation site in the woods. She (and later Gard) dug up the ship in the earth.

DOW AIR FORCE BASE The Bangor base that was closed down in the late sixties.

DOWNEAST SCUBADIVE Ev was referred to these people for his respirator needs.

DUGOUT ROAD The road where Chip McCausland and his common-law wife lived. They had henhouses.

EASTERN MAINE MEDICAL Maine hospital. When Hilly Brown was found to be missing from Derry Home Hospital, the hospital's head of administrative services wished the Browns had taken Hilly to Eastern Maine instead.

ENRICO FERMI BREEDER REACTOR IN MICHIGAN Nuclear power plant where there was a partial nuclear meltdown on October 5, 1966. The engineer who was called in took one look, said "You guys almost lost Detroit," and fainted.

FALL RIVER Jim Gardener did a poetry reading in Fall River on June 24.

FLORIDA For a week and half in 1957, a family in Charlotte, North Carolina, picked up a classical music station from Florida on the drinking glasses in their home.

FRIDAY, NORTH DAKOTA, AND ARNETTE, TEXAS Radio stations that Andy Torgeson and Claudell Weems heard on their police radios during the fire in Big Injun Woods.

FRYEBURG FAIR Gard had gone to the Fryeburg Fair when he was ten years old, and had gotten lost in the Mirror Maze.

THE GENERAL MERCANTILE The store across the road from Cooder's Tavern in 1826. It was owned and operated by Hiram Cooder's nephew.

GREENVILLE In 1973, Moss Harlingen murdered his father in Greenville.

HALIFAX The town where John Leandro's nephew Tony lived.

HAMMOND AND UNION STREETS The Bangor intersection where Anne Anderson stopped to ask a cop for directions to the best hotel in town.

HAMPDEN The mathematician's destination. Also, the town where the Purple Cow bar was located.

HANGAR 18 Gard thought that the ship in the earth would end up in Hangar 18 if they reported it. (Hangar 18 is allegedly the location where the government has hidden the remains of a crashed UFO — and the bodies of aliens — from the public.) Gard felt that no matter who they called, they'd be calling the "Dallas Police." [NOTE: See the entry THE DALLAS POLICE.]

HAVEN, MAINE The town where Bobbi Anderson lived, wrote, and first discovered the ship in the earth. The town was eventually "invaded" and destroyed by the Tommyknockers. [NOTE: Actually, the townsfolk "became" Tommyknockers, and when Gard took off in the ship, a large portion (mostly the western half) of the town burned.]

THE HAVEN COMMUNITY LIBRARY The library started in the Methodist Parsonage by Ruth McCausland.

HAVEN GRAMMAR SCHOOL The school where Alice Kimball, a lesbian, taught.

HAVEN HARDWARE Town hardware store.

THE HAVEN LUNCH Town diner.

HAVEN VILLAGE Haven Village was five miles north of of Bobbi's place, which was located in the geographic center of the Haven township.

THE HOSTELRY AND FEED STORE In 1830, Hiram Cooder's cousin, George, opened a hostelry and feed store in the south end of Montville Plantation.

ILIUM In 1878, Montgomery's name was changed to Ilium. (At the time, there was a trend towards giving cities classical names like Sparta, Carthage, Athens, and Troy.)

INCORPORATED MAINE TOWN #193 Ilium, Maine. In 1900, Preacher Colson put forth Article 14, to change the name of Incorporated Maine Town #193 from Ilium to Haven.

THE IROQUOIS NUCLEAR POWER FACILITY The power plant that was a favorite of Ted the Power Man.

THE JUNQUE-A-TORIUM The shop owned and operated by Mabel Noyes.

KENNEBUNK The location of the Trolley Museum.

KOREA Hank Buck had served in the army in Korea.

L.L. BEAN Camping supplies company.

LEIGHTON STREET Bobbi and Anne Anderson's father owned a house on Leighton Street.

LIMESTONE, PRESQUE ISLE, BRUNSWICK, AND PORT-LAND National guardsmen were sent to Haven from these towns after the fire, and after it was "discovered" that something strange was happening there.

LIMESTONE AIR FORCE BASE Gard at first thought Bobbi should report the ship in the earth to Limestone, but then changed his mind.

LOURDES, FRANCE A place where miracles happened.

LOWER MAIN STREET, DERRY In order to be near his grandson Hilly, Ev Hillman took a room on Lower Main Street when the boy was in Derry Home Hospital.

MAINE MEDICAL SUPPLIES The store in Derry industrial park that specialized in respiration supplies and therapy.

MAP 23 The map in Ev Hillman's atlas that listed Haven.

MASSACHUSETTS, NEW JERSEY, AND NEW YORK Hunters from these three states had once gotten lost in Big Injun Woods.

THE METHODIST PARSONAGE The parsonage where Ruth McCausland started the Haven Community Library.

MILLER BOG ROAD The road where Benny and Iva Jorgenson lived.

MIT The school the mathematician was from.

MIT, CAL TECH, BELL LABS, AND THE SHOP These labs studied the mechanics of the Tommyknocker machine that had changed the Haven air.

THE MOBIL STATION The bellman at the Alhambra told Gard that there was a pay phone at the Mobil station at the intersection of U.S. 1 and Route 26.

MONMOUTH Mrs. Leandro visited her sister in Monmouth.

MONTGOMERY On July 4, 1864, Coodersville's name was changed to Montgomery, in honor of Ellis Montgomery, a local boy who fell at Gettysburg.

MONTVILLE PLANTATION Haven began as Montville Plantation in 1816. It was owned by Hugh Crane, who bought it in 1813 from the Commonwealth of Massachusetts. Montville Plantation was about 22,000 acres. Derry was twenty miles away, so that plantation lumber could be floated downriver. Hugh Crane bought what eventually became Haven for 1800 pounds.

MR. PAPERBACK The bookstore where Ev Hillman bought an atlas for nine dollars.

NAN'S TAVERN The bar in Bangor where John Leandro spoke to Alvin Rutledge.

NEBRASKA The state where Annabelle grew up.

NEW GLOUCESTER 'Becka and Corinne Bouchard had grown up on a sheep farm in New Gloucester.

NEW HAVEN Part of Gard's New England Poetry Caravan tour. [NOTE: New Haven is my hometown, and I am truly sorry I missed Gard when he was here. I would have loved to have heard him read. —sjs]

NEWPORT, UNITY, CHINA, AND WOOLWICH Engines from these towns were sent to the fire in Big Injun Woods.

NEWPORT-DERRY TOWNLINE AUTO SUPPLY The store on Route 7 where Hester Brookline and Tommy Jacklin bought three car batteries and one good used truck battery.

NISTA ROAD The road to the west of the Brown home. It was where the Paulsons lived.

NORTHERN NATIONAL Bangor bank.

NOVA SCOTIA The place where John Leandro's Aunt Megan lived.

THE NUCLEAR PLANT AT WICASSET After the "animal fight" incident in Dr. Etheridge's waiting room, Mrs. Alden told Bobbi she thought the nuclear power plant was too close for comfort.

THE OLD DERRY ROAD IN TROY This was where two of Mary Jacklin's teeth fell out.

OLD SCHOOLHOUSE ROAD On its way to the fire in Big Injun Woods, a pumper ran off the road here and crashed into the woods.

OLDTOWN, SKOWHAGEN, GREAT WOODS, AND LUDLOW The areas where large groups of the Micmac tribe had been centered.

117 MYSTIC AVENUE, MEDFORD, MASSACHUSETTS A holdup took place there, and the request for help came in on Maine police radios.

PAUL'S DOWN-EAST SUPERMART Haven grocery store.

PENOBSCOT COUNTY The Micmac tribe once inhabited most of this county.

PENOBSCOT COUNTY JAIL The jail where Gard spent time after the Famous Thanksgiving Jag of 1980, during which he shot his wife Nora.

PENOBSCOT RIVER Maine river near the Derry Home Hospital.

THE PENTAGON Hilly Brown thought he would give his "invention" (the one that made things *really* disappear) to the Pentagon after he got his picture on the cover of *Newsweek*.

PINELAND Pineland was where the Maine State Institute for the Severely Retarded was located.

POLLOCK'S, G.M. Bangor jewelry store.

PORTSMOUTH The town where 'Becka Paulson's older sister, Corinne, lived.

PRESTON STREAM Ev Hillman's compass hit Preston Stream after he circled Haven on Map 23.

PROVIDENCE One of the stops on Gard's New England Poetry Caravan tour.

THE PURPLE COW Bar in Hampden.

QUADRANT G-3 Maine air space where pilots always reported trouble with their radar.

RADIO SHACK Store in the Capitol Mall. Hilly asked his mother to stop there and buy him some things he needed for his Magic Show.

RHODE ISLAND Moss Harlingen's mother went to Rhode Island one winter, and her husband Abel used the opportunity to commit sodomy with his son Moss.

ROOM 371 Hilly Brown's room in the Derry Home Hospital.

ROUTE 9 The road between Derry and Haven and Bangor.

ROW 5, SEAT 3 Bobbi's seat in Gard's college English class.

SAND HILL COUNTRY The area in Bobbi Anderson's novel *The Buffalo Soldiers* where Robert Howell camped on August 24, 1848.

SEARS The store where Hester Brookline and Tommy Jacklin bought six Allstate batteries.

THE SHED Bobbi's shed was a nasty place. When Gard finally got into it, he found a washing machine, an Electrolux vacuum, Radio Shack smoke detectors, kerosene drums, shower stalls, and computers. Eventually, Anne Anderson, Peter the beagle, and Ev Hillman ended up in those shower stalls, suspended in some viscous liquid, with coaxial cables coming out of their brains.

THE SHELL STATION The station owned and operated by Elt Barker. Elt inspected vehicles.

SING'S Polynesian restaurant. Gard had once heard a commercial for Sing's after he stuck his finger in a socket and somehow turned the steel plate in his head into a radio receiver.

SMITH BROTHERS The bar where Gard had argued with Ron Cummings about Wallace Stevens.

SPLENDID SHOE The Derry company where both of Darla Gaines's parents worked.

THE STARLITE DRIVE-IN Derry drive-in movie. Gard remembered going there with Bobbi in her truck.

STONE COUNTRY BAR AND GRILLE The bar where Gard had gotten into an argument with some guys.

STORROW DRIVE After arriving at Bobbi's house, Gard had a dream that Arberg really *did* have a heart attack and died at a stoplight on Storrow Drive.

STRAIGHT ARROW The intermediate ski trail at Victory Mountain, Vermont, where Gard had his skiing accident when he was seventeen.

SUNDAY RIVER Gard's skiing accident when he was seventeen had been at Sunday River. Ever since then he had nosebleeds.

THE TOMMYKNOCKERS SHIP When Gard actually entered the ship in the earth he saw a hexagonal room with no chairs, no pictures of Niagara Falls, and no pictures of the Cygnus-B Falls either. The walls of the ship became transparent when the ship was activated.

TROY GENERAL STORE The store that sold t-shirts that said "Where the Hell is Troy, Maine?," "I Got the Best Piece of Tail I Ever Got in Troy, Maine," and "The Maine State Bird" (this one sported a picture of a blackfly). This was also the store where Hester Brookline bought sanitary napkins.

THE TROY PARSONAGE Emory Crowell hung himself in the cellar of the parsonage around the turn of the century.

UNITY The town where Gard lived before he came to Haven to help Bobbi.

THE UNIVERSITY OF MAINE The school Ruth McCausland had attended.

THE UNIVERSITY OF NEBRASKA Bobbi read a master's thesis from the University of Nebraska called "Range War and Civil War."

UTICA Bobbi's family hometown. She realized that if she had spent a few more years in Utica with her sister Anne, she would have definitely gone nuts.

UTICA SOLDIER'S HOSPITAL The hospital where Bobbi's father was brought after his stroke.

VICTORY MOUNTAIN, VERMONT The ski slope where Gard had his skiing accident when he was seventeen. He was on Straight Arrow, the intermediate ski trail.

VILLAGE SUBARU Car dealer. Gard had once heard a commercial for the dealership after he stuck his finger in a socket and somehow turned the steel plate in his head into a radio receiver.

WALLY'S SPA The Derry bar where Ev Hillman drank beer. Ev called David Bright from this bar.

WEST MINOT A small press in West Minot once gave Gard a half-cord of ash wood as an advance against publication of a book of Gard's poems. The publisher was from Connecticut, and didn't know the wood was ash.

WESTERN AUTO The store where Beach Jernigan bought the doorbell that he used to blow up the two cops.

(26)
THE TOMMYKNOCKERS
Things

AN ACT OF IMMACULATE EXCRETION Gard felt that if Pat McCardle ever had to shit, she would perform an "Act of Immaculate Excretion."

AIR FORCE ONE The president's plane.

"ALFRED HITCHCOCK PRESENTS" TV show.

THE AMERICAN CANCER SOCIETY Alice Kimball went door-to-door in Haven collecting for the society.

ANACIN Ruth McCausland took two for a headache.

"THE ANSWER TO EVERYTHING" For a moment, Gard thought that the ship in the earth was the "answer to everything." He soon learned differently.

ARTICLE 14 In 1900, Preacher Colson put forth Article 14 to change the name of Incorporated Maine Town #193 from Ilium to Haven.

ASH A small press in West Minot once gave Gard a half cord of ash wood as an advance against publication of a book of Gard's poems. The publisher was from Connecticut, and didn't know the wood was ash.

"ASSHOLE" Bobbi told Gard that if he commited suicide, she'd have "asshole" written on his tombstone.

ATARIS, APPLE II'S AND III'S, TRS-80'S AND COMMODORES The mix of home computers hooked into cassette recorders in Bobbi's shed.

AN ATLAS Ev Hillman bought an atlas at Mr. Paperback for nine dollars.

AUGUST 14 August 14 was forty-one days since "The Dig" began.

AUGUST 24, 1848 The date Robert Howell made camp in Sand Hill Country in Bobbi Anderson's novel *The Buffalo Soldiers*.

"BABY MAKES HER BLUEJEANS TALK" Dr. Hook song that Gard heard in his head.

"BANGOR 'DAILY NEWS' REPORTER ARRESTED ON ILLEGAL WEAPONS CHARGE" John Leandro imagined this headline would appear in the paper if he got caught with the Smith & Wesson .38 in his glove compartment.

"BARNEY MILLER" TV sitcom.

THE BEACH BOYS Bobbi listened to them.

"THE BEATITUDES" Ruth McCausland's favorite scripture.

BENSOHN Brush-trimmer.

BIG DITCH CONSTRUCTION Moss Harlingen's business.

A BIRTHDAY SONNET Gard had once traded a birthday sonnet for a farmer's wife in exchange for three shopping bags of new potatoes. The farmer insisted that the sonnet rhyme.

"BITCHIN' REEFER" Darla had a half-ounce of grass under her mattress. She smoked it with her boyfriend every day after school, and then they did the "horizontal bop" on Darla's bed.

BOBBI'S BOOKCASE Bobbi Anderson's bookcase was indicative of the research needs of a working genre writer: She wrote westerns for a living, and her bookcase reflected that. Her bookcase contained:

- —The Time-Life series on the Old West;
- —Brian Garfield's early westerns;
- —Humbert Hampton's *Western Territories Examined;*
- —Louis L'Amour's Sackett novels;
- —Richard Marius's books *The Coming of the Rain* and *Bound for the Promised Land;*
- —Jay R. Nash's *Bloodletters and Badmen;*
- —Richard F.K. Mudgett's *Westward Expansion;*
- —paperbacks by Ray Hogan, Archie Jocelyn, Max Brand and Ernest Haycox;
- —Zane Grey's novel *Riders of the Purple Sage.*

BOBBI'S GARDEN Bobbi's garden consisted of one and a half acres of beans, cucumbers, peas, corn, radishes, and potatoes. There were no carrots, cabbage, zucchini or squash. (Bobbi didn't grow what she didn't like.)

"BOBBI'S IN TROUBLE" Gard's thought after his binge and beating in the Stone Country Bar and Grille.

BOBBI'S MAIL One day shortly after Bobbi discovered the ship in the earth, her mail consisted of a flyer from Radio Shack, and a bill from Central Maine Power. Her mail often consisted of a K-Mart flyer, and a Procter & Gamble sample.

BOBBI'S "MODIFICATIONS" After Gard arrived at Bobbi's house, he noticed that Bobbi had made the following "improvements" in her surroundings: She put bright fluorescent lighting in the basement; she installed a new strong bannister going downstairs; the cellar had a new dirt floor; she had built a new work table; and she had installed a doorbell with eighteen programmable melodies. She had also installed a new furnace rebreather, and modified her water heater so that it ran on batteries.

BOBBI'S POEM ABOUT HER GRANDFATHER Bobbi thought that the only poem that was any good in her book of poetry, *Boxing the Compass,* was the one she had written in March of 1972, a month after her grandfather had died of cancer.

BOBBI'S PUBLISHING RECORD At the time she discovered the ship in the earth, Bobbi had published eleven books: ten westerns, and one book of poetry. Her first novel was *Hangtown,* which was published in 1975, her latest was *The Long Ride Back,* which came out in 1986. Her westerns also included a novel called *Rimfire Christmas,* and she had a new novel called *Massacre Canyon* coming out in September.

BOBBI'S TRUCK It used to be a Country Squire station wagon.

BOLOGNA, BERMUDA ONION, AND OLIVE OIL John Leandro's favorite sandwich since grade school.

THE BOSTON FIRE DEPARTMENT Lester Moran applied to the department when he was twenty-one years old, but was rejected because of a steel plate in his head.

BOXING THE COMPASS Bobbi Anderson's only book of poetry. It was published in 1974, and the dedication read "This book is for James Gardener."

BRAIN WAVE A novel by Poul Anderson. Bobbi thought that as she uncovered the ship in the earth, a very thin layer of the ship's hull – a molecule or two – was oxidizing as it was uncovered and came in contact with the air. She compared the process with what happened in Peter Straub's novel *Floating Dragon,* and with Anderson's novel.

BRYLCREEM The 3-D Jesus on 'Becka Paulson's TV taught her how to solder by using the example of Brylcreem: "A little dab'll do ya." 'Becka thought it was a little peculiar hearing Jesus talk about Brylcreem.

BUDWEISER The beer that Joe Paulson drank.

THE BUFFALO SOLDIERS The novel that Bobbi mentally dictated into a "modified" typewriter. It was four hundred pages long, and she had computer paper hanging on the wall over the typewriter like paper towels.

BURMA-SHAVE Shaving cream.

CAHOOLAWASSEE The subject of a James Dickey novel.

"CALLERS" Simple electronic devices that were mentally activated.

CAMELS The cigarettes Gard and Bobbi smoked.

CENTRAL MAINE POWER The electric company that serviced Haven.

CESSNA HAWK XP Peter Bailey's plane.

CHEVY VEGA Nancy Voss's car.

THE COKE MACHINE The Coke machine in front of Cooder's market. It rose up eighteen inches off the ground and attacked John Leandro. It broke his shin, crushed his skull, snapped his spine, and left him dead on the road.

COKES The sodas Bobbi and Gard drank.

COLEMAN LANTERN The lantern Bobbi used when she lost power.

CRAZY MAGAZINE The magazine read by the nose-picking deputy who guarded Gard at the Penobscot County Jail following Gard's "Famous Thanksgiving Jag of 1980," during which he shot his wife, Nora.

"CREATIVE PEOPLE HAVE CREATIVE BREAKDOWNS" Gard thought this after seeing all the "modifications" Bobbi had made in her house. He thought she had gone off the deep end.

CUTLASS SUPREME The car Anne Anderson rented from the Bangor Avis agency.

CUTTY SARK. DOUBLE. WATER BACK. The drink Bobbi ordered at the Big Lost Weekend Bar and Grille.

"DAVID BROWN IS ON ALTAIR-4" The message Ruth Mc-Causland found written on the blackboard in her "schoolroom."

DELTA FLIGHT 230 Bobbi's sister Anne Anderson took this flight to Bangor.

DELTA TAU DELTA Gard's college fraternity.

"DERRY STATE POLICEMAN APPARENT SUICIDE, WAS IN CHARGE OF TROOPER DISAPPEARANCE INVESTIGATION" Front page Bangor *Daily News* story by John Leandro that ran on Friday, July 29, 1988.

DES Jim Gardener's ex-mother-in-law had taken this drug.

DETECTIVE BOOK CLUB BOOKS AND READER'S DIGEST CONDENSED BOOKS Some of the books in the Haven Community Library.

THE DISAPPEARING COINS One of the tricks in Hilly Brown's magic set.

DIXIE FIELD-BOSS TIRES Monster Dugan said that these were the wrong tires for a Farmall tractor.

A DODGE John Leandro's car.

A DODGE CARAVEL VAN WITH DELAWARE PLATES After awakening on Arcadia Beach, Gard hitched a ride with the Eddie Parker Band. They drove a Dodge Caravel.

A DODGE DART Ruth McCausland's car.

THE DOLLS Ruth McCausland had a doll collection that included a doll from pre-Communist China, one of Chief Justice John Marshall's daughter's dolls, a genuine Haitian voodoo doll, one of Anna Roosevelt's dolls, Raggedy Ann and Andy dolls, and a Mrs. Beasley doll. Her collection also included a German boy, Effanbee Lady, a Japanese doll, an Indian doll, a Hopi Kachina, a Russian Moss-Man, a China Bisque doll, a French Poupée doll, a Nixon doll, and a Kewpie doll. After Ruth found the message on her blackboard that David Brown was on Altair-4, she heard some of her dolls speaking with the voices of the townspeople: The China Bisque doll spoke in the voice of Beach Jernigan, the French Poupé doll spoke in the voice of Hazel McCready, the Nixon doll, John Enders, and the Kewpie doll, Justin Hurd.

"DON'T BLAME ME; I VOTED FOR HOWARD THE DUCK" The saying written on the visor of Eddie Parker's hat.

A DOORBELL WITH EIGHTEEN PROGRAMMABLE MELODIES One of the improvements Bobbi made in her house after she began to feel the influence of the Tommyknockers. [N OTE: See the entry BOBBI'S "MODIFICATIONS."]

DRINKING GLASSES For a week and a half in 1957, an unnamed family in Charlotte, North Carolina, picked up a classical music station from Florida on the drinking glasses in their home.

DYMOTAPES The labels on the calculators in the Haven selectman's office.

1800 POUNDS The price Hugh Crane paid for Montville Plantation.

1878 The year Montgomery's name was changed to Ilium. (At the time, there was a trend towards giving cities classical names like Sparta, Carthage, Athens, and Troy.)

1816 The year Haven began as Montville Plantation.

1862 The year Albion Cooder, the last surviving Cooder, went bankrupt and commited suicide.

1813 The year Hugh Crane bought Montville Plantation from the Commonwealth of Massachusetts.

1830 The year Hiram Cooder's cousin, George, opened a hostelry and feed store in the south end of Haven village.

1831 In 1831, Montville Plantation became Coodersville.

1828 The year Hiram Cooder's cousin opened the Barber Shop and Small Surgery next to the General Mercantile.

1826 The year Hugh Crane died.

EVEREADY ALKALINE D BATTERIES/EVEREADY LONG-LIFE D-CELL BATTERIES The batteries Bobbi used to run her water heater after she "modified" it. Also, at one point Ruth McCausland dreamed Bobbi Anderson was digging up Eveready batteries.

EX-LAX Hank Buck put a half-box of Ex-Lax in Paul's McDonald's chocolate shake. Paul, Hank's boss, owned Paul's Down-East SuperMart, and Hank hated him. The 3-D Jesus on 'Becka Paulson's TV told her all about it.

EXTRAPOLATING Bobbi knew that extrapolating was part of a fiction writer's business – like trying to fill in the spaces of what happened to the people who had colonized Roanoke Island, North Carolina, when they disappeared from the world with only the word CROATOAN left written on a tree; where the Easter Island monoliths came from; and why, in Blessing, Utah, in 1884, everyone went nuts at the same time.

FAA MAP ECUS-2 The ship in the earth was in the exact middle of square G-3 on this map.

"THE FAMOUS THANKSGIVING JAG OF 1980" Gard's most famous drinking bout. This one ended with him shooting his wife Nora.

THE FAO SCHWARTZ CATALOGUE Marie and Bryant Brown ordered Hilly's birthday gifts from this catalogue.

A FARMALL TRACTOR The tractor Ev Hillman thought of to prove to Monster Dugan that Dugan could read Ev's mind.

FEBRUARY 1972 The month and year Bobbi's grandfather had died of cancer.

FIFTH BUSINESS The first book in Robertson Davies' *Deptford Trilogy.*

THE FIRST GALA MAGIC SHOW Hilly Browns' first backyard magic show.

FLEXIBLE FLYER Hilly Brown's sled.

FLOATING DRAGON A novel by Peter Straub. Bobbi thought that as she uncovered the ship, a very thin layer of the ship's hull – a molecule or two – was oxidizing as it was uncovered. She compared what happened with something in Straub's novel, and in Poul Anderson's novel *Brain Wave.*

A FLYING SAUCER The ship in the earth was a flying saucer. Gard thought that flying saucers had gone out of vogue in the sci-fi genre about the same time as Edgar Rice Burroughs or Otis Adelbert Kline.

A FORCE FIELD A force field kept Gard's fingers out of the chamber where the D batteries ran Bobbi's water heater.

A FORD WAGON Lester Moran's car.

A .45 CALIBER The gun Ev Hillman gave to Monster Dugan.

FOUR BABY TEETH A little boy from Quebec on his way to Old Orchard Beach lost four baby teeth in ten minutes while passing through Haven.

THE FOURTEENTH ANNUAL STATE O' MAINE PHOTOG-RAPHY COMPETITION Photography competition. Christina Lindley won second place.

A FURNACE REBREATHER One of the improvements Bobbi made in her house after she began to feel the influence of the Tommyknockers. [NOTE: See the entry BOBBI'S "MODIFICA-TIONS."]

G.I. JOE, SNAKE EYES, CRYSTAL BALL, MOBAT, AND TERRORDOME Some of Hilly Brown's toys.

GAINES MEAL Peter's previous food. [NOTE: See the entry PETER'S DIET.]

GALLERY A magazine Al Barfield read.

GARD'S VISION OF BOBBI Before Gard's poetry reading at Northeastern, Gard had a vision of Bobbi in her chair with Dean Koontz's *Watchers* open on her lap.

GARDENER'S FIRST RULE FOR TOURING POETS "If it's gratis, grab it."

"GENERAL HOSPITAL" Soap opera 'Becka Paulson watched on TV.

"A GENUINE WORLD CLASS-A THUMPER & WORLD BEATER" Gard's headache the day of his poetry reading at Northeastern University.

THE GIRL'S MILE RACE Event at the Methodist Summer Picnic. Ruth won this race when she was eleven years old, and fainted after she won.

THE GRANGE STATE SPECTACULAR An annual event where Buck Peters did his Jimmy Cagney and John Wayne impersonations.

GRAVY TRAIN Peter's food.

THE GREAT MCDONALD'S EAT OUT A competition Gard participated in in college. He ate six Big Macs.

THE GREAT WHEEL OF KARMA When Gard woke up on Arcadia Beach with the worst hangover of his life, he thought about jumping into the ocean and commiting suicide until the "Great Wheel of Karma" turned in to the next life. He figured "he would just belly flop into the dead zone." [NOTE: See Doug

Winter's insightful analysis of King's use of the image of the Wheel of Karma/Wheel of Fortune in *The Dead Zone* in Doug Winter's *Stephen King: The Art of Darkness* (NAL paperback). Also, see my interview with Doug Winter in this volume.]

A GREEN LIGHT After Bobbi began working at the dig, a green light came out of Peter's cataract. Also, after Gard arrived at Bobbi's house, he thought he saw a green light coming from Bobbi's eyes and from inside Bobbi's typewriter. Gard also dreamt of the green light coming from Bobbi's shed. Gard thought that if cancer had a color, the green light would be its color.

GRIMOIRE Gard's first book of poetry.

HAMILTON BEACH 'Becka Paulson's blender.

HANGTOWN Bobbi's first western novel. It was published in 1975.

"THE HARVEST HOME REVIVAL OF 1900" Illium town celebration which took place on September 7, 1900, after which Preacher Colson fled town. He had impregnated six town girls that night.

"HAVEN CONSTABLE KILLED IN FREAK ACCIDENT— WAS COMMUNITY LEADER" Front page story in the Bangor *Daily News* after Ruth McCausland's death. The story was by John Leandro.

HIDDEN VALLEY RANCH DRESSING A commercial on 'Becka Paulson's Sony.

A HILLCREST FARMS GRADE A JUMBO EGG CARTON The carton Bobbi used to cradle the Eveready Alkaline D batteries she used to run her water heater.

HILLY'S MAGIC SHOW SUPPLIES Hilly asked his mother to buy him the following items at the Radio Shack in the Capitol Mall:

> Ten (10) spring-type contact points @ $.70 each (No. 1334567)
> Three (3) "T" contacts (spring type) @ $1.00 ea (No. 1334709);
> One (1) coaxial cable "barrier" plug @ $2.40 ea (No. 19776-C)

"THE HISTORIC BATTERY RUN OF 1988" Bobbi's battery shopping spree after she was influenced by the Tommyknockers. She hit seven stores.

"HOMEMADE SHIT" Upon awakening on the Arcadia Beach, Gard said, "Kid, in the immortal words of Ed Sanders and Tuli Kupferberg, I feel like homemade shit." [NOTE: In King's long 1969 poem called "Harrison State Park '68," one of the epigraphs he begins the poem with is "And I feel like homemade shit," attributed to Ed Sanders. See the article by Michael Collings in this volume called "The Radiating Pencils of His Bones: The Poetry of Stephen King."]

A HOOVERVILLE STOVE When Bobbi tripped over the ship in the earth, she at first thought it was a tin can (B & M beans or Campbell's soup), or the edge of a Hooverville stove.

HOT TALK A magazine Elmer Haney read.

HOT WATER HEATER Before Bobbi "tommyknockered" her water heater, it had been on the verge of going bad.

HUMPTY DUMPTY Potato chips.

HUSH PUPPIES Shoes.

AN IDIOT SAVANT After Bobbi began to be influenced by the Tommyknockers, she thought her new skills and abilities were evidence that she was an idiot savant.

"IF THE RAPTURE'S TODAY, SOMEBODY GRAB MY STEER-ING WHEEL" A bumper sticker on Frank Garrick's truck.

THE INVENTION Using the guts of an old Texas Instruments calculator, Hilly Brown invented a device that actually made things disappear

JOHN LEANDRO'S FAVORITE SANDWICH SINCE GRADE SCHOOL Bologna, bermuda onion, and olive oil.

JULY 4, 1864 The date Coodersville's name was changed to Montgomery, in honor of Ellis Montgomery, a local boy who fell at Gettysburg.

JULY 4, 1988 The day Gard woke up on Arcadia Beach, New Hampshire, not far from the Arcadia Funworld Amusement Park. He had a hangover so bad that he thought he was having a stroke. The hangover followed his confrontation with Ted the Power Man at the reception following the Northeastern University poetry reading.

JULY 7 The day the picture of Jesus on 'Becka Paulson's Sony TV began to speak to her.

JULY 25, 1988 The day the story by David Bright about the two missing state police officers ran in the Bangor *Daily News.*

JULY 29, 1988 The day a story by John Leandro titled "Derry State Policeman Apparent Suicide, Was In Charge of Trooper Disappearance Investigation" ran on the front page of the Bangor *Daily News.*

JULY 26 John Leandro found out that Ev Hillman had rented a "flat-pack" (for breathing) on July 26.

JUNE 28 Bobbi told Gard that Peter died on June 28. Actually, he was in the shed.

JUNE 25 The date Gard gave a poetry reading at Boston University.

JUNE 21, 1988 The day Bobbi "stumbled over her destiny": The day she tripped over the protruding nosecone of the ship in the earth.

JUNE 24 The day Gard gave a poetry reading in Fall River.

JUNE 27 The date of Gard's reading at Northeastern University.

KREIG PADLOCK Bobbi had one on her shed door.

KYLE-I The vanity plate on Kyle Archinbourg's Cadillac.

"LA GUERRE EST FINI" The phrase that Ev Hillman thought of to prove to Monster Dugan that Dugan could read Ev's mind.

A LATE-FORTIES HUDSON HORNET Bobbi had once found a Hornet buried on New England Paper Company's land.

"LEIGHTON STREET" A poem by Jim Gardener from his book of poetry, *Grimoire.* It was dedicated to Bobbi Anderson.

THE "LEIGHTON STREET" DEDICATION Gard dedicated what he thought was probably his best poem – "Leighton Street" – to Bobbi: "For Bobbi, who first smelled sage in New York."

A LOADED .45 Gard was once arrested in a Seabrook demonstration with a loaded .45 in his backpack.

THE LONG RIDE BACK At the time of the discovery of the ship in the earth, *The Long Ride Back* was Bobbi's latest western novel. It had been published in 1986.

THE LUBBOCK LIGHTS A UFO scare that turned out to be moths.

M-16 The firecracker Ruth McCausland took from Hump Jernigan.

A MAGIC SET Bryant Brown bought Hilly a magic set as a birthday gift from his grandfather.

"MAGNUM" AND "MIAMI VICE" TV shows Joe Paulson watched.

THE MAINE STATE BIRD According to a t-shirt Bobbi wore, the Maine State Bird was a blackfly.

"MAKE LOVE NOT WAR, BE READY FOR BOTH – NRA" The bumpersticker on Beach Jernigan's Chevy truck.

MARCH 1972 The month and year Bobbi wrote the only poem in *Boxing the Compass* that she thought was any good. March 1972 was a month after her grandfather died of cancer.

MARCH 29, 1901 The date Faith Clarendon gave birth to a boy. Preacher Colson was the father. Cora Simard was the midwife. Paul Clarendon cut the baby's throat, then his wife's, then his own. Irwin Simard found the bodies.

MARCH 27, 1901 Ilium's head selectman, Luther Ruvall, proctored the vote to change the name of Ilium to Haven on March 27, 1901.

MASSACRE CANYON At the time of the discovery of the ship in the earth, *Massacre Canyon* was Bobbi Anderson's forthcoming novel. It was due out in September.

MAXI-PADS The pads Bobbi used.

THE MAYFLOWER Patricia McCardle's ancestry was traced to the Mayflower.

MIDOL For period relief.

MILLER LITE The beer Elmer Haney drank.

A MINT GREEN OLDS-88 Newt Berringer's car.

MULTIPLYING COINS AND THE MAGIC GUILLOTINE Two of the tricks in Hilly Brown's magic set.

MUNCHIE MONEY The trade name for chocolate coins.

MUSCULAR DYSTROPHY Vera Anderson had MS, and wore braces on her legs.

"THE NASHVILLE KITTY-CATS THIS FRI AND SAT" Sign at the Big Lost Weekend Bar and Grille.

A NEW DIRT FLOOR IN THE BASEMENT One of the improvements Bobbi made in her house after she began to feel the influence of the Tommyknockers. [NOTE: See the entry (BOBBI'S "MODIFICATIONS."]

THE NEW ENGLAND CONFERENCE OF SMALL TOWNS One of the committees that Ruth McCausland served on.

THE NEW ENGLAND PAPER COMPANY They owned miles of wilderness beyond the wall at the western edge of Bobbi's land. The land they owned was called Burning Woods on the map.

THE NEW ENGLAND POETRY CARAVAN A poet's tour that Jim Gardener participated in that was run by Patricia McCardle. Beginning June 24, Gard was to read in Fall River, followed by two readings in Boston, followed by readings and lectures in Providence and New Haven.

NEW FLUORESCENT LIGHTING IN THE BASEMENT One of the improvements Bobbi made in her house after she began to feel the influence of the Tommyknockers. [NOTE: See the entry BOBBI'S "MODIFICATIONS."]

A NEW, STRONG BANNISTER One of the improvements Bobbi made in her house after she began to feel the influence of the Tommyknockers. [NOTE: See the entry BOBBI'S "MODIFICA-TIONS."]

A NEW WORK TABLE One of the improvements Bobbi made in her house after she began to feel the influence of the Tommyknockers. [NOTE: See the entry BOBBI'S "MODIFICATIONS."]

NEWSWEEK Weekly magazine.

1900 The year Preacher Bradley (Cooder) Colson came to Haven.

1986 The year Bobbi's latest (at the time of the discovery of the ship in the earth) western novel, *The Long Ride Back,* was published.

1959 The year Ruth and Ralph McCausland were married.

1957 For a week and half in 1957, a family in Charlotte, North Carolina, picked up a classical music station from Florida on the drinking glasses in their home.

1975 The year Bobbi's first western novel, *Hangtown,* was published.

1974 The year Bobbi's book of poetry, *Boxing the Compass,* was published.

1973 The year Moss Harlingen murdered his father in Greenville.

A 1930'S VINTAGE UNDERWOOD TYPEWRITER The typewriter Bobbi used to write her first western novel, *Hangtown.*

A NOBEL PRIZE The mathematician from MIT who grasped a new way of looking at mathematics while passing through Haven envisioned winning a Nobel Prize for his insights.

NOSEBLEEDS Gard's skiing accident when he was seventeen had been at Sunday River. Ever since then he had nosebleeds.

THE NUKES Whenever Gard got into trouble, it was always after he had been drinking, and it was always an argument about "the nukes": Seabrook, Chernobyl, Maine Yankee in Wicasset, and Hanford Plant in Washington State.

OCTOBER 5, 1966 The date there was a partial nuclear meltdown of the Enrico Fermi breeder reactor in Michigan. The engineer who was called in took one look, said "You guys almost lost Detroit," and fainted.

103 RESIDENTS When Hugh Crane died in 1826, Haven had 103 residents.

AN "OPUS FOR PRESIDENT T-SHIRT" One of Bobbi's t-shirts.

PEPSI-COLA AND REESE'S PIECES The snack given to Hilly Brown after he was found in the Derry Home Hospital when he was five.

PETER'S CATARACT After Bobbi began working at the dig, Peter's cataract disappeared.

PETER'S DIET At the time of the discovery of the ship in the earth, Peter's latest food was Gravy Train. Previously, when his teeth were able to handle the crunching, his meals had consisted of Gaines Meal in the morning, and then one half can of Rival at night.

"POSTAL WORKERS DO IT BY EXPRESS MAIL" Bumper sticker on Nancy Voss's Chevy Vega.

"THE PRINCIPLE OF COLLAPSING-MOLECULE-FUSION" The principle on which Bobbi's inventions operated. It was nonatomic and totally clean.

A PSYCHOLOGY DEPARTMENT SEMINAR ON CREATIVITY A seminar Bobbi had participated in. It was taught by Dr. Klingerman.

THE PULSE Electromagnetic phenomenon that was theorized to follow big nuclear explosions. Cars and radios stopped dead.

PYORRHEA A gum disease.

THE RADIATION CYCLE Several poems by Jim Gardener about nuclear power. *The Radiation Cycle* had been rejected by five publishers. One editor had written "Poetry and politics rarely mix, poetry and propaganda, never."

"RANGE WAR AND CIVIL WAR" A master's thesis from the University of Nebraska that Bobbi read as part of her continuing research into the Old West.

READINGS AND POETRY WORKSHOPS Gard did poetry readings and workshops to support himself.

A RED SOX GAME Joe Paulson had planned on watching a Red Sox game on the afternoon his wife electrocuted him.

REMINGTON .30-06 Ruth McCausland's shotgun.

THE RIDERS OF THE PURPLE SAGE Bobbi's favorite book as a child.

RIMFIRE CHRISTMAS The title of one of Bobbi Anderson's westerns.

RIVAL Peter's previous food. [NOTE: See the entry PETER'S DIET.]

ROLEX Ron Cummings' watch.

RUBIK'S CUBE The puzzle Hilly Brown got for his ninth birthday.

RUTH'S "PARTY" At the "party" in the town library following Ruth McCausland's funeral, the following food and drink were served:

—coffee;	—cream cheese
—iced tea;	and olive sandwiches;
—Coca-Cola;	—cream cheese and
—ginger-ale;	pimento sandwiches;
—cold cuts;	—Jell-O salad.
—tuna fish sandwiches;	

RUTH'S FUNERAL The following people were among the Havenites who attended Ruth McCausland's funeral:

—Frank Spruce;	—Dick Allison;
—John Mumphrey;	—John Harley;
—Ashley Ruvall;	—the Tremains;
—Doc Warwick;	—the Thurlows;
—Jud Tarkington;	—the Applegates;
—Adley McKeen;	—the Goldmans;
—Hazel McCready;	—the Duplisseys;
—Newt Berringer;	—the Archinbourgs.

A "SCHOOL-LUNCH VICTIM" T-SHIRT T-shirt worn by Jack on Arcadia Beach.

A SEABROOK DEMONSTRATION Gard had once been arrested at Seabrook with a loaded .45 in his backpack.

THE SECOND GALA MAGIC SHOW Hilly Brown's backyard magic show, during which he successfully transported his brother David to Altair-4.

SEPTEMBER 7, 1900 The night of the "Harvest Home Revival of 1900," and the night Preacher Colson fled Haven (after impregnating six girls that night.)

"SESAME STREET" TV show David Brown watched.

A SETH THOMAS CLOCK The clock donated to the library by the grammar school.

SHERRY FENDERSON'S POSTCARD TO BOBBI After Bobbi published *Hangtown*, she wrote Sherry a long letter. Sherry sent her back a postcard that said: "Please don't write me anymore. I don't know you." Sherry felt Bobbi had denied her true artistry by writing a western, and so rejected her.

THE SHOP The special department that investigated happenings in Haven, Maine.

A SHOTGUN As Gard decided what to do about the ship in the earth, Bobbi had a shotgun pointed at the back of his head. If he made the wrong decision, goodbye.

SILVA COMPASS Bobbi's compass.

A SILVERCHIME DIGITAL DOORBELL The programmable doorbell Bobbi installed after she started to feel the influence of the Tommyknockers. Some of the programmable tunes included "Raindrops Keep Fallin' On My Head," "New York, New York," and "Lara's Theme."

A SIMON POCKETWATCH Bobbi's Uncle Frank had once given her a Simon pocketwatch.

"SIX-YEAR-OLD PREGNANT BY SAUCER ALIEN, TEARFUL MOTHER REVEALS" Tabloid headline. Gard thought the tabloids were the only place flying saucers were still in vogue. The stories all seemed to take place in either Brazil or New Hampshire.

A SMITH & WESSON .38 John Leandro's gun.

SOLDIER OF FORTUNE Magazine that Elmer Haney read.

A SOMBRERO The drink Anne Anderson ordered at the Cityscape Hotel. As she put it to the waiter, "A sombrero has Kahlua and cream in it. *Cream*. If you bring me a sombrero with milk in it, chum, you're going to be shampooing with the motherfucker."

A SONY The Paulsons' TV.

A SONY TAPE RECORDER AND A NIKON CAMERA John Leandro put these two things in his car when he set out to Haven.

A STANDING OVATION Gard got a standing ovation for his reading of "Leighton Street" at Northeastern University.

"THE STAPLES" Bobbi's basic booze supply. She kept them in a cabinet behind the pots and pans. The staples included a bottle of gin, Scotch, bourbon, and vodka.

STARTLING STORIES After a force field kept Gard's finger's out of the chamber in Bobbi's water heater where the D batteries sat, Gard felt like he'd walked in to a sci-fi story from *Startling Stories,* circa 1947.

A STEEL PLATE Gard had one in his head. He got it from a skiing accident that almost killed him when he was seventeen.

"STEM CHRISTIE" Annmarie told Gard to "stem christie" as she saw him skiing towards a tree on Victory Mountain in Vermont.

A SUBARU The mathematician's car.

THE SYMBOL The "almost Chinese symbol" on the hatchway of the ship in the earth. "It was pressed into the metal of the ship like bas-relief." Gard wondered what it meant: No Trespassing? We Came in Peace? Abandon Hope, All Ye Who Enter Here?

THE TAB Expenses incurred by poets while on the New England Poetry Caravan. The Tab was picked up by the Caravan. While in New York, Gard watched *Emmanuelle, Indiana Jones and the Temple of Doom,* and *Rainbow Brite and the Star-Stealer.* He charged them to the Caravan.

TAMPAX, MODESS, AND STAY-FREE After the discovery of the ship in the earth, and its subsequent influence of the Tommyknockers on Haven and its residents, Cooder's General Store was completely bought out of these sanitary products.

"THE TELL-TALE HEART" After Bobbi tripped over the ship in the earth, she had a dream of Poe's "The Tell-Tale Heart." She dreamt of a green beam of light, and her teeth falling out.

THE TEXTILE BUSINESS Ron Cummings' family was in the

textile business. Consequently, Ron had loads of money and could afford to be a fulltime poet/playboy/partyer.

"THEY CALL ME DR. LOVE" Legend written on David Brown's t-shirt.

THIRTY POUNDS When Gard finally got to Bobbi's house after hearing the voice that told him "Bobbi's in trouble," Bobbi had already lost thirty pounds.

A 3-D PICTURE OF JESUS The picture that sat on top of the Paulsons' Sony TV. One day, it began speaking to 'Becka Paulson.

A .357 MAGNUM Monster Dugan's gun.

300 YARDS IN CIRCUMFERENCE By extrapolating from the visible part of the ship in the earth, Bobbi figured that the craft had to be three hundred yards in circumference.

A THREE-INCH PIECE OF METAL The tip of the ship in the earth. Bobbi tripped over it.

3:05 P.M. The time the tower blew off the Haven town hall.

THREE SHOPPING BAGS OF NEW POTATOES Gard had once traded a birthday sonnet for a farmer's wife in exchange for three shopping bags of new potatoes. The farmer insisted that the sonnet rhyme.

TIMEX Gard and Bobbi's watch.

A TOMCAT Bobbi's tractor. It cost her $2,500, and had a 4cc engine. Bobbi "modified" it so that it also had an "Up" gear and flew.

THE TOMMYKNOCKERS RHYMES:

> Late last night and the night before,
> Tommyknockers, Tommyknockers,
> knocking at the door.
> I want to go out, don't know if I can,
> 'cause I'm so afraid
> of the Tommyknocker man.
> —Traditional

> Late last night and the night before,
> Tommyknockers, Tommyknockers,
> Knocking at the door.
> I was crazy and Bobbi was sane
> But that was before the Tommyknockers came.
> —Jim Gardener

THE TOMPALL IQ TEST Intelligence test that Hilly Brown was given. It determined that he was a genius.

A TRUCKLOAD OF LOAM Bobbi got the loam for her new cellar floor in Albion.

TUESDAY, NOVEMBER 10, 1947 The day Delbert McCready went into Big Injun Woods and got lost.

TWO MONTHS IN JAIL Gard had spent two months in jail for having a concealed and unlicensed handgun at the Seabrook demonstration.

"TWO STATE POLICE DISAPPEAR IN DERRY – AREA-WIDE MANHUNT BEGINS" The lead story in the Bangor *Daily News* on July 25, 1988. The story was by David Bright.

TYPE "O" Gard's blood.

AN UNDERWOOD Bobbi's typewriter was an old black Underwood.

VALIANT Ev Hillman's car.

VALIUM Gard found a bottle of Valium with his name on it in Bobbi's medicine chest. As Bobbi became more and more controlled by the Tommyknockers, she wanted to keep Gard quiet by feeding him Valium. He flushed one a night down the toilet instead of taking it.

"VIET CONG," "HOOCH," OR "MY LAI" Peter the beagle would play dead if Bobbi said any of these words.

THE VOICES Bobbi knew that most people didn't like to live alone because the voices from the right side of their brain demanded attention and, to many people, it was too easy to be frightened of the voices. Often, people thought they were going mad.

A WATER HEATER THAT RAN ON BATTERIES One of the improvements Bobbi made in her house after she began to feel the influence of the Tommyknockers. [NOTE: See the entry BOBBI'S "MODIFICATIONS."]

A "WAYLON JENNINGS FOR PRESIDENT" BUMPER-STICKER Bumpersticker over the bar in the Stone Country Bar and Grille.

A WEBBER FUEL TRUCK A driver crashed this fuel truck trying to avoid Hilly Brown's sled, thinking that Hilly was on the sled. He didn't know Hilly had fallen off.

THE WECHSLER TEST IQ test. Mrs. Underhill told the Browns to take Hilly to Bangor to have this test administered in order to find out what Hilly's IQ was.

"WHAT A FRIEND WE HAVE IN JESUS" AND "THIS IS MY FATHER'S WORLD" Two hymns Reverend Goohringer programmed into the carillon for Ruth McCausland's funeral. They were Ruth's favorites.

"WHEN WE MEET AT JESUS' FEET" Hymn programmed into Reverend Goohringer's carillon.

"WHERE DO YOU WANT TO PUT HIM?" The question that the computer in the shed asked Gard about what to do with David Brown.

"THE WHOLE BODY TRIP" Bobbi's term for the type of hangover Gard had when he woke up on Arcadia Beach on July 4, 1988.

"WHOPPER SPARERIBS OUR SPECIALTY" Sign at the Big Lost Weekend Bar and Grille.

WZON The Rock Zone. A radio station in Bangor. Once, Gard stuck his finger in a socket, and the plate in his head allowed him to pick up WZON for a week. [NOTE: WZON really exists, and was once owned by Stephen King.]

THE YALE YOUNGER POETS COMPETITION Annual literary competition.

A YELLOW CHALLENGER Bobby Tremain's car.

"YOU GUYS ALMOST LOST DETROIT." On October 5, 1966, there was a partial nuclear meltdown of the Enrico Fermi breeder reactor in Michigan. The engineer who was called in took one look, said "You guys almost lost Detroit," and fainted.

YOUNG MEN FOR CHRIST John Leandro belonged to this church group.

THE DARK HALF

DEDICATION

This book is for Shirley Sonderegger.
who helps me mind my business,
and for her husband, Peter

[No CONTENTS PAGE]

BOOK BREAKDOWN

Author's Note—(Untitled section consisting of two sentences, signed "S.K.")

Prologue—(One unnumbered, untitled section preceded by a paragraph from *Machine's Way* by George Stark as an epigraph)

PART ONE
FOOL'S STUFFING
(Preceded by an excerpt from
Riding to Babylon by George Stark as an epigraph)

Chapter 1:   PEOPLE WILL TALK—(Two untitled

(27)
THE DARK HALF
People

ADDAMS, CHARLES Cartoonist.

ALBERTSON, DR. LESTER The physician who assisted Dr. Pritchard during Thad Beaumont's childhood operation to determine the cause of Todd's headaches.

ARSENAULT, DOLLY Dolly told Norris Ridgewick that she had seen Homer Gamache stop his truck and pick up a man in a suit near Homeland Cemetery on the night Homer was found murdered.

BANNERMAN, GEORGE The Castle Rock sheriff before Pangborn. He had survived a series of rape-strangulations by one of his own men (Frank Dodd), only to be killed by Joe Camber's rabid dog, Cujo. [NOTE: See the sections on *The Dead Zone* and *Cujo* in this volume.]

BARRINGER, FRANKLIN The author of *Folklore in America*.

BATMAN Warren Hamilton became a cop because of Batman.

BEAR, YOGI He hung out (with Boo-Boo) in Jellystone Park.

BEAUMONT, GLEN Thad Beaumont's father.

BEAUMONT, LIZ Elizabeth Stephens Beaumont. Thad's wife, and the mother of William and Wendy Beaumont.

BEAUMONT, SHAYLA Thad Beaumont's mother.

BEAUMONT, THAD Thaddeus Beaumont. Writer, teacher, author of two novels as Thad Beaumont, *The Sudden Dancers* and *Purple Haze*, and four novels as "George Stark," *Machine's Way*, *Oxford Blues*, *Sharkmeat Pie*, and *Riding to Babylon*. Thad was the "father" of his dark half, George Stark (who was actually an unabsorbed twin). At the time of George Stark's "resurrection," Thad was working on a novel called *The Golden Dog*, and he briefly collaborated on the aborted fifth "George Stark" novel called *Steel Machine*. Thad's first short story was called "Outside Marty's House," for which he won honorable mention in an *American Teen* magazine writing contest.

BEAUMONT, WENDY Thad and Liz Beaumont's daughter. She was a twin to her brother Wendy.

BEAUMONT, WILLIAM Thad and Liz Beaumont's son. He was a twin to his sister Wendy.

THE BERGENFIELD HOSPITAL WOMAN Sheriff Pangborn got Hugh Pritchard's home address and phone number from an unnamed woman at Bergenfield Hospital.

"BILLIE" Wilhelmina Burks.

BLACK, HARRY One of Thad Beaumont's childhood friends. Harry was swimming with Thad the day that Thad almost drowned in Lake Davis.

THE BLACK DETECTIVE A black detective who wore a "Property of the N.Y. Yankees" t-shirt was sent to protect Mike Donaldson after Phyllis Myers was murdered.

THE BLUE-HAIRED LADIES While ditching the Suburban, Thad saw a car filled with blue-haired ladies almost crash into a couple in a Datsun Z.

BOOKER, LOUISE The woman at *Publisher's Weekly* who was given the "George Stark" scoop by Rick Cowley (with Thad's approval).

BOWIE, DAVID Liz Beaumont thought that her husband Thad would look like David Bowie if he wore a blonde wig.

BOX, EDGAR A pseudonym.

BRADFORD, DEKE One of Digger Holt's co-workers on the Castle Rock groundskeeping crew. Bradford was the head of the public works department.

BRANNIGAN, OSSIE He owned a '59 T-bird and stored it in Fuzzy Martin's barn.

BRIGGS, MRS. Norton Briggs's wife. He hit her with a frying pan. Thinking she was dead, he then killed himself with a .38 caliber revolver. Mrs. Briggs wasn't dead, however, and when she woke up and saw her dead husband, she tried to kill herself by sticking her head in a gas oven. She was revived by the Oxford Rescue Services paramedics.

BRIGGS, NORTON Norton Briggs hit his wife with a frying pan. Thinking she was dead, he then killed himself with a .38 caliber revolver. Mrs. Briggs wasn't dead, however, and when she woke up and saw her dead husband, she tried to kill herself by sticking her head in a gas oven. She was revived by the Oxford Rescue Services paramedics.

BRIGHAM, SHEILA The Castle Rock daytime police dispatcher.

BUNDY, TED The serial killer who passed a lie detector test.

BURKS, WILHELMINA Rawlie DeLesseps' girlfriend. She worked in the history department at the university. She told everyone to "Just call me Billie, everyone does." Thad Beaumont called her "The Wicked Witch of the East." [NOTE: See the section on "The Crate" in the *Creepshow* section in this volume.]

BURRETTS, ROLAND Darwin Press's chief comptroller.

BURROUGHS, WILLIAM Author. Thad had once been on a panel with Burroughs at the New School in New York.

CARROLL, LEWIS A pseudonym.

CARROLL, TOM The guest of honor at Thad and Liz's party on May 31. It was a retirement party for Tom, who had been in the English department for nineteen years, and who had retired on May 27.

CARSON, JOHNNY The host of "The Tonight Show."

CASPER The Friendly Ghost.

"CAUTIOUS" One of the police officers sent to protect Phyllis Myers after Miriam Cowley's murder.

CHALMERS, POLLY The owner of You Sew and Sew, the shop where Annie Pangborn worked part-time.

CHATTERTON, OFFICER One of the Maine state police officers assigned to guard Thad and his family. Chatterton was killed by Stark.

THE CHIEF COMPTROLLER'S EX-SECRETARY The girl who used to work at Darwin Press. She gave Fred Clawson copies of George Stark's royalty statements.

THE CHIEF OF DETECTIVES After Rick Cowley told the cops guarding him about Stark's phone call, one of them told him that the chief of detectives wanted to see him down at One Police Plaza.

THE CLARKS The Beaumonts' neighbors.

CLAWSON, FREDERICK The "smarmy little prick" who discovered that Beaumont and Stark were the same writer. Clawson was later killed by Stark. Dodie Eberhart called him "Mr. Bigshot." At the time of his death, Clawson was a law student.

THE CLERK The stationery store clerk who sold Thad a box of Berol Black Beauty pencils, and let him use their pencil sharpener.

CLUTTERBACK, ANDY A Castle Rock police officer.

COE, TUCKER A pseudonym.

THE COMEDIAN The May 23 issue of *People* magazine reported the story of a comedian who was fighting a palimony suit.

COMMUNICATIONS TECHNICIAN #1 One of the two cops who put the tracer equipment on Rick Cowley's phones after his call from Stark. He was found with a note tacked to his forehead that said "The Sparrows Are Flying Again." The other was also found with a note tacked to his forehead that said "More Fool's Stuffing. Tell Thad."

COMMUNICATIONS TECHNICIAN #2 One of the two cops who put the tracer equipment on Rick Cowley's phones after his call from Stark. He was found with a note tacked to his forehead that said "The Sparrows Are Flying Again." The other was also found

with a note tacked to his forehead that said "More Fool's Stuffing. Tell Thad."

COP #1 One of the cops who was assigned to protect Rick Cowley after Miriam Cowley was murdered.

COP #2 One of the cops who was assigned to protect Rick Cowley after Miriam Cowley was murdered.

THE COUNTY CORONER He was called in on the murder of Homer Gamache.

THE COUPLE IN THE DATSUN Z While ditching the Suburban, Thad saw a car filled with blue-haired ladies almost crash into a couple in a Datsun Z.

COWLEY, MIRIAM Rick Cowley's ex-wife and a partner in his literary agency. Miriam was killed by George Stark for her role in "killing him off."

COWLEY, MR. Rick's father.

COWLEY, RICK Thad Beaumont's agent.

CURIOUS TOWN RESIDENTS Some of the people who just "dropped by" the Beaumont house after the *People* magazine article about George Stark's "demise" ran.

DAISY George Stark's fictitious dog. Stark told officers "Cautious" and "Extremely" that someone had killed Daisy. It was a ruse to get at Phyllis Myers. It worked.

DAVE One of the two telephone technicians sent to Thad Beaumont's house to place recording and trace-back equipment on Thad's phone lines.

"THE DEAN OF THE DEAD PIPE" Rawlie DeLesseps.

DeLESSEPS, RAWLIE The English professor who was one of Thad's best friends at the university. Rawlie lent Thad his car for Thad's final confrontation with Stark.

THE DEMOCRATIC SENATOR One of the two Washington men (the other was a Republican representative) who gave Dodie Eberhart enough money to retire from hooking.

DONALDSON, MIKE The writer who did the story about Thad Beaumont's "George Stark" alias for *People* magazine.

THE DRIVE-UP GIRL When Warren Hamilton saw the blood in Homer Gamache's truck, he wondered what the driver of the truck had told the McDonald's drive-up girl about the blood.

EBERHART, DODIE Fred Clawson's landlady. She used to be a high-priced call girl in Washington, DC, before she retired.

EDDINGS, JACK One of the Maine state police officers assigned to guard Thad and his family. Eddings was killed by Stark.

ELIOT, GEORGE A pseudonym.

EVELYN One of the characters in Thad Beaumont's novel *The Sudden Dancers*.

"EXTREMELY" One of the police officers sent to protect Phyllis Myers after Miriam Cowley's murder.

FARMER JOHN A character in Thad Beaumont's novel, *Purple Haze*. Farmer John had to shoot a horse that had two broken legs. Dodie Eberhart thought that this scene was written by George Stark rather than Beaumont, like some "literary Rumpelstilskin."

FENTON, MRS. The University of Maine's English department secretary who had died in April of the year in which Thad had to deal with George Stark.

FIFE, DEPUTY BARNEY Norris Ridgewick looked like Barney.

THE FIRST BEAUMONT TWINS Before Wendy and William were born, Liz Beaumont had miscarried twins in her third month.

THE FISHERMAN As part of Alan Pangborn's problems with "summer in Vacationland," a fisherman tore off half of his own right ear while trying to make a fancy fishing cast.

FORTIN, CHARLIE Charlie occasionally did odd jobs for the Beaumonts at their house.

FREIDA A woman who worked for Rick Cowley.

GAMACHE, ELLEN Homer's wife. She called the police when Homer didn't come home from bowling.

GAMACHE, HOMER The man found murdered in his truck on Route 35. He was murdered by George Stark, even though Thad

Beaumont's fingerprints were all over the truck.

GATES, DARLA The girl who gave Fred Clawson information about Thad's pseudonym. She ended up a victim of George Stark.

GAVINEAUX, FRANK Frank was the boy who found Homer Gamache's body after Homer was murdered by George Stark.

GOLDEN, ELLIE Thad Beaumont's Darwin Press "George Stark" editor.

"GONZO TOM" Tom Carroll. (Tom was a big admirer of Hunter Thompson's essays.)

GOODIS, DAVID One of Dodie Eberhart's favorite writers.

GRIFFITHS, NONIE The character in *Machine's Way* who used a straight razor to cut Alexis Machine.

HALSTEAD, JACK One of the characters in the George Stark novel *Riding to Babylon*. Alexis Machine stabbed him in the eye with a small steel rod, as Maureen Romano did to the Greek in "The Wedding Gig." [NOTE: See the "People" entry JACK RANGELY, as well as the section on "The Wedding Gig" (in the *Skeleton Crew* section) in this volume.]

HAMILTON, WARREN A Connecticut state trooper.

"HANSEL" AND "GRETEL" The two kids who got lost in the woods the summer Alan Pangborn was confronted with Thad Beaumont's George Stark problems.

HARKAVAY, JERRY Jerry was the entire staff of Associated Press's Waterville office.

HARRISON, GEORGE Ex-Beatle.

HARRISON, STEVE Maine state police officer. He guarded Thad's house.

HARTLAND, TREVOR Castle Rock's fire chief.

THE HEAD RANGER Alan Pangborn asked Henry Payton if he would call the Yellowstone National Park head ranger regarding Hugh Pritchard.

HENRY One of the characters in Thad Beaumont's novel *The Sudden Dancers*.

HILARY The assisting operating room nurse who screamed and ran from the room when she saw what was in Thad Beaumont's head. Dr. Pritchard had her fired.

HOLT, DIGGER Steven Holt.

HOLT, STEVEN (DIGGER) The head of Castle Rock's three-man groundskeeping crew. He was sixty-one.

HUME, DR. The doctor Thad consulted about the return of the bird noises in his head. Hume sent Thad for a series of cranial x-rays and a CAT scan at the Eastern Maine Medical Center.

THE HUSBAND Sheriff Pangborn remembered a situation involving a husband who swore he'd shoot his wife if she got a divorce. She was assigned police protection. The husband borrowed a laundry truck, dressed in fatigues, walked up to her door, rang the bell, and shot her dead when she answered. The police didn't even know what was happening.

JACKETT, SONNY The owner of a Castle Rock Sunoco station.

JOHN A man who worked for Rick Cowley.

JOHN A Castle Rock police officer.

JOHN WESLEY HARDING Thad Beaumont's pet raccoon when he was an Appalachian Trail guide in Maine, New Hampshire, and Vermont.

KEETON, "BUSTER" Danforth Keeton.

KEETON, DANFORTH ("BUSTER") Castle Rock's first selectman.

LaPOINTE, JOHN Alan Pangborn's #2 deputy. He got poison ivy while searching for the two lost kids ("Hansel" and "Gretel") in the woods.

LENNON, JOHN The murdered Beatle.

LETTERMAN, DAVID The host of "Late Night with David Letterman." [NOTE: Now's as good a time as any to insert the following "Stephen King Top Ten" list that Dave did on "Late Night" on Thursday, April 27, 1989:

TOP TEN LINES FROM STEPHEN KING NOVELS

10. "Oh, there's nothing in the attic."

9. "I know it sounds crazy but that Water Pik is after me!"

8. Stop making fun of my ability to levitate butcher knives—or you'll be sorry."

7. "I've got a feeling that small green dot on your skin will be larger by Chapter 8."

6. "This is a losing battle. Let's just paint the walls red."

5. "This seems awfully large for just a turkey leg."

4. "I've bought a lot of suits in thrift shops before – but this was the first one that ever tried to strangle me."

3. "Since my wife died, our love life has been great."

2. "The company's been sold. You're working for General Electric now."

and the Number One Line from Stephen King's novels…

1. "I've been a veterinarian for thirty years and I'm telling you—that's no ordinary Poodle."]

LORING, DR. The anesthesiologist during the operation on Thad Beaumont's head to determine the cause of his headaches.

MACHINE, ALEXIS The main character of George Stark's novels.

THE MAINTENANCE MEN After the sparrows flew into the west side of Bergenfield County Hospital (following Thad's brain surgery, and while he lay in the intensive care unit), maintenance men cleaned up more than three hundred dead birds.

MALONE One of the FBI men who questioned Thad after Miriam Cowley's murder.

A MAN IN GREEN FATIGUES The man who drove the beer truck that Alan Pangborn saw parked at the Route 5 rest area.

THE MAN IN GREY MECHANICS COVERALLS He saw the thousands of sparrows in Gold's junkyard take flight when Thad told them to go find George Stark.

MARX, GROUCHO The host of "You Bet Your Life."

MARY LOU One of the characters in Thad Beaumont's novel *The Sudden Dancers*.

THE MARYLAND HOUSEWIFE The May 23 issue of *People* magazine reported the story of a Maryland housewife who grew a squash that looked like a bust of Jesus.

THE MASSENBURGS Neighbors of the Beaumonts.

McCOY, HORACE One of Dodie Eberhart's favorite writers.

THE MEDICAL EXAMINER He determined that Homer Gamache was killed between 1:00 and 3:00 a.m. on June 1.

MYERS, PHYLLIS The *People* magazine photographer who shot the photo of Liz and Thad Beaumont "burying" George Stark.

NIXON, RICHARD George Stark told Liz Beaumont that Tolstoy and Richard Nixon were both crazy.

THE NURSE Thad's intensive care unit nurse after his brain surgery. She believed that Thad woke up from his anesthesia about five minutes after the sparrows attacked the hospital building.

OLLINGER One of Rick Cowley's author clients. Ollinger wrote bad science fiction novels.

THE ORNITHOLOGIST The expert quoted in the article in the Bergenfield *Courier* about the sparrows who flew into the west side of the Bergenfield County Hospital. He said the birds were attracted by the bright sunlight reflected on the glass windows.

THE OXFORD RESCUE SERVICES PARAMEDICS Norton Briggs hit his wife with a frying pan. Thinking she was dead, he then killed himself with a .38 caliber revolver. Mrs. Briggs wasn't dead, however, and when she woke up and saw her dead husband, she tried to kill herself by sticking her head in a gas oven. She was revived by the Oxford Rescue Services paramedics.

PANGBORN, ANNIE Sheriff Pangborn's wife.

PANGBORN, SHERIFF ALAN The Castle Rock sheriff.

PANGBORN, TOBY One of Alan and Annie Pangborn's sons.

PANGBORN, TODD One of Alan and Annie Pangborn's sons.

A PARAPLEGIC GIRL The May 23 issue of *People* magazine reported the story of a paraplegic girl who was training for the Big Apple Bike-A-Thon.

PARKER The main character of Donald Westlake's "Richard Stark" novels. Parker was a professional thief.

THE PAYNES Neighbors of the Beaumonts.

PAYTON, HENRY The state cop from the Oxford state police barracks who was called in to investigate the murder of Homer Gamache. He was Oxford's O.C. and C.I.D. man.

PENDER, JUDGE Judge Pender gave a woman who had beaten her husband to death six months in the women's correctional institution, and six years probation. (Pangborn believed that the judge should have given her a medal, instead.)

PENNINGTON, MR. Miriam Cowley's father.

PENNINGTON, MRS. Miriam Cowley's mother.

PHILLIPS, DAVE One of Digger Holt's co-workers on the Castle Rock groundskeeping crew. Dave occasionally did odd jobs for the Beaumonts at their house.

PREBBLE, BILL One of the FBI men who questioned Thad after Miriam Cowley's murder.

PRITCHARD, HELGA Dr. Hugh Pritchard's wife.

PRITCHARD, HUGH The best neurologist in New Jersey. He ordered x-rays of Thad Beaumont's head after Thad went into convulsions while waiting for the school bus. Dr. Pritchard later performed the surgery to excise the parts of "George Stark" that were in Thad's brain.

RAINS, CLAUDE Actor who played the title role in "The Invisible Man."

RANGELY, JACK One of Alexis Machine's "assistants" in the murder of Halstead in *Riding to Babylon*. (Jack held Halstead's head while Machine stabbed Halstead in the left eye with a small steel rod.) [NOTE: This harkens back to the Stephen King short story "The Wedding Gig." Maureen Rico Romano did away with her enemy, the Greek, by sticking a piece of piano wire through his left eye.]

REARDON, LIEUTENANT The New York cop with whom Sheriff Pangborn consulted many times regarding George Stark.

REED, MR. The school bus driver who saved Thad Beaumont's life as a child when Thad had a convulsion on the sidewalk. Reed had been a medic in Korea.

THE REPORTER The reporter who wrote the story for the Bergenfield *Courier* about the sparrows flying into the windows of the Bergenfield County Hospital.

THE REPUBLICAN REPRESENTATIVE One of the two Washington men (the other was a Democratic senator) who gave Dodie Eberhart enough money to retire from hooking.

RIDGEWICK, NORRIS The officer who was at the scene of Homer Gamache's murder with Sheriff Pangborn. (Ridgewick looked like Barney Fife on "The Andy Griffith Show.")

THE ROBERTS Thad had once read an account of two twins who had been separated at birth. It was later learned that they had both married on the same day, both had married women with the same first name and similar looks, and both had named their first sons Robert. Also, the two Roberts had both been born in the same month and year.

RODWAY, JOE The Castle Rock man who blew his wife's brains out and then fled. He was picked up by police in Kingston, Rhode Island.

RODWAY, MRS. Joe's wife. Joe blew her brains out.

ROLLICK One of the characters in *Steel Machine*. He was armed with a Steyr-Aug semi-automatic machine gun.

ROSALIE The girl who worked behind the counter in Dave's Market.

THE SADDLERS Neighbors of the Beaumonts.

"SECRET AGENT X-9" Fred Clawson, according to Thad Beaumont.

SEWARD, DR. The doctor who told Thad's parents that Thad's childhood headaches were migraines. Little did he know.

THE SHULMANS Two of Dodie Eberhart's tenants. Mr. Shulman was a corporate lawyer. The Shulmans liked Guns 'n Roses.

SIS Miriam Cowley, according to George Stark.

SIXTY STUDENTS Sixty students applied for Thad's honors course in creative writing.

STARK, GEORGE Thad Beaumont's dark half. Thad had written one bestseller and three successful follow-up novels using this pseudonym. (Stark was one of Dodie Eberhart's favorite writers.)

STARK, RICHARD The pseudonym Donald Westlake used to write a series of crime novels. Thad Beaumont acknowledged that "George Stark" was a nod to Westlake.

THE STATIONER A stationer on Houston Street in New York City sold George Stark three boxes of Berol Black Beauty pencils.

STEVENS One of the state troopers who was stationed in front of Thad's house after Stark began calling Thad.

TELLFORD, MARTHA Liz Beaumont's aunt. Martha lived in Castle Rock.

THOMPSON, JIM One of Dodie Eberhart's favorite writers.

THE THREE ELDERLY LADIES The three ladies who spoke with Pangborn at the Route 5 rest area. One of the ladies owned the Ford Escort parked there.

TOLSTOY George Stark told Liz Beaumont that Tolstoy and Richard Nixon were both crazy.

TOOMEY, CHARLES F., JR. The Washington, DC, police officer who was the first to arrive at Dodie's apartment house after she called about Fred Clawson's murder.

TOOMEY, STEPHANIE Washington, DC, police officer Charles F. Toomey, Jr.'s wife.

TOTAL STRANGERS Some of the people who just "dropped by" the Beaumont house after the *People* magazine article about George Stark's "demise" ran.

TWAIN, MARK A pseudonym.

THE TWIN BOYS Thad had once read an account of twin boys who had been separated by an entire continent. When one of the boys broke his left leg, the other twin felt excruciating pain in *his* left leg.

THE TWIN FATHERS OF ROBERT Thad had once read an account of two twins who had been separated at birth. It was later learned that they had both married on the same day, both had married women with the same first name and similar looks, and both had named their first sons Robert. Also, the two Roberts had both been born in the same month and year.

THE TWIN GIRLS Thad had once read an account of twin girls who had developed their own special language, which could be understood by no one else on earth.

THE TWO BROKERS Two of Dodie Eberhart's "johns." She wished she had held onto them after she retired from hooking.

THE TWO DEAD PEOPLE Just before Norton Briggs hit his wife with a frying pan, there had been "a gaudy four-car smashup" on Route 117 that left two people dead.

TWO GIRLS Thad noticed two girls on their way to the East Annex to sign up for summer courses at the university.

TWO STATE TROOPERS Two state troopers accompanied Sheriff Pangborn to Thad Beaumont's house when Thad was under suspicion for Homer Gamache's murder.

TWO SUMMER PEOPLE Two Castle Rock summer people got into a fist fight at Nan's Luncheonette over the last copy of the New York *Times*.

THE UTAH ENTREPENEUR The May 23 issue of *People* magazine reported the story of a Utah entrepeneur who was marketing a doll called "Yo Mamma!" The doll was guaranteed to look like "everyone's favorite (?) mother-in-law."

"VAGUE ACQUAINTANCES" Some of the people who just "dropped by" the Beaumont house after the *People* magazine article about George Stark's "demise" ran.

VAN ALLEN, RAY Castle County's medical examiner and coroner.

WES One of the two telephone technicians sent to Thad Beaumont's house to place recording and trace-back equipment on Thad's phone lines.

WESTERMAN, TONY One of the characters in *Steel Machine*. He was armed with a Steyr-Aug semi-automatic machine gun.

WESTLAKE, DONALD E. The crime writer who also wrote a series of novels under the name of Richard Stark.

"THE WICKED WITCH OF THE EAST" Wilhelmina Burks, according to Thad Beaumont.

"THE WICKED WITCH OF L STREET" Dodie Eberhart, according to her tenants, the Shulmans.

THE WIFE Pangborn remembered the situation involving a husband who swore he'd shoot his wife if she got a divorce. She was assigned police protection. The husband borrowed a laundry truck, dressed in fatigues, walked up to her door, rang the bell, and shot her dead when she answered. The police didn't even know what was happening.

WILLEFORD, CHARLES One of Dodie Eberhart's favorite writers.

THE WILLIAMS Castle Rock summer people from Lynn, Massachusetts. They had a house near Thad's.

WILMOT, GASPARD The inventor of the "Yo Mamma!" doll. (Mr. Wilmot had once been indicted for tax evasion, but the charges had been dropped.)

WISTER, RANDY One of Thad Beaumont's childhood friends. Harry was swimming with Thad the day Thad almost drowned in Lake Davis.

THE WOMAN WHO BEAT HER HUSBAND TO DEATH Judge Pender gave her six months in the women's correctional institution, and six months probation. Pangborn believed the judge should have given the woman a medal.

A WRESTLER The May 23 issue of *People* magazine reported the story of a wrestler who was recovering from a heart attack.

THE YOUNG BLONDE STATE TROOPER One of the state troopers who was stationed in front of Thad's house after Stark began calling Thad.

(27)

THE DARK HALF
Places

THE AGENCY LIQUOR STORE Booze emporium about a half-mile from the Beaumont house in Castle Rock.

AMES, IOWA Miriam Cowley believed that you could leave your front door unlocked in either Fargo, North Dakota, or Ames, Iowa, but not in the Big Apple. That's why she had a Kreig lock on her apartment door.

ARMED SERVICES RECORDS AND IDENTIFICATIONS The Washington department that determined that the fingerprints found in Homer Gamache's truck were Thad Beaumont's.

AN ARMY-NAVY STORE George Stark bought a few things at an army-navy store in New York City. He bought Levi's, underwear, socks, and handkerchiefs.

AN AUGUSTA SERVICE STATION On the way to his final confrontation with George Stark, Thad stopped at an Augusta service station and poured three quarts of Sapphire motor oil into Rawlie DeLesseps' Volkswagen.

BERGENFIELD, NEW JERSEY The town where Thad Beaumont was born. Bergenfield was also one of the places where Dr. Hugh Pritchard practiced "doctoring."

BERGENFIELD COUNTY HOSPITAL The hospital where Thad Beaumont was taken after he had a convulsion as a child.

THE BOROUGH OF MANHATTAN MORGUE The morgue where Rick Cowley went to identify Miriam Cowley's body after she was murdered by George Stark.

BOSTON Liz Beaumont was pushed down an escalator in Filene's in Boston. This caused her to miscarry her first twins.

THE BREWER POST OFFICE Fred Clawson staked out the Brewer post office, and watched for Thad Beaumont to pick up George Stark's mail.

CASTLE ROCK, MAINE The town where Thad and Liz Beaumont had their summer home.

CASTLE VIEW The location of one of the two little league baseball fields tended by Digger Holt. (The other was between Castle Rock and Harlow.)

DAVE'S MARKET A "Mom & Pop" store a half-mile from Thad's house.

DEVIL'S KNOB When Alan Pangborn tracked down Hugh Pritchard in Yellowstone, the doctor was at Devil's Knob.

DUKE AND MARLBOROUGH LANE An intersection in the Ridgeway section of Bergenfield, New Jersey, where stood a big blue mailbox. Before his first George Stark "automatic writing" session, Thad saw the Ridgeway suburb in a vision, and the mailbox was covered with sparrows.

THE DUKE STREET CONVENIENCE STORE A store where Thad had gone to buy milk and bread as a child.

THE EAST ANNEX Thad noticed two girls on their way to the East Annex to sign up for summer courses at the university.

IN THE EAST VILLAGE OFF AVENUE B The apartment Stark rented in New York City was in the East Village off Avenue B. He awoke there after Thad had managed to psychically "capture" him with his writing.

THE EASTERN MAINE MEDICAL CENTER The hospital where Dr. Hume sent Thad for x-rays and a CAT scan.

ENDSVILLE "The place where all rail service terminates."

ENGLEWOOD One of the places where Dr. Hugh Pritchard practiced "doctoring."

ENGLEWOOD HEIGHTS One of the places where Dr. Hugh Pritchard practiced "doctoring."

THE FAMOUS ARTISTS SCHOOL A school supposedly based in New Haven. [NOTE: I live in New Haven, and I couldn't find it. Maybe it's in the Dead Zone?]

FARGO, NORTH DAKOTA Miriam Cowley believed that you could leave your front door unlocked in either Fargo, North Dakota, or Ames, Iowa, but not in the Big Apple. That's why she had a Kreig lock on her apartment door.

FILENE'S The store in Boston where Liz Beaumont was once pushed down an escalator, causing her to lose her first set of twins.

FOLE The Federal Office of Law Enforcement. Richard Nixon created this office while he was in the White House.

FORT LARAMIE, WYOMING Dr. Pritchard retired to Fort Laramie after leaving Bergenfield Hospital.

A GAS OVEN Norton Briggs hit his wife with a frying pan. Thinking she was dead, he then killed himself with a .38 caliber revolver. Mrs. Briggs wasn't dead, however, and when she woke up and saw her dead husband, she tried to kill herself by sticking her head in a gas oven. She was revived by the Oxford Rescue Services paramedics.

GOLD'S JUNKYARD The junkyard where Thad hid the Suburban.

GRACE CEMETERY One of the three Castle Rock cemeteries tended by Digger Holt.

GRANT'S DAIRY A Grant's Dairy tanker truck blocked off the view of the cops in the Plymouth who were following Thad.

HACKENSACK One of the places where Dr. Hugh Pritchard practiced "doctoring."

HISTORY DEPARTMENT The department at the university where Wilhelmina Burks worked.

THE HOLIDAY INN Fred Clawson stayed at the Brewer, Maine, Holiday Inn while on his "stakeout" to prove that Thad Beaumont was George Stark.

HOMELAND CEMETERY The cemetery where the pictures of George Stark's "burial" were taken. Homeland was one of the three Castle Rock cemeteries tended by Digger Holt.

HOUSTON STREET A stationer on Houston Street in New York City sold George Stark three boxes of Berol Black Beauty pencils.

JELLYSTONE The park where Yogi Bear hung out.

432

JUNIPER HILL Dolly Arsenault thought that the man Homer Gamache picked up might have been from the Juniper Hill mental asylum. (The man was George Stark, and he was actually from the Homeland Cemetery.)

KINGSTON, RHODE ISLAND Joe Rodway was picked up by police in Kingston when he fled Castle Rock after killing his wife.

KOREA Mr. Reed, Thad's school bus driver, had been a medic in Korea.

L STREET The Washington street where Dodie Eberhart's last surviving apartment building was located.

LAKE DAVIS A little pond a mile from Thad's childhood home in Bergenfield. He swam there when he was ten.

MAINE Thad Beaumont had once been an Appalachian Trail guide in Maine, New Hampshire, and Vermont.

MANCHESTER, NEW HAMPSHIRE George Stark's birthplace, according to his Darwin Press author bio sheet.

THE MELLOW TIGER Right after the fistfight at Nan's Luncheonette, there had been another fistfight in the parking lot of The Mellow Tiger. [NOTE: See the "Places" entry NAN'S LUNCHEONETTE, and the "Things" entry THE NEW YORK *TIMES*. The Mellow Tiger also appears in *Cujo,* and was said to be the only tavern in Castle Rock. (George Meara had two beers there.) See the section on *Cujo* in this volume.]

NAN'S LUNCHEONETTE Two Castle Rock summer people got into a fistfight at Nan's Luncheonette over the last copy of the New York *Times.*

NEBRASKA The May 23 issue of *People* magazine reported the story of nine unsolved sex murders in Nebraska.

NEW HAMPSHIRE Thad Beaumont had once been an Appalachian Trail guide in Maine, New Hampshire, and Vermont.

THE NEW SCHOOL Thad had once been on a panel with William Burroughs at the New School in New York.

THE NEW YORK PUBLIC LIBRARY After his psychic "capture" by Thad, George Stark went to the New York Public Library and rented an hour's time on an IBM electric typewriter in the Writing Room.

ONE POLICE PLAZA After Rick Cowley told the cops guarding him about Stark's phone call, one of them told him down at One Police Plaza.

THE ORONO STATE POLICE BARRACKS When Thad was questioned at his home about the murder of Homer Gamache, Sheriff Pangborn told him they'd like to question him further at the Orono state police barracks. Thad wouldn't go.

OXFORD, MISSISSIPPI George Stark's final residence, according to his Darwin Press author bio sheet.

P.O. BOX 1642, BREWER, MAINE 04412 George Stark's address.

PATERSON One of the places where Dr. Hugh Pritchard practiced "doctoring."

PENN STATION One of Stark's calls to Thad came from a telephone kiosk in Penn Station.

THE PLACES DR. PRITCHARD PRACTICED "DOCTORING." They included Bergenfield, Tenafly, Hackensack, Englewood, Englewood Heights, and Paterson.

PORTLAND JETPORT The airport where Phyllis Myers rented the station wagon she drove to the Homeland Cemetery for George Stark's "burial."

PUSAN Homer Gamache had lost one arm in Pusan during the war.

RADIO SHACK Even the CIA bought at Radio Shack.

THE RAMADA INN Sheriff Pangborn stayed at the Ramada Inn while visiting Thad Beaumont about Homer Gamache's murder.

A ROUTE 5 REST AREA Alan Pangborn stopped at a rest area on Route 5 in his pursuit of Thad and Stark.

ROUTE 117 Just before Norton Briggs hit his wife with a frying pan, there had been "a gaudy four-car smashup" on Route 117 that left two people dead.

SAN LUIS OBISPO Mr. and Mrs. Pennington (Mirian Cowley's

parents) lived in San Luis Obispo.

SCHOOLHOUSE MEADOW As Thad prepared for "the revels" with George Stark, he noticed that Schoolhouse Meadow near his house was completely covered with sparrows.

STACKPOLE CEMETERY One of the three Castle Rock cemeteries tended by Digger Holt.

TENAFLY One of the places where Dr. Hugh Pritchard practiced "doctoring."

TRACK #3 When Stark called Thad from Penn Station, a Pilgrim train that boarded on Track #3 could be heard on the tape of the phone call.

TUCSON Rick Cowley's father lived in Tucson.

TWO LITTLE LEAGUE FIELDS There were two Castle Rock little league baseball fields tended by Digger Holt. One was between Castle Rock and Harlow, the other was in Castle View.

UNIVERSE Castle Rock's billiard parlor and video game arcade. As part of Alan Pangborn's problems with "summer in Vacationland," there was a small dope bust at Universe.

VERMONT Thad Beaumont had once been an Appalachian Trail guide in Maine, New Hampshire, and Vermont.

WASHINGTON, D.C. Dodie Eberhart had been one of Washington's most popular call girls before she retired.

THE WESTPORT I-95 McDONALD'S Homer Gamache's pickup truck was found by Connecticut State Trooper Warren Hamilton in the Westport I-95 McDonald's.

WOMEN'S CORRECTIONAL The prison where the woman who beat her husband to death was sent by Judge Pender.

THE WRITING ROOM After his psychic "capture" by Thad, Stark went to the New York Public Library and rented an hour's time on an IBM electric typewriter in the Writing Room.

YELLOWSTONE PARK Dr. Pritchard was vacationing in Yellowstone Park when Sheriff Pangborn first called him about Thad Beaumont.

YOU SEW AND SEW The sewing shop where Annie Pangborn worked part-time. The shop was owned by Polly Chalmers.

(27)
THE DARK HALF
Things

AMERICAN TEEN The magazine that ran a writing contest in 1960 when Thad Beaumont was eleven years old. He won an honorable mention for his short story, "Outside Marty's House." Later, the first short story for which Thad got paid was bought by *American Teen*.

AN APPALACHIAN TRAIL GUIDE Thad Beaumont had once been an Appalachian Trail guide in Maine, New Hampshire, and Vermont.

THE ATTORNEY GENERAL'S CAPITAL CRIMES DIVISION The office of the attorney general that was called in to investigate the murder of Homer Gamache.

BATMAN'S "TOOLS" The Batpole, the Batarang, the Batmobile, and the Utility Belt. The Utility Belt was Warren Hamilton's favorite Bat accessory.

"BEAT THE CLOCK" Alan Pangborn thought that talking to an answering machine made him feel like a contestant on "Beat The Clock."

A BEER TRUCK As Alan Pangborn pursued Stark and Thad, he stopped at a rest area on Route 5, looking for a ditched vehicle. There was a beer truck, a Ford Escort, and a Volvo parked there.

THE BERGENFIELD *COURIER* After the sparrows flew into the west side of Bergenfield County Hospital (following Thad's brain surgery, and while he lay in the intensive care unit), a story and picture appeared on the front page of the *Courier*.

BEROL BLACK BEAUTY The pencils "George Stark" used to write his novels.

BETWEEN MEMORIAL DAY AND LABOR DAY The period between these two holidays was very stressful for Alan Pangborn and other law enforcement officers.

BETWEEN 1:00 AND 3:00 A.M. ON JUNE 1 Homer Gamache's time of death, according to the medical examiner who did the autopsy.

A BIC PEN After Thad managed to psychically "capture" George Stark with his writing, Stark awoke from a trance with a Bic pen sticking out of the back of his hand.

THE BIG APPLE BIKE-A-THON The May 23 issue of *People* magazine reported the story of a paraplegic girl who was training for the Big Apple Bike-A-Thon.

"BILLIE" Wilhelmina Burks's nickname.

A BIRD CALL, A PAIR OF SUNGLASSES AND A BOSTON RED SOX BASEBALL CAP The things Rawlie DeLesseps gave to Thad as Thad set off for his final confrontation with George Stark.

A BLACK TORONADO George Stark's car. There was a bumper sticker on the car that said "High-Toned Son of a Bitch."

A BLIND, MALFORMED EYE, PART OF A NOSTRIL, THREE FINGERNAILS, AND TWO TEETH These unabsorbed parts of Thad Beaumont's dead, in utero twin (who later came to life as George Stark) were found in Thad's brain during the operation to determine the cause of his headaches. (One of the two teeth had a small cavity.)

THE "BONANZA" THEME SONG While operating on Thad Beaumont's head, Dr. Pritchard hummed the "Bonanza" theme.

A BRONZE STAR Homer Gamache had received a Bronze Star for losing his arm in Korea.

THE BUSY DAYS AT THE HOMELAND CEMETERY Memorial Day, July 4, Mother's Day, and Father's Day.

THE CASTLE ROCK *CALL* The Castle Rock newspaper.

A CERTIFICATE OF MERIT Thad Beaumont received a certificate of merit when he won an honorable mention in the *American Teen* writing contest when he was eleven years old.

A CR-14 A "shot(s) fired form" that had to be filled out by the state police when ever they discharged their weapons.

CRANIAL X-RAYS AND A CAT SCAN When Thad began to hear the bird noises in his head again as an adult, Dr. Hume sent him to the Eastern Maine Medical Center for a series of cranial x-rays and a CAT scan.

"CREATIVE MODES" A three-week block course Thad had once taught.

"THE CREEPAZOIDS" A horror film. The title of this movie gave Liz Beaumont the word "creepazoid," with which she described Fred Clawson.

A CUTLASS SUPREME Thad hid his Suburban in front of a junked Cutlass in Gold's junkyard.

A DARK BROWN PLYMOUTH The car driven by Thad Beaumont's protective "police escort."

DARWIN PRESS The publishing company that published Thad Beaumont's "George Stark" novels.

DEAD SPARROWS After the sparrows flew into the west side of Bergenfield County Hospital (following Thad's brain surgery, and while he lay in the intensive care unit), maintenance men cleaned up more than three hundred dead sparrows.

DEATH AND TEDDY BEARS A book of photographs by Phyllis Myers. It consisted of teddy bears in coffins dressed in children's clothes. She wanted Thad Beaumont to write the text.

DEJA VU The sense of having experienced something before.

DOWN, HOUND! A battery-powered canister that emitted an ultrasonic whistle that "sedated" dogs.

DUTTON Thad Beaumont's publisher (as Thad Beaumont).

EH-7A The university English department's honors course in creative writing.

EIGHT MONTHS The ex-Darwin Press secretary who gave Fred Clawson George Stark's royalty statements worked for Darwin for only eight months in 1985 and 1986.

"EMPLOYEES ONLY BEYOND THIS POINT" The sign on the chain link fence that ran across the driveway to Gold's junkyard.

ENGLISH Thad Beaumont taught English.

THE ENGLISH DEPARTMENT Tom Carroll had been with the University of Maine's English department for nineteen years when he retired.

ENGLISH LEATHER The cologne George Stark used to hide the stench of his festering sores as he began to "lose cohesion."

THE FACULTY DIRECTORY Thad's phone number was listed in the university's faculty directory.

A '59 T-BIRD A car owned by Ossie Brannigan. It was one of the cars stored in Fuzzy Martin's barn.

A FILET-O-FISH BOX Warren Hamilton thought someone was approaching him in the parking lot of the Westport I-95 McDonald's, but it was only a McDonald's Filet-O-Fish box scraping across the lot in the wind.

THE FLAT EARTH SOCIETY As Thad Beaumont protested his innocence during the initial phases of Stark's murderous rampage, he felt like he was the only person at a meeting of the Flat Earth Society who believed that the world was round. [NOTE: See "The Mist" in the *Skeleton Crew* section of this volume.]

THE FLATIRON BUILDING Thad Beaumont had a poster of New York's Flatiron Building in his office. The Flatiron was his very favorite structure in the world.

A FOLK MYTH SEMINAR A seminar taught by Rawlie DeLesseps.

FOLKLORE OF AMERICA A book on superstitions and other folk myths by Franklin Barringer.

A FORD ESCORT As Alan Pangborn pursued Stark and Thad, he stopped at a rest area on Route 5, looking for a ditched vehicle. There was a beer truck, a Ford Escort, and a Volvo parked there.

A FORD WOODY WAGON Thad's station wagon. He kept it stored in Fuzzy Martin's barn.

FOSTER GRANTS The sunglasses worn by George Stark to hide his festering face.

FRED CLAWSON'S MURDER SCENE Dodie Eberhart found Fred Clawson naked, sitting in one of his two living room chairs. His penis had been cut off and stuffed into his mouth. His tongue had been cut out and tacked (with a yellow push pin) to the living room wall. The "George Stark" *People* magazine article was tacked to his chest. Above his tongue on the wall were the words "The Sparrows Are Flying Again" written in blood.

A FRYING PAN Norton Briggs hit his wife with a frying pan. Thinking she was dead, he then killed himself with a .38 caliber revolver. Mrs. Briggs wasn't dead, however, and when she woke up and saw her dead husband, she tried to kill herself by sticking her head in a gas oven. She was revived by the Oxford Rescue Services paramedics.

A GAS CHROMATOGRAPH One of the machines used to remove blood from clothing for analysis.

GEORGE STARK'S ADDRESS Darwin Press's royalty statements for "George Stark" were addressed to:

> Mr. George Stark
> P.O. Box 1642
> Brewer, Maine 04412

This told Fred Clawson all he needed to know about Thad Beaumont's alter ego.

GEORGE STARK'S EPITAPH *People* magazine ran a posed picture of Thad and Liz in a graveyard. They were standing over a grave holding a pick and a spade. The caption to the photo said:

> GEORGE STARK
> 1975-1988
> Not a Very Nice Guy

GLENLIVET After Thad "wrote" the account of Miriam Cowley's murder, he almost took a shot of Glenlivet. He drank milk instead, even though he very badly wanted a drink.

THE GOLDEN DOG Thad Beaumont's novel-in-progress at the time he "buried" George Stark and retired him as a pseudonym.

"GONZO TOM" Tom Carroll's nickname at the university. Tom was a big admirer of Hunter Thompson's essays.

"GUESS WHERE I CALLED FROM, THAD?" The words Thad typed on his IBM typewriter "via" George Stark. He also typed "Tell Anybody and They Die."

THE GUINNESS BOOK OF WORLD RECORDS Sheriff Pangborn said that two people with identical fingerprints belonged in the *Guinness Book* after he determined that Thad Beamont could not have murdered Homer Gamache.

GUNS 'N ROSES Dodie Eberhart's tenants, the Shulmans, liked GNR.

HALF OF HIS RIGHT EAR As part of Alan Pangborn's problems with "summer in Vacationland," a fisherman tore off half of his own right ear while trying to make a fancy fishing cast.

A HANDI-WIPE Alan Pangborn found a Handi-Wipe on the floor of the Volvo parked at the rest area on Route 5.

A HEART ATTACK The May 23 issue of *People* magazine reported the story of a wrestler who was recovering from a heart attack.

"HIGH-TONED SON OF A BITCH" The bumper sticker on George Stark's Toronado.

HONORABLE MENTION Thad Beamont won an honorable mention in the *American Teen* writing contest held in 1960. Thad didn't win the second prize because he was only eleven years old, and not technically a "teen."

THE HONORS COURSE IN CREATIVE WRITING The English course that Thad helmed at the university. In the semester that Thad had to deal with Stark, sixty students applied for the course.

THE IRS Dodie Eberhart had lost one of her three apartment buildings after a disastrous 1986 IRS audit.

JACK DANIELS AND SLEEPING PILLS Three years before his "burial" of George Stark, Thad Beamont washed down a handful of sleeping pills with half a bottle of Jack Daniels in a suicide attempt.

JUNE 1 According to the medical examiner who performed the autopsy, Homer Gamache was murdered between 1:00 and 3:00 a.m. on June 1.

JUNE 10 The date that Thad got a call from Stark while Thad was in Dave's Market.

A KREIG LOCK The lock on Miriam Cowley's apartment door. Also, Fuzzy Martin used a Kreig padlock on his barn door.

A LAWS ID NUMBER Alan Pangborn told the Fort Laramie dispatcher to call the Maine state police barracks to verify his name and LAWS ID number. The number was 109-44-205-ME.

LEVI'S The jeans George Stark wore in New York.

LITERARY MARKET PLACE A digest of names, addresses, and business phone numbers for everyone (writers, editors, agents, publishers, etc.) in the publishing field.

A LITTON LIGHT TEST The test given to Thad Beamont as a child to determine if he was an epileptic.

MACHINE'S WAY Thad Beamont's 1975 first "George Stark" novel.

MAY 31 The day that Homer Gamache was murdered, and the day the Beaumonts had a party at their house, thus giving Thad his ironclad alibi.

MAY 27 The day Tom Carroll retired from the University of Maine's English department after twenty-seven years.

THE MAY 23 ISSUE OF *PEOPLE* MAGAZINE In addition to the article about the "demise" and burial of George Stark, this issue contained the following stories:

The story of nine unsolved murders in Nebraska;
the story of a health food guy busted for kiddie porn;
the story of the Maryland housewife who grew a squash that looked like a bust of Jesus;
the story of the paraplegic girl who was training for the Big Apple Bike-A-Thon;
the story of the wrestler who was recovering from a heart

attack;
the story of the comedian who was fighting a palimony suit;
the story of the Utah entrepeneur who was marketing a doll called Yo Mamma!, which had been invented by Gaspard Wilmot.

THE MEGABUCKS COMPUTER The lottery machine in Dave's Market.

MEL BLANC'S VOICES Mel used to do Elmer Fudd, Daffy Duck, Bugs Bunny, Tweetie Bird, and Foghorn Leghorn. They all mourned his passing.

MIRIAM COWLEY'S PRINTS Miriam Cowley had French Impressionist prints on her apartment walls, as well as a "Cats: Now and Forever" framed poster.

"MR. BLANDINGS BUILDS HIS DREAM HOUSE" The movie that was playing on the "Early Show" on TV the day Thad almost drowned as a child.

"NAME IT AND CLAIM IT" An old radio quiz show.

NARTEX From the first chapter of *Steel Machine,* a high-class cardboard used in the construction of the wedding cake

A NATIONAL BOOK AWARD Thad Beamont was nominated for a National Book Award for his novel *The Sudden Dancers* .

A NEGLI SAW The saw used to cut open Thad Beamont's head as a child.

THE NEW YORK *TIMES* Two Castle Rock summer people got into a fistfight at Nan's Luncheonette over the last copy of the New York *Times* .

A NEW YORK YANKEES BASEBALL CAP The cap worn by George Stark to hide his festering face and bandages.

96529Q The license plate number of Homer Gamache's 1971 Chevrolet pickup truck.

NINE UNSOLVED SEX MURDERS The May 23 issue of *People* magazine reported the story of nine unsolved sex murders in Nebraska.

1988 The year that Thad Beamont "buried" George Stark and retired him as a pseudonym. (That's when the fun really started.)

1978 The year that Dr. Hugh Pritchard retired.

1975 The year that Thad Beamont "gave birth" to the George Stark pseudonym.

A 1971 CHEVY PICKUP Homer Gamache's truck. He was found murdered in it.

1973 The year that Thad and Liz Beamont bought their place in Castle Rock.

1972 The year that Thad Beamont's first novel, *The Sudden Dancers*, was published.

1960 The year that Thad Beamont entered the *American Teen* writing contest.

A 1967 GMC TRUCK George Stark's truck, according to his Darwin Press author bio sheet.

THE NRA (THE NATIONAL RIFLE ASSOCIATION) Liz Beamont's Aunt Martha was a dues-paying member of the NRA, and would shoot rats at the Castle Rock dump when she visited Thad and Liz.

OCTOBER 28, 1960 The day the sparrows flew into the west side of Bergenfield County Hospital. At the time, Thad was in the intensive care unit at the hospital following his brain surgery.

109-44-205-ME Alan Pangborn's LAWS ID number.

THE ONLY TWO NIGHTS THE HOMELAND CEMETERY GATE WAS LOCKED Digger Holt kept the cemetery locked on Graduation night, and on Halloween night.

AN ORINCO TRUCK After Thad's first "automatic writing session" with George Stark, he walked outside and found two dead sparrows on his front walk. As he stood there, an Orinco truck sped past him. [NOTE: Could it have been the truck that killed Gage Creed in *Pet Sematary*?]

"OUTSIDE MARTY'S HOUSE" The story Thad Beamont submitted to *American Teen* magazine's writing contest.

OXFORD BLUES Thad Beamont's second "George Stark" novel.

A PALIMONY SUIT The May 23 issue of *People* magazine reported the story of a comedian who was fighting a palimony suit.

PALL MALL Thad Beaumont smoked Pall Malls before he quit.

PANCAKE MAKEUP George Stark took to wearing pancake makeup as his flesh began to deteriorate and fall off when he scratched. He was "losing cohesion" because Thad refused to write as Stark anymore.

A PAPERWEIGHT As their "co-writing" of *Steel Machine* reached a climax, Thad used a paperweight to break George Stark's wrist.

A PAPIER-MACHE TOMBSTONE Phyllis Myers had brought a papier-mache tombstone with her for the photo shoot that "buried" George Stark.

***PEOPLE* MAGAZINE** The magazine that ran the article about the "demise" of George Stark.

A PERCODAN After George Stark forced Thad to stab himself in his own hand, Thad took a Percodan for the pain.

A PILGRIM TRAIN When Stark called Thad from Penn Station, a Pilgrim train that boarded on Track #3 could be heard on the recording of the phone call.

PRESQUE VU The sense of experiencing something which has not happened, but will.

PSYCHOPOMPS "From the Greek, meaning those who conduct human souls back and forth between the land of the living and the land of the dead." Rawlie DeLesseps explained to Thad that loons and whippoorwills (according to Barringer) were outriders of the living; sparrows were outriders of the deceased.

THE *PUBLISHER'S WEEKLY* "PEOPLE" COLUMN Using the *PW* "People" column, Fred Clawson was able to isolate six Darwin Press employees who had left the company between 1986 and 1987. From there he was able to persuade the chief comptroller's ex-secretary to provide him with royalty statements for Thad's "George Stark" novels. He was able to then conclude it was Beaumont writing under a pseudonym.

PURPLE HAZE Thad Beaumont's second novel.

AN R.O.T.C. CARD Liz Beaumont told Sheriff Pangborn that he could have found out Thad's blood type from Thad's R.O.T.C. card.

RED CROSS ADHESIVE TAPE The tape George Stark used to bind Liz's wrists and ankles.

A REMINGTON 32 TYPEWRITER The "get-well" present bought for Thad by his mother after his brain operation.

A REMINGTON TYPEWRITER The typewriter Thad used to write his "Thad Beaumont" novels. (He wrote his "George Stark" novels longhand with Berol Black Beauty pencils.)

RIDING TO BABYLON Thad Beaumont's fourth "George Stark" novel.

A ROSS TRAY The tray into which Dr. Pritchard dropped what he removed from Thad Beaumont's head.

A SCRIPTO PEN The pen that Thad Beaumont used to edit his "Thad Beaumont" manuscripts.

THE "SEE-THE-LIVING-CROCODILES" SYNDROME Thad Beaumont's interpretation of crazed fans.

SHARKMEAT PIE Thad Beaumont's third "George Stark" novel.

"SIS" When George Stark first took over Thad's body, he made him write an account of Miriam Cowley's murder. The first word he wrote was "Sis." After that came...

> "The woman began to step away from the door. She did this almost at once, even before the door had stopped its short inward swing, but it was too late. My hand shot out through the two-inch gap between the door and the jamb and clamped over her hand."

After writing this, the sparrows in his vision of Bergenfield all took flight at once. He then continued...

> "Miriam Cowley opened her mouth to scream. I had been standing just inside the door, waiting patiently for just over four hours, not drinking coffee, not smoking cigarettes (I'd wanted one, and would have one as soon as it was over, but before, the smell might have alerted her). I

reminded myself to close her eyes after cutting her throat."

The account of her murder ended with...

> "'You're thinking you could brain me with that thing, aren't you, Sis?' I asked her. 'Let me tell you something – that's not a happy thought. And you know what happens to people who lose their happy thoughts, don't you?' The tears were running down her cheeks now."

A SIX-PACK The second time Sheriff Pangborn visited the Beaumonts, he brought a six-pack, sort of as a peace offering. Thad had Pepsi, while Liz and Pangborn drank beer.

A SIX PACK OF PEPSI, CHIPS, AND SOME DIP The items Thad was buying on June 10 at Dave's Market when he got a call from Stark at the store.

62284 The license plate number of George Stark's black Toronado.

THE SOUND OF SPARROWS Before Thad's unabsorbed twin was excised from his brain, he would hear the sounds of sparrows in his head before his headaches. After he was told of Homer Gamache's murder, the sounds came back: "Thousands of birds, all cheeping and twittering at once..."

"THE SPARROWS ARE FLYING AGAIN" This was written in blood on the wall above Fred Clawson's tongue in his Washington apartment.

SPECTROSCOPES One of the machines used to remove blood from clothing for analysis.

A SQUASH THAT LOOKED LIKE A BUST OF JESUS The May 23 issue of *People* magazine reported the story of a Maryland housewife who grew a squash that looked like a bust of Jesus.

STEEL MACHINE Initially, Thad thought that if he was ever going to write another novel as George Stark after *Riding to Babylon*, the title of the book would be *Steel Machine*. He did end up writing part of the novel in actual collaboration with George Stark.

STEYR-AUG SEMI-AUTOMATIC MACHINE GUNS The characters in *Steel Machine*—Jack Rangely, Tony Westerman, and Rollick—were armed with Steyr-Aug semi-automatic machine guns.

THE SUDDEN DANCERS Thad Beaumont's first novel. It was published in 1972, and Thad was nominated for a National Book Award for the novel.

A TANKER TRUCK A Grant's Dairy tanker truck blocked the view of the cops in the Plymouth who were following Thad.

TECHNICIAN #1'S NOTE The two cops who put the tracer equipment on Rick Cowley's phones after Rick's call from Stark. Both cops were found dead in Cowley's apartment. One had a note tacked to his forehead that said "The Sparrows Are Flying Again," and the other was also found with a note tacked to his forehead that said "More Fool's Stuffing. Tell Thad."

TECHNICIAN #2'S NOTE The two cops who put the tracer equipment on Rick Cowley's phones after Rick's call from Stark. Both cops were found dead in Cowley's apartment. One had a note tacked to his forehead that said "The Sparrows Are Flying Again," and the other was also found with a note tacked to his forehead that said "More Fool's Stuffing. Tell Thad."

THE TELEPHONE VAN As Stark escalated his murder spree, a blue-and-white panel truck was sent to Thad's house to place recording and trace-back equipment on Thad's phone lines.

"TELL ANYBODY AND THEY DIE." The words Thad typed on his IBM typewriter "via" George Stark. He also typed "Guess Where I Called From, Thad?"

"THERE ARE NO BIRDS." The first real sentence George Stark ever wrote as a physical being.

THE THINGS FOUND IN FRED CLAWSON'S APARTMENT Dodie Eberhart saw the following things when she opened the door to Clawson's apartment: two bottles of Amstel beer, a Chicagoland ashtray, two cigarette butts, a box of push pins, and the issue of *People* magazine that contained the story about

George Stark's "burial."

THE THINGS WARREN HAMILTON SAW IN HOMER GAMACHE'S TRUCK When Warren found the truck in the Westport I-95 McDonald's parking lot, inside the truck's cab were beer cans, soft drink cans, potato chip bags, pork rind bags, Big Mac and Whopper boxes, bubble gum, unfiltered cigarette butts, and blood.

A .38 CALIBER REVOLVER Norton Briggs hit his wife with a frying pan. Thinking she was dead, he then killed himself with a .38 caliber revolver. Mrs. Briggs wasn't dead, however, and when she woke up and saw her dead husband, she tried to kill herself by sticking her head in a gas oven. She was revived by the Oxford Rescue Services paramedics.

THREE APARTMENT HOUSES Dodie Eberhart bought three apartment houses with the money given to her from two of her "johns." One was lost in '84, the other in '86 following a disastrous IRS audit.

THREE BOXES OF BEROL BLACK BEAUTY PENCILS A stationer on Houston Street in New York City sold George Stark three boxes of Berol Black Beauty pencils.

THREE QUARTS OF SAPPHIRE MOTOR OIL On his way to his confrontation with George Stark, Thad stopped at an Augusta service station and poured three quarts of Sapphire motor oil into Rawlie DeLesseps Volkswagen.

"TRANSFORMATIONAL GRAMMAR" The Gospel according to Noam Chomsky.

TWENTY-SEVEN YEARS Tom Carroll had been with the University of Maine's English department for twenty-seven years when he retired.

(207) 866-2121 The phone number of the Orono state police barracks.

A VOLKSWAGEN Rawlie DeLessep's car. Thad borrowed it to go and meet Stark.

A VOLVO As Alan Pangborn pursued Stark and Thad, he stopped at a rest area on Route 5, looking for a ditched vehicle. There was a beer truck, a Ford Escort, and a Volvo parked there.

THE WASHINGTON *POST* BESTSELLER LIST Dodie Eberhart felt that the bestseller list indicated that most people favored romance and spy novels.

"THE WEDDING" The first chapter of *Steel Machine*.

THE "WILLIAM WILSON COMPLEX" Thad decided to call his dream about Stark and Endsville his "William Wilson Complex."

A WOK Miriam Cowley hid extra cash in her wok.

WORDS AND PHRASES While working on something for his classes, Thad experienced an incident in which he heard the sparrows in his head and then went into some kind of trance. During the trance, he scribbled various words and phrases that related to Miriam Cowley's murder on the back of an order form for complimentary American literature textbooks. He burned the paper in an incinerator.

WYOMING DIRECTORY ASSISTANCE Sheriff Pangborn called Wyoming directory assistance to get the phone number of the Fort Laramie sheriff's office.

YO MAMMA! The May 23 issue of *People* magazine reported the story of a Utah entrepeneur who was marketing a doll called "Yo Mamma!" The doll was supposed to look like "everyone's favorite (?) mother-in-law."

FOUR PAST MIDNIGHT

CONTENTS PAGE

STRAIGHT UP MIDNIGHT:
    An Introductory Note
THE LANGOLIERS
SECRET WINDOW, SECRET GARDEN
THE LIBRARY POLICEMAN
THE SUN DOG

BOOK BREAKDOWN

STRAIGHT UP MIDNIGHT
An Introductory Note
(One section signed "Bangor, Maine July, 1989")

"THE LANGOLIERS"

DEDICATION

This is for Joe,
Another White-
Knuckle Flier.

ONE PAST MIDNIGHT
A Note on "The Langoliers"
(Introductory Note)

CHAPTER ONE: (Eight sections numbered 1-8 with the following headnotes leading off the chapter: "Bad News for Captain Engle. The Little Blind Girl. The Lady's Scent. The Dalton Gang Arrives in Tombstone. The Strange Plight of Flight 29.")

CHAPTER TWO: (Ten sections numbered 1-10 with the following headnotes leading off the chapter: "Darkness and Mountains. The Treasure Trove. Crew-Neck's Nose. The Sound of No Dogs Barking. Panic is Not Allowed. A Change of Destination.")

CHAPTER THREE: (Eight sections numbered 1-8 with the following headnotes leading off the chapter: "The Deductive Method. Accidents and Statistics. Speculative Possibilities. Pressure in the Trenches. Bethany's Problem. The Descent Begins.")

CHAPTER FOUR: (Twelve sections numbered 1-12 with the following headnotes leading off the chapter: "In the Clouds. Welcome to Bangor. A Round of Applause. The Slide and the Conveyor Belt. The Sound of No Phones Ringing. Craig Toomy Makes a Side-Trip. The Little Blind Girl's Warning.")

CHAPTER FIVE: (Nine sections numbered 1-9 with the following headnotes leading off the chapter: "A Book of Matches. The Adventure of the Salami Sandwich. Another Example of the Deductive Method. The Arizona Jew Plays the Violin. The Only Sound in Town.")

CHAPTER SIX: (Thirteen sections numbered 1-13 with the following headnotes leading off the chapter: "Stranded. Bethany's Matches. Two-Way Traffic Ahead. Albert's

Experiment. Nightfall. The Dark and the Blade.")

CHAPTER SEVEN: (Seventeen sections numbered 1-17 with the following headnotes leading off the chapter: "Dinah in the Valley of the Shadow. The Fastest Toaster East of the Mississippi. Racing Against Time. Nick Makes a Decision.")

CHAPTER EIGHT: (Twenty-six sections numbered 1-26 with the following headnotes leading off the chapter: "Refuelling. Dawn's Early Light. The Approach of the Langoliers. Angel of the Morning. The Time-Keepers of Eternity. Take-Off.")

CHAPTER NINE: (Thirty-two sections numbered 1-32 with the following headnotes leading off the chapter: "Goodbye to Bangor. Heading West Through Days and Nights. Seeing Through the Eyes of Others. The Endless Gulf. The Rip. The Warning. Brian's Decision. The Landing. Shooting Stars Only.")

"SECRET WINDOW, SECRET GARDEN"

DEDICATION

This is for
Chuck Verrill.

TWO PAST MIDNIGHT
A Note on "Secret Window, Secret Garden"
(Introductory Note)

(Fifty chapters numbered 1-50)
Epilogue

"THE LIBRARY POLICEMAN"

DEDICATION

This is for the
Staff and
Patrons of the
Pasadena Public
Library.

THREE PAST MIDNIGHT
A Note on "The Library Policeman"
(Introductory Note)

CHAPTER ONE: "The Stand-In" (Four untitled sections numbered 1-4)

CHAPTER TWO: "The Library" (I) (Five untitled sections numbered 1-5)

CHAPTER THREE: "Sam's Speech" (Four untitled sections numbered 1-4)

CHAPTER FOUR: "The Missing Books" (Four untitled sections numbered 1-4)

CHAPTER FIVE: "Angle Street" (I) (Two untitled sec-

tions numbered 1-2)

CHAPTER SIX: "The Library" (II) (Four untitled sections numbered 1-4)

CHAPTER SEVEN: "Night Terrors" (Five untitled sections numbered 1-5)

CHAPTER EIGHT: "Angle Street" (II) (Four untitled sections numbered 1-4)

CHAPTER NINE: "The Library Policeman" (I) (One untitled section)

CHAPTER TEN: "Chron-ø-Lodge-Ick-A-Lee Speaking" (Eight untitled sections numbered 1-8)

CHAPTER ELEVEN: "Dave's Story" (Ten untitled sections numbered 1-10)

CHAPTER TWELVE: "By Air to Des Moines" (Eight untitled sections numbered 1-8)

CHAPTER THIRTEEN: "The Library Policeman" (II) (Two untitled sections numbered 1-2)

CHAPTER FOURTEEN: "The Library" (III) (Eleven untitled sections numbered 1-11)

CHAPTER FIFTEEN: "Angle Street" (III) (Three untitled sections numbered 1-3)

"THE SUN DOG"

DEDICATION

This is in memory
of John D.
MacDonald. I miss
you, old friend
—and you were
right about the
tigers.

FOUR PAST MIDNIGHT
A Note on "The Sun Dog"
(Introductory Note)

(Twenty-four chapters numbered 1-24)
Epilogue

(28a)
FOUR PAST MIDNIGHT
"The Langoliers"
People

"ACE" Albert Kaussner.

THE ARIZONA JEW How Albert Kaussner was known from Sedalia to Steamboat Springs. (In his western dream, that is.)

BELLMAN, DINAH One of the survivors on the time-traveling Flight 29 to Boston. She was blind and psychic.

BELLMAN, MRS. Dinah's mother. Dinah had heard her and Aunt Vicky discussing traveler's checks.

BERLITZ, CHARLES The author of a book about the Bermuda Triangle.

THE BLACK-BEARDED MAN One of the survivors of the time-traveling Flight 29. He had a hangover, and slept through everything. [NOTE: Could this guy have been a certain writer we all know and love?]

BRIAN ENGLE'S LAWYER He paid Brian's monthly bills, including his mortgage payment, his electric bill, and his $2,000-a-month alimony payment to Anne.

BRIGGS One of the people who was scheduled to rent a Budget rental car at the deserted Bangor airport. Albert Kaussner saw a folder with his or her name on it behind the Budget counter.

THE CLANTONS In Albert Kaussner's western dream, Wyatt Earp called The Daltons "The Clantons." Albert corrected him.

"CREW-NECK" Craig Toomy.

CROSBY, DARREN The "blind date" Laurel Stevenson was on her way to meet when Flight 29 went through the rip in time. Through their correspondence, Laurel knew that he was six-foot-one, weighed 180 pounds, had dark blue eyes, and drank Scotch. His cat's name was Stanley.

CRYSTAL, BILLY Harry in "When Harry met Sally," the in-flight movie on the time-traveling flight to Boston.

DALTON, EMMETT One of the Daltons in the western dream that Albert Kaussner had while Flight 29 went through the rip in time. Emmett looked like Donald Sutherland.

DALTON, IKE One of the Daltons in the western dream that Albert Kaussner had while Flight 29 went through the rip in time.

DALTON, PAW One of the Daltons in the western dream that Albert Kaussner had while Flight 29 went through the rip in time. Paw looked like Slim Pickens.

THE DALTON GANG The gang that rode into Dodge (which was really Tombstone) in the western dream that Albert Kaussner had while Flight 29 went through the rip in time.

DEEGAN, JOHN OR JAMES The deputy chief of operations for American Pride Airlines at Los Angeles LAX airport.

DICKEY, JAMES Poet.

DVORAK When Bob Jenkins asked Albert Kaussner to play something on his violin, Albert considered Ralph Vaughan Williams, Stravinsky, Mozart, and Dvořák, but rejected them all in favor of "Someone's in the Kitchen with Dinah."

EARHART, AMELIA The aviatrix who disappeared over the Pacific Ocean.

EARP, VIRGIL One of the Earp brothers who Albert Kaussner drank with in the western dream he had while Flight 29 went through the rip in time.

EARP, WYATT One of the Earp brothers who Albert Kaussner drank with in the western dream he had while Flight 29 went through the rip in time.

ENGLE, ANNE QUINLAN Brian Engle's ex-wife. She died when the building she was living in burned down. She had been living in a brand-new condo.

ENGLE, BRIAN The American Pride pilot who took a side-trip through time.

THE FAT MAN IN A BLUE SUIT During Craig Toomy's hallucinated Prudential Center bond meeting, a fat man in a blue suit asked him how he had checked out the brokers with whom he had done his junk bond business.

FELDMAN, DR. Dina Bellman's doctor.

FENWICK One of the people who was scheduled to rent a Budget rental car at the deserted Bangor airport. Albert Kaussner saw a folder with his or her name on it behind the Budget counter.

THE FLIGHT ATTENDANT A flight attendant on Brian Engle's Flight 7 from Tokyo stood by the hatch after Brian landed and wished the deplaning passengers a pleasant evening in Los Angeles.

GAFFNEY, DON One of the survivors of Flight 29. He wore a red flannel shirt.

THE GHOSTS IN THE BOARDING LOUNGE After Flight 29

returned through the rip in time and landed in the Los Angeles airport, everyone (except Toomy and Nick Hopewell) had to wait for time to "catch up" with them. While they waited, they saw men in business suits, women in traveling dresses, teenagers in Levis and t-shirts, and a father leading two small children. They also saw ghosts sitting in chairs reading transparent copies of *Cosmopolitan, Esquire,* and *U.S. News & World Report.*

THE GRAND HIGH-POOBAH OF CREATION After Craig Toomy began trying to push his weight around on the "diverted" Flight 29, Nick Hopewell told him that he had obviously mistaken himself for the High-Poobah of Creation.

HALLIDAY, DOC One of the guys who Albert Kaussner drank with in the western dream he had while Flight 29 went through the rip in time.

HANDLEFORD One of the people who was scheduled to rent a Budget rental car at the deserted Bangor airport. Albert Kaussner saw a folder with his or her name on it behind the Budget counter.

"HER MAJESTY'S MECHANIC" Nick Hopewell's "title." He fixed things that needed fixing.

HOLBY, TOM The senior vice president of the Desert Sun Banking Corporation.

HOPEWELL, MR. Nick's father.

HOPEWELL, NICK One of the survivors of Flight 29 after it went through the rip in time (the first time). The second time, he chose to sacrifice himself so that the others could live. He was a British secret agent, thirty-five-years-old, and wore bluejeans and an Oxford shirt.

JAMES, FRANK One of the guys who rode with the Dalton gang in the western dream Albert Kaussner had while Flight 29 went through the rip in time.

JENKINS, ROBERT One of the survivors of Flight 29. He was a mystery writer.

KAUSSNER, ALBERT The young, Jewish violin player who was on the time-traveling Flight 29 to Boston.

KEENE, DANNY Brian Engle's co-pilot on Flight 7 from Tokyo to Los Angeles.

THE LANGOLIERS There were actually two types of langoliers: the first were fish that lived deep in the trenches carved into the floor of the Pacific and Indian Oceans. If they were trapped and drawn towards the surface, they exploded. These langoliers became the archetypal symbol for the "time-eating" monstrous beings that were responsible for "eating" yesterday and sending the dead time into "sunless endless gulfs of forever." [NOTE: It makes sense in the book, honest.]

LARSON, GARY Cartoonist. Brain Engle thought that "Pilot Ghost Stories" sounded like a caption for a "Far Side" cartoon.

LEE, MISS Dinah Bellman's therapist.

THE MAN WITH NO NAME A man in Albert Kaussner's dreams. [NOTE: Could the man's name have been Flagg?]

MARCHANT One of the people who was scheduled to rent a Budget rental car at the deserted Bangor airport. Albert Kaussner saw a folder with his or her name on it behind the Budget counter.

MARKEY Craig Toomy found Markey's service revolver in the airport security office at the Bangor Airport.

MOZART When Bob Jenkins asked Albert Kaussner to play something on his violin, Albert considered Ralph Vaughan Williams, Stravinsky, Mozart, and Dvořák, but rejected them all in favor of "Someone's in the Kitchen with Dinah."

"MR. TOOMS OR MR. TUNNEY" Dinah Bellman psychically sensed that Craig Toomy's name was either "Mr. Tooms" or "Mr. Tunney."

MUFFIN The guy in Albert Kaussner's western dream who told Albert that the Dalton gang had ridden into Dodge (which was really Tombstone). Albert had the dream while Flight 29 was going through the rip in time.

O'BANION, MR. A very rich politician and supporter of the Irish Republican Army. Nick Hopewell was assigned to fly to Boston and "fluff" (kill) O'Banion's lady friend as a warning.

O'BANION'S LADY FRIEND Nick Hopewell was assigned to fly to Boston and "fluff" (kill) O'Banion's lady friend as a warning. [NOTE: See the "People" entry MR. O'BANION.]

PARKER, MR. The president of the bank that handled Craig Toomy's side of the South American junk bond transactions.

PESTLEMEN One of the people who was scheduled to rent a Budget rental car at the deserted Bangor airport. Albert Kaussner saw a folder with his or her name on it behind the Budget counter.

"ROBINSON BLOODY CRUSOE" After landing in Bangor and finding the airport deserted, Nick Hopewell said he was beginning to feel like "Robinson Bloody Crusoe."

RYAN, MEG Sally in "When Harry met Sally," the in-flight movie on the time-traveling flight to Boston.

SEARLES, STEVE Brian Engle's navigator on Flight 7 from Tokyo to Los Angeles.

SHAWNA, AUNT Bethany Simms was on her way to spend two weeks with her Aunt Shawna when Flight 29 went through the rip in time.

SIMMS, BETHANY One of the survivors of Flight 29. She was a teenager. She smoked Marlboros.

STANLEY Darren Crosby's cat.

STEVENSON, LAUREL One of the survivors of Flight 29. She was young, dark-haired, and pretty. She took over the guardianship of Dinah Bellman.

STRAVINSKY When Bob Jenkins asked Albert Kaussner to play something on his violin, Albert considered Ralph Vaughan Williams, Stravinsky, Mozart, and Dvorák, but rejected them all in favor of "Someone's in the Kitchen with Dinah."

TOOMY, CATHERINE Craig's mother; Roger's wife. She was an alcoholic.

TOOMY, CRAIG Crew-Neck. The bad guy on Flight 29. He was a twisted psychotic whose career was doomed because of his fraudulent mismanagement of a junk bond transaction. He didn't make Flight 29's trip back through the rip in time.

TOOMY, ROGER Craig's father.

TREVOR, MELANIE The flight attendant on the time-traveling Flight 29 who told Brian that there had been reports of the aurora borealis over the Mojave Desert. She was one of the people who disappeared.

VANCE, PHILO A fictional detective created by S.S. Van Dyne.

VICKY, AUNT Dinah Bellman's aunt. She boarded Flight 29 with Dinah, but wasn't one of the people who survived the trip through the rip.

WARWICK, RUDY One of the survivors of Flight 29. He was a bald, older man wearing a brown three-piece suit.

"THE WHEELHORSE" Craig Toomy, as he was known at the Desert Sun Banking Corporatation.

WILLIAMS, RALPH VAUGHAN When Bob Jenkins asked Albert Kaussner to play something on his violin, Albert considered Ralph Vaughan Williams, Stravinsky, Mozart, and Dvorák, but rejected them all in favor of "Someone's in the Kitchen with Dinah."

(28a)

FOUR PAST MIDNIGHT
"The Langoliers"
Places

AIRPORT SECURITY The room where Craig Toomy found Markey's service revolver.

ATLANTIC AVENUE The street where Anne Engle's condo building was located before it burned down.

BANGOR, MAINE Brian Engle landed Flight 29 in Bangor instead of Boston. [NOTE: Stephen King lives in Bangor, Maine.]

THE BANGOR INTERNATIONAL AIRPORT The BIA, which used to be Dow Air Force Base, had the longest commercial

runway on the East Coast of the United States.

BEIRUT Nick Hopewell had been shot in the leg in Beirut. He ended up with a Teflon knee from the injury.

BELFAST Before Nick sacrificed himself for the rest of the passengers on Flight 29's return trip, he told Laurel Stevenson to track down his father and to tell him that Nick had tried his best "to atone for the day behind the church in Belfast."

THE BERKLEE COLLEGE OF MUSIC Albert Kaussner was on his way to study music at Berklee when Flight 29 went through the rip in time.

THE BERMUDA TRIANGLE An area in the Atlantic where air force planes have been known to unexplainedly disappear.

A BOSTON AGENCY Before her death, Anne Engle had been an advertising executive with a Boston agency.

THE CLOUD NINE RESTAURANT An empty restaurant in the Bangor airport.

COLORADO SPRINGS After failing to reach Denver Center from Flight 29, Brian Engle tried Colorado Springs and Omaha, but got the same results.

DENVER CENTER After Flight 29 went through the rip in time, Brian Engle tried to reach Denver Center, setting 7700, on the plane's radio.

THE DESERT SUN BANKING CORPORATION The company Craig Toomy went to work for right out of UCLA.

DODGE The Dalton gang rode into Dodge (which was really Tombstone) in the western dream that Albert Kaussner had while Flight 29 was going through the rip in time.

THE DOW AIR FORCE BASE The Bangor International Airport, which used to be Dow Air Force Base, has the longest commercial runway on the East Coast of the United States.

DUKE'S MERCANTILE One of the stores in Tombstone in the western dream Albert Kaussner had while Flight 29 was going through the rip in tiime.

THE FALKLANDS Nick Hopewell had seen men die in the Falklands.

5A Brian Engle's seat on the ill-fated time-traveling Flight 29 out of Los Angeles.

FLUTING A village south of London where Nick Hopewell's father lived.

GATE 22 Brian Engle pulled up to Gate 22 at Los Angeles LAX airport with Flight 7, flagship service from Tokyo to LA.

THE HOLIDAY INN Brian Engle saw a Holiday Inn sign as he approached the Bangor Airport with Flight 29.

THE LASALLE BUSINESS SCHOOL There was an advertisement for the LaSalle School on the matches that were in a bowl in the Cloud Nine Restaurant in the Bangor Airport.

LAX AIRPORT The Los Angeles airport where Brian Engle landed Flight 7 from Tokyo.

THE LONGHORN HOTEL In the western dream Albert Kaussner had while Flight 29 was going through the rip in time, a little girl standing in front of the Longhorn Hotel began to scream. It was actually Dinah Bellman screaming on the plane.

MAIN STREET In the western dream Albert Kaussner had while Flight 29 went through the rip in time, the Daltons came riding down Main Street in Tombstone at full gallop.

MASSACHUSETTS Brian Engle's ex-wife Anne lived (and died) in Massachusetts.

MCDONALD'S The summer before his time-travelling plane trip, Albert Kaussner had worked at a McDonald's.

OMAHA After failing to reach Denver Center from Flight 29, Brian Engle tried Colorado Springs and Omaha, but got the same results.

THE ORPHAN'S HOME Catherine Toomy often threatened to send Craig to the orphan's home when he was a child.

PASADENA HIGH SCHOOL Albert Kaussner's high school.

PORTLAND, MAINE While trying to land the "diverted" Flight 29, Brian Engle decided that if they couldn't land in Bangor, they would go on to Portland.

THE PRUDENTIAL CENTER After Flight 29 went through the rip in time, Craig Toomy told Brian Engle that he was supposed to be at a meeting at the Prudential Center in Boston with representatives of Bankers International at nine o'clock.

THE RED BARON An empty bar in the Bangor International Airport.

RELIABLE GUN REPAIR One of the stores in Tombstone in the western dream Albert Kaussner had while Flight 29 was going through the rip in tiime.

ROANOKE ISLAND Roanoke Island, an island off the coast of North Carolina, where an entire colony of settlers simply disappeared.

THE ROCKIES Robert Jenkins saw the Rockies outside a portside window of Flight 29 after all the other passengers (except for himself and other survivors) disappeared.

SAN GABRIELS Nick Hopewell had been backpacking in San Gabriels when he was contacted and told to fly to Boston. He was supposed to "fluff" Mr. O'Banion's lady friend.

SEDALIA In the western dream he had while Flight 29 was going through the rip in time, Albert Kaussner was known as "The Arizona Jew" from Sedalia to Steamboat Springs.

THE SERGIO LEONE SALOON The bar where Albert Kaussner drank in the western dream he had while Flight 29 was going through the rip in time.

STEAMBOAT SPRINGS In the western dream he had while Flight 29 was going through the rip in time, Albert Kaussner was known as "The Arizona Jew" from Sedalia to Steamboat Springs.

TOMBSTONE Albert Kaussner was dreaming he was in Tombstone while Flight 29 was going through the rip in time.

THE TOMBSTONE BAPTIST CHURCH In the western dream Albert Kaussner had while Flight 29 was going through the rip in time, the Tombstone Baptist Church bell tolled high noon.

THE UCLA GRADUATE SCHOOL OF MANAGEMENT Craig Toomy graduated ninth in his class from this UCLA school.

THE UNIVERSITY OF CALIFORNIA Laurel Stevenson was a graduate of the University of California, with a master's degree in library science.

VIETNAM Brain Engle had served two terms in Nam.

WESTWOOD Brian Engle lived in Westwood, California.

(28a)

FOUR PAST MIDNIGHT
"The Langoliers"
Things

AIR NATIONAL GUARD SKIDMARKS As Brian landed Flight 29 in Bangor, he flew over skidmarks made by air national guard jets.

ALBERT KAUSSNER'S NICKNAME IN HIS WESTERN DREAM Wyatt Earp called Albert "Ace."

ALL-NITE TO XANAX Robert Jenkins had researched sleeping pills and sedatives from All-Night to Xanax, because murder by poison was a favorite in his profession (mystery writer).

AMERICAN PRIDE AIRLINES The airline Brian Engle flew for.

ANNE'S PERFUME After his ex-wife Anne died, Brian tried to remember the name of her perfume while sitting on the ill-fated Flight 29. Was it Lissome? Lithsome? Lithium? Lawnboy? Lifebuoy? Lovebite? Lovelorn? Love Boy? (It was L'Envoi.)

ARMY .44S Albert Kaussner heard the firing of army .44s and Garand rifles outside the Sergio Leone Saloon in the western dream he had while Flight 29 was going through the rip in tiime.

THE BIG PICTURE Craig Toomy's father Roger tried to make Craig understand the concept of "THE BIG PICTURE." It worked a little too well.

THE BONUS MYSTERY QUESTION After awakening from his western dream and finding that almost all the passengers had disappeared, Albert Kaussner came up with the Bonus Mystery Question: "Who's flying the plane?"

BRANDING IRON The whiskey that Albert Kaussner drank in the western dream he had while Flight 29 was going through the rip in time.

BRIAN ENGLE'S INSTRUCTIONS TO THE FLIGHT 29 FLIGHT COMPUTER In order to fly back to Los Angeles on the same route he took to Bangor (so as to find the rip in time) Brian told the computer to "REVERSE AP29 = LAXLOGAN." The computer then asked "INCLUDE DIVERSION IN REVERSE PROGRAM AP29," and Brian typed "Y" for Yes. The plane was then able to exactly duplicate in reverse the original flight.

A BUDWEISER Don Gaffney tasted a Budweiser beer in the restaurant in the Bangor Airport, and said it was flat and tasteless.

A BUNTLINE SPECIAL Albert Kaussner's gun in the western dream he had while Flight 29 was going through the rip in time.

"BUY MAINE LOBSTERS" A sign that hung over a huge empty lobster tank in the deserted Bangor Airport.

A C-12 AND A DELTA 727 When Brian Engle landed Flight 29 in Bangor, Nick Hopewell looked out the window and saw a C-12 and a Delta 727 parked in the airport, "as still as statues."

CARLTONS Bethany Simms said her Marlboros tasted like Carltons.

CRAIG TOOMY'S SPECIALTY Foreign, junk, and bad-debt bonds.

"CRAIGGY-WEGGY" The name Craig Toomy's mother used to call Craig.

A DAISY AIR RIFLE When Craig Toomy shot at Albert Kaussner with the gun he got from the Bangor Airport security office, the noise the gun made sounded like the small pop of a Daisy air rifle.

DIAZALINE An odorless, hypnotic drug.

THE FAA Brian Engle knew he could be reported to the FAA for trying to reach the SAC radio band from Flight 29, but he tried anyway.

4:07 A.M. EASTERN DAYLIGHT TIME The time the clocks stopped in the Bangor Airport. (It was 1:07 a.m. Pacific Daylight Time.)

FRIENDS AND LOVERS The magazine through which Laurel Stevenson "met" Darren Crosby. (She saw his ad in the "Personals" column.)

GARAND RIFLES Albert Kaussner heard the firing of army .44s and Garand rifles outside the Sergio Leone Saloon in the western dream he had while Flight 29 was going through the rip in tiime.

A GRETCH Albert Kaussner's violin.

GUCCI Craig Toomy's loafers.

A HARD ROCK CAFE T-SHIRT Albert Kaussner's t-shirt.

HARLEQUIN ROMANCES The romance novels that Laurel Stevenson sometimes read.

L'ENVOI Anne Engle's perfume.

L1011 The number of Brian Engle's American Pride airplane on his flight from Tokyo to Los Angeles.

LED ZEPPELIN SONGS Albert Kaussner admitted that he sometimes played Zeppelin on his violin when his music teacher wasn't around.

LITTLE LEAGUE Albert Kaussner was not allowed to play baseball when he was a kid for fear he might hurt his hands.

MARLBORO Bethany Simms' cigarettes.

A MASTER'S DEGREE IN LIBRARY SCIENCE Laurel Stevenson was a graduate of the University of California, with a master's degree in library science.

METHOPROMINOL An odorless, hypnotic drug.

"MY DOG HAS FLEAS" The tune Brian Engle plucked out on Albert Kaussner's violin.

NEWSWEEK, TIME, **AND** ***U.S. NEWS & WORLD REPORT*** Craig Toomy had been known to buy these magazines, take them home, and sit and shred them into thin strips for over six hours.

THE PENOBSCOT RIVER Brian Engle took Flight 29 over the Penobscot on his approach to the Bangor Airport.

THE REJECTED COMPOSERS When Bob Jenkins asked Albert

Kaussner to play something on his violin, Albert considered Ralph Vaughan Williams, Stravinsky, Mozart, and Dvořák, but rejected them all in favor of "Someone's in the Kitchen with Dinah."

RICE KRISPIES Dinah Bellman heard the approach of the langoliers before anyone else in the Bangor Airport. She said it sounded like the snap, crackle, and pop of Rice Krispies after you pour in the milk.

ROBERT JENKINS FIRST COAST-TO-COAST TRIP Jenkins told Albert Kaussner that his first coast-to-coast airplane trip had been in a TWA prop-job that had made two stops to refuel.

A SALAMI AND CHEESE SANDWICH Rudy Warwick tasted a salami and cheese sandwich in the restaurant in the Bangor Airport. He spit it out, saying it had gone bad.

A 767 The time-traveling Flight 29 was a 767.

"SHOOTING STARS ONLY" On the flight to Boston that took a detour, Brian Engle dreamt of his late wife Anne. In the dream, she dressed in an American Pride uniform and was standing by a cabin window on his flight from Tokyo. Written over the window was "Shooting Stars Only." In the dream, Anne's body began to be pulled outside through a crack in the plane.

THE SHOP A secret government organization that performed experiments and operated clandestinely. [NOTE: The Shop also appears in *Firestarter*. See the section on *Firestarter* in this volume.]

THE SLEEPING MADONNA One of Robert Jenkins's mystery novels. Newgate Callender called it "a masterpiece of logic."

"SOMEONE'S IN THE KITCHEN WITH DINAH" When Bob Jenkins asked Albert Kaussner to play something on his violin, Albert considered Ralph Vaughan Williams, Stravinsky, Mozart, and Dvořák, but rejected them all in favor of "Someone's in the Kitchen with Dinah."

SOP Standard operating procedure. The security procedure that allowed the pilot's cabin on a plane to be opened only from the inside.

SOUTH AMERICAN BONDS Craig Toomy had developed a project to buy a limited number of these bad-debt bonds on a carefully set schedule.

SPECIAL OPERATIONS Nick Hopewell's branch of clandestine undercover service.

THE STRATEGIC AIR COMMAND MILITARY AIRCRAFT BAND After failing to reach Denver, Colorado Springs, and Omaha from Flight 29, Brian Engle tried – against regulations – to reach the SAC band, but got no response.

TAE KWAN DO A defensive karate discipline. Nick Hopewell was a Tae Kwan Do expert.

"TEACUP" Nick Hopewell taught Bethany Simms to say "teacup" when she felt herself losing control.

A TEFLON KNEE Nick Hopewell had been shot in the leg in Beirut, and ended up with a Teflon knee from the injury.

A TEXACO FUEL TRUCK When the langoliers attacked Bangor International Airport, Brian Engle and Nick Hopewell saw them pounce on and eat a Texaco fuel truck.

THE THINGS ALBERT FOUND ON THE SEATS OF FLIGHT 29 AFTER IT WENT THROUGH THE RIP IN TIME He found: wedding rings, diamonds, emeralds, rubies, earrings, studs, necklaces, cufflinks, ID bracelets, watches (from Timex to Rolex). There were Ray-Ban, Polaroid, and Foster Grant eyeglasses. He also found belt buckles and service pins, $400 in quarters, dimes, nickels, and pennies, wallets, pocket knives, calculators, a dildo, a small gold spoon on a gold chain, dental caps and fillings, surgical pins, and a pacemaker.

THE THINGS DINAH FELT ON THE EMPTY SEATS After Dinah woke up on Flight 29 and found Aunt Vicky gone, she felt around on the plane's seats and touched two purses, a briefcase, a pen, a pad, two earpieces, and a wig.

A TOASTER To defend himself and the others against Craig Toomy, Albert Kaussner tied a toaster in a tablecloth and made a weapon.

A TWA OR MONARCH COMMERCIAL PASSENGER PLANE A plane bound for Denver out of San Francisco in 1955 or '56 that disappeared with over one hundred people aboard.

UNICOM The radio band where private pilots obtained landing advisories at small airports.

THE VOR BEACON After trying unsuccessfully to raise Denver on Flight 29's radio, Brian Engle deduced that there was no VOR beacon coming out of Denver Center. This meant no radio.

A WOODEN KITCHEN MATCH On Craig Toomy's tenth birthday, his mother placed a wooden kitchen match between two of Craig's toes, lit it, and then sang "Happy Birthday" to him.

"WORK IS THE CURSE OF THE DRINKING CLASS" A poster on the wall of the Bangor Airport services room.

ZIPPO Don Gaffney's lighter.

❖❖❖

(28b)
FOUR PAST MIDNIGHT
"Secret Window, Secret Garden"
People

ABBY One of the characters in a new novel that Mort Rainey was working on when he first met John Shooter.

ALFALFA When Mort Rainey caught his wife Amy in bed with Ted Milner, he thought that Ted looked like Alfalfa of the Little Rascals because of the way Ted's hair stuck up.

BASSINGER, DON A year-round Tashmore resident. He was an alcoholic.

BLOCK, LAWRENCE One of the writers featured in the June 1980 issue of *Ellery Queen's Mystery Magazine*.

BOWIE, GERDA The owner of Bowie's General Store.

BRADLEY, DETECTIVE The Derry officer who met Mort and Amy (and Ted) at the "site" the day after their house had burned down.

BRUNO Patty Champion's dog.

BUMP Mort Rainey's cat. Shooter killed him.

CARSTAIRS, GREG Morton Rainey's caretaker at the cottage on Tashmore Lake. Mort found him dead behind the wheel of his Scout, with a Phillips screwdriver buried in his forehead.

CARSTAIRS, MRS. Greg's wife.

CHAMPION, PATTY The Raineys' next-door neighbor in Derry.

"CRAZY FOLKS" A "fabled tribe": The people who fixated on, and subsequently annoyed (and sometimes threatened) famous writers.

CREEKMORE, HERB Morton Rainey's literary agent.

THE DAIRY FARMER A dairy farmer in Jackson, Mississippi, who John Shooter once went to see about buying his farm.

DELORES Herb Creekmore's lady friend.

DOWNEY, TODD The main character in John Shooter's short story "Secret Window, Secret Garden."

EVANS, FRED The Consolidated Assurance Company field investigator who specialized in arson crimes. He worked with Dan Strick when Mort and Amy Rainey's Derry house burned down.

EVANS'S SECRETARY The unnamed woman who brought three mugs of coffee into Fred Evans's office when Amy and Ted went there to discuss Mort's death.

FAULKNER, WILLIAM When Morton Rainey first met John Shooter, he thought that John looked like a character out of a Faulkner novel.

THE FIRE CHIEF The Derry fire chief told Amy Rainey that the fire that burned down their house was probably started by gasoline on the dry wood of the house.

5,000 PEOPLE Mechanic Falls consisted of a textile mill that had closed in 1971, 5,000 people, and a yellow blinker at the intersection of Routes 23 and 7.

THE FIVE-YEAR-OLD One of Greg Carstairs' kids.

FORTIN, ISABELLE One of Amy Rainey's Derry neighbors.

GAVIN, MRS. Mort Rainey's cleaning woman. She came in on Tuesdays.

GEORGE One of the characters in a new novel Mort Rainey was working on when he first met John Shooter.

GREENLEAF, MRS. Tom's wife. She died of Alzheimer's disease.

GREENLEAF, TOM The caretaker who took care of the Tashmore Lake cottages on the side of the lake that Greg Carstairs didn't handle. Mort found Tom in the back seat of Greg Carstairs' Scout with a hatchet in his head.

HAVELOCK, TOMMY The lead character in Morton Rainey's short story "Sowing Season."

HIGHSMITH, PATRICIA One of the writers featured in the June 1980 issue of *Ellery Queen's Mystery Magazine*.

HOCH, EDWARD D. One of the writers featured in the June 1980 issue of *Ellery Queen's Mystery Magazine*.

THE HOUSEKEEPER Mort Rainey had kept the wine cellar in his Derry house locked because he thought the housekeeper was stealing wine.

JAFFERY, MARIANNE The woman that Herb Creekmore called at *Ellery Queen's Mystery Magazine*. Herb requested a copy of "Sowing Season" for Mort Rainey.

KINTNER, JOHN The classmate who Mort Rainey plagiarized from in college. Mort submitted Kintner's story "Crowfoot Mile" as his own story, retitled "Eye of the Crow."

THE LIBRARY CURATOR The guy in charge of the back issues of *Ellery Queen's Mystery Magazine*.

A MAN On the night the Raineys' Derry house burned down, Patty Champion saw a man run out of the house right after the fire broke out.

MCBAIN, ED One of the writers featured in the June 1980 issue of *Ellery Queen's Mystery Magazine*.

MILNER, TED Amy Rainer's lover (and later, husband). He was a real estate agent.

MORT'S ROOMMATES While attending Bates College, Mort Rainey shared an apartment in Lewiston with two other students.

NEWSOME, DAVE The Tashmore constable.

PALMER, CHARLES The assistant editor of the *Aspen Quarterly*.

PERKINS, RICHARD The teacher of the creative writing course that Mort Rainey took when he was a junior at Bates College. John Kintner was one of his classmates.

RAINEY, AMY DOWD Morton Rainey's ex-wife. She was born in Portland, Maine.

RAINEY, MORTON The bestselling author who was visited by his past one day...a past he thought was dead and buried. [NOTE: Any more detail than that would be revealing more of the story than I would feel comfortable doing, since I'm sure there will be readers who will be going through these entries *before* reading them. Don't. Read the King tales first, and use these concordances for enhancement. These entries are not meant to be a substitute for the stories themselves. "Secret Window, Secret Garden" is one of those "layered" Stephen King tales that reveal more and more when thought and consideration are given to it. And since that kind of "self-deduction" is one of the primary joys of reading, I will leave the pleasures of finding out more about Mr. Rainey – and his past – to all you Stephen King Constant Readers out there. Enjoy!]

RENDELL, RUTH One of the writers featured in the June 1980 issue of *Ellery Queen's Mystery Magazine*.

THE SEVEN-YEAR-OLD One of Greg Carstairs' kids.

SHOOTER, JOHN The Mississippi author who terrorized Morton Rainey for plagiarism. He claimed Rainey's story "Sowing Season" was actually his own "Secret Window, Secret Garden."

STOKER, JULIET A woman who worked at the Tashmore post office.

STRICK, DAN The Consolidated Assurance Company agent who handled the claim when Mort and Amy Rainey's Derry house burned down.

THE TASHMORE PUBLIC WORKS DEPARTMENT EMPLOY-

EES Most of them ate breakfast in Bowie's General Store.

TROTTS, SONNY Tashmore painter, carpenter, and caretaker. Sonny helped Tom Greenleaf paint the Methodist parish hall.

THE TWO LESBIANS Everybody in Tashmore suspected two women from Camp Wigmore to be lesbians...albeit discreet ones.

WICKERSHAM, MR. The Derry fire chief.

YOUNG, HENRY A friend of Mort Rainey's. It had been Henry who called Mort one day and asked him who the guy was he had seen Amy with at the mall...some relative, perhaps?

(28b)
FOUR PAST MIDNIGHT
"Secret Window, Secret Garden"
Places

AN AMISH GIFT SHOP At the end, Amy Rainey remembered that Mort had bought "Shooter's" black hat at an Amish gift shop in Pennsylvania.

AMY'S OFFICE Before the Derry house burned down, Amy Rainey's office had been a little room that had overlooked the flower garden.

AUGUSTA After Mort Rainey received a twenty-five dollar check for "Eye of the Crow," the story he plagiarized from John Kintner, he put the money in the poorbox at St. Catherine's Church in Augusta. Also, Mort stopped at a tollbooth pay phone in Augusta to call Greg Carstairs and Herb Creekmore. Mort wanted to tell Greg about Shooter, and tell Herb about Shooter, Bump, and the fire in Derry.

BATES COLLEGE Mort Rainey's alma mater.

BILL'S CHEVRON On his way to meet Amy at Marchman's Restaurant, Mort stopped for gas at Bill's Chevron.

BOWIE'S GENERAL STORE The Tashmore mercantile.

CAMP WIGMORE Everybody in Tashmore suspected two women from Camp Wigmore of being lesbians...albeit discreet ones.

THE CENTRAL IDEA DUMP Mort Rainey thought that people assumed that writers had a "Central Idea Dump" where all the ideas for stories came from.

DERRY, MAINE The Maine town where Mort and Amy had lived before their divorce. [Note: Derry also figures prominently in Stephen King's magnum opus *It*. See the section on *It* in this volume.]

A FLOWER GARDEN Before the Derry house burned down, Amy Rainey's office had been a little room that had overlooked the flower garden.

THE GARBAGE CABINET Mort Rainey found Bump the cat nailed to the top of his garbage cabinet with a screwdriver. Shooter did it.

THE INTERSECTION OF ROUTES 23 AND 7 Mechanic Falls consisted of a textile mill that had closed in 1971, 5,000 people, and a yellow blinker at the intersection of Routes 23 and 7.

JACKSON The Mississippi town where the dairy farmer lived who John Shooter went to see about selling his farm. On his way to Jackson, Shooter read "Sowing Season," and realized Rainey had stolen Shooter's own story "Secret Window, Secret Garden."

LAKE DRIVE A road near Mort Rainey's Tashmore house that spilled out onto Route 23.

LEWISTON While attending Bates College, Mort Rainey shared an apartment in Lewiston with two other students.

MARCHMAN'S RESTAURANT After the fire in Derry that burned down their house, Mort told Amy he'd meet her at Marchman's Restaurant, a coffee shop on Witcham Street, the following morning at 9:30.

MEHCANIC FALLS Amy Rainey had once bought a little antique desk at a flea market in Mechanic Falls.

THE METHODIST PARISH HALL The Tashmore church building painted by Sonny Trotts and Tom Greenleaf.

MISSISSIPPI, ALABAMA, LOUISIANA OR FLORIDA Mort Rainey couldn't remember what state John Kintner had come from, but thought that it was one of these Deep South states.

PARAMOUNT The studio which took the option (which it later dropped) on Mort Rainey's novel *The Delacourt Family*. [NOTE: See the "Things" entry THE HOME TEAM.]

PENNSYLVANIA Back issues of *Ellery Queen's Mystery Magazine* were stored in Pennsylvania.

PERKINSBURG John Shooter told Mort Rainey that he had a little farm twenty miles south of Perkinsburg, Mississippi.

THE PERKINSBURG REXALL PHARMACY John Shooter bought his copy of *Everybody Drops the Dime* at a Rexall drugstore while on his way to see a diary farmer in Jackson, Mississippi.

PORTLAND, MAINE Amy Rainey's hometown.

ROCKLAND Mort Rainey worked in Rockland as a waiter one summer.

ROUTE 23 The road that connected to Lake Drive near Mort Rainey's Tashmore house.

SHOOTER'S KNOB, TENNESSEE The town where Ted Milner grew up.

ST. CATHERINE'S After Mort received a twenty-five dollar check for "Eye of the Crow," the story he plagiarized from John Kintner, he put the money in the poorbox at St. Catherine's Church in Augusta.

ST. MARTIN'S PRESS The publishing company that released Mort Rainey's collection *Everybody Drops the Dime* in 1983.

TASHMORE GLEN The region in Maine where Mort Rainey was living when he met John Shooter. He had been there since October because of his divorce.

TASHMORE LAKE There were twenty cottages on Tashmore Lake in the Tashmore Glen region of Maine. One of them was Mort Rainey's.

A TEXTILE MILL Mechanic Falls consisted of a textile mill that had closed in 1971, 5,000 people, and a yellow blinker at the intersection of Routes 23 and 7.

VIETNAM Mort Rainey thought that John Kintner had disappeared to Vietnam at the end of the sixties.

WITCHAM STREET After the fire in Derry that burned down their house, Mort told Amy he'd meet her at Marchman's Restaurant, a coffee shop on Witcham Street, the following morning at 9:30.

(28b)

FOUR PAST MIDNIGHT
"Secret Window, Secret Garden"
Things

ALZHEIMER'S DISEASE Tom Greenleaf had nursed his wife through Alzheimer's disease.

AMY'S MOTHER'S BIBLE Amy Rainey's mother's bible was on the nighstand in the bedroom when their Derry house burned down.

AN ANTIQUE ARMOIRE Part of the list of items lost in the fire at the Raineys' Derry house.

APPROXIMATELY 7500 WORDS The length of John Shooter's short story "Secret Window, Secret Garden."

THE ASPEN QUARTERLY The literary magazine that rejected a story Mort Rainey had submitted to them when he was a sophomore. They later published the story "Crowfoot Mile," which he stole from John Kintner. (He retitled it "Eye of the Crow.")

"AVERAGE HEIGHT, BLONDE HAIR, ROUND WIRE-FRAMED 'JOHN LENNON' GLASSES, WEARING A DARK GREY OR BLACK CAP" Mort Rainey's fictitious description of John Shooter to Derry's Detective Bradley.

A BLACKSTONE JERSEY STOVE A Blackstone Jersey stove plugged up the fireplace in Mort Rainey's living room in his cottage on Tashmore Lake.

BRIGHT BLUE BREEZE Mort Rainey knew that most of his fellow students in the creative writing course he took in college would end up writing items for the newspaper's "Community Calendar" section, or advertising copy for Bright Blue Breeze dishwashing detergent.

A BUICK Mort Rainey's vehicle.

A CADILLAC Don Bassinger's car.

A CELESTRON TELESCOPE Part of the list of items lost in the fire at the Raineys' Derry house.

THE CHAMBERMAID'S PASSKEY The key that Mort Rainey had used to unlock the motel room door the day he found Amy in bed with Ted Milner.

CHANNEL 5 Greg Carstairs had seen coverage of the fire at Mort Rainey's Derry house on the Channel 5 news.

THE CONSOLIDATED ASSURANCE COMPANY The insurance company that insured Mort and Amy Rainey's Derry house.

"CONSTIPATED – CANNOT PASS" A bumpersticker Mort Rainey remembered seeing once on a very old Volkswagen.

"THE COUCH OF THE COMATOSE WRITER" One of the titles Mort bestowed upon his sofa. (The other was "The World-Famous Mort Rainey Sofa.")

COUGH SYRUP, IODINE, AND LISTERINE The things that fell out of Mort Rainey's medicine chest when he smashed the mirror with a poker. (He thought Shooter was hiding in his bathroom.)

"CROWFOOT MILE" The short story that John Kintner submitted in his creative writing class at Bates College when he was a freshman. Mort Rainey later plagiarized the story, and submitted it to the *Aspen Quarterly* as his own "Eye of the Crow."

THE DELACOURT FAMILY A novel written by Morton Rainey. Paramount optioned the book for $75,000 on a pick-up price of $750,000.

"DERRY FIRE INSPECTORS REPORT NO LEADS IN RAINEY ARSON" The headline on page 3 of the newspaper a couple of days after Mort and Amy's Derry house burned down.

$800,000 The value of the restored Victorian owned by Mort and Amy Rainey.

ELLERY QUEEN'S MYSTERY MAGAZINE Morton Rainey's short story "Sowing Season" had been published in the June 1980 issue of *Ellery Queen's Mystery Magazine*, pages 83-97.

EVERYBODY DROPS THE DIME Morton Rainey's short story collection. It collected his earlier work.

"EYE OF THE CROW" The new title of John Kintner's short story "Crowfoot Mile." Mort stole it, renamed it, and submitted it to *The Aspen Quarterly* as his own work.

FEDERAL EXPRESS Herb Creekmore promised he'd send Mort a photocopy of "Sowing Season" out of *Ellery Queen's Mystery Magazine* by Federal Express.

FLORIDA PLATES One of the lies Mort Rainey told Detective Bradley after the Raineys' Derry house burned down was that John Shooter drove a Ford sedan with Florida plates.

A FORD BRONCO Sonny Trotts's vehicle.

A FORD SEDAN One of the lies Mort Rainey told Detective Bradley after the Raineys' Derry house burned down was that John Shooter drove a Ford sedan.

FOUR TVS Part of the list of items lost in the fire at the Raineys' Derry house.

A GREYHOUND BUS The bus John Shooter took to see the dairy farmer in Jackson about buying his farm.

HARPER'S A magazine Mort Rainey tried to read; instead, he kept nodding off.

A HATCHET Mort Rainey found Tom Greenleaf in the back seat of Greg Carstairs' Scout with a hatchet in Tom's head. It was Mort's hatchet.

A HEFTY TRASH BAG After Rainey found Bump the cat dead, he put Bump's body on top of a Hefty trash bag in his garbage cabinet.

"HOME TEAM WRITING TEAM/PROF. DELLACOURT" Mort Rainey had a dream, and these words were on the door of the

444

world's biggest classroom. In the dream, Mort had to write "I Will Not Copy from John Kintner" 5000 times on the blackboard.

THE HOME TEAM An old script at Paramount which was very similar to Mort's story *The Delacourt Family*. *The Home Team* caused the studio to drop the option on Mort's novel for fear of legal problems if they ever released a film.

J. PRESS Ted Milner's shirt.

JOHN SHOOTER'S ADDRESS General Delivery, Delacourt, Mississippi.

JUNE 1980 The month and year that Mort Rainey's short story "Sowing Season" was originally published in *Ellery Queen's Mystery Magazine*.

L & M The cigarettes that Mort Rainey found while rummaging through his desk drawer. They were under a photocopy of his novel *The Organ-Grinder's Boy*.

"A MESSAGE FROM A GHOST" After Mort Rainey was dead, Amy received the following letter:

Missus—I am sorry for all the trouble. Things got out of hand. I am going back to my home now. I got my story, which is all I came for in the first place. It is called "Crowfoot Mile," and it is a crackerjack./Yours truly,..."

"The signature was a bald scrawl below the neat lines of script." It was not Mort Rainey's writing.

MOET ET CHANDON The bottle of champagne used to start the fire at Mort and Amy Rainey's Derry house.

A MOLOTOV COCKTAIL Amy Rainey thought that their Derry house was burned by a Molotov cocktail because she saw fire in the window of the house right after she heard the sound of breaking glass.

AN N.C. WYETH LINE DRAWING Part of the list of items lost in the fire at the Raineys' Derry house.

1983 The year that Mort Rainey's collection *Everybody Drops the Dime* was published by St. Martin's Press.

1982 The year that John Shooter wrote "Secret Window, Secret Garden." This was also the year that Herb Creekmore became Morton Rainey's literary agent.

1979 The year that Mort Rainey wrote "Sowing Season."

92 KANSAS STREET Mort and Amy Rainey's Derry address. (Before it burned down, the house had stood there for 136 years.)

124 BOTTLES OF WINE Part of the list of items lost in the fire at the Raineys' Derry house.

THE ORGAN-GRINDER'S BOY Morton Rainey's third novel. It was an instant bestseller.

PAGES 83-97 The pages in the June 1980 issue of *Ellery Queen's Mystery Magazine* that contained Mort Rainey's short story "Sowing Season."

PALL MALL John Shooter's cigarettes.

A PHILLIPS SCREWDRIVER Mort Rainey found Greg Carstairs behind the wheel of his Scout with a Phillips screwdriver buried in his forehead.

PLANTER'S PEANUTS CAN LID Mort Rainey used it for an ashtray.

POLAROIDS Fred Evans took some Polaroids of the "site" after Mort and Amy Rainey's Derry house burned down.

A PUZZLE QUILT Part of the list of items lost in the fire at the Raineys' Derry house.

THE RAINEY'S INSURED PROPERTY LOST IN THE FIRE The following items were lost when the Raineys' house in Derry burned down: seven major appliances, four TVs (one with a videotape editing hookup), Spode china, an antique armoire worth $14,000, twelve pieces of original art worth $22,000 (including an original N.C. Wyeth line drawing), Waterford glassware, skis, ten-speed bikes, a canoe, three furs, a Celestron telescope, a puzzle quilt, and 124 bottles of wine worth $4,900.

REDI-WHIP During his final disintegration, Mort Rainey used a can of Redi-Whip to write "Shooter" on one of the windows in his Tashmore cottage. He also wrote it elsewhere in the house – on

the walls, the kitchen counters, and the support posts of the deck.

"REMEMBER, YOU HAVE 3 DAYS. I AM NOT JOKING." The note that John Shooter left Mort Rainey on top of his garbage cabinet. Shooter had killed Bump the cat, and nailed him to the roof of the cabinet with a screwdriver.

A RESTORED VICTORIAN Mort and Amy Rainey owned a restored Victorian in Derry, Maine, that burned to the ground. It had been worth $800,000.

A ROYAL TYPEWRITER Mort Rainey's typewriter. Before he got the word processor, he had typed most of his manuscripts on the old Royal. When he came back from the post office with the mutilated issue of *Ellery Queen's Mystery Magazine,* his VDT was smashed and the old Royal, with a copy of "Secret Window, Secret Garden" propped up on top of it, was sitting on his desk.

A SCOUT Tom Greenleaf's vehicle.

A SCREWDRIVER After a confrontation with Shooter, Rainey found Bump the cat nailed to the top of the garbage cabinet with a screwdriver.

THE "SECRET WINDOW, SECRET GARDEN" TITLE PAGE The title page of Shooter's story said:

John Shooter
General Delivery
Dellacourt, Mississippi

30 pages
approximately 7500 words

Selling 1st serial rights, North America

"Secret Window, Secret Garden"
By John Shooter

"SECRET WINDOW, SECRET GARDEN" The short story by John Shooter that Shooter claimed Mort Rainey plagiarized for his own story, "Sowing Season."

SEVEN MAJOR APPLIANCES Part of the list of items lost in the fire at the Raineys' Derry house.

SHOOTER'S HAT Mort Rainey found John Shooter's hat on his back stoop after the Derry house burned down. He put it on and thought he looked like the guy in the painting "American Gothic," even though the guy in the painting was not wearing a hat.

SILEX Mort Rainey's coffeemaker.

SKIS, TEN-SPEED BIKES, AND A CANOE Part of the list of items lost in the fire at the Raineys' Derry house.

"SOWING SEASON" A short story by Morton Rainey that had been published in *Ellery Queen's Mystery Magazine*. John Shooter claimed the story plagiarized his own story, "Secret Window, Secret Garden."

SPEAK NOW, THINK LATER Mort Rainey always felt that his ex-wife Amy "had a bit of a dead-short between her brain and her mouth." He thought she should have a t-shirt that said "Speak Now, Think Later."

SPODE CHINA Part of the list of items lost in the fire at the Raineys' Derry house.

A STATION WAGON John Shooter's car. It had Mississippi plates.

A SUBARU Amy Rainey's car.

SWEDENBORGIANS An obscure religious sect that Greg Carstairs had converted to not long after Woodstock.

THIRTY PAGES The length of John Shooter's short story "Secret Window, Secret Garden."

THREE FURS Part of the list of items lost in the fire at the Raineys' Derry house.

TUPPERWARE The containers in Mort Rainey's refrigerator in the cottage on Tashmore Lake.

TWELVE PIECES OF ORIGINAL ART Part of the list of items lost in the fire at the Raineys' Derry house.

A TWENTY-FIVE DOLLAR CHECK After Mort received a twenty-five dollar check for "Eye of the Crow," the story he plagiarized from John Kintner, he put the money in the poorbox at St. Catherine's Church in Augusta.

WATERFORD GLASSWARE Part of the list of items lost in the fire at the Raineys' Derry house.

"THE WORLD-FAMOUS MORT RAINEY SOFA" One of the titles Mort bestowed upon his sofa. (The other was "The Couch of the Comatose Writer.")

A YELLOW BLINKER Mechanic Falls consisted of a textile mill that had closed in 1971, 5,000 people, and a yellow blinker at the intersection of Routes 23 and 7.

❖❖❖

(28c)

FOUR PAST MIDNIGHT
"The Library Policeman"
People

ADELMAN, KENT The editor of *The Speaker's Companion.*

THE AMAZING JOE Joseph Randowski. The acrobat with Curry & Trembo's All-Star Circus and Travelling Carnival who was scheduled to speak at the Junction City Rotarian's meeting, but had to bow out after he got drunk, fell, and broke his neck.

ANDREWS, V.C. Ardelia Lortz told Sam Peebles that she had no desire to read any novels by Robert McCammon, Stephen King, or V.C. Andrews.

BASKIN, ELMER The Junction City banker who helped float a loan to build a strip shoppng center in Beaverton. Elmer was a Rotarian who wasn't at the Rotary meeting when Sam gave his speech. Baskin called Sam the next day to congratulate him, though.

BEEMAN, NORMAN The Homestead county sheriff.

BERRIGAN, CYNTHIA One of the Junction City public library assistants. She drove a Yugo.

BILLY One of the children that Ardelia Lortz told stories to in the children's room at the library. If one of the children cried, Ardelia would make the other kids put their heads down on their desk while she took the crying child to the bathroom. When they came back, the kid was no longer crying. She had sucked out their fear. Literally.

BLAKE, JENNIFER One of the romance novelists whose books Naomi Higgins borrowed from the library for her mother.

BLUME, JUDY When Sam Peebles was a child, Dr. Seuss was King of the Library, and Judy Blume was Queen.

BRAKEMAN, PHIL When Phil ran for the Iowa state house, Naomi Higgins typed up his speeches.

BRIGHT, BILLY The Curry & Trembo circus employee who called Craig Jones and told him that the Amazing Joe had broken his neck.

A BUNCH OF KIDS When Sam Peebles was a kid, a bunch of kids played a prank on Tommy Reed by stuffing a wad of modeling clay from the art room into the tailpipe of Reed's Pontiac. His muffler blew apart in two pieces.

CANDY, GEORGE A Junction City Rotarian who could produce three million dollars of development money with one phone call.

CARL A Junction City resident who no longer belonged to the local Rotary club.

THE CARTER BOY The Carter boy would babysit Stan Soames' farm while Stan flew charter flights.

THE CHILDREN'S LIBRARY COMMITTEE A group comprised of nine children: four high school students, three middle-school students, and two grammar-school students.

COLLEGE KIDS When Ardelia Lortz was head librarian of the Junction City public library, she used to hire college kids for the circulation room, the reference room, and the main desk – but never for the children's room.

CULPEPPER, FELICIA The Junction City head librarian until 1951.

DAWSON The fuel truck driver who let Stan Soames borrow his car to take Sam and Naomi into Des Moines.

DUNCAN, DAVE "Dirty Dave Duncan." The alcoholic who picked up Sam Peebles' newspapers. Dave was a gifted artist, and Sam Peebles heard the true story of Ardelia Lortz from Dave. Dave died at the hands of the Library Policeman/Ardelia-thing.

DUNCAN, MR. Dave Duncan's father left his mother when Dave was one year old.

DUNCAN, MRS. Dave Duncan's father left his mother when Dave was one year old.

"EARTH PEOPLE" The name Naomi Higgins gave to people who had no problem with booze, pills, pot, or cough medicine.

AN ELDERLY WOMAN At the reception at the Angel Street Homeless Shelter following Dave Duncan's funeral, Sam Peebles saw Burt Iverson and Elmer Baskin listening to an elderly woman who Sam did not know.

EMERSON, RALPH WALDO On the wall of the Junction City library was a motto by Ralph Waldo Emerson: It said: "If you would know how a man treats his wife and his children, see how he treats his books."

ENGALLS, BRUCE The Rotarian who guided Sam Peebles to the bar for a drink after Sam gave his Rotary speech.

FELLEMAN, HELEN The woman who selected the poems that comprised the *Best Loved Poems of the American People.*

FRAME, RUSS A physicians' assistant in Dr. Melden's office. Sam Peebles had made friends with Russ.

FRANK STEPHENS' NIECE FROM OMAHA She was visiting Frank and his wife; they invited Sam Peebles to dinner when she visited.

FREE, SPENCER MICHAEL Poet. Sam Peebles used one of his poems about "the human touch" to finish off his Rotary speech.

GIBSON, TOM One of the two children (the other was Patsy Harrigan) that Ardelia Lortz killed in the library.

GLASTERS, MRS. Sam Peebles' fourth-grade teacher.

GORGO, HIGH EMPEROR OF PELLUCIDAR Sam thought that if he could create an hallucination as real as the "old" library and Ardelia Lortz, the next time he might call to life Gorgo, the High Emperor of Pellucidar.

GUNS 'N ROSES The favorite rock group of the kids who took the poll in the Junction City summer reading program.

THE GUY FROM THE TRUCKING UNION A guy from the trucking union was scheduled to speak at the Junction City Rotary meeting, but he couldn't make it because he was indicted for fraud. Frank Stephens stepped in and spoke in his place.

HARRIGAN, PATSY One of the two children (the other was Tom Gibson) that Ardelia Lortz killed in the library.

HIGGINS, MRS. Naomi Higgins' mother.

HIGGINS, NAOMI The young woman from Proverbia who worked for Sam Peebles on Friday mornings from ten until noon. Naomi had a second life as "Sarah," the woman who ran the Angel Street Homeless Shelter. Naomie and Sam banded together to defeat Ardelia Lortz and the Library Policeman.

HUMPE, BILL One of the farmers (the other was Sam Orday) who used to have cornfields on either side of Truman Road near Ardelia Lortz's house.

IKE President Dwight D. Eisenhower. Dave Duncan told Sam Peebles that he was drunk for the last two-and-a-half years that Ike was president.

THE INSTRUCTOR After his "Children Dinner" dream, Sam remembered one of his college biology instructors lecturing about how the body dealt with the invasion of an alien organism.

IVERSON, BURT After his Rotary speech, Burt called Sam Peebles about a huge insurance deal. Also, Sam later found out that Burt attended Naomi's Alcoholics Anonymous meetings at the Angel Street Homeless Shelter.

JOHN A man who attended one of Naomi's Alcoholics Anonymous meetings at the Angel Street Homeless Shelter. He wore a Cincinnati Bengals sweatshirt.

JONES, CRAIG The head of the Junction City Rotarian's speaker's committee. He called Sam and told him that the Amazing Joe had broken his neck and couldn't speak at the Rotary meeting. He asked Sam to fill in.

JORDAN, KEITH Sam Peebles' twelve-year-old paperboy.

KELLY, BRIAN The man who was the freightmaster at the loading dock at the railroad station at the time when Dave Duncan was sexually involved with Ardelia Lortz. Dave once begged money from Brian.

KENNY A Junction City resident who no longer belonged to the local Rotary club.

KING, STEPHEN Ardelia Lortz told Sam Peebles that she had no desire to read any novels by Robert McCammon, Stephen King, or V.C. Andrews.

KLEMMART, WILLY When Willy was a little boy, Ardelia Lortz showed him her Little Red Riding Hood poster, and frightened him. Willy also became hysterical during Ardelia's retelling of the "Hansel and Gretel" story. Willy was later killed in Vietnam.

LAVIN, CHRISTOPHER The Junction City head librarian who took over for Felicia Culpepper in 1951. Lavin had a degree in library science.

THE LIBRARY POLICEMAN A seven-foot-tall man in a trench-coat and a gray felt hat who spoke with a lisp, and who showed up at Sam Peebles' house looking for Sam's overdue library books. The Library Policeman was an emissary of Ardelia Lortz (and also a manifestation of Ardelia), and had been "fashioned" to reflect one of Sam's worst experiences, being sexually abused as a child outside the library by a man with a lisp.

"LITTLE WHITE WALKING SAM" On his way back from Des Moines, Sam Peebles dreamt of the day he was raped by *his* Library Policeman back in St. Louis. In his dream, Little White Walking Sam replaced Little Red Riding Hood, and the Library Wolf replaced the Big Bad Wolf.

THE LORD OF LICORICE Sam Peebles. A Piggly Wiggly clerk called Sam this when Sam bought twenty packages of Bull's Eye red licorice for his final confrontation with Ardelia Lortz.

LORTZ, ARDELIA The Junction City librarian who appeared to Sam Peebles years after she was dead, and who sent him a Library Policeman. Ardelia was some sort of shape-changing alien who could transform into an "Ardelia-thing" with a huge funnel-shaped proboscis that could suck *fear* out of people's eyes. The fear looked like bloody snot. Ardelia exploded when Sam stuffed a wad of red licorice up her Ardelia-thing snout, but she later came back in embryonic form as a growth on the back of Naomi Higgins' neck. Sam removed the lump with more licorice, and placed it on the railroad tracks where it was run over. As far as we know, that did Ardelia in for good.

LUKEY One of Dave Duncan's friends at the Angel Street Homeless Shelter. Lukey was a wino.

McCAMMON, ROBERT Ardelia Lortz told Sam Peebles that she had no desire to read any novels by Robert McCammon, Stephen King, or V.C. Andrews.

McGILL, DOREEN A chubby sixty-year-old woman who worked at the *Gazette* , and who showed Sam to the newspaper's morgue where the back issues of the newspaper were kept on microfilm.

MEECHAM, ARTHUR The last person to visit the *Gazette*'s morgue before Sam Peebles.

MELDEN, DR. A doctor Sam Peebles knew.

MIKE The Pell's bookstore employee who put aside *Best Loved Poems of the American People* and *The Speaker's Companion* for Naomi.

MOGGINS, IRA The Junction City boy who came home from World War II "all funny in the head," killed his whole family, and then killed himself.

THE MOGGINS FAMILY The entire Moggins family was killed by Ira Moggins when he came home from the Pacific after World War II "all funny in the head." Ira also killed himself.

MOM The driver of the "Mom's Taxi" van. As Sam sat outside the Junction City library and waited for it to close on the night of his

final confrontation with Ardelia Lortz, three junior-high-schoolers came out of the library and ran for a van that had a "Mom's Taxi" sign on it.

THE MUSLIM KNIGHTS The Muslim Knights carried Maltese Stars when they went into battle during the Crusades.

THE 1980 KANSAS CITY ROYALS When Joey Soames was dying of leukemia, Dave Duncan painted the faces of the entire 1980 Kansas City Royals baseball team on baseballs, and then had each player autograph "their" ball for Joey. The players included Willie Aikens, Frank White, U.L. Washington, George Brett, Willie Wilson, Amos Otis, Dan Quisenberry, Paul Splittorff, Ken Brett, Jim Frey, and Darrell Porter.

"OMES" Naomi Higgins. (It was Sam Peebles' nickname for her. She didn't like it.)

ORDAY, SAM One of the farmers (the other was Bill Humpe) who used to have cornfields on either side of Truman Road near Ardelia Lortz's house.

OSBOURNE, OZZY The runner-up (to Guns 'N Roses) for favorite rocker by the kids who took the poll in the Junction City summer reading program.

PEARLMAN, RUDY A Rotarian who told Sam Peebles that his speech was so good that he darn near cried over the Spencer Michael Frees poem Sam used to "finish them off."

PECKHAM, MR. The part-time janitor at the Junction City public library.

PEEBLES, MR. Sam Peebles' father. He died young.

PEEBLES, MRS. Sam's mother. She was widowed young, and had to work to support and raise Sam.

PEEBLES, SAM The Junction City, Iowa, realtor and insurance man who lost two of Ardelia Lortz's library books, and subsequently met the Library Policeman. Sam defeated the Library Policeman/Ardelia Lortz-thing in a final battle in the library.

POWER, DEPUTY SHERIFF JOHN The man who finally found out the truth about Ardelia Lortz. He died of a heart attack.

POWER, TANSY Deputy Sheriff John Power's daughter. Dave Duncan was supposed to kill her on Ardelia Lortz's orders. He didn't, and she grew up, married, and became Tansy Ryan. She worked for the post office.

PRICE, RICHARD The Junction City librarian. He drove an Impala.

THE PRINCE OF PIGGLY WIGGLY The Piggly Wiggly clerk who sold Sam Peebles twenty packages of Bull's Eye red licorice for his final confrontation with Ardelia Lortz. (The Prince liked Mars Bars.)

PUBLIC, JOHN Q. Ardelia Lortz told Sam Peebles that most of the library's funding came from John Q. Public – regular citizens like Sam.

RANDOWSKI, JOSEPH The Amazing Joe.

REED, TOMMY When Sam Peebles was a kid, a bunch of kids played a prank on Tommy Reed by stuffing a wad of modelling clay from the art room into the tailpipe of Reed's Pontiac. His muffler blew apart in two pieces.

ROGERS, ROSEMARY One of the romance novelists whose books Naomi Higgins borrowed from the library for her mother.

RUDOLPH One of Dave Duncan's friends at the Angel Street Homeless Shelter. Rudolph was a wino.

RYAN, TANSY The former Tansy Power.

SAM PEEBLES' LIBRARY POLICEMAN "The Library Wolf." Sam's personal Library Policeman was a man of medium height who wore an overcoat and little round black glasses. This Library Policeman raped Sam when Sam was a child because Sam was overdue in returning Robert Louis Stevenson's *The Black Arrow* to the St. Louis Public Library. The Library Policeman had a slight lisp, and throughout his life Sam remembered hearing the words *"Come with me son...I'm a poleethman."*

SANDRA One of the children Ardelia Lortz told stories to in the children's room at the library. If one of the children cried, Ardelia would make the other kids put their heads down on their desk while she took the crying child to the bathroom. When they came back, the kid was no longer crying. She would suck out their fear. Literally.

SARAH Naomi Higgins' name at the Angel Street Homeless Shelter.

SEGER, MRS. A woman who worked in the Junction City five-and-dime on O'Kane Street at the time when Dave Duncan was sexually involved with Ardelia Lortz.

SEUSS, DR. When Sam was a child, Dr. Seuss was King of the Library, and Judy Blume was Queen.

SHELDON, PAUL One of the romance novelists whose books Naomi Higgins borrowed from the library for her mother. [NOTE: Paul Sheldon was the author of the "Misery Chastain" series in the Stephen King novel *Misery*. See the section on *Misery* in this volume.]

SIMPLE SIMON The kidnapped child in Ardelia Lortz's "Never Take Rides from Strangers" poster. (The kids who frequented the children's library christened him with that name.) He also appeared in a variety of other scary posters. [NOTE: See the "Things" entry DAVE DUNCAN'S POSTERS FOR ARDELIA.]

SOAMES, JOEY Stan and Laura Soames' son. Joey died of leukemia.

SOAMES, LAURA Stan's wife. She left him for another man.

SOAMES, STAN The pilot who operated Western Iowa Air Charter. Stan flew Sam to Des Moines.

SONJA One of the children who Ardelia Lortz told stories to in the children's room at the library.

ST. JOHN, TOMMY The guy who painted the "Angle Street" street sign. (It was supposed to say "Angel Street.")

STANFORD, TOM One of the Junction City library assistants.

STEPHENS, FRANK The Junction City Rotarian who spoke in place of a guy from the trucking union who was indicted for fraud. After Sam Peebles' successful Rotary speech, Frank called Sam and asked him to dinner with Mrs. Stephens and their niece from Omaha.

STEPHENS, MRS. Frank Stephens' wife.

THREE KIDS As Sam sat outside the Junction City library and waited for it to close on the night of his final confrontation with Ardelia Lortz, three junior-high-schoolers came out of the library and ran for a van that had a "Mom's Taxi" sign on it.

TOM GIBSON'S UNCLE Tom Gibson had a no-account uncle in Nebraska and, when Tom and Patsy Harrington were discovered missing, some people thought that they were headed to the uncle's house.

TOMMY One of the children who Ardelia Lortz told stories to in the children's room at the library.

A TOWN OFFICIAL The April 1, 1981, issue of the *Gazette* headlined the surprise resignation of a Junction City town official.

TWO KIDS WEARING "JCHS" JACKETS At the library, after it changed to the "now" version, Sam Peebles saw two kids wearing jackets with "JCHS" stitched on them.

TWO LAWYERS, ONE BANKER, AND TWO REALTORS Naomi Higgins worked mornings five days a week for two lawyers, one banker, and two realtors. (They were four men and one woman.)

VASSER, MARY Sam Peebles' housekeeper. She came in on Thursday mornings.

VERRILL, HANNAH The dispatcher at the Junction City sheriff's office at the time when Dave Duncan was sexually involved with Ardelia Lortz.

WHISTLER, JAMES The review in the *Democrat* of Dave Duncan's art show in Des Moines made him sound like the second coming of James Whistler.

WYCLIFFE, TOM One of Sam Peebles' friends. Tom Wycliffe was a cop who had been overseeing the Iowa state patrol's traffic control board since January of 1989.

YOUNGMAN, STU On the Monday afternoon after Sam Peebles' successful Rotary speech, Stu Youngman called Sam about buying a large homeowner's policy.

(28c)

FOUR PAST MIDNIGHT
"The Library Policeman"
Places

AMES, IOWA The town where Sam Peebles lived before moving to Junction City in 1984.

THE ANGEL STREET HOMELESS SHELTER The shelter run by Naomi "Sarah" Higgins. It was on Angle Street in Junction City. [NOTE: Even though the name of the street was officially "Angle Street," throughout this concordance I use "Angel Street Homeless Shelter" when referring to the shelter because that's how Naomi had the name of the place appear when they put up signs for their benefit chicken dinner.]

"ANGLE STREET" The misspelled name for Angel Street in Junction City.

THE ARCHIE PELLIGAS Dave Duncan's term for the Archipelagos Islands in the Pacific.

THE ART ROOM When Sam Peebles was a kid, a bunch of kids played a prank on Tommy Reed by stuffing a wad of modeling clay from the art room in the tailpipe of his Pontiac. His muffler blew apart in two pieces.

BEAVERTON The location of a strip shopping center built with the help of a loan from banker Elmer Baskin.

BRADY'S RIB The restaurant where Sam Peebles had dinner with Frank Stephens, Frank's wife, and their niece from Omaha.

THE BRIGGS AVENUE BRANCH As a child, Sam Peebles was raped by "The Library Wolf" (his own personal Library Policeman) in the bushes outside the Briggs Avenue branch of the St. Louis Public Library.

BRUCE'S VIDEO STOP A Junction City video rental store. Sam Peebles was a customer.

CEDAR RAPIDS Dave Duncan had once had an art show of his own work in Cedar Rapids. Also, the Amazing Joe ended up in a hospital in Cedar Rapids after he fell and broke his neck.

CHAPELTON JUNIOR COLLEGE Cynthia Berrigan and Tom Stanford both attended Chapelton while working as library assistants at the Junction City Public Library..

THE CHILDREN'S LIBRARY Sam Peebles first met Ardelia Lortz in the children's section of the Junction City Public Library.

CHINA LIGHT A Junction City Chinese restaurant.

THE COUNTY FAIR Dave Duncan said he couldn't go near the cotton candy stand at the county fair because the candy reminded him of Ardelia Lortz's skin as she changed into the Ardelia-thing.

DES MOINES Dave Duncan had once had an art show of his own work in Des Moines.

THE DES MOINES COUNTY AIRPORT The airport where Stan Soames landed with Sam and Naomi. He taxied to the Civil Air Terminal.

THE DOMINO A Junction City roadhouse that burned down.

THE DUNBAR STREET NEWS The St. Louis newsstand where Little White Walking Sam stopped and bought a package of Bull's Eye red licorice for a nickel on his way to the library to return his overdue copy of Robert Louis Stevenson's *The Black Arrow*.

DUNBAR STREET AND JOHNSTOWN AVENUE The intersection where Little White Walking Sam waited for the light to change on his way back to the Briggs Avenue branch of the St. Louis Public Library to return the overdue Stevenson novel, *The Black Arrow*. The Library Wolf raped Sam for not returning the book on time.

'58 OR EARLY 59 The year Dave Duncan got his third OUI (Operating Under the Influence) arrest, and lost his driver's license.

THE 1ST METHODIST CHURCH The location of the April 8 chicken dinner benefit for the Angel Street Homeless Shelter.

THE FIVE-AND-DIME A Junction City business on O'Kane Street.

GARSON ROAD John Power was found dead on Garson Road.

GRAND ISLAND, NEBRASKA Back issues of the Junction City *Gazette* were sent to Grand Island (in six month lots) to be transferred to microfilm.

GRAYLING'S STREAM A stream where Dave Duncan fished.

HUGHIE'S BARBER SHOP Norman Beeman died of a stroke in Hughie's Barber Shop in 1963.

THE IOWA CITY BUSINESS COLLEGE Naomi Higgins' alma mater.

JUNCTION CITY, IOWA The town where Sam Peebles had his real estate and insurance business, and where he met Ardelia Lortz and the Library Policeman.

THE JUNCTION CITY PUBLIC LIBRARY Ardelia Lortz's domain.

JUNCTION CITY REALTY AND INSURANCE Sam Peebles' business.

KELTON AVENUE, JUNCTION CITY, IOWA Sam Peebles owned a house and lived on Kelton Avenue in Junction City.

THE LORILLARD SCHOOL The art school in Des Moines that Dave Duncan had attended on full scholarship.

McKENNA'S A Junction City restaurant. Sam invited Naomi Higgins there for lunch on the Friday after his successful Rotary speech. She declined. Sam had a big breakfast at McKenna's the next morning (Saturday).

THE MORGUE The room at the *Gazette* where Sam looked through back issues of the newspaper on microfilm.

O'KANE STREET A street in Junction City where the five-and-dime was located. This was the last business on the street before you entered the residential district.

OMAHA, NEBRASKA Dave Duncan had once painted a Lucky Strike ad on the right-field wall of the minor-league baseball park in Omaha, Nebraska.

PELL'S The bookstore in Des Moines where Sam Peebles bought the new copies of *Best Loved Poems of the American People* and *The Speaker's Companion*.

A PIGGLY-WIGGLY The Junction City business that used to be a Texaco station.

PROVERBIA Naomi Higgins lived in Proverbia.

THE PROVERBIA AIRPORT The airport where Stan Soames operated Western Iowa Air Charters. Stan flew Sam to Des Moines to buy replacement copies of the library books he'd lost.

THE PROVERBIA FEED COMPANY The Proverbia Feed Company grain elevator could be seen from the front porch of the Angel Street Homeless Shelter.

THE PROVERBIA RIVER Naomi Higgins lived in a house by the Proverbia River with her mother.

PROVIDENCE, RHODE ISLAND Cynthia Berrigan lived in Providence when she was a little girl.

RAILROAD AVENUE The street that intersected with Angle Street in Junction City.

THE RECYCLING CENTER This was the place where Dave Duncan would bring all the old newspapers he had picked up around town. Sam found the jacket of *Best Loved Poems of the American People* on the ground at the recycling center.

THE RIGHT-FIELD WALL OF A MINOR-LEAGUE BASE-BALL PARK Dave Duncan had once painted a Lucky Strike ad on the right-field wall of the minor-league baseball park in Omaha, Nebraska.

THE ROUTE 32 DINER A diner on Route 32 where Dave Duncan ate once in a while when he was still drinking.

SAM'S HOUSE OF PIZZA A Junction City restaurant. Sam Peebles particularly liked their pepperoni-and-double-mushroom pie.

THE SPECIAL REFERENCE SECTION The library section where *The Speaker's Companion* was kept.

ST. LOUIS Sam Peebles lived in St. Louis with his mother after his father died.

THE ST. LOUIS PUBLIC LIBRARY As a child, Sam Peebles was raped by "The Library Wolf" (his own personal Library Police-

man) in the bushes outside the Briggs Avenue branch of the St. Louis Public Library.

ST. MARTIN'S CATHOLIC CHURCH The church that buried Dave Duncan on April 11.

STATE STREET AND MILLER AVENUE The Junction City Public Library stood at the intersection of these two streets.

A TEXACO STATION The Junction City business that became a Piggly-Wiggly.

TRUMAN ROAD Ardelia Lortz used to live on Truman Road.

VIET NAM Willy Klemmart was killed in Viet Nam.

THE WAYVERN HILL CEMETERY The Junction City cemetery.

WEGMAN STREET The Junction City street that led to the back entrance of the public library.

(28c)
FOUR PAST MIDNIGHT
"The Library Policeman"
Things

AN ALCOHOLICS ANONYMOUS MEETING The meetings held at the Angel Street Homeless Shelter. They were run by Naomi "Sarah" Higgins."

AN AMANA The refrigerator at the Angel Street Homeless Shelter.

THE ANGEL STREET HOMELESS SHELTER SIGN It said:

"NO DRINKING ALLOWED
AT THIS SHELTER!
IF YOU HAVE A BOTTLE, IT MUST GO HERE
BEFORE YOU ENTER!"

The sign was nailed to a porch suppport above a rusty barrel.

APRIL 11 The day Dave Duncan was buried by St. Martin's Catholic Church.

APRIL 1, 1981 The date of the article in the *Gazette* about the surprise resignation of a Junction City town official.

APRIL 7 The day Ardelia Lortz left a message on Sam's answering machine about his overdue library books.

APRIL 6 The date Sam's library books were due back.

APRIL 6, 1981 The April 6, 1981, issue of the *Gazette* had a "Special Library Supplement" enclosed in the paper. The supplement covered National Library Week, the summer reading program, and the Junction County bookmobile.

BAPTIST Naomi and Mrs. Higgins' religion.

THE BAPTIST YOUTH PICNIC Naomi Higgins helped at the Baptist Youth Picnic on the Sunday after the Angel Street Shelter benefit chicken dinner.

BEST LOVED POEMS OF THE AMERICAN PEOPLE The book that Sam Peebles used as a resource for his Rotary speech. It accidentally ended up in the dump, and Ardelia Lortz sent the Library Policeman to Sam because he didn't return the book.

BETWEEN 1960 AND 1990 Dave Duncan converted to Catholicism between 1960 and 1990.

BULL'S EYE RED LICORICE On his way to the library to return his overdue copy of Robert Louis Stevenson's *The Black Arrow*, Little White Walking Sam stopped and bought a package of Bull's Eye red licorice for a nickel at the Dunbar Street News in St. Louis.

CATHOLICISM Dave Duncan converted to Catholicism between 1960 and 1990.

A CINCINNATI BENGALS SWEATSHIRT John, a man at one of Naomi's Alcoholics Anonymous meetings at the Angel Street Homeless Shelter, wore a Cincinnati Bengals sweatshirt.

THE CRUSADES The Muslim Knights carried Maltese Stars when they went into battle during the Crusades.

CURRY & TREMBO'S ALL-STAR CIRCUS AND TRAV-ELLING CARNIVAL The Amazing Joe worked for Curry & Trembo's.

A DATSUN Naomi Higgins' car.

DAVE DUNCAN'S POSTERS FOR ARDELIA Dave Duncan painted posters for Ardelia's children's room at the library. They included a poster that said LIBRARY POLICEMEN GO ON VACATION, TOO, showing the Library Policeman fishing with Simple Simon as the bait, and a poster that said LEARN MORE ABOUT SCIENCE AND TECHNOLOGY AT THE LIBRARY – BUT BE SURE TO DO RIGHT AND GET YOUR BOOKS BACK ON TIME, showing Simple Simon strapped to the nosecone of a rocket. Ardelia would replace these scary posters with READ BOOKS JUST FOR THE FUN OF IT when she knew parents would be visiting the children's room.

DECEMBER 27, 1989 The date that Arthur Meecham had visited the *Gazette*'s newspaper morgue.

THE *DEMOCRAT* The newspaper that gave a positive review to Dave Duncan's art show in Des Moines.

DIRTY DAVE DUNCAN'S "CHICKEN DINNER" POSTER It showed a smiling woman holding a platter of fried chicken. It read:

CHICKEN DINNER AT THE
1ST METHODIST CHURCH
TO BENEFIT
"ANGEL STREET HOMELESS SHELTER"
SUNDAY APRIL 8TH
6:00 TO 8:00 P.M.
COME ONE COME ALL

$800 Ardelia Lortz told Sam Peebles that she used to have an all-day assistant at the library until the town council cut the library's budget by $800.

A FIRE EXTINGUISHER When the Library Cop threw Sam down an aisle in the 1960 version of the Junction City Public Library, Sam collided with a fire extinguisher.

572-8699 Sam Peebles' home phone number.

FLOWERS IN THE ATTIC The runner-up for favorite novel in the Junction City summer reading program poll. [NOTE: Rick McCammon's *Swan Song* was the favorite, and *Peyton Place* was also mentioned. See my interview with Robert R. McCammon in this volume.]

A FORD Sam Peebles' car.

"FRIENDS OF BILL ENTER HERE!" The sign that Sam saw when he went to the homeless shelter to see Naomi following his "Children Dinner" dream.

"FROM THE DESK OF SAMUEL PEEBLES" The note pad Sam used for minor correspondence.

"FUIMUS, NON SUMUS" The Latin inscription carved in a semicircle over the green doors of the Briggs Avenue branch of the St. Louis Public Library.

THE *GAZETTE* The Junction City newspaper.

GIRL SCOUT COOKIES Naomi Higgins remembered that her mother was the only one who ever bought Girl Scout cookies from her as a child.

GLASS GLOBES When Sam Peebles first went to the Junction City Public Library, he saw unlit glass globes hanging from the library ceiling.

A "GOD BLESS OUR BOOZELESS HOME" MAGNETIZED PLAQUE Sam saw a "God Bless Our Boozeless Home" magnetized plaque on the refrigerator door at the Angel Street Homeless Shelter.

A GOLD EARRING The only thing left of the Ardelia-thing after it exploded (thanks to Sam Peebles) in the library was a gold earring.

"GOLDILOCKS AND THE THREE BEARS" One of the stories Ardelia would change into a horror story when she told it to the children in the children's room at the library.

A "GOOD-BABY" The name Ardelia Lortz called the children who helped her change the posters in the children's room.

THE GOSPEL ACCORDING TO MATTHEW Dave Duncan was sure that when Ardelia Lortz was teaching Sunday school in Proverbia, she wasn't teaching the Gospel according to Matthew.

THE GROWTH ON NAOMI'S NECK Even though Sam thought that Ardelia was dead after she exploded in the library, a blistery growth – a lump of pinkish jelly – soon appeared on the back of Naomi's neck. It pulsated to the beat of her heart. It was the Ardelia-thing trying for a comeback. Sam removed the growth with a wad of Bull's Eye red licorice, and placed it on the train tracks where it was run over. Ardelia was gone...for good. [NOTE: Or so we think.]

THE "HASTE MAKES WASTE" POSTER Ardelia Lortz once told Dave Duncan to make her a poster for the children's room. It was to read "HASTE MAKES WASTE! GET YOUR LIBRARY BOOKS BACK IN PLENTY OF TIME!" and was to show "a little kid flattened by a steamroller in the middle of the street."

A HUEY, DEWEY, AND LOUIE POSTER A Huey, Dewey, and Louie poster replaced the Little Red Riding Hood poster in the "1990" version of the Junction City children's library on Sam's second visit.

"I CANNOT LIVE WITHOUT BOOKS." The Thomas Jefferson quotation that replaced the "SILENCE!" sign in the "1990" version of the Junction City Public Library.

AN IMPALA Richard Price's car.

THE IOWA LIBRARY ASSOCIATION The posters that Sam saw in the "Ardelia Lortz" version of the Junction City children's library all came from the Iowa Library Asociation, which was a member of the Midwest Library Association, which was a member of the National Library Association.

JANUARY 1989 Tom Wycliffe was the cop who had been overseeing the Iowa state patrol's traffic control board since January of 1989.

"JCHS" JACKETS At the library, after it changed to the "1990" version, Sam Peebles saw two kids wearing jackets with "JCHS" stitched on them.

A JOHNNIE WALKER CARTON The carton in which Sam Peebles' stored his old newspapers until Dave Duncan picked them up.

JOLT "All the sugar and twice the caffeine." The cola Sam Peebles' drank while writing his Rotary speech.

JUNCTION CITY'S SUMMER SIZZLERS The annual Junction City summer reading program. It included a poll.

A KENMORE DRIER The clothes dryer at the Angel Street Homeless Shelter.

KENT Sam Peebles' cigarettes.

LAVENDER SACHET The smell that emanated from Ardelia Lortz during Sam's final confrontation with her in the library.

"LET GO AND LET GOD" A bumpersticker on Naomi Higgins' car.

THE LIBRARY DEFENSE FUND Sam planned on sending twenty dollars to Ardelia Lortz (via the book drop) with his overdue library books. He thought that if she didn't keep the money, then she could put it in the "Library Defense Fund," if there was such a fund.

THE "LIBRARY POLICE" POSTER On the checkout desk of the "Lortz" version of the Junction City children's library, there was a poster of a boy and girl about eight years old cringing away from a man in a trenchcoat and a gray hat who was showing them an ID folder with a star pinned to it. The message beneath read: "AVOID THE LIBRARY POLICE! GOOD GIRLS AND BOYS RETURN THEIR BOOKS *ON TIME!*"

A LITTLE RED RIDING HOOD POSTER A Little Red Riding Hood poster hung on the door of the "Lortz" version of the Junction City Public Library children's library.

"LIVELY SPEAKING" The section of *The Speakers' Companion* that Ardelia Lortz suggested to Sam for help with his Rotary speech. It was divided into three section: "Easing Them In," "Softening Them Up," and "Finishing Them Off."

A LUCKY STRIKE AD Dave Duncan had once painted a Lucky

Strike ad on the right-field wall of the minor-league baseball park in Omaha, Nebraska.

A MALTESE STAR The badge that the Library Policeman carried was a Maltese Star.

MAPLE TREES A grove of maple trees surrounded the Junction City Public Library.

MARCH 1990 The month that the Amazing Joe was scheduled to speak at the Junction City Rotarian's meeting. He couldn't make it: He got drunk and fell and broke his neck.

A MAYTAG WASHER The washing machine at the Angel Street Homeless Shelter.

"MIDWESTERN UGLY" The name Sam Peebles gave to the common style of Iowa architecture, of which the public library was an example.

MODELING CLAY When Sam Peebles was a kid, a bunch of kids played a prank on Tommy Reed by stuffing a wad of modeling clay from the art room into the tailpipe of his Pontiac. His muffler blew apart in two pieces.

THE "MOM'S TAXI" VAN As Sam sat outside the Junction City library and waited for it to close on the night of his final confrontation with Ardelia Lortz, three junior-high-schoolers came out of the library and ran for a van that had a "Mom's Taxi" sign on it.

MUSTEROLE The common room at the Angel Street Homeless Shelter smelled of Musterole.

"MY FACE IS LEAVING IN 5 MINUTES/BE ON IT"! The button worn by the Piggly Wiggly clerk who sold Sam Peebles twenty packages of Bull's Eye red licorice.

A NAVAJO Stan Soames' plane.

A "NEVER TAKE RIDES FROM STRANGERS" POSTER On the wall of the Junction City children's library, Sam Peebles saw a poster of a little boy looking out of the passenger window of a dark car as it sped away from the school. The message said: "NEVER TAKE RIDES FROM STRANGERS!"

"A NIGHTMARE ON ELM STREET, PART 5" The favorite movie of the kids who took the poll in the Junction City summer reading program.

1984 The year that Sam Peebles moved to Junction City.

1970 The year of the Junction City library's renovation project.

1960 When Sam and Naomi went to the Junction City Public Library for their final confrontation with the Ardelia Lortz-thing, they somehow ended up back in the 1960 version of the library.

1960 The year Ardelia Lortz killed two children, and then herself.

1964 The year that Richard Price became the Junction City head librarian.

ORANGE JUICE AND AN OAT BRAN MUFFIN Sam Peebles' regular Monday through Friday breakfast.

THE OXFORD ENGLISH DICTIONARY The "T" volume of the *OED* flew at Sam and Naomi as they knelt by Dave Duncan in the 1960 version of the Junction City Public Library during their final confrontation with the Ardelia Lortz-thing.

THE PAINTED BASEBALLS When Joey Soames was dying of leukemia, Dave Duncan painted the faces of the entire 1980 Kansas City Royals baseball team on baseballs, and then had each player autograph the balls for Joey. The players included Willie Aikens, Frank White, U.L. Washington, George Brett, Willie Wilson, Amos Otis, Dan Quisenberry, Paul Splittorff, Ken Brett, Jim Frey, and Darrell Porter.

"PAPERBOY" While hunting for Ardelia Lortz's library books, Sam came across an envelope with "Paperboy" written across the front.

A PEPPERONI-AND-DOUBLE-MUSHROOM PIZZA The night Sam Peebles worked on his Rotary speech, he ate a pepperoni-and-double-mushroom pie from Sam's House of Pizza.

A PONTIAC When Sam Peebles was a kid, a bunch of kids played a prank on Tommy Reed by stuffing a wad of modeling clay from the art room in the tailpipe of his Pontiac. His muffler blew apart in two pieces.

"THE PRINCESS AND THE PEA" One of the stories Ardelia Lortz would read to the children in the children's room at the library when parents came to visit.

A PROBOSCIS Ardelia Lortz's mouth and nose could turn into a funnel shape called a proboscis.

"READ A BEST SELLER JUST FOR THE FUN OF IT!" The sign in the "1990" version of the library that replaced the "7-DAY RENTALS" sign.

RICHARD PRICE'S NATIONAL LIBRARY WEEK AD In the April 1, 1989, issue of the *Gazette*, Richard Price ran an ad that read:

> RICHARD PRICE AND THE ENTIRE STAFF OF
> THE JUNCTION CITY PUBLIC LIBRARY
> REMIND YOU THAT
> APRIL 6TH-13TH IS
> NATIONAL LIBRARY WEEK
> COME AND SEE US!

THE ROYALS AND THE CUBS Joey Soames' favorite baseball teams.

SAM'S BRUNCH When Sam awoke at 11:00 a.m. from his "Children Dinner" dream, he made himself a brunch consisting of orange juice, a three-egg omelette with green onions, and strong coffee.

SAM'S "'CHILDREN DINNER' SIGN" It read:

> CHILDREN DINNER IN THE
> PUBLIC LIBRARY BUSHES
> TO BENEFIT THE LIBRARY POLICE FUND
> SATURDAY APRIL 19 AND SUNDAY APRIL 20
> MIDNITE TO 2 A.M.
> COME ONE COME ALL
> "THAT'S CHOW-DE-DOW!"

[NOTE: See the "Things" entry SAM'S "CHILDREN DINNER" DREAM.]

SAM'S "CHILDREN DINNER" DREAM Sam Peebles had a dream that Simple Simon from the poster in the children's library was impaled in a pit over an open fire, and that he was the main course at a dinner to benefit the Library Police fund. [NOTE: See the "Things" entry SAM'S "'CHILDREN DINNER' SIGN."]

SAM'S NICKNAME FOR NAOMI It was "Omes." She didn't like it.

SATURDAY APRIL 19 AND SUNDAY APRIL 20 The dates of the "Children Dinner" in Sam's dream.

"THE SEARCH FOR MISSING CHILDREN CONTINUES" The headline in the *Gazette* on the Wednesday after Tom Gibson and Patsy Harrington were discovered missing. An accompanying headline said "COUNTY CORONER SAYS DEPUTY DIED OF HEART ATTACK." The story was about John Power.

SLIM JIMS When Sam Peebles went looking for Dave Duncan at the Angel Street Homeless Shelter, he met a wino named Lukey who asked Sam if he had any Slim Jims.

"SMALL-TOWN BUSINESSES: THE LIFEBLOOD OF AMERICA" The title of Sam Peebles' Rotary speech.

THE SPEAKER'S COMPANION The book that Ardelia Lortz suggested to Sam as an aid to writing his Rotary speech.

SPEAKER'S NIGHT The last Friday of every month was Speaker's Night at the Junction City Rotarian's hall.

THE STATUE OF LIBERTY When Dave Duncan was sexually involved with Ardelia Lortz, he said he was horny enough to rape the Statue of Liberty.

STEAK AND EGGS Sam Peebles' usual Saturday morning breakfast.

THE STORY HOUR The time when Ardelia Lortz would tell children "stories" in the children's room of the library.

STOUFFER'S LASAGNE OR LEAN CUISINE One of Naomi Higgins' two choices for supper the night after Sam Peebles' successful Rotary speech.

SUNDAY SCHOOL Ardelia Lortz taught Sunday school at the Baptist Church in Proverbia.

SUNDAY, APRIL 8 The date of the chicken dinner benefit for the Angel Street Homeless Shelter at the Junction City 1st Methodist Church.

THE SUNNYLAND EXPRESS The train that had once made its only Iowa stop in Junction City.

SWAN SONG The favorite novel of the kids who took the poll in the Junction City summer reading program. [NOTE: See my interview with *Swan Song* author Robert R. McCammon in this volume.]

"SWEET SUE" AND "THE SIDEWALKS OF NEW YORK" The songs Stan Soames sang while flying Sam and Naomi to Des Moines.

"TIME TAKES TIME" A sign that Sam saw at the Angel Street Homeless Shelter on the door that opened into the common room. The message "seemed at once utterly sensible and exquisitely dumb to Sam."

THE TOWN COUNCIL Ardelia Lortz told Sam Peebles that she used to have an all-day assistant at the library until the town council cut the library's budget by $800.

THE TRAFFIC CONTROL BOARD Tom Wycliffe was the cop who had been overseeing the Iowa state patrol's traffic control board since January of 1989.

TUMS The antacids Sam Peebles kept in his desk drawer.

TWENTY DOLLARS Sam planned on sending twenty dollars to Ardelia Lortz (via the book drop) with his overdue library books. He thought that if she didn't keep the money, then she could put it in the "Library Defense Fund," if there was such a fund.

A TWENTY DOLLAR BONUS After his successful Rotary speech, Sam gave Naomi Higgins a twenty dollar bonus.

$22.57 The combined price of *Best Loved Poems of the American People* and *The Speaker's Companion* that Sam Peebles bought at Pell's bookstore.

TWO DOLLARS The charge for issuing an adult library card at the Junction City Public Library. [NOTE: The "Ardelia Lortz" version of the library, that is.]

TWO SKYLIGHTS Two skylights provided light for the Junction City Public Library lobby.

U.S. NEWS & WORLD REPORT When Sam visited the library the second time and saw that it had changed, he picked up a copy of *U.S. News & World Report* because everyone was watching him.

VINABOND Ardelia Lortz had had Robert McCammon's novel *Swan Song* bound in Vinabind. It was the library children's favorite novel. (V.C. Andrews' *Flowers in the Attic* was the runner-up, and *Peyton Place* was also mentioned.)

A WAD OF RED LICORICE During his final battle with the Ardelia Lortz-thing, Sam Peebles stuffed a wad of Bull's eye red licorice up her proboscis. She exploded.

THE WELCOME MAT The night that Sam gave his Rotary speech, he had six drinks, all of them forced upon him free by grateful Rotarians. He went home and puked on his welcome mat.

A YUGO Cynthia Berrigan's car.

❖❖❖

(28d)
FOUR PAST MIDNIGHT
"The Sun Dog"
People

ARMSTRONG, NEIL An astronaut who landed on the moon.

BAKER, MR. One of Kevin Delevan's teachers. Kevin asked Mr. Baker if he knew anyone who repaired cameras after the Polaroid Sun camera Kevin got for his fifteenth birthday kept taking the same picture over and over.

BANNERMAN, BIG GEORGE The Castle Rock sheriff killed by Cujo. [NOTE: See the section on *Cujo* in this volume.]

THE BLACK CHAUFFEUR The Pus Sisters' chauffeur. She was almost as old as they were.

CAMBER, JOE The Castle Rock man killed by his own St. Bernard dog, Cujo. [NOTE: See the section on *Cujo* in this volume.]

CHAFFEE, EMORY The last of Pop Merrill's Mad-Hatters, to whom he tried to sell Kevin's Polaroid Sun camera.

CHALMERS, EVVIE Evvie's granddaughter Polly ran the dress-and-notions shop, You Sew and Sew.

CHALMERS, POLLY The Castle Rock woman who was sweeping the sidewalk next to the Emporium Galorium when John and Kevin Delevan went to the shop to show Pop Merrill Kevin's "haunted" Polaroid. Polly ran the Castle Rock dress-and-notions shop, You Sew and Sew.

CLAUDETTE Pop Merrill knew of an old lady who was in Massachusetts Memorial Hospital because her cat, Claudette, went on a rampage during a séance. The woman lost most of one ear.

THE CLERK The unnamed clerk in Twin City Camera and Video to whom Pop Merrill spoke when Pop went to Lewiston to buy a video cassette and a Polaroid Sun 660.

CLUTTERBUCK, ANDY A Castle Rock police officer.

CONSTANTINE, MR. The LaVerdiere's Super Drug Store pharmacist.

CUJO A Castle Rock St. Bernard that killed Joe Camber, Gary Pervier, and George Bannerman, and then trapped Donna and Tad Trenton in their car. [NOTE: See the section on *Cujo* in this volume.]

DEERE, MISS ELEUSIPPUS One of the Pus Sisters. She was eighty-three years old when Pop Merrill tried to sell her and her twin sister, Meleusippus, Kevin's Polaroid Sun camera.

DEERE, MR. The Pus Sisters' father. He had named his daughters Eleusippus and Meleusippus for two of three triplets who had all become saints.

DELEVAN, JOHN Kevin and Meg's father; Mary's husband.

DELEVAN, KEVIN The fifteen-year old Castle Rock boy who got a Polaroid Sun 660 for his birthday, and soon after met the Sun Dog. Kevin prevented the birth of the dog by taking its picture. On his sixteenth birthday, Kevin got a message from "Polaroidsville" that the dog was still alive, and was coming after him. Inasmuch as "The Sun Dog" is intended to act as something of a prologue to King's long novel *Needful Things*, it's a safe bet that we'll be meeting the Sun Dog again very soon.

DELEVAN, MARY Meg and Kevin's mother; John's wife.

DELEVAN, MEGAN Kevin's sister Meg. She gave him mittens for his fifteenth birthday.

DONAHUE An antiques dealer from Boston who got fifty dollars more than he should have from Pop for a 1915 Victor-Graff gramophone.

DOYON, JANE A lady at Mary Delevan's bridge game who invited Mary and Meg to have dinner with her at Bonanza.

DOYON, MR. Jane's husband. He went to Pittsburgh on business.

DURHAM, MOLLY A salesclerk at LaVerdiere's Super Drug Store.

ELLEN Molly Durham's five-year-old niece.

THE ENGINEER The man who John Delevan bet $400 on the outcome of the Celtics vs. Seventy-Sixers game.

FATHER CHRISTMAS Kevin Delevan thought that Pop Merrill looked like Father Christmas when Pop smiled at them with a twinkle in his eye.

THE FOREMAN He rang the back-to-work bell as John Delevan was discussing his $400 bet with the engineer. Delevan was offered two-to-one odds, and he took the bet.

THE GAME WARDEN He took Bill Roberson's picture after Bill shot a deer.

A GENTLEMAN FARMER A gentleman farmer had eaten between twelve and thirty-five young vagabond men in the

Tecumseh House.

GRANDMOTHER Kevin's grandmother. She lived in Des Moines, and sent him ten dollars for his fifteenth birthday.

GREER, HAL The Philadelphia Seventy-Sixers player who lost the basketball to a Celtic for the winning basket in the game in which John Delevan had bet $400 that he didn't have.

THE HEAD OF AN ENGLISH HOUSE Pop Merrill told Kevin the story of a lady in England who had taken a picture of fox-hunters returning home from a hunt. In the picture was a lady in a long dress wearing a veil, carrying a pocketbook over her arm. The head of the English house where the photographer was staying thought the lady was his great-grandmother.

HILDA, AUNT Kevin Delevan's aunt. She lived in Portland, and sent Kevin a string tie with a horrible clasp for his birthday. She had begun sending the ties when Kevin was three. He was not allowed to throw any of them away. After Kevin's final battle with the Sun Dog, Aunt Hilda died quietly in her sleep, and "[Did] Quite a Lot for the Whole Family."

JACKETT, SONNY The owner/operator of Sonny's Texaco on the road outside of Castle Rock. Pop Merrill had gotten Sonny out of a "desperate scrape" in New Hampshire in 1969.

JOE Cedric McCarty's pilot. Pop Merrill drove to a private airstrip just north of Boothbay Harbor, from where Joe flew him in Cedric McCarty's private Beechcraft plane to McCarty's private island. Pop wanted to sell McCarty Kevin's Polaroid Sun camera.

KEETON, MR. He worked in the Castle Rock selectmen's office.

A LADY IN A LONG DRESS Pop Merrill told Kevin the story of a lady in England who had taken a picture of fox-hunters returning home from a hunt. In the picture was a lady in a long dress wearing a veil, carrying a pocketbook over her arm. The head of the English house where the photographer was staying thought the lady was his great-grandmother.

THE LADY PHOTOGRAPHER IN ENGLAND Pop Merrill told Kevin the story of a lady in England who had taken a picture of fox-hunters returning home from a hunt. In the picture was a lady in a long dress wearing a veil, carrying a pocketbook over her arm. The head of the English house where the photographer was staying thought the lady was his great-grandmother.

LINDEN, MRS. ALTHEA After he purchased two rolls of Polaroid film at LaVerdiere's, Pop Merrill came out of Althea's backyard and onto Mulberry Street. John and Kevin Delevan were waiting for him at the Emporium Galorium.

THE MAD-HATTER WHO BOUGHT A SPIRIT TRUMPET Pop Merrill once sold a Mad-Hatter in Dunwich, Massachusetts, a "spirit trumpet" for ninety dollars.

THE MAD-HATTER WHO HUNG HIMSELF Pop Merrill knew of a Mad-Hatter who hanged himself in the Tecumseh House. The Tecumseh House was where a gentleman farmer had eaten between twelve and thirty-five young vagabond men.

THE MAD-HATTER WHO SPOKE WITH HITLER Pop Merrill knew a Mad-Hatter in Vermont who had twice-weekly conversations with Adolph Hitler.

THE MAD-HATTERS Pop Merrill's term for the people who believed in an unseen world, and who used Ouija boards or other occult and paranormal paraphanelia.

THE MAN WHO KILLED HIS WIFE IN BATH Pop Merrill told Kevin about a man who killed his wife in Bath in 1946. Pop heard the word "basin" on a recording made later in the house. (The man had cut his wife's throat and drained her blood into a basin.)

THE MAN WHO LOST THREE FINGERS Pop Merrill knew of a man in Kingston, Rhode Island, who lost three fingers of his right hand when the rear door of a car in which two teenagers had committed suicide closed on his hand.

McCARTY, CEDRIC A retired industrialist who was the richest of Pop Merrill's Mad-Hatters.

MERRILL, MRS. Pop Merrill's mother. She didn't raise any fools.

MERRILL, REGINALD "POP" The owner and operator of the Emporium Galorium. He stole Kevin Delevan's Polaroid Sun

camera, and paid for it with his life.

NED, UNCLE Cedric McCarty would often spend the afternoon with someone who would try to conjure up the spirit of Cedric's departed Uncle Ned.

NEWMAN, PAUL Adolph Hitler told the Mad-Hatter with whom he spoke twice a week that Paul Newman was a space alien who had been born in a cave on the moon.

THE OLD LADY WHO LOST AN EAR Pop Merrill knew of an old lady who was in Massachusetts Memorial Hospital because her cat, Claudette, went on a rampage during a séance. The woman lost most of one ear.

PANGBORN, MRS. Sheriff Pangborn's wife. She and their son both died in a a car accident.

PANGBORN, SHERIFF ALAN The Castle Rock police officer who arrested Pop Merrill's nephew. [NOTE: Sheriff Pangborn also appears in the novels *The Dark Half*, and *Needful Things*. See the section on *The Dark Half* in this volume.]

THE PANGBORNS' YOUNGEST SON Sheriff Pangborn lost his wife and youngest son in a car accident.

PAULETTE Ellen's big panda bear toy. (Ellen was Molly Durham's niece.)

PERVIER, GARY A Castle Rock man killed by Cujo. [NOTE: See the section on *Cujo* in this volume.]

POP MERRILL'S NEPHEW Pop Merrill's nephew, Ace Merrill (from "The Body"), was serving four years in Shawshank prison for breaking into the Mellow Tiger. [NOTE: See the section on "The Body" (*Different Seasons*) in this volume.]

THE PROPRIETOR The owner of Twin City Camera and Video. Pop Merrill had known him "probably since Homer sailed the wine-dark sea."

THE PUS SISTERS Miss Eleusippus Deere and Mrs. Meleusippus Verrill. Identical twin sisters who lived in Portland, and who were two of Pop Merrill's Mad-Hatters.

RANDY Mary Delevan's brother; Kevin's uncle.

REED, BRANDON John Delevan's boss. John called him and told him he'd be late for work. He called at Kevin's request.

RIDGEWICK, NORRIS A Castle Rock police officer.

ROBERSON, BILL A friend of John Delevan. Bill once shot a deer and had the game warden take his picture.

SHYLOCK John Delevan told his son Kevin that Pop Merrill was Castle Rock's version of Shylock (from the Shakespeare play *The Merchant of Venice*.)

SIMINEAUX, COLETTE The Portland woman who lost an eye when a Ouija board session went wrong.

THE SUN DOG Kevin Delevan's Polaroid kept taking pictures of a large black dog in front of a white picket fence. A red rubber ball was in the grass at the far left of the picture. The Sun Dog eventually tried to be born out of Polaroidsville, but Kevin killed it by taking its picture. (Or so he thought. On his sixteenth birthday, Kevin got a message from Polaroidsville that the Sun Dog was alive and coming to get him.)

TOMBAUGH, CLYDE The first man to calculate the location of Pluto.

THE TWO TEENAGERS Pop Merrill knew of a man in Kingston, Rhode Island, who lost three fingers of his right hand when the rear door of a car in which two teenagers had committed suicide closed on his hand.

UNTERMEYER, BILL The engineer who won the Celtics bet with John Delevan lost twenty dollars to Bill Untermeyer when John paid off the bet the next morning. The engineer had bet he wouldn't pay.

THE VAN DRIVER On his way out of the Pus Sisters' driveway, a van swerved around Pop Merrill's sedan. The driver gave Pop the finger.

VERRILL, MR. Meleusippus Verrill's husband. He was killed in the Battle of Leyte Gulf in 1944.

VERRILL, MELEUSIPPUS DEERE One of the Pus Sisters. She was eighty-three years old when Pop Merrill tried to sell her and her twin sister, Eleusippus, Kevin's Polaroid Sun camera.

WHITTAKER, MRS. Kevin Delevan's algebra teacher.

THE WINO A character in Kevin's nightmare. [NOTE: See the "Things" entry KEVIN'S NIGHTMARE.]

THE WOMAN KILLED IN BATH Pop Merrill told Kevin about a man who killed his wife in Bath in 1946. Pop heard the word "basin" on a recording made later in the house. (The man had cut his wife's throat and drained her blood into a basin.)

A WOMAN PUSHING A SHOPPING CART FILLED WITH POLAROID SUNS A character in Kevin's nightmare. [NOTE: See the "Things" entry KEVIN'S NIGHTMARE.]

THE YOUNG VAGABONDS A gentleman farmer had eaten between twelve and thirty-five young vagabond men in the Tecumseh House.

(28d)
FOUR PAST MIDNIGHT
"The Sun Dog"
Places

ARKHAM The Mad-Hatter to whom Pop Merrill sold a "spirit trumpet" ended up in a padded cell in Arkham.

BATH Pop Merrill told Kevin about a man who killed his wife in Bath in 1946. Pop heard the word "basin" on a recording made later in the house. (The man had cut his wife's throat and drained her blood into a basin.)

A BEN FRANKLIN STORE Castle Rock's real five-and-dime was a Ben Franklin store that folded in 1978.

BONANZA Mary and Meg Delevan had dinner at Bonanza with Jane Doyon.

BOOTHBAY HARBOR Pop Merrill drove to a private airstrip just north of Boothbay Harbor, from where a pilot flew him in Cedric McCarty's private Beechcraft plane to McCarty's private island. Pop wanted to sell McCarty Kevin's Polaroid Sun camera.

BOSTON Donahue, the antiques dealer, was from Boston.

THE BRAMHALL DISTRICT The upper class residential district in Portland where the Pus Sisters lived.

CASTLE HILL On their way to Pop Merrill's, John and Kevin Delevan walked down a street called Castle Hill.

CASTLE ROCK, MAINE The Delevans lived in Castle Rock, which was fifty miles from Portland.

THE CASTLE STREAM A stream in Castle Rock crossed by the Tin Bridge.

A COLONIAL MANSION The Pus Sisters lived in a red brick mansion in Portland.

DES MOINES Kevin Delevan's grandmother lived in Des Moines.

DUNWICH, MASSACHUSETTS Pop Merrill once sold a Mad-Hatter in Dunwich, Massachusetts, a "spirit trumpet" for ninety dollars.

E-Z VIDEO RENTALS One of the stores that took over the defunct Ben Franklin store's space. (The other was a Galaxia.)

THE EMPORIUM GALORIUM Pop Merrill's antique/junk shop.

GALAXIA One of the stores that took over the defunct Ben Franklin store's space. (The other was an E-Z Video Rentals.)

HARRINGTON STREET On their way to Pop Merrill's to show him Kevin's Polaroid, John and Kevin saw a police cruiser drive down Harrington Street.

HILDASVILLE A town in Kevin's nightmare. [NOTE: See the "Things" entry KEVIN'S NIGHTMARE.]

HIROSHIMA The first A-bomb was dropped on Hiroshima by the Enola Gay.

J.C. PENNEY The store where Mr. and Mrs. Delevan purchased Kevin's Polaroid Sun camera.

JUNIPER HILL An insane asylum.

KINGSTON, RHODE ISLAND Pop Merrill knew of a man in Kingston, Rhode Island, who lost three fingers of his right hand when the rear door of a car in which two teenagers had committed suicide closed on the hand.

LaVERDIERE'S SUPER DRUG STORE A Castle Rock drug store that was really more like a "jumped-up five-and-dime."

LEWISTON The town where Twin City Camera and Video was located. Pop Merrill bought a video cassette and a new Polaroid Sun 660 camera at the shop.

LEYTE GULF Meleusippus Verrill's husband was killed in the Battle of Leyte Gulf in 1944.

LOWER MAIN STREET AND WATERMILL LANE Castle Rock's single signal light was at this intersection.

MASSACHUSETTS MEMORIAL HOSPITAL Pop Merrill knew of an old lady who was in Massachusetts Memorial Hospital because her cat, Claudette, went on a rampage during a séance. The woman lost most of one ear.

McCARTY'S PRIVATE ISLAND Pop Merrill drove to a private airstrip just north of Boothbay Harbor, from where a pilot flew him in Cedric McCarty's private Beechcraft plane to McCarty's private island. Pop wanted to sell McCarty Kevin's Polaroid Sun camera.

THE MELLOW TIGER Pop Merrill's nephew, Ace Merrill, was serving four years in Shawshank prison for breaking into the Mellow Tiger. [NOTE: Shawshank prison appears in the *Different Seasons* novella "Rita Hayworth and Shawshank Redemption," and The Mellow Tiger appears in *The Dead Zone* . See the sections on those works in this volume.]

THE MIDWEST Cedric McCarty hailed from the Midwest.

MULBERRY STREET After he purchased two rolls of Polaroid film at LaVerdiere's, Pop Merrill came out of Althea's backyard and onto Mulberry Street. John and Kevin Delevan were waiting for him at the Emporium Galorium.

NAN'S LUNCHEONETTE A Castle Rock coffee shop. The shop was one of Pop Merrill's neighbors.

NEW HAMPSHIRE Pop Merrill had gotten Sonny Jackett out of a "desperate scrape" in New Hampshire in 1969.

OATLEY A town in Kevin's nightmare. [NOTE: See the "Things" entry KEVIN'S NIGHTMARE.]

OXFORD To help pay off Pop Merrill's $400 loan, John Delevan got a job in a mill in Oxford on the three-to-eleven shift.

PITTSBURGH Jane Doyon's husband went to Pittsburgh on business, so Jane invited Mary and Meg Delevan to have dinner with her at Bonanza.

PLUTO Clyde Tombaugh was the first man to calculate its location.

POLAROIDSVILLE The town in Kevin's nightmare…and where the sun Dog lived. [NOTE: See the "Things" entry KEVIN'S NIGHTMARE.]

PORTLAND Colette Simineaux lived in Portland. She lost an eye when a Ouija board session went wrong.

PORTLAND Kevin and Meg Delevan's Aunt Hilda lived in Portland, Maine.

PROVIDENCE, RHODE ISLAND The location of the New England Psychic and Tarot Convention that the Pus Sisters attended.

SCHENECTADY In Kevin's nightmare, the "Polaroid Pop" told Kevin that the dog in Kevin's Polaroid pictures had torn up a a kid in Schenectady. The Polaroid factory was in Schenectady.

SEBAGO LAKE Emory Chaffee lived on Sebago Lake.

SHAWSHANK PRISON Pop Merrill's nephew, Ace Merrill, was serving four years in Shawshank prison for breaking into the Mellow Tiger. [NOTE: Shawshank prison appears in the *Different Seasons* novella "Rita Hayworth and Shawshank Redemption," and The Mellow Tiger appears in *The Dead Zone* . Also, Ace Merrill appears in the *Different Seasons* novella "The Body." See the sections on those works in this volume.]

SONNY'S TEXACO A service station on the road outside of Castle Rock. It was owned and operated by Sonny Jackett, who maintained Pop Merrill's car free of charge because of a loan Pop had made to Sonny in 1969.

THE TECUMSEH HOUSE The house where a gentleman farmer had eaten between twelve and thirty-five vagabond young men.

THE TIN BRIDGE The bridge that crossed the Castle Stream in Castle Rock.

THE TRENTON FARM A Camberville farm. The fat lady from Polaroidsville in Kevin's dream told him that the dog in his Polaroid pictures had broken his leash and tore up three or four people on the Trenton farm.

TWIN CITY CAMERA AND VIDEO The Lewiston shop where Pop Merrill bought a video cassette and a Polaroid Sun 660.

THE VILLAGE WASHTUB A vacant building next to the Emporium Galorium used to be occupied by the Village Washtub.

WARDELL'S COUNTRY STORE A Castle Rock business that had gone bankrupt two years prior to Kevin Delevan's fifteenth birthday. The store had been vacant ever since.

THE WOLF JAW LUMBER COMPANY Castle Rock lumber company on Mulberry Street.

YOU SEW AND SEW One of Pop Merrill's business neighbors.

THE YWCA Meg Delevan took ballet lessons at the YWCA three afternoons a week.

(28d)
FOUR PAST MIDNIGHT
"The Sun Dog"
Things

"BASIN" Pop Merrill told Kevin about a man who killed his wife in Bath in 1946. Pop heard the word "basin" on a recording made later in the house. (The man had cut his wife's throat and drained her blood into a basin.)

THE BATTLE OF LEYTE GULF Meleusippus Verrill's husband was killed in the Battle of Leyte Gulf in 1944.

A BEECHCRAFT PLANE Pop Merrill drove to a private airstrip just north of Boothbay Harbor, from where a pilot flew him in Cedric McCarty's private Beechcraft plane to McCarty's private island. Pop wanted to sell McCarty Kevin's Polaroid Sun camera.

THE BEST AND THE BRIGHTEST A book John Delevan read.

THE BROWNIE BOX CAMERA A camera introduced by Kodak.

CAMELS The cigarettes smoked by the Pus Sisters. They did six packs a day between the two of them.

THE CELTICS VS. THE PHILADELPHIA SEVENTY-SIXERS The basketball game John Delevan bet on and lost, necessitating the $400 loan from Pop Merrill.

"CHILD'S PLAY" A movie Meg Delevan played on the VCR.

CHRISTMAS DAY The Delevans attended church only every third year when Aunt Hilda spent the holidays with them.

A COIN COLLECTION One of the items in Pop Merrill's worktable drawer. It was worth $19,000.

A CRISCO CAN When John Delevan went to Pop Merrill for the $400 loan that he needed to pay off the engineer on the bad Celtics game bet, Pop took forty ten dollar bills out of a Crisco can.

DIAMOND BLUE TIP MATCHES The matches that Pop Merrill used to light his pipe.

AN EAR Pop Merrill knew of an old lady who was in Massachusetts Memorial Hospital because her cat, Claudette, went on a rampage during a séance. The woman lost most of one ear.

"EVIL WEED" The words stamped on Pop Merrill's leather tobacco pouch.

FALL FOTO FESTIVAL A promotion that LaVerdiere's Super Drug Store ran that offered "Super Reductions On All Polaroid Cameras & Accessories."

A FORD The car John Delevan had when he was first married.

FORTUNE MAGAZINE For twelve years in a row, *Fortune* magazine named Cedric McCarty one of the richest men in America.

$400 Pop Merrill once lent John Delevan $400 to cover a bet on a basketball game.

FOUR YEARS Pop Merrill's nephew, Ace Merrill, was serving four years in Shawshank prison for breaking into the Mellow Tiger.

[NOTE: Shawshank prison appears in the *Different Seasons* novella "Rita Hayworth and Shawshank Redemption," and The Mellow Tiger appears in *The Dead Zone*. Also, Ace Merrill appears in the *Different Seasons* novella "The Body." See the sections on those works in this volume.]

A GERMAN CUCKOO CLOCK While in some sort of a "Polaroidsville-induced" trance, Pop Merrill smashed his own German cuckoo clock with a sledgehammer instead of Kevin's Polaroid Sun camera.

GREAT EXPECTATIONS One of the books on Kevin Delevan's summer reading list.

A GROSS JOKES PAPERBACK One of the things in the bottom drawer of Kevin Delevan's desk.

JUST OVER $2,000 IN CASH One of the items in Pop Merrill's worktable drawer.

KEVIN'S GRANDFATHER'S POCKETWATCH One of the things in the bottom drawer of Kevin Delevan's desk.

KEVIN'S NIGHTMARE Kevin dreamt he was on the bum in Oatley, which was either in Vermont or New York. He passed a wino who told him that the name of the place was really Hildasville, but when Kevin saw a woman pushing a shopping cart filled with Polaroid cameras disappear as he passed her, he knew he was in Polaroidsville. He then came to the fence and the dog from his Sun photos, and knew that the photographer was Pop Merrill.

KODAK The company that introduced the Brownie box camera.

KRUGERANDS Pop Merrill had a number of gold Krugerands in his worktable drawer.

A MAGNIFYING GLASS Pop Merrill studied Kevin's Polaroid pictures with a magnifying glass.

MASTERCARD Kevin's parents bought him a Polaroid Sun 660 camera at J.C. Penney's for his birthday, and charged it on a Mastercard.

A MITSUBISHI Pop Merrill had a twenty-five-inch Mitsubishi color TV in his living room.

THE NEW ENGLAND PSYCHIC AND TAROT CONVENTION A convention in Providence, Rhode Island, that the Pus Sisters had attended.

NIKONS, MINOLTAS, AND LEICAS Cameras that didn't take instant photos like Polaroids did.

A 1915 VICTOR-GRAFF GRAMOPHONE An antiques dealer from Boston named Donahue got fifty dollars more than he should have from Pop for a 1915 Victor-Graff gramophone.

A 1958 LINCOLN CONTINENTAL The Pus Sisters were driven around in a 1958 Lincoln Continental by a black woman almost as old as they were.

A 1959 CHEVROLET Pop Merrill's car. It was maintained free of charge at Sonny's Texaco, the fallout of a loan Pop had once made to the proprietor, Sonny Jackett.

1946 Pop Merrill told Kevin about a man who killed his wife in Bath in 1946. Pop heard the word "basin" on a recording made later in the house. (The man had cut his wife's throat and drained her blood into a basin.)

1978 The year the Castle Rock Ben Franklin store went out of business.

1969 Pop Merrill had gotten Sonny Jackett out of a "desperate scrape" in New Hampshire in 1969.

NINETY DOLLARS Pop Merrill once sold a Mad-Hatter in Dunwich, Massachusetts, a "spirit trumpet" for ninety dollars.

$116 A WEEK John Delevan's salary at the time he bet an engineer $400 on the Celtics vs. the Seventy-Sixers game.

A PENTHOUSE GATEFOLD One of the things in the bottom drawer of Kevin Delevan's desk.

PHOTOGRAPHS OF A WOMAN HAVING SEX WITH A SHETLAND PONY Some of the items in Pop Merrill's worktable drawer.

POP MERRILL'S WORKTABLE DRAWER It contained "a number of gold Krugerands; a stamp album in which the least valuable stamp was worth six hundred dollars in the latest

National Philatelist Catalogue; a coin collection worth approximately nineteen thousand dollars; two dozen glossy photographs of a bleary-eyed woman having sexual congress with a Shetland pony; and an amount of cash totalling just over two thousand dollars."

POP'S PAPERBACKS Pop Merrill had a quarter paperback rack in his Emporium Galorium. Some of the titles included *After Dark My Sweet, Fire in the Flesh,* and *The Brass Cupcake.*

PRINCE ALBERT TOBACCO Pop Merrill's tobacco of choice. He usually bought it from Molly Durham at LaVerdiere's Super Drug Store.

A QUEEN ANNE SOFA Pop Merrill posed the Pus Sisters on a Queen Anne sofa in their mansion's living room for a demonstration picture taken with Kevin's Polaroid Sun.

A RAIN-BO SKOOL PAD A pad Kevin used when in grade school.

A RED RUBBER BALL Kevin Delevan's Polaroid kept taking pictures of a large black dog in front of a white picket fence. A red rubber ball was in the grass at the far left of the picture.

A SEIKO Kevin Delevan's watch.

SEPTEMBER 15 Kevin Delevan's birthday.

SHOOT-OUT AT LAREDO A book that Kevin Delevan read.

A SONY WALKMAN One of the things in the bottom drawer of Kevin Delevan's desk.

SPAM Emory Chaffee offered Pop Merrill a Spam and Bermuda onion sandwich. Pop passed.

A SPIRIT TRUMPET Pop Merrill once sold a Mad-Hatter in Dunwich, Massachusetts, a "spirit trumpet" for ninety dollars.

A STAMP COLLECTION One of the items in Pop Merrill's worktable drawer.

A STEINWAY The Pus Sisters had a Steinway grand piano in their living room.

A SUN 660 The Polaroid instant camera Kevin Delevan received for his fifteenth birthday.

SURVEYOR'S ASSISTANT John Delevan's job at the time he bet an engineer $400 on the Celtics vs. the Seventy-Sixers game. He was making $116 a week.

TAPE RECORDERS When Kevin brought his "haunted" Polaroid Sun to Pop Merrill, Pop told him that many people claimed to have captured the voices of dead people with tape recorders.

TAREYTONS Before he quit, John Delevan smoked Tareytons.

THE THINGS IN KEVIN'S BOTTOM DESK DRAWER Besides Aunt Hilda's thirteen string ties, there was also his grandfather's pocketwatch, two sets of matching cufflinks, a *Penthouse* gatefold, a *Gross Jokes* paperback, and a Sony Walkman.

THIRTEEN STRING TIES Kevin had thirteen string ties in his drawer, all birthday gifts from Aunt Hilda. He was not allowed to throw them away. She had begun sending them on his third birthday.

THREE FINGERS Pop Merrill knew of a man in Kingston, Rhode Island, who lost three fingers of his right hand when the rear door of a car in which two teenagers had committed suicide closed on the hand.

TWO SETS OF MATCHING CUFFLINKS Two of the things in the bottom drawer of Kevin Delevan's desk.

A VCR Pop Merrill had a VCR on the end table in his living room.

A VIDEO CASSETTE AND A POLAROID SUN 660 CAMERA The two items Pop Merrill purchased at Twin City Camera and Video in Lewiston.

WEIRD TALES AND FANTASTIC UNIVERSE MAGAZINES During the final moments of the Sun Dog's "birth," John Delevan banged into a table in Pop Merrill's Emporium Galorium and knocked over a pile of *Weird Tales* and *Fantastic Universe* magazines.

A WOODPECKER CLASP The string tie that Aunt Hilda sent Kevin for his fifteenth birthday had a woodpecker clasp.

A WORDSTAR 70 PC Kevin Delevan's sixteenth birthday present. When Kevin typed in "The quick brown fox jumped over the lazy sleeping dog," what printed out was:

> "The dog is loose again.
> It is not sleeping.
> It is not lazy.
> It's coming for you, Kevin.
> It's very hungry.
> And it's very angry."

AN X-ACT-O KNIFE Pop Merrill used an X-Act-O knife to carve lines in the new Polaroid Sun he bought so that when he dropped it, it would make the same chink in the case as the one on Kevin's camera.

Unpublished & Uncollected Works

Chronological Index to Unpublished & Uncollected Works by Stephen King

Three Unpublished Novels
(University of Maine Special Collections Library)

Unpublished & Uncollected Shorter Works

Alphabetical Index to Unpublished & Uncollected Works by Stephen King

PPT=People, Places, and Things

THE AFTERMATH
[An unpublished novel by Stephen King]

What were you doing when you were a teenager?
Stephen King was writing novels.
Think about it.

The Aftermath was Stephen King's "first" novel, or at least the first of the unpublished manuscripts that has survived. It consists of seventy-six single-spaced pages in pica type, totaling close to fifty thousand words.

The Aftermath is science fiction, and takes place after an "Atomic War" that has destroyed a large part of the world's population.

A paramilitary organization known as the Sun Corps has risen to power, and it is the quest of one young survivor named Larry Talman to infiltrate the Corps and destroy the omniscient computer known as DRAC (Digital Relay Analogue Computer) that is running the show.

After Talman succeeds in destroying DRAC (and killing the girl he loved, Reina Durrel, in the process), the truth comes out: The Sun Corps was a front for spies from the planet Deneb IV who had moved in following the "Atomic War" in order to take over the Earth. But to do so, they had to first wipe out the Espers, a group of psychics who threatened their domination.

The Aftermath is broken into the following manuscript sections:

Part I:
    Chapter 1:   pages 1-4
    Chapter 2:   pages 4-10
    Chapter 3:   pages 10-20

Part II:
    Chapter 1:   pages 20-23
    Chapter 2:   pages 23-28
    Chapter 3:   pages 28-32
    Chapter 4:   pages 32-36
    Chapter 5:   pages 36-41
    Chapter 6:   pages 41-46
    Chapter 7:   pages 46-50
    Chapter 8:   pages 50-55
    Chapter 9:   pages 55-60
    Chapter 10:   pages 60-64
    Chapter 11:   pages 64-69
    Chapter 12:   pages 69-74

Part III:
    Chapter 1:   pages 74-76

George Beahm, author of *The Stephen King Companion*, and my source for the information on the three unpublished King novels, had this to say about *The Aftermath*:

"It is important to note that at the same time that King was writing *The Aftermath*, he also began *Getting It On*, which was later retitled *Rage* and almost bought by Doubleday two years before they bought *Carrie*. *Rage* was subsequently published in 1977 – the first Richard Bachman book.

In style, *The Aftermath* is very much a Bachman book.

Despite King's youth, this first novel-length manuscript shows many of his skills: the ability to tell a story, an almost instinctual skill; his ability to create vivid characters, quickly and economically; his ability to develop motivation in his characters. And King trademarks: colloqualisms in dialect; the use of brand names; in science fiction, pseudo-scientific language that sounds convincing.

The Aftermath also contains key King elements that would crop up in his later fiction: This first book shows a typical King character – an ordinary man in extraordinary situations, the standard King plot. There is a rite of passage – a child's loss of innocence through experience. A child is the protagonist in the novel. The novel holds a dark view of the world manifested via the technological horror – the ultimate hard weapon, the nuclear weapon. (King, a byproduct of the fifties when bomb scares were a fact of life, would find it easy to draw on the paranoia of the times.) Fiction reflects the individual writing the story and the age in which it was written; King is very much a creature of his time – and writes accordingly. Also, the presence of Espers – people with extraordinary abilities ("wild talents," a la Carrie and Charlie McGee later), and plagues.

The theme is one used throughout much of his fiction: The destruction of the world. Also, the novel contains the trappings of science fiction: A Lovecraftian race from another planet moves in after the detonation of the 'big one' and uses a computer to devise a game plan.

My summation: *The Aftermath* is a narrative that yanks the reader through the story. The novel begins *in medias res*, then flashes back and rejoins as the character, changed by his experience, realizes the truth that men being what they are, human nature being what it is, people will always band together. The novel asks the questions 'Is government better than anarchy, or are they two sides of the same coin?' and leaves the answer up to the reader."

Doug Winter had this to say about *The Aftermath*:

"[*The Aftermath*] is remarkably mature, and demonstrates King's storytelling talents even at an early age."

The following concordance may seem a bit bewildering, since only a handful of people have actually read the novel. Nonetheless, I think this glimpse at King's early work, as superficial as it must, by necessity, be, will show you the nascent workings of the mind that would eventually conceive and deliver the stories we've come to know and love.

The entries are alphabetical, and the parenthetical code after the entry proper refers to the novel ("A" for *The Aftermath*), the section of the book in which the entry is found (Part 1, 2, or 3) and the individual chapter within the section. Thus "(A; 2: 5)" tells you that the entry comes from *The Aftermath*, Part 2, Chapter 5.

For a detailed synopsis of each of the three unpublished Stephen King novels in the University of Maine's Special Collections Library, I heartily and unreservedly recommend George Beahm's indispensable book, *The Stephen King Companion*.

Many, many thanks to George for his performance above and beyond, and for his help with the compilation of this section. —**sjs**

THE AFTERMATH
People

BRALLY, MR. (A; 2:5) When they got to Eustus, Talman and Vannerman witnessed Lt. Yaeger trying to convince a general store owner named Mr. Brally to give up his Laser Plate cooking device because it "could be used for anything from cooking eggs to igniting an atomic weapon."

CARVEL, MR. (A; 2:8) Talman's teacher at the Sun Corp Statistics & Logistics School. He was an Esper, and he helped Talman destroy DRAC.

CARVER, LT. (A; 2:10) Talman, Lt. Carver, and Reina discussed how the Sun Corps could have built a computer as big as DRAC. (The Corps didn't; The Denebians did.)

THE DAYTIME KEEPER (A; 2:8) The "Daytime Keeper" of DRAC was Reina Durrel. As the "Technican-On-Duty," she activated DRAC with a carefully-positioned palm-print.

THE DENEBIAN (A; 2:12) After DRAC is destroyed, the only Denebian on earth shows up and is shot dead.

DURREL, IRIS (A; 1:3) Reina's sister. Iris was raped in New York by looters.

DURREL, REINA (A; 1:3) The sixteen-year-old girl who Talman met in Graybill, South Carolina. Her parents were killed in the initial atomic blast. She and Talman became lovers, but she left him in the winter of 1969. She eventually became the "Daytime Keeper" of the Sun Corps computer, DRAC. She was killed by a sonic Ear-hum set by Talman.

ESPERS (A; 2:9) Psychics.

FIFTY SUN CORPSMEN (A; 2:6) Eustus's only defense against looters was twelve machine guns and eight "Sonics." Reinforcements arrived from the Village, though, consisting of twenty men and fifty Sun Corpsmen. They used "Molitov" cocktails to defend the town, and the looters' attack was repelled.

GUNTZ, LT (A; 2:2) The Sun Corps officer who interviewed Talman and Vannerman for admission to the Corps.

HITLER, ADOLPH (A; 2:2) The Sun Corps was based on the teachings of its "spiritual founder," Adolph Hitler.

JANIS (A; 1:2) Larry Talman's girlfriend in "The Time Before."

JONESY (A; 1:3) One of the looters who shot and killed Jimmy Tomlinson.

KELLY (A; 1:1) An eighteen-year-old blonde male survivor of the Atomic War. Kelly was shot in the guts in Chapter 1 by looters with deer rifles. He died in Graybill, South Carolina. Kelly tried to defend himself with a Gunnar-Hellman Bolt Pistol.

KRITZMAN, LT. (A; 2:11) A Sun Corps Esper who pumped Talman for information.

MONK (A; 1:3) One of the looters who shot and killed Jimmy Tomlinson.

AN OLD MAN (A; 1:3) After the war, while Reina and Iris Durrel were hitchhiking north, they got picked up by an old man who tried to bargain a ride for sex. They hit him on the head with a purse, and he crashed and died.

THE RELATIVES (A; 1:3) Iris and Reina Durrel headed for New York after the atomic blast because they had relatives there.

ROGER (A; 2:5) The driver who took Vannerman and Talman to Eustus. On the way, they were ambushed by five men, but fought them off.

STOWE, ARNIE (A; 2:3) A Sun Corpsman who had been a member of the Corps three weeks when Talman and Vannerman were inducted.

TALMAN, LARRY (A; 1:1) The eighteen-year-old hero of *The Aftermath*.

THE THIRD LOOTER (A; 1:3) Jimmy Tomlinson was shot and killed by three looters.

TOMLINSON, JIMMY (A; 1:3) A farmer's son. Jimmy joined forces with Talman, but was ambushed and killed by looters (Monk and Jonesy) at a gas station.

TWENTY MEN (A; 2:6) Eustus's only defense against looters was twelve machine guns and eight "Sonics." Reinforcements arrived from the Village, though, consisting of twenty men and fifty Sun Corpsmen. They used "Molitov" cocktails to defend the town, and the looters' attack was repelled.

VANNERMAN, IAN (A; 2:1) After Reina left Talman in the winter of 1969, Talman met Ian Vannerman, who told him that there was "anthrax" in Red Camp, that he had heard stories about "bubonic out West," and a "plague in the towns." Vannerman was an Esper.

YAEGER, LT (A; 2:5) When they got to Eustus, Talman and Vannerman witnessed Lt. Yaeger trying to convince a general store owner named Mr. Brally to give up his Laser Plate cooking device because it "could be used for anything from cooking eggs to igniting an atomic weapon."

THE AFTERMATH
Places

CHICAGO (A; 2:12) After the downfall of the Sun Corps, Talman remained behind in Los Angeles while Carvel and the other survivors left in a heli for Chicago. Talman was upset because he knew everything would start all over again. He believed the goal of mankind should be "making a future of the Aftermath."

DENEB IV (A; 2:12) After DRAC was destroyed, Talman learned that the inhabitants of the planet Deneb IV moved in after the atomic blast that destroyed most of the Earth's population.

EURASIA (A; 2:8) DRAC revealed that two-thirds of Eurasia's population died in the initial atomic blast. DRAC then used "Asimov-Seldon-Theorems" to compute the possibility of continuing democratic systems in Eurasia at 2.041 percent.

EUSTUS, TENNESSEE (A; 2:4) A town a week away from the Nashville Sun Corps Garrison Complex.

THE GENERAL STORE (A; 2:5) A Eustus, Tennessee, store owned by Mr. Brally. In the Aftermath, Brally didn't have any electricity.

GRAYBILL, SOUTH CAROLINA (A; 1:1) Kelly, one of the survivors of the Atomic War, was shot and killed by looters with deer rifles in Graybill, South Carolina. Kelly tried to defend himself with a Gunnar-Hellman Bolt Pistol.

THE LIBRARY (A; 1:3) Talman buried Jimmy Tomlinson in the library because "Books...had been Tomlinson's last wish."

LOS ANGELES (A; 2:7) After the battle at Eustus, Talman took his first plane ride to Los Angeles to attend Sun Corps Statistics & Logistics School.

MANCHESTER (A; 1:2) *The Aftermath* takes place after an Atomic War. On August 14, 1967, a "small tactical atomic warhead hit the Nike-Zeus base outside of [Manchester]."

MECHANICS & WEAPONRY (A; 2:6) After the battle to defend Eustus, Talman and Vannerman were given their battle assignments: Talman went to Statistics & Logistics School; Vannerman to Mechanics & Weaponry.

THE NASHVILLE SUN CORPS GARRISON COMPLEX (A; 2:2) After Talman and Vannerman decided to destroy the Sun Corps, they headed for the Nashville Complex, which was twenty buildings surrounded by an electrified fence, where they joined the Corps as spies.

NEW YORK (A; 1:3) Iris Durrel was raped by looters in New York.

THE NIKE-ZEUS BASE (A; 1:2) *The Aftermath* takes place after an Atomic War. On August 14, 1967, a "small tactical atomic warhead hit the Nike-Zeus base outside of [Manchester]."

STATISTICS & LOGISTICS SCHOOL (A; 2:6) After the battle to defend Eustus, Talman and Vannerman were given their battle assignments: Talman went to Statistics & Logistics School; Vannerman to Mechanics & Weaponry.

SUN CORPS HEADQUARTERS (A; 2:1) There was one in New York and one in Los Angeles.

WOOLWORTHS (A; 1:2) While in Graybill, Talman flashed back to before Armageddon, "The Time Before," when he was in Woolworth's buying his girlfriend Janis a scarf. The bomb went off when he was in the store, and afterward, there was nothing but wreckage: "...for they were not men and women, but fresh hamburger."

(UP1)
THE AFTERMATH
Things

"AMBER GOLD" (A; 1:2) Gasoline, after the Atomic War.

ASIMOV-SELDON-THEOREMS (A; 2:8) DRAC revealed that two-thirds of Eurasia's population died in the initial Atomic blast. DRAC then used "Asimov-Seldon-Theorems" to compute the possibility of continuing democratic systems in Eurasia at 2.041 percent.

AN ATOMIC WAR (A; 1:1) *The Aftermath* takes place after an Atomic War. On August 14, 1967, a "small tactical atomic warhead hit the Nike-Zeus base outside of [Manchester]."

AUGUST 14, 1967 (A; 1:2) The date of Armageddon.

BEEF STEW (A; 2:3) Talman and Vannerman's breakfast the morning after their induction into the Sun Corps.

DRAC (A; 2:8) The Digital Relay Analogue Computer; the Sun Corps massive all-powerful computer. There were seven stories of the computer above ground, and seven stories below.

EIGHT "SONICS" (A; 2:6) Eustus's only defense against looters was twelve machine guns and eight "Sonics." Reinforcements arrived from the Village, though, consisting of twenty men, and fifty Sun Corpsmen. They used "Molitov" cocktails to defend the town, and the looters' attack was repelled.

THE EVILS OF GOVERNMENT" (A; 3:1) In the fall following the downfall of the Sun Corps, Talman wondered "are the evils of government any worse than the evils of anarchy?" He decided to go to Chicage where the Espers were, but he had learned a lesson: "Government is wrong! He shouted in his mind. The War showed that. The Sun Corps showed that!...But he could see all the flaws in his argument now. His eyes were open, for better or worse."

AN EXPLOSIVE CUBE (A; 2:9) Vannerman planned on destroying DRAC by using a cube of plastic explosive (about the size of a sugar cube, but heavier.)

A GUNNAR-HELLMAN BOLT PISTOL (A; 1:1) Kelly, one of the survivors of the Atomic War, was shot and killed by looters with deer rifles in Graybill, South Carolina. He had tried to defend himself with a Gunnar-Hellman Bolt Pistol. The Bolt Pistol used "ultrasonic cartridges" that could make "fist-sized holes."

A LASER PLATE COOKING DEVICE (A; 2:5) A cooking plate that "could be used for anything from cooking eggs to igniting an atomic weapon."

"MOLITOV" COCKTAILS (A; 2:6) Eustus's only defense against looters was twelve machine guns and eight "Sonics." Reinforcements arrived from the Village, though , consisting of twenty men, and fifty Sun Corpsmen. They used "Molitov" cocktails to defend the town, and the looters' attack is repelled.

99.988 PERCENT (A; 2:11) Talman made Reina ask DRAC what would happen to the Sun Corps if DRAC were destroyed? The answer was a 99.988 percent probability that the Corps would collapse.

OCTOBER 1968 (A; 1:2) The time period of *The Aftermath*.

AN OLD FORD (A; 1:1) After the Atomic War, Kelly and Talman drove an old Ford into Graybill, South Carolina. The car was not in very good shape, and the first line of the novel tells us that "The engine of the old Ford died, for the third time that morning."

THE RHINE ESP TEST (A; 2:3) One of the tests given to Vannerman and Talman during their induction into the Sun Corps.

A SCARF (A; 1:2) Talman was in Woolworth's buying his girlfriend Janis a scarf when the bomb went off.

SONIC BADGES (A; 2:8) Access to the room in which DRAC was housed was only by the use of "sonic badges" that emitted "subsonic vibrations."

"A SONIC EAR-HUM" (A; 2:9) Vannerman planned on disabling the people around DRAC by using a "sonic Ear-hum that'll rupture every brain within a twenty-foot span."

A STANDARDIZED IQ TEST (A; 2:3) One of the tests given to Vannerman and Talman during their induction into the Sun Corps.

THE SUN CORPS (A; 1:3) A paramilitary organization that came to power in the fourteen months following the atomic blast. The Sun Corps was based on the teachings of its "spiritual founder," Adolph Hitler. The Corps was actually "A Denebian Front organization to wipe out the Esper menace."

THE SUN CORPS SYMBOL (A; 2:2) A golden sunburst on a green field.

"A SURVIVOR TYPE" (A; 2:2) Ian Vannerman told Talman that he must be "a pretty good survivor type to have made it as long as you have, on your own." [NOTE: The term "survivor type" appears later in King's work as the title of a particularly gnarly short story in *Skeleton Crew*. See the section on "Survivor Type" (21p) in this volume.]

TEN KEYS (A; 2:8) Reina Durrel, as the Daytime Keeper of DRAC, used ten keys to enter data into the computer. Each key was a "basic semantic combination."

"THE TIME BEFORE" (A; 1:2) Talman's term for the time before Armageddon.

TWELVE MACHINE GUNS (A; 2:6) Eustus's only defense against looters was twelve machine guns and eight "Sonics." Reinforcements arrived from the Village, though, consisting of twenty men, and fifty Sun Corpsmen. They used "Molitov" cocktails to defend the town, and the looters' attack was repelled.

SWORD IN THE DARKNESS
[An unpublished novel by Stephen King]

Sword in the Darkness is a 150,000-word novel written by Stephen King between 1968 and 1970. It was completed in Orono, Maine, on April 30, 1970 (a Thursday). It consists of 485 double-spaced manuscript pages in elite typeface, with approximately 300 words per page.

It is ostensibly the story of a race riot in a city called Harding, but the story is actually about a high school boy named Arnie Kalowski who sees his mother and sister die early on in the novel, and who must then care for his father, who has a nervous breakdown. All the while, Arnie watches the sleazy underside of life unfolding in the city around him. The story is about racism, violence, incest, deceit, blackmail, and lust, and was Stephen King's naive attempt to write something about which he had no first-hand knowledge, having grown up in a small town of 900 people and having never even seen a race riot, much less participated in one.

Doug Winter, in *Stephen King: The Art of Darkness*, had this to say about *Sword in the Darkness* :

"Heavily indebted to the "Harrison High" novels of sometime horror novelist John Farris – who, along with Don Robertson, author of *The Greatest Thing Since Sliced Bread* (1965), *Paradise Falls* (1968), and other novels, was a major influence upon the maturing King – this lengthy tale of a race riot at an urban high school was rejected an even dozen times on Publishers' Row. King reflects: 'I had lost my girlfriend of four years, and this book seemed to be constantly, ceaselessly pawing over that relationship and trying to make some sense of it. And that doesn't make for good fiction'."

Sword in the Darkness doesn't have any horror or supernatural elements in it at all. It was Stephen King's attempt at writing a mainstream novel about something that intrigued him: the layers of human behavior, and the secrets in an urban high school and town. Even though he considers it a failed novel, it nonetheless tells a story, and was one more step in the development of a writer.

Sword in the Darkness is broken into four parts as follows:

Part I: Prologue/Good Day, Sunshine
Part II: Late Afternoon
Part III: Full Dark
Part IV: Epilogue/Good Mornin', Blues

The parenthetical notes following the entries refer to the title of the novel ("SD" = *Sword in the Darkness*) and the number following the "SD" is the section of the book from which the entry was drawn. — **sjs**

(UP2)
SWORD IN THE DARKNESS
People

BULL RUN (SD; 3) One of the gang members who worked with Webs McCullough to plan the rioting in Harding when Marcus Slade visited the town.

COOLIDGE, HENRY (SD; 2) Kit Longtin's uncle, the principal of Harding High. She seduced Henry and was photographed naked with him. She let him have sex with her anyway because, she reasoned, he *is* paying for it. (She and Earl Neiman blackmailed Uncle Hank for $10,000.)

COX, MAYOR (SD; 2) The mayor of Harding.

CROSS, JANET (SD; 2) "[H]onor student, potential saluditorian, loudmouth, dream destroyer, rotten-hearted, ugly, stupid, stinking *bitch*." Janet saw Meg and John Edgar together.

CROSS, MRS. (SD; 3) Janet's mother. She was a whore, pimped by Gumbo.

DANNING, BILL (SD; 2) A CPA. Bill was Miriam Kalowski's boss, lover, and father of her unborn child. When he refused to marry her, she commited suicide.

DeCLANCY, MEG (SD; 1) The Harding High student who cried rape at the hands of the high school teacher John Edgars. (She actually tried to seduce him.)

DELANEY, SAMUEL P. (SD; 3) One of Arnie Kalowski's friends. Arnie got drunk with Sam. "Arnie Kalowski was drunk as a lord."

THE DOCK STREET SOCIALIZERS (SD; 2) One of the Harding street gangs. The Socializers were mostly comprised of Jewish and white males.

EDGARS, JOHN (SD; 2) The Harding High teacher who was falsey accused of rape by Meg DeClancy.

GUMBO (SD; 3) Janet Cross's mother's pimp.

HAIGHT, ALEXANDER (SD; 3) Henry Coolidge woke from an erotic dream and saw Alexander Haight coming into his office. Coolidge used a BB pistol to shoot out one of Haight's eyes.

HASH (SD; 3) One of the gang members who worked with Webs McCullough to plan the rioting in Harding when Marcus Slade visited the town.

JIG (SD; 2) One of the gang members who worked with Webs McCullough to plan the rioting in Harding when Marcus Slade visited the town. Jig was a member of the Turner Street Trades street gang.

KALOWSKI, ARNIE (SD; 1) The teenage boy who attended Harding High, and who is the protagonist of *Sword in the Darkness*. At the beginning of the novel, Arnie's mother Rita dies of a brain tumor, and his pregnant sister Miriam commits suicide. Arnie eventually loses his virginity to Kit Longtin.

KALOWSKI, FRANK (SD; 1) Arnie's father. After the deaths of his wife and daughter, he suffers a nervous breakdown on June 20. Arnie cared for him at home.

KALOWSKI, MIRIAM RACHAEL (SD; 1) Arnie's sister; Frank and Rita's daughter. She became pregnant by her boss, Bill Danning, and committed suicide when he told her he wouldn't marry her, didn't love her, and that she should get an abortion.

KALOWSKI, RITA (SD; 1) Arnie and Miriam's mother; Frank's wife. She dies of a brain tumor at the beginning of the novel.

LONGTIN, KIT (SD; 2) A "professional seductress." Kit was a sexy young blond who kept a running tally of how many guys she had slept with, and how many times she had had sex. At the beginning of the novel, she had made it 175 times with "not quite fifty males." Kit's uncle Hank was the principal of Harding High, and had made a pass at her when she was thirteen. She blackmailed him by setting up a situation where the two of them could be photographed naked together.

THE MARKHAM AVENUE CHIEFTAINS (SD; 2) One of the Harding street gangs.

MARTY (SD;3) One of the gang members who worked with Webs McCullough to plan the rioting in Harding when Marcus Slade visited the town.

McCULLOUGH, WEBS (SD; 2) The gang member who planned the rioting that occurred when Marcus Slade came to Harding.

NEIMAN, EARL (SD; 2) A Harding High bully. Earl collaborated with Kit Longtin to blackmail her uncle Henry Coolidge, the principal of Harding High, so Coolidge wouldn't throw him out of school.

PETER (SD; 3) One of the gang members who worked with Webs McCullough to plan the rioting in Harding when Marcus Slade visited the town.

PROBY, LT. (SD; 2) The Harding police officer who told Arnie Kalowski about the death of Arnie's sister.

ROWSMITH, MISS EDIE (SD; 1) The Harding High French teacher. She believed John Edgars when he told her that he was set up by Meg DeClancy.

ROY (SD; 2) One of Marcus Slade's old friends and personal assistants.

SLADE, MARCUS (SD; 2) The crippled black activist whose arrival in Harding sparked the race riot that destroyed the town.

SLADE, MR. (SD; 2) Marcus Slade's father. He was lynched.

SPOONER (SD; 3) One of the gang members who worked with Webs McCullough to plan the rioting in Harding when Marcus Slade visited the town.

THE TURNER STREET TRADES (SD; 2) One of the Harding street gangs. The Trades were mostly comprised of black males.

WOMACK, GALEY (SD; 3) The hunchback who developed the naked photos of Kit Longtin and her Uncle Hank. Galey took pictures of "girls with their snatches spread for high school freshmen to masturbate on."

(UP2)
SWORD IN THE DARKNESS
Places

THE ARCADE (SD; 2) Miriam Kalowski's body was found near the Arcade.

CARLTON STREET (SD; 1) The Harding street where the Kalowskis lived.

THE CLUB (SD; 1) A walkdown bar on Turner Street in Harding.

DOCK STREET (SD; 3) Arnie Kalowski and Kit Longtin went to a fleabag hotel on Dock Street in Harding to have sex.

HARDING (SD; 1) "It is sprawled along the verge of the lake like a string of dirty pearls made clean with the dawn." The major, fictional American city in which *Sword in the Darkness* takes place.

HARDING HIGH SCHOOL (SD; 1) The high school setting for *Sword in the Darkness*. (The novel also focusses on another school, South City Manual Trades, where Slade was scheduled to speak.)

THE MERTON APARTMENT COMPLEX (SD; 1) The building where the Kalowskis lived.

MICHIGAN CIRCLE (SD; 1) An area of discos and theaters in Harding's theater district.

MIKE'S PLACE (SD; 2) A Harding pizza place. Earl Neiman met Kit Longtin at Mike's to plan the blackmail of Kit's Uncle Henry.

MIT (SD; 2) The college Arnie Kalowski hoped to attend.

ROBARD STREET (SD; 1) The Harding street where the Salten Brothers department store was located.

SALTEN BROTHERS (SD; 1) A department store in Harding. They sold mink coats.

SAN FRANCISCO (SD; 2) Marcus Slade planned his Harding visit while he was in San Francisco.

SOUTH CITY MANUAL TRADES (SD; 1) One of the schools that is the focus of *Sword in the Darkness*. (The other is Harding High School.)

TURNER STREET (SD; 1) The Harding street where the Club bar was located.

(UP2)
SWORD IN THE DARKNESS
Things

$5,400 A YEAR (SD; 2) A white man's pay in Harding.

JUNE 20 (SD; 2) The date that Frank Kalowski had a nervous breakdown.

JUNE 29 (SD; 2) The date that Marcus Slade visited Harding.

A 1956 FORD (SD; 2) The car Arnie Kalowski bought for $350.

THE OIL TANKS (SD; 3) As part of the racially-based rioting that took place in Harding when Marcus Slade visited town, the gang members blew up the town's oil tanks: "It went with a... *whoosh* that lit the sky like Judgement Day." [NOTE: King (well, actually, Trashcan Man) also blew up oil tanks later on in *The Stand*. See the section on *The Stand* in this volume. Also see my interview with Richard Christian Matheson in which he discusses the oil tank scene in *The Stand*.]

THE PHOTOS (SD; 2) In order to blackmail Kit's Uncle Hank, Earl Neiman took pictures of Kit and her uncle naked together.

$350 (SD; 2) The price Arnie Kalwoski paid for his 1956 Ford.

$3,000 OR LESS A YEAR (SD; 2) A black man's pay in Harding.

TWO WEEKS PAY AND A BONUS (SD; 2) Following Bill Danning's refusal to marry Miriam Kalowski after getting her pregnant, he gave her two weeks pay and a bonus for "fine secretarial work."

broken into twenty unnumbered chapters. The original manuscript was completed on February 15, 1973 (a Thursday).

The original manuscript also has an accompanying 106-page rewrite, after which the rewrite ends. The novel is paginated, and is in elite typeface until page 50, at which point it goes into pica type.

The chapter/page breakdown of the manuscript is as follows:

Chapter 1	Pages 1-4
Chapter 2	Pages 5-10
Chapter 3	Pages 11-14
Chapter 4	Pages 15-17
Chapter 5	Pages 18-22
Chapter 6	Pages 23-26
Chapter 7	Pages 27-28
Chapter 8	Pages 29-45 (Flashback)
Chapter 9	Pages 46-49
Chapter 10	Pages 50-61
Chapter 11	Pages 62-74 (Flashback)
Chapter 12	Pages 75-86
Chapter 13	Pages 87-96 (with Interlude)
Chapter 14	Pages 102-111
Chapter 15	Pages 112-127 (Flashback)
Chapter 16	Pages 128-127
Chapter 17	Pages 134-139 (Flashback)
Chapter 18	Pages 140-151
Chapter 19	Pages 152-165 (Flashback)
Chapter 20	Pages 166-171
Epilogue	Pages 172-173

George Beahm says *Blaze* has a "distinctive Bachman flavor, a downbeat ending, and no supernatural presence." He also called it "an entertaining read" that unfortunately contains major flaws in logic. (See Beahm's *The Stephen King Companion* for George's analysis of the plot's weaknesses and strengths.)

Once again, my sincerest thanks go out to George Beahm for taking the time to go to Maine, spend a week reading these three unpublished manuscripts and take notes on them, and then allow me total access to, and use of, his research. These three concordances could not have been done were it not for George's superb scholarship and attention to detail regarding these works.

Entries below again feature the story designation – in this case "B" – followed by chapter references. — **sjs**

BLAZE
[An unpublished novel by Stephen King]

Blaze is Stephen King's seventh novel. (The first six were *The Aftermath, The Long Walk, Sword in the Darkness, Getting It On (Rage), The Running Man,* and *Carrie.* Following *Blaze* came *Second Coming*, which later became *'Salem's Lot.*)

King has described *Blaze* as a "literary imitation" of Steinbeck's *Of Mice and Men.* In King's words, *Blaze* was "a melodrama about a huge, almost retarded criminal who kidnaps a baby, planning to ransom it back to the child's rich parents...and then falls in love with the child instead."

The dedication reads "This book is for my mother, Ruth Pillsbury King," and the novel consists of 173 pages

(UP3)
BLAZE
People

ANNIE BRADSTAY'S BOYFRIEND (B; 15) He was an arsonist. He burned down six potato warehouses in Morin.

ARCH George Rockley's name was changed to Arch in the rewrite of the *Blaze* manuscript that was not completed.

BETTS, ADELAIDE (B; 6) The Hager's Mammoth Department Store saleslady who worked in the baby department (The Baby Shoppe), and who sold Blaze $221.55 worth of supplies for the Gerard baby. Adelaide worked on commission.

BLAISDELL, CLAIBORNE, SR. (B; 3) Blaze's father. One day, when Blaze was a child, Sr. threw Jr. down the stairs three times. Blaze had been watching Huckleberry Hound.

BLAZE (B; 1) Claiborne Blaisdell, Jr. The mildly retarded giant who kidnaped a baby, held him for ransom, and ended up getting shot to death during the ransom drop.

BLAZE'S SON (B; 15) Annie Bradstay gave birth to Blaze's son in May of 1950. The child was ten pounds, four ounces. The kid was adopted by the Wyatts from Kittery, Maine, and grew up to attend Boston University and major in English literature.

BLUENOTE, HARRY (B; 15) As a child, Blaze was hired by Bluenote to pick blueberries. Bluenote died of a heart attack.

THE BOOGEYMAN (B; 19) Blaze, according to Henry Melcher, George Rockley's brother-in-law.

BOWIE, MR. (B; 8) The farmer who took in Blaze as a ward of the state.

BOWIE, MRS. (B; 8) The farmer's wife who took in Blaze as a ward of the state.

BRADSTAY, ANNIE (B; 15) The girl who was paid four dollars to have sex with Blaze when Blaze was fifteen years old.

BRIAN (B; 15) One of the boys who watched Blaze have sex with Annie Bradstay.

BURGESS, JOHN (B; 19) A high school teacher who George Rockley met while in prison. Burgess was in for manslaughter and suggested to George, "Kidnap a baby."

CARLTON, JOSEPH (B; 10) The fictitious name that Blaze used to sneak into the Gerard Estate.

CHELTZMAN, JOHN (B; 8) The Chase Home student who did Blaze's homework in exchange for protection from the bullies. John once tried his hand at writing: He wrote a vampire story called *The Eyes of Yurdlak are Upon You*.

CHRIS (B; 15) One of the boys who watched Blaze have sex with Annie Bradstay.

CLAY (B; 8) Blaze's nickname at school.

THE COUNTERMAN (B; 11) The counterman at Lindy's Steak House. After he heard how Blaze and John were able to buy steaks, he befriended them, gave them free steaks, and set them up at the YMCA.

ELTZMAN, MARTIN (B; 8) In 1946, the Sister Mary Dean Chase Home got a new head man, a "short, bald-headed little prick named Martin Eltzman." Blaze hated him.

GERARD, JOSEPH II (B; 16) The Gerard baby's father.

GERARD, JOSEPH III (B; 2) The baby kidnapped by Blaze.

GERARD, MRS. (B; 20) Joseph Gerard II's wife; Joseph Gerard III's mother.

GERARD, NORMA (B; 10) While attempting to escape with the kidnapped Gerard baby, Blaze was surprised by an old woman in the kitchen. It was Norma Gerard. She later died. She was sixty-two.

GLEN (B; 8) The school bully. Blaze beat him up when he hit Marjorie Turlow on her vaccination spot.

GRAINGER, AGENT (B; 18) The police officer who saw Blaze go into the cave with the Gerard baby.

HOLLOWAY (B; 17) The assistant district attorney who tried Blaze for beating Martin Eltzman.

A MALE COLLEGE STUDENT (B; 4) When Blaze was holding up Tim & Janet's Quik-Pik, a male college student walked in with his girlfriend. Blaze robbed him, too. (He got forty-six dollars from the kid's wallet.)

THE MALE COLLEGE STUDENT'S GIRLFRIEND (B; 4) The girlfriend of the guy Blaze robbed at Tim & Janet's Quik-Pik.

MELCHER, HENRY (B; 19) George Rockley's brother-in-law.

"MIGHTY MARTY" (B; 8) Martin Eltzman.

MONAHAN, DAN J. (B; 11) The detective who questioned Blaze and John after they ordered steaks at Lindy's Steak House.

THE NIGHTMAN (B; 4) The unnamed clerk at Tim & Janet's Quik-Pik when Blaze held up the store. The nightman had been reading a porno novel titled *Big and Hard*. The nightman attended UMO in Portland.

THE OPERATOR (B; 16) When Blaze called Joseph Gerard from a pay phone, he gave the operator his full name.

RANDY (B; 8) The dog on the Bowie farm that "scared the shit out of Blaze." Blaze killed him.

ROCKLEY, GEORGE (B; 1) Blaze's mentor and inner guide. We found out that George is dead in Chapter 1. In Chapter 18, George and Blaze have the following conversation:

> "Christ, George, are you in my head?"
> *"I always was, asshole. Now GO!"*

George was "knifed in the area of a floating crap game on the Portland dock."

ST. PIERRE, BILLY (B; 17) One of the low-lifes that Blaze hooked up with after getting out of prison in 1953.

STERLING, ALBERT (B; 16) The man that the telephone operator contacted after Blaze gave him her real name.

THE STORE DETECTIVE (B; 19) The Hardy's Discount store detective whose attention was diverted when Blaze attacked a man who picked up Blaze's phony wallet. (George was robbing the cash register during the commotion.)

TOE-JAM (B; 15) One of the boys who paid Annie Bradstay four dollars to have sex with Blaze when Blaze was fifteen.

A TRUCKER (B; 13) After giving the ransom demand, Blaze hitched a ride into town with a trucker who brought up the subject of the kidnapping. Blaze slipped and revealed that the ransom was $1 million, which no one but the kidnapper and the police could know.

TURLOW, MARJORIE (B; 8) The blonde seventh-grader who was the first girl Blaze ever fell in love with.

WALSH, MR. (B; 12) The night attendant at Oak Hill Arms, which was a quarter-mile from the Gerard mansion. He provided the police with a visual description of Blaze.

THE WYATTS (B; 15) Annie Bradstay gave birth to Blaze's son in May of 1950. He was ten pounds, four ounces. The kid was adopted by the Wyatts from Kittery, Maine, and grew up to attend Boston University and major in English literature.

(UP3)

BLAZE
Places

APEX, MAINE (B; 1) The town where the Bag, a college bar, was located. Blaze stole a dark green Ford from the Bag's parking lot.

THE BABY SHOPPE (B; 6) The baby department of Hager's Mammoth Department Store. Blaze bought $221.55 worth of baby supplies there from Adelaide Betts, who worked on commission.

THE BAG (B; 1) The bar where Blaze stole the dark green Ford.

BOSTON (B; 3) Blaze first met George Rockley in the fall of 1956 in Boston.

THE CAVE (B; 18) The cave where Blaze hid out with the Gerard baby.

CUMBERLAND (B; 8) The Bowies lived on a farm in Cumberland.

CUMBERLAND VILLAGE (B; 20) Blaze was buried in Cumberland Village, one-and-a-half miles from the Sister Mary Dean Chase Home for Boys.

THE GERARD ESTATE (B; 10) The Gerard Estate was in Ocoma Heights. Blaze lied his way in, and kidnapped the Gerard baby.

HAGER'S MAMMOTH DEPARTMENT STORE (B; 6) Blaze bought $221.55 worth of baby supplies from the Baby Shoppe (the baby department of Hager's), from Adelaide Betts, who worked on commission.

HARDY'S DISCOUNT (B; 19) A store in Lynn, Maine, that Blaze and George robbed.

KITTERY, MAINE (B; 15) Annie Bradstay gave birth to Blaze's son in May of 1950. He was ten pounds, four ounces. The kid was adopted by the Wyatts from Kittery, Maine, and grew up to attend Boston University and major in English literature.

LINDY'S STEAK HOUSE (B; 11) The Boston restaurant where Blaze and John ate steaks with the money they found in the theater bathroom.

LYNN, MAINE (B; 19) The town where Hardy's Discount store was located.

MOOCHIE'S DRUGSTORE (B; 19) The drugstore where Henry Melcher first introduced Blaze to his brother-in-law, George Rockley.

MORIN (B; 15) Annie Bradstay's arsonist boyfriend burned down six potato warehouses in Morin.

OCOMA HEIGHTS (B; 10) The Gerard Estate was in Ocoma Heights.

PORTLAND DISTRICT COURT (B; 17) After beating Martin Eltzman "unconscious" for sending John Cheltzman – sick with rheumatic fever – out to pick pumpkins, Blaze was tried in a Portland district court and sentenced to five years in the South Portland Correctional Facility.

THE SHITHOLE (B; 8) The Sister Mary Dean Chase Home for Boys, according to Blaze.

THE SISTER MARY DEAN CHASE HOME FOR BOYS (B; 3) The home where Blaze was placed after his father abused him. He called it "The Shithole."

SIX POTATO WAREHOUSES (B; 15) Annie Bradstay's arsonist boyfriend burned down six potato warehouses in Morin.

THE SOUTH PORTLAND CORRECTIONAL FACILITY (B; 17) After beating Martin Eltzman "unconscious" for sending John Cheltzman – sick with rheumatic fever – out to pick pumpkins, Blaze was tried in a Portland district court and sentenced to five years in the South Portland Correctional Facility.

A THEATER (B; 11) When Blaze was thirteen, he worked in a theater twenty hours a week for twenty-five cents an hour.

TIM & JANET'S (B; 4) The "mom & pop" store Blaze held up after he kidnapped the Gerard baby. Blaze needed baby supplies. It was a Quik-Pik.

THE YMCA (B; 11) When Blaze and John were in Boston partying with the money they'd found, they stayed at the YMCA.

(UP3)
BLAZE
Things

AUGUST 14, 1933 (B; 20) The day that Blaze was born.

AUGUST 15, 1948 (B; 18) The date Blaze and John Cheltzman wrote their names in candlesmoke on a cave wall.

BIG AND HARD (B; 4) The porno novel the nightman at Tim & Janet's Quik-Pik was reading when Blaze held up the store.

BUTCH BALLERINAS (B; 7) The title of the porno novel the nightman was reading at the second store that Blaze robbed.

THE EYES OF YURDLAK ARE UPON YOU (B; 11) The vampire story written as a kid by John Cheltzman.

FALL 1956 (B; 3) Blaze first met George Rockley in the fall of 1956 in Boston.

FEBRUARY 1, 1974 (B; 20) The day that Blaze was shot to death.

FEBRUARY 10 (B; 20) The date Joseph Gerard II held a news conference announcing that his son was all right after the kidnapping, and that he and his wife were leaving for a vacation.

"THE FOREHEADS" (B; 20) After the Gerard baby was returned to his parents, the baby saw "the wrong face" as he lay in his crib: "They were all the wrong faces. He knew; their foreheads were wrong."

FORTY-SIX DOLLARS (B; 5) The amount of money that Blaze got by robbing the male college student who walked into Tim & Janet's Quik-Pik during Blaze's hold-up.

$43.12 (B; 17) The amount that Blaze had in his pocket when he was released from the South Portland Correctional Facility in 1953.

FOUR DOLLARS (B; 15) When Blaze was fifteen, three boys paid Annie Bradstay four dollars to have sex with him.

HUCKELBERRY HOUND (B; 3) The cartoon show that Blaze was watching when his father picked him up and threw him down the stairs three times. Blaze was in the second grade at the time.

I WAS A TEENAGE WEREWOLF AND I WAS A TEENAGE FRANKENSTEIN (B; 19) The two movies that Blaze and George saw after robbing Hardy's Discount store.

MAY 1950 (B; 15) The month and year Annie Bradstay gave birth to Blaze's son. The Wyatts adopted him. He grew up to attend Boston University, majoring in English literature. "He particularly enjoyed Shelley and Keats."

$9,000 (B; 3) After his father died, Blaze was left $9,000 of insurance money, but "somewhere along the line it disappeared."

1953 (B; 17) The year that Blaze was released from the South Portland Correctional Facility.

1946 (B; 8) The year that the Sister Mary Dean Chase Home for Boys got a new head man, a "short, bald-headed little prick named Martin Eltzman."

1965 (B; 18) The year that the Sister Mary Dean Chase School for Boys went broke.

1936 (B; 13) The year that Blaze was born.

$114 (B; 19) The amount of money George and Blaze robbed from Hardy's Discount store in Lynn, Maine.

$107 (B; 11) When Blaze was working in the theater as a kid, he and his friend John found a wallet in the bathroom with $107 in it. They used the money to go to Boston, eat, and go to a baseball game.

$160 (B; 5) The amount of money that Blaze got by robbing Tim & Janet's Quik-Pik.

$1,000,000 (B; 12) Blaze's ransom request for the Gerard baby.

SEPTEMBER 1957 (B; 19) The month and year that Blaze and George robbed Hardy's Discount Store in Lynn, Maine.

$700,000 (B; 9) After a long talk with the long-dead George, Blaze decided that the Gerard kid's ransom should be $700,000, but not less than $400,000.

THE SIX BULLETS THAT HIT BLAZE (B; 20) While attempting to escape from Agent Grainger with the Gerard baby, Blaze was shot with six rounds of .38 caliber bullets. He was hit as follows:

1. In the right calf.
2. In the back of the knee.
3. In the right hip.
4. The fourth shattered his spinal cord.
5. In the back of the neck.
6. The sixth "blew the back of his head off."

SIXTY DOLLARS A MONTH (B; 8) The state paid the Bowies sixty-dollars-a-month to keep Blaze. They used him as cheap labor around the farm.

THE SUNDAY TELEGRAM (B; 19) The newspaper where George read a story about the Gerards.

TWENTY-FIVE CENTS AN HOUR (B; 11) As a kid, Blaze worked in a theater twenty hours a week for twenty-five cents an hour.

TWENTY HOURS A WEEK (B; 11) As a kid, Blaze worked in a theater twenty hours a week for twenty-five cents an hour.

PEOPLE, PLACES AND THINGS: VOLUME I
by Steve King and Chris Chesley

People, Places and Things is the rarest piece of Stephen King material in existence.

There is one surviving original, which is owned by Mr. King, and there probably aren't more than a dozen people in the United States who have a copy. Doug Winter describes this slim compendium as "devoted entirely to tales of horror and black irony," and as unsophisticated and juvenile as the tales are, they are nonetheless (to this reader anyway) amazing examples of a nascent talent. I periodically find some of my early writings...and I usually cringe at the first two lines. King and Chesley's efforts here are remarkably self-assured for two writers so young. Most of these stories bear the unmistakable influence of "E.C. Comics," and the majority of them are just begging to be illustrated – preferrably in loud, garish tones and colors.

In this section of *The Shape Under the Sheet*, I will give you a look at this piece of Stephen King fiction – a collection of writings that makes the availability of *The Plant* seem like mass market.

People, Places and Things is a collection of eighteen one-page short stories written by Steve King and Chris Chesley between 1960 and 1963.

Today, such brief tomes are known as "short-shorts," but back then, they were just known as "stories."

Eight were written by King, nine by Chesley, and one by both of them.

The cover reads:

People, Places, and Things
Volume I

Below the title, on the left of the page are the authors' names: Steve King and Chris Chesley.

At the bottom of the page, on two lines, and aligned with the authors' names is typed "Second Edition/Complete and Unabridged," and below that is the line "Triad Publishing Company."

Below is a reproduction of the Table of Contents page of the collection. Please note that all spelling errors and inconsistencies are "as written" by King and Chesley. I didn't want to insert a bunch of "[sics]," instead preferring to let you see the contents page as it originally appeared – warts and all!)

❖❖❖

Copyright 1963, by
Steve King and Chris Chesley

First Printing, 1960
Second Printing, 1963

(all rights reserved)

TABLE OF CONTENTS

Produced in Assosiation
with the Triad Publishing Company

❖❖❖

For ease of reference, I have abstracted King's contributions to this collection in the following list (in order of appearance). The two stories marked with an asterisk ("The Dimension Warp" and "I'm Falling") have been lost through the years, and no details could be unearthed regarding their contents. In the Foreword to the collection, however, we are told to "[l]et Steve King's I'M FALLING transport you into a world of dreams."

1. "The Hotel at the End of the Road"
2. "I've Got To Get Away!"
3. "The Dimension Warp"*
4. "The Thing At the Bottom of the Well"
5. "The Stranger"
6. "I'm Falling"*
7. "The Cursed Expedition"
8. "The Other Side of the Fog"
9. "Never Look Behind You" (with Chris Chesley)

In the following section are specific details on the characters, locales, and storylines of the Stephen King stories in the collection, my commentary and reactions to the tales, and a combined concordance to all the characters in the stories. — **sjs**

1. "The Hotel at the End of the Road"

•*PLOT SUMMARY*: As the story opens, two punks named Tommy Riviera and Kelso Black are fleeing from the cops in a high-speed chase. They take a side road (described as a "wagon track") where they find an old hotel, which, according to King, "looked just like a scene out of the early 1900's." The two hoods demand a room – at gunpoint – from the old hotel clerk, and are given Room Five. Room Five "was barren except for an iron double bed, a cracked mirror, and soiled wallpaper." They fall alseep, and when they awake the next morning they are paralyzed. The two punks have stumbled onto a macabre museum of the living dead, and they are its first additions in twenty-five years. As the clerk puts it, "you'll be well preserved. And you won't die." The story ends with the reader being told that "Tommy Riviera couldn't even express his horror."

•*CHARACTERS*:   Tommy Riviera
               Kelso Black
               The Hotel Clerk (An unnamed old man)
               Two unnamed police officers

•*LOCALES*:   The highway
               An unnamed side road
               An old hotel
               Room Five in the hotel

NOTES: This "hotel at the end of the road" seems to be the great grandaddy of the Overlook, and the "living mummies" King's first use of zombies. This story was also King's first use of the character of Kelso Black, a guy who would be whisked off to Hell by Satan himself in a later story in this collection, "The Stranger." There really isn't too much in the way of plot development in this story, and there are a few unanswered questions, such as what the clerk does with his "nice specimens," and how Kelso Black manages to get away from either the Hotel or Satan so that he could pull off a robbery and kill a guard? Additionally, why did he leave Tommy Riviera behind? But, again, for all its flaws, we can't help but be amazed by the sophisticated narrative and the sheer unstoppable story-telling powers of Stephen King at such an early age.

2. "I've Got To Get Away!"

•*PLOT SUMMARY*: Denny Phillips can't get the thought out of his head that he has "got to get away." One day he finds himself working on the assembly line of an "atomic factory," and decides that he – and his fellow workers (who King describes as looking "like zombies") – are prisoners of some sort, and that he must try to escape. There are guards everywhere, and Denny is shot during his escape attempt. Instead of being taken away by an ambulance, however, Denny is carted away in a truck with a sign on its side that reads ACME ROBOT REPAIR. Denny is really Robot Number x-238A, and for some unknown reason, he has achieved a sort of human-like consciousness. Two weeks later he is back on the job, but once again a thought begins to race through his mind: "I'VE GOT TO GET AWAY!!"

•*CHARACTERS*:   Denny Phillips, Robot Number x-238A
               Joe, a guard
               Various unnamed guards

•*LOCALES*:   An "atomic factory"

NOTES: Here we have an early science fiction piece by King that takes up all of a half-page, but which is surprisingly well done. King has repeatedly used the theme of out-of-control technology, and here he seems to be exploring ideas that he reworked later in "The Mangler," "Trucks," *Christine*, and "Maximum Overdrive," ideas about machines achieving consciousness. Good story.

4. "The Thing At the Bottom of the Well"

•*PLOT SUMMARY*: The story begins with the reader being told that "Oglethorpe Crater was an ugly, mean little wretch." And King's not kidding either. Some of the tortures this little creep inflicts upon both people and pets include sticking pins in cats and dogs, pulling the wings from flies, pulling worms apart and watching them squirm (although his fun with the worms lost its appeal when he learned that they don't feel any pain), and tying a rope across the top of the cellar stairs so that the maid would trip and fall. One day when Oglethorpe was out "looking for more things to torture," he spotted a well. He yelled "Hello" down into it, and heard a voice reply "Hello, Oglethorpe. Come on down, [a]nd we'll have jolly fun." Oglethorpe went down into the well, and wasn't found for a month. Then one day, the manhunt finally found his body in the well. His arms and legs had been pulled out, and pins had been stuck in his eyes. As they took away his remains, they heard laughter coming from the bottom of the well.

•*CHARACTERS*:   Oglethorpe Crater
               Mrs. Crater, his mother
               The Cook
               Spotty, Oglethorpe's dog
               The Thing in the Well
               Unnamed members of the manhunt

•*LOCALES*:   The Crater house
               A field
               A well

NOTES: "The Thing At the Bottom of the Well" is a very significant early Stephen King story for one important reason: This story seems to be King's first use of the "thing in the sewers" monster that later became Pennywise the Clown in *It*. The monster under the bed, the boogeyman in the closet – this thing at the bottom of the well appears to be the ancestral grandfather of all these bad guys. Also, in this story, we have King using the naturalistic theme that he would re-visit later in countless other stories, the idea that fate rules man, but that we, as rational beings, have the ability to make moral choices. It was fate that Oglethorpe stumbled upon the monster in the well, yet his decisions to act in such a morally reprehensible way were his own choices. The universe turned in such a way as to put things right. The Wheel spun, and Crater paid the price for his terrible behavior. "The Thing At the Bottom of the Well" is a well-done tale that hints at the writer Stephen King would become.

5. "The Stranger"

•*PLOT SUMMARY*: Once again, we meet Kelso Black from "The Hotel At the End of the Road," only this time he's holed up in an attic after a robbery in which he stole fifty grand and killed a guard. He's drinking cheap whiskey from a bottle, and laughing at the "dumb cops" when he's visited by a stranger who "wore a black coat and [had] a hat pulled over his eyes." The stranger tells Black that he's been watching him, and that they'd made a pact about an hour ago when he shot the guard. The stranger has come for Kelso Black. "The stranger took off his coat and hat. Kelso Black looked into that Face." As Kelso screamed and screamed, the stranger just laughed, and in a moment the room was empty...but it smelled of brimstone.

•*CHARACTERS*:   Kelso Black
               The Stranger
               An unnamed guard

•*LOCALES*:   An attic

NOTES: This is another half-page story that packs an amazing wallop. It's not clear when the story takes place, although we've already been told that Kelso Black was turned into a living mummy in "The Hotel At the End of the Road." Now, in this story, we have him being carted off to hell by Lucifer himself. What a week Kelso's having, huh? But, in any case, here we have King's first use of the Dark Man – the personification of evil – who would later become Randall Flagg in *The Stand, The Drawing of the Three,* and *The Eyes of the Dragon.* King has very rarely used demons or demonic intervention as a plot device (although *Night Shift*'s "The Mangler" is one notable exception), but in "The Stranger," he has Satan himself come for Kelso Black. "The Stranger" shows King's narrative powers, even at an early age. In a story written with the grand total of 234 words, King develops his characters, gives us background needed for the story, and delivers one "hell" of a climax. "The Stranger" is an amazing effort for a boy in his mid-teens, and a clear indication of what was to come.

7. "The Cursed Expedition"

•*PLOT SUMMARY:* Jimmy Keller and Hugh Bullford touch down on Venus, and are overwhelmed by its beauty. The air is breathable, everything is "lush and green," and "the fruits were exotic and delicious." Keller was so enthusiastic about the place that he declared "I'm going to call it the Garden of Eden." Bullford, however, is skeptical, and senses something wrong. The morning after the landing, Bullford finds Keller dead. He also realizes that he can no longer contact Earth. That's when the ground suddenly begins to open up. Bullford seeks safety and shelter in the space ship, where he analyzes a piece of the planet's soil. He learns, to his horror, that Venus is alive – a living planet – and at that very moment the ground opens up once again and swallows both Bullford and his ship. The planet "almost seemed to lick its lips." The story ends with the planet resetting itself to "[wait] for the next victim."

•*CHARACTERS:*   Jimmy Keller, an astronaut
Hugh Bullford, an astronaut
Venus, a living planet

•*LOCALES:*   A desert
A rocket ship
The planet Venus

NOTES: Here we have a story that is ostensibly science fiction, but like "The Jaunt," "Beachworld," and "I Am the Doorway," the science fiction settings and trappings just serve as devices to allow King to get to the horror of the story. Interestingly, he uses Venus as the villain, just as he did later in "I Am the Doorway." This story is his first use of the horror of being consumed by a living planet – a fate that later also proves to be the fate of Rand in *Skeleton Crew*'s "Beachworld." The one flaw in the tale is that we're never told how Keller died. All we're told is that "There was a look of horror on [Keller's] face that Bullford never hoped to see again." Did Keller see the planet "open its mouth" during the night, and be so horrified by the sight that he died of fright? Perhaps. Bullford screams at the planet: "You killed him! I know it!" In any case, "The Cursed Expedition" is a tale that shows King's early use of ideas that he would later re-work in future stories – stories that must be considered unique in that they show King's ability to still work within the horror genre while utilizing the specifics of science fiction.

8. "The Other Side of the Fog"

•*PLOT SUMMARY:* Pete Jacobs steps out of his front door and is swallowed up by a strange fog that sends him in to the year 2007. He realizes what has happened, and runs back into the fog, trying to get back home. This time he ends up in the prehistoric past, where he is menaced by a huge brontosaurus. He once again runs back into the fog, and the story ends with us being asked to listen for "footsteps running through the whiteness" the next time we ourselves are caught in the fog. The footsteps would be those of Pete Jacobs, "trying to find his side of the fog." The last line of the story is a plaintive plea: "Help the poor guy."

•*CHARACTERS:*   Pete Jacobs, reluctant time-traveler
A Cop from the future
An unnamed brontosaurus

•*LOCALES:*   Pete Jacob's house
The Fog
An unnamed city in the year 2007
An unnamed locale in the prehistoric past

NOTES: This is a terrific story that I, for one, would love to see King expand into a novel. The time-travel device is admittedly a little hackneyed, but the focus of the tale is not the travel…it's the horror of this poor guy being thrust into a situation he cannot escape. King offers no explanations for why the fog suddenly becomes a time machine. But the horror is very real, and the concept hits home: Imagine being trapped in any time but your own. Putting ordinary people in extraordinary situations has always been King's forté, and in "The Other Side of the Fog," he does a superb job of immediately thrusting us into the heart of the action. This is a very well-done story, and its narrative sophistication and strength belie the age of its author. Just as "Night Surf" was King's first version of *The Stand,* so is "The Other Side of the Fog" his first version of "The Mist."

9. "Never Look Behind You"
(Written with Chris Chesley)

•*PLOT SUMMARY:* George Jacobs – who we are told had been "[picking] the people's pockets clean of money" for fifteen years – is counting money in his office one day with his back to the door. An old woman dressed in rags comes in and speaks to him, saying "Indeed a lot of money. Too bad you won't be able to spend it." She then points her hand at him, a flash of fire blooms on his throat, and George Jacobs dies "with a final gurgle." Later, a young man wonders what killed him. The young man's companion replies "I'm glad he's gone." The story ends with the lines "That one was lucky. He didn't look behind him."

•*CHARACTERS:*   George Jacobs
An old woman, some sort of supernatural being
An unnamed young man
Another unnamed young man

•*LOCALES:*   George Jacobs' office

NOTES: This is a confusing story that doesn't seem to make much sense. The only interpretation I can come up with is that the old woman is a supernatural being who was sent to do away with Jacobs – a man who had been evil all his life. The story's title and last lines would seem to indicate that her power only "kicked in" if she was looked upon, thus the warning "Never Look Behind You." And if that analysis is correct, then King and Chesley seem to be telling us that the young man who was glad Jacobs was dead was also in danger, but in a sense saved himself by not looking behind him where, we must assume, the woman was waiting to exact her "fee." If this interpretation jibes with the authors' intentions, it would seem to fit with King's ubiquitous naturalistic theme of man having to "pay the price" for incorrect moral judgements. This almost karmic view of man's role in the universe was very effectively developed in the Bachman novel *Thinner,* in which Billy Halleck has to pay for his mistakes with the lives – and souls – of his wife and daughter. As King said in an interview with Larry King regarding *Thinner,* "Someone has to eat the pie." We must pay for our erroneous ways. And, interestingly, another similarity to *Thinner* in the "Never Look Behind You" is the unnamed woman who points her hand at Jacobs. The story says "She held up her boney hand," foreshadowing the gypsy's boney finger scratching Halleck's cheek in the opening scene of *Thinner.*

(U1)
PEOPLE, PLACES, AND THINGS, VOLUME 1

[The following is a concordance to Stephen King's characters in Steve King and Chris Chesley's collection "People, Places, and Things." The numbers in parentheses refer to the story number within the collection. ("U1," of course, denotes "Uncollected 1," my master code number for the collection.)

For the titles of the specific stories and details on the places and plots of the tales, refer to the introductory feature preceding this concordance. – **sjs**]

People

BLACK, KELSO (U1-1, 5) A punk turned into a living mummy in U1-1, and a robber who is taken to Hell by Satan in U1-5.

A BRONTOSAURUS (U1-8) The beast Pete Jacobs met when the Fog took him to prehistoric times.

BULLFORD, HUGH (U1-7) Astronaut eaten by Venus.

A COOK (U1-4) The Craters' cook. She fell down the cellar stairs when Oglethorpe tied a rope across the top of the stairs.

CRATER, MRS. (U1-4) Oglethorpe's mother.

CRATER, OGLETHORPE (U1-4) Sadistic creep who delighted in torture, but who got his due at the hands of "the thing at the bottom of the well."

A FUTURE COP (U1-8) The cop that Pete Jacobs met when the Fog took him to April 17, 2007.

THE GUARD (U1-5) Unnamed guard shot by Kelso Black.

THE GUARDS (U1-2) Unnamed guards at the atomic factory where Denny Phillips worked.

THE HOTEL CLERK (U1-1) Unnamed clerk who turned Kelso Black and Tommy Riviera into living mummies.

JACOBS, GEORGE (U1-9) Evil man who had been robbing people for years, but on whom a charge had never stuck. He had $50,973.62 in cash when he was killed by an old woman who sent a flash of fire to his throat.

JACOBS, PETE (U1-8) Reluctant time traveler who, thanks to a mysterious Fog, could not get back to his own time.

JOE (U1-2) A guard at the atomic factory where Denny Phillips worked.

KELLER, JIMMY (U1-7) Astronaut eaten by Venus.

THE MANHUNT MEMBERS (U1-4) Unnamed members of the search team who looked for Oglethorpe Crater.

AN OLD WOMAN (U1-9) An old woman in rags who was some sort of supernatural agent sent to do away with George Jacobs.

PHILLIPS, DENNY (U1-2) Robot Number x-238A, a factory worker who suddenly became conscious, and realized that he "HAD TO GET AWAY!"

RIVIERA, TOMMY (U1-1) A punk turned into a living mummy.

SPOTTY (U1-4) Oglethorpe Crater's dog. Oglethorpe delighted in sticking pins in Spotty.

THE STRANGER (U1-5) Satan. He came and took Kelso Black to hell for killing a guard during a robbery.

THE THING IN THE WELL (U1-4) A monster who exacted revenge against Oglethorpe Crater for his sadistic ways by doing to Oglethorpe what he used to do to animals.

TWO POLICE OFFICERS (U1-1) Two unnamed cops who chased Tommy Riviera and Kelso Black.

TWO YOUNG MEN (U1-9) Two unnamed men who were glad that George Jacobs was dead.

VENUS (U1-7) A living planet that ate Jimmy Keller and Hugh Bullford.

x-238A (U1-2) Denny Phillips, a robot factory worker.

"The Star Invaders"

"The Star Invaders" is Stephen King's second oldest existing short story. (The collection *People, Places, and Things* is the oldest.)

It was published in 1964 as a "Gaslight Book," under the aegis of King's publishing company, Triad, Inc.

"The Star Invaders" is another early attempt by Stephen King at writing science fiction. (His first attempts were the one-page science fiction stories "I've Got to Get Away!," "The Cursed Expedition," and "The Other Side of the Fog" from the *People, Places, and Things* collection.)

I was not able to obtain a copy of "The Star Invaders" in time for me to do the research and the concordance for *The Shape Under the Sheet*.

But, nonetheless, I think the following feature is as complete and thorough as any that I might have hoped to do. I have one person to thank for this: The ever-effervescent "Dr. C," Michael R. Collings.

Yes, Michael came through for me by writing the concordance to "The Star Invaders," as well as giving me background on the piece, details on the physical makeup of the booklet, and a very accurate summary of the story.

My undying thanks and appreciation go out to Dr. Collings for his help and honest enthusiasm for *The Shape Under the Sheet*.

Now, without any further ado...I turn the microphone over to Dr. Michael R. Collings. (The following synopsis is from Dr. Collings brilliant study *The Shorter Works of Stephen King* (Starmont, 1985.) – **sjs**

❖❖❖

"The Star Invaders"
Commentary and Concordance
by Michael R. Collings

"*Synopsis*: In Part I [of "The Star Invaders"], Jerry Hiken, one of the last defenders of Earth, has been captured by the Star Invaders and tortured to force him to reveal the location of Jed Pierce, the brilliant mind behind the Counter weapon. When Hiken resists, they use psychological torture; he breaks, tells everything he knows, then kills himself.

Part II shifts to Pierce's hideout, where work on the Weapon is nearly finished. The Invaders attack. Pierce destroys ship after ship, ignoring the increasing danger as machinery overheats. When the last ship is destroyed, Pierce races to the atomic pile and single-handedly averts a melt-down. The Weapon works; Earth now has a defense against the Invaders."

"The Star Invaders" consists of seventeen pages of text, typed, 1 1/2 spaced on 8 1/2 X 5 1/2 half sheets. The "book" also includes a title page (spatial relationships not exact):

A GASLIGHT BOOK

The

S
T
A
R

INVADERS

By Steve King

At the bottom of the title page is a hand-drawn logo reading "Triad."

The verso of the title page is the copyright page (spatial relationships not exact). It reads:

The Star Invaders, Copyright 1964 by Triad, Inc., and Gaslight Books

FIRST PRINTING
June, 1964

To Johnny, Who wanted one like this

All characters are fictitious.

There are few specifics in the tale, and the story itself is short.

"The Star Invaders" is highly abstracted; there are few specific references to people, places, or things – certainly nothing to suggest King's later "brand name" approach to creating verisimilitude. References to the nuclear reactor are equally vague, and the resolution to the story (that Pierce's Counter Weapon frightens off a vastly superior Invader fleet) is abrupt and unconvincing.

The great strength of the story is its nascent characterization, coupled with an occasional image that would resonate through much of King's fiction.

(U2)
"The Star Invaders"
People

CALLAHAN, BROCK Brock Callahan was one of Jed Pierce's lieutenants.

HIKEN, JERRY Jerry Hiken was one of Jed Pierce's lieutenants. He was responsible for initially betraying Pierce's location to the aliens.

PIERCE, JED The hero of the story. Pierce was Earth's "last hope" for withstanding the Star Invaders.

THE STAR INVADERS Aliens intent upon taking over the earth. They wore armored uniforms with "three curved claws protrud[ing] from each metal cuff."

Places

HIROSHIMA Hiroshima was used as an image for destruction should the placer rods go. [NOTE: See the entry PLACER RODS.]

THE KREMLIN One of the cities (the Kremlin is an ancient "walled city" within the city of Moscow) destroyed by the Star Invaders.

LONDON One of the cities destroyed by the Star Invaders.

STOCKHOLM One of the cities destroyed by the Star Invaders.

WASHINGTON, D.C. One of the cities destroyed by the Star Invaders.

Things

ALTERNATING ELECTROMAGNETIC PRINCIPAL [sic] The assumed power structure in the Star Invaders' ships.

CHAIN REACTION (NUCLEAR) The primary danger posed to the Earth forces by Jed Pierce's Counter Weapon.

THE CLOSET As a child, Jerry Hiken was locked in his father's closet for punishment. [NOTE: This compares with Margaret White's similar use of the closet in *Carrie*, as well as events in the short story "Here There Be Tygers."] Here, Hiken remembers back to the early childhood torture that had created this horrible fear:

"Lord, they had locked him in a small room! It seemed even smaller than before. Jerry felt a cold sweat break out on his brow. He remembered back thirty years. He had been a kid then, a really small kid. His father had been a bear on discipline, and every time he'd done something wrong, he was locked in the closet to meditate...

He had gotten to hate that closet. It was small and stuffed with clothes. The arid smell of moth-balls made him cough, and to his terrified four-year-old mind, it always seemed that a tiger crouched in the corner."

[NOTE: This early "imprisonment" gave the Star Invaders the "weapon" they needed to break Jerry – knowledge of his worst fear. As they explained to him, "You see, earth-creature, each being has his own devils...things that have horrified him always." They tell him "We can lock you in again...Only this time the walls will squeeze until the blood runs from your ears and your nose and even the little black holes in the center of your eyes. It can squeeze you into just a blob of shrieking protoplasm, if we so desire."

This concept of a "monster" that feeds on our fears was later developed to its pentultimate realization as Pennywise the Clown in King's masterwork *It*. –sjs]

THE COUNTER WEAPON The device brought against the Star Invaders by Pierce's forces. It was developed by Pierce.

ELECTROLYSIS SLAB The torture device employed by the Star Invaders against Jerry Hiken.

FORCE SCREENS Devices on the Star Invaders' ships that protected the invaders against Earth attack.

GREEN FIRE The fire that was associated with the Star Invaders' ships – either as weapons or when the ships crashed – was green. [NOTE: Compare this with King's association of green/fire and evil in both *The Eyes of the Dragon* and *The Tommyknockers*.]

NUCLEAR REACTOR The power source for the turbines that would in turn power the Counter Weapon developed by Jed Pierce.

OBSIDIAN (SLAB) Obsidian was part of the electrolysis slab torture instrument used by the Star Invaders against Jerry Hiken.

PLACER RODS Components in Pierce's nuclear reactor. An explosion of the placer rods threatened to blow up the Earth's stronghold.

"SCANNER" The title given to one of Jed Pierce's soldiers. Scanner alerted Pierce's forces to the presence of the Star Invaders.

THE STAR INVADERS Aliens intent upon taking over the earth. They wore armored uniforms with "three curved claws protrud[ing] from each metal cuff."

A TIGER Jerry Hiken recalled being locked in a closet by his father as punishment. While imprisoned, he imagined tigers crouching in the corner. [NOTE: This foreshadows King's later use of the same image of a "tiger in the corner" in the short story "Here There Be Tygers."]

THE TRANSLATOR An unidentified device that allowed the Star Invaders to communicate directly with humans.

TUNGSTEN An element critical to completion of construction of the Counter Weapon. Tungsten was the immediate cause of Jerry Hiken's capture by the Star Invaders.

TURBINES (ELECTRIC) The power source for the Counter Weapon.

"I Was a Teenage Grave Robber"
(Reprinted as: "In A Half-World of Terror")

"I Was a Teenage Grave Robber" (to which I've assigned the code "U3a" for purposes of this work) is divided into nine chapters. Entries below are keyed to the specific chapter in "U3a" from which the piece of data was drawn, except when I refer specifically to the work under its reprint title, "In A Half-World of Terror," designated "(U3b)."

(See the "Things" section of this concordance for details on both printings of this story.)

Story Summary: "I Was a Teenage Grave Robber" is the story of young Danny Gerad, a stone-broke orphan who is recruited by a guy named Rankin to work as a grave robber for a mad scientist named Steffen Weinbaum. Unbeknownst to Danny, Weinbaum is doing experiments on corpses. He has been exposing them to radioactivity, thereby causing the maggots on the bodies to mutate into grotesque globules the size of a Buick. One night, while driving home, Danny stumbles onto a family squabble: He sees a girl running on the highway, and an obviously drunk guy chasing her. Turns out the guy is the girl's legal guardian, her Uncle David, and that he is also a former employee of Weinbaum's. (Uncle Dave, too, was in the Grave Robbing Division.) Danny rescues the girl (whose name was Vicki Pickford), takes her to a movie, and falls in love with her. While at the movies, Danny gets a call to get to Weinbaum's Victorian mansion immediately: It's a life-or-death situation. When he arrives, he discovers that the maggots – weird and pissed-off as maggots can be – are wrecking Weinbaum's lab. Danny saves the day by burning down the house (and fifteen acres of the palatial residential district of Belwood California as well), and rescuing the lovely Miss Vicki again in the process. As an extra added attraction, Danny gets to see Weinbaum be devoured by a giant maggot.

The story ends with our hero resolving himself to whatever role he may have played in Rankin's death, and becoming a "Significant Other" to Vicki Pickford. — **sjs**

(U3a & U3b)
"I Was A Teenage Grave Robber"
People

THE BURSAR (Chapter I) The Bursar told Danny that the school couldn't give him any more time to pay his tuition, and that he would have to leave college.

THE CARETAKER (Chapter I) As Rankin and Danny were robbing Daniel Wheatherby's grave, Danny tripped over a gravestone and almost went sprawling. Rankin then hissed at him, "Do you want to wake up the caretaker, you fool?"

CHARLIE, GREAT-UNCLE (Chapter V) When the usher told Danny there was a "life or death" phone call, Danny thought there might have been trouble with one of his remaining living relatives, such as his Great-Uncle Charlie.

DAVID, UNCLE (Chapter IV) Vicki Pickford's legal guardian. When Danny and Vicki first meet, Vicki is trying to escape from David. Uncle David was killed in a truck accident while attempting to run down Danny. Vicki said of David, "He was my guardian. He was also a drunkard and an all-around crumb. I hated him and I'm glad he's dead."

ERWIN, ERWIN, & BRADSTREET (Chapter II) The phony law firm that tricked Danny into turning over all his money – $15,000.00 – by telling him that his father had embezzled that much, and that Danny was responsible for the loss.

GERAD, DANNY (Chapters I, IV) The narrator of "I Was a Teenage Grave Robber." After being forced to leave college, he took a job as a grave robber for a mad scientist. We first meet him in Chapter I, although we don't learn his name until Chapter IV. Danny destroys the giant maggots created by Dr. Weinbaum from dead human flesh, and saves – and falls in love with – Vicki Pickford.

GERAD, MR. AND MRS. (Chapter II) Danny's parents. They were killed in an auto accident when Danny was thirteen.

THE HIGHWAY PATROLMAN (Chapter IV) An unnamed officer who arrived at the scene of the accident in which Vicki's Uncle David was killed.

PHIBBS, GRANDMA (Chapter V) When the usher told Danny there was a "life or death" phone call, Danny thought there might have been trouble with one of his remaining living relatives, such as Grandma Phibbs.

PICKFORD, VICKI (Chapter IV) The eighteen-year-old girl that Danny Gerad rescued from her guardian, the drunken, evil Uncle David, and then later saved from being eaten by giant maggots. He also fell in love with her.

POLLY, AUNT (Chapter V) When the usher told Danny there was a "life or death" phone call, Danny thought there might have been trouble with one of his remaining living relatives, such as Aunt Polly.

RANKIN (Chapter I) Steffen Weinbaum's assistant. He inducted Danny Gerad into the fine art of grave robbing.

THE USHER (Chapter V) An unnamed usher who came and got Danny in the movie theater, telling him that there was a "life or death" phone call for him.

WEINBAUM, STEFFEN (Chapter I) Mad scientist. He was doing experiments on corpses. This was how Stephen King described him: "Steffen Weinbaum's face was much like a skull; his eyes were deep-set and the skin was stretched so tautly over his cheekbones that his flesh was almost transparent." Weinbaum was eaten by one of the giant maggots he had created.

WHEATHERBY, DANIEL (Chapter I) Dead guy. Danny and Rankin robbed his corpse for Steffen Weinbaum.

WHEATHERBY, MRS. (Chapter I) Daniel's wife. She had predeceased her husband.

Places

THE BELWOOD DISTRICT (Chapter IV) The area where Weinbaum's mansion was located. Danny told the police officer that he had been driving out of the district when he came upon Vicki trying to escape from her Uncle David.

THE BONAVENTURE MOTEL (Chapter IV) The motel where Vicki had been living with her Uncle David.

THE COMPANY (Chapter VI) The unnamed company that Vicki's Uncle David worked for as a night-watchman. They folded, and Uncle David ended up on unemployment. It was then that he took a job with Weinbaum as a grave robber.

THE CRESTWOOD CEMETERY (Chapter III) The cemetery where Daniel Wheatherby was buried, and where Rankin and Danny went to rob his grave.

A VICTORIAN MANSION (Chapter I) The house where Steffen Weinbaum lived, and where Rankin and Dan brought Wheatherby's body. It was the place where Danny killed the giant maggot that ate Weinbaum.

Things

THE ANATOMY OF A GIANT MAGGOT (Chapter VIII) "Veins, red and pulsing, showed under its slimy flesh and millions of squirming tiny maggots in the blood vessels in the skin, even forming a huge eye that stared out at me. A huge maggot, made up of hundreds of millions of maggots, the feasters on the dead flesh that Weinbaum had used so freely."

"BY STEVE KING" The first page of the typed story read:

IN A HALF-WORLD OF TERROR
BY STEVE KING

The copy I had was signed "Steve King 7/24/82"

COMICS REVIEW (U3a) The fanzine which contained Stephen King's first professionally published short story, "I Was a Teenage Grave Robber." It appeared in 1965.

THE COVER PAGE OF THE STORY (U3b) In the *Stories of Suspense* edition of the story (the one I used for my research), the title page of the story showed four disembodied eyes, a running woman, and a man pointing a gun at a skull. The title "In A Half-World of Terror" was hand-lettered.

DANIEL WHEATHERBY'S GRAVESTONE (Chapter I) It read:

DANIEL WHEATHERBY
1899-1962
He has joined his beloved wife in a better land.

EARLY SEPTEMBER (Chapter II) This was when Danny Gerad got the phony letter from the law firm claiming that his father had embezzeled $15,000.00 from a store where he had worked.

"8:00 O'CLOCK SHARP" (Chapter III) The time Danny started "work." He was on the "night shift," so to speak.

THE FEARS OF CHILDHOOD (Chapter V) In a remarkable foreshadowing of King's magnum opus, *It*, King has Danny Gerad expressing his thoughts on the nightmares of childhood as he walks into the "Stygian blackness" of Weinbaum's garage: "All my childish fears of the dark returned. Once again I entered the realm of terror that only a child can know."

FIFTEEN SQUARE MILES OF WOODS AND HOMES (Chapter IX) The land and houses that were destroyed in the fire that burned down Weinbaum's house, lab, and the three giant maggots.

$15,000 (Chapter II) The amount of money that the phony law firm of Erwin, Erwin, & Bradstreet claimed Danny's father had embezzled from a department store where he had worked before his death. They told Danny that he (Danny) was responsible for the "theft."

FIRE (Chapter VIII) To kill the three giant maggots, Danny set fire to Weinbaum's lab.

$500 PER JOB (Chapter II) The fee that Rankin offered Danny to come to work for Weinbaum. He didn't tell him the work was robbing graves.

"FORGIVENESS" (Chapter IX) As Danny reflected on what had happened with Rankin and Weinbaum, he thought "In a way, I suppose, I assisted in Rankin's death; the flesh of the body whose grave I had robbed had fed perhaps the very creature that had killed him. I live with that thought. But I believe that there can be forgiveness. I'm working for it. Or, rather, we're working for it. Vicki and I. Together."

THE GERAD HOUSE (Chapter II) Danny's parents left Danny the Gerad house in their will.

"THE GO-PEDDLE" (Chapters III, V) The gas peddle. [NOTE: Stephen King must have liked this way of describing the gas pedal when he wrote this story because he used the image again in Chapter V.]

"GOODBYE DR. WEINBAUM" (Chapter VIII) This was how King described Weinbaum's death scene: "A huge, white maggot twisted on the garage floor, holding Weinbaum with long suckers, raising him towards its dripping, pink mouth from which horrid mewing sounds came."

"THE HALF-WORLD OF PHANTOM-PEOPLED SHADOWS" (Chapter V) The place where Danny felt he was when he received

a phone call from Weinbaum.

"I'LL PICK YOU UP AT 7:30." (Chapters IV, V) Danny said this to Vicki in Chapter IV. Then, in Chapter V, King had him picking her up at 7:30 *in the morning* for a movie. The passage reads "The next morning at 7:30 sharp, I picked up Vicki at the Bonaventure Motel. The movie was good and we held hands part of the time, ate popcorn part of the time and kissed once or twice. All in all a pleasant evening."

"IN A HALF-WORLD OF TERROR" (Chapter VIII) The place where Danny was as he shot the giant maggot. Here's how King described the moment: "In a half-world of terror I fired the revolver again and again, It mewed and twitched."

THE OPENING LINE OF THE STORY (Chapter I) "In a Half-World of Terror" begins "It was like a nightmare, like some unreal dream that you wake up from the next morning."

RANKIN'S "LIFE OR DEATH" PHONE CALL (Chapter V) The call Danny received while in the movie theater with Vicki. As Danny put it, "You could have knocked me over with a feather when I picked up the telephone and heard Rankin's voice."

RANKIN'S HEAD (Chapter VI) When Danny and Vicki arrived at Weinbaum's mansion, they found Rankin's head bashed in.

SIX O'CLOCK TRAIN (Chapter I) Rankin and Danny joined the stream of commuters hurrying for the six o'clock train after they put Wheatherby's body in the trunk of their car.

STEPHEN KING'S FIRST USE OF RATS (Chapter VI) "I was cut off by a sound that has hounded me through nightmares ever since, a hideous mewing sound, like that of some gigantic rat in pain." It wasn't a rat, though. It was a giant maggot bred in the dead flesh of Daniel Wheatherby. [NOTE: For a look at a particularly effective use of rats by King, see the discussion of "Graveyard Shift" (5b), in the *Night Shift* section in this volume.]

STORIES OF SUSPENSE (U3b) The fanzine published by Marvin Wolfman. In 1966, it published the second appearance of King's short story "I Was a Teenage Grave Robber," reprinting it as "In A Half-World of Terror."

THE *STORIES OF SUSPENSE* COVER (U3b) The cover had "STORIES OF SUSPENSE" above three drawn panels depicting what looked like an astronaut looking at three alien trees, disembodied skulls, and a guy who looked remarkably like Max Headroom. The top two panels had a box in which was written "The fanzine that dares to be different." The monster was saying "Okay Fiends! Here are some scenes from our second issue!" Marv Wolfman signed his name at the bottom of the cover.

A TAVERN (Chapter II) A bar where Danny first met Rankin. He got in using a forged driver's license. This was where Rankin offered Danny the job of robbing graves for Weinbaum, although he didn't tell him what the work involved. All he told Danny was that the pay was $500 per job.

$10,000 (Chapter II) At the age of eighteen, Danny sold the house his parents left him for $10,000.

THIRTY STEPS (Chapter VI) The number of steps down to Weinbaum's laboratory.

THE THREE GIANT MAGGOTS (Chapter VII) Weinbaum bred three giant maggots in tanks filled with a green liquid. [NOTE: Stephen King did not approve of such behavior. He wrote "The three cases had contained three somethings from the darkest pits of a twisted mind."]

THREE LEDGERS (Chapter IX) Danny found three of Weinbaum's ledgers in a metal cabinet that survived the fire. Weinbaum's diary "cleared up a lot."

TRAIN WRECK (Chapter VI) Vicki's parents were killed in a train wreck. Her Uncle David then became her legal guardian. Her Uncle was one of Weinbaum's grave robbers.

$250 (Chapter IV) The amount of the bill to repair Danny's car following his run-in with Vicki's Uncle David.

"THE VELVET DARKNESS OF THE NIGHT" (Chapter VI) An appropriately "King-ish" image, and a surprisingly deft one for such a young writer.

WEINBAUM'S EXPERIMENTS (Chapter III) After Danny met Weinbaum, the scientist told him "my experiments are too complicated to explain in any detail, but they concern human flesh. *Dead* human flesh."

"The Glass Floor"

"The Glass Floor" holds the distinction of being the very first short story Stephen King ever sold.

The story was published in the Fall 1967 edition of *Startling Mystery Stories*, and echoes his second professional sale, "The Reaper's Image," which later appeared in a revised form in *Skeleton Crew*.

The central image of the "The Glass Floor" is, appropriately, a glass floor. (The central image of "The Reaper's Image" is a mirror in which certain people can see the "reaper" – Death himself.)

The story was introduced by the boxed-in line "Why was the old man so reluctant to let him see the room in which his sister had died?"

On the second page of the published story, a column is interrupted with the following blurb:

"STEPHEN KING has been sending us stories for some time, and we returned one of them most reluctantly, since it would be far too long before we could use it, due to its length. But patience may yet bring him his due reward on that tale; meanwhile, here is a chiller whose length allowed us to get it into print much sooner."

The story concerns the death of Charles Wharton's sister, Janine. Determined to see the room in which she died (and possibly get an explanation for her untimely death), Wharton visits the old mansion where his sister lived with her husband, Anthony Reynard, and forces Reynard to allow him into the room. Reynard reluctantly consents, and Wharton ends up meeting the same fate as his sister.

The story begins:

"Wharton moved slowly up the wide steps, hat in hand, craning his neck to get a better look at the Victorian monstrosity that his sister had died in."

The story has an evocative mood and some very "King-ish" images, particularly in the character of the housekeeper, Louise: "She was old, hideously old. Her face hung like limp dough on her skull, and the hand on the door above the chain was grotesquely twisted by arthritis."

The following concordance gives details on the people, places, and things of "The Glass Floor." — **sjs**

(U4)
"The Glass Floor"
People

THE COUNTY COMMISSIONER Wharton threatened to go to the county commissioner if Reynard didn't let him see the room in which Janine died.

LOUISE Anthony Reynard's housekeeper. She was "hideously old. Her face hung like limp dough on her skull."

REYNARD, ANTHONY Charles Wharton's brother-in-law; the husband of Wharton's sister Janine. He owned the "Victorian monstrosity" of a house in which there was a room with a glass floor.

REYNARD, JANINE WHARTON Charles Wharton's sister, and the wife of Anthony Reynard. She fell to her death from a ladder in the room with the glass floor.

THE SHERIFF Wharton threatened to go to the sheriff if Reynard didn't let him see the room in which Janine died.

WHARTON, CHARLES The man who attempted to discover why his sister fell to her death in the house of her husband, Anthony Reynard.

Places

THE EAST ROOM The room with the glass floor in Reynard's house.

THE ROOM WITH THE GLASS FLOOR The East Room in Reynard's house. After his wife Janine's death, he had the room boarded up.

"THE VICTORIAN MONSTROSITY" Anthony Reynard's home, and the place where Charles Wharton's sister died. The house contained the room with the glass floor.

THE VILLAGE Reynard's house was located on the outskirts of an unnamed village. He told Louise to reveal to Wharton the truth about the East Room: "'Go ahead,' Reynard said tiredly. 'He'll find out in the village if he doesn't up here.'"

Things

A BUST OF CICERO Reynard had a bust of Cicero in the corner of his living room.

THE FIRE-DOG An ebony iron fire-dog that stood in Reynard's parlor, "a carven gargoyle that stared at Wharton with Toad's eyes."

"THE GLASS FLOOR" TEASER On the title page of the original appearance of "The Glass Floor" in the Fall 1967 edition of *Startling Mystery Stories,* the following teaser appeared:

"Why was the old man so reluctant to let him see the room in which his sister had died?"

The "old man" was Anthony Reynard," "him" was Charles Wharton, and "his sister" was Janine Wharton Reynard, Anthony's wife and Charles's sister.

"GO AWAY FROM HERE" Wharton heard a voice from inside his head telling him to leave Reynard's house.

A HOOK-ENDED POLE A pole Reynard had at the ready with which to drag out the dead from the room with the glass floor. He used it when Wharton fell to his death from the ladder.

THE LADDER Janine fell to her death from a ladder in the room with the glass floor in Reynard's house.

"A MIRROR" Louise the housekeeper told Wharton about the East Room, the room with the glass floor: "The floor's glass. It's a mirror. The whole floor's a mirror."

POE'S "THE BLACK CAT" When Wharton saw the trowel with which Reynard had sealed off the room with the glass floor, "a straggling remnant of Poe's 'Black Cat' clanged through his mind: '…I had walled the monster up within the tomb…'"

1770 The date that was chiseled into the glass on the door of Anthony Reynard's house.

STARTLING MYSTERY STORIES "The Glass Floor" appeared in the Fall 1967 edition of *Startling Mystery Stories*.

STEPHEN KING'S BIOGRAPHICAL BLURB Accompanying the appearance of "The Glass Floor" in the Fall 1967 edition of *Startling Mystery Stories* was the following blurb:

"STEPHEN KING has been sending us stories for

some time, and we returned one of them most reluctantly, since it would be far too long before we could use it, due to its length. But patience may yet bring him his due reward on that tale; meanwhile, here is a chiller whose length allowed us to get it into print much sooner."

A TROWEL Reynard had used a trowel to plaster off the East Room.

WHARTON'S LAST WORDS While on the ladder in the room with the glass floor, Wharton swooned and screamed "Reynard! I'm falling!" He was history.

"Slade"

"Slade" is "Comedy by Stephen King."

In the summer of 1970 (the summer following his graduation from the University of Maine), King wrote an eight-installment story that can only be described as a "comic western."

"Slade" concerned Jack Slade, a gunslinger with a grim face and "two sinister .45's." Slade was in perpetual mourning for his lost love, the comely Polly Peachtree of Paduka, killed in an untimely accident. A flaming Montgolfier balloon crashed into her barn as she was milking the cows.

Always politically-minded, King used "Slade" as a forum for a few digs at the then-reigning political and social hierarchy, including characters such as Hunchback Fred Agnew, Deputy Marshall Hoagy Carmichael, Mose Hart, Sunrise Jackson, John "Quick Draw" Mitchell, Big Frank Nixon, Shifty Ron Ziegfield, and Slade's "huge black stallion," Stokely.

"Slade" (as well as all the "King's Garbage Truck" columns) has been available only on reversed-image microfiche at the University of Maine Special Collections library. The library made photocopies of the installments available to Michael Collings in 1985, and "Dr. C." did a transcription of the text. He gave copies of the transcribed serial to Stephen King, and my copy of "Slade" came from King's office. The title page of Dr. Collings' transcription describes "Slade" as "A parody of the traditional Western. About 6,500 words; published in eight installments."

It's a good thing Michael Collings did the transcription of this material. In the fall of 1989, I learned that all the *original* copies of *The Maine Campus* in which Stephen King's columns appeared had been stolen from the University of Maine's library.

My disgust and disdain for the thief or thieves knows no bounds.

But, at least we have the words themselves, even though the original pages may now be lost to us. For the record, those pages (keyed to the number of the chapter in the series) were as follows:

Legend

(1) = "Slade" (Chapter 1), *The Maine Campus*, June 11, 1970, page 4.
(2) = "Slade" (Chapter 2), *The Maine Campus*, June 18, 1970, page 4.
(3) = "Slade" (Chapter 3), *The Maine Campus*, June 25, 1970, page 5.
(4) = "Slade" (Chapter 4), *The Maine Campus*, July 2, 1970, page 5, 7.
(5) = "Slade" (Chapter 5), *The Maine Campus*, July 9, 1970, page 5, 7.
(6) = "Slade" (Chapter 6), *The Maine Campus*, July 23, 1970, page 5.
(7) = "Slade" (Chapter 7), *The Maine Campus*, July 30, 1970, page 6.
(8) = "Slade" (Chapter 8), *The Maine Campus*, August 6, 1970, page 5.

The following concordance gives details on the People, Places, and Things in "Slade." As is consistent with my editorial stance in *The Shape Under the Sheet*, I do not spend too much time on interpretation, analysis, or criticism of King's works. For those readers of King's who want analysis, I can recommend *all* of Michael Collings' Starmont books, Tyson Blue's *The Unseen King*, and, of course, Doug Winter's *Stephen King: The Art of Darkness*. (See Part VII, the section on books about King, in this volume.)

I prefer to let the details of the stories and novels speak for themselves. It is my hope that by assembling the specifics of the tales into alphabetical entries, the gist of the story will be communicated to you, King's Constant Reader, and that when used in conjunction with the more interpretative texts available about King's work, you will be enlightened, entertained and, most importantly, scared stupid! —**sjs**

(U5)
"Slade"
People

AGNEW, HUNCHBACK FRED (4, 5) The most detested killer in the American Southwest. Fred was two-foot-three, and had a three-foot Arabian skinning knife. He snuck into Slade's hotel room with his snake, Sadie Hawkins. In Chapter 5 we find out that there was talk that Hunchback Fred might end up the next vice president of the American Southwest.

THE BARTENDER (1) The unnamed barkeep in the Brass Cuspidor Saloon. When Slade walked through the batwing doors, the bartender dropped the knife he was using to cut off the foamy beer-heads.

A BLACK STALLION (1) Slade's horse. In Chapter 3 we learn that it was "huge," and that his name was Stokely.

CARMICHAEL, DEPUTY MARSHALL HOAGY (5) Dead Steer Spring's deputy sheriff. After Slade drank three Zombies, Carmichael arrested the gunslinger for public intoxication.

COLUMBINE, SAM (1) The bad guy. He was trying to get Miss Sandra off the Bar-T ranch.

CUSTER, GENERAL (1) The Brass Cuspidor's bartender's dog. When Slade walked into the saloon, General Custer ran and hid under a table.

DAWSON, MISS SANDRA (1) The woman who owned the Bar-T ranch. Her father died and left it to her.

DAWSON, MR. (1) Miss Sandra's father. He died and left her the Bar-T ranch.

THE FANCY-DAN GAMBLER (1) A gambler playing cards in the Brass Cuspidor when Slade walked in. He was so shaken that he dropped three aces out of his sleeve. (Two of the aces were clubs.)

A GUARD (7) Pinky Lee tortured a guard and forced him to say he was Randolph P. Sorghum.

HART, MOSE (2) Miss Sandra Dawson's top hand on the Bar-T ranch. He came in to town looking for Slade: The Bar-T bunkhouse was on fire.

HASKELL, BOB (6) Real-life *Maine Campus* editor. He was involved in censoring the love scene King wrote for Chapter 6. King decided to change the love scene to a violent scene, "while editor Bob Haskell [was] drunk in the corner."

HAWKINS, SADIE (4) Hunchback Fred Agnew's twelve-foot python. He kept her in a large box made out of woven river reeds.

THE HOTEL CLERK (4) The unnamed Dead Steer Springs Hotel clerk. Slade made him tremble. The clerk gave Slade the second floor suite.

HUGHES, STEVE (6) A real-life University of Maine person. King wrote that Steve was up in the security office playing cutthroat poker with Chief Tynan, Charles Ludwig, and Marge Rode.

AN INDIAN PONY (3) After Slade shot Sunrise Jackson and Shifty Jack Mulloy, Doc Logan got away on an Indian pony with a shifty eye.

JACKSON, SUNRISE (3) One of Sam Columbine's gunmen. He burned the Bar-T bunkhouse. Slade shot him for it. Jackson carried sinister .50 caliber horse pistols.

LEE, "PINKY" (7) Columbine's A-No-1 Top Gun. Pinky had ridden with Captain Quantrill and his Regulators during the Civil War. While passed out in a bordello in Bleeding Heart, Kansas, a Union officer named Randolph P. Sorghum dropped a homemade bomb down a chimney. Pinky lost all his hair, and all the fingers on his left hand except for his pinky.

LOGAN, DOC (3) One of Sam Columbine's gunmen. He burned the Bar-T bunkhouse. It was rumored that Doc Logan had sent twelve sheep ranchers to Boot Hill in the Abilene Range War. After Slade shot Sunrise Jackson and Shifty Jack Mulloy, Doc Logan got away on an Indian pony with a shifty eye.

LUDWIG, CHARLES (6) Real-life University of Maine person. King wrote that he was up in the security office playing cutthroat poker with Chief Tynan, Marge Rode, and Steve Hughes.

MEXICAN BORDER GUARDS (6) While Sandra Dawson was being guarded by Columbine's henchmen, Big Frank Nixon, "Quick-Draw" John Mitchell, and Shifty Ron Ziegfield, Columbine was off torturing a few Mexican border guards.

MITCHELL, JOHN ("QUICK-DRAW") (6) One of Sam Columbine's henchmen. He guarded Sandra Dawson while Columbine was off torturing a few Mexican border guards.

MULLOY, SHIFTY JACK (3) One of Sam Columbine's gunmen. He burned the Bar-T bunkhouse. Slade shot him for it.

NIXON, BIG FRANK (6) One of Sam Columbine's henchmen. He guarded Sandra Dawson while Columbine was off torturing a few Mexican border guards.

AN OLD LADY FROM BOSTON (4) Hunchback Fred Agnew had changed the faces of three U.S. marshals, two county sheriffs, and an old lady from Boston who was on her way to Arizona to recuperate from Parkinson's disease.

THE OLD MAN (1) An old man "either the town drunk or the village idiot" dressed in a Confederate cap, dusty jeans, and suspenders, asked Slade if Miss Sandra had hired Slade to help her with Sam Columbine. When the old man started asking too many questions, "Slade sighted carefully along the barrel of his sinister .45 and winded him once, just for luck."

OLD MEN AND PREGNANT WOMEN (4) They all crossed the street when they saw Slade coming.

PARKMAN, JOHN (THE BACKSHOOTER) (1) One of Sam Columbine's top guns. When Slade entered the Brass Cuspidor, Parkman was at the bar doing shots. In Chapter 2, Slade shot Parkman in the heart six times.

PEACHTREE, MISS POLLY (1, 8) Jack Slade's lost lover. Supposedly, she died when a flaming Montgolfier balloon crashed into the Peachtree barn in Paduka. In Chapter 8, however, we learn that Miss Sandra Dawson was in actuality Miss Polly wearing a blonde wig.

THE PIANO PLAYER (1) The piano player in the Brass Cuspidor Saloon was so shaken when Slade walked in that he fell off his stool.

QUANTRILL, CAPTAIN, AND HIS REGULATORS (7) Columbine's Top Gun, Pinky Lee, had ridden with Captain Quantrill and his Regulators during the Civil War. While Pinky was passed out in a bordello in Bleeding Heart, Kansas, a Union

officer named Randolph P. Sorghum dropped a homemade bomb down a chimney. Pinky lost all his hair, and all the fingers on his left hand except for his pinky.

RODE, MARGIE (6) Real-life *Maine Campus* staff member. King wrote that she was up in the security office playing cutthroat poker with Chief Tynan, Charles Ludwig, and Steve Hughes.

THE SCREAMER (1) When Slade entered the Brass Cuspidor, someone ran down the street screaming that Slade was in town.

SING-LOO (3) The Chinese cook on the Bar-T ranch. Slade accidentally shot him.

SLADE, JACK (1) He rode "tall in the saddle, a grim-faced man dressed all in black." At the beginning of the story, we learn that Slade is mourning the death of his sweetheart, Miss Polly Peachtree of Paduka. There were rumors about Slade: one was that he wore black because he mourned Polly, the second was that he was the Grim Reaper's agent in the American Southwest, and the third was that he was queerer than a three-dollar bill. Slade carried two "sinister .45's," and rode a black stallion named Stokely.

A SMALL BOY (4) A small boy asked Slade for an autograph. Slade shot him in the leg instead. (He didn't want to encourage that kind of thing.)

SORGHUM, RANDOLPH P. (7) The Union officer who dropped a homemade bomb down a chimney while Pinky Lee was asleep in a bordello in Bleeding Heart, Kansas. Pinky lost all his hair, and all the fingers on his left hand except for his pinky.

STOKELY (3) Slade's "huge black stallion."

THREE U.S. MARSHALLS (4) Hunchback Fred Agnew had changed the faces of three U.S. marshals, two county sheriffs, and an old lady from Boston who was on her way to Arizona to recuperate from Parkinson's disease.

TWELVE SHEEP RANCHERS (3) It was rumored that Doc Logan had sent twelve sheep ranchers to Boot Hill in the Abilene Range War.

TWO COUNTY SHERIFFS (4) Hunchback Fred Agnew had changed the faces of three U.S. marshals, two county sheriffs, and an old lady from Boston who was on her way to Arizona to recuperate from Parkinson's disease.

TYNAN, CHIEF (6) Real-life University of Maine security chief.

THE UNDERTAKER (2) The unnamed Dead Steer Springs undertaker who came for the body of John "The Backshooter" Parkman after Slade put six bullets in Parkman's heart.

WHOMPER (7) Pinky Lee's trained bear. To torture a guard, Pinky tied the guard to a chair, put honey on his bare feet, and let Whomper lick off the honey.

A WOUNDED COWPOKE (3) He told Slade that the Bar-T bunkhouse was burned on Sam Columbine's orders. Logan finished off the talkative cowpoke.

ZIEGFIELD, SHIFTY RON (6) One of Sam Columbine's henchmen. He guarded Sandra Dawson while Columbine was off torturing a few Mexican border guards.

Places

THE AMERICAN SOUTHWEST (2) Slade was the most feared gunslinger in the American Southwest.

THE BAR-T BUNKHOUSE (2) At the end of Chapter 2, Mose Hart, Miss Sandra's top hand at the Bar-T ranch, came into town looking for Slade: The Bar-T bunkhouse was on fire.

BLEEDING HEART, KANSAS (7) Columbine's Top Gun, Pinky Lee, had ridden with Captain Quantrill and his Regulators during the Civil War. While Pinky was passed out in a bordello in Bleeding Heart, Kansas, a Union officer named Randolph P. Sorghum dropped a homemade bomb down a chimney. Pinky lost all his hair, and all the fingers on his left hand (except his pinky).

BOOT HILL (3) It was rumored that Doc Logan had sent twelve sheep ranchers to Boot Hill in the Abilene Range War.

THE BRASS CUSPIDOR SALOON (1) The bar in Dead Steer Springs.

DEAD STEER SPRINGS (1) A small western town. "It was almost dark when Slade rode into Dead Steer Springs."

THE DEAD STEER SPRINGS HOTEL (4) After the fire at the Bar-T, Slade checked into the Dead Steer Springs Hotel for a rest.

THE DEAD STEER SPRINGS JAIL (5) The jail where Slade was taken after he was arrested for public intoxication.

PADUKA, ILLINOIS (1) The home town of Slade's lost lover, Miss Polly Peachtree.

ROTTEN VULTURE RANCH (5) Sam Columbine's ranch.

THE SECOND FLOOR SUITE (4) The unnamed Dead Steer Springs Hotel clerk gave Slade the second floor suite in the hotel.

WINDING BLUFF ROAD (3) The road that led to the Bar-T ranch.

Things

THE ABILENE RANGE WAR (3) It was rumored that Doc Logan had sent twelve sheep ranchers to Boot Hill in the Abilene Range War.

ACAPULCO GOLD (6) The pot that Slade smoked.

AN ARABIAN SKINNING KNIFE (4) Hunchback Fred Agnew carried a three-foot Arabian skinning knife. Fred was only two-foot-three.

A BARREL OF TACO CHIPS (7) While in a gunfight with Sam Columbine, Slade hid behind a barrel of taco chips.

BLOOD BRIDES OF SITTING BULL (5) The Western novel that the Brass Cuspidor bartender read behind the bar.

BONANZA COWBOY BOOTS WITH LIFTS (4) The boots Slade wore. He was very sensitive about his height. Slade always slept with his boots on.

BULLETPROOF UNDERWEAR (8) After Slade rescued Sandra Dawson and learned that she was actually his lost love, Miss Polly Peachtree of Paduka, Sam Columbine snuck up and shot him in the back three times. But not to fear: Slade was wearing his bulletproof underwear, and was able to hear Polly express her devotion to Columbine. Slade blasted them both, and rode off with Stokely, his only true friend.

A BUNTLINE SPECIAL (7) Pinky Lee's gun.

THE CIVIL WAR (7) Columbine's Top Gun, Pinky Lee, had ridden with Captain Quantrill and his Regulators during the Civil War. While Pinky was passed out in a bordello in Bleeding Heart, Kansas, a Union officer named Randolph P. Sorghum dropped a homemade bomb down a chimney. Pinky lost all his hair, and all the fingers on his left hand except for his pinky.

A CONFEDERATE CAP, DUSTY JEANS AND SUSPENDERS (1) The clothing worn by the old man who asked Slade if he had been hired by Miss Sandra.

DIGGER'S RYE (2, 5) After Slade shot John "The Backshooter" Parkman in the heart six times, he poured himself a shot of Digger's Rye, which was 190 proof. In Chapter 5, however, we find out that Digger's Rye was 206 Proof.

THE EARLY 1870'S (1) In the early 1870's, Slade's name had begun to strike fear in people's hearts. [NOTE: See the entry THE RUMORS ABOUT SLADE.]

A FLAMING MONTGOLFIER BALLOON (1) Supposedly, Slade's sweetheart Miss Polly Peachtree was killed when a flaming Montgolfier balloon crashed into the Peachtree barn in Paduka.

THE FORT BRAGG BREAKOUT (5) One of the mixed drinks offered at the Brass Cuspidor Saloon.

A GENE McCARTHY BUTTON (3) Just before Slade shot Shifty Jack Mulloy for calling him a Republican, Slade showed Shifty his Gene McCarthy button.

THE GERONIMO (5) One of the mixed drinks offered at the Brass Cuspidor Saloon.

A GIANT BOTTLE OF MAYONNAISE (7) While in a gunfight with Slade, Sam Columbine hid behind a giant bottle of mayonnaise that had been air-dropped a month before after the worst flood disaster in the American Southwest. "(Why drop mayonnaise after a flood disaster? None of your damn business.)"

THE GREAT SOUTHWESTERN RAILROAD (2) Sam Columbine wanted to get the Bar-T away from Miss Sandra so that he could sell it to the Great Southwestern Railroad when the railroad decided to put a branch line there.

HONEY (7) To torture a guard, Pinky tied him to a chair, put honey on his bare feet, and let his bear, Whomper, lick off the honey.

HUNCHBACK FRED AGNEW'S "RECORD" (4) Hunchback Fred Agnew had changed the faces of three U.S. marshalls, two county sheriffs, and an old lady from Boston who was on her way to Arizona to recuperate from Parkinson's disease.

A JOINT (3) After accidentally shooting Sing-Loo, the Chinese cook, Slade rolled himself a joint instead of smoking one of his famous Mexican cigars.

A LARGE BOX MADE OUT OF WOVEN RIVER REEDS (4) The box that Hunchback Fred Agnew kept with him. It contained a twelve-foot python named Sadie Hawkins.

MEXICAN CIGARS (1) Slade's cigars.

"OH THEM GOLDEN SLIPPERS" (1) The song that was being played on the piano just before Slade entered the Brass Cuspidor Saloon.

A PICTURE OF NIAGARA FALLS (4) When Slade shot Hunchback Fred Agnew in the Dead Steer Springs Hotel, Fred fell against the wall and knocked a picture of Niagara Falls off the dresser.

THE POPSKULL PETE (5) One of the mixed drinks offered at the Brass Cuspidor Saloon.

PUBLIC INTOXICATION (5) After Slade drank three Zombies, Dead Steer Spring's Deputy Sheriff Hoagy Carmichael arrested the gunslinger for public intoxication.

A REPUBLICAN (3) Slade shot Shifty Jack Mulloy because Jack called him a Republican.

THE RUMORS ABOUT SLADE (1) In the early 1870's, Slade's name had begun to strike fear in people's hearts. There were three rumors about Slade: one was that he wore black because he was in a state of perpetual mourning for his lost love Miss Polly Peachtree of Paduka, the second was that he was the Grim Reaper's agent in the American Southwest, and the third was that he was queerer than a three-dollar bill.

A SINISTER DERRINGER (4) Slade always kept a sinister derringer strapped to his ankle.

SINISTER .50 CALIBER HORSE PISTOLS (3) Sunrise Jackson's guns.

A SINISTER .44 (1) The gun that John "The Backshooter" Parkman carried.

SIX SHOTS IN THE HEART (2) In Chapter 2, Slade shot John "The Backshooter" Parkman in the heart six times.

SMITH & WESSON (8) Sam Columbine's pistol.

SOLARCAINE (4) After the fire at the Bar-T, Slade checked into the Dead Steer Springs Hotel for a rest. He asked for Solarcaine because he had blisters on his trigger finger.

THE SOURDOUGH ARMPIT (5) One of the mixed drinks offered at the Brass Cuspidor Saloon.

THE SYNOPSES (1-8) The following are King's summations of the "action so far":

THE CHAPTER 1 "TO BE CONTINUED" NOTE (1) "(Will Slade down "Backshooter" Parkman? Will Sandra Dawson take the place of Polly Peachtree in Slade's stony heart? Is Slade really queerer than a three-dollar bill? Do you think anyone really gives a damn? Stick around until next week and find out the answers to these and other equally ridiculous questions in Chapter Two of "A Man Called Slade!")"

THE CHAPTER 2 SYNOPSIS (2) "(What has already happened, if you were smart enough to miss it: Jack Slade, the most feared gunslinger in the American

Southwest, has ridden into Dead Steer Springs. He is in the employ of Miss Sandra Dawson, who has hired him to help get rid of the sinister Sam Columbine, who is trying to steal her land. When we left our hero, he was facing one of Columbine's top guns, John "The Backshooter" Parkman in the Brass Cuspidor Saloon.)"

THE CHAPTER 3 SYNOPSIS (3) "(These ridiculous things have already happened: Slade, the fastest gun in the American Southwest, has been hired by Sandra Dawson to put a crimp in the style of Sam Columbine, who is trying to make her sell her ranch, the Bar-T. When we left Slade, he was racing toward the Bar-T, where the bunkhouse is on fire.)"

THE CHAPTER 4 SYNOPSIS (4) "(What has already happened. Slade, everybody's favorite gunslinger, has just returned from Sandra Dawson's Bar-T ranch to discover that Sandra herself has been kidnapped by Sam Columbine, who is out to get her land by fair means or foul – mostly foul.)"

THE CHAPTER 5 SYNOPSIS (5) "(What has happened so far. Slade, the roughest, toughest (queerest?) gunslinger in the American Southwest has just outwitted Hunchback Fred Agnew at the last possible second when Fred's boss, Sam Columbine, tried to put Slade out of the way. Now Slade is ready to find the ranch of the evil Columbine, where Sandra Dawson is being held prisoner. And if you understand all this, you are two jumps ahead of me already.)"

THE CHAPTER 6 SYNOPSIS (6) [King used the synopsis section of Chapter 6 to rail against the editorial staff of the *Maine Campus* for censoring what he called "a pretty damn good love scene" from his story. — **sjs**]

THE CHAPTER 7 SYNOPSIS (7) "(In our last episode – or at least you were probably hoping it was the last – Slade finally staggered out to Sam Columbine's Rotten Vulture Ranch and freed the fair Sandra Dawson after mowing down the three hardcases Columbine left to guard her. Incidentally, if you've been wondering where Sam Columbine hires all his gunmen, the answer is simple enough – where did you think construction workers get jobs when they go West?

Be that as it may (or may not, for that matter), Slade beat off an attack of gratefulness from the super-sexed Sandra Dawson and then left to find the evil Columbine and put a crimp in his bippy for once and ever.)"

THE CHAPTER 8 SYNOPSIS (8) "(When we last left Slade, he had finally cornered Sam Columbine at the Mexican border where he and his top gun, "Pinky" Lee had been torturing Mexican border guards. Using a clever ruse, Slade lured Lee into the open and ended his career. And now it's just Slade and Columbine...in a fight to the finish.)"

THREE ACES (1) The fancy-dan gambler who was playing cards in the Brass Cuspidor when Slade walked in was so shaken that he dropped three aces out of his sleeve. (Two of them were clubs.)

THREE SHOTS IN THE BACK (8) After Slade rescued Sandra Dawson and learned that she was actually his lost love, Miss Polly Peachtree of Paduka, Sam Columbine snuck up and shot him in the back three times. But not to fear: Slade was wearing his bulletproof underwear and was able to hear Polly express her devotion to Columbine. Slade blasted them both, and rode off with Stokely, his only true friend.

TWO FEET, THREE INCHES (4) Hunchback Fred Agnew's

height.

TWO SINISTER .45'S (1) Jack Slade's guns. He wore them low on his hips. Even the handles were black.

THE VICE PRESIDENT OF HELL (5) After Slade heard the rumor that Hunchback Fred Agnew might be the next vice president of the American Southwest, he remarked that now (after Slade shot him), Fred could be the next vice president of Hell.

THE ZOMBIE (5) One of the mixed drinks offered at the Brass Cuspidor Saloon. Slade ordered three.

"The Blue Air Compressor"

"The Blue Air Compressor" first appeared in *Onan*, the University of Maine student literary magazine, in January of 1971. A revised version appeared ten years later in the July 1981 issue of *Heavy Metal* magazine.

"The Blue Air Compressor" is a strange, experimental story that owes its genesis to a similarly-plotted E.C. Comics story, as well as to the work of Edgar Allan Poe.

A writer named Gerald Nately takes a seaside cottage owned by Mrs. Leighton, the wife of a deceased friend of his. Mrs. L. is fat. Very fat. Very, very fat. And Gerald Nately becomes so obsessed with her size that he attempts to capture the magnificence of her girth in his writing. She discovers his story about her (originally called "The Hog," but later retitled "The Blue Air Compressor"), and begins to mock him, taunting him about his inability to successfully "capture" her on paper:

"Oh, Gerald, [t]his is such a bad story. I don't blame you for using a pen-name. It's – it's *abominable*!

You haven't made me *big* enough, Gerald. That's the trouble. I'm too big for you. Perhaps Poe, or Dostoyevsky, or Melville...but not *you*, Gerald. Not even under your royal pen-name. Not *you*. Not *you.*'

She began to laugh again, huge racking explosions of sound.

'Don't you laugh,' Gerald said stiffly."

Gerald ends up killing Mrs. Leighton by shoving the hose of a blue air compressor down her throat and turning it on: "She seemed to explode all at once." He then buries her dismembered body beneath the floor boards of the shed...Poe's "The Tell-Tale Heart" with a surprise ending:

"When he notified the police that she had been missing for a week, the local constable and a State Policeman came at once. Gerald entertained them quite naturally, even offering them coffee. He heard no beating heart, but then – the interview was conducted in the big house."

The story consists of twenty-nine sections in which King combines straight narrative, stream of consciousness imagery, and authorial intrusion.

The *Onan* version is essentially impossible to find, so your best bet is to try and track down the *Heavy Metal* version, which, while still difficult to locate, is somehat more accessible through used bookstores and dealers.

If you can't find it anywhere, though, the following concordance should at least give you a pretty good feel for the tale, and for what Stephen King was trying to accomplish by telling it. — **sjs**

(U6)
"The Blue Air Compressor"
People

DOSTOYVESKY After reading Gerald Nately's short story about herself called "The Hog," Mrs. Leighton laughed and told him that he hadn't made her big enough, that she was too big for him to handle. Perhaps, Poe, Dostoyevsky, or Melville could handle her, she said, but not Gerald Nately.

KING, STEPHEN King intrudes upon his own story by announcing "My own name, of course, is Steve King, and you'll pardon my intrusion on your mind – or I hope you will." He then goes on to define "Rule One for all writers." [NOTE: See the "Things" entry RULE ONE FOR ALL WRITERS.]

LEIGHTON, MR. Mrs. Leighton's dead husband. Gerald Nately rented his cottage from September until December.

LEIGHTON, MRS. The wife of a friend of Gerald Nately's. After her husband died, Nately rented a cottage from her in which to write. Mrs. Leighton was fat. Upon first seeing her, Nately thought to himself

> "this woman is so goddamn fucking big and old she looks like oh jesus christ print dress she must be six-six and *fat* my god shes fat as a hog..."

Gerald Nately killed Mrs. Leighton after she laughed at his short story, "The Hog." He pole-axed her with a Winchester rifle, and then over-inflated her with a blue air compressor until she exploded. He then cut up her body and buried the pieces in the sand beneath her tool-shed. He didn't hear her heart beating when the police came.

THE LOCAL CONSTABLE The local constable questioned Gerald Nately about Mrs. Leighton's disappearance. (There was no beating heart to be heard.)

MELVILLE After reading Gerald Leighton's short story about herself called "The Hog," Mrs. Leighton laughed and told him that he hadn't made her big enough, that she was too big for him to handle. Perhaps, Poe, Dostoyevsky, or Melville could handle her, she said, but not Gerald Nately.

NATELY, GERALD Writer. Nately was the author of the short story "The Blue Air Compressor" (retitled from its original title "The Hog"), and four "twisted, monumental misunderstood novels." He murdered Mrs. Leighton, the wife of his friend, by over-inflating her with a blue air compressor, and then dismembering her body and burying the pieces in the sand beneath a tool-shed behind her beach house. He killed himself later in Kowloon by cutting off his own head with an ivory-figured guillotine.

POE After reading Gerald Leighton's short story about herself called "The Hog," Mrs. Leighton laughed and told him that he hadn't made her big enough, that she was too big for him to handle. Perhaps, Poe, Dostoyevsky, or Melville could handle her, she said, but not Gerald Nately.

A STATE POLICEMAN A state policeman questioned Gerald Nately about Mrs. Leighton's disappearance. (There was no beating heart to be heard.)

TERRELL, CARROLL F. A member of the University of Maine's English faculty. Stephen King was in Terrell's class one morning when he invented the character of Gerald Nately. Terrell had been talking about Edgar Allan Poe. In one of his "Garbage Truck" columns, King wrote that Terrell was "an excellent critic [who] understands almost everything..."

Places

BENEATH THE TOOL-SHED Gerald Nately cut up Mrs. Leighton's body and buried her in the sand beneath the floor boards of the tool-shed.

BOMBAY Gerald Nately rewrote his story "The Hog" (retitled as "The Blue Air Compressor") in a hotel room in Bombay.

THE COTTAGE A cottage that had been previously used by Mr. Leighton, and that was part of the property later owned by his widow, Mrs. Leighton. Gerald Nately rented the cottage in order to write. (He had known Mr. Leighton.)

"A COUNTRY OF TISSUE" An image Gerald Nately used to describe Mrs. Leighton.

HONG KONG After rewriting his short story in a hotel room in Bombay, Nately then went on to Hong Kong.

KOWLOON A peninsula in southeast China opposite Hong Kong. Kowloon was where Gerald Nately killed himself.

A LISBON FALLS DRUGSTORE In "The Blue Air Compressor," Stephen King tells the reader that the inspiration for the story came from an E.C comic book that he bought as a child at a Lisbon Falls drugstore.

MRS. LEIGHTON'S HOUSE Mrs. Leighton owned a big house on the water that had a detached cottage with a tool-shed.

> "The house was tall, with an incredible slope of shingled roof. The roof dipped and rose at varying angles above the main building and two strangely-angled wings; a widow's walk skirted a mushroom-shaped cupola which looked toward the sea..."

PORTLAND The Stowe Travel Agency was in Portland.

SHORE ROAD The road that led to Mrs. Leighton's house. Nately couldn't see the cottage as he approached the house. Mrs. Leighton later told him that you could only see the cottage from the road when walking, not driving.

STOWE TRAVEL AGENCY The travel agency in Portland that Gerald Nately used to book his "escape" flight to Bombay, Hong Kong, and Kowloon.

THE TOOL-SHED The shed attached to Mr. Leighton's cottage. The tool-shed was where Nately killed Mrs. Leighton with the blue air compressor.

THE UNIVERSITY OF MAINE Stephen King's alma mater. King was in an English class taught by Carroll F. Terrell one morning when he came up with the kernel images for the short story "The Blue Air Compressor."

Things

"AGE" Gerald Nately thought to himself that in Mrs. Leighton "age had run riot in her with luxuriant fleshiness."

"A BAPTIST GRANDFATHER OF A HOUSE" Nately described Mrs. Leighton's house as a "Baptist grandfather of a house."

"THE BLUE AIR COMPRESSOR" The revised title of the short story Gerald Nately wrote about Mrs. Leighton. Its original title was "The Hog."

THE BLUE AIR COMPRESSOR A four-hp. blue air compressor that Gerald Nately used to overinflate Mrs. Leighton, causing her to explode.

COCA-COLA Upon first arriving at Mrs. Leighton's house, she offered Nately Coca-Cola, which he accepted. She had tea.

DECEMBER 5 The day that Gerald Nately was supposed to vacate Mr. Leighton's cottage.

A DISMANTLED CARBURETOR There was a dismantled carburetor for a 1949 Packard on the workbench in the tool-shed that was attached to Mr. Leighton's cottage.

EIGHT O'CLOCK The time of day that Stephen King invented Gerald Nately. King was in an English class taught by Carroll F. Terrell, a member of the University of Maine English faculty, at the time.

FOUR BALD TIRES Four of the items that were in the tool-shed that was attached to Mr. Leighton's cottage.

FOUR NOVELS After writing the short story "The Blue Air Compressor" (which had originally been titled "The Hog"), Gerald Nately went on to write four "twisted, monumental, misunderstood novels."

A GREEN HOSE One of the items that was in the tool-shed that

479

was attached to Mr. Leighton's cottage.

HEDGE-CLIPPERS One of the items that was in the tool-shed that was attached to Mr. Leighton's cottage.

"THE HOG" The original title of the short story that Gerald Nately wrote about Mrs. Leighton. He later retitled it "The Blue Air Compressor."

AN IVORY-FIGURED GUILLOTINE The device with which Gerald Nately killed himself. He commited suicide in Kowloon, China.

THE LOST SENTENCE In the original *Onan* version of "The Blue Air Compressor," during King's first authorial intrusion into the story (and after explaining the genesis of the story), the last paragraph read "The blue air compressor did not come until later. It is desperately important that the reader be made cognizant of these facts." In the revised *Heavy Metal* version ten years later, King eliminated the last sentence.

NATELY'S CRIME Nately's murder of Mrs. Leighton was never discovered. "Gerald Nately was never brought to the dock; his crime was not discovered."

NATELY'S WRITING After settling himself in Mr. Leighton's cottage, Nately showed some of his work to Mrs. Leighton. He showed her some fragments of poetry, the "spine of a novel," and four essays.

A 1949 PACKARD CONVERTIBLE There was a dismantled carburetor for a 1949 Packard on the workbench in the tool-shed that was attached to Mr. Leighton's cottage.

"A PULLMAN CAR" The porch on Mrs. Leighton's house was "longer than a Pullman car."

RABBIT-TRAPS One of the items that was in the tool-shed that was attached to Mr. Leighton's cottage.

RAKES One of the items that was in the tool-shed that was attached to Mr. Leighton's cottage.

RULE ONE FOR ALL WRITERS "The teller is not worth a tin tinker's fart when compared to the listener." This was King's "first draft version" of his now-legendary credo "It is the tale, not he who tells it."

SEPTEMBER The month Gerald Nately rented Mr. Leighton's cottage.

A SHOVEL One of the items that was in the tool-shed that was attached to Mr. Leighton's cottage.

SNOW-SHOES One of the items that was in the tool-shed that was attached to Mr. Leighton's cottage.

A SPACE-HEATER One of the items that was in the tool-shed that was attached to Mr. Leighton's cottage.

STEPHEN KING ON PLAGIARISM In "The Blue Air Compressor," when discussing the inspiration for the story, King tells the reader, "Any author who tells you he has never plagiarized is a liar. A good author begins with bad ideas and improbabilities and fashions them into comments on the human condition."

SYMBOLISM On page 76 of the *Onan* version of the story, Stephen King breaks into the narrative to explain the symbolism in the tale. He begins by informing us that "Most horror stories are sexual in nature." He then goes on to tell us that the conclusion of "The Blue Air Compressor" "is (at least psychologically) a clear metaphor for fears of sexual impotence on my part." He then explains that Mrs. Leighton's large mouth is a symbol for the vagina, and the hose of the compressor is a symbol for the penis. He continues:

> "In the works of Edgar A. Poe, Stephen King, Gerald Nately and others [who write horror], we are apt to find locked rooms, dungeons, empty mansions (all symbols of the womb); scenes of living burial (sexual impotence); the dead returned from the grave (necrophilia); grotesque monsters or human beings (externalized fear of the sexual act itself); torture and/or murder (a viable alternative to the sexual act)."

He posits that these possiblities may not always be valid, but theorizes that the "post-Freudian" reader and writer must consider them. He concludes by stating that "Abnormal psychology has become a part of the human experience."

"THE TELL-TALE HEART" A short story by Edgar Allan Poe. As Nately's obsession with Mrs. Leighton became "increasingly unhealthy," he began to feel like the young man in the Poe story. At the conclusion of "The Blue Air Compressor," neither the local constable nor the state policeman who questioned Nately about Mrs. Leighton's disappearance heard her beating heart. [NOTE: See the Poe story for clarification and amplification.]

THE THREE IMAGES In an early morning English class taught by Carroll F. Terrell, King came up with the three images that evolved into the short story "The Blue Air Compressor":

> ivory guillotine Kowloon
> twisted woman of shadows, like a pig
> some big house

A TWO-HANDED SAW One of the items that was in the tool-shed that was attached to Mr. Leighton's cottage. This item (and a Winchester rifle) only appeared in the *Onan* version. They were deleted from the *Heavy Metal* version. Michael Collings wrote that these deletions "heightened the sense of objectivity, since the '4 hp. air-compressor painted electric blue' now appears in a catalogue that avoids overt images of potential death."

A WINCHESTER RIFLE One of the items in the tool-shed that was attached to Mr. Leighton's cottage. This item (and a two-handed saw) only appeared in the *Onan* version. They were deleted from the *Heavy Metal* version. Michael Collings wrote that these deletions "heightened the sense of objectivity, since the '4 hp. air-compressor painted electric blue' now appears in a catalogue that avoids overt images of potential death." [NOTE: There was one problem, however, with eliminating the rifle from the *Heavy Metal* version. Gerald Nately killed Mrs. Leighton with the rifle before inflating her. Where did the rifle come from?]

A WORKBENCH One of the items that was in the tool-shed that was attached to Mr. Leighton's cottage. The workbench was covered with nails, screws, bolts, washers, two hammers, a plane, a broken level, a dismantled 1949 Packard carburetor, and a four-hp. blue air compressor.

"The Fifth Quarter"

"The Fifth Quarter" first appeared in *Cavalier* magazine in April of 1972. It bore the byline of "John Swithen." The story was reprinted with Stephen King's byline in February of 1986 in a special Stephen King issue of *Twilight Zone* magazine.

"The Fifth Quarter," like "Dolan's Cadillac," is a story of revenge, crime, and dark justice. The narrator (unnamed throughout the story) works diligently and with determination to track down the killers of his friend, Barney. The friend (again, like Robinson in "Dolan's Cadillac") maintains a single-minded coolness throughout his encounter and, in the end, succeeds in recovering the money taken in the Brinks armored car robbery, in which Barney drove the getaway car.

The story ends with Barney's friend satisfied that "The debt had been paid," but also realizing "[He] had a lot to be careful for."

"The Fifth Quarter" is hard to find in the original *Cavalier* edition, but the *Twilight Zone* appearance is still relatively easy to locate. Try the Overlook Connection.
—sjs

(U7)
"The Fifth Quarter"
People

BARNEY An ex-con who got involved in an armored car robbery, and who ended up shot in the stomach, floating in a boat for two days. When his friend found him, Barney lived long enough to tell him the whole story. Barney's friend then went after The Sarge, Keenan, Cappy MacFarland, and Jagger. He ended up with three quarters of the map that showed where the money was buried.

BARNEY'S FRIEND The narrator of "The Fifth Quarter." He chose to even the score after he found Barney, shot in the stomach, in a boat where Barney had been afloat for two days. He took on The Sarge, Keenan, Cappy MacFarland, and Jagger, and ended up with three quarters of the map that showed where the money was buried.

DAVIS, MILES The night Barney's friend went to Keenan's house, Keenan was listening to Miles Davis and drinking a gin fizz.

A FAT YELLOW TOMCAT Sarge's cat.

HEMINGWAY, ERNEST Barney's friend thought that Keenan's living room was done by some pansy decorator who had never gotten over his crush on Ernest Hemingway.

JAGGER Jagger was part of the gang that robbed the Brinks armored truck. It was his idea to bury the money for ten years.

KEENAN A member of the gang that robbed the Brinks truck on April 5, 1972. He participated in the burial of the money, and kept two quarters of the map. Barney's friend shot him.

KEENAN'S SLEEP-IN MAID Keenan's domestic. She was at "a Tupperware party" the night Barney's friend went to Keenan's house.

MacFARLAND, CAPPY Cappy was part of the gang that robbed the armored truck. Cappy buried the money, and made a map.

THE PANSY DECORATOR Barney's friend thought that Keenan's living room was done by some pansy decorator who had never gotten over his crush on Ernest Hemingway.

THE SARGE One of the gang that robbed the Brinks armored car and made off with $180,000 in cash. Sarge lived in a backwoods shack. Sarge weighed in at about two-seventy, and had been a commando in World War II. Barney's friend shot him.

SWITHEN, JOHN Folksinger and writer. Swithen (Stephen King) was the author of "The Fifth Quarter," which first appeared in *Cavalier* magazine in April 1972. John Swithen was also a folksinger who made an appearance at Carrie White's prom. He performed with Maureen Cowan, and they did three songs: "500 Miles," "Lemon Tree," and "Mr. Tambourine Man."

THREE GUARDS Sarge and company robbed the Portland-Bangor Brinks armored truck on April 5, 1972, just outside of Carmel. They made off with $180,000, and killed three guards.

WILSON, FLIP When Keenan asked Barney's friend who he was, he replied "Flip Wilson."

Places

A BACKWOODS SHACK The place where Sarge lived. He said it was better than living raw. After seeing the place, Barney's friend wasn't sure he agreed with him.

BAR HARBOR The $180,000 that Sarge and company stole in the armored car holdup on April 5, 1972, was buried on an island called Carmen's Folly off Bar Harbor, Maine.

THE BOAT Barney's friend found Barney adrift in a boat. He had been shot in the stomach.

CARMEL Sarge and company robbed the Portland-Bangor Brinks armored truck just outside of Carmel. They made off with $180,000, and killed three guards.

CARMEN'S FOLLY The island off Bar Harbor, Maine, where the $180,000 taken in the armored car holdup was buried.

COLEMAN, MASSACHUSSETTS Sarge told Barney's friend that Jagger was at a ski lodge in Coleman, Massachusetts.

A COTTAGE ON THE COAST While putting together files on The Sarge and Keenan, Barney's friend leased a cottage on the coast.

IN THE BASE OF A LAMP The place where Sarge kept his piece of the treasure map.

JOLIET PENITENTIARY Cappy had had some draftsman training in Joliet, so he drew the map that showed where the money was buried.

KEENAN'S HOUSE The house where Barney's friend confronted The Sarge and Keenan. It was "an architectural monstrosity spread over half an acre of land, all slanting angles and steep-sloped roofs behind an iron fence." [NOTE: Compare this description with the houses in "The Glass Floor" and "The Blue Air Compressor."]

KEENAN'S LIVING ROOM Barney's friend thought that Keenan's living room was done by some pansy decorator who had never gotten over his crush on Ernest Hemingway.

A SKI LODGE Sarge told Barney's friend that Jagger was at a ski lodge in Coleman, Massachusetts.

Things

APRIL 5, 1972 The day Sarge and company robbed the Portland-Bangor Brinks armored truck just outside of Carmel. They made off with $180,000, and killed three guards.

BARNEY'S .45 The gun Barney's friend used to shoot Keenan and The Sarge. Barney had kept it hidden – wrapped in a waterproof pouch in a small compartment aft – in the boat where he was shot.

BARNEY'S MIDDLE NAME After the Brinks robbery, May 6, 1972, Barney's friend got a postcard from Barney. It read: "Mom and family fine, store doing good. See you in July." It was signed with Barney's middle name.

BARNEY'S POSTCARD After the Brinks robbery, May 6, 1972, Barney's friend got a postcard from Barney. It read: "Mom and family fine, store doing good. See you in July." It was signed with Barney's middle name.

THE FIFTH QUARTER Jagger was the fifth quarter. Keenan had had two pieces of the map, Sarge had one, and Jagger had the fourth quarter. Jagger himself was the fifth quarter.

A GIN FIZZ The night Barney's friend went to Keenan's house, Keenan was listening to Miles Davis and drinking a gin fizz.

THE HEAP Barney's friend's car.

AN IMPALA Keenan's car.

JAGGER'S ADDRESS After Barney's friend killed Keenan, the Sarge, and Jagger, he kept Jagger's address in case he needed the fourth quarter of the map.

JANUARY The month that Barney's friend went to Keenan's house to even the score and collect the pieces of the map.

JULY 4, 1982 The gang scheduled a reunion on this date. They would all go and dig up the money.

A LITTLE .32 WITH A BRASS-INLAID STOCK Keenan's gun.

MAY 6, 1972 The day Barney's friend got a postcard from Barney. [NOTE: See the entry BARNEY'S POSTCARD.]

A 1943-MODEL DOUBLE-BREASTED SUIT The Sarge's suit. (He kept a razor in the collar.)

$180,000 Barney's friend was after the $180,000 that was buried on an island called Carmen's Folly off Bar Harbor, Maine.

THE PORTLAND-BANGOR BRINKS ARMORED TRUCK Sarge and company robbed the Portland-Bangor Brinks armored truck on April 5, 1972, just outside of Carmel. They made off with $180,000, and killed three guards.

SIX MONTHS It took six months for Barney's friend to get a file on The Sarge and Keenan.

A SOUPED-UP '58 FORD Barney's car. He used it in the Brinks armored car robbery.

THE STOMACH When Barney's friend found Barney floating in the boat, Barney had been shot in the stomach, and had been adrift for two days.

A STUDEBAKER There was a Studebaker in the gully in front of

Sarge's backwoods shack.

A STUDEBAKER LARK Jagger's car.

10:20 P.M. The time that The Sarge showed up at Keenan's house.

"THERE'S ONE BORN EVERY MINUTE" The epitaph that Barney's friend thought should have been on Barney's grave. [NOTE: The phrase was originally coined by P.T. Barnum.]

A THURSDAY NIGHT The January night Barney's friend went to Keenan's house.

TWO ROADBLOCKS Sarge and company robbed the Portland-Bangor Brinks armored truck on April 5, 1972, just outside of Carmel. They made off with $180,000, and killed three guards. After the robbery, they ran two roadblocks in Barney's souped-up '58 Ford.

A VAN GOGH PRINT Keenan's safe was behind a Van Gogh print in his living room.

A VIDEOMASTER TV Sarge had an "ancient" Videomaster TV.

A VOLKSWAGEN Sarge's car.

"Suffer the Little Children"

"Terror rises up from the chaos of feelings of doubt and uncertainty about man's place in the universe; horror frequently follows the recognition that greater powers than man can exert the force of violence and pain on him. The fear of the biblical Job, then, comes from terror; his punishment at the hand of God is horrible. Because man is human and finite, he can bear more terror than horror, more emotional feeling than actual physical pain."

From the "General Introduction" to
The Evil Image: Two Centuries of Gothic Short Fiction and Poetry,
eds. Patricia L. Skarda and Nora Crow Jaffee
(New York: New American Library, Meridian, 1981)

"Suffer the little children to come unto me, and forbid them not: for of such is the kingdom of God.

Verily I say unto you, Whosoever shall not receive the kingdom of God as a little child shall in no wise enter therein."

—Jesus Christ
(The Gospel According to St. Luke: Chapter 18, Verse 16)

"Yea, young children despised me; I arose, and they spake against me."

(The Book of Job: Chapter 19, Verse 18)

"Stephen King is in a unique position to comment on the teacher's frequently-held opinion that her pupils are 'little monsters.'"

From the Introduction to "Suffer the Little Children" in
The Evil Image: Two Centuries of Gothic Short Fiction and Poetry
eds. Patricia L. Skarda and Nora Crow Jaffee
(New York: New American Library, Meridian, 1981)

"Miss Sidley was her name, and teaching was her game."

Thus begins a short story by Stephen King that poses the question all teachers ask themselves at one time or another throughout their career: "Do we *really* know what goes on behind our back when we're writing at the blackboard?" (And I suppose the corollary to that query is, "Do we really *want* to know?")

"Suffer the Little Children" is an enormously effective tale of shape-changing grammar school children that operates on two distinctly independent thematic levels.

The story originally appeared in *Cavalier* magazine in February of 1972. It was reprinted twice: the first time in *The Evil Image: Two Centuries of Gothic Short Fiction and Poetry*, eds. Patricia L. Skarda and Nora Crow Jaffee (New York: New American Library, Meridian, 1981), and

the second time in *65 Great Spine Chillers*, ed. Mary Danby (New York, London: Octpous, 1982.)

Miss Sidley teaches little kids.

And like any classroom full of youngsters, mischief is ever-present. Miss Sidley, however, always prided herself on being in total control of her classroom: through little tricks and manipulations, she always "knew instictively who was chewing gum at the back of the room, who had a beanshooter in his pocket, who wanted to go to the bathroom to trade baseball cards rather than use the facilities."

But one day, as Miss Sidley is writing at the blackboard, out of the corner of her eye, she sees one of her students *change*:

"The reflection was small, ghostly, and distorted. And she had all but the barest corner of her eye on the word she was writing.
Robert changed.
She caught just a corner of it, just a frightening glimpse of Robert's face changing into something...different."

Miss Sidley begins to read new meaning into looks the children give her: "[L]ooks that said: *we have a secret, don't we?*" [NOTE: See the "People" entry THE OTHER ROBERT.]

Miss Sidley eventually becomes convinced that all of her students are monsters – shape-changing, diabolic monsters that only she can recognize as they "[hide] behind masks."

One day, she takes her students to the school mimeograph room, where she deliberately and methodically shoots them one at a time.

There is no trial, and Miss Sidley ends up locked away in an institution for the criminally insane (an "antiseptic madhouse in the next state"). A year later, her doctors allow her to participate in a strictly-controlled group therapy session with mindless retarded children, watching her "for the first sign of an aggressive move."

During one of these sessions, Miss Sidley "seemed to see something which disturbed her; a frown creased her brow and she looked away from the children." She asks to be taken away from them, and later that night she cuts her own throat with a piece of a broken mirror. The story ends with the psychiatrist, Buddy Jenkins, beginning to watch the children.

"Suffer the Little Children" is so effective because we never know if Miss Sidley's visions are real.

The children never change in front of other witnesses. We're never sure if Miss Sidley is experiencing degenerative delusional thinking...or if the children are really shape-changing monsters.

What do you think? —**sjs**

(U8)
"Suffer the Little Children"
People

THE BUS DRIVER The driver who almost hit Miss Sidley after she fled from Robert, whom she had seen "change."

CROSSEN, MARGARET Woman who gave Miss Sidley smelling salts after she fainted.

A DEAD GERMAN Jim Sidley took a gun off a dead German in the Battle of the Bulge.

EDWARD One of Miss Sidley's students. She told him to use "vacation" in a sentence. Edward said "I went on a vacation to New York City."

A GROUP OF RETARDED CHILDREN The children surround Miss Sidley during a group therapy session in the madhouse where she was put after killing twelve students.

HANNING, MR. The school principal.

JANE One of Miss Sidley's students. She had to stay after class.

JENKINS, BUDDY "Buddy Jenkins was his name, psychiatry was his game." Miss Sidley's doctor.

"THE OTHER ROBERT" According to Robert, the "other Robert... liked Show and Tell. He's still hiding 'way, 'way down in my head. Sometimes he runs around...it itches. He wants me to let him out."

THE RETARDED BOY During the encounter session at the madhouse, Miss Sidley picked up this boy when he fell over.

THE RETARDED GIRL Miss Sidley stroked her head during the encounter session in the madhouse.

ROBERT One of Miss Sidley's students. She asked him to use "tomorrow" in a sentence, and he said "Tomorrow a bad thing will happen." Then, he changed.

ROBERT'S FATHER Miss Sidley told Robert to bring him to school.

ROBERT'S MOTHER Miss Sidley told Robert to bring her to school.

SIDLEY, EMILY "Teaching was her game." The third-grade teacher who saw her students "change" one day and, after holding it in as long as she could, took them to the mimeograph room one at a time and shot them.

SIDLEY, JIM Emily's brother. He had taken a gun off a dead German in the Battle of the Bulge. This was the gun Miss Sidley used on her students.

TWELVE CHILDREN Miss Sidley shot twelve children in the mimeograph room at the Summer Street School.

TWO UNNAMED GIRLS Two students who talked about Miss Sidley in the bathroom.

Places

"AN ANTISEPTIC MADHOUSE IN THE NEXT STATE" The institution where Miss Sidley was placed after she murdered twelve students.

THE MIMEOGRAPH ROOM The room to which Miss Sidley took her students for their "very special Test." She shot them with a gun her brother had taken off a dead German.

SUMMER STREET SCHOOL The school where Miss Emily Sidley taught. The school was closed for one week of mourning after she shot the twelve children.

Things

THE BATTLE OF THE BULGE Jim Sidley took a gun off a dead German in this battle.

"THE CROWD" The Ray Bradbury short story that King echoes in "Suffer the Little Children." The students that gather around Sidley after she is almost hit by a bus parallels scenes in "The Crowd," where the "crowd" gathers around accident victims.

"MASKS" Miss Sidley felt that her students were "hiding behind masks."

MISS SIDLEY'S "TEST RESULTS" Miss Sidley shot twelve children in the mimeograph room during her "very special Test." The reason? "They are all monsters. I found out."

"A PIECE OF BROKEN MIRROR" The tool Miss Sidley used to cut her own throat in the madhouse.

POACHED EGGS ON TOAST Miss Sidley's dinner. She ate at 5:00 p.m.

THE READER The text Miss Sidley used in her third-grade class.

"A VERY SPECIAL TEST" The euphemism Miss Sidley used to get twelve students into the mimeograph room, where she then shot them one by one.

"It Grows on You"

"It Grows on You" first appeared in the University of Maine student literary magazine *Marshroots* in the fall of 1973. It was later reprinted in Stuart Schiff's *Whispers* in August of 1982, and the Playboy anthology *Death*, also in 1982.

The story concerns a macabre house owned by Joe Newall that eventually begins to "grow" by itself, adding on cupolas and wings.

The house overlooks the town of Harlow, Maine, much the way the Marsten House overlooked Jeruslaem's Lot and, in a more recent example, the way the house rented by John and Elise in "Rainy Season" overlooked the town of Willow, Maine.

"It Grows on You" is an atmospheric piece that is brooding, quiet, and slowly-paced.

The following concordance details the people, place, and things of the story, and relates the events that lead up to the house taking on a "life of its own."

("It Grows on You" is a relatively difficult piece to locate. The *Whispers* appearance or the Playboy *Death* appearance are probably the two most accessible. Try the usual dealers. —**sjs**

(U9)
"It Grows On You"
People

BOWEN, JOHN He sat by the stove in McKissick's general store with his feet up. He drove a pickup.

BURDEAU, PHIL Joe Newall bought Phil's land from the First Bank in Lewiston. Phil slunk away to Kittery, where he worked as a mechanic specializing in Ford A's and T's.

CORLISS, PAUL He leaned against the counter in the general store.

COUNTY CORONER Lewiston coroner who cut down Joe Newall's dead body.

COY, ALVIN He drove the Hay & Peabody funeral hack. He was the only person from Harlow to attend Joe Newall's funeral.

A FELLOW IN MECHANIC FALLS Unnamed guy who sold Joe Newall sixteen cows.

GATES, GABE Carl Stowe's partner at the Gates Mill. Gabe died of Parkinson's disease and uremic poisoning at the age of seventy-nine. At the time of his death, he was still the town's head selectman and overseer of the poor.

A HALF-WIT Man from Gates Falls who Joe Newall hired to care for his cows.

"THE JAZZ BABY" Unnamed woman who attended Joe Newall's funeral. She was a "young, shapely woman who wore a raccoon coat with a black fur collar." She didn't close her eyes during the prayer.

LEONARD, CORA Joe Newall's first wife. She was a "grain-bag of a woman, moonlike and silent. Her face was clay." She first got pregnant in 1920.

THE MASSACHUSETTS COUPLE The last people to lease (with an option) the Newall house. They were from Auburn.

MATTERLY, JOHN He sat by the stove in the general store with his feet up. He had a huge dent in his forehead just to the right of his left temple from a 1953 car accident. The dent held the contents of a medium-sized water glass.

McKISSICK, HARLEY Irv KcKissick's son. He "presided" over the general store. He was "corpulent" and "red-faced."

McKISSICK, IRV Harley's dad. Irv owned the general store.

METHODIST LADIES AID Ladies group that may have started the rumor that Cora Newall was naked when she fell down the stairs and broke her neck in 1924.

NEWALL, JOE Joe was scrawny. He came to Newall in 1904. He hung himself in November 1929. He made his fortune in Gates Falls, and in 1914 he married Cora Leonard.

NEWALL, SARAH TAMSON Cora and Joe Newall's daughter. She was born January 14, 1921. She was a "mewling monstrosity with no arms." She died when she was six hours old.

PAULSON, GARY Drove an old Chevy. He caned chairs. [NOTE: He carried a cane with a white bicycle grip, just like Mrs. Leighton did in "The Blue Air Compressor."]

THE PAULSON BOYS Gary Paulson had three sons: Two were killed in World War II, and the third was "a no-good." He died in a car accident on the Maine Turnpike near Clinton in 1955.

ROY, DANA He may have been the one who threw the dead chicken at Joe Newall's house. He died of intestinal cancer in 1971. He had been an electrician for Gates Mill until 1930, and then for U.S. Gypsum until his 1956 retirement.

ROY, MRS. Dana's wife. She died in childbirth in 1948.

STOWE, CARL Co-founder of the Gates Mill.

"THAT CRAZY WOP FROM PENNSYLVANIA" Guy who bought the old Wing farm to raise racing horses. He went bankrupt.

THREE YOUNG GIRLS Unnamed girls from South Harlow. Gary Paulson was banging all three in 1922.

TORBUTT, CLEVE The man who found Joe after he had hung himself. It was rumored that Cleve and Joe were financial partners.

TWO SMALL CHILDREN Unnamed children who rolled a red toy fire truck on the Harlow bandstand.

UPSHAW, CLEM The Harlow health officer. He was from Bowie Hill. He got a court order to see Joe's dead cows. He had been elected with Irv McKissick's help.

WING, BENNY He read horror pulps. Benny claimed that Joe Newall had gouged out the eyes of his dead daughter, wife, and cows, and kept them in a jar.

Places

BATES WOOLEN The factory where many Harlow men worked.

CENTRAL MAINE GENERAL HOSPITAL The hospital where Dana Roy died.

FIRST BANK The Lewiston bank that foreclosed on Phil Burdeau's land. Joe Newall bought the land from the bank.

GATES FALLS The town where Joe Newall made his fortune. He lived there in a rented house while the land he bought in South Harlow went fallow.

GATES MILL & WEAVING INC. Joe Newall became foreman of the mill in 1908. The mill owned the Newall House from 1929 on.

THE GENERAL STORE The town's gathering place. It was owned by Irv McKissick, and presided over by his kid, Harley. It had an "ancient" smell: salami, flypaper, coffee, tobacco, sweat, brown Coca-Cola, pepper, cloves, and bay rum. There were announcements of old town meetings on the walls, and a 1962 beanhole bean supper poster in the window.

HARLOW, MAINE The setting for "It Grows on You."

HARLOW METHODIST CHURCH Joe Newall wanted nothing to do with them.

HAY & PEABODY The funeral parlor that handled Joe Newall's funeral.

KITTY KORNER STORE The store in Gates Center where Cora Newall did her shopping every Thursday.

MECHANIC FALLS The fellow who sold Joe Newall sixteen cows lived in Mechanic Falls.

THE NEWALL HOUSE The house was on Stackpole Road overlooking Southwest Bend. It was built by Joe Newall in 1916. Newall added to the house periodically, usually after some trag-

edy. At the conclusion of "It Grows on You," the house had begun adding to itself. In speaking of the house, John Bowen remarked that "it grows on you."

SEARS AND ROEBUCK The half-wit Joe Newall hired got his overalls from the Sears mail-order catalogue.

SOUTHWEST BEND Where the general store was located.

WALKER BROTHERS, INC. The real estate firm representing the Newall House. They were known as "those goddamn sheenies from Gates."

Things

ANTHRAX Joe Newall's sixteen cows died of anthrax in the summer of 1927.

AUGUST 14, 1922 The day that Gary Paulson saw Cora Leonard's naked ass.

AUGUST 1929 The month the second wing on the Newall House was completed.

DANA ROY'S THREE TRIPS OUTSIDE MAINE When he was ten years old, he went to visit an aunt in Indiana; when he was twenty-five, he went to see the Boston Red Sox play in Boston; and when he was forty-seven, he went to an electrician's convention in Portsmouth, New Hampshire.

A DEAD CHICKEN A dead chicken was thrown at the Newall House in 1929, two days after the second wing was completed. It may have been hurled by Dana Roy.

DECEMBER 1, 1929 The day Joe Newall was buried.

EIGHTY-THREE YEARS OLD Gary Paulson's age at death, which took place nineteen days after the action in "It Grows on You" took place. He died of a brain hemorrhage, and he had a hard-on at the time of death. He had been dreaming of Cora Leonard's naked ass.

FORD A'S AND T'S Phil Burdeau's specialty.

GLASS FREEZER Freezer in the back of the general store. It came from New York in 1923.

"GOING BEFORE" The inscription on Sarah Newall's grave marker. She died six hours old on January 14, 1921.

JANUARY 14, 1921 The day Cora Newall gave birth to a daughter that died six hours later. [NOTE: See the "People" entry SARAH TAMSON NEWALL.]

KINGSTON SCALE The scale in the back of the general store.

MEAT GRINDER The machine in the back of the general store.

A NEW CUPOLA Two days after Gary Paulson's death, a new cupola started going up on the Newall House.

NEW ENGLAND AUTUMN The time of year in "It Grows on You."

A NEW WING In 1971, a new wing had started to go up on the Newall House. No one knew where it came from. It was forty feet long by twenty feet wide.

1955 The year that Gary Paulson's third son got killed in a car accident on the Maine Turnpike near Clinton.

1951 The last year that the Mill had a possible buyer for the Newall House.

1953 CAR ACCIDENT The accident that injured John Matterly.

1914 The year that Joe married Cora Leonard.

1908 The year that Joe Newall became foreman of the Gates Mill.

1904 The year Joe Newall came to Harlow.

1971 The year that "It Grows on You" takes place.

1916 The year that Joe Newall completed the construction of the Newall House. It was painted white and had twelve rooms.

1920 The year that Joe Newall added the first wing to the Newall House. It was the year Cora got pregnant.

1928 The year that Joe Newall began adding another wing to his house.

1924 The year that Cora Newall fell down the stairs and broke her neck. There was a rumor – which may have been started by the Methodist Ladies' Aid – that Cora was completely naked at the time. Cora was buried next to her daughter Sarah.

1929 The year that Joe Newall died.

1927 The year that Joe Newall completed construction of a new barn.

1922 The year that Joe Newall added a cupola to the house. His daughter Sarah had died at birth the previous January.

NOVEMBER 1929 The month that Joe Newall hung himself in an unfinished bedroom of the new wing of his house.

ORANGE CRUSH Paul Corliss bought one. It cost twelve cents.

PAULSON'S CANE Gary Paulson used a cane with a white bicycle grip. [NOTE: Mrs. Leighton from "The Blue Air Compressor" also had one.]

PAULSON'S SIGN Gary Paulson had the following sign on his car:

"Gary Paulson Chairs Caned Antiques 353-8972"

A PICKUP John Bowen drove one.

PRINCE ALBERT John Bowen's tobacco.

"QUAINT" What outsiders thought of the Harlow townsfolk.

SEPTEMBER 1929 The month a fire raced through the carding room at the Gates Mill. The fire did $500,000 worth of damage.

SEVENTY-NINE The age at which Gabe Gates died.

SIXTEEN COWS Joe Newall bought the cows from a fellow in Mechanic Falls.

353-8792 Gary Paulson's phone number.

A TURKEY Gary Paulson won one at the Grange.

VITALIS Hair tonic that the crazy wop from Pennsylvania used.

WHAT OUTSIDERS THINK What they think is in the first line of "It Grows on You": "Outsiders think they are always the same, these small towns – that they don't change."

WINSTON THERMOMETER Thermometer in the general store. At the time of the story, it read eighty-two degrees.

"The Cat from Hell"

"The Cat from Hell" has been published five times:

1. *Cavalier* magazine (June, 1977).
2. *Tales of Unknown Horror*, ed. Peter Haining (London: New English Library, 1978).
3. *The Year's Finest Fantasy*, ed. Terry Carr (New York: Putnam, 1978; New York: Berkley, 1979).
4. *Magicats!* eds. Jack Dann and Gardner Dozois (New York: Ace, 1984).
5. *New Bern Magazine* (March-April, 1984); *Top Horror*, ed. Josh Pachter (Munich, West Germany: Wilhelm Heyne Verlag).

Of these five appearances, the second through fifth publications were in the form we now accept as the Stephen King short story "The Cat from Hell." The first appearance – in *Cavalier* magazine in 1977 – was as part of a "Do-It-Yourself" writing contest.

Cavalier editor Nye Willden asked King to write the beginnning of a short story, with his *Cavalier* readers submitting their own conclusions to the story.

Willden published the first five hundred words of the story in the March 1977 issue, and King's conclusion to the story appeared alongside the winning contest entry in the June 1977 issue.

The story was based on a photograph of a cat given to King, and concerns a hit man who is commissioned to "rub out" a cat. Seems as though our protagonist, Drogan, has killed off a lot of our kitty's feline brothers and cousins developing his incredibly lucrative line of pharmaceuticals, and now the "cat from hell" is killing off Drogan's family. Drogan fears he's next, so he hires John Halston to do away with his cat.

The story's conclusion has a terrifically gross stom-ach-bursting scene *very* similar to the dining-room scene in the film "Alien." [NOTE: Was the idea "borrowed" from "The Cat from Hell?"]

As of this writing (winter 1989), the *Magicats* anthology is still in print, and should be very easy to find. — **sjs**

(U10)
"The Cat from Hell"
People

ALICE'S CHESHIRE CAT Halston felt that Sam was grinning at him like Alice's Cheshire.

BROADMOOR, CAROLYN Carolyn was of the Westchester Broadmoors, and she was Amanda Drogan's lifelong friend. She was seventy, and had emphysema. Drogan believed that Carolyn died when Sam stole her breath.

THE CAT FROM HELL The cat owned by Drogan. It was named Sam by Drogan's sister Amanda. "It's face was an even split: half black, half white." According to Drogan, Sam was responsible for three deaths: His sister Amanda, her friend Carolyn Broadmoor (of the Westchester Broadmoors), and the hired man, Dick Gage. Sam eventually got Halston, too.

THE CORONER He told Drogan that Amanda's death was an accident.

THE DAY-MAID The unnamed woman who came into the Drogan house every day.

DROGAN The seventy-two-year old wheelchair-bound old man who hired Halston to "hit" his cat. Drogan owned Drogan Pharmaceuticals.

DROGAN, AMANDA Drogan's seventy-four old sister. Amanda took in the cat from hell, and named him Sam. Amanda died when she fell down the stairs and broke her back, both legs, and her neck. She was found in the Little Friskies.

EIGHTEEN MEN The eighteen unnamed men John Halston had "brought death to" in his career.

15,000 CATS The number of cats killed by Drogan Pharmaceuticals during their testing of Tri-Dormal-G.

GAGE, DICK Drogan's hired man. He was past sixty, and had been with Drogan more than twenty years. He was killed in a car accident on his way to a vet in Milford. Drogan had told him to have the cat put to sleep.

HALSTON, JOHN Hit man, professional murderer. "Death was Halston's business; he had brought it to eighteen men and six women in his career as an independent hitter." He met his doom when he met Sam, the cat from hell.

A HARTFORD MEDIUM She told Carolyn Broadmoor that Amanda's soul had entered Sam the cat. She charged Carolyn twenty dollars for this information.

LOGGIA, SAUL Loggia referred Drogan to John Halston.

REUSS, WILL The farmer who found Halston's car and his cat-ravaged body – complete with the hole in his stomach where Sam had clawed his way out after forcing himself down Halston's throat.

SAM The cat from hell.

SIX WOMEN The six unnamed women John Halston had "brought death to" in his career.

THE VET Veterinarian in Milford. Drogan gave Dick Gage the task of bringing Sam the cat to this vet to be put to sleep. Gage was killed in a car accident on the way there.

THE WESTCHESTER BROADMOORS The family from which Carolyn Broadmoor came.

Places

DROGAN PHARMACEUTICALS The company founded by Drogan. It was one of the biggest drug companies in the world.

The cornerstone of their financial success was the drug Tri-Dormal phenobarbin – a synthetic painkiller, tranquilizer, and mild hallucinogen known as Tri-Dormal-G. It was developed in the 1950s.

NEW JERSEY The Drogan Pharmaceutical labs in New Jersey developed Tri-Dormal-G. The testing on the drug involved the extermination of 15,000 cats, although Drogan said that the cats "expired" during testing.

PLACER'S GLEN Placer's Glen was where Halston left the turnpike with Sam the cat in the car.

Things

CALO When Drogan first saw the cat near his house, he instructed Gage to put out Calo spiked with Tri-Dormal-G. Sam ignored the food.

DROGAN'S ENVELOPE Drogan gave Halston an envelope containing the "hit money": $6,000 in cash. There would be another $6,000 when the cat was dead. (Halston's usual fee was $12,000).

"AN EDGAR GUEST POEM" Halston thought of these lines by Guest when he saw Sam sitting contentedly on Drogan's lap: "The cat on my lap, the hearth's good fire/...A happy man, should you enquire."

HALSTON'S ACCIDENT Halston had an accident while taking Sam to his death. The car ended up in a ravine. The firewall had caved in, and the engine block had smashed into his legs, pinning him.

HALSTON'S GUN A "short-barrelled .45 hybrid." It hung below his armpit in a spring-loaded holster.

"THE HOLLYWOOD SQUARES" The TV show everyone in the Drogan household watched.

JOHN HALSTON'S USUAL FEE A routine hit cost $12,000.

JULY 1 The date of Carolyn Broadmoor's funeral.

LINCOLN MARK IV The car Dick Gage drove. He had an accident in the car on his way to a vet in Milford.

LITTLE FRISKIES Sam didn't like them unless they were wetted down with a little milk.

SAM'S REVENGE After Halston's car accident, the cat from hell did away with the hit man in the following way: "The cat was forcing its way into his mouth, flattening its body, squirming, working itself further and further in." Later, "above Halston's navel, a ragged hole had been clawed in his flesh. Looking out was the gore-streaked black-and-white face of a cat, its eyes huge and glaring. The cat forced its body out." [NOTE: Interestingly, this form of "execution" would later be re-enacted – although in a slightly more "spacey" setting – in the 1979 film, "Alien," although not by Ripley's cat, Jones.)

SEVEN MONTHS The length of time that Sam the cat had been in Drogan's house when Drogan called in John Halston.

'73 PLYMOUTH John Halston's car. It had a custom Cyclone Spoiler engine, a Pensy shift, Hearst linkage, and sat on Bobby Unser Wide Oval tires. Halston had rebuilt the differential and rear end himself.

TRI-DORMAL-G Tri-Dormal-phenobarbin. A synthetic painkiller, tranquilizer, and mild hallucinogen developed in the 1950s in the New Jersey labs of Drogan Pharmaceuticals.

(U11)
"Man With a Belly"
People

THE BEAT COP The beat cop was due at 11:20 p.m. on the night that John Bracken waited for his "target," Norma Correzente, in James Memorial Park.

"BENNY THE BULL" Benito Torreos.

THE BLUE-EYED SON OF BRACKEN AND NORMA The baby that was the offspring of Bracken and Norma Correzente. He had blue eyes, and Don Vittorio was suspicious because there were no blue-eyed Sicilians. Bracken told him the eyes would change. [NOTE: See the "Things" entry THE QUESTION.]

THE BOSTON WHITES Norma Correzente's family.

BRACKEN, JOHN The "hitman" hired by Vito Correzente to rape (and hurt) his wife Norma. Bracken's price was thirty thousand before the hit, and twenty thousand after.

CORREZENTE, NORMA Norma White Correzente. She was John Bracken's "target." Bracken was hired by Norma's husband Vito to rape and hurt her. She was from the Boston Whites, and Don Vittorio thought of her as a rich society bitch. She died giving birth to her and John Bracken's child.

CORREZENTE, VITTORIO Don Vittorio; Vito the Wop. He was the aging Don of an organized crime family. He was "the iron fist inside the glove. He was "a man with a belly in the Sicilian argot." He was married to Norma White, a woman who he felt disgraced him with her ways.

"THE MAN WITH A BELLY" Don Vito Correzente.

THE PITMAN Bracken bribed the Pitman at Jarvis's to find out that Norma Correzente was losing $8-10,000 a week gambling.

SILLS, BENNY The contact man who had put Vito Correzente in touch with John Bracken. Sills ran a hockshop.

TORREOS, BENITO Benny the Bull. He was consigliare to Vito Correzente. He called John Bracken about the hit on Vito's wife.

"VITO THE WOP" Don Vittorio Correzente.

Places

BOSTON The town where Norma White Correzente's family was firmly entrenched.

400 MEEGAN BOULEVARD The address of the Graymoor Arms, Vito Correzente's residence.

THE GRAYMOOR ARMS Vito Correzente's residence. The building was at 400 Meegan Boulevard.

THE HAMMOND AND PARDIS AVENUE INTERSECTION

The intersection where Norma Correzente paused on the night Bracken made his "hit."

HAMMOND STREET James Memorial Park bordered the south side of Hammond Street.

A HOCKSHOP Benny Sills ran a hockshop.

JAMES MEMORIAL PARK John Bracken sat on a bench in this park waiting for Norma Correzente to walk by.

JARVIS'S The most opulent gambling den in the city. Norma Correzente went there every night.

NORMA'S SECOND APARTMENT Norma Correzente's secret second apartment. She took John Bracken there after he raped her.

PALM SPRINGS After Bracken impregnated Norma Correzente, he went to Palm Springs.

TWO $1,000-A-MONTH SUITES Vito Correzente had had two $1,000-a-month suites in the Graymoor Arms converted into a single monolith.

Things

BRACKEN'S PRICE TO MAKE NORMA CORREZENTE PREGNANT He wanted $100,000: $40,000 before conception, and $60,000 after. Norma was doing this to disgrace her husband, whom she hated.

$8-10,000 A WEEK Norma Correzente was losing $8-10,000 a week at Jarvis's.

11:20 P.M. The time the beat cop made his rounds in James Memorial Park.

A LARGE RUBY Vito Correzente wore a large ruby on his fourth finger.

NORMA CORREZENTE'S OPINION OF HER HUSBAND Don Vittorio was "a wop, a stinking spic, a lover of sheep, a crude bludgeoner who went to chic restaurants and ate pie with his fingers, an afficionado of Norman Rockwell, a pedarist..."

$100,000 John Bracken's price to impregnate Norma Correzente.

PASTA AND OREGANO The odors John Bracken thought he could smell when he entered Vito Correzente's monolithic suite at the Graymoor Arms.

A QUESTION Nine months after Bracken impregnated Norma Correzente, Don Vittorio called him to ask him a question: Did he get Norma pregnant? The baby was born with blue eyes, and there were no blue-eyed Sicialians. John told the old man he wouldn't take his own leavings (he wouldn't have had sex with Norma after raping her); and he let the old man die thinking he had a son. Bracken had a belly, too.

A ROUND-TRIP PLANE TICKET AND A CHECK FOR $1,000 John found these two items in his hotel room after he received the call from Benny the Bull requesting his presence at Don Vittorio's suite.

A STROKE Don Vittorio had a stroke after having sex with Norma.

TEN WEEKS Ten weeks after Bracken raped Norma Correzente, she was pregannt with his child.

$30,000 BEFORE THE HIT, $20,000 AFTER John Bracken's price for raping Norma Correzente.

A .25 CALIBER SWEDISH PISTOL The gun carried by Norma Correzente.

(U12)
"The Night of the Tiger"
People

BAILY, CHIPS The circus barker. Chips had malaria and "sometimes had to go someplace far away and holler." Occasionally, the cotton candy salesman would fill in for Chips, and Eddie would fill in selling the cotton candy.

COTTON CANDY SALESMAN The unnamed man who would occasionally have to bark for Chips Baily. [NOTE: See the above CHIPS BAILY entry.]

EBONY VELVET A docile black panther that was so expensive "it had set the circus back almost one season's receipts."

EDMONT, MR. Eddie's high school principal. Eddie was afraid of him.

FARNUM, MR. The ringmaster and half-owner of the circus.

GREEN TERROR The Farnum & Williams' circus's only tiger.

HIGH SCHOOL BOY A sweaty high school kid with books in his arms was the only person at Green Terror's cage when the tornado warnings were announced. He split.

INDRASIL, JASON The circus lion tamer. He looked like Rudolph Valentino.

JOHNSTON, EDDIE Circus roustabout. He was born and raised in Sauk City.

JOHNSTON, MR. Eddie's father. Eddie was afraid of him.

LEGERE, MR. The mysterious man who visited the circus and stood and watched Green Terror, the tiger.

"LEOPARD MAN" Chips Baily's nickname for Indrasil.

LILLIE, MR. He owned a five-and-dime in Sauk City. Eddie worked for him...and was afraid of him.

McGREGOR, MIKE One of the circus roustabouts.

NIXON, KELLY One of the circus roustabouts.

O'HARA, SALLY The Farnum & Williams' circus's red-headed wire walker.

THE SANDMAN Eddie tossed and turned, chasing him during the heat wave.

SOLIENNI, ANDREA The circus's bareback rider. She fell off a horse, got kicked, and was knocked unconscious.

Places

CHICAGO, ILLINOIS One of the circus's stops.
DANVILLE, INDIANA One of the circus's stops.
FLORIDA The circus went there by train from Little Rock, Arkansas.
ILLINOIS AND INDIANA The circus swung through both states.
INDEPENDENCE, KANSAS One of the circus's stops.
LITTLE ROCK, ARKANSAS The town where the circus caught the train to Florida.
ST. LOUIS, MISSOURI One of the circus's stops.
STEUBENVILLE The circus stop where Eddie Johnston first saw Mr. Legere.
WILDWOOD GREEN, OKLAHOMA One of the circus's stops.

Things

THE CIRCUS'S STOPS The Farnum & Williams' Circus made the following stops:

    Steubenville, Ohio
    Danville, Indiana
    Chicago, Illinois
    St. Louis, Missouri
    Independence, Kansas
    Wildwood Green, Oklahoma...and then to
    Little Rock, Arkansas, where they caught the train to
    Florida.

"THE DEMON CAT CAGE" How Indrasil's cat show was billed.
FARNUM & WILLIAMS' ALL-AMERICAN 3-RING CIRCUS AND SIDE SHOW The circus Eddie joined, and which Mr. Legere followed from town to town.
THE FINAL BATTLE The final battle was between Indrasil, Green Terror, and Legere. Green Terror leaped at Indrasil and, later, two dead tigers were found. The "strange" tiger had a long scar at the back of his neck. The assumption is that Green Terror and Legere became one tiger; Indrasil transformed himself into a tiger, and then they fought to the death to settle some ancient battle between them.
GRISGRIS A person of magic. Legere was one, according to Indrasil.
THE HEAT WAVE As the circus moved through the midwest, they were hit by a heat wave that sent temperatures into the nineties every day.
INDRASIL'S SCAR Jason Indrasil had a long scar at the back of his neck.
JUJU A person of magic. Legere was one, according to Indrasil.
1958 According to Indrasil "[Legere] [t]urned the cat against me, back in '58. Always had the power more'n me."
"A POLICEMAN" How Legere described himself.
RAW MEAT Indrasil fed the cats raw meat during the heat wave.
REAR AXLE Chips had to check the rear axle of his U-Haul.
RINGLING BROTHERS CIRCUS Indrasil was with them before he joined Farnum & Williams.
SEVENTY-FIVE FEET In Independence, Kansas, Sally O'Hara fell seventy-five feet off the wire into the net, fracturing her shoulder.
U-HAUL Chips Baily hauled one.
"THE WRATH OF INDRASIL" Indrasil's anger. On one occasion, Legere saved Eddie from this wrath.

"Crouch End"

"All my stories...are based on the fundamental lore or legend that this world was inhabited at one time by another race who, in practising black magic, lost their foothold and were expelled, yet live on outside ever ready to take possession of this earth again."

        H.P. Lovecraft

"'Ever read Lovecraft?'
'Never heard of him.'
'Well, this fellow Lovecraft was always writing about Dimensions,' Vetter said, producing his box of railway matches. 'Dimensions close to ours. Full of these immortal monsters that would drive a man mad at one look. Frightful rubbish, what? Except, whenever one of these people straggles in, I think it all might just be true. I say to myself then – when it's quiet and late at night, like it is now – that our whole world, everything we think of as nice and normal and sane, is like a big leather ball filled with air. Only in some places, the leather's scuffed almost down to nothing. Places where...the barriers are thinner. Do you get me?'"

        From "Crouch End"
        by Stephen King

"Ph'nglui mglw'nafh Cthulhu R'lyeh wgah'nagl fhtagn."

        From "The Call of Cthulhu"
        by H.P. Lovecraft

"Crouch End" is Stephen King's *homage* to H.P. Lovecraft.

The genesis of the story involved an actual trip to London by Stephen and Tabitha King. The Kings went overseas to visit Peter Straub in London, and actually did get lost in the Crouch End section of the city...as did Doris and Lonnie Freeman in "Crouch End." The Freemans got lost, and found themselves in a strange, macabre area of London where the signboards announced weird, guttural names, and tentacles appeared from the darkness beneath the street.

It is indicative of Stephen King's prowess with fiction that a story intended as a nod to a horror master is elevated beyond pastiche into something completely self-contained, something perfect in and of itself.

David Hartwell, in his Introduction to "The Call of Cthulhu" in *The Dark Descent*, says that "Between Poe and King, the great American master of horror is H. P. Lovecraft." Think about that. There, in one sentence – and three writers – is the pantheon of American horror fiction: Edgar Allan Poe, H.P. Lovecraft, and Stephen King. Through his fiction, King has readily acknowledged the work and influence of Poe ("The Blue Air Compressor," "Dolan's Cadillac," and *The Dark Half* come immediately to mind); with "Crouch End," he pays tribute to the other arm of the triumvirate.

"Crouch End" was written for a collection of "Cthulhu Mythos" stories called *New Tales of the Cthulhu Mythos*, which was edited by Ramsey Campbell and appeared from Arkham House in 1980.

It was recently reprinted in the aforementioned Tor hardcover, *The Dark Descent*, edited by David Hartwell.
—sjs

"Crouch End"
People

"THE BLIND PIPER WHO IS NOT NAMED FOR A THOU-SAND YEARS" The ruler of the "thin part" of Crouch End.

THE CABBY The unnamed cab driver who picked up the Freemans. He was an elderly man in a grey suit.

THE EATER OF DIMENSIONS The ruler of the "thin part" of Crouch End.

EVVIE Woman of about sixty who Doris saw talking to a man of about the same age. Evvie gave Doris the fork sign of the evil eye because Doris had been to Crouch End Towen.

EVVIE'S FRIEND Man of about sixty who Doris saw talking to Evvie.

FARNHAM, PC ROBERT Cop; age twenty-seven. He worked in Crouch End Station with PC Vetter. He was lost in Crouch End Towen while looking for Lonnie Freeman. His wife divorced him on grounds of desertion, in order to marry Frank Hobbs. Hobbs worked where Sheila wanted him to: on the Ford assembly line.

FARNHAM, SHEILA Robert's wife. She wanted him off the force.

THE FARNHAM KIDS Two unnamed children of Robert Farnham. They survived him when he didn't return from Crouch End Towen after he went looking for Lonnie Freeman.

FREEMAN, DANNY Lonnie and Doris's son.

FREEMAN, DORIS American woman who lost her husband in Crouch End. She was twenty-six, and had two children.

FREEMAN, LEONARD "Lonnie" Freeman; a lawyer from Millwaukee. He got "lost" in Crouch End Towen. He actually was taken to "Him Who Waits."

FREEMAN, NORMA Lonnie and Doris's daughter.

GORDON, SERGEANT Crouch End officer; his hair went dead-white at the age of forty.

HACKETT Fellow who worked for the BBC; he took dangerous assignments.

"HIM WHO WAITS" The ruler of the weird part of Crouch End. Lonnie went to him.

HOBBS, FRANK Man who married Sheila Farnham after Robert was lost in Crouch End. To Sheila's delight, he worked on Ford assembly line. Because Farnham was never found, she had to divorce him on grounds of desertion.

KIDS AND FATHERS Unnamed people who sat at the entrance to Crouch End. To Lonnie, they "looked reassuringly normal."

LOVECRAFT, H.P. Farnham had never heard of him.

THE MONSTER IN CROUCH END It was black, and it sloshed. It attacked Lonnie Freeman.

A NURSE Unnamed nurse who went back to the hotel with Doris.

A ONE-EYED CAT Grey cat that sat on a ledge next to a restaurant call box (phone).

A PAKISTANI WOMAN Unnamed woman whose purse had been nicked on Hillfield Avenue.

PETTY Officer who commited suicide in the summer of 1976.

RAYMOND, SERGEANT SID He liked to break the fingers of pickpockets.

THE SITTER Unnamed baby sitter watching the Freeman kids.

A SMALL BOY Unnamed child who Doris saw sitting on a curb. He was striking matches.

SQUALES, JOHN Lonnie Freeman's lawyer colleague. The Freemans were on their way to see him.

A TEENAGE BOY AND GIRL Two unnamed kids who passed Doris after she came to. They were talking about a Francis Ford Coppola film.

THE THREE BOYS Doris saw three unnamed boys standing beside their motorcycles. For a moment, she thought that they had rat's heads.

TWO KIDS Two unnamed kids, a boy with a deformed hand, and a girl of about five. The boy made an obscene gesture at the Freemans with his claw-like hand.

VETTER, PC TED Cop, almost fifty-four, who had spent his whole career in Crouch End. After Lonnie Freeman was lost in Crouch End Towen, Vetter took an early retirement, moving into council housing in Frimley. Six months later, he was found dead of a heart attack, a can of Harp's Lager in his hand.

THE WHISTLER FROM THE STARS The two kids told Doris that she had found the Whistler from the Stars in the "thin part" of Crouch End.

Places

"ANOTHER PLANET" As Doris walked through the weird part of Crouch End, she felt like she was on another planet: "The angles seemed different...the colors seemed different."

ARCHWAY AND FINSBURY PARK The border of Crouch End.

BLACKPOOL The porcelain cup came from Blackpool.

BRASS END John Squales lived in Brass End.

CAMBRIDGE CIRCUS Foyle's bookshop was near Cambridge Circus.

CROUCH END A quiet six or eight blocks of London streets. It was a "thin place." [NOTE: See VETTER'S EXPLANATION.]

CROUCH END POLICE STATION Station on Tottenham Lane where Doris Freeman came after she lost her husband in Crouch End Towen.

CROUCH HILL ROAD The entrance to Crouch End.

THE FORD ASSEMBLY LINE Sheila Farnham wanted her husband Robert to work on the Ford assembly line instead of at Crouch End Police Station.

FOYLE'S BOOKSHOP A shop near Cambridge Circus.

FRIMLEY After his retirement, Vetter moved into council housing in Frimley.

HIGHGATE A place that was "mostly all right." [NOTE: See VETTER'S EXPLANATION.]

HILLFIELD AVENUE The avenue where a Pakistani woman's purse had been nicked. It was also one of the roads you took to get to John Squales' house in Brass End.

HOTEL INTER-CONTINENTAL London hotel where the Freemans were staying.

LONDON According to Doris, the city was "a great big sprawling warren of Roads and Mews and Hills and Closes (and even Inns)."

McDONALD'S One of the restaurants in London.

MUSWELL HILL One of the places that was all right. [NOTE: See VETTER'S EXPLANATION.]

MUSWELL HILL POLICE STATION The station to the north of Crouch End where Farnham came from.

NEWSAGENT'S DOORWAY The place where Doris kind of "came to" after Lonnie disappeared and the street opened up.

NORRIS ROAD There was also a Norris Road in Basingstok.

PETRIE STREET The second left off Petrie Street was Brass End.

SLAUGHTER TOWEN The "thin place" in Crouch End. Crouch End Towen. As explained by Sergeant Raymond, "towen" was druidic for a place of ritual sacrifice.

SUSSEX After Robert Farnham was lost in Crouch End, his wife Sheila moved back to Sussex.

TOTTENHAM LANE The Crouch End Police Station was located on Tottenham Lane.

AN UNDERPASS Lonnie and Doris had to go beneath an underpass. A hairy hand grabbed Doris, and pushed Lonnie aside.

VICKERS LANE One of the roads you took to get to John Squales' house in Brass End.

Things

"ALHAZRED" The sign on a warehouse in the "thin part" of Crouch End. Beneath the word were "a series of Arabian pot-hooks and dashes."

AUGUST 19, 1974 The night that Doris Freeman told her story.

THE BACK FILE The unsolved cases file. Lonnie and Farnham were together there.

COKE Farnham drank it.

CONCORDE Doris flew home – without Lonnie – on the Concorde.

THE CROUCH END POLICE STATION POSTERS The old one was "Have you room in your heart for an unwanted child?" and the new one was "Six Rules for Safe Night Cycling."

"CTHULU KRYON" A sign in the "thin part" of Crouch End.

DAWGLISH & SONS A sign on a deserted warehouse in the "thin part" of Crouch End.

"DIMENSIONS" Vetter wondered about science fiction "dimensions."

DIRECTIONS TO JOHN SQUALE'S HOUSE Crouch Hill Road to Hillfield Avenue, left onto Vickers Lane, left onto Petrie Street, to Brass End.

DORIS'S SUICIDE ATTEMPT A month after returning home from London without Lonnie, Doris attempted suicide. She then spent a year in a rest home.

FAG A cigarette.

FORK SIGN The sign of the evil eye. Evvie gave it to Doris because Doris had been to Crouch End Towen.

A FRANCIS FORD COPPOLA FILM The two unnamed kids who passed Doris after she came to were talking about a Francis Ford Coppola film.

THE FREEMANS' VACATION Two weeks in London, and one week in Spain.

"FUCK YOU, JOE!" What the unnamed five-year-old girl yelled at the Freemans.

A HAIRY HAND A hairy hand grabbed Doris, and pushed Lonnie ahead.

HARP LAGER PC Vetter's beer. He drank six cans a night.

"JESUS CHRIST SUPERSTAR" It had been playing at Cambridge Circus for eight years.

THE LONDON STREETFINDER All the cabbies kept it beneath their dash.

A MAN-SHAPED HOLE IN THE LAWN Moaning came out of it, and then a black, sloshing monster.

THE NATIONAL HEALTH Doris thought the National Health took care of kids like the one with the claw hand.

"NRTESN NYARLAHOTEP" A sign in the "thin part" of Crouch End. Doris particularly remembered this one.

PALMISTRY, PHRENOLOGY, AND THE ROSICRUCIANS After hearing Vetter's talk about "dimensions," Farnham figured he probably believed in these, too.

PORCELAIN CUP A cup in the Crouch End station. It was from Blackpool.

"R'YELEH" A sign in the "thin part" of Crouch End.

SILK CUT CIGARETTES Farnham smoked them.

"SIXTY LOST IN UNDERGROUND HORROR" A sign in a newsagent's window. [NOTE: "Underground" means tube or subway.]

"STRANGE THINGS" As the story ends, we are told "And in Crouch End, which is really a quiet suburb of London, strange things still happen. From time to time."

THE SUMMER OF '76 According to PC Vetter, "It was quite bad that summer. Quite bad. There were a lot of us who were afraid they might break through."

TENTACLES When Doris was searching for Lonnie in Crouch End, the street opened up and tentacles came out.

TWO POUNDS FIVE The amount on the meter when the cab abandoned the Freemans.

VETTER'S EXPLANATION "…[O]ur whole world is like a big leather ball filled with air. Only in some places, the leather's scuffed almost down to nothing. Places where…the barriers are thinner."

VETTER'S NIGHTLY DRINKS He drank six cans of Harp lager a night.

YAMAHA BIKE It stood on Norris Road.

"YOGSOGGOTH" A sign in the "thin part" of Crouch End.

"Before The Play"

"Before the Play" is the Prologue to *The Shining*.

It consists of five parts, and its only other appearance was in a limited edition of Stuart Schiff's *Whispers* magazine in August 1982. (That issue also contained one of the three appearances of King's short story, "It Grows on You." The other two appearances of that story were in the literary magazine *Marshroots* in the fall of 1973, and in the anthology *Death*, published by Playboy Press in 1982.)

For the publication in the August 1982 issue of *Whispers*, Stephen King also supplied an essay called "On The Shining and Other Perpetrations," in which he detailed some of the background of "Before the Play." The following excerpts from "On The Shining" are the most relevant passages:

> "The book proper ended with Danny, his mother, and Hallorann, the cook, riding away from the burning Overlook on a snowmobile. It seemed a dubious ending at best; there were too many loose ends to suit me. So I added an epilogue, most of which has now been lost, titled, "After the Play." At this point I became unhappy (there's no pleasing writers, ever; one psychiatrist has even gone so far as to suggest that, in the author's mind, the book is a failure as soon as the first paragraph has been written, because the actuality of words on paper can never live up to the dream of the book which the writer has held in his or her head for weeks, months, or years) again, because the book's form seemed unbalanced. I decided I needed a prologue to balance off the rather lengthy epilogue. Accordingly, I wrote "Before the Play," which was a sketchy history of the Overlook's construction, and a number of terrible events that had occurred there before the events I really wanted to relate.
>
> I liked the prologue so well that I could feel it wanting to become a book in itself; enough energy was left from the novel I had just written to make me feel as if I had just landed a powerful jet which still had enough fuel to take off again and do a few loops, power-turns, and barrel rolls. The feeling of my editor at Doubleday was that both the prologue and most of the epilogue could be cut, with the result that we could offer the book for sale at a dollar less than if we included them (they would have brought the page total of *The Shining* to over five hundred). I agreed willingly enough, and although I don't regret the decision, I'm pleased that Stuart Schiff has elected to publish the prologue here (for the curious, the only part of the epilogue which remains in the book is the final chapter, set in Maine during the summer after the events at the Overlook). I hope you like it too, Gentle Reader."

Concordance entries below are keyed to the sections of "Before the Play" identified in the following list:

Legend

(1) = Scene I: "The Third Floor of a Resort Hotel Fallen Upon Hard Times"

(2) = Scene II: "A Bedroom in the Wee Hours of the Morning"

(3) = Scene III: "On the Night of the Grand Masquerade"

(4) = Scene IV: "And Now this Word from New Hampshire"

(5) = Scene V: "The Overlook, Third Floor, 1958"

The text of "Before the Play" was originally scheduled to be reprinted in this volume; unfortunately, it was simply not possible to include it. A few of the drawings commissioned to accompany it appear hereafter. — **sjs**

(U14)
"Before the Play"
People

ABRUZZI, WALT (5) The New York mobster who loaned two guards to the hood who was holed up in the Presidential Suite of the Overlook.

THE ALBUQUERQUE NEWSPAPER PUBLISHER (1) To stave off the bankruptcy of the Overlook, Bob T. had threatened this publisher (who had a penchant for little girls) with exposure if he didn't pay off an old debt to the Overlook.

ANASTASIO, ALBERT (5) A hood who was dead and in hell. One of the hit men told the hood in the Presidential Suite to say hello to him.

ARKINBAUER, MR. (1) The meat-packing king. While at the Overlook, his wife slipped while getting out of her bath, fell, and broke her wrist.

ARKINBAUER, MRS. (1) The wife of the meat-packing king, Arkinbauer. While at the Overlook, she slipped getting out of her bath, fell, and broke her wrist.

THE BELL-CAPTAIN (1) One of the Overlook's employees after Parris bought the hotel and Bob T. was reduced to being a maintenance man.

BRANDYWINE, CECIL (1) When the Overlook reopened in May of 1923, it was under the ownership of Clyde and Cecil Brandywine, two good old boys from Texas who had bought the hotel from James Parris.

BRANDYWINE, CLYDE (1) When the Overlook reopened in May of 1923, it was under the ownership of Clyde and Cecil Brandywine, two good old boys from Texas who had bought the hotel from James Parris.

BURREY (3) An executive in the Aircrafts Division of Derwent Enterprises. Burrey told Toner that Derwent had bought the Overlook.

THE CHIEF OF POLICE (3) The official who inquired about fingerprints at the scene of Lewis Toner's death.

THE CHIEF OF POLICE'S SISTER (3) She had cleaned Lewis Toner's room in the Overlook before the Grand Masquerade.

THE COMPSONS (2) The Pillsburys' bridge partners.

THE CORONER (3) The official who questioned Horace Derwent about Lewis Toner's death.

DERWENT, HORACE (3) The owner of the Overlook in the thirties. He "kept" Lewis Toner as a lover. Derwent went to the Grand Masquerade dressed as a circus ringmaster.

DERWENT, MRS. (3) Horace Derwent's mother. She died from cancer when she was forty-six years old.

DERWENT'S FOUR GRANDPARENTS (3) They all died from cancer.

A DISHONEST ACCOUNTANT (1) The unnamed accountant in the timbering end of Watson's business who did half a million dollars damage to the organization before being sent to prison for twenty years.

DURKER, HARRY (1) James Parris's groundskeeper.

THE ELEVATOR OPERATOR (2) Lottie Kilgallon Pillsbury had a dream that an elevator operator took her to hell. The elevator operator was a corpse.

GEROUX (1) The Overlook's head cook in 1914.

GIORGIO, TONY (5) A West Coast hood.

THE GOVERNOR (1) Bob T. Watson had "bought" the governor while deciding to build the Overlook.

THE GREY OLD MEN (5) The New York hoods.

GRONDIN (1) The contractor who Bob Watson hired to pave twenty miles from Estes Park to Sidewinder

HANNEMAN (3) A board member for Derwent Enterprises. When Hanneman had a heart attack, Toner was up for his position. He didn't get the job.

HART (3) Horace Derwent's social secretary. He was British, and ten years younger than Toner. He went to the Grand Masquerade dressed as the devil.

THE HEAD HOUSEKEEPER (1) The Overlook's chief of housekeeping.

THE HEAD HOUSEKEEPER'S SISTER (1) She sent out a gossip paper regarding James Parris's divorce.

THE HOOD IN THE PRESIDENTIAL SUITE (5) An unnamed mobster who was blown away by the three hit men. He was thirty-five years old.

KILGALLON, LOTTIE (2) In August of 1929, she was on her honeymoon at the Overlook. She was a very strong, manipulative woman who one night felt a hand grab her wrist from beneath her bed. In 1949, in a Yonkers Holiday Inn, she commited suicide. She left a note that said, "I wish we had gone to Rome."

A MAN (1) To stave off the Overlook's bankruptcy, Bob T. had actually gotten on his knees and begged an unnamed man for money. The man was so revolted that he gave Bob a check for $10,000.

MR. WATSON'S KILLER (1) Bob T. Watson's father was gunned down in Denver by a man suspected of "organizing."

NORMAN (3) A bright young subaltern for Derwent Enterprises. Toner caught him and Patty-Sherry-Merry in a heated clinch in a second floor hallway of the Overlook. Patty-Sherry-Merry was naked from the waist down.

AN OLD WIDOW (1) To stave off bankruptcy, Bob T. had browbeaten an old widow who owed a past-due debt to the hotel.

106 GUESTS (1) The Overlook only had 106 guests for its entire 1911 season.

PARRIS, JAMES (1) One of the Overlook's owners. He owned the hotel until 1915, when he sold it to Clyde and Cecil Brandywine from Texas. Parris's wife left him in 1920, and he later died of a heart attack.

PARRIS, MRS. (1) James Parris's wife. She left him in 1920.

PARRIS'S ACCOUNTANT (1) The unnamed man who worked for Parris after he bought the Overlook.

PARRIS'S MANAGER (1) He was offered a job by the Brandywine brothers when Parris sold the Overlook, but he turned it down.

PATTY-SHERRY-MERRY (3) A secretary for Derwent Enterprises who Toner came upon in the second floor hall of the Overlook. She was in an embrace with Norman, a young subaltern. Patty-Sherry-Merry was naked from the waist down.

THE PERSON WITH THE PALLID FACE (5) After the hood in the Presidential Suite was blown away, a pallid face peeked out of a room, and then slammed the door shut.

PILLSBURY, HAROLD M. (2) William Pillsbury's father; Lottie Kilgallon's father-in-law.

PILLSBURY, WILLIAM (2) Lottie Kilgallon's husband. He was of the Westchester Pillsburys. His family was in publishing; they owned a chain of textile mills, a foundry in Ohio, and extensive agricultural holdings in the South.

RASCAL (1) Boyd Watson's pony.

A REPRESENTATIVE TO THE U.S. CONGRESS (1) Bob T. Watson had bought the representative while deciding to build the Overlook. The representative choked to death on opening day after cutting the opening ribbon. It was as though Poe's "Masque

Under Lottie's Bed

Original drawings by Katherine Flickinger.

Lottie's Elevator Dream

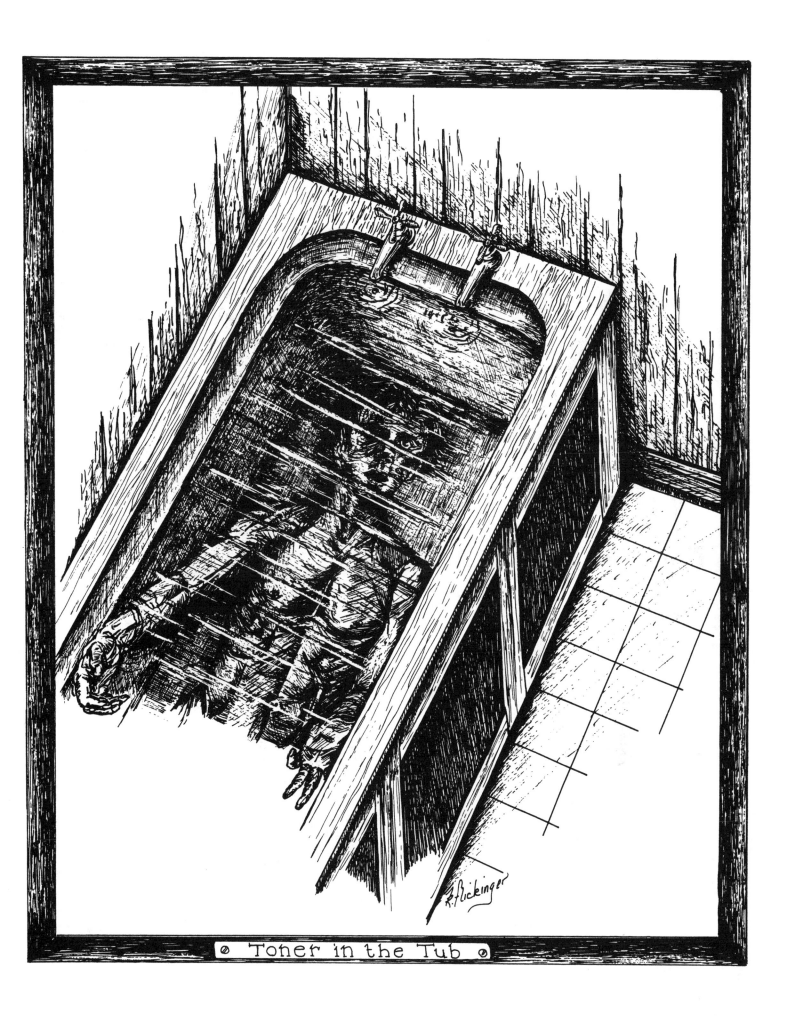

Toner in the Tub

Lottie Kilgallon
Original drawing by Katherine Flickinger.

of the Red Death" had come to life.

RONNIE (3) The San Diego Dago. Lewis Toner's first lover.

RUTHERFORD (1) The Overlook's head accountant for the years 1912 through 1914. He broke the news to Bob T. of the Overlook's dire financial situation.

THE SAN DIEGO DAGO (3) Ronnie. Lewis Toner's first lover.

SARAH WATSON'S MOTHER (1) Boyd Watson was buried next to her.

THE SON OF A GUEST (1) The unnamed man who did an emergency tracheotomy on the choking congressman.

SPECIALLY TRAINED DOMESTICS (1) The Overlook's staff consisted of specially trained maids and servants who were capable of tending to the needs of the hotel's elite clientele.

THE STATE POLICE OFFICER (3) He dusted for fingerprints in Toner's room after Toner's death.

STEEVES, BILL (1) Banker. While considering the Overlook's financial situation, Watson felt that Steeves would give him a third mortgage.

TESSIE (2) A bay mare that Bill Pillsbury rode on the Overlook's grounds.

THE THREE GUNMEN (5) They snuck up to the Presidential Suite on stocking feet to gun down a hood who was hiding out in the Overlook.

"THE TOAST OF BROADWAY" (3) The woman who Horace Derwent kept in a Fifth Avenue penthouse.

TONER, LEWIS (3) Horace Derwent's scorned homosexual lover. Toner attended the Grand Masquerade dressed as a dog, and then commited suicide in his hotel room's bathtub. He used pills that were conveniently placed in his medicine cabinet by the spirits that ruled the hotel. It was discovered during the autopsy that there were no drugs in his body.

TORRANCE, JACKY (4) In "Before the Play," this was the youngest son of Mr. Torrance. In *The Shining,* this character was, of course, Jack Torrance.

TORRANCE, MR. (4) Jacky Torrance's father. He broke his son's arm in the summer of 1953.

TORRANCE, MRS. (4) Jacky Torrance's mother. She was scared to death of her husband.

THE TORRANCE CHILDREN (4) Jacky's siblings. They were scared to death of their father.

THE TWO FRENCH CHEFS (1) The Overlook's kitchen staff. One of the chefs scalded his arm on opening day.

THE TWO GUARDS (5) The two men armed with .357 Magnums who were on loan from Walt Abruzzi in New York City to guard the hood in the Presidential Suite of the Overlook.

THE TWO NEW CHEFS (1) Bob hired two new chefs for the Overlook's 1911 season. The original two would not return.

THE TWO UPSTAIRS MAIDS (1) They had heard Parris's wife begging to leave.

VERECKER, DR. (2) A retired surgeon in his early seventies who played bridge with the Pillsburys at the Overlook.

VERECKER, MALVINA (2) Dr. Verecker's wife. She played bridge with the Pillsburys at the Overlook.

WATSON, BOB T. (1) Bob T. Watson owned the Overlook Hotel until 1915, when he sold it to James Parris.

WATSON, BOYD (1) Bob T.'s son. He broke his neck in a riding accident while jumping his pony, and was buried in Denver.

WATSON, RICHARD (1) Bob T.'s younger son.

WATSON, SARAH (1) Bob Watson's wife. She hated the Overlook.

THE WESTCHESTER PILLSBURYS (2) William Pillsbury's family.

THE WIFE OF A GUEST (1) A woman who fainted after she saw something in the lobby of the Overlook. She said "It didn't look like a man."

WILSON, WOODROW (1) President Wilson had slept in the Overlook's Presidential Suite in 1922.

Bob T. Watson
Original drawing by Katherine Flickinger.

Places

THE AMERICAN HOTEL (2) The hotel in Rome where William Pillsbury had wanted to spend his honeymoon.

THE BERLIN COMMUNITY HOSPITAL (4) The hospital where Jacky Torrance's father worked as an orderly.

A BUNGALOW IN HOLLYWOOD (3) While he was Derwent's lover, Toner had an apartment on the east side of New York, as well as a bungalow in Hollywood.

DENVER, COLORADO (1) Bob T. Watson's father was gunned down in Denver by a man suspected of "organizing." Also, Boyd Watson was buried in Denver after he was killed in a riding accident.

THE EAST SIDE OF NEW YORK CITY (3) While he was Derwent's lover, Toner had an apartment on the east side of New York, as well as a bungalow in Hollywood.

A FIFTH AVENUE PENTHOUSE (3) Horace Derwent kept a woman ("the toast of Broadway") in a Fifth Avenue penthouse.

THE FIRST MERCANTILE BANK OF DENVER (1) Bill Steeves was president of the First Mercantile.

FORTY MILES WEST OF SIDEWINDER, COLORADO (1) The construction site of the Overlook Hotel.

A FOUNDRY IN OHIO (2) One of the Pillsbury's business interests.

HAGGLE NOTCH (1) In 1914, Bob T. Watson had a mining interest in Haggle Notch that closed out.

THE HOUSE OF A THOUSAND THRILLS (3) On Lewis Toner's and Ronnie's first date, they went to the House of a Thousand Thrills.

THE LOBBY (1) The lobby of the Overlook was as wide as three Pullman cars.

THE LONGHORN HOUSE (1) After Parris bought the Overlook, he added a limo from the Longhorn House to the Overlook.

NEW ENGLAND TEXTILE MILLS (2) One of the Pillsbury's business interests.

PLACER, COLORADO (1) Bob T. Watson's family made their fortune in silver from 1870 through 1905 around Placer, Colorado.

THE PRESIDENTIAL SUITE (1) A room in the Overlook that looked out at the Rockies.

ROME (2) William Pillsbury had wanted to go to the American Hotel in Rome for his and Lottie's honeymoon.

A SKI-LODGE IN ASPEN (3) The Sidewinder police chief bought a ski-lodge in Aspen, thanks to the generosity of Horace Derwent (and to keeping his own mouth shut about Lewis Toner's death.)

THE SOUTH (2) The Pillsburys had extensive agricultural (cotton, citrus and fruit) holdings in the South.

ST. PETERSBURG, FLORIDA (3) The Sidewinder coroner retired there, thanks to the generosity of Horace Derwent (and to keeping his own mouth shut about Lewis Toner's death).

TEXAS (1) The home state of Clyde and Cecil Brandywine.

THE TREEHOUSE (4) Jacky escaped up into the treehouse in his yard when his father chased him. His father eventually pulled him out of the treehouse, and broke the boy's arm.

A YONKERS HOLIDAY INN (2) In 1949, Lottie Kilgallon commited suicide in a Yonkers Holiday Inn.

Things

AMERICAN MERCURY (2) One of the magazines in which the Overlook advertised.

AUGUST 1929 (2) The month and year that Lottie and William Pillsbury honeymooned at the Overlook.

THE AUTOMATIC SERVICE COMPANY OF AMERICA (3) The parent company of The Automatic Service Company of Colorado. The Automatic Service Company of America was owned by Derwent Enterprises.

THE AUTOMATIC SERVICE COMPANY OF COLORADO (3)

Jacky's Treehouse
Original drawing by Katherine Flickinger.

The company that donated a library to Sidewinder to hush up Toner's death at the Overlook. (The Automatic Service Company of Colorado was owned by the Automatic Service Company of America, which was owned by Derwent Enterprises.)

BLACK SNOW (1) Snow in August. The black snow contributed to the Overlook's first season being a failure.

THE BOILER (2) A thought kept running through Lottie Kilgallon's head: You had to keep an eye on the Overlook's boiler...or else she'd creep on you.

BRIDGE (2) Lottie Kilgallon Pillsbury was a barracuda at bridge.

A BUILDING MAINTENANCE BILL (1) In September of 1914, the Overlook owed an outstanding building maintenance bill. This bill was one of the outstanding debts that prompted Rutherford to suggest to Bob T. that he file for bankruptcy.

A "COMBAT CASEY" COMICBOOK (4) The comic book Jacky Torrance was reading the day his father came home drunk and broke his arm.

DENVER ELECTRICAL OUTFITTERS, INC. (1) In September of 1914, the Overlook owed Denver Electrical $18,000. This bill was one of the outstanding debts that prompted Rutherford to suggest to Bob T. that he file for bankruptcy.

THE *DENVER POST* (1) They took "'Tis a privilege to live in Colorado" as their motto.

THE DEPRESSION OF 1893-1894 (1) The Watson family lost most of their silver-generated fortune in the depression of '93-'94.

DERWENT ENTERPRISES (3) Horace Derwent's company.

"DERWENT'S FOLLY" (3) The name that people gave to the movie studio Derwent bought on the depression market.

1880 (1) The year that James Parris began his professional life. He began it as a common shyster.

1895-1905 (1) The years in which Bob T. rebuilt the fortune that his family had lost in the depression of 1893-1894.

1870-1905 (1) These were the years that Bob Watson's family made their fortune in silver around Placer, Colorado.

$18,000 (1) In September of 1914, the Overlook owed Denver Electrical Outfitters $18,000. This bill was one of the outstanding debts that prompted Rutherford to suggest to Bob T. that he file for bankruptcy.

$80,000 IN THE RED (1) The Overlook was $80,000 in the red in its 1912 season.

THE ELEVATOR (1) An elevator was installed in the Overlook in 1917.

$50,000 IN LOSSES (1) The Overlook had $50,000 in losses in its 1913 season.

THE FIRE HOSE (2) Lottie Kilgallon had a dream that one of the Overlook's fire hoses came alive and attacked her.

FORTY-FIVE (1) Bob T. Watson's age in 1909, the year that construction of the Overlook Hotel was completed. The Overlook had made him old: he was now bald, and had an ulcer.

FORTY-THREE (1) Bob T. Watson's age in 1907, the year that construction on the Overlook began.

THE GRAND MASQUERADE (3) The masked ball put on by Horace Derwent at the Overlook.

A HAND (2) One night in August of 1929, Lottie Kilgallon reached down to pick up her cigarettes from the floor next to her honeymoon bed in the Overlook Hotel. As she reached for the pack, a hand reached out from beneath the bed and grabbed her wrist.

THE HEALTH ROOM (1) In September of 1914, the Overlook owed an outstanding contractor's bill for the addition of a health room. This bill was one of the outstanding debts that prompted Rutherford to suggest to Bob T. that he file for bankruptcy.

THE HOOD'S GENITALS (5) After the three gunmen blew away the hood in the Presidential Suite, they cut off his testicles.

KEYSTONE PAVING WORKS OF GOLDEN (1) In September of 1914, the Overlook owed Keystone $70,000. This bill was one of the outstanding debts that prompted Rutherford to suggest to Bob T. that he file for bankruptcy.

A LANDSCAPING BILL (1) In September of 1914, the Overlook

owed an outstanding landscaping bill. This bill was one of the outstanding debts that prompted Rutherford to suggest to Bob T. that he file for bankruptcy.

A LIMO (1) After Parris bought the Overlook, he added a limo from the Longhorn House to the Overlook.

LOTTIE'S NOTE (2) In 1949, Lottie Kilgallon Pillsbury commited suicide in a Yonkers Holiday Inn. She left a note that said, "I wish we had gone to Rome."

LOTTIE'S OVERLOOK INSIGHT (2) "It does creep, the whole place – like it was alive!"

MAY 1923 (1) When the Overlook reopened in May of 1923, it was under the ownership of Clyde and Cecil Brandywine, two good old boys from Texas who had bought the hotel from James Parris.

THE MECHANICAL CLOWN (3) The mechanical clown at the House of A Thousand Thrills had laughed at Lewis Toner in the same way Norman and Patty-Sherry-Merry had when they saw him in his dog costume.

THE *NEW YORKER* (2) One of the magazines in which the Overlook advertised.

THE 1911 SEASON (1) The Overlook only had 106 guests for its entire 1911 season.

1909 (1) The year that construction of the Overlook was completed.

1907 (1) The year construction on the Overlook Hotel began, forty miles west of Sidewinder, Colorado.

1917 (1) The year that the elevator was installed in the Overlook.

THE 1913 SEASON (1) The Overlook had $50,000 in losses in its 1913 season.

1910 (1) The year the doors of the Overlook opened.

1936 (3) The year Lewis Toner joined Derwent Enterprises as a bookkeeper.

1939 (3) Lewis Toner had been Horace Derwent's lover since 1939.

THE 1912 SEASON (1) The Overlook was $80,000 in the red in the 1912 season.

1920 (1) The year that Parris's wife left him.

1922 (1) The year that President Woodrow Wilson slept in the Overlook's Presidential Suite.

OCTOBER 7TH, 1922 (1) Closing day at the Overlook Hotel. This was the last day of operation under the ownership of James Parris.

$180,000 (1) The price that James Parris paid for the Overlook.

110 ROOMS (1) The number of rooms in the Overlook Hotel.

135 POUNDS (3) Lewis Toner's weight.

THE OVERLOOK FESTIVAL (1) The closing three nights of the Overlook's season.

"THE OVERLOOK WAS AT HOME WITH THE DEAD" (5) The last line of "Before the Play."

THE OVERLOOK'S ATTRACTIONS (1) The hotel's amenities included a playground, a croquet course, a putting green, tennis courts, shuffleboard courts, a dining room, and a swimming pool that was added later. (These attractions were in addition, of course, to the view of the Rockies, and the hedge topiary.)

THE OVERLOOK'S BILLS (1) The following bills were what prompted Rutherford to suggest bankruptcy for the Overlook to Bob T.:

> Keystone Paving works of Golden—$70,000;
> Denver Electrical Outfitters, Inc.—$18,000;
> a building maintenance bill;
> a landscaping bill;
> the bill for a second well;
> the contractors' bills for the health room;
> the contractors' bills for the two greenhouses;
> outstanding salaries.

THE OVERLOOK'S DECOR (1) The hotel had a grand staircase, neo-Victorian furniture, and a crystal chandelier.

THE OVERLOOK'S FIRST SEASON (1) It was a failure. They had a black snow (snow in August), and the season ended with the hotel in the red.

THE PILLSBURY BUSINESS INTERESTS (2) The Pillsburys were into publishing, they owned a chain of New England textile mills, a foundry in Ohio, and had cotton, citrus, and fruit holdings in the South.

SALARIES OUTSTANDING (1) In September of 1914, the Overlook owed its employees "salaries outstanding." The amount due was one of the outstanding debts that prompted Rutherford to suggest to Bob T. that he file for bankruptcy.

SECONALS (3) During the Grand Masquerade, Toner found a bottle of Seconals in the medicine cabinet of his room in the Overlook. He used them to overdose on.

THE SECOND WELL (1) In September of 1914, the Overlook owed an outstanding bill for a second well. This bill was one of the outstanding debts that prompted Rutherford to suggest to Bob T. that he file for bankruptcy.

SEPTEMBER 1914 (1) By September of 1914, the Overlook was $200,000 in debt. Rutherford recommended bankruptcy to Bob T.

$70,000 (1) In September of 1914, the Overlook owed Keystone Paving Works of Golden $70,000. This bill was one of the outstanding debts that prompted Rutherford to suggest to Bob T. that he file for bankruptcy. Also, the amount that Grondin charged Bob Watson to pave twenty miles from Estes park to Sidewinder. He used substandard materials.

"SOMETHING IN THE LOBBY" (1) The wife of a guest fainted after she claimed she saw something in the lobby of the Overlook that she said did not look like a man.

SUBSTANDARD MATERIALS (1) Grondin the contractor charged Bob Watson $70,000 to pave twenty miles from Estes Park to Sidewinder. He used substandard materials for the job.

SUMMER 1953 (4) This was when Mr. Torrance broke his son Jacky Torrance's arm.

$10,000 (1) To stave off the Overlook's bankruptcy, Bob T. had actually gotten on his knees and begged an unnamed man for money. The man was so revolted that he gave Bob a check for $10,000.

THREE MILLION DOLLARS A YEAR (3) Horace Derwent figured he could make $3 million a year if the country went to war.

A TOPIARY OF HEDGE ANIMALS (1, 2) One of the chief attractions on the grounds of the Overlook Hotel. It was comprised of "lions, buffalo, a rabbit, a cow." Lottie Kilgallon had a dream that the topiary was alive and moving menacingly towards her.

THE TORRANCES' CAR (4) Mr. Torrance had wrecked it when drunk.

$20,000 IN THE RED (1) While reviewing the Overlook's financial situation, Rutherford determined that the 1914 season would end $20,000 in the red.

TWO GREENHOUSES (1) In September of 1914, the Overlook owed an outstanding contractor's bill for the addition of two greenhouses. This bill was one of the outstanding debts that prompted Rutherford to suggest to Bob T. that he file for bankruptcy.

259 POUNDS (3) Horace Derwent's weight.

$200,000 (1) The Overlook was $200,000 in debt in September of 1914.

WATSON'S MINING INTEREST (1) In 1914, Bob T. had a mining interest in Haggle Notch that closed out unsuccessfully.

"WHAT YOU SEE IS WHAT YOU'LL BE" (4) Jacky Torrance's last thought before he blacked out after his father broke his arm.

WINTER 1910 (1) The season that Sarah Watson died.

THE PLANT

"What's happening with *The Plant*? *The Plant*'s a little book that I gave up – 'gave up'...that's a Freudian slip – it's a little book that I gave out to friends as a Christmas card, and what happened was, I went to see "The Little Shop of Horrors" between the second and third installment and realized that's what I was writing and decided I better stop right away. So that's what I did."

Stephen King at a lecture given on April 26, 1989
at the Pasadena Library, in Pasadena, California

The Plant has withered and died.

As you read in the lecture excerpt above, Stephen King has abandoned *The Plant*. Now, to most fans, that development really won't mean too much, since probably 99.4% of King's readers have never even heard of this work, let alone read it. (Actually it's probably much higher than that, but I couldn't resist using the Captain Trips stat from *The Stand*!) But, for those of us who have seen the three installments, we grieve for a Stephen King story lost.

Originally, *The Plant* was intended to be a yearly event. King was always bothered by the notion of pre-printed Christmas cards. He felt they were too impersonal. So, he decided to do something a little bit more special. He came up with the idea of an epistolary novel-in-progress called *The Plant*. He planned on writing one chapter a year, publishing and printing them himself through his own company, Philtrum Press, and using the installments as an opportunity to greet friends at Christmas and, at the same time, tell a new story, which, as we all know, is what Signore King lives for.

Three chapters of *The Plant* were published: The first installment (which I have designated "U15" for purposes of this book) appeared in 1982. There were two hundred signed, numbered copies.

The second installment ("U17") appeared in 1983, and consisted of twenty-six signed, lettered copies, and two hundred signed, numbered copies.

The third, and apparently final, installment ("U21") appeared in 1985. Again, there were twenty-six signed, lettered copies, and two hundred signed, numbered copies.

Chapter One is currently (late 1989-early 1990) selling for $1,500-$2,000.

Chapters Two and Three are currently selling for $2,000-$3,000 for the lettered, and $1,500-$2,000 for the numbered.

The Plant is unique among King's work. It is, as mentioned, an epistolary work: It is told entirely in the form of letters, interoffice memos, journal entries, etc. (See the listing of *The Plant*'s correspondence immediately prior to the "People" section.)

John Kenton, a beleaguered editor at failing Zenith House publishers, receives a query letter from a "writer" named Carlos Detweiller. Carlos has written a book called *True Tales of Demon Infestations*, and wishes to have it published by Zenith House (since they did such a good job with *Bloody Houses*, he tells them.) Kenton decides on a whim to look at a proposal, but instead Carlos sends him the entire manuscript, which includes photos of what appears to be an actual human sacrifice. Kenton calls the police, Carlos is brought in for questioning, and when the photos turn out to be fakes, he is released, but vowing revenge on Kenton. Kenton begins to receive letters from a "Roberta Solrac" ("Carlos" spelled backwards), and one day a mysterious plant appears in the mail for Kenton.

Details on whatever plot developments took place in Chapters One through Three can be found in the following "People," "Places," and "Things" concordance. Entries are again keyed to the sections in which they appear using the following designations:

Legend

(U15 = Part One;
U17 = Part Two; U21 = Part Three)

My special thanks must go out to George Beahm and Barry Levin for their outstanding work on compiling an authoritative price guide to King's published books for George's excellent *The Stephen King Companion* . (Interestingly, George Beahm feels that " *The Plant* very likely will see print as a separate book, as part of a collection, or as a small-press book (a limited edition book or, perhaps, a chapbook).") I hope he's right. *The Plant* is a lot of fun, and it would be terrific if more Stephen King fans could get a chance to read it. — **sjs**

THE PLANT
An Epistolary Work-in-Progress
*A listing of all the correspondence
comprising the collection*

Part One

1. *LETTER*
   To: Zenith House Publishers
   From: Carlos Detweiller
   Date: January 4, 1981
2. *INTEROFFICE MEMO*
   To: Roger
   From: John
   Re: Submissions/January 11-15, 1981
3. *MEMO FROM THE OFFICE OF THE EDITOR-IN-CHIEF*
   To: John Kenton
   From: Roger
   Date: January 15, 1981
4. *LETTER*
   To: Carlos Detweiller
   From: John Kenton
   Date: January 16, 1981
5. *INTEROFFICE MEMO*
   To: Roger
   From: John
   Re: Upon further study
6. *LETTER*
   To: John Kenton
   From: Carlos Detweiller
   Date: January 21, 1981
7. *INTEROFFICE MEMO*
   To: Roger
   From: John
8. *MEMO FROM THE OFFICE OF THE EDITOR-IN-CHIEF*
   To: John
   Date: January 23, 1981

9. *LETTER*
   To: Ruth
   From: John
   Date: January 25, 1981
10. *INTEROFFICE MEMO*
    To: Roger
    From: John
    Re: *True Tales of Demon Infestations,* by Carlos Detweiller
11. *LETTER*
    To: Ruth
    From: John
    Date: January 30, 1981

Part Two

11. *LETTER* (Same Letter from Part One, Continued)
    To: Ruth
    From: John
    Date: January 30, 1981
12. *MEMO FROM THE OFFICE OF THE EDITOR-IN-CHIEF*
    To: John Kenton
    From: Roger
    Date: February 2, 1981
13. *INTEROFFICE MEMO*
    To: Roger
    From: John
    Re: Tree-shaking
14. *MEMO FROM THE OFFICE OF THE EDITOR-IN-CHIEF*
    To: John Kenton
    From: Roger
    Date: February 3, 1981
15. *LETTER*
    To: John "Judas Priest" Kenton
    From: Carlos Detweiller
    Date: February 4, 1981
16. *LETTER*
    To: Ruth
    From: John
    Date: February 7, 1981
17. *LETTER*
    To: John Kenton
    From: Roberta Solrac
    Date: February 19, 1981
18. *INTEROFFICE MEMO*
    To: Roger
    From: John
    Re: Ongoing Sanity
19. *MEMO FROM THE OFFICE OF THE EDITOR-IN - CHIEF*
    To: John Kenton
    From: Roger
    Date: February 23, 1981
20. *INTEROFFICE MEMO*
    To: Roger
    From: John
    Re: Roberta Solrac
21. *MEMO FROM THE OFFICE OF THE EDITOR-IN-CHIEF*
    To: John Kenton
    From: Roger
    Date: February 23, 1981
22. *INTEROFFICE MEMO*
    To: Riddley
    From: John Kenton
    Re: Possible incoming package

(U15, U17, U21)

THE PLANT
People

ABELSON, NORMAN (U21) The twenty-six-year-old Oak Cove Asylum orderly killed by Major "Iron Gut" Hecksler.

ALBANY BUS DRIVER (U15) The unnamed driver stabbed by Major Hecksler.

ANDERSON, TOBY (U21) Ruth Tanaka left John Kenton to be with Toby. She met Anderson in one of her two English Restoration drama classes. Toby gave her a diamond, and Ruth told John that she and Toby would be married in June of 1981.

BARFIELD, TINA (U15) Carlos Detweiller's boss. She owned the Central Falls House of Flowers.

BARKER, OLIVE (U15) Zenith House author. She wrote the Windhover series.

A BUM (U21) The body found in the Shady Grove Crematorium that was presumed to be Hecksler's. It was actually the body of an unnamed bum.

A CAB DRIVER (U21) An unnamed Nigerian or Somalian who drove a Plymouth. Roger Wade puked out of his cab.

CARLYLE (U17) John told Ruth that Detweiller's "warped plank" line was a phrase even Carlyle would admire. [NOTE: See the entry THE GREAT FLOOR OF THE UNIVERSE (U17).]

A DEAD FLY (U21) Riddley found one in Zenith the Plant.

A DECOMPOSED BABY SPIDER (U21) Riddley found one in Zenith the Plant.

"THE DESIGNATED JEW" (U15) Herb Porter, according to Major Hecksler.

DETWEILLER, CARLOS (U15) Author of *True Tales of Demon Infestations*. Carlos sent a query for *True Tales* to Zenith House publisher, John Kenton, who decided on a whim to look at the proposal. Instead, Detweiller sent the entire manuscript, which contained photos of what looked like a real human sacrifice. John went to the police, and Carlos was brought in for questioning. The photos were fakes, and Carlos was released. He was furious, however, and began to write to John as "Roberta Solrac." He also sent John an ivy plant that ended up in the mailroom with the Zenith House janitor, Riddley Walker. Detweiller was, in the meantime, "In Transit." Detweiller was twenty-three years old. At the conclusion of Part Three of *The Plant*, Major "Iron Gut" Hecklser has dreamt of Carlos as the Voice of God, and was plotting a dastardly scheme called "Operation Bookworm."

EDDIE (U15) Riddley's cousin. He was a lawyer.

AN EDITORIAL ASSISTANT (U15) The unnamed assistant who first read the unsolicited manuscript of *Ordinary People*.

ENDERS, HARLOW (U15) The chief comptroller for the Apex Corporation. Apex owned Zenith House. In Part 2 (U17), Roger referred to Harlow as "The Axeman Cometh" Enders.

THE FLORIST (U21) A florist told Riddley that the only plant that smelled like pot was dark columbine.

FORD, STATE POLICE LT. ARTHUR P. (U21) Ford didn't have much hope of catching Hecksler after the major escaped from the Oak Cove Asylum. Ford described Hecksler as "extremely clever, extremely dangerous, and extremely paranoid."

FOSTER, JODIE (U17) After John started hearing from "Roberta Solrac," he told Ruth that if he knew Jody [sic] Foster's number, he'd call her, referring to the period when Jodie was the object of an obsessive fan.

THE "GASH ME" AUTHOR (U15) Zenith House author of *Gash Me, My Darling*. John Kenton helped her through her latest writer's block.

GELB, BILL (U15) A Zenith House editor.

THE GERMANS (U21) They captured Hecksler in November of 1944, and yanked out two of his teeth during interrogation.

GINELLI (U21) A Mafioso who owned the Four Fathers bar. Ginelli played a major role in Stephen King's Richard Bachman novel *Thinner* as well. [NOTE: See the section on *Thinner* in this volume.]

A GRAD STUDENT (U21) The unnamed student who taught the course called "The Psychology of Human Stress," which Roger Wade took in college. Roger got an A: he banged the teacher.

A GUY (U17) The unnamed man who was on the receiving end of Bill Gelb's "Basketball" joke. Bill thought the guy had a good tan, but he was actually black. The guy threw his drink in Bill's face. [NOTE: See the "Things" entry GELB'S JOKE (U17).]

HAMMER, BILL (U15) A former Zenith House editor. He quit after rejecting Major Hecksler's *Twenty Psychic Garden Flowers*. The Major came after him.

HECKLSER, MAJOR GENERAL ANTHONY R., (RETIRED) (U15, 21) "Iron Gut" Hecksler. Lunatic general who wrote *Twenty Psychic Garden Flowers*. In Part One of *The Plant*, Hecksler is in Oak Cove Asylum. He later escaped, and was thought to have commited suicide when three bodies and two gold teeth were found in the Shady Rest Mortuary Crematorium. It wasn't Iron Gut, though; just part of his plan "Operation Hotfoot." He served in France during WWII. In 1981, he was seventy-two years old.

HECKSLER'S SISTER (U15) The unnamed woman who had Hecksler commited to an asylum.

IVERSON, CHIEF BARTON (U15) The Central Falls police chief. He looked into the authenticity of Detweiller's "Human Sakrifice" photos.

JACKSON, SANDRA (U15) A Zenith House editor. She was having an affair with the black janitor, Riddley Walker. [NOTE: See the "Things" entry RIDDLEY AND SANDRA'S FANTASY GAMES]

JOHN KENTON'S THREE SISTERS (U21) Two were married, and one lived at home. The one at home would graduate in June from Sanford High School.

KEEN, MR. NORVILLE (U15, 17) A man in Detweiller's building. Carlos tried to instruct him in the "deeper mysteries." Keen was the guy in the "sakrifice" photos having the impromptu heart surgery.

KENTON, JOHN EDWARD (U15, 17, 21) The twenty-six-year-old editor at Zenith House publishers in New York City. Kenton received Carlos Detweiller's *True Tales of Demon Infestations* query. John's girlfriend was Ruth Tanaka. She was attending college in California. Ruth dropped John for a guy named Toby Anderson. John's father was dead, and his mother lived in Sanford, Maine. John went to Brown University, where he majored in English. He had three sisters, two married, one lived at home. John lived in a two-room Soho apartment.

KENTON, MR. (U21) John's dead father.

KENTON, MRS. (U21) John's mother. She lived in Sanford, Maine.

LASCORBIA, ANTHONY (U15) Zenith House author. He was known for his "From Hell" series. His titles included *Rats from Hell, Scorpions from Hell, Wasps from Hell,* and *Flies from Hell.*

LEEKSTODDER, MR. HUBERT D. (U21) The co-owner of the Shady Rest Mortuary. His ashes were found in the crematorium oven, along with his wife's, and with what were presumed to be those of Major Hecksler.

LEEKSTODDER, MRS. (21) The co-owner of the Shady Rest Mortuary. Her ashes were found in the crematorium oven, along with her husband's, and with what were presumed to be those of Major "Iron Gut" Hecksler.

THE LIBRARIAN FROM MINNESOTA (U15) The bad-tempered woman who wrote bodice rippers for Zenith House.

LINCOLN, PRESIDENT (U17) According to John, Lincoln spoke the immortal words "Good fucking luck, turkey." [NOTE: See the "Things" entry $2,500.]

MARKSLAND, POLICE LIEUTENANT RODNEY (U21) The Long Island cop who investigated the murders at the Shady Rest Mortuary.

THE MIDDLE-AGED MAN (U15) The man seen in the Black Mass photos included with Detweiller's manuscript. He had a knife in his chest. He was actually Mr. Norville Keen, a man who lived in Carlos Detweiller's building.

MOORS, ELLEN K. (U21) The doctor in charge of Iron Gut Hecksler at the Oak Cove Asylum.

"MR. TRUCK-DRIVER" (U21) One of Riddley's roles. [NOTE: See RIDDLEY AND SANDRA'S FANTASY GAMES]

NEWMAN, PAUL (U21) After begging Ruth to come back, John fantasized himself as Paul Newman in "Cool Hand Luke," sitting in his cell after his mother's death, playing his banjo and crying soundlessly.

OLYMPIA, AUNT (U21) Riddley's aunt from Babylon, Alabama. She called Riddley to tell him his mother had died of a heart attack during a nap.

PENBROKE, ALICIA (U21) The thirty-four year old Oak Cove Asylum nurse killed by Iron Gut Hecksler.

PIET, JOHN (U21) The forty-year-old Oak Cove Asylum orderly killed by Iron Gut Hecksler.

PORTER, HERB (U15) Zenith House editor. He enjoyed sneaking into Sandra Jackson's office and sniffing her seat. Riddley Walker described Herb as fat, slovenly, and smoking a cigar. He was five-foot-seven.

"RICHARD GEAR" (U17) In Detweiller's "Dear Judas" letter to John, he told John that he wouldn't fuck him if he was a girl and John was "Richard Gear."

RILEY (U17) The cop sent to check out the House of Flowers.

RUTH'S ROOMMATE (U15, 21) The unnamed girl who wanted to manufacture the world's largest edible Frisbee. John talked to her in an attempt to track down Ruth.

SAVINI, TOM (U17) Special effects expert. Tyndale told John Kenton that the "sakrifice" pictures did look real – like some of Savini's work.

SCHNEUR, HERMAN T. (U21) Albany bus driver. Hecksler tried to kill him, but was acquitted by reason of insanity on charges of assault with a deadly weapon and assault with intent to kill.

SOLRAC, ROBERTA (U17) The alter ego of Carlos Detweiller? After Detweiller's "Judas Priest" letter to John, John began to receive letters from a "Roberta Solrac" ("Solrac" is Carlos spelled backwards). Solrac was a fan of the LaScorbia novels, and agreed that ecology was about to revolt. She told John that she sent LaScorbia a dozen roses after he replied to her letter. She also told John that he, too, would be receiving a gift from her: a small plant.

THE SUPER (U21) The superintendent of Ruth Tanaka's building. John called him to track down Ruth.

SUSAN, AUNT (U21) John Kenton's aunt. She once gave him a pocket diary.

TANAKA, RUTH (U15) John Kenton's lost girlfriend. She was in California studying for her PhD. While there she met Toby Anderson, got engaged, and wrote John a, yes, "Dear John" letter. Ruth did yoga and the Jane Fonda workout, and studied Transformational Grammar, Noam Chomsky and deep structure, and English Restoration drama.

THE TWO DISTRIBUTORS (U15) Two unnamed book dealers that Roger Wade met with. He sent one back to Queens, and one back to Brooklyn.

TYNDALE, SERGEANT (U15) The cop from the 31st precinct who worked with Chief Iverson to verify Detweiller and his photos.

WADE, ROGER (U15) Zenith House's forty-five-year-old editor-in-chief. John thought he looked eight to ten years older. Roger smoked too much, and was three times divorced. Roger taught school for six years – four high school and two elementary.

WALKER, DEIDRE (U21) Riddley's sister. In order to be able to function sexually with Sandra Jackson, Riddley would fantasize about Deidre diapering him, and then "doing him" after he wet himself.

WALKER, FLOYD (U17) Riddley's brother. Riddley felt that Floyd would call Riddley's panic at receiving Solrac's package a "nigger reaction."

WALKER, MRS. (U21) Riddley's mother. She died of a heart attack during a nap. His journal entry after hearing the news read: "Oh, bullshit, my mother. I loved her. I did love her my sweet fat uncomplaining mother who saw so much more than she said and knew so much more than she let on. Oh I did love her and I love her."

WALKER, RIDDLEY (U15) The Zenith House janitor. He was a graduate of Cornell, was writing a novel, and yet talked like a "Nigger Jim" character out of a Southern slave novel. He was having an affair with one of Zenith House's editors, the lovely Sandra Jackson, and he also ended up as sole caretaker of Zenith, the carnivorous ivy plant, sent to John Kenton by Roberta Solrac.

WESTMORELAND, GENERAL (U21) Hecksler was consulted by the general during the war in Viet Nam.

WILSON, GAHAN AND NANCY (U21) They had a house in Connecticut, and that was where Ruth Tanaka first met Roger Wade.

Places

APEX CORPORATION (U15) The company that owned Zenith House. They were thinking of selling off the publishing house.

BROWN UNIVERSITY (U15, 21) John Kenton's alma mater. He majored in English.

BURGER HEAVEN (U15) The restaurant where John lunched with Anthony LaScorbia, the author of *Rats from Hell*, among others. [NOTE: See the "Things" entry THE LaSCORBIA BOOKS.]

CENTRAL FALLS HOUSE OF FLOWERS (U15) The flower shop owned by Tina Barfield. Carlos Detweiller worked there.

CUTLERSVILLE (U21) The town where the Oak Cove Asylum was located.

DOBBS FERRY (U21) The town where Riddley Walker lived.

FALL RIVER, MASSACHUSETTS (U15) Detweiller supposedly attended the meeting of a black coven in Fall River.

FLAGSTAFF, ARIZONA (U15) Detweiller supposedly attended the meeting of a black coven in Flagstaff.

A FLORIST (U21) Riddley stopped in a flower shop; he smelled a Boston plant, and a hybrid called Marion Ivy – neither smelled like pot, as Zenith did.

FOUR FATHERS (U21) A bar where John and Roger drank. It was owned by a man named Ginelli, who Roger said was mafioso.

"THE GREAT PLAINS OF AMERICAN PUBLISHING" (U17) When Roger told John that he "should start shaking the trees" because they needed books that would make some noise by summer, John replied "What trees?" He felt that Zenith House existed on the Great Plains of American Publishing. Roger's reply was to find a tree or find a job.

"IN TRANSIT" (U17) Detweiller's "Dear Judas" letter to John Kenton was signed "In Transit, U.S. of A."

"AN INVISIBLE WORLD" (U21) Riddley wanted to know if there was an invisible world, a place where things like the Shroud of Turin lived.

"THE ISLE OF FORGOTTEN NOVELS" (U21) The place where the old manuscripts that were received at Zenith House without proper return postage were deposited. They were relegated to a moldy back corner of the basement. After Ruth left John, he began going through the pile, returning them at his own expense.

THE MAILROOM (U17) Riddley Walker's kingdom.

THE NINTH FLOOR (U21) The floor where Zenith House was located.

OAK COVE ASYLUM (U21) Asylum from which Iron Gut Hecksler escaped. It was in Cutlersville.

OMAHA, NEBRASKA (U15) Detweiller supposedly attended the meeting of a black coven in Omaha.

PASADENA (U17) The town where Ruth Tanaka lived.

THE RIDDLEY WALKER CASINO (U21) Riddley's mailroom. Gelb visited there. Gelb owed Riddley $192.50.

SANFORD HIGH SCHOOL (U21) The school that John Kenton's youngest sister attended.

SCOURBY'S (U17) A bar where Roger and John often drank.

THE SHADY REST, LONG ISLAND MORTUARY (U21) The crematorium where it was presumed Hecksler and two other people had perished in the oven.

SPORTING GOODS STORE (U21) When Herb Porter wanted to buy a gun, John suggested he try this store at Park and 32nd Streets, which was five blocks away from Zenith House.

THE 31ST PRECINCT (U15) Chief Iverson told John to bring Detweiller's photos to this precinct.

20TH AND PARK AVENUE SOUTH (U21) Where Roger Wade lived.

A TWO-ROOM SOHO APARTMENT (U21) Apartment where John Kenton lived.

ZENITH HOUSE (U15) New York publishing house. The editor-in-chief was Roger Wade, and the editorial staff was made up of John Kenton, Herb Porter, Bill Gelb, and Sandra Jackson. The janitor was Riddley Walker. Apex Corporation owned Zenith. Apex's chief comptroller was Harlow Enders.

Things

ALL RIGHTS (U15) Carlos wanted to sell all rights of his *True Tales,* except for the movie rights. He told John Kenton that he himself would direct the film.

"THE AMITYVILLE HORROR AUDIENCE" (U15) John figured they could sell *True Tales* to this group of readers.

"AN ANCIENT ROYAL" (U15) John Kenton's typewriter.

ANTS FROM HELL (U15) A book by Anthony LaScorbia.

BARBER'S SHEARS (U21) The tool thought to have been used ("in the throat commando-style") by Hecksler on his three victims at the Oak Cove Asylum.

BATTERY ACID (U21) After Ruth broke up with him, John dreamed that he threw battery acid in her face.

BLACK COVENS (U15) Detweiller had stories of coven meetings that he had attended.

BLACK MASS PHOTOS (U15) The photos enclosed with Detweiller's manuscript. They seemed to show an actual human sacrifice.

BLOODY HOUSES (U15) A book published by Zenith House. Everything in the book, including the photos, came right out of the New York Public Library.

BROWN UNIVERSITY MILTON SOCIETY (U15) John was head of this society when in college.

BRUT (U21) When John called Ruth and begged her to come back, he imagined he could smell Toby's Brut over the phone.

BY REASON OF INSANITY (U21) Hecksler was acquitted by reason of insanity after he tried to kill Herman T. Schneur, an Albany bus driver he claimed "one of the twelve North American foremen of the Antichrist."

CANNIBIS SATIVA (U21) Riddley thought that Zenith smelled like pot.

CHAPTERS 1-3, AND A SYNOPSIS (U15) The *True Tales* material John Kenton asked Detweiller to send in. Carlos instead sent the whole manuscript.

COCKROACHES IN THE WATER COOLER (U15) Zenith House's biggest in-house problem.

"COLORFUL CAREER OF IRON-GUTS [sic] HECKSLER RECALLED" (U21) One of the related stories in the *New York Post* after the murders at the Shady Rest Mortuary. It was in the centerfold.

"CRAZY FEVER" (U21) John Kenton told his diary that there was an outbreak of "Crazy fever" at work.

"A DEAR JOHN" SOCIETY" (U21) Society John thought about forming after Ruth broke up with him.

"THE DEEPER MYSTERIES" (U15) Carlos tried to instruct Mr. Keen in these mysteries.

DETWEILLER'S ADDRESS (U15) 147 East 14th Street, Apartment E., Central Falls, Rhode Island 40222.

DETWEILLER'S "DEAR JUDAS" LETTER TO JOHN KENTON (U17) After Carlos was questioned regarding his "sakrifice" photos, he sent a letter to John addressed as follows:

> Mr. John "Judas Priest" Kenton
> Zenith Asshole-House, Publishers of Kaka
> 490 Avenue of Dogshit
> New York, New York 10017

DETWEILLER'S "POOP-SHIT" LETTER TO JOHN KENTON (U21) On March 21, 1981, Detweiller wrote John another letter: It was addressed:

> Mr. John Poop-Shit Kenton
> Zenith House Publishers, Home of the Pus-Bags
> 490 Kaka Avenue South
> New York, New York 10017

The salutation was "Dear Poop-Shit," and in the letter Carlos told John that "You and all your fellow 'Pus-Bags' will soon feel the WRATH!! of CARLOS!!" Apparently, Carlos had "convened the powers of Hell."

DICE (U17) Riddley threw dice with Bill Gelb.

A DOZEN ROSES (U17) Roberta Solrac sent Anthony LaScorbia a dozen roses after he replied to her letter.

ECOLOGY (U17) Roberta Solrac agreed with LaScorbia that ecology was about to revolt.

$81.50 (U21) On March 5, 1981, Gelb owed Riddley $81.50 in gambling losses.

FEDERAL EXPRESS (U21) John Kenton felt that Federal Express made long distance look like an austerity measure.

FIFTY PAGES (U17) Riddley had completed fifty pages of his novel by the end of the weekend just prior to the close of Part Two of *The Plant*.

FIVE DOLLARS (U15) Carlos told John that Tine Barfield owed him five dollars from playing the lottery.

FIVE SECONDS (U17) The length of time Riddley Walker panicked when Roberta Solrac's package for John was received in his mailroom.

FLIES FROM HELL (U17) In Part Two of *The Plant*, this was a forthcoming Zenith House title by Anthony LaScorbia.

FRUSTRATED SURGEONS (U17) John felt that all special effects wizards were "frustrated surgeons."

GASH ME, MY DARLING (U15) A Zenith House title.

GELB'S JOKE (U17) Bill Gelb told the following joke to an unnamed guy at a cocktail party: "How do you stop five black guys from raping a white chick? Answer: Give them a basketball." The guy turned out to be black.

"A GODDAMNED ARCHETYPE" (U15) In a letter to Ruth, John said he felt like he was in the middle of a goddamned archetype: sections of the Sunday New York *Times*, an old Simon & Garfunkel album on the stereo, and a Bloody Mary nearby.

"THE GREAT AMERICAN MEDIAN" (U21) Riddley felt that Herb Porter was an evocation of the Median.

"THE GREAT FLOOR OF THE UNIVERSE" (U17) In Detweiller's "Dear Judas" letter to John, he called John a "warped plank" in the "Great Floor of the Universe."

GROLLIER'S AND COLLIER'S (U21) The encyclopedias Riddley used to look up Zenith the Ivy. He also used Floyd's college botany books.

GUERILLA UNITS (U21) Hecksler trained these units in WWII and Korea.

HEARST SHIFTER (U21) Riddley's erection, during "The Truckdriver and the Hitchhiker." [NOTE: See RIDDLEY AND SANDRA'S FANTASY GAMES]

HEART (U15) In one of the Black Mass photos included with Detweiller's manuscript, Carlos was seen holding up what looked like a human heart.

HECKSLER'S DISPATCH (U21) After he was presumed dead, Hecksler wrote a dispatch dated as follows:

Mar 29 81
1990 hrs
Location Classified

HECKSLER'S DREAM (U21) After Operation Hotfoot, Hecksler dreamt of Carlos, and wondered if he was the voice of God.

HECKLSER'S LETTER TO HERB PORTER (U21) It was addressed:

> Mr. Herbert Porter
> Designated Jew
> Zenith House
> 490 Park Avenue
> New York, NY 10017

Hecksler told Porter he was coming to cut off his penis and put it in his ear. Hecksler claimed that Porter stole the good parts of his book. The P.S. read:

> Roses are red
> Violets are blue
> I am coming to castrate
> A Designated Jew.

HECKSLER'S ZIPPO (U21) Hecksler had a platinum-plated Zippo with the Army emblem on it. It was engraved:

> To Tony from Doug
> Aug. 7th, 1945.

The "Doug" was General Douglas MacArthur.

HERB PORTER'S SOLUTIONS TO THE PROBLEMS OF THE WORLD (U21) Close the borders and keep out the spies and wetbacks! End abortion on demand! Build more prisons! Upgrade possession of marijuana to a felony once again! Sell biochemical stocks! Buy cable-TV issues!

HI-PRO-GAS (U21) A hopped-up version of Mace. Sandra Jackson used it in her "Rainy Night Friend."

HIS FLAMING KISSES (U15) The last book by the librarian from Minnesota. It did not sell well.

THE HORTICULTURAL CONVERGENCE (U21) The nonexistent Robert Ludlum novel jokingly suggested by John when he and Roger discussed "the revenge of the flower people": Detweiller and Hecksler.

JANUARY 11-15, 1981 SUBMISSIONS (U15) John told Roger that he was returning fifteen unsolicited book-length manuscripts; seven outlines and sample chapters; and four unidentifiable blobs, including a book of "gay event poetry" called *Suck My Big Black Cock*. He asked to see outlines and sample chapters on five books, including the latest bodice ripper from "that bad-tempered librarian in Minnesota."

JOHN KENTON'S POSTCARD TO CARLOS (U21) After John received Carlos's "WRATH!!" letter, he mused in a letter to Ruth that he should send Detweiller a postcard reading: "Dear Carlos—I know all about convening the powers of Hell. Your Ob'd Servent, Poop-Shit Kenton."

JOHN'S SELF PITY (U21) John thought his self pity sounded "Byronic-Keatsian-Sorrows-of-Young-Werther."

JOHN'S SIGNATURE (U17) John signed one of his letters to Ruth "Your admiring horse's ass, John."

JUNE OF 1980 (U21) The month when Ruth Tanaka first met Roger Wade. They met at Gahan and Nancy Wilson's place in Connecticut.

THE LaSCORBIA BOOKS (U15) Anthony LaScorbia was a Zenith House author known for his "From Hell" series. His titles included *Rats from Hell, Scorpions from Hell, Wasps from Hell,* and *Flies from Hell.*

"LET SLEEPING WEIRDOS LIE." (U17) Iverson's advice regarding Detweiller.

A LOS ANGELES RAMS UNIFORM (U21) John imagined Toby

Anderson in this uniform.

THE "MACHO MAN" SERIES (U15) Zenith House's biggest steady seller.

"MAD GENERAL DIES IN MORTUARY HORROR!" (U21) The headline of the *New York Post* page 1 article of March 27, 1981.

MARCH 4, 1981 (U21) The date of the *New York Post* article about Hecksler's escape from Oak Cove Asylum.

MARCH 24 (U15) Carlos Detweiller's birthday. He was an Aries on the cusp of Pisces.

MAYMONTH (U21) The title of the novel John Kenton was writing. He scrapped it after Ruth broke up with him. He told his diary that *Maymonth* "sucked that fabled hairy bird."

"THE NECRONOMICON" (U15) Detweiller compared his *True Tales of Demon Infestations* with H.P. Lovecraft's *The Necronomicon.*

NEW YORK POST (U21) The newspaper that ran the article titled "Insane General Escapes Oak Cove Asylum, Kills Three!" about Major General (Ret.) Anthony R. Hecksler. Herb Porter read the *Post.*

"NEW YORKERS BREATHE SIGH OF RELIEF" (U21) One of the related stories in the *New York Post* after the murders at the Shady Rest Mortuary. It was on Page 4.

"NEXT YEAR'S NATIONAL BOOK AWARD WINNER" (U15) John Kenton's sarcastic reference to Carlos Detweiller.

NIKON BLACK-AND-WHITE GLOSSIES (U15) The photos that were enclosed with Detweiller's manuscript.

NIKON COLOR SLIDES (U15) The slides that were enclosed with Detweiller's manuscript.

1979 (U15) The year that John started at Zenith House.

"ONE OF THE TWELVE NORTH AMERICAN FOREMEN OF THE ANTICHRIST." (U21) Herman T. Schneur, according to Hecksler. Hecksler also believed that the two owners of the Shady Rest Mortuary, Mr. and Mrs. Hubert D. Leekstodder were "foremen" as well. He burned them to ashes in their own crematorium to make the world a safer place.

$1,800 (U15) The largest advance Zenith House could offer.

"ONGOING SANITY" (U17) After John received a letter from a "Roberta Solrac" ("Carlos" spelled backwards), he sent a memo to Roger regarding his "ongoing sanity."

"OPERATION BOOKWORM" (U21) Hecksler's plan to unjacket the "designated Jew" from his "bag of guts and waters."

"OPERATION HOTFOOT" (U21) The name Hecksler gave to his plan to murder the Leekstodders and lead people to believe that he'd committed suicide.

ORDINARY PEOPLE (U15) An unsolicited novel that was read by an editorial assistant. This was a million to one shot.

OUIJA BOARD (U15) Detweiller told John he got most of his information from the Ouija board. He did the Ouija with his mother, Tina Barfield, Don Barfield, and Herb Hagstrom. Things he found out included the fact that the disappearance of Amelia Earhart was the work of demons, that there were demonic forces at work on the Titanic, that a "tulpa" infested Richard Nixon, and much more.

"PERSONAL REASONS" (U21) The reason John gave Roger for resigning from Zenith House. It was actually because Ruth broke up with him.

A PHD (U15) Ruth Tanaka was in California working towards her PhD.

THE PHILOSOPHY OF ROGER WADE (U21) "Life without a woman, even if she's a shrew and a nag, sours a man. It turns an essential part of his soul into a pimple."

THE PLANT (U17) John was worried that the plant that Roberta Solrac would be sending him was either deadly nightshade or belladonna. It was actually a small ivy with four yellow-edged leaves.

THE PLANT'S SIGN (U17) A small plastic sign was stuck in the dirt. It read:

HI!
MY
NAME IS ZENITH
I AM A GIFT TO JOHN
FROM ROBERTA

PLANTS FROM HELL (U17) John told Ruth that if LaScorbia's next novel was *Plants from Hell,* he was quitting Zenith House.

PLYMOUTH (U21) The cab that Roger and John took home after they got drunk was a Plymouth. Roger puked out the car window.

POLAROID SX-70 SHOTS (U15) The photos enclosed with Detweiller's *True Tales* manuscript. They were shots of plants: deadly nightshade, belladonna, virgin's hair, etc.

PRE-WWI XEROX MACHINE (U17) Zenith House's copy machine, according to John Kenton.

"THE PSYCHOLOGY OF HUMAN STRESS" (U21) A course that Roger Wade took in college. He got an A; he banged the grad student who taught the course.

QUAALUDES (U15) John suggested that Roger take four Quaaludes for his tension headache.

RAINY NIGHT FRIEND (U21) Sandra Jackson's weapon of defense. It was a silver-plated tear gas cannister, but she had replaced the tear gas with Hi-Pro-Gas, a hopped-up version of Mace.

RATS FROM HELL (U15) A book by Anthony LaScorbia. He followed it up with *Scorpions from Hell.*

REWRITE FEES (U15) If Zenith bought Detweiller's *True Tales of Demon Infestations,* John figured he'd pay a ghost writer $600 to rewrite the book. When he saw Roger wince, he lowered it to $400.

RIDDLEY AND SANDRA'S FANTASY GAMES (U21) Riddley Walker was having an affair with Sandra Jackson, and the fantasy role-playing games they played included "The Truckdriver and the Hitchhiker," "The Virgin and the Chauffeur," and of course, "The Lady Editor and the Nigger Janitor."

RIDDLEY'S NOVEL (U21) The untitled novel that Walker was writing. At the end of Part Two, he had completed fifty pages; during the week of March 5, 1981, he had completed another twenty pages.

RIDDLEY'S "PACKAGED" FEARS (U17) When Riddley received the package from Roberta Solrac, he feared the following: That the package would contain high explosive rigged to special pressure-tapes, noxious floods of black widow spiders, or a litter of baby copperheads.

RIDDLEY'S REPLY (U17) When John sent Riddley a memo telling him to throw away the plant that Roberta Solrac would be sending him, Riddley replied "Yassuh, Mist Kenton!"

ROGER'S BRAIN TUMOR (U15) John wrote Roger a memo telling him that Roger's "brain tumor" sounded like a tension headache. He advised him to take four Quaaludes.

RUTH TANAKA'S ANSWERING MACHINE (U21) John hated it.

S & H GREEN STAMP BOOK (U21) Hecksler wrote his "dispatches" in a stamp book after he was presumed dead.

"THE SAKRED SEANCE" (U15) Six photos enclosed with Detweiller's manuscript. They showed middle-aged men and women in black robes or wearing nothing. The photos included faked plasmic manifestations (a balloon frosted with day-Glo paint).

SANDRA JACKSON'S CHAIR SEAT (U17) Herb Porter would sneak into Jackson's office when she went to the ladies' room and sniff her seat.

SCORPIONS FROM HELL (U15) A book by Anthony LaScorbia. It was Zenith's lead title for February 1981.

SEVEN YEARS (U15) Carlos Detweiller started working on *True Tales* when he was sixteen, and worked on it for seven years before submitting it to Zenith House.

$75.40 (U17) At the end of Part Two of *The Plant,* Bill Gelb owed

Riddley Walker $75.40. This was the amount of his loss from playing dice with Riddley.

A SILVER TOOTH (U21) Riddley Walker had one in the back of his mouth.

THE STANDARD CAVEATS (U15) When John asked Carlos to send in his *True Tales* materials, he included the standard caveats in his letter: enclose adequate postage, Zenith accepted no responsibility for the manuscript, and an agreement to look at the text was not a covenant to publish the book. John said this letter to Carlos looked like a synopsis of *The Naked and the Dead*.

STRANGE PLANTS (U15) Carlos told John that he was very good with plants, especially growing "strange" plants.

SUCK MY BIG BLACK COCK (U15) A book of gay event poetry that John Kenton rejected.

SUPPOSITORIES (U21) Hecksler decided that he and Carlos would destroy the foremen of the Antichrist, but first he needed to get some suppositories. [NOTE: With that, Stephen King concluded Part Three of *The Plant*, which, we are now told, will be the final installment of the work, leaving the novel uncompleted.]

SWEDA CASH REGISTERS (U17) Riddley Walker felt that John Kenton's openness towards Detweiller's *True Tales of Demon Infestations* indicated that his "editorial ears [were] still open and working towards" Sweda cash registers ringing.

THIRTY TO FORTY UNSOLICITED MANUSCRIPTS (U15) John told Ruth that Zenith got thirty to forty unsolicited manuscripts a week.

3,000 DEGREES SPOT HEAT (U21) The Long Island cops figured that Hecksler crawled into the oven at the Shady Rest Mortuary and flicked his Bic, triggering 3000 degrees of spot heat. Actually, he flicked his platinum-plated Zippo with the Army emblem on it.

THE *TOYS IN THE ATTIC* SERIES (U21) Roger Wade felt that Herb Porter or Bill Gelb would have rejected V.C. Andrews very successful series.

TRUE TALES OF DEMON INFESTATIONS (U15) Manuscript written by Carlos Detweiller. Contents included "The World of Voodoo," "The World of the Aether," "The World of the Living Dead," and "The World of Spells." The proposal included "Sakrifice" photos which seemed to show an actual human sacrifice.

TUMS (U15) John Kenton's antacid of choice.

TWENTY PSYCHIC GARDEN FLOWERS (U15) A book by Major General Anthony R. Hecksler (Ret.)

TWENTY-SEVEN MONTHS (U21) In March of 1981, it had been twenty seven months since Hecksler had been commited to the Oak Cove Asylum.

TWO GOLD TEETH (U21) The police found two gold teeth in the crematorium at the Shady Rest Mortuary. Hecksler had been captured by the Germans in November 1944, and two teeth had been yanked out during interrogation.

$2,500 (U17) John Kenton told Ruth he needed to buy a bestseller for $2,500. Regarding the possibility of finding a bestseller for this sum, Kenton quoted the immortal words of President Lincoln: "Good fucking luck, turkey." [Note: The amount of the advance that Stephen King received for his first novel, *Carrie*, was $2,500.]

TYPES OF IVY (U21) Riddley discovered that there was no such thing as "common ivy." He learned that ivy was categorized as poison, Virginia Creeper, Ground, Boston, Japanese, and English. Riddley decided that Zenith looked like a cross between Japanese and poison ivy.

UNITED NEWS DEALERS (U15) A syndicate that handled the distribution of some of Zenith House's titles.

VOGUE OR *BETTER HOMES AND GARDENS* (U21) The magazines that Sandra Jackson took into the bathroom every morning.

"WAKE OF THE RED WITCH" (U17) A John Wayne movie John Kenton watched.

WASPS FROM HELL (U15) A book by Anthony LaScorbia.

LaScorbia was encouraged by John Kenton to write it.

WEDNESDAY (U15) Carlos told John he'd come to New York any Wednesday for his "publishing luncheon."

WHISKEY (U21) Riddley had two big gulps of whiskey after hearing that his mother had died, and before he could tell his journal that Zenith the Ivy was carnivorous.

THE *WINDHOVER* SERIES (U15) Zenith House series written by Olive Barker.

WINGO (U21) Herb Porter played WINGO in the *New York Post*, and said that if he won, he'd buy a Winnebago and paint "WIN-GOBAGO" on the side and tour the country.

"THE WORLD OF SPELLS" (U15) One of the chapters in Carlos Detweiller's manuscript *True Tales of Demon Infestations*.

"THE WORLD OF THE AETHER" (U15) One of the chapters in Carlos Detweiller's manuscript *True Tales of Demon Infestations*.

"THE WORLD OF THE LIVING DEAD" (U15) One of the chapters in Carlos Detweiller's manuscript *True Tales of Demon Infestations*.

"THE WORLD OF VOODOO" (U15) One of the chapters in Carlos Detweiller's manuscript *True Tales of Demon Infestations*.

"YOUR NEW AUTHOR" (U15) How Detweiller signed his second letter to John – even though John had not agreed to publish Detweiller's book.

ZENITH HOUSE'S ADDRESS (U15) 490 Park Avenue South, New York, New York 10017.

ZENITH HOUSE'S NEWSPAPER HABITS (U21) Porter read the *New York Post*, Kenton and Wade read the New York *Times*, and Gelb and Jackson brought the New York *Times*, but secretly read the New York *Daily News*.

ZENITH HOUSE'S POLICY (U15) They didn't read unsolicited manuscripts. This policy was stated in *Writer's Market*, *The Writer's Yearbook*, *The Freelance*, and *The Pen Newsletter*.

ZENITH HOUSE'S POSITION (U15) They had two percent of the paperback market, and they were fifteenth in a field of fifteen.

ZENITH THE IVY'S GROWTH RECORD (U21) It grew very fast: On 2/23, Riddley thought it would die; on 3/4, it was healthier, with four open leaves, two unfurling, and one tendril reaching to the edge of the pot; and, on 3/25, the plant had almost two dozen leaves, a tendril running six inches up the wall, and a single blue flower in the pot.

"Skybar"

"Skybar" is a "Do-It-Yourself" short story. It is one of several story beginnings and endings contributed to a collection called *The Do-It-Yourself Bestseller—A Workbook*, edited by Tom Silberkleit and Jerry Biederman (Doubleday Dolphin trade paperback, 1982.)

The idea was that professional writers (including Isaac Asimov, Robin Cook, Irving Wallace, Colin Wilson, and King) would give the student the beginnings of a story and the last few paragraphs, and the object was for the student to "fill in the blanks" – to write the middle section of the story.

King contributed four paragraphs that began: "There were twelve of us when we went in that night, but only two of us came out – my friend Kirby and me. And Kirby was insane."

King also gave the hopeful writer the last paragraph that ended: "These things happened to me when I was young."

Since the story is incomplete, the following concordance only details the people, places, and things found in King's five paragraphs. — **sjs**

(U16)
"Skybar"
People

CALLAHAN, BRENT One of the kids who went into the Skybar Amusement Park – and didn't come out. He said that the freaks in the Adults Only Freak Tents were fakes.

DUPREE, POP Proprietor of Pop Dupree's Dead-Eye Shootin' Gallery, one of the attractions at the Skybar Amusement Park. Pop used .22's in the Gallery.

KIRBY The ten-year-old fifth-grader who went into the Amusement Park with the narrator and ten other kids. Only the narrator and Kirby came out, and Kirby was insane. [NOTE: At the time of the publication of "Skybar," Stephen King's agent was his longtime friend, Kirby McCauley. McCauley no longer represents King.]

THE NARRATOR The eleven-year-old sixth-grader who went into the Amusement Park with Kirby and ten others. Only the narrator and Kirby came out – and Kirby was insane.

THE NARRATOR'S WIFE The unnamed spouse of the narrator.

STAYNER, RANDY A seventh-grader who was in junior high school, and who was thrown from the highest part of the SkyCoaster rollercoaster.

THE TWELVE The kids that went in to the Skybar Amusement Park. Only two came out: the narrator and Kirby – and Kirby was insane.

Places

DEWEY'S SUNOCO Gas station. They sold Hi-Test for 31.9¢, and gave double S & H Green Stamps.

AN INSANE ASYLUM The place where Kirby lived after his experiences in the Skybar Amusement Park.

THE NARRATOR'S HOUSE It was five miles inland from the Skybar Amusement Park.

THE SKYBAR AMUSEMENT PARK The amusement park where twelve kids went in and only two came out: the narrator and Kirby – and Kirby was insane. Skybar had a double ferris wheel, a fun-house clown, a Shooting Gallery, The Whip, The Mirror Labryinth, The Skycoaster, and an Adults Only Freak Tent.

Things

THE ADULTS ONLY FREAK TENT One of the attractions at the Skybar Amusement Park.

A DOUBLE FERRIS WHEEL One of the attractions at the Skybar Amusement Park.

DOUBLE S & H GREEN STAMPS The stamps given out at Dewey's Sunoco.

THE FIFTH GRADE The grade Kirby was in.

A FUN-HOUSE CLOWN One of the attractions at the Skybar Amusement Park.

THE MIRROR LABYRINTH One of the attractions at the Skybar Amusement Park.

THE MURDERS After the murders at the Skybar Amusement Park began, it was shut down.

POP DUPREE'S DEAD-EYE SHOOTIN' GALLERY One of the attractions at the Skybar Amusement Park. They used .22's.

RANDY STAYNER'S CORPSE As an adult, the narrator dreamt of Randy's corpse getting out of the SkyCoaster.

THE SIXTH GRADE The grade the narrator was in when he went into the Skybar Amusement Park.

THE SKYCOASTER Roller coaster at the Skybar Amusement Park. Randy Stayner was thrown from the highest part of the ride

"THESE THINGS HAPPENED TO ME WHEN I WAS YOUNG." The narrator's unexplained accounting of what went on in the Skybar Amusement Park. [NOTE: "Skybar" was a "reader partici-pation" story of which King wrote the beginning and the end. It was up to the reader/writer to fill in what actually happened in the Park.]

31.9¢ The price of Hi-Test at Dewey's Sunoco.

THE WHIP One of the attractions at the Skybar Amusement Park.

> ## "The Revelations of 'Becka Paulson"
>
> The following concordance entries are the items of fact that are unique to "The Revelations of 'Becka Paulson," the original version of which appeared in *Rolling Stone* magazine, #426/427, July 19/August 2, 1984. The story eventually appeared in a drastically revised form as a chapter of *The Tommyknockers*. See the section on *The Tommyknockers* in this volume for more information. —sjs

(U18)
"The Revelations of 'Becka Paulson"
People

JESUS After shooting herself in the head, Jesus told 'Becka things for three days.

JOE PAULSON'S GRANDDAD Jesus told 'Becka that Joe's granddad was a whoremaster, and that rather than being in heaven, he was with Mr. Splitfoot.

MARGOLIES, VINNIE Vinnie picked up the Paulsons' trash.

"OZZIE NELSON" Joe and Rebecca Paulson's cat. [NOTE: In *The Tommyknockers*, the cat's name is only given as "Ozzie."]

REBECCA'S FATHER He was dead.

REBECCA'S OLDER BROTHER When Rebecca pushed an eyebrow pencil into the hole in her head and poked her brain, memories came back to her, including one of sledding at the age of four while wearing her older brother's snowsuit.

ROLAND Rebecca's brother. He grew up on a sheep farm in New Gloucester.

UNCLE BILL When Rebecca pushed an eyebrow pencil into the hole in her head and poked her brain, memories came back to her, including a '59 Impala her Uncle Bill had owned.

Places

FALMOUTH The town from which Nancy Voss came. [NOTE: In *The Tommyknockers*, she came from Augusta.]

NEW GLOUCESTER Rebecca's brother, Roland, grew up on a sheep farm in New Gloucester.

WEST GERMANY Joe Paulson toured West Germany when he was in the army.

Things

"ANOTHER WORLD" One of the soap operas watched by Rebecca Paulson.

DERRY ELKS RAFFLE The raffle at which Joe Paulson won the .22 caliber target pistol. It was the third prize. The first prize was a Bombardier Ski-Doo; the second prize, an Evinrude motor.

AN EYEBROW PENCIL After shooting herself in the forehead with Joe's .22 caliber target pistol, Rebecca pushed an eyebrow pencil five inches into the hole.

"GENERAL HOSPITAL" One of 'Becka's favorite soaps.

A HAIR DRYER AND A GARNET RING Joe had bought Rebecca a hair dryer and a garnet ring with his poker winnings.

THE JESUS PICTURE After 'Becka shot herself in the head, the Jesus picture on top of her Zenith began to speak to her.

JULY 10 The day that Joe Paulson slept outside in a hammock.

"MARCUS WELBY, M.D." A TV show 'Becka Paulson watched.

READER'S DIGEST CONDENSED BOOKS 'Becka Paulson had a *Reader's Digest Condensed Book* from Autumn 1955 in her downstairs hall closet. It contained *Run Silent, Run Deep,* and *Here's Goggle.*

REBECCA'S MEMORIES When Rebecca pushed an eyebrow pencil into the hole in her head and poked her brain, memories came back to her, including sledding at the age of four wearing her older brother's snowsuit; washing high school blackboards; a '59 Impala her Uncle Bill had owned; and, the smell of cut hay.

REBECCA'S SNACK During "General Hospital," Rebecca ate half a coffee cake, and drank a beer stein filled with Kool-Aid.

REBECCA'S SUPPER 'Becka ate four hot dogs, beans, and ketchup for supper, all mixed together with grape juice as her beverage. "The result looked a bit like the aftermath of a bad motorcycle accident."

A SEARS WASHER The Paulsons' washer.

SPORTS ILLUSTRATED A magazine that Joe Paulson read.

SWANSON HUNGRY MAN FROZEN DINNERS Rebecca Paulson ate two Swanson Hungry Man frozen dinners for lunch.

A .22 CALIBER TARGET PISTOL Joe Paulson's gun. Rebecca accidentally shot herself in the forehead with it.

A WAGONEER Joe Paulson's vehicle.

"WHEEL OF FORTUNE" One of 'Becka Paulson's favorite TV shows.

A ZENITH The Paulsons' TV set. [NOTE: In *The Tommyknockers,* it became a Sony.]

"Dolan's Cadillac"

"Dolan's Cadillac" is a tale of sorrow and revenge, and is told in a manner and tone very similar to Stephen King's other forays into the "crime story" genre: "Man With a Belly," "The Fifth Quarter," and in some ways (other than the intrusion of the supernatural in these tales), "The Cat from Hell" and "Battleground."

Robinson's wife witnessed a crime commited by Dolan, spoke out, and was murdered for her "good citizenship."

Robinson plots the ultimate revenge: He tracks Dolan's every move and decides on a Fourth of July weekend to carry out his plan. He will dig a grave in the highway on which Dolan travels back and forth from Los Angeles to Las Vegas, trap Dolan and his Cadillac in the grave, and bury him alive.

The plan works, and Dolan's body is never found.

Michael Collings criticizes the story for its weak characterization, and on the basis of its overwhelming similarity to Edgar Allan Poe's short story "The Cask of Amontillado." Collings argues that "the similarities [to Poe's story] work more against King's story than in support of it," but acknowledges that "If the reader can ignore Poe and listen only to King, the story has passages of some strength."

I like the story because of its verisimilitude, and its inevitable conclusion. But then again, there isn't too much of King that I *don't* like.

"Dolan's Cadillac" originally appeared as a five-part series in *Castle Rock: The Stephen King Newsletter* from February 1985 through June of 1985. Concordance entries are keyed to the following installment list:

Legend

1 = The first installment of "Dolan's Cadillac"; *Castle Rock: The Stephen King Newsletter* : February 1985

2 = The second installment of "Dolan's Cadillac"; *Castle Rock: The Stephen King Newsletter* : March 1985

3 = The third installment of "Dolan's Cadillac"; *Castle Rock: The Stephen King Newsletter* : April 1985

4 = The fourth installment of "Dolan's Cadillac"; *Castle Rock: The Stephen King Newsletter* : May 1985

5 = The fifth installment of "Dolan's Cadillac"; *Castle Rock: The Stephen King Newsletter* : June 1985

"Dolan's Cadillac" was later published by Lord John Press in two limited editions: one signed edition of 1,000 copies, and one deluxe signed edition of 100 copies. Both are out of print. —**sjs**

(U19)
"Dolan's Cadillac"
People

THE ANESTHETIST (U19-5) He put the gas mask over Robinson's face for his back surgery. As Robinson went out, he heard Dolan laughing.

BIG JOE'S TEAM (U19-2) The four women who arrived at Dolan's to clean. They were two white women, one black, and one chicano.

BILL (U19-2) Robinson pretended he was Bill from Dunny's Catering when he called Big Joe's Cleaning Service to get information about when Dolan would be returning home.

BLOCKER, HARVEY (U19-1) The district foreman for the Las Vegas streets and highways department.

"BUBBA" (U19-1) The nickname that Harvey Blocker called Robinson.

THE BULLDOZER OPERATOR (U19-5) The man who worked on U.S. 71 after Robinson buried Dolan there. The 'dozer operator never said anything about the geometrically-broken asphalt. He may have been dreaming of stepping out with his baby that night.

THE BULLDOZER OPERATOR'S BABY (U19-5) His girlfriend.

THE CHIROPRACTOR (U19-5) The doctor who Robinson saw after burying Dolan. [NOTE: See the "Things" entry ROBINSON'S INJURIES]

THE COLUMNIST (U19-5) The Las Vegas *Sun* columnist who suggested that Dolan may have discovered "the Jimmy Hoffa version of immortality."

THE DISC JOCKEY (U19-5) The WKXR deejay that Robinson heard give the weather.

DOLAN, JAMES (JIM) (U19-1) The hood who had Robinson's wife, Elizabeth, killed.

DOLAN'S BABES (U19-1) Dolan was usually seen with either an "arrogant, icy blonde," or a "laughing redhead."

THE DRIVER (U19-4) Dolan's driver. After he and Dolan were trapped in Robinson's grave, the driver had bones sticking out of his legs. Dolan shot him. (The backseat guard was already dead.)

DUNNY'S CATERING (U19-2) The firm that Robinson pretended he worked for when he called Big Joe's Cleaning Service to get information about Dolan's whereabouts.

GREAT-GRANDFATHER (U19-1) Robinson's. He had his great-grandfather's pocketwatch.

THE LINING MACHINE DRIVER (U19-5) The man who was "unaware he was passing over a fog-gray Cadillac with three people inside."

THE MATH TEACHER (U19-2) Robinson's friend. He helped Robinson calculate the design of the grave/trap he was planning for Dolan.

THE NURSE (U19-5) After his back surgery, a nurse told Robinson that he had spoken while under anesthesia. He had said "It's dark in here. Let me out."

"OLE BLOCKHEAD" (U19-1) The nickname that Tinker called Harvey Blocker.

THE OVERWEIGHT SCREENWRITER (U19-1) Robinson thought that the plot to the "detour" movie he remembered was dreamed up by an overweight screenwriter lying next to a swimming pool, a pina colada in his hand, a supply of Pentel pens, and an Edgar Wallace plot wheel.

A PAIR OF BODYGUARDS (U19-1) Dolan never left home without them.

ROBINSON (U19-4) The narrator of "Dolan's Cadillac." His wife, Elizabeth, was killed by Dolan.

ROBINSON, ELIZABETH (U19-1) Robinson's wife. She testified at Dolan's trial, and she was later killed by dynamite wired to the ignition of her car. Dolan either killed her himself, or had her killed.

THE SECURITY GUARD (U19-2) The uniformed man who entered Dolan's property as Robinson watched.

THIRD-GRADERS (U19-5) After burying Dolan, Robinson taught third-graders.

TINKER (U19-1) One of Harvey Blocker's men. Robinson gave his great-grandfather's pocketwatch to Tinker to hold until he proved himself on the highway crew.

URICH, TIMOTHY (U19-2) One of Robinson's students.

"WHITE-BREAD" (U19-3) How Tinker referred to Robinson.

THE YOUNG MAN WITH A PONYTAIL (U19-2) The boy who cleaned Dolan's pool.

Places

FIRST GRADE (U19-1) The grade that Elizabeth Robinson taught.

GENERAL MOTORS (U19-2) Robinson wrote to GM pretending to be a research writer. They sent him an operator's manual and spec sheet for Dolan's Cadillac.

GLENDALE (U19-2) Robinson's fictitious big punchbowl was at a fictitious wedding reception in Glendale.

HOLLYWOOD HILLS (U19-1) Where Dolan lived.

THE INTERSTATE (U19-5) After burying Dolan, Robinson took the Interstate west instead of Route 71.

KANSAS CITY (U19-5) The place where Robinson had his back surgery after he buried Dolan.

LAS VEGAS TO THE WEST COAST (U19-1) Dolan's regular route in his Cadillac.

THE NINTH STREET HEALTH CLUB (U19-1) After Robinson decided to seek revenge on Dolan, he joined this health club in order to get in shape for the summer job on the highway crew.

1121 ASTER DRIVE, HOLLYWOOD HILLS (U19-2) Dolan's address.

ROUTE 71 (U19-1) The road Dolan took to Los Angeles.

THE SCHOOL (U19-1) Where Robinson met Elizabeth, who later became his wife. They worked at the same school.

THE SPOT (U19-5) After burying Dolan, Robinson once went back out to the highway and pissed on the spot where Dolan was buried.

Things

BIG JOE'S CLEANING SERVICE (U19-2) The cleaning service that cared for Dolan's house.

THE BIG PUNCHBOWL (U19-2) Robinson told Big Joe's that his big punchbowl would be coming back from a wedding reception in Glendale on Sunday.

BIJAN SHIRTS (U19-1) Part of Dolan's wardrobe.

BINOCULARS (U19-3) Robinson watched the three-mile stretch that led to the trap through binoculars.

BUICK RIVIERA (U19-1) Robinson's car. It was "aging."

A CADILLAC SEDAN DeVILLE (U19-1) Dolan's car. It was silver grey, the "same color as his hair." Over the years that Robinson watched him, Dolan had had four Cadillacs.

THE CALENDAR (U19-2) The last page or two of *Nevada Road Signs*. It listed the dates and sites of the roadwork in the coming month.

A CASE-JORDAN BUCKET-LOADER (U19-3) The $55,000 piece of heavy equipment that Robinson used to dig Dolan's grave. It had a grapple and pincers attachment.

A COMPRESSOR AND A JACKHAMMER (U19-3) The tools Robinson used for his first stage of work in digging Dolan's grave.

"DETOUR 5 MILES" (U19-1) Sign on Route 71.

DETOUR SIGNS (U19-2) A car almost caught Robinson removing some detour signs.

"DETOUR 3 MILES BLASTING AREA AHEAD, TURN OFF 2-WAY RADIO" (U19-1) Sign on Route 71 after the "Detour 5 Miles" sign. Robinson saw the signs as he was following Dolan back from Los Angeles.

DIESEL FUEL (U19-3) It cost $1.05 a gallon.

DOLAN'S GRAVE (U19-3) It was a rectangle "not quite five feet wide by forty-two long." Robinson dug it up in forty-two individual rectangles.

DOLAN'S LAST WORDS (U19-5) "For the love of God! For the love of God, Richardson!" [NOTE: Dolan couldn't even correctly remember Robinson's name.]

DOLAN'S SMELL (U19-3) As Robinson waited for Dolan, he thought: "I didn't know if he could smell me, but *I* could smell *him*.

DOLAN'S WINDSHIELD (U19-4) Robinson had worried that the windshield of Dolan's Cadillac would break, but the car had been built to the specifications of dictators' cars, and the glass wouldn't break.

DUNNY'S CATERING (U19-2) The company that Robinson pretended he worked for when he called Big Joe's Cleaning Service to get information about Dolan's arrival time.

DYNAMITE (U19-1) After Elizabeth testified against Dolan, dynamite was wired to the ignition of her car.

ELIZABETH'S HAND (U19-2) As Robinson began digging Dolans' grave, he whispered "Here we go, Elizabeth. It seemed I felt a cold hand stroke the back of my neck."

ELIZABETH'S VOICE (U19-3) Throughout the digging of Dolan's grave, Robinson heard Elizabeth speaking to him: "It's not as bad as you thought, is it, darling? Please – go on. You can do it darling – I know you can."

THE FALSE ALARMS (U19-3) Before Dolan hit the trap, Robinson saw the following vehicles: a Subaru with a woman driver, a pick-up driven by a guy, an Escort, a Plymouth, a Winnebago full of kids having a pillowfight, a late-model Chevrolet, a black hearse, and a mint-green Cadillac loaded with twelve Vegas chorines and an old boy wearing a cowboy hat and Foster Grants.

525 CUBIC FEET OF DIRT (U19-3) The amount of dirt Robinson would have to remove from Dolan's grave.

$5 MILLION (U19-4) Dolan raised his offer to $5 million after Robinson turned down $1 million to release him.

THE FLASHING ARROW (U19-3) After Robinson placed the canvas over the grave, he turned off the flashing light.

A FLAT (U19-1) On his way back from Los Angeles, Dolan got a flat on U.S. 71. Robinson watched Dolan's man change it.

A FORD VAN (U19-2) The battered vehicle that Robinson bought.

FORTY-TWO FEET OF CANVAS (U19-3) Robinson unrolled forty-two feet of canvas that looked like Route 71.

FOUR EMPIRIN, DRIED FRUIT, AND COLD POP-TARTS (U19-3) Robinson's breakfast on the morning after the night he began work digging Dolan's grave.

THE FRONT-END LOADER (U19-1) Tinker taught Robinson how to run it.

"GOD SAYS, 'TAKE WHAT YOU WANT. AND PAY FOR IT.'" (U19-2) Spanish proverb. The epigraph to Part 2.

A GOLD ROLEX (U19-1) Dolan's watch.

HOW TO JUMPSTART A BUCKET-LOADER (U19-3) Tinker taught Robinson the trick: wire the red and green wires together, "like Christmas," and then touch the blue and yellow wires together.

"I AM A HEATHEN" (U19-1) T-shirt worn by Harvey Blocker.

THE JUNE CALENDAR ENTRY (U19-2) The entry on the calendar in *Nevada Road Signs* that gave Robinson the chance to start his plan of revenge on Dolan:

> JULY 1-JULY 2—(tent.).
> U.S. 71 MI 440-472 (WESTBND) RPAV

JUNE 13 (U19-2) The last day of school.

THE LAS VEGAS STREETS AND HIGHWAYS DEPARTMENT (U19-1) Robinson applied for a job with this department as part of his plan of revenge on Dolan.

THE LAS VEGAS SUN (U19-5) The newspaper that did a blurb about Dolan's disappearance.

LOS ANGELES SECURITY SERVICES (U19-2) The company that guarded Dolan's property.

MASTERCARD (U19-2) Robinson had one. He used it as collateral to rent a portable air compressor.

"MEET REVENGE IS PROPER AND JUST." (U19-4) The Koran. The epigraph to Part 4.

THE MOVIE (U19-1) Seeing the detour signs on U.S. 71, Robinson remembered a movie in which armed robbers put up false detour signs in the desert and trapped an armored car.

NAUTILUS MACHINE (U19-1) To get in shape for the summer highway job, Robinson bought a Nautilus machine.

NEVADA ROAD SIGNS (U19-2) The monthly bulletin sent out by the state highway commission.

AN OLD BUICK (U19-3) A car that approached the detour sign.

$1 MILLION (U19-4) As Robinson began to shovel dirt onto Dolan's Cadillac, Dolan offered him $1 million to let him go.

"PLEASE, DARLING." (U19-3) The words that Robinson heard Elizabeth say to him the morning after he began digging Dolan's grave.

"PLEASE, PLEASE...FOR ME." (U19-3) Words Elizabeth said to Robinson (in his head).

POCKETWATCH (U19-1) Robinson had his great-grandfather's pocketwatch. He gave it to Tinker to hold until he proved himself to Blocker on the highway road crew.

A PORTABLE AIR COMPRESSOR (U19-2) Robinson rented an air compressor using his Mastercard as collateral.

A REAL DETOUR (U19-1) Robinson decided not to put up a fake detour, as was done in the movie he remembered, but instead to take away a real one.

"REVENGE IS A DISH BEST EATEN COLD." (U19-1) Spanish proverb. The opening epigraph to Part 1 of "Dolan's Cadillac."

ROADS TO EVERYWHERE (U19-2) The third-grade reading textbook that Robinson used.

ROBINSON'S INJURIES (U19-5) After burying Dolan, Robinson saw a chiropractor who determined that Robinson had three slipped discs, and a serious lower spinal dislocation.

"RPAV" (U19-2) This stood for "repaving" in *Nevada Road Signs*.

A SCIENCE FICTION STORY (U19-2) In order to get the dimensions of the grave/trap that Robinson was designing for Dolan, he pretended he was writing a sci-fi story, and asked his math teacher friend for help. He told his teacher friend that the alien scout vehicle (actually Dolan's Cadillac) would be traveling at "twenty rull," which was equal to fifty miles an hour.

A SEAT BELT (U19-4) Dolan always sat in the backseat, and wore his seatbelt.

SEVEN YEARS (U19-1) Robinson "waited and watched" for seven years before he began his plan of revenge on Dolan.

6:00 P.M., SUNDAY (U19-2) The time and day that Dolan was expected home, according to Big Joe's Cleaning Service.

A '68 CHEVY (U19-4) Elizabeth Robinson's car.

THE STATE HIGHWAY COMMISSION'S MAILING LIST (U19-2) Robinson was on it.

THIRTY POUNDS (U19-5) After his back surgery, Robinson couldn't lift anything over thirty pounds without help.

THREE O'CLOCK IN THE MORNING (U19-3) By 3:00 a.m. on the night he began work, Robinson had dug up twenty-eight squares. He had fourteen to go.

THREE SECONDS (U19-4) The length of time it took to trap Dolan's car.

THREE YEARS OLD (U19-2) At the time Robinson began his plan of revenge, Dolan's latest Cadillac was three years old.

$257 (U19-2) After Robinson bought the Ford van, he was left with $257 in his savings.

"VENGEANCE AND PITY DO NOT MIX." (U19-5) Sheridan. The epigraph to Part 5.

"VENGEANCE IS MINE, SAITH THE LORD." (U19-3) Old Testament. The epigraph to Part 3.

WKXR (U19-5) Radio station that broadcast out of Las Vegas. Before he finished burying Dolan, Robinson listened to WKXR and heard a Barry Manilow song.

"THE WORST DESERT WINDSTORM IN LAS VEGAS HISTORY" (U19-5) After burying Dolan, Robinson woke up in his sleeping bag to the worst desert windstorm in Vegas's history.

"Heroes for Hope Starring the X-Men"

"Heroes for Hope Starring the X-Men," Vol. 1, No, 1, 1985, bears a message on its cover that reads "ALL PROCEEDS FROM THIS COMIC BOOK ARE BEING DONATED TO FAMINE RELIEF AND RECOVERY IN AFRICA." The magazine sold for a dollar-fifty, and all proceeds went to the appropriate charity organizations trying to fight the famine in Africa.

The idea was suggested by Bernie Wrightson, who envisioned the project as a "jam," with artists and writers coming together and contributing their time and creative efforts to the cause. The comic book ran forty-eight pages. Eighteen writers, twenty pencilers, twenty-one inkers, fifteen letterers, and thirteen colorists participated. The front cover was drawn by Arthur Adams, the back cover was drawn by Jim Starlin, and the logo design was drawn by Janet Jackson. The magazine was published by the Marvel Comics Group in 1985.

Stephen King agreed to participate, and his segment was drawn by Wrightson.

The credits for the book were given on the inside front cover. Stephen King's segment was credited as follows:

Pages	10-12
Colorist	Christie Steele
Writer	Stephen King
Penciler	Tom Wrightson
Inker	Jeff Jones
Letterer	Tom Orzechowski

Stephen King's segment consisted of three pages, with a total of seventeen panels of art. King's segment ran 320 words.

Here is a complete list of the writers who participated in "Heroes for Hope Starring the X-Men":

"HEROES FOR HOPE
STARRING THE X-MEN"
Story by
Chris Claremont, Ann Nocenti, Berni Wrightson, Jim
Starlin, and Jim Shooter
Edited by
Ann Nocenti and Chris Claremont
Assistant Editors
Pat Blevins and Terry Kavanagh

WRITERS
STAN LEE (Pages 1-4)
ED BRYANT (Pages 5, 9, & 15)
LOUISE SIMONSON (Pages 6-8)
STEPHEN KING (Pages 10-12)
BILL MANTLO (Pages 13-14)
ALAN MOORE (Pages 16-18)
ANN NOCENTI (Pages 19-21)
HARLAN ELLISON (Pages 22-24)
CHRIS CLAREMONT (Pages 25-26)
JO DUFFY (Pages 27-28)
MIKE BARON (Pages 29-30)
DENNY O'NEIL (Pages 31-32)
GEORGE MARTIN (Pages 33-35)
BRUCE JONES (Pages 36-37)
STEVE ENGLEHART (Pages 38-39)
JIM SHOOTER (Pages 40-41)
MIKE GRELL (Pages 42-44)
ARCHIE GOODWIN (Pages 45-48)

The Story

The X-Men one day face an onslaught by some bizarre, macabre enemy who seems to be able to mentally cut through their defenses and expose them each to their worst fears. It turns out that this enemy is world hunger, come to life as a demonic force determined to destroy mankind and the world with its merciless horrors.

The X-Men fight back with all their abilities, traveling to Africa to unload planes, feed the hungry, and bury the dead.

The story ends as it does in the real world: no end to hunger and famine, but with an eye to the future...and hope.

In Stephen King's segment, King adds depth to the character of Hungry (the personification of world hunger), by having him pervert the recitation of "grace" by saying "Good food, good meat, good God, let's eat!" as he taunts Kitty Pryde with rotten meat. In Stephen King's short story "Cain Rose Up," the college student Curt Garrish said "Good drink, good meat, good God, let's eat" as he began shooting people from his dorm window, symbolically "feeding" on the lives of the innocent, exactly as world hunger "feeds" on the lives of the starving innocents in "Heroes for Hope." — **sjs**

(U20)
"Heroes for Hope
Starring the X-Men"
People

"THE CHEF OF STARVATION" One of the ways Hungry described himself to Kitty Pryde.

"HASH-SLINGER TO THE HOMELESS" One of the ways Hungry described himself to Kitty Pryde.

HUNGRY Hunger. Famine. Starvation. Pestilence. Desolation.

Hungry was the personification of these blights upon mankind. He appeared to Kitty Pryde as a hooded skeletal figure. He described himself to Kitty as "Misery's maitre d'," "the Chef of Starvation," "Waiter to the Waifs of the World," and "Hash-slinger to the Homeless."

"MISERY'S MAITRE D'" One of the ways Hungry described himself to Kitty Pryde.

NIGHTCRAWLER X-Man. He found Kitty Pryde's emaciated body in the kitchen after she was attacked by Hungry.

PRYDE, KITTY X-Man. She was attacked by Hunger when she went into the kitchen to eat. He transformed her into a starving waif, and when he offered her a plate of steak and corn, "the food melt[ed] into a sickening slush of putridity." Nightcrawler came in later and found her emaciated body.

"WAITER TO THE WAIFS OF THE WORLD" One of the ways Hungry described himself to Kitty Pryde.

Places

THE KITCHEN The room where Kitty Pryde was attacked by Hungry, and where Nightcrawler later found her emaciated body.

Things

HOT BUTTERED CORN One of the food items Hungry offered to a starving Kitty Pryde. It turned to maggot-ridden slush before she could eat it.

MAGGOTS Maggots squirmed in the remains of the sirloin and buttered corn that Hungry offered to Kitty Pryde. He turned it rotten before she could eat it.

MEDIUM RARE STEAK One of the food items Hungry offered to a starving Kitty Pryde. It turned to maggot-ridden slush before she could eat it.

"A SICKENING SLUSH OF PUTRIDITY" Hungry offered Kitty Pryde a steak and some buttered corn that turned into a "sickening slush of putridity" as her fingers touched the plate. "Maggots squirm[ed] in the rotted remains of the sirloin."

"The End of the Whole Mess"

"The End of the Whole Mess" is one of Stephen King's infrequent forays into science fiction. Appropriately, it was published in the October 1986 issue of *Omni* magazine.

The story concerns two brothers, one of whom is a genius, the other a freelance writer. The brothers, Bobby and Howard Fornoy, were born gifted and lived intellectually stimulating childhoods, so it is no surprise that they embarked on careers that utilized their many talents.

Bobby Fornoy became fascinated with a small town in Texas called La Plata, a place that had virtually no crime. Bobby traces the cause of this isolated peace to, literally, "something in the water." He dubs this chemical compound "The Calmative," and decides that if a small amount of the chemical in the water of one town works so well, then a huge amount of it distilled and spread all over the globe by a volcanic eruption would bring about total global peace.

Makes sense, right?

There was one little catch, though. The Calmative, in addition to causing a lessening of violent tendencies in people, also brought about premature senility – specifically, a form of Alzheimer's disease.

"The End of the Whole Mess" takes the form of a letter to the future written by the surviving brother, Howard "Bow Wow" Fornoy, telling the story of what happened. The only problem is that Howard has also been "calmified," and he has to write everything down before he, too, becomes a drooling, blithering idiot like the rest of the world's population.

King shows the progressive deterioration in Howard's mental state by misspelling words, mixing things up, and just generally having Bow Wow get more and more stupid as the letter (and the story) nears its completion. The last few paragraphs bear almost no resemblance at all to normal writing.

"The End of the Whole Mess" is a very well done look at what *Omni* called "good intentions gone awry."

The issue of *Omni* containing the magazine is still very easy to locate and, inasmuch as the story has never been reprinted, you'll have to buy an issue if you want to read it. Most of the usual sources should have it. — **sjs**

(U22)
"The End of the Whole Mess"
People

THE ALBANIANS In the year 2004, Albanians tried to air-spray the AIDS virus over West Berlin.

THE BEEKEEPER When Bobby put his hand in the bee's box, it brought back a memory to Howard of once seeing a beekeeper on TV allow bees to crawl all over his face.

THE DEPUTY La Plata's only deputy was the sheriff's nephew: "[H]e bore an uncanny resemblance to Barney Fife on the old Andy Griffith show."

THE DOCTOR The doctor who determined that Bobby Fornoy's headaches at the age of three were from not being able to physically express what his mind wanted to say.

FENDER BENDER DRIVER #1 Bobby saw a fender bender in La Plata. Both drivers were male, drunk, and twenty-four years old. Instead of fighting, though, they simply shook hands and exchanged insurance information.

FENDER BENDER DRIVER #2 Bobby saw a fender bender in La Plata. Both drivers were male, drunk, and twenty-four years old. Instead of fighting, though, they simply shook hands and exchanged insurance information.

15,000 RED CHINESE ADVISORS In the year 2004, the U.S. blockaded the Phillipines after the Cedeno administration accepted fifteen thousand Red Chinese advisors.

FORNOY, BOBBY Robert Fornoy. The Messiah. Bobby discovered the "Calmative" in the waters of La Plata, Texas.

FORNOY, BOW-WOW Howard Fornoy. Bow-Wow was Bobby's nickname for his brother.

FORNOY, HOWARD The narrator of "The End of the Whole Mess," the story of The Calmative. Howard was a former freelance writer, the brother of Bobby Fornoy (The Messiah).

FORNOY, INDIA Howard and Bobby's mother. She graduated cum laude from Drew in business administration, and became a successful CPA in D.C.

FORNOY, RICHARD Howard and Bobby's father. He was a history major who became a full professor at Hofstra at the age of thirty. At the age of forty, he was one of six vice administrators of the National Archives in Washington, D.C.

A FULL PROFESSOR OF GEOLOGY Bobby went to Waco with two sociology grad students and one full professor of geology in order to study the effects of the water.

GOULD, JAY Jay Gould once furnished the parlor car of his private train with fake Manets.

HOWARD'S LANDLORD Howard's landlord was a pussycat.

HOWARD'S SUPER She was a big bulldyke who smoked Odie Perodie cigarettes. She had thirty pounds on Howard.

THE INDIANS By the age of fifteen, Bobby Fornoy was into

archaeology: He combed the White Mountain foothills and reconstructed the history of the Indians who had once lived there.

THE INDIANS AND THE PAKISTANIS Bobby pointed to the following as evidence that the world was going crazy, and as good reasons to use the La Plata water to try and make things better: The Indians and the Pakistanis were poised on the brink, as were the Russians and the Chinese; one half of Africa was starving, the other half was on fire; there had been border skirmishes along the Tex-Mex border since Mexico went Communist.

THE LOCAL INSURANCE LADY Bobby had hitched a ride from La Plata to Waco with the local insurance lady in her Piper Cub.

THE LOCAL SHERIFF The La Plata sheriff was a fat old Republican with a pretty fair Rodney Dangerfield imitation and the beginnings of Alzheimer's disease.

THE MESSIAH Bobby Fornoy.

NEWTON, EINSTEIN, DA VINCI, EDISON (MAYBE) Howard figured that guys like Bobby Fornoy, Newton, et al, only came along once every two or three generations.

AN OLD GUY IN A WALKER When Bobby took off in his homemade airplane in D.C.'s Grant Park, he just missed an old guy in a walker.

AN OLD LADY When Bobby took off in his homemade airplane in D.C.'s Grant Park, an old lady had to jump out of his way.

ONE CRAZY GUY As Howard wrote the story of Bobby and the Calmative, he dialed through four bands on the radio. He found one crazy guy raving, and turned it off.

THE PEOPLE IN GRANT PARK When Bobby took off in his homemade airplane in D.C.'s Grant Park, the following people stopped what they were doing to watch: startled chess players, Frisbee throwers, book readers, lovers, and joggers.

ROGERS, DUKE John Paul Rogers.

ROGERS, JOHN PAUL The geology professor who told Bobby that the volcano on Gulandio was ready to explode.

THE RUSSIANS AND THE CHINESE Bobby pointed to the following as evidence that the world was going crazy, and as good reasons to use the La Plata water to try and make things better: The Indians and the Pakistanis were poised on the brink, as were the Russians and the Chinese; one half of Africa was starving, the other half was on fire; there were border skirmishes along the Tex-Mex border since Mexico went Communist.

THE SCIENTISTS FOR NUCLEAR RESPONSIBILITY On New Year's Eve, the Scientists for Nuclear Responsibility set their Doomsday clock to fifteen seconds before midnight.

THE SONS OF THE JIHAD In the year 2003, a PLO splinter group, the Sons of the Jihad, set off a squirt bomb in London, polluting sixty percent of the city for the next seventy years.

TWO SOCIOLOGY GRADUATE STUDENTS Bobby went to Waco with two sociology grad students and one full professor of geology in order to study the effects of the water.

A YOUNG FELLOW IN A NEAT THREE-PIECE SUIT When Bobby took off in his homemade airplane in D.C.'s Grant Park, he passed a young fellow in a neat three-piece suit who thought he was having an acid flashback.

Places

AFRICA Bobby pointed to the following as evidence that the world was going crazy, and as good reasons to use the La Plata water to try and make things better: The Indians and the Pakistanis were poised on the brink, as were the Russians and the Chinese; one half of Africa was starving, the other half was on fire; there were border skirmishes along the Tex-Mex border since Mexico went Communist.

CARRIGAN'S HILL Howard pushed Bobby down D.C.'s Carrigan's Hill in Bobby's homemade airplane. Carrigan's Hill was the steepest grade in Grant Park.

D STREET When Bobby took off in his homemade airplane in D.C.'s Grant Park, Howard though he'd end up splattered all over D Street.

DREW UNIVERSITY India Fornoy graduated cum laude in business administration from Drew.

THE FORT WORTH BARS The Fort Worth, Texas, bars were like shooting galleries on Saturday nights.

A FOUR-BLOCK RADIUS OF GEORGETOWN Bobby Fornoy once blocked out all the televisions and radios within a four-block radius of Georgetown by using an old black-and-white Zenith, twelve feet of hi-flex, and a coat hanger mounted on the roof of their house. For two hours he broadcast WBOB, which consisted of Bobby reading some of Howard's short stories, telling moron jokes, and explaining why his dad farted in church every Sunday.

GEORGETOWN UNIVERSITY By the age of nine, Bobby Fornoy was attending quantum physics and advanced algebra classes at Georgetown University.

GRANT PARK Howard pushed Bobby down D.C.'s Carrigan's Hill in Bobby's homemade airplane. Carrigan's Hill was the steepest grade in Grant Park.

GULANDIO An island to the west of Borneo. Bobby dropped the La Plata water into a volcano on this island.

HOFSTRA UNIVERSITY Richard Fornoy, Howard and Bobby's father, was a history major who became a full professor at Hofstra at the age of thirty.

LA PLATA, TEXAS A little town forty miles east of Waco that had a remarkably nonviolent history. Bobby Fornoy discovered that it was because of "something in the water." He called his discovery the Calmative, and seeded a volcano with it. The volcano erupted, spreading the Calmative throughout the world. For three years, there was peace. Then, everyone got Alzheimer's disease, and civilization died. La Plata's population was fifteen thousand, twenty-four percent of whom were Indios – people of mixed blood. La Plata's industries included a moccasin factory, two little motor courts, and a couple of scrub farms. For entertainment, there were a couple of dance halls ("where you [could] hear any kind of music you want[ed] as long as it sound[ed] like George Jones"), two drive-ins, and a bowling alley. There was also a still in La Plata.

LONDON In the year 2003, a PLO splinter group, the Sons of the Jihad, set off a squirt bomb in London, polluting sixty percent of the city for the next seventy years.

THE NATIONAL ARCHIVES, WASHINGTON, D.C. At the age of forty, Richard Fornoy was one of six vice administrators of the National Archives in Washington, D.C.

NORTH CONWAY, NEW HAMPSHIRE Howard wrote the story of Bobby and the Calmative in a cabin just north of North Conway, New Hampshire. He could see the White Mountains from the window.

THE PHILIPPINES In the year 2004, the U.S. blockaded the Philippines after the Cedeno administration accepted fifteen thousand Red Chinese advisors.

PUBLIC SCHOOLS As a child, Howard Fornoy had gone to public schools.

RUTGERS Howard Fornoy graduated cum laude from Rutgers.

SHOP-RITE Howard's mother used to shop at Shop-Rite when Howard was a baby.

SOUTH AMERICA At the age of sixteen, Bobby Fornoy went to South America with a group of New England anthropologists.

TEXAS The most violent state in the union – except for the La Plata area.

WACO, TEXAS Bobby spent a summer in Waco reading sociology and geology texts. He then took the water out of an artesian well in La Plata, Texas, a little town forty miles east of Waco, and used it to prove the effects of the Calmative. It really was "something in the water" that made the area so nonviolent.

WASHINGTON, D.C. India Fornoy was a successful CPA in D.C.

WEST BERLIN In the year 2004, Albanians tried to air-spray the AIDS virus over West Berlin.

THE WHITE MOUNTAIN FOOTHILLS By the age of fifteen, Bobby Fornoy was into archaeology: He combed the White Moun-

tain foothills, and reconstructed the history of the Indians who had once lived there.

THE WHITE MOUNTAINS Howard wrote the story of Bobby and the Calmative in a cabin just north of North Conway, New Hampshire. He could see the White Mountains from the window.

Things

A AND B AVERAGES As a child, Howard Fornoy had gone to public schools and gotten A's and B's.

THE ACNE STOPPER An acne stopper had been synthesized that caused cancer and heart attacks in thirty-year-olds. Howard used this information to try and influence Bobby against seeding the Gulandio volcano.

THE AIDS VACCINE In 1994, an AIDS vaccine had been tested that turned the test subjects into epileptics. Howard used this information to try and influence Bobby against seeding the Gulandio volcano.

THE AIDS VIRUS In the year 2004, Albanians tried to air-spray the AIDS virus over West Berlin.

AN AIRLINE MAGAZINE At the age of twenty, Howard Fornoy sold his first magazine piece to an airline magazine.

ALL THE TELEVISIONS AND RADIOS Bobby Fornoy once blocked out all the televisions and radios within a four-block radius of Georgetown by using an old black-and-white Zenith, twelve feet of hi-flex, and a coat hanger mounted on the roof of their house. For two hours he broadcast WBOB, which consisted of Bobby reading some of Howard's short stories, telling moron jokes, and explaining why his dad farted in church every Sunday.

AN AMERICAN FLYER SLED The base of Bobby's reverse-wing airplane.

ARCHAEOLOGY By the age of fifteen, Bobby Fornoy was into archaeology: He combed the White Mountain foothills and reconstructed the history of the Indians who had once lived there.

BOBBY FORNOY'S EVIDENCE THAT THE WORLD WAS GOING CRAZY Bobby pointed to the following as evidence that the world was going crazy, and as good reasons to use the La Plata water to try and make things better: The Indians and the Pakistanis were poised on the brink, as were the Russians and the Chinese; one half of Africa was starving, the other half was on fire; there were border skirmishes along the Tex-Mex border since Mexico went Communist.

BOBBY'S AIRPLANE At the age of eight, Bobby Fornoy invented an airplane. He put a plywood contraption on top of his American Flyer sled. The wings raked forward instead of backwards. (He had seen a show about hawks on "Wild Kingdom." Hawks reversed their wings coming up, so he used them as a model. When Howard asked him why the air force wasn't building them that way, Bobby didn't know that, indeed, they were doing just that.)

A BOX OF CHOCOLATE-COVERED CHERRIES AND A COUPLE OF MALLOW CREMES To sweeten his sweat for his bees and wasps experiment, on the way back from Waco, Bobby ate these sweets.

THE CALMATIVE The chemical compound that Bobby Fornoy discovered in the waters of La Plata, Texas. (His brother Howard thought it should have been called A Real Big Mistake.) One of the first symptoms of the deterioration that came with use of the Calmative was a noticeable drying of the membranes of the throat, along with a groping for words. Then came Alzheimer's disease.

A CALMQUAKE Bobby Fornoy constructed a computer program that showed a seismographic picture of a calmquake in the Waco/La Plata area. He drew forty concentric rings, each having a diameter of six-miles each. Waco was in the eighth, ninth, and tenth rings. An overlay showed the incidence of violent crimes (the computer assigned a number to the ring by a formula that took population density into account). The crimes considered included murders, rapes, assaults and batteries, and vandalism. The numbers read as follows:

40th circle–471
39th circle–420
38th circle–418
27th circle–204

The twenty-seventh ring was an area of fewer than nine hundred people. It reported only three or four cases of spouse abuse, a couple of barroom brawls, and one case of animal cruelty (a farmer got pissed at a pig, and hit it with a shovel). The center of the grid was La Plata. Its number was zero. There were fifteen thousand people in La Plata, twenty-four percent of whom were Indios – people of mixed blood. The center circles of the grid read as follows:

Center circle–Zero
1st circle–5
2nd circle–21
3rd circle–40
4th circle–63
5th circle–70
6th circle–81
7th circle–83

THE CEDENO ADMINISTRATION In the year 2004, the U.S. blockaded the Phillipines after the Cedeno administration accepted fifteen thousand Red Chinese advisors.

A CHUCK BERRY COLLECTION Richard Fornoy had a Chuck Berry collection.

A COMMODORE 64 COMPUTER WITH WORDSTAR Bobby's parents bought him an IBM typewriter and, a year later, a Commodore computer with Wordstar because the doctor had said that his headaches at the age of three were from trying to pass a "mental kidney stone": he couldn't physically express what his mind wanted to say.

A CURTIS-MATHIS TV After Howard Fornoy became a freelance writer, he bought a Curtis-Mathis TV, a Mitsubishi stereo, and published two novels that did pretty well.

DILANTIN The drug that Howard took to try and finish the "End of the Whole Mess" manuscript.

THE DOOMSDAY CLOCK On New Year's Eve, the Scientists for Nuclear Responsibility set their Doomsday clock to fifteen seconds before midnight.

EIGHT The age at which Bobby Fornoy invented an airplane. [NOTE: See the "Things" entry BOBBY'S AIRPLANE.]

EIGHT MONTHS It took Bobby eight months to fully seed the Gulandio volcano with the La Plata water.

"THE END OF WAR," ETC. As Bobby Fornoy's "Calmative" began to destroy Howard Fornoy, he decided to write down what happened. He began: "I want to tell you about the end of war, the degeneration of mankind, and the death of the messiah…"

FAKE MANETS Jay Gould had once furnished the parlor car of his private train with fake Manets.

FIFTEEN SECONDS BEFORE MIDNIGHT On New Year's Eve, the Scientists for Nuclear Responsibility set their Doomsday clock to fifteen seconds before midnight.

FORTY At the age of forty, Richard Fornoy was one of six vice administrators of the National Archives in Washington, D.C.

$450.00 The amount that Howard received for his first magazine piece. His father bought the check from Howard and framed it.

FOUR RADIO BANDS As Howard wrote the story of Bobby and the Calmative, he dialed through four bands on the radio. He found one crazy guy raving, and turned it off.

A FREELANCE WRITER After graduating cum laude from Rutgers, Howard Fornoy became a freelance writer.

THE FREEZE-DRIED VERSON Howard Fornoy had to give his readers the "freeze-dried version" of the end of mankind because

his brother's Calmative was slowly destroying his mind.

THE GULANDIO VOLCANO The volcano into which Bobby dropped the distilled La Plata water. The volcano had been dormant since 1804, except for a few puffs in 1938.

HAWKS They reversed their wings coming up after diving on their prey (they were double-jointed). Bobby built his own airplane modeled after their wing design. (He had seen a show about hawks on "Wild Kingdom.")

HEADACHES Soon after Bobby Fornoy began writing (at the age of three), he began getting headaches. The doctor said it was stress from not being able to physically express what his mind wanted to say. The doctor said he was trying to pass a "mental kidney stone."

HOW THE CONTINENTAL ARMY WINTERED AT VALLEY FORGE Howard Fornoy sold his first magazine piece at the age of twenty. The piece was on how the Continental Army wintered at Valley Forge. He sold it to an airline magazine for $450.

HOWARD'S PIECE ON ART FORGERY Howard Fornoy had written twenty pages on art forgery for *Vanity Fair*. Bobby read it in three minutes.

"HUGE COMPASSES SEARCHING FOR SOME TRUE NORTH" Howard thought that guys like Bobby were huge compasses searching for some true north, and that when they found it they homed in on it with "fearful force."

AN IBM ELECTRIC TYPEWRITER Howard Fornoy typed the story of Bobby and the Calmative on Bobby's electric typewriter after Bobby died. (Bobby's parents had bought him the IBM typewriter after he started getting headaches at the age of three from not being able to physically express what he wanted to say.)

LA PLATA'S CRIME HISTORY In the five years prior to Bobby's arrival and experiments in La Plata, their crime history had consisted of one murder, two cases of assault, and a number of armed robberies. Those involved were all transients, however.

THE LA PLATA WATER The water contained a protein found only in the human brain, and it had such a calming effect on people's violent tendencies that Bobby called it the Calmative. He seeded a volcano with Calmative so that it would spread throughout the world when the volcano erupted. There was only one problem: the water also brought on premature senility.

MENSA CARDS Richard and India Fornoy both had MENSA cards.

A MENTAL KIDNEY STONE The doctor said that Bobby Fornoy's headaches at the age of three were from trying to pass a "mental kidney stone": he couldn't physically express what his mind wanted to say. So, his parents bought him an IBM typewriter and, a year later, a Commodore 64 computer with Wordstar.

A MITSUBISHI STEREO After Howard Fornoy became a freelance writer, he bought a Curtis-Mathis TV, a Mitsubishi stereo, and published two novels that did pretty well.

MORE THAN FIFTY SCHOLARLY PAPERS More than fifty scholarly papers had been written about the nonviolent tendencies in Waco, Texas.

A MUMFORD PHYS. ED T-SHIRT When Bobby Fornoy showed up at his brother Bobby's apartment with the two glass boxes to illustrate the effects of the Calmative, he was wearing a Mumford Phys. Ed. t-shirt.

NATURE'S KAMIKAZE PILOTS Bees. They disemboweled themselves when they pulled their stingers out.

NEW YEAR'S EVE On New Year's Eve, the Scientists for Nuclear Responsibility set their Doomsday clock to fifteen seconds before midnight.

1980 The year Howard Fornoy was born.

1987 The year Bobby Fornoy was born.

NOXON The tranquilizer Bobby used to transport the wasps out of La Plata.

ODIE PERODIE CIGARETTES The cigarettes smoked by the super in Howard's building.

OVER $4 MILLION DOLLARS The cost to seed the Gulandio

volcano with La Plata water. (It was still less than one quarter of one percent of what America spent on defense that year, which was approximately $1.6 billion.)

OVER 60,000 GALLONS Bobby synthesized over sixty thousand gallons of the La Plata water and dropped it into the Gulandio volcano.

OVER 12,000 FIVE-GALLON CONTAINERS Bobby seeded the Gulandio volcano with over 12,000 five-gallon containers of La Plata water.

"PACIFIST WHITE LIGHTNING" Bobby called the distilled, more potent La Plata water "pacifist white lightning."

A PADDINGTON BEAR One of Howard's childhood toys.

PEOPLE'S AIRLINE Bobby had flown People's out of Waco to get to Howard's apartment.

A PIPER CUB The local insurance lady who gave Bobby a ride from La Plata to Waco had a Piper Cub airplane.

A PROTEIN The La Plata water contained a protein found only in the human brain.

QUANTUM PHYSICS AND ADVANCED ALGEBRA CLASSES By the age of nine, Bobby Fornoy was attending quantum physics and advanced algebra classes at Georgetown University.

"A REAL BIG MISTAKE" The Calmative, according to Howard Fornoy.

SIXTEEN At the age of sixteen, Bobby Fornoy went to South America with a group of New England anthropologists.

SMOOTH STINGERS Wasps had smooth stingers so they could sting over and over, unlike bees, whose stingers were barbed. (Bees disemboweled themselves when they pulled out their stingers.)

A SQUIRT BOMB In the year 2003, a PLO splinter group, the Sons of the Jihad, set off a squirt bomb in London, polluting sixty percent of the city for the next seventy years.

THE SYMPTOMS One of the first symptoms of the deterioration that came with use of the Calmative was a noticeable drying of the membranes of the throat, along with a groping for words. Then came Alzheimer's disease.

TEN The age at which Bobby Fornoy graduated high school.

THE TEN-FINGERS METHOD OF HAIR GROOMING Bobby Fornoy used the Ten-Fingers Method of Hair-Grooming: He held his head under the faucet and then raked his fingers through his hair.

A TENSOR LAMP The lamp that Howard Fornoy had on his desk.

THIRTY The age at which Richard Fornoy became a full professor at Hofstra.

THREE Bobby Fornoy began writing at the age of three.

A TIME CAPSULE Bobby asked Howard to write down what happened, and put it in a box that would last a million years so that people would know.

TWO Bobby Fornoy began reading at the age of two.

TWO GLASS BOXES Howard Fornoy showed up at his brother Bobby's apartment with two glass boxes: One contained a wasp's nest, the other contained a bee's nest. He used them to show his brother the effects of the Calmative that he had discovered in the La Plata waters.

TWO NOVELS After Howard Fornoy became a freelance writer, he bought a Curtis-Mathis TV, a Mitsubishi stereo, and published two novels that did pretty well.

2004 In the year 2004, the U.S. blockaded the Phillipines after the Cedeno administration accepted fifteen thousand Red Chinese advisors. Also, in the same year, Albanians tried to air-spray the AIDS virus over West Berlin.

2003 In the year 2003, a PLO splinter group, the Sons of the Jihad, set off a squirt bomb in London, polluting sixty percent of the city for the next seventy years.

TYPE A Howard thought his blood type was A.

WBOB Bobby Fornoy once blocked out all the televisions and radios within a four-block radius of Georgetown by using an old black-and-white Zenith, twelve feet of hi-flex, and a coat hanger mounted on the roof of their house. For two hours he broadcast WBOB, which consisted of Bobby reading some of Howard's short stories, telling moron jokes, and explaining why his dad farted in church every Sunday.

"WILD KINGDOM" Bobby had seen a show about hawks on "Wild Kingdom," and built his own airplane modeled after the hawks' wing design.

A ZENITH Bobby Fornoy once blocked out all the televisions and radios within a four-block radius of Georgetown by using an old black-and-white Zenith, twelve feet of hi-flex, and a coat hanger mounted on the roof of their house. For two hours he broadcast WBOB, which consisted of Bobby reading some of Howard's short stories, telling moron jokes, and explaining why his dad farted in church every Sunday.

"For the Birds"

"For the Birds" is a one-page Stephen King "science-fiction joke," a short anecdote that was written for a collection called *Bred Any Good Rooks Lately?* (Doubleday trade paperback, 1986). The common thread running through each story in the book is that they all end with a pun, usually a horrible one (a real groaner), the pun coming after an unbelievably lengthy set-up.

The result is a hilarious collection that includes such writers as King, Annie Dillard, Roy Blount, Jr., Isaac Asimov, John D. MacDonald, Lawrence Block, Madeleine Engel, Peter Straub, Robert Bloch, and thirty-six others.

In the Acknowledgments, the "Gatherer" (*not* the Editor), James Charlton, expresses his "appreciation to Steve King for letting me use his punchline for the title."

As of this writing, the volume is still available. (The Overlook Connection listed it in a recent catalogue for $9.95.)

The following concordance will fill you in on details from the "joke," but the basic premise is that by 1995, the air in London has gotten so bad that all the rooks are dying off, thereby jeopardizing London's tourist trade, inasmuch as the "Yanks with their Kodaks" love to see London's pigeons. The London City Council hires a guy to raise rooks in Bangor, Maine, which has a similar climate to London's, but without the pollution. The guy loves his job, but for the fact that, every day, London sends him a telegram saying…well, you know what the telegram said, don't you? —sjs

---

(U23)
"For The Birds"
People

THE ORNITHOLOGIST The guy who accompanied the rook raiser to Maine with two cases of rook eggs.

THE ROOK RAISER The guy who the London city government hired to raise rooks in Bangor. They paid him $50,000 a year, and he formed his own company, North American Rook Farms, Inc.

THE ROOKS The pigeons of London. The London city government was very concerned about the disappearance of the rooks because the Yanks with their Kodaks were attracted to all the rooks roosting on the public buildings.

THE YANKS The American tourists. They were particularly attracted to the rooks roosting in the cornices and "odd little crannies" of London's public buildings.

Places

BANGOR, MAINE The London city government discovered that Bangor, Maine, had a similar climate to London, but without the pollution. They paid a guy $50,000 a year to raise rooks in Bangor.

LONDON In 1995, the rooks in London were dying off from the pollution in the atmosphere.

Things

AN AD After the London City Council decided to hire someone to raise rooks for London (so it wouldn't become a "rookless city"), they placed an ad in the paper soliciting bird fanciers.

"BRED ANY GOOD ROOKS LATELY?" After the rook raiser began raising rooks in Bangor, Maine, the London City Council would send him a telegram every day that said "Bred Any Good Rooks Lately?"

THE CONCORDE The plane on which the ornithologist and the rook raiser flew to the United States with the two case of rook eggs.

$50,000 A YEAR The amount that the London city government paid the rook raiser to raise rooks for London in Bangor, Maine.

KODAKS The cameras the Yanks used in London.

THE LONDON CITY COUNCIL After the rook raiser began raising rooks in Bangor, Maine, the London City Council would send him a telegram every day that said "Bred Any Good Rooks Lately?"

1995 The year that the London atmosphere got bad enough to kill off all the rooks.

NORTH AMERICAN ROOK FARMS, INC. The company that the rook raiser formed in Bangor, Maine.

POLLUTION In 1995, the pollution in London's atmosphere was so bad, it was killing off all the rooks.

"A SCIENCE-FICTION JOKE" Stephen King describes the story "For the Birds" as a "science-fiction joke."

A TELEGRAM After the rook raiser began raising rooks in Bangor, Maine, the London City Council would send him a telegram every day that said "Bred Any Good Rooks Lately?"

TWO CASES OF ROOK EGGS The start-up materials for North American Rook Farms, Inc.

"The Doctor's Case"

"The Doctor's Case" is Stephen King writing a true Sherlock Holmes mystery tale – and doing it quite well, thank you very much.

The story was written for *The New Adventures of Sherlock Holmes*, a 1987 Carroll & Graf collection published to commemorate the 100th anniversary of the first Sherlock Holmes' stories.

The tale centers around what Inspector Lestrade describes to Holmes and Watson as "the perfect locked-room mystery," and it is Watson who ends up solving the case – not the legendary Mr. Holmes.

This story proves, once again, that Stephen King can do it all – that he can write many other things besides strictly-defined horror – and that he can do it all well.

He's done crime stories ("Man With a Belly," "The Fifth Quarter," "Dolan's Cadillac"), a gothic romance (*Misery's Return*), science fiction (*The Tommyknockers*, "The Jaunt," "The End of the Whole Mess"), the coming-of-age tale ("The Body," "My Pretty Pony"), humor ("Slade," "For the Birds"), epic fantasy (*The Stand*, *The Talisman*, the Dark Tower series), poetry (from "Harrison State Park '68" in 1968 through *Skeleton Crew*'s "Paranoid: A

Chant" and "For Owen"), and now, with "The Doctor's Case," a masterfully-crafted mystery.

"The Doctor's Case" should be readily available through the major dealers in the field, and probably even in some libraries. It's well worth tracking down and reading if you only know Stephen King as the "King of Horror."

There's more to the Boogeyman than just "Boo!" Read some of the other stuff, and watch the man boogey!

—sjs

(U24)
"The Doctor's Case"
People

THE ASSISTANT Lord Hull's solicitor, Mr. Barnes, and one assistant witnessed Lord Hull's new will, in which he disinherited his family.

BARNES, MR. Lord Hull's solicitor. He and one assistant witnessed Lord Hull's new will, in which he disinherited his family.

THE CHIEF ACCOUNTANT Lord Hull's chief accountant visited the Hull house quarterly to detail the balance sheets of Hull Shipping.

THE EVIL KILLER On their way to Lord Hull's house, Holmes asked Watson if he remembered the "Case of the Speckled Band." There had been a locked room in that case as well, "but there had also been a ventilator, a snake full of poison, and a killer evil enough to allow the one into the other."

A GIRL Lestrade admitted that he once almost kept quite about a case: there was a girl involved.

HOLMES, SHERLOCK Detective extraordinaire, known for his incredible facility to solve cases through logic and observation. There was one occasion, however, where Holmes was "beat to the punch," so to speak: "The Doctor's Case."

HUDSON, MRS. Sherlock Holmes' housekeeper.

HULL, JORY Lord and Lady Hull's middle son. Jory was the one who actually stabbed his father in the back, although the rest of the family was in on it. Jory was short, and looked like Algernon Swinburne. According to his father's first will, Jory would have inherited £40,000 at the time of Lord Hull's death. Jory was born dead. His mother revived him by putting his legs into hot water. His father called him "fish-face," "keg-legs," and "stoat-belly."

HULL, LADY REBECCA Lord Hull's forty-five-year-old wife, and the mother of William, Jory, and Stephen Hull. Lady Hull was terrified of her husband, who used to beat her. She was to receive £150,000 at the time of Lord Hull's death, until she attempted to disinherit her. Watson considered her a "perplexity": "A man who would beat his wife is an abomination; a woman who would allow it an abomination and a perplexity."

HULL, LORD ALBERT The sixty-five-year-old husband of Lady Rebecca Hull, and the father of William, Jory, and Stephen Hull. He was also the founder of Hull Shipping. Hull was "a tyrant in business and a despot at home." Hull was found stabbed to death in his study. He had been stabbed by his middle son, Jory, and the rest of the family had been in on the scheme.

HULL, MR. Lord Hull's brother in Wales. According to Lord Hull's will, he was to inherit £7,500 at the time of Lord Hull's death.

HULL, STEPHEN Lord and Lady Hull's youngest son. He was twenty-eight years old at the time of his father's murder. According to his father's first will, he would have inherited £30,000 at the time of Lord Hull's death.

HULL, WILLIAM Lord and Lady Hull's eldest son. At the time of his father's murder he was thirty-six years old. According to his father's first will, he would have inherited £50,000 at the time of Lord Hull's death.

A LARGE SCARRED TOMCAT When Holmes and Watson

arrived at Lord Hull's house, a large scarred tomcat twined around Holmes' legs, making him sneeze.

LESTRADE, INSPECTOR The London detective who never liked Holmes, but who had a "queer respect" for him. Lestrade used Holmes on occasion to help solve a case.

LORD HULL'S AUNT Lord Hull's aunt in Brittany. According to Lord Hull's will, she was to inherit £7,500 at the time of Lord Hull's death.

THE SERVANTS Lord Hull's servants at the town-house and his place in the country were to receive £5,000 at the time of his death.

STANLEY, MR. OLIVER Lord Hull's valet.

SWINBURNE, ALGERNON Jory Hull was short, and looked like Algernon Swinburne.

TEN CATS The Hulls had ten cats.

TWO CONSTABLES Two constables guarded the Hull house after Lord Hull's murder.

THE WAGGON DRIVER The driver who brought Inspector Lestrade to Sherlock Holmes' residence. Lestrade tossed him a coin.

WATSON, DOCTOR Sherlock Holmes' friend, companion, and colleague. He solved the case of Lord Hull's murder before Sherlock Holmes did.

Places

BEECHWOOD MANOR "Cut-Purse Palace." A prison for women. If Watson revealed the truth about Lord Hull's murder, then Lady Hull would probably have gone to Beechwood for five years.

BRITTANY Lord Hull had an aunt in Brittany.

BROADMOOR If Watson revealed the truth about Lord Hull's murder, William Hull would probably have gone to Broadmoor prison for twenty years,

"CUT-PURSE PALACE" Beechwood Manor. The ladies' prison.

THE EAST END In the Eastcheap or Piccadilly areas of the East End of London, cruel boys would often taunt starving dogs with a sweet, and then eat the candy themselves.

EASTCHEAP In the Eastcheap or Piccadilly areas of the East End of London, cruel boys would often taunt starving dogs with a sweet, and then eat the candy themselves.

HYDE PARK Jory Hull would quick-sketch people in Hyde Park for money. This embarrassed his father, but Jory wouldn't stop until his father agreed to an allowance of thirty-five pounds a week.

INDIA Watson once had a fever in India.

THE LEFT SIDE Sherlock Holmes always sat on the left side of hansom cabs.

MRS. HEMPHILL'S HOME FOR ABANDONED PUSSIES A home for orphaned kitties. Lord Hull's first will bequeathed £10,000 to the home. After he decided to disinherit his family, he chose to will the home £270,000 instead.

PICCADILLY In the Eastcheap or Piccadilly areas of the East End of London, cruel boys would often taunt starving dogs with a sweet, and then eat the candy themselves.

THE PLACE IN THE COUNTRY Lord Hull had a place in the country, fully staffed with servants.

ROTTEN ROW An area of London that Holmes, Watson, and Lestrade passed through on their way to Lord Hull's house.

SAVILLE ROW The street where Lord Hull's house was located.

221B BAKER STREET Sherlock Holmes' residence.

WALES Lord Hull's brother lived in Wales.

Things

THE CANVAS Jory Hull painted a canvas that matched the legs of, and the rug beneath, Lord Hull's study coffee table. Jory then hid behind the painting, snuck out and stabbed his father in the back. Watson discovered the canvas when he noticed that the coffee table legs threw shadows when there was no sun.

£50,000 According to Lord Hull's first will, William Hull was to inherit £50,000 at the time of his father's death.

£5,000 According to Lord Hull's will, his servants at his town-house and his place in the country were to inherit £5,000 at the time of Lord Hull's death.

£40,000 According to Lord Hull's first will, Jory Hull was to inherit £40,000 at the time of his father's death.

"FORTY YEARS IN THE GRAVE" At the time Watson told the story of how he solved Lord Hull's murder, Sherlock Holmes had been forty years in the grave.

GOUT AND ANGINA Lord Hull had always been "a heavy drinker and a champion diner." At the age of sixty, he developed gout and angina.

A HANSOM CAB Watson and Holmes took a hansom cab to Lord Hull's house.

HOLMES' COCAINE DAYS At the time the murder of Lord Hull took place, Watson said that Sherlock Holmes' "cocaine days" were behind him. Watson said that "There were times, especially after his cocaine days were behind him, when Holmes could grow moody to the point of surliness when the skies remained stubbornly gray for a week or more..."

HULL SHIPPING Lord Hull's business.

LORD HULL'S WILL Lord Hull had been stabbed in the back as he sat in his study, his will on the blotter before him. Hull's worth at the time of his death was £300,000, to be divided as follows:

> Lady Rebecca Hull–£150,000
> William Hull–£50,000
> Jory Hull–£40,000
> Stephen Hull–£30,000

The remaining £30,000 was to be divided in the following manner:

> £7,500 for Lord Hull's brother in Wales,
> £7,500 for his aunt in Brittany,
> £5,000 to the servants at Lord Hull's town-house and his place in the country,
> £10,000 to Mrs. Hemphill's Home for Abandoned Pussies.

His revised will disinherited everyone except the distant relatives and the servants, and left £270,000 to the Home for Abandoned Pussies.

NOVEMBER 1899 The month and year that Lord Hull was murdered.

£150,000 According to Lord Hull's first will, Lady Rebecca Hull was to inherit £150,000 at the time of her husband's death.

THE ONLY CASE WATSON EVER SOLVED The only case Watson ever solved was the murder of Lord Hull. His retelling of the incident begins: "I believe there was only one occasion upon which I actually solved a crime before my slightly fabulous friend, Mr. Sherlock Holmes."

"THE PERFECT LOCKED ROOM MYSTERY" Lestrade came for Holmes with the case of the murder of Lord Hull, what he called "the perfect locked room mystery."

THE PROBABLE SENTENCES After Watson discovered Jory Hull's canvas, Lestrade detailed the probable resolution of the case: Jory Hull would swing for his crime; Stephen would go to gaol for life; William would probably get twenty years in Broadmoor; and Lady Hull would go to Beechwood Manor – "Cut-Purse Palace" – for five years. But all this was moot because Watson, Holmes, and Lestrade all agreed not to reveal the truth. They figured Lord Albert Hull got what was coming to him.

"QUICK, WATSON! THE GAME'S AFOOT!" When Holmes decided to visit the site of the murder of Lord Hull, "the perfect-locked room mystery," he said to Watson "Quick, Watson! The game's afoot!" Watson said that that was the only time he had ever heard Holmes actually say the phrase, "despite the countless times the phrase has been attributed to him." [NOTE: Apparently, Stephen King has never been able to find the phrase in the

Sherlock Holmes stories. Has anyone out there ever seen the phrase actually spoken by Sherlock Holmes in one of the tales? If you have, write to me in care of Popular Culture, Ink., and let me know where, would you? Although I've enjoyed the stories, I'm not a Holmes expert, and this would require the assistance of a true Sherlock Holmes afficionado. Can anyone help with this?]

£7,500 According to Lord Hull's will, his brother in Wales and his aunt in Brittany were each to inherit £7,500 at the time of Lord Hull's death.

A SNAKE FULL OF POISON On their way to Lord Hull's house, Holmes asked Watson if he remembered the "Case of the Speckled Band." There had been a locked room in that case as well, "but there had also been a ventilator, a snake full of poison, and a killer evil enough to allow the one into the other."

"THE SPECKLED BAND" On their way to Lord Hull's house, Holmes asked Watson if he remembered the "Case of the Speckled Band." There had been a locked room in that case as well, "but there had also been a ventilator, a snake full of poison, and a killer evil enough to allow the one into the other."

£10,000 According to Lord Hull's will, Mrs. Hemphill's Home for Abandoned Pussies was to inherit £10,000 at the time of Lord Hull's death.

THIRTY-FIVE POUNDS A WEEK Jory Hull would quick-sketch people in Hyde Park for money. This embarrassed his father, but Jory wouldn't stop until his father agreed to an allowance of thirty-five pounds a week.

£30,000 According to Lord Hull's first will, Stephen Hull was to inherit £30,000 at the time of his father's death.

£300,000 The amount of Lord Hull's worth at the time of his death.

£270,000 After Lord Hull decided to disinherit his family, he had a new will drafted that gave Mrs. Hemphill's Home for Abandoned Pussies £270,000 instead of £10,000.

VENTILATOR On their way to Lord Hull's house, Holmes asked Watson if he remembered the "Case of the Speckled Band." There had been a locked room in that case as well, "but there had also been a ventilator, a snake full of poison, and a killer evil enough to allow the one into the other."

A WAGGON Inspector Lestrade arrived at Holmes' residence in the back of an open waggon.

"Popsy"

"Popsy" led off the second volume of J.N. Williamson's Masques series (*Masques II*).

The story concerns one Briggs Sheridan, a small-time hood who is trying to earn enough to pay back a gambling debt by stealing children for "The Turk." And what happened to the children that he kidnapped? "Dey goo on a bot-rahd, Meestait Shurdone." ("They go on a boat ride, Mr. Sheridan.")

Sheridan makes a successful score at the Cousintown Mall, preying on a little boy who was obviously alone, and obviously ready to take the advice of an adult...any adult.

After the child realizes that he's been kidnapped, he warns Sheridan that his "Popsy" is going to find him: "You'll be sorry. When my *Popsy* finds you you'll be sorry. Popsy can fly."

Turns out the kid was right. Both Popsy and his kidnapped grandson are vampires, and when Popsy eventually tracks Sheridan's van, he lands on the roof of the vehicle, rips the driver's side door off its hinges, slits open Sheridan's neck, and he and his grandson drink:

"[Sheridan] saw Popsy's thumbnail for just a second before it disappeared under the shelf of

his chin, the nail ragged and thick and brutal. His throat was cut with that nail before he realized what was happening, and the last things he saw before his sight dimmed to black were the kid, cupping his hands to catch the flow the way Sheridan himself had cupped his hands under the backyard faucet for a drink on a hot summer day, and Popsy, stroking the boy's hair gently, with great love."

Jerry Williamson describes the story as "unaffected, a bit tongue-in-cheek, and different from most of what he's written."

Masques II is out of print, but not too difficult to locate. (The Overlook Connection recently listed it for $29.95.) If you can't afford the hardcover, there is also a $4.95 paperback called *The Best of Masques* that collects stories from *Masques I* and *II*, including "Popsy." Again, try the Overlook Connection. — **sjs**

(U25)
"Popsy"
People

THE GIRL IN THE INFORMATION BOOTH A pretty, dark-haired girl of about twenty-five who worked the Cousintown Mall information booth, and who called the Rent-a-Cop over to the booth.

THE KID Popsy's grandson. He was kidnapped by Sheridan, and rescued by his Popsy. Sheridan thought the kid looked like a "big three...no more than five." The kid wore Tuffskin jeans and a Pittsburgh Penguins tee-shirt.

THE MALL RENT-A-COP A sandy blonde guy with a moustache who caused Sheridan to cancel his first approach to the kid. The guard was too close.

A MOTHER The kid told Sheridan that he had never had a mother.

"MR. REGGIE" Proprietor of the "casino" where Sheridan played cards.

"MR. WIZARD" The name the "big, greasy Turk" called himself. Sheridan stole children for him. When pressed about the fate of the kids, the Turk replied they went on a "boat ride."

POPSY Giant human vampire bat. Popsy rescued the kid from Sheridan, and then let the kid feed on Sheridan.

THE SECOND KID The second kid Sheridan had kidnapped had been six years old, and had kicked him in the balls.

SHERIDAN, BRIGGS Gambler, creep, kidnapper. He stole kids for the Turk in order to pay off gambling debts. He stole the wrong kid, however, when he coerced Popsy's grandson into his van.

SHERIDAN, MRS. Briggs's mother. She willed him her house. He lost it gambling.

THE TWO GORILLAS Two of Mr. Reggie's "workers." They had brought Sheridan into Mr. Reggie's office after Sheridan had ended up owing Reggie $17,000.

THE WOMAN Unnamed mall shopper who saw the kid crying and Sheridan talking to him.

Places

COUSINTOWN MALL One of the malls where Briggs Sheridan looked for kids for the Turk.

HAMMERTON BAY Prison location. Sheridan thought he'd be spending twenty years there if he got caught snatching the kid.

HIGHWAY 41 The road that led to Taluda Heights.

THE INFORMATION BOOTH A booth in the Cousintown Mall. It was run by a pretty, dark-haired girl who looked about twenty-five years old.

McDONALD'S Sheridan told the kid he saw his Popsy at McDonald's.

MR. REGGIE'S The place where Sheridan gambled (cards), and had markers he had to cover within twenty-four hours on the day he kidnapped the kid.

SCOTERVILLE MALL For a moment, Sheridan thought about hitting the Scoterville Mall instead of Cousintown.

SHERIDAN'S HOUSE From gambling, Sheridan had lost the house his mother had left him.

STATE ROAD 28 Sheridan pulled on to this road after leaving the Cousintown Mall.

TALUDA HEIGHTS The Turk had a big ranch-style house in Taluda Heights.

Things

A BLACK SUIT The suit Popsy wore. (He also wore some kind of pendant, and a blue tie.)

"A BOAT RIDE" The kids Sheridan stole for the Turk went on a "boat ride." Sheridan didn't know to where, or what happened to them once they got to their destination.

"A CRIP PLATE" Sheridan usually stole a handicapped person's license plate for his van so he could use the handicapped parking spaces while he was out hunting for kids.

$40,000 The Turk had promised Sheridan $40,000 for the kid.

THE HYPODERMIC NEEDLE The Turk had given Sheridan a hypo to use on the kids only when absolutely necessary. "Drucks could demmege the merchandise."

KHAKI PANTS Pants worn by Sheridan.

KOCH HANDCUFFS The handcuffs Sheridan used on the kid.

THE METAL STRUT After Sheridan handcuffed the kid, the kid began to pull on the metal strut on the side of the passenger seat. The strut ended up all twisted out of shape.

A PITTSBURGH PENGUINS TEE-SHIRT The shirt that the kid was wearing when he was kidnapped by Sheridan.

A "SALEM SPIRIT" OR "LIGHT MY LUCKY" AD Sheridan thought that the Rent-a-Cop and the girl in the information booth looked like the people in these ads.

$17,000 The amount Sheridan owed Mr. Reggie the first night he gambled in Reggie's "club."

SHERIDAN'S THROAT After Popsy rescued the kid, he slit Sheridan's throat and let the kid drink the blood.

TED LAPIDUS COLOGNE The cologne worn by Mr. Reggie.

"THANK YOU FOR SHOPPING THE BEAUTIFUL COUSIN-TOWN MALL!" The sign that Sheridan saw upon leaving the mall.

$35,000 When Sheridan kidnapped the kid, his debt with Mr. Reggie was up to $35,000.

TRANSFORMER FIGURES Popsy had taken the kid to the mall because the kid had wanted some Transformer figures.

TUFFSKIN JEANS The jeans that the kid was wearing when he was kidnapped by Sheridan.

THE VAN Sheridan's van was four years old, and blue. Popsy ripped the driver's side door off when he rescued his grandson from Sheridan.

VAN HUESEN SHIRT The shirt worn by Sheridan.

"The Reploids"

"The Reploids" was one of three Stephen King contributions to the Dark Harvest anthology *Night Visions 5.* (The other two were "Sneakers" (U27), and "Dedication" (U28). See the sections below on those stories.)

One night, a stranger walks out on to Johnny Carson's "Tonight" show stage, and begins doing a monologue...as though he's done exactly the same thing for decades.

When the guy, whose name was Edward Paladin, was taken into custody, he behaved exactly like Johnny Carson would if Johnny was arrested for doing his own show. He was furious.

But apparently, he was also legit.

A parallel dimension to ours had somehow leaked open, and Paladin ended up in our world, while Johnny, it must be assumed, ended up in Paladin's world, hosting that world's version of "The Tonight Show."

The story ends a little bit up in the air, with no firm resolution as to what happened or what would happen. (One critic commented that the story reads like the opening chapter of a novel.)

Whatever the case, the story is a huge amount of fun and, as always, King excels in capturing the realities of our world with incredible accuracy.

Night Visions 5 (edited and introduced by Douglas E. Winter) also contained work by Dan Simmons ("Metastasis," "Vanni Fucci is Alive and Well and Living in Hell," and "Iverson's Pits"), and George R.R. Martin ("The Skin Trade").

Night Visions 5 is still available from many dealers. (I saw it recently for $34.95.) There is also a Berkley paperback of the collection under a different title, *The Skin Trade.* Check with your favorite Purveyor of Phantasies. —**sjs**

(U26)
"The Reploids"
People

THE AUDIENCE There were 150 people in the audience the night Ed Paladin took over for Johnny.

BRYNNER, YUL Paladin said he hadn't smoked a Kent since Yul Brynner died.

THE BUSLOAD OF KIDS They were buried alive in Chowchilla in 1979.

CHEYNEY, DETECTIVE RICHARD "Detective to the Stars." The detective assigned to investigate Edward Paladin, the "imposter" who took over the "The Tonight Show." [NOTE: Cheyney was mistakenly identified as "Dave Cheyney" on page 22 of the story in the hardcover edition.]

DELLUMS, ALBERT K. Ed Paladin's lawyer.

DELLUMS, CARTHAGE, STONEHAM, AND TAYLOR Albert K. Dellum's law firm.

DILLON, ALBERT This was the closest name to Albert Dellums in the Yellow Pages.

THE DRUMMER Doc Severinsen's drummer. He kept his eyes on the Floor Manager for the cue that taping had started.

THE FLOOR MANAGER The unnamed manager who cued the 5:00 p.m. taping of "The Tonight Show."

THE FLYING SCHNAUZERS They were guests on "The Tonight Show" the night Ed Paladin took over for Johnny Carson.

FRED The Director of "The Tonight Show."

HENNING, DOUG He was a guest on "The Tonight Show" the

night Ed Paladin took over for Johnny Carson.

HERMAN, PEE WEE He was a guest on "The Tonight Show" the night Ed Paladin took over for Johnny Carson.

THE INTERN The USC student who was interning on "The Tonight Show." He was afraid of Fred the Director.

JACOBY, PETE Detective 2nd Grade. Rich Cheyney's partner. He did routines. Once, he got a man who beat his wife and son to death laughing so hard, the man signed a confession.

"JOAN RAIFORD" How Paladin identified Joan Rivers.

THE L.A.P.D. CHIEF OF POLICE He was on his way to Burbank as Paladin was being questioned.

THE LAUGHING MAN Man who beat his wife and son to death. Pete Jacoby got him laughing so hard, he signed a confession.

THE MAYOR OF L.A. He was on his way to Burbank as Paladin was being questioned.

McEACHERN, LIEUTENANT He watched the interrogation of Paladin from behind a one-way mirror.

McMAHON, ED Johnny's sidekick. On November 30, 1989, however, Ed Paladin walked out instead of Johnny.

MOORE, HOWLANDA Dellums' home phone number belonged to Howlanda. She'd had the number for three years.

PALADIN, EDWARD A Reploid. He replaced Johnny Carson on "The Tonight Show" on November 30, 1989.

PALADIN, MRS. Ed Paladin's mother. Cheyney threatened that he and two other motorcycle cops would rape her.

THE PRODUCTION ASSISTANT He comforted the Intern after his encounter with Fred the Director.

THE REPLOIDS The parallel beings who inhabited a universe amazingly similar to Earth's. On November 30, 1989, the barriers separating the two worlds somehow "leaked," and suddenly Edward Paladin was hosting "The Tonight Show."

SHEPHERD, CYBILL She was a guest on "The Tonight Show" the night Ed Paladin took over for Johnny Carson.

THE SPECIAL SECURITY GUESTS The coke-snorting movie star whose last picture grossed $70 million; the battered wife of a powerful film producer. [NOTE: See the "Things" entry SPECIAL SECURITY FUNCTIONS.]

THE TWO BURIERS Two people who buried alive a busload of kids in 1979.

Places

BURBANK, CALIFORNIA "Beautiful downtown Burbank." This was where "The Tonight Show" was taped.

CHOWCHILLA The place where two people buried alive a busload of kids in 1979.

THE FIFTH FLOOR HOLDING CELL The normal holding cell in the police station.

STUDIO C The studio where "The Tonight Show" was taped.

WATTS Paladin threatened Cheyney and Jacoby with a beat in Watts for arresting him.

Things

DELLUMS' HOME PHONE NUMBER It belonged to Howlanda Moore.

DELLUMS' OFFICE PHONE NUMBER His office number was a ConTel recording. The number was that of a fairly large stock brokerage firm.

5:00 O'CLOCK Taping time of "The Tonight Show."

THE GUEST LIST The "Tonight Show's" guest list the night Ed Paladin took over for Johnny consisted of Cybill Shepherd of "Moonlighting," Magician Doug Henning, Pee Wee Herman, From Germany, the Flying Schnauzers, the world's only canine acrobats (and Doc Severinsen, the world's only Flying Bandleader, and his Canine Band).

KENTS Cheyney's cigarettes.

THE *L.A. TIMES-MIRROR* AND THE *NATIONAL ENQUIRER*

Two of the media publications that would cover the Carson/Paladin story.

A LIZARD-SKIN WALLET Paladin's wallet.

NOVEMBER 30, 1989 The day the Reploids became news. That was the day Edward Paladin hosted the first two minutes of "The Tonight Show."

THE ONE-DOLLAR BILLS Paladin's single was bright blue, and instead of "Federal Reserve Note," it read "Currency of Government." Instead of the letter A was the letter F. And instead of George Washington, there was a picture of James Madison.

PALADIN'S "GOLF CLUB SWING" Instead of swinging a golf club, Ed Paladin's trademark was juggling.

PALADIN'S IDENTIFICATION When he was arrested, Paladin had on him a California driver's license, a Blue Cross/Blue Shield card, an American Express card, and a Diner's Club card.

PALADIN'S NBC PERFORMER'S PASS It had the peacock in the corner (which only longtimers had), and there was no weight, height, hair, or eye color given. Paladin's pass was salmon pink, NBC's performer passes were bright red. [NOTE: NBC was dealing with rather large egos here. As King put it, "Walk softly, stranger, for here there be tygers."]

THE REPLACEMENT SHOW After Paladin was arrested for taking over "The Tonight Show," Fred the Director ordered a replacement show featuring Don Rickles. He didn't want a show with Joan Rivers, and he said that if he saw Totie Fields, someone would get fired.

ROLEX MIDNIGHT STAR Ed Paladin's watch.

RULE ONE Special Security Functions' Rule One was "You don't shit where you eat."

A RYDER VAN Jacoby threatened to widen the crack in Paladin's ass enough to drive a Ryder van up it.

SPECIAL SECURITY FUNCTIONS This was "Tinsel Town" law enforcement. High profile people got special treatment by the police due to Rule One: "You don't shit where you eat."

THE SPECIAL SECURITY FUNCTIONS ROOM In this room were Dunhill cigarettes, *Fortune, Variety, Vogue, Billboard,* and *Cableview* magazines.

"Sneakers"

"Sneakers" is about a haunted toilet stall. (Actually, Stephen King has talked about how he'd written about haunted houses, so he figured the time was right to write about a haunted *shit*house.)

John Tell takes a job working at a music studio called Tabori Studios. One day, while using the mens' room, he notices a ratty old pair of sneakers beneath the door of the first stall. He discovers that the sneakers belonged to the ghost of a dead delivery boy who was offed while delivering cocaine to someone in the building. The story's resolution allows "Sneakers" to go to his final rest, and John Tell to go on with his life as a "regular man."

"Sneakers" is the middle Stephen King story in *Night Visions 5,* between "The Reploids" and "Dedication." Appropriately, it's the second best of King's three stories in the collection. ("Dedication" is the best.) It's a very contemporary tale, and there are a few puns that add to the fun. (The characters consist of JOHN Tell, PAUL Janning, and GEORGE Ronkler. I kept hoping King would find a way to work Ringo into the mix, but alas, he didn't.) —**sjs**

(U27)
"Sneakers"
People

CREEDENCE CLEARWATER REVIVAL Most of the four or five rock records John Tell owned were by Creedence.

THE DEAD BEATS Heavy metal group. John Tell and Paul Janning were mixing their album in Studio F at Tabori Studios. The Beats consisted of "four dull bastards and one dull bitch," and they were "personally repulsive and professionally incompetent." Their album was called "Beat It 'Til It's Dead."

THE DEAD KENNEDYS Paul Janning said the Dead Beats made the Dead Kennedys sound like the Beatles.

THE DELIVERY BOY The guy who became Sneakers. He had a topcoat slung over his arm to hide the handcuff holding his alligator-skin briefcase. He was offed in the first stall of the third floor men's room in the Tabori Studio building. The rumor was that someone stuck a yellow Eberhard-Faber #2 pencil in his eye.

THE FAT GUY FROM JANUS MUSIC The unnamed guy who used the same men's room that John Tell (and Sneakers) did. After the fat guy was in there, the room was uninhabitable.

THE FIRST BAR GUY The first guy who John Tell met in a bar wanted to talk about the Yankees, Billy Martin, and George Steinbrenner.

A FLY John Tell noticed that a fly crawled into Sneakers' stall and simply fell over dead.

"THE INVISIBLE MEN OF THE ROCK WORLD" Bassists were almost always invisible, except for Paul McCartney.

JANNING, PAUL The man who hired John Tell for the job at Tabori Studios. Janning may have been the best friend Tell had. Paul was a producer.

THE MAN WHO USED A URINAL An unnamed man who used the urinal while John was in a stall in the third floor men's room.

McCARTNEY, PAUL The only rock bassist who was not invisible.

THE MUSIC MIXER ON "KARATE MASTERS OF MASSACRE" The unnamed studio man who had a coronary near the end of May. Because of this poor guy's misfortune, John Tell got two week's work at the Brill Building.

THE OLIVE GUY A musician who used to get a jar of olives delivered backstage before every gig. The olives were packed in cocaine. He put them in his drinks and called them "blast-off martinis." The Olive Guy died in 1978.

RECORD COMPANY EXECS They used to deliver cocaine backstage before concerts.

RONKLER, GEORGIE Tabori producer. His karma didn't allow him to deal with strong emotion. He had been working with Paul Janning for seven years.

THE SATIN SATURNS' BASSIST John Tell's high school bandmate. He had once gotten salmonella.

THE SATIN SATURNS' LEAD GUITARIST John Tell's high school bandmate. He was big and violent.

THE SATIN SATURNS' RHYTHM GUITARIST When the Saturns broke up, John Tell formed a band with the rhythm guitarist.

THE SECOND BAR GUY The second guy John Tell met in a bar was a construction worker and a Mets fan who drank Black Russians.

SNEAKERS The name by which John Tell began thinking of the guy with the sneakers in the third floor men's room.

SNEAKER'S KILLER Sneakers told Tell that his killer went to a hardware store five blocks over and bought a hacksaw with which to cut off Sneaker's left hand.

SNEAKS The name by which John Tell began thinking of the guy with the sneakers in the third floor men's room.

"SOME DOPE PUSHER" The supposed ghost who occupied the stall in the third floor mens' room. He was killed in the stall in 1972 or 1973.

"SOME JANITOR" An imaginary guy who John made up so

George would tell him the "Sneakers" story.

TELL, JOHN He worked at Tabori Studios. He first noticed the sneakers after he'd been working at Tabori a month.

TELL, MR. John's father. He had sayings: "A regular man is a happy man," and "Clean your hands and then clean your plate."

THE THIN GUY FROM JANUS MUSIC John bet that the thin guy and Paul Janning were in on the "sneakers" scam.

THE THIRD FLOOR RECEPTIONIST An unnamed male who smoked Camels and read *Krrang!*

THE WAITER An unnamed waiter at McManus's Pub who picked up the candle that John knocked over after Paul Janning made a gay pass at him.

WYMAN, BILL Rolling Stone. He fell asleep once during a gig and broke his collarbone.

Places

BREW 'N BURGER A restaurant where John made a "pit stop" at lunch.

THE BRILL BUILDING The building that used to be called Tin Pan Alley. John Tell got two week's work at the Brill Building after the music mixer on "Karate Master of Massacre" had a coronary.

CARTIN'S A deli-restaurant on Sixth Avenue.

DESMOND'S STEAK HOUSE A restaurant frequented by workers at Tabori Studios and Janus Music.

THE DONUT SHOP A shop where John occasionally pissed.

THE FIRST STALL OF THE MEN'S ROOM ON THE THIRD FLOOR Sneakers' home.

THE HARDWARE STORE Sneakers told Tell that his killer went to a hardware store five blocks over and bought a hacksaw with which to cut off Sneakers' left hand.

JANUS MUSIC Music company down the hall from Tabori Studios.

MCMANUS'S PUB The bar where Paul Janning made a gay pass at John Tell.

MUSIC CITY Tabori Studios was in a building that used to be called Music City.

PENNSYLVANIA John Tell had come to New York from Pennsylvania four years prior to seeing the sneakers.

STUDIO F The studio in Tabori where Paul Janning and John Tell were working when John first noticed the sneakers. They were mixing an album by a heavy metal group called The Dead Beats.

TABORI STUDIOS The studio where Paul Janning and John Tell were working when John first noticed the sneakers. They were mixing an album by a heavy metal group called The Dead Beats.

Things

"ANSWER TO YOU, ANSWER TO ME" A new Roger Daltrey song that John and Paul were working on.

ATLANTIC The record company that was paying for the Dead Beats studio time.

"BEAT IT 'TILL IT'S DEAD" The Dead Beats' album.

BELL-BOTTOM PANTS AND A BLUE CHAMBRAY SHIRT WITH A PEACE SYMBOL ON EACH POCKET Sneakers' outfit.

BLACK RUSSIANS The drink favored by "the second bar guy."

"BLAST-OFF MARTINIS" Martinis made with olives that had been packed in cocaine. [NOTE: See the "People" entry THE OLIVE GUY.]

THE BRIEFCASE When the delivery boy who became "Sneakers" was killed in the first stall of the third-floor men's room, his briefcase was gone and his left hand was floating in the toilet bowl.

CAMELS The cigarettes smoked by the third-floor receptionist.

COCAINE Rock stars used to get coke deliveries backstage from record company execs before gigs.

A CORNED BEEF SANDWICH AND A CREAM SODA George Ronkler's lunch at Cartin's.

THE DELIVERY BOY'S LEFT HAND When the delivery boy who became "Sneakers" was killed in the first stall of the third-floor men's room, his briefcase was gone and his left hand was floating in the toilet bowl.

"DIVING IN THE DIRT" The first single off the Dead Beats' album. It entered the *Billboard* chart at Number 71 with a bullet.

EVERYTHING THAT RISES MUST CONVERGE The book that John read while he sat on his own toilet at home. He had Vivaldi playing at the same time.

FOUR OR FIVE ROCK RECORDS John Tell only owned four or five rock records, most of them by Creedence Clearwater Revival.

GUCCI LOAFERS Paul Jannings' shoes. One day John saw Paul's Guccis in Sneakers' stall. Paul couldn't see the sneaks – only John could.

A HACKSAW Sneakers told Tell that his killer went to a hardware store five blocks over and bought a hacksaw with which to cut off Sneakers' left hand.

JOHN'S IMAGINARY CARD John imagined the following verse:

"Roses are red and violets are blue!
You thought I was dead but that wasn't true!
I just deliver my mail at the same time as you!"

"KARATE MASTERS OF MASSACRE" Movie. John Tell got two weeks work at the Brill Building after the music mixer on "Karate Masters" had a coronary.

KRRANG! Music magazine read by the third-floor receptionist.

MR. TELL'S SAYINGS "A regular man is a happy man," and "Clean your hands and then clean your plate."

1975-1980 During these years, the rock industry "lay becalmed in the horse latitudes."

#41 The Daltrey album entered the *Billboard* chart at Number 41.

#71 WITH A BULLET The entry position of the single "Diving in the Dirt" off the Dead Beats' album "Beat It 'Til It's Dead." When the Roger Daltrey album entered the chart at Number 41, "Diving" was up to Number 17.

ONE MONTH Tell had been working at Tabori Studios a month when he first noticed the sneakers.

A ROGER DALTREY ALBUM Paul Janning hired John Tell to work on the new Daltrey album after John worked on the Dead Beats' album

THE SATIN SATURNS John Tell's high school band. John played bass.

THE SNEAKERS Tell had been working at Tabori Studios a month when he first noticed the sneakers. They were under the door of the first stall of the men's room on the third floor.

VIVALDI The music that played while John sat on his own toilet at home.

A YELLOW EBERHARD-FABER #2 PENCIL The "weapon" that killed the delivery boy who became "Sneakers." Someone stuck it in his eye.

"Dedication"

Nothing makes me gag.

I've always been able to relate to Stephen King's remark that he has watched "Blood Feast" while eating hamburgers.

But "Dedication" made me gag.

The premise is so gross that for the first time when reading a Stephen King tale, I had an actual physical gastrointestinal reaction to the text.

King has always appealed to me on a vicarious level; essentially an intellectual response. Horror and terror seemed to exist in my mind, rather than my gut.

But, as King has said, if he can't terrify, he'll horrify. And if he can't horrify, then he'll gladly go for the gross-out.

In "Dedication," he does just that.

The premise is neither terrifying nor horrifying: As the jacket blurb describes the story, "A desperate woman is driven to witchcraft to change the natural father of her unborn child."

But the way she goes about it...

Martha Rosewall is a maid in a hotel. One of the regular tenants of the hotel is a writer named Peter Jefferies. Martha is able, through witchcraft and the help of *bruja* woman named Mama Delorme, to make Peter Jefferies the natural father of her unborn son – even though Martha's husband is the *biological* father. And how does she go about it? (*This* is the gross part.) Jefferies is a regular masturbator. Martha knows this because she's the one who changes his sheets. One day, after her visit with the *bruja* woman, Martha gets the urge to scrape Jefferies' dried come off the sheets...and eat it. Apparently, this will allow Jefferies' "genetic soul" (for lack of a better term) to enter Martha's unborn son, gifting him with Jefferies' wonderful writing talents.

It works, and Martha's son goes on to write a superb first novel that he dedicates to his mother.

When I was working on *The Shape Under the Sheet*, I was talking to Jessie Horsting about some of the different uncollected stories I had been researching, and I mentioned "Dedication," telling her it grossed me out. She said she had never heard of it...until I started telling her what it was about. As soon as she heard the premise, she asked me "Is that the one about a maid in a hotel?" It seems that the reputation of "Dedication" had preceded its publication.

Nonetheless, it's a terrific story, and I must extend my professional congratulations to Stephen King for making me skip dinner one night. — **sjs**

(U28)
"Dedication"
People

AARONSON, BEDELIA A woman who worked in the Le Palais kitchen. Bedelia told Martha that she'd seen an old Negro woman in the hotel who got lost looking for the john. The woman was Mama Delorme planting a magic mushrooom on Peter Jefferies' breakfast plate.

BECK, BILLY The doorman at Le Palais during the "Peter Jefferies years." Beck was majoring in English at Fordham.

BILLY BECK'S PROFESSOR Beck's English professor had once told him that a pen to fellows like Thomas Wolfe and Peter

Jefferies was like a telephone booth to Clark Kent. He said they were "divine wind chimes."

BRADFORD Martha Rosewall's oldest brother. He was killed in a car accident in Biloxi twenty years prior to the publication of Peter Rosewall's novel.

BUCKLEY, MR. The Le Palais desk clerk.

THE CHICKEN GEEKER Martha remembered a traveling show that used to come to Babylon, Alabama, every August. The show featured a guy who would be in a hole, and who would geek the head off a chicken thrown down to him.

THE CLEANIN FAIRY Martha figured that Peter Jefferies thought she was the Cleanin Fairy because she cleaned his room when he was not there.

DELORES'S FIRST CHILD The child had fallen from a stair landing, lingered four days in intensive care, and then finally died.

DELORES'S FIVE CHILDREN Delores Williams had five children: One died after falling from a stair landing, and one was the head pediatrics nurse in a Cleveland hospital.

DELORME, MAMA The *bruja* woman who made the novelist Peter Jefferies become Peter Rosewall's "natural" father.

THE ELEVEN CHIEFS OF HOUSEKEEPING Le Palais had eleven Chiefs of Housekeeping, one of whom was Martha Rosewall.

THE HEAD PEDIATRICS NURSE One of Delores Williams' five children was the head pediatrics nurse in a Cleveland hospital.

JEFFERIES, ALTHEA DIXMONT Peter Jefferies' mother. He dedicated *Blaze of Heaven* to her.

JEFFERIES, MR. Peter's father. He had been a big landowner in Alabama.

JEFFERIES, PETER The novelist who was the "natural" father of Peter Rosewall. Jefferies was the author of *Blaze of Heaven* and *Boys in the Mist.*

JOHNNY ROSEWALL'S TWO FRIENDS Johnny and two friends had once tried to hold up a liquor store on lower 49th Street. Johnny's nickel-plated .32 had blown up and killed him.

KENNEDY, JOHN F. Peter Jefferies hated blacks so much that when JFK was shot, he threw a party.

KINSOLVING, MRS. 'Tavia's mother.

KINSOLVING, 'TAVIA One of Martha Rosewall's Harlem neighbors. Tavia had been to Julliard, but lived in Harlem because she was supporting her mother and three younger brothers. 'Tavia told Martha about Mama Delorme, the *bruja* woman.

THE KINSOLVING BOYS 'Tavia Kinsolving's three younger brothers. 'Tavia was supporting them and her mother.

KISSY Martha Rosewall's older sister. When Kissy heard about Martha's troubles with her husband, Johnny, she sent Martha a Greyhound bus ticket with GO NOW written on the envelope in pink crayon.

MARTHA'S FIRST CHILD Martha Rosewall had lost her first child in the third month of her pregnancy.

MARTHA'S MOTHER Martha wrote to her mother about her trouble with Johnny Rosewall, and her mother told her to leave him.

NORAH One of the characters in Peter Jefferies novel *Blaze of Heaven.* At the end of the book, she was hit and killed by a taxi.

PARKER, MRS. Martha Rosewall's Stanton Street Harlem neighbor. On the night of the day that Martha ate Jefferies' dried come off his sheets, Mrs. Parker heard Martha vomiting in the bathroom.

THE PARKER KID After Martha's visit to Mama Delorme, she went home and was in the hall bathroom when one of the Parker kids started banging on the door.

PETER JEFFERIES' NEW MAN The last time Martha saw Peter Jefferies was in February of 1971. He had a new man with him – the old one had quit.

PETER JEFFERIES' OLD MAN The last time Martha saw Peter Jefferies was in February of 1971. He had a new man with him

– the old one had quit.

PROULX, MRS. Le Palais' head of housekeeping. She let Martha have her job back after Martha had Peter.

RAY The bartender at Le Cinq, the Le Palais bar.

ROSEWALL, JOHNNY Martha Rosewall's deceased husband. He was Peter's biological father, but not his *natural* father.

ROSEWALL, MARTHA The chief housekeeper for the tenth, eleventh and twelfth floors at the Le Palais hotel. Martha was the mother of author Peter Rosewall.

ROSEWALL, PETER Martha's son. He was the author of the novel *Blaze of Glory.*

WILLIAMS, DELORES One of Martha Rosewall's best friends. Delores also worked at Le Palais.

WILLIAMS, HARVEY Delores Williams' husband. He was an alcoholic who had made it to sobriety.

YVONNE The Le Palais housekeepr that came on at three o'clock.

Places

BABYLON, ALABAMA Martha Rosewall grew up in Babylon.

BILOXI Martha Rosewall's oldest brother, Bradford, was killed in a car accident in Biloxi twenty years prior to the publication of Peter Rosewall's first novel.

BIRMINGHAM Peter Jefferies came from Birmingham.

THE CHRYSLER BUILDING Peter Jefferies' room in Le Palais looked toward the Chrysler Building.

A CLEVELAND HOSPITAL One of Delores Williams' five children was the head pediatrics nurse in a Cleveland hospital.

THE ELEVENTH FLOOR Peter Jefferies always stayed on the eleventh floor of Le Palais in Room 1163.

FLOORS 10-12 Martha Rosewall was chief housekeeper of the tenth, eleventh, and twelfth floors at Le Palais.

FORDHAM Billy Beck majored in English at Fordham.

HARLEM Martha Rosewall lived in Harlem on Stanton Street, which crossed 119th up by Station Park.

INTENSIVE CARE Delores's first child had fallen from a stair landing, lingered four days in intensive care, and then finally died.

LE CINQ The Le Palais bar.

LE PALAIS One of New York's oldest and grandest hotels. Martha Rosewall was the chief housekeeper of the tenth, eleventh, and twelfth floors at Le Palais.

A LIQUOR STORE ON LOWER 49TH STREET Johnny Rosewall and two friends had once tried to hold up a liquor store on lower 49th Street. Johnny's nickel-plated .32 had blown up and killed him.

OHIO Martha Rosewall's son Peter lived, and wrote, in Ohio.

THE PATISSERIE The Le Palais coffee shop.

ROOM 1163 Peter Jefferies always stayed on the eleventh floor of Le Palais in Room 1163.

THE SERVICE ENTRANCE Martha Rosewall entered Le Palais via the service entrance, around the corner from the main entrance.

A STAIR LANDING Delores Williams's first child had fallen from a stair landing, lingered four days in intensive care, and then finally died.

STANTON STREET Martha Rosewall lived in Harlem on Stanton Street, which crossed 119th up by Station Park.

WEST POINT Peter Jefferies had gone to West Point, and come out a major.

Things

ASSISTANT CHIEF HOUSEKEEPER FROM TEN TO TWELVE Before Peter Jefferies went back to Alabama, there was talk of giving Martha Rosewall this position.

AUGUST The month the traveling show came to Babylon, Alabama.

"THE BIG TWO" Peter Jefferies and his friends used to have drinking parties and talk about the War – "The Big Two." Martha Rosewall remarked to Delores Williams, "For men who seemed like they loved it s'much, they sure-God puked a lot when they talked about it."

A BLACK TRANS-AM FINANCED AT TWENTY-FOUR PERCENT Johnny Rosewall's car.

BLAZE OF GLORY Peter Rosewall's first novel. It was dedicated to his mother.

THE *BLAZE OF GLORY* DEDICATION This was how Peter Rosewall dedicated his first novel:

> "This book is dedicated to my mother, Martha Rosewall. Mom, I couldn't have done it without you."

Beneath the printed dedication, Peter wrote,

> "I really couldn't have done it without you! I love you, Pete."

He then signed it and dated it "April, '85." Martha said the dedication was more than sweet – it was true.

BLAZE OF HEAVEN Peter Jefferies' first novel. It was published in 1946, and was about five men and the war, and what happened to their wives and girlfriends.

THE *BLAZE OF HEAVEN* DEDICATION Peter Jefferies dedication read as follows:

> "This book is dedicated to my mother
> ALTHEA DIXMONT JEFFERIES
> The finest woman I have ever known."

THE *BLAZE OF HEAVEN* INSCRIPTION Peter Jefferies wrote the following inscription in Martha Rosewall's copy of his novel *Blaze of Heaven*:

> "For Martha Rosewall,
> who cleans up my leavings
> and never complains."

He then signed it and dated it "August, '60."

THE BOOK-OF-THE-MONTH CLUB BOMC had taken Peter Rosewall's *Blaze of Glory* as a selection.

A BOTTLE OF PERRIER-JOUET CHAMPAGNE At Le Cinq, Delores ordered a bottle of this champagne to celebrate the release of Peter Rosewall's first novel.

A BOX WITH A DRIED-UP MUSHROOM IN IT Mama Delorme gave Martha a box with a dried-up mushroom in it. She put the box in the back of one of her cabinets.

BOYS IN THE MIST Peter Jefferies biggest-selling novel. It was the story of twin brothers who ended up fighting in World War II on opposite sides.

A BROOM HANDLE Johnny Rosewall had tried to make Martha miscarry Peter by poking her in the stomach with a broom handle.

BRUJA Magic. Martha Rosewall felt that Mama Delorme was probably one of the few *true* witches practicing *bruja*. She felt that people who didn't need *bruja* could afford to laugh at it, like people who didn't need prayer could afford to laugh at that.

A CASSEROLE AND A SIX PACK Martha Rosewall invited Delores Williams home after work for a casserole and a six pack so she could finish telling her the "Peter Jefferies" story.

COLD CREAM Peter Jefferies used cold cream to masturbate with in his Le Palais hotel room. He would leave his semen on the sheets for Martha to clean up.

THE COVER OF *BLAZE OF GLORY* The cover of the novel showed three Marines (one with a bandaged head) charging up a hill.

DANDUX LAUNDRY CARTS The laundry carts used by the Le Palais housekeeping staff.

DELORES'S THREE TOASTS Delores made three champagne toasts to Martha Rosewall in Le Cinq to celebrate the release of Peter Rosewall's first novel:

1. "To your son's first book,"
2. "To your son,"
3. "To a mother's love."

DRESSES MADE FROM FLOUR SACKS When Martha Rosewall was growing up, she wore homemade dresses in Babylon, Alabama.

FEBRUARY 1971 The last time Martha Rosewall saw Peter Jefferies.

FOUR DAYS Delores's first child had fallen from a stair landing, lingered four days in intensive care, and then finally died.

A GREYHOUND BUS TICKET When Martha's older sister, Kissy, heard about Martha's troubles with her husband Johnny, she sent Martha a Greyhound bus ticket with GO NOW written on the envelope in pink crayon.

J. PRESS SLACKS The pants Johnny Rosewall wore.

MARTHA'S BOOKS On Martha Rosewall's three bookshelves were the following books and authors: Alice Walker, Rita Mae Brown, *Yellowback Radio Broke Down* by Ishmael Reed, a couple of books by Kurt Vonnegut, some paperback romances, and some Agatha Christie mysteries.

MARTHA'S TEA Mama Delorme put something in Martha's tea to initiate the process whereby Peter Jefferies would become Peter Rosewall's "natural" father.

A MUSHROOM After Martha had been scraping up Peter Jefferies' dried come and eating it for a while, she saw that there was a mushroom on his breakfast plate that looked like the mushroom that Mama Delorme had given Martha. Jefferies had eaten half of it.

MUZAK Muzak played in the lobby of Le Palais.

A NATIONAL BOOK AWARD One of Peter Jefferies' books had won a National Book Award.

THE NEW YORKER Peter Jefferies once told Martha that he had an idea that he thought he could sell to the *New Yorker* as a short story. It was the story of twin brothers who ended up fighting in World War II on opposite sides. This story idea became Jefferies' biggest-selling novel, *Boys in the Mist*.

A NICKEL-PLATED .32 Johnny and two friends had once tried to hold up a liquor store on lower 49th Street. Johnny's nickel-plated .32 had blown up and killed him. It blew up because Martha had squeezed the mushroom given her by Mama Delorme onto the gun, and the mushroom had bled onto the weapon.

1946 The year that Peter Jefferies' first novel, *Blaze of Heaven*, was published.

1957 The year that Martha Rosewall started working at Le Palais.

PETER JEFFERIES AND PETER ROSEWALL'S HANDWRITING It was identical.

PETER JEFFERIES LE PALAIS TIP HISTORY Jefferies left the following tips for Martha for cleaning his room:

1957-1960—A two dollar tip
1960-1964—A three dollar tip
1964-1971—A five dollar tip

PETER JEFFERIES' SHEETS Jefferies would masturbate onto his sheets in his Le Palais hotel room, and leave the mess for Martha to clean up. After her visit to the *bruja* woman, Mama Delorme, she felt a compulsion come over her when she saw the dried come on the sheets: She found herself scraping the come off the sheets and eating it. This was part of the *bruja* that resulted in Jefferies becoming Peter Rosewall's "natural" father.

PETER JEFFERIES' TIE TYING Martha told Delores that Peter Jefferies could tie his tie four different ways.

PICTURES OF JESUS AND NICODEMUS The pictures on the wall of Mama Delorme's apartment.

A PINK LADY One the day Martha received her son's first book, she and Delores had a drink in Le Cinq, the Le Palais bar. Delores had a Singapore Sling; Martha had a Pink Lady.

A PULITZER PRIZE At one point, there was talk that Peter Jefferies might have been receiving a Pulitzer for his work.

"RASTUS THE COON" JOKES Peter Jefferies used to tell Rastus jokes because he hated blacks. When JFK was shot, Jefferies threw a party.

SEVEN POUNDS Peter Rosewall's birth weight.

SEVEN TO THREE The shift that Martha and Delores worked at Le Palais.

A SINGAPORE SLING One the day Martha received her son's first book, she and Delores had a drink in Le Cinq, the Le Palais bar. Delores had a Singapore Sling; Martha had a Pink Lady.

THE SOUTHERN FLYER The train Peter Jefferies used to take from Birmingham.

THE THIRD MONTH Martha Rosewall had lost her first child in the third month of her pregnancy.

THE THREE THINGS MAMA DELORME TOLD MARTHA When Martha first went to visit Mama Delorme, the *bruja* woman told her three things:

1. You don't believe in me.
2. The bottle from your husband's coat is White Angel heroin.
3. You are three weeks pregnant with a boy you'll name for his natural father.

THE TRAVELING SHOW Martha remembered a traveling show that came to Babylon, Alabama, every August. In the show was a man who would geek the head off a chicken.

TU-TONE AIRTIP SHOES The shoes Johnny Rosewall wore.

TWENTY DOLLARS Martha Rosewall gave Mama Delorme twenty dollars for her "help" with Johnny Rosewall and Peter Jefferies.

A TWO-GRAM BOTTLE Before Johnny died, Martha found a two-gram bottle in his pocket. She brought it with her to Mama Delorme's. [NOTE: See the "Things" entry THE THREE THINGS MAMA DELORME TOLD MARTHA.]

UNIVERSAL PICTURES Universal had bought the film rights to Peter Rosewall's novel *Blaze of Glory*.

"WHAT CAN'T BE CURED MUST BE ENDURED." One of Martha Rosewall's mother's sayings.

"The Night Flier"

"The Night Flier" is Stephen King's eighties spin on the vampire myth. How else, King figures, would a modern-day, happening bloodsucker get around but in his own private plane, right?

The vampire in "Night Flier" goes by the name of Dwight Renfield. ("Dwight" is the first name of Dwight Frye, the actor who played Renfield, the lunatic who idolized Dracula. Dwight is not only a private pilot, he's got a sense of humor, too!)

The story brings back our favorite sleaze-ball, Richard Dees, that intrepid *Inside View* reporter from *The Dead Zone*, and it also takes us back, briefly, to Jerusalem's Lot.

There is an image in "The Night Flier" that is quintessential King, an image that is so blatantly visual, that you can't help but see it in your mind's eye. Even so, it's an image with which everyone might not necessarily be familiar. (Lemme see if I can explain this discretely.)

For those of you out there who have never seen the inside of a men's lavatory, the stalls are usually only used for...ahem..."Number 2."

"Number 1" is performed standing up at a wall urinal, a fixture that looks somewhat like a bathtub standing on its side (although lately they've been reduced to little tiny toilet bowls jutting out from the wall.)

Now, when a man urinates into a men's room urinal – (goodbye discretion) – the stream is not aimed at the bottom of the urinal, but rather against the back wall of the fixture, where it then slides down into the drain.

Every man who has ever used a men's room urinal is familiar with the way the urine looks when it hits the back wall of the urinal.

It fans out at the point of contact with the porcelain, and flows down the wall in a much wider stream than the actual flow hitting the wall.

As J.N. Williamson so insightfully remarked in an interview for this volume, Stephen King is a noticer.

And being a noticer, sometimes you notice things that might slip right by the average homo sapien.

But who ever said Stephen King was average?

In "The Night Flier," King uses this fan-like appearance of the urine as the critical element in Dees' sudden realization that he is seeing (or *not* seeing, actually), an honest-to-badness bloodsucking vampire:

"That was when he heard the sound.

It was a sound he had heard a thousand times before, or maybe ten thousand, a sound that was commonplace in any American man's life...but now it filled him with a dread and a creeping terror beyond all his experience or belief.

It was the sound of a man voiding into a urinal.

There were three urinals. He could see them in the vomit-splattered mirror.

There was no one at any of the urinals.

Dees thought: Vampires. They. Don't. Cast. Reflec–

Then he saw reddish liquid striking the porcelain of the center urinal, saw it running down that porcelain, saw it swirling into the geometric arrangement of holes.

There was no stream in the air.

He saw it only when it struck the dead porcelain.

That was when it became visible.

When it struck the lifeless porcelain.

It seemed that the bloody urine went on striking the porcelain, becoming visible, and swirling down the curved surface of the urinals to the holes forever."

I can *see* that red stream, and I can conjure up the scene in almost-photographic perfection.

Like I said...quintessential King. Mind movies. Skull cinema.

"The Night Flier" is a contemporary chiller that is truly frightening, and one of King's better short stories.

It is available in both the hardcover and paperback editions of Douglas E. Winter's state-of-the-art horror anthology *Prime Evil*. —**sjs**

(U29)
"The Night Flier"
People

THE BLACK DAHLIA Dees believed that the Night Flier – when caught – would be right up there with Jack the Ripper, the Cleveland Torso Murderer, and the Black Dahlia.

BOWIE, CLAIRE The murdered Cumberland County Airport night air traffic controller. He was a bachelor who had worked at the airfield since 1954. He was a victim of the Night Flier. Almost every drop of Bowie's blood was gone when his body was found.

BRIGGS, MELANIE One of the *Inside View* editors that Dees had served under. She was "delectable but inept." Dees had had an affair with her.

A CARNY GUY Buck Kendall once boxed a carny guy for two hundred dollars so they wouldn't repossess his Piper Cub airplane.

THE CLEVELAND TORSO MURDERER Dees believed that the Night Flier – when caught – would be right up there with Jack the Ripper, the Cleveland Torso Murderer, and the Black Dahlia.

THE COP Dees was arrested by a Wilmington cop for the Night Flier's airport murders.

"COUNT DRACULA WITH A PRIVATE PILOT'S LICENSE" The Night Flier, according to Dees. Dees had to admit that the idea was elegant.

THE COUNTRY-AND-WESTERN SINGER WITH AIDS While Dees was stalking the Night Flier, a stringer for *Inside View*, Gloria Swett, was in Nashville interviewing a country-and-western singer with AIDS.

THE D.E.A. GUYS The drug agents who found Doug Sarch's body.

DEES, RICHARD The *Inside View* reporter who tracked the Night Flier and got a story he never wanted.

DEES, RICK The disk jockey who Richard Dees hated.

THE DUFFREY DEPUTY A Duffrey deputy took twenty-five dollars from Dees to tell him about the Sarches.

EIGHT CHILDREN "Mr. Down Home America" and his AIDS-infected wife had had eight children together.

EZRA The mechanic at the Cumberland County Airport in Maine. Ezra found a pile of dirt underneath the Night Flier's plane. The dirt was squirming with worms and maggots.

THE FALMOUTH COPS The cops in Cumberland, Maine, didn't think they were hicks...but they were.

"FARMER JOHN" The Wilmington air traffic controller, according to Dees. (Although he never actually addressed the guy by this derogatory appellation.)

FIVE DRUG SMUGGLERS The Sarches had brought the Maryland state police out to the Duffrey airport four times on false alarms, but they had actually been right five times: They had caught three small drug transporters and two very big ones.

FRYE, DWIGHT The actor who played Renfield, the lunatic who idolized Dracula.

"GLORIA SUET" Gloria Swett.

HERRIOTT, JAMES Richard Dees thought that there was probably still an audience for "All Things Bright and Beautiful," but the one for "All Shit Grim and Gory" had become a growth stock once again:

> "Those in favor of the former had James Herriott. Those in favor of the latter had Stephen King and *Inside View*. The difference, Dees thought, was that King made *his* stuff up."

AN *INSIDE VIEW* REPORTER The AIDS-infected country-and-western singer told an *Inside View* reporter that she had signed a $3 million deal to write her memoirs.

JACK THE RIPPER Dees believed that the Night Flier would be right up there with Jack the Ripper, the Cleveland Torso Murderer, and the Black Dahlia.

KENDALL, GERALD ("BUCK") The Night Flier's victim in Alderton, New York. Buck was 220 pounds, and once boxed a carny guy for two hundred dollars so they wouldn't repossess his Piper Cub airplane. Renfield spiked both sides of Buck's neck and drank his blood.

KENDALL, JENNA Buck's wife. She came by the Alderton airport around 5:00 a.m. to bring Buck a waffle, and discovered his body.

KING, STEPHEN Richard Dees thought that there was probably still an audience for "All Things Bright and Beautiful," but the one for "All Shit Grim and Gory" had become a growth stock once again.

> "Those in favor of the former had James Herriott. Those in favor of the latter had Stephen King and *Inside View*. The difference, Dees thought, was that King made *his* stuff up."

THE MARYLAND STATE POLICE The Sarches had brought the Maryland state police out to the Duffrey Airport four times on false alarms, but they had actually been right five times: They had caught three small drug transporters and two very big ones.

MCCAMMON, SELIDA Before she died, Ellen Sarch had told Selida the story of the Night Flier's arrival at the Duffrey Airport.

MORRISON, MERTON Richard Dees' *Inside View* editor. Morrison was the ninth editor Dees had served under at *Inside View*.

"MR. DOWN HOME AMERICA" The AIDS-infected country-and-western singer's husband. He had given the disease to his wife.

THE NIGHT FLIER The airplane-flying vampire who flew into airports and "had lunch." Reporter Richard Dees was eventually arrested for the Night Flier's Wilmington murders. (Dees was in the wrong place at the wrong time.)

A PART-TIMER at the Alderton Airport told Dees about Buck Kendall's murder.

RAYLENE Ellen Sarch's sister. She was a pretty good mechanic.

RENFIELD The lunatic who idolized Dracula. He was played by the actor Dwight Frye.

RENFIELD, DWIGHT The name that the Night Flier used to land at Cumberland County Airport. He said his place of origin was Bangor, Maine. ("Dwight" was the first name of Dwight Frye, the actor who played Renfield, the lunatic who idolized Dracula.)

RENFIELD'S THREE WILMINGTON VICTIMS Dees saw three bodies when he got to the Wilmington airport: One man, one woman, and a girl of about thirteen or so.

RICE, ANNE The author of *The Vampire LeStat*.

THE RICH SUMMER RESIDENTS The Cumberland County Airport existed on the landing fees paid by the rich summer residents who found the airport easier to use than the Portland Jetport. (The Cumberland County fees were also twenty-five percent less than in Portland.)

SARCH, DOUG Ray and Ellen's only son, Doug, died in the Florida Everglades trying to land with better than a ton of Acapulco Gold in a stolen Beech 18. Doug hit a stump, was thrown from the plane, and eaten by alligators.

SARCH, ELLEN Ray's wife. She was one of the Night Flier's victims in Duffrey, Maryland. Ellen was found dead with *The Vampire LeStat* by Anne Rice open on her stomach.

SARCH, RAY One of the Night Flier's victims in Duffrey, Maryland.

SMITH, JOHNNY Richard Dees thought that the only truly honest man he'd ever met was a psychic named Johnny Smith. They had tried to recruit Smith for *Inside View*, but Johnny turned them down. Johnny was shot while attempting to assassinate presidential candidate Greg Stillson. [NOTE: See the section on *The Dead Zone* in this volume.]

SWETT, GLORIA A stringer for *Inside View*. While Dees was stalking the Night Flier, Swett was in Nashville interviewing the country-and-western singer with AIDS. Gloria weighed two hundred pounds, and was known as "Gloria Suet."

TWO GROUND CONTROLLERS In high summer, Cumberland County Airport employed two mechanics and two ground controllers.

TWO MECHANICS In high summer, Cumberland County Airport employed two mechanics and two ground controllers.

WEBSTER, JOHN Doug Winter led off the section of *Prime Evil* called "In the Court of the Crimson King" with an epigraph from John Webster:

> "The element of water moistens the earth,
> But blood flies upward and bedews the heavens."

KENNY RAY LINKOUS

The Shape Under the Sheet was published in spring 1991, and Kenny Ray Linkous came on board in December of 1990. I was able to include art by Kenny Ray thanks to the efforts of a friend and true fan named Larry Fire.

I met Larry at NECON 1990 in Rhode Island in the summer of that year, and he had kept in touch thereafter. Sometime towards the end of the year, he met Kenny Ray, mentioned *The Shape,* and Kenny offered to contribute a piece. Kenny Ray was put in touch with me via Larry, and "Ricky Oates After His Jaunt" is the artwork Kenny Ray was able to do for the book on *very* short notice (see page 356). Additionally, we were able to include four other previously published drawings by Kenny Ray (one of them to the right).

Kenny Ray Linkous is well-known to Stephen King aficionados. He illustrated the Philtrum Press limited edition of Stephen King's novel *The Eyes of the Dragon.*

Kenny Ray Linkous is thirty-three years old, a self-taught artist, and his *first* professional illustrating job was Stephen King's *Eyes of the Dragon.* (A somewhat heady beginning to a career, wouldn't you say?!) Kenny Ray was born in Tams, West Virginia, and in 1980, moved to Maine, where he now lives and works. His art has appeared in George Beahm's *The Stephen King Companion,* the accompanying special volume *Grimoire* (available only to purchasers of the limited edition of the *Companion*), and, most recently, *Steve King: Man and Artist* by King's University of Maine professor Carroll F. Terrell. Kenny Ray also did art for the special Stephen King section of Barry Hoffman's annual *Gauntlet* (which also contained excerpts from *The Shape Under the Sheet.*) Also, Tyson Blue used one of Kenny Ray's most haunting *Eyes of the Dragon* illustrations, "Flagg Walking Down the Corridor" as the cover for his 1989 Starmont House release *The Unseen King.*

I suggest that anyone needing commercial art include Kenny Ray Linkous on their list of people to talk to. I think you'll enjoy working with this truly gifted artist. Contact Kenny Ray Linkous at 141 Spring Street, Apartment #9, Portland, Maine 04101. —**sjs**

"The Night Flier"
Original drawing by Kenny Ray Linkous.

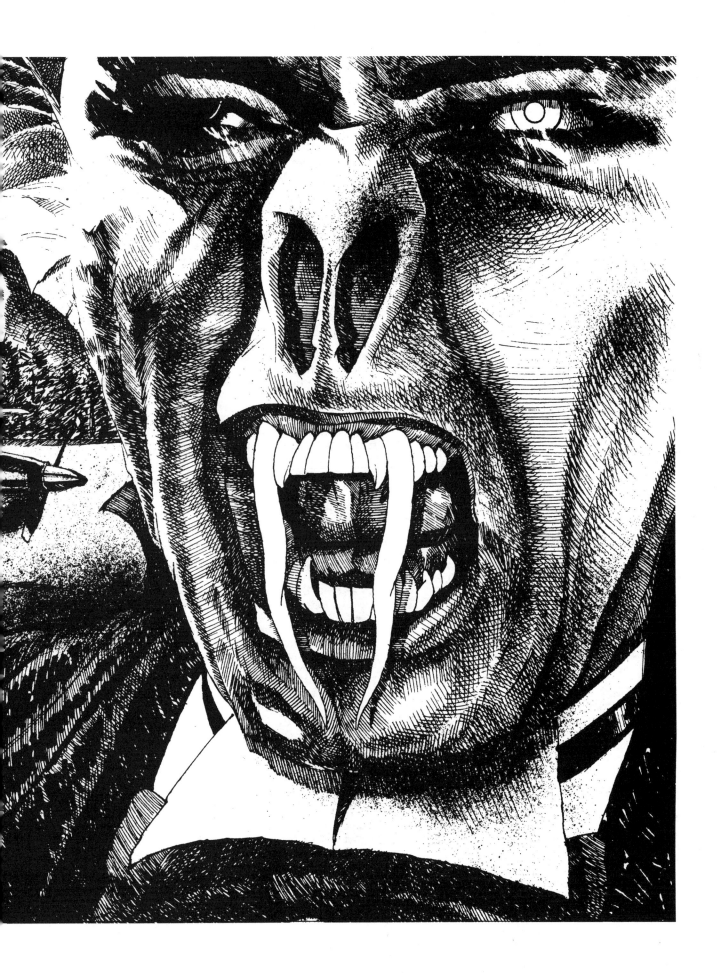

THE WILMINGTON CONTROLLER After Dees almost collided with a Piedmont 727 over Wilmington, he blasted the controller for not giving him clearance to land. Another controller then came on the air and gave him the okay to land.

WILMINGTON CONTROLLER #2 After Dees almost collided with a Piedmont 727 over Wilmington, he blasted the controller for not giving him clearance to land. Another controller then came on the air and gave him the okay to land.

Places

ALDERTON, NEW YORK The Night Flier's stop after Cumberland County, Maine. It was a one-night stand.

BIJAN'S, NEW YORK Doug Sarch was wearing a sportcoat from Bijan's in New York when his body was found.

THE CESSNA'S BELLY HOLD The Night Flier's Cessna had a belly hold that could fit a man.

CUMBERLAND COUNTY, MAINE Cumberland County, Maine sat between a "smaller (and mostly deserted) town with the unlikely name of Jerusalem's Lot" and the town of Falmouth. [NOTE: See the section on 'Salem's Lot in this volume. Also, see the interview with Tobe Hooper in this volume.]

THE CUMBERLAND COUNTY AIRPORT One of the Night Flier's "rest stops." While there he killed Claire Bowie, the Cumberland night air traffic controller.

DAYS INN The motel that Dees stayed at in Maryland.

DUFFREY, MARYLAND The Night Flier had commited a pair of murders at a "mud-hole airport" in Duffrey, Maryland.

THE DUFFREY BEAUTY SHOPPE The place where Ellen Sarch told Selida McCammon the story of the Night Flier's arrival at the Duffrey airport. [NOTE: I don't know if "Selida McCammon" was named for either Rick or Sally McCammon, but I will use this as an excuse to refer you to my interview with Robert R. McCammon in this volume.]

FALMOUTH, MAINE Cumberland County, Maine, sat between a "smaller (and mostly deserted) town with the unlikely name of Jerusalem's Lot" and the town of Falmouth. [NOTE: See the section on 'Salem's Lot in this volume. Also, see the interview with Tobe Hooper in this volume.]

THE FLORIDA EVERGLADES Ray and Ellen's only son, Doug, died in the Florida Everglades trying to land with better than a ton of Acapulco Gold in a stolen Beech 18. Doug hit a stump, was thrown from the plane, and eaten by alligators.

JERUSALEM'S LOT, MAINE Cumberland County, Maine, sat between a "smaller (and mostly deserted) town with the unlikely name of Jerusalem's Lot" and the town of Falmouth. [NOTE: See the section on 'Salem's Lot in this volume. Also, see the interview with Tobe Hooper in this volume.]

NASHVILLE While Dees was stalking the Night Flier, a stringer for *Inside View*, Gloria Swett, was in Nashville interviewing a country-and-western singer with AIDS.

THE PORTLAND JETPORT The Cumberland County Airport existed on the landing fees paid by the rich summer residents who found the airport easier to use than the Portland Jetport. (The Cumberland County fees were also twenty-five percent less than in Portland.)

RUNWAY 34 The runway that Dees used at the Wilmington, North Carolina, airport.

A TOLEDO HOCKSHOP Dees had bought his Nikon at a Toledo hockshop when he was seventeen. The camera was the closest thing Dees had to a wife.

WASHINGTON NATIONAL The airport that Dees flew out of to Wilmington.

WILMINGTON, NORTH CAROLINA Dees confronted the Night Flier in the Wilmington, North Carolina, airport – and ended up being arrested for the vampire's slayings.

Things

"THE AFTER-SUNSET RULE" Even though Dees didn't believe the Night Flier was a vampire, he figured the killer would play by the "After-Sunset Rule" when it came to leaving his stronghold in his plane.

AIDS While Dees was stalking the Night Flier, a stringer for *Inside View*, Gloria Swett, was in Nashville interviewing a country-and-western singer with AIDS.

"ALL SHIT GRIM AND GORY" Richard Dees thought that there was probably still an audience for "All Things Bright and Beautiful," but the one for "All Shit Grim and Gory" had become a growth stock once again:

> "Those in favor of the former had James Herriott. Those in favor of the latter had Stephen King and *Inside View*. The difference, Dees thought, was that King made *his* stuff up."

ALL THINGS BRIGHT AND BEAUTIFUL" Richard Dees thought that there was probably still an audience for "All Things Bright and Beautiful," but the one for "All Shit Grim and Gory" had become a growth stock once again. [NOTE: See the excerpt included in the "ALL SHIT GRIM AND GORY" entry.]

BUCKETS OF BLOOD AND HANDFULS OF GUTS The two things that made *Inside View* a success.

CALVIN KLEIN JEANS The jeans that Doug Sarch was wearing when his body was found.

A CESSNA SKYMASTER 337 The Night Flier's plane. Its tail number was N101BL.

CHESTERFIELDS Ezra's cigarettes.

DEES' HUNCHES ABOUT THE NIGHT FLIER Dees figured that the Night Flier could be in the belly of the Cessna if:

a) He was sleeping in the fetal position with his knees drawn up to his chin
b) He was crazy enought to think he was a real vampire
c) Both of the above.

Dees had his money on C.

DEES' TWO SPEEDS Richard Dees only had two speeds: totally off, and overdrive.

AN FCC FINE As Dees circled the Wilmingtion Airport waiting for clearance to land, he questioned "Farmer John" the air-traffic controller about the Night Flier's plane. Farmer John threatened Dees with an FCC fine if he didn't get off the air. (John had a lot of traffic that night and couldn't talk.)

4:49 A.M. The time that the Night Flier landed at the Cumberland County Airport on the night of July 9.

FOUR MURDERS When Dees began actively pursuing the Night Flier, the vampire had already killed four people.

THE FOUR THINGS DEES WANTED Dees wanted only four things:

1. To not want wanting.
2. Photographs.
3. Dirt. Filth. Horror.
4. To uncover them before anyone else.

4:36 A.M. The time that Claire Bowie gave the Night Flier clearance to land at the Cumberland County Airport.

4:32 A.M. The time that Claire Bowie got his first radio call from the Night Flier.

FOURTEEN YEARS At the time Dees began stalking the Night Flier, he had been working at *Inside View* for fourteen years.

"GUNSMOKE" The Night Flier had watched "Gunsmoke" with the Sarches before he killed them.

"HEROIC REPORTER SAVES (FILL IN A NUMBER) FROM CRAZED NIGHT FLIER" The headline Dees imagined that convinced him to land in the darkened Wilmington airport, even though he faced an FCC violation and a heavy fine.

A HIGH BURNOUT RATE There was a high burnout rate in the tabloid reporter field: After all, how long could you write about UFO's carrying off whole Brazilian villages?

"IN THE COURT OF THE CRIMSON KING" The section of *Prime Evil* which is led off by Stephen King's story "The Night Flier."

INSIDE VIEW The weekly tabloid that Richard Dees worked for. It was "mind-meatloaf that overweight hausfraus bought at the checkout counter and ate in front of the soap operas along with their favorite ice cream."

THE INSIDE VIEW HEADLINES THAT DEES IMAGINED Dees imagined that the following headlines would run in the tabloid when he caught the Night Flier:

> "INSIDE VIEW REPORTER APPREHENDS
> CRAZED NIGHT FLIER."
> "EXCLUSIVE STORY ON HOW BLOOD-DRINKING
> NIGHT FLIER WAS FINALLLY CAUGHT."
> "'NEEDED TO HAVE IT,' DEADLY DRACULA
> DECLARES."

Later, he also imagined a headline that said "THE NIGHT FLIER: COMING SOON TO A CHECKOUT COUNTER NEAR YOU."

JULY 19 The day that the Night Flier flew into the Alderton airport.

JULY 9 The night that the Night Flier arrived in Maine.

"A KILLER INSTINCT" Dees believed in his "killer instinct" when tracking a story.

MORRISON'S PERSONAL FAVORITE INSIDE VIEW STORY "Over Half of Russian Politburo Infected With AIDS, Defector Confides in Top-Secret CIA Memo."

"MY TWINS ARE ALIENS, RAPED WOMAN CRIES" One of the stories in *Inside View.*

N471B Dees' plane number. It was a twin-engine Beechcraft.

N101BL The Night Flier's plane number. It was a Cessna Skymaster 337.

THE NATIONAL ENQUIRER BELUSHI-SMITH SCOOP Dees thought that if he "caught" the Night Flier (on film), the story would be bigger than the Belushi story.

THE NEW REPUBLIC OR ATLANTIC MONTHLY Dees thought that *The New Republic* or the *Atlantic Monthly* could have his story on Ezra's neglect (in not following up on Renfield's missing flight plan). Dees wanted Renfield.

A NIKON Dees' camera. He had bought it a Toledo hockshop when he was seventeen. The camera was the closest thing Dees had to a wife.

1954 The year Claire Bowie started working at the Cumberland County Airport as a night air traffic controller.

PIEDMONT The Wilmington, North Carolina, airport served only Piedmont Airlines.

A PIEDMONT 727 While circling the Wilmington airport, Dees almost hit a Piedmont 727 in mid-air.

A PIPER CUB Buck Kendall's airplane.

RED URINE The Night Flier pissed blood. Dees saw it only when it hit the dead porcelain of the urinal.

A SATELLITE DISH The Alderton, New York, airport had a satellite dish so that none of the "flying farmers" would miss "Dallas" or "Wheel of Fortune."

SEVENTEEN Dees' age when he bought his Nikon camera.

SEVENTY ZILLION COPIES Dees figured *Inside View* would sell seventy zillion copies of the issue that featured his scoop on the Night Flier.

SHORTLY AFTER 10:30 The Night Flier flew into the Alderton, New York, airport shortly after 10:30 on July 19.

A STOLEN BEECH 18 Ray and Ellen's only son, Doug, died in the Florida Everglades trying to land with better than a ton of

Acapulco Gold in a stolen Beech 18. Doug hit a stump, was thrown from the plane, and eaten by alligators.

A STUMP Ray and Ellen's only son, Doug, died in the Florida Everglades trying to land with better than a ton of Acapulco Gold in a stolen Beech 18. Doug hit a stump, was thrown from the plane, and eaten by alligators.

TEN DOLLARS Dees had to bribe Ezra with ten dollars in order to get information about the NIght Flier.

$3 MILLION The AIDS-infected country-and-western singer signed a $3 million deal to write her memoirs.

A TUX WITH A RED-LINED CAPE Ezra told Dees that Renfield was dressed in a tux with a red-lined cape when Renfield landed at the Cumberland County Airport.

TWENTY-SEVEN POUNDS OF PURE BOLIVIAN COCAINE The last drug transporter caught by the Sarches had been carrying twenty-seven pounds of pure Bolivina coke.

A TWIN-ENGINE BEECHCRAFT Dees' plane. Its tail number was N471B.

A $200 PAIR OF PANTS When Dees almost collided with a Piedmont 727 over the Wilmington airport, he ruined a $200 pair of pants by pissing in them.

TWO OUNCES OF PURE COKE Doug Sarch had two ounces of pure coke on him when his body was found.

"THE TWO THINGS THAT MADE INSIDE VIEW A SUCCESS" Merton remembered that the following two things kept the tabloid in the black:

1. Buckets of blood.
2. Handfuls of guts.

THE VAMPIRE LeSTAT A book by Anne Rice. Ellen Sarch was found dead with this book open on her stomach.

A "VAMPIRE STALKS SMALL TOWN STORY" When Dees heard the story of Bowie's death, he recognized a "Vampire Stalks Small Maine Town" story as well as a "Bigfoot Stole My Baby! Anguished Mother Cries" story.

"WOMAN EATS ABUSING HUBBY" A story from *Inside View.*

WORMS AND MAGGOTS Ezra, the mechanic at the Cumberland County Airport in Maine, found a pile of dirt underneath the Night Flier's plane. The dirt was squirming with worms and maggots.

"My Pretty Pony"

In conversation, Stan Wiater once described "My Pretty Pony" to me as "though Ernest Hemingway and Ray Bradbury had collaborated on a story."

In a way, he's right: there is nothing even remotely horrifying about this tale, and I for one consider it a major story from Stephen King.

"My Pretty Pony" is a gentle story of a grandfather and his grandson. The old man, George Banning, is trying to explain the concept of time (and its "relativity") to the young boy, Clivey Banning. Time is a "pretty pony," and Grandpa tries to make the boy understand that "Time ain't got nothin' to do with how fast you can count." He tries to make the boy see that there are two kinds of time: Both were real, but only one was *really* real.

King does an excellent job at communicating the frustration we have all felt waiting for the school bell to ring towards the end of the day — how time stretched and stretched and stretched and seemed like it would go on forever. And he also makes us see how time can run like the wind when we're on vacation, or doing something we enjoy: Then time flies, doesn't it?

King donated "My Pretty Pony" to the Whitney

Museum of Modern Art, and it was published in a limited edition with lithographs by Barbara Kruger. The original Whitney Museum edition was bound in stainless steel, and sold for $2,200. An oversized hardcover was published in a 15,000-copy trade edition by Alfred A. Knopf. That one sold for fifty dollars. As of this writing (late 1989, early 1990), the Knopf edition was still available from most, if not all, of the usual dealers. If you can't afford the fifty dollar edition, try your local library. I'm sure that some of the libraries in the United States purchased the book, and that it is available for borrowing through the inter-library loan. —sjs

(U30)
"My Pretty Pony"
People

THE BAILIFF The court officer who swore Grandpa in when he had jury duty.

BANNING, BILLY Grandpa's son. He was killed in a road accident in 1958. A stone fell off a gravel truck and hit Billy's Ford's windshield. Billy drove into a telephone pole and was electrocuted.

BANNING, CLIVE Clivey. He was ten or eleven years old, and he took "instruction" from his Grandpa, George Banning.

BANNING, GEORGE Clivey Banning's seventy-two-year-old grandfather. Grandpa gave "instruction" to Clivey.

BANNING, GRAMMA SARAH George's wife; Clivey's grandmother. Clivey's mother and father, his Gramma, and his Uncle Don all said things to Clivey that he was supposed to take to heart, although they rarely made sense to him.

BANNING, MR. Clivey's father. He sold insurance and appliances on the road. Clivey's mother and father, his Gramma, and his Uncle Don all said things to Clivey that he was supposed to take to heart, although they rarely made sense to him.

BANNING, MRS. Clivey's mother. She drank all day and then went visiting " a sick friend" at night. Clivey's mother and father, his Gramma, and his Uncle Don all said things to Clivey that he was supposed to take to heart, although they rarely made sense to him.

BANNING, PATTY Clivey's nine-year-old sister. Patty would give Clivey "Peter-Pinches" – vicious little pinches on his penis that sometimes weren't pinches, but strokes.

BRANDY Patty Banning's half-breed poodle.

BRINKMAYER, JOHNNY He used to own the grocery store (the mercantile) before he died of liver cancer. Grandpa had once remarked of Johnny that "that man smells like a nigger."

DAVIS, FRANK He ran Davis Drug.

DAVIS, MR. Frank Davis's father. He opened up Davis Drug in 1910.

THE DOG Clivey liked to feed the dog under the table.

DON, UNCLE Clivey's mother and father, his Gramma, and his Uncle Don all said things to Clivey that he was supposed to take to heart, although they rarely made sense to him.

FILLER, TIM A guy from Schenectady that Grandpa had hired to pick apples. Grandpa was considering offering Tim the foreman's job.

GOD Grandpa thought that God must be "one mean son-of-a-bitch. If He needed something to piss on, why couldn't He have just made Him some sumac bushes and left it at that?"

HAYDEN The old man who lived down the road from the Banning farm. He was senile.

OSGOOD, ARTHUR One of Clive Banning's "friends." Arthur cheated at hide and seek.

OSGOOD, MR. Arthur's father. Grandpa considered him a "stupid son-of-a-bitch," and Arthur to be "the son of that stupid son-of-a-bitch."

A PRETTY PONY "It was from [Grandpa] that Clive Banning had learned the importance of having a pretty pony in your life." The pretty pony was time – the pony was pretty, but had a wicked heart. Really real time was Clivey's pretty pony. Grandpa told him that when people get old, regular time – my pretty pony time – changes to short time.

PUNKIN Patty Banning.

RADWICK THE BUTCHER He always used to keep his finger on the scale.

"A SICK FRIEND" Clivey's Ma used to drink all day, and then go out at night and visit "a sick friend."

SIXTEEN GRANDCHILDREN Grandpa and Gramma Banning had sixteen grandchildren.

TODDMAN, REVEREND The local clergyman.

THE VANCHOCKSTRAW TRIPLETS Clivey, his father, and his sister Patty. His father called them the "Vanchockstraw triplets" because they always ordered the same thing at Davis Drug's ice cream counter: Clivey ordered strawberry, his father would order vanilla, and Patty would order chocolate.

Places

THE BARN DOORWAY As Clivey played hide and seek with his friends, Grandpa "sat in the barn doorway in the smell of apples."

A BEERJOINT IN UTICA The pocketwatch Grandpa gave Clivey had once been stepped on in a beerjoint in Utica, but it still ran.

THE CORNER TAVERN Sometimes Clivey's father went down to the corner tavern for a couple of beers, and to watch the wrestling matches on the TV over the bar.

DAVIS DRUG The drugstore/ice cream parlor where time changed for Grandpa when he was forty.

THE MERCANTILE The local grocery store. It had been owned by Johnny Brinkmayer before he died of liver cancer.

TROY, NEW YORK The town where the Bannings had their farm.

THE WEST ORCHARD The area of the Banning farm where Clivey took instruction from his grandfather.

Things

"ADVICE" By the time Clivey Banning was ten, his Grandpa had stopped giving advice, and switched to "instruction": "Only fools gave [advice] and only fools took it."

AMALGAMATED LIFE AND PROPERTY OF AMERICA The company Clivey's dad worked for. (He had his own franchise.)

APPLIANCES AND INSURANCE Clivey's dad sold appliances and insurance on the road. He had a franchise with Amalgamated Life and Property of America.

BILLY BANNING'S ACCIDENT Grandpa's son Billy was killed in a road accident in 1958. A stone fell off a gravel truck and hit Billy's Ford's windshield. Billy drove into a telephone pole and was electrocuted.

BITCHING Clivey didn't do no bitching and "that was right, because a man never does no bitching – they call it bitching because it ain't for men or even boys smart enough to know better and brave enough to do better."

A BOTTOMLESS GLASS OF WINE Clivey's mother had a glass of wine that was never empty after eleven o'clock in the morning.

CHOCOLATE Patty Banning's ice cream of choice.

"DIFFERENT SEASONS" Grandpa told Clivey that the "way the seasons change [was] the worst. Different seasons stop being different seasons."

FIVE HUNDRED HANDBILLS Grandpa had once put up five hundred handbills over the border in Canada advertising for apple-pickers.

FIVE POCKETS Grandpa Banning had five pockets in his overalls.

A FORD Billy Banning's car.

GRAMMA'S MOTTO "Use it, use it, and don't, for heaven's sake,

My Pretty Pony is the sixth book in the Artists and Writers Series of fine press books published by the Library Fellows of the Whitney Museum of American Art. Barbara Kruger has contributed artwork to accompany a previously unpublished short story by Stephen King. The edition is two hundred and fifty, plus thirty artists' copies, signed by the artist and the author.

The book was designed by Barbara Kruger and produced by May Castleberry, Artists and Writers Series Editor at the Whitney Museum of American Art. Nine lithographs have been proofed and printed on Rives paper by Maurice Sánchez and James Miller at Derrière L'Étoile Studios in New York. The text has been set by hand and printed by letterpress in twenty-four point Century Schoolbook at A.Colish in Mount Vernon, New York, under the supervision of Jerry Kelly. Sixteen pages, including the title and colophon in Helvetica Bold, have been printed by silkscreen by Pinwheel in New York. The book has been bound in leather, cloth, and metal at BookLab in Austin, Texas, under the supervision of Craig Jensen. The stain-

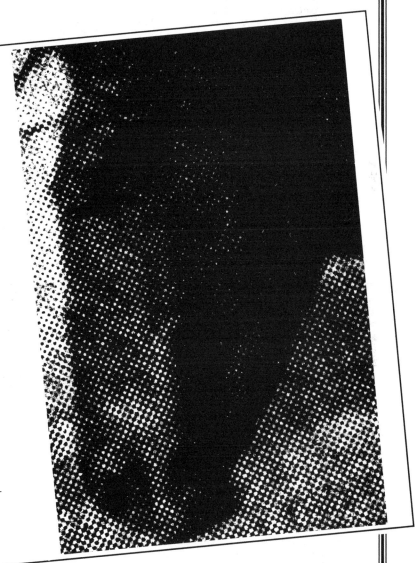

Pages from the Whitney Museum flyer
describing the limited edition of "My Pretty Pony."

ever dare to lose it! Keep it up! Use it up! Break it in, and never pout! Do it in or do without!"

"GRANDPA'S FENCES" A month after Grandpa explained time to Clivey, the old man was found dead of his third and final heart attack:

> "Grandpa's pony had kicked down Grandpa's fences and gone over all the hills of the world."

A HALLOWEEN DISPLAY AND A PENNY CANDY DISPLAY Grandpa remembered seeing a Halloween display and a penny candy display in Davis's Drug. The candy included candy corn, root-beer barrels, and niggerbabies.

HIDE AND SEEK The game Clivey played with his friends. Arthur Osgood cheated at it.

THE "HIGHWAY OF DAYS" As Grandpa explained the difference between the two kinds of time, Clivey thought about "that highway of days" stretching across the plains of June and July and over the unimaginable horizon of August."

"INSTRUCTION" Grandpa Banning gave Clivey "instruction" in Troy, New York, in the West Orchard in 1962. (Grandpa had stopped giving "advice" because "only fools gave it and only fools took it.") Instruction was different: "Smart men give some from time to time and smart men take a little from time to time." Grandpa said that instruction was "remembrance."

"JEW-PANTS" Grandpa called his bluejeans "Jew-pants" or "Joozers."

"JOOZERS" Grandpa called his bluejeans "Jew-pants" or "Joozers."

JURY DUTY When Grandpa was near fifty years old, he got called for jury duty. When the bailiff swore him in, he forgot his age for a moment.

"THE MYSTIC AND UNQUESTIONED FORMULA OF ELIMINATION" Hide and seek's end-all: "I see Clive, my gool-one-two-three!"

1958 The year that Billy Banning was killed in a road accident.

1962 The year that Clive Banning took "instruction" in the West Orchard from his grandfather.

1910 The year that Frank Davis's father opened up Davis Drug.

"PETER-PINCHES" Clivey's sister Patty would give Clivey "Peter-pinches" – vicious little pinches on his penis that sometimes weren't pinches, but masturbatory strokes. Clivey was sworn to secrecy about the "Pinches."

"PUNKIN" Clivey's father's nickname for Clivey's sister Patty.

A SILVER POCKETWATCH Grandpa gave Clivey a tarnished silver pocketwatch. The watch had once been stepped on in a beerjoint in Utica, but it still ran.

"A STRAP-UNDERSHIRT MAN" Grandpa Banning would be a "strap-undershirt man" to the end.

STRAWBERRY Clive Banning's ice cream of choice.

THIRTY-FIVE SECONDS To show Clivey the nature of time, Grandpa counted to sixty in thirty-five seconds. He told Clivey "Time ain't got nothing to do with how fast you can count."

TIME To show Clivey the nature of time, Grandpa counted to sixty in thirty-five seconds. He told Clivey "Time ain't got nothing to do with how fast you can count." He explained that there were two kinds of time: Both were real, but only one was really real.

TWO HEART ATTACKS By 1962, Grandpa Banning had had two heart attacks.

"UNDERSTANDING AND INSTRUCTION" They were cousins who didn't kiss.

UNFILTERED KOOLS Grandpa Banning's cigarettes.

VANILLA Clivey's father's ice cream of choice.

"THE WEATHER OF ITS HEART" Clivey almost missed the last words his Grandpa said to him about the pony's wicked heart:

> "[H]aving a pony to ride was better than having no pony at all, no matter how the weather of its heart may lie."

"Rainy Season"

"Rainy Season" is about toads.

Mean, razor-toothed, killer toads.

And it's about a town called Willow, Maine. Willow was a town with a curse. A curse that meant that every seven years it "rained" the aforementioned killer toads, and that the only way for the rain of toads to stop was for the town to sacrifice two outsiders to the malevolent force that apparently required periodic feeding.

And yet, believe it or not, "Rainy Season" is hugely entertaining, not at all dark, but still good and scary. (And, as Stephen King described it in his cover letter, "pretty gross.")

"Rainy Season" appeared in the Spring 1989 issue of *Midnight Graffiti* magazine (an issue that also contained an article by yours truly called "The Unwritten King," excerpted from the book you now hold in your hands).

Stephen King sent the story off to editors Jessie Horsting and Jim Van Hise for their basic pay rates. This allowed Jessie and Jim to build an entire "Stephen King" issue around the story, and the result is a real collector's item, containing all sorts of terrific features.

The issue is still available and, inasmuch as this was the only appearance of the story, if you want to read it, you'll have to buy the issue.

Better yet, place a subscription to *MG*. (Jesse'll be glad I said that.) Also, see my interviews with both Jessie Horsting and James Van Hise in this volume. — **sjs**

(U31)
"Rainy Season"
People

COUSINS, MILLY A friend of the Grahams'. Milly was Lucy Ducet's grandniece, and had told the Grahams' about the Willow Mercantile.

DUCET, LUCY Milly Cousins' great aunt, and a resident of Willow, Maine. She lived down at the foot of the hill in Willow, and called Henry Eden to tell him that she had seen the Grahams drive by.

EDEN, HENRY The Willow, Maine, resident who owned the Willow Mercantile. He was married, although his wife was never seen. Henry and Laura Stanton tried to convince John and Elise Graham to stay out of Willow on the night the Rainy Season began. Their persuading didn't work, and the Grahams ended up toad food.

EDEN, MRS. Henry Eden's wife. She was never seen. She wanted Henry to quit smoking.

GRAHAM, ELISE A young woman from the University of Missouri who had planned on spending the summer in Willow, Maine, researching a book on the in-migration of the French during the seventeenth century. She and her husband, John, were eaten by toads with razor teeth their first night in town.

GRAHAM, JOHN A young man from the University of Missouri who had planned on spending the summer in Willow, Maine, researching a book on the in-migration of the French during the seventeenth century. He and his wife, Elise, were eaten by toads with razor teeth their first night in town.

THE MANAGER OF THE CASTLE MOTEL Laura Stanton's cousin. He reserved a room for the Grahams even though the motel was all filled up.

STANTON, LAURA A resident of Willow, Maine, and a friend of

Henry Eden's. She tried, with Henry, to convince the Grahams to stay out of Willow on the night of the Rainy Season. She drank a whole six-pack of Dawson's Ale the night it rained toads. Laura drove a Volvo.

TOBY Henry Eden's dog. He was a big, yellow dog of no particular make or model. Toby tended to fart a lot.

Places

THE CASTLE MOTEL A motel on Route 130 just outside of Willow, Maine. Laura Stanton reserved a room there for the Grahams on the night of the Rainy Season. (The motel was booked solid, but the manager was Laura's cousin.) The Grahams refused the offer, opting instead to stay at the Hempstead Place and be eaten alive by toads that had razor blades for teeth.

THE CELLAR John and Elise Graham tried to escape the rain of toads by taking refuge in the cellar of the Hempstead Place. It almost worked, but they forgot about the coal-chute.

A CLAM-STAND IN AUGUSTA As Henry Dean and Laura Stanton told the Grahams about Willow's Rainy Season, John found himself wishing they had stopped at a clam-stand in Augusta instead of driving to the Mercantile for supplies.

A CLAM-STAND IN WOOLRICH After hearing Henry Eden's and Laura Stanton's seemingly ludicrous story of an imminent rain of toads, John and Elise Graham ate at a clam-stand in Woolrich, rather than shop at the Willow Mercantile.

THE HEMPSTEAD PLACE The house in Willow, Maine, that John and Elise Graham rented (thanks to a grant from the University of Missouri) for the summer to research a book. It was a big old house that overlooked the town. It had a coal-chute. [NOTE: See the "Things" entry THE COAL-CHUTE.]

IN A PINE TREE BY THE LAKE At 1:30 a.m. on the morning of June 18, the last toad of Willow's Rainy Season landed in a pine tree by the lake.

LAKE WILLOW On the morning of June 18, toads sat on the rafts in Lake Willow. (Only the heartiest of swimmers dared the waters of Lake Willow before July 4.)

MAIN STREET, WILLOW Upon arriving in Willow, John and Elise Graham ended up on Main Street because they took two wrong turns on their way to the Hempstead Place.

THE POSTAL SUBSTATION The Willow Mercantile was a postal substation.

ROUTE 9 There was a "Welcome to Willow" sign on Route 9 in Willow that had holes in it made by flying toads.

ROUTE 130 The location of the Castle Motel.

ST. LOUIS, MISSOURI John and Elise Graham drove to Willow, Maine, from St. Louis, Missouri. They both attended the University of Missouri.

SONNY'S SUNOCO On the morning of June 18, toads sat on the gas pumps at Sonny's Sunoco.

THE UNIVERSITY OF MISSOURI The school that was paying for the Grahams' summer research project in Maine. They were researching a book on the in-migration of the French during the seventeenth century.

"VACATIONLAND" Upon seeing Willow's Main Street, Elise Graham wondered what happened to the adage that Maine turned into Vacationland in the summer.

WILLOW, MAINE The small Maine town where John and Elise Graham were supposed to spend a summer researching a book on a grant by the University of Missouri. They just so happened to hit Willow on the day the "rainy season" started. Their first night in town, they were both eaten alive by razor-toothed toads that rained from the sky.

THE WILLOW GENERAL MERCANTILE AND HARDWARE The Willow Mercantile, Willow's general store It was owned by Henry Eden (and his never-seen wife). They sold Italian sandwiches, pizza, and groceries. They were also a postal substation, and issued fishing licenses.

THE WILLOW HARDWARE STORE On the morning of June 18, two toads sat on the iron arm of the weathervane atop the Willow Hardware Store.

Things

A BEAN SUPPER AT THE GRANGE OR THE EASTERN STAR On the evening of June 17, Elise asked John where everyone in Willow could be. John said they were all probably at a bean supper at the Grange or the Eastern Star.

BLACK FLUID When a toad fell through the front window of the Hempstead Place and was impaled on a shard of glass, black fluid "burst from its body in thick ropes."

BLACKFLIES People slapped blackflies while waiting for their orders at the clam-stand in Woolrich where John and Elise Graham had dinner on their first night in Willow.

THE BOARD OF SELECTMEN John Graham sarcastically wondered if Henry Eden had gotten permission from the Willow Board of Selectmen before putting in his neon beer sign.

A BOOK John and Elise Graham were on a summer sabbatical in Maine to research a book they were writing on the in-migration of the French during the seventeenth century.

THE COAL-CHUTE In an attempt to escape the rain of razor-toothed toads, John and Elise Graham took refuge in the cellar of the Hempstead Place. They boarded up the cellar windows with plywood to prevent the toads from breaking through, but they forgot about the coal-chute, which "suddenly swung open under the weight of all the toads which had fallen or hopped into it, and thousands of them poured out in a high-pressure jet. It did not last long for the Grahams in the cellar after the coal-chute gave way...."

FISHING LICENSES The Willow Mercantile issued fishing licenses.

A FORD The Grahams' car. The car's air conditioner had died on the trip to Willow from St. Louis.

GROCERIES Some of the items sold at the Willow Mercantile.

HALF PAST FIVE IN THE AFTERNOON The time John and Elise Graham finally found their way into Willow, Maine.

HOME-MADE CIGARETTES Henry Eden rolled his own.

"THE IN-MIGRATION OF THE FRENCH DURING THE SEVENTEENTH CENTURY" The subject John and Elise Graham were researching on their summer sabbatical in Willow, Maine. They were writing a book.

THE IRON ARM OF THE WEATHERVANE On the morning of June 18, two toads sat on the iron arm of the weathervane atop the Willow Hardware Store.

ITALIAN SANDWICHES One of the items sold at the Willow Mercantile.

JULY 4 Only the heartiest of swimmers dared the waters of Lake Willow before July 4.

JUNE 17 The day that the Rainy Season began in Willow, Maine, every seven years.

THE LARGE DAIRY HERDS The large dairy herds in Willow had all been locked up before June 17.

THE MERCANTILE'S CHESTERFIELD SIGN There was a sign on the door of the Willow Mercantile that said:

CHESTERFIELD CIGARETTES
TWENTY-ONE GREAT TOBACCOS
MAKE TWENTY WONDERFUL SMOKES

MIDNIGHT By midnight, the rain of toads on Willow, Maine, had slacked off to a drizzle.

NEARLY FIFTEEN HUNDRED MILES The Grahams had driven nearly fifteen hundred miles from St. Louis, Missouri to Willow, Maine.

A NEON BEER SIGN There was a neon beer sign in the front window of the Willow Mercantile.

1:30 A.M. At 1:30 a.m. on the morning of June 18, the last toad of

Willow's Rainy Season landed in a pine tree by the lake.

PIZZA One of the items sold at the Willow Mercantile.

A QUARTER PAST FIVE At 5:15 a.m. on the morning of June 18, first light began to touch the toads in Willow, Maine.

THE RAINY SEASON An every-seven-years event in Willow, Maine. It took place on the night of June 17, and on that night, it rained toads in Willow. The toads had razor sharp teeth, and were vicious little mothers. It seemed as though part of the seven-year cycle involved the ritual sacrifice of out-of-towners. The ritual consisted of Henry Dean and Laura Stanton trying their darndest to convince the strangers not to stay in Willow on the night of June 17. The strangers (always two) never listened, and ended up being eaten by the savage toads. The next morning, the toads would melt upon being touched by sunlight, and the rainy season would be over for another seven years. Henry Dean thought that if the strangers weren't sacrificed, the toads might not go away with the morning light.

THE REPAIRS By 6:45 a.m. on the morning of June 18, Willow's Rainy Season was over...except for the repairs.

6:05 A.M. At 6:05 a.m. on the morning of June 18, the sun cleared the horizon in Willow, and all the toads began to melt.

SNIPE HUNTS John Graham felt that the "rain of toads" story was probably a joke, as were the snipe hunts from John's summer camp days.

TOADS Every seven years in Willow, Maine, on the night of June 17, it rained toads. The toads had razor-sharp teeth, and were savage. The toads melted upon being touched by the next morning's first light.

TOP TOBACCO The tobacco Henry Eden used to roll his own cigarettes.

A VOLVO Laura Stanton's car.

"WELCOME TO WILLOW, MAINE, THE FRIENDLY PLACE" A sign on Route 9 in Willow. After the Rainy Season, there were holes in it left by flying toads.

THE WILLOW MERCANTILE SIGN The Willow Mercantile had a sign in front of the store that said:

ITALIAN SANDWICHES PIZZA GROCERIES
FISHING LICENSES

WOODEN MATCHES Henry Eden used wooden matches to light his hand-rolled cigarettes.

"Home Delivery"

"Home Delivery" is Stephen King's contribution to a very bizarre anthology, *The Book of the Dead* (John Skipp and Craig Spector, eds; Bantam paperback, 1989).

The Book of the Dead consists of sixteen stories concerning zombies – our friends, the living dead.

"Home Delivery" is a tale that King fans will take a quick liking to: It reads quickly and smoothly, and is one of the grosser, more disgusting tales that King has been generous enough to share with us.

The premise of the anthology is that, yes, one day, the dead get up and start walking around.

And as all good students of Professor George Romero know, when the dead wake up, they're hungry.

And what are they hungry for?

All together now, class: THE LIVING!

That's right. The dead eat the living, and the only way to stop them is to either cut them up so that they can't function as a single unit, or shoot them in the brain and then burn them. (Ideally, you should really do all three: shoot them to shit, chop them up into little pieces, and then burn them up. That sort of guarantees they won't

pester you anymore.)

"Home Delivery" is a fun story, told a little tongue-in-cheek (or in the living dead's case, tongue-out-of-cheek), and it poses a question most of us have probably never considered: "Is it possible for a severed penis to have an orgasm?"

And if that makes you squirm a little, wait until you *really* get into this story: It's best described by a word used by John Skipp and Craig Spector in the Introduction: Overt.

Look it up: It works.

Oh, and if you bought *The Book of the Dead* just for the King story and ignored the other tales within, you are indeed missing out. Take a look at the some of the other stories in this collection: After a Foreword by George Romero, there's Chan McConnell's "Blossom," Richard Laymon's "Mess Hall," "It Helps If You Sing" by Ramsey Campbell, Philip Nutman's "Wet Work," and eleven more (not counting "Home Delivery").

There is some brilliant writing between these covers, and even – if you can imagine this when talking about the cannabalistic living dead – sensitivity. (If you can read Rick McCammon's "Eat Me" without crying, read it again. You're missing something.) Consider "zombie-ism" as an archetype for the state of modern man. Aren't we all really "living dead?" Desensitization, depersonalization, stress, fatigue, and nuclear nightmares have all contributed to our social and psychological putrefication. With all that as a basis for perspective, *The Book of the Dead* may very well be one of the most important anthologies of the twentieth century.

And it's scary and gross as hell, too!

What more could you ask, huh? — **sjs**

(U32)
"Home Delivery"
People

THE ALTONS Maddie's Jenny Island neighbors. They had a woodlot on which there was a lightning-struck pine tree.

THE AMERICANS The Americans blamed the Russians for the dead folks that were up and about.

ARSENAULT, MATT A Jenny Island resident. Matt was on welfare. He offered to stand watch on Zombie Patrol longer than four hours.

CAMPBELL, MRS. Orrin's wife.

CAMPBELL, ORRIN One of the Jenny Island townsmen who showed up at the town (zombie) meeting. Orrin had a wife and two children. [NOTE: Wonder if he was related to Mayberry's Otis Campbell?]

THE CAMPBELL CHILDREN Orrin Campbell and his wife had two children.

THE CHESS TEACHER When relations between the U.S. and the U.S.S.R. fell apart after the dead woke up, the president expelled all Soviet personnel from the United States except for the young Russian who was teaching him to play chess – and who was not averse to a grope under the table now and then.

A CNN NEWS CORRESPONDENT After the dead got up and started walking around, Russia and the U.S. almost blew each other up, each blaming the other for the zombies. A CNN news correspondent wondered how close they had actually come to doing it.

COOK, POP The old guy who owned the two acres of land that bordered George Sullivan's land on Deer Isle. George eventually bought the land.

CRANE, JOHNNY The eighteen-year-old boy who showed up at Jenny Island's town (zombie) meeting.

DAGBOLT, HUMPHREY The British astronomer from Hinchly-on-Strope who discovered the living satellite Star Wormwood. Dagbolt had a deviated septum, fallen arches, balls the size of acorns, was going bald, and had psoriasis.

DAGGETT, BOB Jenny Island's head selectman. He drew up the "Zombie Watch" roster. Daggett was forty-nine years and nine months old.

DAGGETT, FRANK Bob Daggett's great-uncle. He showed up at Jenny Island's town (zombie) meeting. He had a heart attack while on Zombie Patrol, and made his friends blow him to pieces so he would stay down when he died. [NOTE: See the "Things" entry FRANK DAGGETT'S ANTI-ZOMBIE GUARANTEE.]

DAGGETT'S ISLAND DAUGHTER Bob Daggett had four daughters: one was on Jenny Island, and three were on the mainland.

DAGGETT'S THREE MAINLAND DAUGHTERS Bob Daggett had four daughters: one was on Jenny Island, and three were on the mainland.

A DECAYING MAN IN A BROOKS BROTHERS SUIT A photo of this guy grabbing at the breast of a girl wearing a "Property of the Houston Oilers" t-shirt ran in *People* magazine.

DORFMAN, BURT The only Jew on Jenny Island. He was an electrician, and he rigged lights off the island's five generators as the men went on Zombie Patrol.

DOTSON, SONNY He ran Island Amoco, the only gas station on Jenny Island.

EAMONS, DAVE When Jack Pace fell overboard, Dave had seen him pop to the surface before the boat hit him in the head. Dave also participated in Frank Daggett's Anti-Zombie Guarantee. [NOTE: See the "Things" entry FRANK DAGGETT'S ANTI-ZOMBIE GUARANTEE.]

THE EMIR OF KUWAIT A young boy recruited as an INS reporter described how the president, the first lady, the secretary of state, the honorable senator from Oregon, and the emir of Kuwait had all been eaten alive by zombies in the White House ballroom.

THE FIRST LADY A young boy recruited as an INS reporter described how the president, the first lady, the secretary of state, the honorable senator from Oregon, and the emir of Kuwait had all been eaten alive by zombies in the White House ballroom.

FOURNIER, MICHAEL The only child of Mr. and Mrs. Fournier. He had died of leukemia at the age of seventeen. He was one of the first to come back from the dead in the Jenny Island graveyard.

FOURNIER, MR. Michael's father.

FOURNIER, MRS. Michael's mother.

"THE GOTROCKS FAMILY" The Sullivans were never the Gotrocks family...but they made out.

HARKNESS, BUCK One of the Jenny Island men on Zombie Patrol. He fainted when the men had to shoot his dead wife.

HARKNESS, MRS. Buck's wife. She came back from the dead and had to be shot. Buck fainted when he saw it happen.

THE HONORABLE SENATOR FROM OREGON A young boy recruited as an INS reporter described how the president, the first lady, the secretary of state, the honorable senator from Oregon, and the emir of Kuwait had all been eaten alive by zombies in the White House ballroom.

THE INS REPORTER A young boy recruited as an INS reporter described how the president, the first lady, the secretary of state, the honorable senator from Oregon, and the emir of Kuwait had all been eaten alive by zombies in the White House ballroom.

KATINYA, OLGA The Russian cosmonaut on the Gorbachev/Truman spacecraft. (The worms ate her eyes.)

KINSOLVING, ANDY Jenny Islander. He had heard on the news that if you shot the living dead in the head, sometimes they would stay down. [NOTE: It wasn't said if he was related to 'Tavia Kinsolving from Stanton Street in Harlem. See the section on the

short story "Dedication" in this volume for info on the "other" Kinsolvings.]

MADDIE AND JACK'S BABY After Maddie chopped up the body of her dead husband (who had come back to life), she planned on having a home delivery for their still in utero child.

MCELWAIN, DR. Maddie's doctor on the mainland.

MEECHUM, BUD One of the Jenny Island men on Zombie Patrol. He found a bullet hole in his shirt from when the "patrol" was shooting the dead Michael Fournier.

MIKE, UNCLE Jack Pace's uncle. Jack inherited his boat, My Lady-Love, from Uncle Mike.

NEDEAU, BOB He owned the island market (Nedeau's Market?) where Maddie did her shopping.

NEDEAU, CHARLENE Bob Nedeau's teenage daughter. She worked in Bob Nedeau's market. She asked Maddie if she could help her pick out some soup.

NEDEAU, MARGARET Bob Nedeau's wife.

19,000 HAM OPERATORS Nineteen thousand ham operators taped the final sixty-one seconds of transmission from the Gorbachev/Truman spacecraft.

PACE, JACK Maddie's husband. He was a lobsterman who was going to night school because he wanted to be more than a lobsterman. He fell overboard, and was then fatally struck in the head by the boat. Maddie had to kill him again and chop up his body when he came back from the dead. She put the pieces in an unused basement cistern with a concrete cover.

PACE, MADDIE Jack Pace's widow. At the time of Jack's death (his first death, that is), Maddie was pregnant and surprised that she was coping.

PACE, MR. Jack's father. He didn't think Jack should be anything but a lobsterman.

PARTRIDGE, CAL A Jenny Island townsman who showed up at the town (zombie) meeting.

PEEBLES, REVEREND TOM The Jenny Island clergyman. He showed up at the town (zombie) meeting.

THE PRESIDENT A young boy recruited as an INS reporter described how the president, the first lady, the secretary of state, the honorable senator from Oregon, and the emir of Kuwait had all been eaten alive by zombies in the White House ballroom.

PULSIFER, BILL Candi's husband; Cheyne and Brian's father.

PULSIFER, BRIAN Candi Pulsifer's dead son. The Pulsifers offered his room to Maddie.

PULSIFER, CANDI Cheyne's mother.

PULSIFER, CHEYNE The young Pulsifer boy who watched the INS reporter describe how zombies ate the president.

THE PULSIFERS Maddie's Jenny Island neighbors. They had a satellite dish, and it was on their TV that Maddie had seen the dead residents of Wet Noggin, Australia, walking around.

RATHER, DAN The TV anchor who showed the news footage of the zombies in Thumper, Florida. (He suggested "You may want to ask your children to leave the room.")

THE RUSSIANS The Russians blamed the United States for the dead folks that were up and about.

THE SECRETARY OF STATE A young boy recruited as an INS reporter described how the president, the first lady, the secretary of state, the honorable senator from Oregon, and the emir of Kuwait had all been eaten alive by zombies in the White House ballroom.

SEVENTY MEN Seventy men showed up at Jenny Island's town (zombie) meeting.

SULLIVAN, GEORGE Maddie's father. He died of a massive coronary.

SULLIVAN, MADDIE Maddie Pace's maiden name.

SULLIVAN, MRS. Maddie's mother. She came into better than a hundred thousand dollars when her husband George died.

TASK, CAPTAIN VASSILY The Russian commander on the Gorbachev/Truman spacecraft.

Places

THE ALTONS' WOODLOT There was a lightning-struck pine tree on the woodlot.

BIG DUKE'S BIG TEN LANES The bowling alley in Yarmouth where George Sullivan had the massive coronary that killed him.

BITERAD, GERMANY One of the places where "dead people started to get up and walk around."

BUSTER'S TAVERN A bar frequented by George Sullivan.

CALIFORNIA Telescopes in California and Siberia were trained on Star Wormwood after its discovery by Humphrey Dagbolt.

CRICKET'S LEDGE An area on the coast of Jenny Island.

DAGGETT'S BARBER SHOP The Deer Isle barber shop.

DEER ISLE A small island off the coast of Maine where Maddie Pace lived as a child.

ELMIRA, ILLINOIS One of the places where "dead people started to get up and walk around."

FLORIDA One of the places where "dead people started to get up and walk around."

GENNESAULT ISLAND A small island off the coast of Maine. (It was commonly known as "Jenny Island.") Jack and Maddie Pace moved there after they were married.

HINCHLY-ON-STROPE Humphrey Dagbolt was from Hinchly-on-Strope, England.

ISLAND AMOCO The only gas station on Jenny Island. Island Amoco was run by Sonny Dotson, and the station sponsored George Sullivan's bowling team.

JENNY ISLAND Gennesault Island.

THE JENNY ISLAND GRAVEYARD The island menfolk stood watch with shotguns and gasoline at the graveyard, and shot up and burned any dead folk that got up and started walking around.

LENINGRAD One of the places where "dead people started to get up and walk around."

MINSK One of the places where "dead people started to get up and walk around."

MURMANSK One of the places where "dead people started to get up and walk around."

NEW DELHI, INDIA One of the places where "dead people started to get up and walk around."

NIGHT SCHOOL Before he died, Jack Pace was attending night school three nights a week.

OUT THERE The living satellite Star Wormwood had come from the big darkness Out There.

POP COOK'S LAND Two acres that bounded George Sullivan's land on the left. It had plenty of good hardwood left on it, and George eventually bought the acreage from Pop Cook.

RIO DE JANEIRO One of the places where "dead people started to get up and walk around."

A ROADSIDE STAND Maddie's mother sold vegetables from a roadside stand.

SIBERIA Telescopes in California and Siberia were trained on Star Wormwood after its discovery by Humphrey Dagbolt.

THUMPER A small Florida town on the Tamiami trail from where the first news of the zombies was reported.

THE TOWN LIBRARY Maddie was working at the town library when her father died of a massive coronary.

AN UNUSED CISTERN After Maddie cut up Jack Pace's dead body, she put the pieces in an unused basement cistern that had a concrete cover.

WET NOGGIN, AUSTRALIA One of the places where "dead people started to get up and walk around."

THE WHITE HOUSE BALLROOM A young boy recruited as an INS reporter described how the president, the first lady, the secretary of state, the honorable senator from Oregon, and the emir of Kuwait had all been eaten alive by zombies in the White House ballroom.

YARMOUTH The town where Big Duke's Big Ten Bowling Lanes was located.

YARMOUTH ACADEMY The school that Michael Fournier had attended before he died of leukemia at the age of seventeen.

Things

AN AXE When Jack Pace came back from the dead, Maddie cleaved his skull with an axe and then cut him into pieces.

BEANO Frank Daggett suggested that the women and children on Jenny Island play Beano while the men hunted down the living dead.

BOXCAR WILLY RECORDS The TV station cut off the INS reporter who was reporting that the president and others had been eaten by zombies in the White House ballroom with an ad for Boxcar Willy records.

BRAISED VEAL OR LAMB CHOPS Maddie Pace couldn't make up her mind. Sometimes her husband Jack would go through five bottles of beer in a restaurant waiting for her to make up her mind between the braised veal and the lamb chops. No matter what she chose, though, she always wondered if she should have picked the other.

A CHAINSAW George Sullivan had wanted – and had known how to work for – a chainsaw.

CHICKEN NOODLE Jack Pace's favorite soup. When Maddie found this out, she bought the four cans that Bob Nedeau had on his shelf, as well as a whole case he had out back.

A D-9 CATERPILLAR After the Jenny Island men shot and chopped up the living dead, they doused the body parts with diesel fuel, and burned them up. Then, Matt Arsenault plowed the mess under with his D-9 caterpillar.

"DEAD COME TO LIFE IN SMALL FLORIDA TOWN!" The *Inside View* headline reporting the rise of the dead in Thumper, Florida.

DEFCON-2 Norad went to Defcon-2 after relations between the U.S. and the U.S.S.R. deteriorated in the wake of the zombie accusations.

AN EMPTY CASKET At Jack Pace's funeral, they buried an empty casket.

"THE END OF EVERYTHING" Maddie Pace figured that when the dead started getting out of their graves and began eating the living, it was the End of Everything.

THE FINAL SIXTY-ONE SECONDS Nineteen thousand ham operators taped the final sixty-one seconds of transmission from the Gorbachev/Truman spacecraft.

FIVE GENERATORS There were five generators on Jenny island when the men went on patrol. Burt Dorfman, the electrician, rigged lights to run off of them.

A FORD PICK-UP George Sullivan's truck. He had wanted – and had known how to work for – the pick-up.

$41.50 Maddie's starting salary for minding the Deer Isle town library weekday evenings.

FOUR HUNDRED GALLONS OF GAS Sonny Dotson had four hundred gallons of gas, mostly diesel, in his Island Amoco tanks.

FOUR MONTHS Four months after Jack Pace died, "dead folks started to come out of their graves and walk around."

FOUR SDI SATELLITES The United States made a final effort to destroy Star Wormwood at a cost of just under $600 million. Four SDI satellites, each equipped with two six-megaton warheads, were fired (after the Russians agreed to their use) at the living satellite. They all malfunctioned.

FRANK DAGGETT'S ANTI-ZOMBIE GUARANTEE Frank had a heart attack while out shooting and chopping up zombies. In order to be sure he'd stay down once he died, he had Cal Partridge put his rifle in his left ear, Dave Eamons put his .30-.30 in his left armpit, and his great-nephew Bobby Daggett put his rifle over his heart. When Frank hit "Amen" after reciting "The Lord's Prayer," they all pulled their triggers.

GEORGE SULLIVAN'S INSURANCE When George died of a massive coronary during the tie-breaker frame of the League

Bowl-Off at Big Duke's Big Ten lanes in Yarmouth, he left his wife (and his daughter Maddie) better than one hundred thousand dollars in life insurance.

THE GORBACHEV/TRUMAN The spacecraft launched with six Russians, three Americans, and Humphrey Dagbolt on board to investigate Star Wormwood.

THE GULL The ferry boat to the mainland.

A HOME DELIVERY Maddie was very grateful that all the Jenny Island men took care of the living dead, making the island safe for her and her baby. She thought to herself: "It will be a home delivery...and it will be fine."

"HORROR MOVIE COMES TO LIFE!" The subhead to the *Inside View* article "Dead Come to Life in Small Florida Town!" [NOTE: This subhead referred to the George Romero movie "Night of the Living Dead," a film Maddie had never seen. But we all have, haven't we?]

INSIDE VIEW The tabloid that first reported the zombies from Thumper, Florida. [NOTE: See the section on "The Night Flier" in this volume.]

JIFFY POP Maddie Pace and the Pulsifers ate Jiffy Pop popcorn while they watched the INS reporter describe how the president had been eaten by zombies.

THE L.L. BEAN SHIRT When Jack Pace came back from the dead, he was wearing the black-and-red checkered shirt that Maddie had bought him at Bean's one Christmas.

THE LEAGUE BOWL-OFF George Sullivan died of a coronary during the tie-breaker frame of the League Bowl-Off at Big Duke's Lanes in Yarmouth.

LEUKEMIA Michael Fournier died of leukemia at age seventeen.

A LIGHTNING-STRUCK PINE TREE Maddie's Jenny Island neighbors the Altons had a woodlot on which there was a lightning-struck pine tree.

"THE LORD'S PRAYER" Frank Daggett said "The Lord's Prayer" before his friends shot him. [NOTE: See the "Things" entry FRANK DAGGETT'S ANTI-ZOMBIE GUARANTEE.]

"MACUMBA LOVE" *Inside View* ran a photo from "Macumba Love" with their "zombie" article.

A MASSIVE CORONARY George Sullivan died of a massive coronary.

METHODIST OR METHODIST "[O]n Jenny Island you had your choice when it came to religion: you could be a Methodist, or if that didn't suit you, you could be a Methodist."

"MY LADY-LOVE" Jack Pace's boat. He inherited it from his Uncle Mike.

NINETEEN Maddie's age when her father died.

NORAD Norad went to Defcon-2 after relations between the U.S. and the U.S.S.R. deteriorated in the wake of the zombie accusations.

AN OLDSMOBILE Jack Pace had aspirations in life: He wanted an Oldsmobile – not a Chevrolet.

PEOPLE **MAGAZINE** The week the zombies came to Thumper, Florida, *People* magazine ran stills in that week's issue. The issue was wrapped in shrinkwrap, and had a sticker on it that said "Not For Sale To Minors!"

POACHED SALMON AND CHERRIES JUBILEE The original menu at the White House dinner where the president, first lady, secretary of state, senator from Oregon, and the emir of Kuwait ended up being the main course instead.

POLIDENT Frank Daggett held in his Roebuckers false teeth with Polident.

"PREG" Before the dead rose, Maddie discovered that she was pregnant with Jack's child.

ROEBUCKERS Frank Daggett's false teeth. He held them in with Polident.

THE SALYUT-EAGLE-I The rocket that launched the spacecraft Gorbachev/Truman with six Russians, three Americans, and Humphrey Dagbolt on board to investigate Star Wormwood.

A SATELLITE DISH The Pulsifers' had one on Jenny Island.

$600 MILLION The United States made a final effort to destroy Star Wormwood at a cost of just under $600 million. Four SDI satellites each equipped with two six-megaton warheads were fired (after the Russians agreed to their use) at the living satellite. They all malfunctioned.

STAR WORMWOOD The living satellite discovered by the British astronomer Humphrey Dagbolt.

TASS The Soviet news agency. They said the zombies were the result of U.S. chemical warfare against the U.S.S.R.

THE TIE-BREAKER FRAME George Sullivan died of a coronary during the tie-breaker frame of the League Bowl-Off at Big Duke's Lanes in Yarmouth.

TWENTY-SEVEN DAYS Jack Pace found out that he was going to be a father only twenty-seven days before he fell overboard and drowned.

TWENTY-TWO Maddie Pace's age at the time of her husband Jack's death.

TWO NO-DOZ WITH COFFEE Jack Pace's evening regimen before he took the ferry to the mainland for night school three nights a week.

TWO WOODSTOVES The hardwood from Pop Cook's two acres fed two woodstoves in the Sullivan house.

"THE WHEEL" Maddie couldn't find The Wheel after her father George died: George had been the one to tell Maddie and her mother where to squat and lean to the Wheel.

WORMS The Gorbachev/Truman spacecraft was invaded by worms that secreted acid.

"An Evening at God's"

In early 1990, Stephen King was asked to contribute a one-minute play to an American Repertory Theater benefit evening for the repertory's Institute for Advanced Theater Training.

He jumped at the idea (likening it to "the literary equivalent of a doodle"), and came up with "An Evening at God's." The play was auctioned off at the Hasty Pudding Theater on the evening of April 23, 1990.

King was in good company: the fourteen other writers approached to contribute a "playlet" for the benefit were:

William Alfred	David Lodge
Art Buchwald	David Mamet
Don DeLillo	Robert & Joan Parker
Christopher Durang	David Rabe
John Kenneth Gailbraith	Ronald Ribman
Larry Gelbart	John Updike
Arthur Kopit	Wendy Wasserstein

The signed manuscripts were auctioned off at the benefit following a six o'clock dinner at Upstairs at the Pudding.

A lengthy interview with King by Gail Caldwell called "Stephen King: Bogeyman As Family Man" was published in the Boston *Sunday Globe* on April 15, 1990. In the interview, King discussed the benefit and the play. King described it briefly:

"God's sitting at home and drinking a few beers and St. Peter comes in with papers to pass, and God's watching a sitcom on TV. And the earth is sort of hanging in the way of the TV, and he keeps trying to look around the world to see the television.

"So I sat down and wrote it. And it may have been a critical comment: The typewriter broke while I was working on this, and I had to redo it."

In the interview King mentioned that he had been following the superb David Lynch series "Twin Peaks" on TV, that he considered it "the right thing at the right time," and he also said that "As a little kid, I was scared a lot of the time. My imagination was too big for my head at that point, and so I spent a lot of miserable hours. And I feel like I'm getting back at everybody else now."

King also revealed that "What I'd like to do at some point in the next year – this has never really let go of me – is to write a novel about Jonestown."

"An Evening at God's" is a very powerful piece and, to me, just more evidence of the incredible storytelling abilities of Stephen King. Throughout the play, we're fascinated by this glimpse into the workings of the divine, and we are moved by the nonchalance with which God destroys the earth. For me, the icing on the cake is God's last question, "My son got back, didn't he?"

"An Evening at God's" is a terrific detour for Stephen King, and a brilliant addition to his lifelong body of work.
—sjs

"An Evening at God's"
The Play

"An Evening at God's" consists of two-and-one-half pages of typescript in play format. King provides stage instructions, and the play has two characters, God and St. Peter.

The play opens with God sitting in an easy chair in a living room. There is a table beside the chair, on which there is an open bottle of beer. A picnic cooler full of beer is beneath the table, and there are a "great many" empties lying about. "God is feeling pretty good." Across from the chair is a console TV on which is playing a sitcom. The earth is suspended in the air between God and the TV, blocking his line of vision. God is alternately watching TV and reading the book *When Bad Things Happen to Good People*.

There is a knock at the door. God bellows "Come in!," and St. Peter enters carrying a briefcase.

St. Peter, who is leaving on vacation in half an hour, has brought "letters of transmission from hell" for God to sign. St. Peter inquires after God's well-being, and God tells him that he's feeling better, but that he should know better than to eat chili peppers: "They burn me at both ends."

God signs the papers, and St. Peter remarks that the earth is still around after all these years. God says, "Yes, the housekeeper is the most forgetful bitch in the universe."

There is laughter from the television, and God asks if that was Alan Alda. St. Peter replies that it might have been, but that he couldn't see.

God replies "Me, either" and reaches forward and crushes the earth to powder.

Sadly, St. Peter remarks "I believe that was Alan Alda's world, God."

God is unfazed by this revelation, instead chuckling at Robin Williams on the tube. After all, he says, he has all the videotapes. God offers St. Peter a beer.

As St. Peter takes the beer, the stage-lights begin to dim. A spotlight shines on the remains of the earth.

St. Peter tells God that he "actually sort of liked that one."

God, still unfazed, says "It wasn't bad," but that there were "more where that came from."

As the lights continue to dim (and a slight numbus appears around God's head), he now sees Richard Pryor on the set ("That guy kills me!") and then asks "I suppose he was..."

St. Peter replies in the affirmative, and God says "Shit. Maybe I better cut down on my drinking. Still...it WAS in the way."

The stage goes black except for the spotlight on the ruins of the earth.

God then asks St. Peter "My son got back, didn't he?"

St. Peter tells him, yes, some time ago, and God replies "Good. Everything's hunky-dory, then."

The light on the earth goes out.

(U33)
"An Evening at God's"
People

ALDA, ALAN One of God's favorite sitcom stars.

GOD The Creator. In Stephen King's play "An Evening at God's," God is described as "a big guy with a white beard" who signs documents sending people to hell, reads his creations' books, and drinks beer to excess.

GOD'S SON After God destroyed the Earth, he asked St. Peter if his son had gotten back yet.

THE HOUSEKEEPER God's housekeeper. "[T]he most forgetful bitch in the universe." God was apparently pissed-off at her for not moving the earth out of the way of his TV. While drunk, he destroyed the earth so he could watch sitcoms.

PRYOR, RICHARD A favorite of God's. Pryor "killed" God. God, as it happens, also ended up killing Pryor. For real.

ST. PETER God's right-hand man. He dressed in a "snazzy white robe," and carried a briefcase. Peter had liked the Earth before God destroyed it.

WILLIAMS, ROBIN A favorite of God's. God had Robin on videotape.

Places

EARTH God's creation. He destroyed it when drunk because it was in the way of his TV.

GOD'S LIVING ROOM The room where God drank beer, read books, watched TV, and kept his Earth.

HEAVEN The setting of the play "An Evening at God's."

HELL St. Peter brought God "letters of transmission from hell" for God to sign.

Things

BEER God drank it. A lot.

CHILI PEPPERS God ate them, and they didn't agree with him. He told St. Peter "they burned [him] at both ends."

GOD'S TV SET It was a console.

GOD'S VIDEOTAPES God had Alan Alda, Robin Williams, and Richard Pryor tapes in his collection.

LETTERS OF TRANSMISSION FROM HELL The documents St. Peter brought God to sign the day God destroyed the Earth.

A VACATION St. Peter was leaving on vacation when he brought God "letters of transmission from hell" to sign.

WHEN BAD THINGS HAPPEN TO GOOD PEOPLE The book that God was reading when St. Peter visited him with some papers to sign.

[NOTE: Special thanks to Michael J. Autrey for his assistance with the compilation of this feature.]

"The Moving Finger"

"The Moving Finger" was published in a special "Stephen King" issue of *Fantasy & Science Fiction* magazine in December of 1990. It appeared with "The Bear," the opening segment of the third part of King's *Dark Tower* series, *The Waste Lands*.

"The Moving Finger" is notable for a couple of reasons: First, it adds another story to King's use of the "Bathroom Motif." He has set stories in bathrooms twice before: *IT* contained an exploding toilets scene, and "Sneakers" was about a haunted toilet stall. The second remarkable thing about "The Moving Finger" is that it is absolutely hilarious.

"The Moving Finger" is about a guy named Howard Mitla who is, as are many of King's characters, an ordinary man thrust into an extraordinary situation. He hears a noise in his apartment bathroom one night. The noise turns out to be a dismembered human finger crawling around the inside of his bathroom sink. It hides in the drain pipes, you see, and only comes out when Howard is in the bathroom. His wife Vi doesn't see a thing; she can use the bathroom sink with impunity and not encounter "the finger." The finger comes out only when her husband is in the room, and Howard the CPA freaks. He takes to urinating in the alleyway next to his building when Vi is home, and in the kitchen sink when she's not. He doesn't understand why the finger is there, but he accepts it – after he decides that he is not hallucinating from epilepsy or a brain tumor.

He decides to go "*mano a finger*" with the dastardly digit, and so arms himself for the battle: He buys liquid drain cleaner and electric hedge clippers, and stays home from work one day to get the job done.

Only one problem crops up: The finger has now grown – to a length of seven feet. As you can imagine, the hedge clippers come in handy.

I'll leave my summation of the narrative there so as not to spoil the story for you, but I *can* tell you that a toilet bowl plays a pivotal role in the narrative's resolution, as does an young police officer named O'Bannion. And lest we forget: There are five fingers on a hand, right?

I promise you this: After reading "The Moving Finger," you will never watch "Jeopardy" the same way again. —**sjs**

(U34)
"The Moving Finger"
People

THE BLACK-AND-WHITE CAMERAMAN In Howard's "Jeopardy" dream, everything was in black-and-white, including the cameraman.

THE CLERK The toothpick-chewing clerk in the Queen's Boulevard Happy Handyman Hardware Store who sold Howard the Drain-Eze and electric hedge clippers. The clerk was "a bald man with lots of warts on his forehead."

DEAN, MR. One of the partners in the accounting firm Dean, Green, and Lathrop.

DeHORNE, MR. Vi Mitla's father. He had gotten Howard a job with his firm, Dean, Green, and Lathrop.

DeHORNE, MRS. Vi Mitla's mother.

DETTLEBAUM, MRS. She stood outside Howard's apartment

while Officer O'Bannion decided what to do. Inside, Howard was battling the moving finger.

THE DETTLEBAUMS Howard and Vi's neighbors in apartment 3-F.

FEENY, DENNIS One of the Mitlas' neighbors. It was Feeny who called the cops during Howard's battle with the seven-foot acid-burned moving finger.

FENSTER, ALICIA She lived in apartment 2-C.

THE FENSTERS Howard and Vi's neighbors in apartment 2-C.

FLEMING, ART The day Howard stayed home from work, he dreamt he was on "Jeopardy." In his dream, though, Alex Trebek had been replaced by Art Fleming.

GREEN, MR. One of the partners in the firm Dean, Green, and Lathrop.

JAVIER, MRS. A woman who lived on the seventh floor of the Mitlas' apartment building.

KATZ, ARLENE One of Vi Mitla's friends.

LAH, MRS. She was olive-skinned, and owned the market where Howard and Vi shopped.

THE LAHS The Vietnamese people who owned the corner market where Vi bought cherry-vanilla ice cream and a six-pack of American Grain beer on the night Howard discovered the moving finger in his bathroom sink.

LATHROP, JOHN Howard Mitla's boss.

MILDRED One of the "Jeopardy" contestants on the night Howard discovered the moving finger in his bathroom. She wore a hearing aid that looked like a "microwave oven" in her ear.

MITLA, HOWARD Howard was "one of New York's lesser-known certified public accountants," and the gentleman who discovered a moving finger scritch-scratching around his bathroom sink one day. Howard was married to Vi. He eventually waged battle against the finger…and its owner.

MITLA, VIOLET Howard's wife, Vi. Violet was "one of New York's lesser-known dental assistants." She liked beer. "Vi Mitla was one of those large women who move with such dainty precision that they seem almost fragile…"

A *NEW YORK* RAT Before he found out that the thing in his bathroom was actually a finger, Howard was afraid it would be a *New York* rat – a "subway-bred super-rat."

O'BANNION, OFFICER The police officer who reported to the Mitlas' apartment. Dennis Fenny had called the police.

PANG, MRS. When Mrs. Lah asked after Howard's health, he thought to himself, "Oh, yes, I'm fearing just fine, thank you, Mrs. Pang."

A POLITICIAN After Mildred's Daily Double "Jeopardy" failure, a politician came on and began explaining why he should be reelected to run the Nassau County Bureau of Taxation.

STONE, DR. The dentist Vi Mitla worked for.

TREBEK, ALEX The host of "Jeopardy." Vi Mitla thought he looked like a crooked evangelist.

THE TWO MEN CONTESTANTS Mildred's fellow "Jeopardy" players.

Places

THE ALLEY Howard urinated in the alley next to his apartment building after the moving finger pushed up the drain plug in his bathroom sink.

THE BATHROOM The room where Howard Mitla discovered the moving finger.

CAMP HIGH PINES Howard had attended Camp High Pines when he was twelve. His mother had forgotten to pack his toothbrush, and he had gone the whole two weeks without brushing his teeth.

CON ED Howard and Vi Mitla's electric company.

THE CORNER OF HAWKING AND QUEENS BOULEVARD The location of Lah's Twenty-Four-Hour Delicatessen and Convenience Market.

"A DARK HOLE" The brass crosshatch in Howard's bathroom sink had disappeared years ago, and there was only a "dark hole rimmed by a circle of tarnished steel." [NOTE: This echoes the scene in *IT* where Beverly hears voices coming from *her* bathroom drain. See the section on *IT* in this volume.]

THE FOURTH FLOOR Howard and Vi's apartment was on the fourth floor of a nine-story building on Hawking Street.

HAWKING STREET The Mitlas' apartment building was on Hawking Street in Queens.

HELL'S KITCHEN Howard Mitla grew up in New York's Hell's Kitchen area.

LAH'S TWENTY-FOUR-HOUR DELICATESSEN AND CONVENIENCE MARKET A market owned by the Vietnamese people, the Lahs. It was on the corner of Hawking and Queens Boulevard.

THE QUEEN'S BOULEVARD HAPPY HANDYMAN HARDWARE STORE The store where Howard bought the Drain-Eze and electric hedge clippers.

QUEENS Howard and Violet Mitla's apartment was in Queens.

ST. ANNE'S HOSPITAL One of Howard's new tax accounts. It was "a rat's nest." Howard thought that nuns shouldn't be allowed to do bookkeeping.

3-F The Dettlebaums' apartment number.

THE TOILET Howard cut up the finger and put the pieces in the toilet. Officer O'Bannion found him in the bathroom, and Howard asked O'Bannion how much he wished to wager: There were "plop" noises coming from the toilet. "O'Bannion thought about it for a moment...then grasped the toilet seat and wagered it all."

2-C The Fensters' apartment number.

Things

AMERICAN GRAIN The new beer Vi Mitla bought when she went to the store for a pint of ice cream. It was on sale for $1.67, and she bought a six-pack. It gave her a hangover.

"THE BEST WAY TO GET RID OF THOSE TROUBLESOME FINGERS IN YOUR BATHROOM DRAIN" The "Pests and Vipers" answer in Howard's "Jeopardy" dream. Howard knew the correct question was "What is liquid drain cleaner?"

A BROOM Howard's first weapon of choice for his attack on what he thought was a mouse in his bathroom.

"CON BRIO" The way Vi Mitla ate, drank, worked, danced, and made love.

A DELIVERY TRUCK During Howard's "Jeopardy" dream, a delivery truck backfired on the street below, waking him just as he realized the correct question to the answer "The best way to get rid of thiose troublesome fingers in your bathroom drain" was "What is liquid drain cleaner?"

DRAIN-EZE The liquid drain cleaner Howard poured on the moving finger.

ELECTRIC HEDGE CLIPPERS The garden tool Howard used to battle the moving finger.

EPILEPSY OR A BRAIN TUMOR Howard figured he had one or the other after his "moving finger" hallucination. (He had almost convinced himself that the dancing digit *was* an hallucination.)

"THE FIRST MAN TO SET FOOT ON THE MOON" One of the "Jeopardy" answers on the night Howard discovered the moving finger in his bathroom sink. Mildred asked "Who was Neil Aldrin?," but Howard knew the correct question was "Who was Neil Armstrong?"

HEAVY-GAUGE MESH Howard had installed heavy-gauge mesh over all the apartment windows two years prior to his discovery of the moving finger. Because of the mesh, he knew that the noises he heard in the bathroom could not be a burglar. A mouse, maybe. Or even a rat. But not a burglar. It was actually none of the above.

"THE INEXPLICABLE" The "Final Jeopardy" category. The Final Jeopardy answer was "Because they can." Howard asked

Officer O'Bannion if he knew the question. He didn't. The Final Jeopardy question was "Why do terrible things like cancer and murder and fingers in the drain sometimes happen to the nicest people?"

"JEOPARDY" Vi Mitla didn't like "Jeopardy." She said it was because Alex Trebek looked like a crooked evangelist, but Howard knew it was because the show made her feel dumb.

"A MOMENTARY HALLUCINATION" Howard's feeble attempt at explaining the human finger in his bathroom sink.

THE MOVING FINGER A human finger that one day crawled up out of Howard Mitla's bathroom sink drain. It grew when it hit the air. Howard attacked it with Drain-Eze liquid drain cleaner, and then cut it up with electric hedge clippers. He put the pieces in the toilet, where either it grew back together, or where the *other* fingers from the same hand came to join it...and get even. With Howard.

THE NASSAU COUNTY BUREAU OF TAXATION After Mildred's Daily Double "Jeopardy" failure, a politician came on and began explaining why he should be reelected to run the Nassau County Bureau of Taxation.

$1.67 The price of a six-pack of American Grain beer.

A PEPSI In order to urinate in the alley next to his apartment building, Howard told Vi that he was going down to Lah's to get a Pepsi.

"PESTS AND VIPERS" One of the "Jeopardy" categories in Howard's dream.

A PINT OF ICE CREAM Vi Mitla wasn't home when Howard discovered the moving finger. She had gone down to the corner store to get a pint of ice cream. She came home with cherry-vanilla.

PRIME NUMBERS Howard recited prime numbers in his mind as a distracting device when he was attempting to urinate. Howard had a "bashful bladder."

"SCRATCH, SCRATCH, SCRITCHY-SCRATCH" The noise the moving finger made in Howard Mitla's bathroom sink.

"THE SIXTIES" One of the "Jeopardy" categories on the night Howard discovered the moving finger in his bathroom sink.

"SPACE AND AVIATION" One of the "Jeopardy" categories on the night Howard discovered the moving finger in his bathroom sink.

"THIS AIR FORCE TEST SITE WAS ORIGINALLY KNOWN AS MIROC PROVING GROUND" Mildred's Daily Double answer. She asked "What is Vandenberg Air Base?," and lost five hundred dollars. Howard knew the correct question was "What is *Edwards* Air Base?"

"THIS GROUP OF HIPPIES CROSSED THE UNITED STATES IN A BUS WITH WRITER KEN KESEY" The Final Jeopardy answer on the night Howard discovered the moving finger in his bathroom sink. Mildred incorrectly asked "Who were the Merry Men?," but Howard knew the correct question was "Who were the Merry Pranksters?"

"THIS RUSSIAN MADMAN WAS SHOT, STABBED, AND STRANGLED...ALL IN THE SAME NIGHT" One of the "Jeopardy" questions Howard heard on the night he discovered the moving finger. The contestant answered "Who was Lenin?," but Howard knew the correct question was "Who was Rasputin?"

THREE CANS Howard drank three cans of American Grain beer on the night he discovered the moving finger in his bathroom sink.

TWENTY-ONE YEARS When Howard discovered the moving finger in his bathroom sink, he and Vi and been married for twenty-one years.

VITAMIN PEE Beer was full of Vitamin Pee.

"WHEEL OF FORTUNE" On the night Howard discovered the moving finger, his wife Vi had gone down to the corner store for a pint of ice cream. She had waited for "Wheel of Fortune" to be over before she left.

"WHEW!" One of Vi Mitla's favorite exclamations.

"Squad D"

It's very difficult to talk about an unpublished story.

There are several reasons, but probably the most significant reason is that when, and if, the story ever does appear in print, what you see may bear little or no resemblance to the original version.

"Squad D" was written by Stephen King for Harlan Ellison's third "Dangerous Visions" anthology, *The Last Dangerous Visions*, which has yet to be published. (The anthology was scheduled for publication in the late seventies.)

In a 1989 interview with George Beahm for *The Stephen King Companion*, (Andrews and McMeel, trade paperback, 1989), Ellison had the following to say about the story:

> "Stephen's sent me a story for *Last Dangerous Visions* that needs to be rewritten. The problem is, when you say, I'm going to talk to Stephen about rewriting, I'm going to make suggestions, it sounds as if you are trying to blow your own horn: Well, here I am, the smart, clever fellow who is going to teach Stephen King how to write. Well, I don't mean any such thing as that. What I mean is that I was sent a short story, and I think there's a lot more in it than Stephen had time to develop. The story deserves better, the work deserves better, and Stephen's reputation deserves better."

And, in a 1989 telephone conversation with Tyson Blue, Ellison had this to say about "Squad D":

> "The story is currently in preparation. When it appears, it will not be in the form it is in now, and a story should not be critiqued until it's in its final form. Other persons who have discussed the story before this have just jumped the gun."

Therefore, the question I had to face was, is it valid to talk about the story as it now stands (in what is apparently a first-draft version), or should discussion of the piece wait until it is in its final form?

I think the answer lies in whether or not you'll accept Ellison's assertion that "Squad D" is in first-draft form.

Stephen King wrote the story and submitted it to Ellison for publication in *The Last Dangerous Visions*.

He apparently felt it was suitable for publication as is.

I would therefore have to say that the story is worthy of seeing print in the form in which it was written, and that whether or not it is substantially changed before it finally sees print, it is valid to talk about it in its current incarnation.

I am a fan of Harlan Ellison's. I think his story "The Whimper of Whipped Dogs" is a masterpiece. I also think his nonfiction is insightful, astute, and that he is a shrewd observer of contemporary literature and culture. I think Harlan Ellison is fiercely intelligent: He has a red-hot mind – stand close enough to that skull of his and you'll get blisters.

But I am a bigger fan of Stephen King's.

I have always respected Stephen King's judgement when it comes to writers, writing, and stories. Open any page of *Danse Macabre* and you'll find books worth tracking down and reading. King has steered me in the direction of many a writer I may have overlooked, and thus, I hold great store in his opinions. Don Robertson, John D. MacDonald, Jim Thompson, Joseph Payne Brennan...the list goes on and on.

So, if King felt "Squad D" was worthy of being read by his readers, then I think it's fair to at least fill you in on this version of the tale.

"Squad D" is a touching and sad story that seems to stand just fine as is, but apparently Ellison feels it could be better. He's probably right: I'm sure that if King decided to rewrite the story, it would become even more powerful.

But, as is, it is a very moving story of redemption. Michael Collings, in *The Shorter Works of Stephen King* (Starmont House, 1985), had the following to say about the story:

> "Squad D" is a story of guilt and forgiveness, of peace growing out of turmoil. Josh Bortman finds the peace he has sought, among his only friends. Dale Clewson becomes reconciled to his son's death – and to the tragedy that took the lives of too many sons.
>
> While not a particularly 'dangerous' vision, "Squad D" does deserve to be seen. With "The Reach," it is one of King's most penetrating statements on the relationship of life and death – and the tenuous border separating them."

If it ever does appear in print, and it *is* in a different form than it is now, then at least we'll have some details for the record about the story King originally told. — **sjs**

Squad D
The Story

"Squad D" has attained an almost mythic reputation among King fans: it is the story that was supposed to be published, but has not been; it is the story that Harlan Ellison refuses to publish as is; it is one of Stephen King's only attempts at writing about the Viet Nam war.

"Squad D" is about a father. Dale Clewson is the father of Billy Clewson, a young soldier killed in Viet Nam while crossing a bridge that had been booby-trapped by the Viet Cong. Billy was a member of D Squad, a squad that had ten members, nine of which were killed that day on the bridge. The tenth member, Josh Bortman of Castle Rock, Maine, was in the hospital that day with bleeding hemorrhoids, and was thus spared. From his hospital bed, he wrote letters to each surviving family, and with the letter, he enclosed a photograph – enlarged and framed at his own expense – of the nine squad members killed. Josh hadn't been with them when the picture was taken, and he hadn't been with them when they all died.

Eleven years and one day after Squad D was wiped out, Josh Bortman's image appears in the nine Squad D pictures.

Dale Clewson questions his own senses – Were there always nine in the picture?

He decides to call Josh, only to find out that Josh had finally caught up with his friends – he had hung himself the day before in the garage.

(UUP1)
"Squad D"
People

ANDERSON, LIEUTENANT The officer who sent the Clewsons the letter informing them of Billy's death in Viet Nam.

BORTMAN, JOSH A member of Squad D. He was not killed in Ky Doc when a bridge that the Squad was crossing blew up. He was in the hospital with bleeding hemorrhoids. Bortman was from Castle Rock, Maine, and hung himself eleven years later (to the day) that the Squad was killed. His image then appeared in all the Squad D photographs. He had finally caught up with his friends.

BORTMAN, MR. Josh's father.

BORTMAN, MRS. Josh's mother.

BRADLEY, JACK A member of Squad D. He was killed in Ky Doc when a bridge that the squad was crossing blew up. Bradley was from Omaha, Nebraska.

CLEWSON, ANDREA Billy Clewson's mother. She started drinking on the day she and her husband got the telegram informing them that their son Billy had been killed in a bridge explosion in Ky Doc, Viet Nam. She died two years later of liver dysfunction and renal failure.

CLEWSON, BILLY Andrea and Dale Clewson's son, and a member of Squad D. He died at Ky Doc in Viet Nam with Squad D on April 8, 1974, when a bridge the squad was crossing blew up. His family was from Binghampton, New York.

CLEWSON, DALE Billy Clewson's father. He saw Josh Bortman appear in the photograph of D Squad eleven years after nine members of the Squad were killed in a bridge explosion in Ky Doc, Viet Nam. He called Bortman's father, and learned that Josh had killed himself the day he appeared in the picture.

DOTSON, RIDER A member of Squad D. He was killed in Ky Doc when a bridge that the squad was crossing blew up. Dotson was from Oneonta, New York.

DOTSON'S BROTHER Rider Dotson's brother. He, too, called Mr. Bortman about Josh's appearance in the Squad D picture.

GIBSON, CHARLIE A member of Squad D. He was killed in Ky Doc when a bridge the squad was crossing blew up. Gibson played the guitar, and was from Payson, North Dakota.

KALE, BOBBY A member of Squad D. He was killed in Ky Doc when a bridge the squad was crossing blew up. Kale was from Henderson, Iowa.

KALE, MRS. Bobby Kale's mother. She, too, called Mr. Bortman about Josh's appearance in the Squad D picture.

KIMBERLEY, JACK A member of Squad D. He was killed in Ky Doc when a bridge the squad was crossing blew up. Kimberley told lots of dirty jokes, and was from Truth or Consequences, New Mexico.

MOULTON, ANDY A member of Squad D. He was killed in Ky Doc when a bridge the squad was crossing blew up. Moulton was the Squad's staff sergeant, and was from Faraday, Louisiana.

MOULTON, PETER Andy Moulton's father. He, too, called Mr. Bortman about Josh's appearance in the Squad D picture.

AN OLIPHANT An unnamed member of Jimmy Oliphant's family who called Mr. Bortman about Josh's appearance in the Squad D picture.

OLIPHANT, JIMMY A member of Squad D. He was killed in Ky Doc when a bridge the squad was crossing blew up. Oliphant was from Beson, Delaware.

ST. THOMAS, ASLEY A member of Squad D. He was killed in Ky Doc when a bridge the squad was crossing blew up. St. Thomas was from Anderson, Indiana.

Places

ANDERSON, INDIANA Asley St. Thomas's hometown.

BESON, DELAWARE Jimmy Oliphant's hometown.

BINGHAMTON, NEW YORK Billy Clewson's hometown.

CASTLE ROCK, MAINE Josh Bortman's hometown.

FARADAY, LOUISIANA Andy Moulton's hometown.

HENDERSON, IOWA Bobby Kale's hometown.

HOMAM The location of the American base in Viet Nam.

KY DOC Squad D was killed in Ky Doc, Viet Nam, when a bridge they were crossing exploded.

THE KY RIVER The river under the bridge on which the members of Squad D were killed. Squads A and C had waded across the river. Squad D had used the bridge.

OMAHA, NEBRASKA Jack Bradley's hometown.

ONEONTA, NEW YORK Rider Dotson's hometown.

PAYSON, NORTH DAKOTA Charlie Gibson's hometown.

TRUTH OR CONSEQUENCES, NEW MEXICO Jack Kimberley's hometown.

VIET NAM Squad D was killed in Ky Doc, Viet Nam, when a bridge they were crossing exploded.

Things

APRIL 8, 1985 The day that Josh Bortman hung himself in his garage.

APRIL 9, 1985 The day that Dale Clewson called Mr. Bortman about Josh's appearance in the Squad D picture.

AN ASTERISK Josh Bortman had put an asterisk next to his name on the back of the Squad D picture. Dale Clewson thought it meant "still alive" and "don't hate me."

BLEEDING HEMORRHOIDS Josh Bortman had been in the army hospital with bleeding hemorrhoids instead of with his Squad D pals the day they were killed.

D SQUAD It consisted of ten members, nine of which were killed by the Viet Cong in a bridge explosion in Ky Doc, Viet Nam, on April 8, 1974. Squad D consisted of:

Jack Bradley	Jack Kimberley
Billy Clewson	Andy Moulton
Rider Dotson	Jimmy Oliphaunt
Charlie Gibson	Asley St. Thomas
Bobby Kale	Josh Bortman.

A FLYING "O" Lieutenant Anderson's typewriter had a flying O.

JOSH BORTMAN'S DOG TAGS They weren't visible in the picture of Squad D.

THE JUMBLE DRAWERS The drawers in the Clewsons' kitchen that had a lot of junk in them.

LIVER DYSFUNCTION AND RENAL FAILURE The causes of Andrea Clewson's death.

THE MANTEL CLOCK A clock in the Clewson living room. It stopped ticking when Dale Clewson found out about Josh Bortman's suicide.

MAY 1974 The month and year that Dale Clewson received the framed picture of Squad D from Josh Bortman.

SQUAD A They had waded across the Ky River instead of using the bridge. They survived; Squad D did not.

SQUAD C They had waded across the Ky River instead of using the bridge. They survived; Squad D did not.

THE SQUAD D PICTURE After his squad members were killed, Josh Bortman had had nine copies of the squad picture made and sent one to each of the families of the nine guys killed. The framed picture had made its way from Homam to Saigon to San Francisco to the hometowns of the deceased soldiers.

"THE THREE-PART PRESCRIPTION" Dale Clewson felt that the army followed a three-part "prescription" when a young boy was killed: First, the telegram, second, the follow-up letter from the boy's Lieutenant, and third, the coffin, one boy enclosed.

A YAMAHA 500 At the age of eighteen, Billy Clewson had brought home a Yamaha 500.

MOTION PICTURE
ADAPTATIONS

Stephen King at the "Graveyard Shift"
press conference, October 1990.
Photos courtesy George Beahm.

WHAT A LONG, STRANGE TRIP IT'S BEEN
An Interview with Jessie Horsting

Jessie Horsting worked for ten years as an auto mechanic and, at the time I spoke with her, the last book she had read was *Famous Murderers of History*.

Interesting as those credits may be, Jessie's most significant accomplishment for Stephen King fans was authoring a book considered to be the definitive look at the films of Stephen King—although now she describes herself as a somewhat apathetic Stephen King fan who is very often surprised that there's so much material (such as *Castle Rock*) out there about King.

Jessie is the author of *Stephen King at the Movies* (Starlog/Signet, 1986), an oversized trade paperback loaded with everything you could possibly want to know about the film adaptations of Steve's work, as well as stuff you probably never even imagined you wanted to know. (Such as the fact that 9,000 giant cockroaches were imported from Trinidad especially for your viewing pleasure in the "Creepshow" segment called "They're Creeping Up On You," that their biological name is Blaberus Giganticus, and that they were gassed after the filming.)

Jessie has had a varied and fascinating career, doing everything from working in a garage to helming her own magazine, *Midnight Graffiti*. As she puts it, "Boy, I don't even know how to describe myself." She may think she can't do an adequate job, but let her try:

"I actually did work for ten years in a garage – and, in fact, I'm a pretty darn good mechanic —but I also have most of my master's in philosophy. I really don't know how those two combined to make me what I am, but they did. I'd always been pretty interested in writing, but then I just got sidetracked. I got delayed. I guess I like to think of myself as a "character"...a character in a play, maybe?

I worked on the magazine *Fantastic Films* as an assistant editor until that magazine folded. And I also worked for a very short time for a publishing company I'm embarrassed to have worked for, so I won't mention their name.

As a freelance writer, I've written for *Cinefantastique*, *American Film*, *McGill Cinema Annual*, *Starlog*, and *Fangoria*, and right now I'm the chief cook and bottlewasher for my own magazine *Midnight Graffiti*, which we hope will be a roaring success.

I'm currently working on two novels. One is called *Tricks*, which has fantasy elements, although it's not a fantasy novel, and another called *Small Change*, which is definitely mainstream.

I've also been working on short stories—all of which are definitely genre—and as soon as I have time, one will be appearing soon."

Jessie tells me that she prefers Thai food over Chinese, and even though it's not her favorite ethnic food, it's the one she eats the most, since there are about fifteen Thai restaurants within walking distance of her home in Sherman Oaks, California.

I also found out that she loves all kinds of music, particularly rock 'n roll, country, and classical, and that "every form of music has been important to me at one time or another."

She also revealed that one thing she and I have in common is a passionate love for, and appreciation of Kate Bush's "Hounds of Love" album.

Also, Jessie was very encouraging regarding *The Shape Under the Sheet*, reminding me that if I become known as *The* Stephen King authority, "then at least you can look forward to, like, free passes to cons."

I like Jessie Horsting.

She is friendly, fiercely intelligent, and an easy conversationalist who can switch in midstream from talk of the shower scene in "Psycho" and Virgil's role in Dante's *Inferno*, to an explanation of Stephen King as an Aristotelian catalyst in contemporary culture.

Her work in *Stephen King at the Movies* is very impressive, and it's obvious that she not only has an in-depth knowledge of filmmaking and all that it entails, but that she also has a clear grasp of the difficulties and complexities in attempting to successfully translate books to film.

I talked to Jessie on a Monday afternoon in August, a couple of hours after I had interviewed horror writer Ray Garton.

I found her thoughts about Stephen King and his work enlightening and informed, and I think you will, too.

Here is my talk with Jessie "I Have An Immense Irreverence For Everything" Horsting. —**sjs**

WHAT A LONG, STRANGE TRIP IT'S BEEN
An Interview with Jessie Horsting

STEVE SPIGNESI: Let's start off by talking about your Starlog book *Stephen King at the Movies*. There are currently three books available that cover the film adaptations of Stephen King's stories: Yours, Underwood-Miller's *Stephen King Goes to Hollywood* by Jeff Conner, and Michael Collings's Starmont book *The Films of Stephen King*.

JESSIE HORSTING: That's right.

STEVE SPIGNESI: The Starmont book by Michael Collings is criticism—it consists of very insightful critical interpretation. But in terms of a pop culture look at the films, there's only your book and the Underwood-Miller book.

JESSIE HORSTING: Right.

STEVE SPIGNESI: It's my opinion that yours is the superior work. I have nothing against the Underwood-Miller book, but I think it's a bit redundant. Your book has everything. You obviously put a lot into it. How did *Stephen King at the Movies* come about?

JESSIE HORSTING: No one's ever asked me that before. I had had the idea for a book on the films for a long time. I happened to be working at a publisher that was doing entertainment-related things, and I suggested it to him, but he didn't think it was a very good idea, and he didn't want to do it.

I continued to think it was a good idea, so I approached Dave McDonnell at *Starlog*. They had done a film series in trade size. They *did* think it was a good idea, and so approached NAL (New American Library) to distribute it. NAL also liked the idea, and the deal was done. That's how it came about. I had written several articles about Stephen King movies, and the more articles I wrote the more I thought to myself that the market was right for a book covering the films. Also, as his fandom developed, it became more obvious.

When I started writing about him, which was in 1979, 1980, he wasn't the phenomena he grew to be. But by 1985 or so, it seemed to me that there was a screaming need for this type of book.

STEVE SPIGNESI: At last count, the book had sold around 50,000 copies, right?

JESSIE HORSTING: Yes, that's right.

STEVE SPIGNESI: So you were obviously right. The market *is* out there. There *are* people interested in this type of look at King's films. I find it fascinat-

ing that the focus of the book is Stephen King who, "Maximum Overdrive" notwithstanding, is *not* a director—he's a writer. Offhand, I can't think of this type of coverage for adaptations of any other writer's work.

JESSIE HORSTING: Well, there are a lot of people who have had a lot of stories adapted. Ray Bradbury has been real active in this area. My idea for a second book would have been the adaptations of Ray Bradbury's films. There was "The Illustrated Man," "The Martian Chronicles"...he wrote the screenplay for "Moby Dick," there's "Ray Bradbury Theater"...there's plenty of material out there. But it's also the same kind of stories – stories that are very well-constructed. That's the one comment I've heard time and time again from directors. The construction of King's stories is very easily adaptable.

STEVE SPIGNESI: The structure is very cinematic.

JESSIE HORSTING: I think that's one thing that Ray Bradbury showed us as well—the extreme visual nature of it, you know?

First I was a reader of Stephen King's stuff, and then I became a film fan of his. And because he is so extremely visual, it always seemed to me that his stories screamed to be films. And a lot of filmmakers have apparently felt the same way.

When the hardback of *Carrie* came out, the manuscript was sent out to Hollywood simply because it was very visual. It had these extreme images that were very new to horror at the time. And that's what pumped the paperback sale up to $400,000.

STEVE SPIGNESI: Tell me about your personal favorite King films.

JESSIE HORSTING: Well, the one I hated the most is now the one that, all things considered, is among my favorites. "The Shining." (Laughs.) Isn't that weird?

STEVE SPIGNESI: You hated it but now you like it?

JESSIE HORSTING: Yes. Now I really do. For a long time I had a lot of trouble—as many people did—divorcing Stephen King's story from Stanley Kubrick's story.

STEVE SPIGNESI: That's understandable. Even King has said that perhaps it should have been called "Stanley Kubrick's 'The Shining'."

JESSIE HORSTING: We all want all of our favorite images and people and scenes to be part of a film adaptation. And that's what gets in the way of enjoying the film or seeing it for its own merit. I loathed "The Shining" when it first came out—as

Stephen still does. And the principal reason is that in the film, you knew from the start that Jack was crazy. And that, to me, killed the suspense. It killed the entire subtext of the book. It ruined it, and I hated it. But when I was able to divorce my expectations from what was on film there, I realized that it's stylish, it is extremely well-photographed and well-thought out, and it has its own tension. It's just not the tension I expected, you know?

STEVE SPIGNESI: Yes. How about films you liked from the start?

JESSIE HORSTING: I really liked "Cujo." And what is it? As I said in my book, it's a novel about a 200-pound St. Bernard waiting for a woman to get out of a Pinto, you know? And given that that's what the director had to work with, and what the film was, I thought Lewis Teague did a brilliant job. [NOTE: See the interview with Lewis Teague in this volume.]

Teague was forced by the events of the book to have the climactic scenes of the film take place in an open area. And in the horror movie, having an open area in daylight is probably the least likeliest place to foster the development of "surprising" circumstances. Yet Lew managed to make surprises.

STEVE SPIGNESI: Talking about daylight in the horror movie, I recently interviewed horror writer Ray Garton, and he brought up something that I hadn't thought of. In "The Shining," Kubrick tries to scare you in broad daylight. [NOTE: See the interview with Ray Garton in this volume.]

JESSIE HORSTING: Yes! And he does. (Laughs)

STEVE SPIGNESI: He certainly does!

JESSIE HORSTING: And what's very interesting about all that is that all that daylight was false. I talked to John Alcott, the cinematographer on the film, and he told me that all that sunlight was entirely staged. And I thought that was pretty amazing.

STEVE SPIGNESI: That's interesting. I didn't know that, and apparently Ray Garton didn't either, because he said to me that the light in the film had a fluorescent quality to it. I agreed with him, and now I know why it looked that way.

JESSIE HORSTING: That look came from two reasons. In addition to the light being artificial, sections of the film were a little overburned.

STEVE SPIGNESI: Intentionally?

JESSIE HORSTING: Yes. They did that when they wanted that effect. One particular scene I remember was that one shot of him simply looking out the window.

STEVE SPIGNESI: Yes, I know that shot. Nicholson never looked more demented.

JESSIE HORSTING: Well, that was overburned. And a lot of the close face shots in the lobby where he was typing were overburned. They did it just to give the scene that pale quality it had. It's something they do in development on director's instructions. It's just a gimmick.

STEVE SPIGNESI: I thought that that was daylight, and now to find out that it was staged just adds to the visual impact of the film. You're right —it is amazing.

JESSIE HORSTING: Sure is.

STEVE SPIGNESI: My opinions change, but today, my personal favorite King films are "The Dead Zone" and "Stand By Me." Actually, it's a tie, although if I had to flip the coin, I'd probably lean towards "The Dead Zone" simply because it is more of a quintessential King tale.

JESSIE HORSTING: Right. Well, I think "Stand By Me" is certainly the best adaptation. It's the film that really did read between the lines of the story. I think that the great flaw with a lot of the adaptations is that most of them don't read between the lines. It's a flaw insofar as King's fans go.

I think one of the reasons we're fans is because of the sensibilities of Steve's stories – sensibilioties which rarely ends up on the screen. I think it did in "Stand By Me."

I liked "The Dead Zone" as well, but for me it just missed the mark. I thought for what it was, it was terrific. But I don't think that it accurately portrayed Johnny Smith. To me, Johnny Smith was a much more tortured character than Christopher Walken gave us. He did a terrific job, but it was more of a transition in the film. And in the novel, he woke up tortured. In my opinion, it was in some ways the same mistake that Kubrick made – although to be fair we should really call it interpretation. In the film, Johnny Smith's doom is no surprise.

STEVE SPIGNESI: Valid point.

JESSIE HORSTING: And I think that was an important element in the book.

STEVE SPIGNESI: Speaking of the books, what are your favorites?

JESSIE HORSTING: All of them. (Laughs.)

STEVE SPIGNESI: (Laughs.) Good answer!

JESSIE HORSTING: Well, every one has a lot of merit and uniqueness. *The Stand* is the one I've reread the most times.

STEVE SPIGNESI: Are you looking forward to the unabridged version of *The Stand*? [NOTE: This interview was conducted before the release of *The Stand: The Complete & Uncut Edition.*]

JESSIE HORSTING: Yes, I am. I'm very excited. I'm really looking forward to it. Everytime I read *The Stand*, I devour the first two-thirds of it, and then I have to slow down because it's going to be over soon. The unabridged will take some of the edge off that.

STEVE SPIGNESI: Did you screen "Maximum Overdrive" for your book?

JESSIE HORSTING: No. It wasn't out when I was writing my book so I had to rely pretty much on what Stephen told me about it. That film was one that I did a direct interview with Steve on behalf of *Starlog* and for my book.

STEVE SPIGNESI: What are your thoughts on adapting King to film?

JESSIE HORSTING: What certainly has happened with me is that there have been so many disappointments that now I've gotten to the point where I'm not anxious to run out and have my visions abused.

STEVE SPIGNESI: King has said that, in "Maximum Overdrive" he achieved his goal of making a "moron movie." I guess he's decided that, among his many talents, directing is not one of them.

JESSIE HORSTING: Right. But that's one way we find out what we can and cannot do—by trying.

STEVE SPIGNESI: I personally didn't like the soundtrack. AC/DC scored the film. I think that the impact of the film would have been stronger if he had made it more of a "pop soundtrack"—by that I mean a melange of different artists, different songs—something like the "Top Gun" soundtrack, or even "Dirty Dancing."

JESSIE HORSTING: Sure.

STEVE SPIGNESI: Songs that commented on what was happening in the film.

JESSIE HORSTING: Well, AC/DC has always been a pretty one-dimensional band, and asking them to score – or do the majority of scoring on a film—you're going to get a very one-dimensional track.

STEVE SPIGNESI: What can you tell us about "Rainy Season"? [NOTE: The short story "Rainy Season" ran in a special Stephen King Issue of *Midnight Graffiti* released in January 1989, and this interview was conducted before the issue's release.]

JESSIE HORSTING: It's a real fun story. It has very much the same sensibility as "Trucks" did. It made me laugh. I thought it was very funny. It has to do with frogs, and everybody dies. (Laughs.) And it's really designed to be gory and funny. It's very much like an "E.C. Comics" story.

STEVE SPIGNESI: You're the editor of the story?

JESSIE HORSTING: Yes. Although we've only had to make one editing choice so far. It was our consensus that the dog farted once too many times.

STEVE SPIGNESI: The dog farted...

JESSIE HORSTING: ...once too many times. Yes.

STEVE SPIGNESI: Speaking of farts (I can't believe I said that), have you heard of a short story called "The King Family and the Farting Cookie?"

JESSIE HORSTING: No! (Laughs.) Where did you hear about it?

STEVE SPIGNESI: (Laughs.) I found out about it from Doug Winter, who has had a copy of it. It's a short story that King wrote, and it's been circulating only among the real inner circle of King family and friends. I haven't seen it but I thought I'd ask if you had.

JESSIE HORSTING: No! But Steve should share this little gem! I know Harlan (Ellison) is good pals with him, and Harlan has certainly never mentioned it, and I think Harlan *would* talk about it because he loves to rub my nose in any advantage he has on me. We have a hostile truce all the time. (Laughs.) [NOTE: A new short story by Harlan Ellison called "The Function of Dream Sleep" appeared in the premiere issue of *Midnight Graffiti*.] Harlan's the greatest, he really is, but he takes great glee in any little torments.

STEVE SPIGNESI: No kidding?

JESSIE HORSTING: Oh, sure. That's why we get along so well.

STEVE SPIGNESI: What's Harlan up to lately, beside tormenting you?

JESSIE HORSTING: He's been shooting a commercial. For Chevy.

STEVE SPIGNESI: Harlan Ellison is shooting a commercial for Chevy?!

JESSIE HORSTING: I don't know what it means. That's all the information I have. He won't tell me any more.

STEVE SPIGNESI: He's directing it, or writing it?

JESSIE HORSTING: I think he's appearing in it, but he's being really cryptic. I can't imagine the ad campaign that would need a writer of the stature of Harlan Ellison.

STEVE SPIGNESI: That'll be interesting to look for.

JESSIE HORSTING: If you could get Ray Bradbury to say "I've never driven my entire life, but when I do start driving, it'll be a Chevy," or something like that, then you've got something.

STEVE SPIGNESI: Do you think *IT* can ever be successfully made into a film?

JESSIE HORSTING: I think it'd make a great film, but I'd change one thing in it though.

"...[John Wayne] Gacy used to dress up as Pogo the Clown. I did an interview with Steve in 1982 where part of the discussion, part of the conversation, was about John Wayne Gacy....I think that's where Steve's image of Pennywise came from."

STEVE SPIGNESI: What's that?

JESSIE HORSTING: Instead of having them meet the giant spider when they go in, I'd have them meet Pennywise. And then Pennywise could change into something. I think the most chilling image in that book is Pennywise.

And speaking of Pennywise, here's an interesting aside. In the next issue of *Midnight Graffiti,* [Number 2] we're running paintings done by John Wayne Gacy. Gacy used to dress up as Pogo the Clown. I did an interview with Steve in 1982 where part of the discussion, part of the conversation, was about John Wayne Gacy.

STEVE SPIGNESI: That's weird.

JESSIE HORSTING: This is just my guess, but I think that's where Steve's image of Pennywise came from.

STEVE SPIGNESI: The evil clown who beckons the children.

JESSIE HORSTING: Right.

STEVE SPIGNESI: I like your idea of the kids meeting Pennywise, and then having him trans-

form into the giant spider.

JESSIE HORSTING: I don't know why Steve chose to have the climactic confrontation be with this huge evil. From my experience with storytelling, that's usually an error. It's the same error that "Star Trek: The Motion Picture" made. V'ger was just incomprehensible. It was an incomprehensible evil, and so it wasn't very threatening to people. And because Steve's trying to describe the indescribable, it doesn't have the impact. In fact, I think that's where *IT* fails. Had the kids met Pennywise in there, I think it would have been more chilling. Yes, we would have expected it, but nothing could have been more chilling.

STEVE SPIGNESI: Do you write fiction?

JESSIE HORSTING: Yes. Mostly what I've been doing is working on a novel with Steve Boyett.

STEVE SPIGNESI: The one you mentioned in the back of the movie book?

JESSIE HORSTING: Yes. But Steve Boyett did something else, and so we've decided that I'm going to write the book. I also do short stories, but I've just been too busy to concentrate on them. I did *Stephen King at the Movies,* and then I got involved in this magazine.

STEVE SPIGNESI: Will we see a Jessie Horsting short story in *Midnight Graffiti*?

JESSIE HORSTING: Oh, I don't know. I think that's too self-serving. It would accomplish a lot more for me to just sell it to somebody else.

STEVE SPIGNESI: Are your stories horror?

JESSIE HORSTING: Dark fantasy. My writing isn't very graphic, or what you'd call "traditional" horror. To me, there are masters of horror, and I'm not swimming in their pool.

STEVE SPIGNESI: Well, what is horror? What does horror mean to you? Where does it come from?

JESSIE HORSTING: Oh boy! In twenty-five words or less? (Laughs.)

STEVE SPIGNESI: Of course! (Laughs.)

JESSIE HORSTING: Well, it's different for me now then it was even seven years ago. I didn't even watch a horror film until I was twenty-eight. I wouldn't. Just the idea—the whole notion of "Psycho" scared me. All I knew about "Psycho" was the shower scene. Kids threatened me with that for years. "Wait'll you see it, wait'll you see it!" So, my whole answer to that was never to see it – or anything else that might keep me up at night. And then I remember sitting in my living room and asking myself "What the hell are you scared of?" And "Psycho" was on TV, so I watched it, and that was one of the films that hooked me, because unbeknownst to me, Alfred Hitchcock had cleverly not shown any actual stabbings, you know?

STEVE SPIGNESI: That's right.

JESSIE HORSTING: And so I understood number one, that they had put a lot of fear in my mind that didn't exist there, and then I also learned that horror's real personal. I find Anthony Perkins's face a lot more disturbing then the entire shower scene.

So, horror to me is personal—it's your interpretation of the images and the situations, and good horror relies heavily on universal experiences and fears. I guess what I'm saying is that I just know it when I point at it. (Laughs.)

STEVE SPIGNESI: Like that Chief Justice's...

JESSIE HORSTING: Yeah!

STEVE SPIGNESI: ...definition of obscenity.

JESSIE HORSTING: Yeah, that was funny! (Laughs.)

STEVE SPIGNESI: I know what *that* is! (Laughs.) Do you have in your own mind a reason why you think Stephen King has become what he's become? It seems ridiculous that one writer, writing in what had been a bastard genre, would become the industry and the worldwide phenomena that he's become. What's the secret?

JESSIE HORSTING: Well, I think it's two part. You're probably aware of Steve's theory—and belief —that horror is cyclical, and that it is one of the ways society responds to events. Horror is often in response to a period of time when nothing is happening, and it's a way to purge fears that don't have any focus.

STEVE SPIGNESI: It acts as a catharsis.

JESSIE HORSTING: Right.

STEVE SPIGNESI: That doesn't say much for the seventies, then.

JESSIE HORSTING: Well, it says that we're out of Vietnam, and it says that the Cold War with the Soviets was breaking down—and this was even before Gorbachev. There was much more conversation between our two countries, and we were starting to see that "the face of the beast" was not very much different from ours.

And now, the Middle East is a situation so far removed and so detached from us by television that it really doesn't have any impact. We don't have a focus for our fears.

And I really think that's what created the environment for a guy like Stephen King. And then for other writers in the same field like Dean Koontz, V.C. Andrews, and others. We always have fear and we just need a place to focus it. We always need that Aristotelian catalyst.

"Steve's like Virgil was to Dante in Hell. Dante didn't want to go to Hell, and he especially didn't want to go there by himself, but there was this presence that forced him to confront this and to evaluate it and to purge it, and to me that's been Stephen King's role for the public at large."

STEVE SPIGNESI: An outlet that will cleanse – and flense – the soul?

JESSIE HORSTING: Yes. And I think if it wasn't him, someone else would have had major success.

But Stephen King is one of the most unique persons ever to have breathed—his whole sensibility. I think he has great compassion, I think he has great heart, and I think his object is not to see how much he can shock us and frighten us, but instead, to act as our guide.

Steve's like Virgil was to Dante in Hell. Dante didn't want to go to Hell, and he especially didn't want to go there by himself, but there was this presence that forced him to confront this and to evaluate it and to purge it, and to me that's been Stephen King's role for the public at large.

STEVE SPIGNESI: That's interesting. Do you really think that if there were no Stephen King, that the time was right for another writer to have achieved big success—that somebody could have stepped in to fill the need?

JESSIE HORSTING: I think that, yes. I think that if William Peter Blatty was a better writer, he would have been that person.

STEVE SPIGNESI: Do you keep in regular touch with Steve?

JESSIE HORSTING: Not really. Not unless I have a reason to. And I don't really see him that much. I remember one time I saw him at a deep south convention—I think it was one of the last Cons that he appeared at. It was either 1982 or 1983. It was very strange. I got a look at a guy who had stopped smoking and stopped drinking before he got down there. And I saw him start smoking and drinking again that weekend. He hid in his room, and he couldn't walk across the lobby without being mobbed.

Here's a strange scene. They had a book-signing at this Con with Whitley Streiber, Charlie Grant, Dennis Etchison, Stephen King—about five or six guys all in the same room.

About two o'clock in the afternoon people started to get in line to get their books signed. When they started the official signing at two o'clock, there was a guy that continued to say, "Okay, line up in front of the author you want a signature from." And no one moved. There were about four hundred people in line to have Stephen sign their books, and Peter Straub and Dennis Etchison and all these others—really fine writers who had books out at the same time—were sitting there whittling on their pencils.

And that was how the day went. After Stephen had signed four or five books, then the people would go to Peter Straub, or to Dennis, or to Whitley Streiber and get something signed, but I would say that ninety percent of them got Stephen to sign a book and then they left.

The demand for Steve was so great that even though it was supposed to be a two-hour signing, he continued to sign books until about seven or eight o'clock at night. He went out and had some dinner and he came back and then did two more hours of signing in the lobby.

This said two things to me: What a wonderful guy he is—how patient, how understanding, and how sensitive to what people want from him. But number two, how impossible it was going to be for him to ever do it again. And I don't think he ever did. I think he went down to one in Florida after that, but this was basically the last announced appearance.

STEVE SPIGNESI: It's odd that you bring up that story because I think Jerry Williamson was at that Con, and he told me the same story. It stuck with him, too. [NOTE: See the interview with J.N. Williamson in this volume.]

JESSIE HORSTING: It was a horrible scene.

STEVE SPIGNESI: According to what I've heard, it was.

JESSIE HORSTING: Here's an incident that happened in the hall. I was talking to Steve for a moment when a girl came up and just interrupted. He had a beard at the time. And this girl went up

to him, without introducing herself, and said, "Guys are so lucky because they can grow beards

> **"...something unique to Stephen King is that he expresses his instincts for people in his books. There's that aspect of him that seems so understanding and so insightful and so astute, that people go up to him and say, 'Fix me, Stephen,'...."**

to change the way they look" – which said volumes about this gal. And Stephen looked at her and just said, "I'm very sorry I can't do anything to change the way you look." It just killed him, you know? And he said to me later that they think that because they read a certain writer, that that writer understands them, and can solve their problems.

And what I think is something unique to Stephen King is that he expresses his instincts for people in his books. There's that aspect of him that seems so understanding and so insightful and so astute, that people go up to him and say, "Fix me, Stephen," you know? And who can take that?

STEVE SPIGNESI: Do you think that this kind of mind-boggling, overwhelming attention has contributed to his decisions to not only not go to conventions, but to sort of back away from publishing for a while?

JESSIE HORSTING: I don't know. I'm not really privy to whatever has formed that decision, and I really wouldn't want to conjecture. I don't know why. I think he loves to write and I think he probably has a few novels in a trunk someplace. Why he hasn't delivered them to publishers I don't know. But I find it very unlikely to think that he's not writing at all. I think he's continuing to write.

STEVE SPIGNESI: What are your thoughts on the idea of King being what he's called a "brand name?"

JESSIE HORSTING: Well, that's an unfortunate cliche in public life – in any sort of celebrity. Something that I've noticed in the last fifteen years is that we increasingly dispose of our heroes. And it's as predictable as the sun coming up. We identify our heroes, we log them, and then we eat them. And I know Steve is smart enough to anticipate that, and I think that may be part of his "hiatus" —to avoid being eaten.

STEVE SPIGNESI: You think that as a culture, as a society, we tend to devour our favorites?

JESSIE HORSTING: We start to look for the new flavor. And I know Steve's certainly wise enough to undertand that, and it may be very calculated on his part to choreograph that a little bit—to withhold his name and his books for a year or so—so that he's not consumed.

STEVE SPIGNESI: How did you become A Stephen King fan?

JESSIE HORSTING: I was in the hospital. I had been in the hospital for a long time. I had developed peritonitis, and one of the most horrible things was not being able to sleep and not being able to read. And one of the reasons I couldn't read was because nothing held my interest. It's very hard to pull yourself out of your body if you're very sick. All your attention is on being sick, and if you're going to live or not. And my dad was desperately trying to find things for me to get interested in, and he brought me *Carrie*. And that was the first book that I couldn't wait to finish, and that I read all the way through. And I said, "Get me more books by this guy, dad, because you're saving me from going insane."

STEVE SPIGNESI: Steve will probably be pleased to hear that story!

JESSIE HORSTING: I hope so. (Laughs.) ❑

"Misery" Update

Kathy Bates won the 1990 "Best Actress" Oscar for her portrayal of Stephen King's Annie Wilkes in the Castle Rock Entertainment film "Misery."
Photo copyright © 1990 by Castle Rock Entertainment. All Rights Reserved.

CHRONOLOGICAL INDEX TO MOTION PICTURE ADAPTATIONS OF STEPHEN KING'S WORKS

Alphabetical Index to Motion Picture Adaptations of Stephen King's Works

"CARRIE"

"...a journey into unholy places..."

Released November 1976, by United
Artists.
Videotape released in 1984 by CBS/Fox
Video.
Running Time: 98 minutes
Rated R

Director: Brian De Palma
Screenplay by: Lawrence D. Cohen
Based on the Novel by: Stephen King
Producer: Paul Monash
Associate Producer: Louis Stroller
Editor: Paul Hirsch
Director of Photography: Mario Tosi
Music: Pino Donaggio
Art Directors: William Kenney & Jack Fisk

Budget: $1.8 million
Gross Box-Office Receipts: $30 million

CAST

Carrie White	Sissy Spacek
Margaret White	Piper Laurie
Sue Snell	Amy Irving
Tommy Ross	William Katt
Chris Hargensen	Nancy Allen
Billy Nolan	John Travolta
Miss Collins	Betty Buckley
Norma Watson	P.J. Soles
Mr. Fromm	Sydney Lassick
Mr. Morton	Stefan Gierasch
Mrs. Snell	Priscilla Pointer
Freddy	Michael Talbot
The Beak	Doug Cox
George	Harry Gold
Frieda	Noelle North
Cora	Cindy Daly
Rhonda	Dierdre Berthrong
Ernest	Anson Downes
Kenny	Rory Stevens
Helen	Edie McClurg
Boy on Bicycle	Cameron De Palma

"CARRIE"

Brian De Palma's 1976 "Carrie" was the first film adaptation of Stephen King's work, and it was the movie that began King's ascent to popular culture stardom in America.

It still holds up well today, even with the presence of elements that, to me, now seem somewhat dated, such as use of a split-screen and the speeded-up "tuxedo" scene.

The performances are uniformly superb, and Sissy Spacek and Piper Laurie were nominated for Academy Awards for their roles as Carrie and Margaret White. I particularly enjoyed Betty Buckley as Miss Collins, and P.J. Soles interpretation of Norma Watson exquisitely captured that viscious and nasty mien that seems to be manifested most perfectly in that somewhat complicated creature, the teenage girl. Girls that age – in the rigid and harsh social structure of a coed high school – can be wicked: their teeth are long...and they bite. (David Letterman – who considers show business a cruel, sleazy, back-stabbing world peopled by "money-grubbing slime" and creeps – frequently refers to a line he once heard that, to him, described that industry perfectly: "High school with money.")

Both versions of Carrie's story seem to capture the essence of what, for many people, are the worst four years of their life. Stephen King took the high school story one step further (using his cherished "Wouldn't it be funny if...?" device). He populated this vile landscape with stereotypical bitches and jocks (jocks who, in King's world, would likely grow up to be wife-beaters and alcoholics, such as Milt Sturmfuller in *Cycle of the Werewolf*). They all end up paying dearly for their abuses, because this time they screwed around with a telekinetic innocent who had no choice but to use her powers for defense, but not revenge.

The film is fairly faithful to King's novel, although King has remarked that he wishes De Palma had had the budget for Carrie to blow up the whole town, rather than just the gymnasium and a vehicle or two.

Also, one big difference from novel to film was made with purely cinematic considerations in mind: In the book, King has Carrie kill her mother by psychically squeezing her heart to a "full stop." De Palma, instead, has Carrie impale her mother with flying kitchen utensils, leaving her hanging from the wall "crucified," like the religious icons she maniacally worshipped, thereby re-emphasizing and finalizing the religious imagery carried throught the film. (Interestingly, 1988's "Carrie: The Musical" returned to the novel's original means of matricide. At the conclusion of the musical, Carrie places her hand over her mother's heart as they ascend the stairway to heaven – and death. See the feature on "Carrie: The Musical" in this volume.)

(Also, for a somewhat different take on the themes explored in "Carrie," check out the 1989 film "Heathers," which one critic called "The 'Carrie' of the 80's." After seeing it, you'll know what he meant.)

Here are a few of my favorite moments from the film:

1. *The Shower Scene*: First off, I've got to admit that any movie that gives us the talents of Amy Irving, Nancy Allen, and Sissy Spacek (all in various stages of undress in the first few minutes to boot), can't be all bad, right? (I'll bet Joe Bob Briggs *loved* this movie.) But, sexist remarks aside, the opening sequence of "Carrie" fulfilled every high school male's ultimate fantasy: to be inside the girl's locker room while they're all showering and getting dressed. This fantasy was used in a far more trivial manner in "Porky's" later on, but here, De Palma uses the "visit" to set us up for some very serious business: the dark side of the blatant sexuality present in the premise of the girl's inner sanctum: Carrie White's first menstrual period. The horror of the scene comes from the fact that Carrie didn't know what was happening: She thought she was bleeding to death, and her classmates, rather than sympathizing and helping her, treat her like the pariah she obviously is: they hurl

"CARRIE: THE MUSICAL"
The Biggest Flop In Broadway History

"This is the biggest flop in the world history of the theater, going all the way back to Aristophanes."
—Rocco Landesman
(President of Jujamcyn Theaters, and disgruntled (to the tune of $500,000) "Carrie: The Musical" investor.

CARRIE: THE MUSICAL

Based on the Novel *Carrie* by Stephen King
Directed by Terry Hands
Produced by Friedrich Kurz of the Royal Shakespeare Company
Book by Lawrence D. Cohen
Music by Michael Gore
Lyrics by Dean Pitchford
Sets by Ralph Koltai
Costumes by Alexander Reid
Choreography by Debbie Allen

CAST

Margaret White	Betty Buckley
Carrie White	Linzi Hateley
Chris	Charlotte d'Amboise
Tommy	Paul Gyngell
Miss Gardner	Darlene Love
Billy	Gene Anthony Ray
Sue	Sally Ann Triplett

Ensemble

Jamie	Jamie Beth Chandler
Cath	Catherine Coffey
Michèle	Michèle Du Verney
Shelley	Michelle Hodgson
Rose	Rosemarie Jackson
Kelly	Kelly Littlefield
Maddy	Madeleine Loftin
Michelle	Michelle Nelson
Mary Ann	Mary Ann Oedy
Squeezie	Suzanne Maria Thomas
Gary	Gary Co-Burn
Kevin	Kevin Coyne
David	David Danns
Matthew	Matthew Dickens
Eric	Eric Gilliom
Kenny	Kenny Linden
Joey	Joey McKneely
Mark	Mark Santoro
Chris	Christopher Solari
Scott	Scott Wise

Scenes and Musical Numbers

Act I
Prologue: THE GYMNASIUM
"In"................................Miss Gardner and Girls

Scene 1: THE SHOWERS
"Dream On"................................Girls and Carrie
Scene 2: THE LOCKER ROOM
"Carrie"..Carrie
Scene 3: THE WHITE HOME
"Open Your Heart".............Margaret and Carrie
"And Eve Was Weak".........Margaret and Carrie
Scene 4: THE DRIVE-IN
"Don't Waste the Moon"..............Sue, Tommy, Chris, Billy, Girls, Boys
Scene 5: THE WHITE HOME
"Evening Prayers"...............Carrie and Margaret
Scene 6: THE GYMNASIUM
"Unsuspecting Hearts"....................Miss Gardner and Carrie
Scene 7: THE NIGHT SPOT
"Do Me A Favor"..............................Sue, Tommy, Chris, Billy, Girls, Boys
Scene 8: THE WHITE HOME
"I Remember How Those Boys Could Dance"....... Margaret

Intermission

Act II
Scene 1: THE PIG FARM
"Out for Blood"....................................Chris, Billy and Boys
Scene 2: THE GYMNASIUM
"It Hurts to be Strong"....................................Sue
Scene 3: CARRIE'S ROOM
"I'm Not Alone"..Carrie
"When There's No One".........................Margaret
Scene 4: THE PROM
"Wotta Night!".............................Girls and Boys
"Unsuspecting Hearts" (reprise)....................Miss Gardner and Carrie
"Heaven" ....Tommy, Sue, Miss Gardner, Carrie, Margaret, Girls, Boys
"Alma Mater"............Girls, Boys, Miss Gardener
"The Destruction".....................................Carrie
Scene 5: EPILOGUE
"Carrie" (reprise)...................................Margaret

"Carrie: The Musical" opened on Broadway at the Virginia Theater on Thursday, May 12, 1988, and closed after five performances Sunday, May 15, 1988. So, as Bill Murray's character in "Tootsie" said about his own play, "What happened?"

The reviews were brutal, that's what happened. Several positive reviews that I've read (many of which appeared in *Castle Rock*) said that standing ovations were given at the performances they attended. But the critics lambasted it, and "Carrie: The Musical" now has the distinction of being the most costly Broadway failure ever. The show, which was originally produced at Great Britain's Stratford-on-Avon, was initially budgeted at $7 million, a cost which was eventually pushed to $8 million. In the May 30, 1988 issue of *Time* magazine, William A. Henry, III, did an article on the show's closing called "The Biggest All-Time Flop Ever."

Here's a "Carrie: The Musical" diary:

• NOVEMBER 1985: the *New York Times* runs an article revealing that Terry Hands of the Royal Shakespeare Company planned on bringing a musical production of the Stephen King novel *Carrie* to the stage.
• MARCH 1986: *Castle Rock*, "Carrie to be Musical": This reprint of the *New York Times* article was one of the first mentions of the production.
• SUNDAY, JANUARY 3, 1988: The *New York Daily News*, "Entertainment Tomorrow and for the next 12 months of 1988": Blurb about the scheduled production of the show. Also, a sidebar accompanied this feature called "Hot Prospects," which said that Linzi Hateley would be one of the "brightest new stars this year."
• FEBRUARY 1988: *Castle Rock*, "Carrie as a Musical": Details on one of the first stories about the musical, an article by *Chicago Tribune* reporter Howard Reich. This *Castle Rock* piece was by Tim Foster.
• MONDAY, FEBRUARY 22, 1988: *USA Today*, "*Annie* It Ain't": Blurb about the British production of the musical with quotations from director Trevor Hand: "'It's Cinderella, but also Samson. It breaks a number of barriers. It begins with menstruation and ends with mother-killing."
• MARCH 1988: *Castle Rock*, "Carrie to Open at the Virginia Theater": Article about the then-scheduled April 27 opening of the show. This piece revealed that Lawrence Cohen, the show's librettist, was currently working on a television mini-series of Stephen King's novel *IT*.
• MARCH 1988: The *New York Daily News*, "Apple Sauce" by Betty Liu Ebron: "Is something supernatural haunting *Carrie*'s debut?" Blurb that begins "Horrible rumors about *Carrie* are flying all over town. Seem's Stephen King's supernatural tale of prom night teenage revenge is having terrible delays getting to Broadway." The blurb revealed that the cast was making a "low" rehearsal rate of $740 a week until the show moved into previews.
• TUESDAY, MARCH 22, 1988: *USA Today*, "Name Game": Blurb annnouncing that Betty Buckley had taken over the role of Margaret White in the musical. The last line was "King, who's lying low, resting his twisted brain, is, however, expected to show up for the May 4 opening."

• TUESDAY, MARCH 29, 1988: The *New York Daily News*, "Buckley Carries on in *Carrie*," by Phil Roura and Tom Poster: Article about Betty Buckley taking over the role of Margaret White after Barbara Wood withdrew following the London opening. The article ran with a Richard Corkery picture of Buckley, Bridget her dog, choreographer Debbie Allen, and star Linzi Hateley.
• APRIL 1988: *Castle Rock*, "Musical *Carrie* is Strange Spectacle": Richard Mills' positive review of the London production.
• APRIL 1988: *Castle Rock*, "What a Carrie On": Synopsis and commentary on the London reviews of the musical.
• MAY/JUNE 1988: *Castle Rock*, "More *Carrie*-ing On": Review by Brian Osborne of the press night performance of the London production.
• THURSDAY, MAY 5, 1988: *USA Today*, "Sneaks" by Jeannie Williams: "A certain vulture element of New York audiences is waiting gleefully for *Carrie* to open on Broadway. Some who have seen it say it's terrible beyond their wildest dreams, and will enter the folklore with such bombs as *Moose Murders* and *Frankenstein*."
• SUNDAY, MAY 8, 1988: The *New York Daily News*, "Stage Fright" by Patricia O'Haire: Article about the musical's debut the following Thursday, containing an interview with Stephen King.
• THURSDAY, MAY 12, 1988: The *New York Post*, "Warming up for *Carrie*": Biographical profile of Betty Buckley by Diana Maychick. Buckley, who took over for Barbara Cook in the role of Margaret White, revealed that "I gave Margaret a history. Although it's not clear in the book or the movie, I chose to believe that Margaret wasn't married when she had Carrie." Buckley played the role of the sympathetic gym teacher Miss Collins in Brian De Palma's film version of the novel.
• FRIDAY, MAY 13, 1988: The *New York Post*, "Musical *Carrie* soars on blood, guts and gore": Review by Clive Barnes. Barnes starts off his review with "Surprise, surprise! Terry Hands' blood, sweat and tears staging of *Carrie* for his Royal Shakespeare Company works." One of the few positive reviews of the show, Barnes raved about the "marvelous high-tech environments" and a "spartan epic directness that rushes to the heart of any dramatic action and stresses the momentum of each and every moment." However, his review didn't negate the many negative appraisals of the production.
• SATURDAY, MAY 14, 1988: The *New York Times*, Theater Directory:

TODAY AT 2 & 8, TOM'W AT 3
BETTY BUCKLEY
in
CARRIE
The Musical
Tue.-Sat. at 8, Mats. Wed & Sat. 2, Sun. 3.
CALL TELETRON: (212) 246-0102
24 Hours a Day • 7 Days a Week
Groups: (212) 398-8383 • Also at Ticketron
Virginia Theatre, 245 West 52nd St.

"CARRIE: THE MUSICAL"
(continued)

- TUESDAY, MAY 17, 1988: The *New York Post,* "Carrie proves costly failure": Article about the Sunday, May 15th closing of the show. The article revealed that "Carrie" tied "Phantom of the Opera" and "Starlight Express" as the most expensive shows on record. "Phantom of the Opera" and "Starlight Express" were, and still are, huge hits.
- MONDAY, MAY 23, 1988: *Newsweek,* "Shakespeare to Stephen King: The Sins of *Carrie*": Review by Jack Kroll. Review that begins "After the first nuclear explosion, J. Robert Oppenheimer said that the atomic scientists had known sin. It may be that with *Carrie* the directors of the Royal Shakespeare Company have known sin." Kroll wrote "the show's narrative is oddly pointless and unfocussed" and that the "prom-apocalypse" was "just sound and fury signifying silly."
- MONDAY, MAY 23, 1988: *Time,* "Getting All Fired Up Over Nothing": Review by William A. Henry, III. A review that asserted that "What finally opened last week was two musicals lumped together, one compellingly written and overpoweringly performed, the other so ditzily conceived and garishly staged that it deflates the first." He also described the staging as "ludicrously campy high school scenes featuring girls who look and dress like 28-year-old hookers" and proclaims that "[a]s gross-out entertainment, *Carrie* fails to deliver."
- MONDAY, MAY 30, 1988: *Time,* "The Biggest All-Time Flop Ever – *Carrie*'s $7 million close shows why musicals are like dinosaurs": Article by William A. Henry, III. Piece about the closing of the show. Information on the financing of the show, with details on the lack of a reserve
fund which would have carried the production over until word-of-mouth began boosting weekly receipts. Costs involved $4 million for design elements, including $1 million for costumes, $500,000 for a print, poster, and TV ad campaign that was "teasingly mysterious" rather than hard sell, and twenty percent of the week's box-office income to the creative team, "including Novelist King, who otherwise had no role in the show." Henry concluded that "As a result of all these costs, *Carrie* barely had carfare home after its Broadway opening night."
- JULY 1988: *Castle Rock,* "You Read the Book, Saw the Movie, But What About the Show" by Bill Munster: Lenghty in-depth review/analysis of the Broadway production, with suggestions on changes that could be made to improve the show.
- JULY 1988: *Castle Rock,* "Black and White and Read All Over – *Carrie* on Broadway" by Craig Goden: A positive review of what Goden describes as "Medea and Child Meet the Solid Gold Dancers from Hell." The performance Goden attended got a standing ovation and he feels the failure of the production was due to the critics' lambasting of the show. "The whole production deserved a better fate than it was handed by the critics."
- AUGUST 1988: *Castle Rock,* "One Last Time: *Carrie* Reviewed – Buckets of Talent Wasted in *Carrie,*" by Dan Czirasky: A review that asserts that "some real, genuine talent…was horrendously wasted in this ill-conceived production."
- THURSDAY, DECEMBER 29, 1988: The *New York Post*: Clive Barnes gives his "Rags" award (named in honor of the failed Charles Strouse musical) to "Carrie: The Musical." He wrote "This musical attempt to stage a modern horror movie as if it were a Jacobean bloodbath was conceivably ill-advised, but its aspiring talent should not have gone unnoticed. This was the only musical of the year to show ambition and imagination."

sanitary napkins at her in a ritual "stoning of the outcast" while yelling "Plug it up, plug it up." This brings about one of the first manifestations of her telekinetic powers, accompanied by "'Psycho'-like" strings. It's a very effective scene, and a landmark in that a previously taboo subject – menstruation – was not only discussed, but graphically shown on screen.

2. *The Cruising Scene*: In John Travolta's first onscreen appearance, he's seen cruising the boulevard, beer can en-crotched, with a preening Nancy Allen beside him. As is very often the case in films, the music contributes enormously to the effectiveness of this scene: their ride is accompanied by Martha and the Vandella's "Heat Wave," an absolutely perfect choice. In addition to being a great tune, it also sets us up for the final "heat wave" of the film – Carrie's psychic Bic-flicking after her bloodbath. Travolta plays the role of the grinning idiot Billy Nolan, a dumb smirk on his face, and Nancy Allen is despicable the way she insults him, and the way she can't take her eyes off herself in her mirror. Haven't we guys all known girls like Chris Hargensen – girls who won't let you touch their hair because you might mess it? An uncomfortable scene with hints of mold around the edges.

3. *The Hand from the Grave Scene*: This scene scares the bejesus out of people the first time they see it, and it still makes me jump everytime I see it again. I know it's coming, I can describe it almost by the frame, but still my heart gives a leap when that bloody arm pushes through the earth and grabs Amy Irving.

Stephen King has been known to tell the story of the first time he saw the movie "Carrie." He and his wife went to a theater that was filled with black people.

The theatergoer in front of King, a black man, had been relatively quiet throughout the film until the very last scene, when Sissy Spacek grabs Amy Irving's arm from the grave. The guy in front of King stood up and said "Thass it, thass it! The bitch ain't never gone be right now! Uh, uh, no sir. That bitch ain't *never* gone be right!"

From that moment, and that gentleman's reaction, King knew the movie would be a hit.

He was right.

Now, here are some of my least favorite moments:

1. The slapstick/goofy tone to the girl's exercise scene.
2. The speeded-up tuxedo rental scene.
3. William Katt's hairstyle. (I know that was the style in the late seventies, but now it aggravates me.)

What the Critics Had to Say...

"Combining Gothic horror, offhand misogyny and an air of studied triviality, 'Carrie' is De Palma's most enjoyable movie in a long while, and also his silliest. —Janet Maslin, *Newsweek.*

"The horror is effective only once, and the attempts at humor are never very successful and come almost when one is inclined to be moved by somebody's plight, so that the non-jokes yield authentic bad taste. —John Simon, *New York.*

"Stylish but unattractive shocker which works its way up to a fine climax of gore and frenzy, and takes care to provide a final frisson just when the audience thinks it can safely go home." —Leslie Halliwell, *Halliwell's Film Guide,* Fourth Edition.

"'Carrie' is the ultimate revenge tale for the person who remembers high school as a time of rejection and ridicule. Many cruel self-important high-school big shots get their just desserts, and 'Carrie' does it as completely and frighteningly as only Brian De Palma could envision it. ☆☆☆ 1/2." —Mick Martin & Marsha Porter, *Video Movie Guide 1988.*

"Brian De Palma did a nice job with 'Carrie.' When you think of all the terrible movies made of recent books, I have this basic feeling that mine wasn't screwed up too badly." —Stephen King, *Bare Bones.*

"Brian De Palma's first big hit, and his best effort to date. Cleverly designed to appeal to its target teenage audience, "Carrie" finally synthesized all of De Palma's on-and-off real talents for intense, stylish, visual filmmaking. While De Palma has his legion of fans, he seems to be a marginal talent (a lack of intellectual insight into his characters hampers taking his stylistic rip-offs of Hitchcock and Hawks seriously) and a sexist, empty stylist." —*The Motion Picture Guide,* Vol. 2: C-D (Cinebooks, 1985).

" 'SALEM'S LOT"

"Try the cross, Ben."

Broadcast as a made-for-TV miniseries by CBS on November 17 & 24, 1979.
A Warner Brothers film.
Videotape released by Warner Home Video; $89.95.
Running Times:
 Original miniseries: 210 minutes.
 TV movie: 150 minutes
 European Theatrical Release:
  112 minutes
 Home Video: 112 minutes
Rated: Unrated

Director: Tobe Hooper
Producer: Richard Kobritz
Executive Producer: Stirling Silliphant
Teleplay By: Paul Monash
Based On The Novel By: Stephen King
Music Composed By: Harry Sukman
Director of Photography: Jules Brenner
Associate Producer: Anne Cottle
Production Design: Mort Rabinowitz
Editor: Carroll Sax
Special Effects: Frank Torro

Budget: $4 million

CAST

Ben Mears	David Soul
Straker	James Mason
Mark Petrie	Lance Kerwin
Susan Norton	Bonnie Bedelia
Jason Burke	Lew Ayres
Bonnie Sawyer	Julie Cobb
Weasel	Elisha Cook
Cully Sawyer	George Dzundas
Dr. Bill Norton	Ed Flanders
Marjorie Glick	Clarissa Kaye
Mike Ryerson	Geoffrey Lewis

Ned Tebbets	Barney McFadden
Barlow	Reggie Nalder
Larry Crockett	Fred Willard
Parkins Gillespie	Kenneth McMillan
Eva	Marie Windsor
Danny Glick	Brad Savage
Ralphie Glick	Ronnie Scribner
June Petrie	Barbara Babcock
Father Callahan	James Gallery
Ted Petrie	Joshua Bryant
Ann Norton	Bonnie Bartlett
Nolly	Robert Lussier
Henry Glick	Ned Wilson
Royal Snow	Ernie Phillips
Guard	Joe Brooks

" 'SALEM'S LOT"

Stephen King on television? Yup. And because everyone involved in this project took seriously one of King's greatest novels, the Tobe Hooper miniseries that was the original incarnation of the film is a good example of how successfully horror can be interpreted for the tube as a large-scale film WITHOUT gushers of blood, putrefying corpses, or amputated limbs.

But, things were different back then. And that's why I'm afraid of what is going to happen with the miniseries version of King's magnum opus, *It*. Back then, in 1979, before the Reagan years, even though there was a Standards & Practices shadow over everything that creative people did, there was also a willingness to dig deeper, to try harder to create a more textured film with depth and sincerity – which is exactly what "Salem's Lot" is. Now, everyone is so paranoid about the fundamentalist radical right that what has happened is that artistic materials for TV have become so bland, insipid, uninspired, and boring that by trying not to offend anyone, the networks offend the people they should really be trying to please: the fans of the work they are adapting for the tube.

But, in any case, we do have a successful translation from book to screen with "Salem's Lot."

The film does not move quickly, nor does it superficially "collapse" King's brilliant book into something to run between commercials. The film demands your attention, and then pays off in spades.

For me, one more proof that Tobe and company did it right is the fact that all three versions of the film that I have seen (I have not been able to screen the European theatrical version), work. It's like attending a huge banquet: If you've got ten terrific courses as your meal, and you only partake of two or three, the odds are that you're going to greatly enjoy the stuff you did eat. The edited versions of the film stand up to the cutting, and are enjoyable and entertaining versions.

Overall, I think "Salem's Lot" must be counted as one of the better adaptations of King for the screen. Ideally, of course, the best way to have done the film would have been as a big-budget theatrical release, but that was not to be. What we do have, though, is just fine.

[NOTE: See my interview with director Tobe Hooper in this volume.]

Here are a few of my favorite moments from the film:

1. *The Mood*: From the opening shots right through the whole four hours, the feel of the film is appropriate to the dark and somber town itself. Very spooky, and thankfully, not lighted like a fluorescent headache, as are most made-for-TV movies.

2. *David Soul*: I *believe* he is tortured and haunted by what he knows is going on in the Lot, and with this performance he foreshadows Christopher Walken's stunning performance as another King "hero" in "The Dead Zone." (Although, to be frank, there has not been, nor will there probably ever be, as superb a performance as a King character as Walken's Johnny Smith). I did not expect much from Soul. His previous TV credits included the character of Joshua Bolt on the 1968 series "Here Comes the Brides"; the character of Ted Warrick in the 1974 season of "Owen Marshall, Counselor at Law"; and, of course, the co-starring role of Hutch on the so-cool "Starsky and Hutch." His films weren't much better: Before "Salem's Lot," he had done the morbid 1971 release "Johnny Got His Gun," the not-bad (but not good either) 1973 "Dirty Harry" film "Magnum Force," the miserable 1974 film "Dogpound Shuffle," the 1977 TV-sexploitation film, "Little Ladies of the Night," and the almost invisible 1977 British film, "The Stick-Up." He delivered in "Salem's Lot," however, and his performance contributed to the overall feel of this imaginative and scary film.

3. *James Mason*: What can possibly said about this legend of film? His performances throughout the years have been, to the role, excellent, and nothing's different here. Every line is delivered in a manner that makes you hold your breath so as not to miss an inflection or a syllable. A brilliant performance by a greatly-missed master of acting.

4. *Fred Willard*: I wasn't sure that I'd be able to watch Willard in a straight role after seeing him as the ludicrous Jerry Hubbard on Martin Mull's hilarious, but short-lived, "Fernwood 2-Night." But, to Willard's credit, he does a commendable job as the sleazy Larry Crockett in "Salem's Lot."

Now, here are some of my least favorite moments:

I like this movie, and I'd have to nit-pick to find stuff I didn't like about it. So, I'm going to leave my "criticism" at that!

What the Critics Had To Say...

"More than anything, 'Salem's Lot' indicates the difficulty of translating Stephen King's works to television. The words are frequently there; the characters (or facsimiles of them) are present; the narrative line continues largely undisturbed. But Stephen King is missing. The interest he generates, the sense of realism that underlies his every narrative...have disappeared. In this case, it's easy to stipulate a cause: the sanitizing effect of commercial television. In spite of the care expended on it, in spite of the time allowed to present the story, in spite of the special effects, 'Salem's Lot' fails to rise above the crowd. It remains one of many vampire films, no less interesting than most, but no more exciting, either." —Michael R. Collings, from *The Films of Stephen King* (Starmont House, 1986).

"This story of vampires in modern-day New England is one of the better adaptations of Stephen King's novels on film. Some real chills go along with an intelligent script... ☆☆☆☆" —Mick Martin & Marsha Porter, *Video Movie Guide 1990* .

"☆☆☆." —The (Philadelphia) *Inquirer Movie Guide for VCRs.*

"Tobe Hooper...was an unlikely but inspired choice to direct "Salem's Lot." His elegant tracking shots and fondness for gruesome atmospherics stand out among the usual zoom-happy television horrors, and he gets fine performances out of a large cast." — Kim Newman, from a review in *The Penguin Encyclopedia of Horror and the Supernatural* (Viking Penguin, 1986).

"Over an hour has been cut from the original miniseries version of this picture to make a two-hour videocassette. The cuts have resulted in a couple of gaping plot-holes but they have also given this

A STOP AT THE MARSTEN HOUSE
An Interview With Tobe Hooper

In 1974, a low-budget film opened involving a cannibalistic madman who wore a mask of human skin.

This movie went pretty much unnoticed—except, that is, by horror fans who had been waiting since 1968 for something to watch besides "Night of the Living Dead."

The film was Tobe Hooper's "Texas Chainsaw Massacre," and it introduced America to Leatherface and his charming, flesh-eating family.

In *Fangoria*'s 1988 special edition "*Fangoria* Presents Best & Bloodiest Horror Video", the review of "Chainsaw" began: "Perhaps the best compliment that can be paid Tobe Hooper's horror debut—aside from the fact that it's the best cannibal picture ever made in this country, and indisputable proof that *suggestive* horror films can still work in this day and age —is that it never gets easier to watch." That's a keen appraisal of the power of this film: You know what's going on, and yet you really don't ever see "the main event," so to speak.

Now, almost two decades later, "Texas Chainsaw Massacre" is still a hot item in video rental stores. It has spawned a decent sequel (containing one of the grossest scenes on film —the scene where Stretch uses the skin of a human face as a disguise. You cringe when she puts it on, you can almost feel the warm, damp stickiness on your own face!). The film has elevated Leatherface into the pantheon of pop cult heroes, subspecies Nasty. Leatherface is as loved and cherished as Jason from "Friday The 13th" and Freddy Kreuger from "Nightmare On Elm Street." (Well, maybe not quite as loved as Freddy!) And, interestingly, both Jason and Freddy are supernatural villains. As far as we know, Leatherface (and his family for that matter) are nothing more than just plain old cannibalistic American psychotics. Is this a great country, or what? And speaking of Freddy, Tobe Hooper recently returned to television as director of the premiere episode of the TV version of the "Nightmare on Elm Street" films.

As Tobe details in the following interview, after "Chainsaw," he got the job of directing Stephen King's "'Salem's Lot." The film was originally broadcast as a four-hour miniseries, and then cut and released as a two-hour videotape. The four-hour original version is far superior to the videotape version, but the only way you're going to see it is in syndication. The week of July 10, 1988, WPIX, Channel 11 in New York City ran a "Stephen King Film Week," showing an S.K. film every night (except for Thursday, when a debatably more important baseball game took place). On Tuesday and Wednesday of that week, they showed the uncut "'Salem's Lot." Having had the two-hour version for a while, it was enlightening to see the original version, inasmuch as I didn't get to see it when it was first broadcast.

Even though "Chainsaw" has achieved cult status, Tobe is probably best known for his 1982 blockbuster "Poltergeist" – that rollercoaster ride of a movie about your basic all-American family who just so happen to live on top of a graveyard filled with rather restless souls. (Would you believe that the first time I called Tobe's house, I got his answering machine? The recording said "I'm not heeeeere!" You wouldn't believe it? I don't blame you, but I couldn't resist the joke.)

Jody Rein, a friend of mine and an editor at Dell, called me one day to ask about my help in getting an interview with Ron Howard for John Russo, author of the "Night of the Living Dead" screenplay and the accompanying filmbook. John was working on a new book about filmmaking for Dell, and he wanted to talk to Ron Howard. Unfortunately, Ron couldn't do the interview, but in my conversations with Jody, she revealed that John had interviewed Tobe Hooper for his book.

Intrepid (and shameless) journalist that I am, I immediately pounced upon Jody for a phone number. Jody was kind enough to help me out with the number of Tobe's publicist, Scott Holton. Scott was terrific in keeping me informed as to the vagaries of Tobe's schedule, and I eventually interviewed Mr. Hooper on a sunny Monday in March of 1988.

Tobe Hooper is a very nice guy.

He is modest and quiet, and for a man who makes, shall we say, somewhat "raw" films, the closest I've heard him get to using profanity is "Gosh." But, gentle manner notwithstanding, Tobe must have a particular affection for bloodsuckers: He returned to telling a story about vampires—all right, they were *space* vampires, and they were hungry for people's souls instead of their blood, but the idea was the same—in 1985's underrated "Lifeforce."

Here's a list of Tobe's film credits (Those marked with an asterisk are my personal favorites):

1974 – "The Texas Chainsaw Massacre"*
1976 – "Eaten Alive"
1979 – "'Salem's Lot"*
1981 – "The Funhouse"
1982 – "Poltergeist"*
1985 – "Lifeforce"*
1986 – "Invaders from Mars" (Remake)
    [NOTE: Ray Garton did the novelization for this film. See my interview with Ray in this volume.]
1986 – "The Texas Chainsaw Massacre 2"*

Here's my talk with Tobe "Chainsaw Massacre" Hooper. —sjs

A STOP AT THE MARSTEN HOUSE
An Interview With Tobe Hooper

STEVE SPIGNESI: Stephen King's novel *'Salem's Lot* was optioned in 1975 for theatrical release, and after scripts by Sterling Sillphant, Robert Getchell, and Lawrence Cohen were rejected, the project was turned over to Warner Brothers. How did you get the job of directing the film?

TOBE HOOPER: Right after I finished the first "Texas Chainsaw Massacre" film, I moved to Los Angeles. At that time, I was involved with Bill Friedkin. Bill had done "The Exorcist" in 1973 for Warner Brothers. Bill was now at Universal, and since "Salem's Lot" was at Warner Brothers, I now had a choice. I could either go with Warner's and work on "Salem's Lot," or go to Universal and start developing pictures with Bill—kind of under his wing.

"'Salem's Lot" was one of the first things that I was introduced to after "Chainsaw." I read the novel and absolutely loved it. But Warner Brothers simply didn't know what to do with it because it would obviously be such a big budget picture. In fact, they really didn't know that they would *ever* do anything with it.

Then Bill Friedkin left Universal, moved over to Warner's, and got involved with "'Salem's Lot." He was going to produce it, and he wanted me to direct it—as a feature film for theatrical release. And the process of trying to put that project together went on and on. There was even some talk at that time of casting Jon Voight as Ben Mears, but nothing happened. It sometimes take years to get things off the ground out here, and it was no different with "Salem's Lot." It was four years later from the time that I was introduced to the novel before things began to happen.

It finally went to television, and when it did, I was one of the directors under consideration for the project. I met with Richard Kobritz, the producer, and we got along very well. We both saw films in sort of the same way. We both loved Hitchcock and David Lean, and we spoke about Hitchcock's visual style, and how we could use that approach for "'Salem's Lot." We weren't talking about Hitchcock's approach to the interior of the material, but just basically the way his films moved and the way they looked.

At that time Paul Monash had done a 200- or 225-page script—a four-hour miniseries script. And, in spirit, his script was close to King's novel. "Salem's Lot" could have easily run ten hours, there was so much there. The fact that the book was such an epic made squeezing it into a ninety-minute package very difficult, and I suspect this was one of the reasons it didn't go as a theatrical.

I knew that other scripts existed, but I did not read these other scripts. I only read the Monash script, and knowing the novel very well, I tried to stay true to—as best I could—the spirit of Stephen's book. I tried to capture what I felt from the novel. I wish there'd been everything from the novel in the film, because the book is such a magical, fantastic thing.

But I think I was able to capture a lot of it. At least I got the town. I got "Salem's Lot"—a place which I thought of as a blend of Peyton Place and Nosferatu.

But since I only had four hours, there just wasn't time to find a way to correctly insert a lot of the extremely valuable back stories. Nor was there the budget. "Salem's Lot" was a $4 million production, and we built the Marsten House overlooking Ferndale—this little town in northern California—and it was very much like I'd envisioned it from the novel. And that's roughly how the film came about.

STEVE SPIGNESI: What were your thoughts when

you realized that you'd have to work within the constraints of television, especially with a novel as graphic and violent as "Salem's Lot"?

TOBE HOOPER: Well, this was my first television experience, and I was made extremely aware of the restrictions. At that time, Standards & Practices was a lot tougher than it is right now. So, it was a pretty incredible thing to have to deal with —to have to fashion what I actually needed to do, not just what I wanted to do.

For instance, in the novel, the Cullen Sawyer character—played by George Dzundza in the film —puts a shotgun in the mouth of the Larry Crockett character (who was played by Fred Willard). Crockett had been running around behind Sawyer's back, screwing Sawyer's wife Bonnie.

At first, Standards & Practices wasn't even going to allow me to point the gun at Fred Willard's head. Maybe at his chest, but not at his head. And there was a bargaining that went on that eventually allowed me to put the shotgun up to his head —but the gun, the end of the gun, could get no closer than twelve inches. So, I'd have to put a ruler up there when we slated the dailies to prove that it was twelve inches from his head. And it was difficult.

STEVE SPIGNESI: How would your directing have changed if you were working on a theatrical release?

TOBE HOOPER: I shot a second, more graphic version for the European theatrical release, which was like "Take 2," and the gun would go in Fred's mouth, like in the novel. But we only had another $100,000 or so to shoot the second version for foreign release, so there wasn't a lot of that. There wasn't that much time in a thirty-seven-day shoot to really get anything as spectacular as I would have liked.

But, nonetheless, the piece works. I was very happy with the piece because Stephen King's basic story is so strong and the characters are wonderful. I did have characters to deal with which, thank God, were wonderful. The film was mostly there – it was mostly a character piece.

But if I had had a choice, I would have gone for a feature.

STEVE SPIGNESI: What else couldn't you show on TV?

TOBE HOOPER: There was also a problem then in showing a corpse with his eyes open. It was forbidden on television. But I was able to kind of talk and finesse my way around that by explaining to Standards & Practices that vampires are not dead – they're the Undead. So, if they're the Undead, and they're in the "Undead mode"— which means that they have been transformed into a vampire —then they could have their eyes open, so long as it was understood that they were the Undead.

Like when Straker, who was played by James Mason, gets shot at the end of the film. I couldn't have James die with his eyes open, as he did in the novel, even though this was a part of the tone and atmosphere that I would have loved to have seen. Especially in wide screen Panavision!

I definitely would have taken that approach in a feature, because the material had that kind of spectacular quality to it. I would have loved to have shot it in wide screen Panavision, and of course, had a real budget. We could have then have afforded more updated special effects, although the special effects were good in "Salem's Lot."

STEVE SPIGNESI: How involved were you with the special effects?

TOBE HOOPER: I designed the flying rigs where Danny Glick floats through the window. Those things were very important to me, since I don't think there were more then six or seven big special effects numbers in the four hours.

But it was television, so I had to accept it, and be realistic and do my best—accepting that as a given. I had to try to get as much as I could from the work, and I'm very grateful for the characters that Paul Monash scripted and I felt that all of it was really in keeping with the novel.

But the novel would have been just wonderful as a four-hour horror epic in the theater on a, back then, say, at least a $9 or $10 million dollar budget. But it was destined to be a miniseries. I was fortunate to do it and I'm still pleased with it.

STEVE SPIGNESI: Speaking of the characters, you really worked with some terrific character actors. How involved were you with the casting?

TOBE HOOPER: Oh, I was involved totally with the casting. Richard Kobritz and I would meet with all the potential actors and narrow it down from there. We were in collaboration on the casting, and we didn't really have problems casting the picture.

We did need someone with a high TV rating, though, to do Ben Mears, so we went with David Soul, who was very popular at the time because of "Starsky & Hutch."

And I believe "Salem's Lot" was James Mason's first or second appearance as an television actor.

He had had a taste of television, and it got back to me that he would love to do "Salem's Lot." And he came over for it and played Richard Straker.

I really loved working with the cast, and since the film was light on special effects, and since I only had thirty-seven days, I spent most of my time working with the actors, which is something I surely love to do. Especially in this case, with these people. I'm happy with ninety-five percent of the cast, even to now. I loved Kenny McMillan as the Constable.

STEVE SPIGNESI: Chief Gillespie.

TOBE HOOPER: Yes, right. Chief Gillespie. And I loved working with Elisha Cook and Marie Windsor—bringing them back together after twenty-three years. They had done the Stanley Kubrick film "The Killing," back in 1956. And Kobritz and I deliberately brought those guys back together because the parts they played in "'Salem's Lot"—as Weasel Philips and Eva Miller—were so close to the parts they had played in the early Kubrick film. Richard and I love movies, and casting Elisha and Marie was an homage to, I guess to Kubrick, or to the arts—and to what should be.

And the rest of the cast were a fine lot, and I was very happy with it. It was a large cast, and I liked that. I really loved the Peyton Place aspect, too, how the town had an initial seed of darkness that was spreading through the psyche of the community without them really being aware of it.

STEVE SPIGNESI: Let's talk about Barlow. Your final film characterization of Barlow used Max Schreck's Graf Orlock as its model, and this interpretation is markedly different from King's more "textural" description in the novel. In the novel, King describes Barlow in the following manner on page 352 (paperback edition):

> "His face was strong and intelligent and handsome in a sharp forbidding way—yet, as the light shifted, it seemed almost effeminate."

And from page 353:

> "His hair, swept back from his brow in the European manner, seemed to float around his skull. He was wearing a dark suit and wine-colored tie, impeccably knotted, and to Callahan he seemed part and parcel of the darkness that surrounded him. His eyes glared out of their sockets like sly and sullen embers."

This has a very glamorous "Count Dracula" sort-of feel to it, and instead you went with the Nosferatu look. Reportedly, this was Richard Kobritz's decision. What are your thoughts on this different interpretation?

TOBE HOOPER: Well, I went with Kobritz's feeling on that. I was in synch with him on that decision, and right or wrong, whenever you're making a movie, the worst thing you can do is to be indecisive.

It was a big decision, and a big choice. And it would either work or not work, and much would depend on whether or not, of course, one had read the novel.

And in terms of the television audience as a whole, we had some statistics as to how far the novel had gone into that market.

Another factor that played a part in the decision was the fact that the film was light on horror, and Kobritz felt we truly needed a monster. I felt we needed something, too, and that was the genesis of it.

I didn't have Hubie Marsten hanging by his neck puffed up and dead, and I didn't have Ben Mears as a child going into the Marsten House. I didn't have some of those wonderful textures from Steve's book that give you all those things that really allowed Barlow to be that kind of Frank Langella-type character that he is in the novel.

And even now, I don't know whether it was right or wrong, but now it's done, and if I was doing it again, and I had a hundred percent free rein to deal with the situation, I frankly don't know what I would do.

I've heard that Stephen did not care for that approach, but I think he understood the why, but...it's done.

STEVE SPIGNESI: Speaking of Stephen King, do you stay in touch with him?

TOBE HOOPER: We haven't kept in touch in the last couple of years. We used to talk now and again, but it just hasn't happened recently.

"I read Stephen's adaptation to *Pet Sematary,* and think it's one of the most frightening, fantastic screenplays that I've ever read. It is totally Stephen King, and it's the way Stephen King's work should be transposed into screenplay form."

STEVE SPIGNESI: Have you got any thoughts on some of the other film adaptations of King's novels, specifically favorites and failures?

TOBE HOOPER: Yeah gosh, there is an adaptation —gosh, I don't even know if I should be saying this because it hasn't been filmed. [NOTE: The following exchange involving the film adaptations of Stephen King's work took place before the filming of "Pet Sematary" began in August 1988, with Mary Lambert directing.]

I read Stephen's adaptation to "Pet Sematary," and think it's one of the most frightening, fantastic screenplays that I've ever read. It is totally Stephen King, and it's the way Stephen King's work should be transposed into screenplay form.

It is extremely effective. It is for me, without a doubt, one of the top ten screenplays I've ever read, just on its workability. It's really a master-work—even in screenplay form, and with the re-straints of 110 pages or so.

It's alive with Stephen King's atmosphere and mood and the feelings that are so much a part of Stephen's work. You know you're there: He really places you in that special spooky place.

That's my favorite. Without a doubt, Stephen's "Pet Sematary" screenplay is my favorite.

STEVE SPIGNESI: Were you offered a shot at directing it?

TOBE HOOPER: It's complicated. I don't know who is going to direct it, or when it will be made, or *if* it will be made.

There's some complex business dealing in the background to it that is preventing it from cur-rently being produced....I don't know what will become of the piece. I don't know if it will ever be made. It may be one of those things that'll take years to untangle.

So, I'm not sure. I'm not sure that anybody really knows right now what's going on with it.

STEVE SPIGNESI: That's too bad. It sounds like an impressive piece.

TOBE HOOPER: God, I'd love to direct it. I'd do it in a minute. So far, to my knowledge, it's on a shelf.

STEVE SPIGNESI: Are there any particular film adaptations of King's work that you've seen that you consider to be downright failures?

TOBE HOOPER: That I've seen? Well, no, because I've seen some of the films, but then I haven't read the novel. So I can't really make that kind of judgement.

STEVE SPIGNESI: David Croneberg's "Dead Zone" is almost unanimously considered to be one of the better adaptations. Have you seen that?

TOBE HOOPER: Yes, I have.

STEVE SPIGNESI: Have you read *The Dead Zone*?

TOBE HOOPER: No, I haven't.

STEVE SPIGNESI: Okay. How about Stanley Kubrick's "The Shining"?

TOBE HOOPER: Well you know, that was a curious one. I was disappointed by the film and at the same time recognized that it was a really good film, a very well-made film.

Perhaps it should have been called something else, and not "The Shining," the film. I just expected more, that's all. But I liked the film. I just think there's a real separation there in what King's thing was, and the script. The film is cer-tainly inspired by the novel, and is from the novel, but it doesn't go as far as say, I would have gone, or would liked to have seen.

"I find that Stephen really has a direct tap into that thing that really chills us. And I think the way Stephen sits and works every day at it, and that he's really stayed in that, and kept exploring in that zone, and that level of conscious-ness – it just makes him better and better and better....Stephen really knows what he's doing. He's the best at that."

STEVE SPIGNESI: What are your favorite Stephen King novels?

TOBE HOOPER: *Pet Sematary* is one of my favor-ites. And of course 'Salem's Lot was a favorite. And, oh, gosh, I mean, whatever I have in the bookcase in there that I've read – I love all of them.

I find that Stephen really has a direct tap into that thing that really chills us. And I think the way Stephen sits and works every day at it, and that he's really stayed in that, and kept exploring in that zone, and that level of consciousness – it just makes him better and better and better.

His work in that area is sophisticating natu-rally. Stephen really knows what he's doing. He's the best at that.

STEVE SPIGNESI: Have you had a chance to see Steve's first film "Maximum Overdrive"?

TOBE HOOPER: I've seen "Maximum Overdrive" broken up—I've seen it piecemeal on cable. I'll always come in and catch a few minutes of it, but I just haven't had a chance yet to see it all the way through. What's funny is that the way I've seen it makes me think I've seen it, but I haven't seen it, because I've just seen pieces of it.

STEVE SPIGNESI: Any thoughts on his directorial debut?

TOBE HOOPER: Well, I think he did all right. From what I've seen, it was fine. I have nothing negative to say at all about it.

I would have thought, though, that Stephen would have gone for one of the spookier pieces— one of his more spooky inventions. But it's a matter of personal choice, actually. It's the only— I can't say problem, because it's not a problem (it's none of my business for one thing)—but I would have liked to have seen him do one of his stranger, spookier nightmares.

STEVE SPIGNESI: Such as?

TOBE HOOPER: Gosh, I don't want to say because he may do one of them and I won't get a chance to direct it! (Laughs.)

But "Maximum Overdrive" seems like a big picture, with a big cast, and from what I saw he had a special effects nightmare on his hands with all these mechanical things.

I was thinking in terms of something a little more ghostly or bump-in-the-night when I was referring to the spooky stuff, because "Maximum Overdrive" is big and it's broad and it's in the daylight, and it's massive and it's undeniably powerful. I like more isolation...the nighttime...spooky atmospherics...all the things at which Stephen is just the absolute best alive at.

And it was just simply curious to me that he selected this one to do, but then, of course, that's the way the business is. Who knows what happened? I sure don't.

STEVE SPIGNESI: Let's wind it up with one last, very broad, general question. Any final thoughts on King, his successes, his work, his films, or anything at all to do with him?

TOBE HOOPER: Stephen's the tops in my book. He's the focus of all of that. He's the superstar of what he's into, and I admire him a lot.

There's an interesting story about the way Stephen and I met. One of Stephen's best friends —a guy he grew up with—moved across the street from my mother's house in Texas. So, Stephen got my telephone number from across the street to call me. I was making "Salem's Lot," and Stephen had gone and gotten my phone number in L.A. from my mother.

But what was really interesting about that house is that *my* best friend—a guy that *I* grew up with—lived across the street in the same house. He was killed in a car accident, and his wife later remarried and his family moved away.

And then the family of Steve's friend moved into that same house. Steve's friend that he had grown up with on the east coast moved into the house across the street from my mother!

And I've always thought that that set of circumstances—that bit of business—had an almost "Stephen King-like" flavor to it, don't you think?

STEVE SPIGNESI: Yes. It almost sounds like a Stephen King short story.

TOBE HOOPER: I've always thought so. But anyway...God, it's hard to say anything new about Stephen because he's all over. Next month there'll be a new book out, and he's way ahead of most of us. He produces tons of material, and it's all good stuff. At least for me. I think he's great!

STEVE SPIGNESI: I agree. Well, Tobe, I think that caps off the interview nicely. I appreciate your taking the time to talk to me for *The Shape Under the Sheet.* I've always loved your stuff, and I want to express my sincere thanks to you—for every horror fan on the planet—for "The Texas Chainsaw Massacre." George Romero's "Night of the Living Dead" and your "Chainsaw Massacre" started a great twenty years of horrible delights!

TOBE HOOPER: Well, that's great. Thank you, Steve. ❑

Tobe Hooper TV-movie the sort of fast pacing that the original broadcast lacked. ... This videocassette version has little of the variety and depth of character found in King's book, but the pacing caused by the many cuts creates much headlong, unrelenting suspense and terror." —From a review in *Fangoria Presents Best & Bloodiest Horror Video* (O'Quinn Studios, 1988).

"The major emotion that went through my mind [as I watched "'Salem's Lot"] was relief, because TV is this magic medium which seems to turn almost everything it touches into shit, and I felt that "'Salem's Lot" mostly survived that. ... I didn't particularly approve of them turning Barlow into a Nosferatu, who says nothing at all and becomes sort of minor by comparison. That's a different concept than mine altogether, and I think it's one that's a little bit empty." —Stephen King, in an interview with Freff called "The Dark Beyond the Door: Walking (Nervously) into Stephen King's World" from *Tomb of Dracula*, Issues No. 4 and 5.

"Considering the medium, they did a real good job. TV is death to horror. When it went to TV a lot of people moaned and I was one of the moaners." —Stephen King, from an interview with Chris Palmer in the Bangor *Daily News,* November 17, 1979.

"THE SHINING"

"...a fluorescent nightmare..."

Released June 1980, by Warner Brothers/ Hawks Films.
Videotape released by Warner Home Video.
Running Time: 146 minutes in preview, 119 minutes in general release.
Rated R

Director: Stanley Kubrick
Screenplay by: Stanley Kubrick and Diane Johnson
Produced in Association with: The Producer Circle Company; Robert Fryer, Martin Richards, Mary Lea Johnson
Based on The Novel by: Stephen King
Producer: Stanley Kubrick
Executive Producer: Jan Harlan
Assistant Director: Brian Cook
Film Editor: Ray Lovejoy
Director of Photography: John Alcott
Music:　Wendy Carlos,
　　Bela Bartok,
　　Krysztof Penderecki,
　　Gyorgy Ligeti,
　　Rachel Elkin,
　　and Henry Hall
Specific Compositions:
　"The Shining" by Wendy Carlos and Rachel Elkind
　"Rocky Mountains" by Wendy Carlos and Rachel Elkind

"Lontano" by Gyorgy Ligeti
"Utrenja, The Awakening of Jacob" by Krysztof Penderecki
"De Natura Sonoris N. 2" by Krysztof Penderecki
"Music for Strings, Percussion and Celesta" by Bela Bartok
"Home" by Henry Hall

"Music for Strings, Percussion and Celesta"
Conducted By: Herbert Von Karajan
Music Recorded By:
　Deutsche Grammophon
　Wendy Carlos
　Rachel Elkind
　Gyorgy Ligeti
　Krysztof Penderecki
Costumes by: Milena Canonera
Production Designer: Roy Walker
Production Manager: Douglas Twiddy

Budget: $19 million

CAST

Jack Torrance	Jack Nicholson
Wendy Torrance	Shelly Duvall
Danny Torrance	Danny Lloyd
Hallorann	Scatman Crothers
Ullmann	Barry Nelson
Grady	Phillip Stone
Lloyd	Joe Turkel
Doctor	Anne Jackson
Durkin	Tony Burton
Young Woman in Bathtub	Lia Beldam
Old Woman in Bathtub	Billie Gibson
Watson	Barry Dennen
Forest Ranger #1	David Baxt
Forest Ranger #2	Manning Redwood
The Grady Girls	Lisa and Louise Burn
Nurse	Robin Pappas
Secretary	Alison Coleridge
Policeman	Burnell Tucker
Stewardess	Jana Sheldon
Overlook Receptionist	Kate Phelps
Axe Head (Injured Guest)	Norman Gay

"THE SHINING"

"I have my days when I think that I gave Kubrick a live grenade which he heroically threw his body on."
—*Stephen King.*

"The Shining" is a peculiar film, and a strange entry in the catalogue of Stephen King film adaptations.

Personally, I find it watchable, interesting, mostly enjoyable, and a worthwhile viewing experience, but there are a few factors that influence those feelings: First, I am a major Jack Nicholson fan. I think that he sometimes transcends his roles and actually becomes transmuted on some spiritual level in his characters. It's a process we can't perhaps understand, but can only recognize the results of. Secondly, I enjoy seeing Stephen King's works on film. Yes, I'm aware that some of them don't survive the translation from page to film, but generally this is not something that causes me to be completely turned off to a King film. And, lastly, I love movies. Even rotten movies. But, because I don't claim credentials as a critic (I leave that field to people who study film – it's their job after all) and I instead approach this material as a fan, I can't find it in me to blast the films (or even the lesser King works) simply because the general critical consensus is that certain films don't work.

Okay. That out of the way and on the record, let's look at "The Shining."

You'd think it would have worked, wouldn't you? The word was that the legendary Stanley Kubrick had chosen to direct King's novel *The Shining*. The word was that Jack Nicholson would star (in a role that Stephen King wanted Michael Moriarity to play). And the advance expectations were high.

Stephen King has told the story about Kubrick calling him one day from London during the production of "The Shining."

Kubrick called King one morning and asked him if he believed in an afterlife. After a few seconds of thought, King replied that he did. Kubrick then asked King if that didn't mean that all horror stories were ultimately optimistic. His reasoning was, where's the horror of death if we live on? And King replied, "But, Stanley, what about Hell?" There was a moment of silence and then Kubrick said, "I don't believe in Hell," and hung up.

Here are a few of my favorite moments from the film:

1. *The lighting*. Jessie Horsting told me that all the lighting in the film was artificial. This gives the film the "fluorescent nightmare" quality I referred to earlier, and adds, I think, to the eerie sense of "displacement" one gets while watching the film.

2. *Jack Nicholson's off-the-wall performance*: Many critics have faulted the film specifically *for* this performance. The point often made is that in the novel, Jack Torrance was a vessel through which the evil of the Overlook could work its malefic ways. Because of Jack's personal weaknesses and his refusal to accept his responsibilities (to his family, his work, and himself), he became vulnerable, a ready target for dominance by the evil spirit of the hotel. In the film version, that subtext almost doesn't exist. In fact, many people have (correctly) noticed that you know Jack's loopy from the first moment he appears on screen. The evil that lives in the hotel's black heart is ignored, and, instead, "The Shining" turns into just another slasher film. But nonetheless, Jack Nicholson is compellingly watchable, and if there is one single element that makes "The Shining" a worthwhile viewing experience (at least for me), it's ole Jackie boy havin' a high old time with the role. (I think Nicholson's Jack Torrance is probably second only to his portrayal of The Joker in "Batman" for sheer manic power.)

3. *The music*: Totally weird, almost totally electronic, and totally appropriate.

4. *Scatman Crothers*: Aren't you glad Dick Hallorann survived the fire at the Black Spot so we'd get to meet him at the Overlook? But, geez, Dick: How the hell could you pick up on Danny in Florida, but yet not know that Jack was hiding behind a pillar with an axe?

Now here are some of my least favorite moments:

1. *Danny Torrance's finger-puppet, Tony*: I thought this particular "device" was stupid, and didn't work at all.

2. *The script*: The connection made throughout the movie between Jack and the Overlook was too vague to suddenly zoom in on a picture of Jack in the hallway after he was dead, with the expectation that the audience would understand what had happened.

3. *The pacing*: Was this supposed to be a horror film or an existential meditation on man's search for meaning in Colorado? Half of the scares didn't scare me, and most of the time, I wasn't sure Kubrick even *wanted* to scare me. I got the sense throughout the film that Kubrick somehow felt that horror was beneath him, and that it was his responsibility to somehow "elevate" the novel into something vague and "deep." No thanks. I'll take my Stephen King, straight up, thank you very much.

What the Critics Had To Say...

"...perhaps the best approach to Kubrick's 'The Shining' is to divorce it from connections with Stephen King – not because Kubrick failed to do justice to King's narrative, but simply because it has ceased to *be* King's." —Michael R. Collings, from *The Films of Stephen King* (Starmont House, 1986)

"Uninteresting ghost story sparked by meticulous detail and sets but finally vitiated by overlength and over-the-top star performance."
—Leslie Halliwell, *Halliwell's Film Guide,* Fourth Edition.

"[Why would] a director of Kubrick's stature spend his time and effort on a novel that he changes so much it's barely recognizeable?"
—*Variety.*

"Stanley Kubrick keeps things at a snail's pace, and Nicholson's performance approaches high camp. ☆☆ 1/2."
—Mick Martin & Marsha Porter, *Video Movie Guide 1990* .

"I tried very hard to get Warner Bros. and Stanley not to cast Jack Nicholson. I think that Jack Nicholson is an excellent actor and I think he did everything Stanley asked him to in the movie and did a tremendous job, but he's a man who comes across as crazy. Look at those eyes and you see Randall Patrick McMurphy."
—Stephen King, in *Stephen King At the Movies* by Jessie Horsting.

"Style over content, form over function, intellect over belief; whatever the case, most will agree that Kubrick's film is the most beautiful and stylish of the King adaptations."
—Jeff Conner, from *Stephen King Goes to Hollywood.*

"CREEPSHOW"

"[My hope was that] the audience would be
screaming and laughing at the same time."
—Stephen King

Released October 1982, Laurel Show, Inc.,
from Warner Bros.
Videotape released by New World Video;
$69.95.
Running Time: 120 minutes.
Rated R

Director: George A. Romero
Producer: Richard Rubenstein
Screenplay by: Stephen King
Executive Producer: Salah M. Hassanein
Music: John Harrison
Director of Photography: Michael Gornick
Makeup Special Effects: Tom Savini
Production Design &
  Scenic Special Effects: Cletus Anderson
Costume Design: Barbara Anderson
Editors: Michael Spolan, Pasquale Buba,
  George A. Romero, Paul Hirsch
Comic Book Art: Jack Kamen

Budget: $8,000,000

CAST

"Prologue"

Billy	Joe King
Billy's Mother	Iva Jean Saraceni

1. "Father's Day"
(17 minutes)
Edited by Michael Spolan

Sylvia Grantham	Carrie Nye
Aunt Bedelia	Viveca Lindfors
Hank Blaine	Ed Harris
Richard Grantham	Warner Shook
Cass Blaine	Elizabeth Regan
Nathan Grantham	Jan Lormer
Nathan Grantham's Corpse	John Amplas
Mrs. Danvers	Nann Mogg
Yarbro	Peter Messer

2. "The Lonesome Death of Jordy Verrill"
(14 minutes)
Edited by Pasquale Buba

Jordy Verrill	Stephen King
Jordy's Father	Bingo O' Malley
The Professor	Bingo O' Malley
The Doctor	Bingo O' Malley

3. "Something To Tide You Over"
(25 minutes)
Edited by George A. Romero

Richard Vickers	Leslie Nielsen
Harry Wentworth	Ted Danson
Becky Vickers	Gaylen Ross

4. "The Crate"
(37 minutes)
Edited by Paul Hirsch

Harry Northrup	Hal Holbrook
Wilma Northrup	Adrienne Barbeau
Dexter Stanley	Fritz Weaver
Charlie Gereson	Robert Harper
Mike the Janitor	Don Keefer
Tabitha Raymond	Christine Forrest
Richard Raymond	Chuck Aber
Host	Cletus Anderson
Maid	Katie Karlovitz

5. "They're Creeping Up On You"
(14 minutes)
Edited by Michael Spolan

Upson Pratt	E.G. Marshall
White	David Early
The 25,000 Cockroaches	16,000 domestic Blaberus Blaberus and 9,000 Blaberus Giganticus imported from Trinidad

"Epilogue"

Billy	Joe King
Billy's Mother	Iva Jean Saraceni
Garbage Man #1	Marti Schiff
Garbage Man #2	Tom Savini

"CREEPSHOW"

"Creepshow" plays better than it sounds: The whole idea of trying to bring a comic book to life would have seemed to have been doomed from the start. Anyone who has spent any time watching horror movies knows how easy it is to cross the line from terror to parody, so the entire concept of attempting to bring an E.C. Comic to life would initially elicit a groan and shudder. As has been so often noted, horror and comedy can very rarely be combined successfully. The best attempts usually bring with it a black humor that is dark enough to work: "Re-Animator" and "Heathers" come immediately to mind.

But "Creepshow" must also be included in any mention of films that work in combining horror and humor, and the credit must go first to the creative elements behind the project, George A. Romero and Stephen King, and then to the superb cast who were able to portray King's sometimes broadly-drawn characters without smirking.

The film is wonderfully watchable: The wrap-around story (starring a Voodoo-wielding Joe King, Stephen's son) and comic book splash pages work effectively to move us from segment to segment.

I think the reason why "Creepshow" works, and works so well, is because everyone – from the behind-the-camera people to the cast – took the project seriously, and the result is a film that succeeds at, yes, bringing a comic book to life.

Here are a few of my favorite moments from the film:

1. *The performances*: The cast is really terrific in "Creepshow," and kudos must go to the casting people for being able to assemble such filmic luminaries as E.G. Marshall, Hal Holbrook, Viveca Lindfors, and Carrie Nye for the movie. And for a horror flick, yet! Some of my favorite characters include Viveca Lindfors' wild Aunt Bedelia, E.G. Marshall's flawless Howard Hughes-ish Upson Pratt, and Leslie Nielsen's straightfaced Richard Vickers. Honorable mention must also go to Adrienne Barbeau for her Queen Bitch "Billy" Northrup, and John Amplas for his sensitive portrayal of Nathan Grantham's corpse.

2. *Stephen King's "Jordy Verrill" segment*: I'd have to say that the "Verrill" segment is my favorite "Creepshow" story (with "They're Creeping Up On You" a close second). For me, everything works in this sequence. "Verrill" was based on a short story by King called "Weeds," which was supposed to be the opening sequence of a novel. After King finished the story, he realized that he'd said everything he wanted to say in the story, and so left it alone. The "Creepshow" version of this story is scary, funny, and – as the weeds end up devouring our world – ultimately very disturbing. King's performance is completely believeable, if a bit broad. But it works, and I think it's one of the better segments in the film.

3. *The lunch scene in the "The Crate"*: The scene in which Mike the janitor gets eaten by the thing in the crate is perfect. The blood flows down Mike's shirt as he's pulled up into the crate, and you know that his head is gone and that the monster is now beginning to consume the rest of ole' Mike. A close second to this scene would be the stomach-bursting scene in "They're Creeping Up On You." After all, how often do you get to see thousands of cockroaches eating their way up out of a guy's body? A great moment in film history, don't you think?

Now here are some of my least favorite moments:

1. *"Father's Day"*: Even though there are a couple of performances in this segment that partially redeem it, I didn't like it. It seemed overdrawn, overwritten, and badly acted (except for Lindfors).

2. *The comic art effects in some of the live action scenes*: Sometimes I found the switch to garish lighting and color during peak moments distracting. I understand the intent, but I wonder what the film would have been like if they had limited the comic book "feel" to the segues between the segments?

3. *Billy's father*: He was a real asshole, don't you think? The kind of thinking that led this guy to throw out his son's comic book is the same kind of mentality that leads to banning books in libraries.

What the Critics Had To Say...

"[A]...funny and scary...anthology of ghoulish bedtime stories. ☆☆☆☆." —Mick Martin & Marsha Porter, *Video Movie Guide 1990*.

"If there is a movie that best represents Stephen King's roots and macabre sense of humor, the nod has to go to 'Creepshow'..." —*Stephen King At the Movies* by Jessie Horsting.

"'Creepshow' plays like an anthology of human phobias. Romero and King have approached this movie with humor and affection, as well as with an appreciation of the macabre." —Roger Ebert, from *Roger Ebert's Movie Home Companion*.

"Supposedly funny but mainly rather nasty recreation of a famous 'comic' style; far too extended for its own good." —Leslie Halliwell, *Halliwell's Film Guide*, Fourth Edition.

"Robert Bloch and Freddie Francis did it all so much better in 'Torture Garden'." —Tom Milne, *MFB*.

"As a movie 'Creepshow' is negligible, but as a cultural indicator, it's terrific – a big clue to what even the most skillful and likable schlock-horror purveyors have been up to in all those years since 1957's 'I Was a Teenage Werewolf'." —Michael Sragow, from a review called "'Creepshow': The Aesthetics of the Gross-Out" in *Rolling Stone*, November 25, 1982.

"As a film it is ultimately uneven. Some episodes work on entirely different levels from others; treatments vary from the broadly (almost painfully) comic to the supremely disgusting to the superlatively horrifying. Yet to say so is not to condemn the film, since that range of possibilities suggests precisely what King and Romero set out to create. 'Creepshow' was intended as fun – but in a special E.C. sense of the word. To that extent, it succeeds." —Michael R. Collings, from *The Films of Stephen King* (Starmont House, 1986)

"Better-than-adequate entertainment for an undemanding mood, [but] one tends to expect much better work from almost everyone involved." —*Fangoria Presents Best & Bloodiest Horror Video*.

"'Creepshow' is perhaps one of the most unabashed grabs for cash ever to hit your local theater, but there's such innocent greed about it all that it's hard to take offense. I mean, these folks are *desperate* to get rich! It is pure and simple entertainment of a wild and raucous nature with no aspirations outside of trying to give the audience the wild and wooliest roller coaster ride it can arrange." —Gahan Wilson, from a review in *Twilight Zone* magazine, April 1983.

1 "Must See" rating;
2 "Excellent" ratings;
3 "Good" ratings;
1 "Worthless" rating.
—"Film Ratings," *Cinefantastique*, June-July 1983.

"CUJO"

"Once upon a time...a monster came to the small town of Castle Rock, Maine."

Released June 1983, by Warner Brothers, Taft Entertainment.
Videotape released by Warner Home Video; $69.95; CED, $29.95
Running Time: 93 minutes.
Rated R

Directed By: Lewis Teague
Produced By: Daniel H. Blatt, Robert Singer
Screenplay By: Don Carlos Dunaway, Lauren Currier (Barbara Turner)
Based On The Novel By: Stephen King
Associate Producer: Neil A. Machlis
Director of Photography: Jan De Bont
Production Designer: Guy Comtois
Music By: Charles Bernstein
Animal Action By: Karl Lewis Miller
Special Visual Effects Makeup By: Peter Knowlton
Animal Handlers: Glen Garner, Jackie Martin

Budget: $5 million

CAST

Donna Trenton	Dee Wallace
Tad Trenton	Danny Pintauro
Vic Trenton	Daniel Hugh-Kelly
Steve Kemp	Christopher Stone
Joe Camber	Ed Lauter
Charity Camber	Kaiulani Lee
Brett Camber	Billy Jacoby
Gary Pervier	Mills Watson
Sheriff Bannerman	Sandy Ward
Masen	Jerry Hardin
The Sharp Cereal Professor	Merritt Olsen
Roger Breakstone	Arthur Rosenberg
Harry	Harry Donovan-Smith
Meara	Robert Elross
Fournier	Robert Behling
Lady Reporter	Claire Nono
Dr. Merkatz	Daniel H. Blatt

"CUJO"

"Cujo" was the first of a triple-decker "Stephen King Movie" year. (The other two King-based films released in 1983 were "The Dead Zone" and "Christine"). The film version of the novel virtually eliminates the "Frank Dodd's ghost" element from the story, and instead concentrates on the fears of a family in decay.

Lewis Teague did a superb job in working with what is essentially a "woman trapped in a car" story. He was able to generate tension, fear, and an insinuative sense of "unease" throughout the film. I am uncomfortable when I watch this film. The obvious – and painfully cold – distance that is evident in Donna and Vic's deteriorating relationship is difficult to watch. You almost start to wish for a vampire or two to bring us back to the horror genre.

But what makes the film sometimes disconcerting also contributes to its strengths. Stephen King has called this a great big "Sonny Liston" of a movie that just keeps slugging away at the viewer until the climactic (and newly upbeat) ending. With "Cujo," King explored the real fears of daily life, suggesting that we sometimes can create our own reality, and that the "what if" fears that we dwell on can eventually work to destroy us. We can bring on our own doom, King seems to be saying, and Teague visually illustrates this theme by showing Cujo becoming sicker and sicker as the Trentons' situation gets closer and closer to completely falling apart. This paralleling of the two stories – Cujo representing the manifestation of the Trentons' horrible domestic situation – is resolved when Donna triumphs over the insane and murderous dog and saves her son's (and symbolically her family's) life.

This film was shot in California, and did well at the box office. [NOTE: For added insight into Lewis Teague's interpretation of this film, see my interview with Teague in this volume.]

Here are a few of my favorite moments from the film:

1. *Dee Wallace*: I never once did not believe that Dee was the ultimate "thirtysomething" mother. King has remarked that Wallace should have been nominated for an Academy Award for her performance, and to tell the truth, I can't think of too many actresses who could have been as convincing in this role. I particularly love her reading of one particular line: Right after she and Tad are first trapped in Camber's yard, Donna waits a while for the engine to cool down, and then, on her first try, the car starts. Tad cheers and Donna looks out her window at a now-livid Cujo, and says very calmly, "Fuck you, dog." The car immediately stalling after this just adds to the frustration and mounting suspense on the part of the viewer. Great job, Dee.

2. *The Gary Pervier Character and Mills Watson's Performance as Gary*: Admit it: You just gotta love a guy whose entire philosophy of life can be summed up as "I don't give a shit." Also worth mentioning is the over-the-edge depiction of Gary's house: His living quarters are in such bad shape that you can't help but admire his consistency in giving in to total sloth and apathy.

3. *The Cujo Attack Scenes*: The scenes in which Cujo attacks the car are shot with such a claustrophobic intensity that you almost feel like the dog's going to leap right off the screen at you. Kudos must go to wrangler Karl Miller (and the five St. Bernards who played Cujo in varying states of collapse) for eliciting such fine canine performances.

4. *The Music*: As it often does, the soundtrack to this film contributes enormously to the overall mood and tone of the movie.

5. *The Camera Work*: One particular favorite is the revolving camera scene immediately after the first time Donna is physically attacked by Cujo. The camera spins and spins and spins around and around in the Pinto from Donna to Tad until it culminates with Vic suddenly waking up in his hotel room, knowing something is wrong. Very effective.

DOG (AND CAT) DAYS
An Interview With Lewis Teague

So far, Lewis Teague is one of only two directors to have directed two Stephen King films. (The other is Rob Reiner, who directed the film versions of "The Body" ("Stand By Me"), and "Misery." By the way, "Stand By Me" is one of Lewis Teague's favorite King film adaptations.)

Teague first came to Stephen King's attention with his feature "Alligator." In an interview with Charles Grant, King referred to Teague as one "the most unsung directors in America." King also said that Teague "has absolutely no shame and no moral sense. He just wants to go get ya and I relate to that!"

Teague came to "Cujo" after Peter Medak left the project following one day's shooting. Because he came in late, he was hampered by being handed a cast, script, and production he essentially had nothing to do with.

Nonetheless, he pulled it off.

"Cujo" is a terrific film, and a film that even Stephen King has raved about.

Because of Teague's successful handling of "Cujo," he later was given the director's job on another King film, "Cat's Eye." Due to extensive deletions from the final film, the movie bombed, but is nevertheless watchable.

Lewis Teague is usually on the receiving end of favorable reviews. Since 1979, he has directed the following films:

"Lady in Red" – 1979
"Alligator" – 1980
"Fighting Back" – 1982
"Cujo" – 1983
"Cat's Eye" – 1985
"The Jewel of the Nile" – 1985

Here's my talk with Lewis Teague. — **sjs**

DOG (AND CAT) DAYS
An Interview With Lewis Teague

STEVE SPIGNESI: Let's start off with what is probably one of the most discussed aspects of your film version of King's novel *Cujo*: its ending. King is a naturalistic writer. Naturalism is that school of literature that espouses the idea that fate rules man, but that moral choices can be made. King often shows that when responsibilities are not fulfilled, ruin can result. It's been noted that King seemed to be illustrating this theme by having Tad die in the book—the boy paid with his life for Donna's adulterous behavior. The film, however, opted for the more "up" ending of Tad surviving. Why did you go for that ending and do you think it betrayed King's intentions in the novel?

LEWIS TEAGUE: First of all, I don't know if that was Stephen King's intent. I never read that into the book, that Donna had to pay for her adulterous behavior with her son's life.

I see an entirely different theme at work in the book. I felt that *Cujo,* the novel, had to do with fear and our reaction to fear. And I felt that the film was likewise about fear. I see them both as showing that most of our fears are imaginary, and that when we give credence to imaginary fears, they can then become self-fulfilling prophecies. Most of the fears that the family were suffering from in the story were imaginary. The husband was afraid of financial ruin because he'd lost one of his clients. The woman was afraid of growing old and wasting her life away in this rural town after they moved out there from New York. And all these fears were filtering down to the son, who began imagining that he could see monsters in the closet.

I think the film shows what happens when people start believing in imaginary fears. And because these fears all had to do with the future—and no one can predict the future—none of those fears were real. But the family believed the fears and began to act on them as if they were real.

For example, Donna Trenton, being afraid of growing old and wasting away her life, seeks out this affair with a young tennis bum to try to cling desperately to her youth, to desperately seek out some kind of excitement that she feels is lacking in this rural environment. She actually begins to precipitate her own destruction. And the same thing happens with the husband when he allows his fears of financial ruin (which have not come true), and his fear of abandonment (when he discovers that his wife is having the affair), to take over, forcing him to flee to the city and abandon his wife to the fate that befalls her and Tad on the farm, where they're menaced by the rabid Cujo.

And it's not until they face a real fear at the end—the fear of the rabid dog that's attacking the car—and face up to that, that they can put the rest of their fears in perspective, and restore the integrity of the family.

That's basically what I found interesting in the material. That was the way I read the material, and that was the theme that I saw there. And if you view the material that way, then Tad's death is gratuitous.

STEVE SPIGNESI: Did you choose to eliminate the supernatural Frank Dodd/Cujo connection simply because it wouldn't have worked in a film of 120 minutes?

LEWIS TEAGUE: Well, that connection was a literary conceit to begin with. In order to really understand who Frank Dodd was, you had to have read *The Dead Zone.*

Secondly, I felt that within the time span that we had to tell the story, it would have been difficult to create that supernatural thread. Now, when I look back on the material, dropping the supernatural element may have been a mistake.

I came on to the film rather late. I was originally asked to direct the script and since I was not available, they hired another director, Peter Medak, who then either left the picture—or was taken off the picture—within a couple of days after they started shooting.

At that point, I then came back. So, I only had the time to do a limited amount of rewriting in order to tell the story that I wanted to tell. And, now, when I look back on dropping the Dodd business, I think that that may have been a mistake.

By losing the mysterious element of the supernatural, and trying to root the story entirely in reality, I may have made the story just a little pedestrian and lost the thread between the fears that are permeating the family and what eventually happens in the barnyard.

STEVE SPIGNESI: So, your input into the final script was pretty limited then?

LEWIS TEAGUE: To a degree. My input was limited by the amount of time that we had available.

STEVE SPIGNESI: How about the casting? Did you have any say as to who played who?

LEWIS TEAGUE: Well, once again, because I came in late, most of the casting had already been done. Dee Wallace, Daniel Hugh-Kelly, and Danny Pintauro had already been cast for the picture.

STEVE SPIGNESI: How about Stephen King? How much input did he have into the casting and script?

LEWIS TEAGUE: Steve was hardly involved in the production at all. He initially did have some input though—he originally recommended me to direct the picture on the basis of my film "Alligator." But he was really not too involved in the writing of the screenplay.

STEVE SPIGNESI: The lighting in "Cujo" was brilliant, especially the scenes in Tad's room, and the scenes in the barnyard. I thought it added enormously to the overall mood and impact of the film. How much did you have to do with the lighting?

LEWIS TEAGUE: Most of that was the work of the cinematographer, Jan De Bonts. We did discuss the lighting in certain areas, especially towards the end, during the action in the barnyard where the time of day and the passage of time were important elements of the story. We discussed using the lighting to reflect the time of day, and also to create the sense of heat that they were supposed to be enduring. In actuality, we were shooting that scene in freezing weather. It was about 40 degrees out and raining most of the time, so most of the sun and the sunlight had to be created with artificial light.

At times it was horrible for poor little Danny. He was five years old at that time but even then, he was a real trooper. With the temperatures in the forties, we would have to spray him down with water so it would look like he was sweating, and he would actually be freezing.

STEVE SPIGNESI: Let's talk about "Cat's Eye." I know that there was an opening funeral sequence that was cut, and it's generally acknowledged that it would have made the film a bit easier to understand right off the bat—it would have made it more accessible. I've heard that Frank Yablans cut it.

LEWIS TEAGUE: That's correct.

STEVE SPIGNESI: My question is, why didn't you fight him and insist on keeping it?

LEWIS TEAGUE: Actually, I did, but he had more power than I did. He had a little bit more clout since he was running MGM at the time. And he was adamant. He had a real hair up his ass about that scene.

STEVE SPIGNESI: Because of the death of the child?

LEWIS TEAGUE: That was part of it. The scene was very black humor, which I thought was appropriate for the material. He thought it was just too macabre.

STEVE SPIGNESI: Let's talk about your personal favorite King works. Do you have favorite King novels and short stories?

LEWIS TEAGUE: No, I don't, to be real honest with you. I haven't read all of Stephen King's work, so I don't have any real favorites.

STEVE SPIGNESI: Of the stuff that you've read, is there a dream project that you'd like to tackle?

LEWIS TEAGUE: I loved his fairy tale *The Eyes of the Dragon*. That'd be a wonderful movie to make.

STEVE SPIGNESI: How about the other Stephen King film adaptations? Any thoughts on successes and failures?

LEWIS TEAGUE: "Carrie" was great. I loved that. And the one about the body—"Stand By Me." "Stand By Me" was terrific. Those are the only two that I really like.

STEVE SPIGNESI: "Dead Zone" is generally considered to be a decent adaptation. What'd you think of that?

LEWIS TEAGUE: It was a nice film.

STEVE SPIGNESI: How much are you in contact, if at all, with King?

LEWIS TEAGUE: I haven't heard from him recently. We exchanged a few letters, but I haven't talked to him in quite a while.

STEVE SPIGNESI: Have you got any final thoughts on what's come to be known as the "Stephen King Phenomena"—this "industry" that Stephen King

"...I think his success is due largely to the fact that he's a terrific writer and a great storyteller....here's a guy who has a lot of integrity, and he's very unpretentious. And because he's doing exactly what he always wanted to do is why he can do it so well."

has become?

LEWIS TEAGUE: I'm amazed by it, I'm impressed by it, and I think his success is due largely to the fact that he's a terrific writer and a great storyteller. I I really admire the guy. Once, we were in New York together when we were working on "Cat's Eye" and we were talking about either the Great American Novel or art films versus genre films. And I remember that as part of that conversation he said something about how he's doing what he's always wanted to do—in fact, he's doing *exactly* what he always wanted to do. He said he didn't want to go out and write "The Great American Novel," he just wanted to write exciting suspense and horror stories. And I was very impressed with that, because here's a guy who has a lot of integrity, and he's very unpretentious. And because he's doing exactly what he always wanted to do is why he can do it so well. ❏

Now here are some of my least favorite moments:

1. *The Total Elimination of Any Supernatural Element* : I'm sure a script could have been written that acknowledged the possibility that Dodd's ghost was inhabiting the rabid Cujo. You almost get the feeling that they were flirting with the "monster in the closet" subtext from the opening scenes in Tad's room that utilized a shifting perspective and a very spooky depiction of the closet itself. But instead they went with the rabid dog (and his representational and symbolic impact) as the primary catalyst. Remember: In Stephen King's novel, the Trentons moved into Frank Dodd's house. For the film, this element was rejected as "unworkable." Other than this minor complaint, though, I feel that overall "Cujo" is a successful adaptation of a Stephen King novel.

What the Critics Had To Say...

"Sickening adaptation of the Stephen King best seller about a cuddly family pet that turns into a rabid, savage killer. ☆." —The (Philadelphia) *Inquirer Movie Guide for VCRs.*

"Stephen King's story of a mother and son terrorized by a rabid Saint Bernard results in a movie that keeps viewers on the edge of their seats. ☆☆☆ 1/2." —Mick Martin & Marsha Porter, *Video Movie Guide 1990.*

"As a film, 'Cujo' seems intermediate. It avoids the excesses of "Salem's Lot' and the idiosyncratic approach of Kubrick's 'The Shining.' It modifies King's narrative to fit the restraints of...film, but avoids as much as possible altering the characters and situations without reason. The dialogue remains true to the novel, as do characters and settings. At the same time, it has lost the sharpness of King's prose, the indefinable element that his references to Castle Rock and Frank Dodd brought the novel. It has, in fact, become an exploration of true horror, the horror we may confront at any time. There are no vampires or haunted hotels or psychokinetic adolescents in 'Cujo'; there is only a big, friendly dog that contracts rabies, or a wife who makes a mistake and risks losing her husband, or a little boy terrified of shadows who nearly dies.

But he doesn't – and that may be the final strength of 'Cujo.'
In Teague's vision, the family survives." —Michael R. Collings, from *The Films of Stephen King* (Starmont House, 1986)

"[Cujo] keeps the spirit and the flavor of the work; it's this big dumb slugger of a movie. It stands there and keeps on punching. It has no finesse; it has no pretensions. I thought Dee Wallace should have been nominated for an Academy Award." —Stephen King, from *Stephen King at the Movies,* by Jessie Horsting (Starlog Press, 1986)

"WHAT WORKED: The cruel simplicity of the plot, a kind of landlocked 'Jaws.' Dee Wallace as the plucky, heroic mother (though her powers of survival seem little short of miraculous). The dog, who at all times is both scary and pitiable.
WHAT DIDN'T: The attempt (à la 'Dunwich Horror') to make California's seacoast for Maine. The predictable last-minute resurrection of the supposedly dead St. Bernard. The film's evasive p.r. campaign, whose poster, trailer, and press stills never so much as hint that 'Cujo' is about a dog." — *Twilight Zone*, February 1984.

1 "Must See" rating;
2 "Excellent" ratings;
1 "Good" rating;
1 "Mediocre" rating.
1 "Worthless" rating.
—"Film Ratings," *Cinefantastique,* May 1984.

"Questions of morals and ethics aside, it is the visceral punch of a film like 'Cujo' that ultimately makes or breaks it, and 'Cujo' does deliver a sufficient number of scares and shocks. But it doesn't illuminate the lives of its characters in doing so, and may in fact only be successful in reinforcing a fear of dogs in the minds of certain audience members." —From a review by Kyle Counts in *Cinefantastique,* December/January 1983/1984.

"THE DEAD ZONE"

"...an American tragedy..."

Released October 1983, by Paramount Pictures.
Videotape released by Paramount Home Video.
Running Time: 103 minutes.
Rated R

Director: David Cronenberg
Producer: Debra Hill
Screenplay By: Jeffrey Boam
Based on the Novel By: Stephen King
Director of Photography: Mark Irwin, C.S.C.
Production Designer: Carol Spier
Music Composed and
    Arranged By: Michael Kamen
Costume Designer: Olga Dimitrov R.C.A.
Associate Producer: Jeffrey Chernov
Film Editor: Ronald Sanders

Budget: $10 million

CAST

Johnny Smith	Christopher Walken
Sarah Bracknell	Brooke Adams
Sheriff Bannerman	Tom Skerritt
Dr. Sam Weizak	Herbert Lom
Roger Stuart	Anthony Zerbe
Henrietta Dodd	Colleen Dewhurst
Greg Stillson	Martin Sheen
Frank Dodd	Nicholas Campbell
Herb Smith	Sean Sullivan
Vera Smith	Jackie Burroughs
Sonny Elliman	Geza Kovacs
Alma Frechette	Roberta Weiss
Chris Stuart	Simon Craig
Dardis	Peter Dvorsky
Amy	Julie-Ann Heathwood
Walt	Barry Flatman
Denny #1	Raffi Tchalikian
Vice President	Ken Pogue

Five Star General	Gordon Jocelyn
Secretary of State	Bill Copeland
Therapist	Jack Messinger
Nurse	Chapelle Jaffe
Natalie	Cindy Hines
Weisak's Mother	Helene Udy
Teenage Boy With Camera	Ramon Estevez
Young Weizak	Joseph Domenenchini
Reporters	Roger Dunn
	Wally Bondarenko
	Claude Rae
TV Anchorman	John Koensgen
Brenner	Les Carlson
Deputy #1	Jim Bearden
Deputy #2	Hardee Lineham
Ambulance Driver	William Davis
Denny #2	Sierge LeBlanc
Polish Peasants	Vera Winiauski
	Joe Kapnaiko
Truck Driver	Dave Rigby

"THE DEAD ZONE"

David Cronenberg's "The Dead Zone" is unanimously considered to be one of the two best adaptations of a Stephen King work. (Rob Reiner's "Stand By Me" is the other.)

The film is a masterpiece of mood, tone, and atmosphere, and while all the performances are superb, it must be acknowledged that Christopher Walken's portrayal of Johnny Smith achieves an excellence that is almost transcendent. Walken *becomes* Johnny Smith: he literally wears on his face the torture Johnny must live through after awakening from his "trance" (as his fanatically religious mother called it).

The story is, as has been noted, an American tragedy. But the film version of this story achieves a level of emotional depth that is enhanced and amplified by the visual nature of the translation. You shiver from the cold of a New England winter, you sense Johnny's agony as he swallows a painkiller, you can feel the ambivalence Johnny must work through as he realizes that his new psychic abilities can do good, and so must be used to do that good.

"The Dead Zone" is my favorite of King's films. I feel it comes closest to achieving what at times seems to be an impossible task: taking Stephen King's words and turning them into visual images. It was a struggle for me to decide between "Stand By Me" and "The Dead Zone," but in the end I opted for "The Dead Zone" because it is more in the tradition of classic Stephen King.

It is a film that bears repeated watchings, too, and much of that is due to the bleak, snowy, winter mood achieved throughout the film. While watching "The Dead Zone," I am often reminded of the opening lines to Simon & Garfunkel's "I Am a Rock": "A winter's day, in a deep and dark December. I am alone." (And, later on, Johnny voices this sentiment when talking to Weiszak: "Nothing can touch me here. I'm alone.") Johnny's involuntary isolation becomes even more poignant.

"The Dead Zone" *works* and (with "Stand By Me") proves, once and for all, that Stephen King's work *can* be successfully adapted for the screen. All you need is the perfect combination of screenwriter, director, and cast. No problem, right?

Here are a few of my favorite moments from the film:

1. *The "Winter in New England" feel to the film* : The bleak, snow-covered landscapes of mid-winter in New England are perfectly captured in "The Dead Zone." (The film was shot in Canada, which looks very much like New England, especially in the winter months.)

2. *Putting Johnny into his visions* : First, he's in a burning bed in a little girl's bedroom, then he's on the gazebo watching Alma Frechette murdered by Dodd. These scenes were eerie, surrealistic, and very frightening: they seemed to allow a shift of consciousness on the part of the viewer that made the film even more believeable. "The Dead Zone" never once makes you doubt the validity of what happens to Johnny Smith, or that the paranormal exists.

3. *Colleen Dewhurst's death scene* : She made me believe she was shot in the stomach.

Now here are some of my least favorite moments:

There isn't anything I don't like about the film version of "The Dead Zone."

What the Critics Had To Say...

"Almost every character in the film brings to his or her role an authenticity that subsumes personal identity to the character portrayed. As a result, 'The Dead Zone' convinces on multiple levels, an achievement attained by few adaptations of King's work."
—Michael R. Collings, from *The Films of Stephen King* (Starmont House, 1986).

"...an exciting adaptation of the Stephen King suspense novel... ☆☆☆☆." —Mick Martin & Marsha Porter, *Video Movie Guide 1990.*

"'The Dead Zone' does what only a good supernatural thriller can do: it makes us forget it is supernatural. Like 'Rosemary's Baby' and 'The Exorcist,' it tells its story so strongly through the lives of sympathetic, believable people that we not only forgive the gimmicks, we accept them. No other King novel has been better filmed (certainly not the dreadful 'Cujo'), and Cronenberg, who knows how to handle terror, also knows how to create three-dimensional, fascinating characters." —Roger Ebert, from *Roger Ebert's Movie Home Companion.*

"[A] wan and moody adaptation of Stephen King's chiller..." —The (Philadelphia) *Inquirer Movie Guide for VCRs.*

"In almost every way and on many levels, 'The Dead Zone' is a glowing success. Tapping into new resources, Cronenberg proves he's an insightful director of *people,* and not simply a visceral manipulator of intriguing ideas." —David J. Hogan, from a review in *Cinefantastique,* December-January 1983-1984.

2 "Must See" ratings;
1 "Excellent" rating;
4 "Good" ratings.
—"Film Ratings," *Cinefantastique,* May 1984.

Ellie	Keri Montgomery
The Librarian	Jan Burrell
Pepper Boyd	Richard Collier

"CHRISTINE"

"...bad to the bone..."

Released December 1983, by Columbia Pictures.
Videotape released by RCA/Columbia Home Video; $79.95.
Running Time: 110 minutes.
Rated R

Director: John Carpenter
Producer: Richard Kobritz
Screenplay By: Bill Phillips
Based Upon the Novel By: Stephen King
Director of Photography: Donald M. Morgan, A.S.C.
Production Designer: Daniel Lomino
Edited by: Marion Rothman
Executive Producers: Kirby McCauley & Mark Tarlov
Music By: John Carpenter
In Association With: Alan Howarth
Casting By: Karen Rea
Special Effects Supervisor: Roy Arbogast

Budget: $10 million ($500,000 for special effects)

CAST

Arnie Cunningham	Keith Gordon
Dennis Guilder	John Stockwell
Leigh Cabot	Alexandra Paul
Will Darnell	Robert Prosky
Rudolph Junkins	Harry Dean Stanton
Regina Cunningham	Christine Belford
Michael Cunningham	Robert Darnell
Buddy Repperton	William Ostrander
George LeBay	Roberts Blossom
Mr. Casey	David Spielberg
Moochie Morgan	Malcolm Danare
Rich	Steven Tash
Vandenberg	Stuart Charno
Roseanne	Kelly Preston
Chuck	Marc Poppel
Bemis	Douglas Warhit
Mr. Smith	Bruce French

"CHRISTINE"

I like "Christine." I think it is a decent adaptation of a King novel – even though it has its problems in plot and character development. Much as Kubrick did in "The Shining" with the Overlook Hotel, John Carpenter makes Christine supernaturally and intrinsically evil. As Michael Collings so astutely notes in his book, *The Films of Stephen King,* the film ignores the possibility that Roland LeBay may have imbued the car with his own personal evil. In the film, Christine is "bad to the bone" even before she comes off the assembly line. This tends to distance the viewer, creating, essentially, a haunted house on wheels that Arnie Cunningham had the misfortune to "bump into" one day, becoming swallowed up in its malefic aura. Much of this truncation of the novel's subtext is due to the rushed nature of the film's production. It was released within a year of the novel's release, and much had to be eliminated from the story.

Nonetheless, the movie is an enjoyable experience. The car takes on a life and personality of its own and, somehow, Carpenter makes it all seem plausible. The special effects are terrific, and even after several viewings I find myself still caught up in the story each time I watch it again.

Much of the problem with filming King is the fact that Stephen King has already created the "movie of the book" in the Skull Cinema: his writing is so overwhelmingly cinematic that we literally "see" the book as we read. When attempts are made to tranfer his stories to film, the end result is often an abbreviated "mutation": It's the same thing that happens when food manufacturers try to produce a perfect four course frozen meal: the final product is certainly edible, but it sure as hell ain't the same as fresh.

Here are a few of my favorite moments from the film:

1. *Carpenter's direction* : I've always liked John Carpenter's work. I think "Halloween" and "The Thing" are classics. "Christine" is similarly appealing, in that it bears all of his trademarks: brilliant use of dark and light, terrific special effects, and Carpenter's own eerie electronic music. I would have loved to have seen what Carpenter could have done with "Firestarter."

2. *Keith Gordon's performance* : He *becomes* Arnie Cunningham, and never once do I not believe in his characterization. A superb portrayal.

3. *The "Healing Car" scenes* : Great special effects that used up twenty-three 1958 Plymouth Furies to create the seventeen used in the film. (Two survived in mint condition.) Again, Carpenter makes it believeable.

4. *The "Choking Dad" scene* : After Repperton and company destroy Christine, Arnie descends into complete and final obsession with the car. In a conversation with his parents, he tells his mother, "Fuck you," after his father tells them they've decided to help him buy a new car. Michael Cunningham follows Arnie to the stairs and demands that he go back and apologize to his mother. In a chilling moment, Michael grabs Arnie, and Arnie says "You take your mitts off me, motherfucker." Michael then throws Arnie against the staircase and, in a moment of unbelievable strength (obviously "Christine-ly" inspired) Arnie grabs his father by the throat and almost picks him up off the ground with one hand. Michael immediately surrenders to Arnie's superior strength and makes it clear that he suddenly realizes this monster is not his son anymore. This

scene emphasizes the total control Christine now has over Arnie, and is very effective. Arnie's little laugh, followed by "I'm hittin' the sack" ices the cake. Carpenter's music in this scene is poignant and complements the developments nicely.

Now here are some of my least favorite moments:

1. *Alexandra Paul's performance* : It's too wooden at times. She's a stunning girl, but sometimes she acts like a talking Barbie doll in this film.

2. *The stereotypical villains* : Repperton, Moochie, and the rest of the gang are a bunch of idiots. They're so stupid and consistently nasty that you never really take them seriously. These guys are portrayed almost as caricatures of "The high school bad guy." There's no depth to their characters, and we're glad when they're killed off, not so much because they've gotten their just rewards (which is the response the comeuppance of a richly-developed evil character would elicit), but because we're sick of spending (movie) time with them. Arnie underscores this ambivalence during a scene in the hospital room when, talking about Moochie's death, he says to Dennis "*Almost* makes you feel kinda sorry for the little bastard, huh?" (Emphasis mine.)

What the Critics Had To Say...

"The entire movie depends on our willingness to believe that a car can have a mind of its own. The car is another inspiration from Stephen King, the horror novelist who specializes in thrillers about everyday objects. [A]ny day now I expect him to announce 'Amityville IV: The Garage Door-Opener'." —Roger Ebert, from *Roger Ebert's Movie Home Companion* .

"[T]op-flight tasteful terror...about a 1958 Plymouth Fury with spooky powers. It's scary without being gory; a triumph of suspense and atmosphere. ☆☆☆ 1/2." —Mick Martin & Marsha Porter, *Video Movie Guide 1990.*

"As a film 'Christine' works. It is not fully successful; neither is it a complete failure. It tried to accomplish too much. It succeeded on some levels, faltered on others. Visually, it excites and stimulates; in terms of narrative, it assumes too much from the novel, while failing to establish its own rationale for characters and motives. It certainly ranks in the upper-middle ranges of King's films – interesting, at times exciting, pleasant entertainment that neither demands too much from the viewer nor distorts King's narrative beyond description." —Michael R. Collings, from *The Films of Stephen King* (Starmont House, 1986)

"Unfortunately what sinks 'Christine' is the very problem that shot down 'The Thing' and 'Escape from New York': Carpenter's obliviousness to the need for empathetic characters. On a technical level, though, 'Christine' is splendid. A highly skilled *visual* storyteller, Carpenter creates arresting images: A series of tremendous explosions at a dark service station is particularly exciting and well-staged. 'Christine' is fun, I suppose, but it's also an empty, gimmick-filled movie." —David J. Hogan, from a review in *Cinefantastique* , May 1984.

"THE WOMAN IN THE ROOM"

Granite Entertainment, 1983, 1986.
Running Time: 32 minutes

Directed By: Frank Darabont
Screenplay By: Frank Darabont
Based On The Story By: Stephen King
Produced By: Gregory Melton
Associate Producer: Mark Vance
Executive Producer: Douglas Venturelli
Art Director: Gregory Melton
Editors: Frank Darabont and Kevin Rock
Cinematographer: Juan Ruiz Anchia
Production Manager: Michael Sloane

CAST

John Elliott	Michael Cornelison
Mother (Donna Elliott)	Dee Croxton
Prisoner	Brian Libby
Guard #1	Bob Brunson
Guard #2	George Russell

"THE WOMAN IN THE ROOM"

"There are no coincidences."
——Carl Gustav Jung [paraphrased]

"The Woman in the Room" is one of two films comprising *Stephen King's Night Shift Collection* (The other is "The Boogeyman.")

A couple of days before I was to begin working on this feature, a friend of mine gave me some literature on the Hemlock Society, an organization that works to gain social, legal, and medical acceptance for what they term "self-deliverance": autoeuthanasia. Suicide. Their position is that when people are terminally ill, suffering intractable pain and destined for more of the same, that they should be able to peacefully, painlessly, and nonviolently end their life. When *they* decide it's time to die. Sounds humane, doesn't it? Well, the problem is that if anyone even lifts a finger to help the patient with their goal, they are committing an act of murder, regardless of the fact that the action was requested by the patient.

I read through the literature, and it got me thinking about assisted suicide, the subject of King's story, and Darabont's film.

Frank Darabont's film version of "The Woman in the Room" is probably, as King himself put it, "...Clearly the best of the short films made from my stuff."

It is a powerful and horrific look at being terminally ill and trapped in a hospital bed, and it does an excellent job of showing us the quandry family members are in when they know there's no hope, but they can't stand to just sit and watch a loved one "suffer to death."

The most important change in Darabont's screenplay from

King's original story is the addition of a new character, identified simply as "The Prisoner."

John Elliott is a lawyer representing a murderer up for the death sentence. During a lawyer/client discussion, the talk comes around to John's ailing mother. The Prisoner reveals that he once killed a friend of his who was suffering from gangrene after having his legs blown off in Viet Nam. As he says to John, "Hell, he saved my life once. I owed him." John is, of course, considering feeding his mother an overdose of Darvon Complex capsules to put her out of *her* misery. The Prisoner's inescapable logic convinces John to help his mother commit suicide, which is how the film – and the short story – ends.

"The Woman in the Room" is a masterful adaptation of Stephen King's work. It has a somber, dirgelike quality to it, and I say that with the best sense of the words "somber" and "dirgelike" in mind. King's "The Woman in the Room" *is* a somber story, and Darabont gives it the tone and pacing it deserves.

The film also contains a very frightening dream sequence not in King's story, during which John sees the corpse of his mother chasing him in a wheelchair down the hospital corridor.

"The Woman in the Room" is a heartwrenching short story that was successfully translated into a heartwrenching short film. It's reported that Stephen King had to endure his own mother's painful, protracted death from cancer, and the story "The Woman in the Room" was his response to that experience. It is a mark of King's genius that he successfully communicated to us the agony of the situation – both his mother's and his own.

If you haven't seen this film, I suggest you find a copy. It should be available for rental in most video stores. It's well worth your time and effort, and I highly recommend it.

"CHILDREN OF THE CORN"

"Outlander! We have your woman!"

Released June 1984, by New World Pictures.
Videotape released by New World Pictures,
$69.95; Laser, $34.95; CED, $19.95.
Running Time: 93 minutes.
Rated R

Director: Fritz Kiersch
Executive Producers: Earl Glick and
  Charles J. Weber
Producers: Donald P. Borchers and
  Terence Kirby
Screenplay By: George Goldsmith
Based On A Story By: Stephen King
Music: Jonathan Elias
Director of Photography: Raoul Lomas
Associate Producer: Mark Lipson
Editor: Harry Keramidas
Art Director: Craig Stearns
Special Visual Effects: Max. W. Anderson
Wardrobe: Barbara Scott
Makeup: Erica Ueland
First Assistant Director: Susan Gelb
Stunt Coordinator: Bruce Paul Barbour
Stunts: Kerry Cullen

Special Effects: SPFX, Inc.

Budget: $3 million

CAST

Dr. Burt Stanton	Peter Horton
Vicky Baxter	Linda Hamilton
Diehl	R.G. Armstrong
Isaac	John Franklin
Malachai	Courtney Gains
Job	Robby Kiger
Sarah	Annemarie McEvoy
Rachel	Julie Maddalena
Joseph	Jonas Marlowe
Amos	John Philbin
Boy	Dan Snook
Dad	David Cowan
Mom	Suzy Southam
Mr. Hansen	D.G. Johnson
Hansen Customer	Patrick Boylan
Hansen Customer	Elmer Soderstrom
Hansen Customer	Teresa Toigo
Radio Preacher	Mitch Carter

AND...

The following young people from Sioux City, Iowa, who portray the Children of the Corn:

Malachai's Gang:

Mike Altman	Michele Ryan
Ron Altman	Mike Ryan
Peggy Cole	Robin Southam
Mark Cord	Knox Thompson
Jennifer Jackson	Dan Witt
Angie Neimeier	Tim Roberts
Dennis Poppenga	

Rachel's Gang:

Kim Adams	Tim Mook
Deborah Bernstein	Melissa Neimeier
Bill Eckman	Doug Port
Jill Fisher	Jeff Rabbitt
Kathleen Hamm	Russell Roach
Stacey Herbst	Ann Schaffausen
Jodie Kleinberg	Robby Sievers
Duffy Lehmberg	Richard Stabe

"CHILDREN OF THE CORN"

"Children of the Corn" is dangerous. Why? Because, as Michael Collings points out in his essay on the film in his book *The Films of Stephen King,* there are people who will think that this film represents what Stephen King is all about; that Stephen King is responsible for this vapid mutilation because it is, after all, based on one of his short stories.

Well, for all you out there who think that if you've seen the movie, then you don't have to read the book (or the story)...you're wrong.

"Children of the Corn" is *not* the Stephen King story of the same name.

More accomplished film critics than I'll ever be have gone into great detail as to why the film's a failure, and so I will not rehash their views here but, instead, refer you to their works, particularly the aforementioned essay by Michael Collings, as well as Harlan Ellison's essay "In Which We Discover Why The Children Don't Look Like Their Parents," included in *Harlan Ellison's Watching* and elsewhere.

That aside, let me tell you how I *feel* about the film.

My thoughts on "Children of the Corn" can be summed up in one word: Boring. It drags, the dialogue reeks, the story is ridiculous (bearing very little resemblance to King's minor masterpiece of a short story), and the few times I've seen it, I've been restless as hell waiting for it to end.

It's not bad as background, but I'd suggest you take a pass on it if you want something entertaining and scary.

"Children of the Corn," while ostensibly setting out to be both, ends up being neither.

Here are a few of my favorite moments from the film:

1. *Linda Hamilton's "Birthday Serenade" to Peter Horton* : This is a neat scene, if only because Linda Hamilton puts her all into it, and doesn't camp it up. Her peformance in this scene (and, to be fair, throughout the film) makes us believe she's a real person, not just an actor in a role in the way most of the kid actors in this film make you feel.

2. *The music*: It's not bad, and is appropriately eerie when it needs to be. It would have been great in another film.

3. *The special effects*: They're not bad either. I can't rave about them, but they're at least professionally pulled off.

Now here are some of my least favorite moments:

There were a lot. See my comments above, or just watch the movie and make up your own list of "groaners."

What the Critics Had To Say...

"[A] turkey. [A] total mess." —Mick Martin & Marsha Porter, *Video Movie Guide 1990.*

"Utterly humorless, as ineptly directed as a film school freshman's class project, acted with all the panache of a grope in the backseat of a VW..." —Harlan Ellison, "In Which We Discover Why The Children Don't Look Like Their Parents," from *Harlan Ellison's Watching.*

"Cheapo adaptation of a Stephen King short story... ☆"—(The Philadelphia) *Inquirer Movie Guide for VCRs 1988.*

"...[G]enerally considered to be the worst film adaptation of King's work." —George Beahm, *The Stephen King Companion.*

"[T]he picture was a dog: it was a shuck-and-jive situation." —Stephen King.

"...[A] clumsy string of cliched horror film situations..." —Jeff Conner, *Stephen King Goes to Hollywood.*

"Even at the level of horror itself, 'Children of the Corn' proves remarkably inconsistent. The early attempts at inculcating fear rely entirely on startling images, often telegraphed so early that by the time the image actually appears, the viewers have already stifled any reactions and find the image itself tedious." —Michael R. Collings, *The Films of Stephen King* (Starmont House, 1986).

5 "Mediocre" ratings;
2 "Worthless" ratings;
—"Film Ratings" *Cinefantastique,* September 1984.

"...[T]he lack of planning, the lack of imagination, and the hurry-up pressure certainly contributed to the silly half-assed 93 minutes that ended up on-screen." —Jessie Horsting, *Stephen King at the Movies.*

"And for those of us who like a little logic with their hokum, there are those nagging, unanswered questions: why does little Kiger seem so unaffected by the slaughter he witnessed at the diner? Just how has pipsqueak Franklin managed to brainwash so many kids? (Did he spike their Kool-Aid?)

"What *is* the monster behind the rows – a giant gopher, an energy form, or what? And where does it come from? Whatever happened to the dead body in Horton and Hamilton's car? And, finally, how is it possible to prop up a dead body in the middle of the road so that it is *standing*?

"I suggest that all such queries be directed to Stephen King. He must have the answers; after all, that *is* his name above the title." —Kyle Counts, *Cinefantastique,* September 1984.

"FIRESTARTER"

"Wood chips. They should have given me something harder."
—Charlie McGee

Released October 1984, by Universal Pictures.
Videotape released by MCA Home Video, $79.95.
Running Time: 115 minutes.
Rated R

Director: Mark L. Lester
Produced By: Frank Capra, Jr.
Screenplay By: Stanley Mann
Associate Producer: Martha Schumacher
Editor: David Rawlins
Co-Editor: Ron Sanders
Based On The Novel By: Stephen King
Music Composed and
   Performed By: Tangerine Dream
Director of Photography: Guiseppe Ruzzolini
Art Director: Giorgio Postiglione
Stunt Coordinator: Glenn Randall
Special Effects: Mike Wood and Jeff Jarvis
Makeup Effects: Jose Sanchez
Optical Effects: Van der Veer Photo Effects

Budget: $15 million

CAST

Andrew McGee	David Keith
Charlie McGee	Drew Barrymore
Dr. Joseph Wanless	Freddie Jones
Vicky McGee	Heather Locklear
Captain Hollister	Martin Sheen
John Rainbird	George C. Scott
Irv Manders	Art Carney
Norma Manders	Louise Fletcher
Dr. Pynchot	Moses Gunn
Taxi Driver	Antonio Vargas
Drew Snyder	Orville Jamieson
Bates	Curtis Credel
Mayo	Keith Colbert
Knowles	Richard Warlock
Steinowitz	Jeff Ramsey
Young Serviceman	Jack Manger
Young Serviceman's Girl	Lisa Ann Barnes
Security Guard	Larry Sprinkle
Woman In Stall	Cassandra Ward-Freeman
Bearded Student	Scott R. Davis
Grad Assistant	Nina Jones
Proprietor	William Alspaugh
Old Man	Laurens Moore
Old Lady	Anne Fitzgibbon
Mailman	Steve Boles
Motel Owner	Stanley Mann
Blinded Agent #1	Robert Miano
Blinded Agent #2	Leon Rippy
Joan Dugan	Carole Francisco
Josie	Wendie Womble
DSI Technician #1	Etan Boritzer
DSI Technician #2	Joan Foley
Albright	John Sanderford
DSI Orderly #1	Orwin Hardy
DSI Orderly #2	George Wilbur
Agent Hunt	Carey Fox

"FIRESTARTER"

"Firestarter" is not one of my personal favorites among Stephen King film adaptations. I think it begins with excellent intentions but, as is often the case with King adaptations, the end result reminds one (as Richard Christian Matheson put it) of what a novel would look like if you tried to squeeze it through a funnel. That observation is something of a paradox with "Firestarter," though, since Stanley Mann's screenplay stays remarkably close to King's novel. But, even with this seemingly faithful adherence to the book, something is missing in the film version. Watching it gives me a somewhat restless feeling, as though I'm sitting through a made-for-TV movie at times. Why? I'm not sure. I think part of it is the fact that sometimes, for me, King's dialogue doesn't work when spoken.

On the page, it seems fine, but then when spoken aloud, there are times when it sounds borderline corny. I've noticed this in other King film adaptations, and I guess what it means is that King is a novelist and short story writer and that the expanse of these written forms brings with them a certain intellectual shift that makes King's use of language work.

How about the acting? Well, it's a mixed bag. Drew Barrymore's performance is not very good. She seems to be consciously "acting" throughout the entire film. David Keith gives it a world-class try, he really does. He makes the absolute best out of his material, and deserves praise for taking it seriously. George C. Scott is good, as usual, even with a role lacking in much real definition. Martin Sheen likewise does a superb job. He brings a little bit of Greg Stillson to his role as Captain Hollister, and he is a joy to watch.

Overall, the film is watchable, but not something I'd choose from my video library when I'm in the mood for a King Thing. I'll give it a C–.

Here are a few of my favorite moments from the film:

1. *The "You're Blind" Scene*: When Andy McGee comes home to find his daughter gone and his wife dead, he tracks down the Shop agents who took Charlie from his friend Joan's house and, after rescuing her, he tells both agents "You're blind." And they go blind. Very effective, quite scary, and an excellent illustration of what Andy could do when he really got pissed off.

2. *Dr. Wanless's "China Plate" Speech*: I really like this speech. Freddie Jones plays it somberly, and with just enough anger at Sheen's out-of-hand rejection of the idea of Charlie being able to destroy the world, that Wanless becomes a sympathetic – and obviously doomed – character. You really believe his rage at Sheen's suggestion that they use Charlie as a weapon, and your feelings about this man – who has been painted as a "mad scientist" (thanks to the college "experiment" scenes where he seems maniacal and somewhat mad) – change from animosity to sympathy in one scene.

3. *Art Carney*: No matter what role he plays, there always seems to be a little bit of Ed Norton in it. And we're all the better for it.

4. *Tangerine Dream's Score*: I've liked their soundtracks ever since "Risky Business," and they don't disappoint here.

Now here are some of my least favorite moments:

1. *Drew Barrymore's Performance*: As already noted, it's not very good and. at times, it's downright unwatchable.

2. *Louise Fletcher*: She was totally wasted in this film, and that's a shame. The lines written for her character were terrible, and she had nowhere to go with them. A pity.

3. *The "Made-For-TV" Feel*: The film doesn't have enough texture or scope for my taste. It's bland, flat and, at times, boring. It's like moviemaking "by the numbers," and there isn't enough grit to it.

What the Critics Had To Say...

"'Firestarter' is one of the worst of the Stephen King film adaptations. ...[T]he endless FX and stunts are used monotonously and pointlessly." —*Fangoria Presents Best & Bloodiest Horror Video*, 1988, O'Quinn Sudios.

"Stephen King writhes again. ...'Firestarter' is suspenseful, poignant, and sometimes frightening entertainment that goes beyond its genre. ☆☆☆1/2." —Mick Martin & Marsha Porter, *Video Movie Guide 1990.*

"'Firestarter' contains a little girl who can start fires with her mind; her father, whose own ESP causes him to have brain hemorrhages; an Indian child molester who is a CIA killer; a black scientist; a kindly farmer; a government bureaucrat; and a brilliant scientist whose experiments kill 75 percent of his subjects but leave

"DEATH SCENES"
Going to the Movies With Steve King

With this personal essay, "Death Scenes" (published here for the first time), Chris Chesley, Stephen King's childhood friend and *People, Places, and Things* co-author, attempts to make some sense (both for us and for himself) out of his early years with Stephen King.

Chris explained his intentions and hopes for "Death Scenes" in a cover letter that accompanied this piece: "I want to accomplish at least one thing with this essay, and that is to spare the reader my own conclusions about the time I am recounting. Instead of cutting these images to fit a personal frame, I am trying to take the reader into them, so to speak; to give as vivid a sense of their actual presence as possible, and so to place the reader, with a few picked words, at the beginning itself. If I have succeeded, these images will offer their own conclusion. If I have failed, the reader is still there: at the end of the essay, he can bring his or her own interpretation to bear."

"Death Scenes" moves from "reel" life to "real" life and back again as Chris takes us through the years when he and "Steve" King hung out, went to movies, wrote together, and tried to find some answers. I think you'll find some of the real-life incidents Chris recounts quite interesting when taken in the context of Stephen King's writings. And I think you'll recognize a moment or two that ended up transmuted into a scene from King's work.

Chris Chesley has spent a great deal of time and has expended a great deal of emotional effort and energy trying to help me (and my *Shape Under the Sheet* readers) truly "see" the development of a writer. I think he has succeeded in showing us just how the tiny individual moments that make up a single life can be transformed into the universal moments of fiction when "funnelled" through the mind and creative sensibility of such a person as Stephen King.

I think you'll agree that the following essay, "Death Scenes", takes us one step closer to truly understanding just how the creative process works. —**sjs**

"DEATH SCENES"
by Christopher Chesley

(1)

Saturday matinee at the Ritz: a children's asylum, as much delirium in the seats as on the screen. The little kids milled aimlessly down in front or drifted up and down the middle and side aisles. There was a six-year-old getting up from the steps. The kid had been tripped by a hood with a DA who was sitting on the aisle. The kid called the hood a bastard and ran down front. The hood's friends loved it. How could he let his little sister talk to him like that? The hood and his friends all had wavy, high, combed-back hair, and the screen-light gave it a good sheen, like the shine on the perms of that group of girls who craned their necks, looking for any excuse to turn around and be seen by the boys up back, any reason to get somebody to take them home. A girl up in back gave a shriek, and you could hear the girls down by us answer with laughter, but you could also feel them sigh. A white arc of popcorn blasted down from the balcony snipers, and a shotgun spray of candy pounded the seats just down the row. Audience manners were screen manners. Talking in the movie, talking in the seats; noise in the movie, noise in the seats, a peaking raucous matinee voice. And in the very middle of it, about twelfth row and center, he sat, his own raptness setting him apart, untouched by the wild Saturday around him, and he was one with the image. Stephen King was watching a show. Now he slowly leaned forward in his seat, and he seemed to give the crowd a subconscious cue. Suddenly, a sinister pall calmed them. They somberly awaited the worst to happen to Ray Milland. With his X ray eyes, he saw too much. This crowd of kids put on its best behavior: dead quiet in the seats, death scene on the screen.

(2)

Lurid pastorale: a normal day but cold, the empty sky letting some wind blow through frigid high clouds. Steve and I had just started down the hill from my house, on our way to his house so he could get his money. We were going to hitch in to the Ritz. We were walking along the dirt road when a car stopped. The man said he would give us a ride. It was a neighbor, a man we knew. We got in the back seat and shut the doors. The car was warm. Then this man turned and looked at us. The light from the snowbank on the side of the road shone in the car window, giving his face a strange cast. His eyes looked like stones smashed by a mad cutter. He said: Come on in boys, nothing in back but dead bodies. We did not laugh. We knew immediately not to. But it turned out to be a normal ride. He dropped us where we wanted. After we got out, Steve and I looked at each other. I asked Steve what he thought. He said he thought something was going on. We found out a few days later that they had had to come and take that guy away.

(3)

Steve and I looked at each other in the dim light of the Ritz. He was ghastly, motioning with his arm at the rest of the crowd, pointing out how subdued they were as they shared Vincent Price's dilemma. The anxiety danced up and down the rows, the desire to *look* grinding against the desire to look away. And slowly the heart of the audience sank. Vincent Price was giving in, and all the children in the seats knew that they, too, would give in. Vincent Price was surrendering to his obsession. He was in the crypt. He must see the face of the dead, or he would never believe it. And all of us children, too, needed to see to believe. Was the Usher woman really dead? The risk of seeing too much had to be taken. The children readied themselves silently as Vincent Price put his hand on the coffin lid. Even oppressed by this much crypt-shadow, we had to know.

(4)

It had a name, but we all usually called it the river, because it was a wide place *in* a river, fed by cold springs down in its muddy bottom, down where the big snapping turtles and the greasy eels swam. We swam there sometimes, but only from a boat or a homemade raft out in the middle. The shallow water close in was warm, and that was where the bloodsuckers drifted. Every summer there was always some kid who didn't know, and his friends would tell him to just wade in, go on, the water is nice and warm, and soon he would come out, and his friends would watch his face turn the same color as the lily pads the bullfrogs sunned themselves on as he stabbed and picked at the gray-black things clinging to him, finding out how sinuous they were, how hard to remove. But the river was a quiet spot, a good place to go on a summer evening and put a boat in the water and fish a little and drink a little in the twilight.

One night a friend of mine came by and asked Steve and I if we wanted to go see a dead body.

He had heard about somebody who had gone down to the river one summer evening—a guy who had never learned to swim.

When we got to the river it was already dark. We sat on some rocks set back from the scene, but close enough to see down to the low place where people usually put their boats in the water. The gathering had chased the whippoorwills away, and the lights placed to advantage were bright. No one was in a hurry. They looked like men searching for some reason to stand around, as if something in the back of their minds slowed them down. The photographer seemed to be taking too many pictures. The men did official things, but beyond that there was an air of lingering in order to find out a secret. They made small, restrained gestures at the shape, moved toward it, moved away. The body was inhuman; its sense of extreme difference and distance was subduing and forbidding. We looked and looked at its sunken mystery, but in some strange way it was in vain. Then they covered up the body and we went home.

(5)

The stillness in the theatre spread like a dark net. It smothered the little kids at the front, stopped the snickering of their mouths and candy wrappers, and behind us the couples drew apart and kept their hands to themselves. They had seen the body; seen the rigor of its hideous, glaring face. Now the woman who had prepared the body for burial was back in her own rooms, having brought with her a ring she had coveted and so had screwed off one of the body's dead fingers. The woman went to bed but she could not sleep: the dripping of the kitchen tap was too loud, then the bath faucet, and then there was the buzzing of a fly. These irritating effects on the unimaginative, headstrong woman brought the audience up short. They waited for the claim of death to come due. The woman had had no respect. She had ignored the occult reputation of the person she had dressed for the grave. The question of the right of haunted inheritance must be settled.

(6)

At midnight, I climbed out the window of my room into the light of a sinking moon that showed the way down the ladder where Steve was waiting. The cemetery a hundred yards away from my house was the property of the dead alone. We were sneaking out, to pry into the way death disposes of itself. We went over the low stone wall, and walked around the graves, their epitaphs—their last true wills—legible in the white-lit summer air. One large monument mothered a brood of small ones, on it the dates of all those in the plot, tersely showing how dying used to make sweeping claims: the parents had lived to bury all of their seven children. We moved from grave to grave, reading. Here, a grave for an infant, a hand carved in relief on the slab, forefinger pointing up toward immortality; there, a marker for a girl of only twelve years, like us, some weeping, morbid lines of verse on it to mourn her, our dearest too soon angel in heaven. Old-fashioned death liked children. The cemetery had as many young in the rows as old. It was an archive of eighteenth century acceptance. At last we sat down on some broken stones, feeling the resigned departure of the place. The children in here seemed almost to have been let go, helplessly given up, now resting in foundling sadness. The people of the last century must have thought of their graveyard as the doorstep to the rich house of God, leaving their young for the first to open the door at dawn, the epitaphs telling the last parental desire: please take care of our child. Burial was to win heaven over, to gain orphans good will. We looked at more monuments for children who were now near Jesus in some way, as angels around his head, or in his arms, or resting at his feet, and how they died so young surprised us simply because we were so well, and as we left the cemetery, it seemed that the moon would shine forever.

(7)

The matinee children around us were shrinking and cringing. They had seen too much of Hill House and its perverted, demonic atmosphere. They did not want to, but they had to look—at the woman gracefully climbing the circular stairs, her eyes severe and bleak, her rope carried in a neat coil—at the gouged hole in the dark wall sending out the sound of a child stricken with hysteria—at the bedroom door bulging inward under the weight of an overwhelming ferocity. While the children were in this house, they were very quiet, as misunderstood and as lonely as Eleanor, a child with the special gift for approaching the terror of death. By now we all knew who was guilty: the cold place was just outside the nursery door, and in the nursery the insane father infused his children with spiritual madness. Our suspicion grew deeper, more horrifying. Parents stalked us. No home was safe, if you could not look away.

(8)

There was a house down the road from Steve's. It sat on the side of a hill, exhaling emptiness. Even outside the decrepit shadows of its walls, its smell of time hung in the air. We got in through a broken window. Steve showed me around the rooms. Some of them had picked-over junk in the corners, but most were empty, except for dust-motes and cobwebs and age. The house's past was almost a low sound whispering in the corners, a barely-heard mutter hiding away in the farthest room—the last room upstairs at the end of the hall. The house felt uneasy: not quite unoccupied. Open doors did not lie flat against walls; windowsills creaked; the eaves talked in the afternoon wind. Over and over, echoes suggested the question: Is anybody here? The light was deterred, the sound of our steps on the stairs enhanced, and the whole house crouched over us, shadowy and barren, decaying to its death. Steve said: Would you dare to spend the night in here by yourself? I said: Well Jesus, I guess not.

(9)

The boys are sleeping out:

Hey Steve. Tell us a horror story.

Yeah. That one about the guy with the axe, and the woman strips and gets in the pond and he gets her coming out and the axe comes down and splits her.

No. I want to hear the vampire one, Dracula and his vampire women, and the guy comes to visit and the vampire women come into his room—

I heard that one. How about the one where they dig up these bodies, and they aren't really dead.

We know all that stuff. Tell something new.

You wrote anything good lately, Steve?

Yeah, tell us something new.

Make it up. You can do that.

Tell us one of yours, Steve.

the others with powers beyond the imagination of mortal man. The most astonishing thing in the movie, however, is how boring it is." —*Roger Ebert's Home Movie Companion,* 1985.

"Middling adaptation of Stephen King's best seller..." —(The Philadelphia) *InquirerMovie Guide for VCRs.*

"In a last analysis, 'Firestarter' is flawed by being too obviously a 'careful' movie. The script follows King's text carefully. The stunts are staged carefully (not that carelessness or blatant disregard for safety would have made a better film, of course). Characters move through their roles carefully. And the film suffers for it; it seems static, careful, and safe." —Michael R. Collings, from *The Films of Stephen King* (Starmont House, 1986).

"It seems unlikely with such an ample budget, talented cast, and expert crew, that 'Firestarter' should have failed – but letting a $15 million feature rest on the shoulders of a seven-year-old actress and an unproven director proved to be an overwhelming obstacle." —Jessie Horsting, from *Stephen King at the Movies* (Starlog Press, 1986).

"Getting a girl hot takes on a whole new meaning in this eighth adaptation of a Stephen King work. Drew Barrymore does her damndest to screw up her face and somehow carry the torch for this thinly-conceived tale of an 8-year-old pyrotechnic *femme fatale*, but the film never warms above the staleness of microwaved leftovers. It's also uninvolving and unimaginative." —Steven Dimeo, from a review in *Cinefantastique*, September 1984.

3 "Good" ratings;
2 "Mediocre" ratings.
—"Film Ratings," *Cinefantastique*, September 1984.

"CAT'S EYE"

"Forget the cat, you hemorrhoid!
Get the gun!"
–Dr. Donatti

Released April 1985, by MGM/United Artists.
Videotape released by CBS/Fox Home Video; $79.95.
Running Time: 94 minutes.
1. "Quitter's, Inc.": 38 minutes
2. "The Ledge": 26 minutes
3. "The General": 30 minutes
Rated PG-13

Directed By: Lewis Teague
Produced By: Martha J. Schumacher
Screenplay By: Stephen King
Co-Producer: Milton Subotsky
Director of Photography: Jack Cardiff
Film Editor: Scott Conrad, A.C.E.
Production Designer: Giorgio Postiglione
Costume Designer: Clifford Capone
Creatures Created By: Carlo Rambaldi
Music By: Alan Silvestri
Casting By: Howard Feuer & Jeremy Ritzer
Art Director: Jeffrey Ginn

Set Designer: E.C. Chen
Storyboard Artists: Kirk Thatcher and Mentor Huebner
Make-Up: Sandi Duncan
Special Visual Effects: Barry Nolan
Creature Operators: Paolo Scipione, Frank Schepler, Steven Willis

Songs

"Every Breath You Take"
Composed by The Police

"Twist and Shout"
Composed by Phil Medley

"96 Tears"
Composed by R. Martinez

"Cat's Eye"
Composed by
J. Morall/F. Zarr/B. Valanch
Sung by Ray Stevens

Budget: $7 million

CAST

Our Girl/Amanda	Drew Barrymore
Morrison	James Woods
Dr. Donatti	Alan King
Cressner	Kenneth McMillan
Norris	Robert Hays
Sally Ann	Candy Clark
Hugh	James Naughton
Junk	Tony Munafo
Mr. McCann	Court Miller
Mr. Milquetoast	Russell Horton
Mrs. Milquetoast	Patricia Benson
Cindy	Mary D'Arcy
Drunk Businessman	James Rebhorn
Janitor	Jack Dillon
Mrs. McCann	Susan Hawes
Jerrilyn	Shelly Burch
Westlake	Sal Richards
Albert	Jesse Doran
Marcia	Patricia Kalember
Ducky	Mike Starr
Dom	Charles Dutton

"CAT'S EYE"

"Cat's Eye" could also be called a Stephen King" *Night Shift* film," since two of the stories in the film are based on stories from that collection. But the stories used are "Quitters, Inc.," and "The Ledge," two of the tamer, more humorous tales from King's 1978 book. (The third "Cat's Eye" segment is an original story called "The General," written by King for the film.)

Overall, the film is not bad. It's certainly watchable, although I would have liked to have seen the film as King originally wrote it. An opening segment that took place at the funeral of a little girl was cut from the final version, on the orders of Frank Yablans (then the head of MGM/United Artists). The mother of the dead girl becomes fixated on the idea that a cat stole her daughter's breath, but the ghost of the girl appears to the cat and implores him to go find the real creature (one of Carlo Rambaldi's trolls) that killed her. This omission left the viewer wondering why certain things happened, since the final version never clearly establishes that the cat is on a mission.

Of the three segments, "The Ledge" seems to me to be the strongest. There is something universally terrifying about heights, and Lew Teague does a superb job of capturing the giddy vertigo that Robert Hays's character experiences. This segment really seems *dangerous* – even though it was filmed on forced-perspective miniatures on a soundstage. If you didn't know that, you'd find yourself thinking that these people are really crazy for even *trying* to film such a sequence, and hoping like hell that they've got a net down below.

Other than the existence of the Troll, and an occasional ghostly appearance by Amanda, there are no overt supernatural elements in "Cat's Eye," and maybe that's why the film really doesn't interest me enough to watch and re-watch. I like Stephen King's dark side – his sense of humor often doesn't do too much for me.

Nonetheless, "Cat's Eye" (even though it was a commercial and critical flop due, I think, in large part to the mutilation of King's original framing story) is a decent way to spend an hour and a half when there's nothing on cable, and you're between King book releases.

[NOTE: See my interview with director Lewis Teague in this volume.]

Here are a few of my favorite moments from the film:

1. *Alan King*: King gives a tremendous performance as the sadistic anti-smoker, Dr. Donatti. He wears a malicious smirk throughout the segment, and delivers the terrific line I used as the epigraph to this overview ("Forget the cat, you hemorrhoid! Get the gun!"). I think it's wonderful that dramatic actor James Woods gave a superb comic performance, and that the comic Alan King gave a serious performance that effectively communicated Donatti's bizarre cigarette obsession.

2. *The Cat*: I love cats. You got a problem with that?

3. *The Special Visual Effects* : The already-noted forced-perspective miniature sets for "The Ledge" were very effective, Carlo Rambaldi's creature was, as usual, excellent, and the giant bedroom set constructed for the final segment, "The General" is a lot of fun.

4. *Drew Barrymore* : Her performance here is heads above her catatonic, lackluster acting in "Firestarter," and closer to her charming portrayal of Gertie in Steven Spielberg's "E.T.—The Extra-Terrestrial."

5. *The In-Jokes* : Lew Teague and Stephen King have fun with Stephen King's role as pop culture guru by sprinkling "Stephen King" references throughout "Cat's Eye." Some of theses references included appearances by both Cujo and Christine; James Woods watching "The Dead Zone" on TV and telling his wife, "I don't know who writes this crap!"; Candy Clark reading *Pet Sematary* ; the private school Morrison's daughter attends is called Saint Stephen's School for the Exceptional; in "The Ledge," a copy of *Penthouse* is on the coffee table (and, as we all know, *Penthouse* is where the short story "The Ledge" first appeared); and, one sort-of "reverse" reference: In the opening segment of Stephen King's film "Maximum Overdrive" (aside from it containing one of the few screen appearances of Marla Maples – she's a screaming babe in a car), King has a drawbridge open while cars are still on it. (The machines have already taken over.) In the "Quitters, Inc." segment of "Cat's Eye," James Woods sneaks a cigarette while waiting in a line of cars as, you guessed it, a drawbridge opens.

Now here are some of my least favorite moments:

1. *The Choice of Stories* : If it was a given that they were going to use stories from *Night Shift*, I would have preferred to see them take on something with a little more bite and grue. I would love to see a big-budget production of "One for the Road," Gray Matter," "The Mangler," "I Am the Doorway," or even "Battleground." To me, there's Stephen King when he's in his prime (as he was with the stories I mentioned), and then there's King doing other things. I prefer horrific King, rather than the tamer tales used for this film. I've heard that every story in *Night Shift* (except, I think, for "Jerusalem's Lot") has been optioned for the movies. An anthology of King films that is true to the essence of King's stories would be welcome indeed.

2. *The Elimination of Part of King's Framing Story* : As already noted, this did not help the continuity or clarity of the final version of the film.

3. *The Padding of "The Ledge" Story* : I did not like the scene added to the film in which Cressner bets that the cat will make it across the street without getting killed. It seemed gratuitous, cruel, and unneccessary.

What the Critics Had To Say...

"[A] trilogy of terror in the much-missed 'Night Gallery' anthology style...good old-fashioned tell-me-a-scary-story fun. ☆☆☆1/2" —Mick Martin & Marsha Porter, *Video Movie Guide 1990*.

"'Cat's Eye' is an entertaining film. 'Cat's Eye' does indicate several degrees of improvement over 'Creepshow'; and it does argue for King's increasing sense of ease in working with film." —Michael R. Collings, from *The Films of Stephen King* (Starmont House, 1986).

"...[A] crippled thing – though, in many respects, a lively, funny, scary 94 minutes." —Jessie Horsting, from *Stephen King at the Movies* (Starlog Press, 1986).

"The special effects are effective and understated, allowing the foreground to be occupied by some of our basic human fears, of pain for loved ones, of falling from a great height, of suffocation. Stephen King seems to be working his way through the reference books of human phobias, and 'Cat's Eye' is one of his most effective films. ☆☆☆." —Roger Ebert, from *Roger Ebert's Movie Home Companion*.

"King quickly sets up the film's sly undercurrent of sly humor, but as handled by director Lewis Teague, the right balance of comedy and terror is never quite established. ... The cat as a linking device in two of King's stories proves not only pointless but actually lessens suspense." —Lawrence French, from a review in the October 1985 issue of *Cinefantastique* .

0 "Must See" ratings;
1 "Excellent" rating;
3 "Good" ratings;
2 "Mediocre" ratings;
1"Worthless rating.
—"Film Ratings," *Cinefantastique*, October 1985.

"SILVER BULLET"

"You should have left me alone, Marty."
—Reverend Lowe

Released October 1985, by Paramount Pictures.
Videotape released by Paramount Home Video; $79.95.
Running Time: 95 minutes.
Rated R

Directed By: Daniel Attias
Produced By: Martha Schumacher
Associate Producer: John M. Eckert
Screenplay By: Stephen King
Based on the novelette "Cycle of the Werewolf" By: Stephen King
Music By: Jay Chattaway
Film Editor: Daniel Loewenthal
Director of Photography: Armando Nannuzzi
Costume Designer: Clifford Capone
Creatures Created By: Carlo Rambaldi
Production Designer: Giorgio Postiglione

Budget: $7 million

CAST

Uncle Red	Gary Busey
Reverend Lowe	Everett McGill
Marty Coslaw	Corey Haim
Jane Coslaw	Megan Follows
Nan Coslaw	Robin Groves
Bob Coslaw	Leo Rossom
Sheriff Joe Haller	Terry O'Quinn
Andy Fairton	Bill Smitrovich
Brady Kincaid	Joe Wright
Herb Kincaid	Kent Broadhurst
Arnie Westrum	James Gammon
Tammy Sturmfuller	Heather Simmons
Milt Sturmfuller	James A. Baffico
Mrs. Sturmfuller	Rebecca Fleming
Owen Knopfler	Lawrence Tierney
Virgil Cuts	William Newman
Mayor O'Banion	Sam Stoneburner
Billy McLaren	Lonnie Moore
Aspinall	Rick Pasotto
Girl	Cassidy Eckert
Stella Randolph	Wendy Walker
Stella's Boyfriend	Michael Lague
Stella's Mother	Myra Mailloux
Bobby Robertson	William Brown
Elmer Zinneman	Herb Harton
Pete Sylvester	David Hart
Porter Zinneman	Graham Smith
Edgar Rounds	Paul Butler
Maggie Andrews	Crystal Field
Smokey	Julius Leflore
Uncle Red's Girl	Roxanne Aalam
Mrs. Thayer	Pearl Jones
Mr. Thayer	Ish Jones, Jr.
Outfielder	Steven White
Mac	Conrad McLaren
Voice of Older Jane	Tovah Feldshuh
The Werewolf	Everett McGill

"SILVER BULLET"

As most King fans know by now, *Cycle of the Werewolf,* the novelette on which the film "Silver Bullet" is based, was originally proposed to Stephen King as a calendar idea. In his Foreword to the omnibus edition of *Cycle of the Werewolf* and the "Silver Bullet" screenplay, King put it this way:

> "The proposal was made to me in the lobby of a hotel in Providence, Rhode Island, during the World Fantasy Convention in 1979, by a young man from Michigan named Christopher Zavisa. One of the reasons I agreed to at least consider Zavisa's proposal was that I was drunk."

(Regarding his willingness to jump right into the project, King also remembered his mother's admonition, "If you were a girl, Stephen, you'd always be pregnant.")

To cut to the chase, the calendar idea didn't work out for one very good reason: King could not keep the story reined in. It wanted to grow and, wisely, he let it. The result was the slim volume *Cycle of the Werewolf,* which was translated, by King, to the screen as "Silver Bullet," the film under consideration here.

So, how is "Silver Bullet" as a movie? It's okay, but nothing special. It's a standard werewolf movie that assumes knowledge of some things really needed explanation. Jeff Conner, in *Stephen King Goes to Hollywood,* correctly notes that there should have been something in the script that explained how the Reverend became a werewolf: "King's script...offers no explanation for Reverend Lowe's condition. Lowe seems just to have somehow contracted a dose of lycanthropy..." Also, how did Marty end up in a wheelchair? These faults aside, the film works on a few basic levels, and is worth watching. At least once, possibly twice...but "Silver Bullet" unfortunately won't make it into my "Stephen King Screening Overdose Hall of Fame" currently occupied by "IT," "The Dead Zone" and "Stand By Me," with "Pet Sematary" and "Misery" waiting outside in the lobby. [NOTE: In my section on the "Stephen King Notebook" in this volume, I give details on King's handwritten, first-draft screenplay for "Silver Bullet." See that section and then compare it with the actual film.]

Here are a few of my favorite moments from the film:

1. *Megan Follows*: King is right. This girl is going to be a star. She is superb.
2. *Gary Busey*: I went back and forth on Busey: I almost included his performance in my "Least Favorite Moments" section,

but in the end decided I liked his Uncle Red more than I disliked him. Busey gives an over-the-edge performance here that sometimes grates on the nerves, but overall he's very effective.

3. *The Werewolves in Church Dream Sequence*: Terrific fun as all the parishioners begin to change into werewolves in what has to be the largest transformation scene ever filmed. Very well done, and very scary.

4. *Everett McGill*: I like his understated reading and interpretation of this role. And his physical degeneration (the beard stubble, the rumpled clothes and hair, the eye patch) as he begins to lose control of his "dark half" works quite well.

Now here are some of my least favorite moments:

1. *The Music*: I don't know why, but some of the background music for this film (most notably during the "speeding wheelchair" scenes) reminds me of the corny musical porridge that we used to hear under action-and-chase scenes during old "Mod Squad" episodes and bad B-movies. Also, the spooky music is standard fare and doesn't contribute too much to the overall mood of the film, although it was nice to hear a riff of "Psycho" strings during Marty's escape from the werewolf after his lone fireworks session.

2. *The Mood*: Sometimes Attias lets things get a little bit too corny. The whole film should have had the dark feel of the scene where Megan Follows first discovers the true identity of the werewolf. Her face is half in shadows and is really eerie.

3. *The "Silver Bullet" Wheelchair*: Gimme a break, huh? This just seems like a device to allow Marty a way to get around after it was decided that he was crippled. You can't have chase scenes if you can't run or walk, right?

4. *The False Ending*: Overuse of this tired cliche is what gives horror movies a bad name, know whadda mean?

What the Critics Had To Say...

"A superior Stephen King film, this release moves like the projectile for which it was named. ...an edge of your seat winner. ☆☆☆☆." —Mick Martin & Marsha Porter, *Video Movie Guide 1990*.

"['Silver Bullet'] is by no means a definitive statement on werewolf culture; nor is it a very imaginative horror film. ... Still, [the film] is an entertaining and unpretentious picture and despite the R rating for violence it works well as a kid's adventure (especially given the family subplot.)" —Jeff Conner, *Stephen King Goes to Hollywood* (Plume, 1987).

"As werewolf film, 'Silver Bullet' is curiously old-fashioned, almost nostalgic. It concentrates on character more than on special effects. ... All in all an enjoyable film." —Michael R. Collings, from *The Films of Stephen King* (Starmont House, 1986).

"☆." —(The Philadelphia) *Inquirer Movie Guide for VCRs*.

"Although 'Silver Bullet' was Daniel Attias' first feature, the young director shows a sure hand and a sense of style." —Jessie Horsting, from *Stephen King At the Movies* (Starlog Press, 1986).

"[T]his is, I fear, one more in the litany of misses made from King product. Not as bad as 'Cujo' or 'Children of the Corn' or 'Christine,' but as emptyheaded as any of the films I've reviewed this time, 'Silver Bullet' hasn't much to recommend it save a few nice insights by Steve, two extraordinary performances by a young woman named Megan Follows and a little boy named Corey Haim, who play brother and sister, and a scene in a foggy forest that is cinematically enthralling." —Harlan Ellison, from the "Harlan Ellison's Watching" column in *The Magazine of Fantasy and Science Fiction*, October 1985.

"King's script needed a heavy rewrite; there's much that's good in it, but also too much repetition, some bad laughs...and overly-tidy

coincidences. But even this script deserved a better director than Attias, who has no new ideas and doesn't know how to deliver old-fashioned shocks. Even when they look like they should work, the numerous sudden-shock scenes fall flat because of Attias's lack of understanding of the crucial importance of timing and camera angle. A better director – even a slightly better director – would have made a much better film." —Bill Warren in "The Movies and Mr. King: Part II" from *Reign of Fear* (Underwood-Miller, 1988).

"THE BOOGEYMAN"

Granite Entertainment, 1983, 1986.
Running Time: 29 minutes.

Directed By: Jeffrey C. Schiro
Produced By: Jeffrey C. Schiro
Teleplay By: Jeffrey C. Schiro
Based On The Short Story By: Stephen King
Original Score By: John Cote
Director of Photography: Douglas Meltzer

CAST

Lester Billings	Michael Reid
Dr. Harper	Bert Linder
Sgt. Gurland	Terence Brady
Rita Billings	Mindy Silverman
The Coroner	Jerome Bynder
Denny	Bobby Persicheth
Andy	Michael Dagostino
The Neighbor	Nancy Lindeberg
The Husband	James Holmes
Cop #1	John Macdonald
Cop #2	Dave Buff
Attendant #1	Rich West
Attendant #2	John Coté
Dispatch Voice	Brooke Trivas

"THE BOOGEYMAN"

"The Boogeyman" is one of two films comprising *Stephen King's Night Shift Collection* (the other is "The Woman in the Room," discussed above.)

The short story "The Boogeyman," when taken in concert with "The Body," *Cujo*, and *It*, epitomizes Stephen King's thematic approach to childhood fears and, in fact, childhood and the path to maturity itself. The story is about the monster in the closet, the archetypal "thing under the bed" that King has been working with since he began writing. (And I mean that literally: His *People, Places, and Things* story "The Thing At the Bottom of the Well" is about the boogeyman, the monster in the closet, It...the monster that can literally become the embodiment of our worst fear.) King's idea is that "maybe if you think of a thing long enough...it becomes real."

This film adaptation is essentially a very strong rendering of the tale, but nonetheless has a few problem areas. It's a little slow-paced during the scenes where Billings just sits and talks. The sound is a bit muddy at times, and this can be distracting. The lighting, on the other hand, is phenomenal: lots of shadows and darkness that contribute to the mood of the piece. The score is also very effective: It's a combination of sound effects and eerie music that works quite well (the film's composer, John Coté, makes an appearance in the film as an ambulance attendant.)

Michael Reed has a disturbing presence; he looks like a living skull. There's also a nice touch during Billings' emotional collapse. As Billings weeps and raves about the boogeyman, and how he couldn't prevent the death of his children, there's a nice little smirk on the face of Dr. Harper (who is himself, as we all know, the Boogeyman).

Overall, this is a well-done adaptation of an important Stephen King story.

"THE WORD PROCESSOR OF THE GODS"

An episode of the syndicated TV series "Tales from the Darkside"
Based on Stephen King's short story "Word Processor of the Gods"
Broadcast Friday, November 19, 1985.
Running Time: 30 minutes (including commercials).

Directed By: Michael Gornick
Produced By: William Teitler
Teleplay By: Michael McDowell
Based On A Story By: Stephen King
Director of Photography: Ernest Dickerson
Editor: Scott Vickrey
Story Consultant: Tom Allen
Original Music By: Tom Pile & Bill Gordon
Executive Producers: Richard P. Rubinstein, George A. Romero, Jerry Golod

CAST

Richard Hagstrom	Bruce Davison
Lina Hagstrom	Karen Shallo
Seth Hagstrom	Patrick Piccinini
Mr. Nordhoff	William Cain
Jonathan	Jon Matthews
Belinda	Miranda Beeson
Narrator	Paul Sparer

"THE WORD PROCESSOR OF THE GODS"

Stephen King's short fiction translates very well to film, and "The Word Processor of the Gods" is no exception.

This tale of the ultimate fantasy works well on television, and Michael McDowell's screenplay is not the least of the reasons why.

As we all know from our reading, Richard Hagstrom is a failed writer, a failed husband, and a failed father. He married poorly because he didn't have the courage to propose to Belinda, the woman he truly loved. His no-account drunkard brother had no such qualms, and ended up married to Belinda, with whom they had Jonathan, the son Richard should have had.

Richard, in the meantime, ended up with Lina, a fat, lazy mean-spirited bitch, and they had a son, Seth, a fat, lazy creep.

After Richard's brother's family is all killed when his drunken brother drives their van off a cliff, Richard receives a final birthday gift from Jonathan: a cobbled-together word processor that, amazingly, works. But it works in ways Richard would have never believed. The machine has the power to delete from the real world – or create in the real world – whatever is typed on its screen. So, what does Richard do with this newfound power "of the gods"? What would you do? He first creates a sack of gold coins. Then, he types in that he has the idea for twenty bestselling novels, only to have Seth blow the house fuses with his guitar-playing. Richard, naturally, simply deletes Seth. He then deletes Lina, and, as the machine is in overload and on fire, types in that he lives alone except for his beloved wife Belinda and their son Jonathan.

It works.

The cast is very good in this piece. Especially interesting is Mr. Nordhoff, a character who seems to know that the word processor has a power, since he calls Richard and warns him to be careful with it. Also, Karen Shallo is deliciously repulsive as Richard's detestable wife, and Seth is a slug heard mostly offscreen.

McDowell has included a couple of very effective hallucination scenes, one of which has Jonathan appearing to his uncle and telling him he'll build him a word processor, but that he'll have to hurry, because he doesn't have much time.

A decent interpretation of a fascinating Stephen King short story.

"MAXIMUM OVERDRIVE"

"Come on over here, sugarbuns. This machine just called me an asshole."
—Stephen King as an unnamed character in "Maximum Overdrive"

Released August 1986, by MGM/United Artists (De Laurentiis Entertainment Group).
Videotape released by Karl-Lorimar Home Video.
Running Time: 95 minutes.
Rated R

Written For The Screen And Directed By: Stephen King
Produced By: Martha Schumacher
Executive Producers: Mel Pearl, Don Levin
Director of Photography: Armando Nannuzzi
Music By: AC/DC
Production Designer: Giorgio Postiglione
Film Editor: Evan Lottman, A.C.E.
Costume Designer: Clifford Capone

Special Effects Makeup: Dean Gates
Assistant to Stephen King: Stephanie Fowler
Translation By: Roberto Croci/Mara Trovato

Budget: $10 million

CAST

Bill Robinson	Emilio Estevez
Hendershot	Pat Hingle
Brett	Laura Harrington
Connie	Yeardley Smith
Curt	John Short
Wanda June	Ellen McElduff
Duncan	J.C. Quinn
Camp Loman	Christopher Murney
Deke	Holter Graham
Handy	Frankie Faison
Joe	Pat Miller
Max	Jack Canon
Steve	Barry Bell
Frank	John Brasington
Andy	J. Don Ferguson
Brad	Leon Rippy
Barry	Bob Gooden
Rolf	R. Pickett Bugg
Videoplayer	Giancarlo Esposito
Second Man	Martin Tucker
Second Woman	Marla Maples
Bridgemaster	Ned Austin
Helper	Richard Chapman, Jr.
Coach	Bob Gunter
Umpire	Bill Huggins

"MAXIMUM OVERDRIVE"

Okay, let me piss off everybody right from the start: "Maximum Overdrive" is not as bad as you have been led to believe. I, of course, have certainly seen better films, but believe me when I tell you, I have *definitely* seen worse.

Granted, "Maximum Overdrive" has some problems. Based on his *Night Shift* short story "Trucks," and then expanded for the screenplay, the characterization is not up to King's usual standards, the pacing is a bit plodding, and the music is too one-dimensional. But the story's good, the performances aren't bad, and the special effects and gross-out scenes are cool.

In 1989, a documentary on Stephen King called "He Who Writes Will Be Remembered" was produced for Belgian Television's monthly literary program. In the program, Stephen King talked about what went wrong with the film:

MARTIN COENEN: Was directing 'Maximum Overdrive' difficult?
STEPHEN KING: It was very difficult. I made a lot of mistakes, all of which were forgiveable except for one. That is, I went against the way that I've worked all my

life. I'm a very intuitive writer, and I tend to create on the spur of the moment. That is to say that when I sit down at the typewriter, I'm never entirely sure what's going to come out. And I'd read a book about how Alfred Hitchcock worked. And it said that he arranged everything in advance. He knew what every shot was going to look like, what every shot was going to be, with the result that, for him, pre-production was the most exciting time of a film, and everything that happened during shooting was sort-of a bore. And I was scared. And the idea of having a boring shooting schedule sounded wonderful to me. So I went in with every shot mapped out. There are places in the film where I allowed for spur-of-the-moment creativity to creep in. They were the exceptions; and they're the best parts of the film. The rest of it's got sort a stiffish, set-up feel. When I went in, I didn't know what cutaways were, I didn't know what wild sound was, I didn't know what pickup shots were. None of these things. [These were] things that I learned sort-of on-the-run.
MARTIN COENEN: Can I say this movie 'Maximum Overdrive' is about trucks and cars rising against the human race?
STEPHEN KING: Yeah, and it's about 87 minutes long.

[NOTE: In our never ending mission to provide you with more information than you can possibly ever use or want, here are definitions for the film terms Stephen King refered to in the above interview excerpt:

CUTAWAY SHOT: A separate action shot that is not part of the principal action being filmed, but is significant and relevant to it and occurs simultaneously.
WILD SOUND: Recordings made of related material independent of the actual sound recording made during the shooting of a scene.
PICKUP SHOTS: A scene or shot inserted later in a film, after principal photography of the scene has been shot.]

"Maximum Overdrive" is, by King's own admission, a "moron movie." But methinks he doth protest too much. The film is definitely watchable, and it's got a "rough-and-tumble" feel to it that makes for a nice ninety-minute diversion.

Also, it now has a special collector's appeal: It contains one of the first (possibly the first, last, and only) feature film appearances of Marla Maples. Marla is credited as the "Second Woman" (hmmm) and, basically, she gets to function in the role of the "screaming babe in a car." She gets stuck on the drawbridge as it opens on its own at the beginning of the film, and shrieks "The bridge is going up. Stop the car!" Good job, Marla! Later on, she screams "Oh, my God!" as a watermelon comes flying towards the front window of the car she's in. Then, when the watermelon hits, Marla gets slimed, her boyfriend bails out (with "No Excuses") and, a few seconds later, the watermelon truck flips over and crushes the car with poor Marla still inside. An auspicious debut, and one that will definitely achieve true trash-class status, if it hasn't already.

In my interview with Jessie Horsting for this volume, she and I discussed the "failure" of King as a director, and I made the point (which King confirmed in the above interview) that he took on "Maximum Overdrive" not knowing how to direct. I said "I guess he's decided that he may have a lot of talents, but directing is not one of them." Her reply was right on the money: "Right," she said. "But that's one way we find out what we can and cannot do – by trying."

King tried.

And, when you consider the complexities, problems, roadblocks, and financial hassles of writing and directing a major motion picture (especially for someone who's more accustomed to sitting at a typewriter or wordprocessor every day), you come to the realization that "Maximum Overdrive" really isn't that bad at all.

And speaking of problems, one major snafu King had to contend with on the set of "Maximum Overdrive" was the injury of Armando Nannuzzi, his director of photography. On July 31, 1985, King and company were shooting a scene that had an operator-less lawnmower chasing a young boy. After the scene was over, the lawnmower kept heading for the camera instead of being stopped by stagehands. The blades of the lawnmower struck a wooden camera support, and sharp wood splinters flew at Nannuzzi. He was struck in the face and the right eye, and his doctors said he basically lost his "shooting eye." Nannuzzi filed a lawsuit on February 18, 1987, against Stephen King for damages in the amount of $18 million. I don't know the outcome of the suit.

Here are a few of my favorite moments from the film:

1. *The Attack of the Soda Cans* : Soda cans as projectiles launched from a "grenade-launching" soda machine. Who could ask for more?

2. *The Attack of the Steamroller* : A little kid gets run over by a steamroller, and you see it from the kid's point-of-view. Very gross, and a scene that had to be trimmed to get the movie an R rating.

3. *The Opening "Drawbridge" Montage* : A chance to see what we've all thought about as we've driven across these bizarre inventions. Lots of slow motion shots of people and vehicles falling into the river. Plus a glimpse of the soon-to-be-notorious Marla Maples.

4. *The Cast*: To an actor, they all give it their best shot. They all seemed to pick up on the broad characterization King scripted, using it to the advantage, rather than the detriment, of the film. True professionals.

Now here are some of my least favorite moments:

1. *The Music*: As noted, it's too one-dimensional. AC/DC would have been a good choice to do *some* of the music for the film...but ALL of it??!

2. *Stephen King's Displeasure At The Whole Directing Process* : My hope is that this film didn't sour him on trying directing again. I'd love to see him attempt something small and dark (perhaps something like "Suffer the Little Children" or even "Squad D?"). "Maximum Overdrive" was a huge logistical nightmare, and we can only hope that it didn't make King decide never to direct again.

What the Critics Had To Say...

"[A] boring, turgid chaotic mess. ... As a director, King hasn't the faintest idea how to elicit good performances from his cast, and the picture is paced abysmally. A turkey." —Mick Martin and Marsha Porter, *Video Movie Guide 1990.*

"☆." —(The Philadelphia) *Inquirer Movie Guide for VCRs* .

"King has gone on record as saying he meant to make a simple 'moron movie.' ... As 'Maximum Overdrive' was a crash course in the directorial process...it is just as well for King that his sights weren't aimed higher." —Jeff Conner, from *Stephen King Goes to Hollywood* (Plume, 1987).

"Stephen King *can* direct, and 'Maximum Overdrive' comes across as a mechanical version of 'Night of the Living Dead,' with machines supplying the unthinking violence displayed by zombies in Romero's film. ... 'Maximum Overdrive' is a directorial debut to be proud of, and a film which will certainly do well with genre fans." —Judith P. Harris, from a review in *Cinefantastique* , July 1986.

0 "Must See" ratings;
0 "Excellent" rating;
1 "Good" ratings;
3 "Mediocre" ratings;
2 "Worthless ratings.
—"Film Ratings," *Cinefantastique*, October 1986.

"STAND BY ME"

"I was twelve going on thirteen the first time I saw a dead human being."

Released September 1986, by Columbia Pictures.

Videotape released by RCA/Columbia Home Video.

Running Time: 110 minutes.

Rated R

Directed By: Rob Reiner

Screenplay By: Raynold Gideon & Bruce A. Evans

Produced By: Andrew Scheinman, Bruce A. Evans, and Raynold Gideon

Based Upon the Novella "The Body" By: Stephen King

Director of Photography: Thomas del Ruth

Production Designed By: Dennis Washington

Film Editor: Robert Leighton

Original Music: Jack Nitzsche

Set Design: Richard MacKenzie

Budget: $8 million

Gross Box-Office Receipts: $46 million (in the first seventeen weeks of release)

CAST

Gordie Lachance	Wil Wheaton
Gordie (Adult)	Richard Dreyfuss
Chris Chambers	River Phoenix
Teddy Duchamp	Corey Feldman
Vern Tessio	Jerry O'Connell
Ace Merrill	Kiefer Sutherland
Billy Tessio	Casey Siemaszko
Charlie Hogan	Gary Riley
Eyeball Chambers	Bradley Gregg
Vince Desjardins	Jason Oliver
Mr. Lachance	Marshall Bell
Mrs. Lachance	Frances Lee McCain
Mr. Quidacioluo	Bruce Kirby
Milo Pressman	William Bronder
Mayor Grundy	Scott Beach
Denny Lachance	John Cusack
Waitress	Madeline Swift
Chopper	Popeye
Mayor's Wife	Geanette Bobst

Principal Wiggins	Art Burke
Bob Cormier	Matt Williams
Lardass Hogan	Andy Lindberg
Bill Travis	Dick Durock
Lardass Heckler #1	O.B. Babbs
Lardass Heckler #2	Charlie Owens
Donelly Twins	Kenneth & John Hodges
Fat Lady	Susan Thorpe
Moke	Korey Scott Pollard
Jack Mudgett	Rick Elliott
Ray Brower	Kent Lutrell
Gordon's Son	Chance Quinn
His Friend	Jason Naylor

"STAND BY ME"

Throughout the past several years, I've often come upon people to whom I would be introduced as a "writer doing a book about Stephen King." Very often, the response was something along the lines of "I never read that stuff," or "I hate horror." I took great delight in shooting down their misconceptions by asking the simple question, "Have you seen the movie "Stand By Me"? When they responded that they had, and that they absolutely loved it (and they *always* loved it), I would then casually say, "That was a Stephen King story, you know."

The surprise on their faces never fails to amuse me, for their's is the kind of preconceived stereotypical rejection of any popular culture art form that limits people, and keeps them locked into a mundane, boring rut void of the entertainment and growth that can come from experiencing a new (to them) writer, artist, musician, etc.

"Stand By Me" is a quintessential coming-of-age tale about four boys on a journey towards adulthood; a journey that takes the guise of a trip to see a dead body.

You would think the story was autobiographical, but it is not. King has told a couple of different versions of where the tale came from and, as with all writers of fiction, I'm sure there is truth to both versions. (One story he tells details the day his mother told him about a kid who had gotten hit by a train and torn apart. They put the pieces in a basket. Another credits a college roommate with telling King about a dog that had been hit by a train.) Nonetheless, the film (and source novella, "The Body") *are* autobiographical, but only in the sense that the experiences and emotions delineated in the film are elevated to archetypes that trigger memories in our collective consciousness. From such re-experiencing comes growth.

"Stand By Me" is my second favorite King film (after "The Dead Zone"), and I think it just proves – once and for all – that King can tap into places in our hearts that we have perhaps ignored for too long, and thus show us the shape under the sheet, the face behind the mask, the real us. And we're all much better off for the journey.

Here are a few of my favorite moments from the film:

1. *The perfect recreation of the fifties* : The film literally captures a moment in time, a moment of treehouses, small towns, and backyard campouts.

2. *The direction* : Rob Reiner did a magnificent job in eliciting flawless performances from his young cast. I guess Reiner remembers childhood almost as well as King does, wouldn't you say?

3. *The art direction and photography* : The film teems with brilliant locations and sets, and the colors and light warm us with soft and honest hues.

Now here are some of my least favorite moments:

As with "The Dead Zone," I can't find anything wrong with "Stand By Me."

What the Critics Had To Say...

"If there is any justice left in the world, ['Stand By Me'] should be the first King film to win an Oscar." —Tyson Blue, "'Stand By Me': The Best King Film Ever," *Castle Rock* , October 1986.

"Morbid as it may sound, this is not a horror movie. Rather, it is a story of ascending to manhood. Sometimes sad and often funny. ☆☆☆☆ 1/2." —Mick Martin & Marsha Porter, *Video Movie Guide 1990*.

"To the numerous disappointing adaptations of King's work to the screen, 'Stand By Me' is a refreshing exception. King's authorial voice, wonderfully preserved in this movie, goes to show that, despite what everyone believed, King's work can be successfully adapted to the screen." —George Beahm, from *The Stephen King Companion*.

"Simply put, it is *King,* on screen, carefully choreographed and lovingly translated, containing all the rare, quirky wisdom that informs King's characterizations. This may seem like enough adjectives to make even a publicist blush, but after a long dry stretch of near misses and some definite clunkers...'Stand By Me' is an oasis." —Jessie Horsting, from *Stephen King At the Movies*.

"GRAMMA"

An episode of the CBS TV series "The New Twilight Zone"
Based on Stephen King's short story "Gramma"
Broadcast Friday, February 14, 1986.
Running Time: 30 minutes (including commercials).

Directed By: Bradford May
Produced By: Harvey Frand
Teleplay By: Harlan Ellison
Based On A Story By: Stephen King
Director of Photography: Bradford May
Story Editor: Rockne S. O'Bannon
Executive Story Consultant: Alan Brennert
Music By: Mickey Hart (of the Grateful Dead)
Executive Producer: Philip de Guere
Supervising Producer: James Crocker

CAST

George	Barret Oliver
Mother	Darlanne Fluegel
Gramma	Frederick Long

"GRAMMA"

"Gramma" works.

This is a spooky, atmospheric adaptation of one of Stephen King's most frightening stories, and once again shows just how effective King can be on screen when done properly.

Georgie has to stay home alone with his invalid grandmother. Who just so happens to be a witch. And who just so happens to die while he's alone with her.

Harlan Ellison pulls out all the stops with his teleplay, and the special effects contribute to the overall intensity of the production.

"Gramma" was an excellent episode of this reincarnation of Rod Serling's classic series, and although this episode is not available on videotape, the series itself is syndicated in certain areas.

"CREEPSHOW 2"

"It hurts!"
–Page Hannah as Rachel in "The Raft"

Released May 1987, by New World Pictures.
Running Time: 89 minutes.
1. Wraparound Segment #1 and Credits: 5 minutes, 10 seconds
2. "Old Chief Wood'nhead": 28 minutes, 40 seconds
3. Wraparound Segment #2: 1 minute, 17 seconds
4. "The Raft": 21 minutes, 22 seconds
5. Wraparound Segment #3: 1 minute, 42 seconds
6. "The Hitchhiker": 24 minutes, 37 seconds
7. Final Wraparound Segment and Credits: 5 minutes, 56 seconds
Rated R

Directed By: Michael Gornick
Produced By: David Ball
Screenplay By: George A. Romero
Based On Stories By: Stephen King
Executive Producer: Richard P. Rubenstein
Associate Producer: Mitchell Galin
Make-Up Effects Created By: Howard Berger, Ed French
Costume Designer: Eileen Sieff
Production Designer: Bruce Miller
Directors of Photography: Richard Hart, Tom Hurwitz
Film Editor: Peter Weatherley
Music Composed By: Les Reed
Additional Music By: Rick Wakeman

CAST

Billy	Domenick John
Annie Lansing	Lois Chiles
Ray Spruce	George Kennedy
Martha Spruce	Dorothy Lamour
Old Chief Wood'nhead	Dan Kamin
Carly	Philip Doré
Randy	Daniel Beer
Rachel	Page Hannah
The Truckdriver	Stephen King
George Lansing	Richard Parks
Deke	Paul Satterfield
Mr. Cavanaugh	Deane Smith
Mrs. Cavanaugh	Shirley Sonderegger
"The Hitchhiker"	Tom Wright
"The Creep"	Tom Savini
Voice Of The Creep	Joe Silver

Also...

Frank S. Salsedo, Holt McCallany, Don Harvey, David Holbrook, and Jeremy Green.

"CREEPSHOW 2"

"Creepshow 2" in no way lives up to the standards of the original Stephen King/George Romero collaboration, "Creepshow," but it's watchable...in the way that some run-of-the-mill television show is watchable when you've got nothing better to do. Everything about this film seems done on the cheap.

The original screenplay contained a segment called "Pinfall," which is rumored to now be a part of the "Creepshow 3" screenplay. If so, we can look forward to seeing what I think was one of the strongest parts of the "Creepshow 2" screenplay.

The three segments of "Creepshow 2" are "Old Chief Wood'nhead," "The Raft," and "The Hitchhiker," with a wraparound story that is mostly animated. I like "The Raft" the best, perhaps because it comes from very strong source material, one of King's best short stories, also called "The Raft."

The cast and performances are good, but overall, "Creepshow 2" deserves a C, with some moments (such as "The Raft") rating a B.

Here are a few of my favorite moments from the film:

1. *Page Hannah*: Yup, it's Daryl's kid sister. She plays Rachel in "The Raft," and has the distinction of being the first kid to get eaten by the blob in the water. Pretty as a picture, at times she almost looks like a young Sissy Spacek when she played Carrie White.

2. *The Blob Special Effects in "The Raft"*: The scene where Rachel is pushed up out of the blob screaming "It hurts!" is very effective and quite scary. It worked.

3. *Shirley Sonderegger and Stephen King In Cameos*: King plays a shit-kicking truck driver in "The Hitchhiker," and Shirley (King's secretary) plays a crocheting Mrs. Cavanaugh in "Old Chief Wood'nhead."

THE KING OF BOWLING
An Introduction to "Pinfall"

The bowling King?

Yup.

Did you know that Stephen King used to bowl in a league?

Ever since I first heard that, I've always wondered what it would be like for Stephen King to write a bowling horror story. After all, he's written about small towns, cars, a hotel, teachers, kids, growing up, pets, and countless other varied everyday topics. And when you think about it, what's more homely and average than a smalltown bowling league? The weekly ritual, the garish shirts, the beer and pizza afterwards...the very stuff that make up the fabric of much of Stephen King's stories: the nuts and bolts of everyday life in America.

Well, I—and the rest of us King fans—need wonder no more, for such a bowling story exists. It's called "Pinfall" and it's a story about a couple of bowling teams who suddenly enter that macabre and ghastly land known as the Stephen Kingdom.

"Pinfall" is an unfilmed segment of the film "Creepshow 2." "Pinfall" appeared in the first draft script of the film, and was written for the screen by George Romero. "Pinfall" was based on a short story (still unpublished) by Stephen King.

"Pinfall" is Stephen King having fun. The story is an E.C. Comics tale come to life, and the rumor is that one of the reasons it wasn't included in the final version of the film is that the gruesome special effects would have pushed the production way over budget.

In the final version of the film, the segments ran as follows:

1. "Old Chief Woodn'head"
2. "The Raft"
3. "The Hitchhiker"

In the first draft of the script, the sequence ran:

1. "The Raft"
2. "The Hitchhiker"
3. "Pinfall"
4. "Old Chief Woodn'head"

Pinfall is the story of two bowling teams, the prim, proper, and Yuppyish Regi-Men, and the loud, blue-collar, beer-drinking, cigar-smoking Bad News Boors. The Regi-Men "look like junior executives from the Silicone [sic] Valley, late thirties to early forties with neat razor-cuts blown dry, and each with a Tom Selleck moustache." The Boors, on the other hand, "look like the bowlers we might have pictured in our minds. All five of them have pear-shaped torsos and orang-utan [sic] arms. They look like Jack Davis drawings. They all have terminal beard shadow and they're swilling Utica Club beer and smoking hand-shaped Parodi's that look (and smell) like poodle turds."

The "Pinfall" section of the script ran from page 72 through page 103 consisting of Scenes 206 through 242, and the segment was introduced by the Creep:

> CREEP
> ...a gruesome little revenge story,
> short, sweet and...heh, heh, heh...
> striking! I call this one...PINFALL.

The segment begins at Scene 207:

> 207 EFX
> As the Creep finished his introduction, we MOVE IN to an ECU of the splash-panel drawing, which DISSOLVES into a FROZEN LIVE-ACTION FRAME of a....
>
> 208 INT. BIG TEN LANES - EVENING
> ...CLOSE-UP of bowling pins. A ball has hit just to the right of center. We HEAR the familiar thunder of a pinstrike, then the FRAME UN-FREEZES and the action completes itself. All ten of the pins go down.

The Big Ten Lanes is the setting for league bowling. As we enter the Lanes, we hear the noise and see the teams. The first team we see is the Regi-Men. As described in the script, they are insufferable. And particulary unbearable is the Regi-Men's team captain Reggie Rambeaux. Reggie, the ultimate pompous asshole, is "clearly pleased with himself, and not just because he bowled a strike. He's always pleased with himself. He likes himself a lot, and that, in part, makes us not like him at all."

The Regi-Men "study and practice," and take the game—and themselves—very seriously. To these guys, bowling is a fine art...a precision sport, and they do not take kindly to interruptions or distractions when they're playing.

The Bad News Boors, on the other hand, are your basic all-American blue-collar bowling team. They drink beer, smoke cigars, high-five their asses off, and generally have a great time on their one night a week out. They don't practice, they're all overweight, and yet they're consistently in the lead among the leagues' teams.

On the night "Pinfall" opens, the two teams are at it hot and heavy when Reggie Rambeaux, the captain of the Regi-Men, is interrupted during his shot by an old guy who is bowling by himself on the lane next to the Regi-Men.

This is J. Fred MacDugal, an "old geezer," who has bowled at at least two games a night for seventy years.

The Regi-Men immediately pounce on the vulnerable old man, and the Boors, seeing an innocent being pummeled by bullies, jump to his defense. They give MacDugal a shirt, a beer, and make him an honorary member of the Bad News Boors.

The Regi-Men are incensed, yet they stop short of an actual fistfight, instead choosing to pary and jab with prissy verbal assaults:

> REGGIE
> Why is it that lazy, illiterate, slovenly, good-for-nothing imbeciles are always so righteously proud of their stations in life?

The Regi-Men agree:

> REGI-MEN
> How true, how true. Don't waste your time on these slobs, Reggie. Don't waste your breath. Don't let them sucker you into something you'll regret. They're beneath you, they're cretins, animals.

After Reggie rants and raves in a high-pitched voice about wanting to win the championship, Chooch Mandolino coalesces the philosophy of the Boors (and Stephen King??):

> CHOOCH
> Maybe the rest of us don't give a shit about a lousy little statue from a Poduck bowling league. Maybe we think it's more important to have a good time with some good buddies, drink a few beers, have a couple laffs.

The Boors let MacDugal throw a couple of balls, and on his last shot he has a massive coronary, and ends up flying down the lane with the ball and finally making the 7-10 split...the hard way.

The next day, the papers reveal that MacDugal was worth billions of dollars and that in his will, he had bequeathed $1 million to the Big Ten Lanes team that ended up in first place at the end of the season in which he expired.

The competition boils down to the Boors vs. the Regi-Men. The Regi-Men realize that the Boors are their only real competition for the money, but the Boors, as usual, don't take either the competition—or the money—very seriously.

The Regi-Men, on the other hand, take the whole thing *very* seriously...seriously enough in fact to take steps to make sure that they are the *guaranteed* winners of MacDugal's million.

A few nights before the final games, while the Boors are pouring down a few cold ones in Tony's Temporary Work-Stoppage, Reggie loosens the bolts of the right front wheel of the Boors' old Econoline van.

On their way home, the wheel flies off, the van goes off a cliff and explodes, and the next day the Regi-Men show up at the Big Ten Lanes wearing black armbands in mourning for their fallen comrades. They diligently play the part of saddened warriors who are nonetheless continuing on because they know that their colleagues would have wanted them to.

Only the Regi-Men—and the now-dead Boors—know the truth.

Late one night, after all the teams have finished bowling, Reggie keeps his teammates at the Lanes practicing. After all, you can't get ahead without "study and practice", study and practice", study and..."

Suddenly, the lights go out.

The Regi-Men are all alone in a darkened bowling alley in the wee hours of the morning.

And they've got blood on their hands.

And now they've also got visitors.

They're baaaaack! (Sorry, Tobe. Couldn't help it.)

That's right, the Boors are back in town, folks.

Yes, the Bad News Boors returned from the dead to exact revenge from the Regi-Men, and also to bowl one last game...this time using the arms and legs of the Regi-Men as the pins, and Reggie Rambeaux' head as the ball. (See the entries below for details on the deaths of the Regi-Men and the Boors final game).

"Pinfall" is a fun piece, an honest tribute to E.C. Comics, and we can only lament the vagaries of film production budgets, and hope that someday Stephen King will choose to publish "Pinfall" as a real short story.

But in the meantime, it is my hope that this introductory summation, and the entries that follow, will at least give you a taste of a Stephen King pie that you probably would not have been able to enjoy any other way.

"PINFALL"

[An unfilmed segment of the film "Creepshow 2"]
People

BAD NEWS BOOR #5 Unnamed member of the Boors. If the Boors won the $1 million, he couldn't decide whether to buy a hundred-dollar hooker every night for 2,000 nights, or a twenty-five-dollar floozy for 8,000 nights.

BAD NEWS BOOR #4 Unnamed member of the Boors.

BAD NEWS BOOR #3 Unnamed member of the Boors. If the Boors won the $1 million, he wanted to buy five season tickets for the Miami Dolphins.

THE BAD NEWS BOORS Big Ten Lanes bowling team. They adopted J. Fred MacDugal after he was tormented by the Regi-Men. They were later killed by the Regi-Men in a van accident. They all returned from the dead and wreaked their revenge on Reggie's team.

THE CHAUFFEUR The unnamed chauffeur who drove C. Hamilton Wilburforce.

THE CLEANUP CREW Three unnamed men who cleaned up the Big Ten Lanes after closing.

THE DEAD CHOOCH Here's how the script described him:

> "[He] looks more like an overcooked roast with nothing but black sockets running dark-colored fluids where its eyes and nose should be. The teeth make us realize that it is a face. The grinning teeth that seem to be trying to shape the rotting flesh around them, trying to speak, but just rasping, gurgling."

HOUSEMAN, JOHN C. Hamilton Wilburforce is described as looking "somewhat like John Houseman."

THE JANITOR The Big Ten Lanes janitor. He had to wait to lock up the Lanes while the Regi-Men practiced.

LOUIE Bad News Boor team member. He looked like "Tough" Tony Gallento from "On The Waterfront." Louie was Chooch Mandolino's right hand man. All he ever said was "Definitely!" – a total of eighteen times in the segment. He said one of these "definitely's" after he came back from the dead.

MacDUGAL, J. FREDERICK The script described him as "an old Scot who would have died years ago but wasn't willing to pay the stiff rates for a funeral. We're talkin' *old*, friends." Turns out he was a "billionaire bowler." MacDugal was in the Big Tens on team night, and after he interrupted one of Reggie's shots, he was "adopted" by the Boors. He died later that night and left "upwards of three billion dollars." He left $1 million to the Big Ten Lanes bowling team with the highest score at the end of the season. This triggered a rivalry between the Bad News Boors and the Regi-Men, which ended up with the Regi-Men sabotaging the Boors' van and sending the team to a fiery death off a cliff.

THE MAINTENANCE MAN Unnamed worker at the bowling alley who told the Bad News Boors that J. Fred MacDugal was dead.

MANDOLINO, CHOOCH The captain of the Bad News Boors. He was a "Donkey Kong look-alike" with a "Neanderthal brow."

A NEWS CREW A news crew from 2-VU covered the final games of the million dollar tournament.

THE OFFICIAL SCOREKEEPER A "Don Knotts look-alike," the scorekeeper was a little guy who wore a sweatshirt with "Official Scorekeeper" written across its front.

ONE BIG FATSO An unnamed bowler who "look[ed] and sound[ed] like Ralph Cramden [sic]." In the following dignified manner, he queried Wilburforce as to the specifics of MacDugal's bequest:

> FATSO
> "Hey, hold it, hold it. You mean to say that the team wid the best score at the end o' dis season gets a million clams?"

RAMBEAUX, REGGIE Captain of the Regi-Men and owner of Reggie's Computer Supermarket.

REGI-MAN #4 Unnamed member of the Regi-Men.

REGI-MAN #1 Unnamed member of the Regi-Men.

REGI-MAN #3 Unnamed member of the Regi-Men.

REGI-MAN #2 Unnamed member of the Regi-Men.

THE REGI-MEN Five-man bowling team helmed by Reggie Rambeaux.

THE ROVING REPORTER The reporter from 2-VU who covered the final games of the million dollar tournament, as well as the original coverage of MacDugal's bequest. The script described him as a "Bill Murray type."

TWO OTHER OFFICIALS Two unnamed Big Ten Lanes officials who stood with Wilburforce as he revealed details about MacDugal's will to the bowlers.

WILBURFORCE, C. HAMILTON C. Hamilton Wilburforce, Esquire. Attorney for MacDugal and the executor of his estate after his death. He was "a snooty old-schooler in a three-piece pinstripe. His hair is slicked down and he actually wears pince-nez, low on his nose, just above an eyebrow-pencil moustache."

Places

BIG TEN LANES PRO SHOP Shop in the Lanes. On team night after the Boors' death, Reggie was polishing his ball in the shop when the lights went out.

BIG TEN LANES The bowling alley where the Regi-Men and the Bad News Boors bowled on team night.

BIG TEN LANES PARKING LOT The bowling alley's parking lot was filled with K-cars and Datsuns.

EVERYTOWN The setting for "Pinfall."

HIGHTOP ROAD The road where the Boors went off the cliff.

INDUSTRIAL PARK This was where the Regi-Men worked.

"NORMAN BATES LAND" See the "Things" entry "REGGIE'S EYES."

THE SHARPER IMAGE Company where the Regi-Men bought their combination-lock attache cases.

THE STEEL MILL This was where the Bad News Boors worked.

"THREE RIVERS STADIUM AFTER A STEELER LOSS" This was how the script described what the Big Ten Lanes looked like after team night.

TONY'S TEMPORARY WORK-STOPPAGE Blue collar bar "In the Hills Above the Mills." The nightspot of choice for the Bad News Boors. They usually drank shots and beers.

2-VU TV station that sent a news crew to cover the final games of the million dollar tournament.

Things

"THE BEER BARREL POLKA" Song sung by the Bad News Boors. They didn't sing any words, though, instead choosing to write their own lyrics, which consisted mainly of "Da Da, Da Da Da, Da Da Da Da Da, Da Da Da Da Da Da, Daaaaaaaaaaaa."

BIG LEAGUE BOWLATHON VIDEO GAME Regi-Man #3 was killed by being thrown into the screen of this game by one of the dead Bad News Boors.

BLACK ARMBANDS The Regi-Men wore black armbands on the team night following the death of the Bad News Boors.

A BLACK SIXTEEN-POUNDER Chooch Mandolino's bowling ball.

THE BOORS' ATTIRE For work, the Boors dressed in hardhats, biballs, and Levi jackets.

THE BOORS' CRASH When the wheel loosened by Reggie flew off the Boors' van, the van went over a cliff and exploded. The explosion was described in Scene 225 of the script as follows:

> "KA-BLOOOOOOOOOOOOOOOOOOOEY! An enormous explosion occurs halfway down the cliffside and an orange and black cloud that looks like napalm appears. That cloud seems to roll like a runaway beachball down, down, down toward the valley where other orange clouds are belching out of the smokestacks and furnaces of the steel mills."

THE BOORS' SPENDING SPREE In Tony's Temporary Work-Stoppage, after the game in which Reggie Rambeaux threw a gutter ball for a final score of 209, the Boors – now the new favorites to win MacDugal's money – talked about how they would spend their winnings:

> BOOR #3
> I'm gonna buy me some season football tickets...five o' dem, so we can all go.
>
> BOOR #4
> Hey. There's no football teams around here.
>
> BOOR #3
> I know. I'm gonna buy these tickets for the Miami Dolphins.

A big, rowdy, hooting, back-slapping cheer goes up from everyone in the bar. The regular patrons are living out their own fantasies through the "celebrity bowlers."

BOOR #5
I can't decide if I should get me a hundred-dollar hooker for two thousand nights...(a big howl interrupts him and he has to shout over it)...OR A TWENTY-FIVE DOLLAR FLOOZY FOR EIGHT THOUSAND NIGHTS!

BRUNSWICK BLACK J. Fred MacDugal's bowling ball – an old Brunswick black.

BUICK Reggie Rambeaux's car.

THE CREEP'S SUMMATION After the Boors bowled one last game with the Regi-Men's arms and legs, and using Reggie's head as the ball, the Creep said "Oh, well, Reggie Rambeaux always was a...pin-head. Heh, heh, heh."

THE "DAILY BLAB" The newspaper that announced the death of J. Fred MacDugal.

THE DEATH OF REGGIE RAMBEAUX Reggie was killed by the dead Chooch. Chooch used his "charred but powerful hand to push Reggie's head down onto the iron framework of the ball-drill." He then drilled "three holes, about size nine right into Reggie Rambeaux' skull."

THE DEATH OF REGI-MAN #4 Regi-Man #4 was killed by being flung face first into the hot dog rotisserie. The rotisserie prongs bit into his head and his face was then melted by the microwaves.

THE DEATH OF REGI-MAN #3 Regi-Man #3 was killed by being flung head first into the giant video screen of the Big League Bowlathon bowling game. His head bowled a strike. Smoke leaked out of the guy's pores. The Boor that did away with him looked like he'd "been blow-dried by the main jets of a Titan-three rocket."

THE DEATH OF REGI-MAN #2 When the Boors came back from the dead to get even, Regi-Man #2 was killed by having his neck torn open. When he was found by Regi-Man #3, blood was pumping out of his neck. Regi-Man #2 was the first to die.

"DEFINITELY!" The only word Tony Gallento said in all of "Pinfall." He said it seventeen times alive, and one time after he was dead.

DESINEX CANS The cans that were in the Big Ten Lanes lockerroom.

DURABEAM FLASHLIGHT This was the flashlight held by Regi-Man #4 as Reggie Rambeaux loosened the bolts on the wheel of the Boors' Econoline van.

EIGHTY-TWO YEARS OLD MacDugal's age when he died at the bowling alley.

"A FEW BOLTS" Reggie "simply...loosened a few bolts, that's all." He emphasized this to his team members to convince himself that he didn't kill the Boors, that it was the "luck of the draw" that killed the team.

GUTTER BALL Reggie threw a gutter ball the night the crew from 2-VU reported on the million dollar tournament.

HEADSTONES Reggie told a reporter that if the Regi-Men won the tournament, they would buy each of the Boors a "specially designed" headstone to commemorate them properly."

HONORARY MEMBER After MacDugal is harassed by the Regi-Men, the Boors make him an honorary member of their team.

"IN THE HILLS ABOVE THE MILLS" The sign above the the huge gingerbread mirror behind the bar in Tony's Temporary Work-Stoppage.

"JACK DAVIS DRAWINGS" This was how the script described the Bad News Boors.

K-CARS AND DATSUNS The Big Ten Lanes parking lot was filled with K-cars and Datsuns.

THE LAST GAME After the dead Bad News Boors did away with the Regi-Men in a variety of juicy ways, they bowled one last game. This scene occurs in Scene 241 and an EFX shot in Scene 242:

241 INT. BIG TEN LANES - NIGHT

The director (and the effects people) will have to choreograph this final shot for the best effect, so I won't describe it in too much detail.

What we see, basically, is a parody of team-night, with the BAD NEWS BOORS, each charred to a flaking, decaying crisp, drinking bloody beers, giving each other the high-fives (and losing a few over-cooked fingers each time).

The pins are the arms and legs of the REGI-MEN. The ball, of course, is Reggie Rambeaux' head!

As that head bowls a strike, the picture FREEZES, and DISSOLVES TO:

242 EFX

A DRAWING of the head among the flying pins, the closing panel of the story as it appears in CREEPSHOW COMICS. THE CAMERA PULLS BACK and we begin to HEAR THE CACKLING of the Creepshow Creep punching over the music score.

CREEP
Remember, kiddies, bad luck always comes to the greedy.

[NOTE: See THE CREEP'S SUMMATION for the final word on the fate of Reggie Rambeaux. — sjs]

LEMON BLEND COOLER MACHINE It was next to the hot dog rotisserie in the Big Ten Lanes snack counter.

THE LIMOUSINE When C. Hamilton Wilburforce, Esquire, went to the Big Ten Lanes to inform the teams of MacDugal's bequest, he arrived in "the largest automobile ever seen by the clientele of the Big Ten Lanes. It seemed "about the size of the Goodyear Blimp...mainly because its superstructure was so far off the ground." It was "three steps up from the pave to the small studio-apartment that [was] the driver's cockpit."

MacDUGAL'S ESTATE When MacDugal died, he left "upwards of three billion dollars."

"MILLION BUCK BOWLERS KILLED IN FREAK CRASH!" The headline of the newspaper story detailing the fiery death of the Bad News Boors.

"MR. MUGGS, I PRESUME" The way Reggie addressed J. Fred MacDugal.

NIKE SWEATSUITS AND ADIDAS The Regi-Men's warm-up attire.

1968 DODGE ECONOLINE VAN The Boors van. It was rusty. Reggie loosened the bolts on one of the wheels of the van, causing it to fly off, sending the Boors to a fiery death. [NOTE: See the entry THE BOORS' CRASH.] After the van went off the cliff, "the fireball that once was the BOORS' Econoline...spread, when it hit the valley floor, like one of those super slow-motion drops of water you see on NOVA."

"NUMBER TEN DIES AT BIG TEN" Newspaper headline that announced MacDugal's death at the Big Ten Lanes. It was a front page story in the "Daily Blab."

$1 MILLION DOLLAR ESCROW ACCOUNT MacDugal left a provision in his will that gave $1 million to the Big Ten bowling team with the highest score at the end of the season in which he died.

PAGE 72 The page of the first draft script on which "Pinfall" begins.

PARODI CIGARS The smoke of choice for the Bad News Boors.

REGGIE'S BOWLING BALL Reggie used a marbleized blue ball with custom-drilled holes.

REGGIE'S DRILL LIMERICK Reggie and his men chanted the following while jogging:

"There was an old guy named Dave
Who kept a dead whore in a cave
He'd often admit
'I'm a bit of a shit
but think of the money I save'."

REGGIE'S EYES As the Regi-Men watched the Boors' van go off the cliff in a fireball, Reggie's eyes...

"[had] that psychotic glaze that we saw earlier when the quartz light drove him to distraction. A switch thrown somewhere inside his brain has left him in Norman Bates Land. The mill-furnace flames reflecting in the windshield look like the fires of hell and they seem to be consuming the wide-eyes Reggie, who is now in a CLOSE-UP on the other side of the glass."

REGGIE'S MANTRA "Study and practice, study and practice, study and practice."

REGGIE'S QUESTION ABOUT "STATIONS IN LIFE" Reggie Rambeaux wanted to know "Why is it that lazy, illiterate, slovenly good-for-nothing imbeciles are always so righteously proud of their stations in life?" This seems to be a statement by Stephen King (via George Romero) in which he takes a stand against the self-righteous, pompous assholes in the world like Reggie Rambeaux. There was an interview King once did about *Cujo* in which he said something along the lines of "Yeah, Joe Camber's an asshole, but he's MY asshole." Also, in "Pinfall," Chooch asks "Why is it that smart guys is always such shits?" King has always railed against the kind of attitudes that he gave Reggie, and in fact, has defended his own status as a "hick." In an interview he did with *Inside,* the Orono High School student newspaper, when asked "Why do you stay in Maine?," King said: "I'm a hick. I grew up here. I went to one-room schoolhouses. There were outhouses. I am a hick and this is where I feel at home."

THE REGI-MEN'S ATTIRE At the Industrial Park, as the Regi-Men read about MacDugal's death, they were "each in a suit and tie, each with a combination-lock attache from the Sharper Image."

RIGHT FRONT WHEEL The wheel of the Bad News Boors' van. The wheel that was loosened by Reggie Rambeaux. It separated from the axle, sending the Boors to a fiery death.

SCENE 206 The opening scene of "Pinfall" in the "Creepshow 2" script.

SECOND PLACE The night MacDugal died, the Boors ended up in second place.

THE 7-10 SPLIT J. Fred MacDugal had bowled at least twenty frames a day for seventy years and had never made the 7-10 split. However, on the day he died he achieved his dream by going down the lane head first after he had a heart attack in the middle of a swing. Here's how the script captured the moment:

"He slides over the slick boards, reaching the end of the alley, and for the first time in his life, he makes a seven-ten spare. His ball takes out the ten, his head takes out the seven." The reaction among his "adopted team members was so:

CHOOCH
Holy shit! That's what you call makin' it the hard way!

LOUIE
Definitely!

MacDugal's body then gets stuck in the pin sweeping machinery:

"The sweep comes down from overhead and it jams against J. Fred's stiff body. A safety mechanism kicks in and the unit starts to spasm the way an elevator does when something is stuck in its bumper. BARRRAAAAACK, BARRRAAAAACK, BARRRAAAAACK! The jammed sweep makes a hideous noise."

SEVENTY YEARS J. Fred MacDugal had bowled at least twenty frames a day for seventy years and had never made the 7-10 split.

TEAM SHIRTS The Regi-Men's team shirts said "Sponsored by Reggie's Computer Supermarket."

THIRTY-FOUR PINS The Boors were in second place going into the "Million Dollar" playoff. They were thirty-four pins behind the Regi-Men.

TWENTY FRAMES A DAY J. Fred MacDugal had bowled at least twenty frames a day for seventy years. He had never made the 7-10 split.

TWENTY TEAMS The roster that made up team night at the Big Ten Lanes.

2:00 A.M. The time of night the Regi-Men stopped practicing, and the time the dead Boors decided to exact their own revenge.

209 The Regi-Men's final score on the night that Reggie Rambeaux bowled a gutterball. This dropped their lead to twenty-four pins. After this game there was something written on his face: "Something has to be done about this."

222 Reggie Rambeaux's final score the night J. Fred MacDugal was "adopted" by the Boors.

UTICA CLUB BEER The beer of choice for the Boors.

VITAMINS AND GATORADE Reggie passed these out among his team members during practice.

THE WORLD'S TENTH WEALTHIEST MAN J. Fred MacDugal at the time of his death.

4. *Lois Chiles*: She's really good in "The Hitchhiker."

Now here are some of my least favorite moments:

1. *The Music*: It's bland, uninspired, and ignorable.
2. *The Animated Wraparound Segments*: I hate animated sequences. (Although one notable feature of the "Creepshow 2" animated sequences is the presence of Stephen King's house in the background of one scene.)

What the Critics Had To Say...

"Sequels rarely equal the original, which is the case with this movie." —George Beahm, in *The Stephen King Companion* (Andrews and McMeel, 1989)

"...this collaboration has none of the inventive wit of the original King-Romero joint project...most of the goings-on in this film suggest routine movie-making. ... [T]hose who want to keep up with the King ouevre may want to bring a flashlight so they can read one of his novels while watching this film. It's hardly worth devoting a whole attention span to." —Ralph Novak, from a review in *People* magazine, May 25, 1987.

"The trouble with anthology films, even good ones, is that one lousy episode can sink the entire package. "Creepshow 2" – subpar to so-so, but marginally better than expected – never fully recovers from its deadly, barrel-bottom opener. ☆☆." —Mike Clark, from a review in *USA Today,* May 1987.

"'Creepshow 2'...has three suitably grisly ideas that are only glancingly developed. The episodes are marginally interesting, but each is a little too long. And each can be fully explained in a one-sentence synopsis." —Janet Maslin, from a review in the New York *Times*, Monday, May 4, 1987.

"Three tales of horror and terror based on short stories by Stephen King and a screenplay by George Romero should have turned out a lot better than this. ☆☆." —Mick Martin and Marsha Porter, *Video Movie Guide 1990.*

"This film is no masterpiece, by horror or any other standard, but it isn't horrible either. ... 'Creepshow 2' is a nice diversion for a hungry horror fan's night out." —Daniel Aquilante, from a review in the New York *Post,* Monday, May 4, 1987.

"SORRY, RIGHT NUMBER"

An episode of the syndicated TV series
    "Tales from the Darkside"
Broadcast Friday, November 20, 1987.
Running Time: 30 minutes (including commercials).

Directed By: John Sutherland
Produced By: Anthony Santa Croce
Written By: Stephen King
Associate Producer: Erica Fox
Supervising Producer: T.J. Castronova
Executive Producers: Richard P. Rubinstein, George A. Romero, Jerry Golod
Director of Photography: Joseph D. Urbanczyk

Editor: Seth Gaven
Music Composed By: Ken Lauber

CAST

Bill Weiderman	Arthur Taxier
Katie Weiderman	Deborah Harmon
Dawn	Rhonda Dotson
Polly	Katherine Britton
Jeff	Brandon Stewart
Connie	Nicole Huntington
Voice On Phone	Catherine Battistone
Narrator	Paul Sparer

"SORRY, RIGHT NUMBER"

"Sorry, Right Number" is an original screenplay by Stephen King written as an episode for George Romero's TV series "Tales from the Darkside."

The episode opens with Katie Weiderman, the wife of successful horror novelist William Weiderman, talking on the phone with her sister Lois. The conversation is the usual sisterly talk – the kids, which one needed dental work, the fact that Katie's eldest daughter was away at college, and that Katie didn't like having her children so far away from her, etc. But Katie also mentions that her husband hasn't been feeling well lately, and that he couldn't sleep. He'd been having headaches, and thought each one was "the start of a brain tumor." But, she blew it off, saying that he was always like this between books. During the conversation, their son Jeff comes into the kitchen and asks if he can watch the movie version of his dad's first book, *Spider's Kiss*. His sister Connie tells him it's too gory for him, but Katie says his father will tape it for him...but he has to edit out the gory parts.

While she's talking to Lois, the other line rings, and Katie puts Lois on hold to take the call. She hears a sobbing woman, someone who is obviously emotionally distraught, trying to say something, trying to tell her something. Katie thinks it's her daughter Polly calling from school with yet another crisis. Suddenly, the phone goes dead.

The rest of the episode, up until the climax, is Katie trying to track down the caller, and Bill going along and humoring her.

Throughout the evening, though, every now and then...Bill flinches.

After ascertaining that her daughter was all right, and her own mother likewise, and that the reason her sister's phone was off the hook was because she fell asleep, Katie feels better, but still has a disoncerting sense that the caller was "one of mine."

Bill calms her, and sends her to bed. He'll finish taping "Spider's Kiss" for Jeffy, and then he'll be up to bed. Maybe she'll still be awake, she tells him. When she leaves the room, he flexes his left hand.

Time: 10:31 P.M.

The clock changes, and we see it's now 2:30 in the morning.

The TV screen is snow, and Bill is slumped in his easy chair. It's a scene that refers back to the earlier scene when Katie and Bill went to Dawn's house and Dawn was also slumped in the chair. Katie approached her sister expecting the worst. Then, she got off easy. Dawn was asleep. Now, with Bill, she doesn't get off that easily.

She has come down to wake him and bring him to bed, and she

finds that Bill has had a massive heart attack and died.

Fade out.

Fade in ten years later.

It's the tenth anniversary of Bill's death.

It's also Polly's wedding day.

Polly comes into the study where Katie is writing a thank-you note to her sister. Mother and daughter talk about the wedding, and Polly mentions her father, saying she knows her mother still misses him.

Katie cries, and sends Polly out, promising she'll be right out to have some champagne and dance with Jack, Polly's new husband.

Katie finishes the thank-you note and, while rummaging through Bill's desk for a stamp, comes across the video of "Spider's Kiss" that Bill was taping for Jeff the night he died.

She puts the tape in the VCR and, while watching scenes from the movie, goes into some sort of trance in which she reaches out, dials a phone number and sobs into the phone, "take him to the hospital, he's going to have a heart attack."

The line disconnects, and she realizes that she has called her old phone number. She tries it again and it's not in service.

Katie drops the phone and we fade to black.

Katie had called herself from the future to try and warn her younger self that Bill was in trouble. The power of love can transit not only distance, but time as well, it seems.

I like "Sorry, Right Number" very much. It is an emotionally powerful piece with just the right touch of eerie "Twilight Zone" mood to it.

It is currently not available on videotape, but I believe it is broadcast as a "Tales from the Darkside" episode on those syndicated stations that carry the show.

Here are a few notable facts from the episode:

•The first time we see Bill, who is doomed to die from a massive heart attack, we hear a heart beat on the soundtrack.

•*Spider's Kiss* was the title of Bill's first book, and apparently one of his most memorable, since Dawn had it in hardcover, and the operator mentioned that title specifically when she heard his name.

•The Weiderman's phone number was 555-4408.

•The Weiderman's second line – the number Katie gets the call from the future on – was 555-4409.

•Ronnie Hansen, one of Polly's college classmates, asked Polly to the dance Saturday night.

•Dawn was Katie's youngest sister.

•Jerry was Dawn's husband, and the night Bill and Katie went to her house, he was in Burlington on business.

•After Katie called her mother and ascertained that she was all right, she told her mother that she had a little diarrhea and couldn't talk to her.

•Lois was Katie's sister, and Polly, Connie, and Jeffy's aunt.

•The telephone operator loved Bill's books. Bill hung up on her as she was asking if she could send him a book for an autograph.

•Dawn's phone number was 555-6169.

•Bill had bought a gun the previous month after all those murders in Coleville. He brought it with him to Dawn's house.

•Bill says "I heard some people just eat up my books, but this is ridiculous" when he goes to Dawn's and finds that Dawn's baby Dustin had been teething on a hardcover copy of *Spider's Kiss*.

•When Dawn apologizes for the baby eating up the book, Bill says "I know some critics who would say he made a good choice."

•Jack was Polly's husband.

"THE RUNNING MAN"

"I choose Ben Richards. That boy's one mean motherfucker."

—Agnes McArdle

Released November 1987, by Tri-Star/Taft Entertainment.
Videotape released by Vestron Video; $79.98.
Running Time: 101 minutes.
Rated R

Directed By: Paul Michael Glaser
Producers: Tim Zinneman, George Linder
Screenplay By: Steven E. deSouza
Based On The Novel
The Running Man By: Richard Bachman (Stephen King)
Executive Producers: Keith Barish, Rob Cohen
Photography: Thomas Del Ruth
Editors: Mark Roy Warner, Edward A. Warschilka, John Wright
Music: Harold Faltermeyer
Costumes: Robert Blackman
Choreography: Paula Abdul

Songs

"Running Away With You"
Music & Lyrics by
Harold Faltermeyer and John Parr

"The Death March"
/ "Paula's Theme"
By Jackie Jackson and Glen Barbee

"The Theme from
'Gilligan's Island'"

CAST

Ben Richards	Arnold Schwarzenegger
Amber Mendez	Maria Conchito Alonso
Laughlin	Yaphet Kotto
Fireball	Jim Brown
Captain Freedom	Jesse Ventura
Dynamo	Erland Van Lidth
Weiss	Marvin J. McIntyre
Buzzsaw	Gus Rethwisch
Subzero	Professor Toru Tanaka

Mic	Mick Fleetwood
Stevie	Dweezil Zappa
Damon Killian	Richard Dawson
Brenda	Karen Leigh Hopkins
Sven	Sven Thorsen
Lenny	Eddie Bunker
Med Tech	Bryan Kestner
Valdez	Anthony Penya
Tony	Kurt Fuller
Agent	Kenneth Lerner
Amy	Dey Young
Phil Hilton	Roger Bumpass
Announcer	Don Pardo
Mrs. Agnes McArdle	Dona Hardy
Edith Wiggins	Lynne Stewart
Leon	Bill Margolin
Narrator	Joe Leahy
Lieutenant Sanders	George P. Wilbur
Chico	Tom Rosales, Jr.
Suzie Checkpoint	Sondra Holt

Also...

Anthony Brubaker, Joel Kramer, Billy Lucas, Daniel Celario, Mario Celario, Sidney Chankin, Kim Pawlik, Roger Kern, Barbara Lux, Franco Columbu, Lin Shaye, Boyd R. Kestner, Wayne Grace, Charlie Phillips, Greg Lewis, John William James, Jon Cutler, Kerry Brennan, Paula Brown, Megan Gallivan, Suzie Hardy, Debby Harris, Melissa Hurley, Marlene Lange, Morgan Lawley, Cindy Millican, Andrea Moen, Mary Ann Oedy, Karen Owens, Sharon Owens, Pamela Rossi, Mia Togo.

"THE RUNNING MAN"

You can't sit down to watch "The Running Man" expecting to see a Stephen King film. It just ain't the same. I enjoy watching the film, but it never fails to bewilder me when screenwriters "adapt" a novel to the point where it's barely recognizable when compared with the original work.

Ben Richards is still the center of the story, but now he works for the government rather than being a desperate father driven to appearing on "The Running Man" TV game show on the slim chance he'll survive and be able to save his family.

Also, de Souza populated the film with live cartoon characters whose job it was to hunt down the "running men" and do them in as violently as possible. So, if we put aside any preconceived expectations as King fans, the question remains, "Is the film any good?" And thankfully, we can say, yes, it is. If you can forget the novel and just screen it as a science fiction film, you'll have a good time. The film is fast-paced, exciting, and has a snotty sense of humor. Richard Dawson is superb as sleaze-ball game show host Damon Killian, and

Schwarzenegger is...well, he's Schwarzenegger.

The real-life cartoon characters are so bizarre that they're fascinating, and the film's premise of a population that has resorted to blood sports in the wake of an economic collapse is believable and well-developed. (Just watch the news. Especially the reports of soccer matches.)

If someone wanted to film another Bachman novel, I'd love to see either *Thinner* or *The Long Walk* attempted. And since *Rage* was essentially a rehearsal for *Misery*, perhaps Rob Reiner might consider taking on that peculiar psychodrama next?

Overall, "The Running Man," directed by "Starsky and Hutch" alumni Paul Michael Glaser, is an entertaining contribution to genre films.

Here are a few of my favorite moments from the film:

1. *The Jet Sled*: These scenes are genuinely exciting and filmed with edge-of-your-seat tension. Them suckers move!

2. *Maria Conchita Alonso*: Ever since "Moscow on the Hudson," I have admired this Latin beauty. In "The Running Man," she takes her role seriously while giving it just enough hysteria to make the character believable. (And she's better-looking in a body suit than Arnold, too.)

3. *Richard Dawson*: Sleaze personified. A perfect caricature of every treacly, obnoxious game-show host we've ever had the bad fortune to be subjected to on American TV (including, I'm sorry, his own "Family Feud" persona...yuck!). (Richard's performance in "The Running Man" was recognized at the 15th Annual Saturn Awards given by the Academy of Science Fiction, Fantasy, and Horror Films in August of 1988. Dawson won Best Supporting Actor for his role as Killian. Jack Nicholson won Best Actor for his role as a "horny little Devil" in "The Witches of Eastwick.")

4. *The Exploding Neck Collars*: Yup. Those collars are probably exactly what the penal institutions in this country would implement if things got as bad as imagined in the film.

5. *Paula Abdul's Choreography*: Paula, the winner of the Biggest Smile Award (she shows twenty-one-and-a-half teeth with each smile), does a great job of providing the "Solid Gold"-clone dancers with all the right moves.

Now here are some of my least favorite moments:

1. *The Opera-Singing Dynamo*: This character is just plain ridiculous. I'm sorry, but they went off the deep end with this guy.

2. *The Future Yuppies Watching the Chase*: The cuts back to some party room where these future creeps watched the goings-on just distracted and interrupted the pace. A few more reaction shots of the studio audience would probably have worked to better effect.

3. *The Music*: It could have been better; more forceful. It seemed vacant and almost invisible at times; like something from television rather than from a film. If this was intentional, it didn't work.

What the Critics Had To Say...

"It's lights, camera, and action, action, action, as this movie follows the basic Schwarzenneger formula – pain is given and returned, frequently, while Arnold lets his trademark one-liners thud to the ground." —Jami Bernard, from a video review in the New York *Post*, Friday, May 20, 1988.

"[A] ludicrous movie which, while pretending to condemn this country's increasing appetite for blood sports, revels in violence. ☆." —Kathleen Carroll, from a film review in the New York *Daily News*, Saturday, November 14, 1987.

"This just misses trash-classic status, but even 'Murder, She Wrote' can't give you Don Pardo, Jim Brown, Mick Fleetwood, Jesse 'The Body' Ventura, Dweezil Zappa, and Richard Dawson in a single

STUDENT CINEMA FOCUSES ON STEPHEN KING
"The Last Rung On The Ladder" and "The Lawnmower Man"

"THE LAST RUNG ON THE LADDER"

An independent production of Talisman
Films, 1987
(Currently unavailable on videotape)
Running Time: 12 minutes 20 seconds

Directed By: James Cole & Dan Thron
Produced By: James Cole
Screenplay By: James Cole & Dan Thron
Based On The Short Story By: Stephen King
Edited By: James Cole
Director of Photography: Dan Thron
Music By: Anne Livermore
Music Recorded By: Thom Untersee
Sound By: James Cole & Dan Thron
Technical Assistance: Bill Elliott
Special Thanks To: Whitfield Johnson

CAST

Larry	Adam Houhoulis
Kitty	Melissa Whelden
Father	Nat Wordell
Older Larry	Adam Howes

"The Last Rung on the Ladder" is a student film that was completed on a miniscule budget of between $1500 and $1600, shot in Super 8mm, and yet is suprisingly effective for the amount of money the director and producer had to work with.

The film is obviously a non-professional production, but the screenplay, the direction, and yes, even the acting (all amateurs) all contribute to a faithful adaptation of one of Stephen King's most poignant short stories.

I like this film very much, and I can only imagine what young director Cole could do with the right money and equipment.

In conversation, Cole mentioned to me that he had to make one minor change in the story before he could use Melissa Whelden, the young actress who played Kitty. In King's short story, Kitty ends up becoming a call-girl who commits suicide. In Cole's adaptation, the final newspaper headline reads "Young Girl Swan-Dives To Her Death" rather than "Call-Girl..."—one of those creative concessions amateur filmmakers have to make when dealing with people who are essentially not in the film business. Out of res-

pect for Melinda's parents, Cole and Thron decided to eliminate the prostitution reference from the script.

There is a fun "insider" reference in the film for King fans, too. Larry's character says that his mother is over at "Miss Abagail's," a nod to Mother Abagail in *The Stand*. (Jim Gonis did the same thing with his "Lawnmower Man." In that film, he had a rookie cop named "Bannerman.")

Jim Cole wrote a piece for the September, 1988 issue of *Castle Rock* called "The Good and Bad of Film Adaptation" in which he detailed the long road from the idea of making the film to the final product.

Here are a few excerpts from Jim's article:

"The Last Rung on the Ladder'...does not lend itself to the screen as easily as one might think. Hollywood, for the most part, has not made completely faithful adaptations of Mr. King's novels, so how can two students with no budgets and no equipment do any better? Yet, my partner Dan Thron and I believed anything was possible with enough enthusiasm.

June, 1986: After almost a month of searching, I find a genuine post and beam barn in Dennis, Massachusetts. Permission to use for filming is given by the owner, a 91-year-old lawyer who mentioned nothing about liability!

June 21: Principle photography begins. My 1730 house is used for the interior shots. Gathered on the set are co-director Dan Thron, 15, and the two leads, Larry (Adam) and Kitty (Melissa), a bubbly 11-year-old who so matches the story's description it's almost scary.

July 8: Barn interior shots begin. To simulate the deep hay pile, two layers of empty boxes are positioned on the barn floor, with a mattress on top. Lighting is the worst. The dark, cavernous interiors cause internal light meters to not register, when the light on the actors is often overexposed. A lot of guessing comes in handy.

July 29: We only have this last day to use the barn...and the list of required shots is enormous. I have to be serious with the kids and tell them there's no time to goof off today. Within the afternoon, everything is shot. All the pickup shots, the climbing, jumping, falling shots...everything we can think of is shot. All the possible accidents have been avoided, save the time Adam brushed against a hot light and burnt his hand.

August 4: I film the credits in the Berkshires,

The
Last
Rung
on the
Ladder

Directors Jim Gonis (left) and Jim Cole (right).

250 miles away. The magic of film.

August 9: We complete the prologue and epilogue. A grown-up Larry contemplates the letter he has just received from his sister. To make her letter as readable as possible, the actual letter is nearly two feet wide, with oversized handwriting.

August 12-November 22: The first stage of post-production. Even in the rough cut, I see the film is coming together.

April 23, 1987: We record Anne Livermore's original piano score.

October 2: After months of editing and reshooting, the film is transferred down to VHS. Our true goal is achieved, for this Super-8 film looks just as good on video as a bigger budget 16 mm film.

October 14: We send a copy to Stephen King. If Stephen actually saw the film, I only hope he enjoyed it."

Tyson Blue reviewed both "Last Rung" and "Lawnmower Man" in the January 1989 issue of *Castle Rock,* and acknowledged the excellence these young student filmmakers achieved with a small budget and non-professional equipment. Ty's right. Both films are testaments to what dedication and commitment can accomplish.

There are currently no plans for a home video release of either film, although both Jim Cole and Jim Gonis have expressed the hope that they can occasionally show their films at conventions and film festivals.

If you're lucky, maybe you'll get a chance to see either of these two fine short films.

Adam Houhoulis and Melissa Whelden of "Last Rung"

"THE LAWNMOWER MAN"

An unreleased student film, June 1987
(Currently unavailable on videotape)
Running time: 12 minutes
Filmed entirely on location in Dix Hills, Long Island
  and Flushing, New York.

Directed By: Jim Gonis
Produced By: Jim Gonis
Screenplay By: Mike De Luca
Based On The Short Story By: Stephen King
Cinematographer: Ethan Reiff
Edited By: Andy Huelsebusch
Sound By: Jim Calciano
Music By: Charles Nieland
Additional Sound and Production Management:
  Mike De Luca
Boom Man: Matt Rosenfeld
Assistant Camera and Gaffer: Barry Sherman
Hoof Effects Created By: Craig Lindberg
Mower and Makeup Effects By: Ethan Reiff, Barry
  Sherman, Jim Gonis

Andy Clark ("Karras") in "Lawnmower Man"

CAST

Parkette	E.D. Phillips
Karras	Andy Clark
Mrs. Parkette	Helen Hanft
Cop	Tony Di Sante
Rookie Cop ("Bannerman")	Robert Tossberg
Castonmeyer the neighbor	Neil Schimmel
Little Girl	Becky Taub
Sheila	Fayth Schlossberg
Kid	Michael Albert
Gas Jockey	Jim Gonis
Dog	Misha
Cat	Poochi
Critter	Pap

E.D. Phillips ("Parkette") in "Lawnmower Man."

"The Lawnmower Man" is a fun film. Jim Cole, the director of the other student film reviewed in this section, "The Last Rung on the Ladder," sent me a videotape with both his film and Jim Gonis's on it, and thus I was able to review them both for *The Shape Under the Sheet*. "The Lawnmower Man," while obviously a student production, is nonetheless a close-to-professional job. I enjoyed watching it, and asked Jim Gonis to contribute something on the making of the film for my readers.

Here's what he had to say:

"In 1985, I was in a junior-level NYU film class and I wanted to direct a short. I didn't have a script.

"Lawnmower Man" director, Jim Gonis.

"The Lawnmower Man" came to mind first. The crew liked the idea and we went with it.

The story had already been simplified and visualized by Stephen King and Walt Simonson in the *Marvel Comics* "Bizarre Adventures" adaptation, so we started there and worked out a storyboard.

We found the perfect house in Dix Hills, Long Island. It took some nerve to ask the owners if they'd let us use their house for exteriors, but they were very willing and considerate. (The homeowner, Neil Schimmel, has a brief spot in the film as Castonmeyer the neighbor.)

Casting the film looked to be a potential problem: No large-sized men had answered our "Backstage" newspaper ad for the role of Karras (but we did get fifty resumes for the bit role of the rookie cop.) Luckily, a friend of mine introduced us to an actor friend, Andrew Clark, who could look the part and was willing to do it. For the role of Parkette, we chose E.D. Phillips, and he brought on his friend Helen Hanft for the role of Mrs. Parkette.

The project was ambitious for all of us, but the shoot went smoothly thanks to ample preparation.

On Mr. Clark's first shooting day, he asked how Karras should speak. Should he adopt a barrel-chested, salt-o'-the-earth voice, or should he take on the demeanor of a simpleton (a la Jordy Verrill)? After much debate, we went with the latter.

Thanks to the perfectionism of first-time cameraman Ethan Reiff and his assistant Barry Sherman, the rushes looked great. Upon seeing them, I remember us jumping up and down with enthusiasm, wondering how our peers could present such blasé attitudes about their own work. On the basis of the unfinished footage, we did well in class. But I wanted to finish the film.

Working with a core crew of four or five, and during a heat wave (my cat nearly died), we fin

ished shooting.

Not wanting to ever remove all his clothing (understandably; this was after all, just a student film), Mr. Clark's near-naked Karras scenes were usually cheated with camera angles or obstructions. What he had to chew down was pre-cut, pre-washed grass; what appears to be a dead mole was actually boiled liver, food coloring, and a rabbit pelt.

The lawnmower used was long dead; we would tape smoke bombs inside it for the appearance of exhaust. When it seems to eat its way through a chair, what shoots out are shavings that came with the guinea pig I'd borrowed. (I couldn't get a real mole.) Some of these innovations work better than others, but it goes by so fast nobody seems to mind.

I found a good composer named Charles Nieland to do a synth score, and my friend Craig Lindberg constructed Karras's cloven hooves (used in a tight insert shot).

After months in various stages of edit, "The Lawnmower Man" was completed in June, 1987 at a length of twelve minutes and $4,000 over budget.

The film was kindly reviewed by Tyson Blue in *Castle Rock* and shown at the Horrorfest '89 film festival. I've been informed by Milton Subotsky that he holds the rights to the story, so apart from an occasional festival screening, the film, unfortunately, won't be very widely seen. But as an educational exercise that became a labor of love, I feel it was well worth the effort that went into it."

Jim also told me that he heard that there is now talk that Milton Subotsky is planning to build a feature film around the story, and that it may get produced in Los Angeles.

It's too bad that more people won't get to see this adaptation of "The Lawnmower Man." It really is very well done and deserves a wider audience.

unified experience." —Mike Clark, from a video review in *USA Today*, Friday, May 13, 1988.

"All movies like this need a Girl, whose function is to be pulled helplessly behind the hero as he attempts his escape. By casting Maria Conchita Alonso in the role, the filmmakers got more than they bargained for; she remains one of Hollywood's undaunted high spirits, a nice comic counterfoil for Schwarzenneger." —Roger Ebert, from a film review in the New York *Post*, Friday, November 13, 1987.

"[T]he film does have a sense of humor (are you listening, Sly and Chuck?), and some apt subtext about the dangers of edited TV footage passing for truth." —Mike Clark, from a film review in *USA Today*, Friday, November 13, 1987.

"The film tries to have it both ways, not always successfully. Like many such sci-fi movies, it's also loaded with tantalizingly subversive reflections on the state of contemporary society. It's the supposition of 'The Running Man' that we could advance from this era of blissful, Government-approved deregulation to a police state within the professional lifetime of one Johnny Carson. You could almost say that 'The Running Man' makes you stop and think." —Vincent Canby, from a film review in the New York *Times*, Friday, November 13, 1987.

"[A] silly but exciting outing...[a]nother successful variation on the big guy's standard film formula. ☆☆☆ 1/2." —Mick Martin & Marsha Porter, *Video Movie Guide 1990*.

"PET SEMATARY"

"Let God get his own cat."
–Naomi King

Released April 1989, by Paramount Pictures.
Videotape released by Paramount Home Video.
Running Time: 95 minutes.
Rated R

Directed By: Mary Lambert
Produced By: Richard P. Rubenstein
Based Upon The Novel By: Stephen King
Screenplay By: Stephen King
Associate Producer: Ralph S. Singleton
Music By: Elliot Goldenthal
Costume Designer: M. Stewart
Edited By: Michael Hill and Daniel Hanley
Production Designer: Michael Z. Hanan
Director of Photography: Peter Stein
Co-Producer: Mitchell Galin
Executive Producer: Tim Zinnemann
Assistant to Stephen King: Shirley Sonderegger
Special Make-up Designs By: Lance Anderson
Song "Pet Sematary" By Dee Dee Ramone & Daniel Rey. Performed By The Ramones

"No animals were harmed in any way during the making of this film."

Budget: $11.5 million
Gross Box-Office Receipts: $56 million (in the first thirteen weeks in release)

CAST

Louis Creed	Dale Midkiff
Jud Crandall	Fred Gwynne
Rachel Creed	Denise Crosby
Victor Pascow	Brad Greenquist
Irwin Goldman	Michael Lombard
Gage Creed	Miko Hughes
Ellie Creed	Blaze Berdahl
Missy Dandridge	Susan Blommaert
Marcy Charlton	Mara Clark
Steve Masterton	Kavi Raz
Dory Goldman	Mary Louise Wilson
Zelda	Andrew Hubatsek
Girl at Infirmary	Liz Davies
Candystriper	Kara Dalke
Jud as a Child	Matthew August Ferrell
Jud's Mother	Lisa Stathoplos
Minister	Stephen King
Rachel as a Child	Elizabeth Lireneck
Bill Baterman	Chuck Courtney
Timmy Baterman	Peter Stader
Young Jud	Richard Collier
Cop	Chuck Shaw
Seatmate #1	Dorothy McCabe
Seatmate #2	Mary R. Hughes
Logan Gate Agent	Eleanor Grace Courtemanche
Orinco Driver	Donnie Green
Budget Clerk	Lila Duffy
Hitchhike Driver	John David Moore
Ellie Creed #2	Beau Berdahl

"PET SEMATARY"

"Pet Sematary" must be counted as one of the more successful adaptations of a Stephen King work, and part of the reason might be because Stephen King wrote the screenplay from his own novel. The screenplay for "Pet Sematary" had been in circulation since 1985. As is common knowledge by now, the film was originally supposed to be a Laurel Production, with George A. Romero directing. Apparently, Romero was busy with "Monkey Shines: An Experiment in Fear" when everything started happening with "Pet Sematary," and so the directing job went to Mary Lambert, a director whose previous credits consisted of a couple of Madonna videos and the 1987 film "Siesta."

Her previous limited feature-length directorial experience notwithstanding, Lambert did a superb job with "Pet Sematary." The film is at times paralyzingly frightening, and at other times touchingly poignant. (At the screening I attended, there were audible "Awwws" when the resurrected Gage Creed said "No fair," after his father stabbed him in the neck with a hypodermic.)

Dale Midkiff and Denise Crosby are appealing in their respective roles as Louis and Rachel Creed, but the film belongs to Fred Gwynne. His Jud Crandall is flawless: He combines a perfect Maine accent with the proper demeanor to carry it off. And you thought he'd been spending all his time on Mockingbird Lane, now didn't you? (That's a genre joke for those of you who are experiencing this book – and perhaps the entire horror genre – as newcomers. Fred Gwynne, of course, played Herman Munster on the beloved TV series "The Munsters" from 1964 through 1966. And where did Herman and his family live? Why, 1313 Mockingbird Lane in Mockingbird Heights!)

"Pet Sematary" did extremely well at the box office, too. In fact, it set a box office record: The film grossed $12 million its very first weekend in release (the weekend beginning Friday, April 21, 1989), which was the highest opener ever for a movie released in the first half of the year.

Overall, I think the film succeeds on several levels: It is a faithful translation of a masterful novel, it is a competently-acted, well-produced film, and probably most important...it's scary as hell!

Here are a few of my favorite moments from the film:

1. *Fred Gwynne as Jud Crandall* : As I've already said, I think he steals the film. A terrific job by a consummate pro and acting veteran.

2. *The Zelda Goldman scenes* : If those scenes don't scare you, then you definitely have ice water pumping through your veins. Seeing the effects of spinal meningitis was bad enough, but then having Zelda appear after her death to Rachel was almost unwatchable. And here's a piece of trivia for you: Did you know that Zelda was played by a man? Yup. Check out the credits above and you'll see that she was portrayed by an actor named Andrew Hubatsek. Hell of a job, too.

3. *The manifestations in Jud's house after Gage kills him* : When Louis goes to Jud's house looking for his alive-again son, the house *changes*: the walls ooze some kind of gooey ectoplasm, distances shift in Louis's perception, and the sounds of hell can be heard from the walls. Nice special effects and very spooky, too.

4. *The Ramones' and their song "Pet Sematary"* : What can you say about a band who's previous work included starring in the classic film "Rock 'n' Roll High School," and writing and performing a song called "I Wanna Be Sedated"? They were a terrific choice to do the title cut, and they did a great job with the song. Okay, everybody, sing: "I don't wanna be buried in a Pet Sematary. I don't want to live my life again." Talk about angst, huh?

Now here are some of my least favorite moments:

1. *Dale Midkiff*: Occasionally, he's just a little bit too laid back – especially in the film's final scenes, where: 1. He discovers his reanimated son has killed his wife and eaten part of her; 2. He has to re-kill his son and set fire to his body; and, 3. He has to then carry his wife's corpse to the Wendigo Burial Ground in hopes that she's still "fresh enough" to come back okay. And yet, throughout much of this, he wears this look of "Christopher Walken" detachment that really isn't very appropriate. Was he supposed to be in shock? If he was, fine. But I didn't get that from Midkiff's acting in these scenes. Overall, though, he did a good job, although I would have liked to have seen a little more of the emotion he let out when he knelt in the highway after Gage was killed and screamed "No!" to an uncaring, unflinching God.

2. *Gage's Death Scene*: The way that truck was barrel-assing down the highway, Gage should have *exploded* from the impact, but instead, when he comes back from the dead, he's still as cute as a button. No undertaker is *that* good, you know? That truck ended up on its side, for goodness sake, and Gage was literally knocked out of his shoes! How did he come through looking so good? Either they should have pulled back a little on showing the speed of the oncoming truck, or they should have made the reanimated Gage look a lot worse.

3. *Some of the dialogue* : Some of it sounds forced and a bit stilted. For instance, during Rachel's soul-bearing to her husband about the death of her sister Zelda, she admits that after her sister's death, she ran from the house screaming that Zelda was dead, and the neighbors all thought she was crying. She admits to Louis that she was actually laughing, and he comes back with, "Well, if you were, then I salute you for it." That just doesn't sound right. I've never heard someone actually say in conversation, "I salute you for it." But, it's a small point: Generally, the dialogue rings true, except for small lapses – but after all, King's forte is novels, right?

4. *The Graveyard Blooper* : In the section where Louis goes to the cemetery to steal the body of his son, the grave is covered in one scene with flowers from the funeral, and then moments later – with no movement or action on the part of Louis – the flowers are all gone. That kind of lack of continuity should have been caught in post-production.

What the Critics Had To Say...

"Anybody who wants to see anything more vile and scummy than this movie will have to check out a neighborhood septic tank." —Ralph Novak, from a review in *People* magazine, May 15, 1989.

"A good horror film is supposed to scandalize somebody, hit you in an area that you keep walled-off, an area that's taboo. And to see the little kid eating his mother, not only killing her, but *eating* her, is pretty far out in tabooland." —Stephen King, from an interview with Mike Cidoni in the New Haven *Register,* Friday, October 6, 1989.

"There are some truly frightening moments, and Fred Gwynne gives an excellent reading of the neighbor. But there also are too many irrelevant subplots and secondary characters. So nobody's perfect." —V.A. Musetto, from a review of the "Pet Sematary" videotape in the New York *Post,* Sunday, October 15, 1989.

"Another plodding Stephen King movie. King has written a clunky screenplay, and the director, Mary Lambert, comes from rock videos. Her work has no texture, no tease. The film is all pop-out scares and wooden acting." —From the "First-Run Movies" capsule summary feature in the New York *Post.*

"Mary Lambert's film of Stephen King's *Pet Sematary* is ineptly cast (with the solitary exception of Fred Gwynne), poorly paced, directed with a thoroughly uninspired eye and, saddest of all, superficially scripted – by Stephen King himself. "Pet Sematary" is a bad movie. In fairness, however, I must report that its denouement left me with a full load of anxiety. [P]erhaps there is some vestigial visceral hook built into this inept piece of work." —John Boonstra, from a review in the New Haven *Advocate*, May 1, 1989.

"Probably the high point of the whole movie experience was the brief but trademark appearance of King in the movie. As the audience applauded, my friend sat in bewilderment at the commonness and almost forgive-me-dorkiness of Stephen King's appearance." —From a review by "Siskle E. Bert" in New Haven's South Central Community College's *The Raven*, April 25, 1989.

"'Pet Sematary,' based on one of King's better novels, is smoothly made and watchable, but it's totally impersonal. Mary Lambert has a lot of energy, and she isn't afraid of messiness and jarring tones. But she's too solemn and over-explicit for this movie, which needs much fewer literal-minded shocks. King should never write his own screenplays. He doesn't know how to conceal the wheels and pulleys of his plotting, and he relies too much on boring flashbacks and little kids with second sight. His one weird stroke is the friendly, campy ghost [Victor Pascow]. The guy keeps popping up to warn the family of danger – the top of his head gone, his eyes milky, the capillaries gray on his face. He makes the afterlife look much jollier than the dreary here-and-now." —From a review by David Edelstein in the New York *Post*, Saturday, April 22, 1989.

"[I]f 'Pet Sematary' is more memorable than most of its ilk, it's because the material is so gruesomely unflinching. [But if] 'Pet Sematary' could have boasted more authentic details in telling its devastating story, it might have been a classic instead of just another pet peeve. ☆☆." —From a review by Matt Roush in *USA Today*, Tuesday, April 25, 1989.

"...derivative and predictable . . . tasteless in the extreme . . . ☆1/2." —From a review by James Verniere in the Boston *Herald*, Friday, April 21, 1989.

"I think ['Pet Sematary'] could be [King's] best film. I was afraid it would be turned into some sort of slasher film for teens in editing, but I was pleasantly surprised. It's much more of a morality tale, which makes it stronger." —Fred Gwynne, from an interview with Marilyn Beck that appeared in Beck's "From Hollywood" column in the New York *Daily News*, Wednesday, April 5, 1989.

"This scarefest is the most faithful film adaptation of a Stephen King novel yet. [Y]ou'll love the all-out terror... ☆☆☆ 1/2." —Mick Martin & Marsha Porter, *Video Movie Guide 1990*.

"TALES FROM THE DARKSIDE THE MOVIE"

"Evisceration takes at least an hour."
—Betty the Cannibal, from
"The Wraparound Story"

Released May 1990, by Paramount.
Videotape released by Paramount Home Video.
Running Time: 93 minutes ("Cat From Hell," 23 minutes).
1. The Wraparound Story (Written by Michael McDowell.)
2. "Lot 249" (Inspired by a story by Sir Arthur Conan Doyle. Screenplay by Michael McDowell.)
3. "Cat From Hell" (Based on a story by Stephen King. Screenplay by George A. Romero.)
4. "Lover's Vow" (Written by Michael McDowell.)
Rated R

Director: John Harrison
Produced by: Richard P. Rubinstein, Mitchell Galin
Make-Up Effects Consultant: Dick Smith

CAST

"The Wraparound Story"

Betty	Deborah Harry
Priest	David Forrester
Timmy	Matthew Lawrence

"Lot 249"

Andy	Christian Slater
Lee	Robert Sedgwick
Bellingham	Steve Buscemi
Moving Man	Donald Van Horn
Mummy	Michael Deak
Susan	Julianne Moore
Museum Director	George Guidall
Dean	Kathleen Chalfant
Cabbie	Ralph Marrero

"Cat From Hell"

Halston	David Johansen
Cabbie	Paul Greeno
Drogan	William Hickey
Carolyn	Allice Drummond
Amanda	Delores Sutton
Gage	Mark Margolis

"Lover's Vow"

Preston	James Remar
Jer	Ashton Wise
Maddox	Philip Lenkowsky
Wyatt	Robert Klein
Carola	Rae Dawn Chong
Cop #1	Joe DaBenigno
Cop #2	Larry Silvestri
Gallery Patron	Donna Davidge
Margaret	Nicole Leach
John	Daniel Harrison

"TALES FROM THE DARKSIDE THE MOVIE"

"Tales from the Darkside: The Movie" is one of those periodic anthology movies that seem only to exist in the horror genre. Overall, the film is watchable, but nothing I'd go out of my way to see more than twice. (I saw it in the theater when it was released, and then I rented it when it came out on video so that I could write this section. I don't think I'll watch it when it hits cable, but I'll tape it for my collection.)

The wraparound story concerns a cannibalistic housewife (played smoothly by Blondie's Deborah Harry) who is in the midst of preparing a young boy as the main course for a dinner party that evening. The little boy forestalls the evisceration and roasting by reading her stories from a book called, yup, *Tales from the Darkside*.

The first story, which moves rather leadenly, is the segment "Lot 249," based on a short story by Sir Arthur Conan Doyle. The final scene of this segment is very reminiscent of the "Something To Tide You Over" segment from "Creepshow," but it isn't really scary or disturbing. I'd give it a C.

The second segment is the King story "Cat From Hell," and is a routine, vapid adaptation. This deserves a C+. It's kind of slow-paced, and there's no real emotional involvement with any of the characters. As with many of the film versions of King's stories, the characters end up coming off like cartoon characters.

The final segment, "Lover's Vow," is the only original story in the film (other than the wraparound.) It was written by Michael McDowell, and is the best one of the bunch. This one comes off as a real movie, rather than a slapped-together adaptation. The denouement is telegraphed a little bit before the actual climax, but for most of the story the suspense holds. The transformation special effects are incredible, and the ending is truly heartwrenching. A definite B+.

Here are a few of my favorite moments from the "Cat From Hell" segment:

1. *The direction*: It's interesting, and Harrison makes good use of the Steadicam. This contributes somewhat to the overall tone and mood of the segment, but doesn't really redeem it.

2. *The "Creepshow" feel to the segment*: It's visually obvious that Romero wrote (and possibly made some directorial suggestions about) "Cat From Hell."

Now here are some of my least favorite moments:

1. *David Johansen's performance*: It's a little affected and wooden. Why do rockers want to act?

2. *William Hickey's performance*: It's overblown, exaggerated, and cartoonish. (He was much better in "Prizzi's Honor.") (And he blinks after he's dead, too!)

3. *The changes in the story*: Romero changed the story in a couple of places: First, he had Drogan leave the house and Halston stay there with the cat, rather than have Halston take the cat in the car as in the text; and, for the climactic attack by the cat, he had the feline crawl down Halston's throat, spend some time in his stomach, and then, when Drogan returns, crawl back up out of Halston's mouth. Why? Why didn't he include the effect of the cat digging itself out of Halston's stomach as in the story?

4. *Cat-Scratch Fever*: The cat cuts Halston to ribbons on his back, and yet the guy doesn't realize it until he finds blood on his hands, and *then* he laments "This is a hundred dollar shirt." Anyone who's been deeply slashed by a cat knows the instantaneous burning that comes with it. Why didn't he feel it immediately?

What the Critics Had To Say...

"'Tales from the Darkside: The Movie' purports to be a collection of horror playlets that 'frankly, we couldn't make for television.' That's producer Richard P. Rubinstein talking through his hat." — John Boonstra, from a review in the New Haven *Advocate;* Monday, May 14, 1990.

"The collection is strangely likable but far from galvanizing. I suspect the under-17s with a budding taste for gore will be entertained, but the parents who have to deposit them in the theater will groan." —Jami Bernard, from a review in the New York *Post;* Saturday, May 5, 1990.

"A more imaginative script might have put this merely okay fright anthology over the top." —The Phantom of the Movies, from a review in the New York *Daily News,* Tuesday, May 15, 1990.

"STEPHEN KING'S 'GRAVEYARD SHIFT' "

Released October 26, 1990, by Paramount.
Videotape released by Paramount Home Video.
Running Time: 86 minutes.
Rated R

Director: Ralph S. Singleton
Producer: Ralph S. Singleton
Written by: John Esposito
Based on a Short Story by: Stephen King

Budget: $10.5 million

CAST

John Hall	David Andrews
Warwick	Stephen Macht
The Exterminator	Brad Dourif
Jane Wisconsky	Kelly Wolf
Jason Reed	Jonathan Emerson

and...
Andrew Divoff, Vic Polizas.

"STEPHEN KING'S 'GRAVEYARD SHIFT' "

"Stephen King's 'Graveyard Shift'" was the first of three King films released in the fall of 1990. (The second was the "IT" miniseries on ABC on November 18 and 20, and the third was Rob Reiner's big-screen adaptation of *Misery* at Christmas.)

The reviews for "Graveyard Shift" were not good and, to be frank, I did not go to see the film expecting much. I had heard that there were substantial changes to the original *Night Shift* story, and this always aggravates me. (I guess "faithful to the text" doesn't have much meaning any more, huh?) And I also heard – from people who had read (and really liked) John Esposito's original screenplay – that the final version had been substantially changed from what John had written.

So, I went because I had to see it, but I was not looking forward to the experience. (On the other hand, I couldn't wait to see "IT" and "Misery." See my reviews of those films in this volume.)

My "Graveyard Shift" verdict? Well, lemme put it this way. I arrived at the theater a half-hour early, and was thus able to catch the first twenty minutes or so of Martin Scorsese's "Goodfellas," which was playing in the theater next door. After seeing "Graveyard Shift," I now think I should have stayed for the entire Scorsese film and just pretended I never got to see "Shift" in time for inclusion of a review in this volume.

But I'm probably being overly harsh. There *were* some redeeming qualities to the film. The sets were absolutely incredible. The mill where the rats lived took on a personality of its own, and the set designers deserve kudos for their work. In fact, the sets alone are worth the price of admission.

Also, I really liked Kelly Wolf's and Brad Dourif's performances. The scene where Dourif (as the Exterminator) tells David Andrews' character, Hall, about how the Viet Cong used to torture GIs by letting hungry rats burrow into their stomachs is mesmerizing.

The big problem with the film is that it's too slow-paced. Also, King's characters again come off like cartoon people, and I found myself checking my watch throughout the seemingly interminable eighty-six-minute running time of the film.

Overall, I'd call the film a qualified failure (some of the performances and the sets redeem it), but its final grade can't be more than a C–.

"MISERY"

"I'll get you your Novril, Paul. Forgive me for prattling away and making you feel all oogie."
—Annie Wilkes

Released November 1990, by Columbia Pictures.
Castle Rock Entertainment in Association with Nelson Entertainment.
Running Time: 105 minutes.
Rated R

Directed By: Rob Reiner
Screenplay By: William Goldman
Based On The Novel By: Stephen King
Produced By: Andrew Scheinman, Rob Reiner
Music By: Marc Shaiman
Costumes Designed By: Gloria Gresham
Production Designer: Norman Garwood
Edited By: Robert Leighton
Director of Photography: Barry Sonnenfeld
Special Make-Up Effects By: K.N.B. EFX GROUP, Robert Kurtzman, Greg Nicotero, Howard Berger, Rick LaLonde, Bruce S. Fuller
Special Effects Supervisor: Phil Cory
Book Cover Illustrator: Rob Rupple

Budget: $20 million
Gross Box-Office Receipts (the first weekend of release): $10 million

CAST

Paul Sheldon	James Caan
Annie Wilkes	Kathy Bates
Buster	Richard Farnsworth
Virginia	Frances Sternhagen
Marcia Sindell	Lauren Bacall
Libby	Graham Jarvis
Pete	Jerry Potter
Anchorman	Tom Brunelle
Anchorwoman	June Christopher
Reporter #1	Julie Payne
Reporter #2	Archie Hahn III
Reporter #3	Gregory Snegoff
Waitress	Wendy Bowers
Misery the Pig	Herself

SONG CREDITS

"Shotgun"
Performed by Junior Walker & The Allstars
Written by Autry DeWalt

"Tchaikovsky Piano Concerto #1"
Performed by Liberace
Arranged by Liberace

"Moonlight Sonata"
By Ludwig Van Beethoven
Performed by Liberace
Arranged by Liberace

"I'll Be Seeing You"
Performed by Liberace
Written by Irving Kahal and Sammy Fain

"Love Connection"
Written by Larry Grossman

Additional Liberace Dialogue
Courtesy of AVI Record Productions, Inc.

"MISERY"

If I wasn't so cynical, I'd suspect that Hollywood is figuring out what to do with Stephen King's stories. In the month of November 1990, we were treated to the superb ABC miniseries adaptation of *IT* and Rob Reiner's big-screen version of *Misery*. I hope my cynicism is misplaced and that future King adaptations will be of the calibre of these two fine productions.

"Misery" must now be considered one of the five best interpretations of a Stephen King story. (The other four are, of course, "Carrie," "The Dead Zone," "Stand By Me," and "IT.") Rob Reiner seems to have become the King director of choice. In addition to two successes in a row, word has it that he has already optioned the film rights to King's 1991 novel *Needful Things* (described as a "Satan-in-a-smalltown" story.) Since we know from the introduction to *Four Past Midnight* that *Needful Things* will write the final chapter on Castle Rock, Maine, it will be interesting to first, see how Reiner handles what sounds like a *supernatural* horror story, and second, if he'll change the name of his production company!

Everything about "Misery" works: the performances, the script, the direction. Kathy Bates as Annie Wilkes is absolutely astounding. She can change from a demure schoolgirl into a raving beast within the blink of an eye. James Caan wears pain very well, and Richard Farnsworth is perfect as another of King's shrewd, crotchety, yet witty and warm old men (a la Fred Gwynne's Jud Crandall in "Pet Sematary.")

All in all, "Misery" is a project the creative people involved should be proud of, and a film that will undoubtedly do huge box office, and rightfully so. It is brilliant.

Here are a few of my favorite moments from the film:

1. *William Goldman's script:* It is absolutely superb—a top-notch rendering of an already powerful novel, and as good as the screenplays for "IT," "The Dead Zone", and "Stand By Me." Future King adaptors take notice: This is how it's done. (Also, making Annie a Liberace freak was the perfect, bizarre touch.)

2. *Kathy Bates:* An Oscar-winning performance if ever there was one. [NOTE: See "Misery' Update," page 622.]

3. *Richard Farnsworth and Frances Sternhagen:* The perfect couple. I've liked Frances Sternhagen ever since I saw her in 1983's "Romantic Comedy," and here she is the perfect foil to Farnsworth. Terrific casting.

4. *The "Hobbling" Scene:* In its new "sledgehammer" version, it works. At first, I was a little leery about such a drastic change in the story. After all, Annie's axe amputation of Paul's foot (complete with blowtorch cauterization) was an important moment in the story. It helped convince us just how psychotic this woman was. But in the film, thanks to Kathy Bates's magnificent performance, we're convinced of her insanity the first time we see that awesome sea-change in her facial expression the first time she goes over the edge. Here, the move away from the gore of the novel did not detract from the film at all.

5. *Paul Sheldon's "Finger Out the Window" Scene:* Up until Annie broke his ankles, Paul never showed any animosity or anger towards his "nurse." He humored her, patronized her, flattered her, and generally played along, all the while plotting his escape. But after she put him through her special sledgehammer technique, he lost all will for pretense. In this scene, Annie comes home with a big bag of feed for Misery, her pig (played by Misery, the pig), waves hello to Paul, and he returns her wave with a frown and his middle finger. Annie's response? Instead of snapping (since Annie is now in her "sane" mode), she just laughs and says, "What a kidder." A funny, yet revealing scene that sets the stage, and gives Paul's character the motivation for, his final confrontation with Ms. Wilkes.

6. *James Caan:* His best performance since Sonny Corleone in "The Godfather."

7. *Rob Reiner's direction:* It's terrific. I, for one, wish he would first, *read* more of Stephen King, and then immediately thereafter, *direct* more of Stephen King. Reiner definitely has the touch for King's use of characters and the general tone and texture of his stories. Rob Reiner is the best Stephen King director yet.

Now here are some of my least favorite moments:

Nope. Nothing wrong here.

What the Critics Had To Say...

"Rob Reiner's competent-plus wax job on William Goldman's script is keenly orchestrated manipulation; it seems less sturdy upon two minutes reflection than Stanley Kubrick's take on 'The Shining' does after an entire decade. Yet while it unfolds, 'Misery' is a robust audience-participation pic. Reiner's cat-and-mouse (squashed cat-and-mouse actually) will freak us quite nicely until Jonathan Demme's movie of [Thomas Harris's] *The Silence of the Lambs* arrive in February [1991]. ☆☆☆"—Mike Clark, from a review in *USA Today* titled "Reiner's 'Misery' makes scary company"; Friday, November 30, 1990.

"A landmark psychological thriller." —Vernon Scott, UPI.

"A chilling charmer of a thriller...Hitchcock suspense with Rob Reiner wit." —Patrick Stoner, "PBS Flicks."

"Bates' performance is simply spectacular. She can accelerate from simpering girlishness to looming monstrosity with head-spinning—possibly Oscar-winning—speed. Caan partners her with edgy smarts, and their deadly game does something more than pit temporary weakness against sociopathic passion. It also places ironic literary intelligence in conflict with the whacked-out innocence of fandom, and has a smart subtext of class warfare about it too. The actors are supported by the best kind of writerly craft and directorial technique, the kind that refuses to call attention to itself, never gets caught straining for scares or laughs. Popular moviemaking—elegantly economical, artlessly artful—doesn't get much better than this." —Richard Schickel, from a review titled "Deadly Game of Nursing Care" in *Time* magazine, December 10, 1990.

"'Misery' is an effective movie version of the Stephen King best seller...Bates is uncanny in her ability to switch between sweetness and sadism, and Caan does a sound job of playing the long and deeply suffering writer. ☆☆☆." —Roger Ebert.

"'Misery' deals with obsession, insanity, and murder. One of the film's memorable moments occurs when a demented woman takes a sledgehammer to the damaged legs of the bedridden hero. This, you may ask, is a movie fit for the holidays? Indeed, it it. Rob Reiner's skillfully crafted version of Stephen King's novel...is suspenseful, darkly humorous and completely entertaining. It's the perfect chaser to holiday frivolity. ... As a study of obsessive love...'Misery' is more frightening than 'Fatal Attraction' and a great deal more fun." —Philip Wuntch; Dallas *Morning News,* Friday, November 30, 1990.

"The chief limitation of William Goldman's screenplay is that Annie's reverence for the *Misery* books is presented in a completely generic way. The satire exists on a comedy-sketch level. It never extends beyond the most stereotypical idea of why lonely people are drawn to the reassuring banalities of schlock literature. And Rob Reiner's direction is a bit on the poky side. 'Misery' is clever yet pedestrian. Much of the time, we could be watching a first-rate episode of 'Alfred Hitchcock Presents.' Yet the movie has a real kick to it. B+" —Owen Gleiberman, from a review in *Entertainment Weekly,* November 30, 1990.

"Kathy Bates gives an Oscar calibre performance." —Eleanor O'Sullivan, Asbury Park *Press.*

"It's a definite winner. 'Misery' keeps you at the edge of your seat. Sheer entertainment!" —Marilyn Beck; Chicago *Tribune* Syndicate.

"In the original King novel, Annie was a larger-than-life character—a full-blown female Cujo who mutilated Paul. The movie, like the gothic thriller 'What Ever Happened to Baby Jane?' is more of a two-way contest, an increasingly nasty battle of cutting remarks and physical torture. For all of Reiner's efforts to lighten the mood with humor, the movie is ultimately just as sadistic and mean-spirited as last year's comedy 'The War of the Roses.' ☆☆1/2" —Kathleen Carroll, from a review titled "'Misery' checks in at Kathy Bates' motel" in the New York *Daily News,* Friday, November 30, 1990.

"This is one of the best films made from a Stephen King book and marks Reiner's second such success, coming after his film 'Stand By Me,' which was based on King's story 'The Body.' This obviously could have been routine thriller material, but is enlivened by a wonderful performance by Kathy Bates as the crazed fan who alternates between compassion and violent kookiness—all the while smiling beatifically with a little gold cross hanging from her necklace. ☆☆☆" —Gene Siskel.

IT IS THE TALE *AND* HE WHO TELLS IT
A Review of "Misery" (The Movie)
by George Beahm

Early on in King's career, Bill Thompson—King's editor at Doubleday—expressed his concerns about King getting typecast as a horror writer. King's response was that he didn't care what labels people put on him; and besides, he was in fine company.

Years later, King's name has become inextricably linked to the horror genre, a place out in the badlands next to science fiction, and the sales figures have proven that King's fans will buy anything he writes...but what they *really* want is more horror fiction.

It's every popular writer's greatest fear: Though the writer grows, the reader does not; he or she is content with the familiar and wants more of the same.

Misery is at heart a writer's horror story—a riveting read, a suspense and psychological thriller; a story with a dark theme uncomfortably close to King, it's great fiction that begged to be made into a movie.

Rob Reiner—more concerned with character and story than the traditional trappings of horror—has chosen well and wisely in drawing from the King canon "The Body" and *Misery,* both faithfully adapted to the screen. "The Body," adapted as "Stand By Me" with its memorable Ben E. King title song, proved to movie-goers that—as King reminds us—it's the tale and not the teller. "Stand By Me," released without fanfare and without King's name, was both a critical and financial success. "Misery," I believe, ranks up there with "Stand By Me" and "Carrie" in terms of movie adaptations; and Reiner has done what no other film director who has worked with King has done: Reiner is batting a thousand. (Food for thought: Reiner has already optioned the film rights to *Needful Things,* King's "Castle Rock" novel to be published in the fall of 1991.)

Though "Misery" differs from the book, the differences are necessary to make an effective transition from the book to the screen; in the process, the essence of the book—the heart of darkness in Annie Wilkes—remains the essence of the film. William Goldman ("The Princess Bride," "Butch Cassidy and the Sundance Kid," "All the President's Men," "Marathon Man," "Magic"), who wrote the screenplay, did an admirable job, especially with a secondary character in the book who assumes a greater role in the movie, opening up the storyline so it takes the viewer outside of Annie's house, focusing on the hunt for Sheldon.

Rob Reiner, as director, wisely chose to downplay the traditional blood-and-guts motif of the contemporary horror film in two critical instances: In the book, Annie Wilkes uses an axe and Bernz-O-MatiC blowtorch on Sheldon in the gruesome "hobbling" scene, but in the movie she uses a sledgehammer. Also, in the book Trooper Duane Kushner is messily dispatched (finally) with a lawnmower, suggesting "Maximum Overdrive" with its motif of machines run amuck; in the movie, however, the snooping local policeman (Buster) is shot-gunned in the back by Wilkes. King—whose work shows a tendency toward excess at times—is better served by these changes, whereas a straightforward translation of those two scenes would have made the audience moan in revulsion instead of screaming in horror. (Anyone who saw "Graveyard Shift" and heard the audience moan throughout the film knows *exactly* what I mean.)

Rob Reiner's great skill as a director, I think, is that he recognizes King's power as a writer is based on the ability to play on *contemporary* fears, instead of the traditional (and cliched) reworkings of another vampire, werewolf, or mummy tale. With the latter, you know in the back of your mind that it can't really happen; but with the former, *it just might happen,* and it might happen to *you.*

With "Stand By Me" a resounding success, and "Misery" a critical and almost surely a financial success, Reiner has done a rare and wonderful thing: He has given us King on the screen, the way the *author* intended.

I look forward to Reiner's adaptation of *Needful Things.*

"I play a guy with two broken legs. I'm not the leading man, I'm the victim. Usually I'm the one dishing it out so, during the shooting, I wasn't the most wonderful person to be around. I had prosthetic legs. My arms were bloody. I had just dislocated my own shoulder, and I had a 3-inch screw in it. On my way home, mass murder was not out of the question." —James Caan, from an interview in *Details* magazine, December, 1990.

"Ah, misery. The book made me miserable. The movie made me sick. I highly recommend both. ☆☆☆" —Jami Bernard, from a review titled "The Joy of 'Misery'" in the New York *Post*, Friday, November 30, 1990.

"The premise is amusing, and the tale unfolds smoothly on screen, with the jolts coming at just the right intervals. Unlike other Stephen King adaptations, 'Misery' is a tasteful scare show. The gore is downplayed, which may give the movie a broader appeal than many horror films. But that's also what keeps it from being truly memorable. It doesn't have the intense, horrific images to stir nightmares. Reiner doesn't come anywhere near the nasty, erotic charge of Brian De Palma's 'Carrie' or the gleefully perverse sadism of 'Psycho.'" —Stephen Farber, from a review in *Movieline* magazine, December 1990.

"STEPHEN KING'S 'IT'"

"Chief, there's something terribly wrong here in Derry, and you know it."

—Mike Hanlon

An ABC Novel For Television Miniseries.
A Production of the Konigsberg/Sanitsky Company In Association with Lorimar Television.
Broadcast 9-11 P.M., Sunday, November 18, and 9-11 P.M., Tuesday, November 20, 1990.
Running Time: 4 hours (including commercials).

Director: Tommy Lee Wallace
Teleplay: Lawrence D. Cohen (Part 1); Lawrence D. Cohen & Tommy Lee Wallace (Part 2)
Based On The Novel By: Stephen King
Music: Richard Bellis
Director of Photography: Richard Leiterman
Production Designer: Douglas Higgins
Editors: Robert F. Shugrue & David Blangsted, A.C.E.
Supervising Producer: Matthew O'Connor
Executive Producers: Jim Green & Allen Epstein
Associate Producer: Mark Bacino
Special Visual Effects Supervisor: Gene Warren Jr.; Fantasy II
Costume Designer: Monique Stranan
Special Effects Make-Up: Bart J. Mixon
Art Director: Eric Fraser

CAST

Bill Denbrough	Richard Thomas
Beverly Marsh	Annette O'Toole
Ben Hanscom	John Ritter
Mike Hanlon	Tim Reid
Richie Tozier	Harry Anderson
Eddie Kaspbrak	Dennis Christopher
Stan Uris	Richard Masur
Young Bill	Jonathan Brandis
Young Ben	Brandon Crane
Young Bev	Emily Perkins
Young Eddie	Adam Faraizl
Young Richie	Seth Green
Young Stan	Ben Heller
Young Mike	Marlon Taylor
Audra	Olivia Hussey
Mrs. Kaspbrak	Sheila Moore
Young Henry Bowers	Jarred Blancard
Adult Henry Bowers	Michael Cole
Belch Huggins	Drum Garrett
Patrick Hockstetter	Gabe Khouth
Tom Rogan	Ryan Michael
Nat	Charles Siegel
Cyndi	Venus Terzo
Al Marsh	Frank C. Turner
Patti Uris	Caitlin Hicks
Georgie Denbrough	Tony Dakota
Mr. Denbrough	Steven Hilton
Sharon Denbrough	Sheelah Megill
Joey	Kim Kondrashoff
Bradley	Noel Geer
Laurie Anne Winterbarger	Chelan Simmons
Mrs. Winterbarger	Merrilyn Gann
Mr. Gedreau	William B. Davis
Aunt Jean	Susan Astley
Arlene Hanscomb [sic]	Claire Brown
Coach	Garry Chalk
Officer Nell	Terence Kelly
Miss Douglas	Donna Peerless
Ben's Father	Stephen Makaj
Chief Rademacher	Scott Swanson
Mrs. Kersh	Florence Patterson
Derry Cab Driver	Jay Brezeau
Derry Inn Desk Clerk	Nicola Cavendish
Mr. Keene	Tom Heaton
Pharmacist	Paul Batten
Greco	Russell Roberts
Koontz	Bill Croft
Chubby Kid	Amos Hertzman
Gas Station Attendant	Boyd Norman
Rose	Helena Yee
Female Cabbie	Suzie Payne

Library Aide	Megan Leitch
Bum	Deva Neil DePodesta
TV Announcer	Katherine Banwell
Doctor	Douglas Newell

"STEPHEN KING'S 'IT' "

Since *IT* is my favorite Stephen King novel, I had a protective attitude about the book. I honestly did not believe that a novel running 1,090 pages (in paperback) could be successfully adapted as a six or eight hour miniseries. When I heard that the film had been reduced to *four* hours, I was absolutely convinced that it couldn't be done.

There ain't a shoehorn that big, you know?

Well, I was wrong.

Dead wrong.

The "IT" miniseries is terrific. After the first installment ran, I received phone calls from people who had not read the novel telling me that they were going to run out and get the book. Their thinking was, anything this good on film has to be a hell of a lot better as a book.

Of course they're right, but that does not lessen the impact the miniseries has, nor does it negate the excellence of the overall production.

There had been a lot of talk about this adaptation before it became a reality. King himself noted that in the beginning there were problems with the story because the TV networks object to showing children in jeopardy. And as we King fans know, *IT* is basically about kids in *serious* jeopardy. Double jeopardy, you might say, where the answers are more difficult and the scores are doubled.

But things got resolved, and the film was made. The script was by Lawrence D. Cohen (Part 1) and by Cohen and director Tommy Lee Wallace (Part 2). Cohen is familiar to us all for his "Carrie" screenplay, and Tommy Lee Wallace's previous credits include "Halloween III: Season of the Witch", and "Fright Night 2." (Special mention must be made of Richard Bellis's music for "IT." It is perfect, and I congratulate him for choosing a simple, disturbing piano melody as the main theme for the film.)

So, how was it done?

What sleight-of-hand writing wizardry allowed Cohen and Wallace to turn a gargantuan story into a manageable four hours of TV movie?

Basically, what they did was reduce the novel to its absolute bare bones story. There are countless scenes and characters deleted from the script, but those scenes that did remain are true to the underlying story structure. Much of what is missing is not crucial to the primary story, which is the seven Losers' battle with IT. That story remains, and is told brilliantly. I am very impressed with Cohen and Wallace's work on this film. "IT" must be counted as one of those rare King films that succeeds on almost all levels. (What was left out? A lot, including the death of Adrian Mellon, the Turtle, the execution of the Bradley Gang, the House on Neibolt Street, The Other, the Leper, the baseball game of the dead in the Trackers' lot, the Creature from the Black Lagoon, the arrival of IT, the entire "Love and Desire" storyline, the coming to life of the Paul Bunyan statue, the giant Eye, the Smoke-Hole Ritual, the destruction of Derry, the crushing of ITs eggs, Tom Rogan's pursuit of Beverly, Bill's journeys into the Void, and except for a brief mention, the Fire at the Black Spot, and the explosion of the Ironworks. Also, the film's time frame is 1960-1990, not 1958-1985 as in the book.)

"IT" did very well in the ratings: The first two hours of the adaptation averaged a 19.5 rating and a 29 share. The last two hours averaged a 20.6 rating and a 33 share. (One ratings point represents one percent of the 93.1 million TV households in the United States; the "share" represents the percentage of sets turned to the show.)

There was also quite a bit of media coverage, including a lengthy article about the cast in *TV Guide* (the November 17, 1990 issue) called "How to make a monster hit...feed it lots of series stars" by Susan Litwin. It revealed, among other things, that on the set the kidding was "world-class: practiced, lightning-fast, poker-faced...ricocheting without warning from half-serious to wildly funny." We also learned that at one point the "normally shy [Annette] O'Toole sprawl[ed] on the piano and [did] a sexy cabaret rendition of "Big Spender." (I guess she's seen "The Fabulous Baker Boys," huh?) There was also an article by Kit Boss in the November 16, 1990, issue of *Entertainment Weekly* (which coincidentally had Michelle Pfeiffer on the cover) accompanied by some nice photos and a review by Ken Tucker that gave the miniseries a B- grade.)

What the Critics Had To Say...

"The ABC two-parter 'Stephen King's It' is as chilling an original horror flick as network television has unveiled. A well-acted, bonafide skin-crawler, this four hour creepshow may change the way you look at clowns forever. I know I'm never letting one near my kids again. ...What truly elevates 'It' above the chiller-thriller crowd is its dogged emphasis on character and relationships above the lurid trappings that so often bog down the genre. ...'It' is a class act all the way..." —Ray Richmond, from a review titled "'It': 'Stand By Me' meets 'Godzilla'" that originally ran in the Orange County Register, and which was reprinted in the New Haven *Register* on Friday, November 16, 1990.

"By now, one of my deepest fears is having to sit through another horrifyingly bad adaptation of a Stephen King novel—but ABC's four hour 'Stephen King's It' isn't all bad. Just half bad. In the pantheon of movies and miniseries made from King's stories, 'It' falls way below 'Carrie,' 'Stand By Me,' 'The Shining,' (except for that ending) and TV's 'Salem's Lot,' but way above everything else. As with 'Stand By Me,' ['It's] strength is characterization, especially of the bonding that takes place when kids are young. ...'It' comes out better than many dramatizations of King's works. 'It' is no 'Carrie'—but it's no 'Christine' or "Pet Sematary,' either. ☆☆1/2 stars." —Dave Bianculli, from a review titled "Bozo's Evil Twin," in the New York Post, Thursday, November 15, 1990.

"The chief problem faced by director Tommy Lee Wallace is that King's book takes too long getting the grownups back together—we have to see what every character is doing for a living, and what his or her It-inspired neuroses are. This is tedious in both the novel and the miniseries. Once the adults are assembled, though, 'It' features a high level of ensemble acting rare for any horror film. ...In addition to 'It's' slow pace, I found the ending a big letdown—unimaginative special effects animate the monster in its final incarnation. But the cast is terrific, Curry's cackle is chilling, and King's usual buried theme—about the pain adults inflict on children without even realizing it (It?)—is always worth pondering." —Ken Tucker in *Entertainment Weekly*; November 16, 1990.

"'IT' worked on television—a real surprise, and pleasure, considering the content of the novel and the subject matter. The TV climax, however, was anti-climactic: IT finally appeared and was underwhelming." —George Beahm, author of *The Stephen King Companion*.

THE ART OF ADAPTATION
A Synoptic Comparison of "IT" And *IT*

"IT" was broadcast in two, two-hour sections. The following overview of the film, with comments and analysis, will essentially reconstruct the basic outline of the script. I think that this type of in-depth look at the miniseries is justified since *IT* is unquestionably one of King's most important novels, and the miniseries is an example of how to successfully translate horror to the screen. (Even if it is just the TV screen.) This outline will allow you to compare the TV version of the novel with the actual text of King's story.

PART 1

The film opens (both parts) with shots of the pages of a photo album running under the credits. The pictures are from the fifties, and are mostly of the Losers as children. As the credits roll, we see a photo of the Paramount theater (it was the Alladin in the book), and the marquee announces the theater is showing "I Was a Teenage Werewolf." The picture changes to a scene of the actual theater front, now in the 1980s, but the marquee now reads, "Retail space for lease."

The first sequence is the death of Laurie Anne Winterbarger. There's a storm coming up, and her mother hollers for her to come inside. Laurie is playing on her bike in the yard, and she hears a voice coming from the sheets drying on the clothesline. For a split second, in a very frightening scene, we suddenly see Pennywise the clown hiding in the sheets. Laurie's mother comes out of the house shortly thereafter, and screams when she sees Laurie's mutilated body (which we do *not* see.) The police come. The rain pours down. Chief Rademacher tells Mike Hanlon to get lost. Hanlon asks him if he doesn't think six missing or dead kids in Derry is peculiar. Rademacher blows him off, and as the ambulance pulls away, Mike finds a picture of Georgie Denbrough at the scene. He returns to the library and enters what happened in his dairy.

The next series of sequences (and almost the entire first half of the film), is basically a reconstruction of "Part 1: The Shadow Before," "Part 2: June of 1958," and "Part 4: July of 1958" of the novel. The segments follow the "Six Phone Calls" chapter structure, except all of the stories of the Losers' 1990 life is drastically compressed into brief vignettes that lead into the flashbacks that are essentially the stories told in the "June of 1958" section.

In the novel, the six phone calls were in this order:

1. Stan
2. Richie
3. Ben
4. Eddie
5. Bev
6. Bill

In the film, the six phone calls were in this order:

1. Bill
2. Ben
3. Bev
4. Eddie
5. Richie
6. Stan

Here's a synopsis of the "six phone calls":

1. *BILL:* England. We first see Bill Denbrough writing at his word processor. He is working on the screenplay of one of his (unnamed) novels. (In the book, it's *The Black Rapids.*) Denbrough, played by a ponytailed Richard Thomas, is married to Audra, played by Olivia Hussey. After Mike's call, Bill begins to stutter again, already regressing to the childhood state necessary to battle IT. There is a flashback to the Losers swearing they'll return if IT resurfaces. We then see a lengthy scene that is essentially the first chapter ("After the Flood (1957)") in the book: Georgie floating the boat Bill made for him, the boat falling in the sewer, and Georgie getting his arm pulled off by Pennywise. We don't see the amputation, but we do see Pennywise change into his "Killer Clown" persona, complete with razor-sharp fangs and demonic eyes. We then see Georgie's burial, which takes place in the rain. The flashback to 1960 continues with Bill looking through Georgie's photo album. When he gets to the photo of Georgie (the same one Mike Hanlon found at the site of Laurie Anne Winterbarger's death), the photo winks at Bill. Bill throws it across the room where the book's pages begin to turn by themselves. The book stops at Georgie's photo, which now begins to bleed. Bill screams, his parents come into the room, and, you guessed it, *don't see the blood.* Insensitive as usual, the Denbroughs tell Bill to stay out of Georgie's room. The flashback returns to 1990, as Bill leaves Audra in England. Bill tells Audra he loves her. She tells him he's crazy.

(In this segment, I don't like Olivia Hussey in the role of Audra. She plays it cold and somewhat meanspirited. I envisioned Audra as warmer. Her function is Part 2 is basically to "hang around": she spends much of the last half hour wrapped in a cocoon dangling from the wall in ITs chamber. After her rescue, she is catatonic for a while, and then Bill brings her back to life by taking her for a ride on Silver, as in the novel. They kiss in the middle of a Derry intersection (still intact, unlike the novel) as cars blow their horns and the camera pulls back. End of story.)

Commercial Break

2. *BEN:* New York. The second phone call is made to Ben Hanscom, played by a bearded John Ritter. We first see Ben coming back from an awards ceremony where he was presented with an architect's award. He's drunk and has a honey on (and in) his arm(s). Right after he asks the girl "Would you believe I used to be fat?," Mike calls. We immediately jump to a flashback of Henry Bowers getting ready to carve an "H" into Ben's belly. We come back to 1990, where we see Ben pour himself a drink and take an elevator to the top of the building. (He had taken the girl to a loft office in one of his buildings under construction.) He stares out at the city and we wonder if he's going to throw himself off the roof. He begins to remember, and we flashback to Ben as a child introducing himself to his new class. He and his mother have come to Derry to live with their relatives (Arlene's sister) because, after his father's death, his mother would have had to go on welfare if her sister didn't take her in. Henry Bowers calls him names. Ben first notices Bev Marsh and after school she introduces herself. On the way home, Bowers attacks Ben and attempts to carve the "H" in Ben's belly. Ben kicks him in the balls and escapes into the Barrens where he hides in a sewer pipe. Belch and Bowers chase him, see Eddie and Bill, and kick down a "baby dam" they had made. They leave. Ben comes out of the pipe, and after introductions are made, Bill goes off to get Eddie Kaspbrak his aspirator medicine. Bill returns, and a bond has been forged between the three. Later, Ben writes Bev his haiku postcard ("Your hair is winter fire,/January embers./My heart burns there, too."), his cousin teases him about it, they fight, and Ben runs off to the Barrens after his mother insists *he* apologize. In the Barrens, Ben's dead father appears to him (it's actually Pennywise) and tells him the pumping station is his home now. His father transforms into Pennywise, and then disappears. A skeleton covered in moss rears up from the pond and grabs at Ben. We return to 1990 where Ben is still on the roof of the building. He is crying and we hear him whisper, "Please."

Commercial Break

3. *BEV:* Chicago. Bev Marsh, played by Annette O'Toole, is in her office at Beverly By Hand fashions. Her secretary tells her there's a call from Maine. Tom Drogan (her abusive "partner") won't let her take the call because they have a meeting with some Japanese buyers. Bev says she'd take the call anyway, but Tom overrules her and tells her never to contradict him in front of Pam again. Later that night, while the two of them are in bed, the phone rings while Tom is down-

stairs fetching more champagne. It's Mike. Tom comes upstairs and sees Bev packing. She disobeys his orders and continues to pack. He gets the strap. But Mike's call has triggered a resolve in her: Her vow to return if IT resurfaced is stronger than her fear of Tom. She fights him off and throws a bottle of cold cream at his head. It knocks him woozy and she leaves. In the cab, she remembers back to 1960. We flashback to her making breakfast for her father. The doorbell rings. It's Ben secretly dropping off his haiku postcard. Her father takes it from her and asks what she's been doing with boys. He "worries about her. A lot." He slaps her. She runs away, meets Ben, and he asks her to go to the Barrens. There, we meet Richie Tozier and Stan Uris for the first time. Richie does imitations, and Stan is a Boy Scout. They all decide to build the Dam in the Barrens (as per Ben's design) while "It's Alright" plays on the soundtrack. They all return to town. Bill leaves on Silver, and for the first time, we hear him say "Hi-Yo, Silver, Awaaaay!" As Bill leaves, Bev whispers, "My heart burns there, too." Later that night, Bev hears voices coming from her bathroom sink drain, and suddenly a red bubble (balloon?) bursts in the sink, filling the basin with blood and splattering red all over Bev. She screams and when her father comes in the bathroom (after asking if someone was "peeking" in at her), he, like the Denbroughs, doesn't see the blood. Bev fakes it and tells him she saw a spider. We return to 1990, where Bev is lost in thought in the back seat of the cab on the way to the airport.

Commercial Break

4. *EDDIE:* Great Neck, New York. Eddie Kaspbrak, played by Dennis Christopher, is packing his medicines. In a marked departure from the book, Eddie still lives with his mother, rather than being married to Myra. His mother is exactly the same now as she was when Eddie was a child: Overprotective, domineering, and smothering. A limo waits for Eddie. (He owns a limousine company, as in the novel.) He and his driver discuss the "Pacino" job (that's also in the book), and we flashback to 1960, the Paramount theater. "I Was a Teenage Werewolf" is showing, and the gang—Eddie, Bill, Bev, Ben, Richie, and Stan— are together in the balcony. Eddie accidentally kicks popcorn on Henry Bowers, Belch Huggins, and Patrick Hockstetter. Richie then intentionally pours soda on them as well. They flee the theater and go to the Barrens where Ben stares at the pumphouse. They walk Eddie home. His mother is terrible to them and tells them all to go away. When Eddie protests that they're his friends, she replies he doesn't need any friends, all he needs is his ma. His mother tells him not to shower at school. She doesn't want him catching

any of the other boy's germs. His coach makes him shower anyway, and while all alone in the shower room (in a scene not in the novel), all the shower faucets turn themselves on, start growing out of the wall, and fence Eddie in. Pennywise then pops up out of the drain in the floor, changes into a monster clown, and Eddie snaps back to 1990, where he is boarding a train on his way back to Derry.

Commercial Break

5. *RICHIE:* California. Richie Tozier, comedian extraordinaire (in the novel he was a disk jockey), is on a talk show, doing a routine. Tozier, played by comedian Harry Anderson, finishes his bit, and in his dressing room, answers the phone. It's Mike. Richie decides to leave for Maine, and his manager can't understand. He asks Richie, "Who's gonna do Carson?" and Richie responds, "Get Leno." His manager storms out, and Richie flashes back to being attacked by the Teenage Werewolf in the Derry High School basement. Richie runs to the bathroom and pukes his brains out. We then flashback to Bill reading a story to the gang about magic stones and dragons. Bill begins to tell them about what happened with Georgie's photo album when Officer Nell arrives hollering about the dam they built. Nell then tells them there'd been another murder, and the kids—and Officer Nell—all grasp hands in solidarity. The next segment takes place in the high school cafeteria. After being confronted by Bowers and company and having mashed potatoes smeared on his glasses, Richie dumps his whole food tray on Bowers and when Henry chases him and trips, Richie calls him "Banana-Heels." Richie is sent down to the basement to get a mop to clean up the mess, and while down there, he is attacked by the Teenage Werewolf, who then changes into Pennywise. Everyone in the cafeteria laughs at him when he comes back upstairs and tells them there's a werewolf in the basement. We then return to 1990 where Richie is still in the bathroom lying with his head on the toilet bowl lid.

Commercial Break

Interlude: *MIKE:* Derry. Mike Hanlon, played by Tim Reid, writes in his journal in the library. He remembers back to a "Show and Tell" day at school. He had brought his father's photo album to school and showed the class photos of the Ironworks, the Standpipe, and other Derry locales. After school, he is stopped on the street by Bowers and his boys. Bowers is preparing to put a lit cherry bomb in Mike's pocket when a storekeeper yells at them to stop what they're doing. Mike seizes the moment and escapes. Bowers

and company chase him and he runs to the dump where the rest of the Losers are. They side with Mike and defend him with rocks. (This scene is the book's thirteenth chapter, "The Apocalyptic Rockfight" in "Part 4: July of 1958.") After the battle is over, Mike takes a picture of the whole crew (his camera has a timer on it), now christened "The Losers' Club," and then they all look through Mike's father's photo album. The album flips by itself (as Georgie's did for Bill), and a photo of Main Street comes to life. Only this time, they all see it. (This scene is the book's fourteenth chapter, "The Album" in "Part 4: July of 1958.") Pennywise speaks to them from the photo, says "I'll kill you all" (which were the last words Bowers said after the rockfight), and actually thrusts a hand out of the picture at them. Stan freaks. He keeps denying what they all saw. ("No! No! No!"— Twice in the first half of the film, Stan remarks that these happenings are not "empirically possible.") The rest of the Losers insist to him that he saw what he saw. ("Yes. Yes. Yes.") After Stan has calmed down, Bill speaks to Pennywise/IT: "You killed my brother, you bastard," and he decides he will kill the creature. They form a huddle and agree that that is what must be done. Mike then wakes up in the library in 1990. He sees muddy footprints on the floor and next to him is a big yellow balloon. As he retreats from it in horror, it explodes.

Commercial Break

6. *STAN:* Atlanta, Georgia. Stan and his wife Patti are watching "Perfect Strangers" (instead of "Family Feud"). Mike calls. Once again, Stan freaks. He reverts to a childish, disaffected manner. He tells his wife he's going to take a bath. We flashback to the Losers shooting at bottles and cans with a slingshot ("The Bullseye") in order to see who will be given the duty of shooting IT. Stan is reciting his Boy Scout oath like a prayer, like a mantra. Bev hits ten out of ten, and it is decided that she will be the one to shoot. In another marked departure from the book, instead of melting down Ben's silver dollars, Richie hands over a pair of his mother's "solid silver" earrings. These will be the bullets. Before they enter the pumping station, they each take a hit on Eddie's aspirator. They go into the pumphouse, while Bowers, Huggins, and Hockstetter watch. And then follow them in. (There are a couple of King references in this segment: Mike says that his father told him you have to know when to take a *stand*; and Bowers asks Stan, what are you afraid of, *the boogeyman*?) IT, now in his purest, vilest form, approaches through the sewer pipes as a bright light. IT first gets Patrick Hockstetter. The Losers come to ITs chamber. A sewer pipe explodes as Henry is

getting ready to kill Stan. IT takes Belch Huggins: IT squeezes him into a pipe (he is folded in half) and then IT eats him. IT returns and Bowers hair turns white. IT comes to the Losers. They join hands as a giant white thing that looks like a sea manta ray hovers over them. A white mist comes up from the floor. The Losers form a circle. Bill sees Georgie. Bevvie sees her father. The Werewolf grabs Richie's shoulders. (The hands leave when Richie repeats that there is nothing there.) Stan recites the Boy Scout oath. Pennywise appears and takes Stan. He tells him to fear—he'll taste better. Eddie sprays his aspirator in Pennywise's face, telling him it's battery acid. The clown's face begins to melt. Bev shoots him with her "silver bullet." She hits his head and puts a hole in it. Light streams out. Pennywise somersaults into the sewer drain and collapses inward. As he's sliding into the drain, IT grabs Bill. The Losers pull him back. Pennywise's hand turns into claws. They flee the sewers, and Bill makes them swear that they'll all come back if IT isn't dead. (No cutting of the palms with a piece of broken Coke bottle, though. And no gang sex with Beverly either.) They all swear—Stan at the last second. They grab hands and huddle. We return to 1990. Patti Uris goes upstairs to check on Stan. She finds him dead in the tub. Stan has killed himself by slitting his wrists with a razor blade. We see the blades, and we see blood dripping from his fingers. Before Stan died, though, he wrote "IT" on the bathroom wall in his own blood. We hear Pennywise cackling, and Part 1 comes to a conclusion.

PART 2

The second half of "IT" isn't quite as good as the first half, but the segment is still heads above normal TV fare. The Losers as kids are rarely seen, and the story focuses on the group as adults. (There's an occasional (very brief) flashback to a scene from the first half, but essentially, the kids are nowhere to be seen. It's grownup time.)

As in the first half, the performances are superb. The kids were terrific in Part 1, and Richard Thomas, John Ritter, Annette O'Toole, Harry Anderson, Dennis Christopher, and Tim Reid are great in Part 2. (Richard Masur's head is also very good.)

Part 2 is drawn from several different sections and chapters of *IT* the novel, including the chapters "The Reunion" and "Walking Tours" in "Part 3: Grownups," and sections of "Part 5: The Ritual of Chüd." In the following synopsis, I will refer to the book where appropriate, and also make note of the differences. Part 1 was broken into seven sections (one for each "away" character, and one for Mike), and Part 2 is

likewise in seven sections, although each section doesn't really have a character focal point as did Part 1.

The response I got both from people who had read the novel and those who didn't is that they loved the miniseries—up until the last fifteen minutes. And I think what they're saying is that they were able to recognize that 1) the producers ran out of money, and 2) they rushed to get a lot of story told in a too-brief period of time. The first three and a half hours or so were patient with the tale: They took their time letting us get to know the Losers, and as with Rob Reiner's "Stand By Me," it wasn't long before we cared about the characters as people. Character development and story were skillfully interwoven in the first ninety percent of the four hour film. But then we get the final battle with IT (which in the novel resulted in the destruction of Derry), Eddie's death, the rescue of Audra, and her final resurrection from catatonia (thanks to Bill and Silver), all crammed into the final fifteen or twenty minutes. I got the impression that Wallace and company suddenly realized they had a lot of story to catch up with, and a lot of loose ends to tie up, and by this time, there *was* no time. And since the miniseries was supposed to be much longer (I read reports that pegged it at both six and eight hours) this final compression and hurried winding-up can be understood. Also, the special effects left a little bit to be desired. In the book, IT was at least fifteen feet high, and yet in the film, Bill, Bev, and Richie were able to push IT on ITs side and rip ITs heart out. The final manifestation wasn't as frightening as some of the spookier Pennywise moments earlier on, and I think IT should have been more "smoke and mirrors" (perhaps with glimpses of Pennywise buried beneath the face of the Spider?) instead of just a big arachnid.

But these are small points, and overall I was very pleased to see this adaptation of a Stephen King work done so well. And on TV yet!

Segment 1. The first segment of Part 2 opens with Bill Denbrough arriving at the Derry Inn. The desk clerk remarks how happy she is to see him ("hometown boy makes good"), and Bill then takes a cab to the cemetry to visit Georgie's grave. While Bill is at the grave, Pennywise appears to him in a scene not in the book: The clown has dug seven graves, and is standing in the seventh one, telling Bill that one is already taken. (Stan's grave is filled.) Bill tells him we beat you and we're not afraid of you. Pennywise—and the graves—disappear. Bill then goes to the library to see Mike for the first time. When he walks in, he sees a display of his own books. They are titled *Highway, Gargoyles Dance, Gnaw, The Smile,* and *The Glowing.* [NOTE: Whoever wrote the titles for these nonexistent books should have been a little more imaginative. They're terrible, don't you think? *"Gnaw"*?] Bill tells Mike he doesn't remember anything, but then the phrase "Lucky Seven" leaps into his mind. They go to Mike's house ("clean and paid for") where Mike brings out Silver. He had found it in a pawnshop and couldn't *not* buy it. (In the novel, Bill bought the bike himself when he returned to Derry.) Mike tells Bill that he had bought a bike tire repair kit three months before he found Silver. We then flashback to Bill riding Stan away from the haunted house.

The next part of this section begins with Richie Tozier driving through Derry. He, too, has just arrived. As he drives by the Paramount theater, he sees the marquee change. It now reads "Rest In Peace/ Richie Tozier/Born 1950-Died 1990." He goes to the library. Mike is away with Bill, so Richie decides to wait for him. A cute, young librarian brings him a cup of water. He looked like he needed it, she says. As she walks away, he checks out the sashay in her gitalong, and that's when he first hears Pennywise. The clown appears in the balcony and throws balloons around the library. They all burst and spray blood all over the patrons, which, of course, they don't see. (Except in one "blooper" instance when a woman noticeably flinches when the balloon breaks on her face.) Richie boogeys on out of there.

We return to Mike's backyard. Mike comes out of the house changed into dressier clothes for the Losers' reunion Chinese dinner. (In the book, it was a reunion lunch.) He finds Bill fixing Silver. They both take turns riding the bike, while we also see flashbacks to when they rode together as kids. This is a very engaging scene that is played to the accompaniment of "The Way You Do The Things You Do" on the soundtrack. After the rides , Mike gives Bill a deck of Bicycle playing cards. (They make the best noise when clothespinned to the spokes.) Bill drops the deck and two cards land face up—two Aces of Spades, and Pennywise's face is now on the back of the other cards in the deck. (In the novel, the Aces were red and blue.)

Commercial Break

Segment 2. Ben is in a cab talking on a cellular phone. He tells the cabbie to pull over. He goes down into the Barrens where he sees a fat kid being chased by a bunch of bullies. For a second he flashes back to himself being chased by Bowers and company down the same hill. But the kid is real. Ben washes off the kid's cut and gives him a "hankie thing" to wrap around the cut. We then flashback to Ben hearing his dead father's voice in the swamp in the Barrens in front of the pumping-station. He then sees his father's corpse speaking with Pennywise's voice. We see Ben

as a child running towards the voice and then we see Ben as an adult saying, you're only in my mind. A bum touches Ben the adult on the shoulder and asks for spare change. Ben freaks and also boogeys on out of there. The woman cabbie asks Ben if he was reliving his childhood, and Ben responds that he was just saying hi to some old ghosts. As they drive away, Ben sees Pennywise standing by the side of the road holding balloons. A balloon suddenly appears in Ben's cab. On it is written "Turn Back Now."

The next part of this section begins with Eddie arriving in front of a pharmacy to pick up his Hydrox prescription. We then flashback to Mr. Keene trying to tell Eddie that his Hydrox is nothing but water and camphor. Eddie as an adult then sees himself running out of the store after his "talk" with Keene, and he hears the now aged Mr. Keene asking his son (?) the pharmacist for a cigar. Eddie goes into the back room and thanks Mr. Keene for trying to tell him the truth when he was a kid. Keene's hand turns into Pennywise's claws, and the clown's voice comes out of Keene. It tells him to get out of Derry while you still can.

The last part of this section has Beverly arriving in Derry and going to visit her old house. She sees "Marsh" on the door and rings the bell (it's actually the word "Kersh"). The old lady says she knew Bev's father and invites her in. Bev goes in the bathroom, but there's no blood to be found. Mrs. Kersh brings Bev tea. Kersh slurps hers down, and her teeth turn all black. Bev's tea turns to blood. She drops the cup and when Mrs. Kersh is on her knees cleaning up the mess, she turns into Al Marsh's corpse. Bev flees the house. Her father's corpse turns into Pennywise, and she almost gets hit by a truck. She suddenly sees that the house is deserted and boarded up. As she stands there, a balloon floats down the street.

Commercial Break

Segment 3. This section begins in England where we see Greco (the director of the film Bill was writing in Part 1) for the first time. A typical showbiz weasel, he is bitching to Audra about Bill's departure and he tells her to not even think about leaving England. Later that night a violent storm wakes Audra up, and the next thing we know, she's dialing International Reservations for a flight to the United States.

The film then moves back to Derry, specifically the Chinese restaurant where Mike has arranged the reunion dinner. (Here it's called the Chop Suey Chinese Restaurant; in the book it's the Jade of the Orient.) Eddie arrives at the restaurant, reunites with Mike and Ben. Richie arrives, is overwhelmed when he catches a glimpse of the three guys, and runs into the bathroom where he tells himself to get a grip. Bev finally arrives. She says, "What a bunch of handsome old men," and passes out. She wakes up, hugs the guys, and Eddie tells them all that he doesn't remember anything from the summer of 1960. We then immediately flashback to the scene where Eddie sprayed his aspirator (which he told Pennywise was filled with battery acid) at the clown, and much of what happened floods back. Richie asks about Stan, they all feel he'll show, but decide to get started. They all eat dinner, obviously having a good time, while "It's Alright" plays on the soundtrack. After dinner, they chat. Richie reveals he's been married four or five times. He mentions Henry Bowers, and Mike tells them Henry is in Juniper Hills, the mental hospital (the same as in the book). Henry confessed to all the 1960 Derry murders, and after his commitment the murders stopped.

We then see Henry in bed at Juniper Hills. Pennywise speaks to Henry from the full moon and tells him to go back and "finish the job."

Back at the restaurant, dinner is over and Rose brings out the fortune cookies. As in the book, these are *nasty* fortune cookies. Richie tells them he's leaving. Bev objects, and Richie asks her if she has some "high-toned" idea about reliving an old nightmare. (This is a reference to King's novel *The Dark Half*, in which Thad Beaumont's alter ego George Stark drives a black Toronado with a bumpersticker on it that reads "HIGH-TONED SON OF A BITCH.") Eddie suggests that maybe Richie's right. Mike picks up the check against the other's protests, and then they open the fortune cookies. Bev's bleeds. Eddie's contains a giant cockroach. Richie's has a human eye in it. Ben's has claws protruding that open and close. Mike's contains a chicken fetus. And Bill's begins to give birth to a giant fly. They freak, Rose comes in, she doesn't see anything, and they leave the restaurant. (This scene is very similar to the book except for a couple of differences. In the novel, Bev's sprayed blood, Eddie's contained something like a "mutated cricket," and Richie's contained an eye. Ben's, however, contained two human teeth and Bill's gave birth to a fly the size of a baby sparrow from a yellow fluid that looked like pus.)

Commercial Break

Segment 4. It's later that evening and they have all adjourned to the Derry library. Mike calls Stan. We then see a flashback to Bev cleaning up the blood in her bathroom when she was a kid. Back at the library, Richie makes jokes while they wait for Stan to get on the phone and speak to Mike. Mike finds out that Stan is dead and Bill remembers back to his "seven graves" hallucination at the cemetery. We then

flashback to Bill riding down Chestnut Street on Silver. Stan comes running out of the park, and Bill rides him away. Stan tells him he was down in the park "collecting birds" when he heard someone calling him from a big house on the outskirts of the park. (In the book, Stan heard voices coming from the Standpipe. They obviously didn't have the budget to create a realistic 1.75 million gallon water standpipe.) Stan went into the house, the door closed and locked behind him, and the Mummy (wearing clown's pom-poms) came down the stairs after him. (In the novel, it was dead kids.) Stan held out his bird book and recited bird names and the Mummy retreated. The power of belief was able to fend off the demon.

Back at the library, Eddie tells them that Stan saw what was "behind the clown": He looked into "IT's deadlights." Stan had said he had looked there and wanted to be there. For a brief moment, Bill remembers the light in the sewer as Pennywise manifested himself as an energy force back in 1960.

They all decide they need a drink. Mike opens the refrigerator and dozens of balloons fly out. They see Stan's head in the refrigerator. It speaks and makes fun of Bill's stuttering, Richie's nose job, Ben's weight, Bev's choice in men, and Eddie's sex life. (There were no feathers in Stan's mouth, though.) He also mocks Mike for not leaving Derry. The refrigerator door closes, and there is then a huge manifestation scene. The library doors slam shut, the windows break, and books fly off the shelves by the hundreds. It begins to rain inside the library. The Losers form a circle for power and the typewriter begins to type by itself. It reads "He thrusts his fists against the posts and still insists he sees the ghosts." Bill is shocked and haltingly tells the group that his mother had given him that sentence as a speaking exercie to help with his stuttering. In a very funny scene, Richie then says, "No offense, pal, it ain't helping." Bill laughs.

We then go to Juniper Hills where the moon is setting on Henry. The dead Belch Huggins appears to Henry and tells him that they have to pay them (The Losers) back. Belch tells Henry that he himself can get them if they only *half* believe, but that Henry can get them with no conditions—after all, he's still alive. Belch gives Henry his old switchblade. Henry approaches the guard gate. (Koontz is on duty. As in the novel, this is a nod to King's colleague Dean Koontz.) The guard comes after Henry with a roll of coins in his fist (as in the novel) and the clown suddenly appears to Koontz with a Doberman's head (also as in the novel. The Doberman was one of Koontz's biggest, secret fears.) It gets Koontz and Henry escapes Juniper Hills.

Commercial Break

Segment 5. The Derry Inn. The Losers are "gearing up" for their descent into the sewers. Eddie tells them all that he saw himself as a child in the drugstore. He admits he knows that Hydrox is only camphor water. Bev tells him that if he believes in it and it works, then it's good medicine. Mike then tells the history of Derry in thirty year increments. He mentions the 1960 Fire at the Black Spot (in the book it was in 1930), the 1930 explosion at the Ironworks (in the book it happened on Easter Sunday, 1906), and the 1900 massacre at Dred's Creek (not in the book at all). We then see a flashback of Mike telling his class about the disappearance of the Derry settlers, and we also see Mr. Ross, the guy who lived across the street from Beverly Marsh, going into his house while Henry Bowers and company harassed Bev after school one day. Mike then tells them about finding Georgie's picture at the site of Laurie Anne Winterbarger's death, and he makes the point that none of the Losers have kids. Also, that they're all successful—except Mike, the only one who stayed in Derry.

The next segment shows Audra, now in Maine, pulling up at a gas station on the outskirts of Derry. She asks the gas station attendant for directions to the town and he tells her it's right up the road. The guy then begins speaking with Pennywise's voice, and asks her, "Don't you want your balloon, Miss Denbrough?"

Back at the Derry Inn, Ben tells the others about the "fat-paddling" incident from when he was a kid. We then see a flashback to Bev cleaning up the blood in her bathroom. After she was all done, there was a malicious laugh from the drain and all the blood came back in a second. We then see her bringing the guys into the house to see if they, too, see the blood. They do. They all help to clean it up. (In the book, they then brought the bloody rags down to the Kleen-Kloze Washateria.) Back at the Derry Inn, Bev tells them that she fell in love with all of them that day. She says she's cold. Ben says he'll go get her shawl in her room. A brief flashback shows Bill going into the sewers. Back at the Derry Inn, Ben, Mike, and Eddie go upstairs. Ben goes into Bev's room. After Mike closes the window in one of the other's rooms, he is attacked by Henry Bowers and stabbed. Bev comes into her room. Ben is fetching her shawl. She recites his "January embers" haiku to him. They kiss. He sees her back in the mirror as they embrace. She's wearing clown's pants. She was actually Pennywise manifesting himself as Bev. (This is reminiscent of the scene in Kubrick's "The Shining" where Jack Torrance kisses the naked girl from the bathtub and when he looks in

the mirror as they embrace, he sees that she's all rotten and generally dead.) Meanwhile, Henry is trying to finish off Mike in the other room. Eddie and Ben rush in and pull Henry off and Henry is stabbed to death during the scuffle. Henry dies. They take Mike to the hospital.

Commercial Break

Segment 6. The Derry Hospital. Bev, Richie, Eddie, and Bill wait for word on Mike. Ben is outside the hospital. Bev comes out. She says that if Mike dies there will only be five left. Distraught, she wonders why IT hates so much, "Why is it so mean?" Bev tells Ben about her husband Tom, that she married a man just like her father. (Tom's pursuit of Bev to Derry has been eliminated.) Bev then recites Ben's haiku to him, and he is afraid she is another manifestation of Pennywise. But it's really Bev. They kiss. Eddie comes out of the hospital. Mike is going to make it. Bill goes in to see Mike and tells him Henry Bowers is dead. Mike instructs Bill to get the two "silver bullets" out of his sportcoat. Ten years earlier, Mike had gone back in the sewers to retrieve them. He thought they might be needed. He was pretty sure IT was asleep but his hair turned grey overnight. Mike tells Bill he'll understand if he leaves Derry.

The Derry Inn. They cover Bowers's body and leave him in the room. Bill tells the others that the whole town is IT. Bev remembers back to Mr. Ross going in his house while she was being assaulted. They turn on the TV in the room and hear that another little girl was found mutilated. Richie, the last out of the room, sees the report and changes his mind about leaving Derry. As Bill leaves the lobby, he hears "Für Elise" being played on a piano; he sees his mother and either himself or Georgie sitting at the piano in the common room of the hotel. Outside the hotel, he tells the others he's going back in. We suddenly flashback to a sobbing Bill as a child asking the others, "Help me." They huddle. Richie doesn't join the huddle...but he stays and has obviously agreed to join them in the final assault.

On the road outside the Barrens. They "suit up." Bill gives Ben the silver earrings, tells him one is for Mike, and one is for Stan, and that now they're all together again. Lucky Seven. Bill, Ben, Bev, and Eddie grasp hands, and then (in a line of dialogue that strikes me as hilarious every time I hear it), Richie asks, "What the hell you gonna do now? Sing 'Kumbaya?'" Richie says he smells death. And he also says they should have brought a machine gun. They go into the pumphouse and down into the sewers. The first thing they find is Audra's purse. Bill runs into the tunnels screaming Audra's name.

Commercial Break

Segment 7. The sewers. Emotionally spent, Bill sits down, totally devastated by the fact that Audra followed him to Derry and that she is a prisoner of IT. Bev straightens him out and makes him realize that they're all counting on him. They follow the blueprints and end up in the chamber where they first fought IT (as Pennywise). Georgie's paper boat comes floating at them down a culvert. Suddenly Georgie appears and blames Bill for his death. Bill fights the vision, refusing to accept it as his brother, and Georgie disappears. There is a flashback to Bill as a child saying, "You killed my brother, you bastard, let's see you now." Back in the sewers, the Losers hear a voice telling them to get out while they still can. Pennywise's face appears as a giant transparent manifestation, and then disappears. Bill tells the others IT feeds every thirty years. He puts the boat back in the culvert and follows it. The boat stops outside a small door. There are bones and skulls everywhere. Before they enter, Eddie tells them he lied about seeing someone, and that he's actually a virgin. (This completely disregards the "Love and Desire" storyline, since if that element of the story was acknowledged, then Eddie would have made love at least once—to Beverly.) Richie says he can't help Eddie with the fact that he's a virgin, but thanks for sharing. They go through the door. They're in ITs lair. They find Audra wrapped in a cocoon suspended from the ceiling. IT shows up as ITs true earthly corporeal manifestation: a giant spider/crab. Bev shoots and misses. Bill recites his "He thrusts his fists against the posts" mantra. Bev shoots and hits. ITs eyes become the deadlights and hypnotize Ben, Bill, and Richie. Bev goes after the bullet that missed IT. Eddie cries out, "What am I gonna do?," and flashes back to the "This is battery acid"/aspirator scene. Eddie then says, I believe in Santa Claus, the Easter Bunny, and the Tooth Fairy...but I don't believe in you. He tells IT again, this is battery acid and now you disappear. Only this time, IT picks up Eddie in one of his claws. Bev uses the opportunity to shoot the silver bullet at ITs underbelly. She hits. IT drops Eddie. Ben, Bill, and Richie come out of their trance. Eddie is hurt bad. The Spider retreats and Eddie dies. Richie gets pissed. They decide to finish IT off. They chase it, knock the creature over, and Bill rips out ITs heart. IT dies. Bill goes back for Audra. She's catatonic.

Outside. The Barrens. Richie carries Eddie's body. (In the novel, they left his body in the sewers.) Bill tends to Audra. There is a flashback to the huddle that concluded Part 1.

Mike in the hospital. It's a few weeks later and he narrates a final journal entry before all his memories fade. He's thinking about moving out of Derry. Richie is now in a movie—with a guy who reminds Mike of Eddie. Ben and Bev are married and pregnant. (Another curse gone, he says.) Bill and Audra are staying at Mike's house. Audra is still living in catatonia. Bill visits Mike every day. We then see Bill leaving Mike's house. Bill is profoundly sad. As he's putting Audra in a cab, he decides to take her for a ride on Silver. As they ride, he tells her, "Beat it, beat it." It works. Audra comes back to Bill. She has been resurrected by the power of belief and love. They stop and kiss in the middle of a Derry intersection.

THE END

JUMP START By Robb Armstrong

Reprinted by permission of UFS, Inc.

Miscellaneous Formats: Spoken Word Recordings & Poetry

THE AUDIO KING
The Audiotape Versions of Stephen King's Work

The following feature by George Beahm (which originally appeared in George's *The Stephen King Companion*) gives details on the audiotape versions of Stephen King's works.

I'd like to express my sincerest thanks and appreciation to George for contributing this feature, and for his scholarship and attention to detail. —**sjs**

THE AUDIO KING
The Audiotape Versions of Stephen King's Work

1. "Apt Pupil" (from *Different Seasons*), #84065, Recorded Books, Inc. An unabridged recording read by Frank Muller on five cassettes; 7 1/2 hours. Available for purchase ($34.95) or rental. (All Recorded Books tapes are rented for thirty days; this tape rents for $11.50).

2. "Ballad of the Flexible Bullet" (from *Skeleton Crew)*, #85330, Recorded Books, Inc. An unabridged recording read by Frank Muller on two cassettes; 3 hours. Available for purchase ($15.95) or rental ($7.50).

3. "The Body" (from *Different Seasons*), #84064, Recorded Books, Inc. An unabridged recording read by Frank Muller on four cassettes; 6 hours. Available for purchase ($26.95) or rental ($10.50).

4. "The Breathing Method" (from *Different Seasons*), #84066, Recorded Books, Inc. An unabridged recording read by Frank Muller on two cassettes; 3 hours. Available for purchase ($15.95) or rental ($7.50).

5. *The Dark Tower: The Gunslinger,* NAL, 1988. An unabridged recording read by Stephen King on four cassettes; 6 hours, 16 minutes. Credits: Produced by Nancy Fisher, Creative Programming, Inc., New York; engineers, Mark Wellman, John Ciglia, and Marcelo-Gandela; cover illustration by Michael Whelan; photograph by James Salzano; handlettering by Ed Rouya (credited to "Es Rouya"). ISBN 0-453-00636-1, Book Number: H636; $29.95.

Also, a limited edition was produced: $100 (perhaps numbered, but signed by King).

6. *The Dark Tower II: The Drawing of the Three,* NAL, 1989. An unabridged recording read by Stephen King on eight cassettes; 12 hours, 16 minutes. Credits: Produced and edited by Mark Wellman of Marketing, Media & Wellman; engineer, Mark Wellman; cover illustration by Phil Hale; photograph by James Salzano; handlettering by Ed Rouya. ISBN 0-453-00643-4, Book Number: H643; $34.95.

Also, a limited edition was produced: $125 (perhaps numbered, but signed by King).

7. "The Mist" (from *Skeleton Crew*), ZBS Foundation. A dramatization recorded in 3-D sound utilizing the Kunstkopf binaural recording method; 1 hour, 20 minutes. Credits: Directed by Bill Raymond; story adaptation by M. Fulton; assistance provided by Dennis Etchison; musical score by Tim Clark. (Included is a fifteen-minute documentary demonstrating how the special sound effects were created using the Kunstkopf system, "The Making of 'The Mist'.")
   a. real-time chrome cassette, $15
   b. normal low-noise with Dolby B, $10 (O.P.)
   c. high-speed duplication, $9.95, the ZBS 3-D version licensed to Simon & Schuster audioworks; ISBN 0-671-62138-6

8. "The Mist" (from *Skeleton Crew*), #85230, Recorded Books, Inc. An unabridged recording read by Frank Muller on three cassettes; 4 1/2 hours. Available for purchase ($19.95) or rental ($9.50).

9. "Prime Evil: A Taste for Blood" (from *Prime Evil*), Simon & Schuster Audioworks. An unabridged recording read by Ed Begley, Jr. on two cassettes; 150 minutes, with an introduction by editor Douglas E. Winter. $14.95. Three stories: "The Night Flier" by Stephen King, "Food" by Thomas Tessier, and "Having a Woman to Lunch" by Paul Hazel.

10. "Rita Hayworth & Shawshank Redemption" (from *Different Seasons*), #84063, Recorded Books, Inc. An unabridged recording read by Frank Muller on three cassettes; 4 1/2 hours. Available for purchase ($19.95) or rental ($9.50).

11. *Skeleton Crew: Book One* (from *Skeleton Crew*), #85210 (the set), Recorded Books, Inc. Unabridged recordings read by Frank Muller on six cassettes; 9 hours. Available for purchase ($37.95) or rental ($12.50). Stories include:
    * "The Man Who Wouldn't Shake Hands" and "Word Processor of the Gods" (#85320).
    * "Morning Delivery," "Big Wheels," "For Owen," and "Survivor Type" (#85250).
    * "The Jaunt" and "Beachworld" (#85260).
    * "The Raft" and "The Reaper's Image" (#85280).
    * "The Monkey" and "Cain Rose Up" (#85290).
    * "The Reach" and "Uncle Otto's Truck" (#85330).

12. *Skeleton Crew: Book Two* (from *Skeleton Crew*), #85220 (the set), Recorded Books, Inc. Unabridged recordings read by Frank Muller on five cassettes; 7 1/2 hours. Available for purchase ($34.95) or rental ($11.50). Stories include:
    * "The Ballad of the Flexible Bullet" (two cassettes, #85240).
    * "Nona," "Paranoid: A Chant" and "Here There Be Tygers" (#85270).
    * "Mrs. Todd's Shortcut" and "The Wedding Gig" (#85310).
    * "Gramma" (#85340).

13. *Stories from Night Shift* (from *Night Shift*). From Warner Audio Publishing, available as a boxed set and, in some instances, separately. These recordings were also licensed to Waldenbooks for the Waldentapes series (O.P.). A small booklet, reprinting the introduction by John D. MacDonald that appeared in the book, is enclosed with the boxed package. Price: $34.95. Running time: 6 hours. Stories include:
    * "Jerusalem's Lot" (sides 1 and 2), read by Colin Fox.
    * "I Am the Doorway" (side 3), read by Fox.
    * "Night Surf" (side 4), read by David Purdham.
    * "I Know What You Need" (sides 5 and 6), read by Deidre Westervelt.
    * "The Last Rung on the Ladder" (side 7) read by Purdham.
    * "The Boogeyman" (side 8), read by Purdham.
    * "Graveyard Shift" (sides 9 and 10), read by Purdham.
    * "One for the Road" (sides 11 and 12), read by Fox.
    * "The Man Who Loved Flowers" (side 12), read by Purdham.

14. *Stories from Skeleton Crew* (from *Skeleton Crew*). From Warner Audio Publishing, available as a boxed set and, in some instances, separately. These recordings were also licensed to Waldenbooks for the Waldentapes series (O.P.). Price: $34.95. Running time: 6 hours. Stories include:
    * "The Monkey," read by David Purdham.
    * "Mrs. Todd's Shortcut," read by Purdham.
    * "The Reaper's Image," read by Purdham.
    * "Gramma," read by Gale Garnett.

15. *Thinner* by Stephen King (writing as Richard Bachman). From Durkin•Hayes Publishing Ltd. (incorporating the original publisher, LFP, Listen for Pleasure), LFP 7127, an abridged recording read by Paul Sorvino on two cassettes; 2 1/2 hours. Credits: abridged by Sue Dawson, produced by Graham Goodwin. $14.95.

Miscellaneous Material

* "The Author Talks: Stephen King," #87380, Recorded Books, Inc. One cassette, 1 hour, $5.50 (for purchase only; no rental available). A sampler, this has a short reading by King of "Mrs. Todd's Shortcut," and readings by Frank Muller from *Skeleton Crew* and *Night Shift*, interspersed with an interview with King, conducted by Muller, and a short overview of King's writing career.

* "Stephen King," from "The Larry King Show," April 10, 1986. Lion Recording Service (P.O. Box 962, Washington, D.C. 20044). One cassette, 2 hours, $4.95. (A fascinating, illuminating interview, this recording is flawed by poor sound reproduction, perhaps because it was a high-speed duplication.)

AUDIOTAPE UPDATE

Two stories from *Four Past Midnight* are also now on bookstore shelves: "The Langoliers" read by Willem Dafoe (1990), and "Secret Window, Secret Garden" read by James Woods (1991). The remaining two stories from *Four Past Midnight* are also scheduled for audiotape release.

THE RADIATING PENCILS OF HIS BONES
The Poetry of Stephen King

Dr. Michael Collings is the most astute Stephen King critic writing in the field today. He is a brilliant academic who has written extensively on King's work. (See the selected Collings' bibliography following this introduction.) He is a Full Professor of English at Pepperdine University, where he is the Director of the Creative Writing Program. He holds a B.A. and M.A. in English, and a Ph.D. in Renaissance Literature. He is a prolific writer, poet, critic, reviewer, scholar, and novelist. He is also a helluva nice guy whose literary output boggles the mind.

His Starmont volumes take a serious, insightful look at Stephen King's writing and acknowledge that there is *much* more to King's work than many critics will admit, and that there is much more to Stephen King himself than his popularity. I, personally, have learned a lot from Michael Collings. He has taught me to read more deeply and to think more clearly, and he has also shown me how to enhance my enjoyment and understanding of literature. He is a consummate teacher and I highly recommend his work.

"The Radiating Pencils of His Bones" is Dr. Collings' look at the small collection of poetry Stephen King has published over the past twenty-three years. Even if you haven't read some of the rarer poems Dr. Collings discusses in his essay, just reading his piece will help you better appreciate *all* of King's writings, not just his poetry.

I'd like to express my sincerest thanks to Michael for his help over the years; for "Radiating Pencils," for his "Star Invaders" feature in this volume, for his poem, "You, Stephen King," also in this volume, and for his scholarship and dedication to literature and teaching.
—sjs

A Selective
Michael R. Collings Bibliography

Books

- *A Season of Calm Weather* (poems), Hawkes, 1974.
- *The Boundaries of Choice: Moral Freedom in Milton's Poetic Universe*, DAI, 1977.
- *Whole Wheat Harvest* (cookbook), Hawkes, 1980.
- *Piers Anthony* (criticism), Starmont, 1983.
- *The Many Facets of Stephen King* (criticism), Starmont, 1985.
- *The Shorter Works of Stephen King* (with David A. Engebretson; criticism), Starmont, 1985.
- *Stephen King as Richard Bachman* (criticism), Starmont, 1985.
- *The Annotated Guide to Stephen King: A Primary and Secondary Bibliography of the Works of America's Premier Horror Writer* (bibliography), Starmont, 1986.
- *Brian W. Aldiss* (criticism), Starmont, 1986.
- *Reflections on the Fantastic* (edited collection), Greenwood, 1986.
- *The Films of Stephen King* (criticism), Starmont, 1987.
- *Card Catalogue: The Science Fiction and Fantasy of Orson Scott Card* (bibliography), Hypatia, 1987.
- *The Stephen King Phenomenon* (criticism), Starmont, 1987.
- *In the Image of God: Theme, Characterization, and Landscape in the Fiction of Orson Scott Card* (criticism), Greenwood, 1989.

Forthcoming Book

- *Infinite Explorations: Art and Artifice in Stephen King's It, Misery, and The Tommyknockers* (criticism), Starmont, 1991.

Contributor to Many
Journals, Magazines, and Periodicals

- *Castle Rock: The Stephen King Newsletter*
- *Contemporary Literary Criticism*
- *Fantasy Newsletter*
- *Fantasy Review*
- *Footsteps*
- *International Association for the Fantastic in the Arts Newsletter*
- *Mystery Scene*
- *Science Fiction and Fantasy Book Review*
- *Science Fiction and Fantasy Annual Review*
- *Space & Time*
- *West Coast Review of Books*

THE RADIATING PENCILS OF HIS BONES
The Poetry of Stephen King
by Dr. Michael R. Collings

As a writer, Stephen King is not well-known for his poetry; virtually lost among the million-copy novels, the short stories, the reviews and interviews and articles King's readers read, discuss, and anatomize are eight short published poems, most dating from his college years and appearing in esoteric arts magazines published by the University of Maine, Orono. More recently, two poems were included in his 1985 collection, *Skeleton Crew*. Although difficult to find, the early poems are nonetheless worth the effort, if for no other reason than that they provide interesting and valuable insights into the development of King's imagination and his art.

Poetry is a precise form; the limitations of line length, stanza form, rhymical and verbal patterning all lend a sense of focus to poetry. It is characterized by compression of idea and image, by exploration of the possibilities of language. More than any other literary genre—short fiction, screenplay, especially the diffuse bulk of the novel (to say nothing of the long novel, a form that King has frequent recourse to)—poetry requires careful control of every element. A single false word in a 150,000-word novel may not even be noticed; a single false word, even a false sound pattern, however, may destroy the cumulative effect of a ten-line poem.

In addition, poetry lays additional constraints on the writer in terms of coherence, development, and the ability to communicate elliptically. The single image succinctly described must be capable of unfolding, of inviting the reader into the experience of the poem, and of repaying with continual depth and expressiveness as the reader returns to the poem again and again.

Poetry, then, is a difficult form. A number of major novelists began their careers intending to be poets. C.S. Lewis's first books were collections of poetry; Faulkner had aspirations to being a poet; more recently—and in an allied form to King's—Orson Scott Card worked extensively with poetry and poetic drama before turning to science fiction and fantasy. In each case, forays into poetry became part of the writers' apprenticeship, providing opportunities to develop linguistic skills, imagery, rhythms, and discipline that would prove invaluable in later works.

In addition, of course, early poems frequently incorporate ideas and images that will recur in more extended forms later in a writer's career. This is particularly true with King, whose handful of published poems are often of interest less for their inherent value as poems than as indices to King's development. Although the poems may demonstrate what King's critics might consider unusual perceptivity and sensitivity in a writer whose fiction has earned him a reputation as the "king of horror," the poems do not rivet the reader's attention to the same extent as his stories and novels, in part simply because King's many strengths are most apparent in longer forms—particularly his unique narrative stance, that half-familiar colloquial voice that engages readers' imaginations and makes it almost impossible for them to break away from the stories he tells. The more formal distancing and verbal texture of poetry often comes between King as poet and his audience.

By virtue of their form, his poems work against King's colloquial narrative approach. Rather than encompassing the fate of the world, or even the fate of a complex cast of intriguing characters whose stories are told over the expanse of three hundred, or five hundred, or eight hundred pages or more, the poems concentrate on the small, the minute. They are not themselves trivial, but they carry an implicit sense of triviality when considered next to the bulk of *The Stand* or *IT*, for example, or even the lesser weight of *Carrie, 'Salem's Lot,* and the other novels. Yet the poems—especially the earliest of them—fascinate because of the light they shed on King's interests and imagination.

In fact, his earliest published poem, when viewed through the superior vision of hindsight, becomes virtually a catalogue of themes and techniques that will become increasingly important.

"Harrison State Park '68"

By 1968, King had already professionally published four stories and completed the manuscript for *The Long Walk* (published essentially unrevised eleven years later). In the fall of that year, "Harrison State Park '68" appeared under King's name in *Ubris,* a publication of the University of Maine at Orono. It is a long elliptical poem of 100 free verse lines, with stanzas scattered across the page, incorporating white space as well as text into the visual effect of the poetry. "Harrison State Park '68" is, at first glance, obviously experimental and exploratory, as befits the time and situation of its composition—the work of socially- and literarily-aware college student in the late sixties. The subject is a murder in Harrison State Park, a location in Maine mentioned in several of King's later novels.

As a poem, "Harrison State Park '68" is not particularly strong. It relies on verbal cliches ("If you can't be an athlete,/be an athletic supporter"), on overt puns ("call me Ishmael/i am a semen") that sometimes establish only marginal connections with the remainder of the poem, and on elliptical images that disintegrate rather than integrate the communication. Even by the time the poem was written, the use of fragmented white space to create poetic texture had become a visual cliche, while the text often shifts from full conventional use of capitals to erratic use of lower case *i* for the first person pronoun. In addition, it is equally erratic in ignoring punctuational devices: *"can't"* appears conventionally spelled in one stanza, while *"dont"*—without the apostrophe—appears in another. Such inconsistencies of usage occasionally impede the movement of the poem.

However, in spite of these difficulties—which should not be considered surprising in the work of a twenty-year-old neophyte poet—"Harrison State Park '68" repays reading. It begins with what will become a trademark in King's fictions: headnote quotations to suggest the direction of the story to follow. In this case —as with *IT*, which pairs a quotation from William Carlos Williams' *Patterson* with a line from Bruce Springsteen – the passages are carefully juxtaposed to create a sense of internal tension: Thomas Szasz's "All mental disorders are simply defective strategies for handling difficult life situations" collides in context, vocabulary, structure, and meaning, with Ed Sanders' "And I feel like homemade shit."

Yet the headnotes—and their conscious juxtaposition—are effective and appropriate. The poem deals with tension, with conflict, with juxtaposition of images. The early lines *"Modern Screen Romances* is a tent on the grass/Over a dozen condoms/In a quiet box,"* with their quiescent evocation of sexuality and illusion, clash with the poem's horrific conclusion:

> oh don't
> don't
> please touch me
> but don't
> don't
> and i reach for your hand
> but touch only the radiating five pencils
> of your bones:
> —Can you do it?

In addition, throughout the poem there are suggestions of devices that will become vintage King. The repetition of "—Can you do it?" throughout the poem adumbrates the incessant "Do you love?" that helps establish atmosphere and texture in "The Raft" and "The Reach" (originally published as "Do the Dead Sing?"). Several stanzas in "Harrison State Park '68" include brand-name references—Sony, Westinghouse, Playtex living bras, Fig Newtons—as well as refer-

ences to cultural icons such as the Doors and Sonny and Cher. Even the topic, with its implied social criticism and obvious connections to fear, terror, and horror, foreshadows King's later preoccupation with death in its multifarious manifestations. The sense of isolation, fragmentation, and disintegration that the form, structure, and content of the poem communicate will find themselves repeated and expanded in virtually every story King will tell.

"The Dark Man"

More successful as an independent poem and more indicative of the directions King's imagination will follow, however, is "The Dark Man," published in the Spring 1969 issue of *Ubris* and the 1970 issue of *Moth* (also a publication of UMO, with Burton Hatlen as advisor). The differences between "Harrison State Park '68" and "The Dark Man" are striking. The earlier poem is verbally and visually diffuse, lacks a clear focus in its elliptical and imagistic approach to violence, and echoes content through its explicit visual arrangement of seemingly unrelated stanzas. The later poem, on the other hand, is from first glance more tightly focused, with its lines and stanzas shaped into conventional format that is clearly a poem. It begins with a strong, almost stridently abrupt image:

> i have stridden the fuming way
> of sun-hammered tracks and
> smashed cinders...

Subsequent stanzas repeat the initial syntactical structure, "i have...i have...i have," using that repitition to create an undercurrent of rhythm and power. King's images are implicitly and explicitly violent, rough, often verging on the horrific: "desperate houses with counterfeit chimneys"; "glaring swamps/where musk-reek rose/to mix with the sex smell of rotting cypress stumps..."; and

> i forced a girl in a field of wheat
> and left her sprawled with the virgin bread
> a savage sacrifice...

The poem concludes with a simple, understated assertion of the speaker's ultimate identity: "i am a dark man."

To King's later readers, of course, that phrase will resonate with meaning that far exceeds the confines of a single poem. The "dark man" is nearly as consistent a motif in King's fictions as the "monstrous woman." One dark man, Roland, is the key figure in the Dark Tower cycle, while another, Randall Flagg, forms the evil center of *The Stand* and *Eyes of the Dragon*. More specifically—and more interestingly in terms of "The

Dark Man" as suggestive of King's later works—his initial description of Flagg in *The Stand* echoes the atmosphere and feeling, and at times even the specific rhythms and vocabulary, of the poem. In the five pages of Chapter 17, King's paragraphs incessantly repeat similar syntactical openings: "Randall Flagg, the dark man, strode south..."; "He walked rapidly...," "He walked south...," "He moved on...," "He hammered along...," "He rocked along...," "The dark man walked and smiled," "He strode on...," and "He stopped." Only in the final three paragraphs does King shift to another structural form – and the shift is significant because Flagg suddenly becomes aware that "His time of transfiguration was at hand. He was going to be born for the second time..." He becomes, as does the speaker of the final line of the poem, the archetypal Dark Man.

In addition, the images in *The Stand* echo those sketched in the poem. In a sequence that builds on the rape imagery of the final stanza of the poem, King writes of Flagg that

> The women he took to bed with him, even if they had reduced intercourse to something as casual as getting a snack from the refrigerator, accepted him with a stiffening of the body, a turning away of the countenance. Sometimes they accepted him with tears. They took him the way they might take a ram with golden eyes of a black dog—and when it was done they were *cold,* so *cold,* it seemed impossible they could ever be warm again. (Ch. 17)

And, as with the speaker of the poem, Randall Flagg's world is replete with violence and terror:

> He hammered along, arms swinging by his sides. He was known, well known, along the highways in hiding that are traveled by the poor and the mad, by the professional revolutionaries and by those who have been taught to hate so well that their hate shows on their faces like harelips and they are unwelcome except by others like them who welcome them to cheap rooms with slogans and posters on the walls, to basements where lengths of sawed-off pipe are held in padded vises while they are stuffed with high explosives, to back rooms where lunatic plans are laid: to kill a cabinet member, to kidnap the child of a visiting dignitary, or to break into a boardroom meeting of Standard Oil with grenades and machine guns and murder in the name of the people. (Ch. 17)

Even in the rhythms, alliterations, and periods of that final extended sentence, one can hear echoes of similar lines in "The Dark Man," down to and including portions that virtually scan as iambic/dactylic units. The poem is forty-two lines long, divided into five stanzas of increasingly dark imagery that ultimately have required portions of five novels for King to explore more fully.

"Silence" and "Donovan's Brain"

The other two poems published in *Moth* have less impact and are less relevant to his later career, perhaps because they are substantially narrower in focus. "Silence" is a twelve-line monologue, superficially suggestive of King's later poem "Paranoid: A Chant" in its obsession with "the feary silence of fury." Other than that single line, there is little in the poem that is memorable or suggestive. "Donovan's Brain," as the title indicates, reflects the horror film by that title and is again an exercise in obsession and terror—the latter signalled by typographical placement of a single word in the center of the page between lines of asterisks:

****

horror

****

In its combination of filmic echoes and strident imagery—"warped and sucked by desert wine/raped by the brain of that monstrous man"—the poem moves King a step closer to devices that will help form the texture of his subsequent fictions.

"In the key-chords of dawn..."

A year later, another short poem appeared, an untitled work in the January 1971 issue of *Onan,* also published in Orono. There is even less here that looks forward to King's enormous impact as a novelist, in part perhaps because of the subject: fishing. At a time when King was involved in writing not only tales of horror and terror for *Cavalier* and *Startling Mystery Stories* but also more generally mainstream and mostly unpublishable novels—the opening chapters of *Rage, The Long Walk, Sword in the Darkness* (an unpublished race-riot novel), and *Blaze* (an unpublished reworking of Steinbeck's *Of Mice and Men*)—it should not suprise that his poetic imagination might turn to mainstream images as well. [NOTE: See the section on King's unpublished novels, *The Aftermath, Sword in the Darkness,* and *Blaze* in this volume.—sjs] Beginning "In the key-chords of dawn," the poem is a twenty-four line meditation on sport and responsibility; it concludes with the awareness that when the second overwhelms the first, it is time to "put away our poles." Even in a work as insubstantial as this, however, there are indications of growth and maturity through an increasing sense of verbal and visual control in the lines. The images are less violent, less vigorous, but more disciplined than those in "Harrison State Park '68," for example.

"Brooklyn August"

The sense of maturity continues in the next poem, a paean to baseball called "Brooklyn August." Dedicated to Jim Bishop, one of King's instructors at UMO, it appeared in *Io* in 1971. Again, the subject vitiates any sense of direct influence on King's major novels, except that baseball touches the lives of later characters in *IT* and elsewhere. Of some interest, however, is the overt structure of the piece, a blend of traditional poetry and the rhythms of prose. Three rhyming sequences of lines (all with terminal long- *O* rhymes) are interrupted by free-verse descriptive stanzas that move baseball from an idealized national pasttime to a sometimes dark reality. The snap back from prosaic texture to carefully rhyming couplets reminiscent of Eliot's famous

> In the room the women come and go
> Talking of Michelangelo

from "The Love Song of J. Alfred Prufrock" (and in fact using the same terminal rhyme sound) suggests a dissociation of perception as the poem shifts from repetitive, formalistic statements couched in rhyming couplets to the minutiae of observation expressed through free verse and the rhythms of prose. [NOTE: Tyson Blue, in *The Unseen King*, also makes note of King's "Ebbets Fields" stanzas in "Brooklyn August," positing that King's own

> In Ebbets Field the crab-grass grows
> (where Alston managed) row on row

as well as the other similarly rhymed stanzas, are a variation on the opening lines of John McCrae's poem "In Flanders Fields" which begins

> In Flanders fields the poppies blow
> Between the crosses, row on row

a stanza which may very well owe *its* genesis to the T.S. Eliot lines Dr. Collings refers to. — sjs] The poet's vision is expanding, incorporating not only his own observations and interests but also tags of literary heritage as well, a tendency already suggested by echoes of Poe in "The Glass Floor" (1967) and "The Blue Air Compressor" (1971). In later works, King's use of literary allusions and structures would become increasingly complex and important, from the multiple literary references in *The Shining*, to the assertion of an essentially Lovecraftian universe in *IT*, to the unabashed assumption of the guise of genre-romance in *Misery*. King's arsenal of direct allusions would ultimately incorporate Herman Melville, H.P. Lovecraft, W.B. Yeats, Robert Frost, Ernest Hemingway, William Faulkner, John Milton, George Orwell,

J.R.R. Tolkien, H.G. Wells, Bram Stoker, Charles Dickens, William Shakespeare, William Golding, Samuel Coleridge, Sean O'Casey, and others—a tempering of classical and traditional literary elements to counter stridently contemporary and pop-culture references to Bob Dylan, The Who, John Jakes, Bruce Springsteen. "Brooklyn August" lies a long way from the focus of King's major works, but even in its distancing, the poem demonstrates one of his fundamental structural devices.

The *Skeleton Crew* poems: "Paranoid: A Chant" and "For Owen"

Following the appearance of "Brooklyn August," King seemed to have abandoned poetry for the less restrictive, freer, more expansive (and—to be honest—more profitable) possibilities of short story and novel. His list of publications during the next fourteen years includes dozens of short stories; every novel through *The Talisman, The Eyes of the Dragon,* and the final Bachman novel, *Thinner;* and his non-fiction study of horror in film and television, *Danse Macabre.* During the same period, over a dozen films based on his works appeared, many of which he had a hand in developing. Then, when *Skeleton Crew* appeared in 1985, King surprised many of his readers by including two more poems: "Paranoid: A Chant" and "For Owen." Both differ radically from the earlier poems; both show advances in tone and voice that might be expected from a novelist of King's stature.

"Paranoid: A Chant" is an internal monologue, told in colloquial vocabulary and rhythms through the perceptions of a speaker whose own grasp on reality and truth is at best shaky. The speaker is presented as marginally uneducated ("I can't go out no more"), obsessed by fear, and communicating that fear in staccatto bursts of accusation and self-revelation. Verbal and syntactical structures collapse onto themselves; punctuation and other conventional means of establishing order and coherence are absent. The reader is forced to question the narrator's sanity, while the speaker continually, obsessively asserts that he is sane: *these things are happening,* he says, *believe me, I know.* In the warped perceptions of the narrator, luncheonette salt becomes arsenic, "greeting cards are letter bombs," scholars are suborned by the FBI, and "a dark man with no face" crawls "through nine miles/of sewer to surface in my toilet, listening..."

With the inexorable logic-not-logic of madness, the poem ends where it began, with an offer of coffee to the unnamed listener (an offer anyone with any intelligence would refuse) and a return to the opening stanza of the poem. Nothing has changed. Nothing more is known about reality or truth. The circle of madness is closed and the chant resumes.

"For Owen" is less threatening, in part because the narrative voice more closely approximates King's own. The poem is apparently directed toward King's younger son, focusing on the fears and frustrations of a child attending school. Both poems are written in the first person, but where "Paranoid: A Chant" generates an increasing sense of unease and discomfort as the reader discovers what lies in the speaker's mind, "For Owen" soothes and expands metaphorically to suggest the universal experience of death, not in terms of the terror defined in the more horrific stories in *Skeleton Crew*—"The Mist," "Gramma," "The Raft," or "Nona"— but rather in terms of the gentle awakening and understanding that Stella Flanders attains in "The Reach." The poem is admittedly cryptic, reaching for meaning through references to schoolchildren as fruit: watermelons, bananas, plums. But by the final lines, the speaker penetrates the metaphors and deals with death, noting that just as a schoolchild must learn to write, he must also learn the art of dying. In the context of *Skeleton Crew,* "For Owen" seems unusually gentle.

Almost lost in the millions of words that comprise King's thirty-three book-length publications and his nearly two hundred published stories, articles, and reviews; virtually buried in university archives and special-collections rooms; reviving echoes of a young King self-consciously exploring the power of words— in spite of the circumstances militating against easy access and easy reading, these eight short poems nonetheless suggest, foreshadow, resonate. Each represents a small fragment of King's imagination; each expands that fragment into something larger, more complex than it had been. As poems, none will probably endure as acknowledged masterworks of twentieth-century literature; as integral elements in King's development and growth, however, each retains both interest and importance.

Stephen King's Poetry: A Checklist

"Brooklyn August." *Io* 10, 1971: 147; *The Unseen King,* Blue, Tyson. Mercer Island, Washington: Starmont House, 1989: 107-108.
"The Dark Man." *Ubris,* Spring 1969; *Moth,* 1970: [n.p.]
"Donovan's Brain." *Moth,* 1970: [n.p.]
"For Owen." *Skeleton Crew.* New York: Putnam, 1985: 350-360.
"Harrison State Park '68." *Ubris,* Fall 1968: 25-26.
"Paranoid: A Chant." *Skeleton Crew.* New York: Putnam, 1985: 241-244.
"Silence." *Moth,* 1970: [n.p.]
Untitled Poem ["In the key-chords of dawn"]. *Onan,* January 1971: 69.

"You, Stephen King"
by Michael R. Collings

You, Stephen King,
Smiling behind Coke-bottle lenses,
Bushy beard, New England dialect,

And sixty-million copies of your words

How does it work that you,
So distant and removed
(We shared a table once in a hotel bar
But I know you no more now
Than then)
Can touch the deep-springs of *my* fears?

The strongest human coil is fear—
And when its tensions birth
They tear through bowel and gut
Erupt an alien spray
Adrenalin and blood

Fear—

And more.

I cried, you know,
When Stella Flanders crossed the Reach.
I tried to read it to my wife.
We sat beneath the elms
Where the scratch of rusty lawn-swing hinges
Echoed an early sparrow's song—
I read cold death,
Ravenous cancers,
Immutable ice.
The sparrow sang, but the hinges strangled
Into silence.
We stopped.
Stella saw the cap—
My voice broke like too-thin ice
Along a rushing river's bank—a lacy rime
That cannot bear...

I cried. She finished reading
When my voice thawed
And waters gushed beneath
And through the ice.

Stella Flanders crossed the reach,
Reached across to slip her icy fingernail
Along my grandmother's withered neck,
A point of blood welling
Where the cold laid siege
To blood-press ninety years and more.
And the waters thawed and gushed
Beneath my voice.

When ghosts join hands and sing of joy
The coils of fear
Petal
Like the first elusive rose
of June.

A STROLL AMONG THE HEADSTONES: A GUIDED TOUR

THE DREAD ZONE: MY SCARIEST STEPHEN KING MOMENTS
A Few of Tyson Blue's "Favorite Kings"

Tyson Blue has taken his shots from the critics. He's been accused of being self-serving, and (as he acknowledged in a brief bio note written but not reprinted here) of inserting too many details of his own life into his work.

Maybe so.

But I think his occasional over-indulgence in self-rumination simply comes from a very powerful sense of personal excitement and glee about the subjects he's writing about.

Tyson's sort of like this big "little kid" who gets so wrapped up in what he's doing that sometimes he forgets that there are people who will not understand his rapture, and will, instead, fault him for not being clinically detached 100% of the time.

Be that as it may, the ultimate truth of the matter when it comes to a judgement about Tyson's work on Stephen King is that this guy knows Stephen King's work.

Inside and out.

Upside down and sideways.

And his thoughts on King's stuff are insightful, interesting, and valuable.

I spoke with Tyson about doing something for *The Shape Under the Sheet,* and as he relates in the Introduction, he was initially blocked as to the subject of the piece. But after a brief discussion of an idea I had had (and which Tyson graciously acknowledges in the Intro), he went at the essay with a vengeance.

I really liked "The Dread Zone: My Scariest Stephen King Moments" the first time I read it.

And the second time I read it, I liked it even more.

Yes, there are personal details of Tyson Blue's life in the piece, but they are appropriate to the piece: After all, I *did* ask him to detail for you *Shape* readers his scariest Stephen King moments, and I *did* ask him to tell us why they work, and so, in terms of the premise of the essay, the personal details are absolutely necessary.

I think you'll find "The Dread Zone" to be enlightening, funny, and informative.

It's a mature look at childhood moments recaptured in the fiction of the most popular American writer of the twentieth century.

(In addition to my appreciation for "The Dread Zone," I'd also like to offer my special thanks to Tyson for his work in the late, great *Castle Rock: The Stephen King Newsletter,* and for his book on rare King material, *The Unseen King.*)

For your reading pleasure, I have made note of the page numbers (in the *paperback editions*) of the scenes that Tyson comments on in the following essay. Have a ball!) — **sjs**

THE DREAD ZONE:
MY SCARIEST STEPHEN KING MOMENTS
by Tyson Blue

Introduction

The Dread Zone:
What It Is, and How It Came To Be

In a very real way, this essay can be credited as much to Steve Spignesi, its editor, as it is to me, its author, even though I wrote it. The words are mine, but the genesis is Steve's. Here's the story:

A while back—a *long* while, by the time this actually sees print—I had approached Steve about contributing an article or an interview to *The Shape Under the Sheet,* and found him to be very receptive to the idea. Well and good; I've done this a hundred times, and the next thing to do is to come up with an idea and sit down in front of the old VideoWriter and pound the damn thing out.

Except that I found myself completely roadblocked. I could not come up with a topic for a King essay to save my life. Finally, after about a month and a half, I called Steve up and asked him a single question: "If there was one essay you'd like to see in your book about Stephen King which no one has thought of, what would it be?"

The answer, when Steve called back with it, was so simple that I can't see why I never thought of it. What Steve asked me to do was to come up with those scenes in King's work which really got to me, and to explain why they worked on me the way they did. He even had a title for it—"The Dread Zone." So, that's why what you're about to read is partly mine and partly Steve Spignesi's—the actual moments are mine, the reasons why they work for me are also my own, but the skeleton upon which they are hung is his. We hope you enjoy the monster we've created for you.

Dedication

This essay is dedicated to the memory of my golden retriever, Farley, who died when she was struck by lightning one rainy Saturday night last summer. She spent the restful last afternoon of her life curled up by my chair while I wrote what you have just read.

A MAP OF THE DREAD ZONE

•A gravedigger engaged in burying a young man who has died mysteriously feels the dead child staring at him through the lid of the coffin as the sun sets.

•Four young men are crossing a railroad trestle, when a train comes along.

•A young boy runs gleefully away from his frantic parents and into the path of an oncoming truck.

•A mother tries frantically to revive her son, who has succumbed to heat stroke.

•A writer, bedridden, pleads frantically with a madwoman who holds his destiny in her hands—along with an ax and a blowtorch.

•A man makes his way through an unlighted tunnel filled with rotting corpses.

•A boy on his way home one winter's evening sees a mummy walking across a frozen canal towards him.

These, to paraphrase the old show tune, are a few of my favorite Kings. To be more specific (and make my old fourth-grade teacher, Mr. White, pacific), the above scenes are some of the moments in Stephen King's vast oeuvre in which he absolutely, positively, above and beyond the call of duty, scared the flying fuck out of me.

For the next few pages, we'll take a look at these scenes, along with some of my thoughts on just why it is that I found them so powerful, and why they scared me so much more than others might have.

In almost all of these scenes, the common denominator running through them is that they resonate off of events which actually took place in my own life, so that when I read the scene, not only am I affected by King's storytelling, but also bring to it the subliminal impact of this personal memory, thus making it even more effective.

'SALEM'S LOT

"He had a sudden mental image of Danny Glick lying on that little satin pillow with his eyes open. No—that was stupid. They closed the eyes. He had watched Carl Foreman do it enough times. *Course we gum 'em,* Carl had said once. *Wouldn't want the corpse winkin' at the congregation, would we?*

—*'Salem's Lot,* pages 130-135

Oddly enough, the only real exception to this is the first scenes in King's writing which really got to me, which is the burial scene in *'Salem's Lot.* I remember the circumstances very well: I was on an early-morning Greyhound bus, going from Reading, Pennsylvania, where I had gone to visit my friend Jim Steranko [the editor of *Prevue* magazine], back to Philadelphia, where my family was visiting relatives. I had been up most of the night, and was having a tough time staying awake, reading the novel. In fact, I was dozing off a lot, and even dropped the book on the floor a couple of times.

Then, I came to the climactic scene where the Glick boy is getting buried, and the gravedigger can feel the boy's eyes staring at him through the closed lid of the coffin, the pull getting stronger as the sun gets lower. For some reason, the scene scared me so badly that I found myself wide awake—and in broad daylight, yet!

I don't honestly know precisely why this particular scene got to me. At the time, I had only attended three funerals, all closed casket, had never been to a graveside service, and had only seen one dead human being. There was really very little in my personal experience for this scene to resonate off of. One thing which comes to mind might be a youth ill-spent reading EC horror comics and watching Hammer films about vampires leaping out of coffins, or maybe subliminal memories of the unknown monster which hid in the shadows behind the open doors of my room (I've never had monsters in my closet; at my house, they always hid behind the doors).

Perhaps that's it: at this point in the novel, it had not been definitely established that the monsters in the novel were, in fact, vampires. It may have been the very unknown nature of the menace which was luring that man to his death which made the scene so powerful. One thing which supports this is that once I was certain that the creatures were vampires, much of the menace went out of the story for me (I've written about this before, so if you've read that before, bear with me!). There have been so many novels, films, stories and whatnot written about the vampire and the various means by which they can be dispatched that they are, ironically, almost a conventional, a "safe" type of horror, one which can be easily dealt with; granted, it might be a rocky road for the beleagured heroes—especially if they haven't read many vampire novels!—but it can be done.

Another childhood memory which vibrates sympathetically with this scene is one which is, I imagine, common to many of you out there – the occasional feeling, while you are playing all by yourself, that someone is watching you. This happened to me twice that I can recall, and both times under circumstances in which rational thought would have told me my fears were groundless and absurd, if only I had listened to them.

One time when I was four, my mother left me alone in the house while she walked down the hill to get something at the A & P. This was no big deal back then —it was a small town and nothing bad ever happened. Except that that morning I had seen a Little Rascals film on television where the gang had been chased by an African native, and for some reason I became convinced that he was now after me. My mother came home to find me sitting on top of our steps, refusing to go into the house alone.

Another time, years later, I was playing with a friend on a gloomy, cloudy day in my own backyard, and we so thoroughly convinced ourselves that we were being watched by ghostly figures that we ran screaming into the house, even though we both knew we were making the whole thing up and that there was no one there.

Take this primordial fear, the fear of being watched by unseen beings who wish us harm, and throw in the hint that perhaps the unknown watcher is a dead boy in a coffin, and it is not hard to figure out where this scene gets its hair-raising impact.

Another contributing factor to the power of this scene is the sheer storytelling ability of Stephen King. Get the book and reread that scene when you get done with this: look at how marvelously slowly King builds the tension and the suspense, how the power of the pull on Mike Ryerson strengthens as the sun slowly sinks, how his resistance falters more and more until he is compelled to leap into the grave and open the casket even though he half expects what lies within.

"THE BODY"

"An image of Ray Brower, dreadfully mangled and thrown into a ditch somewhere like a ripped-open laundry bag, reeled before my eyes. We would join him, or at least Vern and I would, or at least I would. We had invited ourselves to our own funerals."
—"The Body," *Different Seasons*, pages 351-358

Most of the rest of the scenes I've selected for this essay are not so hard to figure out. Take, for example, my second favorite, the trestle scene from the novella, "The Body."

The scene is already a classic. Four young boys from Castle Rock, Maine, set out on an epic journey to find the body of a young boy who has been struck and killed by a train. At about the midpoint of their journey, they are crossing a long trestle over a river when a train comes along, forcing them to race frantically to make it to the other side.

I can tell you exactly why this scene got to me so strongly, and it has a lot in common with my reasons for choosing "The Body" as my all-time favorite King story. Put simply, this is my youth.

I grew up in New Hampshire at roughly the same time as Stephen King was growing up in Maine, and so shared many of the broad-based, almost generic, growing-up rituals required of boys in the region. The railroad tracks ran right by my house, and were an irresistible temptation to me and my friends when we wanted to go adventuring. They led by the dump, where we sometimes went rummaging for salvageable junk, and just as often were run off by the caretaker, although he didn't have a dog with him, legendary or otherwise.

And, at one time or another, everyone in my circle of friends had to walk across the railroad bridge which spanned the Winnepesaukee River. Granted, there was a pedestrian sidewalk on the bridge right next to the trestle, but the true test was to walk across the river on the tracks. For one thing, the trestle was much, much higher than the other bridge, with rushing water and rocks below.

I remember the day I elected to do it. It was a Sunday, and no trains were running. From the safety of the bank, the bridge, which was at least six feet wide, seemed almost as secure as a highway. It was, I figured, a cinch. As I set out to cross the bridge, however, I soon noticed two phenomena. The first was how rapidly the bridge seemed to shrink as we got farther out, going from six feet to around three. The other was how easy it was to see down between the ties, and just how far down it was.

Did I mention that I have acrophobia?

I was about halfway out on the bridge when I began wondering what would happen if this was the day the Boston & Maine Railroad decided to send a work train out to check the roadbed or something, and happened to get to this trestle about now. The only thing that line of thought did for my peace of mind was to keep it off the fact that I was a hundred feet or so in the air walking along on what seemed to be a single rail hung out over a rushing, dizzying stream of water. There were platforms spaced here and there along the bridge, where persons could presumably stand while trains went by, but somehow they seemed awfully rickety.

Suffice to say that I made it across, and that no trains came, but I doubt that I could have been much more terrified if one *had* come along. And when, years later, I read that scene in "The Body," I knew exactly what Gordie Lachance was going through because I had been there. King's prose accesses my own memories of this event, and I underpinned the experience of the characters in the story with my own, making it doubly effective. This is, I think, a prime factor in King's success, this ability to touch upon the common ground we share as reader and writer.

PET SEMATARY

(1)

"Gage seemed to realize that the game was over, that your parents didn't *scream* at you when it was just a game, and he had tried to put on the brakes, and by then the sound of the truck was *very* loud, the sound of it filled the world."

—*Pet Sematary,* pages 351-358

(2)

SCENE 363 EXTERIOR: GAGE, IN THE ROAD
As he reaches the broken white line he grabs the ball of string.

SOUND OF THE ONCOMING TRUCK
GAGE turns his head.
GAGE (not afraid): *Druck!*

SCENE 364 EXTERIOR: THE ONCOMING TRUCK AND THE DRIVER, GAGE'S POINT OF VIEW
Suddenly THE DRIVER'S face turns into a Halloween mask of horror.
He BLASTS THE AIR-HORN.

SCENE 365 EXTERIOR: LOUIS, ON THE VERGE OF THE ROAD
LOUIS (shrieks): *NO!!*

—*Pet Sematary* screenplay
by Stephen King, pages 82-83

This happens again in my next scene, Gage's death in *Pet Sematary.* Is there a parent alive who has read this novel, or, for that matter, seen the film version, who does not feel the sheer, paralyzing terror it evokes to the very center of themselves?

I doubt it. As King himself admits, the greatest fear a parent has is losing a child. Perhaps some parents do not feel it as strongly as I do, since I have always had a phobia about one of my children getting run over by a car or truck. It is this, coupled with the fear of losing a child in any manner whatsoever, that makes this scene work so effectively for me.

When I was four, I was visiting with my grandmother on her small farm outside a small town in rural southern Alabama. My parents were occupied with something or other, and no one was paying much attention to me. The place was set back off the main road about five hundred feet, so I guess they didn't think they had anything to worry about. I wandered down the dirt road leading to the house, out into the road, and was hit by a car.

I remember nothing of the accident itself, but I remember the car—it was black, with a huge chromed grille (or so it would certainly have seemed to me!) The driver of the car was not wearing a shirt, and had a St. Christopher's medal on a silver chain around his neck. To this day, I dislike men without shirts, and can't abide masculine neckwear of any kind.

Needless to say, I am already predisposed to give roads a healthy respect. They scare the shit out of me. In fact, since reading *Pet Sematary,* I have never let my children get any nearer the road alongside our house than halfway down the yard when they're playing. My youngest son has *never* been allowed to play in the yard unsupervised.

And once, long after I had read the novel, my youngest son began runnning toward the road at a park where we were picknicking. A car was coming toward him, and I was so scared at the thought of what was going to happen that I couldn't move. Luckily, nothing happened, he's fine, but...

That the novel is more effective on parents than on people without children is borne out, at least for me, by a little research I've done. My daughter read the novel, and said that it was good, but didn't indicate to me that it scared her in any way out of the ordinary. And when I've talked with friends of mine who've read the novel who are not parents, their reactions are much the same. But whenever I've talked with other parents about the novel, the almost-universal reaction has been that it was the whole notion of losing a child which terrified them most about the whole thing. Again, King has taken a universal fear and put it to work for him in a sort of writer's shorthand which lessens the work he has to do while at the same time boosting it's power.

CUJO

"Vic put his head on Tad's chest. He looked up at Donna. His face was white but calm enough.
'How long has he been dead, Donna?'"

—*Cujo,* pages 290-292

Young Tad Trenton's death at the end of *Cujo* works in much the same way. It plays on the related fear that sometimes, no matter what hardships you have overcome or what heroic measures you undertake, you simply cannot save your child. Donna Trenton endures days of hell, cooped up in blistering heat in a car, does battle with a rabid St. Bernard which has killed half of Castle Rock, and when she and her son are out of the woods, he stops breathing, and not all the CPR in the world can bring him back.

This is not as powerful a scene for me as Gage's death in *Pet Sematary,* and I think that this is simply because it does not resonate off as many chords in my own experience as does that scene. I have never had to fight for my child's life, or defend any of them from an attacking outside force. I can picture what that is like, and react to it somewhat. On the other hand, I've had first-hand experience with getting hit by a car, it terrifies me, and I know how easy it is for children to get away from adults and how quickly they can get into that danger.

King has referred in interviews to "pressing the fear-buttons" in his readers. The first of these scenes works more powerfully than does the second simply because it presses more buttons at once, playing a chord rather than a single note.

MISERY

"Annie Annie oh Annie please please no please don't Annie I swear to you I'll be good I swear to God I'll be good please give me a chance to be good OH ANNIE PLEASE LET ME BE GOOD—"

"Just a little pain. Then this nasty business will be behind us for good, Paul."   —*Misery,* pages 217-225

A more universal fear-button is pressed in the climactic central scene of King's recent bestseller, the Stoker Award-winning *Misery.* I am referring, of course, to the scene wherein the demented Annie Wilkes hacks off Paul Sheldon's foot with an ax and then cauterizes the wound with a blowtorch.

I vividly remember the first time I read that scene. It was a Sunday night in February of the year the novel was released, and I was reading it in galleys. I was in bed, reading the novel just before going to sleep. I usually sleep with one foot sticking out from under the blankets, but after reading that scene, both feet were tucked securely within the covers, and right up close to me.

What is, I think, most terrifying about the scene is not the actual events which take place, however Grand Guignol they might be, but the dialogue which precedes them. Anyone who has read it cannot help but remember how Sheldon pleads frantically with Annie Wilkes not to maim him, promising to be good, if only she will not hurt him. Annie, on the other hand, remains implacable, and maintains that she is doing it for his own good, and to teach him a lesson.

There is hardly anyone who has managed to make it to adulthood—and probably more than a few unfortunate wives for whom the nightmare goes on—who cannot identify with this. Sheldon's cries are those of a child pleading not to be punished, against an implacable authority figure who will not be reasoned with under any circumstances, leaving the child begging frantically to avert the spanking—or worse—which is inevitably to come.

I remember having a similar conversation with my father once about some uneaten baked beans.

God, How I absofuckinglutely despise baked beans.

THE STAND

"It was much blacker inside than he had imagined..."
—*The Stand,* pages 201-209

Another favorite scene of mine is from the original version of *The Stand* (although the galleys are not even available as I write this, by the time it sees print you will all most likely have read *The Stand: The Complete & Uncut Edition*). For many fans, the scariest part of the novel is Larry Underwood's escape from New York through the Holland Tunnel, which is completely unlighted and choked with wrecked cars and rotted corpses.

The scare here for me was a little less than it was for some of the scenes I've dealt with earlier, but it was still an effective one.

When I was a kid, I spent a lot of summers in Alabama, with friends and relatives who really knew how to cook up a good homemade house of horrors, the equal or better of any carnival ride I've ever seen. And of course, you had to go through the whole thing blindfolded, and never knew what was being placed in your hand, or what you were going to step into. This is precisely the feeling King generates in this scene, and readers who have been through something like it, as I have, already have a reference to help put it in context.

These are the King scenes that really scared me, many of them to the point where it was no longer fun —no fair, Steve, I know this is a horror novel, but that was *really* scary! But there are scares of a different kind in his work as well, the kind which are fun to read, and I thought that I'd throw a few of those in here as well.

IT

"And in spite of his fear, Ben found that part of him did want a balloon. Who in all the world owned a balloon which would float into the wind? Who had even heard of such a thing? Yes...he wanted a balloon, and he wanted to see the clown's face, which was bent down toward the ice, as if to keep it out of that killer wind."
—*IT,* pages 202-207

My favorite scene of this type is the scene in *IT* where Ben Hanscom, one of the Losers, sees the Mummy, dressed in tattered rags, walk slowly towards him across a frozen canal. I especially like the subtle *wrongnesses* King has built into the scene, the things which are out of whack—the Mummy first appears dressed in Pennywise's clown costume, holding a string of balloons which are blowing toward the boy, but against the wind.

Then, there is the slow, measured pace at which

the Mummy approaches, with a steady, relentless stride which seems impossible since he is walking on glare ice. All of this, coupled with the dramatic sunset lighting and the glowing orange eyes of the creature, lend the entire scene an air of unreality and eerieness which is almost perfect.

Reading it, I recalled the two classic scenes from the Disney Studios' "Darby O'Gill and the Little People" (starring a very young, pre-Bond Sean Connery) in which Darby O'Gill confronts banshees. The figures in the film moved with the same slow, fluid grace which made them even more spooky than they might otherwise have been to me when I first saw the film at age seven or so.

CHRISTINE

"Sitting on the passenger side like a grotesque life-sized doll was Michael Cunningham."
—*Christine*, pages 483-490

"THE MONKEY"

"...there was Amos Culligan's Studebaker, and Hal's mother was behind its slimy wheel, a grinning skeleton with a lake bass staring coldly from one fleshless eye socket."
—"The Monkey," *Skeleton Crew*, page 194

Christine is full of scenes like this—but my favorite is near the end, when the Fury shows up filled with dead people, an image King uses again in the *Skeleton Crew* short story, "The Monkey," when the narrator sees the old car full of mossy skeletons buried in the depths of a lake. The scenes involving the deaths of Moochie Welch and Buddy Repperton work especially well, too, as the two thugs are chased by an empty car through a deserted part of a city (for Mocchie), and a desolate stretch of country road (for Repperton). And of course, you already know how I feel about cars...

THE DARK HALF

"Suddenly he passed from the world he had always known to an alien one which was populated only by these sentinels which guarded the border between the land of the living and that of the dead."
—*The Dark Half*, pages 389-393 (hardcover)

A more recent favorite of mine was the scene near the end of *The Dark Half*, in which Thad Beaumont is headed for his final confrontation with George Stark, and he finds that the grounds around his summer home are carpeted with sparrows, which move aside just enough to let him pass, biding their time, waiting for the right moment. This is a fine example of how King uses popular cultural icons to resonate off his

prose, making the reader do some of his work. Anyone who has seen Alfred Hitchcock's "The Birds" will recall the scene where Rod Taylor leads Tippi Hendren, Jessica Tandy, and a very young Veronica Cartwright out of their besieged home to a car in which they hope to escape, passing through a living carpet of birds, who move just enough to avoid the car and let them leave. It is basically the same scene as King's, only done backwards. But in both cases, the scenes play on the inherent menace of this multitude of ordinarily harmless creatures, made menacing both by their numbers and their brooding, silent waiting.

"GRAMMA"

"He looked at the hand dangling down, unburied, and discovered now that he could touch it, he could tuck it under and bury it with the rest of Gramma.
He bent, grasped the cool hand, and lifted it.
The hand twisted in his hand and clutched his wrist."
—"Gramma," *Skeleton Crew*, pages 486-493

I suppose that, in closing, I should return to one final scene which really and truly gave me the Willies. That would be the long sequence in the middle of "Gramma" where George is screwing up his nerve to cover his dead (?) grandmother's face. The resonances here are varied, depending on the reader's experience —if he has seen any of countless horror films where a character approaches a supposedly dead monster, only to have it abruptly spring to life and grab him, it will work on one level. If he has ever had to actually approach a dead person, in the funeral home, say, then the resonance will be even more intense, especially if he is one of those people for whom, the longer they look at a dead person, the more it seems that they are just sleeping. And for those who have been to a crime scene, and seen the body of a crime victim before it is cleaned up or moved away, the referent is even stronger and provides even more creeps.

This scene also works on the fear inherent in being alone in an old, creaky house at night. Add childhood and the presence of a dead, feared relative to the mix, and the resultant terrors are fine indeed.

With that I conclude my look at some of my favorite scary moments from the works of Stephen King. I could go on and on, culling hundreds of such scenes from the books and stories, but I think the points have all been made, and besides, this thing is about a week past deadline as it is! Some of the scenes I have chosen for this essay are doubtless some of the same scenes you would have chosen, while others of you would select different scenes. But I think that your reasons, once you examined them, would be similar to mine.

Tyson Blue.
Photo courtesy Tyson Blue.

What all of the scenes examined here have in common is that they echo or recall events from my own life, or scenes from films I have seen. In short, they resonate within my own experience in such a way as to increase the effect the scene has upon me as a reader, to amplify its power until it has infinitely more impact that it would have had otherwise.

This happens far too often in King's fiction to be mere coincidence. One of King's strengths as a writer is his instinct for tapping into those kinds of experiences which lurk in the depths of our shared cultural pool of experiences, or which recall iconic moments from popular films or television shows, or events which everyone recalls. In this way, he not only pushes our fear buttons, he boosts the power of his signal. In his essay "The Horror Writer and the Ten Bears," he touches on this by listing ten basic fears (bugs, the dark, etc.) which he uses in his work to evoke fright in the readers, but I think that in the essay he merely scratches the surface.

In truth, King's "ten bears" breed "cubs" in the reader's own mind, offspring which are in some way related to or recalled by the bugaboos in the story, but which, because they are *our* personal fears, are much more powerful to us. That is, I submit, a major reason why King's stories and novels terrify us as they do, and is also a reason why he seems to do it so effortlessly.

TYSON BLUE'S TOP TEN STEPHEN KING NOVELS AND SHORT STORIES

NOVELS & NOVELLAS

1. *Pet Sematary*: A novel in the classic tragic mold, not just every parent's nightmare; easily the finest horror novel of the last fifty years.
2. *Misery*: Every writer's worst fantasy, sure, but also a fascinating look at the relationship of writers to fans, as well as the relationship of writers to writing.
3. "The Body": Put simply, this is *my* youth as well.
4. *The Stand: The Complete & Uncut Edition* : Always a favorite, this new incarnation is even better. I've always been a sucker for "ultimate battle" stories.
5. *The Drawing of the Three* : I like this one for its complexity; nothing is quite what it seems at first, but all seems right at the end.
6. *IT*: Again, a lot of my youth echoes through this book; I wish it had been twice as long.
7. *The Dead Zone* : Again, a classic Shakespearean tragedy; I was especially touched by John Smith's plight in losing most of his life.
8. *Firestarter*: In a way, this is a liberal's nightmare/fantasy; Charlie ultimately wins, in one of the few King novels I'd really like a sequel to.
9. *The Dark Half*: Another look at writing and writers, with a nice Hitchcockian twist at the end.
10. *The Long Walk* : My favorite of the Bachmans. I especially liked the way King generates suspense in a novel where very little actually happens.

SHORT STORIES

1. "The Last Rung on the Ladder": Just about perfect; a fine short story.
2. "Gramma": A deliciously scary look at the way children see old people.
3. "The Reach": A profoundly moving story about the bridge between life and death.
4. "Strawberry Spring": I like this one for its use of mood; of weather as a metaphor.
5. "Trucks": A nice film-noir story, which, as "Maximum Overdrive," enabled me to meet Stephen King for the first time.
6. "Dolan's Cadillac": A nice modern variation on Poe's "The Cask of Amontillado"; predictable, sure, but fun to read nevertheless.
7. "The Monkey": Although a little long, I love the way this story imbues a simple toy we've all seen so many times with such malevolence. Nice father-and-son stuff, too.
8. "Mrs. Todd's Shortcut": A perfect Maine folktale, nicely told, and great fun to read aloud—if you can get the Down-East accent right.
9. "Uncle Otto's Truck": I like this one because it's set over near the New Hampshire line, and for the quiet menace of the old truck.
10. "Morning Deliveries": I like the surrealy sinister aspect of this one, as that macabre milkman drops his gruesome goodies off along his way.

HOW KING KILLS
A Gory Guide to the Killer King

"I'm not afraid of dying – I'm afraid of
how I'm gonna die." —Paul Winnick, 8/8/89

"O death, where is thy sting?
O, grave, where is thy victory?"
—1 Corinthians 15:55

O, death, where is thy sting, huh?

Lemme tellya: It's in the work of Stephen King.

When I began *The Shape Under the Sheet,* I already knew that Stephen King used various and nefarious ways of killing off his characters...but to be honest, I had no *idea.*

Initially, my editor Tom Schultheiss had suggested a guide to the ways in which King did away with his characters as a sort-of-fun (yes, that's what he said) overview of the King of Horror's ultimate tool: putting somebody six feet under—and letting us watch him do it.

But like I said...I had no *idea!*

After compiling the complete 18,000-entry concordance, I was able to go back and review the individual "People" sections of every novel and short story, and pull out the characters that died during the telling of the tale. After working for several hours on this section, I called my editor and told him that I didn't think I could finish it: So many people die in King's stories that the section looked like it was going to end up bigger than either of us wanted it. Tom suggested (with a straight face, I'll have you know) that I instead break down the modes of death into categories, so that instead of having a separate category that read "Being Decapitated and Disemboweled by a Werewolf and Propped Against a War Memorial" (as was Brady Kincaid in *Cycle of the Werewolf*), I could simply include this demise in the category "Death From Amputation(s), Decapitation, or Loss of Bodily Parts or Fluids." See how much simpler?

With this in mind, I decided on my editorial slant for this section: I would detail the various means of death within a general grouping of headings, without referencing the individual characters or works in which the death took place.

Now let me give you a rundown of Stephen King's "Top Nine" individual categories of death that I've come up with. They are:

1. DEATH FROM AMPUTATION(S), DE-CAPITATION, OR LOSS OF BODILY PARTS OR FLUIDS
2. DEATH FROM BEING EATEN (BY ANYTHING, INCLUDING ANIMALS AND/OR BUGS)
3. DEATH FROM DISEASE
4. DEATH BY MONSTERS
5. DROWNING DEATHS
6. MOST BIZARRE DEATHS
7. GENTLEST DEATH
8. NONSUPERNATURAL DEATHS (NON-SPECIFIC, BUT INCLUDING MURDERS & VEHICULAR DEATHS)
9. SUICIDES

(By the way, the individual modes of death within each particular category are in no particular chronological, bibliographic, or alphabetical order.)

Are you ready? Barf bags in place? Seat belts, airbags, and helmets on line?

"IT'S SHOWTIME, FOLKS!!!"

1. DEATH FROM AMPUTATION(S), DECAPITATION, OR LOSS OF BODILY PARTS OR FLUIDS

This is an all-purpose general category covering any demise due to losing something important. King is especially inventive with the body parts and/or fluids one can lose resulting in death. They include:

•being torn apart in a cabin
•being decapitated in the sewers
•being decapitated in an ironworks explosion
•being killed in a torture murder and then dissected and left in a 1959 Mercury
•being murdered by and having her brains eaten by her son
•dying from having her throat cut and her blood drained into a basin
•being torn apart
•being decapitated by a werewolf
•being decapitated by a werewolf and propped against a war memorial
•being pulled apart by a thing at the bottom of a well
•castrating a classmate with a piece of rusty metal
•clawing out his own eyes
•death from a cat stealing her breath
•being decapitated
•being decapitated and having her head used as the centerpiece for a cake
•being decapitated and having her head taken away

642

•being cut up and left in various parts of an automobile
•having her head and hand shot off with one shot
•having their heads ripped off and used as bowling balls and their arms and legs ripped off and used as pins
•decapitation by the Frankenstein monster
•being hacked to pieces
•death from having her insides ripped out
•being decapitated by a flying manhole cover during freak weather accompanying the death throes of a giant alien spider
•being torn open
•being torn to pieces
•gouging out the eyes of his dead daughter, wife, and cows and keeping same peepers in a jar
•having every drop of his blood drained
•having his arm ripped out of the socket
•having his legs ripped off by a giant alien spider (but actually dying of fear)
•having his legs ripped off and seven of his toes jammed into his mouth
•having a finger severed off in a gym door
•having her fingernails pulled out
•losing all the fingers on his left hand (except for his pinky) when a homemade bomb was dropped down his chimney
•losing an arm in a shirt-folding machine
•having his left hand sawed off with a hacksaw

2. DEATH FROM BEING EATEN (BY ANYTHING, INCLUDING ANIMALS AND/OR BUGS)

This category consists of those King characters who were doomed to be consumed. King has used the archetypal fear of being "eaten up" in a couple of ways: overtly, as in this category, and then symbolically, as when a character is eaten up by cancer or some other ravaging disease from within. This category includes:

•being eaten by "Him Who Waits"
•being eaten by a monster in a crate
•being eaten by Venus (used twice; once in the *People, Places, and Things* story "The Cursed Expedition," and in "Beachworld")
•being eaten by alligators after being thrown from a plane that crashed during a landing attempt in the Florida Everglades
•being eaten by a giant maggot
•being eaten alive by zombies
•being eaten by alien worms
•being eaten by a rabid dog
•being eaten by a Queen rat
•being eaten by bats

•being eaten by a giant mutant slug amoeba
•being eaten by a lawnmower
•being eaten by a tiger
•death by self-cannibalization
•being eaten by a St. Bernard
•being eaten by a blob in the water
•being eaten by toads with razor-sharp teeth
•being eaten from within by cockroaches

3. DEATH FROM DISEASE

This is the one that hits home: This is the category that could *really happen,* you know? Let's face it, the odds are against us being eaten by a giant mutant slug amoeba, or being decapitated by a werewolf, but heart disease? Cancer? Now, that's really scary! This category (which also includes other forms of physical handicaps and deformities) includes:

•death from a heart attack (used several times)
•death from a massive heart attack
•death from a Jaunt-induced massive heart attack
•death from the superflu (used billions of times)
•death from a massive coronary
•being born a "mewling monstrosity" with no arms, and then dying six hours later
•blindness due to optic nerve degeneration
•breaking his back
•death by disease carried by fleas in blankets given to them by Christian missionaries
•death from emphysema
•death from Parkinson's disease
•death from leukemia (used three times)
•death from pleurisy
•death from Sudden Infant Death syndrome
•death from crib death (used several times)
•death from becoming stupid (premature Alzheimer's, in "The End of the Whole Mess")
•death from Alzheimer's disease
•death from explosive brain hemorrhages caused by a toy monkey
•death from a massive coronary thrombosis while running
•miscarriage
•death from shock and blood loss after trying to amputate his own gangrenous (from stepping on a rusty nail) foot
•death from a fractured skull
•death from an embolism
•death from cancer (nonspecific; used many times)
•death from intestinal cancer
•death from cancer of the esophagus
•death from breast cancer
•death from cancer of the larynx
•death from lung cancer

•death from cancer of the stomach
•death from a brain tumor (used twice)
•death from congestive heart failure
•death from spinal meningitis
•death from a burst appendix
•dying during childbirth (used several times)
•going hopelessly insane
•having the Shaking Disease
•torture by emaciation
•death from Hansen's disease (leprosy)
•death from "A Long Illness"
•death from a stroke (used several times)
•death from a broken neck
•death from puking down his own throat and suffocating to death
•death from a brain hemorrhage
•death from mutilation

4. DEATH BY MONSTERS

This category covers supernatural killers. You've got your werewolves, vampires, and aliens here; and you've also got a prehistoric monster, sentient planets, and zombies. (Since some of these monsters ate their victims, there is some duplication of some of the categories in the "Being Eaten" section.) These "bad guys" include:

•being eaten by Venus
•being eaten by a monster in a crate
•being gutted by a werewolf and hung face down over a church pulpit
•being killed by a werewolf (used several times)
•being killed by a giant alien spider
•being turned into a living mummy
•being turned into a vampire (used several times)
•being killed by her dead father
•being eaten by a giant maggot
•being exsanguinated by a vampire (used several times)
•being decapitated by the Creature from the Black Lagoon
•being partially eaten by something that looked like black smoke
•being killed by the Boogeyman
•being killed by living toy soldiers
•being eaten by a giant mutant slug amoeba
•being physically invaded by aliens
•being attacked by a demonic shirt-folding machine
•being killed by ghosts
•being crucified as a sacrifice to a Corn God
•being killed by The Worm that lived beneath an abandonded church
•being killed by a possessed mirror
•being killed by a funnel-snouted, eye-sucking, shape-changing alien librarian (phew!)
•being killed by giant prehistoric mutant insects
•being killed by supernaturally-sent wolves
•being eaten by the blob in the water
•being eaten by supernatural razor-toothed toads

5. DROWNING DEATHS

This category is self-explanatory. King doesn't drown people too often, but he has turned to this form of death as an old standby. (As you'd expect, the *Creepshow* story "Something To Tide You Over" is the best example of the Drowning King):

•death by drowning (used several times)
•being drowned as an infant
•death by drowning after being buried up to her head in the sand on the beach
•death by drowning after being buried up to his head in the sand on the beach
•death by drowning after being buried up to his head in the sand on the beach by two corpses
•death by drowning in quicksand
•death by drowning at sea
•death by drowning after falling through a frozen Reach
•drowning after falling overboard, then coming back to life, and being chopped up with an axe
•death from a flood
•death by drowning in a toilet and then being partially eaten by a thing that looked like black smoke
•death by drowning on a sand planet (although this can also be considered a "Being Eaten" demise)

6. MOST BIZARRE DEATHS

This is a fun category, a category where Stephen King shows what he's made of. King has come up with some beauts throughout his career, and this is a sampling of his best. (For obvious reasons, this category also includes choice injuries and suicides):

•being absorbed into a tiger
•being eaten by a giant maggot
•death by having thousands of cockroaches invade his body
•death from a wide-awake Jaunt
•dying in a nuclear explosion ignited by a ball of blue fire flicked from Flagg's hand
•death by being shot with a death ray (only lethal to Fornits)
•death by "Territory-initiated" electrocution
•death from having a piece of piano wire stuck in his left eye and into his brain
•being frightened to death in the night after seeing his wife getting out of the bath

- death from a Gramma-induced burst appendix
- death from being Jaunted when all emergence portals had been erased
- death from being filled with motor oil and having a spark plug stuck in his mouth
- dying in a freak Territory earthquake
- death by a cat forcing its way into his mouth, worming his way down his throat, and then eating itself out of the guy's stomach
- death from having their heads ripped off and used as bowling balls and their arms and legs used as pins
- being eaten up by, and then carried away by, sparrows
- death by decapitation (with her head then used as the centerpiece of a cake)
- death by having a flash of fire shot at his throat
- death by being run through a crusher and compacted into a cube
- death when a car burst into his livingroom and ran him over
- being deleted by a word processor
- death when a car burst into a snack bar and ran him over
- being killed by a sonic Ear-hum
- death from exploding after being over-inflated with a blue air compressor
- death when the toilet bowl she was sitting on exploded
- death from an ancient gear-wheel catapulting out of her toilet and cutting her throat in the shower
- death from decapitation by a flying manhole cover during freak weather accompanying the death throes of a giant alien spider
- died frigging with a chainsaw while drunk
- being eaten alive by zombies
- being killed by having its picture taken while trying to escape Polaroidsville
- being eaten by a gentleman farmer
- dying (supposedly) when a flaming Montgolfier balloon crashed into a barn
- having every drop of his blood drained
- having his legs ripped off by a giant alien spider (but actually dying of fear)
- suicide by shotgun after being turned into a living weed by "meteor shit"
- suicide by sticking his right arm down a garbage disposal
- suicide by drinking lye and gin
- sustaining a broken leg and a punctured testicle during freak weather accompanying the death throes of a giant alien spider
- being locked in a refrigerator
- being blown up in a miniature nuclear explosion by living toy soldiers

- being eaten by a giant mutant slug amoeba
- being buried alive in a Cadillac
- being buried alive in a bus
- death from being stabbed in the eye with a yellow Eberhard-Faber #2 pencil
- died chasing a UFO that turned out to be a reflection of Venus
- being "erased" by staying awake during a plane's trip through a time warp
- being "plugged in" in The Shed
- committing suicide with ghost Seconals
- death by crucifixion
- death by a voodoo-caused car accident
- being eaten by a lawnmower
- death from shaking his own cursed hands
- death after looking into a cursed mirror
- death after looking into a cursed floor
- death by self-cannibalization

And the winner for Most Bizarre Death is...
It's a tie.
John Halston's macabre death in "Cat from Hell," in which a cat forced its way into his mouth, wormed his way down his throat, and then ate itself out of Halston's stomach ties with Mrs. Leighton's particularly gross death in "The Blue Air Compressor" (she exploded after being over-inflated with a blue air compressor).

Now aren't you glad you know this?

7. GENTLEST DEATH

But King can be gentle, too. This category is short and sweet. Probably the gentlest (and also most touching) death in the whole of King's lexicon of dying would probably be Stella Flanders's walk across the Reach to meet her dead husband Bill and the other dead of Goat Island. Yes, she was suffering from cancer, but her actual moment of crossing over was sublime and peaceful, and King successfully communicated Stella's moment of attaining a higher state of being.

The actor Anthony Quinn was hospitalized in 1990 just moments away from a massive heart attack and, after he was successfully treated for heart trouble, he said something that has stayed with me, something that can also apply to Stella's own personal "Long Walk": He said he wasn't afraid of dying when he was in the hospital because he didn't believe in death. He thought of death as nothing more than a change, and in "The Reach" King succeeds in showing us the ecstasy that occurs at the moment of transition.

Remember Stephen King's credo: "Faith and power are interchangeable."
Dig it.

8. NONSUPERNATURAL DEATHS (NONSPECIFIC, BUT INCLUDING MURDERS & VEHICULAR DEATHS)

This is a catch-all category; sort of King as Death-master General. Horror doesn't just require bizarre, supernatural agents to kill somebody off. Being shot in the heart six times or being stabbed thirty-seven times will do quite nicely, thank you very much.

- being burned to death
- being beaten into a hole and set afire with gasoline
- being blown away by the army
- death during "homemade" appendix surgery
- being killed in an auto accident (used many times)
- being hit and killed by the Drunk Man Who Had to Go to Jail
- being killed in a van accident
- being killed in a plane crash
- being killed in a motorcycle accident
- being executed in the middle of the street by townsfolk
- being killed with an axe
- being killed with a recoilless hammer
- being beaten to death by his wife
- having her brains blown out
- being killed in a house explosion
- dying in a "gaudy four-car smashup"
- being killed in a jeep accident
- being gunned down by hoods
- being shot dead while answering the front door
- driving a van off a ninety-foot drop
- being killed with two silver bullets
- death from having a piece of piano wire stuck in his left eye and into his brain
- being brained with a gas pump nozzle (he didn't die though)
- being stabbed to death
- death from slipping, falling, breaking his neck and bashing in his head
- being shot by the police
- being murdered by a former Nazi
- being killed by a UPS truck
- being killed by a drunken boyfriend
- being shot in the butt
- being a murderer and necrophiliac
- being run over by a train
- being knocked unconscious by a falling milk bucket and then being burned to death
- being killed in a truck accident
- being killed by being struck with an ashtray
- being killed by a falling grave headstone
- being killed (murdered) in a hunting accident
- being shot in the heart six times
- dying when his nickel-plated .32 blew up in his hands

- death from falling from a stair landing
- being shot in the leg
- being killed in World War II
- being stabbed thirty-seven times
- being lost forever in an amusement park
- death by having a steak knife plunged into the base of his neck and a meat fork into his back
- death from falling down a flight of stairs and breaking her back, both legs, and her neck
- death by professional execution
- being shot with an Uzi
- death from smothering
- death from choking on a piece of apple
- death from falling in a dry well, breaking both legs, and suffering shock, hunger, and dehydration
- death from being scragged by his own men
- being stabbed to death in a truck
- being stabbed in the eye with a small steel rod
- death during drug experimentation
- death by electrocution after driving into a telephone pole
- death from a bridge explosion
- being shot to death during a ransom drop
- death by falling off a porch and breaking his neck
- death from gunshot (used several times)
- death after being shot in the stomach and floating in a boat for two days
- death by having the plug of her respirator pulled after being in a coma from an auto accident
- being killed in a hunting accident
- death by electrocution trying to start up a gasoline generator hooked to every electrical outlet in the house
- death from starvation after accidentally locking herself in a walk-in freezer with the corpses of her husband and son
- dying after injecting himself with ninety-six percent pure heroin
- death when her father's pistol exploded in her hand
- dying after being bitten by a rattlesnake
- death from suffocation after his mouth and nose were taped shut
- being shot to death during a game of Pokeno
- death in a house fire (used several times)
- death by choking to death
- being crushed to death under barrels of Kingsland Ale in a cart accident
- death from electrocution
- death from being stabbed and burned
- death by explosion from a bomb wired to the ignition of his car
- death by explosion from a bomb wired to the ignition of her car
- death by strangulation (used several times)

- death from being shot in the head
- death from lynching (used twice)
- death by poisoning
- death by suicide from eating "white nightshade" mushrooms
- death from being shot by an arrow
- died in a fire (used several times)
- dying in a condominium fire
- being stabbed with a screwdriver
- dying in Vietnam
- dying in a car crash after being hit in the head with a purse
- dying from being shot in the guts with deer rifles
- being stabbed in the forehead with a screwdriver
- dying during childbirth (used several times)
- falling to her death from a ladder
- dying in a car accident that was almost certainly suicide
- falling off Drunk's Leap
- going hopelessly insane
- leaping from the roof of the Cleveland post office
- death by stabbing (used many times)
- being shot in the head and left with a chicken cut open on his lap (Also, the word "Never" was written on his forehead in blood. See *Thinner*.)
- death from falling into an abyss
- death from hanging
- death from a train derailment
- death in a boiler explosion
- being shot by Guards while Walking
- being shot by her boyfriend in an argument over who would go out for Chinese food
- being murdered in the hospital
- being killed by a speeding car
- death from falling from a treehouse
- dying in an apartment house fire
- being stabbed in the back with a cross and being run over by a Lawnboy
- died falling down the stairs
- death from a skull fracture, complicated by being struck in the back by a hurled Royal typewriter and having flaming manuscript pages shoved down her throat
- being buried alive
- dying during the Tap explosion in Oatley

- being killed in the Battle of Leyte Gulf
- dying during a plane explosion while flying the plane into a building
- death from having his throat cut
- death from a broken neck sustained during a horseback riding accident
- being killed by a drunk driver
- being shot in the back
- being shot by a sniper
- being burned to death
- dying quietly in her sleep
- being shot in the throat

9. SUICIDES

And lastly, we come to suicide.

Many of King's characters shuffle off this mortal coil completely on their own, not needing to wait for a vampire (or even a rabid dog) to do them in. Choices for self-cessation include:

- clawing out his own eyes
- committing suicide (nonspecific; used several times)
- suicide from eating "white nightshade" mushrooms
- leaping from the roof of the Cleveland post office
- suicide by sticking his right arm down a garbage disposal
- suicide by hanging
- suicide by shooting himself in the head
- suicide by gunshot (used several times)
- suicide by shotgun after being turned into a living weed by "meteor shit"
- suicide by drug overdose
- suicide by overdose with Veronal
- suicide by slitting his wrists
- suicide by drinking lye and gin
- suicide by stopping walking
- suicide by flying a plane into a building
- suicide by swallowing Drano
- suicide by killing himself with a .38 caliber revolver
- suicide by overdosing on ghost Seconals
- suicide by leaping from the top floor of an insurance building
- suicide by overdosing on Darvon Complex
- suicide by self-cannibalization

PAGE NUMBER KEY TO MASTER CODES
CITED IN THE CHARACTER INDEXES

CS=Creepshow; DS=Different Seasons; FPM=Four Past Midnight; NS=Night Shift; PPT=People, Places and Things; SC=Skeleton Crew

PAGE NUMBER KEY TO MASTER CODES
CITED IN CHARACTER INDEXES
(continued)

CS=Creepshow; DS=Different Seasons; FPM=Four Past Midnight; NS=Night Shift; PPT=People, Places and Things; SC=Skeleton Crew

AN INDEX TO CHARACTERS IN
THE NOVELS OF STEPHEN KING

The following index is Part 1 of a four-part Character Index: Novels, Collections, The Bachman Novels, and Uncollected Short Stories. The Novels Index consists of all the characters in those Stephen King novels originally published under his own name. The Master Number(s) following each character's name correspond to the number(s) of the work(s) in which the character appears. Further information on the character can be obtained by consulting the main concordance section, wherein King's published/collected works are arranged in a chronological, numbered sequence by Master Number.

A

ABELSON, DOC 22
ABELSON, PETER 18
ABLANAP, MRS. 8
A.C. 6A
ACE HIGH 6
ACKERMAN 16
"ADAM SWALLOW" 11
ADAMS, BILLY 18
ADDAMS, CHARLES 27
ADLER 22
ADLER 23
ADULT AND TWO
    CHILDREN IN THE
    RENAULT, THE 18
AGE FAIRY, THE 22
AGING SERGEANT, THE 6A
AHAZ 6
AIDE, THE 27
AILEEN 4
AIR FORCE COLONEL, THE
    22
AL 6A
AL, UNCLE 19
"ALBERT THE BLOB" 18
ALBERTSON, DR. LESTER
    27
ALBRECHT, LISA 22
ALBRECHT GIRL, THE 22
ALBRIGHT, DICK 9
ALDEN, MRS. 27
ALEXANDER, TRUMAN 23
ALFALFA 9
ALFIE 27
ALHAZRED 24
ALICE UNDERWOOD'S
    BROTHER-IN-LAW 6A
ALICE UNDERWOOD'S
    SISTER 6A
ALLEGEHNY AIRLINES
    TICKET CLERK, THE 9
ALLEN, WOODY 23
ALLIBURTON, GEOFFREY
    25
ALLIE 23
ALLISON, DICK 27
ALLISON, HAROLD 1
ALLISON, JUDITH
    BRIGHAM 1
ALVAREZ, BONITA 8
AMBERSON, HENRY 27
AMBULANCE DRIVER, THE
    22
ANDEEN, OFFICER BRUCE
    22
ANDERS 6A
ANDERS 18
ANDERSON, BOBBI 6A
ANDERSON, BOBBI 27
ANDERSON, GEORGE 17
ANDERSON, PAUL 22
ANDERSON, PAULA 27
ANDERSON, POUL 27
ANDERSON, MR. 27
ANDERSON, VERA 27
ANDERSONS, THE 27
ANDI 22
ANDOLINI, CLAUDIO 23
ANDOLINI, JACK 23
ANDREW, UNCLE 6A
ANDREWS, POLEY 27
ANDROS, MR. 6
ANDROS, MRS. 6
ANDROS, NICK 6

ANDUAN PIRATES, THE 24
ANDY 4
ANGEL 6A
ANGEL-FACE 6A
ANGSTROM, BUDDY 22
ANNA CROOKBROWS' SON
    24
ANNABELLE 27
ANNE 23
ANNE 27
ANNIE 22
ANNIE'S BROTHER 25
ANNMARIE 27
ANSON, STORK 22
ANTHROPOLOGISTS, THE
    27
ANUBIS 6
APPLEGATE, BARNEY 27
APPLEGATE, HENRY 27
APPLEGATE'S GRAND-
    MOTHER, HENRY 27
APPLEGATES, THE 27
ARBERG 27
ARCHINBOURG, KYLE 27
ARCHINBOURGS, THE 27
"ARGLEBARGLE" 27
ARIZONA TROOPER #1 6
ARIZONA TROOPER #2 6
ARLEN 24
ARLENE 6
ARMY DRIVER, THE 6
ARMY MAJOR, THE 6A
ARNOLD, BILL 6A
ARNOLD, GRESHAM 22
ARNOLDS, THE 6
ARROWAY, DR. 16
ARROWSMITH, BRENDA 22
ARSENAULT, DOLLY 27
ART TEACHER, THE 22
ASHFORD 2
"ASSHOLE WHO WALKS
    LIKE A MAN, THE" 22
ASSISTANT DISTRICT AT-
    TORNEY, THE 6
ASTAROTH 6
ATLANTIC, CHIEF 27
ATOMIC ENERGY COMMIS-
    SION OFFICIALS 6
ATWELL, CARLTON
    (DIGGER) 18
ATWELL, DIGGER 18
AUBREY 18
AUDEN, W.H. 27
AUDRA'S GRANDFATHER
    22
AUDRA'S YOUNGER SISTER
    22
"AUNT BLUE" 23
"AUNT EVVIE" 11
AURLETTE, ROGER 22
AVARINO, OFFICER
    CHARLES 22
AVIS CLERK, THE 27
AYATOLLAH KHOMEINI,
    THE 9

B

BABALUGAH 6A
BABYSITTER, THE 22
BACH 4
BACON, EILEEN 9
BAEDECKER 4
BAEZ, JOAN 17
BAILEY, PETER 27

BAILEY, STAN 6
BAILLINGS, MRS. 17
BAKER, ANDY 27
BAKER, JANE 6
BAKER, JORY 6A
BAKER, SHERIFF JOHN 6
BAKER STREET PROSTI-
    TUTE, THE 22
BAKERY TRUCK DRIVER, A
    22
BALAZAR, EMILIO ("RICO")
    23
BALGO, MR. 18
BALL, BRIAN 6
BALLINGER, MR. 6
"BANANA-HEELS" 22
BANBERRY, MINETTE 18
BANKER, THE 22
BANKSON, J.W. 22
BANNERMAN, GEORGE 8
BANNERMAN, GEORGE 27
BANNERMAN, KATRINA 8
BANNERMAN, SHERIFF 11
BANNOCK, JOHN 2
BARBER, THE 25 (Misery's
    Return, Version 2)
BARCLAY, DAVIE 2
BARCLAY, HORTENSE 9
BARFIELD, DUKE 27
BARFIELD, "PITS" 27
BARKER, BOB 18
BARKER, ELT 27
BARKERS, THE 18
BARLOW, KURT 2
"BARON BUTTONHOLE" 22
BARONGG, LENNY 16
BARR, MR. 22
BARRETT, DON 1
BARRINGER, FRANKLIN 27
BARTENDER, THE 6
BARTENDER, THE 27
BARTOK 4
BASALE, MIGUEL 23
BASCOMB, BUDDY 2
BASS, CHIEF 8
BAST, HECTOR 18
BATEMAN, GLEN 6
BATEMAN'S NEIGHBOR 6
BATEMAN, BILL 17
BATERMAN, TIMMY 17
BATES, NORVILLE 9
BATMAN 27
BATS, THE 11
BATTAGLIA, CHARLES
    "BABY CHARLIE" 4
BAXTER, RALPH 9
BAYNES, DR. 22
BEAME, ABE 6
BEAR, YOGI 27
BEASLEY, MRS. 11
BEAST, THE 19
BEATRICE, SISTER 4
BEAULIEU, BENNY 22
BEAULIEU, STRINGER 11
BEAULIFANT, HESTER
    "QUEENIE" 25
BEAUCHAMP, CURTIS 6A
BEAUMONT, GLEN 27
BEAUMONT, LIZ 27
BEAUMONT, SHAYLA 27
BEAUMONT, THAD 27
BEAUMONT, WENDY 27
BEAUMONT, WILLIAM 27
BEAUMONT TWINS, THE
    27

BEAVER 27
BECK, DAVE 16
BEE-PEOPLE, THE 25
BEETHOVEN 6
BELASCO, MR. 11
BELL, BRYCE 25
BELLAMY, BILLY 11
BELLBOYS, THE 4
BELLERMAN, MARTY 16
BELLMAN, THE 27
BELLWOOD, JERRY 22
BEN'S FOREMAN 22
BEN'S SECRETARY 22
BENEDIX, TOMMY 8
BENSON, CLIFF 6
BENSON, GARY 4
BENSON, HANNIBAL 17
BENTON, TONY 17
BERGEN, EDGAR 27
BERGERON, DAVE 11
BERGENFIELD HOSPITAL
    WOMAN, THE 27
BERNHARDT, STEVE 8
BERNSTEIN 25
BERRINGER, NEWT 27
BERRINGER, RICKY 27
BERRYMAN, CRYSILDA 25
BERTOLY, ANDREA 22
BESON, ARON 24
BESS 6A
BESSEY, ARLENE 19
BESSEY, MR. 19
BETTE DAVIS AND ALI
    MCGRAW 11
BETTS, RICHARD 6A
BETTY 27
BETTY, AUNT 6
BEWILDERED MAN, THE 2
BICENTE, MRS. 1
BICKFORD, AMSEL 22
BIG BOYS, THE 6A
BIG MAN WITH HIS FISTS,
    THE 6
BIG STEVE 6
BIGGERS, CHARLEY 6A
"BIGGY" 6A
BILL DENBROUGH'S
    CLASSMATES AT THE
    UNIVERSITY OF MAINE
    22
BILLFORD, DR. 25 (Misery's
    Return, Version 2)
"BILLIE" 27
BILLINGS, FRANK 22
BILLY 22
BILLY, UNCLE 1
BILLY THE KID 23
BIMBO 9
BIONDI, GEORGE 23
BIP 22
BISSON, LOUELLA 17
BISSONETTE, FATHER
    RAYMOND 2
BITER-SNAKE 24
BIXBY, JEROME 9
BLACK, COACH 22
BLACK, HARRY 27
BLACK DETECTIVE, THE
    27
BLACK MAN, THE 1
BLACK MAN IN A LOIN-
    CLOTH, THE 6A
BLACK MAN IN THE
    CONTROL ROOM, THE
    6A

BLACK VIETNAM VET, A 6
BLACK WOMAN SHOP-
    LIFTER, THE 6
BLACKFORD 16
BLACKSNAKE, A 27
BLACKY 27
BLAKE, HENRY 1
BLAKE, KEVIN 23
BLAKE, TINA 1
BLAKELY, MRS. 6
BLAKEMOOR, HARRY 6
BLAKEMOOR, RITA 6
BLEDSOE, JERRY 18
BLEDSOE, NITA 18
BLISS, P.P. 1
BLOCK, HARRY 1
BLODWIN, CAL 19
BLONDE GIRL, THE 6
BLONDIE 22
BLUE, DON 27
BLUE WOMAN, THE 23
BLUE-HAIRED LADIES 27
BLUM, HERBERT 22
BLUM, MR. 22
BLUM, PATTY 22
BLUM, RUTH 22
BO DONALDSON AND THE
    HEYWOODS 6
BOBBI'S GRANDFATHER 27
BOBBY 22
BODDIN, DEREK 2
BODDIN, FRANKLIN 2
BODDIN, RICHIE 2
BOGART, HUMPHREY 22
BOK, HANNES 27
BOLLES, DON 8
BOLTON, SKIPPER 22
BONASARO, TONY 25
BOND, JAMES 27
BONNIE 6
BONO, SONNY 9
"BOOGERS" TALIENDO'S
    SISTER 22
BOOGEYMAN, THE 6A
BOOKER, LOUISE 27
BOOKINGS, DR. 25 (Misery's
    Return, Version 2)
BOORMAN, VICTOR T. 4
BOOTH, RAY 6
BOP 22
BORDEAUX, CARLA 22
BORENTZ, HELMUT 8
BORENTZ, JOHANNA 8
BORNS, DR. 27
BORTON, CHIEF 22
BORTON, KENNY 22
"BOSS, THE" 6
BOSSIE 25
BOSTON RED SOX 11
BOSTON STRANGLER, THE
    4
BOUCHARD, STANNY 17
BOUCHARD, STANLEY 17
BOURKAS, THE 25
BOUTILLIER, TOM 22
BOWDENS, MARSTENS,
    AND PILLSBURYS 8
BOWERS, BUTCH 22
BOWERS, HENRY 22
BOWES, DAVID 8
BOWIE, CLAUDE 2
BOWIE, DAVID 27
BOWIE, GRETA 22
BOWIE, RICHARD 22
BOWIE, STEPHEN 22

AN INDEX TO CHARACTERS IN
THE STEPHEN KING COLLECTONS

The following index is Part 2 of a four-part Character Index: Novels, Collections, The Bachman Novels, and Uncollected Short Stories. The Collections Index consists of all the characters in those Stephen King shorter works in collections originally published under his own name. These include *Night Shift, The Dark Tower: The Gunslinger, Creepshow, Different Seasons, Skeleton Crew,* and *Four Past Midnight.* The Master Number(s) following each character's name correspond to the number(s) of the work(s) in which the character appears. Further information on the character can be obtained by consulting the main concordance section, wherein the published/collected works are arranged in chronological, numbered sequence by Master Number.

A

ABBY 28b
ABEL 21d
ABERSHAM, CARL 21v
ACE 28a
ACKERMAN, HARRY 15b
ACKERMAN, SANDRA 5o
ACKERMAN, SHARON 15b
ADELMAN, KENT 28c
ADLEY, DAVID 15d
ADLEY, DAVID 21k
ADLEY, ELLEN 15d
AGELESS STRANGER, THE 14 (5)
AHAZ, CURSED OF GOD 5p
AILEEN 14 (2)
ALFALFA 28b
ALICE 5o
ALICE 14 (1)
ALICE'S PARENTS 5o
ALLIE 14 (1)
ALVIN'S GRANDMOTHER 5c
AMALARA, CARL 5k
AMAZING JOE, THE 28c
AMBULANCE ATTENDANT 15d
ANDERS 5d
ANDERSON, MRS. 15b
ANDREWS, PETER 15d
ANDREWS, PETER 21k
ANDREWS, V.C. 28c
"ANOTHER GUY" 5j
ARIZONA JEW, THE 28a
ARLINDER, DR. 21t
ARMED GUARDS 21f
ARMITAGE, ELMORE 15a
ARMSTRONG, NEIL 28d
ARTHUR 5d
ARTHUR 14 (2)
ARTHUR'S AUNT 5d
ATLANTA BRAVES, THE 15b
AUCTIONEER, THE 21e
AUTOMATED FEMALE ANNOUNCER, THE 21f
AZTECS, THE 21a

B

BABY, THE 5r
BABY HORTENSE, THE SINGING MARVEL 5p
BABY HORTENSE'S DADDY 5p
BABY PIGEONS, THE 5l
BACK-COUNTRY FUCKHEAD DOCTOR, A 5f
BACKWOODS DEEJAY, THE 5c
BADLINGER 12c1
BAILEY 21d
BAKER 21q
BAKER, DARREL 21k
BAKER, JARED 21u
BAKER, MR. 28d
BALLANGER, DR. 5d
BANCICHEK, MR. 15c ("The Revenge of Lard-Ass Hogan")

BANNER, PROFESSOR 5o
BANNERMAN, BIG GEORGE 28d
BANNERMAN, CONSTABLE 15c
BARGER, CHUCKIE 21q
BASCOMB, GEORGE 21e
BASEBALL PLAYER, THE 5l
BASKIN, ELMER 28c
BASSINGER, DON 28b
BAT, A 12b1
BATES, CALVIN 5h
BATES, MISS SANDRA 21m
BATES BOY, THE 21m
BATMAN AND ROBIN 21i
BATS, THE 5b
BEACH BOYS, THE 21l
BEAGLEMEN, HUGH 15d
BEAST, THE 14 (5)
BEAUTY CONTEST JUDGE, THE 5q
BEEFY GUY, THE 21a
BEEMAN, NORMAN 28c
BELLIS 21u
BELLMAN, DINAH 28a
BELLMAN, MRS. 28a
BENSHON, JOHN 21v
BERLITZ, CHARLES 28a
BERNIE 5c
BERRIGAN, CYNTHIA 28c
BESPECTACLED MAN, THE 21a
BETTS, DICKIE 15a
BETTY AND HENRY 5r
BIBBER, AGGIE 21a
BIBBERS, THE 21a
BIFF 21g
BIG CHINK, THE 21p
"BIG GEORGE" 21v
BIGELOW, MR. 5a
BILKMORE, MR. 12b
BILL 21b
BILL GIOSTI'S NIECE 21a
BILLIE 12c1
BILLINGS, ANDY (ANDREW LESTER) 5f
BILLINGS, DENNY 5f
BILLINGS, LESTER 5f
BILLINGS, RITA 5f
BILLINGS, SHIRL 5f
BILLY 15c ("Stud City")
BILLY 28c
BILLY-BOY 21g
BIRD, MISS 21b
"BIRDMAN OF ALCATRAZ, THE" 15a
BLACK OAK ARKANSAS 5t
BLACK-BEARDED MAN, THE 28a
BLACK-HAIRED SWEDE, THE 5m
BLAKE, JENNIFER 28c
BLANCHETTE, NORMAN 21n
BLATCH, ELWOOD 15a
BLIER, ROCKY 21s
BLIND EDDIE 5g
BLOCK, LAWRENCE 28b
BLOND COED, A 21d
BLOND COED'S MOTHER, THE 21d
BLOND COED'S FATHER, THE 21d

BLONDE WOMAN, THE 21a
BLONDI 15b
BLOOD, HARLEY 21v
BLUE MAN, THE 5p
BLUME, JUDY 28c
BOARDMAN, CRAIG 5p
BOARDMAN, MALACHI 5p
BOBBY 5c
BOGART, HUMPHREY 21d
BOLTON, SHERWOOD 15a
BONES 5a
BONSAINT, PAUL 15a
BOOGEYMAN, THE 5f
BOON, JAMES 5a
BOONE, AUNT JUDITH 5a
BOONE, CHARLES 5a
BOONE, GRANDFATHER ROBERT 5a
BOONE, JAMES ROBERT 5a
BOONE, KENNETH 5a
BOONE, MARCELLA 5a
BOONE, PHILLIP 5a
BOONE, RANDOLPH 5a
BOONE, SARAH 5a
BOONE, STEPHEN 5a
BOONE, UNCLE HENRY 5a
BOOTH 5s
BOOTH'S MOTHER 5s
BORDER DWELLERS, THE 14 (1)
BORMAN 5d
BOWDEN, MONICA 15b
BOWDEN, RICHARD 15b
BOWDEN, TODD 15b
BOWDEN, VIC 15b
BOWIE, GERDA 28b
BOWIE, RUSSELL 21v
BOY, A 21r
BOY, THE 21k
BOY, THE 5p
BOY, THE 5d
BOY DOWN THE STREET, THE 5m
BOY DOWN THE STREET'S MOTHER, THE 5m
BOY IN A MADRAS SHIRT, A 21d
BOY IN NEW MEXICO 21j
BOYS WHO TOOK VICKY, THE 5p
BOZEMAN, DAN 15b
BRACKETT, CHARLES "SONNY" 15b
BRACOWICZ, NORMAN "FUZZY" 15c
BRADHSAW, TERRY 21s
BRADLEY, DETECTIVE 28b
BRAKEMAN, PHIL 28c
BRAY, ANN 5k
BRAZZI, RICKY 21p
BRIAN ENGLE'S LAWYER 28a
BRIGGS 28a
BRIGHT, BILLY 28c
BROCHU, CHARLIE 5b
BROCKETT, CLIFTON 5a
BROCKWAY, MRS. 15c ("The Revenge of Lard-Ass Hogan")
BRODY, JIMMY 21d
BROGAN 5b
BROTHER MELVIN 12b
BROWER, HENRY 21k

BROWER, RAY 15c
BROWN 14 (1)
BROWN, BARBARA 5a
BROWN, BUD 21a
BRUCKNER, BUDDY 21t
BRUCKNER, GEORGE 21t
BRUCKNER, MR. 21t
BRUCKNER, RUTH 21t
BRUGGER, HENRY 21e
BRUNO 28b
BUCKLAND, FRANKLIN 21e
BUCKLAND, HOMER 21e
BUCKLAND, MEGAN 21e
BUFFINGTON 21f
BUILDING SUPERINTENDENT, THE 21k
BUM, THE 15b
BUMP 28b
BUNCH OF KIDS, A 5c
BUNCH OF KIDS, A 28c
BURDON, MR. 21t
BURKES, DAVID 15a
BURNT MAN, THE 21p
BURROUGHS, MRS. 15c
BURT'S MOTHER 5p
BUSINESSMAN, THE 21f
BYRON HADLEY'S BROTHER 15a

C

CAB DRIVER 15d
CABBAGE AND TURNIP GIRL, THE 15c
CADILLAC'S OWNER, THE 5i
CAIN 21d
CALHOUN, MR. 5a
CALIFORNIA EXECUTIVE, THE 21a
CALLAHAN, JOHNNY 15a
CAMBER, JOE 21e
CAMBER, JOE 21t
CAMBER, JOE 28d
CAMPANELLA, ROY 15c
CAMPUS COP, A 5k
CANDY, GEORGE 28c
CAPTAIN, THE 21l
"CAPTAIN FUTURE" 21u
CARDEN, ROBERT 15d
CARL 28c
CARL AMALARA'S ROOMMATE 5k
CARLA PARKETTE'S MOTHER 5m
CARLIN, MR. 21m
CARMICHAEL 5b
CARMODY, MRS. 21a
CARPENTER, JULIA 12c1
CARRUTHERS, LATHROP 15d
CARSON 21f
CARSON, JOHNNY 15b
CARSTAIRS, GREG 28b
CARSTAIRS, MRS. 28b
CARTER, DANNY 15c ("Stud City")
CARTER BOY, THE 28c
CARTOON GRAMMA, THE 21t
CARUNE, VICTOR 21f
CARVER, MISSUS 12b1
CASH, JOHNNY 21n

CASTELLANO, FIONA 15b
CASTNER 14 (1)
CASTNER, MRS. 14 (1)
CASTONMEYER, JACK 5m
CASTONMEYER, LENORE 12e
CASTONMEYER, NORMAN 12e
CASTONMEYER'S DOG, THE 5m
CASTONMEYERS, THE 5m
CAVELLA, STEVE 15c
CERMAN, GAIL 5k
CHAFFEE, EMORY 28d
CHALMERS, EVVIE 28d
CHALMERS, MRS. 28d
CHALMERS, POLLY 28d
CHAMBERS, CHRIS 15c
CHAMBERS, EYEBALL 15c
CHAMBERS, FRANK 15c
CHAMBERS, JAKE (JOHN) 14 (2)
CHAMBERS, MR. 14 (2)
CHAMBERS, MRS. 14 (2)
CHAMBERS, RANDY 15b
CHAMPION, PATTY 28b
CHARBONNEAU, MARGUERITE 15c ("The Revenge of Lard-Ass Hogan")
CHARBONNEAU, MAYOR 15c ("The Revenge of Lard-Ass Hogan")
CHARLES 21b
"CHARLIE" 14 (1)
CHARLIE 21g
CHEAP LITTLE CORNER-WALKERS 21t
CHERINIKOU, MRS. 5e
CHESTER 15a
CHESTER 15b
CHICO 15c ("Stud City")
CHILD, FRANK 21v
CHILD WITH NO EYES, A 5a
CHILDREN'S LIBRARY COMMITTEE, THE 28c
CHOPPER 15c
CHRISTIAN MISSIONARIES 12c1
CHUBBY BOY, A 21a
CISCO 21i
CLAGGERT, SAMUEL 21m
CLANTONS, THE 28a
CLAPHAM, MRS. 21a
CLARKSON, DR. 15c
CLARY, MR. 5a
CLAUDETTE 28d
CLAWSON, RUTH 5p
CLAWSON, SANDRA 5p
CLERK, THE 28d
CLORIS, MR. 5a
CLUTTERBUCK, ANDY 28d
COLLEGE KIDS 28c
COLLEGE KIDS NEXT DOOR, THE 21r
COLLINS, THE 21r
COMPANY PRESIDENT, THE 5q
CONANT 5i
CONDON, DOC 12b1
CONNORS, BERTIE 5g
CONSTANTINE, MR. 28d

AN INDEX TO CHARACTERS IN
THE BACHMAN NOVELS

The following index is Part 3 of a four-part Character Index: Novels, Collections, The Bachman Novels, and Uncollected Short Stories. The Bachman Novels Index consists of all the characters in those Stephen King novels originally published under the name Richard Bachman. The Master Number(s) following each character's name correspond to the number(s) of the work(s) in which the character appears. Further information on the character can be obtained by consulting the main concordance section, wherein the published/collected works are arranged in chronological, numbered sequence by Master Number.

A

AARONSON 7
ABRAHAM 7
ABRAHAM'S GIRLFRIEND 7
ABRAHAM'S GRANDFA-THER 7
ADAMS, NICK 10
ADDERLY, CANNONBALL 7
AHAB 20
AIRLINE POLICE, THE 13
ALAN 10
ALBERT, DAVE 10
ALBERT, HANK 10
ALBERTSON, RALPH 10
ALICE 7
AMOS 20
ANDERSON, DR. 3
ANDERSON, WARNER 20
ANDREA 10
ANDREISSEN, DANA 3
ANDY 10
ANGIE 10
ANNMARIE 3
ARNCASTER, LARS 20
ATTLEBORO BULLY, THE 20

B

BAKER, ART 7
BAKER, ARTHUR 7
BAKER, JAMES 7
BAKER OR BARKER 10
BAKER'S AUNT 7
BAKER'S AUNT HATTIE 7
BAKER'S AUNT HATTIE'S KIDS 7
BAKER'S BROTHER 7
BAKER'S GIRL 7
BAKER'S GRANDFATHER 7
BAKER'S UNCLE 7
BALDING WHGH MAN, THE 7
BANK GUARD, THE 10
BANK MANAGER, THE 10
BANNED NOISEMAKERS, THE 7
BARKOVITCH, GARY 7
BART AND MARY'S FIRST CHILD 10
BARTON DETECTIVE SERVICES 20
BASEBALL BAT BOY, THE 3
BASTARD IN AN ARMY COAT, THE 7
BATES, IRMA 3
BEA 10
BEAN, MRS. 20
BEARDED FARMER, THE 7
BEATLES, THE 3
BETTY 10
"BIFF" 20
BIG BLONDE KID, A 7
BIG FAT HOOCHIE-KOOCHIE MAMA, THE 7
BILL 10
BLACK MAN, THE 7
BLACK WOMAN WITH AN AFRO, A 10
BLOCK POLICE, THE 13
BOY, THE 13
BOY AFTER LARSON, THE 7

BOY BEHIND OLSON AND GARRATY, THE 7
BOY IN A BLACK TURTLENECK, A 7
BOY IN A BLUE SWEATER, THE 7
BOY RAY DIDN'T KNOW, THE 7
BOY WHO HAD A CONVULSION, THE 7
BOY WHO RAN INTO THE WOODS, THE 7
BOY WITH SUNSTROKE, THE 7
BOYFRIEND OF THE GIRL WITH LARGE BREASTS, THE 7
BOYNTON, JUDGE HILMER 20
BRADBURY, RAY 7
BRENNER, OLIVIA 10
BRONTICELLI, LUIGI 10
BROOKS, SUSAN 3
BROWNMILLER, SUSAN 3
BRUBECK, DAVE 7
BURLY MAN, A 7
BURNS, ARTHUR M. 13
BUSINESS ASSOCIATE, A 20

C

CAB DRIVER, THE 13
CABLE, DICKY 3
CALLAGHEE, MRS. 20
CALLOWAY, JEAN 10
CALLOWAY, LESTER 10
CANNING, VICTOR 3
CARLISLE, KITTY 10
CARLSON, JOHN 3
CAROL GRANGER'S SISTER 3
CAROLYN 7
CARPENTER, KAREN 20
CARRADINE, JOHN 3
CASKIN, NANCY 3
CASTINGUAY, MRS. 3
CASTINGUAY, SAM 3
CATHY SCRAMM'S PARENTS 7
CHALKER, ALLEN 20
CHALMERS, HENRY 10
CHASE VEHICLE GUARDS, THE 7
CHILDREN, THE 7
CHRISTIE, AGATHA 3
CINDY 10
CLERK, THE 10
CLUMP OF CHEERING HOUSEWIVES, THE 7
COCKER, ANDY 10
COLLETTE, DANA 3
COLLINS, WILKIE 3
COLTER, REGGIE 7
COMPLAINING LADY, THE 10
CONLEY 20
CONNIE 10
COP, A 7
COP, THE 13
COSELL, HOWARD 10
COULSON, MR. 3
COVEY OF HIGH SCHOOL BOYS, THE 7

COWLES, BOBBY 13
COWLES, MARY 13
CRAGER, JACK 13
CRANSTON, LAMONT 3
CROSS, SANDRA 3
CROSSKILL, RICHARD 20
CROSSKILLS, THE 20
CULLEN, BILL 10
CURLEY 7
CURRY 13

D

D'ALLESSIO, GEORGE (FREAKY) 7
DAHL, ARLENE 10
DALLAS COWGIRLS 20
DANKMANS, THE 10
DANO, JOHN ("PIG PEN") 3
DANO, LILLY 3
DANO, MRS. 3
DARBYS, THE 10
DAVIDSON 7
DAWES, BART 10
DAWES, CHARLIE 10
DAWES, CHARLES FREDERICK 10
DAWES, MARY 10
DEBBINS, ROSEANNE 3
DECKER, CARL 3
DECKER, CHARLIE 3
DECKER, RITA 3
DECKER, TOM 3
DEEGAN, JOHN 13
DEEVER, GEORGIA 20
DELEAVNEY, JUDGE SAMUEL K.N. 3
DENCH, CARLA 3
DENVER, MR. 3
DICKY 13
DIEHARDS, THE 7
DIMENT, ETHEL 10
DIOR 20
DOG, A 7
DOG'S OWNER, THE 7
DONAHUE, ROBERT S. 13
DONNIGAN, FLAPPER 13
DORGENS, MRS. AMELIA 7
DRAKE 10
DRAKE, PHIL 10
DRUNK FELLA, THE 7
DUGANFIELD, DAVID 20
DUNCAN 10
DUNINGER, WAYNE 13
DUNKIN DONUTS PEOPLE, THE 7
"DUSSETTES, AUBUCHONS, AND LAVESQUES" 7

E

EARL, RANDY 3
EASTWOOD, CLINT 20
EINSTEIN, ALBERT 20
ELDERLY WOMAN WITH AN ELASTIC BANDAGE AROUND ONE LEG, AN 10
ELLEN HOBART'S MOTHER 10
ELWELL, MR. 7
ELWELL, MRS. 7
ENDERS, LON 20
EV 7

EWING 7

F

FABULOUS OYSTERS, THE 10
FAMILY OF FIVE, THE 7
FAMILY OF FOUR AND THEIR CAT, A 7
FAMILY THAT WATCHED, THE 7
FANDER 20
FAT, BALD MAN, THE 7
FAT MAN, THE 20
FAT NEWSPAPERMAN, THE 7
FAT WOMAN, A 7
FAZIO, MR. 3
FEDNACH, HUGH 10
FENNER, PHILIP T. 10
FENTNER 7
FENUM, ROGER 7
FIEDLER, GEORGE 7
FIELD, CHARLIE 7
FITZGERALD, PAT 3
FIVE POLICEMEN, THE 13
FIVE RICH KIDS, THE 20
"FLASH" 20
FLOREN, MYRON 3
FLOYD, GRACE 10
FOSTER, STEPHEN AND EDGAR ALLAN POE 7
FOUR LITTLE BOYS 7
FOXWORTH, RAND 20
FRANKEL, MR. 3
FRANKIE 13
FRANKLIN, PETER 3
FREDDY 10
FRIEDMAN, KIPPY 13

G

GALLANT 7
GANNON, TANIS 3
GARRATY, JEFF 7
GARRATY, JIM 7
GARRATY, MR. 7
GARRATY, MRS. 7
GARRATY, RAY (RAYMOND DAVIS) 7
GARRATY'S LITTLE BROTHER 7
GAS STATION ATTENDANT, THE 7
GAVIN 3
GAVIN, MIKE 3
GAYLE 10
GEORGIE 10
GIBBS, ETHEL 10
GILLY 13
GINA 20
GINELLI, RICHARD 20
GIRL BEAT WITH A BASEBALL BAT, THE 3
GIRL WITH LARGE BREASTS, THE 7
GOLDMAN, JACK 3
GOLEON, RICH 13
GORDON, JOHN T. 10
GOSSAGE, RICH 3
GOVERNOR, THE 10
GRACE, DON 3
GRADY, CHARLIE 13
GRANGER, CAROL 3

GRANGER, MRS. 3
GRANGER, TOM 10
GRANGER, VERNA 10
GRASSNER, OGDEN FATHER 13
GREELY, PENSCHLEY, KINDER, AND HALLECK 20
GREEN, MRS. 3
GREENBERGER, WILL 3
GREENBRIAR BOYS, THE 3
GREENE, LORNE 10
GRIBBLE 7
GRIFFEN, JOHN 13
GRIFFEN, MERV 10
GROUP OF LITTLE GIRLS, A 7
GROUP OF MEN AROUND A FORD PICKUP, THE 7
GROUP OF TEENAGERS, A 7
GROUP OF WORKERS, A 7
GUARD, THE (#1) 7
GUARD, THE (#2) 7
GUIDANCE COUNSELOR, THE 7

H

HALLECK, HEIDI 20
HALLECK, LINDA JOAN 20
HALLECK, WILLIAM "BILLY" 20
HAMNER, WALLY 10
HANK 10
HANNAFORD, BRIAN 3
HANNAFORD, JESSIE DECKER 3
HANRAHAN, GERRY 13
HARKNESS 7
HARLAN 7
HARRIS 13
HEAD, EDITH 3
HEIDI'S MOTHER 20
HEILIG, MAMMA 20
HEILIG, TREY 20
HELL'S ANGELS BOY, THE 7
HERALD, CORKY 3
HIGH SCHOOL BAND, A 7
HISTORY TEACHER, THE 7
HIZZONER 13
HOBART, ELLEN 10
HOBART, JACK 10
HOBART, LINDA 10
HOBARTS, THE 10
HOLLOW-CHEEKED MAN WITH NO TEETH IN AN UNCLE SAM SUIT, THE 7
HOLLOWAY, DON 13
HOPI INDIANS, THE 7
HOPLEY, DUNCAN 20
HOTEL CLERK, THE 20
HOUGH, BILL 7
HOUSTON, DR. MICHAEL 20
HOUSTON, MRS. 20
HOUSTON, SAMANTHA 20
HOWARD, RON 7
HUMAN SUBMARINE, THE 7
HUNTERS, THE 13

(continued on page 669)

AN INDEX TO CHARACTERS IN
UNCOLLECTED SHORT STORIES

The following index is Part 4 of a four-part Character Index: Novels, Collections, The Bachman Novels, and Uncollected Short Stories. The Uncollected Short Stories Index consists of all the characters in those Stephen King short stories which are either unpublished or published but uncollected. The Master Number(s) following each character's name correspond to the number(s) of the work(s) in which the character appears. Further information on the character can be obtained by consulting the concordance section, wherein the unpublished/uncollected works are arranged in a separate (from the main concordance) chronological, numbered sequence by Master Number.

A

AARONSON, BEDELIA U28
ABELSON, NORMAN U21
ABRUZZI, WALT U14 (5)
AGNEW, HUNCHBACK FRED U5 (4, 5)
ALBANIANS, THE U22
ALBANY BUS DRIVER U15
ALBUQUERQUE NEWSPAPER PUBLISHER, THE U14 (1)
ALDA, ALAN U33
ALICE'S CHESHIRE CAT U10
ALTONS, THE U32
AMERICANS, THE U32
ANASTASIO, ALBERT U14 (5)
ANDERSON, LIEUTENANT UUP1
ANDERSON, TOBY U21
ANESTHETIST, THE U19-5
ARKINBAUER, MR. U14 (1)
ARKINBAUER, MRS. U14 (1)
ARSENAULT, MATT U32
ASSISTANT, THE U24
AUDIENCE, THE U26

B

BAILIFF, THE U30
BAILY, CHIPS U12
BANNING, BILLY U30
BANNING, CLIVE U30
BANNING, GEORGE U30
BANNING, GRAMMA SARAH U30
BANNING, MR. U30
BANNING, MRS. U30
BANNING, PATTY U30
BARFIELD, TINA U15
BARKER, OLIVE U15
BARNES, MR. U24
BARNEY U7
BARNEY'S FRIEND U7
BARTENDER, THE U5 (1)
BEAT COP, THE U11
BECK, BILLY U28
BEEKEEPER, THE U22
BELL-CAPTAIN, THE U14 (1)
BENNY THE BULL U11
BIG JOE'S TEAM U19-2
BILL U19-2
BILLY BECK'S PROFESSOR U28
BLACK, KELSO U1-1, 5
BLACK DAHLIA, THE U29
BLACK STALLION, A U5 (1)
BLACK-AND-WHITE CAMERAMAN, THE U34
"BLIND PIPER WHO IS NOT NAMED FOR A THOUSAND YEARS, THE" U13
BLOCKER, HARVEY U19-1
BLUE-EYED SON OF BRACKEN AND NORMA, THE U11
BORTMAN, JOSH UUP1
BORTMAN, MR. UUP1
BORTMAN, MRS. UUP1
BOSTON WHITES, THE U11

BOWEN, JOHN U9
BOWIE, CLAIRE U29
BRACKEN, JOHN U11
BRADFORD U28
BRADLEY, JACK UUP1
BRANDY U30
BRANDYWINE, CECIL U14 (1)
BRANDYWINE, CLYDE U14 (1)
BRIGGS, MELANIE U29
BRINKMAYER, JOHNNY U30
BROADMOOR, CAROLYN U10
BRONTOSAURUS, A U1-8
BRYNNER, YUL U26
"BUBBA" U19-1
BUCKLEY, MR. U28
BULLDOZER OPERATOR, THE U19-5
BULLDOZER OPERATOR'S BABY, THE U19-5
BULLFORD, HUGH U1-7
BUM, A (U21)
BURDEAU, PHIL U9
BURREY U14 (3)
BURSAR, THE U3b, Chapter I
BUS DRIVER, THE U8
BUSLOAD OF KIDS, THE U26

C

CAB DRIVER U21
CABBY, THE U13
CALLAHAN, BROCK U2
CALLAHAN, BRENT U16
CAMPBELL, ORRIN U32
CAMPBELL, MRS. U32
CAMPBELL CHILDREN, THE U32
CARETAKER U3b, Chapter I
CARLYLE (U17)
CARMICHAEL, DEPUTY MARSHALL HOAGY U5 (5)
CARNY GUY, A U29
CAT FROM HELL, THE U10
CHARLIE, GREAT-UNCLE U3b, Chapter V
"CHEF OF STARVATION, THE" U20
CHESS TEACHER, THE U32
CHEYNEY, DETECTIVE RICHARD U26
CHICKEN GEEKER, THE U28
CHIEF ACCOUNTANT, THE U24
CHIEF OF POLICE, THE U14 (3)
CHIEF OF POLICE'S SISTER, THE U14 (3)
CHIROPRACTOR, THE U19-5
CLEANIN FAIRY, THE U28
CLERK, THE U34
CLEVELAND TORSO MURDERER, THE U29
CLEWSON, ANDREA UUP1
CLEWSON, BILLY UUP1

CLEWSON, DALE UUP1
CNN NEWS CORRESPONDENT, A U32
COLUMBINE, SAM U5 (1)
COLUMNIST, THE U19-5
COMPSONS, THE U14 (2)
COOK, A U1-4
COOK, POP U32
COP, THE U29
CORLISS, PAUL U9
CORONER, THE U10
CORONER, THE U14 (3)
CORREZENTE, NORMA U11
CORREZENTE, VITTORIO U11
COTTON CANDY SALESMAN U12
"COUNT DRACULA WITH A PRIVATE PILOT'S LICENSE" U29
COUNTRY & WESTERN SINGER WITH AIDS, THE U29
COUNTY COMMISSIONER, THE U4
COUNTY CORONER U9
COUSINS, MILLY U31
COY, ALVIN U9
CRANE, JOHNNY U32
CRATER, MRS. U1-4
CRATER, OGLETHORPE U1-4
"CRAZY WOP FROM PENNSYLVANIA, THAT" U9
CREEDENCE CLEARWATER REVIVAL U27
CROSSEN, MARGARET U8
CUSTER, GENERAL U5 (1)

D

DAGBOLT, HUMPHREY U32
DAGGETT, BOB U32
DAGGETT, FRANK U32
DAGGETT'S ISLAND DAUGHTER U32
DAGGETT'S THREE MAINLAND DAUGHTERS U32
DAVID, UNCLE U3b, Chapter IV
DAVIS, FRANK U30
DAVIS, MILES U7
DAVIS, MR. U30
DAWSON, MISS SANDRA U5 (1)
DAWSON, MR. U5 (1)
DAY-MAID, THE U10
DEA GUYS U29
DEAD BEATS, THE U27
DEAD FLY, A U21
DEAD GERMAN, A U8
DEAD KENNEDYS, THE U27
DEAN, MR. U34
DECAYING MAN IN A BROOKS BROTHERS SUIT, A U32
DECOMPOSED BABY SPIDER, A U21
DEES, RICHARD U29
DEES, RICK U29
DeHORNE, MR. U34
DeHORNE, MRS. U34

DEIDRE U21
DELIVERY BOY, THE U27
DELLUMS, ALBERT K. U26
DELLUMS, CARTHAGE, STONEHAM, AND TAYLOR U26
DELORES'S FIRST CHILD U28
DELORES'S FIVE CHILDREN U28
DELORME, MAMA U28
DEPUTY, THE U22
DERWENT, HORACE U14 (3)
DERWENT, MRS. U14 (3)
DERWENT'S FOUR GRANDPARENTS U14 (3)
"DESIGNATED JEW, THE" U15
DETTLEBAUM, MRS. U34
DETTLEBAUMS, THE U34
DETWEILLER, CARLOS U15
DILLON, ALBERT U26
DISC JOCKEY, THE U19-5
DISHONEST ACCOUNTANT, A U14 (1)
DOCTOR, THE U22
DOG, THE U30
DOLAN, JAMES (JIM) U19-1
DOLAN'S BABES U19-1
DON, UNCLE U30
DORFMAN, BURT U32
DOSTEYVESKY U6
DOTSON, RIDER UUP1
DOTSON, SONNY U32
DOTSON'S BROTHER UUP1
DOWN HOME AMERICA, MR. U29
DRIVER, THE U19-4
DROGAN U10
DROGAN, AMANDA U10
DRUMMER, THE U26
DUCET, LUCY U31
DUFFREY DEPUTY, THE U29
DURKER, HARRY U14 (1)

E

EAMONS, DAVE U32
EATER OF DIMENSIONS, THE U13
EBONY VELVET U12
EDDIE (U15)
EDEN, HENRY U31
EDEN, MRS. U31
EDITORIAL ASSISTANT U15
EDMONT, MR. U12
EDWARD U8
EIGHT CHILDREN U29
EIGHTEEN MEN U10
ELEVATOR OPERATOR, THE U14 (2)
ELEVEN CHIEFS OF HOUSEKEEPING, THE U28
EMIR OF KUWAIT, THE U32
ENDERS, HARLOW U15
ERWIN, ERWIN, & BRADSTREET U3b, Chapter II
EVIL KILLER, THE U24

EVVIE U13
EVVIE'S FRIEND U13
EZRA U29

F

FALMOUTH COPS, THE U29
FANCY-DAN GAMBLER, THE U5 (1)
"FARMER JOHN" U29
FARNHAM, PC ROBERT U13
FARNHAM, SHEILA U13
FARNHAM KIDS, THE U13
FARNUM, MR. U12
FAT GUY FROM JANUS MUSIC, THE U27
FAT YELLOW TOMCAT, A U7
FELLOW IN MECHANIC FALLS, A U9
FENDER BENDER DRIVER #1 U22
FENDER BENDER DRIVER #2 U22
FENNY, DENNIS U34
FENSTER, ALICIA U34
FENSTERS, THE U34
FIFTEEN THOUSAND CATS U10
FIFTEEN THOUSAND RED CHINESE ADVISORS U22
FILLER, TIM U30
FIRST BAR GUY, THE U27
FIRST LADY, THE U32
FIVE DRUG SMUGGLERS U29
FLEMING, ART U34
FLOOR MANAGER, THE U26
FLORIST, THE U21
FLY, A U27
FLYING SCHANUZERS, THE U26
FORD, STATE POLICE LT. ARTHUR P. U21
FORNOY, BOBBY U22
FORNOY, BOW-WOW U22
FORNOY, HOWARD U22
FORNOY, INDIA U22
FORNOY, RICHARD U22
FOSTER, JODIE U17
FOURNIER, MICHAEL U32
FOURNIER, MR. U32
FOURNIER, MRS. U32
FRED U26
FREEMAN, DANNY U13
FREEMAN, DORIS U13
FREEMAN, LEONARD U13
FREEMAN, NORMA U13
FRYE, DWIGHT U29
FULL PROFESSOR OF GEOLOGY, A U22
FUTURE COP, A U1-8

G

GAGE, DICK U10
"GASH ME" AUTHOR, THE U15

(continued from page 666)

PART VI

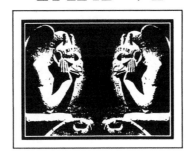

BENEATH THE SHEET

Commentary on King's "Marketable Obsessions"

"HE WHO TELLS IT"
An Annotated Bibliography of Books & Articles
About Stephen King and His Work

The following bibliography includes all the books currently available about Stephen King, as well as a couple of titles (*Danse Macabre* by King himself, and *Faces of Fear* by Doug Winter) which, while not specifically about King, are valuable resources nonetheless, and should be given consideration. *Danse Macabre* contains revealing autobiographical information about King and the influences on his writing, and *Faces of Fear* contains a very important interview with King.

Following the book bibliography is a bibliography of selected issues of *Twilight Zone*, *Cinefantastique* and other magazines containing significant articles about King and/or his work.

BOOKS

Alphabetical Checklist of Titles

1. *The Annotated Guide to Stephen King*, by Michael R. Collings.
2. *Bare Bones: Conversations on Terror With Stephen King*, edited by Tim Underwood and Chuck Miller.
3. *Danse Macabre*, by Stephen King
4. *Discovering Stephen King*, edited by Darrell Schweitzer.
5. *Enterprise Incidents Presents Stephen King*, by James Van Hise.
6. *Faces of Fear: Encounters With the Creators of Modern Horror*, by Douglas E. Winter.
7. *Fear Itself: The Horror Fiction of Stephen King*, edited by Tim Underwood and Chuck Miller.
8. *Feast of Fear: Conversations With Stephen King*, edited by Tim Underwood and Chuck Miller
9. *The Films of Stephen King*, by Michael R. Collings.
10. *The Gothic World of Stephen King: Landscape of Nightmares*, edited by Gary Hoppenstand and Ray B. Browne.
11. *Kingdom of Fear: The World of Stephen King*, edited by Tim Underwood and Chuck Miller.
12. *Landscape of Fear: Stephen King's American Gothic*, by Tony Magistrale.
13. *The Many Facets of Stephen King*, by Michael R. Collings.
14. *The Moral Voyages of Stephen King*, by Tony Magistrale.
15. *Reign of Fear: Fiction and Film of Stephen King*, edited by Don Herron.
16. *The Shape Under the Sheet: The Complete Stephen King Encyclopedia*, by Stephen J. Spignesi.
17. *The Shorter Works of Stephen King*, by Michael Collings & David Engebretson.
18. *Stephen King: The Art of Darkness*, by Douglas E. Winter.
19. *Stephen King As Richard Bachman*, by Michael R. Collings.
20. *Stephen King At the Movies*, by Jessie Horsting.
21. *The Stephen King Companion*, by George Beahm.
22. *Stephen King: The First Decade, Carrie to Pet Sematary*, by Joseph Reino.
23. *Stephen King Goes to Hollywood*, by Jeff Conner.
24. *The Stephen King Phenomenon*, by Michael R. Collings.
25. *The Stephen King Quiz Book*, by Stephen Spignesi.
26. *Teacher's Manual: Novels of Stephen King*, by Edward J. Zagorski.
27. *The Unseen King*, by Tyson Blue.

Annotations

1. *THE ANNOTATED GUIDE TO STEPHEN KING*, by Michael R. Collings (Starmont House, 1987).
   This is a detailed primary and secondary bibliography of the works of Stephen King. A very valuable resource. An update is currently in the works.

2. *BARE BONES: CONVERSATIONS ON TERROR WITH STEPHEN KING*, edited by Tim Underwood and Chuck Miller (Underwood-Miller, 1987; McGraw-Hill).
   This books contains thirty interviews with Stephen King, the majority of them previously published. It's a good value, though, for those fans who haven't been able to get their hands on some of the major King interviews, most of which are included here. The most significant are the 1981 *High Times* Interview, the 1982 *Penthouse* Interview, and the 1983 *Playboy* Interview.

3. *DANSE MACABRE*, by Stephen King (Berkley paperback, 1981).
   What a book! Imagine being in a booth in a bar somewhere in Maine during a snowstorm with six or twenty pitchers of beer on the table and Stephen King sitting across from you. Now imagine that Stephen King has decided to tell you literally *everything* he knows about the horror genre. OK? Now write down everything he says, and at the end of the month (year) (decade), you'll have *Danse Macabre*. That's what this book is: *Everything* Stephen King knows about horror, from books, to television, to movies, and back again. This guy has very obviously studied widely in the genre and can speak with impeccable credentials. His two appendices in the back of the book where he details the best films and books in the horror field are alone worth the price of admission. *Danse Macabre* was on the *New York Times* hardcover bestseller list for ten weeks in the spring of 1981. And with good reason: This nonfiction study of what had previously been considered a bastard genre is a masterpiece. It is a definitive look at the horror field; and it was penned by the definitive author in the field. If you haven't read this Kingly opus...Shame On You! (And if you have read it...go read it again!)

4. *DISCOVERING STEPHEN KING*, edited by Darrell Schweitzer (Starmont House, 1985).
   This—along with *Fear Itself*—was one of the first collections of critical studies of King's work. A well-balanced anthology, *Discovering Stephen King* contains some exceptional essays, some of which include Collings' look at *The Stand*, Heldreth's "The Dead Child," Schweitzer's "Collecting Stephen King," and Price's look at "King and the Lovecraft Mythos." This collection is an excellent place to start for the student interested in a scholarly look at the work of Stephen King.

5. *ENTERPRISE INCIDENTS PRESENTS STEPHEN KING*, by James Van Hise (New Media, 1984).
   This was a magazine-type look at King, his novels, his films, and several uncollected (at the time) stories. (Several of these uncollected tales ended up in *Skeleton Crew* the following year.) The book is an interesting read and offers varied and diverse opinions and insights on King and his impact as a writer and on popular culture. [NOTE: See my interview with editor Jim Van Hise, and a reproduction of the book's cover illustration, "Staircase O' Monsters" by Steve Fiorilla and Jim McDermott, in this volume.]

6. *FACES OF FEAR: ENCOUNTERS WITH THE CREATORS OF MODERN HORROR*, by Douglas E. Winter (Berkley trade paperback, 1985).

Although not solely about Stephen King, I have included *Faces of Fear* in this bibliography for a few reasons. First, is that it is by Douglas Winter, author of the definitive critical biography, *Stephen King: The Art of Darkness,* second, because it contains an interview with Stephen King that must be considered one of the most important in print, and third, it is a very valuable contribution to the field. *Faces of Fear* is a terrific collection of interviews with horror writers, and is an excellent anthology for those interested in the particular work of one of the included authors, or for those with an overall interest in the horror genre. In the interview with King, he discusses *Pet Sematary,* one of the few times he's consented to talk about the book. In addition to the interview with King, *Faces of Fear* also contains lengthy interviews with Robert Bloch, Richard Matheson, William P.Blatty, Dennis Etchison, Ramsey Campbell, David Morrell, James Herbert, Charles L. Grant, T.E.D. Klein, Alan Ryan, John Coyne, V.C. Andrews, Michael McDowell, and Whitley Strieber.

7. *FEAR ITSELF: THE HORROR FICTION OF STEPHEN KING,* edited by Tim Underwood and Chuck Miller (Signet paperback, 1982).

This was the very first collection of critical essays about Stephen King's work. The roster of writers who participated is a literal "who's who" of contemporary supernatural horror writers. Also, the inclusion of King's own "On Becoming A Brand Name" makes this anthology a must. Essays to note are the ones by Chelsea Quinn Yarbro, Fritz Lieber, Charles L. Grant, Douglas E. Winter, and, of course, *Night Of The Living Dead*'s George Romero. By now, the bibliography is terribly dated, but it still contains some good information about first editions of the novels. *Fear Itself* is a very worthwhile general introduction to King criticism.

8. *FEAST OF FEAR: CONVERSATIONS WITH STEPHEN KING,* edited by Tim Underwood and Chuck Miller (Underwood-Miller, 1989, Limited Edition only).

I guess *Bare Bones* did well enough for Tim Underwood and Chuck Miller that they decided to compile *another* collection of reprinted interviews with Stephen King. The book contains forty-seven talks with King, and once again, is broken down into sections such as "Genesis," "Early Years," "Going Hollywood," etc. For the King fan, these two collections are goldmines of information straight from the horse's mouth, so to speak. It's not clear how King feels about this type of "packaging" of his words, but these tomes do serve a purpose in that they assemble in two places a well-organized collection of important King interviews.

9. *THE FILMS OF STEPHEN KING,* by Michael R. Collings (Starmont House, 1986).

This is a well-thought out overview and analysis of the film interpretations of Stephen King's works. Unlike the Starlog book, Collings looks at themes, and the difficulty in translating fiction to film. As Collings states in the Foreword, " *The Films of Stephen King* concerns the inevitable seesaw between author and filmmaker, with narrative as the fulcrum separating them." This book is a very intelligent analysis of the attempts by many and varied directors and film production people to convert the printed word to the visual image. This process becomes even more fascinating when the printed word is that of such a visual writer. Collings acknowledges King's use of visual imagery in his prose and helps the reader understand that having such "film-ready" novels available to the filmmaker is not often the blessing it would seem.

10. *THE GOTHIC WORLD OF STEPHEN KING: LANDSCAPE OF NIGHTMARES,* edited by Gary Hoppenstand and Ray B. Browne (Bowling Green State University Popular Press, 1987).

Academics *love* to analyze Stephen King, and this volume is yet another collection of scholarly articles about King and his work.

11. *KINGDOM OF FEAR: THE WORLD OF STEPHEN KING,* edited by Tim Underwood and Chuck Miller (NAL/Plume Trade Paperback, 1986).

Underwood and Miller decided that *Fear Itself* only scratched the surface of King criticism, and so compiled this 1986 collection of essays. The writers are even more stellar in this book, and included are such legends as Robert Bloch, Ramsey Campbell, Whitley Strieber, Clive Barker, and Harlan Ellison. There isn't a clunker in the bunch, except for Don Herron's notorious "anti-King" bias. (One wonders why he even bothers reading the guy if his reaction to King's work is so uniformly and consistently negative.) Thompson's "A Girl Named Carrie" tells us how Stephen King sold his first novel (Thompson was his editor at the time), and King's own "The Horror Writer And The Ten Bears" gives us added insight into the creation of modern horror.

12. *LANDSCAPE OF FEAR: STEPHEN KING'S AMERICAN GOTHIC,* by Tony Magistrale (Bowling Green State University Popular Press, 1988).

See my remarks for book number 10 above.

13. *THE MANY FACETS OF STEPHEN KING,* by Michael R. Collings (Starmont House, 1985).

The Many Facets of Stephen King explores *other* approaches to the work of Stephen King than simply as a writer of supernatural horror. From the Foreword: "In Stephen King's writing, we explore many 'facets' of horror as they glint from widely divergent perspectives. King's writing is not straight-line in the sense that he went through a 'mainstream phase,' a separate 'horror phase,' or a distinct 'epic-fantasy quest' phase. Instead, his forms and themes intertwine, reflecting each other, glittering like the continuous movement of light around a brilliantly set gem-stone." *The Many Facets of Stephen King* is an enlightening look at the other sides of Stephen King, and it is a book which will help readers "approach King from multiple directions, just as he approaches his craft from multiple directions."

14. *THE MORAL VOYAGES OF STEPHEN KING,* by Tony Magistrale (Starmont House, 1989).

An insightful analysis of King's "moral voyages," those excursions into the human soul taken by his many and varied characters. Magistrale does a good job of recognizing the subtext implicit in King's major "decision-making" characters, and explores how King works with his main credo (from *Danse Macabre*): "[M]orality is telling the truth as your heart knows it." An excellent interpretative study of a side of King's work too many critics ignore.

15. *REIGN OF FEAR: FICTION AND FILM OF STEPHEN KING,* edited by Don Herron (Underwood-Miller, 1988).

I think Don Herron should make his own personal "Stand": Quit writing about Stephen King. In his whiny "Summation" at the end of *Reign of Fear,* he moans that he had so looked forward to "quitting" his job as a "published Stephen King critic" when he heard that there was talk of a "satisfactory retirement" by Stephen King. In his listing of the reasons why he even deigned to critique King with his blisteringly brilliant insights, he admitted that the job was "fairly lucrative," and "some fun." I don't think it was an accident that he put the money part of the job at the front of the list. But, regardless of Herron's obvious dislike for anything by King other than *The Shining, The Dead Zone,* "Apt Pupil," and "The Body," the purpose of this review is to look at the overall effectiveness and value of the entire *Reign of Fear* collection. Overall, it's not bad. It's a mixed bag, actually. There are some pieces that are strong, honest, and contribute to our understanding of King and his work. But then there are essays that seem to exist for no reason other than to make the author feel like a bigshot because he shit on Stephen King in print. Herron must be included in the latter category. He described *IT,* the novel that I—and countless others (including the renowned Michael R. Collings)—consider to be King's magnum opus, as "two tons of crap in a five-ton crate." When I consider Don Herron's editorial position regarding Stephen King, I'm reminded of two adages that are particularly appropriate to his self-inflated "critique": One is the old one about those who can't do, teach (or try to), and the other is a line from John Travolta's sequel to "Saturday Night Fever," "Staying Alive." Travolta's character—cocky, arrogant, and a know-it-all—walks off the production. The choreographer confronts him in the hallway and blasts him with the question, "What'd you ever do that means anything?" I ask Herron the same question. As an epigraph to his "Summation," he quotes King as saying "Everybody has an opinion, but nobody's opinion is better than anybody else's," and the placement of the quote carries with it an almost-perceptible smirk. From his tone in the following essay, you can almost hear Herron saying, "Wrong, Steve-o. *My* opinion is better than most. And here it is." Well, my reply to that is that *that* sounds like "two tons of crap in a five-ton crate." And you know what crap smells like.

16. *THE SHAPE UNDER THE SHEET: THE COMPLETE STEPHEN KING ENCYCLOPEDIA,* by Stephen J. Spignesi (Popular Culture, Ink., 1991).

The book you now hold in your hands.

17. *THE SHORTER WORKS OF STEPHEN KING,* by Michael Collings & David Engebretson (Starmont House, 1985).

From the Foreword: *The Shorter Works of Stephen King* "is a comprehensive study of King's short fiction, from the level of individual stories to full collections, including not only plot summaries but critical approaches to each story, identifying themes, symbols, and relationships between the story and the rest of King's work." This book is an excellent companion to the work covered, whether you read Collings' analyses before or after you read (or reread) the actual stories.

18. *STEPHEN KING: THE ART OF DARKNESS,* by Douglas E. Winter (Signet paperback, 1986).

This is the one book every Stephen King fan, student or scholar must have. Winter is one of the world's leading critics of Stephen King's work and in *The Art of Darkness,* he takes the reader on a guided tour of everything King had written through 1986. Winter gives detailed analyses of every book, including specifics on rare King material such as *The Dark Tower* books and *The Plant,* as well as the pseudonymous Richard Bachman books. *The Art of Darkness* also includes a detailed bibliography, comprehensive plot summaries for every piece of shorter fiction (including juvenilia), and very informative footnotes for every chapter, many of which lead the student to other sources of King information. This book could also be called the only currently existing Stephen King biography, since Winter details King's life in chronological form, as well as through interviews with King, many of which are exclusive to this book. This is a book written by a serious Stephen King *fan,* and as such, you won't find much real criticism of either King or his writing. Analysis, yes. Complaints, no. Winter admits as much in the Foreword: "What you hold in your hands, then is best described as a critical appreciation; it is an intermingling of biography, literary analysis, and unabashed enthusiasm, spiced with commentary by Stephen King transcribed from our more than twelve hours of recorded conversations." *The Art of Darkness* is one of the few truly indispensable Stephen King studies available today.

19. *STEPHEN KING AS RICHARD BACHMAN,* by Michael R. Collings (Starmont House, 1985).

The first—and so far only—book-length study of Stephen King's pseudonymous work. Collings looks at Richard Bachman as an alter ego of Stephen King, and analyzes him as an author who primarily published *non*-supernatural/horror novels (with the exception of *Thinner.*) The "Speculations" chapter looks at the possible existence of other King pseudonyms.

20. *STEPHEN KING AT THE MOVIES,* by Jessie Horsting (Starlog/Signet Trade Paperback, 1986).

This is a terrific oversized paperback that will really appeal to fans or students of the film adaptations of King's work. It's filled with interviews with the people involved in each film, and *loaded* with pictures. Not really a critical study, this glossy full-color trade book is nonetheless an excellent addition to any King fan's library. A lot of the text is background material on how each film became a reality. The "Film Credits" section is very thorough, and the essay by Harlan Ellison rounds out the book nicely. *Stephen King at the Movies* is a Starlog/Signet production, so if you're familiar with *Starlog* magazine, then you'll immediately recognize and be familiar with the same approach to this material.

21. *THE STEPHEN KING COMPANION,* by George Beahm (Andrews and McMeel, 1989).

A superb sourcebook detailing every book, videotape, and audiotape of King's work. Also contains many interviews, sidebars, and articles about the King phenomenon. I'm on record as stating that if you could only own three books about Stephen King, *The Stephen King Companion* should be one of them. (The other two are Doug Winter's *Stephen King: The Art of Darkness* and my own *The Shape Under the Sheet.*) *The Companion* is an excellent introductory volume for the King reader. (George Beahm is also the author of a forthcoming Stephen King biography.)

22. *STEPHEN KING: THE FIRST DECADE, CARRIE TO PET SEMATARY,* by Joseph Reino (Twayne Publishers, 1988).

A study of King's novels written between 1974 and 1983.

23. *STEPHEN KING GOES TO HOLLYWOOD,* by Jeff Conner (New American Library, 1987).

This is a glossy look at the film adaptations of King's work that doesn't quite measure up to the standards set by Jessie Horsting with her own earlier *Stephen King At the Movies.* Conner, the publisher of Scream Press, seems to spend an awful lot of time talking about how the film deals were made, and while this is no doubt of interest to the people involved, it holds little entertainment or enlightenment for the average King fan. If you're looking for details on the making of the films, interviews with the principals, and definitive cast and crew credits, check out Horsting's book. If you'd like information on how movie deals are made in Hollywood – specifically Stephen King movies – then Conner's book is a good complementary volume to own.

24. *THE STEPHEN KING PHENOMENON,* by Michael R. Collings (Starmont House, 1987).

This looks at just what the title indicates: The Stephen King Phenomenon. And Phenomenon it is! Starting off with a brilliant analysis of King's magnum opus, *IT,* Collings then takes the reader through King's bestseller stats, and then looks at his track record with the critics. There is material here that will entertain and enlighten, while at the same time helping the reader understand this Phenomenon called Stephen King. This book is a self-contained education on the nature of literary popularity in the world today.

25. *THE STEPHEN KING QUIZ BOOK,* by Stephen J. Spignesi (New American Library, 1990).

This is the authorized quiz book. It contains 107 quizzes comprising 1,510 questions covering every novel, all the short stories, and even some of the uncollected pieces.

26. *TEACHER'S MANUAL: NOVELS OF STEPHEN KING,* by Edward J. Zagorski (New American Library, 1981).

This is just what the title says: a Teacher's Manual to aid in the teaching of Stephen King's earlier work. Because of its publication date (1981), the manual ends with *Firestarter* and *Night Shift,* but is important for its insightful look at the themes Stephen King works with in his fiction. The pamphlet contains a good overview of horror fiction and also takes a look at Stephen King's role in the horror genre.

27. *THE UNSEEN KING,* by Tyson Blue (Starmont House, 1989).

The Unseen King, by Tyson Blue, the former *Castle Rock* contributing editor, deals with rare King: works of King's which have not been seen by a mass audience, including juvenilia, college writings, *The Plant*, uncollected short stories and other such items. Blue sometimes is a bit more visible in his critique than is usual for this type of overview, but he is a King expert nonetheless, and this volume is well-organized and insightful.

Forthcoming Books

1. *"The Shining" Reader*, by Tony Magistrale (Starmont House).
2. *Infinite Explorations: Art and Artifice In Stephen King's IT, Misery, and The Tommyknockers*, by Michael R. Collings (Starmont House).
3. *The Stephen King Bibliography*, by Douglas E. Winter (Donald M. Grant).
4. *The Stephen King Story*, by George Beahm (Andrews and McMeel).

SELECTIVE MAGAZINE BIBLIOGRAPHY

1. Notable Issues of *Twilight Zone* Magazine

- APRIL 1981; "Premiere Issue"
  ◊ "Stephen King: "I Like To Go For The Jugular." (Interview by Charles L. Grant.)
- MAY 1982
  ◊ "Front-Row Seats At The 'Creepshow'" (Article by Ed Naha.)
- JULY 1982
  ◊ "Digging *The Boogens*" (Film review by Stephen King.)
- SEPTEMBER 1982
  ◊ "TZ Screen Preview: *Creepshow*" (Film preview by Robert Martin.)
- NOVEMBER 1982
  ◊ *The Evil Dead:* Why You Haven't Seen It Yet...And Why You Ought To" (Film review by Stephen King.)
- DECEMBER 1983
  ◊ "TZ Screen Preview: *Dead Zone*" (Film preview by James Verniere.)
- FEBRUARY 1984
  ◊ "Screen Preview: *Christine*" (James Verniere.)
  ◊ "Stephen King Talks About *Christine*" (Randy Lofficier.)
- FEBRUARY 1985
  ◊ "Stephen King, Peter Straub, & The Quest For 'The Talisman'" (Interview by Douglas E. Winter.)
- DECEMBER 1985
  ◊ "New Adventures In The Screen Trade: A Non-Stop King Takes On TV" (Interview by Ben Herdon.)
- FEBRUARY 1986 "Stephen King Special"
  ◊ "The Fifth Quarter" (A short story by Stephen King, originally published as by "John Swithen.")
  ◊ "Talking Terror With Stephen King" (Douglas E. Winter.)
  ◊ "King Directs 'Overdrive'" (Tyson Blue.)
  ◊ "Collecting King" (Douglas E. Winter.)
- DECEMBER 1986 "Halloween Horror Special"
  ◊ "Stephen King: The Truth about *IT*" (Interview by Tyson Blue.)

2. Notable Issues of *Fantastic Films* Magazine

- NOVEMBER 1982; 5th Anniversary Issue
  ◊ "*Creepshow*" (Article by J. Stein.)
- FEBRUARY 1983; #32
  ◊ "*Fantastic Films* Interviews Stephen King" (Michael Stein & Jessie Horsting.)
  ◊ "Director George Romero Talks About *Creepshow*" (Interview by Blake Mitchell & Jim Ferguson.)

- NOVEMBER 1983; #36
  ◊ "*Cujo:* Director Lewis Teague Reveals The Difficulties Of Adapting The Best-Selling Novel For The Screen" (Article and interview by Jessie Horsting.)
- JUNE 1985; #44
  ◊ "A Director's Eye View Of Stephen King's *Cat's Eye*" (Article and interview by Jessie Horsting.)

3. Notable Issues of *Cinefantastique* Magazine

- SEPTEMBER/OCTOBER 1982; VOLUME 13, NO. 1 "Are These The Scariest Men In America?"
  ◊ "*Creepshow:* It's An $8 Million Comic Book From George Romero & Friends" (Article by Paul Gagne.)
- NOVEMBER/DECEMBER 1982; VOLUME 13, NO. 2/VOLUME 13, NO. 3; Special Double Issue
  ◊ "*Dead Zone:* David Cronenberg To Direct Stephen King's Chilling ESP Saga For Dino DeLaurentis" (Preview by Tim Lucas.)
- APRIL/MAY 1983; VOLUME 13, NO. 4
  ◊ "*Creepshow:* Romero, King Bring Back The Gory Glory Days Of E.C. Comics" (Review by David J. Hogan.)
- JUNE/JULY 1983; VOLUME 13, NO. 5
  ◊ "*Dead Zone:* David Cronenberg Shuns The Auteur Route To Adapt Stephen King's ESP Novel To The Screen" (Preview by Tim Lucas.)
- AUGUST/SEPTEMBER 1983; VOLUME 13, NO. 6/VOLUME 14, NO. 1; Special Double Issue
  ◊ "John Carpenter's *Christine:* Bringing Stephen King's Bestseller To The Screen" (Article by Bill Kelley.)
- DECEMBER 1983/JANUARY 1984; VOLUME 14, NO. 2
  ◊ "Stephen King: With *Cujo, The Dead Zone* And *Christine,* He Just Might Be The Most Bankable Name In Hollywood" (Profile by Paul Gagne.)
  ◊ "David Cronenberg's *The Dead Zone:* Horror Film Auteur David Cronenberg Takes A Brief Hiatus In Stephen King Territory" (Article by Tim Lucas.)
  ◊ "*Cujo:* King's Shaggy Dog Thriller Only Succeeds At The Shock Level" (Review by Kyle Counts.)
  ◊ "*The Dead Zone:* King & Cronenberg: It's The Best Of Both Worlds" (Review by David J. Hogan.)
- MAY 1984; VOLUME 14, NO. 3
  ◊ "*Firestarter:* ET's Drew Barrymore Gets Scary As The Title Character in Stephen King's Bestseller" (Article by David J. Hogan.)
  ◊ "*Christine:* Carpenter Borrowed King's Car, But Doesn't Know How To Drive" (Review by David J. Hogan.)
  ◊ "Effects Man Roy Arbogast Was In Charge Of The Film's Amazing Automotive Star" (Article by Bill Kelley.)
- SEPTEMBER 1984; VOLUME 14, NO. 4 & 5; Special Double Issue
  ◊ "*Firestarter*" (Article by David J. Hogan.)
- MAY 1985; VOLUME 15, NO. 2
  ◊ "*Cat's Eye:* Horror Master Stephen King Blends Stories From *Night Shift* With A Dash Of Macabre Humor" (Article by Tim Hewitt.)
  ◊ "King's Eye: An Author's-Eye-View Of Scriptwriting, Working For Dino DeLaurentis, And Horror" (Interview by Tim Hewitt.)
  ◊ "*Silver Bullet:* Stephen King Tale Pits Werewolf Against Wheelchair Hotrodder" (Preview by Tim Hewitt.)
  ◊ "The Night Of The Horror King" (Profile by Ray and Katalin Ellis.)
- JULY 1985; VOLUME 15, NO. 3
  ◊ "Stephen King's *Night Shift:* Student Shorts Of King Tales Headed For VideoCassette Release" (Preview by Janrae Frank.)
- OCTOBER 1985; VOLUME 15, NO. 4
  ◊ "Stephen King's *Cat's Eye:* Director Lewis Teague And Effects

Expert Carlo Rambaldi On Filming Stephen King's Imaginative Horror Anthology" (Article by Tim Hewitt.)

◊ *"Cat's Eye:* The Cat As A Linking Device In Two Of King's Stories Proves Not Only Pointless But Actually Lessens Suspense" (Review by Lawrence French.)

•JULY 1986; VOLUME 16, NO. 3

◊ *"Maximum Overdrive:* Sneak Preview Of Rampaging Truck Shocker Shows Stephen King Knows How To Direct" (Preview by Judith P. Harris.)

•OCTOBER 1986; VOLUME 16, NO. 3/VOLUME 16, NO. 4

◊*"Maximum Overdrive:* Stephen King Rises From The Ashes Of His Latest Adaptation In The Driver's Seat" (Article by Tim Hewitt.)

◊ "The Subotsky-King Connection" (Article by Alan Jones.)

•JANUARY 1990; VOLUME 20, NO. 3.

◊ "Stephen King Strikes Back!" (Article on the *Pet Sematary* film by Gary L. Wood.)

•DECEMBER 1990; Volume 21, No. 3.

◊ "Stephen King's *Graveyard Shift*" (Article on the forthcoming film by Gary Wood.)

◊ "Stephen King's *IT*" (Article on the forthcoming miniseries by Gary Wood.)

◊ "Stephen King's *Misery*" (Article on the forthcoming film by Gary Wood.)

•FEBRUARY 1991; VOLUME 21, NO. 4. (Special Stephen King Issue)

◊ "Directing the Blood and Gore: 'Misery'" (Article by Gary Wood on Rob Reiner's direction of "Misery.")

◊ "Horror King, Stephen King" (Biographical article by Stephen Spignesi.)

◊ "Rob Reiner on Stephen King" (Interview with Reiner by Gary Wood.)

◊ "Hard Hitting Makeup Effects" (Article by Gary Wood on the special effects in "Misery.")

◊ "Read the Book, Forget the Film: Stephen King & Hollywood" (Article by Gary Wood on why King adaptations go wrong.)

◊ "Night of the Living King: 'The Dark Half'" (Article by Gary Wood on George Romero's adaptation of King's novel.)

◊ "King in Development: 'The Stand'" (Article by Gary Wood on the ten-year history of the filming of King's novel.)

◊ "On Spielberg: A Tale of Two Steves" (Article by Gary Wood on Steven Spielberg's adaptation of King and Straub's novel *The Talisman.*)

◊ "Upcoming Horrors, 'Thinner' & Others" (Article by Gary Wood on forthcoming King film projects.)

◊ "Eyeing the Movie Menu: What's Wrong with Stephen King?" (Article by Thomas Doherty on King film adaptations.)

◊ "Blasting Stephen King: 'Firestarter'" (Interview with 'Firestarter' director Mark Lester by Gary Wood.)

◊ "King on 'Firestarter': Who's to Blame?" (Article by Stephen King responding to Mark Lester's criticism of King's public response to Lester's film "Firestarter.")

◊ "Whatever Happened to 'Apt Pupil'" (Article by Gary Wood on a dead King film project.)

◊ "King's Boxoffice Bite" (Article by Gary Wood on the financial success of King films.)

◊ "King's Vision on the Screen" 'Pet Sematary'" (Article by Gary Wood on King's own adaptation of his novel.)

◊ "On Moviemaking with Dino DeLaurentiis" (Article by Gary Wood on King's work with DeLaurentiis.)

◊ "Animal Lovers Vs. Pets Run Amuck" (Article by Gary Wood on the use of animals in King's films.)

◊ "'Shotgunners': King & Peckinpah" (Article by Gary Wood on the unfilmed original King screenplay "The Shotgunners.")

◊ "Shooting It in Maine" (Article by Gary Wood on King's use of Maine locales for films.)

◊ "To Direct, or Not to Direct" (Article by Gary Wood on King's second thoughts about directing after "Maximum Overdrive.")

◊ "Visualizing Stephen King: 'It'" (Article by Gary Wood on the ABC miniseries.)

◊ "Another King Movie Mistake: 'Graveyard Shift'" (Article by Charles Leayman on the King film based on the *Night Shift* short story.)

4. Other Notable Magazine Coverage of Stephen King

•*PREVUE;* April/May 1982

◊ "The Once And Future King" (Profile by David McDonnell.)

◊ "The First Look Inside George Romero's New Bestiary *Creepshow*" (Film preview by David McDonnell and John Sayers.)

•*PLAYBOY;* June 1983

◊ *"Playboy* Interview: Stephen King: A Candid Conversation With The Author Of *Carrie* And *The Shining* About Ghosts, Vampires, Big Bucks And Other Gruesome Tales Of Horror" (Interview by Eric Norden.)

•*FANGORIA;* October 1983

◊ *"Cujo:* Lewis Teague, The *Alligator* Director, Talks About Bringing Stephen King's Rabid Saint Bernard To The Screen" (Interview by David Everitt.)

•*PREVUE;* December/January 1984

◊ *"Christine:* Stephen King And John Carpenter Take A Joy Ride To Terror!" (Film preview by Kim Johnson.)

•*TIME MAGAZINE;* October 6, 1986

◊ "Cover Story: "King Of Horror: The Master Of Pop Dread Writes On...And On...And On...And On" (Profile by Stefan Kanfor.)

◊ "The Novelist Sounds Off" (Interview by Cathy Booth.)

•*THE BLOODY BEST OF FANGORIA;* Volume #5, 1986

◊ "Horror Partners: Bestselling Novelists Stephen King And Peter Straub On Their Long-Awaited Collaboration, *The Talisman*" (Interview by Stanley Wiater and Roger Anker.)

•*THE BLOODY BEST OF FANGORIA;* Volume #6, 1987

◊ "Stephen King Takes A Vacation: The Bestselling Author Unleashes *IT*" (Interview by Edward Gross.)

•*OMNI;* February 1987

◊ "Forum: "What's Scaring Stephen King" (Essay by Stephen King.)

•*MAD MAGAZINE;* March 1987, Number 269

◊ "Stand But Me" (A MAD Movie Satire written by Dick Debartolo; drawn by Mort Drucker.)

•*CRACKED;* April 1989; Number 4

◊ "You Can Write Like Stephen King!" (Satirical flowchart written by Doug Martin; drawn by Peter Mulligan.)

•*FEAR;* August 1989

◊ "The Maine Man, Part 1" (Article by Paddy McKillop.)

•*FEAR;* September 1989

◊ "The Maine Man, Part 2" (Article by Paddy McKillop.)

•*MYSTERY SCENE;* Number 10

◊ "Interview: Stephen King" (Interview by Ed Gorman.)

•*W•B: WALDENBOOKS' NEWS, REVIEWS & EXCLUSIVE INTERVIEWS WITH TODAY'S HOTTEST AUTHORS;* November/December 1989, Number 10

◊ "Stephen King" (*Dark Half* interview by A.T.)

•*MYSTERY SCENE;* Number 27

◊ "An Interview About Stephen King With Stephen Spignesi" (Interview by Barry Hoffman.)

•*GAUNTLET;* Number 2, 1991

◊ Contains a special Stephen King section, with articles by Stephen King (an update of "The Dreaded X"), Michael Collings (a comparison of the two versions of *The Stand*), George Beahm (a market update), Howard Wornom (on King censorship), and Stephen Spignesi (a roundtable discussion with Richard Matheson, Richard Christian Matheson, Douglas Winter, J.N. Williamson, Joe Lansdale, Ray Garton, and Robert R. McCammon on "The Stephen King Influence.")

A GATHERING OF KINGS
A Valuable Addition to the Stephen King Bibliography

THE LARRY KING INTERVIEW WITH STEPHEN KING

Originally broadcast on the Mutual Broadcasting Network on April 10, 1986.
Available on cassette from:
Lion Recordings
P.O. Box 962
Washington, D.C. 20044

This is a terrific interview with Stephen King which was originally heard on radio all over the country. It runs about ninety minutes, and S.K. covers everything from whether or not his house is haunted, to *The Plant* and the *Dark Tower* books. A *must* interview for S.K. fans, collectors, and/or students. Here's an excerpt from the tape where S.K. discusses the genesis of *IT*:

Larry King: When you sit down to write a book, is the idea already there?

Stephen King: No, sometimes an idea will bounce around for a long time. This novel *IT* that's coming out in the fall percolated, I think, for about three years. You know, the idea just sort of "pogo-ed" into my mind, all at once. I was walking over a bridge and it was almost dark and I was wearing a pair of boots and it was a wooden bridge and I could hear my footsteps on the bridge and I flashed on this story "Billy Goats Gruff" with the troll under the bridge. "Who's that trip-trapping over my bridge?" And I thought OK, that's what I want to write about. I want to write about a real troll under a real bridge. And so two or three years went by, and after awhile the bad ideas just fell out. I just didn't think about them anymore. But the good ones came up. Maybe I'd be riding somewhere to pick up my kids from school when I'd say well, yeah, I could do *this* with it, and then I forgot about it for a week and then it would come back. But it wouldn't go away. It just stayed. And finally I sat down to write it and about four years and about sixteen hundred pages later, it was done. And that's all.

THE STEPHEN KING COMPANION
Author George Beahm Discusses His King Volume

Let's say you could only afford to buy three books about Stephen King, and you wanted those three to give you as wide-ranging an understanding of King and his work as possible. What three should you buy?

There's a whole slew of titles out there, isn't there? You've got all those Starmont titles, all those Underwood-Miller tomes, the movie books, the university press stuff, the books of interviews...well, you get the picture.

But there is an answer.

If you really couldn't buy any more than three titles, then those three books should be the following:

1. *The Stephen King Companion*, by George Beahm.
2. *Stephen King: The Art of Darkness*, by Douglas E. Winter.
3. *The Shape Under the Sheet: The Complete Stephen King Encyclopedia*, by Stephen J. Spignesi.

And I've listed them in that order for a very specific reason: That's how you should read them.

George Beahm's *The Stephen King Companion* gives the novice King reader a complete and accurate introduction to Stephen King and his work. It is the *perfect* introductory volume.

Doug Winter's *Stephen King: The Art of Darkness* takes you further. It helps the reader explore the themes King uses, and offers insightful analysis of all of King's novels, adding a deeper understanding. *Art* also offers a detailed and valuable bibliography.

And my own book, *The Shape Under the Sheet*, is for the King reader who wants to know literally everything they possibly can about the World of King.

With that out of the way, I now would like to introduce you to George Beahm and his *Stephen King Companion*.

George speaks eloquently of his intentions in writing the *Companion* in his essay "Why I Wrote *The Stephen King Companion*" in this section, so I won't rehash what George has already said so well.

Instead, I will offer my own thoughts about the book.

The *Companion* has become a valuable addition to my King library—and let's face it: I am not your ordinary King fan! When George very kindly sent me a set of the *Companion*'s galleys before publication for my thoughts and opinions, I eagerly read through it.

I came away pleased.

I admitted to George that there was nothing in the book that I didn't already know, but the vast majority of his readers will not have spent the previous three years *studying* King's work. To the King reader who knows nothing of King but the titles he or she can find in the bookstores, the *Companion* will appear as a godsend.

George spent a lot of time making the book as accurate as possible, and there are many features in the book guaranteed to open the eyes of the average King reader.

Open it to any page and there will bound to be something of interest for the King fan.

I, for one, was delighted to see Charles McGrath's *IT* parody, *ID*, reprinted here. This piece kills me. The first time I read the opening lines...

> The terror, which has already lasted fifteen weeks and which may never end, for all I know, began with the men and the chainsaws.
> *The men*
> *The chainsaws*

...I had to put it down I was laughing so hard. It is to George's credit that he recognized the brilliance of this parody and reprinted it for us to have at our disposal.

Also, the *Companion* contains the first ever transcript of Stephen King's Virginia Beach lecture on censorship, and for that alone, King fans should have this book.

Reading *The Stephen King Companion* is like eating potato chips.

Barbecue potato chips.

With french onion dip.

And ice cold white wine on the side.

It's irresistible.

Now let me tell you about George. George Beahm is the guy who spent a week in a motel in Orono just so he could read and take notes on the three unpublished King novels in the University of Maine's Special Collections Library. And after all that, he was remarkably restrained in writing about these "finds," refusing to even give the *impression* of being presumptuous with material that was not his own.

George is also the guy who called me almost daily to make sure the information he had about my two King books was accurate.

And George is also the guy who sent me a picture of him and Goofy at Disneyworld, claiming that the photo showed the "real" George.

If you don't have a copy of the *Companion*, read over the book's Table of Contents which follows.

After you do, I think you'll agree the book is something you have to have.

I can hear you out there: Hey, Steve. What are *you* getting out of this plug?

Absolutely nothing, other than the satisfaction in knowing that I am turning people on to something I know they will enjoy, *and* get a lot out of.

Okay. I'm done.

It's time for another barbecue potato chip.

—sjs

WHY I WROTE
THE STEPHEN KING COMPANION
by George Beahm

"I had never attempted a book-length nonfiction project, and the idea was intimidating....With nonfiction, there's all that bothersome business of making sure your facts are straight, that the dates jibe, that the names are spelled right...and worst of all, it means being out front. ....The writer of nonfiction is all too visible."
—From the forenote to Stephen King's *Danse Macabre*

It's a longstanding tradition that insofar as a writer and his body of work are concerned, literary autopsies are preferable to biopsies. After all, when the body is laid out on the examination table, it's easier to touch the shape under the sheet.

What, then, accounts for the sheer number of books about King, and why would I want to add my own? (By my count, there were twenty books about King in print when I made the decision to write *The Stephen King Companion*—and another ten that would appear within the year.)

The sheer number of books about King is easily explained: King's mass and specialized appeal is such that books will inevitably be written, each reflecting the author's specific point of view. For academicians, a raft of books—notably Winter's, Collings's many titles, three collections from Underwood-Miller, and university press material. For researchers and students, primary and secondary bibliographies from Winter, Collings, and Murphy. For the die-hard King fan, a trivia quiz book and a concordance, both from Spignesi. And for anyone wanting to read King's own thoughts, there's two collections of interviews from Underwood-Miller.

What, I asked myself, hadn't been done?

At that time a good friend of mine, Howard "Rusty" Wornom, came up with a terrific idea for a companion book. After I saw his proposal, inspired by *Murder Ink* and *The Agatha Christie Companion,* the idea struck me: Why not a companion book on King and his work? The more I thought of it, the more it made perfect sense. After all, every conceivable book about King had been written, *except* a book that would talk to King's largest audience—the mainstream reader. What, I asked myself, would that reader want to know about King and his work?

The Stephen King Companion is my partial answer to that question. The publisher and I agreed the book had to be published in the fall of 1989 – less than a year after the signing of the contract. This meant that rights and permissions, research, writing, and editing had to be done within six months, at which point the manuscript would be turned over to the book editor. As anyone with even a passing familiarity in the book industry will tell you, only a gol-durned fool who wouldn't mind working seven days a week, eighteen hours a day, would commit to such a project. Fortunately, I had done two other book-length studies on contemporary artists, so I knew exactly what was involved and how to accelerate the initial research; unfortunately, I had prior commitments that had to be honored, time and work intensive book-related projects that sucked away all my free time, and a part-time obligation with the federal government that became a full-time commitment.

The experience of rushing to go to print reminded me of nothing so much as an old-fashioned potato-bag race. I put one leg in the bag; the publisher put in the other. Then off we went to the finish line, working in tandem, galumphing across the field, hoping not to fall flat on our faces...or asses.

The general tenor of the reviews from the magazines in the book trade, library trade, as well as newspaper reviews, and especially letters from readers, happily confirmed what I had hoped: that King's general reader found my book to be useful, entertaining, and informative.

(continued)

The front cover of George Beahm's bestselling paperback
The Stephen King Companion (Andrews & McMeel, 1989).
Cover photo credit: *Bangor Daily News.* Photo by Carroll Hall.

George Beahm.
Photo courtesy George Beahm.

THE STEPHEN KING COMPANION
by George Beahm
(Andrews and McMeel, trade paperback, 1989)

As with any book project written under such constraints, there were regrets. I would have liked to have had the opportunity to reread all of King's fiction—something I think goes with the territory. (I'm catching up on the re-reading now, of course.) I would have liked to have incorporated selected passages from reviews on King's books—something I hope to do in a future edition. I would have liked to have gotten an illustrator to render appropriately macabre art for chapter headings, sidebars, and for specific articles—again, something I hope to correct in a future edition. I would have liked to have interviewed more writers in and outside the horror field—something that would have given the book more depth. I would have liked to expand the discussions on each of King's books, supplemented with sidebars about the movies. Most of all, I would have liked to have had the time to finish some of the articles that never saw print: a narrative snapshot of Maine, and, most especially, Bangor; an expanded overview to King's career, a long essay about King's values and background as they shaped his fiction; studies of Tabitha King's work; and other articles too numerous to mention.

A nonfiction book also presents another problem: the book, once published, is fixed in time; but the world, as King reminds us, moves on...and my book became history. My initial response to this was to update the book with each new printing, an utterly impractical notion. The six months that followed the book's publication was enough to show me that updating it would be a Sisyphean task—partly due to King's prolificity.

I'm now making detailed notes so that at some point in the future, I can incorporate several years of updates, corrections, and deletions into a revised edition – the new! improved! version.

Aside from the practicalities of publishing, a book once written is, creatively speaking, stone-cold dead to its author. Publishing it is simply laying out the corpse in a coffin for all to see—it means being out front. All that's left is for you to file into the funeral house and be handed one of those neatly printed death announcements for which someone made sure the facts were straight, the dates jibed...and the names were spelled right.

GEORGE BEAHM'S TOP TEN

As you know, Gentle Reader, scattered throughout *The Shape Under the Sheet* are various and sundry sidebars containing all sorts of nifty information, the most common being an informal look at personal favorite King works, all contributed by the many fine folks who have participated in this project.

Here is a look at George Beahm's faves. George is the author of the amazingly complete and absolutely invaluable *Stephen King Companion,* and I thought his personal choices for King's best stuff would be of interest to all you "Shapies" out there.

George wrote, "Generally, I find King's Doubleday titles (*Carrie,* *'Salem's Lot,* *The Shining,* *Night Shift,* and *The Stand*) to be his most powerful work—King in rare form, writing with a sense of urgency. Also, I generally prefer his novellas to his novels, where King has enough room to tell the story—and then stops. (Some of his novels could have been condensed to a novella and, in the process, become more powerful and memorable.") —**sjs**

George Beahm's Top 5 King Books

1. *'SALEM'S LOT*
    • My favorite King novel. King got it right here—the small town atmosphere, the original retelling of the vampire myth, and the story's vivid imagery.
2. *THE STAND*
    • A magnificent epic tale.
3. *THE SHINING*
    • This novel is King in his prime. *The Shining* is a classic *genus loci* story with elements of Greek tragedy.
4. *DIFFERENT SEASONS*
    • I think King is at his best in the novella length. "Apt Pupil" and "The Body" stand out—(and they appear in my Top 5 Short Story list as well)—"Apt Pupil" because of its depiction of innocence corrupted, and "The Body" because of its realistic evocation of childhood. "The Body" is King's ultimate rite of passage story.

5. *DANSE MACABRE*
    • *Danse Macabre*—King's only (to date) book-length work of nonfiction—is informal, chatty, and informative. This is a good overview of the horror field, and especially accessible to those outside of the field.

George Beahm's Top 5 Shorter Works

1. "The Mist"
    • This novella is the perfect example of what King can do best—a story rich in imagery and ordinary people in extraordinary situations. Especially effective is the notion of the mist as an outside evil, so large that it cannot be confined to the limits of the story.
2. "The Reach"
    • This is an elegaic tale that, more than any of his other stories, shows us what Faulkner said was the only thing worth writing about: the human heart in conflict with itself. This, my friends, is literature. (Give "The Reach" to your teacher who, nose in air, sniffs with disdain because King writes "all those horror stories." Then watch him or her gasp with delight after reading *this* short, plaintive tale.)
3. "Big Wheels: A Tale of the Laundry Game (Milkman #2)"
    • This story is a personal favorite because of its evocation of small-town Maine and because of the ominous intrusion of the milkman who is much, much more than a mere deliveryman. King is at his colloquial best with this story, and I especially like his handling of the gradual shift from a real world into an unreal world.
4. "The Body"
    • "The Body" is again King at his best: King makes us young again. (As King reminds us, when we grow up, we forget how to see the world as innocents: we lose our sense of wonder. Writers keep it alive for us. In this story, we are children again.)
5. "Apt Pupil"
    • "Apt Pupil" is a brilliant story in which a parasitic relationship (Todd "feeding" on the memories of Dussander) becomes symbiotic: both Todd and Dussander consider the other the true monster...and both become apt pupils.

"AND HIS KINGDOM WAS FULL OF DARKNESS..."
An Interview With Douglas E. Winter

The title of this interview is from *Revelations* (16:10), and it serves two purposes: it describes the realm in which Stephen King works—the kingdom of darkness—and it also serves as an apt job description for Douglas E. Winter, the authorized chronicler of King's travels in that land.

Even though Doug is best-known to Stephen King fans as the author of the definitive biographical study of our favorite writer, *Stephen King: The Art of Darkness,* (see the Doug Winter bibliography included in this section), he is also an attorney and a partner in —as the jacket copy for *Prime Evil* says—the busy "internationally-based law firm of Bryan, Cave, McPheeters & McRoberts."

Doug usually puts in a good fifty-hour work week, and then on most nights comes home, "ignores his wife and kids" (those are Doug's words, folks, honest), and spends another few hours sitting in front of his word processor, working on any number of writing projects.

Current projects include a novel called *From Parts Unknown* co-authored with Charles Grant; a novel of his own, tentatively entitled *Argento;* and a rather secret new anthology.

After a few false starts and a bunch of scheduling mix-ups, Doug and I finally got to talk on a steamy hot Sunday afternoon in July. Doug did the interview from his law office in Washington. He was behind in his legal work, having spent part of the prior week in New York overseeing the audio tape versions of the first stories from *Prime Evil,* including the recording of Stephen King's short story "The Night Flier." On a day when temperatures hit the high nineties, and the humidity withered even tough guys with tattoos, Doug Winter and I discussed the chilling horrors of the work of Stephen King.

I learned a lot from Doug. He has an intimidating intelligence about him—and by that I don't mean he himself is personally foreboding or intimidating. Far from it: he's such a nice and "regular" guy, that after talking to him for a few minutes, you forget his cum laude Harvard law degree and his reputation as a superb writer, and you also try to ignore the fact that he has had Stephen King over to his house for hotdog roasts.

If you talk with Doug for awhile, you quickly realize two things: One is the fact that Doug has read—in his own words—"mercilessly" since he was a very young boy, and the second is that you yourself haven't read nearly as much as you should have! (That's an opinion Doug holds about many of the current crop of horror writers. He discusses his feelings about some younger writers' lack of awareness of horror fiction classics in the following interview.)

I had a lot of fun talking with Doug. And, in addition to gaining new insight into the nature of horror fiction as well as the writing of Stephen King, I also learned about the Stephen King short story called "The King Family and the Farting Cookie!" (And no, it's never been anthologized.)

Before we get started with the interview, though, I'd like to take this opportunity to express my sincerest thanks to both Doug and Lynne Winter for their continued interest, support, and help with this interview, and with *The Shape Under the Sheet.* Right at the time when I needed Doug's editorial changes and suggestions, he found himself in the middle of a particularly complex legal case that literally took every moment he had. (And it also moved him to Detroit for months on end!) At one point during this period, he told me "my life is not my own," and yet he found the time to make extensive changes and expansions in our first draft interview. Also, his charming wife Lynne went out of her way to relay messages from me when Doug was incommunicado. Lynne was consistently patient, good-spirited and helpful whenever I needed an answer or a piece of information from Doug.

Yup. Them Winters is shure 'nuff nice folks.

No wonder Stephen King goes to their house for hotdogs, y'know? — **sjs**

Before my interview with Doug Winter here's a brief listing of some of his work:

Selective Listing of Writings by Douglas E. Winter

BOOKS

- *Stephen King.* Starmont House, 1982 (hardcover and trade paperback).
- *Shadowings: The Reader's Guide to Horror Fiction.* Starmont House, 1983 (hardcover and paperback).
- *Stephen King: The Art of Darkness.*
  1. NAL Books, 1984 (hardcover);
  2. NAL/Plume, 1985 (trade paperback, revised edition);
  3. NAL/Signet, 1986 (paperback);
  4. New English Library, 1989 (trade paperback, revised edition).
- *Faces of Fear.*
  1. Berkley, 1985 (trade paperback);
  2. Pan, 1990 (paperback, revised edition).
- *Black Wine* (editor). Dark Harvest, 1986 (hardcover).
- *Splatter: A Cautionary Tale.* Footsteps Press, 1987 (limited edition hardcover and trade paperback).
- *Prime Evil.*
  1. NAL Books, 1988 (hardcover);
  2. Donald M. Grant, 1988 (limited edition hardcover);
  3. Bantam UK, 1988 (hardcover);
  4. NAL/Signet, 1989 (paperback);
  5. Bantam UK, 1989 (paperback);
     ...also translated editions in France, Germany, Holland, Italy, Japan, Norway, Spain, and Sweden.

NONFICTION APPEARANCES
Newspapers

- The *Washington Post;* The *Washington Times;* The *Philadelphia Inquirer;* The *Cleveland Plain Dealer.*

Magazines

- *Saturday Review; Harpers Bazaar; Gallery; Twilight Zone; Fear; Fangoria; Mystery Scene; L'Ecran Fantastique* (France); *El Gobo* (Spain).

Books

- *Clive Barker: Shadows in Eden;*
- *The Encyclopedia of Horror and the Supernatural;*
- *Fear Itself;*
- *Horror: 100 Best Books;*
- *Night Visions 5* (aka *The Skin Trade*);
- *Das Jahre Der Wehrwolfs* (Germany);
- *Das Stephen King Buch* (Germany).

SHORT STORY APPEARANCES

- *Book of the Dead;*
- *Fly In My Eye;*
- *Greystone Bay;*
- *Masques II;*
- *Masques III;*
- *Midnight;*
- *Shadows 10;*
- *Silver Scream;*
- *Splatterpunks;*
- *The Year's Best Fantasy and Horror Stories.*

"AND HIS KINGDOM WAS FULL OF DARKNESS..."
An Interview With Douglas E. Winter

1. *KING ANALYSIS*

STEVE SPIGNESI: As you know, my first book, *Mayberry, My Hometown* was an "Andy Griffith Show" encyclopedia. I spent an enormous amount of time studying the show, and after the book was published, I discovered that I had lost a small part of my "sense of wonder"—that sense of pure joy— regarding the show. So far that hasn't happened to me with the work of Stephen King, even though I'm studying his stuff with as much intensity as I did the show. After *Stephen King: The Art of Darkness*—which obviously required a similiar level of "immersion"—do you find yourself reading Stephen King's work now as though you're still examining something under a microscope, or is there still a pure, non-analytical thrill?

DOUG WINTER: Actually I find that there's still a little bit of both—I read him analytically, and yet there's still the sheer enjoyment of the work. I suppose I've always been an analytical kind of reader. I can't help but read any fiction with a certain sense of analysis. I think that's just been ingrained in me since a fairly early age. When I first came to Steve's work, I had something of that analytical kind of approach and I certainly think that's one of the reasons why a lot my early criticism of Steve's fiction was interesting to people. I was treating what people had previously liked to think of as popular entertainment, in a serious fashion. But I'd always had that bent—particularly toward horror fiction.

Steve often sends me manuscripts, and each time I get something like that, I still am drawn to read it with a real sense of enthusiasm, a sense of anticipation. So, I can't say that I've become jaded in any way. I've read his books over and over again. And still, each time there's a new one, I look forward to reading it with great joy, and great anticipation.

2. *THE TIME WAS RIGHT FOR STEPHEN KING?*

STEVE SPIGNESI: Recently, I interviewed both Richard Matheson and his son Richard Christian Matheson for *The Shape Under the Sheet.* Richard Matheson Senior told me that he thinks that one of the *primary* reasons for Stephen King's success over the last fifteen years or so, is that the "Time" —with a capital T—was right, and that if Stephen

King himself had come about in the sixties, Matheson didn't feel that he would have had the success he's had, nor would he have been welcomed by the public the way he was after *Carrie* and *'Salem's Lot.* [NOTE: See the interview with Richard Matheson in this volume.] What are your thoughts on his opinion that King was in the "right place at the right time," so to speak, and that he was a "product of his times"?

DOUG WINTER: Stephen King is, to a certain extent, like any other person, a product of his times. And his writing is a product of *its* times. Because of that, you can't have a Stephen King writing *Carrie* or *'Salem's Lot* in 1963 or '64. It just doesn't work out that way. But if you want to hypothesize that you have Stephen King—with his tremendous talents—writing in the 1960's rather than in the 1970's—it's a complete speculation of course—my view tends to be that it is ultimately talent and persistence that win out. And I believe that he certainly would have found his niche as a popular novelist.

As to his writing, it may be that he would have involved himself with different thematic concerns and would have been working with different sociopolitical perspectives. There are just so many variables that it's impossible to say, except that I don't think the time in and of itself would have had an effect on his capability of becoming a very popular novelist.

3. *PERSONAL FAVORITES*

STEVE SPIGNESI: Let's talk about your personal "Stephen King" favorites.

DOUG WINTER: Well, unfortunately I don't like to answer those questions because my favorites tend to vary over time. If someone says to me "What are your ten favorite horror novels?," I don't like to answer, because, you know, you ask me now, and then six months from now, I'm likely to give you a different list.

STEVE SPIGNESI: Well, for the record, you gave the following ten works (alphabetically) as your personal favorites in horror fiction in J.N. Williamson's *How To Write Tales of Horror, Fantasy & Science Fiction* (Writer's Digest Books, 1987):

> J.G. Ballard, *The Atrocity Exhibition*
> J.G. Ballard, *Crash*
> William Peter Blatty, *The Exorcist*
> Thomas Harris, *Red Dragon*
> Shirley Jackson, *The Haunting of Hill House*
> Stephen King, "The Body"
> Stephen King, *The Dead Zone*
> Stephen King, *'Salem's Lot*

> Richard Matheson, *I Am Legend*
> Peter Straub, *Ghost Story*

DOUG WINTER: Well, I'd give you a different list today. With me oftentimes it tends to be *moments* in fiction that are memorable. When I look back at Steve's work, I guess I would still say that among my favorite novels are *'Salem's Lot, The Dead Zone,* and *Misery. Cujo* is also a particular favorite, interestingly enough. A lot of people don't particularly like that book. But my views change from here to there. *'Salem's Lot* is an example of a book I'll read again and again. *The Dead Zone* also. But with some of Steve's books, I'll read them and I'll enjoy them, but I won't be as interested in coming back to them.

4. *EDITING KING &* *STEPHEN KING, CHEF EXTRAORDINAIRE*

STEVE SPIGNESI: Let's talk about Steve's most recent short stories. You were editor of the three

Douglas E. Winter
Photo courtesy George Beahm.

King stories in *Night Visions 5* (Dark Harvest, 1988) "The Reploids," "Sneakers," and "Dedication," as well as the Stephen King short story "The Night Flier" in your anthology *Prime Evil*.

DOUG WINTER: Well, in point of fact, of those four stories, the only one that I actually edited in the classic sense of the word, is "The Night Flier." I'm more or less just the "host" of *Night Visions 5*. I wished that I'd asked them to make it clear that, like Clive Barker in *Night Visions 4*, I really only wrote the Introduction to the book. (This was in fact corrected for the Berkley paperback edition of *Night Visions 5, The Skin Trade*.)

I wrote letters to Steve, Dan Simmons, and George R.R. Martin telling them about problems that I saw in the stories, but I didn't edit them in the classical sense of saying, "You really ought to do this," or "This needs to be fixed," or "Hey, I can't use this story." I didn't act as a line editor. I actually exercised the function of a copy editor.

STEVE SPIGNESI: But you did do the hands-on editing of "The Night Flier"?
DOUG WINTER: Yes.

STEVE SPIGNESI: How often are you in touch with King?
DOUG WINTER: It depends. It depends on the time and what's going on. It's varied over the years.

STEVE SPIGNESI: I've got to ask this. In *Faces of Fear*, your collection of interviews with horror writers, you talked about Stephen King making you hamburgers. What kind of a cook is Stephen King?
DOUG WINTER: He's good. He made us some pretty good and pretty big hamburgers. And I've made *him* "poopdogs." That's where you take these wonderful hot dogs that have been stuffed with chili, pop them into the microwave, and zap them till they burst.

5. THE FORMAT OF DARKNESS

STEVE SPIGNESI: I found the format of *Stephen King: The Art of Darkness* very, very appealing. The combination of biography, critical interpretation, bibliography, and index just worked perfectly. How did you come upon that particular layout?
DOUG WINTER: It just seemed like a good idea at the time. I like to think of myself as a writer first. Criticism is an aspect of my writing, but I'm a writer first. I want to entertain my readers while hopefully enlightening them. Most academics, that is, most people who are critics, are not writers

first. They are academics first. And they really don't understand—although they should—how much one's life affects one's writing. It should be hitting them right in the face since it's somewhat equivalent to what they do for a living—but they really don't understand.

You can't divorce the two. And if you know Steve's fiction at all, you know how very personal it is, and how very much that his life and his experiences are tied up in his fiction. When I was writing *Art of Darkness*, it struck me that in order to understand fairly what Stephen King did as a writer, and also in order to understand why it had an importance and meaning beyond entertainment, you had to have two things in particular in mind. You had to have an overview and an understanding of what horror fiction was really about. And second, you had to have an overview and some understanding of what Stephen King's life had been like. As a result, the organization of *Art of Darkness* was manifest.

I had to provide a thematic and conceptual introduction that talked about horror fiction and what it's supposed to do. And I'm still not very happy with the opening chapter of *Art of Darkness* because it *is* very abstract and conceptual and I imagine not the sort of thing that a lot of popular readers would want to read—unless they're Stephen King fans.

So, it just came very naturally to have a conceptual and somewhat abstract introduction, and then follow that with a biographical interlude before going on to the novels themselves in sequence. I can state all those things now but it wasn't the sort of thing I had to think about very long.

6. STEPHEN KING UNDER THE MICROSCOPE

STEVE SPIGNESI: There are a number of critical interpretations of King's fiction on the market, including *Kingdom of Fear, Fear Itself, Reign of Fear*, and a number of University Press studies. What do you think of the slew of interpretive books on King and also, do you know what Stephen King thinks of these "under the microscope" analyses of his work?
DOUG WINTER: Well, I'm in a funny place, right? It's tough to criticize other things that have been done because it sounds like I'm picking on them because of what I've done. It seems like I'm giving somebody else a hard time because they're in my territory—and it's *not* my territory.

Steve wrote to *Locus* recently that he was kind

of tired of these things. The letter was about the Underwood/Miller book *Bare Bones*. And, in fact, I pulled my work out of *Bare Bones* because they were trying to pass it off as a book *by* Steve, when it wasn't anything but a collection of reprint interviews.

I was very disturbed by this notion and I know Steve was also, so I just pulled all my material out of the book. I didn't want to be part of it.

Also, I was asked to edit the book that became *Kingdom of Fear,* and I turned that down, despite some very good money. Regarding Steve's work, It seems to me that there are books that can be written—as with any contemporary writer—and that those books will address that writer and his concerns in different ways.

Then there are the books that have nothing to do with the writer. They really have nothing at all to do with the writer who's under the microscope. They have to do with the fellow who's writing the book. And they have to do with economics. And a lot of what we are seeing has to do with economics—certainly the Underwood-Miller stuff. I mean, Underwood-Miller aren't doing those books because of a deep-seated love and affection for Stephen King and his work. And the books themselves are not very good. Even *Fear Itself*—which I'm in—is just not a very good book. The books are done because people buy them. Now, that's not a criticism—that's the reality of the marketplace. But sometimes you begin to get the feeling that Steve or his name is being used. And that's a shame.

There is also the aspect to it of...what's the point? How many books can really be written about Stephen King that will say anything new, and that will have any particular meaning to his readers? And that's the important thing. Academic books can be written ad nauseum. Lord knows how many books have been written about Joseph Conrad. And they'll continue to be written. But they rarely have much significance to Conrad's readers.

I suspect that the books that are being written now about Steve's work—and I've sampled them pretty well—don't have a great deal of meaning for King's readers. Many of them are moving off into that realm of academic abstraction where it's of interest to the person who's writing that book, and it's of interest to fellow academicians, but it just doesn't have much meaning for the readers.

There's one other point:

You've seen my books like *Faces of Fear*. I'm interested in championing a lot of different things about horror fiction. Stephen King is one of them,

but he's not the end-all and be-all.

And what I have found particularly disturbing is the inability that's reflected in these books—both from the writers of the books as well as their publishers—to accept or to recognize that there are other writers out there. It's almost as if these books are being written in a vacuum, and the writers don't realize the degree to which King himself has been affected by people like Matheson, and by film.

They refuse to acknowledge the presence of other writers. It's as if Peter Straub, for example, were only someone who happened to write this book with Stephen King called *The Talisman,* you know?

"You have to look at Steve as part of a 'field.' He is born of that field. There's no doubt about it. It was a very rich and very fertile field before he was there, and it will continue to be so after he's gone. Hopefully that will be later rather than sooner."

STEVE SPIGNESI: Yes, I know what you mean. I've seen a lot of that kind of "tunnel vision" in books and articles about King.

DOUG WINTER: And you kind of scratch your head. You have to look at Steve as part of a "field." He is born of that field. There's no doubt about it. It was a very rich and very fertile field before he was there, and it will continue to be so after he's gone. Hopefully that will be later rather than sooner.

And there are a lot of other damn good people who are working out there in it. And one of the things that offends me about these books is the fact that these books almost proceed from the assumption that nobody else exists.

When I wrote *Art of Darkness,* among the messages that I was trying to communicate—to both the mass audience as well as that kind of critical literary establishment—was to say look, here is another reason why horror fiction is important to us, and why it's historically always been important to us.

I wanted to show that there are explanations for why Stephen King has been so phenomenally successful that have nothing to do with the things that people typically point to, such as the easy edibility of his fiction, its pop cult surfaces, and all the rest of the "King cliches."

With *Art of Darkness,* I wanted to get at the real thematic concerns that seem to be lying out there, and to get at the reasons why Steve has touched so many people in so many different ways.

And, now on the other end of the spectrum, it's almost as if the message is kind of running back in the other direction, and maybe that's the danger of literary acceptability. I've never wanted horror to be entirely literarily acceptable.

The thinking now seems to be that this thing known as "Stephen King" may really be a phenomenon which the critical academic establishment can not only look at but perhaps be the only people capable of understanding, and that there's a need now for these "scholars" to re-translate it for the average reader. I don't know. I know that's a pretty harsh indictment. I suspect that a lot of this stuff is being written by people who genuinely enjoy Steve's writing and genuinely want to write about it. So, they find their own ways of making it acceptable.

6. *STEPHEN KING FANDOM*

STEVE SPIGNESI: Well, as an ancillary question to the subject of critical acceptance and analysis, what are your thoughts on the fact that a "dark side" of fandom has developed regarding Stephen King and his work?

DOUG WINTER: Well, I think it's always been there. An inevitable part of any fandom is the dark side. So, it's not as though Steve were an atypical recipient of this kind of attention. High profile people know it's there and that it affects most of them who obtain this kind of status. And it's an unfortunate thing.

STEVE SPIGNESI: All of celebrity brings with it this kind of "attention"?

DOUG WINTER: Yeah, I think it does. It is a necessary evil of celebrity. And you hear horror stories from all sorts of different people.

I was in New York on Thursday and Friday, July 28th and 29th, 1988, for the taping of the audiocassette versions of *Prime Evil.* Ed Begley Jr. was reading "The Night Flier," and we were talking during one of the breaks. Ed had been a delegate to the Democratic National Convention, and he said it was one of the worst things he's ever done in his life.

He went there with genuine political ideals, and he was just hounded to death by people wanting autographs, and photos. They just wouldn't leave him alone. He spent most of his time locked in his hotel room.

7. *THE INFLUENCE OF STEPHEN KING*

STEVE SPIGNESI: Many current writers of horror and dark fantasy obviously show the unmistakable influence of King. One of them is Robert McCammon. I've read reviews where McCammon's *Swan Song* has been likened to *The Stand.* I've even heard it called a *Stand*-clone. Personally, I loved both books, but I do see many similarities. Do you have any thoughts on McCammon's work as it relates to King and King's influence on his writing?

DOUG WINTER: Rick McCammon is a talented and energetic writer who's fiction, unfortunately, and intentionally or not, sometimes seems to "mime" a lot of Steve King's work. The parallels are unmistakable. And you can't say—it's just impossible to say that *Swan Song* is anything other than a *Stand*-clone. And it can't be unintentional. I mean, you cannot be *un*aware of *The Stand.*

You cannot work in this field and be unaware of *The Stand.* If you're going to write a post-apocalyptic novel, then you better damn well be aware of *The Stand.* And when you read *Swan Song,* you can't help but see *The Stand.* You can see the same kind of landscapes, you can see the same kind of characters. So, I think it's unfortunate, and although Rick seems to be tremendously successful, I think it ultimately has to work against him.

Also, what staggers me is the occasional inability of readers to "notice." In fact, I read a lot of reviews of *Swan Song* that just sort of ignored or downplayed the similarities. It could possibly be because Rick's very well-liked, and he seems to be a tremendously nice fellow.

I just wish that he could throw off this kind of shadow. His short fiction particularly *is* original, and his more recent novels show that he seems finally to have found his voice.

T.E.D. Klein once said that he wrote *The Ceremonies* because it was almost like reading pornography and wanting to write it to get yourself off. T.E.D. loved Arthur Machen so much he just asked himself what would have happened if Arthur Machen wrote a big novel? And he just wanted to do this, so he deliberately wrote *The Ceremonies* as an "Arthur Machen novel." And maybe that's what it is with Rick? Maybe he just loved Steve's stuff so much that it was almost like automatic writing?

8. WILL HISTORY REMEMBER STEPHEN KING?

STEVE SPIGNESI: Let's talk about "literary longevity." In your opinion, will Stephen King's work survive? And if so, why; and if not, why not?

DOUG WINTER: A few months ago, they had a big get-together up in New York of some of the lions of contemporary fiction. A lot of the literati, basically. And at this gathering, Leslie Fiedler's on the record as saying, "Look, you guys know that fifty years from now, the guy who's going to be remembered is Stephen King." (Laughs.)

STEVE SPIGNESI: That's great!

DOUG WINTER: And the truth is, *of course* his work will survive, and of course he'll be remembered.

All you have to do is look at history. You don't even have to look at Stephen King. Put aside who Stephen King is, and what he is, and what his writing has meant to the current decade. Just look back over history. Or go into the bookstores and look at what kind of books you can buy from the 1880's and 1890's. So many of them are horror stories.

And for that reason alone, I think that he is going to be remembered. Just from the twentieth century, you can go out to the bookstores today and buy Poe, Lovecraft, you can buy the work of a lot of people who were writing in the twenties, thirties, and forties. And it sure is hard to find anything by anybody else who was writing popular fiction during that time period. Likewise, it's also hard to find people who were writing so-called "serious fiction" during that time period.

So, from the view of history, that would be enough. But wholly apart from that, Stephen King is very much the writer of his time. The obvious parallel is Charles Dickens. Steve is a writer whose fiction is about the 1970's and 1980's. It's about the time in which he works.

And another interesting aspect of literary history is that it is usually the fiction that's about its time that survives. We tend to read a lot of things because of their setting in place or time. And Steve's fiction is very much a part of this culture. And as a result, his work will be remembered for that alone—wholly separate from being horror fiction.

9. WHICH ROAD WILL STEPHEN KING TAKE?

STEVE SPIGNESI: What direction do you think King's writing will take? Do you think he'll con-

tinue to work in horror? Or do you think he'll continue to write more mainstream? He's a young man. He's got another forty or fifty years ahead of him if he wants.

DOUG WINTER: Yes, he's got a lot of writing time ahead of him.

STEVE SPIGNESI: From your personal knowledge of King, do you think he's getting to a point, or has gotten to a point where he's saying "I've done this, and now I want to do something else." In *Misery,* he included parts of a completely valid Gothic romance within the main novel, and he did it very well.

DOUG WINTER: Well, I think that his novel *IT* is precisely about that. It's essentially saying, I've done this, and now I'm doing it on the big canvas, and maybe, in a way, this is an end to some of these things. *IT* is very much a landmark book in that regard.

If you look at the books that Steve's written after that, I think that you tend to see two things. I think you tend to see an effort to write what you might call more imaginative fables—things like *Eyes of the Dragon* and *The Tommyknockers.*

Misery and *The Dark Half* are examples of another direction that I think has always been more or less implicit in a lot of his writing, and one that I think we're likely to see more of, and that is the movement into a more, I suppose, outward-looking kind of fiction that is about a different kind of horror. And I realize that's a peculiar thing to say about *Misery,* which is a very insular, "one-act play" kind of book.

But it's about...a different kind of horror. It's about a less elemental horror, and a more *human* kind of horror.

It's hard to predict what any writer is going to do. But in the past twenty years in horror fiction, I feel that we have gone through not only an explosion in popularity, but at the same time, almost a definitional phase. It's almost as if someone has been out there trying to put down picket fences—brought on in part by its popularity. Certainly publishers tempted to cash in on it are now coming out with their own horror lines, much as one has science fiction lines.

And there's been something of an effort to try and define the turf—to say, "this is what horror is all about," and I think you're going to find that writers—especially conscientious writers and imaginative writers like Steve—are going to be pushing at that.

Misery is purely a psychological novel. Twenty

years ago, no one—except for a few people—would have thought of it as a horror novel. It would have been considered a suspense novel.

But now you see people pushing against the fences. Peter Straub's novels *Koko* and *Mystery* are good examples of that—a sweeping "thriller," or suspense novel. I suppose those are the best words for them, but they are filled with the aesthestics of horror.

Thomas Harris is another good example of somebody who works that area, who's really best considered either a mystery or suspense novelist, and yet his stories just seem imbued with the aesthestics of horror.

STEVE SPIGNESI: King has always been very vocal in his praise of Harris's *Red Dragon*.

DOUG WINTER: Yes, he has. And I think that's one possible direction for Steve's work. He has always been interested in mystery and crime fiction, and some of his recent stuff is reminescent to me, in an odd way, of Jim Thompson. I told Steve that *The Drawing of the Three* read like Jim Thompson on acid. (Laughs.) It's got this very concrete feeling of a real world that lies just beneath the dark shadow of a soulless insanity.

And you feel that also in *Misery*. And in *The Dark Half*. You feel that we're moving off into new realms that are less defined by creatures, and defined more by what is really loose in the world today.

10. *HAS STEPHEN KING INFLUENCED DOUG WINTER'S FICTION?*

STEVE SPIGNESI: Let's talk about your fiction. Whenever I ask writers "Has Stephen King influenced your own fiction?," almost a stock answer is "How could he have not?" Does this apply to your work? If so, *how* has King has influenced your own writing?

DOUG WINTER: Well, certainly, he is one of a number of people who has influenced me. I think anyone who's a writer can not help but be influenced in some way by what they read. And certainly my first recommendation to anyone who wants to write is just to read mercilessly.

For me it's a little bit difficult sometimes to divorce Steve's influence from the influence of the people who have influenced him. Richard Matheson is a good example. I didn't grow up reading Stephen King. I grew up reading Matheson, Bradbury, Thompson and others, because essentially Steve and I are of the same generation.

STEVE SPIGNESI: So, by the time you began writing, you had already found your voice?

DOUG WINTER: All of the formative aspects of my writing really came from the writers I mentioned, as well as from many, many other people. Conrad. Ballard. The list goes on and on.

There's a story I did called "Masks," which was a Stephen King pastiche. It was intentionally done that way. I wrote it after finishing *Art of Darkness*. And after "Masks," I did a story called "Streetlife" which was intended to be sort of a Ray Bradbury story. I had a couple of people say to me, "Gee, you know your writing is pretty obviously influenced by Steve." And my immediate reaction was to kind of draw up and say, "How could you say that kind of thing?"

But it became obvious to me that people were inevitably going to do that because of the fact that I'd written a book about Steve—because of my connection with him. It became clear that this was going to be inevitable.

So, what I had to do—and what I then set about doing—was to consciously avoid sounding like, feeling like, or doing anything like Stephen King might do it. And I think I've had fairly good success doing that. Regarding my story "Masks," *Twilight Zone* asked Ramsey Campbell if he'd read anything recently that had impressed him, and he said, "Well, I read this story by Doug Winter, which strangely enough sounded like what would happen if Stephen King tried to write a Ramsey Campbell story." (Laughs.)

[NOTE: Campbell's remark appears in the April 1987 edition of *Twilight Zone*, where Campbell was interviewed by Stan Wiater. — **sjs**]

STEVE SPIGNESI: I'd say Campbell and King add up to quite a lineage!

DOUG WINTER: I thought that was a pretty damn good recommendation.

So, what I have consciously done—in my short fiction at least—is to write experimentally. Things like "Splatter" and "Less Than Zombie." These are *completely* different.

I was very glad to see Bill Munster of *Footsteps* advertise "Splatter" in *Castle Rock* because I originally thought, geez, this story may turn some people off. But it'd be really nice to get some of Steve's readers reading something of mine just because they happened to know I've written about Steve, and then finding something completely different, and hopefully enjoying it. And perhaps this will help readers recognize that writers are their own personalities.

STEVE SPIGNESI: I was going to bring up "Splatter." I've read it three or four times in the last few days to prepare for this interview, and I was struck by what I saw as...let's call it a "determined originality"...and so now it's a bit of a revelation to me to hear you say that it *was* an experiment. I just read it as another piece of fiction. Right or wrong, I tend to avoid things that are presented as being blatantly experimental. I'm almost afraid of them somehow, and yet "Splatter" worked for me. Richard Christian Matheson and I talked about that type of experimentation when we were discussing some of his stories, particularly "Conversation Piece" and "Graduation." He told me that his father sort of "flicked the switch" in his brain that allowed him to work with these odd formats. And then his "prose poem" "Vampire" came out of that. [NOTE: See the interview with Richard Christian Matheson in this volume.] For me, the message of "Splatter" was of course, very, very important and quite significant. I thought the story worked, and I'd love to see you do more in that direction.

DOUG WINTER: Well, that's great. I did an even more depressing story, "Less Than Zombie," for Skipp and Spector's *Book of the Dead*.

11. *LITERARY IMITATION AND STEPHEN KING*

DOUG WINTER: The other aspect of all this is that there are good and bad influences that Stephen King can have. And most people tend to see the bad ones. When you read things, you tend to see the surfaces.

Now, a lot of people love to imitate H.P. Lovecraft. And a lot of film directors imitate Hitchcock. Now, what I'm about to say is not original with me—Ramsey Campbell said it in *Faces of Fear*. It's the notion that surfaces are much easier to imitate than substance. So, a writer can write stories that immediately will knock people as being Lovecraft-like, and directors can make movies that immediately will knock people as being Hitchcock-like, and writers can also write stories that will immediately touch the reader as being King-like.

But people don't seem to understand that that in and of itself is not enough. If you've got the surface—the style but not the substance—you're not going to deliver.

We've been seeing a lot of paperback originals recently that use the King surface—that kind of a high pop culture feel. There's a lot of brand names,

> **"We've been seeing a lot of paperback originals recently that use the King surface—that kind of a high pop culture feel. There's a lot of brand names, a lot of wise-cracking style, a lot of internalized dialogue....And yet, unless you've got that heart and soul which Steve has—it just doesn't come across. You're not being King-like—you're not even in the ballpark."**

a lot of wise-cracking style, a lot of internalized dialogue.

STEVE SPIGNESI: Yes, many of these "production line" novels seem to make a point of using *tons* of contemporaneous cultural references.

DOUG WINTER: And yet, unless you've got that heart and soul which Steve has—it just doesn't come across. You're not being King-like—you're not even in the ballpark. And, unfortunately, people don't understand that. A lot of writers don't understand that, and they don't know that imitation is *not* the sincerest form of flattery.

STEVE SPIGNESI: Right. It's the easiest way out.

DOUG WINTER: It's the easiest way out.

12. *THE STEPHEN KING BIBLIOGRAPHY: AFGHANISTAN IN VIRGINIA*

STEVE SPIGNESI: Tell us about the legendary Stephen King bibliography you're doing for Donald Grant.

DOUG WINTER: Steve once said that *The Stand* was his Vietnam. Well, this book is my Afghanistan. (Laughs.)

STEVE SPIGNESI: (Laughs.) We've been hearing about this volume now for...how long?

DOUG WINTER: Decades. I tell myself it only *seems* like my entire life.

I've got this huge data base which I started back at the time I did *Art of Darkness*. I have a monster bibliography of everything that Steve's written, and everything that's been written about him, and it's just become so huge that I'm afraid to look at it.

I do not have a great deal of time to devote to

it, and as time passes, this thing just... *grows*. It's in my office and it keeps growing on its own. It's like [the creature in the film] "Alien"—it keeps transforming, you know?

But, Don and I are talking about it again. It's really just a question of my time. I have been unable, because of my writing obligations and my legal work, to get to it. It really needs about a week to ten days of my full attention and devotion. And I just don't have that. I've tried everything. I hired a research assistant. Then I hired another research assistant. It's nearly impossible, but I think it's going to be done. The question is when. Hopefully, soon. I'd like to get it finished by the end of this year. But I just don't know if I'm going to have the time to turn my attention to it.

STEVE SPIGNESI: I had the same problem with this book. I had thought that I would stop at a particular point with the short fiction, and yet, more and more stuff kept coming out. Tappan King at *Twilight Zone* told me I should just stop with "The Night Flier" and leave everything that's released after that for the second edition. The question that kept running through my head regarding your King bibliography was "Where would *you* stop?" Where will you draw the line as to what piece or what time period the bibliography will run up through?

DOUG WINTER: Well, I'm just not sure. It's going to have to depend on where I finally end up. And of course, it's going to take some time in production and stuff will come out. This bibliography is going to be like a computer—it's going to be obsolete the moment it's published.

13. *GOING TO THE MOVIES*

STEVE SPIGNESI: What are your thoughts on the film adaptations of King's work?

DOUG WINTER: There really isn't much to say that a thousand people haven't said already. There are some things that have been good, there have been some things that have been awful, and I think that this is pretty much par for the movie business. You have to sort of try and step back and look at the movie as if a book didn't exist.

STEVE SPIGNESI: Which admittedly is difficult with a film that has the "Stephen King" name attached to it.

DOUG WINTER: Yes, but it has to be judged on that ground—on its own. It's a difficult thing, I think, to adapt most books—particularly a very popular one—into a film.

I talk about this in the Introduction of *Prime Evil*—how very difficult it is to make horror films. Good horror films. From books.

Once a reader reads a book, they set in their own mind the images that ought to be up on the screen. Most good horror fiction deals with the imagination, and Steve's is no different. It is the function of a motion picture, generally, to deny imagination. To entertain with images. In other words, to *produce* images, rather than to encourage the viewer to produce them in his or her own mind. As a result, now the director's dictating what the pictures look like, and you're going to be a little bit disappointed of how the director chooses to tell the story because of his or her telling it in a way that Steve didn't, and in a way that you didn't experience when you read the book. Sometimes they've done a good job. Rob Reiner, certainly, did a good job in "Stand By Me."

STEVE SPIGNESI: "Stand By Me" is my personal favorite film adaptation, although Cronenberg's "Dead Zone" runs a close second.

DOUG WINTER: Yes, I thought "Dead Zone" was very good. And despite most everyone's grousings, I thought "The Shining" wasn't bad. And, of course, Brian DePalma's "Carrie" is probably still the best.

But then you've got some things that are just God-awful. You've got "Children of the Corn" which no one should have made into a movie in the first place. And you've got "Creepshow 2."

It's not as if it's something that movie people are necessarily doing to Steve. It's difficult to make good horror fiction on film. That's "Given Number One." And, Number Two, it's even more difficult to try to take a very popular book and make it into a movie. And, let's face it, there's a rush to do a lot of Stephen King films because of the popularity of his fiction, and his name.

STEVE SPIGNESI: What did you think of the unfilmed "Creepshow 2" story "Pinfall"? [NOTE: See the section on "Pinfall" in Part V of this volume. —**sjs**]

DOUG WINTER: I saw it as a satire. I think "Pinfall" is really a true E.C. Comics story.

STEVE SPIGNESI: Any ideas as to why it wasn't filmed?

DOUG WINTER: Who knows? "Creepshow 2" was obviously a pretty low-budget movie. Maybe it would have been too costly to do some of the effects —to do them well? I don't know.

STEVE SPIGNESI: I thought the story was very

funny, but my thoughts were that Gornick would have had a real problem with the special effects required—specifically the scenes of the Regi-Men's arms and legs becoming bowling pins, and their heads being used for bowling balls.

DOUG WINTER: After seeing "Creepshow 2," I think Gornick would have had a real problem doing anything. Sorry, but it was one of the least impressive motion pictures I've ever seen.

STEVE SPIGNESI: I guess you didn't like it, huh?

DOUG WINTER: I think it was a waste of good time and good money.

14. *PRIME EVIL*

STEVE SPIGNESI: Let's talk about your anthology *Prime Evil.* I once taught a course on King, and my students ranged from teenagers up through eighty-year-olds. One of my students asked a question that I hadn't thought of. He made the point that horror anthologies are usually released in trade paperback editions, and yet *Prime Evil* was initially released as a hardcover. He wanted to know if this was simply because of the inclusion of the "name brands" of Stephen King and Clive Barker. Did the publisher say, "Hey, we've got hardcover sales here"?

DOUG WINTER: No. I don't know how else to say this—I don't want it to sound egotistical. *Prime Evil* was sold to NAL on proposal. The deal was that I would put together a collection of state-of-the-art horror fiction that I would edit, and that it was a hard/soft deal. It would be a hardcover book. And those were the terms. And I told them that I would try to have Steve in the book, but when the book was sold, I didn't have Steve; I didn't have any stories. The book was just sold on the idea of me putting this thing together. And NAL gave me the time to do it, and to do it the way I wanted.

STEVE SPIGNESI: So the "name brand" of Doug Winter got the hardcover deal?

DOUG WINTER: I don't think I'm a name brand but yes, it was a hardcover deal.

STEVE SPIGNESI: How many copies of *Prime Evil* did you sign for Don Grant?

DOUG WINTER: In addition to all the limited editions, I signed twelve hundred copies of the NAL hardcover edition in four hours. And my arm was sore the day after. But it was fun. *Prime Evil* set a record for the largest first printing of an anthology of any kind.

STEVE SPIGNESI: How many copies was the first printing?

DOUG WINTER: 85,000.

STEVE SPIGNESI: That's a huge first printing for a horror anthology.

DOUG WINTER: Yes, but if you consider a novel, it's small. Tom Clancy's novel *The Cardinal of the Kremlin* had a first printing of a million copies or so in hardcover. So, that shows you something, relatively speaking. *The Dark Half* had a first printing of 1.5 million copies. The anthology is still the weak sister, or weak brother, as they say, in fiction. A lot of people think it's going the way of poetry. *Prime Evil* was an effort to show otherwise, but we'll see.

15. *DOUG'S STRAWBERRY SPRING*

STEVE SPIGNESI: In *Art of Darkness,* you tell how King's short story "Strawberry Spring" was your first exposure to Stephen King. Was it that particular tale that did it, or was it King's writing?

DOUG WINTER: Well, I think it was the story's effect, as well as a lot of other things. It was the fact that I was very much a fan of horror fiction, and it was the fact that there wasn't a great deal of original horror fiction to be found in that time period. So, "Strawberry Spring" sort of leapt out at me. It was a good story, and all those things kind of clicked together at once.

STEVE SPIGNESI: I just re-read it this morning before I called you and I was struck by how so very accomplished the writing is. He was only twenty-one when he wrote it, and yet it reads like the work of a much more mature writer. It's a superb story.

DOUG WINTER: It really is.

STEVE SPIGNESI: The imagery, the writing, the language—everything worked. What are your thoughts on the fact that the horror fiction market was so depressed at the time that a story as good as "Strawberry Spring" had to make its initial appearance in a skin mag?

DOUG WINTER: Well, that goes to another aspect of my view about horror fiction. I've recently heard a lot of interesting comments from people about "The Night Flier." Ed Begley was commenting on how grotesque it was, and yet how funny at the same time. And he was howling with laughter. He'd try to read some of these lines very seriously, and then he'd break up. And people have said to me, "You know, that Stephen King story is just really in bad taste, you know?"

STEVE SPIGNESI: The reaction you've been getting

is that "Night Flier" was in bad taste?

DOUG WINTER: Oh, yes. People have said that to me, sure.

STEVE SPIGNESI: I wonder what they say about "Dedication," then! (Laughs.)

16. *HORROR AS AN OUTLAW: BAD TASTE CAN BE GOOD*

DOUG WINTER: (Laughs.) Well, yes. What's interesting to see about those things is that I really do think that horror fiction is ultimately an outlaw form of literature.

We've always wanted to strive for literary acceptability, and that certainly is something that I was trying for with *Art of Darkness*. But we don't actually want horror to be part of the establishment. And that's why I don't like all the various academic books that are now starting to come out on Steve, because the premise then is that he is part of the establishment.

It's a very subversive fiction and at heart, it's really closer to pornography than anything else. And it ought to be. Because its concerns are the things that we don't like to think about. The things we want to repress.

"...it continues to be, to me, very refreshing to find Steve striking out into these areas like he has in 'The Night Flier.' Moving off into the realms of poor taste, perhaps— although I certainly don't think so. I think it's a riot. But definitely moving off to those regions—and not allowing himself to be co-opted in any way."

STEVE SPIGNESI: The "dark half?"

DOUG WINTER: Yes. And that's why it continues to be, to me, very refreshing to find Steve striking out into these areas like he has in "The Night Flier." Moving off into the realms of poor taste, perhaps— although I certainly don't think so. I think it's a riot. But definitely moving off to those regions— and not allowing himself to be co-opted in any way. And that's important to maintaining the freshness of horror fiction—for it to move into those kind of dire directions every once in a while.

17. *SPLATTERPUNKING*

STEVE SPIGNESI: Now that brings up an interesting point. I think you'd agree that Stephen King is part of a handful of writers that make up – for want of a better term—"the horror establishment." Writers such as Stephen King, Peter Straub, Dean Koontz, Ramsey Campbell, Dennis Etchison, Charles Grant, and lately Clive Barker, as well as a few others. The major names in the field. And now with stories such as "The Night Flier" and "Dedication," King is moving off into these new "regions," as you put it. Do you think that the younger generation of horror writers—the "splatterpunk" writers, the writers of the New Horror such as Joe Lansdale, Ray Garton, Skipp and Spector and others—are in their own way responding to (or rebelling against?) the commercial acceptance of horror writers such as King, and saying, "Hey, you're not shocked by Stephen King, you're gonna buy a million copies of his book...well, I'll show you something that'll *really* shock you?" And where do you fit in this pantheon? Are you a splatterpunker, Doug?

DOUG WINTER: No, although one of my stories has been reprinted in the *Splatterpunks* anthology. And I was supposed to be in that picture that was in *Twilight Zone* of all the people in Nashville.

[NOTE: The picture Doug is referring to ran in the October 1988 issue of *Twilight Zone* magazine. The photo accompanied an article called "Inside the New Horror" by Philip Nutman. The photos by Beth Gwinn were of John Skipp, Craig Spector, J.K. Potter, David J. Schow, Jeff Conner, Joe Lansdale, Richard Christian Matheson, Ray Garton, and Robert R. McCammon. — **sjs**]

Fortunately, I was somewhere else at the time.

STEVE SPIGNESI: Fortunately?

DOUG WINTER: Yes, because I have trouble enough belonging to the Horror Writers of America, let alone a "literary movement." It's nice, but what does a splatterpunk do when he's forty, you know? He becomes a splatterfart? (Laughs.)

STEVE SPIGNESI: (Laughs.)

DOUG WINTER: The titles are nice and everything else, but I'm not a joiner, and I don't think it's a good idea to tie what you do to a *kind* of fiction. But, to answer your question, I know most of those guys personally, and they all very much like and admire Stephen King. And they all very much like and admire traditional horror. Not all of them want to be called splatterpunks. Unfortunately, though, some so-called "splatterpunks" haven't read enough—they don't know as much about it as they should, but essentially, they are really people who love the form.

Their aesthetic may be a little bit angrier, but oddly enough most of so-called "splatterpunk" is really very reactionary fiction. It's not radical fiction at all. It's radical in its violence and in its explicitness, but at heart it's—to use Steve's phrase —as conservative as a Republican in a suit, because it is all openly about putting things back to right.

"A lot of Steve's fiction is like that....at once subversive, and at the same time, conservative because really, part of its message is to hold the reader's hand and to say, look, everything's going to be all right. No matter how bad it is, everything's gonna be all right."

I've always been more interested in putting things to wrong. (Laughs.) But in any event, I guess what I'm saying is that it's a very conservative kind of fiction. And there's nothing wrong with that. A lot of Steve's fiction is like that, too. And you can see the ins and outs. It's horror being at once subversive, and at the same time, conservative because really, part of its message is to hold the reader's hand and to say, look, everything's going to be all right. No matter how bad it is, everything's gonna be all right. And ultimately, bad ending or good in horror, it does that, because you're going to be able to quit at some point.

STEVE SPIGNESI: I was a little surprised to see R.C. Matheson included in that group with writers like Ray Garton and Joe Lansdale, who are much more graphic and visceral.

DOUG WINTER: Yes.

STEVE SPIGNESI: To me R. C.'s writing doesn't fit in the same category as, for instance, Joe Lansdale's early novel *Act of Love*. *Act of Love* was Joe's first novel, it was originally released in the early eighties, and yet it has the Hacker sauteeing breaded slices of a woman's breasts in a frying pan. It has some of the most graphic violence that I've ever read. R.C's work doesn't have anywhere near the explicitness of many of these writers.

DOUG WINTER: Right.

STEVE SPIGNESI: But I don't know. Am I being too picky in making gradations within horror, in the sense that there's the Horror Elite, comprised of Matheson, Bloch, Bradbury and the other legends, and then there's the Horror Establishment consisting of King and the other big names, and then there's the New Horror, consisting of the guys profiled in the *Twilight Zone* piece and other younger writers? With the gradations separating the groups being marked by the increasing use of graphic violence, with the newer writers being the most explicit?

DOUG WINTER: Well, yes, I do think you're making a mistake because I think a lot of things that Steve has done have been incredibly graphic.

STEVE SPIGNESI: Maybe I'm getting jaded myself, but I don't think he comes close to some of what these new guys are doing.

DOUG WINTER: Well, I think Steve tends to write less about *sexual* violence than writers like, say, Skipp and Spector, or Clive.

STEVE SPIGNESI: That's true.

DOUG WINTER: But I think it's a mistake to try to lump different people together in that fashion because you do what you've got to do. What I dislike are the people who do it when they don't have to do it—whose only interest is in the explicitness of their work. Whose only interest is in the excessiveness of their imagery.

And certainly you can make great arguments for that as an art form in and of itself. Some of the things that Clive has done show that you can use excessiveness in and of itself as an art form. But, he is more of a genuine intellectual in what he does and he is doing it for reasons, whereas a lot of other people just aren't. They're just doing it to be explicit.

18. *WHAT'S A LITTLE GRATUITOUS VIOLENCE BETWEEN FRIENDS?*

STEVE SPIGNESI: Justifiable violence versus gratuitous violence and explicitness?

DOUG WINTER: Right. To be really crass – you can thrust sharp objects into genitals, for example...you can do that—as I did, for instance in "Splatter"— and it's justifiable, I think, even though a lot of people didn't like it there. And then you can do it in another context, and it's completely unjustifiable.

The writer has to sit back and question himself at every turn: "Why am I doing this?" And it seems to me that anytime you are indulging in explicit images, you ought to sit back and ask yourself that question. Why am I doing this? Is it because I get off on it? And I think a lot of people do.

Is it because there is a reason to it, is it because there is something I wanted to do to the reader at this time, in this place? There are all kinds of reasons to do these things. And some of those reasons are good reasons, and some of them aren't. But ultimately it depends upon the writer and the reader. And the marketplace. I mean, if the marketplace wants it, the marketplace oughtta get it.

19. *DO COOKIES FART?*

STEVE SPIGNESI: Let's talk about King collectibles. As you know, rare Stephen King items—especially the very early stuff—are commanding all kinds of prices in the collecting market today. Is there an elusive piece of King material that you haven't been able to get your hands on? [NOTE: See the interviews with dealers Craig Goden, Dave Hinchberger, and Michael Autrey in this volume. — sjs]

DOUG WINTER: Well, I'm not a collector.

STEVE SPIGNESI: Well, can we assume that you— since you're probably the ultimate Stephen King insider—have seen most of what Stephen King has written?

DOUG WINTER: I've seen a lot. And I've seen some pretty weird stuff. I've seen "The King Family and the Farting Cookie." Do you know "The Farting Cookie" story?

STEVE SPIGNESI: No.

DOUG WINTER: I once held a copy of it in my hands...but let's face it, the thrill is in *reading* something, not owning it.

There are things that come my way just because of my position in the field of King study. I have some nice books—but I've never considered them "investments."

This Stephen King collecting craze—whatever it is—has become very much a concern to me. I've never been too excited by the notion.

STEVE SPIGNESI: I guess essentially what King fans want to know is, do you have everything you

covered in *Art of Darkness*? I mean, you reported on some very rare materials in that book. How did you come across "Star Invaders," "People, Places, and Things," "Harrison State Park '68"—the really, really difficult to find pieces?

DOUG WINTER: There's a network. Somebody'll send you a photocopy of something. Bookdealers will occasionally have obscure things that they offer for sale, and they send photocopies my way. For example, some guy had one of the poems and he was selling the thing for something like $500, but he was all too happy to let me borrow it. Somebody just sent me a notice that they were offering a copy of *Moth* for sale at auction.

STEVE SPIGNESI: James Dourgarian has one, signed by Steve and Tabitha, and he's asking $950 for it. I find it fascinating that Stan Wiater bought a copy of *Moth* for $30 at a paper convention in Hartford two years ago. The pricing of King materials seems to have gotten totally out of control. [NOTE: See the interview with Stan Wiater in this volume. —sjs]

DOUG WINTER: And that's an understatement.

STEVE SPIGNESI: I'm not a collector either. I'm interested in the text. It's the words that count for me. And based on your remarks in your article "Collecting King" in the special Stephen King issue of *Twilight Zone* (February 1986), you seem to be of the same philosophy. And I think King's inscription to you on the first edition of *The Shining* that he gave you says it all: "Here's a True Fact collectors don't seem to know—it's the same story even if you print it on shopping bags..."

DOUG WINTER: Right.

STEVE SPIGNESI: As does the epigraph to *Different Seasons*: "It is the tale, not he who tells it." And yet I come across collectors all the time because of this book, and to be honest, some of these completists are off the wall!

DOUG WINTER: I know. Regarding my hunt for this rare stuff, though, a couple of people helped me a lot. Roger Anker was one of them. He did the Dark Harvest book *Charles Beaumont: Selected Stories*. He was a big help back in the early eighties – he had a lot of stuff. So, completists have a role, too.

❏

TAKING NOTICE OF "THE NOTICER"
An Interview With J. N. Williamson

I was first introduced to J.N. (Jerry) Williamson through a fortuitous set of circumstances involving my literary agent John White, the UFO experience, astrology, and the principle of sychronicity. (Trust me: It's not as complicated as it might sound!)

My agent John—as well as being the prolific author of *Pole Shift, The Practical Guide to Death and Dying,* and *Everything You Want To Know About TM*—is also an editor in his own right, having helmed such anthologies as *The Highest State of Consciousness, What Is Meditation?, Frontiers of Consciousness, Psychic Exploration, Future Science,* and *Kundalini, Evolution and Enlightenment.* John is very involved in the study of the UFO "experience," and after having read J.N. Williamson's science fiction novel *Brotherkind,* he felt intrigued enough about Jerry's UFO theories to contact him about possibly working together on a project involving UFO percipients/contactees and the entire UFO experience in general.

John was kind enough to photocopy his and Jerry's correspondence for me on the chance that I might find talking to Jerry useful. Now here's where the sychronicity comes in. I had just finished working my way through a brand new anthology that J.N. had edited called *How To Write Tales of Horror, Fantasy & Science Fiction,* and I had recently purchased Jerry's latest anthology *Masques II,* in which there appeared a chilling new Stephen King short story called "Popsy."

I've often heard it said that "There are no coincidences." (Was it Freud or Jung who said that? Or was it Moe Howard? Whatever. The point is that whoever said it was right!) Well, to make a long story short (if that's even possible at this point) I contacted Jerry, queried him about doing an interview for this book, and the rest, as they say, is history.

We did the interview by phone on a cold gray January day—Martin Luther King's birthday. There were still mountains of snow on the front lawn from a recent blizzard, and I had spent the morning bitching to myself about how cold my feet were.

One thing I must say about Jerry Williamson up front is that he's got class. Even though he remarked that he was sorry for being "occasionally verbose" during our interview, I found his answers insightful, to the point, and I also found that Jerry was a keen judge of not only the dark fantasy genre, but of other writers, and the publishing industry in general. He went out of his way to be helpful, and in fact, upon reading over the transcripts of our talk, I found myself realizing I should have followed up certain of Jerry's answers with other specific questions—but I didn't. Jerry was kind enough, though, to address these questions in a follow-up letter and I was then able to work these new remarks into the interview.

Regarding Jerry's career: As the flap copy of his *How To* succinctly puts it "Ask J. N. Williamson for his credits and stand back."

He has written or edited thirty-five books, including the following (as author, and in no particular order):

> *The Houngan* (Best Fantasy Novel, *West Coast Review of Books*)
> *The Tulpa*
> *The Longest Night*
> *Premonition*
> *Playmates*
> *Wards of Armageddon* (with John Maclay)
> *Brotherkind*
> *The Offspring*
> *Evil Offspring*
> *Ghost* (Nominated for 1984 Balrog Best Novel)
> *Horror House*
> *Horror Mansion*
> *The Ritual*
> *The Black School*
> *The Banished*
> *Babel's Children*
> *Death-Coach*
> *Death-Angel*
> *Death-School*
> *Death-Doctor*
> *Noonspell*

Jerry also edited the following books:

> *Masques* (Balrog for Best Professional Achievement; Runnerup for the World Fantasy Award in 1985)
> *Masques II*
> *Masques III*
> *How To Write Tales of Horror, Fantasy & Science Fiction*

Also, Jerry has written more than 75 short stories, including the Nebula Award-recommended "The Night Seasons" and "The Book of Webster's."

J.N. has been a drummer, an astrologer, an original member of the Sherlock Holmes "Baker Street Irregulars," a Fuller Brush Man, a professional recording vocalist, and an insurance investigator.

From his introduction to his short story "Wordsong" in *Masques II* and from talking to Jerry about his fascinating life, I learned that he has met Spike Jones, James Garner, Barry Goldwater, and Annette Funicello, that he has conversed with Donald Duck, Walt Disney, August Derleth, Shelley Berman, and Coach "Bear" Bryant, and that he has corresponded with J. Edgar Hoover, Andy Rooney, Bob Newhart, and J.D. Salinger.

Also, he has slept with Mary Williamson.

Here is my talk with J.N. "It's Almost Time For My Second Childhood!" Williamson.
—sjs

TAKING NOTICE OF "THE NOTICER"
An Interview With J. N. Williamson

STEVE SPIGNESI: Jerry, I really appreciate your taking the time to talk to me about Stephen King.

J. N. WILLIAMSON: Oh, it's my pleasure, although I don't know how wonderful the interview will be. I really don't consider myself an expert on Steve's work, but I've certainly read most of it, and I certainly do have views, so hopefully that'll be helpful.

STEVE SPIGNESI: OK, terrific. Why don't we start with how you met him and your first impression of him?

J. N. WILLIAMSON: I first met Stephen King in Ottawa at the World Fantasy Convention in 1984 and, like everyone else, I was curious to know what kind of a fellow he would appear to be. And, like everyone else, I knew he was, of course, infinitely famous, and so on and so forth. But I was completely unprepared for the fan reaction to him. Even though we are all aware by now that he's one of the few physically identifiable writers (thanks to his commercials, and appearances and his movies and so on), I'm not sure—unless you've been to a convention or someplace where lots of his readers are present—that you can understand or even begin to anticipate the sort-of reception he got.

STEVE SPIGNESI: Can you describe how he was received by the fans?

J. N. WILLIAMSON: Well, I remember one incident that stands out in my mind. I was sitting at a table with several other writers, two of whom I would say are very famous and very successful—in a room full of writers of one kind or another, and of one degree of success or another. They had set up a table for Steve and Peter Straub, who were there to sign *The Talisman*. Some 700 people were in attendance and I fully expected that there would be big crowds around Stephen and around Peter. But what still staggers me when I think about it is the fact that I'd say 90% of the fans in attendance immediately queued up in the King-Straub line. And this wasn't done with any sort of disrespect towards the other writers—eventually the other people at my table and I ended up signing a lot of books. But it was the first time I realized just how successful and important Steve and, of course, Peter Straub, are.

STEVE SPIGNESI: Did you meet King that first day?

J. N. WILLIAMSON: No. It was basically impossible to approach him the first couple of days of the convention. I had a desire, of course, to meet Steve and Peter, along with many other writers. And I

J. N. Williamson.
Photo courtesy Mark Savo.

really wanted to form many dear friendships. (Laughs.) But getting up—getting *to* King is simply a damn good trick. And if you're a professional writer yourself, you're not really inclined to get in a line. It seems fairly ridiculous!

STEVE SPIGNESI: Who else was at your table?

J. N. WILLIAMSON: Some of the other writers who were present included F. Paul Wilson, who wrote *The Keep*, Bill Nolan—William F. Nolan—who wrote *Logan's Run;* and Robert R. McCammon, who at the time had a bestseller in *Mystery Walk*, and since has written *Usher's Passing* and *Swan Song*. There were many, many notable writers...outstanding writers...but, like I said, it was really impossible those first couple of days to get near King.

STEVE SPIGNESI: I understand the first *Masques* anthology had just been released at this time?

J. N. WILLIAMSON: Yes, the first *Masques* anthology, which I edited, made its debut at that convention. And I was there primarily to sign the book.

STEVE SPIGNESI: So, how did you finally end up getting to meet Messrs. King and Straub?

J. N. WILLIAMSON: When I finally had the chance to meet both Stephen and Peter it was sort of an amusing situation. I had gone down to the book room to meet John Maclay, who's the publisher of the *Masques* books and a very dear friend of mine, as well my collaborator on our novel *Wards of Armageddon*. John was coming out of the dealers room when across the hall, out of a small room, stepped Peter Straub. So, Peter said to me "I've been wanting to meet you and say hello, and tell you that I wish Stephen King would buy his own books." (Laughs.) And I said "What do you mean?" And he said "I just bought a copy of *Masques,* and damned if Stephen didn't just take it away from me. He's sitting in there reading it." So, I stuck my nose in the door and was immediately aware not just of Steve, but of, as I recall, at least one bodyguard and maybe two. And that absolutely floored me. I've seen a lot of famous writers, but I can't remember seeing any other writers with bodyguards.

STEVE SPIGNESI: Do you think it was necessary for King to have bodyguards?

J. N. WILLIAMSON: In retrospect I think probably it was a very good idea for King and Straub to have them there.

So, Steve looked up and said "Looks like a fine book, wish I'd been in it." And I discovered then that invitations I'd given to King had never reached

him because he was out of the country at the time. And I don't know why, but nobody at his place bothered to notify me of that. I had written him three letters and made a couple of phone calls, but hadn't been told that Steve was out of the country.

So, I immediately felt better about Steve. My assumption at that point had been that he doesn't even bother to answer letters from other writers—which was absolutely dead wrong. He was very friendly, and he was engrossed in my book. And then Peter said, "Let's go buy another copy of *Masques.*" I said fine. Now this is, I think, kind of an amusing anecdote about Peter Straub. We went to the dealer's room and I led him up to the book table where John Maclay and his wife Joyce were sitting and, of course, John and Joyce immediately wanted to give Peter a copy of the book. And Peter said "No, no, I'm quite capable of paying for it," but John and Joyce insisted. Peter asked me to sign it to him, and as I was, I looked up and the dealers room was suddenly filled with people making a beeline for us, or putting it more precisely, for Peter Straub. And he said, "Oh, God," and I said, "There's an exit over there, Peter, run for it, I'll block for you." (Laughs.) And we had this absurd scene where dignified Peter Straub was jogging through the dealers room. (Laughs.)

STEVE SPIGNESI: It must have been funny to see Peter Straub fleeing like that.

J. N. WILLIAMSON: It was kind of a riot! By the way, Peter's a very nice man—a very pleasant guy and an outstanding writer. But, again, I was foiled at any chance of really exchanging any more than a few words with Steve. I went back to the little anteroom and he had disappeared from there.

Then I learned an anecdote from the Maclays that was kind of neat, and I think says something interesting about Steve. Steve had come to buy a copy of *Masques* that morning, and a comedy of errors transpired in which Joyce Maclay, the wife of the publisher, tried to give him a copy. Like Straub, King wanted to pay for it, and again, Joyce wouldn't hear of it. Finally, Steve offered her five dollars for a copy because she absolutely refused to take the full amount. And during this transaction, at some point, King was spotted and he had to take off. So, the whole thing was kind of ridiculous.

STEVE SPIGNESI: Did Steve do anything publicly at this convention?

J. N. WILLIAMSON: Yes. That Sunday the World Fantasy Con honored one of my two or three favorite living writers—Richard Matheson—with the World Fantasy Award for Lifetime Achievement. Matheson was not there, and so Steve accepted the award for him. You know, I turn into a little boy around Dick Matheson and Ray Bradbury and Robert Bloch. I simply admire them endlessly!

STEVE SPIGNESI: That's understandable.

J. N. WILLIAMSON: (Laughs.) I was just tickled to death for Matheson. I badly wanted him to be there. Happily, he did attend the next convention and we had a wonderful time.

STEVE SPIGNESI: Did you ever get a chance to finally talk with King?

J. N. WILLIAMSON: Yes. At the end of the banquet, as we were both preparing to leave, I was sort-of just standing by myself, waiting for my wife, who had gone somewhere.

It should be noted that at *this* banquet we had primarily writers and their families, agents, editors and so on, attending, and so, for once, King wasn't besieged. So, as I was standing there, King looked up over the crowd. I was standing by the doors waiting for my wife to come back.

Now, Steve is quite tall, and actually turned out to be much taller than I'd realized, and so he was looking over the heads of people. Our gazes met, and he said "Hi, J.N." And I said, "Hi Steve, I'm thrilled to death about Matheson." And he said, "So am I. He's a cardinal influence. Wonderful man." And I said, "I couldn't agree more." And then he started to try to reach me through the crowd. But people and fans outside the banquet hall had seen him, and you could hear people saying, "There's Stephen King! There's Stephen King!" (Laughs.) And King said, "Oh, God!," and that sort of cut our conversation short. But before we parted he said, "Gosh, I'd like to be in another anthology of yours." And I said, "I'd love to have you." And he said, "Are you gonna do another one?" And I said, "Probably, I'm not sure yet," and that was the end of that.

So, then, when I was asked by John Maclay to edit *Masques II*, I fully intended to again contact King, and this time I hoped I would have better luck. But before I ever even had a chance to write him, in came a story from Steve's agent Kirby McCauley, a story that King had written expressly for *Masques II*.

STEVE SPIGNESI: "Popsy."

J. N. WILLIAMSON: Yes.

STEVE SPIGNESI: What were your feelings about King after receiving the story?

J. N. WILLIAMSON: He kept his word and didn't

even have to be asked. I think that says a great deal about him. And considering what a dilemma he has in simply moving from room to room—and the kind of ego I've seen in other writers—I've had problems with it at times myself, to be honest—I think Stephen King handles himself very well.

STEVE SPIGNESI: An obvious gentleman. That's terrific. Tell me, why did you thank Stephen King on the Acknowledgments page of your novel *Noonspell*?

J. N. WILLIAMSON: That was an effort I made to thank several writers who had specifically cooperated with me in my editing of my book *How To Write Tales of Horror, Fantasy & Science Fiction* for *Writer's Digest*. I had dropped a line to Steve and asked him if he would supply me with a list of some of his favorite horror novels and short stories, and he had.

STEVE SPIGNESI: It's an interesting list. His favorite horror novels included Ray Bradbury's *Something Wicked This Way Comes*, Richard Matheson's *I Am Legend*, and Ramsey Campbell's *The Doll Who Ate His Mother*.

J. N. WILLIAMSON: Yes, it is interesting. And that sort of cooperation was what I had gotten from the other people that I cited as well, and I hoped he would know what I meant by that "Thank You," because after I wrote it I got to thinking "You know, it'll be six months to a year before this comes out and nobody'll really know why it's there." But I didn't want to mention the *How To* because it would look like I was plugging it. But, then, I said the hell with it. I'll just let it stand and let them figure it out.

STEVE SPIGNESI: I've been reading quite a bit of your work lately, and I was wondering if King has influenced *your* writing at all? Have you ever found yourself doing something that was specifically influenced by King? He and his work are so prevalent, so ubiquitous in contemporary pop culture. Have you ever found yourself using more brand names, for instance, or doing something you can directly attribute to King?

J. N. WILLIAMSON: Yes, in only one instance. And I guess you have a bit of a scoop of sorts here.

STEVE SPIGNESI: I'm glad I asked.

J. N. WILLIAMSON: I've been kind of wanting to tell this story anyway. I wrote a 33,000-word novella called "The Night Seasons," which ran for a year in *Night Cry* magazine and was then nominated for a World Fantasy Award in 1987 in the novella category. Its derivation is kind of wild. The novella is unlike anything else I've ever written, because it deals with—if I was writing this I would say it much more tactfully—it deals with an alcoholic who ends up in a drunk tank in the County Jail. I very rarely drink, and happily I have never ended up in the drunk tank or in jail. (Laughs.)

STEVE SPIGNESI: That's good to hear. (Laughs.)
J. N. WILLIAMSON: And I certainly don't mean to imply that Stephen King has! God knows I don't mean that! But when I began to write the novella, what I had in my mind privately, all by my little self in my little room, was trying to write something between a parody and a pastiche of Stephen King.

I began it for my own amusement—*entirely* for my own amusement. I didn't think I would ever send it out to anybody and I certainly didn't think I was writing anything that was particularly good, to be honest with you. I finished about a third of it, and realized that, inescapably, my own voice had begun to creep in greatly, and then I saw a way to go on with it and write a work I thought was publishable.

Up until then I had had King's novella "The Mist" in mind and was—without using the same setting—creating basically the same kind of format as "The Mist." As a matter of fact, "The Night Seasons" remains, for better or worse, structured much the way "The Mist" is. So, what happened was that I suddenly realized that I wanted to finish this, and make it serious, and I then thought that the piece was publishable. So, I went back and started scratching out things that seemed to me to be peculiarly like Stephen King.

STEVE SPIGNESI: Such as?
J. N. WILLIAMSON: An awful lot of brand names went out, and some swearing that customarily isn't in my fiction unless it's entirely justified, went out. Other things I don't think I even want to detail went out. But, nonetheless, the structuring remained consciously like that of "The Mist," without there being any other similarities that I'm aware of at all. In no way do I think it's a King rip-off as it finally appeared in print...and as it now stands.

But the other thing I'm trying to say is that Steve is an extraordinarily contemporaneous writer to me. I'm quite sure he has written—and can write—in any doggone period he feels like writing about and write it well. But that level of society, and the concerns of the characters in "The Night Seasons" are not usually nor customarily mine at all. So what floored me, frankly, was when the

novella sold the first time out. Novellas are very difficult to place. And then when I was nominated for a World Fantasy Award, I didn't know whether to feel good about it, laugh, contact King, or...

STEVE SPIGNESI: ...just leave it alone?
J. N. WILLIAMSON: Yeah! And I've never quite gotten over the fact that "The Night Seasons" and another short story of mine called "The Book of Webster's" which *Night Cry* also published— received several recommendations for the Nebula Award from Science Fiction Writers of America. The reason I mention "The Book of Webster's" is that, while it has absolutely nothing whatsoever to do with King, it is, again, a very contemporaneous story that involves serial killers. It's a very hip story, a very glib story, and this seems to tell me something about Stephen King and about current general reader interest in horror that equates with some of the successes King and some other writers have had.

STEVE SPIGNESI: To go on with that just a little bit: How do you think the horror/dark fantasy genre has changed since King published *Carrie* in 1974? Can you summarize what his influence has been?
J. N. WILLIAMSON: It's been profound mostly, I believe, in opening doors for other writers of grue. I don't think it would have ever been a bona fide genre—a genre with dozens of successful practitioners in it as it has now—if it hadn't been for Stephen King.

I'm very tired of, and disgusted with, writers who specifically knock Stephen King. I am not one of those and I'm also not one who says that King is the greatest writer who ever lived. I don't believe that at all. But to knock him either on the grounds of his writing, which is excellent by and large, or to say that he hasn't had an immense helpful influence—including for me personally—would be just ridiculous. It would be a lie.

STEVE SPIGNESI: It's more than obvious that Stephen King has had a major impact on publishing, the horror genre, popular culture, films, and literature in general. But I think a key question that must be asked is do you personally think Stephen King's work will survive? For instance, do you think that 150 years from now, Stephen King's work will still be read, let alone be considered classic horror?
J. N. WILLIAMSON: I know only one writer whose work seems to me bound to survive and be read 150 years from now—speaking in terms of the "fan-

tasy" genre as an "umbrella", that is—and that is Ray Bradbury.

Frankly, I doubt many authors working today give much thought to the long-range survival of their work. I have no idea whether Ray or Steve give a hoot. Even for a John Simon, a guess about whose fiction will survive must necessarily be a guess, since I don't know of any time machines offering us a ride into the future.

STEVE SPIGNESI: It sounds like you're saying that most professional writers "seize the day" and sort of write for the moment.

J. N. WILLIAMSON: It does seem to me a likelihood that most contemporary writers think less about immortality than authors of fifty to seventy-five years ago, for a host of reasons: First, getting published at all today is such a competitive matter that the tendency when we start out—a tendency that may well become habitual—is to please acquiring editors. Since it may well be that most editors are well under thirty-five years of age, and have grown up—in common with numerous successful writers *in horror particularly*—during a period when the past was viewed as an enemy—or as a time when all the mistakes were made—what we write is often meant to be modern. Contemporary.

STEVE SPIGNESI: Is this good or bad?

J. N. WILLIAMSON: Well, it's historians and sociologists who want to read that which was modern *yesterday*.

STEVE SPIGNESI: If today's readers want blatantly *contemporary* fiction, then is that the kind of work that you think is destined to survive?

J. N. WILLIAMSON: We bandy words around too much these days—use them far too loosely. A writer of Ray Bradbury's stripe—or Ray Russell's, or William F. Nolan's (and there are, mercifully, others)—frequently is said to have created "timeless" fiction, and that is largely true in their instances.

But then the same word is applied to a large number of stories and novels which writer and publisher alike intended to be an entertaining yarn, even a potboiler—and no more than that. I'm far more in favor of there being more entertaining potboilers written than self-consciously pretentious fiction, pompous stuff filled with Portent and Meaning (even though I sometimes do that myself). The point then becomes that many writers in many fields at this point in time are either trying to get published and survive as creative

artists, or, having achieved that, write much the same thing over and over, for fear of otherwise rocking the boat. To reach that achievement, many of those writers have attempted to be as modern as they can possibly be.

> **"...Stephen King's difference from these other writers is that he is *always* entertaining, does not pad potboilers or pretend they're anything but that.**
>
> **I think that the fault—if he and other contemporary writers, including myself, don't survive—doesn't lie with him, it lies with the hard sell of commercial types and with readers who would deify him."**

STEVE SPIGNESI: Where does Stephen King fit in this scheme of things?

J. N. WILLIAMSON: Well, Stephen King's difference from these other writers is that he is *always* entertaining, does not pad potboilers or pretend they're anything but that.

I think that the fault—if he and other contemporary writers, including myself, don't survive—doesn't lie with him, it lies with the hard sell of commercial types and with readers who would deify him. In that process, I believe, it becomes exceedingly difficult to judge which stories and novels any writer has written which are truly first-rate and deserving to survive the years. I do not believe for a minute that anyone creative, including the more innovative basketball stars, performs at the same level every time out. I see nothing wrong with a "little" story, a "little" novel, if it's well-crafted and does what the storyline and theme of that particular work called for. It's my hope that your *The Shape Under the Sheet* will so effectively catalogue Mr. K's writing for those that care about it fifty or one-hundred years from now, that they will be able to separate Stephen's first-rate stuff from the lesser stuff.

STEVE SPIGNESI: Your confidence in me and my book is flattering, and I appreciate it. Since we're talking about King's tales, I've got to ask if you've got a favorite Stephen King novel?

J. N. WILLIAMSON: Actually it's pretty much of a toss-up, and I'm not at all sure that Steve himself would agree with me, but what the heck. I think his *Pet Sematary* is—for nine-tenths of the book—one of the finest horror novels I've ever read. I'd *love* to see him revise the last chapter or two.

STEVE SPIGNESI: Do you think that because *Pet Sematary* is your personal favorite, do you therefore think it's King's best novel?

J. N. WILLIAMSON: Oh, good question, good question. No. Probably *Misery* is.

STEVE SPIGNESI: That's interesting, especially since *Misery* is basically a novel of *psychological* terror.

J. N. WILLIAMSON: Yes, but in terms of sheer storytelling and originality, I like *Pet Sematary* better. I also admired tremendously—and still do—the nerve it took to attempt to make a character sympathetic who's going into a graveyard to dig up his dead son. And he did it, he succeeded. I think it's the most skillful thing Stephen King has ever done.

I like to think that I'll accept writing challenges almost anytime, but I'm not sure I would have accepted that one, except maybe in short story form, where I could have just sort of written it and forgotten about it. Most of the time anybody attempting that kind of a scene would have the character become so unsympathetic, so neurotic—or worse—that you'd blow the rest of the book. And instead of that, you wind up feeling...well, I will admit—he almost made me cry. I thought it was terribly sad, and as a father, I found myself thinking, yeah...I'd probably do that. In some other writers hands – in a *lot* of other writers' hands—I would have either not liked his protagonist, or felt he was very sick, and the whole thing might have become laughable. It was never laughable.

STEVE SPIGNESI: That's interesting. I have a stock answer when people ask me for my personal "Stephen King" favorite: It's the one I'm reading at the moment. But I think if I really had to pick one, it would probably be *IT*. With all the knocks it's taken, and even with King's criticism of it himself, I consider that book his ultimate achievement in storytelling. I can't really see where the critics are on the money when it comes to what they're saying about *IT*. Even though King has called the book rather unorganized, to me, it flowed perfectly. I just flew through it and absolutely adored it. And I also found *The Drawing of the Three* just brilliant, a real page-turner.

J. N. WILLIAMSON: I agree. I liked that, too.

STEVE SPIGNESI: What did you think of *IT*?

J. N. WILLIAMSON: I liked it very much and I think it's an example of the special kind of gift—not unique, thank God!—but the special kind of gift that Steve has—the sheer storytelling gift. I remember when I was once "damned with faint praise," so to speak. A review of one of my books several years ago said, "Basically all Williamson is is a storyteller." And I took those words out and told everybody about it. Because I think that's one of the neatest things you can possibly be in this world.

STEVE SPIGNESI: I agree. I envy storytellers. I enjoy writing nonfiction, but I just haven't yet found a voice for longer works of fiction. Recently on the phone my brother asked me, "When are you going to write a novel?" I told him, "When it comes!"

J. N. WILLIAMSON: That's a good answer, Steve! You know, there's an aspect of writing a long novel—and I've now written thirty of them—comparable to a marathon running. It's seen as a curse when a writer is called prolific, and King has been called prolific. Dean Koontz has been called prolific. God knows *I'm* prolific. And again, that's not usually meant as a compliment. But anybody's who set out to write his first novel has some idea of how tough it is.

"I've never really tried to understand Stephen King's great accomplishments. I think that to attempt to get too involved with analyzing the 'why' of it all it seems almost to amount to dissecting the living, and that makes me uncomfortable because I have no urge whatsoever for Stephen to write or to sell less than he is now....yet the fact remains that King is the most successful wordworker we have, and unless we know why, the suspicion can grow that he is somehow undeserving of his achievements."

STEVE SPIGNESI: I think you're right. King's first novel *Carrie* was a "stalled" short story he expanded by padding it with fictitious excerpts from journals, magazines, and newspaper articles. And *Carrie* started King's incredible "reign of horror." Have you any thoughts on the "secret of his success"?

J. N. WILLIAMSON: I've never really tried to understand Stephen King's great accomplishments. I think that to attempt to get too involved with analyzing the "why" of it all it seems almost to amount to dissecting the living, and that makes me uncomfortable because I have no urge whatsoever for Stephen to write or to sell less than he is now.

So far as I know, he hasn't asked for this kind of in-depth thinking, yet the fact remains that King is the most successful wordworker we have, and unless we know why, the suspicion can grow that he is somehow undeserving of his achievements.

I don't believe that he has ever consciously sought comparison to any preexisting standards of writing, and therefore logically he has no reason to expect any other writers to follow him or to be like him. If he was ever what Colin Wilson called an "outsider," he appears to me be an insider now...but deep inside, never insisting that he lead. If we're not careful, we can do to him what has been done to J.D. Salinger and others. And I think that would be a shame. Not a major tragedy, maybe, but a shame.

STEVE SPIGNESI: A shame, yes, but also dangerous, in that he *could* end up like Salinger if we're not careful.

J. N. WILLIAMSON: Right. The author of *Catcher in the Rye* and the *Franny and Zooey* novellas recorded the whole feeling of a particular corner of his time faithfully, yet always with his idiosyncratic talents busy identifying those little things that were painfully wrong, even horrifying about his society, period, and place.

We tried to create a cult around Jerry Salinger, but he, too, didn't wish to lead any revolutions or fight a "Don Quixote" kind of war. Basically, I think that Salinger wanted two things: first, to show that he *noticed* what was wrong (and also knew what was right), and, secondly, that he wanted to write. Then, when we pantingly yearned for him to go on with the first, to tell us about all the rest of it, we kept him publicly from doing the second...writing. I don't think that should happen to King. I don't see why—even while I sympathize

with the need to figure out why certain successes are achieved—we should expect our storytellers to do what our statesmen seldom even begin to do.

A better question, perhaps, than why Steve King hit the jackpot, might well be, why haven't other writers with greater talent, perception or knowledge struck it rich? Ultimately, I believe *that* question would explain utterly Mr. King's marvelous accomplishments, but suggest a great many of the things that J.D. Salinger and others found as good and bad in our society.

STEVE SPIGNESI: I understand that. During the writing of this book, people would often ask me what I was working on, and when I'd tell them I was working on a book about Stephen King, in many instances it was very clear to me by some of their responses just how that "cult of celebrity" could develop. King and his work are not a cult obsession with me, but with many people they are. I can truly understand where *Misery* came from. And I like the idea that in Bangor they tend to leave him alone.

J. N. WILLIAMSON: Yes, I do too.

STEVE SPIGNESI: I have friends in Bangor who say that King often goes for long walks, and very often they'll see him in a package store buying his beer, and it's always "Hello, Mr. King, how are you?" And that's it. There isn't that kind of "swarming" that you described at the conventions, which I can imagine must really be rough. It's a given that we all work towards that kind of acclaim, but, nonethless, I'm sure it can be difficult to deal with the constant demands for a piece of you.

J. N. WILLIAMSON: You touch on an aspect that is absolutely right. I know when I was a kid and first began to write, I thought I wanted just what King has. And now, apart from the money, I don't really think I do. Because the scene at the convention was really kind of a sad picture. I mean, here's this tall, strapping still-young man who'd like to say something to various people, and being basically unable to do it—unless he wants to invite them all to his room. And the truth of the matter is at that time he didn't know me from Adam except that he was nice enough in a letter to say he had read a couple of novels of mine.

There are all kinds of crackpots in the world. He didn't know that I wasn't going to bring twenty-seven fans up to his room! Another incident I remember with fondness of King was one involving my friend Bill Nolan. One of the people who was sitting at that autograph table I mentioned was Bill Nolan. Bill is a very dear friend of mine, and a fine, versatile writer, author, poet, screenwriter...whatever! So, while we were sitting there, Bill said, "King looks like he's falling asleep over there. I'm gonna go over there and wake him up."

Now, Bill is positively irrepressible—he's about sixty going on nine! A wonderful guy. So, he makes a beeline for King, just gets up and boldly walks over to where King and Straub are sitting. He then remarked loudly to whomever was listening that he had taught King everything he knows, or something of that sort. Now some people are so pompous and basically stuck on themselves that they'd resent that kind of an intrusion. But Steve looked up with a big grin and said, "Bill, you old sonofabitch!" and clapped him on the shoulder. A very different kind of a thing than you might have expected.

STEVE SPIGNESI: He seems to be able to take all of this much less seriously than a lot of his fans do. I have a taped radio interview that King did with Larry King in 1986, and what's most interesting is that during the interview a lot of King's fans were calling up and saying things like, "You're my favorite writer, you're books are the best books I've ever read in my life...," and so forth and so on. And during the entire ninety minutes Steve King is just so laid-back, so relaxed, that he obviously just doesn't take himself or the fandom too seriously. He can look at it all with a wry smile.

J. N. WILLIAMSON: Basically, I think what you see of Stephen King is what you get. That's nice in this day and age.

STEVE SPIGNESI: It really is. Getting back to *Masques II*—what did you do when you first received "Popsy" in the mail?

J. N. WILLIAMSON: I called Kirby McCauley, King's agent. I read "Popsy" and phoned Kirby. I mean it was that simple. You don't let these get away. When I got him on the phone, I said, "Kirby, this is Jerry Williamson. The story came from Steve. I think it's terrific and I want it."

And Kirby said, "Stephen wrote it especially for you, but he said to tell you that there's one catch." And my stomach sank.

Let's go off on a tangent here. When I was putting the first *Masques* together, I became aware of what any new anthologist quickly learns. Unless you have a big reputation as an anthologist yourself, to get people into an anthology that's basically your first one, you've just about got to get a couple of writers whom other writers admire.

Ray Bradbury basically made it possible for me to edit the first *Masques*. Because Ray agreed to be in the book, I was then able to say, "Oh by the way, Ray Bradbury's gonna be in it," and people said, "Oh, that's fine. If Ray's gonna be in it, it must be all right." So, that's what King's story arriving meant to me for *Masques II*. Now I could not only go back to any of the talented people in the first one that I wanted to, but I could talk to other people whom I didn't yet know, or hadn't yet met.

So, my stomach sank when Kirby said there was a catch. And I said, "Well, what is it?" And Kirby said, "Stephen does not want his name to be the only name on the cover of that book." And I remember exactly what McCauley said next. He said "Stephen does not want to be an anthology leader."

STEVE SPIGNESI: That's very interesting, because McCauley's *Dark Forces* anthology uses King's name very prominently, although to be fair to Kirby, he only uses all caps on the cover for the two novellas in the anthology, one of which happens to be King's "The Mist." The other is T.E.D. Klein's "Children of the Kingdom."

J. N. WILLIAMSON: *Dark Forces* is a fine, fine anthology, but I don't think King had the clout in 1980 when *Dark Forces* was released that he would have a year or so later.

So, you can imagine the reaction when I mentioned King's condition to my friend John Maclay, the publisher of *Masques I* and *II*. He said, "Oh God! I can't mention King?!" And I said, "No, no, that's not what he said. He said he's not supposed to be the *only* writer you mention." (Laughs.)

So, I remembered King's injunction when we did the *Best of Masques* with Berkley, and both Mr. Maclay and I made it clear to Berkley that Steve really did not want to be the only writer mentioned. So, at the top of the cover, it says "Featuring Stephen King, Robert R. McCammon, Robert Bloch, Ray Bradbury and more." And certainly in that company, he *shouldn't* want to be the only writer mentioned. Actually, I feel badly that they didn't put *more* names down, notably Richard Matheson and Ray Russell. But in any case, they did put Steve with these other people, too.

STEVE SPIGNESI: OK, let's shift lanes for a moment. Honestly now, did you have any inkling that King was using the "Richard Bachman" pseudonym?

J. N. WILLIAMSON: Yes, I did.

STEVE SPIGNESI: How did you find out?

J. N. WILLIAMSON: I found out during a conversation with Kirby McCauley on the phone. At that point I didn't suspect Bachman was King for the simple reason that I hadn't gotten around to reading a Richard Bachman novel yet. But the Bachman books had taken off by then.

I really don't remember why I was talking to Kirby at the time—I guess we probably talk two or three times a year for one reason or another. And he represents, or has represented, some other writers, too, like Robert Bloch, and he also represents Gahan Wilson and on and on. Since then, Bob Bloch has become a personal friend, so I can just work with him that way. But at this time, when I was talking with Kirby, one of us brought up Bachman, and Kirby said, "Well, you do know about Richard Bachman don't you?" And I said, "No, no I don't. What do you mean?" And he said, "Well there are these rumors going around that Steve is Bachman...," and then he said, "But in reality Richard Bachman is...," and he told me some wonderful concoction of notions that he obviously didn't mean for me to take seriously—something like Bachman was an aged recluse living in northern Canada, or some such thing. A bunch of ridiculous stuff. Also, that Bachman had never written anything before, and had spent his life fishing, or something like that.

It was Kirby's way of saying, "We know perfectly well who Bachman is, don't we?" And I said "You're saying it's...you're saying it's Steve!" And he said, "Why...I didn't say that, did I?! I just told you...he is an old recluse, blah, blah, blah, blah!" (Laughs.)

STEVE SPIGNESI: (Laughs.) That's a great story!

J. N. WILLIAMSON: I seem to remember almost his exact words because he was very droll about it.

STEVE SPIGNESI: So, the word *was* beginning to leak a little bit.

J. N. WILLIAMSON: Yeah, I think he knew the lid wasn't going to be kept on much longer.

STEVE SPIGNESI: In talking about King's work in general, if you were given the task of describing Steve's work to the Martian who knew nothing about our planet...

J. N. WILLIAMSON: (Laughs.)...Good question!

STEVE SPIGNESI: ...what would you tell him?

J. N. WILLIAMSON: Oh, gee whiz. No, I don't think I'd say gee whiz. I haven't met any Martians lately. I've met Whitley Strieber, though! (Laughs.) Isn't *Communion* fascinating!?

STEVE SPIGNESI: Yes, it is. In fact, it could almost be read as a contemporary horror story, if it wasn't written as nonfiction. Do you believe Whitley?

J. N. WILLIAMSON: I believe that Whitley is sincere. And I think I'm one of the few writers who does believe he's sincere. I wrote about this in my column in *2AM* magazine. I had wanted to get Whitley into the first *Masques*. I liked his *The Wolfen* and *The Hunger* very much. Stu Schiff, who's the editor of *Whispers* magazine, gave me Whitley's phone number, and I made a phone call during the period that Whitley swears he was first, uh...

STEVE SPIGNESI: ...contacted?...

J. N. WILLIAMSON: Contacted, yeah. I'm not quite sure about these words. Even though I'm a UFO buff, his book is a startling thing coming from a successful novelist. When I called Whitley's residence, a woman answered the phone and I asked for him, and she said, "Well, who is this?" And I told her, and told her that I wanted to talk to Whitley about a story for an anthology I was editing. And she said, "Whitley will not be doing any more horror writing." Click. And the phone hangs up.

Then I met Whitley at the same World Fantasy Convention the following year. I didn't know what Whitley looked like. But someone must have pointed me out to him because he came up to me, this very dignified, nice-looking gentleman. I remember he had a three-piece suit on and looked like a million bucks. He introduced himself, and I said "Well, Whitley, hi, how are you?" And he said —very directly—"Why didn't you ask me into *Masques*?" It was almost the first thing he said to me. And I said, "I did. I wanted you very badly in *Masques.*" And I told him what had happened. And he said, "Oh, that's really very interesting," and sort of wandered away.

He seemed then to be *enormously* preoccupied, to put it mildly. I couldn't say that more definitely. I remember he appeared on a panel, and he made some very intelligent observations about his views on horror, and he and I had two or three other chats, but he always seemed so very preoccupied. All along I've been one of his defenders. I think— without having any idea whether or not he actually had these experiences—I believe that he thinks that he did. I do want to make myself clear. I believe he thinks he did.

STEVE SPIGNESI: That's very interesting. For the most part Stephen King seems to stay away from science fiction. Other than a handful of works, he really hasn't done too much with sci-fi or the UFO experience. Of course, there are the short stories "Beachworld," "I Am the Doorway," and "The Jaunt," as well as *The Stand, Firestarter,* and the two Bachman novels *The Long Walk* and *The Running Man.* And I find it interesting that IT came from outer space, and that now King has written what is probably his final statement on alien intrusions with *The Tommyknockers.*

J. N. WILLIAMSON: And if there's a difference King and I have in our approaches to writing, it's largely —at least under his real name—our treatment of the icons of metaphysical and supernatural stuff. As a matter of fact I've always wanted to ask him why he seems to avoid them—if he just simply has no capacity for believing in them, or that he has no interest...whatever it is. It's kind of a consuming interest of mine—not that I believe everything I read—but I find it wonderful source material for ideas—particularly Colin Wilson's books.

STEVE SPIGNESI: What else have you been reading?

J. N. WILLIAMSON: If you haven't read Dan Simmons' *The Song of Kali,* do yourself a favor. It's a wonderful book.

STEVE SPIGNESI: I'll make a point of it. [NOTE: I have since read *Kali.* J.N. was right. Read it. It's an experience.]

J. N. WILLIAMSON: In a way, I feel a sort of sympathy for Dan. It's as if Steve had written *The Shining* or *'Salem's Lot* first, and then had to wonder, "God, what do I do for an encore?" That's what I'm trying to say about Simmons and his *Song of Kali.* Let me tell you how I heard of the book. I like to boost other writers when they aren't terribly well-known.

I was putting my *How To* together and the first time I heard of *Song of Kali* was when Harlan Ellison called me to tell me a bunch of his favorite stories and novels and said, "Williamson, run out right now and buy and read *Song of Kali* by Dan Simmons. You're gonna love it."

And the reason he put it that way was that he was on my answering machine. I finally realized dimly in my room that that voice yelling at me on the machine was Harlan Ellison, but by the time I got there he was gone. So, I hung up the phone and about another minute or two passed and then Dean Koontz called. And he said "Have you heard of *The Song of Kali* by Dan Simmons?" I said, "What *is* this!?"

So, then I exchanged letters with F. Paul Wilson, who wrote one of my, I guess, three or four all-time favorite horror novels, *The Keep.* And Paul said, "You have got to read *The Song of Kali.*" And I said, "My God...this is unheard of."

I mean, this was high praise. And of course *Song of Kali* did win the World Fantasy Award for Best Novel in 1986. When I finally started reading it, I couldn't put it down.

> **"Stephen King is a 'noticer.' He has an eye for detail that's expressed in writing that he reads. And these details—both the names of products and how they're packaged and marketed—seem to stick with him....King sees the artifacts of his time clearly and they're important to him at some unconscious level, I believe, the way they are to those who make and market them. So, when he writes about them, we see them very clearly."**

STEVE SPIGNESI: Before we call it quits, do you have any last thoughts about Stephen King and his work? Is there anything else you want to say? That Martian is still waiting!

J. N. WILLIAMSON: Yes, there is. Stephen King is a "noticer." He has an eye for detail that's expressed in writing that he reads. And these details —both the names of products and how they're packaged and marketed—seem to stick with him. Many admirers of his have tried to imitate this facility, but it doesn't work because it isn't necessarily natural to them.

King sees the artifacts of his time clearly and they're important to him at some unconscious level, I believe, the way they are to those who make and market them. So, when he writes about them, we see them very clearly.

Last night I was reading a book containing some comments about writers, and it was said that most writers want to reform and to improve the world. And I believe Steve has used what might be seen as an apparent lack as a strength, and that where he does want reforms, they're the ordinary and common desires of his readers—and they're founded on fear.

> **"From King's work, I have the impression that he was an outsider, too, but that he either hasn't gotten around to criticizing those forces that made him that way, or that he has done whatever he could to make himself accepted, or at least acceptable."**

Let me explain this. I believe that most creative people are outsiders and tend to resent it, brood about what makes them different, and find fault in everything and everybody but themselves. From King's work, I have the impression that he was an outsider, too, but that he either hasn't gotten around to criticizing those forces that made him that way, or that he has done whatever he could to make himself accepted, or at least acceptable.

If this is right, it seems to me to mean that he tried living in the middle-class world of the American sixties and seventies, and that he tried to become accepted by other young people who saw cars as power symbols, loved rock music almost indiscriminately, feared the existence of nuclear weapons more than they did God or evil, and truly and always put peer acceptances and the friendship of the "in" group above acceptances by their superiors within their own individual fields. Or even, it appears, the standards by which their predecessors were judged. And to that degree only, perhaps Stephen can be seen as a rebel.

But, otherwise, basically he seems to me to have become a part of an in group that he's very, very comfortable with. This reverts to what I was saying earlier about the idea that he really doesn't seem to have any desire to have this mantle of leadership and power thrust on him, and I don't see why he should, if he doesn't want it.

STEVE SPIGNESI: Jerry, thanks for sharing your thoughts on Stephen King. Your time—and your work—is much appreciated.

J.N. WILLIAMSON: Glad I could help. In its own way, I think your book is essential. ❏

PRESENTING STEPHEN KING
An Interview with James Van Hise,
editor of *Midnight Graffiti* magazine

James Van Hise has been in the dark fantasy and comics publishing business for many years. He began the "Enterprise Incidents" series, conceptualized and wrote the special edition *Enterprise Incidents Presents Stephen King*, the *Illustrated Guide to The Masters of the Macabre*, and is currently (with Jessie Horsting) the editor of *Midnight Graffiti* magazine.

James was one of the first people I interviewed for *The Shape Under the Sheet*, and I found him to be very helpful. Thanks to him, I was able to get in touch with Steve Fiorilla, the artist who did the original *Enterprise Incidents* "Staircase O' Monsters" cover illustration and obtain the rights to reprint the drawing in this volume. [NOTE: The drawing appears in the *Creepshow* section of the published works concordance in Part V.]

Also, *Midnight Graffiti* was one of the first publications to publish an excerpt from *The Shape Under the Sheet* ("The Unwritten King," *MG*#3, Spring 1989), and for that kindness I am very grateful to both Jim and Jessie. (*Midnight Graffiti* #3, still available for $8.50 from *Midnight Graffiti*, can be obtained from the address given below.)

I heartily recommend finding a copy of *Enterprise Incidents Presents Stephen King*, as well as Jim's *Illustrated Guide to the Masters of the Macabre*, which not only updates *Enterprise Incidents*, but also comprehensively covers Clive Barker's work. Also not to be missed is Jim and Jessie's latest venture, *Midnight Graffiti* magazine. For *Enterprise Incidents*, try the usual dealers, and for back issues of (and subscriptions to) *Midnight Graffiti*, as well as copies of *The Illustrated Guide to the Masters of the Macabre* ($14.95), write to:

> *Midnight Graffiti*
> 13101 Sudan Road
> Poway, California, 92064

Now stop listening to me and listen to Mr. Van Hise.

Sweet dreams! —**sjs**

PRESENTING STEPHEN KING
An Interview with James Van Hise

STEVE SPIGNESI: Where did the idea for a "Stephen King" magazine come from?

JAMES VAN HISE: At the time, no one had done any kind of overview like that. Now there's volumes and volumes of them, most of which consist of people retreading the same ground over and over. But, at the time, no one had done anything like *Enterprise Incidents*, and I really wanted to do it. I suggested it to Hal Schuster, and he agreed it would be a good idea. Hal's the one who put the "Enterprise Incidents" title on it when he published it just as some sort of odd marketing tool whose reason and logic still defy me. I was just going to call it "The Stephen King Review," but it ended up as part of the "Enterprise" series. It took me a few months to do all the writing and pull it all together.

STEVE SPIGNESI: Where'd the artwork come from?

JAMES VAN HISE: A lot of the artwork in there I specifically solicited for that book. There are a lot of drawings based on King's stories, and there were a couple of things that already existed that I thought would be interesting to use.

STEVE SPIGNESI: As part of your research for the magazine, did you track down all the stories in their original appearances, specifically the (then-uncollected) *Skeleton Crew* stuff?

JAMES VAN HISE: Yes. I had read almost all of them already, as they were published. The only ones I had to track down, which of course had never been reprinted, were "The Glass Floor," and "I Was a Teenage Grave Robber."

STEVE SPIGNESI: By using the "Enterprise Incidents" title, were you and Hal suggesting that this was part of that series, even though it had nothing to do with the other titles in the series?

JAMES VAN HISE: At the time, Hal was publishing "Enterprise Incidents" monthly, it was on the national newsstands, and so he was just tying into something which was already existing just so the dealers wouldn't overlook it. He was more in the comic fandom distribution market, and he wasn't sure whether a lot of people in comics read Stephen King. I told him, well, yes, they do. He wasn't sure, but it turned out that all the dealers who bought it sold out of it real fast.

STEVE SPIGNESI: How many copies were printed?

JAMES VAN HISE: I don't think there were more than 3,000 copies printed.

STEVE SPIGNESI: How many are left?

JAMES VAN HISE: Not even twenty. Hal might have a handful left, but that's about it.

"...anything that has something to do with Stephen King that has anywhere near a quality approach to it is going to remain a collectible because the Stephen King fan can never get enough. Even though King has an incredible amount of fiction out there, they want more."

STEVE SPIGNESI: What are your thoughts on the fact that this is now a collector's item, and that it is selling for sometimes five or six times the cover price? Or more?

JAMES VAN HISE: Well, I've done things in the past that have become collector's items. I was the original publisher of *Enterprise Incidents* and *Enterprise Incidents 1* now goes for about twenty-five dollars. Also, I'm not surprised because anything that has something to do with Stephen King that has anywhere near a quality approach to it is going to remain a collectible because the Stephen King fan can never get enough. Even though King has an incredible amount of fiction out there, they want more.

STEVE SPIGNESI: Did King have any reaction to the magazine at all?

JAMES VAN HISE: No. I did send a copy to his office after it was published, but I never got any specific comment on it or anything.

STEVE SPIGNESI: What are your personal favorite King stories and novels?

JAMES VAN HISE: My favorite novel is *'Salem's Lot;* my favorite stories are "Children of the Corn," and "The Mangler." Also, "The Word Processor of the Gods" is a story I really liked a lot.

STEVE SPIGNESI: What are your thoughts on his more recent stories?

JAMES VAN HISE: I've liked them. I thought "The Night Flier" was pretty interesting. He seems to be trying to move into different areas. If anything, his stories are becoming even *more* modern. He's always done modern horror, but he's also sometimes explored the traditional aspects as well. But he knows what's going on out there and he's not trying to do the same thing over and over again.

STEVE SPIGNESI: Doug Winter told me that some people have expressed to him a shocked sensibility about some of the more graphic scenes in "Night Flier."

JAMES VAN HISE: But King has done *very* graphic things before. If you go back to "The Mangler"—it describes people *caught in machinery.* Of King's early stories, that's one of his most graphic.

STEVE SPIGNESI: That's true, although now it seems as though he's getting more sexually explicit. He always seemed to avoid that area.

JAMES VAN HISE: True. In fact, for a long time he said he wasn't comfortable writing about sex, but

James Van Hise.
Photo courtesy James Van Hise.

The Stephen King special issue of
Midnight Graffiti (Spring 1989).

I think he finally decided it wasn't something he should avoid; rather, I think he's trying to explore it and incorporate it more naturally into his writing.

STEVE SPIGNESI: What are your thoughts on the phenomenon Stephen King has become? He burst on the scene with *Carrie,* and from that point on, it has seemed he can do no wrong.

JAMES VAN HISE: Steve's an overnight success who had been writing for several years before he *became* an overnight success. He became a big success with his novels, but he had been doing short stories for several years before that. His background is that of a struggling writer and he understands what all the other writers are going through. Basically, Steve has achieved what every writer hopes to achieve.

"...King's a nice guy, too. He uses his position to try and help people. He sent 'Rainy Season' to us for *Midnight Graffiti*. He knows very well that a story from him can help a small magazine not just get established, but stay in existence."

My feeling about all this is, gee, a best-selling writer who can write. I think that a lot of best-selling writers tend to do a lot of ephemeral things. If you look back to what the best-sellers were ten, fifteen years ago, none of them are in print anymore. King's stuff remains in print, people collect it, and follow it, and I'm glad to see it happen.

And King's a nice guy, too. He uses his position to try and help people. He sent "Rainy Season" to us for *Midnight Graffiti*. He knows very well that a story from him can help a small magazine not just get established, but stay in existence.

STEVE SPIGNESI: I've interviewed quite a few writers for this book, and no one has ever had a bad word to say about Stephen King. Do you find that?

JAMES VAN HISE: Oh, yeah. There are other writers who had been in the business a long time before they achieved any kind of measure of success, and it kind of made them either reclusive, or it went to their head. Suddenly, after being dirt-poor for twenty-five years of writing, they have money, and they take themselves more seriously than they

ever did before. With King, maybe it's because he came up through different routes. And he also has his family, which helps him keep more of a perspective on things. But everybody's different, and he just seems to be able to handle his success better than many other people tend to.

STEVE SPIGNESI: Tell us about *Midnight Graffiti*.

JAMES VAN HISE: We wanted to do a dark fantasy magazine that would try to do different things from what other magazines were doing.

We wanted to not just deal with what's going on in the genre now, but explore things that other magazines are just not bothering with, like humor. Most other magazines are just very straightforward...it's like they're trying to make people take them seriously. We're willing to take some chances and do different things; explore different facets that other people might not want to touch on.

As you've seen over the past couple of years, each issue of *Midnight Graffiti* is in a different format. For instance, our second issue had three short stories, an excerpt from an unpublished satirical screenplay called *Zombies on Broadway*, excerpts from seven of the stories from Skipp and Spector's *Book of the Dead*, and a portfolio of paintings by John Wayne Gacy (which I found disturbing, dark, and unpalatable.)

STEVE SPIGNESI: Then, *Midnight Graffiti* aims to be the "different" horror magazine on the market?

JAMES VAN HISE: Yes. We're trying to surprise people with each issue. We're trying to come up with stuff that people just wouldn't find somewhere else. We're trying to bring imagination to the whole process of publishing a dark fantasy magazine. We published Steve Boyett's "Emerald City Blues," a story that was rejected elsewhere. We published it uncut. And it got a lot of attention. We've also done a "Stephen King" issue, a "Psychos" issue, and a "Dinosaurs" issue.

STEVE SPIGNESI: I—along with many others— greatly enjoy the magazine, and wish you and Jessie many years of "Happy Publishing!"

JAMES VAN HISE: Thanks.   ❐

ON THE TRAIL OF THE BOOGEYMAN
An Interview With Stanley Wiater

Stan Wiater collects skulls.

He says they're all plastic...but I'm not sure I believe him.

I once saw a worm crawl out of the eye socket of a "plastic" skull he keeps on top of his word processor.

I first met Stan through my friend Jerry (J.N.) Williamson. Jerry recommended that I talk to Stan for *The Shape Under the Sheet* because of Stan's record of having interviewed Stephen King more times than any other journalist. Jerry also made mention of the fact that Stan was a very bright guy, and that I would probably enjoy speaking with him.

Jerry was right.

Stan "The Man" Wiater (pronounced wee-ott'-er) is my kind of guy. He's incredibly well-read, and, for the past several years, has made his living as a freelance writer.

Stan and I did a lengthy telephone interview in early 1988 for this volume, and then kept up a somewhat irregular correspondence by mail and on the phone. We finally met in the summer of 1989 at NECON IX at Roger Williams College in Bristol, Rhode Island. Stan was toastmaster, and, for the first time, I got to see The Man in his element.

Well, like I told him...he's missed his calling.

Forget all this horror stuff.

Stan should be in stand-up.

Stan was superb throughout the weekend. One particular panel I attended consisted of Lucius Shepard, Chet Williamson, and Stan, and was billed as a Guest of Honor dialogue. It was an informative experience and I learned a lot by watching Stan apply his very proficient interviewing skills to a three-man dialogue format. Stan was even able to intersperse the talking with a few very dry, deadpan one-liners that had us laughing one moment, and then immediately shutting up so we could hear the writers talk about their craft.

Stan also writes fiction, and he graciously (and generously) allowed me to reprint his short story "The Toucher" in *The Shape Under the Sheet*. "The Toucher" was chosen by Stephen King as the winning entry in the *Boston Phoenix* Short Story Competition in 1980. His other fiction work includes the Stephen King pastiche "The Man Who Would Not Be King," which appeared in the June 1986 issue of *Castle Rock*, and the incredible short story "Moist Dreams," one of the more memorable tales from J. N. Williamson's *Masques II* anthology. Stan's stories have also appeared in *Cavalier* magazine (by Nye Willden, the same editor who bought King's early stories!), and the late, great *Twilight Zone*. His infrequent stories are beginning to turn up in more and more anthologies, though as of late he has switched hats and is editing a few anthologies on his own.

Like some kind of twisted Boy Scout, Stan is helpful, courteous, kind, and generous—all while working on shining a light on the dark side of the human psyche. He has been writing about horror for more than fifteen years, in numerous publications. He was a regular contributor to both *Horrorstruck* amd *Twilight Zone*. He is currently a contributing editor to no less than three magazines—*Fangoria*, *New Blood*, and England's *Fear*. Along the way, he has carved out an enviable niche for himself as the premier interviewer in the field. To that end, Stan's most recent contributions are two huge collections of interviews, *Dark Dreamers: Conversations with the Masters of Horror*, and *Dark Visions: Conversations with the Masters of the Horror Film*, both of which were published by Avon. — sjs

Selective Listing of Writings by Stanley Wiater

BOOKS
- *Dark Dreamers* (Avon, 1990)
- *Dark Visions* (Avon, 1991)
- *Night Visions 7* (editor) (Dark Harvest, 1989)

BOOK & ANTHOLOGY APPEARANCES
- *Kingdom of Fear*, edited by Chuck Miller and Tim Underwood.
- *Masques II*, edited by J.N. Williamson.
- *Bare Bones*, edited by Chuck Miller and Tim Underwood.
- *Teenage Mutant Ninja Turtles*, by Eastman and Laird.
- *Reign of Fear*, edited by Don Herron.
- *The Shape Under the Sheet: The Complete Stephen King Encyclopedia*, by Stephen J. Spignesi (A reprinting of "The Toucher," a short story).
- *Feast of Fear*, edited by Tim Underwood and Chuck Miller.
- *Masques III*, edited by J.N. Williamson.

• *Obsessions*, edited by Gary Raisor.
• *Fly In My Eye #2*, edited by Steve Niles.
• *Shriek* (comic book adaptation of "End of the Line").
• *Shriek #2* (comic book adaptation of "The Toucher").
• *Clive Barker's Shadows in Eden*, by Stephen Jones.
• *James Herbert: By Horror Haunted*, by Stephen Jones.

ARTICLES AND INTERVIEWS
ON STEPHEN KING

The Springfield Morning Union
(Springfield, Massachusetts)
1. "Halloween Made for Horror Writers" (10/31/79)
2. An article on Stephen King at the University of Massachusetts (4/2/85)

The Valley Advocate
(Hatfield, Massachusetts)
1. "King's *Shining* – Very Bright" (6/25/80)
2. "Dark Stars Rising" (4/8/81)
3. "Just Your Average Guy" (5/27/81)
4. "Stephen King's *Danse Macabre*" (5/27/81)
5. An article on Stephen King and Peter Straub at the World Fantasy Convention (10/31/84)
6. "The Stephen King Phenomenon" (7/21/86)

Fangoria magazine
1. Issue #6 – "Stephen King & George Romero: Collaboration in Terror" (6/80)
2. Issues #42 & #43 – "Horror Partners: King & Straub" (with Roger Anker) (2/85 & 3/85)

Prevue magazine
1. Issue #64 – "Stephen King: The Maximum Overdrive Interview" (May/July 1986)

Castle Rock: The Stephen King Newsletter
1. June 1986 – "The Man Who Would Not Be King" (short story)
2. October 1986 – "The Toucher" (short story)
3. March 1987 – "The Horror, The Horror"
4. July 1988 – "Reach Out and Touch Some Thing: Blurbs and Stephen King"

Stan is a graduate of the University of Massachusetts with a double major in writing and cinema. He graduated magna cum laude. (I told you this kid was no slouch.) He was a panelist at NECON in 1982, 1983, 1984, 1985, and 1987, and at the World Fantasy Convention in 1985, 1986, and 1987. He has lectured on horror and cinema, and been a guest and occasional on-air host for talk radio.

Stan lives in Massachusetts with his wife, Iris. They recently had their first child.

Here is my talk with Stan "The Man" Wiater. —**sjs**

ON THE TRAIL OF THE BOOGEYMAN
An Interview With Stanley Wiater

STEVE SPIGNESI: Why don't we start out with how you first met Stephen King, and how you got involved with interviewing him?

STANLEY WIATER: That's an easy story. Back in October of 1979, I was writing for a newspaper in Springfield, Massachusetts, called *The Springfield Morning Union*, and I asked them if I could do a story on the World Fantasy Convention that was being held that year in Providence, Rhode Island. Of course, Providence, Rhode Island has absolutely nothing to do with Springfield, Massachusetts, but I convinced them that it was vitally important that I go down there.

It was the second "horror" convention to be held in Providence, Rhode Island, and it was really my first introduction to the whole idea of conventions, at least those that focussed on horror as a specific genre. I had been more familiar with comic book and science fiction conventions.

So, I went down there, showed them my press card, and I was let in by the people who ran the thing, two guys named Bob Booth and Bob Plante, who are now very dear friends.

At the time, Stephen King was there, along with Peter Straub, Ramsey Campbell, and Charles L. Grant. We watched Stephen King participate in a couple of panels, and then, after his last panel for the day was over, I went up to him and said "I'm Stan Wiater from the Springfield newspapers, and I'd like to do an interview with you." He says, "I'm not doing any interviews." I said "Fine." I found out, though, that he was heading towards the bar because he'd been talking all day, so naturally, being a reporter, I followed him there.

King sat down at a table with Peter Straub and George Romero, and Romero's partner and producer Richard Rubenstein. Now, since I'm an extremely *polite* reporter, I sat down with them. King ordered a round of drinks, and I just sat there, but I did take out my tape recorder. I bought myself a drink, and I said, "Well since you're not going to give me an interview, I'll just have to talk to you and let the tape recorder run."

Stephen King and Peter Straub gave me this wonderful look of...shall we say "endearment," and we've been good friends ever since. Basically what I did was sit at the table with them for about two hours with a tape recorder going, talking to all four gentlemen. A very small part of that interview was later published in *Fangoria #6*. All the interviews I've done with King have since been published either in newspaper or magazine form, and were eventually collected in the Underwood-Miller books, *Bare Bones* and *Feast of Fear*. For reasons that would take too long to explain, one of the interviews was published twice in the two Underwood-Miller collections, but never in the mass market editions of *Bare Bones*.

STEVE SPIGNESI: Why don't you fill us in a little bit on some memorable interview moments with King...perhaps some anecdotes that you feel show the "real" Stephen King?

STANLEY WIATER: I think the situation with that first interview reveals a lot about King. Instead of blowing me off or throwing me out like anybody could—and should—have done, he was courteous enough—after we started our conversation—to realize that I was a fan and not just an obnoxious reporter. Sometimes I have to be agressive as a reporter to get my story, but after sitting with them for just fifteen minutes or so, both King and Straub realized that I'd read all their books, I'd seen all of Romero's films, and their whole attitude changed.

STEVE SPIGNESI: What do your remember about King's appearance? Was he bearded? Was he in a shirt and tie? Or was he "dressing down" even back then?

STANLEY WIATER: King was as impeccably dressed as he always is: he had on bluejeans and a sportcoat. He always wears a sportcoat to social functions. He was also wearing a motorcycle t-shirt that I believe said "Number One." And, of course, that was because this convention took place on the same weekend that his novel *The Dead Zone* had gone to Number One on the *New York Times* bestseller list. That was his first Number One bestseller.

STEVE SPIGNESI: What is your impression of King's feelings about book collecting, limited editions, and the sometimes shameless exploitation of his name?

STANLEY WIATER: I remember that in the course of our discussion that day I had mentioned that his first novel *Carrie,* which was supposedly already out of print, was being sold for fifty dollars a copy in the dealers' room. This upset King then as it still does now. He's always very upset at his books being treated like they were platinum or gold commodities.

After I mentioned this, he told me that *Carrie* was still in print—even in 1979. So, I had a friend who worked in a bookstore order three copies of the book from the publisher, just to see if it was in print. Of course, we know a book in print does not necessarily make it a first edition, but I got three copies back from the Doubleday warehouse and they were all first editions for the grand sum of $5.95 apiece. So, even then, King was being "exploited." You could buy one of Peter Straub's books for the cover price, but *Carrie,* and of course *'Salem's Lot* which was soon to follow, were both going to be—by King's perspective—outrageously overpriced.

STEVE SPIGNESI: I love the inscription King wrote on a first edition of *The Shining* he gave to Doug Winter: "Doug—Here's a True Fact collectors don't seem to know—it's the same story even if you print it on a shopping bag..."

STANLEY WIATER: That's right. And I've used that line in articles of my own—the words *are* still the same whether they're printed on a shopping bag, or printed in blood or gold ink. The words don't change any. He really can't believe that people pay the prices they do for his books.

Stephen King does have his own private publishing company, Philtrum Press, but that's simply a man who has the money wanting to create an artistic product, a beautiful product. We all know that books can be beautiful things. Donald M. Grant's books are a good example of that. But King still feels that people should not pay the prices the dealers charge. He really can't see anyone paying, say, a thousand dollars for a first edition of *'Salem's Lot,* when they can go out and buy the paperback for $2.95.

STEVE SPIGNESI: I can understand King's aversion to that kind of inflation, but it might be an unavoidable "by-product" of his own success. What are your thoughts on the fact that supply and demand are nowhere more prevalent than in rare King things? I mean, if King's books are produced in limited quantity—"X"—and there are a certain number of people—"Y"—that want them, and "Y" is greater than "X," then price is going to go up. That's just cause and effect. That's business.

STANLEY WIATER: Yeah, but I think King legitimately makes an effort to make all of his work—except for the very minor stuff—available in millions of easily-affordable copies. It's like the Richard Bachman stuff. He had a reason for being Richard Bachman, so therefore there were "Richard Bachman" novels. But did people go crazy about them? No, they didn't go crazy about them until they knew it was Stephen King.

Stanley Wiater.
Photo courtesy Iris Wiater.

Likewise, *The Plant.* I think he considers *The Plant* basically a gift and not a commercial writing. With *The Eyes of the Dragon,* he did a limited edition for his own "amusement," so to speak, and then sold it to Viking so there could be a million copies available to his fans. And it's the same thing with *The Dark Tower.* He did that book as sort of a favor to Donald M. Grant, whom he admired for years. Donald had asked him if he could have something that no one else had, and King said sure, you can have this, but at the same time, it was always in the back of King's head that eventually millions of people were going to see the *Dark Tower* books. And of course, *The Dark Tower* was published worldwide in a trade paperback series, so it's not like the fans could never see it.

Now, admittedly the average fan may have to wait a couple of years for some of this stuff as compared to the so-called "hardcore" collectors, but the vast amount of King's fans can't really miss something that they're not really aware of. I think only the hardcore fans are the ones really going for the rare King materials. *The Dark Tower* is the exception because, of course, he or his

publisher listed it on the "Other Works by Stephen King" page in one of his mainstream books, and then of course the whole world knew about it.

STEVE SPIGNESI: Being in the field, I know you talk to a lot of King fans on a fairly regular basis. What do they want to know? What do they ask you about?

STANLEY WIATER: Well, it's the old story: What is King really like? I subscribed to, and wrote for, *Castle Rock,* and I read the so-called "fan" articles and it kind of boggled my mind that people seemed to worship the ground he walks on. Now, this isn't unique to King, of course. There are people who worship Chuck Norris and Michael Jackson. A celebrity's a celebrity.

I know that King didn't plan to be a celebrity. I've asked him about this, and he says he never planned to be. He feels as though you can't control your own life. The fans want to know literally *everything.* Does he breathe, does he fart, does he burp, does he put on his pants one leg at a time, and of course he does all those things. He is about as normal and regular as you can imagine.

How many celebrity writers can you name? There are very few. King purposely makes a point of not getting carried away by the idea of being a celebrity. He is very sure of himself, very confident in his abilities as a writer, and he sees the celebrity as an unnatural by-product of being a successful writer.

But in terms of people asking what is he really like—if he wasn't a world-famous writer, you wouldn't think he was anybody. If you saw him on the street, you'd think, well, there's a guy who's truck has broken down. Or there's a guy who should be sweeping the floors of a high school. I mean, he's very unassuming.

STEVE SPIGNESI: How so?

STANLEY WIATER: He doesn't wear thousand dollar suits, he doesn't wear a Rolex watch. I remember at one convention he had bought a twenty-five-dollar pen to sign autographs with, and the thing wasn't working right so he ended up using a ninety-eight-cent Bic to sign all the books. Whatever works for him is what works.

His only extravagance that I'm aware of— outside of the fact that he has two beautiful houses in Maine—is a couple of Mercedes-Benzes he bought back, I'd say, about 1980 or '81. And yet when he came to the NECON Horror Convention in '82, he couldn't park one of them properly. NECON's held every year on the Roger Williams College campus in Bristol, Rhode Island. Steve came to it one summer to sign the so-called *limited,* limited editions of *The Dark Tower* for Don Grant, and he just drove there in one of his new Mercedes. I remember he was trying to park it between two cars and couldn't do it, so he ended up parking it up over the curb. And he just left it there. He was like, "It's just a car." Other people were saying my God, that's a fifty-thousand-dollar automobile. King's attitude was, well, I got it parked, that's all that counts. And he left it there. If memory serves, I was bold enough to ask why he bought such a car in the first place, and King's answer was something to the effect that he just wanted a car that was known to be dependable, and would start on cold mornings.

STEVE SPIGNESI: He *is* very unassuming. One of the most memorable interviews with King I've ever heard was the one with Larry King in April 1986. He was on TV first, and then he did the two-hour Larry King radio show.

STANLEY WIATER: Yes, I saw and heard both. King was really "on" that night, and very much himself.

STEVE SPIGNESI: I was really impressed with just how natural, relaxed, and laid-back he was. He was getting calls from fans who were, as you say, worshipping the ground he walked on. And his obviously sincere attitude was "I am a regular guy." Do you think he has to work at that?

STANLEY WIATER: I think at this point he does, yeah. He can do pretty much whatever he wants. He's very rich. Estimates of his worth run between thirty and fifty million dollars because of all the movies sales, and I'm sure if there were Stephen King dolls, he could make a couple of million off of those, too.

But I think what he really works on is the fact that it happened so quickly. If people go back to his history, and look up the articles he has written about his life, or turn to Doug Winter's *Art of Darkness,* they'll see that before *Carrie* hit, he was living in a trailer, teaching at a school, and then working at a laundromat at night to make ends meet. He and Tabitha had a car that was just about ready to die, and they had no phone because they couldn't afford one, and then he went from that to selling the paperback rights to *Carrie* for $400,000.

This all happened in the early seventies, so it's not like King has to go back to his very early youth to remember how rough he had it. For most people, a decade is nothing. I can think back a decade easily.

I think that King always has in the back of his mind that he's a professional *working* writer. Most of my dealings with King have been as a fellow professional—either as a a reporter interviewing a writer, or as a fellow horror writer in a social setting.

STEVE SPIGNESI: What is your perception of your relationship with King?

STANLEY WIATER: King has always dealt with me either as a member of the press, or just as a fellow writer. It's much more professional a relationship than personal, though he's never been less than kind or friendly. At the conventions, which sadly he no longer attends, when we're all sitting around drinking, we will invariably make Stephen King pay for the drinks. Or we'll make him go get the pitcher of beer because we know King's good for it.

He never puts on airs. We never sense that he's thinking, "I outsell every one of you sitting at this table." His attitude is always "You're a good writer, I'm a good writer, and we're all writers." And I suppose it would be the same if there were a bunch of plastic surgeons sitting at that table. When you're together with your peers, you don't talk about how many plastic surgery jobs you do, or how much you get paid for a job. King never does that.

"Stephen King likes to wear bluejeans, and t-shirts, and work shoes—shit-kickers as we call 'em —and he likes to drink his Budweiser out of a can, and he likes to see slimy, grade Z movies, and put his feet up on the chair like anybody else."

STEVE SPIGNESI: You know, R.C. Matheson told me that he thinks that King would be the kind of guy that in high school would put cherry bombs in the cheerleaders' lockers, blow them up and go, "Yeah, all right!"

STANLEY WIATER: Oh, definitely. Like all of us, there's a vulgar side to King that you never see.. King is very earthy, and that "quality" is just part of his natural ability. When I compare him to a truckdriver or a janitor, it's not to denigrate either position, it's simply to say that a truckdriver uses language in a certain way, and it's perfectly acceptable, and King is exactly that way.

He doesn't put on any pretensions. Believe me, if Stephen King wanted to be pretentious, he could be the most pretentious fop in the world. He is, after all, a former English teacher, and he possesses an incredible intelligence and command of the English language.

But Stephen King likes to wear bluejeans, and t-shirts, and work shoes—shit-kickers as we call 'em—and he likes to drink his Budweiser out of a can, and he likes to see slimy, grade Z movies, and put his feet up on the chair like anybody else.

STEVE SPIGNESI: I think you're right about King's amazing intelligence. Some of the references in his novels are to subjects that show an obvious wide-ranging knowledge of a great many things, including mathematics, chemistry, and even ornithology. And speaking of his novels, what would you pick as your favorite King novel? Let's break the question into two parts. What's your *favorite* King novel, and do you think it's also his best?

STANLEY WIATER: That's well put, because people are able to do that with King's work.

My favorite is *The Shining,* because of all his works, that is the one that literally scared me. I think we can count on one hand the stories or novels or movies that have physically scared us. And *The Shining* did that for me, and, of course, as a horror writer, and a horror fan, that is as good as sex. You say, "My God, I've just had an orgasm." The French call it "frisson," or the act of sheer fright. To get that from a printed page, in a lighted room, is just fantastic.

For the best written, I think that award must go to *The Dead Zone.* Because it's just basically a one-character novel, for it to work, you really have to have total confidence that the writer is going to make this character 110% believeable all the way throughout the novel. There are no sidebars or side plots to go with: You just have Johnny Smith for the whole length of the book. And I think it succeeds brilliantly. You're completely enraptured in that total world vision. I think *The Dead Zone* is technically his best work to date. *The Shining* will always be my favorite, though, because I'll always remember reading the chapter where Danny goes into the bathroom and finds what's in the bathtub. That's such a wonderful moment in literary history.

STEVE SPIGNESI: King is on record, I believe, as saying that the bathtub scene in *The Shining* and the blowtorch scene in *Misery* were the only two scenes *that scared him* as he was writing them.

Had you heard that?

STANLEY WIATER: It's possible. I know he had problems with *Pet Sematary.* When I interviewed him in 1979, I believe I was the first print reporter to ask King, "Have you ever written anything that has scared you or that you found too scary to publish?" And that's when he mentioned *Pet Sematary.* At that point, he had literally just finished the manuscript a few months before, and the only two people who had seen it were his wife and Peter Straub. So, that's another possibility right there.

STEVE SPIGNESI: How about King's shorter works. What are your favorite short stories, and what do you think are his most technically proficient short stories?

STANLEY WIATER: One of my personal favorites is "The Man Who Loved Flowers." I asked him about that one. I said, "Why do you prefer to write supernatural short stories over psychological stories?," because "Flowers" is so well done. I told him that I really enjoyed the dark psychological element and change in that story. We just have a man who, we ultimately discover, is deranged. He told me that that he found it easier to have a supernatural story work for him rather than focus strictly on psychological horror. He mentioned Straub's *Shadowland* at the time. I should mention that most of my interviews with King were also conducted simultaneously with Peter Straub. I always like to get the sparks going between these two writers.

King mentioned a scene in *Shadowland* that was set in the boy's school where one of the kids levitates a pencil out of boredom. He's just sitting there in class and he levitates a pencil in front of him. And he said, "That's what I like. I love the idea of creating the impossible, and not having any restraints."

So, that was his rationale for why he didn't really go for the psychological short stories. So, that story always stands out in my mind. "Nona" is another one, because again, my personal interests in horror have a tendency towards the psychological and when King goes into that level, I just have a personal preference towards it.

STEVE SPIGNESI: "Nona" is R.C. Matheson's favorite King short story.

STANLEY WIATER: Yeah. There are levels to that story that keep coming back to me.

STEVE SPIGNESI: What are your thoughts on the film versions of King's stuff? Successes, failures?

"King saw it [the film 'Creepshow'] that day for probably the fiftieth time, and he and I walked back to the hotel after the showing. We were discussing the film and other matters, and he asked me what I thought of his part. I told him not to give up his day job."

STANLEY WIATER: In 1982 the World Fantasy Convention was held in your hometown New Haven, Connecticut. Stephen King had arranged to have a private showing of "Creepshow" at a nearby theater.

Of course, "Creepshow" is most humorous when you're with five hundred other horror and fantasy fans, rather than with a mainstream audience. King saw it that day for probably the fiftieth time, and he and I walked back to the hotel after the showing. We were discussing the film and other matters, and he asked me what I thought of his part. I told him not to give up his day job.

STEVE SPIGNESI: Do you think there are films that are going to be remembered ten years from now, other than by hardcore Stephen King fans?

STANLEY WIATER: "The Dead Zone" will probably be remembered. David Cronenberg did a wonderful job. I think he really captured the essence of the novel very well.

"The Shining" is going to be remembered simply because it's Stanley Kubrick. I think if it was any other director's vision behind it, the film would probably already be forgotten. But because Kubrick has been recognized—and I think rightfully so—as a cinematic genius, people are always going to go back and refer to that particular adaptation. Those two are the only ones that I see right now as really being important King adaptations. I know King is very fond of "Cujo," but I've never been fond of it myself, so it's hard for me to see where he finds the greatness in that particular work.

STEVE SPIGNESI: A lot of critics that I've read look at De Palma's "Carrie" as one of the more successful translations from book to film. What do you think?

STANLEY WIATER: It works very well. I know King was very happy with it. A lot of that has to do with Sissy Spacek. Again, it's a simple film, in terms of the plot. Brian De Palma tries to bring more to it than there is, but again there are different ways of looking at it. Is it faithful to King's vision? Yes. Is it a great film? It's not *that* great a film, but for anyone who watches horror films, the biggest flaw of 99% of them is not the special effects, of course, it's the *acting*. Usually the acting is abominable. And if you look at "Carrie," "The Shining," and "The Dead Zone," you're talking about films that have acting equal to any other so-called great mainstream film like "Terms of Endearment" or something along those lines. What makes it successful is that you believe the actors believe their characters, and therefore you can believe the film.

STEVE SPIGNESI: *Christine* has always been a personal favorite of mine. I really enjoyed the film version. What do you think of it?

STANLEY WIATER: I wasn't fond of the book, and I had trouble with the film. The film was very faithful to the book, but again we're talking apples and oranges. It's very difficult. I can see someone liking the film and then not liking the book after they've gone to the book from seeing the film. But having always read the book first, I did not think much of *Christine* as a novel, so therefore, I did not think much of the film. But, in defense, it *is* faithful to King's vision. And for King fans I think that's the important thing.

STEVE SPIGNESI: What didn't you like about *Christine*?

STANLEY WIATER: Well, basically, just the premise. I just couldn't buy the premise of a haunted car. That's all. I thought there was a nice little short story in there—a 5,000-word short story about a haunted car. But to have a full novel, and then to have a full-blown film wrapped around it, it just didn't reach me.

STEVE SPIGNESI: Tell us about "The Toucher."

STANLEY WIATER: Stephen King picked my story "The Toucher" as the First Place winner of the *Boston Phoenix* Short Story Competition in 1980. "The Toucher" was the first short story I ever sold, and the first I had ever had published professionally, not counting a few small press things in high school. I had seen the ad for the Competition in *The Boston Phoenix*, entered the story—which had been rejected by everyone else, by the way—and I won. Stephanie Leonard later reprinted the story in the October 1986 issue of *Castle Rock*. Stephen King wrote me a letter dated April 13, 1980, informing me that I won. [NOTE: The letter is reproduced below. —**sjs**]

721

Dear Mr. Wiater,

I am pleased to tell you that I have picked your story "The Toucher" as the winner of the *Boston Phoenix* Short Story Contest. You'll notice that I haven't said "You've won." I'm a cautious bastard. But it is my understanding that I'm the final judge, and so I imagine you have. Just save the celebration until you get notification from the *Boston Phoenix.*

I thought the story was very good, although the West Virginia dialect seemed a little thick in some places. It rang very true in most. The story reminded me a little of the work of Davis Grubb. It is a sort of story that might be published in one of the mystery magazines, if not for the sexual overtones. As you probably know, those magazines are usually favored by blue-haired old ladies, and they are not into sex.

Anyway, congratulations, and please drop me a line if you'd like following the notification by the *Boston Phoenix.*

Sincerely,
Stephen King

I have several letters from King but that, of course, was the first—and in many ways, most important—one. He had forgotten our encounter several months earlier, which is understandable. As I say, even back in '79, the media avalanche was starting to engulf him.

In terms of King's influence on my fiction, that's how I was fated. It's not a thematic thing, it's not a stylistic thing—it's the impetus that for years I'd been trying to sell my fiction, and everybody had been turning it down as too graphic, or not graphic enough, or too sexy, or not sexy enough. And I was saying, geez, am I ever going to be a fiction writer?—which has been, and still is, one of my primary goals.

And then to send out a story to this competition—one of something like five hundred submissions by the way—and to have Stephen King say "You're a talented writer," which he's told me in letters and to my face...well, I don't have to say anything more.

It's as if someone was gonna take a sword and tap me on either shoulder and say "Rise, Sir Stanley. You have slayed the mighty dragon of rejection," and it's all because of Stephen King.

STEVE SPIGNESI: How often do you keep in touch with King?

STANLEY WIATER: About once or twice a year, I'm afraid. I wish I could say it was more, but lately it's just a couple of times a year. I've seen him once or twice a year from '79 up to about '85 or '86. And then he stopped going to the conventions. He no longer goes to the conventions and as you know, he's gotten more and more insulated from the press. He's stopped doing major interviews. He's

pretty well talked-out. So, unfortunately, I can't sit and say I have a running correspondence with King, but I am confident that when the time comes he will be there if I need something. I know I can state without embarrassment that even though I'm presently an unpublished novelist, King has read my novel-length work and been very supportive of my fiction in general. He knows I'm in this for as long as it takes, and respects me all the more for it.

As a writer, King will help you...he knows what it's like to be out there and to be unknown, but this is not to say that he reads everything that comes down the pike. I can only say in my own case that when I got to know King personally he was always there to lend some kind of moral support and I think to this day he still does so.

STEVE SPIGNESI: Any last thoughts? Any little "Stephen King Vignettes" that stick out in your mind?

STANLEY WIATER: Yes, two. One took place at the 1981 World Fantasy Convention in Baltimore, Maryland. My wife and I had arrived from Massachusetts by train at about eleven o'clock at night. The ride was hell on earth, but we both love trains anyway. We got to the hotel about eleven, and I immediately ran into some friends of mine who directed me to Kirby McCauley's party. Kirby goes to the World Fantasy Convention almost every year and always has a private party.

I went to the party, saw King—who had a few drinks in him—and I said, let's go down to the bar. This was Halloween night, by the way. So myself, another reporter—I think it was someone from the *Boston Phoenix,* as a matter of fact—we all went down to the bar with King, and we ordered drinks. As we're listening to the music, we notice that the entire hotel staff is dressed in Halloween costumes—and yet they're hosting the World Fantasy Convention. What's funny about that is that all the men who go to the World Fantasy Convention dress up in suits and ties, and all the women wear dresses.

So, the three of us are sitting there, talking about rock and roll and I remember talking specifically about "96 Tears" by ? and the Mysterians, and what a great rock and roll song that was. King loves rock and roll, and while he's writing he listens to it—loud.

I started talking about Tim Buckley, who is a semi-obscure folk/rock artist of the sixties. King said he felt that you really have to be a writer to appreciate that kind of singer/songwriter. Buckley was kind of like a Tom Rush-Bob Dylanish writer who was reportedly murdered by his manager.

So, at the end of an evening where we have even more and more drinks, King, of course, picks up the tab, as he almost always did in the times that we were together. The waitress came and I'm not sure if he signed his hotel card or a credit card slip, but she saw "Stephen King" and even though she didn't really recognize him, she saw "Stephen King" on the signature and she said "Are you *the* Stephen King?" And he just said, "Yes, I am." You know, very laidback, not bragging at all, as if people come up to me everyday and say "Are you *the* Stanley Wiater?"—as if we all go through that in our lives. But this was back in 1981 and Stephen King was already getting "Are you *the* Stephen King?" in a bar.

For the next story, we'll flash forward to April of '85 when Stephen King came to the University of Massachusetts as part of the Distinguished Visitors Program.

King had no official association with the university, but he has relatives in the nearby town of Pelham, and Pelham is close to Amherst where the University is located, and somehow they got him to go out there.

King wasn't really giving a speech—it was more like an informal series of anecdotes. You couldn't buy tickets for it, but you had to have a ticket to go in.

I was still stringing for the same newspaper, *The Springfield Morning Union,* and I had the assignment to cover his appearance. Of course, his coming to the university made front page news everywhere because by this time he was so famous.

About fourteen hundred people showed up to hear King, and after his talk, he went to a semi-private reception. Now, I had to finish my article on King for a ten o'clock deadline that night. The event got over at 9:30 and I had a ten-mile drive to make it to the nearest newspaper office to use their word processor and modem to send them my story.

But I knew this before I even went there. So, like all good reporters, I wrote my story on King before I even went to the speech. When I got to the reception after, there were about half a dozen people there waiting for King. It wasn't really a public thing, it was mostly for the press and the people who had organized Stephen King's appearance.

I was looking at my watch constantly because I still had to send the story—I still had to press the button at 10:00 to send the story from Northampton, Massachusetts to Springfield, which is about thirty miles away.

Finally, King comes in. I'm not sure if he knew Iris and I were in the audience or not.

We immediately went up to him and told him some good news about Iris and I. He gives me a hug, he gives my wife a hug and a kiss, we say see you later, we gotta go, and we walk out of the room.

And before we go, we turn, and there were about ten people who had come in behind King with their jaws on the floor saying "Who the hell was that?," because King was very affectionate to both of us.

It was unfortunate that we couldn't spend the evening with him because I had to work. But the point I'm making is that there was that instant recognition on his part, and his genuine interest in us and our lives. That's always a great feeling, and we've experienced this at other conventions where there will be hundreds of people around and he'll see me and go out of his way to say hello. Even if we're not doing a formal interview, he'll go out of his way to come and talk to me or my wife.

And that's a great feeling of satisfaction for myself – that I'm not just someone who has "used" King and then I've forgotten him and he's forgotten me.

I like to think of him as a true friend—not just a name on the end of a letter.

So, I really think our friendship continues to this day, at least in the sense that if it wasn't for King's kindness and professionalism towards me, I probably wouldn't have ever come this far on my own. He opened a lot of doors for me, for which I'll always be grateful. It's just very rewarding to keep those emotions going, however infrequent they may be. ❑

STAN WIATER'S "TOP 5"

Novels
1. *THE SHINING*
2. *THE DEAD ZONE*
3. *PET SEMATARY*
4. *MISERY*
5. *THE DARK HALF*

Short Stories
1. "The Man Who Loved Flowers"
2. "Nona"
3. "Apt Pupil"
4. "Survivor Type"
5. "The Mist"

"THE TOUCHER"
by Stanley Wiater

I only reveals this when boys the likes of you starts to getting ideas about girls the likes of me. I know it is popular talk all about that the bigger girls becomes on certain areas of her tops and bottoms, the littler our brains becomes, but that ain't always truth, though sometimes I will declare some of us likes to act that it is.

Which is why I carry this small leather pouch in my ladie's bag whenever I'm none sure about the gentlemanly intentions of my present company.

A good luck charm, you say? You could say that, if you was one to go and believe in luck. I just believes in knowing what there is to knows, and when the time comes, how to rightly use what you knows. No, sir, what's in this pouch used to belong to the Toucher.

Now, you never heard of him, and I don't think any of the menfolk knew him around here—least not by what we called him, as the Toucher. I was a sight lesser of age then, though my kin would say I was always pleasant to rest eyes upon. An I wasn't under-developed under the top of my head back then, neither. I don't deny I'm still developing in some of them other places, from the way I keep pushing through my clothes before I wear them out.

Anyways, when I was a little one, 'bout eleven, twelve years, I was still a mite older than my girl friends, and I don't mean just by calendar reckoning. Even then, I was interested in more than dolls, dressing up frilly, and seeing how many wrapped sweets I could make disappear in a sitting. Don't you laugh, but I actually desired to learn about things when I was small, and enjoyed sitting near the elders and listening to them tell grown-up talk about grown-up matters, and such. I figure they never gave me no mind, sitting so close ear-shot—they probably figured I didn't understand most of the adult talk they was speaking.

Well, some I truly did not—like discussing whether to bring in that electricity stuff on wires—but some I did. The few books and magazines I came across in the attics and sitting rooms helped me a little, but not always much. And what I was learning in the school then couldn't help a blind coalminer stumble. But like I says, I did like to listen; I enjoyed trying to puzzle out the things we little ones was not supposed to be interested in. Or be able to understand right off and then refigure what they really mean.

Anyhows, it was late one summer that the Toucher came into our lives.

That was not his real name, of course not. If I tell you his Christian name, you'd mayhaps have heard of it, it being the same as some of his relations that still live on abouts the vicinity. He was a real person, mark for certain he was, and he had come to this town to visit with these relatives of his.

He was the quiet type, as you might have figured. He didn't have to do anything while he was here, on accounts of he was just supposed to be visiting, and none of us knew where he had comes from or what he did while he was back there. Mayhaps he had had to come here 'cause of things that had gone on before in his home town. He didn't look like no coal digger's son, for certain. But naturally, the grown-ups never told us a thing, one way or the other. And most of us just thought he was another new grown-up, kind of nice looking, kind of quiet, like I says.

It was only after Mary Louise Jennings got hurt by him that we started to call him that name.

I suppose 'hurt' is not exactly the true and proper word, not seeing she was cut up or shot or run over or anything like that kind of hurt. But she running to me near twilight that muddy August day, with her eyes real red and puffy from crying out all her tears, and it was a long long time before she was able to cry again afters, Truth was, she'd been too afraid to go to her folks after it happened, and seeing how her and the other girls kind of looked to me as understanding things they did not, she drew out for me the whole reoccurance of the sad events.

I told her then what I figured had happened to her, and calmed her into not worrying, that certain things had been left untouched so she wouldn't have to go to Doc Fitchatt or the pastor about anything unless she really wanted to. She was still unsure if she should tell her folks what this man had done to her, but I warned her that the man—the Toucher—would go and deny the sad event, and then might be fit to call Mary Louise a liar. And worse things than that. I told her just to keep it to us girls and hope real real hard that such a sad occurance would not reoccur again.

But you know that, except for some finicky weather, things don't change all that much during the long and dry summer days up here. And nights.

Things was quiet for a few weeks, and we had good times about; swimming, camping, going to the dances overseed by chaperones. But you know too, sometimes people don't always choose the chaperones too smartly—the Toucher happened to be one of them that was overseeing the dance held at the school assembly hall. I was home that night with a poison sumac rash I should've had the fair sense not to obtain in the first place, but that was how I myself was not there.

724

Like the Toucher was.

Leaving out the grimy details, it then so happened that Debra Ann Marples was chasing fireflies out back that night when he went to chasing her when nobody was about. And caught her. Considering the indecent condition her lacy Sunday best dress was in when she shows it to me the following morning, I knew then that the Toucher had pleased his hands and fingers a whole lot. His mouth, too, Debra Ann said, who to this day can't let anyone kiss her there.

Debra Ann told me she had fibbed that big raccoon had come startled her, and she'd fallen down and spoilt her dress that way, and her folks had believed this. She knowed too that her family would be severely taken in hurt and embarrassment if they really had refigured the truth, and also because the grown-ups seemed to like the Toucher so much who didn't know what he was really like, that they mightn't not believe the clear truth either. She believed and agreed with me, though, after I told her about Mary Louise that she was still okay deep inside which would for a long time show she had ever been touched like that.

Now sure, I was getting worried myself meanwhiles, having this kind of bad knowledge filling my head and not having anyone, young as or older than me, to let off with some of the pressures I was getting put on me. By then I knews what the Toucher was doing wasn't right or natural, but didn't see how I could tell anyone about it—anyone who could put a halt on his doing it anymore, that is. But he was hurting my friends, that was clear for certain, and I didn't like it at all.

Or him.

So we began to play together more and more often, in the manner that we didn't go around by ourselves alone as much like we used to have done. We never knew when the Toucher would be around, seeing as he didn't have no job or missus or anything that tied him to being someplace for sure at any particular time. He could walk around anywheres, be out at all hours, and was still always grownup respectable, being as we also never saw him at Miss Olivia's sportin' house or near any of the gin mills and saloons. While we was at the age when most folks still looked at us as little girls who were slowly growing up into blossoming women. So we didn't have to act overly respectable and timid-tame either, and could wanders about pretty much where we pleased without anyone worrying where we was or if we was out alone.

So, when Abigal Carathews was out picking wild flowers for her momma's birthday, it was one of those times when she was alone. And when the Toucher just happened to have been trailing her for awhiles—all the way from the main road out to the fields on Old Man Carter's property.

He had her out there in the tall grass for several hours, at least that is how long Abigal said it seemed like when I went to visit at her house after not seeing her outside for a fair number of days. She had told her folks she's gotten ahold of a summer sickness, and since school was out anyways, they hadn't been too upset about her milingering in bed for awhiles in case she was just making it up out of whole cloth, her being unhealthy in the first place.

None of us had had what they nowadays call a 'hygenic education' then, and Abigal, she was ascared of what had happened, but not as ascared as she would've been if she had understood what the Toucher was truly after, but only found relief instead with us young ones. As I says, the reading I did on my own, and the big ears I would grow whenever my folks or other grown-ups thought they was alone, taught me more about such personal things than anybody I'd ever talked to or had told to me. Personal things about girls and boys, so don't think for a silvery moon minute I am unawares why you asked me to walk out all this way just because the band's taking a breather.

Well, we was all getting pretty bad frights by now, and it was decided to let every girl we knew in on what had really happened to Abigal and the others, so that they could be on their guard against the Toucher from now on. They all didn't understand right off what it was they had to be 'fraid of, and a couple of them thought the man was fair looking and kind of nice, and said they didn't understand what they was supposed to be ascared of if they ever found themselves alone with him anyhows.

Trouble there was, I didn't knows enough about regular menfolk to explain what they was like, let alone a man who wasn't at all regular in his womanly desires.

Those who'd been touched now took to carrying knives and razor shaving handles hawked from kitchen drawers and their daddies' dressing tables. Most of the other girls in town did, too, seeing how four of us was awares of what was going on, and we all couldn't be capable of making up such a nasty and terrible tale if some parts of it was not near to true. And we had to tell them the Toucher never went back to the same girl twice, so it wasn't those who had been touched who had to worry, but those who had not.

That summer, our kinfolk never noticed no changes in any of us, but that's the way it is with grown-ups, who just 'bout ignore your living existence until you do something they don't wish to see or hear tell about. But we was afraid, we purely was, and we carried sharp things in our ladie's bags, and in our pants and dress pockets; things that could hurt back if someone came too close with their touching. And we didn't play much out of doors any time, though we had several weeks of playing out of doors weather still due us.

My daddy had been working on the porch of our house during that same time—this was before he got sent overseas to fight—and he had sent me into town to pick up a carton of newfangled roofing nails he had ordered. I would've taken my bike, see, but one of the tires was newly flat, and I hadn't gotten around to fixing it, so when my daddy sent me on the errand, my own two feet was the main source of transportation in getting there.

Now our town has not growed all that much since these events took place, so you don't have to strain your brain too far to imagine how quiet things can get when it's too hot for anyone but a young tyke to be doing business downtown when everyone else is inside drinking beer or catching an extra twenty winks. I remembers it seemed more like a Sunday morning than a Saturday afternoon, is how still and quiet was everything.

Anyways, the Toucher must have been watching before I entered the hardware store, and knowed I would cut through the back alleyways as a shorter route back to the main road and home. Because he was standing there—big as life like they says in the magazines—his grimy smile and hands ready for me just as I reached the deserted lot behind the store.

I'd never seen him so close up before, and at first look he was not nothing scary to look at. Truth to tell, you look a little like him yourself in this moonlight. But anyways, I knew who this man truly was, and I was remembering what he'd done to my friends, so I sure as hell wasn't going to be fooled into letting him get me on the ground so he could do whatever he wanted to my untouched person.

But I had the carton of nails, which was heavy, but not that heavy, sitting inside the paper bag. I don't recollect what told me to to this, but when the Toucher started to bend down and reach for me with those longer fingery hands, I swung the bag of nails as fierce as I could against his face. He went down to the dirt without uttering a word, and I wasn't sure if I had knocked him proper or just stunned him like, so before he could get to his feet again I swung that bag of nails a few more times against the back of his skull just to make for sure. The carton of nails had broken open by now and with the bare nails sticking out all wet and strained, the bag felt heavier by the time I was done, as I recalls.

That was the last and final occasion the Toucher ever bothered any of us, and being it was some summers back, you probably had yet to move here to knows about the big scandal which followed and about all the questions that went unanswered. Unanswered for the grown-ups, that is, who never suspected any of us when it was finally over.

You see, we each got something to remember the Toucher by, me and the girls I got together quick and gathered in that deserted back lot while he was still breathing. We didn't bury him alive, if that's your thinking. None of us are like that, and you're more the fool to think such a thing if you do. But like I says, we all got things from him to remember what he had done to us, before he was finally put away in the ground by the grown-ups.

Which is why I carry this pouch when I foresee my beaus might try something a few beats too fast for my maiden heart.

Take a look inside.

That was one of the things he touched us with that dark, long ago summer. You see now? He ain't going to be touching any girls anywhere anymore with what we let him retain. I got the biggest part 'cause of my being the only one who knew what counted most. I forgets if all the others have kept theirs, but last time I gossiped with Mary Louise, she still had his left thumb. And Debra Ann his tongue...

Copyright © 1980 by Stanley Wiater.
Reprinted by permission of the author.

HIS FATHER'S SON
An Interview with Richard Christian Matheson

In the October 1981 issue of *Twilight Zone* magazine, Richard Matheson, Senior said: "Giving [my son] my name was a mistake on my part. No one should ever name their son after themselves. It's a horrible thing to do to somebody." [Note: See the interview with Richard Matheson, Sr., earlier in this volume.]

But being named Richard Christian Matheson has not hindered this very talented, and extremely affable writer, editor, producer, and soon-to-be director.

Over the years, Matheson has worked for virtually every studio in Los Angeles as an executive story editor, scripting hundreds of episodes for some twenty-plus TV shows, including everything from "The Incredible Hulk," "B.J. and The Bear," and "Simon and Simon," to "The Rockford Files," "Hardcastle and McCormack," and "Hunter." More recently, his focus has shifted away from TV—except for occasional freelance scripting, such as a Steven Spielberg episode for "Amazing Stories"—to writing and producing feature films, and writing horror-fantasy short fiction.

"R.C.," as he is known, called me one March afternoon to tell me he'd be delighted to participate in *The Shape Under the Sheet*. My contact with R.C. had been made through J.N. Williamson, and I was surprised at how promptly he responded to my request for an interview.

I had just finished reading R.C.'s new collection of horror short stories called *Scars and Other Distinguishing Marks* (Scream Press, 1987). *Scars* was of particular interest to me: Stephen King wrote the Introduction to the collection, and in it he said that R.C. was a writer who, while still developing, was an artist to enjoy *now*. That recommendation was good enough for me.

I greatly enjoyed R.C.'s short stories, but I was more interested in one particular piece of nonfiction he had done for J.N. Williamson's *How To Write Tales of Horror, Science Fiction & Fantasy* called "They Laughed When I Howled At the Moon." This piece on the techniques of writing horror bore the unmistakable influence of Stephen King. In fact—as

I mentioned to R.C. during our talk—if there were no byline on the essay, one could easily (and justifiably) claim King had written it.

We talked about King's influence on his own writing, as well as his father's influence on King, and we also discussed specific short-shorts R.C. had written.

Richard Christian Matheson is in his mid-thirties, single ("I just haven't had time to get married," he said, laughingly, "Too many television shows!"), and lives on the West Coast.

He is a charming, literate gentleman, and he's drop-dead good-looking enough to warrant being in front of the camera, as well as behind it.

Here's our talk. —sjs

HIS FATHER'S SON
An Interview with
Richard Christian Matheson

STEVE SPIGNESI: Thanks for taking the time to talk to me, Richard. I'm a great admirer of your new book of short stories *Scars and Other Distinguishing Marks*.

RICHARD CHRISTIAN MATHESON: Thank you. I'm happy to do it. I truly hope I've got a point of view that's somewhat different from what you've been getting. I would assume that many of the people you're talking to about Stephen are saying much of the same stuff. It's interesting when you deal with a writer with the kind of accomplishment and style that Steve has—in a way you're almost wedged into a certain kind of reaction...much of which has been said before. And a lot of the critique has been done by people considerably more articulate than myself. I think Steve has taken a style for himself that is "repetitive" enough or "permanent" enough that anything I would have said about him five years ago, I'd probably still say about him now. So, with all that in mind, let's get started and hope I don't mortify the both of us!

STEVE SPIGNESI: OK. Let's start with a piece of nonfiction that you did. "They Laughed When I Howled At the Moon" was written for J.N. Williamson for his anthology *How To Write Tales of Horror, Fantasy, & Science Fiction*. Frankly, if I didn't know who wrote that piece, I would have said that it might have been written by Stephen King.

RICHARD CHRISTIAN MATHESON: Now that's interesting.

STEVE SPIGNESI: Do you think that your colloquial and very contemporaneous use of language is a result of working in television and films, or has it been primarily influenced by your reading, and if so, by the work of Stephen King in particular?

RICHARD CHRISTIAN MATHESON: I would say it's been influenced by three separate voices. Three separate writers. One of them is Raymond Chandler, who was great at that stuff. I mean, he came up with the most "demented" kind of metaphors, and while I don't know that people really spoke that way, I always hoped that people did, you know? As invented as these characters were, Chandler managed to make them sound somehow real—they sounded natural, and they just jumped out at you.

Another major influence on my writing was Stephen Cannell, who I worked with for about three or four years. Cannell was a big admirer of Chandler's. And Cannell was really the first guy I worked with—certainly in television—who had influenced not so much my plotting style, but my dialogue style. My "people" style. My characters and my approach to them. And it was the same kind of thinking. It was coming up with those strange turns of phrase. It was "let's not kill somebody, let's drop a house on 'em." Those kind-of weird ideas where you realized that you could really play with the situation. It was kind of a pop poetry.

And with Stephen King, to me it's like Springsteen. So much of his stuff to me is like he's riffing. I don't know if Steve's a Chandler person or not, but King's language is real gonzo. He was the first writer in the prose field other than gonzo journalists like John Rechy, Hunter Thompson, Ben Fong-Torres, and P.J. O'Rourke, who brought sort of the rock sensibility to contemporary fiction.

STEVE SPIGNESI: The Rolling Stone School of Journalism.

RICHARD CHRISTIAN MATHESON: Yeah! And he sort of tipped the flashlight in a direction that would allow me my own use of this style.

A lot of my style came from the years that I'd spent in rock and roll as a drummer. And I learned a sort of "idea anarchy" from my dad. And then I learned this kind-of lawless use of language and eccentric references, and also these strange rhythm

> **"Stephen King should have a shoulder strap holding that word processor. It's like he's picking off these strange sort of fahrenheit solos and just zapping, and it's very rock—it's very rock-oriented. So, I got a lot of my playfulness with language from King. He convinced me that you could do it....can we call it 'heavy-metal language?'"**

patterns of rock from King. Stephen King should have a shoulder strap holding that word processor. It's like he's picking off these strange sort of fahrenheit solos and just zapping, and it's very rock—it's very rock-oriented. So, I got a lot of my playfulness with language from King. He convinced me that you could do it. That you could do that...can we call it "heavy-metal language?" I don't know. But that's not fair to Steve either because then he does these great elegant interplays in a paragraph that are very poetic and beautifully written. What makes his writing so extraordinary to me is that he mixes—he mixes this stuff together, like that scene in *The Stand*, where the guy is blowing up the refinery. [NOTE: Book One, Chapter 26 — sjs] That whole description is amazing to me...the way he just kind of weaves that all together. With King, it's like Springsteen and Lovecraft had a child or something.

STEVE SPIGNESI: Your father Richard Matheson was one of the three cardinal influences on King's work – he talks about your dad all the time. And now Stephen King is, admittedly, an influence on your writing. What are your thoughts on the fact that your father has ended up influencing *your* writing "channelled," so to speak, through Stephen King?

RICHARD CHRISTIAN MATHESON: It's strange, isn't it?

STEVE SPIGNESI: Yes, it is.

RICHARD CHRISTIAN MATHESON: Well, I think King took the best of my father, which was a very strong narrative and character kind of "drive," and then he added something which I think my father did less of, which was a much more in-depth search of his characters. And King also did a *lot more* characters. My father tended to orient his stuff toward one guy. When Stephen King is involved in idea formation—that process when he begins to develop story ideas and characters—he calls the character he sees "The I-Guy." And then this I-Guy becomes a bunch of other people as time goes on and he begins to name the characters in the story. I think my father stuck much more with that I-Guy. With King, it was almost like having a teacher that loves F. Scott Fitzgerald showing you things about Fitzgerald that you never saw. And in his case, the way he showed you was through his writing.

Because I knew that my father was an influence, I could see that seminal patchcord to my dad. I'd see my dad in King's writing, and I was very well aware of the dynamic between the two of them. King would send letters to my dad occasionally and say "I'd like you to read my new book." Not that my dad was a present-day mentor, but he had really been a voice that King had paid attention to. And I looked at what King did, and could see the directions my father had kind-of laid down. And I liked it. It appealed to me. Not so much the ideas. I never thought King's ideas were anything different than what was going on out there. I guess a lot of people have discussed all that. I never looked at King's ideas and went "wow." But I always looked at the characters and thought "wow!" So, I guess what I learned from King was characters, and I think had my father approached his fiction with more of a "people" fabric rather than the "individual man" fabric, an "idea" fabric, you probably would have seen work that was a lot like King's.

STEVE SPIGNESI: Let's talk about your favorite King novels.

RICHARD CHRISTIAN MATHESON: *The Stand.*

STEVE SPIGNESI: How about a second choice?

RICHARD CHRISTIAN MATHESON: Probably either *Pet Sematary* or *The Shining.* But to me, Number One is *The Stand.* He makes these enormous ideas very accessible, and he takes, again, these corrosive sort of extortive people, and he just—boom!—you know, there they are sitting right in front of you talking to you right off that page.

STEVE SPIGNESI: It's interesting that your choices are his early stuff.

RICHARD CHRISTIAN MATHESON: Yeah! I like the early stuff. It seems to me that *The Stand*—in a funny sort of a way—and this returns to your question—is like the outgrowth of *I Am Legend.* It's like an outgrowth...with character overlays. And yet, of course, it's totally different, and there's a whole other kind of other "migratory" thing going on, and the whole concept is different, but the feeling to me is very similar. It's as though the world has been strip-mined, and there's almost nothing left, and it's like, what do the few people that have survived do?

STEVE SPIGNESI: What are your favorites among King's shorter pieces?

RICHARD CHRISTIAN MATHESON: My favorite short story is "Nona." I think it's a wonderful story. To me "Nona" is like this "bubbling wound" love story. The logic gets suffocated by obsession, and reason gets burned down. This vulnerable soul, this guy, is skinned alive. And the writing is some of King's best. He makes you see this guy's mind stabbed, and you just see all of his reason and all of his logic running down his temples. And he's been destroyed by a woman who doesn't care. Maybe she doesn't even exist. I don't know. In a funny way I couldn't tell you exactly what's going on in that story.

Richard Christian Matheson.
Photo courtesy Richard Christian Matheson.

STEVE SPIGNESI: I agree. I also think that King's use of imagery is absolutely stunning in this piece. There's a great line from the beginning of the story ("She comes to me across a dark room with a stone floor and I smell dry October roses.") that seems to capture the darkness of the story.

RICHARD CHRISTIAN MATHESON: Interestingly, part of what I like about King's writing is when I know precisely what's going on. But "Nona" is a pretty surrealistic piece. It has this sort of borderline hallucinatory quality to it. There she is. This gentle kiss turns into this horrible illness that overtakes this guy. I love that story. I think it's wonderful.

I was taking a shower this morning, and I got "image-flu." You know, you read too much King, and see too much Cannell, and it just drives you nuts after awhile. I was thinking—in a very simple sense—of an image that really struck me regarding King's fiction in general, and particularly in something like *The Stand* or "Nona." With King, it's like the news sensibly playing on the radio of a car that's burning and overturning. The narrative drive is unrelenting. That's how it strikes me. That the narrative drive is still there. You can still hear "well in New York today, da, da, da, da," and here's the weather..." and meanwhile you've got these bodies that are being, you know...

STEVE SPIGNESI: Yes.

RICHARD CHRISTIAN MATHESON: I don't know why that popped into my mind. I must be using the right kind of soap or something.

STEVE SPIGNESI: How about honorable mentions in King's shorter pieces?

RICHARD CHRISTIAN MATHESON: Well, I like "Survivor Type." "Survivor Type" is more like one of my father's stories. I mean, you got this one guy.

STEVE SPIGNESI: To me, your short story "Conversation Piece" is as viscerally graphic as King's "Survivor Type," if a bit more understated. How gross would you get for a story idea?

RICHARD CHRISTIAN MATHESON: I don't think I would get gross at all. The grossest I ever got was a story called "Goosebumps." To me that story was really beyond what I was comfortable with. I get ideas all the time that I could swing more graphically if I wanted to. And I don't know if it's because I'm getting older—in terms of my taste changing—or if it's because I just don't enjoy that kind of stuff myself, but it doesn't challenge me to do that. To me, it's pretty easy to do that.

Clive [Barker] goes into descriptive passages that are remarkable—you can taste it and smell it and everything. But as wonderful a writer as Clive is, that type of writing just doesn't give me any insight. It's really easy for this kind of fiction to become immature because the images of horror that seem to delight the readers are often the immature images. This can happen in any kind of fiction, but it's easier in horror. It can so easily become immature.

So, what I try to do if I think of an image that I suspect is an immature one is look for a subtler way of achieving the same effect. For instance, imagine that a guy decides to *literally* eat his wife on their wedding night. Well, there's a subtle way to do that. She wakes up, and there's just a little tiny notch on her arm, and there's a pen knife that his best friend gave him for the wedding on the night table, and she looks at the knife, puts the two together, and you end the story on that.

STEVE SPIGNESI: The implications are more horrific than actually seeing the "meal," so to speak.

RICHARD CHRISTIAN MATHESON: Right, whereas somebody else might go with a bite mark, and somebody else might go with a whole arm missing. To me the suggestion of what's gonna happen is much more disturbing.

STEVE SPIGNESI: Why are we more frightened by what we don't see, and why are you more geared towards "cerebral" terrors?

RICHARD CHRISTIAN MATHESON: I don't know why that is. My dad didn't do a whole lot of graphic stuff, if any, and to me [Ray] Bradbury's and my father's restraint appeals to me a lot. In certain cases, they were a little more "reigned in" with their language.

STEVE SPIGNESI: As you know, "Survivor Type" was Stephen King's "unpublishable" story—until he published it himself in *Skeleton Crew*. Do you think King has ever gone too far for the purpose of the story that he's telling?

RICHARD CHRISTIAN MATHESON: No, I don't think so. I don't think a writer can go too far. I think it's just an individual decision. Maybe Clive probably looks at his stuff and thinks "I really went down on this passage—I should have gone more." I'm picking on Clive only because he's sort of the current "target"—much more than King, really. But even Steve may look at his stuff and just say the same thing – that he could have gone farther. But it depends on what you're after. I'm trying to create a reflective surface when it comes to a story. It's like those projection screen systems.

On a good one, you send an image onto the screen at one, and it bounces back at two. So, what *I'm* trying to do is have the story bouncing back at the reader two times louder—*after* they finish the story. And for me, it can be done without all that stuff. But, that's just me. I don't think I can write —what I call at it's worst—"vivi-fiction."

STEVE SPIGNESI: That type of stunningly graphic, visceral writing that a lot of people simply can't stomach.

RICHARD CHRISTIAN MATHESON: Yes. But I don't think King's gone too far, and I don't think Clive's gone too far. And I think that if somebody said, well, R.C. Matheson didn't go far enough—I don't think any of those comments would be valid because you do what you think is right about the story. And that's what makes it your story.

STEVE SPIGNESI: Your father told me he considers your story "Vampire" "incredible." He said, "Who would dare do a story in which each sentence is one word!" But that type of avant-garde approach to fiction can confuse some people. I personally think "Mugger" is brilliant.

RICHARD CHRISTIAN MATHESON: Sometimes I think maybe I went too far in "Mugger."

STEVE SPIGNESI: Really?

RICHARD CHRISTIAN MATHESON: But see, I'm very drawn to the psychological. My whole bent is the psychological, so whenever I stumble onto an idea that has a physical nature to it—like "Conversation Piece"—I prefer to handle it psychologically. Look at my dad's *The Shrinking Man*. It's really a psychological study, you know? It's like a case history on the psychological aspects of what happens to this guy, and in a way, it's like the play *Equus*. As the viewer, you're focusing on a physical peculiarity, and yet the author really doesn't even dwell all that much on the physicality of it. He certainly has to deal with it, but what makes it such a mature piece of work is the psychological nature of it.

It's the same thing with my father's *I Am Legend*. When I look at horror that I like, and that I think is worthwhile, it's because there's a psychological component that is very challenging, and somewhat evocative, and it makes me think. And if the premise happens to be attached to something graphic, then it doesn't bother me. But when it's just graphic—or even when it's just purely subtle and there's nothing psychological there—then I feel like the writer has not turned over any stones I hadn't already been aware of.

STEVE SPIGNESI: Since we're talking about your book, perhaps you could tell how you got Stephen King to write the Foreword to *Scars*?

RICHARD CHRISTIAN MATHESON: I just asked him. And he said sure. At the time, he was busy directing "Maximum Overdrive," the film version of his short story "Trucks."

STEVE SPIGNESI: Yes, I did notice that the Foreword was dated Wilmington, North Carolina, where King directed "Overdrive."

RICHARD CHRISTIAN MATHESON: Right. At the time, he had read quite a bit of my stuff, but hadn't seen the whole book, simply because I didn't have all the stories together yet.

But while I was putting *Scars* together, I was still producing TV and writing my ass off—really turning out scripts like crazy. I really wanted to bulk the book out because with my stuff, you could run fifty stories and the book would be fifty-one pages long! So, I had a length problem to a degree. I had, geez, I don't know, fifteen stories, and I didn't think it really was sufficient to make the book worth doing—even though Scream Press was prepared to do it.

So, I would work on them, then I would send them to him, and so he ended up reading them a bit at a time. And the Foreword's kind of a funny thing because I think it's almost—on some very subtle level—an inside joke because it, too, has a kind of quickness to it. It's almost like a short-short Intro.

STEVE SPIGNESI: That's true. It's quite unlike King's usual Introductions. His Intro to Harlan Ellison's *Stalking the Nightmare,* for instance, runs ten pages in paperback.

RICHARD CHRISTIAN MATHESON: Right. It's almost as though he picked up on the cadence of the stuff, and just said, you know, it would be funny to do that kind of a Foreword. Where as Dennis Etchison's Introduction seemed more on the longish side. I do wonder if King wasn't subconsciously kind of thinking that way.

STEVE SPIGNESI: Either that or he was just so busy.

RICHARD CHRISTIAN MATHESON: You know what? Sometimes I think, Jesus Christ, he was as busy as *I* was. We would exchange these letters that were just, you know, covered with blood. I could see that we were both just hanging on.

STEVE SPIGNESI: Well, he was working on *IT* at the same time.

RICHARD CHRISTIAN MATHESON: That's right, he was.

STEVE SPIGNESI: I read that he was working twelve hours a day directing, and then writing until he fell asleep in the chair. I heard he didn't even have the time to spend the money that was doled out to him every day for expenses, and that by the end of the shoot, he had, literally, thousands of dollars in cash in his pockets.

RICHARD CHRISTIAN MATHESON: I was delighted that he agreed to do it. I had asked him to do it because—in sort of a paraphrase motive to your question—I was interested to see what he would say about the "migration" of an influence from my father to him, and from him to me. He didn't really touch on it, but I thought the idea of presenting the situation where he could say something might appeal to him. But he was real gracious to do it, and I was delighted he took the time because, let's face it, the guy barely has time to take a shower.

STEVE SPIGNESI: Let's talk about your first published effort, "Graduation." It's written in the epistolary form, and in a sense, it's almost a nod to Stephen King's short story "Strawberry Spring." Why did you use the epistolary form as your debut, and, as a corollary to that question, what do you think of King's epistolary novel-in-progress *The Plant*? What are your thoughts on writing in "entry" form?

RICHARD CHRISTIAN MATHESON: I love it. I absolutely love it. King's "Survivor Type" was a journal, and that's one of my favorites of King's shorter pieces. Actually the epistolary form of "Graduation" was a suggestion my father made, because I wrote it when I literally didn't know *anything*. I was seventeen, and I sat down—it's odd that we should be talking about it now on Valentine's Day night—and I just wrote it. [Note: This interview was conducted on Valentine's Day, 1988. —sjs]

I had previously toyed around with all kinds of little story ideas. I loved to just sit in front of my typewriter and sort of "intellectually doodle." But other than comedy sketches I'd written, and the occasional, very bizarre little story that was a page or two long, I'd never really sat down and written something. And I don't know why it popped into my head.

I got about halfway through it—really blazing along for two or three hours—and I showed it to my dad, and he said, "Oh God, you should do the *whole thing* as a correspondence. Do the whole thing

that way." And I said, "You can do that?" And he whispered "You can do anything you want." So, that's what I did. I hadn't realized that you could do that. I didn't realize that you could, date stuff, you know. That you could make it a log.

STEVE SPIGNESI: It hadn't registered yet that you could have fun with it.

RICHARD CHRISTIAN MATHESON: Yeah. I didn't really know that. I should have, because I'd read enough stuff, but I didn't. It's like "Star Trek," you know, like "Stardate"? I suddenly realized that there are different ways you can encapsulate a story approach.

Regarding King's *The Plant*—I thought it worked like a charm. But with King, had he not taken it that way, I think it still would have worked. I don't know exactly what he would have done, but I know how I could have done "Graduation," and it still would have worked. There have been a number of "epistolary" novels that have come out in recent years that I've been aware of. I'm sure there's a rich tradition of them.

STEVE SPIGNESI: As a screenwriter, what are your thoughts on the film adaptations of King's stuff?

RICHARD CHRISTIAN MATHESON: I knew we'd probably get to that. I think they've been very disappointing. Very disappointing. But I think it's not unusual when that happens. The books and stories seem not to translate as powerfully onto the screen. I think it's a malaise common to the film business. I think it's almost impossible to attempt the emotional reconstruction of a novel on a visual and aural medium, and to take that material—which is rich with all these tributaries and nuances and history—and try and get that across when you've only got a hundred twenty-five pages to do it in.

The average script—which is actually a shooting script—is a hundred pages long. And you've got virtually no words on the page at all. So, of fifty pages, let's say seventy percent of it's dialogue, and the other thirty percent is montage, action, so forth. Let's be generous, let's say eighty-five percent is dialogue—and that *is* being generous. A portion of that dialogue is designed merely to entertain—not to be informative. So, look at what you're trying to do with about a seventy percent representation of dialogue.

Dialogue is the clearest and most immediate way you can get characterization across—I mean real rich, complex characterization. The only way you can *really* get it across is by what people say to one another.

And in the case of King, you're trying to take a novel and reduce that—shove it through a funnel —and you can't do it. There's just no way you can do it. That's why the miniseries is sort of the "bastard" novel form in the visual media.

It's possible sometimes to take a smaller idea, a smaller "backdrop," if you will, something with fewer characters... I think some of the adaptations of his short stories have been done pretty well. But even there, something went wrong. Something goes wrong, and I don't know what it is.

The first time I saw "The Shining," I thought it was just awful. But somehow it's worn well, and I like it more and more. I think there's only one film that I really thought turned out well. That was "The Dead Zone" with Christopher Walken.

STEVE SPIGNESI: That's one of my favorites. I've seen it at least a dozen times.

RICHARD CHRISTIAN MATHESON: I liked it a lot. And a lot of it was because of Christopher Walken. They chose an actor—who directed that?

STEVE SPIGNESI: David Cronenberg.

RICHARD CHRISTIAN MATHESON: Right, Cronenberg. Cronenberg and Walken. They made a wise move with the choice of Walken in particular. He has a very textured and "creased" kind-of a process that comes across just on his face. He's really a fine actor, and he gave a much more textured performance, than, say, Nicholson gave in "The Shining."

You began to get some of the quality of King's writing. You began to get to some of it because you look at this guy—forget for the moment what Cronenberg did, which was excellent—but in Walken you have an actor who could give you the richness that King put into the work. I think that that "richness" is usually what gets lost. I think it's just that simple.

You can't take five, six, seven, eight hundred pages of detailed characterization and jam it into a hundred pages. How do you do it? There's just no way. Something's gonna suffer. And with King, so much of the fun is in his characters. Again, I don't think his ideas are anything revolutionary, but I think his characters are superb.

What happens in the film format, is that you have to read a lot into it. And as a person who deals with this stuff everyday, I know that you have to get as many ideas into one line as you possibly can. You've got to get a lot of stories for the amount of space you're given. It's sort of like a highly elongated haiku form. And it's very difficult. I know my father has been asked to adapt many, many

novels and ultimately turned down ninety percent of them because he said, I just can't do them justice. There's just no way to do it.

And while there have been great moments— some radiant moments—in King's films, in general I think he's too fine a novelist to have the films convey that.

STEVE SPIGNESI: I tend to agree.

RICHARD CHRISTIAN MATHESON: I don't mean that as a left-handed compliment either. What I've always hoped, is that *The Stand* would be done as a ten part miniseries. I'll tell you another film that I liked. I liked *'Salem's Lot*, which was done by Tobe Hooper.

"Part of King's whole charisma as a writer—what really hooks you in—is that you kind of relax a little bit, you know? It's like, 'Have a Michelob, and then let me tell ya.'"

STEVE SPIGNESI: He was given four hours for that, which allowed him to be a bit more expansive.

RICHARD CHRISTIAN MATHESON: Tobe's a friend of mine and I spoke with him about that a little bit. I think that he sensed the same thing. It can stretch out a little bit. Part of King's whole charisma as a writer—what really hooks you in— is that you kind of relax a little bit, you know? It's like, "Have a Michelob, and then let me tell ya."

But there's no time to have a Michelob when you're in the theater. You just have to get to it. It's like commando storytelling. You just have to get in and get out. That's why—no joke intended— that's why a guy like Sylvester Stallone makes better films. His films are better. It's because he's saying the least amount, and in a form that really benefits from that.

I was reading an article about Sonny Bono in *Vanity Fair*, and he was talking about Phil Spector, the record producer known for "the Wall of Sound." I guess Bono did backup singing for Phil Spector for awhile—he was one of the "bricks" in the wall of sound. And he was saying that when he was writing songs for Phil Spector, Spector's big phrase was "Is it dumb enough?"

And what he meant by that was, is it gonna hit all the emotions quickly enough? Are people gonna get it fast enough? And that's the whole point with films. And God knows television is even worse, because you've got to structure your story to the commercial so you're tethered by even more restrictions other than just time. You're really stuck.

STEVE SPIGNESI: If you could adapt any Stephen King novel to the screen, what would it be?

RICHARD CHRISTIAN MATHESON: I'd pick *The Stand.*

STEVE SPIGNESI: Do you think you could do a good job on reducing that to something feasible? Would you use a ten part miniseries?

RICHARD CHRISTIAN MATHESON: Yeah, I would not try and do it as a film. You could only take a small aspect of the novel and do it as a feature film. For instance, you could take The Walkin Dude and you could almost do that aspect of the book as a film, but the whole book would require a longer form. The ideas are so resonant, and there's such a selection of characters and ways to go, that to me it would really feel like I was trying to jam an elephant into a coffee cup.

I think it would hurt it, and even using every trick in the book I could think of, it just wouldn't work. The best trick I could think of would be to say to the people making it, "make it longer." Give me more money, give the project more money. I know George Romero has *The Stand,* but I don't know what his plans are. You know, it would be like trying to do *Ulysses* as a half-hour "Growing Pains" episode. (Laughs.)

Believe me, there's no shortage of people in this town who would agree to do it. People who would agree to do anything. They'd just say, "Oh, Stephen King? Yeah!" On the other hand, there are people who would make a similar error in the other direction, too. They would say, "Oh, we got the rights to 'Nona?' Great, let's make it a miniseries."

STEVE SPIGNESI: It's time for your basic "Obligatory Question," Rich. I've been asking everybody this simply to get as broad a range of answers as possible.

RICHARD CHRISTIAN MATHESON: Should Stephen keep the beard or should he shave it?

STEVE SPIGNESI: No, it's not that. It's even more cliched than that!

RICHARD CHRISTIAN MATHESON: OK.

STEVE SPIGNESI: What is Stephen King really like? Gut reaction.

RICHARD CHRISTIAN MATHESON: Irreverent is the first word that comes to my mind, and yet I can't say I really know him. We've really only "side-swiped" over the years. It's funny how you get to know somebody through reading their stuff, you know? My father's personality is not presented in his writing. If you spent your whole life with him, as I have, you'd have a difficult time connecting up the guy with the work.

"...with King—from all the people I know that do spend time with him, and the mutual friends we have—I think that what you see on the page is a lot of what you get. I'm half guessing and yet I sort of half know this to be true. I think that guy is not distancing himself very much from his work."

STEVE SPIGNESI: That's interesting, because when I asked your father what King was really like, he said: "Read his work."

RICHARD CHRISTIAN MATHESON: Well, in some cases, such as my father's, I think it's a mistake to assume a complete knowledge of the writer simply by being very familiar with their work.

I know a couple of real luminaries in pop music. Their work is classic American songwriting in rock and roll. I mean stuff that our children will be talking about. And yet, when you meet these people, in some cases, they're incommunicative, they're insensitive, they're cold, they're judgemental. Anything other than what their art conveys.

And yet with King—from all the people I know that do spend time with him, and the mutual friends we have—I think that what you see on the page is a lot of what you get. I'm half guessing and yet I sort of half know this to be true. I think that guy is not distancing himself very much from his work.

STEVE SPIGNESI: In a sense he is his work?

RICHARD CHRISTIAN MATHESON: Well, in a way. I mean, we're all our work.

STEVE SPIGNESI: Sounds like your short story "Incorporation." (Laughs.)

RICHARD CHRISTIAN MATHESON: (Laughs.) We're all our work, but if you have enough of a technique and a style, you can shroud yourself. It becomes like an extension cord—you can be ten feet from the wall. But I don't think Stephen King uses an extension cord. I think he's the wall and the socket, and that he sticks his finger in when he feels like it.

STEVE SPIGNESI: So, what's your capsule personality blurb for Stephen King?

RICHARD CHRISTIAN MATHESON: My impression of him—and I'm picking up a little bit on what Doug Winter said in his *Art of Darkness*—is that he just seems like a guy you'd hang out with in high school. A guy that would put cherry bombs in the cheerleaders' lockers, and he would be, like, "Yeah!"

So, there's that "high school-type" guy, and yet, in a way, I think the truth is that King is deceptive—as my father is deceptive.

My father doesn't seem like the guy that comes through in his books. My father seems like the Dean of Students. Not that he's a strict personality type. He isn't. But he's very taciturn to a degree, and fairly conservative in his mien. And yet, there again both my dad and Stephen King are fishing out of the same pond that we all do, but it's like they're each using some kind of weird bait, 'cause they both catch some really strange stuff.

So, with King, my feeling again is that the line is closer, that he is that voice that he uses so often. The voice that says "Boy, this is going to blow your mind! Why don't you sit down and hang around for a couple of hours because I've got something now that's just gonna fuckin' make your dick fall off!"

And perhaps it's also a regional effect. I have friends that are from Ireland, and I have friends that are from France, and they are two distinctly different personalities. It seems there is a personality, and a technique of communicating that each country, each region if you will, seems to breed, or seems to cause or influence. So, that may have something to do with it, too.

STEVE SPIGNESI: Let's talk about your short story "Goosebumps." There's a rather bizarre character in the story named Mr. McCauley who keeps sending out a particularly nasty short story. I was wondering if this reference to Kirby McCauley—King's agent for many years—was meant as a tribute, or as a veiled response to the work he does?

RICHARD CHRISTIAN MATHESON: (Laughs.) No, it's a total tribute. You know, he used to be my agent, too.

STEVE SPIGNESI: How did that come about?

RICHARD CHRISTIAN MATHESON: When I first started out, Kirby and I came together quickly, and then I got totally besieged and marooned in television, and I really wasn't able to pursue a novel career. I never really have been able to. This whole direction in my life has just made it damn near impossible.

People ask me why I write short-shorts. And I tell them it's because I've only got like eight minutes a month left to write. I think it's amazing that I don't write Hallmark cards.

Kirby was great. He was supportive, he was unfailingly sensitive, and considerate. I only got to see him when he was out on this coast which, at the time, was quite often. I just thought the world of him. I thought he was a great guy.

STEVE SPIGNESI: Let's talk about the creative process, and how you think King manages to keep generating so much material. Is the creative response to life an escape from, and yet at the same time, a magnification of reality?

RICHARD CHRISTIAN MATHESON: Yes. One of the things about writing short-shorts is that it's the perfect vehicle for capturing—there's that word again—capturing a moment, an attention span, or a thought span. An idea span. It's like a candle. A candle's just going to melt down after an hour or two. So, I try and get it while it's there. At this seminar I did at UCLA, someone asked me, "How do you rewrite?" Do you have any tips for rewriting?" And other than standing in an oil pan to collect my blood and drinking Bactine, I said wait until your mood changes, because with every mood change you go through, you'll see something different in a piece.

"...his output amazes me. And one of the reasons it amazes me is that I'm sure that as a creative guy, he is afflicted by mood changes. And how he governs his output and is able to find that positive conjunction of mood and creation is just fascinating."

STEVE SPIGNESI: I, too, have found that that's very true.

RICHARD CHRISTIAN MATHESON: One of the things I've learned about writing is to know your own mood, and to know which project you want to direct that mood toward. To return to the original subject: Mr. King. Like everybody else, his output amazes me. And one of the reasons it amazes me is that I'm sure that as a creative guy, he is afflicted by mood changes. And how he governs his output and is able to find that positive conjunction of mood and creation is just fascinating.

STEVE SPIGNESI: The way he taps into it.

RICHARD CHRISTIAN MATHESON: Yeah. And doesn't let up. I mean, what does he do if he gets depressed for three days?

STEVE SPIGNESI: I would guess he writes.

RICHARD CHRISTIAN MATHESON: It seems like he just keeps going, but what happens to the writing? Does the writing reflect that? That is to say, does he have some kind of protective shield that allows him to keep moving forward? I don't know. But I know when I'm in the right spirit to write comedy. Or to write horror. Sometimes I'm wrong. Sometimes when I'm in a wonderful mood to write, it's just junk. And other times when I'm terribly dispirited, I do stuff that I think is terrific.

So, even with your understanding of yourself, you can be bewildered by it all. But King does so much, it interests me that he doesn't seem to ever be..."stuck."

I think that when people talk about writer's block, I don't think that it's writer's block at all. I think it's just moodiness. Sometimes a mood can span a month or two. I think that writers tend to be pretty moody people. After all, how could you not be moody if you're sensitized to all these things around you? It's as though you're walking around with fifty satellite dishes surrounding you. And then, as a professional writer, you train yourself to pick up even more stuff—you actually look for it. It's no longer that you're answering the door when it gets there. You're out there with a flashlight looking around for it.

"Nobody writes as much as Stephen King. And the success that he's had, the meteor that he's been sitting on—it's like Mighty Mouse sitting on the end of that rocket. That's Steve King....how does he modulate all this stuff? I don't know, maybe for him writing is how he modulates it."

STEVE SPIGNESI: Yes, Stephen King seems to have never been afflicted with writer's block in his life. Or if he has, he seems to have been able to conquer it.

RICHARD CHRISTIAN MATHESON: How does he deal with that? I know Steve Cannell was running his production company, and also trying to write every day. He was writing three or four hours every morning. But he was writing in a given format. I don't think he was writing from as personal a place. In some cases, he was. He's had ups and downs in his life, and often he wrote about them through his work.

But he wasn't writing as much as King. Nobody writes as much as Stephen King. And the success that he's had, the meteor that he's been sitting on—it's like Mighty Mouse sitting on the end of that rocket. That's Steve King.

And how does he modulate all this stuff? I don't know, maybe for him writing is how he modulates it. Maybe when he stops writing for two or three days, that's when it all catches up with him.

Maybe he's running. Maybe him and that typewriter are a couple of feet ahead of whatever's chasing him. I don't know. But it's a very complicated mindset to be doing what he's doing, and to do it as frequently as he does it. I'm impressed, and I don't know exactly what's going on inside that head of his. And then you add to that the fact that he doesn't have to do it, and then perhaps that's where the answer is. Maybe the ultimate reply to my speculations is that he does it because if he didn't do it, he'd freak.

STEVE SPIGNESI: People are always asking him, "Why do you write so much, and why do you write horror?" And his stock answer to those questions is usually: "What makes you think I have a choice?"

RICHARD CHRISTIAN MATHESON: Yeah, but my parenthetical question to that would be, "Yeah, but Steve, what do you do when you don't feel like writing? I mean, there's gotta be days you don't feel like writing. What do you do when you're in a terrible mood?"

STEVE SPIGNESI: I heard he bakes bread.

RICHARD CHRISTIAN MATHESON: Well, he could probably sell his bread to Bantam. He could probably sell "Stephen King Bread" for fifty dollars a loaf.

But what do you do when you've just had an argument with your wife? What do you do when you think you've made some terrible mistake and fucked up your kid's life by doing something stupid? Do you always, always find yourself able to sit down at the typewriter and in some poised yet explosive way, organize all that angst and tumult, and turn it into this—what's Clive Barker's word? —"frisson?"

I guess he can do it. I know I can write comedy in any frame of mind. It startled me. I don't even know how it works, except that it's some sort of weird subconscious algebra that I know how to do. And I don't just mean set a punchline. I mean I can find ironies and paradoxes and odd sort of comic inferences no matter what my frame of mind. But I'm not doing it as often as King is doing it either. He's turning the stuff out with such volume...it's interesting to me. I find it quite amazing.

And also, a lot of horror writers seem not only sort of traditional, if not parochial in their work, but even in their thinking. But Steve King...he's snapping bra straps while he's writing. He's knocking ashes all over everything.

"There isn't one emotion that he doesn't seem to be able to turn inside out and back out again at will. Whatever it happens to be...greed, or pity, or desperation. He understands all that. It's like he's got some bizarre telescope that he put together up in fucking Bangor out of beer and snow and rock and roll, and he can see the dark side of the moon."

And yet I know he sees all kind of emotional twists and turns. You can see it in his characters. There isn't one emotion that he doesn't seem to be able to turn inside out and back out again at will. Whatever it happens to be...greed, or pity, or desperation. He understands all that. It's like he's got some bizarre telescope that he put together up in fucking Bangor out of beer and snow and rock and roll, and he can see the dark side of the moon.

STEVE SPIGNESI: And then show it to us.

RICHARD CHRISTIAN MATHESON: Right. He can track these weird, senseless patterns of thought.

STEVE SPIGNESI: Why do you think his particular vision is so appealing?

RICHARD CHRISTIAN MATHESON: I can best answer that by telling you a story. People talk about how there's certain writers you can read, and there's certain writers you can't.

People say, "Yeah, I try and read John Barth, and I read a page and I can't get any further. Then there are other writers like Ludlum—I'm making this up—but "Boy I can't stop reading him."

I was reading the *TV Guide* one day. And I was reading this Letter to the Editor. And I'm reading, maybe, one sentence, and I'm going "This is fucking great." One sentence! Then I read the second sentence, and I'm saying to myself, "This is getting even better." And I finish this letter, and I go, "This is really something."

And at the bottom it said: "Stephen King, Bangor, Maine." And I thought to myself, I don't know what this guy's doing, but you can't *not* read him. I mean, even a fucking letter to the *TV Guide*. I'm reading a fucking letter to the *TV Guide* and I'm hooked.

He has a highly magnetic prose style, and yet I don't know exactly what he's doing, because he does many different things. Anybody who has said, "Oh, well Stephen King...it's the MacDonald's approach to prose," well, that's bullshit. That's stupid. That's a very naive overview, as though he's just some clown sitting in Pizza Hut.

STEVE SPIGNESI: That letter was about Elvis and rock and roll.

RICHARD CHRISTIAN MATHESON: Right! And it hooked me. And I don't know what he said. I mean, I don't remember it. But I remember smiling. I remember just going, "Oh, there you go."

STEVE SPIGNESI: Without knowing it was King, right?

RICHARD CHRISTIAN MATHESON: Yeah. Sure. You know what it's like? It's like when you hear a song with a great hook. A couple of years back the English singer Paul Young did a song called "Everytime You Go Away." It had a real hook. I don't know if you like the song or not...

STEVE SPIGNESI: Yeah, I do.

RICHARD CHRISTIAN MATHESON: Well, it was written by Hall & Oates. And it's the same kind of thing. I mean Liza Minelli—who's not my idea of rock and roll—could have done "Every Breath You Take," and it would have been good.

It's like what the Bee Gees used to do. The Bee Gees used to write songs for other people. And again, I'm picking people whose songwriting I responded to. Lennon & McCartney used to write songs for people. And there was something going on. There's some kind of a hook that artists hear, and I don't know where that comes from. I have no idea. I know there are people now who say they can read my stuff and know it's mine. They claim that a certain tendency has turned into a recognizable style. This came as a total shock to me.

STEVE SPIGNESI: No kidding?

RICHARD CHRISTIAN MATHESON: Yeah. And I said to them "I have no idea what you're talking about." And they said, "You never will." So, I guess I'd say that Stephen King has this rhythm you just can't turn away from.

STEVE SPIGNESI: Terrific. Well, we've worked through all my questions and now...

RICHARD CHRISTIAN MATHESON: Now it's time for a song. (Laughs.)

STEVE SPIGNESI: (Laughs.) That'd be nice...perhaps some AC/DC, in honor of Stephen King?

RICHARD CHRISTIAN MATHESON: (Laughs.) I'm glad I could come up with something you could use in your book. It's always amazing to me when I do these interviews, because I think to myself, Jesus Christ, I've got like, half a bowl of small curd here in my mind. And yet you managed to pull it together. You asked some very insightful questions, so I thank you.

STEVE SPIGNESI: Oh, it was my pleasure. It was a great interview, and again, your fiction is terrific. I like the short works, and I just hope you do a lot more.

RICHARD CHRISTIAN MATHESON: Well, thank you. I'm getting a lot of encouragement, and I hope I can find the time to keep doing it. I do have some stories coming out this year in various books, and so there's just cause to keep at it, and I probably will. What I imagine I'll do for the coming year is to link them together, and try and find a novel format for them, but once you get this deep into the short-short form, it's pretty hard to back out. ❐

ONE LIVE GUY
An Interview With Ray Garton

I don't think I'd be overstating the issue if I said that Ray Garton brings a somewhat peculiar personal mythology to his career as a horror writer.

Ray was born and raised a Seventh Day Adventist, a religion that bans, among other things, movies and books.

So, how did Ray end up writing horror novels?

To do so, it was necessary for him to make a complete break from the church, a decision that resulted in him having his tires slashed, having shit put in his car, getting theological obscene phone calls, and even being shot at. (The Adventists do not take well to one of their sheep deciding to stray from the herd. Especially if this sheep decides to dye his wool black, if you know what I mean.)

But Ray has survived this trial by bullshit remarkably centered, and able to not only talk about his problems with the Adventists, but to actually laugh about them.

Here are some things you should know about Ray Garton:

1. Ray is a young man.

While still in his twenties, he has already published four novels, two novelizations, and a bunch of shorter works.

His novels include *Seductions* and *Darklings* (both from Pinnacle Books, a defunct company whose catalog is now owned by Zebra Books), *Live Girls* (Avon), and *Crucifax Autumn* (from Dark Harvest). Ray also did the novelizations of *Invaders from Mars* and *Warlock*. His novella *In the Blood* was in *Night Visions 6*, and his short story "Sinema" was one of the superb contributions to the *Silver Scream* anthology. His tastes run towards the erotic, and much of his work reflects the dark and nasty side of physical/social intercourse. *Warlock*, for instance, is about a male warlock so beloved by Satan that the Dark Lord gave him (as Redferne in *Warlock* described it) "his member." Inside my copy of *Warlock*, Ray put it this way:

"For Steve,
    The tender, heartwarming story of a colonial warlock who walks softly and carries a big, um...stick."

Ray was being discreet. Actually, the warlock does a hell of a lot more with his, um...stick, than carry it!

2. Ray Garton is a nice guy.

I was introduced to him—as I've been introduced to so many other horror notables—by my good friend, Dave Hinchberger.

Ray made my sister Janet's year by talking to her on her birthday. I called my sister at work, put her on hold, called Ray, and then turned the two calls into a transcontinental conference call. You could hear the shriek on Altair-4 when Ray said, "Hi, Janet. This is Ray Garton." Ray said he had fun talking to her, and I personally was very impressed with his generosity with his time.

Ray gave me a lengthy interview for *The Shape Under the Sheet*, and I think you *will* find his thoughts on King significant, enlightening, and interesting. Ray—like R.C. Matheson—is of the first generation to have King as a major influence, unlike writers King's age who have been influenced by the same writers who influenced King. (Such as Bradbury, Bloch, Matheson, et al.) The resulting style and delivery is, as Sara Wood in *Midnight Graffiti* put it, "pure Sam Kinison." Ray hits early, hard, and usually below the belt.

Remember the "Star Trek" episode in which Captain Kirk got split into two people, one good and one bad, and the only way to fix things was to run both Kirks through the transporter again—sort of using it like some high-tech blender—and make Captain Kirk one guy again? To me, if you took MTV and ran it through the transporter on the Enterprise with David Cronenberg and the psychosexual tension of the films "Blue Velvet" and "Taxi Driver," you might get some idea of Ray's stuff. (How's that for high concept?)

A better way is to read the suckers.

3. Ray has been censored.

The abortion scene from *Crucifax Autumn* was cut from the Avon paperback (although it did appear in its original form in the Dark Harvest hardcover edition of the novel.) If you can't afford the Dark Harvest edition and all you can get your hands on is the Avon edition, look for the Fall 1988 issue of *Midnight Graf-*

fiti. (Try the Overlook Connection or write the magazine itself.) To their credit, editors Jessie Horsting and James Van Hise reprinted the original scene as written, although they did warn readers not to read it if they were squeamish. (Squeamish??!! Horror fans? Shit!)

And lastly...

4. Ray Garton is a writer with a long future ahead of him.

His work is accomplished, stylish, and intelligent, and the dude ain't thirty yet!

Here's my talk with Brother Garton. — **sjs**

ONE LIVE GUY
An Interview With Ray Garton

STEVE SPIGNESI: I appreciate your taking the time to talk with me for *The Shape Under the Sheet,* Ray. I know time is a very valuable commodity for working writers.

RAY GARTON: Thanks for including me. I really appreciate it.

STEVE SPIGNESI: You've said that if it wasn't for Stephen King, you wouldn't be doing what you're doing. Why don't we start off with you explaining what you meant by that?

RAY GARTON: I grew up as a Seventh Day Adventist, and to this day, I don't know where I got my love for the horror genre because I wasn't able to watch movies when I was a kid. I didn't really start reading horror novels until just before *Carrie* came out. I'd read a couple of Thomas Tryon novels and, for some reason, I had this love of horror even before I was sure what it was. When I was a little kid I would draw these pictures of people with horrible things happening to them— their heads getting chopped off, people getting stabbed—and my parents wondered where they went wrong. And then I read *Carrie,* and I don't know what it was about that book that hit me so hard, but I thought to myself, yeah, this is the way it should be. Why isn't everybody else like this? And the more books of King's that I read, the more I began to realize that maybe I could try my own hand at writing this kind of stuff. I really think that if there hadn't been a horror novel to impress me as much as *Carrie* did—which showed me how good a horror novel could be—I don't think I would have done it.

STEVE SPIGNESI: Is *Carrie* your favorite King novel?

RAY GARTON: No, *The Shining* is my favorite.

STEVE SPIGNESI: How about the short fiction?

RAY GARTON: That's not easy. I like "Gray Matter" a lot. I don't think it's his best story, but personally I like it a lot.

STEVE SPIGNESI: Let's talk about splatterpunk. What does the term "splatterpunk" mean to you?

RAY GARTON: You know, I was there when they first coined the word. It was in a hotel room in Providence, Rhode Island, at the World Fantasy Convention. At the time, it was a joke – sort of a backlash aimed at the older cast of writers who go to every single one of these conventions without fail, and who sometimes go out of their way on panels and things to slam any writer under the age of forty. So, I guess when we started talking about it over a few drinks—more like a lot of drinks actually—we meant it to include all the younger writers, the newer writers, who aren't afraid to get really gory and really sexually explicit. And it turned out that that included a lot of writers who aren't necessarily so young, and who don't really like the label. I don't think that we intended it to be the label that it turned out to be. It's not like we need any more labels. There're plenty of them out there now. It sort of no-holds-barred horror fiction.

STEVE SPIGNESI: Speaking of labels, how has the presence of Stephen King—who has metamorphosed into a brand name for horror fiction— changed people's perception of horror?

RAY GARTON: When people meet me and find out that I'm a writer, they always ask, "Well what do you write?" When I say I write horror novels, they invariably say, "Oh, you mean you're like Stephen King?" That's like going up to a Christian minister and saying, "Oh, you teach the word of God? Are you like Jesus Christ?" (Laughs.) People keep asking me if I hope to have the success of King. *Nobody* hopes to have the success of King. King didn't hope to have the success of King. It's something that you don't expect—it's something that happens to you right out of the blue.

STEVE SPIGNESI: When did you first meet Stephen King?

RAY GARTON: The first time I ever met him was at a convention. I was really excited about meeting him, and so I kept putting off going to his table. I kept going to other writers first, because I was really nervous. When I finally got up my nerve, I told myself just keep your mouth shut and don't say a thing, because most of all, I did not want to be disillusioned about King. Even though he was supposed to be a nice guy, I didn't want to give him a chance to shatter my illusion of him. So, I went up to him, put the books I wanted signed on the table, and didn't say a word. He kept looking at my name tag. And then he said, "Ray Garton, Ray Garton, I know you. You wrote something and I read it. What was it? *Seductions*, it was *Seductions*. Yeah, that was good. I read that. That was really good." And I made like Ralph Kramden, you know...homina, homina, homina, homina.

STEVE SPIGNESI: You must have felt like a million bucks.

RAY GARTON: I did. I felt wonderful.

STEVE SPIGNESI: I'm not surprised at the response you got from King. Everyone I've talked to has unfailingly praised him for just being a regular guy. Stan Wiater made the point that King could rub every writer's nose in it if he wanted to. [NOTE: See the interview with Stan Wiater in this volume. —sjs]

RAY GARTON: He could. The man loans God money. He doesn't have to be as nice as he is. I mean if anybody has an excuse not to be nice, he does. And yet, he's such a great guy. And this is comforting. I guess this keeps me from entirely losing faith in the whole business. I've found that the writers who make it big in this field, like Stephen King and Dean Koontz and Robert McCammon—they're really nice guys. They would never think of turning someone away in a rude manner. I can't imagine any of them doing it. They're all so nice. They would go out of their way to sign a book, to say hi to a fan. And I don't think that it has anything to do with their success. I mean I don't think that they're a success because they're nice people. I think they're successful because they're very talented and they deserve their success. But it's nice to know that these nice guys make it big. There are a lot of jerks in this business who make a point of being rude and arrogant, and yet when you say their name outside of a convention, more people go "Who?" than know who they are.

STEVE SPIGNESI: How do you think King has changed the horror genre since *Carrie*?

RAY GARTON: He has shown us that in order for a horror story to really work, you have to have not only characters that you like, but characters that you know. I think that's one of the things that makes his stuff so scary, and why my fingerprints

are on all the covers of his books from clutching them so hard. I really like the people in his books —and I've met them before. A lot of people think that in a horror story, all the stuff that comes first is the blood, the gore, the monsters, the occult, whatever. Just like a lot of science fiction people

> **"...he's broadened the readership of horror. There are people who would never think of reading a horror novel who read everything Stephen King writes....I ask people, 'Do you read horror fiction?,' and they usually reply, 'Oh, no. I read Stephen King but I don't read any of that horror stuff.' He's transcended the genre and interested a lot more people in it."**

think that you need aliens, and spaceships, and funny gadgets to make it work. But none of that stuff is what comes first. You have to have believable people, and I think he's showed everybody that. (Of course, after *Carrie,* there were a lot of evil teenager books and after *The Shining,* there were more gerund titles than you could keep track of—the "This-ing" and the "That-ing" and on and on.)

I also think he's broadened the readership of horror. There are people who would never think of reading a horror novel who read everything Stephen King writes. And they will tell you they don't read horror. I ask people, "Do you read horror fiction?," and they usually reply, "Oh, no. I read Stephen King but I don't read any of that horror stuff." He's transcended the genre and interested a lot more people in it. Also, a lot of people who didn't read it before started reading King and then began looking around for other writers in the field.

STEVE SPIGNESI: He's kind of like the crossover artist who can move from the soul charts to the pop charts?

RAY GARTON: Exactly.

STEVE SPIGNESI: My favorite King novel is *IT,* and that book has taken its slams in the past couple of years. The criticism has been that it's a third longer than it should be, that it's extremely self-indulgent, that it's almost a pastiche of King—that it's sort of like King parodying himself at times, what with the brand names and the double column exclamation points and all the interior dialogue. What are your thoughts on *IT*?

RAY GARTON: I enjoyed it. I have to admit I was really intimidated by its size and was afraid to read it in bed in hardcover for fear of hurting myself, but I really liked it. I don't have any complaints about it at all. I've heard all that criticism, too, and I don't necessarily agree with it. I figure at this point King can pretty much do whatever he wants and it's fine with me.

STEVE SPIGNESI: Right. I personally think it's probably his best work ever, or at least one of the two or three best things he's ever done. When I talk to writers about their favorite King works, many times they insist on differentiating between what they consider to be their favorites, and what they consider to be King's best work. Your favorite novel is *The Shining*. Do you also think it's his *best* novel as well?

RAY GARTON: I was really impressed with *Misery*. I thought he did an amazing job with that. When you consider that the book was as limited as it was in scope—it didn't feel like it. He did wonders with that story. But in my opinion, I'd have to say that *The Shining* is his best work.

STEVE SPIGNESI: What'd you think of the movie?

RAY GARTON: I hated the movie. I left the theater angry. I vowed never to go see another Stanley Kubrick movie as long as I live.

STEVE SPIGNESI: No kidding?

RAY GARTON: I did. I vowed at the time that I wouldn't.

STEVE SPIGNESI: Well, Stan did make some changes!

RAY GARTON: I was very upset. I thought Jack Nicholson was crazy from the beginning, which was a mistake. And he tried too hard to make us scared in broad daylight, which I know is what he wanted to do—but that's not *The Shining*. *The Shining* had some really dark corners and some dark rooms, and it should have been left that way. It shouldn't have been so bright. The whole movie looked fluorescent. It was really too bright. And I don't know whose idea it was to cast Shelly Duvall as the wife. I think Shelly Duvall is a fine actress, but I don't think she was right for that role. But I do think that Nicholson was great.

STEVE SPIGNESI: Do you think "The Shining" is the worst Stephen King film adaptation?

RAY GARTON: "Children of the Corn" is probably the worst.

STEVE SPIGNESI: I agree. "Children of the Corn" seems to be a very frivolous attempt. But In terms of the *serious* attempts at translating King to film, do you think "The Shining" fails the most noticeably?

RAY GARTON: Yeah, I think so.

STEVE SPIGNESI: And on the other end of the scale, what are your favorite film versions? What do you think are the best adaptations?

RAY GARTON: I loved "Carrie"—I thought it was fantastic. I though "The Dead Zone" was wonderful, and I liked "Cujo" a lot. I think I'm in the minority there, but I liked "Cujo" a lot. Now that I think about it, there have been more really good ones than I seemed to think before. "Stand By Me" is great.

STEVE SPIGNESI: I really enjoyed "Christine."

RAY GARTON: Yes, "Christine" is very good.

STEVE SPIGNESI: I think that the films have sort of taken a bad rap. The critics have all come down on them as not being very good, but, like you said, if you look at the list, there are more winners than losers.

RAY GARTON: Yes, there are.

STEVE SPIGNESI: Let's talk about some of the newer King stuff. What did you think of the *Night Visions 5* stories? Specifically, "Dedication," the tender story of a mother's devotion that was considered unpublishable until *NV5*?

RAY GARTON: That's the one about the hotel maid who licks the writer's cum off the sheets and eats it, right?

STEVE SPIGNESI: That's the one!

RAY GARTON: That is disgusting!

STEVE SPIGNESI: That story was rejected by quite a few magazine editors until they finally went with it for *Night Visions 5*. Doug Winter edited that volume and wrote the intro. Doug is great with the turn of the phrase. He described it as Stephen King's "least palatable story" (Laughs.)

RAY GARTON: (Laughs.)

STEVE SPIGNESI: How graphic, how gross, how disgusting can "mainstream" horror get—and by that I mean legitimate, mass market releases? Stuff that's on the newsstand and in the bookstores.

RAY GARTON: I don't think there should be any

limit as long as that's not all there is in the piece. I hate it when someone says "This is just too much."

My most recent experience with that was with my novel *Crucifax Autumn*. *Crucifax* contains an abortion scene that is rather brutal, because the guy who performs the abortion has this very long tongue, and he does the abortion with the tongue, and then eats the fetus. And the editor at Pocket Books who was working on it was eight months pregnant at the time that she read it, and she went through the roof. She told me, "This is too much. You can't do this." They made me cut it. And it was very important to the story. I know everybody says that, but it was. You'll just have to take my word for it. And there are a lot of people who think that there should be some sort of lid on mainstream horror, but I don't think there should be any differentiation between different kinds of horror. Mainstream is a word that confuses me. I think that anybody can be mainstream as long as enough people read them. And I think that one of the things that keeps a lot of writers from being mainstream is either that they don't get enough exposure, or maybe their stuff is too gory and there aren't enough people interested in it. I think a story can get as graphic as a writer wants it to get as long as its good. I thought "Dedication" was very good, but I kept thinking to myself, what was Steve thinking when he was writing this? What kind of mood was he in?

STEVE SPIGNESI: So, it can go as far as necessary for the point of the story?

RAY GARTON: Right.

STEVE SPIGNESI: You know that things happen in waves, and that trends happen everywhere in popular culture—in politics, in fashion, in music, and in literature. Do you think that there will eventually be a return to a subtler, less-graphic, less-sexually-explicit form of storytelling that still uses the supernatural and the occult?

RAY GARTON: Yes, I do. And I think it's already starting in the movies. I think all the mad slasher movies have gotten very old. In fact, I think they got old long before they started to die out. It seems that horror is getting less graphic in the movies. It's hard to tell in fiction. But I do somehow feel that it's going to become more subtle, and a little less extreme.

STEVE SPIGNESI: Do you think Stephen King's work will survive?

RAY GARTON: Oh, absolutely. I think he's the Charles Dickens of our time. I think he'll be around for a long time.

STEVE SPIGNESI: Can you see him changing his focus over the years? Personally, I think King will be all over the block in the future. I don't think you're going to see King writing in any identifiable genre as he gets older. He's only forty. He's got decades of writing ahead of him, and I think his intellect is too vibrant, and his imagination too fertile to be locked into a genre. He's shown that over the years. He's done mainstream, he's done sci-fi, he's done fantasy. I can see him turning out a serious crime novel, and I can see him doing a mainstream love story. What do you think?

RAY GARTON: I've thought that for years. It's not that I want him to leave the genre of horror, but I hate it when people say, "He's too talented to be writing that stuff." But I can see him doing a lot of other things.

"...there's still going to be some dark shadows in whatever he writes. Even when he's being funny...the darkness is there. He's got this way of looking at things that is not so optimistic—he never does entirely look away from the bad stuff. And I don't think he ever will, no matter what he's writing."

STEVE SPIGNESI: Exactly. I think King is going to get restless. Take *Misery,* for example. I don't think it's an accident that Paul Sheldon's self-contained *Misery* novel was "reproduced" so extensively in the text. He also seems to like Westerns.

RAY GARTON: I suspect, though, that maybe there's still going to be some dark shadows in whatever he writes. Even when he's being funny...the darkness is there. He's got this way of looking at things that is not so optimistic—he never does entirely look away from the bad stuff. And I don't think he ever will, no matter what he's writing. But I don't know. I don't think he'll always be writing horror.

STEVE SPIGNESI: Are you in touch with King at all?

RAY GARTON: We wrote a couple of times and met at that convention and that's about it. I don't even try anymore to get in touch with him. (Laughs.) It just seems so pointless. We don't know each other well enough for me to expect him to ever be able to respond to me. I realize that this man is not just busy, he is a *business*.

STEVE SPIGNESI: Who else are you reading?

RAY GARTON: I like Robert McCammon. And there's a guy out there that nobody seems to have heard of who I think is incredible named Thomas Tessier.

STEVE SPIGNESI: Oh, sure. He's got a short story called "Food" in *Prime Evil*.

RAY GARTON: Is he in *Prime Evil*? Oh, that's great. That'll give him some exposure. He wrote two books that really hit me over the head. One was *Finishing Touches*, and one was *Rapture*. And they're both very dry, normal, average books that don't even read like horror. In fact, you have to get pretty far into them before you realize that you're reading a horror novel. They were recommended to me by my editor at Avon, and they're very disturbing. *Finishing Touches* is extremely graphic. The last half of the book is shocking. I couldn't believe what I was reading. There were a couple of times that I put the book down and didn't know if I was going to go on, it was that bad. But he has a nice relaxed style that creeps up on you. He doesn't let you know what you're in for before you get there.

STEVE SPIGNESI: Have you read a horror novel called *The Jade Unicorn*? That was an Avon paperback release after the Macmillan hardcover. It was written by a good friend of mine named Jay Halpern. I've been suggesting it to people.

RAY GARTON: Yeah, I'm familiar with that. I've never read it, but I think I have a copy of it. But then again, I've got a lot of books I haven't read. One of the rotten things about writing is that I don't have a lot of time to read anymore. But, I'll have to go look for that. I know I have it somewhere.

STEVE SPIGNESI: What's your workday like?

RAY GARTON: Well, I sleep late because I go to bed really late. I do most of my work at night, so I sleep from anywhere from eight 'till noon, unless I go to bed at eight in the morning, and then I'll sleep until later in the afternoon. During the day I try to get things like research done, which is difficult here because I'm living in what is probably the only county in the free world which doesn't have a library system. I do try to get some reading done, but it just takes me forever to get through a book now. Right now I'm reading a book called *The Predators*, and I just finished *The Tommyknockers* not long ago.

STEVE SPIGNESI: What did you think?

RAY GARTON: I loved it. I really enjoyed it. It wasn't what I expected, but I like that. I thought it was fun.

STEVE SPIGNESI: I'm in the middle of *Swan Song* and *Catcher in the Rye* again.

RAY GARTON: (Laughs.) You've got varied reading tastes, I guess. What do you think of *Swan Song*?

STEVE SPIGNESI: I am in love with it. I can't wait to get back to it when I put it down. I've been recommending it to all kinds of people. It's like watching a movie in your head. McCammon is a very visual writer.

RAY GARTON: I know exactly what you mean. He's very cinematic and forceful. He writes in 3-D. His novel *They Thirst* is among the best vampire novels I have ever read. It's outstanding. He's really good. I like him a lot. Nice guy, too.

STEVE SPIGNESI: Do you think I like McCammon because he reminds me of King?

RAY GARTON: That could very well be. He reminds me of King, too. I think that he has his own style, but he has the same relaxed, almost conversational style that puts me at ease and lets me really get cozy with a book. That's one of the reasons I like King so much, and it's also one of the reasons I like McCammon as much as I do. ❐

TEXAS HORRORS
A Talk With Joe Lansdale

There's a duality in most horror writers, a compromise between the dark and the light, what Joe Lansdale calls "the feeding of the alligators" that live in our subconscious.

Joe Lansdale's theory is that horror works, and is necessary, because if we don't feed the alligators, someday they might get so hungry they'll come out and bite someone. Like me—or you. Joe believes that when you don't explore the dark side, you starve the little critters and they'll become so enraged that one day society will wake up and find that we have a John Wayne Gacy or a Richard Speck on our hands. Or a Jim Bakker, for that matter.

It must work: I have many times remarked, both in print and in conversation, that horror writers are, to a man or woman, the nicest, gentlest bunch of folks I've ever had the pleasure to know and work with.

Joe Lansdale is the kind of interview subject writers love: He speaks in complete sentences, answers questions with complete thoughts, and doesn't go off on tangents when responding to a question.

He's also one helluva nice guy.

He's serious-minded about his work, and has obviously read wide and deep in many genres.

He is best-known to horror/dark fantasy fans for his novels *Act of Love, The Nightrunners, Dead in the West, The Magic Wagon, The Drive-In,* and *The Drive-In II.* Joe has also written several novels under pseudonyms.

He is also a master of the short story, and if you haven't read his post-nuclear war tale "Tight Little Stitches in a Dead Man's Back," do it soon: it is a brilliant story that will not disappoint you. Guaranteed.

I think you'll agree after you read the following interview that Joe's wide-ranging knowledge of, and proficiency in, the horror genre gives him a special insight into the phenomenon known as "Stephen King."

Joe is married to Karen, and lives in East Texas with their son, Keith, and their daughter, Kasey.

Here's my talk with Joe Lansdale. — **sjs**

TEXAS HORRORS
A Talk With Joe Lansdale

STEVE SPIGNESI: How do you think Stephen King has influenced the horror genre?

JOE LANSDALE: I think that he's probably given it a broader outlook. By that I mean that before Stephen King came along, there were some people —Richard Matheson comes immediately to mind— who were doing some of the things that he was doing, but he gave horror a more "popular" voice.

There had certainly been bestsellers in horror before, like *The Exorcist,* and *Rosemary's Baby,* and some of Thomas Tryon's early stuff, but I think that what King did was to give the field a more "real-world" focus.

Stephen King has a very popular voice, a sort of an everyday man's voice. And I think that that voice—combined with the fact that he mixed in a lot of the elements of the bestseller and broadened the characterization—opened up the possiblities of the horror novel. The horror in his stories seemed to represent more than just monsters, at least in his earlier stories and novels.

King's "monsters" were representative of the problems that we all face. They weren't just things like being afraid of the dark, or primal things like that. Those are basic fears and they're certainly in his novels, but there are so many other things as well.

In *The Shining,* he dealt with alcoholism and child abuse, and what I think are the *real* horrors in life. And he was able to use the horror "furniture" as a sort of metaphor for all of these bad things that we worry about...all of these fears that we all have as parents, or just as people existing in modern times.

And then he was able to give it a special twist in his own unique way. I think that that's been his major influence on the field.

STEVE SPIGNESI: The last time we spoke, you said "Stephen King has given us all a meal ticket." What did you mean by that, and has King influenced your own work, and if so, how?

JOE LANSDALE: That's true. He *has* given a lot of us horror writers a meal ticket.

I don't know that I've been influenced by him so much stylistically, but I don't think that there is any writer working now that is in my age bracket that hasn't been influenced by him in some way or another. He's influenced us all in that

Joe R. Lansdale.
Photo courtesy Joe R. Lansdale.

he has encouraged us to make a living doing what we're now doing. And he has provided us with a meal ticket because he was so successful that he created an entire field. Horror was here before, but not in a marketing sense. There were a few little bitty magazines off in the background that usually paid in copies or a quarter cent a word, but things changed after King. So, in that sense, we do all owe him a career.

I also think he showed me that you could do something with horror besides just tell a booger tale—that you could really have some significance to what you were doing without necessarily being arty-farty. I think he belittles himself a bit too much in that area.

STEVE SPIGNESI: He does seem to be very self-effacing, and he doesn't take himself very seriously. I agree that his work is much more significant than he gives himself credit for—at least publicly. Do you think that he might be using that sort of self-deprecation as a defense?

JOE LANSDALE: Yeah, it could well be. He once said in an interview that any resemblance to his work and literature was purely an accident. And I certainly don't think that all of his work matches up to literature, but then again, a lot of the work of the people who are considered literary doesn't match up to literature either.

STEVE SPIGNESI: Regarding that quotation, do

you think he was serious? Do you think he believes that?

JOE LANSDALE: I think he has come to believe it more and more. I think he has probably been affected by the critics more than he likes to admit, because I think his more recent work is just more and more booger tales. His later short stories have disappointed me.

I think Stephen King is a major talent, but I'm wondering if he's tired and worn down from being "Stephen King," and having to produce more and more work to a demanding audience.

He seems to write more and more for his audience and less and less for himself. When he wrote for himself, I actually think he was more successful. I believe that the only way you can write is to write for yourself.

When I'm writing, I just say, "Fuck the reader." It's not that I don't care about the reader, it's just that it's impossible for me to guess what other readers want, and what they expect, and if I try to do that, I'm gonna end up being like television, where I try to please everyone and end up pleasing no one.

STEVE SPIGNESI: Are you talking specifically about King's stories in *Night Visions 5* and *Prime Evil*?

JOE LANSDALE: I haven't read the *Prime Evil* story ["The Night Flier"], but I am talking about the *Night Visions* stories, ["The Reploids," "Sneakers," and "Dedication"] plus some individual things I've seen.

I've also been disappointed with some of his later novels, but I think that may just be me in that case. I couldn't finish *IT*, for example. It just didn't work for me. I thought it was rather boring. But I did feel he was trying for deeper thematic levels with that novel.

But some of his more recent short stories seemed to me to be empty and hollow, and to be kind of like the booger stories that people would have written back in the forties or the fifties.

STEVE SPIGNESI: That's an interesting viewpoint, because other writers and critics have told me that they think that King seems to be writing more modern fiction, more graphic fiction, and that he seems to understand where the field is headed, and is responding to that.

JOE LANSDALE: I couldn't disagree more. I don't think that's true at all. I think that his recent fiction is just lukewarm—not because he doesn't have the talent, but just because being "Stephen King" is such a "burden."

> **"What I'm saying is that I think Stephen King is moving in new directions, and that those directions are not horror. And I also think that he's still trying to write horror fiction because it's what is expected of him – but he may well have had his say there."**

I think Stephen King is a brilliant writer, and I don't want what I'm saying here to sound like I'm trying to put the man down, or put myself on some pedestal. I should be so lucky to be as successful and talented as Stephen King.

What I'm saying is that I think Stephen King is moving in new directions, and that those directions are not horror. And I also think that he's still trying to write horror fiction because it's what is expected of him—but he may well have had his say there.

I don't think that means that he doesn't respect horror anymore. But I think a writer may well have only so many stories in him or her in a particular field.

I personally think that things like "The Body" and stories like that are more where he is going.

As to King becoming more graphic—I think he's always been graphic. He may not have been as "splatterpunky" as some of the writers now, but I think he's always been graphic. In fact, that was one of the things that impressed me about his work early on: he didn't flinch, although sometimes the editors made him take things out. I remember him talking about the censored scene from 'Salem's Lot where he originally had rats burrowing out of a guy's mouth. Doubleday absolutely refused to print it.

So, no, I don't really see that he's becoming more graphic. The newer stories to me read more "old-fashioned" then new.

STEVE SPIGNESI: Doug Winter has told me that he thinks King might be moving more towards the hardcore realistic crime stories of Ed McBain and Jim Thompson.

JOE LANSDALE: Yeah, I do, too. I think that's probably correct. That's where I'm going, too. In fact, that's where I've been.

STEVE SPIGNESI: Doug told me he thought that

The Drawing of the Three read "like Jim Thompson on acid."

JOE LANSDALE: I don't know if I agree with that. I think Jim Thompson's an overrated writer. He's underrated in the sense that he's been ignored far too long, but now I think he's going through a period of being overrated.

But I do think that Doug's right in that King is moving in that direction, but I see him moving in a dual direction. I think you're going to see him working more in the literary mainstream—away from the supernatural. There's only so much you can do with boogers and bears, and after a point—doing anything over and over and over—I think you get to where you start to repeat yourself.

In fact, I feel that the whole horror field is moving in that direction. I don't think it's just King. I think that it has been changing for quite some time.

STEVE SPIGNESI: King's recent releases seem to bear you out. *The Tommyknockers* is science fiction, *Misery* and *The Dark Half* are psychological horror (although *Dark Half* has a definite supernatural catalyst), and *The Eyes of the Dragon* is fantasy. *IT*, which I consider to be his magnum opus, seemed to be the coda to his "monster period," if we can call it that.

JOE LANSDALE: But I think *IT* also showed, at the same time, that he was moving in the direction of what I call literary mainstream: In that novel, he greatly broadened the characterization, and the story was more and more about people, which is really where he started. Still, it's not a book that I felt was successful.

STEVE SPIGNESI: Can you give us some specific examples of early works that you consider to be King at the top of his game?

JOE LANSDALE: My favorite books by King are what I call the "S" books: *'Salem's Lot, The Shining,* and *The Stand.* In those books, he dealt with characters very, very strongly, and yet he still had the supernatural elements—which seemed fresh and new because they didn't override the story. I also liked *Night Shift.* A lot of the stories there are *Weird Tales*-type stories, but the best of them had another dimension to them, greater thematic depth, and those that were less that way were just so goddamned energetic.

STEVE SPIGNESI: What did you think of *Misery*?

JOE LANSDALE: I think *Misery* is the best of his books since the early days.

STEVE SPIGNESI: What about King's short stories? Do you have any personal favorites?

JOE LANSDALE: I like his short stories a lot. I liked all the ones, except for a couple, in *Night Shift*, even though they were very much, in many ways, traditional stories. But they had a feel for characterization, and they had a lot of heart in them.

I think that some of his later ones—in *Skeleton Crew*, for example—are professional, but they lack the heart.

Skeleton Crew does contain some excellent stories, though, like "The Mist," which is a favorite of mine. I like that, and I like the really raw, clever ones like "The Mangler" from *Night Shift*.

I think that what he—and a lot of the rest of us—are doing—is showing the influence of growing up in the era of the *Weird Tales* story. Even though we weren't reading *Weird Tales* per se, that kind of story was carried over into collections, and what I—and a lot of my contemporaries—were reading were stories collected from *Weird Tales* and other pulps.

And you have to add to that the influence of "Twilight Zone." Every story back then seemed to have a twist in it, or the story led to a twist.

In the beginning, a lot of us felt like we weren't writing a "real" story unless it had a kicker in the end. And as time passes, the field is moving away from leading up to the surprise ending and focussing more on the characters and the prose and the thing that happened along the way. Stories can still have surprises, but now we're seeing stories not written purely for surprise ending.

I think that that's one of the biggest changes in the field in the last few years, and King had a lot to do with it. Those types of stories are still written, and they will continue to be written, but I think that their heyday has passed. Unless everything kind of cycles back around again years from now.

But more and more now, stories tend to mix genres, and they tend to be interested in literary concerns. This is not to knock horror and say that the literary people always know what they're doing, either. But I think that we're having a period where we're melding a lot of different genres. Literary's a genre, too, you know.

STEVE SPIGNESI: Jerry Williamson told me that mainstream was a genre, too.

JOE LANSDALE: Sure. He's right.

STEVE SPIGNESI: That leads me to the question of what is horror to you, and where does it come from?

JOE LANSDALE: Horror to me is representative of day-to-day problems and day-to-day fears.

It's not so much stuff like vampires and ghosts anymore—stuff that used to scare me when I was a kid. I suppose those things could certainly scare me now if somebody did it right or did it differently, but generally, they don't work for me anymore.

What is scary in *The Shining* isn't that there are ghosts, but that those ghosts represent Jack Torrance's weaknesses and fears. Alcoholism and child abuse—or at least a moment when he may have gotten out of hand because he was drunk—are both hinted at, and those are both scary. That's what I got from the book, and I think that that's what the book's about—it's about the real fears that people have.

I'm a parent now. I have two kids, and you worry about what people can do to your children. You worry about what you yourself can do in a moment of anger.

You read in the papers everyday about people that are killing folks for no reason other than the fact that they want to do it. Mass murderers, serial killers, things like that.

That's the kind of thing, to me, that is horror, and I think that that's why you're seeing more and more realistic horror because the monsters just don't match up to reality anymore.

A lot of this was here before—it isn't like it just occurred in the last few years or anything—but I think we're much more aware of it now. I was born in 1951, and when I was growing up as a kid in the fifties, it was nothing for one of us to go down to somebody's house, or to go off by ourselves all day around town. Kidnappings and mass murders happened, I suppose; it just didn't happen often, and it didn't happen around us.

But as time has gone on, we've become much more aware of those things because there are more people, and for whatever reasons, it is definitely happening more often.

So, the result is that we have more fears—real fears. We read about these things in the paper everyday, we see it on television. It used to be that the idea of child molestation or mass murder was something that really was bizarre and unusual when it happened. I remember when Richard Speck killed all those nurses. Back then, it was just incredible news. But now you see that kind of shit in the paper everyday. Those are real fears for me, and that's horror to me.

STEVE SPIGNESI: Do you subscribe to the theory that horror fiction can act as a catharsis for society in general?

JOE LANSDALE: I think that to some extent it is a catharsis, because sometimes you can read really disgusting stuff, and it can do you good.

I've always said that you have to feed the alligators in the pit of the subconscious, and if you don't feed those little buddies, they might just crawl out.

But then there are some people who can feed them and feed them, but those alligators are so hungry that they crawl out anyway.

The kind of people who worry me—and I've said this in interviews before—are the people who say that they don't need any of that sort of thing. And by that I don't mean a person that doesn't read horror fiction. Not everybody's gonna need that. But everybody, I think, has to have some sort of release. I believe that somebody who doesn't feed the gators is breeding a big batch of them babies. And someday, when he or she least expects it, they just might come crawling out. In fact, they might bite *me*.

STEVE SPIGNESI: I've often thought that as scary as something supernatural can be, probably the scariest thing that could ever happen to me would be finding a lump in my body, or meeting an actual unrepentant child molester or serial murderer. You know, *real* scary stuff. There was a liquor store holdup in New Haven a few years back. Everything went fine for the robbers—in fact, they were on their way out the door with the money when one of them turned around, looked at the store owner's wife, and said, "You look like you could use some time in the hospital," and then shot her twice in the stomach. That kind of hardcore evil is hard for me to comprehend.

JOE LANSDALE: Sure, that's exactly it. And I find that the older I get, the less I believe in God, and the supernatural. I can't fall back on that stuff anymore. I can't say, "Oh, yes, God's waiting for me on the other side," or that there are ghosts and spirits.

It just seems to me more and more that we're out here alone and you do the best you can. I believe that a lot of it is just like the Wheel of Fortune in *The Dead Zone*. That baby spins and spins and wherever that old ball ends up, Jack, that's where it is.

And as I get older, it's hard for me to continue to believe in spooks and boogers. It's hard for them to scare me. A really incredible genius of a writer can do it, though—exactly the way King did in *'Salem's Lot*. I didn't believe in vampires, but King

scared the shit out of me. And I went into that book thinking that no one could do it with vampires anymore. But he wrote it with such conviction, that he did it—he scared me.

So, it can be done. But because a lot of us are getting older—and finding it harder to see a booger under the bed when there's so many boogers out there walking around—horror fiction is moving away from that whole arena.

I think we're all realizing that if you see a booger under the bed, you can almost bet it's a real booger—it's *somebody*.

It's getting harder and harder to say, "I don't want to dangle my foot off the side of the bed because a monster might get me."

The shadows don't worry me. It's the flesh and blood that worries me.

STEVE SPIGNESI: Splatterpunk.

JOE LANSDALE: It's a shitty term. I hate it and I don't like being called that.

STEVE SPIGNESI: What does it mean, and why do you hate it?

JOE LANSDALE: I hate it because it's narrow. I think David Schow invented the term kind of as a joke, and I think Skipp and Spector have perpetuated it. John and Craig are nice guys, and I like them and I have nothing bad to say about their work, but as a term, I think it's limiting them, and all of us. They're having a lot of fun with it. It's a big joke to them—sort of like a rock and roll branch of literature or something.

With splatters, the writing is very vicious and it shows a lot of blood. I don't like it because even though I'm graphic sometimes, I don't necessarily think that splash and blood are scary. It's what's inside of people—and I don't mean guts and blood. I mean what they think, and what they plan, that can be very, very frightening.

I certainly believe in being graphic when you need to be, and I have been in the past. Some of the things that I was doing were splattery well before that term came into effect. When you go back to *Act of Love*—that's a pretty nasty book. It shows some things that I don't think were particularly popular in books at that time, nor had they been done that often. [NOTE: Joe Lansdale's *Act of Love* is about a serial killer who murders and mutilates women. After he kills them, he hacks off their breasts, takes the body parts home, breads and fries them, and then eats them. —**sjs**]

I'm not trying to say that I'm the only person to be that graphic—nor am I the first person that has ever done work like this. But I'm just saying that I don't shy away from it. I never have.

But my point is that I've also written a lot of other things, and if you get that kind of label, then people constantly look for you to do a certain thing, and that just won't work for me.

So, I don't like the term. I think it's limiting.

STEVE SPIGNESI: So, essentially, splatterpunk is a violent and graphic "branch" of horror that, in your opinion, shoots for shock value, rather than the terror of the soul?

JOE LANSDALE: I certainly think shock value is part of it, and I think that that's fine.

I think a lot of people believe that some of my stuff is bloodier than it is. If they go back and re-read it, they'll find that a lot of times it isn't that bloody. It just gave you the feeling that it was.

On the other hand, I'm not defending the "quiet" school of horror, either. I don't really like either school by itself. I like a mixture of both elements.

To go back to King: He's always mixed them.

STEVE SPIGNESI: The second issue of *Midnight Graffiti* printed paintings by John Wayne Gacy, and Jim Van Hise, the editor, told me that even though there's nothing overt in them, they're so disturbing that he can't study them. There's a darkness to them that is just very disturbing, and the art seems to act as an amplifier for Gacy's buried urges. It's fascinating that Gacy is so disturbed, so innately evil, that even a drawing of something as innocent as the Seven Dwarfs could come across to a viewer as threatening.

JOE LANSDALE: The thing that's scarier than that is that I don't think that the term "evil" works. Evil is supposed to be recognizable. "Evil" is one of those things we've made up: he is *evil*—He's a slinking guy, he looks nasty.

What is scary is people like John Wayne Gacy and Ted Bundy, who look pretty goddamned normal, and in many ways may not be evil. They may like dogs, or give to the United Way, or something of that nature. But inside them there's this confusion.

And the scariest part about all this is that there is not one thing, not one horrible crime that can be committed, or a horrible thing that can be thought, that we ourselves don't have in us.

I think what makes the difference between you and me and John Wayne Gacy and Ted Bundy is that we also have other things that balance these things out—positive things that override these negative things.

But we all have those negative thoughts. Sometimes they're just little flashes.

STEVE SPIGNESI: The "dark half."

JOE LANSDALE: That's right. The dark half. I think that by writing about it and reading about it, you explore it, and in some way gain an understanding of it. And I think it's good to understand it—and this goes back to what I was saying about the alligators.

STEVE SPIGNESI: What are your thoughts on the film versions of King's stories? You're a very visual writer yourself and I'm sure you've seen millions of movies.

JOE LANSDALE: Yeah, I've seen a lot of movies. "Stand By Me" is just about my favorite. I also liked "The Dead Zone" and "Carrie." I was reasonably entertained by "'Salem's Lot," but that could have been a much better movie. That was kind of like the cartoon or comic book version of the novel.

Karen gives me a hard time about this. She liked "Firestarter."

STEVE SPIGNESI: Okay, it's on the record. Karen Lansdale liked the film version of "Firestarter." What about "The Shining?"

JOE LANSDALE: I hated it.

STEVE SPIGNESI: I usually get either love or hate answers on that one.

JOE LANSDALE: I think that the reason I hated it is because Kubrick had a lot to work with there, and he missed the whole point.

STEVE SPIGNESI: It did seem to be a betrayal of the novel.

JOE LANSDALE: And it's not just that it wasn't like the novel. I think Kubrick didn't understand what makes horror work. There are so many things in there that are just not scary. They don't work. There are countless set-ups that don't work. I think it's just a failure. It is pretty, though.

STEVE SPIGNESI: Can you give us an example of a set-up in the film that you think bombed?

JOE LANSDALE: Sure. The Dick Halloran character, for instance. He has this little ESP flash that Danny Torrance needs him, and so he goes back to Colorado. But when he gets there, he doesn't have enough sense to know that Jack Nicholson is hiding behind a pillar with an axe. (Laughs.) There are just a lot of things like that.

STEVE SPIGNESI: He could pick up messages is Florida...

JOE LANSDALE: ...but he couldn't pick up messages in the hallway. Right.

STEVE SPIGNESI: Kubrick certainly took his share of negative critical reviews for the film.

JOE LANSDALE: Yeah, most of the things I've seen have been pretty negative, although there are some people who really liked it, and who are defenders of it. I don't think there is *any* defense for that movie.

STEVE SPIGNESI: Okay, let's get a glimpse inside Joe Lansdale. What have you been reading?

JOE LANSDALE: I've been reading Charles Bukowski, and an excellent crime writer who died just recently named Charles Wileford. I also recently read Thomas Harris's *Silence of the Lambs,* and *Die Hard* by Roderick Thorpe. And I'm currently re-reading *All My Friends Are Gonna Be Strangers* by Larry McMurty.

STEVE SPIGNESI: What was the last book you read?

JOE LANSDALE: That would be *Post Office* by Charles Bukowski.

STEVE SPIGNESI: Who are some of the contemporary horror writers that you like?

JOE LANSDALE: Stephen King is obvious. And even though I wouldn't exactly call him a horror writer, I'm very impressed with Thomas Harris.

STEVE SPIGNESI: I thought *Red Dragon* was brilliant, and I also thought the film version, "Manhunter," was excellent.

JOE LANSDALE: I liked the film. I didn't like it as much as the book, but I did like it.

I like Dean Koontz—especially when he does psychological horror.

I think K.W. Jeter's *Dark Seeker* is good. I think Jeter is interesting.

I think Kelley Wilde's *The Suiting* is *damn* interesting. That's one of the better horror novels I've read in a while. He's an interesting guy and I think he's a talent to watch. He did some fun things with what could have been a silly idea. I like David Schow's short stories.

But to be perfectly honest, I'm pretty tired of horror, and I don't read much of it anymore.

I used to go through periods where I'd read nothing but science fiction. For years I wouldn't read it, and then I'd go through periods where I'd come back and read tons of it. It's the same with mystery, suspense, western, literary and horror. I'll take a break from it, then glut again.

Right now, the kind of fiction that stays with me the most is sort-of oddball mainstream stuff. Harry Crews is a favorite of mine. I love Flannery O'Connor. And I re-read those things. And I like suspense fiction and crime fiction—I feel that that's the direction that I'm going anyway.

STEVE SPIGNESI: Have you seen R.C. Matheson's *Scars*?

JOE LANSDALE: Yes, I'm very impressed with Richard Christian. I think he's the best short story writer in the field.

STEVE SPIGNESI: High praise. What did you think Ray Garton's *Live Girls* and *Crucifax Autumn*?

JOE LANSDALE: I liked *Live Girls* real well...I was a little disappointed in *Crucifax Autumn*. *Trade Secrets* is great! Ray's young...I think he's got a good career ahead of him.

STEVE SPIGNESI: McCammon?

JOE LANSDALE: I like Rick McCammon's stuff. I think he's good. I'm very entertained by him. I liked *They Thirst,* but my favorite McCammon novel is probably *Mystery Walk.*

STEVE SPIGNESI: What kind of music do you listen to?

JOE LANSDALE: Country and western, rock and roll, classical, and mixtures of those things. Rockabilly. Lately, I've been listening mostly to country & western, though.

STEVE SPIGNESI: I'll bet your area [Nacogdoches, Texas] is real strong in country.

JOE LANSDALE: Yeah, but it's also strong in rock & roll.

STEVE SPIGNESI: What are your personal favorites of your own short stories?

JOE LANSDALE: "The Pit" in *The Black Lizard Anthology of Crime;* "Tight Little Stiches in a Dead Man's Back" which was in *Nukes* and also *The Year's Best Horror;* "The Night They Missed the Horror Show" in *Silver Scream.*

One that I think works real great sometimes, and is a failure other times is "On the Far Side of the Cadillac Desert with Dead Folks" in *The Book of the Dead.*

Also, one of my more "old-fashioned" stories, "Fish Night" that was in *Fears.*

STEVE SPIGNESI: Give us a rundown of your novels and any forthcoming works.

JOE LANSDALE: *Act of Love, The Nightrunners, Dead in the West, The Magic Wagon, The Drive-In,* (A B Movie with Blood and Popcorn), *The Drive-In II* (Not Just One of Them Sequels), and *Cold in*

July (a suspense novel).

I also have another untitled suspense novel sold. My short story collection *By Bizarre Hands* was recently published.

"King had a sixties voice, and was especially appealing to people about my age, but somehow was able to grab the younger ones coming up, too.

There is something about that voice, and I think that's why he crosses over so much. He gets the younger readers, as well as people our age and a little bit older, because he does seem to be able to capture the sensibility of what people are calling 'The Big Chill' generation."

STEVE SPIGNESI: Did you know that Stephen King was Richard Bachman before everyone else knew?

JOE LANSDALE: I didn't know for sure, but I had suspicions when I read *The Running Man.*

I didn't really know it was King, but I said to myself that this guy is the best Stephen King "imitator" around. *Running Man* doesn't have the depth of the 'real" King novels, but it reminds me of King—which, of course, in a way is what it is. It's sort-of King's approach—stripped down.

I didn't know it was King, but I found out before it was announced, probably like most people in the field did.

STEVE SPIGNESI: Richard Matheson told me that he didn't think King would have made it if it wasn't the right time.

JOE LANSDALE: I think that's a good point, and I agree with that.

I think he would have made it, but I don't think he would have been the big-time writer he's become. Everything was just right. Everything.

First of all, *The Exorcist* and Thomas Tryon and all that stuff had showed that this type of material could sell. Add to that the fact that King had a sixties voice, and was especially appealing to people about my age, but somehow was able to grab the younger ones coming up, too.

There is something about that voice, and I think that's why he crosses over so much. He gets the younger readers, as well as people our age and a little bit older, because he does seem to be able to capture the sensibility of what people are calling "The Big Chill" generation.

Again, to me, labels seem kind of narrowminded, but that's us, supposedly.

That's what really appealed to me—that's what struck me when I was reading his work. I said, my God, this is the first writer that I have read that sounds like my generation.

There had been other people that also had the "voice" of my generation, but King was also a *genre* writer.

He had that real informal storytelling style which I appreciate—probably because I have that kind of approach, too. East Texas is noted for its storytellers.

I grew up with those kind of people and I think that's another appeal of his work to me. ❏

"IN THE LIGHT"
An Interview With Robert R. McCammon

How good is Robert R. McCammon? This good:

"He listened to the rhythm of the hospital – the polite bing-bonging of signal bells through the intercom system, followed by requests for various doctors; the quiet, intense conversations of other people, friends and relatives of patients, in the seating area; the squeak of a nurse's shoes on the linoleum; the constant opening and closing of elevator doors. An ambulance's siren wailed from the emergency entrance on the west side of the hospital. A wheelchair creaked past, a black nurse pushing a pregnant dark-haired woman to the elevators en route to the maternity ward on the second floor. Two austere doctors in white coats stood talking to an elderly man, his face gray and stricken; they all entered an elevator together, and the numbers marched upward. The daily patterns of life and death were in full motion here, Jack mused. A hospital seemed to be a universe in itself, teeming with small comedies and tragedies, an abode of miracles and secrets from the morgue in its chill basement to the eight-floor's wide corridors where mental patients paced like caged tigers."
    —From the short story "Best Friends"

And this good:

"Through the diner's plate-glass windows, a dense curtain of rain flapped across the Gulf gas pumps and continued across the parking lot."
    —From the short story "Nightcrawlers"

And this good:

"The wind churned, threw them one way and then the other—and as it withdrew from Brenda's apartment it took the two bodies with it, into the charged air over the city's roofs.
    They flew, buffeted higher and higher, bone locked to bone. The city disappeared beneath them, and they went up into the clouds where the blue lightning danced.
    They knew great joy, and at the upper limits of the clouds where the lightning was hottest, they thought they could see the stars."
    —From the short story "Eat Me"

As Joe Lansdale put it so aptly in his introduction to an interview with McCammon for *Twilight Zone* magazine, Robert R. "Rick" McCammon is "the embodiment of the perfect Southern gentleman, the kind of guy you wouldn't mind your daughter bringing home." He is gracious, modest, and very soft-spoken, and his quiet persona belies the sheer power of his fiction. From his writing, you'd almost expect Rick to be like his "Nightcrawlers" character Big Bob Clayton, a redneck who drinks "Rebel Yell whiskey straight," and

whose "favorite songs are about good women gone bad and trains on the long track to nowhere."

McCammon's work has found a ready and eager audience since the publication of his first novel, *Baal*, in 1978, and even he recently had to admit that, yes, he is now collectible.

I was introduced to Rick by Dave Hinchberger, head honcho (when Laurie's not around) and chief cook and bottle-washer at the Overlook Connection. Rick was more than happy to talk to me for *The Shape Under the Sheet*, and we did an hour-long interview on an October Wednesday, just days before Halloween.

The title of this interview—"In the Light"—comes from Rick's magnificent short story "Nightcrawlers," which appeared in J.N. Williamson's first *Masques* anthology, and which was later made into a superb (new) "Twilight Zone" episode. Stephen King has named "Nightcrawlers" as one of his ten favorite horror short stories of all time.

The Los Angeles *Times* hailed Rick's novel *Usher's Passing* with the blurb "King, Straub, and now Robert McCammon." This association has not always been good for Rick. He has been accused of being overly influenced by King and even trying to infringe on King and Straub's "territory"—a ridiculous idea to begin with, but one which has somehow lingered. All of these issues are discussed in the following interview, but before we get to that, I've included a rudimentary bibliography of some of the important novels and short stories by Robert R. McCammon. (Works marked with an asterisk (*) are my personal favorites and especially recommended.) — sjs

Selective Listing of Writings by Robert R. McCammon

NOVELS

SHORT STORIES

- "Makeup" (In *Modern Masters of Horror*, an Ace paperback, 1982)
- "Nightcrawlers" (In *Masques*, published by Maclay, 1984)**
- "The Red House" (In *Greystone Bay*, a Tor paperback, 1985)
- "He'll Come Knocking At Your Door" (In *Halloween Horrors*, Charter paperback, 1986)
- "Yellow Jacket Summer" (In the October 1986 issue of *Twilight Zone* magazine)*
- "The Deep End" (In *Night Visions Hardshell*, a Berkley paperback, 1988)
- "A Life in the Day of" (In *Night Visions Hardshell*, a Berkley paperback, 1988)*
- "Best Friends" (In *Night Visions Hardshell*, a Berkley paperback, 1988)*
- "Doom City" (In *Doom City*, a Tor paperback, 1988)
- "Night Calls the Green Falcon" (In *Silver Scream*, a Tor paperback, 1988)
- "I Scream Man" (In the Winter 1985 issue of *The Horror Show*)
- "Eat Me" (In *Book of the Dead*, a Bantam paperback, 1989)**

"IN THE LIGHT"
An Interview With Robert R. McCammon

STEVE SPIGNESI: Let's start off with this: What were your thoughts upon hearing that your story "Nightcrawlers" was one of Stephen King's ten favorite horror short stories of all time?

ROBERT McCAMMON: I didn't know that.

STEVE SPIGNESI: For his collection *How To Write Tales of Horror, Fantasy, and Science Fiction*, Jerry Williamson asked a number of genre writers to contribute lists of their favorite stories and novels. Your story "Nightcrawlers" was included in King's Top Ten.

ROBERT McCAMMON: I've seen the book, but I didn't know that was in there. I think that's great. I think Stephen King is a fantastic writer. And I think his influence in the field is huge, and it's going to continue to be huge for a long time to come. It really makes me feel very good that he liked the story that much. I'm very pleased.

STEVE SPIGNESI: How well do you know Stephen King?

ROBERT McCAMMON: We've met just briefly, and it was a long time ago. It was the sort of situation where I would have liked very much to have been able to say hello and talk, but he's always surrounded by people, so you can't really get a chance to spend much time with him.

I really don't know him, and I don't think he really knows me.

STEVE SPIGNESI: Have you got a favorite King novel?

ROBERT McCAMMON: *The Shining* is definitely my favorite King novel.

STEVE SPIGNESI: Why?

ROBERT McCAMMON: Because it is a brilliantly realized piece.

If somebody had said to me, "I'm going to write a four-hundred page novel that's basically about three people in a haunted house, and it will sustain your interest on every page, and it's going to be tight and great," I would have said, "Gee, that's kind of stretching it a bit, because with only three characters, you have some limitations."

But in *The Shining*, Stephen King is able to take those characters and create a fully-realized, fantastic world within the Overlook.

To me, the book is so tight and so fresh. I think it's an incredibly keen vision of one man's mental breakdown, and how he's influenced by his past and how these evil spirits find the cracks in his soul and get to him through those cracks. It's so brilliantly done that it's definitely my favorite.

I think *The Shining* is the definitive haunted house horror novel. It's wonderful.

Robert R. McCammon.
Photo courtesy Sheri Vann.

STEVE SPIGNESI: What are your thoughts about his shorter work? Do you have any favorites among the short stories?

ROBERT McCAMMON: I think his shorter work is good but I really tend to like the novels better. I really like "Quitters, Inc." I enjoyed that one because it was kind of offbeat. I think that story is a good example of what King is famous for—taking an ordinary situation and giving it a very violent and strange twist. I think "Quitters, Inc." is a prime example of what he does best.

STEVE SPIGNESI: What is horror? Where does it come from and what does it mean to you?

ROBERT McCAMMON: I think that that goes back to the question that people ask all horror writers: why do you write this stuff? And there was a time when I thought, well, people write horror because it's fun. But that's a very superficial answer.

I think it's something we feel. I think it's something that's inside us that we feel we have to get out—that we have to purge. I think horror writers, most of all, are really nice people, and I think a large part of that is because they're able to purge this kind of violence that is in us all.

I think that a lot of these people—myself included—are very lucky that we can write, because if we couldn't write, how would we get rid of these impulses? How would we get rid of these thoughts? How would we deal with all the things that we need to get out?

I think we're all pretty fortunate that we can get these things down on paper. I'm not really sure where it comes from. It may come from something in our childhood—something that happened to us...I'm not really sure.

STEVE SPIGNESI: What frightens you?

ROBERT McCAMMON: My biggest fear is being trapped in a particular situation and not being able to get out of it.

For instance, before I became a writer, I was working in a couple of real dead-end jobs, and I was in a situation where someone was over me, telling me what I could and couldn't do. I was working in the advertising department of a department store, and all I was doing was taking ads round to all the different departments and getting okays for the newspaper.

Basically I was told that this was all I could do, even though I wanted to write ad copy.

After I left that job, I worked on a newspaper on the copy desk for a very short time. I wanted to be a reporter, but I was told I couldn't be one. I was told I had to stay on the copy desk and write headlines. If I couldn't write—if I hadn't taken a chance and written *Baal*—I would probably be stuck there today.

You know what terrifies me? To have somebody sit over you like a dumb overlord who squats on your back, and says "This is where you're going to remain for the rest of your life, and there's no escape." That, to me, is pretty bad.

STEVE SPIGNESI: Who are your literary influences?

ROBERT McCAMMON: Ray Bradbury, for one. I grew up reading Bradbury, and I think his work is just great. As I go on, I'm beginning to see the influences of Bradbury more and more in my work.

Also, the old guys—Edgar Allan Poe in particular, because as a kid I really loved Poe. This was strange because at that time my friends were reading comic books and I was reading Edgar Allan Poe. His stuff seemed to strike a responsive chord in me.

I also read Edgar Rice Burroughs. I loved the Tarzan books and the "Mars" series.

I was also influenced by H.P. Lovecraft, though not as much as by Poe and Burroughs. There are probably a lot of other people who influenced me as well, and I'm sure there are a lot of other things—even comic books—thrown into the stew that I'm not even aware of.

STEVE SPIGNESI: It seems as though many of the so-called "name brand" horror writers today are approximately our age—mid-thirties to mid-forties or so—and you all seem to have been influenced by the same writers. I seem to be hearing over and over the same names when it comes to the writers the major names feel have influenced them.

ROBERT McCAMMON: Right.

STEVE SPIGNESI: However, now I'm starting to see people who are telling me that Stephen King is now an *influence*. I find it interesting that King's contemporaries have been telling me that they have been influenced by the same guys that King read—Bradbury, Bloch, Poe, Matheson, etc. The younger generation of writers—writers in their mid twenties or so—are now saying that *Stephen King* is their major influence. What are your thoughts on this development?

ROBERT McCAMMON: Well, I would have to say that Stephen King has influenced me, too. I think that's obvious.

I think that because his books are everywhere, and also because he's such a fantastic writer, it

> "It would be almost impossible to work in a literary 'vacuum,' so to speak, and not have read King, not have admired his work, not have admired his vision of things and his craft, and the way he puts things together....it would be almost impossible to be working in the horror genre and not have somebody compare you to King....[b]ecause that's just the standard. It's a very high standard, but Stephen King *is* the standard."

would be very difficult to work in this field and not be influenced, in some way, by The King.

It would be almost impossible to work in a literary "vacuum," so to speak, and not have read King, not have admired his work, not have admired his vision of things and his craft, and the way he puts things together.

For a while there, everywhere you looked, you saw King's name. He was doing interviews, he was doing two books a year, he was doing short story collections—he was really flooding the field.

And frankly, it would be almost impossible to be working in the horror genre and not have somebody compare you to King—to have somebody say, "Oh, you want to be the next Stephen King," or, "You're as good as King," or, "You're not as good as King." Because that's just the standard. It's a very high standard, but Stephen King *is* the standard.

So, certainly, King has influenced me.

STEVE SPIGNESI: So, Stephen King is horror's "long distance runner"?

ROBERT McCAMMON: Absolutely. And speaking of longevity, I find it interesting that every six or seven years, it seems that there is a new wave of writers coming into the field of horror writing. Most of them will write one or two books and then they'll be gone, but there'll be a few who will stick around, and they'll continue to work.

STEVE SPIGNESI: How do you feel personally when you see a dustjacket blurb such as the one your publishers have used that read "King, Straub, and now, McCammon?"

ROBERT McCAMMON: It's a way to sell books. And again, that strictly speaks to the power of Stephen King in the marketplace. You see that on a lot of people's books, and if there were somebody else that the publishers felt was very successful and had a huge readership, it would not be King's name on there, it would be Edith Schwartz's, or whomever. It's simply a marketing ploy. I appreciate it, but in some ways, it's a detriment because I think it can hurt a writer to say "this person's going to be the next Stephen King," or "this person writes like King," or anything along those lines.

STEVE SPIGNESI: If you could rewrite any of your books, which would you choose?

ROBERT McCAMMON: I'd probably rewrite all of them. I'm never satisfied with them when I'm through—in fact, I can't stand to look at them when I get through with them because I can see all the seams and all the mistakes, and I end up thinking, God, why didn't I take care of that when I had a chance? So, I'd probably rewrite all of them. It's probably better that I usually don't even pick them up and look at them again.

STEVE SPIGNESI: I have been known to cringe when I read through things I've written in the past.

ROBERT McCAMMON: Oh, yeah. Six months or a year after I've written something and it's out on the marketplace, I'll pick it up and kind of page through it—just to torture myself, I guess—and I'll instantly see something, and I'll say, "Oh God, that's awful. That sentence is awful. Why did I do that?"

But I think that kind of self-criticism is a good sign in a way because it's an indication that you've progressed beyond where you were when you wrote that book, which I think is very, very important.

STEVE SPIGNESI: I do exactly the same thing with my first book. I open it up and almost start editing it.

ROBERT McCAMMON: Yeah, I know what you mean. And that can be a maddening thing to do, and it's probably not good to do because I really think that when you write a book you do the best you can at the time. You do the very best that you can at the time, and then you've got to put it aside and move on. And if you look back at that book years later and you cringe, then you've just got to accept that as a fact.

STEVE SPIGNESI: You're an extremely visual writer. Reading your stuff is true "skull cinema": it's like watching a movie in your head.

ROBERT McCAMMON: Well, that's good, because that's what I want to do.

STEVE SPIGNESI: Do you watch a lot of TV, and/or movies?

ROBERT McCAMMON: No, I don't, although I tend to plan out scenes visually, because I really do think of writing as creating a movie in your mind. I think a writer does the casting and the lighting and the sets and the costumes and everything else as well. I think it's more a matter of detail—of throwing in detail when and where you need it to highlight particular things in the scene.

That's always appealed to me. The visual quality of fiction always appeals to me, and that in particular is what appeals to me about King's work—right down to the roses in the carpet of the Overlook: you can see them, I can see them, and I can also feel that carpet. That's what I really like about Steve's work, and that's what appeals to me about any good writer's work—that you can see it, that you can walk through it and be there, and it's immediate.

STEVE SPIGNESI: Have you read much of King's later stuff?

ROBERT McCAMMON: Some. I probably don't read as much now as I used to. The last King novel I read was *The Tommyknockers.*

STEVE SPIGNESI: What'd you think?

ROBERT McCAMMON: I think it's a great idea, but I think it was overwritten. I read that King has said of himself that he has a tendency to spill his guts and let everything come out. I think the idea was super, but I got tired of reading. It wore me out. I ended up just sort of plodding through to get to the end. But I think the idea was very, very good.

STEVE SPIGNESI: Did you know about the Richard Bachman pseudonym?

ROBERT McCAMMON: Yes, I did.

STEVE SPIGNESI: How'd you find out?

ROBERT McCAMMON: To me, it was obvious. NAL had given a super advance to this relative unknown named Richard Bachman.

STEVE SPIGNESI: And how did you hear about the big advance?

ROBERT McCAMMON: I read about it in *Publisher's Weekly.* I read that New American Library was giving this super huge advance to "Richard Bach-man"—whom I had never heard of before—for a book called *Thinner.*

I remember I was at the ABA convention, and I saw this NAL promotional literature for *Thinner,* and the first thing that came into my mind was, why are they giving this guy this huge amount of money to compete with Stephen King? It's the same house. Why are they going to do this? Then I realized that this was a steam valve.

If *The Talisman* didn't do well, then they were going to release *Thinner* and say it wasn't King. *The Talisman* was a gamble. I think the pseudonym idea was a steam valve, but I also think it was a brilliant thing that somebody put together.

I went up to one of the salespeople at the NAL booth and asked her "Is Richard Bachman Stephen King?," and she looked at me and said, "No!," and laughed. But I knew it.

STEVE SPIGNESI: So, you became aware of the connection with *Thinner,* which was 1985. Had you been aware of the Bachman paperback originals prior to that?

ROBERT McCAMMON: No. I had never heard the name before.

So, when I saw this huge advance being given to somebody I had never heard of, and from the same house, and I saw that the novel was written in the same style...well, my goodness, it wasn't too difficult to see right through them.

NAL was giving away promo copies, so I got one, and there was King's style all over the place: the italics, the parenthetical asides, the interior dialogue. And I thought, well, if this isn't King, this guy is going to get into a lot of trouble for ripping off Stephen King's style.

STEVE SPIGNESI: I love the Literary Guild Magazine's one-line "review" of *Thinner.* The reviewer said, "*Thinner* is what Stephen King would write like if Stephen King could write."

ROBERT McCAMMON: (Laughs.) Oh, really? I think the creation of "Richard Bachman" was a very smart move, but to me it was obvious. But it worked.

STEVE SPIGNESI: What are your thoughts on being called a splatterpunker? What does that "literary movement" mean to you, and do you like being considered one?

ROBERT McCAMMON: It really doesn't matter to me.

What we're basically talking about here is an abundance of gore and violence and gut-slashings —the kind of graphic tone and style that was spearheaded by Clive Barker.

I don't think I write that way. I have done some work that is in that genre, but I don't like labeling—even though in this profession, we're going to label things.

There's quiet horror, there's psychological horror, and then there's splatterpunk. It doesn't matter to me because I think there's room for different "schools," and I also think there's an audience for everything.

It certainly doesn't offend me. I don't pick up the splatterpunk work and say this is the most horrible thing and should be banned. I think some of it is very, very good, and I really enjoy it. But I enjoy any good writing. And it seems to me that if violence and gore are necessary in the story, then it's fine. I see no problem with it at all.

STEVE SPIGNESI: Some of King's more recent short stories—"The Night Flier" and "Home Delivery" immediately come to mind—have been pretty graphic. Do you think he might be responding to the splatterpunker's tendency to be more "overt," to show more blood and guts, so to speak?

ROBERT McCAMMON: I think every author should try to do different things, and it may be that King is not going to necessarily stay with psychological horror and he's not going to necessarily stay with a splatterpunk story, but I do think it's good for all writers to try different things.

I'm working on a short story now called "Dark Eye" that I think is very graphic—but I think it adds to the story.

My next novel will probably be a psychological novel, and it won't be graphic at all. There may be some graphic scenes, but the whole tone is not going to be graphic.

I think it's to the benefit of the author to go back and forth and not do one particular type of novel and be typecast as doing only splatterpunk, or doing only psychological horror, or whatever.

STEVE SPIGNESI: I think *Swan Song* is a masterwork.

ROBERT McCAMMON: Well, thank you, I appreciate it—but I hope it's *not* a masterwork, though, because when you say "masterwork," it usually means it was the cap of your career.

STEVE SPIGNESI: Well, then, I consider it a *major* work, and it's my personal favorite of your novels. Now, I'm not telling you anything new when I tell you that people have compared it to *The Stand.*

ROBERT McCAMMON: Absolutely.

STEVE SPIGNESI: And some of them have come down hard on you for supposedly "ripping off" Stephen King. What is your response to this kind of criticism?

ROBERT McCAMMON: Well, first of all I think that Stephen King's fans are extremely loyal. He has legions of loyal fans. And if these legions of fans feel that somebody is kind of trading on King's territory, they're gonna jump hard.

Somebody once wrote me a letter about treading on King and Straub's turf—but not for *Swan Song.* They were criticizing me for *Usher's Passing.*

I took the heat for *Swan Song* because there was a disaster involved on a worldwide scale. I kept saying "Mine is a nuclear disaster and King's was a plague," but it didn't seem to make any difference.

Their thinking was, "it's still a disaster—and Stephen King has written the ultimate disaster novel, so therefore anything from *The Stand* on has no validity." I just had to do the best I could do at the time.

STEVE SPIGNESI: How conscious were you of *The Stand* when you were writing *Swan Song*?

ROBERT McCAMMON: I was very aware of *The Stand,* and that made writing *Swan Song* difficult because I had had this idea about a nuclear holocaust novel for several years.

It was hard—with *The Stand* out there—to realize that what I wanted to do had to do with a disaster, and that it also had to do with a demonic force that was roaming the country reveling in this ultimate disaster.

I knew that when the book came out I was gonna get slammed. But I'd had this idea and it was a good idea, and if I didn't do it, then what would that be saying? So, I felt like I could take the heat, and it really has not been as bad as I thought it might be. I've gotten a few letters, but generally people really like the book, and most readers do seem to understand that the disaster is different.

STEVE SPIGNESI: What were the last books you read?

ROBERT McCAMMON: I recently read *The Prince of Tides* by Pat Conroy, *Silence of the Lambs* by Thomas Harris, and *Koko* by Peter Straub. Basically I read a lot of biographies and a lot of histories and nonfiction. I cut down on my reading of fiction when I'm working because I really don't want to be influenced or swayed in any way.

STEVE SPIGNESI: Speaking of being influenced,

Douglas E. Winter, the author of *Stephen King: The Art of Darkness,* has, on occasion, been a bit hard on you in print. In an interview I did with Doug for *The Shape Under the Sheet,* he said, "Rick McCammon is a talented and energetic writer who's fiction unfortunately, and intentionally or not, seems to mime a lot of Steve King's work." [NOTE: See my interview with Doug Winter in this volume. —sjs] Do you think his accusations are justified or unjustified, and what is your response to his assertions?

> **"...it's very difficult to be in this genre and not see King everywhere, and when people compare me to King, it makes it even more difficult. But then again, that can work both ways because if people are comparing me to King, then the thinking sometimes goes, well, maybe I *am* doing good."**

ROBERT McCAMMON: Oh, I think that Winter's justified. I think that I have been influenced by Stephen King to a great extent, and probably more so then I should have been. I think I'm working out of that now. As I said, I think it's very difficult to be in this genre and not see King everywhere, and when people compare me to King, it makes it even more difficult. But then again, that can work both ways because if people are comparing me to King, then the thinking sometimes goes, well, maybe I *am* doing good.

But King's loyal fans get very upset when that happens because they don't really want anyone to be compared to King. And Doug Winter is a loyal King fan.

STEVE SPIGNESI: That brings up an interesting question. What is the perception—by his fellow horror writers—of Stephen King as an influence on the market?

ROBERT McCAMMON: I think there's an undercurrent in the field that King is so huge that a lot of very, very good writers don't get much of a chance.

STEVE SPIGNESI: Is it envy?

ROBERT McCAMMON: I'm not sure if it's envy as much as it is a recognition that if somebody goes into a bookstore with five dollars and they're interested in horror fiction, they're going to buy a Stephen King book. Out of the whole shelf of people who do this type of writing, they're going to buy a King book.

I can understand the reasons for that because King is really such a fantastic writer. There are other really good writers in the field, but King is just wonderful. I do think, though, that his later work is overloaded just a bit. I really like his early work better, but that's neither here nor there.

It interests me that King is not working as much as he has been, and that when he slacked off a bit, Dean Koontz became very popular. Dean was not popular when King was in his greatest heyday.

King has been such a huge force that there's really been very little room for anybody else to get any publicity or for anybody else to get anywhere.

What really helped Clive Barker was that King said Clive was "the future of horror." That *really* helped Clive. If Stephen King had said, "I don't like Clive Barker," where would Clive be today? It's an interesting situation, it really is.

STEVE SPIGNESI: Do you agree with the theory that horror runs in cycles—that horror fiction and films are only popular in the good times because society needs a focus for its fears?

ROBERT McCAMMON: Yeah, that's probably true. And it's certainly true that people would rather have light entertainment when their lives are in bad shape.

On a deep level, I think horror fiction may be trying to say something about humanity—it may be trying to say something about people. But, basically, I think most people read it as an entertainment, as an escape, as a way to channel aggressions, and as a way to come to grips with some of their fears. I think most people read horror for fun.

It's kind of like going to the amusement park and riding on a rollercoaster that you know is going to scare the hell out of you, but you want to do it because you enjoy it.

STEVE SPIGNESI: It's a safe threat.

ROBERT McCAMMON: It's a safe threat, because you can always close the book and put it away.

STEVE SPIGNESI: What are your thoughts on the film adaptations of King's stories?

ROBERT McCAMMON: I think the reason why the "Stephen King" movies haven't been successful is because King's work is already so visual and so great as it is between the covers: it's already there, and anything a director does is not going to be as good.

I think the detail is there, and the great visual qualities are already there for you to see in your mind, and so seeing it on film is a letdown.

STEVE SPIGNESI: Specific failures?

ROBERT McCAMMON: "The Shining." Of course, I would say "The Shining."

I remember watching "The Shining" with a friend of mine who said, "Boy, I really thought that was a good movie." And I said, "Have you read the book?," and he hadn't and *that's* why he liked it. Maybe it *was* a good movie for somebody who hadn't read the book, but if you read the novel and really get into that world, then the movie, of course, would be a disappointment.

Regarding the others, I thought "The Dead Zone" was probably better than most.

STEVE SPIGNESI: I really enjoyed "Stand By Me."

ROBERT McCAMMON: Yes, but that was a totally different thing.

I've noticed that movies with King's name on them haven't done very well, so they consciously downplayed King's involvement with "Stand By Me." It seemed like they were saying, "This is not a horror piece and we don't want people to even *think* it's a horror piece, so let's bury King's name in the credits somewhere"—which was a smart move.

STEVE SPIGNESI: How about your stories? If I were you I'd be trembling in my boots over what Hollywood might do to your work.

ROBERT McCAMMON: Yeah, I know, I know.

STEVE SPIGNESI: Have you sold any of the film rights?

ROBERT McCAMMON: Yes. Somebody's already done the script for *They Thirst*, but it was so terrible, it probably won't get done.

STEVE SPIGNESI: You had final approval?

ROBERT McCAMMON: Yeah, but it's still floating around.

I don't care really about the film versions, though. My child is the book, and I feel that as long as I'm creating a modest, decent child, then that's fine with me.

If something gets made into a movie, fine, but I think it might just as easily be a disaster.

I'd hate for the day to come when I could say, "Yeah, they made a movie out of one of my books...but don't go see it!" (Laughs.)

People are always asking me "When are you going to have a movie made out of one of your books?" I tell them, "I've already made a movie. The movies are in the pages, and you see the movie in your mind."

STEVE SPIGNESI: You had to be pleased with "Nightcrawlers," though.

ROBERT McCAMMON: I was very pleased with that. "Twilight Zone" did a very good job, and William Friedkin did a great job directing. That was exciting.

STEVE SPIGNESI: We talked about fans and their perception of their "heroes" a while back, and it occurred to me that I hadn't asked you what you thought of *Misery*?

ROBERT McCAMMON: *Misery* seems to me to be a scream of "I'd like to do another kind of writing but my fans want me to continue to do horror novels."

STEVE SPIGNESI: I've done several "favorite novel and story" surveys for this book, and "The Body" was almost always one of the top three favorite King stories. It seems that the fans might accept other types of writing from "The King," don't you think?

ROBERT McCAMMON: But "The Body" is a novella. I wonder what the reaction would be if King were to do an entirely *different* type of novel? I wonder what his fans' reaction would be then? I think that maybe he would like to do that, but that he might feel that he's not being allowed to. □

JOSEPH PAYNE BRENNAN
A Living Legend Is Dead

"Over the ground on the gravesite
in which I will soon be interred
November winds touch down...

The scene will not change,
I presume,
after the pious procession,
with precise impatience
puts me under the earth."
—From the poem "City Cemetery,"
by Joseph Payne Brennan (1984)

The last image I'll ever have of my friend Joseph Payne Brennan is that of two dark-suited men closing the cover of his coffin.

I first met Joe Brennan in the summer of 1989. At NECON IX, Stan Wiater showed me a picture of Joe taken at the 1979 World Fantasy Convention and mentioned to me that Brennan lived in New Haven, Connecticut, (my hometown). So a couple of days after the convention, I tracked down his phone number, called him, and asked him for an interview for this book. I felt that his thoughts on King would be very insightful, and since King had written the introduction to Joe's brilliant collection *The Shapes of Midnight*, I knew that a talk with Joe would be very appropriate for inclusion in *The Shape Under the Sheet*.

The best he could do, he told me, was to answer a few written questions. He had just been told that he had a possibly fatal illness and he was preparing to begin a series of treatments that were sure to sap him of both time and energy.

I sent him a few questions, and within two weeks, he had returned his answers with a cover letter:

Dear Stephen:
　Enclosed is a brief and I fear totally inadequate reply to your queries. I wish I were in better shape so that I might plunge into some hasty reading and research which would enable me to answer all your queries at length. Alas, I've been seriously 'under the weather' for months and even now am awaiting word as to the specific nature of the illness—whether malignant and finally fatal, or only serious and curable.

Joe's illness was leukemia. He referred to it as his "infection." Throughout the remainder of 1989, we kept in touch either by phone or mail. The last time I spoke with Joe was just after Christmas. He called me to ask if I would bring *The Shape* limited edition signature sheets to his house and then pick them up so that he wouldn't have to worry about packing them up and shipping them off to the next person. (He had given me permission to reprint his classic story "Canavan's Back Yard" in *The Shape,* and so had agreed to sign the limited.)

The next thing I knew, he was dead. The Tuesday after Joe died, my mother called me and asked if I had seen that morning's New Haven *Register.* I hadn't. I don't get the paper at home, and I usually don't get a chance to read the copy I buy until late in the afternoon.

"Your friend Joe Brennan died," she said.

I felt like I had been punched in the heart.

The day of his funeral was a bright, cold day, and the services were held in a funeral parlor in Hamden. The priest's eulogy started off in the usual manner, but then quickly shifted gears. For anyone who has any doubts, you definitely know you're at the funeral of a horror writer when you hear the priest say, "I first read "Slime" in *Weird Tales* magazine in 1953." As sad as the day was, there were more than a few smiles at that line.

Joe was born in 1918 in Bridgeport, Connecticut, but lived in New Haven since he was a few weeks old.

Joseph Payne Brennan was, literally, a "living legend"—only in Joe's case, that description was not just overblown hyperbole: It was a legitimate—and earned—title.

He wrote poetry and fiction, and he edited the small press magazine *Macabre* and the poetry magazine *Essence.*

His work still stands as classic, quintessential horror, and no less a luminary that Stephen King has said that "Joseph Payne Brennan is one of the most effective writers in the horror genre, and he is certainly one of the writers I have patterned my own career upon; one of the writers whom I studied and with whom I kept school." (From King's introduction to *The Shapes of Midnight.*) King has also compared Joe's stories to those of William Faulkner and Charlotte Perkins Gilman.

Selected List of Writings by
Joseph Payne Brennan

POETRY COLLECTIONS
Heart of Earth (1950)
The Humming Stair (1953)
The Wind of Time (1962)
Nightmare Need (1964)
Death Poems (1974)
Edges of Night (1974)
A Sheaf of Snow Poems (1974)
As Evening Advances (1978)
Webs of Time (1979)
Creep to Death (1981)
Sixty Selected Poems (1985)
Look Back On Laurel Hills (1989)

SHORT STORY COLLECTIONS
Nine Horrors and a Dream (1958)
The Dark Returners (1959)
Scream at Midnight (1963)
Stories of Darkness and Dread (1973)
The Casebook of Lucius Leffing (1973)
The Chronicles of Lucius Leffing (1973)
The Shapes of Midnight (1980)
The Adventures of Lucius Leffing (1990)

NOVELETTE
Act of Providence (Written with Donald M. Grant) (1979)

Joe's death had quite an effect on me, and I only knew him a short time. I think it was a combination of several factors: First was his incredible generosity with his time and his willingness to help me at a time when I'm sure answering questions and corresponding were the last things he had the energy for; second, his dignity in the face of doom and his amazing acceptance of his own mortality (he often spoke as though his death was no more than a trivial inconvenience that he had to get by and then move on to other things); third, his sheer storytelling brilliance; and last, the unjust and cruel hand dealt a man of such kindness, warmth, and good nature.

Joe was a sweetheart of a guy, and I am a better person for having known him.

Mark in your memory well the date of Sunday, January 28, 1990, for that, my friends, was the day the stories died.

Here is Joseph Payne Brennan's last interview. —**sjs**

JOSEPH PAYNE BRENNAN
The Last Interview With A Legend

STEVE SPIGNESI: How did you first meet Stephen King?

JOSEPH PAYNE BRENNAN: In 1979, the organizers of the Fifth World Fantasy Convention invited me to attend as a guest. Don Higgins, a friend who drove me up to Providence, urged that I introduce myself to Stephen King. When I hesitated, Don took the initiative. He reported back that King was not only willing, but eager, to meet me. And although he was surrounded by a crush of fans, King took time out to shake hands and talk.

STEVE SPIGNESI: How did it come about that King agreed to write the introduction to your short story collection *The Shapes of Midnight*?

JOSEPH PAYNE BRENNAN: During the convention, without hesitation, King told my friend Don that he would be glad to write the introduction to the collection, which was due to be published by Berkley Books. Stephen's introduction, in the opinion of some readers, is one of his best. Of course, I agree!

STEVE SPIGNESI: Have you followed King's career at all?

JOSEPH PAYNE BRENNAN: I have followed Stephen's career, but somewhat as an amateur astronomer follows the course of a brand-new blazing comet. I must admit, though, that I am by no means a King specialist.

STEVE SPIGNESI: Are you familiar enough with his work to come up with opinions of his best and worst stories?

JOSEPH PAYNE BRENNAN: Not really. I don't read many novels and I rarely watch movies. An appalling confession, I admit, but there it is. This limitation makes it impossible for me to reply adequately to questions such as "What is King's best novel, Is his style plain or ornate?," etc.

STEVE SPIGNESI: Of the stuff that you have read...why do you think it works?

JOSEPH PAYNE BRENNAN: Let me say this. Whenever I've picked up a book by Stephen King, he's kept me turning the pages. I'm not sure why— style, plot content, atmosphere, descriptive power? Maybe it's a mixture of all of these. And perhaps, in addition, it's the sheer energy and strength of the author shining through the pages. That's my gut-level response. I'll leave the more detailed analyses to the other commentators in your book who are better qualified to supply them.

STEVE SPIGNESI: Stephen King's publishing history has been dubbed by many "The Stephen King Phenomenon." What do you think King's impact has been on the genre?

JOSEPH PAYNE BRENNAN: King's impact has been massive and far-reaching. It revolutionized the genre, increased the audience by fiftyfold and virtually created a separate industry. The Stephen King Phenomenon will easily continue through this century and decades into the next.

STEVE SPIGNESI: I guess you've already answered my last question, Joe: Do you think Stephen King's work will survive?

JOSEPH PAYNE BRENNAN: I think the *best* of Stephen King's work will most definitely survive—unless, that is, the books of all we scribblers are left in ashes by the inferno of a coming Armageddon. ❏

Joseph Payne Brennan at home, February 1989.
Photo courtesy Mrs. Joseph Payne Brennan.

JOSEPH PAYNE BRENNAN
The Nature of the Man
by Donald M. Grant

For all of you people who have never met him, contrary to rumor and popular belief, Joseph Payne Brennan doesn't even look like his famous character, Canavan. When I first knew him—and it's closing on forty years now!—he was a little pudgy after gold-bricking for a couple of years in George Patton's Third Army. That puts some dates on the two of us, for which I apologize to Joe—but has it really been *that* long?

I remember Joe visiting me in the '50s. I was living in a wonderful, rural, woodsy town called Exeter, in the state of Rhode Island, where the nearest house was more than a quarter of a mile away. Joe came over from the neighboring state of Connecticut to talk publications. Part of his visit—and he was most adamant on this score—had to be devoted to a long and rambling walk on the narrow, tree-covered road that passed by our house. After that, every time he used a rural area in one of the Leffing stories or other strange tales, I recalled his lengthy tramp through Exeter's woods and swamps. I wonder how many stories had their genesis in that traverse? Neither am I so sure that I'm not the model for the "unspeakable butcher" found in "Diary of a Werewolf"!

Whether it was Joe's visit or other forces (perhaps malignant), I packed my family out of Exeter soon after. I leave the cause of that hurried retreat to the speculation of the reader.

Joe's literary career is not a little amazing. He has been represented in more than 100 anthologies, is the author of 20 books, approximately 500 short stories, and several *thousand* poems.

Bookwise, we first got together in producing *The Dark Returners* which was published in 1959 under Joe's Macabre House imprint. It was followed in 1963 by a little book called *Scream at Midnight*. Subsequently, we combined in publishing several other titles including four books about Brennan's psychic detective, Lucius Leffing, beginning with *The Casebook of Lucius Leffing* in 1973. Three more Leffing books followed: *The Chronicles of Lucius Leffing* (1977), *Act of Providence* (1979), and *The Adventures of Lucius Leffing* (1989).

I had the great pleasure of collaborating with him on *Act of Providence,* which happened to be set at the First World Fantasy Convention in Providence, Rhode Island, in 1975. It was a vastly successful and marvelously charismatic convention, yet behind the scenes lurked a dark evil, and we set out to chronicle the events as they took place. With this in mind, I want to share with you one little incident that occurred during the writing. It points up the kind of person Joe really is.

In one scene in the book, a little knot of convention officials are gathered in the hotel lobby, animatedly discussing the disappearance of one of its members. Brennan, of course, is the teller of tales and the confidant of Lucius Leffing himself. As such, Brennan is a fixture in all of the Leffing stories. Here, he is an unintentional eavesdropper who accidentally hears a member of the convention committee utter rather naively: "What we need is Brennan's fictional detective, Lucius Leffing."

The person who uttered those words and demonstrated a complete lack of understanding, even a bungling ineptitude, was I. Indeed, it was I who penned that particular manuscript response that ushered from Brennan's lips.

What was written in the manuscript was: "The ass!"

Considering that I was the party labeling himself as an ass without offending another, I must admit that it tickled my sense of humor.

Up to this point, the story had taken shape rather effortlessly. We had each written portions of the book and then passed them back and forth with gently noted editorial changes on both our parts. But when this particular episode came back to me from Joe, it was flagged and noted with what had to have been a 3" paint brush. "NO!" it fairly shrieked at me. "TOO STRONG." Then, written in pen in a hand far less demonstrative: "Make this 'Damnation!'"

I didn't give up without a fight, but eventually Joe won out and "Damnation!" was used.

It wasn't that Joe didn't see the humor of the situation, or at least the fact that I was trying to pass myself off as a bungler (when everyone knows that I am a warrior-hero out of the Conan mold). He well knew what I was about. I know because we talked about it. It was simply a case where he didn't want to see a person as the target for laughter, in spite of the fact that I had engineered the situation and purported to make myself the target. Joe simply didn't want anyone hurt.

Such is the nature of the man!

Donald Grant's remembrance of Joseph Payne Brennan and introduction to "Canavan's Back Yard" was written in September of 1989, four months before Joe died. After talking it over, Don and I agreed to run it as originally written, since it captured his feelings at the time he wrote it. — sjs

"CANAVAN'S BACK YARD"
by Joseph Payne Brennan

I first met Canavan over twenty years ago shortly after he had emigrated from London. He was an antiquarian and a lover of old books; so he quite naturally set up shop as a second-hand book dealer after he settled in New Haven.

Since his small capital didn't permit him to rent premises in the center of the city, he rented combined business and living quarters in an isolated old house near the outskirts of town. The section was sparsely settled, but since a good percentage of Canavan's business was transacted by mail, it didn't particularly matter.

Quite often, after a morning spent at my typewriter, I walked out to Canavan's shop and spent most of the afternoon browsing among his old books. I found it a great pleasure, especially because Canavan never resorted to high-pressure methods to make a sale. He was aware of my precarious financial situation; he never frowned if I walked away empty-handed.

In fact, he seemed to welcome me for my company alone. Only a few book buyers called at his place with regularity, and I think he was often lonely. Sometimes when business was slow, he would brew a pot of English tea and the two of us would sit for hours, drinking tea and talking about books.

Canavan even looked like an antiquarian book dealer—or the popular caricature of one. He was small of frame, somewhat stoop-shouldered, and his blue eyes peered out from behind archaic spectacles with steel rims and square-cut lenses.

Although I doubt if his yearly income ever matched that of a good paperhanger, he managed to "get by" and he was content. Content, that is, until he began noticing his back yard.

Behind the ramshackle old house in which he lived and ran his shop, stretched a long, desolate yard overgrown with brambles and high brindle-colored grass. Several decayed apple trees, jagged and black with rot, added to the scene's dismal aspect. The broken wooden fences on both sides of the yard were all but swallowed up by the tangle of coarse grass. They appeared to be literally sinking into the ground. Altogether, the yard presented an unusually depressing picture, and I often wondered why Canavan didn't clean it up. But it was none of my business; I never mentioned it.

One afternoon when I visited the shop, Canavan was not in the front display room, so I walked down a narrow corridor to a rear storeroom where he sometimes worked, packing and unpacking book shipments. When I entered the storeroom, Canavan was standing at the window, looking out at the back yard.

I started to speak and then for some reason didn't. I think what stopped me was the look on Canavan's face. He was gazing out at the yard with a peculiar intense expression, as if he were completely absorbed by something he saw there. Varying, conflicting emotions showed on his strained features. He seemed both fascinated and fearful, attracted and repelled. When he finally noticed me, he almost jumped. He stared at me for a moment as if I were a total stranger.

Then his old easy smile came back, and his blue eyes twinkled behind the square spectacles. He shook his head. "That back yard of mine sure looks funny sometimes. You look at it long enough, you think it runs for miles!"

That was all he said at the time, and I soon forgot about it. I didn't know that was just the beginning of the horrible business.

After that, whenever I visited the shop, I found Canavan in the rear storeroom. Once in a while he was actually working, but most of the time he was simply standing at the window looking out at that dreary yard of his.

Sometimes he would stand there for minutes completely oblivious to my presence. Whatever he saw appeared to rivet his entire attention. His countenance at these times showed an expression of fright mingled with a queer kind of pleasurable expectancy. Usually it was necessary for me to cough loudly or shuffle my feet before he turned from the window.

Afterward, when he talked about books, he would seem to be his old self again, but I began to experience the disconcerting feeling that he was merely acting, that while he chatted about incunabula, his thoughts were actually still dwelling on that infernal back yard.

Several times I thought of questioning him about the yard, but whenever words were on the tip of my tongue, I was stopped by a sense of embarrassment. How can one admonish a man for looking out of a window at his own back yard. What does one say and how does one say it?

I kept silent. Later I regretted it bitterly.

Canavan's business, never really flourishing, began to diminish. Worse than that, he appeared to be failing physically. He grew more stooped and gaunt. Though his eyes never lost their sharp glint, I began to believe it was more the glitter of fever than the twinkle of healthy enthusiasm which animated them.

One afternoon when I entered the shop, Canavan was nowhere to be found. Thinking he might be just outside the back door engaged in some household chore, I leaned against the rear window and looked out.

I didn't see Canavan, but as I gazed out over the yard I was swept with a sudden inexplicable sense of desolation which seemed to roll over me like the wave of an icy sea. My initial impulse was to pull away from the window, but something held me. As I stared out over that miserable tangle of briars and brindle grass, I experienced what for want of a better word I can only call *curiosity*. Perhaps some cool, analytical, dispassionate part of my brain simply wanted to discover what had caused my sudden feeling of acute depression. Or possibly some feature of that wretched vista attracted me on a subconscious level which I had never permitted to crowd up into my sane and waking hours.

In any case, I remained at the window. The long dry brown grass wavered slightly in the wind. The rotted black trees reared motionless. Not a single bird, not even a butterfly, hovered over that bleak expanse. There was nothing to be seen except the stalks of long brindle grass, the decayed trees, and scattered clumps of low-growing briars.

Yet there was something about that particular isolated slice of landscape which I found intriguing. I think I had the feeling that it presented some kind of puzzle, and that if I gazed at it long enough, the puzzle would resolve itself.

After I had stood looking out at it for a few minutes, I experienced the odd sensation that its perspective was subtly altering. Neither the grass nor the trees changed, and yet the yard itself seemed to expand its dimensions. At first I merely reflected that the yard was actually much longer than I had previously believed. Then I had an idea that in reality it stretched for several acres. Finally, I became convinced that it continued for an interminable distance and that, if I entered it, I might walk for miles and miles before I came to the end.

I was seized by a sudden almost overpowering desire to rush out the back door, plunge into that sea of wavering brindle grass, and stride straight ahead until I had discovered for myself just how far it did extend. I was, in fact, on the point of doing so – when I saw Canavan.

He appeared abruptly out of the tangle of tall grass at the near end of the yard. For at least a minute he seemed to be completely lost. He looked at the back of his own house as if he had never in his life seen it before. He was disheveled and obviously excited. Briars clung to his trousers and jacket, and pieces of grass were stuck in the hooks of his old-fashioned shoes. His eyes roved around wildly; he seemed about to turn and bolt back into the tangle from which he had just emerged.

I rapped loudly on the window pane. He paused in a half turn, looked over his shoulder, and saw me.

Gradually an expression of normality returned to his agitated features. Walking in a weary slouch, he approached the house. I hurried to the door and let him in. He went straight to the front display room and sank down in a chair.

He looked up when I followed him into the room. "Frank," he said in a half whisper, "would you make some tea?"

I brewed tea, and he drank it scalding hot without saying a word. He looked utterly exhausted; I knew he was too tired to tell me what had happened.

"You had better stay indoors for a few days," I said as I left.

He nodded weakly, without looking up, and bade me good day.

When I returned to the shop the next afternoon, he appeared rested and refreshed but nevertheless moody and depressed. He made no mention of the previous day's episode. For a week or so it seemed as if he might forget about the yard. But one day when I went into the shop, he was standing at the rear window, and I could see that he tore himself away only with the greatest reluctance. After that, the pattern began repeating itself with regularity. I knew that that weird tangle of brindle grass behind his house was becoming an obsession.

Because I feared for his business as well as for his fragile health, I finally remonstrated with him. I pointed out that he was losing customers; he had not issued a book catalogue in months. I told him that the time spent in gazing at that witch's half acre he called his back yard would be better spent in listing his books and filling his orders. I assured him that an obsession such as his was sure to undermine his health. And finally I pointed out the absurd and ridiculous aspects of the affair. If people knew he spent hours in staring out of his window at nothing more than a miniature jungle of grass and briars, they might think he was actually mad.

I ended by boldly asking him exactly what he had experienced that afternoon when I had seen him come out of the grass with a lost bewildered expression on his face.

He removed his square spectacles with a sigh.

"Frank," he said, "I know you mean well. But there's something about that backyard—some secret—that I've got to find out. I don't know what it is exactly—something about distance and dimensions and perspectives, I think. But whatever it is, I've come to consider it—well, a challenge. I've got to get to the root of it. If you think I'm crazy, I'm sorry. But I'll have no rest until I solve the riddle of that piece of ground."

He replaced his spectacles with a frown. "That afternoon," he went on, "when you were standing at the window, I had a strange and frightening experience out there. I had been watching at the window, and finally I felt myself drawn irresistibly outside. I plunged into the grass with a feeling of exhilaration, of adventure, of expectancy. As I advanced into the yard, my sense of elation quickly changed to a mood of black depression. I turned around, intending to come right out—but I couldn't. You won't believe this, I know—but I was lost! I simply lost all sense of direction and couldn't decide which way to turn. That grass is taller than it looks! When you get into it, you can't see anything beyond it."

"I know this sounds incredible—but I wandered out there for an hour. The yard seemed fantastically large—it almost seemed to alter its dimensions as I moved, so that a large expanse of it lay always in front of me. I must have walked in circles. I swear I trudged miles!"

He shook his head. "You don't have to believe me. I don't expect you to. But that's what happened. When I finally found my way out, it was by the sheerest accident. And the strangest part of it is that once I got out, I felt suddenly terrified without the tall grass all around me and I wanted to rush back in again! This in spite of the ghastly sense of desolation which the place aroused in me.

"But I've got to go back. I've got to figure the thing out. There's something out there that defies the laws of earthly nature as we know them. I mean to find out what it is. I think I have a plan and I mean to put it into practice."

His words stirred me strangely and when I uneasily recalled my own experience at the window that afternoon, I found it difficult to dismiss his story as sheer nonsense. I did—half-heartedly—try to dissuade him from entering the yard again, but I knew even as I spoke that I was wasting my breath.

I left the shop that afternoon with a feeling of oppression and foreboding which nothing could remove.

When I called several days later, my worst fears were realized—Canavan was missing. The front door of the shop was unlatched as usual, but Canavan was not in the house. I looked in every room. Finally, with a feeling of infinite dread, I opened the back door and looked out toward the yard.

The long stalks of brown grass slid against each other in the slight breeze with dry sibilant whispers. The dead trees reared black and motionless. Although it was late summer, I could hear neither the chirp of a bird nor the chirr of a single insect. The yard itself seemed to be listening.

Feeling something against my foot, I glanced down and saw a thick twine stretching from inside the door,

across the scant cleared space immediately adjacent to the house and thence into the wavering wall of grass. Instantly I recalled Canavan's mention of a "plan." His plan, I realized immediately, was to enter the yard trailing a stout cord behind him. No matter how he twisted and turned, he must have reasoned, he could always find his way out by following back along the cord.

It seemed like a workable scheme, so I felt relieved. Probably Canavan was still in the yard. I decided I would wait for him to come out. Perhaps if he were permitted to roam around in the yard long enough, without interruption, the place would lose its evil fascination for him, and he would forget about it.

I went back into the shop and browsed among the books. At the end of an hour I became uneasy again. I wondered how long Canavan had been in the yard. When I began reflecting on the old man's uncertain health, I felt a sense of responsibility.

I finally returned to the back door, saw that he was nowhere in sight, and called out his name. I experienced the disquieting sensation that my shout carried no further than the very edge of that whispering fringe of grass. It was as if the sound had been smothered, deadened, nullified as soon as the vibrations of it reached the border of that overgrown yard.

I called again and again, but there was no reply. At length I decided to go in after him. I would follow along the cord, I thought, and I would be sure to locate him. I told myself that the thick grass undoubtedly did stifle my shout and possibly, in any case, Canavan might be growing slightly deaf.

Just inside the door, the cord was tied securely around the leg of a heavy table. Taking hold of the twine, I crossed the cleared area back of the house and slipped into the rustling expanse of grass.

The going was easy at first, and I made good progress. As I advanced, however, the grass stems became thicker, and grew closer together, and I was forced to shove my way through them.

When I was no more than a few yards inside the tangle, I was overwhelmed with the same bottomless sense of desolation which I had experienced before. There was certainly something uncanny about the place. I felt as if I had suddenly veered into another world—a world of briars and brindle grass whose ceaseless half-heard whisperings were somehow alive with evil.

As I pushed along, the cord abruptly came to an end. Glancing down, I saw that it had caught against a thorn bush, abraded itself, and had subsequently broken. Although I bent down and poked in the area for several minutes, I was unable to locate the piece from which it had parted. Probably Canavan was unaware that the cord had broken and was now pulling it along with him.

I straightened up, cupped my hands to my mouth, and shouted. My shout seemed to be all but drowned in my throat by that dismal wall of grass. I felt as if I were down at the bottom of a well, shouting up.

Frowning with growing uneasiness, I tramped ahead. The grass stalks kept getting thicker and tougher, and at length I needed both hands to propel myself through the matted growth. I began to sweat profusely; my head started to ache, and I imagined that my vision was beginning to blur. I felt the same tense, almost unbearable oppression which one experiences on a stifling summer's day when a storm is brewing and the atmosphere is charged with static electricity.

Also, I realized with a slight qualm of fear that I had got turned around and didn't know which part of the yard I was in. During an objective half-minute in which I reflected that I was actually worried about getting lost in someone's back yard, I almost laughed— almost. But there was something about the place which didn't permit laughter. I plodded ahead with a sober face.

Presently I began to feel that I was not alone. I had a sudden hair-raising conviction that someone—or something—was creeping along in the grass behind me. I cannot say with certainty that I heard anything, although I may have, but all at once I was firmly convinced that some creature was crawling or wriggling a short distance to the rear.

I felt that I was being watched and that the watcher was wholly malignant.

For a wild instant I considered headlong flight. Then, unaccountably, rage took possession of me. I was suddenly furious with Canavan, furious with the yard, furious with myself. All my pent-up tension exploded in a gust of rage which swept away fear. Now, I vowed, I would get to the root of the weird business. I would be tormented and frustrated by it no longer.

I whirled without warning and lunged into the grass where I believed my stealthy pursuer might be hiding.

I stopped abruptly; my savage anger melted into inexpressible horror.

In the faint but brassy sunlight which filtered down through the towering stalks, Canavan crouched on all fours like a beast about to spring. His glasses were gone, his clothes were in shreds and his mouth was twisted into an insane grimace, half smirk, half snarl.

I stood petrified, staring at him. His eyes, queerly out of focus, glared at me with concentrated hatred and without any glimmer of recognition. His gray hair was matted with grass and small sticks; his entire body, in fact, including the tattered remains of his clothing, was covered with them as if he had grovelled or rolled on the ground like a wild animal.

After the first throat-freezing shock, I finally found my tongue.

"Canavan!" I screamed at him. "Canavan, for God's sake don't you know me?"

His answer was a low throaty snarl. His lips twisted back from his yellowish teeth, and his crouching body tensed for a spring.

Pure terror took possession of me. I leaped aside and flung myself into that infernal wall of grass an instant before he lunged.

The intensity of my terror must have given me added strength. I rammed headlong through those twisted stalks which before I had laboriously pulled aside. I could hear the grass and briar brushes crashing behind me, and I knew that I was running for my life.

I pounded on as in a nightmare. Grass stalks snapped against my face like whips, and thorns gnashed me like razors, but I felt nothing. All my physical and mental resources were concentrated in one frenzied resolve: I must get out of that devil's field of grass and away from the monstrous thing which followed swiftly in my wake.

My breath began coming in great shuddering sobs. My legs felt weak and I seemed to be looking through spinning saucers of light. But I ran on.

The thing behind me was gaining. I could hear it growling, and I could feel it lunge against the earth only inches behind my flying feet. And all the time I had the maddening conviction that I was actually running in circles.

At last, when I felt that I must surely collapse in another second, I plunged through a final brindle thicket into the open sunlight. Ahead of me lay the cleared area at the rear of Canavan's shop. Just beyond was the house itself.

Gasping and fighting for breath, I dragged myself toward the door. For no reason that I could explain, then or afterwards, I felt absolutely certain that the horror at my heels would not venture into the open area. I didn't even turn around to make sure.

Inside the house I fell weakly into a chair. My strained breathing slowly returned to normal, but my mind remained caught up in a whirlwind of sheer horror and hideous conjecture.

Canavan, I realized, had gone completely mad. Some ghastly shock had turned him into a ravening bestial lunatic thirsting to savagely destroy any living thing that crossed his path. Remembering the oddly-focused eyes which had glared at me with a glaze of animal ferocity, I knew that his mind had not been merely unhinged—it was totally gone. Death could be the only possible release.

But Canavan was still at least the shell of a human being, and he had been my friend. I could not take the law into my own hands.

With many misgivings I called the police and an ambulance.

What followed was more madness, plus a session of questions and demands which left me in a state of near nervous collapse.

A half dozen burly policemen spent the better part of an hour tramping through that wavering brindle grass without locating any trace of Canavan. They came out cursing, rubbing their eyes and shaking their heads. They were flushed, furious—and ill at ease. They announced that they had seen nothing and heard nothing except some sneaking dog which stayed always out of sight and growled at them at intervals.

When they mentioned the growling dog, I opened my mouth to speak, but thought better of it and said nothing. They were already regarding me with open suspicion as if they believed my own mind might be breaking.

I repeated my story at least twenty times, and still they were not satisfied. They ransacked the entire house. They inspected Canavan's files. They even removed some loose boards in one of the rooms and searched underneath.

At length they grudgingly concluded that Canavan had suffered total loss of memory after experiencing some kind of shock and that he had wandered off the premises in a state of amnesia shortly after I had encountered him in the yard. My own description of his appearance and actions they discounted as lurid exaggeration. After warning me that I would probably be questioned further and that my own premises might be inspected, they reluctantly permitted me to leave.

Their subsequent searches and investigations revealed nothing new and Canavan was put down as a missing person, probably afflicted with acute amnesia.

But I was not satisfied, and I could not rest.

Six months of patient, painstaking, tedious research in the files and stacks of the local university library finally yielded something which I do not offer as an explanation, nor even as a definite clue, but only as a fantastic near-impossiblity which I ask no one to believe.

One afternoon, after my extended research over a period of months had produced nothing of significance, the Keeper of Rare Books at the library triumphantly bore to my study niche a tiny, crumbling pamphlet which had been printed in New Haven in 1695. It mentioned no author and carried the stark title, *Death of Goodie Larkins, Witche.*

Several years before, it revealed, an ancient crone, one Goodie Larkins, had been accused by neighbors of turning a missing child into a wild dog. The Salem madness was raging at the time, and Goodie Larkins had been summarily condemned to death. Instead of being burned, she had been driven into a marsh deep in the woods where seven savage dogs, starved for a fortnight, had been turned loose on her trail. Apparently her accusers felt that this was a touch of truly poetic justice.

As the ravening dogs closed in on her, she was heard by her retreating neighbors to utter a frightful curse:

"Let this lande I fall upon lye alle the way to Hell!" she had screamed. *"And they who tarry here be as these beasties that rende me dead!"*

A subsequent inspection of old maps and land deeds satisfied me that the marsh in which Goodie Larkins was torn to pieces by the dogs after uttering her awful curse—originally occupied the same lot or square which now enclosed Canavan's hellish back yard!

I say no more. I returned only once to that devilish spot. It was a cold desolate autumn day, and a keening wind rattled the brindle stalks. I cannot say what urged me back to that unholy area; perhaps it was some lingering feeling of loyalty toward the Canavan I had known. Perhaps it was even some last shred of hope. But as soon as I entered the cleared area behind Canavan's boarded-up house, I knew I had made a mistake.

As I stared at the stiff waving grass, the bare trees and the black ragged briars, I felt as if I, in turn, were being watched. I felt as if something alien and wholly evil were observing me, and though I was terrified, I experienced a perverse, insane impulse to rush headlong into that whispering expanse. Again I imagined I saw that monstrous landscape subtly alter its dimensions and perspective until I was staring at a stretch of blowing brindle grass and rotted trees which ran for miles. Something urged me to enter, to lose myself in the lovely grass, to roll and grovel at its roots, to rip off the foolish encumbrances of cloth which covered me and run howling and ravenous, on and on, on and on...

Instead, I turned and rushed away. I ran through the windy autumn streets like a madman. I lurched into my rooms and bolted the door.

I have never gone back since. And I never shall.

THE END

SPIGNESI'S FAVORITES
Novels, Novellas, Short Stories, Poetry & Films

NOVELS

1. *IT*
2. *The Long Walk*
3. *The Stand: The Complete & Uncut Edition*
4. *Misery*
5. *The Dark Half*
6. *The Dark Tower II: The Drawing of the Three*
7. *Thinner*
8. *The Shining*
9. *Pet Sematary*
10. *The Dead Zone*

5. "The Last Rung on the Ladder"
6. "Home Delivery"
7. "The Mangler"
8. "The Jaunt"
9. "Survivor Type"
10. "Nona"
11. "The Plant" (Part 1)
12. "Gramma"
13. "Graveyard Shift"
14. "Dolan's Cadillac"
15. "The Reach"

NOVELLAS

1. "Secret Window, Secret Garden"
2. "The Langoliers"
3. "The Body"
4. "Apt Pupil"
5. "The Breathing Method"

SHORT STORIES

1. "One for the Road"
2. "Gray Matter"
3. "Squad D"
4. "My Pretty Pony"

POETRY

1. "Paranoid: A Chant"
2. "For Owen"
3. "Leighton Street"
4. "Brooklyn August"
5. "The Dark Man"

FILMS

1. "Misery"
2. "Stand By Me"
3. "IT"
4. "The Dead Zone"
5. "Carrie" & "The Shining" (Tie)

PART VII

IN A REGION WITH NO PROPER NAME

The Hidden Horrors of Stephen King

THE UNWRITTEN KING
Stories Stephen King Has Thought Of,
But Just Hasn't Written Down (Yet)

Did you know that in some dark corner of the Stephen Kingdom there is a crepuscular zone where the Lost and Unwritten Stories live?

The Lost Stories have disappeared over the years, much like little David Brown did during his brother Hilly's magic show in *The Tommyknockers*. These Lost Tales include King's first short story (something to do with dinosaurs that were allergic to leather), and another one about an asteroid miner and a pink cube. The Lost Stories also include the two tales, "The Dimension Warp" and "I'm Falling," from the 1963 Stephen King/Chris Chesley collaborative collection *People, Places, and Things*.

These stories are gone forever, and we can only mourn their loss. They could have been and always would have been...our friends.

The Unwritten Stories, however, are another...er, story altogether.

The Unwritten King consists of those stories that Stephen King has thought of—and actually described in interviews—but hasn't yet taken the time to *write down*.

Hearing King describe these tales only whets our appetite for the real thing. It's like his Afterword to *The Drawing of the Three*. Now that we know that the next two volumes of *The Dark Tower* series are *The Waste Lands* and *Wizard and Glass*, we anxiously await any and every pronouncement from the King as to just where he is in Roland's story, and how close Roland—and Stephen King—are to the Dark Tower.

Here is a look at five notable tales that have been crawling around up in that attic where King hides his goblins. (I've heard that this attic is somewhere between his two ears, just due north of the room where he keeps his joke inventory.)

My sources were interviews with King—one talk with Douglas Winter, one with Julie Washington, one with Bryan Miller; and an article by King called "Stephen King's Desert Island," which appeared in the July 1990 issue of *Conde Nast Traveler* magazine. Only one of the four stories is titled—"The Rats Are Loose on Flight 74"—although for the Miller story, King made up his own dustjacket blurb.

"The Rats Are Loose on Flight 74" is King's version of *The Fear of Flying*:

"The Rats Are Loose on Flight 74"

"I worry about airplanes. I can remember being on a transcontinental flight and getting to the halfway point—which the stewardesses always announce with great cheer—although what they are saying is that you are now too far to turn back. You either have to go ahead or die. And I thought, what if somebody said, 'I need a pillow,' and the stewardess opened the overhead rack and all these rats came out into her face, and she started to scream, and the rats were biting off her nose and everything else, and one of the people in first class opened up a pouch to get an airsick bag because this was so gross, and rats came out of there, rats came out of everywhere. And the name of this story was going to be 'The Rats Are Loose on Flight 74.' I just haven't gotten around to writing it yet, but I probably will."

—From an interview with
Douglas E. Winter, *Faces of Fear*, pg. 239

David Letterman notwithstanding, Stephen King also has his own Top Ten list, made up of his Top Ten Fears—which he calls "Bears." "The Rats Are Loose on Flight 74" once again shows King working with his Number 5 "Bear," the fear of rats. King has used rats as a horror device in the past, most notably in the *Night Shift* story "Graveyard Shift," in which our friend Hall becomes a late supper for mutant rats in the sub-basement of the Gates Falls mill:

"Something had happened to the rats back here, some hideous mutation that never could have survived under the eye of the sun; nature would have forbidden it. But down here, nature had taken on another ghastly face.

"The rats were gigantic, some as high as three feet. But their rear legs were gone and they were blind as moles, like their flying cousins."

—"Graveyard Shift" From *Night Shift*

Another notable use of rats by King was in a segment from *'Salem's Lot* that never appeared in print. Doubleday vetoed the scene and King was forced to censor himself. King described the "lost scene" in an interview with *Playboy* magazine:

"I had a scene in which Jimmy Cody, the

local doctor, is devoured in a boardinghouse basement by a horde of rats summoned from the town dump by the leader of the vampires. They swarm all over him like a writhing, furry carpet, biting and clawing, and when he tries to scream a warning to his companion upstairs, one of them scurries into his open mouth and squirms there as it gnaws out his tongue. I loved the scene, but my editor made it clear that *no way* would Doubleday publish something like that, and I came around eventually and impaled poor Jimmy on knives. But, shit, it just wasn't the same."

> —From "Playboy Interview:
> Stephen King," *Playboy,* June 1983

There's no doubt that "The Rats Are Loose on Flight 74" would be a terrific story in King's hands. The only question is, of course, how would it end? Would King kill everybody, sending the plane and its passengers down to a fiery death after, say, a rat chews out the eyes of the pilot? Or would he have the passengers triumph over the invasion by killing the rats and surviving the flight? Who knows? If and when King gets around to writing this story, that's when we'll find out.

❖❖❖

In an interview with Julie Washington called "If You're Scared Silly, then Stephen King is Happy," which originally appeared in the Cleveland, Ohio *Plain Dealer* on January 31, 1988, and which was reprinted in the April 1988 *Castle Rock,* King described two story ideas that he hadn't gotten around to writing down yet. He didn't mention titles, so I will just describe them by their subject matter: The "Kiddie Ride" Story, and The "Airport Ladies Room" Story.

The "Kiddie Ride" Story

"You know those kiddie rides in malls? Well, what would happen if a mother put her kid inside a ride, dropped in a quarter and watched the thing spin around a few times, and when it stopped, she discovered her son had disappeared?"

> —From "If You're Scared Silly,
> then Stephen King is Happy,"
> by Julie Washington

Where'd the kid go? To Altair-4 with the Lost Stories and David Brown? This is an eerie idea that has a real "Twilight Zone" feel to it. King uses this motif in the following story idea as well, (also from the Washington article):

The "Airport Ladies' Room" Story

"Or how about this: Husband and wife are at the airport to board a plane. The woman has to go to the ladies' room, so the man waits outside for her. And waits. She never comes out. Pretty soon he notices that other women are going in, but not coming out. Boyfriends and husbands accumulate outside the bathroom, all feeling uneasy but reluctant to talk to each other. Eventually they alert airport security, then the governor and ultimately the president in an effort to deal with the mystery."

This sounds like a fun idea, most notably because here King is toying with the idea of setting another story in a bathroom. King's most memorable uses of bathrooms occur in *IT* (the exploding toilets), in "Sneakers" from *Night Visions 5* (the haunted toilet stall), and in the 1990 story "The Moving Finger."

Interestingly, with this unwritten story, King turns a public ladies' rest room into something opening onto another dimension, again much like Hilly Brown's magic table in *The Tommyknockers.*

There appear to be a lot of doorways that open on to Altair-4.

❖❖❖

On Wednesday, October 26, 1988, the New York *Times* ran an interview with King by Bryan Miller called "Writer Eats Steak Before It Eats Him" as part of their "Eating Out With..." column.

King had dinner with Miller and King's business manager, Arthur Greene.

King, drinking a Bloody Mary, split the house-special steak with Greene, along with fried potatoes and creamed spinach on the side.

King talked about the different uses of food in his work, mentioning specifically *Thinner,* as well as *Carrie, 'Salem's Lot, The Shining, Cujo,* and *Pet Sematary.*

King also discussed his own culinary interests, and said he often cooked for his children. He described one of his specialties: "[G]round chuck with canned spaghetti, jazzed up with cayenne and other peppers." He admitted "It's awful stuff, but they gobble it up." After the meal was over, Miller and King chatted about King being "forever on the lookout for ghoulish new plots." Miller revealed that "[King] even devised one on the spot when I mentioned that I had once worked for a newspaper in Connecticut."

Let's call this one...

The "Werewolves in Connecticut" Story

"I can see it now. You go up there and take this job because, well, either your wife died or you had some terrible debilitating illness. That's when the werewolves show up. You know it, but nobody else will believe you and your editor won't publish any of these things.

"It was a quiet little New England town, until *he* came."

—From "Writer Eats Steak Before
It Eats Him," by Bryan Miller
New York *Times,* October 26, 1988

This sounds like "Tarker's Mills Comes To 'Salem's Lot," doesn't it?

King's most notable use of werewolves, of course, is in *Cycle of the Werewolf,* and in that book, there's only *one* werewolf terrorizing the town. I think it would be terrific to have a whole swarm (flock?) (pack?) of lycanthropes wreaking havoc on "a quiet little New England town."

❖❖❖

The last Unwritten Story we'll look at is a tale that King actually wrote part of for an article called "Stephen King's Desert Island," which appeared in the July 1990 issue of *Conde Nast Traveler* magazine.

In the article, King talked about the question he's asked "every three months or so": "If you were stranded on a desert island, what one book would you take with you?"

He makes the point that he has no survival skills, and that "the concept of living off the land belongs only in robust, self-congratulatory novels like *Robinson Crusoe,* allegories like *Lord of the Flies,* or those mindlessly cheerful novels of boys' adventures written in the last quarter of the nineteenth century and the first quarter of the twentieth."

King then gives us three paragraphs of literary imitation of these types of novels, involving three characters, Richard, Thomas, and Little Toby. Thomas suggests that "[i]f we stretch our shirts over those fallen logs...we shall catch each morning's fall of dew! We can drink that!" Richard then exclaims "Rather!" and tells the boys that he can make a "whizzer heliograph" with a piece of broken mirror because, he, of course, remembers his "Morse from the Scouts." The excerpt from this nonexistent work ends with "'Hurrah for the adventure!' cried Little Toby, causing them all to laugh indulgently."

I think Stephen King is incredibly well-read, don't you? But in any case, King does answer the question...sort-of. He states that "[he] would much more likely be sitting on that bone-white beach for the next twenty years with a copy of *Killer Crabs from Hell* than *Remembrance of Things Past.*"

He emphasized that "You don't *set out* to be marooned, that's the point." And then he changes the original question to a more logical "What would you *write* if you were marooned on a desert island?" King's answer? "Everything I could."

Amen.

(And get that boy a rescue ship.)

The unwritten tales lurking in the dark corners of his imagination just re-emphasize the sheer storytelling powers possessed by Stephen King. I once read that the music of Beethoven that survived on paper was only ten percent of what he actually wrote. I've seen accounts that told of old Lud playing original music in public for hours on end...and never writing any of it down.

For now, we can only imagine the countless untold stories hidden somewhere behind those glasses, but what is really more important is that we revel in the tales told.

THE UNFINISHED KING
The Stephen King Notebook

In Michael J. Autrey's Spring 1989 Stephen King/Clive Barker catalogue, an item was listed that immediately started me salivating and piqued my King-sized interest:

STEPHEN KING HOLOGRAPHIC—Handwritten manuscript to an unfinished, unpublished short story titled "Keyholes" written in a 8 1/2x11" composition notebook. Also included is the outline to the movie Silver Bullet, 20 pages of King solving math equations and a personal note to his wife. This is definitely a one of a kind item. Call or write for details on this one...
....NM–$6,000.00

An unfinished, unpublished Stephen King short story!? I had to have it. But $6,000 was a little steep for me. ($6.00 would have been more in the ballpark.)

I wrote to Michael Autrey, and just simply asked for it. To cut right to the chase, he agreed to help, first, because he wanted to be involved in this book, and secondly, because Michael's basically a pretty nice guy.

Thanks to Michael's support, and his belief in *The Shape Under the Sheet,* a photocopy of the entire notebook was made available to me for research.

In this section, I'll take you on a tour through what has to be one of the most unique Stephen King items in existence. But let me clarify what I mean when I say that: I'm sure that King has countless notebooks strewn throughout his home and offices filled with all kinds of ephemera: stalled stories, outlines, notes, poems, jottings, doodles, beginnings of novels...what have you. But the reason this particular notebook is such a rarity is that King personally donated it to a charity auction. King donated it for the American Repertory Theatre's annual benefit auction. It was auctioned off on May 1, 1988.

It has since traded hands a few times, and Michael ended up offering it in his catalogue at the price of $6,000.

I will now go through *The Stephen King Notebook* page by page, and give details on "Keyholes," the "Silver Bullet" outline, and other items contained within.

The Stephen King Notebook consists of thirty-five pages, all in King's hand, and contains a few personal notes to himself, the manuscript to the unfinished story "Keyholes," the revised outline to the film "Silver Bullet," twenty pages of King working through a textbook and solving algebraic equations, notes about two sports teams, a list of actors and actresses, and a full-page note to his wife Tabitha.

The first page contains the following notes King made to himself:

Copy-edit <u>Skeleton Crew</u>
"Momilies" for Michelle Slung, plus picture
   of Mom
Short summary of <u>Christine</u> for same mag—
   V.F.?
Pack!

These notes can allow us to date the notebook. Since *Skeleton Crew* was released in hardcover in 1985 (and copy-editing of galleys is usually done in the eight-to-ten month period prior to publication), and since the revised "Silver Bullet" outline in the notebook is dated "3/14/84," we can date the notebook somewhere in early 1984, probably the first six months.

The "Momilies" reference was King reminding himself to come up with some memorable "homilies" from his mother for inclusion in Slung's book *Momilies.* In the June 1985 issue of *Castle Rock,* Stephanie Leonard said the following about King's participation in the book:

[*Momilies*] is special to us because it contains some of Stephen King's mother's wisdom, as well as her photograph. Examples of Nellie Ruth King's words to her children: "You'll never be hung for your beauty." "He's no better than you – we all stand naked inside our clothes," and "Keep all string a' drawing."

It's not clear what King was referring to when he mentioned the "short summary of *Christine* for same mag," nor what the initials V.F. stood for, unless he was thinking of writing something about *Christine* for *Vanity Fair* magazine.

And, from his last one-line note—"Pack!"—I guess King was going "on the road again," transforming himself into Travelin' Steve! (Or, as his son Owen once said, "[Daddy's] going off to be Stephen King." Or, maybe he was just going on vacation. Who knows?)

The next section of the notebook is the most important: the handwritten manuscript to the unfinished short story "Keyholes."

The story consists of two-and-one-half handwritten pages comprising twenty-six paragraphs and 768 words.

It begins:

"Conklin's first, snap, judgement was that this man, Michael Briggs, was not the sort of fellow who usually sought psychiatric help."

"Keyholes" is important for a couple of reasons: one, it shows us how King writes, and two, it shows us how King can create mood, tone, and immediately memorable characters in a few short paragraphs.

The story, such as it is, is brief: It all takes place in Dr. Conklin's office. Conklin is preparing to have a session with a man named Michael Briggs, a construction worker, who wants to talk to the doctor about his son, Jeremy.

At first, Conklin had told his nurse, Nancy Adrian, to refer Briggs to another doctor, Milton Abrams, in Albany. But Briggs refused to see Abrams because he vaguely knew him, and he felt that had to tell his story to a complete stranger first. As he put it, "I'd tell a priest if I was Catholic."

There is something going on with Briggs's son Jeremy, and Briggs isn't sure exactly what is happening. He tells Conklin, "I just want to know what's going on with my kid—if it's me or what."

The characters in "Keyholes" immediately spring to life: we can see Dr. Conklin, an older, dignified gentleman living a very nice life thanks to his practice. His nurse describes him as an "expensive New York psychiatrist," with the emphasis on "expensive." Conklin is trying to quit smoking. Every morning he filled his cigarette case with exactly ten Winston 100's, and when the cigarettes were gone, he was through smoking for the day.

Nancy Adrian is a strong character in the piece; in fact, she's the one who convinces Conklin to finally see Briggs. King describes her as "forty-five, but when she grinned she looked twenty." A simple phrase, but oh so "on." King can throw a picture up onto the movie screen of your mind with a few precisely chosen words. We're told that Conklin and Adrian might have been an item once: "[O]nce, over drinks, he had called her the Della Street of psychiatry, and she had almost hit him."

Michael Briggs is very reminiscent of another Stephen King troubled father character: Lester Billings, from King's seminal *Night Shift* short story, "The Boogeyman." As in that story, Briggs is a single parent, only in "Keyholes," Briggs is a widower, while Billings was divorced.

King describes Briggs as having long, "almost shoulder-length" hair, and that "[h]is large hands were chapped, scabbed in a number of places, and

when he reached over the desk to shake, [Conklin] felt the rasp of rough callouses."

As to what is going on with Jeremy...we're never told in this brief opening segment. King sets the stage, introduces the characters, and then simply stops writing. (In this notebook, that is. He may have transcribed this opening segment, completed the story, and have it stored on disk, waiting for the right time and place to release it.) At one point, Nurse Adrian remarks that "[Briggs] sounded like a man who thinks there's something physical wrong with his son." Except that he's telling his story to a psychiatrist.

After the expositional opening paragraphs that set the stage, we're back in the present time (story time, that is), and the piece ends with "And here it was, Wednesday afternoon...and here was Mr. Briggs sitting opposite him with his work-reddened hands folded in his lap and looking warily at Conklin."

There is one clue early on in the piece where King describes the wary look Briggs gives the psychiatric couch in Conklin's office. But whether or not that actually means anything is never confirmed. All we're told is that Jeremy is seven, something is going on with him, and Briggs is very distraught about it. We can wonder if the title "Keyholes" would have revealed something about the situation but unless King completes the story, we can only speculate.

I found it very interesting to see how King works when he writes by hand.

He apparently just sat down and began writing. The story segment reads remarkably "finished" for a first draft. There are only eight or nine cross-outs, and all the dialogue reads like a final draft.

I did a transcription of the handwritten manuscript to make it easier to work with, and the story looks good in typescript.

There are a couple of errors in terms of King remembering names: Twice he refers to Nurse Adrian as "Nurse Abrams," confusing the doctor he referred to once with the nurse, but that would have been easily corrected in second draft.

The manuscript of "Keyholes" is a fascinating glimpse at the working habits of one of the world's most popular writers, and we can only hope that someday he'll finish the story and make it available to his readers.

Following the manuscript of "Keyholes" is King's handwritten revision of the outline of his screenplay for the film "Silver Bullet" (which was based on his novella *Cycle of the Werewolf*). [NOTE: See the section on *Cycle of the Werewolf* in this volume.]

The revision is dated 3/14/84; the actual film—with substantial changes even from this revision—was released in October of 1985.

King has the outline broken up by month, and the outline ends at August.

Here is a rundown of King's outline and what takes place in the individual sections:

I.) *JANUARY*

1. The murder of Arnie Westrum.
2. We meet Marty; find out that his mother is displeased with her brother ("Uncle Al," which was changed to "Uncle Red" in the final film version).
3. We meet Reverend Lowe and Stella Randolph. King makes a note that "In the book Stella is fat; here she is plain and tired-looking..." Lowe, instead of helping her deal with her illicit pregnancy, gives her a "self-righteous sermon."

II.) *FEBRUARY*

1. We see Tarker's Mills; we see Brady Kincaid pulling Marty on a sled. King makes a note that "still no sign that Marty is a cripple.")
2. We see a newspaper headline "Hope for Early Arrest Dims in Westrum Murder Case."
3. Stella Randolph picks up a prescription, goes home, writes a suicide note, and takes "about forty sleeping pills." The Werewolf bursts in and "saves her immortal soul by turning suicide into murder."

III.) *MARCH*

1. We see Sheriff Neary plodding along with "his mostly useless investigation" into the town's deaths.
2. We see Marty for the first time in his motor-driven wheelchair. A girl he likes tells him she's nervous about the noises coming from a shed near her house.
3. We see Marty and Uncle Al playing cards. Marty's mother comes in "looking as if she just swallowed a peeled lemon." She tells Al if he can't stop drinking, he has to stop coming around.
4. The girl's father goes into the shed and the Werewolf gets him.
5. A collecting the corpse scene.
6. Marty watches the police taking away the dead man.

IV.) *APRIL*

1. Marty and Brady fly kites.
2. We meet the town vigilantes in Alfie

Knopfler's bar.

3. Marty climbs a tree to retrieve Brady's kite. His mother freaks.
4. Back to the bar. The vigilantes are getting all worked up.
5. The Werewolf gets Brady Kincaid in the park.
6. Andy Kincaid finds "what's left" of Brady.
7. Brady's funeral. Mrs. Kincaid spills water and flowers on Marty's head when she leans down to kiss him.

V.) *MAY*

1. The vigilantes "appear in all their dubious glory."
2. Marty suggests to Uncle Al that the killings might be the work of a Werewolf. Uncle Al replies, "You've been watching too many monster movies, Marty. It'll turn out to be your ordinary, garden-variety psycho—you'll see. Norman Bates, Tarker's Mills style."
3. The first vigilante manhunt.
4. The Werewolf gets four vigilantes.

VI.) *JUNE*

1. A town in panic.
2. People begin leaving town.
3. Reverend Lester Lowe's "everyone becomes a were-something" dream.
4. We learn scene 3 was a dream; we discover the church custodian "horribly massacred."

VII.) *JULY*

1. The Coslaw house; we learn the fireworks have been cancelled.
2. A TV crew—"professional ghouls"—waits for the next murder.
3. Uncle Al gives Marty fireworks. Marty confronts and injures the Werewolf. King notes that "His confrontation with the wolf should follow the book exactly..."
4. The injured Wolf bursts into the parsonage and wrecks stuff because his "eyesocket [is] a bleeding hole."
5. The full moon sets.
6. We learn that Lowe is the Werewolf. (We see the Reverend on the floor with a bloody eye hole.)

VIII.) *AUGUST*

1. Marty at a camp for crippled children. He reads a letter from Uncle Al telling him that the only one in town wearing an eyepatch was "puny 138-pound Lester Lowe," and that

Marty certainly couldn't believe that Lowe was a Werewolf!

2. Marty writing a letter to Lowe.

3. A discussion at Knopfler's Bar ("or maybe at the barber shop!")

And that is where the revision stops.

Following the "Silver Bullet" revision is perhaps the strangest assemblage of pages in the notebook: twenty pages of King solving algebraic equations, obviously taken from a textbook.

Following the algebra, there is one page that contains a win/loss/average tabulation comparing the Louisiana Shooting Stars and the S.F. Golddiggers.

The next page, written in King's hand in cursive script, consists of the following list:

> Lee Marvin
> Peter Falk
> Robert Redford
> William Shatner
> Elizabeth Montgomery
>
> Patrick O'Neil in "A Short Drink
>   from a Certain Fountain"

And the last page of *The Stephen King Notebook* contains a large, block-printed note from King to his wife, Tabitha:

> Tabby,
> In case I should
> forget to remind you later.
> I must record on The Gunslinger
> with Mark Wellman tonight
> at the Z from 6 p.m., or 8 p.m.,
> or until my voice gives out—
>   Steve

And that, my friends, is *The Stephen King Notebook.*

Page Number Key to Master Codes
Cited in the Concordance Sections

CS=Creepshow; DS=Different Seasons; FPM=Four Past Midnight; NS=Night Shift; PPT=People, Places and Things; SC=Skeleton Crew

Page Number Key to Master Codes
Cited in Concordance Sections
(continued)

CS=Creepshow; DS=Different Seasons; FPM=Four Past Midnight; NS=Night Shift; PPT=People, Places and Things; SC=Skeleton Crew